*Presented to*

BY

ON

*Your word is a lamp to my feet*
*and a light for my path.*

PSALM 119:105

# My Family Tree

NAME

BIRTHPLACE DATE

BROTHERS & SISTERS

CHURCH EVENT DATE

CHURCH EVENT DATE

## FATHER

NAME

BIRTHPLACE DATE

## MOTHER

NAME

BIRTHPLACE DATE

## GRANDPARENTS

GRANDFATHER'S NAME

BIRTHPLACE DATE

GRANDMOTHER'S NAME

BIRTHPLACE DATE

## GRANDPARENTS

GRANDFATHER'S NAME

BIRTHPLACE DATE

GRANDMOTHER'S NAME

BIRTHPLACE DATE

# Aspire

# Aspire

the new

# WOMEN of COLOR STUDY BIBLE

ZONDERVAN®
.com

ZONDERVAN®

*NIV Aspire: The New Women of Color Study Bible*


Published by Zondervan
*Grand Rapids, Michigan 49530, U.S.A.*

ISBN: 978-0-310-93478-3



*Printed in the United States of America*

International Bible Society
www.ibs.org

The purpose and passion of International Bible Society is to faithfully translate, publish and reach out with God's Word so that people around the world may become disciples of Jesus Christ and members of his Body.

# TABLE OF CONTENTS

# WOMEN OF THE BIBLE NOTES TABLE OF CONTENTS

# ALPHABETICAL LIST AND ABBREVIATIONS

*Alphabetical List*—The books of the New Testament are in *italic*.


*Acts* ... *1274*
Amos ... 1041
1 Chronicles ... 467
2 Chronicles ... 505
*Colossians* ... *1402*
*1 Corinthians* ... *1343*
*2 Corinthians* ... *1363*
Daniel ... 1001
Deuteronomy ... 202
Ecclesiastes ... 771
*Ephesians* ... *1386*
Esther ... 580
Exodus ... 70
Ezekiel ... 946
Ezra ... 546
*Galatians* ... *1377*
Genesis ... 2
Habakkuk ... 1077
Haggai ... 1091
*Hebrews* ... *1444*
Hosea ... 1020
Isaiah ... 796
*James* ... *1461*
Jeremiah ... 869
Job ... 592
Joel ... 1034
*John* ... *1237*
*I John* ... *1481*
*2 John* ... *1488*
*3 John* ... *1492*
Jonah ... 1057
Joshua ... 244
*Jude* ... *1495*
Judges ... 273
1 Kings ... 392
2 Kings ... 430
Lamentations ... 937
Leviticus ... 119
*Luke* ... *1191*
Malachi ... 1107
*Mark* ... *1159*
*Matthew* ... *1114*
Micah ... 1062
Nahum ... 1071
Nehemiah ... 561
Numbers ... 153
Obadiah ... 1053
*1 Peter* ... *1468*
*2 Peter* ... *1476*
*Philemon* ... *1440*
*Philippians* ... *1394*
Proverbs ... 733
Psalms ... 632
*Revelation* ... *1499*
*Romans* ... *1320*
Ruth ... 308
1 Samuel ... 317
2 Samuel ... 357
Song of Songs ... 784
*1 Thessalonians* ... *1409*
*2 Thessalonians* ... *1416*
*1 Timothy* ... *1420*
*2 Timothy* ... *1428*
*Titus* ... *1435*
Zechariah ... 1095
Zephaniah ... 1084


| | |
|---|---|
| Genesis | Ge |
| Exodus | Ex |
| Leviticus | Lev |
| Numbers | Nu |
| Deuteronomy | Dt |
| Joshua | Jos |
| Judges | Jdg |
| Ruth | Ru |
| 1 Samuel | 1Sa |
| 2 Samuel | 2Sa |
| 1 Kings | 1Ki |
| 2 Kings | 2Ki |
| 1 Chronicles | 1Ch |
| 2 Chronicles | 2Ch |
| Ezra | Ezr |
| Nehemiah | Neh |
| Esther | Est |
| Job | Job |
| Psalms | Ps |
| Proverbs | Pr |
| Ecclesiastes | Ecc |
| Song of Songs | SS |
| Isaiah | Isa |
| Jeremiah | Jer |
| Lamentations | La |
| Ezekiel | Eze |
| Daniel | Da |
| Hosea | Hos |
| Joel | Joel |
| Amos | Am |
| Obadiah | Ob |
| Jonah | Jnh |
| Micah | Mic |
| Nahum | Na |
| Habakkuk | Hab |
| Zephaniah | Zep |
| Haggai | Hag |
| Zechariah | Zec |
| Malachi | Mal |
| Matthew | Mt |
| Mark | Mk |
| Luke | Lk |
| John | Jn |
| Acts | Ac |
| Romans | Ro |
| 1 Corinthians | 1Co |
| 2 Corinthians | 2Co |
| Galatians | Gal |
| Ephesians | Eph |
| Philippians | Php |
| Colossians | Col |
| 1 Thessalonians | 1Th |
| 2 Thessalonians | 2Th |
| 1 Timothy | 1Ti |
| 2 Timothy | 2Ti |
| Titus | Tit |
| Philemon | Phm |
| Hebrews | Heb |
| James | Jas |
| 1 Peter | 1Pe |
| 2 Peter | 2Pe |
| 1 John | 1Jn |
| 2 John | 2Jn |
| 3 John | 3Jn |
| Jude | Jude |
| Revelation | Rev |

Welcome to *Aspire: The New Women of Color Study Bible.* You may be familiar with the *Women of Color Study Bible*; in fact, you may own one. What's different about this Bible? How is it "new"? *Aspire: The New Women of Color Study Bible* takes some of its content from the previous Bible, but all of that content is completely revised and updated. Many of the same contributors are included, but other women have also been added to the list. This Bible offers more notes and features (see the list below), and it places the notes in the Scripture text where you can conveniently find them. *Aspire: The New Women of Color Study Bible* will aid your study of God's Word, encourage your faith and renew your spirit each day.

## FEATURES OF *ASPIRE: THE NEW WOMEN OF COLOR STUDY BIBLE*

### *The New International Version of the Bible*

The most important part of any Bible is the Scripture itself. This Bible uses the New International Version (NIV). Trusted by scholars and used by millions of readers, the New International Version is the most read, most trusted translation in the world.

### *Women of the Bible Notes*

What can you learn from women who lived so long ago? Plenty! A variety of women of color have written on the lives of women of the Bible. You'll recognize Biblical women such as Sarah, Rachel, Ruth and Lydia. You'll gain insight into your life today by reading about The Woman of Thebez and Candace. There is much to learn from women who lived so long ago.

### *Inspire Notes*

Do you wonder if the Bible is relevant to the issues you're facing today? As you read the Inspire notes, written by women of color, you'll find that the Bible has a lot to say about the topics that are important to you. Also, some of the Inspire Notes were written with a specific focus on the needs of leaders. These notes are indicated with a different heading and the words "leadership focus" to set these types of notes apart.

### *The African Presence Notes*

Originally called "The Black Presence Notes" in the Women of Color Study Bible, these notes have been completely revised and rewritten to be even more helpful and accurate. With a new introduction (see page xii), these notes will open your eyes to the importance Africa and Africans played in the ancient Biblical world.

*From God Notes*

God is madly in love with you! Sometimes you need a reminder of his love. A completely new feature, these notes are taken from Scripture and include thoughts of affirmation and encouragement for you from God.

*Prayers to God Notes*

Tied to Scripture, these notes offer prayers to God that you can read as personal thoughts or use to prompt your own prayers to your God and Father.

*Quotes*

Some days you need a thought of inspiration or encouragement. These quotes from a variety of women give you something to think about as you go about your day.

*Book Introductions*

Each of the 66 books of the Bible begins with an introduction that gives an overview of the book. The overview gives some basic content information and background, then a simple and useful outline gives you a sense of the structure of the book. Also, there is a box of facts for easy and quick reference.

*Subject Index*

Looking for information on a particular topic? The subject index guides you to those notes that address your area of interest.

*Study Helps*

A Bible concordance, center-column reference system and color maps are included in this Bible to assist you in your study of God's Word.

## NOTE FROM THE GENERAL EDITOR

I must give glory and honor to God for the completion of this project. While completing this special Bible project was a challenge, I was revived each time I sat down to edit a piece. I constantly prayed that God would inspire the readers as much as I was inspired when I read each word.

And naturally, a project of this magnitude involves many gifted people, to whom I owe much gratitude. Thank you, Mel Banks II for following your dream and pushing to have your concept become a reality. Thank you, Cheryl Wilson, Victoria Christopher Murray, and Crystal McDowell for your talents, dedication, and willingness to work at a moment's notice. Thank you, Vanessa Lovelace for your editorial review. Thank you, Marjorie H. Lawson, editor of the original project, and all of the contributors. Thank you, Shari Vanden Berg, Mike Vander Klipp, and all of the staff at Zondervan—your expertise and patience have been greatly appreciated.

Lastly, I'd like to thank my dear mother, Mrs. Ernestine C. Washington, who taught me by example to love the word of God. She died suddenly just as I was completing this project; the lessons she taught me will remain a part of my ministry and work always. Thank you, Mama.

To our readers, I continue to pray that you will draw nearer to God through reading his word.

Katara A. Washington, General Editor

## ABOUT THE CREATOR

Urban Spirit creates, publishes and distributes fine inspirational books, Bibles and gifts for urban America. The company was founded by Mel Banks II in 1993 as Children of Color Publishing after the success of the *Children of Color Holy Bible*—the first Bible of its kind featuring uniquely authentic illustrations of Bible characters who are "people of color." Because of an even greater need for Bibles targeting the specific needs of African Americans, the company transformed into Nia Publishing Co. Inc and developed the popular *Women of Color Study Bible* and the *Men of Color Study Bible*. The publisher has also created Bibles for young teens (*Wisdom and Grace* for girls and *Strength and Honor* for boys).

Today our work includes the same quality craftsmanship and the same desire to match the needs of the individual with answers from the word of God that resonate with the unique experiences of African Americans, people of color everywhere and now urban America.

The notes of this Bible interchangeably refer to the "African Presence in the Bible," "Africans in the Bible" and "The Black Presence." We chose to use the first two terms to help identify the presence of Africans in the Biblical times geographically, collectively and individually. We include the latter term to make the connection with those individuals or groups of individuals whose ancestry is linked to the peoples identified in modern terms as "Blacks."

Geographically, the African presence can be identified with the Egyptian empire that was the dominant kingdom in the ancient Near East during the Late Bronze Age (about 1550–1200 B.C.). Egypt's control and influence stretched from the northernmost region of Palestine (Canaan), the homeland of Israel and Judah, to Cush (Nubia/Ethiopia) in the south. Cush, located in northeastern Africa in today's southern Egypt and northern Sudan, is mentioned in relation to the location of one of the rivers flowing from the Garden of Eden (see Ge 2:13), as well as the personal name of the progenitor of the Cushites (see Ge 10:6). Put or Phut is the eponym of Lybia (Cyrene), located in northern Africa, west of Egypt.

Egyptians, Cushites, Ethiopians and Cyrenes are mentioned throughout the Bible. The Egyptian dominance, while on the decline during the period of Israel's emergence, is attested by its more than 100 occurrences of "Egyptians" or "Egyptian" in the Bible. Cushites, often used interchangeably with Ethiopians in the Bible, are mentioned in the history of the Israelites as family members, soldiers and allies.

As long as cultures have existed, there has been contact between different ethnic groups as a result of migration, trade, wars, etc. For example, interaction between the Cushites and the Egyptians was extensive, and intermarriage was frequent. The population of Palestine was heterogeneous, making it difficult to define any group by modern racial categories of "black," "white," "Hispanic" and "Asian." A study of art from ancient cultures shows people who varied in color complexions, from light brown to black. The population that departed Egypt with Moses and the Israelites is described as a "mixed multitude," which likely included the dark brown Cushites, the light brown Egyptians, and every other color variation in between (see Ex 12:38). In other words, they represent the many hues that present day Blacks comprise.

One of the difficulties of identifying the African presence in the Bible is distinguishing between the terms "ethnicity" and "race." The English terms "ethnic" and "ethnicity" are derived from the Greek word *ethnos*. In its simplest form, ethnicity is "a relationship between two contrasting individuals and groups of people," which is differentiated by the groups' respective culture, ancestry, religion or language.[1] Race, on the other hand is a system of human classification based on observable characteristics such as skin color, facial features, hair texture and body proportion. Individuals could belong to the same racial group, like the Hutus and Tutsis in central Africa, but different ethnic groups.

The Bible refers to people based on their ethnicity, not race. This invariably masks the racial character of the Africans in the Bible, diminishing their contributions to or role in the Biblical story. The result too often is the lack of connection of modern day Blacks to the lands and people of the Bible.

Vanessa Lovelace

---

[1] Gay Byron. *Symbolic Blackness and Ethnic Difference in Early Christian Literature*. New York: Routledge, 2002.

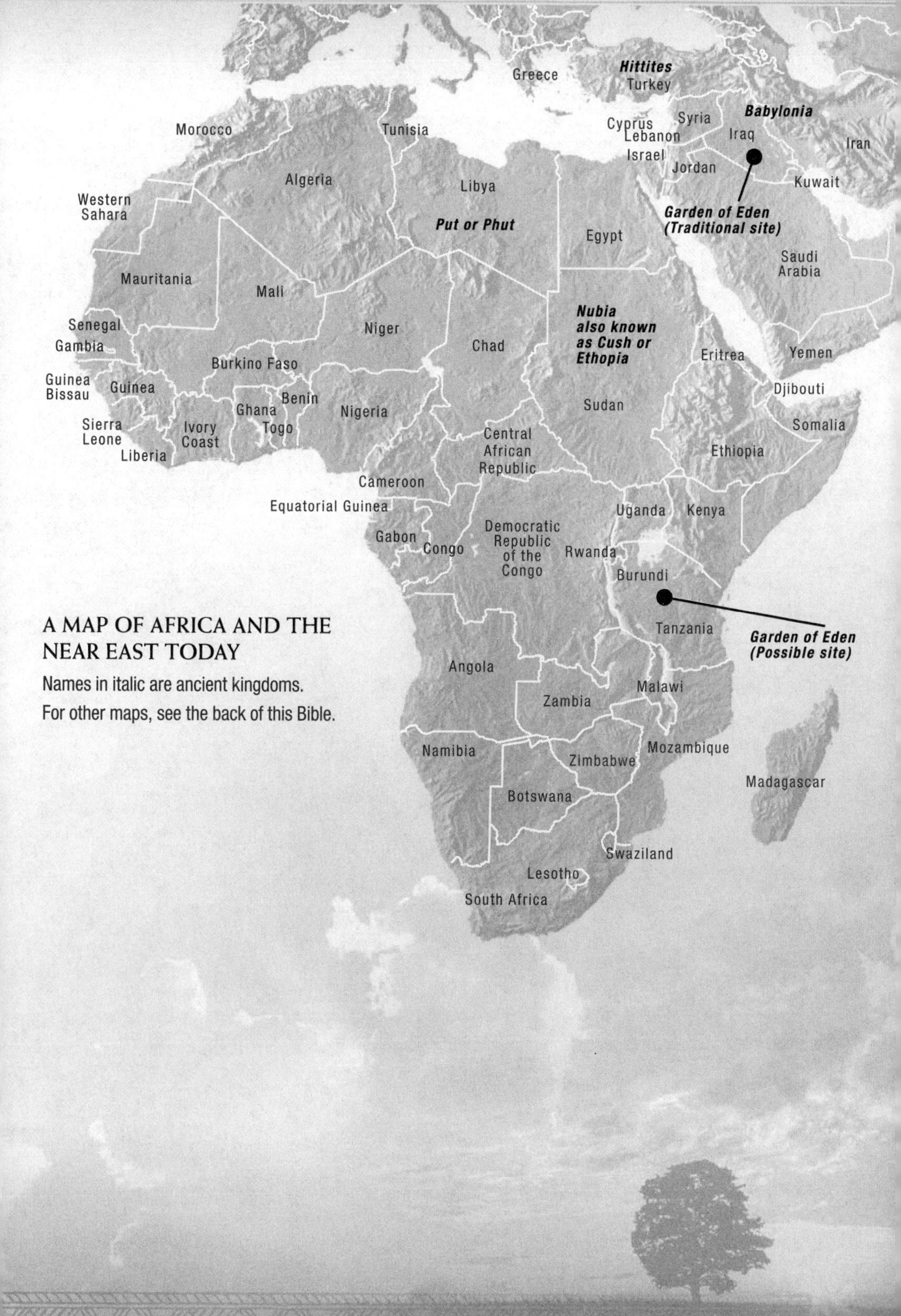


## A MAP OF AFRICA AND THE NEAR EAST TODAY

Names in italic are ancient kingdoms.

For other maps, see the back of this Bible.

# PREFACE TO THE NIV

THE NEW INTERNATIONAL VERSION is a completely new translation of the Holy Bible made by over a hundred scholars working directly from the best available Hebrew, Aramaic and Greek texts. It had its beginning in 1965 when, after several years of exploratory study by committees from the Christian Reformed Church and the National Association of Evangelicals, a group of scholars met at Palos Heights, Illinois, and concurred in the need for a new translation of the Bible in contemporary English. This group, though not made up of official church representatives, was transdenominational. Its conclusion was endorsed by a large number of leaders from many denominations who met in Chicago in 1966.

Responsibility for the new version was delegated by the Palos Heights group to a self-governing body of fifteen, the Committee on Bible Translation, composed for the most part of biblical scholars from colleges, universities and seminaries. In 1967 the New York Bible Society (now the International Bible Society) generously undertook the financial sponsorship of the project—a sponsorship that made it possible to enlist the help of many distinguished scholars. The fact that participants from the United States, Great Britain, Canada, Australia and New Zealand worked together gave the project its international scope. That they were from many denominations—including Anglican, Assemblies of God, Baptist, Brethren, Christian Reformed, Church of Christ, Evangelical Free, Lutheran, Mennonite, Methodist, Nazarene, Presbyterian, Wesleyan and other churches—helped to safeguard the translation from sectarian bias.

How it was made helps to give the New International Version its distinctiveness. The translation of each book was assigned to a team of scholars. Next, one of the Intermediate Editorial Committees revised the initial translation, with constant reference to the Hebrew, Aramaic or Greek. Their work then went to one of the General Editorial Committees, which checked it in detail and made another thorough revision. This revision in turn was carefully reviewed by the Committee on Bible Translation, which made further changes and then released the final version for publication. In this way the entire Bible underwent three revisions, during each of which the translation was examined for its faithfulness to the original languages and for its English style.

All this involved many thousands of hours of research and discussion regarding the meaning of the texts and the precise way of putting them into English. It may well be that no other translation has been made by a more thorough process of review and revision from committee to committee than this one.

From the beginning of the project, the Committee on Bible Translation held to certain goals for the New International Version: that it would be an accurate translation and one that would have clarity and literary quality and so prove suitable for public and private reading, teaching, preaching, memorizing and liturgical use. The Committee also sought to preserve some measure of continuity with the long tradition of translating the Scriptures into English.

In working toward these goals, the translators were united in their commitment to the authority and infallibility of the Bible as God's Word in written form. They believe that it contains the divine answer to the deepest needs of humanity, that it sheds unique light on our path in a dark world, and that it sets forth the way to our eternal well-being.

The first concern of the translators has been the accuracy of the translation and its fidelity to the thought of the biblical writers. They have weighed the significance of the lexical and grammatical details of the Hebrew, Aramaic and Greek texts. At the same time, they have striven for more than a word-for-word translation. Because thought patterns and syntax differ from language to language, faithful communication of the meaning of the writers of the Bible demands frequent modifications in sentence structure and constant regard for the contextual meanings of words.

A sensitive feeling for style does not always accompany scholarship. Accordingly the Committee on Bible Translation submitted the developing version to a number of stylistic consultants. Two of them read every book of both Old and New Testaments twice—once before and once after the last major revision—and made invaluable suggestions. Samples of the translation were tested for clarity and ease of reading by various kinds of people—young and old, highly educated and less well educated, ministers and laymen.

Concern for clear and natural English—that the New International Version should be idiomatic but not idiosyncratic, contemporary but not dated—motivated the translators and consultants. At the same time, they tried to reflect the differing styles of the biblical writers. In view of the international use of English, the translators sought to avoid obvious Americanisms on the one hand and obvious Anglicisms on the other. A British edition reflects the comparatively few differences of significant idiom and of spelling.

As for the traditional pronouns "thou," "thee" and "thine" in reference to the Deity, the translators judged that to use these archaisms (along with the old verb forms such as "doest," wouldest" and "hadst") would violate accuracy in translation. Neither Hebrew, Aramaic nor Greek uses special pronouns for the persons of the Godhead. A present-day translation is not enhanced by forms that in the time of the King James Version were used in everyday speech, whether referring to God or man.

For the Old Testament the standard Hebrew text, the Masoretic Text as published in the latest editions of *Biblia Hebraica*, was used throughout. The Dead Sea Scrolls contain material bearing on an earlier stage of the Hebrew text. They were consulted, as were the Samaritan Pentateuch and the ancient scribal traditions relating to textual changes. Sometimes a variant Hebrew reading in the margin of the Masoretic Text was followed instead of the text itself. Such instances, being variants within the Masoretic tradition, are not specified by footnotes. In rare cases, words in the consonantal text were divided differently from the way they appear in the Masoretic Text. Footnotes indicate this. The translators also consulted the more important early versions—the Septuagint; Aquila, Symmachus and Theodotion; the Vulgate; the Syriac Peshitta; the Targums; and for the Psalms the *Juxta Hebraica* of Jerome. Readings from these versions were occasionally followed where the Masoretic Text seemed doubtful and where accepted principles of textual criticism showed that one or more of these textual witnesses appeared to provide the correct reading. Such instances are footnoted. Sometimes vowel letters and vowel signs did not, in the judgment of the translators, represent the correct vowels for the original consonantal text. Accordingly some words were read with a different set of vowels. These instances are usually not indicated by footnotes.

The Greek text used in translating the New Testament was an eclectic one. No other piece of ancient literature has such an abundance of manuscript witnesses as does the New Testament. Where existing manuscripts differ, the translators made their choice of readings according to accepted principles of New Testament textual criticism. Footnotes call attention to places where there was uncertainty about what the original text was. The best current printed texts of the Greek New Testament were used.

There is a sense in which the work of translation is never wholly finished. This applies to all great literature and uniquely so to the Bible. In 1973 the New Testament in the New International Version was published. Since then, suggestions for corrections and revisions have been received from various sources. The Committee on Bible Translation carefully considered the suggestions and adopted a number of them. These were incorporated in the first printing of the entire Bible in 1978. Additional revisions were made by the Committee on Bible Translation in 1983 and appear in printings after that date.

As in other ancient documents, the precise meaning of the biblical texts is sometimes uncertain. This is more often the case with the Hebrew and Aramaic texts than with the Greek text. Although archaeological and linguistic discoveries in this century aid in understanding difficult passages, some uncertainties remain. The more significant of these have been called to the reader's attention in the footnotes.

In regard to the divine name *YHWH*, commonly referred to as the *Tetragrammaton*, the translators adopted the device used in most English versions of rendering that name as "LORD" in capital letters to distinguish it from

*Adonai*, another Hebrew word rendered "Lord," for which small letters are used. Wherever the two names stand together in the Old Testament as a compound name of God, they are rendered "Sovereign LORD."

Because for most readers today the phrases "the LORD of hosts" and "God of hosts" have little meaning, this version renders them "the LORD Almighty" and "God Almighty." These renderings convey the sense of the Hebrew, namely, "he who is sovereign over all the 'hosts' (powers) in heaven and on earth, especially over the 'hosts' (armies) of Israel." For readers unacquainted with Hebrew this does not make clear the distinction between *Sabaoth* ("hosts" or "Almighty") and *Shaddai* (which can also be translated "Almighty"), but the latter occurs infrequently and is always footnoted. When *Adonai* and *YHWH Sabaoth* occur together, they are rendered "the Lord, the LORD Almighty."

As for other proper nouns, the familiar spellings of the King James Version are generally retained. Names traditionally spelled with "ch," except where it is final, are usually spelled in this translation with "k" or "c," since the biblical languages do not have the sound that "ch" frequently indicates in English—for example, in chant. For well-known names such as Zechariah, however, the traditional spelling has been retained. Variation in the spelling of names in the original languages has usually not been indicated. Where a person or place has two or more different names in the Hebrew, Aramaic or Greek texts, the more familiar one has generally been used, with footnotes where needed.

To achieve clarity the translators sometimes supplied words not in the original texts but required by the context. If there was uncertainty about such material, it is enclosed in brackets. Also for the sake of clarity or style, nouns, including some proper nouns, are sometimes substituted for pronouns, and vice versa. And though the Hebrew writers often shifted back and forth between first, second and third personal pronouns without change of antecedent, this translation often makes them uniform, in accordance with English style and without the use of footnotes.

Poetical passages are printed as poetry, that is, with indentation of lines and with separate stanzas. These are generally designed to reflect the structure of Hebrew poetry. This poetry is normally characterized by parallelism in balanced lines. Most of the poetry in the Bible is in the Old Testament, and scholars differ regarding the scansion of Hebrew lines. The translators determined the stanza divisions for the most part by analysis of the subject matter. The stanzas therefore serve as poetic paragraphs.

As an aid to the reader, sectional headings are inserted in most of the books. They are not to be regarded as part of the NIV text, are not for oral reading, and are not intended to dictate the interpretation of the sections they head.

The footnotes in this version are of several kinds, most of which need no explanation. Those giving alternative translations begin with "Or" and generally introduce the alternative with the last word preceding it in the text, except when it is a single-word alternative; in poetry quoted in a footnote a slant mark indicates a line division. Footnotes introduced by "Or" do not have uniform significance. In some cases two possible translations were considered to have about equal validity. In other cases, though the translators were convinced that the translation in the text was correct, they judged that another interpretation was possible and of sufficient importance to be represented in a footnote.

In the New Testament, footnotes that refer to uncertainty regarding the original text are introduced by "Some manuscripts" or similar expressions. In the Old Testament, evidence for the reading chosen is given first and evidence for the alternative is added after a semicolon (for example: Septuagint; Hebrew *father*). In such notes the term "Hebrew" refers to the Masoretic Text.

It should be noted that minerals, flora and fauna, architectural details, articles of clothing and jewelry, musical instruments and other articles cannot always be identified with precision. Also measures of capacity in the biblical period are particularly uncertain (see the table of weights and measures following the text).

Like all translations of the Bible, made as they are by imperfect man, this one undoubtedly falls short of its goals. Yet we are grateful to God for the extent to which he has enabled us to realize these goals and for the strength he has given us and our colleagues to complete our task. We offer this version of the Bible to him in whose name and for whose glory it has been made. We pray that it will lead many into a better understanding of the Holy Scriptures and a fuller knowledge of Jesus Christ the incarnate Word, of whom the Scriptures so faithfully testify.

*The Committee on Bible Translation*
June 1978
(Revised August 1983)

Names of the translators and editors may be secured
from the International Bible Society,
translation sponsors of the New International Version,
1820 Jet Stream Drive, Colorado Springs, CO 80921-3696 U.S.A.

# Old Testament

# Genesis

## OVERVIEW

The first book of the Bible, Genesis, covers the period from God's creation of the heavens and the earth through the Israelites' entrance into Egypt.

The first Hebrew word of this book means "beginning," and Genesis records a number of beginnings—that of the universe, the earth, plants, animals, humankind, sin, judgment, redemption and more. While women many times are listed as secondary players in the drama of Genesis, they actually play key roles in this book of beginnings and often shed light on the humanness of God's chosen people.

Adam and Eve failed the test of obedience to God, and each one incurred different consequences. God told Adam that the ground would be cursed because of his actions. And God announced to Eve that she would have pain in childbearing. Both consequences are just as evident today as they were then!

The Hebrew nation began with the call of Abram (see Ge 12), who was later renamed Abraham (see Ge 17). His wife, Sarai, renamed Sarah, served as the matriarch of the Hebrew race. It was through the Hebrews that God would introduce salvation to humanity.

God rewarded the elderly Abraham's faith with the birth of his promised son, Isaac. Sarah was overjoyed and laughed with delight (see Ge 21:6). Isaac grew up and married Rebekah. After a struggle with infertility, God blessed the couple with twin sons—Jacob and Esau. God selected the younger twin, Jacob (later renamed Israel), to become the progenitor of the covenant people—the Israelites. Jacob and his wives, Leah and Rachel, and their servants, Zilpah and Bilhah, had a total of 12 sons and 1 daughter. The book climaxes with Israel and his family in Egypt, where God used Israel's son Joseph to provide for their survival; from this family came the 12 tribes of Israel.

## OUTLINE

The phrase "the generations of," repeated 11 times, points us to the outline of the book of Genesis. This phrase can be understood as the "record" or "story of."

I. The Story of Creation (1:1—2:3)
II. The Story of Adam and Eve (2:4—4:26)
III. The Story of Adam's Descendants (5:1—6:8)
IV. The Story of Noah (6:9—9:17)
V. The Story of Noah's Descendants (9:18—11:9)
VI. The Story of Shem's Descendants (11:10–26)
VII. The Story of Abraham and Sarah (11:27—25:11)
VIII. The Story of Ishmael, Hagar's Son (25:12–18)
IX. The Story of Isaac and Rebekah (25:19—27:40)
X. The Story of Esau, Jacob, Leah and Rachel (27:41—33:20)
XI. The Story of Dinah and the Shechemites (34:1–31)
XII. The Story of Jacob, Esau and Joseph Continued (35:1—37:36)
XIII. The Story of Judah and Tamar (38:1–30)
XIV. The Completion of the Story of Joseph (39:1—50:26)

## SCANNABLE FACTS:

**Author:** Moses

**Time Written:** 1446 to 1406 B.C.

**Themes to Note:** Creation, Flood, Beginning of the Hebrew Nation

**Notable Women:** Eve, Sarah, Hagar, Lot's Wife, Rebekah, Rachel, Leah, Dinah, Tamar

**1:1** a Jn 1:1–2 b Isa 42:5; 44:24; 45:12,18
**1:3** c Ps 33:6,9 d 2Co 4:6*
**1:5** e Ps 74:16
**1:6** f Jer 10:12
**1:7** g Ps 148:4
**1:9** h Ps 104:6–9; Jer 5:22; 2Pe 3:5
**1:14** i Ps 74:16 j Ps 104:19
**1:16** k Ps 136:8 l Ps 136:9 m Ps 8:3; Isa 40:26

## The Beginning

1 In the beginning[a] God created the
heavens and the earth.[b] 2 Now the
earth was[a] formless and empty, dark-
ness was over the surface of the deep,
and the Spirit of God was hovering
over the waters.

3 And God said,[c] "Let there be light," and
there was light.[d] 4 God saw that the light
was good, and he separated the light
from the darkness. 5 God called the
light "day," and the darkness he called
"night."[e] And there was evening, and
there was morning—the first day.
6 And God said, "Let there be an expanse[f]
between the waters to separate water
from water." 7 So God made the ex-
panse and separated the water under
the expanse from the water above it.[g]
And it was so. 8 God called the expanse
"sky." And there was evening, and
there was morning—the second day.
9 And God said, "Let the water under the
sky be gathered to one place,[h] and let
dry ground appear." And it was so.
10 God called the dry ground "land,"
and the gathered waters he called
"seas." And God saw that it was good.
11 Then God said, "Let the land pro-
duce vegetation: seed-bearing plants
and trees on the land that bear fruit
with seed in it, according to their var-
ious kinds." And it was so. 12 The land
produced vegetation: plants bearing
seed according to their kinds and trees
bearing fruit with seed in it according
to their kinds. And God saw that it was
good. 13 And there was evening, and
there was morning—the third day.
14 And God said, "Let there be lights[i] in the
expanse of the sky to separate the day
from the night, and let them serve as
signs to mark seasons[j] and days and
years, 15 and let them be lights in the
expanse of the sky to give light on
the earth." And it was so. 16 God made
two great lights—the greater light to
govern[k] the day and the lesser light to
govern[l] the night. He also made the
stars.[m] 17 God set them in the expanse
of the sky to give light on the earth,
18 to govern the day and the night, and
to separate light from darkness. And
God saw that it was good. 19 And there
was evening, and there was morn-
ing—the fourth day.
20 And God said, "Let the water teem with
living creatures, and let birds fly above
the earth across the expanse of the
sky." 21 So God created the great crea-
tures of the sea and every living and
moving thing with which the water
teems, according to their kinds, and
every winged bird according to its
kind. And God saw that it was good.
22 God blessed them and said, "Be fruit-
ful and increase in number and fill the
water in the seas, and let the birds in-
crease on the earth." 23 And there was
evening, and there was morning—the
fifth day.
24 And God said, "Let the land produce
living creatures according to their
kinds: livestock, creatures that move
along the ground, and wild animals,
each according to its kind." And it
was so. 25 God made the wild animals
according to their kinds, the livestock
according to their kinds, and all the
creatures that move along the ground
according to their kinds. And God saw
that it was good.
26 Then God said, "Let us make man
in our image, in our likeness, and let
them rule over the fish of the sea and
the birds of the air, over the livestock,
over all the earth,[b] and over all the crea-
tures that move along the ground."

27 So God created man in his own image,
in the image of God he created him;
male and female[n] he created them.

28 God blessed them and said to
them, "Be fruitful and increase in
number; fill the earth[o] and subdue it.
Rule over the fish of the sea and the
birds of the air and over every living
creature that moves on the ground."
29 Then God said, "I give you every
seed-bearing plant on the face of the
whole earth and every tree that has

**1:27** n Ge 5:2; Mt 19:4*; Mk 10:6*
**1:28** o Ge 9:1,7; Lev 26:9

[a]2 Or possibly *became* [b]26 Hebrew; Syriac *all the wild animals*

1:29 p Ps 104:14
1:30 q Ps 145:15
1:31 r Ps 104:24
2:2 s Ex 20:11; Heb 4:4*

fruit with seed in it. They will be yours
for food.[p] [30]And to all the beasts of
the earth and all the birds of the air
and all the creatures that move on
the ground—everything that has the
breath of life in it—I give every green
plant for food.[q]" And it was so.

[31]God saw all that he had made,[r]
and it was very good. And there was
evening, and there was morning—the
sixth day.

2 Thus the heavens and the earth
were completed in all their vast array.

[2]By the seventh day God had finished the
work he had been doing; so on the sev-
enth day he rested[a] from all his work.[s]

[3]And God blessed the seventh day and
made it holy, because on it he rested
from all the work of creating that he
had done.

## Adam and Eve

[4]This is the account of the heavens and
the earth when they were created.

When the LORD God made the earth and
the heavens— [5]and no shrub of the field
had yet appeared on the earth[b] and no plant
of the field had yet sprung up,[t] for the LORD
God had not sent rain on the earth[b] and
there was no man to work the ground, [6]but
streams[c] came up from the earth and wa-
tered the whole surface of the ground— [7]the
LORD God formed the man[d] from the dust[u]
of the ground and breathed into his nostrils
the breath of life, and the man became a liv-
ing being.[v]

[8]Now the LORD God had planted a gar-
den in the east, in Eden; and there he put
the man he had formed. [9]And the LORD
God made all kinds of trees grow out of the
ground—trees that were pleasing to the eye
and good for food. In the middle of the gar-
den were the tree of life[w] and the tree of the
knowledge of good and evil.

[10]A river watering the garden flowed from
Eden; from there it was separated into four
headwaters. [11]The name of the first is the
Pishon; it winds through the entire land

2:5 t Ge 1:11
2:7 u Ge 3:19 v 1Co 15:45*
2:9 w Ge 3:22,24; Rev 2:7; 22:2,14,19

[a]2 Or *ceased*; also in verse 3 [b]5 Or *land*; also in verse 6 [c]6 Or *mist* [d]7 The Hebrew for *man (adam)* sounds like and may be related to the Hebrew for *ground (adamah)*; it is also the name *Adam* (see Gen. 2:20).

## *The African Presence*

### Genesis 2:8

The earliest remains of humankind were found in Tanzania; it is believed that humankind began here and migrated up the Nile River to other parts of the world. Before recent discoveries of humankind's origin in Africa, archaeological academics suggested Mesopotamia as the most likely location for the Garden of Eden. The etymology of the word *eden* strongly indicates that it is derived from the Sumerian word for "plain," "steppe" or "fertile plain." There are scholars (such as J. G. Jackson and James G. Frazer) who claim that the early Sumerians originated from Africa (Ethiopia) and migrated to Mesopotamia. The Sumerians are described as "black-headed ones." It is debated whether this refers to their hair color (*Yamauchi*) or their hair and skin color (*Copher*).

Also, according to African scholar Cheikh Anta Diop, a noted but sometimes controversial historian, and George Rawlinson, another historian and author of many books on ancient history, the Sumerian people originally settled in Mesopotamia around 5000 to 2500 B.C. These two scholars also claim that the Sumerians migrated to Mesopotamia from Africa. Rawlinson reports that inscriptions, dialect and tradition all point to these early inhabitants as being originally from Africa.

# Inspire

## THE CREATION OF WOMAN

When God created woman, he created her equal to man, not inferior or superior. She was created for a purpose and for greatness! How was the woman created? It began with God putting Adam into a deep sleep, taking out one of his ribs, and closing the place up with flesh (see Ge 2:21–24). The word "flesh" represents life itself—created life. God had to remove something "out of" Adam to create and make room for what he was bringing back to him—another life: woman.

God created the woman from the rib of man. In Hebrew, the language of the Old Testament, the word for *rib* signifies the side of something—more often the side of a building than of a person. Therefore, the woman is at the man's side: as his confidante, encourager and inward strength. She is his "helper" (see Ge 2:20), the one most appropriate for his life. The word "helper" does not imply inferiority. It describes a function and not worth. Women do not lose their worth when they assume the role of a helper. Adam expressed Eve's purpose when he said, "This is now bone of my bones and flesh of my flesh" (v. 23). He was saying that the woman was literally a part of him.

When God brought the woman to Adam, God brought into Adam's life a trusted friend and a wife. She became something that nothing else or no one else could be to him. When Adam said, "She shall be called 'woman' " (Ge 2:23), he was declaring her existence. Adam was also praising and celebrating her creation. The woman became Adam's spiritual partner in the task of obedience to God, dominion over the earth and procreation of the generations.

Adam represents all humanity, and the woman was named Eve because she was the mother of all humanity (see Ge 3:20). She was created with life, to bring life, to nurture life and to be an example of life. Every human life has received a woman's touch.

Woman was fearfully and wonderfully made (see Ps 139:14), purposefully saved (see Jn 15:16), gifted for greatness (see 1Co 12:4–7), empowered to accomplish God's will (see Eph 1:17–21), assigned to do great things (see Mt 28:1–10). She is a crown of glory (see Pr 12:4; Isa 62:3) and the Lord's own treasured possession (see Mal 3:17). The woman was created for greatness!

—G. London

### read

Genesis 1:27–28; 2:18–24.

**See also** the Inspire Notes "Marriage" and "The Image of God and the Beauty of the Heart," and the Women of the Bible Note "Eve: The First African Woman."

### WOMAN of COLOR

Do you honestly believe you were created for greatness? Are you living like God's gifted and great creation? What will you do today to live as God has created you to live?

For the next Inspire note, go to page 43.

2:14
x Da 10:4
2:17
y Ro 5:12; 6:23

of Havilah, where there is gold. 12(The gold
of that land is good; aromatic resin[a] and
onyx are also there.) 13The name of the sec-
ond river is the Gihon; it winds through
the entire land of Cush.[b] 14The name of the
third river is the Tigris;[x] it runs along the
east side of Asshur. And the fourth river is
the Euphrates.

15The LORD God took the man and
put him in the Garden of Eden to work
it and take care of it. 16And the LORD God
commanded the man, "You are free to eat
from any tree in the garden; 17but you must
not eat from the tree of the knowledge of
good and evil, for when you eat of it you
will surely die."[y]

18The LORD God said, "It is not good for
the man to be alone. I will make a helper
suitable for him."

19Now the LORD God had formed out of
the ground all the beasts of the field and all
the birds of the air. He brought them to the
man to see what he would name them; and
whatever the man called each living crea-
ture, that was its name. 20So the man gave
names to all the livestock, the birds of the
air and all the beasts of the field.

But for Adam[c] no suitable helper was
found. 21So the LORD God caused the man
to fall into a deep sleep; and while he was
sleeping, he took one of the man's ribs[d] and
closed up the place with flesh. 22Then the
LORD God made a woman from the rib[e] he
had taken out of the man, and he brought
her to the man.

23The man said,

"This is now bone of my bones
and flesh of my flesh;[z]
she shall be called 'woman,[f]'
for she was taken out of man."

24For this reason a man will leave his father
and mother and be united to his wife, and
they will become one flesh.[a]

25The man and his wife were both naked,[b]
and they felt no shame.

2:23
z Eph 5:28–30
2:24
a Mt 19:5*; Mk 10:7–8*; 1Co 6:16*; Eph 5:31*
2:25
b Ge 3:7,10–11

[a]12 Or *good; pearls* [b]13 Possibly southeast Mesopotamia [c]20 Or *the man* [d]21 Or *took part of the man's side*
[e]22 Or *part* [f]23 The Hebrew for *woman* sounds like the Hebrew for *man.*

## The African Presence

### Genesis 2:10–14

Archaeological evidence points to the African continent as the place where human life began and from where people migrated to other parts of the earth. Thus, Africa would be the location of the Garden of Eden—but how do we reconcile the descriptions of the rivers related to the garden? In Genesis 2:10–14 we read that a river went out of Eden and parted into four heads: the Pishon, the Gihon, the Tigris and the Euphrates. Most scholars place the Tigris and Euphrates in Mesopotamia, where the rivers still exist today. However, the other descriptions make locating the Garden of Eden there difficult (for example, relating the four rivers to a single river that flowed through Eden, implying that all four rivers shared a common source).

It is possible that the geographic descriptions have been marred by time. And it is indeed possible that the garden was located in Africa. Recent aerial photographs of North Africa indicate ancient riverbeds buried beneath the earth's surface. If these were the Pishon and the Gihon, and a common source of the four rivers can be determined in Africa, the African location of the Garden of Eden would indeed be possible, given the other anthropological and archaeological evidence that points to Africa as the birthplace of humanity.

# Eve

## *The First African Woman*

The story of Eve is relevant to women of color for several reasons. It is no secret that women of color have reigned throughout history as the first women to do many things in God's world. The creation of Eve, the first woman of color, occurred on the sixth day of creation.

In the first chapters of Genesis, the story of the creation of Eve demonstrates the importance of men and women complementing one another, supporting one another and empowering one another. When women of color develop and nurture relationships—whether intimate, professional, familial or social—we must remember the importance of embracing and empowering through our role as "helper" (Ge 2:20). I define helper not only in the sense of a husband-wife team or a male-female relationship, but also inclusively from a Biblical stance: women helping women, women helping men, women helping children, women helping the community and women helping others who may or may not be like them.

Eve's story also shows the challenge of listening and hearing God when God speaks to us. When we fail to hear God's voice, we move in the wrong direction, and we commit sin. Eve first sinned when she listened to the serpent instead of God (see Ge 3:1–8). There will be times when we listen to the wrong voice, but it's important to remember that we can always go to God and seek forgiveness. There is no need to hide from God. God wants us to confess our wrongs to him. In fact, in Genesis 3:9 God asked Adam and Eve, "Where are you?" The question "Where are we in our relationship to God?" should be ever before us.

The story of Eve should remind women of color that God has created each of us in his image. We know that God has empowered and inspired many women of color to be pioneers, to be helpers and to be women who listen to the voice of God.

—P. Turner Williams

### reflection

*Where are you in your relationship with God?*

*Whose voice are you listening to?*

### read

Genesis 1:27; 2:18—4:25; Romans 5:18–19; 2 Corinthians 11:3.

**See also** the Inspire Notes "The Creation of Woman" and "The Image of God and the Beauty of the Heart."

For the next Women of the Bible note, go to page 22.

3:1 c 2Co 11:3; Rev 12:9; 20:2
3:6 d 1Ti 2:14
3:8 e Job 31:33

## The Fall of Man

3 Now the serpent[c] was more crafty than
any of the wild animals the LORD God
had made. He said to the woman, "Did God
really say, 'You must not eat from any tree
in the garden'?"
2The woman said to the serpent, "We may
eat fruit from the trees in the garden, 3but
God did say, 'You must not eat fruit from the
tree that is in the middle of the garden, and
you must not touch it, or you will die.'"
4"You will not surely die," the serpent
said to the woman. 5"For God knows that
when you eat of it your eyes will be opened,
and you will be like God, knowing good
and evil."
6When the woman saw that the fruit of
the tree was good for food and pleasing to
the eye, and also desirable for gaining wis-
dom, she took some and ate it. She also gave
some to her husband, who was with her, and
he ate it.[d] 7Then the eyes of both of them
were opened, and they realized they were
naked; so they sewed fig leaves together and
made coverings for themselves.

*Lord,*

*I'm stuck. I'm falling into temptation that I can't handle. I need escape and relief. I need the assurance that you know and understand how I'm feeling. Since you have been tempted just as I'm now being tempted, I know that your compassion for me will bring your love and power to bear in my life today, right now. In the name of Jesus, the overcomer,*

*Amen*

GENESIS 3:1–7

8Then the man and his wife heard the
sound of the LORD God as he was walking in
the garden in the cool of the day, and they
hid[e] from the LORD God among the trees of
the garden. 9But the LORD God called to the
man, "Where are you?"
10He answered, "I heard you in the gar-
den, and I was afraid because I was naked;
so I hid."
11And he said, "Who told you that you
were naked? Have you eaten from the tree
that I commanded you not to eat from?"
12The man said, "The woman you put
here with me—she gave me some fruit from
the tree, and I ate it."
13Then the LORD God said to the woman,
"What is this you have done?"
The woman said, "The serpent deceived
me, and I ate."
14So the LORD God said to the serpent, "Be-
cause you have done this,

"Cursed are you above all the livestock
and all the wild animals!
You will crawl on your belly
and you will eat dust
all the days of your life.
15 And I will put enmity
between you and the woman,
and between your offspring[a][f] and hers;
he will crush[b] your head,[g]
and you will strike his heel."

16To the woman he said,

"I will greatly increase your pains in
childbearing;
with pain you will give birth to
children.
Your desire will be for your husband,
and he will rule over you."

17To Adam he said, "Because you listened
to your wife and ate from the tree about
which I commanded you, 'You must not eat
of it,'

"Cursed[h] is the ground because of you;
through painful toil you will eat of it
all the days of your life.[i]
18 It will produce thorns and thistles for you,
and you will eat the plants of the field.
19 By the sweat of your brow
you will eat your food
until you return to the ground,
since from it you were taken;
for dust you are
and to dust you will return."[j]

3:15 f 1Jn 3:8 g Ro 16:20
3:17 h Ro 8:20–22 i Ecc 2:23
3:19 j Ge 2:7; Ps 90:3; Ecc 12:7

[a] 15 Or *seed* [b] 15 Or *strike*

> *"Next to God we are indebted to women, first for life itself, and then for making it worth living."*
> —MARY MCLEOD BETHUNE, EDUCATOR

[20]Adam[a] named his wife Eve,[b] because she would become the mother of all the living.

[21]The LORD God made garments of skin for Adam and his wife and clothed them. [22]And the LORD God said, "The man has now become like one of us, knowing good and evil. He must not be allowed to reach out his hand and take also from the tree of life[k] and eat, and live forever." [23]So the LORD God banished him from the Garden of Eden to work the ground from which he had been taken. [24]After he drove the man out, he placed on the east side[c] of the Garden of Eden cherubim and a flaming sword flashing back and forth to guard the way to the tree of life.

3:22
k Rev 22:14

4:4
l Heb 11:4

## Cain and Abel

**4** Adam[a] lay with his wife Eve, and she became pregnant and gave birth to Cain.[d] She said, "With the help of the LORD I have brought forth[e] a man." [2]Later she gave birth to his brother Abel.

Now Abel kept flocks, and Cain worked the soil. [3]In the course of time Cain brought some of the fruits of the soil as an offering to the LORD. [4]But Abel brought fat portions from some of the firstborn of his flock. The LORD looked with favor on Abel and his offering,[l] [5]but on Cain and his offering he did not look with favor. So Cain was very angry, and his face was downcast.

[6]Then the LORD said to Cain, "Why are you angry? Why is your face downcast? [7]If you do what is right, will you not be accepted? But if you do not do what is right, sin is crouching at your door; it desires to have you, but you must master it."

[8]Now Cain said to his brother Abel, "Let's go out to the field."[f] And while they were in the field, Cain attacked his brother Abel and killed him.[m]

[9]Then the LORD said to Cain, "Where is your brother Abel?"

"I don't know," he replied. "Am I my brother's keeper?"

[10]The LORD said, "What have you done? Listen! Your brother's blood cries out to me from the ground. [11]Now you are under a curse and driven from the ground, which opened its mouth to receive your brother's blood from your hand. [12]When you work the ground, it will no longer yield its crops for you. You will be a restless wanderer on the earth."

[13]Cain said to the LORD, "My punishment is more than I can bear. [14]Today you are driving me from the land, and I will be hidden from your presence;[n] I will be a restless wanderer on the earth, and whoever finds me will kill me."[o]

[15]But the LORD said to him, "Not so[g]; if anyone kills Cain[p], he will suffer vengeance seven times over." Then the LORD put a mark on Cain so that no one who found him would kill him. [16]So Cain went out from the LORD's presence and lived in the land of Nod,[h] east of Eden.

[17]Cain lay with his wife, and she became pregnant and gave birth to Enoch. Cain was then building a city, and he named it after his son Enoch. [18]To Enoch was born Irad, and Irad was the father of Mehujael, and Mehujael was the father of Methushael, and Methushael was the father of Lamech.

[19]Lamech married two women, one named Adah and the other Zillah. [20]Adah gave birth to Jabal; he was the father of those who live in tents and raise livestock. [21]His brother's name was Jubal; he was the

4:8
m Mt 23:35; 1Jn 3:12

4:14
n Ps 51:11
o Nu 35:19, 21,27,33

4:15
p Eze 9:4,6

*Woman of color.*

*When you do your best, you don't have to compete with, or become jealous of, your sister or brother.*

*Father of All*

GENESIS 4:1–7

[a]20,1 Or *The man* [b]20 *Eve* probably means *living.* [c]24 Or *placed in front* [d]1 *Cain* sounds like the Hebrew for *brought forth* or *acquired.* [e]1 Or *have acquired* [f]8 Samaritan Pentateuch, Septuagint, Vulgate and Syriac; Masoretic Text does not have *"Let's go out to the field."* [g]15 Septuagint, Vulgate and Syriac; Hebrew *Very well* [h]16 *Nod* means *wandering* (see verses 12 and 14).

4:24 q ver 15
4:25 r Ge 5:3
4:26 s Ge 12:8; 1Ki 18:24; Joel 2:32; Zep 3:9; 1Co 1:2
5:1 t Ge 1:27; Eph 4:24; Col 3:10
5:2 u Ge 1:27
5:5 v Ge 3:19

father of all who play the harp and flute. 22 Zillah also had a son, Tubal-Cain, who forged all kinds of tools out of[a] bronze and iron. Tubal-Cain's sister was Naamah.

23 Lamech said to his wives,

"Adah and Zillah, listen to me;
 wives of Lamech, hear my words.
I have killed[b] a man for wounding me,
 a young man for injuring me.
24 If Cain is avenged seven times,[q]
 then Lamech seventy-seven times."

25 Adam lay with his wife again, and she gave birth to a son and named him Seth,[c r] saying, "God has granted me another child in place of Abel, since Cain killed him." 26 Seth also had a son, and he named him Enosh.

At that time men began to call on[d] the name of the LORD.[s]

## From Adam to Noah

5 This is the written account of Adam's line.

When God created man, he made him in the likeness of God.[t] 2 He created them male and female[u] and blessed them. And when they were created, he called them "man.[e]"

3 When Adam had lived 130 years, he had a son in his own likeness, in his own image; and he named him Seth. 4 After Seth was born, Adam lived 800 years and had other sons and daughters. 5 Altogether, Adam lived 930 years, and then he died.[v]

6 When Seth had lived 105 years, he became the father[f] of Enosh. 7 And after he became the father of Enosh, Seth lived 807 years and had other sons and daughters. 8 Altogether, Seth lived 912 years, and then he died.

9 When Enosh had lived 90 years, he became the father of Kenan. 10 And after he became the father of Kenan, Enosh lived 815 years and had other sons and daughters. 11 Altogether, Enosh lived 905 years, and then he died.

12 When Kenan had lived 70 years, he became the father of Mahalalel. 13 And after he became the father of Mahalalel, Kenan lived 840 years and had other sons and daughters. 14 Altogether, Kenan lived 910 years, and then he died.

15 When Mahalalel had lived 65 years, he became the father of Jared. 16 And after he became the father of Jared, Mahalalel lived 830 years and had other sons and daughters. 17 Altogether, Mahalalel lived 895 years, and then he died.

18 When Jared had lived 162 years, he became the father of Enoch. 19 And after he became the father of Enoch, Jared lived 800 years and had other sons and daughters. 20 Altogether, Jared lived 962 years, and then he died.

21 When Enoch had lived 65 years, he became the father of Methuselah. 22 And after he became the father of Methuselah, Enoch walked with God[w] 300 years and had other sons and daughters. 23 Altogether, Enoch lived 365 years. 24 Enoch walked with God; then he was no more, because God took him away.[x]

25 When Methuselah had lived 187 years, he became the father of Lamech. 26 And after he became the father of Lamech, Methuselah lived 782 years and had other sons and daughters. 27 Altogether, Methuselah lived 969 years, and then he died.

28 When Lamech had lived 182 years, he had a son. 29 He named him Noah[g] and said, "He will comfort us in the labor and painful toil of our hands caused by the ground the LORD has cursed.[y]" 30 After Noah was born, Lamech lived 595 years and had other sons and daughters. 31 Altogether, Lamech lived 777 years, and then he died.

32 After Noah was 500 years old, he became the father of Shem, Ham and Japheth.

## The Flood

6 When men began to increase in number on the earth and daughters were born to them, 2 the sons of God saw that the daughters of men were beautiful, and they married any of them they chose. 3 Then the LORD said, "My Spirit will not contend with[h] man forever, for he is mortal[i]; his days will be a hundred and twenty years."

4 The Nephilim were on the earth in those days—and also afterward—when the sons

5:22 w ver 24; Ge 6:9; Mic 6:8
5:24 x 2Ki 2:1,11; Heb 11:5
5:29 y Ge 3:17

[a] 22 Or *who instructed all who work in* [b] 23 Or *I will kill* [c] 25 *Seth* probably means *granted.* [d] 26 Or *to proclaim*
[e] 2 Hebrew *adam* [f] 6 *Father* may mean *ancestor*; also in verses 7–26. [g] 29 *Noah* sounds like the Hebrew for *comfort.*
[h] 3 Or *My spirit will not remain in* [i] 3 Or *corrupt*

of God went to the daughters of men and had children by them. They were the heroes of old, men of renown.

[5]The LORD saw how great man's wickedness on the earth had become, and that every inclination of the thoughts of his heart was only evil all the time.[z] [6]The LORD was grieved[a] that he had made man on the earth, and his heart was filled with pain. [7]So the LORD said, "I will wipe mankind, whom I have created, from the face of the earth—men and animals, and creatures that move along the ground, and birds of the air—for I am grieved that I have made them." [8]But Noah found favor in the eyes of the LORD.[b]

[9]This is the account of Noah.

Noah was a righteous man, blameless among the people of his time,[c] and he walked with God.[d] [10]Noah had three sons: Shem, Ham and Japheth.

[11]Now the earth was corrupt in God's sight and was full of violence. [12]God saw how corrupt the earth had become, for all the people on earth had corrupted their ways.[e] [13]So God said to Noah, "I am going to put an end to all people, for the earth is filled with violence because of them. I am surely going to destroy both them and the earth. [14]So make yourself an ark of cypress[*a*] wood; make rooms in it and coat it with pitch[f] inside and out. [15]This is how you are to build it: The ark is to be 450 feet long, 75 feet wide and 45 feet high.[*b*] [16]Make a roof for it and finish[*c*] the ark to within 18 inches[*d*] of the top. Put a door in the side of the ark and make lower, middle and upper decks. [17]I am going to bring floodwaters on the earth to destroy all life under the heavens, every creature that has the breath of life in it. Everything on earth will perish. [18]But I will establish my covenant with you, and you will enter the ark—you and your sons and your wife and your sons' wives with you. [19]You are to bring into the ark two of all living creatures, male and female, to keep them alive with you. [20]Two[g] of every kind of bird, of every kind of animal and of every kind of creature that moves along the ground will come to you to be kept alive. [21]You are to take every kind of food that is to be eaten and store it away as food for you and for them."

[22]Noah did everything just as God commanded him.[h]

7 The LORD then said to Noah, "Go into the ark, you and your whole family, because I have found you righteous[i] in this generation. [2]Take with you seven[*e*] of every kind of clean[j] animal, a male and its mate, and two of every kind of unclean animal, a male and its mate, [3]and also seven of every kind of bird, male and female, to keep their various kinds alive throughout the earth. [4]Seven days from now I will send rain on the earth for forty days and forty nights, and I will wipe from the face of the earth every living creature I have made."

[5]And Noah did all that the LORD commanded him.

[6]Noah was six hundred years old when the floodwaters came on the earth. [7]And Noah and his sons and his wife and his sons' wives entered the ark to escape the waters of the flood. [8]Pairs of clean and unclean animals, of birds and of all creatures that move along the ground, [9]male and female, came to Noah and entered the ark, as God had commanded Noah. [10]And after the seven days the floodwaters came on the earth.

[11]In the six hundredth year of Noah's life, on the seventeenth day of the second month—on that day all the springs of the great deep[k] burst forth, and the floodgates of the heavens[l] were opened. [12]And rain fell on the earth forty days and forty nights.

[13]On that very day Noah and his sons, Shem, Ham and Japheth, together with his wife and the wives of his three sons, entered the ark. [14]They had with them every wild animal according to its kind, all livestock according to their kinds, every creature that moves along the ground according to its kind and every bird according to its kind, everything with wings. [15]Pairs of all creatures that have the breath of life in them came to Noah and entered the ark. [16]The animals going in were male and female of every living thing, as God had commanded Noah. Then the LORD shut him in.

[17]For forty days the flood kept coming on

**6:5** z Ge 8:21
**6:6** a Isa 63:10
**6:8** b Ge 19:19; Ex 33:12,13,17; Lk 1:30; Ac 7:46
**6:9** c Heb 11:7; 2Pe 2:5 d Ge 5:22
**6:12** e Ps 14:1-3
**6:14** f Ex 2:3
**6:20** g Ge 7:15
**6:22** h Ge 7:5,9,16
**7:1** i Ge 6:9
**7:2** j Lev 10:10; 11:1-47
**7:11** k Eze 26:19 l Ge 8:2

*a* 14 The meaning of the Hebrew for this word is uncertain. *b* 15 Hebrew *300 cubits long, 50 cubits wide and 30 cubits high* (about 140 meters long, 23 meters wide and 13.5 meters high) *c* 16 Or *Make an opening for light by finishing* *d* 16 Hebrew *a cubit* (about 0.5 meter) *e* 2 Or *seven pairs*; also in verse 3

**7:21**
m Ge 6:7,13

**7:23**
n Mt 24:39; Lk 17:27; 2Pe 2:5

the earth, and as the waters increased they lifted the ark high above the earth. 18The waters rose and increased greatly on the earth, and the ark floated on the surface of the water. 19They rose greatly on the earth, and all the high mountains under the entire heavens were covered. 20The waters rose and covered the mountains to a depth of more than twenty feet.[a,b] 21Every living thing that moved on the earth perished—birds, livestock, wild animals, all the creatures that swarm over the earth, and all mankind.[m] 22Everything on dry land that had the breath of life in its nostrils died. 23Every living thing on the face of the earth was wiped out; men and animals and the creatures that move along the ground and the birds of the air were wiped from the earth.[n] Only Noah was left, and those with him in the ark.

24The waters flooded the earth for a hundred and fifty days.

8 But God remembered Noah and all the wild animals and the livestock that were with him in the ark, and he sent a wind over the earth, and the waters receded. 2Now the springs of the deep and the floodgates of the heavens had been closed, and the rain had stopped falling from the sky. 3The water receded steadily from the earth. At the end of the hundred and fifty days the water had gone down, 4and on the seventeenth day of the seventh month the ark came to rest on the mountains of Ararat. 5The waters continued to recede until the tenth month, and on the first day of the tenth month the tops of the mountains became visible.

6After forty days Noah opened the window he had made in the ark 7and sent out a raven, and it kept flying back and forth until the water had dried up from the earth. 8Then he sent out a dove to see if the water had receded from the surface of the ground. 9But the dove could find no place to set its feet because there was water over all the surface of the earth; so it returned to Noah in the ark. He reached out his hand and took the dove and brought it back to himself in the ark. 10He waited seven more days and again sent out the dove from the ark. 11When the dove returned to him in the evening, there in its beak was a freshly plucked olive leaf! Then Noah knew that the water had receded from the earth. 12He waited seven more days and sent the dove out again, but this time it did not return to him.

13By the first day of the first month of Noah's six hundred and first year, the water had dried up from the earth. Noah then removed the covering from the ark and saw that the surface of the ground was dry. 14By the twenty-seventh day of the second month the earth was completely dry.

15Then God said to Noah, 16"Come out of the ark, you and your wife and your sons and their wives. 17Bring out every kind of living creature that is with you—the birds, the animals, and all the creatures that move along the ground—so they can multiply on the earth and be fruitful and increase in number upon it."[o]

18So Noah came out, together with his sons and his wife and his sons' wives. 19All the animals and all the creatures that move along the ground and all the birds—everything that moves on the earth—came out of the ark, one kind after another.

20Then Noah built an altar to the LORD[p] and, taking some of all the clean animals and clean birds, he sacrificed burnt offerings[q] on it. 21The LORD smelled the pleasing aroma[r] and said in his heart: "Never again will I curse the ground[s] because of man, even though[c] every inclination of his heart is evil from childhood. And never again will I destroy all living creatures,[t] as I have done.

22 "As long as the earth endures,
seedtime and harvest,
cold and heat,
summer and winter,
day and night
will never cease."

## God's Covenant With Noah

9 Then God blessed Noah and his sons, saying to them, "Be fruitful and increase in number and fill the earth.[u] 2The fear and dread of you will fall upon all the beasts of the earth and all the birds of the air, upon every creature that moves along the ground, and upon all the fish of the sea; they are given into your hands. 3Everything

**8:17**
o Ge 1:22

**8:20**
p Ge 12:7–8
q Ge 22:2,13; Ex 10:25

**8:21**
r Lev 1:9,13; 2Co 2:15
s Ge 3:17
t Ge 9:11,15; Isa 54:9

**9:1**
u Ge 1:22

[a]20 Hebrew *fifteen cubits* (about 6.9 meters) [b]20 Or *rose more than twenty feet, and the mountains were covered*
[c]21 Or *man, for*

that lives and moves will be food for you.[v] Just as I gave you the green plants, I now give you everything.

4"But you must not eat meat that has its lifeblood still in it.[w] 5And for your lifeblood I will surely demand an accounting. I will demand an accounting from every animal.[x] And from each man, too, I will demand an accounting for the life of his fellow man.[y]

6"Whoever sheds the blood of man,
by man shall his blood be shed;[z]
for in the image of God[a]
has God made man.

7As for you, be fruitful and increase in number; multiply on the earth and increase upon it."[b]

8Then God said to Noah and to his sons with him: 9"I now establish my covenant with you[c] and with your descendants after you 10and with every living creature that was with you—the birds, the livestock and all the wild animals, all those that came out of the ark with you—every living creature on earth. 11I establish my covenant with you: Never again will all life be cut off by the waters of a flood; never again will there be a flood to destroy the earth."

12And God said, "This is the sign of the covenant[d] I am making between me and you and every living creature with you, a covenant for all generations to come: 13I have set my rainbow in the clouds, and it will be the sign of the covenant between me and the earth. 14Whenever I bring clouds over the earth and the rainbow appears in the clouds, 15I will remember my covenant[e] between me and you and all living creatures of every kind. Never again will the waters become a flood to destroy all life. 16Whenever the rainbow appears in the clouds, I will see it and remember the everlasting covenant[f] between God and all living creatures of every kind on the earth."

17So God said to Noah, "This is the sign of the covenant[g] I have established between me and all life on the earth."

## The Sons of Noah

18The sons of Noah who came out of the ark were Shem, Ham and Japheth. (Ham was the father of Canaan.) 19These were the three sons of Noah, and from them came the people who were scattered over the earth.

20Noah, a man of the soil, proceeded[a] to plant a vineyard. 21When he drank some of its wine, he became drunk and lay uncovered inside his tent. 22Ham, the father of Canaan, saw his father's nakedness and told his two brothers outside. 23But Shem and

9:3 v Ge 1:29
9:4 w Lev 3:17; 17:10–14; Dt 12:16,23–25; 1Sa 14:33
9:5 x Ex 21:28–32 y Ge 4:10
9:6 z Ex 21:12,14; Lev 24:17; Mt 26:52 a Ge 1:26
9:7 b Ge 1:22
9:9 c Ge 6:18
9:12 d Ge 17:11
9:15 e Lev 26:42,45
9:16 f Ge 17:7,13,19
9:17 g ver 12; Ge 17:11

[a]20 Or *soil, was the first*

## The African Presence

### Genesis 9:18–27

**When Noah learned what his son Ham had done, he cursed Canaan, Ham's son. Exegetes first tried to reconcile the curse on Canaan instead of Ham by arguing that Canaan was actually Noah's fourth and youngest son, making him Ham's brother rather than his son. Others tried to resolve the problem by removing "Ham, the father of" from verse 22, making Canaan the perpetrator of the act. Medieval Jewish, Christian and Muslim theologians misinterpreted Noah's statement, transferring the curse from Canaan to Ham. The misnomer "the Curse of Ham," which became the common misconception, took on racial implications in the Middle Ages. Some justified the African slave trade on the basis that God had ordained that Ham's black descendants be slaves to the descendants of Shem and Japheth on account of Ham's sin.**

9:25
h ver 18
i Ge 25:23

Japheth took a garment and laid it across
their shoulders; then they walked in back-
ward and covered their father's nakedness.
Their faces were turned the other way so that
they would not see their father's nakedness.
24 When Noah awoke from his wine and
found out what his youngest son had done
to him, 25 he said,

"Cursed be Canaan![h]
The lowest of slaves
will he be to his brothers.[i]"

26 He also said,

"Blessed be the LORD, the God of Shem!
May Canaan be the slave of Shem.[a]
27 May God extend the territory of Japheth[b];
may Japheth live in the tents of Shem,
and may Canaan be his[c] slave."

28 After the flood Noah lived 350 years.
29 Altogether, Noah lived 950 years, and then
he died.

## The Table of Nations

**10** This is the account of Shem, Ham and Japheth, Noah's sons, who themselves had sons after the flood.

### The Japhethites

2 The sons[d] of Japheth:
Gomer, Magog, Madai, Javan, Tubal, Meshech and Tiras.

3 The sons of Gomer:
Ashkenaz, Riphath and Togarmah.[j]

4 The sons of Javan:
Elishah, Tarshish,[k] the Kittim and
the Rodanim.[e] 5 (From these the mar-
itime peoples spread out into their territories by their clans within their nations, each with its own language.)

### The Hamites

6 The sons of Ham:
Cush, Mizraim,[f] Put and Canaan.[l]

7 The sons of Cush:
Seba, Havilah, Sabtah, Raamah and Sabteca.

The sons of Raamah:
Sheba and Dedan.

8 Cush was the father[g] of Nimrod, who
grew to be a mighty warrior on the earth.
9 He was a mighty hunter before the LORD;
that is why it is said, "Like Nimrod, a mighty
hunter before the LORD." 10 The first centers
of his kingdom were Babylon,[m] Erech, Ak-
kad and Calneh, in[h] Shinar.[i] 11 From that
land he went to Assyria,[n] where he built
Nineveh, Rehoboth Ir,[j] Calah 12 and Resen,
which is between Nineveh and Calah; that
is the great city.

13 Mizraim was the father of
the Ludites, Anamites, Lehabites,

10:3
j Eze 38:6
10:4
k Jnh 1:3
10:6
l ver 15; Ge 9:18
10:10
m Ge 11:9
10:11
n Mic 5:6

[a]26 Or *be his slave* [b]27 *Japheth* sounds like the Hebrew for *extend.* [c]27 Or *their* [d]2 *Sons* may mean *descendants* or *successors* or *nations*; also in verses 3, 4, 6, 7, 20–23, 29 and 31. [e]4 Some manuscripts of the Masoretic Text and Samaritan Pentateuch (see also Septuagint and 1 Chron. 1:7); most manuscripts of the Masoretic Text *Dodanim* [f]6 That is, Egypt; also in verse 13 [g]8 *Father* may mean *ancestor* or *predecessor* or *founder*; also in verses 13, 15, 24 and 26. [h]10 Or *Erech and Akkad—all of them in* [i]10 That is, Babylonia [j]11 Or *Nineveh with its city squares*

## The African Presence

### Genesis 10

After the Genesis flood, the sons of Noah migrated in several directions: Japheth and his children represent nations to the north and west of Canaan (including present-day Europe and northeastern Asia); Ham and his children represent nations in Mesopotamia/Asia as well as the continent of Africa; Shem and his children represent nations in Mesopotamia/Asia. The story of Nimrod, grandson of Ham and son of Cush, establishes the African presence in Mesopotamia: "The first centers of [Nimrod's] kingdom were Babylon, Erech, Akkad and Calneh, in Shinar. From that land he went to Assyria, where he built Nineveh" (vv. 10–11).

**10:15** o ver 6; Ge 9:18
**10:19** p Ge 13:12; 17:8
**10:21** q ver 24; Nu 24:24
**10:23** r Job 1:1
**10:24** s ver 21

Naphtuhites, [14]Pathrusites, Casluhites (from whom the Philistines came) and Caphtorites.

[15]Canaan[o] was the father of
Sidon his firstborn,[a] and of the Hittites, [16]Jebusites, Amorites, Girgashites, [17]Hivites, Arkites, Sinites, [18]Arvadites, Zemarites and Hamathites.

Later the Canaanite clans scattered [19]and the borders of Canaan[p] reached from Sidon toward Gerar as far as Gaza, and then toward Sodom, Gomorrah, Admah and Zeboiim, as far as Lasha.

[20]These are the sons of Ham by their clans and languages, in their territories and nations.

### The Semites

[21]Sons were also born to Shem, whose older brother was[b] Japheth; Shem was the ancestor of all the sons of Eber.[q]

[22]The sons of Shem:
Elam, Asshur, Arphaxad, Lud and Aram.

[23]The sons of Aram:
Uz,[r] Hul, Gether and Meshech.[c]

[24]Arphaxad was the father of[d] Shelah,
and Shelah the father of Eber.[s]

[25]Two sons were born to Eber:
One was named Peleg,[e] because in his time the earth was divided; his brother was named Joktan.

[26]Joktan was the father of
Almodad, Sheleph, Hazarmaveth, Jerah, [27]Hadoram, Uzal, Diklah, [28]Obal, Abimael, Sheba, [29]Ophir, Havilah and Jobab. All these were sons of Joktan.

[30]The region where they lived stretched from Mesha toward Sephar, in the eastern hill country.

[31]These are the sons of Shem by their clans and languages, in their territories and nations.

[32]These are the clans of Noah's sons,[t] according to their lines of descent, within their nations. From these the nations spread out over the earth[u] after the flood.

### The Tower of Babel

11 Now the whole world had one language and a common speech. [2]As men moved eastward,[f] they found a plain in Shinar[g] and settled there.

[3]They said to each other, "Come, let's make bricks and bake them thoroughly."

**10:32** t ver 1
u Ge 9:19

[a]15 Or *of the Sidonians, the foremost* [b]21 Or *Shem, the older brother of* [c]23 See Septuagint and 1 Chron. 1:17; Hebrew *Mash* [d]24 Hebrew; Septuagint *father of Cainan, and Cainan was the father of* [e]25 *Peleg* means *division.* [f]2 Or *from the east*; or *in the east* [g]2 That is, Babylonia

## *The African Presence*

### Genesis 10:6

Mizraim/Egypt/Egyptians are mentioned some 100 times in Genesis (see chs. 10; 12–13; 15–16; 21; 25–26; 37; 39–43; 45–50). *Mizraim* is the Hebrew word designating the people who were otherwise called Egyptians.

Prior to Alexander the Great conquering the land in 332 B.C., the people along the Nile River called themselves *Kemet.*

*KMT* or *kemet* is the Egyptian word, a combination of *km* ("black") and the suffix *t* (literally "thing" or "land"). *Kemet* can mean "black land" or sometimes "people of the black land." It is generally assumed to reference the dark soil of the Nile Valley. The term *KMM.W* or *kememew* was a term also sometimes used by the Egyptians; it means "the black people."

The ancient Egyptians traced their origins to a land they called Punt, or "Ta Neteru" ("Land of the Gods"), believed to be located in the Ethiopian Highlands.

**11:4** v Dt 1:28
**11:5** w ver 7; Ge 18:21
**11:7** x Ge 1:26 y Ge 42:23
**11:8** z Lk 1:51

They used brick instead of stone, and tar for mortar. 4Then they said, "Come, let us build ourselves a city, with a tower that reaches to the heavens,[v] so that we may make a name for ourselves and not be scattered over the face of the whole earth."

5But the LORD came down[w] to see the city and the tower that the men were building. 6The LORD said, "If as one people speaking the same language they have begun to do this, then nothing they plan to do will be impossible for them. 7Come, let us[x] go down and confuse their language so they will not understand each other."[y]

8So the LORD scattered them from there over all the earth,[z] and they stopped building the city. 9That is why it was called Babel[a]—because there the LORD confused the language of the whole world. From there the LORD scattered them over the face of the whole earth.

## From Shem to Abram

10This is the account of Shem.

Two years after the flood, when Shem was 100 years old, he became the father[b] of Arphaxad. 11And after he became the father of Arphaxad, Shem lived 500 years and had other sons and daughters.

12When Arphaxad had lived 35 years, he became the father of Shelah. 13And after he became the father of Shelah, Arphaxad lived 403 years and had other sons and daughters.[c]

14When Shelah had lived 30 years, he became the father of Eber. 15And after he became the father of Eber, Shelah lived 403 years and had other sons and daughters.

16When Eber had lived 34 years, he became the father of Peleg. 17And after he became the father of Peleg, Eber lived 430 years and had other sons and daughters.

18When Peleg had lived 30 years, he became the father of Reu. 19And after he became the father of Reu, Peleg lived 209 years and had other sons and daughters.

20When Reu had lived 32 years, he became the father of Serug. 21And after he became the father of Serug, Reu lived 207 years and had other sons and daughters.

22When Serug had lived 30 years, he became the father of Nahor. 23And after he became the father of Nahor, Serug lived 200 years and had other sons and daughters.

[a]9 That is, Babylon; *Babel* sounds like the Hebrew for *confused.* [b]10 *Father* may mean *ancestor*; also in verses 11–25. [c]12,13 Hebrew; Septuagint (see also Luke 3:35, 36 and note at Gen. 10:24) *35 years, he became the father of Cainan.* 13*And after he became the father of Cainan, Arphaxad lived 430 years and had other sons and daughters, and then he died. When Cainan had lived 130 years, he became the father of Shelah. And after he became the father of Shelah, Cainan lived 330 years and had other sons and daughters*

## The African Presence

### Genesis 10:6–12

Several geographic locations and people group names indicate the presence of people of color in these chapters. They represent the peoples and nations south and southwest of Biblical Israel. Among them are: (1) Ham or Hamites. *Ham* is the Hebrew adjective for "warm" or "hot." The word is used in the Psalms to collectively represent the Egyptians or the land of Egypt (see Ps 105:23,27; 106:22). Ham's name could refer to the warmth of the geographic region attributed to him. (2) Cush or Cushites, called "Ethiopians" in some Bible translations. Biblical Ethiopia is not present-day Ethiopia, but a region located south of Egypt (see the African Presence note on Ex 5:1–5). (3) Mizraim or Mizraimites. The word means "two Egypts," referring to Upper and Lower Egypt. (4) Put (either Libya or modern Somalia). (5) Canaan or Canaanites (Babylon and Assyria). It is not necessary to assert that all these people were "coal" black to establish that they had ties to African heritage.

11:26
a Jos 24:2

11:27
b ver 31; Ge 12:4

11:29
c Ge 17:15

11:30
d Ge 16:1

11:31
e Ge 15:7; Ne 9:7; Ac 7:4

12:1
f Ac 7:3*; Heb 11:8

24 When Nahor had lived 29 years, he
became the father of Terah. 25 And after he
became the father of Terah, Nahor lived 119
years and had other sons and daughters.
26 After Terah had lived 70 years, he became
the father of Abram, Nahor[a] and Haran.

27 This is the account of Terah.

Terah became the father of Abram, Nahor
and Haran. And Haran became the father of
Lot.[b] 28 While his father Terah was still alive,
Haran died in Ur of the Chaldeans, in the
land of his birth. 29 Abram and Nahor both
married. The name of Abram's wife was
Sarai,[c] and the name of Nahor's wife was
Milcah; she was the daughter of Haran, the
father of both Milcah and Iscah. 30 Now Sarai
was barren; she had no children.[d]
31 Terah took his son Abram, his grand-
son Lot son of Haran, and his daughter-in-
law Sarai, the wife of his son Abram, and
together they set out from Ur of the Chalde-
ans[e] to go to Canaan. But when they came to
Haran, they settled there.
32 Terah lived 205 years, and he died in
Haran.

## The Call of Abram

12 The LORD had said to Abram, "Leave
your country, your people and your
father's household and go to the land I will
show you.[f]

2 "I will make you into a great nation[g]
and I will bless you;
I will make your name great,
and you will be a blessing.
3 I will bless those who bless you,
and whoever curses you I will curse;[h]
and all peoples on earth
will be blessed through you.[i]"

4 So Abram left, as the LORD had told him;
and Lot went with him. Abram was seventy-
five years old when he set out from Haran. 5 He
took his wife Sarai, his nephew Lot, all the pos-
sessions they had accumulated and the people[j]
they had acquired in Haran, and they set out
for the land of Canaan, and they arrived there.
6 Abram traveled through the land as far
as the site of the great tree of Moreh at She-
chem. At that time the Canaanites were in
the land. 7 The LORD appeared to Abram[k]
and said, "To your offspring[a] I will give this
land."[l] So he built an altar there to the LORD,
who had appeared to him.
8 From there he went on toward the hills
east of Bethel[m] and pitched his tent, with
Bethel on the west and Ai on the east. There
he built an altar to the LORD and called on
the name of the LORD. 9 Then Abram set out
and continued toward the Negev.

## Abram in Egypt

10 Now there was a famine in the land, and
Abram went down to Egypt to live there for

12:2
g Ge 17:2,4; 18:18

12:3
h Ge 27:29; Nu 24:9
i Ge 22:18; 26:4; Ac 3:25; Gal 3:8*

12:5
j Ge 14:14

12:7
k Ge 17:1
l Ge 13:15,17; Ps 105:9–11

12:8
m Ge 13:3

[a]7 Or *seed*

## The African Presence

### Genesis 12:10

Historical records indicate that people of African descent can be identified all the way from the southern coasts of Africa into Asia and all around the Pacific Rim. Archaeological findings, such as inscriptions and paintings on walls, pottery and tombs in Mesopotamia and Egypt, show people with African features.

The name "Egypt" is a Greek term. Before the arrival of Greeks, the native people called their land *Kemet* (see the African Presence note on Ge 10:6). Some scholars have argued that *kemet* is a reference to both the land and its people, while others claim that the term refers only to the black soil.

a while because the famine was severe. 11 As he was about to enter Egypt, he said to his wife Sarai, "I know what a beautiful woman you are. 12 When the Egyptians see you, they will say, 'This is his wife.' Then they will kill me but will let you live. 13 Say you are my sister, so that I will be treated well for your sake and my life will be spared because of you."

14 When Abram came to Egypt, the Egyptians saw that she was a very beautiful woman. 15 And when Pharaoh's officials saw her, they praised her to Pharaoh, and she was taken into his palace. 16 He treated Abram well for her sake, and Abram acquired sheep and cattle, male and female donkeys, menservants and maidservants, and camels.

17 But the LORD inflicted serious diseases on Pharaoh and his household[n] because of Abram's wife Sarai. 18 So Pharaoh summoned Abram. "What have you done to me?" he said. "Why didn't you tell me she was your wife? 19 Why did you say, 'She is my sister,' so that I took her to be my wife? Now then, here is your wife. Take her and go!" 20 Then Pharaoh gave orders about Abram to his men, and they sent him on his way, with his wife and everything he had.

## Abram and Lot Separate

**13** So Abram went up from Egypt to the Negev, with his wife and everything he had, and Lot went with him. 2 Abram had become very wealthy in livestock and in silver and gold.

3 From the Negev he went from place to place until he came to Bethel, to the place between Bethel and Ai where his tent had been earlier 4 and where he had first built an altar.[o] There Abram called on the name of the LORD.

5 Now Lot, who was moving about with Abram, also had flocks and herds and tents. 6 But the land could not support them while they stayed together, for their possessions were so great that they were not able to stay together. 7 And quarreling[p] arose between Abram's herdsmen and the herdsmen of Lot. The Canaanites and Perizzites were also living in the land at that time.

8 So Abram said to Lot, "Let's not have any quarreling between you and me, or between your herdsmen and mine, for we are brothers. 9 Is not the whole land before you? Let's part company. If you go to the left, I'll go to the right; if you go to the right, I'll go to the left."

10 Lot looked up and saw that the whole plain of the Jordan was well watered, like the garden of the LORD,[q] like the land of Egypt, toward Zoar.[r] (This was before the LORD destroyed Sodom and Gomorrah.)[s] 11 So Lot chose for himself the whole plain of the Jordan and set out toward the east. The two men parted company: 12 Abram lived in the land of Canaan, while Lot lived among the cities of the plain and pitched his tents near Sodom. 13 Now the men of Sodom were wicked and were sinning greatly against the LORD.[t]

14 The LORD said to Abram after Lot had parted from him, "Lift up your eyes from where you are and look north and south, east and west. 15 All the land that you see I will give to you and your offspring[a] forever.[u] 16 I will make your offspring like the dust of the earth, so that if anyone could count the dust, then your offspring could be counted. 17 Go, walk through the length and breadth of the land,[v] for I am giving it to you."

18 So Abram moved his tents and went to live near the great trees of Mamre[w] at Hebron, where he built an altar to the LORD.

## Abram Rescues Lot

**14** At this time Amraphel king of Shinar,[b] Arioch king of Ellasar, Kedorlaomer king of Elam and Tidal king of Goiim 2 went to war against Bera king of Sodom, Birsha king of Gomorrah, Shinab king of Admah, Shemeber king of Zeboiim, and the king of Bela (that is, Zoar). 3 All these latter kings joined forces in the Valley of Siddim (the Salt Sea[c][x]). 4 For twelve years they had been subject to Kedorlaomer, but in the thirteenth year they rebelled.

5 In the fourteenth year, Kedorlaomer and the kings allied with him went out and defeated the Rephaites in Ashteroth Karnaim, the Zuzites in Ham, the Emites in Shaveh Kiriathaim 6 and the Horites[y] in the hill country of Seir, as far as El Paran near

**12:17** n 1Ch 16:21
**13:4** o Ge 12:7
**13:7** p Ge 26:20,21
**13:10** q Ge 2:8–10 r Ge 19:22,30 s Ge 19:17–29
**13:13** t Ge 18:20; 2Pe 2:8
**13:15** u Ge 12:7; Gal 3:16*
**13:17** v Nu 13:17–25
**13:18** w Ge 14:13,24
**14:3** x Nu 34:3,12; Jos 3:16
**14:6** y Dt 2:12,22

[a] 15 Or *seed*; also in verse 16 [b] 1 That is, Babylonia; also in verse 9 [c] 3 That is, the Dead Sea

the desert. 7 Then they turned back and went to En Mishpat (that is, Kadesh), and they conquered the whole territory of the Amalekites, as well as the Amorites who were living in Hazazon Tamar.

8 Then the king of Sodom, the king of Gomorrah, the king of Admah, the king of Zeboiim and the king of Bela (that is, Zoar) marched out and drew up their battle lines in the Valley of Siddim 9 against Kedorlaomer king of Elam, Tidal king of Goiim, Amraphel king of Shinar and Arioch king of Ellasar—four kings against five. 10 Now the Valley of Siddim was full of tar pits, and when the kings of Sodom and Gomorrah fled, some of the men fell into them and the rest fled to the hills. 11 The four kings seized all the goods of Sodom and Gomorrah and all their food; then they went away. 12 They also carried off Abram's nephew Lot and his possessions, since he was living in Sodom.

13 One who had escaped came and reported this to Abram the Hebrew. Now Abram was living near the great trees of Mamre[z] the Amorite, a brother[a] of Eshcol and Aner, all of whom were allied with Abram. 14 When Abram heard that his relative had been taken captive, he called out the 318 trained men born in his household[a] and went in pursuit as far as Dan. 15 During the night Abram divided his men to attack them and he routed them, pursuing them as far as Hobah, north of Damascus. 16 He recovered all the goods and brought back his relative Lot and his possessions, together with the women and the other people.

17 After Abram returned from defeating Kedorlaomer and the kings allied with him, the king of Sodom came out to meet him in the Valley of Shaveh (that is, the King's Valley).[b]

18 Then Melchizedek[c] king of Salem[b][d] brought out bread and wine. He was priest of God Most High, 19 and he blessed Abram, saying,

"Blessed be Abram by God Most High,
  Creator[c] of heaven and earth.[e]
20 And blessed be[d] God Most High,[f]
  who delivered your enemies into your
    hand."

Then Abram gave him a tenth of everything.[g]

21 The king of Sodom said to Abram, "Give me the people and keep the goods for yourself."

22 But Abram said to the king of Sodom, "I have raised my hand to the LORD, God Most High, Creator of heaven and earth, and have taken an oath 23 that I will accept nothing belonging to you, not even a thread or the thong of a sandal, so that you will never be able to say, 'I made Abram rich.' 24 I will accept nothing but what my men have eaten and the share that belongs to the men who went with me—to Aner, Eshcol and Mamre. Let them have their share."

## God's Covenant With Abram

15 After this, the word of the LORD came to Abram in a vision:

"Do not be afraid,[h] Abram.
  I am your shield,[e][i]
  your very great reward.[f]"

2 But Abram said, "O Sovereign LORD, what can you give me since I remain childless and the one who will inherit[g] my estate is Eliezer of Damascus?" 3 And Abram said, "You have given me no children; so a servant in my household will be my heir."

*Lord,*

*I pray that I will clearly hear your unique and distinctive call on my life. Don't let me get sidetracked with things that are nonessential to your purpose. Lift my eyes above my circumstances so I will not become discouraged by temporary inconveniences. Give me patience to wait for your perfect timing.*

*Amen*

GENESIS 15:1–6

**14:13** z ver 24; Ge 13:18
**14:14** a Ge 15:3
**14:17** b 2Sa 18:18
**14:18** c Ps 110:4; Heb 5:6 d Heb 7:2
**14:19** e ver 22
**14:20** f Ge 24:27
**14:20** g Heb 7:4
**15:1** h Ge 21:17; 26:24; Isa 41:10,13–14 i Dt 33:29

[a]13 Or *a relative*; or *an ally* [b]18 That is, Jerusalem [c]19 Or *Possessor*; also in verse 22 [d]20 Or *And praise be to*
[e]1 Or *sovereign* [f]1 Or *shield; / your reward will be very great* [g]2 The meaning of the Hebrew for this phrase is uncertain.

**15:5** j Ro 4:18*; Heb 11:12
**15:6** k Ro 4:3*,20–24*; Gal 3:6*; Jas 2:23*
**15:12** l Ge 2:21
**15:13** m Ex 12:40; Ac 7:6,17
**15:14** n Ac 7:7* o Ex 12:32–38
**15:15** p Ge 25:8

4Then the word of the LORD came to him: "This man will not be your heir, but a son coming from your own body will be your heir." 5He took him outside and said, "Look up at the heavens and count the stars—if indeed you can count them." Then he said to him, "So shall your offspring be."[j]

6Abram believed the LORD, and he credited it to him as righteousness.[k]

7He also said to him, "I am the LORD, who brought you out of Ur of the Chaldeans to give you this land to take possession of it."

8But Abram said, "O Sovereign LORD, how can I know that I will gain possession of it?"

9So the LORD said to him, "Bring me a heifer, a goat and a ram, each three years old, along with a dove and a young pigeon."

10Abram brought all these to him, cut them in two and arranged the halves opposite each other; the birds, however, he did not cut in half. 11Then birds of prey came down on the carcasses, but Abram drove them away.

12As the sun was setting, Abram fell into a deep sleep,[l] and a thick and dreadful darkness came over him. 13Then the LORD said to him, "Know for certain that your descendants will be strangers in a country not their own, and they will be enslaved and mistreated four hundred years.[m] 14But I will punish the nation they serve as slaves, and afterward they will come out[n] with great possessions.[o] 15You, however, will go to your fathers in peace and be buried at a good old age.[p] 16In the fourth generation your descendants will come back here, for the sin of the Amorites has not yet reached its full measure."

17When the sun had set and darkness had fallen, a smoking firepot with a blazing torch appeared and passed between the pieces. 18On that day the LORD made a covenant with Abram and said, "To your descendants I give this land, from the river[a] of Egypt to the great river, the Euphrates— 19the land of the Kenites, Kenizzites, Kadmonites, 20Hittites, Perizzites, Rephaites, 21Amorites, Canaanites, Girgashites and Jebusites."

## Hagar and Ishmael

**16** Now Sarai, Abram's wife, had borne him no children. But she had an Egyptian maidservant named Hagar; 2so she said to Abram, "The LORD has kept me from having children. Go, sleep with my maidservant; perhaps I can build a family through her."[q]

Abram agreed to what Sarai said. 3So after Abram had been living in Canaan[r] ten years, Sarai his wife took her Egyptian maidservant Hagar and gave her to her husband to be his wife. 4He slept with Hagar, and she conceived.

When she knew she was pregnant, she began to despise her mistress. 5Then Sarai said to Abram, "You are responsible for the wrong I am suffering. I put my servant in your arms, and now that she knows she is pregnant, she despises me. May the LORD judge between you and me."[s]

6"Your servant is in your hands," Abram said. "Do with her whatever you think best."

**16:2** q Ge 30:3–4, 9–10
**16:3** r Ge 12:5
**16:5** s Ge 31:53

[a]18 Or *Wadi*

## The African Presence

### Genesis 16:1

Notable people of African descent are: (1) Hagar (see Ge 16:1; 21:9); (2) Hagar's son Ishmael, who was Egyptian and Israelite (see Ge 16:15); (3) Ishmael's unnamed Egyptian wife (see Ge 21:21); and (4) Ephraim and Manasseh, sons of Joseph by Asenath, the daughter of Potiphera, the Egyptian priest of On (see Ge 41:50–52).

# Hagar

## Battered, Beaten and Rejected—but Not Abandoned

Given her story, it's no surprise that women of color find a kindred spirit in the person of Hagar. She was a young slave from Egypt who found herself in the midst of a foreign, nomadic people. She was forced to give her body to her master, Abram—an idea first proposed by his wife, Sarai (see Ge 16:1–3). But once she obeyed her mistress and master, she was rejected and scorned.

Sarai's mistreatment of the pregnant Hagar forced the young woman to run away. Hagar fled into the desert where she met the angel of God. He told her to return to Sarai and give birth to Abram's son, Ishmael, who would become the father of a nation. Hagar was amazed that the living God saw her. Filled with hope, Hagar returned and gave birth to her son (see Ge 16:4–15).

In God's time and by God's grace, the promised son, Isaac, was born to Sarah and Abraham (see Ge 21:1–7), whose names were changed by God before Isaac's birth. After Isaac's birth Sarah saw Hagar's child as a threat to Isaac's position as heir, so she implored Abraham to expel them (see Ge 21:8–13).

Hagar and Ishmael were sent into the desert with a meager supply of food and water. When the water ran out, Hagar sat apart from her son so as not to witness his death. Again the angel of God appeared to reassure her of God's plan and to reveal to her a well of drinking water. Refreshed, renewed and redirected, Hagar raised her son alone. Ishmael grew to be a strong, powerful man and founder of the Arab nations (see Ge 21:14–21; 25:13–18).

Disadvantaged and dispossessed women today can relate to Hagar. Many have experienced estrangement, prejudice, hardship, hopelessness, grief and despair. Many have known the fear that accompanies being an abandoned, pregnant woman alone in the world. Regardless of your circumstances, your social status, or how many times you've been knocked down, battered and beaten by life, you cannot escape God's care. God provided for Hagar and her son, and he can and will provide for you.

—T. Wade

### reflection

*Reflect on a time when you felt battered, beaten and rejected. How did God refresh, renew and redirect you?*

*Consider sharing your testimony with a woman who is experiencing rejection.*

### read

Genesis 16; 21; 25:12–18.

**See also** the Inspire Notes "Single Mothers," "Overcoming Abuse," "Single Parenting" and "Abandonment."

For the next Women of the Bible note, go to page 27.

**16:12** t Ge 25:18
**17:1** u Ge 28:3; v Dt 18:13
**17:5** w ver 15; Ne 9:7; x Ro 4:17*
**17:6** y Ge 35:11

Then Sarai mistreated Hagar; so she fled
from her.
7 The angel of the LORD found Hagar near
a spring in the desert; it was the spring that
is beside the road to Shur. 8 And he said, "Ha-
gar, servant of Sarai, where have you come
from, and where are you going?"
"I'm running away from my mistress
Sarai," she answered.
9 Then the angel of the LORD told her, "Go
back to your mistress and submit to her."
10 The angel added, "I will so increase your
descendants that they will be too numerous
to count."
11 The angel of the LORD also said to her:

"You are now with child
and you will have a son.
You shall name him Ishmael,[a]
for the LORD has heard of your misery.
12 He will be a wild donkey of a man;
his hand will be against everyone
and everyone's hand against him,
and he will live in hostility
toward[b] all his brothers.[t]"

13 She gave this name to the LORD who
spoke to her: "You are the God who sees
me," for she said, "I have now seen[c] the One
who sees me." 14 That is why the well was
called Beer Lahai Roi[d]; it is still there, be-
tween Kadesh and Bered.
15 So Hagar bore Abram a son, and Abram
gave the name Ishmael to the son she had
borne. 16 Abram was eighty-six years old
when Hagar bore him Ishmael.

## The Covenant of Circumcision

17 When Abram was ninety-nine years
old, the LORD appeared to him and
said, "I am God Almighty[e];[u] walk before me
and be blameless.[v] 2 I will confirm my cov-
enant between me and you and will greatly
increase your numbers."
3 Abram fell facedown, and God said to
him, 4 "As for me, this is my covenant with
you: You will be the father of many nations.
5 No longer will you be called Abram[f]; your
name will be Abraham,[g][w] for I have made
you a father of many nations.[x] 6 I will make
you very fruitful;[y] I will make nations of
you, and kings will come from you. 7 I will
establish my covenant as an everlasting
covenant between me and you and your de-
scendants after you for the generations to
come, to be your God and the God of your
descendants after you.[z] 8 The whole land of
Canaan, where you are now an alien, I will
give as an everlasting possession to you and
your descendants after you;[a] and I will be
their God."
9 Then God said to Abraham, "As for you,
you must keep my covenant, you and your
descendants after you for the generations to
come. 10 This is my covenant with you and
your descendants after you, the covenant
you are to keep: Every male among you
shall be circumcised.[b] 11 You are to undergo
circumcision, and it will be the sign of the
covenant[c] between me and you. 12 For the
generations to come every male among you
who is eight days old must be circumcised,[d]
including those born in your household
or bought with money from a foreigner—
those who are not your offspring. 13 Whether
born in your household or bought with your
money, they must be circumcised. My cov-
enant in your flesh is to be an everlasting
covenant. 14 Any uncircumcised male, who
has not been circumcised in the flesh, will
be cut off from his people; he has broken
my covenant."
15 God also said to Abraham, "As for Sarai
your wife, you are no longer to call her Sarai;
her name will be Sarah. 16 I will bless her and
will surely give you a son by her. I will bless
her so that she will be the mother of nations;
kings of peoples will come from her."
17 Abraham fell facedown; he laughed[e]
and said to himself, "Will a son be born to a
man a hundred years old? Will Sarah bear a
child at the age of ninety?" 18 And Abraham
said to God, "If only Ishmael might live un-
der your blessing!"
19 Then God said, "Yes, but your wife
Sarah will bear you a son,[f] and you will
call him Isaac.[h] I will establish my cov-
enant with him as an everlasting covenant
for his descendants after him. 20 And as
for Ishmael, I have heard you: I will surely
bless him; I will make him fruitful and will

**17:7** z Ro 9:8; Gal 3:16
**17:8** a Ge 12:7
**17:10** b ver 23; Ac 7:8
**17:11** c Ro 4:11
**17:12** d Lev 12:3
**17:17** e Ge 18:12; 21:6
**17:19** f Ge 18:14; 21:2

[a]11 *Ishmael* means *God hears.* [b]12 Or *live to the east / of* [c]13 Or *seen the back of* [d]14 *Beer Lahai Roi* means *well of the Living One who sees me.* [e]1 Hebrew *El-Shaddai* [f]5 *Abram* means *exalted father.* [g]5 *Abraham* means *father of many.* [h]19 *Isaac* means *he laughs.*

greatly increase his numbers.[g] He will be the father of twelve rulers,[h] and I will make him into a great nation.[i] 21But my covenant I will establish with Isaac, whom Sarah will bear to you by this time next year." 22When he had finished speaking with Abraham, God went up from him.

23On that very day Abraham took his son Ishmael and all those born in his household or bought with his money, every male in his household, and circumcised them, as God told him. 24Abraham was ninety-nine years old when he was circumcised, 25and his son Ishmael was thirteen; 26Abraham and his son Ishmael were both circumcised on that same day. 27And every male in Abraham's household, including those born in his household or bought from a foreigner, was circumcised with him.

## The Three Visitors

**18** The LORD appeared to Abraham near the great trees of Mamre[j] while he was sitting at the entrance to his tent in the heat of the day. 2Abraham looked up and saw three men[k] standing nearby. When he saw them, he hurried from the entrance of his tent to meet them and bowed low to the ground.

3He said, "If I have found favor in your eyes, my lord,[a] do not pass your servant by. 4Let a little water be brought, and then you may all wash your feet[l] and rest under this tree. 5Let me get you something to eat, so you can be refreshed and then go on your way—now that you have come to your servant."

"Very well," they answered, "do as you say."

6So Abraham hurried into the tent to Sarah. "Quick," he said, "get three seahs[b] of fine flour and knead it and bake some bread."

7Then he ran to the herd and selected a choice, tender calf and gave it to a servant, who hurried to prepare it. 8He then brought some curds and milk and the calf that had been prepared, and set these before them. While they ate, he stood near them under a tree.

9"Where is your wife Sarah?" they asked him.

"There, in the tent," he said.

10Then the LORD[c] said, "I will surely return to you about this time next year, and Sarah your wife will have a son."[m]

Now Sarah was listening at the entrance to the tent, which was behind him. 11Abraham and Sarah were already old and well advanced in years,[n] and Sarah was past the age of childbearing.[o] 12So Sarah laughed[p] to herself as she thought, "After I am worn out and my master[d][q] is old, will I now have this pleasure?"

13Then the LORD said to Abraham, "Why did Sarah laugh and say, 'Will I really have a child, now that I am old?' 14Is anything too hard for the LORD?[r] I will return to you at the appointed time next year and Sarah will have a son."

15Sarah was afraid, so she lied and said, "I did not laugh."

But he said, "Yes, you did laugh."

## Abraham Pleads for Sodom

16When the men got up to leave, they looked down toward Sodom, and Abraham walked along with them to see them on their way. 17Then the LORD said, "Shall I hide from Abraham what I am about to do? 18Abraham will surely become a great and powerful nation,[s] and all nations on earth will be blessed through him. 19For I have chosen him, so that he will direct his children[t] and his household after him to keep the way of the LORD by doing what is right and just, so that the LORD will bring about for Abraham what he has promised him."

20Then the LORD said, "The outcry against Sodom and Gomorrah is so great and their sin so grievous 21that I will go down and see if what they have done is as bad as the outcry that has reached me. If not, I will know."

22The men turned away and went toward Sodom, but Abraham remained standing before the LORD.[e] 23Then Abraham approached him and said: "Will you sweep away the righteous with the wicked?[u] 24What if there are fifty righteous people in the city? Will you really sweep it away and not spare[f] the place for the sake of the fifty righteous people in it?[v] 25Far be it from you to do such a thing—to kill the righteous with the

[a] 3 Or *O Lord* [b] 6 That is, probably about 20 quarts (about 22 liters) [c] 10 Hebrew *Then he* [d] 12 Or *husband* [e] 22 Masoretic Text; an ancient Hebrew scribal tradition *but the LORD remained standing before Abraham* [f] 24 Or *forgive*; also in verse 26

**17:20** g Ge 16:10 h Ge 25:12–16 i Ge 21:18
**18:1** j Ge 13:18; 14:13
**18:2** k ver 16,22; Heb 13:2
**18:4** l Ge 19:2; 43:24
**18:10** m Ro 9:9*
**18:11** n Ge 17:17 o Ro 4:19
**18:12** p Ge 17:17; 21:6 q 1Pe 3:6
**18:14** r Jer 32:17,27; Lk 1:37
**18:18** s Gal 3:8*
**18:19** t Dt 4:9–10; 6:7
**18:23** u Nu 16:22
**18:24** v Jer 5:1

wicked, treating the righteous and the wicked alike. Far be it from you! Will not the Judge[a] of all the earth do right?"[w]

26 The LORD said, "If I find fifty righteous people in the city of Sodom, I will spare the whole place for their sake."

27 Then Abraham spoke up again: "Now that I have been so bold as to speak to the Lord, though I am nothing but dust and ashes,[x] 28 what if the number of the righteous is five less than fifty? Will you destroy the whole city because of five people?"

"If I find forty-five there," he said, "I will not destroy it."

29 Once again he spoke to him, "What if only forty are found there?"

He said, "For the sake of forty, I will not do it."

30 Then he said, "May the Lord not be angry, but let me speak. What if only thirty can be found there?"

He answered, "I will not do it if I find thirty there."

31 Abraham said, "Now that I have been so bold as to speak to the Lord, what if only twenty can be found there?"

He said, "For the sake of twenty, I will not destroy it."

32 Then he said, "May the Lord not be angry, but let me speak just once more. What if only ten can be found there?"

He answered, "For the sake of ten, I will not destroy it."

33 When the LORD had finished speaking with Abraham, he left, and Abraham returned home.

## Sodom and Gomorrah Destroyed

19 The two angels arrived at Sodom in the evening, and Lot was sitting in the gateway of the city. When he saw them, he got up to meet them and bowed down with his face to the ground. 2 "My lords," he said, "please turn aside to your servant's house. You can wash your feet and spend the night and then go on your way early in the morning."

"No," they answered, "we will spend the night in the square."

3 But he insisted so strongly that they did go with him and entered his house. He prepared a meal for them, baking bread without yeast, and they ate.[y] 4 Before they had gone to bed, all the men from every part of the city of Sodom—both young and old—surrounded the house. 5 They called to Lot, "Where are the men who came to you tonight? Bring them out to us so that we can have sex with them."[z]

6 Lot went outside to meet them and shut the door behind him 7 and said, "No, my friends. Don't do this wicked thing. 8 Look, I have two daughters who have never slept with a man. Let me bring them out to you, and you can do what you like with them. But don't do anything to these men, for they have come under the protection of my roof."

9 "Get out of our way," they replied. And they said, "This fellow came here as an alien, and now he wants to play the judge![a] We'll treat you worse than them." They kept bringing pressure on Lot and moved forward to break down the door.

10 But the men inside reached out and pulled Lot back into the house and shut the door. 11 Then they struck the men who were at the door of the house, young and old, with blindness so that they could not find the door.

12 The two men said to Lot, "Do you have anyone else here—sons-in-law, sons or daughters, or anyone else in the city who belongs to you?[b] Get them out of here, 13 because we are going to destroy this place. The outcry to the LORD against its people is so great that he has sent us to destroy it."[c]

14 So Lot went out and spoke to his sons-in-law, who were pledged to marry[b] his daughters. He said, "Hurry and get out of this place, because the LORD is about to destroy the city![d]" But his sons-in-law thought he was joking.

15 With the coming of dawn, the angels urged Lot, saying, "Hurry! Take your wife and your two daughters who are here, or you will be swept away when the city is punished."

16 When he hesitated, the men grasped his hand and the hands of his wife and of his two daughters and led them safely out of the city, for the LORD was merciful to them.

[a] 25 Or *Ruler* [b] 14 Or *were married to*

**18:25** w Job 8:3,20; Isa 3:10–11
**18:27** x Ge 2:7; 3:19
**19:3** y Ge 18:6
**19:5** z Jdg 19:22; Ro 1:24–27
**19:9** a Ex 2:14
**19:12** b Ge 7:1
**19:13** c 1Ch 21:15
**19:14** d Nu 16:21

**19:17** e ver 26
**19:24** f Dt 29:23; Isa 1:9; 13:19 g Lk 17:29
**19:26** h ver 17 i Lk 17:32
**19:27** j Ge 18:22
**19:28** k Rev 18:9

17 As soon as they had brought them out, one of them said, "Flee for your lives! Don't look back,[e] and don't stop anywhere in the plain! Flee to the mountains or you will be swept away!"

18 But Lot said to them, "No, my lords,[a] please! 19 Your[b] servant has found favor in your[b] eyes, and you[b] have shown great kindness to me in sparing my life. But I can't flee to the mountains; this disaster will overtake me, and I'll die. 20 Look, here is a town near enough to run to, and it is small. Let me flee to it—it is very small, isn't it? Then my life will be spared."

21 He said to him, "Very well, I will grant this request too; I will not overthrow the town you speak of. 22 But flee there quickly, because I cannot do anything until you reach it." (That is why the town was called Zoar.[c])

23 By the time Lot reached Zoar, the sun had risen over the land. 24 Then the LORD rained down burning sulfur on Sodom and Gomorrah[f]—from the LORD out of the heavens.[g] 25 Thus he overthrew those cities and the entire plain, including all those living in the cities—and also the vegetation in the land. 26 But Lot's wife looked back,[h] and she became a pillar of salt.[i]

27 Early the next morning Abraham got up and returned to the place where he had stood before the LORD.[j] 28 He looked down toward Sodom and Gomorrah, toward all the land of the plain, and he saw dense smoke rising from the land, like smoke from a furnace.[k]

29 So when God destroyed the cities of the plain, he remembered Abraham, and he brought Lot out of the catastrophe that overthrew the cities where Lot had lived.

## Lot and His Daughters

30 Lot and his two daughters left Zoar and settled in the mountains, for he was afraid to stay in Zoar. He and his two daughters lived in a cave. 31 One day the older daughter said to the younger, "Our father is old, and there is no man around here to lie with us, as is the custom all over the earth. 32 Let's get our father to drink wine and then lie with him and preserve our family line through our father."

33 That night they got their father to drink wine, and the older daughter went in and lay with him. He was not aware of it when she lay down or when she got up.

34 The next day the older daughter said to the younger, "Last night I lay with my father. Let's get him to drink wine again tonight, and you go in and lie with him so we can preserve our family line through our father." 35 So they got their father to drink wine that night also, and the younger daughter went and lay with him. Again he was not aware of it when she lay down or when she got up.

36 So both of Lot's daughters became pregnant by their father. 37 The older daughter had a son, and she named him Moab[d]; he is the father of the Moabites[l] of today. 38 The younger daughter also had a son, and she named him Ben-Ammi[e]; he is the father of the Ammonites[m] of today.

## Abraham and Abimelech

20 Now Abraham moved on from there[n] into the region of the Negev and lived between Kadesh and Shur. For a while he stayed in Gerar, 2 and there Abraham said of his wife Sarah, "She is my sister.[o]" Then Abimelech king of Gerar sent for Sarah and took her.

3 But God came to Abimelech in a dream one night and said to him, "You are as good as dead because of the woman you have taken; she is a married woman."

4 Now Abimelech had not gone near her, so he said, "Lord, will you destroy an innocent nation? 5 Did he not say to me, 'She is my sister,' and didn't she also say, 'He is my brother'? I have done this with a clear conscience and clean hands."

6 Then God said to him in the dream, "Yes, I know you did this with a clear conscience, and so I have kept you from sinning against me. That is why I did not let you touch her. 7 Now return the man's wife, for he is a prophet, and he will pray for you[p] and you will live. But if you do not return her, you may be sure that you and all yours will die."

**19:37** l Dt 2:9
**19:38** m Dt 2:19
**20:1** n Ge 18:1
**20:2** o ver 12; Ge 12:13; 26:7
**20:7** p ver 17; 1Sa 7:5; Job 42:8

[a] 18 Or *No, Lord*; or *No, my lord* [b] 19 The Hebrew is singular. [c] 22 *Zoar* means *small.* [d] 37 *Moab* sounds like the Hebrew for *from father.* [e] 38 *Ben-Ammi* means *son of my people.*

# Lot's Wife

## *Why Look Back?*

We know the story of Lot's wife, who disobeyed God by looking back at the of Sodom and Gomorrah and, consequently, turned into a pillar of salt (see 19:15–26). This woman was the spouse of a rich and influential man. Yet the tures do not record Lot's wife's name or any information regarding her family of origin. While we don't know her name, we know her story.

Lot, Abraham's nephew, was a man of substance. He had done well in the sinful city of Sodom and was held in some respect. Genesis 19:1 says that Lot was "sitting in the gateway of the city." Such a position would indicate that Lot was probably a member of Sodom's ruling council. Because of Lot's power and respect, his wife, Mrs. Lot, also received some level of respect in their community. She enjoyed the comforts afforded her because of her relationship with her husband.

Lot's wife is a perfect example of the principle "Where your treasure is, there your heart will be also" (Mt 6:21). When the angels told her family to leave, she started out in the right direction and followed Lot outside the city, yet she was destroyed because she looked back. She was not totally committed to giving up her old ways in obedience to God.

Think about all that we as women/sisters have willingly put up with in those times when we have allowed ourselves to be belittled, put down and mistreated (verbally and physically) just to have a man, a job, material possessions, a certain lifestyle or something else we thought we needed so badly. Lord, help us! When God releases us from that foolishness and makes a way out of no way, we dare to look back with some regret, some desire for what was—to a moment when things were "good."

Those who put their hand to the gospel plow have no reason to look back now.

—M. Allen Bellinger

### reflection

*Use the story of Lot's wife as a reminder to keep looking forward to all God has in store for you. Do not let your past keep you from moving forward.*

### read

Genesis 18–19; Luke 9:62; 17:28–32.

**See also** the Inspire Notes "Self-Control" and "Temptation."

For the next Women of the Bible note, go to page 29.

**20:11** q Ps 36:1 r Ge 12:12; 26:7
**20:14** s Ge 12:16
**20:15** t Ge 13:9
**20:18** u Ge 12:17
**21:2** v Gal 4:22; Heb 11:11
**21:3** w Ge 17:19
**21:4** x Ge 17:10,12; Ac 7:8

8 Early the next morning Abimelech summoned all his officials, and when he told them all that had happened, they were very much afraid. 9 Then Abimelech called Abraham in and said, "What have you done to us? How have I wronged you that you have brought such great guilt upon me and my kingdom? You have done things to me that should not be done." 10 And Abimelech asked Abraham, "What was your reason for doing this?"

11 Abraham replied, "I said to myself, 'There is surely no fear of God[q] in this place, and they will kill me because of my wife.'[r] 12 Besides, she really is my sister, the daughter of my father though not of my mother; and she became my wife. 13 And when God had me wander from my father's household, I said to her, 'This is how you can show your love to me: Everywhere we go, say of me, "He is my brother." ' "

14 Then Abimelech brought sheep and cattle and male and female slaves and gave them to Abraham,[s] and he returned Sarah his wife to him. 15 And Abimelech said, "My land is before you; live wherever you like."[t]

16 To Sarah he said, "I am giving your brother a thousand shekels[a] of silver. This is to cover the offense against you before all who are with you; you are completely vindicated."

17 Then Abraham prayed to God, and God healed Abimelech, his wife and his slave girls so they could have children again, 18 for the LORD had closed up every womb in Abimelech's household because of Abraham's wife Sarah.[u]

## The Birth of Isaac

**21** Now the LORD was gracious to Sarah as he had said, and the LORD did for Sarah what he had promised. 2 Sarah became pregnant and bore a son to Abraham in his old age,[v] at the very time God had promised him. 3 Abraham gave the name Isaac[b][w] to the son Sarah bore him. 4 When his son Isaac was eight days old, Abraham circumcised him,[x] as God commanded him. 5 Abraham was a hundred years old when his son Isaac was born to him.

6 Sarah said, "God has brought me laughter,[y] and everyone who hears about this will laugh with me." 7 And she added, "Who would have said to Abraham that Sarah would nurse children? Yet I have borne him a son in his old age."

## Hagar and Ishmael Sent Away

8 The child grew and was weaned, and on the day Isaac was weaned Abraham held a great feast. 9 But Sarah saw that the son whom Hagar the Egyptian had borne to Abraham was mocking, 10 and she said to Abraham, "Get rid of that slave woman and her son, for that slave woman's son will never share in the inheritance with my son Isaac."[z]

11 The matter distressed Abraham greatly because it concerned his son.[a] 12 But God said to him, "Do not be so distressed about the boy and your maidservant. Listen to whatever Sarah tells you, because it is through Isaac that your offspring[c] will be reckoned.[b] 13 I will make the son of the maidservant into a nation also, because he is your offspring."

14 Early the next morning Abraham took some food and a skin of water and gave them to Hagar. He set them on her shoulders and then sent her off with the boy. She went on her way and wandered in the desert of Beersheba.

15 When the water in the skin was gone, she put the boy under one of the bushes. 16 Then she went off and sat down nearby, about a bowshot away, for she thought, "I cannot watch the boy die." And as she sat there nearby, she[d] began to sob.

17 God heard the boy crying,[c] and the angel of God called to Hagar from heaven and said to her, "What is the matter, Hagar? Do not be afraid; God has heard the boy crying as he lies there. 18 Lift the boy up and take him by the hand, for I will make him into a great nation."

19 Then God opened her eyes and she saw a well of water. So she went and filled the skin with water and gave the boy a drink.

20 God was with the boy[d] as he grew up. He lived in the desert and became an archer. 21 While he was living in the Desert of Paran, his mother got a wife for him[e] from Egypt.

**21:6** y Ge 17:17
**21:10** z Gal 4:30*
**21:11** a Ge 17:18
**21:12** b Ro 9:7*; Heb 11:18*
**21:17** c Ex 3:7
**21:20** d Ge 28:15
**21:21** e Ge 24:4,38

[a]16 That is, about 25 pounds (about 11.5 kilograms) [b]3 *Isaac* means *he laughs.* [c]12 Or *seed* [d]16 Hebrew; Septuagint *the child*

# Sarah

## Is Anything Too Hard for God?

Sarah was a woman after my own heart; in many ways, she represents women of faith who step out on God's Word—even when they don't understand how things will work out.

When God instructed Abraham to leave his father's household and go to the country of God's choosing, Sarah was 65 years old and Abraham was 75. God promised that he would make Abraham and his descendants a blessing to many. Abraham obeyed God and took Sarah, Lot (his nephew) and all of their possessions and headed for Canaan (see Ge 12:1–5).

God spoke directly to Abraham and indirectly to Sarah. Sarah obeyed God by supporting her husband's plans for the move. It is not said very often, but there are many African American women who love their husbands, move when they say it's time to go, and happily follow their leadership. Many of us are blessed to have strong men who listen to God and obey his Word. The Bible gives wonderful examples of good marriages and provides guidance on how to experience a blessed marriage.

Just like many women of faith—married and single—Sarah began an awesome journey based on God's promises. However, many years passed and Sarah and Abraham still did not have their promised child. Sarah began to believe that she would never have a child of her own for Abraham. So she persuaded Abraham to take her Egyptian servant girl as a surrogate wife, and Ishmael was born to Hagar (see Ge 16). Both Sarah and Abraham forgot God's ability to fulfill his promises. Sarah's attempt at assisting God had dire consequences for the descendants of Ishmael (Arabs) and Isaac (Israelites/Jews).

Sarah's bitter jealousy and anger toward Hagar destroyed the family unit. "A woman's family is held together by her wisdom, but it can be destroyed by her foolishness" (Pr 14:1, paraphrased). Sister Sarah did mess up, just as we sometimes mess up. But God keeps his promises! At age 90, Sarah became pregnant by Abraham when he was 100 years old (see Ge 21). Is anything too hard for God?

Sarah gave birth to a son, Isaac, through whom all nations have been blessed in the person of the Messiah, our Lord and Savior, Jesus Christ. Sarah's story reminds women of faith that we are not perfect; however, we can trust God's promises as we journey along the path of life. God will deliver—even when we don't understand how.

—B. Yates

### reflection

*Reflect on a time you tried to "assist" God in bringing about his promises, as Sarah did by giving Hagar to Abraham. What were the results?*

*How has this lesson reminded you to wait on God's timing for the fulfillment of his promises?*

### read

Genesis 16; 18:1–15; 21:1–7; Hebrews 11:8–12.

See also the Inspire Notes "Infertility," "Submission," "Waiting on God" and "Commitment to God."

For the next Women of the Bible note, go to page 35.

**21:25** f Ge 26:15,18, 20–22
**21:27** g Ge 26:28,31
**21:30** h Ge 31:44,47, 48,50,52
**22:1** i Dt 8:2,16; Heb 11:17; Jas 1:12–13
**22:2** j Jn 3:16

## The Treaty at Beersheba

22 At that time Abimelech and Phicol the commander of his forces said to Abraham, "God is with you in everything you do. 23 Now swear to me here before God that you will not deal falsely with me or my children or my descendants. Show to me and the country where you are living as an alien the same kindness I have shown to you."

24 Abraham said, "I swear it."

25 Then Abraham complained to Abimelech about a well of water that Abimelech's servants had seized.[f] 26 But Abimelech said, "I don't know who has done this. You did not tell me, and I heard about it only today."

27 So Abraham brought sheep and cattle and gave them to Abimelech, and the two men made a treaty.[g] 28 Abraham set apart seven ewe lambs from the flock, 29 and Abimelech asked Abraham, "What is the meaning of these seven ewe lambs you have set apart by themselves?"

30 He replied, "Accept these seven lambs from my hand as a witness[h] that I dug this well."

31 So that place was called Beersheba,[a] because the two men swore an oath there.

32 After the treaty had been made at Beersheba, Abimelech and Phicol the commander of his forces returned to the land of the Philistines. 33 Abraham planted a tamarisk tree in Beersheba, and there he called upon the name of the LORD, the Eternal God. 34 And Abraham stayed in the land of the Philistines for a long time.

## Abraham Tested

22 Some time later God tested[i] Abraham. He said to him, "Abraham!"

"Here I am," he replied.

2 Then God said, "Take your son[j], your only son, Isaac, whom you love, and go to the region of Moriah. Sacrifice him there as a burnt offering on one of the mountains I will tell you about."

3 Early the next morning Abraham got up and saddled his donkey. He took with him two of his servants and his son Isaac. When he had cut enough wood for the burnt offering, he set out for the place God had told him about. 4 On the third day Abraham looked up and saw the place in the distance. 5 He said to his servants, "Stay here with the donkey while I and the boy go over there. We will worship and then we will come back to you."

6 Abraham took the wood for the burnt offering and placed it on his son Isaac,[k] and he himself carried the fire and the knife. As the two of them went on together, 7 Isaac spoke up and said to his father Abraham, "Father?"

"Yes, my son?" Abraham replied.

"The fire and wood are here," Isaac said, "but where is the lamb for the burnt offering?"

8 Abraham answered, "God himself will provide the lamb for the burnt offering, my son." And the two of them went on together.

9 When they reached the place God had told him about, Abraham built an altar there and arranged the wood on it. He bound his son Isaac and laid him on the altar, on top of the wood. 10 Then he reached out his hand and took the knife to slay his son. 11 But the angel of the LORD called out to him from heaven, "Abraham! Abraham!"

"Here I am," he replied.

12 "Do not lay a hand on the boy," he said. "Do not do anything to him. Now I know that you fear God, because you have not withheld from me your son, your only son.[l]"

13 Abraham looked up and there in a thicket he saw a ram[b] caught by its horns. He went over and took the ram and sacrificed it as a burnt offering instead of his son.[m] 14 So Abraham called that place The LORD Will Provide. And to this day it is said, "On the mountain of the LORD it will be provided."

15 The angel of the LORD called to Abraham from heaven a second time 16 and said, "I swear by myself,[n] declares the LORD, that because you have done this and have not withheld your son, your only son, 17 I will surely bless you and make your descendants[o] as numerous as the stars in the sky[p] and as the sand on the seashore.[q] Your descendants will take possession of the cities of their enemies,[r] 18 and through your offspring[c] all

**22:6** k Jn 19:17
**22:12** l ver 2; Jn 3:16
**22:13** m Ro 8:32
**22:16** n Heb 6:13
**22:17** o Heb 6:14* p Ge 15:5 q Ge 26:24 r Ge 24:60

[a]31 *Beersheba* can mean *well of seven* or *well of the oath.* [b]13 Many manuscripts of the Masoretic Text, Samaritan Pentateuch, Septuagint and Syriac; most manuscripts of the Masoretic Text *a ram behind ⌊him⌋* [c]18 Or *seed*

**22:18** s Ac 3:25*; Gal 3:8*
**22:23** t Ge 24:15
**23:2** u Jos 14:15
**23:4** v Ps 105:12; Heb 11:9,13
**23:6** w Ge 14:14–16; 24:35
**23:10** x Ru 4:4

nations on earth will be blessed,[s] because you have obeyed me."

[19]Then Abraham returned to his servants, and they set off together for Beersheba. And Abraham stayed in Beersheba.

## Nahor's Sons

[20]Some time later Abraham was told, "Milcah is also a mother; she has borne sons to your brother Nahor: [21]Uz the firstborn, Buz his brother, Kemuel (the father of Aram), [22]Kesed, Hazo, Pildash, Jidlaph and Bethuel." [23]Bethuel became the father of Rebekah.[t] Milcah bore these eight sons to Abraham's brother Nahor. [24]His concubine, whose name was Reumah, also had sons: Tebah, Gaham, Tahash and Maacah.

## The Death of Sarah

**23** Sarah lived to be a hundred and twenty-seven years old. [2]She died at Kiriath Arba[u] (that is, Hebron) in the land of Canaan, and Abraham went to mourn for Sarah and to weep over her.

[3]Then Abraham rose from beside his dead wife and spoke to the Hittites.[a] He said, [4]"I am an alien and a stranger[v] among you. Sell me some property for a burial site here so I can bury my dead."

[5]The Hittites replied to Abraham, [6]"Sir, listen to us. You are a mighty prince[w] among us. Bury your dead in the choicest of our tombs. None of us will refuse you his tomb for burying your dead."

[7]Then Abraham rose and bowed down before the people of the land, the Hittites. [8]He said to them, "If you are willing to let me bury my dead, then listen to me and intercede with Ephron son of Zohar on my behalf [9]so he will sell me the cave of Machpelah, which belongs to him and is at the end of his field. Ask him to sell it to me for the full price as a burial site among you."

[10]Ephron the Hittite was sitting among his people and he replied to Abraham in the hearing of all the Hittites who had come to the gate[x] of his city. [11]"No, my lord," he said. "Listen to me; I give[b] you the field, and I give[b] you the cave that is in it. I give[b] it to you in the presence of my people. Bury your dead."

[12]Again Abraham bowed down before the people of the land [13]and he said to Ephron in their hearing, "Listen to me, if you will. I will pay the price of the field. Accept it from me so I can bury my dead there."

[14]Ephron answered Abraham, [15]"Listen to me, my lord; the land is worth four hundred shekels[c] of silver, but what is that between me and you? Bury your dead."

[16]Abraham agreed to Ephron's terms and weighed out for him the price he had named in the hearing of the Hittites: four hundred shekels of silver,[y] according to the weight current among the merchants.

[17]So Ephron's field in Machpelah near Mamre[z]—both the field and the cave in it, and all the trees within the borders of the field—was deeded [18]to Abraham as his property in the presence of all the Hittites who had come to the gate of the city. [19]Afterward Abraham buried his wife Sarah in the cave in the field of Machpelah near Mamre (which is at Hebron) in the land of Canaan. [20]So the field and the cave in it were deeded to Abraham by the Hittites as a burial site.

## Isaac and Rebekah

**24** Abraham was now old and well advanced in years, and the LORD had blessed him in every way.[a] [2]He said to the chief[d] servant in his household, the one in charge of all that he had, "Put your hand under my thigh. [3]I want you to swear by the LORD, the God of heaven and the God of earth,[b] that you will not get a wife for my son from the daughters of the Canaanites, among whom I am living, [4]but will go to my country and my own relatives[c] and get a wife for my son Isaac."

[5]The servant asked him, "What if the woman is unwilling to come back with me to this land? Shall I then take your son back to the country you came from?"

[6]"Make sure that you do not take my son back there," Abraham said. [7]"The LORD, the God of heaven, who brought me out of my father's household and my native land and who spoke to me and promised me on oath, saying, 'To your offspring[e][d] I will give this

**23:16** y Jer 32:9
**23:17** z Ge 25:9; 49:30–32; 50:13
**24:1** a ver 35
**24:3** b Ge 14:19
**24:4** c Ge 12:1
**24:7** d Gal 3:16*

[a]3 Or *the sons of Heth*; also in verses 5, 7, 10, 16, 18 and 20 [b]11 Or *sell* [c]15 That is, about 10 pounds (about 4.5 kilograms) [d]2 Or *oldest* [e]7 Or *seed*

land'[e]—he will send his angel before you[f] so that you can get a wife for my son from there. 8 If the woman is unwilling to come back with you, then you will be released from this oath of mine. Only do not take my son back there." 9 So the servant put his hand under the thigh of his master Abraham and swore an oath to him concerning this matter.

10 Then the servant took ten of his master's camels and left, taking with him all kinds of good things from his master. He set out for Aram Naharaim[a] and made his way to the town of Nahor. 11 He had the camels kneel down near the well outside the town; it was toward evening, the time the women go out to draw water.[g]

12 Then he prayed, "O LORD, God of my master Abraham,[h] give me success today, and show kindness to my master Abraham. 13 See, I am standing beside this spring, and the daughters of the townspeople are coming out to draw water. 14 May it be that when I say to a girl, 'Please let down your jar that I may have a drink,' and she says, 'Drink, and I'll water your camels too'—let her be the one you have chosen for your servant Isaac. By this I will know that you have shown kindness to my master."

15 Before he had finished praying, Rebekah[i] came out with her jar on her shoulder. She was the daughter of Bethuel son of Milcah, who was the wife of Abraham's brother Nahor. 16 The girl was very beautiful,[j] a virgin; no man had ever lain with her. She went down to the spring, filled her jar and came up again.

17 The servant hurried to meet her and said, "Please give me a little water from your jar."

18 "Drink, my lord," she said, and quickly lowered the jar to her hands and gave him a drink.

19 After she had given him a drink, she said, "I'll draw water for your camels too, until they have finished drinking." 20 So she quickly emptied her jar into the trough, ran back to the well to draw more water, and drew enough for all his camels. 21 Without saying a word, the man watched her closely to learn whether or not the LORD had made his journey successful.

22 When the camels had finished drinking, the man took out a gold nose ring weighing a beka[b] and two gold bracelets weighing ten shekels.[c] 23 Then he asked, "Whose daughter are you? Please tell me, is there room in your father's house for us to spend the night?"

24 She answered him, "I am the daughter of Bethuel, the son that Milcah bore to Nahor." 25 And she added, "We have plenty of straw and fodder, as well as room for you to spend the night."

26 Then the man bowed down and worshiped the LORD,[k] 27 saying, "Praise be to the LORD, the God of my master Abraham, who has not abandoned his kindness and faithfulness to my master. As for me, the LORD has led me on the journey to the house of my master's relatives."

28 The girl ran and told her mother's household about these things. 29 Now Rebekah had a brother named Laban,[l] and he hurried out to the man at the spring. 30 As soon as he had seen the nose ring, and the bracelets on his sister's arms, and had heard Rebekah tell what the man said to her, he went out to the man and found him standing by the camels near the spring. 31 "Come, you who are blessed by the LORD,"[m] he said. "Why are you standing out here? I have prepared the house and a place for the camels."

32 So the man went to the house, and the camels were unloaded. Straw and fodder were brought for the camels, and water for him and his men to wash their feet.[n] 33 Then food was set before him, but he said, "I will not eat until I have told you what I have to say."

"Then tell us," ⌊Laban⌋ said.

34 So he said, "I am Abraham's servant. 35 The LORD has blessed my master abundantly,[o] and he has become wealthy. He has given him sheep and cattle, silver and gold, menservants and maidservants, and camels and donkeys. 36 My master's wife Sarah has borne him a son in her[d] old age,[p] and he has given him everything he owns.[q] 37 And my master made me swear an oath, and said, 'You must not get a wife for my son

**24:7** e Ge 12:7; 13:15 f Ex 23:20,23
**24:11** g ver 13; 1Sa 9:11
**24:12** h ver 27,42,48; Ge 26:24; Ex 3:6,15,16
**24:15** i Ge 22:23
**24:16** j Ge 26:7
**24:26** k ver 48,52
**24:29** l ver 4; Ge 29:5,12,13
**24:31** m Ge 26:29
**24:32** n Ge 43:24; Jdg 19:21
**24:35** o ver 1
**24:36** p Ge 21:2,10 q Ge 25:5

[a]10 That is, Northwest Mesopotamia [b]22 That is, about 1/5 ounce (about 5.5 grams) [c]22 That is, about 4 ounces (about 110 grams) [d]36 Or *his*

from the daughters of the Canaanites, in whose land I live,[r] 38but go to my father's family and to my own clan, and get a wife for my son.'

39"Then I asked my master, 'What if the woman will not come back with me?'[s]

40"He replied, 'The LORD, before whom I have walked, will send his angel with you[t] and make your journey a success, so that you can get a wife for my son from my own clan and from my father's family. 41Then, when you go to my clan, you will be released from my oath even if they refuse to give her to you—you will be released from my oath.'[u]

42"When I came to the spring today, I said, 'O LORD, God of my master Abraham, if you will, please grant success[v] to the journey on which I have come. 43See, I am standing beside this spring;[w] if a maiden comes out to draw water and I say to her, "Please let me drink a little water from your jar," 44and if she says to me, "Drink, and I'll draw water for your camels too," let her be the one the LORD has chosen for my master's son.'

45"Before I finished praying in my heart,[x] Rebekah came out, with her jar on her shoulder.[y] She went down to the spring and drew water, and I said to her, 'Please give me a drink.'

46"She quickly lowered her jar from her shoulder and said, 'Drink, and I'll water your camels too.' So I drank, and she watered the camels also.

47"I asked her, 'Whose daughter are you?'

"She said, 'The daughter of Bethuel son of Nahor, whom Milcah bore to him.'

"Then I put the ring in her nose and the bracelets on her arms, 48and I bowed down and worshiped the LORD.[z] I praised the LORD, the God of my master Abraham, who had led me on the right road to get the granddaughter of my master's brother for his son. 49Now if you will show kindness and faithfulness[a] to my master, tell me; and if not, tell me, so I may know which way to turn."

50Laban and Bethuel answered, "This is from the LORD;[b] we can say nothing to you one way or the other.[c] 51Here is Rebekah; take her and go, and let her become the wife of your master's son, as the LORD has directed."

52When Abraham's servant heard what they said, he bowed down to the ground before the LORD.[d] 53Then the servant brought out gold and silver jewelry and articles of clothing and gave them to Rebekah; he also gave costly gifts to her brother and to her mother. 54Then he and the men who were with him ate and drank and spent the night there.

When they got up the next morning, he said, "Send me on my way[e] to my master."

55But her brother and her mother replied, "Let the girl remain with us ten days or so; then you[a] may go."

56But he said to them, "Do not detain me, now that the LORD has granted success to my journey. Send me on my way so I may go to my master."

57Then they said, "Let's call the girl and ask her about it." 58So they called Rebekah and asked her, "Will you go with this man?"

"I will go," she said.

59So they sent their sister Rebekah on her way, along with her nurse[f] and Abraham's servant and his men. 60And they blessed Rebekah and said to her,

"Our sister, may you increase
to thousands upon thousands;[g]
may your offspring possess
the gates of their enemies."[h]

61Then Rebekah and her maids got ready and mounted their camels and went back with the man. So the servant took Rebekah and left.

62Now Isaac had come from Beer Lahai Roi,[i] for he was living in the Negev. 63He went out to the field one evening to meditate,[b][j] and as he looked up, he saw camels approaching. 64Rebekah also looked up and saw Isaac. She got down from her camel 65and asked the servant, "Who is that man in the field coming to meet us?"

"He is my master," the servant answered. So she took her veil and covered herself.

66Then the servant told Isaac all he had done. 67Isaac brought her into the tent of his mother Sarah, and he married Rebekah.

**24:37** r ver 3
**24:39** s ver 5
**24:40** t ver 7
**24:41** u ver 8
**24:42** v ver 12
**24:43** w ver 13
**24:45** x 1Sa 1:13 y ver 15
**24:48** z ver 26
**24:49** a Ge 47:29; Jos 2:14
**24:50** b Ps 118:23 c Ge 31:7,24, 29,42
**24:52** d ver 26
**24:54** e ver 56,59
**24:59** f Ge 35:8
**24:60** g Ge 17:16 h Ge 22:17
**24:62** i Ge 16:14; 25:11
**24:63** j Ps 1:2; 77:12; 119:15,27,48,97, 148; 143:5

[a]55 Or *she* [b]63 The meaning of the Hebrew for this word is uncertain.

25:5 k Ge 24:36
25:8 l Ge 15:15 m Ge 35:29; 49:29,33
25:10 n Ge 23:16
25:12 o Ge 16:15

So she became his wife, and he loved her; and Isaac was comforted after his mother's death.

## The Death of Abraham

**25** Abraham took[a] another wife, whose name was Keturah. [2]She bore him Zimran, Jokshan, Medan, Midian, Ishbak and Shuah. [3]Jokshan was the father of Sheba and Dedan; the descendants of Dedan were the Asshurites, the Letushites and the Leummites. [4]The sons of Midian were Ephah, Epher, Hanoch, Abida and Eldaah. All these were descendants of Keturah.

[5]Abraham left everything he owned to Isaac.[k] [6]But while he was still living, he gave gifts to the sons of his concubines and sent them away from his son Isaac to the land of the east.

[7]Altogether, Abraham lived a hundred and seventy-five years. [8]Then Abraham breathed his last and died at a good old age,[l] an old man and full of years; and he was gathered to his people.[m] [9]His sons Isaac and Ishmael buried him in the cave of Machpelah near Mamre, in the field of Ephron son of Zohar the Hittite, [10]the field Abraham had bought from the Hittites.[b][n] There Abraham was buried with his wife Sarah. [11]After Abraham's death, God blessed his son Isaac, who then lived near Beer Lahai Roi.

## Ishmael's Sons

[12]This is the account of Abraham's son Ishmael, whom Sarah's maidservant, Hagar the Egyptian, bore to Abraham.[o]

[13]These are the names of the sons of Ishmael, listed in the order of their birth: Nebaioth the firstborn of Ishmael, Kedar, Adbeel, Mibsam, [14]Mishma, Dumah, Massa, [15]Hadad, Tema, Jetur, Naphish and Kedemah. [16]These were the sons of Ishmael, and these are the names of the twelve tribal rulers[p] according to their settlements and camps. [17]Altogether, Ishmael lived a hundred and thirty-seven years. He breathed his last and died, and he was gathered to his people.[q] [18]His descendants settled in the area from Havilah to Shur, near the border of Egypt, as you go toward Asshur. And they lived in hostility toward[c] all their brothers.[r]

## Jacob and Esau

[19]This is the account of Abraham's son Isaac.

Abraham became the father of Isaac, [20]and Isaac was forty years old when he married Rebekah daughter of Bethuel the Aramean from Paddan Aram[d] and sister of Laban[s] the Aramean.

[21]Isaac prayed to the LORD on behalf of his wife, because she was barren. The LORD answered his prayer, and his wife Rebekah became pregnant. [22]The babies jostled each other within her, and she said, "Why is this happening to me?" So she went to inquire of the LORD.

[23]The LORD said to her,

"Two nations are in your womb,
and two peoples from within you will be separated;
one people will be stronger than the other,
and the older will serve the younger.[t]"

[24]When the time came for her to give birth, there were twin boys in her womb. [25]The first

25:16 p Ge 17:20
25:17 q ver 8
25:18 r Ge 16:12
25:20 s Ge 24:29
25:23 t Ge 27:29,40; Mal 1:3; Ro 9:11–12*

[a]1 Or *had taken* [b]10 Or *the sons of Heth* [c]18 Or *lived to the east of* [d]20 That is, Northwest Mesopotamia

### The African Presence

**Genesis 25:1–2**

The name *Keturah* is derived from the root word "qatar," which means "thick smoke" or "incense." Her descendants with Abraham are associated with Arabian and Aramean tribes or cities situated along the "incense route" through western Arabia.

# Rebekah

## A Woman of Obsessive Love

Rebekah was unable to have children for nearly 20 years after marrying Isaac. But Isaac prayed for his wife, and finally Rebekah conceived twin boys—Jacob and Esau (see Ge 25:19–26). Although Esau was the eldest and entitled to his father's inheritance and blessing, Rebekah favored her younger son, Jacob, and desired that he take the place of Esau as the inheritor. When the opportunity arose, Rebekah helped Jacob deceive his father. Isaac, who had become old, feeble and blind, bestowed upon Jacob the family blessing and inheritance that was intended for Esau (see Ge 27:1–30).

Rebekah later protected Jacob from Esau's wrath by sending him to stay with her brother Laban in Haran. Unfortunately, Rebekah and Jacob were never reunited, and upon her death, Rebekah was buried in the family burial ground at Machpelah.

It is instinctive and proper for a woman—a wife and mother—to love passionately. But Rebekah's love for Jacob became a selfish, jealous love that led to favoritism of one child over another. Her love for Jacob also led her to compromise her love for, and loyalty to, her husband. She was determined to do what she thought would help Jacob, at the expense of both Esau and Isaac.

Unlike Rebekah's case, sometimes we hear that crimes of passion have ultimately led to the deaths of innocent people. As mothers and spouses, we must take care that our love for our children and our spouses does not become an obsessive love—a love that would allow us to succumb to the temptation of Satan, to betray moral ethics, covenant relationships and spiritual commitments. As women of God, our love should always be pure and subject to the Spirit of God.

God's love for us serves as the ultimate, true example of a pure love—a love that is unconditional, shows no bias or favoritism and is not jealous or boastful. Unselfish motives or desires define pure love: It always protects, always trusts, always hopes, always perseveres and, above all, never fails (see 1Co 13:7–8).

—T. Harrison-Dixon

### reflection

*Evaluate the love you have for family members. How can you make sure your love is pure and subject to God's Spirit?*

### read

Genesis 24–27;
1 Corinthians 13.
**See also** the Inspire Notes "Infertility," "Marriage" and "Love," and the Women of the Bible Note "The Bridegroom and His Bride: Soul Mates in Life."

For the next Women of the Bible note, go to page 41.

**25:25** u Ge 27:11
**25:26** v Hos 12:3 w Ge 27:36
**25:33** x Heb 12:16
**26:1** y Ge 12:10 z Ge 20:1
**26:2** a Ge 12:7 b Ge 12:1
**26:3** c Ge 12:2; 22:16–18 d Ge 12:7; 13:15
**26:4** e Ge 15:5; 22:17
**26:7** f Ge 12:13; 20:2,12

to come out was red, and his whole body was
like a hairy garment;[u] so they named him
Esau.[a] 26 After this, his brother came out,
with his hand grasping Esau's heel;[v] so he
was named Jacob.[b w] Isaac was sixty years
old when Rebekah gave birth to them.

27 The boys grew up, and Esau became a
skillful hunter, a man of the open country,
while Jacob was a quiet man, staying among
the tents. 28 Isaac, who had a taste for wild
game, loved Esau, but Rebekah loved Jacob.

29 Once when Jacob was cooking some
stew, Esau came in from the open country,
famished. 30 He said to Jacob, "Quick, let me
have some of that red stew! I'm famished!"
(That is why he was also called Edom.[c])

31 Jacob replied, "First sell me your birth-
right."

32 "Look, I am about to die," Esau said.
"What good is the birthright to me?"

33 But Jacob said, "Swear to me first." So
he swore an oath to him, selling his birth-
right[x] to Jacob.

34 Then Jacob gave Esau some bread and
some lentil stew. He ate and drank, and then
got up and left.

So Esau despised his birthright.

## Isaac and Abimelech

26 Now there was a famine in the
land[y]—besides the earlier famine
of Abraham's time—and Isaac went to
Abimelech king of the Philistines in Gerar.[z]
2 The LORD appeared[a] to Isaac and said, "Do
not go down to Egypt; live in the land where
I tell you to live.[b] 3 Stay in this land for a
while, and I will be with you and will bless
you.[c] For to you and your descendants I will
give all these lands[d] and will confirm the
oath I swore to your father Abraham. 4 I will
make your descendants as numerous as the
stars in the sky[e] and will give them all these
lands, and through your offspring[d] all na-
tions on earth will be blessed, 5 because
Abraham obeyed me and kept my require-
ments, my commands, my decrees and my
laws." 6 So Isaac stayed in Gerar.

7 When the men of that place asked him
about his wife, he said, "She is my sister,[f]"
because he was afraid to say, "She is my
wife." He thought, "The men of this place
might kill me on account of Rebekah, be-
cause she is beautiful."

8 When Isaac had been there a long time,
Abimelech king of the Philistines looked
down from a window and saw Isaac caress-
ing his wife Rebekah. 9 So Abimelech sum-
moned Isaac and said, "She is really your
wife! Why did you say, 'She is my sister'?"

Isaac answered him, "Because I thought I
might lose my life on account of her."

10 Then Abimelech said, "What is this you
have done to us?[g] One of the men might well
have slept with your wife, and you would
have brought guilt upon us."

11 So Abimelech gave orders to all the peo-
ple: "Anyone who molests this man or his
wife shall surely be put to death."

12 Isaac planted crops in that land and the
same year reaped a hundredfold, because
the LORD blessed him.[h] 13 The man became
rich, and his wealth continued to grow until
he became very wealthy. 14 He had so many
flocks and herds and servants that the Phi-
listines envied him. 15 So all the wells[i] that
his father's servants had dug in the time of
his father Abraham, the Philistines stopped
up, filling them with earth.

16 Then Abimelech said to Isaac, "Move
away from us; you have become too power-
ful for us."

17 So Isaac moved away from there and
encamped in the Valley of Gerar and settled
there. 18 Isaac reopened the wells that had
been dug in the time of his father Abraham,
which the Philistines had stopped up after
Abraham died, and he gave them the same
names his father had given them.

19 Isaac's servants dug in the valley and
discovered a well of fresh water there. 20 But
the herdsmen of Gerar quarreled with
Isaac's herdsmen and said, "The water is
ours!" So he named the well Esek,[e] because
they disputed with him. 21 Then they dug
another well, but they quarreled over that
one also; so he named it Sitnah.[f] 22 He moved
on from there and dug another well, and
no one quarreled over it. He named it Reho-
both,[g] saying, "Now the LORD has given us
room and we will flourish[j] in the land."

**26:10** g Ge 20:9
**26:12** h ver 3
**26:15** i Ge 21:30
**26:22** j Ge 17:6

[a] 25 *Esau* may mean *hairy*; he was also called Edom, which means *red.* [b] 26 *Jacob* means *he grasps the heel* (figuratively, *he deceives*). [c] 30 *Edom* means *red.* [d] 4 Or *seed* [e] 20 *Esek* means *dispute.* [f] 21 *Sitnah* means *opposition.* [g] 22 *Rehoboth* means *room.*

**26:24** k Ge 24:12 l Ge 17:7
**26:25** m Ge 12:7,8; 13:4,18; Ps 116:17
**26:26** n Ge 21:22
**26:28** o Ge 21:22
**26:31** p Ge 21:31
**26:34** q Ge 36:2
**26:35** r Ge 27:46
**27:3** s Ge 25:27

23 From there he went up to Beersheba.
24 That night the LORD appeared to him and
said, "I am the God of your father Abra-
ham.[k] Do not be afraid, for I am with you; I
will bless you and will increase the number
of your descendants for the sake of my ser-
vant Abraham."[l]

25 Isaac built an altar[m] there and called on
the name of the LORD. There he pitched his
tent, and there his servants dug a well.

26 Meanwhile, Abimelech had come to
him from Gerar, with Ahuzzath his personal
adviser and Phicol the commander of his
forces.[n] 27 Isaac asked them, "Why have you
come to me, since you were hostile to me
and sent me away?"

28 They answered, "We saw clearly that the
LORD was with you;[o] so we said, 'There ought
to be a sworn agreement between us'—be-
tween us and you. Let us make a treaty with
you 29 that you will do us no harm, just as we
did not molest you but always treated you
well and sent you away in peace. And now
you are blessed by the LORD."

30 Isaac then made a feast for them, and
they ate and drank. 31 Early the next morn-
ing the men swore an oath[p] to each other.
Then Isaac sent them on their way, and they
left him in peace.

32 That day Isaac's servants came and told
him about the well they had dug. They said,
"We've found water!" 33 He called it Shibah,[a]
and to this day the name of the town has
been Beersheba.[b]

34 When Esau was forty years old, he mar-
ried Judith daughter of Beeri the Hittite,
and also Basemath daughter of Elon the Hit-
tite.[q] 35 They were a source of grief to Isaac
and Rebekah.[r]

## Jacob Gets Isaac's Blessing

27 When Isaac was old and his eyes
were so weak that he could no lon-
ger see, he called for Esau his older son and
said to him, "My son."

"Here I am," he answered.

2 Isaac said, "I am now an old man and
don't know the day of my death. 3 Now
then, get your weapons—your quiver and
bow—and go out to the open country[s] to
hunt some wild game for me. 4 Prepare me
the kind of tasty food I like and bring it to
me to eat, so that I may give you my blessing
before I die."

5 Now Rebekah was listening as Isaac
spoke to his son Esau. When Esau left for
the open country to hunt game and bring it
back, 6 Rebekah said to her son Jacob, "Look,
I overheard your father say to your brother
Esau, 7 'Bring me some game and prepare
me some tasty food to eat, so that I may give
you my blessing in the presence of the LORD
before I die.' 8 Now, my son, listen carefully
and do what I tell you:[t] 9 Go out to the flock
and bring me two choice young goats, so I
can prepare some tasty food for your father,
just the way he likes it. 10 Then take it to your
father to eat, so that he may give you his
blessing before he dies."

11 Jacob said to Rebekah his mother, "But
my brother Esau is a hairy man,[u] and I'm a
man with smooth skin. 12 What if my father
touches me?[v] I would appear to be tricking
him and would bring down a curse on my-
self rather than a blessing."

13 His mother said to him, "My son, let the
curse fall on me. Just do what I say; go and
get them for me."

14 So he went and got them and brought
them to his mother, and she prepared some
tasty food, just the way his father liked it.
15 Then Rebekah took the best clothes[w] of
Esau her older son, which she had in the
house, and put them on her younger son
Jacob. 16 She also covered his hands and the
smooth part of his neck with the goatskins.
17 Then she handed to her son Jacob the tasty
food and the bread she had made.

18 He went to his father and said, "My fa-
ther."

"Yes, my son," he answered. "Who is it?"

19 Jacob said to his father, "I am Esau your
firstborn. I have done as you told me. Please
sit up and eat some of my game so that you
may give me your blessing."[x]

20 Isaac asked his son, "How did you find
it so quickly, my son?"

"The LORD your God gave me success,"
he replied.

21 Then Isaac said to Jacob, "Come near so
I can touch you,[y] my son, to know whether
you really are my son Esau or not."

**27:8** t ver 13,43
**27:11** u Ge 25:25
**27:12** v ver 22
**27:15** w ver 27
**27:19** x ver 4
**27:21** y ver 12

[a]33 *Shibah* can mean *oath* or *seven.* [b]33 *Beersheba* can mean *well of the oath* or *well of seven.*

**27:23** z ver 16
**27:25** a ver 4
**27:27** b Heb 11:20; c SS 4:11
**27:28** d Dt 33:13; e Dt 33:28
**27:29** f Isa 49:7,23; g Ge 9:25; 25:23; h Ge 12:3
**27:31** i ver 4
**27:33** j Ge 28:3,4; Ro 11:29
**27:34** k Heb 12:17

22 Jacob went close to his father Isaac, who touched him and said, "The voice is the voice of Jacob, but the hands are the hands of Esau." 23 He did not recognize him, for his hands were hairy like those of his brother Esau;[z] so he blessed him. 24 "Are you really my son Esau?" he asked.

"I am," he replied.

25 Then he said, "My son, bring me some of your game to eat, so that I may give you my blessing."[a]

Jacob brought it to him and he ate; and he brought some wine and he drank. 26 Then his father Isaac said to him, "Come here, my son, and kiss me."

27 So he went to him and kissed him.[b] When Isaac caught the smell of his clothes,[c] he blessed him and said,

"Ah, the smell of my son
is like the smell of a field
that the LORD has blessed.
28 May God give you of heaven's dew[d]
and of earth's richness—
an abundance of grain and new
wine.[e]
29 May nations serve you
and peoples bow down to you.[f]
Be lord over your brothers,
and may the sons of your mother bow
down to you.[g]
May those who curse you be cursed
and those who bless you be blessed.[h]"

30 After Isaac finished blessing him and Jacob had scarcely left his father's presence, his brother Esau came in from hunting. 31 He too prepared some tasty food and brought it to his father. Then he said to him, "My father, sit up and eat some of my game, so that you may give me your blessing."[i]

32 His father Isaac asked him, "Who are you?"

"I am your son," he answered, "your firstborn, Esau."

33 Isaac trembled violently and said, "Who was it, then, that hunted game and brought it to me? I ate it just before you came and I blessed him—and indeed he will be blessed![j]"

34 When Esau heard his father's words, he burst out with a loud and bitter cry[k] and said to his father, "Bless me—me too, my father!"

35 But he said, "Your brother came deceitfully and took your blessing."

36 Esau said, "Isn't he rightly named Jacob[a]?[l] He has deceived me these two times: He took my birthright,[m] and now he's taken my blessing!" Then he asked, "Haven't you reserved any blessing for me?"

37 Isaac answered Esau, "I have made him lord over you and have made all his relatives his servants, and I have sustained him with grain and new wine.[n] So what can I possibly do for you, my son?"

38 Esau said to his father, "Do you have only one blessing, my father? Bless me too, my father!" Then Esau wept aloud.[o]

39 His father Isaac answered him,

"Your dwelling will be
away from the earth's richness,
away from the dew[p] of heaven above.
40 You will live by the sword
and you will serve your brother.[q]
But when you grow restless,
you will throw his yoke
from off your neck.[r]"

## Jacob Flees to Laban

41 Esau held a grudge against Jacob because of the blessing his father had given him. He said to himself, "The days of mourning for my father are near; then I will kill my brother Jacob."

42 When Rebekah was told what her older son Esau had said, she sent for her younger son Jacob and said to him, "Your brother Esau is consoling himself with the thought of killing you. 43 Now then, my son, do what I say: Flee at once to my brother Laban in Haran.[s] 44 Stay with him for a while until your brother's fury subsides. 45 When your brother is no longer angry with you and forgets what you did to him, I'll send word for you to come back from there. Why should I lose both of you in one day?"

46 Then Rebekah said to Isaac, "I'm disgusted with living because of these Hittite women. If Jacob takes a wife from among the women of this land, from Hittite women like these, my life will not be worth living."[t]

**27:36** l Ge 25:26; m Ge 25:33
**27:37** n ver 28
**27:38** o Heb 12:17
**27:39** p ver 28
**27:40** q Ge 25:23; r 2Ki 8:20–22
**27:43** s Ge 11:31
**27:46** t Ge 26:35

[a] 36 *Jacob* means *he grasps the heel* (figuratively, *he deceives*).

**28:1** u Ge 24:3
**28:3** v Ge 17:1; w Ge 17:6
**28:4** x Ge 12:2,3; y Ge 17:8
**28:8** z Ge 26:35
**28:12** a Jn 1:51
**28:13** b Ge 26:24; c Ge 13:15
**28:14** d Ge 26:4

28 So Isaac called for Jacob and blessed[a] him and commanded him: "Do not marry a Canaanite woman.[u] 2Go at once to Paddan Aram,[b] to the house of your mother's father Bethuel. Take a wife for yourself there, from among the daughters of Laban, your mother's brother. 3May God Almighty[c][v] bless you and make you fruitful[w] and increase your numbers until you become a community of peoples. 4May he give you and your descendants the blessing given to Abraham,[x] so that you may take possession of the land where you now live as an alien,[y] the land God gave to Abraham." 5Then Isaac sent Jacob on his way, and he went to Paddan Aram, to Laban son of Bethuel the Aramean, the brother of Rebekah, who was the mother of Jacob and Esau.

6Now Esau learned that Isaac had blessed Jacob and had sent him to Paddan Aram to take a wife from there, and that when he blessed him he commanded him, "Do not marry a Canaanite woman," 7and that Jacob had obeyed his father and mother and had gone to Paddan Aram. 8Esau then realized how displeasing the Canaanite women were to his father Isaac;[z] 9so he went to Ishmael and married Mahalath, the sister of Nebaioth and daughter of Ishmael son of Abraham, in addition to the wives he already had.

## Jacob's Dream at Bethel

10Jacob left Beersheba and set out for Haran. 11When he reached a certain place, he stopped for the night because the sun had set. Taking one of the stones there, he put it under his head and lay down to sleep. 12He had a dream in which he saw a stairway[d] resting on the earth, with its top reaching to heaven, and the angels of God were ascending and descending on it.[a] 13There above it[e] stood the LORD, and he said: "I am the LORD, the God of your father Abraham and the God of Isaac.[b] I will give you and your descendants the land[c] on which you are lying. 14Your descendants will be like the dust of the earth, and you[d] will spread out to the west and to the east, to the north and to the south. All peoples on earth will be blessed through you and your offspring.[e] 15I am with you and will watch over you wherever you go, and I will bring you back to this land. I will not leave you until I have done what I have promised you."

16When Jacob awoke from his sleep, he thought, "Surely the LORD is in this place, and I was not aware of it." 17He was afraid and said, "How awesome is this place![f] This is none other than the house of God; this is the gate of heaven."

18Early the next morning Jacob took the stone he had placed under his head and set it up as a pillar and poured oil on top of it. 19He called that place Bethel,[f] though the city used to be called Luz.[g]

20Then Jacob made a vow,[h] saying, "If God will be with me and will watch over me[i] on this journey I am taking and will give me food to eat and clothes to wear 21so that I return safely[j] to my father's house, then the LORD[g] will be my God[k] 22and[h] this stone that I have set up as a pillar will be God's house,[l] and of all that you give me I will give you a tenth.[m]"

## Jacob Arrives in Paddan Aram

29 Then Jacob continued on his journey and came to the land of the eastern peoples. 2There he saw a well in the field, with three flocks of sheep lying near it because the flocks were watered from that well. The stone over the mouth of the well was large. 3When all the flocks were gathered there, the shepherds would roll the stone away from the well's mouth and water the sheep. Then they would return the stone to its place over the mouth of the well.

4Jacob asked the shepherds, "My brothers, where are you from?"

"We're from Haran," they replied.

5He said to them, "Do you know Laban, Nahor's grandson?"

"Yes, we know him," they answered.

6Then Jacob asked them, "Is he well?"

"Yes, he is," they said, "and here comes his daughter Rachel with the sheep."

7"Look," he said, "the sun is still high; it is not time for the flocks to be gathered.

**28:14** e Ge 12:3; 18:18; 22:18; Gal 3:8
**28:17** f Ex 3:5; Jos 5:15
**28:19** g Jdg 1:23,26
**28:20** h Ge 31:13; i ver 15
**28:21** j Jdg 11:31; k Dt 26:17
**28:22** l Ge 35:7,14; m Ge 14:20; Lev 27:30

[a]1 Or *greeted* [b]2 That is, Northwest Mesopotamia; also in verses 5, 6 and 7 [c]3 Hebrew *El-Shaddai* [d]12 Or *ladder* [e]13 Or *There beside him* [f]19 *Bethel* means *house of God.* [g]20,21 Or *Since God . . . father's house, the LORD* [h]21,22 Or *house, and the LORD will be my God, 22then*

**29:12** n Ge 24:28
**29:13** o Ge 24:29
**29:14** p Jdg 9:2
**29:21** q Jdg 15:1
**29:22** r Jdg 14:10; Jn 2:1–2

Water the sheep and take them back to pasture.”

[8]“We can’t,” they replied, “until all the flocks are gathered and the stone has been rolled away from the mouth of the well. Then we will water the sheep.”

[9]While he was still talking with them, Rachel came with her father’s sheep, for she was a shepherdess. [10]When Jacob saw Rachel daughter of Laban, his mother’s brother, and Laban’s sheep, he went over and rolled the stone away from the mouth of the well and watered his uncle’s sheep. [11]Then Jacob kissed Rachel and began to weep aloud. [12]He had told Rachel that he was a relative of her father and a son of Rebekah. So she ran and told her father.[n]

[13]As soon as Laban[o] heard the news about Jacob, his sister’s son, he hurried to meet him. He embraced him and kissed him and brought him to his home, and there Jacob told him all these things. [14]Then Laban said to him, “You are my own flesh and blood.”[p]

## Jacob Marries Leah and Rachel

After Jacob had stayed with him for a whole month, [15]Laban said to him, “Just because you are a relative of mine, should you work for me for nothing? Tell me what your wages should be.”

[16]Now Laban had two daughters; the name of the older was Leah, and the name of the younger was Rachel. [17]Leah had weak[a] eyes, but Rachel was lovely in form, and beautiful. [18]Jacob was in love with Rachel and said, “I’ll work for you seven years in return for your younger daughter Rachel.”

[19]Laban said, “It’s better that I give her to you than to some other man. Stay here with me.” [20]So Jacob served seven years to get Rachel, but they seemed like only a few days to him because of his love for her.

[21]Then Jacob said to Laban, “Give me my wife. My time is completed, and I want to lie with her.[q]”

[22]So Laban brought together all the people of the place and gave a feast.[r] [23]But when evening came, he took his daughter Leah and gave her to Jacob, and Jacob lay with her. [24]And Laban gave his servant girl Zilpah to his daughter as her maidservant.

[25]When morning came, there was Leah! So Jacob said to Laban, “What is this you have done to me?[s] I served you for Rachel, didn’t I? Why have you deceived me?[t]”

[26]Laban replied, “It is not our custom here to give the younger daughter in marriage before the older one. [27]Finish this daughter’s bridal week; then we will give you the younger one also, in return for another seven years of work.”

[28]And Jacob did so. He finished the week with Leah, and then Laban gave him his daughter Rachel to be his wife. [29]Laban gave his servant girl Bilhah to his daughter Rachel as her maidservant. [30]Jacob lay with Rachel also, and he loved Rachel more than Leah. And he worked for Laban another seven years.[u]

## Jacob’s Children

[31]When the LORD saw that Leah was not loved,[v] he opened her womb,[w] but Rachel was barren. [32]Leah became pregnant and gave birth to a son. She named him Reuben,[b] for she said, “It is because the LORD has seen my misery.[x] Surely my husband will love me now.”

[33]She conceived again, and when she gave birth to a son she said, “Because the LORD heard that I am not loved, he gave me this one too.” So she named him Simeon.[c]

[34]Again she conceived, and when she gave birth to a son she said, “Now at last my husband will become attached to me, because I have borne him three sons.” So he was named Levi.[d][y]

[35]She conceived again, and when she gave birth to a son she said, “This time I will praise the LORD.” So she named him Judah.[e][z] Then she stopped having children.

**30** When Rachel saw that she was not bearing Jacob any children,[a] she became jealous of her sister. So she said to Jacob, “Give me children, or I’ll die!”

[2]Jacob became angry with her and said, “Am I in the place of God, who has kept you from having children?”[b]

[3]Then she said, “Here is Bilhah, my maidservant. Sleep with her so that she can bear

**29:25** s Ge 12:18 t Ge 27:36
**29:30** u Ge 31:41
**29:31** v Dt 21:15–17 w Ge 11:30; 30:1; Ps 127:3
**29:32** x Ge 16:11; 31:42
**29:34** y Ge 49:5–7
**29:35** z Ge 49:8; Mt 1:2–3
**30:1** a Ge 29:31; 1Sa 1:5–6
**30:2** b Ge 16:2; 29:31

[a]17 Or *delicate* [b]32 *Reuben* sounds like the Hebrew for *he has seen my misery*; the name means *see, a son.* [c]33 *Simeon* probably means *one who hears.* [d]34 *Levi* sounds like and may be derived from the Hebrew for *attached.* [e]35 *Judah* sounds like and may be derived from the Hebrew for *praise.*

# Rachel

## Taking Care of Business

What was Rachel doing when she met Jacob, the man who fell in love with her? We often hear about how Jacob was smitten with Laban's pretty daughter; we read how he told Laban that he would work seven years for Rachel's hand in marriage; we remember how Jacob served that seven years, and then Laban tricked him and gave him Leah, Rachel's older sister. Because Jacob desired to have Rachel, he worked for Laban another seven years (see Ge 29:16–30). But what made Rachel so attractive that she was worth 14 years of labor? Was it simply her beauty? Or did Jacob see something else in the young woman?

Perhaps Jacob realized that Rachel was a woman who was taking care of business. When Jacob met Rachel, she was not sitting around waiting to be rescued from her single life. Rachel was working. She was taking care of her father's sheep (see Ge 29:6–12). In fact, her future husband rolled away the stone of a well to aid her in her work. Jacob not only looked upon Rachel's physical beauty, but he likely also noted her dedication and commitment to her father's sheep.

Women who are waiting for their future mates should be taking care of their own business; they should not be idly waiting for someone to make their lives complete or happy. No matter what our situation, we need to understand that we are complete in Christ and that true joy comes from our relationship with him. We should be taking care of God's sheep and living out the purposes God has placed in our hearts. Then when our mates come along, they will be willing to help us continue taking care of the business God has given us charge over—they will not want to hinder us.

—K. Washington

### reflection

*How are you living out the purposes God has placed in your life?*

### read

Genesis 29:1—30:26; 31:4,14–19,32–35; 33:2,7; 35:16–20.

**See also** the Inspire Notes "The Gift of Aloneness" and "Singleness—A Stage of Life," and the Women of the Bible Note "Leah: Courage, Resistance and Struggle."

For the next Women of the Bible note, go to page 46.

**30:3** c Ge 16:2
**30:4** d Ge 16:3–4
**30:9** e ver 4
**30:13** f Lk 1:48

children for me and that through her I too
can build a family."[c]
4So she gave him her servant Bilhah as
a wife. Jacob slept with her,[d] 5and she be-
came pregnant and bore him a son. 6Then
Rachel said, "God has vindicated me; he has
listened to my plea and given me a son." Be-
cause of this she named him Dan.[a]
7Rachel's servant Bilhah conceived again
and bore Jacob a second son. 8Then Rachel
said, "I have had a great struggle with my
sister, and I have won." So she named him
Naphtali.[b]
9When Leah saw that she had stopped
having children, she took her maidservant
Zilpah and gave her to Jacob as a wife.[e] 10Le-
ah's servant Zilpah bore Jacob a son. 11Then
Leah said, "What good fortune!"[c] So she
named him Gad.[d]
12Leah's servant Zilpah bore Jacob a sec-
ond son. 13Then Leah said, "How happy I
am! The women will call me happy."[f] So she
named him Asher.[e]
14During wheat harvest, Reuben went out
into the fields and found some mandrake
plants, which he brought to his mother
Leah. Rachel said to Leah, "Please give me
some of your son's mandrakes."
15But she said to her, "Wasn't it enough
that you took away my husband? Will you
take my son's mandrakes too?"
"Very well," Rachel said, "he can sleep
with you tonight in return for your son's
mandrakes."
16So when Jacob came in from the fields
that evening, Leah went out to meet him.
"You must sleep with me," she said. "I have
hired you with my son's mandrakes." So he
slept with her that night.
17God listened to Leah, and she became
pregnant and bore Jacob a fifth son. 18Then
Leah said, "God has rewarded me for giving
my maidservant to my husband." So she
named him Issachar.[f]
19Leah conceived again and bore Jacob
a sixth son. 20Then Leah said, "God has
presented me with a precious gift. This
time my husband will treat me with honor,
because I have borne him six sons." So she
named him Zebulun.[g]
21Some time later she gave birth to a
daughter and named her Dinah.
22Then God remembered Rachel;[g] he
listened to her and opened her womb.[h]
23She became pregnant and gave birth to a
son and said, "God has taken away my dis-
grace."[i] 24She named him Joseph,[h] and said,
"May the LORD add to me another son."[j]

## Jacob's Flocks Increase

25After Rachel gave birth to Joseph, Jacob
said to Laban, "Send me on my way[k] so I can
go back to my own homeland. 26Give me my
wives and children, for whom I have served
you,[l] and I will be on my way. You know how
much work I've done for you."
27But Laban said to him, "If I have found
favor in your eyes, please stay. I have learned
by divination that[i] the LORD has blessed me
because of you."[m] 28He added, "Name your
wages,[n] and I will pay them."
29Jacob said to him, "You know how I
have worked for you and how your livestock
has fared under my care. 30The little you had
before I came has increased greatly, and the
LORD has blessed you wherever I have been.
But now, when may I do something for my
own household?"
31"What shall I give you?" he asked.
"Don't give me anything," Jacob replied.
"But if you will do this one thing for me, I will
go on tending your flocks and watching over
them: 32Let me go through all your flocks to-
day and remove from them every speckled
or spotted sheep, every dark-colored lamb
and every spotted or speckled goat.[o] They
will be my wages. 33And my honesty will
testify for me in the future, whenever you
check on the wages you have paid me. Any
goat in my possession that is not speckled
or spotted, or any lamb that is not dark-
colored, will be considered stolen."
34"Agreed," said Laban. "Let it be as you
have said." 35That same day he removed all
the male goats that were streaked or spot-
ted, and all the speckled or spotted female
goats (all that had white on them) and all
the dark-colored lambs, and he placed them
in the care of his sons. 36Then he put a three-
day journey between himself and Jacob,

**30:22** g 1Sa 1:19–20 h Ge 29:31
**30:23** i Isa 4:1; Lk 1:25
**30:24** j Ge 35:17
**30:25** k Ge 24:54
**30:26** l Ge 29:20,30; Hos 12:12
**30:27** m Ge 26:24; 39:3,5
**30:28** n Ge 29:15
**30:32** o Ge 31:8,12

[a]6 *Dan* here means *he has vindicated.* [b]8 *Naphtali* means *my struggle.* [c]11 Or *"A troop is coming!"* [d]11 *Gad* can mean *good fortune* or *a troop.* [e]13 *Asher* means *happy.* [f]18 *Issachar* sounds like the Hebrew for *reward.* [g]20 *Zebulun* probably means *honor.* [h]24 *Joseph* means *may he add.* [i]27 Or possibly *have become rich and*

Inspire

# INFERTILITY

**Infertility is often a hidden problem in the church. In Biblical times barrenness, or infertility, was viewed as a stigma and a curse. Thus both Rachel in the Old Testament and Elizabeth in the New Testament exclaimed that their "disgrace" had been removed when they became pregnant (see Ge 30:23; Lk 1:25).**

Although there are an equal number of male and female factors involved in infertility, many times women today continue to feel stigmatized and cursed because of it. Infertility can also cause a crisis of faith for many women. It violates our sense of femininity and infringes on God's calling to "be fruitful and increase in number" (Ge 1:28). Infertility can cause us to feel that we have failed our spouses and our ancestors. Sometimes we may even feel cursed by God: If children are a gift and we cannot have children, then we must be undeserving of the gift. Some women feel they are being punished for previous transgressions (e.g., abortions) or are suffering because they were "selfish" for delaying child bearing because of educational or career goals.

Infertility also makes us question the nature of the God we serve. If God is the provider and divine healer, then why doesn't he heal our barrenness? And if God will not bless us with a child, then why doesn't he at least take away our intense desire for one? Sometimes well-meaning folks in church make it worse by asking if we have fasted and prayed like Hannah—as if we haven't taken our desires to the altar numerous times. Church folk can sometimes be insensitive to the fact that certain holidays (e.g., Christmas and Mother's Day) are painful reminders of unwanted childlessness for women with infertility.

The good news is that God does hear the cries of those who suffer from infertility. God provides us with several models of how to keep our faith even when we don't receive the desires of our hearts (e.g., Job and Paul). Women can also redefine what it means to "be fruitful and increase in number" by recognizing that we can help bring forth the next generation through other activities besides parenting (e.g., teaching, mentoring and loving children).

—S. Davis Molock

## read

Genesis 18:1–15; 30:1–24; Job 1; Psalm 113:9; Luke 1:5–7,23–25.

**See also** Inspire Notes "Motherhood," "Suffering," "Waiting on God" and "The Paradox of Life and Suffering," and the Women of the Bible Notes "Sarah: Is Anything Too Hard for God?" "Rebekah: A Woman of Obsessive Love," "Rachel: Taking Care of Business" and "Hannah: What Do You Do When God Says 'No.'"

## WOMAN of COLOR

How will you be fruitful today?

For the next Inspire note, go to page 91.

while Jacob continued to tend the rest of La-
ban's flocks.
37 Jacob, however, took fresh-cut branches
from poplar, almond and plane trees and
made white stripes on them by peeling the
bark and exposing the white inner wood of
the branches. 38 Then he placed the peeled
branches in all the watering troughs, so that
they would be directly in front of the flocks
when they came to drink. When the flocks
were in heat and came to drink, 39 they
mated in front of the branches. And they
bore young that were streaked or speckled
or spotted. 40 Jacob set apart the young of the
flock by themselves, but made the rest face
the streaked and dark-colored animals that
belonged to Laban. Thus he made separate
flocks for himself and did not put them with
Laban's animals. 41 Whenever the stronger
females were in heat, Jacob would place the
branches in the troughs in front of the ani-
mals so they would mate near the branches,
42 but if the animals were weak, he would not
place them there. So the weak animals went
to Laban and the strong ones to Jacob. 43 In
this way the man grew exceedingly prosper-
ous and came to own large flocks, and maid-
servants and menservants, and camels
and donkeys.[p]

## Jacob Flees From Laban

31 Jacob heard that Laban's sons were
saying, "Jacob has taken everything
our father owned and has gained all this
wealth from what belonged to our father."
2 And Jacob noticed that Laban's attitude to-
ward him was not what it had been.
3 Then the LORD said to Jacob, "Go back[q]
to the land of your fathers and to your rela-
tives, and I will be with you."[r]
4 So Jacob sent word to Rachel and Leah to
come out to the fields where his flocks were.
5 He said to them, "I see that your father's at-
titude toward me is not what it was before,
but the God of my father has been with
me.[s] 6 You know that I've worked for your fa-
ther with all my strength,[t] 7 yet your father
has cheated me by changing my wages ten
times.[u] However, God has not allowed him
to harm me. 8 If he said, 'The speckled ones
will be your wages,' then all the flocks gave
birth to speckled young; and if he said, 'The
streaked ones will be your wages,'[v] then all
the flocks bore streaked young. 9 So God has
taken away your father's livestock and has
given them to me.
10 "In breeding season I once had a dream
in which I looked up and saw that the male
goats mating with the flock were streaked,
speckled or spotted. 11 The angel of God said
to me in the dream, 'Jacob.' I answered,
'Here I am.' 12 And he said, 'Look up and
see that all the male goats mating with the
flock are streaked, speckled or spotted, for
I have seen all that Laban has been doing to
you.[w] 13 I am the God of Bethel,[x] where you
anointed a pillar and where you made a vow
to me. Now leave this land at once and go
back to your native land.' "
14 Then Rachel and Leah replied, "Do we
still have any share in the inheritance of our
father's estate? 15 Does he not regard us as
foreigners? Not only has he sold us, but he
has used up what was paid for us.[y] 16 Surely
all the wealth that God took away from our
father belongs to us and our children. So do
whatever God has told you."
17 Then Jacob put his children and his
wives on camels, 18 and he drove all his live-
stock ahead of him, along with all the goods
he had accumulated in Paddan Aram,[a] to go
to his father Isaac[z] in the land of Canaan.
19 When Laban had gone to shear his
sheep, Rachel stole her father's household
gods.[a] 20 Moreover, Jacob deceived[b] Laban
the Aramean by not telling him he was run-
ning away. 21 So he fled with all he had, and
crossing the River,[b] he headed for the hill
country of Gilead.

## Laban Pursues Jacob

22 On the third day Laban was told that Ja-
cob had fled. 23 Taking his relatives with him,
he pursued Jacob for seven days and caught
up with him in the hill country of Gilead.
24 Then God came to Laban the Aramean in
a dream at night and said to him,[c] "Be care-
ful not to say anything to Jacob, either good
or bad."[d]
25 Jacob had pitched his tent in the hill
country of Gilead when Laban overtook
him, and Laban and his relatives camped

[a] 18 That is, Northwest Mesopotamia [b] 21 That is, the Euphrates

**30:43** p Ge 12:16; 13:2; 24:35; 26:13–14
**31:3** q Ge 32:9 r Ge 21:22; 26:3; 28:15
**31:5** s Ge 21:22; 26:3
**31:6** t Ge 30:29
**31:7** u ver 41
**31:8** v Ge 30:32
**31:12** w Ex 3:7
**31:13** x Ge 28:10–22
**31:15** y Ge 29:20
**31:18** z Ge 35:27
**31:19** a ver 30,32,34–35; Ge 35:2; Jdg 17:5; 1Sa 19:13; Hos 3:4
**31:20** b Ge 27:36
**31:24** c Ge 20:3 d Ge 24:50

**31:28** e ver 55
**31:30** f ver 19
**31:32** g Ge 44:9
**31:35** h Lev 19:3,32
**31:37** i ver 23

there too. 26 Then Laban said to Jacob, "What
have you done? You've deceived me, and
you've carried off my daughters like cap-
tives in war. 27 Why did you run off secretly
and deceive me? Why didn't you tell me, so I
could send you away with joy and singing to
the music of tambourines and harps? 28 You
didn't even let me kiss my grandchildren
and my daughters good-by.[e] You have done
a foolish thing. 29 I have the power to harm
you; but last night the God of your father
said to me, 'Be careful not to say anything
to Jacob, either good or bad.' 30 Now you
have gone off because you longed to return
to your father's house. But why did you steal
my gods?[f]"

31 Jacob answered Laban, "I was afraid, be-
cause I thought you would take your daugh-
ters away from me by force. 32 But if you find
anyone who has your gods, he shall not live.[g]
In the presence of our relatives, see for your-
self whether there is anything of yours here
with me; and if so, take it." Now Jacob did
not know that Rachel had stolen the gods.

33 So Laban went into Jacob's tent and
into Leah's tent and into the tent of the two
maidservants, but he found nothing. Af-
ter he came out of Leah's tent, he entered
Rachel's tent. 34 Now Rachel had taken the
household gods and put them inside her
camel's saddle and was sitting on them. La-
ban searched through everything in the tent
but found nothing.

35 Rachel said to her father, "Don't be angry,
my lord, that I cannot stand up in your pres-
ence;[h] I'm having my period." So he searched
but could not find the household gods.

36 Jacob was angry and took Laban to
task. "What is my crime?" he asked Laban.
"What sin have I committed that you hunt
me down? 37 Now that you have searched
through all my goods, what have you found
that belongs to your household? Put it here
in front of your relatives[i] and mine, and let
them judge between the two of us.

38 "I have been with you for twenty years
now. Your sheep and goats have not mis-
carried, nor have I eaten rams from your
flocks. 39 I did not bring you animals torn by
wild beasts; I bore the loss myself. And you
demanded payment from me for whatever
was stolen by day or night.[j] 40 This was my
situation: The heat consumed me in the
daytime and the cold at night, and sleep
fled from my eyes. 41 It was like this for the
twenty years I was in your household. I
worked for you fourteen years for your two
daughters[k] and six years for your flocks,
and you changed my wages ten times.[l] 42 If
the God of my father, the God of Abraham
and the Fear of Isaac,[m] had not been with
me, you would surely have sent me away
empty-handed. But God has seen my hard-
ship and the toil of my hands,[n] and last
night he rebuked you."

43 Laban answered Jacob, "The women
are my daughters, the children are my chil-
dren, and the flocks are my flocks. All you
see is mine. Yet what can I do today about
these daughters of mine, or about the chil-
dren they have borne? 44 Come now, let's
make a covenant,[o] you and I, and let it serve
as a witness between us."[p]

45 So Jacob took a stone and set it up as
a pillar.[q] 46 He said to his relatives, "Gather
some stones." So they took stones and piled
them in a heap, and they ate there by the
heap. 47 Laban called it Jegar Sahadutha,[a]
and Jacob called it Galeed.[b]

48 Laban said, "This heap is a witness be-
tween you and me today." That is why it was
called Galeed. 49 It was also called Mizpah,[c][r]
because he said, "May the LORD keep watch
between you and me when we are away from
each other. 50 If you mistreat my daughters or
if you take any wives besides my daughters,
even though no one is with us, remember
that God is a witness[s] between you and me."

51 Laban also said to Jacob, "Here is this
heap, and here is this pillar I have set up be-
tween you and me. 52 This heap is a witness,
and this pillar is a witness, that I will not go
past this heap to your side to harm you and
that you will not go past this heap and pil-
lar to my side to harm me. 53 May the God of
Abraham and the God of Nahor, the God of
their father, judge between us."[t]

So Jacob took an oath in the name of the
Fear of his father Isaac.[u] 54 He offered a sac-
rifice there in the hill country and invited
his relatives to a meal. After they had eaten,
they spent the night there.

**31:39** j Ex 22:13
**31:41** k Ge 29:30 l ver 7
**31:42** m ver 53 n Ge 29:32
**31:44** o Ge 21:27; 26:28 p Jos 24:27
**31:45** q Ge 28:18
**31:49** r Jdg 11:29; 1Sa 7:5–6
**31:50** s Jer 29:23; 42:5
**31:53** t Ge 16:5 u ver 42

[a] 47 The Aramaic *Jegar Sahadutha* means *witness heap.* [b] 47 The Hebrew *Galeed* means *witness heap.* [c] 49 *Mizpah* means *watchtower.*

# Leah

## Courage, Resistance and Struggle

Leah's story is one that many women can relate to. It is the story of a woman longing to be loved, looking for validation, yearning to be affirmed. Women who recognize they're on a dead-end road and who therefore desire to know what to do next and how to find a new way can learn from Leah's experiences.

"Leah girl" came to my church last Sunday with her six children. She was tall and lanky and had pretty eyes, but no other feature distinguished her from most "sistas." A member invited "Leah girl" because "Leah girl" had been drawn by her testimony. While on her post as a security guard, "Leah girl" overheard the lament of another young woman. This young woman had been dissed by her man again. Their relationship was a series of broken promises. "Leah girl" walked up and said, "Excuse me, it sounds like you're where I just left."

"Leah girl" had just found the courage to break free from the married man with whom she'd been involved. I bet the first five of her children are named, "This time he'll love me." I get the feeling, however, that the youngest is named, "Now I will praise the Lord."

"Leah girl" came to my church last Sunday. She was hungry, thirsty and looking for a relationship with the Lord. She had come to terms with the fact that validation, affirmation and confirmation are gifts from the Lord and not empty promises from immoral brothers. "Leah girl" lifted her face to praise God.

"Leah girl" represents thousands of women looking for love in all the wrong places. The Biblical Leah spent many years competing for Jacob's love, but one day she decided to look to the Lord instead. For many years Leah struggled to feel fulfilled through her relationship with her husband. During some of those years, she found the strength to rely on the Lord; at other times, she fell victim to the trap of looking for validation through another. If your name is "Leah girl," take the first step today to develop a relationship with Christ. Let the Lord create in you that which will bring eternal satisfaction.

—E. Walters

### reflection

*Have you had the courage to leave unhealthy patterns in the past?*

*What got you through?*

*Use your past successes to help break other unhealthy patterns or share your testimony with someone who needs to hear it.*

### read

Genesis 29:16–17, 31–35; 30:9–21; 35:23; Ruth 4:11.

**See also** the Inspire Notes "Courage to Heal" and "The Paradox of Life and Suffering," and the Women of the Bible Note "Rachel: Taking Care of Business."

For the next Women of the Bible note, go to page 49.

32:3 v Ge 25:30; 36:8,9
32:5 w Ge 12:16; 30:43 x Ge 33:8,10,15
32:6 y Ge 33:1
32:9 z Ge 31:13
32:10 a Ge 24:27
32:11 b Ge 27:41
32:12 c Ge 28:13–15; Hos 1:10
32:13 d Ge 43:11,15, 25,26; Pr 18:16

55 Early the next morning Laban kissed his grandchildren and his daughters and blessed them. Then he left and returned home.

## Jacob Prepares to Meet Esau

**32** Jacob also went on his way, and the angels of God met him. 2 When Jacob saw them, he said, "This is the camp of God!" So he named that place Mahanaim.[a]

3 Jacob sent messengers ahead of him to his brother Esau in the land of Seir, the country of Edom.[v] 4 He instructed them: "This is what you are to say to my master Esau: 'Your servant Jacob says, I have been staying with Laban and have remained there till now. 5 I have cattle and donkeys, sheep and goats, menservants and maidservants.[w] Now I am sending this message to my lord, that I may find favor in your eyes.[x]' "

6 When the messengers returned to Jacob, they said, "We went to your brother Esau, and now he is coming to meet you, and four hundred men are with him."[y]

7 In great fear and distress Jacob divided the people who were with him into two groups,[b] and the flocks and herds and camels as well. 8 He thought, "If Esau comes and attacks one group,[c] the group[c] that is left may escape."

9 Then Jacob prayed, "O God of my father Abraham, God of my father Isaac, O LORD, who said to me, 'Go back to your country and your relatives, and I will make you prosper,'[z] 10 I am unworthy of all the kindness and faithfulness[a] you have shown your servant. I had only my staff when I crossed this Jordan, but now I have become two groups. 11 Save me, I pray, from the hand of my brother Esau, for I am afraid he will come and attack me, and also the mothers with their children.[b] 12 But you have said, 'I will surely make you prosper and will make your descendants like the sand of the sea, which cannot be counted.[c]' "

13 He spent the night there, and from what he had with him he selected a gift[d] for his brother Esau: 14 two hundred female goats and twenty male goats, two hundred ewes and twenty rams, 15 thirty female camels with their young, forty cows and ten bulls, and twenty female donkeys and ten male donkeys. 16 He put them in the care of his servants, each herd by itself, and said to his servants, "Go ahead of me, and keep some space between the herds."

17 He instructed the one in the lead: "When my brother Esau meets you and asks, 'To whom do you belong, and where are you going, and who owns all these animals in front of you?' 18 then you are to say, 'They belong to your servant Jacob. They are a gift sent to my lord Esau, and he is coming behind us.' "

19 He also instructed the second, the third and all the others who followed the herds: "You are to say the same thing to Esau when you meet him. 20 And be sure to say, 'Your servant Jacob is coming behind us.' " For he thought, "I will pacify him with these gifts I am sending on ahead; later, when I see him, perhaps he will receive me." 21 So Jacob's gifts went on ahead of him, but he himself spent the night in the camp.

## Jacob Wrestles With God

22 That night Jacob got up and took his two wives, his two maidservants and his eleven sons and crossed the ford of the Jabbok.[e] 23 After he had sent them across the stream, he sent over all his possessions. 24 So Jacob was left alone, and a man wrestled with him till daybreak. 25 When the man saw that he could not overpower him, he touched the socket of Jacob's hip so that his hip was wrenched as he wrestled with the man. 26 Then the man said, "Let me go, for it is daybreak."

But Jacob replied, "I will not let you go unless you bless me."[f]

27 The man asked him, "What is your name?"

"Jacob," he answered.

28 Then the man said, "Your name will no longer be Jacob, but Israel,[d][g] because you have struggled with God and with men and have overcome."

29 Jacob said, "Please tell me your name."

But he replied, "Why do you ask my name?" Then he blessed him there.

30 So Jacob called the place Peniel,[e] saying, "It is because I saw God face to face,[h] and yet my life was spared."

32:22 e Dt 2:37; 3:16
32:26 f Hos 12:4
32:28 g Ge 17:5; 35:10
32:30 h Ge 16:13; Ex 24:11; Jdg 6:22

[a] 2 *Mahanaim* means *two camps.* [b] 7 Or *camps*; also in verse 10 [c] 8 Or *camp* [d] 28 *Israel* means *he struggles with God.* [e] 30 *Peniel* means *face of God.*

31 The sun rose above him as he passed Peniel,[a] and he was limping because of his hip. 32 Therefore to this day the Israelites do not eat the tendon attached to the socket of the hip, because the socket of Jacob's hip was touched near the tendon.

## Jacob Meets Esau

33 Jacob looked up and there was Esau, coming with his four hundred men;[i] so he divided the children among Leah, Rachel and the two maidservants. 2 He put the maidservants and their children in front, Leah and her children next, and Rachel and Joseph in the rear. 3 He himself went on ahead and bowed down to the ground[j] seven times as he approached his brother.

4 But Esau ran to meet Jacob and embraced him; he threw his arms around his neck and kissed him. And they wept.[k] 5 Then Esau looked up and saw the women and children. "Who are these with you?" he asked.

Jacob answered, "They are the children God has graciously given your servant.[l]"

6 Then the maidservants and their children approached and bowed down. 7 Next, Leah and her children came and bowed down. Last of all came Joseph and Rachel, and they too bowed down.

8 Esau asked, "What do you mean by all these droves I met?"[m]

"To find favor in your eyes, my lord," he said.

9 But Esau said, "I already have plenty, my brother. Keep what you have for yourself."

10 "No, please!" said Jacob. "If I have found favor in your eyes, accept this gift from me. For to see your face is like seeing the face of God, now that you have received me favorably. 11 Please accept the present[n] that was brought to you, for God has been gracious to me and I have all I need." And because Jacob insisted, Esau accepted it.

12 Then Esau said, "Let us be on our way; I'll accompany you."

13 But Jacob said to him, "My lord knows that the children are tender and that I must care for the ewes and cows that are nursing their young. If they are driven hard just one day, all the animals will die. 14 So let my lord go on ahead of his servant, while I move along slowly at the pace of the droves before me and that of the children, until I come to my lord in Seir.[o]"

15 Esau said, "Then let me leave some of my men with you."

"But why do that?" Jacob asked. "Just let me find favor in the eyes of my lord."

16 So that day Esau started on his way back to Seir. 17 Jacob, however, went to Succoth,[p] where he built a place for himself and made shelters for his livestock. That is why the place is called Succoth.[b]

18 After Jacob came from Paddan Aram,[c] he arrived safely at the[d] city of Shechem[q] in Canaan and camped within sight of the city. 19 For a hundred pieces of silver,[e] he bought from the sons of Hamor, the father of Shechem,[r] the plot of ground[s] where he pitched his tent. 20 There he set up an altar and called it El Elohe Israel.[f]

## Dinah and the Shechemites

34 Now Dinah,[t] the daughter Leah had borne to Jacob, went out to visit the women of the land. 2 When Shechem son of Hamor the Hivite, the ruler of that area, saw her, he took her and violated her. 3 His heart was drawn to Dinah daughter of Jacob, and he loved the girl and spoke tenderly to her. 4 And Shechem said to his father Hamor, "Get me this girl as my wife."

5 When Jacob heard that his daughter Dinah had been defiled, his sons were in the fields with his livestock; so he kept quiet about it until they came home.

6 Then Shechem's father Hamor went out to talk with Jacob.[u] 7 Now Jacob's sons had come in from the fields as soon as they heard what had happened. They were filled with grief and fury, because Shechem had done a disgraceful thing in[g] Israel[v] by lying with Jacob's daughter—a thing that should not be done.

8 But Hamor said to them, "My son Shechem has his heart set on your daughter. Please give her to him as his wife. 9 Intermarry with us; give us your daughters and take our daughters for yourselves. 10 You can settle among us;[w] the land is open

**33:1** i Ge 32:6
**33:3** j Ge 42:6
**33:4** k Ge 45:14–15
**33:5** l Ge 48:9; Ps 127:3; Isa 8:18
**33:8** m Ge 32:14–16
**33:11** n 1Sa 25:27
**33:14** o Ge 32:3
**33:17** p Jdg 8:5,6,8,14–16
**33:18** q Jos 24:1; Jdg 9:1
**33:19** r Jos 24:32; s Jn 4:5
**34:1** t Ge 30:21
**34:6** u Jdg 14:2–5
**34:7** v Dt 22:21; Jdg 20:6; 2Sa 13:12
**34:10** w Ge 47:6,27

[a]31 Hebrew *Penuel,* a variant of *Peniel* [b]17 *Succoth* means *shelters.* [c]18 That is, Northwest Mesopotamia
[d]18 Or *arrived at Shalem, a* [e]19 Hebrew *hundred kesitahs*; a kesitah was a unit of money of unknown weight and value.
[f]20 *El Elohe Israel* can mean *God, the God of Israel* or *mighty is the God of Israel.* [g]7 Or *against*

# Dinah

## *An Abused Woman*

Dinah is a forgotten woman of the Bible. While we know much about her brothers, Jacob's 12 sons, we know very little about this female child, Jacob's only daughter mentioned in Scripture.

Genesis 34 tells the story of Dinah, the daughter of Jacob and Leah. Dinah left the Hebrew campsite to visit the women in the land. Away from the protection of her family enclave, Dinah was taken by Shechem, the son of a local ruler, and raped.

When Jacob learned of his daughter's rape, he was silent. He did not protest against her treatment; instead he listened to the appeals of Dinah's rapist in the interest of political harmony between the Hebrews and the Hivites. While Jacob continued to negotiate, Dinah's brothers began plotting against the Hivites; meanwhile, Dinah was noticeably absent from the proceedings. According to the story, her feelings and views were never taken into consideration. And not until verse 26 does the reader learn that Dinah had been in Shechem's house all along.

As women of color, we may relate to Dinah's story. We may have been devalued simply for being born female in a culture in which male children are granted more prestige and promise. Perhaps we've been abused in the name of love in so-called loving relationships, while those around us ignored our pain. Perhaps family members and friends are fully aware of the abuse but have chosen to turn away in silence.

This chapter tells a tragic story. Is there any redemption here? First, we can relate to the anger of Dinah's brothers when they learned of her rape. They declared that the rape should not have been done (see Ge 34:7). They declared that a violation of one woman is an affront to the entire community. And while their methods of revenge are abhorrent to us, they ultimately removed Dinah from her place of violation. We need to have the same anger as Dinah's brothers had when we hear of violence toward our abused sisters. We, too, can declare that physical and mental abuse are unacceptable and offend the entire community. We must not be silent!

—M. Coleman

### reflection

*When have you seen another woman mistreated?*

*When have you experienced abuse?*

*How can you take action against the wrongs done to you and your sisters?*

### read

Genesis 34.

**See also** the Inspire Notes "Commitment to Community," "Sexual Abuse" and "Overcoming Abuse," and the Women of the Bible Notes "The Levite's Concubine: Broken Pieces" and "Tamar: A Violated Woman."

For the next Women of the Bible note, go to page 55.

**34:10** x Ge 13:9; 20:15 y Ge 42:34
**34:12** z Ex 22:16; Dt 22:29; 1Sa 18:25
**34:14** a Ge 17:14
**34:15** b Ex 12:48
**34:25** c Ge 49:5 d Ge 49:7

to you.[x] Live in it, trade[a] in it,[y] and acquire
property in it."
11 Then Shechem said to Dinah's father
and brothers, "Let me find favor in your
eyes, and I will give you whatever you ask.
12 Make the price for the bride[z] and the gift I
am to bring as great as you like, and I'll pay
whatever you ask me. Only give me the girl
as my wife."

13 Because their sister Dinah had been
defiled, Jacob's sons replied deceitfully as
they spoke to Shechem and his father Ha-
mor. 14 They said to them, "We can't do such
a thing; we can't give our sister to a man
who is not circumcised.[a] That would be a
disgrace to us. 15 We will give our consent to
you on one condition only: that you become
like us by circumcising all your males.[b]
16 Then we will give you our daughters and
take your daughters for ourselves. We'll set-
tle among you and become one people with
you. 17 But if you will not agree to be circum-
cised, we'll take our sister[b] and go."

18 Their proposal seemed good to Hamor
and his son Shechem. 19 The young man,
who was the most honored of all his father's
household, lost no time in doing what they
said, because he was delighted with Jacob's
daughter. 20 So Hamor and his son Shechem
went to the gate of their city to speak to their
fellow townsmen. 21 "These men are friendly
toward us," they said. "Let them live in our
land and trade in it; the land has plenty of
room for them. We can marry their daugh-
ters and they can marry ours. 22 But the men
will consent to live with us as one people
only on the condition that our males be cir-
cumcised, as they themselves are. 23 Won't
their livestock, their property and all their
other animals become ours? So let us give
our consent to them, and they will settle
among us."

24 All the men who went out of the city gate
agreed with Hamor and his son Shechem,
and every male in the city was circumcised.

25 Three days later, while all of them were
still in pain, two of Jacob's sons, Simeon and
Levi, Dinah's brothers, took their swords[c]
and attacked the unsuspecting city, killing
every male.[d] 26 They put Hamor and his son
Shechem to the sword and took Dinah from
Shechem's house and left. 27 The sons of Ja-
cob came upon the dead bodies and looted
the city where[c] their sister had been defiled.
28 They seized their flocks and herds and
donkeys and everything else of theirs in
the city and out in the fields. 29 They carried
off all their wealth and all their women and
children, taking as plunder everything in
the houses.

30 Then Jacob said to Simeon and Levi,
"You have brought trouble on me by mak-
ing me a stench to the Canaanites and Per-
izzites, the people living in this land. We
are few in number, and if they join forces
against me and attack me, I and my house-
hold will be destroyed."

31 But they replied, "Should he have
treated our sister like a prostitute?"

## Jacob Returns to Bethel

35 Then God said to Jacob, "Go up
to Bethel[e] and settle there, and
build an altar there to God, who appeared
to you when you were fleeing from your
brother Esau."[f]

2 So Jacob said to his household[g] and to
all who were with him, "Get rid of the for-
eign gods[h] you have with you, and purify
yourselves and change your clothes.[i] 3 Then
come, let us go up to Bethel, where I will
build an altar to God, who answered me in
the day of my distress[j] and who has been
with me wherever I have gone." 4 So they
gave Jacob all the foreign gods they had and
the rings in their ears, and Jacob buried
them under the oak at Shechem. 5 Then they
set out, and the terror of God fell upon the
towns all around them so that no one pur-
sued them.

6 Jacob and all the people with him came
to Luz[k] (that is, Bethel) in the land of Ca-
naan. 7 There he built an altar, and he called
the place El Bethel,[d] because it was there
that God revealed himself to him when he
was fleeing from his brother.

8 Now Deborah, Rebekah's nurse,[l] died
and was buried under the oak below Bethel.
So it was named Allon Bacuth.[e]

9 After Jacob returned from Paddan
Aram,[f] God appeared to him again and
blessed him.[m] 10 God said to him, "Your

**35:1** e Ge 28:19 f Ge 27:43
**35:2** g Ge 18:19; Jos 24:15 h Ge 31:19 i Ex 19:10,14
**35:3** j Ge 32:7
**35:6** k Ge 28:19
**35:8** l Ge 24:59
**35:9** m Ge 32:29

[a] 10 Or *move about freely*; also in verse 21 [b] 17 Hebrew *daughter* [c] 27 Or *because* [d] 7 *El Bethel* means *God of Bethel.*
[e] 8 *Allon Bacuth* means *oak of weeping.* [f] 9 That is, Northwest Mesopotamia; also in verse 26

35:10 n Ge 17:5
35:11 o Ge 17:1 p Ge 28:3 q Ge 17:6
35:12 r Ge 13:15; 28:13
35:13 s Ge 17:22
35:14 t Ge 28:18
35:15 u Ge 28:19
35:17 v Ge 30:24
35:20 w 1Sa 10:2

name is Jacob,[a] but you will no longer be
called Jacob; your name will be Israel.[b]"[n] So
he named him Israel.
11And God said to him, "I am God Al-
mighty[c];[o] be fruitful and increase in num-
ber. A nation[p] and a community of nations
will come from you, and kings will come
from your body.[q] 12The land I gave to Abra-
ham and Isaac I also give to you, and I will
give this land to your descendants after
you.[r]" 13Then God went up from him[s] at the
place where he had talked with him.
14Jacob set up a stone pillar at the place
where God had talked with him, and he
poured out a drink offering on it; he also
poured oil on it.[t] 15Jacob called the place
where God had talked with him Bethel.[d][u]

*Daughter,*

*I know exactly where you are and how you are doing. Please trust me with every detail of your life.*

*With all my love,*

*Your Father, God*

GENESIS 35:14–15

## The Deaths of Rachel and Isaac

16Then they moved on from Bethel. While
they were still some distance from Ephrath,
Rachel began to give birth and had great
difficulty. 17And as she was having great
difficulty in childbirth, the midwife said to
her, "Don't be afraid, for you have another
son."[v] 18As she breathed her last—for she
was dying—she named her son Ben-Oni.[e]
But his father named him Benjamin.[f]
19So Rachel died and was buried on the
way to Ephrath (that is, Bethlehem). 20Over
her tomb Jacob set up a pillar, and to this
day that pillar marks Rachel's tomb.[w]
21Israel moved on again and pitched his
tent beyond Migdal Eder. 22While Israel was
living in that region, Reuben went in and
slept with his father's concubine[x] Bilhah,
and Israel heard of it.

Jacob had twelve sons:

23The sons of Leah:
Reuben the firstborn of Jacob,
Simeon, Levi, Judah, Issachar and
Zebulun.
24The sons of Rachel:
Joseph[y] and Benjamin.[z]
25The sons of Rachel's maidservant Bil-
hah:
Dan and Naphtali.
26The sons of Leah's maidservant Zil-
pah:
Gad and Asher.

These were the sons of Jacob, who were
born to him in Paddan Aram.
27Jacob came home to his father Isaac
in Mamre,[a] near Kiriath Arba (that is,
Hebron), where Abraham and Isaac had
stayed. 28Isaac lived a hundred and eighty
years. 29Then he breathed his last and died
and was gathered to his people,[b] old and full
of years.[c] And his sons Esau and Jacob bur-
ied him.[d]

## Esau's Descendants

36 This is the account of Esau (that is,
Edom).[e]
2Esau took his wives from the
women of Canaan:[f] Adah daughter
of Elon the Hittite,[g] and Oholibamah
daughter of Anah and granddaughter
of Zibeon the Hivite— 3also Basemath
daughter of Ishmael and sister of Ne-
baioth.
4Adah bore Eliphaz to Esau, Base-
math bore Reuel,[h] 5and Oholibamah
bore Jeush, Jalam and Korah. These
were the sons of Esau, who were born
to him in Canaan.
6Esau took his wives and sons and
daughters and all the members of his
household, as well as his livestock
and all his other animals and all the
goods he had acquired in Canaan,[i] and
moved to a land some distance from
his brother Jacob. 7Their possessions

35:22 x Ge 49:4; 1Ch 5:1
35:24 y Ge 30:24 z ver 18
35:27 a Ge 13:18
35:29 b Ge 25:8 c Ge 15:15 d Ge 25:9
36:1 e Ge 25:30
36:2 f Ge 28:8–9 g Ge 26:34
36:4 h 1Ch 1:35
36:6 i Ge 12:5

[a]10 *Jacob* means *he grasps the heel* (figuratively, *he deceives*). [b]10 *Israel* means *he struggles with God.* [c]11 Hebrew *El-Shaddai* [d]15 *Bethel* means *house of God.* [e]18 *Ben-Oni* means *son of my trouble.* [f]18 *Benjamin* means *son of my right hand.*

**36:7**
j Ge 13:6
**36:8**
k Dt 2:4
l Ge 32:3
**36:12**
m Ex 17:8,16; Nu 24:20; 1Sa 15:2
n ver 16
**36:15**
o Ex 15:15
**36:17**
p 1Ch 1:37

were too great for them to remain
together; the land where they were
staying could not support them both
because of their livestock.[j] 8 So Esau[k]
(that is, Edom) settled in the hill country of Seir.[l]

9 This is the account of Esau the father of
the Edomites in the hill country of Seir.

10 These are the names of Esau's sons:
Eliphaz, the son of Esau's wife Adah, and Reuel, the son of Esau's wife Basemath.
11 The sons of Eliphaz:
Teman, Omar, Zepho, Gatam and Kenaz.
12 Esau's son Eliphaz also had a concubine named Timna, who bore him Amalek.[m] These were grandsons of Esau's wife Adah.[n]
13 The sons of Reuel:
Nahath, Zerah, Shammah and Mizzah. These were grandsons of Esau's wife Basemath.
14 The sons of Esau's wife Oholibamah
daughter of Anah and granddaughter
of Zibeon, whom she bore to Esau:
Jeush, Jalam and Korah.

15 These were the chiefs[o] among Esau's descendants:
The sons of Eliphaz the firstborn of Esau:
Chiefs Teman, Omar, Zepho, Kenaz,
16 Korah,[a] Gatam and Amalek.
These were the chiefs descended from Eliphaz in Edom; they were grandsons of Adah.
17 The sons of Esau's son Reuel:[p]
Chiefs Nahath, Zerah, Shammah and Mizzah. These were the chiefs descended from Reuel in Edom; they were grandsons of Esau's wife Basemath.
18 The sons of Esau's wife Oholibamah:
Chiefs Jeush, Jalam and Korah. These were the chiefs descended from Esau's wife Oholibamah daughter of Anah.
19 These were the sons of Esau (that is,
Edom), and these were their chiefs.

20 These were the sons of Seir the Horite,[q]
who were living in the region:
Lotan, Shobal, Zibeon, Anah,
21 Dishon, Ezer and Dishan. These sons of Seir in Edom were Horite chiefs.
22 The sons of Lotan:
Hori and Homam.[b] Timna was Lotan's sister.
23 The sons of Shobal:
Alvan, Manahath, Ebal, Shepho and Onam.
24 The sons of Zibeon:
Aiah and Anah. This is the Anah who discovered the hot springs[c] in the desert while he was grazing the donkeys of his father Zibeon.
25 The children of Anah:
Dishon and Oholibamah daughter of Anah.
26 The sons of Dishon[d]:
Hemdan, Eshban, Ithran and Keran.
27 The sons of Ezer:
Bilhan, Zaavan and Akan.
28 The sons of Dishan:
Uz and Aran.
29 These were the Horite chiefs:
Lotan, Shobal, Zibeon, Anah,
30 Dishon, Ezer and Dishan. These were the Horite chiefs, according to their divisions, in the land of Seir.

## The Rulers of Edom

31 These were the kings who reigned in
Edom before any Israelite king[r] reigned[e]:
32 Bela son of Beor became king of Edom. His city was named Dinhabah.
33 When Bela died, Jobab son of Zerah from Bozrah succeeded him as king.
34 When Jobab died, Husham from the land of the Temanites succeeded him as king.
35 When Husham died, Hadad son of Bedad, who defeated Midian in the country of Moab,[s] succeeded him as king. His city was named Avith.
36 When Hadad died, Samlah from Masrekah succeeded him as king.

**36:20**
q Ge 14:6; Dt 2:12,22
**36:31**
r 1Ch 1:43
**36:35**
s Ge 19:37; Ru 1:1,6

[a] 16 Masoretic Text; Samaritan Pentateuch (see also Gen. 36:11 and 1 Chron. 1:36) does not have *Korah.* [b] 22 Hebrew *Hemam,* a variant of *Homam* (see 1 Chron. 1:39) [c] 24 Vulgate; Syriac *discovered water;* the meaning of the Hebrew for this word is uncertain. [d] 26 Hebrew *Dishan,* a variant of *Dishon* [e] 31 Or *before an Israelite king reigned over them*

[37] When Samlah died, Shaul from Rehoboth on the river[a] succeeded him as king.
[38] When Shaul died, Baal-Hanan son of Acbor succeeded him as king.
[39] When Baal-Hanan son of Acbor died, Hadad[b] succeeded him as king. His city was named Pau, and his wife's name was Mehetabel daughter of Matred, the daughter of Me-Zahab.

[40] These were the chiefs descended from Esau, by name, according to their clans and regions:

Timna, Alvah, Jetheth, [41] Oholibamah, Elah, Pinon, [42] Kenaz, Teman, Mibzar, [43] Magdiel and Iram. These were the chiefs of Edom, according to their settlements in the land they occupied.

This was Esau the father of the Edomites.

## Joseph's Dreams

37 Jacob lived in the land where his father had stayed,[t] the land of Canaan.

[2] This is the account of Jacob.

Joseph, a young man of seventeen, was tending the flocks[u] with his brothers, the sons of Bilhah and the sons of Zilpah, his father's wives, and he brought their father a bad report[v] about them.

[3] Now Israel loved Joseph more than any of his other sons, because he had been born to him in his old age;[w] and he made a richly ornamented[c] robe for him. [4] When his brothers saw that their father loved him more than any of them, they hated him[x] and could not speak a kind word to him.

[5] Joseph had a dream, and when he told it to his brothers, they hated him all the more. [6] He said to them, "Listen to this dream I had: [7] We were binding sheaves of grain out in the field when suddenly my sheaf rose and stood upright, while your sheaves gathered around mine and bowed down to it."[y]

[8] His brothers said to him, "Do you intend to reign over us? Will you actually rule us?"[z] And they hated him all the more because of his dream and what he had said.

[9] Then he had another dream, and he told it to his brothers. "Listen," he said, "I had another dream, and this time the sun and moon and eleven stars were bowing down to me."

[10] When he told his father as well as his brothers, his father rebuked him and said, "What is this dream you had? Will your mother and I and your brothers actually come and bow down to the ground before you?"[a] [11] His brothers were jealous of him,[b] but his father kept the matter in mind.[c]

## Joseph Sold by His Brothers

[12] Now his brothers had gone to graze their father's flocks near Shechem, [13] and Israel said to Joseph, "As you know, your brothers are grazing the flocks near Shechem. Come, I am going to send you to them."

"Very well," he replied.

[14] So he said to him, "Go and see if all is well with your brothers and with the flocks, and bring word back to me." Then he sent him off from the Valley of Hebron.

When Joseph arrived at Shechem, [15] a man found him wandering around in the fields and asked him, "What are you looking for?"

[16] He replied, "I'm looking for my brothers. Can you tell me where they are grazing their flocks?"

[17] "They have moved on from here," the man answered. "I heard them say, 'Let's go to Dothan.[d]'"

So Joseph went after his brothers and found them near Dothan. [18] But they saw him in the distance, and before he reached them, they plotted to kill him.[e]

[19] "Here comes that dreamer!" they said to each other. [20] "Come now, let's kill him and throw him into one of these cisterns and say that a ferocious animal devoured him. Then we'll see what comes of his dreams."[f]

[21] When Reuben heard this, he tried to rescue him from their hands. "Let's not take his life," he said.[g] [22] "Don't shed any blood. Throw him into this cistern here in the desert, but don't lay a hand on him." Reuben said this to rescue him from them and take him back to his father.

**37:1** t Ge 17:8
**37:2** u Ps 78:71 v 1Sa 2:24
**37:3** w Ge 44:20
**37:4** x Ge 27:41
**37:7** y Ge 42:6,9; 43:26,28; 44:14; 50:18
**37:8** z Ge 49:26
**37:10** a Ge 27:29
**37:11** b Ac 7:9 c Lk 2:19,51
**37:17** d 2Ki 6:13
**37:18** e Mk 14:1
**37:20** f Ge 50:20
**37:21** g Ge 42:22

[a] 37 Possibly the Euphrates [b] 39 Many manuscripts of the Masoretic Text, Samaritan Pentateuch and Syriac (see also 1 Chron. 1:50); most manuscripts of the Masoretic Text *Hadar* [c] 3 The meaning of the Hebrew for *richly ornamented* is uncertain; also in verses 23 and 32.

**37:25** h ver 28
**37:26** i ver 20; Ge 4:10
**37:27** j Ge 42:21
**37:28** k Jdg 6:1–3 l Ge 45:4–5; Ps 105:17; Ac 7:9
**37:29** m Job 1:20
**37:30** n ver 22; Ge 42:13,36
**37:31** o ver 3,23
**37:33** p ver 20
**37:35** q Ge 42:38; 44:22,29,31
**37:36** r Ge 39:1

23 So when Joseph came to his brothers, they stripped him of his robe—the richly ornamented robe he was wearing— 24 and they took him and threw him into the cistern. Now the cistern was empty; there was no water in it.

25 As they sat down to eat their meal, they looked up and saw a caravan of Ishmaelites coming from Gilead. Their camels were loaded with spices, balm and myrrh, and they were on their way to take them down to Egypt.[h]

26 Judah said to his brothers, "What will we gain if we kill our brother and cover up his blood?[i] 27 Come, let's sell him to the Ishmaelites and not lay our hands on him; after all, he is our brother,[j] our own flesh and blood." His brothers agreed.

28 So when the Midianite[k] merchants came by, his brothers pulled Joseph up out of the cistern and sold him for twenty shekels[a] of silver to the Ishmaelites, who took him to Egypt.[l]

29 When Reuben returned to the cistern and saw that Joseph was not there, he tore his clothes.[m] 30 He went back to his brothers and said, "The boy isn't there! Where can I turn now?"[n]

31 Then they got Joseph's robe,[o] slaughtered a goat and dipped the robe in the blood. 32 They took the ornamented robe back to their father and said, "We found this. Examine it to see whether it is your son's robe."

33 He recognized it and said, "It is my son's robe! Some ferocious animal[p] has devoured him. Joseph has surely been torn to pieces."

34 Then Jacob tore his clothes, put on sackcloth and mourned for his son many days. 35 All his sons and daughters came to comfort him, but he refused to be comforted. "No," he said, "in mourning will I go down to the grave[b][q] to my son." So his father wept for him.

36 Meanwhile, the Midianites[c] sold Joseph in Egypt to Potiphar, one of Pharaoh's officials, the captain of the guard.[r]

## Judah and Tamar

**38** At that time, Judah left his brothers and went down to stay with a man of Adullam named Hirah. 2 There Judah met the daughter of a Canaanite man named Shua.[s] He married her and lay with her; 3 she became pregnant and gave birth to a son, who was named Er.[t] 4 She conceived again and gave birth to a son and named him Onan. 5 She gave birth to still another son and named him Shelah. It was at Kezib that she gave birth to him.

6 Judah got a wife for Er, his firstborn, and her name was Tamar. 7 But Er, Judah's firstborn, was wicked in the LORD's sight; so the LORD put him to death.[u]

8 Then Judah said to Onan, "Lie with your brother's wife and fulfill your duty to her as a brother-in-law to produce offspring for your brother."[v] 9 But Onan knew that the offspring would not be his; so whenever he lay with his brother's wife, he spilled his semen on the ground to keep from producing offspring for his brother. 10 What he did was wicked in the LORD's sight; so he put him to death also.[w]

11 Judah then said to his daughter-in-law Tamar, "Live as a widow in your father's house until my son Shelah grows up."[x] For he thought, "He may die too, just like his brothers." So Tamar went to live in her father's house.

12 After a long time Judah's wife, the daughter of Shua, died. When Judah had recovered from his grief, he went up to Timnah, to the men who were shearing his sheep, and his friend Hirah the Adullamite went with him.

13 When Tamar was told, "Your father-in-law is on his way to Timnah to shear his sheep," 14 she took off her widow's clothes, covered herself with a veil to disguise herself, and then sat down at the entrance to Enaim, which is on the road to Timnah. For she saw that, though Shelah[y] had now grown up, she had not been given to him as his wife.

15 When Judah saw her, he thought she was a prostitute, for she had covered her face. 16 Not realizing that she was his daughter-in-law, he went over to her by the roadside and said, "Come now, let me sleep with you."

"And what will you give me to sleep with you?" she asked.

**38:2** s 1Ch 2:3
**38:3** t ver 6; Ge 46:12
**38:7** u 1Ch 2:3
**38:8** v Dt 25:5–6; Mt 22:24–28
**38:10** w Ge 46:12
**38:11** x Ru 1:13
**38:14** y ver 11

[a] 28 That is, about 8 ounces (about 0.2 kilogram) [b] 35 Hebrew *Sheol* [c] 36 Samaritan Pentateuch, Septuagint, Vulgate and Syriac (see also verse 28); Masoretic Text *Medanites*

# Tamar

## *The Link Between Judah and Jesus*

Tamar is a forgotten heroine in the Bible. Tamar's story begins with the loss of two husbands, Er and Onan (see Ge 38:6–10), sons of Judah. Childless, her future was questionable. Tamar had two choices: (1) she could accept her lot in life; or (2) she could take action. Tamar made the second choice and became her own advocate.

Bound by what was known as "levirate law" to either marry another son of Judah or be liberated by Judah to marry another man, Tamar used her femininity and played on his manliness, dressing as a prostitute (see Ge 38:13–15). Her goal was security by any means necessary, even a pregnancy when she was unmarried. And, though she risked death if found guilty of adultery, she acquired Judah's personal pledge by obtaining his seal, cord and staff as proof of his participation in this sexually immoral act. Not only did Judah's personal items implicate him, they forced him to fulfill his responsibility to her as the father of her child.

When Judah realized that he had denied her justice under levirate law, he could only say, "She is more righteous than I" (Ge 38:26).

Tamar gave birth to twins, Perez and Zerah (see Ge 38:27–30). Critics may ask, "Why is this story found in the middle of Joseph's story?" One reason is that it prepares us for Genesis 49, a chapter in which Jacob blesses Judah, his fourth son, with his scepter, a symbol of birthright and kingship traditionally given to the firstborn. The immoral and violent behavior of his three older brothers (Reuben, Simeon and Levi) set the stage for this blessing to be passed to Judah. Thus, it was through the "Lion of Judah" that the house of David was established. David's ancestry is traced back to Perez, one of the twins fathered by Judah through his daughter-in-law Tamar (see Ru 4:18–22; Mt 1:1–3). Here we have the link between Judah and Jesus.

God works in amazing ways. Despite Tamar and Judah's immoral acts, God sovereignly worked out his good plan. No human frailty can thwart his purposes.

—K. Worrill Johnson

### reflection

*How has God used one of your so-called mistakes to accomplish his purpose in your life or in the lives of others?*

*Share your testimony with a sister who is beating herself up about one of her mistakes.*

### read

Genesis 38; Deuteronomy 25:5–6. See also the Inspire Notes "God Is Immutable," "Omniscience: God Is All Knowing" and "Abandonment."

For the next Women of the Bible note, go to page 73.

17 “I’ll send you a young goat from my flock,” he said.

“Will you give me something as a pledge[z] until you send it?” she asked.

18 He said, “What pledge should I give you?”

“Your seal[a] and its cord, and the staff in your hand,” she answered. So he gave them to her and slept with her, and she became pregnant by him. 19 After she left, she took off her veil and put on her widow’s clothes[b] again.

20 Meanwhile Judah sent the young goat by his friend the Adullamite in order to get his pledge back from the woman, but he did not find her. 21 He asked the men who lived there, “Where is the shrine prostitute who was beside the road at Enaim?”

“There hasn’t been any shrine prostitute here,” they said.

22 So he went back to Judah and said, “I didn’t find her. Besides, the men who lived there said, ‘There hasn’t been any shrine prostitute here.’ ”

23 Then Judah said, “Let her keep what she has, or we will become a laughingstock. After all, I did send her this young goat, but you didn’t find her.”

24 About three months later Judah was told, “Your daughter-in-law Tamar is guilty of prostitution, and as a result she is now pregnant.”

Judah said, “Bring her out and have her burned to death!”[c]

25 As she was being brought out, she sent a message to her father-in-law. “I am pregnant by the man who owns these,” she said. And she added, “See if you recognize whose seal and cord and staff these are.”[d]

26 Judah recognized them and said, “She is more righteous than I,[e] since I wouldn’t give her to my son Shelah.[f]” And he did not sleep with her again.

27 When the time came for her to give birth, there were twin boys in her womb. 28 As she was giving birth, one of them put out his hand; so the midwife took a scarlet thread and tied it on his wrist and said, “This one came out first.” 29 But when he drew back his hand, his brother came out, and she said, “So this is how you have broken out!” And he was named Perez.[a][g] 30 Then his brother, who had the scarlet thread on his wrist, came out and he was given the name Zerah.[b]

## Joseph and Potiphar’s Wife

39 Now Joseph had been taken down to Egypt. Potiphar, an Egyptian who was one of Pharaoh’s officials, the captain of the guard,[h] bought him from the Ishmaelites who had taken him there.[i]

2 The LORD was with Joseph and he prospered, and he lived in the house of his Egyptian master. 3 When his master saw that the LORD was with him[j] and that the LORD gave him success in everything he did,[k] 4 Joseph found favor in his eyes and became his attendant. Potiphar put him in charge of his household, and he entrusted to his care everything he owned. 5 From the time he put him in charge of his household and of all that he owned, the LORD blessed the household of the Egyptian because of Joseph. The blessing of the LORD was on everything Potiphar had, both in the house and in the field. 6 So he left in Joseph’s care everything he had; with Joseph in charge, he did not concern himself with anything except the food he ate.

Now Joseph was well-built and handsome, 7 and after a while his master’s wife took notice of Joseph and said, “Come to bed with me!”

8 But he refused.[l] “With me in charge,” he told her, “my master does not concern himself with anything in the house; everything he owns he has entrusted to my care. 9 No one is greater in this house than I am. My master has withheld nothing from me except you, because you are his wife. How then could I do such a wicked thing and sin against God?”[m] 10 And though she spoke to Joseph day after day, he refused to go to bed with her or even be with her.

11 One day he went into the house to attend to his duties, and none of the household servants was inside. 12 She caught him by his cloak[n] and said, “Come to bed with me!” But he left his cloak in her hand and ran out of the house.

13 When she saw that he had left his cloak

**38:17** z ver 20
**38:18** a ver 25
**38:19** b ver 14
**38:24** c Lev 21:9; Dt 22:21,22
**38:25** d ver 18
**38:26** e 1Sa 24:17 f ver 11
**38:29** g Ge 46:12; Nu 26:20,21; Mt 1:3
**39:1** h Ge 37:36 i Ge 37:25; Ps 105:17
**39:3** j Ge 21:22; 26:28 k Ps 1:3
**39:8** l Pr 6:23–24
**39:9** m Ge 20:6; 42:18; 2Sa 12:13
**39:12** n Pr 7:13

[a]29 *Perez* means *breaking out.* [b]30 *Zerah* can mean *scarlet* or *brightness.*

39:14 o Dt 22:24,27
39:17 p Ex 23:1,7
39:19 q Pr 6:34
39:20 r Ps 105:18
39:21 s Ex 3:21
39:23 t ver 3
40:3 u Ge 39:20

in her hand and had run out of the house, 14she called her household servants. "Look," she said to them, "this Hebrew has been brought to us to make sport of us! He came in here to sleep with me, but I screamed.[o] 15When he heard me scream for help, he left his cloak beside me and ran out of the house."

16She kept his cloak beside her until his master came home. 17Then she told him this story:[p] "That Hebrew slave you brought us came to me to make sport of me. 18But as soon as I screamed for help, he left his cloak beside me and ran out of the house."

19When his master heard the story his wife told him, saying, "This is how your slave treated me," he burned with anger.[q] 20Joseph's master took him and put him in prison,[r] the place where the king's prisoners were confined.

But while Joseph was there in the prison, 21the LORD was with him; he showed him kindness and granted him favor in the eyes of the prison warden.[s] 22So the warden put Joseph in charge of all those held in the prison, and he was made responsible for all that was done there. 23The warden paid no attention to anything under Joseph's care, because the LORD was with Joseph and gave him success in whatever he did.[t]

## The Cupbearer and the Baker

40 Some time later, the cupbearer and the baker of the king of Egypt offended their master, the king of Egypt. 2Pharaoh was angry with his two officials, the chief cupbearer and the chief baker, 3and put them in custody in the house of the captain of the guard,[u] in the same prison where Joseph was confined. 4The captain of the guard assigned them to Joseph, and he attended them.

After they had been in custody for some time, 5each of the two men—the cupbearer and the baker of the king of Egypt, who were being held in prison—had a dream the same night, and each dream had a meaning of its own.

6When Joseph came to them the next morning, he saw that they were dejected. 7So he asked Pharaoh's officials who were in custody with him in his master's house, "Why are your faces so sad today?"

8"We both had dreams," they answered, "but there is no one to interpret them."[v]

Then Joseph said to them, "Do not interpretations belong to God?[w] Tell me your dreams."

9So the chief cupbearer told Joseph his dream. He said to him, "In my dream I saw a vine in front of me, 10and on the vine were three branches. As soon as it budded, it blossomed, and its clusters ripened into grapes. 11Pharaoh's cup was in my hand, and I took the grapes, squeezed them into Pharaoh's cup and put the cup in his hand."

12"This is what it means,[x]" Joseph said to him. "The three branches are three days. 13Within three days Pharaoh will lift up your head and restore you to your position, and you will put Pharaoh's cup in his hand, just as you used to do when you were his cupbearer. 14But when all goes well with you, remember me and show me kindness;[y] mention me to Pharaoh and get me out of this prison. 15For I was forcibly carried off from the land of the Hebrews, and even here I have done nothing to deserve being put in a dungeon."

16When the chief baker saw that Joseph had given a favorable interpretation, he said to Joseph, "I too had a dream: On my head were three baskets of bread.[a] 17In the top basket were all kinds of baked goods for Pharaoh, but the birds were eating them out of the basket on my head."

18"This is what it means," Joseph said. "The three baskets are three days.[z] 19Within three days Pharaoh will lift off your head[a] and hang you on a tree.[b] And the birds will eat away your flesh."

20Now the third day was Pharaoh's birthday, and he gave a feast for all his officials. He lifted up the heads of the chief cupbearer and the chief baker in the presence of his officials: 21He restored the chief cupbearer to his position, so that he once again put the cup into Pharaoh's hand,[b] 22but he hanged[c] the chief baker,[c] just as Joseph had said to them in his interpretation.[d]

23The chief cupbearer, however, did not remember Joseph; he forgot him.

40:8 v Ge 41:8,15 w Ge 41:16; Da 2:22,28,47
40:12 x Da 2:36; 4:19
40:14 y Jos 2:12
40:18 z ver 12
40:19 a ver 13
40:21 b ver 13
40:22 c ver 19 d Ps 105:19

[a]16 Or *three wicker baskets* [b]19 Or *and impale you on a pole* [c]22 Or *impaled*

**41:8**
e Da 2:1,3; 4:5,19
f Ex 7:11,22; Da 2:2,27; 4:7

**41:10**
g Ge 40:2

*God,*

*I get very upset when I've been wronged. Please help me to find and utilize the pause button. No matter what someone else does to me or says about me, don't let it interfere with my relationship with you. I want you to be pleased with me, Lord. Let me feel your presence in and around me so that the negative feelings I experience may be swallowed up in your love. Thank you.*

*Amen.*

GENESIS 40:20–23

## Pharaoh's Dreams

**41** When two full years had passed, Pharaoh had a dream: He was standing by the Nile, 2when out of the river there came up seven cows, sleek and fat, and they grazed among the reeds. 3After them, seven other cows, ugly and gaunt, came up out of the Nile and stood beside those on the riverbank. 4And the cows that were ugly and gaunt ate up the seven sleek, fat cows. Then Pharaoh woke up.

5He fell asleep again and had a second dream: Seven heads of grain, healthy and good, were growing on a single stalk. 6After them, seven other heads of grain sprouted—thin and scorched by the east wind. 7The thin heads of grain swallowed up the seven healthy, full heads. Then Pharaoh woke up; it had been a dream.

8In the morning his mind was troubled,[e] so he sent for all the magicians[f] and wise men of Egypt. Pharaoh told them his dreams, but no one could interpret them for him.

9Then the chief cupbearer said to Pharaoh, "Today I am reminded of my shortcomings. 10Pharaoh was once angry with his servants,[g] and he imprisoned me and the chief baker in the house of the captain of the guard. 11Each of us had a dream the same night, and each dream had a meaning of its own.[h] 12Now a young Hebrew was there with us, a servant of the captain of the guard. We told him our dreams, and he interpreted them for us, giving each man the interpretation of his dream.[i] 13And things turned out exactly as he interpreted them to us: I was restored to my position, and the other man was hanged.[a][j]"

14So Pharaoh sent for Joseph, and he was quickly brought from the dungeon.[k] When he had shaved and changed his clothes, he came before Pharaoh.

15Pharaoh said to Joseph, "I had a dream, and no one can interpret it. But I have heard it said of you that when you hear a dream you can interpret it."[l]

16"I cannot do it," Joseph replied to Pharaoh, "but God will give Pharaoh the answer he desires."[m]

17Then Pharaoh said to Joseph, "In my dream I was standing on the bank of the Nile, 18when out of the river there came up seven cows, fat and sleek, and they grazed among the reeds. 19After them, seven other cows came up—scrawny and very ugly and lean. I had never seen such ugly cows in all the land of Egypt. 20The lean, ugly cows ate up the seven fat cows that came up first. 21But even after they ate them, no one could tell that they had done so; they looked just as ugly as before. Then I woke up.

22"In my dreams I also saw seven heads of grain, full and good, growing on a single stalk. 23After them, seven other heads sprouted—withered and thin and scorched by the east wind. 24The thin heads of grain swallowed up the seven good heads. I told this to the magicians, but none could explain it to me."

25Then Joseph said to Pharaoh, "The dreams of Pharaoh are one and the same. God has revealed to Pharaoh what he is about to do.[n] 26The seven good cows are seven years, and the seven good heads of grain are seven years; it is one and the same dream. 27The seven lean, ugly cows that came up afterward are seven years, and so are the seven worthless heads of grain scorched by the east wind: They are seven years of famine.[o]

[a]13 Or *impaled*

**41:11**
h Ge 40:5

**41:12**
i Ge 40:12

**41:13**
j Ge 40:22

**41:14**
k Ps 105:20; Da 2:25

**41:15**
l Da 5:16

**41:16**
m Ge 40:8; Da 2:30; Ac 3:12; 2Co 3:5

**41:25**
n Da 2:45

**41:27**
o 2Ki 8:1

28 “It is just as I said to Pharaoh: God
has shown Pharaoh what he is about to do.
29 Seven years of great abundance[p] are com-
ing throughout the land of Egypt, 30 but
seven years of famine[q] will follow them.
Then all the abundance in Egypt will be for-
gotten, and the famine will ravage the land.
31 The abundance in the land will not be re-
membered, because the famine that follows
it will be so severe. 32 The reason the dream
was given to Pharaoh in two forms is that
the matter has been firmly decided by God,
and God will do it soon.

33 “And now let Pharaoh look for a discern-
ing and wise man and put him in charge of
the land of Egypt. 34 Let Pharaoh appoint
commissioners over the land to take a fifth
of the harvest of Egypt during the seven
years of abundance. 35 They should collect
all the food of these good years that are
coming and store up the grain under the
authority of Pharaoh, to be kept in the cit-
ies for food.[r] 36 This food should be held in
reserve for the country, to be used during
the seven years of famine that will come
upon Egypt, so that the country may not be
ruined by the famine.”

37 The plan seemed good to Pharaoh and
to all his officials. 38 So Pharaoh asked them,
“Can we find anyone like this man, one in
whom is the spirit of God[a]?”[s]

39 Then Pharaoh said to Joseph, “Since
God has made all this known to you, there is
no one so discerning and wise as you. 40 You
shall be in charge of my palace, and all my
people are to submit to your orders.[t] Only
with respect to the throne will I be greater
than you.”

## Joseph in Charge of Egypt

41 So Pharaoh said to Joseph, “I hereby put
you in charge of the whole land of Egypt.”[u]
42 Then Pharaoh took his signet ring[v] from
his finger and put it on Joseph’s finger. He
dressed him in robes of fine linen and put
a gold chain around his neck.[w] 43 He had
him ride in a chariot as his second-in-
command,[b] and men shouted before him,
“Make way[c]!” Thus he put him in charge of
the whole land of Egypt.

44 Then Pharaoh said to Joseph, “I am
Pharaoh, but without your word no one will
lift hand or foot in all Egypt.” 45 Pharaoh
gave Joseph the name Zaphenath-Paneah
and gave him Asenath daughter of Potiph-
era, priest of On,[d] to be his wife. And Joseph
went throughout the land of Egypt.

46 Joseph was thirty years old when he en-
tered the service of Pharaoh king of Egypt.
And Joseph went out from Pharaoh’s pres-
ence and traveled throughout Egypt. 47 Dur-
ing the seven years of abundance the land
produced plentifully. 48 Joseph collected
all the food produced in those seven years
of abundance in Egypt and stored it in the
cities. In each city he put the food grown in
the fields surrounding it. 49 Joseph stored up
huge quantities of grain, like the sand of the
sea; it was so much that he stopped keeping
records because it was beyond measure.

50 Before the years of famine came, two
sons were born to Joseph by Asenath daugh-
ter of Potiphera, priest of On. 51 Joseph
named his firstborn Manasseh[e] and said,
“It is because God has made me forget all
my trouble and all my father’s household.”
52 The second son he named Ephraim[f] and
said, “It is because God has made me fruit-
ful[x] in the land of my suffering.”

53 The seven years of abundance in Egypt
came to an end, 54 and the seven years of fam-
ine began,[y] just as Joseph had said. There
was famine in all the other lands, but in the
whole land of Egypt there was food. 55 When
all Egypt began to feel the famine, the peo-
ple cried to Pharaoh for food. Then Pharaoh
told all the Egyptians, “Go to Joseph and do
what he tells you.”

56 When the famine had spread over the
whole country, Joseph opened the store-
houses and sold grain to the Egyptians, for
the famine was severe throughout Egypt.
57 And all the countries came to Egypt to buy
grain from Joseph, because the famine was
severe in all the world.

## Joseph’s Brothers Go to Egypt

42 When Jacob learned that there
was grain in Egypt,[z] he said to his
sons, “Why do you just keep looking at each

**41:29** p ver 47
**41:30** q ver 54; Ge 47:13
**41:35** r ver 48
**41:38** s Nu 27:18; Job 32:8; Da 4:8–9,18; 5:11,14
**41:40** t Ps 105:21–22; Ac 7:10
**41:41** u Ge 42:6
**41:42** v Est 3:10 w Da 5:7,16,29
**41:52** x Ge 17:6; 49:22
**41:54** y ver 30; Ps 105:11; Ac 7:11
**42:1** z Ac 7:12

[a] 38 Or *of the gods* [b] 43 Or *in the chariot of his second-in-command*; or *in his second chariot* [c] 43 Or *Bow down*
[d] 45 That is, Heliopolis; also in verse 50 [e] 51 *Manasseh* sounds like and may be derived from the Hebrew for *forget.*
[f] 52 *Ephraim* sounds like the Hebrew for *twice fruitful.*

**42:2** a Ge 43:8
**42:4** b ver 38
**42:5** c Ac 7:11
**42:6** d Ge 41:41 e Ge 37:7–10
**42:9** f Ge 37:7
**42:13** g Ge 37:30,33; 44:20
**42:15** h 1Sa 17:55
**42:18** i Lev 25:43

other?" 2He continued, "I have heard that there is grain in Egypt. Go down there and buy some for us, so that we may live and not die."[a]

3Then ten of Joseph's brothers went down to buy grain from Egypt. 4But Jacob did not send Benjamin, Joseph's brother, with the others, because he was afraid that harm might come to him.[b] 5So Israel's sons were among those who went to buy grain, for the famine was in the land of Canaan also.[c]

6Now Joseph was the governor of the land,[d] the one who sold grain to all its people. So when Joseph's brothers arrived, they bowed down to him with their faces to the ground.[e] 7As soon as Joseph saw his brothers, he recognized them, but he pretended to be a stranger and spoke harshly to them. "Where do you come from?" he asked.

"From the land of Canaan," they replied, "to buy food."

8Although Joseph recognized his brothers, they did not recognize him. 9Then he remembered his dreams[f] about them and said to them, "You are spies! You have come to see where our land is unprotected."

10"No, my lord," they answered. "Your servants have come to buy food. 11We are all the sons of one man. Your servants are honest men, not spies."

12"No!" he said to them. "You have come to see where our land is unprotected."

13But they replied, "Your servants were twelve brothers, the sons of one man, who lives in the land of Canaan. The youngest is now with our father, and one is no more."[g]

14Joseph said to them, "It is just as I told you: You are spies! 15And this is how you will be tested: As surely as Pharaoh lives,[h] you will not leave this place unless your youngest brother comes here. 16Send one of your number to get your brother; the rest of you will be kept in prison, so that your words may be tested to see if you are telling the truth. If you are not, then as surely as Pharaoh lives, you are spies!" 17And he put them all in custody for three days.

18On the third day, Joseph said to them, "Do this and you will live, for I fear God:[i] 19If you are honest men, let one of your brothers stay here in prison, while the rest of you go and take grain back for your starving households. 20But you must bring your youngest brother to me,[j] so that your words may be verified and that you may not die." This they proceeded to do.

21They said to one another, "Surely we are being punished because of our brother. We saw how distressed he was when he pleaded with us for his life, but we would not listen; that's why this distress[k] has come upon us."

22Reuben replied, "Didn't I tell you not to sin against the boy?[l] But you wouldn't listen! Now we must give an accounting[m] for his blood." 23They did not realize that Joseph could understand them, since he was using an interpreter.

24He turned away from them and began to weep, but then turned back and spoke to them again. He had Simeon taken from them and bound before their eyes.

25Joseph gave orders to fill their bags with grain, to put each man's silver back in his sack, and to give them provisions for their journey.[n] After this was done for them, 26they loaded their grain on their donkeys and left.

27At the place where they stopped for the night one of them opened his sack to get feed for his donkey, and he saw his silver in the mouth of his sack. 28"My silver has been returned," he said to his brothers. "Here it is in my sack."

Their hearts sank and they turned to each other trembling and said, "What is this that God has done to us?"

29When they came to their father Jacob in the land of Canaan, they told him all that had happened to them. They said, 30"The man who is lord over the land spoke harshly to us[o] and treated us as though we were spying on the land. 31But we said to him, 'We are honest men; we are not spies. 32We were twelve brothers, sons of one father. One is no more, and the youngest is now with our father in Canaan.'

33"Then the man who is lord over the land said to us, 'This is how I will know whether you are honest men: Leave one of your brothers here with me, and take food for your starving households and go. 34But bring your youngest brother to me so I will know that you are not spies but honest men. Then

**42:20** j ver 15,34; Ge 43:5
**42:21** k Hos 5:15
**42:22** l Ge 37:21–22 m Ge 9:5
**42:25** n Ro 12:17,20–21
**42:30** o ver 7

**42:34** p Ge 34:10
**42:36** q Ge 43:14
**42:38** r Ge 37:33 s Ge 37:35
**43:1** t Ge 12:10; 41:56–57
**43:3** u Ge 42:15; 44:23
**43:7** v Ge 42:13

I will give your brother back to you, and you
can trade[a] in the land.[p]'"
35As they were emptying their sacks,
there in each man's sack was his pouch
of silver! When they and their father saw
the money pouches, they were frightened.
36Their father Jacob said to them, "You
have deprived me of my children. Joseph is
no more and Simeon is no more, and now
you want to take Benjamin.[q] Everything is
against me!"
37Then Reuben said to his father, "You
may put both of my sons to death if I do not
bring him back to you. Entrust him to my
care, and I will bring him back."
38But Jacob said, "My son will not go
down there with you; his brother is dead[r]
and he is the only one left. If harm comes
to him on the journey you are taking, you
will bring my gray head down to the grave[b][s]
in sorrow."

## The Second Journey to Egypt

43 Now the famine was still severe in
the land.[t] 2So when they had eaten
all the grain they had brought from Egypt,
their father said to them, "Go back and buy
us a little more food."
3But Judah said to him, "The man warned
us solemnly, 'You will not see my face again
unless your brother is with you.'[u] 4If you will
send our brother along with us, we will go
down and buy food for you. 5But if you will
not send him, we will not go down, because
the man said to us, 'You will not see my face
again unless your brother is with you.'"
6Israel asked, "Why did you bring this
trouble on me by telling the man you had
another brother?"
7They replied, "The man questioned us
closely about ourselves and our family. 'Is
your father still living?' he asked us. 'Do you
have another brother?'[v] We simply answered
his questions. How were we to know he
would say, 'Bring your brother down here'?"
8Then Judah said to Israel his father,
"Send the boy along with me and we will go
at once, so that we and you and our children
may live and not die. 9I myself will guaran-
tee his safety; you can hold me personally
responsible for him. If I do not bring him
back to you and set him here before you, I
will bear the blame before you all my life.[w]
10As it is, if we had not delayed, we could
have gone and returned twice."
11Then their father Israel said to them,
"If it must be, then do this: Put some of the
best products of the land in your bags and
take them down to the man as a gift[x]—a lit-
tle balm[y] and a little honey, some spices and
myrrh, some pistachio nuts and almonds.
12Take double the amount of silver with you,
for you must return the silver that was put
back into the mouths of your sacks.[z] Per-
haps it was a mistake. 13Take your brother
also and go back to the man at once. 14And
may God Almighty[c] grant you mercy be-
fore the man so that he will let your other
brother and Benjamin come back with you.
As for me, if I am bereaved, I am bereaved."
15So the men took the gifts and double
the amount of silver, and Benjamin also.
They hurried down to Egypt and presented
themselves to Joseph. 16When Joseph saw
Benjamin with them, he said to the steward
of his house,[a] "Take these men to my house,
slaughter an animal and prepare dinner;
they are to eat with me at noon."
17The man did as Joseph told him and
took the men to Joseph's house. 18Now
the men were frightened when they were
taken to his house. They thought, "We were
brought here because of the silver that was
put back into our sacks the first time. He
wants to attack us and overpower us and
seize us as slaves and take our donkeys."
19So they went up to Joseph's steward and
spoke to him at the entrance to the house.
20"Please, sir," they said, "we came down
here the first time to buy food. 21But at the
place where we stopped for the night we
opened our sacks and each of us found his
silver—the exact weight—in the mouth of
his sack. So we have brought it back with
us.[b] 22We have also brought additional silver
with us to buy food. We don't know who put
our silver in our sacks."
23"It's all right," he said. "Don't be afraid.
Your God, the God of your father, has given
you treasure in your sacks; I received
your silver." Then he brought Simeon out
to them.

**43:9** w Ge 42:37; 44:32; Phm 1:18–19
**43:11** x Ge 32:20; Pr 18:16 y Ge 37:25; Jer 8:22
**43:12** z Ge 42:25
**43:16** a Ge 44:1,4,12
**43:21** b ver 15; Ge 42:27,35

[a]34 Or *move about freely* [b]38 Hebrew *Sheol* [c]14 Hebrew *El-Shaddai*

**43:24** c ver 16 d Ge 18:4; 24:32
**43:26** e Ge 37:7,10
**43:28** f Ge 37:7
**43:29** g Ge 42:13
**43:30** h Ge 42:24; 45:2,14,15; 46:29
**43:32** i Ge 46:34
**43:34** j Ge 37:3; 45:22

24 The steward took the men into Joseph's house,[c] gave them water to wash their feet[d] and provided fodder for their donkeys. 25 They prepared their gifts for Joseph's arrival at noon, because they had heard that they were to eat there.

26 When Joseph came home, they presented to him the gifts they had brought into the house, and they bowed down before him to the ground.[e] 27 He asked them how they were, and then he said, "How is your aged father you told me about? Is he still living?"

28 They replied, "Your servant our father is still alive and well." And they bowed low to pay him honor.[f]

29 As he looked about and saw his brother Benjamin, his own mother's son, he asked, "Is this your youngest brother, the one you told me about?"[g] And he said, "God be gracious to you, my son." 30 Deeply moved at the sight of his brother, Joseph hurried out and looked for a place to weep. He went into his private room and wept[h] there.

31 After he had washed his face, he came out and, controlling himself, said, "Serve the food."

32 They served him by himself, the brothers by themselves, and the Egyptians who ate with him by themselves, because Egyptians could not eat with Hebrews, for that is detestable to Egyptians.[i] 33 The men had been seated before him in the order of their ages, from the firstborn to the youngest; and they looked at each other in astonishment. 34 When portions were served to them from Joseph's table, Benjamin's portion was five times as much as anyone else's.[j] So they feasted and drank freely with him.

## A Silver Cup in a Sack

**44** Now Joseph gave these instructions to the steward of his house: "Fill the men's sacks with as much food as they can carry, and put each man's silver in the mouth of his sack. 2 Then put my cup, the silver one, in the mouth of the youngest one's sack, along with the silver for his grain." And he did as Joseph said.

3 As morning dawned, the men were sent on their way with their donkeys. 4 They had not gone far from the city when Joseph said to his steward, "Go after those men at once, and when you catch up with them, say to them, 'Why have you repaid good with evil? 5 Isn't this the cup my master drinks from and also uses for divination? This is a wicked thing you have done.' "

6 When he caught up with them, he repeated these words to them. 7 But they said to him, "Why does my lord say such things? Far be it from your servants to do anything like that! 8 We even brought back to you from the land of Canaan the silver we found inside the mouths of our sacks.[k] So why would we steal silver or gold from your master's house? 9 If any of your servants is found to have it, he will die;[l] and the rest of us will become my lord's slaves."

10 "Very well, then," he said, "let it be as you say. Whoever is found to have it will become my slave; the rest of you will be free from blame."

11 Each of them quickly lowered his sack to the ground and opened it. 12 Then the steward proceeded to search, beginning with the oldest and ending with the youngest. And the cup was found in Benjamin's sack. 13 At this, they tore their clothes.[m] Then they all loaded their donkeys and returned to the city.

14 Joseph was still in the house when Judah and his brothers came in, and they threw themselves to the ground before him.[n] 15 Joseph said to them, "What is this you have done? Don't you know that a man like me can find things out by divination?[o]"

16 "What can we say to my lord?" Judah replied. "What can we say? How can we prove our innocence? God has uncovered your servants' guilt. We are now my lord's slaves[p]—we ourselves and the one who was found to have the cup."

17 But Joseph said, "Far be it from me to do such a thing! Only the man who was found to have the cup will become my slave. The rest of you, go back to your father in peace."

18 Then Judah went up to him and said: "Please, my lord, let your servant speak a word to my lord. Do not be angry[q] with your servant, though you are equal to Pharaoh himself. 19 My lord asked his servants, 'Do you have a father or a brother?' 20 And we answered, 'We have an aged father, and there is a young son born to him in his old

**44:8** k Ge 42:25; 43:21
**44:9** l Ge 31:32
**44:13** m Ge 37:29; Nu 14:6
**44:14** n Ge 37:7,10
**44:15** o ver 5
**44:16** p ver 9
**44:18** q Ge 18:30; Ex 32:22

**44:20** r Ge 37:3 s Ge 37:33 t Ge 42:13
**44:21** u Ge 42:15
**44:23** v Ge 43:5
**44:27** w Ge 46:19
**44:28** x Ge 37:33
**44:29** y Ge 42:38
**44:30** z 1Sa 18:1
**44:32** a Ge 43:9

age.[r] His brother is dead,[s] and he is the only one of his mother's sons left, and his father loves him.'[t]

21 "Then you said to your servants, 'Bring him down to me so I can see him for myself.'[u] 22 And we said to my lord, 'The boy cannot leave his father; if he leaves him, his father will die.' 23 But you told your servants, 'Unless your youngest brother comes down with you, you will not see my face again.'[v] 24 When we went back to your servant my father, we told him what my lord had said.

25 "Then our father said, 'Go back and buy a little more food.' 26 But we said, 'We cannot go down. Only if our youngest brother is with us will we go. We cannot see the man's face unless our youngest brother is with us.'

27 "Your servant my father said to us, 'You know that my wife bore me two sons.[w] 28 One of them went away from me, and I said, "He has surely been torn to pieces."[x] And I have not seen him since. 29 If you take this one from me too and harm comes to him, you will bring my gray head down to the grave[a] in misery.'[y]

30 "So now, if the boy is not with us when I go back to your servant my father and if my father, whose life is closely bound up with the boy's life,[z] 31 sees that the boy isn't there, he will die. Your servants will bring the gray head of our father down to the grave in sorrow. 32 Your servant guaranteed the boy's safety to my father. I said, 'If I do not bring him back to you, I will bear the blame before you, my father, all my life!'[a]

33 "Now then, please let your servant remain here as my lord's slave in place of the boy, and let the boy return with his brothers. 34 How can I go back to my father if the boy is not with me? No! Do not let me see the misery that would come upon my father."

## Joseph Makes Himself Known

**45** Then Joseph could no longer control himself before all his attendants, and he cried out, "Have everyone leave my presence!" So there was no one with Joseph when he made himself known to his brothers. 2 And he wept so loudly that the Egyptians heard him, and Pharaoh's household heard about it.

3 Joseph said to his brothers, "I am Joseph! Is my father still living?"[b] But his brothers were not able to answer him, because they were terrified at his presence.

4 Then Joseph said to his brothers, "Come close to me." When they had done so, he said, "I am your brother Joseph, the one you sold into Egypt![c] 5 And now, do not be distressed and do not be angry with yourselves for selling me here, because it was to save lives that God sent me ahead of you.[d] 6 For two years now there has been famine in the land, and for the next five years there will not be plowing and reaping. 7 But God sent me ahead of you to preserve for you a remnant on earth and to save your lives by a great deliverance.[b]

8 "So then, it was not you who sent me here, but God. He made me father[e] to Pharaoh, lord of his entire household and ruler of all Egypt.[f] 9 Now hurry back to my father and say to him, 'This is what your son Joseph says: God has made me lord of all Egypt. Come down to me; don't delay. 10 You shall live in the region of Goshen[g] and be near me—you, your children and grandchildren, your flocks and herds, and all you have. 11 I will provide for you there, because five years of famine are still to come. Otherwise you and your household and all who belong to you will become destitute.'

12 "You can see for yourselves, and so can my brother Benjamin, that it is really I who am speaking to you. 13 Tell my father about all the honor accorded me in Egypt and about everything you have seen. And bring my father down here quickly.[h]"

14 Then he threw his arms around his brother Benjamin and wept, and Benjamin embraced him, weeping. 15 And he kissed all his brothers and wept over them. Afterward his brothers talked with him.

16 When the news reached Pharaoh's palace that Joseph's brothers had come, Pharaoh and all his officials were pleased. 17 Pharaoh said to Joseph, "Tell your brothers, 'Do this: Load your animals and return to the land of Canaan, 18 and bring your father and your families back to me. I will give

**45:3** b Ac 7:13
**45:4** c Ge 37:28
**45:5** d ver 7–8; Ge 50:20; Ps 105:17
**45:8** e Jdg 17:10 f Ge 41:41
**45:10** g Ge 47:1
**45:13** h Ac 7:14

[a] 29 Hebrew *Sheol*; also in verse 31 [b] 7 Or *save you as a great band of survivors*

**45:18** i Ge 27:28; 46:34; 47:6,11,27
**45:19** j Ge 46:5
**45:27** k ver 19
**46:2** l Ge 15:1; Job 33:14–15
**46:3** m Ge 28:13 n Ge 12:2
**46:4** o Ge 28:15; 48:21; Ex 3:8 p Ge 50:1,24

you the best of the land of Egypt[i] and you can enjoy the fat of the land.’

19 “You are also directed to tell them, ‘Do this: Take some carts[j] from Egypt for your children and your wives, and get your father and come. 20 Never mind about your belongings, because the best of all Egypt will be yours.’ ”

21 So the sons of Israel did this. Joseph gave them carts, as Pharaoh had commanded, and he also gave them provisions for their journey. 22 To each of them he gave new clothing, but to Benjamin he gave three hundred shekels[a] of silver and five sets of clothes. 23 And this is what he sent to his father: ten donkeys loaded with the best things of Egypt, and ten female donkeys loaded with grain and bread and other provisions for his journey. 24 Then he sent his brothers away, and as they were leaving he said to them, “Don’t quarrel on the way!”

25 So they went up out of Egypt and came to their father Jacob in the land of Canaan. 26 They told him, “Joseph is still alive! In fact, he is ruler of all Egypt.” Jacob was stunned; he did not believe them. 27 But when they told him everything Joseph had said to them, and when he saw the carts[k] Joseph had sent to carry him back, the spirit of their father Jacob revived. 28 And Israel said, “I’m convinced! My son Joseph is still alive. I will go and see him before I die.”

## Jacob Goes to Egypt

46 So Israel set out with all that was his, and when he reached Beersheba, he offered sacrifices to the God of his father Isaac.

2 And God spoke to Israel in a vision at night[l] and said, “Jacob! Jacob!”

“Here I am,” he replied.

3 “I am God, the God of your father,”[m] he said. “Do not be afraid to go down to Egypt, for I will make you into a great nation[n] there. 4 I will go down to Egypt with you, and I will surely bring you back again.[o] And Joseph’s own hand will close your eyes.[p]”

5 Then Jacob left Beersheba, and Israel’s sons took their father Jacob and their children and their wives in the carts that Pharaoh had sent to transport him. 6 They also took with them their livestock and the possessions they had acquired in Canaan, and Jacob and all his offspring went to Egypt.[q] 7 He took with him to Egypt his sons and grandsons and his daughters and granddaughters—all his offspring.

8 These are the names of the sons of Israel (Jacob and his descendants) who went to Egypt:

Reuben the firstborn of Jacob.

9 The sons of Reuben:
Hanoch, Pallu, Hezron and Carmi.

10 The sons of Simeon:
Jemuel,[r] Jamin, Ohad, Jakin, Zohar and Shaul the son of a Canaanite woman.

11 The sons of Levi:
Gershon, Kohath and Merari.

12 The sons of Judah:
Er, Onan, Shelah, Perez and Zerah (but Er and Onan had died in the land of Canaan).
The sons of Perez:[s]
Hezron and Hamul.

13 The sons of Issachar:
Tola, Puah,[b] Jashub[c] and Shimron.

14 The sons of Zebulun:
Sered, Elon and Jahleel.

15 These were the sons Leah bore to Jacob in Paddan Aram,[d] besides his daughter Dinah. These sons and daughters of his were thirty-three in all.

16 The sons of Gad:
Zephon,[e][t] Haggi, Shuni, Ezbon, Eri, Arodi and Areli.

17 The sons of Asher:[u]
Imnah, Ishvah, Ishvi and Beriah.
Their sister was Serah.
The sons of Beriah:
Heber and Malkiel.

18 These were the children born to Jacob by Zilpah, whom Laban had given to his daughter Leah—sixteen in all.

19 The sons of Jacob’s wife Rachel:
Joseph and Benjamin. 20 In Egypt, Manasseh[v] and Ephraim were born

**46:6** q Dt 26:5; Jos 24:4; Ps 105:23; Isa 52:4; Ac 7:15
**46:10** r Ex 6:15
**46:12** s 1Ch 2:5
**46:16** t Nu 26:15
**46:17** u Ge 30:13; 1Ch 7:30–31
**46:20** v Ge 41:51

[a] 22 That is, about 7 1/2 pounds (about 3.5 kilograms) [b] 13 Samaritan Pentateuch and Syriac (see also 1 Chron. 7:1); Masoretic Text *Puvah* [c] 13 Samaritan Pentateuch and some Septuagint manuscripts (see also Num. 26:24 and 1 Chron. 7:1); Masoretic Text *Iob* [d] 15 That is, Northwest Mesopotamia [e] 16 Samaritan Pentateuch and Septuagint (see also Num. 26:15); Masoretic Text *Ziphion*

to Joseph by Asenath daughter of
Potiphera, priest of On.[a]

21 The sons of Benjamin:[w]
Bela, Beker, Ashbel, Gera, Naaman,
Ehi, Rosh, Muppim, Huppim and
Ard.

22 These were the sons of Rachel who were born to Jacob—fourteen in all.

23 The son of Dan:
Hushim.

24 The sons of Naphtali:
Jahziel, Guni, Jezer and Shillem.

25 These were the sons born to Jacob by Bilhah,[x] whom Laban had given to his daughter Rachel[y]—seven in all.

26 All those who went to Egypt with Jacob—those who were his direct descendants, not counting his sons' wives—numbered sixty-six persons.[z] 27 With the two sons[b] who had been born to Joseph in Egypt, the members of Jacob's family, which went to Egypt, were seventy[c] in all.[a]

28 Now Jacob sent Judah ahead of him to Joseph to get directions to Goshen. When they arrived in the region of Goshen, 29 Joseph had his chariot made ready and went to Goshen to meet his father Israel. As soon as Joseph appeared before him, he threw his arms around his father[d] and wept for a long time.[b]

30 Israel said to Joseph, "Now I am ready to die, since I have seen for myself that you are still alive."

31 Then Joseph said to his brothers and to his father's household, "I will go up and speak to Pharaoh and will say to him, 'My brothers and my father's household, who were living in the land of Canaan, have come to me.[c] 32 The men are shepherds; they tend livestock, and they have brought along their flocks and herds and everything they own.' 33 When Pharaoh calls you in and asks, 'What is your occupation?'[d] 34 you should answer, 'Your servants have tended livestock from our boyhood on, just as our fathers did.' Then you will be allowed to settle in the region of Goshen, for all shepherds are detestable to the Egyptians.[e]"

47 Joseph went and told Pharaoh, "My father and brothers, with their flocks and herds and everything they own, have come from the land of Canaan and are now in Goshen."[f] 2 He chose five of his brothers and presented them before Pharaoh.

3 Pharaoh asked the brothers, "What is your occupation?"[g]

"Your servants are shepherds," they replied to Pharaoh, "just as our fathers were." 4 They also said to him, "We have come to live here awhile,[h] because the famine is severe in Canaan[i] and your servants' flocks have no pasture. So now, please let your servants settle in Goshen."[j]

5 Pharaoh said to Joseph, "Your father and your brothers have come to you, 6 and the land of Egypt is before you; settle your father and your brothers in the best part of the land. Let them live in Goshen. And if you know of any among them with special ability, put them in charge of my own livestock."

7 Then Joseph brought his father Jacob in and presented him before Pharaoh. After Jacob blessed[e] Pharaoh, 8 Pharaoh asked him, "How old are you?"

9 And Jacob said to Pharaoh, "The years of my pilgrimage are a hundred and thirty.[k] My years have been few and difficult, and they do not equal the years of the pilgrimage of my fathers.[l]" 10 Then Jacob blessed[f] Pharaoh[m] and went out from his presence.

11 So Joseph settled his father and his brothers in Egypt and gave them property in the best part of the land, the district of Rameses,[n] as Pharaoh directed. 12 Joseph also provided his father and his brothers and all his father's household with food, according to the number of their children.

## Joseph and the Famine

13 There was no food, however, in the whole region because the famine was severe; both Egypt and Canaan wasted away because of the famine.[o] 14 Joseph collected all the money that was to be found in Egypt and Canaan in payment for the grain they were buying, and he brought it to Pharaoh's palace.[p] 15 When the money of the people of Egypt and Canaan was gone, all Egypt came

**46:21** w 1Ch 7:6–12
**46:25** x Ge 30:8; y Ge 29:29
**46:26** z Ex 1:5; Dt 10:22
**46:27** a Ac 7:14
**46:29** b Ge 45:14–15
**46:31** c Ge 47:1
**46:33** d Ge 47:3
**46:34** e Ge 43:32; Ex 8:26

**47:1** f Ge 46:31
**47:3** g Ge 46:33
**47:4** h Ge 15:13; Dt 26:5; i Ge 43:1; j Ge 46:34
**47:9** k Ge 25:7; l Ge 35:28
**47:10** m ver 7
**47:11** n Ex 1:11; 12:37
**47:13** o Ge 41:30; Ac 7:11
**47:14** p Ge 41:56

[a] 20 That is, Heliopolis [b] 27 Hebrew; Septuagint *the nine children* [c] 27 Hebrew (see also Exodus 1:5 and footnote); Septuagint (see also Acts 7:14) *seventy-five* [d] 29 Hebrew *around him* [e] 7 Or *greeted* [f] 10 Or *said farewell to*

to Joseph and said, "Give us food. Why should we die before your eyes? Our money is used up."

16 "Then bring your livestock," said Joseph. "I will sell you food in exchange for your livestock, since your money is gone." 17 So they brought their livestock to Joseph, and he gave them food in exchange for their horses, their sheep and goats, their cattle and donkeys. And he brought them through that year with food in exchange for all their livestock.

18 When that year was over, they came to him the following year and said, "We cannot hide from our lord the fact that since our money is gone and our livestock belongs to you, there is nothing left for our lord except our bodies and our land. 19 Why should we perish before your eyes—we and our land as well? Buy us and our land in exchange for food, and we with our land will be in bondage to Pharaoh. Give us seed so that we may live and not die, and that the land may not become desolate."

20 So Joseph bought all the land in Egypt for Pharaoh. The Egyptians, one and all, sold their fields, because the famine was too severe for them. The land became Pharaoh's, 21 and Joseph reduced the people to servitude,[a] from one end of Egypt to the other. 22 However, he did not buy the land of the priests, because they received a regular allotment from Pharaoh and had food enough from the allotment[q] Pharaoh gave them. That is why they did not sell their land.

23 Joseph said to the people, "Now that I have bought you and your land today for Pharaoh, here is seed for you so you can plant the ground. 24 But when the crop comes in, give a fifth of it to Pharaoh. The other four-fifths you may keep as seed for the fields and as food for yourselves and your households and your children."

25 "You have saved our lives," they said. "May we find favor in the eyes of our lord; we will be in bondage to Pharaoh."

26 So Joseph established it as a law concerning land in Egypt—still in force today—that a fifth of the produce belongs to Pharaoh. It was only the land of the priests that did not become Pharaoh's.[r]

27 Now the Israelites settled in Egypt in the region of Goshen. They acquired property there and were fruitful and increased greatly in number.

28 Jacob lived in Egypt seventeen years, and the years of his life were a hundred and forty-seven. 29 When the time drew near for Israel to die,[s] he called for his son Joseph and said to him, "If I have found favor in your eyes, put your hand under my thigh[t] and promise that you will show me kindness and faithfulness. Do not bury me in Egypt, 30 but when I rest with my fathers, carry me out of Egypt and bury me where they are buried."[u]

"I will do as you say," he said.

31 "Swear to me," he said. Then Joseph swore to him, and Israel worshiped as he leaned on the top of his staff.[b]

## Manasseh and Ephraim

48 Some time later Joseph was told, "Your father is ill." So he took his two sons Manasseh and Ephraim along with him. 2 When Jacob was told, "Your son Joseph has come to you," Israel rallied his strength and sat up on the bed.

3 Jacob said to Joseph, "God Almighty[c] appeared to me at Luz[v] in the land of Canaan, and there he blessed me[w] 4 and said to me, 'I am going to make you fruitful and will increase your numbers. I will make you a community of peoples, and I will give this land as an everlasting possession to your descendants after you.'

5 "Now then, your two sons born to you in Egypt[x] before I came to you here will be reckoned as mine; Ephraim and Manasseh will be mine,[y] just as Reuben and Simeon are mine. 6 Any children born to you after them will be yours; in the territory they inherit they will be reckoned under the names of their brothers. 7 As I was returning from Paddan,[d] to my sorrow Rachel died in the land of Canaan while we were still on the way, a little distance from Ephrath. So I buried her there beside the road to Ephrath" (that is, Bethlehem).[z]

8 When Israel saw the sons of Joseph, he asked, "Who are these?"

**47:22** q Dt 14:28–29; Ezr 7:24
**47:26** r ver 22
**47:29** s Dt 31:14 t Ge 24:2
**47:30** u Ge 49:29–32; 50:5,13
**48:3** v Ge 28:19 w Ge 28:13; 35:9–12
**48:5** x Ge 41:50–52; 46:20 y Jos 14:4
**48:7** z Ge 35:19

[a] 21 Samaritan Pentateuch and Septuagint (see also Vulgate); Masoretic Text *and he moved the people into the cities*
[b] 31 Or *Israel bowed down at the head of his bed* [c] 3 Hebrew *El-Shaddai* [d] 7 That is, Northwest Mesopotamia

48:9 a Ge33:5
48:10 b Ge27:1 c Ge27:27
48:15 d Ge17:1
48:16 e Heb11:21
48:17 f ver14
48:19 g Ge25:23

9 "They are the sons God has given me here,"[a] Joseph said to his father.

Then Israel said, "Bring them to me so I may bless them."

10 Now Israel's eyes were failing because of old age, and he could hardly see.[b] So Joseph brought his sons close to him, and his father kissed them[c] and embraced them.

11 Israel said to Joseph, "I never expected to see your face again, and now God has allowed me to see your children too."

12 Then Joseph removed them from Israel's knees and bowed down with his face to the ground. 13 And Joseph took both of them, Ephraim on his right toward Israel's left hand and Manasseh on his left toward Israel's right hand, and brought them close to him. 14 But Israel reached out his right hand and put it on Ephraim's head, though he was the younger, and crossing his arms, he put his left hand on Manasseh's head, even though Manasseh was the firstborn.

15 Then he blessed[d] Joseph and said,

"May the God before whom my fathers
Abraham and Isaac walked,
the God who has been my shepherd
all my life to this day,
16 the Angel who has delivered me from all harm
—may he bless these boys.[e]
May they be called by my name
and the names of my fathers Abraham and Isaac,
and may they increase greatly
upon the earth."

17 When Joseph saw his father placing his right hand on Ephraim's head[f] he was displeased; so he took hold of his father's hand to move it from Ephraim's head to Manasseh's head. 18 Joseph said to him, "No, my father, this one is the firstborn; put your right hand on his head."

19 But his father refused and said, "I know, my son, I know. He too will become a people, and he too will become great. Nevertheless, his younger brother will be greater than he,[g] and his descendants will become a group of nations." 20 He blessed them that day and said,

"In your[a] name will Israel pronounce this blessing:
'May God make you like Ephraim and Manasseh.' "

So he put Ephraim ahead of Manasseh.

21 Then Israel said to Joseph, "I am about to die, but God will be with you[b][h] and take you[b] back to the land of your[b] fathers.[i] 22 And to you, as one who is over your brothers, I give the ridge of land[c][j] I took from the Amorites with my sword and my bow."

## Jacob Blesses His Sons

49 Then Jacob called for his sons and said: "Gather around so I can tell you what will happen to you in days to come.[k]

2 "Assemble and listen, sons of Jacob;
listen to your father Israel.

3 "Reuben, you are my firstborn,[l]
my might, the first sign of my strength,[m]
excelling in honor, excelling in power.
4 Turbulent as the waters, you will no longer excel,
for you went up onto your father's bed,
onto my couch and defiled it.[n]

5 "Simeon and Levi are brothers—
their swords[d] are weapons of violence.
6 Let me not enter their council,
let me not join their assembly,[o]
for they have killed men in their anger[p]
and hamstrung oxen as they pleased.
7 Cursed be their anger, so fierce,
and their fury, so cruel!
I will scatter them in Jacob
and disperse them in Israel.[q]

8 "Judah,[e] your brothers will praise you;
your hand will be on the neck of your enemies;
your father's sons will bow down to you.[r]
9 You are a lion's[s] cub, O Judah;
you return from the prey, my son.
Like a lion he crouches and lies down,
like a lioness—who dares to rouse him?
10 The scepter will not depart from Judah,[t]

48:21 h Ge26:3; 46:4 i Ge28:13; 50:24
48:22 j Jos24:32; Jn4:5
49:1 k Nu24:14
49:3 l Ge29:32 m Dt21:17
49:4 n Ge35:22; Dt27:20
49:6 o Pr1:15; Eph5:11 p Ge34:26
49:7 q Jos19:1,9
49:8 r 1Ch5:2
49:9 s Nu24:9
49:10 t Nu24:17,19; Ps60:7

[a]20 The Hebrew is singular. [b]21 The Hebrew is plural. [c]22 Or *And to you I give one portion more than to your brothers—the portion* [d]5 The meaning of the Hebrew for this word is uncertain. [e]8 *Judah* sounds like and may be derived from the Hebrew for *praise.*

nor the ruler's staff from between his feet,
until he comes to whom it belongs[a]
and the obedience of the nations is his.[u]
11 He will tether his donkey to a vine,
his colt to the choicest branch;
he will wash his garments in wine,
his robes in the blood of grapes.
12 His eyes will be darker than wine,
his teeth whiter than milk.[b]

13 "Zebulun[v] will live by the seashore
and become a haven for ships;
his border will extend toward Sidon.

14 "Issachar is a rawboned[c] donkey
lying down between two saddlebags.[d]
15 When he sees how good is his resting place
and how pleasant is his land,
he will bend his shoulder to the burden
and submit to forced labor.

16 "Dan[e][w] will provide justice for his people
as one of the tribes of Israel.
17 Dan[x] will be a serpent by the roadside,
a viper along the path,
that bites the horse's heels
so that its rider tumbles backward.

18 "I look for your deliverance, O LORD.

19 "Gad[f][y] will be attacked by a band of raiders,
but he will attack them at their heels.

20 "Asher's[z] food will be rich;
he will provide delicacies fit for a king.

21 "Naphtali[a] is a doe set free
that bears beautiful fawns.[g]

22 "Joseph[b] is a fruitful vine,
a fruitful vine near a spring,
whose branches climb over a wall.[h]
23 With bitterness archers attacked him;
they shot at him with hostility.
24 But his bow remained steady,
his strong arms[c] stayed[i] limber,
because of the hand of the Mighty One of Jacob,[d]
because of the Shepherd, the Rock of Israel,[e]
25 because of your father's God,[f] who helps you,
because of the Almighty,[j] who blesses you
with blessings of the heavens above,
blessings of the deep that lies below,[g]
blessings of the breast and womb.
26 Your father's blessings are greater
than the blessings of the ancient mountains,
than[k] the bounty of the age-old hills.
Let all these rest on the head of Joseph,
on the brow of the prince among[l] his brothers.[h]

27 "Benjamin is a ravenous wolf;
in the morning he devours the prey,
in the evening he divides the plunder."

28 All these are the twelve tribes of Israel,
and this is what their father said to them
when he blessed them, giving each the blessing appropriate to him.

## The Death of Jacob

29 Then he gave them these instructions:
"I am about to be gathered to my people.[i]
Bury me with my fathers in the cave in the
field of Ephron the Hittite, 30 the cave in the
field of Machpelah, near Mamre in Canaan,
which Abraham bought as a burial place
from Ephron the Hittite, along with the field.
31 There Abraham[j] and his wife Sarah[k] were
buried, there Isaac and his wife Rebekah[l]
were buried, and there I buried Leah. 32 The
field and the cave in it were bought from
the Hittites.[m]"

33 When Jacob had finished giving instructions to his sons, he drew his feet up into the
bed, breathed his last and was gathered to
his people.[m]

50 Joseph threw himself upon his father and wept over him and kissed
him.[n] 2 Then Joseph directed the physicians
in his service to embalm his father Israel.
So the physicians embalmed him,[o] 3 taking
a full forty days, for that was the time required for embalming. And the Egyptians
mourned for him seventy days.

**49:10** u Ps 2:9; Isa 42:1,4
**49:13** v Dt 33:18–19
**49:16** w Dt 33:22
**49:17** x Jdg 18:27
**49:19** y Dt 33:20
**49:20** z Dt 33:24
**49:21** a Dt 33:23
**49:22** b Dt 33:13–17
**49:24** c Ps 18:34 d Ps 132:2,5; Isa 1:24; 41:10 e Isa 28:16
**49:25** f Ge 28:13 g Ge 27:28
**49:26** h Dt 33:15–16
**49:29** i Ge 25:8
**49:31** j Ge 25:9 k Ge 23:19 l Ge 35:29
**49:33** m ver 29; Ge 25:8; Ac 7:15
**50:1** n Ge 46:4
**50:2** o ver 26; 2Ch 16:14

[a]10 Or *until Shiloh comes*; or *until he comes to whom tribute belongs* [b]12 Or *will be dull from wine, / his teeth white from milk* [c]14 Or *strong* [d]14 Or *campfires* [e]16 *Dan* here means *he provides justice.* [f]19 *Gad* can mean *attack* and *band of raiders.* [g]21 Or *free; / he utters beautiful words* [h]22 Or *Joseph is a wild colt, / a wild colt near a spring, / a wild donkey on a terraced hill* [i]23,24 Or *archers will attack… will shoot… will remain… will stay* [j]25 Hebrew *Shaddai* [k]26 Or *of my progenitors, / as great as* [l]26 Or *the one separated from* [m]32 Or *the sons of Heth*

**50:5** p Isa 22:16 q Ge 47:31
**50:10** r Ac 8:2 s 1Sa 31:13; Job 2:13
**50:13** t Ge 23:20; Ac 7:16
**50:15** u Ge 37:28

[4]When the days of mourning had passed, Joseph said to Pharaoh's court, "If I have found favor in your eyes, speak to Pharaoh for me. Tell him, [5]'My father made me swear an oath and said, "I am about to die; bury me in the tomb I dug for myself[p] in the land of Canaan."[q] Now let me go up and bury my father; then I will return.'"

[6]Pharaoh said, "Go up and bury your father, as he made you swear to do."

[7]So Joseph went up to bury his father. All Pharaoh's officials accompanied him—the dignitaries of his court and all the dignitaries of Egypt— [8]besides all the members of Joseph's household and his brothers and those belonging to his father's household. Only their children and their flocks and herds were left in Goshen. [9]Chariots and horsemen[a] also went up with him. It was a very large company.

[10]When they reached the threshing floor of Atad, near the Jordan, they lamented loudly and bitterly;[r] and there Joseph observed a seven-day period[s] of mourning for his father. [11]When the Canaanites who lived there saw the mourning at the threshing floor of Atad, they said, "The Egyptians are holding a solemn ceremony of mourning." That is why that place near the Jordan is called Abel Mizraim.[b]

[12]So Jacob's sons did as he had commanded them: [13]They carried him to the land of Canaan and buried him in the cave in the field of Machpelah, near Mamre, which Abraham had bought as a burial place from Ephron the Hittite, along with the field.[t] [14]After burying his father, Joseph returned to Egypt, together with his brothers and all the others who had gone with him to bury his father.

## Joseph Reassures His Brothers

[15]When Joseph's brothers saw that their father was dead, they said, "What if Joseph holds a grudge against us and pays us back for all the wrongs we did to him?"[u] [16]So they sent word to Joseph, saying, "Your father left these instructions before he died: [17]'This is what you are to say to Joseph: I ask you to forgive your brothers the sins and the wrongs they committed in treating you so badly.' Now please forgive the sins of the servants of the God of your father." When their message came to him, Joseph wept.

[18]His brothers then came and threw themselves down before him.[v] "We are your slaves," they said.

[19]But Joseph said to them, "Don't be afraid. Am I in the place of God?[w] [20]You intended to harm me, but God intended it for good[x] to accomplish what is now being done, the saving of many lives.[y] [21]So then, don't be afraid. I will provide for you and your children.[z]" And he reassured them and spoke kindly to them.

*My child,*

*I can take the evil done to you and use it for your good—just think about how I worked out the details of Joseph's story. I am always at work to build up my children.*

*Your Loving "Abba"*

GENESIS 50:15–21

## The Death of Joseph

[22]Joseph stayed in Egypt, along with all his father's family. He lived a hundred and ten years [23]and saw the third generation of Ephraim's children. Also the children of Makir son of Manasseh were placed at birth on Joseph's knees.[c]

[24]Then Joseph said to his brothers, "I am about to die. But God will surely come to your aid and take you up out of this land to the land he promised on oath to Abraham, Isaac and Jacob."[a] [25]And Joseph made the sons of Israel swear an oath and said, "God will surely come to your aid, and then you must carry my bones up from this place."

[26]So Joseph died at the age of a hundred and ten. And after they embalmed him, he was placed in a coffin in Egypt.

**50:18** v Ge 37:7
**50:19** w Ro 12:19; Heb 10:30
**50:20** x Ro 8:28 y Ge 45:5
**50:21** z Ge 45:11
**50:24** a Ge 12:7; 26:3; 28:13; 35:12

[a]9 Or *charioteers* [b]11 *Abel Mizraim* means *mourning of the Egyptians.* [c]23 That is, were counted as his

# Exodus

## OVERVIEW

The book of Exodus continues the story begun in Genesis and goes on to record the oppression and liberation of the Israelites from slavery in Egypt. African American preachers used this book as a favorite sermon source during and after slavery.

The first two chapters of Exodus reveal the faith and courage of the Hebrew women. The Hebrew midwives Shiphrah and Puah feared God more than the pharaoh of Egypt and rescued many male babies from death, for Pharaoh had ordered that all male babies be killed at birth. Jochebed also defied the decree from Pharaoh and risked her life to hide her baby, Moses, in the reeds along the Nile River, where Pharaoh's daughter found him and then adopted him as her son.

Moses grew up in the Egyptian royal household, but he never forgot his roots or the oppression of his people. As a young man, Moses witnessed an Egyptian beating an Israelite worker. He killed the Egyptian and hid his body. Despite covering his tracks, the murder was discovered, and in the face of Pharaoh's wrath, Moses fled to Midian for safety.

The rest of the book of Exodus highlights other major events in Israel's history. After Moses began a new life as a shepherd, the Lord God, Yahweh, met him at the burning bush and sent him back to Egypt as a liberator (see Ex 3–4). Despite this great commission, God was prepared to kill Moses while he was on his way to Egypt. Moses' life was again spared because of a woman—Zipporah saved her husband's life by circumcising their son (see Ex 4:24–26).

Pharaoh finally agreed to set the Israelites free, but not until after God afflicted the land with ten plagues (see Ex 7–12). After miraculously crossing the Red Sea, Moses' sister, Miriam, led the people in praising God for his intervention (see Ex 13–15). At Mount Sinai, God gave Moses the Ten Commandments and instructions for constructing his tabernacle, along with laws for worship and community living.

Women today can look to Exodus for inspiration on how God answers prayers and sends deliverers to free us from the things and people who bind us. As you read this book, ask God to free you from the bondage that enslaves you and to give you courage to help free others. Look to the stories of Shiphrah and Puah, Jochebed and Miriam—as well as Miriam's brothers, Moses and Aaron—as inspirational examples of how God used ordinary women and men to set his people free.

## OUTLINE

I. The Oppression of the Israelites (1:1–22)
II. The Birth and Preservation of Moses (2:1–25)
III. The Commission of Moses (3:1—6:30)
IV. The Judgment of Plagues on Egypt (7:1—11:10)
V. The Passover (12:1–30)
VI. The Exodus From Egypt and the Crossing of the Red Sea (12:31—14:31)
VII. The Celebration of Freedom (15:1–21)
VIII. The Provision of God for the Journey (15:22—18:27)
IX. The Covenant of God With the Israelites (19:1—24:18)
X. Instructions for the Tabernacle and the Priests (25:1—31:18)
XI. The Great Sin of Idolatry (32:1—33:6)
XII. The Tent of Meeting and God's Glory (33:7–23)
XIII. Renewal of the Covenant (34:1–35)
XIV. Tabernacle Instructions (35:1—40:38)

## SCANNABLE FACTS:

**Author:** Moses

**Time Written:** During the 1400s B.C., while the Israelites were traveling in the desert

**Theme to Note:** God intervenes for the liberation of his people

**Notable Women:** Shiphrah and Puah (Hebrew midwives), Jochebed, Miriam, Pharaoh's daughter, Zipporah

## The Israelites Oppressed

1 These are the names of the sons of Israel[a] who went to Egypt with Jacob, each with his family: [2]Reuben, Simeon, Levi and Judah; [3]Issachar, Zebulun and Benjamin; [4]Dan and Naphtali; Gad and Asher. [5]The descendants of Jacob numbered seventy[a] in all;[b] Joseph was already in Egypt.

[6]Now Joseph and all his brothers and all that generation died,[c] [7]but the Israelites were fruitful and multiplied greatly and became exceedingly numerous,[d] so that the land was filled with them.

[8]Then a new king, who did not know about Joseph, came to power in Egypt. [9]"Look," he said to his people, "the Israelites have become much too numerous[e] for us. [10]Come, we must deal shrewdly with them or they will become even more numerous and, if war breaks out, will join our enemies, fight against us and leave the country."

[11]So they put slave masters[f] over them to oppress them with forced labor,[g] and they built Pithom and Rameses[h] as store cities for Pharaoh. [12]But the more they were oppressed, the more they multiplied and spread; so the Egyptians came to dread the Israelites [13]and worked them ruthlessly. [14]They made their lives bitter with hard labor in brick and mortar and with all kinds of work in the fields; in all their hard labor the Egyptians used them ruthlessly.[i]

[15]The king of Egypt said to the Hebrew midwives, whose names were Shiphrah and Puah, [16]"When you help the Hebrew women in childbirth and observe them on the delivery stool, if it is a boy, kill him; but if it is a girl, let her live." [17]The midwives, however, feared[j] God and did not do what the king of Egypt had told them to do; they let the boys live. [18]Then the king of Egypt summoned the midwives and asked them, "Why have you done this? Why have you let the boys live?"

[19]The midwives answered Pharaoh, "Hebrew women are not like Egyptian women; they are vigorous and give birth before the midwives arrive."

[20]So God was kind to the midwives and the people increased and became even more numerous. [21]And because the midwives feared God, he gave them families[k] of their own.

[22]Then Pharaoh gave this order to all his people: "Every boy that is born[b] you must throw into the Nile, but let every girl live."[l]

## The Birth of Moses

2 Now a man of the house of Levi married a Levite woman,[m] [2]and she became pregnant and gave birth to a son. When she saw that he was a fine child, she hid him for three months.[n] [3]But when she could hide him no longer, she got a papyrus basket for him and coated it with tar and pitch. Then she placed the child in it and put it among the reeds along the bank of the Nile. [4]His sister[o] stood at a distance to see what would happen to him.

[5]Then Pharaoh's daughter went down to the Nile to bathe, and her attendants were walking along the river bank. She saw the basket among the reeds and sent her slave girl to get it. [6]She opened it and saw the baby. He was crying, and she felt sorry for

**1:1** a Ge 46:8
**1:5** b Ge 46:26
**1:6** c Ge 50:26
**1:7** d Ge 46:3; Ac 7:17
**1:9** e Ps 105:24–25
**1:11** f Ex 3:7 g Ge 15:13 h Ge 47:11
**1:14** i Ex 2:23; Nu 20:15
**1:17** j ver 21; Pr 16:6
**1:21** k 1Sa 2:35
**1:22** l Ac 7:19
**2:1** m Ex 6:20
**2:2** n Ac 7:20; Heb 11:23
**2:4** o Ex 15:20; Nu 26:59

[a]5 Masoretic Text (see also Gen. 46:27); Dead Sea Scrolls and Septuagint (see also Acts 7:14 and note at Gen. 46:27) *seventy-five* [b]22 Masoretic Text; Samaritan Pentateuch, Septuagint and Targums *born to the Hebrews*

### The African Presence

**Exodus 1**

Based on geography, historical evidence and Biblical references, the events recorded in Exodus occurred in Egypt and surrounding areas, places occupied and influenced by people of African descent.

# Jochebed

## *She Knew It Would Take a Village*

Somehow Jochebed knew it would take a village not only to raise her child, but also to save his life. So she started calling on that village from the day of his birth.

The first two village members introduced in the story are midwives named Shiphrah and Puah, who were ordered to kill all male babies born to Hebrew women. But these midwives lied to the king in order to spare the babies' lives (see Ex 1:15–19). Their refusal to kill the male babies was the first step in saving Moses, Jochebed's son.

Jochebed herself performed the second step by managing to conceal her baby for three months, defying the order to throw him into the Nile River. During that time she carefully constructed a basket of papyrus and coated it with tar and pitch for waterproofing (see Ex 2:3); she observed the bathing patterns of Pharaoh's daughter, the princess; and she coached her daughter, Miriam (another village member), so she would know what to say and do when the princess found the baby. Jochebed also knew that Miriam fully grasped the plan and understood how to suddenly appear and suggest the appropriate nurse for the discovered child.

The next step involved an unsuspecting village member: Pharaoh's daughter. She discovered the beautiful baby who had cried at just the right moment and, at Miriam's prompting, the princess hired Jochebed to take care of the child. The princess raised this Hebrew boy in luxury as her own son, naming him Moses.

Yes, Jochebed knew that it would take a village to raise her child, and she used that village well. She was a loving, caring, concerned, resourceful, determined mother. And she was faithful. God heard her prayers and intervened on her behalf. He honored her steadfast purpose by using all her children—Aaron, Miriam and Moses—to lead his people out of bondage.

Jochebed was a woman of courage who feared only God, not people. She had an unwavering faith in God's promises. She teaches us that it doesn't matter who we are or what our circumstances are; it's how we deal with the lumps and bumps—the challenges and responsibilities that come with being a woman and a mother—that really matters.

—M. Kimbrough

### reflection

*Think about the lumps and bumps—the challenges and responsibilities—that stand before you in this season of your life.*

*How can Jochebed's faith and works inspire you to handle your situation?*

### read

Exodus 1:8—2:10; Numbers 26:59; Hebrews 11:23–29.

See also the Inspire Notes "Motherhood," "Confidence" and "Faith" and the Women of the Bible Notes "Rahab: Willing to Be Used by God" and "The Revelation 12 Woman: A Woman of Focus."

For the next Women of the Bible note, go to page 77.

him. "This is one of the Hebrew babies," she said.

7 Then his sister asked Pharaoh's daughter, "Shall I go and get one of the Hebrew women to nurse the baby for you?"

8 "Yes, go," she answered. And the girl went and got the baby's mother. 9 Pharaoh's daughter said to her, "Take this baby and nurse him for me, and I will pay you." So the woman took the baby and nursed him. 10 When the child grew older, she took him to Pharaoh's daughter and he became her son. She named him Moses,[a] saying, "I drew him out of the water."

## Moses Flees to Midian

11 One day, after Moses had grown up, he went out to where his own people[p] were and watched them at their hard labor. He saw an Egyptian beating a Hebrew, one of his own people. 12 Glancing this way and that and seeing no one, he killed the Egyptian and hid him in the sand. 13 The next day he went out and saw two Hebrews fighting. He asked the one in the wrong, "Why are you hitting your fellow Hebrew?"[q]

14 The man said, "Who made you ruler and judge over us?[r] Are you thinking of killing me as you killed the Egyptian?" Then Moses was afraid and thought, "What I did must have become known."

15 When Pharaoh heard of this, he tried to kill Moses, but Moses fled from Pharaoh and went to live in Midian, where he sat down by a well. 16 Now a priest of Midian[s] had seven daughters, and they came to draw water[t] and fill the troughs to water their father's flock. 17 Some shepherds came along and drove them away, but Moses got up and came to their rescue and watered their flock.[u]

18 When the girls returned to Reuel[v] their father, he asked them, "Why have you returned so early today?"

19 They answered, "An Egyptian rescued us from the shepherds. He even drew water for us and watered the flock."

20 "And where is he?" he asked his daughters. "Why did you leave him? Invite him to have something to eat."

21 Moses agreed to stay with the man, who gave his daughter Zipporah[w] to Moses in marriage. 22 Zipporah gave birth to a son, and Moses named him Gershom,[b] saying, "I have become an alien in a foreign land."

23 During that long period, the king of Egypt died. The Israelites groaned in their slavery and cried out, and their cry[x] for help because of their slavery went up to God. 24 God heard their groaning and he remembered his covenant[y] with Abraham, with Isaac and with Jacob. 25 So God looked on the Israelites and was concerned[z] about them.

## Moses and the Burning Bush

3 Now Moses was tending the flock of Jethro his father-in-law, the priest of Midian, and he led the flock to the far side

**2:11** p Ac 7:23; Heb 11:24–26
**2:13** q Ac 7:26
**2:14** r Ac 7:27*
**2:16** s Ex 3:1 t Ge 24:11
**2:17** u Ge 29:10
**2:18** v Nu 10:29
**2:21** w Ex 18:2
**2:23** x Ex 3:7,9; Dt 26:7; Jas 5:4
**2:24** y Ps 105:10,42
**2:25** z Ex 3:7; 4:31

[a] 10 *Moses* sounds like the Hebrew for *draw out.* [b] 22 *Gershom* sounds like the Hebrew for *an alien there.*

## The African Presence

### Exodus 2:1–10

Although her name is not mentioned, Pharaoh's daughter (see vv. 5–10), an Egyptian, rescued Moses despite Pharaoh's mandate that all Hebrew infant males be slaughtered. God used this princess to take in Moses so that he would be nurtured and educated in the courts of Egypt before he was appointed leader of the Hebrews.

Pharaoh's daughter gave Moses an Egyptian name that in Hebrew means "to draw out" or "take out" because she "drew him out of the water" (v. 10). However, the name *Mose* in Egyptian etymology is a compound name usually combined with the name of an Egyptian deity.

3:2 a Dt33:16; Ac7:30
3:6 b Mt22:32* Ac7:32*
3:7 c Ex2:25

of the desert and came to Horeb, the moun-
tain of God. 2There the angel of the LORD ap-
peared to him in flames of fire from within
a bush.[a] Moses saw that though the bush
was on fire it did not burn up. 3So Moses
thought, "I will go over and see this strange
sight—why the bush does not burn up."

4When the LORD saw that he had gone
over to look, God called to him from within
the bush, "Moses! Moses!"

And Moses said, "Here I am."

5"Do not come any closer," God said.
"Take off your sandals, for the place where
you are standing is holy ground." 6Then he
said, "I am the God of your father, the God
of Abraham, the God of Isaac and the God of
Jacob."[b] At this, Moses hid his face, because
he was afraid to look at God.

7The LORD said, "I have indeed seen the
misery of my people in Egypt. I have heard
them crying out because of their slave
drivers, and I am concerned[c] about their
suffering. 8So I have come down to rescue
them from the hand of the Egyptians and to
bring them up out of that land into a good
and spacious land, a land flowing with milk
and honey[d]—the home of the Canaanites,
Hittites, Amorites, Perizzites, Hivites and
Jebusites. 9And now the cry of the Israelites
has reached me, and I have seen the way the
Egyptians are oppressing them. 10So now,
go. I am sending you to Pharaoh to bring my
people the Israelites out of Egypt."[e]

11But Moses said to God, "Who am I, that
I should go to Pharaoh and bring the Israel-
ites out of Egypt?"

12And God said, "I will be with you. And
this will be the sign to you that it is I who
have sent you: When you have brought the
people out of Egypt, you[a] will worship God
on this mountain."

13Moses said to God, "Suppose I go to the
Israelites and say to them, 'The God of your
fathers has sent me to you,' and they ask
me, 'What is his name?' Then what shall I
tell them?"

3:8 d ver 17
3:10 e Mic6:4

[a]12 The Hebrew is plural.

## The African Presence

### Exodus 2:16–22

While in Midian, Moses worked as a shepherd. There he met and married Zipporah, one of the daughters of Reuel (also called Jethro, see Ex 3:1; also, different translations refer to Hobab the Kenite as both Moses' brother-in-law and father-in-law, see Nu 10:29; Jdg 4:11), a Midianite priest (see Ex 2:16–22). The Midianites were descendants of Abraham's union with Keturah (see Ge 25:1–2; 1Ch 1:32; see also the African Presence note on Ge 25:1–2).

Later, Moses had a wife referred to as a Cushite (see Nu 12:1). A major question concerning Moses' wife is her ethnic identity. Was she a Midianite? Was she a Cushite? Is Zipporah to be identified with the Cushite woman or did Moses have more than one wife? Arguments are advanced on both sides. On the one hand, some scholars claim the Cushite woman in Numbers 12 is to be identified with Zipporah on the basis of the parallelism between Cushan and Midian in Habakkuk 3:7. On the other hand, some scholars believe that the Cushite woman was a second wife. Due to the large numbers of Cushites, or Nubians, present in Egypt as both slaves and members of the royal household, the Cushite woman could have been among the mixed multitude that departed Egypt with the Israelites during the exodus. An alternative theory is that Moses' Midianite wife in Exodus 2 represents one tradition and the Cushite wife in Numbers 12 represents a second tradition, similar to the differences in the names of Moses' father-in-law (see paragraph above).

**3:14** f Ex 6:2–3; Jn 8:58; Heb 13:8
**3:15** g Ps 135:13
**3:17** h Ge 15:16
**3:18** i Ex 4:1,8,31 j Ex 5:1,3
**3:20** k Ex 6:1,6; 9:15 l Dt 6:22; Ne 9:10 m Ex 12:31–33
**3:22** n Ex 11:2
**4:2** o ver 17,20

14 God said to Moses, "I AM WHO I AM.[a] This is what you are to say to the Israelites: 'I AM[f] has sent me to you.' "

15 God also said to Moses, "Say to the Israelites, 'The LORD,[b] the God of your fathers—the God of Abraham, the God of Isaac and the God of Jacob—has sent me to you.' This is my name[g] forever, the name by which I am to be remembered from generation to generation.

16 "Go, assemble the elders of Israel and say to them, 'The LORD, the God of your fathers—the God of Abraham, Isaac and Jacob—appeared to me and said: I have watched over you and have seen what has been done to you in Egypt. 17 And I have promised to bring you up out of your misery in Egypt[h] into the land of the Canaanites, Hittites, Amorites, Perizzites, Hivites and Jebusites—a land flowing with milk and honey.'

18 "The elders of Israel will listen[i] to you. Then you and the elders are to go to the king of Egypt and say to him, 'The LORD, the God of the Hebrews, has met with us. Let us take a three-day journey into the desert to offer sacrifices[j] to the LORD our God.' 19 But I know that the king of Egypt will not let you go unless a mighty hand compels him. 20 So I will stretch out my hand[k] and strike the Egyptians with all the wonders[l] that I will perform among them. After that, he will let you go.[m]

21 "And I will make the Egyptians favorably disposed toward this people, so that when you leave you will not go empty-handed. 22 Every woman is to ask her neighbor and any woman living in her house for articles of silver and gold[n] and for clothing, which you will put on your sons and daughters. And so you will plunder the Egyptians."

## Signs for Moses

4 Moses answered, "What if they do not believe me or listen to me and say, 'The LORD did not appear to you'?"

2 Then the LORD said to him, "What is that in your hand?"

"A staff,"[o] he replied.

3 The LORD said, "Throw it on the ground."

Moses threw it on the ground and it became a snake, and he ran from it. 4 Then the LORD said to him, "Reach out your hand and take it by the tail." So Moses reached out and took hold of the snake and it turned back into a staff in his hand. 5 "This," said the LORD, "is so that they may believe that the LORD, the God of their fathers—the God of Abraham, the God of Isaac and the God of Jacob—has appeared to you."

6 Then the LORD said, "Put your hand inside your cloak." So Moses put his hand into his cloak, and when he took it out, it was leprous,[c] like snow.[p]

7 "Now put it back into your cloak," he said. So Moses put his hand back into his cloak, and when he took it out, it was restored, like the rest of his flesh.

8 Then the LORD said, "If they do not believe you or pay attention to the first miraculous sign, they may believe the second. 9 But if they do not believe these two signs or listen to you, take some water from the Nile and pour it on the dry ground. The water you take from the river will become blood[q] on the ground."

10 Moses said to the LORD, "O Lord, I have never been eloquent, neither in the past nor since you have spoken to your servant. I am slow of speech and tongue."

11 The LORD said to him, "Who gave man his mouth? Who makes him deaf or mute? Who gives him sight or makes him blind?[r] Is it not I, the LORD? 12 Now go; I will help you speak and will teach you what to say."[s]

13 But Moses said, "O Lord, please send someone else to do it."

14 Then the LORD's anger burned against Moses and he said, "What about your brother, Aaron the Levite? I know he can speak well. He is already on his way to meet[t] you, and his heart will be glad when he sees you. 15 You shall speak to him and put words in his mouth;[u] I will help both of you speak and will teach you what to do. 16 He will speak to the people for you, and it will be as if he were your mouth and as if you were God to him. 17 But take this staff[v] in your hand so you can perform miraculous signs with it."

**4:6** p Nu 12:10; 2Ki 5:1,27
**4:9** q Ex 7:17–21
**4:11** r Ps 94:9
**4:12** s Isa 50:4; Jer 1:9; Mt 10:19–20; Mk 13:11; Lk 12:12
**4:14** t ver 27
**4:15** u Nu 23:5,12,16
**4:17** v ver 2

[a] 14 Or *I WILL BE WHAT I WILL BE* [b] 15 The Hebrew for *LORD* sounds like and may be derived from the Hebrew for *I AM* in verse 14.
[c] 6 The Hebrew word was used for various diseases affecting the skin—not necessarily leprosy.

# Zipporah

## *Fulfilling Her Purpose*

The African American woman of today has the potential to carry out the purpose for which she was created. It is not necessary that she live in the shadow of another person in order to establish a spiritual legacy. Historically, many women have faded into the background of stories, unnamed and unnoticed. Often, tradition and culture dictated that a woman's identity be connected to someone else. Such was the case for Zipporah, the daughter of Jethro and the wife of Moses. We can only surmise about her character from the few times she is mentioned and the one time she is quoted (see Ex 2:15–22; 4:24–26; 18:1–6).

Zipporah is introduced as one of seven daughters, possibly the oldest, of the Midianite priest Jethro (also known as Reuel). Moses met this family after fleeing from Egypt. As shepherds, Jethro's daughters courageously faced daily harassment by other shepherds when watering their father's flocks. Moses helped them, and their father repaid him with hospitality and, eventually, with permission to marry Zipporah.

As the wife of Moses and mother of Gershom and Eliezer, Zipporah did not share the same spiritual heritage as her husband. Perhaps this is the reason that the sacred tradition of circumcision had been neglected. While Moses was returning to Egypt, God "was about to kill him," and his life was spared only after one of the boys was circumcised (Ex 4:24–25). A wife's resistance to God's will not only endangers God's divine purpose for the couple's lives, but it also places her family in spiritual jeopardy. Zipporah's action and her words of reproach to Moses lead us to assume that her sons likely remained uncircumcised due to her prejudice against a rite not practiced among her people. However, her actions saved her husband's life. She gave in to what she apparently came to realize was the will of God, which brought about a positive result from a frightening situation.

Women of color must be like Zipporah and follow God's will—when we agree and when we do not. We must remember that we see only a portion; God sees the entire picture and knows what is best for us.

—A. Aubry

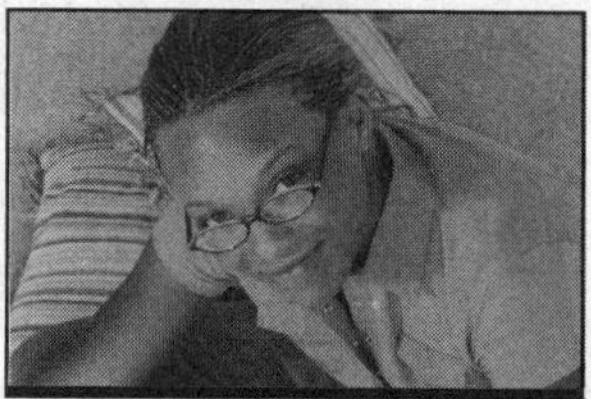

### reflection

*What is God asking you to do that you do not agree with?*

*How will you submit to the will of God?*

### read

Exodus 2:15–22; 4:18–26; 18:2–6.

**See also** the Inspire Notes "Motherhood," "Submission" and "Omniscience: God Is All-Knowing" and the Women of the Bible Notes "Tamar: The Link Between Judah and Jesus" and "Fortune-Telling Slave Girl: A Surprising Testimony to God's Work."

For the next Women of the Bible note, go to page 171.

**4:19** w Ex 2:15 x Ex 2:23
**4:21** y Ex 7:3,13; 9:12,35; Dt 2:30; Jn 12:40
**4:22** z Jer 31:9; Hos 11:1; Ro 9:4
**4:23** a Ex 12:12,29
**4:24** b Nu 22:22
**4:25** c Jos 5:2,3

## Moses Returns to Egypt

18Then Moses went back to Jethro his
father-in-law and said to him, "Let me go
back to my own people in Egypt to see if any
of them are still alive."

Jethro said, "Go, and I wish you well."

19Now the LORD had said to Moses in
Midian, "Go back to Egypt, for all the men
who wanted to kill[w] you are dead.[x]" 20So
Moses took his wife and sons, put them on
a donkey and started back to Egypt. And he
took the staff of God in his hand.

21The LORD said to Moses, "When you re-
turn to Egypt, see that you perform before
Pharaoh all the wonders I have given you
the power to do. But I will harden his heart[y]
so that he will not let the people go. 22Then
say to Pharaoh, 'This is what the LORD says:
Israel is my firstborn son,[z] 23and I told you,
"Let my son go, so he may worship me." But
you refused to let him go; so I will kill your
firstborn son.'"[a]

24At a lodging place on the way, the LORD
met ⌊Moses⌋[a] and was about to kill[b] him.
25But Zipporah took a flint knife, cut off her
son's foreskin[c] and touched ⌊Moses'⌋ feet
with it.[b] "Surely you are a bridegroom of
blood to me," she said. 26So the LORD let him
alone. (At that time she said "bridegroom of
blood," referring to circumcision.)

27The LORD said to Aaron, "Go into the
desert to meet Moses." So he met Moses
at the mountain[d] of God and kissed him.
28Then Moses told Aaron everything the
LORD had sent him to say, and also about all
the miraculous signs he had commanded
him to perform.

29Moses and Aaron brought together all
the elders[e] of the Israelites, 30and Aaron
told them everything the LORD had said to
Moses. He also performed the signs before
the people, 31and they believed.[f] And when
they heard that the LORD was concerned
about them and had seen their misery, they
bowed down and worshiped.

## Bricks Without Straw

5 Afterward Moses and Aaron went to
Pharaoh and said, "This is what the
LORD, the God of Israel, says: 'Let my people
go, so that they may hold a festival to me in
the desert.'"

2Pharaoh said, "Who is the LORD,[g] that I
should obey him and let Israel go? I do not
know the LORD and I will not let Israel go."[h]

3Then they said, "The God of the Hebrews
has met with us. Now let us take a three-day
journey into the desert to offer sacrifices to
the LORD our God, or he may strike us with
plagues or with the sword."

4But the king of Egypt said, "Moses and
Aaron, why are you taking the people away
from their labor?[i] Get back to your work!"

**4:27** d Ex 3:1
**4:29** e Ex 3:16
**4:31** f Ex 3:18
**5:2** g Job 21:15 h Ex 3:19
**5:4** i Ex 1:11

[a]24 Or ⌊*Moses' son*⌋; Hebrew *him* [b]25 Or *and drew near* ⌊*Moses'*⌋ *feet*

## The African Presence

### Exodus 5:1–5

Egypt played an important role in the Biblical narrative and especially in the story of Moses and the exodus. Closely associated with Egypt during this time was the ancient kingdom of Nubia. The exact geographic region is disputed; however, most scholars generally agree that the area of Nubia included the middle of the Nile from what is present-day southern Egypt and northern Sudan. Nubia is the Biblical "Cush," which is often "Ethiopia" in the English Bible, following the Greek translation. Biblical "Ethiopia" is therefore not to be confused with present-day Ethiopia.

Nubia and Egypt shared a long history of interaction. At times Nubia was under Egyptian rule, allowing an intermingling of trade, resources and culture.

5 Then Pharaoh said, "Look, the people of the land are now numerous, and you are stopping them from working."

6 That same day Pharaoh gave this order to the slave drivers and foremen in charge of the people: 7 "You are no longer to supply the people with straw for making bricks; let them go and gather their own straw. 8 But require them to make the same number of bricks as before; don't reduce the quota. They are lazy; that is why they are crying out, 'Let us go and sacrifice to our God.' 9 Make the work harder for the men so that they keep working and pay no attention to lies."

10 Then the slave drivers and the foremen went out and said to the people, "This is what Pharaoh says: 'I will not give you any more straw. 11 Go and get your own straw wherever you can find it, but your work will not be reduced at all.'" 12 So the people scattered all over Egypt to gather stubble to use for straw. 13 The slave drivers kept pressing them, saying, "Complete the work required of you for each day, just as when you had straw." 14 The Israelite foremen appointed by Pharaoh's slave drivers were beaten and were asked, "Why didn't you meet your quota of bricks yesterday or today, as before?"

15 Then the Israelite foremen went and appealed to Pharaoh: "Why have you treated your servants this way? 16 Your servants are given no straw, yet we are told, 'Make bricks!' Your servants are being beaten, but the fault is with your own people."

17 Pharaoh said, "Lazy, that's what you are—lazy! That is why you keep saying, 'Let us go and sacrifice to the LORD.' 18 Now get to work. You will not be given any straw, yet you must produce your full quota of bricks."

19 The Israelite foremen realized they were in trouble when they were told, "You are not to reduce the number of bricks required of you for each day." 20 When they left Pharaoh, they found Moses and Aaron waiting to meet them, 21 and they said, "May the LORD look upon you and judge you! You have made us a stench to Pharaoh and his officials and have put a sword in their hand to kill us."

## God Promises Deliverance

22 Moses returned to the LORD and said, "O Lord, why have you brought trouble upon this people? Is this why you sent me? 23 Ever since I went to Pharaoh to speak in your name, he has brought trouble upon this people, and you have not rescued your people at all."

6 Then the LORD said to Moses, "Now you will see what I will do to Pharaoh: Because of my mighty hand[j] he will let them go;[k] because of my mighty hand he will drive them out of his country."[l]

2 God also said to Moses, "I am the LORD. 3 I appeared to Abraham, to Isaac and to Jacob as God Almighty,[a][m] but by my name[n] the LORD[b][o] I did not make myself known to them.[c] 4 I also established my covenant[p] with them to give them the land of Canaan, where they lived as aliens.[q] 5 Moreover, I have heard the groaning[r] of the Israelites, whom the Egyptians are enslaving, and I have remembered my covenant.

6 "Therefore, say to the Israelites: 'I am the LORD, and I will bring you out from under the yoke of the Egyptians. I will free you from being slaves to them, and I will redeem[s] you with an outstretched arm and with mighty acts of judgment. 7 I will take you as my own people, and I will be your God.[t] Then you will know that I am the LORD your God, who brought you out from under the yoke of the Egyptians. 8 And I will bring

*Daughter,*

*I am whatever you need.*

*Remember that I know exactly what you need and will always be your provider.*

*Your God and Father*

EXODUS 6:1–8

6:1 j Ex 3:19 k Ex 3:20 l Ex 12:31,33,39
6:3 m Ge 17:1 n Ps 83:18; Isa 52:6 o Ex 3:14
6:4 p Ge 15:18 q Ge 28:4,13
6:5 r Ex 2:23
6:6 s Dt 7:8; 1Ch 17:21
6:7 t Dt 4:20; 2Sa 7:24

[a] 3 Hebrew *El-Shaddai* [b] 3 See note at Exodus 3:15. [c] 3 Or *Almighty, and by my name the LORD did I not let myself be known to them?*

6:8
u Ge 15:18

you to the land[u] I swore with uplifted hand to give to Abraham, to Isaac and to Jacob. I will give it to you as a possession. I am the LORD.'"

9 Moses reported this to the Israelites, but they did not listen to him because of their discouragement and cruel bondage.

10 Then the LORD said to Moses, 11 "Go, tell Pharaoh king of Egypt to let the Israelites go out of his country."

12 But Moses said to the LORD, "If the Israelites will not listen to me, why would Pharaoh listen to me, since I speak with faltering lips[a]?"

*Dear Heavenly Father,*

*whose omniscience directs me, you have blessed me with gifts that remain unopened. Sometimes I'm so caught up in my daily routine that I lose sight of my God-honoring hopes and dreams. They seem so distant and unattainable. Help me each day to grow in the knowledge that I can trust you as I anticipate the fulfillment of your promises. In Jesus' blessed name,*

*Amen*

EXODUS 6:2–12

## Family Record of Moses and Aaron

13 Now the LORD spoke to Moses and Aaron about the Israelites and Pharaoh king of Egypt, and he commanded them to bring the Israelites out of Egypt.

14 These were the heads of their families[b]:

The sons of Reuben the firstborn son of Israel were Hanoch and Pallu, Hezron and Carmi. These were the clans of Reuben.

15 The sons of Simeon were Jemuel, Jamin, Ohad, Jakin, Zohar and Shaul the son of a Canaanite woman. These were the clans of Simeon.

16 These were the names of the sons of Levi according to their records: Gershon,[v] Kohath and Merari.[w] Levi lived 137 years.

17 The sons of Gershon, by clans, were Libni and Shimei.[x]

18 The sons of Kohath were Amram, Izhar, Hebron and Uzziel.[y] Kohath lived 133 years.

19 The sons of Merari were Mahli and Mushi.[z]

These were the clans of Levi according to their records.

20 Amram married his father's sister Jochebed, who bore him Aaron and Moses.[a] Amram lived 137 years.

21 The sons of Izhar[b] were Korah, Nepheg and Zicri.

22 The sons of Uzziel were Mishael, Elzaphan[c] and Sithri.

23 Aaron married Elisheba, daughter of Amminadab and sister of Nahshon, and she bore him Nadab and Abihu, Eleazar and Ithamar.

24 The sons of Korah were Assir, Elkanah and Abiasaph. These were the Korahite clans.

25 Eleazar son of Aaron married one of the daughters of Putiel, and she bore him Phinehas.[d]

These were the heads of the Levite families, clan by clan.

26 It was this same Aaron and Moses to whom the LORD said, "Bring the Israelites out of Egypt by their divisions." 27 They were the ones who spoke to Pharaoh king of Egypt about bringing the Israelites out of Egypt. It was the same Moses and Aaron.

## Aaron to Speak for Moses

28 Now when the LORD spoke to Moses in Egypt, 29 he said to him, "I am the LORD. Tell Pharaoh king of Egypt everything I tell you."

30 But Moses said to the LORD, "Since I speak with faltering lips, why would Pharaoh listen to me?"

6:16
v Ge 46:11
w Nu 3:17

6:17
x 1Ch 6:17

6:18
y 1Ch 6:2,18

6:19
z 1Ch 6:19

6:20
a Ex 2:1–2

6:21
b 1Ch 6:38

6:22
c Lev 10:4

6:25
d Nu 25:7,11; Jos 24:33

[a] 12 Hebrew *I am uncircumcised of lips*; also in verse 30 [b] 14 The Hebrew for *families* here and in verse 25 refers to units larger than clans.

## The African Presence

### Exodus 6:25

Aaron's son Eleazar married one of the daughters of Putiel, and she gave birth to a son named Phinehas. *Putiel* in Hebrew literally means "my God is Put." *Put* is the Hebrew word for Libya. The Hebrew name *Phinehas* means "the Nubian." Marriage to Cushites in Moses' family is a recurring theme (see Nu 12).

**7:1** e Ex4:16
**7:3** f Ex4:21
**7:4** g Ex11:9
**7:5** h Ex3:20
**7:6** i ver2
**7:7** j Dt34:7; Ac7:23,30
**7:9** k Isa7:11 l Ex4:2–5
**7:11** m Ge41:8 n ver22; Ex8:7,18

**7** Then the LORD said to Moses, "See, I have made you like God[e] to Pharaoh, and your brother Aaron will be your prophet. 2You are to say everything I command you, and your brother Aaron is to tell Pharaoh to let the Israelites go out of his country. 3But I will harden Pharaoh's heart,[f] and though I multiply my miraculous signs and wonders in Egypt, 4he will not listen[g] to you. Then I will lay my hand on Egypt and with mighty acts of judgment I will bring out my divisions, my people the Israelites. 5And the Egyptians will know that I am the LORD when I stretch out my hand[h] against Egypt and bring the Israelites out of it."

6Moses and Aaron did just as the LORD commanded[i] them. 7Moses was eighty years old[j] and Aaron eighty-three when they spoke to Pharaoh.

### Aaron's Staff Becomes a Snake

8The LORD said to Moses and Aaron, 9"When Pharaoh says to you, 'Perform a miracle,[k]' then say to Aaron, 'Take your staff and throw it down before Pharaoh,' and it will become a snake."[l]

10So Moses and Aaron went to Pharaoh and did just as the LORD commanded. Aaron threw his staff down in front of Pharaoh and his officials, and it became a snake. 11Pharaoh then summoned wise men and sorcerers, and the Egyptian magicians[m] also did the same things by their secret arts:[n] 12Each one threw down his staff and it became a snake. But Aaron's staff swallowed up their staffs. 13Yet Pharaoh's heart became hard and he would not listen to them, just as the LORD had said.

### The Plague of Blood

14Then the LORD said to Moses, "Pharaoh's heart is unyielding; he refuses to let the people go. 15Go to Pharaoh in the morning as he goes out to the water. Wait on the bank of the Nile to meet him, and take in your hand the staff that was changed into a snake. 16Then say to him, 'The LORD, the God of the Hebrews, has sent me to say to you: Let my people go, so that they may worship[o] me in the desert. But until now you have not listened. 17This is what the LORD says: By this you will know that I am the LORD: With the staff that is in my hand I will strike the water of the Nile, and it will be changed into blood.[p] 18The fish in the Nile will die, and the river will stink; the Egyptians will not be able to drink its water.'"[q]

19The LORD said to Moses, "Tell Aaron, 'Take your staff and stretch out your hand[r] over the waters of Egypt—over the streams and canals, over the ponds and all the reservoirs'—and they will turn to blood. Blood will be everywhere in Egypt, even in the wooden buckets and stone jars."

20Moses and Aaron did just as the LORD had commanded. He raised his staff in the presence of Pharaoh and his officials and struck the water of the Nile, and all the water was changed into blood.[s] 21The fish in the Nile died, and the river smelled so bad that the Egyptians could not drink its water. Blood was everywhere in Egypt.

22But the Egyptian magicians did the same things by their secret arts,[t] and Pharaoh's heart became hard; he would not listen to Moses and Aaron, just as the LORD had said. 23Instead, he turned and went into his

**7:16** o Ex3:18
**7:17** p Ex4:9; Rev16:4
**7:18** q ver21,24
**7:19** r Ex14:21
**7:20** s Ps78:44; 105:29
**7:22** t ver11

palace, and did not take even this to heart. [24]And all the Egyptians dug along the Nile to get drinking water, because they could not drink the water of the river.

## The Plague of Frogs

[25]Seven days passed after the LORD struck

# 8

the Nile. [1]Then the LORD said to Moses, "Go to Pharaoh and say to him, 'This is what the LORD says: Let my people go, so that they may worship me. [2]If you refuse to let them go, I will plague your whole country with frogs. [3]The Nile will teem with frogs. They will come up into your palace and your bedroom and onto your bed, into the houses of your officials and on your people, and into your ovens and kneading troughs. [4]The frogs will go up on you and your people and all your officials.'"

[5]Then the LORD said to Moses, "Tell Aaron, 'Stretch out your hand with your staff[u] over the streams and canals and ponds, and make frogs come up on the land of Egypt.'"

[6]So Aaron stretched out his hand over the waters of Egypt, and the frogs[v] came up and covered the land. [7]But the magicians did the same things by their secret arts;[w] they also made frogs come up on the land of Egypt.

[8]Pharaoh summoned Moses and Aaron and said, "Pray[x] to the LORD to take the frogs away from me and my people, and I will let your people go to offer sacrifices to the LORD."

[9]Moses said to Pharaoh, "I leave to you the honor of setting the time for me to pray for you and your officials and your people that you and your houses may be rid of the frogs, except for those that remain in the Nile."

[10]"Tomorrow," Pharaoh said.

Moses replied, "It will be as you say, so that you may know there is no one like the LORD our God.[y] [11]The frogs will leave you and your houses, your officials and your people; they will remain only in the Nile."

[12]After Moses and Aaron left Pharaoh, Moses cried out to the LORD about the frogs he had brought on Pharaoh. [13]And the LORD did what Moses asked. The frogs died in the houses, in the courtyards and in the fields. [14]They were piled into heaps, and the land reeked of them. [15]But when Pharaoh saw that there was relief, he hardened his heart and would not listen to Moses and Aaron, just as the LORD had said.

## The Plague of Gnats

[16]Then the LORD said to Moses, "Tell Aaron, 'Stretch out your staff and strike the dust of the ground,' and throughout the land of Egypt the dust will become gnats." [17]They did this, and when Aaron stretched out his hand with the staff and struck the dust of the ground, gnats[z] came upon men and animals. All the dust throughout the land of Egypt became gnats. [18]But when the magicians tried to produce gnats by their secret arts,[a] they could not. And the gnats were on men and animals.

[19]The magicians said to Pharaoh, "This is the finger of God." But Pharaoh's heart was hard and he would not listen, just as the LORD had said.

## The Plague of Flies

[20]Then the LORD said to Moses, "Get up early in the morning[b] and confront Pharaoh as he goes to the water and say to him, 'This is what the LORD says: Let my people go, so that they may worship me. [21]If you do not let my people go, I will send swarms of flies on you and your officials, on your people and into your houses. The houses of the Egyptians will be full of flies, and even the ground where they are.

[22]"'But on that day I will deal differently with the land of Goshen, where my people live;[c] no swarms of flies will be there, so that you will know that I, the LORD, am in this land. [23]I will make a distinction[a] between my people and your people. This miraculous sign will occur tomorrow.'"

[24]And the LORD did this. Dense swarms of flies poured into Pharaoh's palace and into the houses of his officials, and throughout Egypt the land was ruined by the flies.[d]

[25]Then Pharaoh summoned Moses and Aaron and said, "Go, sacrifice to your God here in the land."

[26]But Moses said, "That would not be right. The sacrifices we offer the LORD our God would be detestable to the Egyptians.

[a]23 Septuagint and Vulgate; Hebrew *will put a deliverance*

**8:5** u Ex7:19
**8:6** v Ps78:45; 105:30
**8:7** w Ex7:11
**8:8** x Ex9:28; 10:17
**8:10** y Ex9:14; Dt33:26; Isa46:9; Jer10:6
**8:17** z Ps105:31
**8:18** a Ex7:11
**8:20** b Ex7:15
**8:22** c Ex9:4,6,26; 10:23; 11:7
**8:24** d Ps78:45; 105:31

**8:27** e Ex 3:18
**8:28** f ver 8
**8:29** g ver 15
**8:32** h Ex 4:21
**9:1** i Ex 8:1
**9:4** j Ex 8:22
**9:7** k Ex 7:14; 8:32

And if we offer sacrifices that are detestable in their eyes, will they not stone us? 27 We must take a three-day journey into the desert to offer sacrifices[e] to the LORD our God, as he commands us."

28 Pharaoh said, "I will let you go to offer sacrifices to the LORD your God in the desert, but you must not go very far. Now pray[f] for me."

29 Moses answered, "As soon as I leave you, I will pray to the LORD, and tomorrow the flies will leave Pharaoh and his officials and his people. Only be sure that Pharaoh does not act deceitfully[g] again by not letting the people go to offer sacrifices to the LORD."

30 Then Moses left Pharaoh and prayed to the LORD, 31 and the LORD did what Moses asked: The flies left Pharaoh and his officials and his people; not a fly remained. 32 But this time also Pharaoh hardened his heart[h] and would not let the people go.

## The Plague on Livestock

9 Then the LORD said to Moses, "Go to Pharaoh and say to him, 'This is what the LORD, the God of the Hebrews, says: "Let my people go, so that they may worship[i] me." 2 If you refuse to let them go and continue to hold them back, 3 the hand of the LORD will bring a terrible plague on your livestock in the field—on your horses and donkeys and camels and on your cattle and sheep and goats. 4 But the LORD will make a distinction between the livestock of Israel and that of Egypt,[j] so that no animal belonging to the Israelites will die.' "

5 The LORD set a time and said, "Tomorrow the LORD will do this in the land." 6 And the next day the LORD did it: All the livestock of the Egyptians died, but not one animal belonging to the Israelites died. 7 Pharaoh sent men to investigate and found that not even one of the animals of the Israelites had died. Yet his heart was unyielding and he would not let the people go.[k]

## The Plague of Boils

8 Then the LORD said to Moses and Aaron, "Take handfuls of soot from a furnace and have Moses toss it into the air in the presence of Pharaoh. 9 It will become fine dust over the whole land of Egypt, and festering boils[l] will break out on men and animals throughout the land."

10 So they took soot from a furnace and stood before Pharaoh. Moses tossed it into the air, and festering boils broke out on men and animals. 11 The magicians could not stand before Moses because of the boils that were on them and on all the Egyptians. 12 But the LORD hardened Pharaoh's heart[m] and he would not listen to Moses and Aaron, just as the LORD had said to Moses.

## The Plague of Hail

13 Then the LORD said to Moses, "Get up early in the morning, confront Pharaoh and say to him, 'This is what the LORD, the God of the Hebrews, says: Let my people go, so that they may worship me, 14 or this time I will send the full force of my plagues against you and against your officials and your people, so you may know[n] that there is no one like me in all the earth. 15 For by now I could have stretched out my hand and struck you and your people with a plague that would have wiped you off the earth. 16 But I have raised you up[a] for this very purpose, that I might show you my power[o] and that my name might be proclaimed in all the earth. 17 You still set yourself against my people and will not let them go. 18 Therefore, at this time tomorrow I will send the worst hailstorm that has ever fallen on Egypt, from the day it was founded till now. 19 Give an order now to bring your livestock and everything you have in the field to a place of shelter, because the hail will fall on every man and animal that has not been brought in and is still out in the field, and they will die.' "

20 Those officials of Pharaoh who feared the word of the LORD hurried to bring their slaves and their livestock inside. 21 But those who ignored the word of the LORD left their slaves and livestock in the field.

22 Then the LORD said to Moses, "Stretch out your hand toward the sky so that hail will fall all over Egypt—on men and animals and on everything growing in the fields of Egypt." 23 When Moses stretched out his staff toward the sky, the LORD sent

**9:9** l Rev 16:2
**9:12** m Ex 4:21
**9:14** n Ex 8:10
**9:16** o Ro 9:17*

[a] 16 Or *have spared you*

**9:23**
p Ps 18:13
q Jos 10:11; Ps 78:47; Eze 38:22; Rev 8:7; 16:21

**9:25**
r Ps 105:32–33

**9:26**
s ver 4
t Ex 8:22; 10:23; 11:7

**9:27**
u Ex 10:16
v 2Ch 12:6; La 1:18

**9:28**
w Ex 8:8

**9:29**
x 1Ki 8:22,38; Ps 143:6
y Ps 24:1

**9:35**
z Ex 4:21

**10:1**
a Ex 4:21

**10:2**
b Dt 4:9; Ps 44:1

thunder[p] and hail,[q] and lightning flashed
down to the ground. So the LORD rained hail
on the land of Egypt; 24hail fell and light-
ning flashed back and forth. It was the worst
storm in all the land of Egypt since it had
become a nation. 25Throughout Egypt hail
struck everything in the fields—both men
and animals; it beat down everything grow-
ing in the fields and stripped every tree.[r]
26The only place it did not hail was the land
of Goshen,[s] where the Israelites were.[t]

27Then Pharaoh summoned Moses and
Aaron. "This time I have sinned,"[u] he said
to them. "The LORD is in the right,[v] and I
and my people are in the wrong. 28Pray to
the LORD, for we have had enough thunder
and hail. I will let you go;[w] you don't have to
stay any longer."

29Moses replied, "When I have gone out
of the city, I will spread out my hands[x] in
prayer to the LORD. The thunder will stop
and there will be no more hail, so you may
know that the earth[y] is the LORD's. 30But I
know that you and your officials still do not
fear the LORD God."

31(The flax and barley were destroyed,
since the barley had headed and the flax was
in bloom. 32The wheat and spelt, however,
were not destroyed, because they ripen
later.)

33Then Moses left Pharaoh and went out
of the city. He spread out his hands toward
the LORD; the thunder and hail stopped, and
the rain no longer poured down on the land.
34When Pharaoh saw that the rain and hail
and thunder had stopped, he sinned again:
He and his officials hardened their hearts.
35So Pharaoh's heart[z] was hard and he would
not let the Israelites go, just as the LORD had
said through Moses.

## The Plague of Locusts

10 Then the LORD said to Moses, "Go
to Pharaoh, for I have hardened his
heart[a] and the hearts of his officials so that
I may perform these miraculous signs of
mine among them 2that you may tell your
children[b] and grandchildren how I dealt
harshly with the Egyptians and how I per-
formed my signs among them, and that you
may know that I am the LORD."

3So Moses and Aaron went to Pharaoh
and said to him, "This is what the LORD, the
God of the Hebrews, says: 'How long will
you refuse to humble[c] yourself before me?
Let my people go, so that they may worship
me. 4If you refuse to let them go, I will bring
locusts into your country tomorrow. 5They
will cover the face of the ground so that it
cannot be seen. They will devour what little
you have left[d] after the hail, including every
tree that is growing in your fields. 6They
will fill your houses and those of all your
officials and all the Egyptians—something
neither your fathers nor your forefathers
have ever seen from the day they settled in
this land till now.'" Then Moses turned and
left Pharaoh.

7Pharaoh's officials said to him, "How
long will this man be a snare[e] to us? Let
the people go, so that they may worship the
LORD their God. Do you not yet realize that
Egypt is ruined?"[f]

8Then Moses and Aaron were brought
back to Pharaoh. "Go, worship the LORD
your God," he said. "But just who will be
going?"

9Moses answered, "We will go with our
young and old, with our sons and daugh-
ters, and with our flocks and herds, because
we are to celebrate a festival to the LORD."

10Pharaoh said, "The LORD be with you—
if I let you go, along with your women and
children! Clearly you are bent on evil.[a] 11No!
Have only the men go; and worship the LORD,
since that's what you have been asking for."
Then Moses and Aaron were driven out of
Pharaoh's presence.

12And the LORD said to Moses, "Stretch
out your hand[g] over Egypt so that locusts
will swarm over the land and devour every-
thing growing in the fields, everything left
by the hail."

13So Moses stretched out his staff over
Egypt, and the LORD made an east wind
blow across the land all that day and all that
night. By morning the wind had brought the
locusts; 14they invaded all Egypt and settled
down in every area of the country in great
numbers. Never before had there been such
a plague of locusts,[h] nor will there ever be
again. 15They covered all the ground until it

**10:3**
c Jas 4:10

**10:5**
d Joel 1:4

**10:7**
e Ex 23:33; Jos 23:13
f Ex 8:19

**10:12**
g Ex 7:19

**10:14**
h Joel 2:1–11,25

[a]10 Or *Be careful, trouble is in store for you!*

10:15 i Ps 105:34–35
10:16 j Ex 9:27
10:20 k Ex 4:21
10:22 l Ps 105:28
10:24 m ver 8–10
10:29 n Heb 11:27

was black. They devoured[i] all that was left after the hail—everything growing in the fields and the fruit on the trees. Nothing green remained on tree or plant in all the land of Egypt.

16 Pharaoh quickly summoned Moses and Aaron and said, "I have sinned[j] against the LORD your God and against you. 17 Now forgive my sin once more and pray to the LORD your God to take this deadly plague away from me."

18 Moses then left Pharaoh and prayed to the LORD. 19 And the LORD changed the wind to a very strong west wind, which caught up the locusts and carried them into the Red Sea.[a] Not a locust was left anywhere in Egypt. 20 But the LORD hardened Pharaoh's heart,[k] and he would not let the Israelites go.

## The Plague of Darkness

21 Then the LORD said to Moses, "Stretch out your hand toward the sky so that darkness will spread over Egypt—darkness that can be felt." 22 So Moses stretched out his hand toward the sky, and total darkness[l] covered all Egypt for three days. 23 No one could see anyone else or leave his place for three days. Yet all the Israelites had light in the places where they lived.

24 Then Pharaoh summoned Moses and said, "Go, worship the LORD. Even your women and children[m] may go with you; only leave your flocks and herds behind."

25 But Moses said, "You must allow us to have sacrifices and burnt offerings to present to the LORD our God. 26 Our livestock too must go with us; not a hoof is to be left behind. We have to use some of them in worshiping the LORD our God, and until we get there we will not know what we are to use to worship the LORD."

27 But the LORD hardened Pharaoh's heart, and he was not willing to let them go. 28 Pharaoh said to Moses, "Get out of my sight! Make sure you do not appear before me again! The day you see my face you will die."

29 "Just as you say," Moses replied, "I will never appear[n] before you again."

## The Plague on the Firstborn

11 Now the LORD had said to Moses, "I will bring one more plague on Pharaoh and on Egypt. After that, he will let you go from here, and when he does, he will drive you out completely. 2 Tell the people that men and women alike are to ask their neighbors for articles of silver and gold."[o] 3 (The LORD made the Egyptians favorably disposed toward the people, and Moses himself was highly regarded in Egypt by Pharaoh's officials and by the people.)

4 So Moses said, "This is what the LORD says: 'About midnight[p] I will go throughout Egypt. 5 Every firstborn son in Egypt will die, from the firstborn son of Pharaoh, who sits on the throne, to the firstborn son of the slave girl, who is at her hand mill, and all the firstborn of the cattle as well. 6 There will be loud wailing[q] throughout Egypt—worse than there has ever been or ever will be again. 7 But among the Israelites not a dog will bark at any man or animal.' Then you will know that the LORD makes a distinction[r] between Egypt and Israel. 8 All these officials of yours will come to me, bowing down before me and saying, 'Go,[s] you and all the people who follow you!' After that I will leave." Then Moses, hot with anger, left Pharaoh.

9 The LORD had said to Moses, "Pharaoh will refuse to listen[t] to you—so that my wonders may be multiplied in Egypt." 10 Moses and Aaron performed all these wonders before Pharaoh, but the LORD hardened Pharaoh's heart,[u] and he would not let the Israelites go out of his country.

## The Passover

12 The LORD said to Moses and Aaron in Egypt, 2 "This month is to be for you the first month,[v] the first month of your year. 3 Tell the whole community of Israel that on the tenth day of this month each man is to take a lamb[b] for his family, one for each household. 4 If any household is too small for a whole lamb, they must share one with their nearest neighbor, having taken into account the number of people there are. You are to determine the amount of lamb needed in accordance with what each person

11:2 o Ex 3:21,22
11:4 p Ex 12:29
11:6 q Ex 12:30
11:7 r Ex 8:22
11:8 s Ex 12:31–33
11:9 t Ex 7:4
11:10 u Ex 4:21
12:2 v Ex 13:4; Dt 16:1

[a] 19 Hebrew *Yam Suph*; that is, Sea of Reeds [b] 3 The Hebrew word can mean *lamb* or *kid*; also in verse 4.

**12:5** w Lev 22:18–21
**12:6** x Lev 23:5; Nu 9:1–3,5,11 y Dt 16:4,6
**12:8** z Ex 34:25 a Dt 16:7
**12:10** b Ex 34:25
**12:11** c Dt 16:3
**12:12** d Ex 11:4 e Nu 33:4
**12:14** f Ex 13:9 g Ex 13:5,10
**12:15** h Ex 23:15; Lev 23:6; Dt 16:3 i Nu 9:13
**12:17** j Ex 13:3
**12:18** k ver 2; Lev 23:5–8

will eat. 5 The animals you choose must be year-old males without defect,[w] and you may take them from the sheep or the goats. 6 Take care of them until the fourteenth day of the month,[x] when all the people of the community of Israel must slaughter them at twilight.[y] 7 Then they are to take some of the blood and put it on the sides and tops of the doorframes of the houses where they eat the lambs. 8 That same night[z] they are to eat the meat roasted[a] over the fire, along with bitter herbs, and bread made without yeast. 9 Do not eat the meat raw or cooked in water, but roast it over the fire—head, legs and inner parts. 10 Do not leave any of it till morning;[b] if some is left till morning, you must burn it. 11 This is how you are to eat it: with your cloak tucked into your belt, your sandals on your feet and your staff in your hand. Eat it in haste;[c] it is the LORD's Passover.

12 "On that same night I will pass through[d] Egypt and strike down every firstborn—both men and animals—and I will bring judgment on all the gods[e] of Egypt. I am the LORD. 13 The blood will be a sign for you on the houses where you are; and when I see the blood, I will pass over you. No destructive plague will touch you when I strike Egypt.

14 "This is a day you are to commemorate;[f] for the generations to come you shall celebrate it as a festival to the LORD—a lasting ordinance.[g] 15 For seven days you are to eat bread made without yeast.[h] On the first day remove the yeast from your houses, for whoever eats anything with yeast in it from the first day through the seventh must be cut off[i] from Israel. 16 On the first day hold a sacred assembly, and another one on the seventh day. Do no work at all on these days, except to prepare food for everyone to eat—that is all you may do.

17 "Celebrate the Feast of Unleavened Bread, because it was on this very day that I brought your divisions out of Egypt.[j] Celebrate this day as a lasting ordinance for the generations to come. 18 In the first month[k] you are to eat bread made without yeast, from the evening of the fourteenth day until the evening of the twenty-first day. 19 For seven days no yeast is to be found in your houses. And whoever eats anything with yeast in it must be cut off from the community of Israel, whether he is an alien or native-born. 20 Eat nothing made with yeast. Wherever you live, you must eat unleavened bread."

21 Then Moses summoned all the elders of Israel and said to them, "Go at once and select the animals for your families and slaughter the Passover lamb. 22 Take a bunch of hyssop, dip it into the blood in the basin and put some of the blood[l] on the top and on both sides of the doorframe. Not one of you shall go out the door of his house until morning. 23 When the LORD goes through the land to strike down the Egyptians, he will see the blood on the top and sides of the doorframe and will pass over[m] that doorway, and he will not permit the destroyer to enter your houses and strike you down.

24 "Obey these instructions as a lasting ordinance for you and your descendants. 25 When you enter the land that the LORD will give you as he promised, observe this ceremony. 26 And when your children ask you, 'What does this ceremony mean to you?' 27 then tell them, 'It is the Passover[n] sacrifice to the LORD, who passed over the houses of the Israelites in Egypt and spared our homes when he struck down the Egyptians.'" Then the people bowed down and worshiped. 28 The Israelites did just what the LORD commanded Moses and Aaron.

29 At midnight[o] the LORD struck down all the firstborn[p] in Egypt, from the firstborn of Pharaoh, who sat on the throne, to the firstborn of the prisoner, who was in the dungeon, and the firstborn of all the livestock as well. 30 Pharaoh and all his officials and all the Egyptians got up during the night, and there was loud wailing[q] in Egypt, for there was not a house without someone dead.

## The Exodus

31 During the night Pharaoh summoned Moses and Aaron and said, "Up! Leave my people, you and the Israelites! Go, worship the LORD as you have requested. 32 Take your flocks and herds, as you have said, and go. And also bless me."

33 The Egyptians urged the people to hurry and leave the country. "For otherwise," they

**12:22** l ver 7
**12:23** m ver 13
**12:27** n ver 11
**12:29** o Ex 11:4 p Ex 4:23
**12:30** q Ex 11:6

said, "we will all die!" 34 So the people took their dough before the yeast was added, and carried it on their shoulders in kneading troughs wrapped in clothing. 35 The Israelites did as Moses instructed and asked the Egyptians for articles of silver and gold[r] and for clothing. 36 The LORD had made the Egyptians favorably disposed toward the people, and they gave them what they asked for; so they plundered[s] the Egyptians.

37 The Israelites journeyed from Rameses to Succoth.[t] There were about six hundred thousand men[u] on foot, besides women and children. 38 Many other people went up with them, as well as large droves of livestock, both flocks and herds. 39 With the dough they had brought from Egypt, they baked cakes of unleavened bread. The dough was without yeast because they had been driven out of Egypt and did not have time to prepare food for themselves.

40 Now the length of time the Israelite people lived in Egypt[a] was 430 years.[v] 41 At the end of the 430 years, to the very day, all the LORD's divisions left Egypt. 42 Because the LORD kept vigil that night to bring them out of Egypt, on this night all the Israelites are to keep vigil to honor the LORD for the generations to come.[w]

## Passover Restrictions

43 The LORD said to Moses and Aaron, "These are the regulations for the Passover:

"No foreigner is to eat of it. 44 Any slave you have bought may eat of it after you have circumcised[x] him, 45 but a temporary resident and a hired worker may not eat of it.

46 "It must be eaten inside one house; take none of the meat outside the house. Do not break any of the bones.[y] 47 The whole community of Israel must celebrate it.

48 "An alien living among you who wants to celebrate the LORD's Passover must have all the males in his household circumcised; then he may take part like one born in the land.[z] No uncircumcised male may eat of it. 49 The same law applies to the native-born and to the alien[a] living among you."

50 All the Israelites did just what the LORD had commanded Moses and Aaron. 51 And on that very day the LORD brought the Israelites out of Egypt by their divisions.

## Consecration of the Firstborn

13 The LORD said to Moses, 2 "Consecrate to me every firstborn male.[b] The first offspring of every womb among the Israelites belongs to me, whether man or animal."

3 Then Moses said to the people, "Commemorate this day, the day you came out of Egypt, out of the land of slavery, because the LORD brought you out of it with a mighty hand. Eat nothing containing yeast. 4 Today, in the month of Abib, you are leaving. 5 When the LORD brings you into the land of the Canaanites, Hittites, Amorites, Hivites and Jebusites[c]—the land he swore to your forefathers to give you, a land flowing with milk and honey—you are to observe this ceremony[d] in this month: 6 For seven days eat bread made without yeast and on the seventh day hold a festival[e] to the LORD. 7 Eat unleavened bread during those seven days; nothing with yeast in it is to be seen among you, nor shall any yeast be seen anywhere within your borders. 8 On that day tell your son, 'I do this because of what the LORD did for me when I came out of Egypt.' 9 This observance will be for you like a sign on your hand and a reminder on your forehead[f] that the law of the LORD is to be on your lips. For the LORD brought you out of Egypt with his mighty hand. 10 You must keep this ordinance at the appointed time year after year.

11 "After the LORD brings you into the land of the Canaanites and gives it to you, as he promised on oath to you and your forefathers, 12 you are to give over to the LORD the first offspring of every womb. All the firstborn males of your livestock belong to the LORD.[g] 13 Redeem with a lamb every firstborn donkey, but if you do not redeem it, break its neck.[h] Redeem every firstborn among your sons.[i]

14 "In days to come, when your son asks you, 'What does this mean?' say to him, 'With a mighty hand the LORD brought us out of Egypt, out of the land of slavery. 15 When Pharaoh stubbornly refused to let us go, the LORD killed every firstborn in

**12:35** r Ex3:22
**12:36** s Ex3:22
**12:37** t Nu33:3–5 u Nu11:13,21
**12:40** v Ge15:13; Ac7:6; Gal3:17
**12:42** w Dt16:1,6
**12:44** x Ge17:12–13
**12:46** y Nu9:12; Jn19:36*
**12:48** z Nu9:14
**12:49** a Nu15:15–16,29
**13:2** b ver12,13,15; Ex22:29; Lk2:23*
**13:5** c Ex3:8 d Ex12:25–26
**13:6** e Ex12:15–20
**13:9** f Dt6:8
**13:12** g Lk2:23*
**13:13** h Ex34:20 i Nu18:15

[a]40 Masoretic Text; Samaritan Pentateuch and Septuagint *Egypt and Canaan*

**13:16** j ver 9
**13:17** k Ex 14:11; Nu 14:1–4; Dt 17:16
**13:19** l Jos 24:32 m Ge 50:24–25
**13:20** n Nu 33:6
**13:21** o Ex 14:19,24; Ps 78:14; 1Co 10:1
**14:2** p Nu 33:7
**14:4** q Ex 4:21 r Ro 9:17,22–23

Egypt, both man and animal. This is why I sacrifice to the LORD the first male offspring of every womb and redeem each of my firstborn sons.' [16]And it will be like a sign on your hand and a symbol on your forehead[j] that the LORD brought us out of Egypt with his mighty hand."

## Crossing the Sea

[17]When Pharaoh let the people go, God did not lead them on the road through the Philistine country, though that was shorter. For God said, "If they face war, they might change their minds and return to Egypt."[k] [18]So God led the people around by the desert road toward the Red Sea.[a] The Israelites went up out of Egypt armed for battle.

[19]Moses took the bones of Joseph[l] with him because Joseph had made the sons of Israel swear an oath. He had said, "God will surely come to your aid, and then you must carry my bones up with you from this place."[b][m]

[20]After leaving Succoth they camped at Etham on the edge of the desert.[n] [21]By day the LORD went ahead of them in a pillar of cloud[o] to guide them on their way and by night in a pillar of fire to give them light, so that they could travel by day or night. [22]Neither the pillar of cloud by day nor the pillar of fire by night left its place in front of the people.

**14** Then the LORD said to Moses, [2]"Tell the Israelites to turn back and encamp near Pi Hahiroth, between Migdol[p] and the sea. They are to encamp by the sea, directly opposite Baal Zephon. [3]Pharaoh will think, 'The Israelites are wandering around the land in confusion, hemmed in by the desert.' [4]And I will harden Pharaoh's heart,[q] and he will pursue them. But I will gain glory[r] for myself through Pharaoh and all his army, and the Egyptians will know that I am the LORD." So the Israelites did this.

[5]When the king of Egypt was told that the people had fled, Pharaoh and his officials changed their minds about them and said, "What have we done? We have let the Israelites go and have lost their services!" [6]So he had his chariot made ready and took his army with him. [7]He took six hundred of the best chariots, along with all the other chariots of Egypt, with officers over all of them. [8]The LORD hardened the heart[s] of Pharaoh king of Egypt, so that he pursued the Israelites, who were marching out boldly.[t] [9]The Egyptians—all Pharaoh's horses and chariots, horsemen[c] and troops—pursued the Israelites and overtook[u] them as they camped by the sea near Pi Hahiroth, opposite Baal Zephon.

[10]As Pharaoh approached, the Israelites looked up, and there were the Egyptians, marching after them. They were terrified and cried[v] out to the LORD. [11]They said to Moses, "Was it because there were no graves in Egypt that you brought us to the desert to die? What have you done to us by bringing us out of Egypt? [12]Didn't we say to you in Egypt, 'Leave us alone; let us serve the Egyptians'? It would have been better for us to serve the Egyptians than to die in the desert!"

[13]Moses answered the people, "Do not be afraid. Stand firm and you will see[w] the deliverance the LORD will bring you today. The Egyptians you see today you will never see[x] again. [14]The LORD will fight[y] for you; you need only to be still."[z]

[15]Then the LORD said to Moses, "Why are you crying out to me? Tell the Israelites to move on. [16]Raise your staff and stretch out your hand over the sea to divide the water so that the Israelites can go through the sea on dry ground. [17]I will harden the hearts of the Egyptians so that they will go in after them.[a] And I will gain glory through Pharaoh and all his army, through his chariots and his horsemen. [18]The Egyptians will know that I am the LORD when I gain glory through Pharaoh, his chariots and his horsemen."

[19]Then the angel of God, who had been traveling in front of Israel's army, withdrew and went behind them. The pillar of cloud[b] also moved from in front and stood behind them, [20]coming between the armies of Egypt and Israel. Throughout the night the cloud brought darkness to the one side and light to the other side; so neither went near the other all night long.

[21]Then Moses stretched out his hand over

**14:8** s ver 4 t Nu 33:3
**14:9** u Ex 15:9
**14:10** v Ne 9:9
**14:13** w 2Ch 20:17; Isa 41:10,13–14 x ver 30
**14:14** y Ex 15:3; Dt 1:30; 2Ch 20:29 z Ps 46:10; Isa 30:15
**14:17** a ver 4
**14:19** b Ex 13:21

[a]18 Hebrew *Yam Suph*; that is, Sea of Reeds [b]19 See Gen. 50:25. [c]9 Or *charioteers*; also in verses 17, 18, 23, 26 and 28

14:21 c Isa 63:12
14:22 d Heb 11:29
14:27 e Ex 15:1,21; Ps 106:11

the sea, and all that night the LORD drove the sea back with a strong east wind and turned it into dry land. The waters were divided,[c] 22and the Israelites went through the sea on dry ground,[d] with a wall of water on their right and on their left.

23The Egyptians pursued them, and all Pharaoh's horses and chariots and horsemen followed them into the sea. 24During the last watch of the night the LORD looked down from the pillar of fire and cloud at the Egyptian army and threw it into confusion. 25He made the wheels of their chariots come off[a] so that they had difficulty driving. And the Egyptians said, "Let's get away from the Israelites! The LORD is fighting for them against Egypt."

26Then the LORD said to Moses, "Stretch out your hand over the sea so that the waters may flow back over the Egyptians and their chariots and horsemen." 27Moses stretched out his hand over the sea, and at daybreak the sea went back to its place. The Egyptians were fleeing toward[b] it, and the LORD swept them into the sea.[e] 28The water flowed back and covered the chariots and horsemen—the entire army of Pharaoh that had followed the Israelites into the sea. Not one of them survived.

29But the Israelites went through the sea on dry ground, with a wall of water on their right and on their left. 30That day the LORD saved[f] Israel from the hands of the Egyptians, and Israel saw the Egyptians lying dead on the shore. 31And when the Israelites saw the great power the LORD displayed against the Egyptians, the people feared the LORD and put their trust[g] in him and in Moses his servant.

*Lord,*

*open my eyes. Let me see your hosts, your chariots of fire, your horses and your provision for me and my life. I believe that you love me enough to deliver me from all my enemies—or to keep me secure in the midst of trouble—if that is part of your master plan. Lord, please help me to trust you more. In the precious name of Jesus, my example,*

*Amen*

EXODUS 14:29–31

## The Song of Moses and Miriam

15 Then Moses and the Israelites sang this song to the LORD:

"I will sing[h] to the LORD,
for he is highly exalted.
The horse and its rider
he has hurled into the sea.
2 The LORD is my strength and my song;
he has become my salvation.
He is my God, and I will praise him,
my father's God, and I will exalt[i] him.
3 The LORD is a warrior;[j]
the LORD is his name.
4 Pharaoh's chariots and his army[k]
he has hurled into the sea.
The best of Pharaoh's officers
are drowned in the Red Sea.[c]
5 The deep waters have covered them;
they sank to the depths like a stone.[l]
6 "Your right hand,[m] O LORD,
was majestic in power.
Your right hand, O LORD,
shattered the enemy.
7 In the greatness of your majesty
you threw down those who opposed you.
You unleashed your burning anger;
it consumed them like stubble.
8 By the blast of your nostrils[n]
the waters piled up.[o]
The surging waters stood firm like a wall;
the deep waters congealed in the heart of the sea.

9 "The enemy boasted,
'I will pursue,[p] I will overtake them.
I will divide the spoils;
I will gorge myself on them.
I will draw my sword
and my hand will destroy them.'

14:30 f Ps 106:8,10,21
14:31 g Jn 2:11
15:1 h Ps 106:12
15:2 i Ex 3:6,15–16
15:3 j Rev 19:11
15:4 k Ex 14:6–7
15:5 l Ne 9:11
15:6 m Ps 118:15
15:8 n Ex 14:21 o Ps 78:13
15:9 p Ex 14:5–9

[a]25 Or *He jammed the wheels of their chariots* (see Samaritan Pentateuch, Septuagint and Syriac) [b]27 Or *from* [c]4 Hebrew *Yam Suph*; that is, Sea of Reeds; also in verse 22

**15:10**
q Ex 14:27–28

**15:11**
r Ex 8:10
s Isa 6:3
t Ps 8:1

**15:13**
u Ne 9:12
v Ps 78:54

**15:14**
w Dt 2:25

**15:15**
x Nu 22:3
y Jos 5:1

**15:16**
z Ps 74:2

**15:17**
a Ps 44:2
b Ps 78:54,68

10 But you blew with your breath,
and the sea covered them.
They sank like lead
in the mighty waters.[q]

11 "Who among the gods is like you,[r]
O LORD?
Who is like you—
majestic in holiness,[s]
awesome in glory,[t]
working wonders?
12 You stretched out your right hand
and the earth swallowed them.

13 "In your unfailing love you will lead[u]
the people you have redeemed.
In your strength you will guide them
to your holy dwelling.[v]
14 The nations will hear and tremble;[w]
anguish will grip the people of
Philistia.
15 The chiefs of Edom will be terrified,
the leaders of Moab will be seized with
trembling,[x]
the people[*a*] of Canaan will melt[y] away;
16 terror and dread will fall upon them.
By the power of your arm
they will be as still as a stone—
until your people pass by, O LORD,
until the people you bought[*b*][z]
pass by.
17 You will bring them in and plant[a] them
on the mountain[b] of your
inheritance—
the place, O LORD, you made for your
dwelling,
the sanctuary, O Lord, your hands
established.

18 The LORD will reign
for ever and ever."

19 When Pharaoh's horses, chariots and
horsemen[*c*] went into the sea,[c] the LORD
brought the waters of the sea back over
them, but the Israelites walked through
the sea on dry ground. 20 Then Miriam[d]
the prophetess, Aaron's sister, took a tam-
bourine in her hand, and all the women fol-
lowed her, with tambourines and dancing.[e]
21 Miriam sang to them:

"Sing to the Lord,
for he is highly exalted.
The horse and its rider
he has hurled into the sea."

## The Waters of Marah and Elim

22 Then Moses led Israel from the Red Sea
and they went into the Desert of Shur. For
three days they traveled in the desert with-
out finding water. 23 When they came to Ma-
rah, they could not drink its water because
it was bitter. (That is why the place is called
Marah.[*d*][f]) 24 So the people grumbled against
Moses, saying, "What are we to drink?"
25 Then Moses cried out to the LORD, and
the LORD showed him a piece of wood. He
threw it into the water, and the water be-
came sweet.

There the LORD made a decree and a law
for them, and there he tested them. 26 He
said, "If you listen carefully to the voice
of the LORD your God and do what is right
in his eyes, if you pay attention to his com-
mands and keep all his decrees,[g] I will not
bring on you any of the diseases[h] I brought

**15:19**
c Ex 14:28

**15:20**
d Nu 26:59
e 1Sa 18:6;
Ps 150:4

**15:23**
f Nu 33:8

**15:26**
g Dt 7:12
h Dt 28:27,58–60

[a] 15 Or *rulers* [b] 16 Or *created* [c] 19 Or *charioteers* [d] 23 *Marah* means *bitter.*

## The African Presence

### Exodus 15:20

Miriam—Aaron and Moses' sister—is described here as a prophetess. Of note is Miriam's Egyptian connection. Not only was Miriam a resident alien of Egypt, but her name is Egyptian. The exact etymology is undetermined, but the first three letters appear to be derived from an Egyptian root word for "love" or "beloved" that is often combined with the name of a deity.

# Inspire

## DANCE, SISTERS, DANCE

Dance is an art form used to express and stir our emotions and the emotions of others. In many countries—especially in Africa—dance is an important part of the culture as well as an intricate part of all celebrations.

Our sister Miriam, the prophetess, called the women together to dance and sing after the victory of crossing the Red Sea (see Ex 15:20). Miriam led the way for the women to engage in dancing. Yes! They danced because of the powerful intervention of the almighty and merciful God who had made a way out of no way. Because of this intervention, they lifted this song: "Sing to the Lord, for he is highly exalted. The horse and its rider he has hurled into the sea" (Ex 15:21).

The Old Testament Scriptures record several instances in which dance was used to express joy and praise to the Lord (see 2Sa 6:14; Ps 149:3; 150:4; Jer 31:4). Dancing before the Lord corporately was generally done by the women (see Ex 15:20; Jdg 21:19–21; Ps 68:24–25). But in a story recorded in 2 Samuel 6:1–23, King David worshiped God with dance. The Bible tells us he "danced before the Lord with all his might." David's wife Michal saw his exuberant behavior and was humiliated and embarrassed. She thought that David should have acted with more dignity before the people. But David didn't care about the opinions of others. He only cared about God's opinion. His dancing brought glory to God, and he refused to be embarrassed by his praise.

Today we can sing our own victory song and dance before God. God has done great things for us! Like the people of Israel, he has brought us through our own "Red Sea" experiences. Like David, he has restored us to wholeness. He has brought us through sickness, pain, suffering, trials, tribulation, abuse and unpleasant situations. Sisters, stop right now and just rejoice in the Lord and dance before him!

—C. Bracey

### read

Exodus 15:19–21; Psalm 30:11–12.

See also the Inspire Note "True Joy," and the Women of the Bible Note "Miriam: Plagued by Jealousy."

### WOMAN of COLOR

What "Red Sea" has God allowed you to cross as an individual? What "Red Sea" has God allowed your family, community or race to cross? Celebrate God's victory through praise and dance.

For the next Inspire note, go to page 109.

on the Egyptians, for I am the LORD, who heals you."

27 Then they came to Elim, where there were twelve springs and seventy palm trees, and they camped[i] there near the water.

## Manna and Quail

16 The whole Israelite community set out from Elim and came to the Desert of Sin,[j] which is between Elim and Sinai, on the fifteenth day of the second month after they had come out of Egypt. 2 In the desert the whole community grumbled[k] against Moses and Aaron. 3 The Israelites said to them, "If only we had died by the LORD's hand in Egypt! There we sat around pots of meat and ate all the food[l] we wanted, but you have brought us out into this desert to starve this entire assembly to death."

4 Then the LORD said to Moses, "I will rain down bread from heaven[m] for you. The people are to go out each day and gather enough for that day. In this way I will test them and see whether they will follow my instructions. 5 On the sixth day they are to prepare what they bring in, and that is to be twice[n] as much as they gather on the other days."

6 So Moses and Aaron said to all the Israelites, "In the evening you will know that it was the LORD who brought you out of Egypt, 7 and in the morning you will see the glory of the LORD, because he has heard your grumbling against him. Who are we, that you should grumble against us?"[o] 8 Moses also said, "You will know that it was the LORD when he gives you meat to eat in the evening and all the bread you want in the morning, because he has heard your grumbling against him. Who are we? You are not grumbling against us, but against the LORD."

9 Then Moses told Aaron, "Say to the entire Israelite community, 'Come before the LORD, for he has heard your grumbling.' "

10 While Aaron was speaking to the whole Israelite community, they looked toward the desert, and there was the glory[p] of the LORD appearing in the cloud.

11 The LORD said to Moses, 12 "I have heard the grumbling of the Israelites. Tell them, 'At twilight you will eat meat, and in the morning you will be filled with bread. Then you will know that I am the LORD your God.' "

13 That evening quail[q] came and covered the camp, and in the morning there was a layer of dew around the camp. 14 When the dew was gone, thin flakes like frost[r] on the ground appeared on the desert floor. 15 When the Israelites saw it, they said to each other, "What is it?" For they did not know what it was.

Moses said to them, "It is the bread the LORD has given you to eat. 16 This is what the LORD has commanded: 'Each one is to gather as much as he needs. Take an omer[a] for each person you have in your tent.' "

17 The Israelites did as they were told; some gathered much, some little. 18 And when they measured it by the omer, he who gathered much did not have too much, and he who gathered little did not have too little.[s] Each one gathered as much as he needed.

19 Then Moses said to them, "No one is to keep any of it until morning."[t]

20 However, some of them paid no attention to Moses; they kept part of it until morning, but it was full of maggots and began to smell. So Moses was angry with them.

21 Each morning everyone gathered as much as he needed, and when the sun grew hot, it melted away. 22 On the sixth day, they gathered twice as much—two omers[b] for each person—and the leaders of the community came and reported this to Moses. 23 He said to them, "This is what the LORD commanded: 'Tomorrow is to be a day of rest, a holy Sabbath[u] to the LORD. So bake what you want to bake and boil what you want to boil. Save whatever is left and keep it until morning.' "

24 So they saved it until morning, as Moses commanded, and it did not stink or get maggots in it. 25 "Eat it today," Moses said, "because today is a Sabbath to the LORD. You will not find any of it on the ground today. 26 Six days you are to gather it, but on the seventh day, the Sabbath, there will not be any."

27 Nevertheless, some of the people went out on the seventh day to gather it, but they found none. 28 Then the LORD said to Moses,

**15:27** i Nu 33:9
**16:1** j Nu 33:11,12
**16:2** k 1Co 10:10
**16:3** l Nu 11:4,34
**16:4** m Dt 8:3; Jn 6:31*
**16:5** n ver 22
**16:7** o Nu 16:11
**16:10** p ver 7
**16:13** q Nu 11:31; Ps 78:27–28; 105:40
**16:14** r Nu 11:7–9
**16:18** s 2Co 8:15*
**16:19** t Ex 12:10
**16:23** u Ge 2:3; Ex 20:8; 23:12

[a]16 That is, probably about 2 quarts (about 2 liters); also in verses 18, 32, 33 and 36 [b]22 That is, probably about 4 quarts (about 4.5 liters)

"How long will you[a] refuse to keep my commands[v] and my instructions? 29 Bear in mind that the LORD has given you the Sabbath; that is why on the sixth day he gives you bread for two days. Everyone is to stay where he is on the seventh day; no one is to go out." 30 So the people rested on the seventh day.

31 The people of Israel called the bread manna.[b][w] It was white like coriander seed and tasted like wafers made with honey. 32 Moses said, "This is what the LORD has commanded: 'Take an omer of manna and keep it for the generations to come, so they can see the bread I gave you to eat in the desert when I brought you out of Egypt.' "

33 So Moses said to Aaron, "Take a jar and put an omer of manna[x] in it. Then place it before the LORD to be kept for the generations to come."

34 As the LORD commanded Moses, Aaron put the manna in front of the Testimony,[y] that it might be kept. 35 The Israelites ate manna forty years, until they came to a land that was settled; they ate manna until they reached the border of Canaan.[z]

36 (An omer is one tenth of an ephah.)

## Water From the Rock

17 The whole Israelite community set out from the Desert of Sin,[a] traveling from place to place as the LORD commanded. They camped at Rephidim, but there was no water for the people to drink. 2 So they quarreled with Moses and said, "Give us water[b] to drink."

Moses replied, "Why do you quarrel with me? Why do you put the LORD to the test?"[c]

3 But the people were thirsty for water there, and they grumbled[d] against Moses. They said, "Why did you bring us up out of Egypt to make us and our children and livestock die of thirst?"

4 Then Moses cried out to the LORD, "What am I to do with these people? They are almost ready to stone[e] me."

5 The LORD answered Moses, "Walk on ahead of the people. Take with you some of the elders of Israel and take in your hand the staff with which you struck the Nile, and go. 6 I will stand there before you by the rock at Horeb. Strike the rock, and water[f] will come out of it for the people to drink." So Moses did this in the sight of the elders of Israel. 7 And he called the place Massah[c] and Meribah[d] because the Israelites quarreled and because they tested the LORD saying, "Is the LORD among us or not?"

## The Amalekites Defeated

8 The Amalekites[g] came and attacked the Israelites at Rephidim. 9 Moses said to Joshua, "Choose some of our men and go out to fight the Amalekites. Tomorrow I will stand on top of the hill with the staff of God in my hands."

10 So Joshua fought the Amalekites as Moses had ordered, and Moses, Aaron and Hur went to the top of the hill. 11 As long as Moses held up his hands, the Israelites were winning, but whenever he lowered his hands, the Amalekites were winning. 12 When Moses' hands grew tired, they took a stone and put it under him and he sat on it. Aaron and Hur held his hands up—one on one side, one on the other—so that his hands remained steady till sunset. 13 So Joshua overcame the Amalekite army with the sword.

14 Then the LORD said to Moses, "Write[h] this on a scroll as something to be remembered and make sure that Joshua hears it, because I will completely blot out the memory of Amalek from under heaven."

15 Moses built an altar and called it The LORD is my Banner. 16 He said, "For hands were lifted up to the throne of the LORD. The[e] LORD will be at war against the Amalekites from generation to generation."

## Jethro Visits Moses

18 Now Jethro, the priest of Midian[i] and father-in-law of Moses, heard of everything God had done for Moses and for his people Israel, and how the LORD had brought Israel out of Egypt.

2 After Moses had sent away his wife Zipporah,[j] his father-in-law Jethro received her 3 and her two sons.[k] One son was named Gershom,[f] for Moses said, "I have become an alien in a foreign land";[l] 4 and the other was named Eliezer,[g] for he said, "My father's

16:28 v Ps78:10
16:31 w Nu11:7–9
16:33 x Heb9:4
16:34 y Ex25:16,21,22
16:35 z Jos5:12
17:1 a Ex16:1
17:2 b Nu20:2 c Dt6:16; Ps78:18,41; 1Co10:9
17:3 d Ex15:24; 16:2–3
17:4 e Nu14:10
17:6 f Nu20:11; 1Co10:4
17:8 g Dt25:17–19
17:14 h Ex34:27
18:1 i Ex2:16; 3:1
18:2 j Ex4:25
18:3 k Ac7:29 l Ex2:22

a 28 The Hebrew is plural. b 31 *Manna* means *What is it?* (see verse 15). c 7 *Massah* means *testing.* d 7 *Meribah* means *quarreling.* e 16 Or *"Because a hand was against the throne of the LORD, the* f 3 *Gershom* sounds like the Hebrew for *an alien there.* g 4 *Eliezer* means *my God is helper.*

**18:5** m Ex3:1
**18:7** n Ge43:28
**18:10** o Ps68:19–20
**18:11** p Lk1:51

God was my helper; he saved me from the sword of Pharaoh."

5 Jethro, Moses' father-in-law, together with Moses' sons and wife, came to him in the desert, where he was camped near the mountain[m] of God. 6 Jethro had sent word to him, "I, your father-in-law Jethro, am coming to you with your wife and her two sons."

7 So Moses went out to meet his father-in-law and bowed down[n] and kissed him. They greeted each other and then went into the tent. 8 Moses told his father-in-law about everything the LORD had done to Pharaoh and the Egyptians for Israel's sake and about all the hardships they had met along the way and how the LORD had saved them.

9 Jethro was delighted to hear about all the good things the LORD had done for Israel in rescuing them from the hand of the Egyptians. 10 He said, "Praise be to the LORD,[o] who rescued you from the hand of the Egyptians and of Pharaoh, and who rescued the people from the hand of the Egyptians. 11 Now I know that the LORD is greater than all other gods, for he did this to those who had treated Israel arrogantly."[p] 12 Then Jethro, Moses' father-in-law, brought a burnt offering and other sacrifices to God, and Aaron came with all the elders of Israel to eat bread with Moses' father-in-law in the presence of God.

13 The next day Moses took his seat to serve as judge for the people, and they stood around him from morning till evening. 14 When his father-in-law saw all that Moses was doing for the people, he said, "What is this you are doing for the people? Why do you alone sit as judge, while all these people stand around you from morning till evening?"

15 Moses answered him, "Because the people come to me to seek God's will.[q] 16 Whenever they have a dispute, it is brought to me, and I decide between the parties and inform them of God's decrees and laws."

17 Moses' father-in-law replied, "What you are doing is not good. 18 You and these people who come to you will only wear yourselves out. The work is too heavy for you; you cannot handle it alone.[r] 19 Listen now to me and I will give you some advice, and may God be with you. You must be the people's representative before God and bring their disputes[s] to him. 20 Teach them the decrees and laws,[t] and show them the way to live[u] and the duties they are to perform.[v] 21 But select capable men[w] from all the people—men who fear God, trustworthy men who hate dishonest gain[x]—and appoint them as officials[y] over thousands, hundreds, fifties and tens. 22 Have them serve as judges for the people at all times, but have them bring every difficult case[z] to you; the simple cases they can decide themselves. That will make your load lighter, because they will share[a] it with you. 23 If you do this and God so commands, you will be able to stand the strain, and all these people will go home satisfied."

24 Moses listened to his father-in-law and did everything he said. 25 He chose capable men from all Israel and made them leaders of the people, officials over thousands, hundreds, fifties and tens.[b] 26 They served as judges for the people at all times. The difficult cases they brought to Moses, but the simple ones they decided themselves.[c]

27 Then Moses sent his father-in-law on his way, and Jethro returned to his own country.[d]

**18:15** q Nu9:6,8; Dt17:8–13
**18:18** r Nu11:11,14,17
**18:19** s Nu27:5
**18:20** t Dt5:1 u Ps143:8 v Dt1:18
**18:21** w Ac6:3 x Dt16:19 y Dt1:13,15; 2Ch19:5–10
**18:22** z Dt1:17–18 a Nu11:17
**18:25** b Dt1:13–15
**18:26** c ver22
**18:27** d Nu10:29–30

## *The African Presence*

### Exodus 18:1

Jethro, father of Zipporah, mentored Moses and advised him to appoint officials to ease his workload. Moses was then able to delegate the people's numerous complaints. Jethro, as a wise man of African-Asiatic descent, assisted Moses in his difficult task.

**19:2** e Ex 17:1
**19:3** f Ac 7:38
**19:4** g Dt 29:2
**19:5** h Dt 5:2 i Dt 10:14
**19:6** j 1Pe 2:5 k Dt 7:6
**19:8** l Ex 24:3,7

*Dear God,*

*I have gotten so caught up in* doing *that I am no longer truly* being. *I know that means that I can't be what you want me to be. Please teach me temperance and restore balance to my life. Show me how to yoke up with you, for your yoke is easy and your burden is light. Thank you, Jesus, my brother and companion!*

*Amen*

EXODUS 18:17–24

## At Mount Sinai

**19** In the third month after the Israelites left Egypt—on the very day—they came to the Desert of Sinai. 2 After they set out from Rephidim,[e] they entered the Desert of Sinai, and Israel camped there in the desert in front of the mountain.

3 Then Moses went up to God, and the LORD called[f] to him from the mountain and said, "This is what you are to say to the house of Jacob and what you are to tell the people of Israel: 4 'You yourselves have seen what I did to Egypt,[g] and how I carried you on eagles' wings and brought you to myself. 5 Now if you obey me fully and keep my covenant,[h] then out of all nations you will be my treasured possession. Although the whole earth[i] is mine, 6 you[a] will be for me a kingdom of priests[j] and a holy nation.'[k] These are the words you are to speak to the Israelites."

7 So Moses went back and summoned the elders of the people and set before them all the words the LORD had commanded him to speak. 8 The people all responded together, "We will do everything the LORD has said."[l] So Moses brought their answer back to the LORD.

9 The LORD said to Moses, "I am going to come to you in a dense cloud,[m] so that the people will hear me speaking with you and will always put their trust in you." Then Moses told the LORD what the people had said.

10 And the LORD said to Moses, "Go to the people and consecrate[n] them today and tomorrow. Have them wash their clothes 11 and be ready by the third day, because on that day the LORD will come down on Mount Sinai in the sight of all the people. 12 Put limits for the people around the mountain and tell them, 'Be careful that you do not go up the mountain or touch the foot of it. Whoever touches the mountain shall surely be put to death. 13 He shall surely be stoned[o] or shot with arrows; not a hand is to be laid on him. Whether man or animal, he shall not be permitted to live.' Only when the ram's horn sounds a long blast may they go up to the mountain."

14 After Moses had gone down the mountain to the people, he consecrated them, and they washed their clothes. 15 Then he said to the people, "Prepare yourselves for the third day. Abstain from sexual relations."

16 On the morning of the third day there was thunder and lightning, with a thick cloud over the mountain, and a very loud trumpet blast.[p] Everyone in the camp trembled. 17 Then Moses led the people out of the camp to meet with God, and they stood at the foot of the mountain. 18 Mount Sinai was covered with smoke,[q] because the LORD descended on it in fire. The smoke billowed up from it like smoke from a furnace, the whole mountain[b] trembled[r] violently, 19 and the sound of the trumpet grew louder and louder. Then Moses spoke and the voice[s] of God answered[t] him.[c]

20 The LORD descended to the top of Mount Sinai and called Moses to the top of the mountain. So Moses went up 21 and the LORD said to him, "Go down and warn the people so they do not force their way through to see[u] the LORD and many of them perish. 22 Even the priests, who approach[v] the LORD, must consecrate themselves, or the LORD will break out against them."

23 Moses said to the LORD, "The people cannot come up Mount Sinai, because you

**19:9** m ver 16; Ex 24:15–16
**19:10** n Lev 11:44
**19:13** o Heb 12:20*
**19:16** p Heb 12:18–19; Rev 4:1
**19:18** q Ps 104:32 r Ps 68:8
**19:19** s Ne 9:13 t Ps 81:7
**19:21** u Ex 3:5; 1Sa 6:19
**19:22** v Lev 10:3

[a] 5,6 Or *possession, for the whole earth is mine.* 6 *You* [b] 18 Most Hebrew manuscripts; a few Hebrew manuscripts and Septuagint *all the people* [c] 19 Or *and God answered him with thunder*

**19:23** w ver 12
**20:3** x Jer 35:15
**20:5** y Dt 4:24; z Jer 32:18
**20:6** a Dt 7:9
**20:7** b Lev 19:12
**20:8** c Ex 31:13–16
**20:9** d Lk 13:14
**20:11** e Ge 2:2

yourself warned us, 'Put limits[w] around the mountain and set it apart as holy.'"

[24]The LORD replied, "Go down and bring Aaron up with you. But the priests and the people must not force their way through to come up to the LORD, or he will break out against them."

[25]So Moses went down to the people and told them.

## The Ten Commandments

**20** And God spoke all these words:

[2]"I am the LORD your God, who brought you out of Egypt, out of the land of slavery.

[3]"You shall have no other gods before[a] me.[x]

[4]"You shall not make for yourself an idol in the form of anything in heaven above or on the earth beneath or in the waters below. [5]You shall not bow down to them or worship them; for I, the LORD your God, am a jealous God,[y] punishing the children for the sin of the fathers to the third and fourth generation[z] of those who hate me, [6]but showing love to a thousand[a] ⌞generations⌟ of those who love me and keep my commandments.

[7]"You shall not misuse the name of the LORD your God, for the LORD will not hold anyone guiltless who misuses his name.[b]

[8]"Remember the Sabbath[c] day by keeping it holy. [9]Six days you shall labor and do all your work,[d] [10]but the seventh day is a Sabbath to the LORD your God. On it you shall not do any work, neither you, nor your son or daughter, nor your manservant or maidservant, nor your animals, nor the alien within your gates. [11]For in six days the LORD made the heavens and the earth, the sea, and all that is in them, but he rested[e] on the seventh day. Therefore the LORD blessed the Sabbath day and made it holy.

[12]"Honor your father and your mother,[f] so that you may live long in the land the LORD your God is giving you.

[13]"You shall not murder.[g]

[14]"You shall not commit adultery.

[15]"You shall not steal.[h]

[16]"You shall not give false testimony against your neighbor.[i]

[17]"You shall not covet[j] your neighbor's house. You shall not covet your neighbor's wife, or his manservant or maidservant, his ox or donkey, or anything that belongs to your neighbor."

*My child,*

*I give you guidelines and commandments for a reason. I know what lies ahead, so trust me and do what I say. I would never lead you astray.*

*In changeless love,*
*God*

EXODUS 20:1–17

[18]When the people saw the thunder and lightning and heard the trumpet[k] and saw the mountain in smoke, they trembled with fear. They stayed at a distance [19]and said to Moses, "Speak to us yourself and we will listen. But do not have God speak to us or we will die."[l]

[20]Moses said to the people, "Do not be afraid. God has come to test you, so that the fear of God will be with you to keep you from sinning."[m]

[21]The people remained at a distance, while Moses approached the thick darkness where God was.

**20:12** f Mt 15:4*; Eph 6:2
**20:13** g Ro 13:9*
**20:15** h Mt 19:18*
**20:16** i Ex 23:1,7
**20:17** j Ro 7:7*; 13:9*; Eph 5:3
**20:18** k Ex 19:16–19; Heb 12:18–19
**20:19** l Dt 5:5,23–27
**20:20** m Pr 16:6

[a]3 Or *besides*

## Idols and Altars

[22]Then the LORD said to Moses, "Tell the Israelites this: 'You have seen for yourselves that I have spoken to you from heaven: [23]Do not make any gods to be alongside me; do not make for yourselves gods of silver or gods of gold.

[24]" 'Make an altar of earth for me and sacrifice on it your burnt offerings and fellowship offerings,[a] your sheep and goats and your cattle. Wherever I cause my name to be honored, I will come to you and bless[n] you. [25]If you make an altar of stones for me, do not build it with dressed stones, for you will defile it if you use a tool on it. [26]And do not go up to my altar on steps, lest your nakedness be exposed on it.'

# 21

"These are the laws[o] you are to set before them:

## Hebrew Servants

[2]"If you buy a Hebrew servant, he is to serve you for six years. But in the seventh year, he shall go free, without paying anything. [3]If he comes alone, he is to go free alone; but if he has a wife when he comes, she is to go with him. [4]If his master gives him a wife and she bears him sons or daughters, the woman and her children shall belong to her master, and only the man shall go free.

[5]"But if the servant declares, 'I love my master and my wife and children and do not want to go free,'[p] [6]then his master must take him before the judges.[b] He shall take him to the door or the doorpost and pierce his ear with an awl. Then he will be his servant for life.[q]

[7]"If a man sells his daughter as a servant, she is not to go free as menservants do. [8]If she does not please the master who has selected her for himself,[c] he must let her be redeemed. He has no right to sell her to foreigners, because he has broken faith with her. [9]If he selects her for his son, he must grant her the rights of a daughter. [10]If he marries another woman, he must not deprive the first one of her food, clothing and marital rights.[r] [11]If he does not provide her with these three things, she is to go free, without any payment of money.

## Personal Injuries

[12]"Anyone who strikes a man and kills him shall surely be put to death.[s] [13]However, if he does not do it intentionally, but God lets it happen, he is to flee to a place[t] I will designate. [14]But if a man schemes and kills another man deliberately, take him away from my altar and put him to death.[u]

[15]"Anyone who attacks[d] his father or his mother must be put to death.

[16]"Anyone who kidnaps another and either sells him or still has him when he is caught must be put to death.[v]

[17]"Anyone who curses his father or mother must be put to death.[w]

[18]"If men quarrel and one hits the other with a stone or with his fist[e] and he does not die but is confined to bed, [19]the one who struck the blow will not be held responsible if the other gets up and walks around outside with his staff; however, he must pay the injured man for the loss of his time and see that he is completely healed.

[20]"If a man beats his male or female slave with a rod and the slave dies as a direct result, he must be punished, [21]but he is not to be punished if the slave gets up after a day or two, since the slave is his property.

[22]"If men who are fighting hit a pregnant woman and she gives birth prematurely[f] but there is no serious injury, the offender must be fined whatever the woman's husband demands and the court allows. [23]But if there is serious injury, you are to take life for life, [24]eye for eye, tooth for tooth,[x] hand for hand, foot for foot, [25]burn for burn, wound for wound, bruise for bruise.

[26]"If a man hits a manservant or maidservant in the eye and destroys it, he must let the servant go free to compensate for the eye. [27]And if he knocks out the tooth of a manservant or maidservant, he must let the servant go free to compensate for the tooth.

[28]"If a bull gores a man or a woman to death, the bull must be stoned to death,[y] and its meat must not be eaten. But the owner of the bull will not be held responsible. [29]If, however, the bull has had the habit of goring and the owner has been warned but has not kept it penned up and it kills

**20:24** n Ge 12:2
**21:1** o Dt 4:14
**21:5** p Dt 15:16
**21:6** q Ne 5:5
**21:10** r 1Co 7:3–5
**21:12** s Ge 9:6
**21:13** t Nu 35:10–34; Dt 19:2–13
**21:14** u Dt 19:11–12; 1Ki 2:28–34
**21:16** v Dt 24:7
**21:17** w Mk 7:10*
**21:24** x Mt 5:38*
**21:28** y Ge 9:5

[a]24 Traditionally *peace offerings* [b]6 Or *before God* [c]8 Or *master so that he does not choose her* [d]15 Or *kills*
[e]18 Or *with a tool* [f]22 Or *she has a miscarriage*

**21:32**
z Zec 11:12–13; Mt 26:15

**22:1**
a 2Sa 12:6

**22:2**
b Mt 24:43

**22:3**
c Ex 21:2

a man or woman, the bull must be stoned and the owner also must be put to death. 30 However, if payment is demanded of him, he may redeem his life by paying whatever is demanded. 31 This law also applies if the bull gores a son or daughter. 32 If the bull gores a male or female slave, the owner must pay thirty shekels[a][z] of silver to the master of the slave, and the bull must be stoned.

33 "If a man uncovers a pit or digs one and fails to cover it and an ox or a donkey falls into it, 34 the owner of the pit must pay for the loss; he must pay its owner, and the dead animal will be his.

35 "If a man's bull injures the bull of another and it dies, they are to sell the live one and divide both the money and the dead animal equally. 36 However, if it was known that the bull had the habit of goring, yet the owner did not keep it penned up, the owner must pay, animal for animal, and the dead animal will be his.

## Protection of Property

22 "If a man steals an ox or a sheep and slaughters it or sells it, he must pay back[a] five head of cattle for the ox and four sheep for the sheep.

2 "If a thief is caught breaking in[b] and is struck so that he dies, the defender is not guilty of bloodshed; 3 but if it happens[b] after sunrise, he is guilty of bloodshed.

"A thief must certainly make restitution, but if he has nothing, he must be sold[c] to pay for his theft.

4 "If the stolen animal is found alive in his possession—whether ox or donkey or sheep—he must pay back double.

5 "If a man grazes his livestock in a field or vineyard and lets them stray and they graze in another man's field, he must make restitution from the best of his own field or vineyard.

6 "If a fire breaks out and spreads into thornbushes so that it burns shocks of grain or standing grain or the whole field, the one who started the fire must make restitution.

7 "If a man gives his neighbor silver or goods for safekeeping and they are stolen from the neighbor's house, the thief, if he is caught, must pay back double. 8 But if the thief is not found, the owner of the house must appear before the judges[c] to determine whether he has laid his hands on the other man's property. 9 In all cases of illegal possession of an ox, a donkey, a sheep, a garment, or any other lost property about which somebody says, 'This is mine,' both parties are to bring their cases before the judges.[d] The one whom the judges declare[d] guilty must pay back double to his neighbor.

10 "If a man gives a donkey, an ox, a sheep or any other animal to his neighbor for safekeeping and it dies or is injured or is taken away while no one is looking, 11 the issue between them will be settled by the taking of an oath[e] before the LORD that the neighbor did not lay hands on the other person's property. The owner is to accept this, and no restitution is required. 12 But if the animal was stolen from the neighbor, he must make restitution to the owner. 13 If it was torn to pieces by a wild animal, he shall bring in the remains as evidence and he will not be required to pay for the torn animal.[f]

14 "If a man borrows an animal from his neighbor and it is injured or dies while the owner is not present, he must make restitution. 15 But if the owner is with the animal, the borrower will not have to pay. If the animal was hired, the money paid for the hire covers the loss.

## Social Responsibility

16 "If a man seduces a virgin[g] who is not pledged to be married and sleeps with her, he must pay the bride-price, and she shall be his wife. 17 If her father absolutely refuses to give her to him, he must still pay the bride-price for virgins.

18 "Do not allow a sorceress to live.

19 "Anyone who has sexual relations with an animal[h] must be put to death.

20 "Whoever sacrifices to any god other than the LORD must be destroyed.[e][i]

21 "Do not mistreat an alien or oppress him, for you were aliens[j] in Egypt.

22 "Do not take advantage of a widow or an orphan. 23 If you do and they cry out[k] to me, I will certainly hear their cry.[l] 24 My anger

**22:9**
d Dt 25:1

**22:11**
e Heb 6:16

**22:13**
f Ge 31:39

**22:16**
g Dt 22:28

**22:19**
h Lev 18:23

**22:20**
i Dt 17:2–5

**22:21**
j Dt 10:19

**22:23**
k Lk 18:7
l Ps 18:6

[a]32 That is, about 12 ounces (about 0.3 kilogram) [b]3 Or *if he strikes him* [c]8 Or *before God*; also in verse 9 [d]9 Or *whom God declares* [e]20 The Hebrew term refers to the irrevocable giving over of things or persons to the LORD, often by totally destroying them.

will be aroused, and I will kill you with the sword; your wives will become widows and your children fatherless.[m]

25"If you lend money to one of my people among you who is needy, do not be like a moneylender; charge him no interest.[a] 26If you take your neighbor's cloak as a pledge, return it to him by sunset, 27because his cloak is the only covering he has for his body. What else will he sleep in? When he cries out to me, I will hear, for I am compassionate.

28"Do not blaspheme God[b] or curse the ruler of your people.[n]

29"Do not hold back offerings[o] from your granaries or your vats.[c]

"You must give me the firstborn of your sons.[p] 30Do the same with your cattle and your sheep.[q] Let them stay with their mothers for seven days, but give them to me on the eighth day.[r]

31"You are to be my holy people.[s] So do not eat the meat of an animal torn by wild beasts; throw it to the dogs.

## Laws of Justice and Mercy

23 "Do not spread false reports. Do not help a wicked man by being a malicious witness.

2"Do not follow the crowd in doing wrong. When you give testimony in a lawsuit, do not pervert justice by siding with the crowd, 3and do not show favoritism to a poor man in his lawsuit.

4"If you come across your enemy's ox or donkey wandering off, be sure to take it back to him. 5If you see the donkey[t] of someone who hates you fallen down under its load, do not leave it there; be sure you help him with it.

6"Do not deny justice to your poor people in their lawsuits. 7Have nothing to do with a false charge[u] and do not put an innocent or honest person to death, for I will not acquit the guilty.

8"Do not accept a bribe,[v] for a bribe blinds those who see and twists the words of the righteous.

9"Do not oppress an alien;[w] you yourselves know how it feels to be aliens, because you were aliens in Egypt.

## Sabbath Laws

10"For six years you are to sow your fields and harvest the crops, 11but during the seventh year let the land lie unplowed and unused. Then the poor among your people may get food from it, and the wild animals may eat what they leave. Do the same with your vineyard and your olive grove.

12"Six days do your work, but on the seventh day do not work, so that your ox and your donkey may rest and the slave born in your household, and the alien as well, may be refreshed.

13"Be careful to do everything I have said to you. Do not invoke the names of other gods; do not let them be heard on your lips.

## The Three Annual Festivals

14"Three times[x] a year you are to celebrate a festival to me.

15"Celebrate the Feast of Unleavened Bread;[y] for seven days eat bread made without yeast, as I commanded you. Do this at the appointed time in the month of Abib, for in that month you came out of Egypt.

"No one is to appear before me empty-handed.[z]

16"Celebrate the Feast of Harvest with the firstfruits[a] of the crops you sow in your field.

"Celebrate the Feast of Ingathering at the end of the year, when you gather in your crops from the field.

17"Three times[b] a year all the men are to appear before the Sovereign LORD.

18"Do not offer the blood of a sacrifice to me along with anything containing yeast.

"The fat of my festival offerings must not be kept until morning.

19"Bring the best of the firstfruits of your soil to the house of the LORD your God.

"Do not cook a young goat in its mother's milk.[c]

## God's Angel to Prepare the Way

20"See, I am sending an angel ahead of you to guard you along the way and to bring you to the place I have prepared. 21Pay attention to him and listen to what he says. Do not rebel against him; he will not forgive your rebellion,[d] since my Name is in him.

[a]25 Or *excessive interest* [b]28 Or *Do not revile the judges* [c]29 The meaning of the Hebrew for this phrase is uncertain.

**22:24** m Ps69:24; 109:9
**22:28** n Ac23:5*
**22:29** o Ex23:15,16,19 p Ex13:2
**22:30** q Ex13:12; Dt15:19 r Lev22:27
**22:31** s Lev19:2
**23:5** t Dt22:4
**23:7** u Eph4:25
**23:8** v Dt10:17
**23:9** w Ex22:21
**23:14** x Ex34:23,24
**23:15** y Ex12:17 z Ex34:20
**23:16** a Ex34:22
**23:17** b Dt16:16
**23:19** c Dt14:21
**23:21** d Ps78:8,40,56

**23:23**
e Jos 24:8,11
**23:24**
f Ex 20:5
g Dt 12:30–31
**23:25**
h Dt 6:13; Mt 4:10
i Dt 28:1–14
j Ex 15:26
**23:26**
k Dt 7:14
**23:27**
l Dt 7:23
**23:28**
m Jos 24:12
**23:29**
n Dt 7:22
**23:31**
o Ge 15:18
p Jos 21:44
**24:1**
q Nu 11:16

22 If you listen carefully to what he says and
do all that I say, I will be an enemy to your
enemies and will oppose those who oppose
you. 23 My angel will go ahead of you and
bring you into the land of the Amorites,
Hittites, Perizzites, Canaanites, Hivites
and Jebusites,[e] and I will wipe them out.
24 Do not bow down before their gods or
worship[f] them or follow their practices.[g]
You must demolish them and break their
sacred stones to pieces. 25 Worship the LORD
your God,[h] and his blessing[i] will be on your
food and water. I will take away sickness[j]
from among you, 26 and none will miscarry
or be barren[k] in your land. I will give you a
full life span.

27 "I will send my terror ahead of you
and throw into confusion[l] every nation you
encounter. I will make all your enemies
turn their backs and run. 28 I will send the
hornet[m] ahead of you to drive the Hivites,
Canaanites and Hittites out of your way.
29 But I will not drive them out in a single
year, because the land would become deso-
late and the wild animals[n] too numerous for
you. 30 Little by little I will drive them out be-
fore you, until you have increased enough to
take possession of the land.

31 "I will establish your borders from the
Red Sea[a] to the Sea of the Philistines,[b] and
from the desert to the River.[c][o] I will hand
over to you the people who live in the land
and you will drive them out[p] before you.
32 Do not make a covenant with them or with
their gods. 33 Do not let them live in your
land, or they will cause you to sin against
me, because the worship of their gods will
certainly be a snare to you."

## The Covenant Confirmed

24 Then he said to Moses, "Come up
to the LORD, you and Aaron, Nadab
and Abihu, and seventy of the elders[q] of
Israel. You are to worship at a distance, 2 but
Moses alone is to approach the LORD; the oth-
ers must not come near. And the people may
not come up with him."

3 When Moses went and told the people all
the LORD's words and laws, they responded
with one voice, "Everything the LORD has
said we will do."[r] 4 Moses then wrote[s] down
everything the LORD had said.

He got up early the next morning and
built an altar at the foot of the mountain
and set up twelve stone pillars representing
the twelve tribes of Israel. 5 Then he sent
young Israelite men, and they offered burnt
offerings and sacrificed young bulls as fel-
lowship offerings[d] to the LORD. 6 Moses took
half of the blood[t] and put it in bowls, and the
other half he sprinkled on the altar. 7 Then
he took the Book of the Covenant and read it
to the people. They responded, "We will do
everything the LORD has said; we will obey."

8 Moses then took the blood, sprinkled it
on the people and said, "This is the blood
of the covenant that the LORD has made with
you in accordance with all these words."

9 Moses and Aaron, Nadab and Abihu,
and the seventy elders of Israel went up
10 and saw the God of Israel. Under his feet
was something like a pavement made of sap-
phire,[e][u] clear as the sky[v] itself. 11 But God did
not raise his hand against these leaders of
the Israelites; they saw[w] God, and they ate
and drank.

12 The LORD said to Moses, "Come up to
me on the mountain and stay here, and
I will give you the tablets of stone,[x] with
the law and commands I have written for
their instruction."

13 Then Moses set out with Joshua his
aide, and Moses went up on the mountain
of God. 14 He said to the elders, "Wait here
for us until we come back to you. Aaron and
Hur are with you, and anyone involved in a
dispute can go to them."

15 When Moses went up on the mountain,
the cloud[y] covered it, 16 and the glory of the
LORD settled on Mount Sinai. For six days
the cloud covered the mountain, and on
the seventh day the LORD called to Moses
from within the cloud. 17 To the Israelites the
glory of the LORD looked like a consuming
fire[z] on top of the mountain. 18 Then Moses
entered the cloud as he went on up the moun-
tain. And he stayed on the mountain forty[a]
days and forty nights.

**24:3**
r Ex 19:8
**24:4**
s Dt 31:9
**24:6**
t Heb 9:18
**24:10**
u Eze 1:26
v Rev 4:3
**24:11**
w Ge 32:30
**24:12**
x Ex 32:15–16
**24:15**
y Ex 19:9
**24:17**
z Heb 12:18,29
**24:18**
a Dt 9:9

[a] 31 Hebrew *Yam Suph*; that is, Sea of Reeds [b] 31 That is, the Mediterranean [c] 31 That is, the Euphrates [d] 5 Traditionally *peace offerings* [e] 10 Or *lapis lazuli*

## Offerings for the Tabernacle

25 The LORD said to Moses, 2"Tell the Israelites to bring me an offering. You are to receive the offering for me from each man whose heart prompts[b] him to give. 3These are the offerings you are to receive from them: gold, silver and bronze; 4blue, purple and scarlet yarn and fine linen; goat hair; 5ram skins dyed red and hides of sea cows[a]; acacia wood; 6olive oil[c] for the light; spices for the anointing oil and for the fragrant incense; 7and onyx stones and other gems to be mounted on the ephod[d] and breastpiece.[e]

8"Then have them make a sanctuary[f] for me, and I will dwell[g] among them. 9Make this tabernacle and all its furnishings exactly like the pattern[h] I will show you.

## The Ark

10"Have them make a chest of acacia wood—two and a half cubits long, a cubit and a half wide, and a cubit and a half high.[b] 11Overlay it with pure gold, both inside and out, and make a gold molding around it. 12Cast four gold rings for it and fasten them to its four feet, with two rings on one side and two rings on the other. 13Then make poles of acacia wood and overlay them with gold. 14Insert the poles into the rings on the sides of the chest to carry it. 15The poles are to remain in the rings of this ark; they are not to be removed. 16Then put in the ark the Testimony,[i] which I will give you.

17"Make an atonement cover[c] of pure gold—two and a half cubits long and a cubit and a half wide.[d] 18And make two cherubim out of hammered gold at the ends of the cover. 19Make one cherub on one end and the second cherub on the other; make the cherubim of one piece with the cover, at the two ends. 20The cherubim are to have their wings spread upward, overshadowing[j] the cover with them. The cherubim are to face each other, looking toward the cover. 21Place the cover on top of the ark[k] and put in the ark the Testimony,[l] which I will give you. 22There, above the cover between the two cherubim[m] that are over the ark of the Testimony, I will meet[n] with you and give you all my commands for the Israelites.

## The Table

23"Make a table of acacia wood—two cubits long, a cubit wide and a cubit and a half high.[e] 24Overlay it with pure gold and make a gold molding around it. 25Also make around it a rim a handbreadth[f] wide and put a gold molding on the rim. 26Make four gold rings for the table and fasten them to the four corners, where the four legs are. 27The rings are to be close to the rim to hold the poles used in carrying the table. 28Make the poles of acacia wood, overlay them with gold and carry the table with them. 29And make its plates and dishes of pure gold, as well as its pitchers and bowls for the pouring out of offerings.[o] 30Put the bread of the Presence[p] on this table to be before me at all times.

## The Lampstand

31"Make a lampstand of pure gold and hammer it out, base and shaft; its flowerlike cups, buds and blossoms shall be of one piece with it. 32Six branches are to extend from the sides of the lampstand—three on one side and three on the other. 33Three cups shaped like almond flowers with buds and blossoms are to be on one branch, three on the next branch, and the same for all six branches extending from the lampstand. 34And on the lampstand there are to be four cups shaped like almond flowers with buds and blossoms. 35One bud shall be under the first pair of branches extending from the lampstand, a second bud under the second pair, and a third bud under the third pair—six branches in all. 36The buds and branches shall all be of one piece with the lampstand, hammered out of pure gold.

37"Then make its seven lamps and set them up on it so that they light the space in front of it. 38Its wick trimmers and trays are to be of pure gold. 39A talent[g] of pure gold is to be used for the lampstand and all these accessories. 40See that you make them according to the pattern[q] shown you on the mountain.

**25:2** b Ex 35:21; 2Co 8:11–12; 9:7
**25:6** c Ex 27:20; 30:22–32
**25:7** d Ex 28:4,6–14 e Ex 28:15–30
**25:8** f Ex 36:1–5 g Ex 29:45; Rev 21:3
**25:9** h ver 40
**25:16** i Dt 31:26; Heb 9:4
**25:20** j 1Ki 8:7; Heb 9:5
**25:21** k Ex 26:34 l ver 16
**25:22** m Nu 7:89; Ps 80:1
**25:22** n Ex 29:42–43
**25:29** o Nu 4:7
**25:30** p Lev 24:5–9
**25:40** q Ex 26:30; Ac 7:44; Heb 8:5*

[a] 5 That is, dugongs [b] 10 That is, about 3 3/4 feet (about 1.1 meters) long and 2 1/4 feet (about 0.7 meter) wide and high
[c] 17 Traditionally *a mercy seat* [d] 17 That is, about 3 3/4 feet (about 1.1 meters) long and 2 1/4 feet (about 0.7 meter) wide
[e] 23 That is, about 3 feet (about 0.9 meter) long and 1 1/2 feet (about 0.5 meter) wide and 2 1/4 feet (about 0.7 meter) high
[f] 25 That is, about 3 inches (about 8 centimeters) [g] 39 That is, about 75 pounds (about 34 kilograms)

**26:14**
r Ex36:19

## The Tabernacle

**26** "Make the tabernacle with ten curtains of finely twisted linen and blue, purple and scarlet yarn, with cherubim worked into them by a skilled craftsman. [2]All the curtains are to be the same size—twenty-eight cubits long and four cubits wide.[a] [3]Join five of the curtains together, and do the same with the other five. [4]Make loops of blue material along the edge of the end curtain in one set, and do the same with the end curtain in the other set. [5]Make fifty loops on one curtain and fifty loops on the end curtain of the other set, with the loops opposite each other. [6]Then make fifty gold clasps and use them to fasten the curtains together so that the tabernacle is a unit.

[7]"Make curtains of goat hair for the tent over the tabernacle—eleven altogether. [8]All eleven curtains are to be the same size—thirty cubits long and four cubits wide.[b] [9]Join five of the curtains together into one set and the other six into another set. Fold the sixth curtain double at the front of the tent. [10]Make fifty loops along the edge of the end curtain in one set and also along the edge of the end curtain in the other set. [11]Then make fifty bronze clasps and put them in the loops to fasten the tent together as a unit. [12]As for the additional length of the tent curtains, the half curtain that is left over is to hang down at the rear of the tabernacle. [13]The tent curtains will be a cubit[c] longer on both sides; what is left will hang over the sides of the tabernacle so as to cover it. [14]Make for the tent a covering of ram skins dyed red, and over that a covering of hides of sea cows.[d][r]

[15]"Make upright frames of acacia wood for the tabernacle. [16]Each frame is to be ten cubits long and a cubit and a half wide,[e] [17]with two projections set parallel to each other. Make all the frames of the tabernacle in this way. [18]Make twenty frames for the south side of the tabernacle [19]and make forty silver bases to go under them—two bases for each frame, one under each projection. [20]For the other side, the north side of the tabernacle, make twenty frames [21]and forty silver bases—two under each frame. [22]Make six frames for the far end, that is, the west end of the tabernacle, [23]and make two frames for the corners at the far end. [24]At these two corners they must be double from the bottom all the way to the top, and fitted into a single ring; both shall be like that. [25]So there will be eight frames and sixteen silver bases—two under each frame.

[26]"Also make crossbars of acacia wood: five for the frames on one side of the tabernacle, [27]five for those on the other side, and five for the frames on the west, at the far end of the tabernacle. [28]The center crossbar is to extend from end to end at the middle of the frames. [29]Overlay the frames with gold and make gold rings to hold the crossbars. Also overlay the crossbars with gold.

[30]"Set up the tabernacle according to the plan[s] shown you on the mountain.

[31]"Make a curtain[t] of blue, purple and scarlet yarn and finely twisted linen, with cherubim[u] worked into it by a skilled craftsman. [32]Hang it with gold hooks on four posts of acacia wood overlaid with gold and standing on four silver bases. [33]Hang the curtain from the clasps and place the ark of the Testimony behind the curtain.[v] The curtain will separate the Holy Place from the Most Holy Place.[w] [34]Put the atonement cover[x] on the ark of the Testimony in the Most Holy Place. [35]Place the table outside the curtain on the north side of the tabernacle and put the lampstand[y] opposite it on the south side.

[36]"For the entrance to the tent make a curtain of blue, purple and scarlet yarn and finely twisted linen—the work of an embroiderer. [37]Make gold hooks for this curtain and five posts of acacia wood overlaid with gold. And cast five bronze bases for them.

## The Altar of Burnt Offering

**27** "Build an altar of acacia wood, three cubits[f] high; it is to be square, five cubits long and five cubits wide.[g] [2]Make a horn at each of the four corners, so that the horns and the altar are of one piece, and

**26:30**
s Ex25:9,40; Ac7:44; Heb8:5

**26:31**
t Mt27:51; Heb9:3
u Ex36:35

**26:33**
v Ex40:3,21
w Heb9:2–3

**26:34**
x Ex25:21; 40:20

**26:35**
y Ex40:22,24

[a]2 That is, about 42 feet (about 12.5 meters) long and 6 feet (about 1.8 meters) wide [b]8 That is, about 45 feet (about 13.5 meters) long and 6 feet (about 1.8 meters) wide [c]13 That is, about 1 1/2 feet (about 0.5 meter) [d]14 That is, dugongs [e]16 That is, about 15 feet (about 4.5 meters) long and 2 1/4 feet (about 0.7 meter) wide [f]1 That is, about 4 1/2 feet (about 1.3 meters) [g]1 That is, about 7 1/2 feet (about 2.3 meters) long and wide

**27:8** z Ex25:9,40

overlay the altar with bronze. 3 Make all its utensils of bronze—its pots to remove the ashes, and its shovels, sprinkling bowls, meat forks and firepans. 4 Make a grating for it, a bronze network, and make a bronze ring at each of the four corners of the network. 5 Put it under the ledge of the altar so that it is halfway up the altar. 6 Make poles of acacia wood for the altar and overlay them with bronze. 7 The poles are to be inserted into the rings so they will be on two sides of the altar when it is carried. 8 Make the altar hollow, out of boards. It is to be made just as you were shown[z] on the mountain.

## The Courtyard

9 "Make a courtyard for the tabernacle. The south side shall be a hundred cubits[a] long and is to have curtains of finely twisted linen, 10 with twenty posts and twenty bronze bases and with silver hooks and bands on the posts. 11 The north side shall also be a hundred cubits long and is to have curtains, with twenty posts and twenty bronze bases and with silver hooks and bands on the posts.

12 "The west end of the courtyard shall be fifty cubits[b] wide and have curtains, with ten posts and ten bases. 13 On the east end, toward the sunrise, the courtyard shall also be fifty cubits wide. 14 Curtains fifteen cubits[c] long are to be on one side of the entrance, with three posts and three bases, 15 and curtains fifteen cubits long are to be on the other side, with three posts and three bases.

16 "For the entrance to the courtyard, provide a curtain twenty cubits[d] long, of blue, purple and scarlet yarn and finely twisted linen—the work of an embroiderer—with four posts and four bases. 17 All the posts around the courtyard are to have silver bands and hooks, and bronze bases. 18 The courtyard shall be a hundred cubits long and fifty cubits wide,[e] with curtains of finely twisted linen five cubits[f] high, and with bronze bases. 19 All the other articles used in the service of the tabernacle, whatever their function, including all the tent pegs for it and those for the courtyard, are to be of bronze.

## Oil for the Lampstand

20 "Command the Israelites to bring you clear oil of pressed olives for the light so that the lamps may be kept burning. 21 In the Tent of Meeting,[a] outside the curtain that is in front of the Testimony,[b] Aaron and his sons are to keep the lamps burning before the LORD from evening till morning. This is to be a lasting ordinance[c] among the Israelites for the generations to come.

## The Priestly Garments

28 "Have Aaron[d] your brother brought to you from among the Israelites, along with his sons Nadab and Abihu, Eleazar and Ithamar, so they may serve me as priests.[e] 2 Make sacred garments[f] for your brother Aaron, to give him dignity and honor. 3 Tell all the skilled men[g] to whom I have given wisdom[h] in such matters that they are to make garments for Aaron, for his consecration, so he may serve me as priest. 4 These are the garments they are to make: a breastpiece,[i] an ephod, a robe,[j] a woven tunic,[k] a turban and a sash. They are to make these sacred garments for your brother Aaron and his sons, so they may serve me as priests. 5 Have them use gold, and blue, purple and scarlet yarn, and fine linen.

## The Ephod

6 "Make the ephod of gold, and of blue, purple and scarlet yarn, and of finely twisted linen—the work of a skilled craftsman. 7 It is to have two shoulder pieces attached to two of its corners, so it can be fastened. 8 Its skillfully woven waistband is to be like it—of one piece with the ephod and made with gold, and with blue, purple and scarlet yarn, and with finely twisted linen.

9 "Take two onyx stones and engrave on them the names of the sons of Israel 10 in the order of their birth—six names on one stone and the remaining six on the other. 11 Engrave the names of the sons of Israel on the two stones the way a gem cutter engraves a seal. Then mount the stones in gold filigree settings 12 and fasten them on the shoulder pieces of the ephod as memorial stones for the sons of Israel. Aaron is to bear

**27:21** a Ex28:43 b Ex26:31,33 c Lev3:17; 16:34

**28:1** d Heb5:4 e Nu18:1–7; Heb5:1

**28:2** f Ex29:5,29; 31:10

**28:3** g Ex31:6 h Ex31:3

**28:4** i ver15–30 j ver31–35 k ver39

[a] 9 That is, about 150 feet (about 46 meters); also in verse 11 [b] 12 That is, about 75 feet (about 23 meters); also in verse 13 [c] 14 That is, about 22 1/2 feet (about 6.9 meters); also in verse 15 [d] 16 That is, about 30 feet (about 9 meters) [e] 18 That is, about 150 feet (about 46 meters) long and 75 feet (about 23 meters) wide [f] 18 That is, about 7 1/2 feet (about 2.3 meters)

the names on his shoulders as a memorial before the LORD. 13 Make gold filigree settings 14 and two braided chains of pure gold, like a rope, and attach the chains to the settings.

## The Breastpiece

15 "Fashion a breastpiece for making decisions—the work of a skilled craftsman. Make it like the ephod: of gold, and of blue, purple and scarlet yarn, and of finely twisted linen. 16 It is to be square—a span[a] long and a span wide—and folded double. 17 Then mount four rows of precious stones on it. In the first row there shall be a ruby, a topaz and a beryl; 18 in the second row a turquoise, a sapphire[b] and an emerald; 19 in the third row a jacinth, an agate and an amethyst; 20 in the fourth row a chrysolite, an onyx and a jasper.[c] Mount them in gold filigree settings. 21 There are to be twelve stones, one for each of the names of the sons of Israel, each engraved like a seal with the name of one of the twelve tribes.

22 "For the breastpiece make braided chains of pure gold, like a rope. 23 Make two gold rings for it and fasten them to two corners of the breastpiece. 24 Fasten the two gold chains to the rings at the corners of the breastpiece, 25 and the other ends of the chains to the two settings, attaching them to the shoulder pieces of the ephod at the front. 26 Make two gold rings and attach them to the other two corners of the breastpiece on the inside edge next to the ephod. 27 Make two more gold rings and attach them to the bottom of the shoulder pieces on the front of the ephod, close to the seam just above the waistband of the ephod. 28 The rings of the breastpiece are to be tied to the rings of the ephod with blue cord, connecting it to the waistband, so that the breastpiece will not swing out from the ephod.

29 "Whenever Aaron enters the Holy Place, he will bear the names of the sons of Israel over his heart on the breastpiece of decision as a continuing memorial before the LORD. 30 Also put the Urim and the Thummim[l] in the breastpiece, so they may be over Aaron's heart whenever he enters the presence of the LORD. Thus Aaron will always bear the means of making decisions for the Israelites over his heart before the LORD.

## Other Priestly Garments

31 "Make the robe of the ephod entirely of blue cloth, 32 with an opening for the head in its center. There shall be a woven edge like a collar[d] around this opening, so that it will not tear. 33 Make pomegranates of blue, purple and scarlet yarn around the hem of the robe, with gold bells between them. 34 The gold bells and the pomegranates are to alternate around the hem of the robe. 35 Aaron must wear it when he ministers. The sound of the bells will be heard when he enters the Holy Place before the LORD and when he comes out, so that he will not die.

36 "Make a plate of pure gold and engrave on it as on a seal: HOLY TO THE LORD.[m] 37 Fasten a blue cord to it to attach it to the turban; it is to be on the front of the turban. 38 It will be on Aaron's forehead, and he will bear the guilt[n] involved in the sacred gifts the Israelites consecrate, whatever their gifts may be. It will be on Aaron's forehead continually so that they will be acceptable to the LORD.

39 "Weave the tunic of fine linen and make the turban of fine linen. The sash is to be the work of an embroiderer. 40 Make tunics, sashes and headbands for Aaron's sons,[o] to give them dignity and honor. 41 After you put these clothes on your brother Aaron and his sons, anoint and ordain them. Consecrate them so they may serve me as priests.[p]

42 "Make linen undergarments[q] as a covering for the body, reaching from the waist to the thigh. 43 Aaron and his sons must wear them whenever they enter the Tent of Meeting[r] or approach the altar to minister in the Holy Place, so that they will not incur guilt and die.[s]

"This is to be a lasting ordinance for Aaron and his descendants.

## Consecration of the Priests

29 "This is what you are to do to consecrate them, so they may serve me as priests: Take a young bull and two rams without defect. 2 And from fine wheat flour, without yeast, make bread, and cakes

**28:30** l Lev 8:8; Nu 27:21
**28:36** m Zec 14:20
**28:38** n Lev 10:17; Nu 18:1
**28:40** o ver 4
**28:41** p Ex 29:7–9; 30:30; Lev 8:1–36
**28:42** q Lev 6:10; Eze 44:18
**28:43** r Ex 27:21 s Ex 20:26

[a]16 That is, about 9 inches (about 22 centimeters) [b]18 Or *lapis lazuli* [c]20 The precise identification of some of these precious stones is uncertain. [d]32 The meaning of the Hebrew for this word is uncertain.

mixed with oil, and wafers spread with oil.[t] 3Put them in a basket and present them in it—along with the bull and the two rams. 4Then bring Aaron and his sons to the entrance to the Tent of Meeting and wash them with water.[u] 5Take the garments and dress Aaron with the tunic, the robe of the ephod, the ephod itself and the breastpiece. Fasten the ephod on him by its skillfully woven waistband.[v] 6Put the turban on his head and attach the sacred diadem[w] to the turban. 7Take the anointing oil[x] and anoint him by pouring it on his head. 8Bring his sons and dress them in tunics 9and put headbands on them. Then tie sashes on Aaron and his sons.[a][y] The priesthood is theirs by a lasting ordinance.[z] In this way you shall ordain Aaron and his sons.

10"Bring the bull to the front of the Tent of Meeting, and Aaron and his sons shall lay their hands on its head. 11Slaughter it in the LORD's presence at the entrance to the Tent of Meeting. 12Take some of the bull's blood and put it on the horns[a] of the altar with your finger, and pour out the rest of it at the base of the altar. 13Then take all the fat[b] around the inner parts, the covering of the liver, and both kidneys with the fat on them, and burn them on the altar. 14But burn the bull's flesh and its hide and its offal outside the camp.[c] It is a sin offering.

15"Take one of the rams, and Aaron and his sons shall lay their hands on its head. 16Slaughter it and take the blood and sprinkle it against the altar on all sides. 17Cut the ram into pieces and wash the inner parts and the legs, putting them with the head and the other pieces. 18Then burn the entire ram on the altar. It is a burnt offering to the LORD, a pleasing aroma,[d] an offering made to the LORD by fire.

19"Take the other ram, and Aaron and his sons shall lay their hands on its head. 20Slaughter it, take some of its blood and put it on the lobes of the right ears of Aaron and his sons, on the thumbs of their right hands, and on the big toes of their right feet. Then sprinkle blood against the altar on all sides. 21And take some of the blood[e] on the altar and some of the anointing oil[f] and sprinkle it on Aaron and his garments and on his sons and their garments. Then he and his sons and their garments will be consecrated.[g]

22"Take from this ram the fat, the fat tail, the fat around the inner parts, the covering of the liver, both kidneys with the fat on them, and the right thigh. (This is the ram for the ordination.) 23From the basket of bread made without yeast, which is before the LORD, take a loaf, and a cake made with oil, and a wafer. 24Put all these in the hands of Aaron and his sons and wave them before the LORD as a wave offering.[h] 25Then take them from their hands and burn them on the altar along with the burnt offering for a pleasing aroma to the LORD, an offering made to the LORD by fire. 26After you take the breast of the ram for Aaron's ordination, wave it before the LORD as a wave offering, and it will be your share.

27"Consecrate those parts of the ordination ram that belong to Aaron and his sons:[i] the breast that was waved and the thigh that was presented. 28This is always to be the regular share from the Israelites for Aaron and his sons. It is the contribution the Israelites are to make to the LORD from their fellowship offerings.[b]

29"Aaron's sacred garments will belong to his descendants so that they can be anointed and ordained in them.[j] 30The son who succeeds him as priest and comes to the Tent of Meeting to minister in the Holy Place is to wear them seven days.

31"Take the ram for the ordination and cook the meat in a sacred place. 32At the entrance to the Tent of Meeting, Aaron and his sons are to eat the meat of the ram and the bread that is in the basket. 33They are to eat these offerings by which atonement was made for their ordination and consecration. But no one else may eat[k] them, because they are sacred. 34And if any of the meat of the ordination ram or any bread is left over till morning, burn it up. It must not be eaten, because it is sacred.

35"Do for Aaron and his sons everything I have commanded you, taking seven days to ordain them. 36Sacrifice a bull each day[l] as a sin offering to make atonement. Purify the altar by making atonement for it, and anoint it to consecrate it. 37For seven days

**29:2** t Lev 6:19–23
**29:4** u Ex 40:12
**29:5** v Ex 28:8
**29:6** w Lev 8:9
**29:7** x Ex 30:25,30,31; Lev 8:12; 21:10
**29:9** y Ex 28:40 z Nu 18:7
**29:12** a Ex 27:2
**29:13** b Lev 3:3,5,9
**29:14** c Lev 4:11–12,21; Heb 13:11
**29:18** d Ge 8:21
**29:21** e Heb 9:22 f Ex 30:25,31
**29:21** g ver 1
**29:24** h Lev 7:30
**29:27** i Lev 7:31,34
**29:29** j Nu 20:26,28
**29:33** k Lev 10:14; 22:10,13
**29:36** l Heb 10:11

[a]9 Hebrew; Septuagint *on them* [b]28 Traditionally *peace offerings*

**29:37** m Ex40:10
**29:38** n Nu28:3–8
**29:42** o Ex30:8 p Ex25:22
**29:43** q 1Ki8:11
**29:45** r Ex25:8; Lev26:12 s 2Co6:16; Rev21:3
**29:46** t Ex20:2
**30:6** u Ex25:22

make atonement for the altar and consecrate it. Then the altar will be most holy, and whatever touches it will be holy.[m]

38"This is what you are to offer on the altar regularly each day:[n] two lambs a year old. 39Offer one in the morning and the other at twilight. 40With the first lamb offer a tenth of an ephah[a] of fine flour mixed with a quarter of a hin[b] of oil from pressed olives, and a quarter of a hin of wine as a drink offering. 41Sacrifice the other lamb at twilight with the same grain offering and its drink offering as in the morning—a pleasing aroma, an offering made to the LORD by fire.

42"For the generations to come[o] this burnt offering is to be made regularly at the entrance to the Tent of Meeting before the LORD. There I will meet you and speak to you;[p] 43there also I will meet with the Israelites, and the place will be consecrated by my glory.[q]

44"So I will consecrate the Tent of Meeting and the altar and will consecrate Aaron and his sons to serve me as priests. 45Then I will dwell[r] among the Israelites and be their God.[s] 46They will know that I am the LORD their God, who brought them out of Egypt so that I might dwell among them. I am the LORD their God.[t]

## The Altar of Incense

**30** "Make an altar of acacia wood for burning incense. 2It is to be square, a cubit long and a cubit wide, and two cubits high[c]—its horns of one piece with it. 3Overlay the top and all the sides and the horns with pure gold, and make a gold molding around it. 4Make two gold rings for the altar below the molding—two on opposite sides—to hold the poles used to carry it. 5Make the poles of acacia wood and overlay them with gold. 6Put the altar in front of the curtain that is before the ark of the Testimony—before the atonement cover[u] that is over the Testimony—where I will meet with you.

7"Aaron must burn fragrant incense on the altar every morning when he tends the lamps. 8He must burn incense again when he lights the lamps at twilight so incense will burn regularly before the LORD for the generations to come. 9Do not offer on this altar any other incense[v] or any burnt offering or grain offering, and do not pour a drink offering on it. 10Once a year Aaron shall make atonement[w] on its horns. This annual atonement must be made with the blood of the atoning sin offering for the generations to come. It is most holy to the LORD."

## Atonement Money

11Then the LORD said to Moses, 12"When you take a census[x] of the Israelites to count them, each one must pay the LORD a ransom[y] for his life at the time he is counted. Then no plague will come on them when you number them. 13Each one who crosses over to those already counted is to give a half shekel,[d] according to the sanctuary shekel,[z] which weighs twenty gerahs. This half shekel is an offering to the LORD. 14All who cross over, those twenty years old or more, are to give an offering to the LORD. 15The rich are not to give more than a half shekel and the poor are not to give less when you make the offering to the LORD to atone for your lives. 16Receive the atonement money from the Israelites and use it for the service of the Tent of Meeting. It will be a memorial for the Israelites before the LORD, making atonement for your lives."

## Basin for Washing

17Then the LORD said to Moses, 18"Make a bronze basin,[a] with its bronze stand, for washing. Place it between the Tent of Meeting and the altar, and put water in it. 19Aaron and his sons are to wash their hands and feet[b] with water from it. 20Whenever they enter the Tent of Meeting, they shall wash with water so that they will not die. Also, when they approach the altar to minister by presenting an offering made to the LORD by fire, 21they shall wash their hands and feet so that they will not die. This is to be a lasting ordinance[c] for Aaron and his descendants for the generations to come."

## Anointing Oil

22Then the LORD said to Moses, 23"Take the following fine spices: 500 shekels[e] of liquid

**30:9** v Lev10:1
**30:10** w Lev16:18–19,30
**30:12** x Nu1:2,49 y Nu31:50
**30:13** z Mt17:24
**30:18** a Ex38:8; 40:7,30
**30:19** b Ex40:31–32
**30:21** c Ex27:21; 28:43

[a]40 That is, probably about 2 quarts (about 2 liters) [b]40 That is, probably about 1 quart (about 1 liter) [c]2 That is, about 1 1/2 feet (about 0.5 meter) long and wide and about 3 feet (about 0.9 meter) high [d]13 That is, about 1/5 ounce (about 6 grams); also in verse 15 [e]23 That is, about 12 1/2 pounds (about 6 kilograms)

**30:25** d Ex37:29
**30:26** e Lev8:10
**30:30** f Lev8:2,12,30
**30:33** g ver38

myrrh, half as much (that is, 250 shekels) of fragrant cinnamon, 250 shekels of fragrant cane, [24]500 shekels of cassia—all according to the sanctuary shekel—and a hin[a] of olive oil. [25]Make these into a sacred anointing oil, a fragrant blend, the work of a perfumer.[d] It will be the sacred anointing oil. [26]Then use it to anoint[e] the Tent of Meeting, the ark of the Testimony, [27]the table and all its articles, the lampstand and its accessories, the altar of incense, [28]the altar of burnt offering and all its utensils, and the basin with its stand. [29]You shall consecrate them so they will be most holy, and whatever touches them will be holy.

[30]"Anoint Aaron and his sons and consecrate[f] them so they may serve me as priests. [31]Say to the Israelites, 'This is to be my sacred anointing oil for the generations to come. [32]Do not pour it on men's bodies and do not make any oil with the same formula. It is sacred, and you are to consider it sacred. [33]Whoever makes perfume like it and whoever puts it on anyone other than a priest must be cut off[g] from his people.' "

## Incense

[34]Then the LORD said to Moses, "Take fragrant spices—gum resin, onycha and galbanum—and pure frankincense, all in equal amounts, [35]and make a fragrant blend of incense, the work of a perfumer. It is to be salted and pure and sacred. [36]Grind some of it to powder and place it in front of the Testimony in the Tent of Meeting, where I will meet with you. It shall be most holy to you. [37]Do not make any incense with this formula for yourselves; consider it holy to the LORD. [38]Whoever makes any like it to enjoy its fragrance must be cut off from his people."

## Bezalel and Oholiab

**31** Then the LORD said to Moses, [2]"See, I have chosen Bezalel[h] son of Uri, the son of Hur, of the tribe of Judah, [3]and I have filled him with the Spirit of God, with skill, ability and knowledge in all kinds of crafts— [4]to make artistic designs for work in gold, silver and bronze, [5]to cut and set stones, to work in wood, and to engage in all kinds of craftsmanship. [6]Moreover, I have appointed Oholiab son of Ahisamach, of the tribe of Dan, to help him. Also I have given skill to all the craftsmen to make everything I have commanded you: [7]the Tent of Meeting,[i] the ark of the Testimony[j] with the atonement cover[k] on it, and all the other furnishings of the tent— [8]the table[l] and its articles, the pure gold lampstand[m] and all its accessories, the altar of incense, [9]the altar of burnt offering and all its utensils, the basin with its stand— [10]and also the woven garments, both the sacred garments for Aaron the priest and the garments for his sons when they serve as priests, [11]and the anointing oil[n] and fragrant incense for the Holy Place. They are to make them just as I commanded you."

## The Sabbath

[12]Then the LORD said to Moses, [13]"Say to the Israelites, 'You must observe my Sabbaths. This will be a sign[o] between me and you for the generations to come, so you may know that I am the LORD, who makes you holy.[b]

**31:2** h Ex36:1,2
**31:7** i Ex36:8–38 j Ex37:1–5 k Ex37:6
**31:8** l Ex37:10–16 m Ex37:17–24
**31:11** n Ex30:22–32
**31:13** o Eze20:12,20

[a]24 That is, probably about 4 quarts (about 4 liters) [b]13 Or *who sanctifies you*; or *who sets you apart as holy*

## The African Presence

**Exodus 31:1–10**

God gave Bezalel and Oholiab exceptional giftedness to oversee and carry out projects for the tabernacle. It is likely that they learned much of their skill while working as slaves in Egypt. The Egyptians were known for their ability to work with metals and other materials.

14 "'Observe the Sabbath, because it is holy to you. Anyone who desecrates it must be put to death;[p] whoever does any work on that day must be cut off from his people. 15 For six days, work[q] is to be done, but the seventh day is a Sabbath of rest, holy to the LORD. Whoever does any work on the Sabbath day must be put to death. 16 The Israelites are to observe the Sabbath, celebrating it for the generations to come as a lasting covenant. 17 It will be a sign[r] between me and the Israelites forever, for in six days the LORD made the heavens and the earth, and on the seventh day he abstained from work and rested.[s]'"

18 When the LORD finished speaking to Moses on Mount Sinai, he gave him the two tablets of the Testimony, the tablets of stone inscribed by the finger of God.[t]

## The Golden Calf

32 When the people saw that Moses was so long in coming down from the mountain, they gathered around Aaron and said, "Come, make us gods[a] who will go before us. As for this fellow Moses who brought us up out of Egypt, we don't know what has happened to him."

2 Aaron answered them, "Take off the gold earrings that your wives, your sons and your daughters are wearing, and bring them to me." 3 So all the people took off their earrings and brought them to Aaron. 4 He took what they handed him and made it into an idol cast in the shape of a calf,[u] fashioning it with a tool. Then they said, "These are your gods,[b] O Israel, who brought you up out of Egypt."

5 When Aaron saw this, he built an altar in front of the calf and announced, "Tomorrow there will be a festival to the LORD." 6 So the next day the people rose early and sacrificed burnt offerings and presented fellowship offerings.[c] Afterward they sat down to eat and drink and got up to indulge in revelry.[v]

7 Then the LORD said to Moses, "Go down, because your people, whom you brought up out of Egypt, have become corrupt.[w] 8 They have been quick to turn away from what I commanded them and have made themselves an idol[x] cast in the shape of a calf. They have bowed down to it and sacrificed to it and have said, 'These are your gods, O Israel, who brought you up out of Egypt.'[y]

9 "I have seen these people," the LORD said to Moses, "and they are a stiff-necked[z] people. 10 Now leave me alone so that my anger may burn against them and that I may destroy them. Then I will make you into a great nation."[a]

11 But Moses sought the favor[b] of the LORD his God. "O LORD," he said, "why should your anger burn against your people, whom you brought out of Egypt with great power and a mighty hand? 12 Why should the Egyptians say, 'It was with evil intent that he brought them out, to kill them in the mountains and to wipe them off the face of the earth'?[c] Turn from your fierce anger; relent and do not bring disaster on your people. 13 Remember your servants Abraham, Isaac and Israel, to whom you swore by your own self:[d] 'I will make your descendants as numerous as the stars in the sky and I will give your descendants all this land[e] I promised them, and it will be their inheritance forever.'" 14 Then the LORD relented[f] and did not bring on his people the disaster he had threatened.

15 Moses turned and went down the mountain with the two tablets of the Testimony in his hands.[g] They were inscribed on both sides, front and back. 16 The tablets were the work of God; the writing was the writing of God, engraved on the tablets.

17 When Joshua heard the noise of the people shouting, he said to Moses, "There is the sound of war in the camp."

18 Moses replied:

"It is not the sound of victory,
it is not the sound of defeat;
it is the sound of singing that I hear."

19 When Moses approached the camp and saw the calf[h] and the dancing, his anger burned and he threw the tablets out of his hands, breaking them to pieces[i] at the foot of the mountain. 20 And he took the calf they had made and burned it in the fire; then he ground it to powder, scattered it on the water[j] and made the Israelites drink it.

21 He said to Aaron, "What did these

**31:14** p Nu 15:32–36
**31:15** q Ex 20:8–11
**31:17** r ver 13; s Ge 2:2–3
**31:18** t Ex 32:15–16
**32:4** u Dt 9:16; Ac 7:41
**32:6** v 1Co 10:7*
**32:7** w Ge 6:11–12; Dt 9:12
**32:8** x Ex 20:4; y 1Ki 12:28
**32:9** z Ex 33:3,5; 34:9; Isa 48:4; Ac 7:51
**32:10** a Nu 14:12; Dt 9:14
**32:11** b Dt 9:18
**32:12** c Nu 14:13–16
**32:13** d Ge 22:16; Heb 6:13; e Ge 12:7
**32:14** f Ps 106:45
**32:15** g Dt 9:15
**32:19** h Dt 9:16; i Dt 9:17
**32:20** j Dt 9:21

[a] 1 Or *a god*; also in verses 23 and 31 [b] 4 Or *This is your god*; also in verse 8 [c] 6 Traditionally *peace offerings*

32:22 k Dt9:24

people do to you, that you led them into
such great sin?"
[22]"Do not be angry, my lord," Aaron an-
swered. "You know how prone these people
are to evil.[k] [23]They said to me, 'Make us
gods who will go before us. As for this fellow
Moses who brought us up out of Egypt, we
don't know what has happened to him.' [24]So
I told them, 'Whoever has any gold jewelry,
take it off.' Then they gave me the gold,
and I threw it into the fire, and out came
this calf!"

Inspire

# THE FAITHFULNESS OF GOD

Faithfulness is an attribute that the Bible applies to both God and humans. As it applies to God, it means that God is absolutely reliable. He is not fickle but is steadfast and constant in his dealings with his creation, which, of course, includes us. The word *faithfulness* is used to convey to us how unchanging and loyal God is in his love for us. He does not love us one day and change his mind another day. His love for us does not change when we fail him. God may discipline us when we go astray, but his love does not change.

In the book of Exodus, we see that God was faithful to his people time and again—even though they were continually whining about how they were better off back in Egypt. When they worshiped the golden calf, God planned to destroy them all and start again with Moses (see Ex 32:7–10). But Moses had faith in the love and faithfulness of God. Moses reminded God of his promise to Abraham, Isaac and Jacob/Israel (see Ex 32:13). What faith and courage it takes to talk to our angry Father and know that he will keep his promises—even when we truly deserve his wrath and not his favor!

The Old and New Testaments praise God for his faithfulness, and Scripture challenges us as his children to develop faithfulness in our lives. Unwavering trust and steadfast loyalty are two virtues essential for our personal and spiritual growth.

Women of color, we must hold fast to our faithfulness as mothers, friends and leaders. God's faithfulness toward humans mirrors how faithfulness leads to productivity, resulting in the fruit of diligence, security and reliability. It also creates an atmosphere of stability—not only for one's self, but also for others. Our dependability and commitment to others will manifest itself in our faithfulness, love and service to them. And our unfailing faith will be rewarded for all eternity.

—T. Byrd

For the next Inspire note, go to page 140.

**read**

Exodus 32.
See also the Inspire Note "Commitment to Community," and the Women of the Bible Notes "Ruth: A Model of Friendship and Sisterhood" and "Naomi: Call Me Bitter."

**WOMAN of COLOR**

How faithful are you to God and to others?

**32:30** l 1Sa 12:20
**32:31** m Ex 20:23
**32:32** n Ps 69:28; Da 12:1; Rev 3:5; 21:27

25 Moses saw that the people were running
wild and that Aaron had let them get out of
control and so become a laughingstock to
their enemies. 26 So he stood at the entrance
to the camp and said, "Whoever is for the
LORD, come to me." And all the Levites ral-
lied to him.
27 Then he said to them, "This is what
the LORD, the God of Israel, says: 'Each
man strap a sword to his side. Go back and
forth through the camp from one end to the
other, each killing his brother and friend
and neighbor.' " 28 The Levites did as Moses
commanded, and that day about three thou-
sand of the people died. 29 Then Moses said,
"You have been set apart to the LORD today,
for you were against your own sons and
brothers, and he has blessed you this day."
30 The next day Moses said to the people,
"You have committed a great sin.[l] But now I
will go up to the LORD; perhaps I can make
atonement for your sin."
31 So Moses went back to the LORD and
said, "Oh, what a great sin these people have
committed! They have made themselves
gods of gold.[m] 32 But now, please forgive
their sin—but if not, then blot me out of the
book[n] you have written."
33 The LORD replied to Moses, "Whoever
has sinned against me I will blot out of my
book. 34 Now go, lead the people to the place
I spoke of, and my angel will go before you.
However, when the time comes for me to
punish, I will punish them for their sin."
35 And the LORD struck the people with a
plague because of what they did with the
calf Aaron had made.
33 Then the LORD said to Moses, "Leave
this place, you and the people you
brought up out of Egypt, and go up to the
land I promised on oath to Abraham, Isaac
and Jacob, saying, 'I will give it to your de-
scendants.'[o] 2 I will send an angel before you
and drive out the Canaanites, Amorites, Hit-
tites, Perizzites, Hivites and Jebusites. 3 Go
up to the land flowing with milk and honey.[p]
But I will not go with you, because you are a
stiff-necked people and I might destroy you
on the way."
4 When the people heard these distressing
words, they began to mourn[q] and no one put
on any ornaments. 5 For the LORD had said to
Moses, "Tell the Israelites, 'You are a stiff-
necked people. If I were to go with you even
for a moment, I might destroy you. Now take
off your ornaments and I will decide what to
do with you.' " 6 So the Israelites stripped off
their ornaments at Mount Horeb.

## The Tent of Meeting

7 Now Moses used to take a tent and pitch
it outside the camp some distance away,
calling it the "tent of meeting." Anyone in-
quiring of the LORD would go to the tent of
meeting outside the camp. 8 And whenever
Moses went out to the tent, all the people
rose and stood at the entrances to their
tents, watching Moses until he entered the
tent. 9 As Moses went into the tent, the pillar
of cloud would come down and stay at the
entrance, while the LORD spoke[r] with Moses.
10 Whenever the people saw the pillar of
cloud standing at the entrance to the tent,
they all stood and worshiped, each at the en-
trance to his tent. 11 The LORD would speak
to Moses face to face,[s] as a man speaks with
his friend. Then Moses would return to the
camp, but his young aide Joshua son of Nun
did not leave the tent.

**33:1** o Ge 12:7
**33:3** p Ex 3:8
**33:4** q Nu 14:39
**33:9** r Ps 99:7
**33:11** s Nu 12:8; Dt 34:10

### *The African Presence*

**Exodus 33:1**

Egypt, located in northern Africa, was a powerful and thriving nation during the time of Moses. Egyptian relics from this time period are renowned for their beauty and creativity, and give modern people a glimpse of the intelligence and ingenuity of this culture.

## Moses and the Glory of the LORD

12Moses said to the LORD, "You have been telling me, 'Lead these people,' but you have not let me know whom you will send with me. You have said, 'I know you by name[t] and you have found favor with me.' 13If you are pleased with me, teach me your ways[u] so I may know you and continue to find favor with you. Remember that this nation is your people."[v]

14The LORD replied, "My Presence[w] will go with you, and I will give you rest."

15Then Moses said to him, "If your Presence does not go with us, do not send us up from here. 16How will anyone know that you are pleased with me and with your people unless you go with us? What else will distinguish me and your people from all the other people on the face of the earth?"

17And the LORD said to Moses, "I will do the very thing you have asked, because I am pleased with you and I know you by name."

18Then Moses said, "Now show me your glory."

19And the LORD said, "I will cause all my goodness to pass in front of you, and I will proclaim my name, the LORD, in your presence. I will have mercy on whom I will have mercy, and I will have compassion on whom I will have compassion.[x] 20But," he said, "you cannot see my face, for no one may see me and live."

21Then the LORD said, "There is a place near me where you may stand on a rock. 22When my glory passes by, I will put you in a cleft in the rock and cover you with my hand until I have passed by. 23Then I will remove my hand and you will see my back; but my face must not be seen."

## The New Stone Tablets

34 The LORD said to Moses, "Chisel out two stone tablets like the first ones, and I will write on them the words that were on the first tablets, which you broke.[y] 2Be ready in the morning, and then come up on Mount Sinai.[z] Present yourself to me there on top of the mountain. 3No one is to come with you or be seen anywhere on the mountain;[a] not even the flocks and herds may graze in front of the mountain."

4So Moses chiseled out two stone tablets like the first ones and went up Mount Sinai early in the morning, as the LORD had commanded him; and he carried the two stone tablets in his hands. 5Then the LORD came down in the cloud and stood there with him and proclaimed his name, the LORD. 6And he passed in front of Moses, proclaiming, "The LORD, the LORD, the compassionate and gracious God, slow to anger, abounding in love[b] and faithfulness, 7maintaining love to thousands,[c] and forgiving wickedness, rebellion and sin.[d] Yet he does not leave the guilty unpunished; he punishes the children and their children for the sin of the fathers to the third and fourth generation."

8Moses bowed to the ground at once and worshiped. 9"O Lord, if I have found favor in your eyes," he said, "then let the Lord go with us. Although this is a stiff-necked people, forgive our wickedness and our sin, and take us as your inheritance."

10Then the LORD said: "I am making a covenant[e] with you. Before all your people I will do wonders never before done in any nation in all the world.[f] The people you live among will see how awesome is the work that I, the LORD, will do for you. 11Obey what I command you today. I will drive out before you the Amorites, Canaanites, Hittites, Perizzites, Hivites and Jebusites.[g] 12Be careful not to make a treaty with those who live in the land where you are going, or they will be a snare[h] among you. 13Break down their altars, smash their sacred stones and cut down their Asherah poles.[a][i] 14Do not worship any other god,[j] for the LORD, whose name is Jealous, is a jealous God.

15"Be careful not to make a treaty with those who live in the land; for when they prostitute themselves to their gods and sacrifice to them, they will invite you and you will eat their sacrifices.[k] 16And when you choose some of their daughters as wives[l] for your sons and those daughters prostitute themselves to their gods, they will lead your sons to do the same.

> *"Positive anything is better than negative nothing."*
> —LORRAINE HANSBERRY, PLAYWRIGHT AND ACTIVIST

**33:12** t ver 17
**33:13** u Ps 25:4; v Dt 9:26,29
**33:14** w Isa 63:9
**33:19** x Ro 9:15*
**34:1** y Ex 32:19
**34:2** z Ex 19:11
**34:3** a Ex 19:12–13,21
**34:6** b Ne 9:17
**34:7** c Ex 20:6; d Ps 103:3
**34:10** e Dt 5:2–3; f Dt 4:32
**34:11** g Ex 33:2
**34:12** h Ex 23:32–33
**34:13** i 2Ki 18:4
**34:14** j Ex 20:3
**34:15** k Nu 25:2
**34:16** l Dt 7:3

[a]13 That is, symbols of the goddess Asherah

**34:18** m Ex 12:15
**34:19** n Ex 13:2
**34:20** o Ex 13:13,15
**34:21** p Ex 20:9
**34:22** q Ex 23:16
**34:23** r Ex 23:14
**34:26** s Ex 23:19
**34:28** t Ex 24:18; u ver 1; Ex 31:18; v Dt 4:13; 10:4
**34:29** w Ex 32:15; x Mt 17:2; 2Co 3:7,13

17“Do not make cast idols.

18“Celebrate the Feast of Unleavened Bread. For seven days eat bread made without yeast,[m] as I commanded you. Do this at the appointed time in the month of Abib, for in that month you came out of Egypt.

19“The first offspring[n] of every womb belongs to me, including all the firstborn males of your livestock, whether from herd or flock. 20Redeem the firstborn donkey with a lamb, but if you do not redeem it, break its neck.[o] Redeem all your firstborn sons.

“No one is to appear before me empty-handed.

21“Six days you shall labor, but on the seventh day you shall rest;[p] even during the plowing season and harvest you must rest.

22“Celebrate the Feast of Weeks with the firstfruits of the wheat harvest, and the Feast of Ingathering[q] at the turn of the year.[a] 23Three times[r] a year all your men are to appear before the Sovereign LORD, the God of Israel. 24I will drive out nations before you and enlarge your territory, and no one will covet your land when you go up three times each year to appear before the LORD your God.

25“Do not offer the blood of a sacrifice to me along with anything containing yeast, and do not let any of the sacrifice from the Passover Feast remain until morning.

26“Bring the best of the firstfruits of your soil to the house of the LORD your God.

“Do not cook a young goat in its mother's milk.”[s]

27Then the LORD said to Moses, “Write down these words, for in accordance with these words I have made a covenant with you and with Israel.” 28Moses was there with the LORD forty days and forty nights[t] without eating bread or drinking water. And he wrote on the tablets[u] the words of the covenant—the Ten Commandments.[v]

## The Radiant Face of Moses

29When Moses came down from Mount Sinai with the two tablets of the Testimony in his hands,[w] he was not aware that his face was radiant[x] because he had spoken with the LORD. 30When Aaron and all the Israelites saw Moses, his face was radiant, and they were afraid to come near him. 31But Moses called to them; so Aaron and all the leaders of the community came back to him, and he spoke to them. 32Afterward all the Israelites came near him, and he gave them all the commands the LORD had given him on Mount Sinai.

33When Moses finished speaking to them, he put a veil[y] over his face. 34But whenever he entered the LORD's presence to speak with him, he removed the veil until he came out. And when he came out and told the Israelites what he had been commanded, 35they saw that his face was radiant. Then Moses would put the veil back over his face until he went in to speak with the LORD.

## Sabbath Regulations

35 Moses assembled the whole Israelite community and said to them, “These are the things the LORD has commanded[z] you to do: 2For six days, work is to be done, but the seventh day shall be your holy day, a Sabbath of rest to the LORD. Whoever does any work on it must be put to death. 3Do not light a fire in any of your dwellings on the Sabbath day.[a]”

## Materials for the Tabernacle

4Moses said to the whole Israelite community, “This is what the LORD has commanded: 5From what you have, take an offering for the LORD. Everyone who is willing is to bring to the LORD an offering of gold, silver and bronze; 6blue, purple and scarlet yarn and fine linen; goat hair; 7ram skins dyed red and hides of sea cows[b]; acacia wood; 8olive oil for the light; spices for the anointing oil and for the fragrant incense; 9and onyx stones and other gems to be mounted on the ephod and breastpiece.

10“All who are skilled among you are to come and make everything the LORD has commanded:[b] 11the tabernacle[c] with its tent and its covering, clasps, frames, crossbars, posts and bases; 12the ark with its poles and the atonement cover and the curtain that shields it; 13the table[d] with its poles and all its articles and the bread of the Presence; 14the lampstand that is for light with its ac-

**34:33** y 2Co 3:13
**35:1** z Ex 34:32
**35:3** a Ex 16:23
**35:10** b Ex 31:6
**35:11** c Ex 26:1-37
**35:13** d Ex 25:23-30

[a]22 That is, in the fall [b]7 That is, dugongs; also in verse 23

**35:15** e Ex30:1–6
**35:19** f Ex28:2; 31:10
**35:29** g ver21; 1Ch29:9 h ver4–9; Ex25:1–7; 36:3; 2Ki12:4

cessories, lamps and oil for the light; 15 the
altar[e] of incense with its poles, the anoint-
ing oil and the fragrant incense; the curtain
for the doorway at the entrance to the taber-
nacle; 16 the altar of burnt offering with its
bronze grating, its poles and all its utensils;
the bronze basin with its stand; 17 the cur-
tains of the courtyard with its posts and
bases, and the curtain for the entrance to the
courtyard; 18 the tent pegs for the tabernacle
and for the courtyard, and their ropes; 19 the
woven garments worn for ministering in the
sanctuary—both the sacred garments[f] for
Aaron the priest and the garments for his
sons when they serve as priests."

20 Then the whole Israelite community
withdrew from Moses' presence, 21 and every-
one who was willing and whose heart moved
him came and brought an offering to the
LORD for the work on the Tent of Meeting, for
all its service, and for the sacred garments.
22 All who were willing, men and women
alike, came and brought gold jewelry of all
kinds: brooches, earrings, rings and orna-
ments. They all presented their gold as a
wave offering to the LORD. 23 Everyone who
had blue, purple or scarlet yarn or fine linen,
or goat hair, ram skins dyed red or hides of
sea cows brought them. 24 Those presenting
an offering of silver or bronze brought it as
an offering to the LORD, and everyone who
had acacia wood for any part of the work
brought it. 25 Every skilled woman spun with
her hands and brought what she had spun—
blue, purple or scarlet yarn or fine linen.
26 And all the women who were willing and
had the skill spun the goat hair. 27 The lead-
ers brought onyx stones and other gems to
be mounted on the ephod and breastpiece.
28 They also brought spices and olive oil for
the light and for the anointing oil and for
the fragrant incense. 29 All the Israelite men
and women who were willing[g] brought to
the LORD freewill offerings[h] for all the work
the LORD through Moses had commanded
them to do.

## Bezalel and Oholiab

30 Then Moses said to the Israelites, "See,
the LORD has chosen Bezalel son of Uri, the
son of Hur, of the tribe of Judah, 31 and he
has filled him with the Spirit of God, with
skill, ability and knowledge in all kinds of
crafts[i]— 32 to make artistic designs for work
in gold, silver and bronze, 33 to cut and set
stones, to work in wood and to engage in
all kinds of artistic craftsmanship. 34 And
he has given both him and Oholiab[j] son of
Ahisamach, of the tribe of Dan, the ability
to teach[k] others. 35 He has filled them with
skill to do all kinds of work[l] as craftsmen,
designers, embroiderers in blue, purple and
scarlet yarn and fine linen, and weavers—
all of them master craftsmen and designers.

36 1 So Bezalel, Oholiab and every
skilled person[m] to whom the LORD
has given skill and ability to know how to
carry out all the work of constructing the
sanctuary[n] are to do the work just as the
LORD has commanded."

2 Then Moses summoned Bezalel[o] and
Oholiab[p] and every skilled person to whom
the LORD had given ability and who was
willing[q] to come and do the work. 3 They
received from Moses all the offerings[r] the
Israelites had brought to carry out the work
of constructing the sanctuary. And the peo-
ple continued to bring freewill offerings
morning after morning. 4 So all the skilled
craftsmen who were doing all the work
on the sanctuary left their work 5 and said
to Moses, "The people are bringing more
than enough[s] for doing the work the LORD
commanded to be done."

6 Then Moses gave an order and they sent
this word throughout the camp: "No man
or woman is to make anything else as an
offering for the sanctuary." And so the peo-
ple were restrained from bringing more,
7 because what they already had was more[t]
than enough to do all the work.

## The Tabernacle

8 All the skilled men among the workmen
made the tabernacle with ten curtains of
finely twisted linen and blue, purple and
scarlet yarn, with cherubim worked into
them by a skilled craftsman. 9 All the cur-
tains were the same size—twenty-eight
cubits long and four cubits wide.[a] 10 They
joined five of the curtains together and did
the same with the other five. 11 Then they

**35:31** i ver35; 2Ch2:7,14
**35:34** j Ex31:6 k 2Ch2:14
**35:35** l ver31; Ex31:3,6
**36:1** m Ex28:3 n Ex25:8
**36:2** o Ex31:2 p Ex31:6 q Ex25:2; 35:21,26; 1Ch29:5
**36:3** r Ex35:29
**36:5** s 2Ch24:14; 31:10; 2Co8:2–3
**36:7** t 1Ki7:47

[a]9 That is, about 42 feet (about 12.5 meters) long and 6 feet (about 1.8 meters) wide

made loops of blue material along the edge of the end curtain in one set, and the same was done with the end curtain in the other set. 12They also made fifty loops on one curtain and fifty loops on the end curtain of the other set, with the loops opposite each other. 13Then they made fifty gold clasps and used them to fasten the two sets of curtains together so that the tabernacle was a unit.[u]

14They made curtains of goat hair for the tent over the tabernacle—eleven altogether. 15All eleven curtains were the same size—thirty cubits long and four cubits wide.[a] 16They joined five of the curtains into one set and the other six into another set. 17Then they made fifty loops along the edge of the end curtain in one set and also along the edge of the end curtain in the other set. 18They made fifty bronze clasps to fasten the tent together as a unit.[v] 19Then they made for the tent a covering of ram skins dyed red, and over that a covering of hides of sea cows.[b]

20They made upright frames of acacia wood for the tabernacle. 21Each frame was ten cubits long and a cubit and a half wide,[c] 22with two projections set parallel to each other. They made all the frames of the tabernacle in this way. 23They made twenty frames for the south side of the tabernacle 24and made forty silver bases to go under them—two bases for each frame, one under each projection. 25For the other side, the north side of the tabernacle, they made twenty frames 26and forty silver bases—two under each frame. 27They made six frames for the far end, that is, the west end of the tabernacle, 28and two frames were made for the corners of the tabernacle at the far end. 29At these two corners the frames were double from the bottom all the way to the top and fitted into a single ring; both were made alike. 30So there were eight frames and sixteen silver bases—two under each frame.

31They also made crossbars of acacia wood: five for the frames on one side of the tabernacle, 32five for those on the other side, and five for the frames on the west, at the far end of the tabernacle. 33They made the center crossbar so that it extended from end to end at the middle of the frames. 34They overlaid the frames with gold and made gold rings to hold the crossbars. They also overlaid the crossbars with gold.

35They made the curtain[w] of blue, purple and scarlet yarn and finely twisted linen, with cherubim worked into it by a skilled craftsman. 36They made four posts of acacia wood for it and overlaid them with gold. They made gold hooks for them and cast their four silver bases. 37For the entrance to the tent they made a curtain of blue, purple and scarlet yarn and finely twisted linen—the work of an embroiderer;[x] 38and they made five posts with hooks for them. They overlaid the tops of the posts and their bands with gold and made their five bases of bronze.

## The Ark

37 Bezalel[y] made the ark[z] of acacia wood—two and a half cubits long, a cubit and a half wide, and a cubit and a half high.[d] 2He overlaid it with pure gold,[a] both inside and out, and made a gold molding around it. 3He cast four gold rings for it and fastened them to its four feet, with two rings on one side and two rings on the other. 4Then he made poles of acacia wood and overlaid them with gold. 5And he inserted the poles into the rings on the sides of the ark to carry it.

6He made the atonement cover[b] of pure gold—two and a half cubits long and a cubit and a half wide.[e] 7Then he made two cherubim[c] out of hammered gold at the ends of the cover. 8He made one cherub on one end and the second cherub on the other; at the two ends he made them of one piece with the cover. 9The cherubim had their wings spread upward, overshadowing[d] the cover with them. The cherubim faced each other, looking toward the cover.[e]

## The Table

10They[f] made the table[f] of acacia wood—two cubits long, a cubit wide, and a cubit

**36:13** u ver 18
**36:18** v ver 13
**36:35** w Ex 39:38; Mt 27:51; Lk 23:45; Heb 9:3
**36:37** x Ex 27:16
**37:1** y Ex 31:2 z Ex 30:6; 39:35; Dt 10:3
**37:2** a ver 11,26
**37:6** b Ex 26:34; 31:7; Heb 9:5
**37:7** c Eze 41:18
**37:9** d Heb 9:5 e Dt 10:3
**37:10** f Heb 9:2

[a]15 That is, about 45 feet (about 13.5 meters) long and 6 feet (about 1.8 meters) wide [b]19 That is, dugongs [c]21 That is, about 15 feet (about 4.5 meters) long and 2 1/4 feet (about 0.7 meter) wide [d]1 That is, about 3 3/4 feet (about 1.1 meters) long and 2 1/4 feet (about 0.7 meter) wide and high [e]6 That is, about 3 3/4 feet (about 1.1 meters) long and 2 1/4 feet (about 0.7 meter) wide [f]10 Or *He*; also in verses 11–29

**37:11** g ver 2
**37:14** h ver 27
**37:17** i Heb 9:2; Rev 1:12
**37:22** j ver 17; Nu 8:4
**37:23** k Ex 40:4,25
**37:25** l Ex 30:34–36; Lk 1:11; Heb 9:4; Rev 8:3 m Ex 27:2; Rev 9:13

and a half high.[a] 11Then they overlaid it with
pure gold[g] and made a gold molding around
it. 12They also made around it a rim a hand-
breadth[b] wide and put a gold molding on
the rim. 13They cast four gold rings for the
table and fastened them to the four corners,
where the four legs were. 14The rings[h] were
put close to the rim to hold the poles used
in carrying the table. 15The poles for carry-
ing the table were made of acacia wood and
were overlaid with gold. 16And they made
from pure gold the articles for the table—its
plates and dishes and bowls and its pitchers
for the pouring out of drink offerings.

## The Lampstand

17They made the lampstand[i] of pure gold
and hammered it out, base and shaft; its
flowerlike cups, buds and blossoms were of
one piece with it. 18Six branches extended
from the sides of the lampstand—three
on one side and three on the other. 19Three
cups shaped like almond flowers with buds
and blossoms were on one branch, three
on the next branch and the same for all six
branches extending from the lampstand.
20And on the lampstand were four cups
shaped like almond flowers with buds and
blossoms. 21One bud was under the first
pair of branches extending from the lamp-
stand, a second bud under the second pair,
and a third bud under the third pair—six
branches in all. 22The buds and the branches
were all of one piece with the lampstand,
hammered out of pure gold.[j]

23They made its seven lamps,[k] as well as
its wick trimmers and trays, of pure gold.
24They made the lampstand and all its acces-
sories from one talent[c] of pure gold.

## The Altar of Incense

25They made the altar of incense[l] out of
acacia wood. It was square, a cubit long
and a cubit wide, and two cubits high[d]—its
horns[m] of one piece with it. 26They overlaid
the top and all the sides and the horns with
pure gold, and made a gold molding around
it. 27They made two gold rings below the
molding—two on opposite sides—to hold
the poles used to carry it. 28They made the
poles of acacia wood and overlaid them
with gold.[n]

29They also made the sacred anointing
oil[o] and the pure, fragrant incense[p]—the
work of a perfumer.

## The Altar of Burnt Offering

38 They[e] built the altar of burnt offer-
ing of acacia wood, three cubits[f]
high; it was square, five cubits long and five
cubits wide.[g] 2They made a horn at each of
the four corners, so that the horns and the
altar were of one piece, and they overlaid the
altar with bronze. 3They made all its uten-
sils of bronze—its pots, shovels, sprinkling
bowls, meat forks and firepans. 4They made
a grating for the altar, a bronze network,
to be under its ledge, halfway up the altar.
5They cast bronze rings to hold the poles for
the four corners of the bronze grating. 6They
made the poles of acacia wood and overlaid
them with bronze. 7They inserted the poles
into the rings so they would be on the sides
of the altar for carrying it. They made it hol-
low, out of boards.

## Basin for Washing

8They made the bronze basin[q] and its
bronze stand from the mirrors of the women[r]
who served at the entrance to the Tent of
Meeting.

## The Courtyard

9Next they made the courtyard. The south
side was a hundred cubits[h] long and had cur-
tains of finely twisted linen, 10with twenty
posts and twenty bronze bases, and with sil-
ver hooks and bands on the posts. 11The north
side was also a hundred cubits long and had
twenty posts and twenty bronze bases, with
silver hooks and bands on the posts.

12The west end was fifty cubits[i] wide and
had curtains, with ten posts and ten bases,
with silver hooks and bands on the posts.
13The east end, toward the sunrise, was also
fifty cubits wide. 14Curtains fifteen cubits[j]
long were on one side of the entrance, with

**37:28** n Ex 25:13
**37:29** o Ex 31:11 p Ex 30:1,25
**38:8** q Ex 30:18 r Dt 23:17; 1Sa 2:22

[a]10 That is, about 3 feet (about 0.9 meter) long, 1 1/2 feet (about 0.5 meter) wide, and 2 1/4 feet (about 0.7 meter) high [b]12 That is, about 3 inches (about 8 centimeters) [c]24 That is, about 75 pounds (about 34 kilograms) [d]25 That is, about 1 1/2 feet (about 0.5 meter) long and wide, and about 3 feet (about 0.9 meter) high [e]1 Or *He*; also in verses 2–9 [f]1 That is, about 4 1/2 feet (about 1.3 meters) [g]1 That is, about 7 1/2 feet (about 2.3 meters) long and wide [h]9 That is, about 150 feet (about 46 meters) [i]12 That is, about 75 feet (about 23 meters) [j]14 That is, about 22 1/2 feet (about 6.9 meters)

**38:21** s Nu 1:50,53; 9:15; 10:11; 17:7; 2Ch 24:6; Ac 7:44; Rev 15:5 t Nu 4:28,33
**38:22** u Ex 31:2
**38:24** v Ex 30:13
**38:25** w Ex 30:12
**38:26** x Ex 30:12 y Ex 30:13 z Ex 30:14 a Ex 12:37; Nu 1:46
**38:27** b Ex 26:19

three posts and three bases, 15and curtains fifteen cubits long were on the other side of the entrance to the courtyard, with three posts and three bases. 16All the curtains around the courtyard were of finely twisted linen. 17The bases for the posts were bronze. The hooks and bands on the posts were silver, and their tops were overlaid with silver; so all the posts of the courtyard had silver bands.

18The curtain for the entrance to the courtyard was of blue, purple and scarlet yarn and finely twisted linen—the work of an embroiderer. It was twenty cubits[a] long and, like the curtains of the courtyard, five cubits[b] high, 19with four posts and four bronze bases. Their hooks and bands were silver, and their tops were overlaid with silver. 20All the tent pegs of the tabernacle and of the surrounding courtyard were bronze.

## The Materials Used

21These are the amounts of the materials used for the tabernacle, the tabernacle of the Testimony,[s] which were recorded at Moses' command by the Levites under the direction of Ithamar[t] son of Aaron, the priest. 22(Bezalel[u] son of Uri, the son of Hur, of the tribe of Judah, made everything the LORD commanded Moses; 23with him was Oholiab son of Ahisamach, of the tribe of Dan—a craftsman and designer, and an embroiderer in blue, purple and scarlet yarn and fine linen.) 24The total amount of the gold from the wave offering used for all the work on the sanctuary was 29 talents and 730 shekels,[c] according to the sanctuary shekel.[v]

25The silver obtained from those of the community who were counted in the census[w] was 100 talents and 1,775 shekels,[d] according to the sanctuary shekel— 26one beka per person,[x] that is, half a shekel,[e] according to the sanctuary shekel,[y] from everyone who had crossed over to those counted, twenty years old or more,[z] a total of 603,550 men.[a] 27The 100 talents[f] of silver were used to cast the bases[b] for the sanctuary and for the curtain—100 bases from the 100 talents, one talent for each base. 28They used the 1,775 shekels[g] to make the hooks for the posts, to overlay the tops of the posts, and to make their bands.

29The bronze from the wave offering was 70 talents and 2,400 shekels.[h] 30They used it to make the bases for the entrance to the Tent of Meeting, the bronze altar with its bronze grating and all its utensils, 31the bases for the surrounding courtyard and those for its entrance and all the tent pegs for the tabernacle and those for the surrounding courtyard.

## The Priestly Garments

39 From the blue, purple and scarlet yarn[c] they made woven garments for ministering in the sanctuary.[d] They also made sacred garments[e] for Aaron, as the LORD commanded Moses.

## The Ephod

2They[i] made the ephod of gold, and of blue, purple and scarlet yarn, and of finely twisted linen. 3They hammered out thin sheets of gold and cut strands to be worked into the blue, purple and scarlet yarn and fine linen—the work of a skilled craftsman. 4They made shoulder pieces for the ephod, which were attached to two of its corners, so it could be fastened. 5Its skillfully woven waistband was like it—of one piece with the ephod and made with gold, and with blue, purple and scarlet yarn, and with finely twisted linen, as the LORD commanded Moses.

6They mounted the onyx stones in gold filigree settings and engraved them like a seal with the names of the sons of Israel. 7Then they fastened them on the shoulder pieces of the ephod as memorial[f] stones for the sons of Israel, as the LORD commanded Moses.

## The Breastpiece

8They fashioned the breastpiece[g]—the work of a skilled craftsman. They made it like the ephod: of gold, and of blue, purple and scarlet yarn, and of finely twisted linen. 9It was square—a span[j] long and a

**39:1** c Ex 35:23 d Ex 35:19 e ver 41; Ex 28:2
**39:7** f Lev 24:7; Jos 4:7
**39:8** g Lev 8:8

[a]18 That is, about 30 feet (about 9 meters) [b]18 That is, about 7 1/2 feet (about 2.3 meters) [c]24 The weight of the gold was a little over one ton (about 1 metric ton). [d]25 The weight of the silver was a little over 3 3/4 tons (about 3.4 metric tons). [e]26 That is, about 1/5 ounce (about 5.5 grams) [f]27 That is, about 3 3/4 tons (about 3.4 metric tons) [g]28 That is, about 45 pounds (about 20 kilograms) [h]29 The weight of the bronze was about 2 1/2 tons (about 2.4 metric tons). [i]2 Or *He*; also in verses 7, 8 and 22 [j]9 That is, about 9 inches (about 22 centimeters)

**39:14** h Rev 21:12

span wide—and folded double. 10Then they mounted four rows of precious stones on it. In the first row there was a ruby, a topaz and a beryl; 11in the second row a turquoise, a sapphire[a] and an emerald; 12in the third row a jacinth, an agate and an amethyst; 13in the fourth row a chrysolite, an onyx and a jasper.[b] They were mounted in gold filigree settings. 14There were twelve stones, one for each of the names of the sons of Israel, each engraved like a seal with the name of one of the twelve tribes.[h]

15For the breastpiece they made braided chains of pure gold, like a rope. 16They made two gold filigree settings and two gold rings, and fastened the rings to two of the corners of the breastpiece. 17They fastened the two gold chains to the rings at the corners of the breastpiece, 18and the other ends of the chains to the two settings, attaching them to the shoulder pieces of the ephod at the front. 19They made two gold rings and attached them to the other two corners of the breastpiece on the inside edge next to the ephod. 20Then they made two more gold rings and attached them to the bottom of the shoulder pieces on the front of the ephod, close to the seam just above the waistband of the ephod. 21They tied the rings of the breastpiece to the rings of the ephod with blue cord, connecting it to the waistband so that the breastpiece would not swing out from the ephod—as the LORD commanded Moses.

## Other Priestly Garments

22They made the robe of the ephod entirely of blue cloth—the work of a weaver— 23with an opening in the center of the robe like the opening of a collar,[c] and a band around this opening, so that it would not tear. 24They made pomegranates of blue, purple and scarlet yarn and finely twisted linen around the hem of the robe. 25And they made bells of pure gold and attached them around the hem between the pomegranates. 26The bells and pomegranates alternated around the hem of the robe to be worn for ministering, as the LORD commanded Moses.

27For Aaron and his sons, they made tunics of fine linen—the work of a weaver— 28and the turban of fine linen, the linen headbands and the undergarments of finely twisted linen. 29The sash was of finely twisted linen and blue, purple and scarlet yarn—the work of an embroiderer—as the LORD commanded Moses.

30They made the plate, the sacred diadem, out of pure gold and engraved on it, like an inscription on a seal: HOLY TO THE LORD. 31Then they fastened a blue cord to it to attach it to the turban, as the LORD commanded Moses.

## Moses Inspects the Tabernacle

32So all the work on the tabernacle, the Tent of Meeting, was completed. The Israelites did everything just as the LORD commanded Moses.[i] 33Then they brought the tabernacle to Moses: the tent and all its furnishings, its clasps, frames, crossbars, posts and bases; 34the covering of ram skins dyed red, the covering of hides of sea cows[d] and the shielding curtain; 35the ark of the Testimony with its poles and the atonement cover; 36the table with all its articles and the bread of the Presence; 37the pure gold lampstand with its row of lamps and all its accessories, and the oil for the light; 38the gold altar, the anointing oil, the fragrant incense, and the curtain for the entrance to the tent; 39the bronze altar with its bronze grating, its poles and all its utensils; the basin with its stand; 40the curtains of the courtyard with its posts and bases, and the curtain for the entrance to the courtyard; the ropes and tent pegs for the courtyard; all the furnishings for the tabernacle, the Tent of Meeting; 41and the woven garments worn for ministering in the sanctuary, both the sacred garments for Aaron the priest and the garments for his sons when serving as priests.

42The Israelites had done all the work just as the LORD had commanded Moses. 43Moses inspected the work and saw that they had done it just as the LORD had commanded. So Moses blessed[j] them.

## Setting Up the Tabernacle

40 Then the LORD said to Moses: 2"Set up the tabernacle, the Tent of Meeting,[k] on the first day of the first month.[l] 3Place the ark[m] of the Testimony in it and

**39:32** i ver 42–43; Ex 25:9

**39:43** j Lev 9:22,23; Nu 6:23–27; 2Sa 6:18; 1Ki 8:14,55; 2Ch 30:27

**40:2** k Nu 1:1 l ver 17; Ex 12:2

**40:3** m Ex 26:33

[a]11 Or *lapis lazuli* [b]13 The precise identification of some of these precious stones is uncertain. [c]23 The meaning of the Hebrew for this word is uncertain. [d]34 That is, dugongs

**40:4** n Ex 25:30
**40:7** o Ex 30:18
**40:9** p Ex 30:26
**40:10** q Ex 29:36
**40:12** r Lev 8:1–13
**40:13** s Ex 28:41 t Lev 8:12
**40:15** u Ex 29:9; Nu 25:13
**40:17** v Nu 7:1 w ver 2
**40:20** x Ex 16:34; 25:16; Heb 9:4
**40:21** y Ex 26:33
**40:22** z Ex 26:35

shield the ark with the curtain. 4 Bring in the
table and set out what belongs on it.[n] Then
bring in the lampstand and set up its lamps.
5 Place the gold altar of incense in front of
the ark of the Testimony and put the curtain
at the entrance to the tabernacle.

6 "Place the altar of burnt offering in front
of the entrance to the tabernacle, the Tent of
Meeting; 7 place the basin[o] between the Tent
of Meeting and the altar and put water in it.
8 Set up the courtyard around it and put the
curtain at the entrance to the courtyard.

9 "Take the anointing oil and anoint[p] the
tabernacle and everything in it; consecrate
it and all its furnishings, and it will be holy.
10 Then anoint the altar of burnt offering and
all its utensils; consecrate[q] the altar, and it
will be most holy. 11 Anoint the basin and its
stand and consecrate them.

12 "Bring Aaron and his sons to the en-
trance to the Tent of Meeting and wash
them with water.[r] 13 Then dress Aaron in
the sacred garments,[s] anoint him and con-
secrate[t] him so he may serve me as priest.
14 Bring his sons and dress them in tunics.
15 Anoint them just as you anointed their
father, so they may serve me as priests.
Their anointing will be to a priesthood that
will continue for all generations to come.[u]"
16 Moses did everything just as the LORD
commanded him.

17 So the tabernacle[v] was set up on the first
day of the first month[w] in the second year.
18 When Moses set up the tabernacle, he
put the bases in place, erected the frames,
inserted the crossbars and set up the posts.
19 Then he spread the tent over the taberna-
cle and put the covering over the tent, as the
LORD commanded him.

20 He took the Testimony[x] and placed it
in the ark, attached the poles to the ark and
put the atonement cover over it. 21 Then he
brought the ark into the tabernacle and hung
the shielding curtain[y] and shielded the ark of
the Testimony, as the LORD commanded him.

22 Moses placed the table[z] in the Tent
of Meeting on the north side of the taber-
nacle outside the curtain 23 and set out the
bread on it before the LORD, as the LORD com-
manded him.

24 He placed the lampstand[a] in the Tent of
Meeting opposite the table on the south side
of the tabernacle 25 and set up the lamps[b] be-
fore the LORD, as the LORD commanded him.

26 Moses placed the gold altar[c] in the Tent
of Meeting in front of the curtain 27 and
burned fragrant incense on it, as the LORD
commanded him. 28 Then he put up the cur-
tain at the entrance to the tabernacle.

29 He set the altar of burnt offering near
the entrance to the tabernacle, the Tent of
Meeting, and offered on it burnt offerings
and grain offerings,[d] as the LORD command-
ed him.

30 He placed the basin between the Tent
of Meeting and the altar and put water in it
for washing, 31 and Moses and Aaron and his
sons used it to wash their hands and feet.
32 They washed whenever they entered the
Tent of Meeting or approached the altar, as
the LORD commanded Moses.

33 Then Moses set up the courtyard around
the tabernacle and altar and put up the cur-
tain at the entrance to the courtyard. And so
Moses finished the work.

## The Glory of the LORD

34 Then the cloud[e] covered the Tent of
Meeting, and the glory of the LORD filled
the tabernacle. 35 Moses could not enter the
Tent of Meeting because the cloud had set-
tled upon it, and the glory of the LORD filled
the tabernacle.

36 In all the travels of the Israelites, when-
ever the cloud lifted from above the taber-
nacle, they would set out;[f] 37 but if the cloud
did not lift, they did not set out—until the
day it lifted. 38 So the cloud[g] of the LORD was
over the tabernacle by day, and fire was in
the cloud by night, in the sight of all the
house of Israel during all their travels.

**40:24** a Ex 26:35
**40:25** b Ex 25:37
**40:26** c ver 5; Ex 30:6
**40:29** d ver 6
**40:34** e Nu 9:15–23
**40:36** f Nu 9:17–23; Ne 9:19
**40:38** g Ex 13:21; Nu 9:15

# Leviticus

## OVERVIEW

The book of Leviticus provides instructions for presenting God with various kinds of offerings, including the five main offerings described in chapters 1–7: burnt, grain, fellowship, sin and guilt offerings. These offerings were required for the people to approach the holy God who delivered them from bondage and established a covenant with them.

Leviticus also includes a number of miscellaneous regulations regarding how the people were to live and worship God. There are instructions for purity for women with regard to childbirth and menstruation (see Lev 12; 15), as well as prohibitions against improper sexual relations (see Lev 18). These mandates were given to lead the people and priests to live holy lives and to dictate how special days were to be conducted.

The Israelites understood that God could only be approached as he directed. Aaron's sons were instantly killed for disregarding God's holiness (see Lev 10). The son of Shelomith, an Israelite woman, was publicly killed for blaspheming God (see Lev 24).

Even in the time of grace, God will not tolerate sin. A woman can only find acceptance from God through the atoning work of Jesus Christ. By confessing that "Jesus is Lord" and believing that God raised him from the dead, a woman can be saved and boldly approach the throne of grace (see Ro 10:9–10; Heb 4:16).

# Leviticus

## OUTLINE

I. Instructions for the Five Main Offerings (1:1—7:38)
II. Instructions for the Priesthood (8:1—10:20)
III. Instructions for the People Concerning Clean and Unclean (11:1—15:33)
IV. Instructions for the Day of Atonement (16:1–34)
V. Instructions for Religious and Ethical Living (17:1—26:46)
VI. Instructions Regarding Vows (27:1–34)

## SCANNABLE FACTS:

**Author:** Moses

**Time Written:** During the 1400s B.C., while the Israelites were traveling in the desert

**Themes to Note:** The holiness of God; instructions for religious and ethical daily life

**Notable Woman:** Shelomith, daughter of Dibri the Danite (see Lev 24:11)

1:1 a Ex 19:3 b Nu 7:89
1:2 c Lev 22:18–19
1:3 d Dt 15:21; Heb 9:14; 1Pe 1:19
1:4 e Ex 29:10,15; Lev 3:2 f 2Ch 29:23–24
1:5 g Heb 12:24
1:9 h Ge 8:21; Eph 5:2
1:10 i ver 3

## The Burnt Offering

1 The LORD called to Moses[a] and spoke to him from the Tent of Meeting.[b] He said, 2"Speak to the Israelites and say to them: 'When any of you brings an offering to the LORD, bring as your offering an animal from either the herd or the flock.[c]

3" 'If the offering is a burnt offering from the herd, he is to offer a male without defect.[d] He must present it at the entrance to the Tent of Meeting so that it[a] will be acceptable to the LORD. 4He is to lay his hand on the head[e] of the burnt offering, and it will be accepted on his behalf to make atonement[f] for him. 5He is to slaughter the young bull before the LORD, and then Aaron's sons the priests shall bring the blood and sprinkle it against the altar on all sides[g] at the entrance to the Tent of Meeting. 6He is to skin the burnt offering and cut it into pieces. 7The sons of Aaron the priest are to put fire on the altar and arrange wood on the fire. 8Then Aaron's sons the priests shall arrange the pieces, including the head and the fat, on the burning wood that is on the altar. 9He is to wash the inner parts and the legs with water, and the priest is to burn all of it on the altar. It is a burnt offering, an offering made by fire, an aroma pleasing to the LORD.[h]

10" 'If the offering is a burnt offering from the flock, from either the sheep or the goats,[i] he is to offer a male without defect. 11He is to slaughter it at the north side of the altar before the LORD, and Aaron's sons the priests shall sprinkle its blood against the altar on all sides. 12He is to cut it into pieces, and the priest shall arrange them, including the head and the fat, on the burning wood that is on the altar. 13He is to wash the inner parts and the legs with water, and the priest is to bring all of it and burn it on the altar. It is a burnt offering, an offering made by fire, an aroma pleasing to the LORD.

14" 'If the offering to the LORD is a burnt offering of birds, he is to offer a dove or a young pigeon.[j] 15The priest shall bring it to the altar, wring off the head and burn it on the altar; its blood shall be drained out on the side of the altar. 16He is to remove the crop with its contents[b] and throw it to the east side of the altar, where the ashes[k] are. 17He shall tear it open by the wings, not severing it completely,[l] and then the priest shall burn it on the wood that is on the fire on the altar. It is a burnt offering, an offering made by fire, an aroma pleasing to the LORD.

## The Grain Offering

2 " 'When someone brings a grain offering[m] to the LORD, his offering is to be of fine flour. He is to pour oil on it, put incense on it 2and take it to Aaron's sons the priests. The priest shall take a handful of the fine flour and oil, together with all the incense, and burn this as a memorial portion[n] on the altar, an offering made by fire, an aroma pleasing to the LORD. 3The rest of the grain offering belongs to Aaron and his sons;[o] it is a most holy part of the offerings made to the LORD by fire.

4" 'If you bring a grain offering baked in an oven, it is to consist of fine flour: cakes made without yeast and mixed with oil, or[c] wafers made without yeast and spread with oil. 5If your grain offering is prepared on a griddle, it is to be made of fine flour mixed

1:14 j Lev 5:7
1:16 k Lev 6:10
1:17 l Ge 15:10
2:1 m Lev 6:14–18
2:2 n ver 9,16; Lev 5:12; 6:15; Ac 10:4
2:3 o Lev 10:12,13

[a]3 Or *he* [b]16 Or *crop and the feathers*; the meaning of the Hebrew for this word is uncertain. [c]4 Or *and*

## The African Presence

### Leviticus 1–8

The Lord gave specific instructions concerning how acceptable offerings were to be presented. The use of altars and offerings were common among the people of Africa and northeast Africa/Asia prior to these instructions.

with oil, and without yeast. [6]Crumble it and pour oil on it; it is a grain offering. [7]If your grain offering is cooked in a pan, it is to be made of fine flour and oil. [8]Bring the grain offering made of these things to the LORD; present it to the priest, who shall take it to the altar. [9]He shall take out the memorial portion[p] from the grain offering and burn it on the altar as an offering made by fire, an aroma pleasing to the LORD. [10]The rest of the grain offering belongs to Aaron and his sons;[q] it is a most holy part of the offerings made to the LORD by fire.

[11]" 'Every grain offering you bring to the LORD must be made without yeast,[r] for you are not to burn any yeast or honey in an offering made to the LORD by fire. [12]You may bring them to the LORD as an offering of the firstfruits,[s] but they are not to be offered on the altar as a pleasing aroma. [13]Season all your grain offerings with salt. Do not leave the salt of the covenant[t] of your God out of your grain offerings; add salt to all your offerings.

[14]" 'If you bring a grain offering of firstfruits[u] to the LORD, offer crushed heads of new grain roasted in the fire. [15]Put oil and incense on it; it is a grain offering. [16]The priest shall burn the memorial portion[v] of the crushed grain and the oil, together with all the incense, as an offering made to the LORD by fire.

## The Fellowship Offering

**3** " 'If someone's offering is a fellowship offering,[a][w] and he offers an animal from the herd, whether male or female, he is to present before the LORD an animal without defect.[x] [2]He is to lay his hand on the head of his offering and slaughter it[y] at the entrance to the Tent of Meeting. Then Aaron's sons the priests shall sprinkle the blood against the altar on all sides. [3]From the fellowship offering he is to bring a sacrifice made to the LORD by fire: all the fat that covers the inner parts or is connected to them, [4]both kidneys with the fat on them near the loins, and the covering of the liver, which he will remove with the kidneys. [5]Then Aaron's sons are to burn it on the altar on top of the burnt offering[z] that is on the burning wood, as an offering made by fire, an aroma pleasing to the LORD.

[6]" 'If he offers an animal from the flock as a fellowship offering[a] to the LORD, he is to offer a male or female without defect. [7]If he offers a lamb, he is to present it before the LORD. [8]He is to lay his hand on the head of his offering and slaughter it in front of the Tent of Meeting. Then Aaron's sons shall sprinkle its blood against the altar on all sides. [9]From the fellowship offering he is to bring a sacrifice made to the LORD by fire: its fat, the entire fat tail cut off close to the backbone, all the fat that covers the inner parts or is connected to them, [10]both kidneys with the fat on them near the loins, and the covering of the liver, which he will remove with the kidneys. [11]The priest shall burn them on the altar as food,[b] an offering made to the LORD by fire.

[12]" 'If his offering is a goat, he is to present it before the LORD. [13]He is to lay his hand on its head and slaughter it in front of the Tent of Meeting. Then Aaron's sons shall sprinkle its blood against the altar on all sides. [14]From what he offers he is to make this offering to the LORD by fire: all the fat that covers the inner parts or is connected to them, [15]both kidneys with the fat on them near the loins, and the covering of the liver, which he will remove with the kidneys. [16]The priest shall burn them on the altar as food, an offering made by fire, a pleasing aroma. All the fat is the LORD's.

[17]" 'This is a lasting ordinance for the generations to come, wherever you live: You must not eat any fat or any blood.[c] ' "

## The Sin Offering

**4** The LORD said to Moses, [2]"Say to the Israelites: 'When anyone sins unintentionally[d] and does what is forbidden in any of the LORD's commands—

[3]" 'If the anointed priest sins, bringing guilt on the people, he must bring to the LORD a young bull without defect as a sin offering for the sin he has committed. [4]He is to present the bull at the entrance to the Tent of Meeting before the LORD.[e] He is to lay his hand on its head and slaughter it before the

**2:9** p ver 2
**2:10** q ver 3
**2:11** r Lev 6:16
**2:12** s Lev 23:10
**2:13** t Nu 18:19
**2:14** u Lev 23:10
**2:16** v ver 2
**3:1** w Lev 7:11-34 x Lev 22:21
**3:2** y Lev 1:5
**3:5** z Ex 29:13,38-42
**3:6** a ver 1
**3:11** b Lev 21:6,17
**3:17** c Lev 7:25-26; 17:10-16
**4:2** d Lev 5:15-18; Heb 9:7
**4:4** e Lev 1:3

[a]1 Traditionally *peace offering*; also in verses 3, 6 and 9

LORD. 5 Then the anointed priest shall take some of the bull's blood and carry it into the Tent of Meeting. 6 He is to dip his finger into the blood and sprinkle some of it seven times before the LORD, in front of the curtain of the sanctuary. 7 The priest shall then put some of the blood on the horns of the altar of fragrant incense that is before the LORD in the Tent of Meeting. The rest of the bull's blood he shall pour out at the base of the altar[f] of burnt offering[g] at the entrance to the Tent of Meeting. 8 He shall remove all the fat[h] from the bull of the sin offering—the fat that covers the inner parts or is connected to them, 9 both kidneys with the fat on them near the loins, and the covering of the liver, which he will remove with the kidneys— 10 just as the fat is removed from the ox[a] sacrificed as a fellowship offering.[b] Then the priest shall burn them on the altar of burnt offering. 11 But the hide of the bull and all its flesh, as well as the head and legs, the inner parts and offal[i]— 12 that is, all the rest of the bull—he must take outside the camp[j] to a place ceremonially clean,[k] where the ashes are thrown, and burn it in a wood fire on the ash heap.

13 " 'If the whole Israelite community sins unintentionally[l] and does what is forbidden in any of the LORD's commands, even though the community is unaware of the matter, they are guilty. 14 When they become aware of the sin they committed, the assembly must bring a young bull[m] as a sin offering[n] and present it before the Tent of Meeting. 15 The elders of the community are to lay their hands on the bull's head[o] before the LORD, and the bull shall be slaughtered before the LORD. 16 Then the anointed priest is to take some of the bull's blood into the Tent of Meeting. 17 He shall dip his finger into the blood and sprinkle it before the LORD[p] seven times in front of the curtain. 18 He is to put some of the blood on the horns of the altar that is before the LORD in the Tent of Meeting. The rest of the blood he shall pour out at the base of the altar of burnt offering at the entrance to the Tent of Meeting. 19 He shall remove all the fat from it and burn it on the altar, 20 and do with this bull just as he did with the bull for the sin offering. In this way the priest will make atonement for them, and they will be forgiven.[q] 21 Then he shall take the bull outside the camp and burn it as he burned the first bull. This is the sin offering for the community.

22 " 'When a leader sins unintentionally[r] and does what is forbidden in any of the commands of the LORD his God, he is guilty. 23 When he is made aware of the sin he committed, he must bring as his offering a male goat without defect. 24 He is to lay his hand on the goat's head and slaughter it at the place where the burnt offering is slaughtered before the LORD. It is a sin offering. 25 Then the priest shall take some of the blood of the sin offering with his finger and put it on the horns of the altar of burnt offering and pour out the rest of the blood at the base of the altar.[s] 26 He shall burn all the fat on the altar as he burned the fat of the fellowship offering. In this way the priest will make atonement for the man's sin, and he will be forgiven.

27 " 'If a member of the community sins unintentionally[t] and does what is forbidden in any of the LORD's commands, he is guilty. 28 When he is made aware of the sin he committed, he must bring as his offering for the sin he committed a female goat without defect. 29 He is to lay his hand on the head[u] of the sin offering[v] and slaughter it at the place of the burnt offering. 30 Then the priest is to take some of the blood with his finger and put it on the horns of the altar of burnt offering and pour out the rest of the blood at the base of the altar. 31 He shall remove all the fat, just as the fat is removed from the fellowship offering, and the priest shall burn it on the altar as an aroma pleasing to the LORD.[w] In this way the priest will make atonement for him, and he will be forgiven.

32 " 'If he brings a lamb as his sin offering, he is to bring a female without defect. 33 He is to lay his hand on its head and slaughter it for a sin offering at the place where the burnt offering is slaughtered. 34 Then the priest shall take some of the blood of the sin offering with his finger and put it on the horns of the altar of burnt offering and pour out the rest of the blood at the base of the

**4:7** f Lev 8:15 g Lev 5:9; 9:9; 16:18
**4:8** h Lev 3:3–5
**4:11** i Nu 19:5
**4:12** j Heb 13:11 k Lev 6:11
**4:13** l ver 2; Lev 5:2–4,17; Nu 15:24–26
**4:14** m ver 3 n ver 23,28
**4:15** o Lev 1:4; 8:14,22; Nu 8:10
**4:17** p ver 6
**4:20** q Nu 15:25
**4:22** r ver 2
**4:25** s ver 7,18,30,34; Lev 9:9
**4:27** t ver 2; Nu 15:27
**4:29** u ver 4,24 v Lev 1:4
**4:31** w Ge 8:21

[a] 10 The Hebrew word can include both male and female. [b] 10 Traditionally *peace offering*; also in verses 26, 31 and 35

**4:35** x ver 26,31
**5:1** y Pr 29:24
**5:2** z Lev 11:11, 24–40
**5:3** a Nu 19:11–16
**5:5** b Lev 16:21; 26:40; Nu 5:7
**5:7** c Lev 12:8
**5:9** d Lev 4:7,18
**5:10** e Lev 1:14–17

altar. 35 He shall remove all the fat, just as the fat is removed from the lamb of the fellowship offering, and the priest shall burn it on the altar[x] on top of the offerings made to the LORD by fire. In this way the priest will make atonement for him for the sin he has committed, and he will be forgiven.

5 "'If a person sins because he does not speak up when he hears a public charge to testify[y] regarding something he has seen or learned about, he will be held responsible.

2 "'Or if a person touches anything ceremonially unclean—whether the carcasses of unclean wild animals or of unclean livestock or of unclean creatures that move along the ground[z]—even though he is unaware of it, he has become unclean and is guilty.

3 "'Or if he touches human uncleanness[a]—anything that would make him unclean—even though he is unaware of it, when he learns of it he will be guilty.

4 "'Or if a person thoughtlessly takes an oath to do anything, whether good or evil—in any matter one might carelessly swear about—even though he is unaware of it, in any case when he learns of it he will be guilty.

5 "'When anyone is guilty in any of these ways, he must confess[b] in what way he has sinned 6 and, as a penalty for the sin he has committed, he must bring to the LORD a female lamb or goat from the flock as a sin offering; and the priest shall make atonement for him for his sin.

7 "'If he cannot afford[c] a lamb, he is to bring two doves or two young pigeons to the LORD as a penalty for his sin—one for a sin offering and the other for a burnt offering. 8 He is to bring them to the priest, who shall first offer the one for the sin offering. He is to wring its head from its neck, not severing it completely, 9 and is to sprinkle some of the blood of the sin offering against the side of the altar; the rest of the blood must be drained out at the base of the altar.[d] It is a sin offering. 10 The priest shall then offer the other as a burnt offering in the prescribed way[e] and make atonement for him for the sin he has committed, and he will be forgiven.

11 "'If, however, he cannot afford two doves or two young pigeons, he is to bring as an offering for his sin a tenth of an ephah[a] of fine flour for a sin offering. He must not put oil or incense on it, because it is a sin offering. 12 He is to bring it to the priest, who shall take a handful of it as a memorial portion and burn it on the altar on top of the offerings made to the LORD by fire. It is a sin offering. 13 In this way the priest will make atonement for him for any of these sins he has committed, and he will be forgiven. The rest of the offering will belong to the priest,[f] as in the case of the grain offering.'"

## The Guilt Offering

14 The LORD said to Moses: 15 "When a person commits a violation and sins unintentionally in regard to any of the LORD's holy things, he is to bring to the LORD as a penalty a ram from the flock, one without defect and of the proper value in silver, according to the sanctuary shekel.[b] It is a guilt offering. 16 He must make restitution[g] for what he has failed to do in regard to the holy things, add a fifth of the value[h] to that and give it all to the priest, who will make atonement for him with the ram as a guilt offering, and he will be forgiven.

17 "If a person sins and does what is forbidden in any of the LORD's commands, even though he does not know it,[i] he is guilty and will be held responsible. 18 He is to bring to the priest as a guilt offering a ram from the

**5:13** f Lev 2:3
**5:16** g Lev 6:4 h Lev 22:14; Nu 5:7
**5:17** i Lev 4:2

*Lord,*

*where I have stumbled, forgive me.*

*Allow your Spirit to convict me in the areas in which I need to be purified.*

*In Jesus' perfect name I pray,*

*Amen*

LEVITICUS 5:14–19

[a] 11 That is, probably about 2 quarts (about 2 liters) [b] 15 That is, about 2/5 ounce (about 11.5 grams)

**5:18** j ver 15
**6:2** k Ex 22:7
**6:3** l Dt 22:1–3
**6:5** m Nu 5:7; n Lev 5:15
**6:6** o Lev 5:15
**6:10** p Ex 28:39–42,43

flock, one without defect and of the proper
value. In this way the priest will make atone-
ment for him for the wrong he has commit-
ted unintentionally, and he will be forgiven.[j]
19 It is a guilt offering; he has been guilty of[a]
wrongdoing against the LORD."

6 The LORD said to Moses: 2 "If anyone sins
and is unfaithful to the LORD by deceiv-
ing his neighbor about something entrusted
to him or left in his care[k] or stolen, or if he
cheats him, 3 or if he finds lost property and
lies about it,[l] or if he swears falsely, or if he
commits any such sin that people may do—
4 when he thus sins and becomes guilty, he
must return what he has stolen or taken by
extortion, or what was entrusted to him, or
the lost property he found, 5 or whatever it
was he swore falsely about. He must make
restitution[m] in full, add a fifth of the value
to it and give it all to the owner on the day
he presents his guilt offering.[n] 6 And as a
penalty he must bring to the priest, that is,
to the LORD, his guilt offering,[o] a ram from
the flock, one without defect and of the
proper value. 7 In this way the priest will
make atonement for him before the LORD,
and he will be forgiven for any of these
things he did that made him guilty."

## The Burnt Offering

8 The LORD said to Moses: 9 "Give Aaron
and his sons this command: 'These are
the regulations for the burnt offering: The
burnt offering is to remain on the altar
hearth throughout the night, till morning,
and the fire must be kept burning on the al-
tar. 10 The priest shall then put on his linen
clothes, with linen undergarments next to
his body,[p] and shall remove the ashes of the
burnt offering that the fire has consumed
on the altar and place them beside the altar.
11 Then he is to take off these clothes and put
on others, and carry the ashes outside the
camp to a place that is ceremonially clean.
12 The fire on the altar must be kept burning;
it must not go out. Every morning the priest
is to add firewood and arrange the burnt
offering on the fire and burn the fat of the
fellowship offerings[b] on it. 13 The fire must
be kept burning on the altar continuously;
it must not go out.

## The Grain Offering

14 "'These are the regulations for the grain
offering: Aaron's sons are to bring it before
the LORD, in front of the altar. 15 The priest is to
take a handful of fine flour and oil, together
with all the incense on the grain offering,
and burn the memorial portion on the altar
as an aroma pleasing to the LORD. 16 Aaron
and his sons[q] shall eat the rest of it, but it is to
be eaten without yeast[r] in a holy place; they
are to eat it in the courtyard of the Tent of
Meeting. 17 It must not be baked with yeast;
I have given it as their share of the offerings
made to me by fire. Like the sin offering and
the guilt offering, it is most holy. 18 Any male
descendant of Aaron may eat it.[s] It is his reg-
ular share of the offerings made to the LORD
by fire for the generations to come. Whatever
touches them will become holy.[c]'"

19 The LORD also said to Moses, 20 "This is
the offering Aaron and his sons are to bring
to the LORD on the day he[d] is anointed: a
tenth of an ephah[e] of fine flour as a regular
grain offering,[t] half of it in the morning and
half in the evening. 21 Prepare it with oil on
a griddle;[u] bring it well-mixed and present
the grain offering broken[f] in pieces as an
aroma pleasing to the LORD. 22 The son who is
to succeed him as anointed priest shall pre-
pare it. It is the LORD's regular share and is
to be burned completely. 23 Every grain offer-
ing of a priest shall be burned completely; it
must not be eaten."

## The Sin Offering

24 The LORD said to Moses, 25 "Say to Aaron
and his sons: 'These are the regulations for
the sin offering: The sin offering is to be
slaughtered before the LORD in the place[v] the
burnt offering is slaughtered; it is most holy.
26 The priest who offers it shall eat it; it is to
be eaten in a holy place,[w] in the courtyard
of the Tent of Meeting. 27 Whatever touches
any of the flesh will become holy, and if any
of the blood is spattered on a garment, you
must wash it in a holy place. 28 The clay pot[x]
the meat is cooked in must be broken; but if
it is cooked in a bronze pot, the pot is to be
scoured and rinsed with water. 29 Any male

**6:16** q Lev 2:3; r Lev 2:11
**6:18** s ver 29; Nu 18:9–10
**6:20** t Ex 29:2
**6:21** u Lev 2:5
**6:25** v Lev 1:5,11
**6:26** w ver 16
**6:28** x Lev 11:33; 15:12

[a]19 Or *has made full expiation for his* [b]12 Traditionally *peace offerings* [c]18 Or *Whoever touches them must be holy*; similarly in verse 27 [d]20 Or *each* [e]20 That is, probably about 2 quarts (about 2 liters) [f]21 The meaning of the Hebrew for this word is uncertain.

in a priest's family may eat it;[y] it is most
holy. 30 But any sin offering whose blood is
brought into the Tent of Meeting to make
atonement in the Holy Place must not be
eaten; it must be burned.

## The Guilt Offering

7 " 'These are the regulations for the guilt
offering,[z] which is most holy: 2 The guilt
offering is to be slaughtered in the place
where the burnt offering is slaughtered,
and its blood is to be sprinkled against the
altar on all sides. 3 All its fat shall be offered:
the fat tail and the fat that covers the inner
parts, 4 both kidneys with the fat on them
near the loins, and the covering of the liver,
which is to be removed with the kidneys.
5 The priest shall burn them on the altar as
an offering made to the LORD by fire. It is a
guilt offering. 6 Any male in a priest's family
may eat it,[a] but it must be eaten in a holy
place; it is most holy.[b]

7 " 'The same law applies to both the sin
offering and the guilt offering: They belong
to the priest[c] who makes atonement with
them. 8 The priest who offers a burnt offer-
ing for anyone may keep its hide for him-
self. 9 Every grain offering baked in an oven
or cooked in a pan or on a griddle[d] belongs
to the priest who offers it, 10 and every grain
offering, whether mixed with oil or dry, be-
longs equally to all the sons of Aaron.

## The Fellowship Offering

11 " 'These are the regulations for the fel-
lowship offering[a] a person may present to
the LORD:

12 " 'If he offers it as an expression of
thankfulness, then along with this thank
offering he is to offer cakes of bread made
without yeast and mixed with oil, wafers[e]
made without yeast and spread with oil, and
cakes of fine flour well-kneaded and mixed
with oil. 13 Along with his fellowship offering
of thanksgiving he is to present an offering
with cakes of bread made with yeast.[f] 14 He
is to bring one of each kind as an offering,
a contribution to the LORD; it belongs to the
priest who sprinkles the blood of the fellow-
ship offerings. 15 The meat of his fellowship
offering of thanksgiving must be eaten on
the day it is offered; he must leave none of
it till morning.[g]

16 " 'If, however, his offering is the result
of a vow or is a freewill offering, the sacri-
fice shall be eaten on the day he offers it, but
anything left over may be eaten on the next
day.[h] 17 Any meat of the sacrifice left over till
the third day must be burned up. 18 If any
meat of the fellowship offering is eaten on
the third day, it will not be accepted.[i] It will
not be credited to the one who offered it, for
it is impure; the person who eats any of it
will be held responsible.

19 " 'Meat that touches anything ceremo-
nially unclean must not be eaten; it must
be burned up. As for other meat, anyone
ceremonially clean may eat it. 20 But if any-
one who is unclean eats any meat of the
fellowship offering belonging to the LORD,
that person must be cut off from his people.[j]
21 If anyone touches something unclean—
whether human uncleanness or an unclean
animal or any unclean, detestable thing—
and then eats any of the meat of the fellow-
ship offering belonging to the LORD, that
person must be cut off from his people.' "

## Eating Fat and Blood Forbidden

22 The LORD said to Moses, 23 "Say to the
Israelites: 'Do not eat any of the fat of cat-
tle, sheep or goats.[k] 24 The fat of an animal
found dead or torn by wild animals may be
used for any other purpose, but you must
not eat it. 25 Anyone who eats the fat of an an-
imal from which an offering by fire may be[b]
made to the LORD must be cut off from his
people. 26 And wherever you live, you must
not eat the blood[l] of any bird or animal. 27 If
anyone eats blood,[m] that person must be cut
off from his people.' "

## The Priests' Share

28 The LORD said to Moses, 29 "Say to the
Israelites: 'Anyone who brings a fellowship
offering to the LORD is to bring part of it
as his sacrifice to the LORD. 30 With his own
hands he is to bring the offering made to the
LORD by fire; he is to bring the fat, together
with the breast, and wave the breast before
the LORD as a wave offering.[n] 31 The priest
shall burn the fat on the altar, but the breast

**6:29** y ver 18
**7:1** z Lev 5:14–6:7
**7:6** a Lev 6:18 b Lev 2:3
**7:7** c Lev 6:17,26
**7:9** d Lev 2:5
**7:12** e Lev 2:4
**7:13** f Am 4:5
**7:15** g Lev 22:30
**7:16** h Lev 19:5–8
**7:18** i Lev 19:7
**7:20** j Lev 22:3–7
**7:23** k Lev 3:17; 17:13–14
**7:26** l Ge 9:4
**7:27** m Lev 17:10–24; Ac 15:20,29
**7:30** n Nu 6:20

[a] 11 Traditionally *peace offering*; also in verses 13–37 [b] 25 Or *fire is*

**7:31** o ver 34
**7:34** p Ex 29:27; Nu 18:18–19
**7:38** q Lev 1:2
**8:2** r Ex 30:23–25,30 s Ex 29:2–3
**8:3** t Nu 8:9
**8:6** u Ex 29:4
**8:8** v Ex 28:30
**8:9** w Ex 28:36

belongs to Aaron and his sons.[o] 32You are to give the right thigh of your fellowship offerings to the priest as a contribution. 33The son of Aaron who offers the blood and the fat of the fellowship offering shall have the right thigh as his share. 34From the fellowship offerings of the Israelites, I have taken the breast that is waved and the thigh that is presented and have given them to Aaron the priest and his sons[p] as their regular share from the Israelites.' "

35This is the portion of the offerings made to the LORD by fire that were allotted to Aaron and his sons on the day they were presented to serve the LORD as priests. 36On the day they were anointed, the LORD commanded that the Israelites give this to them as their regular share for the generations to come.

37These, then, are the regulations for the burnt offering, the grain offering, the sin offering, the guilt offering, the ordination offering and the fellowship offering, 38which the Lord gave Moses on Mount Sinai on the day he commanded the Israelites to bring their offerings to the Lord,[q] in the Desert of Sinai.

## The Ordination of Aaron and His Sons

8 The LORD said to Moses, 2"Bring Aaron and his sons, their garments, the anointing oil,[r] the bull for the sin offering, the two rams and the basket containing bread made without yeast,[s] 3and gather the entire assembly[t] at the entrance to the Tent of Meeting." 4Moses did as the LORD commanded him, and the assembly gathered at the entrance to the Tent of Meeting.

5Moses said to the assembly, "This is what the LORD has commanded to be done." 6Then Moses brought Aaron and his sons forward and washed them with water.[u] 7He put the tunic on Aaron, tied the sash around him, clothed him with the robe and put the ephod on him. He also tied the ephod to him by its skillfully woven waistband; so it was fastened on him. 8He placed the breastpiece on him and put the Urim and Thummim[v] in the breastpiece. 9Then he placed the turban on Aaron's head and set the gold plate, the sacred diadem,[w] on the front of it, as the LORD commanded Moses.

10Then Moses took the anointing oil[x] and anointed the tabernacle and everything in it, and so consecrated them. 11He sprinkled some of the oil on the altar seven times, anointing the altar and all its utensils and the basin with its stand, to consecrate them. 12He poured some of the anointing oil on Aaron's head and anointed him to consecrate him.[y] 13Then he brought Aaron's sons forward, put tunics on them, tied sashes around them and put headbands on them, as the LORD commanded Moses.

14He then presented the bull[z] for the sin offering,[a] and Aaron and his sons laid their hands on its head. 15Moses slaughtered the bull and took some of the blood, and with his finger he put it on all the horns of the altar[b] to purify the altar.[c] He poured out the rest of the blood at the base of the altar. So he consecrated it to make atonement for it.[d] 16Moses also took all the fat around the inner parts, the covering of the liver, and both kidneys and their fat, and burned it on the altar. 17But the bull with its hide and its flesh and its offal[e] he burned up outside the camp,[f] as the LORD commanded Moses.

18He then presented the ram for the burnt offering, and Aaron and his sons laid their hands on its head. 19Then Moses slaughtered the ram and sprinkled the blood against the altar on all sides. 20He cut the ram into pieces and burned the head, the pieces and the fat. 21He washed the inner parts and the legs with water and burned the whole ram on the altar as a burnt offering, a pleasing aroma, an offering made to the LORD by fire, as the LORD commanded Moses.

22He then presented the other ram, the ram for the ordination, and Aaron and his sons laid their hands on its head. 23Moses slaughtered the ram and took some of its blood and put it on the lobe of Aaron's right ear, on the thumb of his right hand and on the big toe of his right foot. 24Moses also brought Aaron's sons forward and put some of the blood on the lobes of their right ears, on the thumbs of their right hands and on the big toes of their right feet. Then he sprinkled blood against the altar on all sides. 25He took the fat, the fat tail, all the fat around the inner parts, the covering of the liver, both kidneys and their fat and the

**8:10** x ver 2
**8:12** y Ex 30:30
**8:14** z Lev 4:3 a Ps 66:15; Eze 43:19
**8:15** b Lev 4:7 c Heb 9:22 d Eze 43:20
**8:17** e Lev 4:11 f Lev 4:12

8:34
g Heb 7:16

right thigh. [26]Then from the basket of bread made without yeast, which was before the LORD, he took a cake of bread, and one made with oil, and a wafer; he put these on the fat portions and on the right thigh. [27]He put all these in the hands of Aaron and his sons and waved them before the LORD as a wave offering. [28]Then Moses took them from their hands and burned them on the altar on top of the burnt offering as an ordination offering, a pleasing aroma, an offering made to the LORD by fire. [29]He also took the breast—Moses' share of the ordination ram—and waved it before the LORD as a wave offering, as the LORD commanded Moses.

[30]Then Moses took some of the anointing oil and some of the blood from the altar and sprinkled them on Aaron and his garments and on his sons and their garments. So he consecrated Aaron and his garments and his sons and their garments.

[31]Moses then said to Aaron and his sons, "Cook the meat at the entrance to the Tent of Meeting and eat it there with the bread from the basket of ordination offerings, as I commanded, saying,[a] 'Aaron and his sons are to eat it.' [32]Then burn up the rest of the meat and the bread. [33]Do not leave the entrance to the Tent of Meeting for seven days, until the days of your ordination are completed, for your ordination will last seven days. [34]What has been done today was commanded by the LORD[g] to make atonement for you. [35]You must stay at the entrance to the Tent of Meeting day and night for seven days and do what the LORD requires,[h] so you will not die; for that is what I have been commanded." [36]So Aaron and his sons did everything the LORD commanded through Moses.

*Woman of color,*

*Remember that I gave the ultimate sacrifice: my Son, Jesus.*

*Because I love you,*
*God*

LEVITICUS 8:34–36

## The Priests Begin Their Ministry

9 On the eighth day[i] Moses summoned Aaron and his sons and the elders of Israel. [2]He said to Aaron, "Take a bull calf for your sin offering and a ram for your burnt offering, both without defect, and present them before the LORD. [3]Then say to the Israelites: 'Take a male goat for a sin offering, a calf and a lamb—both a year old and without defect—for a burnt offering, [4]and an ox[b] and a ram for a fellowship offering[c] to sacrifice before the LORD, together with a grain offering mixed with oil. For today the LORD will appear to you.[j]'"

[5]They took the things Moses commanded to the front of the Tent of Meeting, and the entire assembly came near and stood before the LORD. [6]Then Moses said, "This is what the LORD has commanded you to do, so that the glory of the LORD[k] may appear to you."

[7]Moses said to Aaron, "Come to the altar and sacrifice your sin offering and your burnt offering and make atonement for yourself and the people; sacrifice the offering that is for the people and make atonement for them, as the LORD has commanded.[l]"

[8]So Aaron came to the altar and slaughtered the calf as a sin offering[m] for himself. [9]His sons brought the blood to him, and he dipped his finger into the blood and put it on the horns of the altar; the rest of the blood he poured out at the base of the altar. [10]On the altar he burned the fat, the kidneys and the covering of the liver from the sin offering, as the LORD commanded Moses; [11]the flesh and the hide[n] he burned up outside the camp.[o]

[12]Then he slaughtered the burnt offering. His sons handed him the blood, and he sprinkled it against the altar on all sides. [13]They handed him the burnt offering piece by piece, including the head, and he burned them on the altar. [14]He washed the inner parts and the legs and burned them on top of the burnt offering on the altar.

[15]Aaron then brought the offering that

8:35
h Nu 3:7; Dt 11:1; 1Ki 2:3

9:1
i Eze 43:27

9:4
j Ex 29:43

9:6
k ver 23

9:7
l Heb 5:1,3; 7:27

9:8
m Lev 4:1–12

9:11
n Lev 4:11
o Lev 8:17

[a]31 Or *I was commanded:* [b]4 The Hebrew word can include both male and female; also in verses 18 and 19.
[c]4 Traditionally *peace offering*; also in verses 18 and 22

**9:16** p Lev 1:1–13
**9:17** q Lev 2:1–2
**9:18** r Lev 3:1–11
**9:21** s Lev 7:30–34
**9:22** t Nu 6:23; Dt 21:5; Lk 24:50
**9:23** u ver 6
**9:24** v Jdg 6:21; 2Ch 7:1 w 1Ki 18:39
**10:1** x Nu 3:2–4 y Lev 16:12
**10:3** z Ex 19:22 a Ex 30:29; Lev 21:6; Eze 28:22

was for the people. He took the goat for the people's sin offering and slaughtered it and offered it for a sin offering as he did with the first one.

[16]He brought the burnt offering and offered it in the prescribed way.[p] [17]He also brought the grain offering, took a handful of it and burned it on the altar in addition to the morning's burnt offering.[q]

[18]He slaughtered the ox and the ram as the fellowship offering for the people.[r] His sons handed him the blood, and he sprinkled it against the altar on all sides. [19]But the fat portions of the ox and the ram—the fat tail, the layer of fat, the kidneys and the covering of the liver— [20]these they laid on the breasts, and then Aaron burned the fat on the altar. [21]Aaron waved the breasts and the right thigh before the LORD as a wave offering,[s] as Moses commanded.

[22]Then Aaron lifted his hands toward the people and blessed them.[t] And having sacrificed the sin offering, the burnt offering and the fellowship offering, he stepped down.

[23]Moses and Aaron then went into the Tent of Meeting. When they came out, they blessed the people; and the glory of the LORD[u] appeared to all the people. [24]Fire[v] came out from the presence of the LORD and consumed the burnt offering and the fat portions on the altar. And when all the people saw it, they shouted for joy and fell facedown.[w]

## The Death of Nadab and Abihu

**10** Aaron's sons Nadab and Abihu[x] took their censers, put fire in them[y] and added incense; and they offered unauthorized fire before the LORD, contrary to his command. [2]So fire came out from the presence of the LORD and consumed them, and they died before the LORD. [3]Moses then said to Aaron, "This is what the LORD spoke of when he said:

"'Among those who approach me[z]
I will show myself holy;[a]
in the sight of all the people
I will be honored.'"

Aaron remained silent.

[4]Moses summoned Mishael and Elzaphan,[b] sons of Aaron's uncle Uzziel, and said to them, "Come here; carry your cousins outside the camp, away from the front of the sanctuary." [5]So they came and carried them, still in their tunics, outside the camp, as Moses ordered.

[6]Then Moses said to Aaron and his sons Eleazar and Ithamar, "Do not let your hair become unkempt,[a][c] and do not tear your clothes, or you will die and the LORD will be angry with the whole community.[d] But your relatives, all the house of Israel, may mourn for those the LORD has destroyed by fire. [7]Do not leave the entrance to the Tent of Meeting or you will die, because the LORD's anointing oil[e] is on you." So they did as Moses said.

[8]Then the LORD said to Aaron, [9]"You and your sons are not to drink wine or other fermented drink[f] whenever you go into the Tent of Meeting, or you will die. This is a lasting ordinance for the generations to come. [10]You must distinguish between the holy and the common, between the unclean and the clean, [11]and you must teach the Israelites all the decrees the LORD has given them through Moses."

[12]Moses said to Aaron and his remaining sons, Eleazar and Ithamar, "Take the grain offering left over from the offerings made to the LORD by fire and eat it prepared without yeast beside the altar,[g] for it is most holy. [13]Eat it in a holy place, because it is your share and your sons' share of the offerings made to the LORD by fire; for so I have been commanded. [14]But you and your sons and your daughters may eat the breast that was waved and the thigh that was presented. Eat them in a ceremonially clean place; they have been given to you and your children as your share of the Israelites' fellowship offerings.[b] [15]The thigh[h] that was presented and the breast that was waved must be brought with the fat portions of the offerings made by fire, to be waved before the LORD as a wave offering. This will be the regular share for you and your children, as the LORD has commanded."

[16]When Moses inquired about the goat of the sin offering[i] and found that it had been burned up, he was angry with Eleazar and Ithamar, Aaron's remaining sons, and

**10:4** b Ex 6:22
**10:6** c Lev 21:10 d Nu 16:22; Jos 7:1
**10:7** e Lev 21:12
**10:9** f Eze 44:21; Lk 1:15; 1Ti 3:3; Tit 1:7
**10:12** g Lev 6:14–18
**10:15** h Lev 7:34
**10:16** i Lev 9:3

[a]6 Or *Do not uncover your heads* [b]14 Traditionally *peace offerings*

**10:17** j Lev 6:24–30
**10:18** k Lev 6:26,30
**10:19** l Lev 9:12
**11:7** m Isa 65:4
**11:8** n Heb 9:10

asked, 17 "Why didn't you eat the sin offering[j] in the sanctuary area? It is most holy; it was given to you to take away the guilt of the community by making atonement for them before the LORD. 18 Since its blood was not taken into the Holy Place,[k] you should have eaten the goat in the sanctuary area, as I commanded."

19 Aaron replied to Moses, "Today they sacrificed their sin offering and their burnt offering[l] before the LORD, but such things as this have happened to me. Would the LORD have been pleased if I had eaten the sin offering today?" 20 When Moses heard this, he was satisfied.

## Clean and Unclean Food

**11** The LORD said to Moses and Aaron, 2 "Say to the Israelites: 'Of all the animals that live on land, these are the ones you may eat: 3 You may eat any animal that has a split hoof completely divided and that chews the cud.

4 " 'There are some that only chew the cud or only have a split hoof, but you must not eat them. The camel, though it chews the cud, does not have a split hoof; it is ceremonially unclean for you. 5 The coney,[a] though it chews the cud, does not have a split hoof; it is unclean for you. 6 The rabbit, though it chews the cud, does not have a split hoof; it is unclean for you. 7 And the pig,[m] though it has a split hoof completely divided, does not chew the cud; it is unclean for you. 8 You must not eat their meat or touch their carcasses; they are unclean for you.[n]

9 " 'Of all the creatures living in the water of the seas and the streams, you may eat any that have fins and scales. 10 But all creatures in the seas or streams that do not have fins and scales—whether among all the swarming things or among all the other living creatures in the water—you are to detest. 11 And since you are to detest them, you must not eat their meat and you must detest their carcasses. 12 Anything living in the water that does not have fins and scales is to be detestable to you.

13 " 'These are the birds you are to detest and not eat because they are detestable: the eagle, the vulture, the black vulture, 14 the red kite, any kind of black kite, 15 any kind of raven, 16 the horned owl, the screech owl, the gull, any kind of hawk, 17 the little owl, the cormorant, the great owl, 18 the white owl, the desert owl, the osprey, 19 the stork, any kind of heron, the hoopoe and the bat.[b]

20 " 'All flying insects that walk on all fours are to be detestable to you. 21 There are, however, some winged creatures that walk on all fours that you may eat: those that have jointed legs for hopping on the ground. 22 Of these you may eat any kind of locust,[o] katydid, cricket or grasshopper. 23 But all other winged creatures that have four legs you are to detest.

24 " 'You will make yourselves unclean by these; whoever touches their carcasses will be unclean till evening. 25 Whoever picks up one of their carcasses must wash his clothes, and he will be unclean till evening.

26 " 'Every animal that has a split hoof not completely divided or that does not chew the cud is unclean for you; whoever touches ⌞the carcass of⌟ any of them will be unclean. 27 Of all the animals that walk on all fours, those that walk on their paws are unclean for you; whoever touches their carcasses will be unclean till evening. 28 Anyone who picks up their carcasses must wash his clothes, and he will be unclean till evening. They are unclean for you.

29 " 'Of the animals that move about on the ground, these are unclean for you: the weasel, the rat, any kind of great lizard, 30 the gecko, the monitor lizard, the wall lizard, the skink and the chameleon. 31 Of all those that move along the ground, these are unclean for you. Whoever touches them when they are dead will be unclean till evening. 32 When one of them dies and falls on something, that article, whatever its use, will be unclean, whether it is made of wood, cloth, hide or sackcloth.[p] Put it in water; it will be unclean till evening, and then it will be clean. 33 If one of them falls into a clay pot, everything in it will be unclean, and you must break the pot.[q] 34 Any food that could be eaten but has water on it from such a pot is unclean, and any liquid that could be drunk from it is unclean. 35 Anything that one of their carcasses falls on becomes

**11:22** o Mt 3:4; Mk 1:6
**11:32** p Lev 15:12
**11:33** q Lev 6:28; 15:12

[a]5 That is, the hyrax or rock badger [b]19 The precise identification of some of the birds, insects and animals in this chapter is uncertain.

**11:40** r Lev 17:15; 22:8
**11:44** s Ex 19:6 t Lev 19:2; 1Pe 1:15,16*
**11:45** u Ex 6:7; 20:2 v Ex 19:6; 1Pe 1:16*
**11:47** w Lev 10:10
**12:2** x Lev 15:19; 18:19
**12:3** y Ge 17:12; Lk 1:59; 2:21

unclean; an oven or cooking pot must be broken up. They are unclean, and you are to regard them as unclean. [36]A spring, however, or a cistern for collecting water remains clean, but anyone who touches one of these carcasses is unclean. [37]If a carcass falls on any seeds that are to be planted, they remain clean. [38]But if water has been put on the seed and a carcass falls on it, it is unclean for you.

[39]" 'If an animal that you are allowed to eat dies, anyone who touches the carcass will be unclean till evening. [40]Anyone who eats some of the carcass must wash his clothes, and he will be unclean till evening.[r] Anyone who picks up the carcass must wash his clothes, and he will be unclean till evening.

[41]" 'Every creature that moves about on the ground is detestable; it is not to be eaten. [42]You are not to eat any creature that moves about on the ground, whether it moves on its belly or walks on all fours or on many feet; it is detestable. [43]Do not defile yourselves by any of these creatures. Do not make yourselves unclean by means of them or be made unclean by them. [44]I am the LORD your God; consecrate yourselves and be holy,[s] because I am holy.[t] Do not make yourselves unclean by any creature that moves about on the ground. [45]I am the LORD who brought you up out of Egypt[u] to be your God; therefore be holy, because I am holy.[v]

[46]" 'These are the regulations concerning animals, birds, every living thing that moves in the water and every creature that moves about on the ground. [47]You must distinguish between the unclean and the clean, between living creatures that may be eaten and those that may not be eaten.[w]' "

## Purification After Childbirth

**12** The LORD said to Moses, [2]"Say to the Israelites: 'A woman who becomes pregnant and gives birth to a son will be ceremonially unclean for seven days, just as she is unclean during her monthly period.[x] [3]On the eighth day the boy is to be circumcised.[y] [4]Then the woman must wait thirty-three days to be purified from her bleeding. She must not touch anything sacred or go to the sanctuary until the days of her purification are over. [5]If she gives birth to a daughter, for two weeks the woman will be unclean, as during her period. Then she must wait sixty-six days to be purified from her bleeding.

[6]" 'When the days of her purification for a son or daughter are over,[z] she is to bring to the priest at the entrance to the Tent of Meeting a year-old lamb for a burnt offering and a young pigeon or a dove for a sin offering.[a] [7]He shall offer them before the LORD to make atonement for her, and then she will be ceremonially clean from her flow of blood.

" 'These are the regulations for the woman who gives birth to a boy or a girl. [8]If she cannot afford a lamb, she is to bring two doves or two young pigeons, one for a burnt offering and the other for a sin offering.[b] In this way the priest will make atonement for her, and she will be clean.[c]' "

## Regulations About Infectious Skin Diseases

**13** The LORD said to Moses and Aaron, [2]"When anyone has a swelling or a rash or a bright spot on his skin that may become an infectious skin disease,[a] he must be brought to Aaron the priest[d] or to one of his sons[b] who is a priest. [3]The priest is to examine the sore on his skin, and if the hair in the sore has turned white and the sore appears to be more than skin deep,[c] it is an infectious skin disease. When the priest examines him, he shall pronounce him ceremonially unclean. [4]If the spot on his skin is white but does not appear to be more than skin deep and the hair in it has not turned white, the priest is to put the infected person in isolation for seven days. [5]On the seventh day the priest is to examine him, and if he sees that the sore is unchanged and has not spread in the skin, he is to keep him in isolation another seven days. [6]On the seventh day the priest is to examine him again, and if the sore has faded and has not spread in the skin, the priest shall pronounce him clean; it is only a rash.

**12:6** z Lk 2:22 a Lev 5:7
**12:8** b Lev 5:7; Lk 2:22–24* c Lev 4:26
**13:2** d Dt 24:8

[a]2 Traditionally *leprosy*; the Hebrew word was used for various diseases affecting the skin—not necessarily leprosy; also elsewhere in this chapter. [b]2 Or *descendants* [c]3 Or *be lower than the rest of the skin*; also elsewhere in this chapter

**13:6** e Lev 11:25 f Lev 14:8,9,20,48
**13:7** g Lk 5:14
**13:18** h Ex 9:9

The man must wash his clothes,[e] and he will be clean.[f] 7But if the rash does spread in his skin after he has shown himself to the priest to be pronounced clean, he must appear before the priest again.[g] 8The priest is to examine him, and if the rash has spread in the skin, he shall pronounce him unclean; it is an infectious disease.

9"When anyone has an infectious skin disease, he must be brought to the priest. 10The priest is to examine him, and if there is a white swelling in the skin that has turned the hair white and if there is raw flesh in the swelling, 11it is a chronic skin disease and the priest shall pronounce him unclean. He is not to put him in isolation, because he is already unclean.

12"If the disease breaks out all over his skin and, so far as the priest can see, it covers all the skin of the infected person from head to foot, 13the priest is to examine him, and if the disease has covered his whole body, he shall pronounce that person clean. Since it has all turned white, he is clean. 14But whenever raw flesh appears on him, he will be unclean. 15When the priest sees the raw flesh, he shall pronounce him unclean. The raw flesh is unclean; he has an infectious disease. 16Should the raw flesh change and turn white, he must go to the priest. 17The priest is to examine him, and if the sores have turned white, the priest shall pronounce the infected person clean; then he will be clean.

18"When someone has a boil[h] on his skin and it heals, 19and in the place where the boil was, a white swelling or reddish-white spot appears, he must present himself to the priest. 20The priest is to examine it, and if it appears to be more than skin deep and the hair in it has turned white, the priest shall pronounce him unclean. It is an infectious skin disease that has broken out where the boil was. 21But if, when the priest examines it, there is no white hair in it and it is not more than skin deep and has faded, then the priest is to put him in isolation for seven days. 22If it is spreading in the skin, the priest shall pronounce him unclean; it is infectious. 23But if the spot is unchanged and has not spread, it is only a scar from the boil, and the priest shall pronounce him clean.

24"When someone has a burn on his skin and a reddish-white or white spot appears in the raw flesh of the burn, 25the priest is to examine the spot, and if the hair in it has turned white, and it appears to be more than skin deep, it is an infectious disease that has broken out in the burn. The priest shall pronounce him unclean; it is an infectious skin disease. 26But if the priest examines it and there is no white hair in the spot and if it is not more than skin deep and has faded, then the priest is to put him in isolation for seven days. 27On the seventh day the priest is to examine him,[i] and if it is spreading in the skin, the priest shall pronounce him unclean; it is an infectious skin disease. 28If, however, the spot is unchanged and has not spread in the skin but has faded, it is a swelling from the burn, and the priest shall pronounce him clean; it is only a scar from the burn.

29"If a man or woman has a sore on the head or on the chin, 30the priest is to examine the sore, and if it appears to be more than skin deep and the hair in it is yellow and thin, the priest shall pronounce that person unclean; it is an itch, an infectious disease of the head or chin. 31But if, when the priest examines this kind of sore, it does not seem to be more than skin deep and there is no black hair in it, then the priest is to put the infected person in isolation for seven days. 32On the seventh day the priest is to examine the sore, and if the itch has not spread and there is no yellow hair in it and it does not appear to be more than skin deep, 33he must be shaved except for the diseased area, and the priest is to keep him in isolation another seven days. 34On the seventh day the priest is to examine the itch, and if it has not spread in the skin and appears to be no more than skin deep, the priest shall pronounce him clean. He must wash his clothes, and he will be clean. 35But if the itch does spread in the skin after he is pronounced clean, 36the priest is to examine him, and if the itch has spread in the skin, the priest does not need to look for yellow hair; the person is unclean.[j] 37If, however, in his judgment it is unchanged and black hair has grown in it, the itch is healed. He is clean, and the priest shall pronounce him clean.

**13:27** i ver 5
**13:36** j ver 30

**13:40** k 2Ki 2:23; Isa 15:2; Eze 29:18; Am 8:10
**13:45** l Eze 24:17,22; Mic 3:7 m La 4:15
**13:46** n Nu 5:1–4; 12:14; 2Ki 7:3; 15:5; Lk 17:12
**13:50** o Eze 44:23
**13:51** p Lev 14:44

38“When a man or woman has white spots on the skin, 39the priest is to examine them, and if the spots are dull white, it is a harmless rash that has broken out on the skin; that person is clean.

40“When a man has lost his hair and is bald,[k] he is clean. 41If he has lost his hair from the front of his scalp and has a bald forehead, he is clean. 42But if he has a reddish-white sore on his bald head or forehead, it is an infectious disease breaking out on his head or forehead. 43The priest is to examine him, and if the swollen sore on his head or forehead is reddish-white like an infectious skin disease, 44the man is diseased and is unclean. The priest shall pronounce him unclean because of the sore on his head.

45“The person with such an infectious disease must wear torn clothes, let his hair be unkempt,[a] cover the lower part of his face[l] and cry out, ‘Unclean! Unclean!’[m] 46As long as he has the infection he remains unclean. He must live alone; he must live outside the camp.[n]

## Regulations About Mildew

47“If any clothing is contaminated with mildew—any woolen or linen clothing, 48any woven or knitted material of linen or wool, any leather or anything made of leather— 49and if the contamination in the clothing, or leather, or woven or knitted material, or any leather article, is greenish or reddish, it is a spreading mildew and must be shown to the priest. 50The priest is to examine the mildew[o] and isolate the affected article for seven days. 51On the seventh day he is to examine it, and if the mildew has spread in the clothing, or the woven or knitted material, or the leather, whatever its use, it is a destructive mildew; the article is unclean.[p] 52He must burn up the clothing, or the woven or knitted material of wool or linen, or any leather article that has the contamination in it, because the mildew is destructive; the article must be burned up.

53“But if, when the priest examines it, the mildew has not spread in the clothing, or the woven or knitted material, or the leather article, 54he shall order that the contaminated article be washed. Then he is to isolate it for another seven days. 55After the affected article has been washed, the priest is to examine it, and if the mildew has not changed its appearance, even though it has not spread, it is unclean. Burn it with fire, whether the mildew has affected one side or the other. 56If, when the priest examines it, the mildew has faded after the article has been washed, he is to tear the contaminated part out of the clothing, or the leather, or the woven or knitted material. 57But if it reappears in the clothing, or in the woven or knitted material, or in the leather article, it is spreading, and whatever has the mildew must be burned with fire. 58The clothing, or the woven or knitted material, or any leather article that has been washed and is rid of the mildew, must be washed again, and it will be clean.”

59These are the regulations concerning contamination by mildew in woolen or linen clothing, woven or knitted material, or any leather article, for pronouncing them clean or unclean.

## Cleansing From Infectious Skin Diseases

14 The LORD said to Moses, 2“These are the regulations for the diseased person at the time of his ceremonial cleansing, when he is brought to the priest:[q] 3The priest is to go outside the camp and examine him. If the person has been healed of his infectious skin disease,[b] 4the priest shall order that two live clean birds and some cedar wood, scarlet yarn and hyssop be brought for the one to be cleansed.[r] 5Then the priest shall order that one of the birds be killed over fresh water in a clay pot. 6He is then to take the live bird and dip it, together with the cedar wood, the scarlet yarn and the hyssop, into the blood of the bird that was killed over the fresh water. 7Seven times he shall sprinkle[s] the one to be cleansed of the infectious disease and pronounce him clean. Then he is to release the live bird in the open fields.

8“The person to be cleansed must wash his clothes,[t] shave off all his hair and bathe with water; then he will be ceremonially

**14:2** q Mt 8:2–4; Mk 1:40–44; Lk 5:12–14; 17:14
**14:4** r Nu 19:6
**14:7** s 2Ki 5:10,14
**14:8** t Lev 11:25; 13:6

[a]45 Or *clothes, uncover his head* [b]3 Traditionally *leprosy*; the Hebrew word was used for various diseases affecting the skin—not necessarily leprosy; also elsewhere in this chapter.

clean. After this he may come into the camp, but he must stay outside his tent for seven days. 9On the seventh day he must shave off all his hair; he must shave his head, his beard, his eyebrows and the rest of his hair. He must wash his clothes and bathe himself with water, and he will be clean.

10"On the eighth day he must bring two male lambs and one ewe lamb a year old, each without defect, along with three-tenths of an ephah[a] of fine flour mixed with oil for a grain offering, and one log[b] of oil. 11The priest who pronounces him clean shall present both the one to be cleansed and his offerings before the LORD at the entrance to the Tent of Meeting.

12"Then the priest is to take one of the male lambs and offer it as a guilt offering,[u] along with the log of oil; he shall wave them before the LORD as a wave offering.[v] 13He is to slaughter the lamb in the holy place[w] where the sin offering and the burnt offering are slaughtered. Like the sin offering, the guilt offering belongs to the priest;[x] it is most holy. 14The priest is to take some of the blood of the guilt offering and put it on the lobe of the right ear of the one to be cleansed, on the thumb of his right hand and on the big toe of his right foot.[y] 15The priest shall then take some of the log of oil, pour it in the palm of his own left hand, 16dip his right forefinger into the oil in his palm, and with his finger sprinkle some of it before the LORD seven times. 17The priest is to put some of the oil remaining in his palm on the lobe of the right ear of the one to be cleansed, on the thumb of his right hand and on the big toe of his right foot, on top of the blood of the guilt offering. 18The rest of the oil in his palm the priest shall put on the head of the one to be cleansed and make atonement for him before the LORD.

19"Then the priest is to sacrifice the sin offering and make atonement for the one to be cleansed from his uncleanness. After that, the priest shall slaughter the burnt offering 20and offer it on the altar, together with the grain offering, and make atonement for him, and he will be clean.

21"If, however, he is poor[z] and cannot afford these, he must take one male lamb as a guilt offering to be waved to make atonement for him, together with a tenth of an ephah[c] of fine flour mixed with oil for a grain offering, a log of oil, 22and two doves or two young pigeons, which he can afford, one for a sin offering and the other for a burnt offering.

23"On the eighth day he must bring them for his cleansing to the priest at the entrance to the Tent of Meeting, before the LORD.[a] 24The priest is to take the lamb for the guilt offering, together with the log of oil,[b] and wave them before the LORD as a wave offering.[c] 25He shall slaughter the lamb for the guilt offering and take some of its blood and put it on the lobe of the right ear of the one to be cleansed, on the thumb of his right hand and on the big toe of his right foot.[d] 26The priest is to pour some of the oil into the palm of his own left hand, 27and with his right forefinger sprinkle some of the oil from his palm seven times before the LORD. 28Some of the oil in his palm he is to put on the same places he put the blood of the guilt offering—on the lobe of the right ear of the one to be cleansed, on the thumb of his right hand and on the big toe of his right foot. 29The rest of the oil in his palm the priest shall put on the head of the one to be cleansed, to make atonement for him before the LORD. 30Then he shall sacrifice the doves or the young pigeons, which the person can afford, 31one[d] as a sin offering and the other as a burnt offering,[e] together with the grain offering. In this way the priest will make atonement before the LORD on behalf of the one to be cleansed."

32These are the regulations for anyone who has an infectious skin disease and who cannot afford the regular offerings for his cleansing.

## Cleansing From Mildew

33The LORD said to Moses and Aaron, 34"When you enter the land of Canaan, which I am giving you as your possession,[f] and I put a spreading mildew in a house in that land, 35the owner of the house must go and tell the priest, 'I have seen something that looks like mildew in my house.' 36The priest is to order the house to be emptied before

**14:12** u Lev 5:18; 6:6–7 v Ex 29:24
**14:13** w Ex 29:11 x Lev 6:24–30; 7:7
**14:14** y Ex 29:20; Lev 8:23
**14:21** z Lev 5:7; 12:8
**14:23** a ver 10,11
**14:24** b ver 10 c ver 12
**14:25** d ver 14
**14:31** e Lev 5:7
**14:34** f Ge 17:8; Nu 32:22; Dt 7:1; 32:49

[a]10 That is, probably about 6 quarts (about 6.5 liters) [b]10 That is, probably about 2/3 pint (about 0.3 liter); also in verses 12, 15, 21 and 24 [c]21 That is, probably about 2 quarts (about 2 liters) [d]31 Septuagint and Syriac; Hebrew *31such as the person can afford, one*

**14:44** g Lev 13:51
**14:49** h ver 4
**14:51** i Ps 51:7
**14:53** j ver 20

he goes in to examine the mildew, so that nothing in the house will be pronounced unclean. After this the priest is to go in and inspect the house. 37 He is to examine the mildew on the walls, and if it has greenish or reddish depressions that appear to be deeper than the surface of the wall, 38 the priest shall go out the doorway of the house and close it up for seven days. 39 On the seventh day the priest shall return to inspect the house. If the mildew has spread on the walls, 40 he is to order that the contaminated stones be torn out and thrown into an unclean place outside the town. 41 He must have all the inside walls of the house scraped and the material that is scraped off dumped into an unclean place outside the town. 42 Then they are to take other stones to replace these and take new clay and plaster the house.

43 "If the mildew reappears in the house after the stones have been torn out and the house scraped and plastered, 44 the priest is to go and examine it and, if the mildew has spread in the house, it is a destructive mildew; the house is unclean.[g] 45 It must be torn down—its stones, timbers and all the plaster—and taken out of the town to an unclean place.

46 "Anyone who goes into the house while it is closed up will be unclean till evening. 47 Anyone who sleeps or eats in the house must wash his clothes.

48 "But if the priest comes to examine it and the mildew has not spread after the house has been plastered, he shall pronounce the house clean, because the mildew is gone. 49 To purify the house he is to take two birds and some cedar wood, scarlet yarn and hyssop.[h] 50 He shall kill one of the birds over fresh water in a clay pot. 51 Then he is to take the cedar wood, the hyssop,[i] the scarlet yarn and the live bird, dip them into the blood of the dead bird and the fresh water, and sprinkle the house seven times. 52 He shall purify the house with the bird's blood, the fresh water, the live bird, the cedar wood, the hyssop and the scarlet yarn. 53 Then he is to release the live bird in the open fields outside the town. In this way he will make atonement for the house, and it will be clean.[j]"

54 These are the regulations for any infectious skin disease,[k] for an itch, 55 for mildew[l] in clothing or in a house, 56 and for a swelling, a rash or a bright spot,[m] 57 to determine when something is clean or unclean.

These are the regulations for infectious skin diseases and mildew.

## Discharges Causing Uncleanness

15 The LORD said to Moses and Aaron, 2 "Speak to the Israelites and say to them: 'When any man has a bodily discharge,[n] the discharge is unclean. 3 Whether it continues flowing from his body or is blocked, it will make him unclean. This is how his discharge will bring about uncleanness:

4 " 'Any bed the man with a discharge lies on will be unclean, and anything he sits on will be unclean. 5 Anyone who touches his bed must wash his clothes[o] and bathe with water, and he will be unclean till evening. 6 Whoever sits on anything that the man with a discharge sat on must wash his clothes and bathe with water, and he will be unclean till evening.

7 " 'Whoever touches the man who has a discharge must wash his clothes and bathe with water, and he will be unclean till evening.

8 " 'If the man with the discharge spits on someone who is clean, that person must wash his clothes and bathe with water, and he will be unclean till evening.

9 " 'Everything the man sits on when riding will be unclean, 10 and whoever touches any of the things that were under him will be unclean till evening; whoever picks up those things must wash his clothes and bathe with water, and he will be unclean till evening.

11 " 'Anyone the man with a discharge touches without rinsing his hands with water must wash his clothes and bathe with water, and he will be unclean till evening.

12 " 'A clay pot[p] that the man touches must be broken, and any wooden article[q] is to be rinsed with water.

13 " 'When a man is cleansed from his discharge, he is to count off seven days[r] for his ceremonial cleansing; he must wash his clothes and bathe himself with fresh water, and he will be clean. 14 On the eighth day he

**14:54** k Lev 13:2,30
**14:55** l Lev 13:47–52
**14:56** m Lev 13:2
**15:2** n Lev 22:4; Nu 5:2; 2Sa 3:29; Mt 9:20
**15:5** o Lev 11:25
**15:12** p Lev 6:28 q Lev 11:32
**15:13** r Lev 8:33

**15:14** s Lev 14:22
**15:15** t Lev 5:7 u Lev 14:31 v Lev 14:18,19
**15:16** w Lev 22:4; Dt 23:10
**15:18** x 1Sa 21:4
**15:19** y Lev 12:2
**15:24** z Lev 20:18
**15:25** a Mt 9:20; Mk 5:25; Lk 8:43

must take two doves or two young pigeons[s] and come before the LORD to the entrance to the Tent of Meeting and give them to the priest. 15 The priest is to sacrifice them, the one for a sin offering[t] and the other for a burnt offering.[u] In this way he will make atonement before the LORD for the man because of his discharge.[v]

16 “‘When a man has an emission of semen,[w] he must bathe his whole body with water, and he will be unclean till evening. 17 Any clothing or leather that has semen on it must be washed with water, and it will be unclean till evening. 18 When a man lies with a woman and there is an emission of semen,[x] both must bathe with water, and they will be unclean till evening.

19 “‘When a woman has her regular flow of blood, the impurity of her monthly period[y] will last seven days, and anyone who touches her will be unclean till evening.

20 “‘Anything she lies on during her period will be unclean, and anything she sits on will be unclean. 21 Whoever touches her bed must wash his clothes and bathe with water, and he will be unclean till evening. 22 Whoever touches anything she sits on must wash his clothes and bathe with water, and he will be unclean till evening. 23 Whether it is the bed or anything she was sitting on, when anyone touches it, he will be unclean till evening.

24 “‘If a man lies with her and her monthly flow[z] touches him, he will be unclean for seven days; any bed he lies on will be unclean.

25 “‘When a woman has a discharge of blood for many days at a time other than her monthly period[a] or has a discharge that continues beyond her period, she will be unclean as long as she has the discharge, just as in the days of her period. 26 Any bed she lies on while her discharge continues will be unclean, as is her bed during her monthly period, and anything she sits on will be unclean, as during her period. 27 Whoever touches them will be unclean; he must wash his clothes and bathe with water, and he will be unclean till evening.

28 “‘When she is cleansed from her discharge, she must count off seven days, and after that she will be ceremonially clean. 29 On the eighth day she must take two doves or two young pigeons and bring them to the priest at the entrance to the Tent of Meeting. 30 The priest is to sacrifice one for a sin offering and the other for a burnt offering. In this way he will make atonement for her before the LORD for the uncleanness of her discharge.

31 “‘You must keep the Israelites separate from things that make them unclean, so they will not die in their uncleanness for defiling my dwelling place,[a][b] which is among them.’”

32 These are the regulations for a man with a discharge, for anyone made unclean by an emission of semen,[c] 33 for a woman in her monthly period, for a man or a woman with a discharge, and for a man who lies with a woman who is ceremonially unclean.[d]

## The Day of Atonement

16 The LORD spoke to Moses after the death of the two sons of Aaron who died when they approached the LORD.[e] 2 The LORD said to Moses: “Tell your brother Aaron not to come whenever he chooses[f] into the Most Holy Place behind the curtain in front of the atonement cover on the ark, or else he will die, because I appear[g] in the cloud over the atonement cover.

3 “This is how Aaron is to enter the sanctuary area: with a young bull for a sin offering and a ram for a burnt offering. 4 He is to put on the sacred linen tunic, with linen undergarments next to his body; he is to tie the linen sash around him and put on the linen turban.[h] These are sacred garments;[i] so he must bathe himself with water before he puts them on. 5 From the Israelite community[j] he is to take two male goats[k] for a sin offering and a ram for a burnt offering.

6 “Aaron is to offer the bull for his own sin offering to make atonement for himself and his household.[l] 7 Then he is to take the two goats and present them before the LORD at the entrance to the Tent of Meeting. 8 He is to cast lots for the two goats—one lot for the LORD and the other for the scapegoat.[b] 9 Aaron shall bring the goat whose lot falls

**15:31** b Nu 19:13,20; Eze 5:11; 23:38
**15:32** c ver 2
**15:33** d ver 19,24,25
**16:1** e Lev 10:1
**16:2** f Ex 30:10; Heb 9:7 g Ex 25:22
**16:4** h Ex 28:39 i Ex 28:42
**16:5** j Lev 4:13–21 k 2Ch 29:23
**16:6** l Lev 9:7; Heb 5:3; 7:27; 9:7,12

[a] 31 Or *my tabernacle* [b] 8 That is, the goat of removal; Hebrew *azazel*; also in verses 10 and 26

**16:12**
m Lev 10:1
n Ex 30:34–38
**16:14**
o Heb 9:7,13,25
p Lev 4:6
**16:15**
q Heb 9:7,12
**16:16**
r Ex 29:36

to the LORD and sacrifice it for a sin offering.
[10]But the goat chosen by lot as the scapegoat
shall be presented alive before the LORD to
be used for making atonement by sending it
into the desert as a scapegoat.
[11]"Aaron shall bring the bull for his own
sin offering to make atonement for himself
and his household, and he is to slaughter
the bull for his own sin offering. [12]He is to
take a censer full of burning coals[m] from
the altar before the LORD and two handfuls
of finely ground fragrant incense[n] and take
them behind the curtain. [13]He is to put the
incense on the fire before the LORD, and the
smoke of the incense will conceal the atone-
ment cover above the Testimony, so that he
will not die. [14]He is to take some of the bull's
blood[o] and with his finger sprinkle it on the
front of the atonement cover; then he shall
sprinkle some of it with his finger seven
times before the atonement cover.[p]
[15]"He shall then slaughter the goat for
the sin offering for the people[q] and take its
blood behind the curtain and do with it as
he did with the bull's blood: He shall sprin-
kle it on the atonement cover and in front of
it. [16]In this way he will make atonement[r] for
the Most Holy Place because of the unclean-
ness and rebellion of the Israelites, whatever
their sins have been. He is to do the same for
the Tent of Meeting, which is among them
in the midst of their uncleanness. [17]No one
is to be in the Tent of Meeting from the time
Aaron goes in to make atonement in the
Most Holy Place until he comes out, having
made atonement for himself, his household
and the whole community of Israel.
[18]"Then he shall come out to the altar
that is before the LORD and make atonement
for it. He shall take some of the bull's blood
and some of the goat's blood and put it on
all the horns of the altar. [19]He shall sprinkle
some of the blood on it with his finger seven
times to cleanse it and to consecrate it from
the uncleanness of the Israelites.
[20]"When Aaron has finished making
atonement for the Most Holy Place, the Tent
of Meeting and the altar, he shall bring for-
ward the live goat. [21]He is to lay both hands
on the head of the live goat and confess over
it all the wickedness and rebellion of the
Israelites—all their sins—and put them
on the goat's head. He shall send the goat
away into the desert in the care of a man
appointed for the task. [22]The goat will carry
on itself all their sins to a solitary place; and
the man shall release it in the desert.
[23]"Then Aaron is to go into the Tent of
Meeting and take off the linen garments he
put on before he entered the Most Holy
Place, and he is to leave them there.[s] [24]He
shall bathe himself with water in a holy
place and put on his regular garments.[t]
Then he shall come out and sacrifice the
burnt offering for himself and the burnt of-
fering for the people, to make atonement for
himself and for the people. [25]He shall also
burn the fat of the sin offering on the altar.
[26]"The man who releases the goat as a
scapegoat must wash his clothes and bathe
himself with water; afterward he may come
into the camp. [27]The bull and the goat for
the sin offerings, whose blood was brought
into the Most Holy Place to make atone-
ment, must be taken outside the camp;[u]
their hides, flesh and offal are to be burned
up. [28]The man who burns them must wash
his clothes and bathe himself with water; af-
terward he may come into the camp.
[29]"This is to be a lasting ordinance for
you: On the tenth day of the seventh month
you must deny yourselves[a][v] and not do any
work—whether native-born or an alien
living among you— [30]because on this day
atonement will be made for you, to cleanse
you. Then, before the LORD, you will be clean
from all your sins. [31]It is a sabbath of rest,
and you must deny yourselves; it is a lasting
ordinance. [32]The priest who is anointed and
ordained to succeed his father as high priest
is to make atonement. He is to put on the
sacred linen garments[w] [33]and make atone-
ment for the Most Holy Place, for the Tent
of Meeting and the altar, and for the priests
and all the people of the community.
[34]"This is to be a lasting ordinance for
you: Atonement is to be made once a year[x]
for all the sins of the Israelites."

And it was done, as the LORD commanded
Moses.

**16:23**
s Eze 42:14; 44:19
**16:24**
t ver 3–5
**16:27**
u Heb 13:11
**16:29**
v Lev 23:27,32; Nu 29:7; Isa 58:3
**16:32**
w ver 4
**16:34**
x Heb 9:7,25

[a]29 Or *must fast*; also in verse 31

## Eating Blood Forbidden

**17** The LORD said to Moses, 2 "Speak to Aaron and his sons and to all the Israelites and say to them: 'This is what the LORD has commanded: 3 Any Israelite who sacrifices an ox,[a] a lamb or a goat in the camp or outside of it 4 instead of bringing it to the entrance to the Tent of Meeting to present it as an offering to the LORD in front of the tabernacle of the LORD[y]—that man shall be considered guilty of bloodshed; he has shed blood and must be cut off from his people. 5 This is so the Israelites will bring to the LORD the sacrifices they are now making in the open fields. They must bring them to the priest, that is, to the LORD, at the entrance to the Tent of Meeting and sacrifice them as fellowship offerings.[b] 6 The priest is to sprinkle the blood against the altar of the LORD at the entrance to the Tent of Meeting and burn the fat as an aroma pleasing to the LORD.[z] 7 They must no longer offer any of their sacrifices to the goat idols[c][a] to whom they prostitute themselves.[b] This is to be a lasting ordinance for them and for the generations to come.'

8 "Say to them: 'Any Israelite or any alien living among them who offers a burnt offering or sacrifice 9 and does not bring it to the entrance to the Tent of Meeting to sacrifice it to the LORD—that man must be cut off from his people.

10 " 'Any Israelite or any alien living among them who eats any blood—I will set my face against that person who eats blood[c] and will cut him off from his people. 11 For the life of a creature is in the blood, and I have given it to you to make atonement for yourselves on the altar; it is the blood that makes atonement for one's life.[d] 12 Therefore I say to the Israelites, "None of you may eat blood, nor may an alien living among you eat blood."

13 " 'Any Israelite or any alien living among you who hunts any animal or bird that may be eaten must drain out the blood and cover it with earth,[e] 14 because the life of every creature is its blood. That is why I have said to the Israelites, "You must not eat the blood of any creature, because the life of every creature is its blood; anyone who eats it must be cut off."[f]

15 " 'Anyone, whether native-born or alien, who eats anything found dead or torn by wild animals[g] must wash his clothes and bathe with water, and he will be ceremonially unclean till evening; then he will be clean. 16 But if he does not wash his clothes and bathe himself, he will be held responsible.' "

## Unlawful Sexual Relations

**18** The LORD said to Moses, 2 "Speak to the Israelites and say to them: 'I am the LORD your God.[h] 3 You must not do as they do in Egypt, where you used to live, and you must not do as they do in the land of Canaan, where I am bringing you. Do not follow their practices. 4 You must obey my laws and be careful to follow my decrees. I am the LORD your God. 5 Keep my decrees and laws, for the man who obeys them will live by them.[i] I am the LORD.

6 " 'No one is to approach any close relative to have sexual relations. I am the LORD.

7 " 'Do not dishonor your father[j] by having sexual relations with your mother. She is your mother; do not have relations with her.

8 " 'Do not have sexual relations with your father's wife; that would dishonor your father.

9 " 'Do not have sexual relations with your sister,[k] either your father's daughter or your mother's daughter, whether she was born in the same home or elsewhere.

10 " 'Do not have sexual relations with your son's daughter or your daughter's daughter; that would dishonor you.

11 " 'Do not have sexual relations with the daughter of your father's wife, born to your father; she is your sister.

12 " 'Do not have sexual relations with your father's sister;[l] she is your father's close relative.

13 " 'Do not have sexual relations with your mother's sister, because she is your mother's close relative.

14 " 'Do not dishonor your father's brother by approaching his wife to have sexual relations; she is your aunt.[m]

**17:4** y Dt12:5–21
**17:6** z Nu18:17
**17:7** a 2Ch11:15 b Ex32:8; 34:15; Dt32:17; 1Co10:20
**17:10** c Dt12:16,23
**17:11** d Heb9:22
**17:13** e Dt12:16
**17:14** f ver11
**17:15** g Ex22:31
**18:2** h Ex6:7
**18:5** i Eze20:11; Ro10:5*; Gal3:12*
**18:7** j Lev20:11
**18:9** k Lev20:17
**18:12** l Lev20:19
**18:14** m Lev20:20

a3 The Hebrew word can include both male and female. b5 Traditionally *peace offerings* c7 Or *demons*

**18:17** n Lev 20:14
**18:19** o Lev 15:24; 20:18
**18:20** p Ex 20:14; Lev 20:10; Mt 5:27,28; 1Co 6:9; Heb 13:4
**18:21** q Lev 20:2–5 r Lev 19:12
**18:22** s Lev 20:13
**18:23** t Ex 22:19
**18:30** u Dt 11:1

15"'Do not have sexual relations with
your daughter-in-law. She is your son's wife;
do not have relations with her.
16"'Do not have sexual relations with
your brother's wife; that would dishonor
your brother.
17"'Do not have sexual relations with
both a woman and her daughter.[n] Do not
have sexual relations with either her son's
daughter or her daughter's daughter; they
are her close relatives. That is wickedness.
18"'Do not take your wife's sister as a
rival wife and have sexual relations with her
while your wife is living.
19"'Do not approach a woman to have
sexual relations during the uncleanness of
her monthly period.[o]
20"'Do not have sexual relations with
your neighbor's wife[p] and defile yourself
with her.
21"'Do not give any of your children to be
sacrificed[a] to Molech,[q] for you must not profane
the name of your God.[r] I am the LORD.
22"'Do not lie with a man as one lies with
a woman;[s] that is detestable.
23"'Do not have sexual relations with an
animal and defile yourself with it. A woman
must not present herself to an animal to
have sexual relations with it; that is a perversion.[t]
24"'Do not defile yourselves in any of
these ways, because this is how the nations
that I am going to drive out before you became
defiled. 25Even the land was defiled;
so I punished it for its sin, and the land
vomited out its inhabitants. 26But you must
keep my decrees and my laws. The nativeborn
and the aliens living among you must
not do any of these detestable things, 27for
all these things were done by the people who
lived in the land before you, and the land became
defiled. 28And if you defile the land, it
will vomit you out as it vomited out the nations
that were before you.
29"'Everyone who does any of these detestable
things—such persons must be cut
off from their people. 30Keep my requirements[u]
and do not follow any of the detestable
customs that were practiced before you
came and do not defile yourselves with
them. I am the LORD your God.'"

## Various Laws

**19** The LORD said to Moses, 2"Speak to
the entire assembly of Israel and say
to them: 'Be holy because I, the LORD your
God, am holy.
3"'Each of you must respect his mother
and father,[v] and you must observe my Sabbaths.
I am the LORD your God.
4"'Do not turn to idols or make gods of
cast metal for yourselves.[w] I am the LORD
your God.
5"'When you sacrifice a fellowship offering[b]
to the LORD, sacrifice it in such a way
that it will be accepted on your behalf. 6It
shall be eaten on the day you sacrifice it or
on the next day; anything left over until the
third day must be burned up. 7If any of it is
eaten on the third day, it is impure and will
not be accepted. 8Whoever eats it will be
held responsible because he has desecrated
what is holy to the LORD; that person must be
cut off from his people.
9"'When you reap the harvest of your
land, do not reap to the very edges of your
field or gather the gleanings of your harvest.[x]
10Do not go over your vineyard a second
time or pick up the grapes that have
fallen. Leave them for the poor and the
alien. I am the LORD your God.
11"'Do not steal.[y]
"'Do not lie.[z]
"'Do not deceive one another.
12"'Do not swear falsely by my name[a]
and so profane the name of your God. I am
the LORD.
13"'Do not defraud your neighbor or rob
him.
"'Do not hold back the wages of a hired
man overnight.
14"'Do not curse the deaf or put a stumbling
block in front of the blind,[b] but fear
your God. I am the LORD.
15"'Do not pervert justice; do not show
partiality to the poor or favoritism to the
great, but judge your neighbor fairly.
16"'Do not go about spreading slander
among your people.
"'Do not do anything that endangers
your neighbor's life. I am the LORD.
17"'Do not hate your brother in your
heart.[c] Rebuke your neighbor frankly[d] so
you will not share in his guilt.

**19:3** v Ex 20:12
**19:4** w Ex 20:4,23
**19:9** x Dt 24:19–22
**19:11** y Ex 20:15 z Eph 4:25
**19:12** a Ex 20:7; Mt 5:33
**19:14** b Dt 27:18
**19:17** c 1Jn 2:9; 3:15 d Mt 18:15; Lk 17:3

[a]21 Or *to be passed through* ⌊*the fire*⌋ [b]5 Traditionally *peace offering*

# Inspire

## LET'S TALK ABOUT SEX

We live in a society saturated with sexual images. Every time we turn on the TV, go to see a movie or listen to music, we hear and see sexual images. Products are sold using sex, ideas are promoted using sex, and standards are set using sex. Just think about the last movie you watched or the TV shows you love. Think of your favorite toothpaste or your favorite car, and remember how those items are advertised. With so much societal emphasis on sex, it's difficult to hear what God has to say about it.

God is not against sex. In fact, sexuality is one of God's gifts to human beings. However, our sex-saturated society has distorted God's original intentions for sex. Most people are looking for love and intimacy and settling for sexual relationships.

Scripture provides insight into God's intentions for sexual relationships. In Genesis 1:28, God gives human beings a command to be fruitful and multiply. His command is given to the first union he blessed—that of Adam and Eve. Sexual intercourse functioned as the seal of their union and still functions as a seal for marriages today.

What often gets left out when we talk about the Bible's view of sex is God's gift of sex for marital pleasure. Hebrews 13:4 says, "Marriage should be honored by all, and the marriage bed kept pure." First Corinthians 7:2–5 expresses the understanding that the sexual act inside of marriage is important, and the husband and wife need to be sure to meet each other's needs in a reasonable manner. The Song of Songs portrays the beauty of the relationship between a husband and wife.

While God's plan has always been for people to fulfill their sexual needs only within the context of marriage and to reject the ways of the world (see Lev 18), God does not say that our sexuality is sinful. What we are admonished to do is control our desires and bring them under the leadership of the Holy Spirit. Singleness and celibacy are gifts from God (see 1Co 7:7–8), and they are no less desirable or important to God than marriage is. Since God created our bodies, our purpose is to honor God with our bodies (see 1Co 6:18–20). We do this by acknowledging the gift of sexuality and using that gift in obedience to our Creator.

—C. Belt

### read

Leviticus 18; see also Genesis 2:18–25; Song of Songs.

**See also** the Inspire Notes "Marriage," "What Is Intimacy?" "Adultery" and "Temptation," and the Women of the Bible Note "The Bridegroom and His Bride: Soul Mates in Life."

### WOMAN of COLOR

Are you using the gift of sexuality in obedience to your Creator? If not, why not? How can you change?

For the next Inspire note, go to page 149.

*"My great hope is to laugh as much as I cry, to get my work done and try to love somebody and have the courage to accept the love in return."*

—MAYA ANGELOU, POET AND WRITER

18" 'Do not seek revenge[e] or bear a grudge[f] against one of your people, but love your neighbor as yourself.[g] I am the LORD.

19" 'Keep my decrees.

" 'Do not mate different kinds of animals.

" 'Do not plant your field with two kinds of seed.[h]

" 'Do not wear clothing woven of two kinds of material.[i]

20" 'If a man sleeps with a woman who is a slave girl promised to another man but who has not been ransomed or given her freedom, there must be due punishment. Yet they are not to be put to death, because she had not been freed. 21The man, however, must bring a ram to the entrance to the Tent of Meeting for a guilt offering to the LORD. 22With the ram of the guilt offering the priest is to make atonement for him before the LORD for the sin he has committed, and his sin will be forgiven.

23" 'When you enter the land and plant any kind of fruit tree, regard its fruit as forbidden.[a] For three years you are to consider it forbidden[a]; it must not be eaten. 24In the fourth year all its fruit will be holy, an offering of praise to the LORD. 25But in the fifth year you may eat its fruit. In this way your harvest will be increased. I am the LORD your God.

26" 'Do not eat any meat with the blood still in it.[j]

" 'Do not practice divination or sorcery.[k]

27" 'Do not cut the hair at the sides of your head or clip off the edges of your beard.[l]

28" 'Do not cut your bodies for the dead or put tattoo marks on yourselves. I am the LORD.

29" 'Do not degrade your daughter by making her a prostitute,[m] or the land will turn to prostitution and be filled with wickedness.

30" 'Observe my Sabbaths and have reverence for my sanctuary. I am the LORD.[n]

31" 'Do not turn to mediums or seek out spiritists, for you will be defiled by them. I am the LORD your God.

32" 'Rise in the presence of the aged, show respect for the elderly and revere your God. I am the LORD.

33" 'When an alien lives with you in your land, do not mistreat him. 34The alien living with you must be treated as one of your native-born. Love him as yourself, for you were aliens in Egypt. I am the LORD your God.

35" 'Do not use dishonest standards when measuring length, weight or quantity. 36Use honest scales and honest weights, an honest ephah[b] and an honest hin.[c] I am the LORD your God, who brought you out of Egypt.

37" 'Keep all my decrees and all my laws and follow them. I am the LORD.' "

## Punishments for Sin

**20** The LORD said to Moses, 2"Say to the Israelites: 'Any Israelite or any alien living in Israel who gives[d] any of his children to Molech must be put to death. The people of the community are to stone him. 3I will set my face against that man and I will cut him off from his people; for by giving his children to Molech, he has defiled my sanctuary and profaned my holy name.[o] 4If the people of the community close their eyes when that man gives one of his children to Molech and they fail to put him to death, 5I will set my face against that man and his family and will cut off from their people both him and all who follow him in prostituting themselves to Molech.

6" 'I will set my face against the person who turns to mediums and spiritists to prostitute himself by following them, and I will cut him off from his people.[p]

7" 'Consecrate yourselves and be holy, because I am the LORD your God. 8Keep my decrees and follow them. I am the LORD, who makes you holy.[e][q]

9" 'If anyone curses his father or mother,[r] he must be put to death.[s] He has cursed his father or his mother, and his blood will be on his own head.

10" 'If a man commits adultery with

**19:18** e Ro 12:19 f Ps 103:9 g Mt 5:43*; 19:16*; 22:39* Ro 13:9*
**19:19** h Dt 22:9 i Dt 22:11
**19:26** j Lev 17:10 k Dt 18:10
**19:27** l Lev 21:5
**19:29** m Dt 23:18
**19:30** n Lev 26:2
**20:3** o Lev 18:21
**20:6** p Lev 19:31
**20:8** q Ex 31:13
**20:9** r Dt 27:16 s Ex 21:17

[a]23 Hebrew *uncircumcised* [b]36 An ephah was a dry measure. [c]36 A hin was a liquid measure. [d]2 Or *sacrifices*; also in verses 3 and 4 [e]8 Or *who sanctifies you*; or *who sets you apart as holy*

**20:13** t Lev 18:22
**20:14** u Dt 27:23
**20:15** v Lev 18:23
**20:17** w Lev 18:9

*Lord,*

*I want to be more like you. I know that I have displeased you in my attitudes and actions. I want to know what holiness means, so that I may glorify you in every aspect of my life. In Jesus' name,*

*Amen*

LEVITICUS 20:7–8

another man's wife—with the wife of his neighbor—both the adulterer and the adulteress must be put to death.

11“‘If a man sleeps with his father's wife, he has dishonored his father. Both the man and the woman must be put to death; their blood will be on their own heads.

12“‘If a man sleeps with his daughter-in-law, both of them must be put to death. What they have done is a perversion; their blood will be on their own heads.

13“‘If a man lies with a man as one lies with a woman, both of them have done what is detestable.[t] They must be put to death; their blood will be on their own heads.

14“‘If a man marries both a woman and her mother, it is wicked. Both he and they must be burned in the fire, so that no wickedness will be among you.[u]

15“‘If a man has sexual relations with an animal,[v] he must be put to death, and you must kill the animal.

16“‘If a woman approaches an animal to have sexual relations with it, kill both the woman and the animal. They must be put to death; their blood will be on their own heads.

17“‘If a man marries his sister[w], the daughter of either his father or his mother, and they have sexual relations, it is a disgrace. They must be cut off before the eyes of their people. He has dishonored his sister and will be held responsible.

18“‘If a man lies with a woman during her monthly period and has sexual relations with her, he has exposed the source of her flow, and she has also uncovered it. Both of them must be cut off from their people.

19“‘Do not have sexual relations with the sister of either your mother or your father,[x] for that would dishonor a close relative; both of you would be held responsible.

20“‘If a man sleeps with his aunt,[y] he has dishonored his uncle. They will be held responsible; they will die childless.

21“‘If a man marries his brother's wife,[z] it is an act of impurity; he has dishonored his brother. They will be childless.

22“‘Keep all my decrees and laws and follow them, so that the land[a] where I am bringing you to live may not vomit you out. 23You must not live according to the customs of the nations[b] I am going to drive out before you. Because they did all these things, I abhorred them. 24But I said to you, “You will possess their land; I will give it to you as an inheritance, a land flowing with milk and honey.” I am the LORD your God, who has set you apart from the nations.[c]

25“‘You must therefore make a distinction between clean and unclean animals and between unclean and clean birds.[d] Do not defile yourselves by any animal or bird or anything that moves along the ground—those which I have set apart as unclean for you. 26You are to be holy to me[*a*] because I, the LORD, am holy, and I have set you apart from the nations to be my own.

27“‘A man or woman who is a medium or spiritist among you must be put to death.[e] You are to stone them; their blood will be on their own heads.’”

## Rules for Priests

**21** The LORD said to Moses, “Speak to the priests, the sons of Aaron, and say to them: ‘A priest must not make himself ceremonially unclean for any of his people who die, 2except for a close relative, such as his mother or father, his son or daughter, his brother, 3or an unmarried sister who is dependent on him since she has no husband—for her he may make himself unclean. 4He must not make himself unclean for people related to him by marriage,[*b*] and so defile himself.

**20:19** x Lev 18:12–13
**20:20** y Lev 18:14
**20:21** z Lev 18:16
**20:22** a Lev 18:25–28
**20:23** b Lev 18:3
**20:24** c Ex 33:16
**20:25** d Lev 11:1–47; Dt 14:3–21
**20:27** e Lev 19:31

[*a*]26 Or *be my holy ones* [*b*]4 Or *unclean as a leader among his people*

5"'Priests must not shave their heads or shave off the edges of their beards[f] or cut their bodies.[g] 6They must be holy to their God and must not profane the name of their God.[h] Because they present the offerings made to the LORD by fire,[i] the food of their God, they are to be holy.

7"'They must not marry women defiled by prostitution or divorced from their husbands,[j] because priests are holy to their God. 8Regard them as holy,[k] because they offer up the food of your God. Consider them holy, because I the LORD am holy—I who make you holy.[a]

9"'If a priest's daughter defiles herself by becoming a prostitute, she disgraces her father; she must be burned in the fire.[l]

10"'The high priest, the one among his brothers who has had the anointing oil poured on his head and who has been ordained to wear the priestly garments, must not let his hair become unkempt[b] or tear his clothes.[m] 11He must not enter a place where there is a dead body. He must not make himself unclean,[n] even for his father or mother, 12nor leave the sanctuary of his God or desecrate it, because he has been dedicated by the anointing oil[o] of his God. I am the LORD.

13"'The woman he marries must be a virgin. 14He must not marry a widow, a divorced woman, or a woman defiled by prostitution, but only a virgin from his own people, 15so he will not defile his offspring among his people. I am the LORD, who makes him holy.[c]'"

16The LORD said to Moses, 17"Say to Aaron: 'For the generations to come none of your descendants who has a defect may come near to offer the food of his God. 18No man who has any defect[p] may come near: no man who is blind or lame, disfigured or deformed; 19no man with a crippled foot or hand, 20or who is hunchbacked or dwarfed, or who has any eye defect, or who has festering or running sores or damaged testicles.[q] 21No descendant of Aaron the priest who has any defect is to come near to present the offerings made to the LORD by fire. He has a defect; he must not come near to offer the food of his God. 22He may eat the most holy food of his God, as well as the holy food; 23yet because of his defect, he must not go near the curtain or approach the altar, and so desecrate my sanctuary. I am the LORD, who makes them holy.[d]'"

24So Moses told this to Aaron and his sons and to all the Israelites.

# 22

The LORD said to Moses, 2"Tell Aaron and his sons to treat with respect the sacred offerings the Israelites consecrate to me, so they will not profane my holy name. I am the LORD.

3"Say to them: 'For the generations to come, if any of your descendants is ceremonially unclean and yet comes near the sacred offerings that the Israelites consecrate to the LORD, that person must be cut off from my presence.[r] I am the LORD.

4"'If a descendant of Aaron has an infectious skin disease[e] or a bodily discharge,[s] he may not eat the sacred offerings until he is cleansed. He will also be unclean if he touches something defiled by a corpse or by anyone who has an emission of semen, 5or if he touches any crawling thing[t] that makes him unclean, or any person who makes him unclean, whatever the uncleanness may be. 6The one who touches any such thing will be unclean till evening. He must not eat any of the sacred offerings unless he has bathed himself with water. 7When the sun goes down, he will be clean, and after that he may eat the sacred offerings, for they are his food.[u] 8He must not eat anything found dead or torn by wild animals,[v] and so become unclean through it. I am the LORD.

9"'The priests are to keep my requirements so that they do not become guilty and die[w] for treating them with contempt. I am the LORD, who makes them holy.[f]

10"'No one outside a priest's family may eat the sacred offering, nor may the guest of a priest or his hired worker eat it. 11But if a priest buys a slave with money, or if a slave is born in his household, that slave may eat his food. 12If a priest's daughter marries anyone other than a priest, she may not eat any of the sacred contributions. 13But if a priest's daughter becomes a widow or is

**21:5** f Eze 44:20 g Lev 19:28
**21:6** h Lev 18:21 i Lev 3:11
**21:7** j ver 13,14
**21:8** k ver 6
**21:9** l Ge 38:24
**21:10** m Lev 10:6
**21:11** n Lev 19:28
**21:12** o Lev 10:7
**21:18** p Lev 22:19–25
**21:20** q Dt 23:1
**22:3** r Lev 7:20,21
**22:4** s Lev 14:1–32
**22:5** t Lev 11:24–28,43
**22:7** u Nu 18:11
**22:8** v Ex 22:31; Lev 17:15
**22:9** w ver 16; Ex 28:43

[a]8 Or *who sanctify you*; or *who set you apart as holy* [b]10 Or *not uncover his head* [c]15 Or *who sanctifies him*; or *who sets him apart as holy* [d]23 Or *who sanctifies them*; or *who sets them apart as holy* [e]4 Traditionally *leprosy*; the Hebrew word was used for various diseases affecting the skin—not necessarily leprosy. [f]9 Or *who sanctifies them*; or *who sets them apart as holy*; also in verse 16

divorced, yet has no children, and she returns to live in her father's house as in her youth, she may eat of her father's food. No unauthorized person, however, may eat any of it.

14"'If anyone eats a sacred offering by mistake, he must make restitution to the priest for the offering and add a fifth of the value[x] to it. 15The priests must not desecrate the sacred offerings the Israelites present to the LORD 16by allowing them to eat the sacred offerings and so bring upon them guilt requiring payment.[y] I am the LORD, who makes them holy.'"

## Unacceptable Sacrifices

17The LORD said to Moses, 18"Speak to Aaron and his sons and to all the Israelites and say to them: 'If any of you—either an Israelite or an alien living in Israel—presents a gift for a burnt offering to the LORD, either to fulfill a vow or as a freewill offering, 19you must present a male without defect from the cattle, sheep or goats in order that it may be accepted on your behalf. 20Do not bring anything with a defect,[z] because it will not be accepted on your behalf. 21When anyone brings from the herd or flock a fellowship offering[a][a] to the LORD to fulfill a special vow or as a freewill offering, it must be without defect or blemish to be acceptable. 22Do not offer to the LORD the blind, the injured or the maimed, or anything with warts or festering or running sores. Do not place any of these on the altar as an offering made to the LORD by fire. 23You may, however, present as a freewill offering an ox[b] or a sheep that is deformed or stunted, but it will not be accepted in fulfillment of a vow. 24You must not offer to the LORD an animal whose testicles are bruised, crushed, torn or cut. You must not do this in your own land, 25and you must not accept such animals from the hand of a foreigner and offer them as the food of your God.[b] They will not be accepted on your behalf, because they are deformed and have defects.'"

26The LORD said to Moses, 27"When a calf, a lamb or a goat is born, it is to remain with its mother for seven days.[c] From the eighth day on, it will be acceptable as an offering made to the LORD by fire. 28Do not slaughter a cow or a sheep and its young on the same day.[d]

29"When you sacrifice a thank offering[e] to the LORD, sacrifice it in such a way that it will be accepted on your behalf. 30It must be eaten that same day; leave none of it till morning. I am the LORD.

31"Keep[f] my commands and follow them. I am the LORD. 32Do not profane my holy name.[g] I must be acknowledged as holy by the Israelites. I am the LORD, who makes[c] you holy[d] 33and who brought you out of Egypt to be your God. I am the LORD."

23 The LORD said to Moses, 2"Speak to the Israelites and say to them: 'These are my appointed feasts,[h] the appointed feasts of the LORD, which you are to proclaim as sacred assemblies.

## The Sabbath

3"'There are six days when you may work,[i] but the seventh day is a Sabbath of rest,[j] a day of sacred assembly. You are not to do any work; wherever you live, it is a Sabbath to the LORD.

*Lord,*

*I want to enjoy sweet Sabbath rest.*
*Help me today to make choices that will*
*prepare my body for true relaxation*
*and rejuvenation. May I then use*
*my strength in testimony for you.*

*Amen*

LEVITICUS 23:3

## The Passover and Unleavened Bread

4"'These are the LORD's appointed feasts, the sacred assemblies you are to proclaim at their appointed times: 5The LORD's Passover begins at twilight on the fourteenth day of

22:14 x Lev 5:15
22:16 y ver 9
22:20 z Dt 15:21; Heb 9:14; 1Pe 1:19
22:21 a Lev 3:6
22:25 b Lev 21:6
22:27 c Ex 22:30
22:28 d Dt 22:6,7
22:29 e Lev 7:12
22:31 f Dt 4:2,40
22:32 g Lev 18:21
23:2 h ver 4,37,44; Nu 29:39
23:3 i Ex 20:9 j Ex 20:10; 31:13–17; Lev 19:3; Dt 5:13; Heb 4:9,10

[a]21 Traditionally *peace offering* [b]23 The Hebrew word can include both male and female. [c]32 Or *made* [d]32 Or *who sanctifies you*; or *who sets you apart as holy*

the first month.[k] 6 On the fifteenth day of that month the LORD's Feast of Unleavened Bread begins; for seven days you must eat bread made without yeast. 7 On the first day hold a sacred assembly and do no regular work. 8 For seven days present an offering made to the LORD by fire. And on the seventh day hold a sacred assembly and do no regular work.' "

## Firstfruits

9 The LORD said to Moses, 10 "Speak to the Israelites and say to them: 'When you enter the land I am going to give you and you reap its harvest, bring to the priest a sheaf of the first grain you harvest. 11 He is to wave the sheaf before the LORD so it will be accepted on your behalf; the priest is to wave it on the day after the Sabbath. 12 On the day you wave the sheaf, you must sacrifice as a burnt offering to the LORD a lamb a year old without defect, 13 together with its grain offering[l] of two-tenths of an ephah[a] of fine flour mixed with oil—an offering made to the LORD by fire, a pleasing aroma—and its drink offering of a quarter of a hin[b] of wine. 14 You must not eat any bread, or roasted or new grain, until the very day you bring this offering to your God. This is to be a lasting ordinance for the generations to come, wherever you live.

## Feast of Weeks

15 " 'From the day after the Sabbath, the day you brought the sheaf of the wave offering, count off seven full weeks. 16 Count off fifty days up to the day after the seventh Sabbath,[m] and then present an offering of new grain to the LORD. 17 From wherever you live, bring two loaves made of two-tenths of an ephah of fine flour, baked with yeast, as a wave offering of firstfruits[n] to the LORD. 18 Present with this bread seven male lambs, each a year old and without defect, one young bull and two rams. They will be a burnt offering to the LORD, together with their grain offerings and drink offerings—an offering made by fire, an aroma pleasing to the LORD. 19 Then sacrifice one male goat for a sin offering and two lambs, each a year old, for a fellowship offering.[c] 20 The priest is to wave the two lambs before the LORD as a wave offering, together with the bread of the firstfruits. They are a sacred offering to the LORD for the priest. 21 On that same day you are to proclaim a sacred assembly[o] and do no regular work.[p] This is to be a lasting ordinance for the generations to come, wherever you live.

22 " 'When you reap the harvest[q] of your land, do not reap to the very edges of your field or gather the gleanings of your harvest. Leave them for the poor and the alien. I am the LORD your God.' "

## Feast of Trumpets

23 The LORD said to Moses, 24 "Say to the Israelites: 'On the first day of the seventh month you are to have a day of rest, a sacred assembly commemorated with trumpet blasts.[r] 25 Do no regular work, but present an offering made to the LORD by fire.' "

## Day of Atonement

26 The LORD said to Moses, 27 "The tenth day of this seventh month[s] is the Day of Atonement. Hold a sacred assembly[t] and deny yourselves,[d] and present an offering made to the LORD by fire. 28 Do no work on that day, because it is the Day of Atonement, when atonement is made for you before the LORD your God. 29 Anyone who does not deny himself on that day must be cut off from his people.[u] 30 I will destroy from among his people[v] anyone who does any work on that day. 31 You shall do no work at all. This is to be a lasting ordinance for the generations to come, wherever you live. 32 It is a sabbath of rest for you, and you must deny yourselves. From the evening of the ninth day of the month until the following evening you are to observe your sabbath."

## Feast of Tabernacles

33 The LORD said to Moses, 34 "Say to the Israelites: 'On the fifteenth day of the seventh month the LORD's Feast of Tabernacles[w] begins, and it lasts for seven days. 35 The first day is a sacred assembly; do no regular work. 36 For seven days present offerings made to the LORD by fire, and on the eighth day hold a sacred assembly and present an

**23:5** k Ex 12:18–19
**23:13** l Lev 2:14–16
**23:16** m Nu 28:26; Ac 2:1
**23:17** n Ex 34:22; Lev 2:12
**23:21** o ver 2 p ver 3
**23:22** q Lev 19:9
**23:24** r Lev 25:9; Nu 29:1
**23:27** s Lev 16:29 t Nu 29:7
**23:29** u Ge 17:14
**23:30** v Lev 20:3
**23:34** w Ex 23:16; Dt 16:13; Jn 7:2

[a] 13 That is, probably about 4 quarts (about 4.5 liters); also in verse 17 [b] 13 That is, probably about 1 quart (about 1 liter)
[c] 19 Traditionally *peace offering* [d] 27 Or *and fast*; also in verses 29 and 32

offering made to the LORD by fire. It is the closing assembly; do no regular work.

37("'These are the LORD's appointed feasts, which you are to proclaim as sacred assemblies for bringing offerings made to the LORD by fire—the burnt offerings and grain offerings, sacrifices and drink offerings required for each day. 38These offerings are in addition to those for the LORD's Sabbaths and[a] in addition to your gifts and whatever you have vowed and all the freewill offerings you give to the LORD.)

39"'So beginning with the fifteenth day of the seventh month, after you have gathered the crops of the land, celebrate the festival to the LORD for seven days;[x] the first day is a day of rest, and the eighth day also is a day of rest. 40On the first day you are to take choice fruit from the trees, and palm fronds, leafy branches and poplars,[y] and rejoice before the LORD your God for seven days. 41Celebrate this as a festival to the LORD for seven days each year. This is to be a lasting ordinance for the generations to come; celebrate it in the seventh month. 42Live in booths for seven days: All native-born Israelites are to live in booths 43so your descendants will know that I had the Israelites live in booths when I brought them out of Egypt. I am the LORD your God.'"

44So Moses announced to the Israelites the appointed feasts of the LORD.

## Oil and Bread Set Before the LORD

24 The LORD said to Moses, 2"Command the Israelites to bring you clear oil of pressed olives for the light so that the lamps may be kept burning continually. 3Outside the curtain of the Testimony in the Tent of Meeting, Aaron is to tend the lamps before the LORD from evening till morning, continually. This is to be a lasting ordinance for the generations to come. 4The lamps on the pure gold lampstand before the LORD must be tended continually.

5"Take fine flour and bake twelve loaves of bread,[z] using two-tenths of an ephah[b] for each loaf. 6Set them in two rows, six in each row, on the table of pure gold[a] before the LORD. 7Along each row put some pure incense as a memorial portion to represent the bread and to be an offering made to the LORD by fire. 8This bread is to be set out before the LORD regularly,[b] Sabbath after Sabbath, on behalf of the Israelites, as a lasting covenant. 9It belongs to Aaron and his sons,[c] who are to eat it in a holy place, because it is a most holy part of their regular share of the offerings made to the LORD by fire."

## A Blasphemer Stoned

10Now the son of an Israelite mother and an Egyptian father went out among the Israelites, and a fight broke out in the camp between him and an Israelite. 11The son of the Israelite woman blasphemed the Name with a curse; so they brought him to Moses. (His mother's name was Shelomith, the daughter of Dibri the Danite.) 12They put him in custody until the will of the LORD should be made clear to them.[d]

13Then the LORD said to Moses: 14"Take the blasphemer outside the camp. All those who heard him are to lay their hands on his head, and the entire assembly is to stone him.[e] 15Say to the Israelites: 'If anyone curses his God, he will be held responsible; 16anyone who blasphemes the name of the LORD must be put to death.[f] The entire assembly must stone him. Whether an alien or native-born, when he blasphemes the Name, he must be put to death.

17"'If anyone takes the life of a human being, he must be put to death.[g] 18Anyone who takes the life of someone's animal must make restitution[h]—life for life. 19If anyone injures his neighbor, whatever he has done must be done to him: 20fracture for fracture, eye for eye, tooth for tooth.[i] As he has injured the other, so he is to be injured. 21Whoever kills an animal must make restitution, but whoever kills a man must be put to death.[j] 22You are to have the same law for the alien[k] and the native-born.[l] I am the LORD your God.'"

23Then Moses spoke to the Israelites, and they took the blasphemer outside the camp and stoned him. The Israelites did as the LORD commanded Moses.

**23:39** x Ex 23:16
**23:40** y Ne 8:14–17
**24:5** z Ex 25:30
**24:6** a Ex 25:23–30

**24:8** b Nu 4:7; 2Ch 2:4
**24:9** c Lev 8:31; Mt 12:4; Mk 2:26; Lk 6:4
**24:12** d Ex 18:16; Nu 15:34
**24:14** e Dt 13:9; 17:5,7
**24:16** f 1Ki 21:10,13
**24:17** g Ex 21:12; Nu 35:30–31
**24:18** h ver 21
**24:20** i Mt 5:38*
**24:21** j ver 17
**24:22** k Ex 12:49 l Nu 15:16

[a]38 Or *These feasts are in addition to the LORD's Sabbaths, and these offerings are* [b]5 That is, probably about 4 quarts (about 4.5 liters)

## The Sabbath Year

**25** The LORD said to Moses on Mount Sinai, 2"Speak to the Israelites and say to them: 'When you enter the land I am going to give you, the land itself must observe a sabbath to the LORD. 3For six years sow your fields, and for six years prune your vineyards and gather their crops. 4But in the seventh year the land is to have a sabbath of rest, a sabbath to the LORD. Do not sow your fields or prune your vineyards. 5Do not reap what grows of itself or harvest the grapes of your untended vines. The land is to have a year of rest. 6Whatever the land yields during the sabbath year will be food for you—for yourself, your manservant and maidservant, and the hired worker and temporary resident who live among you, 7as well as for your livestock and the wild animals in your land. Whatever the land produces may be eaten.

## The Year of Jubilee

8" 'Count off seven sabbaths of years—seven times seven years—so that the seven sabbaths of years amount to a period of forty-nine years. 9Then have the trumpet[m] sounded everywhere on the tenth day of the seventh month; on the Day of Atonement sound the trumpet throughout your land. 10Consecrate the fiftieth year and proclaim liberty[n] throughout the land to all its inhabitants. It shall be a jubilee for you; each one of you is to return to his family property and each to his own clan. 11The fiftieth year shall be a jubilee for you; do not sow and do not reap what grows of itself or harvest the untended vines. 12For it is a jubilee and is to be holy for you; eat only what is taken directly from the fields.

13" 'In this Year of Jubilee[o] everyone is to return to his own property.

14" 'If you sell land to one of your countrymen or buy any from him, do not take advantage of each other. 15You are to buy from your countryman on the basis of the number of years[p] since the Jubilee. And he is to sell to you on the basis of the number of years left for harvesting crops. 16When the years are many, you are to increase the price, and when the years are few, you are to decrease the price, because what he is really selling you is the number of crops. 17Do not take advantage of each other, but fear your God.[q] I am the LORD your God.[r]

18" 'Follow my decrees and be careful to obey my laws, and you will live safely in the land.[s] 19Then the land will yield its fruit, and you will eat your fill and live there in safety. 20You may ask, "What will we eat in the seventh year[t] if we do not plant or harvest our crops?" 21I will send you such a blessing in the sixth year that the land will yield enough for three years. 22While you plant during the eighth year, you will eat from the old crop and will continue to eat from it until the harvest of the ninth year comes in.[u]

23" 'The land must not be sold permanently, because the land is mine[v] and you are but aliens[w] and my tenants. 24Throughout the country that you hold as a possession, you must provide for the redemption of the land.

25" 'If one of your countrymen becomes poor and sells some of his property, his nearest relative[x] is to come and redeem[y] what his countryman has sold. 26If, however, a man has no one to redeem it for him but he himself prospers and acquires sufficient means to redeem it, 27he is to determine the value for the years since he sold it and refund the balance to the man to whom he sold it; he can then go back to his own property. 28But if he does not acquire the means to repay him, what he sold will remain in the possession of the buyer until the Year of Jubilee. It will be returned in the Jubilee, and he can then go back to his property.

29" 'If a man sells a house in a walled city, he retains the right of redemption a full year after its sale. During that time he may redeem it. 30If it is not redeemed before a full year has passed, the house in the walled city shall belong permanently to the buyer and his descendants. It is not to be returned in the Jubilee. 31But houses in villages without walls around them are to be considered as open country. They can be redeemed, and they are to be returned in the Jubilee.

32" 'The Levites always have the right to redeem their houses in the Levitical towns,[z] which they possess. 33So the property of the Levites is redeemable—that is, a house sold in any town they hold—and is to be

**25:9** m Lev 23:24
**25:10** n Jer 34:8,15,17
**25:13** o ver 10
**25:15** p Lev 27:18,23
**25:17** q Lev 19:14 r Lev 19:32
**25:18** s Lev 26:4,5; Dt 12:10
**25:20** t ver 4
**25:22** u Lev 26:10
**25:23** v Ex 19:5 w Ge 23:4; Ps 39:12; Heb 11:13
**25:25** x Ru 2:20 y Ru 4:4
**25:32** z Nu 35:1–8

25:35 a Dt15:8
25:36 b Ex22:25; Dt23:19–20
25:39 c Ex21:2; Dt15:12; 1Ki9:22
25:41 d ver28
25:43 e Ex1:13

returned in the Jubilee, because the houses in the towns of the Levites are their property among the Israelites. 34But the pastureland belonging to their towns must not be sold; it is their permanent possession.

35" 'If one of your countrymen becomes poor and is unable to support himself among you, help him[a] as you would an alien or a temporary resident, so he can continue to live among you. 36Do not take interest[b] of any kind[a] from him, but fear your God, so that your countryman may continue to live among you. 37You must not lend him money at interest or sell him food at a profit. 38I am the LORD your God, who brought you out of Egypt to give you the land of Canaan and to be your God.

39" 'If one of your countrymen becomes poor among you and sells himself to you, do not make him work as a slave.[c] 40He is to be treated as a hired worker or a temporary resident among you; he is to work for you until the Year of Jubilee. 41Then he and his children are to be released, and he will go back to his own clan and to the property[d] of his forefathers. 42Because the Israelites are my servants, whom I brought out of Egypt, they must not be sold as slaves. 43Do not rule over them ruthlessly,[e] but fear your God.

44" 'Your male and female slaves are to come from the nations around you; from them you may buy slaves. 45You may also buy some of the temporary residents living among you and members of their clans born in your country, and they will become your property. 46You can will them to your children as inherited property and can make them slaves for life, but you must not rule over your fellow Israelites ruthlessly.

47" 'If an alien or a temporary resident among you becomes rich and one of your countrymen becomes poor and sells himself to the alien living among you or to a member of the alien's clan, 48he retains the right of redemption after he has sold himself. One of his relatives may redeem him: 49An uncle or a cousin or any blood relative in his clan may redeem him. Or if he prospers, he may redeem himself. 50He and his buyer are to count the time from the year he sold himself up to the Year of Jubilee. The price for his release is to be based on the rate paid to a hired man[f] for that number of years. 51If many years remain, he must pay for his redemption a larger share of the price paid for him. 52If only a few years remain until the Year of Jubilee, he is to compute that and pay for his redemption accordingly. 53He is to be treated as a man hired from year to year; you must see to it that his owner does not rule over him ruthlessly.

54" 'Even if he is not redeemed in any of these ways, he and his children are to be released in the Year of Jubilee, 55for the Israelites belong to me as servants. They are my servants, whom I brought out of Egypt. I am the LORD your God.

*My beloved creation,*

*I want to liberate you from anything that hinders our relationship; I desire above all for you to be free.*

*Love,*
*God*

LEVITICUS 25:54–55

## Reward for Obedience

26 " 'Do not make idols[g] or set up an image or a sacred stone for yourselves, and do not place a carved stone in your land to bow down before it. I am the LORD your God.

2" 'Observe my Sabbaths and have reverence for my sanctuary.[h] I am the LORD.

3" 'If you follow my decrees and are careful to obey[i] my commands, 4I will send you rain in its season, and the ground will yield its crops and the trees of the field their fruit. 5Your threshing will continue until grape harvest and the grape harvest will continue until planting, and you will eat all the food you want[j] and live in safety in your land.[k]

6" 'I will grant peace in the land,[l] and

25:50 f Job7:1
26:1 g Ex20:4; Dt5:8
26:2 h Lev19:30
26:3 i Dt28:1,9
26:5 j Am9:13 k Lev25:18
26:6 l Ps29:11; 147:14

[a]36 Or *take excessive interest*; similarly in verse 37

# Inspire

## REST

We are women of the new millennium: wives, mothers, career women. Every day someone is depending on us, some project needs our focus, some task must be completed. With all that is going on in our lives, there is often no time for us to consider slowing down, let alone taking a little time to rest.

Yet resting is not only a mandate but also a practice that God himself modeled. After God created everything, he rested (see Ge 2:2). And then he made that resting day a holy day (see Ge 2:3; Ex 20:8–11; Lev 23:3). He also commanded the Israelites to observe "sabbath years" so that the land, as well as the workers, could rest (see Lev 25:1–7).

As leaders at work and home who have so much to do, it may seem inconceivable, almost selfish, to take time for ourselves. However, there was a purpose to God's directive. Resting allows us to restore, to heal and to build. It is the same principle that exercise experts suggest. Fitness trainers advise clients to work out for a few days and then rest. During workout times, muscles are broken down. During the resting phase, muscles are built up—they enlarge and become stronger.

That principle is God's plan for our lives. During our resting times, we are revitalized, able to refocus, able to rebuild. We can see things more clearly when our minds and bodies are rested. Without rest, we weaken; and in a weakened state, we're susceptible to sickness, stress and temptation. We are much more likely to fall when our resistance is down—when we are tired from long hours of work or when we've had no rest.

Like the disciples who were told to rest in order to be prepared (see Mk 6:30–31), God wants us, his disciples today, to be prepared for all that he has planned for our lives. This can be accomplished through understanding the principle of rest and by making it as important of a priority in our lives as everything else on our to-do list. If our Creator and Master Teacher took time to rest, surely today's leaders can make the time to be restored, renewed and refreshed. We will all benefit.

—V. Murray

### read

Leviticus 25:1–7; see also Genesis 2:1–3.

See also the Inspire Notes "Coping With Life's Tasks" and "Stress Management: Learning to Say 'No.'"

### WOMAN of COLOR

Look at your calendar and schedule time to rest today! You may want to take a walk, sip a cup of herbal tea or soak in a bubble bath. Find a way to build rest and relaxation into every day.

For the next Inspire note, go to page 176.

you will lie down and no one will make you afraid. I will remove savage beasts[m] from the land, and the sword will not pass through your country. 7 You will pursue your enemies, and they will fall by the sword before you. 8 Five of you will chase a hundred, and a hundred of you will chase ten thousand, and your enemies will fall by the sword before you.[n]

9 " 'I will look on you with favor and make you fruitful and increase your numbers,[o] and I will keep my covenant with you. 10 You will still be eating last year's harvest when you will have to move it out to make room for the new.[p] 11 I will put my dwelling place[a][q] among you, and I will not abhor you. 12 I will walk among you and be your God, and you will be my people.[r] 13 I am the LORD your God, who brought you out of Egypt so that you would no longer be slaves to the Egyptians; I broke the bars of your yoke and enabled you to walk with heads held high.

## Punishment for Disobedience

14 " 'But if you will not listen to me and carry out all these commands,[s] 15 and if you reject my decrees and abhor my laws and fail to carry out all my commands and so violate my covenant, 16 then I will do this to you: I will bring upon you sudden terror, wasting diseases and fever[t] that will destroy your sight and drain away your life.[u] You will plant seed in vain, because your enemies will eat it. 17 I will set my face against you so that you will be defeated by your enemies; those who hate you will rule over you,[v] and you will flee even when no one is pursuing you.[w]

18 " 'If after all this you will not listen to me, I will punish you for your sins seven times over. 19 I will break down your stubborn pride[x] and make the sky above you like iron and the ground beneath you like bronze. 20 Your strength will be spent in vain,[y] because your soil will not yield its crops, nor will the trees of the land yield their fruit.

21 " 'If you remain hostile toward me and refuse to listen to me, I will multiply your afflictions seven times over, as your sins deserve. 22 I will send wild animals against you, and they will rob you of your children, destroy your cattle and make you so few in number that your roads will be deserted.

23 " 'If in spite of these things you do not accept my correction[z] but continue to be hostile toward me, 24 I myself will be hostile toward you and will afflict you for your sins seven times over. 25 And I will bring the sword upon you to avenge the breaking of the covenant. When you withdraw into your cities, I will send a plague among you, and you will be given into enemy hands. 26 When I cut off your supply of bread,[a] ten women will be able to bake your bread in one oven, and they will dole out the bread by weight. You will eat, but you will not be satisfied.

27 " 'If in spite of this you still do not listen to me but continue to be hostile toward me, 28 then in my anger I will be hostile toward you, and I myself will punish you for your sins seven times over. 29 You will eat the flesh of your sons and the flesh of your daughters.[b] 30 I will destroy your high places,[c] cut down your incense altars[d] and pile your dead bodies on the lifeless forms of your idols, and I will abhor you. 31 I will turn your cities into ruins and lay waste your sanctuaries,[e] and I will take no delight in the pleasing aroma of your offerings. 32 I will lay waste the land,[f] so that your enemies who live there will be appalled. 33 I will scatter you among the nations[g] and will draw out my sword and pursue you. Your land will be laid waste, and your cities will lie in ruins. 34 Then the land will enjoy its sabbath years all the time that it lies desolate and you are in the country of your enemies;[h] then the land will rest and enjoy its sabbaths. 35 All the time that it lies desolate, the land will have the rest it did not have during the sabbaths you lived in it.

36 " 'As for those of you who are left, I will make their hearts so fearful in the lands of their enemies that the sound of a windblown leaf will put them to flight.[i] They will run as though fleeing from the sword, and they will fall, even though no one is pursuing them. 37 They will stumble over one another as though fleeing from the sword, even though no one is pursuing them. So you will not be able to stand before your enemies. 38 You will

**26:6** m ver 22
**26:8** n Dt 32:30
**26:9** o Ge 17:6
**26:10** p Lev 25:22
**26:11** q Ex 25:8
**26:12** r 2Co 6:16*
**26:14** s Dt 28:15–68; Mal 2:2
**26:16** t Dt 28:22,35 u 1Sa 2:33
**26:17** v Ps 106:41 w ver 36,37; Ps 53:5
**26:19** x Isa 25:11
**26:20** y Ps 127:1
**26:23** z Jer 2:30
**26:26** a Mic 6:14
**26:29** b Dt 28:53
**26:30** c 2Ch 34:3; Eze 6:3 d Eze 6:6
**26:31** e Ps 74:3–7
**26:32** f Jer 9:11
**26:33** g Dt 4:27; Eze 12:15
**26:34** h 2Ch 36:21
**26:36** i Eze 21:7

a 11 Or *my tabernacle*

**26:40** j 1Jn 1:9
**26:44** k Ro 11:2 l Dt 4:31
**26:45** m Ex 6:8
**26:46** n Lev 7:38; 27:34
**27:3** o Ex 30:13
**27:6** p Nu 18:16

perish among the nations; the land of your
enemies will devour you. [39]Those of you who
are left will waste away in the lands of their
enemies because of their sins; also because
of their fathers' sins they will waste away.

[40]" 'But if they will confess their sins and
the sins of their fathers[j]—their treachery
against me and their hostility toward me,
[41]which made me hostile toward them so
that I sent them into the land of their en-
emies—then when their uncircumcised
hearts are humbled and they pay for their
sin, [42]I will remember my covenant with
Jacob and my covenant with Isaac and my
covenant with Abraham, and I will remem-
ber the land. [43]For the land will be deserted
by them and will enjoy its sabbaths while it
lies desolate without them. They will pay for
their sins because they rejected my laws and
abhorred my decrees. [44]Yet in spite of this,
when they are in the land of their enemies, I
will not reject them or abhor[k] them so as to
destroy them completely,[l] breaking my cov-
enant with them. I am the LORD their God.
[45]But for their sake I will remember the cov-
enant with their ancestors whom I brought
out of Egypt[m] in the sight of the nations to
be their God. I am the LORD.' "

[46]These are the decrees, the laws and the
regulations that the LORD established on
Mount Sinai between himself and the Israel-
ites through Moses.[n]

## Redeeming What Is the LORD's

27 The LORD said to Moses, [2]"Speak to
the Israelites and say to them: 'If
anyone makes a special vow to dedicate per-
sons to the LORD by giving equivalent values,
[3]set the value of a male between the ages of
twenty and sixty at fifty shekels[a] of silver,
according to the sanctuary shekel[b];[o] [4]and
if it is a female, set her value at thirty shek-
els.[c] [5]If it is a person between the ages of five
and twenty, set the value of a male at twenty
shekels[d] and of a female at ten shekels.[e] [6]If
it is a person between one month and five
years, set the value of a male at five shek-
els[f][p] of silver and that of a female at three
shekels[g] of silver. [7]If it is a person sixty years
old or more, set the value of a male at fifteen
shekels[h] and of a female at ten shekels. [8]If
anyone making the vow is too poor to pay
the specified amount, he is to present the
person to the priest, who will set the value
for him according to what the man making
the vow can afford.

[9]" 'If what he vowed is an animal that is ac-
ceptable as an offering to the LORD, such an
animal given to the LORD becomes holy. [10]He
must not exchange it or substitute a good
one for a bad one, or a bad one for a good
one; if he should substitute one animal for
another, both it and the substitute become
holy. [11]If what he vowed is a ceremonially
unclean animal—one that is not acceptable
as an offering to the LORD—the animal must
be presented to the priest, [12]who will judge
its quality as good or bad. Whatever value
the priest then sets, that is what it will be.
[13]If the owner wishes to redeem the animal,
he must add a fifth to its value.

[14]" 'If a man dedicates his house as some-
thing holy to the LORD, the priest will judge
its quality as good or bad. Whatever value
the priest then sets, so it will remain. [15]If
the man who dedicates his house redeems
it,[q] he must add a fifth to its value, and the
house will again become his.

[16]" 'If a man dedicates to the LORD part
of his family land, its value is to be set ac-
cording to the amount of seed required for
it—fifty shekels of silver to a homer[i] of bar-
ley seed. [17]If he dedicates his field during
the Year of Jubilee, the value that has been
set remains. [18]But if he dedicates his field af-
ter the Jubilee, the priest will determine the
value according to the number of years that
remain[r] until the next Year of Jubilee, and
its set value will be reduced. [19]If the man
who dedicates the field wishes to redeem
it, he must add a fifth to its value, and the
field will again become his. [20]If, however, he
does not redeem the field, or if he has sold it
to someone else, it can never be redeemed.
[21]When the field is released in the Jubilee,[s]
it will become holy, like a field devoted to

**27:15** q ver 13,20
**27:18** r Lev 25:15
**27:21** s Lev 25:10

[a]3 That is, about 1 1/4 pounds (about 0.6 kilogram); also in verse 16 [b]3 That is, about 2/5 ounce (about 11.5 grams); also in verse 25 [c]4 That is, about 12 ounces (about 0.3 kilogram) [d]5 That is, about 8 ounces (about 0.2 kilogram) [e]5 That is, about 4 ounces (about 110 grams); also in verse 7 [f]6 That is, about 2 ounces (about 55 grams) [g]6 That is, about 1 1/4 ounces (about 35 grams) [h]7 That is, about 6 ounces (about 170 grams) [i]16 That is, probably about 6 bushels (about 220 liters)

the Lord;[t] it will become the property of the priests.[a]

[22]"'If a man dedicates to the Lord a field he has bought, which is not part of his family land, [23]the priest will determine its value up to the Year of Jubilee, and the man must pay its value on that day as something holy to the Lord. [24]In the Year of Jubilee the field will revert to the person from whom he bought it,[u] the one whose land it was. [25]Every value is to be set according to the sanctuary shekel,[v] twenty gerahs to the shekel.

[26]"'No one, however, may dedicate the firstborn of an animal, since the firstborn already belongs to the Lord;[w] whether an ox[b] or a sheep, it is the Lord's. [27]If it is one of the unclean animals,[x] he may buy it back at its set value, adding a fifth of the value to it. If he does not redeem it, it is to be sold at its set value.

[28]"'But nothing that a man owns and devotes[c][y] to the Lord—whether man or animal or family land—may be sold or redeemed; everything so devoted is most holy to the Lord.

[29]"'No person devoted to destruction[d] may be ransomed; he must be put to death.

[30]"'A tithe[z] of everything from the land, whether grain from the soil or fruit from the trees, belongs to the Lord; it is holy to the Lord. [31]If a man redeems any of his tithe, he must add a fifth of the value to it. [32]The entire tithe of the herd and flock—every tenth animal that passes under the shepherd's rod—will be holy to the Lord. [33]He must not pick out the good from the bad or make any substitution.[a] If he does make a substitution, both the animal and its substitute become holy and cannot be redeemed.'"

[34]These are the commands the Lord gave Moses on Mount Sinai for the Israelites.[b]

27:21 t Nu 18:14; Eze 44:29
27:24 u Lev 25:28
27:25 v Ex 30:13
27:26 w Ex 13:2,12
27:27 x ver 11
27:28 y Jos 6:17–19
27:30 z Ge 28:22; Mal 3:8
27:33 a ver 10
27:34 b Lev 26:46

[a]21 Or *priest* [b]26 The Hebrew word can include both male and female. [c]28 The Hebrew term refers to the irrevocable giving over of things or persons to the Lord. [d]29 The Hebrew term refers to the irrevocable giving over of things or persons to the Lord, often by totally destroying them.

# Numbers

## OVERVIEW

The book of Numbers describes a census of each tribe of Israel. It also highlights the story of the Israelites' journey from Mount Sinai to the border of the promised land. However, after ten spies gave a negative report about the Canaanites, the people's hearts filled with fear, and they grumbled against Moses and Aaron. But it was God who responded to their complaining. As a result of the people's unbelief, they were condemned to wander in the desert until their children were ready to take the land. Only Caleb and Joshua—the only spies who were faithful to God—would accompany the next generation into the promised land.

The Israelites wandered in the desert for 40 years, until the last person who was at least 20 years old at the time of the rebellion died. The book concludes with a new generation of people waiting on the plains of Moab, ready to take the land. It is on these plains that Moses prepared the new generation of Israelites to enter the land promised to their forefather, Abraham (see Nu 27–36).

Upon taking the land, each family would receive a land inheritance. Although women never inherited their father's land, a special case arose: The daughters of Zelophehad appeared before Moses and requested an inheritance because their father died with no male heir. God affirmed their request and these women—Mahlah, Noah, Hoglah, Milcah and Tirzah—were allotted an inheritance that was to stay within their family (see Nu 27:1–11).

Also recorded in the book of Numbers is the account of Miriam and Aaron's grumbling against Moses. The result of their complaint against Moses' Cushite wife (perhaps Zipporah) resulted in Miriam becoming afflicted with leprosy for a brief period.

Many times the circumstances of life may cause a woman to feel like she is wandering in the desert, like the Israelites did. However, just as God led the Israelites through the desert, he will lead those who put their trust in him through the difficulties of life. Study how God met every need of the Hebrew people, and trust him to meet your every need as well.

## OUTLINE

I. The First Census of the People (1:1—4:49)
II. The Commands for Purity of the People (5:1—9:23)
III. God's Discipline and Provision (10:1—12:16)
IV. Finding and Losing the Promised Land (13:1—14:45)
V. Instructions for Offerings and Korah's Rebellion (15:1—16:50)
VI. Aaron's Staff and Priesthood Duties (17:1—19:22)
VII. Moses' Sin and Aaron's Death (20:1–29)
VIII. Journey in the Wilderness (21:1–35)
IX. Balaam's Blessing and Israel's Sin (22:1—25:18)
X. The Second Census of the People (26:1–65)
XI. Instructions for the New Generation (27:1—30:16)
XII. Midianite War (31:1–54)
XIII. Stages in the Journey (32:1—33:56)
XIV. Land Inheritance (34:1—36:13)

### SCANNABLE FACTS:

**Author:** Moses

**Time Written:** During the 1400s B.C., while the Israelites were traveling in the desert

**Themes to Note:** God's punishment and provision

**Notable Women:** Miriam, Zelophehad's daughters

## The Census

1 The LORD spoke to Moses in the Tent of
Meeting[a] in the Desert of Sinai on the
first day of the second month of the second
year after the Israelites came out of Egypt.
He said: 2"Take a census[b] of the whole Israel-
ite community by their clans and families,
listing every man by name, one by one. 3You
and Aaron are to number by their divisions
all the men in Israel twenty years old or
more[c] who are able to serve in the army.
4One man from each tribe, each the head of
his family,[d] is to help you.[e] 5These are the
names of the men who are to assist you:

from Reuben,[f] Elizur son of Shedeur;
6from Simeon, Shelumiel son of Zuri-
shaddai;
7from Judah, Nahshon son of Ammina-
dab;[g]
8from Issachar, Nethanel son of Zuar;
9from Zebulun, Eliab son of Helon;
10from the sons of Joseph:
from Ephraim, Elishama son of
Ammihud;
from Manasseh, Gamaliel son of
Pedahzur;
11from Benjamin, Abidan son of Gid-
eoni;
12from Dan, Ahiezer son of Ammishad-
dai;
13from Asher, Pagiel son of Ocran;
14from Gad, Eliasaph son of Deuel;[h]
15from Naphtali, Ahira son of Enan."

16These were the men appointed from the
community, the leaders[i] of their ancestral
tribes. They were the heads of the clans of
Israel.[j]
17Moses and Aaron took these men whose
names had been given, 18and they called the
whole community together on the first day
of the second month. The people indicated
their ancestry[k] by their clans and families,
and the men twenty years old or more were
listed by name, one by one, 19as the LORD
commanded Moses. And so he counted
them in the Desert of Sinai:

20From the descendants of Reuben[l] the first-
born son of Israel:

All the men twenty years old or
more who were able to serve in
the army were listed by name, one
by one, according to the records
of their clans and families. 21The
number from the tribe of Reuben
was 46,500.

22From the descendants of Simeon:[m]

All the men twenty years old or
more who were able to serve in
the army were counted and listed
by name, one by one, according to
the records of their clans and fami-
lies. 23The number from the tribe of
Simeon was 59,300.

24From the descendants of Gad:[n]

All the men twenty years old or
more who were able to serve in the
army were listed by name, accord-
ing to the records of their clans and
families. 25The number from the
tribe of Gad was 45,650.

26From the descendants of Judah:[o]

All the men twenty years old or
more who were able to serve in the
army were listed by name, accord-
ing to the records of their clans and
families. 27The number from the
tribe of Judah was 74,600.

1:1 a Ex 40:2
1:2 b Ex 30:11–16; Nu 26:2
1:3 c Ex 30:14
1:4 d ver 16 e Dt 1:15
1:5 f Rev 7:5
1:7 g Ru 4:20; 1Ch 2:10; Lk 3:32
1:14 h Nu 2:14
1:16 i Ex 18:25 j ver 4; Nu 7:2
1:18 k Ezr 2:59
1:20 l Nu 26:5–11
1:22 m Nu 26:12–14
1:24 n Nu 26:15–18
1:26 o Nu 26:19–22

### The African Presence

**Numbers 1:10**

Ephraim and Manasseh, the sons of Joseph, were born by his Egyptian wife, Asenath (see Ge 41:45–52).

28 From the descendants of Issachar:[p]

All the men twenty years old or more who were able to serve in the army were listed by name, according to the records of their clans and families. 29 The number from the tribe of Issachar was 54,400.

30 From the descendants of Zebulun:[q]

All the men twenty years old or more who were able to serve in the army were listed by name, according to the records of their clans and families. 31 The number from the tribe of Zebulun was 57,400.

32 From the sons of Joseph:

From the descendants of Ephraim:[r]

All the men twenty years old or more who were able to serve in the army were listed by name, according to the records of their clans and families. 33 The number from the tribe of Ephraim was 40,500.

34 From the descendants of Manasseh:[s]

All the men twenty years old or more who were able to serve in the army were listed by name, according to the records of their clans and families. 35 The number from the tribe of Manasseh was 32,200.

36 From the descendants of Benjamin:[t]

All the men twenty years old or more who were able to serve in the army were listed by name, according to the records of their clans and families. 37 The number from the tribe of Benjamin was 35,400.

38 From the descendants of Dan:[u]

All the men twenty years old or more who were able to serve in the army were listed by name, according to the records of their clans and families. 39 The number from the tribe of Dan was 62,700.

40 From the descendants of Asher:[v]

All the men twenty years old or more who were able to serve in the army were listed by name, according to the records of their clans and families. 41 The number from the tribe of Asher was 41,500.

42 From the descendants of Naphtali:[w]

All the men twenty years old or more who were able to serve in the army were listed by name, according to the records of their clans and families. 43 The number from the tribe of Naphtali was 53,400.

44 These were the men counted by Moses and Aaron and the twelve leaders of Israel, each one representing his family. 45 All the Israelites twenty years old or more who were able to serve in Israel's army were counted according to their families. 46 The total number was 603,550.[x]

47 The families of the tribe of Levi,[y] however, were not counted along with the others. 48 The LORD had said to Moses: 49 "You must not count the tribe of Levi or include them in the census of the other Israelites. 50 Instead, appoint the Levites to be in charge of the tabernacle of the Testimony—over all its furnishings and everything belonging to it. They are to carry the tabernacle and all its furnishings; they are to take care of it and encamp around it. 51 Whenever the tabernacle is to move, the Levites are to take it down, and whenever the tabernacle is to be set up, the Levites shall do it. Anyone else who goes near it shall be put to death. 52 The Israelites are to set up their tents by divisions, each man in his own camp under his own standard.[z] 53 The Levites, however, are to set up their tents around the tabernacle of the Testimony so that wrath will not fall on the Israelite community. The Levites are to be responsible for the care of the tabernacle of the Testimony."

54 The Israelites did all this just as the LORD commanded Moses.

## The Arrangement of the Tribal Camps

2 The LORD said to Moses and Aaron: 2 "The Israelites are to camp around the Tent of Meeting some distance from it, each man under his standard[a] with the banners of his family."

3 On the east, toward the sunrise, the divisions of the camp of Judah are to encamp under their standard. The leader of the people of Judah is

**1:28** p Nu 26:23–25
**1:30** q Nu 26:26–27
**1:32** r Nu 26:35–37
**1:34** s Nu 26:28–34
**1:36** t Nu 26:38–41
**1:38** u Nu 26:42–43
**1:40** v Nu 26:44–47
**1:42** w Nu 26:48–50
**1:46** x Ex 12:37; 38:26; Nu 2:32; 26:51
**1:47** y Nu 2:33; 26:57
**1:52** z Nu 2:2
**2:2** a Nu 1:52

2:3 b Nu 10:14
2:9 c Nu 10:14
2:16 d Nu 10:18
2:20 e Nu 1:10

Nahshon son of Amminadab.[b] 4His division numbers 74,600.

5The tribe of Issachar will camp next to them. The leader of the people of Issachar is Nethanel son of Zuar. 6His division numbers 54,400.

7The tribe of Zebulun will be next. The leader of the people of Zebulun is Eliab son of Helon. 8His division numbers 57,400.

9All the men assigned to the camp of Judah, according to their divisions, number 186,400. They will set out first.[c]

10On the south will be the divisions of the camp of Reuben under their standard. The leader of the people of Reuben is Elizur son of Shedeur. 11His division numbers 46,500.

12The tribe of Simeon will camp next to them. The leader of the people of Simeon is Shelumiel son of Zurishaddai. 13His division numbers 59,300.

14The tribe of Gad will be next. The leader of the people of Gad is Eliasaph son of Deuel.[a] 15His division numbers 45,650.

16All the men assigned to the camp of Reuben,[d] according to their divisions, number 151,450. They will set out second.

17Then the Tent of Meeting and the camp of the Levites will set out in the middle of the camps. They will set out in the same order as they encamp, each in his own place under his standard.

18On the west will be the divisions of the camp of Ephraim under their standard. The leader of the people of Ephraim is Elishama son of Ammihud. 19His division numbers 40,500.

20The tribe of Manasseh will be next to them. The leader of the people of Manasseh is Gamaliel son of Pedahzur.[e] 21His division numbers 32,200.

22The tribe of Benjamin will be next. The leader of the people of Benjamin is Abidan son of Gideoni. 23His division numbers 35,400.

24All the men assigned to the camp of Ephraim,[f] according to their divisions, number 108,100. They will set out third.

25On the north will be the divisions of the camp of Dan, under their standard. The leader of the people of Dan is Ahiezer son of Ammishaddai. 26His division numbers 62,700.

27The tribe of Asher will camp next to them. The leader of the people of Asher is Pagiel son of Ocran.[g] 28His division numbers 41,500.

29The tribe of Naphtali will be next. The leader of the people of Naphtali is Ahira son of Enan. 30His division numbers 53,400.

31All the men assigned to the camp of Dan number 157,600. They will set out last,[h] under their standards.

32These are the Israelites, counted according to their families. All those in the camps, by their divisions, number 603,550.[i] 33The Levites, however, were not counted[j] along with the other Israelites, as the LORD commanded Moses.

34So the Israelites did everything the LORD commanded Moses; that is the way they encamped under their standards, and that is the way they set out, each with his clan and family.

## The Levites

**3** This is the account of the family of Aaron and Moses at the time the LORD talked with Moses on Mount Sinai.

2The names of the sons of Aaron were Nadab the firstborn and Abihu, Eleazar and Ithamar.[k] 3Those were the names of Aaron's sons, the anointed priests, who were ordained to serve as priests. 4Nadab and Abihu, however, fell dead before the LORD[l] when they made an offering with unauthorized fire before him in the Desert of Sinai.[m] They had no sons; so only Eleazar and Ithamar served as priests during the lifetime of their father Aaron.

2:24 f Nu 10:22
2:27 g Nu 1:13
2:31 h Nu 10:25
2:32 i Ex 38:26; Nu 1:46
2:33 j Nu 1:47
3:2 k Ex 6:23
3:4 l Lev 10:2 m Lev 10:1

[a]14 Many manuscripts of the Masoretic Text, Samaritan Pentateuch and Vulgate (see also Num. 1:14); most manuscripts of the Masoretic Text *Reuel*

5 The LORD said to Moses, 6 "Bring the tribe of Levi and present them to Aaron the priest to assist him.[n] 7 They are to perform duties for him and for the whole community at the Tent of Meeting by doing the work of the tabernacle. 8 They are to take care of all the furnishings of the Tent of Meeting, fulfilling the obligations of the Israelites by doing the work of the tabernacle. 9 Give the Levites to Aaron and his sons;[o] they are the Israelites who are to be given wholly to him.[a] 10 Appoint Aaron and his sons to serve as priests;[p] anyone else who approaches the sanctuary must be put to death."[q]

11 The LORD also said to Moses, 12 "I have taken the Levites from among the Israelites in place of the first male offspring[r] of every Israelite woman. The Levites are mine, 13 for all the firstborn are mine.[s] When I struck down all the firstborn in Egypt, I set apart for myself every firstborn in Israel, whether man or animal. They are to be mine. I am the LORD."

14 The LORD said to Moses in the Desert of Sinai, 15 "Count[t] the Levites by their families and clans. Count every male a month old or more." 16 So Moses counted them, as he was commanded by the word of the LORD.

17 These were the names of the sons of Levi:
Gershon, Kohath and Merari.[u]

18 These were the names of the Gershonite clans:
Libni and Shimei.[v]

19 The Kohathite clans:
Amram, Izhar, Hebron and Uzziel.

20 The Merarite clans:
Mahli and Mushi.

These were the Levite clans, according to their families.

21 To Gershon belonged the clans of the Libnites and Shimeites; these were the Gershonite clans. 22 The number of all the males a month old or more who were counted was 7,500. 23 The Gershonite clans were to camp on the west, behind the tabernacle. 24 The leader of the families of the Gershonites was Eliasaph son of Lael. 25 At the Tent of Meeting the Gershonites were responsible for the care of the tabernacle and tent, its coverings, the curtain at the entrance[w] to the Tent of Meeting, 26 the curtains of the courtyard, the curtain at the entrance to the courtyard surrounding the tabernacle and altar, and the ropes—and everything related to their use.

27 To Kohath belonged the clans of the Amramites, Izharites, Hebronites and Uzzielites;[x] these were the Kohathite clans. 28 The number of all the males a month old or more was 8,600.[b] The Kohathites were responsible for the care of the sanctuary. 29 The Kohathite clans were to camp on the south side of the tabernacle. 30 The leader of the families of the Kohathite clans was Elizaphan son of Uzziel. 31 They were responsible for the care of the ark,[y] the table, the lampstand,[z] the altars, the articles of the sanctuary used in ministering, the curtain, and everything related to their use. 32 The chief leader of the Levites was Eleazar son of Aaron, the priest. He was appointed over those who were responsible for the care of the sanctuary.

33 To Merari belonged the clans of the Mahlites and the Mushites; these were the Merarite clans. 34 The number of all the males a month old or more who were counted was 6,200. 35 The leader of the families of the Merarite clans was Zuriel son of Abihail; they were to camp on the north side of the tabernacle. 36 The Merarites were appointed[a] to take care of the frames of the tabernacle, its crossbars, posts, bases, all its equipment, and everything related to their use, 37 as well as the posts of the surrounding courtyard with their bases, tent pegs and ropes.

38 Moses and Aaron and his sons were to camp to the east of the tabernacle, toward the sunrise, in front of the Tent of Meeting. They were responsible for the care of the sanctuary[b] on behalf of the Israelites. Anyone else who approached the sanctuary was to be put to death.[c]

39 The total number of Levites counted at the LORD's command by Moses and Aaron ac-

**3:6** n Nu 8:6–22; 18:1–7
**3:9** o Nu 8:19; 18:6
**3:10** p Ex 29:9 q Nu 1:51
**3:12** r ver 41; Nu 8:16,18
**3:13** s Ex 13:12
**3:15** t ver 39
**3:17** u Ex 6:16
**3:18** v Ex 6:17
**3:25** w Ex 26:36; Nu 4:25
**3:27** x 1Ch 26:23
**3:31** y Ex 25:10–22 z Ex 25:31
**3:36** a Nu 4:32
**3:38** b Nu 18:5 c ver 10

[a] 9 Most manuscripts of the Masoretic Text; some manuscripts of the Masoretic Text, Samaritan Pentateuch and Septuagint (see also Num. 8:16) *to me* [b] 28 Hebrew; some Septuagint manuscripts *8,300*

cording to their clans, including every male a month old or more, was 22,000.[d]

40The LORD said to Moses, "Count all the firstborn Israelite males who are a month old or more and make a list of their names. 41Take the Levites for me in place of all the firstborn of the Israelites,[e] and the livestock of the Levites in place of all the firstborn of the livestock of the Israelites. I am the LORD."

42So Moses counted all the firstborn of the Israelites, as the LORD commanded him. 43The total number of firstborn males a month old or more, listed by name, was 22,273.[f]

44The LORD also said to Moses, 45"Take the Levites in place of all the firstborn of Israel, and the livestock of the Levites in place of their livestock. The Levites are to be mine. I am the LORD. 46To redeem[g] the 273 firstborn Israelites who exceed the number of the Levites, 47collect five shekels[a][h] for each one, according to the sanctuary shekel,[i] which weighs twenty gerahs.[j] 48Give the money for the redemption of the additional Israelites to Aaron and his sons."

49So Moses collected the redemption money from those who exceeded the number redeemed by the Levites. 50From the firstborn of the Israelites he collected silver weighing 1,365 shekels,[b][k] according to the sanctuary shekel. 51Moses gave the redemption money to Aaron and his sons, as he was commanded by the word of the LORD.

## The Kohathites

4 The LORD said to Moses and Aaron: 2"Take a census of the Kohathite branch of the Levites by their clans and families. 3Count all the men from thirty to fifty years of age[l] who come to serve in the work in the Tent of Meeting.

4"This is the work of the Kohathites in the Tent of Meeting: the care of the most holy things. 5When the camp is to move, Aaron and his sons are to go in and take down the shielding curtain and cover the ark of the Testimony with it. 6Then they are to cover this with hides of sea cows,[c] spread a cloth of solid blue over that and put the poles in place.

7"Over the table of the Presence[m] they are to spread a blue cloth and put on it the plates, dishes and bowls, and the jars for drink offerings; the bread that is continually there[n] is to remain on it. 8Over these they are to spread a scarlet cloth, cover that with hides of sea cows and put its poles in place.

9"They are to take a blue cloth and cover the lampstand that is for light, together with its lamps, its wick trimmers and trays,[o] and all its jars for the oil used to supply it. 10Then they are to wrap it and all its accessories in a covering of hides of sea cows and put it on a carrying frame.

11"Over the gold altar[p] they are to spread a blue cloth and cover that with hides of sea cows and put its poles in place.

12"They are to take all the articles used for ministering in the sanctuary, wrap them in a blue cloth, cover that with hides of sea cows and put them on a carrying frame.

13"They are to remove the ashes from the bronze altar[q] and spread a purple cloth over it. 14Then they are to place on it all the utensils used for ministering at the altar, including the firepans, meat forks, shovels and sprinkling bowls. Over it they are to spread a covering of hides of sea cows and put its poles in place.

15"After Aaron and his sons have finished covering the holy furnishings and all the holy articles, and when the camp is ready to move, the Kohathites are to come to do the carrying.[r] But they must not touch the holy things or they will die.[s] The Kohathites are to carry those things that are in the Tent of Meeting.

16"Eleazar son of Aaron, the priest, is to have charge of the oil for the light,[t] the fragrant incense, the regular grain offering[u] and the anointing oil. He is to be in charge of the entire tabernacle and everything in it, including its holy furnishings and articles."

17The LORD said to Moses and Aaron, 18"See that the Kohathite tribal clans are not cut off from the Levites. 19So that they may live and not die when they come near the most holy things,[v] do this for them: Aaron and his sons are to go into the sanctuary and assign to each man his work and what he is to carry. 20But the Kohathites must not

**3:39** d Nu 26:62
**3:41** e ver 12
**3:43** f ver 39
**3:46** g Ex 13:13; Nu 18:15
**3:47** h Lev 27:6 i Ex 30:13 j Lev 27:25
**3:50** k ver 46–48
**4:3** l ver 23; Nu 8:25; 1Ch 23:3,24,27
**4:7** m Lev 24:6 n Ex 25:30
**4:9** o Ex 25:31,37,38
**4:11** p Ex 30:1
**4:13** q Ex 27:1–8
**4:15** r Nu 7:9 s 2Sa 6:6,7
**4:16** t Ex 25:6 u Ex 29:41
**4:19** v ver 15

[a]47 That is, about 2 ounces (about 55 grams) [b]50 That is, about 35 pounds (about 15.5 kilograms) [c]6 That is, dugongs; also in verses 8, 10, 11, 12, 14 and 25

go in to look[w] at the holy things, even for a moment, or they will die."

## The Gershonites

[21]The LORD said to Moses, [22]"Take a census also of the Gershonites by their families and clans. [23]Count all the men from thirty to fifty years of age[x] who come to serve in the work at the Tent of Meeting.

[24]"This is the service of the Gershonite clans as they work and carry burdens: [25]They are to carry the curtains of the tabernacle, the Tent of Meeting,[y] its covering and the outer covering of hides of sea cows, the curtains for the entrance to the Tent of Meeting, [26]the curtains of the courtyard surrounding the tabernacle and altar, the curtain for the entrance, the ropes and all the equipment used in its service. The Gershonites are to do all that needs to be done with these things. [27]All their service, whether carrying or doing other work, is to be done under the direction of Aaron and his sons. You shall assign to them as their responsibility all they are to carry. [28]This is the service of the Gershonite clans at the Tent of Meeting. Their duties are to be under the direction of Ithamar son of Aaron, the priest.

## The Merarites

[29]"Count the Merarites by their clans and families. [30]Count all the men from thirty to fifty years of age who come to serve in the work at the Tent of Meeting. [31]This is their duty as they perform service at the Tent of Meeting: to carry the frames of the tabernacle, its crossbars, posts and bases,[z] [32]as well as the posts of the surrounding courtyard with their bases, tent pegs, ropes, all their equipment and everything related to their use. Assign to each man the specific things he is to carry. [33]This is the service of the Merarite clans as they work at the Tent of Meeting under the direction of Ithamar son of Aaron, the priest."

## The Numbering of the Levite Clans

[34]Moses, Aaron and the leaders of the community counted the Kohathites[a] by their clans and families. [35]All the men from thirty to fifty years of age who came to serve in the work in the Tent of Meeting, [36]counted by clans, were 2,750. [37]This was the total of all those in the Kohathite clans[b] who served in the Tent of Meeting. Moses and Aaron counted them according to the LORD's command through Moses.

[38]The Gershonites[c] were counted by their clans and families. [39]All the men from thirty to fifty years of age who came to serve in the work at the Tent of Meeting, [40]counted by their clans and families, were 2,630. [41]This was the total of those in the Gershonite clans who served at the Tent of Meeting. Moses and Aaron counted them according to the LORD's command.

[42]The Merarites were counted by their clans and families. [43]All the men from thirty to fifty years of age who came to serve in the work at the Tent of Meeting, [44]counted by their clans, were 3,200. [45]This was the total of those in the Merarite clans.[d] Moses and Aaron counted them according to the LORD's command through Moses.

[46]So Moses, Aaron and the leaders of Israel counted all the Levites by their clans and families. [47]All the men from thirty to fifty years of age[e] who came to do the work of serving and carrying the Tent of Meeting [48]numbered 8,580. [49]At the LORD's command through Moses, each was assigned his work and told what to carry.

Thus they were counted, as the LORD commanded Moses.

## The Purity of the Camp

5 The LORD said to Moses, [2]"Command the Israelites to send away from the camp anyone who has an infectious skin disease[a][f] or a discharge[g] of any kind, or who is ceremonially unclean[h] because of a dead body. [3]Send away male and female alike; send them outside the camp so they will not defile their camp, where I dwell among them.[i]" [4]The Israelites did this; they sent them outside the camp. They did just as the LORD had instructed Moses.

## Restitution for Wrongs

[5]The LORD said to Moses, [6]"Say to the Israelites: 'When a man or woman wrongs

4:20 w Ex19:21
4:23 x ver 3
4:25 y Nu3:25
4:31 z Nu3:36
4:34 a ver 2
4:37 b Nu3:27
4:38 c Ge46:11
4:45 d ver29
4:47 e ver 3
5:2 f Lev13:46 g Lev15:2 h Lev13:3; Nu9:6–10
5:3 i Lev26:12; 2Co6:16

[a]2 Traditionally *leprosy*; the Hebrew word was used for various diseases affecting the skin—not necessarily leprosy.

another in any way[a] and so is unfaithful[j] to the LORD, that person is guilty 7 and must confess[k] the sin he has committed. He must make full restitution[l] for his wrong, add one fifth to it and give it all to the person he has wronged. 8 But if that person has no close relative to whom restitution can be made for the wrong, the restitution belongs to the LORD and must be given to the priest, along with the ram with which atonement is made for him.[m] 9 All the sacred contributions the Israelites bring to a priest will belong to him.[n] 10 Each man's sacred gifts are his own, but what he gives to the priest will belong to the priest.[o]' "

## The Test for an Unfaithful Wife

11 Then the LORD said to Moses, 12 "Speak to the Israelites and say to them: 'If a man's wife goes astray and is unfaithful to him 13 by sleeping with another man,[p] and this is hidden from her husband and her impurity is undetected (since there is no witness against her and she has not been caught in the act), 14 and if feelings of jealousy come over her husband and he suspects his wife and she is impure—or if he is jealous and suspects her even though she is not impure— 15 then he is to take his wife to the priest. He must also take an offering of a tenth of an ephah[b] of barley flour on her behalf. He must not pour oil on it or put incense on it, because it is a grain offering for jealousy, a reminder[q] offering to draw attention to guilt.

16 " 'The priest shall bring her and have her stand before the LORD. 17 Then he shall take some holy water in a clay jar and put some dust from the tabernacle floor into the water. 18 After the priest has had the woman stand before the LORD, he shall loosen her hair[r] and place in her hands the reminder offering, the grain offering for jealousy, while he himself holds the bitter water that brings a curse. 19 Then the priest shall put the woman under oath and say to her, "If no other man has slept with you and you have not gone astray and become impure while married to your husband, may this bitter water that brings a curse not harm you. 20 But if you have gone astray while married to your husband and you have defiled yourself by sleeping with a man other than your husband"— 21 here the priest is to put the woman under this curse of the oath[s]—"may the LORD cause your people to curse and denounce you when he causes your thigh to waste away and your abdomen to swell.[c] 22 May this water[t] that brings a curse enter your body so that your abdomen swells and your thigh wastes away.[d]"

" 'Then the woman is to say, "Amen. So be it.[u]"

23 " 'The priest is to write these curses on a scroll and then wash them off into the bitter water. 24 He shall have the woman drink the bitter water that brings a curse, and this water will enter her and cause bitter suffering. 25 The priest is to take from her hands the grain offering for jealousy, wave it before the LORD[v] and bring it to the altar. 26 The priest is then to take a handful of the grain offering as a memorial offering and burn it on the altar; after that, he is to have the woman drink the water. 27 If she has defiled herself and been unfaithful to her husband, then when she is made to drink the water that brings a curse, it will go into her and cause bitter suffering; her abdomen will swell and her thigh waste away,[e] and she will become accursed[w] among her people. 28 If, however, the woman has not defiled herself and is free from impurity, she will be cleared of guilt and will be able to have children.

29 " 'This, then, is the law of jealousy when a woman goes astray[x] and defiles herself while married to her husband, 30 or when feelings of jealousy come over a man because he suspects his wife. The priest is to have her stand before the LORD and is to apply this entire law to her. 31 The husband will be innocent of any wrongdoing, but the woman will bear the consequences of her sin.' "

## The Nazirite

6 The LORD said to Moses, 2 "Speak to the Israelites and say to them: 'If a man or woman wants to make a special vow[y], a vow of separation to the LORD as a Nazirite,[z] 3 he must abstain from wine[a] and other fermented drink and must not drink

**5:6** j Lev 6:2
**5:7** k Lev 5:5; 26:40; Jos 7:19; Lk 19:8 l Lev 6:5
**5:8** m Lev 6:6,7
**5:9** n Lev 6:17
**5:10** o Lev 10:13
**5:13** p Lev 18:20
**5:15** q Eze 29:16
**5:18** r 1Co 11:6
**5:21** s Jos 6:26; 1Sa 14:24; Ne 10:29
**5:22** t Ps 109:18 u Dt 27:15
**5:25** v Lev 8:27
**5:27** w Jer 29:18; 42:18
**5:29** x ver 19
**6:2** y Ac 21:23 z Jdg 13:5; 16:17; Am 2:11,12
**6:3** a Lk 1:15

[a]6 Or *woman commits any wrong common to mankind* [b]15 That is, probably about 2 quarts (about 2 liters) [c]21 Or *causes you to have a miscarrying womb and barrenness* [d]22 Or *body and cause you to be barren and have a miscarrying womb* [e]27 Or *suffering; she will have barrenness and a miscarrying womb*

**6:5** b 1Sa 1:11
**6:6** c Nu 19:11–22
**6:7** d Nu 9:6
**6:10** e Lev 5:7; 14:22
**6:13** f Ac 21:26
**6:14** g Lev 14:10
**6:15** h Ex 29:2

vinegar made from wine or from other fermented drink. He must not drink grape juice or eat grapes or raisins. 4As long as he is a Nazirite, he must not eat anything that comes from the grapevine, not even the seeds or skins.

5" 'During the entire period of his vow of separation no razor may be used on his head.[b] He must be holy until the period of his separation to the LORD is over; he must let the hair of his head grow long. 6Throughout the period of his separation to the LORD he must not go near a dead body.[c] 7Even if his own father or mother or brother or sister dies, he must not make himself ceremonially unclean[d] on account of them, because the symbol of his separation to God is on his head. 8Throughout the period of his separation he is consecrated to the LORD.

9" 'If someone dies suddenly in his presence, thus defiling the hair he has dedicated, he must shave his head on the day of his cleansing—the seventh day. 10Then on the eighth day he must bring two doves or two young pigeons[e] to the priest at the entrance to the Tent of Meeting. 11The priest is to offer one as a sin offering and the other as a burnt offering to make atonement for him because he sinned by being in the presence of the dead body. That same day he is to consecrate his head. 12He must dedicate himself to the LORD for the period of his separation and must bring a year-old male lamb as a guilt offering. The previous days do not count, because he became defiled during his separation.

13" 'Now this is the law for the Nazirite when the period of his separation is over.[f] He is to be brought to the entrance to the Tent of Meeting. 14There he is to present his offerings to the LORD: a year-old male lamb without defect for a burnt offering, a year-old ewe lamb without defect for a sin offering,[g] a ram without defect for a fellowship offering,[a] 15together with their grain offerings and drink offerings, and a basket of bread made without yeast—cakes made of fine flour mixed with oil, and wafers spread with oil.[h]

16" 'The priest is to present them before the LORD and make the sin offering and the burnt offering. 17He is to present the basket of unleavened bread and is to sacrifice the ram as a fellowship offering to the LORD, together with its grain offering and drink offering.

18" 'Then at the entrance to the Tent of Meeting, the Nazirite must shave off the hair that he dedicated.[i] He is to take the hair and put it in the fire that is under the sacrifice of the fellowship offering.

19" 'After the Nazirite has shaved off the hair of his dedication, the priest is to place in his hands a boiled shoulder of the ram, and a cake and a wafer from the basket, both made without yeast. 20The priest shall then wave them before the LORD as a wave offering; they are holy and belong to the priest, together with the breast that was waved and the thigh that was presented. After that, the Nazirite may drink wine.

21" 'This is the law of the Nazirite who vows his offering to the LORD in accordance with his separation, in addition to whatever else he can afford. He must fulfill the vow he has made, according to the law of the Nazirite.' "

## The Priestly Blessing

22The LORD said to Moses, 23"Tell Aaron and his sons, 'This is how you are to bless[j] the Israelites. Say to them:

24" ' "The LORD bless you[k]
   and keep you;
25 the LORD make his face shine upon you[l]
   and be gracious to you;[m]
26 the LORD turn his face[n] toward you
   and give you peace." '

27"So they will put my name[o] on the Israelites, and I will bless them."

## Offerings at the Dedication of the Tabernacle

7 When Moses finished setting up the tabernacle,[p] he anointed it and consecrated it and all its furnishings. He also anointed and consecrated the altar and all its utensils. 2Then the leaders of Israel,[q] the heads of families who were the tribal leaders in charge of those who were counted, made offerings. 3They brought as their gifts

**6:18** i ver 9; Ac 21:24
**6:23** j 1Ch 23:13
**6:24** k Dt 28:3–6
**6:25** l Ps 80:3; 119:135 m Ge 43:29; Ps 25:16; 86:16
**6:26** n Ps 4:6; 44:3
**6:27** o Dt 28:10; 2Ch 7:14
**7:1** p Ex 40:17
**7:2** q Nu 1:5–16

[a]14 Traditionally *peace offering*; also in verses 17 and 18

**7:7** r Nu 4:24–26,28
**7:8** s Nu 4:31–33
**7:9** t Nu 4:15
**7:10** u 2Ch 7:9
**7:16** v Lev 4:3,23
**7:17** w Lev 3:1
**7:18** x Nu 1:8

before the LORD six covered carts and twelve oxen—an ox from each leader and a cart from every two. These they presented before the tabernacle.

4 The LORD said to Moses, 5 "Accept these from them, that they may be used in the work at the Tent of Meeting. Give them to the Levites as each man's work requires."

6 So Moses took the carts and oxen and gave them to the Levites. 7 He gave two carts and four oxen to the Gershonites,[r] as their work required, 8 and he gave four carts and eight oxen to the Merarites,[s] as their work required. They were all under the direction of Ithamar son of Aaron, the priest. 9 But Moses did not give any to the Kohathites, because they were to carry on their shoulders[t] the holy things, for which they were responsible.

10 When the altar was anointed, the leaders brought their offerings for its dedication[u] and presented them before the altar. 11 For the LORD had said to Moses, "Each day one leader is to bring his offering for the dedication of the altar."

12 The one who brought his offering on the first day was Nahshon son of Amminadab of the tribe of Judah.

13 His offering was one silver plate weighing a hundred and thirty shekels,[a] and one silver sprinkling bowl weighing seventy shekels,[b] both according to the sanctuary shekel, each filled with fine flour mixed with oil as a grain offering; 14 one gold dish weighing ten shekels,[c] filled with incense; 15 one young bull, one ram and one male lamb a year old, for a burnt offering; 16 one male goat for a sin offering;[v] 17 and two oxen, five rams, five male goats and five male lambs a year old, to be sacrificed as a fellowship offering.[d][w] This was the offering of Nahshon son of Amminadab.

18 On the second day Nethanel son of Zuar,[x] the leader of Issachar, brought his offering.

19 The offering he brought was one silver plate weighing a hundred and thirty shekels, and one silver sprinkling bowl weighing seventy shekels, both according to the sanctuary shekel, each filled with fine flour mixed with oil as a grain offering; 20 one gold dish weighing ten shekels, filled with incense; 21 one young bull, one ram and one male lamb a year old, for a burnt offering; 22 one male goat for a sin offering; 23 and two oxen, five rams, five male goats and five male lambs a year old, to be sacrificed as a fellowship offering. This was the offering of Nethanel son of Zuar.

24 On the third day, Eliab son of Helon,[y] the leader of the people of Zebulun, brought his offering.

25 His offering was one silver plate weighing a hundred and thirty shekels, and one silver sprinkling bowl weighing seventy shekels, both according to the sanctuary shekel, each filled with fine flour mixed with oil as a grain offering; 26 one gold dish weighing ten shekels, filled with incense; 27 one young bull, one ram and one male lamb a year old, for a burnt offering; 28 one male goat for a sin offering; 29 and two oxen, five rams, five male goats and five male lambs a year old, to be sacrificed as a fellowship offering. This was the offering of Eliab son of Helon.

30 On the fourth day Elizur son of Shedeur,[z] the leader of the people of Reuben, brought his offering.

31 His offering was one silver plate weighing a hundred and thirty shekels, and one silver sprinkling bowl weighing seventy shekels, both according to the sanctuary shekel, each filled with fine flour mixed with oil as a grain offering; 32 one gold dish weighing ten shekels, filled with incense; 33 one young bull, one ram and one male lamb a year old, for a burnt offering; 34 one male goat for a sin offering; 35 and two oxen, five rams, five male goats and five male lambs a year old, to be sacrificed as a fellowship

**7:24** y Nu 1:9
**7:30** z Nu 1:5

[a] 13 That is, about 3 1/4 pounds (about 1.5 kilograms); also elsewhere in this chapter [b] 13 That is, about 1 3/4 pounds (about 0.8 kilogram); also elsewhere in this chapter [c] 14 That is, about 4 ounces (about 110 grams); also elsewhere in this chapter [d] 17 Traditionally *peace offering*; also elsewhere in this chapter

offering. This was the offering of Elizur son of Shedeur.

36 On the fifth day Shelumiel son of Zurishaddai,[a] the leader of the people of Simeon, brought his offering.

37 His offering was one silver plate weighing a hundred and thirty shekels, and one silver sprinkling bowl weighing seventy shekels, both according to the sanctuary shekel, each filled with fine flour mixed with oil as a grain offering; 38 one gold dish weighing ten shekels, filled with incense; 39 one young bull, one ram and one male lamb a year old, for a burnt offering; 40 one male goat for a sin offering; 41 and two oxen, five rams, five male goats and five male lambs a year old, to be sacrificed as a fellowship offering. This was the offering of Shelumiel son of Zurishaddai.

42 On the sixth day Eliasaph son of Deuel,[b] the leader of the people of Gad, brought his offering.

43 His offering was one silver plate weighing a hundred and thirty shekels, and one silver sprinkling bowl weighing seventy shekels, both according to the sanctuary shekel, each filled with fine flour mixed with oil as a grain offering; 44 one gold dish weighing ten shekels, filled with incense; 45 one young bull, one ram and one male lamb a year old, for a burnt offering; 46 one male goat for a sin offering; 47 and two oxen, five rams, five male goats and five male lambs a year old, to be sacrificed as a fellowship offering. This was the offering of Eliasaph son of Deuel.

48 On the seventh day Elishama son of Ammihud,[c] the leader of the people of Ephraim, brought his offering.

49 His offering was one silver plate weighing a hundred and thirty shekels, and one silver sprinkling bowl weighing seventy shekels, both according to the sanctuary shekel, each filled with fine flour mixed with oil as a grain offering; 50 one gold dish weighing ten shekels, filled with incense; 51 one young bull, one ram and one male lamb a year old, for a burnt offering; 52 one male goat for a sin offering; 53 and two oxen, five rams, five male goats and five male lambs a year old, to be sacrificed as a fellowship offering. This was the offering of Elishama son of Ammihud.

54 On the eighth day Gamaliel son of Pedahzur,[d] the leader of the people of Manasseh, brought his offering.

55 His offering was one silver plate weighing a hundred and thirty shekels, and one silver sprinkling bowl weighing seventy shekels, both according to the sanctuary shekel, each filled with fine flour mixed with oil as a grain offering; 56 one gold dish weighing ten shekels, filled with incense; 57 one young bull, one ram and one male lamb a year old, for a burnt offering; 58 one male goat for a sin offering; 59 and two oxen, five rams, five male goats and five male lambs a year old, to be sacrificed as a fellowship offering. This was the offering of Gamaliel son of Pedahzur.

60 On the ninth day Abidan son of Gideoni,[e] the leader of the people of Benjamin, brought his offering.

61 His offering was one silver plate weighing a hundred and thirty shekels, and one silver sprinkling bowl weighing seventy shekels, both according to the sanctuary shekel, each filled with fine flour mixed with oil as a grain offering; 62 one gold dish weighing ten shekels, filled with incense; 63 one young bull, one ram and one male lamb a year old, for a burnt offering; 64 one male goat for a sin offering; 65 and two oxen, five rams, five male goats and five male lambs a year old, to be sacrificed as a fellowship offering. This was the offering of Abidan son of Gideoni.

66 On the tenth day Ahiezer son of Ammishaddai,[f] the leader of the people of Dan, brought his offering.

67 His offering was one silver plate weighing a hundred and thirty shek-

**7:36** a Nu 1:6
**7:42** b Nu 1:14
**7:48** c Nu 1:10
**7:54** d Nu 1:10; 2:20
**7:60** e Nu 1:11
**7:66** f Nu 1:12; 2:25

els, and one silver sprinkling bowl weighing seventy shekels, both according to the sanctuary shekel, each filled with fine flour mixed with oil as a grain offering; 68 one gold dish weighing ten shekels, filled with incense; 69 one young bull, one ram and one male lamb a year old, for a burnt offering; 70 one male goat for a sin offering; 71 and two oxen, five rams, five male goats and five male lambs a year old, to be sacrificed as a fellowship offering. This was the offering of Ahiezer son of Ammishaddai.

72 On the eleventh day Pagiel son of Ocran,[g] the leader of the people of Asher, brought his offering.

73 His offering was one silver plate weighing a hundred and thirty shekels, and one silver sprinkling bowl weighing seventy shekels, both according to the sanctuary shekel, each filled with fine flour mixed with oil as a grain offering; 74 one gold dish weighing ten shekels, filled with incense; 75 one young bull, one ram and one male lamb a year old, for a burnt offering; 76 one male goat for a sin offering; 77 and two oxen, five rams, five male goats and five male lambs a year old, to be sacrificed as a fellowship offering. This was the offering of Pagiel son of Ocran.

78 On the twelfth day Ahira son of Enan,[h] the leader of the people of Naphtali, brought his offering.

79 His offering was one silver plate weighing a hundred and thirty shekels, and one silver sprinkling bowl weighing seventy shekels, both according to the sanctuary shekel, each filled with fine flour mixed with oil as a grain offering; 80 one gold dish weighing ten shekels, filled with incense; 81 one young bull, one ram and one male lamb a year old, for a burnt offering; 82 one male goat for a sin offering; 83 and two oxen, five rams, five male goats and five male lambs a year old, to be sacrificed as a fellowship offering. This was the offering of Ahira son of Enan.

84 These were the offerings of the Israelite leaders for the dedication of the altar when it was anointed:[i] twelve silver plates, twelve silver sprinkling bowls and twelve gold dishes. 85 Each silver plate weighed a hundred and thirty shekels, and each sprinkling bowl seventy shekels. Altogether, the silver dishes weighed two thousand four hundred shekels,[a] according to the sanctuary shekel. 86 The twelve gold dishes filled with incense weighed ten shekels each, according to the sanctuary shekel. Altogether, the gold dishes weighed a hundred and twenty shekels.[b] 87 The total number of animals for the burnt offering came to twelve young bulls, twelve rams and twelve male lambs a year old, together with their grain offering. Twelve male goats were used for the sin offering. 88 The total number of animals for the sacrifice of the fellowship offering came to twenty-four oxen, sixty rams, sixty male goats and sixty male lambs a year old. These were the offerings for the dedication of the altar after it was anointed.[j]

89 When Moses entered the Tent of Meeting to speak with the LORD,[k] he heard the voice speaking to him from between the two cherubim above the atonement cover[l] on the ark of the Testimony. And he spoke with him.

## Setting Up the Lamps

8 The LORD said to Moses, 2 "Speak to Aaron and say to him, 'When you set up the seven lamps, they are to light the area in front of the lampstand.[m]' "

3 Aaron did so; he set up the lamps so that they faced forward on the lampstand, just as the LORD commanded Moses. 4 This is how the lampstand was made: It was made of hammered gold[n]—from its base to its blossoms. The lampstand was made exactly like the pattern the LORD had shown Moses.

## The Setting Apart of the Levites

5 The LORD said to Moses: 6 "Take the Levites from among the other Israelites

7:72 g Nu 1:13
7:78 h Nu 1:15; 2:29
7:84 i ver 1,10
7:88 j ver 1,10
7:89 k Ex 25:21,22 l Ps 80:1; 99:1
8:2 m Ex 25:37
8:4 n Ex 25:18,36

[a] 85 That is, about 60 pounds (about 28 kilograms) [b] 86 That is, about 3 pounds (about 1.4 kilograms)

and make them ceremonially clean.[o] 7To purify them, do this: Sprinkle the water of cleansing[p] on them; then have them shave their whole bodies[q] and wash their clothes, and so purify themselves. 8Have them take a young bull with its grain offering of fine flour mixed with oil;[r] then you are to take a second young bull for a sin offering. 9Bring the Levites to the front of the Tent of Meeting[s] and assemble the whole Israelite community.[t] 10You are to bring the Levites before the LORD, and the Israelites are to lay their hands on them. 11Aaron is to present the Levites before the LORD as a wave offering from the Israelites, so that they may be ready to do the work of the LORD.

12"After the Levites lay their hands on the heads of the bulls,[u] use the one for a sin offering to the LORD and the other for a burnt offering, to make atonement for the Levites. 13Have the Levites stand in front of Aaron and his sons and then present them as a wave offering to the LORD. 14In this way you are to set the Levites apart from the other Israelites, and the Levites will be mine.[v]

15"After you have purified the Levites and presented them as a wave offering,[w] they are to come to do their work at the Tent of Meeting. 16They are the Israelites who are to be given wholly to me. I have taken them as my own in place of the firstborn, the first male offspring[x] from every Israelite woman. 17Every firstborn male in Israel, whether man or animal, is mine. When I struck down all the firstborn in Egypt, I set them apart for myself.[y] 18And I have taken the Levites in place of all the firstborn sons in Israel. 19Of all the Israelites, I have given the Levites as gifts to Aaron and his sons[z] to do the work at the Tent of Meeting on behalf of the Israelites[a] and to make atonement for them[b] so that no plague will strike the Israelites when they go near the sanctuary."

20Moses, Aaron and the whole Israelite community did with the Levites just as the LORD commanded Moses. 21The Levites purified themselves and washed their clothes.[c] Then Aaron presented them as a wave offering before the LORD and made atonement for them to purify them. 22After that, the Levites came to do their work at the Tent of Meeting under the supervision of Aaron and his sons. They did with the Levites just as the LORD commanded Moses.

23The LORD said to Moses, 24"This applies to the Levites: Men twenty-five years old or more[d] shall come to take part in the work at the Tent of Meeting, 25but at the age of fifty, they must retire from their regular service and work no longer. 26They may assist their brothers in performing their duties at the Tent of Meeting, but they themselves must not do the work. This, then, is how you are to assign the responsibilities of the Levites."

## The Passover

9 The LORD spoke to Moses in the Desert of Sinai in the first month of the second year after they came out of Egypt.[e] He said, 2"Have the Israelites celebrate the Passover at the appointed time. 3Celebrate it at the appointed time, at twilight on the fourteenth day of this month, in accordance with all its rules and regulations."

4So Moses told the Israelites to celebrate the Passover, 5and they did so in the Desert of Sinai at twilight on the fourteenth day of the first month.[f] The Israelites did everything just as the LORD commanded Moses.

6But some of them could not celebrate the Passover on that day because they were ceremonially unclean on account of a dead body. So they came to Moses and Aaron[g] that same day 7and said to Moses, "We have become unclean because of a dead body, but why should we be kept from presenting the LORD's offering with the other Israelites at the appointed time?"

8Moses answered them, "Wait until I find out what the LORD commands concerning you."

9Then the LORD said to Moses, 10"Tell the Israelites: 'When any of you or your descendants are unclean because of a dead body or are away on a journey, they may still celebrate the LORD's Passover. 11They are to celebrate it on the fourteenth day of the second month at twilight. They are to eat the lamb, together with unleavened bread and bitter herbs.[h] 12They must not leave any of it till morning or break any of its bones.[i] When they celebrate the Passover, they must fol-

**8:6** o Isa 52:11
**8:7** p Nu 19:9,17 q Lev 14:9
**8:8** r Lev 2:1
**8:9** s Ex 40:12 t Lev 8:3
**8:12** u Ex 29:10
**8:14** v Nu 3:12
**8:15** w Ex 29:24
**8:16** x Nu 3:12
**8:17** y Ex 13:2
**8:19** z Nu 3:9 a Nu 1:53 b Nu 16:46
**8:21** c ver 7
**8:24** d 1Ch 23:3
**9:1** e Nu 1:1
**9:5** f Ex 12:1–13; Jos 5:10
**9:6** g Ex 18:15; Nu 27:2
**9:11** h Ex 12:8
**9:12** i Ex 12:46; Jn 19:36*

**9:13** j Ge 17:14; Ex 12:15
**9:14** k Ex 12:48,49
**9:15** l Ex 40:34 m Ex 13:21
**9:17** n Ex 40:36–38; Nu 10:11,12; 1Co 10:1

low all the regulations. 13 But if a man who is ceremonially clean and not on a journey fails to celebrate the Passover, that person must be cut off from his people[j] because he did not present the LORD's offering at the appointed time. That man will bear the consequences of his sin.

14 "'An alien[k] living among you who wants to celebrate the LORD's Passover must do so in accordance with its rules and regulations. You must have the same regulations for the alien and the native-born.'"

## The Cloud Above the Tabernacle

15 On the day the tabernacle, the Tent of the Testimony, was set up, the cloud[l] covered it. From evening till morning the cloud above the tabernacle looked like fire.[m] 16 That is how it continued to be; the cloud covered it, and at night it looked like fire. 17 Whenever the cloud lifted from above the Tent, the Israelites set out; wherever the cloud settled, the Israelites encamped.[n] 18 At the LORD's command the Israelites set out, and at his command they encamped. As long as the cloud stayed over the tabernacle, they remained in camp. 19 When the cloud remained over the tabernacle a long time, the Israelites obeyed the LORD's order and did not set out. 20 Sometimes the cloud was over the tabernacle only a few days; at the LORD's command they would encamp, and then at his command they would set out. 21 Sometimes the cloud stayed only from evening till morning, and when it lifted in the morning, they set out. Whether by day or by night, whenever the cloud lifted, they set out. 22 Whether the cloud stayed over the tabernacle for two days or a month or a year, the Israelites would remain in camp and not set out; but when it lifted, they would set out. 23 At the LORD's command they encamped, and at the LORD's command they set out. They obeyed the LORD's order, in accordance with his command through Moses.

## The Silver Trumpets

10 The LORD said to Moses: 2 "Make two trumpets of hammered silver, and use them for calling the community together and for having the camps set out. 3 When both are sounded, the whole community is to assemble before you at the entrance to the Tent of Meeting. 4 If only one is sounded, the leaders[o]—the heads of the clans of Israel—are to assemble before you. 5 When a trumpet blast is sounded, the tribes camping on the east are to set out.[p] 6 At the sounding of a second blast, the camps on the south are to set out.[q] The blast will be the signal for setting out. 7 To gather the assembly, blow the trumpets,[r] but not with the same signal.

8 "The sons of Aaron, the priests, are to blow the trumpets. This is to be a lasting ordinance for you and the generations to come.[s] 9 When you go into battle in your own land against an enemy who is oppressing you,[t] sound a blast on the trumpets. Then you will be remembered by the LORD your God and rescued from your enemies.[u] 10 Also at your times of rejoicing—your appointed feasts and New Moon festivals—you are to sound the trumpets[v] over your burnt offerings and fellowship offerings,[a] and they will be a memorial for you before your God. I am the LORD your God."

## The Israelites Leave Sinai

11 On the twentieth day of the second month of the second year, the cloud lifted[w] from above the tabernacle of the Testimony. 12 Then the Israelites set out from the Desert of Sinai and traveled from place to place until the cloud came to rest in the Desert of Paran. 13 They set out, this first time, at the LORD's command through Moses.

14 The divisions of the camp of Judah went first, under their standard.[x] Nahshon son of Amminadab was in command. 15 Nethanel son of Zuar was over the division of the tribe of Issachar, 16 and Eliab son of Helon was over the division of the tribe of Zebulun. 17 Then the tabernacle was taken down, and the Gershonites and Merarites, who carried it, set out.[y]

18 The divisions of the camp of Reuben went next, under their standard.[z] Elizur son of Shedeur was in command. 19 Shelumiel son of Zurishaddai was over the division of the tribe of Simeon, 20 and Eliasaph son of

**10:4** o Ex 18:21
**10:5** p ver 14
**10:6** q ver 18
**10:7** r Joel 2:1
**10:8** s Nu 31:6
**10:9** t Jdg 2:18 u Ps 106:4
**10:10** v Lev 23:24
**10:11** w Nu 9:17
**10:14** x Nu 2:3–9
**10:17** y Nu 4:21–32
**10:18** z Nu 2:10–16

[a] 10 Traditionally *peace offerings*

Deuel was over the division of the tribe of
Gad. 21Then the Kohathites set out, carrying
the holy things.[a] The tabernacle was to be
set up before they arrived.
22The divisions of the camp of Ephraim[b]
went next, under their standard. Elishama
son of Ammihud was in command. 23Ga-
maliel son of Pedahzur was over the divi-
sion of the tribe of Manasseh, 24and Abidan
son of Gideoni was over the division of the
tribe of Benjamin.
25Finally, as the rear guard[c] for all the
units, the divisions of the camp of Dan set
out, under their standard. Ahiezer son of
Ammishaddai was in command. 26Pagiel
son of Ocran was over the division of the
tribe of Asher, 27and Ahira son of Enan was
over the division of the tribe of Naphtali.
28This was the order of march for the Israel-
ite divisions as they set out.
29Now Moses said to Hobab son of Reuel[d]
the Midianite, Moses' father-in-law, "We
are setting out for the place about which the
LORD said, 'I will give it to you.'[e] Come with
us and we will treat you well, for the LORD
has promised good things to Israel."
30He answered, "No, I will not go; I am
going back to my own land and my own
people."
31But Moses said, "Please do not leave us.
You know where we should camp in the des-
ert, and you can be our eyes.[f] 32If you come
with us, we will share with you whatever
good things the LORD gives us."
33So they set out[g] from the mountain of
the LORD and traveled for three days. The
ark of the covenant of the LORD went before
them during those three days to find them
a place to rest. 34The cloud of the LORD was
over them by day when they set out from
the camp.[h]
35Whenever the ark set out, Moses said,

"Rise up, O LORD!
May your enemies be scattered;[i]
may your foes flee before you."

36Whenever it came to rest, he said,

"Return, O LORD,
to the countless thousands of Israel."

10:21 a Nu 4:20
10:22 b Nu 2:24
10:25 c Nu 2:31; Jos 6:9
10:29 d Ex 2:18 e Ge 12:7
10:31 f Job 29:15
10:33 g Dt 1:33
10:34 h Nu 9:15-23
10:35 i Ps 68:1

## Fire From the LORD

11 Now the people complained about
their hardships in the hearing of
the LORD, and when he heard them his an-
ger was aroused. Then fire from the LORD
burned among them[j] and consumed some
of the outskirts of the camp. 2When the
people cried out to Moses, he prayed to the
LORD[k] and the fire died down. 3So that place
was called Taberah,[a] because fire from the
LORD had burned among them.

## Quail From the LORD

4The rabble with them began to crave
other food,[l] and again the Israelites started
wailing[m] and said, "If only we had meat to
eat! 5We remember the fish we ate in Egypt
at no cost—also the cucumbers, melons,
leeks, onions and garlic.[n] 6But now we have
lost our appetite; we never see anything but
this manna!"
7The manna was like coriander seed[o] and
looked like resin. 8The people went around
gathering it, and then ground it in a hand-
mill or crushed it in a mortar. They cooked
it in a pot or made it into cakes. And it tasted
like something made with olive oil. 9When
the dew[p] settled on the camp at night, the
manna also came down.
10Moses heard the people of every family
wailing, each at the entrance to his tent.
The LORD became exceedingly angry, and
Moses was troubled. 11He asked the LORD,
"Why have you brought this trouble on your
servant? What have I done to displease you
that you put the burden of all these people
on me? 12Did I conceive all these people?
Did I give them birth? Why do you tell me
to carry them in my arms, as a nurse carries
an infant,[q] to the land you promised on oath
to their forefathers?[r] 13Where can I get meat
for all these people? They keep wailing to
me, 'Give us meat to eat!' 14I cannot carry
all these people by myself; the burden is too
heavy for me.[s] 15If this is how you are going
to treat me, put me to death right now—if I
have found favor in your eyes—and do not
let me face my own ruin."
16The LORD said to Moses: "Bring me
seventy of Israel's elders who are known
to you as leaders and officials among the

11:1 j Lev 10:2
11:2 k Nu 21:7
11:4 l Ex 12:38 m Ps 78:18
11:5 n Ex 16:3
11:7 o Ex 16:31
11:9 p Ex 16:13
11:12 q Isa 49:23 r Ex 13:5
11:14 s Ex 18:18

[a]3 *Taberah* means *burning.*

people. Have them come to the Tent of Meeting, that they may stand there with you. [17]I will come down and speak with you there, and I will take of the Spirit that is on you and put the Spirit on them.[t] They will help you carry the burden of the people so that you will not have to carry it alone.[u]

[18]"Tell the people: 'Consecrate yourselves[v] in preparation for tomorrow, when you will eat meat. The LORD heard you when you wailed, "If only we had meat to eat! We were better off in Egypt!"[w] Now the LORD will give you meat, and you will eat it. [19]You will not eat it for just one day, or two days, or five, ten or twenty days, [20]but for a whole month—until it comes out of your nostrils and you loathe it[x]—because you have rejected the LORD, who is among you, and have wailed before him, saying, "Why did we ever leave Egypt?" ' "

[21]But Moses said, "Here I am among six hundred thousand men on foot, and you say, 'I will give them meat to eat for a whole month!' [22]Would they have enough if flocks and herds were slaughtered for them? Would they have enough if all the fish in the sea were caught for them?"

[23]The LORD answered Moses, "Is the LORD's arm too short?[y] You will now see whether or not what I say will come true for you."

[24]So Moses went out and told the people what the LORD had said. He brought together seventy of their elders and had them stand around the Tent. [25]Then the LORD came down in the cloud[z] and spoke with him,[a] and he took of the Spirit that was on him and put the Spirit on the seventy elders. When the Spirit rested on them, they prophesied, but they did not do so again.[a]

[26]However, two men, whose names were Eldad and Medad, had remained in the camp. They were listed among the elders, but did not go out to the Tent. Yet the Spirit also rested on them, and they prophesied in the camp. [27]A young man ran and told Moses, "Eldad and Medad are prophesying in the camp."

[28]Joshua son of Nun, who had been Moses' aide since youth, spoke up and said, "Moses, my lord, stop them!"[b]

[29]But Moses replied, "Are you jealous for my sake? I wish that all the LORD's people were prophets[c] and that the LORD would put his Spirit on them!" [30]Then Moses and the elders of Israel returned to the camp.

[31]Now a wind went out from the LORD and drove quail[d] in from the sea. It brought them[b] down all around the camp to about three feet[c] above the ground, as far as a day's walk in any direction. [32]All that day and night and all the next day the people went out and gathered quail. No one gathered less than ten homers.[d] Then they spread them out all around the camp. [33]But while the meat was still between their teeth[e] and before it could be consumed, the anger of the LORD burned against the people, and he struck them with a severe plague.[f] [34]Therefore the place was named Kibroth Hattaavah,[e] because there they buried the people who had craved other food.

[35]From Kibroth Hattaavah the people traveled to Hazeroth[g] and stayed there.

## Miriam and Aaron Oppose Moses

**12** Miriam and Aaron began to talk against Moses because of his Cushite wife,[h] for he had married a Cushite. [2]"Has the LORD spoken only through Moses?" they asked. "Hasn't he also spoken through us?" And the LORD heard this.

[3](Now Moses was a very humble man, more humble than anyone else on the face of the earth.)

[4]At once the LORD said to Moses, Aaron and Miriam, "Come out to the Tent of Meeting, all three of you." So the three of them came out. [5]Then the LORD came down in a pillar of cloud;[i] he stood at the entrance to the Tent and summoned Aaron and Miriam. When both of them stepped forward, [6]he said, "Listen to my words:

"When a prophet of the LORD is among
you,
I reveal myself to him in visions,[j]
I speak to him in dreams.[k]
[7]But this is not true of my servant
Moses;[l]
he is faithful in all my house.[m]
[8]With him I speak face to face,

[a]25 Or *prophesied and continued to do so* [b]31 Or *They flew* [c]31 Hebrew *two cubits* (about 1 meter) [d]32 That is, probably about 60 bushels (about 2.2 kiloliters) [e]34 *Kibroth Hattaavah* means *graves of craving.*

**11:17** t ver 25,29; 1Sa 10:6 u Ex 18:18
**11:18** v Ex 19:10 w Ac 7:39
**11:20** x Ps 78:29
**11:23** y Isa 50:2; 59:1
**11:25** z Nu 12:5 a ver 17
**11:28** b Mk 9:38–40
**11:29** c 1Co 14:5
**11:31** d Ex 16:13; Ps 78:26–28
**11:33** e Ps 78:30 f Ps 106:15
**11:35** g Nu 33:17
**12:1** h Ex 2:21
**12:5** i Nu 11:25
**12:6** j Ge 15:1; 46:2 k Ge 31:10; 1Ki 3:5; Heb 1:1
**12:7** l Ps 105:26 m Heb 3:2,5

12:8 n Dt34:10 o Ps17:15
12:10 p Dt24:9 q 2Ki5:1,27
12:11 r 2Sa19:19; 24:10
12:14 s Lev13:46; Nu5:2–3

clearly and not in riddles;[n]
he sees the form of the LORD.[o]
Why then were you not afraid
to speak against my servant
Moses?"

9 The anger of the LORD burned against them, and he left them.

10 When the cloud lifted from above the Tent, there stood Miriam—leprous,[a] like snow.[p] Aaron turned toward her and saw that she had leprosy;[q] 11 and he said to Moses, "Please, my lord, do not hold against us the sin we have so foolishly committed.[r] 12 Do not let her be like a stillborn infant coming from its mother's womb with its flesh half eaten away."

13 So Moses cried out to the LORD, "O God, please heal her!"

14 The LORD replied to Moses, "If her father had spit in her face, would she not have been in disgrace for seven days? Confine her outside the camp[s] for seven days; after that she can be brought back." 15 So Miriam was confined outside the camp for seven days, and the people did not move on till she was brought back.

16 After that, the people left Hazeroth and encamped in the Desert of Paran.

## Exploring Canaan

13:2 t Dt1:22

13 The LORD said to Moses, 2 "Send some men to explore[t] the land of Canaan, which I am giving to the Israelites. From each ancestral tribe send one of its leaders."

3 So at the LORD's command Moses sent them out from the Desert of Paran. All of them were leaders of the Israelites. 4 These are their names:

from the tribe of Reuben, Shammua son of Zaccur;
5 from the tribe of Simeon, Shaphat son of Hori;
6 from the tribe of Judah, Caleb son of Jephunneh;
7 from the tribe of Issachar, Igal son of Joseph;
8 from the tribe of Ephraim, Hoshea son of Nun;
9 from the tribe of Benjamin, Palti son of Raphu;
10 from the tribe of Zebulun, Gaddiel son of Sodi;
11 from the tribe of Manasseh (a tribe of Joseph), Gaddi son of Susi;
12 from the tribe of Dan, Ammiel son of Gemalli;

[a]10 The Hebrew word was used for various diseases affecting the skin—not necessarily leprosy.

## The African Presence

### Numbers 12

Some scholars suggest that Miriam and Aaron objected to Moses' Cushite wife because of her culture or religion. This wife was most likely Zipporah, daughter of Jethro, a Midianite priest. Habakkuk 3:7 identifies the "tents of Cushan" with the "dwellings of Midian," lending evidence that Zipporah was the wife mentioned here (but see the African Presence note on Ex 2:16–22).

The Lord punished Miriam by inflicting her with a flaky skin disease often translated "leprosy." Many alternative theories have been offered as to why Miriam and Aaron opposed Moses' marriage to the Cushite woman—from disapproval of Moses marrying a foreign woman, to opposition to interracial marriage, to jealousy by Miriam of his new wife, to jealousy of Moses' role as God's spokesperson. Some scholars have contrasted Miriam's flaky skin, which probably appeared white, with the dark skin of the Cushite woman, intimating that her skin color was originally dark.

# Miriam

## *Plagued by Jealousy*

Miriam was the daughter of Amram and Jochebed, and the sister of Aaron and Moses. Bible scholars assume her to be the sister mentioned in Exodus 2 who watched the basket that held baby Moses float through the reeds to the pharaoh's palace. Miriam watched from afar as Pharaoh's daughter retrieved the basket and claimed Moses as her son. Miriam offered to get a wet nurse—the child's own mother, unbeknownst to Pharaoh's daughter (see Ex 2:7–9).

Years later, Moses fled Egypt and settled in Midian. He met Zipporah, the daughter of Jethro, a Midianite priest, and married her (see Ex 2:15–21). Some time later, Miriam and Aaron criticized Moses "because of his Cushite wife" (Nu 12:1). We are not certain if Zipporah is to be identified as this woman that Miriam and Aaron spoke against. It is possible (though not necessarily so) that the Cushite wife mentioned here was another woman Moses had married.

In addition to their criticisms related to Moses' wife, Miriam and Aaron questioned and challenged Moses' sole right to speak for God to the people. As a result of opposing Moses—which stemmed from jealousy—Miriam was stricken with leprosy (see Nu 12:9–10). After Moses and Aaron interceded with God on Miriam's behalf, she was healed of her leprosy after a seven-day confinement (see Nu 12:11–15).

The spirit of Miriam is alive and well in many women today. We daily suffer physical and spiritual calamities as a result of the deeply rooted jealousies that we harbor. It is jealousy that creates criticism and envy of our friends, loved ones and even strangers. Jealousy and the actions that result from it are not of God.

So then, how do we thwart or control jealousy? How do we prevent ourselves from suffering Miriam's plight? We must be "reborn" each day, seeking God in our every thought and action. We need to pray to him for strength to be Spirit-minded, Christ-centered and God-directed in our homes, workplaces, communities and, most of all, in our churches.

—T. Harrison-Dixon

### reflection

*Do you sometimes struggle with jealousy and criticism?*

*Ask God to receive glory from your life as he deals with you.*

### read

Numbers 12:1–16; 20:1; 26:59; see also Exodus 2:4–10; 15:20–21; Deuteronomy 24:9; Micah 6:4.

See also the Inspire Notes "Dance, Sisters, Dance," "Rebellion," "Female Ministers and Evangelists" and "Women in Preaching Ministries."

For the next Women of the Bible note, go to page 191.

**13:20** u Dt 1:25
**13:22** v Jos 15:14 w Ps 78:12,43
**13:27** x Ex 3:8 y Dt 1:25
**13:28** z Dt 1:28

13 from the tribe of Asher, Sethur son of Michael;
14 from the tribe of Naphtali, Nahbi son of Vophsi;
15 from the tribe of Gad, Geuel son of Maki.

16 These are the names of the men Moses sent to explore the land. (Moses gave Hoshea son of Nun the name Joshua.)

17 When Moses sent them to explore Canaan, he said, "Go up through the Negev and on into the hill country. 18 See what the land is like and whether the people who live there are strong or weak, few or many. 19 What kind of land do they live in? Is it good or bad? What kind of towns do they live in? Are they unwalled or fortified? 20 How is the soil? Is it fertile or poor? Are there trees on it or not? Do your best to bring back some of the fruit of the land.[u]" (It was the season for the first ripe grapes.)

21 So they went up and explored the land from the Desert of Zin as far as Rehob, toward Lebo[a] Hamath. 22 They went up through the Negev and came to Hebron, where Ahiman, Sheshai and Talmai,[v] the descendants of Anak, lived. (Hebron had been built seven years before Zoan in Egypt.)[w] 23 When they reached the Valley of Eshcol,[b] they cut off a branch bearing a single cluster of grapes. Two of them carried it on a pole between them, along with some pomegranates and figs. 24 That place was called the Valley of Eshcol because of the cluster of grapes the Israelites cut off there. 25 At the end of forty days they returned from exploring the land.

## Report on the Exploration

26 They came back to Moses and Aaron and the whole Israelite community at Kadesh in the Desert of Paran. There they reported to them and to the whole assembly and showed them the fruit of the land. 27 They gave Moses this account: "We went into the land to which you sent us, and it does flow with milk and honey![x] Here is its fruit.[y] 28 But the people who live there are powerful, and the cities are fortified and very large.[z] We even saw descendants of Anak there. 29 The Amalekites live in the Negev; the Hittites, Jebusites and Amorites live in the hill country; and the Canaanites live near the sea and along the Jordan."

30 Then Caleb silenced the people before Moses and said, "We should go up and take possession of the land, for we can certainly do it."

31 But the men who had gone up with him said, "We can't attack those people; they are stronger than we are."[a] 32 And they spread among the Israelites a bad report[b] about the land they had explored. They said, "The land we explored devours those living in it. All the people we saw there are of great size. 33 We saw the Nephilim there (the descendants of Anak come from the Nephilim). We seemed like grasshoppers in our own eyes, and we looked the same to them."

> *"What we need are mental and spiritual giants who are aflame with a purpose . . . We're a race ready for crusade."*
>
> —NANNIE HELEN BURROUGHS, CIVIL RIGHTS ACTIVIST

## The People Rebel

14 That night all the people of the community raised their voices and wept aloud. 2 All the Israelites grumbled against Moses and Aaron, and the whole assembly said to them, "If only we had died in Egypt! Or in this desert! 3 Why is the LORD bringing us to this land only to let us fall by the sword? Our wives and children will be taken as plunder. Wouldn't it be better for us to go back to Egypt?" 4 And they said to each other, "We should choose a leader and go back to Egypt."

5 Then Moses and Aaron fell facedown[c] in front of the whole Israelite assembly gathered there. 6 Joshua son of Nun and Caleb son of Jephunneh, who were among those who had explored the land, tore their clothes 7 and said to the entire Israelite assembly, "The land we passed through and explored is exceedingly good.[d] 8 If the LORD is pleased with us,[e] he will lead us into that land, a land flowing with milk and honey,[f] and will give it to us. 9 Only do not rebel[g]

**13:31** a Dt 1:28; 9:1; Jos 14:8
**13:32** b Nu 14:36,37
**14:5** c Nu 16:4,22,45
**14:7** d Nu 13:27
**14:8** e Dt 10:15 f Nu 13:27
**14:9** g Dt 9:7,23,24

[a] 21 Or *toward the entrance to* [b] 23 *Eshcol* means *cluster*; also in verse 24.

against the LORD. And do not be afraid of the people of the land,[h] because we will swallow them up. Their protection is gone, but the LORD is with us. Do not be afraid of them."

10 But the whole assembly talked about stoning[i] them. Then the glory of the LORD[j] appeared at the Tent of Meeting to all the Israelites. 11 The LORD said to Moses, "How long will these people treat me with contempt? How long will they refuse to believe in me, in spite of all the miraculous signs I have performed among them? 12 I will strike them down with a plague and destroy them, but I will make you into a nation[k] greater and stronger than they."

13 Moses said to the LORD, "Then the Egyptians will hear about it! By your power you brought these people up from among them.[l] 14 And they will tell the inhabitants of this land about it. They have already heard[m] that you, O LORD, are with these people and that you, O LORD, have been seen face to face, that your cloud stays over them, and that you go before them in a pillar of cloud by day and a pillar of fire by night.[n] 15 If you put these people to death all at one time, the nations who have heard this report about you will say, 16 'The LORD was not able to bring these people into the land he promised them on oath; so he slaughtered them in the desert.'

17 "Now may the Lord's strength be displayed, just as you have declared: 18 'The LORD is slow to anger, abounding in love and forgiving sin and rebellion.[o] Yet he does not leave the guilty unpunished; he punishes the children for the sin of the fathers to the third and fourth generation.'[p] 19 In accordance with your great love, forgive[q] the sin of these people, just as you have pardoned them from the time they left Egypt until now."

20 The LORD replied, "I have forgiven them, as you asked. 21 Nevertheless, as surely as I live and as surely as the glory of the LORD fills the whole earth,[r] 22 not one of the men who saw my glory and the miraculous signs I performed in Egypt and in the desert but who disobeyed me and tested me ten times— 23 not one of them will ever see the land I promised on oath to their forefathers. No one who has treated me with contempt will ever see it. 24 But because my servant Caleb has a different spirit and follows me wholeheartedly,[s] I will bring him into the land he went to, and his descendants will inherit it.[t] 25 Since the Amalekites and Canaanites are living in the valleys, turn back tomorrow and set out toward the desert along the route to the Red Sea.[a]"

26 The LORD said to Moses and Aaron: 27 "How long will this wicked community grumble against me? I have heard the complaints of these grumbling Israelites. 28 So tell them, 'As surely as I live,[u] declares the LORD, I will do to you the very things I heard you say: 29 In this desert your bodies will fall—every one of you twenty years old or more[v] who was counted in the census and who has grumbled against me. 30 Not one of you will enter the land I swore with uplifted hand to make your home, except Caleb son of Jephunneh and Joshua son of Nun. 31 As for your children that you said would be taken as plunder, I will bring them in to enjoy the land you have rejected. 32 But you—your bodies will fall[w] in this desert. 33 Your children will be shepherds here for forty years, suffering for your unfaithfulness, until the last of your bodies lies in the desert. 34 For forty years—one year for each of the forty days you explored the land[x]—you will suffer for your sins and know what it is like to have me against you.' 35 I, the LORD, have spoken, and I will surely do these things[y] to this whole wicked community, which has banded together against me. They will meet their end in this desert; here they will die."

36 So the men Moses had sent to explore the land, who returned and made the whole community grumble against him by spreading a bad report[z] about it— 37 these men responsible for spreading the bad report about the land were struck down and died of a plague before the LORD. 38 Of the men who went to explore the land, only Joshua son of Nun and Caleb son of Jephunneh survived.

39 When Moses reported this to all the Israelites, they mourned[a] bitterly. 40 Early the next morning they went up toward the high hill country. "We have sinned[b]," they said. "We will go up to the place the LORD promised."

[a]25 Hebrew *Yam Suph*; that is, Sea of Reeds

**14:9** h Dt1:21; 7:18; 20:1
**14:10** i Ex17:4 j Lev9:23
**14:12** k Ex32:10
**14:13** l Ex32:11–14; Ps106:23
**14:14** m Ex15:14 n Ex13:21
**14:18** o Ex34:6 p Ex20:5
**14:19** q Ex34:9
**14:21** r Ps72:19
**14:24** s Jos14:8,14 t Nu32:12
**14:28** u ver21
**14:29** v Nu1:45
**14:32** w 1Co10:5
**14:34** x Nu13:25
**14:35** y Nu23:19
**14:36** z Nu13:32
**14:39** a Ex33:4
**14:40** b Dt1:41

[41]But Moses said, "Why are you disobeying the LORD's command? This will not succeed![c] [42]Do not go up, because the LORD is not with you. You will be defeated by your enemies,[d] [43]for the Amalekites and Canaanites will face you there. Because you have turned away from the LORD, he will not be with you and you will fall by the sword."

[44]Nevertheless, in their presumption they went up[e] toward the high hill country, though neither Moses nor the ark of the LORD's covenant moved from the camp. [45]Then the Amalekites and Canaanites who lived in that hill country came down and attacked them and beat them down all the way to Hormah.[f]

## Supplementary Offerings

**15** The LORD said to Moses, [2]"Speak to the Israelites and say to them: 'After you enter the land I am giving you as a home [3]and you present to the LORD offerings made by fire, from the herd or the flock,[g] as an aroma pleasing to the LORD—whether burnt offerings or sacrifices, for special vows or freewill offerings or festival offerings[h]— [4]then the one who brings his offering shall present to the LORD a grain offering[i] of a tenth of an ephah[a] of fine flour mixed with a quarter of a hin[b] of oil. [5]With each lamb for the burnt offering or the sacrifice, prepare a quarter of a hin of wine as a drink offering.

[6]" 'With a ram prepare a grain offering[j] of two-tenths of an ephah[c] of fine flour mixed with a third of a hin[d] of oil, [7]and a third of a hin of wine as a drink offering. Offer it as an aroma pleasing to the LORD.

[8]" 'When you prepare a young bull as a burnt offering or sacrifice, for a special vow or a fellowship offering[e] to the LORD, [9]bring with the bull a grain offering of three-tenths of an ephah[f] of fine flour mixed with half a hin[g] of oil. [10]Also bring half a hin of wine as a drink offering. It will be an offering made by fire, an aroma pleasing to the LORD. [11]Each bull or ram, each lamb or young goat, is to be prepared in this manner. [12]Do this for each one, for as many as you prepare.

[13]" 'Everyone who is native-born must do these things in this way when he brings an offering made by fire as an aroma pleasing to the LORD. [14]For the generations to come, whenever an alien or anyone else living among you presents an offering made by fire as an aroma pleasing to the LORD, he must do exactly as you do. [15]The community is to have the same rules for you and for the alien living among you; this is a lasting ordinance for the generations to come.[k] You and the alien shall be the same before the LORD: [16]The same laws and regulations will apply both to you and to the alien living among you.' "

[17]The LORD said to Moses, [18]"Speak to the Israelites and say to them: 'When you enter the land to which I am taking you [19]and you eat the food of the land,[l] present a portion as an offering to the LORD. [20]Present a cake from the first of your ground meal and present it as an offering from the threshing floor.[m] [21]Throughout the generations to come you are to give this offering to the LORD from the first of your ground meal.

## Offerings for Unintentional Sins

[22]" 'Now if you unintentionally fail to keep any of these commands the LORD gave Moses[n]— [23]any of the LORD's commands to you through him, from the day the LORD gave them and continuing through the generations to come— [24]and if this is done unintentionally without the community being aware of it, then the whole community is to offer a young bull for a burnt offering[o] as an aroma pleasing to the LORD, along with its prescribed grain offering and drink offering, and a male goat for a sin offering. [25]The priest is to make atonement for the whole Israelite community, and they will be forgiven,[p] for it was not intentional and they have brought to the LORD for their wrong an offering made by fire and a sin offering. [26]The whole Israelite community and the aliens living among them will be forgiven, because all the people were involved in the unintentional wrong.

[27]" 'But if just one person sins unintentionally,[q] he must bring a year-old female

**14:41** c 2Ch 24:20
**14:42** d Dt 1:42
**14:44** e Dt 1:43
**14:45** f Nu 21:3; Dt 1:44
**15:3** g Lev 1:2 h Lev 23:1–44
**15:4** i Lev 6:14
**15:6** j Nu 28:12
**15:15** k ver 29; Nu 9:14
**15:19** l Jos 5:11,12
**15:20** m Lev 2:14
**15:22** n Lev 4:2
**15:24** o Lev 4:14
**15:25** p Lev 4:20
**15:27** q Lev 4:27

[a]4 That is, probably about 2 quarts (about 2 liters) [b]4 That is, probably about 1 quart (about 1 liter); also in verse 5 [c]6 That is, probably about 4 quarts (about 4.5 liters) [d]6 That is, probably about 1 1/4 quarts (about 1.2 liters); also in verse 7 [e]8 Traditionally *peace offering* [f]9 That is, probably about 6 quarts (about 6.5 liters) [g]9 That is, probably about 2 quarts (about 2 liters); also in verse 10

goat for a sin offering. 28 The priest is to make atonement before the LORD for the one who erred by sinning unintentionally, and when atonement has been made for him, he will be forgiven.[r] 29 One and the same law applies to everyone who sins unintentionally, whether he is a native-born Israelite or an alien.

30 " 'But anyone who sins defiantly,[s] whether native-born or alien, blasphemes the LORD, and that person must be cut off from his people. 31 Because he has despised the LORD's word and broken his commands,[t] that person must surely be cut off; his guilt remains on him.[u] ' "

## The Sabbath-Breaker Put to Death

32 While the Israelites were in the desert, a man was found gathering wood on the Sabbath day.[v] 33 Those who found him gathering wood brought him to Moses and Aaron and the whole assembly, 34 and they kept him in custody, because it was not clear what should be done to him. 35 Then the LORD said to Moses, "The man must die.[w] The whole assembly must stone him outside the camp.[x]" 36 So the assembly took him outside the camp and stoned him to death, as the LORD commanded Moses.

## Tassels on Garments

37 The LORD said to Moses, 38 "Speak to the Israelites and say to them: 'Throughout the generations to come you are to make tassels on the corners of your garments,[y] with a blue cord on each tassel. 39 You will have these tassels to look at and so you will remember all the commands of the LORD, that you may obey them and not prostitute yourselves by going after the lusts of your own hearts and eyes. 40 Then you will remember to obey all my commands and will be consecrated to your God.[z] 41 I am the LORD your God, who brought you out of Egypt to be your God. I am the LORD your God.' "

## Korah, Dathan and Abiram

**16** Korah[a] son of Izhar, the son of Kohath, the son of Levi, and certain Reubenites—Dathan and Abiram, sons of Eliab, and On son of Peleth—became insolent[a] 2 and rose up against Moses. With them were 250 Israelite men, well-known community leaders who had been appointed members of the council. 3 They came as a group to oppose Moses and Aaron[b] and said to them, "You have gone too far! The whole community is holy,[c] every one of them, and the LORD is with them. Why then do you set yourselves above the LORD's assembly?"

4 When Moses heard this, he fell facedown.[d] 5 Then he said to Korah and all his followers: "In the morning the LORD will show who belongs to him and who is holy, and he will have that person come near him. The man he chooses[e] he will cause to come near him. 6 You, Korah, and all your followers are to do this: Take censers 7 and tomorrow put fire and incense in them before the LORD. The man the LORD chooses will be the one who is holy. You Levites have gone too far!"

8 Moses also said to Korah, "Now listen, you Levites! 9 Isn't it enough for you that the God of Israel has separated you from the rest of the Israelite community and brought you near himself to do the work at the LORD's tabernacle and to stand before the community and minister to them?[f] 10 He has brought you and all your fellow Levites near himself, but now you are trying to get the priesthood too. 11 It is against the LORD that you and all your followers have banded together. Who is Aaron that you should grumble[g] against him?"

12 Then Moses summoned Dathan and Abiram, the sons of Eliab. But they said, "We will not come! 13 Isn't it enough that you have brought us up out of a land flowing with milk and honey to kill us in the desert?

*My child,*

*Check and double-check your motives. I want your heart now and always to be pure.*

*Your Concerned Father*

NUMBERS 16:1–11

**15:28** r Lev 4:35
**15:30** s Dt 17:13; Ps 19:13
**15:31** t 2Sa 12:9; Pr 13:13 u Lev 5:1; Eze 18:20
**15:32** v Ex 31:14,15; 35:2,3
**15:35** w Ex 31:14,15 x Lev 24:14
**15:38** y Dt 22:12; Mt 23:5
**15:40** z Lev 11:44; Ro 12:1; Col 1:22; 1Pe 1:15
**16:1** a Jude 1:11
**16:3** b Ps 106:16 c Ex 19:6
**16:4** d Nu 14:5
**16:5** e Nu 17:5
**16:9** f Dt 10:8
**16:11** g 1Co 10:10

[a]1 Or *Peleth—took* ⌊*men*⌋

Inspire

## REBELLION

Rebellion is defined as open resistance to authority. A rebellious spirit is one that defies and disobeys authority, including the human authority that God has set in place, such as parents, employers, the government and the church. God deals very harshly with those who are rebellious.

The first generation of Israelites died in the desert because they were rebellious and did not trust God to care for them as they stood on the brink of entering the promised land (see Nu 14). And Moses never got to see the promised land because of his rebellion at Meribah (see Nu 20:6–13).

Rebellion often begins with the seeds of discontentment and generally involves envy of someone or something. Korah and some 250 other Israelite leaders were envious of the authority God had given Moses and Aaron (see Nu 16:1–11). As a result of their rebellion, all of them were destroyed (see Nu 16:16–35).

The Bible speaks of several kinds of rebellion. Isaiah 65:2 says that following after one's own thoughts and ways is a form of rebellion. Hebrews 3:8 speaks of hard-heartedness as a form of rebellion. At the center of all rebellion is sin, falling short of God's standard (see Ps 78:17; Ro 3:23). We become frustrated with the way things seem and begin to doubt God's plan. We then decide to follow another plan, which eventually only causes more problems.

The solution to rebellion is trust in God. How do we truly trust in God? Sometimes it is not easy to trust him when things in our lives seem difficult, painful or confusing. When we go through a challenging time, we may not be able to place our good in God's hands. But trust is most meaningful when we chose to trust in the face of difficulties.

If we trust God with all of our hearts to bring about *his* desired end, believing that "in all things God works for the good of those who love him and have been called according to his purpose" (Ro 8:28), then our thoughts of rebellion will fade away.

—J. Thompson

**read**

Numbers 16.
See also the Inspire Note "Submission," and the Women of the Bible Notes "Miriam: Plagued by Jealousy" and "Herodias and Salome: Evil Choices."

**WOMAN of COLOR**

In which areas of your life are you being rebellious against God or against other authority figures?

For the next Inspire note, go to page 182.

And now you also want to lord it over us?[h] 14 Moreover, you haven't brought us into a land flowing with milk and honey[i] or given us an inheritance of fields and vineyards. Will you gouge out the eyes of[a] these men? No, we will not come!"

15 Then Moses became very angry and said to the LORD, "Do not accept their offering. I have not taken so much as a donkey[j] from them, nor have I wronged any of them."

16 Moses said to Korah, "You and all your followers are to appear before the LORD tomorrow—you and they and Aaron. 17 Each man is to take his censer and put incense in it—250 censers in all—and present it before the LORD. You and Aaron are to present your censers also." 18 So each man took his censer, put fire and incense in it, and stood with Moses and Aaron at the entrance to the Tent of Meeting. 19 When Korah had gathered all his followers in opposition to them[k] at the entrance to the Tent of Meeting, the glory of the LORD[l] appeared to the entire assembly. 20 The LORD said to Moses and Aaron, 21 "Separate yourselves from this assembly so I can put an end to them at once."[m]

22 But Moses and Aaron fell facedown and cried out, "O God, God of the spirits of all mankind, will you be angry with the entire assembly when only one man sins?"

23 Then the LORD said to Moses, 24 "Say to the assembly, 'Move away from the tents of Korah, Dathan and Abiram.'"

25 Moses got up and went to Dathan and Abiram, and the elders of Israel followed him. 26 He warned the assembly, "Move back from the tents of these wicked men! Do not touch anything belonging to them, or you will be swept away[n] because of all their sins." 27 So they moved away from the tents of Korah, Dathan and Abiram. Dathan and Abiram had come out and were standing with their wives, children and little ones at the entrances to their tents.

28 Then Moses said, "This is how you will know that the LORD has sent me[o] to do all these things and that it was not my idea: 29 If these men die a natural death and experience only what usually happens to men, then the LORD has not sent me. 30 But if the LORD brings about something totally new, and the earth opens its mouth and swallows them, with everything that belongs to them, and they go down alive into the grave,[b][p] then you will know that these men have treated the LORD with contempt."

31 As soon as he finished saying all this, the ground under them split apart 32 and the earth opened its mouth and swallowed them,[q] with their households and all Korah's men and all their possessions. 33 They went down alive into the grave, with everything they owned; the earth closed over them, and they perished and were gone from the community. 34 At their cries, all the Israelites around them fled, shouting, "The earth is going to swallow us too!"

35 And fire came out from the LORD[r] and consumed the 250 men who were offering the incense.

36 The LORD said to Moses, 37 "Tell Eleazar son of Aaron, the priest, to take the censers out of the smoldering remains and scatter the coals some distance away, for the censers are holy— 38 the censers of the men who sinned at the cost of their lives.[s] Hammer the censers into sheets to overlay the altar, for they were presented before the LORD and have become holy. Let them be a sign[t] to the Israelites."

39 So Eleazar the priest collected the bronze censers brought by those who had been burned up, and he had them hammered out to overlay the altar, 40 as the LORD directed him through Moses. This was to remind the Israelites that no one except a descendant of Aaron should come to burn incense before the LORD,[u] or he would become like Korah and his followers.[v]

41 The next day the whole Israelite community grumbled against Moses and Aaron. "You have killed the LORD's people," they said.

42 But when the assembly gathered in opposition[w] to Moses and Aaron and turned toward the Tent of Meeting, suddenly the cloud covered it and the glory of the LORD appeared. 43 Then Moses and Aaron went to the front of the Tent of Meeting, 44 and the LORD said to Moses, 45 "Get away from this assembly so I can put an end to them at once." And they fell facedown.

[a]14 Or *you make slaves of*; or *you deceive* [b]30 Hebrew *Sheol*; also in verse 33

**16:13** h Ac 7:27,35
**16:14** i Lev 20:24
**16:15** j 1Sa 12:3
**16:19** k ver 42 l Nu 14:10
**16:21** m Ex 32:10
**16:26** n Ge 19:15
**16:28** o Ex 3:12; Jn 5:36; 6:38
**16:30** p Ps 55:15
**16:32** q Nu 26:11
**16:35** r Nu 11:1–3
**16:38** s Pr 20:2 t Nu 26:10; Eze 14:8
**16:40** u 2Ch 26:18 v Nu 3:10
**16:42** w ver 19

46 Then Moses said to Aaron, "Take your censer and put incense in it, along with fire from the altar, and hurry to the assembly to make atonement[x] for them. Wrath has come out from the LORD; the plague[y] has started." 47 So Aaron did as Moses said, and ran into the midst of the assembly. The plague had already started among the people,[z] but Aaron offered the incense and made atonement for them. 48 He stood between the living and the dead, and the plague stopped.[a] 49 But 14,700 people died from the plague, in addition to those who had died because of Korah.[b] 50 Then Aaron returned to Moses at the entrance to the Tent of Meeting, for the plague had stopped.

## The Budding of Aaron's Staff

17 The LORD said to Moses, 2 "Speak to the Israelites and get twelve staffs from them, one from the leader of each of their ancestral tribes. Write the name of each man on his staff. 3 On the staff of Levi write Aaron's name, for there must be one staff for the head of each ancestral tribe. 4 Place them in the Tent of Meeting in front of the Testimony, where I meet with you.[c] 5 The staff belonging to the man I choose[d] will sprout, and I will rid myself of this constant grumbling against you by the Israelites."

6 So Moses spoke to the Israelites, and their leaders gave him twelve staffs, one for the leader of each of their ancestral tribes, and Aaron's staff was among them. 7 Moses placed the staffs before the LORD in the Tent of the Testimony.

8 The next day Moses entered the Tent of the Testimony and saw that Aaron's staff, which represented the house of Levi, had not only sprouted but had budded, blossomed and produced almonds. 9 Then Moses brought out all the staffs from the LORD's presence to all the Israelites. They looked at them, and each man took his own staff.

10 The LORD said to Moses, "Put back Aaron's staff in front of the Testimony, to be kept as a sign to the rebellious. This will put an end to their grumbling against me, so that they will not die." 11 Moses did just as the LORD commanded him.

12 The Israelites said to Moses, "We will die! We are lost, we are all lost! 13 Anyone who even comes near the tabernacle of the LORD will die.[e] Are we all going to die?"

## Duties of Priests and Levites

18 The LORD said to Aaron, "You, your sons and your father's family are to bear the responsibility for offenses against the sanctuary,[f] and you and your sons alone are to bear the responsibility for offenses against the priesthood. 2 Bring your fellow Levites from your ancestral tribe to join you and assist you when you and your sons minister[g] before the Tent of the Testimony. 3 They are to be responsible to you and are to perform all the duties of the Tent, but they must not go near the furnishings of the sanctuary or the altar, or both they and you will die.[h] 4 They are to join you and be responsible for the care of the Tent of Meeting—all the work at the Tent—and no one else may come near where you are.

5 "You are to be responsible for the care of the sanctuary and the altar, so that wrath will not fall on the Israelites again. 6 I myself have selected your fellow Levites from among the Israelites as a gift to you,[i] dedicated to the LORD to do the work at the Tent of Meeting. 7 But only you and your sons may serve as priests in connection with everything at the altar and inside the curtain.[j] I am giving you the service of the priesthood as a gift. Anyone else who comes near the sanctuary must be put to death."

## Offerings for Priests and Levites

8 Then the LORD said to Aaron, "I myself have put you in charge of the offerings presented to me; all the holy offerings the Israelites give me I give to you and your sons as your portion and regular share.[k] 9 You are to have the part of the most holy offerings that is kept from the fire. From all the gifts they bring me as most holy offerings, whether grain or sin[l] or guilt offerings, that part belongs to you and your sons. 10 Eat it as something most holy; every male shall eat it.[m] You must regard it as holy.

11 "This also is yours: whatever is set aside from the gifts of all the wave offerings[n] of the Israelites. I give this to you and your sons and daughters as your regular

**16:46** x Nu 25:13 y Nu 8:19
**16:47** z Nu 25:6–8
**16:48** a Ps 106:30
**16:49** b ver 32
**17:4** c Ex 25:22
**17:5** d Nu 16:5
**17:13** e Nu 1:51
**18:1** f Ex 28:38
**18:2** g Nu 3:10
**18:3** h Nu 4:15
**18:6** i Nu 3:9
**18:7** j Heb 9:3,6
**18:8** k Lev 6:16; 7:6,31–34,36
**18:9** l Lev 6:25
**18:10** m Lev 6:16
**18:11** n Ex 29:26

18:11 o Lev 22:1–16
18:12 p Ex 23:19; Ne 10:35
18:15 q Ex 13:2 r Ex 13:13
18:16 s Lev 27:6
18:17 t Lev 3:2
18:19 u 2Ch 13:5
18:20 v Dt 10:9; 18:1–2; Jos 13:33; Eze 44:28
18:21 w Lev 27:30–33
18:22 x Nu 1:51

share. Everyone in your household who is
ceremonially clean[o] may eat it.
12"I give you all the finest olive oil and all
the finest new wine and grain they give the
LORD as the firstfruits of their harvest.[p] 13All
the land's firstfruits that they bring to the
LORD will be yours. Everyone in your house-
hold who is ceremonially clean may eat it.
14"Everything in Israel that is devoted[a]
to the LORD is yours. 15The first offspring of
every womb, both man and animal, that is
offered to the LORD is yours.[q] But you must
redeem every firstborn son and every first-
born male of unclean animals.[r] 16When they
are a month old, you must redeem them at
the redemption price set at five shekels[b][s] of
silver, according to the sanctuary shekel,
which weighs twenty gerahs.
17"But you must not redeem the first-
born of an ox, a sheep or a goat; they are
holy. Sprinkle their blood[t] on the altar and
burn their fat as an offering made by fire,
an aroma pleasing to the LORD. 18Their
meat is to be yours, just as the breast of the
wave offering and the right thigh are yours.
19Whatever is set aside from the holy offer-
ings the Israelites present to the LORD I give
to you and your sons and daughters as your
regular share. It is an everlasting covenant
of salt[u] before the LORD for both you and
your offspring."
20The LORD said to Aaron, "You will have
no inheritance in their land, nor will you
have any share among them; I am your
share and your inheritance[v] among the Is-
raelites.
21"I give to the Levites all the tithes in
Israel as their inheritance[w] in return for
the work they do while serving at the Tent
of Meeting. 22From now on the Israelites
must not go near the Tent of Meeting, or
they will bear the consequences of their sin
and will die.[x] 23It is the Levites who are to do
the work at the Tent of Meeting and bear the
responsibility for offenses against it. This
is a lasting ordinance for the generations
to come. They will receive no inheritance
among the Israelites. 24Instead, I give to the
Levites as their inheritance the tithes that
the Israelites present as an offering to the
LORD. That is why I said concerning them:
'They will have no inheritance among the Is-
raelites.'"
25The LORD said to Moses, 26"Speak to the
Levites and say to them: 'When you receive
from the Israelites the tithe I give you as
your inheritance, you must present a tenth
of that tithe as the LORD's offering.[y] 27Your
offering will be reckoned to you as grain
from the threshing floor or juice from the
winepress. 28In this way you also will pre-
sent an offering to the LORD from all the
tithes you receive from the Israelites. From
these tithes you must give the LORD's portion
to Aaron the priest. 29You must present as
the LORD's portion the best and holiest part
of everything given to you.'
30"Say to the Levites: 'When you present
the best part, it will be reckoned to you as
the product of the threshing floor or the
winepress. 31You and your households may
eat the rest of it anywhere, for it is your
wages for your work at the Tent of Meeting.
32By presenting the best part[z] of it you will
not be guilty in this matter; then you will
not defile the holy offerings[a] of the Israel-
ites, and you will not die.'"

## The Water of Cleansing

19 The LORD said to Moses and Aaron:
2"This is a requirement of the law
that the LORD has commanded: Tell the Isra-
elites to bring you a red heifer without defect
or blemish and that has never been under a
yoke.[b] 3Give it to Eleazar[c] the priest; it is to
be taken outside the camp[d] and slaughtered
in his presence. 4Then Eleazar the priest is
to take some of its blood on his finger and
sprinkle it seven times toward the front of
the Tent of Meeting. 5While he watches, the
heifer is to be burned—its hide, flesh, blood
and offal.[e] 6The priest is to take some cedar
wood, hyssop and scarlet wool[f] and throw
them onto the burning heifer. 7After that, the
priest must wash his clothes and bathe him-
self with water. He may then come into the
camp, but he will be ceremonially unclean
till evening. 8The man who burns it must
also wash his clothes and bathe with water,
and he too will be unclean till evening.
9"A man who is clean shall gather up
the ashes of the heifer[g] and put them in

18:26 y Ne 10:38
18:32 z Lev 22:15 a Lev 19:8
19:2 b Dt 21:3
19:3 c Nu 3:4 d Lev 4:12,21
19:5 e Ex 29:14
19:6 f Lev 14:4
19:9 g Heb 9:13

[a]14 The Hebrew term refers to the irrevocable giving over of things or persons to the LORD. [b]16 That is, about 2 ounces (about 55 grams)

a ceremonially clean place outside the camp. They shall be kept by the Israelite community for use in the water of cleansing;[h] it is for purification from sin. [10]The man who gathers up the ashes of the heifer must also wash his clothes, and he too will be unclean till evening. This will be a lasting ordinance both for the Israelites and for the aliens living among them.

[11]"Whoever touches the dead body[i] of anyone will be unclean for seven days.[j] [12]He must purify himself with the water on the third day and on the seventh day;[k] then he will be clean. But if he does not purify himself on the third and seventh days, he will not be clean. [13]Whoever touches the dead body of anyone and fails to purify himself defiles the LORD's tabernacle.[l] That person must be cut off from Israel.[m] Because the water of cleansing has not been sprinkled on him, he is unclean; his uncleanness remains on him.

[14]"This is the law that applies when a person dies in a tent: Anyone who enters the tent and anyone who is in it will be unclean for seven days, [15]and every open container without a lid fastened on it will be unclean.

[16]"Anyone out in the open who touches someone who has been killed with a sword or someone who has died a natural death, or anyone who touches a human bone or a grave, will be unclean for seven days.

[17]"For the unclean person, put some ashes[n] from the burned purification offering into a jar and pour fresh water over them. [18]Then a man who is ceremonially clean is to take some hyssop, dip it in the water and sprinkle the tent and all the furnishings and the people who were there. He must also sprinkle anyone who has touched a human bone or a grave or someone who has been killed or someone who has died a natural death. [19]The man who is clean is to sprinkle the unclean person on the third and seventh days, and on the seventh day he is to purify him.[o] The person being cleansed must wash his clothes and bathe with water, and that evening he will be clean. [20]But if a person who is unclean does not purify himself, he must be cut off from the community, because he has defiled the sanctuary of the LORD. The water of cleansing has not been sprinkled on him, and he is unclean. [21]This is a lasting ordinance for them.

"The man who sprinkles the water of cleansing must also wash his clothes, and anyone who touches the water of cleansing will be unclean till evening. [22]Anything that an unclean person touches becomes unclean, and anyone who touches it becomes unclean till evening."

## Water From the Rock

**20** In the first month the whole Israelite community arrived at the Desert of Zin, and they stayed at Kadesh.[p] There Miriam died and was buried.

[2]Now there was no water for the community,[q] and the people gathered in opposition to Moses and Aaron. [3]They quarreled[r] with Moses and said, "If only we had died when our brothers fell dead before the LORD![s] [4]Why did you bring the LORD's community into this desert, that we and our livestock should die here?[t] [5]Why did you bring us up out of Egypt to this terrible place? It has no grain or figs, grapevines or pomegranates. And there is no water to drink!"

[6]Moses and Aaron went from the assembly to the entrance to the Tent of Meeting and fell facedown,[u] and the glory of the LORD appeared to them. [7]The LORD said to Moses, [8]"Take the staff, and you and your brother Aaron gather the assembly together. Speak to that rock before their eyes and it will pour out its water.[v] You will bring water out of the rock for the community so they and their livestock can drink."

[9]So Moses took the staff from the LORD's presence,[w] just as he commanded him. [10]He and Aaron gathered the assembly together in front of the rock and Moses said to them, "Listen, you rebels, must we bring you water out of this rock?"[x] [11]Then Moses raised his arm and struck the rock twice with his staff. Water[y] gushed out, and the community and their livestock drank.

[12]But the LORD said to Moses and Aaron, "Because you did not trust in me enough to honor me as holy[z] in the sight of the Israelites, you will not bring this community into the land I give them."[a]

**19:9** h ver 13
**19:11** i Lev 21:1; Nu 5:2 j Nu 31:19
**19:12** k ver 19; Nu 31:19
**19:13** l Lev 15:31 m Lev 7:20; 22:3
**19:17** n ver 9
**19:19** o Eze 36:25; Heb 10:22

**20:1** p Nu 33:36
**20:2** q Ex 17:1
**20:3** r Ex 17:2 s Nu 14:2; 16:31–35
**20:4** t Ex 14:11; 17:3; Nu 14:3; 16:13
**20:6** u Nu 14:5
**20:8** v Ex 17:6; Isa 43:20
**20:9** w Nu 17:10
**20:10** x Ps 106:32,33
**20:11** y Ex 17:6; 1Co 10:4
**20:12** z Nu 27:14 a Dt 1:37

20:13 b Ex17:7
20:16 c Ex2:23 d Ex14:19
20:17 e Nu21:22
20:19 f Dt2:6,28
20:21 g Dt2:8; Jdg 11:18

13 These were the waters of Meribah,[a][b]
where the Israelites quarreled with the LORD
and where he showed himself holy among
them.

## Edom Denies Israel Passage

14 Moses sent messengers from Kadesh to
the king of Edom, saying:

> "This is what your brother Israel
> says: You know about all the hard-
> ships that have come upon us. 15 Our
> forefathers went down into Egypt, and
> we lived there many years. The Egyp-
> tians mistreated us and our fathers,
> 16 but when we cried out to the LORD, he
> heard our cry[c] and sent an angel[d] and
> brought us out of Egypt.
>
> "Now we are here at Kadesh, a town
> on the edge of your territory. 17 Please
> let us pass through your country. We
> will not go through any field or vine-
> yard, or drink water from any well.
> We will travel along the king's high-
> way and not turn to the right or to
> the left until we have passed through
> your territory.[e]"

18 But Edom answered:

> "You may not pass through here; if
> you try, we will march out and attack
> you with the sword."

19 The Israelites replied:

> "We will go along the main road,
> and if we or our livestock drink any of
> your water, we will pay for it.[f] We only
> want to pass through on foot—noth-
> ing else."

20 Again they answered:

> "You may not pass through."

Then Edom came out against them with
a large and powerful army. 21 Since Edom re-
fused to let them go through their territory,
Israel turned away from them.[g]

## The Death of Aaron

22 The whole Israelite community set out
from Kadesh and came to Mount Hor. 23 At
Mount Hor, near the border of Edom, the
LORD said to Moses and Aaron, 24 "Aaron will
be gathered to his people.[h] He will not enter
the land I give the Israelites, because both
of you rebelled against my command at the
waters of Meribah. 25 Get Aaron and his son
Eleazar and take them up Mount Hor. 26 Re-
move Aaron's garments and put them on his
son Eleazar, for Aaron will be gathered to
his people; he will die there."

27 Moses did as the LORD commanded:
They went up Mount Hor in the sight of
the whole community. 28 Moses removed
Aaron's garments and put them on his son
Eleazar.[i] And Aaron died there[j] on top of the
mountain. Then Moses and Eleazar came
down from the mountain, 29 and when the
whole community learned that Aaron had
died, the entire house of Israel mourned for
him[k] thirty days.

20:24 h Ge25:8
20:28 i Ex29:29 j Nu33:38; Dt10:6
20:29 k Dt34:8
21:1 l Nu33:40
21:4 m Nu20:22
21:5 n Ps78:19
21:6 o Dt8:15 p 1Co10:9
21:7 q Ps78:34 r Ac8:24

## Arad Destroyed

21 When the Canaanite king of Arad,[l]
who lived in the Negev, heard that
Israel was coming along the road to Atha-
rim, he attacked the Israelites and captured
some of them. 2 Then Israel made this vow
to the LORD: "If you will deliver these people
into our hands, we will totally destroy[b] their
cities." 3 The LORD listened to Israel's plea
and gave the Canaanites over to them. They
completely destroyed them and their towns;
so the place was named Hormah.[c]

## The Bronze Snake

4 They traveled from Mount Hor[m] along
the route to the Red Sea,[d] to go around
Edom. But the people grew impatient on the
way; 5 they spoke against God[n] and against
Moses, and said, "Why have you brought us
up out of Egypt to die in the desert? There is
no bread! There is no water! And we detest
this miserable food!"

6 Then the LORD sent venomous snakes[o]
among them; they bit the people and many
Israelites died.[p] 7 The people came to Moses[q]
and said, "We sinned when we spoke against
the LORD and against you. Pray that the
LORD[r] will take the snakes away from us." So
Moses prayed for the people.

8 The LORD said to Moses, "Make a snake
and put it up on a pole; anyone who is bitten

[a] 13 *Meribah* means *quarreling.* [b] 2 The Hebrew term refers to the irrevocable giving over of things or persons to the LORD, often by totally destroying them; also in verse 3. [c] 3 *Hormah* means *destruction.* [d] 4 Hebrew *Yam Suph*; that is, Sea of Reeds

# Inspire

## ANGER: ACT OR REACT

**This scene in Numbers 20:1–13 reminds the reader of what happened 40 years earlier. In Exodus 17:1–7, the Israelites were faced with a water shortage. This was a serious situation in a desert. The people were desperate, and they blamed Moses for taking them from their captivity in Egypt only to die in the desert. At this time, God commanded Moses to strike the rock, and as a result, the community received fresh water. Now, 40 years later, the children of the rebellious people are just as rebellious. With many years of frustration and anger behind him, Moses disobeys God's command to speak to the rock, and he strikes it instead.**

We may feel sympathetic with Moses' situation and feel that his anger was justified, but God did not view it that way. As a result of Moses' lack of trust in, and respect for, the Lord, God forbade Moses to enter the promised land (see Nu 20:2–12).

Anger can be defined as a strong feeling of displeasure aroused by a real or supposed inequity. While the Lord is slow to anger (see Ps 103:8), his anger is expressed as a holy response to our rebellion and sin. The destruction of Sodom and Gomorrah is an example (see Ge 19:1–29; Dt 29:23–28).

As black women, we are confronted with many opportunities to become angry because of real or supposed inequities. Many times we react to an inequity rather than think it through. Too often we allow anger to consume us to the point of not being able to take appropriate action. However, because of God's steadfast love for us, we can step back from the situation and wait for divine leading; we can learn to act and not react.

When confronted by circumstances that you perceive as unjust, don't react too quickly—even though you may feel hurt or threatened. Don't follow your first impulse to curse, seek revenge or do something out of anger or hurt. These angry responses can lead to sin. Wait on the Lord. Anger may boil within, but praise the Lord. Ask yourself if you are willing to trust God enough to release your anger into his care. Focus the energy of your anger into positive action. Pray and meditate on God's Word so that when you are provoked, wisdom is what spills out of you.

A woman who acts instead of reacts is a woman secure in who she is, what she believes and how she is to respond. Her actions are not determined by another's actions. She is guided by the wisdom of the Lord. Our God is glorified when we act rather than react.

—J. Wood

### read

Numbers 20:1–13; see also Proverbs 15:1; Galatians 5:19–23; 6:6–10; Ephesians 4:26–32. See also the Inspire Notes "Rebellion," "Submission" and "Self-Control," and the Women of the Bible Note "Athaliah: An Angry Woman."

### WOMAN of COLOR

How will you act instead of react to inequities today?

For the next Inspire note, go to page 212.

**21:9** s 2Ki 18:4 t Jn 3:14–15
**21:11** u Nu 33:44
**21:12** v Dt 2:13,14
**21:15** w Dt 2:9,18
**21:17** x Ex 15:1
**21:22** y Nu 20:17

can look at it and live." 9So Moses made a
bronze snake[s] and put it up on a pole. Then
when anyone was bitten by a snake and
looked at the bronze snake, he lived.[t]

## The Journey to Moab

10The Israelites moved on and camped
at Oboth. 11Then they set out from Oboth
and camped in Iye Abarim, in the desert
that faces Moab[u] toward the sunrise. 12From
there they moved on and camped in the Ze-
red Valley.[v] 13They set out from there and
camped alongside the Arnon, which is in
the desert extending into Amorite territory.
The Arnon is the border of Moab, between
Moab and the Amorites. 14That is why the
Book of the Wars of the LORD says:

"... Waheb in Suphah[a] and the ravines,
the Arnon 15and[b] the slopes of the
ravines
that lead to the site of Ar[w]
and lie along the border of Moab."

16From there they continued on to Beer, the
well where the LORD said to Moses, "Gather
the people together and I will give them
water."
17Then Israel sang this song:[x]

"Spring up, O well!
Sing about it,
18 about the well that the princes dug,
that the nobles of the people sank—
the nobles with scepters and staffs."

Then they went from the desert to Matta-
nah, 19from Mattanah to Nahaliel, from
Nahaliel to Bamoth, 20and from Bamoth to
the valley in Moab where the top of Pisgah
overlooks the wasteland.

## Defeat of Sihon and Og

21Israel sent messengers to say to Sihon
king of the Amorites:

22"Let us pass through your coun-
try. We will not turn aside into any
field or vineyard, or drink water from
any well. We will travel along the
king's highway until we have passed
through your territory.[y]"

23But Sihon would not let Israel pass
through his territory. He mustered his en-
tire army and marched out into the desert
against Israel. When he reached Jahaz,[z] he
fought with Israel. 24Israel, however, put
him to the sword[a] and took over his land
from the Arnon to the Jabbok, but only as
far as the Ammonites, because their border
was fortified. 25Israel captured all the cities
of the Amorites and occupied them, includ-
ing Heshbon and all its surrounding settle-
ments. 26Heshbon was the city of Sihon king
of the Amorites, who had fought against the
former king of Moab and had taken from
him all his land as far as the Arnon.
27That is why the poets say:

"Come to Heshbon and let it be rebuilt;
let Sihon's city be restored.

28 "Fire went out from Heshbon,
a blaze from the city of Sihon.[b]
It consumed Ar of Moab,
the citizens of Arnon's heights.[c]
29 Woe to you, O Moab!
You are destroyed, O people of
Chemosh![d]
He has given up his sons as fugitives
and his daughters as captives
to Sihon king of the Amorites.

30 "But we have overthrown them;
Heshbon is destroyed all the way to
Dibon.[e]
We have demolished them as far as Nophah,
which extends to Medeba."

31So Israel settled in the land of the Am-
orites.
32After Moses had sent spies to Jazer,[f]
the Israelites captured its surrounding set-
tlements and drove out the Amorites who
were there. 33Then they turned and went up
along the road toward Bashan, and Og king
of Bashan and his whole army marched out
to meet them in battle at Edrei.[g]
34The LORD said to Moses, "Do not be
afraid of him, for I have handed him over to
you, with his whole army and his land. Do to
him what you did to Sihon king of the Amo-
rites, who reigned in Heshbon.[h]"
35So they struck him down, together with

**21:23** z Dt 2:32
**21:24** a Dt 2:33; Ps 135:10–11
**21:28** b Jer 48:45 c Isa 15:2
**21:29** d Jdg 11:24; 1Ki 11:7,33; 2Ki 23:13
**21:30** e Nu 32:3; Jer 48:18,22
**21:32** f Nu 32:1,3,35; Jer 48:32
**21:33** g Dt 3:1,10; Jos 13:12,31
**21:34** h Dt 3:2

[a]14 The meaning of the Hebrew for this phrase is uncertain. [b]14,15 Or *"I have been given from Suphah and the ravines / of the Arnon 15to*

22:1 i Nu 33:48
22:3 j Ex 15:15
22:5 k Dt 23:4
22:6 l Nu 23:7,11,13
22:8 m ver 19

his sons and his whole army, leaving them no survivors. And they took possession of his land.

## Balak Summons Balaam

**22** Then the Israelites traveled to the plains of Moab and camped along the Jordan across from Jericho.[a][i]

2 Now Balak son of Zippor saw all that Israel had done to the Amorites, 3 and Moab was terrified because there were so many people. Indeed, Moab was filled with dread[j] because of the Israelites.

4 The Moabites said to the elders of Midian, "This horde is going to lick up everything around us, as an ox licks up the grass of the field."

So Balak son of Zippor, who was king of Moab at that time, 5 sent messengers to summon Balaam son of Beor,[k] who was at Pethor, near the River,[b] in his native land. Balak said:

> "A people has come out of Egypt; they cover the face of the land and have settled next to me. 6 Now come and put a curse[l] on these people, because they are too powerful for me. Perhaps then I will be able to defeat them and drive them out of the country. For I know that those you bless are blessed, and those you curse are cursed."

7 The elders of Moab and Midian left, taking with them the fee for divination. When they came to Balaam, they told him what Balak had said.

8 "Spend the night here," Balaam said to them, "and I will bring you back the answer the LORD gives me.[m]" So the Moabite princes stayed with him.

9 God came to Balaam and asked, "Who are these men with you?"

10 Balaam said to God, "Balak son of Zippor, king of Moab, sent me this message: 11 'A people that has come out of Egypt covers the face of the land. Now come and put a curse on them for me. Perhaps then I will be able to fight them and drive them away.' "

12 But God said to Balaam, "Do not go with them. You must not put a curse on those people, because they are blessed."

13 The next morning Balaam got up and said to Balak's princes, "Go back to your own country, for the LORD has refused to let me go with you."

14 So the Moabite princes returned to Balak and said, "Balaam refused to come with us."

15 Then Balak sent other princes, more numerous and more distinguished than the first. 16 They came to Balaam and said:

> "This is what Balak son of Zippor says: Do not let anything keep you from coming to me, 17 because I will reward you handsomely and do whatever you say. Come and put a curse[n] on these people for me."

18 But Balaam answered them, "Even if Balak gave me his palace filled with silver and gold, I could not do anything great or small to go beyond the command of the LORD my God.[o] 19 Now stay here tonight as the others did, and I will find out what else the LORD will tell me."

20 That night God came to Balaam and said, "Since these men have come to summon you, go with them, but do only what I tell you."[p]

## Balaam's Donkey

21 Balaam got up in the morning, saddled his donkey and went with the princes of Moab. 22 But God was very angry when he went, and the angel of the LORD[q] stood in the road to oppose him. Balaam was riding on his donkey, and his two servants were with him. 23 When the donkey saw the angel of the LORD standing in the road with a drawn sword in his hand, she turned off the road into a field. Balaam beat her to get her back on the road.

24 Then the angel of the LORD stood in a narrow path between two vineyards, with walls on both sides. 25 When the donkey saw the angel of the LORD, she pressed close to the wall, crushing Balaam's foot against it. So he beat her again.

26 Then the angel of the LORD moved on ahead and stood in a narrow place where there was no room to turn, either to the right or to the left. 27 When the donkey saw

22:17 n ver 6
22:18 o ver 38; Nu 24:13; 1Ki 22:14; 2Ch 18:13
22:20 p ver 35,38; Nu 23:5,12, 16,26; 24:13
22:22 q Ex 23:20

[a] 1 Hebrew *Jordan of Jericho*; possibly an ancient name for the Jordan River [b] 5 That is, the Euphrates

the angel of the LORD, she lay down under Balaam, and he was angry[r] and beat her with his staff. 28 Then the LORD opened the donkey's mouth,[s] and she said to Balaam, "What have I done to you to make you beat me these three times?"

29 Balaam answered the donkey, "You have made a fool of me! If I had a sword in my hand, I would kill you right now.[t]"

30 The donkey said to Balaam, "Am I not your own donkey, which you have always ridden, to this day? Have I been in the habit of doing this to you?"

"No," he said.

31 Then the LORD opened Balaam's eyes,[u] and he saw the angel of the LORD standing in the road with his sword drawn. So he bowed low and fell facedown.

32 The angel of the LORD asked him, "Why have you beaten your donkey these three times? I have come here to oppose you because your path is a reckless one before me.[a] 33 The donkey saw me and turned away from me these three times. If she had not turned away, I would certainly have killed you by now, but I would have spared her."

34 Balaam said to the angel of the LORD, "I have sinned.[v] I did not realize you were standing in the road to oppose me. Now if you are displeased, I will go back."

35 The angel of the LORD said to Balaam, "Go with the men, but speak only what I tell you." So Balaam went with the princes of Balak.

36 When Balak heard that Balaam was coming, he went out to meet him at the Moabite town on the Arnon[w] border, at the edge of his territory. 37 Balak said to Balaam, "Did I not send you an urgent summons? Why didn't you come to me? Am I really not able to reward you?"

38 "Well, I have come to you now," Balaam replied. "But can I say just anything? I must speak only what God puts in my mouth."[x]

39 Then Balaam went with Balak to Kiriath Huzoth. 40 Balak sacrificed cattle and sheep, and gave some to Balaam and the princes who were with him. 41 The next morning Balak took Balaam up to Bamoth Baal,[y] and from there he saw part of the people.[z]

## Balaam's First Oracle

23 Balaam said, "Build me seven altars here, and prepare seven bulls and seven rams for me." 2 Balak did as Balaam said, and the two of them offered a bull and a ram on each altar.[a]

3 Then Balaam said to Balak, "Stay here beside your offering while I go aside. Perhaps the LORD will come to meet with me.[b] Whatever he reveals to me I will tell you." Then he went off to a barren height.

4 God met with him,[c] and Balaam said, "I have prepared seven altars, and on each altar I have offered a bull and a ram."

5 The LORD put a message in Balaam's mouth[d] and said, "Go back to Balak and give him this message."

6 So he went back to him and found him standing beside his offering, with all the princes of Moab. 7 Then Balaam uttered his oracle:[e]

"Balak brought me from Aram,
the king of Moab from the eastern mountains.
'Come,' he said, 'curse Jacob for me;
come, denounce Israel.'[f]
8 How can I curse
those whom God has not cursed?
How can I denounce
those whom the LORD has not denounced?
9 From the rocky peaks I see them,
from the heights I view them.
I see a people who live apart
and do not consider themselves one of the nations.[g]
10 Who can count the dust of Jacob[h]
or number the fourth part of Israel?
Let me die the death of the righteous,
and may my end be like theirs!"

11 Balak said to Balaam, "What have you done to me? I brought you to curse my enemies, but you have done nothing but bless them!"

12 He answered, "Must I not speak what the LORD puts in my mouth?"[i]

## Balaam's Second Oracle

13 Then Balak said to him, "Come with me to another place where you can see them;

[a] 32 The meaning of the Hebrew for this clause is uncertain.

**22:27** r Jas 1:19
**22:28** s 2Pe 2:16
**22:29** t Pr 12:10; Mt 15:19
**22:31** u Ge 21:19
**22:34** v Nu 14:40; 1Sa 15:24,30; 2Sa 12:13
**22:36** w Nu 21:13
**22:38** x Nu 23:5,16,26
**22:41** y Nu 21:28 z Nu 23:13

**23:2** a ver 14,30
**23:3** b ver 15
**23:4** c ver 16
**23:5** d Dt 18:18; Jer 1:9
**23:7** e ver 18; Nu 24:3,21 f Nu 22:6
**23:9** g Dt 32:8; 33:28
**23:10** h Ge 13:16
**23:12** i Nu 22:20,38

**23:19** j 1Sa 15:29; Mal 3:6; Jas 1:17
**23:20** k Ge 22:17; Nu 22:12
**23:21** l Ps 32:2,5; Ro 4:7–8 m Ps 89:15–18
**23:22** n Nu 24:8
**23:24** o Ge 49:9
**23:27** p ver 13

you will see only a part but not all of them.
And from there, curse them for me." 14 So he
took him to the field of Zophim on the top of
Pisgah, and there he built seven altars and
offered a bull and a ram on each altar.

15 Balaam said to Balak, "Stay here beside
your offering while I meet with him over
there."

16 The LORD met with Balaam and put a
message in his mouth and said, "Go back to
Balak and give him this message."

17 So he went to him and found him stand-
ing beside his offering, with the princes
of Moab. Balak asked him, "What did the
LORD say?"

18 Then he uttered his oracle:

"Arise, Balak, and listen;
hear me, son of Zippor.
19 God is not a man, that he should lie,
nor a son of man, that he should
change his mind.[j]
Does he speak and then not act?
Does he promise and not fulfill?
20 I have received a command to bless;
he has blessed,[k] and I cannot change it.

21 "No misfortune is seen in Jacob,[l]
no misery observed in Israel.[a]
The LORD their God is with them;
the shout of the King[m] is among them.
22 God brought them out of Egypt;[n]
they have the strength of a wild ox.
23 There is no sorcery against Jacob,
no divination against Israel.
It will now be said of Jacob
and of Israel, 'See what God has
done!'
24 The people rise like a lioness;
they rouse themselves like a lion[o]
that does not rest till he devours his prey
and drinks the blood of his victims."

25 Then Balak said to Balaam, "Neither
curse them at all nor bless them at all!"

26 Balaam answered, "Did I not tell you I
must do whatever the LORD says?"

## Balaam's Third Oracle

27 Then Balak said to Balaam, "Come, let
me take you to another place.[p] Perhaps it
will please God to let you curse them for me
from there." 28 And Balak took Balaam to the
top of Peor, overlooking the wasteland.

29 Balaam said, "Build me seven altars
here, and prepare seven bulls and seven
rams for me." 30 Balak did as Balaam had
said, and offered a bull and a ram on each
altar.

24 Now when Balaam saw that it
pleased the LORD to bless Israel, he
did not resort to sorcery as at other times,
but turned his face toward the desert.
2 When Balaam looked out and saw Israel
encamped tribe by tribe, the Spirit of God
came upon him[q] 3 and he uttered his oracle:

"The oracle of Balaam son of Beor,
the oracle of one whose eye sees
clearly,
4 the oracle of one who hears the words of
God,
who sees a vision from the Almighty,[b]
who falls prostrate, and whose eyes are
opened:
5 "How beautiful are your tents, O Jacob,
your dwelling places, O Israel!

6 "Like valleys they spread out,
like gardens beside a river,
like aloes planted by the LORD,
like cedars beside the waters.[r]
7 Water will flow from their buckets;
their seed will have abundant water.

"Their king will be greater than Agag;[s]
their kingdom will be exalted.[t]

8 "God brought them out of Egypt;
they have the strength of a wild ox.
They devour hostile nations
and break their bones in pieces;[u]
with their arrows they pierce them.[v]
9 Like a lion they crouch and lie down,
like a lioness[w]—who dares to rouse
them?
"May those who bless you be blessed
and those who curse you be cursed!"[x]

10 Then Balak's anger burned against Ba-
laam. He struck his hands together and said
to him, "I summoned you to curse my ene-
mies, but you have blessed them these three
times. 11 Now leave at once and go home!

**24:2** q Nu 11:25,26
**24:6** r Ps 1:3; 104:16
**24:7** s 2Sa 15:8 t 2Sa 5:12; 1Ch 14:2
**24:8** u Ps 2:9; Jer 50:17 v Ps 45:5
**24:9** w Ge 49:9 x Ge 12:3

[a] 21 Or *He has not looked on Jacob's offenses / or on the wrongs found in Israel.* [b] 4 Hebrew *Shaddai*; also in verse 16

**24:13** y Nu 22:18
**24:14** z Ge 49:1; Mic 6:5
**24:17** a Rev 1:7 b Mt 2:2 c Ge 49:10
**24:19** d Ge 49:10

I said I would reward you handsomely, but the LORD has kept you from being rewarded."

12 Balaam answered Balak, "Did I not tell the messengers you sent me, 13 'Even if Balak gave me his palace filled with silver and gold, I could not do anything of my own accord, good or bad, to go beyond the command of the LORD[y]—and I must say only what the LORD says'? 14 Now I am going back to my people, but come, let me warn you of what this people will do to your people in days to come."[z]

## Balaam's Fourth Oracle

15 Then he uttered his oracle:

"The oracle of Balaam son of Beor,
the oracle of one whose eye sees clearly,
16 the oracle of one who hears the words of God,
who has knowledge from the Most High,
who sees a vision from the Almighty,
who falls prostrate, and whose eyes are opened:

17 "I see him, but not now;
I behold him, but not near.[a]
A star will come out of Jacob;[b]
a scepter will rise out of Israel.[c]
He will crush the foreheads of Moab,
the skulls[a] of[b] all the sons of Sheth.[c]
18 Edom will be conquered;
Seir, his enemy, will be conquered,
but Israel will grow strong.
19 A ruler will come out of Jacob[d]
and destroy the survivors of the city."

## Balaam's Final Oracles

20 Then Balaam saw Amalek and uttered his oracle:

"Amalek was first among the nations,
but he will come to ruin at last."

21 Then he saw the Kenites and uttered his oracle:

"Your dwelling place is secure,
your nest is set in a rock;
22 yet you Kenites will be destroyed
when Asshur takes you captive."

23 Then he uttered his oracle:

"Ah, who can live when God does this?[d]
24 Ships will come from the shores of Kittim;[e]
they will subdue Asshur and Eber,[f]
but they too will come to ruin.[g]"

25 Then Balaam got up and returned home and Balak went his own way.

## Moab Seduces Israel

25 While Israel was staying in Shittim,[h] the men began to indulge in sexual immorality[i] with Moabite women,[j] 2 who invited them to the sacrifices to their gods.[k] The people ate and bowed down before these gods. 3 So Israel joined in worshiping the Baal of Peor.[l] And the LORD's anger burned against them.

4 The LORD said to Moses, "Take all the leaders of these people, kill them and expose them in broad daylight before the LORD,[m] so that the LORD's fierce anger[n] may turn away from Israel."

5 So Moses said to Israel's judges, "Each

**24:24** e Ge 10:4 f Ge 10:21 g ver 20
**25:1** h Jos 2:1 i 1Co 10:8; Rev 2:14 j Nu 31:16
**25:2** k Ex 20:5
**25:3** l Ps 106:28
**25:4** m Dt 4:3 n Dt 13:17

[a] 17 Samaritan Pentateuch (see also Jer. 48:45); the meaning of the word in the Masoretic Text is uncertain.
[b] 17 Or possibly *Moab, / batter* [c] 17 Or *all the noisy boasters* [d] 23 Masoretic Text; with a different word division of the Hebrew *A people will gather from the north.*

## The African Presence

**Numbers 25**

The Midianites were the descendants of Abraham and Keturah (see the African Presence notes on Ge 25:1–2 and Ex 2:16–22).

of you must put to death those of your men who have joined in worshiping the Baal of Peor."

6Then an Israelite man brought to his family a Midianite woman right before the eyes of Moses and the whole assembly of Israel while they were weeping at the entrance to the Tent of Meeting. 7When Phinehas son of Eleazar, the son of Aaron, the priest, saw this, he left the assembly, took a spear in his hand 8and followed the Israelite into the tent. He drove the spear through both of them—through the Israelite and into the woman's body. Then the plague against the Israelites was stopped;[o] 9but those who died in the plague[p] numbered 24,000.

10The LORD said to Moses, 11"Phinehas son of Eleazar, the son of Aaron, the priest, has turned my anger away from the Israelites;[q] for he was as zealous as I am for my honor[r] among them, so that in my zeal I did not put an end to them. 12Therefore tell him I am making my covenant of peace[s] with him. 13He and his descendants will have a covenant of a lasting priesthood, because he was zealous for the honor of his God and made atonement for the Israelites."

14The name of the Israelite who was killed with the Midianite woman was Zimri son of Salu, the leader of a Simeonite family. 15And the name of the Midianite woman who was put to death was Cozbi daughter of Zur, a tribal chief of a Midianite family.[t]

16The LORD said to Moses, 17"Treat the Midianites[u] as enemies and kill them, 18because they treated you as enemies when they deceived you in the affair of Peor and their sister Cozbi, the daughter of a Midianite leader, the woman who was killed when the plague came as a result of Peor."

## The Second Census

**26** After the plague the LORD said to Moses and Eleazar son of Aaron, the priest, 2"Take a census[v] of the whole Israelite community by families—all those twenty years old or more who are able to serve in the army of Israel." 3So on the plains of Moab[w] by the Jordan across from Jericho,[a][x] Moses and Eleazar the priest spoke with them and said, 4"Take a census of the men twenty years old or more, as the LORD commanded Moses."

These were the Israelites who came out of Egypt:

5The descendants of Reuben, the firstborn son of Israel, were:

through Hanoch, the Hanochite clan;
through Pallu, the Palluite clan;
6through Hezron, the Hezronite clan;
through Carmi, the Carmite clan.

7These were the clans of Reuben; those numbered were 43,730.

8The son of Pallu was Eliab, 9and the sons of Eliab were Nemuel, Dathan and Abiram. The same Dathan and Abiram were the community officials who rebelled against Moses and Aaron and were among Korah's followers when they rebelled against the LORD.[y] 10The earth opened its mouth and swallowed them along with Korah, whose followers died when the fire devoured the 250 men. And they served as a warning sign.[z] 11The line of Korah, however, did not die out.

12The descendants of Simeon by their clans were:

through Nemuel, the Nemuelite clan;
through Jamin,[a] the Jaminite clan;
through Jakin, the Jakinite clan;
13through Zerah,[b] the Zerahite clan;
through Shaul, the Shaulite clan.

14These were the clans of Simeon; there were 22,200 men.

15The descendants of Gad by their clans were:

through Zephon,[c] the Zephonite clan;
through Haggi, the Haggite clan;
through Shuni, the Shunite clan;
16through Ozni, the Oznite clan;
through Eri, the Erite clan;
17through Arodi,[b] the Arodite clan;
through Areli, the Arelite clan.

18These were the clans of Gad;[d] those numbered were 40,500.

19Er and Onan were sons of Judah, but they died[e] in Canaan.

**25:8** o Ps 106:30
**25:9** p 1Co 10:8
**25:11** q Ps 106:30 r Ex 20:5
**25:12** s Isa 54:10; Mal 2:4,5
**25:15** t Nu 31:8
**25:17** u Nu 31:1–3
**26:2** v Ex 30:11–16
**26:3** w Nu 33:48

**26:3** x Nu 22:1
**26:9** y Nu 16:2
**26:10** z Nu 16:35,38
**26:12** a 1Ch 4:24
**26:13** b Ge 46:10
**26:15** c Ge 46:16
**26:18** d Nu 1:25
**26:19** e Ge 38:2–10; 46:12

[a]3 Hebrew *Jordan of Jericho*; possibly an ancient name for the Jordan River; also in verse 63 [b]17 Samaritan Pentateuch and Syriac (see also Gen. 46:16); Masoretic Text *Arod*

20 The descendants of Judah by their clans were:
through Shelah,[f] the Shelanite clan;
through Perez, the Perezite clan;
through Zerah, the Zerahite clan.
21 The descendants of Perez were:
through Hezron, the Hezronite clan;
through Hamul, the Hamulite clan.
22 These were the clans of Judah;[g] those numbered were 76,500.

23 The descendants of Issachar by their clans were:
through Tola,[h] the Tolaite clan;
through Puah, the Puite[a] clan;
24 through Jashub, the Jashubite clan;
through Shimron, the Shimronite clan.
25 These were the clans of Issachar;[i] those numbered were 64,300.
26 The descendants of Zebulun by their clans were:
through Sered, the Seredite clan;
through Elon, the Elonite clan;
through Jahleel, the Jahleelite clan.
27 These were the clans of Zebulun; those numbered were 60,500.

28 The descendants of Joseph by their clans through Manasseh and Ephraim were:
29 The descendants of Manasseh:
through Makir,[j] the Makirite clan (Makir was the father of Gilead);
through Gilead, the Gileadite clan.
30 These were the descendants of Gilead:
through Iezer,[k] the Iezerite clan;
through Helek, the Helekite clan;
31 through Asriel, the Asrielite clan;
through Shechem, the Shechemite clan;
32 through Shemida, the Shemidaite clan;
through Hepher, the Hepherite clan.
33 (Zelophehad[l] son of Hepher had no sons; he had only daughters, whose names were Mahlah, Noah, Hoglah, Milcah and Tirzah.)
34 These were the clans of Manasseh; those numbered were 52,700.

35 These were the descendants of Ephraim by their clans:
through Shuthelah, the Shuthelahite clan;
through Beker, the Bekerite clan;
through Tahan, the Tahanite clan.
36 These were the descendants of Shuthelah:
through Eran, the Eranite clan.
37 These were the clans of Ephraim;[m] those numbered were 32,500.

These were the descendants of Joseph by their clans.
38 The descendants of Benjamin[n] by their clans were:
through Bela, the Belaite clan;
through Ashbel, the Ashbelite clan;
through Ahiram, the Ahiramite clan;
39 through Shupham,[b] the Shuphamite clan;
through Hupham, the Huphamite clan.
40 The descendants of Bela through Ard and Naaman were:
through Ard,[c] the Ardite clan;
through Naaman, the Naamite clan.
41 These were the clans of Benjamin;[o] those numbered were 45,600.

42 These were the descendants of Dan by their clans:
through Shuham,[p] the Shuhamite clan.
These were the clans of Dan:
43 All of them were Shuhamite clans; and those numbered were 64,400.

44 The descendants of Asher by their clans were:
through Imnah, the Imnite clan;
through Ishvi, the Ishvite clan;
through Beriah, the Beriite clan;
45 and through the descendants of Beriah:
through Heber, the Heberite clan;
through Malkiel, the Malkielite clan.
46 (Asher had a daughter named Serah.)
47 These were the clans of Asher;[q] those numbered were 53,400.

**26:20** f 1Ch 2:3
**26:22** g Nu 1:27
**26:23** h Ge 46:13
**26:25** i Nu 1:29
**26:29** j Jos 17:1
**26:30** k Jos 17:2; Jdg 6:11
**26:33** l Nu 27:1
**26:37** m Nu 1:33
**26:38** n Ge 46:21
**26:41** o Nu 1:37
**26:42** p Ge 46:23
**26:47** q Nu 1:41

[a] 23 Samaritan Pentateuch, Septuagint, Vulgate and Syriac (see also 1 Chron. 7:1); Masoretic Text *through Puvah, the Punite* [b] 39 A few manuscripts of the Masoretic Text, Samaritan Pentateuch, Vulgate and Syriac (see also Septuagint); most manuscripts of the Masoretic Text *Shephupham* [c] 40 Samaritan Pentateuch and Vulgate (see also Septuagint); Masoretic Text does not have *through Ard.*

48 The descendants of Naphtali by their clans were:

through Jahzeel, the Jahzeelite clan;
through Guni, the Gunite clan;
49 through Jezer, the Jezerite clan;
through Shillem, the Shillemite clan.

50 These were the clans of Naphtali; those numbered were 45,400.

51 The total number of the men of Israel was 601,730.

52 The LORD said to Moses, 53 "The land is to be allotted to them as an inheritance based on the number of names.[r] 54 To a larger group give a larger inheritance, and to a smaller group a smaller one; each is to receive its inheritance according to the number[s] of those listed. 55 Be sure that the land is distributed by lot.[t] What each group inherits will be according to the names for its ancestral tribe. 56 Each inheritance is to be distributed by lot among the larger and smaller groups."

57 These were the Levites[u] who were counted by their clans:

through Gershon, the Gershonite clan;
through Kohath, the Kohathite clan;
through Merari, the Merarite clan.

58 These also were Levite clans:

the Libnite clan,
the Hebronite clan,
the Mahlite clan,
the Mushite clan,
the Korahite clan.
(Kohath was the forefather of Amram; 59 the name of Amram's wife was Jochebed, a descendant of Levi, who was born to the Levites[a] in Egypt. To Amram she bore Aaron, Moses[v] and their sister Miriam. 60 Aaron was the father of Nadab and Abihu, Eleazar and Ithamar.[w] 61 But Nadab and Abihu[x] died when they made an offering before the LORD with unauthorized fire.)[y]

62 All the male Levites a month old or more numbered 23,000. They were not counted[z] along with the other Israelites because they received no inheritance[a] among them.

63 These are the ones counted by Moses and Eleazar the priest when they counted the Israelites on the plains of Moab by the Jordan across from Jericho. 64 Not one of them was among those counted[b] by Moses and Aaron the priest when they counted the Israelites in the Desert of Sinai. 65 For the LORD had told those Israelites they would surely die in the desert,[c] and not one of them was left except Caleb son of Jephunneh and Joshua son of Nun.

## Zelophehad's Daughters

27 The daughters of Zelophehad[d] son of Hepher, the son of Gilead, the son of Makir,[e] the son of Manasseh, belonged to the clans of Manasseh son of Joseph. The names of the daughters were Mahlah, Noah, Hoglah, Milcah and Tirzah. They approached 2 the entrance to the Tent of Meeting and stood before Moses, Eleazar the priest, the leaders and the whole assembly, and said, 3 "Our father died in the desert.[f] He was not among Korah's followers, who banded together against the LORD,[g] but he died for his own sin and left no sons. 4 Why should our father's name disappear from his clan because he had no son? Give us property among our father's relatives."

5 So Moses brought their case before the LORD[h] 6 and the LORD said to him, 7 "What Zelophehad's daughters are saying is right. You must certainly give them property as an inheritance among their father's relatives and turn their father's inheritance over to them.

8 "Say to the Israelites, 'If a man dies and leaves no son, turn his inheritance over to his daughter. 9 If he has no daughter, give his inheritance to his brothers. 10 If he has no brothers, give his inheritance to his father's brothers. 11 If his father had no brothers, give his inheritance to the nearest relative in his clan, that he may possess it. This is to be a legal requirement[i] for the Israelites, as the LORD commanded Moses.'"

## Joshua to Succeed Moses

12 Then the LORD said to Moses, "Go up this mountain in the Abarim range[j] and see the land[k] I have given the Israelites. 13 After you have seen it, you too will be gathered to your people,[l] as your brother Aaron was,

[a]59 Or *Jochebed, a daughter of Levi, who was born to Levi*

**26:53** r Jos 11:23; 14:1
**26:54** s Nu 33:54
**26:55** t Nu 34:14
**26:57** u Ge 46:11
**26:59** v Ex 6:20
**26:60** w Nu 3:2
**26:61** x Lev 10:1–2 y Nu 3:4
**26:62** z Nu 1:47 a Nu 18:23
**26:64** b Dt 2:14–15; Heb 3:17
**26:65** c Nu 14:28; 1Co 10:5
**27:1** d Nu 26:33 e Nu 36:1
**27:3** f Nu 26:65 g Nu 16:2
**27:5** h Nu 9:8
**27:11** i Nu 35:29
**27:12** j Nu 33:47; Jer 22:20 k Dt 32:48–52
**27:13** l Nu 31:2

# Zelophehad's Daughters

## reflection

*What lessons do you learn from Zelophehad's daughters?*

*How can you use these lessons to inspire you and motivate your sisters around you?*

## read

Numbers 27:1–11; 36:1–12.

**See also** the Inspire Notes "Influencing Others," "God's Righteousness" and "Be Focused," and the Women of the Bible Notes "Acsah: A Wise Daughter" and "A Virtuous Woman: A Strong Woman, Dependent on God."

## *Seeking an Inheritance*

The Bible speaks of daughters as well as sons; however, the daughters often appear in the background. The genealogies go on and on as they list the sons, but what about the daughters?

We find one powerful account of daughters in Numbers 27—the daughters of Zelophehad. The Biblical account relates how they courageously requested to receive a family inheritance in anticipation of the Israelites' entrance into the promised land. The tradition was that land allotments remained in the family through a male relative, thus perpetuating the ancestral name. Zelophehad's daughters made a request that not only challenged that tradition but also changed the laws of the community. Their actions were personal, yet the results brought about change in the legal and cultural system by becoming case law.

The five daughters—Mahlah, Noah, Hoglah, Milcah and Tirzah—were amazing women. Because their father had died in the desert leaving no male heir, they realized that his name and their family's portion in Canaan would be lost. They were not trying to be aggressive and annihilate the values and norms of their culture, but they did want to be heard. So they took a risk and made their claim within the context of their religious, cultural and legal system. They put themselves in a position of being rebuffed or blessed. Because they boldly presented a legitimate request, they were blessed, and so, too, were many who came behind them.

The inheritance given to Mahlah, Noah, Hoglah, Milcah and Tirzah demonstrates that God does not give women secondary status and that he is concerned for them. These sisters were rewarded for their faith in God and in his justice for their welfare and personal security. They asked and they received. Often we receive not because we ask not!

The story of Zelophehad's daughters in Numbers 27:1–11 provides the following lesson for women today: Proclaim who you are and that you have God-given rights. Know how your culture constrains or supports you as you claim your rights, and know that asserting yourself can lead to changes in your society that will benefit future generations.

—B. McRipley

For the next Women of the Bible note, go to page 248.

14 for when the community rebelled at the waters in the Desert of Zin, both of you disobeyed my command to honor me as holy[m] before their eyes." (These were the waters of Meribah[n] Kadesh, in the Desert of Zin.)

15 Moses said to the LORD, 16 "May the LORD, the God of the spirits of all mankind,[o] appoint a man over this community 17 to go out and come in before them, one who will lead them out and bring them in, so the LORD's people will not be like sheep without a shepherd."[p]

18 So the LORD said to Moses, "Take Joshua son of Nun, a man in whom is the spirit,[a][q] and lay your hand on him.[r] 19 Have him stand before Eleazar the priest and the entire assembly and commission him in their presence.[s] 20 Give him some of your authority so the whole Israelite community will obey him.[t] 21 He is to stand before Eleazar the priest, who will obtain decisions for him by inquiring of the Urim[u] before the LORD. At his command he and the entire community of the Israelites will go out, and at his command they will come in."

22 Moses did as the LORD commanded him. He took Joshua and had him stand before Eleazar the priest and the whole assembly. 23 Then he laid his hands on him and commissioned him, as the LORD instructed through Moses.

## Daily Offerings

**28** The LORD said to Moses, 2 "Give this command to the Israelites and say to them: 'See that you present to me at the appointed time the food[v] for my offerings made by fire, as an aroma pleasing to me.' 3 Say to them: 'This is the offering made by fire that you are to present to the LORD: two lambs a year old without defect, as a regular burnt offering each day.[w] 4 Prepare one lamb in the morning and the other at twilight, 5 together with a grain offering of a tenth of an ephah[b] of fine flour mixed with a quarter of a hin[c] of oil[x] from pressed olives. 6 This is the regular burnt offering instituted at Mount Sinai as a pleasing aroma, an offering made to the LORD by fire. 7 The accompanying drink offering[y] is to be a quarter of a hin of fermented drink with each lamb. Pour out the drink offering to the LORD at the sanctuary. 8 Prepare the second lamb at twilight, along with the same kind of grain offering and drink offering that you prepare in the morning. This is an offering made by fire, an aroma pleasing to the LORD.

## Sabbath Offerings

9 " 'On the Sabbath day, make an offering of two lambs a year old without defect, together with its drink offering and a grain offering of two-tenths of an ephah[d] of fine flour mixed with oil. 10 This is the burnt offering for every Sabbath, in addition to the regular burnt offering[z] and its drink offering.

## Monthly Offerings

11 " 'On the first of every month,[a] present to the LORD a burnt offering of two young bulls, one ram and seven male lambs a year old, all without defect. 12 With each bull there is to be a grain offering[b] of three-tenths of an ephah[e][c] of fine flour mixed with oil; with the ram, a grain offering of two-tenths of an ephah of fine flour mixed with oil; 13 and with each lamb, a grain offering of a tenth of an ephah of fine flour mixed with oil. This is for a burnt offering, a pleasing aroma, an offering made to the LORD by fire. 14 With each bull there is to be a drink offering of half a hin[f] of wine; with the ram, a third of a hin[g]; and with each lamb, a quarter of a hin. This is the monthly burnt offering to be made at each new moon during the year. 15 Besides the regular burnt offering[d] with its drink offering, one male goat is to be presented to the LORD as a sin offering.

## The Passover

16 " 'On the fourteenth day of the first month the LORD's Passover[e] is to be held. 17 On the fifteenth day of this month there is to be a festival; for seven days eat bread made without yeast.[f] 18 On the first day hold a sacred assembly and do no regular work.[g] 19 Present to the LORD an offering made by

**27:14** m Nu 20:12 n Dt 32:51; Ps 106:32
**27:16** o Nu 16:22
**27:17** p Dt 31:2; Mt 9:36; Mk 6:34
**27:18** q Nu 11:25–29 r Dt 34:9
**27:19** s Dt 31:7
**27:20** t Jos 1:16,17
**27:21** u Ex 28:30
**28:2** v Lev 3:11
**28:3** w Ex 29:38
**28:5** x Lev 2:1
**28:7** y Ex 29:41
**28:10** z ver 3
**28:11** a Nu 10:10
**28:12** b Nu 15:6 c Nu 15:9
**28:15** d ver 3,23,24
**28:16** e Ex 12:6,18; Lev 23:5; Dt 16:1
**28:17** f Lev 23:6
**28:18** g Ex 12:16

[a] 18 Or *Spirit* [b] 5 That is, probably about 2 quarts (about 2 liters); also in verses 13, 21 and 29 [c] 5 That is, probably about 1 quart (about 1 liter); also in verses 7 and 14 [d] 9 That is, probably about 4 quarts (about 4.5 liters); also in verses 12, 20 and 28 [e] 12 That is, probably about 6 quarts (about 6.5 liters); also in verses 20 and 28 [f] 14 That is, probably about 2 quarts (about 2 liters) [g] 14 That is, probably about 1 1/4 quarts (about 1.2 liters)

**28:26** h Ex34:22 i Ex23:16 j Dt16:10
**28:31** k ver 3,19
**29:1** l Lev23:24
**29:6** m Nu28:11 n Nu28:3

fire, a burnt offering of two young bulls, one ram and seven male lambs a year old, all without defect. 20 With each bull prepare a grain offering of three-tenths of an ephah of fine flour mixed with oil; with the ram, two-tenths; 21 and with each of the seven lambs, one-tenth. 22 Include one male goat as a sin offering to make atonement for you. 23 Prepare these in addition to the regular morning burnt offering. 24 In this way prepare the food for the offering made by fire every day for seven days as an aroma pleasing to the LORD; it is to be prepared in addition to the regular burnt offering and its drink offering. 25 On the seventh day hold a sacred assembly and do no regular work.

## Feast of Weeks

26 "'On the day of firstfruits,[h] when you present to the LORD an offering of new grain during the Feast of Weeks,[i] hold a sacred assembly and do no regular work.[j] 27 Present a burnt offering of two young bulls, one ram and seven male lambs a year old as an aroma pleasing to the LORD. 28 With each bull there is to be a grain offering of three-tenths of an ephah of fine flour mixed with oil; with the ram, two-tenths; 29 and with each of the seven lambs, one-tenth. 30 Include one male goat to make atonement for you. 31 Prepare these together with their drink offerings, in addition to the regular burnt offering[k] and its grain offering. Be sure the animals are without defect.

## Feast of Trumpets

29 "'On the first day of the seventh month hold a sacred assembly and do no regular work.[l] It is a day for you to sound the trumpets. 2 As an aroma pleasing to the LORD, prepare a burnt offering of one young bull, one ram and seven male lambs a year old, all without defect. 3 With the bull prepare a grain offering of three-tenths of an ephah[a] of fine flour mixed with oil; with the ram, two-tenths[b]; 4 and with each of the seven lambs, one-tenth.[c] 5 Include one male goat as a sin offering to make atonement for you. 6 These are in addition to the monthly[m] and daily burnt offerings[n] with their grain offerings and drink offerings as specified. They are offerings made to the LORD by fire—a pleasing aroma.

## Day of Atonement

7 "'On the tenth day of this seventh month hold a sacred assembly. You must deny yourselves[d] and do no work.[o] 8 Present as an aroma pleasing to the LORD a burnt offering of one young bull, one ram and seven male lambs a year old, all without defect. 9 With the bull prepare a grain offering of three-tenths of an ephah of fine flour mixed with oil; with the ram, two-tenths; 10 and with each of the seven lambs, one-tenth. 11 Include one male goat as a sin offering, in addition to the sin offering for atonement and the regular burnt offering[p] with its grain offering, and their drink offerings.

## Feast of Tabernacles

12 "'On the fifteenth day of the seventh month, hold a sacred assembly and do no regular work. Celebrate a festival to the LORD for seven days. 13 Present an offering made by fire as an aroma pleasing to the LORD, a burnt offering of thirteen young bulls, two rams and fourteen male lambs a year old, all without defect. 14 With each of the thirteen bulls prepare a grain offering of three-tenths of an ephah of fine flour mixed with oil; with each of the two rams, two-tenths; 15 and with each of the fourteen lambs, one-tenth. 16 Include one male goat as a sin offering, in addition to the regular burnt offering with its grain offering and drink offering.

17 "'On the second day[q] prepare twelve young bulls, two rams and fourteen male lambs a year old, all without defect. 18 With the bulls, rams and lambs, prepare their grain offerings[r] and drink offerings according to the number specified.[s] 19 Include one male goat as a sin offering, in addition to the regular burnt offering with its grain offering, and their drink offerings.

20 "'On the third day prepare eleven bulls, two rams and fourteen male lambs a year old, all without defect. 21 With the bulls, rams and lambs, prepare their grain offerings and drink offerings according to the

**29:7** o Ex31:15; Lev16:29; 23:26-32
**29:11** p Lev16:3; Nu28:3
**29:17** q Lev23:36
**29:18** r ver 9 s Nu15:4-12

[a] 3 That is, probably about 6 quarts (about 6.5 liters); also in verses 9 and 14 [b] 3 That is, probably about 4 quarts (about 4.5 liters); also in verses 9 and 14 [c] 4 That is, probably about 2 quarts (about 2 liters); also in verses 10 and 15
[d] 7 Or *must fast*

number specified. 22 Include one male goat as a sin offering, in addition to the regular burnt offering with its grain offering and drink offering.

23 " 'On the fourth day prepare ten bulls, two rams and fourteen male lambs a year old, all without defect. 24 With the bulls, rams and lambs, prepare their grain offerings and drink offerings according to the number specified. 25 Include one male goat as a sin offering, in addition to the regular burnt offering with its grain offering and drink offering.

26 " 'On the fifth day prepare nine bulls, two rams and fourteen male lambs a year old, all without defect. 27 With the bulls, rams and lambs, prepare their grain offerings and drink offerings according to the number specified. 28 Include one male goat as a sin offering, in addition to the regular burnt offering with its grain offering and drink offering.

29 " 'On the sixth day prepare eight bulls, two rams and fourteen male lambs a year old, all without defect. 30 With the bulls, rams and lambs, prepare their grain offerings and drink offerings according to the number specified. 31 Include one male goat as a sin offering, in addition to the regular burnt offering with its grain offering and drink offering.

32 " 'On the seventh day prepare seven bulls, two rams and fourteen male lambs a year old, all without defect. 33 With the bulls, rams and lambs, prepare their grain offerings and drink offerings according to the number specified. 34 Include one male goat as a sin offering, in addition to the regular burnt offering with its grain offering and drink offering.

35 " 'On the eighth day hold an assembly[t] and do no regular work. 36 Present an offering made by fire as an aroma pleasing to the LORD, a burnt offering of one bull, one ram and seven male lambs a year old, all without defect. 37 With the bull, the ram and the lambs, prepare their grain offerings and drink offerings according to the number specified. 38 Include one male goat as a sin offering, in addition to the regular burnt offering with its grain offering and drink offering.

39 " 'In addition to what you vow and your freewill offerings, prepare these for the LORD at your appointed feasts:[u] your burnt offerings,[v] grain offerings, drink offerings and fellowship offerings.[a]' "

40 Moses told the Israelites all that the LORD commanded him.

## Vows

**30** Moses said to the heads of the tribes of Israel:[w] "This is what the LORD commands: 2 When a man makes a vow to the LORD or takes an oath to obligate himself by a pledge, he must not break his word but must do everything he said.[x]

3 "When a young woman still living in her father's house makes a vow to the LORD or obligates herself by a pledge 4 and her father hears about her vow or pledge but says nothing to her, then all her vows and every pledge by which she obligated herself will stand. 5 But if her father forbids her when he hears about it, none of her vows or the pledges by which she obligated herself will stand; the LORD will release her because her father has forbidden her.

6 "If she marries after she makes a vow or after her lips utter a rash promise by which she obligates herself 7 and her husband hears about it but says nothing to her, then her vows or the pledges by which she obligated herself will stand. 8 But if her husband forbids her when he hears about it, he nullifies the vow that obligates her or the rash promise by which she obligates herself, and the LORD will release her.

9 "Any vow or obligation taken by a widow or divorced woman will be binding on her.

10 "If a woman living with her husband makes a vow or obligates herself by a pledge under oath 11 and her husband hears about it but says nothing to her and does not forbid her, then all her vows or the pledges by which she obligated herself will stand. 12 But if her husband nullifies them when he hears about them, then none of the vows or pledges that came from her lips will stand.[y] Her husband has nullified them, and the LORD will release her. 13 Her husband may confirm or nullify any vow she makes or any sworn pledge to deny herself. 14 But if her husband says noth-

**29:35** t Lev 23:36

**29:39** u Lev 23:2 v 1Ch 23:31; 2Ch 31:3

**30:1** w Nu 1:4

**30:2** x Dt 23:21–23; Ps 50:14

**30:12** y Eph 5:22

[a] 39 Traditionally *peace offerings*

ing to her about it from day to day, then he confirms all her vows or the pledges binding on her. He confirms them by saying nothing to her when he hears about them. 15 If, however, he nullifies them some time after he hears about them, then he is responsible for her guilt."

16 These are the regulations the LORD gave Moses concerning relationships between a man and his wife, and between a father and his young daughter still living in his house.

## Vengeance on the Midianites

31 The LORD said to Moses, 2 "Take vengeance on the Midianites for the Israelites. After that, you will be gathered to your people.[z]"

3 So Moses said to the people, "Arm some of your men to go to war against the Midianites and to carry out the LORD's vengeance on them. 4 Send into battle a thousand men from each of the tribes of Israel." 5 So twelve thousand men armed for battle, a thousand from each tribe, were supplied from the clans of Israel. 6 Moses sent them into battle, a thousand from each tribe, along with Phinehas son of Eleazar, the priest, who took with him articles from the sanctuary and the trumpets[a] for signaling.

7 They fought against Midian, as the LORD commanded Moses, and killed every man.[b] 8 Among their victims were Evi, Rekem, Zur, Hur and Reba[c]—the five kings of Midian. They also killed Balaam son of Beor with the sword.[d] 9 The Israelites captured the Midianite women and children and took all the Midianite herds, flocks and goods as plunder. 10 They burned all the towns where the Midianites had settled, as well as all their camps. 11 They took all the plunder and spoils, including the people and animals,[e] 12 and brought the captives, spoils and plunder to Moses and Eleazar the priest and the Israelite assembly at their camp on the plains of Moab, by the Jordan across from Jericho.[a]

13 Moses, Eleazar the priest and all the leaders of the community went to meet them outside the camp. 14 Moses was angry with the officers of the army—the commanders of thousands and commanders of hundreds—who returned from the battle.

15 "Have you allowed all the women to live?" he asked them. 16 "They were the ones who followed Balaam's advice[f] and were the means of turning the Israelites away from the LORD in what happened at Peor,[g] so that a plague struck the LORD's people. 17 Now kill all the boys. And kill every woman who has slept with a man,[h] 18 but save for yourselves every girl who has never slept with a man.

19 "All of you who have killed anyone or touched anyone who was killed must stay outside the camp seven days. On the third and seventh days you must purify yourselves[i] and your captives. 20 Purify every garment as well as everything made of leather, goat hair or wood."

21 Then Eleazar the priest said to the soldiers who had gone into battle, "This is the requirement of the law that the LORD gave Moses: 22 Gold, silver, bronze, iron, tin, lead 23 and anything else that can withstand fire must be put through the fire,[j] and then it will be clean. But it must also be purified with the water of cleansing.[k] And whatever cannot withstand fire must be put through that water. 24 On the seventh day wash your clothes and you will be clean.[l] Then you may come into the camp."

## Dividing the Spoils

25 The LORD said to Moses, 26 "You and Eleazar the priest and the family heads of the community are to count all the people and animals that were captured. 27 Divide[m] the spoils between the soldiers who took part in the battle and the rest of the community. 28 From the soldiers who fought in the battle, set apart as tribute for the LORD[n] one out of every five hundred, whether persons, cattle, donkeys, sheep or goats. 29 Take this tribute from their half share and give it to Eleazar the priest as the LORD's part. 30 From the Israelites' half, select one out of every fifty, whether persons, cattle, donkeys, sheep, goats or other animals. Give them to the Levites, who are responsible for the care of the LORD's tabernacle.[o]" 31 So Moses and Eleazar the priest did as the LORD commanded Moses.

**31:2** z Nu 20:26; 27:13
**31:6** a Nu 10:9
**31:7** b Dt 20:13; Jdg 21:11; 1Ki 11:15,16
**31:8** c Jos 13:21 d Jos 13:22
**31:11** e Dt 20:14
**31:16** f 2Pe 2:15 g Nu 25:1–9
**31:17** h Dt 7:2; 20:16–18; Jdg 21:11
**31:19** i Nu 19:12
**31:23** j 1Co 3:13 k Nu 19:9,17
**31:24** l Lev 11:25
**31:27** m Jos 22:8
**31:28** n Nu 18:21
**31:30** o Nu 3:7; 18:3

[a] 12 Hebrew *Jordan of Jericho*; possibly an ancient name for the Jordan River

**31:37** p ver 38–41
**31:41** q Nu 18:8
**31:50** r Ex 30:16
**31:53** s Dt 20:14

32 The plunder remaining from the spoils that the soldiers took was 675,000 sheep, 33 72,000 cattle, 34 61,000 donkeys 35 and 32,000 women who had never slept with a man.

36 The half share of those who fought in the battle was:

> 337,500 sheep, 37 of which the tribute for the LORD[p] was 675;
> 38 36,000 cattle, of which the tribute for the LORD was 72;
> 39 30,500 donkeys, of which the tribute for the LORD was 61;
> 40 16,000 people, of which the tribute for the LORD was 32.

41 Moses gave the tribute to Eleazar the priest as the LORD's part,[q] as the LORD commanded Moses.

42 The half belonging to the Israelites, which Moses set apart from that of the fighting men— 43 the community's half—was 337,500 sheep, 44 36,000 cattle, 45 30,500 donkeys 46 and 16,000 people. 47 From the Israelites' half, Moses selected one out of every fifty persons and animals, as the LORD commanded him, and gave them to the Levites, who were responsible for the care of the LORD's tabernacle.

48 Then the officers who were over the units of the army—the commanders of thousands and commanders of hundreds—went to Moses 49 and said to him, "Your servants have counted the soldiers under our command, and not one is missing. 50 So we have brought as an offering to the LORD the gold articles each of us acquired—armlets, bracelets, signet rings, earrings and necklaces—to make atonement for ourselves[r] before the LORD."

51 Moses and Eleazar the priest accepted from them the gold—all the crafted articles. 52 All the gold from the commanders of thousands and commanders of hundreds that Moses and Eleazar presented as a gift to the LORD weighed 16,750 shekels.[a] 53 Each soldier had taken plunder[s] for himself. 54 Moses and Eleazar the priest accepted the gold from the commanders of thousands and commanders of hundreds and brought it into the Tent of Meeting as a memorial for the Israelites before the LORD.

## The Transjordan Tribes

**32** The Reubenites and Gadites, who had very large herds and flocks, saw that the lands of Jazer[t] and Gilead were suitable for livestock.[u] 2 So they came to Moses and Eleazar the priest and to the leaders of the community, and said, 3 "Ataroth, Dibon, Jazer, Nimrah,[v] Heshbon, Elealeh, Sebam, Nebo and Beon[w]— 4 the land the LORD subdued[x] before the people of Israel—are suitable for livestock, and your servants have livestock. 5 If we have found favor in your eyes," they said, "let this land be given to your servants as our possession. Do not make us cross the Jordan."

6 Moses said to the Gadites and Reubenites, "Shall your countrymen go to war while you sit here? 7 Why do you discourage the Israelites from going over into the land the LORD has given them?[y] 8 This is what your fathers did when I sent them from Kadesh Barnea to look over the land.[z] 9 After they went up to the Valley of Eshcol[a] and viewed the land, they discouraged the Israelites from entering the land the LORD had given them. 10 The LORD's anger was aroused that day and he swore this oath: 11 'Because they have not followed me wholeheartedly, not one of the men twenty years old or more who came up out of Egypt will see the land I promised on oath to Abraham, Isaac and Jacob[b]— 12 not one except Caleb son of Jephunneh the Kenizzite and Joshua son of Nun, for they followed the LORD wholeheartedly.'[c] 13 The LORD's anger burned against Israel and he made them wander in the desert forty years, until the whole generation of those who had done evil in his sight was gone.[d]

14 "And here you are, a brood of sinners, standing in the place of your fathers and making the LORD even more angry with Israel. 15 If you turn away from following him, he will again leave all this people in the desert, and you will be the cause of their destruction.[e]"

16 Then they came up to him and said, "We would like to build pens here for our livestock and cities for our women and children. 17 But we are ready to arm ourselves and go ahead of the Israelites[f] until we have brought them to their place. Meanwhile our

**32:1** t Nu 21:32; u Ex 12:38
**32:3** v ver 36; w ver 38
**32:4** x Nu 21:34
**32:7** y Nu 13:27—14:4
**32:8** z Nu 13:3,26; Dt 1:19–25
**32:9** a Dt 1:24
**32:11** b Nu 14:28–30
**32:12** c Nu 14:24,30; Dt 1:36
**32:13** d Nu 14:28–35; 26:64,65
**32:15** e Dt 30:17–18; 2Ch 7:20
**32:17** f Jos 4:12,13

[a] 52 That is, about 420 pounds (about 190 kilograms)

women and children will live in fortified cities, for protection from the inhabitants of the land. [18]We will not return to our homes until every Israelite has received his inheritance.[g] [19]We will not receive any inheritance with them on the other side of the Jordan, because our inheritance has come to us on the east side of the Jordan."[h]

[20]Then Moses said to them, "If you will do this—if you will arm yourselves before the LORD for battle,[i] [21]and if all of you will go armed over the Jordan before the LORD until he has driven his enemies out before him— [22]then when the land is subdued before the LORD, you may return and be free from your obligation to the LORD and to Israel. And this land will be your possession before the LORD.[j]

[23]"But if you fail to do this, you will be sinning against the LORD; and you may be sure that your sin will find you out.[k] [24]Build cities for your women and children, and pens for your flocks,[l] but do what you have promised."

[25]The Gadites and Reubenites said to Moses, "We your servants will do as our lord commands. [26]Our children and wives, our flocks and herds will remain here in the cities of Gilead.[m] [27]But your servants, every man armed for battle, will cross over to fight before the LORD, just as our lord says."

[28]Then Moses gave orders about them[n] to Eleazar the priest and Joshua son of Nun and to the family heads of the Israelite tribes. [29]He said to them, "If the Gadites and Reubenites, every man armed for battle, cross over the Jordan with you before the LORD, then when the land is subdued before you, give them the land of Gilead as their possession. [30]But if they do not cross over with you armed, they must accept their possession with you in Canaan."

[31]The Gadites and Reubenites answered, "Your servants will do what the LORD has said. [32]We will cross over before the LORD into Canaan armed, but the property we inherit will be on this side of the Jordan."

[33]Then Moses gave to the Gadites, the Reubenites and the half-tribe of Manasseh son of Joseph the kingdom of Sihon king of the Amorites and the kingdom of Og king of Bashan—the whole land with its cities and the territory around them.[o]

[34]The Gadites built up Dibon, Ataroth, Aroer,[p] [35]Atroth Shophan, Jazer, Jogbehah, [36]Beth Nimrah[q] and Beth Haran as fortified cities, and built pens for their flocks. [37]And the Reubenites rebuilt Heshbon, Elealeh and Kiriathaim, [38]as well as Nebo and Baal Meon (these names were changed) and Sibmah. They gave names to the cities they rebuilt.

[39]The descendants of Makir[r] son of Manasseh went to Gilead, captured it and drove out the Amorites who were there. [40]So Moses gave Gilead to the Makirites, the descendants of Manasseh, and they settled there. [41]Jair, a descendant of Manasseh, captured their settlements and called them Havvoth Jair.[a][s] [42]And Nobah captured Kenath and its surrounding settlements and called it Nobah after himself.[t]

## Stages in Israel's Journey

33 Here are the stages in the journey of the Israelites when they came out of Egypt by divisions under the leadership of Moses and Aaron. [2]At the LORD's command Moses recorded the stages in their journey. This is their journey by stages:

[3]The Israelites set out from Rameses on the fifteenth day of the first month, the day after the Passover. They marched out boldly[u] in full view of all the Egyptians, [4]who were burying all their firstborn, whom the LORD had struck down among them; for the LORD had brought judgment on their gods.[v]

[5]The Israelites left Rameses and camped at Succoth.

[6]They left Succoth and camped at Etham, on the edge of the desert.[w]

[7]They left Etham, turned back to Pi Hahiroth, to the east of Baal Zephon, and camped near Migdol.[x]

[8]They left Pi Hahiroth[b] and passed through the sea[y] into the desert, and when they had traveled for three days in the Desert of Etham, they camped at Marah.

**32:18** g Jos 22:1–4
**32:19** h Jos 12:1
**32:20** i Dt 3:18
**32:22** j Dt 3:18–20
**32:23** k Ge 4:7
**32:24** l ver 1,16
**32:26** m Jos 1:14
**32:28** n Jos 1:13
**32:33** o Nu 21:24; Jos 12:6
**32:34** p Dt 2:36
**32:36** q ver 3
**32:39** r Ge 50:23
**32:41** s Dt 3:14; Jdg 10:4
**32:42** t 2Sa 18:18; Ps 49:11
**33:3** u Ex 14:8
**33:4** v Ex 12:12
**33:6** w Ex 13:20
**33:7** x Ex 14:2
**33:8** y Ex 14:22

[a]41 Or *them the settlements of Jair* [b]8 Many manuscripts of the Masoretic Text, Samaritan Pentateuch and Vulgate; most manuscripts of the Masoretic Text *left from before Hahiroth*

**33:9** z Ex15:27
**33:11** a Ex16:1
**33:15** b Ex17:1; c Ex19:1
**33:16** d Nu11:34
**33:17** e Nu11:35
**33:30** f Dt10:6

9 They left Marah and went to Elim, where there were twelve springs and seventy palm trees, and they camped[z] there.

10 They left Elim and camped by the Red Sea.[a]

11 They left the Red Sea and camped in the Desert of Sin.[a]

12 They left the Desert of Sin and camped at Dophkah.

13 They left Dophkah and camped at Alush.

14 They left Alush and camped at Rephidim, where there was no water for the people to drink.

15 They left Rephidim[b] and camped in the Desert of Sinai.[c]

16 They left the Desert of Sinai and camped at Kibroth Hattaavah.[d]

17 They left Kibroth Hattaavah and camped at Hazeroth.[e]

18 They left Hazeroth and camped at Rithmah.

19 They left Rithmah and camped at Rimmon Perez.

20 They left Rimmon Perez and camped at Libnah.

21 They left Libnah and camped at Rissah.

22 They left Rissah and camped at Kehelathah.

23 They left Kehelathah and camped at Mount Shepher.

24 They left Mount Shepher and camped at Haradah.

25 They left Haradah and camped at Makheloth.

26 They left Makheloth and camped at Tahath.

27 They left Tahath and camped at Terah.

28 They left Terah and camped at Mithcah.

29 They left Mithcah and camped at Hashmonah.

30 They left Hashmonah and camped at Moseroth.[f]

31 They left Moseroth and camped at Bene Jaakan.

32 They left Bene Jaakan and camped at Hor Haggidgad.

33 They left Hor Haggidgad and camped at Jotbathah.

34 They left Jotbathah and camped at Abronah.

35 They left Abronah and camped at Ezion Geber.[g]

36 They left Ezion Geber and camped at Kadesh, in the Desert of Zin.[h]

37 They left Kadesh and camped at Mount Hor,[i] on the border of Edom. 38 At the LORD's command Aaron the priest went up Mount Hor, where he died[j] on the first day of the fifth month of the fortieth year after the Israelites came out of Egypt.[k] 39 Aaron was a hundred and twenty-three years old when he died on Mount Hor.

40 The Canaanite king of Arad,[l] who lived in the Negev of Canaan, heard that the Israelites were coming.

41 They left Mount Hor and camped at Zalmonah.

42 They left Zalmonah and camped at Punon.

43 They left Punon and camped at Oboth.[m]

44 They left Oboth and camped at Iye Abarim, on the border of Moab.

45 They left Iyim[b] and camped at Dibon Gad.

46 They left Dibon Gad and camped at Almon Diblathaim.

47 They left Almon Diblathaim and camped in the mountains of Abarim, near Nebo.

48 They left the mountains of Abarim and camped on the plains of Moab by the Jordan across from Jericho.[n] 49 There on the plains of Moab they camped along the Jordan from Beth Jeshimoth to Abel Shittim.[o]

50 On the plains of Moab by the Jordan across from Jericho the LORD said to Moses, 51 "Speak to the Israelites and say to them: 'When you cross the Jordan into Canaan, 52 drive out all the inhabitants of the land before you. Destroy all their carved images and their cast idols, and demolish all their high places.[p] 53 Take possession of the land and settle in it, for I have given you the land

**33:35** g Dt2:8
**33:36** h Nu20:1
**33:37** i Nu20:22
**33:38** j Dt10:6; k Nu20:25–28
**33:40** l Nu21:1
**33:43** m Nu21:10
**33:48** n Nu22:1
**33:49** o Nu25:1
**33:52** p Ex23:24; Dt7:2,5

[a] 10 Hebrew *Yam Suph*; that is, Sea of Reeds; also in verse 11 [b] 45 That is, Iye Abarim [c] 48 Hebrew *Jordan of Jericho*; possibly an ancient name for the Jordan River; also in verse 50

to possess. [54]Distribute the land by lot, according to your clans.[q] To a larger group give a larger inheritance, and to a smaller group a smaller one. Whatever falls to them by lot will be theirs. Distribute it according to your ancestral tribes.

[55]"'But if you do not drive out the inhabitants of the land, those you allow to remain will become barbs in your eyes and thorns[r] in your sides. They will give you trouble in the land where you will live. [56]And then I will do to you what I plan to do to them.'"

## Boundaries of Canaan

**34** The LORD said to Moses, [2]"Command the Israelites and say to them: 'When you enter Canaan, the land that will be allotted to you as an inheritance[s] will have these boundaries:

*Daughter,*

*Boundaries are good. Set boundaries in your life according to my Word.*

*With my protective love, God*

NUMBERS 34:2

[3]"'Your southern side will include some of the Desert of Zin[t] along the border of Edom. On the east, your southern boundary will start from the end of the Salt Sea,[a] [4]cross south of Scorpion[b] Pass, continue on to Zin and go south of Kadesh Barnea.[u] Then it will go to Hazar Addar and over to Azmon, [5]where it will turn, join the Wadi of Egypt[v] and end at the Sea.[c]

[6]"'Your western boundary will be the coast of the Great Sea. This will be your boundary on the west.

[7]"'For your northern boundary,[w] run a line from the Great Sea to Mount Hor [8]and from Mount Hor to Lebo[d] Hamath. Then the boundary will go to Zedad, [9]continue to Ziphron and end at Hazar Enan. This will be your boundary on the north.

[10]"'For your eastern boundary, run a line from Hazar Enan to Shepham. [11]The boundary will go down from Shepham to Riblah[x] on the east side of Ain and continue along the slopes east of the Sea of Kinnereth.[e][y] [12]Then the boundary will go down along the Jordan and end at the Salt Sea.

"'This will be your land, with its boundaries on every side.'"

[13]Moses commanded the Israelites: "Assign this land by lot as an inheritance.[z] The LORD has ordered that it be given to the nine and a half tribes, [14]because the families of the tribe of Reuben, the tribe of Gad and the half-tribe of Manasseh have received their inheritance.[a] [15]These two and a half tribes have received their inheritance on the east side of the Jordan of Jericho,[f] toward the sunrise."

[16]The LORD said to Moses, [17]"These are the names of the men who are to assign the land for you as an inheritance: Eleazar the priest and Joshua[b] son of Nun. [18]And appoint one leader from each tribe to help[c] assign the land. [19]These are their names:

Caleb son of Jephunneh,
  from the tribe of Judah;
[20]Shemuel son of Ammihud,
  from the tribe of Simeon;
[21]Elidad son of Kislon,
  from the tribe of Benjamin;
[22]Bukki son of Jogli,
  the leader from the tribe of Dan;
[23]Hanniel son of Ephod,
  the leader from the tribe of Manasseh son of Joseph;
[24]Kemuel son of Shiphtan,
  the leader from the tribe of Ephraim son of Joseph;
[25]Elizaphan son of Parnach,
  the leader from the tribe of Zebulun;
[26]Paltiel son of Azzan,
  the leader from the tribe of Issachar;
[27]Ahihud son of Shelomi,
  the leader from the tribe of Asher;

**33:54** q Nu 26:54
**33:55** r Jos 23:13
**34:2** s Ge 17:8; Dt 1:7–8; Ps 78:54–55
**34:3** t Jos 15:1–3
**34:4** u Nu 32:8
**34:5** v Jos 15:4
**34:7** w Eze 47:15–17
**34:11** x 2Ki 23:33 y Dt 3:17
**34:13** z Jos 14:1–5
**34:14** a Nu 32:33
**34:17** b Jos 14:1
**34:18** c Nu 1:4,16

[a]3 That is, the Dead Sea; also in verse 12 [b]4 Hebrew *Akrabbim* [c]5 That is, the Mediterranean; also in verses 6 and 7 [d]8 Or *to the entrance to* [e]11 That is, Galilee [f]15 *Jordan of Jericho* was possibly an ancient name for the Jordan River.

**35:2** d Lev 25:32–34
**35:6** e Jos 20:7–9; 21:3,13
**35:8** f Nu 26:54
**35:11** g Ex 21:13
**35:12** h Jos 20:3

28 Pedahel son of Ammihud,
the leader from the tribe of Naphtali."

29 These are the men the LORD commanded to assign the inheritance to the Israelites in the land of Canaan.

## Towns for the Levites

35 On the plains of Moab by the Jordan across from Jericho,[a] the LORD said to Moses, 2 "Command the Israelites to give the Levites towns to live in[d] from the inheritance the Israelites will possess. And give them pasturelands around the towns. 3 Then they will have towns to live in and pasturelands for their cattle, flocks and all their other livestock.

4 "The pasturelands around the towns that you give the Levites will extend out fifteen hundred feet[b] from the town wall. 5 Outside the town, measure three thousand feet[c] on the east side, three thousand on the south side, three thousand on the west and three thousand on the north, with the town in the center. They will have this area as pastureland for the towns.

## Cities of Refuge

6 "Six of the towns you give the Levites will be cities of refuge, to which a person who has killed someone may flee.[e] In addition, give them forty-two other towns. 7 In all you must give the Levites forty-eight towns, together with their pasturelands. 8 The towns you give the Levites from the land the Israelites possess are to be given in proportion to the inheritance of each tribe: Take many towns from a tribe that has many, but few from one that has few."[f]

9 Then the LORD said to Moses: 10 "Speak to the Israelites and say to them: 'When you cross the Jordan into Canaan, 11 select some towns to be your cities of refuge, to which a person who has killed someone accidentally[g] may flee. 12 They will be places of refuge from the avenger,[h] so that a person accused of murder may not die before he stands trial before the assembly. 13 These six towns you give will be your cities of refuge. 14 Give three on this side of the Jordan and three in Canaan as cities of refuge. 15 These six towns will be a place of refuge for Israelites, aliens and any other people living among them, so that anyone who has killed another accidentally can flee there.

16 " 'If a man strikes someone with an iron object so that he dies, he is a murderer; the murderer shall be put to death.[i] 17 Or if anyone has a stone in his hand that could kill, and he strikes someone so that he dies, he is a murderer; the murderer shall be put to death. 18 Or if anyone has a wooden object in his hand that could kill, and he hits someone so that he dies, he is a murderer; the murderer shall be put to death. 19 The avenger of blood shall put the murderer to death; when he meets him, he shall put him to death. 20 If anyone with malice aforethought shoves another or throws something at him intentionally[j] so that he dies 21 or if in hostility he hits him with his fist so that he dies, that person shall be put to death; he is a murderer. The avenger of blood shall put the murderer to death when he meets him.

22 " 'But if without hostility someone suddenly shoves another or throws something at him unintentionally 23 or, without seeing him, drops a stone on him that could kill him, and he dies, then since he was not his enemy and he did not intend to harm him, 24 the assembly[k] must judge between him and the avenger of blood according to these regulations. 25 The assembly must protect the one accused of murder from the avenger of blood and send him back to the city of refuge to which he fled. He must stay there until the death of the high priest, who was anointed with the holy oil.[l]

26 " 'But if the accused ever goes outside the limits of the city of refuge to which he has fled 27 and the avenger of blood finds him outside the city, the avenger of blood may kill the accused without being guilty of murder. 28 The accused must stay in his city of refuge until the death of the high priest; only after the death of the high priest may he return to his own property.

29 " 'These are to be legal requirements for you throughout the generations to come, wherever you live.

30 " 'Anyone who kills a person is to be put

**35:16** i Ex 21:12; Lev 24:17
**35:20** j Ex 21:14
**35:24** k ver 12
**35:25** l Ex 29:7

[a] 1 Hebrew *Jordan of Jericho*; possibly an ancient name for the Jordan River [b] 4 Hebrew *a thousand cubits* (about 450 meters) [c] 5 Hebrew *two thousand cubits* (about 900 meters)

to death as a murderer only on the testimony of witnesses. But no one is to be put to death on the testimony of only one witness.[m]

31 "'Do not accept a ransom for the life of a murderer, who deserves to die. He must surely be put to death.

32 "'Do not accept a ransom for anyone who has fled to a city of refuge and so allow him to go back and live on his own land before the death of the high priest.

33 "'Do not pollute the land where you are. Bloodshed pollutes the land,[n] and atonement cannot be made for the land on which blood has been shed, except by the blood of the one who shed it. 34 Do not defile the land[o] where you live and where I dwell, for I, the LORD, dwell among the Israelites.'"

## Inheritance of Zelophehad's Daughters

36 The family heads of the clan of Gilead[p] son of Makir, the son of Manasseh, who were from the clans of the descendants of Joseph, came and spoke before Moses and the leaders, the heads of the Israelite families. 2 They said, "When the LORD commanded my lord to give the land as an inheritance to the Israelites by lot, he ordered you to give the inheritance of our brother Zelophehad[q] to his daughters. 3 Now suppose they marry men from other Israelite tribes; then their inheritance will be taken from our ancestral inheritance and added to that of the tribe they marry into. And so part of the inheritance allotted to us will be taken away. 4 When the Year of Jubilee[r] for the Israelites comes, their inheritance will be added to that of the tribe into which they marry, and their property will be taken from the tribal inheritance of our forefathers."

5 Then at the LORD's command Moses gave this order to the Israelites: "What the tribe of the descendants of Joseph is saying is right. 6 This is what the LORD commands for Zelophehad's daughters: They may marry anyone they please as long as they marry within the tribal clan of their father. 7 No inheritance[s] in Israel is to pass from tribe to tribe, for every Israelite shall keep the tribal land inherited from his forefathers. 8 Every daughter who inherits land in any Israelite tribe must marry someone in her father's tribal clan,[t] so that every Israelite will possess the inheritance of his fathers. 9 No inheritance may pass from tribe to tribe, for each Israelite tribe is to keep the land it inherits."

*My God*

*there are so many injustices to forgive and overlook, so many debts that have not yet been paid. Still, you have fully paid my debt, freeing me to forgive the debts others owe me. In the name of Jesus, my Redeemer,*

*Amen*

NUMBERS 36:1–9

10 So Zelophehad's daughters did as the LORD commanded Moses. 11 Zelophehad's daughters—Mahlah, Tirzah, Hoglah, Milcah and Noah[u]—married their cousins on their father's side. 12 They married within the clans of the descendants of Manasseh son of Joseph, and their inheritance remained in their father's clan and tribe.

13 These are the commands and regulations the LORD gave through Moses to the Israelites on the plains of Moab by the Jordan across from Jericho.[a]

**35:30** m Dt 17:6; 19:15; Mt 18:16; 2Co 13:1
**35:33** n Ge 9:6; Ps 106:38
**35:34** o Lev 18:24,25
**36:1** p Nu 26:29
**36:2** q Nu 26:33; 27:1,7
**36:4** r Lev 25:10
**36:7** s 1Ki 21:3
**36:8** t 1Ch 23:22
**36:11** u Nu 27:1

[a] 13 Hebrew *Jordan of Jericho*; possibly an ancient name for the Jordan River

# Deuteronomy

## OVERVIEW

Deuteronomy consists of several speeches given by Moses on the plains of Moab—speeches in which he restated and renewed God's covenant with the Israelites. Moses reminded the people of where they had come from and where they were going. He emphasized how God's blessings would be upon those who were obedient to his laws. However, Moses also related how God's curses would be on those who forsook him.

Moses wanted the Israelites to pass on a godly heritage to the next generation of Israelites by sharing the testimony of God's deliverance out of Egypt and by teaching them the laws of God.

God's heart for the disenfranchised is evident in his strong admonition for the people to remember those in need. Chapter 24 describes the ways in which the Israelites were to care for aliens, orphans and widows.

Deuteronomy concludes with Moses' commissioning of Joshua as his successor and the story of Moses' death (see Dt 31–34).

Just as the Israelites needed to be reminded of God's blessings, women of our generation also need to look back to see how far he has brought us. Out of grateful hearts, mothers, grandmothers, sisters, aunts and daughters need to pass on their knowledge of God's faithfulness to the generations of sisters following after them. Reflect on Moses' last words as if he were speaking to your family.

# OUTLINE

I. Preamble (1:1–5)
II. Historical Prologue (1:6—4:43)
III. Stipulations of the Covenant (4:44—26:19)
IV. Blessings and Curses (27:1—30:20)
V. Transition of Leadership From Moses to Joshua (31:1—34:12)

## SCANNABLE FACTS:

**Author:** Moses

**Time Written:** Just before the Israelites entered the promised land, about 1406 B.C.

**Themes to Note:** Blessings and curses; remembering God's laws

**Notable Women:** Israelite women who assembled with their families for Moses' addresses

## The Command to Leave Horeb

1 These are the words Moses spoke to all Israel in the desert east of the Jordan—that is, in the Arabah—opposite Suph, between Paran and Tophel, Laban, Hazeroth and Dizahab. 2(It takes eleven days to go from Horeb to Kadesh Barnea[a] by the Mount Seir road.)

3In the fortieth year,[b] on the first day of the eleventh month, Moses proclaimed to the Israelites all that the LORD had commanded him concerning them. 4This was after he had defeated Sihon king of the Amorites, who reigned in Heshbon, and at Edrei had defeated Og[c] king of Bashan, who reigned in Ashtaroth.

5East of the Jordan in the territory of Moab, Moses began to expound this law, saying:

6The LORD our God said to us[d] at Horeb, "You have stayed long enough at this mountain. 7Break camp and advance into the hill country of the Amorites; go to all the neighboring peoples in the Arabah, in the mountains, in the western foothills, in the Negev and along the coast, to the land of the Canaanites and to Lebanon,[e] as far as the great river, the Euphrates. 8See, I have given you this land. Go in and take possession of the land that the LORD swore[f] he would give to your fathers—to Abraham, Isaac and Jacob—and to their descendants after them."

## The Appointment of Leaders

9At that time I said to you, "You are too heavy a burden for me to carry alone.[g] 10The LORD your God has increased your numbers so that today you are as many[h] as the stars in the sky.[i] 11May the LORD, the God of your fathers, increase you a thousand times and bless you as he has promised![j] 12But how can I bear your problems and your burdens and your disputes all by myself? 13Choose some wise, understanding and respected men from each of your tribes, and I will set them over you."

14You answered me, "What you propose to do is good."

15So I took[k] the leading men of your tribes, wise and respected men, and appointed them to have authority over you—as commanders of thousands, of hundreds, of fifties and of tens and as tribal officials. 16And I charged your judges at that time: Hear the disputes between your brothers and judge fairly,[l] whether the case is between brother Israelites or between one of them and an alien. 17Do not show partiality[m] in judging; hear both small and great alike. Do not be afraid of any man, for judgment belongs to God. Bring me any case too hard for you,

**1:2** a Nu 13:26; Dt 9:23
**1:3** b Nu 33:38
**1:4** c Nu 21:33–35
**1:6** d Nu 10:13
**1:7** e Dt 11:24
**1:8** f Ge 12:7; 26:4; 28:13
**1:9** g Ex 18:18
**1:10** h Ge 15:5 i Dt 10:22; 28:62
**1:11** j Ex 32:13
**1:15** k Ex 18:25
**1:16** l Dt 16:18
**1:17** m Jas 2:1

## *The African Presence*

### Deuteronomy 1

The structure of the book of Deuteronomy follows the Hittite treaty format. Hittites were descendants of Ham through Canaan (see Ge 10:15). Archaeological discoveries show that they were a very prominent and populous people. In the Hittite treaty format, a king reviewed what was done for his vassal and commanded his people to loyalty. In the book of Deuteronomy, Moses reviewed what God did for Israel and exhorted the people to remain faithful to *Yahweh* (God). Because Ham's offspring represent the geographic territories once dominated by Egypt—present-day Egypt, Libya and Sudan and into the area today known as Israel—they can claim a relation to African heritage. Since "heritage" is something "passed down" or "inherited," Canaan (Israel or Palestine) most certainly received or was influenced by Egypt culturally, politically, religiously, etc.

and I will hear it.[n] 18 And at that time I told you everything you were to do.

## Spies Sent Out

19 Then, as the LORD our God commanded us, we set out from Horeb and went toward the hill country of the Amorites through all that vast and dreadful desert[o] that you have seen, and so we reached Kadesh Barnea. 20 Then I said to you, "You have reached the hill country of the Amorites, which the LORD our God is giving us. 21 See, the LORD your God has given you the land. Go up and take possession of it as the LORD, the God of your fathers, told you. Do not be afraid;[p] do not be discouraged."

22 Then all of you came to me and said, "Let us send men ahead to spy out the land for us and bring back a report about the route we are to take and the towns we will come to."

23 The idea seemed good to me; so I selected twelve of you, one man from each tribe. 24 They left and went up into the hill country, and came to the Valley of Eshcol[q] and explored it. 25 Taking with them some of the fruit of the land, they brought it down to us and reported, "It is a good land that the LORD our God is giving us."

## Rebellion Against the LORD

26 But you were unwilling to go up;[r] you rebelled against the command of the LORD your God. 27 You grumbled[s] in your tents and said, "The LORD hates us; so he brought us out of Egypt to deliver us into the hands of the Amorites to destroy us. 28 Where can we go? Our brothers have made us lose heart. They say, 'The people are stronger and taller than we are; the cities are large, with walls up to the sky. We even saw the Anakites[t] there.' "

29 Then I said to you, "Do not be terrified; do not be afraid of them. 30 The LORD your God, who is going before you, will fight[u] for you, as he did for you in Egypt, before your very eyes, 31 and in the desert. There you saw how the LORD your God carried[v] you, as a father carries his son, all the way you went until you reached this place."

32 In spite of this, you did not trust[w] in the LORD your God, 33 who went ahead of you on your journey, in fire by night and in a cloud by day,[x] to search out places for you to camp and to show you the way you should go.

34 When the LORD heard what you said, he was angry and solemnly swore:[y] 35 "Not a man of this evil generation shall see the good land I swore to give your forefathers, 36 except Caleb son of Jephunneh. He will see it, and I will give him and his descendants the land he set his feet on, because he followed the LORD wholeheartedly."

37 Because of you the LORD became angry[z] with me also and said, "You shall not enter[a] it, either. 38 But your assistant, Joshua[b] son of Nun, will enter it. Encourage him, because he will lead Israel to inherit it. 39 And the little ones that you said would be taken captive,[c] your children who do not yet know good from bad—they will enter the land. I will give it to them and they will take possession of it. 40 But as for you, turn around and set out toward the desert along the route to the Red Sea.[a][d]"

41 Then you replied, "We have sinned against the LORD. We will go up and fight, as the LORD our God commanded us." So every one of you put on his weapons, thinking it easy to go up into the hill country.

42 But the LORD said to me, "Tell them, 'Do not go up and fight, because I will not be with you. You will be defeated by your enemies.' "[e]

43 So I told you, but you would not listen. You rebelled against the LORD's command and in your arrogance you marched up into the hill country. 44 The Amorites who lived in those hills came out against you; they chased you like a swarm of bees[f] and beat you down from Seir all the way to Hormah. 45 You came back and wept before the LORD, but he paid no attention to your weeping and turned a deaf ear to you. 46 And so you stayed in Kadesh[g] many days—all the time you spent there.

## Wanderings in the Desert

2 Then we turned back and set out toward the desert along the route to the Red Sea,[a] as the LORD had directed me. For a

[a]40,1 Hebrew *Yam Suph*; that is, Sea of Reeds

**1:17** n Ex 18:26
**1:19** o Dt 8:15
**1:21** p Jos 1:6,9,18
**1:24** q Nu 13:21–25
**1:26** r Nu 14:1–4
**1:27** s Dt 9:28
**1:28** t Nu 13:33; Dt 9:1–3
**1:30** u Ex 14:14
**1:31** v Dt 32:10–12; Ac 13:18
**1:32** w Ps 106:24
**1:33** x Ex 13:21
**1:34** y Nu 14:23, 28–30
**1:37** z Dt 3:26; a Nu 20:12
**1:38** b Nu 14:30
**1:39** c Nu 14:3
**1:40** d Nu 14:25
**1:42** e Nu 14:41–43
**1:44** f Ps 118:12
**1:46** g Nu 20:1

**2:4** h Nu 20:14–21
**2:5** i Jos 24:4
**2:7** j Dt 8:2–4
**2:9** k Ge 19:36–38
**2:10** l Ge 14:5
**2:12** m ver 22
**2:14** n Nu 14:29–35; o Dt 1:34–35

long time we made our way around the hill country of Seir.

[2]Then the LORD said to me, [3]"You have made your way around this hill country long enough; now turn north. [4]Give the people these orders:[h] 'You are about to pass through the territory of your brothers the descendants of Esau, who live in Seir. They will be afraid of you, but be very careful. [5]Do not provoke them to war, for I will not give you any of their land, not even enough to put your foot on. I have given Esau the hill country of Seir as his own.[i] [6]You are to pay them in silver for the food you eat and the water you drink.'"

[7]The LORD your God has blessed you in all the work of your hands. He has watched[j] over your journey through this vast desert. These forty years the LORD your God has been with you, and you have not lacked anything.

[8]So we went on past our brothers the descendants of Esau, who live in Seir. We turned from the Arabah road, which comes up from Elath and Ezion Geber, and traveled along the desert road of Moab.

[9]Then the LORD said to me, "Do not harass the Moabites or provoke them to war, for I will not give you any part of their land. I have given Ar to the descendants of Lot[k] as a possession."

[10](The Emites[l] used to live there—a people strong and numerous, and as tall as the Anakites. [11]Like the Anakites, they too were considered Rephaites, but the Moabites called them Emites. [12]Horites used to live in Seir, but the descendants of Esau drove them out. They destroyed the Horites from before them and settled in their place, just as Israel did[m] in the land the LORD gave them as their possession.)

[13]And the LORD said, "Now get up and cross the Zered Valley." So we crossed the valley.

[14]Thirty-eight years passed from the time we left Kadesh Barnea until we crossed the Zered Valley. By then, that entire generation[n] of fighting men had perished from the camp, as the LORD had sworn to them.[o] [15]The LORD's hand was against them until he had completely eliminated them from the camp.

[16]Now when the last of these fighting men among the people had died, [17]the LORD said to me, [18]"Today you are to pass by the region of Moab at Ar. [19]When you come to the Ammonites,[p] do not harass them or provoke them to war, for I will not give you possession of any land belonging to the Ammonites. I have given it as a possession to the descendants of Lot."

[20](That too was considered a land of the Rephaites, who used to live there; but the Ammonites called them Zamzummites. [21]They were a people strong and numerous, and as tall as the Anakites. The LORD destroyed them from before the Ammonites, who drove them out and settled in their place. [22]The LORD had done the same for the descendants of Esau, who lived in Seir,[q] when he destroyed the Horites from before them. They drove them out and have lived in their place to this day. [23]And as for the Avvites[r] who lived in villages as far as Gaza, the Caphtorites[s] coming out from Caphtor[a][t] destroyed them and settled in their place.)

## Defeat of Sihon King of Heshbon

[24]"Set out now and cross the Arnon Gorge.[u] See, I have given into your hand Sihon the Amorite, king of Heshbon, and his country. Begin to take possession of it and engage him in battle. [25]This very day I will begin to put the terror and fear of you on all the nations under heaven. They will hear reports of you and will tremble[v] and be in anguish because of you."

[26]From the desert of Kedemoth I sent messengers to Sihon king of Heshbon offering peace and saying, [27]"Let us pass through your country. We will stay on the main road; we will not turn aside to the right or to the left.[w] [28]Sell us food to eat and water to drink for their price in silver. Only let us pass through on foot[x]— [29]as the descendants of Esau, who live in Seir, and the Moabites, who live in Ar, did for us—until we cross the Jordan into the land the LORD our God is giving us." [30]But Sihon king of Heshbon refused to let us pass through. For the LORD your God had made his spirit stubborn[y] and his heart obstinate in order to give him into your hands, as he has now done.

**2:19** p Ge 19:38
**2:22** q Ge 36:8
**2:23** r Jos 13:3; s Ge 10:14; t Am 9:7
**2:24** u Jdg 11:13,18
**2:25** v Ex 15:14–16
**2:27** w Nu 21:21–22
**2:28** x Nu 20:19
**2:30** y Nu 21:23

[a]23 That is, Crete

**2:32** z Nu 21:23
**2:34** a Dt 3:6; 7:2
**2:36** b Dt 3:12; 4:48
**2:37** c Nu 21:24
**3:1** d Nu 21:33
**3:4** e 1Ki 4:13
**3:6** f Dt 2:24,34

31The LORD said to me, "See, I have begun to deliver Sihon and his country over to you. Now begin to conquer and possess his land."

32When Sihon and all his army came out to meet us in battle[z] at Jahaz, 33the LORD our God delivered him over to us and we struck him down, together with his sons and his whole army. 34At that time we took all his towns and completely destroyed[a][a] them—men, women and children. We left no survivors. 35But the livestock and the plunder from the towns we had captured we carried off for ourselves. 36From Aroer[b] on the rim of the Arnon Gorge, and from the town in the gorge, even as far as Gilead, not one town was too strong for us. The LORD our God gave us all of them. 37But in accordance with the command of the LORD our God, you did not encroach on any of the land of the Ammonites,[c] neither the land along the course of the Jabbok nor that around the towns in the hills.

## Defeat of Og King of Bashan

3 Next we turned and went up along the road toward Bashan, and Og king of Bashan with his whole army marched out to meet us in battle at Edrei.[d] 2The LORD said to me, "Do not be afraid of him, for I have handed him over to you with his whole army and his land. Do to him what you did to Sihon king of the Amorites, who reigned in Heshbon."

3So the LORD our God also gave into our hands Og king of Bashan and all his army. We struck them down, leaving no survivors. 4At that time we took all his cities. There was not one of the sixty cities that we did not take from them—the whole region of Argob, Og's kingdom in Bashan.[e] 5All these cities were fortified with high walls and with gates and bars, and there were also a great many unwalled villages. 6We completely destroyed[a] them, as we had done with Sihon king of Heshbon, destroying[a][f] every city—men, women and children. 7But all the livestock and the plunder from their cities we carried off for ourselves.

8So at that time we took from these two kings of the Amorites the territory east of the Jordan, from the Arnon Gorge as far as Mount Hermon. 9(Hermon is called Sirion[g] by the Sidonians; the Amorites call it Senir.) 10We took all the towns on the plateau, and all Gilead, and all Bashan as far as Salecah and Edrei, towns of Og's kingdom in Bashan. 11(Only Og king of Bashan was left of the remnant of the Rephaites.[h] His bed[b] was made of iron and was more than thirteen feet long and six feet wide.[c] It is still in Rabbah[i] of the Ammonites.)

## Division of the Land

12Of the land that we took over at that time, I gave the Reubenites and the Gadites the territory north of Aroer[j] by the Arnon Gorge, including half the hill country of Gilead, together with its towns. 13The rest of Gilead and also all of Bashan, the kingdom of Og, I gave to the half-tribe of Manasseh. (The whole region of Argob in Bashan used to be known as a land of the Rephaites. 14Jair,[k] a descendant of Manasseh, took the whole region of Argob as far as the border of the Geshurites and the Maacathites; it was named after him, so that to this day Bashan is called Havvoth Jair.[d]) 15And I gave Gilead to Makir.[l] 16But to the Reubenites and the Gadites I gave the territory extending from Gilead down to the Arnon Gorge (the middle of the gorge being the border) and out to the Jabbok River, which is the border of the Ammonites. 17Its western border was the Jordan in the Arabah, from Kinnereth[m] to the Sea of the Arabah (the Salt Sea[e]), below the slopes of Pisgah.

18I commanded you at that time: "The LORD your God has given you this land to take possession of it. But all your able-bodied men, armed for battle, must cross over ahead of your brother Israelites.[n] 19However, your wives, your children and your livestock (I know you have much livestock) may stay in the towns I have given you, 20until the LORD gives rest to your brothers as he has to you, and they too have taken over the land that the LORD your God is giving them, across the

**3:9** g Ps 29:6
**3:11** h Ge 14:5; i 2Sa 12:26; Jer 49:2
**3:12** j Nu 32:32–38; Dt 2:36
**3:14** k Nu 32:41
**3:15** l Nu 32:39–40
**3:17** m Nu 34:11
**3:18** n Nu 32:17

[a]34,6 The Hebrew term refers to the irrevocable giving over of things or persons to the LORD, often by totally destroying them.
[b]11 Or *sarcophagus* [c]11 Hebrew *nine cubits long and four cubits wide* (about 4 meters long and 1.8 meters wide)
[d]14 Or *called the settlements of Jair* [e]17 That is, the Dead Sea

**3:22** o Dt 1:29
**3:24** p Ex 15:11; Ps 86:8
**3:25** q Dt 4:22
**3:26** r Dt 1:37
**3:27** s Nu 27:12
**3:28** t Nu 27:18–23
**3:29** u Dt 34:6
**4:1** v Dt 30:15–20
**4:2** w Dt 12:32; Jos 1:7

Jordan. After that, each of you may go back to
the possession I have given you."

## Moses Forbidden to Cross the Jordan

21 At that time I commanded Joshua: "You
have seen with your own eyes all that the
LORD your God has done to these two kings.
The LORD will do the same to all the king-
doms over there where you are going. 22 Do
not be afraid[o] of them; the LORD your God
himself will fight for you."
23 At that time I pleaded with the LORD:
24 "O Sovereign LORD, you have begun to
show to your servant your greatness and
your strong hand. For what god[p] is there in
heaven or on earth who can do the deeds
and mighty works you do? 25 Let me go over
and see the good land[q] beyond the Jordan—
that fine hill country and Lebanon."
26 But because of you the LORD was angry[r]
with me and would not listen to me. "That is
enough," the LORD said. "Do not speak to me
anymore about this matter. 27 Go up to the
top of Pisgah and look west and north and
south and east. Look at the land with your
own eyes, since you are not going to cross
this Jordan.[s] 28 But commission[t] Joshua, and
encourage and strengthen him, for he will
lead this people across and will cause them
to inherit the land that you will see." 29 So we
stayed in the valley near Beth Peor.[u]

## Obedience Commanded

4 Hear now, O Israel, the decrees and laws
I am about to teach you. Follow them so
that you may live[v] and may go in and take
possession of the land that the LORD, the
God of your fathers, is giving you. 2 Do not
add[w] to what I command you and do not sub-
tract from it, but keep the commands of the
LORD your God that I give you.
3 You saw with your own eyes what the
LORD did at Baal Peor. The LORD your God
destroyed from among you everyone who
followed the Baal of Peor, 4 but all of you who
held fast to the LORD your God are still alive
today.
5 See, I have taught you decrees and laws
as the LORD my God commanded me, so that
you may follow them in the land you are
entering to take possession of it. 6 Observe
them carefully, for this will show your wis-
dom and understanding to the nations, who
will hear about all these decrees and say,
"Surely this great nation is a wise and under-
standing people." 7 What other nation is so
great[x] as to have their gods near[y] them the
way the LORD our God is near us whenever
we pray to him? 8 And what other nation is so
great as to have such righteous decrees and
laws as this body of laws I am setting before
you today?
9 Only be careful,[z] and watch yourselves
closely so that you do not forget the things
your eyes have seen or let them slip from
your heart as long as you live. Teach[a] them
to your children and to their children after
them. 10 Remember the day you stood before
the LORD your God at Horeb, when he said to
me, "Assemble the people before me to hear
my words so that they may learn to revere
me as long as they live in the land and may
teach them to their children." 11 You came
near and stood at the foot of the mountain
while it blazed with fire[b] to the very heav-
ens, with black clouds and deep darkness.
12 Then the LORD spoke to you out of the fire.
You heard the sound of words but saw no
form; there was only a voice. 13 He declared
to you his covenant, the Ten Command-
ments,[c] which he commanded you to follow
and then wrote them on two stone tablets.
14 And the LORD directed me at that time to
teach you the decrees and laws you are to
follow in the land that you are crossing the
Jordan to possess.

## Idolatry Forbidden

15 You saw no form of any kind the day the
LORD spoke to you at Horeb out of the fire.

*Lord,*

*help me to keep the commands that you have given to me and to all your children. Give me a heart that follows you in all ways. In your Son's precious name I pray,*

*Amen.*

DEUTERONOMY 4:1–2

**4:7** x 2Sa 7:23; y Isa 55:6
**4:9** z Pr 4:23; a Eph 6:4
**4:11** b Ex 19:18
**4:13** c Ex 34:28

Therefore watch yourselves very carefully, 16 so that you do not become corrupt and make for yourselves an idol,[d] an image of any shape, whether formed like a man or a woman, 17 or like any animal on earth or any bird that flies in the air, 18 or like any creature that moves along the ground or any fish in the waters below. 19 And when you look up to the sky and see the sun,[e] the moon and the stars—all the heavenly array—do not be enticed into bowing down to them and worshiping things the LORD your God has apportioned to all the nations under heaven. 20 But as for you, the LORD took you and brought you out of the iron-smelting furnace,[f] out of Egypt, to be the people of his inheritance, as you now are.

21 The LORD was angry with me[g] because of you, and he solemnly swore that I would not cross the Jordan and enter the good land the LORD your God is giving you as your inheritance. 22 I will die in this land; I will not cross the Jordan; but you are about to cross over and take possession of that good land.[h] 23 Be careful not to forget the covenant[i] of the LORD your God that he made with you; do not make for yourselves an idol in the form of anything the LORD your God has forbidden. 24 For the LORD your God is a consuming fire,[j] a jealous God.

25 After you have had children and grandchildren and have lived in the land a long time—if you then become corrupt and make any kind of idol, doing evil[k] in the eyes of the LORD your God and provoking him to anger, 26 I call heaven and earth as witnesses against you[l] this day that you will quickly perish from the land that you are crossing the Jordan to possess. You will not live there long but will certainly be destroyed. 27 The LORD will scatter you among the peoples, and only a few of you will survive among the nations to which the LORD will drive you. 28 There you will worship man-made gods[m] of wood and stone, which cannot see or hear or eat or smell.[n] 29 But if from there you seek[o] the LORD your God, you will find him if you look for him with all your heart and with all your soul.[p] 30 When you are in distress and all these things have happened to you, then in later days[q] you will return to the LORD your God and obey him. 31 For the LORD your God is a merciful[r] God; he will not abandon or destroy you or forget the covenant with your forefathers, which he confirmed to them by oath.

## The LORD Is God

32 Ask now about the former days, long before your time, from the day God created man on the earth; ask from one end of the heavens to the other. Has anything so great as this ever happened, or has anything like it ever been heard of? 33 Has any other people heard the voice of God[a] speaking out of fire, as you have, and lived?[s] 34 Has any god ever tried to take for himself one nation out of another nation, by testings, by miraculous signs and wonders,[t] by war, by a mighty hand and an outstretched arm, or by great and awesome deeds, like all the things the LORD your God did for you in Egypt before your very eyes?

35 You were shown these things so that you might know that the LORD is God; besides him there is no other.[u] 36 From heaven he made you hear his voice[v] to discipline you. On earth he showed you his great fire, and you heard his words from out of the fire. 37 Because he loved[w] your forefathers and chose their descendants after them, he brought you out of Egypt by his Presence and his great strength, 38 to drive out before you nations greater and stronger than you and to bring you into their land to give it to you for your inheritance, as it is today.

39 Acknowledge and take to heart this day that the LORD is God in heaven above and on the earth below. There is no other.[x] 40 Keep[y] his decrees and commands, which I am giving you today, so that it may go well with you and your children after you and that you may live long in the land the LORD your God gives you for all time.

## Cities of Refuge

41 Then Moses set aside three cities east of the Jordan, 42 to which anyone who had killed a person could flee if he had unintentionally killed his neighbor without malice aforethought. He could flee into one of these cities and save his life. 43 The cities were these:

[a]33 Or *of a god*

**4:16** d Ex 20:4–5; Dt 5:8
**4:19** e Dt 17:3
**4:20** f 1Ki 8:51; Jer 11:4
**4:21** g Dt 1:37
**4:22** h Dt 3:25
**4:23** i ver 9,16
**4:24** j Ex 24:17; Dt 9:3; Heb 12:29
**4:25** k 2Ki 17:2,17
**4:26** l Dt 30:18–19
**4:28** m Dt 28:36,64 n Ps 115:4–8
**4:29** o 2Ch 15:4; Isa 55:6 p Dt 30:1–3,10
**4:30** q Hos 3:5
**4:31** r 2Ch 30:9; Ps 116:5
**4:33** s Dt 5:24–26
**4:34** t Dt 7:19
**4:35** u Dt 32:39; 1Sa 2:2; Isa 45:5,18
**4:36** v Ex 19:9,19
**4:37** w Dt 10:15
**4:39** x Jos 2:11
**4:40** y Lev 22:31

Bezer in the desert plateau, for the Reubenites; Ramoth in Gilead, for the Gadites; and Golan in Bashan, for the Manassites.

## Introduction to the Law

44 This is the law Moses set before the Israelites. 45 These are the stipulations, decrees and laws Moses gave them when they came out of Egypt 46 and were in the valley near Beth Peor east of the Jordan, in the land of Sihon[z] king of the Amorites, who reigned in Heshbon and was defeated by Moses and the Israelites as they came out of Egypt. 47 They took possession of his land and the land of Og king of Bashan, the two Amorite kings east of the Jordan. 48 This land extended from Aroer[a] on the rim of the Arnon Gorge to Mount Siyon[a] (that is, Hermon), 49 and included all the Arabah east of the Jordan, as far as the Sea of the Arabah,[b] below the slopes of Pisgah.

## The Ten Commandments

5 Moses summoned all Israel and said: Hear, O Israel, the decrees and laws I declare in your hearing today. Learn them and be sure to follow them. 2 The LORD our God made a covenant[b] with us at Horeb. 3 It was not with our fathers that the LORD made this covenant, but with us, with all of us who are alive here today. 4 The LORD spoke[c] to you face to face out of the fire on the mountain. 5 (At that time I stood between the LORD and you to declare to you the word of the LORD, because you were afraid[d] of the fire and did not go up the mountain.) And he said:

6 "I am the LORD your God, who
brought you out of Egypt, out of
the land of slavery.
7 "You shall have no other gods before[c] me.
8 "You shall not make for yourself an
idol in the form of anything in
heaven above or on the earth
beneath or in the waters below.
9 You shall not bow down to them
or worship them; for I, the LORD
your God, am a jealous God, punishing the children for the sin
of the fathers to the third and
fourth generation of those who
hate me,[e] 10 but showing love to a
thousand ⌊generations⌋ of those
who love me and keep my commandments.[f]
11 "You shall not misuse the name of the
LORD your God, for the LORD will
not hold anyone guiltless who
misuses his name.[g]
12 "Observe the Sabbath day by keeping
it holy, as the LORD your God has
commanded you. 13 Six days you
shall labor and do all your work,
14 but the seventh day[h] is a Sabbath to the LORD your God. On
it you shall not do any work, neither you, nor your son or daughter, nor your manservant or
maidservant, nor your ox, your
donkey or any of your animals,
nor the alien within your gates,
so that your manservant and
maidservant may rest, as you do.
15 Remember that you were slaves
in Egypt and that the LORD your
God brought you out of there
with a mighty hand and an outstretched arm. Therefore the
LORD your God has commanded
you to observe the Sabbath day.
16 "Honor your father and your mother,[i]
as the LORD your God has commanded you, so that you may
live long and that it may go well
with you in the land the LORD
your God is giving you.
17 "You shall not murder.[j]
18 "You shall not commit adultery.[k]
19 "You shall not steal.
20 "You shall not give false testimony
against your neighbor.
21 "You shall not covet your neighbor's
wife. You shall not set your desire on your neighbor's house
or land, his manservant or maidservant, his ox or donkey, or
anything that belongs to your
neighbor."[l]

22 These are the commandments the LORD proclaimed in a loud voice to your whole as-

4:46 z Nu 21:26; Dt 3:29
4:48 a Dt 2:36
5:2 b Ex 19:5
5:4 c Dt 4:12,33,36
5:5 d Ex 20:18,21
5:9 e Ex 34:7
5:10 f Jer 32:18
5:11 g Lev 19:12
5:14 h Ge 2:2
5:16 i Eph 6:2–3*
5:17 j Mt 5:21–22*
5:18 k Mt 5:27–30; Lk 18:20*
5:21 l Ro 7:7*

[a]48 Hebrew; Syriac (see also Deut. 3:9) *Sirion* [b]49 That is, the Dead Sea [c]7 Or *besides*

5:22 m Ex31:18; Dt4:13
5:25 n Dt18:16
5:26 o Dt4:33
5:28 p Dt18:17
5:29 q Ps81:8,13 r Isa48:18
5:32 s Dt17:11,20; 28:14; Jos1:7
5:33 t Dt4:40
6:2 u Dt10:12–13

sembly there on the mountain from out of
the fire, the cloud and the deep darkness;
and he added nothing more. Then he wrote
them on two stone tablets[m] and gave them
to me.
23 When you heard the voice out of the
darkness, while the mountain was ablaze
with fire, all the leading men of your tribes
and your elders came to me. 24 And you said,
"The LORD our God has shown us his glory
and his majesty, and we have heard his voice
from the fire. Today we have seen that a man
can live even if God speaks with him. 25 But
now, why should we die? This great fire will
consume us, and we will die if we hear the
voice of the LORD our God any longer.[n] 26 For
what mortal man has ever heard the voice
of the living God speaking out of fire, as we
have, and survived?[o] 27 Go near and listen to
all that the LORD our God says. Then tell us
whatever the LORD our God tells you. We will
listen and obey."
28 The LORD heard you when you spoke to
me and the LORD said to me, "I have heard
what this people said to you. Everything
they said was good.[p] 29 Oh, that their hearts
would be inclined to fear me[q] and keep all
my commands[r] always, so that it might go
well with them and their children forever!
30 "Go, tell them to return to their tents.
31 But you stay here with me so that I may
give you all the commands, decrees and
laws you are to teach them to follow in the
land I am giving them to possess."
32 So be careful to do what the LORD your
God has commanded you; do not turn aside
to the right or to the left.[s] 33 Walk in all the
way that the LORD your God has commanded
you, so that you may live and prosper and
prolong your days[t] in the land that you will
possess.

## Love the LORD Your God

6 These are the commands, decrees and
laws the LORD your God directed me to
teach you to observe in the land that you
are crossing the Jordan to possess, 2 so that
you, your children and their children after
them may fear[u] the LORD your God as long
as you live by keeping all his decrees and
commands that I give you, and so that you
may enjoy long life. 3 Hear, O Israel, and be
careful to obey so that it may go well with
you and that you may increase greatly in
a land flowing with milk and honey,[v] just
as the LORD, the God of your fathers, prom-
ised you.
4 Hear, O Israel: The LORD our God, the
LORD is one.[a][w] 5 Love[x] the LORD your God
with all your heart and with all your soul
and with all your strength. 6 These com-
mandments that I give you today are to be
upon your hearts.[y] 7 Impress them on your
children. Talk about them when you sit at
home and when you walk along the road,
when you lie down and when you get up.[z]
8 Tie them as symbols on your hands and
bind them on your foreheads. 9 Write them
on the doorframes of your houses and on
your gates.[a]
10 When the LORD your God brings you
into the land he swore to your fathers, to
Abraham, Isaac and Jacob, to give you—a
land with large, flourishing cities you did
not build,[b] 11 houses filled with all kinds of
good things you did not provide, wells you
did not dig, and vineyards and olive groves
you did not plant—then when you eat and
are satisfied,[c] 12 be careful that you do not
forget the LORD, who brought you out of
Egypt, out of the land of slavery.
13 Fear the LORD your God, serve him only[d]
and take your oaths in his name. 14 Do not
follow other gods, the gods of the peoples
around you; 15 for the LORD your God[e], who
is among you, is a jealous God and his anger
will burn against you, and he will destroy
you from the face of the land. 16 Do not test
the LORD your God[f] as you did at Massah. 17 Be
sure to keep the commands of the LORD your
God and the stipulations and decrees he has
given you.[g] 18 Do what is right and good in
the LORD's sight, so that it may go well with
you and you may go in and take over the
good land that the LORD promised on oath
to your forefathers, 19 thrusting out all your
enemies before you, as the LORD said.
20 In the future, when your son asks you,[h]
"What is the meaning of the stipulations,
decrees and laws the LORD our God has
commanded you?" 21 tell him: "We were
slaves of Pharaoh in Egypt, but the LORD

6:3 v Ex3:8
6:4 w 1Co8:4
6:5 x Mt22:37*
6:6 y Dt11:18
6:7 z Eph6:4
6:9 a Dt11:20
6:10 b Jos24:13
6:11 c Dt8:10
6:13 d Mt4:10*
6:15 e Dt4:24
6:16 f Mt4:7*
6:17 g Ps119:4
6:20 h Ex13:14

[a] 4 Or *The LORD our God is one LORD*; or *The LORD is our God, the LORD is one*; or *The LORD is our God, the LORD alone*

# Inspire

## A GREAT CHALLENGE: TEACHING OUR CHILDREN

Motivation to strive for academic excellence is one of the greatest challenges facing many African American students today. Several factors may be responsible for this challenge. Perhaps the most paralyzing factor is negative peer pressure. For example, many students try to study and strive for success but are stifled in their efforts by students who are on their way to the big city of Nowhere. Those students who want to excel or have the potential to excel are ostracized and constantly told, "You're trying to act white!"

I have never been able to understand the logic couched in their implication that African Americans are supposed to be ignorant. Admittedly, everyone wants to be accepted, loved and respected. But when human potential is compromised for a "get-by education" and peer acceptance, the result is limited development. This, from an economic perspective, translates into unemployment or limited income—a major step toward poverty. Spiritually and emotionally this compromise stifles growth and can lead to an unsatisfactory life.

Parents should expose their children to positive people who have the opportunity to mold lives and change attitudes on a daily basis. These are people who participate in lifelong learning activities, demand high expectations in educational achievements, enhance self-esteem, volunteer in schools and visit schools to model the importance of education. These are people who exemplify and instill moral and spiritual values. These are people who promote faith development and racial pride by sharing their faith and ancestral stories. These are people who demonstrate the importance of setting goals and reaching them.

The very survival of our race compels us as parents and concerned adults to accept the challenge to help our youth understand that African Americans suffered, bled and died so that we could enter the door to opportunity via education. Because of this, our youth do not have the right to nullify sacrifices made on their behalf. Moreover, we must fulfill the mandates reflected in Deuteronomy 6:5–9 and Psalm 78:1–4. These mandates, coupled with our empowerment efforts, will not only sustain our heritage but also be one of the greatest legacies we can bequeath.

—H. Harris

### read

Deuteronomy 6:1–9; Ephesians 6:4.

**See also** the Inspire Notes "Parenting," "Raising Children: Modeling Discipleship," "Children: A Blessed Heritage From God" and "Nurturing Spiritual Gifts in Our Children," and the Women of the Bible Notes "Daughter of Jairus: A Testament of Faith" and "Mary, the Mother of Jesus: A Model of Motherhood."

### WOMAN of COLOR

What are you sharing with children in your family and community?

For the next Inspire note, go to page 220.

brought us out of Egypt with a mighty hand. 22 Before our eyes the LORD sent miraculous signs and wonders—great and terrible—upon Egypt and Pharaoh and his whole household. 23 But he brought us out from there to bring us in and give us the land that he promised on oath to our forefathers. 24 The LORD commanded us to obey all these decrees and to fear the LORD our God,[i] so that we might always prosper and be kept alive, as is the case today. 25 And if we are careful to obey all this law before the LORD our God, as he has commanded us, that will be our righteousness."

## Driving Out the Nations

7 When the LORD your God brings you into the land you are entering to possess and drives out before you many nations[j]—the Hittites, Girgashites, Amorites, Canaanites, Perizzites, Hivites and Jebusites, seven nations larger and stronger than you— 2 and when the LORD your God has delivered them over to you and you have defeated them, then you must destroy them totally.[a] Make no treaty[k] with them, and show them no mercy. 3 Do not intermarry with them.[l] Do not give your daughters to their sons or take their daughters for your sons, 4 for they will turn your sons away from following me to serve other gods, and the LORD's anger will burn against you and will quickly destroy you. 5 This is what you are to do to them: Break down their altars, smash their sacred stones, cut down their Asherah poles[b] and burn their idols in the fire.[m] 6 For you are a people holy[n] to the LORD your God. The LORD your God has chosen[o] you out of all the peoples on the face of the earth to be his people, his treasured possession.

7 The LORD did not set his affection on you and choose you because you were more numerous than other peoples, for you were the fewest of all peoples.[p] 8 But it was because the LORD loved you and kept the oath he swore to your forefathers that he brought you out with a mighty hand and redeemed you from the land of slavery,[q] from the power of Pharaoh king of Egypt. 9 Know therefore that the LORD your God is God; he is the faithful God,[r] keeping his covenant of love[s] to a thousand generations of those who love him and keep his commands. 10 But

those who hate him he will repay to their
face by destruction;
he will not be slow to repay to their
face those who hate him.

11 Therefore, take care to follow the commands, decrees and laws I give you today.

12 If you pay attention to these laws and are careful to follow them, then the LORD your God will keep his covenant of love with you, as he swore to your forefathers.[t] 13 He will love you and bless you and increase your numbers. He will bless the fruit of your womb, the crops of your land—your grain, new wine and oil—the calves of your herds and the lambs of your flocks in the land that he swore to your forefathers to give you. 14 You will be blessed more than any other people; none of your men or women will be childless, nor any of your livestock without young.[u] 15 The LORD will keep you free from every disease.[v] He will not inflict on you the horrible diseases you knew in Egypt, but he will inflict them on all who hate you. 16 You must destroy all the peoples the LORD your God gives over to you. Do not look on them with pity[w] and do not serve their gods, for that will be a snare to you.

17 You may say to yourselves, "These nations are stronger than we are. How can we drive them out?" 18 But do not be afraid of them; remember well what the LORD your God did to Pharaoh and to all Egypt.[x] 19 You saw with your own eyes the great trials, the miraculous signs and wonders, the mighty hand and outstretched arm, with which the LORD your God brought you out. The LORD your God will do the same to all the peoples you now fear.[y] 20 Moreover, the LORD your God will send the hornet[z] among them until even the survivors who hide from you have perished. 21 Do not be terrified by them, for the LORD your God, who is among you, is a great and awesome God. 22 The LORD your God will drive out those nations before you, little by little.[a] You will not be allowed to eliminate them all at once, or the wild animals will multiply around you. 23 But the LORD your God will deliver them over to

**6:24** i Jer 32:39
**7:1** j Dt 31:3
**7:2** k Ex 23:32
**7:3** l Ex 34:15–16
**7:5** m Ex 23:24
**7:6** n Ex 19:5–6; o Dt 14:2
**7:7** p Dt 10:22
**7:8** q Ex 13:14
**7:9** r 1Co 1:9; s Ne 1:5
**7:12** t Dt 28:1–14
**7:14** u Ex 23:26
**7:15** v Ex 15:26
**7:16** w ver 2
**7:18** x Ps 105:5
**7:19** y Dt 4:34
**7:20** z Jos 24:12
**7:22** a Ex 23:28–30

[a]2 The Hebrew term refers to the irrevocable giving over of things or persons to the LORD, often by totally destroying them; also in verse 26. [b]5 That is, symbols of the goddess Asherah; here and elsewhere in Deuteronomy

you, throwing them into great confusion until they are destroyed. 24 He will give their kings into your hand, and you will wipe out their names from under heaven. No one will be able to stand up against you; you will destroy them. 25 The images of their gods you are to burn[b] in the fire. Do not covet the silver and gold on them, and do not take it for yourselves, or you will be ensnared[c] by it, for it is detestable to the LORD your God. 26 Do not bring a detestable thing into your house or you, like it, will be set apart for destruction. Utterly abhor and detest it, for it is set apart for destruction.

## Do Not Forget the LORD

8 Be careful to follow every command I am giving you today, so that you may live[d] and increase and may enter and possess the land that the LORD promised on oath to your forefathers. 2 Remember how the LORD your God led you all the way in the desert these forty years, to humble you and to test you in order to know what was in your heart, whether or not you would keep his commands. 3 He humbled you, causing you to hunger and then feeding you with manna, which neither you nor your fathers had known, to teach you that man does not live on bread alone but on every word that comes from the mouth of the LORD.[e] 4 Your clothes did not wear out and your feet did not swell during these forty years.[f] 5 Know then in your heart that as a man disciplines his son, so the LORD your God disciplines you.[g]

6 Observe the commands of the LORD your God, walking in his ways and revering him. 7 For the LORD your God is bringing you into a good land—a land with streams and pools of water, with springs flowing in the valleys and hills;[h] 8 a land with wheat and barley, vines and fig trees, pomegranates, olive oil and honey; 9 a land where bread will not be scarce and you will lack nothing; a land where the rocks are iron and you can dig copper out of the hills.

10 When you have eaten and are satisfied,[i] praise the LORD your God for the good land he has given you. 11 Be careful that you do not forget the LORD your God, failing to observe his commands, his laws and his decrees that I am giving you this day. 12 Otherwise, when you eat and are satisfied, when you build fine houses and settle down, 13 and when your herds and flocks grow large and your silver and gold increase and all you have is multiplied, 14 then your heart will become proud and you will forget the LORD your God, who brought you out of Egypt, out of the land of slavery. 15 He led you through the vast and dreadful desert, that thirsty and waterless land, with its venomous snakes[j] and scorpions. He brought you water out of hard rock.[k] 16 He gave you manna to eat in the desert, something your fathers had never known,[l] to humble and to test you so that in the end it might go well with you. 17 You may say to yourself, "My power and the strength of my hands have produced this wealth for me." 18 But remember the LORD your God, for it is he who gives you the ability to produce wealth,[m] and so confirms his covenant, which he swore to your forefathers, as it is today.

19 If you ever forget the LORD your God and follow other gods and worship and bow down to them, I testify against you today that you will surely be destroyed.[n] 20 Like the nations the LORD destroyed before you, so you will be destroyed for not obeying the LORD your God.

## Not Because of Israel's Righteousness

9 Hear, O Israel. You are now about to cross the Jordan to go in and dispossess nations greater and stronger than you, with large cities that have walls up to the sky. 2 The people are strong and tall—Anakites! You know about them and have heard it said: "Who can stand up against the Anakites?"[o] 3 But be assured today that the LORD your God is the one who goes across ahead of you[p] like a devouring fire.[q] He will destroy them; he will subdue them before you. And you will drive them out and annihilate them quickly,[r] as the LORD has promised you.

4 After the LORD your God has driven them out before you, do not say to yourself,[s] "The LORD has brought me here to take possession of this land because of my righteousness." No, it is on account of the wickedness of these nations[t] that the LORD is going to

**7:25** b 1Ch 14:12 c Jdg 8:27
**8:1** d Dt 4:1
**8:3** e Mt 4:4*; Lk 4:4*
**8:4** f Dt 29:5
**8:5** g Pr 3:11–12; Heb 12:5–11
**8:7** h Dt 11:9–12
**8:10** i Dt 6:10–12
**8:15** j Nu 21:6 k Nu 20:11
**8:16** l Ex 16:15
**8:18** m Pr 10:22; Hos 2:8
**8:19** n Dt 4:26; 30:18
**9:2** o Nu 13:22, 28,32–33
**9:3** p Dt 31:3 q Dt 4:24 r Dt 7:23–24
**9:4** s Dt 8:17 t Lev 18:21, 24–30

9:5
u Ge 12:7

9:6
v ver 13

9:9
w Ex 24:12,15,18

9:12
x Ex 32:7–8

9:13
y Ex 32:9

9:14
z Ex 32:10

9:15
a Ex 32:15

drive them out before you. [5]It is not because of your righteousness or your integrity that you are going in to take possession of their land; but on account of the wickedness of these nations, the LORD your God will drive them out before you, to accomplish what he swore[u] to your fathers, to Abraham, Isaac and Jacob. [6]Understand, then, that it is not because of your righteousness that the LORD your God is giving you this good land to possess, for you are a stiff-necked people.[v]

## The Golden Calf

[7]Remember this and never forget how you provoked the LORD your God to anger in the desert. From the day you left Egypt until you arrived here, you have been rebellious against the LORD. [8]At Horeb you aroused the LORD's wrath so that he was angry enough to destroy you. [9]When I went up on the mountain to receive the tablets of stone, the tablets of the covenant that the LORD had made with you, I stayed on the mountain forty days and forty nights; I ate no bread and drank no water.[w] [10]The LORD gave me two stone tablets inscribed by the finger of God. On them were all the commandments the LORD proclaimed to you on the mountain out of the fire, on the day of the assembly.

[11]At the end of the forty days and forty nights, the LORD gave me the two stone tablets, the tablets of the covenant. [12]Then the LORD told me, "Go down from here at once, because your people whom you brought out of Egypt have become corrupt.[x] They have turned away quickly from what I commanded them and have made a cast idol for themselves."

[13]And the LORD said to me, "I have seen this people[y], and they are a stiff-necked people indeed! [14]Let me alone,[z] so that I may destroy them and blot out their name from under heaven. And I will make you into a nation stronger and more numerous than they."

[15]So I turned and went down from the mountain while it was ablaze with fire. And the two tablets of the covenant were in my hands.[a][a] [16]When I looked, I saw that you had sinned against the LORD your God; you had made for yourselves an idol cast in the shape of a calf. You had turned aside quickly from the way that the LORD had commanded you. [17]So I took the two tablets and threw them out of my hands, breaking them to pieces before your eyes.

[18]Then once again I fell[b] prostrate before the LORD for forty days and forty nights; I ate no bread and drank no water, because of all the sin you had committed, doing what was evil in the LORD's sight and so provoking him to anger. [19]I feared the anger and wrath of the LORD, for he was angry enough with you to destroy you. But again the LORD listened to me. [20]And the LORD was angry enough with Aaron to destroy him, but at that time I prayed for Aaron too. [21]Also I took that sinful thing of yours, the calf you had made, and burned it in the fire. Then I crushed it and ground it to powder as fine as dust and threw the dust into a stream that flowed down the mountain.[c]

[22]You also made the LORD angry at Taberah,[d] at Massah[e] and at Kibroth Hattaavah.[f]

[23]And when the LORD sent you out from Kadesh Barnea, he said, "Go up and take possession of the land I have given you." But you rebelled against the command of the LORD your God. You did not trust him or obey him. [24]You have been rebellious against the LORD ever since I have known you.[g]

[25]I lay prostrate before the LORD those forty days and forty nights because the LORD had said he would destroy you.[h] [26]I prayed to the LORD and said, "O Sovereign LORD, do not destroy your people, your own inheritance that you redeemed by your great power and brought out of Egypt with a mighty hand.[i] [27]Remember your servants Abraham, Isaac and Jacob. Overlook the stubbornness of this people, their wickedness and their sin. [28]Otherwise, the country from which you brought us will say, 'Because the LORD was not able to take them into the land he had promised them, and because he hated them, he brought them out to put them to death in the desert.' [29]But they are your people, your inheritance[j] that you brought out by your great power and your outstretched arm."

9:18
b Ex 34:28

9:21
c Ex 32:20

9:22
d Nu 11:3
e Ex 17:7
f Nu 11:34

9:24
g Dt 31:27

9:25
h ver 18

9:26
i Ex 32:11

9:29
j Dt 4:20

[a]15 Or *And I had the two tablets of the covenant with me, one in each hand*

## Tablets Like the First Ones

**10** At that time the LORD said to me, "Chisel out two stone tablets[k] like the first ones and come up to me on the mountain. Also make a wooden chest.[a] 2I will write on the tablets the words that were on the first tablets, which you broke. Then you are to put them in the chest."[l]

3So I made the ark out of acacia wood and chiseled[m] out two stone tablets like the first ones, and I went up on the mountain with the two tablets in my hands. 4The LORD wrote on these tablets what he had written before, the Ten Commandments he had proclaimed[n] to you on the mountain, out of the fire, on the day of the assembly. And the LORD gave them to me. 5Then I came back down the mountain and put the tablets in the ark[o] I had made, as the LORD commanded me, and they are there now.

6(The Israelites traveled from the wells of the Jaakanites to Moserah.[p] There Aaron died and was buried, and Eleazar his son succeeded him as priest. 7From there they traveled to Gudgodah and on to Jotbathah, a land with streams of water.[q] 8At that time the LORD set apart the tribe of Levi[r] to carry the ark of the covenant of the LORD, to stand before the LORD to minister[s] and to pronounce blessings[t] in his name, as they still do today. 9That is why the Levites have no share or inheritance among their brothers; the LORD is their inheritance, as the LORD your God told them.)

10Now I had stayed on the mountain forty days and nights, as I did the first time, and the LORD listened to me at this time also. It was not his will to destroy you. 11"Go," the LORD said to me, "and lead the people on their way, so that they may enter and possess the land that I swore to their fathers to give them."

## Fear the LORD

12And now, O Israel, what does the LORD your God ask of you[u] but to fear the LORD your God, to walk in all his ways, to love him, to serve the LORD your God with all your heart[v] and with all your soul, 13and to observe the LORD's commands and decrees that I am giving you today for your own good?

[a]1 That is, an ark

10:1 k Ex25:10; 34:1–2
10:2 l Ex25:16,21
10:3 m Ex34:4
10:4 n Ex20:1
10:5 o Ex40:20
10:6 p Nu33:30,31,38
10:7 q Nu33:32–34
10:8 r Nu3:6 s Dt18:5 t Dt21:5
10:12 u Mic6:8 v Dt6:5

---

*Child,*

*Honor me by following my Word.*
*I know what I'm doing!*

*Your*
*Loving Guide*

DEUTERONOMY 10:12–13

---

14To the LORD your God belong the heavens, even the highest heavens,[w] the earth and everything in it. 15Yet the LORD set his affection on your forefathers and loved[x] them, and he chose you, their descendants, above all the nations, as it is today. 16Circumcise[y] your hearts, therefore, and do not be stiff-necked[z] any longer. 17For the LORD your God is God of gods and Lord of lords, the great God, mighty and awesome, who shows no partiality[a] and accepts no bribes. 18He defends the cause of the fatherless and the widow,[b] and loves the alien, giving him food and clothing. 19And you are to love those who are aliens, for you yourselves were aliens in Egypt.[c] 20Fear the LORD your God and serve him. Hold fast[d] to him and take your oaths in his name.[e] 21He is your praise; he is your God, who performed for you those great and awesome wonders you saw with your own eyes. 22Your forefathers who went down into Egypt were seventy in all,[f] and now the LORD your God has made you as numerous as the stars in the sky.

## Love and Obey the LORD

**11** Love[g] the LORD your God and keep his requirements, his decrees, his laws and his commands always. 2Remember today that your children were not the ones who saw and experienced the discipline of the LORD your God: his majesty, his mighty hand, his outstretched arm; 3the signs he performed and the things he did in the heart of Egypt, both to Pharaoh king of Egypt and to his whole country; 4what he

10:14 w 1Ki8:27
10:15 x Dt4:37
10:16 y Jer4:4 z Dt9:6
10:17 a Ac10:34
10:18 b Ps68:5
10:19 c Lev19:34
10:20 d Dt11:22 e Ps63:11
10:22 f Ge46:26–27
11:1 g Dt10:12

did to the Egyptian army, to its horses and chariots, how he overwhelmed them with the waters of the Red Sea[a] as they were pursuing you, and how the LORD brought lasting ruin on them. [5]It was not your children who saw what he did for you in the desert until you arrived at this place, [6]and what he did[h] to Dathan and Abiram, sons of Eliab the Reubenite, when the earth opened its mouth right in the middle of all Israel and swallowed them up with their households, their tents and every living thing that belonged to them. [7]But it was your own eyes that saw all these great things the LORD has done.

[8]Observe therefore all the commands I am giving you today, so that you may have the strength to go in and take over the land that you are crossing the Jordan to possess,[i] [9]and so that you may live long[j] in the land that the LORD swore to your forefathers to give to them and their descendants, a land flowing with milk and honey.[k] [10]The land you are entering to take over is not like the land of Egypt, from which you have come, where you planted your seed and irrigated it by foot as in a vegetable garden. [11]But the land you are crossing the Jordan to take possession of is a land of mountains and valleys that drinks rain from heaven.[l] [12]It is a land the LORD your God cares for; the eyes of the LORD your God are continually on it from the beginning of the year to its end.

[13]So if you faithfully obey the commands I am giving you today—to love the LORD your God and to serve him with all your heart and with all your soul— [14]then I will send rain[m] on your land in its season, both autumn and spring rains,[n] so that you may gather in your grain, new wine and oil. [15]I will provide grass in the fields for your cattle, and you will eat and be satisfied.

[16]Be careful, or you will be enticed to turn away and worship other gods and bow down to them. [17]Then the LORD's anger will burn against you, and he will shut[o] the heavens so that it will not rain and the ground will yield no produce, and you will soon perish[p] from the good land the LORD is giving you. [18]Fix these words of mine in your hearts and minds; tie them as symbols on your hands and bind them on your foreheads.[q] [19]Teach them to your children,[r] talking about them when you sit at home and when you walk along the road, when you lie down and when you get up.[s] [20]Write them on the doorframes of your houses and on your gates,[t] [21]so that your days and the days of your children may be many in the land that the LORD swore to give your forefathers, as many as the days that the heavens are above the earth.

[22]If you carefully observe[u] all these commands I am giving you to follow—to love the LORD your God, to walk in all his ways and to hold fast to him— [23]then the LORD will drive out all these nations before you, and you will dispossess nations larger and stronger than you.[v] [24]Every place where you set your foot will be yours:[w] Your territory will extend from the desert to Lebanon, and from the Euphrates River to the western sea.[b] [25]No man will be able to stand against you. The LORD your God, as he promised you, will put the terror and fear of you on the whole land, wherever you go.[x]

[26]See, I am setting before you today a blessing and a curse[y]— [27]the blessing[z] if you obey the commands of the LORD your God that I am giving you today; [28]the curse if you disobey[a] the commands of the LORD your God and turn from the way that I command you today by following other gods, which you have not known. [29]When the LORD your God has brought you into the land you are entering to possess, you are to proclaim on Mount Gerizim the blessings, and on Mount Ebal the curses.[b] [30]As you know, these mountains are across the Jordan, west of the road,[c] toward the setting sun, near the great trees of Moreh,[c] in the territory of those Canaanites living in the Arabah in the vicinity of Gilgal. [31]You are about to cross the Jordan to enter and take possession of the land the LORD your God is giving you. When you have taken it over and are living there, [32]be sure that you obey

*"It's pretty hard for the Lord to guide you if you haven't made up your mind which way you want to go."*

—MADAME C. J. WALKER, FIRST FEMALE AFRICAN AMERICAN MILLIONAIRE

**11:6** h Nu16:1–35
**11:8** i Jos1:7
**11:9** j Dt4:40 k Ex3:8
**11:11** l Dt8:7
**11:14** m Dt28:12 n Joel2:23
**11:17** o 1Ki8:35 p Dt4:26
**11:18** q Dt6:6–8
**11:19** r Dt6:7 s Dt4:9–10
**11:20** t Dt6:9
**11:22** u Dt6:17
**11:23** v Dt9:1
**11:24** w Ge15:18; Ex23:31; Jos1:3
**11:25** x Dt7:24
**11:26** y Dt30:1,15,19
**11:27** z Dt28:1–14
**11:28** a Dt28:15
**11:29** b Dt27:12–13; Jos8:33
**11:30** c Ge12:6

[a]4 Hebrew *Yam Suph*; that is, Sea of Reeds [b]24 That is, the Mediterranean [c]30 Or *Jordan, westward*

**12:1** d Dt4:9–10
**12:7** e ver12,18; Dt14:26
**12:11** f ver5
**12:12** g ver7 h Dt10:9

all the decrees and laws I am setting before you today.

## The One Place of Worship

**12** These are the decrees and laws you must be careful to follow in the land that the LORD, the God of your fathers, has given you to possess—as long as you live in the land.[d] 2 Destroy completely all the places on the high mountains and on the hills and under every spreading tree where the nations you are dispossessing worship their gods. 3 Break down their altars, smash their sacred stones and burn their Asherah poles in the fire; cut down the idols of their gods and wipe out their names from those places.

4 You must not worship the LORD your God in their way. 5 But you are to seek the place the LORD your God will choose from among all your tribes to put his Name there for his dwelling. To that place you must go; 6 there bring your burnt offerings and sacrifices, your tithes and special gifts, what you have vowed to give and your freewill offerings, and the firstborn of your herds and flocks. 7 There, in the presence of the LORD your God, you and your families shall eat and shall rejoice[e] in everything you have put your hand to, because the LORD your God has blessed you.

8 You are not to do as we do here today, everyone as he sees fit, 9 since you have not yet reached the resting place and the inheritance the LORD your God is giving you. 10 But you will cross the Jordan and settle in the land the LORD your God is giving you as an inheritance, and he will give you rest from all your enemies around you so that you will live in safety. 11 Then to the place the LORD your God will choose as a dwelling for his Name[f]—there you are to bring everything I command you: your burnt offerings and sacrifices, your tithes and special gifts, and all the choice possessions you have vowed to the LORD. 12 And there rejoice[g] before the LORD your God, you, your sons and daughters, your menservants and maidservants, and the Levites from your towns, who have no allotment or inheritance[h] of their own. 13 Be careful not to sacrifice your burnt offerings anywhere you please. 14 Offer them only at the place the LORD will choose in one of your tribes, and there observe everything I command you.

15 Nevertheless, you may slaughter your animals in any of your towns and eat as much of the meat as you want, as if it were gazelle or deer,[i] according to the blessing the LORD your God gives you. Both the ceremonially unclean and the clean may eat it. 16 But you must not eat the blood;[j] pour it out on the ground like water. 17 You must not eat in your own towns the tithe of your grain and new wine and oil, or the firstborn of your herds and flocks, or whatever you have vowed to give, or your freewill offerings or special gifts. 18 Instead, you are to eat them in the presence of the LORD your God at the place the LORD your God will choose—you, your sons and daughters, your menservants and maidservants, and the Levites from your towns—and you are to rejoice[k] before the LORD your God in everything you put your hand to. 19 Be careful not to neglect the Levites[l] as long as you live in your land.

20 When the LORD your God has enlarged your territory as he promised[m] you, and you crave meat and say, "I would like some meat," then you may eat as much of it as you want. 21 If the place where the LORD your God chooses to put his Name is too far away from you, you may slaughter animals from the herds and flocks the LORD has given you, as I have commanded you, and in your own towns you may eat as much of them as you want. 22 Eat them as you would gazelle or deer.[n] Both the ceremonially unclean and the clean may eat. 23 But be sure you do not eat the blood,[o] because the blood is the life, and you must not eat the life with the meat. 24 You must not eat the blood; pour it out on the ground like water. 25 Do not eat it, so that it may go well[p] with you and your children after you, because you will be doing what is right in the eyes of the LORD.

26 But take your consecrated things and whatever you have vowed to give, and go to the place the LORD will choose. 27 Present your burnt offerings[q] on the altar of the LORD your God, both the meat and the blood. The blood of your sacrifices must be poured beside the altar of the LORD your God, but you may eat the meat. 28 Be careful to obey

**12:15** i Dt14:5
**12:16** j Lev17:10–12
**12:18** k ver7,12
**12:19** l Dt14:27
**12:20** m Ge15:18; Dt11:24
**12:22** n ver15
**12:23** o ver16; Lev17:11,14
**12:25** p Dt4:40
**12:27** q Lev1:5,9,13

all these regulations I am giving you, so that it may always go well with you and your children after you, because you will be doing what is good and right in the eyes of the LORD your God.

29 The LORD your God will cut off before you the nations you are about to invade and dispossess. But when you have driven them out and settled in their land, 30 and after they have been destroyed before you, be careful not to be ensnared by inquiring about their gods, saying, "How do these nations serve their gods? We will do the same." 31 You must not worship the LORD your God in their way, because in worshiping their gods, they do all kinds of detestable things the LORD hates. They even burn their sons[r] and daughters in the fire as sacrifices to their gods.

32 See that you do all I command you; do not add[s] to it or take away from it.

## Worshiping Other Gods

13 If a prophet,[t] or one who foretells by dreams, appears among you and announces to you a miraculous sign or wonder, 2 and if the sign or wonder of which he has spoken takes place, and he says, "Let us follow other gods" (gods you have not known) "and let us worship them," 3 you must not listen to the words of that prophet or dreamer. The LORD your God is testing[u] you to find out whether you love him with all your heart and with all your soul. 4 It is the LORD your God you must follow,[v] and him you must revere. Keep his commands and obey him; serve him and hold fast to him. 5 That prophet or dreamer must be put to death, because he preached rebellion against the LORD your God, who brought you out of Egypt and redeemed you from the land of slavery; he has tried to turn you from the way the LORD your God commanded you to follow. You must purge the evil from among you.

6 If your very own brother, or your son or daughter, or the wife you love, or your closest friend secretly entices[w] you, saying, "Let us go and worship other gods" (gods that neither you nor your fathers have known, 7 gods of the peoples around you, whether near or far, from one end of the land to the other), 8 do not yield to him or listen to him. Show him no pity. Do not spare him or shield him. 9 You must certainly put him to death.[x] Your hand must be the first in putting him to death, and then the hands of all the people. 10 Stone him to death, because he tried to turn you away from the LORD your God, who brought you out of Egypt, out of the land of slavery. 11 Then all Israel will hear and be afraid,[y] and no one among you will do such an evil thing again.

12 If you hear it said about one of the towns the LORD your God is giving you to live in 13 that wicked men[z] have arisen among you and have led the people of their town astray, saying, "Let us go and worship other gods" (gods you have not known), 14 then you must inquire, probe and investigate it thoroughly. And if it is true and it has been proved that this detestable thing has been done among you, 15 you must certainly put to the sword all who live in that town. Destroy it completely,[a] both its people and its livestock. 16 Gather all the plunder of the town into the middle of the public square and completely burn the town and all its plunder as a whole burnt offering to the LORD your God. It is to remain a ruin[a] forever, never to be rebuilt. 17 None of those condemned things[a] shall be found in your hands, so that the LORD will turn from his fierce anger;[b] he will show you mercy, have compassion on you, and increase your numbers, as he promised on oath to your forefathers, 18 because you obey the LORD your God, keeping all his commands that I am giving you today and doing what is right in his eyes.

## Clean and Unclean Food

14 You are the children[c] of the LORD your God. Do not cut yourselves or shave the front of your heads for the dead, 2 for you are a people holy to the LORD your God. Out of all the peoples on the face of the earth, the LORD has chosen you to be his treasured possession.[d]

3 Do not eat any detestable thing.[e] 4 These are the animals you may eat:[f] the ox, the sheep, the goat, 5 the deer, the gazelle, the roe deer, the wild goat, the ibex, the antelope and the mountain sheep.[b] 6 You may

[a] 15,17 The Hebrew term refers to the irrevocable giving over of things or persons to the LORD, often by totally destroying them. [b] 5 The precise identification of some of the birds and animals in this chapter is uncertain.

- **12:31** r Dt 18:10
- **12:32** s Dt 4:2
- **13:1** t Mt 24:24
- **13:3** u Dt 8:2,16
- **13:4** v 2Ki 23:3
- **13:6** w Dt 17:2–7

- **13:9** x Dt 17:5,7
- **13:11** y Dt 19:20
- **13:13** z ver 2,6
- **13:16** a Jos 8:28
- **13:17** b Nu 25:4
- **14:1** c Lev 21:5; Ro 8:14
- **14:2** d Dt 7:6
- **14:3** e Eze 4:14
- **14:4** f Lev 11:2–45

Inspire

## INFLUENCING OTHERS

As we study the Scriptures, we read of women who had tremendous influence over their families, communities and nations. The same kind of influence is present today among women. Today's women use their influence to lead others, raise children and serve as shepherds of God's flock.

All of us have the ability to affect the actions of others in some way. We must be very sure that we are first being Christ-led ourselves, because those who exercise control over the thoughts and actions of others will be held accountable by God for how they use this influence. And for those of us who have charge over children, we have even more responsibility. We need to help our kids understand not only how they influence others, but also, perhaps more importantly, how others influence them. We need to be vigilant to monitor how those influences (friends, media, advertising) affect our children, and we need to be aware of how our own choices can affect our children.

Deuteronomy 13 gives us some warnings about who we allow to lead and influence us. The Scriptures are clear that even if the person influencing us is someone close to us—a brother or sister, mother or father—we must still weigh their words against what we know is true from the Bible. And even then, if the gift of pleasing and flowing words are from God, we must be sure that those words guide us in the right direction. We must allow those words to steer us toward God and not away from him.

Examine the message of anyone you might think to follow. Are they speaking basic truths? Do their words align with the truths from the Bible? Will following their lead be beneficial for all concerned? Above all, are they sent by Christ to help you on the journey to him and to wholeness?

Be wise in all of your choices. Only those who influence you to live completely for Christ are worth following.

—A. Adams-Morris

### read

Deuteronomy 13;
See also the Inspire Notes "Motherhood," "Women in Preaching Ministries" and "Women in Teaching Ministries," and the Women of the Bible Notes "Samson's Bride: Nothing by Chance," "Delilah: Strength That Builds or Destroys" and "Mary, the Mother of Jesus: A Model of Motherhood."

### WOMAN of COLOR

Whom do you influence? Who influences you? What messages are you giving and receiving?

For the next Inspire note, go to page 230.

14:8 g Lev 11:26–27
14:21 h Lev 17:15 i Ex 34:26
14:22 j Lev 27:30
14:23 k Dt 12:5

eat any animal that has a split hoof divided
in two and that chews the cud. 7However,
of those that chew the cud or that have a
split hoof completely divided you may not
eat the camel, the rabbit or the coney.[a] Al-
though they chew the cud, they do not have
a split hoof; they are ceremonially unclean
for you. 8The pig is also unclean; although
it has a split hoof, it does not chew the
cud. You are not to eat their meat or touch
their carcasses.[g]

9Of all the creatures living in the water,
you may eat any that has fins and scales.
10But anything that does not have fins and
scales you may not eat; for you it is unclean.

11You may eat any clean bird. 12But these
you may not eat: the eagle, the vulture, the
black vulture, 13the red kite, the black kite,
any kind of falcon, 14any kind of raven,
15the horned owl, the screech owl, the gull,
any kind of hawk, 16the little owl, the great
owl, the white owl, 17the desert owl, the os-
prey, the cormorant, 18the stork, any kind of
heron, the hoopoe and the bat.

19All flying insects that swarm are un-
clean to you; do not eat them. 20But any
winged creature that is clean you may eat.

21Do not eat anything you find already
dead.[h] You may give it to an alien living in
any of your towns, and he may eat it, or you
may sell it to a foreigner. But you are a peo-
ple holy to the LORD your God.

Do not cook a young goat in its moth-
er's milk.[i]

## Tithes

22Be sure to set aside a tenth[j] of all that
your fields produce each year. 23Eat the tithe
of your grain, new wine and oil, and the first-
born of your herds and flocks in the pres-
ence of the LORD your God at the place he will
choose as a dwelling for his Name,[k] so that
you may learn to revere the LORD your God
always. 24But if that place is too distant and
you have been blessed by the LORD your God
and cannot carry your tithe (because the
place where the LORD will choose to put his
Name is so far away), 25then exchange your
tithe for silver, and take the silver with you
and go to the place the LORD your God will
choose. 26Use the silver to buy whatever you
like: cattle, sheep, wine or other fermented
drink, or anything you wish. Then you
and your household shall eat there in the
presence of the LORD your God and rejoice.[l]
27And do not neglect the Levites living in
your towns, for they have no allotment or
inheritance of their own.[m]

28At the end of every three years, bring
all the tithes of that year's produce and
store it in your towns,[n] 29so that the Levites
(who have no allotment or inheritance of
their own) and the aliens,[o] the fatherless
and the widows who live in your towns may
come and eat and be satisfied, and so that
the LORD your God may bless[p] you in all the
work of your hands.

## The Year for Canceling Debts

15 At the end of every seven years you
must cancel debts.[q] 2This is how it
is to be done: Every creditor shall cancel the
loan he has made to his fellow Israelite. He
shall not require payment from his fellow Is-
raelite or brother, because the LORD's time for
canceling debts has been proclaimed. 3You
may require payment from a foreigner,[r] but
you must cancel any debt your brother owes
you. 4However, there should be no poor
among you, for in the land the LORD your
God is giving you to possess as your inher-
itance, he will richly bless you, 5if only you
fully obey the LORD your God and are care-
ful to follow all these commands I am giv-
ing you today. 6For the LORD your God will
bless you as he has promised, and you will
lend to many nations but will borrow from
none. You will rule over many nations but
none will rule over you.[s]

7If there is a poor man among your broth-
ers in any of the towns of the land that the
LORD your God is giving you, do not be
hardhearted or tightfisted[t] toward your
poor brother. 8Rather be openhanded[u] and
freely lend him whatever he needs. 9Be care-
ful not to harbor this wicked thought: "The
seventh year, the year for canceling debts, is
near," so that you do not show ill will toward
your needy brother and give him nothing.
He may then appeal to the LORD against you,
and you will be found guilty of sin.[v] 10Give
generously to him and do so without a grudg-

14:26 l Dt 12:7–8
14:27 m Nu 18:20
14:28 n Dt 26:12
14:29 o Dt 26:12 p Dt 15:10
15:1 q Dt 31:10
15:3 r Dt 23:20
15:6 s Dt 28:12–13,44
15:7 t 1Jn 3:17
15:8 u Mt 5:42
15:9 v Dt 24:15

[a]7 That is, the hyrax or rock badger

**15:10**
w 2Co9:5

ing heart;[w] then because of this the LORD
your God will bless you in all your work and
in everything you put your
hand to. 11 There will
always be poor people
in the land. Therefore
I command you to be
openhanded toward
your brothers and
toward the poor and
needy in your land.[x]

> *"We make a living by what we get, but we make a life by what we give."*
>
> —BARBARA HARRIS, FIRST FEMALE AFRICAN AMERICAN EPISCOPAL BISHOP

## Freeing Servants

12 If a fellow Hebrew,
a man or a woman,
sells himself to you and
serves you six years, in
the seventh year you must let him go free.[y]
13 And when you release him, do not send
him away empty-handed. 14 Supply him
liberally from your flock, your threshing
floor and your winepress. Give to him as the
LORD your God has blessed you. 15 Remem-
ber that you were slaves in Egypt and the
LORD your God redeemed you. That is why I
give you this command today.
16 But if your servant says to you, "I do not
want to leave you," because he loves you and
your family and is well off with you, 17 then
take an awl and push it through his ear
lobe into the door, and he will become your
servant for life. Do the same for your maid-
servant.
18 Do not consider it a hardship to set your
servant free, because his service to you these
six years has been worth twice as much as
that of a hired hand. And the LORD your God
will bless you in everything you do.

**15:11**
x Mt26:11; Mk14:7; Jn12:8

**15:12**
y Ex21:2; Lev25:39

**15:19**
z Ex13:2

**15:20**
a Dt12:5–7,17,18

**15:21**
b Lev22:19–25

## The Firstborn Animals

19 Set apart for the LORD your God every
firstborn male[z] of your herds and flocks. Do
not put the firstborn of your oxen to work,
and do not shear the firstborn of your sheep.
20 Each year you and your family are to eat
them in the presence of the LORD your God
at the place he will choose.[a] 21 If an animal
has a defect, is lame or blind, or has any se-
rious flaw, you must not sacrifice it to the
LORD your God.[b] 22 You are to eat it in your
own towns. Both the ceremonially unclean
and the clean may eat it, as if it were gazelle
or deer.[c] 23 But you must not eat the blood;
pour it out on the ground like water.[d]

## Passover

16 Observe the month of Abib[e] and
celebrate the Passover of the LORD
your God, because in the month of Abib he
brought you out of Egypt by night. 2 Sacrifice
as the Passover to the LORD your God an ani-
mal from your flock or herd at the place the
LORD will choose as a dwelling for his Name.
3 Do not eat it with bread made with yeast,
but for seven days eat unleavened bread, the
bread of affliction, because you left Egypt
in haste[f]—so that all the days of your life
you may remember the time of your depar-
ture from Egypt. 4 Let no yeast be found in
your possession in all your land for seven
days. Do not let any of the meat you sacri-
fice on the evening of the first day remain
until morning.
5 You must not sacrifice the Passover in
any town the LORD your God gives you 6 ex-
cept in the place he will choose as a dwelling
for his Name. There you must sacrifice the
Passover in the evening, when the sun goes
down, on the anniversary[a] of your depar-
ture from Egypt. 7 Roast[g] it and eat it at the
place the LORD your God will choose. Then
in the morning return to your tents. 8 For six
days eat unleavened bread and on the sev-
enth day hold an assembly[h] to the LORD your
God and do no work.

## Feast of Weeks

9 Count off seven weeks[i] from the time
you begin to put the sickle to the standing
grain.[j] 10 Then celebrate the Feast of Weeks
to the LORD your God by giving a freewill
offering in proportion to the blessings the
LORD your God has given you. 11 And rejoice[k]
before the LORD your God at the place he will
choose as a dwelling for his Name—you,
your sons and daughters, your menservants
and maidservants, the Levites[l] in your
towns, and the aliens, the fatherless and
the widows living among you. 12 Remember
that you were slaves in Egypt,[m] and follow
carefully these decrees.

**15:22**
c Dt12:15,22

**15:23**
d Dt12:16

**16:1**
e Ex12:2

**16:3**
f Ex12:11,15,19

**16:7**
g Ex12:8

**16:8**
h Ex12:16

**16:9**
i Ex34:22; Lev23:15
j Ex23:16

**16:11**
k Dt12:7
l Dt12:12

**16:12**
m Dt15:15

[a] 6 Or *down, at the time of day*

## Feast of Tabernacles

[13]Celebrate the Feast of Tabernacles for seven days after you have gathered the produce of your threshing floor[n] and your winepress. [14]Be joyful at your Feast—you, your sons and daughters, your menservants and maidservants, and the Levites, the aliens, the fatherless and the widows who live in your towns. [15]For seven days celebrate the Feast to the LORD your God at the place the LORD will choose. For the LORD your God will bless you in all your harvest and in all the work of your hands, and your joy will be complete.

[16]Three times a year all your men must appear before the LORD your God at the place he will choose: at the Feast of Unleavened Bread, the Feast of Weeks and the Feast of Tabernacles.[o] No man should appear before the LORD empty-handed:[p] [17]Each of you must bring a gift in proportion to the way the LORD your God has blessed you.

## Judges

[18]Appoint judges and officials for each of your tribes in every town the LORD your God is giving you, and they shall judge the people fairly. [19]Do not pervert justice[q] or show partiality.[r] Do not accept a bribe, for a bribe blinds the eyes of the wise and twists the words of the righteous. [20]Follow justice and justice alone, so that you may live and possess the land the LORD your God is giving you.

## Worshiping Other Gods

[21]Do not set up any wooden Asherah pole[a] beside the altar you build to the LORD your God, [22]and do not erect a sacred stone, for these the LORD your God hates.

**17** Do not sacrifice to the LORD your God an ox or a sheep that has any defect or flaw in it, for that would be detestable to him.[s]

[2]If a man or woman living among you in one of the towns the LORD gives you is found doing evil in the eyes of the LORD your God in violation of his covenant,[t] [3]and contrary to my command has worshiped other gods, bowing down to them or to the sun or the moon or the stars of the sky, [4]and this has been brought to your attention, then you must investigate it thoroughly. If it is true and it has been proved that this detestable thing has been done in Israel, [5]take the man or woman who has done this evil deed to your city gate and stone that person to death. [6]On the testimony of two or three witnesses a man shall be put to death, but no one shall be put to death on the testimony of only one witness.[u] [7]The hands of the witnesses must be the first in putting him to death, and then the hands of all the people. You must purge the evil[v] from among you.

## Law Courts

[8]If cases come before your courts that are too difficult for you to judge—whether bloodshed, lawsuits or assaults—take them to the place the LORD your God will choose.[w] [9]Go to the priests, who are Levites, and to the judge who is in office at that time. Inquire of them and they will give you the verdict.[x] [10]You must act according to the decisions they give you at the place the LORD will choose. Be careful to do everything they direct you to do. [11]Act according to the law they teach you and the decisions they give you. Do not turn aside from what they tell you, to the right or to the left. [12]The man who shows contempt for the judge or for the priest who stands ministering there to the LORD your God must be put to death. You must purge the evil from Israel. [13]All the people will hear and be afraid, and will not be contemptuous again.

## The King

[14]When you enter the land the LORD your God is giving you and have taken possession of it and settled in it, and you say, "Let us set a king over us like all the nations around us,"[y] [15]be sure to appoint over you the king the LORD your God chooses. He must be from among your own brothers.[z] Do not place a foreigner over you, one who is not a brother Israelite. [16]The king, moreover, must not acquire great numbers of horses for himself[a] or make the people return to Egypt to get more of them,[b] for the LORD has told you, "You are not to go back that way again."

**16:13** n Lev 23:34
**16:16** o Ex 23:14,16 p Ex 34:20
**16:19** q Ex 23:2,8 r Dt 1:17
**17:1** s Dt 15:21
**17:2** t Dt 13:6–11
**17:6** u Nu 35:30; Dt 19:15; Mt 18:16
**17:7** v Dt 13:5,9
**17:8** w Dt 12:5
**17:9** x Dt 19:17
**17:14** y 1Sa 8:5,19–20
**17:15** z Jer 30:21
**17:16** a 1Ki 4:26; 10:26 b 1Ki 10:28; Eze 17:15

[a]21 Or *Do not plant any tree dedicated to Asherah*

**17:17** c 1Ki 11:3
**17:20** d Dt 5:32
**18:1** e Dt 10:9; 1Co 9:13
**18:3** f Lev 7:28–34
**18:4** g Nu 18:12
**18:5** h Dt 10:8
**18:8** i Ne 12:44,47
**18:10** j Dt 12:31

17 He must not take many wives,[c] or his heart will be led astray. He must not accumulate large amounts of silver and gold.

18 When he takes the throne of his kingdom, he is to write for himself on a scroll a copy of this law, taken from that of the priests, who are Levites. 19 It is to be with him, and he is to read it all the days of his life so that he may learn to revere the LORD his God and follow carefully all the words of this law and these decrees 20 and not consider himself better than his brothers and turn from the law to the right or to the left.[d] Then he and his descendants will reign a long time over his kingdom in Israel.

## Offerings for Priests and Levites

**18** The priests, who are Levites—indeed the whole tribe of Levi—are to have no allotment or inheritance with Israel. They shall live on the offerings made to the LORD by fire, for that is their inheritance.[e] 2 They shall have no inheritance among their brothers; the LORD is their inheritance, as he promised them.

3 This is the share due the priests from the people who sacrifice a bull or a sheep: the shoulder, the jowls and the inner parts.[f] 4 You are to give them the firstfruits of your grain, new wine and oil, and the first wool from the shearing of your sheep,[g] 5 for the LORD your God has chosen them and their descendants out of all your tribes to stand and minister[h] in the LORD's name always.

6 If a Levite moves from one of your towns anywhere in Israel where he is living, and comes in all earnestness to the place the LORD will choose, 7 he may minister in the name of the LORD his God like all his fellow Levites who serve there in the presence of the LORD. 8 He is to share equally in their benefits, even though he has received money from the sale of family possessions.[i]

## Detestable Practices

9 When you enter the land the LORD your God is giving you, do not learn to imitate the detestable ways of the nations there. 10 Let no one be found among you who sacrifices his son or daughter in[a] the fire, who practices divination[j] or sorcery, interprets omens, engages in witchcraft, 11 or casts spells, or who is a medium or spiritist or who consults the dead. 12 Anyone who does these things is detestable to the LORD, and because of these detestable practices the LORD your God will drive out those nations before you. 13 You must be blameless before the LORD your God.

## The Prophet

14 The nations you will dispossess listen to those who practice sorcery or divination. But as for you, the LORD your God has not permitted you to do so. 15 The LORD your God will raise up for you a prophet like me from among your own brothers.[k] You must listen to him. 16 For this is what you asked of the LORD your God at Horeb on the day of the assembly when you said, "Let us not hear the voice of the LORD our God nor see this great fire anymore, or we will die."[l]

17 The LORD said to me: "What they say is good. 18 I will raise up for them a prophet like you from among their brothers; I will put my words[m] in his mouth, and he will tell them everything I command him.[n] 19 If anyone does not listen to my words that the prophet speaks in my name, I myself will call him to account.[o] 20 But a prophet who presumes to speak in my name anything I have not commanded him to say, or a prophet who speaks in the name of other gods, must be put to death."

21 You may say to yourselves, "How can we know when a message has not been spoken by the LORD?" 22 If what a prophet proclaims in the name of the LORD does not take place or come true, that is a message the LORD has not spoken.[p] That prophet has spoken presumptuously.[q] Do not be afraid of him.

## Cities of Refuge

**19** When the LORD your God has destroyed the nations whose land he is giving you, and when you have driven them out and settled in their towns and houses, 2 then set aside for yourselves three cities centrally located in the land the LORD your God is giving you to possess. 3 Build roads to them and divide into three parts the land the LORD your God is giving you as an inher-

**18:15** k Ac 3:22*
**18:16** l Ex 20:19
**18:18** m Isa 51:16 n Jn 4:25–26
**18:19** o Ac 3:23*
**18:22** p Jer 28:9 q ver 20

[a] 10 Or *who makes his son or daughter pass through*

**19:9** r Jos 20:7–8
**19:14** s Dt 27:17
**19:15** t Nu 35:30; Dt 17:6; Mt 18:16*; 2Co 13:1*
**19:16** u Ps 27:12

itance, so that anyone who kills a man may flee there.

[4]This is the rule concerning the man who kills another and flees there to save his life—one who kills his neighbor unintentionally, without malice aforethought. [5]For instance, a man may go into the forest with his neighbor to cut wood, and as he swings his ax to fell a tree, the head may fly off and hit his neighbor and kill him. That man may flee to one of these cities and save his life. [6]Otherwise, the avenger of blood might pursue him in a rage, overtake him if the distance is too great, and kill him even though he is not deserving of death, since he did it to his neighbor without malice aforethought. [7]This is why I command you to set aside for yourselves three cities.

[8]If the LORD your God enlarges your territory, as he promised on oath to your forefathers, and gives you the whole land he promised them, [9]because you carefully follow all these laws I command you today—to love the LORD your God and to walk always in his ways[r]—then you are to set aside three more cities. [10]Do this so that innocent blood will not be shed in your land, which the LORD your God is giving you as your inheritance, and so that you will not be guilty of bloodshed.

[11]But if a man hates his neighbor and lies in wait for him, assaults and kills him, and then flees to one of these cities, [12]the elders of his town shall send for him, bring him back from the city, and hand him over to the avenger of blood to die. [13]Show him no pity. You must purge from Israel the guilt of shedding innocent blood, so that it may go well with you.

[14]Do not move your neighbor's boundary stone set up by your predecessors in the inheritance you receive in the land the LORD your God is giving you to possess.[s]

## Witnesses

[15]One witness is not enough to convict a man accused of any crime or offense he may have committed. A matter must be established by the testimony of two or three witnesses.[t]

[16]If a malicious witness[u] takes the stand to accuse a man of a crime, [17]the two men involved in the dispute must stand in the presence of the LORD before the priests and the judges[v] who are in office at the time. [18]The judges must make a thorough investigation, and if the witness proves to be a liar, giving false testimony against his brother, [19]then do to him as he intended to do to his brother.[w] You must purge the evil from among you. [20]The rest of the people will hear of this and be afraid, and never again will such an evil thing be done among you. [21]Show no pity:[x] life for life, eye for eye, tooth for tooth, hand for hand, foot for foot.[y]

## Going to War

**20** When you go to war against your enemies and see horses and chariots and an army greater than yours, do not be afraid[z] of them, because the LORD your God, who brought you up out of Egypt, will be with you. [2]When you are about to go into battle, the priest shall come forward and address the army. [3]He shall say: "Hear, O Israel, today you are going into battle against your enemies. Do not be fainthearted or afraid; do not be terrified or give way to panic before them. [4]For the LORD your God is the one who goes with you to fight[a] for you against your enemies to give you victory."

[5]The officers shall say to the army: "Has anyone built a new house and not dedicated it? Let him go home, or he may die in battle and someone else may dedicate it. [6]Has anyone planted a vineyard and not begun to enjoy it? Let him go home, or he may die in battle and someone else enjoy it. [7]Has anyone become pledged to a woman and not married her? Let him go home, or he may die in battle and someone else marry her.[b]" [8]Then the officers shall add, "Is any man afraid or fainthearted? Let him go home so that his brothers will not become disheartened too."[c] [9]When the officers have finished speaking to the army, they shall appoint commanders over it.

[10]When you march up to attack a city, make its people an offer of peace. [11]If they accept and open their gates, all the people in it shall be subject to forced labor and shall work for you. [12]If they refuse to make peace and they engage you in battle, lay siege to that city. [13]When the LORD your God

**19:17** v Dt 17:9
**19:19** w Pr 19:5,9
**19:21** x ver 13; y Ex 21:24; Lev 24:20; Mt 5:38*
**20:1** z Dt 31:6,8
**20:4** a Dt 1:30
**20:7** b Dt 24:5
**20:8** c Jdg 7:3

**20:13** d Nu 31:7
**20:14** e Jos 8:2
**20:16** f Dt 7:2; Jos 11:14
**20:18** g Ex 23:33
**21:5** h Dt 17:8–11
**21:6** i Mt 27:24

delivers it into your hand, put to the sword all the men in it.[d] [14]As for the women, the children, the livestock[e] and everything else in the city, you may take these as plunder for yourselves. And you may use the plunder the LORD your God gives you from your enemies. [15]This is how you are to treat all the cities that are at a distance from you and do not belong to the nations nearby.

[16]However, in the cities of the nations the LORD your God is giving you as an inheritance, do not leave alive anything that breathes.[f] [17]Completely destroy[a] them—the Hittites, Amorites, Canaanites, Perizzites, Hivites and Jebusites—as the LORD your God has commanded you. [18]Otherwise, they will teach you to follow all the detestable things they do in worshiping their gods, and you will sin[g] against the LORD your God.

[19]When you lay siege to a city for a long time, fighting against it to capture it, do not destroy its trees by putting an ax to them, because you can eat their fruit. Do not cut them down. Are the trees of the field people, that you should besiege them?[b] [20]However, you may cut down trees that you know are not fruit trees and use them to build siege works until the city at war with you falls.

## Atonement for an Unsolved Murder

**21** If a man is found slain, lying in a field in the land the LORD your God is giving you to possess, and it is not known who killed him, [2]your elders and judges shall go out and measure the distance from the body to the neighboring towns. [3]Then the elders of the town nearest the body shall take a heifer that has never been worked and has never worn a yoke [4]and lead her down to a valley that has not been plowed or planted and where there is a flowing stream. There in the valley they are to break the heifer's neck. [5]The priests, the sons of Levi, shall step forward, for the LORD your God has chosen them to minister and to pronounce blessings in the name of the LORD and to decide all cases of dispute and assault.[h] [6]Then all the elders of the town nearest the body shall wash their hands[i] over the heifer whose neck was broken in the valley, [7]and they shall declare: "Our hands did not shed this blood, nor did our eyes see it done. [8]Accept this atonement for your people Israel, whom you have redeemed, O LORD, and do not hold your people guilty of the blood of an innocent man." And the bloodshed will be atoned for. [9]So you will purge[j] from yourselves the guilt of shedding innocent blood, since you have done what is right in the eyes of the LORD.

**21:9** j Dt 19:13
**21:12** k Lev 14:9
**21:13** l Ps 45:10
**21:15** m Ge 29:33
**21:16** n 1Ch 26:10
**21:17** o Ge 49:3

## Marrying a Captive Woman

[10]When you go to war against your enemies and the LORD your God delivers them into your hands and you take captives, [11]if you notice among the captives a beautiful woman and are attracted to her, you may take her as your wife. [12]Bring her into your home and have her shave her head,[k] trim her nails [13]and put aside the clothes she was wearing when captured. After she has lived in your house and mourned her father and mother for a full month,[l] then you may go to her and be her husband and she shall be your wife. [14]If you are not pleased with her, let her go wherever she wishes. You must not sell her or treat her as a slave, since you have dishonored her.

## The Right of the Firstborn

[15]If a man has two wives, and he loves one but not the other, and both bear him sons but the firstborn is the son of the wife he does not love,[m] [16]when he wills his property to his sons, he must not give the rights of the firstborn to the son of the wife he loves in preference to his actual firstborn, the son of the wife he does not love.[n] [17]He must acknowledge the son of his unloved wife as the firstborn by giving him a double share of all he has. That son is the first sign of his father's strength.[o] The right of the firstborn belongs to him.

## A Rebellious Son

[18]If a man has a stubborn and rebellious son who does not obey his father and mother and will not listen to them when they discipline him, [19]his father and mother shall take

[a]17 The Hebrew term refers to the irrevocable giving over of things or persons to the LORD, often by totally destroying them.
[b]19 Or *down to use in the siege, for the fruit trees are for the benefit of man.*

hold of him and bring him to the elders at the gate of his town. 20 They shall say to the elders, "This son of ours is stubborn and rebellious. He will not obey us. He is a profligate and a drunkard." 21 Then all the men of his town shall stone him to death. You must purge the evil from among you. All Israel will hear of it and be afraid.[p]

## Various Laws

22 If a man guilty of a capital offense is put to death and his body is hung on a tree, 23 you must not leave his body on the tree overnight.[q] Be sure to bury him that same day, because anyone who is hung on a tree is under God's curse.[r] You must not desecrate the land the LORD your God is giving you as an inheritance.

22 If you see your brother's ox or sheep straying, do not ignore it but be sure to take it back to him.[s] 2 If the brother does not live near you or if you do not know who he is, take it home with you and keep it until he comes looking for it. Then give it back to him. 3 Do the same if you find your brother's donkey or his cloak or anything he loses. Do not ignore it.

4 If you see your brother's donkey or his ox fallen on the road, do not ignore it. Help him get it to its feet.

5 A woman must not wear men's clothing, nor a man wear women's clothing, for the LORD your God detests anyone who does this.

6 If you come across a bird's nest beside the road, either in a tree or on the ground, and the mother is sitting on the young or on the eggs, do not take the mother with the young.[t] 7 You may take the young, but be sure to let the mother go, so that it may go well with you and you may have a long life.[u]

8 When you build a new house, make a parapet around your roof so that you may not bring the guilt of bloodshed on your house if someone falls from the roof.

9 Do not plant two kinds of seed in your vineyard;[v] if you do, not only the crops you plant but also the fruit of the vineyard will be defiled.[a]

10 Do not plow with an ox and a donkey yoked together.

11 Do not wear clothes of wool and linen woven together.[w]

12 Make tassels on the four corners of the cloak you wear.[x]

## Marriage Violations

13 If a man takes a wife and, after lying with her, dislikes her 14 and slanders her and gives her a bad name, saying, "I married this woman, but when I approached her, I did not find proof of her virginity," 15 then the girl's father and mother shall bring proof that she was a virgin to the town elders at the gate. 16 The girl's father will say to the elders, "I gave my daughter in marriage to this man, but he dislikes her. 17 Now he has slandered her and said, 'I did not find your daughter to be a virgin.' But here is the proof of my daughter's virginity." Then her parents shall display the cloth before the elders of the town, 18 and the elders shall take the man and punish him. 19 They shall fine him a hundred shekels of silver[b] and give them to the girl's father, because this man has given an Israelite virgin a bad name. She shall continue to be his wife; he must not divorce her as long as he lives.

20 If, however, the charge is true and no proof of the girl's virginity can be found, 21 she shall be brought to the door of her father's house and there the men of her town shall stone her to death. She has done a disgraceful thing[y] in Israel by being promiscuous while still in her father's house. You must purge the evil from among you.

22 If a man is found sleeping with another man's wife, both the man who slept with her and the woman must die.[z] You must purge the evil from Israel.

23 If a man happens to meet in a town a virgin pledged to be married and he sleeps with her, 24 you shall take both of them to the gate of that town and stone them to death—the girl because she was in a town and did not scream for help, and the man because he violated another man's wife. You must purge the evil from among you.

25 But if out in the country a man happens to meet a girl pledged to be married and rapes her, only the man who has done this shall die. 26 Do nothing to the girl; she has

**21:21** p Dt13:11
**21:23** q Jos8:29; 10:27; Jn19:31 r Gal3:13*
**22:1** s Ex23:4–5
**22:6** t Lev22:28
**22:7** u Dt4:40
**22:9** v Lev19:19
**22:11** w Lev19:19
**22:12** x Nu15:37–41
**22:21** y Ge34:7; Dt13:5
**22:22** z Lev20:10; Jn8:5

[a] 9 Or *be forfeited to the sanctuary* [b] 19 That is, about 2 1/2 pounds (about 1 kilogram)

committed no sin deserving death. This case is like that of someone who attacks and murders his neighbor, [27]for the man found the girl out in the country, and though the betrothed girl screamed, there was no one to rescue her.

[28]If a man happens to meet a virgin who is not pledged to be married and rapes her and they are discovered,[a] [29]he shall pay the girl's father fifty shekels of silver.[a] He must marry the girl, for he has violated her. He can never divorce her as long as he lives.

[30]A man is not to marry his father's wife; he must not dishonor his father's bed.[b]

## Exclusion From the Assembly

**23** No one who has been emasculated by crushing or cutting may enter the assembly of the LORD.

[2]No one born of a forbidden marriage[b] nor any of his descendants may enter the assembly of the LORD, even down to the tenth generation.

[3]No Ammonite or Moabite or any of his descendants may enter the assembly of the LORD, even down to the tenth generation.[c] [4]For they did not come to meet you with bread and water on your way when you came out of Egypt, and they hired Balaam[d] son of Beor from Pethor in Aram Naharaim[c] to pronounce a curse on you. [5]However, the LORD your God would not listen to Balaam but turned the curse into a blessing for you, because the LORD your God loves you. [6]Do not seek a treaty of friendship with them as long as you live.[e]

[7]Do not abhor an Edomite, for he is your brother.[f] Do not abhor an Egyptian, because you lived as an alien in his country. [8]The third generation of children born to them may enter the assembly of the LORD.

## Uncleanness in the Camp

[9]When you are encamped against your enemies, keep away from everything impure. [10]If one of your men is unclean because of a nocturnal emission, he is to go outside the camp and stay there.[g] [11]But as evening approaches he is to wash himself, and at sunset he may return to the camp.

[12]Designate a place outside the camp where you can go to relieve yourself. [13]As part of your equipment have something to dig with, and when you relieve yourself, dig a hole and cover up your excrement. [14]For the LORD your God moves[h] about in your camp to protect you and to deliver your enemies to you. Your camp must be holy, so that he will not see among you anything indecent and turn away from you.

## Miscellaneous Laws

[15]If a slave has taken refuge with you, do not hand him over to his master.[i] [16]Let him live among you wherever he likes and in whatever town he chooses. Do not oppress him.

[17]No Israelite man or woman is to become a shrine prostitute. [18]You must not bring the earnings of a female prostitute or of a male prostitute[d] into the house of the LORD your God to pay any vow, because the LORD your God detests them both.

[19]Do not charge your brother interest, whether on money or food or anything else that may earn interest.[j] [20]You may charge a foreigner interest, but not a brother Israelite, so that the LORD your God may bless you in everything you put your hand to in the land you are entering to possess.

[21]If you make a vow to the LORD your God, do not be slow to pay it, for the LORD your God will certainly demand it of you and you will be guilty of sin.[k] [22]But if you refrain from making a vow, you will not be guilty. [23]Whatever your lips utter you must be sure to do, because you made your vow freely to the LORD your God with your own mouth.

[24]If you enter your neighbor's vineyard, you may eat all the grapes you want, but do not put any in your basket. [25]If you enter your neighbor's grainfield, you may pick kernels with your hands, but you must not put a sickle to his standing grain.[l]

**24** If a man marries a woman who becomes displeasing to him because he finds something indecent about her, and he writes her a certificate of divorce,[m] gives it to her and sends her from his house, [2]and if after she leaves his house she becomes the wife of another man, [3]and her second husband dislikes her and writes her a certifi-

**22:28** a Ex22:16
**22:30** b Lev18:8; Dt27:20; 1Co5:1
**23:3** c Ne13:2
**23:4** d Nu22:5–6
**23:6** e Ezr9:12
**23:7** f Ge25:26
**23:10** g Lev15:16
**23:14** h Lev26:12
**23:15** i 1Sa30:15
**23:19** j Ex22:25; Lev25:35–37
**23:21** k Nu30:1–2
**23:25** l Mt12:1; Mk2:23; Lk6:1
**24:1** m Mt5:31*; 19:7–9; Mk10:4–5

[a]29 That is, about 1 1/4 pounds (about 0.6 kilogram) [b]2 Or *one of illegitimate birth* [c]4 That is, Northwest Mesopotamia
[d]18 Hebrew *of a dog*

cate of divorce, gives it to her and sends her from his house, or if he dies, [4]then her first husband, who divorced her, is not allowed to marry her again after she has been defiled. That would be detestable in the eyes of the LORD. Do not bring sin upon the land the LORD[n] your God is giving you as an inheritance.

[5]If a man has recently married, he must not be sent to war or have any other duty laid on him. For one year he is to be free to stay at home and bring happiness to the wife he has married.[o]

[6]Do not take a pair of millstones—not even the upper one—as security for a debt, because that would be taking a man's livelihood as security.

[7]If a man is caught kidnapping one of his brother Israelites and treats him as a slave or sells him, the kidnapper must die.[p] You must purge the evil from among you.

[8]In cases of leprous[a] diseases be very careful to do exactly as the priests, who are Levites, instruct you. You must follow carefully what I have commanded them.[q] [9]Remember what the LORD your God did to Miriam along the way after you came out of Egypt.[r]

[10]When you make a loan of any kind to your neighbor, do not go into his house to get what he is offering as a pledge. [11]Stay outside and let the man to whom you are making the loan bring the pledge out to you. [12]If the man is poor, do not go to sleep with his pledge in your possession. [13]Return his cloak to him by sunset[s] so that he may sleep in it. Then he will thank you, and it will be regarded as a righteous act in the sight of the LORD your God.

[14]Do not take advantage of a hired man who is poor and needy, whether he is a brother Israelite or an alien living in one of your towns. [15]Pay him his wages each day before sunset, because he is poor and is counting on it.[t] Otherwise he may cry to the LORD against you, and you will be guilty of sin.[u]

[16]Fathers shall not be put to death for their children, nor children put to death for their fathers; each is to die for his own sin.[v]

[17]Do not deprive the alien or the fatherless of justice, or take the cloak of the widow as a pledge. [18]Remember that you were slaves in Egypt and the LORD your God redeemed you from there. That is why I command you to do this.

[19]When you are harvesting in your field and you overlook a sheaf, do not go back to get it.[w] Leave it for the alien, the fatherless and the widow, so that the LORD your God may bless you in all the work of your hands. [20]When you beat the olives from your trees, do not go over the branches a second time. Leave what remains for the alien, the fatherless and the widow. [21]When you harvest the grapes in your vineyard, do not go over the vines again. Leave what remains for the alien, the fatherless and the widow. [22]Remember that you were slaves in Egypt. That is why I command you to do this.

# 25

When men have a dispute, they are to take it to court and the judges will decide the case,[x] acquitting the innocent and condemning the guilty. [2]If the guilty man deserves to be beaten, the judge shall make him lie down and have him flogged in his presence with the number of lashes his crime deserves, [3]but he must not give him more than forty lashes.[y] If he is flogged more than that, your brother will be degraded in your eyes.

[4]Do not muzzle an ox while it is treading out the grain.[z]

[5]If brothers are living together and one of them dies without a son, his widow must not marry outside the family. Her husband's brother shall take her and marry her and fulfill the duty of a brother-in-law to her.[a] [6]The first son she bears shall carry on the name of the dead brother so that his name will not be blotted out from Israel.[b]

[7]However, if a man does not want to marry his brother's wife, she shall go to the elders at the town gate and say, "My husband's brother refuses to carry on his brother's name in Israel. He will not fulfill the duty of a brother-in-law to me."[c] [8]Then the elders of his town shall summon him and talk to him. If he persists in saying, "I do not want to marry her," [9]his brother's widow shall go up to him in the presence of the elders, take off one of his sandals,[d] spit in his face and

**24:4** n Jer 3:1
**24:5** o Dt 20:7
**24:7** p Ex 21:16
**24:8** q Lev 13:1–46
**24:9** r Nu 12:10
**24:13** s Ex 22:26
**24:15** t Lev 19:13 u Jas 5:4
**24:16** v Jer 31:29–30; Eze 18:20
**24:19** w Lev 19:9; 23:22
**25:1** x Dt 19:17
**25:3** y 2Co 11:24
**25:4** z 1Ti 5:18*
**25:5** a Mt 22:24; Lk 20:28
**25:6** b Ru 4:5,10
**25:7** c Ru 4:1–2,5–6
**25:9** d Ru 4:7–8,11

[a]8 The Hebrew word was used for various diseases affecting the skin—not necessarily leprosy.

# Inspire

## SINGLE MOTHERS

During Biblical times a woman was dependent on her male relatives (father, brothers, husband) for much of her well-being. A woman without the protection of a husband or father was often in a desperate situation. And a woman bearing a child while separated from her husband—or worse, a woman bearing a child outside of a marriage relationship—often faced severe consequences.

In our society, we see a large number of single mothers—women who have children outside of marriage or women who are separated, divorced or widowed. And there are also some married women who are single-handedly taking care of their children's emotional, financial or spiritual needs; these women are, in a sense, single mothers as well.

Like mothers in Biblical times, single mothers today experience shame, ridicule and rejection by friends and family. Due to their circumstances, many find themselves in a cycle of poverty, struggling to provide a decent life for themselves and their children. Although marriage is desirable and ordained by God, the Bible teaches us that, regardless of the circumstances, God values all children and has a divine plan for each child's life. In Deuteronomy 24 we see how God charged the Israelites to care for women who were raising children alone. He commanded justice for those who needed protection (see Dt 24:17), and he also made a way to provide food for the poor (see Dt 24:19–21).

If you are a single mother, you can find comfort in these truths from the Bible:

1. God loves and cares for you and your children (see Mk 10:13–16).
2. God is willing and able to provide for all of your needs according to his glorious riches (see Php 4:19).
3. There is no condemnation for those who are in Christ Jesus (see Ro 8:1).

Are you a single mother? If so, take heart. God sees your situation, and he is interested in justice for you and protection for your children. Do you know any single mothers? Keep in mind that God has spoken to you and commanded you to be a support for your sister in a difficult circumstance. What can you do to help? Offer to watch her kids so she can get out and run some errands. Make her a tasty and nutritious meal or invite her and her family to your house for a meal. Listen and be a friend. God is pleased when we watch over his children.

—J. Thompson

### read

Deuteronomy 24; see also Genesis 16:1–16; 21:8–21; Psalm 68:4–6.

**See also** the Inspire Notes "Motherhood," "Loneliness" and "Single Parenting," and the Women of the Bible Notes "Hagar: Battered, Beaten and Rejected—but Not Abandoned" and "The Prophet's Widow: God Provides."

### WOMAN of COLOR

Remind yourself and others today that God loves and cares for all of his children.

For the next Inspire note, go to page 240.

say, "This is what is done to the man who will not build up his brother's family line." 10 That man's line shall be known in Israel as The Family of the Unsandaled.

11 If two men are fighting and the wife of one of them comes to rescue her husband from his assailant, and she reaches out and seizes him by his private parts, 12 you shall cut off her hand. Show her no pity.

13 Do not have two differing weights in your bag—one heavy, one light.[e] 14 Do not have two differing measures in your house—one large, one small. 15 You must have accurate and honest weights and measures, so that you may live long in the land the LORD your God is giving you. 16 For the LORD your God detests anyone who does these things, anyone who deals dishonestly.[f]

17 Remember what the Amalekites[g] did to you along the way when you came out of Egypt. 18 When you were weary and worn out, they met you on your journey and cut off all who were lagging behind; they had no fear of God. 19 When the LORD your God gives you rest from all the enemies around you in the land he is giving you to possess as an inheritance, you shall blot out the memory of Amalek[h] from under heaven. Do not forget!

## Firstfruits and Tithes

26 When you have entered the land the LORD your God is giving you as an inheritance and have taken possession of it and settled in it, 2 take some of the firstfruits[i] of all that you produce from the soil of the land the LORD your God is giving you and put them in a basket. Then go to the place the LORD your God will choose as a dwelling for his Name 3 and say to the priest in office at the time, "I declare today to the LORD your God that I have come to the land the LORD swore to our forefathers to give us." 4 The priest shall take the basket from your hands and set it down in front of the altar of the LORD your God. 5 Then you shall declare before the LORD your God: "My father was a wandering Aramean, and he went down into Egypt with a few people[j] and lived there and became a great nation, powerful and numerous. 6 But the Egyptians mistreated us and made us suffer,[k] putting us to hard labor. 7 Then we cried out to the LORD, the God of our fathers, and the LORD heard our voice[l] and saw our misery, toil and oppression. 8 So the LORD brought us out of Egypt with a mighty hand and an outstretched arm, with great terror and with miraculous signs and wonders.[m] 9 He brought us to this place and gave us this land, a land flowing with milk and honey;[n] 10 and now I bring the firstfruits of the soil that you, O LORD, have given me." Place the basket before the LORD your God and bow down before him. 11 And you and the Levites[o] and the aliens among you shall rejoice in all the good things the LORD your God has given to you and your household.

12 When you have finished setting aside a tenth of all your produce in the third year, the year of the tithe,[p] you shall give it to the Levite, the alien, the fatherless and the widow, so that they may eat in your towns and be satisfied. 13 Then say to the LORD your God: "I have removed from my house the sacred portion and have given it to the Levite, the alien, the fatherless and the widow, according to all you commanded. I have not turned aside from your commands nor have I forgotten any of them.[q] 14 I have not eaten any of the sacred portion while I was in mourning, nor have I removed any of it while I was unclean, nor have I offered any of it to the dead. I have obeyed the LORD my God; I have done everything you commanded me. 15 Look down from heaven, your holy dwelling place, and bless your people Israel and the land you have given us as you promised on oath to our forefathers, a land flowing with milk and honey."

## Follow the LORD's Commands

16 The LORD your God commands you this day to follow these decrees and laws; carefully observe them with all your heart and with all your soul. 17 You have declared this day that the LORD is your God and that you will walk in his ways, that you will keep his decrees, commands and laws, and that you will obey him. 18 And the LORD has declared this day that you are his people, his treasured possession[r] as he promised, and that you are to keep all his commands. 19 He has declared that he will set you in praise,

**25:13** e Lev 19:35–37
**25:16** f Pr 11:1
**25:17** g Ex 17:8
**25:19** h 1Sa 15:2–3
**26:2** i Ex 23:16,19; Nu 18:13
**26:5** j Ge 43:1–2; 46:27; Dt 10:22
**26:6** k Ex 1:11,14
**26:7** l Ex 2:23–25
**26:8** m Dt 4:34
**26:9** n Ex 3:8
**26:11** o Dt 12:7
**26:12** p Dt 14:28–29
**26:13** q Ps 119:141, 153,176
**26:18** r Dt 7:6

26:19
s Dt28:1,13,44
t Dt7:6

27:2
u Jos8:31

27:5
v Jos8:31
w Ex20:25

*God,*

*I desire to be holy and pure. Cleanse me and make me whole. Give me the strength to follow you, and you alone.*

*Amen*

DEUTERONOMY 26:16–19

fame and honor high above all the nations[s] he has made and that you will be a people holy[t] to the LORD your God, as he promised.

## The Altar on Mount Ebal

27 Moses and the elders of Israel commanded the people: "Keep all these commands that I give you today.
[2]When you have crossed the Jordan into the land the LORD your God is giving you, set up some large stones and coat them with plaster.[u] [3]Write on them all the words of this law when you have crossed over to enter the land the LORD your God is giving you, a land flowing with milk and honey, just as the LORD, the God of your fathers, promised you. [4]And when you have crossed the Jordan, set up these stones on Mount Ebal, as I command you today, and coat them with plaster. [5]Build there an altar[v] to the LORD your God, an altar of stones. Do not use any iron tool[w] upon them. [6]Build the altar of the LORD your God with fieldstones and offer burnt offerings on it to the LORD your God. [7]Sacrifice fellowship offerings[a] there, eating them and rejoicing in the presence of the LORD your God. [8]And you shall write very clearly all the words of this law on these stones you have set up."

## Curses From Mount Ebal

[9]Then Moses and the priests, who are Levites, said to all Israel, "Be silent, O Israel, and listen! You have now become the people of the LORD your God. [10]Obey the LORD your God and follow his commands and decrees that I give you today."

[a]7 Traditionally *peace offerings*

[11]On the same day Moses commanded the people:

[12]When you have crossed the Jordan, these tribes shall stand on Mount Gerizim to bless the people: Simeon, Levi, Judah, Issachar, Joseph and Benjamin.[x] [13]And these tribes shall stand on Mount Ebal to pronounce curses: Reuben, Gad, Asher, Zebulun, Dan and Naphtali.

[14]The Levites shall recite to all the people of Israel in a loud voice:

[15]"Cursed is the man who carves an image or casts an idol[y]—a thing detestable to the LORD, the work of the craftsman's hands—and sets it up in secret."

Then all the people shall say, "Amen!"

[16]"Cursed is the man who dishonors his father or his mother."[z]

Then all the people shall say, "Amen!"

[17]"Cursed is the man who moves his neighbor's boundary stone."

Then all the people shall say, "Amen!"

[18]"Cursed is the man who leads the blind astray on the road."[a]

Then all the people shall say, "Amen!"

[19]"Cursed is the man who withholds justice from the alien,[b] the fatherless or the widow."[c]

Then all the people shall say, "Amen!"

*Woman of color,*

*Remember what I have done for you and your people. Give thanks and celebrate!*

*The God and Father of All*

DEUTERONOMY 27:1–8

27:12
x Jos8:35

27:15
y Ex20:4; 34:17

27:16
z Ex21:17

27:18
a Lev19:14

27:19
b Dt24:19
c Dt10:18

27:20 d Lev 18:7; Dt 22:30
27:21 e Lev 18:23
27:22 f Lev 18:9
27:24 g Lev 24:17; Nu 35:31
27:25 h Ex 23:7–8
27:26 i Gal 3:10*
28:1 j Dt 26:19
28:3 k Ge 39:5
28:6 l Ps 121:8

20“Cursed is the man who sleeps with his father’s wife, for he dishonors his father’s bed.”[d]

Then all the people shall say, “Amen!”

21“Cursed is the man who has sexual relations with any animal.”[e]

Then all the people shall say, “Amen!”

22“Cursed is the man who sleeps with his sister, the daughter of his father or the daughter of his mother.”[f]

Then all the people shall say, “Amen!”

23“Cursed is the man who sleeps with his mother-in-law.”

Then all the people shall say, “Amen!”

24“Cursed is the man who kills[g] his neighbor secretly.”

Then all the people shall say, “Amen!”

25“Cursed is the man who accepts a bribe to kill an innocent person.”[h]

Then all the people shall say, “Amen!”

26“Cursed is the man who does not uphold the words of this law by carrying them out.”[i]

Then all the people shall say, “Amen!”

## Blessings for Obedience

**28** If you fully obey the LORD your God and carefully follow all his commands I give you today, the LORD your God will set you high above all the nations on earth.[j] 2All these blessings will come upon you and accompany you if you obey the LORD your God:

3You will be blessed in the city and blessed in the country.[k]

4The fruit of your womb will be blessed, and the crops of your land and the young of your livestock—the calves of your herds and the lambs of your flocks.

5Your basket and your kneading trough will be blessed.

6You will be blessed when you come in and blessed when you go out.[l]

7The LORD will grant that the enemies who rise up against you will be defeated before you. They will come at you from one direction but flee from you in seven.

8The LORD will send a blessing on your barns and on everything you put your hand to. The LORD your God will bless you in the land he is giving you.

9The LORD will establish you as his holy people,[m] as he promised you on oath, if you keep the commands of the LORD your God and walk in his ways. 10Then all the peoples on earth will see that you are called by the name[n] of the LORD, and they will fear you. 11The LORD will grant you abundant prosperity—in the fruit of your womb, the young of your livestock and the crops of your ground—in the land he swore to your forefathers to give you.

12The LORD will open the heavens, the storehouse of his bounty, to send rain[o] on your land in season and to bless all the work of your hands. You will lend to many nations but will borrow from none. 13The LORD will make you the head, not the tail. If you pay attention to the commands of the LORD your God that I give you this day and carefully follow them, you will always be at the top, never at the bottom. 14Do not turn aside from any of the commands I give you today, to the right or to the left,[p] following other gods and serving them.

## Curses for Disobedience

15However, if you do not obey[q] the LORD your God and do not carefully follow all his commands and decrees I am giving you today, all these curses will come upon you and overtake you:[r]

16You will be cursed in the city and cursed in the country.

17Your basket and your kneading trough will be cursed.

18The fruit of your womb will be cursed, and the crops of your land, and the calves of your herds and the lambs of your flocks.

19You will be cursed when you come in and cursed when you go out.

20The LORD will send on you curses,[s] confusion and rebuke[t] in everything you put

28:9 m Ex 19:6
28:10 n 2Ch 7:14
28:12 o Lev 26:4
28:14 p Dt 5:32
28:15 q Lev 26:14 r Jos 23:15
28:20 s Mal 2:2 t Isa 51:20

**28:21** u Lev 26:25
**28:22** v Lev 26:16 w Am 4:9
**28:25** x Jer 15:4
**28:26** y Jer 7:33; 16:4
**28:30** z Jer 8:10 a Am 5:11
**28:33** b Jer 5:15–17

your hand to, until you are destroyed and come to sudden ruin because of the evil you have done in forsaking him.[a] 21The LORD will plague you with diseases until he has destroyed you from the land you are entering to possess.[u] 22The LORD will strike you with wasting disease, with fever and inflammation, with scorching heat and drought,[v] with blight and mildew, which will plague you until you perish.[w] 23The sky over your head will be bronze, the ground beneath you iron. 24The LORD will turn the rain of your country into dust and powder; it will come down from the skies until you are destroyed.

25The LORD will cause you to be defeated before your enemies. You will come at them from one direction but flee from them in seven, and you will become a thing of horror to all the kingdoms on earth.[x] 26Your carcasses will be food for all the birds of the air and the beasts of the earth, and there will be no one to frighten them away.[y] 27The LORD will afflict you with the boils of Egypt and with tumors, festering sores and the itch, from which you cannot be cured. 28The LORD will afflict you with madness, blindness and confusion of mind. 29At midday you will grope about like a blind man in the dark. You will be unsuccessful in everything you do; day after day you will be oppressed and robbed, with no one to rescue you.

30You will be pledged to be married to a woman, but another will take her and ravish her.[z] You will build a house, but you will not live in it.[a] You will plant a vineyard, but you will not even begin to enjoy its fruit. 31Your ox will be slaughtered before your eyes, but you will eat none of it. Your donkey will be forcibly taken from you and will not be returned. Your sheep will be given to your enemies, and no one will rescue them. 32Your sons and daughters will be given to another nation, and you will wear out your eyes watching for them day after day, powerless to lift a hand. 33A people that you do not know will eat what your land and labor produce, and you will have nothing but cruel oppression all your days.[b] 34The sights you see will drive you mad. 35The LORD will afflict your knees and legs with painful boils that cannot be cured, spreading from the soles of your feet to the top of your head.

36The LORD will drive you and the king[c] you set over you to a nation unknown to you or your fathers.[d] There you will worship other gods, gods of wood and stone.[e] 37You will become a thing of horror and an object of scorn and ridicule to all the nations where the LORD will drive you.[f]

38You will sow much seed in the field but you will harvest little,[g] because locusts will devour[h] it. 39You will plant vineyards and cultivate them but you will not drink the wine or gather the grapes, because worms will eat them. 40You will have olive trees throughout your country but you will not use the oil, because the olives will drop off. 41You will have sons and daughters but you will not keep them, because they will go into captivity. 42Swarms of locusts will take over all your trees and the crops of your land.

43The alien who lives among you will rise above you higher and higher, but you will sink lower and lower.[i] 44He will lend to you, but you will not lend to him.[j] He will be the head, but you will be the tail.

45All these curses will come upon you. They will pursue you and overtake you until you are destroyed, because you did not obey the LORD your God and observe the commands and decrees he gave you. 46They will be a sign and a wonder to you and your descendants forever.[k] 47Because you did not serve the LORD your God joyfully and gladly in the time of prosperity, 48therefore in hunger and thirst, in nakedness and dire poverty, you will serve the enemies the LORD sends against you. He will put an iron yoke[l] on your neck until he has destroyed you.

49The LORD will bring a nation against you from far away, from the ends of the earth,[m] like an eagle[n] swooping down, a nation whose language you will not understand, 50a fierce-looking nation without respect for the old or pity for the young. 51They will devour the young of your livestock and the crops of your land until you are destroyed. They will leave you no grain, new wine or oil, nor any calves of your herds or lambs of your flocks until you are ruined. 52They will lay siege to all the cities throughout your

**28:36** c 2Ki 17:4,6; 24:12,14 d Jer 16:13 e Dt 4:28
**28:37** f Jer 24:9
**28:38** g Mic 6:15; Hag 1:6,9 h Joel 1:4
**28:43** i ver 13
**28:44** j ver 12
**28:46** k Isa 8:18
**28:48** l Jer 28:13–14
**28:49** m Jer 5:15 n Hos 8:1

[a] 20 Hebrew *me*

**28:52** o Zep 1:14–16,17
**28:53** p Lev 26:29; Jer 19:9; La 2:20
**28:62** q Dt 4:27; 10:22
**28:64** r Dt 4:27

land until the high fortified walls in which you trust fall down. They will besiege all the cities throughout the land the LORD your God is giving you.[o]

53 Because of the suffering that your enemy will inflict on you during the siege, you will eat the fruit of the womb, the flesh of the sons and daughters the LORD your God has given you.[p] 54 Even the most gentle and sensitive man among you will have no compassion on his own brother or the wife he loves or his surviving children, 55 and he will not give to one of them any of the flesh of his children that he is eating. It will be all he has left because of the suffering your enemy will inflict on you during the siege of all your cities. 56 The most gentle and sensitive woman among you—so sensitive and gentle that she would not venture to touch the ground with the sole of her foot—will begrudge the husband she loves and her own son or daughter 57 the afterbirth from her womb and the children she bears. For she intends to eat them secretly during the siege and in the distress that your enemy will inflict on you in your cities.

58 If you do not carefully follow all the words of this law, which are written in this book, and do not revere this glorious and awesome name—the LORD your God— 59 the LORD will send fearful plagues on you and your descendants, harsh and prolonged disasters, and severe and lingering illnesses. 60 He will bring upon you all the diseases of Egypt that you dreaded, and they will cling to you. 61 The LORD will also bring on you every kind of sickness and disaster not recorded in this Book of the Law, until you are destroyed. 62 You who were as numerous as the stars in the sky[q] will be left but few in number, because you did not obey the LORD your God. 63 Just as it pleased the LORD to make you prosper and increase in number, so it will please him to ruin and destroy you. You will be uprooted from the land you are entering to possess.

64 Then the LORD will scatter[r] you among all nations, from one end of the earth to the other. There you will worship other gods—gods of wood and stone, which neither you nor your fathers have known. 65 Among those nations you will find no repose, no resting place for the sole of your foot. There the LORD will give you an anxious mind, eyes weary with longing, and a despairing heart.[s] 66 You will live in constant suspense, filled with dread both night and day, never sure of your life. 67 In the morning you will say, "If only it were evening!" and in the evening, "If only it were morning!"—because of the terror that will fill your hearts and the sights that your eyes will see. 68 The LORD will send you back in ships to Egypt on a journey I said you should never make again. There you will offer yourselves for sale to your enemies as male and female slaves, but no one will buy you.

## Renewal of the Covenant

**29** These are the terms of the covenant the LORD commanded Moses to make with the Israelites in Moab, in addition to the covenant he had made with them at Horeb.[t]

2 Moses summoned all the Israelites and said to them:

Your eyes have seen all that the LORD did in Egypt to Pharaoh, to all his officials and to all his land. 3 With your own eyes you saw those great trials, those miraculous signs and great wonders. 4 But to this day the LORD has not given you a mind that understands or eyes that see or ears that hear.[u] 5 During the forty years that I led you through the desert, your clothes did not wear out, nor did the sandals on your feet.[v] 6 You ate no bread and drank no wine or other fermented drink. I did this so that you might know that I am the LORD your God.[w]

7 When you reached this place, Sihon king of Heshbon and Og king of Bashan came out to fight against us, but we defeated them.[x] 8 We took their land and gave it as an inheritance to the Reubenites, the Gadites and the half-tribe of Manasseh.[y]

9 Carefully follow[z] the terms of this covenant, so that you may prosper in everything you do. 10 All of you are standing today in the presence of the LORD your God—your leaders and chief men, your elders and officials, and all the other men of Israel, 11 together with your children and your wives, and the aliens living in your camps who chop your wood and carry your water.[a]

**28:65** s Lev 26:16,36
**29:1** t Dt 5:2–3
**29:4** u Isa 6:10; Ac 28:26–27; Ro 11:8*
**29:5** v Dt 8:4
**29:6** w Dt 8:3
**29:7** x Nu 21:21–24,33–35
**29:8** y Nu 32:33; Dt 3:12–13
**29:9** z Dt 4:6; Jos 1:7
**29:11** a Jos 9:21,23,27

**29:13** b Ge 17:7; Ex 6:7
**29:18** c Heb 12:15
**29:20** d Ps 74:1; 79:5 e Dt 9:14
**29:22** f Jer 19:8
**29:23** g Zep 2:9
**29:24** h Jer 22:8–9

12 You are standing here in order to enter into a covenant with the LORD your God, a covenant the LORD is making with you this day and sealing with an oath, 13 to confirm you this day as his people, that he may be your God[b] as he promised you and as he swore to your fathers, Abraham, Isaac and Jacob. 14 I am making this covenant, with its oath, not only with you 15 who are standing here with us today in the presence of the LORD our God but also with those who are not here today.

16 You yourselves know how we lived in Egypt and how we passed through the countries on the way here. 17 You saw among them their detestable images and idols of wood and stone, of silver and gold. 18 Make sure there is no man or woman, clan or tribe among you today whose heart turns away from the LORD our God to go and worship the gods of those nations; make sure there is no root among you that produces such bitter poison.[c]

19 When such a person hears the words of this oath, he invokes a blessing on himself and therefore thinks, "I will be safe, even though I persist in going my own way." This will bring disaster on the watered land as well as the dry.[a] 20 The LORD will never be willing to forgive him; his wrath and zeal will burn[d] against that man. All the curses written in this book will fall upon him, and the LORD will blot[e] out his name from under heaven. 21 The LORD will single him out from all the tribes of Israel for disaster, according to all the curses of the covenant written in this Book of the Law.

22 Your children who follow you in later generations and foreigners who come from distant lands will see the calamities that have fallen on the land and the diseases with which the LORD has afflicted it.[f] 23 The whole land will be a burning waste of salt and sulfur—nothing planted, nothing sprouting, no vegetation growing on it. It will be like the destruction of Sodom and Gomorrah,[g] Admah and Zeboiim, which the LORD overthrew in fierce anger. 24 All the nations will ask: "Why has the LORD done this to this land?[h] Why this fierce, burning anger?"

25 And the answer will be: "It is because this people abandoned the covenant of the LORD, the God of their fathers, the covenant he made with them when he brought them out of Egypt. 26 They went off and worshiped other gods and bowed down to them, gods they did not know, gods he had not given them. 27 Therefore the LORD's anger burned against this land, so that he brought on it all the curses written in this book. 28 In furious anger and in great wrath the LORD uprooted[i] them from their land and thrust them into another land, as it is now."

29 The secret things belong to the LORD our God, but the things revealed belong to us and to our children forever, that we may follow all the words of this law.

## Prosperity After Turning to the LORD

**30** When all these blessings and curses[j] I have set before you come upon you and you take them to heart wherever the LORD your God disperses you among the nations,[k] 2 and when you and your children return[l] to the LORD your God and obey him with all your heart and with all your soul according to everything I command you today, 3 then the LORD your God will restore your fortunes[b][m] and have compassion on you and gather[n] you again from all the nations where he scattered you.[o] 4 Even if you have been banished to the most distant land under the heavens, from there the LORD your God will gather you and bring you back.[p] 5 He will bring you to the land that belonged to your fathers, and you will take possession of it. He will make you more prosperous and numerous than your fathers. 6 The LORD your God will circumcise your hearts and the hearts of your descendants,[q] so that you may love him with all your heart and with all your soul, and live. 7 The LORD your God will put all these curses on your enemies who hate and persecute you. 8 You will again obey the LORD and follow all his commands I am giving you today. 9 Then the LORD your God will make you most prosperous in all the work of your hands and in the fruit of your womb, the young of your livestock and the crops of your land.[r] The LORD will again delight in you and make you prosper-

**29:28** i 1Ki 14:15; 2Ch 7:20
**30:1** j Dt 11:26 k 1Ki 8:47
**30:2** l Dt 4:30
**30:3** m Ps 126:4 n Jer 32:37; Eze 34:13 o Jer 29:14
**30:4** p Ne 1:8–9; Isa 43:6
**30:6** q Jer 32:39
**30:9** r 32:41

[a]19 Or *way, in order to add drunkenness to thirst."* [b]3 Or *will bring you back from captivity*

ous, just as he delighted in your fathers, 10 if you obey the LORD your God and keep his commands and decrees that are written in this Book of the Law and turn to the LORD your God with all your heart and with all your soul.

## The Offer of Life or Death

11 Now what I am commanding you today is not too difficult for you or beyond your reach. 12 It is not up in heaven, so that you have to ask, "Who will ascend into heaven to get it and proclaim it to us so we may obey it?"[s] 13 Nor is it beyond the sea, so that you have to ask, "Who will cross the sea to get it and proclaim it to us so we may obey it?" 14 No, the word is very near you; it is in your mouth and in your heart so you may obey it.

15 See, I set before you today life and prosperity, death and destruction.[t] 16 For I command you today to love the LORD your God, to walk in his ways, and to keep his commands, decrees and laws; then you will live and increase, and the LORD your God will bless you in the land you are entering to possess.

17 But if your heart turns away and you are not obedient, and if you are drawn away to bow down to other gods and worship them, 18 I declare to you this day that you will certainly be destroyed.[u] You will not live long in the land you are crossing the Jordan to enter and possess.

19 This day I call heaven and earth as witnesses against you[v] that I have set before you life and death, blessings and curses. Now choose life, so that you and your children may live 20 and that you may love the LORD your God, listen to his voice, and hold fast to him. For the LORD is your life, and he will give you many years in the land he swore to give to your fathers, Abraham, Isaac and Jacob.

## Joshua to Succeed Moses

31 Then Moses went out and spoke these words to all Israel: 2 "I am now a hundred and twenty years old[w] and I am no longer able to lead you. The LORD has said to me, 'You shall not cross the Jordan.'[x] 3 The LORD your God himself will cross over ahead of you.[y] He will destroy these nations before you, and you will take possession of their land. Joshua also will cross over ahead of you, as the LORD said. 4 And the LORD will do to them what he did to Sihon and Og, the kings of the Amorites, whom he destroyed along with their land. 5 The LORD will deliver[z] them to you, and you must do to them all that I have commanded you. 6 Be strong and courageous.[a] Do not be afraid or terrified because of them, for the LORD your God goes with you;[b] he will never leave you nor forsake[c] you."

7 Then Moses summoned Joshua and said[d] to him in the presence of all Israel, "Be strong and courageous, for you must go with this people into the land that the LORD swore to their forefathers to give them, and you must divide it among them as their inheritance. 8 The LORD himself goes before you and will be with you; he will never leave you nor forsake you. Do not be afraid; do not be discouraged."

## The Reading of the Law

9 So Moses wrote down this law and gave it to the priests, the sons of Levi, who carried[e] the ark of the covenant of the LORD, and to all the elders of Israel. 10 Then Moses commanded them: "At the end of every seven years, in the year for canceling debts,[f] during the Feast of Tabernacles,[g] 11 when all Israel comes to appear[h] before the LORD your God at the place he will choose, you shall read this law[i] before them in their hearing. 12 Assemble the people—men, women and children, and the aliens living in your towns—so they can listen and learn[j] to fear the LORD your God and follow carefully all the words of this law. 13 Their children, who do not know this law, must hear it and learn to fear the LORD your God as long as you live in the land you are crossing the Jordan to possess."

## Israel's Rebellion Predicted

14 The LORD said to Moses, "Now the day of your death is near. Call Joshua and present yourselves at the Tent of Meeting, where I will commission him." So Moses and Joshua came and presented themselves at the Tent of Meeting.

**30:12** s Ro 10:6*
**30:15** t Dt 11:26
**30:18** u Dt 8:19
**30:19** v Dt 4:26
**31:2** w Dt 34:7 x Dt 3:23,26
**31:3** y Dt 9:3
**31:5** z Dt 7:2
**31:6** a Jos 10:25 b Dt 1:29; 20:4 c Heb 13:5*
**31:7** d Dt 1:38; 3:28
**31:9** e ver 25; Nu 4:15
**31:10** f Dt 15:1 g Lev 23:34
**31:11** h Dt 16:16 i Jos 8:34–35
**31:12** j Dt 4:10

**31:15** k Ex 33:9
**31:16** l Jdg 2:12; m Jdg 10:6,13
**31:17** n Jdg 6:13; o Nu 14:42
**31:20** p Dt 32:15–17
**31:23** q ver 7; r Jos 1:6
**31:27** s Dt 9:6,24

15 Then the LORD appeared at the Tent in a pillar of cloud, and the cloud stood over the entrance to the Tent.[k] 16 And the LORD said to Moses: "You are going to rest with your fathers, and these people will soon prostitute[l] themselves to the foreign gods of the land they are entering. They will forsake[m] me and break the covenant I made with them. 17 On that day I will become angry with them and forsake[n] them; I will hide my face from them, and they will be destroyed. Many disasters and difficulties will come upon them, and on that day they will ask, 'Have not these disasters come upon us because our God is not with us?'[o] 18 And I will certainly hide my face on that day because of all their wickedness in turning to other gods.

19 "Now write down for yourselves this song and teach it to the Israelites and have them sing it, so that it may be a witness for me against them. 20 When I have brought them into the land flowing with milk and honey, the land I promised on oath to their forefathers, and when they eat their fill and thrive, they will turn to other gods[p] and worship them, rejecting me and breaking my covenant. 21 And when many disasters and difficulties come upon them, this song will testify against them, because it will not be forgotten by their descendants. I know what they are disposed to do, even before I bring them into the land I promised them on oath." 22 So Moses wrote down this song that day and taught it to the Israelites.

23 The LORD gave this command[q] to Joshua son of Nun: "Be strong and courageous,[r] for you will bring the Israelites into the land I promised them on oath, and I myself will be with you."

24 After Moses finished writing in a book the words of this law from beginning to end, 25 he gave this command to the Levites who carried the ark of the covenant of the LORD: 26 "Take this Book of the Law and place it beside the ark of the covenant of the LORD your God. There it will remain as a witness against you. 27 For I know how rebellious and stiff-necked[s] you are. If you have been rebellious against the LORD while I am still alive and with you, how much more will you rebel after I die! 28 Assemble before me all the elders of your tribes and all your officials, so that I can speak these words in their hearing and call heaven and earth to testify against them.[t] 29 For I know that after my death you are sure to become utterly corrupt and to turn from the way I have commanded you. In days to come, disaster will fall upon you because you will do evil in the sight of the LORD and provoke him to anger by what your hands have made."

### The Song of Moses

30 And Moses recited the words of this song from beginning to end in the hearing of the whole assembly of Israel:

**32** Listen, O heavens,[u] and I will speak;
hear, O earth, the words of my mouth.
2 Let my teaching fall like rain
and my words descend like dew,[v]
like showers on new grass,
like abundant rain on tender plants.
3 I will proclaim the name of the LORD.[w]
Oh, praise the greatness of our God!
4 He is the Rock, his works are perfect,[x]
and all his ways are just.
A faithful God who does no wrong,
upright and just is he.
5 They have acted corruptly toward him;
to their shame they are no longer his children,
but a warped and crooked generation.[a][y]
6 Is this the way you repay[z] the LORD,
O foolish and unwise people?
Is he not your Father,[a] your Creator,[b]
who made you and formed you?
7 Remember the days of old;
consider the generations long past.
Ask your father and he will tell you,
your elders, and they will explain to you.
8 When the Most High gave the nations their inheritance,
when he divided all mankind,[b]
he set up boundaries for the peoples
according to the number of the sons of Israel.[c]

**31:28** t Dt 4:26; 32:1
**32:1** u Isa 1:2
**32:2** v Isa 55:11
**32:3** w Ex 33:19
**32:4** x 2Sa 22:31
**32:5** y Dt 31:29
**32:6** z Ps 116:12; a Isa 63:16
**32:8** b Ge 11:8; Ac 17:26

[a]5 Or *Corrupt are they and not his children, / a generation warped and twisted to their shame* [b]6 Or *Father, who bought you* [c]8 Masoretic Text; Dead Sea Scrolls (see also Septuagint) *sons of God*

32:9 c Jer 10:16
32:10 d Ps 17:8; Zec 2:8
32:11 e Ex 19:4
32:13 f Isa 58:14
32:14 g Ps 81:16
32:15 h Dt 31:20 i Isa 1:4,28
32:16 j 1Co 10:22
32:17 k Dt 28:64
32:19 l Ps 106:40
32:20 m Dt 31:17,29

9 For the LORD's portion[c] is his people,
Jacob his allotted inheritance.

10 In a desert land he found him,
in a barren and howling waste.
He shielded him and cared for him;
he guarded him as the apple of his eye,[d]
11 like an eagle that stirs up its nest
and hovers over its young,[e]
that spreads its wings to catch them
and carries them on its pinions.
12 The LORD alone led him;
no foreign god was with him.
13 He made him ride on the heights[f] of the land
and fed him with the fruit of the fields.
He nourished him with honey from the rock,
and with oil from the flinty crag,
14 with curds and milk from herd and flock
and with fattened lambs and goats,
with choice rams of Bashan
and the finest kernels of wheat.[g]
You drank the foaming blood of the grape.

15 Jeshurun[a] grew fat[h] and kicked;
filled with food, he became heavy and sleek.
He abandoned[i] the God who made him
and rejected the Rock his Savior.
16 They made him jealous[j] with their foreign gods
and angered him with their detestable idols.
17 They sacrificed to demons, which are not God—
gods they had not known,[k]
gods that recently appeared,
gods your fathers did not fear.
18 You deserted the Rock, who fathered you;
you forgot the God who gave you birth.

19 The LORD saw this and rejected them
because he was angered by his sons and daughters.[l]
20 "I will hide my face[m] from them," he said,
"and see what their end will be;
for they are a perverse generation,
children who are unfaithful.
21 They made me jealous by what is no god
and angered me with their worthless idols.
I will make them envious by those who are not a people;
I will make them angry by a nation
that has no understanding.[n]
22 For a fire has been kindled by my wrath,
one that burns to the realm of death[b] below.[o]
It will devour the earth and its harvests
and set afire the foundations of the mountains.

23 "I will heap calamities[p] upon them
and spend my arrows against them.
24 I will send wasting famine against them,
consuming pestilence[q] and deadly plague;
I will send against them the fangs of wild beasts,[r]
the venom of vipers that glide in the dust.
25 In the street the sword will make them childless;
in their homes terror will reign.[s]
Young men and young women will perish,
infants and gray-haired men.[t]
26 I said I would scatter[u] them
and blot out their memory from mankind,
27 but I dreaded the taunt of the enemy,
lest the adversary misunderstand
and say, 'Our hand has triumphed;
the LORD has not done all this.' "
28 They are a nation without sense,
there is no discernment in them.
29 If only they were wise and would understand this
and discern what their end will be!
30 How could one man chase a thousand,
or two put ten thousand to flight,[v]
unless their Rock had sold them,
unless the LORD had given them up?[w]
31 For their rock is not like our Rock,
as even our enemies concede.
32 Their vine comes from the vine of Sodom
and from the fields of Gomorrah.
Their grapes are filled with poison,
and their clusters with bitterness.

32:21 n Ro 10:19*
32:22 o La 4:11
32:23 p Dt 29:21
32:24 q Dt 28:22 r Lev 26:22
32:25 s Eze 7:15 t 2Ch 36:17
32:26 u Dt 4:27
32:30 v Lev 26:8 w Ps 44:12

[a]15 *Jeshurun* means *the upright one*, that is, Israel. [b]22 Hebrew *to Sheol*

# Inspire

## GOD IS A JEALOUS GOD

As a woman of color and an ordained minister, I have often contemplated the divine attributes of God. My Creator is immutable, omnipotent, omnipresent, omniscient, perfect, holy and infinite—the divine nature! Yet, this unequaled God allows this humble daughter to share in and experience God's attributes of love, goodness, justice, mercy, wisdom and jealousy. Jealousy? Yes, God is jealous!

From a social, cultural, mental, emotional and historical perspective, the term jealousy signals a condition of being possessive, resentful, insecure, distrusting and angry. We see these characteristics displayed even among the Christian sisters—clergy sisters included! However, the divine jealousy is something different. It aligns with the character of God.

Understandably, jealousy is an unusual concept to attribute to a holy God. In the secular sense, the word *jealousy* is negatively defined in terms of human relationships. However, divine jealousy aligns with the character of God. God's divine jealousy does not covet something that belongs to another but covets something that belongs to him. We read in Deuteronomy 32:16, for instance, that the Israelites "made [God] jealous with their foreign gods." The relationship between God and his children is to be exclusive.

The key to understanding God's divine jealousy is in God's covenant: "You shall have no other gods before me. You shall not make for yourself an idol [graven image] . . . You shall not bow down to them or worship them; for I, the Lord your God, am a jealous God" (Ex 20:3–5). And God also said to his people, "Do not worship any other god, for the Lord, whose name is Jealous, is a jealous God" (Ex 34:14).

Yes, God is divinely jealous and madly in love with you! Don't worship anyone or anything other than your God. Honor your relationship with your Creator and Savior more than anything or anyone else.

—W. Blagmond

### read

Deuteronomy 32:15–21; see also Exodus 34:14,27; Deuteronomy 6:14–15; 1 Corinthians 10:18–22; James 4:4–5.

See also the Inspire Notes "The Faithfulness of God" and "Commitment to God."

### WOMAN of COLOR

How are you honoring your relationship with God more than your relationship with anyone or anything else?

For the next Inspire note, go to page 285.

**32:33** x Ps 58:4
**32:35** y Ro 12:19*; Heb 10:30*
**32:36** z Ps 135:14; Joel 2:14
**32:37** a Jdg 10:14; Jer 2:28
**32:39** b Isa 41:4 c Isa 45:5 d Ps 50:22
**32:41** e Isa 66:16 f Jer 50:29
**32:42** g Jer 46:10,14
**32:43** h Ro 15:10* i Ps 85:1; Rev 19:2

33 Their wine is the venom of serpents,
the deadly poison of cobras.[x]
34 "Have I not kept this in reserve
and sealed it in my vaults?
35 It is mine to avenge; I will repay.[y]
In due time their foot will slip;
their day of disaster is near
and their doom rushes upon them."

36 The LORD will judge his people
and have compassion on his servants[z]
when he sees their strength is gone
and no one is left, slave or free.
37 He will say: "Now where are their gods,
the rock they took refuge in,[a]
38 the gods who ate the fat of their sacrifices
and drank the wine of their drink
offerings?
Let them rise up to help you!
Let them give you shelter!

39 "See now that I myself am He![b]
There is no god besides me.[c]
I put to death and I bring to life,
I have wounded and I will heal,
and no one can deliver out of my
hand.[d]
40 I lift my hand to heaven and declare:
As surely as I live forever,
41 when I sharpen my flashing sword[e]
and my hand grasps it in judgment,
I will take vengeance on my adversaries
and repay those who hate me.[f]
42 I will make my arrows drunk with blood,
while my sword devours flesh:[g]
the blood of the slain and the captives,
the heads of the enemy leaders."

43 Rejoice,[h] O nations, with his people,[a,b]
for he will avenge the blood of his
servants;
he will take vengeance on his enemies
and make atonement for his land and
people.[i]

44 Moses came with Joshua[c] son of Nun
and spoke all the words of this song in the
hearing of the people. 45 When Moses fin-
ished reciting all these words to all Israel,
46 he said to them, "Take to heart all the
words I have solemnly declared to you
this day,[j] so that you may command your
children to obey carefully all the words of
this law. 47 They are not just idle words for
you—they are your life. By them you will
live long in the land you are crossing the Jor-
dan to possess."

## Moses to Die on Mount Nebo

48 On that same day the LORD told Moses,
49 "Go up into the Abarim[k] Range to Mount
Nebo in Moab, across from Jericho, and
view Canaan, the land I am giving the Isra-
elites as their own possession. 50 There on
the mountain that you have climbed you
will die and be gathered to your people, just
as your brother Aaron died on Mount Hor
and was gathered to his people. 51 This is
because both of you broke faith with me in
the presence of the Israelites at the waters
of Meribah Kadesh in the Desert of Zin[l] and
because you did not uphold my holiness
among the Israelites. 52 Therefore, you will
see the land only from a distance;[m] you will
not enter the land I am giving to the people
of Israel."

## Moses Blesses the Tribes

33 This is the blessing that Moses the
man of God pronounced on the Isra-
elites before his death. 2 He said:

"The LORD came from Sinai
and dawned over them from Seir;
he shone forth from Mount Paran.[n]
He came with[d] myriads of holy ones[o]
from the south, from his mountain
slopes.[e]
3 Surely it is you who love the people;
all the holy ones are in your hand.
At your feet they all bow down,[p]
and from you receive instruction,
4 the law that Moses gave us,
the possession of the assembly of
Jacob.[q]
5 He was king over Jeshurun[f]
when the leaders of the people
assembled,
along with the tribes of Israel.

6 "Let Reuben live and not die,
nor[g] his men be few."

**32:46** j Eze 40:4
**32:49** k Nu 27:12
**32:51** l Nu 20:11–13
**32:52** m Dt 34:1–3
**33:2** n Hab 3:3 o Da 7:10; Rev 5:11
**33:3** p Lk 10:39
**33:4** q Ps 119:111

[a]43 Or *Make his people rejoice, O nations* [b]43 Masoretic Text; Dead Sea Scrolls (see also Septuagint) *people, / and let all the angels worship him /* [c]44 Hebrew *Hoshea,* a variant of *Joshua* [d]2 Or *from* [e]2 The meaning of the Hebrew for this phrase is uncertain. [f]5 *Jeshurun* means *the upright one,* that is, Israel; also in verse 26. [g]6 Or *but let*

**33:7** r Ge 49:10
**33:8** s Ex 28:30 t Ex 17:7
**33:9** u Ex 32:26–29
**33:10** v Ps 51:19
**33:13** w Ge 49:25 x Ge 27:28

7 And this he said about Judah:[r]

"Hear, O LORD, the cry of Judah;
bring him to his people.
With his own hands he defends his cause.
Oh, be his help against his foes!"

8 About Levi he said:

"Your Thummim and Urim[s] belong
to the man you favored.
You tested him at Massah;
you contended with him at the waters of Meribah.[t]
9 He said of his father and mother,[u]
'I have no regard for them.'
He did not recognize his brothers
or acknowledge his own children,
but he watched over your word
and guarded your covenant.
10 He teaches your precepts to Jacob
and your law to Israel.
He offers incense before you
and whole burnt offerings on your altar.[v]
11 Bless all his skills, O LORD,
and be pleased with the work of his hands.
Smite the loins of those who rise up against him;
strike his foes till they rise no more."

12 About Benjamin he said:

"Let the beloved of the LORD rest secure in him,
for he shields him all day long,
and the one the LORD loves rests between his shoulders."

13 About Joseph[w] he said:

"May the LORD bless his land
with the precious dew from heaven above
and with the deep waters that lie below;[x]
14 with the best the sun brings forth
and the finest the moon can yield;
15 with the choicest gifts of the ancient mountains
and the fruitfulness of the everlasting hills;
16 with the best gifts of the earth and its fullness
and the favor of him who dwelt in the burning bush.[y]
Let all these rest on the head of Joseph,
on the brow of the prince among[a] his brothers.
17 In majesty he is like a firstborn bull;
his horns are the horns of a wild ox.[z]
With them he will gore[a] the nations,
even those at the ends of the earth.
Such are the ten thousands of Ephraim;
such are the thousands of Manasseh."

18 About Zebulun[b] he said:

"Rejoice, Zebulun, in your going out,
and you, Issachar, in your tents.
19 They will summon peoples to the mountain[c]
and there offer sacrifices of righteousness;[d]
they will feast on the abundance of the seas,
on the treasures hidden in the sand."

20 About Gad he said:

"Blessed is he who enlarges Gad's domain!
Gad lives there like a lion,
tearing at arm or head.
21 He chose the best land for himself;
the leader's portion was kept for him.
When the heads of the people assembled,
he carried out the LORD's righteous will,[e]
and his judgments concerning Israel."

22 About Dan[f] he said:

"Dan is a lion's cub,
springing out of Bashan."

23 About Naphtali he said:

"Naphtali is abounding with the favor of the LORD
and is full of his blessing;
he will inherit southward to the lake."

24 About Asher[g] he said:

"Most blessed of sons is Asher;
let him be favored by his brothers,
and let him bathe his feet in oil.[h]

**33:16** y Ex 3:2
**33:17** z Nu 23:22 a Ps 44:5
**33:18** b Ge 49:13–15
**33:19** c Isa 2:3 d Ps 4:5
**33:21** e Jos 4:12
**33:22** f Ge 49:16
**33:24** g Ge 49:21 h Ge 49:20; Job 29:6

[a]16 Or *of the one separated from*

**33:26**
i Ex 15:11
**33:27**
j Ps 90:1
k Jos 24:18
**33:28**
l Ge 27:28
**33:29**
m Ps 144:15
n Ps 115:9–11
**34:1**
o Dt 32:49
p Dt 32:52

25 The bolts of your gates will be iron and
bronze,
and your strength will equal your
days.

26 "There is no one like the God of
Jeshurun,[i]
who rides on the heavens to help you
and on the clouds in his majesty.
27 The eternal God is your refuge,[j]
and underneath are the everlasting
arms.
He will drive out your enemy before you,[k]
saying, 'Destroy him!'
28 So Israel will live in safety alone;
Jacob's spring is secure
in a land of grain and new wine,
where the heavens drop dew.[l]
29 Blessed are you, O Israel![m]
Who is like you,
a people saved by the LORD?
He is your shield and helper[n]
and your glorious sword.
Your enemies will cower before you,
and you will trample down their high
places.[a]"

## The Death of Moses

34 Then Moses climbed Mount Nebo
from the plains of Moab to the top
of Pisgah, across from Jericho.[o] There the
LORD showed[p] him the whole land—from
Gilead to Dan, 2 all of Naphtali, the territory
of Ephraim and Manasseh, all the land of
Judah as far as the western sea,[b][q] 3 the Ne-
gev and the whole region from the Valley
of Jericho, the City of Palms,[r] as far as Zoar.
4 Then the LORD said to him, "This is the land
I promised on oath to Abraham, Isaac and
Jacob when I said, 'I will give it[s] to your de-
scendants.' I have let you see it with your
eyes, but you will not cross over into it."
5 And Moses the servant of the LORD died[t]
there in Moab, as the LORD had said. 6 He bur-
ied him[c] in Moab, in the valley opposite Beth
Peor, but to this day no one knows where his
grave is.[u] 7 Moses was a hundred and twenty
years old[v] when he died, yet his eyes were
not weak[w] nor his strength gone. 8 The Israel-
ites grieved for Moses in the plains of Moab
thirty days, until the time of weeping and
mourning was over.
9 Now Joshua son of Nun was filled with
the spirit[d] of wisdom[x] because Moses had
laid his hands on him.[y] So the Israelites
listened to him and did what the LORD had
commanded Moses.
10 Since then, no prophet has risen in
Israel like Moses,[z] whom the LORD knew
face to face,[a] 11 who did all those miraculous
signs and wonders the LORD sent him to do
in Egypt—to Pharaoh and to all his officials
and to his whole land. 12 For no one has ever
shown the mighty power or performed the
awesome deeds that Moses did in the sight
of all Israel.

**34:2**
q Dt 11:24
**34:3**
r 2Ch 28:15
**34:4**
s Ge 12:7
**34:5**
t Dt 32:50; Jos 1:1–2
**34:6**
u Jude 1:9
**34:7**
v Dt 31:2
w Ge 27:1
**34:9**
x Isa 11:2
y Nu 27:18,23
**34:10**
z Dt 18:15,18
a Ex 33:11; Nu 12:6,8; Dt 5:4

[a] 29 Or *will tread upon their bodies* [b] 2 That is, the Mediterranean [c] 6 Or *He was buried* [d] 9 Or *Spirit*

# Joshua

## OVERVIEW

After the death of Moses, God told Joshua that he would never leave him nor forsake him; therefore, he was to be strong and courageous. Joshua needed this encouragement as the new leader of the Israelites. In conquering the land, Joshua and the Israelites would need persistence and courage.

Joshua secretly sent his spies into the land. They infiltrated Jericho, where Rahab, the prostitute, hid them. She risked her life to save the spies, who faced certain death if they were discovered by the king of Jericho. In return, Joshua spared her life and the lives of her family during the destruction of that great city. Rahab is mentioned in Hebrews 11:31 and James 2:25 for her faith in God during turbulent times. Joshua would also lead the Israelites on amazing adventures that included crossing the flooded Jordan River (see Jos 3) and fighting to save the Gibeonites (see Jos 10).

The book of Joshua also records the land allotment for the people of Israel. Like Moses, his mentor and friend, Joshua encouraged the people to stay true to the one holy God.

There is a Jericho in every woman's life—a time of choosing God's direction and instruction over the influences of the world and the dictates of worldly desires. Sometimes God's ways seem impossible. However, a committed believer will look beyond the "foolishness" of praising God around a fortified city and experience his deliverance, as Joshua and the Israelites did.

## OUTLINE

I. The Entrance Into the Promised Land (1:1—4:24)
II. The Conquest of the Promised Land (5:1—12:24)
III. The Division of the Promised Land (13:1—22:34)
IV. Joshua's Last Words to the People (23:1–16)
V. Renewed Covenant With God (24:1–33)

### SCANNABLE FACTS:

**Author:** Unknown, but Joshua probably wrote much of the book in its earliest form

**Time Written:** Around the time of Joshua's death, about 1390 B.C.

**Themes to Note:** The conquest of the promised land; God keeps his promises

**Notable Women:** Rahab, Acsah

1:1 a Dt34:5
1:2 b ver11
1:3 c Dt11:24
1:4 d Ge15:18
1:5 e Dt7:24 f Dt31:6–8
1:6 g Dt31:23
1:7 h Dt5:32

## The LORD Commands Joshua

1 After the death of Moses the servant of the LORD,[a] the LORD said to Joshua son of Nun, Moses' aide: 2"Moses my servant is dead. Now then, you and all these people, get ready to cross the Jordan River[b] into the land I am about to give to them—to the Israelites. 3I will give you every place where you set your foot,[c] as I promised Moses. 4Your territory will extend from the desert to Lebanon, and from the great river, the Euphrates[d]—all the Hittite country—to the Great Sea[a] on the west. 5No one will be able to stand up against you[e] all the days of your life. As I was with Moses, so I will be with you; I will never leave you nor forsake[f] you.

6"Be strong and courageous, because you will lead these people to inherit the land I swore to their forefathers[g] to give them. 7Be strong and very courageous. Be careful to obey all the law my servant Moses gave you; do not turn from it to the right or to the left,[h] that you may be successful wherever you go. 8Do not let this Book of the Law depart from your mouth; meditate on it day and night, so that you may be careful to do everything written in it. Then you will be prosperous and successful.[i] 9Have I not commanded you? Be strong and courageous. Do not be terrified; do not be discouraged, for the LORD your God will be with you wherever you go."[j]

10So Joshua ordered the officers of the people: 11"Go through the camp and tell the people, 'Get your supplies ready. Three days from now you will cross the Jordan here to go in and take possession of the land the LORD your God is giving you for your own.' "

12But to the Reubenites, the Gadites and the half-tribe of Manasseh,[k] Joshua said, 13"Remember the command that Moses the servant of the LORD gave you: 'The LORD your God is giving you rest[l] and has granted you this land.' 14Your wives, your children and your livestock may stay in the land that Moses gave you east of the Jordan, but all your fighting men, fully armed, must cross over ahead of your brothers. You are to help your brothers 15until the LORD gives them rest, as he has done for you, and until they too have taken possession of the land that the LORD your God is giving them. After that, you may go back and occupy your own land, which Moses the servant of the LORD

1:8 i Ps1:1–3
1:9 j Dt31:7–8; Jer1:8
1:12 k Nu32:20–22
1:13 l Dt3:18–20

[a]4 That is, the Mediterranean

## The African Presence

### Joshua 1:1–5

When the Israelites came into the promised land, it was occupied by the descendants of Ham and Canaan. These people had departed from the moral standards of God and were to be dispossessed.

The name "Canaan" is used interchangeably for all of the ethnic groups residing in this geographic region: the Hittites, Girgashites, Amorites, Canaanites, Perizzites, Hivites and Jebusites. Some of the Canaanites were indigenous to the land, while others migrated to the region (the Sea Peoples). The Egyptians ruled Canaan for over 300 years. The peoples of Canaan represent an amalgam of skin colors.

There are strong arguments (Gottwald, Noth, et al) that Israel emerged from a socio-political peasant upheaval from within Canaan. Conflict between the Israelites in the northern highlands and the occupants of the lowlands (Canaanites) led to the animosity between the two groups. The Canaanites were cursed in Israelite memory because of their antagonistic political relationship.

gave you east of the Jordan toward the sunrise."[m]

16 Then they answered Joshua, "Whatever you have commanded us we will do, and wherever you send us we will go. 17 Just as we fully obeyed Moses, so we will obey you. Only may the LORD your God be with you as he was with Moses. 18 Whoever rebels against your word and does not obey your words, whatever you may command them, will be put to death. Only be strong and courageous!"

## Rahab and the Spies

2 Then Joshua son of Nun secretly sent two spies[n] from Shittim.[o] "Go, look over the land," he said, "especially Jericho." So they went and entered the house of a prostitute[a] named Rahab[p] and stayed there.

2 The king of Jericho was told, "Look! Some of the Israelites have come here tonight to spy out the land." 3 So the king of Jericho sent this message to Rahab: "Bring out the men who came to you and entered your house, because they have come to spy out the whole land."

4 But the woman had taken the two men and hidden them.[q] She said, "Yes, the men came to me, but I did not know where they had come from. 5 At dusk, when it was time to close the city gate, the men left. I don't know which way they went. Go after them quickly. You may catch up with them." 6 (But she had taken them up to the roof and hidden them under the stalks of flax[r] she had laid out on the roof.) 7 So the men set out in pursuit of the spies on the road that leads to the fords of the Jordan, and as soon as the pursuers had gone out, the gate was shut.

8 Before the spies lay down for the night, she went up on the roof 9 and said to them, "I know that the LORD has given this land to you and that a great fear[s] of you has fallen on us, so that all who live in this country are melting in fear because of you. 10 We have heard how the LORD dried up[t] the water of the Red Sea[b] for you when you came out of Egypt, and what you did to Sihon and Og,[u] the two kings of the Amorites east of the Jordan, whom you completely destroyed.[c] 11 When we heard of it, our hearts melted and everyone's courage failed because of you,[v] for the LORD your God is God in heaven above and on the earth[w] below. 12 Now then, please swear to me by the LORD that you will show kindness to my family, because I have shown kindness to you. Give me a sure sign[x] 13 that you will spare the lives of my father and mother, my brothers and sisters, and all who belong to them, and that you will save us from death."

14 "Our lives for your lives!" the men assured her. "If you don't tell what we are doing, we will treat you kindly and faithfully[y] when the LORD gives us the land."

15 So she let them down by a rope through the window, for the house she lived in was part of the city wall. 16 Now she had said to them, "Go to the hills so the pursuers will not find you. Hide yourselves there three days until they return, and then go on your way."

17 The men said to her, "This oath[z] you made us swear will not be binding on us 18 unless, when we enter the land, you have tied this scarlet cord in the window through which you let us down, and unless you have brought your father and mother, your brothers and all your family[a] into your house. 19 If anyone goes outside your house into the street, his blood will be on his own head; we will not be responsible. As for anyone who is in the house with you, his blood will be on our head[b] if a hand is laid on him. 20 But if you tell what we are doing, we will be released from the oath you made us swear."

21 "Agreed," she replied. "Let it be as you say." So she sent them away and they departed. And she tied the scarlet cord in the window.

22 When they left, they went into the hills and stayed there three days, until the pursuers had searched all along the road and returned without finding them. 23 Then the two men started back. They went down out of the hills, forded the river and came to Joshua son of Nun and told him everything that had happened to them. 24 They said to Joshua, "The LORD has surely given the whole land into our hands; all the people are melting in fear because of us."

**1:15** m Jos 22:1–4
**2:1** n Jas 2:25 o Nu 25:1 p Heb 11:31
**2:4** q 2Sa 17:19–20
**2:6** r Jas 2:25
**2:9** s Ex 23:27; Dt 2:25
**2:10** t Ex 14:21 u Nu 21:21,24,34–35
**2:11** v Ex 15:14; Jos 5:1 w Dt 4:39
**2:12** x ver 18
**2:14** y Jdg 1:24
**2:17** z Ge 24:8
**2:18** a ver 12
**2:19** b Mt 27:25

[a]1 Or possibly *an innkeeper* [b]10 Hebrew *Yam Suph*; that is, Sea of Reeds [c]10 The Hebrew term refers to the irrevocable giving over of things or persons to the LORD, often by totally destroying them.

# Rahab

## *Willing to Be Used by God*

Rahab's story shows that God can use anyone. Rahab was a prostitute whose house was part of Jericho's defensive wall. When Joshua sent spies into Jericho, the spies lodged in Rahab's house (see Jos 2:1). When the king of Jericho sent soldiers in search of the spies, Rahab courageously hid them on the rooftop and told the king's soldiers that the spies were not there (see Jos 2:2–6). Because of her great courage and kindness, the spies promised Rahab that her family would not be harmed during the destruction of Jericho.

Just before Rahab helped the spies escape safely through a window, they instructed her to hang a scarlet cord from her window so that the Israelites would be able to identify the family that should be spared (see Jos 2:14–18). Rahab told the spies that she had heard stories about God's miracles and that she recognized their God as the one true God (see Jos 2:8–11).

Rahab's story has taught women throughout time that God uses whomever he chooses to fulfill his mission. God doesn't always choose the most righteous; he chooses those who are the most willing.

Rahab's belief in God gave her the courage to help the spies. The greater news, however, is that in spite of the fact that she was a prostitute, God chose her to assist Joshua in his mission to capture Jericho. Her faith earned her a place in the "Hebrews Hall of Faith" (see Heb 11:31) and a listing in the genealogy of Jesus (see Mt 1:5).

When God comes into our hearts, we can truly become new people. However, we must remain faithful in reaching for the courage and boldness that allows us to take the first steps toward him. And as women of God, we must remember to not discount others who do not act as we do. They, too, may be used by God and can become new creations.

—T. Harrison-Dixon

### reflection

*What is God's plan for you this day?*

*How has God used you in spite of yourself to accomplish his will?*

### read

Joshua 1:2,11; 2:1–24; Matthew 1:5; Hebrews 11:31; James 2:25.

**See also** the Inspire Notes "Responsible Decisions in Leadership," "Confidence" and "Faith," and the Women of the Bible Notes "Jochebed: She Knew It Would Take a Village" and "The Revelation 12 Woman: A Woman of Focus."

For the next Women of the Bible note, go to page 263.

## Crossing the Jordan

3 Early in the morning Joshua and all the Israelites set out from Shittim[c] and went to the Jordan, where they camped before crossing over. 2After three days the officers went throughout the camp,[d] 3giving orders to the people: "When you see the ark of the covenant of the LORD your God, and the priests,[e] who are Levites, carrying it, you are to move out from your positions and follow it. 4Then you will know which way to go, since you have never been this way before. But keep a distance of about a thousand yards[a] between you and the ark; do not go near it."

5Joshua told the people, "Consecrate yourselves,[f] for tomorrow the LORD will do amazing things among you."

6Joshua said to the priests, "Take up the ark of the covenant and pass on ahead of the people." So they took it up and went ahead of them.

7And the LORD said to Joshua, "Today I will begin to exalt you in the eyes of all Israel, so they may know that I am with you as I was with Moses.[g] 8Tell the priests who carry the ark of the covenant: 'When you reach the edge of the Jordan's waters, go and stand in the river.' "

9Joshua said to the Israelites, "Come here and listen to the words of the LORD your God. 10This is how you will know that the living God[h] is among you and that he will certainly drive out before you the Canaanites, Hittites, Hivites, Perizzites, Girgashites, Amorites and Jebusites.[i] 11See, the ark of the covenant of the Lord of all the earth[j] will go into the Jordan ahead of you. 12Now then, choose twelve men[k] from the tribes of Israel, one from each tribe. 13And as soon as the priests who carry the ark of the LORD—the Lord of all the earth—set foot in the Jordan, its waters flowing downstream will be cut off and stand up in a heap."

14So when the people broke camp to cross the Jordan, the priests carrying the ark of the covenant went ahead[l] of them. 15Now the Jordan is at flood stage[m] all during harvest. Yet as soon as the priests who carried the ark reached the Jordan and their feet touched the water's edge, 16the water from upstream stopped flowing.[n] It piled up in a heap a great distance away, at a town called Adam in the vicinity of Zarethan, while the water flowing down to the Sea of the Arabah (the Salt Sea[b]) was completely cut off. So the people crossed over opposite Jericho. 17The priests who carried the ark of the covenant of the LORD stood firm on dry ground in the middle of the Jordan, while all Israel passed by until the whole nation had completed the crossing on dry ground.[o]

> *God,*
>
> *you are awesome. I marvel at what you have done for me and for my people. Help me to live my life as a perpetual thanksgiving offering to you.*
>
> *Amen*
>
> JOSHUA 3:1–5

4 When the whole nation had finished crossing the Jordan,[p] the LORD said to Joshua, 2"Choose twelve men[q] from among the people, one from each tribe, 3and tell them to take up twelve stones[r] from the middle of the Jordan from right where the priests stood and to carry them over with you and put them down at the place where you stay tonight.[s]"

4So Joshua called together the twelve men he had appointed from the Israelites, one from each tribe, 5and said to them, "Go over before the ark of the LORD your God into the middle of the Jordan. Each of you is to take up a stone on his shoulder, according to the number of the tribes of the Israelites, 6to serve as a sign among you. In the future, when your children ask you, 'What do these stones mean?'[t] 7tell them that the flow of the Jordan was cut off[u] before the ark of the covenant of the LORD. When it crossed the Jordan, the waters of the Jordan were cut off. These stones are to be a memorial to the people of Israel forever."

**3:1** c Jos 2:1
**3:2** d Jos 1:11
**3:3** e Dt 31:9
**3:5** f Ex 19:10,14; Jos 7:13
**3:7** g Jos 1:5
**3:10** h Dt 5:26 i Dt 7:1
**3:11** j Zec 6:5
**3:12** k Jos 4:2,4
**3:14** l Ac 7:44–45
**3:15** m Jos 4:18; 1Ch 12:15
**3:16** n Ps 66:6
**3:17** o Ex 14:22,29
**4:1** p Dt 27:2
**4:2** q Jos 3:12
**4:3** r ver 20 s ver 19
**4:6** t Ex 12:26; 13:14
**4:7** u Jos 3:13

[a]4 Hebrew *about two thousand cubits* (about 900 meters) [b]16 That is, the Dead Sea

**4:8** v ver 20
**4:14** w Jos 3:7
**4:20** x ver 3,8

8 So the Israelites did as Joshua commanded them. They took twelve stones from the middle of the Jordan, according to the number of the tribes of the Israelites, as the LORD had told Joshua;[v] and they carried them over with them to their camp, where they put them down. 9 Joshua set up the twelve stones that had been[a] in the middle of the Jordan at the spot where the priests who carried the ark of the covenant had stood. And they are there to this day.

> *"If I can inspire one of these youngsters to develop the talent I know they possess, then my monument will be in their work."*
>
> —AUGUSTA SAVAGE, SCULPTOR

10 Now the priests who carried the ark remained standing in the middle of the Jordan until everything the LORD had commanded Joshua was done by the people, just as Moses had directed Joshua. The people hurried over, 11 and as soon as all of them had crossed, the ark of the LORD and the priests came to the other side while the people watched. 12 The men of Reuben, Gad and the half-tribe of Manasseh crossed over, armed, in front of the Israelites, as Moses had directed them. 13 About forty thousand armed for battle crossed over before the LORD to the plains of Jericho for war.

14 That day the LORD exalted[w] Joshua in the sight of all Israel; and they revered him all the days of his life, just as they had revered Moses.

15 Then the LORD said to Joshua, 16 "Command the priests carrying the ark of the Testimony to come up out of the Jordan."

17 So Joshua commanded the priests, "Come up out of the Jordan."

18 And the priests came up out of the river carrying the ark of the covenant of the LORD. No sooner had they set their feet on the dry ground than the waters of the Jordan returned to their place and ran at flood stage as before.

19 On the tenth day of the first month the people went up from the Jordan and camped at Gilgal on the eastern border of Jericho. 20 And Joshua set up at Gilgal the twelve stones[x] they had taken out of the Jordan. 21 He said to the Israelites, "In the future when your descendants ask their fathers, 'What do these stones mean?' 22 tell them, 'Israel crossed the Jordan on dry ground.'[y] 23 For the LORD your God dried up the Jordan before you until you had crossed over. The LORD your God did to the Jordan just what he had done to the Red Sea[b] when he dried it up before us until we had crossed over.[z] 24 He did this so that all the peoples of the earth might know[a] that the hand of the LORD is powerful[b] and so that you might always fear the LORD your God.[c]"

## Circumcision at Gilgal

**5** Now when all the Amorite kings west of the Jordan and all the Canaanite kings along the coast[d] heard how the LORD had dried up the Jordan before the Israelites until we had crossed over, their hearts melted[e] and they no longer had the courage to face the Israelites.

2 At that time the LORD said to Joshua, "Make flint knives[f] and circumcise the Israelites again." 3 So Joshua made flint knives and circumcised the Israelites at Gibeath Haaraloth.[c]

4 Now this is why he did so: All those who came out of Egypt—all the men of military age—died in the desert on the way after leaving Egypt.[g] 5 All the people that came out had been circumcised, but all the people born in the desert during the journey from Egypt had not. 6 The Israelites had moved about in the desert forty years[h] until all the men who were of military age when they left Egypt had died, since they had not obeyed the LORD. For the LORD had sworn to them that they would not see the land that he had solemnly promised their fathers to give us,[i] a land flowing with milk and honey. 7 So he raised up their sons in their place, and these were the ones Joshua circumcised. They were still uncircumcised because they had not been circumcised on the way. 8 And after the whole nation had been circumcised, they remained where they were in camp until they were healed.

9 Then the LORD said to Joshua, "Today I have rolled away the reproach of Egypt from

**4:22** y Jos 3:17
**4:23** z Ex 14:21
**4:24** a 1Ki 8:42–43; Ps 106:8 b Ex 15:16; 1Ch 29:12; Ps 89:13 c Ex 14:31
**5:1** d Nu 13:29 e Jos 2:9–11
**5:2** f Ex 4:25
**5:4** g Dt 2:14
**5:6** h Dt 2:7 i Nu 14:23,29–35; Dt 2:14

[a] 9 Or *Joshua also set up twelve stones* [b] 23 Hebrew *Yam Suph*; that is, Sea of Reeds [c] 3 *Gibeath Haaraloth* means *hill of foreskins.*

**5:12** j Ex 16:35
**5:13** k Ge 18:2; 32:24
**5:14** l Ge 17:3
**5:15** m Ex 3:5
**6:2** n Dt 7:24

you." So the place has been called Gilgal[a] to this day.

[10]On the evening of the fourteenth day of the month, while camped at Gilgal on the plains of Jericho, the Israelites celebrated the Passover. [11]The day after the Passover, that very day, they ate some of the produce of the land: unleavened bread and roasted grain. [12]The manna stopped the day after[b] they ate this food from the land; there was no longer any manna for the Israelites, but that year they ate of the produce of Canaan.[j]

## The Fall of Jericho

[13]Now when Joshua was near Jericho, he looked up and saw a man[k] standing in front of him with a drawn sword in his hand. Joshua went up to him and asked, "Are you for us or for our enemies?"

[14]"Neither," he replied, "but as commander of the army of the LORD I have now come." Then Joshua fell facedown[l] to the ground in reverence, and asked him, "What message does my Lord[c] have for his servant?"

[15]The commander of the LORD's army replied, "Take off your sandals, for the place where you are standing is holy."[m] And Joshua did so.

**6** Now Jericho was tightly shut up because of the Israelites. No one went out and no one came in.

[2]Then the LORD said to Joshua, "See, I have delivered[n] Jericho into your hands, along with its king and its fighting men. [3]March around the city once with all the armed men. Do this for six days. [4]Have seven priests carry trumpets of rams' horns in front of the ark. On the seventh day, march around the city seven times, with the priests blowing the trumpets. [5]When you hear them sound a long blast on the trumpets, have all the people give a loud shout; then the wall of the city will collapse and the people will go up, every man straight in."

[6]So Joshua son of Nun called the priests and said to them, "Take up the ark of the covenant of the LORD and have seven priests carry trumpets in front of it." [7]And he ordered the people, "Advance! March around the city, with the armed guard going ahead of the ark of the LORD."

[8]When Joshua had spoken to the people, the seven priests carrying the seven trumpets before the LORD went forward, blowing their trumpets, and the ark of the LORD's covenant followed them. [9]The armed guard marched ahead of the priests who blew the trumpets, and the rear guard followed the ark. All this time the trumpets were sounding. [10]But Joshua had commanded the people, "Do not give a war cry, do not raise your voices, do not say a word until the day I tell you to shout. Then shout!" [11]So he had the ark of the LORD carried around the city, circling it once. Then the people returned to camp and spent the night there.

[12]Joshua got up early the next morning and the priests took up the ark of the LORD. [13]The seven priests carrying the seven trumpets went forward, marching before the ark of the LORD and blowing the trumpets. The armed men went ahead of them and the rear guard followed the ark of the LORD, while the trumpets kept sounding. [14]So on the second day they marched around the city once and returned to the camp. They did this for six days.

[15]On the seventh day, they got up at daybreak and marched around the city seven times in the same manner, except that on that day they circled the city seven times. [16]The seventh time around, when the priests sounded the trumpet blast, Joshua commanded the people, "Shout! For the LORD has given you the city! [17]The city and all that is in it are to be devoted[d][o] to the LORD. Only Rahab the prostitute[e] and all who are with her in her house shall be spared, because she hid[p] the spies we sent. [18]But keep away from the devoted things,[q] so that you will not bring about your own destruction by taking any of them. Otherwise you will make the camp of Israel liable to destruction and bring trouble on it. [19]All the silver and gold and the articles of bronze and iron are sacred to the LORD and must go into his treasury."

[20]When the trumpets sounded, the people shouted, and at the sound of the trumpet,

**6:17** o Lev 27:28 p Jos 2:4
**6:18** q Jos 7:1

[a]9 *Gilgal* sounds like the Hebrew for *roll.* [b]12 Or *the day* [c]14 Or *lord* [d]17 The Hebrew term refers to the irrevocable giving over of things or persons to the LORD, often by totally destroying them; also in verses 18 and 21. [e]17 Or possibly *innkeeper*; also in verses 22 and 25

**6:20** r Heb 11:30
**6:21** s Dt 20:16
**6:22** t Jos 2:14; Heb 11:31
**6:23** u Jos 2:13
**6:24** v ver 19
**6:25** w Jos 2:6
**6:26** x 1Ki 16:34
**6:27** y Jos 1:5 z Jos 9:1
**7:1** a Jos 6:18

when the people gave a loud shout, the wall collapsed; so every man charged straight in, and they took the city.[r] 21 They devoted the city to the LORD and destroyed[s] with the sword every living thing in it—men and women, young and old, cattle, sheep and donkeys.

22 Joshua said to the two men who had spied out the land, "Go into the prostitute's house and bring her out and all who belong to her, in accordance with your oath to her."[t] 23 So the young men who had done the spying went in and brought out Rahab, her father and mother and brothers and all who belonged to her.[u] They brought out her entire family and put them in a place outside the camp of Israel.

24 Then they burned the whole city and everything in it, but they put the silver and gold and the articles of bronze and iron[v] into the treasury of the LORD's house. 25 But Joshua spared Rahab the prostitute, with her family and all who belonged to her, because she hid the men Joshua had sent as spies to Jericho[w]—and she lives among the Israelites to this day.

26 At that time Joshua pronounced this solemn oath: "Cursed before the LORD is the man who undertakes to rebuild this city, Jericho:

"At the cost of his firstborn son
    will he lay its foundations;
at the cost of his youngest
    will he set up its gates."[x]

27 So the LORD was with Joshua,[y] and his fame spread[z] throughout the land.

## Achan's Sin

**7** But the Israelites acted unfaithfully in regard to the devoted things[a];[a] Achan son of Carmi, the son of Zimri,[b] the son of Zerah, of the tribe of Judah, took some of them. So the LORD's anger burned against Israel.

2 Now Joshua sent men from Jericho to Ai, which is near Beth Aven to the east of Bethel, and told them, "Go up and spy out the region." So the men went up and spied out Ai.

3 When they returned to Joshua, they said, "Not all the people will have to go up against Ai. Send two or three thousand men to take it and do not weary all the people, for only a few men are there." 4 So about three thousand men went up; but they were routed by the men of Ai,[b] 5 who killed about thirty-six of them. They chased the Israelites from the city gate as far as the stone quarries[c] and struck them down on the slopes. At this the hearts of the people melted and became like water.

6 Then Joshua tore his clothes and fell facedown to the ground before the ark of the LORD, remaining there till evening. The elders of Israel did the same, and sprinkled dust[c] on their heads. 7 And Joshua said, "Ah, Sovereign LORD, why did you ever bring this people across the Jordan to deliver us into the hands of the Amorites to destroy us? If only we had been content to stay on the other side of the Jordan! 8 O Lord, what can I say, now that Israel has been routed by its enemies? 9 The Canaanites and the other people of the country will hear about this and they will surround us and wipe out our name from the earth.[d] What then will you do for your own great name?"

10 The LORD said to Joshua, "Stand up! What are you doing down on your face? 11 Israel has sinned; they have violated my covenant,[e] which I commanded them to keep. They have taken some of the devoted things; they have stolen, they have lied, they have put them with their own possessions. 12 That is why the Israelites cannot stand against their enemies; they turn their backs and run because they have been made liable to destruction. I will not be with you anymore unless you destroy whatever among you is devoted to destruction.

13 "Go, consecrate the people. Tell them, 'Consecrate yourselves[f] in preparation for tomorrow; for this is what the LORD, the God of Israel, says: That which is devoted is among you, O Israel. You cannot stand against your enemies until you remove it.

14 "'In the morning, present yourselves tribe by tribe. The tribe that the LORD takes[g] shall come forward clan by clan; the clan

**7:4** b Lev 26:17; Dt 28:25
**7:6** c Job 2:12; Rev 18:19
**7:9** d Ex 32:12
**7:11** e Jos 6:17–19
**7:13** f Jos 3:5; 6:18
**7:14** g Pr 16:33

[a]1 The Hebrew term refers to the irrevocable giving over of things or persons to the LORD, often by totally destroying them; also in verses 11, 12, 13 and 15. [b]1 See Septuagint and 1 Chron. 2:6; Hebrew *Zabdi*; also in verses 17 and 18.
[c]5 Or *as far as Shebarim*

**7:15** h 1Sa 14:39 i ver 11 j Ge 34:7
**7:19** k Jer 13:16; Jn 9:24* l 1Sa 14:43
**7:24** m Jos 15:7
**7:25** n Jos 6:18 o Dt 17:5

that the LORD takes shall come forward family by family; and the family that the LORD takes shall come forward man by man. 15 He who is caught with the devoted things shall be destroyed by fire, along with all that belongs to him.[h] He has violated the covenant[i] of the LORD and has done a disgraceful thing in Israel!'"[j]

16 Early the next morning Joshua had Israel come forward by tribes, and Judah was taken. 17 The clans of Judah came forward, and he took the Zerahites. He had the clan of the Zerahites come forward by families, and Zimri was taken. 18 Joshua had his family come forward man by man, and Achan son of Carmi, the son of Zimri, the son of Zerah, of the tribe of Judah, was taken.

19 Then Joshua said to Achan, "My son, give glory[k] to the LORD,[a] the God of Israel, and give him the praise.[b] Tell[l] me what you have done; do not hide it from me."

20 Achan replied, "It is true! I have sinned against the LORD, the God of Israel. This is what I have done: 21 When I saw in the plunder a beautiful robe from Babylonia,[c] two hundred shekels[d] of silver and a wedge of gold weighing fifty shekels,[e] I coveted them and took them. They are hidden in the ground inside my tent, with the silver underneath."

22 So Joshua sent messengers, and they ran to the tent, and there it was, hidden in his tent, with the silver underneath. 23 They took the things from the tent, brought them to Joshua and all the Israelites and spread them out before the LORD.

24 Then Joshua, together with all Israel, took Achan son of Zerah, the silver, the robe, the gold wedge, his sons and daughters, his cattle, donkeys and sheep, his tent and all that he had, to the Valley of Achor.[m] 25 Joshua said, "Why have you brought this trouble[n] on us? The LORD will bring trouble on you today."

Then all Israel stoned him,[o] and after they had stoned the rest, they burned them. 26 Over Achan they heaped up a large pile of rocks, which remains to this day. Then the LORD turned from his fierce anger. Therefore that place has been called the Valley of Achor[f] ever since.

## Ai Destroyed

**8** Then the LORD said to Joshua, "Do not be afraid;[p] do not be discouraged.[q] Take the whole army with you, and go up and attack Ai. For I have delivered[r] into your hands the king of Ai, his people, his city and his land. 2 You shall do to Ai and its king as you did to Jericho and its king, except that you may carry off their plunder and livestock for yourselves.[s] Set an ambush behind the city."

*My daughter,*

*Even when you are afraid, remember that I control all things. Whatever the situation, trust me to work it out.*

*The Sovereign One*

JOSHUA 8:1

3 So Joshua and the whole army moved out to attack Ai. He chose thirty thousand of his best fighting men and sent them out at night 4 with these orders: "Listen carefully. You are to set an ambush behind the city. Don't go very far from it. All of you be on the alert. 5 I and all those with me will advance on the city, and when the men come out against us, as they did before, we will flee from them. 6 They will pursue us until we have lured them away from the city, for they will say, 'They are running away from us as they did before.' So when we flee from them, 7 you are to rise up from ambush and take the city. The LORD your God will give it into your hand. 8 When you have taken the city, set it on fire. Do what the LORD has commanded. See to it; you have my orders."

9 Then Joshua sent them off, and they went to the place of ambush and lay in wait between Bethel and Ai, to the west of Ai—but Joshua spent that night with the people.

10 Early the next morning[t] Joshua mustered his men, and he and the leaders of

**8:1** p Dt 31:6 q Dt 1:21; Jos 1:9 r Jos 6:2
**8:2** s ver 27; Dt 20:14
**8:10** t Ge 22:3

[a] 19 A solemn charge to tell the truth [b] 19 Or *and confess to him* [c] 21 Hebrew *Shinar* [d] 21 That is, about 5 pounds (about 2.3 kilograms) [e] 21 That is, about 1 1/4 pounds (about 0.6 kilogram) [f] 26 *Achor* means *trouble.*

Israel marched before them to Ai. 11 The entire force that was with him marched up and approached the city and arrived in front of it. They set up camp north of Ai, with the valley between them and the city. 12 Joshua had taken about five thousand men and set them in ambush between Bethel and Ai, to the west of the city. 13 They had the soldiers take up their positions—all those in the camp to the north of the city and the ambush to the west of it. That night Joshua went into the valley.

14 When the king of Ai saw this, he and all the men of the city hurried out early in the morning to meet Israel in battle at a certain place overlooking the Arabah. But he did not know[u] that an ambush had been set against him behind the city. 15 Joshua and all Israel let themselves be driven back[v] before them, and they fled toward the desert.[w] 16 All the men of Ai were called to pursue them, and they pursued Joshua and were lured away[x] from the city. 17 Not a man remained in Ai or Bethel who did not go after Israel. They left the city open and went in pursuit of Israel.

18 Then the LORD said to Joshua, "Hold out toward Ai the javelin that is in your hand,[y] for into your hand I will deliver the city." So Joshua held out his javelin[z] toward Ai. 19 As soon as he did this, the men in the ambush rose quickly from their position and rushed forward. They entered the city and captured it and quickly set it on fire.[a]

20 The men of Ai looked back and saw the smoke of the city rising against the sky, but they had no chance to escape in any direction, for the Israelites who had been fleeing toward the desert had turned back against their pursuers. 21 For when Joshua and all Israel saw that the ambush had taken the city and that smoke was going up from the city, they turned around and attacked the men of Ai. 22 The men of the ambush also came out of the city against them, so that they were caught in the middle, with Israelites on both sides. Israel cut them down, leaving them neither survivors nor fugitives.[b] 23 But they took the king of Ai alive and brought him to Joshua.

24 When Israel had finished killing all the men of Ai in the fields and in the desert where they had chased them, and when every one of them had been put to the sword, all the Israelites returned to Ai and killed those who were in it. 25 Twelve thousand men and women fell that day—all the people of Ai.[c] 26 For Joshua did not draw back the hand that held out his javelin until he had destroyed[a] all who lived in Ai.[d] 27 But Israel did carry off for themselves the livestock and plunder of this city, as the LORD had instructed Joshua.[e]

28 So Joshua burned Ai and made it a permanent heap of ruins,[f] a desolate place to this day. 29 He hung the king of Ai on a tree and left him there until evening. At sunset,[g] Joshua ordered them to take his body from the tree and throw it down at the entrance of the city gate. And they raised a large pile of rocks over it, which remains to this day.

## The Covenant Renewed at Mount Ebal

30 Then Joshua built on Mount Ebal an altar to the LORD, the God of Israel, 31 as Moses the servant of the LORD had commanded the Israelites. He built it according to what is written in the Book of the Law of Moses—an altar of uncut stones, on which no iron tool[h] had been used. On it they offered to the LORD burnt offerings and sacrificed fellowship offerings.[b][i] 32 There, in the presence of the Israelites, Joshua copied on stones the law of Moses, which he had written.[j] 33 All Israel, aliens and citizens alike, with their elders, officials and judges, were standing on both sides of the ark of the covenant of the LORD, facing those who carried it—the priests, who were Levites.[k] Half of the people stood in front of Mount Gerizim and half of them in front of Mount Ebal,[l] as Moses the servant of the LORD had formerly commanded when he gave instructions to bless the people of Israel.

34 Afterward, Joshua read all the words of the law—the blessings and the curses—just as it is written in the Book of the Law.[m] 35 There was not a word of all that Moses had commanded that Joshua did not read to the whole assembly of Israel, including the women and children, and the aliens who lived among them.[n]

**8:14** u Jdg 20:34
**8:15** v Jdg 20:36 w Jos 15:61; 16:1; 18:12
**8:16** x Jdg 20:31
**8:18** y Ex 17:9–12 z ver 26
**8:19** a ver 8
**8:22** b Dt 7:2
**8:25** c Dt 20:16–18
**8:26** d Ex 17:12
**8:27** e ver 2
**8:28** f Dt 13:16
**8:29** g Dt 21:23
**8:31** h Ex 20:25 i Dt 27:6–7
**8:32** j Dt 27:8
**8:33** k Dt 31:12 l Dt 11:29; 27:11–14
**8:34** m Dt 31:11
**8:35** n Dt 31:12

[a] 26 The Hebrew term refers to the irrevocable giving over of things or persons to the LORD, often by totally destroying them.
[b] 31 Traditionally *peace offerings*

## The Gibeonite Deception

**9** Now when all the kings west of the Jordan heard about these things—those in the hill country, in the western foothills, and along the entire coast of the Great Sea[a][o] as far as Lebanon (the kings of the Hittites, Amorites, Canaanites, Perizzites, Hivites and Jebusites)— [2]they came together to make war against Joshua and Israel.

[3]However, when the people of Gibeon[p] heard what Joshua had done to Jericho and Ai, [4]they resorted to a ruse: They went as a delegation whose donkeys were loaded[b] with worn-out sacks and old wineskins, cracked and mended. [5]The men put worn and patched sandals on their feet and wore old clothes. All the bread of their food supply was dry and moldy. [6]Then they went to Joshua in the camp at Gilgal[q] and said to him and the men of Israel, "We have come from a distant country; make a treaty with us."

[7]The men of Israel said to the Hivites,[r] "But perhaps you live near us. How then can we make a treaty[s] with you?"

[8]"We are your servants," they said to Joshua.

But Joshua asked, "Who are you and where do you come from?"

[9]They answered: "Your servants have come from a very distant country[t] because of the fame of the LORD your God. For we have heard reports[u] of him: all that he did in Egypt, [10]and all that he did to the two kings of the Amorites east of the Jordan—Sihon king of Heshbon, and Og king of Bashan, who reigned in Ashtaroth.[v] [11]And our elders and all those living in our country said to us, 'Take provisions for your journey; go and meet them and say to them, "We are your servants; make a treaty with us."' [12]This bread of ours was warm when we packed it at home on the day we left to come to you. But now see how dry and moldy it is. [13]And these wineskins that we filled were new, but see how cracked they are. And our clothes and sandals are worn out by the very long journey."

[14]The men of Israel sampled their provisions but did not inquire[w] of the LORD. [15]Then Joshua made a treaty of peace with them to let them live, and the leaders of the assembly ratified it by oath.

[16]Three days after they made the treaty with the Gibeonites, the Israelites heard that they were neighbors, living near them. [17]So the Israelites set out and on the third day came to their cities: Gibeon, Kephirah, Beeroth[x] and Kiriath Jearim. [18]But the Israelites did not attack them, because the leaders of the assembly had sworn an oath[y] to them by the LORD, the God of Israel.

The whole assembly grumbled against the leaders, [19]but all the leaders answered, "We have given them our oath by the LORD, the God of Israel, and we cannot touch them now. [20]This is what we will do to them: We will let them live, so that wrath will not fall on us for breaking the oath we swore to them." [21]They continued, "Let them live,[z] but let them be woodcutters and water carriers[a] for the entire community." So the leaders' promise to them was kept.

[22]Then Joshua summoned the Gibeonites and said, "Why did you deceive us by saying, 'We live a long way from you,' while actually you live near[b] us? [23]You are now under a curse:[c] You will never cease to serve as woodcutters and water carriers for the house of my God."

[24]They answered Joshua, "Your servants were clearly told how the LORD your God had commanded his servant Moses to give you the whole land and to wipe out all its inhabitants from before you. So we feared for our lives because of you, and that is why we did this. [25]We are now in your hands.[d] Do to us whatever seems good and right to you."

[26]So Joshua saved them from the Israelites, and they did not kill them. [27]That day he made the Gibeonites woodcutters and water carriers for the community and for the altar of the LORD at the place the LORD would choose.[e] And that is what they are to this day.

## The Sun Stands Still

**10** Now Adoni-Zedek king of Jerusalem heard that Joshua had taken Ai[f] and totally destroyed[c][g] it, doing to Ai

9:1 o Nu 34:6
9:3 p Jos 10:2
9:6 q Jos 5:10
9:7 r Jos 11:19 s Ex 23:32
9:9 t Dt 20:15 u ver 24; Jos 2:9
9:10 v Nu 21:24,35
9:14 w Nu 27:21
9:17 x Jos 18:25
9:18 y Ps 15:4
9:21 z ver 15 a Dt 29:11
9:22 b ver 16
9:23 c Ge 9:25
9:25 d Ge 16:6
9:27 e Dt 12:5
10:1 f Jos 8:1 g Dt 20:16; Jos 8:22

[a]1 That is, the Mediterranean [b]4 Most Hebrew manuscripts; some Hebrew manuscripts, Vulgate and Syriac (see also Septuagint) *They prepared provisions and loaded their donkeys* [c]1 The Hebrew term refers to the irrevocable giving over of things or persons to the LORD, often by totally destroying them; also in verses 28, 35, 37, 39 and 40.

and its king as he had done to Jericho and its king, and that the people of Gibeon had made a treaty of peace[h] with Israel and were living near them. [2]He and his people were very much alarmed at this, because Gibeon was an important city, like one of the royal cities; it was larger than Ai, and all its men were good fighters. [3]So Adoni-Zedek king of Jerusalem appealed to Hoham king of Hebron,[i] Piram king of Jarmuth, Japhia king of Lachish[j] and Debir king of Eglon. [4]"Come up and help me attack Gibeon," he said, "because it has made peace[k] with Joshua and the Israelites."

[5]Then the five kings of the Amorites[l]—the kings of Jerusalem, Hebron, Jarmuth, Lachish and Eglon—joined forces. They moved up with all their troops and took up positions against Gibeon and attacked it.

[6]The Gibeonites then sent word to Joshua in the camp at Gilgal: "Do not abandon your servants. Come up to us quickly and save us! Help us, because all the Amorite kings from the hill country have joined forces against us."

[7]So Joshua marched up from Gilgal with his entire army,[m] including all the best fighting men. [8]The LORD said to Joshua, "Do not be afraid[n] of them; I have given them into your hand. Not one of them will be able to withstand you."

[9]After an all-night march from Gilgal, Joshua took them by surprise. [10]The LORD threw them into confusion before Israel,[o] who defeated them in a great victory at Gibeon. Israel pursued them along the road going up to Beth Horon and cut them down all the way to Azekah and Makkedah. [11]As they fled before Israel on the road down from Beth Horon to Azekah, the LORD hurled large hailstones[p] down on them from the sky, and more of them died from the hailstones than were killed by the swords of the Israelites.

[12]On the day the LORD gave the Amorites over to Israel, Joshua said to the LORD in the presence of Israel:

"O sun, stand still over Gibeon,
O moon, over the Valley of Aijalon."
[13]So the sun stood still,[q]
and the moon stopped,
till the nation avenged itself on[a] its enemies,

as it is written in the Book of Jashar.[r]

The sun stopped in the middle of the sky and delayed going down about a full day. [14]There has never been a day like it before or since, a day when the LORD listened to a man. Surely the LORD was fighting[s] for Israel!

[15]Then Joshua returned with all Israel to the camp at Gilgal.[t]

## Five Amorite Kings Killed

[16]Now the five kings had fled and hidden in the cave at Makkedah. [17]When Joshua was told that the five kings had been found hiding in the cave at Makkedah, [18]he said, "Roll large rocks up to the mouth of the cave, and post some men there to guard it. [19]But don't stop! Pursue your enemies, attack them from the rear and don't let them reach their cities, for the LORD your God has given them into your hand."

[20]So Joshua and the Israelites destroyed them completely[u]—almost to a man—but the few who were left reached their fortified cities. [21]The whole army then returned safely to Joshua in the camp at Makkedah, and no one uttered a word against the Israelites.

[22]Joshua said, "Open the mouth of the cave and bring those five kings out to me." [23]So they brought the five kings out of the cave—the kings of Jerusalem, Hebron, Jarmuth, Lachish and Eglon. [24]When they had brought these kings to Joshua, he summoned all the men of Israel and said to the army commanders who had come with him, "Come here and put your feet[v] on the necks of these kings." So they came forward and placed their feet on their necks.

[25]Joshua said to them, "Do not be afraid; do not be discouraged. Be strong and courageous. This is what the LORD will do to all the enemies you are going to fight." [26]Then Joshua struck and killed the kings and hung them on five trees, and they were left hanging on the trees until evening.

[27]At sunset[w] Joshua gave the order and they took them down from the trees and threw them into the cave where they had been hiding. At the mouth of the cave

[a]13 Or *nation triumphed over*

**10:1** h Jos 9:15
**10:3** i Ge 13:18; j Isa 36:2; 37:8; Jer 34:7
**10:4** k Jos 9:15
**10:5** l Nu 13:29
**10:7** m Jos 8:1
**10:8** n Jos 1:9
**10:10** o Dt 7:23
**10:11** p Ps 18:12
**10:13** q Hab 3:11
**10:13** r 2Sa 1:18
**10:14** s ver 42
**10:15** t ver 43
**10:20** u Dt 20:16
**10:24** v Mal 4:3
**10:27** w Dt 21:23

they placed large rocks, which are there to this day.

[28]That day Joshua took Makkedah. He put the city and its king to the sword and totally destroyed everyone in it. He left no survivors.[x] And he did to the king of Makkedah as he had done to the king of Jericho.[y]

## Southern Cities Conquered

[29]Then Joshua and all Israel with him moved on from Makkedah to Libnah and attacked it. [30]The LORD also gave that city and its king into Israel's hand. The city and everyone in it Joshua put to the sword. He left no survivors there. And he did to its king as he had done to the king of Jericho.

[31]Then Joshua and all Israel with him moved on from Libnah to Lachish; he took up positions against it and attacked it. [32]The LORD handed Lachish over to Israel, and Joshua took it on the second day. The city and everyone in it he put to the sword, just as he had done to Libnah. [33]Meanwhile, Horam king of Gezer had come up to help Lachish, but Joshua defeated him and his army—until no survivors were left.

[34]Then Joshua and all Israel with him moved on from Lachish to Eglon; they took up positions against it and attacked it. [35]They captured it that same day and put it to the sword and totally destroyed everyone in it, just as they had done to Lachish.

[36]Then Joshua and all Israel with him went up from Eglon to Hebron[z] and attacked it. [37]They took the city and put it to the sword, together with its king, its villages and everyone in it. They left no survivors. Just as at Eglon, they totally destroyed it and everyone in it.

[38]Then Joshua and all Israel with him turned around and attacked Debir.[a] [39]They took the city, its king and its villages, and put them to the sword. Everyone in it they totally destroyed. They left no survivors. They did to Debir and its king as they had done to Libnah and its king and to Hebron.

[40]So Joshua subdued the whole region, including the hill country, the Negev, the western foothills and the mountain slopes, together with all their kings.[b] He left no survivors. He totally destroyed all who breathed, just as the LORD, the God of Israel, had commanded.[c] [41]Joshua subdued them from Kadesh Barnea to Gaza and from the whole region of Goshen[d] to Gibeon. [42]All these kings and their lands Joshua conquered in one campaign, because the LORD, the God of Israel, fought[e] for Israel.

[43]Then Joshua returned with all Israel to the camp at Gilgal.

## Northern Kings Defeated

**11** When Jabin king of Hazor heard of this, he sent word to Jobab king of Madon, to the kings of Shimron and Acshaph, [2]and to the northern kings who were in the mountains, in the Arabah[f] south of Kinnereth, in the western foothills and in

**10:28**
x Dt 20:16
y Jos 6:21
**10:36**
z Jos 14:13; 15:13; Jdg 1:10
**10:38**
a Jos 15:15; Jdg 1:11
**10:40**
b Dt 7:24
c Dt 20:16–17
**10:41**
d Jos 11:16
**10:42**
e ver 14
**11:2**
f Jos 12:3

## The African Presence

**Joshua 11**

Israel's conquest of the promised land was a war directed by God as judgment against people whose corruption had crossed the limit of God's patience. Genesis 15:16 notes that the Amorites (descended from Canaan) were sinful in the eyes of God and that Abraham's descendants would return to the land. God's sentence was that all the people were to be wiped out; however, it did not happen that way. Moreover, the Israelites not only intermingled with the people by intermarrying, but they also worshiped Canaanite gods. God's instruction not to intermarry had nothing to do with the races; it was an injunction against the wicked practices of the people.

**11:4** g Jdg 7:12
**11:6** h Jos 10:8 i 2Sa 8:4
**11:8** j Jos 13:6
**11:11** k Dt 20:16–17
**11:12** l Nu 33:50–52; Dt 7:2
**11:15** m Ex 34:11; Jos 1:7
**11:16** n Jos 10:41

Naphoth Dor[a] on the west; 3 to the Canaanites in the east and west; to the Amorites, Hittites, Perizzites and Jebusites in the hill country; and to the Hivites below Hermon in the region of Mizpah. 4 They came out with all their troops and a large number of horses and chariots—a huge army, as numerous as the sand on the seashore.[g] 5 All these kings joined forces and made camp together at the Waters of Merom, to fight against Israel.

6 The LORD said to Joshua, "Do not be afraid of them, because by this time tomorrow I will hand all of them over[h] to Israel, slain. You are to hamstring[i] their horses and burn their chariots."

7 So Joshua and his whole army came against them suddenly at the Waters of Merom and attacked them, 8 and the LORD gave them into the hand of Israel. They defeated them and pursued them all the way to Greater Sidon, to Misrephoth Maim,[j] and to the Valley of Mizpah on the east, until no survivors were left. 9 Joshua did to them as the LORD had directed: He hamstrung their horses and burned their chariots.

10 At that time Joshua turned back and captured Hazor and put its king to the sword. (Hazor had been the head of all these kingdoms.) 11 Everyone in it they put to the sword. They totally destroyed[b] them, not sparing anything that breathed,[k] and he burned up Hazor itself.

12 Joshua took all these royal cities and their kings and put them to the sword. He totally destroyed them, as Moses the servant of the LORD had commanded.[l] 13 Yet Israel did not burn any of the cities built on their mounds—except Hazor, which Joshua burned. 14 The Israelites carried off for themselves all the plunder and livestock of these cities, but all the people they put to the sword until they completely destroyed them, not sparing anyone that breathed. 15 As the LORD commanded his servant Moses, so Moses commanded Joshua, and Joshua did it; he left nothing undone of all that the LORD commanded Moses.[m]

16 So Joshua took this entire land: the hill country, all the Negev, the whole region of Goshen, the western foothills,[n] the Arabah and the mountains of Israel with their foothills, 17 from Mount Halak, which rises toward Seir, to Baal Gad in the Valley of Lebanon[o] below Mount Hermon. He captured all their kings and struck them down, putting them to death.[p] 18 Joshua waged war against all these kings for a long time. 19 Except for the Hivites living in Gibeon,[q] not one city made a treaty of peace with the Israelites, who took them all in battle. 20 For it was the LORD himself who hardened their hearts to wage war against Israel, so that he might destroy them totally, exterminating them without mercy, as the LORD had commanded Moses.

21 At that time Joshua went and destroyed the Anakites[r] from the hill country: from Hebron, Debir and Anab, from all the hill country of Judah, and from all the hill country of Israel. Joshua totally destroyed them and their towns. 22 No Anakites were left in Israelite territory; only in Gaza, Gath[s] and Ashdod did any survive. 23 So Joshua took the entire land,[t] just as the LORD had directed Moses, and he gave it as an inheritance to Israel according to their tribal divisions.

Then the land had rest from war.

## List of Defeated Kings

12 These are the kings of the land whom the Israelites had defeated and whose territory they took over east of the Jordan, from the Arnon Gorge to Mount Hermon,[u] including all the eastern side of the Arabah:

2 Sihon king of the Amorites,
who reigned in Heshbon. He ruled from Aroer on the rim of the Arnon Gorge—from the middle of the gorge—to the Jabbok River, which is the border of the Ammonites. This included half of Gilead. 3 He also ruled over the eastern Arabah from the Sea of Kinnereth[c][v] to the Sea of the Arabah (the Salt Sea[d]), to Beth Jeshimoth,[w] and then southward below the slopes of Pisgah.

4 And the territory of Og king of Bashan,
one of the last of the Rephaites, who

**11:17** o Jos 12:7 p Dt 7:24
**11:19** q Jos 9:3
**11:21** r Nu 13:22,33
**11:22** s 1Sa 17:4
**11:23** t Jos 21:43–45
**12:1** u Dt 3:8
**12:3** v Jos 11:2 w Jos 13:20

[a] 2 Or *in the heights of Dor* [b] 11 The Hebrew term refers to the irrevocable giving over of things or persons to the LORD, often by totally destroying them; also in verses 12, 20 and 21. [c] 3 That is, Galilee [d] 3 That is, the Dead Sea

12:4 x Dt 1:4
12:5 y Dt 3:10
12:6 z Nu 32:29,33
12:7 a Jos 11:17
12:8 b Jos 11:16
12:9 c Jos 6:2 d Jos 8:29
12:12 e Jos 10:33
12:17 f 1Ki 4:10

reigned in Ashtaroth[x] and Edrei. 5 He
ruled over Mount Hermon, Salecah,[y]
all of Bashan to the border of the peo-
ple of Geshur and Maacah, and half of
Gilead to the border of Sihon king of
Heshbon.

6 Moses, the servant of the LORD, and the
Israelites conquered them. And Moses
the servant of the LORD gave their land to the
Reubenites, the Gadites and the half-tribe
of Manasseh to be their possession.[z]

7 These are the kings of the land that
Joshua and the Israelites conquered on
the west side of the Jordan, from Baal Gad
in the Valley of Lebanon[a] to Mount Halak,
which rises toward Seir (their lands Joshua
gave as an inheritance to the tribes of Israel
according to their tribal divisions— 8 the
hill country, the western foothills, the Ar-
abah, the mountain slopes, the desert and
the Negev[b]—the lands of the Hittites, Am-
orites, Canaanites, Perizzites, Hivites and
Jebusites):

| | |
|---|---|
| 9 the king of Jericho[c] | one |
| the king of Ai[d] (near Bethel) | one |
| 10 the king of Jerusalem | one |
| the king of Hebron | one |
| 11 the king of Jarmuth | one |
| the king of Lachish | one |
| 12 the king of Eglon | one |
| the king of Gezer[e] | one |
| 13 the king of Debir | one |
| the king of Geder | one |
| 14 the king of Hormah | one |
| the king of Arad | one |
| 15 the king of Libnah | one |
| the king of Adullam | one |
| 16 the king of Makkedah | one |
| the king of Bethel | one |
| 17 the king of Tappuah | one |
| the king of Hepher[f] | one |
| 18 the king of Aphek | one |
| the king of Lasharon | one |
| 19 the king of Madon | one |
| the king of Hazor | one |
| 20 the king of Shimron Meron | one |
| the king of Acshaph | one |
| 21 the king of Taanach | one |
| the king of Megiddo | one |
| 22 the king of Kedesh[g] | one |
| the king of Jokneam in Carmel | one |
| 23 the king of Dor (in Naphoth Dor[a]) | one |
| the king of Goyim in Gilgal | one |
| 24 the king of Tirzah | one |

thirty-one kings in all.

## Land Still to Be Taken

13 When Joshua was old and well ad-
vanced in years,[h] the LORD said to
him, "You are very old, and there are still
very large areas of land to be taken over.

2 "This is the land that remains: all
the regions of the Philistines and
Geshurites: 3 from the Shihor River
on the east of Egypt to the territory of
Ekron on the north, all of it counted
as Canaanite (the territory of the five
Philistine rulers[i] in Gaza, Ashdod,
Ashkelon, Gath and Ekron—that of
the Avvites);[j] 4 from the south, all the
land of the Canaanites, from Arah of
the Sidonians as far as Aphek, the re-
gion of the Amorites,[k] 5 the area of the
Gebalites[b];[l] and all Lebanon to the
east, from Baal Gad below Mount Her-
mon to Lebo[c] Hamath.

6 "As for all the inhabitants of the moun-
tain regions from Lebanon to Misrephoth
Maim,[m] that is, all the Sidonians, I myself
will drive them out before the Israelites.
Be sure to allocate this land to Israel for an
inheritance, as I have instructed you, 7 and
divide it as an inheritance among the nine
tribes and half of the tribe of Manasseh."

## Division of the Land East of the Jordan

8 The other half of Manasseh,[d] the Reuben-
ites and the Gadites had received the inheri-
tance that Moses had given them east of the
Jordan, as he, the servant of the LORD, had
assigned[n] it to them.

9 It extended from Aroer[o] on the rim of
the Arnon Gorge, and from the town in
the middle of the gorge, and included
the whole plateau of Medeba as far as
Dibon, 10 and all the towns of Sihon king
of the Amorites, who ruled in Heshbon,

12:22 g Jos 19:37
13:1 h Jos 14:10
13:3 i Jdg 3:3 j Dt 2:23
13:4 k Am 2:10
13:5 l 1Ki 5:18
13:6 m Jos 11:8
13:8 n Jos 12:6
13:9 o ver 16

[a] 23 Or *in the heights of Dor* [b] 5 That is, the area of Byblos [c] 5 Or *to the entrance to* [d] 8 Hebrew *With it* (that is, with the other half of Manasseh)

**13:10** p Nu 21:24
**13:12** q Dt 3:11; r Jos 12:4
**13:14** s Dt 18:1–2
**13:16** t ver 9; Jos 12:2
**13:18** u Nu 21:23
**13:19** v Nu 32:37
**13:21** w Nu 31:8
**13:25** x Nu 21:32

out to the border of the Ammonites.[p] 11It also included Gilead, the territory of the people of Geshur and Maacah, all of Mount Hermon and all Bashan as far as Salecah— 12that is, the whole kingdom of Og in Bashan,[q] who had reigned in Ashtaroth[r] and Edrei and had survived as one of the last of the Rephaites. Moses had defeated them and taken over their land. 13But the Israelites did not drive out the people of Geshur and Maacah, so they continue to live among the Israelites to this day.

14But to the tribe of Levi he gave no inheritance, since the offerings made by fire to the LORD, the God of Israel, are their inheritance, as he promised them.[s]

15This is what Moses had given to the tribe of Reuben, clan by clan:

16The territory from Aroer[t] on the rim of the Arnon Gorge, and from the town in the middle of the gorge, and the whole plateau past Medeba 17to Heshbon and all its towns on the plateau, including Dibon, Bamoth Baal, Beth Baal Meon, 18Jahaz,[u] Kedemoth, Mephaath, 19Kiriathaim,[v] Sibmah, Zereth Shahar on the hill in the valley, 20Beth Peor, the slopes of Pisgah, and Beth Jeshimoth— 21all the towns on the plateau and the entire realm of Sihon king of the Amorites, who ruled at Heshbon. Moses had defeated him and the Midianite chiefs, Evi, Rekem, Zur, Hur and Reba[w]—princes allied with Sihon—who lived in that country. 22In addition to those slain in battle, the Israelites had put to the sword Balaam son of Beor, who practiced divination. 23The boundary of the Reubenites was the bank of the Jordan. These towns and their villages were the inheritance of the Reubenites, clan by clan.

24This is what Moses had given to the tribe of Gad, clan by clan:

25The territory of Jazer,[x] all the towns of Gilead and half the Ammonite country as far as Aroer, near Rabbah; 26and from Heshbon to Ramath Mizpah and Betonim, and from Mahanaim to the territory of Debir; 27and in the valley, Beth Haram, Beth Nimrah, Succoth and Zaphon with the rest of the realm of Sihon king of Heshbon (the east side of the Jordan, the territory up to the end of the Sea of Kinnereth[a][y]). 28These towns and their villages were the inheritance of the Gadites, clan by clan.

29This is what Moses had given to the half-tribe of Manasseh, that is, to half the family of the descendants of Manasseh, clan by clan:

30The territory extending from Mahanaim and including all of Bashan, the entire realm of Og king of Bashan—all the settlements of Jair[z] in Bashan, sixty towns, 31half of Gilead, and Ashtaroth and Edrei (the royal cities of Og in Bashan). This was for the descendants of Makir son of Manasseh—for half of the sons of Makir, clan by clan.

32This is the inheritance Moses had given when he was in the plains of Moab across the Jordan east of Jericho. 33But to the tribe of Levi, Moses had given no inheritance; the LORD, the God of Israel, is their inheritance,[a] as he promised them.[b]

## Division of the Land West of the Jordan

**14** Now these are the areas the Israelites received as an inheritance in the land of Canaan, which Eleazar the priest, Joshua son of Nun and the heads of the tribal clans of Israel allotted to them.[c] 2Their inheritances were assigned by lot[d] to the nine-and-a-half tribes, as the LORD had commanded through Moses. 3Moses had granted the two-and-a-half tribes their inheritance east of the Jordan[e] but had not granted the Levites an inheritance among the rest,[f] 4for the sons of Joseph had become two tribes—Manasseh and Ephraim.[g] The Levites received no share of the land but only towns to live in, with pasturelands for their flocks and herds. 5So the Israelites divided the land, just as the LORD had commanded Moses.

**13:27** y Nu 34:11
**13:30** z Nu 32:41
**13:33** a Nu 18:20; b ver 14
**14:1** c Nu 34:17–18
**14:2** d Nu 26:55
**14:3** e Nu 32:33; f Jos 13:14
**14:4** g Ge 48:5

[a]27 That is, Galilee

14:6 h Nu 14:30 i Nu 13:26
14:7 j Nu 13:30; 14:6–9
14:8 k Nu 14:24
14:9 l Dt 1:36
14:11 m Dt 34:7
14:12 n Nu 13:33
14:13 o Jos 22:6,7
14:15 p Jos 11:23
15:1 q Nu 34:3
15:3 r Nu 34:4

## Hebron Given to Caleb

[6]Now the men of Judah approached Joshua at Gilgal, and Caleb son of Jephunneh[h] the Kenizzite said to him, "You know what the LORD said to Moses the man of God at Kadesh Barnea[i] about you and me. [7]I was forty years old when Moses the servant of the LORD sent me from Kadesh Barnea to explore the land. And I brought him back a report according to my convictions,[j] [8]but my brothers who went up with me made the hearts of the people melt with fear. I, however, followed the LORD my God wholeheartedly.[k] [9]So on that day Moses swore to me, 'The land on which your feet have walked will be your inheritance and that of your children[l] forever, because you have followed the LORD my God wholeheartedly.'[a]

[10]"Now then, just as the LORD promised, he has kept me alive for forty-five years since the time he said this to Moses, while Israel moved about in the desert. So here I am today, eighty-five years old! [11]I am still as strong[m] today as the day Moses sent me out; I'm just as vigorous to go out to battle now as I was then. [12]Now give me this hill country that the LORD promised me that day. You yourself heard then that the Anakites[n] were there and their cities were large and fortified, but, the LORD helping me, I will drive them out just as he said."

[13]Then Joshua blessed[o] Caleb son of Jephunneh and gave him Hebron as his inheritance. [14]So Hebron has belonged to Caleb son of Jephunneh the Kenizzite ever since, because he followed the LORD, the God of Israel, wholeheartedly. [15](Hebron used to be called Kiriath Arba after Arba, who was the greatest man among the Anakites.)

Then the land had rest[p] from war.

## Allotment for Judah

15 The allotment for the tribe of Judah, clan by clan, extended down to the territory of Edom,[q] to the Desert of Zin in the extreme south.

[2]Their southern boundary started from the bay at the southern end of the Salt Sea,[b] [3]crossed south of Scorpion[c] Pass,[r] continued on to Zin and went over to the south of Kadesh Barnea. Then it ran past Hezron up to Addar and curved around to Karka. [4]It then passed along to Azmon[s] and joined the Wadi of Egypt, ending at the sea. This is their[d] southern boundary.

[5]The eastern boundary is the Salt Sea as far as the mouth of the Jordan.

The northern boundary started from the bay of the sea at the mouth of the Jordan, [6]went up to Beth Hoglah and continued north of Beth Arabah to the Stone of Bohan[t] son of Reuben. [7]The boundary then went up to Debir from the Valley of Achor[u] and turned north to Gilgal, which faces the Pass of Adummim south of the gorge. It continued along to the waters of En Shemesh and came out at En Rogel. [8]Then it ran up the Valley of Ben Hinnom along the southern slope of the Jebusite[v] city (that is, Jerusalem). From there it climbed to the top of the hill west of the Hinnom Valley at the northern end of the Valley of Rephaim. [9]From the hilltop the boundary headed toward the spring of the waters of Nephtoah,[w] came out at the towns of Mount Ephron and went down toward Baalah[x] (that is, Kiriath Jearim). [10]Then it curved westward from Baalah to Mount Seir, ran along the northern slope of Mount Jearim (that is, Kesalon), continued down to Beth Shemesh and crossed to Timnah.[y] [11]It went to the northern slope of Ekron, turned toward Shikkeron, passed along to Mount Baalah and reached Jabneel. The boundary ended at the sea.

[12]The western boundary is the coastline of the Great Sea.[e][z]

These are the boundaries around the people of Judah by their clans.

[13]In accordance with the LORD's command to him, Joshua gave to Caleb son of Jephunneh a portion in Judah—Kiriath Arba, that is, Hebron. (Arba was the forefather of Anak.)[a] [14]From Hebron Caleb drove out the three Anakites—Sheshai,

15:4 s Nu 34:5
15:6 t Jos 18:17
15:7 u Jos 7:24
15:8 v ver 63
15:9 w Jos 18:15 x 1Ch 13:6
15:10 y Ge 38:12
15:12 z Nu 34:6
15:13 a Jos 14:13–15

[a]9 Deut. 1:36 [b]2 That is, the Dead Sea; also in verse 5 [c]3 Hebrew *Akrabbim* [d]4 Hebrew *your* [e]12 That is, the Mediterranean; also in verse 47

**15:14** b Nu 13:22
**15:16** c Jdg 1:12
**15:17** d Jdg 3:9,11
**15:21** e Ge 35:21
**15:31** f 1Sa 27:6
**15:33** g Jdg 13:25; 16:31
**15:35** h 1Sa 22:1
**15:38** i 2Ki 14:7
**15:39** j Jos 10:3; 2Ki 14:19

Ahiman and Talmai[b]—descendants of Anak. 15 From there he marched against the people living in Debir (formerly called Kiriath Sepher). 16 And Caleb said, "I will give my daughter Acsah[c] in marriage to the man who attacks and captures Kiriath Sepher." 17 Othniel[d] son of Kenaz, Caleb's brother, took it; so Caleb gave his daughter Acsah to him in marriage.

18 One day when she came to Othniel, she urged him[a] to ask her father for a field. When she got off her donkey, Caleb asked her, "What can I do for you?"

19 She replied, "Do me a special favor. Since you have given me land in the Negev, give me also springs of water." So Caleb gave her the upper and lower springs.

20 This is the inheritance of the tribe of Judah, clan by clan:

21 The southernmost towns of the tribe of Judah in the Negev toward the boundary of Edom were:

Kabzeel, Eder,[e] Jagur, 22 Kinah, Dimonah, Adadah, 23 Kedesh, Hazor, Ithnan, 24 Ziph, Telem, Bealoth, 25 Hazor Hadattah, Kerioth Hezron (that is, Hazor), 26 Amam, Shema, Moladah, 27 Hazar Gaddah, Heshmon, Beth Pelet, 28 Hazar Shual, Beersheba, Biziothiah, 29 Baalah, Iim, Ezem, 30 Eltolad, Kesil, Hormah, 31 Ziklag,[f] Madmannah, Sansannah, 32 Lebaoth, Shilhim, Ain and Rimmon—a total of twenty-nine towns and their villages.

33 In the western foothills:

Eshtaol,[g] Zorah, Ashnah, 34 Zanoah, En Gannim, Tappuah, Enam, 35 Jarmuth, Adullam,[h] Socoh, Azekah, 36 Shaaraim, Adithaim and Gederah (or Gederothaim)[b]—fourteen towns and their villages.

37 Zenan, Hadashah, Migdal Gad, 38 Dilean, Mizpah, Joktheel,[i] 39 Lachish,[j] Bozkath, Eglon, 40 Cabbon, Lahmas, Kitlish, 41 Gederoth, Beth Dagon, Naamah and Makkedah—sixteen towns and their villages.

42 Libnah, Ether, Ashan, 43 Iphtah, Ashnah, Nezib, 44 Keilah, Aczib and Mareshah—nine towns and their villages.

45 Ekron, with its surrounding settlements and villages; 46 west of Ekron, all that were in the vicinity of Ashdod, together with their villages; 47 Ashdod, its surrounding settlements and villages; and Gaza, its settlements and villages, as far as the Wadi of Egypt[k] and the coastline of the Great Sea.[l]

48 In the hill country:

Shamir, Jattir, Socoh, 49 Dannah, Kiriath Sannah (that is, Debir), 50 Anab, Eshtemoh, Anim, 51 Goshen,[m] Holon and Giloh—eleven towns and their villages.

52 Arab, Dumah, Eshan, 53 Janim, Beth Tappuah, Aphekah, 54 Humtah, Kiriath Arba (that is, Hebron) and Zior—nine towns and their villages.

55 Maon, Carmel, Ziph, Juttah, 56 Jezreel, Jokdeam, Zanoah, 57 Kain, Gibeah and Timnah—ten towns and their villages.

58 Halhul, Beth Zur, Gedor, 59 Maarath, Beth Anoth and Eltekon—six towns and their villages.

60 Kiriath Baal (that is, Kiriath Jearim[n]) and Rabbah—two towns and their villages.

61 In the desert:

Beth Arabah, Middin, Secacah, 62 Nibshan, the City of Salt and En Gedi—six towns and their villages.

63 Judah could not[o] dislodge the Jebusites[p], who were living in Jerusalem; to this day the Jebusites live there with the people of Judah.

## Allotment for Ephraim and Manasseh

**16** The allotment for Joseph began at the Jordan of Jericho,[c] east of the waters of Jericho, and went up from there through the desert into the hill country of Bethel. 2 It went on from Bethel (that is, Luz[q]),[d] crossed over to the territory of the Arkites in

**15:47** k ver 4; l Nu 34:6
**15:51** m Jos 10:41; 11:16
**15:60** n Jos 18:14
**15:63** o Jdg 1:21; p 2Sa 5:6
**16:2** q Jos 18:13

[a] 18 Hebrew and some Septuagint manuscripts; other Septuagint manuscripts (see also note at Judges 1:14) *Othniel, he urged her* [b] 36 Or *Gederah and Gederothaim* [c] 1 *Jordan of Jericho* was possibly an ancient name for the Jordan River. [d] 2 Septuagint; Hebrew *Bethel to Luz*

# Acsah

## A Wise Daughter

Although she is a little-known woman of the Bible, Acsah is a wonderful role model for women today. She used her wisdom and knowledge to provide for her family.

The story of Acsah is found in the books of Joshua and Judges. Acsah was the daughter of Caleb, who achieved fame as one of the two spies of Israel who gave a good report about the promised land (see Nu 13:26–33). We read that later, at the age of 85, Caleb reminded Joshua of the promise that had been given him by Moses regarding the land of Canaan (see Jos 14:6–15). Caleb had success in driving out some of the inhabitants of the land that he acquired; however, he needed help to conquer the land of Debir. In order to do this, he offered his daughter Acsah in marriage as an incentive (see Jos 15:13–17).

The account of Acsah implies she and Caleb enjoyed a close relationship. Although she was used as a commodity to help her father conquer land, Acsah used her wisdom to make the best of her situation. The Negev, the southern part of Judah, is a hot, dry region with less than eight inches of rainfall annually. Water is a necessity, and springs make life easier in this harsh country. The wording of Acsah's request suggests that she had some knowledge of what life was like in this area. She was wise enough to get her husband's consent before asking her father to give her a dowry of commercial value and productivity (see Jos 15:18–19).

The exchange between Caleb and his nephew Othniel is unknown; however, Caleb respected his daughter enough to want to know her wishes. Acsah's story is an account of an obedient daughter who did not bemoan her fate but utilized wisdom. Her actions possibly allowed her family to become successful and respected in the community, for we later learn that Othniel became the first judge of Israel after Joshua's death (see Jdg 3:9–11).

—M. Copeland

### reflection

*Reflect on a time you used wisdom to make the best of a seemingly bad situation.*

*How does that past experience inspire you to use wisdom in a situation you are dealing with today?*

### read

Joshua 15:13–19; Judges 1:11–15; 3:9–11.

See also the Inspire Notes "Influencing Others," "Discernment" and "Seek Wisdom," and the Women of the Bible Notes "Zelophehad's Daughters: Seeking an Inheritance" and "A Virtuous Woman: A Strong Woman, Dependent on God."

For the next Women of the Bible note, go to page 279.

**16:5** r Jos 18:13
**16:6** s Jos 17:7
**16:8** t Jos 17:9
**16:10** u Jos 17:13; Jdg 1:28–29; 1Ki 9:16
**17:1** v Ge 41:51
**17:2** w Nu 26:30
**17:3** x Nu 27:1 y Nu 26:33

Ataroth, [3]descended westward to the
territory of the Japhletites as far as the
region of Lower Beth Horon and on to
Gezer, ending at the sea.
[4]So Manasseh and Ephraim, the descen-
dants of Joseph, received their inheritance.

[5]This was the territory of Ephraim, clan by
clan:

The boundary of their inheritance
went from Ataroth Addar[r] in the east
to Upper Beth Horon [6]and continued
to the sea. From Micmethath[s] on the
north it curved eastward to Taanath
Shiloh, passing by it to Janoah on the
east. [7]Then it went down from Janoah
to Ataroth and Naarah, touched Jeri-
cho and came out at the Jordan. [8]From
Tappuah the border went west to the
Kanah Ravine[t] and ended at the sea.
This was the inheritance of the tribe
of the Ephraimites, clan by clan. [9]It
also included all the towns and their
villages that were set aside for the
Ephraimites within the inheritance of
the Manassites.
[10]They did not dislodge the Canaanites
living in Gezer; to this day the Canaanites
live among the people of Ephraim but are re-
quired to do forced labor.[u]

17 This was the allotment for the tribe
of Manasseh as Joseph's firstborn,[v]
that is, for Makir, Manasseh's firstborn. Ma-
kir was the ancestor of the Gileadites, who
had received Gilead and Bashan because the
Makirites were great soldiers. [2]So this allot-
ment was for the rest of the people of Manas-
seh—the clans of Abiezer,[w] Helek, Asriel,
Shechem, Hepher and Shemida. These are
the other male descendants of Manasseh
son of Joseph by their clans.

[3]Now Zelophehad son of Hepher,[x] the son
of Gilead, the son of Makir, the son of Manas-
seh, had no sons but only daughters,[y] whose
names were Mahlah, Noah, Hoglah, Mil-
cah and Tirzah. [4]They went to Eleazar the
priest, Joshua son of Nun, and the leaders
and said, "The LORD commanded Moses to
give us an inheritance among our brothers."
So Joshua gave them an inheritance along
with the brothers of their father, according
to the LORD's command.[z] [5]Manasseh's share
consisted of ten tracts of land besides Gilead
and Bashan east of the Jordan, [6]because the
daughters of the tribe of Manasseh received
an inheritance among the sons. The land
of Gilead belonged to the rest of the descen-
dants of Manasseh.

[7]The territory of Manasseh ex-
tended from Asher to Micmethath[a]
east of Shechem. The boundary ran
southward from there to include the
people living at En Tappuah. [8](Ma-
nasseh had the land of Tappuah, but
Tappuah[b] itself, on the boundary of
Manasseh, belonged to the Ephraim-
ites.) [9]Then the boundary continued
south to the Kanah Ravine.[c] There
were towns belonging to Ephraim ly-
ing among the towns of Manasseh, but
the boundary of Manasseh was the
northern side of the ravine and ended
at the sea. [10]On the south the land be-
longed to Ephraim, on the north to
Manasseh. The territory of Manasseh
reached the sea and bordered Asher
on the north and Issachar on the east.

[11]Within Issachar and Asher, Ma-
nasseh also had Beth Shan,[d] Ibleam
and the people of Dor, Endor, Taanach
and Megiddo, together with their sur-
rounding settlements (the third in the
list is Naphoth[a]).
[12]Yet the Manassites were not able[e] to
occupy these towns, for the Canaanites were
determined to live in that region. [13]However,
when the Israelites grew stronger, they
subjected the Canaanites to forced labor but
did not drive them out completely.[f]

[14]The people of Joseph said to Joshua,
"Why have you given us only one allotment
and one portion for an inheritance? We are
a numerous people and the LORD has blessed
us abundantly."[g]

[15]"If you are so numerous," Joshua an-
swered, "and if the hill country of Ephraim
is too small for you, go up into the forest and
clear land for yourselves there in the land of
the Perizzites and Rephaites."

[16]The people of Joseph replied, "The hill
country is not enough for us, and all the
Canaanites who live in the plain have iron

**17:4** z Nu 27:5–7
**17:7** a Jos 16:6
**17:8** b Jos 16:8
**17:9** c Jos 16:8
**17:11** d 1Ch 7:29
**17:12** e Jdg 1:27
**17:13** f Jos 16:10
**17:14** g Nu 26:28–37

[a]11 That is, Naphoth Dor

chariots,[h] both those in Beth Shan and its settlements and those in the Valley of Jezreel."

[17]But Joshua said to the house of Joseph—to Ephraim and Manasseh—"You are numerous and very powerful. You will have not only one allotment [18]but the forested hill country as well. Clear it, and its farthest limits will be yours; though the Canaanites have iron chariots and though they are strong, you can drive them out."

## Division of the Rest of the Land

**18** The whole assembly of the Israelites gathered at Shiloh[i] and set up the Tent of Meeting there. The country was brought under their control, [2]but there were still seven Israelite tribes who had not yet received their inheritance.

[3]So Joshua said to the Israelites: "How long will you wait before you begin to take possession of the land that the LORD, the God of your fathers, has given you? [4]Appoint three men from each tribe. I will send them out to make a survey of the land and to write a description of it, according to the inheritance of each. Then they will return to me. [5]You are to divide the land into seven parts. Judah is to remain in its territory on the south[j] and the house of Joseph in its territory on the north.[k] [6]After you have written descriptions of the seven parts of the land, bring them here to me and I will cast lots for you in the presence of the LORD our God. [7]The Levites, however, do not get a portion among you, because the priestly service of the LORD is their inheritance.[l] And Gad, Reuben and the half-tribe of Manasseh have already received their inheritance on the east side of the Jordan. Moses the servant of the LORD gave it to them."

[8]As the men started on their way to map out the land, Joshua instructed them, "Go and make a survey of the land and write a description of it. Then return to me, and I will cast lots for you here at Shiloh in the presence of the LORD." [9]So the men left and went through the land. They wrote its description on a scroll, town by town, in seven parts, and returned to Joshua in the camp at Shiloh. [10]Joshua then cast lots for them in Shiloh in the presence of the LORD, and there he distributed the land to the Israelites according to their tribal divisions.[m]

## Allotment for Benjamin

[11]The lot came up for the tribe of Benjamin, clan by clan. Their allotted territory lay between the tribes of Judah and Joseph:

[12]On the north side their boundary began at the Jordan, passed the northern slope of Jericho and headed west into the hill country, coming out at the desert[n] of Beth Aven. [13]From there it crossed to the south slope of Luz[o] (that is, Bethel[p]) and went down to Ataroth Addar[q] on the hill south of Lower Beth Horon.

[14]From the hill facing Beth Horon on the south the boundary turned south along the western side and came out at Kiriath Baal (that is, Kiriath Jearim), a town of the people of Judah. This was the western side.

[15]The southern side began at the outskirts of Kiriath Jearim on the west, and the boundary came out at the spring of the waters of Nephtoah.[r] [16]The boundary went down to the foot of the hill facing the Valley of Ben Hinnom, north of the Valley of Rephaim. It continued down the Hinnom Valley[s] along the southern slope of the Jebusite city and so to En Rogel.[t] [17]It then curved north, went to En Shemesh, continued to Geliloth, which faces the Pass of Adummim, and ran down to the Stone of Bohan[u] son of Reuben. [18]It continued to the northern slope of Beth Arabah[a][v] and on down into the Arabah. [19]It then went to the northern slope of Beth Hoglah and came out at the northern bay of the Salt Sea,[b] at the mouth of the Jordan in the south. This was the southern boundary.

[20]The Jordan formed the boundary on the eastern side.

These were the boundaries that marked out the inheritance of the clans of Benjamin on all sides.

**17:16** h Jdg 1:19; 4:3,13
**18:1** i Jos 19:51; Jer 7:12
**18:5** j Jos 15:1 k Jos 16:1–4
**18:7** l Jos 13:33
**18:10** m Jos 19:51
**18:12** n Jos 16:1
**18:13** o Ge 28:19 p Jdg 1:23 q Jos 16:5
**18:15** r Jos 15:9
**18:16** s Jos 15:8; 2Ki 23:10 t Jos 15:7
**18:17** u Jos 15:6
**18:18** v Jos 15:6

[a]18 Septuagint; Hebrew *slope facing the Arabah* [b]19 That is, the Dead Sea

**18:24** w Isa 10:29
**18:28** x 2Sa 21:14; y Jos 15:8
**19:1** z ver 9
**19:11** a Jos 12:22

21 The tribe of Benjamin, clan by clan, had the following cities:

Jericho, Beth Hoglah, Emek Keziz, 22 Beth Arabah, Zemaraim, Bethel, 23 Avvim, Parah, Ophrah, 24 Kephar Ammoni, Ophni and Geba[w]—twelve towns and their villages.

25 Gibeon, Ramah, Beeroth, 26 Mizpah, Kephirah, Mozah, 27 Rekem, Irpeel, Taralah, 28 Zelah,[x] Haeleph, the Jebusite city[y] (that is, Jerusalem), Gibeah and Kiriath—fourteen towns and their villages.

This was the inheritance of Benjamin for its clans.

## Allotment for Simeon

**19** The second lot came out for the tribe of Simeon, clan by clan. Their inheritance lay within the territory of Judah.[z] 2 It included:

Beersheba (or Sheba),[a] Moladah, 3 Hazar Shual, Balah, Ezem, 4 Eltolad, Bethul, Hormah, 5 Ziklag, Beth Marcaboth, Hazar Susah, 6 Beth Lebaoth and Sharuhen—thirteen towns and their villages;

7 Ain, Rimmon, Ether and Ashan—four towns and their villages— 8 and all the villages around these towns as far as Baalath Beer (Ramah in the Negev).

This was the inheritance of the tribe of the Simeonites, clan by clan. 9 The inheritance of the Simeonites was taken from the share of Judah, because Judah's portion was more than they needed. So the Simeonites received their inheritance within the territory of Judah.

## Allotment for Zebulun

10 The third lot came up for Zebulun, clan by clan:

The boundary of their inheritance went as far as Sarid. 11 Going west it ran to Maralah, touched Dabbesheth, and extended to the ravine near Jokneam.[a] 12 It turned east from Sarid toward the sunrise to the territory of Kisloth Tabor and went on to Daberath and up to Japhia. 13 Then it continued eastward to Gath Hepher and Eth Kazin; it came out at Rimmon and turned toward Neah. 14 There the boundary went around on the north to Hannathon and ended at the Valley of Iphtah El. 15 Included were Kattath, Nahalal, Shimron, Idalah and Bethlehem. There were twelve towns and their villages.

16 These towns and their villages were the inheritance of Zebulun, clan by clan.

## Allotment for Issachar

17 The fourth lot came out for Issachar, clan by clan. 18 Their territory included:

Jezreel, Kesulloth, Shunem,[b] 19 Hapharaim, Shion, Anaharath, 20 Rabbith, Kishion, Ebez, 21 Remeth, En Gannim, En Haddah and Beth Pazzez. 22 The boundary touched Tabor,[c] Shahazumah and Beth Shemesh, and ended at the Jordan. There were sixteen towns and their villages.

23 These towns and their villages were the inheritance of the tribe of Issachar, clan by clan.

## Allotment for Asher

24 The fifth lot came out for the tribe of Asher, clan by clan. 25 Their territory included:

Helkath, Hali, Beten, Acshaph, 26 Allammelech, Amad and Mishal. On the west the boundary touched Carmel and Shihor Libnath. 27 It then turned east toward Beth Dagon, touched Zebulun and the Valley of Iphtah El, and went north to Beth Emek and Neiel, passing Cabul[d] on the left. 28 It went to Abdon,[b] Rehob,[e] Hammon and Kanah, as far as Greater Sidon.[f] 29 The boundary then turned back toward Ramah and went to the fortified city of Tyre, turned toward Hosah and came out at the sea in the region of Aczib,[g] 30 Ummah, Aphek and Rehob. There were twenty-two towns and their villages.

31 These towns and their villages were the inheritance of the tribe of Asher, clan by clan.

**19:18** b 1Sa 28:4; 2Ki 4:8
**19:22** c Jdg 4:6,12; Ps 89:12
**19:27** d 1Ki 9:13
**19:28** e Jdg 1:31; f Ge 10:19; Jos 11:8
**19:29** g Jdg 1:31

[a]2 Or *Beersheba, Sheba*; 1 Chron. 4:28 does not have *Sheba*.
[b]28 Some Hebrew manuscripts (see also Joshua 21:30); most Hebrew manuscripts *Ebron*

## Allotment for Naphtali

32 The sixth lot came out for Naphtali, clan by clan:

33 Their boundary went from Heleph and the large tree in Zaanannim, passing Adami Nekeb and Jabneel to Lakkum and ending at the Jordan. 34 The boundary ran west through Aznoth Tabor and came out at Hukkok. It touched Zebulun on the south, Asher on the west and the Jordan[a] on the east. 35 The fortified cities were Ziddim, Zer, Hammath, Rakkath, Kinnereth, 36 Adamah, Ramah, Hazor, 37 Kedesh, Edrei, En Hazor, 38 Iron, Migdal El, Horem, Beth Anath and Beth Shemesh. There were nineteen towns and their villages.

39 These towns and their villages were the inheritance of the tribe of Naphtali, clan by clan.[h]

## Allotment for Dan

40 The seventh lot came out for the tribe of Dan, clan by clan. 41 The territory of their inheritance included:

Zorah, Eshtaol, Ir Shemesh, 42 Shaalabbin, Aijalon,[i] Ithlah, 43 Elon, Timnah, Ekron, 44 Eltekeh, Gibbethon, Baalath, 45 Jehud, Bene Berak, Gath Rimmon, 46 Me Jarkon and Rakkon, with the area facing Joppa.

47 (But the Danites had difficulty taking possession of their territory,[j] so they went up and attacked Leshem, took it, put it to the sword and occupied it. They settled in Leshem and named it Dan after their forefather.)[k]

48 These towns and their villages were the inheritance of the tribe of Dan, clan by clan.

## Allotment for Joshua

49 When they had finished dividing the land into its allotted portions, the Israelites gave Joshua son of Nun an inheritance among them, 50 as the LORD had commanded. They gave him the town he asked for—Timnath Serah[b][l] in the hill country of Ephraim. And he built up the town and settled there.

51 These are the territories that Eleazar the priest, Joshua son of Nun and the heads of the tribal clans of Israel assigned by lot at Shiloh in the presence of the LORD at the entrance to the Tent of Meeting. And so they finished dividing the land.[m]

## Cities of Refuge

**20** Then the LORD said to Joshua: 2 "Tell the Israelites to designate the cities of refuge, as I instructed you through Moses, 3 so that anyone who kills a person accidentally and unintentionally may flee there and find protection from the avenger of blood.

4 "When he flees to one of these cities, he is to stand in the entrance of the city gate[n] and state his case before the elders of that city. Then they are to admit him into their city and give him a place to live with them. 5 If the avenger of blood pursues him, they must not surrender the one accused, because he killed his neighbor unintentionally and without malice aforethought. 6 He is to stay in that city until he has stood trial before the assembly[o] and until the death of the high priest who is serving at that time. Then he may go back to his own home in the town from which he fled."

7 So they set apart Kedesh[p] in Galilee in the hill country of Naphtali, Shechem in the hill country of Ephraim, and Kiriath Arba (that is, Hebron[q]) in the hill country of Judah.[r] 8 On the east side of the Jordan of Jericho[c] they designated Bezer[s] in the desert on the plateau in the tribe of Reuben, Ramoth in Gilead in the tribe of Gad, and Golan in Bashan in the tribe of Manasseh. 9 Any of the Israelites or any alien living among them who killed someone accidentally could flee to these designated cities and not be killed by the avenger of blood prior to standing trial before the assembly.[t]

## Towns for the Levites

**21** Now the family heads of the Levites approached Eleazar the priest, Joshua son of Nun, and the heads of the other tribal families of Israel[u] 2 at Shiloh in Canaan and said to them, "The

[a]34 Septuagint; Hebrew *west, and Judah, the Jordan,* [b]50 Also known as *Timnath Heres* (see Judges 2:9) [c]8 *Jordan of Jericho* was possibly an ancient name for the Jordan River.

**19:39** h Dt33:23
**19:42** i Jdg1:35
**19:47** j Jdg18:1 k Jdg18:27,29
**19:50** l Jos24:30
**19:51** m Jos14:1; 18:10
**20:4** n Ru4:1
**20:6** o Nu35:12
**20:7** p Jos21:32; 1Ch6:76 q Jos21:11 r Lk1:39
**20:8** s Jos21:36
**20:9** t Ex21:13; Nu35:15
**21:1** u Jos14:1

LORD commanded through Moses that you give us towns to live in, with pasturelands for our livestock."[v] 3So, as the LORD had commanded, the Israelites gave the Levites the following towns and pasturelands out of their own inheritance:

4The first lot came out for the Kohathites, clan by clan. The Levites who were descendants of Aaron the priest were allotted thirteen towns from the tribes of Judah, Simeon and Benjamin.[w] 5The rest of Kohath's descendants were allotted ten towns from the clans of the tribes of Ephraim, Dan and half of Manasseh.

6The descendants of Gershon were allotted thirteen towns from the clans of the tribes of Issachar, Asher, Naphtali and the half-tribe of Manasseh in Bashan.

7The descendants of Merari, clan by clan, received twelve towns from the tribes of Reuben, Gad and Zebulun.

8So the Israelites allotted to the Levites these towns and their pasturelands, as the LORD had commanded through Moses.

9From the tribes of Judah and Simeon they allotted the following towns by name 10(these towns were assigned to the descendants of Aaron who were from the Kohathite clans of the Levites, because the first lot fell to them):

> 11They gave them Kiriath Arba (that is, Hebron[x]), with its surrounding pastureland, in the hill country of Judah. (Arba was the forefather of Anak.) 12But the fields and villages around the city they had given to Caleb son of Jephunneh as his possession.
>
> 13So to the descendants of Aaron the priest they gave Hebron (a city of refuge for one accused of murder), Libnah,[y] 14Jattir, Eshtemoa, 15Holon, Debir, 16Ain, Juttah[z] and Beth Shemesh,[a] together with their pasturelands—nine towns from these two tribes.
>
> 17And from the tribe of Benjamin they gave them Gibeon, Geba,[b] 18Anathoth and Almon, together with their pasturelands—four towns.

19All the towns for the priests, the descendants of Aaron, were thirteen, together with their pasturelands.

20The rest of the Kohathite clans of the Levites were allotted towns from the tribe of Ephraim:

> 21In the hill country of Ephraim they were given Shechem[c] (a city of refuge for one accused of murder) and Gezer, 22Kibzaim and Beth Horon, together with their pasturelands—four towns.
>
> 23Also from the tribe of Dan they received Eltekeh, Gibbethon, 24Aijalon and Gath Rimmon, together with their pasturelands—four towns.
>
> 25From half the tribe of Manasseh they received Taanach and Gath Rimmon, together with their pasturelands—two towns.

26All these ten towns and their pasturelands were given to the rest of the Kohathite clans.

27The Levite clans of the Gershonites were given:

from the half-tribe of Manasseh,
  Golan in Bashan[d] (a city of refuge for one accused of murder[e]) and Be Eshtarah, together with their pasturelands—two towns;

28from the tribe of Issachar,
  Kishion, Daberath, 29Jarmuth and En Gannim, together with their pasturelands—four towns;

30from the tribe of Asher,
  Mishal, Abdon, 31Helkath and Rehob, together with their pasturelands—four towns;

32from the tribe of Naphtali,
  Kedesh in Galilee (a city of refuge for one accused of murder[f]), Hammoth Dor and Kartan, together with their pasturelands—three towns.

33All the towns of the Gershonite clans were thirteen, together with their pasturelands.

34The Merarite clans (the rest of the Levites) were given:

from the tribe of Zebulun,[g]
  Jokneam, Kartah, 35Dimnah and Nahalal, together with their pasturelands—four towns;

36from the tribe of Reuben,
  Bezer,[h] Jahaz, 37Kedemoth and Mephaath, together with their pasturelands—four towns;

**21:2** v Nu 35:2–3
**21:4** w ver 19
**21:11** x Jos 15:13; 1Ch 6:55
**21:13** y Jos 15:42; 1Ch 6:57
**21:16** z Jos 15:55 a Jos 15:10
**21:17** b Jos 18:24
**21:21** c Jos 20:7
**21:27** d Jos 12:5 e Nu 35:6
**21:32** f Jos 20:7
**21:34** g 1Ch 6:77
**21:36** h Jos 20:8

**21:38** i Dt4:43
**21:41** j Nu35:7
**21:43** k Dt11:31
**21:44** l Jos1:13; m Dt7:24
**21:45** n Jos23:14; Ne9:8
**22:4** o Dt3:20; p Nu32:18
**22:5** q Dt5:29; r Dt6:6,17
**22:6** s Ex39:43
**22:7** t Nu32:33; u Jos17:2,5

38 from the tribe of Gad,
Ramoth[i] in Gilead (a city of refuge for
one accused of murder), Mahanaim,
39 Heshbon and Jazer, together with
their pasturelands—four towns in
all.
40 All the towns allotted to the Merarite
clans, who were the rest of the Levites,
were twelve.
41 The towns of the Levites in the territory
held by the Israelites were forty-eight in all,
together with their pasturelands.[j] 42 Each of
these towns had pasturelands surrounding
it; this was true for all these towns.

43 So the LORD gave Israel all the land he
had sworn to give their forefathers, and
they took possession[k] of it and settled there.
44 The LORD gave them rest[l] on every side, just
as he had sworn to their forefathers. Not one
of their enemies withstood them; the LORD
handed all their enemies over to them.[m]
45 Not one of all the LORD's good promises[n] to
the house of Israel failed; every one was fulfilled.

## Eastern Tribes Return Home

22 Then Joshua summoned the Reu-
benites, the Gadites and the half-
tribe of Manasseh 2 and said to them, "You
have done all that Moses the servant of the
LORD commanded, and you have obeyed me
in everything I commanded. 3 For a long
time now—to this very day—you have not
deserted your brothers but have carried out
the mission the LORD your God gave you.
4 Now that the LORD your God has given your
brothers rest as he promised, return to your
homes[o] in the land that Moses the servant
of the LORD gave you on the other side of
the Jordan.[p] 5 But be very careful to keep the
commandment and the law that Moses
the servant of the LORD gave you: to love the
LORD your God, to walk in all his ways, to
obey his commands,[q] to hold fast to him
and to serve him with all your heart and all
your soul.[r]"

6 Then Joshua blessed[s] them and sent
them away, and they went to their homes.
7 (To the half-tribe of Manasseh Moses had
given land in Bashan,[t] and to the other half
of the tribe Joshua gave land on the west
side[u] of the Jordan with their brothers.)
When Joshua sent them home, he blessed
them, 8 saying, "Return to your homes with
your great wealth—with large herds of livestock, with silver, gold, bronze and iron,
and a great quantity of clothing—and divide[v] with your brothers the plunder[w] from
your enemies."

9 So the Reubenites, the Gadites and the
half-tribe of Manasseh left the Israelites
at Shiloh in Canaan to return to Gilead,[x]
their own land, which they had acquired in
accordance with the command of the LORD
through Moses.

10 When they came to Geliloth near the Jordan in the land of Canaan, the Reubenites,
the Gadites and the half-tribe of Manasseh
built an imposing altar there by the Jordan.
11 And when the Israelites heard that they
had built the altar on the border of Canaan
at Geliloth near the Jordan on the Israelite
side, 12 the whole assembly of Israel gathered
at Shiloh[y] to go to war against them.

13 So the Israelites sent Phinehas[z] son of
Eleazar, the priest, to the land of Gilead—to
Reuben, Gad and the half-tribe of Manasseh. 14 With him they sent ten of the chief
men, one for each of the tribes of Israel, each
the head of a family division among the Israelite clans.[a]

15 When they went to Gilead—to Reuben,
Gad and the half-tribe of Manasseh—they
said to them: 16 "The whole assembly of the
LORD says: 'How could you break faith with
the God of Israel like this? How could you
turn away from the LORD and build yourselves an altar in rebellion[b] against him
now? 17 Was not the sin of Peor[c] enough for
us? Up to this very day we have not cleansed
ourselves from that sin, even though a
plague fell on the community of the LORD!
18 And are you now turning away from the
LORD?

"'If you rebel against the LORD today,
tomorrow he will be angry with the whole
community of Israel. 19 If the land you possess is defiled, come over to the LORD's land,
where the LORD's tabernacle stands, and
share the land with us. But do not rebel
against the LORD or against us by building
an altar for yourselves, other than the altar
of the LORD our God. 20 When Achan son of
Zerah acted unfaithfully regarding the

**22:8** v Nu31:27; w 1Sa30:16
**22:9** x Nu32:26,29
**22:12** y Jos18:1
**22:13** z Nu25:7
**22:14** a Nu1:4
**22:16** b Dt12:13–14
**22:17** c Nu25:1–9

devoted things,[a][d] did not wrath come upon the whole community of Israel? He was not the only one who died for his sin.'"[e]

21 Then Reuben, Gad and the half-tribe of Manasseh replied to the heads of the clans of Israel: 22 "The Mighty One, God, the LORD! The Mighty One, God,[f] the LORD! He knows![g] And let Israel know! If this has been in rebellion or disobedience to the LORD, do not spare us this day. 23 If we have built our own altar to turn away from the LORD and to offer burnt offerings and grain offerings, or to sacrifice fellowship offerings[b] on it, may the LORD himself call us to account.[h]

24 "No! We did it for fear that some day your descendants might say to ours, 'What do you have to do with the LORD, the God of Israel? 25 The LORD has made the Jordan a boundary between us and you—you Reubenites and Gadites! You have no share in the LORD.' So your descendants might cause ours to stop fearing the LORD.

26 "That is why we said, 'Let us get ready and build an altar—but not for burnt offerings or sacrifices.' 27 On the contrary, it is to be a witness[i] between us and you and the generations that follow, that we will worship the LORD at his sanctuary with our burnt offerings, sacrifices and fellowship offerings.[j] Then in the future your descendants will not be able to say to ours, 'You have no share in the LORD.'

28 "And we said, 'If they ever say this to us, or to our descendants, we will answer: Look at the replica of the LORD's altar, which our fathers built, not for burnt offerings and sacrifices, but as a witness between us and you.'

29 "Far be it from us to rebel against the LORD and turn away from him today by building an altar for burnt offerings, grain offerings and sacrifices, other than the altar of the LORD our God that stands before his tabernacle."[k]

30 When Phinehas the priest and the leaders of the community—the heads of the clans of the Israelites—heard what Reuben, Gad and Manasseh had to say, they were pleased. 31 And Phinehas son of Eleazar, the priest, said to Reuben, Gad and Manasseh, "Today we know that the LORD is with us,[l] because you have not acted unfaithfully toward the LORD in this matter. Now you have rescued the Israelites from the LORD's hand."

32 Then Phinehas son of Eleazar, the priest, and the leaders returned to Canaan from their meeting with the Reubenites and Gadites in Gilead and reported to the Israelites. 33 They were glad to hear the report and praised God.[m] And they talked no more about going to war against them to devastate the country where the Reubenites and the Gadites lived.

34 And the Reubenites and the Gadites gave the altar this name: A Witness Between Us that the LORD is God.

## Joshua's Farewell to the Leaders

23 After a long time had passed and the LORD had given Israel rest[n] from all their enemies around them, Joshua, by then old and well advanced in years,[o] 2 summoned all Israel—their elders, leaders, judges and officials[p]—and said to them: "I am old and well advanced in years. 3 You yourselves have seen everything the LORD your God has done to all these nations for your sake; it was the LORD your God who fought for you. 4 Remember how I have allotted as an inheritance for your tribes all the land of the nations that remain—the nations I conquered—between the Jordan and the Great Sea[c] in the west. 5 The LORD your God himself will drive them out of your way. He will push them out before you, and you will take possession of their land, as the LORD your God promised you.

6 "Be very strong; be careful to obey all that is written in the Book of the Law of Moses, without turning aside to the right or to the left.[q] 7 Do not associate with these nations that remain among you; do not invoke the names of their gods or swear[r] by them. You must not serve them or bow down to them. 8 But you are to hold fast to the LORD[s] your God, as you have until now.

9 "The LORD has driven out before you great and powerful nations;[t] to this day no one has been able to withstand you. 10 One

**22:20** d Jos 7:1 e Jos 7:5
**22:22** f Dt 10:17 g 1Ki 8:39
**22:23** h Dt 18:19; 1Sa 20:16
**22:27** i Jos 24:27 j Dt 12:6
**22:29** k Dt 12:13–14
**22:31** l Lev 26:11–12; 2Ch 15:2
**22:33** m 1Ch 29:20
**23:1** n Jos 21:44 o Jos 13:1
**23:2** p Jos 24:1
**23:6** q Jos 1:7
**23:7** r Ex 23:13
**23:8** s Dt 10:20
**23:9** t Dt 11:23

[a] 20 The Hebrew term refers to the irrevocable giving over of things or persons to the LORD, often by totally destroying them.
[b] 23 Traditionally *peace offerings*; also in verse 27 [c] 4 That is, the Mediterranean

23:10
u Lev 26:8
v Dt 3:22

23:12
w Dt 7:3

23:14
x 1Ki 2:2

23:15
y Dt 28:15

of you routs a thousand,[u] because the LORD your God fights for you,[v] just as he promised. 11 So be very careful to love the LORD your God.

12 "But if you turn away and ally yourselves with the survivors of these nations that remain among you and if you intermarry with them[w] and associate with them, 13 then you may be sure that the LORD your God will no longer drive out these nations before you. Instead, they will become snares and traps for you, whips on your backs and thorns in your eyes, until you perish from this good land, which the LORD your God has given you.

14 "Now I am about to go the way of all the earth.[x] You know with all your heart and soul that not one of all the good promises the LORD your God gave you has failed. Every promise has been fulfilled; not one has failed. 15 But just as every good promise of the LORD your God has come true, so the LORD will bring on you all the evil he has threatened, until he has destroyed you from this good land he has given you.[y] 16 If you violate the covenant of the LORD your God, which he commanded you, and go and serve other gods and bow down to them, the LORD's anger will burn against you, and you will quickly perish from the good land he has given you."

*Thank you, Lord,*

*for my spiritual leaders. Help me to follow you, through their example, as they have followed you. Teach me to share your love with those around me so that they, too, may fall in step.*

*Amen*

JOSHUA 23:14–16

## The Covenant Renewed at Shechem

**24** Then Joshua assembled all the tribes of Israel at Shechem. He summoned the elders, leaders, judges and officials of Israel,[z] and they presented themselves before God.

2 Joshua said to all the people, "This is what the LORD, the God of Israel, says: 'Long ago your forefathers, including Terah the father of Abraham and Nahor, lived beyond the River[a] and worshiped other gods.[a] 3 But I took your father Abraham from the land beyond the River and led him throughout Canaan[b] and gave him many descendants. I gave him Isaac, 4 and to Isaac I gave Jacob and Esau.[c] I assigned the hill country of Seir[d] to Esau, but Jacob and his sons went down to Egypt.[e]

5 " 'Then I sent Moses and Aaron,[f] and I afflicted the Egyptians by what I did there, and I brought you out. 6 When I brought your fathers out of Egypt, you came to the sea, and the Egyptians pursued them with chariots and horsemen[b] as far as the Red Sea.[c] 7 But they cried to the LORD for help, and he put darkness between you and the Egyptians; he brought the sea over them and covered them. You saw with your own eyes what I did to the Egyptians. Then you lived in the desert for a long time.

8 " 'I brought you to the land of the Amorites who lived east of the Jordan. They fought against you, but I gave them into your hands. I destroyed them from before you, and you took possession of their land.[g] 9 When Balak son of Zippor,[h] the king of Moab, prepared to fight against Israel, he sent for Balaam son of Beor to put a curse on you. 10 But I would not listen to Balaam, so he blessed you again and again, and I delivered you out of his hand.

11 " 'Then you crossed the Jordan[i] and came to Jericho.[j] The citizens of Jericho fought against you, as did also the Amorites, Perizzites, Canaanites, Hittites, Girgashites, Hivites and Jebusites, but I gave them into your hands. 12 I sent the hornet[k] ahead of you, which drove them out before you—also the two Amorite kings. You did not do it with your own sword and bow. 13 So I gave you a land on which you did not toil and cities you did not build; and you live in them and eat from vineyards and olive groves that you did not plant.'[l]

14 "Now fear the LORD and serve him with

24:1
z Jos 23:2

24:2
a Ge 11:32

24:3
b Ge 12:1

24:4
c Ge 25:26
d Dt 2:5
e Ge 46:5–6

24:5
f Ex 3:10

24:8
g Nu 21:31

24:9
h Nu 22:2

24:11
i Jos 3:16–17
j Jos 6:1

24:12
k Ex 23:28; Ps 44:3,6–7

24:13
l Dt 6:10–11

[a] 2 That is, the Euphrates; also in verses 3, 14 and 15 [b] 6 Or *charioteers* [c] 6 Hebrew *Yam Suph*; that is, Sea of Reeds

all faithfulness.[m] Throw away the gods your
forefathers worshiped beyond the River
and in Egypt, and serve the LORD. 15 But if
serving the LORD seems undesirable to you,
then choose for yourselves this day whom
you will serve, whether the gods your fore-
fathers served beyond the River, or the gods
of the Amorites, in whose land you are liv-
ing. But as for me and my household, we will
serve the LORD."
16 Then the people answered, "Far be it
from us to forsake the LORD to serve other
gods! 17 It was the LORD our God himself
who brought us and our fathers up out of
Egypt, from that land of slavery, and per-
formed those great signs before our eyes.
He protected us on our entire journey and
among all the nations through which we
traveled. 18 And the LORD drove out before us
all the nations, including the Amorites, who
lived in the land. We too will serve the LORD,
because he is our God."
19 Joshua said to the people, "You are not
able to serve the LORD. He is a holy God; he
is a jealous God.[n] He will not forgive your re-
bellion[o] and your sins. 20 If you forsake the
LORD[p] and serve foreign gods, he will turn
and bring disaster on you and make an end
of you,[q] after he has been good to you."
21 But the people said to Joshua, "No! We
will serve the LORD."
22 Then Joshua said, "You are witnesses
against yourselves that you have chosen[r] to
serve the LORD."
"Yes, we are witnesses," they replied.
23 "Now then," said Joshua, "throw away
the foreign gods that are among you and
yield your hearts to the LORD, the God of
Israel."
24 And the people said to Joshua, "We will
serve the LORD our God and obey him."[s]
25 On that day Joshua made a covenant[t]
for the people, and there at Shechem he
drew up for them decrees and laws. 26 And
Joshua recorded these things in the Book of
the Law of God.[u] Then he took a large stone
and set it up there under the oak near the
holy place of the LORD.
27 "See!" he said to all the people. "This
stone will be a witness[v] against us. It has
heard all the words the LORD has said to us.
It will be a witness against you if you are un-
true to your God."

## Buried in the Promised Land

28 Then Joshua sent the people away, each
to his own inheritance.
29 After these things, Joshua son of Nun,
the servant of the LORD, died at the age of a
hundred and ten. 30 And they buried him in
the land of his inheritance, at Timnath Se-
rah[a][w] in the hill country of Ephraim, north
of Mount Gaash.
31 Israel served the LORD throughout the
lifetime of Joshua and of the elders[x] who out-
lived him and who had experienced every-
thing the LORD had done for Israel.
32 And Joseph's bones, which the Israelites
had brought up from Egypt,[y] were buried
at Shechem in the tract of land[z] that Jacob
bought for a hundred pieces of silver[b] from
the sons of Hamor, the father of Shechem.
This became the inheritance of Joseph's de-
scendants.
33 And Eleazar son of Aaron[a] died and
was buried at Gibeah, which had been allot-
ted to his son Phinehas in the hill country
of Ephraim.

**24:14** m Dt 10:12; 18:13; 1Sa 12:24; 2Co 1:12
**24:19** n Ex 20:5 o Ex 23:21
**24:20** p 1Ch 28:9,20 q Jos 23:15
**24:22** r Ps 119:30,173
**24:24** s Ex 19:8
**24:25** t Ex 24:8
**24:26** u Dt 31:24
**24:27** v Jos 22:27
**24:30** w Jos 19:50
**24:31** x Jdg 2:7
**24:32** y Ge 50:25; Ex 13:19 z Ge 33:19
**24:33** a Jos 22:13

[a]30 Also known as *Timnath Heres* (see Judges 2:9) [b]32 Hebrew *hundred kesitahs*; a kesitah was a unit of money of unknown weight and value.

# Judges

## OVERVIEW

The book of Judges records the repetitive cycles of disobedience (idolatry and immorality) by the Israelites and the resulting judgments of God (carried out by the surrounding nations). Each judgment was followed by a period in which the Israelites cried out to the Lord, who showed pity by sending a judge, or deliverer, to lead them.

One such deliverer was Deborah, a prophetess and judge in Israel during a period of oppression by Jabin, the king of Canaan, whose armies were led by a captain named Sisera. When Deborah approached Barak to fight for the Israelites, he refused to go to battle without her. Deborah then prophesied that God would deliver Jabin into the hands of a woman. With a dramatic twist, Deborah's prophecy was fulfilled when Jael tricked Sisera and killed him while he slept (see Jdg 4).

Another judge, Jephthah, serves as a reminder of the danger of casual promises. He made a vow to God to sacrifice the first thing to emerge from his home if he was given victory over his enemies. Unfortunately, it was his daughter who met him upon his return. Although it is debated whether he sacrificed her life or her future prospect of marriage (see Jdg 11), the point of the story is the same: A rash vow can result in consequences for the person making the vow and also for other people.

After the death of each judge, the people fell back into sin. Each cycle of sin pulled them further away from God. Many women struggle with cycles of sin and seeking God's forgiveness. Godly sorrow results in true repentance (see 2Co 7:10). Every cycle of sin can be broken by faith in Jesus Christ, who delivers believers from the domination of sin. Find true freedom in Christ by accepting his forgiveness and cleansing (see 1Jn 1:9).

## OUTLINE

I. The Incomplete Conquest of the Land (1:1—3:6)
II. Othniel (3:7–11)
III. Ehud (3:12–30)
IV. Shamgar (3:31)
V. Deborah (4:1—5:31)
VI. Gideon (6:1—8:35)
VII. Abimelech's Evil Ways (9:1–57)
VIII. Tola (10:1–2)
IX. Jair (10:3–5)
X. Jephthah (10:6—12:7)
XI. Ibzan (12:8–10)
XII. Elon (12:11–12)
XIII. Abdon (12:13–15)
XIV. Samson (13:1—16:31)
XV. The Moral Collapse of Israel (17:1—21:25)

## SCANNABLE FACTS:

**Author:** Unknown; traditionally ascribed to Samuel

**Time Written:** Probably around 1000 B.C.

**Themes to Note:** Israel's cycles of disobedience; God's judgment and mercy

**Notable Women:** Deborah, Jael, Jephthah's daughter, Samson's mother, Delilah

## Israel Fights the Remaining Canaanites

**1** After the death of Joshua, the Israelites asked the LORD, "Who will be the first[a] to go up and fight for us against the Canaanites?"

2 The LORD answered, "Judah[b] is to go; I have given the land into their hands."

3 Then the men of Judah said to the Simeonites their brothers, "Come up with us into the territory allotted to us, to fight against the Canaanites. We in turn will go with you into yours." So the Simeonites[c] went with them.

4 When Judah attacked, the LORD gave the Canaanites and Perizzites[d] into their hands and they struck down ten thousand men at Bezek. 5 It was there that they found Adoni-Bezek and fought against him, putting to rout the Canaanites and Perizzites. 6 Adoni-Bezek fled, but they chased him and caught him, and cut off his thumbs and big toes.

7 Then Adoni-Bezek said, "Seventy kings with their thumbs and big toes cut off have picked up scraps under my table. Now God has paid me back[e] for what I did to them." They brought him to Jerusalem, and he died there.

8 The men of Judah attacked Jerusalem[f] also and took it. They put the city to the sword and set it on fire.

9 After that, the men of Judah went down to fight against the Canaanites living in the hill country, the Negev and the western foothills. 10 They advanced against the Canaanites living in Hebron (formerly called Kiriath Arba) and defeated Sheshai, Ahiman and Talmai.[g]

11 From there they advanced against the people living in Debir (formerly called Kiriath Sepher). 12 And Caleb said, "I will give my daughter Acsah in marriage to the man who attacks and captures Kiriath Sepher." 13 Othniel son of Kenaz, Caleb's younger brother, took it; so Caleb gave his daughter Acsah to him in marriage.

14 One day when she came to Othniel, she urged him[a] to ask her father for a field. When she got off her donkey, Caleb asked her, "What can I do for you?"

15 She replied, "Do me a special favor. Since you have given me land in the Negev, give me also springs of water." Then Caleb gave her the upper and lower springs.

16 The descendants of Moses' father-in-law,[h] the Kenite,[i] went up from the City of Palms[b][j] with the men of Judah to live among the people of the Desert of Judah in the Negev near Arad.[k]

17 Then the men of Judah went with the Simeonites their brothers and attacked the Canaanites living in Zephath, and they totally destroyed[c] the city. Therefore it was called Hormah.[d][l] 18 The men of Judah also took[e] Gaza, Ashkelon and Ekron—each city with its territory.

19 The LORD was with the men of Judah. They took possession of the hill country, but they were unable to drive the people from the plains, because they had iron chariots.[m] 20 As Moses had promised, Hebron[n] was given to Caleb, who drove from it the three sons of Anak. 21 The Benjamites, however, failed[o] to dislodge the Jebusites, who were living in Jerusalem; to this day the Jebusites live there with the Benjamites.

22 Now the house of Joseph attacked Bethel, and the LORD was with them. 23 When they sent men to spy out Bethel (formerly called Luz),[p] 24 the spies saw a man coming out of the city and they said to him, "Show us how to get into the city and we will see that you are treated well.[q]" 25 So he showed them, and they put the city to the sword but spared[r] the man and his whole family. 26 He then went to the land of the Hittites, where he built a city and called it Luz, which is its name to this day.

27 But Manasseh did not drive out the people of Beth Shan or Taanach or Dor or Ibleam[s] or Megiddo and their surrounding settlements, for the Canaanites were determined to live in that land. 28 When Israel became strong, they pressed the Canaanites into forced labor but never drove them out completely. 29 Nor did Ephraim drive out the Canaanites living in Gezer, but the Canaanites continued to live there among

**1:1** a Nu 27:21
**1:2** b Ge 49:8
**1:3** c ver 17
**1:4** d Ge 13:7
**1:7** e Lev 24:19
**1:8** f ver 21; Jos 15:63
**1:10** g Jos 15:14
**1:16** h Nu 10:29 i Jdg 4:11 j Dt 34:3 k Nu 21:1
**1:17** l Nu 21:3
**1:19** m Jos 17:16
**1:20** n Jos 14:9; 15:13–14
**1:21** o Jos 15:63
**1:23** p Ge 28:19
**1:24** q Jos 2:12,14
**1:25** r Jos 6:25
**1:27** s Jos 17:11

[a] 14 Hebrew; Septuagint and Vulgate *Othniel, he urged her* [b] 16 That is, Jericho [c] 17 The Hebrew term refers to the irrevocable giving over of things or persons to the LORD, often by totally destroying them. [d] 17 *Hormah* means *destruction.* [e] 18 Hebrew; Septuagint *Judah did not take*

**1:29** t Jos 16:10
**1:36** u Jos 15:3
**2:1** v ver 5 w Ex 20:2 x Ge 17:8
**2:3** y Jos 23:13 z Ps 106:36

them.[t] 30Neither did Zebulun drive out the Canaanites living in Kitron or Nahalol, who remained among them; but they did subject them to forced labor. 31Nor did Asher drive out those living in Acco or Sidon or Ahlab or Aczib or Helbah or Aphek or Rehob, 32and because of this the people of Asher lived among the Canaanite inhabitants of the land. 33Neither did Naphtali drive out those living in Beth Shemesh or Beth Anath; but the Naphtalites too lived among the Canaanite inhabitants of the land, and those living in Beth Shemesh and Beth Anath became forced laborers for them. 34The Amorites confined the Danites to the hill country, not allowing them to come down into the plain. 35And the Amorites were determined also to hold out in Mount Heres, Aijalon and Shaalbim, but when the power of the house of Joseph increased, they too were pressed into forced labor. 36The boundary of the Amorites was from Scorpion[a] Pass[u] to Sela and beyond.

## The Angel of the LORD at Bokim

2 The angel of the LORD went up from Gilgal to Bokim[v] and said, "I brought you up out of Egypt[w] and led you into the land that I swore to give to your forefathers.[x] I said, 'I will never break my covenant with you, 2and you shall not make a covenant with the people of this land, but you shall break down their altars.' Yet you have disobeyed me. Why have you done this? 3Now therefore I tell you that I will not drive them out before you;[y] they will be ⌞thorns⌟ in your sides and their gods will be a snare[z] to you."

4When the angel of the LORD had spoken these things to all the Israelites, the people wept aloud, 5and they called that place Bokim.[b] There they offered sacrifices to the LORD.

## Disobedience and Defeat

6After Joshua had dismissed the Israelites, they went to take possession of the land, each to his own inheritance. 7The people served the LORD throughout the lifetime of Joshua and of the elders who outlived him and who had seen all the great things the LORD had done for Israel.

8Joshua son of Nun, the servant of the LORD, died at the age of a hundred and ten. 9And they buried him in the land of his inheritance, at Timnath Heres[c][a] in the hill country of Ephraim, north of Mount Gaash.

10After that whole generation had been gathered to their fathers, another generation grew up, who knew neither the LORD nor what he had done for Israel.[b] 11Then the Israelites did evil in the eyes of the LORD and served the Baals.[c] 12They forsook the LORD, the God of their fathers, who had brought them out of Egypt. They followed and worshiped various gods of the peoples around them.[d] They provoked the LORD to anger 13because they forsook him and served Baal and the Ashtoreths. 14In his anger against Israel the LORD handed them over[e] to raiders who plundered them. He sold them to their enemies all around, whom they were no longer able to resist.[f] 15Whenever Israel went out to fight, the hand of the LORD was against them to defeat them, just as he had sworn to them. They were in great distress.

16Then the LORD raised up judges,[d] who saved[g] them out of the hands of these raiders. 17Yet they would not listen to their judges but prostituted themselves to other gods and worshiped them. Unlike their fathers, they quickly turned from the way in which their fathers had walked, the way of obedience to the LORD's commands.[h] 18Whenever the LORD raised up a judge for them, he was with the judge and saved them out of the hands of their enemies as long as the judge lived; for the LORD had compassion on them as they groaned under those who oppressed and afflicted them. 19But when the judge died, the people returned to ways even more corrupt[i] than those of their fathers, following other gods and serving and worshiping them. They refused to give up their evil practices and stubborn ways.

20Therefore the LORD was very angry[j] with Israel and said, "Because this nation has violated the covenant that I laid down for their forefathers and has not listened to me, 21I will no longer drive out before them any

**2:9** a Jos 19:50
**2:10** b Ex 5:2; 1Sa 2:12
**2:11** c Jdg 3:7
**2:12** d Dt 31:16
**2:14** e Ps 106:41 f Dt 28:25
**2:16** g Ps 106:43
**2:17** h ver 7
**2:19** i Jdg 3:12
**2:20** j ver 14; Jos 23:16

[a]36 Hebrew *Akrabbim* [b]5 *Bokim* means *weepers.* [c]9 Also known as *Timnath Serah* (see Joshua 19:50 and 24:30)
[d]16 Or *leaders*; similarly in verses 17–19

2:22 k Jdg 3:1,14
3:1 l Jdg 2:21–22
3:3 m Jos 13:3
3:5 n Ps 106:35
3:6 o Ex 34:16; Dt 7:3–4
3:7 p Dt 4:9 q Jdg 2:11,13

of the nations Joshua left when he died. 22 I will use them to test[k] Israel and see whether they will keep the way of the LORD and walk in it as their forefathers did." 23 The LORD had allowed those nations to remain; he did not drive them out at once by giving them into the hands of Joshua.

3 These are the nations the LORD left to test[l] all those Israelites who had not experienced any of the wars in Canaan 2 (he did this only to teach warfare to the descendants of the Israelites who had not had previous battle experience): 3 the five[m] rulers of the Philistines, all the Canaanites, the Sidonians, and the Hivites living in the Lebanon mountains from Mount Baal Hermon to Lebo[a] Hamath. 4 They were left to test the Israelites to see whether they would obey the LORD's commands, which he had given their forefathers through Moses.

5 The Israelites lived[n] among the Canaanites, Hittites, Amorites, Perizzites, Hivites and Jebusites. 6 They took their daughters in marriage and gave their own daughters to their sons, and served their gods.[o]

## Othniel

7 The Israelites did evil in the eyes of the LORD; they forgot the LORD[p] their God and served the Baals and the Asherahs.[q] 8 The anger of the LORD burned against Israel so that he sold them into the hands of Cushan-Rishathaim king of Aram Naharaim,[b] to whom the Israelites were subject for eight years. 9 But when they cried out[r] to the LORD, he raised up for them a deliverer, Othniel[s] son of Kenaz, Caleb's younger brother, who saved them. 10 The Spirit of the LORD came upon him,[t] so that he became Israel's judge[c] and went to war. The LORD gave Cushan-Rishathaim king of Aram into the hands of Othniel, who overpowered him. 11 So the land had peace for forty years, until Othniel son of Kenaz died.

## Ehud

12 Once again the Israelites did evil in the eyes of the LORD,[u] and because they did this evil the LORD gave Eglon king of Moab power over Israel. 13 Getting the Ammonites and Amalekites to join him, Eglon came and attacked Israel, and they took possession of the City of Palms.[d][v] 14 The Israelites were subject to Eglon king of Moab for eighteen years.

15 Again the Israelites cried out to the LORD, and he gave them a deliverer—Ehud, a left-handed man, the son of Gera the Benjamite. The Israelites sent him with tribute to Eglon king of Moab. 16 Now Ehud had made a double-edged sword about a foot and a half[e] long, which he strapped to his right thigh under his clothing. 17 He presented the tribute to Eglon king of Moab, who was a very

3:9 r ver 15 s Jdg 1:13
3:10 t Nu 11:25,29; Jdg 6:34
3:12 u Jdg 2:11,14
3:13 v Jdg 1:16

[a] 3 Or *to the entrance to* [b] 8 That is, Northwest Mesopotamia [c] 10 Or *leader* [d] 13 That is, Jericho [e] 16 Hebrew *a cubit* (about 0.5 meter)

## The African Presence

**Judges 3:1–6**

The promised land had been occupied by the people of Hamitic descent: the Canaanites, Amorites, Jebusites, Hivites, Hittites and Perizzites. Because the Israelites never completed God's instruction to drive out the occupants, the Hamitic peoples conquered and oppressed the Israelites. Because Ham's offspring represent the geographic territories once dominated by Egypt—present-day Egypt, Libya and Sudan and into the area today known as Israel—they can claim a relation to African heritage. Since "heritage" is something "passed down" or "inherited," Canaan (Israel or Palestine) most certainly received or was influenced by Egypt culturally, politically, religiously, etc.

fat man. [18]After Ehud had presented the tribute, he sent on their way the men who had carried it. [19]At the idols[a] near Gilgal he himself turned back and said, "I have a secret message for you, O king."

The king said, "Quiet!" And all his attendants left him.

[20]Ehud then approached him while he was sitting alone in the upper room of his summer palace[b] and said, "I have a message from God for you." As the king rose from his seat, [21]Ehud reached with his left hand, drew the sword from his right thigh and plunged it into the king's belly. [22]Even the handle sank in after the blade, which came out his back. Ehud did not pull the sword out, and the fat closed in over it. [23]Then Ehud went out to the porch[c]; he shut the doors of the upper room behind him and locked them.

[24]After he had gone, the servants came and found the doors of the upper room locked. They said, "He must be relieving himself[w] in the inner room of the house." [25]They waited to the point of embarrassment, but when he did not open the doors of the room, they took a key and unlocked them. There they saw their lord fallen to the floor, dead.

[26]While they waited, Ehud got away. He passed by the idols and escaped to Seirah. [27]When he arrived there, he blew a trumpet[x] in the hill country of Ephraim, and the Israelites went down with him from the hills, with him leading them.

[28]"Follow me," he ordered, "for the LORD has given Moab, your enemy, into your hands.[y]" So they followed him down and, taking possession of the fords of the Jordan[z] that led to Moab, they allowed no one to cross over. [29]At that time they struck down about ten thousand Moabites, all vigorous and strong; not a man escaped. [30]That day Moab was made subject to Israel, and the land had peace for eighty years.

## Shamgar

[31]After Ehud came Shamgar son of Anath,[a] who struck down six hundred Philistines with an oxgoad. He too saved Israel.

## Deborah

**4** After Ehud died, the Israelites once again did evil[b] in the eyes of the LORD. [2]So the LORD sold them into the hands of Jabin, a king of Canaan, who reigned in Hazor.[c] The commander of his army was Sisera,[d] who lived in Harosheth Haggoyim. [3]Because he had nine hundred iron chariots[e] and had cruelly oppressed the Israelites for twenty years, they cried to the LORD for help.

[4]Deborah, a prophetess, the wife of Lappidoth, was leading[d] Israel at that time. [5]She held court under the Palm of Deborah between Ramah and Bethel in the hill country of Ephraim, and the Israelites came to her to have their disputes decided. [6]She sent for Barak son of Abinoam[f] from Kedesh in Naphtali and said to him, "The LORD, the God of Israel, commands you: 'Go, take with you ten thousand men of Naphtali and Zebulun and lead the way to Mount Tabor. [7]I will lure Sisera, the commander of Jabin's army, with his chariots and his troops to the Kishon River[g] and give him into your hands.'"

[8]Barak said to her, "If you go with me, I will go; but if you don't go with me, I won't go."

[9]"Very well," Deborah said, "I will go with you. But because of the way you are going about this,[e] the honor will not be yours, for the LORD will hand Sisera over to a woman." So Deborah went with Barak to Kedesh, [10]where he summoned[h] Zebulun and Naphtali. Ten thousand men followed him, and Deborah also went with him.

[11]Now Heber the Kenite had left the other Kenites,[i] the descendants of Hobab, Moses' brother-in-law,[f] and pitched his tent by the great tree in Zaanannim near Kedesh.

[12]When they told Sisera that Barak son of Abinoam had gone up to Mount Tabor, [13]Sisera gathered together his nine hundred iron chariots and all the men with him, from Harosheth Haggoyim to the Kishon River.

[14]Then Deborah said to Barak, "Go! This is the day the LORD has given Sisera into your hands. Has not the LORD gone ahead[j] of you?" So Barak went down Mount Tabor,

**3:24** w 1Sa 24:3
**3:27** x Jdg 6:34
**3:28** y Jdg 7:9,15 z Jdg 7:24; 12:5
**3:31** a Jdg 5:6
**4:1** b Jdg 2:19
**4:2** c Jos 11:1 d ver 13,16; Ps 83:9
**4:3** e Jdg 1:19
**4:6** f Heb 11:32
**4:7** g Ps 83:9
**4:10** h Jdg 5:15,18
**4:11** i Jdg 1:16
**4:14** j Dt 9:3; 2Sa 5:24

[a]19 Or *the stone quarries*; also in verse 26 [b]20 The meaning of the Hebrew for this phrase is uncertain. [c]23 The meaning of the Hebrew for this word is uncertain. [d]4 Traditionally *judging* [e]9 Or *But on the expedition you are undertaking* [f]11 Or *father-in-law*

# Deborah

## *An Uncommon Leader*

Deborah—a strong, courageous leader—serves as a great example for women of color today. Like many women, Deborah lived during a time when there was much unrest in her nation (see Jdg 4:1). Deborah served as a judge and prophetess during Israel's bondage under Jabin, a king of Canaan, who resided in Hazor. Sisera, the captain of Jabin's army, was renowned for having 900 iron chariots. He was also known for his oppression of the Israelites (see Jdg 4:2–3).

Deborah's name means "bee," which is very appropriate. She gathered the people to her as honey, but her sting was most fatal to her enemies. She was a godly woman who wore many hats—that of prophet, poet, encourager, warrior, wife and ruler.

God chose Deborah to minister justice and to lead his people out of bondage into peace. Deborah was one of several women distinguished in Scripture by her ability to discern the purposes of God. When God spoke to her, she took action.

God directed Deborah to speak to one who could deliver the Israelites from their enemies. Deborah sent for Barak, the son of Abinoam, and related the instructions God had for him and the promise of victory if he obeyed. Barak replied that he would lead their army to war only if Deborah would go with him; if she would not go, he would not go. Deborah agreed to go, but she informed Barak that the victory would now be credited to a woman (see Jdg 4:6–10).

It all happened as Deborah said. God delivered Sisera into the hands of Jael, who killed him with a tent peg (see Jdg 4:21 and the Women of the Bible note on Jael). And God rescued the Israelites from their foes. Because of Deborah's obedience and willingness to act, she is remembered today for her leadership and courage.

—J. Josey

### reflection

*How can Deborah's story inspire you to live up to being the woman God has called you to be?*

### read

Judges 4–5.

**See also** the Inspire Notes "Responsible Decisions in Leadership," "Female Ministers and Evangelists," "Servant-Leadership," "Women in Preaching Ministries" and "Character," and the Women of the Bible Notes "Huldah: A Prophetess of God," "Queen Vashti: A Woman of Strength," "A Virtuous Woman: A Strong Woman, Dependent on God" and "Philip's Daughters: Those Preaching Women."

For the next Women of the Bible note, go to page 281.

4:15 k Jos 10:10
4:16 l Ps 83:9
4:19 m Jdg 5:25
4:21 n Jdg 5:26
5:1 o Ex 15:1

followed by ten thousand men. [15]At Barak's
advance, the LORD routed[k] Sisera and all
his chariots and army by the sword, and
Sisera abandoned his chariot and fled on
foot. [16]But Barak pursued the chariots and
army as far as Harosheth Haggoyim. All the
troops of Sisera fell by the sword; not a man
was left.[l]

[17]Sisera, however, fled on foot to the tent
of Jael, the wife of Heber the Kenite, because
there were friendly relations between Jabin
king of Hazor and the clan of Heber the Ke-
nite.

[18]Jael went out to meet Sisera and said to
him, "Come, my lord, come right in. Don't
be afraid." So he entered her tent, and she
put a covering over him.

[19]"I'm thirsty," he said. "Please give me
some water." She opened a skin of milk,[m]
gave him a drink, and covered him up.

[20]"Stand in the doorway of the tent," he
told her. "If someone comes by and asks
you, 'Is anyone here?' say 'No.'"

[21]But Jael, Heber's wife, picked up a tent
peg and a hammer and went quietly to him
while he lay fast asleep, exhausted. She
drove the peg through his temple into the
ground, and he died.[n]

[22]Barak came by in pursuit of Sisera,
and Jael went out to meet him. "Come," she
said, "I will show you the man you're look-
ing for." So he went in with her, and there
lay Sisera with the tent peg through his tem-
ple—dead.

[23]On that day God subdued Jabin, the
Canaanite king, before the Israelites. [24]And
the hand of the Israelites grew stronger and
stronger against Jabin, the Canaanite king,
until they destroyed him.

## The Song of Deborah

**5** On that day Deborah and Barak son of
Abinoam sang this song:[o]

[2]"When the princes in Israel take the lead,
when the people willingly offer
themselves—
praise the LORD!

[3]"Hear this, you kings! Listen, you rulers!
I will sing to[a] the LORD, I will sing;
I will make music to[b] the LORD, the God
of Israel.[p]

[4]"O LORD, when you went out from Seir,[q]
when you marched from the land of
Edom,
the earth shook, the heavens poured,
the clouds poured down water.[r]
[5]The mountains quaked[s] before the LORD,
the One of Sinai,
before the LORD, the God of Israel.

[6]"In the days of Shamgar son of Anath,[t]
in the days of Jael,[u] the roads were
abandoned;
travelers took to winding paths.
[7]Village life[c] in Israel ceased,
ceased until I,[d] Deborah, arose,
arose a mother in Israel.
[8]When they chose new gods,[v]
war came to the city gates,
and not a shield or spear was seen
among forty thousand in Israel.
[9]My heart is with Israel's princes,
with the willing volunteers among the
people.
Praise the LORD!

[10]"You who ride on white donkeys,[w]
sitting on your saddle blankets,
and you who walk along the road,
consider [11]the voice of the singers[e] at the
watering places.
They recite the righteous acts[x] of the
LORD,
the righteous acts of his warriors[f] in
Israel.

"Then the people of the LORD
went down to the city gates.
[12]'Wake up,[y] wake up, Deborah!
Wake up, wake up, break out in song!
Arise, O Barak!
Take captive your captives,[z] O son of
Abinoam.'

[13]"Then the men who were left
came down to the nobles;
the people of the LORD
came to me with the mighty.
[14]Some came from Ephraim, whose roots
were in Amalek;

5:3 p Ps 27:6
5:4 q Dt 33:2 r Ps 68:8
5:5 s Ps 68:8; 97:5
5:6 t Jdg 3:31 u Jdg 4:17
5:8 v Dt 32:17
5:10 w Jdg 10:4; 12:14
5:11 x 1Sa 12:7; Mic 6:5
5:12 y Ps 57:8 z Ps 68:18

[a]3 Or *of* [b]3 Or */ with song I will praise* [c]7 Or *Warriors* [d]7 Or *you* [e]11 Or *archers*; the meaning of the Hebrew for this word is uncertain. [f]11 Or *villagers*

# Jael

## Just Another Woman on the Lord's Side

Jael is clearly a true role model for women of color today—she used what was at her disposal to accomplish what she understood to be her fight.

We don't know much about this woman whose account is found in the book of Judges. We don't know whose daughter she was. She is simply described as the wife of Heber the Kenite. Many years earlier, Moses had married a Kenite woman, and a number of these nomadic people later settled among the Israelites in the promised land (see Jdg 1:16).

Though the Kenites were long-time allies of Israel, Heber was on the side of the enemy. Most likely he told Sisera, the commander of the enemy army, where Israel's army was camped (see Jdg 4:12). Jael, however, had her own thoughts about the matter.

Jael may or may not have known Israel's God. Nevertheless, the sequence of events suggests that Jael knew enough to know that being on the Lord's side was the better choice.

When Israel's victory was certain, Sisera ran for his life to his friend's home. Jael invited him in. She gave the exhausted soldier something to drink and then covered him up. When he fell asleep, Jael took a hammer and used it to drive a tent peg through his skull, killing him instantly.

Although we don't know much about Jael and her motives, we know enough to celebrate this woman of great courage. She was obviously a woman of deep conviction. She had the big picture in view. She realized that helping Israel was the right thing to do.

Womanhood was honored as Deborah and Jael were used by God to accomplish his purpose of delivering his people from their enemies. Although Jael's actions fulfilled Deborah's prophecy, she may have known only that Israel was on the Lord's side. But that was enough.

There are times in a woman's life when she must take a stand. It may mean risking your career, social status or something else more precious. Life will present you with many battles and many decisions, so choose carefully. Never go into battle unless you are on the Lord's side. Never fight for the sake of personal glory. Be certain that your motivation is the liberation and redemption of God's people.

—E. Walters

### reflection

*What have you taken a stand for in life?*

*What have you had to sacrifice?*

*How has God received the glory?*

### read

Judges 4:11–24; 5:24–27.

See also the Inspire Notes "Confidence" and "Be Focused," and the Women of the Bible Note "Deborah: An Uncommon Leader."

For the next Women of the Bible note, go to page 290.

**5:15** a Jdg 4:10
**5:17** b Jos 19:29
**5:18** c Jdg 4:6,10
**5:19** d Jdg 1:27
**5:20** e Jos 10:11
**5:21** f Jdg 4:7

Benjamin was with the people who
followed you.
From Makir captains came down,
from Zebulun those who bear a
commander's staff.
15 The princes of Issachar were with
Deborah;[a]
yes, Issachar was with Barak,
rushing after him into the valley.
In the districts of Reuben
there was much searching of heart.
16 Why did you stay among the campfires[a]
to hear the whistling for the flocks?
In the districts of Reuben
there was much searching of heart.
17 Gilead stayed beyond the Jordan.
And Dan, why did he linger by the
ships?
Asher remained on the coast[b]
and stayed in his coves.
18 The people of Zebulun risked their very
lives;
so did Naphtali on the heights of the
field.[c]

19 "Kings came, they fought;
the kings of Canaan fought
at Taanach by the waters of Megiddo,[d]
but they carried off no silver, no
plunder.
20 From the heavens[e] the stars fought,
from their courses they fought against
Sisera.
21 The river Kishon[f] swept them away,
the age-old river, the river Kishon.
March on, my soul; be strong!
22 Then thundered the horses' hoofs—

*Lord,*

*help me to face my enemies armed with the faith of Deborah. Grant me the assurance that those who would do me harm have already been delivered into your hands.*

*Amen*

JUDGES 5:19–21

galloping, galloping go his mighty
steeds.
23 'Curse Meroz,' said the angel of the LORD.
'Curse its people bitterly,
because they did not come to help the LORD,
to help the LORD against the mighty.'

24 "Most blessed of women be Jael,[g]
the wife of Heber the Kenite,
most blessed of tent-dwelling women.
25 He asked for water, and she gave him
milk;[h]
in a bowl fit for nobles she brought him
curdled milk.
26 Her hand reached for the tent peg,
her right hand for the workman's
hammer.
She struck Sisera, she crushed his head,
she shattered and pierced his temple.
27 At her feet he sank,
he fell; there he lay.
At her feet he sank, he fell;
where he sank, there he fell—dead.

28 "Through the window peered Sisera's
mother;
behind the lattice she cried out,
'Why is his chariot so long in coming?
Why is the clatter of his chariots
delayed?'
29 The wisest of her ladies answer her;
indeed, she keeps saying to herself,
30 'Are they not finding and dividing the
spoils:[i]
a girl or two for each man,
colorful garments as plunder for Sisera,
colorful garments embroidered,
highly embroidered garments for my
neck—
all this as plunder?'

31 "So may all your enemies perish, O LORD!
But may they who love you be like the
sun[j]
when it rises in its strength."

Then the land had peace forty years.

## Gideon

6 Again the Israelites did evil in the eyes of the LORD,[k] and for seven years he gave them into the hands of the Midianites.

**5:24** g Jdg 4:17
**5:25** h Jdg 4:19
**5:30** i Ex 15:9
**5:31** j Ps 19:4
**6:1** k Jdg 2:11

[a]16 Or *saddlebags*

**6:2** l 1Sa 13:6 m Heb 11:38
**6:4** n Lev 26:16; Dt 28:30,51
**6:5** o Jdg 7:12
**6:8** p Jdg 2:1
**6:9** q Ps 44:2
**6:10** r Jer 10:2
**6:11** s Jos 17:2 t Heb 11:32
**6:12** u Jos 1:5
**6:13** v Ps 44:1
**6:14** w Heb 11:34
**6:15** x 1Sa 9:21
**6:16** y Ex 3:12; Jos 1:5

2 Because the power of Midian was so oppressive,[l] the Israelites prepared shelters for themselves in mountain clefts, caves and strongholds.[m] 3 Whenever the Israelites planted their crops, the Midianites, Amalekites and other eastern peoples invaded the country. 4 They camped on the land and ruined the crops[n] all the way to Gaza and did not spare a living thing for Israel, neither sheep nor cattle nor donkeys. 5 They came up with their livestock and their tents like swarms of locusts.[o] It was impossible to count the men and their camels; they invaded the land to ravage it. 6 Midian so impoverished the Israelites that they cried out to the LORD for help.

7 When the Israelites cried to the LORD because of Midian, 8 he sent them a prophet, who said, "This is what the LORD, the God of Israel, says: I brought you up out of Egypt,[p] out of the land of slavery. 9 I snatched you from the power of Egypt and from the hand of all your oppressors. I drove them from before you and gave you their land.[q] 10 I said to you, 'I am the LORD your God; do not worship the gods of the Amorites,[r] in whose land you live.' But you have not listened to me."

11 The angel of the LORD came and sat down under the oak in Ophrah that belonged to Joash the Abiezrite,[s] where his son Gideon[t] was threshing wheat in a winepress to keep it from the Midianites. 12 When the angel of the LORD appeared to Gideon, he said, "The LORD is with you,[u] mighty warrior."

13 "But sir," Gideon replied, "if the LORD is with us, why has all this happened to us? Where are all his wonders that our fathers told[v] us about when they said, 'Did not the LORD bring us up out of Egypt?' But now the LORD has abandoned us and put us into the hand of Midian."

14 The LORD turned to him and said, "Go in the strength you have[w] and save Israel out of Midian's hand. Am I not sending you?"

15 "But Lord,[a]" Gideon asked, "how can I save Israel? My clan is the weakest in Manasseh, and I am the least in my family.[x]"

16 The LORD answered, "I will be with you[y], and you will strike down all the Midianites together."

17 Gideon replied, "If now I have found favor in your eyes, give me a sign[z] that it is really you talking to me. 18 Please do not go away until I come back and bring my offering and set it before you."

And the LORD said, "I will wait until you return."

19 Gideon went in, prepared a young goat, and from an ephah[b] of flour he made bread without yeast. Putting the meat in a basket and its broth in a pot, he brought them out and offered them to him under the oak.[a]

20 The angel of God said to him, "Take the meat and the unleavened bread, place them on this rock,[b] and pour out the broth." And Gideon did so. 21 With the tip of the staff that was in his hand, the angel of the LORD touched the meat and the unleavened bread.[c] Fire flared from the rock, consuming the meat and the bread. And the angel of the LORD disappeared. 22 When Gideon realized[d] that it was the angel of the LORD, he exclaimed, "Ah, Sovereign LORD! I have seen the angel of the LORD face to face!"[e]

23 But the LORD said to him, "Peace! Do not be afraid. You are not going to die."

24 So Gideon built an altar to the LORD there and called it The LORD is Peace. To this day it stands in Ophrah of the Abiezrites.

25 That same night the LORD said to him, "Take the second bull from your father's herd, the one seven years old.[c] Tear down your father's altar to Baal and cut down the Asherah pole[d][f] beside it. 26 Then build a proper kind of[e] altar to the LORD your God on the top of this height. Using the wood of the Asherah pole that you cut down, offer the second[f] bull as a burnt offering."

27 So Gideon took ten of his servants and did as the LORD told him. But because he was afraid of his family and the men of the town, he did it at night rather than in the daytime.

28 In the morning when the men of the town got up, there was Baal's altar, demolished, with the Asherah pole beside it cut down and the second bull sacrificed on the newly built altar!

29 They asked each other, "Who did this?"

**6:17** z ver 36–37
**6:19** a Ge 18:7–8
**6:20** b Jdg 13:19
**6:21** c Lev 9:24
**6:22** d Jdg 13:16,21 e Jdg 13:22
**6:25** f Ex 34:13

[a] 15 Or *sir* [b] 19 That is, probably about 3/5 bushel (about 22 liters) [c] 25 Or *Take a full-grown, mature bull from your father's herd* [d] 25 That is, a symbol of the goddess Asherah; here and elsewhere in Judges [e] 26 Or *build with layers of stone an* [f] 26 Or *full-grown*; also in verse 28

When they carefully investigated, they were told, "Gideon son of Joash did it."

30 The men of the town demanded of Joash, "Bring out your son. He must die, because he has broken down Baal's altar and cut down the Asherah pole beside it."

31 But Joash replied to the hostile crowd around him, "Are you going to plead Baal's cause? Are you trying to save him? Whoever fights for him shall be put to death by morning! If Baal really is a god, he can defend himself when someone breaks down his altar." 32 So that day they called Gideon "Jerub-Baal,[a][g]" saying, "Let Baal contend with him," because he broke down Baal's altar.

33 Now all the Midianites, Amalekites and other eastern peoples joined forces and crossed over the Jordan and camped in the Valley of Jezreel.[h] 34 Then the Spirit of the LORD came upon[i] Gideon, and he blew a trumpet,[j] summoning the Abiezrites to follow him. 35 He sent messengers throughout Manasseh, calling them to arms, and also into Asher, Zebulun and Naphtali, so that they too went up to meet them.

36 Gideon said to God, "If you will save Israel by my hand as you have promised— 37 look, I will place a wool fleece on the threshing floor. If there is dew only on the fleece and all the ground is dry, then I will know[k] that you will save Israel by my hand, as you said." 38 And that is what happened. Gideon rose early the next day; he squeezed the fleece and wrung out the dew—a bowlful of water.

39 Then Gideon said to God, "Do not be angry with me. Let me make just one more request.[l] Allow me one more test with the fleece. This time make the fleece dry and the ground covered with dew." 40 That night God did so. Only the fleece was dry; all the ground was covered with dew.

## Gideon Defeats the Midianites

7 Early in the morning, Jerub-Baal[m] (that is, Gideon) and all his men camped at the spring of Harod. The camp of Midian was north of them in the valley near the hill of Moreh. 2 The LORD said to Gideon, "You have too many men for me to deliver Midian into their hands. In order that Israel may not boast against me that her own strength[n] has saved her, 3 announce now to the people, 'Anyone who trembles with fear may turn back and leave Mount Gilead.[o]'" So twenty-two thousand men left, while ten thousand remained.

4 But the LORD said to Gideon, "There are still too many[p] men. Take them down to the water, and I will sift them for you there. If I say, 'This one shall go with you,' he shall go; but if I say, 'This one shall not go with you,' he shall not go."

5 So Gideon took the men down to the water. There the LORD told him, "Separate those who lap the water with their tongues like a dog from those who kneel down to drink." 6 Three hundred men lapped with their hands to their mouths. All the rest got down on their knees to drink.

7 The LORD said to Gideon, "With the three hundred men that lapped I will save you and give the Midianites into your hands. Let all the other men go, each to his own place."[q] 8 So Gideon sent the rest of the Israelites to their tents but kept the three hundred, who took over the provisions and trumpets of the others.

6:32 g Jdg 7:1; 1Sa 12:11
6:33 h Jos 17:16
6:34 i Jdg 3:10; j Jdg 3:27
6:37 k Ge 24:14
6:39 l Ge 18:32
7:1 m Jdg 6:32
7:2 n Dt 8:17
7:3 o Dt 20:8
7:4 p 1Sa 14:6
7:7 q 1Sa 14:6

[a] 32 *Jerub-Baal* means *let Baal contend.*

*The African Presence*

**Judges 6**

Midianites were the descendants of Abraham and Keturah (see the African Presence notes on Ge 25:1–2 and Ex 2:16–22).

Now the camp of Midian lay below him
in the valley. 9 During that night the LORD
said to Gideon, "Get up, go down against the
camp, because I am going to give it into your
hands.[r] 10 If you are afraid to attack, go down
to the camp with your servant Purah 11 and
listen to what they are saying. Afterward,
you will be encouraged to attack the camp."
So he and Purah his servant went down to
the outposts of the camp. 12 The Midianites,

7:9 r Jos 2:24

# Inspire

## COURAGE TO HEAL

Gideon's story speaks to women and men about courage and overcoming great obstacles. As Judges 6:12 puts it, "The angel of the LORD appeared unto [Gideon], and said unto him, The LORD is with thee, thou mighty man of valour" (KJV). African American women are women of great courage and dedication. We know from experience that it takes great courage to become whole.

Our valor in the face of apparently insurmountable obstacles gives us the ability to heal and be healed. In Jeremiah 30:12, God told his people, "Your wound is incurable, your injury beyond healing." Yet in verse 17 of the same chapter, God said, "But I will restore you to health and heal your wounds."

A person needs courage to choose wholeness. Why else would Jesus have asked a man who was so obviously in need of healing whether he wanted to be healed (see Jn 5:6)? As if Jesus didn't already know! It wasn't for Jesus' own sake that he asked the question, but for the sake of the man in need of healing.

It takes courage to say, "I want to be healed." Some of us have that courage. We are willing to go through the painful process of transformation. We are willing to go through the excruciating elimination of parts of ourselves in order to become who we were created to be. We are willing to have our wounds exposed and cleansed. We come out on the other side of pain and exposure transformed—renewed time and time again. We survive and thrive to show our daughters and sons the way through the underbrush of childhood trauma, addiction, domestic abuse, racism, sexism, oppression, neglect and hurt.

We are mighty women of valor. We have a divine battle plan. We have our troops in place. We have our marching orders, and we are ready to move out for the sake of healing and wholeness—again! Where there's a will, there's a way. If you provide the will, God will provide the way.

—L. LEE

For the next Inspire note, go to page 311.

### read

Judges 6–7.

See also the Inspire Notes "Sexual Abuse," "Overcoming Abuse" and "Help for the Addict," and the Women of the Bible Notes "The Levite's Concubine: Broken Pieces" and "Hemorrhaging Woman: Faith to Press In."

### WOMAN of COLOR

What do you need courage to be healed from today?

**7:12** s Jdg 8:10 t Jdg 6:5 u Jos 11:4
**7:21** v 2Ki 7:7
**7:22** w 1Sa 14:20
**7:23** x Jdg 6:35

the Amalekites[s] and all the other eastern peoples had settled in the valley, thick as locusts.[t] Their camels could no more be counted than the sand on the seashore.[u]

13 Gideon arrived just as a man was telling a friend his dream. "I had a dream," he was saying. "A round loaf of barley bread came tumbling into the Midianite camp. It struck the tent with such force that the tent overturned and collapsed."

14 His friend responded, "This can be nothing other than the sword of Gideon son of Joash, the Israelite. God has given the Midianites and the whole camp into his hands."

15 When Gideon heard the dream and its interpretation, he worshiped God. He returned to the camp of Israel and called out, "Get up! The LORD has given the Midianite camp into your hands." 16 Dividing the three hundred men into three companies, he placed trumpets and empty jars in the hands of all of them, with torches inside.

17 "Watch me," he told them. "Follow my lead. When I get to the edge of the camp, do exactly as I do. 18 When I and all who are with me blow our trumpets, then from all around the camp blow yours and shout, 'For the LORD and for Gideon.' "

19 Gideon and the hundred men with him reached the edge of the camp at the beginning of the middle watch, just after they had changed the guard. They blew their trumpets and broke the jars that were in their hands. 20 The three companies blew the trumpets and smashed the jars. Grasping the torches in their left hands and holding in their right hands the trumpets they were to blow, they shouted, "A sword for the LORD and for Gideon!" 21 While each man held his position around the camp, all the Midianites ran, crying out as they fled.[v]

22 When the three hundred trumpets sounded, the LORD caused the men throughout the camp to turn on each other[w] with their swords. The army fled to Beth Shittah toward Zererah as far as the border of Abel Meholah near Tabbath. 23 Israelites from Naphtali, Asher and all Manasseh were called out,[x] and they pursued the Midianites. 24 Gideon sent messengers throughout the hill country of Ephraim, saying, "Come down against the Midianites and seize the waters of the Jordan[y] ahead of them as far as Beth Barah."

So all the men of Ephraim were called out and they took the waters of the Jordan as far as Beth Barah. 25 They also captured two of the Midianite leaders, Oreb and Zeeb[z]. They killed Oreb at the rock of Oreb,[a] and Zeeb at the winepress of Zeeb. They pursued the Midianites and brought the heads of Oreb and Zeeb to Gideon, who was by the Jordan.[b]

## Zebah and Zalmunna

8 Now the Ephraimites asked Gideon, "Why have you treated us like this? Why didn't you call us when you went to fight Midian?"[c] And they criticized him sharply.

2 But he answered them, "What have I accomplished compared to you? Aren't the gleanings of Ephraim's grapes better than the full grape harvest of Abiezer? 3 God gave Oreb and Zeeb,[d] the Midianite leaders, into your hands. What was I able to do compared to you?" At this, their resentment against him subsided.

4 Gideon and his three hundred men, exhausted yet keeping up the pursuit, came to the Jordan and crossed it. 5 He said to the men of Succoth,[e] "Give my troops some bread; they are worn out, and I am still pursuing Zebah and Zalmunna, the kings of Midian."

6 But the officials of Succoth said, "Do you already have the hands of Zebah and Zalmunna in your possession? Why should we give bread to your troops?"[f]

7 Then Gideon replied, "Just for that, when the LORD has given Zebah and Zalmunna[g] into my hand, I will tear your flesh with desert thorns and briers."

8 From there he went up to Peniel[a][h] and made the same request of them, but they answered as the men of Succoth had. 9 So he said to the men of Peniel, "When I return in triumph, I will tear down this tower."

10 Now Zebah and Zalmunna were in Karkor with a force of about fifteen thousand men, all that were left of the armies of the

**7:24** y Jdg 3:28
**7:25** z Jdg 8:3; Ps 83:11 a Isa 10:26 b Jdg 8:4
**8:1** c Jdg 12:1
**8:3** d Jdg 7:25
**8:5** e Ge 33:17
**8:6** f ver 15
**8:7** g Jdg 7:15
**8:8** h Ge 32:30

[a] 8 Hebrew *Penuel*, a variant of *Peniel*; also in verses 9 and 17

eastern peoples; a hundred and twenty thousand swordsmen had fallen.[i] [11]Gideon went up by the route of the nomads east of Nobah and Jogbehah and fell upon the unsuspecting army. [12]Zebah and Zalmunna, the two kings of Midian, fled, but he pursued them and captured them, routing their entire army.

[13]Gideon son of Joash then returned from the battle by the Pass of Heres. [14]He caught a young man of Succoth and questioned him, and the young man wrote down for him the names of the seventy-seven officials of Succoth, the elders of the town. [15]Then Gideon came and said to the men of Succoth, "Here are Zebah and Zalmunna, about whom you taunted me by saying, 'Do you already have the hands of Zebah and Zalmunna in your possession? Why should we give bread to your exhausted men?[j]' " [16]He took the elders of the town and taught the men of Succoth a lesson by punishing them with desert thorns and briers. [17]He also pulled down the tower of Peniel and killed the men of the town.[k]

[18]Then he asked Zebah and Zalmunna, "What kind of men did you kill at Tabor?[l]"

"Men like you," they answered, "each one with the bearing of a prince."

[19]Gideon replied, "Those were my brothers, the sons of my own mother. As surely as the LORD lives, if you had spared their lives, I would not kill you." [20]Turning to Jether, his oldest son, he said, "Kill them!" But Jether did not draw his sword, because he was only a boy and was afraid.

[21]Zebah and Zalmunna said, "Come, do it yourself. 'As is the man, so is his strength.'" So Gideon stepped forward and killed them, and took the ornaments[m] off their camels' necks.

## Gideon's Ephod

[22]The Israelites said to Gideon, "Rule over us—you, your son and your grandson—because you have saved us out of the hand of Midian."

[23]But Gideon told them, "I will not rule over you, nor will my son rule over you. The LORD will rule[n] over you." [24]And he said, "I do have one request, that each of you give me an earring from your share of the plunder." (It was the custom of the Ishmaelites[o] to wear gold earrings.)

[25]They answered, "We'll be glad to give them." So they spread out a garment, and each man threw a ring from his plunder onto it. [26]The weight of the gold rings he asked for came to seventeen hundred shekels,[a] not counting the ornaments, the pendants and the purple garments worn by the kings of Midian or the chains that were on their camels' necks. [27]Gideon made the gold into an ephod,[p] which he placed in Ophrah, his town. All Israel prostituted themselves by worshiping it there, and it became a snare[q] to Gideon and his family.

## Gideon's Death

[28]Thus Midian was subdued before the Israelites and did not raise its head again. During Gideon's lifetime, the land enjoyed peace forty years.

[29]Jerub-Baal son of Joash went back home to live. [30]He had seventy sons[r] of his own, for he had many wives. [31]His concubine, who lived in Shechem, also bore him a son, whom he named Abimelech.[s] [32]Gideon son of Joash died at a good old age and was buried in the tomb of his father Joash in Ophrah of the Abiezrites.

[33]No sooner had Gideon died than the Israelites again prostituted themselves to the Baals.[t] They set up Baal-Berith[u] as their god[v] and [34]did not remember the LORD their God, who had rescued them from the hands of all their enemies on every side. [35]They also failed to show kindness to the family of Jerub-Baal (that is, Gideon) for all the good things he had done for them.

## Abimelech

**9** Abimelech[w] son of Jerub-Baal went to his mother's brothers in Shechem and said to them and to all his mother's clan, [2]"Ask all the citizens of Shechem, 'Which is better for you: to have all seventy of Jerub-Baal's sons rule over you, or just one man?' Remember, I am your flesh and blood.[x]"

[3]When the brothers repeated all this to the citizens of Shechem, they were inclined to follow Abimelech, for they said, "He is our

**8:10** i Jdg 7:12
**8:15** j ver 6
**8:17** k ver 9
**8:18** l Jdg 4:6
**8:21** m ver 26; Ps 83:11
**8:23** n 1Sa 8:7; 10:19; 12:12
**8:24** o Ge 25:13
**8:27** p Jdg 17:5 q Dt 7:16; Ps 106:39
**8:30** r Jdg 9:2,5,18,24
**8:31** s Jdg 9:1
**8:33** t Jdg 2:11,13,19 u Jdg 9:4 v Jdg 9:27,46
**9:1** w Jdg 8:31
**9:2** x Ge 29:14

[a]26 That is, about 43 pounds (about 19.5 kilograms)

brother." 4They gave him seventy shekels[a] of silver from the temple of Baal-Berith,[y] and Abimelech used it to hire reckless adventurers, who became his followers. 5He went to his father's home in Ophrah and on one stone murdered his seventy brothers, the sons of Jerub-Baal. But Jotham, the youngest son of Jerub-Baal, escaped by hiding.[z] 6Then all the citizens of Shechem and Beth Millo gathered beside the great tree at the pillar in Shechem to crown Abimelech king.

7When Jotham was told about this, he climbed up on the top of Mount Gerizim[a] and shouted to them, "Listen to me, citizens of Shechem, so that God may listen to you. 8One day the trees went out to anoint a king for themselves. They said to the olive tree, 'Be our king.'

9"But the olive tree answered, 'Should I give up my oil, by which both gods and men are honored, to hold sway over the trees?'

10"Next, the trees said to the fig tree, 'Come and be our king.'

11"But the fig tree replied, 'Should I give up my fruit, so good and sweet, to hold sway over the trees?'

12"Then the trees said to the vine, 'Come and be our king.'

13"But the vine answered, 'Should I give up my wine, which cheers both gods and men, to hold sway over the trees?'

14"Finally all the trees said to the thornbush, 'Come and be our king.'

15"The thornbush said to the trees, 'If you really want to anoint me king over you, come and take refuge in my shade;[b] but if not, then let fire come out of the thornbush and consume the cedars of Lebanon!'

16"Now if you have acted honorably and in good faith when you made Abimelech king, and if you have been fair to Jerub-Baal and his family, and if you have treated him as he deserves— 17and to think that my father fought for you, risked his life to rescue you from the hand of Midian 18(but today you have revolted against my father's family, murdered his seventy sons[c] on a single stone, and made Abimelech, the son of his slave girl, king over the citizens of Shechem because he is your brother)— 19if then you have acted honorably and in good faith toward Jerub-Baal and his family today, may Abimelech be your joy, and may you be his, too! 20But if you have not, let fire come out from Abimelech and consume you, citizens of Shechem and Beth Millo, and let fire come out from you, citizens of Shechem and Beth Millo, and consume Abimelech!"

21Then Jotham fled, escaping to Beer, and he lived there because he was afraid of his brother Abimelech.

22After Abimelech had governed Israel three years, 23God sent an evil spirit[d] between Abimelech and the citizens of Shechem, who acted treacherously against Abimelech. 24God did this in order that the crime against Jerub-Baal's seventy sons, the shedding[e] of their blood, might be avenged on their brother Abimelech and on the citizens of Shechem, who had helped him[f] murder his brothers. 25In opposition to him these citizens of Shechem set men on the hilltops to ambush and rob everyone who passed by, and this was reported to Abimelech.

26Now Gaal son of Ebed moved with his brothers into Shechem, and its citizens put their confidence in him. 27After they had gone out into the fields and gathered the grapes and trodden them, they held a festival in the temple of their god.[g] While they were eating and drinking, they cursed Abimelech. 28Then Gaal son of Ebed said, "Who is Abimelech, and who is Shechem, that we should be subject to him? Isn't he Jerub-Baal's son, and isn't Zebul his deputy? Serve the men of Hamor,[h] Shechem's father! Why should we serve Abimelech? 29If only this people were under my command![i] Then I would get rid of him. I would say to Abimelech, 'Call out your whole army!' "[b]

30When Zebul the governor of the city heard what Gaal son of Ebed said, he was very angry. 31Under cover he sent messengers to Abimelech, saying, "Gaal son of Ebed and his brothers have come to Shechem and are stirring up the city against you. 32Now then, during the night you and your men should come and lie in wait in the fields. 33In the morning at sunrise, advance against the city. When Gaal and his men come out

**9:4** y Jdg 8:33
**9:5** z 2Ki 11:2
**9:7** a Dt 11:29; Jn 4:20
**9:15** b Isa 30:2
**9:18** c ver 5–6; Jdg 8:30
**9:23** d 1Sa 16:14,23; 18:10
**9:24** e Nu 35:33 f Dt 27:25
**9:27** g Jdg 8:33
**9:28** h Ge 34:2,6
**9:29** i 2Sa 15:4

[a]4 That is, about 1 3/4 pounds (about 0.8 kilogram) [b]29 Septuagint; Hebrew *him." Then he said to Abimelech, "Call out your whole army!"*

**9:33** j 1Sa 10:7
**9:38** k ver 28–29
**9:45** l ver 20; 2Ki 3:25 m Dt 29:23
**9:46** n Jdg 8:33
**9:48** o Ps 68:14

against you, do whatever your hand finds to do.[j]"

34 So Abimelech and all his troops set out by night and took up concealed positions near Shechem in four companies. 35 Now Gaal son of Ebed had gone out and was standing at the entrance to the city gate just as Abimelech and his soldiers came out from their hiding place.

36 When Gaal saw them, he said to Zebul, "Look, people are coming down from the tops of the mountains!"

Zebul replied, "You mistake the shadows of the mountains for men."

37 But Gaal spoke up again: "Look, people are coming down from the center of the land, and a company is coming from the direction of the soothsayers' tree."

38 Then Zebul said to him, "Where is your big talk now, you who said, 'Who is Abimelech that we should be subject to him?' Aren't these the men you ridiculed?[k] Go out and fight them!"

39 So Gaal led out[a] the citizens of Shechem and fought Abimelech. 40 Abimelech chased him, and many fell wounded in the flight—all the way to the entrance to the gate. 41 Abimelech stayed in Arumah, and Zebul drove Gaal and his brothers out of Shechem.

42 The next day the people of Shechem went out to the fields, and this was reported to Abimelech. 43 So he took his men, divided them into three companies and set an ambush in the fields. When he saw the people coming out of the city, he rose to attack them. 44 Abimelech and the companies with him rushed forward to a position at the entrance to the city gate. Then two companies rushed upon those in the fields and struck them down. 45 All that day Abimelech pressed his attack against the city until he had captured it and killed its people. Then he destroyed the city[l] and scattered salt[m] over it.

46 On hearing this, the citizens in the tower of Shechem went into the stronghold of the temple[n] of El-Berith. 47 When Abimelech heard that they had assembled there, 48 he and all his men went up Mount Zalmon.[o] He took an ax and cut off some branches, which he lifted to his shoulders. He ordered the men with him, "Quick! Do what you have seen me do!" 49 So all the men cut branches and followed Abimelech. They piled them against the stronghold and set it on fire over the people inside. So all the people in the tower of Shechem, about a thousand men and women, also died.

50 Next Abimelech went to Thebez and besieged it and captured it. 51 Inside the city, however, was a strong tower, to which all the men and women—all the people of the city—fled. They locked themselves in and climbed up on the tower roof. 52 Abimelech went to the tower and stormed it. But as he approached the entrance to the tower to set it on fire, 53 a woman dropped an upper millstone on his head and cracked his skull.[p]

54 Hurriedly he called to his armor-bearer, "Draw your sword and kill me,[q] so that they can't say, 'A woman killed him.' " So his servant ran him through, and he died. 55 When the Israelites saw that Abimelech was dead, they went home.

56 Thus God repaid the wickedness that Abimelech had done to his father by murdering his seventy brothers. 57 God also made the men of Shechem pay for all their wickedness.[r] The curse of Jotham son of Jerub-Baal came on them.

## Tola

**10** After the time of Abimelech a man of Issachar, Tola son of Puah, the son of Dodo, rose to save[s] Israel. He lived in Shamir, in the hill country of Ephraim. 2 He led[b] Israel twenty-three years; then he died, and was buried in Shamir.

## Jair

3 He was followed by Jair of Gilead, who led Israel twenty-two years. 4 He had thirty sons, who rode thirty donkeys. They controlled thirty towns in Gilead, which to this day are called Havvoth Jair.[c][t] 5 When Jair died, he was buried in Kamon.

## Jephthah

6 Again the Israelites did evil in the eyes of the LORD. They served the Baals and the Ashtoreths,[u] and the gods of Aram, the gods of

**9:53** p 2Sa 11:21
**9:54** q 1Sa 31:4
**9:57** r ver 20
**10:1** s Jdg 2:16
**10:4** t Nu 32:41
**10:6** u Jdg 2:13

[a] 39 Or *Gaal went out in the sight of* [b] 2 Traditionally *judged*; also in verse 3 [c] 4 Or *called the settlements of Jair*

# The Woman of Thebez

## *Protector of Her People*

She is a nameless woman. Scripture gives no clue concerning her parentage. We only know her as the anonymous woman who killed Abimelech, one of the sons of Gideon, by throwing a millstone from the tower of Thebez (see Jdg 9:52–54).

The people of Thebez were under siege by Abimelech and his men (see Jdg 9:50–51). The people had fled to the tower for safety. Abimelech followed them, intending to set the tower on fire. As he approached the tower, a woman dropped a "millstone on his head and cracked his skull" (Jdg 9:53). Since grinding grain was considered "women's work" during this period, we can see that the woman used what she had on hand—a millstone—to defeat her enemy.

What can we learn from this woman? Obviously, she was a woman who could assess the situation at hand, make a decision and act on that decision with haste. Her immediate response in that moment saved not only her life but also the lives of all those who sought refuge in the tower. Surely the woman understood that in her culture it was unlikely that she would receive any credit for her heroism. God used this unnamed woman to perform a small yet significant act (see Jdg 9:56).

How willing are you to step forward when called upon—without worrying about what's in it for you? Each of us should be willing at any given moment to respond when a situation arises in which God is directing us through the Holy Spirit. God knows the motives of our hearts and will reward us for acts that reflect his glory. God called and the woman responded. This is a reminder to each of us to always be ready when God calls us, no matter what the task. God equips us for every task we are sent to do. All we need to do is be a willing vessel.

—J. Hopkins

### reflection

*How willing are you to perform both little and big tasks for God?*

*Be open to opportunities throughout this day.*

### read

Judges 9; 2 Samuel 11:21.
See also the Inspire Note "Commitment to God."

For the next Women of the Bible note, go to page 295.

**10:6** v Dt 32:15
**10:7** w Dt 31:17
**10:10** x 1Sa 12:10
**10:11** y Nu 21:21; Jdg 3:13
**10:12** z Ps 106:42
**10:15** a 1Sa 3:18
**10:16** b Jos 24:23; Jer 18:8
**10:17** c Jdg 11:29
**11:1** d Heb 11:32
**11:3** e 2Sa 10:6,8
**11:4** f Jdg 10:9

Sidon, the gods of Moab, the gods of the Ammonites and the gods of the Philistines. And because the Israelites forsook the LORD[v] and no longer served him, [7]he became angry[w] with them. He sold them into the hands of the Philistines and the Ammonites, [8]who that year shattered and crushed them. For eighteen years they oppressed all the Israelites on the east side of the Jordan in Gilead, the land of the Amorites. [9]The Ammonites also crossed the Jordan to fight against Judah, Benjamin and the house of Ephraim; and Israel was in great distress. [10]Then the Israelites cried out to the LORD, "We have sinned against you, forsaking our God and serving the Baals."[x]

[11]The LORD replied, "When the Egyptians, the Amorites, the Ammonites,[y] the Philistines, [12]the Sidonians, the Amalekites and the Maonites[a] oppressed you[z] and you cried to me for help, did I not save you from their hands? [13]But you have forsaken me and served other gods, so I will no longer save you. [14]Go and cry out to the gods you have chosen. Let them save you when you are in trouble!"

[15]But the Israelites said to the LORD, "We have sinned. Do with us whatever you think best,[a] but please rescue us now." [16]Then they got rid of the foreign gods among them and served the LORD.[b] And he could bear Israel's misery no longer.

[17]When the Ammonites were called to arms and camped in Gilead, the Israelites assembled and camped at Mizpah.[c] [18]The leaders of the people of Gilead said to each other, "Whoever will launch the attack against the Ammonites will be the head of all those living in Gilead."

## 11

Jephthah[d] the Gileadite was a mighty warrior. His father was Gilead; his mother was a prostitute. [2]Gilead's wife also bore him sons, and when they were grown up, they drove Jephthah away. "You are not going to get any inheritance in our family," they said, "because you are the son of another woman." [3]So Jephthah fled from his brothers and settled in the land of Tob,[e] where a group of adventurers gathered around him and followed him.

[4]Some time later, when the Ammonites[f] made war on Israel, [5]the elders of Gilead went to get Jephthah from the land of Tob. [6]"Come," they said, "be our commander, so we can fight the Ammonites."

[7]Jephthah said to them, "Didn't you hate me and drive me from my father's house?[g] Why do you come to me now, when you're in trouble?"

[8]The elders of Gilead said to him, "Nevertheless, we are turning to you now; come with us to fight the Ammonites, and you will be our head[h] over all who live in Gilead."

[9]Jephthah answered, "Suppose you take me back to fight the Ammonites and the LORD gives them to me—will I really be your head?"

[10]The elders of Gilead replied, "The LORD is our witness;[i] we will certainly do as you say." [11]So Jephthah went with the elders of Gilead, and the people made him head and commander over them. And he repeated all his words before the LORD in Mizpah.[j]

[12]Then Jephthah sent messengers to the Ammonite king with the question: "What do you have against us that you have attacked our country?"

[13]The king of the Ammonites answered Jephthah's messengers, "When Israel came up out of Egypt, they took away my land from the Arnon to the Jabbok,[k] all the way to the Jordan. Now give it back peaceably."

[14]Jephthah sent back messengers to the Ammonite king, [15]saying:

"This is what Jephthah says: Israel did not take the land of Moab or the land of the Ammonites. [16]But when they came up out of Egypt, Israel went through the desert to the Red Sea[b] and on to Kadesh.[l] [17]Then Israel sent messengers to the king of Edom, saying, 'Give us permission to go through your country,' but the king of Edom would not listen. They sent also to the king of Moab, and he refused. So Israel stayed at Kadesh.

[18]"Next they traveled through the desert, skirted the lands of Edom[m] and Moab, passed along the eastern side[n] of the country of Moab, and camped on the other side of the Arnon. They

**11:7** g Ge 26:27
**11:8** h Jdg 10:18
**11:10** i Jer 42:5
**11:11** j Jdg 10:17
**11:13** k Nu 21:24
**11:16** l Nu 20:1
**11:18** m Nu 21:4; n Dt 2:8

[a] 12 Hebrew; some Septuagint manuscripts *Midianites* [b] 16 Hebrew *Yam Suph*; that is, Sea of Reeds

**11:19** o Nu 21:21–22; Dt 2:26–27
**11:22** p Dt 2:36
**11:24** q Nu 21:29; 1Ki 11:7
**11:25** r Nu 22:2 s Jos 24:9
**11:26** t Nu 21:25
**11:27** u Ge 18:25 v Ge 16:5; 31:53; 1Sa 24:12,15
**11:29** w Jdg 3:10

did not enter the territory of Moab, for the Arnon was its border.

19 "Then Israel sent messengers to Sihon king of the Amorites, who ruled in Heshbon, and said to him, 'Let us pass through your country to our own place.'[o] 20 Sihon, however, did not trust Israel[a] to pass through his territory. He mustered all his men and encamped at Jahaz and fought with Israel.

21 "Then the LORD, the God of Israel, gave Sihon and all his men into Israel's hands, and they defeated them. Israel took over all the land of the Amorites who lived in that country, 22 capturing all of it from the Arnon to the Jabbok and from the desert to the Jordan.[p]

23 "Now since the LORD, the God of Israel, has driven the Amorites out before his people Israel, what right have you to take it over? 24 Will you not take what your god Chemosh[q] gives you? Likewise, whatever the LORD our God has given us, we will possess. 25 Are you better than Balak son of Zippor,[r] king of Moab? Did he ever quarrel with Israel or fight with them?[s] 26 For three hundred years Israel occupied[t] Heshbon, Aroer, the surrounding settlements and all the towns along the Arnon. Why didn't you retake them during that time? 27 I have not wronged you, but you are doing me wrong by waging war against me. Let the LORD, the Judge,[b][u] decide[v] the dispute this day between the Israelites and the Ammonites."

28 The king of Ammon, however, paid no attention to the message Jephthah sent him.

29 Then the Spirit[w] of the LORD came upon Jephthah. He crossed Gilead and Manasseh, passed through Mizpah of Gilead, and from there he advanced against the Ammonites. 30 And Jephthah made a vow to the LORD: "If you give the Ammonites into my hands, 31 whatever comes out of the door of my house to meet me when I return in triumph from the Ammonites will be the LORD's, and I will sacrifice it as a burnt offering."

32 Then Jephthah went over to fight the Ammonites, and the LORD gave them into his hands. 33 He devastated twenty towns from Aroer to the vicinity of Minnith,[x] as far as Abel Keramim. Thus Israel subdued Ammon.

34 When Jephthah returned to his home in Mizpah, who should come out to meet him but his daughter, dancing to the sound of tambourines![y] She was an only child. Except for her he had neither son nor daughter. 35 When he saw her, he tore his clothes and cried, "Oh! My daughter! You have made me miserable and wretched, because I have made a vow to the LORD that I cannot break.[z]"

36 "My father," she replied, "you have given your word to the LORD. Do to me just as you promised, now that the LORD has avenged you of your enemies, the Ammonites. 37 But grant me this one request," she said. "Give me two months to roam the hills and weep with my friends, because I will never marry."

38 "You may go," he said. And he let her go for two months. She and the girls went into the hills and wept because she would never marry. 39 After the two months, she returned to her father and he did to her as he had vowed. And she was a virgin.

From this comes the Israelite custom 40 that each year the young women of Israel go out for four days to commemorate the daughter of Jephthah the Gileadite.

## Jephthah and Ephraim

12 The men of Ephraim called out their forces, crossed over to Zaphon and said to Jephthah, "Why did you go to fight the Ammonites without calling us to go with you?[a] We're going to burn down your house over your head."

2 Jephthah answered, "I and my people were engaged in a great struggle with the Ammonites, and although I called, you didn't save me out of their hands. 3 When I saw that you wouldn't help, I took my life in my hands[b] and crossed over to fight the Ammonites, and the LORD gave me the victory over them. Now why have you come up today to fight me?"

4 Jephthah then called together the men

**11:33** x Eze 27:17
**11:34** y Jer 31:4
**11:35** z Nu 30:2; Ecc 5:2,4,5
**12:1** a Jdg 8:1
**12:3** b 1Sa 19:5

[a] 20 Or *however, would not make an agreement for Israel* [b] 27 Or *Ruler*

of Gilead and fought against Ephraim. The Gileadites struck them down because the Ephraimites had said, "You Gileadites are renegades from Ephraim and Manasseh." 5The Gileadites captured the fords of the Jordan[c] leading to Ephraim, and whenever a survivor of Ephraim said, "Let me cross over," the men of Gilead asked him, "Are you an Ephraimite?" If he replied, "No," 6they said, "All right, say 'Shibboleth.' " If he said, "Sibboleth," because he could not pronounce the word correctly, they seized him and killed him at the fords of the Jordan. Forty-two thousand Ephraimites were killed at that time.

7Jephthah led[a] Israel six years. Then Jephthah the Gileadite died, and was buried in a town in Gilead.

## Ibzan, Elon and Abdon

8After him, Ibzan of Bethlehem led Israel. 9He had thirty sons and thirty daughters. He gave his daughters away in marriage to those outside his clan, and for his sons he brought in thirty young women as wives from outside his clan. Ibzan led Israel seven years. 10Then Ibzan died, and was buried in Bethlehem.

11After him, Elon the Zebulunite led Israel ten years. 12Then Elon died, and was buried in Aijalon in the land of Zebulun.

13After him, Abdon son of Hillel, from Pirathon, led Israel. 14He had forty sons and thirty grandsons, who rode on seventy donkeys.[d] He led Israel eight years. 15Then Abdon son of Hillel died, and was buried at Pirathon in Ephraim, in the hill country of the Amalekites.[e]

## The Birth of Samson

**13** Again the Israelites did evil in the eyes of the LORD, so the LORD delivered them into the hands of the Philistines[f] for forty years.

2A certain man of Zorah,[g] named Manoah, from the clan of the Danites, had a wife who was sterile and remained childless. 3The angel of the LORD appeared to her[h] and said, "You are sterile and childless, but you are going to conceive and have a son.[i] 4Now see to it that you drink no wine or other fermented drink and that you do not eat anything unclean,[j] 5because you will conceive and give birth to a son. No razor[k] may be used on his head, because the boy is to be a Nazirite,[l] set apart to God from birth, and he will begin[m] the deliverance of Israel from the hands of the Philistines."

6Then the woman went to her husband and told him, "A man of God[n] came to me. He looked like an angel of God, very awesome. I didn't ask him where he came from, and he didn't tell me his name. 7But he said to me, 'You will conceive and give birth to a son. Now then, drink no wine or other fermented drink and do not eat anything unclean, because the boy will be a Nazirite of God from birth until the day of his death.' "

8Then Manoah prayed to the LORD: "O Lord, I beg you, let the man of God you sent to us come again to teach us how to bring up the boy who is to be born."

9God heard Manoah, and the angel of God came again to the woman while she was out in the field; but her husband Manoah was not with her. 10The woman hurried to tell her husband, "He's here! The man who appeared to me the other day!"

11Manoah got up and followed his wife. When he came to the man, he said, "Are you the one who talked to my wife?"

"I am," he said.

12So Manoah asked him, "When your words are fulfilled, what is to be the rule for the boy's life and work?"

13The angel of the LORD answered, "Your wife must do all that I have told her. 14She must not eat anything that comes from the grapevine, nor drink any wine or other fermented drink nor eat anything unclean.[o] She must do everything I have commanded her."

15Manoah said to the angel of the LORD, "We would like you to stay until we prepare a young goat[p] for you."

16The angel of the LORD replied, "Even though you detain me, I will not eat any of your food. But if you prepare a burnt offering, offer it to the LORD." (Manoah did not realize that it was the angel of the LORD.)

17Then Manoah inquired of the angel of the LORD, "What is your name, so that we may honor you when your word comes true?"

[a]7 Traditionally *judged*; also in verses 8–14

**12:5** c Jdg 3:28
**12:14** d Jdg 5:10
**12:15** e Jdg 5:14
**13:1** f Jdg 2:11
**13:2** g Jos 19:41
**13:3** h ver 10 i Lk 1:13
**13:4** j ver 14; Nu 6:2–4; Lk 1:15
**13:5** k Nu 6:5; 1Sa 1:11 l Nu 6:2,13 m 1Sa 7:13
**13:6** n ver 8; 1Sa 2:27; 9:6
**13:14** o ver 4
**13:15** p Jdg 6:19

**13:19** q Jdg 6:20
**13:20** r Lev 9:24
**13:22** s Dt 5:26 t Jdg 6:22
**13:24** u Heb 11:32 v 1Sa 3:19
**13:25** w Jdg 3:10 x Jdg 18:12
**14:2** y Ge 21:21
**14:3** z Ex 34:16
**14:4** a Jos 11:20 b Jdg 13:1
**14:6** c Jdg 3:10

[18]He replied, "Why do you ask my name? It is beyond understanding.[a]" [19]Then Manoah took a young goat, together with the grain offering, and sacrificed it on a rock[q] to the LORD. And the LORD did an amazing thing while Manoah and his wife watched: [20]As the flame[r] blazed up from the altar toward heaven, the angel of the LORD ascended in the flame. Seeing this, Manoah and his wife fell with their faces to the ground. [21]When the angel of the LORD did not show himself again to Manoah and his wife, Manoah realized that it was the angel of the LORD.

[22]"We are doomed[s] to die!" he said to his wife. "We have seen[t] God!"

[23]But his wife answered, "If the LORD had meant to kill us, he would not have accepted a burnt offering and grain offering from our hands, nor shown us all these things or now told us this."

[24]The woman gave birth to a boy and named him Samson.[u] He grew[v] and the LORD blessed him, [25]and the Spirit of the LORD began to stir[w] him while he was in Mahaneh Dan,[x] between Zorah and Eshtaol.

## Samson's Marriage

14 Samson went down to Timnah and saw there a young Philistine woman. [2]When he returned, he said to his father and mother, "I have seen a Philistine woman in Timnah; now get her for me as my wife."[y]

[3]His father and mother replied, "Isn't there an acceptable woman among your relatives or among all our people? Must you go to the uncircumcised Philistines to get a wife?[z]"

But Samson said to his father, "Get her for me. She's the right one for me." [4](His parents did not know that this was from the LORD, who was seeking an occasion to confront the Philistines;[a] for at that time they were ruling over Israel.)[b] [5]Samson went down to Timnah together with his father and mother. As they approached the vineyards of Timnah, suddenly a young lion came roaring toward him. [6]The Spirit of the LORD came upon him in power[c] so that he tore the lion apart with his bare hands as he might have torn a young goat. But he told neither his father nor his mother what he had done. [7]Then he went down and talked with the woman, and he liked her.

[8]Some time later, when he went back to marry her, he turned aside to look at the lion's carcass. In it was a swarm of bees and some honey, [9]which he scooped out with his hands and ate as he went along. When he rejoined his parents, he gave them some, and they too ate it. But he did not tell them that he had taken the honey from the lion's carcass.

[10]Now his father went down to see the woman. And Samson made a feast there, as was customary for bridegrooms. [11]When he appeared, he was given thirty companions.

[12]"Let me tell you a riddle,[d]" Samson said to them. "If you can give me the answer within the seven days of the feast,[e] I will give you thirty linen garments and thirty sets of clothes.[f] [13]If you can't tell me the answer, you must give me thirty linen garments and thirty sets of clothes."

"Tell us your riddle," they said. "Let's hear it."

[14]He replied,

"Out of the eater, something to eat;
out of the strong, something sweet."

For three days they could not give the answer.

[15]On the fourth[b] day, they said to Samson's wife, "Coax[g] your husband into explaining the riddle for us, or we will burn you and your father's household to death.[h] Did you invite us here to rob us?"

[16]Then Samson's wife threw herself on him, sobbing, "You hate me! You don't really love me.[i] You've given my people a riddle, but you haven't told me the answer."

"I haven't even explained it to my father or mother," he replied, "so why should I explain it to you?" [17]She cried the whole seven days of the feast. So on the seventh day he finally told her, because she continued to press him. She in turn explained the riddle to her people.

[18]Before sunset on the seventh day the men of the town said to him,

"What is sweeter than honey?
What is stronger than a lion?"

**14:12** d Eze 17:2 e Ge 29:27 f Ge 45:22; 2Ki 5:5
**14:15** g Jdg 16:5; Ecc 7:26 h Jdg 15:6
**14:16** i Jdg 16:15

[a]18 Or *is wonderful* [b]15 Some Septuagint manuscripts and Syriac; Hebrew *seventh*

# Samson's Mother

## The Strength of a Wife and Mother

The angel of God appeared to an unnamed woman (see Jdg 13). She was Manoah's wife and soon to be Samson's mother. Though her namelessness might imply that she was insignificant, the angel spoke to the woman and revealed that the Lord would use her to give birth to one who would begin to deliver Israel from the Philistines.

Manoah's wife did not address the angel. Instead she told her husband what the Lord had revealed. The angel appeared to the woman a second time. Although Manoah prayed that the divine messenger would return and give further instructions, God did not send the angel directly to him. Why? We could make a couple assumptions here: (1) God speaks to women who will share with their husbands the plans of God; and (2) women are encouraged to carry the story of God's plan of salvation to others. (In Matthew 28:10, Jesus told the women to "go and tell.")

Manoah's wife was not a woman who aggressively tried to be her own boss. She heard God. She believed God. She led her husband to the angel of God. She willingly kept quiet while her husband questioned the angel. The angel replied, "Your wife must do all that I have told her" (Jdg 13:13). The responsibility was placed on the woman to do God's bidding.

As the vessel to bring forth deliverance for Israel, she was to refrain from certain things while carrying Israel's liberator. She was not to drink alcohol or eat any unclean food. She was told how to nurture the life of this consecrated child. No razor was to come upon her son's head. He was to be set apart and raised to be used for God's purpose. The child, Samson, would bring destruction to those who hated Israel (see Jdg 13:4–7,13–14).

One of the mysteries of people of color has been their ability to survive the hardships of life and still maintain strength of body and mind. The strength of our women has consistently been faith in God. Samson's mother reminds us to listen to God's instructions and obey him. Those who know their purpose can be great weapons against the enemies of God.

—D. L. Shumake JaPhia

### reflection

*How has your faith given you strength?*

*Share your story with a woman who needs strength today.*

### read

Judges 13.

See also the Inspire Notes "Motherhood," "Submission" and "Sacrificial Living," and the Women of the Bible Notes "Samson's Bride: Nothing by Chance," "Delilah: Strength That Builds or Destroys" and "Mary, the Mother of Jesus: A Model of Motherhood."

For the next Women of the Bible note, go to page 297.

**14:19** j Nu 11:25; Jdg 3:10; 6:34; 13:25; 1Sa 11:6; Isa 11:2
**14:20** k Jdg 15:2,6; Jn 3:29
**15:2** l Jdg 14:20
**15:6** m Jdg 14:15
**15:9** n ver 14,17,19

Samson said to them,

> "If you had not plowed with my heifer,
> you would not have solved my riddle."

19 Then the Spirit of the LORD came upon him in power.[j] He went down to Ashkelon, struck down thirty of their men, stripped them of their belongings and gave their clothes to those who had explained the riddle. Burning with anger, he went up to his father's house. 20 And Samson's wife was given to the friend[k] who had attended him at his wedding.

## Samson's Vengeance on the Philistines

**15** Later on, at the time of wheat harvest, Samson took a young goat and went to visit his wife. He said, "I'm going to my wife's room." But her father would not let him go in.

2 "I was so sure you thoroughly hated her," he said, "that I gave her to your friend.[l] Isn't her younger sister more attractive? Take her instead."

3 Samson said to them, "This time I have a right to get even with the Philistines; I will really harm them." 4 So he went out and caught three hundred foxes and tied them tail to tail in pairs. He then fastened a torch to every pair of tails, 5 lit the torches and let the foxes loose in the standing grain of the Philistines. He burned up the shocks and standing grain, together with the vineyards and olive groves.

6 When the Philistines asked, "Who did this?" they were told, "Samson, the Timnite's son-in-law, because his wife was given to his friend."

So the Philistines went up and burned her and her father to death.[m] 7 Samson said to them, "Since you've acted like this, I won't stop until I get my revenge on you." 8 He attacked them viciously and slaughtered many of them. Then he went down and stayed in a cave in the rock of Etam.

9 The Philistines went up and camped in Judah, spreading out near Lehi.[n] 10 The men of Judah asked, "Why have you come to fight us?"

"We have come to take Samson prisoner," they answered, "to do to him as he did to us."

11 Then three thousand men from Judah went down to the cave in the rock of Etam and said to Samson, "Don't you realize that the Philistines are rulers over us?[o] What have you done to us?"

He answered, "I merely did to them what they did to me."

12 They said to him, "We've come to tie you up and hand you over to the Philistines."

Samson said, "Swear to me that you won't kill me yourselves."

13 "Agreed," they answered. "We will only tie you up and hand you over to them. We will not kill you." So they bound him with two new ropes and led him up from the rock. 14 As he approached Lehi, the Philistines came toward him shouting. The Spirit of the LORD came upon him in power.[p] The ropes on his arms became like charred flax, and the bindings dropped from his hands. 15 Finding a fresh jawbone of a donkey, he grabbed it and struck down a thousand men.[q]

16 Then Samson said,

> "With a donkey's jawbone
> I have made donkeys of them.[a]
> With a donkey's jawbone
> I have killed a thousand men."

17 When he finished speaking, he threw away the jawbone; and the place was called Ramath Lehi.[b]

18 Because he was very thirsty, he cried out to the LORD,[r] "You have given your servant this great victory. Must I now die of thirst and fall into the hands of the uncircumcised?" 19 Then God opened up the hollow place in Lehi, and water came out of it. When Samson drank, his strength returned and he revived.[s] So the spring was called En Hakkore,[c] and it is still there in Lehi.

20 Samson led[d] Israel for twenty years[t] in the days of the Philistines.

## Samson and Delilah

**16** One day Samson went to Gaza, where he saw a prostitute. He went in to spend the night with her. 2 The people of Gaza were told, "Samson is here!" So

**15:11** o Jdg 14:4
**15:14** p Jdg 14:19
**15:15** q Lev 26:8; Jos 23:10
**15:18** r Jdg 16:28
**15:19** s Ge 45:27; Isa 40:29
**15:20** t Jdg 13:1; 16:31

[a] 16 Or *made a heap or two*; the Hebrew for *donkey* sounds like the Hebrew for *heap.* [b] 17 *Ramath Lehi* means *jawbone hill.* [c] 19 *En Hakkore* means *caller's spring.* [d] 20 Traditionally *judged*

# Samson's Bride

## Nothing by Chance

It is not by chance that Samson's marriage is the first recorded event of his adult life. Samson's bride is first mentioned in Judges 14:1–3. Interestingly, she is not described in the usual patriarchal Biblical tradition as "the daughter of . . ."; instead she is called "a Philistine woman in Timnah" (Jdg 14:2). She is characterized by the place she lived and, more significantly, by her ethnic background. As a Gentile woman, she was a poor choice for a wife for Samson (see Dt 7:3–4). The marriage was doomed from the beginning. Her loyalty to her past ultimately affected her future.

Samson's bride manipulated him into telling her the secret of a riddle he had presented at their wedding banquet. At the demands of her countrymen and their threats of death, she betrayed Samson. Out of vengeance Samson attacked some of the Philistines, while his wife was given to another (see Jdg 14:19–20). Unfortunately, the sad saga did not end there. After Samson exacted his revenge against the Philistines, his wife and her father were murdered. More deaths followed (see Jdg 15:6–8).

The key to understanding this little-known woman is to look at who brought her into Samson's life. The astonishing thing about this story is that God allowed Samson's relationship with this Philistine woman. Judges 14:4 states that "[Samson's] parents did not know that this was from the LORD." Thus, God was orchestrating the circumstances so that Samson—in spite of, and even through, his sinful and impulsive choices—could confront the Philistines and deliver Israel from them.

How reassuring it is to know that even when we, like the woman of Timnah, don't know what God is doing, his sovereign hand still controls the action. Others may not be able to see God in the situation, but we can be assured that God can use any situation. The Philistine woman's presence in Samson's life provided a turning point for him.

We need to recognize that God has placed us in a position of influence as Christian mothers, daughters, wives, sisters, friends and coworkers. As Christians, we must lead lives strengthened by prayer and enhanced by the Word of God. Though we may not see how God is using us, we can know that wherever God has placed us, we are making a difference.

—S. RILEY

### reflection

*Reflect on a time when God got the glory from even one of your bad decisions.*

*Walk in this day remembering that God is sovereign.*

### read

Judges 14:1—15:8.
See also the Inspire Notes "Rebellion," "Influencing Others," "Bumping Into Omnipotence," "God Is Sovereign" and "Marriage," and the Women of the Bible Notes "Samson's Mother: The Strength of a Wife and Mother" and "Delilah: Strength That Builds or Destroys."

For the next Women of the Bible note, go to page 299.

**16:5** u Jos 13:3 v Jdg 14:15
**16:10** w ver 13

they surrounded the place and lay in wait for him all night at the city gate. They made no move during the night, saying, "At dawn we'll kill him."

[3]But Samson lay there only until the middle of the night. Then he got up and took hold of the doors of the city gate, together with the two posts, and tore them loose, bar and all. He lifted them to his shoulders and carried them to the top of the hill that faces Hebron.

[4]Some time later, he fell in love with a woman in the Valley of Sorek whose name was Delilah. [5]The rulers of the Philistines[u] went to her and said, "See if you can lure[v] him into showing you the secret of his great strength and how we can overpower him so we may tie him up and subdue him. Each one of us will give you eleven hundred shekels[a] of silver."

[6]So Delilah said to Samson, "Tell me the secret of your great strength and how you can be tied up and subdued."

[7]Samson answered her, "If anyone ties me with seven fresh thongs[b] that have not been dried, I'll become as weak as any other man."

[8]Then the rulers of the Philistines brought her seven fresh thongs that had not been dried, and she tied him with them. [9]With men hidden in the room, she called to him, "Samson, the Philistines are upon you!" But he snapped the thongs as easily as a piece of string snaps when it comes close to a flame. So the secret of his strength was not discovered.

[10]Then Delilah said to Samson, "You have made a fool of me;[w] you lied to me. Come now, tell me how you can be tied."

[11]He said, "If anyone ties me securely with new ropes that have never been used, I'll become as weak as any other man."

[12]So Delilah took new ropes and tied him with them. Then, with men hidden in the room, she called to him, "Samson, the Philistines are upon you!" But he snapped the ropes off his arms as if they were threads.

[13]Delilah then said to Samson, "Until now, you have been making a fool of me and lying to me. Tell me how you can be tied."

He replied, "If you weave the seven braids of my head into the fabric ⌊on the loom⌋ and tighten it with the pin, I'll become as weak as any other man." So while he was sleeping, Delilah took the seven braids of his head, wove them into the fabric [14]and[c] tightened it with the pin.

Again she called to him, "Samson, the Philistines are upon you!" He awoke from his sleep and pulled up the pin and the loom, with the fabric.

[15]Then she said to him, "How can you say, 'I love you,'[x] when you won't confide in me? This is the third time you have made a fool of me and haven't told me the secret of your great strength." [16]With such nagging she prodded him day after day until he was tired to death.

[17]So he told her everything.[y] "No razor has ever been used on my head," he said, "because I have been a Nazirite[z] set apart to God since birth. If my head were shaved, my strength would leave me, and I would become as weak as any other man."

[18]When Delilah saw that he had told her everything, she sent word to the rulers of the Philistines, "Come back once more; he has told me everything." So the rulers of the Philistines returned with the silver in their hands. [19]Having put him to sleep on her lap, she called a man to shave off the seven braids of his hair, and so began to subdue him.[d] And his strength left him.[a]

[20]Then she called, "Samson, the Philistines are upon you!"

He awoke from his sleep and thought, "I'll go out as before and shake myself free." But he did not know that the LORD had left him.[b]

[21]Then the Philistines seized him, gouged out his eyes and took him down to Gaza. Binding him with bronze shackles, they set him to grinding in the prison. [22]But the hair on his head began to grow again after it had been shaved.

## The Death of Samson

[23]Now the rulers of the Philistines assembled to offer a great sacrifice to Dagon[c] their god and to celebrate, saying, "Our

**16:15** x Jdg 14:16
**16:17** y Mic 7:5 z Nu 6:2,5; Jdg 13:5
**16:19** a Pr 7:26–27
**16:20** b Nu 14:42; Jos 7:12; 1Sa 16:14; 18:12; 28:15
**16:23** c 1Sa 5:2

[a]5 That is, about 28 pounds (about 13 kilograms) [b]7 Or *bowstrings*; also in verses 8 and 9 [c]13,14 Some Septuagint manuscripts; Hebrew *"⌊I can⌋ if you weave the seven braids of my head into the fabric ⌊on the loom⌋." [14]So she*
[d]19 Hebrew; some Septuagint manuscripts *and he began to weaken*

# Delilah

## *Strength That Builds or Destroys*

The story of Samson and Delilah often generates reflection on the weaknesses of Samson. Many questions arise regarding how Samson could be so clueless about Delilah's agenda to assist the Philistines in his demise. But the story of Samson and Delilah is not necessarily that simple. Delilah has a message for all women to take to heart. Delilah, as many women in the Bible, reminds us of the unusual strength women have—a strength that can either build up or destroy those around us. While women are naturally the weaker sex physically, we possess an exceptional, yet subtle, spiritual and emotional strength.

It is important for women to be conscious of this strength because of its potential to either build up or destroy. Women have the power to build up individuals, families, communities and churches. Likewise, that same power can also destroy. Delilah chose to destroy a man for money. She could have chosen to help build up his character, as Deborah attempted to do with Barak (see Jdg 4:6–7). Instead, as a result of Delilah's decision, at the same time that Samson was destroyed, so were thousands of Delilah's people (see Jdg 16:26–30).

Delilah held a special power over Samson's heart—and it wasn't exclusively the power of sexual attraction. Although Delilah had proved herself untrustworthy, she still was able to make Samson feel comfortable with her. The people in our lives—especially our loved ones—need to feel comfortable around us; they need to feel as if they can trust us. We, in turn, should not use this special power to destroy them but to help them grow into the people God has called them to become. Women must be aware of the strength that God has given us and understand that Satan desires to use this strength for evil. We must choose how this God-given strength will be used—to build up or to destroy.

—B. Whitaker

### reflection

*How will you use your special power to build up those around you rather than to destroy them?*

### read

Judges 16.

See also the Inspire Notes "Influencing Others" and "Temptation," and the Women of the Bible Notes "Samson's Mother: The Strength of a Wife and Mother" and "Samson's Bride: Nothing by Chance."

For the next Women of the Bible note, go to page 301.

**16:24** d Da 5:4 e 1Sa 31:9; 1Ch 10:9
**16:25** f Jdg 9:27
**16:28** g Jdg 15:18 h Jer 15:15
**16:31** i Jdg 15:20

god has delivered Samson, our enemy, into
our hands."
24 When the people saw him, they praised
their god,[d] saying,

"Our god has delivered our enemy
into our hands,[e]
the one who laid waste our land
and multiplied our slain."

25 While they were in high spirits,[f] they
shouted, "Bring out Samson to entertain
us." So they called Samson out of the prison,
and he performed for them.
When they stood him among the pil-
lars, 26 Samson said to the servant who held
his hand, "Put me where I can feel the pil-
lars that support the temple, so that I may
lean against them." 27 Now the temple was
crowded with men and women; all the rulers
of the Philistines were there, and on the roof
were about three thousand men and women
watching Samson perform. 28 Then Samson
prayed to the LORD,[g] "O Sovereign LORD, re-
member me. O God, please strengthen me
just once more, and let me with one blow get
revenge[h] on the Philistines for my two eyes."
29 Then Samson reached toward the two cen-
tral pillars on which the temple stood. Brac-
ing himself against them, his right hand on
the one and his left hand on the other, 30 Sam-
son said, "Let me die with the Philistines!"
Then he pushed with all his might, and
down came the temple on the rulers and all
the people in it. Thus he killed many more
when he died than while he lived.
31 Then his brothers and his father's whole
family went down to get him. They brought
him back and buried him between Zorah
and Eshtaol in the tomb of Manoah his fa-
ther. He had led[a] Israel twenty years.[i]

## Micah's Idols

17 Now a man named Micah from the
hill country of Ephraim 2 said to his
mother, "The eleven hundred shekels[b] of
silver that were taken from you and about
which I heard you utter a curse—I have that
silver with me; I took it."
Then his mother said, "The LORD bless
you, my son!"
3 When he returned the eleven hundred
shekels of silver to his mother, she said, "I
solemnly consecrate my silver to the LORD
for my son to make a carved image and a
cast idol.[j] I will give it back to you."
4 So he returned the silver to his mother,
and she took two hundred shekels[c] of silver
and gave them to a silversmith, who made
them into the image and the idol. And they
were put in Micah's house.
5 Now this man Micah had a shrine, and
he made an ephod[k] and some idols and in-
stalled one of his sons as his priest. 6 In those
days Israel had no king;[l] everyone did as he
saw fit.[m]
7 A young Levite from Bethlehem in Ju-
dah,[n] who had been living within the clan
of Judah, 8 left that town in search of some
other place to stay. On his way[d] he came
to Micah's house in the hill country of
Ephraim.
9 Micah asked him, "Where are you
from?"
"I'm a Levite from Bethlehem in Ju-
dah," he said, "and I'm looking for a place
to stay."
10 Then Micah said to him, "Live with me
and be my father and priest,[o] and I'll give
you ten shekels[e] of silver a year, your clothes
and your food." 11 So the Levite agreed to live
with him, and the young man was to him
like one of his sons. 12 Then Micah installed
the Levite, and the young man became his
priest and lived in his house. 13 And Micah
said, "Now I know that the LORD will be
good to me, since this Levite has become
my priest."

## Danites Settle in Laish

18 In those days Israel had no king.[p]
And in those days the tribe of the
Danites was seeking a place of their own
where they might settle, because they had
not yet come into an inheritance among
the tribes of Israel.[q] 2 So the Danites[r] sent
five warriors from Zorah and Eshtaol to
spy out the land and explore it. These men
represented all their clans. They told them,
"Go, explore the land."
The men entered the hill country of

**17:3** j Ex 20:4,23
**17:5** k Jdg 8:27
**17:6** l Jdg 18:1; 19:1 m Dt 12:8
**17:7** n Jdg 19:1; Ru 1:1–2; Mic 5:2; Mt 2:1
**17:10** o Jdg 18:19
**18:1** p Jdg 17:6 q Jos 19:47
**18:2** r Jdg 13:25

[a] 31 Traditionally *judged* [b] 2 That is, about 28 pounds (about 13 kilograms) [c] 4 That is, about 5 pounds (about 2.3 kilograms) [d] 8 Or *To carry on his profession* [e] 10 That is, about 4 ounces (about 110 grams)

# Micah's Mother

## The Consequences of Ignoring God

Little is known of the mother of this man named Micah (not the Micah who wrote the book of the Old Testament bearing his name) except what is written in Judges 17. She lived with her son in Ephraim.

From her story, women of color who are mothers can learn three things that they *should not* do:

1. *Be dishonest*. Dishonesty leads to negative consequences. When her son returned 1,100 shekels of silver that he had stolen from her, she stated her intention to consecrate the silver to the Lord in order to counteract the curse that she had cast. She announced that she would give the money back to Micah to make a carved image and a cast idol. She then proceeded to contribute only 200 shekels of silver—a small fraction of her initial promise—for the project (see Jdg 17:4).

2. *Disobey the commandments*. By encouraging and participating with her son in making idols, she broke one of God's commandments: "You shall not make for yourself an idol in the form of anything" (Ex 20:4).

3. *Ignore your family's sinfulness*. In addition to participating in the making of idols, there is no indication that Micah's mother tried to stop her son from installing her grandson, and later a Levite who was not a member of the priestly line, as priest. There were rules by which priests were to be chosen, and she and her family ignored God's law. Consequently, her son's actions contributed to his—and Israel's—religious confusion.

We are charged to obey God's commandments in all areas of our lives and to teach—by our words and actions—our families to do the same.

—A. Dise

### reflection

*How do you show those around you that you trust and obey God?*

### read

Judges 17.

See also the Inspire Notes "Motherhood," "Parenting," "Raising Children: Modeling Discipleship" and "Children: A Blessed Heritage From God," and the Women of the Bible Note "Mary, the Mother of Jesus: A Model of Motherhood."

For the next Women of the Bible note, go to page 305.

**18:2** s Jdg 17:1
**18:4** t Jdg 17:12
**18:6** u 1Ki 22:6
**18:7** v Jos 19:47 w ver 28
**18:9** x Nu 13:30; 1Ki 22:3
**18:10** y Dt 8:9
**18:11** z ver 16,17
**18:12** a Jdg 13:25
**18:16** b ver 11

Ephraim and came to the house of Micah,[s] where they spent the night. 3 When they were near Micah's house, they recognized the voice of the young Levite; so they turned in there and asked him, "Who brought you here? What are you doing in this place? Why are you here?"

4 He told them what Micah had done for him, and said, "He has hired me and I am his priest.[t]"

5 Then they said to him, "Please inquire of God to learn whether our journey will be successful."

6 The priest answered them, "Go in peace[u]. Your journey has the LORD's approval."

7 So the five men left and came to Laish,[v] where they saw that the people were living in safety, like the Sidonians, unsuspecting and secure. And since their land lacked nothing, they were prosperous.[a] Also, they lived a long way from the Sidonians[w] and had no relationship with anyone else.[b]

8 When they returned to Zorah and Eshtaol, their brothers asked them, "How did you find things?"

9 They answered, "Come on, let's attack them! We have seen that the land is very good. Aren't you going to do something? Don't hesitate to go there and take it over.[x] 10 When you get there, you will find an unsuspecting people and a spacious land that God has put into your hands, a land that lacks nothing[y] whatever."

11 Then six hundred men[z] from the clan of the Danites, armed for battle, set out from Zorah and Eshtaol. 12 On their way they set up camp near Kiriath Jearim in Judah. This is why the place west of Kiriath Jearim is called Mahaneh Dan[c][a] to this day. 13 From there they went on to the hill country of Ephraim and came to Micah's house.

14 Then the five men who had spied out the land of Laish said to their brothers, "Do you know that one of these houses has an ephod, other household gods, a carved image and a cast idol? Now you know what to do." 15 So they turned in there and went to the house of the young Levite at Micah's place and greeted him. 16 The six hundred Danites,[b] armed for battle, stood at the entrance to the gate. 17 The five men who had spied out the land went inside and took the carved image, the ephod, the other household gods and the cast idol while the priest and the six hundred armed men stood at the entrance to the gate.

18 When these men went into Micah's house and took the carved image, the ephod, the other household gods and the cast idol, the priest said to them, "What are you doing?"

19 They answered him, "Be quiet![c] Don't say a word. Come with us, and be our father and priest.[d] Isn't it better that you serve a tribe and clan in Israel as priest rather than just one man's household?" 20 Then the priest was glad. He took the ephod, the other household gods and the carved image and went along with the people. 21 Putting their little children, their livestock and their possessions in front of them, they turned away and left.

22 When they had gone some distance from Micah's house, the men who lived near Micah were called together and overtook the Danites. 23 As they shouted after them, the Danites turned and said to Micah, "What's the matter with you that you called out your men to fight?"

24 He replied, "You took the gods I made, and my priest, and went away. What else do I have? How can you ask, 'What's the matter with you?'"

25 The Danites answered, "Don't argue with us, or some hot-tempered men will attack you, and you and your family will lose your lives." 26 So the Danites went their way, and Micah, seeing that they were too strong for him, turned around and went back home.

27 Then they took what Micah had made, and his priest, and went on to Laish, against a peaceful and unsuspecting people. They attacked them with the sword and burned down their city.[e] 28 There was no one to rescue them because they lived a long way from Sidon[f] and had no relationship with anyone else. The city was in a valley near Beth Rehob.[g]

The Danites rebuilt the city and settled

**18:19** c Job 21:5; 29:9; 40:4 d Jdg 17:10
**18:27** e Jos 19:47
**18:28** f ver 7 g 2Sa 10:6

[a]7 The meaning of the Hebrew for this clause is uncertain. [b]7 Hebrew; some Septuagint manuscripts *with the Arameans*
[c]12 *Mahaneh Dan* means *Dan's camp.*

18:29 h Jos 19:47
18:30 i Ex 2:22; Jdg 17:3,5
18:31 j Jos 18:1
19:1 k Jdg 18:1
19:5 l ver 8; Ge 18:5
19:10 m 1Ch 11:4–5

there. 29 They named it Dan after their fore-
father Dan, who was born to Israel—though
the city used to be called Laish.[h] 30 There
the Danites set up for themselves the idols,
and Jonathan son of Gershom,[i] the son of
Moses,[a] and his sons were priests for the
tribe of Dan until the time of the captivity of
the land. 31 They continued to use the idols
Micah had made, all the time the house of
God was in Shiloh.[j]

## A Levite and His Concubine

19 In those days Israel had no king.
Now a Levite who lived in a remote
area in the hill country of Ephraim[k] took a
concubine from Bethlehem in Judah. 2 But
she was unfaithful to him. She left him and
went back to her father's house in Bethle-
hem, Judah. After she had been there four
months, 3 her husband went to her to per-
suade her to return. He had with him his
servant and two donkeys. She took him into
her father's house, and when her father saw
him, he gladly welcomed him. 4 His father-
in-law, the girl's father, prevailed upon him
to stay; so he remained with him three days,
eating and drinking, and sleeping there.

5 On the fourth day they got up early and
he prepared to leave, but the girl's father
said to his son-in-law, "Refresh yourself[l]
with something to eat; then you can go." 6 So
the two of them sat down to eat and drink
together. Afterward the girl's father said,
"Please stay tonight and enjoy yourself."
7 And when the man got up to go, his father-
in-law persuaded him, so he stayed there
that night. 8 On the morning of the fifth day,
when he rose to go, the girl's father said, "Re-
fresh yourself. Wait till afternoon!" So the
two of them ate together.

9 Then when the man, with his concubine
and his servant, got up to leave, his father-
in-law, the girl's father, said, "Now look, it's
almost evening. Spend the night here; the
day is nearly over. Stay and enjoy yourself.
Early tomorrow morning you can get up
and be on your way home." 10 But, unwilling
to stay another night, the man left and went
toward Jebus[m] (that is, Jerusalem), with his
two saddled donkeys and his concubine.

11 When they were near Jebus and the day
was almost gone, the servant said to his mas-
ter, "Come, let's stop at this city of the Jebu-
sites and spend the night."

12 His master replied, "No. We won't go
into an alien city, whose people are not Isra-
elites. We will go on to Gibeah." 13 He added,
"Come, let's try to reach Gibeah or Ramah[n]
and spend the night in one of those places."
14 So they went on, and the sun set as they
neared Gibeah in Benjamin. 15 There they
stopped to spend the night. They went and
sat in the city square, but no one took them
into his home for the night.

16 That evening[o] an old man from the
hill country of Ephraim, who was living in
Gibeah (the men of the place were Benja-
mites), came in from his work in the fields.
17 When he looked and saw the traveler in the
city square, the old man asked, "Where are
you going? Where did you come from?"

18 He answered, "We are on our way from
Bethlehem in Judah to a remote area in the
hill country of Ephraim where I live. I have
been to Bethlehem in Judah and now I am
going to the house of the LORD.[p] No one has
taken me into his house. 19 We have both
straw and fodder for our donkeys and bread
and wine for ourselves your servants—me,
your maidservant, and the young man with
us. We don't need anything."

20 "You are welcome at my house," the
old man said. "Let me supply whatever
you need. Only don't spend the night in the
square." 21 So he took him into his house and
fed his donkeys. After they had washed their
feet, they had something to eat and drink.[q]

22 While they were enjoying themselves,
some of the wicked men[r] of the city sur-
rounded the house. Pounding on the door,
they shouted to the old man who owned the
house, "Bring out the man who came to your
house so we can have sex with him.[s]"

23 The owner of the house went outside
and said to them, "No, my friends, don't be
so vile. Since this man is my guest, don't do
this disgraceful thing.[t] 24 Look, here is my
virgin daughter,[u] and his concubine. I will
bring them out to you now, and you can use
them and do to them whatever you wish.
But to this man, don't do such a disgrace-
ful thing."

19:13 n Jos 18:25
19:16 o Ps 104:23
19:18 p Jdg 18:31
19:21 q Ge 24:32–33
19:22 r Dt 13:13 s Ge 19:4–5; Ro 1:26–27
19:23 t Ge 34:7; Dt 22:21; 2Sa 13:12
19:24 u Ge 19:8

[a] 30 An ancient Hebrew scribal tradition, some Septuagint manuscripts and Vulgate; Masoretic Text *Manasseh*

**19:29** v 1Sa 11:7
**19:30** w Jdg 20:7
**20:1** x Jdg 21:5 y 1Sa 7:5
**20:2** z Jdg 8:10
**20:4** a Jdg 19:15
**20:5** b Jdg 19:22 c Jdg 19:25–26
**20:6** d Jdg 19:29 e Jos 7:15
**20:7** f Jdg 19:30

25 But the men would not listen to him. So the man took his concubine and sent her outside to them, and they raped her and abused her throughout the night, and at dawn they let her go. 26 At daybreak the woman went back to the house where her master was staying, fell down at the door and lay there until daylight.

27 When her master got up in the morning and opened the door of the house and stepped out to continue on his way, there lay his concubine, fallen in the doorway of the house, with her hands on the threshold. 28 He said to her, "Get up; let's go." But there was no answer. Then the man put her on his donkey and set out for home.

29 When he reached home, he took a knife and cut up his concubine, limb by limb, into twelve parts and sent them into all the areas of Israel.[v] 30 Everyone who saw it said, "Such a thing has never been seen or done, not since the day the Israelites came up out of Egypt. Think about it! Consider it! Tell us what to do![w]"

## Israelites Fight the Benjamites

**20** Then all the Israelites[x] from Dan to Beersheba and from the land of Gilead came out as one man and assembled[y] before the LORD in Mizpah. 2 The leaders of all the people of the tribes of Israel took their places in the assembly of the people of God, four hundred thousand soldiers[z] armed with swords. 3 (The Benjamites heard that the Israelites had gone up to Mizpah.) Then the Israelites said, "Tell us how this awful thing happened."

4 So the Levite, the husband of the murdered woman, said, "I and my concubine came to Gibeah in Benjamin to spend the night.[a] 5 During the night the men of Gibeah came after me and surrounded the house, intending to kill me.[b] They raped my concubine, and she died.[c] 6 I took my concubine, cut her into pieces and sent one piece to each region of Israel's inheritance,[d] because they committed this lewd and disgraceful act[e] in Israel. 7 Now, all you Israelites, speak up and give your verdict.[f]"

8 All the people rose as one man, saying, "None of us will go home. No, not one of us will return to his house. 9 But now this is what we'll do to Gibeah: We'll go up against it as the lot directs. 10 We'll take ten men out of every hundred from all the tribes of Israel, and a hundred from a thousand, and a thousand from ten thousand, to get provisions for the army. Then, when the army arrives at Gibeah[a] in Benjamin, it can give them what they deserve for all this vileness done in Israel." 11 So all the men of Israel got together and united as one man against the city.

12 The tribes of Israel sent men throughout the tribe of Benjamin, saying, "What about this awful crime that was committed among you? 13 Now surrender those wicked men[g] of Gibeah so that we may put them to death and purge the evil from Israel."

But the Benjamites would not listen to their fellow Israelites. 14 From their towns they came together at Gibeah to fight against the Israelites. 15 At once the Benjamites mobilized twenty-six thousand swordsmen from their towns, in addition to seven hundred chosen men from those living in Gibeah. 16 Among all these soldiers there were seven hundred chosen men who were left-handed,[h] each of whom could sling a stone at a hair and not miss.

17 Israel, apart from Benjamin, mustered four hundred thousand swordsmen, all of them fighting men.

18 The Israelites went up to Bethel[b] and inquired of God.[i] They said, "Who of us shall go first to fight[j] against the Benjamites?"

The LORD replied, "Judah shall go first."

19 The next morning the Israelites got up and pitched camp near Gibeah. 20 The men of Israel went out to fight the Benjamites and took up battle positions against them at Gibeah. 21 The Benjamites came out of Gibeah and cut down twenty-two thousand Israelites on the battlefield that day. 22 But the men of Israel encouraged one another and again took up their positions where they had stationed themselves the first day. 23 The Israelites went up and wept before the LORD until evening,[k] and they inquired of the LORD. They said, "Shall we go up again to battle against the Benjamites, our brothers?"

**20:13** g Dt 13:13
**20:16** h Jdg 3:15; 1Ch 12:2
**20:18** i ver 26–27; Nu 27:21 j ver 23,28
**20:23** k Jos 7:6

[a] 10 One Hebrew manuscript; most Hebrew manuscripts *Geba,* a variant of *Gibeah* [b] 18 Or *to the house of God*; also in verse 26

# The Levite's Concubine

## Broken Pieces

Judges 19 relates the horrific account of a woman's life and death in such graphic detail that it could cause us to think we're reading a grisly novel rather than the Bible.

This anonymous woman was the concubine (a legitimate, but secondary, wife) of a Levite. After being unfaithful to the Levite, she left him and returned to her father's home. Four months later her husband set out on a journey to convince her to come back to him.

The Levite arrived at the home of his concubine's father. There he spent many days conversing with her father, and he repeatedly put off his journey home in order to stay with his host. Like Lot in Genesis 19, the Levite hesitated (see Ge 19:16). His lack of strength of mind set the stage for the ensuing tragedy.

Finally the Levite began the journey home, accompanied by his concubine. We do not know if she was coerced or convinced to go, but she left with the Levite and his servant. When evening came, the travelers stopped in an Israelite town in the territory of Benjamin to find shelter for the night. They were taken in by a hospitable stranger just as it began to look as if they would have to spend the night in the town square. Again, in a story that contains many parallels to that of Lot and Sodom and Gomorrah, men from the town swarmed to the man's door seeking to have sex with the Levite guest. Instead, the man offered his daughter and the Levite's concubine. At first the wicked men of the city refused the offer, but eventually the Levite sent his concubine out to them. Violation and death resulted. The subsequent dismemberment and distribution of the concubine's body led to civil war in Israel.

There are countless women around us today who are broken into many pieces. They have suffered horrors, violence and abuse. Many of these women darken the doors of our churches and ministries; often they remain anonymous, unheard and unspoken to. They literally are standing at the threshold crying out for help, and we step over them and continue on our own journeys, just as the Levite tried to do (see Jdg 19:27).

If you feel broken and wonder if anyone even knows your name, remember that God knows who you are. When society continues to rob you of your dignity, God is able to take every broken piece of your life and bring about wholeness.

—C. Ward

For the next Women of the Bible note, go to page 313.

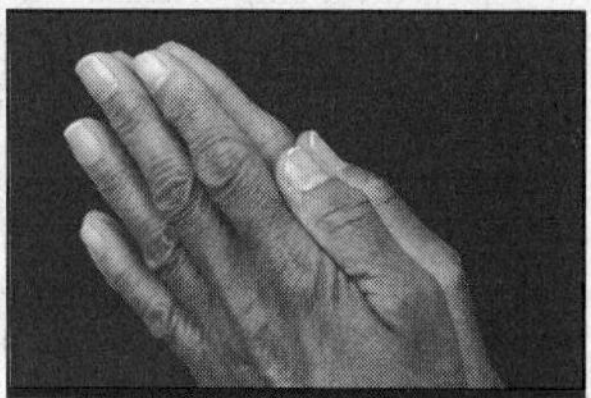

### reflection

*How has God brought about wholeness in your life?*

*Share your story with someone who is broken.*

*If you have not yet experienced wholeness, seek out a sister who has, and ask her to share her story.*

### read

Judges 19.

See also the Inspire Notes "Courage to Heal," "Sexual Abuse," "Suffering," "Overcoming Abuse" and "The Paradox of Life and Suffering," and the Women of the Bible Notes "Dinah: An Abused Woman" and "Tamar: A Violated Woman."

**20:29** l Jos 8:2,4
**20:31** m Jos 8:16
**20:34** n Jos 8:14

The LORD answered, "Go up against them."

24 Then the Israelites drew near to Benjamin the second day. 25 This time, when the Benjamites came out from Gibeah to oppose them, they cut down another eighteen thousand Israelites, all of them armed with swords.

26 Then the Israelites, all the people, went up to Bethel, and there they sat weeping before the LORD. They fasted that day until evening and presented burnt offerings and fellowship offerings[a] to the LORD. 27 And the Israelites inquired of the LORD. (In those days the ark of the covenant of God was there, 28 with Phinehas son of Eleazar, the son of Aaron, ministering before it.) They asked, "Shall we go up again to battle with Benjamin our brother, or not?"

The LORD responded, "Go, for tomorrow I will give them into your hands."

29 Then Israel set an ambush[l] around Gibeah. 30 They went up against the Benjamites on the third day and took up positions against Gibeah as they had done before. 31 The Benjamites came out to meet them and were drawn away[m] from the city. They began to inflict casualties on the Israelites as before, so that about thirty men fell in the open field and on the roads—the one leading to Bethel and the other to Gibeah.

32 While the Benjamites were saying, "We are defeating them as before," the Israelites were saying, "Let's retreat and draw them away from the city to the roads."

33 All the men of Israel moved from their places and took up positions at Baal Tamar, and the Israelite ambush charged out of its place on the west[b] of Gibeah.[c] 34 Then ten thousand of Israel's finest men made a frontal attack on Gibeah. The fighting was so heavy that the Benjamites did not realize[n] how near disaster was. 35 The LORD defeated Benjamin before Israel, and on that day the Israelites struck down 25,100 Benjamites, all armed with swords. 36 Then the Benjamites saw that they were beaten.

Now the men of Israel had given way before Benjamin, because they relied on the ambush they had set near Gibeah. 37 The men who had been in ambush made a sudden dash into Gibeah, spread out and put the whole city to the sword.[o] 38 The men of Israel had arranged with the ambush that they should send up a great cloud of smoke from the city, 39 and then the men of Israel would turn in the battle.

The Benjamites had begun to inflict casualties on the men of Israel (about thirty), and they said, "We are defeating them as in the first battle."[p] 40 But when the column of smoke began to rise from the city, the Benjamites turned and saw the smoke of the whole city going up into the sky. 41 Then the men of Israel turned on them, and the men of Benjamin were terrified, because they realized that disaster had come upon them. 42 So they fled before the Israelites in the direction of the desert, but they could not escape the battle. And the men of Israel who came out of the towns cut them down there. 43 They surrounded the Benjamites, chased them and easily[d] overran them in the vicinity of Gibeah on the east. 44 Eighteen thousand Benjamites fell, all of them valiant fighters. 45 As they turned and fled toward the desert to the rock of Rimmon,[q] the Israelites cut down five thousand men along the roads. They kept pressing after the Benjamites as far as Gidom and struck down two thousand more.

46 On that day twenty-five thousand Benjamite swordsmen fell, all of them valiant fighters. 47 But six hundred men turned and fled into the desert to the rock of Rimmon, where they stayed four months. 48 The men of Israel went back to Benjamin and put all the towns to the sword, including the animals and everything else they found. All the towns they came across they set on fire.

## Wives for the Benjamites

**21** The men of Israel had taken an oath at Mizpah: "Not one of us will give[r] his daughter in marriage to a Benjamite."

2 The people went to Bethel,[e] where they sat before God until evening, raising their voices and weeping bitterly. 3 "O LORD, the God of Israel," they cried, "why has this hap-

**20:37** o Jos 8:19
**20:39** p ver 32
**20:45** q Jos 15:32; Jdg 21:13
**21:1** r ver 7,18

[a] 26 Traditionally *peace offerings* [b] 33 Some Septuagint manuscripts and Vulgate; the meaning of the Hebrew for this word is uncertain. [c] 33 Hebrew *Geba,* a variant of *Gibeah* [d] 43 The meaning of the Hebrew for this word is uncertain.
[e] 2 Or *to the house of God*

**21:4** s Jdg 20:26; 2Sa 24:25
**21:5** t Jdg 5:23
**21:8** u 1Sa 11:1
**21:11** v Nu 31:17–18
**21:13** w Jdg 20:47

pened to Israel? Why should one tribe be
missing from Israel today?"
4 Early the next day the people built an
altar and presented burnt offerings and fel-
lowship offerings.[a][s]
5 Then the Israelites asked, "Who from all
the tribes of Israel[t] has failed to assemble
before the LORD?" For they had taken a
solemn oath that anyone who failed to as-
semble before the LORD at Mizpah should
certainly be put to death.
6 Now the Israelites grieved for their broth-
ers, the Benjamites. "Today one tribe is cut
off from Israel," they said. 7 "How can we pro-
vide wives for those who are left, since we
have taken an oath by the LORD not to give
them any of our daughters in marriage?"
8 Then they asked, "Which one of the tribes
of Israel failed to assemble before the LORD
at Mizpah?" They discovered that no one
from Jabesh Gilead[u] had come to the camp
for the assembly. 9 For when they counted
the people, they found that none of the peo-
ple of Jabesh Gilead were there.
10 So the assembly sent twelve thousand
fighting men with instructions to go to
Jabesh Gilead and put to the sword those
living there, including the women and chil-
dren. 11 "This is what you are to do," they
said. "Kill every male and every woman
who is not a virgin.[v]" 12 They found among
the people living in Jabesh Gilead four hun-
dred young women who had never slept
with a man, and they took them to the camp
at Shiloh in Canaan.
13 Then the whole assembly sent an offer
of peace to the Benjamites at the rock of
Rimmon.[w] 14 So the Benjamites returned at
that time and were given the women of Ja-
besh Gilead who had been spared. But there
were not enough for all of them.
15 The people grieved for Benjamin, be-
cause the LORD had made a gap in the tribes
of Israel. 16 And the elders of the assembly
said, "With the women of Benjamin de-
stroyed, how shall we provide wives for the
men who are left? 17 The Benjamite survivors
must have heirs," they said, "so that a tribe
of Israel will not be wiped out. 18 We can't
give them our daughters as wives, since
we Israelites have taken this oath: 'Cursed
be anyone who gives a wife to a Benjamite.'
19 But look, there is the annual festival of the
LORD in Shiloh, to the north of Bethel, and
east of the road that goes from Bethel to
Shechem, and to the south of Lebonah."
20 So they instructed the Benjamites, say-
ing, "Go and hide in the vineyards 21 and
watch. When the girls of Shiloh come out
to join in the dancing,[x] then rush from
the vineyards and each of you seize a wife
from the girls of Shiloh and go to the land
of Benjamin. 22 When their fathers or broth-
ers complain to us, we will say to them, 'Do
us a kindness by helping them, because we
did not get wives for them during the war,
and you are innocent, since you did not give
your daughters to them.' "
23 So that is what the Benjamites did. While
the girls were dancing, each man caught one
and carried her off to be his wife. Then they
returned to their inheritance and rebuilt the
towns and settled in them.[y]
24 At that time the Israelites left that place
and went home to their tribes and clans,
each to his own inheritance.
25 In those days Israel had no king; every-
one did as he saw fit.[z]

**21:21** x Ex 15:20; Jdg 11:34
**21:23** y Jdg 20:48
**21:25** z Jdg 17:6; 18:1; 19:1

[a] 4 Traditionally *peace offerings*

# Ruth

## OVERVIEW

The book of Ruth opens with the departure of Elimelech and Naomi and their sons, Mahlon and Kilion, from the land of Israel during a time of famine. They settled in Moab, and the sons married Ruth and Orpah, Moabite women. To Naomi's dismay, her husband and both sons died prematurely in the foreign country, and she decided to return to her homeland when she heard that the famine there had ended. While Orpah remained in Moab, Ruth chose to travel with Naomi and accept the Israelite people and their God as her own.

Returning to her homeland alone and without the protection and care of a husband or sons was a bitter experience for Naomi, but as the events unfolded, Ruth married a kind relative (a "kinsman-redeemer") of Naomi's named Boaz. Naomi was redeemed from sorrow, and at the end of the book we see her rejoicing in the birth of a second kinsman-redeemer through Ruth and Boaz. The genealogy of David, the great king of Israel, reveals that David was the great-grandson of Ruth.

The bond of sisterly love is strong and conquers setbacks and struggles. Just as Ruth and Naomi clung to each other during perilous times, women believers can support each other with the same devotion through prayer, words of encouragement and acts of service.

## OUTLINE

I. Naomi Goes to Moab and Back to Israel (1:1–22)
II. Ruth Meets Boaz (2:1–23)
III. Ruth Follows Naomi's Instructions (3:1–18)
IV. Boaz Marries Ruth (4:1–22)

### SCANNABLE FACTS:

**Author:** Unknown

**Time Written:** Probably around the time of David, about 1000 B.C.

**Theme to Note:** Trust in God's provision during difficult times

**Notable Women:** Naomi, Ruth, Orpah

1:1 a Jdg 2:16–18 b Jdg 3:30
1:2 c Ge 35:19
1:6 d Ex 4:31 e Mt 6:11
1:8 f Ru 2:20; 2Ti 1:16
1:9 g Ru 3:1
1:11 h Ge 38:11; Dt 25:5
1:13 i Jdg 2:15; Job 19:21; Ps 32:4

## Naomi and Ruth

1 In the days when the judges ruled,[a][a] there was a famine in the land, and a man from Bethlehem in Judah, together with his wife and two sons, went to live for a while in the country of Moab.[b] 2 The man's name was Elimelech, his wife's name Naomi, and the names of his two sons were Mahlon and Kilion. They were Ephrathites from Bethlehem,[c] Judah. And they went to Moab and lived there.

3 Now Elimelech, Naomi's husband, died, and she was left with her two sons. 4 They married Moabite women, one named Orpah and the other Ruth. After they had lived there about ten years, 5 both Mahlon and Kilion also died, and Naomi was left without her two sons and her husband.

6 When she heard in Moab that the LORD had come to the aid of his people[d] by providing food[e] for them, Naomi and her daughters-in-law prepared to return home from there. 7 With her two daughters-in-law she left the place where she had been living and set out on the road that would take them back to the land of Judah.

8 Then Naomi said to her two daughters-in-law, "Go back, each of you, to your mother's home. May the LORD show kindness[f] to you, as you have shown to your dead and to me. 9 May the LORD grant that each of you will find rest[g] in the home of another husband."

Then she kissed them and they wept aloud 10 and said to her, "We will go back with you to your people."

11 But Naomi said, "Return home, my daughters. Why would you come with me? Am I going to have any more sons, who could become your husbands?[h] 12 Return home, my daughters; I am too old to have another husband. Even if I thought there was still hope for me—even if I had a husband tonight and then gave birth to sons— 13 would you wait until they grew up? Would you remain unmarried for them? No, my daughters. It is more bitter for me than for you, because the LORD's hand has gone out against me!"[i]

14 At this they wept again. Then Orpah kissed her mother-in-law good-by, but Ruth clung to her.

15 "Look," said Naomi, "your sister-in-law is going back to her people and her gods. Go back with her."

16 But Ruth replied, "Don't urge me to leave you[j] or to turn back from you. Where you go I will go, and where you stay I will stay. Your people will be my people and your God my God. 17 Where you die I will die, and there I will be buried. May the LORD deal with me, be it ever so severely,[k] if anything but death separates you and me." 18 When Naomi realized that Ruth was determined to go with her, she stopped urging her.[l]

19 So the two women went on until they came to Bethlehem. When they arrived in Bethlehem, the whole town was stirred[m] because of them, and the women exclaimed, "Can this be Naomi?"

20 "Don't call me Naomi,[b]" she told them. "Call me Mara,[c] because the Almighty[d] has made my life very bitter. 21 I went away full, but the LORD has brought me back empty.[n] Why call me Naomi? The LORD has afflicted[e] me; the Almighty has brought misfortune upon me."

22 So Naomi returned from Moab accompanied by Ruth the Moabitess, her daughter-in-law, arriving in Bethlehem as the barley harvest[o] was beginning.

## Ruth Meets Boaz

2 Now Naomi had a relative[p] on her husband's side, from the clan of Elimelech, a man of standing, whose name was Boaz.

2 And Ruth the Moabitess said to Naomi, "Let me go to the fields and pick up the leftover grain[q] behind anyone in whose eyes I find favor."

Naomi said to her, "Go ahead, my daughter." 3 So she went out and began to glean in the fields behind the harvesters. As it turned out, she found herself working in a field belonging to Boaz, who was from the clan of Elimelech.

4 Just then Boaz arrived from Bethlehem and greeted the harvesters, "The LORD be with you!"[r]

"The LORD bless you!"[s] they called back.

1:16 j 2Ki 2:2
1:17 k 1Sa 3:17; 2Ki 6:31
1:18 l Ac 21:14
1:19 m Mt 21:10
1:21 n Job 1:21
1:22 o Ex 9:31
2:1 p Ru 3:2,12
2:2 q Lev 19:9; Dt 24:19
2:4 r Lk 1:28; 2Th 3:16 s Ps 129:7–8

[a]1 Traditionally *judged* [b]20 *Naomi* means *pleasant*; also in verse 21. [c]20 *Mara* means *bitter.* [d]20 Hebrew *Shaddai*; also in verse 21 [e]21 Or *has testified against*

2:6 t Ru 1:22

5 Boaz asked the foreman of his harvest-
ers, "Whose young woman is that?"
6 The foreman replied, "She is the Moabit-
ess[t] who came back from Moab with Naomi.
7 She said, 'Please let me glean and gather
among the sheaves behind the harvesters.'
She went into the field and has worked
steadily from morning till now, except for a
short rest in the shelter."
8 So Boaz said to Ruth, "My daughter, lis-
ten to me. Don't go and glean in another
field and don't go away from here. Stay
here with my servant girls. 9 Watch the field
where the men are harvesting, and follow
along after the girls. I have told the men not
to touch you. And whenever you are thirsty,
go and get a drink from the water jars the
men have filled."
10 At this, she bowed down with her face
to the ground.[u] She exclaimed, "Why have

2:10 u 1Sa 25:23

Inspire

## INTIMATE FRIENDSHIPS

Naomi and Ruth's story is one of the most intimate portrayals of friendship in the Scriptures. In spite of the fact that staying together meant that Ruth had to leave her home, her family and her country, she clung to Naomi (see Ru 1:14); and her vow to Naomi stands as one of the most beautiful commitments of friendship in history (see Ru 1:16–17).

Ruth and Naomi were more than daughter- and mother-in-law; they were friends that loved at all times—in good and bad situations. Their actions demonstrated the self-sacrificing love that builds intimacy in any relationship. This is the type of love that would lead a person to lay down her life for a friend (see Jn 15:13).

While an intimate friend is a great gift, intimacy bears with it the potential for great pain. Betrayal is so much more hurtful when it comes at the hand of a trusted, intimate friend (see Ps 55:12–14). Intimate friendship can be disrupted by petty disputation, lack of trustworthiness or devotion, withholding kindness and gossip. All of these things can be intimacy breakers.

As women of color, we should cherish the intimate friendships we are blessed to have and guard these valuable relationships against intimacy breakers. Let Ruth and Naomi's difficult, yet mutually rewarding, relationship guide you in your intimate relationships.

—E. Alexander

For the next Inspire note, go to page 321.

**read**

Ruth 1.

**See also** the Inspire Notes "Friendship," "What Is Intimacy?" and "Intimacy: Relationships With Other Christians," and the Women of the Bible Notes "Ruth: A Model of Friendship and Sisterhood," "Naomi: Call Me Bitter" and "Euodia and Syntyche: Women in Conflict."

**WOMAN of COLOR**

How are you cultivating, nurturing or preserving an intimate friendship?

I found such favor in your eyes that you notice me—a foreigner?"

11 "Boaz replied, "I've been told all about what you have done for your mother-in-law[v] since the death of your husband—how you left your father and mother and your homeland and came to live with a people you did not know before.[w] 12 May the LORD repay you for what you have done. May you be richly rewarded by the LORD,[x] the God of Israel, under whose wings[y] you have come to take refuge.[z]"

13 "May I continue to find favor in your eyes, my lord," she said. "You have given me comfort and have spoken kindly to your servant—though I do not have the standing of one of your servant girls."

14 At mealtime Boaz said to her, "Come over here. Have some bread and dip it in the wine vinegar."

When she sat down with the harvesters, he offered her some roasted grain. She ate all she wanted and had some left over.[a] 15 As she got up to glean, Boaz gave orders to his men, "Even if she gathers among the sheaves, don't embarrass her. 16 Rather, pull out some stalks for her from the bundles and leave them for her to pick up, and don't rebuke her."

17 So Ruth gleaned in the field until evening. Then she threshed the barley she had gathered, and it amounted to about an ephah.[a] 18 She carried it back to town, and her mother-in-law saw how much she had gathered. Ruth also brought out and gave her what she had left over[b] after she had eaten enough.

19 Her mother-in-law asked her, "Where did you glean today? Where did you work? Blessed be the man who took notice of you!"

Then Ruth told her mother-in-law about the one at whose place she had been working. "The name of the man I worked with today is Boaz," she said.

20 "The LORD bless him!" Naomi said to her daughter-in-law. "He has not stopped showing his kindness[c] to the living and the dead." She added, "That man is our close relative; he is one of our kinsman-redeemers.[d]"

21 Then Ruth the Moabitess said, "He even said to me, 'Stay with my workers until they finish harvesting all my grain.'"

22 Naomi said to Ruth her daughter-in-law, "It will be good for you, my daughter, to go with his girls, because in someone else's field you might be harmed."

23 So Ruth stayed close to the servant girls of Boaz to glean until the barley and wheat harvests[e] were finished. And she lived with her mother-in-law.

## Ruth and Boaz at the Threshing Floor

3 One day Naomi her mother-in-law said to her, "My daughter, should I not try to find a home[b] for you, where you will be well provided for? 2 Is not Boaz, with whose servant girls you have been, a kinsman of ours? Tonight he will be winnowing barley on the threshing floor. 3 Wash and perfume yourself,[f] and put on your best clothes. Then go down to the threshing floor, but don't let him know you are there until he has finished eating and drinking. 4 When he lies down, note the place where he is lying. Then go and uncover his feet and lie down. He will tell you what to do."

5 "I will do whatever you say," Ruth answered. 6 So she went down to the threshing floor and did everything her mother-in-law told her to do.

7 When Boaz had finished eating and drinking and was in good spirits,[g] he went over to lie down at the far end of the grain pile. Ruth approached quietly, uncovered his feet and lay down. 8 In the middle of the night something startled the man, and he turned and discovered a woman lying at his feet.

9 "Who are you?" he asked.

"I am your servant Ruth," she said. "Spread the corner of your garment over me, since you are a kinsman-redeemer.[h]"

10 "The LORD bless you, my daughter,"

*"It is sometimes assumed that the typical female slave was a house servant . . . either a cook, maid, or mammy . . . The reality is actually the diametrical opposite of the myth . . . Seven out of eight slaves were field workers."*

—ANGELA DAVIS, WRITER AND ACTIVIST

**2:11** v Ru 1:14 w Ru 1:16–17
**2:12** x 1Sa 24:19 y Ps 17:8 z Ru 1:16
**2:14** a ver 18
**2:18** b ver 14
**2:20** c Ru 3:10 d Ru 3:9,12
**2:23** e Dt 16:9
**3:3** f 2Sa 14:2
**3:7** g Jdg 19:6,9,22; 2Sa 13:28
**3:9** h Ru 2:20

[a]17 That is, probably about 3/5 bushel (about 22 liters) [b]1 Hebrew *find rest* (see Ruth 1:9)

# Ruth

## A Model of Friendship and Sisterhood

The book of Ruth and the woman Ruth have provided the Biblical canon with a captivating voice that reaches far beyond what the writer of this book may have intended. This brief account holds more than a sentimental Scriptural reference for a wedding or a life design for single women. This story poignantly highlights many of the issues that African American women struggle with today (e.g., family, security, loss, racism, sexism and survival).

Ruth is best known for marrying Boaz and giving birth to Obed, an ancestor of David and, consequently, Jesus. But before she claimed her place in history as "wife" and "mother," she added a unique imprint as "woman" and "sista." In Ruth 1:14, we find this Moabite widow making an unprecedented choice to "cling" (or "cleave," KJV) to her Israelite mother-in-law.

The relationship between Ruth and Naomi bound two women who could have easily chosen to become estranged. After the death of her husband (Naomi's son), Ruth was left with an uncertain future. She could return to her home, but there was no guarantee that her family would embrace her, since she had married an Israelite. The Israelites were long-time antagonists of her people. She could follow her mother-in-law, but there was uncertainty about how she would be received as a foreigner with scorned ethnic roots. Using her courage and strength, Ruth remained with, or "clung" to, Naomi. As a result, they were able to move beyond their given identities as wives and widows and establish different identities as partners and sojourners.

The return of Naomi to Bethlehem was the beginning of a new life for her and Ruth. Ruth worked in the fields of Naomi's relative, Boaz. Following the advice of Naomi, Ruth eventually won the love of Boaz, who bought the estate of Naomi and married Ruth.

This story's gift to us is a message about the value of collaboration, cooperation, friendship, love and trust between two women. At a turning point in her life, Ruth continued a relationship that would become a great blessing for both women. By taking risks and working together, Ruth and Naomi became a model for future generations of love, trust and loyalty.

—K. Mosby-Avery

### reflection

*How can you work with other women to bring about change for yourself and for others?*

*Is there anything that stands in the way of your cooperating with other women? Seek God's guidance in dealing with your concern.*

### read

Ruth 1–4; see also Leviticus 25:25.

**See also** the Inspire Notes "The Faithfulness of God," "Intimate Friendships," "Commitment to Community," "Friendship" and "Intimacy: Relationships With Other Christians," and the Women of the Bible Note "Naomi: Call Me Bitter."

For the next Women of the Bible note, go to page 315.

he replied. "This kindness is greater than that which you showed earlier: You have not run after the younger men, whether rich or poor. 11 And now, my daughter, don't be afraid. I will do for you all you ask. All my fellow townsmen know that you are a woman of noble character.[i] 12 Although it is true that I am near of kin, there is a kinsman-redeemer nearer than[j] I. 13 Stay here for the night, and in the morning if he wants to redeem,[k] good; let him redeem. But if he is not willing, as surely as the LORD lives I will do it. Lie here until morning."

14 So she lay at his feet until morning, but got up before anyone could be recognized; and he said, "Don't let it be known that a woman came to the threshing floor."[l]

15 He also said, "Bring me the shawl you are wearing and hold it out." When she did so, he poured into it six measures of barley and put it on her. Then he[a] went back to town.

16 When Ruth came to her mother-in-law, Naomi asked, "How did it go, my daughter?"

Then she told her everything Boaz had done for her 17 and added, "He gave me these six measures of barley, saying, 'Don't go back to your mother-in-law empty-handed.'"

18 Then Naomi said, "Wait, my daughter, until you find out what happens. For the man will not rest until the matter is settled today."

## Boaz Marries Ruth

4 Meanwhile Boaz went up to the town gate and sat there. When the kinsman-redeemer he had mentioned[m] came along, Boaz said, "Come over here, my friend, and sit down." So he went over and sat down.

2 Boaz took ten of the elders of the town and said, "Sit here," and they did so. 3 Then he said to the kinsman-redeemer, "Naomi, who has come back from Moab, is selling the piece of land that belonged to our brother Elimelech. 4 I thought I should bring the matter to your attention and suggest that you buy it in the presence of these seated here and in the presence of the elders of my people. If you will redeem it, do so. But if you[b] will not, tell me, so I will know. For no one has the right to do it except you,[n] and I am next in line."

**3:11** i Pr12:4
**3:12** j Ru4:1
**3:13** k Dt25:5; Mt22:24
**3:14** l Ro14:16; 2Co8:21
**4:1** m Ru3:12

"I will redeem it," he said.

5 Then Boaz said, "On the day you buy the land from Naomi and from Ruth the Moabitess, you acquire[c] the dead man's widow, in order to maintain the name of the dead with his property."[o]

6 At this, the kinsman-redeemer said, "Then I cannot redeem[p] it because I might endanger my own estate. You redeem it yourself. I cannot do it."

7 (Now in earlier times in Israel, for the redemption and transfer of property to become final, one party took off his sandal and gave it to the other. This was the method of legalizing transactions in Israel.)[q]

8 So the kinsman-redeemer said to Boaz, "Buy it yourself." And he removed his sandal.

9 Then Boaz announced to the elders and all the people, "Today you are witnesses that I have bought from Naomi all the property of Elimelech, Kilion and Mahlon. 10 I have also acquired Ruth the Moabitess, Mahlon's widow, as my wife, in order to maintain the name of the dead with his property, so that his name will not disappear from among his family or from the town records.[r] Today you are witnesses!"

11 Then the elders and all those at the gate said, "We are witnesses. May the LORD make the woman who is coming into your home like Rachel and Leah,[s] who together built up the house of Israel. May you have standing in Ephrathah and be famous in Bethlehem. 12 Through the offspring the LORD gives you by this young woman, may your family be like that of Perez,[t] whom Tamar bore to Judah."

## The Genealogy of David

13 So Boaz took Ruth and she became his wife. Then he went to her, and the LORD enabled her to conceive,[u] and she gave birth to a son. 14 The women[v] said to Naomi: "Praise be to the LORD, who this day has not left you without a kinsman-redeemer. May he become famous throughout Israel! 15 He will renew your life and sustain you in your old

**4:4** n Lev25:25; Jer32:7–8
**4:5** o Ge38:8; Dt25:5–6
**4:6** p Ru3:13
**4:7** q Dt25:7–9
**4:10** r Dt25:6
**4:11** s Ps127:3
**4:12** t ver18; Ge38:29
**4:13** u Ge29:31; 33:5; Ru3:11
**4:14** v Lk1:58

[a] 15 Most Hebrew manuscripts; many Hebrew manuscripts, Vulgate and Syriac *she* [b] 4 Many Hebrew manuscripts, Septuagint, Vulgate and Syriac; most Hebrew manuscripts *he* [c] 5 Hebrew; Vulgate and Syriac *Naomi, you acquire Ruth the Moabitess,*

# Naomi

## Call Me Bitter

My family left our hometown, Bethlehem, with thoughts of a better life. My husband and I packed up our two sons and moved to the country of Moab because there was a famine in Israel. We became comfortable in Moab. But one day the unthinkable happened: my husband died. The only thing that helped relieve my grief was the marriages of my sons. Although my daughters-in-law were Moabites rather than Israelites, I grew to love them like daughters.

Then, unbelievably, both of my sons died. I was thrown into the depths of despair; and Ruth, Orpah and I were left alone in an unkind world. At the time I thought, *It's funny: while my name means "pleasant," my spirit counters such a lighthearted name. Instead, my spirit says, "Call me bitter."*

When I heard that the famine was over in Israel, I decided to return home. I thought that at least my people were there, and I could wait my time out to die. My daughters-in-law begged to return to Bethlehem with me because they were determined not to leave me alone. But what could I offer them? While we were on the journey to Israel, I convinced Orpah to return to her family in Moab. But Ruth refused to go. She was determined to accompany me. I reluctantly allowed her to do so.

When we arrived in Bethlehem, our status as widows meant we had no one to care for us. We had no food, and I was too old to work. When my friends tried to comfort me, all I could say was, "Call me bitter." Now I realize just how God blessed me by giving me Ruth. She gleaned in the fields so that we could eat. And when she was fortunate enough to work on the property of one of my relatives, Boaz, she followed my advice and eventually married this kind man. Ruth and Boaz then took care of me. But my story does not end there. When Ruth had a son, she brought him to me to care for! Call me bitter? No! God has taken my bitterness and given me a garment of praise! I praise him for Ruth because I now know that she is more valuable to me than seven sons!

—C. Belt

### reflection

*Reflect on a time when God took away your bitterness and gave you a spirit of praise.*

*How can your past experience inspire you to continue to trust in the Lord?*

### read

Ruth 1–4.

See also the Inspire Notes "The Faithfulness of God," "Intimate Friendships," "Friendship," "Intimacy: Relationships With Other Christians" and "Abandonment," and the Women of the Bible Note "Ruth: A Model of Friendship and Sisterhood."

For the next Women of the Bible note, go to page 320.

4:15 w Ru 1:16–17; 2:11–12

4:18 x Mt 1:3–6

age. For your daughter-in-law, who loves you and who is better to you than seven sons,[w] has given him birth."

16 Then Naomi took the child, laid him in her lap and cared for him. 17 The women living there said, "Naomi has a son." And they named him Obed. He was the father of Jesse, the father of David.

18 This, then, is the family line of Perez[x]:

Perez was the father of Hezron,
19 Hezron the father of Ram,
Ram the father of Amminadab,
20 Amminadab the father of Nahshon,
Nahshon the father of Salmon,[a]
21 Salmon the father of Boaz,
Boaz the father of Obed,
22 Obed the father of Jesse,
and Jesse the father of David.

*Woman of color,*

*Look at how I have provided for those in the past, for those in your life—and for you. Just trust me!*

*Your Creator and Provider*

RUTH 4:13–17

[a]20 A few Hebrew manuscripts, some Septuagint manuscripts and Vulgate (see also verse 21 and Septuagint of 1 Chron. 2:11); most Hebrew manuscripts *Salma*

# 1 Samuel

## OVERVIEW

The book of 1 Samuel begins with the miraculous birth of Samuel, the last judge in Israel, and transitions into the establishment of kingship in Israel. Hannah, Samuel's mother, was grieved because of her infertility. God heard her desperate prayer and blessed her with a son. Hannah sacrificially promised to return the child to God for his service. After Samuel was weaned, Hannah fulfilled her promise and took the boy to the Lord's tabernacle in preparation for a lifetime of service to his people (see 1Sa 1–3). Samuel became both a judge and a prophet; however, the people wanted to be like the nations around them. They demanded a king, and God reminded Samuel that they were not rejecting him, but the Lord (see 1Sa 8:7).

The book then goes on to tell the story of Saul, who was appointed the first king. Saul began his reign well, but twice he disobeyed a command from the Lord and therefore was rejected as Israel's leader (see 1Sa 13; 15). God then directed Samuel to anoint David as the new king (see 1Sa 16), even though David was the youngest son of a family in a small town.

Women play a significant role in this book. Hannah's earnest prayers resulted in her giving birth to Samuel, who has been called the last of the judges and the first of the prophets. Michal, one of Saul's daughters, fell in love with David, married him and helped him escape one of Saul's murderous plans (see 1Sa 18–19). Abigail saved an entire household from being slaughtered as a result of the actions of her foolish husband (see 1Sa 25). And the witch of Endor gave Saul his death sentence (see 1Sa 28).

Does God hear the desperate prayers of women like Hannah today? Yes, for "this is the confidence we have in approaching God: that if we ask anything according to his will, he hears us" (1Jn 5:14). Renew your faith in God's ability to hear your prayers as you read about Hannah's faith and see how God went beyond her prayer to mightily use her son Samuel.

## OUTLINE

I. Samuel's Birth and Calling (1:1—3:21)
II. Israel Defeated and the Ark of God Taken (4:1—7:17)
III. The People of Israel Request a King (8:1–22)
IV. Saul Anointed and Rejected (9:1—15:35)
V. Samuel Anoints David (16:1–23)
VI. David and Goliath (17:1–58)
VII. David Becomes Alienated From Saul (18:1—19:24)
VIII. David on the Run (20:1—27:12)
IX. Saul's Last Days (28:1—31:13)

## SCANNABLE FACTS:

**Author:** Unknown

**Time Written:** Unknown

**Theme to Note:** Obedience is greater than sacrifice

**Notable Women:** Hannah, Michal, Abigail, the witch of Endor

## The Birth of Samuel

1 There was a certain man from Ramathaim, a Zuphite[a] from the hill country of Ephraim, whose name was Elkanah[a] son of Jeroham, the son of Elihu, the son of Tohu, the son of Zuph, an Ephraimite. [2]He had two wives; one was called Hannah and the other Peninnah. Peninnah had children, but Hannah had none.

[3]Year after year this man went up from his town to worship[b] and sacrifice to the LORD Almighty at Shiloh,[c] where Hophni and Phinehas, the two sons of Eli, were priests of the LORD. [4]Whenever the day came for Elkanah to sacrifice,[d] he would give portions of the meat to his wife Peninnah and to all her sons and daughters. [5]But to Hannah he gave a double portion because he loved her, and the LORD had closed her womb.[e] [6]And because the LORD had closed her womb, her rival kept provoking her in order to irritate her.[f] [7]This went on year after year. Whenever Hannah went up to the house of the LORD, her rival provoked her till she wept and would not eat. [8]Elkanah her husband would say to her, "Hannah, why are you weeping? Why don't you eat? Why are you downhearted? Don't I mean more to you than ten sons?[g]"

[9]Once when they had finished eating and drinking in Shiloh, Hannah stood up. Now Eli the priest was sitting on a chair by the doorpost of the LORD's temple.[b][h] [10]In bitterness of soul Hannah wept much and prayed to the LORD. [11]And she made a vow, saying, "O LORD Almighty, if you will only look upon your servant's misery and remember me, and not forget your servant but give her a son, then I will give him to the LORD for all the days of his life, and no razor[i] will ever be used on his head."

[12]As she kept on praying to the LORD, Eli observed her mouth. [13]Hannah was praying in her heart, and her lips were moving but her voice was not heard. Eli thought she was drunk [14]and said to her, "How long will you keep on getting drunk? Get rid of your wine."

[15]"Not so, my lord," Hannah replied, "I am a woman who is deeply troubled. I have not been drinking wine or beer; I was pouring[j] out my soul to the LORD. [16]Do not take your servant for a wicked woman; I have been praying here out of my great anguish and grief."

[17]Eli answered, "Go in peace,[k] and may the God of Israel grant you what you have asked of him.[l]"

[18]She said, "May your servant find favor in your eyes.[m]" Then she went her way and ate something, and her face was no longer downcast.

[19]Early the next morning they arose and worshiped before the LORD and then went back to their home at Ramah. Elkanah lay with Hannah his wife, and the LORD remembered[n] her. [20]So in the course of time Hannah conceived and gave birth to a son. She named him Samuel,[c] saying, "Because I asked the LORD for him."

## Hannah Dedicates Samuel

[21]When the man Elkanah went up with all his family to offer the annual[o] sacrifice to the LORD and to fulfill his vow, [22]Hannah did not go. She said to her husband, "After the boy is weaned, I will take him and present[p] him before the LORD, and he will live there always."

[23]"Do what seems best to you," Elkanah her husband told her. "Stay here until you have weaned him; only may the LORD make good[q] his[d] word." So the woman stayed at home and nursed her son until she had weaned him.

[24]After he was weaned, she took the boy with her, young as he was, along with a three-year-old bull,[e][r] an ephah[f] of flour and a skin of wine, and brought him to the house of the LORD at Shiloh. [25]When they had slaughtered the bull, they brought the boy to Eli, [26]and she said to him, "As surely as you live, my lord, I am the woman who stood here beside you praying to the LORD. [27]I prayed for this child, and the LORD has granted me what I asked of him. [28]So now I give him to the LORD. For his whole life he will be given over to the LORD." And he worshiped the LORD there.

**1:1** a 1Ch 6:27,34
**1:3** b Dt 12:5–7 c Jos 18:1
**1:4** d Dt 12:17–18
**1:5** e Ge 16:1; 30:2
**1:6** f Job 24:21
**1:8** g Ru 4:15
**1:9** h 1Sa 3:3
**1:11** i Nu 6:1–21; Jdg 13:5
**1:15** j 62:8
**1:17** k Jdg 18:6; Mk 5:34 l Ps 20:3–5
**1:18** m Ru 2:13
**1:19** n Ge 30:22
**1:21** o ver 3
**1:22** p Lk 2:22
**1:23** q Nu 30:7
**1:24** r Dt 12:5; Jos 18:1

[a]1 Or *from Ramathaim Zuphim* [b]9 That is, tabernacle [c]20 *Samuel* sounds like the Hebrew for *heard of God.*
[d]23 Masoretic Text; Dead Sea Scrolls, Septuagint and Syriac *your* [e]24 Dead Sea Scrolls, Septuagint and Syriac; Masoretic Text *with three bulls* [f]24 That is, probably about 3/5 bushel (about 22 liters)

# Hannah

## What Do You Do When God Says "No"?

We never get used to disappointment. To live the life of an infertile woman is heartbreaking on a monthly basis. Hannah had been infertile for many years. Others scorned her because in her culture having children, especially male children, was a symbol of wholeness. Her husband's other wife, Peninnah, who had children, taunted her. Hannah was made to feel incomplete and inadequate as a wife and as a woman.

Through her situation, Hannah teaches us what to do when our desire does not materialize. She shows us how to handle "no" or "not yet" from God. Though Hannah lived with life's disappointments on a daily basis, she re-emphasizes for us the value of prayer. Hannah continued to go to the tabernacle with her husband, Elkanah, to pray. She continued to worship God even though her prayers went unanswered.

Hannah remained faithful to God when it seemed that God had closed the door to her request for a child. She continued to pray and share her pain and sorrows with him (see 1Sa 1:15–16). Hannah never stopped believing that the God she served was able to help her. She prayed without ceasing and continued to worship the only one who could soothe her soul.

When God did say "yes," Hannah responded with joy and love. And she honored him by offering her son back to him. Hannah realized that her son was a gift from God.

Just because God has said "no" now, he may not mean "no" eternally. Sometimes God has to put things in order before he can say "yes." Perhaps there are people and situations that he must work on before our "yes" can come. And sometimes God's "yes" doesn't look like what we thought we wanted—but even then, honor must be given to the giver of all gifts. When God answers our prayers, we must remember to follow Hannah's model and offer our answered prayer back to God; we must honor God with the people and things he gives us.

—L. Mosley White

### reflection

*Have you committed to praying to God for all your needs and wants?*

*Use Hannah as a model for handling your "no" and "not yet" moments.*

### read

1 Samuel 1:1—2:11.

**See also** the Inspire Notes "Infertility," "Distress," "Waiting on God," "Praying for Patience," "Prayer: A God-Given Promise," "Prayer: The Antidote to Worry," "Peace" and "Prayer," and the Women of the Bible Note "The Persistent Widow: Always Pray."

For the next Women of the Bible note, go to page 342.

2:1 s Lk 1:46–55
t Isa 12:2–3

## Hannah's Prayer

2 Then Hannah prayed and said:[s]
"My heart rejoices in the LORD;
in the LORD my horn[a][t] is lifted high.
My mouth boasts over my enemies,
for I delight in your deliverance.

2 "There is no one holy[b][u] like the LORD;
there is no one besides you;
there is no Rock like our God.

3 "Do not keep talking so proudly
or let your mouth speak such
arrogance,

2:2 u Ex 15:11

[a]1 *Horn* here symbolizes strength; also in verse 10. [b]2 Or *no Holy One*

Inspire

## COMMITMENT TO COMMUNITY

God answered Hannah's fervent prayers for a child, and Hannah pledged to give the child back to God (see 1Sa 1:21–22). Samuel, Hannah's child, went on to become one of God's greatest prophets and helped save the community from the selfish excesses of Eli's sons, who functioned as priests in the house of the Lord. God used Hannah's faithful cry of pain to fulfill God's purpose for the community.

Women of color who believe in Christ are in a special place in this world. We are people of color in a world in which the noncolored population has both political and economic advantage. We are women in a society that continues to be dominated by men. We live under painful double-edged oppression. Despite our own pain, or perhaps because of it, we have the special ability to see and feel the struggles of those around us in a way that those in power cannot.

As believers in Christ, we know that God works through people on the opposite side of the political and economic power structure to create change and to move the world to new levels of civility. When we fervently pray and humble ourselves to God's will for our lives, as Hannah did, we open ourselves to what God would have us give back to our communities. We give back to God by helping others and by becoming engaged in the struggle to create a political and economic system that recognizes the worth of all of God's children. By faithfully offering our best to God, like Hannah did, we become empowered by God to create communities that reflect his love.

—A. DAVIS

**read**

Read 1 Samuel 1:1–28.
**See also** the Inspire Notes "Integrity" and "Sacrificial Living," and the Women of the Bible Notes "Hannah: What Do You Do When God Says 'No'?" "Lydia: A Model for Women in Business," "Phoebe: A Faithful Messenger" and "Priscilla: An Open-Door Policy."

**WOMAN of COLOR**

How are you using your gifts to create communities that reflect God's love?

For the next Inspire note, go to page 331.

**2:3** v 1Sa 16:7 w Pr 16:2
**2:5** x Ps 113:9; Jer 15:9
**2:6** y Dt 32:39
**2:7** z Ps 75:7
**2:8** a Job 36:7 b Job 38:4
**2:9** c Ps 91:12
**2:10** d Ps 2:9 e Ps 18:13 f Ps 96:13 g Ps 89:24
**2:11** h 1Sa 3:1
**2:12** i Jer 2:8

for the LORD is a God who knows,
and by him deeds[v] are weighed.[w]

4 "The bows of the warriors are broken,
but those who stumbled are armed
with strength.
5 Those who were full hire themselves out
for food,
but those who were hungry hunger no
more.
She who was barren[x] has borne seven
children,
but she who has had many sons pines
away.

6 "The LORD brings death and makes alive;[y]
he brings down to the grave[a] and
raises up.
7 The LORD sends poverty and wealth;
he humbles and he exalts.[z]
8 He raises the poor from the dust
and lifts the needy from the ash heap;
he seats them with princes
and has them inherit a throne of
honor.[a]

"For the foundations[b] of the earth are the
LORD's;
upon them he has set the world.
9 He will guard the feet[c] of his saints,
but the wicked will be silenced in
darkness.

"It is not by strength that one prevails;
10 those who oppose the LORD will be
shattered.[d]
He will thunder[e] against them from
heaven;
the LORD will judge[f] the ends of the
earth.

"He will give strength to his king
and exalt the horn[g] of his anointed."

11 Then Elkanah went home to Ramah,
but the boy ministered[h] before the LORD un-
der Eli the priest.

## Eli's Wicked Sons

12 Eli's sons were wicked men; they had no
regard[i] for the LORD. 13 Now it was the practice
of the priests with the people that whenever
anyone offered a sacrifice and while the
meat was being boiled, the servant of the
priest would come with a three-pronged
fork in his hand. 14 He would plunge it into
the pan or kettle or caldron or pot, and the
priest would take for himself whatever the
fork brought up. This is how they treated all
the Israelites who came to Shiloh. 15 But even
before the fat was burned, the servant of the
priest would come and say to the man who
was sacrificing, "Give the priest some meat
to roast; he won't accept boiled meat from
you, but only raw."

16 If the man said to him, "Let the fat be
burned up first, and then take whatever
you want," the servant would then answer,
"No, hand it over now; if you don't, I'll take
it by force."

17 This sin of the young men was very
great in the LORD's sight, for they[b] were treat-
ing the LORD's offering with contempt.[j]

18 But Samuel was ministering[k] before
the LORD—a boy wearing a linen ephod.
19 Each year his mother made him a little
robe and took it to him when she went up
with her husband to offer the annual[l] sacri-
fice. 20 Eli would bless Elkanah and his wife,
saying, "May the LORD give you children by
this woman to take the place of the one she
prayed[m] for and gave to the LORD." Then they
would go home. 21 And the LORD was gracious
to Hannah;[n] she conceived and gave birth to
three sons and two daughters. Meanwhile,
the boy Samuel grew[o] up in the presence of
the LORD.

22 Now Eli, who was very old, heard about
everything his sons were doing to all Israel
and how they slept with the women[p] who
served at the entrance to the Tent of Meet-
ing. 23 So he said to them, "Why do you do
such things? I hear from all the people about
these wicked deeds of yours. 24 No, my sons;
it is not a good report that I hear spreading
among the LORD's people. 25 If a man sins
against another man, God[c] may mediate for
him; but if a man sins against the LORD, who
will[q] intercede for him?" His sons, however,
did not listen to their father's rebuke, for it
was the LORD's will to put them to death.

26 And the boy Samuel continued to grow[r]
in stature and in favor with the LORD and
with men.

**2:17** j Mal 2:7–9
**2:18** k ver 11
**2:19** l 1Sa 1:3
**2:20** m 1Sa 1:11,27–28
**2:21** n Ge 21:1 o ver 26
**2:22** p Ex 38:8
**2:25** q Nu 15:30; Jos 11:20
**2:26** r ver 21; Lk 2:52

[a]6 Hebrew *Sheol* [b]17 Or *men* [c]25 Or *the judges*

**2:27** s Ex 4:14–16
**2:28** t Ex 28:1
**2:29** u Dt 12:5
**2:30** v Ex 29:9; w Mal 2:9
**2:31** x 1Sa 4:11–18; 22:16–20
**2:32** y Zec 8:4
**2:34** z 1Sa 4:11; a 1Ki 13:3
**2:35** b 2Sa 7:11,27; 1Ki 11:38
**3:1** c 1Sa 2:11; d Ps 74:9; e Am 8:11

## Prophecy Against the House of Eli

27 Now a man of God[s] came to Eli and said to him, "This is what the LORD says: 'Did I not clearly reveal myself to your father's house when they were in Egypt under Pharaoh? 28 I chose[t] your father out of all the tribes of Israel to be my priest, to go up to my altar, to burn incense, and to wear an ephod in my presence. I also gave your father's house all the offerings made with fire by the Israelites. 29 Why do you[a] scorn my sacrifice and offering that I prescribed for my dwelling?[u] Why do you honor your sons more than me by fattening yourselves on the choice parts of every offering made by my people Israel?'

30 "Therefore the LORD, the God of Israel, declares: 'I promised that your house and your father's house would minister before me forever.[v]' But now the LORD declares: 'Far be it from me! Those who honor me I will honor, but those who despise[w] me will be disdained. 31 The time is coming when I will cut short your strength and the strength of your father's house, so that there will not be an old man in your family line[x] 32 and you will see distress in my dwelling. Although good will be done to Israel, in your family line there will never be an old man.[y] 33 Every one of you that I do not cut off from my altar will be spared only to blind your eyes with tears and to grieve your heart, and all your descendants will die in the prime of life.

34 "'And what happens to your two sons, Hophni and Phinehas, will be a sign to you—they will both die[z] on the same day.[a] 35 I will raise up for myself a faithful priest, who will do according to what is in my heart and mind. I will firmly establish his house, and he will minister before my anointed[b] one always. 36 Then everyone left in your family line will come and bow down before him for a piece of silver and a crust of bread and plead, "Appoint me to some priestly office so I can have food to eat."'"

## The LORD Calls Samuel

3 The boy Samuel ministered[c] before the LORD under Eli. In those days the word of the LORD was rare;[d] there were not many visions.[e]

2 One night Eli, whose eyes were becoming so weak that he could barely see, was lying down in his usual place. 3 The lamp of God had not yet gone out, and Samuel was lying down in the temple[b] of the LORD, where the ark of God was. 4 Then the LORD called Samuel.

Samuel answered, "Here I am." 5 And he ran to Eli and said, "Here I am; you called me."

But Eli said, "I did not call; go back and lie down." So he went and lay down.

6 Again the LORD called, "Samuel!" And Samuel got up and went to Eli and said, "Here I am; you called me."

"My son," Eli said, "I did not call; go back and lie down."

7 Now Samuel did not yet know the LORD: The word of the LORD had not yet been revealed[f] to him.

8 The LORD called Samuel a third time, and Samuel got up and went to Eli and said, "Here I am; you called me."

Then Eli realized that the LORD was calling the boy. 9 So Eli told Samuel, "Go and lie down, and if he calls you, say, 'Speak, LORD, for your servant is listening.'" So Samuel went and lay down in his place.

10 The LORD came and stood there, calling as at the other times, "Samuel! Samuel!"

Then Samuel said, "Speak, for your servant is listening."

11 And the LORD said to Samuel: "See, I am about to do something in Israel that will make the ears of everyone who hears of it tingle.[g] 12 At that time I will carry out against

**3:7** f Ac 19:12
**3:11** g 2Ki 21:12

*Lord,*

*I want to recognize you whenever and wherever you show up in my life. I want to see your face and respond enthusiastically to your voice. In the mighty name of Jesus,*

*Amen*

1 SAMUEL 3:7–10

[a]29 The Hebrew is plural. [b]3 That is, tabernacle

Eli everything[h] I spoke against his family—from beginning to end. 13 For I told him that I would judge his family forever because of the sin he knew about; his sons made themselves contemptible,[a] and he failed to restrain[i] them. 14 Therefore, I swore to the house of Eli, 'The guilt of Eli's house will never be atoned[j] for by sacrifice or offering.' "

15 Samuel lay down until morning and then opened the doors of the house of the LORD. He was afraid to tell Eli the vision, 16 but Eli called him and said, "Samuel, my son."

Samuel answered, "Here I am."

17 "What was it he said to you?" Eli asked. "Do not hide it from me. May God deal with you, be it ever so severely, if you hide from me anything he told you." 18 So Samuel told him everything, hiding nothing from him. Then Eli said, "He is the LORD; let him do what is good in his eyes."[k]

19 The LORD was with[l] Samuel as he grew[m] up, and he let none[n] of his words fall to the ground. 20 And all Israel from Dan to Beersheba[o] recognized that Samuel was attested as a prophet of the LORD. 21 The LORD continued to appear at Shiloh, and there he revealed himself to Samuel through his word.

4 And Samuel's word came to all Israel.

## The Philistines Capture the Ark

Now the Israelites went out to fight against the Philistines. The Israelites camped at Ebenezer,[p] and the Philistines at Aphek. 2 The Philistines deployed their forces to meet Israel, and as the battle spread, Israel was defeated by the Philistines, who killed about four thousand of them on the battlefield. 3 When the soldiers returned to camp, the elders of Israel asked, "Why did the Lord bring defeat upon us today before the Philistines? Let us bring the ark of the Lord's covenant from Shiloh, so that it[b] may go with us and save us from the hand of our enemies."

4 So the people sent men to Shiloh, and they brought back the ark of the covenant of the LORD Almighty, who is enthroned between the cherubim.[q] And Eli's two sons, Hophni and Phinehas, were there with the ark of the covenant of God.

5 When the ark of the LORD's covenant came into the camp, all Israel raised such a great shout that the ground shook. 6 Hearing the uproar, the Philistines asked, "What's all this shouting in the Hebrew camp?"

When they learned that the ark of the Lord had come into the camp, 7 the Philistines were afraid. "A god has come into the camp," they said. "We're in trouble! Nothing like this has happened before. 8 Woe to us! Who will deliver us from the hand of these mighty gods? They are the gods who struck the Egyptians with all kinds of plagues in the desert. 9 Be strong, Philistines! Be men, or you will be subject to the Hebrews, as they[r] have been to you. Be men, and fight!"

10 So the Philistines fought, and the Israelites were defeated[s] and every man fled to his tent. The slaughter was very great; Israel lost thirty thousand foot soldiers. 11 The ark of God was captured, and Eli's two sons, Hophni and Phinehas, died.[t]

## Death of Eli

12 That same day a Benjamite ran from the battle line and went to Shiloh, his clothes torn and dust[u] on his head. 13 When he arrived, there was Eli[v] sitting on his chair by the side of the road, watching, because his heart feared for the ark of God. When the man entered the town and told what had happened, the whole town sent up a cry.

14 Eli heard the outcry and asked, "What is the meaning of this uproar?"

The man hurried over to Eli, 15 who was ninety-eight years old and whose eyes[w] were set so that he could not see. 16 He told Eli, "I have just come from the battle line; I fled from it this very day."

Eli asked, "What happened, my son?"

17 The man who brought the news replied, "Israel fled before the Philistines, and the army has suffered heavy losses. Also your two sons, Hophni and Phinehas, are dead, and the ark of God has been captured."

18 When he mentioned the ark of God, Eli fell backward off his chair by the side of the gate. His neck was broken and he died,

**3:12** h 1Sa2:27–36
**3:13** i 1Sa2:12,17, 22,29–31
**3:14** j 1Sa2:25
**3:18** k Isa39:8
**3:19** l Ge39:2 m 1Sa2:21 n 1Sa9:6
**3:20** o Jdg20:1
**4:1** p 1Sa7:12
**4:4** q 2Sa6:2
**4:9** r Jdg13:1; 1Co16:13
**4:10** s ver 2; Dt28:25
**4:11** t 1Sa2:34; Ps78:61,64
**4:12** u Jos7:6; 2Sa1:2; Ne9:1
**4:13** v 1Sa1:9
**4:15** w 1Sa3:2

[a]13 Masoretic Text; an ancient Hebrew scribal tradition and Septuagint *sons blasphemed God* [b]3 Or *he*

for he was an old man and heavy. He had led[a] Israel forty years.

[19]His daughter-in-law, the wife of Phinehas, was pregnant and near the time of delivery. When she heard the news that the ark of God had been captured and that her father-in-law and her husband were dead, she went into labor and gave birth, but was overcome by her labor pains. [20]As she was dying, the women attending her said, "Don't despair; you have given birth to a son." But she did not respond or pay any attention.

[21]She named the boy Ichabod,[b] saying, "The glory has departed from Israel"—because of the capture of the ark of God and the deaths of her father-in-law and her husband. [22]She said, "The glory has departed from Israel, for the ark of God has been captured."

## The Ark in Ashdod and Ekron

**5** After the Philistines had captured the ark of God, they took it from Ebenezer[x] to Ashdod. [2]Then they carried the ark into Dagon's temple and set it beside Dagon.[y] [3]When the people of Ashdod rose early the next day, there was Dagon, fallen[z] on his face on the ground before the ark of the LORD! They took Dagon and put him back in his place. [4]But the following morning when they rose, there was Dagon, fallen on his face on the ground before the ark of the LORD! His head and hands had been broken[a] off and were lying on the threshold; only his body remained. [5]That is why to this day neither the priests of Dagon nor any others who enter Dagon's temple at Ashdod step on the threshold.

[6]The LORD's hand[b] was heavy upon the people of Ashdod and its vicinity; he brought devastation[c] upon them and afflicted them with tumors.[cd] [7]When the men of Ashdod saw what was happening, they said, "The ark of the god of Israel must not stay here with us, because his hand is heavy upon us and upon Dagon our god." [8]So they called together all the rulers of the Philistines and asked them, "What shall we do with the ark of the god of Israel?"

They answered, "Have the ark of the god of Israel moved to Gath." So they moved the ark of the God of Israel.

[9]But after they had moved it, the LORD's hand was against that city, throwing it into a great panic.[e] He afflicted the people of the city, both young and old, with an outbreak of tumors.[d] [10]So they sent the ark of God to Ekron.

As the ark of God was entering Ekron, the people of Ekron cried out, "They have brought the ark of the god of Israel around to us to kill us and our people." [11]So they called together all the rulers[f] of the Philistines and said, "Send the ark of the god of Israel away; let it go back to its own place, or it[e] will kill us and our people." For death had filled the city with panic; God's hand was very heavy upon it. [12]Those who did not die were afflicted with tumors, and the outcry of the city went up to heaven.

## The Ark Returned to Israel

**6** When the ark of the LORD had been in Philistine territory seven months, [2]the Philistines called for the priests and the diviners[g] and said, "What shall we do with the ark of the LORD? Tell us how we should send it back to its place."

[3]They answered, "If you return the ark of the god of Israel, do not send it away empty,[h] but by all means send a guilt offering[i] to him. Then you will be healed, and you will know why his hand has not been lifted from you."

[4]The Philistines asked, "What guilt offering should we send to him?"

They replied, "Five gold tumors and five gold rats, according to the number[j] of the Philistine rulers, because the same plague has struck both you and your rulers. [5]Make models of the tumors[k] and of the rats that are destroying the country, and pay honor[l] to Israel's god. Perhaps he will lift his hand from you and your gods and your land. [6]Why do you harden your hearts as the Egyptians and Pharaoh did? When he[f] treated them harshly, did they[m] not send the Israelites out so they could go on their way?

[7]"Now then, get a new cart[n] ready, with two cows that have calved and have never

**5:1** x 1Sa 4:1; 7:12
**5:2** y Jdg 16:23
**5:3** z Isa 19:1; 46:7
**5:4** a Eze 6:6; Mic 1:7
**5:6** b Ex 9:3 c Ps 78:66 d 1Sa 6:5
**5:9** e 1Sa 7:13
**5:11** f ver 6,8–9
**6:2** g Ge 41:8; Ex 7:11
**6:3** h Ex 23:15; Dt 16:16 i Lev 5:15
**6:4** j Jos 13:3; Jdg 3:3
**6:5** k 1Sa 5:6–11 l Jos 7:19; Isa 42:12
**6:6** m Ex 12:31,33
**6:7** n 2Sa 6:3

[a]18 Traditionally *judged* [b]21 *Ichabod* means *no glory.* [c]6 Hebrew; Septuagint and Vulgate *tumors. And rats appeared in their land, and death and destruction were throughout the city* [d]9 Or *with tumors in the groin* (see Septuagint) [e]11 Or *he* [f]6 That is, God

**6:7** o Nu 19:2
**6:9** p ver 3; Jos 15:10
**6:14** q 1Ki 19:21
**6:17** r ver 4
**6:19** s 2Sa 6:7

been yoked.[o] Hitch the cows to the cart, but take their calves away and pen them up. [8]Take the ark of the LORD and put it on the cart, and in a chest beside it put the gold objects you are sending back to him as a guilt offering. Send it on its way, [9]but keep watching it. If it goes up to its own territory, toward Beth Shemesh,[p] then the LORD has brought this great disaster on us. But if it does not, then we will know that it was not his hand that struck us and that it happened to us by chance."

[10]So they did this. They took two such cows and hitched them to the cart and penned up their calves. [11]They placed the ark of the LORD on the cart and along with it the chest containing the gold rats and the models of the tumors. [12]Then the cows went straight up toward Beth Shemesh, keeping on the road and lowing all the way; they did not turn to the right or to the left. The rulers of the Philistines followed them as far as the border of Beth Shemesh.

[13]Now the people of Beth Shemesh were harvesting their wheat in the valley, and when they looked up and saw the ark, they rejoiced at the sight. [14]The cart came to the field of Joshua of Beth Shemesh, and there it stopped beside a large rock. The people chopped up the wood of the cart and sacrificed the cows as a burnt offering[q] to the LORD. [15]The Levites took down the ark of the LORD, together with the chest containing the gold objects, and placed them on the large rock. On that day the people of Beth Shemesh offered burnt offerings and made sacrifices to the LORD. [16]The five rulers of the Philistines saw all this and then returned that same day to Ekron.

[17]These are the gold tumors the Philistines sent as a guilt offering to the LORD—one each[r] for Ashdod, Gaza, Ashkelon, Gath and Ekron. [18]And the number of the gold rats was according to the number of Philistine towns belonging to the five rulers—the fortified towns with their country villages. The large rock, on which[a] they set the ark of the LORD, is a witness to this day in the field of Joshua of Beth Shemesh.

[19]But God struck down[s] some of the men of Beth Shemesh, putting seventy[b] of them to death because they had looked into the ark of the LORD. The people mourned because of the heavy blow the LORD had dealt them, [20]and the men of Beth Shemesh asked, "Who can stand[t] in the presence of the LORD, this holy God? To whom will the ark go up from here?"

[21]Then they sent messengers to the people of Kiriath Jearim, saying, "The Philistines have returned the ark of the LORD. Come

**7** down and take it up to your place." [1]So the men of Kiriath Jearim came and took up the ark of the LORD. They took it to Abinadab's[u] house on the hill and consecrated Eleazar his son to guard the ark of the LORD.

## Samuel Subdues the Philistines at Mizpah

[2]It was a long time, twenty years in all, that the ark remained at Kiriath Jearim, and all the people of Israel mourned and sought after the LORD. [3]And Samuel said to the whole house of Israel, "If you are returning to the LORD with all your hearts, then rid[v] yourselves of the foreign gods and the Ashtoreths[w] and commit[x] yourselves to the LORD and serve him only,[y] and he will deliver you out of the hand of the Philistines." [4]So the Israelites put away their Baals and Ashtoreths, and served the LORD only.

[5]Then Samuel said, "Assemble all Israel at Mizpah and I will intercede with the LORD for you." [6]When they had assembled at Mizpah, they drew water and poured it out before the LORD. On that day they fasted and there they confessed, "We have sinned against the LORD." And Samuel was leader[c][z] of Israel at Mizpah.

[7]When the Philistines heard that Israel had assembled at Mizpah, the rulers of the Philistines came up to attack them. And when the Israelites heard of it, they were afraid[a] because of the Philistines. [8]They said to Samuel, "Do not stop crying[b] out to the LORD our God for us, that he may rescue us from the hand of the Philistines." [9]Then Samuel[c] took a suckling lamb and offered it up as a whole burnt offering to the LORD. He cried out to the LORD on Israel's behalf, and the LORD answered him.

**6:20** t 2Sa 6:9; Mal 3:2
**7:1** u 2Sa 6:3
**7:3** v Jos 24:14; w Jdg 2:12–13; x Joel 2:12; y Dt 6:13; Lk 4:8
**7:6** z Jdg 10:10; Ne 9:1
**7:7** a 1Sa 17:11
**7:8** b Isa 37:4
**7:9** c Ps 99:6

[a] 18 A few Hebrew manuscripts (see also Septuagint); most Hebrew manuscripts *villages as far as Greater Abel, where*
[b] 19 A few Hebrew manuscripts; most Hebrew manuscripts and Septuagint *50,070* [c] 6 Traditionally *judge*

[10]While Samuel was sacrificing the burnt offering, the Philistines drew near to engage Israel in battle. But that day the LORD thundered[d] with loud thunder against the Philistines and threw them into such a panic[e] that they were routed before the Israelites. [11]The men of Israel rushed out of Mizpah and pursued the Philistines, slaughtering them along the way to a point below Beth Car.

[12]Then Samuel took a stone[f] and set it up between Mizpah and Shen. He named it Ebenezer,[a] saying, "Thus far has the LORD helped us." [13]So the Philistines were subdued[g] and did not invade Israelite territory again.

Throughout Samuel's lifetime, the hand of the Lord was against the Philistines. [14]The towns from Ekron to Gath that the Philistines had captured from Israel were restored to her, and Israel delivered the neighboring territory from the power of the Philistines. And there was peace between Israel and the Amorites.

[15]Samuel continued as judge over Israel all the days of his life. [16]From year to year he went on a circuit from Bethel to Gilgal to Mizpah, judging Israel in all those places. [17]But he always went back to Ramah, where his home was, and there he also judged Israel. And he built an altar there to the LORD.

## Israel Asks for a King

8 When Samuel grew old, he appointed[h] his sons as judges for Israel. [2]The name of his firstborn was Joel and the name of his second was Abijah, and they served at Beersheba. [3]But his sons did not walk in his ways. They turned aside after dishonest gain and accepted bribes and perverted justice.

[4]So all the elders of Israel gathered together and came to Samuel at Ramah.[i] [5]They said to him, "You are old, and your sons do not walk in your ways; now appoint a king[j] to lead[b] us, such as all the other nations have."

[6]But when they said, "Give us a king to lead us," this displeased Samuel; so he prayed to the LORD. [7]And the LORD told him: "Listen to all that the people are saying to you; it is not you they have rejected, but they have rejected me as their king.[k] [8]As they have done from the day I brought them up out of Egypt until this day, forsaking me and serving other gods, so they are doing to you. [9]Now listen to them; but warn them solemnly and let them know[l] what the king who will reign over them will do."

[10]Samuel told all the words of the LORD to the people who were asking him for a king. [11]He said, "This is what the king who will reign over you will do: He will take[m] your sons and make them serve with his chariots and horses, and they will run in front of his chariots. [12]Some he will assign to be commanders of thousands and commanders of fifties, and others to plow his ground and reap his harvest, and still others to make weapons of war and equipment for his chariots. [13]He will take your daughters to be perfumers and cooks and bakers. [14]He will take the best of your[n] fields and vineyards[o] and olive groves and give them to his attendants. [15]He will take a tenth of your grain and of your vintage and give it to his officials and attendants. [16]Your menservants and maidservants and the best of your cattle[c] and donkeys he will take for his own use. [17]He will take a tenth of your flocks, and you yourselves will become his slaves. [18]When that day comes, you will cry out for relief from the king you have chosen, and the LORD will not answer[p] you in that day."

[19]But the people refused[q] to listen to Samuel. "No!" they said. "We want a king over us. [20]Then we will be like all the other nations,[r] with a king to lead us and to go out before us and fight our battles."

[21]When Samuel heard all that the people said, he repeated it before the LORD. [22]The LORD answered, "Listen[s] to them and give them a king."

Then Samuel said to the men of Israel, "Everyone go back to his town."

## Samuel Anoints Saul

9 There was a Benjamite, a man of standing, whose name was Kish[t] son of Abiel, the son of Zeror, the son of Becorath, the son of Aphiah of Benjamin. [2]He had a son named Saul, an impressive young man without equal among the Israelites—a head taller[u] than any of the others.

**7:10** d 1Sa 2:10; 2Sa 22:14–15 e Jos 10:10
**7:12** f Jos 4:9
**7:13** g Jdg 13:1,5; 1Sa 13:5
**8:1** h Dt 16:18–19
**8:4** i 1Sa 7:17
**8:5** j Dt 17:14–20
**8:7** k Ex 16:8; 1Sa 10:19
**8:9** l ver 11–18
**8:11** m 1Sa 14:52
**8:14** n Eze 46:18 o 1Ki 21:7,15
**8:18** p Mic 3:4
**8:19** q Jer 44:16
**8:20** r ver 5
**8:22** s ver 7
**9:1** t 1Sa 14:51; 1Ch 9:39
**9:2** u 1Sa 10:23

[a]12 *Ebenezer* means *stone of help.* [b]5 Traditionally *judge*; also in verses 6 and 20 [c]16 Septuagint; Hebrew *young men*

**9:4** v 2Ki 4:42
**9:6** w Dt 33:1 x 1Sa 3:19
**9:7** y 1Ki 14:3; 2Ki 8:8
**9:9** z 2Sa 24:11; 1Ch 26:28; Isa 30:10

3 Now the donkeys belonging to Saul's father Kish were lost, and Kish said to his son Saul, "Take one of the servants with you and go and look for the donkeys." 4 So he passed through the hill country of Ephraim and through the area around Shalisha,[v] but they did not find them. They went on into the district of Shaalim, but the donkeys were not there. Then he passed through the territory of Benjamin, but they did not find them.

5 When they reached the district of Zuph, Saul said to the servant who was with him, "Come, let's go back, or my father will stop thinking about the donkeys and start worrying about us."

6 But the servant replied, "Look, in this town there is a man of God;[w] he is highly respected, and everything[x] he says comes true. Let's go there now. Perhaps he will tell us what way to take."

7 Saul said to his servant, "If we go, what can we give the man? The food in our sacks is gone. We have no gift[y] to take to the man of God. What do we have?"

8 The servant answered him again. "Look," he said, "I have a quarter of a shekel[a] of silver. I will give it to the man of God so that he will tell us what way to take." 9 (Formerly in Israel, if a man went to inquire of God, he would say, "Come, let us go to the seer," because the prophet of today used to be called a seer.)[z]

10 "Good," Saul said to his servant. "Come, let's go." So they set out for the town where the man of God was.

11 As they were going up the hill to the town, they met some girls coming out to draw water, and they asked them, "Is the seer here?"

12 "He is," they answered. "He's ahead of you. Hurry now; he has just come to our town today, for the people have a sacrifice at the high place. 13 As soon as you enter the town, you will find him before he goes up to the high place to eat. The people will not begin eating until he comes, because he must bless the sacrifice; afterward, those who are invited will eat. Go up now; you should find him about this time."

14 They went up to the town, and as they were entering it, there was Samuel, coming toward them on his way up to the high place.

15 Now the day before Saul came, the LORD had revealed this to Samuel: 16 "About this time tomorrow I will send you a man from the land of Benjamin. Anoint[a] him leader over my people Israel; he will deliver[b] my people from the hand of the Philistines. I have looked upon my people, for their cry has reached me."

17 When Samuel caught sight of Saul, the LORD said to him, "This[c] is the man I spoke to you about; he will govern my people."

18 Saul approached Samuel in the gateway and asked, "Would you please tell me where the seer's house is?"

19 "I am the seer," Samuel replied. "Go up ahead of me to the high place, for today you are to eat with me, and in the morning I will let you go and will tell you all that is in your heart. 20 As for the donkeys[d] you lost three days ago, do not worry about them; they have been found. And to whom is all the desire[e] of Israel turned, if not to you and all your father's family?"

21 Saul answered, "But am I not a Benjamite, from the smallest tribe[f] of Israel, and is not my clan the least of all the clans of the tribe of Benjamin?[g] Why do you say such a thing to me?"

22 Then Samuel brought Saul and his servant into the hall and seated them at the head of those who were invited—about thirty in number. 23 Samuel said to the cook, "Bring the piece of meat I gave you, the one I told you to lay aside."

24 So the cook took up the leg with what was on it and set it in front of Saul. Samuel said, "Here is what has been kept for you. Eat, because it was set aside for you for this occasion, from the time I said, 'I have invited guests.'" And Saul dined with Samuel that day.

25 After they came down from the high place to the town, Samuel talked with Saul on the roof[h] of his house. 26 They rose about daybreak and Samuel called to Saul on the roof, "Get ready, and I will send you on your way." When Saul got ready, he and Samuel went outside together. 27 As they were going down to the edge of the town, Samuel said

**9:16** a 1Sa 10:1 b Ex 3:7–9
**9:17** c 1Sa 16:12
**9:20** d ver 3 e 1Sa 8:5; 12:13
**9:21** f 1Sa 15:17 g Jdg 20:35,46
**9:25** h Dt 22:8; Ac 10:9

a 8 That is, about 1/10 ounce (about 3 grams)

to Saul, "Tell the servant to go on ahead of us"—and the servant did so—"but you stay here awhile, so that I may give you a message from God."

**10** Then Samuel took a flask[i] of oil and poured it on Saul's head and kissed him, saying, "Has not the LORD anointed you leader over his inheritance?[a] 2 When you leave me today, you will meet two men near Rachel's tomb,[j] at Zelzah on the border of Benjamin. They will say to you, 'The donkeys you set out to look for have been found. And now your father has stopped thinking about them and is worried about you. He is asking, "What shall I do about my son?"'

3 "Then you will go on from there until you reach the great tree of Tabor. Three men going up to God at Bethel[k] will meet you there. One will be carrying three young goats, another three loaves of bread, and another a skin of wine. 4 They will greet you and offer you two loaves of bread, which you will accept from them.

5 "After that you will go to Gibeah of God, where there is a Philistine outpost.[l] As you approach the town, you will meet a procession of prophets coming down from the high place with lyres, tambourines, flutes and harps[m] being played before them, and they will be prophesying. 6 The Spirit[n] of the LORD will come upon you in power, and you will prophesy with them; and you will be changed into a different person. 7 Once these signs are fulfilled, do whatever your hand finds to do, for God is with[o] you.

8 "Go down ahead of me to Gilgal.[p] I will surely come down to you to sacrifice burnt offerings and fellowship offerings,[b] but you must wait seven days until I come to you and tell you what you are to do."

## Saul Made King

9 As Saul turned to leave Samuel, God changed Saul's heart, and all these signs were fulfilled that day. 10 When they arrived at Gibeah, a procession of prophets met him; the Spirit of God came upon him in power, and he joined in their prophesying.[q] 11 When all those who had formerly known him saw him prophesying with the prophets, they asked each other, "What is this[r] that has happened to the son of Kish? Is Saul also among the prophets?"

12 A man who lived there answered, "And who is their father?" So it became a saying: "Is Saul also among the prophets?" 13 After Saul stopped prophesying, he went to the high place.

14 Now Saul's uncle asked him and his servant, "Where have you been?"

"Looking for the donkeys," he said. "But when we saw they were not to be found, we went to Samuel."

15 Saul's uncle said, "Tell me what Samuel said to you."

16 Saul replied, "He assured us that the donkeys had been found." But he did not tell his uncle what Samuel had said about the kingship.

17 Samuel summoned the people of Israel to the LORD at Mizpah[s] 18 and said to them, "This is what the LORD, the God of Israel, says: 'I brought Israel up out of Egypt, and I delivered you from the power of Egypt and all the kingdoms that oppressed[t] you.' 19 But you have now rejected your God, who saves you out of all your calamities and distresses. And you have said, 'No, set a king[u] over us.' So now present yourselves before the LORD by your tribes and clans."

*Faithful one,*

*I am your King. Serve me and me alone.*

*Love,*
*God*

1 SAMUEL 10:17–19

20 When Samuel brought all the tribes of Israel near, the tribe of Benjamin was chosen. 21 Then he brought forward the tribe of Benjamin, clan by clan, and Matri's clan was chosen. Finally Saul son of Kish was chosen. But when they looked for him, he was not to

**10:1** i 2Ki 9:1,3,6
**10:2** j Ge 35:20
**10:3** k Ge 35:7–8
**10:5** l 1Sa 13:3; m 2Ki 3:15
**10:6** n Nu 11:25; 1Sa 19:23–24
**10:7** o Jdg 6:12
**10:8** p 1Sa 11:14–15
**10:10** q ver 5–6; 1Sa 19:20
**10:11** r Mt 13:54; Jn 7:15
**10:17** s 1Sa 7:5
**10:18** t Jdg 6:8–9
**10:19** u 1Sa 8:5–7

[a] 1 Hebrew; Septuagint and Vulgate *over his people Israel? You will reign over the LORD's people and save them from the power of their enemies round about. And this will be a sign to you that the LORD has anointed you leader over his inheritance:*
[b] 8 Traditionally *peace offerings*

be found. 22 So they inquired further of the LORD, "Has the man come here yet?"

And the Lord said, "Yes, he has hidden himself among the baggage."

23 They ran and brought him out, and as he stood among the people he was a head taller[v] than any of the others. 24 Samuel said to all the people, "Do you see the man the LORD has chosen?[w] There is no one like him among all the people."

Then the people shouted, "Long live[x] the king!"

25 Samuel explained to the people the regulations[y] of the kingship. He wrote them down on a scroll and deposited it before the LORD. Then Samuel dismissed the people, each to his own home.

> *"This is the secret of life, being able to feed off the spirit."*
>
> —TRAMAINE HAWKINS, SINGER

26 Saul also went to his home in Gibeah,[z] accompanied by valiant men whose hearts God had touched. 27 But some troublemakers said, "How can this fellow save us?" They despised him and brought him no gifts. But Saul kept silent.

## Saul Rescues the City of Jabesh

11 Nahash[a] the Ammonite went up and besieged Jabesh Gilead.[b] And all the men of Jabesh said to him, "Make a treaty with us, and we will be subject to you."

2 But Nahash the Ammonite replied, "I will make a treaty with you only on the condition that I gouge out the right eye of every one of you and so bring disgrace[c] on all Israel."

3 The elders of Jabesh said to him, "Give us seven days so we can send messengers throughout Israel; if no one comes to rescue us, we will surrender to you."

4 When the messengers came to Gibeah[d] of Saul and reported these terms to the people, they all wept aloud. 5 Just then Saul was returning from the fields, behind his oxen, and he asked, "What is wrong with the people? Why are they weeping?" Then they repeated to him what the men of Jabesh had said.

6 When Saul heard their words, the Spirit[e] of God came upon him in power, and he burned with anger. 7 He took a pair of oxen, cut them into pieces, and sent the pieces by messengers throughout Israel,[f] proclaiming, "This is what will be done to the oxen of anyone[g] who does not follow Saul and Samuel." Then the terror of the LORD fell on the people, and they turned out as one man. 8 When Saul mustered them at Bezek,[h] the men of Israel numbered three hundred thousand and the men of Judah thirty thousand.

9 They told the messengers who had come, "Say to the men of Jabesh Gilead, 'By the time the sun is hot tomorrow, you will be delivered.'" When the messengers went and reported this to the men of Jabesh, they were elated. 10 They said to the Ammonites, "Tomorrow we will surrender[i] to you, and you can do to us whatever seems good to you."

11 The next day Saul separated his men into three divisions;[j] during the last watch of the night they broke into the camp of the Ammonites and slaughtered them until the heat of the day. Those who survived were scattered, so that no two of them were left together.

## Saul Confirmed as King

12 The people then said to Samuel, "Who[k] was it that asked, 'Shall Saul reign over us?' Bring these men to us and we will put them to death."

13 But Saul said, "No one shall be put to death today,[l] for this day the LORD has rescued[m] Israel."

14 Then Samuel said to the people, "Come, let us go to Gilgal[n] and there reaffirm the kingship." 15 So all the people went to Gilgal and confirmed Saul as king in the presence of the LORD. There they sacrificed fellowship offerings[a] before the LORD, and Saul and all the Israelites held a great celebration.

## Samuel's Farewell Speech

12 Samuel said to all Israel, "I have listened to everything you said to me and have set a king over you. 2 Now you have a king as your leader.[o] As for me, I am old and gray, and my sons are here with you. I

**10:23** v 1Sa 9:2
**10:24** w 2Sa 21:6 x 1Ki 1:25,34,39
**10:25** y 1Sa 8:11–18
**10:26** z 1Sa 11:4
**11:1** a 1Sa 12:12 b Jdg 21:8
**11:2** c 1Sa 17:26
**11:4** d 1Sa 10:5,26
**11:6** e Jdg 3:10
**11:7** f Jdg 19:29 g Jdg 21:5
**11:8** h Jdg 1:4
**11:10** i ver 3
**11:11** j Jdg 7:16
**11:12** k Lk 19:27
**11:13** l 2Sa 19:22 m 1Sa 19:5
**11:14** n 1Sa 10:8
**12:2** o 1Sa 8:5

[a] 15 Traditionally *peace offerings*

12:3
p 1Sa 24:6;
2Sa 1:14

have been your leader from my youth until
this day. 3 Here I stand. Testify against me in
the presence of the LORD and his anointed.p
Whose ox have I taken? Whose donkey
have I taken? Whom have I cheated? Whom
have I oppressed? From whose hand have I
accepted a bribe to make me shut my eyes?
If I have done any of these, I will make
it right."
4 "You have not cheated or oppressed us,"
they replied. "You have not taken anything
from anyone's hand."

# Inspire

## GOD'S RIGHTEOUSNESS

**The judge had been paid off! The criminal was given a light sentence. The victim, a young black woman who had pressed charges against her boss for sexual harassment, sat stunned in the courtroom. She could not believe what she had just heard. Whatever happened to righteousness and justice? How could the judge, who was sworn to uphold the law, take such a stand? Oh, how she longed for a righteous judge!**

Have you ever been in a situation in which you felt that justice and righteousness were thrown out the window? The Bible says, "The LORD is righteous, he loves justice; upright men will see his face" (Ps 11:7). These are words of assurance in a world in which justice is for sale to the highest bidder, and righteousness is a scarce commodity. In such a world, God's righteousness is immovable.

As the prophet Samuel pointed out, God has always acted in a righteous manner in his dealings with his people (see 1Sa 12:6–7). God's standards are nonnegotiable. His righteous nature assures us that he will always do what is right (see Ps 145:17), and God always acts in conformity with his law. In a wishy-washy world, we can take courage in the fact that God never acts against his own nature. In fact, Jesus Christ came, was crucified, was buried and rose again to satisfy the demands of God's righteousness. Christ's sacrifice paid the penalty for our sins.

God's righteousness challenges those who call on God to do what is right. The Bible says that because of the shed blood of Jesus Christ, we have the righteousness of God (see Ro 3:21–26). How is God's righteousness reflected in us? How often do we act contrary to our nature as Christians?

—C. BELT

For the next Inspire note, go to page 349.

### read

1 Samuel 12:1–15;
Psalm 11:1–7; 116:5.

See also the Inspire Notes "The Faithfulness of God," "Bumping Into Omnipotence" and "God Is Immutable," and the Women of the Bible Note "Zelophehad's Daughters: Seeking an Inheritance."

### WOMAN of COLOR

How are you reflecting the righteousness of God?

**12:5** q Ac 23:9 r Ex 22:4
**12:7** s Mic 6:1–5
**12:8** t Ex 2:23 u Ex 3:10
**12:9** v Jdg 3:7 w Jdg 4:2 x Jdg 10:7 y Jdg 3:12
**12:11** z Jdg 6:14,32 a Jdg 4:6 b Jdg 11:1
**12:12** c 1Sa 11:1 d 1Sa 8:6,19
**12:13** e 1Sa 8:5; Hos 13:11
**12:14** f Jos 24:14
**12:15** g Jos 24:20
**12:16** h Ex 14:13
**12:17** i Pr 26:1 j 1Sa 8:6–7

5 Samuel said to them, "The LORD is wit-
ness against you, and also his anointed is
witness this day, that you have not found
anything[q] in my hand.[r]"
"He is witness," they said.
6 Then Samuel said to the people, "It is the
LORD who appointed Moses and Aaron and
brought your forefathers up out of Egypt.
7 Now then, stand here, because I am going
to confront[s] you with evidence before the
LORD as to all the righteous acts performed
by the LORD for you and your fathers.
8 "After Jacob entered Egypt, they cried[t] to
the LORD for help, and the LORD sent[u] Moses
and Aaron, who brought your forefathers
out of Egypt and settled them in this place.
9 "But they forgot[v] the LORD their God;
so he sold them into the hand of Sisera,[w]
the commander of the army of Hazor, and
into the hands of the Philistines[x] and the
king of Moab,[y] who fought against them.
10 They cried out to the LORD and said, 'We
have sinned; we have forsaken the LORD
and served the Baals and the Ashtoreths.
But now deliver us from the hands of our
enemies, and we will serve you.' 11 Then the
LORD sent Jerub-Baal,[a][z] Barak,[b][a] Jephthah[b]
and Samuel,[c] and he delivered you from the
hands of your enemies on every side, so that
you lived securely.
12 "But when you saw that Nahash[c] king
of the Ammonites was moving against you,
you said to me, 'No, we want a king to rule[d]
over us'—even though the LORD your God
was your king. 13 Now here is the king[e] you
have chosen, the one you asked for; see, the
LORD has set a king over you. 14 If you fear[f]
the LORD and serve and obey him and do not
rebel against his commands, and if both
you and the king who reigns over you follow
the LORD your God—good! 15 But if you do
not obey the LORD, and if you rebel against[g]
his commands, his hand will be against
you, as it was against your fathers.
16 "Now then, stand still and see[h] this
great thing the LORD is about to do before
your eyes! 17 Is it not wheat harvest now?
I will call upon the LORD to send thunder
and rain.[i] And you will realize what an evil[j]
thing you did in the eyes of the LORD when
you asked for a king."
18 Then Samuel called upon the LORD, and
that same day the LORD sent thunder and
rain. So all the people stood in awe[k] of the
LORD and of Samuel.
19 The people all said to Samuel, "Pray to
the LORD your God for your servants so that
we will not die, for we have added to all our
other sins the evil of asking for a king."
20 "Do not be afraid," Samuel replied.
"You have done all this evil; yet do not turn
away from the LORD, but serve the LORD with
all your heart. 21 Do not turn away after use-
less[l] idols.[m] They can do you no good, nor
can they rescue you, because they are use-
less. 22 For the sake of his great name[n] the
LORD will not reject his people, because the
LORD was pleased to make[o] you his own. 23 As
for me, far be it from me that I should sin
against the LORD by failing to pray[p] for you.
And I will teach[q] you the way that is good
and right. 24 But be sure to fear[r] the LORD and
serve him faithfully with all your heart;
consider what great[s] things he has done for
you. 25 Yet if you persist in doing evil, both
you and your king will be swept[t] away."

## Samuel Rebukes Saul

13 Saul was ⌊thirty⌋[d] years old when he
became king, and he reigned over
Israel ⌊forty-⌋[e] two years.
2 Saul[f] chose three thousand men from
Israel; two thousand were with him at Mic-
mash and in the hill country of Bethel, and
a thousand were with Jonathan at Gibeah in
Benjamin. The rest of the men he sent back
to their homes.
3 Jonathan attacked the Philistine out-
post[u] at Geba, and the Philistines heard
about it. Then Saul had the trumpet blown
throughout the land and said, "Let the He-
brews hear!" 4 So all Israel heard the news:
"Saul has attacked the Philistine outpost,
and now Israel has become a stench to
the Philistines." And the people were sum-
moned to join Saul at Gilgal.
5 The Philistines assembled to fight Israel,
with three thousand[g] chariots, six thousand

**12:18** k Ex 14:31
**12:21** l Hab 2:18 m Dt 11:16
**12:22** n Jos 7:9 o Dt 7:7
**12:23** p Col 1:9; 2Ti 1:3 q 1Ki 8:36
**12:24** r Ecc 12:13 s Dt 10:21
**12:25** t Jos 24:20
**13:3** u 1Sa 10:5

[a] 11 Also called *Gideon* [b] 11 Some Septuagint manuscripts and Syriac; Hebrew *Bedan* [c] 11 Hebrew; some Septuagint manuscripts and Syriac *Samson* [d] 1 A few late manuscripts of the Septuagint; Hebrew does not have *thirty.* [e] 1 See the round number in Acts 13:21; Hebrew does not have *forty-.* [f] 1,2 Or *and when he had reigned over Israel two years,* [2] *he* [g] 5 Some Septuagint manuscripts and Syriac; Hebrew *thirty thousand*

13:6 v Jdg 6:2
13:8 w 1Sa 10:8
13:13 x 2Ch 16:9 y 1Sa 15:23,24
13:14 z 1Sa 15:28 a Ac 13:22
13:15 b 1Sa 14:2
13:17 c Jos 18:23

charioteers, and soldiers as numerous as
the sand on the seashore. They went up
and camped at Micmash, east of Beth Aven.
6 When the men of Israel saw that their situ-
ation was critical and that their army was
hard pressed, they hid in caves and thickets,
among the rocks, and in pits and cisterns.[v]
7 Some Hebrews even crossed the Jordan to
the land of Gad and Gilead.

Saul remained at Gilgal, and all the
troops with him were quaking with fear.
8 He waited seven[w] days, the time set by
Samuel; but Samuel did not come to Gilgal,
and Saul's men began to scatter. 9 So he said,
"Bring me the burnt offering and the fellow-
ship offerings.[a]" And Saul offered up the
burnt offering. 10 Just as he finished making
the offering, Samuel arrived, and Saul went
out to greet him.

11 "What have you done?" asked Samuel.

Saul replied, "When I saw that the men
were scattering, and that you did not come
at the set time, and that the Philistines were
assembling at Micmash, 12 I thought, 'Now
the Philistines will come down against me
at Gilgal, and I have not sought the LORD's
favor.' So I felt compelled to offer the burnt
offering."

13 "You acted foolishly,[x]" Samuel said.
"You have not kept[y] the command the LORD
your God gave you; if you had, he would
have established your kingdom over Israel
for all time. 14 But now your kingdom[z] will
not endure; the LORD has sought out a man
after his own heart[a] and appointed him
leader of his people, because you have not
kept the LORD's command."

15 Then Samuel left Gilgal[b] and went up to
Gibeah[b] in Benjamin, and Saul counted the
men who were with him. They numbered
about six hundred.

## Israel Without Weapons

16 Saul and his son Jonathan and the
men with them were staying in Gibeah[c] in
Benjamin, while the Philistines camped at
Micmash. 17 Raiding parties went out from
the Philistine camp in three detachments.
One turned toward Ophrah[c] in the vicinity
of Shual, 18 another toward Beth Horon,[d] and
the third toward the borderland overlooking
the Valley of Zeboim[e] facing the desert.

19 Not a blacksmith[f] could be found in the
whole land of Israel, because the Philistines
had said, "Otherwise the Hebrews will make
swords or spears!" 20 So all Israel went down
to the Philistines to have their plowshares,
mattocks, axes and sickles[d] sharpened.
21 The price was two thirds of a shekel[e] for
sharpening plowshares and mattocks, and
a third of a shekel[f] for sharpening forks and
axes and for repointing goads.

22 So on the day of the battle not a soldier
with Saul and Jonathan had a sword or
spear[g] in his hand; only Saul and his son
Jonathan had them.

## Jonathan Attacks the Philistines

23 Now a detachment of Philistines had
14 gone out to the pass at Micmash. 1 One
day Jonathan son of Saul said to the
young man bearing his armor, "Come, let's
go over to the Philistine outpost on the other
side." But he did not tell his father.

2 Saul was staying on the outskirts of
Gibeah[h] under a pomegranate tree in Mig-
ron. With him were about six hundred men,
3 among whom was Ahijah, who was wear-
ing an ephod. He was a son of Ichabod's[i]
brother Ahitub[j] son of Phinehas, the son of
Eli,[k] the LORD's priest in Shiloh. No one was
aware that Jonathan had left.

4 On each side of the pass[l] that Jonathan
intended to cross to reach the Philistine
outpost was a cliff; one was called Bozez,
and the other Seneh. 5 One cliff stood to the
north toward Micmash, the other to the
south toward Geba.

6 Jonathan said to his young armor-
bearer, "Come, let's go over to the outpost of
those uncircumcised[m] fellows. Perhaps the
LORD will act in our behalf. Nothing can hin-
der the LORD from saving, whether by many[n]
or by few."

7 "Do all that you have in mind," his
armor-bearer said. "Go ahead; I am with
you heart and soul."

8 Jonathan said, "Come, then; we will

13:18 d Jos 18:13–14 e Ne 11:34
13:19 f 2Ki 24:14
13:22 g Jdg 5:8
14:2 h 1Sa 13:15
14:3 i 1Sa 4:21 j 1Sa 22:11,20 k 1Sa 2:28
14:4 l 1Sa 13:23
14:6 m Jer 9:26 n Jdg 7:4

[a]9 Traditionally *peace offerings* [b]15 Hebrew; Septuagint *Gilgal and went his way; the rest of the people went after Saul to meet the army, and they went out of Gilgal* [c]16 Two Hebrew manuscripts; most Hebrew manuscripts *Geba,* a variant of *Gibeah* [d]20 Septuagint; Hebrew *plowshares* [e]21 Hebrew *pim*; that is, about 1/4 ounce (about 8 grams) [f]21 That is, about 1/8 ounce (about 4 grams)

**14:10** o Ge 24:14
**14:12** p 2Sa 5:24
**14:15** q Ge 35:5; 2Ki 7:5–7 r 1Sa 13:17
**14:19** s Nu 27:21
**14:20** t Jdg 7:22; 2Ch 20:23

cross over toward the men and let them see us. [9]If they say to us, 'Wait there until we come to you,' we will stay where we are and not go up to them. [10]But if they say, 'Come up to us,' we will climb up, because that will be our sign[o] that the LORD has given them into our hands."

[11]So both of them showed themselves to the Philistine outpost. "Look!" said the Philistines. "The Hebrews are crawling out of the holes they were hiding in." [12]The men of the outpost shouted to Jonathan and his armor-bearer, "Come up to us and we'll teach you a lesson."

So Jonathan said to his armor-bearer, "Climb up after me; the Lord has given them into the hand[p] of Israel."

[13]Jonathan climbed up, using his hands and feet, with his armor-bearer right behind him. The Philistines fell before Jonathan, and his armor-bearer followed and killed behind him. [14]In that first attack Jonathan and his armor-bearer killed some twenty men in an area of about half an acre.[a]

## Israel Routs the Philistines

[15]Then panic[q] struck the whole army—those in the camp and field, and those in the outposts and raiding[r] parties—and the ground shook. It was a panic sent by God.[b]

[16]Saul's lookouts at Gibeah in Benjamin saw the army melting away in all directions. [17]Then Saul said to the men who were with him, "Muster the forces and see who has left us." When they did, it was Jonathan and his armor-bearer who were not there.

[18]Saul said to Ahijah, "Bring the ark of God." (At that time it was with the Israelites.)[c] [19]While Saul was talking to the priest, the tumult in the Philistine camp increased more and more. So Saul said to the priest,[s] "Withdraw your hand."

[20]Then Saul and all his men assembled and went to the battle. They found the Philistines in total confusion, striking[t] each other with their swords. [21]Those Hebrews who had previously been with the Philistines and had gone up with them to their camp went over to the Israelites who were with Saul and Jonathan. [22]When all the Israelites who had hidden[u] in the hill country of Ephraim heard that the Philistines were on the run, they joined the battle in hot pursuit. [23]So the LORD rescued[v] Israel that day, and the battle moved on beyond Beth Aven.[w]

## Jonathan Eats Honey

[24]Now the men of Israel were in distress that day, because Saul had bound the people under an oath,[x] saying, "Cursed be any man who eats food before evening comes, before I have avenged myself on my enemies!" So none of the troops tasted food.

[25]The entire army[d] entered the woods, and there was honey on the ground. [26]When they went into the woods, they saw the honey oozing out, yet no one put his hand to his mouth, because they feared the oath. [27]But Jonathan had not heard that his father had bound the people with the oath, so he reached out the end of the staff that was in his hand and dipped it into the honeycomb. He raised his hand to his mouth, and his eyes brightened.[e] [28]Then one of the soldiers told him, "Your father bound the army under a strict oath, saying, 'Cursed be any man who eats food today!' That is why the men are faint."

[29]Jonathan said, "My father has made trouble[y] for the country. See how my eyes brightened[f] when I tasted a little of this honey. [30]How much better it would have been if the men had eaten today some of the plunder they took from their enemies. Would not the slaughter of the Philistines have been even greater?"

[31]That day, after the Israelites had struck down the Philistines from Micmash to Aijalon, they were exhausted. [32]They pounced on the plunder[z] and, taking sheep, cattle and calves, they butchered them on the ground and ate them, together with the blood.[a] [33]Then someone said to Saul, "Look, the men are sinning against the LORD by eating meat that has blood in it."

"You have broken faith," he said. "Roll a large stone over here at once." [34]Then he said, "Go out among the men and tell them, 'Each of you bring me your cattle and sheep, and slaughter them here and eat them. Do

**14:22** u 1Sa 13:6
**14:23** v Ex 14:30; Ps 44:6–7 w 1Sa 13:5
**14:24** x Jos 6:26
**14:29** y 1Ki 18:18
**14:32** z 1Sa 15:19 a Lev 17:10–14

[a]14 Hebrew *half a yoke*; a "yoke" was the land plowed by a yoke of oxen in one day. [b]15 Or *a terrible panic* [c]18 Hebrew; Septuagint *"Bring the ephod." (At that time he wore the ephod before the Israelites.)* [d]25 Or *Now all the people of the land* [e]27 Or *his strength was renewed* [f]29 Or *my strength was renewed*

not sin against the Lord by eating meat with blood still in it.' "

So everyone brought his ox that night and slaughtered it there. 35 Then Saul built an altar[b] to the Lord; it was the first time he had done this.

36 Saul said, "Let us go down after the Philistines by night and plunder them till dawn, and let us not leave one of them alive."

"Do whatever seems best to you," they replied.

But the priest said, "Let us inquire of God here."

37 So Saul asked God, "Shall I go down after the Philistines? Will you give them into Israel's hand?" But God did not answer[c] him that day.

38 Saul therefore said, "Come here, all you who are leaders of the army, and let us find out what sin has been committed[d] today. 39 As surely as the Lord who rescues Israel lives,[e] even if it lies with my son Jonathan, he must die." But not one of the men said a word.

40 Saul then said to all the Israelites, "You stand over there; I and Jonathan my son will stand over here."

"Do what seems best to you," the men replied.

41 Then Saul prayed to the Lord, the God of Israel, "Give[f] me the right answer."[a] And Jonathan and Saul were taken by lot, and the men were cleared. 42 Saul said, "Cast the lot between me and Jonathan my son." And Jonathan was taken.

43 Then Saul said to Jonathan, "Tell me what you have done."[g]

So Jonathan told him, "I merely tasted a little honey with the end of my staff. And now must I die?"

44 Saul said, "May God deal with me, be it ever so severely,[h] if you do not die, Jonathan."

45 But the men said to Saul, "Should Jonathan die—he who has brought about this great deliverance in Israel? Never! As surely as the Lord lives, not a hair[i] of his head will fall to the ground, for he did this today with God's help." So the men rescued[j] Jonathan, and he was not put to death.

46 Then Saul stopped pursuing the Philistines, and they withdrew to their own land.

47 After Saul had assumed rule over Israel, he fought against their enemies on every side: Moab, the Ammonites, Edom, the kings[b] of Zobah, and the Philistines. Wherever he turned, he inflicted punishment on them.[c] 48 He fought valiantly and defeated the Amalekites,[k] delivering Israel from the hands of those who had plundered them.

## Saul's Family

49 Saul's sons were Jonathan, Ishvi and Malki-Shua.[l] The name of his older daughter was Merab, and that of the younger was Michal. 50 His wife's name was Ahinoam daughter of Ahimaaz. The name of the commander of Saul's army was Abner son of Ner, and Ner was Saul's uncle. 51 Saul's father Kish[m] and Abner's father Ner were sons of Abiel.

52 All the days of Saul there was bitter war with the Philistines, and whenever Saul saw a mighty or brave man, he took him into his service.

## The Lord Rejects Saul as King

15 Samuel said to Saul, "I am the one the Lord sent to anoint[n] you king over his people Israel; so listen now to the message from the Lord. 2 This is what the Lord Almighty says: 'I will punish the Amalekites[o] for what they did to Israel when they waylaid them as they came up from Egypt. 3 Now go, attack the Amalekites and totally destroy[d] everything that belongs to them. Do not spare them; put to death men and women, children and infants, cattle and sheep, camels and donkeys.' "

4 So Saul summoned the men and mustered them at Telaim—two hundred thousand foot soldiers and ten thousand men from Judah. 5 Saul went to the city of Amalek and set an ambush in the ravine. 6 Then he said to the Kenites,[p] "Go away, leave the Amalekites so that I do not destroy you along with them; for you showed kindness to all the Israelites when they came up out

**14:35** b 1Sa 7:17
**14:37** c 1Sa 28:6,15
**14:38** d 1Sa 10:19
**14:39** e 2Sa 12:5
**14:41** f Ac 1:24
**14:43** g Jos 7:19
**14:44** h Ru 1:17
**14:45** i 1Ki 1:52; j 2Sa 14:11
**14:48** k 1Sa 15:2,7
**14:49** l 1Sa 31:2; 1Ch 8:33
**14:51** m 1Sa 9:1
**15:1** n 1Sa 9:16
**15:2** o Ex 17:8–14; Nu 24:20; Dt 25:17–19
**15:6** p Ex 18:10,19; Nu 10:29–32; Jdg 1:16; 4:1

[a] 41 Hebrew; Septuagint *"Why have you not answered your servant today? If the fault is in me or my son Jonathan, respond with Urim, but if the men of Israel are at fault, respond with Thummim."* [b] 47 Masoretic Text; Dead Sea Scrolls and Septuagint *king* [c] 47 Hebrew; Septuagint *he was victorious* [d] 3 The Hebrew term refers to the irrevocable giving over of things or persons to the Lord, often by totally destroying them; also in verses 8, 9, 15, 18, 20 and 21.

of Egypt." So the Kenites moved away from the Amalekites.

7 Then Saul attacked the Amalekites[q] all the way from Havilah to Shur,[r] to the east of Egypt. 8 He took Agag king of the Amalekites alive,[s] and all his people he totally destroyed with the sword. 9 But Saul and the army spared[t] Agag and the best of the sheep and cattle, the fat calves[a] and lambs—everything that was good. These they were unwilling to destroy completely, but everything that was despised and weak they totally destroyed.

10 Then the word of the LORD came to Samuel: 11 "I am grieved[u] that I have made Saul king, because he has turned away from me and has not carried out my instructions."[v] Samuel was troubled, and he cried out to the LORD all that night.

12 Early in the morning Samuel got up and went to meet Saul, but he was told, "Saul has gone to Carmel.[w] There he has set up a monument in his own honor and has turned and gone on down to Gilgal."

13 When Samuel reached him, Saul said, "The LORD bless you! I have carried out the LORD's instructions."

14 But Samuel said, "What then is this bleating of sheep in my ears? What is this lowing of cattle that I hear?"

15 Saul answered, "The soldiers brought them from the Amalekites; they spared the best of the sheep and cattle to sacrifice to the LORD your God, but we totally destroyed the rest."

16 "Stop!" Samuel said to Saul. "Let me tell you what the LORD said to me last night."

"Tell me," Saul replied.

17 Samuel said, "Although you were once small in your own eyes, did you not become the head of the tribes of Israel? The LORD anointed you king over Israel. 18 And he sent you on a mission, saying, 'Go and completely destroy those wicked people, the Amalekites; make war on them until you have wiped them out.' 19 Why did you not obey the LORD? Why did you pounce on the plunder and do evil in the eyes of the LORD?"

20 "But I did obey the LORD," Saul said. "I went on the mission the LORD assigned me. I completely destroyed the Amalekites and brought back Agag their king. 21 The soldiers took sheep and cattle from the plunder, the best of what was devoted to God, in order to sacrifice them to the LORD your God at Gilgal."

22 But Samuel replied:

"Does the LORD delight in burnt offerings
and sacrifices
as much as in obeying the voice of the
LORD?
To obey is better than sacrifice,[x]
and to heed is better than the fat of
rams.
23 For rebellion is like the sin of divination,
and arrogance like the evil of idolatry.
Because you have rejected[y] the word of
the LORD,
he has rejected you as king."

24 Then Saul said to Samuel, "I have sinned. I violated the LORD's command and your instructions. I was afraid[z] of the people and so I gave in to them. 25 Now I beg you, forgive my sin and come back with me, so that I may worship the LORD."

26 But Samuel said to him, "I will not go back with you. You have rejected the word of the LORD, and the LORD has rejected you as king over Israel!"

27 As Samuel turned to leave, Saul caught hold of the hem of his robe, and it tore.[a] 28 Samuel said to him, "The LORD has torn[b] the kingdom of Israel from you today and has given it to one of your neighbors—to one better than you. 29 He who is the Glory of Israel does not lie or change[c] his mind; for he is not a man, that he should change his mind."

30 Saul replied, "I have sinned. But please honor[d] me before the elders of my people and before Israel; come back with me, so that I may worship the LORD your God." 31 So Samuel went back with Saul, and Saul worshiped the LORD.

32 Then Samuel said, "Bring me Agag king of the Amalekites."

Agag came to him confidently,[b] thinking, "Surely the bitterness of death is past."

33 But Samuel said,

**15:7** q 1Sa 14:48 r Ge 16:7; 25:17–18
**15:8** s 1Sa 30:1
**15:9** t ver 3,15
**15:11** u Ge 6:6; 2Sa 24:16 v 1Ki 9:6–7
**15:12** w Jos 15:55
**15:22** x Isa 1:11–15; Hos 6:6; Mic 6:6–8; Mk 12:33; Heb 10:6–9
**15:23** y 1Sa 13:13
**15:24** z Isa 51:12–13
**15:27** a 1Ki 11:11,31
**15:28** b 1Sa 28:17
**15:29** c Nu 23:19; Eze 24:14
**15:30** d Jn 12:43

[a]9 Or *the grown bulls*; the meaning of the Hebrew for this phrase is uncertain. [b]32 Or *him trembling, yet*

15:33 e Jdg 1:7
15:34 f 1Sa 11:4
15:35 g 1Sa 19:24; h 1Sa 16:1
16:1 i 1Sa 15:35; j 1Sa 15:23; k 2Ki 9:1; l Ps 78:70; Ac 13:22
16:3 m Ex 4:15; n 1Sa 9:16
16:4 o 1Ki 2:13; 2Ki 9:17
16:5 p Ex 19:10,22
16:6 q 1Sa 17:13
16:7 r 1Ki 8:39
16:8 s 1Sa 17:13

"As your sword has made women
childless,
so will your mother be childless
among women."[e]

And Samuel put Agag to death before the LORD at Gilgal.

34 Then Samuel left for Ramah, but Saul went up to his home in Gibeah[f] of Saul. 35 Until the day Samuel[g] died, he did not go to see Saul again, though Samuel mourned[h] for him. And the LORD was grieved that he had made Saul king over Israel.

## Samuel Anoints David

16 The LORD said to Samuel, "How long will you mourn[i] for Saul, since I have rejected[j] him as king over Israel? Fill your horn with oil[k] and be on your way; I am sending you to Jesse of Bethlehem. I have chosen[l] one of his sons to be king."

2 But Samuel said, "How can I go? Saul will hear about it and kill me."

The Lord said, "Take a heifer with you and say, 'I have come to sacrifice to the Lord.' 3 Invite Jesse to the sacrifice, and I will show[m] you what to do. You are to anoint[n] for me the one I indicate."

4 Samuel did what the LORD said. When he arrived at Bethlehem, the elders of the town trembled when they met him. They asked, "Do you come in peace?[o]"

5 Samuel replied, "Yes, in peace; I have come to sacrifice to the LORD. Consecrate[p] yourselves and come to the sacrifice with me." Then he consecrated Jesse and his sons and invited them to the sacrifice.

6 When they arrived, Samuel saw Eliab[q] and thought, "Surely the LORD's anointed stands here before the LORD."

7 But the LORD said to Samuel, "Do not consider his appearance or his height, for I have rejected him. The LORD does not look at the things man looks at. Man looks at the outward appearance, but the LORD looks at the heart."[r]

8 Then Jesse called Abinadab[s] and had him pass in front of Samuel. But Samuel said, "The LORD has not chosen this one either." 9 Jesse then had Shammah pass by, but Samuel said, "Nor has the LORD chosen this one." 10 Jesse had seven of his sons pass before Samuel, but Samuel said to him, "The LORD has not chosen these." 11 So he asked Jesse, "Are these all the sons you have?"

"There is still the youngest," Jesse answered, "but he is tending the sheep."

Samuel said, "Send for him; we will not sit down[a] until he arrives."

12 So he[t] sent and had him brought in. He was ruddy, with a fine appearance and handsome features.

Then the Lord said, "Rise and anoint him; he is the one."

13 So Samuel took the horn of oil and anointed him in the presence of his brothers, and from that day on the Spirit of the LORD came upon David in power.[u] Samuel then went to Ramah.

## David in Saul's Service

14 Now the Spirit of the LORD had departed[v] from Saul, and an evil[b] spirit[w] from the LORD tormented him.

15 Saul's attendants said to him, "See, an evil spirit from God is tormenting you. 16 Let our lord command his servants here to search for someone who can play the harp.[x] He will play when the evil spirit from God comes upon you, and you will feel better."

17 So Saul said to his attendants, "Find someone who plays well and bring him to me."

18 One of the servants answered, "I have seen a son of Jesse of Bethlehem who knows how to play the harp. He is a brave man and a warrior. He speaks well and is a fine-looking man. And the LORD is with[y] him."

19 Then Saul sent messengers to Jesse and said, "Send me your son David, who is with the sheep." 20 So Jesse took a donkey loaded with bread,[z] a skin of wine and a young goat and sent them with his son David to Saul.

21 David came to Saul and entered his service.[a] Saul liked him very much, and David became one of his armor-bearers. 22 Then Saul sent word to Jesse, saying, "Allow David to remain in my service, for I am pleased with him."

23 Whenever the spirit from God came upon Saul, David would take his harp and play. Then relief would come to Saul; he

16:12 t 1Sa 9:17
16:13 u 1Sa 10:1,6,9–10; 11:6
16:14 v Jdg 16:20; w Jdg 9:23
16:16 x 2Ki 3:15
16:18 y 1Sa 3:19; 17:32–37
16:20 z 1Sa 10:27
16:21 a Ge 41:46

[a] 11 Some Septuagint manuscripts; Hebrew *not gather around*
[b] 14 Or *injurious*; also in verses 15, 16 and 23

would feel better, and the evil spirit[b] would leave him.

## David and Goliath

**17** Now the Philistines gathered their forces for war and assembled at Socoh in Judah. They pitched camp at Ephes Dammim, between Socoh and Azekah. 2Saul and the Israelites assembled and camped in the Valley of Elah and drew up their battle line to meet the Philistines. 3The Philistines occupied one hill and the Israelites another, with the valley between them.

4A champion named Goliath,[c] who was from Gath, came out of the Philistine camp. He was over nine feet[a] tall. 5He had a bronze helmet on his head and wore a coat of scale armor of bronze weighing five thousand shekels[b]; 6on his legs he wore bronze greaves, and a bronze javelin was slung on his back. 7His spear shaft was like a weaver's rod, and its iron point weighed six hundred shekels.[c] His shield bearer went ahead of him.

8Goliath stood and shouted to the ranks of Israel, "Why do you come out and line up for battle? Am I not a Philistine, and are you not the servants of Saul? Choose[d] a man and have him come down to me. 9If he is able to fight and kill me, we will become your subjects; but if I overcome him and kill him, you will become our subjects and serve us." 10Then the Philistine said, "This day I defy[e] the ranks of Israel! Give me a man and let us fight each other." 11On hearing the Philistine's words, Saul and all the Israelites were dismayed and terrified.

12Now David was the son of an Ephrathite named Jesse,[f] who was from Bethlehem[g] in Judah. Jesse had eight[h] sons, and in Saul's time he was old and well advanced in years. 13Jesse's three oldest sons had followed Saul to the war: The firstborn was Eliab;[i] the second, Abinadab; and the third, Shammah.[j] 14David was the youngest. The three oldest followed Saul, 15but David went back and forth from Saul to tend his father's sheep[k] at Bethlehem.

16For forty days the Philistine came forward every morning and evening and took his stand.

17Now Jesse said to his son David, "Take this ephah[d] of roasted grain and these ten loaves of bread for your brothers and hurry to their camp. 18Take along these ten cheeses to the commander of their unit.[e] See how your brothers[l] are and bring back some assurance[f] from them. 19They are with Saul and all the men of Israel in the Valley of Elah, fighting against the Philistines."

20Early in the morning David left the flock with a shepherd, loaded up and set out, as Jesse had directed. He reached the camp as the army was going out to its battle positions, shouting the war cry. 21Israel and the Philistines were drawing up their lines facing each other. 22David left his things with the keeper of supplies, ran to the battle lines and greeted his brothers. 23As he was talking with them, Goliath, the Philistine champion from Gath, stepped out from his lines and shouted his usual[m] defiance, and David heard it. 24When the Israelites saw the man, they all ran from him in great fear.

25Now the Israelites had been saying, "Do you see how this man keeps coming out? He comes out to defy Israel. The king will give great wealth to the man who kills him. He will also give him his daughter[n] in marriage and will exempt his father's family from taxes in Israel."

26David asked the men standing near him, "What will be done for the man who kills this Philistine and removes this disgrace[o] from Israel? Who is this uncircumcised[p] Philistine that he should defy[q] the armies of the living God?"

27They repeated to him what they had been saying and told him, "This is what will be done for the man who kills him."

28When Eliab, David's oldest brother, heard him speaking with the men, he burned with anger[r] at him and asked, "Why have you come down here? And with whom did you leave those few sheep in the desert? I know how conceited you are and how wicked your heart is; you came down only to watch the battle."

29"Now what have I done?" said David. "Can't I even speak?" 30He then turned away to someone else and brought up the same

**16:23** b ver 14–16
**17:4** c Jos 11:21–22; 2Sa 21:19
**17:8** d 1Sa 8:17
**17:10** e ver 26,45
**17:12** f 1Ch 2:13–15 g Ge 35:19 h 1Sa 16:11
**17:13** i 1Sa 16:6 j 1Sa 16:9
**17:15** k 1Sa 16:19
**17:18** l Ge 37:14
**17:23** m ver 8–10
**17:25** n Jos 15:16
**17:26** o 1Sa 11:2 p 1Sa 14:6 q ver 10
**17:28** r Ge 37:4,8,11

[a]4 Hebrew *was six cubits and a span* (about 3 meters) [b]5 That is, about 125 pounds (about 57 kilograms) [c]7 That is, about 15 pounds (about 7 kilograms) [d]17 That is, probably about 3/5 bushel (about 22 liters) [e]18 Hebrew *thousand* [f]18 Or *some token*; or *some pledge of spoils*

**17:32** s Dt 20:3; 1Sa 16:18
**17:37** t 2Ti 4:17 u 1Sa 20:13; 1Ch 22:11,16

matter, and the men answered him as before. 31 What David said was overheard and reported to Saul, and Saul sent for him.

32 David said to Saul, "Let no one lose heart[s] on account of this Philistine; your servant will go and fight him."

33 Saul replied, "You are not able to go out against this Philistine and fight him; you are only a boy, and he has been a fighting man from his youth."

34 But David said to Saul, "Your servant has been keeping his father's sheep. When a lion or a bear came and carried off a sheep from the flock, 35 I went after it, struck it and rescued the sheep from its mouth. When it turned on me, I seized it by its hair, struck it and killed it. 36 Your servant has killed both the lion and the bear; this uncircumcised Philistine will be like one of them, because he has defied the armies of the living God. 37 The LORD who delivered me from the paw of the lion[t] and the paw of the bear will deliver me from the hand of this Philistine."

Saul said to David, "Go, and the Lord be with[u] you."

38 Then Saul dressed David in his own tunic. He put a coat of armor on him and a bronze helmet on his head. 39 David fastened on his sword over the tunic and tried walking around, because he was not used to them.

"I cannot go in these," he said to Saul, "because I am not used to them." So he took them off. 40 Then he took his staff in his hand, chose five smooth stones from the stream, put them in the pouch of his shepherd's bag and, with his sling in his hand, approached the Philistine.

41 Meanwhile, the Philistine, with his shield bearer in front of him, kept coming closer to David. 42 He looked David over and saw that he was only a boy, ruddy and handsome,[v] and he despised him. 43 He said to David, "Am I a dog,[w] that you come at me with sticks?" And the Philistine cursed David by his gods. 44 "Come here," he said, "and I'll give your flesh to the birds of the air and the beasts of the field![x]"

45 David said to the Philistine, "You come against me with sword and spear and javelin, but I come against you in the name[y] of the LORD Almighty, the God of the armies of Israel, whom you have defied. 46 This day the LORD will hand you over to me, and I'll strike you down and cut off your head. Today I will give the carcasses of the Philistine army to the birds of the air and the beasts of the earth, and the whole world will know that there is a God in Israel.[z] 47 All those gathered here will know that it is not by sword[a] or spear that the LORD saves;[b] for the battle is the LORD's, and he will give all of you into our hands."

48 As the Philistine moved closer to attack him, David ran quickly toward the battle line to meet him. 49 Reaching into his

**17:42** v 1Sa 16:12
**17:43** w 1Sa 24:14; 2Sa 3:8
**17:44** x 1Ki 20:10–11
**17:45** y 2Ch 32:8; Heb 11:32–34
**17:46** z 1Ki 18:36; 2Ki 19:19
**17:47** a Hos 1:7 b 2Ch 14:11

## *The African Presence*

### 1 Samuel 17

The Philistines and Israelites were fierce enemies. Many of the battles described in 1 Samuel were between these two foes. The story of David and Goliath is a story of a Philistine champion, Goliath, and an Israelite shepherd, David. The ancestry of the Philistines can be traced to Ham's son Mizraim (see Ge 10:6,13; see also the African Presence note on Ge 10:6). The Philistines occupied the coastland of Canaan. Because Ham's offspring (the Philistines) represent the geographic territories once dominated by Egypt—present-day Egypt, Libya and Sudan and into the area today known as Israel—they can claim a relation to African heritage. Since "heritage" is something "passed down" or "inherited," Canaan (Israel or Palestine) most certainly received or was influenced by Egypt culturally, politically, religiously, etc.

bag and taking out a stone, he slung it and struck the Philistine on the forehead. The stone sank into his forehead, and he fell facedown on the ground.

50So David triumphed over the Philistine with a sling and a stone; without a sword in his hand he struck down the Philistine and killed him.

51David ran and stood over him. He took hold of the Philistine's sword and drew it from the scabbard. After he killed him, he cut off his head with the sword.

When the Philistines saw that their hero was dead, they turned and ran. 52Then the men of Israel and Judah surged forward with a shout and pursued the Philistines to the entrance of Gath[a] and to the gates of Ekron. Their dead were strewn along the Shaaraim[c] road to Gath and Ekron. 53When the Israelites returned from chasing the Philistines, they plundered their camp. 54David took the Philistine's head and brought it to Jerusalem, and he put the Philistine's weapons in his own tent.

55As Saul watched David[d] going out to meet the Philistine, he said to Abner, commander of the army, "Abner, whose son is that young man?"

Abner replied, "As surely as you live, O king, I don't know."

56The king said, "Find out whose son this young man is."

57As soon as David returned from killing the Philistine, Abner took him and brought him before Saul, with David still holding the Philistine's head.

58"Whose son are you, young man?" Saul asked him.

David said, "I am the son of your servant Jesse of Bethlehem."

## Saul's Jealousy of David

18 After David had finished talking with Saul, Jonathan became one in spirit with David, and he loved[e] him as himself.[f] 2From that day Saul kept David with him and did not let him return to his father's house. 3And Jonathan made a covenant with David because he loved him as himself. 4Jonathan took off the robe he was wearing and gave it to David, along with his tunic, and even his sword, his bow and his belt.

5Whatever Saul sent him to do, David did it so successfully[b] that Saul gave him a high rank in the army. This pleased all the people, and Saul's officers as well.

6When the men were returning home after David had killed the Philistine, the women came out from all the towns of Israel to meet King Saul with singing and dancing,[g] with joyful songs and with tambourines[h] and lutes. 7As they danced, they sang:

"Saul has slain his thousands,
and David his tens[i] of thousands."

8Saul was very angry; this refrain galled him. "They have credited David with tens of thousands," he thought, "but me with only thousands. What more can he get but the kingdom?" 9And from that time on Saul kept a jealous eye on David.

10The next day an evil[c] spirit[j] from God came forcefully upon Saul. He was prophesying in his house, while David was playing the harp, as he usually[k] did. Saul had a spear in his hand 11and he hurled it, saying to himself,[l] "I'll pin David to the wall." But David eluded[m] him twice.

12Saul was afraid of David, because the LORD was with David but had left Saul. 13So he sent David away from him and gave him command over a thousand men, and David led the troops in their campaigns.[n] 14In everything he did he had great success,[d][o] because the LORD was with him. 15When Saul saw how successful[e] he was, he was afraid of him. 16But all Israel and Judah loved David, because he led them in their campaigns.[p]

17Saul said to David, "Here is my older daughter[q] Merab. I will give her to you in marriage; only serve me bravely and fight the battles[r] of the LORD." For Saul said to himself,[s] "I will not raise a hand against him. Let the Philistines do that!"

18But David said to Saul, "Who am I,[t] and what is my family or my father's clan in Israel, that I should become the king's son-in-law?" 19So[f] when the time came for Merab,[u] Saul's daughter, to be given to

**17:52** c Jos 15:36
**17:55** d 1Sa 16:21
**18:1** e 2Sa 1:26 f Ge 44:30
**18:6** g Ex 15:20 h Jdg 11:34
**18:7** i 1Sa 21:11
**18:10** j 1Sa 16:14 k 1Sa 19:7
**18:11** l 1Sa 20:7,33 m 1Sa 19:10
**18:13** n 2Sa 5:2
**18:14** o Ge 39:3
**18:16** p ver 5
**18:17** q 1Sa 17:25 r 1Sa 25:28 s ver 25
**18:18** t 1Sa 9:21; 2Sa 7:18
**18:19** u 2Sa 21:8

[a]52 Some Septuagint manuscripts; Hebrew *a valley* [b]5 Or *wisely* [c]10 Or *injurious* [d]14 Or *he was very wise*
[e]15 Or *wise* [f]19 Or *However,*

**18:19** v Jdg 7:22
**18:20** w ver 28
**18:25** x Ex 22:17; 1Sa 14:24
**18:27** y 2Sa 3:14

David, she was given in marriage to Adriel
of Meholah.[v]
20 Now Saul's daughter Michal[w] was in
love with David, and when they told Saul
about it, he was pleased. 21 "I will give her
to him," he thought, "so that she may be a
snare to him and so that the hand of the Phi-
listines may be against him." So Saul said to
David, "Now you have a second opportunity
to become my son-in-law."
22 Then Saul ordered his attendants:
"Speak to David privately and say, 'Look,
the king is pleased with you, and his atten-
dants all like you; now become his son-in-
law.' "
23 They repeated these words to David.
But David said, "Do you think it is a small
matter to become the king's son-in-law? I'm
only a poor man and little known."
24 When Saul's servants told him what
David had said, 25 Saul replied, "Say to Da-
vid, 'The king wants no other price[x] for the
bride than a hundred Philistine foreskins,
to take revenge on his enemies.' " Saul's
plan was to have David fall by the hands of
the Philistines.
26 When the attendants told David these
things, he was pleased to become the king's
son-in-law. So before the allotted time
elapsed, 27 David and his men went out and
killed two hundred Philistines. He brought
their foreskins and presented the full num-
ber to the king so that he might become the
king's son-in-law. Then Saul gave him his
daughter Michal[y] in marriage.
28 When Saul realized that the LORD was
with David and that his daughter Michal
loved David, 29 Saul became still more afraid
of him, and he remained his enemy the rest
of his days.
30 The Philistine commanders continued
to go out to battle, and as often as they did,
David met with more success[a] than the rest
of Saul's officers, and his name became well
known.

## Saul Tries to Kill David

**19** Saul told his son Jonathan and all
the attendants to kill David. But Jon-
athan was very fond of David 2 and warned
him, "My father Saul is looking for a chance
to kill you. Be on your guard tomorrow
morning; go into hiding and stay there. 3 I
will go out and stand with my father in the
field where you are. I'll speak to him about
you and will tell you what I find out."
4 Jonathan spoke well of David to Saul his
father and said to him, "Let not the king
do wrong[z] to his servant David; he has not
wronged you, and what he has done has
benefited you greatly. 5 He took his life in
his hands when he killed the Philistine. The
LORD won a great victory[a] for all Israel, and
you saw it and were glad. Why then would
you do wrong to an innocent[b] man like Da-
vid by killing him for no reason?"
6 Saul listened to Jonathan and took this
oath: "As surely as the LORD lives, David will
not be put to death."
7 So Jonathan called David and told him
the whole conversation. He brought him to
Saul, and David was with Saul as before.
8 Once more war broke out, and David
went out and fought the Philistines. He
struck them with such force that they fled
before him.
9 But an evil[b] spirit[c] from the LORD came
upon Saul as he was sitting in his house with
his spear in his hand. While David was play-
ing the harp, 10 Saul tried to pin him to the
wall with his spear, but David eluded him
as Saul drove the spear into the wall. That
night David made good his escape.
11 Saul sent men to David's house to watch
it and to kill him in the morning. But Mi-
chal, David's wife, warned him, "If you don't
run for your life tonight, tomorrow you'll be
killed." 12 So Michal let David down through
a window,[d] and he fled and escaped. 13 Then
Michal took an idol[c] and laid it on the bed,
covering it with a garment and putting some
goats' hair at the head.
14 When Saul sent the men to capture Da-
vid, Michal said, "He is ill."
15 Then Saul sent the men back to see Da-
vid and told them, "Bring him up to me in
his bed so that I may kill him." 16 But when
the men entered, there was the idol in the
bed, and at the head was some goats' hair.
17 Saul said to Michal, "Why did you de-
ceive me like this and send my enemy away
so that he escaped?"

**19:4** z Ge 42:22
**19:5** a 1Sa 11:13; 17:49–50 b 1Sa 20:32
**19:9** c 1Sa 16:14; 18:10–11
**19:12** d Jos 2:15; Ac 9:25

[a]30 Or *David acted more wisely* [b]9 Or *injurious* [c]13 Hebrew *teraphim*; also in verse 16

# Michal

## A Disappointed Bride

The story of Michal has a lot to teach women of color. Michal was the daughter of King Saul, but she was in love with a young former shepherd named David. But there was a problem: Her father feared David and was intensely jealous of him. Saul used his daughter as bait, promising her to David in marriage if he would kill a hundred Philistines as a bride price. Saul hoped that young David would himself be killed; but once again David triumphed, and Michal became his wife.

Michal seemed to truly love her husband, even risking her own life to save David's (see 1Sa 19:11–17). However, she soon discovered that her love was not enough to save a marriage besieged by politics and pressure. She was taken from David and given to another man (see 1Sa 25:44). Michal had to learn to lean on God rather than on the things of life.

All of us think that people, things or situations will make us happy. As young girls, we start off early by chasing after designer clothes, popularity and the right relationship. The list can go on and on. Our desires—for material goods, degrees, power and prestige, money, and wonderful, perfect relationships—can become our idols. We dream about obtaining them, and some of us will do anything to get the things we want, the things we think will make us happy and fulfilled.

Michal needed to know that the true God wanted a relationship—in a sense, a "marriage"—with her. If she had known this, she would have been able to rejoice with her husband when he celebrated before the Lord (see 2Sa 6:16–22). As women we need to know that God wants an intimate relationship with us. We shouldn't put any of our desires before God.

Women and girls of African ancestry, what is our destiny? Will we ever be truly happy simply by being married or when we get the many other things we desire? Michal can help us answer that question with a resounding "no." We must have our own relationship with God and understand what destiny God would have us fulfill. Then we will be fulfilled women.

—B. Garvin

### reflection

*Does God fulfill you more than any other person or thing?*

### read

1 Samuel 18:17–29; 19:11–17; 25:44; 2 Samuel 3:12–16; 6:12–23.

See also the Inspire Notes "True Joy," "Marriage" and "What Is Intimacy?"

For the next Women of the Bible note, go to page 351.

**19:20** e Nu 11:25 f 1Sa 10:5

**19:24** g Isa 20:2

**20:1** h 1Sa 24:9

**20:5** i Nu 10:10; 28:11 j 1Sa 19:2

Michal told him, "He said to me, 'Let me get away. Why should I kill you?' "

[18]When David had fled and made his escape, he went to Samuel at Ramah and told him all that Saul had done to him. Then he and Samuel went to Naioth and stayed there. [19]Word came to Saul: "David is in Naioth at Ramah"; [20]so he sent men to capture him. But when they saw a group of prophets prophesying, with Samuel standing there as their leader, the Spirit of God came upon[e] Saul's men and they also prophesied.[f] [21]Saul was told about it, and he sent more men, and they prophesied too. Saul sent men a third time, and they also prophesied. [22]Finally, he himself left for Ramah and went to the great cistern at Secu. And he asked, "Where are Samuel and David?"

"Over in Naioth at Ramah," they said.

[23]So Saul went to Naioth at Ramah. But the Spirit of God came even upon him, and he walked along prophesying until he came to Naioth. [24]He stripped[g] off his robes and also prophesied in Samuel's presence. He lay that way all that day and night. This is why people say, "Is Saul also among the prophets?"

## David and Jonathan

**20** Then David fled from Naioth at Ramah and went to Jonathan and asked, "What have I done? What is my crime? How have I wronged[h] your father, that he is trying to take my life?"

[2]"Never!" Jonathan replied. "You are not going to die! Look, my father doesn't do anything, great or small, without confiding in me. Why would he hide this from me? It's not so!"

[3]But David took an oath and said, "Your father knows very well that I have found favor in your eyes, and he has said to himself, 'Jonathan must not know this or he will be grieved.' Yet as surely as the LORD lives and as you live, there is only a step between me and death."

[4]Jonathan said to David, "Whatever you want me to do, I'll do for you."

[5]So David said, "Look, tomorrow is the New Moon festival,[i] and I am supposed to dine with the king; but let me go and hide[j] in the field until the evening of the day after tomorrow. [6]If your father misses me at all, tell him, 'David earnestly asked my permission to hurry to Bethlehem,[k] his hometown, because an annual sacrifice is being made there for his whole clan.' [7]If he says, 'Very well,' then your servant is safe. But if he loses his temper,[l] you can be sure that he is determined to harm me. [8]As for you, show kindness to your servant, for you have brought him into a covenant[m] with you before the LORD. If I am guilty, then kill[n] me yourself! Why hand me over to your father?"

[9]"Never!" Jonathan said. "If I had the least inkling that my father was determined to harm you, wouldn't I tell you?"

[10]David asked, "Who will tell me if your father answers you harshly?"

[11]"Come," Jonathan said, "let's go out into the field." So they went there together.

[12]Then Jonathan said to David: "By the LORD, the God of Israel, I will surely sound out my father by this time the day after tomorrow! If he is favorably disposed toward you, will I not send you word and let you know? [13]But if my father is inclined to harm you, may the LORD deal with me, be it ever so severely,[o] if I do not let you know and send you away safely. May the LORD be with[p] you as he has been with my father. [14]But show me unfailing kindness like that of the LORD as long as I live, so that I may not be killed, [15]and do not ever cut off your kindness from my family[q]—not even when the LORD has cut off every one of David's enemies from the face of the earth."

[16]So Jonathan made a covenant with the house of David, saying, "May the LORD call David's enemies to account." [17]And Jonathan had David reaffirm his oath[r] out of love for him, because he loved him as he loved himself.

[18]Then Jonathan said to David: "Tomorrow is the New Moon festival. You will be missed, because your seat will be empty.[s] [19]The day after tomorrow, toward evening, go to the place where you hid[t] when this trouble began, and wait by the stone Ezel. [20]I will shoot three arrows to the side of it, as though I were shooting at a target. [21]Then I will send a boy and say, 'Go, find the arrows.' If I say to him, 'Look, the arrows are on this side of you; bring them here,' then come, because, as surely as the LORD lives, you are safe; there is no danger. [22]But if I

**20:6** k 1Sa 17:58

**20:7** l 1Sa 25:17

**20:8** m 1Sa 18:3; 23:18 n 2Sa 14:32

**20:13** o Ru 1:17; 1Sa 3:17 p 1Sa 17:37

**20:15** q 2Sa 9:7

**20:17** r 1Sa 18:3

**20:18** s ver 5,25

**20:19** t 1Sa 19:2

**20:23** u ver 14–15; Ge 31:50
**20:26** v Lev 7:20–21; 15:5
**20:28** w ver 6
**20:32** x 1Sa 19:4; Mt 27:23
**20:33** y ver 7; 1Sa 18:11,17

say to the boy, 'Look, the arrows are beyond you,' then you must go, because the LORD has sent you away. 23And about the matter you and I discussed—remember, the LORD is witness[u] between you and me forever."

24So David hid in the field, and when the New Moon festival came, the king sat down to eat. 25He sat in his customary place by the wall, opposite Jonathan,[a] and Abner sat next to Saul, but David's place was empty. 26Saul said nothing that day, for he thought, "Something must have happened to David to make him ceremonially unclean—surely he is unclean.[v]" 27But the next day, the second day of the month, David's place was empty again. Then Saul said to his son Jonathan, "Why hasn't the son of Jesse come to the meal, either yesterday or today?"

28Jonathan answered, "David earnestly asked me for permission[w] to go to Bethlehem. 29He said, 'Let me go, because our family is observing a sacrifice in the town and my brother has ordered me to be there. If I have found favor in your eyes, let me get away to see my brothers.' That is why he has not come to the king's table."

30Saul's anger flared up at Jonathan and he said to him, "You son of a perverse and rebellious woman! Don't I know that you have sided with the son of Jesse to your own shame and to the shame of the mother who bore you? 31As long as the son of Jesse lives on this earth, neither you nor your kingdom will be established. Now send and bring him to me, for he must die!"

32"Why[x] should he be put to death? What has he done?" Jonathan asked his father. 33But Saul hurled his spear at him to kill him. Then Jonathan knew that his father intended[y] to kill David.

34Jonathan got up from the table in fierce anger; on that second day of the month he did not eat, because he was grieved at his father's shameful treatment of David.

35In the morning Jonathan went out to the field for his meeting with David. He had a small boy with him, 36and he said to the boy, "Run and find the arrows I shoot." As the boy ran, he shot an arrow beyond him. 37When the boy came to the place where Jonathan's arrow had fallen, Jonathan called out after him, "Isn't the arrow beyond you?" 38Then he shouted, "Hurry! Go quickly! Don't stop!" The boy picked up the arrow and returned to his master. 39(The boy knew nothing of all this; only Jonathan and David knew.) 40Then Jonathan gave his weapons to the boy and said, "Go, carry them back to town."

41After the boy had gone, David got up from the south side ⌞of the stone⌟ and bowed down before Jonathan three times, with his face to the ground. Then they kissed each other and wept together—but David wept the most.

42Jonathan said to David, "Go in peace,[z] for we have sworn friendship with each other in the name of the LORD, saying, 'The LORD is witness between you and me, and between your descendants and my descendants forever.'" Then David left, and Jonathan went back to the town.

*Lord,*

*grant me the heart of a friend. I want you to use me to help, and even save, others.*

*Amen*

1 SAMUEL 20:42

## David at Nob

21 David went to Nob, to Ahimelech the priest. Ahimelech trembled[a] when he met him, and asked, "Why are you alone? Why is no one with you?"

2David answered Ahimelech the priest, "The king charged me with a certain matter and said to me, 'No one is to know anything about your mission and your instructions.' As for my men, I have told them to meet me at a certain place. 3Now then, what do you have on hand? Give me five loaves of bread, or whatever you can find."

4But the priest answered David, "I don't have any ordinary bread[b] on hand; however, there is some consecrated[c] bread here—provided the men have kept themselves from women."

**20:42** z 1Sa 1:17
**21:1** a 1Sa 16:4
**21:4** b Lev 24:8–9 c Mt 12:4

[a]25 Septuagint; Hebrew *wall. Jonathan arose*

**21:6** d Lev 24:8–9; Mt 12:3–4
**21:7** e 1Sa 22:9,22
**21:9** f 1Sa 17:51 g 1Sa 17:2
**21:11** h 1Sa 18:7; 29:5
**21:13** i Ps 34 Title
**22:1** j 2Sa 23:13

5David replied, "Indeed women have been kept from us, as usual whenever[a] I set out. The men's things[b] are holy even on missions that are not holy. How much more so today!" 6So the priest gave him the consecrated bread,[d] since there was no bread there except the bread of the Presence that had been removed from before the LORD and replaced by hot bread on the day it was taken away.

7Now one of Saul's servants was there that day, detained before the LORD; he was Doeg[e] the Edomite, Saul's head shepherd.

8David asked Ahimelech, "Don't you have a spear or a sword here? I haven't brought my sword or any other weapon, because the king's business was urgent."

9The priest replied, "The sword[f] of Goliath the Philistine, whom you killed in the Valley of Elah,[g] is here; it is wrapped in a cloth behind the ephod. If you want it, take it; there is no sword here but that one."

David said, "There is none like it; give it to me."

## David at Gath

10That day David fled from Saul and went to Achish king of Gath. 11But the servants of Achish said to him, "Isn't this David, the king of the land? Isn't he the one they sing about in their dances:

> " 'Saul has slain his thousands,
> and David his tens of thousands'?"[h]

12David took these words to heart and was very much afraid of Achish king of Gath. 13So he pretended to be insane[i] in their presence; and while he was in their hands he acted like a madman, making marks on the doors of the gate and letting saliva run down his beard.

14Achish said to his servants, "Look at the man! He is insane! Why bring him to me? 15Am I so short of madmen that you have to bring this fellow here to carry on like this in front of me? Must this man come into my house?"

## David at Adullam and Mizpah

**22** David left Gath and escaped to the cave[j] of Adullam. When his brothers and his father's household heard about it, they went down to him there. 2All those who were in distress or in debt or discontented gathered[k] around him, and he became their leader. About four hundred men were with him.

3From there David went to Mizpah in Moab and said to the king of Moab, "Would you let my father and mother come and stay with you until I learn what God will do for me?" 4So he left them with the king of Moab, and they stayed with him as long as David was in the stronghold.

5But the prophet Gad[l] said to David, "Do not stay in the stronghold. Go into the land of Judah." So David left and went to the forest of Hereth.

## Saul Kills the Priests of Nob

6Now Saul heard that David and his men had been discovered. And Saul, spear in hand, was seated under the tamarisk tree on the hill at Gibeah, with all his officials standing around him. 7Saul said to them, "Listen, men of Benjamin! Will the son of Jesse give all of you fields and vineyards? Will he make all of you commanders[m] of thousands and commanders of hundreds? 8Is that why you have all conspired against me? No one tells me when my son makes a covenant[n] with the son of Jesse. None of you is concerned about me or tells me that my son has incited my servant to lie in wait for me, as he does today."

9But Doeg the Edomite, who was standing with Saul's officials, said, "I saw the son of Jesse come to Ahimelech son of Ahitub at Nob.[o] 10Ahimelech inquired of the LORD for him; he also gave him provisions[p] and the sword of Goliath the Philistine."

11Then the king sent for the priest Ahimelech son of Ahitub and his father's whole family, who were the priests at Nob, and they all came to the king. 12Saul said, "Listen now, son of Ahitub."

"Yes, my lord," he answered.

13Saul said to him, "Why have you conspired against me, you and the son of Jesse, giving him bread and a sword and inquiring of God for him, so that he has rebelled against me and lies in wait for me, as he does today?"

**22:2** k 1Sa 25:13
**22:5** l 2Sa 24:11; 1Ch 21:9; 2Ch 29:25
**22:7** m 1Sa 8:14
**22:8** n 1Sa 18:3
**22:9** o 1Sa 21:1
**22:10** p 1Sa 21:6

[a]5 Or *from us in the past few days since* [b]5 Or *bodies*

14 Ahimelech answered the king, "Who of all your servants is as loyal as David, the king's son-in-law, captain of your bodyguard and highly respected in your household? 15 Was that day the first time I inquired of God for him? Of course not! Let not the king accuse your servant or any of his father's family, for your servant knows nothing at all about this whole affair."

16 But the king said, "You will surely die, Ahimelech, you and your father's whole family."

17 Then the king ordered the guards at his side: "Turn and kill the priests of the LORD, because they too have sided with David. They knew he was fleeing, yet they did not tell me."

But the king's officials were not willing[q] to raise a hand to strike the priests of the Lord.

18 The king then ordered Doeg, "You turn and strike down the priests." So Doeg the Edomite turned and struck them down. That day he killed eighty-five men who wore the linen ephod.[r] 19 He also put to the sword Nob, the town of the priests, with its men and women, its children and infants, and its cattle, donkeys and sheep.

20 But Abiathar,[s] a son of Ahimelech son of Ahitub, escaped and fled to join David.[t] 21 He told David that Saul had killed the priests of the LORD. 22 Then David said to Abiathar: "That day, when Doeg[u] the Edomite was there, I knew he would be sure to tell Saul. I am responsible for the death of your father's whole family. 23 Stay with me; don't be afraid; the man who is seeking your life[v] is seeking mine also. You will be safe with me."

## David Saves Keilah

23 When David was told, "Look, the Philistines are fighting against Keilah[w] and are looting the threshing floors," 2 he inquired[x] of the LORD, saying, "Shall I go and attack these Philistines?"

The Lord answered him, "Go, attack the Philistines and save Keilah."

3 But David's men said to him, "Here in Judah we are afraid. How much more, then, if we go to Keilah against the Philistine forces!"

4 Once again David inquired of the LORD, and the LORD answered him, "Go down to Keilah, for I am going to give the Philistines into your hand." 5 So David and his men went to Keilah, fought the Philistines and carried off their livestock. He inflicted heavy losses on the Philistines and saved the people of Keilah. 6 (Now Abiathar[y] son of Ahimelech had brought the ephod down with him when he fled to David at Keilah.)

## Saul Pursues David

7 Saul was told that David had gone to Keilah, and he said, "God has handed him over to me, for David has imprisoned himself by entering a town with gates and bars." 8 And Saul called up all his forces for battle, to go down to Keilah to besiege David and his men.

9 When David learned that Saul was plotting against him, he said to Abiathar[z] the priest, "Bring the ephod." 10 David said, "O LORD, God of Israel, your servant has heard definitely that Saul plans to come to Keilah and destroy the town on account of me. 11 Will the citizens of Keilah surrender me to him? Will Saul come down, as your servant has heard? O LORD, God of Israel, tell your servant."

And the Lord said, "He will."

12 Again David asked, "Will the citizens of Keilah surrender me and my men to Saul?"

And the Lord said, "They will."

13 So David and his men,[a] about six hundred in number, left Keilah and kept moving from place to place. When Saul was told that David had escaped from Keilah, he did not go there.

14 David stayed in the desert strongholds and in the hills of the Desert of Ziph. Day after day Saul searched[b] for him, but God did not give David into his hands.

15 While David was at Horesh in the Desert of Ziph, he learned that Saul had come out to take his life. 16 And Saul's son Jonathan went to David at Horesh and helped him find strength in God. 17 "Don't be afraid," he said. "My father Saul will not lay a hand on you. You will be king[c] over Israel, and I will be second to you. Even my father Saul knows this." 18 The two of them made a covenant[d] before the LORD. Then Jonathan went home, but David remained at Horesh.

19 The Ziphites[e] went up to Saul at Gibeah

**22:17** q Ex 1:17
**22:18** r 1Sa 2:18,31
**22:20** s 1Sa 23:6,9 t 1Sa 2:32
**22:22** u 1Sa 21:7
**22:23** v 1Ki 2:26
**23:1** w Jos 15:44
**23:2** x ver 4,12
**23:6** y 1Sa 22:20
**23:9** z 1Sa 30:7
**23:13** a 1Sa 22:2; 25:13
**23:14** b Ps 54:3–4
**23:17** c 1Sa 24:20
**23:18** d 1Sa 18:3; 20:16,42; 2Sa 21:7
**23:19** e 1Sa 26:1

and said, "Is not David hiding among us in the strongholds at Horesh, on the hill of Hakilah, south of Jeshimon? 20 Now, O king, come down whenever it pleases you to do so, and we will be responsible for handing him over to the king."

21 Saul replied, "The LORD bless you for your concern[f] for me. 22 Go and make further preparation. Find out where David usually goes and who has seen him there. They tell me he is very crafty. 23 Find out about all the hiding places he uses and come back to me with definite information.[a] Then I will go with you; if he is in the area, I will track him down among all the clans of Judah."

24 So they set out and went to Ziph ahead of Saul. Now David and his men were in the Desert of Maon,[g] in the Arabah south of Jeshimon. 25 Saul and his men began the search, and when David was told about it, he went down to the rock and stayed in the Desert of Maon. When Saul heard this, he went into the Desert of Maon in pursuit of David.

26 Saul[h] was going along one side of the mountain, and David and his men were on the other side, hurrying to get away from Saul. As Saul and his forces were closing in on David and his men to capture them, 27 a messenger came to Saul, saying, "Come quickly! The Philistines are raiding the land." 28 Then Saul broke off his pursuit of David and went to meet the Philistines. That is why they call this place Sela Hammahlekoth.[b] 29 And David went up from there and lived in the strongholds of En Gedi.[i]

*My child,*

*Don't worry. I've got your back!*

*The Omnipotent One*

1 SAMUEL 23:26–29

## David Spares Saul's Life

**24** After Saul returned from pursuing the Philistines, he was told, "David is in the Desert of En Gedi.[j]" 2 So Saul took three thousand chosen men from all Israel and set out to look for David and his men near the Crags of the Wild Goats.

3 He came to the sheep pens along the way; a cave was there, and Saul went in to relieve[k] himself. David and his men were far back in the cave. 4 The men said, "This is the day the LORD spoke of when he said[c] to you, 'I will give your enemy into your hands for you to deal with as you wish.'" Then David crept up unnoticed and cut off a corner of Saul's robe.

5 Afterward, David was conscience-stricken[l] for having cut off a corner of his robe. 6 He said to his men, "The LORD forbid that I should do such a thing to my master, the LORD's anointed,[m] or lift my hand against him; for he is the anointed of the LORD." 7 With these words David rebuked his men and did not allow them to attack Saul. And Saul left the cave and went his way.

8 Then David went out of the cave and called out to Saul, "My lord the king!" When Saul looked behind him, David bowed down and prostrated himself with his face to the ground. 9 He said to Saul, "Why do you listen when men say, 'David is bent on harming you'? 10 This day you have seen with your own eyes how the LORD delivered you into my hands in the cave. Some urged me to kill you, but I spared you; I said, 'I will not lift my hand against my master, because he is the LORD's anointed.' 11 See, my father, look at this piece of your robe in my hand! I cut off the corner of your robe but did not kill you. Now understand and recognize that I am not guilty of wrongdoing or rebellion. I have not wronged you, but you are hunting[n] me down to take my life. 12 May the LORD judge between you and me. And may the LORD avenge[o] the wrongs you have done to me, but my hand will not touch you. 13 As the old saying goes, 'From evildoers come evil deeds,' so my hand will not touch you.

14 "Against whom has the king of Israel come out? Whom are you pursuing? A dead dog?[p] A flea? 15 May the LORD be our judge[q] and decide between us. May he consider my cause and uphold[r] it; may he vindicate me by delivering me from your hand."

16 When David finished saying this, Saul

**23:21** f 1Sa 22:8
**23:24** g Jos 15:55; 1Sa 25:2
**23:26** h Ps 17:9
**23:29** i 2Ch 20:2
**24:1** j 1Sa 23:28–29
**24:3** k Jdg 3:24
**24:5** l 2Sa 24:10
**24:6** m 1Sa 26:11
**24:11** n 1Sa 26:20
**24:12** o Jdg 11:27
**24:14** p 1Sa 17:43
**24:15** q ver 12; r Ps 35:1,23

[a] 23 Or *me at Nacon* [b] 28 *Sela Hammahlekoth* means *rock of parting.* [c] 4 Or *"Today the LORD is saying*

asked, "Is that your voice,[s] David my son?" And he wept aloud. 17 "You are more righteous than I,"[t] he said. "You have treated me well,[u] but I have treated you badly. 18 You have just now told me of the good you did to me; the LORD delivered[v] me into your hands, but you did not kill me. 19 When a man finds his enemy, does he let him get away unharmed? May the LORD reward you well for the way you treated me today. 20 I know that you will surely be king and that the kingdom of Israel will be established in your hands. 21 Now swear[w] to me by the LORD that you will not cut off my descendants or wipe out my name from my father's family."

22 So David gave his oath to Saul. Then Saul returned home, but David and his men went up to the stronghold.[x]

## David, Nabal and Abigail

25 Now Samuel died,[y] and all Israel assembled and mourned[z] for him; and they buried him at his home in Ramah.

Then David moved down into the Desert of Maon.[a] 2 A certain man in Maon,[a] who had property there at Carmel, was very wealthy. He had a thousand goats and three thousand sheep, which he was shearing in Carmel. 3 His name was Nabal and his wife's name was Abigail. She was an intelligent and beautiful woman, but her husband, a Calebite, was surly and mean in his dealings.

4 While David was in the desert, he heard that Nabal was shearing sheep. 5 So he sent ten young men and said to them, "Go up to Nabal at Carmel and greet him in my name. 6 Say to him: 'Long life to you! Good health to you and your household! And good health to all that is yours![b]

7 " 'Now I hear that it is sheep-shearing time. When your shepherds were with us, we did not mistreat[c] them, and the whole time they were at Carmel nothing of theirs was missing. 8 Ask your own servants and they will tell you. Therefore be favorable toward my young men, since we come at a festive time. Please give your servants and your son David whatever[d] you can find for them.' "

9 When David's men arrived, they gave Nabal this message in David's name. Then they waited.

10 Nabal answered David's servants, "Who[e] is this David? Who is this son of Jesse? Many servants are breaking away from their masters these days. 11 Why should I take my bread and water, and the meat I have slaughtered for my shearers, and give it to men coming from who knows where?"

12 David's men turned around and went back. When they arrived, they reported every word. 13 David said to his men, "Put on your swords!" So they put on their swords, and David put on his. About four hundred men went up with David, while two hundred stayed with the supplies.[f]

14 One of the servants told Nabal's wife Abigail: "David sent messengers from the desert to give our master his greetings, but he hurled insults at them. 15 Yet these men were very good to us. They did not mistreat[g] us, and the whole time we were out in the fields near them nothing was missing. 16 Night and day they were a wall[h] around us all the time we were herding our sheep near them. 17 Now think it over and see what you can do, because disaster is hanging over our master and his whole household. He is such a wicked man that no one can talk to him."

18 Abigail lost no time. She took two hundred loaves of bread, two skins of wine, five dressed sheep, five seahs[b] of roasted grain, a hundred cakes of raisins and two hundred cakes of pressed figs, and loaded them on donkeys. 19 Then she told her servants, "Go on ahead;[i] I'll follow you." But she did not tell her husband Nabal.

20 As she came riding her donkey into a mountain ravine, there were David and his men descending toward her, and she met them. 21 David had just said, "It's been useless—all my watching over this fellow's property in the desert so that nothing of his was missing. He has paid[j] me back evil for good. 22 May God deal with David,[c] be it ever so severely,[k] if by morning I leave alive one male[l] of all who belong to him!"

23 When Abigail saw David, she quickly got off her donkey and bowed down before

24:16 s 1Sa 26:17
24:17 t Ge 38:26; u Mt 5:44
24:18 v 1Sa 26:23
24:21 w Ge 21:23; 2Sa 21:1–9
24:22 x 1Sa 23:29
25:1 y 1Sa 28:3; z Dt 34:8
25:2 a Jos 15:55
25:6 b 1Ch 12:18
25:7 c ver 15
25:8 d Ne 8:10
25:10 e Jdg 9:28
25:13 f 1Sa 30:24
25:15 g ver 7
25:16 h Ex 14:22
25:19 i Ge 32:20
25:21 j Ps 109:5
25:22 k 1Sa 3:17; 20:13; l 1Ki 14:10

[a]1 Some Septuagint manuscripts; Hebrew *Paran* [b]18 That is, probably about a bushel (about 37 liters) [c]22 Some Septuagint manuscripts; Hebrew *with David's enemies*

David with her face to the ground. 24She
fell at his feet and said: "My lord, let the
blame be on me alone. Please let your ser-
vant speak to you; hear what your servant
has to say. 25May my lord pay no attention
to that wicked man Nabal. He is just like
his name—his name is Fool, and folly goes
with him. But as for me, your servant, I did
not see the men my master sent.
26"Now since the LORD has kept you, my
master, from bloodshed and from avenging
yourself with your own hands, as surely as
the LORD lives and as you live, may your ene-
mies and all who intend to harm my master

Inspire

## DISCERNMENT

Women have been said to have an innate way of "knowing things." It's often referred to as "mother wit" or "women's intuition." Biblically speaking, this innate way of knowing is called *discernment.* The word *discern* refers to one's ability to distinguish between, recognize and comprehend that which is obscured from vision and reasoning. The Bible speaks of two types of discernment: (1) discerning spirits (see 1Co 12:10; 1Jn 4:1–6) and (2) discerning God's will and that which is morally correct (see 1Co 2:12–14; Php 1:9–11; Heb 5:11–14).

The gift of discernment is best epitomized in the life of Jesus Christ. He was able to discern the thoughts and hearts of those whom he encountered (see Mt 12:24–25; Mk 2:5–11; Jn 1:43–48). The gift of discernment allows one to see beyond words and actions to uncover hidden motivations and intent. Because discernment is a gift from God, it is always subject to the written revelation of God—the Word of God.

Abigail was a women who had the gift of discernment. She exercised wisdom by intervening on behalf of her husband and family with David, the future king of Israel, and averted what could have been destruction for her family (see especially 1Sa 25:32–34). Her special discernment, obedience and wise actions were later rewarded when she became David's wife (see 1Sa 25:39).

You may not have the gift of discernment to the extent that Abigail did, but you can learn from her story to make good decisions, to act in the best interest of others and to look to God for wisdom.

—J. Thompson

### read

1 Samuel 25.

**See also** the Inspire Notes "Seek Wisdom" and "Goodness," and the Women of the Bible Notes "Acsah: A Wise Daughter," "Abigail: A Wise Wife" and "Wisdom Personified: The Cry of Wisdom."

### WOMAN of COLOR

How do you use your intuition or discernment to help others?

For the next Inspire note, go to page 373.

**25:26** m 2Sa 18:32
**25:27** n Ge 33:11; 1Sa 30:26
**25:28** o 2Sa 7:11,26 p 1Sa 18:17 q 1Sa 24:11
**25:29** r Jer 10:18
**25:32** s Ex 18:10
**25:33** t ver 26
**25:35** u Ge 19:21; 1Sa 20:42; 2Ki 5:19

be like Nabal.[m] 27 And let this gift,[n] which your servant has brought to my master, be given to the men who follow you. 28 Please forgive your servant's offense, for the LORD will certainly make a lasting[o] dynasty for my master, because he fights the LORD's battles.[p] Let no wrongdoing[q] be found in you as long as you live. 29 Even though someone is pursuing you to take your life, the life of my master will be bound securely in the bundle of the living by the LORD your God. But the lives of your enemies he will hurl[r] away as from the pocket of a sling. 30 When the LORD has done for my master every good thing he promised concerning him and has appointed him leader over Israel, 31 my master will not have on his conscience the staggering burden of needless bloodshed or of having avenged himself. And when the LORD has brought my master success, remember your servant."

32 David said to Abigail, "Praise[s] be to the LORD, the God of Israel, who has sent you today to meet me. 33 May you be blessed for your good judgment and for keeping me from bloodshed[t] this day and from avenging myself with my own hands. 34 Otherwise, as surely as the LORD, the God of Israel, lives, who has kept me from harming you, if you had not come quickly to meet me, not one male belonging to Nabal would have been left alive by daybreak."

35 Then David accepted from her hand what she had brought him and said, "Go home in peace. I have heard your words and granted[u] your request."

36 When Abigail went to Nabal, he was in the house holding a banquet like that of a king. He was in high spirits and very drunk. So she told him nothing until daybreak. 37 Then in the morning, when Nabal was sober, his wife told him all these things, and his heart failed him and he became like a stone. 38 About ten days later, the LORD struck Nabal and he died.

39 When David heard that Nabal was dead, he said, "Praise be to the LORD, who has upheld my cause against Nabal for treating me with contempt. He has kept his servant from doing wrong and has brought Nabal's wrongdoing down on his own head."

Then David sent word to Abigail, asking her to become his wife. 40 His servants went to Carmel and said to Abigail, "David has sent us to you to take you to become his wife."

41 She bowed down with her face to the ground and said, "Here is your maidservant, ready to serve you and wash the feet of my master's servants." 42 Abigail quickly got on a donkey and, attended by her five maids, went with David's messengers and became his wife. 43 David had also married Ahinoam[v] of Jezreel, and they both were his wives.[w] 44 But Saul had given his daughter Michal, David's wife, to Paltiel[a][x] son of Laish, who was from Gallim.[y]

## David Again Spares Saul's Life

26 The Ziphites[z] went to Saul at Gibeah and said, "Is not David hiding on the hill of Hakilah, which faces Jeshimon?"

2 So Saul went down to the Desert of Ziph, with his three thousand chosen men of Israel, to search there for David. 3 Saul made his camp beside the road on the hill of Hakilah facing Jeshimon, but David stayed in the desert. When he saw that Saul had followed him there, 4 he sent out scouts and learned that Saul had definitely arrived.[b]

5 Then David set out and went to the place where Saul had camped. He saw where Saul and Abner[a] son of Ner, the commander of the army, had lain down. Saul was lying inside the camp, with the army encamped around him.

6 David then asked Ahimelech the Hittite and Abishai son of Zeruiah,[b] Joab's brother, "Who will go down into the camp with me to Saul?"

"I'll go with you," said Abishai.

7 So David and Abishai went to the army by night, and there was Saul, lying asleep inside the camp with his spear stuck in the ground near his head. Abner and the soldiers were lying around him.

8 Abishai said to David, "Today God has delivered your enemy into your hands. Now let me pin him to the ground with one thrust of my spear; I won't strike him twice."

9 But David said to Abishai, "Don't destroy him! Who can lay a hand on the LORD's

**25:43** v Jos 15:56 w 1Sa 27:3
**25:44** x 2Sa 3:15 y Isa 10:30
**26:1** z 1Sa 23:19
**26:5** a 1Sa 17:55
**26:6** b 1Ch 2:16

[a]44 Hebrew *Palti,* a variant of *Paltiel* [b]4 Or *had come to Nacon*

# Abigail

## A Wise Wife

The story of Abigail shows women today how to deal with challenges. As Abigail's story proves, following wisdom and goodness eventually yields great results.

When David journeyed through the desert after Samuel's death, he sent greetings to Nabal, the rich husband of Abigail. David asked Nabal for a customary gift for services rendered while David's men were on Nabal's property. Nabal refused in a very insulting manner. His behavior was not very surprising however. Nabal's name means "fool" and he lived up to that name. David took offense and rounded up 400 men to attack Nabal and his household. In the meantime, a servant who had overheard Nabal's remarks warned Abigail of David's intentions. Abigail, being the intuitive, wise, beautiful woman of color that she was, took bread, wine, sheep and other gifts and loaded them on donkeys to forestall David's assault on her household.

When Abigail approached David, she quickly dismounted and fell on her face in submission, accepting the blame for her husband's foolish remarks. Her actions and words showed great respect for this man of God. She depended not only on her reasoning, but also on God's grace. She began to remind David of who he was. She also reminded him that vengeance belongs to the Lord, who is the captain of the battlefield.

David repented and thanked Abigail for being an instrument of God by reminding him not to take matters into his own hands.

Upon returning home, Abigail found her husband drunk after a feast. She was not able to tell him anything about what had transpired earlier that day. When he awoke the next morning, she shared with him the previous day's events. When she confronted him, his heart became as stone. Ten days later "the LORD struck Nabal and he died" (1Sa 25:38).

When David heard that Nabal was dead, he rejoiced in the judgment of God. Because of his regard for Abigail, he sent for her to be his wife. Abigail earned David's respect. She models for women today wisdom and determination to make the best of a bad situation.

—P. GEORGE

### reflection

*What situations in your life require wisdom and determination to bring about success?*

*Seek God for guidance.*

### read

1 Samuel 25:1–44; 2 Samuel 3:3.

**See also** the Inspire Notes "Discernment," "Responsible Decisions in Leadership" and "Seek Wisdom," and the Women of the Bible Notes "The Queen of Sheba: In Search of True Wisdom" and "Wisdom Personified: The Cry of Wisdom."

For the next Women of the Bible note, go to page 371.

anointed[c] and be guiltless? 10 As surely as the LORD lives," he said, "the LORD himself will strike[d] him; either his time[e] will come and he will die,[f] or he will go into battle and perish. 11 But the LORD forbid that I should lay a hand on the LORD's anointed. Now get the spear and water jug that are near his head, and let's go."

12 So David took the spear and water jug near Saul's head, and they left. No one saw or knew about it, nor did anyone wake up. They were all sleeping, because the LORD had put them into a deep sleep.[g]

13 Then David crossed over to the other side and stood on top of the hill some distance away; there was a wide space between them. 14 He called out to the army and to Abner son of Ner, "Aren't you going to answer me, Abner?"

Abner replied, "Who are you who calls to the king?"

15 David said, "You're a man, aren't you? And who is like you in Israel? Why didn't you guard your lord the king? Someone came to destroy your lord the king. 16 What you have done is not good. As surely as the LORD lives, you and your men deserve to die, because you did not guard your master, the LORD's anointed. Look around you. Where are the king's spear and water jug that were near his head?"

17 Saul recognized David's voice and said, "Is that your voice,[h] David my son?"

David replied, "Yes it is, my lord the king." 18 And he added, "Why is my lord pursuing his servant? What have I done, and what wrong[i] am I guilty of? 19 Now let my lord the king listen to his servant's words. If the Lord has incited you against me, then may he accept an offering.[j] If, however, men have done it, may they be cursed before the Lord! They have now driven me from my share in the Lord's inheritance and have said, 'Go, serve other gods.' 20 Now do not let my blood fall to the ground far from the presence of the Lord. The king of Israel has come out to look for a flea[k]—as one hunts a partridge in the mountains."

21 Then Saul said, "I have sinned.[l] Come back, David my son. Because you considered my life precious[m] today, I will not try to harm you again. Surely I have acted like a fool and have erred greatly."

22 "Here is the king's spear," David answered. "Let one of your young men come over and get it. 23 The LORD rewards every man for his righteousness and faithfulness. The LORD delivered you into my hands today, but I would not lay a hand on the LORD's anointed. 24 As surely as I valued your life today, so may the LORD value my life and deliver me from all trouble."

25 Then Saul said to David, "May you be blessed, my son David; you will do great things and surely triumph."

So David went on his way, and Saul returned home.

## David Among the Philistines

27 But David thought to himself, "One of these days I will be destroyed by the hand of Saul. The best thing I can do is to escape to the land of the Philistines. Then Saul will give up searching for me anywhere in Israel, and I will slip out of his hand."

2 So David and the six hundred men[n] with him left and went[o] over to Achish son of Maoch king of Gath. 3 David and his men settled in Gath with Achish. Each man had his family with him, and David had his two wives:[p] Ahinoam of Jezreel and Abigail of Carmel, the widow of Nabal. 4 When Saul was told that David had fled to Gath, he no longer searched for him.

5 Then David said to Achish, "If I have found favor in your eyes, let a place be assigned to me in one of the country towns, that I may live there. Why should your servant live in the royal city with you?"

6 So on that day Achish gave him Ziklag,[q] and it has belonged to the kings of Judah ever since. 7 David lived in Philistine territory a year and four months.

8 Now David and his men went up and raided the Geshurites, the Girzites and the Amalekites.[r] (From ancient times these peoples had lived in the land extending to Shur and Egypt.) 9 Whenever David attacked an area, he did not leave a man or woman alive, but took sheep and cattle, donkeys and camels, and clothes. Then he returned to Achish.

10 When Achish asked, "Where did you go raiding today?" David would say, "Against the Negev of Judah" or "Against the Negev of Jerahmeel[s]" or "Against the Negev of the

**26:9** c 2Sa 1:14
**26:10** d 1Sa 25:38 e Dt 31:14 f 1Sa 31:6
**26:12** g Ge 2:21; 15:12
**26:17** h 1Sa 24:16
**26:18** i 1Sa 24:9,11–14
**26:19** j 2Sa 16:11
**26:20** k 1Sa 24:14
**26:21** l 1Sa 15:24 m 1Sa 24:17
**27:2** n 1Sa 25:13 o 1Sa 21:10
**27:3** p 1Sa 25:43
**27:6** q Jos 15:31; 19:5
**27:8** r 1Sa 15:7–8
**27:10** s 1Ch 2:9,25

**27:10** t Jdg 1:16
**28:1** u 1Sa 29:1
**28:3** v 1Sa 25:1 w Lev 19:31; Dt 18:10–11
**28:4** x 2Ki 4:8 y 1Sa 31:1,3
**28:6** z 1Ch 10:13–14; Pr 1:28 a Ex 28:30
**28:8** b Dt 18:10–11; Isa 8:19
**28:9** c ver 3

Kenites.[t]" 11 He did not leave a man or woman alive to be brought to Gath, for he thought, "They might inform on us and say, 'This is what David did.'" And such was his practice as long as he lived in Philistine territory. 12 Achish trusted David and said to himself, "He has become so odious to his people, the Israelites, that he will be my servant forever."

## Saul and the Witch of Endor

**28** In those days the Philistines gathered[u] their forces to fight against Israel. Achish said to David, "You must understand that you and your men will accompany me in the army."

2 David said, "Then you will see for yourself what your servant can do."

Achish replied, "Very well, I will make you my bodyguard for life."

3 Now Samuel was dead,[v] and all Israel had mourned for him and buried him in his own town of Ramah. Saul had expelled the mediums and spiritists[w] from the land.

4 The Philistines assembled and came and set up camp at Shunem,[x] while Saul gathered all the Israelites and set up camp at Gilboa.[y] 5 When Saul saw the Philistine army, he was afraid; terror filled his heart. 6 He inquired[z] of the LORD, but the LORD did not answer him by dreams or Urim[a] or prophets. 7 Saul then said to his attendants, "Find me a woman who is a medium, so I may go and inquire of her."

"There is one in Endor," they said.

8 So Saul disguised himself, putting on other clothes, and at night he and two men went to the woman. "Consult[b] a spirit for me," he said, "and bring up for me the one I name."

9 But the woman said to him, "Surely you know what Saul has done. He has cut off[c] the mediums and spiritists from the land. Why have you set a trap for my life to bring about my death?"

10 Saul swore to her by the LORD, "As surely as the LORD lives, you will not be punished for this."

11 Then the woman asked, "Whom shall I bring up for you?"

"Bring up Samuel," he said.

12 When the woman saw Samuel, she cried out at the top of her voice and said to Saul, "Why have you deceived me? You are Saul!"

13 The king said to her, "Don't be afraid. What do you see?"

The woman said, "I see a spirit[a] coming up out of the ground."

14 "What does he look like?" he asked.

"An old man wearing a robe[d] is coming up," she said.

Then Saul knew it was Samuel, and he bowed down and prostrated himself with his face to the ground.

15 Samuel said to Saul, "Why have you disturbed me by bringing me up?"

"I am in great distress," Saul said. "The Philistines are fighting against me, and God has turned[e] away from me. He no longer answers me, either by prophets or by dreams. So I have called on you to tell me what to do."

16 Samuel said, "Why do you consult me, now that the LORD has turned away from you and become your enemy? 17 The LORD has done what he predicted through me. The LORD has torn the kingdom out of your hands and given it to one of your neighbors—to David. 18 Because you did not obey the LORD or carry out his fierce wrath against the Amalekites, the LORD has done this to you today. 19 The LORD will hand over both Israel and you to the Philistines, and tomorrow you and your sons will be with me. The LORD will also hand over the army of Israel to the Philistines."

20 Immediately Saul fell full length on the ground, filled with fear because of Samuel's words. His strength was gone, for he had eaten nothing all that day and night.

21 When the woman came to Saul and saw that he was greatly shaken, she said, "Look, your maidservant has obeyed you. I took my life[f] in my hands and did what you told me to do. 22 Now please listen to your servant and let me give you some food so you may eat and have the strength to go on your way."

23 He refused and said, "I will not eat."

But his men joined the woman in urging him, and he listened to them. He got up from the ground and sat on the couch.

**28:14** d 1Sa 15:27
**28:15** e ver 6; 1Sa 18:12
**28:21** f Jdg 12:3; 1Sa 19:5

[a] 13 Or *see spirits*; or *see gods*

**29:1** g 1Sa 28:1 h 1Sa 4:1
**29:2** i 1Sa 28:2
**29:3** j 1Sa 27:7; Da 6:5
**29:4** k 1Sa 14:21
**29:5** l 1Sa 18:7; 21:11
**29:6** m ver 3
**29:9** n 2Sa 14:17,20; 19:27 o ver 4

24 The woman had a fattened calf at the house, which she butchered at once. She took some flour, kneaded it and baked bread without yeast. 25 Then she set it before Saul and his men, and they ate. That same night they got up and left.

## Achish Sends David Back to Ziklag

**29** The Philistines gathered[g] all their forces at Aphek,[h] and Israel camped by the spring in Jezreel. 2 As the Philistine rulers marched with their units of hundreds and thousands, David and his men were marching at the rear[i] with Achish. 3 The commanders of the Philistines asked, "What about these Hebrews?"

Achish replied, "Is this not David, who was an officer of Saul king of Israel? He has already been with me for over a year,[j] and from the day he left Saul until now, I have found no fault in him."

4 But the Philistine commanders were angry with him and said, "Send the man back, that he may return to the place you assigned him. He must not go with us into battle, or he will turn[k] against us during the fighting. How better could he regain his master's favor than by taking the heads of our own men? 5 Isn't this the David they sang about in their dances:

" 'Saul has slain his thousands,
and David his tens of thousands'?"[l]

6 So Achish called David and said to him, "As surely as the LORD lives, you have been reliable, and I would be pleased to have you serve with me in the army. From the day you came to me until now, I have found no fault in you, but the rulers[m] don't approve of you. 7 Turn back and go in peace; do nothing to displease the Philistine rulers."

8 "But what have I done?" asked David. "What have you found against your servant from the day I came to you until now? Why can't I go and fight against the enemies of my lord the king?"

9 Achish answered, "I know that you have been as pleasing in my eyes as an angel[n] of God; nevertheless, the Philistine commanders[o] have said, 'He must not go up with us into battle.' 10 Now get up early, along with your master's servants who have come with you, and leave[p] in the morning as soon as it is light."

11 So David and his men got up early in the morning to go back to the land of the Philistines, and the Philistines went up to Jezreel.

## David Destroys the Amalekites

**30** David and his men reached Ziklag[q] on the third day. Now the Amalekites[r] had raided the Negev and Ziklag. They had attacked Ziklag and burned it, 2 and had taken captive the women and all who were in it, both young and old. They killed none of them, but carried them off as they went on their way.

3 When David and his men came to Ziklag, they found it destroyed by fire and their wives and sons and daughters taken captive. 4 So David and his men wept aloud until they had no strength left to weep. 5 David's two wives[s] had been captured—Ahinoam of Jezreel and Abigail, the widow of Nabal of Carmel. 6 David was greatly distressed because the men were talking of stoning[t] him; each one was bitter in spirit because of his sons and daughters. But David found strength in the LORD his God.

*Father,*

*when I can't see my way ahead, please remind me that you are in charge of my life, that you guard me and guide my every step. For this I love you and thank you. In Jesus' name,*

*Amen*

1 SAMUEL 30:6

7 Then David said to Abiathar the priest, the son of Ahimelech, "Bring me the ephod.[u]" Abiathar brought it to him, 8 and David inquired[v] of the LORD, "Shall I pursue this raiding party? Will I overtake them?"

"Pursue them," he answered. "You will certainly overtake them and succeed in the rescue."

9 David and the six hundred men with

**29:10** p 1Ch 12:19
**30:1** q 1Sa 29:4,11 r 1Sa 15:7; 27:8
**30:5** s 1Sa 25:43
**30:6** t Ex 17:4
**30:7** u 1Sa 23:9
**30:8** v 1Sa 23:2

**30:10** w ver 9,21
**30:12** x Jdg 15:19
**30:14** y 2Sa 8:18; Eze 25:16 z Jos 14:13
**30:17** a 1Sa 15:3
**30:21** b ver 10

him came to the Besor Ravine, where some stayed behind, [10]for two hundred men were too exhausted[w] to cross the ravine. But David and four hundred men continued the pursuit.

[11]They found an Egyptian in a field and brought him to David. They gave him water to drink and food to eat— [12]part of a cake of pressed figs and two cakes of raisins. He ate and was revived,[x] for he had not eaten any food or drunk any water for three days and three nights.

[13]David asked him, "To whom do you belong, and where do you come from?"

He said, "I am an Egyptian, the slave of an Amalekite. My master abandoned me when I became ill three days ago. [14]We raided the Negev of the Kerethites[y] and the territory belonging to Judah and the Negev of Caleb.[z] And we burned Ziklag."

[15]David asked him, "Can you lead me down to this raiding party?"

He answered, "Swear to me before God that you will not kill me or hand me over to my master, and I will take you down to them."

[16]He led David down, and there they were, scattered over the countryside, eating, drinking and reveling because of the great amount of plunder they had taken from the land of the Philistines and from Judah. [17]David fought them from dusk until the evening of the next day, and none of them got away, except four hundred young men who rode off on camels and fled.[a] [18]David recovered everything the Amalekites had taken, including his two wives. [19]Nothing was missing: young or old, boy or girl, plunder or anything else they had taken. David brought everything back. [20]He took all the flocks and herds, and his men drove them ahead of the other livestock, saying, "This is David's plunder."

[21]Then David came to the two hundred men who had been too exhausted[b] to follow him and who were left behind at the Besor Ravine. They came out to meet David and the people with him. As David and his men approached, he greeted them. [22]But all the evil men and troublemakers among David's followers said, "Because they did not go out with us, we will not share with them the plunder we recovered. However, each man may take his wife and children and go."

[23]David replied, "No, my brothers, you must not do that with what the LORD has given us. He has protected us and handed over to us the forces that came against us. [24]Who will listen to what you say? The share of the man who stayed with the supplies is to be the same as that of him who went down to the battle. All will share alike.[c]" [25]David made this a statute and ordinance for Israel from that day to this.

[26]When David arrived in Ziklag, he sent some of the plunder to the elders of Judah, who were his friends, saying, "Here is a present for you from the plunder of the LORD's enemies."

[27]He sent it to those who were in Bethel, Ramoth[d] Negev and Jattir;[e] [28]to those in Aroer,[f] Siphmoth, Eshtemoa [29]and Racal; to those in the towns of the Jerahmeelites[g] and the Kenites; [30]to those in Hormah,[h] Bor Ashan, Athach [31]and Hebron;[i] and to those in all the other places where David and his men had roamed.

## Saul Takes His Life

**31** Now the Philistines fought against Israel; the Israelites fled before them, and many fell slain on Mount Gilboa.[j] [2]The Philistines pressed hard after Saul and his sons, and they killed his sons Jonathan, Abinadab and Malki-Shua. [3]The fighting grew fierce around Saul, and when the archers overtook him, they wounded[k] him critically.

[4]Saul said to his armor-bearer, "Draw your sword and run me through,[l] or these uncircumcised fellows will come and run me through and abuse me."

But his armor-bearer was terrified and would not do it; so Saul took his own sword and fell on it. [5]When the armor-bearer saw that Saul was dead, he too fell on his sword and died with him. [6]So Saul and his three sons and his armor-bearer and all his men died together that same day.

[7]When the Israelites along the valley and those across the Jordan saw that the Israelite army had fled and that Saul and his sons had died, they abandoned their

**30:24** c Nu 31:27; Jos 22:8
**30:27** d Jos 19:8 e Jos 15:48
**30:28** f Jos 13:16
**30:29** g 1Sa 27:10
**30:30** h Jdg 1:17
**30:31** i Jos 14:13
**31:1** j 1Sa 28:4; 1Ch 10:1–12
**31:3** k 2Sa 1:6
**31:4** l Jdg 9:54

towns and fled. And the Philistines came
and occupied them.
8The next day, when the Philistines
came to strip the dead, they found Saul
and his three sons fallen on Mount Gilboa.
9They cut off his head and stripped off
his armor, and they sent messengers
throughout the land of the Philistines to
proclaim the news[m] in the temple of their
idols and among their people. 10They put
his armor in the temple of the Ashtoreths[n]
and fastened his body to the wall of Beth
Shan.[o]
11When the people of Jabesh Gilead[p] heard
of what the Philistines had done to Saul,
12all their valiant men journeyed through
the night to Beth Shan. They took down the
bodies of Saul and his sons from the wall of
Beth Shan and went to Jabesh, where they
burned them. 13Then they took their bones[q]
and buried them under a tamarisk tree at
Jabesh, and they fasted seven days.

**31:9** m 2Sa 1:20
**31:10** n Jdg 2:12–13
**31:10** o Jos 17:11
**31:11** p 1Sa 11:1
**31:13** q 2Sa 21:12–14

# 2 Samuel

## OVERVIEW

After David became king—first over his own tribe of Judah and then over all of Israel—he captured Jerusalem, making it the capital of Israel and the home of the ark of the covenant (see 2Sa 5–6), received God's promise of an everlasting dynasty (see 2Sa 7) and led the Israelites in military victories over many of their enemies (see 2Sa 8; 10).

Despite all his accomplishments, David had weaknesses and faced difficulties—especially in his family relationships. Michal, Saul's daughter and one of David's wives, had such disdain for David's zealous worship of the Lord that it drove a wedge between them until her death (see 2Sa 6). David even committed adultery and planned the death of loyal Uriah in an attempt to cover up his sin (see 2Sa 11–12). As a result of committing adultery with David, Bathsheba (Uriah's wife) lost her husband and first child to premature deaths, but God restored her and later blessed her when she gave birth to Solomon, who was loved by God. David also responded inadequately to his daughter's rape and her brother Absalom's murderous revenge (see 2Sa 13–14). David then suffered the humiliation of his beloved son Absalom's coup and resulting death (see 2Sa 15–18). As Nathan the prophet had declared, David and his family were plagued by violence and death (see 2Sa 12:10–12).

The suffering of David's family was a direct consequence of his "hidden" sin. The attempt to hide sin only exposes us to worse repercussions. Confessing our sins to each other has positive benefits (see Jas 5:16). Freedom from guilt and shame—coupled with accountability to a wise, loving friend in the Lord—can bring healing. Learn from David's mistakes; expose the sin in your life through confession and reconciliation.

## OUTLINE

I. David's Lament Over Saul and Jonathan (1:1–27)
II. David's Establishment as King (2:1—7:29)
III. David's Victories Over Israel's Enemies (8:1–18)
IV. David's Faithfulness to His Covenant With Jonathan (9:1–13)
V. David Defeats the Ammonites (10:1–19)
VI. David Commits Adultery and Murder (11:1–27)
VII. David Is Rebuked and Repents (12:1–31)
VIII. Amnon Rapes Tamar (13:1–22)
IX. David Loses His Son Amnon (13:23–39)
X. David Loses His Son Absalom (14:1—20:26)
XI. The Last Years of David's Reign (21:1—24:25)

### SCANNABLE FACTS:

**Author:** Unknown

**Time Written:** Unknown

**Theme to Note:** Every hidden sin will be revealed and has its consequences

**Notable Women:** Michal, Bathsheba, Rizpah, Tamar

1:1 a 1Sa 30:17
1:2 b 1Sa 4:12
1:6 c 1Sa 31:2–4
1:8 d 1Sa 15:2
1:10 e Jdg 9:54
1:14 f 1Sa 24:6; 26:9
1:15 g 2Sa 4:12

## David Hears of Saul's Death

1 After the death of Saul, David returned from defeating[a] the Amalekites and stayed in Ziklag two days. 2 On the third day a man arrived from Saul's camp, with his clothes torn and with dust on his head.[b] When he came to David, he fell to the ground to pay him honor.

3 "Where have you come from?" David asked him.

He answered, "I have escaped from the Israelite camp."

4 "What happened?" David asked. "Tell me."

He said, "The men fled from the battle. Many of them fell and died. And Saul and his son Jonathan are dead."

5 Then David said to the young man who brought him the report, "How do you know that Saul and his son Jonathan are dead?"

6 "I happened to be on Mount Gilboa,[c]" the young man said, "and there was Saul, leaning on his spear, with the chariots and riders almost upon him. 7 When he turned around and saw me, he called out to me, and I said, 'What can I do?'

8 "He asked me, 'Who are you?'

"'An Amalekite,[d]' I answered.

9 "Then he said to me, 'Stand over me and kill me! I am in the throes of death, but I'm still alive.'

10 "So I stood over him and killed him, because I knew that after he had fallen he could not survive. And I took the crown[e] that was on his head and the band on his arm and have brought them here to my lord."

11 Then David and all the men with him took hold of their clothes and tore them. 12 They mourned and wept and fasted till evening for Saul and his son Jonathan, and for the army of the LORD and the house of Israel, because they had fallen by the sword.

13 David said to the young man who brought him the report, "Where are you from?"

"I am the son of an alien, an Amalekite," he answered.

14 David asked him, "Why were you not afraid to lift your hand to destroy the LORD's anointed?[f]"

15 Then David called one of his men and said, "Go, strike him down!"[g] So he struck him down, and he died.[h] 16 For David had said to him, "Your blood be on your own head. Your own mouth testified against you when you said, 'I killed the LORD's anointed.'"

## David's Lament for Saul and Jonathan

17 David took up this lament concerning Saul and his son Jonathan, 18 and ordered that the men of Judah be taught this lament of the bow (it is written in the Book of Jashar):[i]

19 "Your glory, O Israel, lies slain on your heights.
How the mighty have fallen![j]

20 "Tell it not in Gath,[k]
proclaim it not in the streets of Ashkelon,
lest the daughters of the Philistines[l] be glad,
lest the daughters of the uncircumcised rejoice.[m]

21 "O mountains of Gilboa,[n]
may you have neither dew nor rain,
nor fields that yield offerings ⌊of grain⌋.
For there the shield of the mighty was defiled,
the shield of Saul—no longer rubbed with oil.[o]

22 From the blood[p] of the slain,
from the flesh of the mighty,
the bow[q] of Jonathan did not turn back,
the sword of Saul did not return unsatisfied.

23 "Saul and Jonathan—
in life they were loved and gracious,
and in death they were not parted.
They were swifter than eagles,[r]
they were stronger than lions.[s]

24 "O daughters of Israel,
weep for Saul,
who clothed you in scarlet and finery,
who adorned your garments with ornaments of gold.

25 "How the mighty have fallen in battle!
Jonathan lies slain on your heights.

26 I grieve for you, Jonathan my brother;
you were very dear to me.
Your love for me was wonderful,[t]
more wonderful than that of women.

1:15 h 2Sa 4:10
1:18 i Jos 10:13
1:19 j ver 27
1:20 k Mic 1:10 l 1Sa 31:8 m Ex 15:20; 1Sa 18:6
1:21 n 1Sa 31:1 o Isa 21:5
1:22 p Isa 34:3,7 q 1Sa 18:4
1:23 r Jer 4:13 s Jdg 14:18
1:26 t 1Sa 18:1

**1:27** u ver 19,25
**2:1** v 1Sa 23:2,11–12 w Ge 13:18; 1Sa 30:31
**2:4** x 2Sa 5:3–5 y 1Sa 31:11–13
**2:5** z 1Sa 23:21
**2:8** a 1Sa 14:50
**2:11** b 2Sa 5:5
**2:12** c Jos 18:25
**2:13** d 1Ch 2:16

[27]"How the mighty have fallen!
The weapons of war have perished!"[u]

## David Anointed King Over Judah

2 In the course of time, David inquired[v] of the LORD. "Shall I go up to one of the towns of Judah?" he asked.

The LORD said, "Go up."

David asked, "Where shall I go?"

"To Hebron,"[w] the LORD answered.

[2]So David went up there with his two wives, Ahinoam of Jezreel and Abigail, the widow of Nabal of Carmel. [3]David also took the men who were with him, each with his family, and they settled in Hebron and its towns. [4]Then the men of Judah came to Hebron and there they anointed[x] David king over the house of Judah.

When David was told that it was the men of Jabesh Gilead[y] who had buried Saul, [5]he sent messengers to the men of Jabesh Gilead to say to them, "The LORD bless[z] you for showing this kindness to Saul your master by burying him. [6]May the LORD now show you kindness and faithfulness, and I too will show you the same favor because you have done this. [7]Now then, be strong and brave, for Saul your master is dead, and the house of Judah has anointed me king over them."

## War Between the Houses of David and Saul

[8]Meanwhile, Abner[a] son of Ner, the commander of Saul's army, had taken Ish-Bosheth son of Saul and brought him over to Mahanaim. [9]He made him king over Gilead, Ashuri[a] and Jezreel, and also over Ephraim, Benjamin and all Israel.

[10]Ish-Bosheth son of Saul was forty years old when he became king over Israel, and he reigned two years. The house of Judah, however, followed David. [11]The length of time David was king in Hebron over the house of Judah was seven years and six months.[b]

[12]Abner son of Ner, together with the men of Ish-Bosheth son of Saul, left Mahanaim and went to Gibeon.[c] [13]Joab[d] son of Zeruiah and David's men went out and met them at the pool of Gibeon. One group sat down on one side of the pool and one group on the other side.

[14]Then Abner said to Joab, "Let's have some of the young men get up and fight hand to hand in front of us."

"All right, let them do it," Joab said.

[15]So they stood up and were counted off—twelve men for Benjamin and Ish-Bosheth son of Saul, and twelve for David. [16]Then each man grabbed his opponent by the head and thrust his dagger into his opponent's side, and they fell down together. So that place in Gibeon was called Helkath Hazzurim.[b]

[17]The battle that day was very fierce, and Abner and the men of Israel were defeated[e] by David's men.

[18]The three sons of Zeruiah were there: Joab, Abishai and Asahel.[f] Now Asahel was as fleet-footed as a wild gazelle.[g] [19]He chased Abner, turning neither to the right nor to the left as he pursued him. [20]Abner looked behind him and asked, "Is that you, Asahel?"

"It is," he answered.

[21]Then Abner said to him, "Turn aside to the right or to the left; take on one of the young men and strip him of his weapons." But Asahel would not stop chasing him.

[22]Again Abner warned Asahel, "Stop chasing me! Why should I strike you down? How could I look your brother Joab in the face?"[h]

[23]But Asahel refused to give up the pursuit; so Abner thrust the butt of his spear into Asahel's stomach,[i] and the spear came out through his back. He fell there and died on the spot. And every man stopped when he came to the place where Asahel had fallen and died.

[24]But Joab and Abishai pursued Abner, and as the sun was setting, they came to the hill of Ammah, near Giah on the way to the wasteland of Gibeon. [25]Then the men of Benjamin rallied behind Abner. They formed themselves into a group and took their stand on top of a hill.

[26]Abner called out to Joab, "Must the sword devour forever? Don't you realize that this will end in bitterness? How long

**2:17** e 2Sa 3:1
**2:18** f 1Ch 2:16 g 1Ch 12:8
**2:22** h 2Sa 3:27
**2:23** i 2Sa 3:27; 4:6

[a]9 Or *Asher* [b]16 *Helkath Hazzurim* means *field of daggers* or *field of hostilities.*

before you order your men to stop pursuing their brothers?"

27Joab answered, "As surely as God lives, if you had not spoken, the men would have continued the pursuit of their brothers until morning.[a]" 28So Joab blew the trumpet, and all the men came to a halt; they no longer pursued Israel, nor did they fight anymore.

29All that night Abner and his men marched through the Arabah. They crossed the Jordan, continued through the whole Bithron[b] and came to Mahanaim.

30Then Joab returned from pursuing Abner and assembled all his men. Besides Asahel, nineteen of David's men were found missing. 31But David's men had killed three hundred and sixty Benjamites who were with Abner. 32They took Asahel and buried him in his father's tomb at Bethlehem. Then Joab and his men marched all night and arrived at Hebron by daybreak.

3 The war between the house of Saul and the house of David lasted a long time.[j] David grew stronger and stronger, while the house of Saul grew weaker and weaker.

2Sons were born to David in Hebron:

His firstborn was Amnon the son of Ahinoam[k] of Jezreel;
3his second, Kileab the son of Abigail the widow of Nabal of Carmel;
the third, Absalom the son of Maacah daughter of Talmai king of Geshur;[l]
4the fourth, Adonijah[m] the son of Haggith;
the fifth, Shephatiah the son of Abital;
5and the sixth, Ithream the son of David's wife Eglah.
These were born to David in Hebron.

## Abner Goes Over to David

6During the war between the house of Saul and the house of David, Abner had been strengthening his own position in the house of Saul. 7Now Saul had had a concubine[n] named Rizpah[o] daughter of Aiah. And Ish-Bosheth said to Abner, "Why did you sleep with my father's concubine?"

8Abner was very angry because of what Ish-Bosheth said and he answered, "Am I a dog's head[p]—on Judah's side? This very day I am loyal to the house of your father Saul and to his family and friends. I haven't handed you over to David. Yet now you accuse me of an offense involving this woman! 9May God deal with Abner, be it ever so severely, if I do not do for David what the LORD promised[q] him on oath 10and transfer the kingdom from the house of Saul and establish David's throne over Israel and Judah from Dan to Beersheba."[r] 11Ish-Bosheth did not dare to say another word to Abner, because he was afraid of him.

12Then Abner sent messengers on his behalf to say to David, "Whose land is it? Make an agreement with me, and I will help you bring all Israel over to you."

13"Good," said David. "I will make an agreement with you. But I demand one thing of you: Do not come into my presence unless you bring Michal daughter of Saul when you come to see me."[s] 14Then David sent messengers to Ish-Bosheth son of Saul, demanding, "Give me my wife Michal,[t] whom I betrothed to myself for the price of a hundred Philistine foreskins."

15So Ish-Bosheth gave orders and had her taken away from her husband Paltiel[u] son of Laish. 16Her husband, however, went with her, weeping behind her all the way to Bahurim.[v] Then Abner said to him, "Go back home!" So he went back.

17Abner conferred with the elders of Israel and said, "For some time you have wanted to make David your king. 18Now do it! For the LORD promised David, 'By my servant David I will rescue my people Israel from the hand of the Philistines[w] and from the hand of all their enemies.[x]'"

19Abner also spoke to the Benjamites in person. Then he went to Hebron to tell David everything that Israel and the whole house of Benjamin[y] wanted to do. 20When Abner, who had twenty men with him, came to David at Hebron, David prepared a feast for him and his men. 21Then Abner said to David, "Let

**3:1** j 1Ki 14:30
**3:2** k 1Sa 25:43; 1Ch 3:1–3
**3:3** l 1Sa 27:8; 2Sa 13:37
**3:4** m 1Ki 1:5,11
**3:7** n 2Sa 16:21–22 o 2Sa 21:8–11
**3:8** p 1Sa 24:14; 2Sa 9:8
**3:9** q 1Sa 15:28; 1Ki 19:2
**3:10** r Jdg 20:1
**3:13** s 1Sa 18:20
**3:14** t 1Sa 18:27
**3:15** u 1Sa 25:44
**3:16** v 2Sa 16:5; 19:16
**3:18** w 1Sa 9:16 x 1Sa 15:28
**3:19** y 1Ch 12:2,16,29

[a]27 Or *spoken this morning, the men would not have taken up the pursuit of their brothers*; or *spoken, the men would have given up the pursuit of their brothers by morning* [b]29 Or *morning*; or *ravine*; the meaning of the Hebrew for this word is uncertain.

**3:21** z ver 10,12 a 1Ki 11:37
**3:27** b 2Sa 2:22; 20:9–10; 1Ki 2:5
**3:29** c 1Ki 2:31–33
**3:31** d Ge 37:34
**3:32** e Pr 24:17

me go at once and assemble all Israel for my lord the king, so that they may make a compact[z] with you, and that you may rule over all that your heart desires."[a] So David sent Abner away, and he went in peace.

## Joab Murders Abner

22 Just then David's men and Joab returned from a raid and brought with them a great deal of plunder. But Abner was no longer with David in Hebron, because David had sent him away, and he had gone in peace. 23 When Joab and all the soldiers with him arrived, he was told that Abner son of Ner had come to the king and that the king had sent him away and that he had gone in peace.

24 So Joab went to the king and said, "What have you done? Look, Abner came to you. Why did you let him go? Now he is gone! 25 You know Abner son of Ner; he came to deceive you and observe your movements and find out everything you are doing."

26 Joab then left David and sent messengers after Abner, and they brought him back from the well of Sirah. But David did not know it. 27 Now when Abner returned to Hebron, Joab took him aside into the gateway, as though to speak with him privately. And there, to avenge the blood of his brother Asahel, Joab stabbed him in the stomach, and he died.[b]

28 Later, when David heard about this, he said, "I and my kingdom are forever innocent before the LORD concerning the blood of Abner son of Ner. 29 May his blood fall upon the head of Joab and upon all his father's house![c] May Joab's house never be without someone who has a running sore or leprosy[a] or who leans on a crutch or who falls by the sword or who lacks food."

30 (Joab and his brother Abishai murdered Abner because he had killed their brother Asahel in the battle at Gibeon.)

31 Then David said to Joab and all the people with him, "Tear your clothes and put on sackcloth and walk in mourning[d] in front of Abner." King David himself walked behind the bier. 32 They buried Abner in Hebron, and the king wept[e] aloud at Abner's tomb. All the people wept also.

33 The king sang this lament for Abner:

"Should Abner have died as the lawless
die?
34 Your hands were not bound,
your feet were not fettered.
You fell as one falls before wicked men."

And all the people wept over him again.

35 Then they all came and urged David to eat something while it was still day; but David took an oath, saying, "May God deal with me, be it ever so severely,[f] if I taste bread[g] or anything else before the sun sets!"

36 All the people took note and were pleased; indeed, everything the king did pleased them. 37 So on that day all the people and all Israel knew that the king had no part in the murder of Abner son of Ner.

38 Then the king said to his men, "Do you not realize that a prince and a great man has fallen in Israel this day? 39 And today, though I am the anointed king, I am weak, and these sons of Zeruiah are too strong for me.[h] May the LORD repay the evildoer according to his evil deeds!"

## Ish-Bosheth Murdered

4 When Ish-Bosheth son of Saul heard that Abner[i] had died in Hebron, he lost courage, and all Israel became alarmed. 2 Now Saul's son had two men who were leaders of raiding bands. One was named Baanah and the other Recab; they were sons of Rimmon the Beerothite from the tribe of Benjamin—Beeroth[j] is considered part of Benjamin, 3 because the people of Beeroth fled to Gittaim[k] and have lived there as aliens to this day.

4 (Jonathan son of Saul had a son who was lame in both feet. He was five years old when the news about Saul and Jonathan came from Jezreel. His nurse picked him up and fled, but as she hurried to leave, he fell and became crippled. His name was Mephibosheth.)[l]

5 Now Recab and Baanah, the sons of Rimmon the Beerothite, set out for the house of Ish-Bosheth, and they arrived there in the heat of the day while he was taking his noonday rest. 6 They went into the inner part of

**3:35** f Ru 1:17 g 2Sa 1:12; 12:17
**3:39** h 2Sa 19:5–7
**4:1** i 2Sa 3:27; Ezr 4:4
**4:2** j Jos 9:17; 18:25
**4:3** k Ne 11:33
**4:4** l 2Sa 9:3,6; 1Ch 8:34; 9:40

[a]29 The Hebrew word was used for various diseases affecting the skin—not necessarily leprosy.

the house as if to get some wheat, and they stabbed[m] him in the stomach. Then Recab and his brother Baanah slipped away.

7They had gone into the house while he was lying on the bed in his bedroom. After they stabbed and killed him, they cut off his head. Taking it with them, they traveled all night by way of the Arabah. 8They brought the head of Ish-Bosheth to David at Hebron and said to the king, "Here is the head of Ish-Bosheth son of Saul, your enemy, who tried to take your life. This day the LORD has avenged my lord the king against Saul and his offspring."

9David answered Recab and his brother Baanah, the sons of Rimmon the Beerothite, "As surely as the LORD lives, who has delivered[n] me out of all trouble, 10when a man told me, 'Saul is dead,' and thought he was bringing good news, I seized him and put him to death in Ziklag.[o] That was the reward I gave him for his news! 11How much more—when wicked men have killed an innocent man in his own house and on his own bed—should I not now demand his blood[p] from your hand and rid the earth of you!"

12So David gave an order to his men, and they killed them.[q] They cut off their hands and feet and hung the bodies by the pool in Hebron. But they took the head of Ish-Bosheth and buried it in Abner's tomb at Hebron.

## David Becomes King Over Israel

5 All the tribes of Israel came to David at Hebron and said, "We are your own flesh and blood. 2In the past, while Saul was king over us, you were the one who led Israel on their military campaigns.[r] And the LORD said to you, 'You will shepherd[s] my people Israel, and you will become their ruler.'"

3When all the elders of Israel had come to King David at Hebron, the king made a compact[t] with them at Hebron before the LORD, and they anointed David king over Israel.

4David was thirty years old[u] when he became king, and he reigned forty[v] years. 5In Hebron he reigned over Judah seven years and six months,[w] and in Jerusalem he reigned over all Israel and Judah thirty-three years.

## David Conquers Jerusalem

6The king and his men marched to Jerusalem[x] to attack the Jebusites, who lived there. The Jebusites said to David, "You will not get in here; even the blind and the lame can ward you off." They thought, "David cannot get in here." 7Nevertheless, David captured the fortress of Zion, the City of David.[y]

8On that day, David said, "Anyone who conquers the Jebusites will have to use the water shaft[a] to reach those 'lame and blind' who are David's enemies.[b]" That is why they say, "The 'blind and lame' will not enter the palace."

9David then took up residence in the fortress and called it the City of David. He built up the area around it, from the supporting terraces[c] inward. 10And he became more and more powerful,[z] because the LORD God Almighty was with him.

11Now Hiram[a] king of Tyre sent messengers to David, along with cedar logs and carpenters and stonemasons, and they built a palace for David. 12And David knew that the LORD had established him as king over Israel and had exalted his kingdom for the sake of his people Israel.

13After he left Hebron, David took more concubines and wives[b] in Jerusalem, and more sons and daughters were born to him. 14These are the names of the children born to him there:[c] Shammua, Shobab, Nathan, Solomon, 15Ibhar, Elishua, Nepheg, Japhia, 16Elishama, Eliada and Eliphelet.

## David Defeats the Philistines

17When the Philistines heard that David had been anointed king over Israel, they went up in full force to search for him, but David heard about it and went down to the stronghold.[d] 18Now the Philistines had come and spread out in the Valley of Rephaim;[e] 19so David inquired[f] of the LORD, "Shall I go and attack the Philistines? Will you hand them over to me?"

The LORD answered him, "Go, for I will surely hand the Philistines over to you."

20So David went to Baal Perazim, and there he defeated them. He said, "As waters break out, the LORD has broken out against

[a]8 Or *use scaling hooks* [b]8 Or *are hated by David* [c]9 Or *the Millo*

**4:6** m 2Sa 2:23
**4:9** n 1Ki 1:29
**4:10** o 2Sa 1:2–16
**4:11** p Ge 9:5
**4:12** q 2Sa 1:15
**5:2** r 1Sa 18:5,13,16 s 1Sa 16:1
**5:3** t 2Sa 3:21
**5:4** u Lk 3:23 v 1Ch 26:31
**5:5** w 2Sa 2:11; 1Ch 3:4
**5:6** x Jdg 1:8
**5:7** y 1Ki 2:10
**5:10** z 2Sa 3:1
**5:11** a 1Ki 5:1,18
**5:13** b Dt 17:17
**5:14** c 1Ch 3:5
**5:17** d 2Sa 23:14; 1Ch 11:16
**5:18** e Jos 15:8
**5:19** f 1Sa 23:2

**5:20** g Isa 28:21
**5:24** h 2Ki 7:6 i Jdg 4:14
**6:2** j 1Sa 4:4 k Lev 24:16
**6:3** l 1Sa 6:7

my enemies before me." So that place was called Baal Perazim.[a][g] 21 The Philistines abandoned their idols there, and David and his men carried them off.

22 Once more the Philistines came up and spread out in the Valley of Rephaim; 23 so David inquired of the LORD, and he answered, "Do not go straight up, but circle around behind them and attack them in front of the balsam trees. 24 As soon as you hear the sound[h] of marching in the tops of the balsam trees, move quickly, because that will mean the LORD has gone out in front[i] of you to strike the Philistine army." 25 So David did as the LORD commanded him, and he struck down the Philistines all the way from Gibeon[b] to Gezer.

## The Ark Brought to Jerusalem

6 David again brought together out of Israel chosen men, thirty thousand in all. 2 He and all his men set out from Baalah of Judah[c] to bring up from there the ark[j] of God, which is called by the Name,[d][k] the name of the LORD Almighty, who is enthroned between the cherubim that are on the ark. 3 They set the ark of God on a new cart[l] and brought it from the house of Abinadab, which was on the hill. Uzzah and Ahio, sons of Abinadab, were guiding the new cart 4 with the ark of God on it,[e] and Ahio was walking in front of it. 5 David and the whole house of Israel were celebrating with all their might before the LORD, with songs[f] and with harps, lyres, tambourines, sistrums and cymbals.

6 When they came to the threshing floor of Nacon, Uzzah reached out and took hold of[m] the ark of God, because the oxen stumbled. 7 The LORD's anger burned against Uzzah because of his irreverent act; therefore God struck him down[n] and he died there beside the ark of God.

8 Then David was angry because the LORD's wrath had broken out against Uzzah, and to this day that place is called Perez Uzzah.[g]

9 David was afraid of the LORD that day and said, "How can the ark of the LORD ever come to me?" 10 He was not willing to take the ark of the LORD to be with him in the City of David. Instead, he took it aside to the house of Obed-Edom the Gittite. 11 The ark of the LORD remained in the house of Obed-Edom the Gittite for three months, and the LORD blessed him and his entire household.[o]

12 Now King David[p] was told, "The LORD has blessed the household of Obed-Edom and everything he has, because of the ark of God." So David went down and brought up the ark of God from the house of Obed-Edom to the City of David with rejoicing. 13 When those who were carrying the ark of the LORD had taken six steps, he sacrificed[q] a bull and a fattened calf. 14 David, wearing a linen ephod,[r] danced[s] before the LORD with all his might, 15 while he and the entire house

**6:6** m Nu 4:15,19–20; 1Ch 13:9
**6:7** n 1Sa 6:19
**6:11** o Ge 39:5
**6:12** p 1Ki 8:1; 1Ch 15:25
**6:13** q 1Ki 8:5,62
**6:14** r 1Sa 2:18 s Ex 15:20

[a]20 *Baal Perazim* means *the lord who breaks out.* [b]25 Septuagint (see also 1 Chron. 14:16); Hebrew *Geba* [c]2 That is, Kiriath Jearim; Hebrew *Baale Judah*, a variant of *Baalah of Judah* [d]2 Hebrew; Septuagint and Vulgate do not have *the Name.* [e]3,4 Dead Sea Scrolls and some Septuagint manuscripts; Masoretic Text *cart* [4]*and they brought it with the ark of God from the house of Abinadab, which was on the hill* [f]5 See Dead Sea Scrolls, Septuagint and 1 Chronicles 13:8; Masoretic Text *celebrating before the LORD with all kinds of instruments made of pine.* [g]8 *Perez Uzzah* means *outbreak against Uzzah.*

## The African Presence

### 2 Samuel 5:17–25

After David became king, he continued to battle the Philistines (see also 2Sa 21:15–22; 23:14–17). The ancestry of the Philistines can be traced to one of Ham's sons, Mizraim (see Ge 10:6,13; see also the African Presence note on Ge 10:6). They occupied the coastland of Canaan. For more on the Philistines, see the African Presence note on 1 Samuel 17.

*God.*

*I thank you for your presence in my life. Help me to commune with you throughout this day, as well as every day. I love you and praise you for remaining with me.*

*Amen.*

2 SAMUEL 6:12–15

of Israel brought up the ark of the LORD with shouts and the sound of trumpets.

16 As the ark of the LORD was entering the City of David, Michal daughter of Saul watched from a window. And when she saw King David leaping and dancing before the LORD, she despised him in her heart.

17 They brought the ark of the LORD and set it in its place inside the tent that David had pitched for it,[t] and David sacrificed burnt offerings[u] and fellowship offerings[a] before the LORD. 18 After he had finished sacrificing the burnt offerings and fellowship offerings, he blessed the people in the name of the LORD Almighty. 19 Then he gave a loaf of bread, a cake of dates and a cake of raisins to each person in the whole crowd of Israelites, both men and women. And all the people went to their homes.

20 When David returned home to bless his household, Michal daughter of Saul came out to meet him and said, "How the king of Israel has distinguished himself today, disrobing[v] in the sight of the slave girls of his servants as any vulgar fellow would!"

21 David said to Michal, "It was before the LORD, who chose me rather than your father or anyone from his house when he appointed[w] me ruler over the LORD's people Israel—I will celebrate before the LORD. 22 I will become even more undignified than this, and I will be humiliated in my own eyes. But by these slave girls you spoke of, I will be held in honor."

23 And Michal daughter of Saul had no children to the day of her death.

## God's Promise to David

7 After the king was settled in his palace[x] and the LORD had given him rest from all his enemies around him, 2 he said to Nathan the prophet, "Here I am, living in a palace[y] of cedar, while the ark of God remains in a tent."[z]

3 Nathan replied to the king, "Whatever you have in mind, go ahead and do it, for the LORD is with you."

4 That night the word of the LORD came to Nathan, saying:

5 "Go and tell my servant David, 'This is what the LORD says: Are you[a] the one to build me a house to dwell in?[b] 6 I have not dwelt in a house from the day I brought the Israelites up out of Egypt to this day. I have been moving from place to place with a tent[c] as my dwelling.[d] 7 Wherever I have moved with all the Israelites, did I ever say to any of their rulers whom I commanded to shepherd my people Israel, "Why have you not built me a house of cedar?[e]" '

8 "Now then, tell my servant David, 'This is what the LORD Almighty says: I took you from the pasture and from following the flock[f] to be ruler over my people Israel. 9 I have been with you wherever you have gone,[g] and I have cut off all your enemies from before you.[h] Now I will make your name great, like the names of the greatest men of the earth. 10 And I will provide a place for my people Israel and will plant[i] them so that they can have a home of their own and no longer be disturbed. Wicked[j] people will not oppress them anymore, as they did at the beginning 11 and have done ever since the time I appointed leaders[b][k] over my people Israel. I will also give you rest from all your enemies.

" 'The LORD declares to you that the LORD himself will establish[l] a house[m] for you: 12 When your days are over and you rest[n] with your fathers, I will raise up your offspring to succeed you, who will come from your own body,

[a] 17 Traditionally *peace offerings*; also in verse 18 [b] 11 Traditionally *judges*

**6:17** t 1Ch 15:1 u 1Ki 8:62–64
**6:20** v ver 14,16
**6:21** w 1Sa 13:14

**7:1** x 1Ch 17:1
**7:2** y 2Sa 5:11 z Ex 26:1
**7:5** a 1Ki 8:19 b 1Ki 5:3–5
**7:6** c Ex 40:18,34 d 1Ki 8:16
**7:7** e Lev 26:11–12
**7:8** f 1Sa 16:11
**7:9** g 2Sa 5:10 h Ps 18:37–42
**7:10** i Isa 5:1–7 j Ps 89:22–23
**7:11** k 1Sa 12:9–11 l 1Sa 25:28 m ver 27
**7:12** n 1Ki 2:1

**7:14** o Heb 1:5* p Ps 89:30–33
**7:19** q Isa 55:8–9
**7:22** r Dt 3:24

and I will establish his kingdom. 13He is the one who will build a house for my Name, and I will establish the throne of his kingdom forever. 14I will be his father, and he will be my son.[o] When he does wrong, I will punish him with the rod[p] of men, with floggings inflicted by men. 15But my love will never be taken away from him, as I took it away from Saul, whom I removed from before you. 16Your house and your kingdom will endure forever before me[a]; your throne will be established forever.'"

*Daughter,*

*Trust all of my promises. I will deliver.*

*Your Ultimate Promise Keeper*

2 SAMUEL 7:8–16

17Nathan reported to David all the words of this entire revelation.

## David's Prayer

18Then King David went in and sat before the LORD, and he said:

"Who am I, O Sovereign LORD, and what is my family, that you have brought me this far? 19And as if this were not enough in your sight, O Sovereign LORD, you have also spoken about the future of the house of your servant. Is this your usual way of dealing with man,[q] O Sovereign LORD?

20"What more can David say to you? For you know your servant, O Sovereign LORD. 21For the sake of your word and according to your will, you have done this great thing and made it known to your servant.

22"How great you are,[r] O Sovereign LORD! There is no one like you, and there is no God but you, as we have heard with our own ears.[s] 23And who is like your people Israel[t]—the one nation on earth that God went out to redeem as a people for himself, and to make a name for himself, and to perform great and awesome wonders by driving out nations and their gods from before your people, whom you redeemed[u] from Egypt?[b] 24You have established your people Israel as your very own[v] forever, and you, O LORD, have become their God.[w]

25"And now, LORD God, keep forever the promise you have made concerning your servant and his house. Do as you promised, 26so that your name will be great forever. Then men will say, 'The LORD Almighty is God over Israel!' And the house of your servant David will be established before you.

27"O LORD Almighty, God of Israel, you have revealed this to your servant, saying, 'I will build a house for you.' So your servant has found courage to offer you this prayer. 28O Sovereign LORD, you are God! Your words are trustworthy,[x] and you have promised these good things to your servant. 29Now be pleased to bless the house of your servant, that it may continue forever in your sight; for you, O Sovereign LORD, have spoken, and with your blessing[y] the house of your servant will be blessed forever."

## David's Victories

8 In the course of time, David defeated the Philistines and subdued them, and he took Metheg Ammah from the control of the Philistines.

2David also defeated the Moabites.[z] He made them lie down on the ground and measured them off with a length of cord. Every two lengths of them were put to death, and the third length was allowed to live. So the Moabites became subject to David and brought tribute.

3Moreover, David fought Hadadezer[a] son of Rehob, king of Zobah, when he went to restore his control along the Euphrates River.

**7:22** s Ps 44:1
**7:23** t Dt 4:32–38 u Dt 9:26
**7:24** v Dt 26:18 w Ps 48:14
**7:28** x Jn 17:17
**7:29** y Nu 6:23–27
**8:2** z Nu 24:17
**8:3** a 2Sa 10:16,19

[a]16 Some Hebrew manuscripts and Septuagint; most Hebrew manuscripts *you* [b]23 See Septuagint and 1 Chron. 17:21; Hebrew *wonders for your land and before your people, whom you redeemed from Egypt, from the nations and their gods.*

8:4 b Jos 11:9
8:5 c 1Ki 11:24
8:7 d 1Ki 10:16
8:11 e 1Ki 7:51
8:13 f 2Ki 14:7
8:14 g Nu 24:17–18 h Ge 27:29,37–40
8:16 i 1Ki 4:3
8:17 j 1Ch 24:3

4 David captured a thousand of his chariots, seven thousand charioteers[a] and twenty thousand foot soldiers. He hamstrung[b] all but a hundred of the chariot horses.

5 When the Arameans of Damascus[c] came to help Hadadezer king of Zobah, David struck down twenty-two thousand of them. 6 He put garrisons in the Aramean kingdom of Damascus, and the Arameans became subject to him and brought tribute. The LORD gave David victory wherever he went.

7 David took the gold shields[d] that belonged to the officers of Hadadezer and brought them to Jerusalem. 8 From Tebah[b] and Berothai, towns that belonged to Hadadezer, King David took a great quantity of bronze.

9 When Tou[c] king of Hamath heard that David had defeated the entire army of Hadadezer, 10 he sent his son Joram[d] to King David to greet him and congratulate him on his victory in battle over Hadadezer, who had been at war with Tou. Joram brought with him articles of silver and gold and bronze.

11 King David dedicated[e] these articles to the LORD, as he had done with the silver and gold from all the nations he had subdued: 12 Edom[e] and Moab, the Ammonites and the Philistines, and Amalek. He also dedicated the plunder taken from Hadadezer son of Rehob, king of Zobah.

13 And David became famous after he returned from striking down eighteen thousand Edomites[f] in the Valley of Salt.[f]

14 He put garrisons throughout Edom, and all the Edomites[g] became subject to David.[h] The LORD gave David victory wherever he went.

## David's Officials

15 David reigned over all Israel, doing what was just and right for all his people. 16 Joab son of Zeruiah was over the army; Jehoshaphat[i] son of Ahilud was recorder; 17 Zadok[j] son of Ahitub and Ahimelech son of Abiathar were priests; Seraiah was secretary; 18 Benaiah son of Jehoiada was over the Kerethites[k] and Pelethites; and David's sons were royal advisers.[g]

## David and Mephibosheth

9 David asked, "Is there anyone still left of the house of Saul to whom I can show kindness for Jonathan's sake?"[l]

2 Now there was a servant of Saul's household named Ziba.[m] They called him to appear before David, and the king said to him, "Are you Ziba?"

"Your servant," he replied.

3 The king asked, "Is there no one still left of the house of Saul to whom I can show God's kindness?"

Ziba answered the king, "There is still a son of Jonathan;[n] he is crippled[o] in both feet."

4 "Where is he?" the king asked.

Ziba answered, "He is at the house of Makir[p] son of Ammiel in Lo Debar."

5 So King David had him brought from Lo Debar, from the house of Makir son of Ammiel.

6 When Mephibosheth son of Jonathan, the son of Saul, came to David, he bowed down to pay him honor.

David said, "Mephibosheth!"

"Your servant," he replied.

7 "Don't be afraid," David said to him, "for I will surely show you kindness for the sake of your father Jonathan. I will restore to you all the land that belonged to your grandfather Saul, and you will always eat at my table.[q]"

8 Mephibosheth bowed down and said, "What is your servant, that you should notice a dead dog[r] like me?"

9 Then the king summoned Ziba, Saul's servant, and said to him, "I have given your master's grandson everything that belonged to Saul and his family. 10 You and your sons and your servants are to farm the land for him and bring in the crops, so that your master's grandson[s] may be provided for. And Mephibosheth, grandson of your master, will always eat at my table." (Now Ziba had fifteen sons and twenty servants.)

8:18 k 1Sa 30:14
9:1 l 1Sa 20:14–17,42
9:2 m 2Sa 16:1–4; 19:17,26,29
9:3 n 1Sa 20:14 o 2Sa 4:4
9:4 p 2Sa 17:27–29
9:7 q 2Sa 19:28
9:8 r 2Sa 16:9
9:10 s ver 7,11,13; 2Sa 19:28

[a] 4 Septuagint (see also Dead Sea Scrolls and 1 Chron. 18:4); Masoretic Text *captured seventeen hundred of his charioteers*
[b] 8 See some Septuagint manuscripts (see also 1 Chron. 18:8); Hebrew *Betah.*
[c] 9 Hebrew *Toi,* a variant of *Tou;* also in verse 10
[d] 10 A variant of *Hadoram*
[e] 12 Some Hebrew manuscripts, Septuagint and Syriac (see also 1 Chron. 18:11); most Hebrew manuscripts *Aram*
[f] 13 A few Hebrew manuscripts, Septuagint and Syriac (see also 1 Chron. 18:12); most Hebrew manuscripts *Aram* (that is, Arameans)
[g] 18 Or *were priests*

**10:4**
t Isa 15:2
u Isa 20:4

**10:6**
v Ge 34:30
w 2Sa 8:5

[11]Then Ziba said to the king, "Your servant will do whatever my lord the king commands his servant to do." So Mephibosheth ate at David's[a] table like one of the king's sons.

[12]Mephibosheth had a young son named Mica, and all the members of Ziba's household were servants of Mephibosheth. [13]And Mephibosheth lived in Jerusalem, because he always ate at the king's table, and he was crippled in both feet.

## David Defeats the Ammonites

**10** In the course of time, the king of the Ammonites died, and his son Hanun succeeded him as king. [2]David thought, "I will show kindness to Hanun son of Nahash, just as his father showed kindness to me." So David sent a delegation to express his sympathy to Hanun concerning his father.

When David's men came to the land of the Ammonites, [3]the Ammonite nobles said to Hanun their lord, "Do you think David is honoring your father by sending men to you to express sympathy? Hasn't David sent them to you to explore the city and spy it out and overthrow it?" [4]So Hanun seized David's men, shaved off half of each man's beard,[t] cut off their garments in the middle at the buttocks,[u] and sent them away.

[5]When David was told about this, he sent messengers to meet the men, for they were greatly humiliated. The king said, "Stay at Jericho till your beards have grown, and then come back."

[6]When the Ammonites realized that they had become a stench[v] in David's nostrils, they hired twenty thousand Aramean[w] foot soldiers from Beth Rehob and Zobah, as well as the king of Maacah with a thousand men, and also twelve thousand men from Tob.

[7]On hearing this, David sent Joab out with the entire army of fighting men. [8]The Ammonites came out and drew up in battle formation at the entrance to their city gate, while the Arameans of Zobah and Rehob and the men of Tob and Maacah were by themselves in the open country.

[9]Joab saw that there were battle lines in front of him and behind him; so he selected some of the best troops in Israel and deployed them against the Arameans. [10]He put the rest of the men under the command of Abishai his brother and deployed them against the Ammonites. [11]Joab said, "If the Arameans are too strong for me, then you are to come to my rescue; but if the Ammonites are too strong for you, then I will come to rescue you. [12]Be strong[x] and let us fight bravely for our people and the cities of our God. The LORD will do what is good in his sight."[y]

[13]Then Joab and the troops with him advanced to fight the Arameans, and they fled before him. [14]When the Ammonites saw that the Arameans were fleeing, they fled before Abishai and went inside the city. So Joab returned from fighting the Ammonites and came to Jerusalem.

[15]After the Arameans saw that they had been routed by Israel, they regrouped. [16]Hadadezer had Arameans brought from beyond the River[b]; they went to Helam, with Shobach the commander of Hadadezer's army leading them.

[17]When David was told of this, he gathered all Israel, crossed the Jordan and went to Helam. The Arameans formed their battle lines to meet David and fought against him. [18]But they fled before Israel, and David killed seven hundred of their charioteers and forty thousand of their foot soldiers.[c] He also struck down Shobach the commander of their army, and he died there. [19]When all the kings who were vassals of Hadadezer saw that they had been defeated by Israel, they made peace with the Israelites and became subject[z] to them.

So the Arameans were afraid to help the Ammonites anymore.

## David and Bathsheba

**11** In the spring,[a] at the time when kings go off to war, David sent Joab out with the king's men and the whole Israelite army.[b] They destroyed the Ammonites and besieged Rabbah. But David remained in Jerusalem.

[2]One evening David got up from his bed

**10:12**
x Dt 31:6; 1Co 16:13
y 1Sa 3:18

**10:19**
z 2Sa 8:6

**11:1**
a 1Ki 20:22,26
b 1Ch 20:1

[a]11 Septuagint; Hebrew *my* [b]16 That is, the Euphrates [c]18 Some Septuagint manuscripts (see also 1 Chron. 19:18); Hebrew *horsemen*

and walked around on the roof[c] of the palace. From the roof he saw[d] a woman bathing. The woman was very beautiful, 3 and David sent someone to find out about her. The man said, "Isn't this Bathsheba, the daughter of Eliam and the wife of Uriah[e] the Hittite?" 4 Then David sent messengers to get her.[f] She came to him, and he slept with her. (She had purified herself from her uncleanness.)[g] Then[a] she went back home. 5 The woman conceived and sent word to David, saying, "I am pregnant."

6 So David sent this word to Joab: "Send me Uriah the Hittite." And Joab sent him to David. 7 When Uriah came to him, David asked him how Joab was, how the soldiers were and how the war was going. 8 Then David said to Uriah, "Go down to your house and wash your feet." So Uriah left the palace, and a gift from the king was sent after him. 9 But Uriah slept at the entrance to the palace with all his master's servants and did not go down to his house.

10 When David was told, "Uriah did not go home," he asked him, "Haven't you just come from a distance? Why didn't you go home?"

11 Uriah said to David, "The ark[h] and Israel and Judah are staying in tents, and my master Joab and my lord's men are camped in the open fields. How could I go to my house to eat and drink and lie with my wife? As surely as you live, I will not do such a thing!"

12 Then David said to him, "Stay here one more day, and tomorrow I will send you back." So Uriah remained in Jerusalem that day and the next. 13 At David's invitation, he ate and drank with him, and David made him drunk. But in the evening Uriah went out to sleep on his mat among his master's servants; he did not go home.

14 In the morning David wrote a letter[i] to Joab and sent it with Uriah. 15 In it he wrote, "Put Uriah in the front line where the fighting is fiercest. Then withdraw from him so he will be struck down[j] and die."

16 So while Joab had the city under siege, he put Uriah at a place where he knew the strongest defenders were. 17 When the men of the city came out and fought against Joab, some of the men in David's army fell; moreover, Uriah the Hittite died.

18 Joab sent David a full account of the battle. 19 He instructed the messenger: "When you have finished giving the king this account of the battle, 20 the king's anger may flare up, and he may ask you, 'Why did you get so close to the city to fight? Didn't you know they would shoot arrows from the wall? 21 Who killed Abimelech son of Jerub-Besheth[b]? Didn't a woman throw an upper millstone on him from the wall,[k] so that he died in Thebez? Why did you get so close to the wall?' If he asks you this, then say to him, 'Also, your servant Uriah the Hittite is dead.'"

22 The messenger set out, and when he arrived he told David everything Joab had sent him to say. 23 The messenger said to David, "The men overpowered us and came out against us in the open, but we drove them back to the entrance to the city gate. 24 Then the archers shot arrows at your servants from the wall, and some of the king's men died. Moreover, your servant Uriah the Hittite is dead."

[a]4 Or *with her. When she purified herself from her uncleanness,* [b]21 Also known as *Jerub-Baal* (that is, Gideon)

**11:2** c Dt 22:8 d Mt 5:28
**11:3** e 2Sa 23:39
**11:4** f Ps 51 Title; Jas 1:14–15 g Lev 15:25–30; 18:19
**11:11** h 2Sa 7:2
**11:14** i 1Ki 21:8
**11:15** j 2Sa 12:9
**11:21** k Jdg 9:50–54

## *The African Presence*

### 2 Samuel 11

David's wife Bathsheba was first married to Uriah the Hittite. Hittites were descendants of Ham through Canaan (see Ge 10:15; 23:10). For more on the Hittities, see the African Presence note on Deuteronomy 1.

25 David told the messenger, "Say this to Joab: 'Don't let this upset you; the sword devours one as well as another. Press the attack against the city and destroy it.' Say this to encourage Joab."

26 When Uriah's wife heard that her husband was dead, she mourned for him. 27 After the time of mourning was over, David had her brought to his house, and she became his wife and bore him a son. But the thing David had done displeased[l] the LORD.

## Nathan Rebukes David

12 The LORD sent Nathan to David.[m] When he came to him,[n] he said, "There were two men in a certain town, one rich and the other poor. 2 The rich man had a very large number of sheep and cattle, 3 but the poor man had nothing except one little ewe lamb he had bought. He raised it, and it grew up with him and his children. It shared his food, drank from his cup and even slept in his arms. It was like a daughter to him.

4 "Now a traveler came to the rich man, but the rich man refrained from taking one of his own sheep or cattle to prepare a meal for the traveler who had come to him. Instead, he took the ewe lamb that belonged to the poor man and prepared it for the one who had come to him."

5 David burned with anger against the man and said to Nathan, "As surely as the LORD lives, the man who did this deserves to die! 6 He must pay for that lamb four times over,[o] because he did such a thing and had no pity."

7 Then Nathan said to David, "You are the man! This is what the LORD, the God of Israel, says: 'I anointed[p] you[q] king over Israel, and I delivered you from the hand of Saul. 8 I gave your master's house to you, and your master's wives into your arms. I gave you the house of Israel and Judah. And if all this had been too little, I would have given you even more. 9 Why did you despise the word of the LORD by doing what is evil in his eyes? You struck down[r] Uriah the Hittite with the sword and took his wife to be your own. You killed him with the sword of the Ammonites. 10 Now, therefore, the sword[s] will never depart from your house, because you despised me and took the wife of Uriah the Hittite to be your own.'

11 "This is what the LORD says: 'Out of your own household I am going to bring calamity upon you.[t] Before your very eyes I will take your wives and give them to one who is close to you, and he will lie with your wives in broad daylight. 12 You did it in secret, but I will do this thing in broad daylight[u] before all Israel.'"

13 Then David said to Nathan, "I have sinned[v] against the LORD."

Nathan replied, "The LORD has taken away your sin.[w] You are not going to die. 14 But because by doing this you have made the enemies of the LORD show utter contempt,[a][x] the son born to you will die."

15 After Nathan had gone home, the LORD struck the child that Uriah's wife had borne to David, and he became ill. 16 David pleaded with God for the child. He fasted and went into his house and spent the nights lying[y] on the ground. 17 The elders of his household stood beside him to get him up from the ground, but he refused, and he would not eat any food with them.

18 On the seventh day the child died. David's servants were afraid to tell him that the child was dead, for they thought, "While the child was still living, we spoke to David but he would not listen to us. How can we tell him the child is dead? He may do something desperate."

19 David noticed that his servants were whispering among themselves and he realized the child was dead. "Is the child dead?" he asked.

"Yes," they replied, "he is dead."

20 Then David got up from the ground. After he had washed, put on lotions and changed his clothes, he went into the house of the LORD and worshiped. Then he went to his own house, and at his request they served him food, and he ate.

21 His servants asked him, "Why are you acting this way? While the child was alive, you fasted and wept, but now that the child is dead, you get up and eat!"

22 He answered, "While the child was still alive, I fasted and wept. I thought, 'Who knows?[z] The LORD may be gracious to me

**11:27** l 2Sa 12:9; Ps 51:4–5
**12:1** m Ps 51 Title n 2Sa 14:4
**12:6** o Ex 22:1; Lk 19:8
**12:7** p 1Sa 16:13 q 1Ki 20:42
**12:9** r 2Sa 11:15
**12:10** s 2Sa 13:28
**12:11** t Dt 28:30; 2Sa 16:21–22
**12:12** u 2Sa 16:22
**12:13** v 1Sa 15:24; 2Sa 24:10 w Pr 28:13; Mic 7:18–19
**12:14** x Isa 52:5; Ro 2:24
**12:16** y 2Sa 13:31
**12:22** z Jnh 3:9

[a] 14 Masoretic Text; an ancient Hebrew scribal tradition *this you have shown utter contempt for the LORD*

# Bathsheba

## A Silent Affair

The story of Bathsheba elicits different kinds of responses from each reader. It is a story of sin, sorrow, redemption and consequence. It is a story of a powerful man who went after what he wanted and a woman who had little power to resist being used by him. We learn of the humanity of King David, the faithfulness of Uriah and the silence of Bathsheba.

Women of color have experienced ultimate powerlessness. With our history of slavery, we understand oppression and male domination. We understand a culture in which women, especially women of color, are treated like pawns in the larger scheme of political progress and ambition.

In Bathsheba's time, women generally had no voice, no power, no place in decision making. Their voices were rarely heard. In this story, the only time we read that Bathsheba spoke was to send word to King David that she was pregnant (see 2Sa 11:5). We hear nothing more from her for the remainder of the story. Like so many other Biblical women, we don't really know Bathsheba's personal perspective. She may have felt reluctant to be with King David; she may have felt that she could not refuse the king; or she may have been a willing partner. Many things are unknown, but we do know that King David went to great lengths to be with Bathsheba and that he plotted her husband's death after learning that she was pregnant.

In this story, we learn that there are consequences for our behavior, that true prophets of God speak the truth even to the king, that sinful behavior is not acceptable to God, and that God forgives us when we confess our sins. Read the story of David and Bathsheba with the knowledge that God loves the people he has created, and he can restore us to wholeness even when we fall from grace. Remember that Bathsheba and David later had a son named Solomon, who became the wisest man of all time. Even in the midst of sin and dysfunction, God receives glory when we confess our sins and return to his path.

—M. Newbern-Williams

### reflection

*Reflect on a time in your life when God received glory in the midst of your sin and dysfunction.*

*Thank God for his grace.*

### read

2 Samuel 11:1—12:25; 1 Kings 1:11–31; 2:13–25.

See also the Inspire Notes "Grace and Mercy," "Adultery" and "Forgiveness: God's Extended Mercy," and the Women of the Bible Notes "The Adulteress of Proverbs: The Path to Death," "Gomer: An Unfaithful Wife" and "The Forgiven Adulteress: Caught but Not Condemned."

For the next Women of the Bible note, go to page 375.

**12:22** a Isa38:1–5
**12:23** b Ge37:35 c Job7:10
**12:24** d 1Ch22:9; Mt1:6
**12:26** e Dt3:11; 1Ch20:1–3
**12:30** f 1Ch20:2
**13:1** g 2Sa3:2 h 1Ch3:9
**13:3** i 1Sa16:9

and let the child live.'[a] 23 But now that he is dead, why should I fast? Can I bring him back again? I will go to him,[b] but he will not return to me."[c]

24 Then David comforted his wife Bathsheba, and he went to her and lay with her. She gave birth to a son, and they named him Solomon.[d] The LORD loved him; 25 and because the LORD loved him, he sent word through Nathan the prophet to name him Jedidiah.[a]

26 Meanwhile Joab fought against Rabbah[e] of the Ammonites and captured the royal citadel. 27 Joab then sent messengers to David, saying, "I have fought against Rabbah and taken its water supply. 28 Now muster the rest of the troops and besiege the city and capture it. Otherwise I will take the city, and it will be named after me."

29 So David mustered the entire army and went to Rabbah, and attacked and captured it. 30 He took the crown[f] from the head of their king[b]—its weight was a talent[c] of gold, and it was set with precious stones—and it was placed on David's head. He took a great quantity of plunder from the city 31 and brought out the people who were there, consigning them to labor with saws and with iron picks and axes, and he made them work at brickmaking.[d] He did this to all the Ammonite towns. Then David and his entire army returned to Jerusalem.

## Amnon and Tamar

**13** In the course of time, Amnon[g] son of David fell in love with Tamar,[h] the beautiful sister of Absalom son of David.

2 Amnon became frustrated to the point of illness on account of his sister Tamar, for she was a virgin, and it seemed impossible for him to do anything to her.

3 Now Amnon had a friend named Jonadab son of Shimeah,[i] David's brother. Jonadab was a very shrewd man. 4 He asked Amnon, "Why do you, the king's son, look so haggard morning after morning? Won't you tell me?"

Amnon said to him, "I'm in love with Tamar, my brother Absalom's sister."

5 "Go to bed and pretend to be ill," Jonadab said. "When your father comes to see you, say to him, 'I would like my sister Tamar to come and give me something to eat. Let her prepare the food in my sight so I may watch her and then eat it from her hand.' "

6 So Amnon lay down and pretended to be ill. When the king came to see him, Amnon said to him, "I would like my sister Tamar to come and make some special bread in my sight, so I may eat from her hand."

7 David sent word to Tamar at the palace: "Go to the house of your brother Amnon and prepare some food for him." 8 So Tamar went to the house of her brother Amnon, who was lying down. She took some dough, kneaded it, made the bread in his sight and baked it. 9 Then she took the pan and served him the bread, but he refused to eat.

"Send everyone out of here,"[j] Amnon said. So everyone left him. 10 Then Amnon said to Tamar, "Bring the food here into my bedroom so I may eat from your hand." And Tamar took the bread she had prepared and brought it to her brother Amnon in his bedroom. 11 But when she took it to him to eat, he grabbed[k] her and said, "Come to bed with me, my sister."

12 "Don't, my brother!" she said to him. "Don't force me. Such a thing should not be done in Israel![l] Don't do this wicked thing.[m] 13 What about me?[n] Where could I get rid of my disgrace? And what about you? You would be like one of the wicked fools in Israel. Please speak to the king; he will not keep me from being married to you." 14 But he refused to listen to her, and since he was stronger than she, he raped her.[o]

15 Then Amnon hated her with intense hatred. In fact, he hated her more than he had loved her. Amnon said to her, "Get up and get out!"

16 "No!" she said to him. "Sending me away would be a greater wrong than what you have already done to me."

But he refused to listen to her. 17 He called his personal servant and said, "Get this woman out of here and bolt the door after her." 18 So his servant put her out and bolted the door after her. She was wearing a richly ornamented[e] robe,[p] for this was the kind of

**13:9** j Ge45:1
**13:11** k Ge39:12
**13:12** l Lev20:17; Jdg20:6 m Jdg19:23
**13:13** n Lev18:9
**13:14** o Dt22:25
**13:18** p Ge37:23

[a]25 *Jedidiah* means *loved by the LORD.* [b]30 Or *of Milcom* (that is, Molech) [c]30 That is, about 75 pounds (about 34 kilograms) [d]31 The meaning of the Hebrew for this clause is uncertain. [e]18 The meaning of the Hebrew for this phrase is uncertain.

# Inspire

## SEXUAL ABUSE

Sexual abuse is probably the most violent, brutal and degrading form of suffering. Flashbacks and night terrors rob you of sleep. Sounds, sights, smells and touches trigger old memories. You might be constantly blamed, shamed, misunderstood or even called demon-possessed. The emotional pain might become so intense that it causes you to consider ending your life or the life of your abuser(s). Yet, you are not alone, and God's Word offers help.

The Bible records acts of sexual abuse. Tamar was raped by her half brother Amnon, who at one time said he loved her (see 2Sa 13:1–22), and Dinah was raped by a Hivite prince, who also said he loved her (see Ge 34:1–4). Regardless of what these violent perpetrators said then and what modern-day perpetrators say today, violence and abuse do not equal love.

Healing from sexual abuse is not an easy process, and it takes time and understanding to stop feeling like a victim. It might take years of crying, praying, journaling, yelling, screaming and counseling to improve your self-esteem and emotional health. During that time, you must find a way to deal with your suffering and anger in a healthy manner. You need to protect your mind, body and soul. You need to nurture yourself. During your time of healing, you can find comfort and encouragement in knowing that God will never leave you nor forsake you (see Dt 31:6; Isa 41:10).

Be assured that God is in control of your life. You can let go of the memories of abuse, and you can become whole. Focus on living one day at a time before your loving God. God will send trustworthy people to journey with you and assist in your healing. Love yourself. Trust yourself. Love and trust God. He is with you and will never leave you. God knows, cares and understands.

The Scriptures do not offer any easy solutions to suffering. However, we should look at the way Christ handled suffering. He should be our model. The suffering he experienced on this earth and the heavenly victory he celebrates today shows us that our suffering is not in vain. With God's help, we also will have the victory!

—M. Taylor

### read

2 Samuel 13:1–22; see also Genesis 34:1–4; Psalm 31. See also the Inspire Notes "Courage to Heal," "Overcoming Abuse," "Fear," "The Paradox of Life and Suffering" and "Domestic Violence," and the Women of the Bible Notes "Dinah: An Abused Woman," "The Levite's Concubine: Broken Pieces" and "Tamar: A Violated Woman."

### WOMAN of COLOR

How will you seek to heal from past abuse—whether it is sexual, physical, verbal or emotional? How can you help others?

For the next Inspire note, go to page 399.

garment the virgin daughters of the king wore. 19 Tamar put ashes[q] on her head and tore the ornamented[a] robe she was wearing. She put her hand on her head and went away, weeping aloud as she went.

20 Her brother Absalom said to her, "Has that Amnon, your brother, been with you? Be quiet now, my sister; he is your brother. Don't take this thing to heart." And Tamar lived in her brother Absalom's house, a desolate woman.

21 When King David heard all this, he was furious. 22 Absalom never said a word to Amnon, either good or bad;[r] he hated[s] Amnon because he had disgraced his sister Tamar.

## Absalom Kills Amnon

23 Two years later, when Absalom's sheepshearers[t] were at Baal Hazor near the border of Ephraim, he invited all the king's sons to come there. 24 Absalom went to the king and said, "Your servant has had shearers come. Will the king and his officials please join me?"

25 "No, my son," the king replied. "All of us should not go; we would only be a burden to you." Although Absalom urged him, he still refused to go, but gave him his blessing.

26 Then Absalom said, "If not, please let my brother Amnon come with us."

The king asked him, "Why should he go with you?" 27 But Absalom urged him, so he sent with him Amnon and the rest of the king's sons.

28 Absalom ordered his men, "Listen! When Amnon is in high[u] spirits from drinking wine and I say to you, 'Strike Amnon down,' then kill him. Don't be afraid. Have not I given you this order? Be strong and brave." 29 So Absalom's men did to Amnon what Absalom had ordered. Then all the king's sons got up, mounted their mules and fled.

30 While they were on their way, the report came to David: "Absalom has struck down all the king's sons; not one of them is left." 31 The king stood up, tore[v] his clothes and lay down on the ground; and all his servants stood by with their clothes torn.

32 But Jonadab son of Shimeah, David's brother, said, "My lord should not think that they killed all the princes; only Amnon is dead. This has been Absalom's expressed intention ever since the day Amnon raped his sister Tamar. 33 My lord the king should not be concerned about the report that all the king's sons are dead. Only Amnon is dead."

34 Meanwhile, Absalom had fled.

Now the man standing watch looked up and saw many people on the road west of him, coming down the side of the hill. The watchman went and told the king, "I see men in the direction of Horonaim, on the side of the hill."[b]

35 Jonadab said to the king, "See, the king's sons are here; it has happened just as your servant said."

36 As he finished speaking, the king's sons came in, wailing loudly. The king, too, and all his servants wept very bitterly.

37 Absalom fled and went to Talmai[w] son of Ammihud, the king of Geshur. But King David mourned for his son every day.

38 After Absalom fled and went to Geshur, he stayed there three years. 39 And the spirit of the king[c] longed to go to Absalom, for he was consoled[x] concerning Amnon's death.

## Absalom Returns to Jerusalem

14 Joab son of Zeruiah knew that the king's heart longed for Absalom. 2 So Joab sent someone to Tekoa[y] and had a wise woman brought from there. He said to her, "Pretend you are in mourning. Dress in mourning clothes, and don't use any cosmetic lotions. Act like a woman who has spent many days grieving for the dead. 3 Then go to the king and speak these words to him." And Joab[z] put the words in her mouth.

4 When the woman from Tekoa went[d] to the king, she fell with her face to the ground to pay him honor, and she said, "Help me, O king!"

5 The king asked her, "What is troubling you?"

She said, "I am indeed a widow; my husband is dead. 6 I your servant had two sons. They got into a fight with each other in the

**13:19** q Jos 7:6; 1Sa 4:12; Est 4:1
**13:22** r Ge 31:24 s Lev 19:17–18; 1Jn 2:9–11
**13:23** t 1Sa 25:7
**13:28** u Jdg 19:6,9,22; 1Sa 25:36
**13:31** v 2Sa 1:11; 12:16
**13:37** w 2Sa 3:3
**13:39** x 2Sa 12:19–23
**14:2** y 2Ch 11:6; Am 1:1
**14:3** z ver 19

[a] 19 The meaning of the Hebrew for this word is uncertain. [b] 34 Septuagint; Hebrew does not have this sentence.
[c] 39 Dead Sea Scrolls and some Septuagint manuscripts; Masoretic Text *But ⌊the spirit of⌋ David the king* [d] 4 Many Hebrew manuscripts, Septuagint, Vulgate and Syriac; most Hebrew manuscripts *spoke*

# Tamar

## A Violated Woman

Tamar is a role model for any woman who has ever tried to do right but was treated wrongly. From the account of Amnon and Tamar, it appears that Tamar was a respectable young woman who wanted to play by the rules. When her father, King David, instructed her to make a meal for her half brother Amnon, Tamar did just as she was told (see 2Sa 13:7–8). When her unscrupulous brother told her to serve him alone in his bedroom, Tamar did as she was instructed (see vv. 8–10). Even as Amnon grabbed her, Tamar pleaded with him to stop and follow the rules (see vv. 12–14). She told him that if he would just ask the king for her hand in marriage, they could be married and have sex "the right way." While Amnon *thought* he was in love with her, we see that Amnon used her to gratify his immediate desires and then despised her.

Many of us are in situations like Tamar's. We've tried to live according to God's Word; we've obeyed the laws of the land, but somehow we still keep getting violated. Someone betrays our trust, someone manipulates our generosity, and before we know it, we're left living with the consequences of other people's poor choices and sinful acts.

Second Samuel 13:20 describes what happened to Tamar after the rape. She could not marry, so she lived with her brother Absalom as a desolate, broken and violated woman. What can we learn from this tragic story?

While it's hard to find anything positive here, it does force us to rethink how we treat victims. Do we cast aside those who struggle in life and live desolate, broken lives? Or do we remind them of the healing power of Christ? Do we share the stories of how Jesus took the time to speak to those who were the castaways of society? Do we show the same love Christ showed to the downtrodden? With the love of Christ, we who try to do right and end up getting wronged do not have to live defeated lives. Our brokenness can be restored and our tragedies can become testimonies of the true, unconditional love of Christ. Let Tamar's story remind us to extend a hand and the love of Jesus to those who have been violated in any way.

—K. Washington

### reflection

*How do you treat your sisters who are struggling?*

*What can you do today to help someone who has been victimized?*

### read

2 Samuel 13.

See also the Inspire Notes "Sexual Abuse" and "Overcoming Abuse," and the Women of the Bible Notes "Dinah: An Abused Woman" and "The Levite's Concubine: Broken Pieces."

For the next Women of the Bible note, go to page 387.

**14:7** a Nu 35:19 b Mt 21:38 c Dt 19:10–13
**14:9** d 1Sa 25:24 e Mt 27:25 f 1Ki 2:33
**14:11** g Nu 35:12,21 h 1Sa 14:45
**14:13** i 2Sa 12:7; 1Ki 20:40 j 2Sa 13:38–39
**14:14** k Heb 9:27 l Nu 35:15,25–28; Job 34:15
**14:17** m ver 20; 2Sa 19:27
**14:19** n ver 3
**14:20** o ver 17; 2Sa 19:27
**14:27** p 2Sa 18:18

field, and no one was there to separate them. One struck the other and killed him. [7]Now the whole clan has risen up against your servant; they say, 'Hand over the one who struck his brother down, so that we may put him to death[a] for the life of his brother whom he killed; then we will get rid of the heir[b] as well.' They would put out the only burning coal I have left,[c] leaving my husband neither name nor descendant on the face of the earth."

[8]The king said to the woman, "Go home, and I will issue an order in your behalf."

[9]But the woman from Tekoa said to him, "My lord the king, let the blame[d] rest on me and on my father's family,[e] and let the king and his throne be without guilt.[f]"

[10]The king replied, "If anyone says anything to you, bring him to me, and he will not bother you again."

[11]She said, "Then let the king invoke the LORD his God to prevent the avenger[g] of blood from adding to the destruction, so that my son will not be destroyed."

"As surely as the LORD lives," he said, "not one hair of your son's head will fall to the ground.[h]"

[12]Then the woman said, "Let your servant speak a word to my lord the king."

"Speak," he replied.

[13]The woman said, "Why then have you devised a thing like this against the people of God? When the king says this, does he not convict himself,[i] for the king has not brought back his banished son?[j] [14]Like water spilled on the ground, which cannot be recovered, so we must die.[k] But God does not take away life; instead, he devises ways so that a banished person[l] may not remain estranged from him.

[15]"And now I have come to say this to my lord the king because the people have made me afraid. Your servant thought, 'I will speak to the king; perhaps he will do what his servant asks. [16]Perhaps the king will agree to deliver his servant from the hand of the man who is trying to cut off both me and my son from the inheritance God gave us.'

[17]"And now your servant says, 'May the word of my lord the king bring me rest, for my lord the king is like an angel[m] of God in discerning good and evil. May the LORD your God be with you.'"

[18]Then the king said to the woman, "Do not keep from me the answer to what I am going to ask you."

"Let my lord the king speak," the woman said.

[19]The king asked, "Isn't the hand of Joab[n] with you in all this?"

The woman answered, "As surely as you live, my lord the king, no one can turn to the right or to the left from anything my lord the king says. Yes, it was your servant Joab who instructed me to do this and who put all these words into the mouth of your servant. [20]Your servant Joab did this to change the present situation. My lord has wisdom like that of an angel of God—he knows everything that happens in the land.[o]"

[21]The king said to Joab, "Very well, I will do it. Go, bring back the young man Absalom."

[22]Joab fell with his face to the ground to pay him honor, and he blessed the king. Joab said, "Today your servant knows that he has found favor in your eyes, my lord the king, because the king has granted his servant's request."

[23]Then Joab went to Geshur and brought Absalom back to Jerusalem. [24]But the king said, "He must go to his own house; he must not see my face." So Absalom went to his own house and did not see the face of the king.

[25]In all Israel there was not a man so highly praised for his handsome appearance as Absalom. From the top of his head to the sole of his foot there was no blemish in him. [26]Whenever he cut the hair of his head—he used to cut his hair from time to time when it became too heavy for him—he would weigh it, and its weight was two hundred shekels[a] by the royal standard.

[27]Three sons[p] and a daughter were born to Absalom. The daughter's name was Tamar, and she became a beautiful woman.

[28]Absalom lived two years in Jerusalem without seeing the king's face. [29]Then Absalom sent for Joab in order to send him to the king, but Joab refused to come to him. So he sent a second time, but he refused to come.

[a]26 That is, about 5 pounds (about 2.3 kilograms)

**14:32** q 1Sa 20:8
**14:33** r Ge 33:4; Lk 15:20
**15:1** s 2Sa 12:11 t 1Ki 1:5
**15:2** u 2Sa 19:8
**15:4** v Jdg 9:29
**15:6** w Ro 16:18
**15:8** x 2Sa 13:37–38 y Ge 28:20

30 Then he said to his servants, "Look, Joab's
field is next to mine, and he has barley there.
Go and set it on fire." So Absalom's servants
set the field on fire.
31 Then Joab did go to Absalom's house
and he said to him, "Why have your ser-
vants set my field on fire?"
32 Absalom said to Joab, "Look, I sent
word to you and said, 'Come here so I can
send you to the king to ask, "Why have I
come from Geshur? It would be better for
me if I were still there!"' Now then, I want
to see the king's face, and if I am guilty of
anything, let him put me to death."[q]
33 So Joab went to the king and told him
this. Then the king summoned Absalom,
and he came in and bowed down with his
face to the ground before the king. And the
king kissed[r] Absalom.

## Absalom's Conspiracy

15 In the course of time,[s] Absalom
provided himself with a chariot[t]
and horses and with fifty men to run ahead
of him. 2 He would get up early and stand by
the side of the road leading to the city gate.[u]
Whenever anyone came with a complaint to
be placed before the king for a decision, Ab-
salom would call out to him, "What town are
you from?" He would answer, "Your servant
is from one of the tribes of Israel." 3 Then Ab-
salom would say to him, "Look, your claims
are valid and proper, but there is no repre-
sentative of the king to hear you." 4 And Ab-
salom would add, "If only I were appointed
judge in the land![v] Then everyone who has
a complaint or case could come to me and I
would see that he gets justice."
5 Also, whenever anyone approached him
to bow down before him, Absalom would
reach out his hand, take hold of him and
kiss him. 6 Absalom behaved in this way
toward all the Israelites who came to the
king asking for justice, and so he stole the
hearts[w] of the men of Israel.
7 At the end of four[a] years, Absalom said
to the king, "Let me go to Hebron and ful-
fill a vow I made to the LORD. 8 While your
servant was living at Geshur[x] in Aram, I
made this vow:[y] 'If the LORD takes me back
to Jerusalem, I will worship the LORD in He-
bron.[b]'"
9 The king said to him, "Go in peace." So
he went to Hebron.
10 Then Absalom sent secret messengers
throughout the tribes of Israel to say, "As
soon as you hear the sound of the trumpets,
then say, 'Absalom is king in Hebron.'"
11 Two hundred men from Jerusalem had ac-
companied Absalom. They had been invited
as guests and went quite innocently, know-
ing nothing about the matter. 12 While Absa-
lom was offering sacrifices, he also sent for
Ahithophel[z] the Gilonite, David's counselor,
to come from Giloh,[a] his hometown. And so
the conspiracy gained strength, and Absa-
lom's following kept on increasing.[b]

## David Flees

13 A messenger came and told David,
"The hearts of the men of Israel are with
Absalom."
14 Then David said to all his officials who
were with him in Jerusalem, "Come! We
must flee,[c] or none of us will escape from Ab-
salom.[d] We must leave immediately, or he
will move quickly to overtake us and bring
ruin upon us and put the city to the sword."
15 The king's officials answered him,
"Your servants are ready to do whatever our
lord the king chooses."
16 The king set out, with his entire house-
hold following him; but he left ten concu-
bines[e] to take care of the palace. 17 So the
king set out, with all the people following
him, and they halted at a place some dis-
tance away. 18 All his men marched past him,
along with all the Kerethites[f] and Pelethites;
and all the six hundred Gittites who had ac-
companied him from Gath marched before
the king.
19 The king said to Ittai[g] the Gittite,
"Why should you come along with us? Go
back and stay with King Absalom. You are
a foreigner, an exile from your homeland.
20 You came only yesterday. And today shall
I make you wander[h] about with us, when I
do not know where I am going? Go back, and
take your countrymen. May kindness and
faithfulness be with you."

**15:12** z ver 31,34 a Jos 15:51 b Ps 3:1
**15:14** c Ps 3 Title d 2Sa 19:9
**15:16** e 2Sa 16:21–22
**15:18** f 2Sa 8:18
**15:19** g 2Sa 18:2
**15:20** h 1Sa 23:13

[a] 7 Some Septuagint manuscripts, Syriac and Josephus; Hebrew *forty* [b] 8 Some Septuagint manuscripts; Hebrew does not have *in Hebron.*

**15:21** i Ru 1:16–17
**15:25** j Ps 43:3
**15:26** k 1Sa 3:18
**15:27** l 1Sa 9:9; m 2Sa 17:17
**15:28** n 2Sa 17:16
**15:30** o Est 6:12; Isa 20:2–4
**15:31** p 2Sa 16:23; 17:14,23
**15:32** q Jos 16:2
**15:33** r 2Sa 19:35

21 But Ittai replied to the king, "As surely as the LORD lives, and as my lord the king lives, wherever my lord the king may be, whether it means life or death, there will your servant be."[i]

22 David said to Ittai, "Go ahead, march on." So Ittai the Gittite marched on with all his men and the families that were with him.

23 The whole countryside wept aloud as all the people passed by. The king also crossed the Kidron Valley, and all the people moved on toward the desert.

24 Zadok was there, too, and all the Levites who were with him were carrying the ark of the covenant of God. They set down the ark of God, and Abiathar offered sacrifices[a] until all the people had finished leaving the city.

25 Then the king said to Zadok, "Take the ark of God back into the city. If I find favor in the LORD's eyes, he will bring me back and let me see it and his dwelling place[j] again. 26 But if he says, 'I am not pleased with you,' then I am ready; let him do to me whatever seems good to him.[k]"

27 The king also said to Zadok the priest, "Aren't you a seer?[l] Go back to the city in peace, with your son Ahimaaz and Jonathan[m] son of Abiathar. You and Abiathar take your two sons with you. 28 I will wait at the fords[n] in the desert until word comes from you to inform me." 29 So Zadok and Abiathar took the ark of God back to Jerusalem and stayed there.

30 But David continued up the Mount of Olives, weeping as he went; his head[o] was covered and he was barefoot. All the people with him covered their heads too and were weeping as they went up. 31 Now David had been told, "Ahithophel[p] is among the conspirators with Absalom." So David prayed, "O LORD, turn Ahithophel's counsel into foolishness."

32 When David arrived at the summit, where people used to worship God, Hushai the Arkite[q] was there to meet him, his robe torn and dust on his head. 33 David said to him, "If you go with me, you will be a burden[r] to me. 34 But if you return to the city and say to Absalom, 'I will be your servant, O king; I was your father's servant in the past, but now I will be your servant,'[s] then you can help me by frustrating Ahithophel's advice. 35 Won't the priests Zadok and Abiathar be there with you? Tell them anything you hear in the king's palace.[t] 36 Their two sons, Ahimaaz son of Zadok and Jonathan[u] son of Abiathar, are there with them. Send them to me with anything you hear."

37 So David's friend Hushai[v] arrived at Jerusalem as Absalom was entering the city.

## David and Ziba

16 When David had gone a short distance beyond the summit, there was Ziba,[w] the steward of Mephibosheth, waiting to meet him. He had a string of donkeys saddled and loaded with two hundred loaves of bread, a hundred cakes of raisins, a hundred cakes of figs and a skin of wine.

2 The king asked Ziba, "Why have you brought these?"

Ziba answered, "The donkeys are for the king's household to ride on, the bread and fruit are for the men to eat, and the wine is to refresh[x] those who become exhausted in the desert."

3 The king then asked, "Where is your master's grandson?"[y]

Ziba said to him, "He is staying in Jerusalem, because he thinks, 'Today the house of Israel will give me back my grandfather's kingdom.' "

4 Then the king said to Ziba, "All that belonged to Mephibosheth is now yours."

"I humbly bow," Ziba said. "May I find favor in your eyes, my lord the king."

## Shimei Curses David

5 As King David approached Bahurim, a man from the same clan as Saul's family came out from there. His name was Shimei[z] son of Gera, and he cursed as he came out. 6 He pelted David and all the king's officials with stones, though all the troops and the special guard were on David's right and left. 7 As he cursed, Shimei said, "Get out, get out, you man of blood, you scoundrel! 8 The LORD has repaid you for all the blood you shed in the household of Saul, in whose place you have reigned. The LORD has handed the

**15:34** s 2Sa 16:19
**15:35** t 2Sa 17:15–16
**15:36** u ver 27
**15:37** v 2Sa 16:16–17; 1Ch 27:33
**16:1** w 2Sa 9:1–13
**16:2** x 2Sa 17:27–29
**16:3** y 2Sa 19:26–27
**16:5** z 2Sa 19:16–23; 1Ki 2:8–9,36,44

[a] 24 Or *Abiathar went up*

kingdom over to your son Absalom. You have come to ruin because you are a man of blood!"

9 Then Abishai son of Zeruiah said to the king, "Why should this dead dog curse my lord the king? Let me go over and cut off his head."

10 But the king said, "What do you and I have in common, you sons of Zeruiah?[a] If he is cursing because the LORD said to him, 'Curse David,' who can ask, 'Why do you do this?' "[b]

11 David then said to Abishai and all his officials, "My son,[c] who is of my own flesh, is trying to take my life. How much more, then, this Benjamite! Leave him alone; let him curse, for the LORD has told him to. 12 It may be that the LORD will see my distress and repay me with good[d] for the cursing I am receiving today."

13 So David and his men continued along the road while Shimei was going along the hillside opposite him, cursing as he went and throwing stones at him and showering him with dirt. 14 The king and all the people with him arrived at their destination exhausted. And there he refreshed himself.

*My beloved child,*

*I'm with you—even when you're experiencing trials. Continue to follow me; don't give up.*

*Love always,*
*Your "Abba"*

2 SAMUEL 16:5–14

## The Advice of Ahithophel and Hushai

15 Meanwhile, Absalom[e] and all the men of Israel came to Jerusalem, and Ahithophel was with him. 16 Then Hushai[f] the Arkite, David's friend, went to Absalom and said to him, "Long live the king! Long live the king!"

17 Absalom asked Hushai, "Is this the love you show your friend? Why didn't you go with your friend?"[g]

18 Hushai said to Absalom, "No, the one chosen by the LORD, by these people, and by all the men of Israel—his I will be, and I will remain with him. 19 Furthermore, whom should I serve? Should I not serve the son? Just as I served your father, so I will serve you."[h]

20 Absalom said to Ahithophel, "Give us your advice. What should we do?"

21 Ahithophel answered, "Lie with your father's concubines whom he left to take care of the palace. Then all Israel will hear that you have made yourself a stench in your father's nostrils, and the hands of everyone with you will be strengthened." 22 So they pitched a tent for Absalom on the roof, and he lay with his father's concubines in the sight of all Israel.[i]

23 Now in those days the advice Ahithophel gave was like that of one who inquires of God. That was how both David[j] and Absalom regarded all of Ahithophel's advice.

17 Ahithophel said to Absalom, "I would[a] choose twelve thousand men and set out tonight in pursuit of David. 2 I would[b] attack him while he is weary and weak.[k] I would[b] strike him with terror, and then all the people with him will flee. I would[b] strike down only the king[l] 3 and bring all the people back to you. The death of the man you seek will mean the return of all; all the people will be unharmed." 4 This plan seemed good to Absalom and to all the elders of Israel.

5 But Absalom said, "Summon also Hushai[m] the Arkite, so we can hear what he has to say." 6 When Hushai came to him, Absalom said, "Ahithophel has given this advice. Should we do what he says? If not, give us your opinion."

7 Hushai replied to Absalom, "The advice Ahithophel has given is not good this time. 8 You know your father and his men; they are fighters, and as fierce as a wild bear robbed of her cubs.[n] Besides, your father is an experienced fighter; he will not spend the night

[a]1 Or *Let me* [b]2 Or *will*

**16:10** a 2Sa 19:22 b Ro 9:20
**16:11** c 2Sa 12:11
**16:12** d Dt 23:5; Ro 8:28
**16:15** e 2Sa 15:37
**16:16** f 2Sa 15:37
**16:17** g 2Sa 19:25
**16:19** h 2Sa 15:34
**16:22** i 2Sa 12:11–12
**16:23** j 2Sa 15:12
**17:2** k 2Sa 16:14 l 1Ki 22:31
**17:5** m 2Sa 15:32
**17:8** n Hos 13:8

with the troops. [9]Even now, he is hidden in a cave or some other place. If he should attack your troops first,[a] whoever hears about it will say, 'There has been a slaughter among the troops who follow Absalom.' [10]Then even the bravest soldier, whose heart is like the heart of a lion, will melt[o] with fear, for all Israel knows that your father is a fighter and that those with him are brave.

[11]"So I advise you: Let all Israel, from Dan to Beersheba—as numerous as the sand on the seashore—be gathered to you, with you yourself leading them into battle. [12]Then we will attack him wherever he may be found, and we will fall on him as dew settles on the ground. Neither he nor any of his men will be left alive. [13]If he withdraws into a city, then all Israel will bring ropes to that city, and we will drag it down to the valley until not even a piece of it can be found."

[14]Absalom and all the men of Israel said, "The advice of Hushai the Arkite is better than that of Ahithophel." For the LORD had determined to frustrate[p] the good advice of Ahithophel in order to bring disaster[q] on Absalom.

[15]Hushai told Zadok and Abiathar, the priests, "Ahithophel has advised Absalom and the elders of Israel to do such and such, but I have advised them to do so and so. [16]Now send a message immediately and tell David, 'Do not spend the night at the fords in the desert;[r] cross over without fail, or the king and all the people with him will be swallowed up.' "

[17]Jonathan[s] and Ahimaaz were staying at En Rogel.[t] A servant girl was to go and inform them, and they were to go and tell King David, for they could not risk being seen entering the city. [18]But a young man saw them and told Absalom. So the two of them left quickly and went to the house of a man in Bahurim.[u] He had a well in his courtyard, and they climbed down into it. [19]His wife took a covering and spread it out over the opening of the well and scattered grain over it. No one knew anything about it.[v]

[20]When Absalom's men came to the woman[w] at the house, they asked, "Where are Ahimaaz and Jonathan?"

The woman answered them, "They crossed over the brook."[b] The men searched but found no one, so they returned to Jerusalem.

[21]After the men had gone, the two climbed out of the well and went to inform King David. They said to him, "Set out and cross the river at once; Ahithophel has advised such and such against you." [22]So David and all the people with him set out and crossed the Jordan. By daybreak, no one was left who had not crossed the Jordan.

[23]When Ahithophel saw that his advice[x] had not been followed, he saddled his donkey and set out for his house in his hometown. He put his house in order[y] and then hanged himself. So he died and was buried in his father's tomb.

[24]David went to Mahanaim,[z] and Absalom crossed the Jordan with all the men of Israel. [25]Absalom had appointed Amasa[a] over the army in place of Joab. Amasa was the son of a man named Jether,[c][b] an Israelite[d] who had married Abigail,[e] the daughter of Nahash and sister of Zeruiah the mother of Joab. [26]The Israelites and Absalom camped in the land of Gilead.

[27]When David came to Mahanaim, Shobi son of Nahash from Rabbah[c] of the Ammonites, and Makir son of Ammiel from Lo Debar, and Barzillai[d] the Gileadite from Rogelim [28]brought bedding and bowls and articles of pottery. They also brought wheat and barley, flour and roasted grain, beans and lentils,[f] [29]honey and curds, sheep, and cheese from cows' milk for David and his people to eat. For they said, "The people have become hungry and tired and thirsty in the desert.[e]"

## Absalom's Death

**18** David mustered the men who were with him and appointed over them commanders of thousands and commanders of hundreds. [2]David sent the troops out[f]—a third under the command of Joab, a third under Joab's brother Abishai son

**17:10** o Jos 2:9,11
**17:14** p 2Sa 15:34 q Ps 9:16
**17:16** r 2Sa 15:28
**17:17** s 2Sa 15:27,36 t Jos 15:7; 18:16
**17:18** u 2Sa 16:5
**17:19** v Jos 2:6
**17:20** w Jos 2:3–5
**17:23** x 2Sa 15:12 y 2Ki 20:1; Mt 27:5
**17:24** z Ge 32:2; 2Sa 2:8
**17:25** a 2Sa 19:13 b 1Ch 2:13–17
**17:27** c 2Sa 10:1–2; 12:26,29 d 2Sa 19:31–39; 1Ki 2:7
**17:29** e 2Sa 16:2
**18:2** f 1Sa 11:11

[a]9 Or *When some of the men fall at the first attack* [b]20 Or *"They passed by the sheep pen toward the water."* [c]25 Hebrew *Ithra,* a variant of *Jether* [d]25 Hebrew and some Septuagint manuscripts; other Septuagint manuscripts (see also 1 Chron. 2:17) *Ishmaelite* or *Jezreelite* [e]25 Hebrew *Abigal,* a variant of *Abigail* [f]28 Most Septuagint manuscripts and Syriac; Hebrew *lentils, and roasted grain*

**18:2** g 2Sa 15:19
**18:3** h 2Sa 21:17
**18:6** i Jos 17:18
**18:9** j 2Sa 14:26

of Zeruiah, and a third under Ittai[g] the Gittite. The king told the troops, "I myself will surely march out with you."

3But the men said, "You must not go out; if we are forced to flee, they won't care about us. Even if half of us die, they won't care; but you are worth ten thousand of us.[a] It would be better now for you to give us support from the city."[h]

4The king answered, "I will do whatever seems best to you."

So the king stood beside the gate while all the men marched out in units of hundreds and of thousands. 5The king commanded Joab, Abishai and Ittai, "Be gentle with the young man Absalom for my sake." And all the troops heard the king giving orders concerning Absalom to each of the commanders.

6The army marched into the field to fight Israel, and the battle took place in the forest[i] of Ephraim. 7There the army of Israel was defeated by David's men, and the casualties that day were great—twenty thousand men. 8The battle spread out over the whole countryside, and the forest claimed more lives that day than the sword.

9Now Absalom happened to meet David's men. He was riding his mule, and as the mule went under the thick branches of a large oak, Absalom's head[j] got caught in the tree. He was left hanging in midair, while the mule he was riding kept on going.

10When one of the men saw this, he told Joab, "I just saw Absalom hanging in an oak tree."

11Joab said to the man who had told him this, "What! You saw him? Why didn't you strike him to the ground right there? Then I would have had to give you ten shekels[b] of silver and a warrior's belt."

12But the man replied, "Even if a thousand shekels[c] were weighed out into my hands, I would not lift my hand against the king's son. In our hearing the king commanded you and Abishai and Ittai, 'Protect the young man Absalom for my sake.[d]' 13And if I had put my life in jeopardy[e]—and nothing is hidden from the king—you would have kept your distance from me."

14Joab[k] said, "I'm not going to wait like this for you." So he took three javelins in his hand and plunged them into Absalom's heart while Absalom was still alive in the oak tree. 15And ten of Joab's armor-bearers surrounded Absalom, struck him and killed him.

16Then Joab[l] sounded the trumpet, and the troops stopped pursuing Israel, for Joab halted them. 17They took Absalom, threw him into a big pit in the forest and piled up[m] a large heap of rocks[n] over him. Meanwhile, all the Israelites fled to their homes.

18During his lifetime Absalom had taken a pillar and erected it in the King's Valley[o] as a monument[p] to himself, for he thought, "I have no son[q] to carry on the memory of my name." He named the pillar after himself, and it is called Absalom's Monument to this day.

## David Mourns

19Now Ahimaaz[r] son of Zadok said, "Let me run and take the news to the king that the LORD has delivered him from the hand of his enemies.[s]"

20"You are not the one to take the news today," Joab told him. "You may take the news another time, but you must not do so today, because the king's son is dead."

21Then Joab said to a Cushite, "Go, tell the king what you have seen." The Cushite bowed down before Joab and ran off.

22Ahimaaz son of Zadok again said to Joab, "Come what may, please let me run behind the Cushite."

But Joab replied, "My son, why do you want to go? You don't have any news that will bring you a reward."

23He said, "Come what may, I want to run."

So Joab said, "Run!" Then Ahimaaz ran by way of the plain[f] and outran the Cushite.

24While David was sitting between the inner and outer gates, the watchman[t] went up to the roof of the gateway by the wall. As he looked out, he saw a man running alone.

**18:14** k 2Sa 14:30
**18:16** l 2Sa 2:28; 20:22
**18:17** m Jos 7:26 n Jos 8:29
**18:18** o Ge 14:17 p 1Sa 15:12 q 2Sa 14:27
**18:19** r 2Sa 15:36 s ver 31
**18:24** t 2Sa 19:8; 2Ki 9:17

[a]3 Two Hebrew manuscripts, some Septuagint manuscripts and Vulgate; most Hebrew manuscripts *care; for now there are ten thousand like us* [b]11 That is, about 4 ounces (about 115 grams) [c]12 That is, about 25 pounds (about 11 kilograms) [d]12 A few Hebrew manuscripts, Septuagint, Vulgate and Syriac; most Hebrew manuscripts may be translated *Absalom, whoever you may be.* [e]13 Or *Otherwise, if I had acted treacherously toward him* [f]23 That is, the plain of the Jordan

## The African Presence

**2 Samuel 18:21–23,31–32**

A Cushite in David's army was sent to bring David the bad news of his son Absalom's demise.

18:32
u 1Sa 25:26

25The watchman called out to the king and reported it.

The king said, "If he is alone, he must have good news." And the man came closer and closer.

26Then the watchman saw another man running, and he called down to the gatekeeper, "Look, another man running alone!"

The king said, "He must be bringing good news, too."

27The watchman said, "It seems to me that the first one runs like Ahimaaz son of Zadok."

"He's a good man," the king said. "He comes with good news."

28Then Ahimaaz called out to the king, "All is well!" He bowed down before the king with his face to the ground and said, "Praise be to the LORD your God! He has delivered up the men who lifted their hands against my lord the king."

29The king asked, "Is the young man Absalom safe?"

Ahimaaz answered, "I saw great confusion just as Joab was about to send the king's servant and me, your servant, but I don't know what it was."

30The king said, "Stand aside and wait here." So he stepped aside and stood there.

31Then the Cushite arrived and said, "My lord the king, hear the good news! The LORD has delivered you today from all who rose up against you."

32The king asked the Cushite, "Is the young man Absalom safe?"

The Cushite replied, "May the enemies of my lord the king and all who rise up to harm you be like that young man."[u]

33The king was shaken. He went up to the room over the gateway and wept. As he went, he said: "O my son Absalom! My son, my son Absalom! If only I had died[v] instead of you—O Absalom, my son, my son!"[w]

18:33
v Ex 32:32
w 2Sa 19:4; Ro 9:3

19:8
x 2Sa 15:2

19 Joab was told, "The king is weeping and mourning for Absalom." 2And for the whole army the victory that day was turned into mourning, because on that day the troops heard it said, "The king is grieving for his son." 3The men stole into the city that day as men steal in who are ashamed when they flee from battle. 4The king covered his face and cried aloud, "O my son Absalom! O Absalom, my son, my son!"

5Then Joab went into the house to the king and said, "Today you have humiliated all your men, who have just saved your life and the lives of your sons and daughters and the lives of your wives and concubines. 6You love those who hate you and hate those who love you. You have made it clear today that the commanders and their men mean nothing to you. I see that you would be pleased if Absalom were alive today and all of us were dead. 7Now go out and encourage your men. I swear by the LORD that if you don't go out, not a man will be left with you by nightfall. This will be worse for you than all the calamities that have come upon you from your youth till now."

8So the king got up and took his seat in the gateway. When the men were told, "The king is sitting in the gateway,[x]" they all came before him.

### David Returns to Jerusalem

Meanwhile, the Israelites had fled to their homes. 9Throughout the tribes of Israel, the people were all arguing with each other, saying, "The king delivered us from the hand of our enemies; he is the one who rescued

**19:9** y 2Sa 8:1–14 z 2Sa 15:14
**19:13** a 2Sa 17:25
**19:15** b Jos 5:9
**19:16** c 2Sa 16:5–13; 1Ki 2:8
**19:17** d 2Sa 16:1–2
**19:19** e 1Sa 22:15; 2Sa 16:6–8
**19:21** f Ex 22:28
**19:22** g 2Sa 16:10 h 1Sa 11:13

us from the hand of the Philistines.[y] But now he has fled the country because of Absalom;[z] 10and Absalom, whom we anointed to rule over us, has died in battle. So why do you say nothing about bringing the king back?"

11King David sent this message to Zadok and Abiathar, the priests: "Ask the elders of Judah, 'Why should you be the last to bring the king back to his palace, since what is being said throughout Israel has reached the king at his quarters? 12You are my brothers, my own flesh and blood. So why should you be the last to bring back the king?' 13And say to Amasa,[a] 'Are you not my own flesh and blood? May God deal with me, be it ever so severely, if from now on you are not the commander of my army in place of Joab.' "

14He won over the hearts of all the men of Judah as though they were one man. They sent word to the king, "Return, you and all your men." 15Then the king returned and went as far as the Jordan.

Now the men of Judah had come to Gilgal[b] to go out and meet the king and bring him across the Jordan. 16Shimei[c] son of Gera, the Benjamite from Bahurim, hurried down with the men of Judah to meet King David. 17With him were a thousand Benjamites, along with Ziba,[d] the steward of Saul's household, and his fifteen sons and twenty servants. They rushed to the Jordan, where the king was. 18They crossed at the ford to take the king's household over and to do whatever he wished.

When Shimei son of Gera crossed the Jordan, he fell prostrate before the king 19and said to him, "May my lord not hold me guilty. Do not remember how your servant did wrong on the day my lord the king left Jerusalem.[e] May the king put it out of his mind. 20For I your servant know that I have sinned, but today I have come here as the first of the whole house of Joseph to come down and meet my lord the king."

21Then Abishai son of Zeruiah said, "Shouldn't Shimei be put to death for this? He cursed[f] the LORD's anointed."

22David replied, "What do you and I have in common, you sons of Zeruiah?[g] This day you have become my adversaries! Should anyone be put to death in Israel today?[h] Do I not know that today I am king over Israel?" 23So the king said to Shimei, "You shall not die." And the king promised him on oath.[i]

24Mephibosheth,[j] Saul's grandson, also went down to meet the king. He had not taken care of his feet or trimmed his mustache or washed his clothes from the day the king left until the day he returned safely. 25When he came from Jerusalem to meet the king, the king asked him, "Why didn't you go with me,[k] Mephibosheth?"

26He said, "My lord the king, since I your servant am lame, I said, 'I will have my donkey saddled and will ride on it, so I can go with the king.' But Ziba[l] my servant betrayed me. 27And he has slandered your servant to my lord the king. My lord the king is like an angel[m] of God; so do whatever pleases you. 28All my grandfather's descendants deserved nothing but death from my lord the king, but you gave your servant a place among those who eat at your table.[n] So what right do I have to make any more appeals to the king?"

29The king said to him, "Why say more? I order you and Ziba to divide the fields."

30Mephibosheth said to the king, "Let him take everything, now that my lord the king has arrived home safely."

31Barzillai[o] the Gileadite also came down from Rogelim to cross the Jordan with the king and to send him on his way from there. 32Now Barzillai was a very old man, eighty years of age. He had provided for the king during his stay in Mahanaim, for he was a very wealthy[p] man. 33The king said to Barzillai, "Cross over with me and stay with me in Jerusalem, and I will provide for you."

34But Barzillai answered the king, "How many more years will I live, that I should go up to Jerusalem with the king? 35I am now eighty[q] years old. Can I tell the difference between what is good and what is not? Can your servant taste what he eats and drinks? Can I still hear the voices of men and women singers? Why should your servant be an added burden to my lord the king? 36Your servant will cross over the Jordan with the king for a short distance, but why should the king reward me in this way? 37Let your servant return, that I may die in my own town near the tomb of my father[r] and mother. But here is your servant Kimham.[s]

**19:23** i 1Ki 2:8,42
**19:24** j 2Sa 9:6–10
**19:25** k 2Sa 16:17
**19:26** l 2Sa 9:2
**19:27** m 2Sa 14:17,20
**19:28** n 2Sa 9:7,13
**19:31** o 1Ki 2:7
**19:32** p 2Sa 17:27
**19:35** q Ps 90:10
**19:37** r 1Ki 2:7 s Jer 41:17

Let him cross over with my lord the king. Do for him whatever pleases you."

[38]The king said, "Kimham shall cross over with me, and I will do for him whatever pleases you. And anything you desire from me I will do for you."

[39]So all the people crossed the Jordan, and then the king crossed over. The king kissed Barzillai and gave him his blessing,[t] and Barzillai returned to his home.

[40]When the king crossed over to Gilgal, Kimham crossed with him. All the troops of Judah and half the troops of Israel had taken the king over.

[41]Soon all the men of Israel were coming to the king and saying to him, "Why did our brothers, the men of Judah, steal the king away and bring him and his household across the Jordan, together with all his men?"

[42]All the men of Judah answered the men of Israel, "We did this because the king is closely related to us. Why are you angry about it? Have we eaten any of the king's provisions? Have we taken anything for ourselves?"

[43]Then the men of Israel answered the men of Judah, "We have ten shares in the king; and besides, we have a greater claim on David than you have. So why do you treat us with contempt? Were we not the first to speak of bringing back our king?"

But the men of Judah responded even more harshly than the men of Israel.

## Sheba Rebels Against David

**20** Now a troublemaker named Sheba son of Bicri, a Benjamite, happened to be there. He sounded the trumpet and shouted,

"We have no share in David,[u]
  no part in Jesse's son![v]
Every man to his tent, O Israel!"

[2]So all the men of Israel deserted David to follow Sheba son of Bicri. But the men of Judah stayed by their king all the way from the Jordan to Jerusalem.

[3]When David returned to his palace in Jerusalem, he took the ten concubines[w] he had left to take care of the palace and put them in a house under guard. He provided for them, but did not lie with them. They were kept in confinement till the day of their death, living as widows.

[4]Then the king said to Amasa,[x] "Summon the men of Judah to come to me within three days, and be here yourself." [5]But when Amasa went to summon Judah, he took longer than the time the king had set for him.

[6]David said to Abishai, "Now Sheba son of Bicri will do us more harm than Absalom did. Take your master's men and pursue him, or he will find fortified cities and escape from us." [7]So Joab's men and the Kerethites[y] and Pelethites and all the mighty warriors went out under the command of Abishai. They marched out from Jerusalem to pursue Sheba son of Bicri.

[8]While they were at the great rock in Gibeon, Amasa came to meet them. Joab was wearing his military tunic, and strapped over it at his waist was a belt with a dagger in its sheath. As he stepped forward, it dropped out of its sheath.

[9]Joab said to Amasa, "How are you, my brother?" Then Joab took Amasa by the beard with his right hand to kiss him. [10]Amasa was not on his guard against the dagger[z] in Joab's[a] hand, and Joab plunged it into his belly, and his intestines spilled out on the ground. Without being stabbed again, Amasa died. Then Joab and his brother Abishai pursued Sheba son of Bicri.

[11]One of Joab's men stood beside Amasa and said, "Whoever favors Joab, and whoever is for David, let him follow Joab!" [12]Amasa lay wallowing in his blood in the middle of the road, and the man saw that all the troops came to a halt there. When he realized that everyone who came up to Amasa stopped, he dragged him from the road into a field and threw a garment over him. [13]After Amasa had been removed from the road, all the men went on with Joab to pursue Sheba son of Bicri.

[14]Sheba passed through all the tribes of Israel to Abel Beth Maacah[a] and through the entire region of the Berites, who gathered together and followed him. [15]All the troops with Joab came and besieged Sheba in Abel Beth Maacah.[b] They built a siege

**19:39** t Ge 31:55
**20:1** u 1Ki 12:16 v 2Ch 10:16
**20:3** w 2Sa 15:16; 16:21–22
**20:4** x 2Sa 19:13
**20:7** y 2Sa 8:18; 1Ki 1:38
**20:10** z 2Sa 2:23 a 1Ki 2:5
**20:15** b 1Ki 15:20; 2Ki 15:29

[a]14 Or *Abel, even Beth Maacah*; also in verse 15

**20:15** c 2Ki 19:32
**20:16** d 2Sa 14:2
**20:19** e 1Sa 26:19; 2Sa 21:3
**20:22** f Ecc 9:13
**20:23** g 2Sa 8:16–18
**20:24** h 1Ki 4:6
**20:25** i 2Sa 8:17
**21:1** j Ge 12:10
**21:2** k Jos 9:15

ramp[c] up to the city, and it stood against
the outer fortifications. While they were
battering the wall to bring it down, 16 a wise
woman[d] called from the city, "Listen! Lis-
ten! Tell Joab to come here so I can speak to
him." 17 He went toward her, and she asked,
"Are you Joab?"

"I am," he answered.

She said, "Listen to what your servant
has to say."

"I'm listening," he said.

18 She continued, "Long ago they used to
say, 'Get your answer at Abel,' and that set-
tled it. 19 We are the peaceful and faithful in
Israel. You are trying to destroy a city that is
a mother in Israel. Why do you want to swal-
low up the LORD's inheritance?"[e]

20 "Far be it from me!" Joab replied,
"Far be it from me to swallow up or de-
stroy! 21 That is not the case. A man named
Sheba son of Bicri, from the hill country
of Ephraim, has lifted up his hand against
the king, against David. Hand over this one
man, and I'll withdraw from the city."

The woman said to Joab, "His head will
be thrown to you from the wall."

22 Then the woman went to all the people
with her wise advice,[f] and they cut off the
head of Sheba son of Bicri and threw it to
Joab. So he sounded the trumpet, and his
men dispersed from the city, each returning
to his home. And Joab went back to the king
in Jerusalem.

23 Joab[g] was over Israel's entire army; Be-
naiah son of Jehoiada was over the Kereth-
ites and Pelethites; 24 Adoniram[a][h] was in
charge of forced labor; Jehoshaphat son of
Ahilud was recorder; 25 Sheva was secretary;
Zadok[i] and Abiathar were priests; 26 and Ira
the Jairite was David's priest.

## The Gibeonites Avenged

21 During the reign of David, there
was a famine[j] for three successive
years; so David sought the face of the LORD.
The LORD said, "It is on account of Saul and
his blood-stained house; it is because he put
the Gibeonites to death."

2 The king summoned the Gibeonites[k]
and spoke to them. (Now the Gibeonites
were not a part of Israel but were survivors
of the Amorites; the Israelites had sworn to
⌞spare⌟ them, but Saul in his zeal for Israel
and Judah had tried to annihilate them.)
3 David asked the Gibeonites, "What shall
I do for you? How shall I make amends so
that you will bless the LORD's inheritance?"[l]

4 The Gibeonites answered him, "We have
no right to demand silver or gold from Saul
or his family, nor do we have the right to put
anyone in Israel to death."

"What do you want me to do for you?"
David asked.

5 They answered the king, "As for the man
who destroyed us and plotted against us so
that we have been decimated and have no
place anywhere in Israel, 6 let seven of his
male descendants be given to us to be killed
and exposed[m] before the LORD at Gibeah of
Saul—the LORD's chosen[n] one."

So the king said, "I will give them to
you."

7 The king spared Mephibosheth[o] son of
Jonathan, the son of Saul, because of the
oath[p] before the LORD between David and
Jonathan son of Saul. 8 But the king took
Armoni and Mephibosheth, the two sons
of Aiah's daughter Rizpah,[q] whom she had
borne to Saul, together with the five sons
of Saul's daughter Merab,[b] whom she had
borne to Adriel son of Barzillai the Meho-
lathite. 9 He handed them over to the Gibe-
onites, who killed and exposed them on a
hill before the LORD. All seven of them fell
together; they were put to death during the
first days of the harvest, just as the barley
harvest was beginning.

10 Rizpah daughter of Aiah took sackcloth
and spread it out for herself on a rock. From
the beginning of the harvest till the rain
poured down from the heavens on the bod-
ies, she did not let the birds of the air touch
them by day or the wild animals by night.
11 When David was told what Aiah's daugh-
ter Rizpah, Saul's concubine, had done,
12 he went and took the bones of Saul[r] and
his son Jonathan from the citizens of Jabesh
Gilead. (They had taken them secretly from
the public square at Beth Shan, where the
Philistines had hung them after they struck

**21:3** l 1Sa 26:19; 2Sa 20:19
**21:6** m Nu 25:4; n 1Sa 10:24
**21:7** o 2Sa 4:4; p 1Sa 18:3; 20:8,15
**21:8** q 2Sa 3:7
**21:12** r 1Sa 31:11–13

[a]24 Some Septuagint manuscripts (see also 1 Kings 4:6 and 5:14); Hebrew *Adoram* [b]8 Two Hebrew manuscripts, some Septuagint manuscripts and Syriac (see also 1 Samuel 18:19); most Hebrew and Septuagint manuscripts *Michal*

**21:14**
s Jos 18:28
t Jos 7:26
u 2Sa 24:25

**21:17**
v 2Sa 18:3

**21:18**
w 1Ch 11:29; 20:4

**22:1**
x Ex 15:1; Jdg 5:1

Saul down on Gilboa.) 13 David brought the
bones of Saul and his son Jonathan from
there, and the bones of those who had been
killed and exposed were gathered up.
14 They buried the bones of Saul and his
son Jonathan in the tomb of Saul's father
Kish, at Zela[s] in Benjamin, and did every-
thing the king commanded. After that,[t] God
answered prayer[u] in behalf of the land.

## Wars Against the Philistines

15 Once again there was a battle between
the Philistines and Israel. David went down
with his men to fight against the Philistines,
and he became exhausted. 16 And Ishbi-
Benob, one of the descendants of Rapha,
whose bronze spearhead weighed three
hundred shekels[a] and who was armed with
a new ⌊sword⌋, said he would kill David.
17 But Abishai son of Zeruiah came to Da-
vid's rescue; he struck the Philistine down
and killed him. Then David's men swore to
him, saying, "Never again will you go out
with us to battle, so that the lamp of Israel
will not be extinguished.[v]"
18 In the course of time, there was another
battle with the Philistines, at Gob. At that
time Sibbecai[w] the Hushathite killed Saph,
one of the descendants of Rapha.
19 In another battle with the Philistines at
Gob, Elhanan son of Jaare-Oregim[b] the Beth-
lehemite killed Goliath[c] the Gittite, who had
a spear with a shaft like a weaver's rod.
20 In still another battle, which took
place at Gath, there was a huge man with
six fingers on each hand and six toes on
each foot—twenty-four in all. He also was
descended from Rapha. 21 When he taunted
Israel, Jonathan son of Shimeah, David's
brother, killed him.
22 These four were descendants of Rapha
in Gath, and they fell at the hands of David
and his men.

## David's Song of Praise

22 David sang[x] to the LORD the words
of this song when the LORD deliv-
ered him from the hand of all his enemies
and from the hand of Saul. 2 He said:

"The LORD is my rock, my fortress and my
deliverer;
3 my God is my rock, in whom I take
refuge,
my shield[y] and the horn[d][z] of my
salvation.
He is my stronghold,[a] my refuge and my
savior—
from violent men you save me.
4 I call to the LORD, who is worthy of praise,
and I am saved from my enemies.

5 "The waves of death swirled about me;
the torrents of destruction
overwhelmed me.
6 The cords of the grave[e][b] coiled around
me;
the snares of death confronted me.
7 In my distress[c] I called[d] to the LORD;
I called out to my God.
From his temple he heard my voice;
my cry came to his ears.

8 "The earth[e] trembled and quaked,
the foundations[f] of the heavens[f] shook;
they trembled because he was angry.
9 Smoke rose from his nostrils;
consuming fire[g] came from his mouth,
burning coals blazed out of it.
10 He parted the heavens and came down;
dark clouds[h] were under his feet.
11 He mounted the cherubim and flew;
he soared[g] on the wings of the wind.[i]
12 He made darkness his canopy around
him—
the dark[h] rain clouds of the sky.
13 Out of the brightness of his presence
bolts of lightning[j] blazed forth.
14 The LORD thundered[k] from heaven;
the voice of the Most High resounded.
15 He shot arrows and scattered ⌊the
enemies⌋,
bolts of lightning and routed them.
16 The valleys of the sea were exposed
and the foundations of the earth laid
bare
at the rebuke of the LORD,
at the blast of breath from his nostrils.

17 "He reached down from on high[l] and took
hold of me;

**22:3**
y Ge 15:1
z Lk 1:69
a Ps 9:9

**22:6**
b Ps 116:3

**22:7**
c Ps 120:1
d Ps 116:4

**22:8**
e Jdg 5:4
f Job 26:11

**22:9**
g Ps 97:3; Heb 12:29

**22:10**
h 1Ki 8:12

**22:11**
i Ps 104:3

**22:13**
j ver 9

**22:14**
k 1Sa 2:10

**22:17**
l Ps 144:7

[a]16 That is, about 7 1/2 pounds (about 3.5 kilograms) [b]19 Or *son of Jair the weaver* [c]19 Hebrew and Septuagint; 1 Chron. 20:5 *son of Jair killed Lahmi the brother of Goliath* [d]3 *Horn* here symbolizes strength. [e]6 Hebrew *Sheol* [f]8 Hebrew; Vulgate and Syriac (see also Psalm 18:7) *mountains* [g]11 Many Hebrew manuscripts (see also Psalm 18:10); most Hebrew manuscripts *appeared* [h]12 Septuagint and Vulgate (see also Psalm 18:11); Hebrew *massed*

# Rizpah

## A Grieving Mother

Rizpah is a relatively unknown woman of the Scriptures, yet her actions speaker louder than words. In Rizpah we see a mother who demonstrated love and compassion in order to preserve the remains of not only her two sons, but also her stepdaughter's five sons. She took sackcloth—a symbol of mourning and distress—and placed it on a rock for herself. The men had been put to death at the beginning of the barley harvest in April (see 2Sa 21:9). Rizpah kept watch over the bodies to protect them from the vultures and jackals "till the rain poured down from the heavens" (2Sa 21:10). Though this may have been a special God-sent rain, marking the end of God's judgment via drought, alternatively this reference could have been to the normal rainy season in October. Seven men were executed for their father's/grandfather's sin; for as long as six months, Rizpah dealt with their deaths, face to face.

When King David heard of Rizpah's vigil, he was moved by her example and provided a proper burial both for these seven men and for Saul and Jonathan. While Rizpah couldn't save her sons' lives, her courageous protection of their bodies after death was rewarded (see 2Sa 21:11–14). Rizpah prompted an act that blessed the entire land.

Mothers all over this nation, especially African American mothers, have found themselves in Rizpah's position. They find themselves taking on the vultures by day and the jackals by night. Today's vultures and jackals include racism and the drug culture that destroys everything that gets in its way. The phenomenon of crack strikes at the central nervous system of our community. It can make African American children turn on their own mothers and African American women give up their children—something even slavery couldn't do.

Statistics continue to knock at the door with tragic news. Each day many of our mothers learn that their children have been harmed in some way—socially, economically, educationally, psychologically, spiritually or physically. We must grieve; we must pick up our sackcloth and grieve over the situations that now confront us. We must keep vigil over the injustice done to our children. Even if and when some die, we must keep pressing for justice and honor. Through the prayers of mothers, through the vigils of mothers and through the fight of mothers, others can be saved, and our land can be healed.

—R. Walker

### reflection

*For what or for whom do you feel compelled to keep a vigil until justice is done?*

*Pray and fight for justice.*

### read

2 Samuel 3:6–11; 21:1–14.

**See also** the Inspire Notes "Commitment to Community," "Motherhood," "Suffering," "Parenting" and "Children: A Blessed Heritage From God," and the Women of the Bible Notes "Bathsheba: A Silent Affair," "The Shunammite Woman: Our Sister's Grief Is Our Grief," "Job's Wife: She Was Tested Too," "Ezekiel's Wife: On God's Stage" and "Mary and Martha: Grieving Sisters."

For the next Women of the Bible note, go to page 411.

**22:19** m Ps 23:4
**22:20** n Ps 31:8
**22:21** o Ps 24:4
**22:22** p Ge 18:19; Ps 128:1
**22:23** q Dt 6:4–9
**22:24** r Eph 1:4
**22:27** s Lev 26:23–24
**22:28** t Ps 72:12–13
**22:31** u Ps 12:6
**22:32** v 1Sa 2:2

he drew me out of deep waters.
18 He rescued me from my powerful enemy,
from my foes, who were too strong
for me.
19 They confronted me in the day of my
disaster,
but the LORD was my support.[m]
20 He brought me out into a spacious[n] place;
he rescued me because he delighted
in me.

21 "The LORD has dealt with me according to
my righteousness;
according to the cleanness of my
hands[o] he has rewarded me.
22 For I have kept[p] the ways of the LORD;
I have not done evil by turning from
my God.
23 All his laws are before me;[q]
I have not turned away from his
decrees.
24 I have been blameless[r] before him
and have kept myself from sin.
25 The LORD has rewarded me according to
my righteousness,
according to my cleanness[a] in his
sight.

26 "To the faithful you show yourself
faithful,
to the blameless you show yourself
blameless,
27 to the pure you show yourself pure,
but to the crooked you show yourself
shrewd.[s]
28 You save the humble,[t]
but your eyes are on the haughty to
bring them low.
29 You are my lamp, O LORD;
the LORD turns my darkness into light.
30 With your help I can advance against a
troop[b];
with my God I can scale a wall.

31 "As for God, his way is perfect;
the word of the LORD is flawless.[u]
He is a shield
for all who take refuge in him.
32 For who is God besides the LORD?
And who is the Rock[v] except our God?
33 It is God who arms me with strength[c]
and makes my way perfect.
34 He makes my feet like the feet of a deer;
he enables me to stand on the
heights.
35 He trains my hands[w] for battle;
my arms can bend a bow of bronze.
36 You give me your shield of victory;
you stoop down to make me great.
37 You broaden the path[x] beneath me,
so that my ankles do not turn.

38 "I pursued my enemies and crushed
them;
I did not turn back till they were
destroyed.
39 I crushed[y] them completely, and they
could not rise;
they fell beneath my feet.
40 You armed me with strength for battle;
you made my adversaries bow at my
feet.[z]
41 You made my enemies turn their backs[a]
in flight,
and I destroyed my foes.
42 They cried for help, but there was no one
to save them—
to the LORD, but he did not answer.
43 I beat them as fine as the dust of the
earth;
I pounded and trampled them like
mud[b] in the streets.

44 "You have delivered[c] me from the attacks
of my people;
you have preserved[d] me as the head of
nations.
People[e] I did not know are
subject to me,
45 and foreigners come
cringing
to me;
as soon as they hear
me, they
obey me.
46 They all lose heart;
they come
trembling[d f]
from their
strongholds.

**22:35** w Ps 144:1
**22:37** x Pr 4:11
**22:39** y Mal 4:3
**22:40** z Ps 44:5
**22:41** a Ex 23:27
**22:43** b Isa 10:6
**22:44** c 2Sa 3:1 d Dt 28:13 e Isa 55:3–5
**22:46** f Mic 7:17

*"I always had only one prayer: 'Lord, just crack the door a little, and I'll kick it open all the way.'"*

—SHIRLEY CAESAR,
SINGER AND PASTOR

[a]25 Hebrew; Septuagint and Vulgate (see also Psalm 18:24) *to the cleanness of my hands* [b]30 Or *can run through a barricade* [c]33 Dead Sea Scrolls, some Septuagint manuscripts, Vulgate and Syriac (see also Psalm 18:32); Masoretic Text *who is my strong refuge* [d]46 Some Septuagint manuscripts and Vulgate (see also Psalm 18:45); Masoretic Text *they arm themselves.*

47 "The LORD lives! Praise be to my Rock!
Exalted be God, the Rock, my Savior![g]
48 He is the God who avenges me,[h]
who puts the nations under me,
49 who sets me free from my enemies.[i]
You exalted me above my foes;
from violent men you rescued me.
50 Therefore I will praise you, O LORD,
among the nations;
I will sing praises to your name.[j]
51 He gives his king great victories;[k]
he shows unfailing kindness to his
anointed,
to David[l] and his descendants forever."[m]

## The Last Words of David

23 These are the last words of David:

"The oracle of David son of Jesse,
the oracle of the man exalted[n] by the
Most High,
the man anointed[o] by the God of Jacob,
Israel's singer of songs[a]:
2 "The Spirit[p] of the LORD spoke
through me;
his word was on my tongue.
3 The God of Israel spoke,
the Rock[q] of Israel said to me:
'When one rules over men in
righteousness,
when he rules in the fear of God,
4 he is like the light of morning at sunrise[r]
on a cloudless morning,
like the brightness after rain
that brings the grass from the earth.'
5 "Is not my house right with God?
Has he not made with me an
everlasting covenant,[s]
arranged and secured in every part?
Will he not bring to fruition my salvation
and grant me my every desire?
6 But evil men are all to be cast aside like
thorns,[t]
which are not gathered with the hand.
7 Whoever touches thorns
uses a tool of iron or the shaft of a
spear;
they are burned up where they lie."

## David's Mighty Men

8 These are the names of David's mighty
men:
Josheb-Basshebeth,[b] a Tahkemonite,[c] was
chief of the Three; he raised his spear against
eight hundred men, whom he killed[d] in one
encounter.
9 Next to him was Eleazar son of Dodai[u]
the Ahohite. As one of the three mighty
men, he was with David when they taunted
the Philistines gathered ⌊at Pas Dammim⌋[e]
for battle. Then the men of Israel retreated,
10 but he stood his ground and struck down
the Philistines till his hand grew tired and
froze to the sword. The LORD brought about
a great victory that day. The troops returned
to Eleazar, but only to strip the dead.
11 Next to him was Shammah son of Agee
the Hararite. When the Philistines banded
together at a place where there was a field
full of lentils, Israel's troops fled from them.
12 But Shammah took his stand in the mid-
dle of the field. He defended it and struck
the Philistines down, and the LORD brought
about a great victory.
13 During harvest time, three of the thirty
chief men came down to David at the cave
of Adullam,[v] while a band of Philistines was
encamped in the Valley of Rephaim.[w] 14 At
that time David was in the stronghold,[x] and
the Philistine garrison was at Bethlehem.
15 David longed for water and said, "Oh, that
someone would get me a drink of water
from the well near the gate of Bethlehem!"
16 So the three mighty men broke through
the Philistine lines, drew water from the
well near the gate of Bethlehem and carried
it back to David. But he refused to drink it;
instead, he poured it out before the LORD.
17 "Far be it from me, O LORD, to do this!" he
said. "Is it not the blood[y] of men who went
at the risk of their lives?" And David would
not drink it.
Such were the exploits of the three mighty
men.
18 Abishai[z] the brother of Joab son of
Zeruiah was chief of the Three.[f] He raised
his spear against three hundred men, whom

**22:47** g Ps 89:26
**22:48** h Ps 144:2
**22:49** i Ps 140:1,4
**22:50** j Ro 15:9*
**22:51** k Ps 144:9–10; l 2Sa 7:13; m Ps 89:24,29
**23:1** n Ps 78:70–71; o 1Sa 16:12–13; Ps 89:20
**23:2** p 2Pe 1:21
**23:3** q Dt 32:4
**23:4** r Jdg 5:31
**23:5** s Ps 89:29
**23:6** t Mt 13:40–41
**23:9** u 1Ch 27:4
**23:13** v 1Sa 22:1; w 2Sa 5:18
**23:14** x 1Sa 22:4–5
**23:17** y Lev 17:10–12
**23:18** z 1Ch 11:20

[a] 1 Or *Israel's beloved singer* [b] 8 Hebrew; some Septuagint manuscripts suggest *Ish-Bosheth,* that is, *Esh-Baal* (see also 1 Chron. 11:11 *Jashobeam*). [c] 8 Probably a variant of *Hacmonite* (see 1 Chron. 11:11) [d] 8 Some Septuagint manuscripts (see also 1 Chron. 11:11); Hebrew and other Septuagint manuscripts *Three; it was Adino the Eznite who killed eight hundred men* [e] 9 See 1 Chron. 11:13; Hebrew *gathered there.* [f] 18 Most Hebrew manuscripts (see also 1 Chron. 11:20); two Hebrew manuscripts and Syriac *Thirty*

he killed, and so he became as famous
as the Three. 19 Was he not held in greater
honor than the Three? He became their com-
mander, even though he was not included
among them.

20 Benaiah son of Jehoiada was a valiant
fighter from Kabzeel,[a] who performed
great exploits. He struck down two of Mo-
ab's best men. He also went down into a pit
on a snowy day and killed a lion. 21 And he
struck down a huge Egyptian. Although the
Egyptian had a spear in his hand, Benaiah
went against him with a club. He snatched
the spear from the Egyptian's hand and
killed him with his own spear. 22 Such were
the exploits of Benaiah son of Jehoiada; he
too was as famous as the three mighty men.
23 He was held in greater honor than any of
the Thirty, but he was not included among
the Three. And David put him in charge of
his bodyguard.

24 Among the Thirty were:
Asahel[b] the brother of Joab,
Elhanan son of Dodo from Beth-
lehem,
25 Shammah the Harodite,[c]
Elika the Harodite,
26 Helez the Paltite,
Ira son of Ikkesh from Tekoa,
27 Abiezer from Anathoth,[d]
Mebunnai[a] the Hushathite,
28 Zalmon the Ahohite,
Maharai the Netophathite,[e]
29 Heled[b] son of Baanah the Netopha-
thite,
Ithai son of Ribai from Gibeah
in Benjamin,
30 Benaiah the Pirathonite,
Hiddai[c] from the ravines of Gaash,[f]
31 Abi-Albon the Arbathite,
Azmaveth the Barhumite,
32 Eliahba the Shaalbonite,
the sons of Jashen,
Jonathan 33 son of[d] Shammah the
Hararite,
Ahiam son of Sharar[e] the Hararite,
34 Eliphelet son of Ahasbai the Maaca-
thite,
Eliam[g] son of Ahithophel[h] the Gilo-
nite,
35 Hezro the Carmelite,
Paarai the Arbite,
36 Igal son of Nathan from Zobah,
the son of Hagri,[f]
37 Zelek the Ammonite,
Naharai the Beerothite, the armor-
bearer of Joab son of Zeruiah,
38 Ira the Ithrite,[i]
Gareb the Ithrite
39 and Uriah[j] the Hittite.
There were thirty-seven in all.

## David Counts the Fighting Men

24 Again the anger of the LORD burned
against Israel, and he incited David
against them, saying, "Go and take a census
of[k] Israel and Judah."

2 So the king said to Joab and the army
commanders[g] with him, "Go throughout
the tribes of Israel from Dan to Beersheba[l]
and enroll the fighting men, so that I may
know how many there are."

3 But Joab replied to the king, "May the
LORD your God multiply the troops a hun-
dred times over, and may the eyes of my
lord the king see it. But why does my lord
the king want to do such a thing?"

4 The king's word, however, overruled
Joab and the army commanders; so they left
the presence of the king to enroll the fight-
ing men of Israel.

5 After crossing the Jordan, they camped
near Aroer,[m] south of the town in the gorge,
and then went through Gad and on to Jazer.[n]
6 They went to Gilead and the region of Tah-
tim Hodshi, and on to Dan Jaan and around
toward Sidon.[o] 7 Then they went toward the
fortress of Tyre and all the towns of the Hi-
vites and Canaanites. Finally, they went on
to Beersheba in the Negev of Judah.

8 After they had gone through the entire
land, they came back to Jerusalem at the
end of nine months and twenty days.

9 Joab reported the number of the fighting
men to the king: In Israel there were eight
hundred thousand able-bodied men who

**23:20** a Jos 15:21
**23:24** b 2Sa 2:18
**23:25** c Jdg 7:1; 1Ch 11:27
**23:27** d Jos 21:18
**23:28** e 2Ki 25:23
**23:30** f Jos 24:30
**23:34** g 2Sa 11:3 h 2Sa 15:12
**23:38** i 1Ch 2:53
**23:39** j 2Sa 11:3
**24:1** k 1Ch 27:23
**24:2** l Jdg 20:1; 2Sa 3:10
**24:5** m Dt 2:36; Jos 13:9 n Nu 21:32
**24:6** o Jos 19:28

[a]27 Hebrew; some Septuagint manuscripts (see also 1 Chron. 11:29) *Sibbecai* [b]29 Some Hebrew manuscripts and Vulgate (see also 1 Chron. 11:30); most Hebrew manuscripts *Heleb* [c]30 Hebrew; some Septuagint manuscripts (see also 1 Chron. 11:32) *Hurai* [d]33 Some Septuagint manuscripts (see also 1 Chron. 11:34); Hebrew does not have *son of.* [e]33 Hebrew; some Septuagint manuscripts (see also 1 Chron. 11:35) *Sacar* [f]36 Some Septuagint manuscripts (see also 1 Chron. 11:38); Hebrew *Haggadi* [g]2 Septuagint (see also verse 4 and 1 Chron. 21:2); Hebrew *Joab the army commander*

could handle a sword, and in Judah five hundred thousand.[p]

10 David was conscience-stricken[q] after he had counted the fighting men, and he said to the LORD, "I have sinned[r] greatly in what I have done. Now, O LORD, I beg you, take away the guilt of your servant. I have done a very foolish thing.[s]"

11 Before David got up the next morning, the word of the LORD had come to Gad[t] the prophet, David's seer:[u] 12 "Go and tell David, 'This is what the LORD says: I am giving you three options. Choose one of them for me to carry out against you.' "

13 So Gad went to David and said to him, "Shall there come upon you three[a] years of famine in your land? Or three months of fleeing from your enemies while they pursue you? Or three days of plague in your land? Now then, think it over and decide how I should answer the one who sent me."

14 David said to Gad, "I am in deep distress. Let us fall into the hands of the LORD, for his mercy[v] is great; but do not let me fall into the hands of men."

15 So the LORD sent a plague on Israel from that morning until the end of the time designated, and seventy thousand of the people from Dan to Beersheba died.[w] 16 When the angel stretched out his hand to destroy Jerusalem, the LORD was grieved[x] because of the calamity and said to the angel who was afflicting the people, "Enough! Withdraw your hand." The angel of the LORD[y] was then at the threshing floor of Araunah the Jebusite.

17 When David saw the angel who was striking down the people, he said to the LORD, "I am the one who has sinned and done wrong. These are but sheep. What have they done? Let your hand fall upon me and my family."[z]

## David Builds an Altar

18 On that day Gad went to David and said to him, "Go up and build an altar to the LORD on the threshing floor of Araunah the Jebusite." 19 So David went up, as the LORD had commanded through Gad. 20 When Araunah looked and saw the king and his men coming toward him, he went out and bowed down before the king with his face to the ground.

21 Araunah said, "Why has my lord the king come to his servant?"

"To buy your threshing floor," David answered, "so I can build an altar to the LORD, that the plague on the people may be stopped."[z]

22 Araunah said to David, "Let my lord the king take whatever pleases him and offer it up. Here are oxen[a] for the burnt offering, and here are threshing sledges and ox yokes for the wood. 23 O king, Araunah gives[b] all this to the king." Araunah also said to him, "May the LORD your God accept you."

24 But the king replied to Araunah, "No, I insist on paying you for it. I will not sacrifice to the LORD my God burnt offerings that cost me nothing."

So David bought the threshing floor and the oxen and paid fifty shekels[b] of silver for them. 25 David built an altar to the LORD there and sacrificed burnt offerings and fellowship offerings.[c] Then the LORD answered prayer[c] in behalf of the land, and the plague on Israel was stopped.

**24:9** p 1Ch 21:5
**24:10** q 1Sa 24:5 r 2Sa 12:13 s 1Sa 13:13
**24:11** t 1Sa 22:5 u 1Sa 9:9; 1Ch 29:29
**24:14** v Ps 103:8,13
**24:15** w 1Ch 27:24
**24:16** x Ge 6:6; 1Sa 15:11 y Ex 12:23
**24:21** z Nu 16:44–50
**24:22** a 1Ki 19:21
**24:23** b Eze 20:40–41
**24:25** c 2Sa 21:14

[a] 13 Septuagint (see also 1 Chron. 21:12); Hebrew *seven* [b] 24 That is, about 1 1/4 pounds (about 0.6 kilogram)
[c] 25 Traditionally *peace offerings*

# 1 Kings

## OVERVIEW

First Kings begins with the death of David and proceeds to give an extensive account of the reign of his son Solomon. As queen mother, Bathsheba was instrumental in gaining the throne for her son (see 1Ki 1). During his 40-year reign, Solomon was blessed with wisdom and material wealth. The first part of his reign was far more prosperous than the latter part. It was during the first part of his reign that he built the temple in Jerusalem (see 1Ki 6–8).

The latter portion of Solomon's reign was marred by his intermarriages with women who served idols, and his heart turned away from God. After his death, ten tribes of Israel revolted, leaving the tribe of Judah (and the tribe of Simeon, which had essentially become absorbed by Judah) under the reign of Davidic kings.

The book of 1 Kings describes how prophets brought God's word to the kings in both the northern and southern kingdoms. Elijah was most outspoken to King Ahab and his wicked wife Jezebel. The ministries of Elijah and many other prophets are covered in the last few chapters of 1 Kings.

As you read this book, reflect on the care God provided for the widow at Zarephath and her son through Elijah (see 1Ki 17:7–24). Meditate on how God doesn't desert his people during difficulty; on the contrary, he says, "Never will I leave you; never will I forsake you" (Heb 13:5).

## OUTLINE

I. Solomon Is Established as David's Successor (1:1—2:46)
II. God Gives Solomon Wisdom (3:1–28)
III. Solomon's Reign and Building Projects (4:1—10:29)
IV. Solomon Makes Poor Choices (11:1–43)
V. Rehoboam's Succession to the Throne (12:1–24)
VI. Israel and Judah From Jeroboam I/Rehoboam to Ahab/Asa (12:25—16:34)
VII. The Ministries of Elijah and Other Prophets (17:1—22:53)

## SCANNABLE FACTS:

**Author:** Unknown

**Time Written:** Probably during the Babylonian exile, around 550 B.C.

**Theme to Note:** Obedience brings blessing, while disobedience brings disaster

**Notable Women:** Bathsheba, the queen of Sheba, Jezebel, the widow at Zarephath

**1:3** a Jos 19:18
**1:5** b 2Sa 3:4
**1:6** c 2Sa 3:3–4
**1:7** d 1Ki 2:22,28 e 2Sa 20:25
**1:8** f 2Sa 23:8
**1:11** g 2Sa 3:4
**1:13** h 1Ch 22:9–13

## Adonijah Sets Himself Up as King

1 When King David was old and well advanced in years, he could not keep warm even when they put covers over him. 2So his servants said to him, "Let us look for a young virgin to attend the king and take care of him. She can lie beside him so that our lord the king may keep warm."

3Then they searched throughout Israel for a beautiful girl and found Abishag, a Shunammite,[a] and brought her to the king. 4The girl was very beautiful; she took care of the king and waited on him, but the king had no intimate relations with her.

5Now Adonijah,[b] whose mother was Haggith, put himself forward and said, "I will be king." So he got chariots and horses[a] ready, with fifty men to run ahead of him. 6(His father had never interfered[c] with him by asking, "Why do you behave as you do?" He was also very handsome and was born next after Absalom.)

7Adonijah conferred with Joab[d] son of Zeruiah and with Abiathar[e] the priest, and they gave him their support. 8But Zadok the priest, Benaiah son of Jehoiada, Nathan the prophet, Shimei and Rei[b] and David's special guard[f] did not join Adonijah.

9Adonijah then sacrificed sheep, cattle and fattened calves at the Stone of Zoheleth near En Rogel. He invited all his brothers, the king's sons, and all the men of Judah who were royal officials, 10but he did not invite Nathan the prophet or Benaiah or the special guard or his brother Solomon.

11Then Nathan asked Bathsheba, Solomon's mother, "Have you not heard that Adonijah,[g] the son of Haggith, has become king without our lord David's knowing it? 12Now then, let me advise you how you can save your own life and the life of your son Solomon. 13Go in to King David and say to him, 'My lord the king, did you not swear[h] to me your servant: "Surely Solomon your son shall be king after me, and he will sit on my throne"? Why then has Adonijah become king?' 14While you are still there talking to the king, I will come in and confirm what you have said."

15So Bathsheba went to see the aged king in his room, where Abishag the Shunammite was attending him. 16Bathsheba bowed low and knelt before the king.

"What is it you want?" the king asked.

17She said to him, "My lord, you yourself swore[i] to me your servant by the LORD your God: 'Solomon your son shall be king after me, and he will sit on my throne.' 18But now Adonijah has become king, and you, my lord the king, do not know about it. 19He has sacrificed[j] great numbers of cattle, fattened calves, and sheep, and has invited all the king's sons, Abiathar the priest and Joab the commander of the army, but he has not invited Solomon your servant. 20My lord the king, the eyes of all Israel are on you, to learn from you who will sit on the throne of my lord the king after him. 21Otherwise, as soon as my lord the king is laid to rest[k] with his fathers, I and my son Solomon will be treated as criminals."

22While she was still speaking with the king, Nathan the prophet arrived. 23And they told the king, "Nathan the prophet is here." So he went before the king and bowed with his face to the ground.

24Nathan said, "Have you, my lord the king, declared that Adonijah shall be king after you, and that he will sit on your throne? 25Today he has gone down and sacrificed great numbers of cattle, fattened calves and sheep. He has invited all the king's sons, the commanders of the army and Abiathar the priest. Right now they are eating and drinking with him and saying, 'Long live King Adonijah!' 26But me your servant, and Zadok the priest, and Benaiah son of Jehoiada, and your servant Solomon he did not invite. 27Is this something my lord the king has done without letting his servants know who should sit on the throne of my lord the king after him?"

## David Makes Solomon King

28Then King David said, "Call in Bathsheba." So she came into the king's presence and stood before him.

29The king then took an oath: "As surely as the LORD lives, who has delivered me out of every trouble,[l] 30I will surely carry out today what I swore[m] to you by the LORD, the

**1:17** i ver 13,30
**1:19** j ver 9
**1:21** k Dt 31:16; 1Ki 2:10
**1:29** l 2Sa 4:9
**1:30** m ver 13,17

[a]5 Or *charioteers* [b]8 Or *and his friends*

God of Israel: Solomon your son shall be
king after me, and he will sit on my throne
in my place."
31Then Bathsheba bowed low with her
face to the ground and, kneeling before the
king, said, "May my lord King David live
forever!"
32King David said, "Call in Zadok the
priest, Nathan the prophet and Benaiah son
of Jehoiada." When they came before the
king, 33he said to them: "Take your lord's
servants with you and set Solomon my son
on my own mule[n] and take him down to
Gihon. 34There have Zadok the priest and
Nathan the prophet anoint[o] him king over
Israel. Blow the trumpet[p] and shout, 'Long
live King Solomon!' 35Then you are to go
up with him, and he is to come and sit on
my throne and reign in my place. I have
appointed him ruler over Israel and Judah."
36Benaiah son of Jehoiada answered the
king, "Amen! May the LORD, the God of my
lord the king, so declare it. 37As the LORD was
with my lord the king, so may he be with[q]
Solomon to make his throne even greater[r]
than the throne of my lord King David!"
38So Zadok the priest, Nathan the prophet,
Benaiah son of Jehoiada, the Kerethites and
the Pelethites went down and put Solomon
on King David's mule and escorted him to
Gihon. 39Zadok the priest took the horn of
oil[s] from the sacred tent and anointed Solo-
mon. Then they sounded the trumpet and
all the people shouted, "Long live King Sol-
omon!" 40And all the people went up after
him, playing flutes and rejoicing greatly, so
that the ground shook with the sound.
41Adonijah and all the guests who were
with him heard it as they were finishing
their feast. On hearing the sound of the
trumpet, Joab asked, "What's the meaning
of all the noise in the city?"
42Even as he was speaking, Jonathan son
of Abiathar the priest arrived. Adonijah
said, "Come in. A worthy man like you must
be bringing good news."[t]
43"Not at all!" Jonathan answered. "Our
lord King David has made Solomon king.
44The king has sent with him Zadok the
priest, Nathan the prophet, Benaiah son of
Jehoiada, the Kerethites and the Pelethites,
and they have put him on the king's mule,
45and Zadok the priest and Nathan the
prophet have anointed him king at Gihon.
From there they have gone up cheering,
and the city resounds with it. That's the
noise you hear. 46Moreover, Solomon has
taken his seat on the royal throne. 47Also,
the royal officials have come to congratulate
our lord King David, saying, 'May your God
make Solomon's name more famous than
yours and his throne greater[u] than yours!'
And the king bowed in worship on his bed
48and said, 'Praise be to the LORD, the God
of Israel, who has allowed my eyes to see a
successor[v] on my throne today.'"
49At this, all Adonijah's guests rose in
alarm and dispersed. 50But Adonijah, in
fear of Solomon, went and took hold of the
horns[w] of the altar. 51Then Solomon was
told, "Adonijah is afraid of King Solomon
and is clinging to the horns of the altar. He
says, 'Let King Solomon swear to me today
that he will not put his servant to death with
the sword.'"
52Solomon replied, "If he shows himself
to be a worthy man, not a hair[x] of his head
will fall to the ground; but if evil is found in
him, he will die." 53Then King Solomon sent
men, and they brought him down from the
altar. And Adonijah came and bowed down
to King Solomon, and Solomon said, "Go to
your home."

## David's Charge to Solomon

2 When the time drew near for David
to die,[y] he gave a charge to Solomon
his son.
2"I am about to go the way of all the
earth,"[z] he said. "So be strong, show your-
self a man, 3and observe what the LORD your
God requires: Walk in his ways, and keep
his decrees and commands, his laws and re-
quirements, as written in the Law of Moses,
so that you may prosper[a] in all you do and
wherever you go, 4and that the LORD may
keep his promise[b] to me: 'If your descen-
dants watch how they live, and if they walk
faithfully[c] before me with all their heart
and soul, you will never fail to have a man
on the throne of Israel.'
5"Now you yourself know what Joab son of
Zeruiah did to me—what he did to the two
commanders of Israel's armies, Abner son

1:33 n 2Sa 20:6–7
1:34 o 1Sa 10:1; 16:3,12 p 2Sa 15:10
1:37 q Jos 1:5,17; 1Sa 20:13 r ver 47
1:39 s Ps 89:20
1:42 t 2Sa 18:26
1:47 u ver 37
1:48 v 1Ki 3:6
1:50 w 1Ki 2:28
1:52 x 1Sa 14:45
2:1 y Ge 47:29; Dt 31:14
2:2 z Jos 23:14
2:3 a 1Ch 22:13
2:4 b 2Sa 7:13,25 c 2Ki 20:3; Ps 132:12

**2:7**
d 2Sa 17:27; 19:31–39
e 2Sa 9:7

**2:8**
f 2Sa 16:5–13
g 2Sa 19:18–23

**2:10**
h Ac 2:29
i 2Sa 5:7

**2:11**
j 2Sa 5:4,5

**2:12**
k 1Ch 29:23
l 2Ch 1:1

**2:13**
m 1Sa 16:4

*Lord,*

*thank you for the gift of eternal life. Make me, along with your other waiting children, ready at a moment's notice to receive your final miracle.*

*Amen.*

1 KINGS 2:1–3

of Ner and Amasa son of Jether. He killed them, shedding their blood in peacetime as if in battle, and with that blood stained the belt around his waist and the sandals on his feet. [6]Deal with him according to your wisdom, but do not let his gray head go down to the grave[a] in peace.

[7]"But show kindness to the sons of Barzillai[d] of Gilead and let them be among those who eat at your table.[e] They stood by me when I fled from your brother Absalom.

[8]"And remember, you have with you Shimei[f] son of Gera, the Benjamite from Bahurim, who called down bitter curses on me the day I went to Mahanaim. When he came down to meet me at the Jordan, I swore[g] to him by the LORD: 'I will not put you to death by the sword.' [9]But now, do not consider him innocent. You are a man of wisdom; you will know what to do to him. Bring his gray head down to the grave in blood."

[10]Then David rested with his fathers and was buried[h] in the City of David.[i] [11]He had reigned[j] forty years over Israel—seven years in Hebron and thirty-three in Jerusalem. [12]So Solomon sat on the throne[k] of his father David, and his rule was firmly established.[l]

## Solomon's Throne Established

[13]Now Adonijah, the son of Haggith, went to Bathsheba, Solomon's mother. Bathsheba asked him, "Do you come peacefully?"[m]

He answered, "Yes, peacefully." [14]Then he added, "I have something to say to you."

"You may say it," she replied.

[15]"As you know," he said, "the kingdom was mine. All Israel looked to me as their king. But things changed, and the kingdom has gone to my brother; for it has come to him from the LORD. [16]Now I have one request to make of you. Do not refuse me."

"You may make it," she said.

[17]So he continued, "Please ask King Solomon—he will not refuse you—to give me Abishag[n] the Shunammite as my wife."

[18]"Very well," Bathsheba replied, "I will speak to the king for you."

[19]When Bathsheba went to King Solomon to speak to him for Adonijah, the king stood up to meet her, bowed down to her and sat down on his throne. He had a throne brought for the king's mother, and she sat down at his right hand.[o]

[20]"I have one small request to make of you," she said. "Do not refuse me."

The king replied, "Make it, my mother; I will not refuse you."

[21]So she said, "Let Abishag the Shunammite be given in marriage to your brother Adonijah."

[22]King Solomon answered his mother, "Why do you request Abishag the Shunammite for Adonijah? You might as well request the kingdom for him—after all, he is my older brother—yes, for him and for Abiathar the priest and Joab son of Zeruiah!"

[23]Then King Solomon swore by the LORD: "May God deal with me, be it ever so severely,[p] if Adonijah does not pay with his life for this request! [24]And now, as surely as the LORD lives—he who has established me securely on the throne of my father David and has founded a dynasty for me as he promised[q]—Adonijah shall be put to death today!" [25]So King Solomon gave orders to Benaiah son of Jehoiada, and he struck down Adonijah and he died.

[26]To Abiathar[r] the priest the king said, "Go back to your fields in Anathoth.[s] You deserve to die, but I will not put you to death now, because you carried the ark[t] of the Sovereign LORD before my father David and shared all my father's hardships." [27]So Solomon removed Abiathar from the priesthood of the LORD, fulfilling[u] the word the

**2:17**
n 1Ki 1:3

**2:19**
o Ps 45:9

**2:23**
p Ru 1:17

**2:24**
q 2Sa 7:11

**2:26**
r 1Sa 22:20
s Jos 21:18
t 2Sa 15:24

**2:27**
u 1Sa 2:27–36

[a]6 Hebrew *Sheol*; also in verse 9

**2:30**
v Ex21:14

**2:31**
w Dt19:13

**2:32**
x Jdg9:57
y Jdg9:24
z 2Ch21:13

**2:37**
a 2Sa15:23
b 2Sa1:16

**2:39**
c 1Sa27:2

LORD had spoken at Shiloh about the house of Eli.

28 When the news reached Joab, who had conspired with Adonijah though not with Absalom, he fled to the tent of the LORD and took hold of the horns of the altar. 29 King Solomon was told that Joab had fled to the tent of the LORD and was beside the altar. Then Solomon ordered Benaiah son of Jehoiada, "Go, strike him down!"

30 So Benaiah entered the tent of the LORD and said to Joab, "The king says, 'Come out![v]'"

But he answered, "No, I will die here."

Benaiah reported to the king, "This is how Joab answered me."

31 Then the king commanded Benaiah, "Do as he says. Strike him down and bury him, and so clear me and my father's house of the guilt of the innocent blood[w] that Joab shed. 32 The LORD will repay[x] him for the blood he shed,[y] because without the knowledge of my father David he attacked two men and killed them with the sword. Both of them—Abner son of Ner, commander of Israel's army, and Amasa son of Jether, commander of Judah's army—were better[z] men and more upright than he. 33 May the guilt of their blood rest on the head of Joab and his descendants forever. But on David and his descendants, his house and his throne, may there be the LORD's peace forever."

34 So Benaiah son of Jehoiada went up and struck down Joab and killed him, and he was buried on his own land[a] in the desert. 35 The king put Benaiah son of Jehoiada over the army in Joab's position and replaced Abiathar with Zadok the priest.

36 Then the king sent for Shimei and said to him, "Build yourself a house in Jerusalem and live there, but do not go anywhere else. 37 The day you leave and cross the Kidron Valley,[a] you can be sure you will die; your blood will be on your own head."[b]

38 Shimei answered the king, "What you say is good. Your servant will do as my lord the king has said." And Shimei stayed in Jerusalem for a long time.

39 But three years later, two of Shimei's slaves ran off to Achish[c] son of Maacah, king of Gath, and Shimei was told, "Your slaves are in Gath." 40 At this, he saddled his donkey and went to Achish at Gath in search of his slaves. So Shimei went away and brought the slaves back from Gath.

41 When Solomon was told that Shimei had gone from Jerusalem to Gath and had returned, 42 the king summoned Shimei and said to him, "Did I not make you swear by the LORD and warn you, 'On the day you leave to go anywhere else, you can be sure you will die'? At that time you said to me, 'What you say is good. I will obey.' 43 Why then did you not keep your oath to the LORD and obey the command I gave you?"

44 The king also said to Shimei, "You know in your heart all the wrong[d] you did to my father David. Now the LORD will repay you for your wrongdoing. 45 But King Solomon will be blessed, and David's throne will remain secure before the LORD forever."

46 Then the king gave the order to Benaiah son of Jehoiada, and he went out and struck Shimei down and killed him.

The kingdom was now firmly established[e] in Solomon's hands.

## Solomon Asks for Wisdom

3 Solomon made an alliance with Pharaoh king of Egypt and married[f] his daughter.[g] He brought her to the City of David until he finished building his palace and the temple of the LORD, and the wall around Jerusalem. 2 The people, however, were still sacrificing at the high places,[h] because a temple had not yet been built for the Name of the LORD. 3 Solomon showed his love[i] for the LORD by walking according to the statutes of his father David, except that he offered sacrifices and burned incense on the high places.

4 The king went to Gibeon[j] to offer sacrifices, for that was the most important high place, and Solomon offered a thousand burnt offerings on that altar. 5 At Gibeon the LORD appeared[k] to Solomon during the night in a dream,[l] and God said, "Ask for whatever you want me to give you."

6 Solomon answered, "You have shown great kindness to your servant, my father David, because he was faithful to you and righteous and upright in heart. You have

**2:44**
d 2Sa16:5–13

**2:46**
e ver 12

**3:1**
f 1Ki7:8
g 1Ki9:24

**3:2**
h Lev17:3–5; Dt12:2,4–5

**3:3**
i Dt6:5

**3:4**
j 1Ch16:39

**3:5**
k 1Ki9:2
l Nu12:6; Mt1:20

[a]34 Or *buried in his tomb*

**3:6** m 1Ki 1:48
**3:7** n Nu 27:17
**3:8** o Dt 7:6; p Ge 15:5
**3:9** q Jas 1:5; r Pr 2:3–9; s Ps 72:1–2
**3:11** t Jas 4:3
**3:12** u 1Jn 5:14–15; v 1Ki 4:29,30,31
**3:13** w Mt 6:33; x 1Ki 4:21–24
**3:14** y Pr 3:1–2,16
**3:15** z Ge 41:7; a 1Ki 8:65

continued this great kindness to him and have given him a son[m] to sit on his throne this very day.

7 "Now, O LORD my God, you have made your servant king in place of my father David. But I am only a little child[n] and do not know how to carry out my duties. 8 Your servant is here among the people you have chosen,[o] a great people, too numerous to count or number.[p] 9 So give your servant a discerning[q] heart to govern your people and to distinguish[r] between right and wrong. For who is able[s] to govern this great people of yours?"

10 The Lord was pleased that Solomon had asked for this. 11 So God said to him, "Since you have asked[t] for this and not for long life or wealth for yourself, nor have asked for the death of your enemies but for discernment in administering justice, 12 I will do what you have asked.[u] I will give you a wise[v] and discerning heart, so that there will never have been anyone like you, nor will there ever be. 13 Moreover, I will give you what you have not[w] asked for—both riches and honor[x]—so that in your lifetime you will have no equal among kings. 14 And if you walk[y] in my ways and obey my statutes and commands as David your father did, I will give you a long life." 15 Then Solomon awoke[z]—and he realized it had been a dream.

He returned to Jerusalem, stood before the ark of the Lord's covenant and sacrificed burnt offerings[a] and fellowship offerings.[a] Then he gave a feast for all his court.

## A Wise Ruling

16 Now two prostitutes came to the king and stood before him. 17 One of them said, "My lord, this woman and I live in the same house. I had a baby while she was there with me. 18 The third day after my child was born, this woman also had a baby. We were alone; there was no one in the house but the two of us.

19 "During the night this woman's son died because she lay on him. 20 So she got up in the middle of the night and took my son from my side while I your servant was asleep. She put him by her breast and put her dead son by my breast. 21 The next morning, I got up to nurse my son—and he was dead! But when I looked at him closely in the morning light, I saw that it wasn't the son I had borne."

22 The other woman said, "No! The living one is my son; the dead one is yours."

But the first one insisted, "No! The dead one is yours; the living one is mine." And so they argued before the king.

23 The king said, "This one says, 'My son is alive and your son is dead,' while that one says, 'No! Your son is dead and mine is alive.' "

24 Then the king said, "Bring me a sword." So they brought a sword for the king. 25 He then gave an order: "Cut the living child in two and give half to one and half to the other."

26 The woman whose son was alive was filled with compassion[b] for her son and said to the king, "Please, my lord, give her the living baby! Don't kill him!"

But the other said, "Neither I nor you shall have him. Cut him in two!"

27 Then the king gave his ruling: "Give the living baby to the first woman. Do not kill him; she is his mother."

28 When all Israel heard the verdict the king had given, they held the king in awe, because they saw that he had wisdom[c] from God to administer justice.

## Solomon's Officials and Governors

4 So King Solomon ruled over all Israel. 2 And these were his chief officials:

Azariah son of Zadok—the priest;
3 Elihoreph and Ahijah, sons of Shisha—secretaries;
Jehoshaphat[d] son of Ahilud—recorder;
4 Benaiah son of Jehoiada—commander in chief;
Zadok and Abiathar—priests;
5 Azariah son of Nathan—in charge of the district officers;
Zabud son of Nathan—a priest and personal adviser to the king;
6 Ahishar—in charge of the palace;
Adoniram son of Abda—in charge of forced labor.

**3:26** b Ge 43:30; Isa 49:15; Jer 31:20; Hos 11:8
**3:28** c ver 9,11–12
**4:3** d 2Sa 8:16

[a] 15 Traditionally *peace offerings*

# Inspire

## MOTHERHOOD

**Motherhood is like a home study course in managing multiple projects. A mother gathers school materials, provides economic stability, finds nutritional subsistence in five minutes and nurtures those entrusted to her care by physical, emotional or spiritual birth. In this course called motherhood, compassion and sacrifice are innate gifts and tools to help our children. Take the example of the woman in 1 Kings 3:16–28. King Solomon knew that the actual mother loved her child so much that she would give her child to the other woman rather than watch her child die. This is the hallmark of sacrificial love.**

We may not understand God's reason for choosing us to sacrifice so much, but it is a call we must answer. God's mothering representatives in our lives have sacrificed over the years, and it is this sacrificial love toward us that drives us to pass on this legacy to our children. So we work to build up our families rather than tear them down with hurtful words and actions. Our children will not remember so much the words we said but how we said them; they will remember what we did for them and with them.

For women who consider motherhood a thankless job because the valleys far outnumber the peaks, we must remember that the valleys are necessary. We will learn more about our purpose in the valleys as we allow God to work out the plan already predestined for our lives. There is value in the valley because God is there with us, and we learn to turn to him for guidance.

Isaiah 49:14–15 uses an illustration of a newborn baby and its mother to remind us that the love we have for those entrusted to our mothering care is like the sacrificial love God has for us. Because there is not a circumstance that can separate us from God's love (see Ro 8:38–39), we ought not to allow anything to separate us from our love for those we care for.

—M. Lawson

### read

1 King 3:16–28.

**See also** the Inspire Notes "Parenting," "Raising Children: Modeling Discipleship," "Children: A Blessed Heritage From God" and "Nurturing Spiritual Gifts in Our Children," and the Women of the Bible Notes "Jochebed: She Knew It Would Take a Village," "Samson's Mother: The Strength of a Wife and Mother" and "Mary, the Mother of Jesus: A Model of Motherhood."

### WOMAN of COLOR

How are you showing sacrificial and compassionate love to your children or to children in your extended family or community?

For the next Inspire note, go to page 427.

7 Solomon also had twelve district gover-
nors over all Israel, who supplied provisions
for the king and the royal household. Each
one had to provide supplies for one month
in the year. 8 These are their names:

Ben-Hur—in the hill country of Ephraim;
9 Ben-Deker—in Makaz, Shaalbim,[e] Beth Shemesh and Elon Bethhanan;
10 Ben-Hesed—in Arubboth (Socoh and all the land of Hepher[f] were his);
11 Ben-Abinadab—in Naphoth Dor[a] (he was married to Taphath daughter of Solomon);
12 Baana son of Ahilud—in Taanach and Megiddo, and in all of Beth Shan[g] next to Zarethan below Jezreel, from Beth Shan to Abel Meholah across to Jokmeam;
13 Ben-Geber—in Ramoth Gilead (the settlements of Jair[h] son of Manasseh in Gilead were his, as well as the district of Argob in Bashan and its sixty large walled cities[i] with bronze gate bars);
14 Ahinadab son of Iddo—in Mahanaim;
15 Ahimaaz—in Naphtali (he had married Basemath daughter of Solomon);
16 Baana son of Hushai[j]—in Asher and in Aloth;
17 Jehoshaphat son of Paruah—in Issachar;
18 Shimei son of Ela—in Benjamin;
19 Geber son of Uri—in Gilead (the country of Sihon king of the Amorites and the country of Og[k] king of Bashan). He was the only governor over the district.

## Solomon's Daily Provisions

20 The people of Judah and Israel were as
numerous as the sand[l] on the seashore; they
ate, they drank and they were happy. 21 And
Solomon ruled[m] over all the kingdoms from
the River[b] to the land of the Philistines, as
far as the border of Egypt. These countries
brought tribute and were Solomon's sub-
jects all his life.

22 Solomon's daily provisions were thirty
cors[c] of fine flour and sixty cors[d] of meal,
23 ten head of stall-fed cattle, twenty of pas-
ture-fed cattle and a hundred sheep and
goats, as well as deer, gazelles, roebucks
and choice fowl. 24 For he ruled over all the
kingdoms west of the River, from Tiphsah
to Gaza, and had peace on all sides. 25 During
Solomon's lifetime Judah and Israel, from
Dan to Beersheba, lived in safety,[n] each man
under his own vine and fig tree.[o]

26 Solomon had four[e] thousand stalls
for chariot horses, and twelve thousand
horses.[f]

27 The district officers, each in his month,
supplied provisions for King Solomon and
all who came to the king's table. They saw
to it that nothing was lacking. 28 They also
brought to the proper place their quotas of
barley and straw for the chariot horses and
the other horses.

## Solomon's Wisdom

29 God gave Solomon wisdom[p] and very
great insight, and a breadth of understand-
ing as measureless as the sand on the sea-
shore. 30 Solomon's wisdom was greater than
the wisdom of all the men of the East, and
greater than all the wisdom of Egypt.[q] 31 He
was wiser[r] than any other man, including
Ethan the Ezrahite—wiser than Heman,
Calcol and Darda, the sons of Mahol. And
his fame spread to all the surrounding na-
tions. 32 He spoke three thousand proverbs[s]
and his songs[t] numbered a thousand and
five. 33 He described plant life, from the

*Lord,*

*I pray for wisdom. Help me to hear your voice and to follow your direction. I thank you for answering my prayer.*

*Amen*

1 KINGS 4:29–34

**4:9** e Jdg 1:35
**4:10** f Jos 12:17
**4:12** g Jos 17:11
**4:13** h Nu 32:41 i Dt 3:4
**4:16** j 2Sa 15:32
**4:19** k Dt 3:8–10
**4:20** l 1Ki 3:8
**4:21** m 2Ch 9:26
**4:25** n Jer 23:6 o Mic 4:4; Zec 3:10
**4:29** p 1Ki 3:12
**4:30** q Ac 7:22
**4:31** r 1Ki 3:12
**4:32** s Pr 1:1; Ecc 12:9 t SS 1:1

[a] 11 Or *in the heights of Dor* [b] 21 That is, the Euphrates; also in verse 24 [c] 22 That is, probably about 185 bushels (about 6.6 kiloliters) [d] 22 That is, probably about 375 bushels (about 13.2 kiloliters) [e] 26 Some Septuagint manuscripts (see also 2 Chron. 9:25); Hebrew *forty* [f] 26 Or *charioteers*

4:34 u 2Ch 9:23
5:1 v 2Sa 5:11
5:3 w 28:3
5:4 x 1Ch 22:9
5:5 y 1Ch 17:12 z 2Sa 7:13
5:9 a Ezr 3:7

cedar of Lebanon to the hyssop that grows out of walls. He also taught about animals and birds, reptiles and fish. 34 Men of all nations came to listen to Solomon's wisdom, sent by all the kings[u] of the world, who had heard of his wisdom.

## Preparations for Building the Temple

5 When Hiram[v] king of Tyre heard that Solomon had been anointed king to succeed his father David, he sent his envoys to Solomon, because he had always been on friendly terms with David. 2 Solomon sent back this message to Hiram:

> 3 "You know that because of the wars[w] waged against my father David from all sides, he could not build a temple for the Name of the LORD his God until the LORD put his enemies under his feet. 4 But now the LORD my God has given me rest[x] on every side, and there is no adversary or disaster. 5 I intend, therefore, to build a temple[y] for the Name of the LORD my God, as the LORD told my father David, when he said, 'Your son whom I will put on the throne in your place will build the temple for my Name.'[z]
>
> 6 "So give orders that cedars of Lebanon be cut for me. My men will work with yours, and I will pay you for your men whatever wages you set. You know that we have no one so skilled in felling timber as the Sidonians."

7 When Hiram heard Solomon's message, he was greatly pleased and said, "Praise be to the LORD today, for he has given David a wise son to rule over this great nation."

8 So Hiram sent word to Solomon:

> "I have received the message you sent me and will do all you want in providing the cedar and pine logs. 9 My men will haul them down from Lebanon to the sea[a], and I will float them in rafts by sea to the place you specify. There I will separate them and you can take them away. And you are to grant my wish by providing food[b] for my royal household."

10 In this way Hiram kept Solomon supplied with all the cedar and pine logs he wanted, 11 and Solomon gave Hiram twenty thousand cors[a] of wheat as food for his household, in addition to twenty thousand baths[b,c] of pressed olive oil. Solomon continued to do this for Hiram year after year. 12 The LORD gave Solomon wisdom,[c] just as he had promised him. There were peaceful relations between Hiram and Solomon, and the two of them made a treaty.

13 King Solomon conscripted laborers from all Israel—thirty thousand men. 14 He sent them off to Lebanon in shifts of ten thousand a month, so that they spent one month in Lebanon and two months at home. Adoniram[d] was in charge of the forced labor. 15 Solomon had seventy thousand carriers and eighty thousand stonecutters in the hills, 16 as well as thirty-three hundred[d] foremen who supervised the project and directed the workmen. 17 At the king's command they removed from the quarry large blocks of quality stone[e] to provide a foundation of dressed stone for the temple. 18 The craftsmen of Solomon and Hiram and the men of Gebal[e] cut and prepared the timber and stone for the building of the temple.

## Solomon Builds the Temple

6 In the four hundred and eightieth[f] year after the Israelites had come out of Egypt, in the fourth year of Solomon's reign over Israel, in the month of Ziv, the second month, he began to build the temple of the LORD.

2 The temple that King Solomon built for the LORD was sixty cubits long, twenty wide and thirty high.[g] 3 The portico at the front of the main hall of the temple extended the width of the temple, that is twenty cubits,[h] and projected ten cubits[i] from the front of the temple. 4 He made narrow clerestory windows[f] in the temple. 5 Against the walls of the main hall and inner sanctuary he built

5:9 b Eze 27:17; Ac 12:20
5:12 c 1Ki 3:12
5:14 d 1Ki 4:6
5:17 e 1Ch 22:2
6:4 f Eze 40:16

[a] 11 That is, probably about 125,000 bushels (about 4,400 kiloliters) [b] 11 Septuagint (see also 2 Chron. 2:10); Hebrew *twenty cors* [c] 11 That is, about 115,000 gallons (about 440 kiloliters) [d] 16 Hebrew; some Septuagint manuscripts (see also 2 Chron. 2:2, 18) *thirty-six hundred* [e] 18 That is, Byblos [f] 1 Hebrew; Septuagint *four hundred and fortieth* [g] 2 That is, about 90 feet (about 27 meters) long and 30 feet (about 9 meters) wide and 45 feet (about 13.5 meters) high [h] 3 That is, about 30 feet (about 9 meters) [i] 3 That is, about 15 feet (about 4.5 meters)

a structure around the building, in which
there were side rooms.[g] [6]The lowest floor
was five cubits[a] wide, the middle floor six
cubits[b] and the third floor seven.[c] He made
offset ledges around the outside of the tem-
ple so that nothing would be inserted into
the temple walls.

[7]In building the temple, only blocks
dressed at the quarry were used, and no
hammer, chisel or any other iron tool[h] was
heard at the temple site while it was be-
ing built.

[8]The entrance to the lowest[d] floor was on
the south side of the temple; a stairway led
up to the middle level and from there to the
third. [9]So he built the temple and completed
it, roofing it with beams and cedar[i] planks.
[10]And he built the side rooms all along the
temple. The height of each was five cubits,
and they were attached to the temple by
beams of cedar.

[11]The word of the LORD came to Solomon:
[12]"As for this temple you are building, if you
follow my decrees, carry out my regulations
and keep all my commands and obey them,
I will fulfill through you the promise[j] I gave
to David your father. [13]And I will live among
the Israelites and will not abandon[k] my peo-
ple Israel."

[14]So Solomon built the temple and
completed it. [15]He lined its interior walls
with cedar boards, paneling them from
the floor of the temple to the ceiling, and
covered the floor of the temple with planks
of pine. [16]He partitioned off twenty cubits[e]
at the rear of the temple with cedar boards
from floor to ceiling to form within the tem-
ple an inner sanctuary, the Most Holy Place.[l]
[17]The main hall in front of this room was
forty cubits[f] long. [18]The inside of the tem-
ple was cedar, carved with gourds and open
flowers. Everything was cedar; no stone was
to be seen.

[19]He prepared the inner sanctuary within
the temple to set the ark of the covenant of
the LORD there. [20]The inner sanctuary was
twenty cubits long, twenty wide and twenty
high.[g] He overlaid the inside with pure gold,
and he also overlaid the altar of cedar. [21]Sol-
omon covered the inside of the temple with
pure gold, and he extended gold chains
across the front of the inner sanctuary,
which was overlaid with gold. [22]So he over-
laid the whole interior with gold. He also
overlaid with gold the altar that belonged to
the inner sanctuary.

[23]In the inner sanctuary he made a pair
of cherubim[m] of olive wood, each ten cubits[h]
high. [24]One wing of the first cherub was
five cubits long, and the other wing five cu-
bits—ten cubits from wing tip to wing tip.
[25]The second cherub also measured ten cu-
bits, for the two cherubim were identical in
size and shape. [26]The height of each cherub
was ten cubits. [27]He placed the cherubim[n] in-
side the innermost room of the temple, with
their wings spread out. The wing of one
cherub touched one wall, while the wing of
the other touched the other wall, and their
wings touched each other in the middle of
the room. [28]He overlaid the cherubim with
gold.

[29]On the walls all around the temple, in
both the inner and outer rooms, he carved
cherubim, palm trees and open flowers. [30]He
also covered the floors of both the inner and
outer rooms of the temple with gold.

[31]For the entrance of the inner sanctuary
he made doors of olive wood with five-sided
jambs. [32]And on the two olive wood doors he
carved cherubim, palm trees and open flow-
ers, and overlaid the cherubim and palm
trees with beaten gold. [33]In the same way he
made four-sided jambs of olive wood for the
entrance to the main hall. [34]He also made
two pine doors, each having two leaves that
turned in sockets. [35]He carved cherubim,
palm trees and open flowers on them and
overlaid them with gold hammered evenly
over the carvings.

[36]And he built the inner courtyard of
three courses[o] of dressed stone and one
course of trimmed cedar beams.

[37]The foundation of the temple of the
LORD was laid in the fourth year, in the
month of Ziv. [38]In the eleventh year in
the month of Bul, the eighth month, the tem-
ple was finished in all its details according

**6:5** g Eze 41:5–6
**6:7** h Dt 27:5
**6:9** i ver 14,38
**6:12** j 2Sa 7:12–16; 1Ki 9:5
**6:13** k Ex 25:8; Dt 31:6
**6:16** l Ex 26:33; Lev 16:2; 1Ki 8:6
**6:23** m Ex 37:1–9
**6:27** n Ex 25:20; 37:9
**6:36** o 1Ki 7:12

[a]6 That is, about 7 1/2 feet (about 2.3 meters); also in verses 10 and 24 [b]6 That is, about 9 feet (about 2.7 meters)
[c]6 That is, about 10 1/2 feet (about 3.1 meters) [d]8 Septuagint; Hebrew *middle* [e]16 That is, about 30 feet (about 9 meters) [f]17 That is, about 60 feet (about 18 meters) [g]20 That is, about 30 feet (about 9 meters) long, wide and high
[h]23 That is, about 15 feet (about 4.5 meters)

to its specifications. He had spent seven years building it.

## Solomon Builds His Palace

7 It took Solomon thirteen years, however, to complete the construction of his palace.[p] 2He built the Palace of the Forest of Lebanon[q] a hundred cubits long, fifty wide and thirty high,[a] with four rows of cedar columns supporting trimmed cedar beams. 3It was roofed with cedar above the beams that rested on the columns—forty-five beams, fifteen to a row. 4Its windows were placed high in sets of three, facing each other. 5All the doorways had rectangular frames; they were in the front part in sets of three, facing each other.[b]

6He made a colonnade fifty cubits long and thirty wide.[c] In front of it was a portico, and in front of that were pillars and an overhanging roof.

7He built the throne hall, the Hall of Justice, where he was to judge, and he covered it with cedar from floor to ceiling.[d][r] 8And the palace in which he was to live, set farther back, was similar in design. Solomon also made a palace like this hall for Pharaoh's daughter, whom he had married.[s]

9All these structures, from the outside to the great courtyard and from foundation to eaves, were made of blocks of high-grade stone cut to size and trimmed with a saw on their inner and outer faces. 10The foundations were laid with large stones of good quality, some measuring ten cubits[e] and some eight.[f] 11Above were high-grade stones, cut to size, and cedar beams. 12The great courtyard was surrounded by a wall of three courses[t] of dressed stone and one course of trimmed cedar beams, as was the inner courtyard of the temple of the LORD with its portico.

## The Temple's Furnishings

13King Solomon sent to Tyre and brought Huram,[g] 14whose mother was a widow from the tribe of Naphtali and whose father was a man of Tyre and a craftsman in bronze. Huram was highly skilled[u] and experienced in all kinds of bronze work. He came to King Solomon and did all[v] the work assigned to him.

15He cast two bronze pillars,[w] each eighteen cubits high and twelve cubits around,[h] by line. 16He also made two capitals of cast bronze to set on the tops of the pillars; each capital was five cubits[i] high. 17A network of interwoven chains festooned the capitals on top of the pillars, seven for each capital. 18He made pomegranates in two rows[j] encircling each network to decorate the capitals on top of the pillars.[k] He did the same for each capital. 19The capitals on top of the pillars in the portico were in the shape of lilies, four cubits[l] high. 20On the capitals of both pillars, above the bowl-shaped part next to the network, were the two hundred pomegranates[x] in rows all around. 21He erected the pillars at the portico of the temple. The pillar to the south he named Jakin[m] and the one to the north Boaz.[n][y] 22The capitals on top were in the shape of lilies. And so the work on the pillars was completed.

23He made the Sea[z] of cast metal, circular in shape, measuring ten cubits[e] from rim to rim and five cubits high. It took a line of thirty cubits[o] to measure around it. 24Below the rim, gourds encircled it—ten to a cubit. The gourds were cast in two rows in one piece with the Sea.

25The Sea stood on twelve bulls,[a] three facing north, three facing west, three facing south and three facing east. The Sea rested on top of them, and their hindquarters were toward the center. 26It was a handbreadth[p] in thickness, and its rim was like the rim of a cup, like a lily blossom. It held two thousand baths.[q]

27He also made ten movable stands[b] of bronze; each was four cubits long, four wide

**7:1** p 1Ki 9:10; 2Ch 8:1
**7:2** q 1Ki 10:17
**7:7** r 1Ki 6:15
**7:8** s 1Ki 3:1; 2Ch 8:11
**7:12** t 1Ki 6:36
**7:14** u Ex 31:2-5; 2Ch 2:14 v 2Ch 4:11,16
**7:15** w 2Ki 25:17; 2Ch 3:15
**7:20** x 2Ch 3:16; 4:13
**7:21** y 2Ch 3:17
**7:23** z 2Ki 25:13
**7:25** a Jer 52:20
**7:27** b 2Ch 4:14

[a]2 That is, about 150 feet (about 46 meters) long, 75 feet (about 23 meters) wide and 45 feet (about 13.5 meters) high [b]5 The meaning of the Hebrew for this verse is uncertain. [c]6 That is, about 75 feet (about 23 meters) long and 45 feet (about 13.5 meters) wide [d]7 Vulgate and Syriac; Hebrew *floor* [e]10,23 That is, about 15 feet (about 4.5 meters) [f]10 That is, about 12 feet (about 3.6 meters) [g]13 Hebrew *Hiram,* a variant of *Huram*; also in verses 40 and 45 [h]15 That is, about 27 feet (about 8.1 meters) high and 18 feet (about 5.4 meters) around [i]16 That is, about 7 1/2 feet (about 2.3 meters); also in verse 23 [j]18 Two Hebrew manuscripts and Septuagint; most Hebrew manuscripts *made the pillars, and there were two rows* [k]18 Many Hebrew manuscripts and Syriac; most Hebrew manuscripts *pomegranates* [l]19 That is, about 6 feet (about 1.8 meters); also in verse 38 [m]21 *Jakin* probably means *he establishes.* [n]21 *Boaz* probably means *in him is strength.* [o]23 That is, about 45 feet (about 13.5 meters) [p]26 That is, about 3 inches (about 8 centimeters) [q]26 That is, probably about 11,500 gallons (about 44 kiloliters); the Septuagint does not have this sentence.

> **7:38** c 2Ch 4:6

and three high.[a] 28 This is how the stands were made: They had side panels attached to uprights. 29 On the panels between the uprights were lions, bulls and cherubim—and on the uprights as well. Above and below the lions and bulls were wreaths of hammered work. 30 Each stand had four bronze wheels with bronze axles, and each had a basin resting on four supports, cast with wreaths on each side. 31 On the inside of the stand there was an opening that had a circular frame one cubit[b] deep. This opening was round, and with its basework it measured a cubit and a half.[c] Around its opening there was engraving. The panels of the stands were square, not round. 32 The four wheels were under the panels, and the axles of the wheels were attached to the stand. The diameter of each wheel was a cubit and a half. 33 The wheels were made like chariot wheels; the axles, rims, spokes and hubs were all of cast metal.

34 Each stand had four handles, one on each corner, projecting from the stand. 35 At the top of the stand there was a circular band half a cubit[d] deep. The supports and panels were attached to the top of the stand. 36 He engraved cherubim, lions and palm trees on the surfaces of the supports and on the panels, in every available space, with wreaths all around. 37 This is the way he made the ten stands. They were all cast in the same molds and were identical in size and shape.

38 He then made ten bronze basins,[c] each holding forty baths[e] and measuring four cubits across, one basin to go on each of the ten stands. 39 He placed five of the stands on the south side of the temple and five on the north. He placed the Sea on the south side, at the southeast corner of the temple. 40 He also made the basins and shovels and sprinkling bowls.

So Huram finished all the work he had undertaken for King Solomon in the temple of the LORD:

41 the two pillars;
the two bowl-shaped capitals on top of the pillars;
the two sets of network decorating the two bowl-shaped capitals on top of the pillars;
42 the four hundred pomegranates for the two sets of network (two rows of pomegranates for each network, decorating the bowl-shaped capitals on top of the pillars);
43 the ten stands with their ten basins;
44 the Sea and the twelve bulls under it;
45 the pots, shovels and sprinkling bowls.

All these objects that Huram made for King Solomon for the temple of the LORD were of burnished bronze. 46 The king had them cast in clay molds in the plain of the Jordan between Succoth and Zarethan.[d] 47 Solomon left all these things unweighed, because there were so many; the weight of the bronze was not determined.

48 Solomon also made all the furnishings that were in the LORD's temple:

the golden altar;
the golden table[e] on which was the bread of the Presence;
49 the lampstands of pure gold (five on the right and five on the left, in front of the inner sanctuary);
the gold floral work and lamps and tongs;
50 the pure gold basins, wick trimmers, sprinkling bowls, dishes and censers;
and the gold sockets for the doors of the innermost room, the Most Holy Place, and also for the doors of the main hall of the temple.

51 When all the work King Solomon had done for the temple of the LORD was finished, he brought in the things his father David had dedicated[f]—the silver and gold and the furnishings—and he placed them in the treasuries of the LORD's temple.

> **7:46** d Jos 3:16
> **7:48** e Ex 37:10
> **7:51** f 2Sa 8:11

## The Ark Brought to the Temple

8 Then King Solomon summoned into his presence at Jerusalem the elders of Israel, all the heads of the tribes and the chiefs of the Israelite families, to bring up

[a] 27 That is, about 6 feet (about 1.8 meters) long and wide and about 4 1/2 feet (about 1.3 meters) high [b] 31 That is, about 1 1/2 feet (about 0.5 meter) [c] 31 That is, about 2 1/4 feet (about 0.7 meter); also in verse 32 [d] 35 That is, about 3/4 foot (about 0.2 meter) [e] 38 That is, about 230 gallons (about 880 liters)

the ark[g] of the LORD's covenant from Zion, the City of David.[h] 2All the men of Israel came together to King Solomon at the time of the festival in the month of Ethanim, the seventh month.[i]

3When all the elders of Israel had arrived, the priests took up the ark, 4and they brought up the ark of the LORD and the Tent of Meeting[j] and all the sacred furnishings in it. The priests and Levites carried them up, 5and King Solomon and the entire assembly of Israel that had gathered about him were before the ark, sacrificing[k] so many sheep and cattle that they could not be recorded or counted.

6The priests then brought the ark of the LORD's covenant to its place in the inner sanctuary of the temple, the Most Holy Place, and put it beneath the wings of the cherubim.[l] 7The cherubim spread their wings over the place of the ark and overshadowed the ark and its carrying poles. 8These poles were so long that their ends could be seen from the Holy Place in front of the inner sanctuary, but not from outside the Holy Place; and they are still there today.[m] 9There was nothing in the ark except the two stone tablets[n] that Moses had placed in it at Horeb, where the LORD made a covenant with the Israelites after they came out of Egypt.

10When the priests withdrew from the Holy Place, the cloud[o] filled the temple of the LORD. 11And the priests could not perform their service because of the cloud, for the glory of the LORD filled his temple.

12Then Solomon said, "The LORD has said that he would dwell in a dark cloud; 13I have indeed built a magnificent temple for you, a place for you to dwell[p] forever."

14While the whole assembly of Israel was standing there, the king turned around and blessed[q] them. 15Then he said:

> "Praise be to the LORD, the God of Israel, who with his own hand has fulfilled what he promised with his own mouth to my father David. For he said, 16'Since the day I brought my people Israel out of Egypt, I have not chosen a city in any tribe of Israel to have a temple built for my Name to be there, but I have chosen[r] David to rule my people Israel.'

17"My father David had it in his heart to build a temple for the Name of the LORD, the God of Israel. 18But the LORD said to my father David, 'Because it was in your heart to build a temple for my Name, you did well to have this in your heart. 19Nevertheless, you[s] are not the one to build the temple, but your son, who is your own flesh and blood—he is the one who will build the temple for my Name.'[t]

20"The LORD has kept the promise he made: I have succeeded David my father and now I sit on the throne of Israel, just as the LORD promised, and I have built[u] the temple for the Name of the LORD, the God of Israel. 21I have provided a place there for the ark, in which is the covenant of the LORD that he made with our fathers when he brought them out of Egypt."

## Solomon's Prayer of Dedication

22Then Solomon stood before the altar of the LORD in front of the whole assembly of Israel, spread out his hands[v] toward heaven 23and said:

> "O LORD, God of Israel, there is no God like you in heaven above or on earth below—you who keep your covenant of love[w] with your servants who continue wholeheartedly in your way. 24You have kept your promise to your servant David my father; with your mouth you have promised and with your hand you have fulfilled it—as it is today.

> 25"Now LORD, God of Israel, keep for your servant David my father the promises you made to him when you said, 'You shall never fail to have a man to sit before me on the throne of Israel, if only your sons are careful in all they do to walk before me as you have done.' 26And now, O God of Israel, let your word that you promised[x] your servant David my father come true.

> 27"But will God really dwell[y] on earth? The heavens, even the highest heaven, cannot contain[z] you. How much less this temple I have built! 28Yet give attention to your servant's

**8:1** g 2Sa 6:17 h 2Sa 5:7
**8:2** i Lev 23:34
**8:4** j 2Ch 1:3
**8:5** k 2Sa 6:13
**8:6** l 1Ki 6:19,27
**8:8** m Ex 25:13–15
**8:9** n Ex 25:21; Dt 10:2–5; Heb 9:4
**8:10** o Ex 40:34–35
**8:13** p Ps 132:13
**8:14** q 2Sa 6:18
**8:16** r 1Sa 16:1
**8:19** s 2Sa 7:5 t 2Sa 7:13
**8:20** u 1Ch 28:6
**8:22** v Ezr 9:5
**8:23** w Dt 7:9,12; Ne 1:5
**8:26** x 2Sa 7:25
**8:27** y Ac 7:48 z 2Ch 2:6; Isa 66:1; Jer 23:24

prayer and his plea for mercy, O LORD my God. Hear the cry and the prayer that your servant is praying in your presence this day. 29 May your eyes be open toward this temple night and day, this place of which you said, 'My Name[a] shall be there,' so that you will hear the prayer your servant prays toward this place. 30 Hear the supplication of your servant and of your people Israel when they pray toward this place. Hear from heaven, your dwelling place, and when you hear, forgive.

31 "When a man wrongs his neighbor and is required to take an oath and he comes and swears the oath[b] before your altar in this temple, 32 then hear from heaven and act. Judge between your servants, condemning the guilty and bringing down on his own head what he has done. Declare the innocent not guilty, and so establish his innocence.[c]

33 "When your people Israel have been defeated[d] by an enemy because they have sinned against you, and when they turn back to you and confess your name, praying and making supplication to you in this temple, 34 then hear from heaven and forgive the sin of your people Israel and bring them back to the land you gave to their fathers.

35 "When the heavens are shut up and there is no rain[e] because your people have sinned against you, and when they pray toward this place and confess your name and turn from their sin because you have afflicted them, 36 then hear from heaven and forgive the sin of your servants, your people Israel. Teach[f] them the right way[g] to live, and send rain on the land you gave your people for an inheritance.

37 "When famine[h] or plague comes to the land, or blight or mildew, locusts or grasshoppers, or when an enemy besieges them in any of their cities, whatever disaster or disease may come, 38 and when a prayer or plea is made by any of your people Israel—each one aware of the afflictions of his own heart, and spreading out his hands toward this temple— 39 then hear from heaven, your dwelling place. Forgive and act; deal with each man according to all he does, since you know[i] his heart (for you alone know the hearts of all men), 40 so that they will fear you all the time they live in the land you gave our fathers.

41 "As for the foreigner who does not belong to your people Israel but has come from a distant land because of your name— 42 for men will hear of your great name and your mighty hand[j] and your outstretched arm—when he comes and prays toward this temple, 43 then hear from heaven, your dwelling place, and do whatever the foreigner asks of you, so that all the peoples of the earth may know[k] your name and fear you, as do your own people Israel, and may know that this house I have built bears your Name.

44 "When your people go to war against their enemies, wherever you send them, and when they pray to the LORD toward the city you have chosen and the temple I have built for your Name, 45 then hear from heaven their prayer and their plea, and uphold their cause.

46 "When they sin against you—for there is no one who does not sin—and you become angry with them and give them over to the enemy, who takes them captive[l] to his own land, far away or near; 47 and if they have a change of heart in the land where they are held captive, and repent and plead[m] with you in the land of their conquerors and say, 'We have sinned, we have done wrong, we have acted wickedly';[n] 48 and if they turn back to you with all their heart and soul in the land of their enemies who took them captive, and pray[o] to you toward the land you gave their fathers, toward the city you have chosen and the temple I have built for your Name; 49 then from heaven, your dwelling place, hear their prayer and their plea, and uphold their cause.

**8:29** a Dt 12:11
**8:31** b Ex 22:11
**8:32** c Dt 25:1
**8:33** d Lev 26:17; Dt 28:25
**8:35** e Lev 26:19
**8:36** f 1Sa 12:23 g Ps 27:11
**8:37** h Lev 26:26
**8:39** i 1Sa 16:7; 1Ch 28:9; Ps 11:4; Jer 17:10
**8:42** j Dt 3:24
**8:43** k 1Sa 17:46
**8:46** l Lev 26:33–39
**8:47** m Ne 1:6 n Ps 106:6
**8:48** o Da 6:10

**8:50** p Ps 106:46
**8:51** q Dt 9:29 r Jer 11:4
**8:53** s Ex 19:5
**8:56** t Dt 12:10 u Jos 23:15
**8:57** v Jos 1:5
**8:58** w Ps 119:36
**8:61** x 1Ki 11:4; 2Ki 20:3

50 And forgive your people, who have
sinned against you; forgive all the
offenses they have committed against
you, and cause their conquerors to
show them mercy;[p] 51 for they are your
people and your inheritance,[q] whom
you brought out of Egypt, out of that
iron-smelting furnace.[r]

52 "May your eyes be open to your
servant's plea and to the plea of your
people Israel, and may you listen to
them whenever they cry out to you.
53 For you singled them out from all
the nations of the world to be your
own inheritance,[s] just as you declared
through your servant Moses when
you, O Sovereign LORD, brought our fa-
thers out of Egypt."

54 When Solomon had finished all these
prayers and supplications to the LORD, he
rose from before the altar of the LORD, where
he had been kneeling with his hands spread
out toward heaven. 55 He stood and blessed
the whole assembly of Israel in a loud
voice, saying:

56 "Praise be to the LORD, who has
given rest[t] to his people Israel just as
he promised. Not one word has failed
of all the good promises[u] he gave
through his servant Moses. 57 May the
LORD our God be with us as he was
with our fathers; may he never leave
us nor forsake[v] us. 58 May he turn our
hearts[w] to him, to walk in all his ways
and to keep the commands, decrees
and regulations he gave our fathers.
59 And may these words of mine, which
I have prayed before the LORD, be near
to the LORD our God day and night,
that he may uphold the cause of his ser-
vant and the cause of his people Israel
according to each day's need, 60 so that
all the peoples of the earth may know
that the LORD is God and that there is
no other. 61 But your hearts must be
fully committed[x] to the LORD our God,
to live by his decrees and obey his com-
mands, as at this time."

## The Dedication of the Temple

62 Then the king and all Israel with him of-
fered sacrifices before the LORD. 63 Solomon
offered a sacrifice of fellowship offerings[a]
to the LORD: twenty-two thousand cattle
and a hundred and twenty thousand sheep
and goats. So the king and all the Israelites
dedicated the temple of the LORD.

64 On that same day the king consecrated
the middle part of the courtyard in front of
the temple of the LORD, and there he offered
burnt offerings, grain offerings and the
fat of the fellowship offerings, because the
bronze altar[y] before the LORD was too small
to hold the burnt offerings, the grain offer-
ings and the fat of the fellowship offerings.

65 So Solomon observed the festival at
that time, and all Israel with him—a vast as-
sembly, people from Lebo[b] Hamath[z] to the
Wadi of Egypt.[a] They celebrated it before
the LORD our God for seven days and seven
days more, fourteen days in all. 66 On the
following day he sent the people away. They
blessed the king and then went home, joyful
and glad in heart for all the good things the
LORD had done for his servant David and his
people Israel.

## The LORD Appears to Solomon

9 When Solomon had finished building
the temple of the LORD and the royal
palace, and had achieved all he had desired
to do, 2 the LORD appeared[b] to him a second
time, as he had appeared to him at Gibeon.
3 The LORD said to him:

"I have heard[c] the prayer and plea
you have made before me; I have
consecrated this temple, which you
have built, by putting my Name there
forever. My eyes[d] and my heart will al-
ways be there.

4 "As for you, if you walk before me
in integrity of heart and uprightness,
as David your father did, and do all I
command and observe my decrees
and laws, 5 I will establish[e] your royal
throne over Israel forever, as I prom-
ised David your father when I said,
'You shall never fail[f] to have a man on
the throne of Israel.'

**8:64** y 2Ch 4:1
**8:65** z Nu 34:8 a Ge 15:18
**9:2** b 1Ki 3:5
**9:3** c 2Ki 20:5 d Dt 11:12
**9:5** e 1Ch 22:10 f 2Sa 7:15; 1Ki 2:4

[a] 63 Traditionally *peace offerings*; also in verse 64 [b] 65 Or *from the entrance to*

**9:7**
g 2Ki17:23
h Jer 7:14
i Dt28:37

**9:8**
j Dt29:24;
Jer 22:8–9

6“But if you[a] or your sons turn
away from me and do not observe the
commands and decrees I have given
you[a] and go off to serve other gods
and worship them, 7then I will cut
off Israel from the land[g] I have given
them and will reject this temple I have
consecrated for my Name.[h] Israel will
then become a byword and an object
of ridicule[i] among all peoples. 8And
though this temple is now imposing,
all who pass by will be appalled and
will scoff and say, ‘Why has the LORD
done such a thing to this land and to
this temple?’[j] 9People will answer, ‘Be-
cause they have forsaken the LORD their
God, who brought their fathers out of
Egypt, and have embraced other gods,
worshiping and serving them—that is
why the LORD brought all this disaster
on them.’ ”

## Solomon’s Other Activities

10At the end of twenty years, during
which Solomon built these two buildings—
the temple of the LORD and the royal pal-
ace— 11King Solomon gave twenty towns
in Galilee to Hiram king of Tyre, because Hi-
ram had supplied him with all the cedar and
pine and gold he wanted. 12But when Hiram
went from Tyre to see the towns that Solo-
mon had given him, he was not pleased with
them. 13“What kind of towns are these you
have given me, my brother?” he asked. And
he called them the Land of Cabul,[b][k] a name
they have to this day. 14Now Hiram had sent
to the king 120 talents[c] of gold.
15Here is the account of the forced labor
King Solomon conscripted[l] to build the
LORD’s temple, his own palace, the support-
ing terraces,[d][m] the wall of Jerusalem, and
Hazor, Megiddo and Gezer. 16(Pharaoh king
of Egypt had attacked and captured Gezer.
He had set it on fire. He killed its Canaanite
inhabitants and then gave it as a wedding
gift to his daughter, Solomon’s wife. 17And
Solomon rebuilt Gezer.) He built up Lower
Beth Horon,[n] 18Baalath, and Tadmor[e] in the
desert, within his land, 19as well as all his
store cities and the towns for his chariots[o]
and for his horses[f]—whatever he desired to
build in Jerusalem, in Lebanon and through-
out all the territory he ruled.
20All the people left from the Amorites,
Hittites, Perizzites, Hivites and Jebusites
(these peoples were not Israelites), 21that
is, their descendants remaining in the
land, whom the Israelites could not extermi-
nate[g][p]—these Solomon conscripted for his
slave labor force,[q] as it is to this day. 22But
Solomon did not make slaves[r] of any of the
Israelites; they were his fighting men, his
government officials, his officers, his cap-
tains, and the commanders of his chariots
and charioteers. 23They were also the chief
officials in charge of Solomon’s projects—

**9:13**
k Jos 19:27

**9:15**
l 1Ki5:13
m 2Sa 5:9

**9:17**
n Jos 16:3;
2Ch 8:5

**9:19**
o 1Ki 4:26

**9:21**
p Jos 15:63;
17:12
q Ezr 2:55,58

**9:22**
r Lev 25:39

[a]6 The Hebrew is plural. [b]13 *Cabul* sounds like the Hebrew for *good-for-nothing.* [c]14 That is, about 4 1/2 tons (about 4 metric tons) [d]15 Or *the Millo*; also in verse 24 [e]18 The Hebrew may also be read *Tamar.* [f]19 Or *charioteers*
[g]21 The Hebrew term refers to the irrevocable giving over of things or persons to the LORD, often by totally destroying them.

## *The African Presence*

### 1 Kings 9:20–21

Solomon enslaved the Amorites, Hittites, Perizzites, Hivites and Jebusites—all were descendants of Canaan, son of Ham. Because Ham’s offspring represent the geographic territories once dominated by Egypt—present-day Egypt, Libya and Sudan and into the area today known as Israel—they can claim a relation to African heritage. Since “heritage” is something “passed down” or “inherited,” Canaan (Israel or Palestine) most certainly received or was influenced by Egypt culturally, politically, religiously, etc.

**9:24** s 1Ki 3:1
t 1Ki 11:27; 2Ch 32:5
**9:26** u 1Ki 22:48
v Nu 33:35
**9:27** w 1Ki 10:11
**10:1** x Mt 12:42

550 officials supervising the men who did the work.

24 After Pharaoh's daughter[s] had come up from the City of David to the palace Solomon had built for her, he constructed the supporting terraces.[t]

25 Three times a year Solomon sacrificed burnt offerings and fellowship offerings[a] on the altar he had built for the LORD, burning incense before the LORD along with them, and so fulfilled the temple obligations.

26 King Solomon also built ships[u] at Ezion Geber,[v] which is near Elath in Edom, on the shore of the Red Sea.[b] 27 And Hiram sent his men—sailors[w] who knew the sea—to serve in the fleet with Solomon's men. 28 They sailed to Ophir and brought back 420 talents[c] of gold, which they delivered to King Solomon.

## The Queen of Sheba Visits Solomon

10 When the queen of Sheba[x] heard about the fame of Solomon and his relation to the name of the LORD, she came to test him with hard questions. 2 Arriving at Jerusalem with a very great caravan—with camels carrying spices, large quantities of gold, and precious stones—she came to Solomon and talked with him about all that she had on her mind. 3 Solomon answered all her questions; nothing was too hard for the king to explain to her. 4 When the queen of Sheba saw all the wisdom of Solomon and the palace he had built, 5 the food on his table, the seating of his officials, the attending servants in their robes, his cupbearers, and the burnt offerings he made at[d] the temple of the LORD, she was overwhelmed.

6 She said to the king, "The report I heard in my own country about your achievements and your wisdom is true. 7 But I did not believe these things until I came and saw with my own eyes. Indeed, not even half was told me; in wisdom and wealth you have far exceeded the report I heard. 8 How happy your men must be! How happy your officials, who continually stand before you and hear[y] your wisdom! 9 Praise[z] be to the LORD your God, who has delighted in you and placed you on the throne of Israel. Because of the LORD's eternal love for Israel, he has made you king, to maintain justice[a] and righteousness."

10 And she gave the king 120 talents[e] of gold, large quantities of spices, and precious stones. Never again were so many spices brought in as those the queen of Sheba gave to King Solomon.

11 (Hiram's ships brought gold from Ophir;[b] and from there they brought great cargoes of almugwood[f] and precious stones. 12 The king used the almugwood to make supports for the temple of the LORD and for the royal palace, and to make harps and lyres for the musicians. So much almugwood has never been imported or seen since that day.)

13 King Solomon gave the queen of Sheba all she desired and asked for, besides what he had given her out of his royal bounty. Then she left and returned with her retinue to her own country.

**10:8** y Pr 8:34
**10:9** z 1Ki 5:7
a 2Sa 8:15; Ps 72:2
**10:11** b 1Ki 9:27-28

[a] 25 Traditionally *peace offerings* [b] 26 Hebrew *Yam Suph*; that is, Sea of Reeds [c] 28 That is, about 16 tons (about 14.5 metric tons) [d] 5 Or *the ascent by which he went up to* [e] 10 That is, about 4 1/2 tons (about 4 metric tons) [f] 11 Probably a variant of *algumwood*; also in verse 12

## The African Presence

**1 Kings 10:1–13**

According to the Coptic church tradition, Solomon fathered a son, Menelek, with the queen of Sheba. Sheba was located in southern Arabia, in present-day Yemen, across the Red Sea from present-day Ethiopia.

10:16 c 1Ki 14:26–28
10:17 d 1Ki 7:2
10:23 e 1Ki 3:13 f 1Ki 4:30

## Solomon's Splendor

14 The weight of the gold that Solomon received yearly was 666 talents,[a] 15 not including the revenues from merchants and traders and from all the Arabian kings and the governors of the land.

16 King Solomon made two hundred large shields[c] of hammered gold; six hundred bekas[b] of gold went into each shield. 17 He also made three hundred small shields of hammered gold, with three minas[c] of gold in each shield. The king put them in the Palace of the Forest of Lebanon.[d]

18 Then the king made a great throne inlaid with ivory and overlaid with fine gold. 19 The throne had six steps, and its back had a rounded top. On both sides of the seat were armrests, with a lion standing beside each of them. 20 Twelve lions stood on the six steps, one at either end of each step. Nothing like it had ever been made for any other kingdom. 21 All King Solomon's goblets were gold, and all the household articles in the Palace of the Forest of Lebanon were pure gold. Nothing was made of silver, because silver was considered of little value in Solomon's days. 22 The king had a fleet of trading ships[d] at sea along with the ships of Hiram. Once every three years it returned, carrying gold, silver and ivory, and apes and baboons.

23 King Solomon was greater in riches[e] and wisdom[f] than all the other kings of the earth. 24 The whole world sought audience with Solomon to hear the wisdom God had put in his heart. 25 Year after year, everyone who came brought a gift—articles of silver and gold, robes, weapons and spices, and horses and mules.

26 Solomon accumulated chariots and horses;[g] he had fourteen hundred chariots and twelve thousand horses,[e] which he kept in the chariot cities and also with him in Jerusalem. 27 The king made silver as common in Jerusalem as stones, and cedar as plentiful as sycamore-fig trees in the foothills. 28 Solomon's horses were imported from Egypt[f] and from Kue[g]—the royal merchants purchased them from Kue. 29 They imported a chariot from Egypt for six hundred shekels[h] of silver, and a horse for a hundred and fifty.[c] They also exported them to all the kings of the Hittites and of the Arameans.

## Solomon's Wives

11 King Solomon, however, loved many foreign women[h] besides Pharaoh's daughter—Moabites, Ammonites, Edomites, Sidonians and Hittites. 2 They were from nations about which the LORD had told the Israelites, "You must not intermarry[i] with them, because they will surely turn your hearts after their gods." Nevertheless, Solomon held fast to them in love. 3 He had seven hundred wives of royal birth and three hundred concubines, and his wives led him astray. 4 As Solomon grew old, his wives turned his heart after other gods, and his heart was not fully devoted to the LORD his God, as the heart of David his father had been. 5 He followed Ashtoreth[j] the goddess of the Sidonians, and Molech[i] the detestable god of the Ammonites. 6 So Solomon did evil in the eyes of the LORD; he did

10:26 g 1Ki 4:26; 2Ch 1:14; 9:25
11:1 h Ne 13:26
11:2 i Ex 34:16; Dt 7:3–4
11:5 j Jdg 2:13

[a]14 That is, about 25 tons (about 23 metric tons) [b]16 That is, about 7 1/2 pounds (about 3.5 kilograms) [c]17,29 That is, about 3 3/4 pounds (about 1.7 kilograms) [d]22 Hebrew *of ships of Tarshish* [e]26 Or *charioteers* [f]28 Or possibly *Muzur,* a region in Cilicia; also in verse 29 [g]28 Probably *Cilicia* [h]29 That is, about 15 pounds (about 7 kilograms) [i]5 Hebrew *Milcom*; also in verse 33

### The African Presence

**1 Kings 11:1**

Solomon married many wives, including Egyptians and Hittites, from among the nations surrounding the Israelites.

# The Queen of Sheba

## In Search of True Wisdom

The queen of Sheba, also known as the Queen of the South (see Mt 12:42; Lk 11:31), was perhaps one of the most powerful women of her day. Scholars generally agree that she reigned over territory in southwest Arabia (modern Yemen), across the Red Sea from northeast Africa. The name *Sheba* (or *Seba*) implies that this queen was a woman of color. Sheba is mentioned as a grandson of Keturah, Abraham's second wife (see Ge 25:1–4; 1Ch 1:32; see the African Presence notes on Genesis 25:1–2 and Exodus 2:16–22).

As we look at the exchange of gifts between the queen of Sheba and Solomon (see 1Ki 10:10–13; 2Ch 9:9–12), several points deserve further consideration. First, she came bearing gifts. The area from which the queen of Sheba came was known for both gold and spices. She gave the king 120 talents (about 4.5 tons) of gold and scores of spices and jewels. Jewish historians give her credit for introducing the cultivation of certain spices, like balsam, to Israel. The kinds of gifts she gave and the quantities of those gifts had never been seen in Israel.

Second, notice the gifts that Solomon gave the queen of Sheba. Though Solomon was known for being generous with his many guests, he was reported to have been exceptionally generous with the queen of Sheba. He gave her anything her heart desired. The total of the gifts he gave her exceeded what she had given him (see 2Ch 9:12). They appear to have made a profound impression upon one another. His wisdom and opulence awed the queen. And even though she was a woman of enormous wealth and wisdom, Solomon's magnificent wealth and wisdom overwhelmed her. And out of respect for him, she gave the highest praise to his God. God later gave the queen of Sheba a great tribute also: He used her to show the Pharisees how foolish they were (see Mt 12:42).

Solomon, who was reported to have had 700 wives and 300 concubines, obviously had special regard for this powerful woman of color who sought out wisdom for herself. Jewish tradition tells us that Solomon and the queen of Sheba parented a son, believed to be King Menelek.

—A. S. Fosua

### reflection

*What price are you willing to pay to gain true wisdom?*

*Are you willing to give up some things to seek God fully?*

### read

1 Kings 10:1–13; 2 Chronicles 9:1–12; Matthew 12:42.

See also the Inspire Notes "Discernment," "Responsible Decisions in Leadership" and "Seek Wisdom," and the Women of the Bible Notes "Abigail: A Wise Wife," "Wisdom Personified: The Cry of Wisdom" and "Candace: Secure Leader."

For the next Women of the Bible note, go to page 436.

not follow the LORD completely, as David his father had done.

7On a hill east[k] of Jerusalem, Solomon built a high place for Chemosh[l] the detestable god of Moab, and for Molech the detestable god of the Ammonites. 8He did the same for all his foreign wives, who burned incense and offered sacrifices to their gods.

9The LORD became angry with Solomon because his heart had turned away from the LORD, the God of Israel, who had appeared[m] to him twice. 10Although he had forbidden Solomon to follow other gods,[n] Solomon did not keep the LORD's command.[o] 11So the LORD said to Solomon, "Since this is your attitude and you have not kept my covenant and my decrees, which I commanded you, I will most certainly tear[p] the kingdom away from you and give it to one of your subordinates. 12Nevertheless, for the sake of David your father, I will not do it during your lifetime. I will tear it out of the hand of your son. 13Yet I will not tear the whole kingdom from him, but will give him one tribe for the sake[q] of David my servant and for the sake of Jerusalem, which I have chosen."

## Solomon's Adversaries

14Then the LORD raised up against Solomon an adversary, Hadad the Edomite, from the royal line of Edom. 15Earlier when David was fighting with Edom, Joab the commander of the army, who had gone up to bury the dead, had struck down all the men in Edom.[r] 16Joab and all the Israelites stayed there for six months, until they had destroyed all the men in Edom. 17But Hadad, still only a boy, fled to Egypt with some Edomite officials who had served his father. 18They set out from Midian and went to Paran. Then taking men from Paran with them, they went to Egypt, to Pharaoh king of Egypt, who gave Hadad a house and land and provided him with food.

19Pharaoh was so pleased with Hadad that he gave him a sister of his own wife, Queen Tahpenes, in marriage. 20The sister of Tahpenes bore him a son named Genubath, whom Tahpenes brought up in the royal palace. There Genubath lived with Pharaoh's own children.

21While he was in Egypt, Hadad heard that David rested with his fathers and that Joab the commander of the army was also dead. Then Hadad said to Pharaoh, "Let me go, that I may return to my own country."

22"What have you lacked here that you want to go back to your own country?" Pharaoh asked.

"Nothing," Hadad replied, "but do let me go!"

23And God raised up against Solomon another adversary, Rezon son of Eliada, who had fled from his master, Hadadezer[s] king of Zobah. 24He gathered men around him and became the leader of a band of rebels when David destroyed the forces[a] ⌞of Zobah⌟; the rebels went to Damascus,[t] where they settled and took control. 25Rezon was Israel's adversary as long as Solomon lived, adding to the trouble caused by Hadad. So Rezon ruled in Aram and was hostile toward Israel.

## Jeroboam Rebels Against Solomon

26Also, Jeroboam son of Nebat rebelled[u] against the king. He was one of Solomon's officials, an Ephraimite from Zeredah, and his mother was a widow named Zeruah.

27Here is the account of how he rebelled against the king: Solomon had built the supporting terraces[b][v] and had filled in the gap in the wall of the city of David his father. 28Now Jeroboam was a man of standing, and when Solomon saw how well the young man did his work, he put him in charge of the whole labor force of the house of Joseph.

29About that time Jeroboam was going out of Jerusalem, and Ahijah[w] the prophet of Shiloh met him on the way, wearing a new cloak. The two of them were alone out in the country, 30and Ahijah took hold of the new cloak he was wearing and tore[x] it into twelve pieces. 31Then he said to Jeroboam, "Take ten pieces for yourself, for this is what the LORD, the God of Israel, says: 'See, I am going to tear[y] the kingdom out of Solomon's hand and give you ten tribes. 32But for the sake of my servant David and the city of Jerusalem, which I have chosen out of all the tribes of Israel, he will have one tribe.

**11:7** k 2Ki 23:13 l Nu 21:29; Jdg 11:24
**11:9** m 1Ki 3:5; 9:2
**11:10** n 1Ki 9:6 o 1Ki 6:12
**11:11** p ver 31; 1Ki 12:15–16
**11:13** q 2Sa 7:15
**11:15** r 2Sa 8:14; 1Ch 18:12
**11:23** s 2Sa 8:3
**11:24** t 2Sa 10:8,18
**11:26** u 2Sa 20:21; 1Ki 12:2; 2Ch 13:6
**11:27** v 1Ki 9:24
**11:29** w 1Ki 14:2
**11:30** x 1Sa 15:27
**11:31** y ver 11

[a]24 Hebrew *destroyed them* [b]27 Or *the Millo*

**11:33** z ver 5–7
**11:36** a 1Ki 15:4; 2Ki 8:19
**11:38** b Jos 1:5; 2Sa 7:11,27

33 I will do this because they have[a] forsaken me and worshiped[z] Ashtoreth the goddess of the Sidonians, Chemosh the god of the Moabites, and Molech the god of the Ammonites, and have not walked in my ways, nor done what is right in my eyes, nor kept my statutes and laws as David, Solomon's father, did.

34 " 'But I will not take the whole kingdom out of Solomon's hand; I have made him ruler all the days of his life for the sake of David my servant, whom I chose and who observed my commands and statutes. 35 I will take the kingdom from his son's hands and give you ten tribes. 36 I will give one tribe to his son so that David my servant may always have a lamp[a] before me in Jerusalem, the city where I chose to put my Name. 37 However, as for you, I will take you, and you will rule over all that your heart desires; you will be king over Israel. 38 If you do whatever I command you and walk in my ways and do what is right in my eyes by keeping my statutes and commands, as David my servant did, I will be with you. I will build you a dynasty[b] as enduring as the one I built for David and will give Israel to you. 39 I will humble David's descendants because of this, but not forever.' "

40 Solomon tried to kill Jeroboam, but Jeroboam fled to Egypt, to Shishak the king, and stayed there until Solomon's death.

## Solomon's Death

41 As for the other events of Solomon's reign—all he did and the wisdom he displayed—are they not written in the book of the annals of Solomon? 42 Solomon reigned in Jerusalem over all Israel forty years. 43 Then he rested with his fathers and was buried in the city of David his father. And Rehoboam his son succeeded him as king.

## Israel Rebels Against Rehoboam

**12:2** c 1Ki 11:40
**12:4** d 1Sa 8:11–18

12 Rehoboam went to Shechem, for all the Israelites had gone there to make him king. 2 When Jeroboam son of Nebat heard this (he was still in Egypt, where he had fled[c] from King Solomon), he returned from[b] Egypt. 3 So they sent for Jeroboam, and he and the whole assembly of Israel went to Rehoboam and said to him: 4 "Your father put a heavy yoke[d] on us, but now lighten the harsh labor and the heavy yoke he put on us, and we will serve you."

5 Rehoboam answered, "Go away for three days and then come back to me." So the people went away.

6 Then King Rehoboam consulted the elders who had served his father Solomon during his lifetime. "How would you advise me to answer these people?" he asked.

7 They replied, "If today you will be a servant to these people and serve them and give them a favorable answer, they will always be your servants."

8 But Rehoboam rejected the advice the elders gave him and consulted the young men who had grown up with him and were serving him. 9 He asked them, "What is your advice? How should we answer these people who say to me, 'Lighten the yoke your father put on us'?"

10 The young men who had grown up with him replied, "Tell these people who have said to you, 'Your father put a heavy yoke on us, but make our yoke lighter'—tell them, 'My little finger is thicker than my father's waist. 11 My father laid on you a heavy yoke; I will make it even heavier. My father

[a]33 Hebrew; Septuagint, Vulgate and Syriac *because he has* [b]2 Or *he remained in*

### *The African Presence*

**1 Kings 11:40**

Jeroboam took refuge in Egypt when Solomon sought to kill him.

**12:15** e 1Ki 11:29
**12:16** f 2Sa 20:1
**12:17** g 1Ki 11:13,36
**12:18** h 1Ki 4:6; 5:14
**12:19** i 2Ki 17:21
**12:20** j 1Ki 11:13,32
**12:21** k 2Ch 11:1

scourged you with whips; I will scourge you with scorpions.' "

[12]Three days later Jeroboam and all the people returned to Rehoboam, as the king had said, "Come back to me in three days." [13]The king answered the people harshly. Rejecting the advice given him by the elders, [14]he followed the advice of the young men and said, "My father made your yoke heavy; I will make it even heavier. My father scourged you with whips; I will scourge you with scorpions." [15]So the king did not listen to the people, for this turn of events was from the LORD, to fulfill the word the LORD had spoken to Jeroboam son of Nebat through Ahijah[e] the Shilonite.

[16]When all Israel saw that the king refused to listen to them, they answered the king:

"What share do we have in David,
what part in Jesse's son?
To your tents, O Israel![f]
Look after your own house, O David!"

So the Israelites went home. [17]But as for the Israelites who were living in the towns of Judah,[g] Rehoboam still ruled over them.

[18]King Rehoboam sent out Adoniram,[a][h] who was in charge of forced labor, but all Israel stoned him to death. King Rehoboam, however, managed to get into his chariot and escape to Jerusalem. [19]So Israel has been in rebellion against the house of David[i] to this day.

[20]When all the Israelites heard that Jeroboam had returned, they sent and called him to the assembly and made him king over all Israel. Only the tribe of Judah remained loyal to the house of David.[j]

[21]When Rehoboam arrived in Jerusalem, he mustered the whole house of Judah and the tribe of Benjamin—a hundred and eighty thousand fighting men—to make war[k] against the house of Israel and to regain the kingdom for Rehoboam son of Solomon.

[22]But this word of God came to Shemaiah the man of God: [23]"Say to Rehoboam son of Solomon king of Judah, to the whole house of Judah and Benjamin, and to the rest of the people, [24]'This is what the LORD says: Do not go up to fight against your brothers, the Israelites. Go home, every one of you, for this is my doing.' " So they obeyed the word of the LORD and went home again, as the LORD had ordered.

## Golden Calves at Bethel and Dan

[25]Then Jeroboam fortified Shechem[l] in the hill country of Ephraim and lived there. From there he went out and built up Peniel.[b][m]

[26]Jeroboam thought to himself, "The kingdom will now likely revert to the house of David. [27]If these people go up to offer sacrifices at the temple of the LORD in Jerusalem,[n] they will again give their allegiance to their lord, Rehoboam king of Judah. They will kill me and return to King Rehoboam."

[28]After seeking advice, the king made two golden calves.[o] He said to the people, "It is too much for you to go up to Jerusalem. Here are your gods, O Israel, who brought you up out of Egypt."[p] [29]One he set up in Bethel,[q] and the other in Dan.[r] [30]And this thing became a sin;[s] the people went even as far as Dan to worship the one there.

[31]Jeroboam built shrines[t] on high places and appointed priests[u] from all sorts of people, even though they were not Levites. [32]He instituted a festival on the fifteenth day of the eighth[v] month, like the festival held in Judah, and offered sacrifices on the altar. This he did in Bethel, sacrificing to the calves he had made. And at Bethel he also installed priests at the high places he had made. [33]On the fifteenth day of the eighth month, a month of his own choosing, he offered sacrifices on the altar he had built at Bethel. So he instituted the festival for the Israelites and went up to the altar to make offerings.

## The Man of God From Judah

**13** By the word of the LORD a man of God[w] came from Judah to Bethel, as Jeroboam was standing by the altar to make an offering. [2]He cried out against the altar by the word of the LORD: "O altar, altar! This is what the LORD says: 'A son named

**12:25** l Jdg 9:45 m Jdg 8:8,17
**12:27** n Dt 12:5–6
**12:28** o Ex 32:4 p Ex 32:8
**12:29** q Ge 28:19 r Jdg 18:27–31
**12:30** s 1Ki 13:34; 2Ki 17:21
**12:31** t 1Ki 13:32 u 2Ki 17:32; 2Ch 11:14–15
**12:32** v Lev 23:33–34; Nu 29:12
**13:1** w 2Ki 23:17

[a]18 Some Septuagint manuscripts and Syriac (see also 1 Kings 4:6 and 5:14); Hebrew *Adoram* [b]25 Hebrew *Penuel,* a variant of *Peniel*

**13:2** x 2Ki 23:15–16,20
**13:6** y Ex 8:8; 9:28; Ac 8:24
**13:7** z 1Sa 9:7; 2Ki 5:15
**13:8** a Nu 22:18; 24:13

Josiah[x] will be born to the house of David.
On you he will sacrifice the priests of the
high places who now make offerings here,
and human bones will be burned on you.'"
[3]That same day the man of God gave a sign:
"This is the sign the LORD has declared: The
altar will be split apart and the ashes on it
will be poured out."

[4]When King Jeroboam heard what the
man of God cried out against the altar at
Bethel, he stretched out his hand from the
altar and said, "Seize him!" But the hand he
stretched out toward the man shriveled up,
so that he could not pull it back. [5]Also, the
altar was split apart and its ashes poured
out according to the sign given by the man
of God by the word of the LORD.

[6]Then the king said to the man of God,
"Intercede[y] with the LORD your God and
pray for me that my hand may be restored."
So the man of God interceded with the LORD,
and the king's hand was restored and be-
came as it was before.

[7]The king said to the man of God, "Come
home with me and have something to eat,
and I will give you a gift."[z]

[8]But the man of God answered the king,
"Even if you were to give me half your posses-
sions,[a] I would not go with you, nor would
I eat bread or drink water here. [9]For I was
commanded by the word of the LORD: 'You
must not eat bread or drink water or return
by the way you came.'" [10]So he took another
road and did not return by the way he had
come to Bethel.

[11]Now there was a certain old prophet
living in Bethel, whose sons came and told
him all that the man of God had done there
that day. They also told their father what he
had said to the king. [12]Their father asked
them, "Which way did he go?" And his
sons showed him which road the man of
God from Judah had taken. [13]So he said to
his sons, "Saddle the donkey for me." And
when they had saddled the donkey for him,
he mounted it [14]and rode after the man of
God. He found him sitting under an oak tree
and asked, "Are you the man of God who
came from Judah?"

"I am," he replied.

[15]So the prophet said to him, "Come
home with me and eat."

[16]The man of God said, "I cannot turn
back and go with you, nor can I eat bread[b] or
drink water with you in this place. [17]I have
been told by the word of the LORD: 'You must
not eat bread or drink water there or return
by the way you came.'"

[18]The old prophet answered, "I too am
a prophet, as you are. And an angel said to
me by the word of the LORD: 'Bring him back
with you to your house so that he may eat
bread and drink water.'" (But he was lying
to him.) [19]So the man of God returned with
him and ate and drank in his house.

[20]While they were sitting at the table, the
word of the LORD came to the old prophet
who had brought him back. [21]He cried out to
the man of God who had come from Judah,
"This is what the LORD says: 'You have de-
fied the word of the LORD and have not kept
the command the LORD your God gave you.
[22]You came back and ate bread and drank
water in the place where he told you not to
eat or drink. Therefore your body will not
be buried in the tomb of your fathers.'"

[23]When the man of God had finished
eating and drinking, the prophet who had
brought him back saddled his donkey for
him. [24]As he went on his way, a lion[c] met him
on the road and killed him, and his body
was thrown down on the road, with both
the donkey and the lion standing beside it.
[25]Some people who passed by saw the body
thrown down there, with the lion standing
beside the body, and they went and reported
it in the city where the old prophet lived.

[26]When the prophet who had brought
him back from his journey heard of it, he
said, "It is the man of God who defied the
word of the LORD. The LORD has given him
over to the lion, which has mauled him
and killed him, as the word of the LORD had
warned him."

[27]The prophet said to his sons, "Saddle
the donkey for me," and they did so. [28]Then
he went out and found the body thrown
down on the road, with the donkey and the
lion standing beside it. The lion had neither
eaten the body nor mauled the donkey. [29]So
the prophet picked up the body of the man
of God, laid it on the donkey, and brought it
back to his own city to mourn for him and
bury him. [30]Then he laid the body in his

**13:16** b ver 8
**13:24** c 1Ki 20:36

13:30 d Jer 22:18
13:31 e 2Ki 23:18
13:32 f 1Ki 16:24,28
13:33 g 1Ki 12:31
13:34 h 1Ki 14:10
14:2 i 1Ki 11:29
14:3 j 1Sa 9:7
14:8 k 1Ki 11:31,33,38

own tomb, and they mourned over him and said, "Oh, my brother!"[d]

31 After burying him, he said to his sons, "When I die, bury me in the grave where the man of God is buried; lay my bones[e] beside his bones. 32 For the message he declared by the word of the LORD against the altar in Bethel and against all the shrines on the high places in the towns of Samaria[f] will certainly come true."

33 Even after this, Jeroboam did not change his evil ways, but once more appointed priests for the high places from all sorts[g] of people. Anyone who wanted to become a priest he consecrated for the high places. 34 This was the sin of the house of Jeroboam that led to its downfall and to its destruction[h] from the face of the earth.

## Ahijah's Prophecy Against Jeroboam

14 At that time Abijah son of Jeroboam became ill, 2 and Jeroboam said to his wife, "Go, disguise yourself, so you won't be recognized as the wife of Jeroboam. Then go to Shiloh. Ahijah[i] the prophet is there—the one who told me I would be king over this people. 3 Take ten loaves of bread[j] with you, some cakes and a jar of honey, and go to him. He will tell you what will happen to the boy." 4 So Jeroboam's wife did what he said and went to Ahijah's house in Shiloh.

Now Ahijah could not see; his sight was gone because of his age. 5 But the LORD had told Ahijah, "Jeroboam's wife is coming to ask you about her son, for he is ill, and you are to give her such and such an answer. When she arrives, she will pretend to be someone else."

6 So when Ahijah heard the sound of her footsteps at the door, he said, "Come in, wife of Jeroboam. Why this pretense? I have been sent to you with bad news. 7 Go, tell Jeroboam that this is what the LORD, the God of Israel, says: 'I raised you up from among the people and made you a leader over my people Israel. 8 I tore[k] the kingdom away from the house of David and gave it to you, but you have not been like my servant David, who kept my commands and followed me with all his heart, doing only what was right in my eyes. 9 You have done more evil than all who lived before you. You have made for yourself other gods, idols[l] made of metal; you have provoked me to anger and thrust me behind your back.[m]

*My own beloved,*

*Follow me with all of your heart—*

*that's my ultimate desire of and for you!*

*Your God*

1 KINGS 14:6–9

10 " 'Because of this, I am going to bring disaster on the house of Jeroboam. I will cut off from Jeroboam every last male in Israel—slave or free.[n] I will burn up the house of Jeroboam as one burns dung, until it is all gone.[o] 11 Dogs[p] will eat those belonging to Jeroboam who die in the city, and the birds of the air will feed on those who die in the country. The LORD has spoken!'

12 "As for you, go back home. When you set foot in your city, the boy will die. 13 All Israel will mourn for him and bury him. He is the only one belonging to Jeroboam who will be buried, because he is the only one in the house of Jeroboam in whom the LORD, the God of Israel, has found anything good.

14 "The LORD will raise up for himself a king over Israel who will cut off the family of Jeroboam. This is the day! What? Yes, even now.[a] 15 And the LORD will strike Israel, so that it will be like a reed swaying in the water. He will uproot Israel from this good land that he gave to their forefathers and scatter them beyond the River,[b] because they provoked[q] the LORD to anger by making Asherah[r] poles.[c] 16 And he will give Israel up because of the sins[s] Jeroboam has committed and has caused Israel to commit."

17 Then Jeroboam's wife got up and left and went to Tirzah.[t] As soon as she stepped over the threshold of the house, the boy died. 18 They buried him, and all Israel mourned

14:9 l 2Ch 11:15 m Ps 50:17
14:10 n Dt 32:36; 2Ki 9:8–9 o 1Ki 15:29
14:11 p 1Ki 16:4; 21:24
14:15 q Jos 23:15–16 r Ex 34:13; Dt 12:3
14:16 s 1Ki 12:30
14:17 t 1Ki 16:6–9

[a] 14 The meaning of the Hebrew for this sentence is uncertain. [b] 15 That is, the Euphrates [c] 15 That is, symbols of the goddess Asherah; here and elsewhere in 1 Kings

14:22
u 2Ch 12:1
v Dt 32:21

14:23
w Dt 12:2; Isa 57:5

14:24
x Dt 23:17; 2Ki 23:7

14:25
y 2Ch 12:2

14:26
z 1Ki 10:17

14:30
a 1Ki 12:21

for him, as the LORD had said through his servant the prophet Ahijah.

19 The other events of Jeroboam's reign, his wars and how he ruled, are written in the book of the annals of the kings of Israel. 20 He reigned for twenty-two years and then rested with his fathers. And Nadab his son succeeded him as king.

## Rehoboam King of Judah

21 Rehoboam son of Solomon was king in Judah. He was forty-one years old when he became king, and he reigned seventeen years in Jerusalem, the city the LORD had chosen out of all the tribes of Israel in which to put his Name. His mother's name was Naamah; she was an Ammonite.

22 Judah[u] did evil in the eyes of the LORD. By the sins they committed they stirred up his jealous anger[v] more than their fathers had done. 23 They also set up for themselves high places, sacred stones and Asherah poles on every high hill and under every spreading tree.[w] 24 There were even male shrine prostitutes[x] in the land; the people engaged in all the detestable practices of the nations the LORD had driven out before the Israelites.

25 In the fifth year of King Rehoboam, Shishak king of Egypt attacked[y] Jerusalem. 26 He carried off the treasures of the temple of the LORD and the treasures of the royal palace. He took everything, including all the gold shields[z] Solomon had made. 27 So King Rehoboam made bronze shields to replace them and assigned these to the commanders of the guard on duty at the entrance to the royal palace. 28 Whenever the king went to the LORD's temple, the guards bore the shields, and afterward they returned them to the guardroom.

29 As for the other events of Rehoboam's reign, and all he did, are they not written in the book of the annals of the kings of Judah? 30 There was continual warfare[a] between Rehoboam and Jeroboam. 31 And Rehoboam rested with his fathers and was buried with them in the City of David. His mother's name was Naamah; she was an Ammonite. And Abijah[*a*] his son succeeded him as king.

## Abijah King of Judah

**15** In the eighteenth year of the reign of Jeroboam son of Nebat, Abijah[*b*] became king of Judah, 2 and he reigned in Jerusalem three years. His mother's name was Maacah[b] daughter of Abishalom.[*c*]

3 He committed all the sins his father had done before him; his heart was not fully devoted[c] to the LORD his God, as the heart of David his forefather had been. 4 Nevertheless, for David's sake the LORD his God gave him a lamp[d] in Jerusalem by raising up a son to succeed him and by making Jerusalem strong. 5 For David had done what was right in the eyes of the LORD and had not failed to keep any of the LORD's commands all the days of his life—except in the case of Uriah[e] the Hittite.

6 There was war[f] between Rehoboam[*d*] and Jeroboam throughout ⌞Abijah's⌟ lifetime. 7 As for the other events of Abijah's reign, and all he did, are they not written in the book of the annals of the kings of Judah? There was war between Abijah and Jeroboam. 8 And Abijah rested with his fathers and was buried in the City of David. And Asa his son succeeded him as king.

## Asa King of Judah

9 In the twentieth year of Jeroboam king of Israel, Asa became king of Judah, 10 and he reigned in Jerusalem forty-one years. His grandmother's name was Maacah daughter of Abishalom.

11 Asa did what was right in the eyes of the LORD, as his father David had done. 12 He expelled the male shrine prostitutes[g] from the land and got rid of all the idols his fathers had made. 13 He even deposed his grandmother Maacah from her position as queen mother, because she had made a repulsive Asherah pole. Asa cut the pole down[h] and burned it in the Kidron Valley. 14 Although he did not remove the high places, Asa's heart was fully committed[i] to the LORD all his life. 15 He brought into the temple of the LORD the

15:2
b 2Ch 11:20

15:3
c 1Ki 11:4

15:4
d 2Ch 21:7

15:5
e 2Sa 11:2–27; 12:9

15:6
f 1Ki 14:30

15:12
g 1Ki 14:24

15:13
h Ex 32:20

15:14
i 1Ki 22:43

[a]31 Some Hebrew manuscripts and Septuagint (see also 2 Chron. 12:16); most Hebrew manuscripts *Abijam* [b]1 Some Hebrew manuscripts and Septuagint (see also 2 Chron. 12:16); most Hebrew manuscripts *Abijam*; also in verses 7 and 8 [c]2 A variant of *Absalom*; also in verse 10 [d]6 Most Hebrew manuscripts; some Hebrew manuscripts and Syriac *Abijam* (that is, Abijah)

15:17 j Jos 18:25; 1Ki 12:27
15:18 k 1Ki 11:23–24
15:20 l Jdg 18:29; 2Sa 20:14
15:22 m Jos 21:17
15:24 n Mt 1:8
15:26 o 1Ki 12:30
15:27 p 1Ki 14:14 q Jos 19:44

silver and gold and the articles that he and his father had dedicated.

16 There was war between Asa and Baasha king of Israel throughout their reigns. 17 Baasha king of Israel went up against Judah and fortified Ramah[j] to prevent anyone from leaving or entering the territory of Asa king of Judah.

18 Asa then took all the silver and gold that was left in the treasuries of the LORD's temple and of his own palace. He entrusted it to his officials and sent them to Ben-Hadad[k] son of Tabrimmon, the son of Hezion, the king of Aram, who was ruling in Damascus. 19 "Let there be a treaty between me and you," he said, "as there was between my father and your father. See, I am sending you a gift of silver and gold. Now break your treaty with Baasha king of Israel so he will withdraw from me."

20 Ben-Hadad agreed with King Asa and sent the commanders of his forces against the towns of Israel. He conquered[l] Ijon, Dan, Abel Beth Maacah and all Kinnereth in addition to Naphtali. 21 When Baasha heard this, he stopped building Ramah and withdrew to Tirzah. 22 Then King Asa issued an order to all Judah—no one was exempt—and they carried away from Ramah the stones and timber Baasha had been using there. With them King Asa built up Geba[m] in Benjamin, and also Mizpah.

23 As for all the other events of Asa's reign, all his achievements, all he did and the cities he built, are they not written in the book of the annals of the kings of Judah? In his old age, however, his feet became diseased. 24 Then Asa rested with his fathers and was buried with them in the city of his father David. And Jehoshaphat[n] his son succeeded him as king.

## Nadab King of Israel

25 Nadab son of Jeroboam became king of Israel in the second year of Asa king of Judah, and he reigned over Israel two years. 26 He did evil in the eyes of the LORD, walking in the ways of his father[o] and in his sin, which he had caused Israel to commit.

27 Baasha son of Ahijah of the house of Issachar plotted against him, and he struck him down[p] at Gibbethon,[q] a Philistine town, while Nadab and all Israel were besieging it. 28 Baasha killed Nadab in the third year of Asa king of Judah and succeeded him as king.

29 As soon as he began to reign, he killed Jeroboam's whole family. He did not leave Jeroboam anyone that breathed, but destroyed them all, according to the word of the LORD given through his servant Ahijah the Shilonite— 30 because of the sins Jeroboam had committed and had caused Israel to commit, and because he provoked the LORD, the God of Israel, to anger.

31 As for the other events of Nadab's reign, and all he did, are they not written in the book of the annals of the kings of Israel? 32 There was war[r] between Asa and Baasha king of Israel throughout their reigns.

## Baasha King of Israel

33 In the third year of Asa king of Judah, Baasha son of Ahijah became king of all Israel in Tirzah, and he reigned twenty-four years. 34 He did evil in the eyes of the LORD, walking in the ways of Jeroboam and in his sin, which he had caused Israel to commit.

16 Then the word of the LORD came to Jehu[s] son of Hanani against Baasha: 2 "I lifted you up from the dust and made you leader[t] of my people Israel, but you walked in the ways of Jeroboam and caused my people Israel to sin and to provoke me to anger by their sins. 3 So I am about to consume Baasha and his house,[u] and I will make your house like that of Jeroboam son of Nebat. 4 Dogs[v] will eat those belonging to Baasha who die in the city, and the birds of the air will feed on those who die in the country."

5 As for the other events of Baasha's reign, what he did and his achievements, are they not written in the book of the annals of the kings of Israel? 6 Baasha rested with his fathers and was buried in Tirzah. And Elah his son succeeded him as king.

7 Moreover, the word of the LORD came through the prophet Jehu[w] son of Hanani to Baasha and his house, because of all the evil he had done in the eyes of the LORD, provoking him to anger by the things he did, and becoming like the house of Jeroboam—and also because he destroyed it.

15:32 r ver 16
16:1 s ver 7; 2Ch 19:2; 20:34
16:2 t 1Ki 14:7–9
16:3 u ver 11; 1Ki 14:10
16:4 v 1Ki 14:11
16:7 w ver 1

**16:9** x 2Ki 9:30–33
**16:13** y Dt 32:21
**16:15** z 1Ki 15:27

## Elah King of Israel

8 In the twenty-sixth year of Asa king of Judah, Elah son of Baasha became king of Israel, and he reigned in Tirzah two years.

9 Zimri, one of his officials, who had command of half his chariots, plotted against him. Elah was in Tirzah at the time, getting drunk[x] in the home of Arza, the man in charge of the palace at Tirzah. 10 Zimri came in, struck him down and killed him in the twenty-seventh year of Asa king of Judah. Then he succeeded him as king.

11 As soon as he began to reign and was seated on the throne, he killed off Baasha's whole family. He did not spare a single male, whether relative or friend. 12 So Zimri destroyed the whole family of Baasha, in accordance with the word of the LORD spoken against Baasha through the prophet Jehu— 13 because of all the sins Baasha and his son Elah had committed and had caused Israel to commit, so that they provoked the LORD, the God of Israel, to anger by their worthless idols.[y]

14 As for the other events of Elah's reign, and all he did, are they not written in the book of the annals of the kings of Israel?

## Zimri King of Israel

15 In the twenty-seventh year of Asa king of Judah, Zimri reigned in Tirzah seven days. The army was encamped near Gibbethon,[z] a Philistine town. 16 When the Israelites in the camp heard that Zimri had plotted against the king and murdered him, they proclaimed Omri, the commander of the army, king over Israel that very day there in the camp. 17 Then Omri and all the Israelites with him withdrew from Gibbethon and laid siege to Tirzah. 18 When Zimri saw that the city was taken, he went into the citadel of the royal palace and set the palace on fire around him. So he died, 19 because of the sins he had committed, doing evil in the eyes of the LORD and walking in the ways of Jeroboam and in the sin he had committed and had caused Israel to commit.

20 As for the other events of Zimri's reign, and the rebellion he carried out, are they not written in the book of the annals of the kings of Israel?

## Omri King of Israel

21 Then the people of Israel were split into two factions; half supported Tibni son of Ginath for king, and the other half supported Omri. 22 But Omri's followers proved stronger than those of Tibni son of Ginath. So Tibni died and Omri became king.

23 In the thirty-first year of Asa king of Judah, Omri became king of Israel, and he reigned twelve years, six of them in Tirzah. 24 He bought the hill of Samaria from Shemer for two talents[a] of silver and built a city on the hill, calling it Samaria,[a] after Shemer, the name of the former owner of the hill.

25 But Omri did evil[b] in the eyes of the LORD and sinned more than all those before him. 26 He walked in all the ways of Jeroboam son of Nebat and in his sin, which he had caused[c] Israel to commit, so that they provoked the LORD, the God of Israel, to anger by their worthless idols.

27 As for the other events of Omri's reign, what he did and the things he achieved, are they not written in the book of the annals of the kings of Israel? 28 Omri rested with his fathers and was buried in Samaria. And Ahab his son succeeded him as king.

## Ahab Becomes King of Israel

29 In the thirty-eighth year of Asa king of Judah, Ahab son of Omri became king of Israel, and he reigned in Samaria over Israel twenty-two years. 30 Ahab son of Omri did more[d] evil in the eyes of the LORD than any of those before him. 31 He not only considered it trivial to commit the sins of Jeroboam son of Nebat, but he also married[e] Jezebel daughter of Ethbaal king of the Sidonians, and began to serve Baal[f] and worship him. 32 He set up an altar for Baal in the temple[g] of Baal that he built in Samaria. 33 Ahab also made an Asherah pole[h] and did more[i] to provoke the LORD, the God of Israel, to anger than did all the kings of Israel before him.

34 In Ahab's time, Hiel of Bethel rebuilt Jericho. He laid its foundations at the cost of his firstborn son Abiram, and he set up its gates at the cost of his youngest son Segub, in accordance with the word of the LORD spoken by Joshua son of Nun.[j]

**16:24** a 1Ki 13:32
**16:25** b Mic 6:16
**16:26** c ver 19
**16:30** d 1Ki 14:9
**16:31** e Dt 7:3 f 2Ki 10:18; 17:16
**16:32** g 2Ki 10:21,27
**16:33** h 2Ki 13:6 i 1Ki 21:25
**16:34** j Jos 6:26

[a] 24 That is, about 150 pounds (about 70 kilograms)

**17:1**
k Jas 5:17
l 2Ki 3:14; Lk 4:25

**17:9**
m Ob 1:20
n Lk 4:26

**17:12**
o 2Ki 4:2

## Elijah Fed by Ravens

17 Now Elijah[k] the Tishbite, from Tishbe[a] in Gilead, said to Ahab, "As the LORD, the God of Israel, lives, whom I serve, there will be neither dew nor rain[l] in the next few years except at my word."

2 Then the word of the LORD came to Elijah: 3 "Leave here, turn eastward and hide in the Kerith Ravine, east of the Jordan. 4 You will drink from the brook, and I have ordered the ravens to feed you there."

5 So he did what the LORD had told him. He went to the Kerith Ravine, east of the Jordan, and stayed there. 6 The ravens brought him bread and meat in the morning and bread and meat in the evening, and he drank from the brook.

## The Widow at Zarephath

7 Some time later the brook dried up because there had been no rain in the land. 8 Then the word of the LORD came to him: 9 "Go at once to Zarephath[m] of Sidon and stay there. I have commanded a widow[n] in that place to supply you with food." 10 So he went to Zarephath. When he came to the town gate, a widow was there gathering sticks. He called to her and asked, "Would you bring me a little water in a jar so I may have a drink?" 11 As she was going to get it, he called, "And bring me, please, a piece of bread."

12 "As surely as the LORD your God lives," she replied, "I don't have any bread—only a handful of flour in a jar and a little oil[o] in a jug. I am gathering a few sticks to take home and make a meal for myself and my son, that we may eat it—and die."

13 Elijah said to her, "Don't be afraid. Go home and do as you have said. But first make a small cake of bread for me from what you have and bring it to me, and then make something for yourself and your son. 14 For this is what the LORD, the God of Israel, says: 'The jar of flour will not be used up and the jug of oil will not run dry until the day the LORD gives rain on the land.' "

15 She went away and did as Elijah had told her. So there was food every day for Elijah and for the woman and her family. 16 For the jar of flour was not used up and the jug of oil did not run dry, in keeping with the word of the LORD spoken by Elijah.

17 Some time later the son of the woman who owned the house became ill. He grew worse and worse, and finally stopped breathing. 18 She said to Elijah, "What do you have against me, man of God? Did you come to remind me of my sin and kill my son?"

19 "Give me your son," Elijah replied. He took him from her arms, carried him to the upper room where he was staying, and laid him on his bed. 20 Then he cried out to the LORD, "O LORD my God, have you brought tragedy also upon this widow I am staying with, by causing her son to die?" 21 Then he stretched[p] himself out on the boy three times and cried to the LORD, "O LORD my God, let this boy's life return to him!"

22 The LORD heard Elijah's cry, and the boy's life returned to him, and he lived. 23 Elijah picked up the child and carried him down from the room into the house. He gave him to his mother and said, "Look, your son is alive!"

24 Then the woman said to Elijah, "Now I know[q] that you are a man of God and that the word of the LORD from your mouth is the truth."

## Elijah and Obadiah

18 After a long time, in the third[r] year, the word of the LORD came to Elijah: "Go and present yourself to Ahab, and I will send rain[s] on the land." 2 So Elijah went to present himself to Ahab.

Now the famine was severe in Samaria, 3 and Ahab had summoned Obadiah, who was in charge of his palace. (Obadiah was a devout believer in the LORD. 4 While Jezebel was killing off the LORD's prophets, Obadiah had taken a hundred prophets and hidden them in two caves, fifty in each, and had supplied them with food and water.) 5 Ahab had said to Obadiah, "Go through the land to all the springs and valleys. Maybe we can find some grass to keep the horses and mules alive so we will not have to kill any of our animals." 6 So they divided the land they were to cover, Ahab going in one direction and Obadiah in another.

7 As Obadiah was walking along, Elijah

**17:21**
p 2Ki 4:34; Ac 20:10

**17:24**
q Jn 3:2; 16:30

**18:1**
r Lk 4:25; Jas 5:17
s Dt 28:12

[a]1 Or *Tishbite, of the settlers*

met him. Obadiah recognized[t] him, bowed down to the ground, and said, “Is it really you, my lord Elijah?”

8“Yes,” he replied. “Go tell your master, ‘Elijah is here.’ ”

9“What have I done wrong,” asked Obadiah, “that you are handing your servant over to Ahab to be put to death? 10As surely as the LORD your God lives, there is not a nation or kingdom where my master has not sent someone to look[u] for you. And whenever a nation or kingdom claimed you were not there, he made them swear they could not find you. 11But now you tell me to go to my master and say, ‘Elijah is here.’ 12I don’t know where the Spirit[v] of the LORD may carry you when I leave you. If I go and tell Ahab and he doesn’t find you, he will kill me. Yet I your servant have worshiped the LORD since my youth. 13Haven’t you heard, my lord, what I did while Jezebel was killing the prophets of the LORD? I hid a hundred of the LORD’s prophets in two caves, fifty in each, and supplied them with food and water. 14And now you tell me to go to my master and say, ‘Elijah is here.’ He will kill me!”

15Elijah said, “As the LORD Almighty lives, whom I serve, I will surely present myself to Ahab today.”

## Elijah on Mount Carmel

16So Obadiah went to meet Ahab and told him, and Ahab went to meet Elijah. 17When he saw Elijah, he said to him, “Is that you, you troubler[w] of Israel?”

18“I have not made trouble for Israel,” Elijah replied. “But you[x] and your father’s family have. You have abandoned the LORD’s commands and have followed the Baals. 19Now summon the people from all over Israel to meet me on Mount Carmel.[y] And bring the four hundred and fifty prophets of Baal and the four hundred prophets of Asherah, who eat at Jezebel’s table.”

20So Ahab sent word throughout all Israel and assembled the prophets on Mount Carmel. 21Elijah went before the people and said, “How long will you waver[z] between two opinions? If the LORD is God, follow him; but if Baal is God, follow him.”

But the people said nothing.

22Then Elijah said to them, “I am the only one of the LORD’s prophets left,[a] but Baal has four hundred and fifty prophets. 23Get two bulls for us. Let them choose one for themselves, and let them cut it into pieces and put it on the wood but not set fire to it. I will prepare the other bull and put it on the wood but not set fire to it. 24Then you call on the name of your god, and I will call on the name of the LORD. The god who answers by fire[b]—he is God.”

Then all the people said, “What you say is good.”

25Elijah said to the prophets of Baal, “Choose one of the bulls and prepare it first, since there are so many of you. Call on the name of your god, but do not light the fire.” 26So they took the bull given them and prepared it.

Then they called on the name of Baal from morning till noon. “O Baal, answer us!” they shouted. But there was no response;[c] no one answered. And they danced around the altar they had made.

27At noon Elijah began to taunt them. “Shout louder!” he said. “Surely he is a god! Perhaps he is deep in thought, or busy, or traveling. Maybe he is sleeping and must be awakened.” 28So they shouted louder and slashed[d] themselves with swords and spears, as was their custom, until their blood flowed. 29Midday passed, and they continued their frantic prophesying until the time for the evening sacrifice. But there was no response, no one answered, no one paid attention.

30Then Elijah said to all the people, “Come here to me.” They came to him, and he repaired the altar[e] of the LORD, which was in ruins. 31Elijah took twelve stones, one for each of the tribes descended from Jacob, to whom the word of the LORD had come, saying, “Your name shall be Israel.”[f] 32With the stones he built an altar in the name[g] of the LORD, and he dug a trench around it large enough to hold two seahs[a] of seed. 33He arranged the wood, cut the bull into pieces and laid it on the wood. Then he said to them, “Fill four large jars with water and pour it on the offering and on the wood.”

**18:7** t 2Ki 1:8
**18:10** u 1Ki 17:3
**18:12** v 2Ki 2:16; Eze 3:14; Ac 8:39
**18:17** w Jos 7:25; 1Ki 21:20
**18:18** x 1Ki 16:31,33
**18:19** y Jos 19:26
**18:21** z Jos 24:15; 2Ki 17:41; Mt 6:24
**18:22** a 1Ki 19:10
**18:24** b ver 38
**18:26** c Ps 115:4–5; Jer 10:5
**18:28** d Lev 19:28
**18:30** e 1Ki 19:10
**18:31** f 2Ki 17:34
**18:32** g Col 3:17

[a]32 That is, probably about 13 quarts (about 15 liters)

*Woman of color,*

*I still specialize in the impossible.*
*Watch me.*

*God*

1 KINGS 18:30–39

34"Do it again," he said, and they did it again.

"Do it a third time," he ordered, and they did it the third time. 35The water ran down around the altar and even filled the trench.

36At the time of sacrifice, the prophet Elijah stepped forward and prayed: "O LORD, God of Abraham, Isaac and Israel, let it be known today that you are God in Israel and that I am your servant and have done all these things at your command.[h] 37Answer me, O LORD, answer me, so these people will know that you, O LORD, are God, and that you are turning their hearts back again."

38Then the fire[i] of the LORD fell and burned up the sacrifice, the wood, the stones and the soil, and also licked up the water in the trench.

39When all the people saw this, they fell prostrate and cried, "The LORD—he is God! The LORD—he is God!"

40Then Elijah commanded them, "Seize the prophets of Baal. Don't let anyone get away!" They seized them, and Elijah had them brought down to the Kishon Valley and slaughtered[j] there.

41And Elijah said to Ahab, "Go, eat and drink, for there is the sound of a heavy rain." 42So Ahab went off to eat and drink, but Elijah climbed to the top of Carmel, bent down to the ground and put his face between his knees.[k]

43"Go and look toward the sea," he told his servant. And he went up and looked.

"There is nothing there," he said.

Seven times Elijah said, "Go back."

44The seventh time the servant reported, "A cloud as small as a man's hand is rising from the sea."

So Elijah said, "Go and tell Ahab, 'Hitch up your chariot and go down before the rain stops you.'"

45Meanwhile, the sky grew black with clouds, the wind rose, a heavy rain came on and Ahab rode off to Jezreel. 46The power of the LORD came upon Elijah and, tucking his cloak into his belt,[l] he ran ahead of Ahab all the way to Jezreel.

## Elijah Flees to Horeb

**19** Now Ahab told Jezebel everything Elijah had done and how he had killed[m] all the prophets with the sword. 2So Jezebel sent a messenger to Elijah to say, "May the gods deal with me, be it ever so severely,[n] if by this time tomorrow I do not make your life like that of one of them."

3Elijah was afraid[a] and ran for his life. When he came to Beersheba in Judah, he left his servant there, 4while he himself went a day's journey into the desert. He came to a broom tree, sat down under it and prayed that he might die. "I have had enough, LORD," he said. "Take my life;[o] I am no better than my ancestors." 5Then he lay down under the tree and fell asleep.

All at once an angel touched him and said, "Get up and eat." 6He looked around, and there by his head was a cake of bread baked over hot coals, and a jar of water. He ate and drank and then lay down again.

7The angel of the LORD came back a second time and touched him and said, "Get up and eat, for the journey is too much for you." 8So he got up and ate and drank. Strengthened by that food, he traveled forty[p] days and forty nights until he reached Horeb,[q] the mountain of God. 9There he went into a cave and spent the night.

## The LORD Appears to Elijah

And the word of the LORD came to him: "What are you doing here, Elijah?"

10He replied, "I have been very zealous for the LORD God Almighty. The Israelites have rejected your covenant, broken down your altars, and put your prophets to death with

**18:36** h Nu 16:28
**18:38** i Lev 9:24; 1Ch 21:26; 2Ch 7:1
**18:40** j Dt 13:5; 18:20; 2Ki 10:24–25
**18:42** k Jas 5:18
**18:46** l 2Ki 4:29
**19:1** m 1Ki 18:40
**19:2** n 1Ki 20:10; 2Ki 6:31
**19:4** o Nu 11:15; Jnh 4:8
**19:8** p Ex 34:28; Dt 9:9–11,18; Mt 4:2 q Ex 3:1

[a]3 Or *Elijah saw*

**19:10** r 1Ki 18:4,22; Ro 11:3*
**19:11** s Ex 24:12 t Eze 1:4
**19:13** u Ex 3:6
**19:15** v 2Ki 8:7–15
**19:17** w 2Ki 8:12,29; 9:14; 13:3,7,22
**19:18** x Ro 11:4* y Hos 13:2
**19:20** z Mt 8:21–22; Lk 9:61
**19:21** a 2Sa 24:22

the sword. I am the only one left,[r] and now they are trying to kill me too."

[11]The LORD said, "Go out and stand on the mountain[s] in the presence of the LORD, for the LORD is about to pass by."

Then a great and powerful wind[t] tore the mountains apart and shattered the rocks before the LORD, but the LORD was not in the wind. After the wind there was an earthquake, but the LORD was not in the earthquake. [12]After the earthquake came a fire, but the LORD was not in the fire. And after the fire came a gentle whisper. [13]When Elijah heard it, he pulled his cloak over his face[u] and went out and stood at the mouth of the cave.

Then a voice said to him, "What are you doing here, Elijah?"

[14]He replied, "I have been very zealous for the LORD God Almighty. The Israelites have rejected your covenant, broken down your altars, and put your prophets to death with the sword. I am the only one left, and now they are trying to kill me too."

[15]The LORD said to him, "Go back the way you came, and go to the Desert of Damascus. When you get there, anoint Hazael[v] king over Aram. [16]Also, anoint Jehu son of Nimshi king over Israel, and anoint Elisha son of Shaphat from Abel Meholah to succeed you as prophet. [17]Jehu will put to death any who escape the sword of Hazael,[w] and Elisha will put to death any who escape the sword of Jehu. [18]Yet I reserve[x] seven thousand in Israel—all whose knees have not bowed down to Baal and all whose mouths have not kissed[y] him."

## The Call of Elisha

[19]So Elijah went from there and found Elisha son of Shaphat. He was plowing with twelve yoke of oxen, and he himself was driving the twelfth pair. Elijah went up to him and threw his cloak around him. [20]Elisha then left his oxen and ran after Elijah. "Let me kiss my father and mother good-by,"[z] he said, "and then I will come with you."

"Go back," Elijah replied. "What have I done to you?"

[21]So Elisha left him and went back. He took his yoke of oxen[a] and slaughtered them. He burned the plowing equipment to cook the meat and gave it to the people, and they ate. Then he set out to follow Elijah and became his attendant.

## Ben-Hadad Attacks Samaria

**20** Now Ben-Hadad[b] king of Aram mustered his entire army. Accompanied by thirty-two kings with their horses and chariots, he went up and besieged Samaria and attacked it. [2]He sent messengers into the city to Ahab king of Israel, saying, "This is what Ben-Hadad says: [3]'Your silver and gold are mine, and the best of your wives and children are mine.'"

[4]The king of Israel answered, "Just as you say, my lord the king. I and all I have are yours."

[5]The messengers came again and said, "This is what Ben-Hadad says: 'I sent to demand your silver and gold, your wives and your children. [6]But about this time tomorrow I am going to send my officials to search your palace and the houses of your officials. They will seize everything you value and carry it away.'"

[7]The king of Israel summoned all the elders of the land and said to them, "See how this man is looking for trouble![c] When he sent for my wives and my children, my silver and my gold, I did not refuse him."

[8]The elders and the people all answered, "Don't listen to him or agree to his demands."

[9]So he replied to Ben-Hadad's messengers, "Tell my lord the king, 'Your servant will do all you demanded the first time, but this demand I cannot meet.'" They left and took the answer back to Ben-Hadad.

[10]Then Ben-Hadad sent another message to Ahab: "May the gods deal with me, be it ever so severely, if enough dust[d] remains in Samaria to give each of my men a handful."

[11]The king of Israel answered, "Tell him: 'One who puts on his armor should not boast[e] like one who takes it off.'"

[12]Ben-Hadad heard this message while he and the kings were drinking in their tents,[a] and he ordered his men: "Prepare to attack." So they prepared to attack the city.

**20:1** b 1Ki 15:18
**20:7** c 2Ki 5:7
**20:10** d 1Ki 19:2
**20:11** e Pr 27:1

[a]12 Or *in Succoth*; also in verse 16

**20:13** f ver 28
**20:16** g ver 12; 1Ki 16:9
**20:22** h 2Sa 11:1

## Ahab Defeats Ben-Hadad

13 Meanwhile a prophet came to Ahab
king of Israel and announced, "This is what
the LORD says: 'Do you see this vast army? I
will give it into your hand today, and then
you will know[f] that I am the LORD.'"
14 "But who will do this?" asked Ahab.

The prophet replied, "This is what the
LORD says: 'The young officers of the provin-
cial commanders will do it.'"

"And who will start the battle?" he
asked.

The prophet answered, "You will."

15 So Ahab summoned the young officers
of the provincial commanders, 232 men.
Then he assembled the rest of the Israel-
ites, 7,000 in all. 16 They set out at noon while
Ben-Hadad and the 32 kings allied with him
were in their tents getting drunk.[g] 17 The
young officers of the provincial command-
ers went out first.

Now Ben-Hadad had dispatched scouts,
who reported, "Men are advancing from
Samaria."

18 He said, "If they have come out for
peace, take them alive; if they have come
out for war, take them alive."

19 The young officers of the provincial
commanders marched out of the city with
the army behind them 20 and each one
struck down his opponent. At that, the Ar-
ameans fled, with the Israelites in pursuit.
But Ben-Hadad king of Aram escaped on
horseback with some of his horsemen. 21 The
king of Israel advanced and overpowered
the horses and chariots and inflicted heavy
losses on the Arameans.

22 Afterward, the prophet came to the
king of Israel and said, "Strengthen your po-
sition and see what must be done, because
next spring[h] the king of Aram will attack
you again."

23 Meanwhile, the officials of the king of
Aram advised him, "Their gods are gods of
the hills. That is why they were too strong
for us. But if we fight them on the plains,
surely we will be stronger than they. 24 Do
this: Remove all the kings from their
commands and replace them with other
officers. 25 You must also raise an army
like the one you lost—horse for horse and
chariot for chariot—so we can fight Israel
on the plains. Then surely we will be stron-
ger than they." He agreed with them and
acted accordingly.

26 The next spring Ben-Hadad mustered
the Arameans and went up to Aphek[i] to
fight against Israel. 27 When the Israelites
were also mustered and given provisions,
they marched out to meet them. The Israel-
ites camped opposite them like two small
flocks of goats, while the Arameans covered
the countryside.

28 The man of God came up and told the
king of Israel, "This is what the LORD says:
'Because the Arameans think the LORD is a
god of the hills and not a god of the valleys, I
will deliver this vast army into your hands,
and you will know[j] that I am the LORD.'"

29 For seven days they camped opposite
each other, and on the seventh day the bat-
tle was joined. The Israelites inflicted a hun-
dred thousand casualties on the Aramean
foot soldiers in one day. 30 The rest of them
escaped to the city of Aphek, where the wall
collapsed on twenty-seven thousand of
them. And Ben-Hadad fled to the city and
hid[k] in an inner room.

31 His officials said to him, "Look, we have
heard that the kings of the house of Israel
are merciful. Let us go to the king of Israel
with sackcloth[l] around our waists and ropes
around our heads. Perhaps he will spare
your life."

32 Wearing sackcloth around their waists
and ropes around their heads, they went to
the king of Israel and said, "Your servant
Ben-Hadad says: 'Please let me live.'"

The king answered, "Is he still alive? He
is my brother."

33 The men took this as a good sign and
were quick to pick up his word. "Yes, your
brother Ben-Hadad!" they said.

"Go and get him," the king said. When
Ben-Hadad came out, Ahab had him come
up into his chariot.

34 "I will return the cities[m] my father took
from your father," Ben-Hadad offered. "You
may set up your own market areas in Damas-
cus, as my father did in Samaria."

⌞Ahab said,⌟ "On the basis of a treaty I
will set you free." So he made a treaty with
him, and let him go.

**20:26** i 2Ki 13:17
**20:28** j ver 13
**20:30** k 1Ki 22:25; 2Ch 18:24
**20:31** l Ge 37:34
**20:34** m 1Ki 15:20

20:35 n 2Ki 2:3–7
20:36 o 1Ki 13:24
20:39 p 2Ki 10:24
20:42 q 1Ki 22:31–37
20:43 r 1Ki 21:4
21:3 s Lev 25:23; Nu 36:7; Eze 46:18

## A Prophet Condemns Ahab

35 By the word of the LORD one of the sons of the prophets said to his companion, "Strike me with your weapon," but the man refused.[n]

36 So the prophet said, "Because you have not obeyed the LORD, as soon as you leave me a lion[o] will kill you." And after the man went away, a lion found him and killed him.

37 The prophet found another man and said, "Strike me, please." So the man struck him and wounded him. 38 Then the prophet went and stood by the road waiting for the king. He disguised himself with his headband down over his eyes. 39 As the king passed by, the prophet called out to him, "Your servant went into the thick of the battle, and someone came to me with a captive and said, 'Guard this man. If he is missing, it will be your life for his life,[p] or you must pay a talent[a] of silver.' 40 While your servant was busy here and there, the man disappeared."

"That is your sentence," the king of Israel said. "You have pronounced it yourself."

41 Then the prophet quickly removed the headband from his eyes, and the king of Israel recognized him as one of the prophets. 42 He said to the king, "This is what the LORD says: 'You have set free a man I had determined should die.[b] Therefore it is your life for his life,[q] your people for his people.' " 43 Sullen and angry,[r] the king of Israel went to his palace in Samaria.

## Naboth's Vineyard

21 Some time later there was an incident involving a vineyard belonging to Naboth the Jezreelite. The vineyard was in Jezreel, close to the palace of Ahab king of Samaria. 2 Ahab said to Naboth, "Let me have your vineyard to use for a vegetable garden, since it is close to my palace. In exchange I will give you a better vineyard or, if you prefer, I will pay you whatever it is worth."

3 But Naboth replied, "The LORD forbid that I should give you the inheritance[s] of my fathers."

4 So Ahab went home, sullen and angry because Naboth the Jezreelite had said, "I will not give you the inheritance of my fathers." He lay on his bed sulking and refused to eat.

5 His wife Jezebel came in and asked him, "Why are you so sullen? Why won't you eat?"

6 He answered her, "Because I said to Naboth the Jezreelite, 'Sell me your vineyard; or if you prefer, I will give you another vineyard in its place.' But he said, 'I will not give you my vineyard.' "

7 Jezebel his wife said, "Is this how you act as king over Israel? Get up and eat! Cheer up. I'll get you the vineyard of Naboth the Jezreelite."

8 So she wrote letters in Ahab's name, placed his seal on them, and sent them to the elders and nobles who lived in Naboth's city with him. 9 In those letters she wrote:

> "Proclaim a day of fasting and seat Naboth in a prominent place among the people. 10 But seat two scoundrels[t] opposite him and have them testify that he has cursed[u] both God and the king. Then take him out and stone him to death."

11 So the elders and nobles who lived in Naboth's city did as Jezebel directed in the letters she had written to them. 12 They proclaimed a fast and seated Naboth in a prominent place among the people. 13 Then two scoundrels came and sat opposite him and brought charges against Naboth before the people, saying, "Naboth has cursed both God and the king." So they took him outside the city and stoned him to death.[v] 14 Then they sent word to Jezebel: "Naboth has been stoned and is dead."

15 As soon as Jezebel heard that Naboth had been stoned to death, she said to Ahab, "Get up and take possession of the vineyard of Naboth the Jezreelite that he refused to sell you. He is no longer alive, but dead." 16 When Ahab heard that Naboth was dead, he got up and went down to take possession of Naboth's vineyard.

17 Then the word of the LORD came to Elijah the Tishbite: 18 "Go down to meet Ahab king of Israel, who rules in Samaria. He is now

21:10 t Ac 6:11 u Ex 22:28; Lev 24:15–16
21:13 v 2Ki 9:26

[a] 39 That is, about 75 pounds (about 34 kilograms) [b] 42 The Hebrew term refers to the irrevocable giving over of things or persons to the LORD, often by totally destroying them.

**21:19** w 1Ki 22:38
**21:20** x 1Ki 18:17 y Ro 7:14
**21:21** z 1Ki 14:10; 2Ki 9:8
**21:22** a 1Ki 15:29
**21:23** b 2Ki 9:10,34–36
**21:24** c 1Ki 14:11; 16:4
**21:26** d Ge 15:16
**21:29** e 2Ki 9:26
**22:3** f Dt 4:43

in Naboth's vineyard, where he has gone to take possession of it. 19 Say to him, 'This is what the LORD says: Have you not murdered a man and seized his property?' Then say to him, 'This is what the LORD says: In the place where dogs licked up Naboth's blood, dogs[w] will lick up your blood—yes, yours!'"

20 Ahab said to Elijah, "So you have found me, my enemy!"[x]

"I have found you," he answered, "because you have sold[y] yourself to do evil in the eyes of the LORD. 21 'I am going to bring disaster on you. I will consume your descendants and cut off from Ahab every last male[z] in Israel—slave or free. 22 I will make your house[a] like that of Jeroboam son of Nebat and that of Baasha son of Ahijah, because you have provoked me to anger and have caused Israel to sin.'

23 "And also concerning Jezebel the LORD says: 'Dogs[b] will devour Jezebel by the wall of[a] Jezreel.'

24 "Dogs[c] will eat those belonging to Ahab who die in the city, and the birds of the air will feed on those who die in the country."

25 (There was never a man like Ahab, who sold himself to do evil in the eyes of the LORD, urged on by Jezebel his wife. 26 He behaved in the vilest manner by going after idols, like the Amorites[d] the LORD drove out before Israel.)

27 When Ahab heard these words, he tore his clothes, put on sackcloth and fasted. He lay in sackcloth and went around meekly.

28 Then the word of the LORD came to Elijah the Tishbite: 29 "Have you noticed how Ahab has humbled himself before me? Because he has humbled himself, I will not bring this disaster in his day, but I will bring it on his house in the days of his son."[e]

## Micaiah Prophesies Against Ahab

**22** For three years there was no war between Aram and Israel. 2 But in the third year Jehoshaphat king of Judah went down to see the king of Israel. 3 The king of Israel had said to his officials, "Don't you know that Ramoth Gilead[f] belongs to us and yet we are doing nothing to retake it from the king of Aram?"

4 So he asked Jehoshaphat, "Will you go with me to fight[g] against Ramoth Gilead?"

Jehoshaphat replied to the king of Israel, "I am as you are, my people as your people, my horses as your horses." 5 But Jehoshaphat also said to the king of Israel, "First seek the counsel of the LORD."

6 So the king of Israel brought together the prophets—about four hundred men—and asked them, "Shall I go to war against Ramoth Gilead, or shall I refrain?"

"Go,"[h] they answered, "for the Lord will give it into the king's hand."

7 But Jehoshaphat asked, "Is there not a prophet[i] of the LORD here whom we can inquire of?"

8 The king of Israel answered Jehoshaphat, "There is still one man through whom we can inquire of the LORD, but I hate him because he never prophesies anything good about me, but always bad. He is Micaiah son of Imlah."

"The king should not say that," Jehoshaphat replied.

9 So the king of Israel called one of his officials and said, "Bring Micaiah son of Imlah at once."

10 Dressed in their royal robes, the king of Israel and Jehoshaphat king of Judah were sitting on their thrones at the threshing floor by the entrance of the gate of Samaria, with all the prophets prophesying before them. 11 Now Zedekiah son of Kenaanah had made iron horns[j] and he declared, "This is what the LORD says: 'With these you will gore the Arameans until they are destroyed.'"

12 All the other prophets were prophesying the same thing. "Attack Ramoth Gilead and be victorious," they said, "for the LORD will give it into the king's hand."

13 The messenger who had gone to summon Micaiah said to him, "Look, as one man the other prophets are predicting success for the king. Let your word agree with theirs, and speak favorably."

14 But Micaiah said, "As surely as the LORD lives, I can tell him only what the LORD tells me."[k]

15 When he arrived, the king asked him, "Micaiah, shall we go to war against Ramoth Gilead, or shall I refrain?"

**22:4** g 2Ki 3:7
**22:6** h 1Ki 18:19
**22:7** i 2Ki 3:11
**22:11** j Dt 33:17; Zec 1:18–21
**22:14** k Nu 22:18

[a] 23 Most Hebrew manuscripts; a few Hebrew manuscripts, Vulgate and Syriac (see also 2 Kings 9:26) *the plot of ground at*

# Inspire

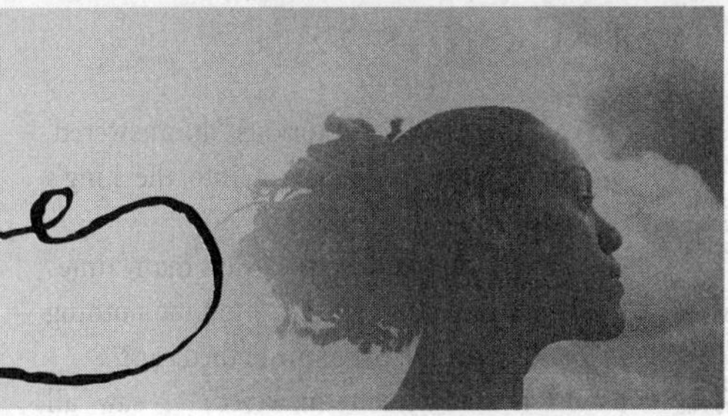

## SUBMISSION

From the creation of Eve, women of color have been created to help meet the Biblical requirements for God-glorifying fruitfulness. People are to submit to God first and then mutually to one another. Otherwise, women of color may experience ethnic- and gender-based impositions. Too often submission implies a superior-inferior, master-slave, head-feet relationship, when, in fact, submission is measured by one's love for God. Submission does not mean subjecting oneself to abuse. Nor does it mean mindless acquiescence to the needs and desires of others.

Some Biblical women shed light on the type of submission women of color, as well as others, should embody. The success of these women was directly related to their submission—first to God and then to the four other types of submission the Bible requires: to one another, to leaders, to government and to husbands. Without exception, spiritually enabled women in the Bible were submissive to God. Esther provides a good example of submission. Even Hagar, a symbol of oppression, had a life-changing, liberating experience when she, as a refugee, submitted to God (see Ge 16:6–15).

On the other hand, spiritually depraved women in the Bible eventually came to naught. Such was the case with Jezebel, who rebelled against submission to God; her refusal cost her everything, including her kingdom and her life (see 1Ki 21:23–25; 2Ki 9:6–10,30–37).

Those who submit to God will be empowered. On the other hand, those who rebel against God will be continually disempowered. We must remember, however, that blind submission or obedience to a man—whether a husband, pastor, boss or bishop—is not Biblical submission. Only those who are submitted to God's will begin submission where God's Word begins. And when this is the case, submission to governments, leaders and husbands, when applicable, will follow.

—P. J. Anderson

For the next Inspire note, go to page 483.

### read

1 Kings 21; see also Genesis 16:6–15; 2 Kings 9.

See also the Inspire Notes "Marriage" and "Commitment to God," and the Women of the Bible Notes "Sarah: Is Anything Too Hard for God?" "Wise and Foolish Virgins: Preparing for Christ" and "Peter's Mother-in-Law: From Suffering to Service."

### WOMAN *of* COLOR

How are you submitting to God in all areas of your life?

**22:17** l Mt 9:36
**22:19** m Isa 6:1; Da 7:9 n Job 1:6
**22:22** o Jdg 9:23; 2Th 2:11
**22:23** p Eze 14:9
**22:25** q 1Ki 20:30
**22:28** r Dt 18:22

"Attack and be victorious," he answered, "for the LORD will give it into the king's hand."

[16]The king said to him, "How many times must I make you swear to tell me nothing but the truth in the name of the LORD?"

[17]Then Micaiah answered, "I saw all Israel scattered on the hills like sheep without a shepherd,[l] and the LORD said, 'These people have no master. Let each one go home in peace.'"

[18]The king of Israel said to Jehoshaphat, "Didn't I tell you that he never prophesies anything good about me, but only bad?"

[19]Micaiah continued, "Therefore hear the word of the LORD: I saw the LORD sitting on his throne[m] with all the host[n] of heaven standing around him on his right and on his left. [20]And the LORD said, 'Who will entice Ahab into attacking Ramoth Gilead and going to his death there?'

"One suggested this, and another that. [21]Finally, a spirit came forward, stood before the LORD and said, 'I will entice him.'

[22]" 'By what means?' the LORD asked.

" 'I will go out and be a lying[o] spirit in the mouths of all his prophets,' he said.

" 'You will succeed in enticing him,' said the LORD. 'Go and do it.'

[23]"So now the LORD has put a lying spirit in the mouths of all these prophets[p] of yours. The LORD has decreed disaster for you."

[24]Then Zedekiah son of Kenaanah went up and slapped Micaiah in the face. "Which way did the spirit from[a] the LORD go when he went from me to speak to you?" he asked.

[25]Micaiah replied, "You will find out on the day you go to hide[q] in an inner room."

[26]The king of Israel then ordered, "Take Micaiah and send him back to Amon the ruler of the city and to Joash the king's son [27]and say, 'This is what the king says: Put this fellow in prison and give him nothing but bread and water until I return safely.'"

[28]Micaiah declared, "If you ever return safely, the LORD has not spoken[r] through me." Then he added, "Mark my words, all you people!"

## Ahab Killed at Ramoth Gilead

**22:30** s 2Ch 35:32
**22:38** t 1Ki 21:19
**22:39** u Am 3:15

[29]So the king of Israel and Jehoshaphat king of Judah went up to Ramoth Gilead. [30]The king of Israel said to Jehoshaphat, "I will enter the battle in disguise,[s] but you wear your royal robes." So the king of Israel disguised himself and went into battle.

[31]Now the king of Aram had ordered his thirty-two chariot commanders, "Do not fight with anyone, small or great, except the king of Israel." [32]When the chariot commanders saw Jehoshaphat, they thought, "Surely this is the king of Israel." So they turned to attack him, but when Jehoshaphat cried out, [33]the chariot commanders saw that he was not the king of Israel and stopped pursuing him.

[34]But someone drew his bow at random and hit the king of Israel between the sections of his armor. The king told his chariot driver, "Wheel around and get me out of the fighting. I've been wounded." [35]All day long the battle raged, and the king was propped up in his chariot facing the Arameans. The blood from his wound ran onto the floor of the chariot, and that evening he died. [36]As the sun was setting, a cry spread through the army: "Every man to his town; everyone to his land!"

[37]So the king died and was brought to Samaria, and they buried him there. [38]They washed the chariot at a pool in Samaria (where the prostitutes bathed),[b] and the dogs[t] licked up his blood, as the word of the LORD had declared.

[39]As for the other events of Ahab's reign, including all he did, the palace he built and inlaid with ivory,[u] and the cities he fortified, are they not written in the book of the annals of the kings of Israel? [40]Ahab rested with his fathers. And Ahaziah his son succeeded him as king.

## Jehoshaphat King of Judah

[41]Jehoshaphat son of Asa became king of Judah in the fourth year of Ahab king of Israel. [42]Jehoshaphat was thirty-five years old when he became king, and he reigned in Jerusalem twenty-five years. His mother's name was Azubah daughter of Shilhi. [43]In

[a]24 Or *Spirit of* [b]38 Or *Samaria and cleaned the weapons*

everything he walked in the ways of his father Asa[v] and did not stray from them; he did what was right in the eyes of the LORD. The high places,[w] however, were not removed, and the people continued to offer sacrifices and burn incense there. 44 Jehoshaphat was also at peace with the king of Israel.

45 As for the other events of Jehoshaphat's reign, the things he achieved and his military exploits, are they not written in the book of the annals of the kings of Judah? 46 He rid the land of the rest of the male shrine prostitutes[x] who remained there even after the reign of his father Asa. 47 There was then no king[y] in Edom; a deputy ruled.

48 Now Jehoshaphat built a fleet of trading ships[a] to go to Ophir for gold, but they never set sail—they were wrecked at Ezion Geber. 49 At that time Ahaziah son of Ahab said to Jehoshaphat, "Let my men sail with your men," but Jehoshaphat refused.

50 Then Jehoshaphat rested with his fathers and was buried with them in the city of David his father. And Jehoram his son succeeded him.

## Ahaziah King of Israel

51 Ahaziah son of Ahab became king of Israel in Samaria in the seventeenth year of Jehoshaphat king of Judah, and he reigned over Israel two years. 52 He did evil[z] in the eyes of the LORD, because he walked in the ways of his father and mother and in the ways of Jeroboam son of Nebat, who caused Israel to sin. 53 He served and worshiped Baal and provoked the LORD, the God of Israel, to anger, just as his father[a] had done.

**22:43**
v 2Ch 17:3
w 1Ki 15:14; 2Ki 12:3

**22:46**
x 1Ki 15:12

**22:47**
y 2Sa 8:14; 2Ki 3:9

**22:52**
z 1Ki 15:26

**22:53**
a 1Ki 16:30–32

[a]48 Hebrew *of ships of Tarshish*

# 2 Kings

## OVERVIEW

The book of 2 Kings begins with the triumph of Elijah being whisked away to heaven by a chariot of fire and the unprecedented ministry of Elisha, who was blessed to inherit Elijah's ministry and prophetic gift. Elisha is credited with several miracles, including parting the Jordan River (see 2Ki 2:13–14) and multiplying bread to feed 100 men (see 2Ki 4:42–44).

Influential women are also highlighted in the book of 2 Kings. Elisha was cared for by a Shunammite woman, and later God brought her son back to life through Elisha (see 2Ki 4:8–37; 8:1–6). A young servant girl from Israel convinced Naaman, who was the commander of the army of the king of Aram, to visit Elisha for healing from leprosy (see 2Ki 5). Athaliah was the only queen to rule in Israel; however, she was wicked and slaughtered all of the royal family of Judah—with the exception of Joash, who was hidden by his aunt, Jehosheba, until he was appointed king at seven years old (see 2Ki 11).

In secular society, the right thing to do is usually not the most popular thing to do. However, as women believers in Jesus Christ, the hope of our blessed destiny with its eternal rewards far outweighs the temporary pleasures of worldly living. Study how Athaliah's life ended in spite of her powerful influence over the kingdom; compare that to the blessing experienced by the Shunammite woman who cared for the prophet Elisha.

## OUTLINE

- I. The Ministries of Elijah and Elisha (1:1—8:15)
- II. Two Kings of Judah (8:16—29)
- III. Jehu's Purging Reign (9:1—10:36)
- IV. Joash's Rescue and Reign (11:1—12:21)
- V. Kings of Israel and Judah (13:1—16:20)
- VI. Israel Exiled to Assyria (17:1—41)
- VII. Kings of Judah (18:1—24:20)
- VIII. The Fall of Jerusalem (25:1—30)

## SCANNABLE FACTS:

**Author:** Unknown

**Time Written:** Probably during the Babylonian exile, around 550 B.C.

**Theme to Note:** God speaks truth through his prophets

**Notable Women:** The Shunammite woman, Naaman's servant girl, Athaliah, Jehosheba, Huldah the prophetess

**1:1** a 2Sa 8:2; 2Ki 3:5
**1:2** b ver 16 c Mk 3:22 d Mt 10:25 e 2Ki 8:7–10
**1:3** f Ge 16:7 g 1Ki 17:1
**1:4** h ver 6,16
**1:8** i Zec 13:4; Mt 3:4; Mk 1:6
**1:10** j 1Ki 18:38; Lk 9:54

## The LORD's Judgment on Ahaziah

1 After Ahab's death, Moab[a] rebelled
against Israel. 2Now Ahaziah had fallen
through the lattice of his upper room in
Samaria and injured himself. So he sent
messengers,[b] saying to them, "Go and con-
sult Baal-Zebub,[c] the god of Ekron,[d] to see if
I will recover[e] from this injury."
3But the angel[f] of the LORD said to Elijah[g]
the Tishbite, "Go up and meet the messen-
gers of the king of Samaria and ask them,
'Is it because there is no God in Israel that
you are going off to consult Baal-Zebub, the
god of Ekron?' 4Therefore this is what the
LORD says: 'You will not leave[h] the bed you
are lying on. You will certainly die!'" So Eli-
jah went.
5When the messengers returned to
the king, he asked them, "Why have you
come back?"
6"A man came to meet us," they replied.
"And he said to us, 'Go back to the king who
sent you and tell him, "This is what the LORD
says: Is it because there is no God in Israel
that you are sending men to consult Baal-
Zebub, the god of Ekron? Therefore you will
not leave the bed you are lying on. You will
certainly die!"'"
7The king asked them, "What kind of
man was it who came to meet you and told
you this?"
8They replied, "He was a man with a gar-
ment of hair[i] and with a leather belt around
his waist."
The king said, "That was Elijah the Tish-
bite."
9Then he sent to Elijah a captain with his
company of fifty men. The captain went up
to Elijah, who was sitting on the top of a hill,
and said to him, "Man of God, the king says,
'Come down!'"
10Elijah answered the captain, "If I am
a man of God, may fire come down from
heaven and consume you and your fifty
men!" Then fire[j] fell from heaven and con-
sumed the captain and his men.
11At this the king sent to Elijah another
captain with his fifty men. The captain said
to him, "Man of God, this is what the king
says, 'Come down at once!'"
12"If I am a man of God," Elijah replied,
"may fire come down from heaven and con-
sume you and your fifty men!" Then the fire
of God fell from heaven and consumed him
and his fifty men.
13So the king sent a third captain with
his fifty men. This third captain went up
and fell on his knees before Elijah. "Man
of God," he begged, "please have respect
for my life[k] and the lives of these fifty men,
your servants! 14See, fire has fallen from
heaven and consumed the first two captains
and all their men. But now have respect for
my life!"
15The angel[l] of the LORD said to Elijah,
"Go down with him; do not be afraid[m] of
him." So Elijah got up and went down with
him to the king.
16He told the king, "This is what the LORD
says: Is it because there is no God in Israel
for you to consult that you have sent mes-
sengers to consult Baal-Zebub, the god of
Ekron? Because you have done this, you will
never leave the bed you are lying on. You will
certainly die!" 17So he died, according to the
word of the LORD that Elijah had spoken.
Because Ahaziah had no son, Joram[a][n]
succeeded him as king in the second year of
Jehoram son of Jehoshaphat king of Judah.
18As for all the other events of Ahaziah's
reign, and what he did, are they not writ-
ten in the book of the annals of the kings
of Israel?

## Elijah Taken Up to Heaven

2 When the LORD was about to take[o] Eli-
jah up to heaven in a whirlwind, Elijah
and Elisha[p] were on their way from Gilgal.
2Elijah said to Elisha, "Stay here; the LORD
has sent me to Bethel."
But Elisha said, "As surely as the LORD
lives and as you live, I will not leave you."[q]
So they went down to Bethel.
3The company of the prophets at Bethel
came out to Elisha and asked, "Do you know
that the LORD is going to take your master
from you today?"
"Yes, I know," Elisha replied, "but do not
speak of it."
4Then Elijah said to him, "Stay here, Eli-
sha; the LORD has sent me to Jericho."

**1:13** k 1Sa 26:21; Ps 72:14
**1:15** l ver 3 m Isa 51:12; Jer 1:17; Eze 2:6
**1:17** n 2Ki 3:1; 8:16
**2:1** o Ge 5:24; Heb 11:5 p 1Ki 19:16,21
**2:2** q Ru 1:16; 1Sa 1:26

[a] 17 Hebrew *Jehoram*, a variant of *Joram*

2:6 r Jos 3:15
2:8 s 1Ki 19:19 t ver 14 u Ex 14:21 v Ex 14:22,29
2:11 w 2Ki 6:17; Ps 104:3,4
2:12 x 2Ki 13:14
2:14 y ver 8
2:15 z ver 7

And he replied, "As surely as the LORD lives and as you live, I will not leave you." So they went to Jericho.

5The company of the prophets at Jericho went up to Elisha and asked him, "Do you know that the LORD is going to take your master from you today?"

"Yes, I know," he replied, "but do not speak of it."

6Then Elijah said to him, "Stay here; the LORD has sent me to the Jordan."[r]

And he replied, "As surely as the LORD lives and as you live, I will not leave you." So the two of them walked on.

7Fifty men of the company of the prophets went and stood at a distance, facing the place where Elijah and Elisha had stopped at the Jordan. 8Elijah took his cloak,[s] rolled it up and struck[t] the water with it. The water divided[u] to the right and to the left, and the two of them crossed over on dry[v] ground.

9When they had crossed, Elijah said to Elisha, "Tell me, what can I do for you before I am taken from you?"

"Let me inherit a double portion of your spirit," Elisha replied.

10"You have asked a difficult thing," Elijah said, "yet if you see me when I am taken from you, it will be yours—otherwise not."

11As they were walking along and talking together, suddenly a chariot of fire[w] and horses of fire appeared and separated the two of them, and Elijah went up to heaven in a whirlwind. 12Elisha saw this and cried out, "My father! My father! The chariots[x] and horsemen of Israel!" And Elisha saw him no more. Then he took hold of his own clothes and tore them apart.

13He picked up the cloak that had fallen from Elijah and went back and stood on the bank of the Jordan. 14Then he took the cloak that had fallen from him and struck[y] the water with it. "Where now is the LORD, the God of Elijah?" he asked. When he struck the water, it divided to the right and to the left, and he crossed over.

15The company[z] of the prophets from Jericho, who were watching, said, "The spirit of Elijah is resting on Elisha." And they went to meet him and bowed to the ground before him. 16"Look," they said, "we your servants have fifty able men. Let them go and look for your master. Perhaps the Spirit[a] of the LORD has picked him up[b] and set him down on some mountain or in some valley."

"No," Elisha replied, "do not send them."

17But they persisted until he was too ashamed to refuse. So he said, "Send them." And they sent fifty men, who searched for three days but did not find him. 18When they returned to Elisha, who was staying in Jericho, he said to them, "Didn't I tell you not to go?"

## Healing of the Water

19The men of the city said to Elisha, "Look, our lord, this town is well situated, as you can see, but the water is bad and the land is unproductive."

20"Bring me a new bowl," he said, "and put salt in it." So they brought it to him.

21Then he went out to the spring and threw[c] the salt into it, saying, "This is what the LORD says: 'I have healed this water. Never again will it cause death or make the land unproductive.' " 22And the water has remained wholesome to this day, according to the word Elisha had spoken.

## Elisha Is Jeered

23From there Elisha went up to Bethel. As he was walking along the road, some youths came out of the town and jeered at him. "Go on up, you baldhead!" they said. "Go on up, you baldhead!" 24He turned around, looked at them and called down a curse on them in the name of the LORD. Then two bears came out of the woods and mauled forty-two of the youths. 25And he went on to Mount Carmel[d] and from there returned to Samaria.

## Moab Revolts

3 Joram[a][e] son of Ahab became king of Israel in Samaria in the eighteenth year of Jehoshaphat king of Judah, and he reigned twelve years. 2He did evil in the eyes of the LORD, but not as his father[f] and mother had done. He got rid of the sacred stone of Baal that his father had made. 3Nevertheless he clung to the sins[g] of Jeroboam son of Nebat, which he had caused Israel to commit; he did not turn away from them.

2:16 a 1Ki 18:12 b Ac 8:39
2:21 c Ex 15:25; 2Ki 4:41; 6:6
2:25 d 1Ki 18:20
3:1 e 2Ki 1:17
3:2 f 1Ki 16:30–32
3:3 g 1Ki 12:28–32

[a]1 Hebrew *Jehoram,* a variant of *Joram*; also in verse 6

**3:4** h Isa 16:1
**3:5** i 2Ki 1:1
**3:7** j 1Ki 22:4
**3:9** k 1Ki 22:47
**3:11** l 1Ki 22:7
**3:15** m 1Sa 16:23; n Eze 1:3

4Now Mesha king of Moab raised sheep, and he had to supply the king of Israel with a hundred thousand lambs[h] and with the wool of a hundred thousand rams. 5But after Ahab died, the king of Moab rebelled[i] against the king of Israel. 6So at that time King Joram set out from Samaria and mobilized all Israel. 7He also sent this message to Jehoshaphat king of Judah: "The king of Moab has rebelled against me. Will you go with me to fight[j] against Moab?"

"I will go with you," he replied. "I am as you are, my people as your people, my horses as your horses."

8"By what route shall we attack?" he asked.

"Through the Desert of Edom," he answered.

9So the king of Israel set out with the king of Judah and the king of Edom.[k] After a roundabout march of seven days, the army had no more water for themselves or for the animals with them.

10"What!" exclaimed the king of Israel. "Has the LORD called us three kings together only to hand us over to Moab?"

11But Jehoshaphat asked, "Is there no prophet of the LORD here, that we may inquire[l] of the LORD through him?"

An officer of the king of Israel answered, "Elisha son of Shaphat is here. He used to pour water on the hands of Elijah.[a]"

12Jehoshaphat said, "The word of the LORD is with him." So the king of Israel and Jehoshaphat and the king of Edom went down to him.

13Elisha said to the king of Israel, "What do we have to do with each other? Go to the prophets of your father and the prophets of your mother."

"No," the king of Israel answered, "because it was the LORD who called us three kings together to hand us over to Moab."

14Elisha said, "As surely as the LORD Almighty lives, whom I serve, if I did not have respect for the presence of Jehoshaphat king of Judah, I would not look at you or even notice you. 15But now bring me a harpist."[m]

While the harpist was playing, the hand[n] of the LORD came upon Elisha 16and he said, "This is what the LORD says: Make this valley full of ditches. 17For this is what the LORD says: You will see neither wind nor rain, yet this valley will be filled with water, and you, your cattle and your other animals will drink. 18This is an easy[o] thing in the eyes of the LORD; he will also hand Moab over to you. 19You will overthrow every fortified city and every major town. You will cut down every good tree, stop up all the springs, and ruin every good field with stones."

20The next morning, about the time[p] for offering the sacrifice, there it was—water flowing from the direction of Edom! And the land was filled with water.

21Now all the Moabites had heard that the kings had come to fight against them; so every man, young and old, who could bear arms was called up and stationed on the border. 22When they got up early in the morning, the sun was shining on the water. To the Moabites across the way, the water looked red—like blood. 23"That's blood!" they said. "Those kings must have fought and slaughtered each other. Now to the plunder, Moab!"

24But when the Moabites came to the camp of Israel, the Israelites rose up and fought them until they fled. And the Israelites invaded the land and slaughtered the Moabites. 25They destroyed the towns, and each man threw a stone on every good field until it was covered. They stopped up all the springs and cut down every good tree. Only Kir Hareseth[q] was left with its stones in place, but men armed with slings surrounded it and attacked it as well.

26When the king of Moab saw that the battle had gone against him, he took with him seven hundred swordsmen to break through to the king of Edom, but they failed. 27Then he took his firstborn[r] son, who was to succeed him as king, and offered him as a sacrifice on the city wall. The fury against Israel was great; they withdrew and returned to their own land.

## The Widow's Oil

4 The wife of a man from the company of the prophets cried out to Elisha, "Your servant my husband is dead, and you know that he revered the LORD. But now his

**3:18** o Ge 18:14; Jer 32:17,27; Mk 10:27
**3:20** p Ex 29:39-40
**3:25** q ver 19; Isa 16:7; Jer 48:31,36
**3:27** r Am 2:1; Mic 6:7

[a]11 That is, he was Elijah's personal servant.

creditor[s] is coming to take my two boys as his slaves."

2Elisha replied to her, "How can I help you? Tell me, what do you have in your house?"

"Your servant has nothing there at all," she said, "except a little oil."[t]

3Elisha said, "Go around and ask all your neighbors for empty jars. Don't ask for just a few. 4Then go inside and shut the door behind you and your sons. Pour oil into all the jars, and as each is filled, put it to one side."

5She left him and afterward shut the door behind her and her sons. They brought the jars to her and she kept pouring. 6When all the jars were full, she said to her son, "Bring me another one."

But he replied, "There is not a jar left." Then the oil stopped flowing.

7She went and told the man of God,[u] and he said, "Go, sell the oil and pay your debts. You and your sons can live on what is left."

## The Shunammite's Son Restored to Life

8One day Elisha went to Shunem.[v] And a well-to-do woman was there, who urged him to stay for a meal. So whenever he came by, he stopped there to eat. 9She said to her husband, "I know that this man who often comes our way is a holy man of God. 10Let's make a small room on the roof and put in it a bed and a table, a chair and a lamp for him. Then he can stay[w] there whenever he comes to us."

11One day when Elisha came, he went up to his room and lay down there. 12He said to his servant Gehazi, "Call the Shunammite." So he called her, and she stood before him. 13Elisha said to him, "Tell her, 'You have gone to all this trouble for us. Now what can be done for you? Can we speak on your behalf to the king or the commander of the army?' "

She replied, "I have a home among my own people."

14"What can be done for her?" Elisha asked.

Gehazi said, "Well, she has no son and her husband is old."

15Then Elisha said, "Call her." So he called her, and she stood in the doorway. 16"About this time[x] next year," Elisha said, "you will hold a son in your arms."

"No, my lord," she objected. "Don't mislead your servant, O man of God!"

17But the woman became pregnant, and the next year about that same time she gave birth to a son, just as Elisha had told her.

18The child grew, and one day he went out to his father, who was with the reapers. 19"My head! My head!" he said to his father.

His father told a servant, "Carry him to his mother." 20After the servant had lifted him up and carried him to his mother, the boy sat on her lap until noon, and then he died. 21She went up and laid him on the bed[y] of the man of God, then shut the door and went out.

22She called her husband and said, "Please send me one of the servants and a donkey so I can go to the man of God quickly and return."

23"Why go to him today?" he asked. "It's not the New Moon[z] or the Sabbath."

"It's all right," she said.

24She saddled the donkey and said to her servant, "Lead on; don't slow down for me unless I tell you." 25So she set out and came to the man of God at Mount Carmel.[a]

When he saw her in the distance, the man of God said to his servant Gehazi, "Look! There's the Shunammite! 26Run to meet her and ask her, 'Are you all right? Is your husband all right? Is your child all right?' "

"Everything is all right," she said.

27When she reached the man of God at the mountain, she took hold of his feet. Gehazi came over to push her away, but the man of God said, "Leave her alone! She is in bitter distress, but the LORD has hidden it from me and has not told me why."

28"Did I ask you for a son, my lord?" she said. "Didn't I tell you, 'Don't raise my hopes'?"

29Elisha said to Gehazi, "Tuck your cloak into your belt,[b] take my staff[c] in your hand and run. If you meet anyone, do not greet him, and if anyone greets you, do not answer. Lay my staff on the boy's face."

30But the child's mother said, "As surely as the LORD lives and as you live, I will not leave you." So he got up and followed her.

31Gehazi went on ahead and laid the staff

**4:1** s Lev 25:39–43; Ne 5:3–5
**4:2** t 1Ki 17:12
**4:7** u 1Ki 12:22
**4:8** v Jos 19:18
**4:10** w Mt 10:41; Ro 12:13
**4:16** x Ge 18:10
**4:21** y ver 32
**4:23** z Nu 10:10; 1Ch 23:31
**4:25** a 1Ki 18:20; 2Ki 2:25
**4:29** b 1Ki 18:46; 2Ki 9:1 c Ex 4:2; 7:19

# The Prophet's Widow

## God Provides

The widow was the least of all people in ancient society. Upon her husband's death, his inheritance passed to his sons. If she had no children, she was returned to her father's household. Thus, her vulnerable state made her easy prey for a creditor or anyone else who wished to take advantage of an already bad situation. Although the Jewish Scriptures clearly called for mercy and justice for widows (see Dt 14:28–29; 24:19–21; Isa 10:1–2), it obviously wasn't always the reality.

Second Kings 4:1–7 records one widow's plight and the miracle of mercy that restored her. This woman's husband had been part of a rather unique and closed community within Israel—that of the prophets. Yet she was no less vulnerable than other widows were. Her back was against the wall, and her creditors were about to take her only means of survival—her two sons. Her story describes a marvelous truth that God works with what we have to do miraculous things! When she appealed to the prophet Elisha, he asked what she had in her house (see 2Ki 4:2). It was from a simple jar of oil that God met her needs. As she poured out the oil—in obedience to Elisha's instruction—she witnessed God's abundant love. God provided her with the means to pay her creditors and to support her family.

How often do we overlook what is in our "house" that God wants to use? We might look for great things and great people to move on our behalf, and yet these things and these people are powerless without God's intervention.

It is interesting that the widow mentioned oil as the one thing of value or usefulness in her house. Oil is a symbol of the indwelling presence of the Holy Spirit. In the parable of the ten virgins, recorded in Matthew 25, we are reminded to keep the lamp of our hearts filled with oil—the Holy Spirit—to ensure that the bridegroom (Jesus) knows that we are prepared and anxiously awaiting his return. Again, God will use what is in our "house" in that final miracle of mercy.

The prophet's widow exemplifies God's concern for women. Through her example, we see our need to have faith and to obey God's will. God will take care of the rest.

—L. D. Caldwell

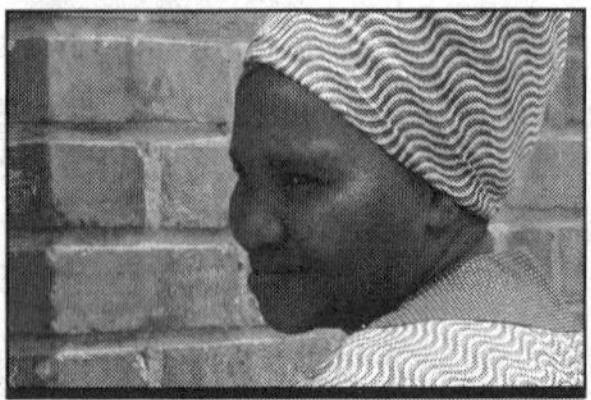

### reflection

*Ask God to show you what you have that he can use to make good out of a bad situation.*

### read

2 Kings 4:1–7.
See also the Inspire Notes "Single Mothers," "Motherhood," "Distress," "Single Parenting" and "Faith," and the Women of the Bible Notes "Wise and Foolish Virgins: Preparing for Christ" and "The Widow's Offering: Selfless Giving."

For the next Women of the Bible note, go to page 438.

**4:33** d 1Ki 17:20; Mt 6:6
**4:34** e 1Ki 17:21; Ac 20:10
**4:35** f 2Ki 8:5
**4:38** g 2Ki 2:1 h 2Ki 8:1
**4:41** i Ex 15:25; 2Ki 2:21
**4:42** j 1Sa 9:4 k 1Sa 9:7

on the boy's face, but there was no sound or response. So Gehazi went back to meet Elisha and told him, "The boy has not awakened."

32 When Elisha reached the house, there was the boy lying dead on his couch. 33 He went in, shut the door on the two of them and prayed[d] to the LORD. 34 Then he got on the bed and lay upon the boy, mouth to mouth, eyes to eyes, hands to hands. As he stretched[e] himself out upon him, the boy's body grew warm. 35 Elisha turned away and walked back and forth in the room and then got on the bed and stretched out upon him once more. The boy sneezed seven times and opened his eyes.[f]

36 Elisha summoned Gehazi and said, "Call the Shunammite." And he did. When she came, he said, "Take your son." 37 She came in, fell at his feet and bowed to the ground. Then she took her son and went out.

## Death in the Pot

38 Elisha returned to Gilgal[g] and there was a famine[h] in that region. While the company of the prophets was meeting with him, he said to his servant, "Put on the large pot and cook some stew for these men."

39 One of them went out into the fields to gather herbs and found a wild vine. He gathered some of its gourds and filled the fold of his cloak. When he returned, he cut them up into the pot of stew, though no one knew what they were. 40 The stew was poured out for the men, but as they began to eat it, they cried out, "O man of God, there is death in the pot!" And they could not eat it.

41 Elisha said, "Get some flour." He put it into the pot and said, "Serve it to the people to eat." And there was nothing harmful in the pot.[i]

## Feeding of a Hundred

42 A man came from Baal Shalishah,[j] bringing the man of God twenty loaves of barley bread[k] baked from the first ripe grain, along with some heads of new grain. "Give it to the people to eat," Elisha said.

43 "How can I set this before a hundred men?" his servant asked.

But Elisha answered, "Give it to the people to eat.[l] For this is what the LORD says: 'They will eat and have some left over.[m]'" 44 Then he set it before them, and they ate and had some left over, according to the word of the LORD.

## Naaman Healed of Leprosy

5 Now Naaman was commander of the army of the king of Aram. He was a great man in the sight of his master and highly regarded, because through him the LORD had given victory to Aram. He was a valiant soldier, but he had leprosy.[a][n]

2 Now bands from Aram had gone out and had taken captive a young girl from Israel, and she served Naaman's wife. 3 She said to her mistress, "If only my master would see the prophet who is in Samaria! He would cure him of his leprosy."

4 Naaman went to his master and told him what the girl from Israel had said. 5 "By all means, go," the king of Aram replied. "I will send a letter to the king of Israel." So Naaman left, taking with him ten talents[b] of silver, six thousand shekels[c] of gold and ten sets of clothing.[o] 6 The letter that he took to the king of Israel read: "With this letter I am sending my servant Naaman to you so that you may cure him of his leprosy."

7 As soon as the king of Israel read the letter,[p] he tore his robes and said, "Am I God?[q] Can I kill and bring back to life?[r] Why does this fellow send someone to me to be cured of his leprosy? See how he is trying to pick a quarrel[s] with me!"

8 When Elisha the man of God heard that the king of Israel had torn his robes, he sent him this message: "Why have you torn your robes? Have the man come to me and he will know that there is a prophet in Israel." 9 So Naaman went with his horses and chariots and stopped at the door of Elisha's house. 10 Elisha sent a messenger to say to him, "Go, wash[t] yourself seven times in the Jordan, and your flesh will be restored and you will be cleansed."

11 But Naaman went away angry and said, "I thought that he would surely come out to me and stand and call on the name of the

**4:43** l Lk 9:13 m Jn 6:12
**5:1** n Lk 4:27
**5:5** o 1Sa 9:7
**5:7** p 2Ki 19:14 q Ge 30:2 r Dt 32:39; 1Sa 2:6 s 1Ki 20:7
**5:10** t Jn 9:7

[a]1 The Hebrew word was used for various diseases affecting the skin—not necessarily leprosy; also in verses 3, 6, 7, 11 and 27. [b]5 That is, about 750 pounds (about 340 kilograms) [c]5 That is, about 150 pounds (about 70 kilograms)

women OF THE Bible

# The Shunammite Woman

## Our Sister's Grief Is Our Grief

How do we share our loss or losses with others? What can this unnamed wealthy woman tell us about faith, humility, hospitality and grace? God had the author of 2 Kings record this woman's story to help us deal with our own losses.

A woman of means, the Shunammite woman showed kindness to the prophet Elisha and his servant Gehazi. She provided a room and provision for the itinerant prophet (see 2Ki 4:10). Her reward for humility, hospitality and grace came in the form of a prophecy; Elisha prophesied that she and her elderly husband would bear a son (see 2Ki 4:15–16). And that prophecy came true. The woman had a baby boy.

In later years, the child died in her arms—the very arms that had held him when he cried, the very arms that had comforted him when he was ill, the very arms that had fed him when he could not feed himself, and the very arms that had taught him to love the Lord. Yet, although filled with grief, she held on to the fact that the prophet of God had foretold the gift of her son. Could we lay our child down and walk away? Could we hold fast to the promises of God? The Shunammite woman's faith and confident determination in the midst of grief resulted in the restoration of her son's life.

Miracles happen to us daily. Our grievous losses are sometimes precursors to hidden miracles yet to be revealed. Our faith unlocks the key to our understanding. As we journey through this story, we can envision the many blessings that unfolded for this Shunammite wife and mother. And we can anticipate our own miracles in the midst of our grief.

—B. Kitt

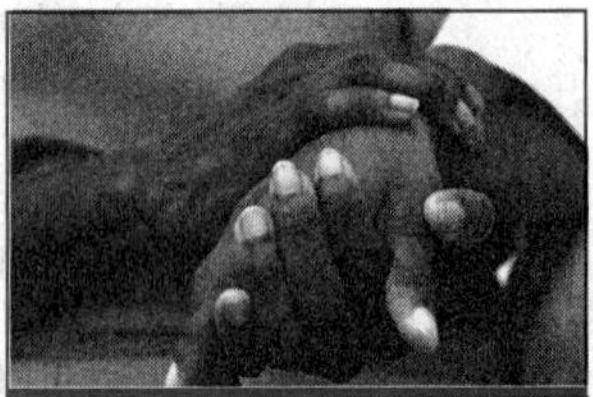

### reflection

*What miracles have come out of grievous situations in your life?*

*Share your testimony with someone who needs to hear it.*

### read

2 Kings 4:8–37; 8:1–6.

See also the Inspire Notes "The Faithfulness of God," "Suffering," "The Paradox of Life and Suffering," "Grieving a Miscarriage or Stillborn Child" and "Faith," and the Women of the Bible Notes "Bathsheba: A Silent Affair," "Rizpah: A Grieving Mother," "Ezekiel's Wife: On God's Stage," "The Canaanite Woman: Persistence Pays Off" and "Mary and Martha: Grieving Sisters."

For the next Women of the Bible note, go to page 445.

5:12
u Pr 14:17,29; 19:11

5:13
v 2Ki 6:21

5:14
w Job 33:25; Lk 4:27

5:15
x Jos 4:24; 1Sa 17:46

5:16
y ver 20,26; Ge 14:23

5:17
z Ex 20:24

5:18
a 2Ki 7:2

5:19
b 1Sa 1:17

*My seeking child,*

*Looking for answers? Consult me.*

*Your*
*Creator Father*

2 KINGS 5:1–10

LORD his God, wave his hand over the spot and cure me of my leprosy. 12 Are not Abana and Pharpar, the rivers of Damascus, better than any of the waters of Israel? Couldn't I wash in them and be cleansed?" So he turned and went off in a rage.[u]

13 Naaman's servants went to him and said, "My father,[v] if the prophet had told you to do some great thing, would you not have done it? How much more, then, when he tells you, 'Wash and be cleansed'!" 14 So he went down and dipped himself in the Jordan seven times, as the man of God had told him, and his flesh was restored and became clean like that of a young boy.[w]

15 Then Naaman and all his attendants went back to the man of God. He stood before him and said, "Now I know[x] that there is no God in all the world except in Israel. Please accept now a gift from your servant."

16 The prophet answered, "As surely as the LORD lives, whom I serve, I will not accept a thing." And even though Naaman urged him, he refused.[y]

17 "If you will not," said Naaman, "please let me, your servant, be given as much earth[z] as a pair of mules can carry, for your servant will never again make burnt offerings and sacrifices to any other god but the LORD. 18 But may the LORD forgive your servant for this one thing: When my master enters the temple of Rimmon to bow down and he is leaning[a] on my arm and I bow there also—when I bow down in the temple of Rimmon, may the LORD forgive your servant for this."

19 "Go in peace,"[b] Elisha said.

After Naaman had traveled some distance, 20 Gehazi, the servant of Elisha the man of God, said to himself, "My master was too easy on Naaman, this Aramean, by not accepting from him what he brought. As surely as the LORD[c] lives, I will run after him and get something from him."

21 So Gehazi hurried after Naaman. When Naaman saw him running toward him, he got down from the chariot to meet him. "Is everything all right?" he asked.

22 "Everything is all right," Gehazi answered. "My master sent me to say, 'Two young men from the company of the prophets have just come to me from the hill country of Ephraim. Please give them a talent[a] of silver and two sets of clothing.' "[d]

23 "By all means, take two talents," said Naaman. He urged Gehazi to accept them, and then tied up the two talents of silver in two bags, with two sets of clothing. He gave them to two of his servants, and they carried them ahead of Gehazi. 24 When Gehazi came to the hill, he took the things from the servants and put them away in the house. He sent the men away and they left. 25 Then he went in and stood before his master Elisha.

"Where have you been, Gehazi?" Elisha asked.

"Your servant didn't go anywhere," Gehazi answered.

26 But Elisha said to him, "Was not my spirit with you when the man got down from his chariot to meet you? Is this the time[e] to take money, or to accept clothes, olive groves, vineyards, flocks, herds, or menservants and maidservants? 27 Naaman's leprosy[f] will cling to you and to your descendants forever." Then Gehazi went from Elisha's presence and he was leprous, as white as snow.[g]

## An Axhead Floats

6 The company of the prophets said to Elisha, "Look, the place where we meet with you is too small for us. 2 Let us go to the Jordan, where each of us can get a pole; and let us build a place there for us to live."

And he said, "Go."

3 Then one of them said, "Won't you please come with your servants?"

"I will," Elisha replied. 4 And he went with them.

5:20
c Ex 20:7

5:22
d ver 5

5:26
e ver 16

5:27
f Nu 12:10
g Ex 4:6

[a]22 That is, about 75 pounds (about 34 kilograms)

6:6 h Ex 15:25; 2Ki 2:21
6:9 i ver 12
6:13 j Ge 37:17

They went to the Jordan and began to cut down trees. [5]As one of them was cutting down a tree, the iron axhead fell into the water. "Oh, my lord," he cried out, "it was borrowed!"

[6]The man of God asked, "Where did it fall?" When he showed him the place, Elisha cut a stick and threw[h] it there, and made the iron float. [7]"Lift it out," he said. Then the man reached out his hand and took it.

## Elisha Traps Blinded Arameans

[8]Now the king of Aram was at war with Israel. After conferring with his officers, he said, "I will set up my camp in such and such a place."

[9]The man of God sent word to the king[i] of Israel: "Beware of passing that place, because the Arameans are going down there." [10]So the king of Israel checked on the place indicated by the man of God. Time and again Elisha warned the king, so that he was on his guard in such places.

[11]This enraged the king of Aram. He summoned his officers and demanded of them, "Will you not tell me which of us is on the side of the king of Israel?"

[12]"None of us, my lord the king," said one of his officers, "but Elisha, the prophet who is in Israel, tells the king of Israel the very words you speak in your bedroom."

[13]"Go, find out where he is," the king ordered, "so I can send men and capture him." The report came back: "He is in Dothan."[j] [14]Then he sent horses and chariots and a strong force there. They went by night and surrounded the city.

*My God,*

*I need your strength to keep going. Renew me and grant me the will and resolve to continue pressing on in the power of your name.*

*Amen*

2 KINGS 6:11–16

[15]When the servant of the man of God got up and went out early the next morning, an army with horses and chariots had surrounded the city. "Oh, my lord, what shall we do?" the servant asked.

[16]"Don't be afraid," the prophet answered. "Those who are with us are more[k] than those who are with them."

[17]And Elisha prayed, "O LORD, open his eyes so he may see." Then the LORD opened the servant's eyes, and he looked and saw the hills full of horses and chariots[l] of fire all around Elisha.

[18]As the enemy came down toward him, Elisha prayed to the LORD, "Strike these people with blindness."[m] So he struck them with blindness, as Elisha had asked.

[19]Elisha told them, "This is not the road and this is not the city. Follow me, and I will lead you to the man you are looking for." And he led them to Samaria.

[20]After they entered the city, Elisha said, "LORD, open the eyes of these men so they can see." Then the LORD opened their eyes and they looked, and there they were, inside Samaria.

[21]When the king of Israel saw them, he asked Elisha, "Shall I kill them, my father?[n] Shall I kill them?"

[22]"Do not kill them," he answered. "Would you kill men you have captured[o] with your own sword or bow? Set food and water before them so that they may eat and drink and then go back to their master." [23]So he prepared a great feast for them, and after they had finished eating and drinking, he sent them away, and they returned to their master. So the bands[p] from Aram stopped raiding Israel's territory.

## Famine in Besieged Samaria

[24]Some time later, Ben-Hadad king of Aram mobilized his entire army and marched up and laid siege to Samaria. [25]There was a great famine in the city; the siege lasted so long that a donkey's head sold for eighty shekels[a] of silver, and a quarter of a cab[b] of seed pods[c] for five shekels.[d]

[26]As the king of Israel was passing by on

6:16 k 2Ch 32:7; Ps 55:18; Ro 8:31; 1Jn 4:4
6:17 l 2Ki 2:11,12; Ps 68:17; Zec 6:1–7
6:18 m Ge 19:11
6:21 n 2Ki 5:13
6:22 o Dt 20:11; Ro 12:20
6:23 p 2Ki 5:2

[a]25 That is, about 2 pounds (about 1 kilogram) [b]25 That is, probably about 1/2 pint (about 0.3 liter) [c]25 Or *of doves' dung* [d]25 That is, about 2 ounces (about 55 grams)

the wall, a woman cried to him, "Help me, my lord the king!"

27 The king replied, "If the LORD does not help you, where can I get help for you? From the threshing floor? From the winepress?" 28 Then he asked her, "What's the matter?"

She answered, "This woman said to me, 'Give up your son so we may eat him today, and tomorrow we'll eat my son.' 29 So we cooked my son and ate[q] him. The next day I said to her, 'Give up your son so we may eat him,' but she had hidden him."

30 When the king heard the woman's words, he tore his robes. As he went along the wall, the people looked, and there, underneath, he had sackcloth[r] on his body. 31 He said, "May God deal with me, be it ever so severely, if the head of Elisha son of Shaphat remains on his shoulders today!"

32 Now Elisha was sitting in his house, and the elders[s] were sitting with him. The king sent a messenger ahead, but before he arrived, Elisha said to the elders, "Don't you see how this murderer[t] is sending someone to cut off my head? Look, when the messenger comes, shut the door and hold it shut against him. Is not the sound of his master's footsteps behind him?"

33 While he was still talking to them, the messenger came down to him. And ⌞the king⌟ said, "This disaster is from the LORD. Why should I wait[u] for the LORD any longer?"

7 Elisha said, "Hear the word of the LORD. This is what the LORD says: About this time tomorrow, a seah[a] of flour will sell for a shekel[b] and two seahs[c] of barley for a shekel[v] at the gate of Samaria."

2 The officer on whose arm the king was leaning[w] said to the man of God, "Look, even if the LORD should open the floodgates[x] of the heavens, could this happen?"

"You will see it with your own eyes," answered Elisha, "but you will not eat[y] any of it!"

## The Siege Lifted

3 Now there were four men with leprosy[d][z] at the entrance of the city gate. They said to each other, "Why stay here until we die? 4 If we say, 'We'll go into the city'—the famine is there, and we will die. And if we stay here, we will die. So let's go over to the camp of the Arameans and surrender. If they spare us, we live; if they kill us, then we die."

5 At dusk they got up and went to the camp of the Arameans. When they reached the edge of the camp, not a man was there, 6 for the Lord had caused the Arameans to hear the sound[a] of chariots and horses and a great army, so that they said to one another, "Look, the king of Israel has hired the Hittite and Egyptian kings to attack us!" 7 So they got up and fled[b] in the dusk and abandoned their tents and their horses and donkeys. They left the camp as it was and ran for their lives.

8 The men who had leprosy reached the edge of the camp and entered one of the tents. They ate and drank, and carried away silver, gold and clothes, and went off and hid them. They returned and entered another tent and took some things from it and hid them also.

9 Then they said to each other, "We're not doing right. This is a day of good news and we are keeping it to ourselves. If we wait until daylight, punishment will overtake us. Let's go at once and report this to the royal palace."

10 So they went and called out to the city gatekeepers and told them, "We went into the Aramean camp and not a man was there—not a sound of anyone—only tethered horses and donkeys, and the tents left just as they were." 11 The gatekeepers shouted the news, and it was reported within the palace.

12 The king got up in the night and said to his officers, "I will tell you what the Arameans have done to us. They know we are starving; so they have left the camp to hide in the countryside, thinking, 'They will surely come out, and then we will take them alive and get into the city.'"

13 One of his officers answered, "Have some men take five of the horses that are left in the city. Their plight will be like that of all the Israelites left here—yes, they will only be like all these Israelites who are doomed.

**6:29** q Lev 26:29; Dt 28:53–55
**6:30** r Ge 37:34; 1Ki 21:27
**6:32** s Eze 8:1; 14:1; 20:1 t 1Ki 18:4
**6:33** u Job 2:9
**7:1** v ver 16
**7:2** w 2Ki 5:18 x ver 19; Ge 7:11; Mal 3:10 y ver 17
**7:3** z Lev 13:45–46; Nu 5:1–4
**7:6** a 2Sa 5:24
**7:7** b Ps 48:4–6; Pr 28:1

[a]1 That is, probably about 7 quarts (about 7.3 liters); also in verses 16 and 18 [b]1 That is, about 2/5 ounce (about 11 grams); also in verses 16 and 18 [c]1 That is, probably about 13 quarts (about 15 liters); also in verses 16 and 18
[d]3 The Hebrew word is used for various diseases affecting the skin—not necessarily leprosy; also in verse 8.

So let us send them to find out what happened."

14 So they selected two chariots with their horses, and the king sent them after the Aramean army. He commanded the drivers, "Go and find out what has happened." 15 They followed them as far as the Jordan, and they found the whole road strewn with the clothing and equipment the Arameans had thrown away in their headlong flight. So the messengers returned and reported to the king. 16 Then the people went out and plundered the camp of the Arameans. So a seah of flour sold for a shekel, and two seahs of barley sold for a shekel,[c] as the LORD had said.

17 Now the king had put the officer on whose arm he leaned in charge of the gate, and the people trampled him in the gateway, and he died,[d] just as the man of God had foretold when the king came down to his house. 18 It happened as the man of God had said to the king: "About this time tomorrow, a seah of flour will sell for a shekel and two seahs of barley for a shekel at the gate of Samaria."

19 The officer had said to the man of God, "Look, even if the LORD should open the floodgates[e] of the heavens, could this happen?" The man of God had replied, "You will see it with your own eyes, but you will not eat any of it!" 20 And that is exactly what happened to him, for the people trampled him in the gateway, and he died.

## The Shunammite's Land Restored

8 Now Elisha had said to the woman[f] whose son he had restored to life, "Go away with your family and stay for a while wherever you can, because the LORD has decreed a famine in the land that will last seven years."[g] 2 The woman proceeded to do as the man of God said. She and her family went away and stayed in the land of the Philistines seven years.

3 At the end of the seven years she came back from the land of the Philistines and went to the king to beg for her house and land. 4 The king was talking to Gehazi, the servant of the man of God, and had said, "Tell me about all the great things Elisha has done." 5 Just as Gehazi was telling the king how Elisha had restored[h] the dead to life, the woman whose son Elisha had brought back to life came to beg the king for her house and land.

Gehazi said, "This is the woman, my lord the king, and this is her son whom Elisha restored to life." 6 The king asked the woman about it, and she told him.

Then he assigned an official to her case and said to him, "Give back everything that belonged to her, including all the income from her land from the day she left the country until now."

## Hazael Murders Ben-Hadad

7 Elisha went to Damascus, and Ben-Hadad[i] king of Aram was ill. When the king was told, "The man of God has come all the way up here," 8 he said to Hazael,[j] "Take a gift[k] with you and go to meet the man of God. Consult the LORD through him; ask him, 'Will I recover from this illness?' "

9 Hazael went to meet Elisha, taking with him as a gift forty camel-loads of all the finest wares of Damascus. He went in and stood before him, and said, "Your son Ben-Hadad king of Aram has sent me to ask, 'Will I recover from this illness?' "

10 Elisha answered, "Go and say to him, 'You will certainly recover'; but[a] the LORD has revealed to me that he will in fact die." 11 He stared at him with a fixed gaze until Hazael felt ashamed. Then the man of God began to weep.[l]

12 "Why is my lord weeping?" asked Hazael.

"Because I know the harm[m] you will do to the Israelites," he answered. "You will set fire to their fortified places, kill their young men with the sword, dash their little children to the ground, and rip open[n] their pregnant women."

13 Hazael said, "How could your servant, a mere dog,[o] accomplish such a feat?"

"The LORD has shown me that you will become king[p] of Aram," answered Elisha.

14 Then Hazael left Elisha and returned to his master. When Ben-Hadad asked, "What did Elisha say to you?" Hazael replied, "He told me that you would certainly recover."

**7:16** c ver 1
**7:17** d ver 2
**7:19** e ver 2
**8:1** f 2Ki 4:8-37 g Ps 105:16; Hag 1:11
**8:5** h 2Ki 4:35
**8:7** i 2Ki 6:24
**8:8** j 1Ki 19:15 k 1Sa 9:7; 2Ki 1:2
**8:11** l Lk 19:41
**8:12** m 1Ki 19:17; 2Ki 10:32; 12:17; 13:3,7 n 2Ki 15:16
**8:13** o 1Sa 17:43 p 1Ki 19:15

[a] 10 The Hebrew may also be read *Go and say, 'You will certainly not recover,' for.*

15 But the next day he took a thick cloth, soaked it in water and spread it over the king's face, so that he died. Then Hazael succeeded him as king.

## Jehoram King of Judah

16 In the fifth year of Joram[q] son of Ahab king of Israel, when Jehoshaphat was king of Judah, Jehoram[r] son of Jehoshaphat began his reign as king of Judah. 17 He was thirty-two years old when he became king, and he reigned in Jerusalem eight years. 18 He walked in the ways of the kings of Israel, as the house of Ahab had done, for he married a daughter of Ahab. He did evil in the eyes of the LORD. 19 Nevertheless, for the sake of his servant David, the LORD was not willing to destroy Judah. He had promised to maintain a lamp[s] for David and his descendants forever.

20 In the time of Jehoram, Edom rebelled against Judah and set up its own king.[t] 21 So Jehoram[a] went to Zair with all his chariots. The Edomites surrounded him and his chariot commanders, but he rose up and broke through by night; his army, however, fled back home. 22 To this day Edom has been in rebellion[u] against Judah. Libnah[v] revolted at the same time.

23 As for the other events of Jehoram's reign, and all he did, are they not written in the book of the annals of the kings of Judah? 24 Jehoram rested with his fathers and was buried with them in the City of David. And Ahaziah his son succeeded him as king.

## Ahaziah King of Judah

25 In the twelfth year of Joram son of Ahab king of Israel, Ahaziah son of Jehoram king of Judah began to reign. 26 Ahaziah was twenty-two years old when he became king, and he reigned in Jerusalem one year. His mother's name was Athaliah, a granddaughter of Omri king of Israel. 27 He walked in the ways of the house of Ahab and did evil in the eyes of the LORD, as the house of Ahab had done, for he was related by marriage to Ahab's family.

28 Ahaziah went with Joram son of Ahab to war against Hazael king of Aram at Ramoth Gilead.[w] The Arameans wounded Joram; 29 so King Joram returned to Jezreel[x] to recover from the wounds the Arameans had inflicted on him at Ramoth[b] in his battle with Hazael king of Aram.

Then Ahaziah son of Jehoram king of Judah went down to Jezreel to see Joram son of Ahab, because he had been wounded.

## Jehu Anointed King of Israel

9 The prophet Elisha summoned a man from the company of the prophets and said to him, "Tuck your cloak into your belt,[y] take this flask of oil with you and go to Ramoth Gilead.[z] 2 When you get there, look for Jehu son of Jehoshaphat, the son of Nimshi. Go to him, get him away from his companions and take him into an inner room. 3 Then take the flask and pour the oil on his head and declare, 'This is what the LORD says: I anoint you king over Israel.' Then open the door and run; don't delay!"

4 So the young man, the prophet, went to Ramoth Gilead. 5 When he arrived, he found the army officers sitting together. "I have a message for you, commander," he said.

"For which of us?" asked Jehu.

"For you, commander," he replied.

6 Jehu got up and went into the house. Then the prophet poured the oil[a] on Jehu's head and declared, "This is what the LORD, the God of Israel, says: 'I anoint you king over the LORD's people Israel. 7 You are to destroy the house of Ahab your master, and I will avenge the blood of my servants the prophets and the blood of all the LORD's servants shed by Jezebel.[b] 8 The whole house of Ahab will perish. I will cut off from Ahab every last male[c] in Israel—slave or free. 9 I will make the house of Ahab like the house of Jeroboam[d] son of Nebat and like the house of Baasha son of Ahijah. 10 As for Jezebel, dogs[e] will devour her on the plot of ground at Jezreel, and no one will bury her.'" Then he opened the door and ran.

11 When Jehu went out to his fellow officers, one of them asked him, "Is everything all right? Why did this madman[f] come to you?"

"You know the man and the sort of things he says," Jehu replied.

12 "That's not true!" they said. "Tell us."

**8:16** q 2Ki 1:17 r 2Ch 21:1–4
**8:19** s 2Sa 7:13; 1Ki 11:36
**8:20** t 1Ki 22:47
**8:22** u Ge 27:40 v Jos 21:13
**8:28** w 1Ki 22:3,29
**8:29** x 2Ki 9:15
**9:1** y 2Ki 4:29 z 2Ki 8:28
**9:6** a 1Ki 19:16; 2Ch 22:7
**9:7** b 1Ki 18:4; 21:15
**9:8** c Dt 32:36; 1Sa 25:22; 1Ki 21:21
**9:9** d 1Ki 14:10; 15:29; 16:3,11
**9:10** e ver 35–36; 1Ki 21:23
**9:11** f Jer 29:26; Jn 10:20; Ac 26:24

[a] 21 Hebrew *Joram,* a variant of *Jehoram*; also in verses 23 and 24 [b] 29 Hebrew *Ramah,* a variant of *Ramoth*

Jehu said, "Here is what he told me: 'This is what the LORD says: I anoint you king over Israel.'"

13 They hurried and took their cloaks and spread[g] them under him on the bare steps. Then they blew the trumpet and shouted, "Jehu is king!"

## Jehu Kills Joram and Ahaziah

14 So Jehu son of Jehoshaphat, the son of Nimshi, conspired against Joram. (Now Joram and all Israel had been defending Ramoth Gilead[h] against Hazael king of Aram, 15 but King Joram[a] had returned to Jezreel to recover[i] from the wounds the Arameans had inflicted on him in the battle with Hazael king of Aram.) Jehu said, "If this is the way you feel, don't let anyone slip out of the city to go and tell the news in Jezreel." 16 Then he got into his chariot and rode to Jezreel, because Joram was resting there and Ahaziah king of Judah had gone down to see him.

17 When the lookout standing on the tower in Jezreel saw Jehu's troops approaching, he called out, "I see some troops coming."

"Get a horseman," Joram ordered. "Send him to meet them and ask, 'Do you come in peace?'"

18 The horseman rode off to meet Jehu and said, "This is what the king says: 'Do you come in peace?'"

"What do you have to do with peace?" Jehu replied. "Fall in behind me."

The lookout reported, "The messenger has reached them, but he isn't coming back."

19 So the king sent out a second horseman. When he came to them he said, "This is what the king says: 'Do you come in peace?'"

Jehu replied, "What do you have to do with peace? Fall in behind me."

20 The lookout reported, "He has reached them, but he isn't coming back either. The driving is like[j] that of Jehu son of Nimshi—he drives like a madman."

21 "Hitch up my chariot," Joram ordered. And when it was hitched up, Joram king of Israel and Ahaziah king of Judah rode out, each in his own chariot, to meet Jehu. They met him at the plot of ground that had belonged to Naboth[k] the Jezreelite. 22 When Joram saw Jehu he asked, "Have you come in peace, Jehu?"

"How can there be peace," Jehu replied, "as long as all the idolatry and witchcraft of your mother Jezebel[l] abound?"

23 Joram turned about and fled, calling out to Ahaziah, "Treachery,[m] Ahaziah!"

24 Then Jehu drew his bow[n] and shot Joram between the shoulders. The arrow pierced his heart and he slumped down in his chariot. 25 Jehu said to Bidkar, his chariot officer, "Pick him up and throw him on the field that belonged to Naboth the Jezreelite. Remember how you and I were riding together in chariots behind Ahab his father when the LORD made this prophecy[o] about him: 26 'Yesterday I saw the blood of Naboth[p] and the blood of his sons, declares the LORD, and I will surely make you pay for it on this plot of ground, declares the LORD.'[b] Now then, pick him up and throw him on that plot, in accordance with the word of the LORD."

27 When Ahaziah king of Judah saw what had happened, he fled up the road to Beth Haggan.[c] Jehu chased him, shouting, "Kill him too!" They wounded him in his chariot on the way up to Gur near Ibleam,[q] but he escaped to Megiddo and died there. 28 His servants took him by chariot[r] to Jerusalem and buried him with his fathers in his tomb in the City of David. 29 (In the eleventh[s] year of Joram son of Ahab, Ahaziah had become king of Judah.)

## Jezebel Killed

30 Then Jehu went to Jezreel. When Jezebel heard about it, she painted[t] her eyes, arranged her hair and looked out of a window. 31 As Jehu entered the gate, she asked, "Have you come in peace, Zimri,[u] you murderer of your master?"[d]

32 He looked up at the window and called out, "Who is on my side? Who?" Two or three eunuchs looked down at him. 33 "Throw her down!" Jehu said. So they threw her down, and some of her blood spattered the wall and the horses as they trampled her underfoot.

**9:13** g Mt 21:8
**9:14** h 2Ki 8:28
**9:15** i 2Ki 8:29
**9:20** j 2Sa 18:27
**9:21** k 1Ki 21:1–7,15–19
**9:22** l 1Ki 18:19
**9:23** m 2Ki 11:14
**9:24** n 1Ki 22:34
**9:25** o 1Ki 21:19–22,24–29
**9:26** p 1Ki 21:19
**9:27** q Jdg 1:27
**9:28** r 2Ki 23:30
**9:29** s 2Ki 8:25
**9:30** t Jer 4:30; Eze 23:40
**9:31** u 1Ki 16:9–10

[a] 15 Hebrew *Jehoram,* a variant of *Joram;* also in verses 17 and 21–24 [b] 26 See 1 Kings 21:19. [c] 27 Or *fled by way of the garden house* [d] 31 Or *"Did Zimri have peace, who murdered his master?"*

# Jezebel

## A Wicked Queen

Evil, idolatrous and an abuser of power are just a few of the descriptions associated with Queen Jezebel. However, even from *her* story, women of color can learn valuable lessons.

Jezebel grew up in a home and community of idol worshipers. She brought her own religious beliefs with her when she married King Ahab, and her influence contributed to the widespread worship of idols in Israel. Jezebel influenced both the king and the country, and Ahab's reign was characterized as evil in part as a result of his reliance on his wife and her views (see 1Ki 16:31; 21:25–26).

Elijah was one of God's prophets during the reign of Ahab and Jezebel. Elijah challenged the 450 prophets of Baal and 400 prophets of Asherah to call on their god to send fire upon an altar; of course they were unsuccessful. Elijah prayed to God to send fire on an altar that Elijah had first soaked in water. The true and living God produced fire. After Elijah won this amazing challenge, he ordered the deaths of all of the prophets of Baal and Asherah (see 1Ki 18:40; 19:1). When Jezebel heard what Elijah had done to the prophets of the gods she worshiped, she sent a message to Elijah, threatening to kill him by the next day (see 1Ki 19:2).

It has been said that the test of a true prophet is that his or her prediction comes true. Jezebel's prediction about taking Elijah's life did not come true. Elijah ran away and hid from Jezebel's wrath, but Yahweh protected, fed and sheltered him (see 1Ki 19:3–9). Conversely, Elijah prophesied about Jezebel's destruction as well as her family's demise (see 1Ki 21:20–24), and she died just as Elijah prophesied: dogs devoured her so that no one could recognize her body (see 2Ki 9:30–37). Ahab and Jezebel's evil choices contributed to their own deaths, the deaths of the prophets of Baal and the deaths of the 70 sons of Ahab (see 1Ki 22:34–38; 2Ki 10:7).

Sometimes it seems like the wicked prosper and the righteous suffer, but this story reminds us that there is a day of judgment coming. Regardless of how things seem, eventually the righteous will receive shelter, as was true with Elijah, and evil will have its own reward, as was seen through the deaths of Ahab, Jezebel and their children.

—D. McCabe

### reflection

*Reflect on times when it looked like the wicked were prospering. How did things turn out?*

*Seek to live life on God's side regardless of how things look around you.*

### read

2 Kings 9:10,22,30–37; see also 1 Kings 16:29–33; 18:16—19:9; 21:4–26.

See also the Inspire Notes "Influencing Others," "Responsible Decisions in Leadership" and "Seek Wisdom," and the Women of the Bible Note "Athaliah: An Angry Woman."

For the next Women of the Bible note, go to page 462.

**9:34** v 1Ki 16:31
**9:36** w 1Ki 21:23
**9:37** x Ps 83:10; Jer 8:2
**10:5** y Jos 9:8
**10:7** z 1Ki 21:21

34 Jehu went in and ate and drank. "Take
care of that cursed woman," he said, "and
bury her, for she was a king's daughter."[v]
35 But when they went out to bury her, they
found nothing except her skull, her feet and
her hands. 36 They went back and told Jehu,
who said, "This is the word of the LORD that
he spoke through his servant Elijah the Tish-
bite: On the plot of ground at Jezreel dogs
will devour Jezebel's flesh.[a][w] 37 Jezebel's
body will be like refuse[x] on the ground in
the plot at Jezreel, so that no one will be able
to say, 'This is Jezebel.' "

## Ahab's Family Killed

10 Now there were in Samaria seventy
sons of the house of Ahab. So Jehu
wrote letters and sent them to Samaria: to
the officials of Jezreel,[b] to the elders and to
the guardians of Ahab's children. He said,
2 "As soon as this letter reaches you, since
your master's sons are with you and you
have chariots and horses, a fortified city
and weapons, 3 choose the best and most
worthy of your master's sons and set him on
his father's throne. Then fight for your mas-
ter's house."

4 But they were terrified and said, "If two
kings could not resist him, how can we?"

5 So the palace administrator, the city gov-
ernor, the elders and the guardians sent this
message to Jehu: "We are your servants[y] and
we will do anything you say. We will not ap-
point anyone as king; you do whatever you
think best."

6 Then Jehu wrote them a second letter, say-
ing, "If you are on my side and will obey me,
take the heads of your master's sons and come
to me in Jezreel by this time tomorrow."

Now the royal princes, seventy of them,
were with the leading men of the city,
who were rearing them. 7 When the letter
arrived, these men took the princes and
slaughtered all seventy[z] of them. They put
their heads in baskets and sent them to Jehu
in Jezreel. 8 When the messenger arrived, he
told Jehu, "They have brought the heads of
the princes."

Then Jehu ordered, "Put them in two
piles at the entrance of the city gate un-
til morning."

9 The next morning Jehu went out. He
stood before all the people and said, "You
are innocent. It was I who conspired against
my master and killed him, but who killed
all these? 10 Know then, that not a word the
LORD has spoken against the house of Ahab
will fail. The LORD has done what he prom-
ised[a] through his servant Elijah."[b] 11 So Jehu
killed everyone in Jezreel who remained of
the house of Ahab, as well as all his chief
men, his close friends and his priests, leav-
ing him no survivor.

12 Jehu then set out and went toward
Samaria. At Beth Eked of the Shepherds,
13 he met some relatives of Ahaziah king of
Judah and asked, "Who are you?"

They said, "We are relatives of Ahaziah,[c]
and we have come down to greet the fami-
lies of the king and of the queen mother."

14 "Take them alive!" he ordered. So they
took them alive and slaughtered them by
the well of Beth Eked—forty-two men. He
left no survivor.

15 After he left there, he came upon Jehon-
adab[d] son of Recab,[e] who was on his way to
meet him. Jehu greeted him and said, "Are
you in accord with me, as I am with you?"

"I am," Jehonadab answered.

"If so," said Jehu, "give me your hand."[f]
So he did, and Jehu helped him up into the
chariot. 16 Jehu said, "Come with me and see
my zeal[g] for the LORD." Then he had him ride
along in his chariot.

17 When Jehu came to Samaria, he killed
all who were left there of Ahab's family;[h] he
destroyed them, according to the word of
the LORD spoken to Elijah.

## Ministers of Baal Killed

18 Then Jehu brought all the people
together and said to them, "Ahab served[i]
Baal a little; Jehu will serve him much.
19 Now summon all the prophets of Baal, all
his ministers and all his priests. See that no
one is missing, because I am going to hold
a great sacrifice for Baal. Anyone who fails
to come will no longer live." But Jehu was
acting deceptively in order to destroy the
ministers of Baal.

20 Jehu said, "Call an assembly[j] in honor of
Baal." So they proclaimed it. 21 Then he sent

**10:10** a 2Ki 9:7–10 b 1Ki 21:29
**10:13** c 2Ki 8:24,29; 2Ch 22:8
**10:15** d Jer 35:6,14–19 e 1Ch 2:55 f Ezr 10:19
**10:16** g 1Ki 19:10
**10:17** h 2Ki 9:8
**10:18** i 1Ki 16:31–32
**10:20** j Ex 32:5; Joel 1:14

[a]36 See 1 Kings 21:23. [b]1 Hebrew; some Septuagint manuscripts and Vulgate *of the city*

**10:24** k 1Ki 20:39
**10:25** l 1Ki 18:40
**10:26** m 1Ki 14:23
**10:29** n 1Ki 12:28–29
**10:30** o 2Ki 15:12
**10:32** p 2Ki 8:12

word throughout Israel, and all the ministers of Baal came; not one stayed away. They crowded into the temple of Baal until it was full from one end to the other. [22]And Jehu said to the keeper of the wardrobe, "Bring robes for all the ministers of Baal." So he brought out robes for them.

[23]Then Jehu and Jehonadab son of Recab went into the temple of Baal. Jehu said to the ministers of Baal, "Look around and see that no servants of the LORD are here with you—only ministers of Baal." [24]So they went in to make sacrifices and burnt offerings. Now Jehu had posted eighty men outside with this warning: "If one of you lets any of the men I am placing in your hands escape, it will be your life for his life."[k]

[25]As soon as Jehu had finished making the burnt offering, he ordered the guards and officers: "Go in and kill them; let no one escape."[l] So they cut them down with the sword. The guards and officers threw the bodies out and then entered the inner shrine of the temple of Baal. [26]They brought the sacred stone[m] out of the temple of Baal and burned it. [27]They demolished the sacred stone of Baal and tore down the temple of Baal, and people have used it for a latrine to this day.

[28]So Jehu destroyed Baal worship in Israel. [29]However, he did not turn away from the sins of Jeroboam son of Nebat, which he had caused Israel to commit—the worship of the golden calves[n] at Bethel and Dan.

[30]The LORD said to Jehu, "Because you have done well in accomplishing what is right in my eyes and have done to the house of Ahab all I had in mind to do, your descendants will sit on the throne of Israel to the fourth generation."[o] [31]Yet Jehu was not careful to keep the law of the LORD, the God of Israel, with all his heart. He did not turn away from the sins of Jeroboam, which he had caused Israel to commit.

[32]In those days the LORD began to reduce the size of Israel. Hazael[p] overpowered the Israelites throughout their territory [33]east of the Jordan in all the land of Gilead (the region of Gad, Reuben and Manasseh), from Aroer by the Arnon Gorge through Gilead to Bashan.

[34]As for the other events of Jehu's reign, all he did, and all his achievements, are they not written in the book of the annals of the kings of Israel?

[35]Jehu rested with his fathers and was buried in Samaria. And Jehoahaz his son succeeded him as king. [36]The time that Jehu reigned over Israel in Samaria was twenty-eight years.

## Athaliah and Joash

**11** When Athaliah the mother of Ahaziah saw that her son was dead, she proceeded to destroy the whole royal family. [2]But Jehosheba, the daughter of King Jehoram[a] and sister of Ahaziah, took Joash[q] son of Ahaziah and stole him away from among the royal princes, who were about to be murdered. She put him and his nurse in a bedroom to hide him from Athaliah; so he was not killed. [3]He remained hidden with his nurse at the temple of the LORD for six years while Athaliah ruled the land.

[4]In the seventh year Jehoiada sent for the commanders of units of a hundred, the Carites[r] and the guards and had them brought to him at the temple of the LORD. He made a covenant with them and put them under oath at the temple of the LORD. Then he showed them the king's son. [5]He commanded them, saying, "This is what you are to do: You who are in the three companies that are going on duty on the Sabbath[s]—a third of you guarding the royal palace, [6]a third at the Sur Gate, and a third at the gate behind the guard, who take turns guarding the temple— [7]and you who are in the other two companies that normally go off Sabbath duty are all to guard the temple for the king. [8]Station yourselves around the king, each man with his weapon in his hand. Anyone who approaches your ranks[b] must be put to death. Stay close to the king wherever he goes."

[9]The commanders of units of a hundred did just as Jehoiada the priest ordered. Each one took his men—those who were going on duty on the Sabbath and those who were going off duty—and came to Jehoiada the priest. [10]Then he gave the commanders the spears and shields[t] that had belonged to King David and that were in the temple

**11:2** q 2Ki 12:1
**11:4** r ver 19
**11:5** s 1Ch 9:25
**11:10** t 2Sa 8:7

[a]2 Hebrew *Joram,* a variant of *Jehoram* [b]8 Or *approaches the precincts*

**11:12**
u Ex 25:16
v 1Sa 10:24

**11:14**
w 2Ki 23:3; 2Ch 34:31
x 1Ki 1:39
y Ge 37:29
z 2Ki 9:23

**11:17**
a 2Sa 5:3; 2Ch 15:12; 34:31

**11:18**
b Dt 12:3
c 1Ki 18:40; 2Ki 10:25

**11:19**
d ver 4

**11:20**
e Pr 11:10

of the LORD. 11 The guards, each with his weapon in his hand, stationed themselves around the king—near the altar and the temple, from the south side to the north side of the temple.

12 Jehoiada brought out the king's son and put the crown on him; he presented him with a copy of the covenant[u] and proclaimed him king. They anointed him, and the people clapped their hands and shouted, "Long live the king!"[v]

13 When Athaliah heard the noise made by the guards and the people, she went to the people at the temple of the LORD. 14 She looked and there was the king, standing by the pillar,[w] as the custom was. The officers and the trumpeters were beside the king, and all the people of the land were rejoicing and blowing trumpets.[x] Then Athaliah tore[y] her robes and called out, "Treason! Treason!"[z]

15 Jehoiada the priest ordered the commanders of units of a hundred, who were in charge of the troops: "Bring her out between the ranks[a] and put to the sword anyone who follows her." For the priest had said, "She must not be put to death in the temple of the LORD." 16 So they seized her as she reached the place where the horses enter the palace grounds, and there she was put to death.

17 Jehoiada then made a covenant[a] between the LORD and the king and people that they would be the LORD's people. He also made a covenant between the king and the people. 18 All the people of the land went to the temple of Baal and tore it down. They smashed[b] the altars and idols to pieces and killed Mattan the priest[c] of Baal in front of the altars.

Then Jehoiada the priest posted guards at the temple of the LORD. 19 He took with him the commanders of hundreds, the Carites,[d] the guards and all the people of the land, and together they brought the king down from the temple of the LORD and went into the palace, entering by way of the gate of the guards. The king then took his place on the royal throne, 20 and all the people of the land rejoiced.[e] And the city was quiet, because Athaliah had been slain with the sword at the palace.

21 Joash[b] was seven years old when he began to reign.

## Joash Repairs the Temple

12 In the seventh year of Jehu, Joash[c] became king, and he reigned in Jerusalem forty years. His mother's name was Zibiah; she was from Beersheba. 2 Joash did what was right in the eyes of the LORD all the years Jehoiada the priest instructed him. 3 The high places,[f] however, were not removed; the people continued to offer sacrifices and burn incense there.

4 Joash said to the priests, "Collect[g] all the money that is brought as sacred offerings[h] to the temple of the LORD—the money collected in the census, the money received from personal vows and the money brought voluntarily[i] to the temple. 5 Let every priest receive the money from one of the treasurers, and let it be used to repair whatever damage is found in the temple."

6 But by the twenty-third year of King Joash the priests still had not repaired the temple. 7 Therefore King Joash summoned Jehoiada the priest and the other priests and asked them, "Why aren't you repairing the damage done to the temple? Take no more money from your treasurers, but hand it over for repairing the temple." 8 The priests agreed that they would not collect any more money from the people and that they would not repair the temple themselves.

9 Jehoiada the priest took a chest and bored a hole in its lid. He placed it beside the altar, on the right side as one enters the temple of the LORD. The priests who guarded the entrance put into the chest all the money[j] that was brought to the temple of the LORD. 10 Whenever they saw that there was a large amount of money in the chest, the royal secretary and the high priest came, counted the money that had been brought into the temple of the LORD and put it into bags. 11 When the amount had been determined, they gave the money to the men appointed to supervise the work on the temple. With it they paid those who worked on the temple of the LORD—the carpenters and builders, 12 the masons and stonecutters. They purchased

**12:3**
f 2Ki 14:4; 15:35

**12:4**
g 2Ki 22:4
h Ex 35:5
i 1Ch 29:3-9

**12:9**
j Mk 12:41; Lk 21:1

[a]15 Or *out from the precincts* [b]21 Hebrew *Jehoash,* a variant of *Joash* [c]1 Hebrew *Jehoash,* a variant of *Joash*; also in verses 2, 4, 6, 7 and 18

timber and dressed stone for the repair of the temple of the LORD, and met all the other expenses of restoring the temple.

[13]The money brought into the temple was not spent for making silver basins, wick trimmers, sprinkling bowls, trumpets or any other articles of gold[k] or silver for the temple of the LORD; [14]it was paid to the workmen, who used it to repair the temple. [15]They did not require an accounting from those to whom they gave the money to pay the workers, because they acted with complete honesty.[l] [16]The money from the guilt offerings[m] and sin offerings was not brought into the temple of the LORD; it belonged to the priests.

[17]About this time Hazael[n] king of Aram went up and attacked Gath and captured it. Then he turned to attack Jerusalem. [18]But Joash king of Judah took all the sacred objects dedicated by his fathers—Jehoshaphat, Jehoram and Ahaziah, the kings of Judah—and the gifts he himself had dedicated and all the gold found in the treasuries of the temple of the LORD and of the royal palace, and he sent[o] them to Hazael king of Aram, who then withdrew from Jerusalem.

[19]As for the other events of the reign of Joash, and all he did, are they not written in the book of the annals of the kings of Judah? [20]His officials[p] conspired against him and assassinated[q] him at Beth Millo, on the road down to Silla. [21]The officials who murdered him were Jozabad son of Shimeath and Jehozabad son of Shomer. He died and was buried with his fathers in the City of David. And Amaziah his son succeeded him as king.

## Jehoahaz King of Israel

**13** In the twenty-third year of Joash son of Ahaziah king of Judah, Jehoahaz son of Jehu became king of Israel in Samaria, and he reigned seventeen years. [2]He did evil[r] in the eyes of the LORD by following the sins of Jeroboam son of Nebat, which he had caused Israel to commit, and he did not turn away from them. [3]So the LORD's anger[s] burned against Israel, and for a long time he kept them under the power of Hazael king of Aram and Ben-Hadad his son.

[4]Then Jehoahaz sought the LORD's favor, and the LORD listened to him, for he saw[t] how severely the king of Aram was oppressing[u] Israel. [5]The LORD provided a deliverer[v] for Israel, and they escaped from the power of Aram. So the Israelites lived in their own homes as they had before. [6]But they did not turn away from the sins of the house of Jeroboam, which he had caused Israel to commit; they continued in them. Also, the Asherah pole[a][w] remained standing in Samaria.

[7]Nothing had been left of the army of Jehoahaz except fifty horsemen, ten chariots and ten thousand foot soldiers, for the king of Aram had destroyed the rest and made them like the dust at threshing time.

[8]As for the other events of the reign of Jehoahaz, all he did and his achievements, are they not written in the book of the annals of the kings of Israel? [9]Jehoahaz rested with his fathers and was buried in Samaria. And Jehoash[b] his son succeeded him as king.

## Jehoash King of Israel

[10]In the thirty-seventh year of Joash king of Judah, Jehoash son of Jehoahaz became king of Israel in Samaria, and he reigned sixteen years. [11]He did evil in the eyes of the LORD and did not turn away from any of the sins of Jeroboam son of Nebat, which he had caused Israel to commit; he continued in them.

[12]As for the other events of the reign of Jehoash, all he did and his achievements, including his war against Amaziah[x] king of Judah, are they not written in the book of the annals of the kings of Israel? [13]Jehoash rested with his fathers, and Jeroboam succeeded him on the throne. Jehoash was buried in Samaria with the kings of Israel.

[14]Now Elisha was suffering from the illness from which he died. Jehoash king of Israel went down to see him and wept over him. "My father! My father!" he cried. "The chariots[y] and horsemen of Israel!"

[15]Elisha said, "Get a bow and some arrows," and he did so. [16]"Take the bow in

**12:13** k 1Ki 7:48–51; 2Ch 24:14
**12:15** l 2Ki 22:7
**12:16** m Nu 18:9
**12:17** n 2Ki 8:12
**12:18** o 1Ki 15:18
**12:20** p 2Ki 14:5 q 2Ch 24:25
**13:2** r 1Ki 12:26–33
**13:3** s Jdg 2:14
**13:4** t Ex 3:7 u 2Ki 14:26
**13:5** v ver 25; 2Ki 14:25,27
**13:6** w 1Ki 16:33
**13:12** x 2Ki 14:15
**13:14** y 2Ki 2:12

[a]6 That is, a symbol of the goddess Asherah; here and elsewhere in 2 Kings [b]9 Hebrew *Joash,* a variant of *Jehoash*; also in verses 12–14 and 25

your hands," he said to the king of Israel. When he had taken it, Elisha put his hands on the king's hands.

17"Open the east window," he said, and he opened it. "Shoot!" Elisha said, and he shot. "The LORD's arrow of victory, the arrow of victory over Aram!" Elisha declared. "You will completely destroy the Arameans at Aphek."[z]

18Then he said, "Take the arrows," and the king took them. Elisha told him, "Strike the ground." He struck it three times and stopped. 19The man of God was angry with him and said, "You should have struck the ground five or six times; then you would have defeated Aram and completely destroyed it. But now you will defeat it only three times."[a]

20Elisha died and was buried.

Now Moabite raiders used to enter the country every spring. 21Once while some Israelites were burying a man, suddenly they saw a band of raiders; so they threw the man's body into Elisha's tomb. When the body touched Elisha's bones, the man came to life[b] and stood up on his feet.

22Hazael king of Aram oppressed[c] Israel throughout the reign of Jehoahaz. 23But the LORD was gracious to them and had compassion and showed concern for them because of his covenant[d] with Abraham, Isaac and Jacob. To this day he has been unwilling to destroy them or banish them from his presence.

24Hazael king of Aram died, and Ben-Hadad his son succeeded him as king. 25Then Jehoash son of Jehoahaz recaptured from Ben-Hadad son of Hazael the towns he had taken in battle from his father Jehoahaz. Three times[e] Jehoash defeated him, and so he recovered[f] the Israelite towns.

## Amaziah King of Judah

14 In the second year of Jehoash[a] son of Jehoahaz king of Israel, Amaziah son of Joash king of Judah began to reign. 2He was twenty-five years old when he became king, and he reigned in Jerusalem twenty-nine years. His mother's name was Jehoaddin; she was from Jerusalem. 3He did what was right in the eyes of the LORD, but not as his father David had done. In everything he followed the example of his father Joash. 4The high places,[g] however, were not removed; the people continued to offer sacrifices and burn incense there.

5After the kingdom was firmly in his grasp, he executed the officials[h] who had murdered his father the king. 6Yet he did not put the sons of the assassins to death, in accordance with what is written in the Book of the Law of Moses where the LORD commanded: "Fathers shall not be put to death for their children, nor children put to death for their fathers; each is to die for his own sins."[b][i]

7He was the one who defeated ten thousand Edomites in the Valley of Salt[j] and captured Sela in battle, calling it Joktheel, the name it has to this day.

8Then Amaziah sent messengers to Jehoash son of Jehoahaz, the son of Jehu, king of Israel, with the challenge: "Come, meet me face to face."

9But Jehoash king of Israel replied to Amaziah king of Judah: "A thistle[k] in Lebanon sent a message to a cedar in Lebanon, 'Give your daughter to my son in marriage.' Then a wild beast in Lebanon came along and trampled the thistle underfoot. 10You have indeed defeated Edom and now you are arrogant.[l] Glory in your victory, but stay at home! Why ask for trouble and cause your own downfall and that of Judah also?"

11Amaziah, however, would not listen, so Jehoash king of Israel attacked. He and Amaziah king of Judah faced each other at Beth Shemesh in Judah. 12Judah was routed by Israel, and every man fled to his home. 13Jehoash king of Israel captured Amaziah king of Judah, the son of Joash, the son of Ahaziah, at Beth Shemesh. Then Jehoash went to Jerusalem and broke down the wall of Jerusalem from the Ephraim Gate[m] to the Corner Gate[n]—a section about six hundred feet long.[c] 14He took all the gold and silver and all the articles found in the temple of the LORD and in the treasuries of the royal palace. He also took hostages and returned to Samaria.

**13:17** z 1Ki 20:26
**13:19** a ver 25
**13:21** b Mt 27:52
**13:22** c 1Ki 19:17; 2Ki 8:12
**13:23** d Ex 2:24
**13:25** e ver 18,19 f 2Ki 10:32

**14:4** g 2Ki 12:3
**14:5** h 2Ki 12:20
**14:6** i Jer 31:30; Eze 18:4,20
**14:7** j 2Sa 8:13; 2Ch 25:11
**14:9** k Jdg 9:8–15
**14:10** l Dt 8:14; 2Ch 26:16; 32:25
**14:13** m Ne 8:16; 12:39 n Jer 31:38; Zec 14:10

[a]1 Hebrew *Joash*, a variant of *Jehoash*; also in verses 13, 23 and 27 [b]6 Deut. 24:16 [c]13 Hebrew *four hundred cubits* (about 180 meters)

**14:15** o 2Ki 13:12
**14:22** p 2Ki 16:6
**14:25** q Dt 3:17 r Jnh 1:1; Mt 12:39
**14:26** s Dt 32:36 t 2Ki 13:4

15 As for the other events of the reign of Jehoash, what he did and his achievements, including his war[o] against Amaziah king of Judah, are they not written in the book of the annals of the kings of Israel? 16 Jehoash rested with his fathers and was buried in Samaria with the kings of Israel. And Jeroboam his son succeeded him as king.

17 Amaziah son of Joash king of Judah lived for fifteen years after the death of Jehoash son of Jehoahaz king of Israel. 18 As for the other events of Amaziah's reign, are they not written in the book of the annals of the kings of Judah?

19 They conspired against him in Jerusalem, and he fled to Lachish, but they sent men after him to Lachish and killed him there. 20 He was brought back by horse and was buried in Jerusalem with his fathers, in the City of David.

21 Then all the people of Judah took Azariah,[a] who was sixteen years old, and made him king in place of his father Amaziah. 22 He was the one who rebuilt Elath[p] and restored it to Judah after Amaziah rested with his fathers.

## Jeroboam II King of Israel

23 In the fifteenth year of Amaziah son of Joash king of Judah, Jeroboam son of Jehoash king of Israel became king in Samaria, and he reigned forty-one years. 24 He did evil in the eyes of the LORD and did not turn away from any of the sins of Jeroboam son of Nebat, which he had caused Israel to commit. 25 He was the one who restored the boundaries of Israel from Lebo[b] Hamath to the Sea of the Arabah,[c][q] in accordance with the word of the LORD, the God of Israel, spoken through his servant Jonah[r] son of Amittai, the prophet from Gath Hepher.

26 The LORD had seen how bitterly everyone in Israel, whether slave or free,[s] was suffering;[t] there was no one to help them. 27 And since the LORD had not said he would blot out the name of Israel from under heaven, he saved them by the hand of Jeroboam son of Jehoash.

28 As for the other events of Jeroboam's reign, all he did, and his military achievements, including how he recovered for Israel both Damascus[u] and Hamath,[v] which had belonged to Yaudi,[d] are they not written in the book of the annals of the kings of Israel? 29 Jeroboam rested with his fathers, the kings of Israel. And Zechariah his son succeeded him as king.

## Azariah King of Judah

**15** In the twenty-seventh year of Jeroboam king of Israel, Azariah[w] son of Amaziah king of Judah began to reign. 2 He was sixteen years old when he became king, and he reigned in Jerusalem fifty-two years. His mother's name was Jecoliah; she was from Jerusalem. 3 He did what was right in the eyes of the LORD, just as his father Amaziah had done. 4 The high places, however, were not removed; the people continued to offer sacrifices and burn incense there.

5 The LORD afflicted the king with leprosy[e] until the day he died, and he lived in a separate house.[f][x] Jotham the king's son had charge of the palace and governed the people of the land.

6 As for the other events of Azariah's reign, and all he did, are they not written in the book of the annals of the kings of Judah? 7 Azariah rested with his fathers and was buried near them in the City of David. And Jotham his son succeeded him as king.

## Zechariah King of Israel

8 In the thirty-eighth year of Azariah king of Judah, Zechariah son of Jeroboam became king of Israel in Samaria, and he reigned six months. 9 He did evil in the eyes of the LORD, as his fathers had done. He did not turn away from the sins of Jeroboam son of Nebat, which he had caused Israel to commit.

10 Shallum son of Jabesh conspired against Zechariah. He attacked him in front of the people,[g] assassinated him and succeeded him as king. 11 The other events of Zechariah's reign are written in the book of the annals of the kings of Israel. 12 So the word of the LORD spoken to Jehu was fulfilled:[y]

**14:28** u 2Sa 8:5; 1Ki 11:24 v 2Ch 8:3
**15:1** w 2Ki 14:21
**15:5** x Lev 13:46
**15:12** y 2Ki 10:30

[a] 21 Also called *Uzziah* [b] 25 Or *from the entrance to* [c] 25 That is, the Dead Sea [d] 28 Or *Judah* [e] 5 The Hebrew word was used for various diseases affecting the skin—not necessarily leprosy. [f] 5 Or *in a house where he was relieved of responsibility* [g] 10 Hebrew; some Septuagint manuscripts *in Ibleam*

15:13 z ver 1,8
15:14 a 1Ki 14:17
15:16 b 1Ki 4:24 c 2Ki 8:12; Hos 13:16
15:19 d 1Ch 5:6,26

"Your descendants will sit on the throne of
Israel to the fourth generation."[a]

## Shallum King of Israel

13 Shallum son of Jabesh became king in
the thirty-ninth year of Uzziah king of Ju-
dah, and he reigned in Samaria[z] one month.
14 Then Menahem son of Gadi went from Tir-
zah[a] up to Samaria. He attacked Shallum
son of Jabesh in Samaria, assassinated him
and succeeded him as king.

15 The other events of Shallum's reign,
and the conspiracy he led, are written in the
book of the annals of the kings of Israel.

16 At that time Menahem, starting out
from Tirzah, attacked Tiphsah[b] and ev-
eryone in the city and its vicinity, because
they refused to open[c] their gates. He sacked
Tiphsah and ripped open all the pregnant
women.

## Menahem King of Israel

17 In the thirty-ninth year of Azariah king
of Judah, Menahem son of Gadi became
king of Israel, and he reigned in Samaria ten
years. 18 He did evil in the eyes of the LORD.
During his entire reign he did not turn away
from the sins of Jeroboam son of Nebat,
which he had caused Israel to commit.

19 Then Pul[b][d] king of Assyria invaded the
land, and Menahem gave him a thousand
talents[c] of silver to gain his support and
strengthen his own hold on the kingdom.
20 Menahem exacted this money from Israel.
Every wealthy man had to contribute fifty
shekels[d] of silver to be given to the king of
Assyria. So the king of Assyria withdrew
and stayed in the land no longer.

21 As for the other events of Menahem's
reign, and all he did, are they not written in
the book of the annals of the kings of Israel?
22 Menahem rested with his fathers. And
Pekahiah his son succeeded him as king.

## Pekahiah King of Israel

23 In the fiftieth year of Azariah king of
Judah, Pekahiah son of Menahem became
king of Israel in Samaria, and he reigned
two years. 24 Pekahiah did evil in the eyes
of the LORD. He did not turn away from the
sins of Jeroboam son of Nebat, which he had
caused Israel to commit. 25 One of his chief
officers, Pekah son of Remaliah, conspired
against him. Taking fifty men of Gilead with
him, he assassinated Pekahiah, along with
Argob and Arieh, in the citadel of the royal
palace at Samaria. So Pekah killed Pekahiah
and succeeded him as king.

26 The other events of Pekahiah's reign,
and all he did, are written in the book of the
annals of the kings of Israel.

## Pekah King of Israel

27 In the fifty-second year of Azariah king
of Judah, Pekah[e] son of Remaliah became
king of Israel in Samaria, and he reigned
twenty years. 28 He did evil in the eyes of the
LORD. He did not turn away from the sins of
Jeroboam son of Nebat, which he had caused
Israel to commit.

15:27 e 2Ch 28:6; Isa 7:1

[a] 12 2 Kings 10:30 [b] 19 Also called *Tiglath-Pileser* [c] 19 That is, about 37 tons (about 34 metric tons) [d] 20 That is, about 1 1/4 pounds (about 0.6 kilogram)

## The African Presence

### 2 Kings 15:19; 17:1–6

King Pul is the Babylonian name of the Assyrian ruler Tiglath-Pileser III. He exacted tribute from King Menahem, the ruler of Israel. Later, King Shalmaneser V, who ruled Assyria from 727 to 722 B.C. (see 2Ki 17:1–6), continued the domination of the nation of Israel. These eastern kings were from the region of Mesopotamia (north of Babylonia), an area some argue was originally settled by the black Sumerians (see the African Presence note on Ge 2:8).

29 In the time of Pekah king of Israel, Tiglath-Pileser[f] king of Assyria came and took Ijon,[g] Abel Beth Maacah, Janoah, Kedesh and Hazor. He took Gilead and Galilee, including all the land of Naphtali,[h] and deported the people to Assyria. 30 Then Hoshea[i] son of Elah conspired against Pekah son of Remaliah. He attacked and assassinated him, and then succeeded him as king in the twentieth year of Jotham son of Uzziah.

31 As for the other events of Pekah's reign, and all he did, are they not written in the book of the annals of the kings of Israel?

## Jotham King of Judah

32 In the second year of Pekah son of Remaliah king of Israel, Jotham son of Uzziah king of Judah began to reign. 33 He was twenty-five years old when he became king, and he reigned in Jerusalem sixteen years. His mother's name was Jerusha daughter of Zadok. 34 He did what was right[j] in the eyes of the LORD, just as his father Uzziah had done. 35 The high places, however, were not removed; the people continued to offer sacrifices and burn incense there. Jotham rebuilt the Upper Gate of the temple of the LORD.

36 As for the other events of Jotham's reign, and what he did, are they not written in the book of the annals of the kings of Judah? 37 (In those days the LORD began to send Rezin[k] king of Aram and Pekah son of Remaliah against Judah.) 38 Jotham rested with his fathers and was buried with them in the City of David, the city of his father. And Ahaz his son succeeded him as king.

## Ahaz King of Judah

16 In the seventeenth year of Pekah son of Remaliah, Ahaz son of Jotham king of Judah began to reign. 2 Ahaz was twenty years old when he became king, and he reigned in Jerusalem sixteen years. Unlike David his father, he did not do what was right in the eyes of the LORD his God. 3 He walked in the ways of the kings of Israel and even sacrificed his son[l] in[a] the fire, following the detestable[m] ways of the nations the LORD had driven out before the Israelites. 4 He offered sacrifices and burned incense at the high places, on the hilltops and under every spreading tree.[n]

5 Then Rezin[o] king of Aram and Pekah son of Remaliah king of Israel marched up to fight against Jerusalem and besieged Ahaz, but they could not overpower him. 6 At that time, Rezin king of Aram recovered Elath[p] for Aram by driving out the men of Judah. Edomites then moved into Elath and have lived there to this day.

7 Ahaz sent messengers to say to Tiglath-Pileser[q] king of Assyria, "I am your servant and vassal. Come up and save me out of the hand of the king of Aram and of the king of Israel, who are attacking me." 8 And Ahaz took the silver and gold found in the temple of the LORD and in the treasuries of the royal palace and sent it as a gift[r] to the king of Assyria. 9 The king of Assyria complied by attacking Damascus and capturing it. He deported its inhabitants to Kir[s] and put Rezin to death.

10 Then King Ahaz went to Damascus to meet Tiglath-Pileser king of Assyria. He saw an altar in Damascus and sent to Uriah[t] the priest a sketch of the altar, with detailed plans for its construction. 11 So Uriah the priest built an altar in accordance with all the plans that King Ahaz had sent from Damascus and finished it before King Ahaz returned. 12 When the king came back from Damascus and saw the altar, he approached it and presented offerings[b][u] on it. 13 He offered up his burnt offering and grain offering, poured out his drink offering, and sprinkled the blood of his fellowship offerings[c] on the altar. 14 The bronze altar[v] that stood before the LORD he brought from the front of the temple—from between the new altar and the temple of the LORD—and put it on the north side of the new altar.

15 King Ahaz then gave these orders to Uriah the priest: "On the large new altar, offer the morning[w] burnt offering and the evening grain offering, the king's burnt offering and his grain offering, and the burnt offering of all the people of the land, and their grain offering and their drink offering. Sprinkle on the altar all the blood of the burnt offerings and sacrifices. But I will

**15:29** f 2Ki 17:6; 1Ch 5:26 g 1Ki 15:20 h 2Ki 16:9; 17:24; 2Ch 16:4; Isa
**15:30** i 2Ki 17:1
**15:34** j ver 3; 2Ch 26:4–5
**15:37** k 2Ki 16:5; Isa 7:1
**16:3** l Lev 18:21 m Dt 12:31
**16:4** n Dt 12:2
**16:5** o 2Ki 15:37; Isa 7:1,4
**16:6** p 2Ki 14:22
**16:7** q 2Ki 15:29
**16:8** r 2Ki 12:18
**16:9** s Am 1:5
**16:10** t Isa 8:2
**16:12** u 2Ch 26:16
**16:14** v 2Ch 4:1
**16:15** w Ex 29:38–41

[a] 3 Or *even made his son pass through* [b] 12 Or *and went up* [c] 13 Traditionally *peace offerings*

use the bronze altar for seeking guidance." 16 And Uriah the priest did just as King Ahaz had ordered.

17 King Ahaz took away the side panels and removed the basins from the movable stands. He removed the Sea from the bronze bulls that supported it and set it on a stone base.[x] 18 He took away the Sabbath canopy[a] that had been built at the temple and removed the royal entryway outside the temple of the LORD, in deference to the king of Assyria.

19 As for the other events of the reign of Ahaz, and what he did, are they not written in the book of the annals of the kings of Judah? 20 Ahaz rested with his fathers and was buried with them in the City of David. And Hezekiah his son succeeded him as king.

## Hoshea Last King of Israel

17 In the twelfth year of Ahaz king of Judah, Hoshea[y] son of Elah became king of Israel in Samaria, and he reigned nine years. 2 He did evil in the eyes of the LORD, but not like the kings of Israel who preceded him.

3 Shalmaneser[z] king of Assyria came up to attack Hoshea, who had been Shalmaneser's vassal and had paid him tribute. 4 But the king of Assyria discovered that Hoshea was a traitor, for he had sent envoys to So[b] king of Egypt, and he no longer paid tribute to the king of Assyria, as he had done year by year. Therefore Shalmaneser seized him and put him in prison. 5 The king of Assyria invaded the entire land, marched against Samaria and laid siege to it for three years. 6 In the ninth year of Hoshea, the king of Assyria captured Samaria and deported the Israelites to Assyria. He settled them in Halah, in Gozan on the Habor River and in the towns of the Medes.

## Israel Exiled Because of Sin

7 All this took place because the Israelites had sinned[a] against the LORD their God, who had brought them up out of Egypt from under the power of Pharaoh king of Egypt. They worshiped other gods 8 and followed the practices of the nations[b] the LORD had driven out before them, as well as the practices that the kings of Israel had introduced. 9 The Israelites secretly did things against the LORD their God that were not right. From watchtower to fortified city[c] they built themselves high places in all their towns. 10 They set up sacred stones and Asherah poles[d] on every high hill and under every spreading tree.[e] 11 At every high place they burned incense, as the nations whom the LORD had driven out before them had done. They did wicked things that provoked the LORD to anger. 12 They worshiped idols,[f] though the LORD had said, "You shall not do this."[c] 13 The LORD warned Israel and Judah through all his prophets and seers:[g] "Turn from your evil ways.[h] Observe my commands and decrees, in accordance with the entire Law that I commanded your fathers to obey and that I delivered to you through my servants the prophets."

14 But they would not listen and were as stiff-necked as their fathers, who did not trust in the LORD their God. 15 They rejected his decrees and the covenant[i] he had made with their fathers and the warnings he had given them. They followed worthless idols[j] and themselves became worthless. They imitated the nations[k] around them although the LORD had ordered them, "Do not do as they do," and they did the things the LORD had forbidden them to do.

16 They forsook all the commands of the LORD their God and made for themselves two idols cast in the shape of calves,[l] and an Asherah pole. They bowed down to all the starry hosts, and they worshiped Baal. 17 They sacrificed[m] their sons and daughters in[d] the fire. They practiced divination and sorcery and sold[n] themselves to do evil in the eyes of the LORD, provoking him to anger.

18 So the LORD was very angry with Israel and removed them from his presence. Only the tribe of Judah was left, 19 and even Judah did not keep the commands of the LORD their God. They followed the practices Israel had introduced. 20 Therefore the LORD rejected all the people of Israel; he afflicted them and gave them into the hands of plun-

**16:17** x 1Ki 7:27
**17:1** y 2Ki 15:30
**17:3** z 2Ki 18:9–12
**17:7** a Jos 23:16
**17:8** b Lev 18:3; Dt 18:9
**17:9** c 2Ki 18:8
**17:10** d Ex 34:13; Mic 5:14 e 1Ki 14:23
**17:12** f Ex 20:4
**17:13** g 1Sa 9:9 h Jer 18:11
**17:15** i Dt 29:25 j Dt 32:21 k Dt 12:30–31
**17:16** l 1Ki 12:28
**17:17** m Dt 18:10–12; 2Ki 16:3 n 1Ki 21:20

[a] 18 Or *the dais of his throne* (see Septuagint) [b] 4 Or *to Sais, to the*; *So* is possibly an abbreviation for *Osorkon.*
[c] 12 Exodus 20:4,5 [d] 17 Or *They made their sons and daughters pass through*

derers,[o] until he thrust them from his presence.

21When he tore[p] Israel away from the house of David, they made Jeroboam son of Nebat their king.[q] Jeroboam enticed Israel away from following the LORD and caused them to commit a great sin. 22The Israelites persisted in all the sins of Jeroboam and did not turn away from them 23until the LORD removed them from his presence, as he had warned through all his servants the prophets. So the people of Israel were taken from their homeland into exile in Assyria, and they are still there.

## Samaria Resettled

24The king of Assyria[r] brought people from Babylon, Cuthah, Avva, Hamath and Sepharvaim[s] and settled them in the towns of Samaria to replace the Israelites. They took over Samaria and lived in its towns. 25When they first lived there, they did not worship the LORD; so he sent lions among them and they killed some of the people. 26It was reported to the king of Assyria: "The people you deported and resettled in the towns of Samaria do not know what the god of that country requires. He has sent lions among them, which are killing them off, because the people do not know what he requires."

27Then the king of Assyria gave this order: "Have one of the priests you took captive from Samaria go back to live there and teach the people what the god of the land requires." 28So one of the priests who had been exiled from Samaria came to live in Bethel and taught them how to worship the LORD.

29Nevertheless, each national group made its own gods in the several towns where they settled, and set them up in the shrines the people of Samaria had made at the high places. 30The men from Babylon made Succoth Benoth, the men from Cuthah made Nergal, and the men from Hamath made Ashima; 31the Avvites made Nibhaz and Tartak, and the Sepharvites burned their children in the fire as sacrifices to Adrammelech and Anammelech, the gods of Sepharvaim.[t] 32They worshiped the LORD, but they also appointed all sorts[u] of their own people to officiate for them as priests in the shrines at the high places. 33They worshiped the LORD, but they also served their own gods in accordance with the customs of the nations from which they had been brought.

34To this day they persist in their former practices. They neither worship the LORD nor adhere to the decrees and ordinances, the laws and commands that the LORD gave the descendants of Jacob, whom he named Israel.[v] 35When the LORD made a covenant with the Israelites, he commanded them: "Do not worship[w] any other gods or bow down to them, serve them or sacrifice to them. 36But the LORD, who brought you up out of Egypt with mighty power and outstretched arm,[x] is the one you must worship. To him you shall bow down and to him offer sacrifices. 37You must always be careful[y] to keep the decrees and ordinances, the laws and commands he wrote for you. Do not worship other gods. 38Do not forget[z] the covenant I have made with you, and do not worship other gods. 39Rather, worship the LORD your God; it is he who will deliver you from the hand of all your enemies."

40They would not listen, however, but persisted in their former practices. 41Even while these people were worshiping the LORD, they were serving their idols. To this day their children and grandchildren continue to do as their fathers did.

## Hezekiah King of Judah

**18** In the third year of Hoshea son of Elah king of Israel, Hezekiah[a] son of Ahaz king of Judah began to reign. 2He was twenty-five years old when he became king, and he reigned in Jerusalem twenty-nine years. His mother's name was Abijah[a] daughter of Zechariah. 3He did what was right in the eyes of the LORD, just as his father David had done. 4He removed[b] the high places, smashed the sacred stones and cut down the Asherah poles. He broke into pieces the bronze snake[c] Moses had made, for up to that time the Israelites had been burning incense to it. (It was called[b] Nehushtan.[c])

5Hezekiah trusted[d] in the LORD, the God

**17:20** o 2Ki 15:29
**17:21** p 1Ki 11:11; q 1Ki 12:20
**17:24** r Ezr 4:2,10; s 2Ki 18:34
**17:31** t ver 24
**17:32** u 1Ki 12:31
**17:34** v Ge 32:28; 35:10
**17:35** w Ex 20:5; Jdg 6:10
**17:36** x Ex 6:6
**17:37** y Dt 5:32
**17:38** z Dt 4:23
**18:1** a 2Ch 28:27
**18:4** b 2Ch 31:1; c Nu 21:9
**18:5** d 2Ki 19:10; 23:25

[a]2 Hebrew *Abi,* a variant of *Abijah* [b]4 Or *He called it* [c]4 *Nehushtan* sounds like the Hebrew for *bronze* and *snake* and *unclean thing.*

of Israel. There was no one like him among all the kings of Judah, either before him or after him. 6He held fast[e] to the LORD and did not cease to follow him; he kept the commands the LORD had given Moses. 7And the LORD was with him; he was successful[f] in whatever he undertook. He rebelled[g] against the king of Assyria and did not serve him. 8From watchtower to fortified city,[h] he defeated the Philistines, as far as Gaza and its territory.

9In King Hezekiah's fourth year, which was the seventh year of Hoshea son of Elah king of Israel, Shalmaneser king of Assyria marched against Samaria and laid siege to it. 10At the end of three years the Assyrians took it. So Samaria was captured in Hezekiah's sixth year, which was the ninth year of Hoshea king of Israel. 11The king of Assyria deported Israel to Assyria and settled them in Halah, in Gozan on the Habor River and in towns of the Medes. 12This happened because they had not obeyed the LORD their God, but had violated his covenant—all that Moses the servant of the LORD commanded.[i] They neither listened to the commands[j] nor carried them out.

13In the fourteenth year of King Hezekiah's reign, Sennacherib king of Assyria attacked all the fortified cities of Judah[k] and captured them. 14So Hezekiah king of Judah sent this message to the king of Assyria at Lachish: "I have done wrong. Withdraw from me, and I will pay whatever you demand of me." The king of Assyria exacted from Hezekiah king of Judah three hundred talents[a] of silver and thirty talents[b] of gold. 15So Hezekiah gave[l] him all the silver that was found in the temple of the LORD and in the treasuries of the royal palace.

16At this time Hezekiah king of Judah stripped off the gold with which he had covered the doors and doorposts of the temple of the LORD, and gave it to the king of Assyria.

## Sennacherib Threatens Jerusalem

17The king of Assyria sent his supreme commander,[m] his chief officer and his field commander with a large army, from Lachish to King Hezekiah at Jerusalem. They came up to Jerusalem and stopped at the aqueduct of the Upper Pool,[n] on the road to the Washerman's Field. 18They called for the king; and Eliakim[o] son of Hilkiah the palace administrator, Shebna[p] the secretary, and Joah son of Asaph the recorder went out to them.

19The field commander said to them, "Tell Hezekiah:

"'This is what the great king, the king of Assyria, says: On what are you basing this confidence of yours? 20You say you have strategy and military strength—but you speak only empty words. On whom are you depending, that you rebel against me? 21Look now, you are depending on Egypt,[q] that splintered reed of a staff,[r] which pierces a man's hand and wounds him if he leans on it! Such is Pharaoh king of Egypt to all who depend on him. 22And if you say to me, "We are depending on the LORD our God"—isn't he the one whose high places and altars Hezekiah removed, saying to Judah and Jerusalem, "You must worship before this altar in Jerusalem"?

23"'Come now, make a bargain with my master, the king of Assyria: I will give you two thousand horses—if you can put riders on them! 24How can you repulse one officer of the least of my master's officials, even though you are depending on Egypt for chariots and horsemen[c]? 25Furthermore, have I come to attack and destroy this place without word from the LORD? The LORD himself told me to march against this country and destroy it.'"

26Then Eliakim son of Hilkiah, and Shebna and Joah said to the field commander, "Please speak to your servants in Aramaic,[s] since we understand it. Don't speak to us in Hebrew in the hearing of the people on the wall."

27But the commander replied, "Was it only to your master and you that my master sent me to say these things, and not to the men sitting on the wall—who, like you, will

**18:6** e Dt 10:20
**18:7** f Ge 39:3; 1Sa 18:14 g 2Ki 16:7
**18:8** h 2Ki 17:9; Isa 14:29
**18:12** i Da 9:6,10 j 1Ki 9:6
**18:13** k 2Ch 32:1
**18:15** l 1Ki 15:18; 2Ki 16:8
**18:17** m Isa 20:1
**18:17** n 2Ki 20:20
**18:18** o 2Ki 19:2; Isa 22:20 p Isa 22:15
**18:21** q Eze 29:6 r Isa 30:5,7
**18:26** s Ezr 4:7

[a] 14 That is, about 11 tons (about 10 metric tons) [b] 14 That is, about 1 ton (about 1 metric ton) [c] 24 Or *charioteers*

have to eat their own filth and drink their own urine?"

28Then the commander stood and called out in Hebrew: "Hear the word of the great king, the king of Assyria! 29This is what the king says: Do not let Hezekiah deceive you. He cannot deliver you from my hand. 30Do not let Hezekiah persuade you to trust in the LORD when he says, 'The LORD will surely deliver us; this city will not be given into the hand of the king of Assyria.'

31"Do not listen to Hezekiah. This is what the king of Assyria says: Make peace with me and come out to me. Then every one of you will eat from his own vine and fig tree[t] and drink water from his own cistern, 32until I come and take you to a land like your own, a land of grain and new wine, a land of bread and vineyards, a land of olive trees and honey. Choose life[u] and not death!

"Do not listen to Hezekiah, for he is misleading you when he says, 'The LORD will deliver us.' 33Has the god[v] of any nation ever delivered his land from the hand of the king of Assyria? 34Where are the gods of Hamath[w] and Arpad? Where are the gods of Sepharvaim, Hena and Ivvah? Have they rescued Samaria from my hand? 35Who of all the gods of these countries has been able to save his land from me? How then can the LORD deliver Jerusalem from my hand?"

36But the people remained silent and said nothing in reply, because the king had commanded, "Do not answer him."

37Then Eliakim son of Hilkiah the palace administrator, Shebna the secretary and Joah son of Asaph the recorder went to Hezekiah, with their clothes torn, and told him what the field commander had said.

## Jerusalem's Deliverance Foretold

19 When King Hezekiah heard this, he tore[x] his clothes and put on sackcloth and went into the temple of the LORD. 2He sent Eliakim the palace administrator, Shebna the secretary and the leading priests, all wearing sackcloth, to the prophet Isaiah son of Amoz. 3They told him, "This is what Hezekiah says: This day is a day of distress and rebuke and disgrace, as when children come to the point of birth and there is no strength to deliver them. 4It may be that the LORD your God will hear all the words of the field commander, whom his master, the king of Assyria, has sent to ridicule[y] the living God, and that he will rebuke[z] him for the words the LORD your God has heard. Therefore pray for the remnant that still survives."

5When King Hezekiah's officials came to Isaiah, 6Isaiah said to them, "Tell your master, 'This is what the LORD says: Do not be afraid of what you have heard—those words with which the underlings of the king of Assyria have blasphemed me. 7Listen! I am going to put such a spirit in him that when he hears a certain report, he will return to his own country, and there I will have him cut down with the sword.[a]'"

8When the field commander heard that the king of Assyria had left Lachish,[b] he withdrew and found the king fighting against Libnah.

9Now Sennacherib received a report that Tirhakah, the Cushite[a] king ⌞of Egypt⌟, was marching out to fight against him. So he again sent messengers to Hezekiah with this word: 10"Say to Hezekiah king of Judah: Do not let the god you depend[c] on deceive you when he says, 'Jerusalem will not be handed over to the king of Assyria.' 11Surely you have heard what the kings of Assyria have done to all the countries, destroying them completely. And will you be delivered? 12Did the gods of the nations that were destroyed by my forefathers deliver[d] them: the gods of Gozan, Haran, Rezeph and the people of Eden who were in Tel Assar? 13Where is the king of Hamath, the king of Arpad, the king of the city of Sepharvaim, or of Hena or Ivvah?"[e]

## Hezekiah's Prayer

14Hezekiah received the letter from the messengers and read it. Then he went up to the temple of the LORD and spread it out before the LORD. 15And Hezekiah prayed to the LORD: "O LORD, God of Israel, enthroned between the cherubim, you alone are God over all the kingdoms of the earth. You have made heaven and earth. 16Give ear,[f] O LORD, and hear; open your eyes,[g] O LORD, and see;

**18:31** t 1Ki 4:25
**18:32** u Dt 8:7–9
**18:33** v 2Ki 19:12
**18:34** w 2Ki 17:24; 19:13
**19:1** x Ge 37:34; 1Ki 21:27; 2Ch 32:20–22
**19:4** y 2Ki 18:35 z 2Sa 16:12
**19:7** a ver 37
**19:8** b 2Ki 18:14
**19:10** c 2Ki 18:5
**19:12** d 2Ki 18:33
**19:13** e 2Ki 18:34
**19:16** f Ps 31:2 g ver 4; 2Ch 6:40

[a]9 That is, from the upper Nile region

The African Presence

**2 Kings 19:9–13**

**Tirhakah, a Cushite king of Egypt, attempted to defend Egypt against Assyria, but he was defeated (see also Isa 37:9).**

listen to the words Sennacherib has sent to
insult the living God.
[17]"It is true, O LORD, that the Assyrian
kings have laid waste these nations and
their lands. [18]They have thrown their gods
into the fire and destroyed them, for they
were not gods[h] but only wood and stone,
fashioned by men's hands. [19]Now, O LORD
our God, deliver us from his hand, so that
all kingdoms on earth may know[i] that you
alone, O LORD, are God."

## Isaiah Prophesies Sennacherib's Fall

[20]Then Isaiah son of Amoz sent a mes-
sage to Hezekiah: "This is what the LORD,
the God of Israel, says: I have heard your
prayer concerning Sennacherib king of
Assyria. [21]This is the word that the LORD has
spoken against him:

"'The Virgin Daughter[j] of Zion
despises you and mocks you.
The Daughter of Jerusalem
tosses her head as you flee.
[22] Who is it you have insulted and
blasphemed?

*God,*

*Thank you for blessing me while I'm here on earth. Help me to remember and believe that when the wicked come upon me to eat up my flesh, they will only stumble and fall (see Ps 27:2).*

*Amen*

2 KINGS 19:14–19

Against whom have you raised your
voice
and lifted your eyes in pride?
Against the Holy One of Israel!
[23] By your messengers
you have heaped insults on the Lord.
And you have said,
"With my many chariots[k]
I have ascended the heights of the
mountains,
the utmost heights of Lebanon.
I have cut down its tallest cedars,
the choicest of its pines.
I have reached its remotest parts,
the finest of its forests.
[24] I have dug wells in foreign lands
and drunk the water there.
With the soles of my feet
I have dried up all the streams of
Egypt."

[25] "'Have you not heard?
Long ago I ordained it.
In days of old I planned[l] it;
now I have brought it to pass,
that you have turned fortified cities
into piles of stone.
[26] Their people, drained of power,
are dismayed and put to shame.
They are like plants in the field,
like tender green shoots,
like grass sprouting on the roof,
scorched[m] before it grows up.

[27] "'But I know[n] where you stay
and when you come and go
and how you rage against me.
[28] Because you rage against me
and your insolence has reached my
ears,
I will put my hook[o] in your nose
and my bit in your mouth,

**19:18** h Jer 10:3–10
**19:19** i Ps 83:18
**19:21** j La 2:13
**19:23** k Ps 20:7
**19:25** l Isa 10:5; 45:7
**19:26** m Ps 129:6
**19:27** n Ps 139:1–4
**19:28** o Eze 29:4

and I will make you return[p]
by the way you came.'

29"This will be the sign[q] for you, O Hezekiah:

"This year you will eat what grows by
itself,
and the second year what springs from
that.
But in the third year sow and reap,
plant vineyards and eat their fruit.
30 Once more a remnant of the house of
Judah
will take root[r] below and bear fruit
above.
31 For out of Jerusalem will come a remnant,
and out of Mount Zion a band of
survivors.

The zeal[s] of the LORD Almighty will accom-
plish this.

32"Therefore this is what the LORD says
concerning the king of Assyria:

"He will not enter this city
or shoot an arrow here.
He will not come before it with shield
or build a siege ramp against it.
33 By the way that he came he will return;[t]
he will not enter this city,
declares the LORD.
34 I will defend[u] this city and save it,
for my sake and for the sake of David[v]
my servant."

35That night the angel of the LORD went out
and put to death a hundred and eighty-five
thousand men in the Assyrian camp. When
the people got up the next morning—there
were all the dead bodies! 36So Sennacherib
king of Assyria broke camp and withdrew.
He returned to Nineveh and stayed there.
37One day, while he was worshiping in the
temple of his god Nisroch, his sons Adram-
melech and Sharezer cut him down with
the sword,[w] and they escaped to the land of
Ararat. And Esarhaddon[x] his son succeeded
him as king.

19:28 p ver 33
19:29 q Lk 2:12
19:30 r 2Ch 32:22–23
19:31 s Isa 9:7
19:33 t ver 28
19:34 u 2Ki 20:6; v 1Ki 11:12–13
19:37 w ver 7; x Ezr 4:2

## Hezekiah's Illness

20 In those days Hezekiah became ill
and was at the point of death. The
prophet Isaiah son of Amoz went to him and
said, "This is what the LORD says: Put your
house in order, because you are going to die;
you will not recover."
2Hezekiah turned his face to the wall and
prayed to the LORD, 3"Remember,[y] O LORD,
how I have walked before you faithfully and
with wholehearted devotion and have done
what is good in your eyes." And Hezekiah
wept bitterly.
4Before Isaiah had left the middle court,
the word of the LORD came to him: 5"Go back
and tell Hezekiah, the leader of my people,
'This is what the LORD, the God of your fa-
ther David, says: I have heard[z] your prayer
and seen your tears;[a] I will heal you. On the
third day from now you will go up to the
temple of the LORD. 6I will add fifteen years
to your life. And I will deliver you and this
city from the hand of the king of Assyria. I
will defend[b] this city for my sake and for the
sake of my servant David.'"
7Then Isaiah said, "Prepare a poultice of
figs." They did so and applied it to the boil,
and he recovered.
8Hezekiah had asked Isaiah, "What will
be the sign that the LORD will heal me and
that I will go up to the temple of the LORD on
the third day from now?"
9Isaiah answered, "This is the LORD's
sign to you that the LORD will do what he has
promised: Shall the shadow go forward ten
steps, or shall it go back ten steps?"
10"It is a simple matter for the shadow
to go forward ten steps," said Hezekiah.
"Rather, have it go back ten steps."
11Then the prophet Isaiah called upon
the LORD, and the LORD made the shadow go
back the ten steps it had gone down on the
stairway of Ahaz.

## Envoys From Babylon

12At that time Merodach-Baladan son
of Baladan king of Babylon sent Hezekiah
letters and a gift, because he had heard of
Hezekiah's illness. 13Hezekiah received the
messengers and showed them all that was
in his storehouses—the silver, the gold,
the spices and the fine oil—his armory
and everything found among his treasures.
There was nothing in his palace or in all his
kingdom that Hezekiah did not show them.
14Then Isaiah the prophet went to King

20:3 y Ne 13:22
20:5 z 1Sa 9:16; 1Ki 9:3; 2Ki 19:20; a Ps 39:12
20:6 b 2Ki 19:34

Hezekiah and asked, "What did those men
say, and where did they come from?"
"From a distant land," Hezekiah replied.
"They came from Babylon."
15 The prophet asked, "What did they see
in your palace?"
"They saw everything in my palace,"
Hezekiah said. "There is nothing among my
treasures that I did not show them."
16 Then Isaiah said to Hezekiah, "Hear
the word of the LORD: 17 The time will surely
come when everything in your palace, and
all that your fathers have stored up until
this day, will be carried off to Babylon.[c]
Nothing will be left, says the LORD. 18 And
some of your descendants,[d] your own flesh
and blood, that will be born to you, will be
taken away, and they will become eunuchs
in the palace of the king of Babylon."
19 "The word of the LORD you have spoken
is good," Hezekiah replied. For he thought,
"Will there not be peace and security in
my lifetime?"
20 As for the other events of Hezekiah's
reign, all his achievements and how he
made the pool[e] and the tunnel by which
he brought water into the city, are they not
written in the book of the annals of the
kings of Judah? 21 Hezekiah rested with his
fathers. And Manasseh his son succeeded
him as king.

## Manasseh King of Judah

21 Manasseh was twelve years old
when he became king, and he
reigned in Jerusalem fifty-five years. His
mother's name was Hephzibah. 2 He did evil
in the eyes of the LORD, following the detest-
able practices[f] of the nations the LORD had
driven out before the Israelites. 3 He rebuilt
the high places[g] his father Hezekiah had
destroyed; he also erected altars to Baal[h]
and made an Asherah pole, as Ahab king of
Israel had done. He bowed down to all the
starry hosts[i] and worshiped them. 4 He built
altars[j] in the temple of the LORD, of which
the LORD had said, "In Jerusalem I will put
my Name."[k] 5 In both courts of the temple
of the LORD, he built altars to all the starry
hosts. 6 He sacrificed his own son[l] in[a] the
fire, practiced sorcery and divination, and
consulted mediums and spiritists.[m] He did
much evil in the eyes of the LORD, provoking
him to anger.
7 He took the carved Asherah pole he had
made and put it in the temple, of which the
LORD had said to David and to his son Sol-
omon, "In this temple and in Jerusalem,
which I have chosen out of all the tribes of
Israel, I will put my Name[n] forever. 8 I will
not again[o] make the feet of the Israelites
wander from the land I gave their fore-
fathers, if only they will be careful to do
everything I commanded them and will
keep the whole Law that my servant Moses
gave them." 9 But the people did not listen.
Manasseh led them astray, so that they did
more evil[p] than the nations the LORD had de-
stroyed before the Israelites.
10 The LORD said through his servants the
prophets: 11 "Manasseh king of Judah has
committed these detestable sins. He has
done more evil[q] than the Amorites[r] who
preceded him and has led Judah into sin
with his idols. 12 Therefore this is what the
LORD, the God of Israel, says: I am going to
bring such disaster on Jerusalem and Judah
that the ears of everyone who hears of it will
tingle.[s] 13 I will stretch out over Jerusalem
the measuring line used against Samaria
and the plumb line[t] used against the house
of Ahab. I will wipe out Jerusalem as one
wipes a dish, wiping it and turning it upside
down. 14 I will forsake[u] the remnant[v] of my
inheritance and hand them over to their
enemies. They will be looted and plundered
by all their foes, 15 because they have done
evil in my eyes and have provoked me to an-
ger from the day their forefathers came out
of Egypt until this day."
16 Moreover, Manasseh also shed so much
innocent blood[w] that he filled Jerusalem
from end to end—besides the sin that he
had caused Judah to commit, so that they
did evil in the eyes of the LORD.
17 As for the other events of Manasseh's
reign, and all he did, including the sin he
committed, are they not written in the book
of the annals of the kings of Judah? 18 Manas-
seh rested with his fathers and was buried
in his palace garden, the garden of Uzza.
And Amon his son succeeded him as king.

[a] 6 Or *He made his own son pass through*

**20:17** c 2Ki 24:13; 25:13; Jer 52:17–23
**20:18** d 2Ki 24:15; 2Ch 33:11
**20:20** e Ne 3:16
**21:2** f 2Ki 16:3
**21:3** g 2Ki 18:4 h 1Ki 16:32 i Dt 17:3; 2Ki 17:16
**21:4** j Jer 32:34 k 2Sa 7:13; 1Ki 8:29
**21:6** l Lev 18:21; Dt 18:10; 2Ki 16:3; 17:17
**21:6** m Lev 19:31
**21:7** n 1Ki 8:29; 9:3
**21:8** o 2Sa 7:10
**21:9** p Pr 29:12
**21:11** q 2Ki 24:3–4 r 1Ki 21:26
**21:12** s 1Sa 3:11; Jer 19:3
**21:13** t Isa 34:11; Am 7:7–9
**21:14** u Ps 78:58–60 v 2Ki 19:4
**21:16** w 2Ki 24:4

## Amon King of Judah

19 Amon was twenty-two years old when he became king, and he reigned in Jerusalem two years. His mother's name was Meshullemeth daughter of Haruz; she was from Jotbah. 20 He did evil[x] in the eyes of the LORD, as his father Manasseh had done. 21 He walked in all the ways of his father; he worshiped the idols his father had worshiped, and bowed down to them. 22 He forsook the LORD, the God of his fathers, and did not walk[y] in the way of the LORD.

23 Amon's officials conspired against him and assassinated the king in his palace. 24 Then the people of the land killed all who had plotted against King Amon, and they made Josiah his son king in his place.

25 As for the other events of Amon's reign, and what he did, are they not written in the book of the annals of the kings of Judah? 26 He was buried in his grave in the garden of Uzza. And Josiah his son succeeded him as king.

## The Book of the Law Found

22 Josiah was eight years old when he became king, and he reigned in Jerusalem thirty-one years. His mother's name was Jedidah daughter of Adaiah; she was from Bozkath.[z] 2 He did what was right in the eyes of the LORD and walked in all the ways of his father David, not turning aside to the right[a] or to the left.

3 In the eighteenth year of his reign, King Josiah sent the secretary, Shaphan son of Azaliah, the son of Meshullam, to the temple of the LORD. He said: 4 "Go up to Hilkiah the high priest and have him get ready the money that has been brought into the temple of the LORD, which the doorkeepers have collected[b] from the people. 5 Have them entrust it to the men appointed to supervise the work on the temple. And have these men pay the workers who repair[c] the temple of the LORD— 6 the carpenters, the builders and the masons. Also have them purchase timber and dressed stone to repair the temple. 7 But they need not account for the money entrusted to them, because they are acting faithfully."[d]

8 Hilkiah the high priest said to Shaphan the secretary, "I have found the Book of the Law[e] in the temple of the LORD." He gave it to Shaphan, who read it. 9 Then Shaphan the secretary went to the king and reported to him: "Your officials have paid out the money that was in the temple of the LORD and have entrusted it to the workers and supervisors at the temple." 10 Then Shaphan the secretary informed the king, "Hilkiah the priest has given me a book." And Shaphan read from it in the presence of the king.

11 When the king heard the words of the Book of the Law, he tore his robes. 12 He gave these orders to Hilkiah the priest, Ahikam[f] son of Shaphan, Acbor son of Micaiah, Shaphan the secretary and Asaiah the king's attendant: 13 "Go and inquire of the LORD for me and for the people and for all Judah about what is written in this book that has been found. Great is the LORD's anger[g] that burns against us because our fathers have not obeyed the words of this book; they have not acted in accordance with all that is written there concerning us."

14 Hilkiah the priest, Ahikam, Acbor, Shaphan and Asaiah went to speak to the prophetess Huldah, who was the wife of Shallum son of Tikvah, the son of Harhas, keeper of the wardrobe. She lived in Jerusalem, in the Second District.

15 She said to them, "This is what the LORD, the God of Israel, says: Tell the man who sent you to me, 16 'This is what the LORD says: I am going to bring disaster on this place and its people, according to everything written in the book[h] the king of Judah has read. 17 Because they have forsaken[i] me and burned incense to other gods and provoked me to anger by all the idols their hands have made,[a] my anger will burn against this place and will not be quenched.' 18 Tell the king of Judah, who sent you to inquire of the LORD, 'This is what the LORD, the God of Israel, says concerning the words you heard: 19 Because your heart was responsive and you humbled[j] yourself before the LORD when you heard what I have spoken against this place and its people, that they would become accursed[k] and laid waste,[l] and because you tore your robes and wept in my presence, I have heard you, declares the LORD.

[a] 17 Or *by everything they have done*

**21:20** x ver 2–6
**21:22** y 1Ki 11:33
**22:1** z Jos 15:39
**22:2** a Dt 5:32
**22:4** b 2Ki 12:4–5
**22:5** c 2Ki 12:5,11–14
**22:7** d 2Ki 12:15
**22:8** e Dt 31:24
**22:12** f 2Ki 25:22
**22:13** g Dt 29:24–28
**22:16** h Dt 29:27; Da 9:11
**22:17** i Dt 29:25–27
**22:19** j 1Ki 21:29; Ps 51:17; Isa 57:15 k Jer 26:6 l Lev 26:31

# Huldah

## A Prophetess of God

One of the great stories of a woman prophet in the Bible is found in 2 Kings 22. The prophet's name was Huldah. Not much is recorded of her life, but the story of one event in her life serves to create an unforgettable profile of a woman called by God.

Huldah lived in Jerusalem during the reign of Josiah. This king of Judah, unlike his father and grandfather, "did what was right in the eyes of the LORD" (2Ki 22:2). Hilkiah, the high priest, discovered the Book of the Law in the temple. When King Josiah heard the neglected words of Scripture, he responded with grief and repentance. Josiah then sent members of his cabinet to inquire of the Lord's pending judgment on his people. They sought counsel from the prophetess Huldah. God used Huldah to deliver messages to the king (see 2Ki 22:14–20). It is noteworthy that Huldah was consulted rather than Jeremiah, the well-known prophet who also ministered at this time (compare 2Ki 22:3–4 and Jer 1:2). This demonstrates that God doesn't assign women secondary status, nor does he use women for ministry only when there are no men available.

Huldah's brief biography mentions only that she was married to a man named Shallum and that she lived in the Second District of Jerusalem (see 2Ki 22:14; see also 2Ch 34:22). That's all! Yet the king's men sought her for counsel. The common cord that linked Huldah with the leader of the country and members of the king's cabinet was that they wanted to do what was pleasing in God's sight.

While little else is known about Huldah, we know the most important thing about her: She desired to do God's will. When people think of you, will they remember you as a Huldah? Will they say you wanted to follow God?

—M. ARMSTEAD

### reflection

*Reflect on a time when others sought you out for counsel. Did you share God's Word with them or did you tell them what they wanted to hear?*

### read

2 Kings 22:1–20; 2 Chronicles 34:14–28.

**See also** the Inspire Notes "Responsible Decisions in Leadership," "Female Ministers and Evangelists," "Servant-Leadership," "Women in Preaching Ministries" and "Character," and the Women of the Bible Notes "Deborah: An Uncommon Leader," "Queen Vashti: A Woman of Strength," "A Virtuous Woman: A Strong Woman, Dependent on God" and "Philip's Daughters: Those Preaching Women."

For the next Women of the Bible note, go to page 527.

20 Therefore I will gather you to your fathers, and you will be buried in peace. Your eyes will not see all the disaster I am going to bring on this place.' "

So they took her answer back to the king.

## Josiah Renews the Covenant

**23** Then the king called together all the elders of Judah and Jerusalem. 2 He went up to the temple of the LORD with the men of Judah, the people of Jerusalem, the priests and the prophets—all the people from the least to the greatest. He read[m] in their hearing all the words of the Book of the Covenant, which had been found in the temple of the LORD. 3 The king stood by the pillar and renewed the covenant[n] in the presence of the LORD—to follow[o] the LORD and keep his commands, regulations and decrees with all his heart and all his soul, thus confirming the words of the covenant written in this book. Then all the people pledged themselves to the covenant.

4 The king ordered Hilkiah the high priest, the priests next in rank and the doorkeepers to remove from the temple of the LORD all the articles made for Baal and Asherah and all the starry hosts. He burned them outside Jerusalem in the fields of the Kidron Valley and took the ashes to Bethel. 5 He did away with the pagan priests appointed by the kings of Judah to burn incense on the high places of the towns of Judah and on those around Jerusalem—those who burned incense to Baal, to the sun and moon, to the constellations and to all the starry hosts. 6 He took the Asherah pole from the temple of the LORD to the Kidron Valley outside Jerusalem and burned it there. He ground it to powder and scattered the dust over the graves of the common people. 7 He also tore down the quarters of the male shrine prostitutes,[p] which were in the temple of the LORD and where women did weaving for Asherah.

8 Josiah brought all the priests from the towns of Judah and desecrated the high places, from Geba[q] to Beersheba, where the priests had burned incense. He broke down the shrines[a] at the gates—at the entrance to the Gate of Joshua, the city governor, which is on the left of the city gate. 9 Although the priests of the high places did not serve[r] at the altar of the LORD in Jerusalem, they ate unleavened bread with their fellow priests.

10 He desecrated Topheth,[s] which was in the Valley of Ben Hinnom, so no one could use it to sacrifice his son[t] or daughter in[b] the fire to Molech. 11 He removed from the entrance to the temple of the LORD the horses that the kings of Judah had dedicated to the sun. They were in the court near the room of an official named Nathan-Melech. Josiah then burned the chariots dedicated to the sun.

12 He pulled down the altars the kings of Judah had erected on the roof[u] near the upper room of Ahaz, and the altars Manasseh had built in the two courts[v] of the temple of the LORD. He removed them from there, smashed them to pieces and threw the rubble into the Kidron Valley. 13 The king also desecrated the high places that were east of Jerusalem on the south of the Hill of Corruption—the ones Solomon[w] king of Israel had built for Ashtoreth the vile goddess of the Sidonians, for Chemosh the vile god of Moab, and for Molech[c] the detestable god of the people of Ammon. 14 Josiah smashed[x] the sacred stones and cut down the Asherah poles and covered the sites with human bones.

15 Even the altar at Bethel, the high place made by Jeroboam[y] son of Nebat, who had caused Israel to sin—even that altar and high place he demolished. He burned the high place and ground it to powder, and burned the Asherah pole also. 16 Then Josiah[z] looked around, and when he saw the tombs that were there on the hillside, he had the bones removed from them and burned on the altar to defile it, in accordance with the word of the LORD proclaimed by the man of God who foretold these things.

17 The king asked, "What is that tombstone I see?"

The men of the city said, "It marks the tomb of the man of God who came from Judah and pronounced against the altar of Bethel the very things you have done to it."

18 "Leave it alone," he said. "Don't let anyone disturb his bones[a]." So they spared his bones and those of the prophet who had come from Samaria.

**23:2** m Dt 31:11; 2Ki 22:8
**23:3** n 2Ki 11:14,17 o Dt 13:4
**23:7** p 1Ki 14:24; 15:12; Eze 16:16
**23:8** q 1Ki 15:22
**23:9** r Eze 44:10–14
**23:10** s Isa 30:33; Jer 7:31,32 t Lev 18:21
**23:12** u Jer 19:13; Zep 1:5 v 2Ki 21:5
**23:13** w 1Ki 11:7
**23:14** x Ex 23:24; Dt 7:5,25
**23:15** y 1Ki 12:33
**23:16** z 1Ki 13:2
**23:18** a 1Ki 13:31

[a]8 Or *high places* [b]10 Or *to make his son or daughter pass through* [c]13 Hebrew *Milcom*

19 Just as he had done at Bethel, Josiah
removed and defiled all the shrines at the
high places that the kings of Israel had built
in the towns of Samaria that had provoked
the LORD to anger. 20 Josiah slaughtered[b] all
the priests of those high places on the altars
and burned human bones on them. Then he
went back to Jerusalem.

21 The king gave this order to all the peo-
ple: "Celebrate the Passover[c] to the LORD
your God, as it is written in this Book of
the Covenant." 22 Not since the days of the
judges who led Israel, nor throughout the
days of the kings of Israel and the kings of
Judah, had any such Passover been ob-
served. 23 But in the eighteenth year of King
Josiah, this Passover was celebrated to the
LORD in Jerusalem.

24 Furthermore, Josiah got rid of the me-
diums and spiritists,[d] the household gods,
the idols and all the other detestable things
seen in Judah and Jerusalem. This he did to
fulfill the requirements of the law written
in the book that Hilkiah the priest had dis-
covered in the temple of the LORD. 25 Neither
before nor after Josiah was there a king like
him who turned[e] to the LORD as he did—
with all his heart and with all his soul and
with all his strength, in accordance with all
the Law of Moses.

26 Nevertheless, the LORD did not turn
away from the heat of his fierce anger, which
burned against Judah because of all that
Manasseh[f] had done to provoke him to an-
ger. 27 So the LORD said, "I will remove[g] Judah
also from my presence[h] as I removed Israel,
and I will reject Jerusalem, the city I chose,
and this temple, about which I said, 'There
shall my Name be.'[a]"

28 As for the other events of Josiah's reign,
and all he did, are they not written in the
book of the annals of the kings of Judah?

29 While Josiah was king, Pharaoh Neco
king of Egypt went up to the Euphrates
River to help the king of Assyria. King Josiah
marched out to meet him in battle, but Neco
faced him and killed him at Megiddo. 30 Josi-
ah's servants brought his body in a chariot
from Megiddo to Jerusalem and buried him
in his own tomb. And the people of the land
took Jehoahaz son of Josiah and anointed
him and made him king in place of his fa-
ther.

## Jehoahaz King of Judah

31 Jehoahaz was twenty-three years old
when he became king, and he reigned in Je-
rusalem three months. His mother's name
was Hamutal daughter of Jeremiah; she
was from Libnah. 32 He did evil in the eyes
of the LORD, just as his fathers had done.
33 Pharaoh Neco put him in chains at Rib-
lah in the land of Hamath[b] so that he might
not reign in Jerusalem, and he imposed on
Judah a levy of a hundred talents[c] of silver
and a talent[d] of gold. 34 Pharaoh Neco made
Eliakim[i] son of Josiah king in place of his
father Josiah and changed Eliakim's name
to Jehoiakim. But he took Jehoahaz and car-
ried him off to Egypt, and there he died.[j]
35 Jehoiakim paid Pharaoh Neco the silver
and gold he demanded. In order to do so,
he taxed the land and exacted the silver and
gold from the people of the land according
to their assessments.[k]

## Jehoiakim King of Judah

36 Jehoiakim was twenty-five years old
when he became king, and he reigned in
Jerusalem eleven years. His mother's name
was Zebidah daughter of Pedaiah; she was
from Rumah. 37 And he did evil in the eyes of
the LORD, just as his fathers had done.

24 During Jehoiakim's reign, Nebu-
chadnezzar[l] king of Babylon in-
vaded the land, and Jehoiakim became his
vassal for three years. But then he changed
his mind and rebelled against Nebuchadnez-
zar. 2 The LORD sent Babylonian,[e] Aramean,
Moabite and Ammonite raiders against
him. He sent them to destroy Judah, in accor-
dance with the word of the LORD proclaimed
by his servants the prophets. 3 Surely these
things happened to Judah according to the
LORD's command, in order to remove them
from his presence because of the sins of
Manasseh[m] and all he had done, 4 including
the shedding of innocent blood.[n] For he had
filled Jerusalem with innocent blood, and
the LORD was not willing to forgive.

**23:20** b 2Ki 11:18
**23:21** c Ex 12:11; Nu 9:2
**23:24** d Dt 18:11
**23:25** e 2Ki 18:5
**23:26** f 2Ki 21:12; Jer 15:4
**23:27** g 2Ki 21:13 h 2Ki 18:11
**23:34** i 2Ch 36:5–8 j Jer 22:12; Eze 19:3–4
**23:35** k ver 33
**24:1** l Jer 25:1,9
**24:3** m 2Ki 23:26
**24:4** n 2Ki 21:16

[a]27 1 Kings 8:29 [b]33 Hebrew; Septuagint (see also 2 Chron. 36:3) *Neco at Riblah in Hamath removed him*
[c]33 That is, about 3 3/4 tons (about 3.4 metric tons) [d]33 That is, about 75 pounds (about 34 kilograms) [e]2 Or *Chaldean*

**24:6** o Jer 22:19
**24:7** p Jer 37:5–7; 46:2
**24:12** q Jer 24:1; 29:2
**24:13** r 2Ki 20:17 s Isa 39:6
**24:14** t Jer 24:1; 52:28 u 2Ki 25:12; Jer 40:7; 52:16
**24:15** v Jer 22:24–28
**24:17** w 2Ch 36:11; Jer 37:1
**24:18** x Jer 52:1

[5]As for the other events of Jehoiakim's reign, and all he did, are they not written in the book of the annals of the kings of Judah? [6]Jehoiakim rested[o] with his fathers. And Jehoiachin his son succeeded him as king.

[7]The king of Egypt did not march out from his own country again, because the king of Babylon[p] had taken all his territory, from the Wadi of Egypt to the Euphrates River.

## Jehoiachin King of Judah

[8]Jehoiachin was eighteen years old when he became king, and he reigned in Jerusalem three months. His mother's name was Nehushta daughter of Elnathan; she was from Jerusalem. [9]He did evil in the eyes of the LORD, just as his father had done.

[10]At that time the officers of Nebuchadnezzar king of Babylon advanced on Jerusalem and laid siege to it, [11]and Nebuchadnezzar himself came up to the city while his officers were besieging it. [12]Jehoiachin king of Judah, his mother, his attendants, his nobles and his officials all surrendered[q] to him.

In the eighth year of the reign of the king of Babylon, he took Jehoiachin prisoner. [13]As the LORD had declared,[r] Nebuchadnezzar removed all the treasures[s] from the temple of the LORD and from the royal palace, and took away all the gold articles that Solomon king of Israel had made for the temple of the LORD. [14]He carried into exile[t] all Jerusalem: all the officers and fighting men, and all the craftsmen and artisans—a total of ten thousand. Only the poorest[u] people of the land were left.

[15]Nebuchadnezzar took Jehoiachin captive to Babylon. He also took from Jerusalem to Babylon the king's mother,[v] his wives, his officials and the leading men of the land. [16]The king of Babylon also deported to Babylon the entire force of seven thousand fighting men, strong and fit for war, and a thousand craftsmen and artisans. [17]He made Mattaniah, Jehoiachin's uncle, king in his place and changed his name to Zedekiah.[w]

## Zedekiah King of Judah

[18]Zedekiah[x] was twenty-one years old when he became king, and he reigned in Jerusalem eleven years. His mother's name was Hamutal[y] daughter of Jeremiah; she was from Libnah. [19]He did evil in the eyes of the LORD, just as Jehoiakim had done. [20]It was because of the LORD's anger that all this happened to Jerusalem and Judah, and in the end he thrust them from his presence.

## The Fall of Jerusalem

Now Zedekiah rebelled against the king of Babylon.

**25** So in the ninth year of Zedekiah's reign, on the tenth day of the tenth month, Nebuchadnezzar king of Babylon marched against Jerusalem with his whole army. He encamped outside the city and built siege works[z] all around it. [2]The city was kept under siege until the eleventh year of King Zedekiah. [3]By the ninth day of the ⌞fourth⌟[a] month the famine in the city had become so severe that there was no food for the people to eat. [4]Then the city wall was broken through,[a] and the whole army fled at night through the gate between the two walls near the king's garden, though the Babylonians[b] were surrounding the city. They fled toward the Arabah,[c] [5]but the Babylonian[d] army pursued the king and overtook him in the plains of Jericho. All his soldiers were separated from him and scattered, [6]and he was captured. He was taken to the king of Babylon at Riblah,[b] where sentence was pronounced on him. [7]They killed the sons of Zedekiah before his eyes. Then they put out his eyes, bound him with bronze shackles and took him to Babylon.

[8]On the seventh day of the fifth month, in the nineteenth year of Nebuchadnezzar king of Babylon, Nebuzaradan commander of the imperial guard, an official of the king of Babylon, came to Jerusalem. [9]He set fire to the temple of the LORD, the royal palace and all the houses of Jerusalem. Every important building he burned down.[c] [10]The whole Babylonian army, under the commander of the imperial guard, broke down the walls[d] around Jerusalem. [11]Nebuzaradan the commander of the guard carried into exile the people who remained in the city, along with the rest of the populace

**24:18** y 2Ki 23:31
**25:1** z Eze
**25:4** a Eze 33:21
**25:6** b 2Ki 23:33
**25:9** c Ps 74:3–8; Am 2:5
**25:10** d Ne 1:3

[a]3 See Jer. 52:6. [b]4 Or *Chaldeans*; also in verses 13, 25 and 26 [c]4 Or *the Jordan Valley* [d]5 Or *Chaldean*; also in verses 10 and 24

**25:12** e 2Ki 24:14
**25:17** f 1Ki 7:15–22
**25:18** g 1Ch 6:14; Ezr 7:1 h Jer 21:1; 29:25

and those who had gone over to the king of Babylon. [12]But the commander left behind some of the poorest people[e] of the land to work the vineyards and fields.

*Woman of color,*

*Even when you are in exile,*
*I'll take care of you. I don't, won't*
*and can't forget about you—ever.*

*Love always,*
*God*

2 KINGS 25:8–12

[13]The Babylonians broke up the bronze pillars, the movable stands and the bronze Sea that were at the temple of the LORD and they carried the bronze to Babylon. [14]They also took away the pots, shovels, wick trimmers, dishes and all the bronze articles used in the temple service. [15]The commander of the imperial guard took away the censers and sprinkling bowls—all that were made of pure gold or silver.

[16]The bronze from the two pillars, the Sea and the movable stands, which Solomon had made for the temple of the LORD, was more than could be weighed. [17]Each pillar[f] was twenty-seven feet[a] high. The bronze capital on top of one pillar was four and a half feet[b] high and was decorated with a network and pomegranates of bronze all around. The other pillar, with its network, was similar.

[18]The commander of the guard took as prisoners Seraiah[g] the chief priest, Zephaniah[h] the priest next in rank and the three doorkeepers. [19]Of those still in the city, he took the officer in charge of the fighting men and five royal advisers. He also took the secretary who was chief officer in charge of conscripting the people of the land and sixty of his men who were found in the city. [20]Nebuzaradan the commander took them all and brought them to the king of Babylon at Riblah. [21]There at Riblah, in the land of Hamath, the king had them executed.

So Judah went into captivity, away from her land.[i]

[22]Nebuchadnezzar king of Babylon appointed Gedaliah[j] son of Ahikam, the son of Shaphan, to be over the people he had left behind in Judah. [23]When all the army officers and their men heard that the king of Babylon had appointed Gedaliah as governor, they came to Gedaliah at Mizpah—Ishmael son of Nethaniah, Johanan son of Kareah, Seraiah son of Tanhumeth the Netophathite, Jaazaniah the son of the Maacathite, and their men. [24]Gedaliah took an oath to reassure them and their men. "Do not be afraid of the Babylonian officials," he said. "Settle down in the land and serve the king of Babylon, and it will go well with you."

[25]In the seventh month, however, Ishmael son of Nethaniah, the son of Elishama, who was of royal blood, came with ten men and assassinated Gedaliah and also the men of Judah and the Babylonians who were with him at Mizpah. [26]At this, all the people from the least to the greatest, together with the army officers, fled to Egypt[k] for fear of the Babylonians.

## Jehoiachin Released

[27]In the thirty-seventh year of the exile of Jehoiachin king of Judah, in the year Evil-Merodach[c] became king of Babylon, he released Jehoiachin[l] from prison on the twenty-seventh day of the twelfth month. [28]He spoke kindly to him and gave him a seat of honor[m] higher than those of the other kings who were with him in Babylon. [29]So Jehoiachin put aside his prison clothes and for the rest of his life ate regularly at the king's table.[n] [30]Day by day the king gave Jehoiachin a regular allowance as long as he lived.

**25:21** i Dt 28:64; 2Ki 23:27
**25:22** j Jer 40:5,7
**25:26** k Jer 43:7
**25:27** l 2Ki 24:12; Jer 52:31–34
**25:28** m Ezr 5:5; Da 2:48
**25:29** n 2Sa 9:7

[a]17 Hebrew *eighteen cubits* (about 8.1 meters) [b]17 Hebrew *three cubits* (about 1.3 meters) [c]27 Also called *Amel-Marduk*

# 1 Chronicles

## OVERVIEW

The book of 1 Chronicles begins with a genealogy of the patriarchs, from Adam to Jacob (Israel), and then continues with genealogical records of the tribes of Israel. Most of 1 Chronicles is devoted to describing David's reign. Much of the material in 1 and 2 Chronicles is similar to the books of Samuel and Kings, with the primary difference being a matter of emphasis. While the writer of Kings focused on the exile of Israel and Judah as judgment for apostasy, the writer of Chronicles focused on the faithfulness of God in preserving his covenant with Abraham and David.

Women believers can study how God kept his promise to Abraham and David as proof that he continues to keep his word. God doesn't lie (see Tit 1:2), like sinful people do, and those who put their trust in him will never be disappointed. As you study 1 Chronicles, make note of how God continued to keep his covenant in spite of David's setbacks.

## OUTLINE

I. Genealogies: Creation to Restoration (1:1—9:44)
II. Saul's Death and David's Reign (10:1—22:19)
III. Divisions of Levites, Priests and Officials (23:1—27:34)
IV. End of the Reign of David (28:1—29:30)

### SCANNABLE FACTS:

**Author:** Unknown; possibly Ezra

**Time Written:** About 450 B.C.

**Theme to Note:** God's faithfulness to his covenant

**Notable Woman:** Michal (see 1Ch 15:29)

1:1
a Ge 5:1–32; Lk 3:36–38

1:2
b Ge 5:9
c Ge 5:12
d Ge 5:15

1:3
e Ge 5:18; Jude 1:14
f Ge 5:21
g Ge 5:25
h Ge 5:29

1:4
i Ge 6:10; 10:1
j Ge 5:32

1:24
k Ge 10:21–25; Lk 3:34–36

## Historical Records From Adam to Abraham

### To Noah's Sons

1 Adam,[a] Seth, Enosh, 2 Kenan,[b] Mahalalel,[c] Jared,[d] 3 Enoch,[e] Methuselah,[f] Lamech,[g] Noah.[h]

4 The sons of Noah:[a][i]
Shem, Ham and Japheth.[j]

### The Japhethites

5 The sons[b] of Japheth:
Gomer, Magog, Madai, Javan, Tubal, Meshech and Tiras.

6 The sons of Gomer:
Ashkenaz, Riphath[c] and Togarmah.

7 The sons of Javan:
Elishah, Tarshish, the Kittim and the Rodanim.

### The Hamites

8 The sons of Ham:
Cush, Mizraim,[d] Put and Canaan.

9 The sons of Cush:
Seba, Havilah, Sabta, Raamah and Sabteca.

The sons of Raamah:
Sheba and Dedan.

10 Cush was the father[e] of
Nimrod, who grew to be a mighty warrior on earth.

11 Mizraim was the father of
the Ludites, Anamites, Lehabites, Naphtuhites, 12 Pathrusites, Casluhites (from whom the Philistines came) and Caphtorites.

13 Canaan was the father of
Sidon his firstborn,[f] and of the Hittites, 14 Jebusites, Amorites, Girgashites, 15 Hivites, Arkites, Sinites, 16 Arvadites, Zemarites and Hamathites.

### The Semites

17 The sons of Shem:
Elam, Asshur, Arphaxad, Lud and Aram.

The sons of Aram:[g]
Uz, Hul, Gether and Meshech.

18 Arphaxad was the father of Shelah,
and Shelah the father of Eber.

19 Two sons were born to Eber:
One was named Peleg,[h] because in his time the earth was divided; his brother was named Joktan.

20 Joktan was the father of
Almodad, Sheleph, Hazarmaveth, Jerah, 21 Hadoram, Uzal, Diklah, 22 Obal,[i] Abimael, Sheba, 23 Ophir, Havilah and Jobab. All these were sons of Joktan.

24 Shem,[k] Arphaxad,[j] Shelah,
25 Eber, Peleg, Reu,

[a]4 Septuagint; Hebrew does not have this line. [b]5 *Sons* may mean *descendants* or *successors* or *nations*; also in verses 6–10, 17 and 20. [c]6 Many Hebrew manuscripts and Vulgate (see also Septuagint and Gen. 10:3); most Hebrew manuscripts *Diphath* [d]8 That is, Egypt; also in verse 11 [e]10 *Father* may mean *ancestor* or *predecessor* or *founder*; also in verses 11, 13, 18 and 20. [f]13 Or *of the Sidonians, the foremost* [g]17 One Hebrew manuscript and some Septuagint manuscripts (see also Gen. 10:23); most Hebrew manuscripts do not have this line. [h]19 *Peleg* means *division.* [i]22 Some Hebrew manuscripts and Syriac (see also Gen. 10:28); most Hebrew manuscripts *Ebal* [j]24 Hebrew; some Septuagint manuscripts *Arphaxad, Cainan* (see also note at Gen. 11:10)

## The African Presence

### 1 Chronicles 1:1–27

The genealogies listed in 1 Chronicles include references to Adam through Noah and the sons of Noah: Shem, Ham and Japheth. After the Genesis flood, the sons of Noah migrated in several directions: Japheth and his children represent nations to the north and west of Canaan (including present-day Europe and northeastern Asia); Ham and his children represent nations in Mesopotamia/Asia as well as the continent of Africa; Shem and his children represent nations in Mesopotamia/Asia.

1:32 l Ge 22:24 m Ge 10:7
1:34 n Lk 3:34 o Ge 21:2–3; Mt 1:2; Ac 7:8 p Ge 17:5; 25:25–26
1:35 q Ge 36:19 r Ge 36:4

26 Serug, Nahor, Terah
27 and Abram (that is, Abraham).

## The Family of Abraham

28 The sons of Abraham:
Isaac and Ishmael.

### Descendants of Hagar

29 These were their descendants:
Nebaioth the firstborn of Ishmael, Kedar, Adbeel, Mibsam, 30 Mishma, Dumah, Massa, Hadad, Tema, 31 Jetur, Naphish and Kedemah. These were the sons of Ishmael.

### Descendants of Keturah

32 The sons born to Keturah, Abraham's concubine:[l]
Zimran, Jokshan, Medan, Midian, Ishbak and Shuah.
The sons of Jokshan:
Sheba and Dedan.[m]
33 The sons of Midian:
Ephah, Epher, Hanoch, Abida and Eldaah.
All these were descendants of Keturah.

### Descendants of Sarah

34 Abraham[n] was the father of Isaac.[o]
The sons of Isaac:
Esau and Israel.[p]

## Esau's Sons

35 The sons of Esau:[q]
Eliphaz, Reuel,[r] Jeush, Jalam and Korah.
36 The sons of Eliphaz:
Teman, Omar, Zepho,[a] Gatam and Kenaz;
by Timna: Amalek.[b][s]
37 The sons of Reuel:[t]
Nahath, Zerah, Shammah and Mizzah.

### The People of Seir in Edom

38 The sons of Seir:
Lotan, Shobal, Zibeon, Anah, Dishon, Ezer and Dishan.
39 The sons of Lotan:
Hori and Homam. Timna was Lotan's sister.
40 The sons of Shobal:
Alvan,[c] Manahath, Ebal, Shepho and Onam.
The sons of Zibeon:
Aiah and Anah.[u]
41 The son of Anah:
Dishon.
The sons of Dishon:
Hemdan,[d] Eshban, Ithran and Keran.
42 The sons of Ezer:
Bilhan, Zaavan and Akan.[e]
The sons of Dishan[f]:
Uz and Aran.

### The Rulers of Edom

43 These were the kings who reigned in Edom before any Israelite king reigned[g]:
Bela son of Beor, whose city was named Dinhabah.

1:36 s Ex 17:14
1:37 t Ge 36:17
1:40 u Ge 36:2

[a]36 Many Hebrew manuscripts, some Septuagint manuscripts and Syriac (see also Gen. 36:11); most Hebrew manuscripts *Zephi* [b]36 Some Septuagint manuscripts (see also Gen. 36:12); Hebrew *Gatam, Kenaz, Timna and Amalek* [c]40 Many Hebrew manuscripts and some Septuagint manuscripts (see also Gen. 36:23); most Hebrew manuscripts *Alian* [d]41 Many Hebrew manuscripts and some Septuagint manuscripts (see also Gen. 36:26); most Hebrew manuscripts *Hamran* [e]42 Many Hebrew and Septuagint manuscripts (see also Gen. 36:27); most Hebrew manuscripts *Zaavan, Jaakan* [f]42 Hebrew *Dishon,* a variant of *Dishan* [g]43 Or *before an Israelite king reigned over them*

## The African Presence

**1 Chronicles 1:28–33**

The genealogy of Chronicles includes Abraham's children Isaac and Ishmael. Two of Abraham's mates were Hagar and Keturah. Hagar was an Egyptian (see Ge 16:1). Midian, one of Abraham's children by Keturah, was an ancestor of Zipporah (Moses' wife). For more on Keturah, see the African Presence notes on Genesis 25:1–2 and Exodus 2:16–22.

44 When Bela died, Jobab son of Zerah from Bozrah succeeded him as king.
45 When Jobab died, Husham from the land of the Temanites[v] succeeded him as king.
46 When Husham died, Hadad son of Bedad, who defeated Midian in the country of Moab, succeeded him as king. His city was named Avith.
47 When Hadad died, Samlah from Masrekah succeeded him as king.
48 When Samlah died, Shaul from Rehoboth on the river[a] succeeded him as king.
49 When Shaul died, Baal-Hanan son of Acbor succeeded him as king.
50 When Baal-Hanan died, Hadad succeeded him as king. His city was named Pau,[b] and his wife's name was Mehetabel daughter of Matred, the daughter of Me-Zahab. 51 Hadad also died.

The chiefs of Edom were:
Timna, Alvah, Jetheth, 52 Oholibamah, Elah, Pinon, 53 Kenaz, Teman, Mibzar, 54 Magdiel and Iram. These were the chiefs of Edom.

## Israel's Sons

2 These were the sons of Israel:
Reuben, Simeon, Levi, Judah, Issachar, Zebulun, 2 Dan, Joseph, Benjamin, Naphtali, Gad and Asher.

## Judah

### To Hezron's Sons

3 The sons of Judah:[w]
Er, Onan and Shelah. These three were born to him by a Canaanite woman, the daughter of Shua. Er, Judah's firstborn, was wicked in the LORD's sight; so the LORD put him to death. 4 Tamar, Judah's daughter-in-law, bore him Perez[x] and Zerah. Judah had five sons in all.

5 The sons of Perez:[y]
Hezron and Hamul.
6 The sons of Zerah:
Zimri, Ethan, Heman, Calcol and Darda[c]—five in all.
7 The son of Carmi:
Achar,[d][z] who brought trouble on Israel by violating the ban on taking devoted things.[e][a]
8 The son of Ethan:
Azariah.
9 The sons born to Hezron were:
Jerahmeel, Ram and Caleb.[f]

### From Ram Son of Hezron

10 Ram was the father of
Amminadab, and Amminadab the father of Nahshon, the leader of the people of Judah. 11 Nahshon was the father of Salmon,[g] Salmon the father of Boaz, 12 Boaz the father of Obed and Obed the father of Jesse.
13 Jesse was the father of
Eliab[b] his firstborn; the second son was Abinadab, the third Shimea, 14 the fourth Nethanel, the fifth Raddai, 15 the sixth Ozem and the seventh David. 16 Their sisters were Zeruiah and Abigail. Zeruiah's[c] three sons were Abishai, Joab and Asahel. 17 Abigail was the mother of Amasa,[d] whose father was Jether the Ishmaelite.

### Caleb Son of Hezron

18 Caleb son of Hezron had children by his wife Azubah (and by Jerioth). These were her sons: Jesher, Shobab and Ardon. 19 When Azubah died, Caleb[e] married Ephrath, who bore him Hur. 20 Hur was the father of Uri, and Uri the father of Bezalel.[f]
21 Later, Hezron lay with the daughter of Makir the father of Gilead[g] (he had married her when he was sixty years old), and she bore him Segub. 22 Segub was the father of Jair, who controlled twenty-three towns in Gilead. 23 (But Geshur and Aram

**1:45** v Ge 36:11
**2:3** w Ge 38:2–10
**2:4** x Ge 38:29
**2:5** y Ge 46:12
**2:7** z Jos 7:1 a Jos 6:18
**2:13** b 1Sa 16:6
**2:16** c 2Sa 2:18
**2:17** d 2Sa 17:25
**2:19** e ver 42,50
**2:20** f Ex 31:2
**2:21** g Nu 27:1

[a]48 Possibly the Euphrates [b]50 Many Hebrew manuscripts, some Septuagint manuscripts, Vulgate and Syriac (see also Gen. 36:39); most Hebrew manuscripts *Pai* [c]6 Many Hebrew manuscripts, some Septuagint manuscripts and Syriac (see also 1 Kings 4:31); most Hebrew manuscripts *Dara* [d]7 *Achar* means *trouble*; *Achar* is called *Achan* in Joshua. [e]7 The Hebrew term refers to the irrevocable giving over of things or persons to the LORD, often by totally destroying them. [f]9 Hebrew *Kelubai,* a variant of *Caleb* [g]11 Septuagint (see also Ruth 4:21); Hebrew *Salma*

**2:23** h Nu 32:41; Dt 3:14; Jos 13:30
**2:24** i 1Ch 4:5
**2:36** j 1Ch 11:41

captured Havvoth Jair,[a][h] as well as Kenath with its surrounding settlements—sixty towns.) All these were descendants of Makir the father of Gilead.

24 After Hezron died in Caleb Ephrathah, Abijah the wife of Hezron bore him Ashhur[i] the father[b] of Tekoa.

## Jerahmeel Son of Hezron

25 The sons of Jerahmeel the firstborn of Hezron:
Ram his firstborn, Bunah, Oren, Ozem and[c] Ahijah.
26 Jerahmeel had another wife, whose name was Atarah; she was the mother of Onam.
27 The sons of Ram the firstborn of Jerahmeel:
Maaz, Jamin and Eker.
28 The sons of Onam:
Shammai and Jada.
The sons of Shammai:
Nadab and Abishur.
29 Abishur's wife was named Abihail, who bore him Ahban and Molid.
30 The sons of Nadab:
Seled and Appaim. Seled died without children.
31 The son of Appaim:
Ishi, who was the father of Sheshan.
Sheshan was the father of Ahlai.
32 The sons of Jada, Shammai's brother:
Jether and Jonathan. Jether died without children.
33 The sons of Jonathan:
Peleth and Zaza.
These were the descendants of Jerahmeel.
34 Sheshan had no sons—only daughters.
He had an Egyptian servant named Jarha.
35 Sheshan gave his daughter in marriage to his servant Jarha, and she bore him Attai.
36 Attai was the father of Nathan,
Nathan the father of Zabad,[j]
37 Zabad the father of Ephlal,
Ephlal the father of Obed,
38 Obed the father of Jehu,
Jehu the father of Azariah,
39 Azariah the father of Helez,
Helez the father of Eleasah,
40 Eleasah the father of Sismai,
Sismai the father of Shallum,
41 Shallum the father of Jekamiah,
and Jekamiah the father of Elishama.

## The Clans of Caleb

42 The sons of Caleb the brother of Jerahmeel:
Mesha his firstborn, who was the father of Ziph, and his son Mareshah,[d] who was the father of Hebron.
43 The sons of Hebron:
Korah, Tappuah, Rekem and Shema.
44 Shema was the father of Raham, and Raham the father of Jorkeam. Rekem was the father of Shammai.
45 The son of Shammai was Maon, and Maon was the father of Beth Zur.
46 Caleb's concubine Ephah was the mother of Haran, Moza and Gazez. Haran was the father of Gazez.
47 The sons of Jahdai:
Regem, Jotham, Geshan, Pelet, Ephah and Shaaph.
48 Caleb's concubine Maacah was the mother of Sheber and Tirhanah.
49 She also gave birth to Shaaph the father of Madmannah and to Sheva the father of Macbenah and Gibea. Caleb's daughter was Acsah.
50 These were the descendants of Caleb.

The sons of Hur the firstborn of Ephrathah:
Shobal the father of Kiriath Jearim,
51 Salma the father of Bethlehem, and Hareph the father of Beth Gader.
52 The descendants of Shobal the father of Kiriath Jearim were:
Haroeh, half the Manahathites,
53 and the clans of Kiriath Jearim: the Ithrites, Puthites, Shumathites and Mishraites. From these descended the Zorathites and Eshtaolites.
54 The descendants of Salma:

[a] 23 Or *captured the settlements of Jair* [b] 24 *Father* may mean *civic leader* or *military leader*; also in verses 42, 45, 49–52 and possibly elsewhere. [c] 25 Or *Oren and Ozem, by* [d] 42 The meaning of the Hebrew for this phrase is uncertain.

**2:55**
k Jdg 1:16
l Jer 35:2–19

**3:1**
m Jos 15:56

**3:4**
n 2Sa 2:11; 5:5

**3:5**
o 2Sa 11:3; 12:24

Bethlehem, the Netophathites, Atroth Beth Joab, half the Manahathites, the Zorites, 55 and the clans of scribes[a] who lived at Jabez: the Tirathites, Shimeathites and Sucathites. These are the Kenites[k] who came from Hammath, the father of the house of Recab.[b][l]

## The Sons of David

3 These were the sons of David born to him in Hebron:

The firstborn was Amnon the son of Ahinoam of Jezreel;[m]
the second, Daniel the son of Abigail of Carmel;
2 the third, Absalom the son of Maacah daughter of Talmai king of Geshur;
the fourth, Adonijah the son of Haggith;
3 the fifth, Shephatiah the son of Abital;
and the sixth, Ithream, by his wife Eglah.
4 These six were born to David in Hebron, where he reigned seven years and six months.[n]

David reigned in Jerusalem thirty-three years, 5 and these were the children born to him there:

Shammua,[c] Shobab, Nathan and Solomon. These four were by Bathsheba[d][o] daughter of Ammiel. 6 There

*Lord,*

*I thank you for my family—for those in my bloodline and for those who have become my family by their choice to follow you. Teach me to love them, each one, just as you love me. In your precious name,*

*Amen.*

1 CHRONICLES 3:1–9

were also Ibhar, Elishua,[e] Eliphelet, 7 Nogah, Nepheg, Japhia, 8 Elishama, Eliada and Eliphelet—nine in all. 9 All these were the sons of David, besides his sons by his concubines. And Tamar[p] was their sister.

## The Kings of Judah

10 Solomon's son was Rehoboam,[q]
Abijah his son,
Asa his son,
Jehoshaphat his son,
11 Jehoram[f][r] his son,
Ahaziah[s] his son,
Joash[t] his son,
12 Amaziah his son,
Azariah his son,
Jotham[u] his son,
13 Ahaz[v] his son,
Hezekiah his son,
Manasseh his son,
14 Amon his son,
Josiah[w] his son.

15 The sons of Josiah:
Johanan the firstborn,
Jehoiakim the second son,
Zedekiah[x] the third,
Shallum the fourth.

16 The successors of Jehoiakim:
Jehoiachin[g][y] his son,
and Zedekiah.[z]

## The Royal Line After the Exile

17 The descendants of Jehoiachin the captive:
Shealtiel his son, 18 Malkiram, Pedaiah, Shenazzar,[a] Jekamiah, Hoshama and Nedabiah.

19 The sons of Pedaiah:
Zerubbabel[b] and Shimei.

The sons of Zerubbabel:
Meshullam and Hananiah.
Shelomith was their sister.
20 There were also five others:
Hashubah, Ohel, Berekiah, Hasadiah and Jushab-Hesed.

21 The descendants of Hananiah:
Pelatiah and Jeshaiah, and the sons of Rephaiah, of Arnan, of Obadiah and of Shecaniah.

**3:9**
p 2Sa 13:1

**3:10**
q 1Ki 11:43

**3:11**
r 2Ki 8:16–24; 2Ch 21:1
s 2Ch 22:1–10
t 2Ki 11:1–12:21

**3:12**
u Isa 1:1; Hos 1:1

**3:13**
v Isa 7:1

**3:14**
w Jer 1:2; 25:3

**3:15**
x Jer 37:1

**3:16**
y Mt 1:11
z 2Ki 24:18

**3:18**
a Ezr 1:8

**3:19**
b Ezr 5:2

[a]55 Or *of the Sopherites* [b]55 Or *father of Beth Recab* [c]5 Hebrew *Shimea,* a variant of *Shammua* [d]5 One Hebrew manuscript and Vulgate (see also Septuagint and 2 Samuel 11:3); most Hebrew manuscripts *Bathshua* [e]6 Two Hebrew manuscripts (see also 2 Samuel 5:15 and 1 Chron. 14:5); most Hebrew manuscripts *Elishama* [f]11 Hebrew *Joram,* a variant of *Jehoram* [g]16 Hebrew *Jeconiah,* a variant of *Jehoiachin*; also in verse 17

3:22 c Ezr 8:2–3
4:1 d Ge 46:12; 1Ch 2:3
4:4 e 1Ch 2:50
4:5 f 1Ch 2:24

[22] The descendants of Shecaniah:
Shemaiah and his sons:
Hattush,[c] Igal, Bariah, Neariah and Shaphat—six in all.
[23] The sons of Neariah:
Elioenai, Hizkiah and Azrikam—three in all.
[24] The sons of Elioenai:
Hodaviah, Eliashib, Pelaiah, Akkub, Johanan, Delaiah and Anani—seven in all.

## Other Clans of Judah

4 The descendants of Judah:[d]
Perez, Hezron, Carmi, Hur and Shobal.
[2] Reaiah son of Shobal was the father of Jahath, and Jahath the father of Ahumai and Lahad. These were the clans of the Zorathites.
[3] These were the sons[a] of Etam:
Jezreel, Ishma and Idbash. Their sister was named Hazzelelponi.
[4]Penuel was the father of Gedor, and Ezer the father of Hushah.
These were the descendants of Hur,[e] the firstborn of Ephrathah and father[b] of Bethlehem.
[5] Ashhur[f] the father of Tekoa had two wives, Helah and Naarah.
[6] Naarah bore him Ahuzzam, Hepher, Temeni and Haahashtari. These were the descendants of Naarah.
[7] The sons of Helah:
Zereth, Zohar, Ethnan, [8]and Koz, who was the father of Anub and Hazzobebah and of the clans of Aharhel son of Harum.

[9]Jabez was more honorable than his brothers. His mother had named him Jabez,[c] saying, "I gave birth to him in pain." [10]Jabez cried out to the God of Israel, "Oh, that you would bless me and enlarge my territory! Let your hand be with me, and keep me from harm so that I will be free from pain." And God granted his request.

[11] Kelub, Shuhah's brother, was the father of Mehir, who was the father of Eshton. [12]Eshton was the father of Beth Rapha, Paseah and Tehinnah the father of Ir Nahash.[d] These were the men of Recah.

[13] The sons of Kenaz:
Othniel[g] and Seraiah.
The sons of Othniel:
Hathath and Meonothai.[e] [14]Meonothai was the father of Ophrah.
Seraiah was the father of Joab,
the father of Ge Harashim.[f] It was called this because its people were craftsmen.
[15] The sons of Caleb son of Jephunneh:
Iru, Elah and Naam.
The son of Elah:
Kenaz.
[16] The sons of Jehallelel:
Ziph, Ziphah, Tiria and Asarel.
[17] The sons of Ezrah:
Jether, Mered, Epher and Jalon. One of Mered's wives gave birth to Miriam, Shammai and Ishbah the father of Eshtemoa. [18](His Judean wife gave birth to Jered the father of Gedor, Heber the father of Soco, and Jekuthiel the father of Zanoah.) These were the children of Pharaoh's daughter Bithiah, whom Mered had married.
[19] The sons of Hodiah's wife, the sister of Naham:
the father of Keilah the Garmite, and Eshtemoa the Maacathite.
[20] The sons of Shimon:
Amnon, Rinnah, Ben-Hanan and Tilon.
The descendants of Ishi:
Zoheth and Ben-Zoheth.
[21] The sons of Shelah[h] son of Judah:
Er the father of Lecah, Laadah the father of Mareshah and the clans of the linen workers at Beth Ashbea, [22]Jokim, the men of Cozeba, and Joash and Saraph, who ruled in Moab and Jashubi Lehem. (These records are from ancient times.) [23]They were the potters who lived at

4:13 g Jos 15:17
4:21 h Ge 38:5

[a]3 Some Septuagint manuscripts (see also Vulgate); Hebrew *father* [b]4 *Father* may mean *civic leader* or *military leader*; also in verses 12, 14, 17, 18 and possibly elsewhere. [c]9 *Jabez* sounds like the Hebrew for *pain.* [d]12 Or *of the city of Nahash* [e]13 Some Septuagint manuscripts and Vulgate; Hebrew does not have *and Meonothai.* [f]14 *Ge Harashim* means *valley of craftsmen.*

Netaim and Gederah; they stayed
there and worked for the king.

## Simeon

24 The descendants of Simeon:[i]
Nemuel, Jamin, Jarib,[j] Zerah and
Shaul;
25 Shallum was Shaul's son, Mibsam
his son and Mishma his son.
26 The descendants of Mishma:
Hammuel his son, Zaccur his son
and Shimei his son.
27 Shimei had sixteen sons and six daugh-
ters, but his brothers did not have many
children; so their entire clan did not be-
come as numerous as the people of Judah.
28 They lived in Beersheba, Moladah, Hazar
Shual, 29 Bilhah, Ezem,[k] Tolad, 30 Bethuel,
Hormah, Ziklag, 31 Beth Marcaboth, Ha-
zar Susim, Beth Biri and Shaaraim. These
were their towns until the reign of David.
32 Their surrounding villages were Etam,
Ain, Rimmon, Token and Ashan—five
towns— 33 and all the villages around these
towns as far as Baalath.[a] These were their
settlements. And they kept a genealogical
record.

34 Meshobab, Jamlech, Joshah son of
Amaziah, 35 Joel, Jehu son of Joshibiah,
the son of Seraiah, the son of Asiel,
36 also Elioenai, Jaakobah, Jeshohaiah,
Asaiah, Adiel, Jesimiel, Benaiah, 37 and
Ziza son of Shiphi, the son of Allon,
the son of Jedaiah, the son of Shimri,
the son of Shemaiah.

38 The men listed above by name were
leaders of their clans. Their families in-
creased greatly, 39 and they went to the out-
skirts of Gedor to the east of the valley in
search of pasture for their flocks. 40 They
found rich, good pasture, and the land was
spacious, peaceful and quiet.[l] Some Ham-
ites had lived there formerly.
41 The men whose names were listed came
in the days of Hezekiah king of Judah. They
attacked the Hamites in their dwellings
and also the Meunites who were there and
completely destroyed[b] them, as is evident
to this day. Then they settled in their place,
because there was pasture for their flocks.
42 And five hundred of these Simeonites, led
by Pelatiah, Neariah, Rephaiah and Uzziel,
the sons of Ishi, invaded the hill country of
Seir. 43 They killed the remaining Amalek-
ites[m] who had escaped, and they have lived
there to this day.

## Reuben

5 The sons of Reuben[n] the firstborn of
Israel (he was the firstborn, but when
he defiled his father's marriage bed,[o] his
rights as firstborn were given to the sons
of Joseph[p] son of Israel; so he could not be
listed in the genealogical record in accor-
dance with his birthright, 2 and though Ju-
dah[q] was the strongest of his brothers and
a ruler[r] came from him, the rights of the
firstborn belonged to Joseph)— 3 the sons
of Reuben[s] the firstborn of Israel:
Hanoch, Pallu, Hezron and Carmi.
4 The descendants of Joel:
Shemaiah his son, Gog his son,
Shimei his son, 5 Micah his son,
Reaiah his son, Baal his son,
6 and Beerah his son, whom Tiglath-
Pileser[c] king of Assyria took into
exile. Beerah was a leader of the
Reubenites.
7 Their relatives by clans,[t] listed according
to their genealogical records:
Jeiel the chief, Zechariah, 8 and
Bela son of Azaz, the son of Shema,
the son of Joel. They settled in the
area from Aroer[u] to Nebo and Baal
Meon. 9 To the east they occupied
the land up to the edge of the des-
ert that extends to the Euphrates
River, because their livestock had
increased in Gilead.[v]
10 During Saul's reign they waged
war against the Hagrites, who were
defeated at their hands; they occupied
the dwellings of the Hagrites through-
out the entire region east of Gilead.

## Gad

11 The Gadites[w] lived next to them in Ba-
shan, as far as Salecah:[x]
12 Joel was the chief, Shapham the

**4:24** i Ge 29:33 j Nu 26:12
**4:29** k Jos 15:29
**4:40** l Jdg 18:7–10
**4:43** m 1Sa 15:8; 30:17; 2Sa 8:12
**5:1** n Ge 29:32 o Ge 35:22; 49:4 p Ge 48:16,22
**5:2** q Ge 49:10,12 r Ps 60:7; Mic 5:2; Mt 2:6
**5:3** s Ge 46:9; Ex 6:14; Nu 26:5–11
**5:7** t ver 17
**5:8** u Nu 32:34
**5:9** v Jos 22:9
**5:11** w Jos 13:24–28 x Jos 13:11

[a] 33 Some Septuagint manuscripts (see also Joshua 19:8); Hebrew *Baal* [b] 41 The Hebrew term refers to the irrevocable giving over of things or persons to the LORD, often by totally destroying them. [c] 6 Hebrew *Tilgath-Pilneser*, a variant of *Tiglath-Pileser*; also in verse 26

5:17
y 2Ki 15:32
z 2Ki 14:16,28

5:19
a Ge 25:15; 1Ch 1:31

5:20
b 2Ch 14:11; Ps 22:5

5:22
c 2Ki 15:29; 17:6

second, then Janai and Shaphat, in
Bashan.
13 Their relatives, by families, were:
Michael, Meshullam, Sheba, Jorai,
Jacan, Zia and Eber—seven in all.
14 These were the sons of Abihail son
of Huri, the son of Jaroah, the son of
Gilead, the son of Michael, the son
of Jeshishai, the son of Jahdo, the
son of Buz.
15 Ahi son of Abdiel, the son of Guni,
was head of their family.
16 The Gadites lived in Gilead, in Bashan
and its outlying villages, and on all
the pasturelands of Sharon as far as
they extended.
17 All these were entered in the genealog-
ical records during the reigns of Jotham[y]
king of Judah and Jeroboam[z] king of Israel.

18 The Reubenites, the Gadites and the
half-tribe of Manasseh had 44,760 men
ready for military service—able-bodied
men who could handle shield and sword,
who could use a bow, and who were trained
for battle. 19 They waged war against the Hag-
rites, Jetur,[a] Naphish and Nodab. 20 They
were helped in fighting them, and God
handed the Hagrites and all their allies over
to them, because they cried[b] out to him dur-
ing the battle. He answered their prayers,
because they trusted in him. 21 They seized
the livestock of the Hagrites—fifty thou-
sand camels, two hundred fifty thousand
sheep and two thousand donkeys. They also
took one hundred thousand people captive,
22 and many others fell slain, because the bat-
tle was God's. And they occupied the land
until the exile.[c]

## The Half-Tribe of Manasseh

23 The people of the half-tribe of Manas-
seh were numerous; they settled in the land
from Bashan to Baal Hermon, that is, to Se-
nir (Mount Hermon).

24 These were the heads of their fami-
lies: Epher, Ishi, Eliel, Azriel, Jeremiah,
Hodaviah and Jahdiel. They were brave
warriors, famous men, and heads of their
families. 25 But they were unfaithful to the
God of their fathers and prostituted them-
selves to the gods of the peoples of the land,
whom God had destroyed before them. 26 So
the God of Israel stirred up the spirit of Pul[d]
king of Assyria (that is, Tiglath-Pileser[e]
king of Assyria), who took the Reubenites,
the Gadites and the half-tribe of Manasseh
into exile. He took them to Halah, Habor,
Hara and the river of Gozan, where they are
to this day.

## Levi

6 The sons of Levi:[f]
Gershon, Kohath and Merari.
2 The sons of Kohath:
Amram, Izhar, Hebron and Uzziel.
3 The children of Amram:
Aaron, Moses and Miriam.
The sons of Aaron:
Nadab, Abihu,[g] Eleazar and Itha-
mar.
4 Eleazar was the father of Phinehas,
Phinehas the father of Abishua,
5 Abishua the father of Bukki,
Bukki the father of Uzzi,
6 Uzzi the father of Zerahiah,
Zerahiah the father of Meraioth,
7 Meraioth the father of Amariah,
Amariah the father of Ahitub,
8 Ahitub the father of Zadok,[h]
Zadok the father of Ahimaaz,
9 Ahimaaz the father of Azariah,
Azariah the father of Johanan,
10 Johanan the father of Azariah[i] (it
was he who served as priest in the
temple Solomon built in Jerusa-
lem),
11 Azariah the father of Amariah,
Amariah the father of Ahitub,
12 Ahitub the father of Zadok,
Zadok the father of Shallum,
13 Shallum the father of Hilkiah,[j]
Hilkiah the father of Azariah,
14 Azariah the father of Seraiah,[k]
and Seraiah the father of Jehoz-
adak.
15 Jehozadak[l] was deported when the
LORD sent Judah and Jerusalem into ex-
ile by the hand of Nebuchadnezzar.

16 The sons of Levi:[m]
Gershon,[a] Kohath and Merari.

5:26
d 2Ki 15:19
e 2Ki 15:29

6:1
f Ge 46:11; Ex 6:16

6:3
g Lev 10:1

6:8
h 2Sa 8:17; 15:27

6:10
i 1Ki 6:1; 2Ch 3:1; 26:17–18

6:13
j 2Ki 22:1–20

6:14
k Ezr 2:2; Ne 11:11

6:15
l 2Ki 25:18; Hag 1:1,14; Zec 6:11

6:16
m Ge 29:34; Ex 6:16

[a]16 Hebrew *Gershom*, a variant of *Gershon*; also in verses 17, 20, 43, 62 and 71

6:19 n 1Ch 23:21
6:24 o 1Ch 15:5
6:28 p ver 33; 1Sa 8:2
6:31 q 1Ch 15:19
6:37 r Ex 6:24
6:49 s Ex 27:1–8

17 These are the names of the sons of Gershon:
Libni and Shimei.
18 The sons of Kohath:
Amram, Izhar, Hebron and Uzziel.
19 The sons of Merari:[n]
Mahli and Mushi.
These are the clans of the Levites listed according to their fathers:
20 Of Gershon:
Libni his son, Jehath his son,
Zimmah his son, 21 Joah his son,
Iddo his son, Zerah his son
and Jeatherai his son.
22 The descendants of Kohath:
Amminadab his son, Korah his son,
Assir his son, 23 Elkanah his son,
Ebiasaph his son, Assir his son,
24 Tahath his son, Uriel[o] his son,
Uzziah his son and Shaul his son.
25 The descendants of Elkanah:
Amasai, Ahimoth,
26 Elkanah his son,[a] Zophai his son,
Nahath his son, 27 Eliab his son,
Jeroham his son, Elkanah his son
and Samuel his son.[b]
28 The sons of Samuel:
Joel[c][p] the firstborn
and Abijah the second son.
29 The descendants of Merari:
Mahli, Libni his son,
Shimei his son, Uzzah his son,
30 Shimea his son, Haggiah his son
and Asaiah his son.

### The Temple Musicians

31 These are the men David put in charge of the music[q] in the house of the LORD after the ark came to rest there. 32 They ministered with music before the tabernacle, the Tent of Meeting, until Solomon built the temple of the LORD in Jerusalem. They performed their duties according to the regulations laid down for them.

33 Here are the men who served, together with their sons:
From the Kohathites:
Heman, the musician,
the son of Joel, the son of Samuel,
34 the son of Elkanah, the son of Jeroham,
the son of Eliel, the son of Toah,
35 the son of Zuph, the son of Elkanah,
the son of Mahath, the son of Amasai,
36 the son of Elkanah, the son of Joel,
the son of Azariah, the son of Zephaniah,
37 the son of Tahath, the son of Assir,
the son of Ebiasaph, the son of Korah,[r]
38 the son of Izhar, the son of Kohath,
the son of Levi, the son of Israel;
39 and Heman's associate Asaph, who served at his right hand:
Asaph son of Berekiah, the son of Shimea,
40 the son of Michael, the son of Baaseiah,[d]
the son of Malkijah, 41 the son of Ethni,
the son of Zerah, the son of Adaiah,
42 the son of Ethan, the son of Zimmah,
the son of Shimei, 43 the son of Jahath,
the son of Gershon, the son of Levi;
44 and from their associates, the Merarites, at his left hand:
Ethan son of Kishi, the son of Abdi,
the son of Malluch, 45 the son of Hashabiah,
the son of Amaziah, the son of Hilkiah,
46 the son of Amzi, the son of Bani,
the son of Shemer, 47 the son of Mahli,
the son of Mushi, the son of Merari,
the son of Levi.

48 Their fellow Levites were assigned to all the other duties of the tabernacle, the house of God. 49 But Aaron and his descendants were the ones who presented offerings on the altar[s] of burnt offering and on the altar

[a] 26 Some Hebrew manuscripts, Septuagint and Syriac; most Hebrew manuscripts *Ahimoth* [26] *and Elkanah. The sons of Elkanah:* [b] 27 Some Septuagint manuscripts (see also 1 Samuel 1:19,20 and 1 Chron. 6:33,34); Hebrew does not have *and Samuel his son.* [c] 28 Some Septuagint manuscripts and Syriac (see also 1 Samuel 8:2 and 1 Chron. 6:33); Hebrew does not have *Joel.* [d] 40 Most Hebrew manuscripts; some Hebrew manuscripts, one Septuagint manuscript and Syriac *Maaseiah*

**6:49** t Ex 30:1–7,10
**6:56** u Jos 14:13; 15:13
**6:58** v Jos 10:3
**6:60** w Jer 1:1
**6:64** x Nu 35:1–8; Jos 21:3,41–42

of incense[t] in connection with all that was
done in the Most Holy Place, making atone-
ment for Israel, in accordance with all that
Moses the servant of God had commanded.

50 These were the descendants of Aaron:
Eleazar his son, Phinehas his son,
Abishua his son, 51 Bukki his son,
Uzzi his son, Zerahiah his son,
52 Meraioth his son, Amariah his son,
Ahitub his son, 53 Zadok his son
and Ahimaaz his son.

54 These were the locations of their settle-
ments allotted as their territory (they were
assigned to the descendants of Aaron who
were from the Kohathite clan, because the
first lot was for them):

55 They were given Hebron in Judah
with its surrounding pasturelands.
56 But the fields and villages around
the city were given to Caleb son of Je-
phunneh.[u]

57 So the descendants of Aaron were
given Hebron (a city of refuge), and
Libnah,[a] Jattir, Eshtemoa, 58 Hilen,
Debir,[v] 59 Ashan, Juttah[b] and Beth
Shemesh, together with their pasture-
lands. 60 And from the tribe of Benja-
min they were given Gibeon,[c] Geba,
Alemeth and Anathoth,[w] together
with their pasturelands.

These towns, which were distribut-
ed among the Kohathite clans, were
thirteen in all.

61 The rest of Kohath's descendants were
allotted ten towns from the clans of half the
tribe of Manasseh.

62 The descendants of Gershon, clan by
clan, were allotted thirteen towns from the
tribes of Issachar, Asher and Naphtali, and
from the part of the tribe of Manasseh that
is in Bashan.

63 The descendants of Merari, clan by
clan, were allotted twelve towns from the
tribes of Reuben, Gad and Zebulun.

64 So the Israelites gave the Levites these
towns[x] and their pasturelands. 65 From the
tribes of Judah, Simeon and Benjamin they
allotted the previously named towns.

66 Some of the Kohathite clans were given
as their territory towns from the tribe of
Ephraim.

67 In the hill country of Ephraim
they were given Shechem (a city of
refuge), and Gezer,[d] 68 Jokmeam, Beth
Horon,[y] 69 Aijalon and Gath Rimmon,
together with their pasturelands.

70 And from half the tribe of Ma-
nasseh the Israelites gave Aner and
Bileam, together with their pasture-
lands, to the rest of the Kohathite
clans.

71 The Gershonites received the follow-
ing:
From the clan of the half-tribe of Ma-
nasseh
they received Golan in Bashan
and also Ashtaroth, together with
their pasturelands;
72 from the tribe of Issachar
they received Kedesh, Daberath,
73 Ramoth and Anem, together with
their pasturelands;
74 from the tribe of Asher
they received Mashal, Abdon, 75 Hu-
kok and Rehob,[z] together with
their pasturelands;
76 and from the tribe of Naphtali
they received Kedesh in Galilee,
Hammon and Kiriathaim, together
with their pasturelands.

77 The Merarites (the rest of the Levites)
received the following:
From the tribe of Zebulun
they received Jokneam, Kartah,[e]
Rimmono and Tabor, together with
their pasturelands;
78 from the tribe of Reuben across the
Jordan east of Jericho
they received Bezer in the desert,
Jahzah, 79 Kedemoth[a] and Mepha-
ath, together with their pasture-
lands;
80 and from the tribe of Gad
they received Ramoth in Gilead,
Mahanaim, 81 Heshbon and Jazer,
together with their pasturelands.[b]

**6:68** y Jos 10:10
**6:75** z Nu 13:21
**6:79** a Dt 2:26
**6:81** b 2Ch 11:14

[a]57 See Joshua 21:13; Hebrew *given the cities of refuge: Hebron, Libnah.* [b]59 Syriac (see also Septuagint and Joshua 21:16); Hebrew does not have *Juttah.* [c]60 See Joshua 21:17; Hebrew does not have *Gibeon.* [d]67 See Joshua 21:21; Hebrew *given the cities of refuge: Shechem, Gezer.* [e]77 See Septuagint and Joshua 21:34; Hebrew does not have *Jokneam, Kartah.*

7:1
c Nu 26:23
d Ge 46:13

7:6
e Ge 46:21;
Nu 26:38;
1Ch 8:1–40

## Issachar

7 The sons of Issachar:[c]
Tola, Puah,[d] Jashub and Shimron
—four in all.
2 The sons of Tola:
Uzzi, Rephaiah, Jeriel, Jahmai, Ib-
sam and Samuel—heads of their
families. During the reign of Da-
vid, the descendants of Tola listed
as fighting men in their genealogy
numbered 22,600.
3 The son of Uzzi:
Izrahiah.
The sons of Izrahiah:
Michael, Obadiah, Joel and Isshiah.
All five of them were chiefs. 4 Ac-
cording to their family genealogy,
they had 36,000 men ready for bat-
tle, for they had many wives and
children.
5 The relatives who were fighting men
belonging to all the clans of Issa-
char, as listed in their genealogy,
were 87,000 in all.

## Benjamin

6 Three sons of Benjamin:[e]
Bela, Beker and Jediael.
7 The sons of Bela:
Ezbon, Uzzi, Uzziel, Jerimoth and
Iri, heads of families—five in all.
Their genealogical record listed
22,034 fighting men.
8 The sons of Beker:
Zemirah, Joash, Eliezer, Elioenai,
Omri, Jeremoth, Abijah, Anathoth
and Alemeth. All these were the
sons of Beker. 9 Their genealogical
record listed the heads of families
and 20,200 fighting men.
10 The son of Jediael:
Bilhan.
The sons of Bilhan:
Jeush, Benjamin, Ehud, Kenaa-
nah, Zethan, Tarshish and Ahish-
ahar. 11 All these sons of Jediael
were heads of families. There were
17,200 fighting men ready to go out
to war.
12 The Shuppites and Huppites were the
descendants of Ir, and the Hushites
the descendants of Aher.

## Naphtali

13 The sons of Naphtali:[f]
Jahziel, Guni, Jezer and Shillem[a]—
the descendants of Bilhah.

## Manasseh

14 The descendants of Manasseh:
Asriel was his descendant through
his Aramean concubine. She gave
birth to Makir the father of Gilead.[g]
15 Makir took a wife from among the
Huppites and Shuppites. His sister's
name was Maacah.
Another descendant was named Ze-
lophehad,[h] who had only daughters.
16 Makir's wife Maacah gave birth
to a son and named him Peresh. His
brother was named Sheresh, and his
sons were Ulam and Rakem.
17 The son of Ulam:
Bedan.
These were the sons of Gilead[i] son of
Makir, the son of Manasseh. 18 His
sister Hammoleketh gave birth to
Ishhod, Abiezer and Mahlah.
19 The sons of Shemida were:
Ahian, Shechem, Likhi and Aniam.

## Ephraim

20 The descendants of Ephraim:[j]
Shuthelah, Bered his son,
Tahath his son, Eleadah his son,
Tahath his son, 21 Zabad his son
and Shuthelah his son.
Ezer and Elead were killed by the
native-born men of Gath, when they
went down to seize their livestock.
22 Their father Ephraim mourned for
them many days, and his relatives
came to comfort him. 23 Then he lay
with his wife again, and she became
pregnant and gave birth to a son. He
named him Beriah,[b] because there
had been misfortune in his family.
24 His daughter was Sheerah, who built
Lower and Upper Beth Horon[k] as well
as Uzzen Sheerah.
25 Rephah was his son, Resheph his son,[c]

7:13
f Ge 46:24

7:14
g Nu 26:30

7:15
h Nu 36:1–12

7:17
i 1Sa 12:11

7:20
j Nu 26:35

7:24
k Jos 16:3,5

[a]13 Some Hebrew and Septuagint manuscripts (see also Gen. 46:24 and Num. 26:49); most Hebrew manuscripts *Shallum*
[b]23 *Beriah* sounds like the Hebrew for *misfortune.* [c]25 Some Septuagint manuscripts; Hebrew does not have *his son.*

7:28 l Jos 16:7
7:29 m Jos 17:11
7:30 n Ge 46:17; Nu 26:44
8:1 o Ge 46:21; 1Ch 7:6

Telah his son, Tahan his son,
26 Ladan his son, Ammihud his son,
Elishama his son, 27 Nun his son
and Joshua his son.
28 Their lands and settlements included
Bethel and its surrounding villages, Naaran
to the east, Gezer[l] and its villages to the
west, and Shechem and its villages all
the way to Ayyah and its villages. 29 Along
the borders of Manasseh were Beth Shan,[m]
Taanach, Megiddo and Dor, together with
their villages. The descendants of Joseph
son of Israel lived in these towns.

## Asher

30 The sons of Asher:[n]
Imnah, Ishvah, Ishvi and Beriah.
Their sister was Serah.
31 The sons of Beriah:
Heber and Malkiel, who was the father of Birzaith.
32 Heber was the father of Japhlet, Shomer and Hotham and of their sister Shua.
33 The sons of Japhlet:
Pasach, Bimhal and Ashvath.
These were Japhlet's sons.
34 The sons of Shomer:
Ahi, Rohgah,[a] Hubbah and Aram.
35 The sons of his brother Helem:
Zophah, Imna, Shelesh and Amal.
36 The sons of Zophah:
Suah, Harnepher, Shual, Beri, Imrah, 37 Bezer, Hod, Shamma, Shilshah, Ithran[b] and Beera.
38 The sons of Jether:
Jephunneh, Pispah and Ara.
39 The sons of Ulla:
Arah, Hanniel and Rizia.
40 All these were descendants of Asher—
heads of families, choice men, brave warriors and outstanding leaders. The number
of men ready for battle, as listed in their
genealogy, was 26,000.

## The Genealogy of Saul the Benjamite

8 Benjamin[o] was the father of Bela his firstborn,
Ashbel the second son, Aharah the third,
2 Nohah the fourth and Rapha the fifth.
3 The sons of Bela were:
Addar, Gera, Abihud,[c] 4 Abishua,
Naaman, Ahoah,[p] 5 Gera, Shephuphan and Huram.
6 These were the descendants of Ehud,[q]
who were heads of families of those living in Geba and were deported to Manahath:
7 Naaman, Ahijah, and Gera, who deported them and who was the father of Uzza and Ahihud.
8 Sons were born to Shaharaim in Moab
after he had divorced his wives Hushim and Baara. 9 By his wife Hodesh he had Jobab, Zibia, Mesha,
Malcam, 10 Jeuz, Sakia and Mirmah.
These were his sons, heads of families. 11 By Hushim he had Abitub
and Elpaal.
12 The sons of Elpaal:
Eber, Misham, Shemed (who built
Ono[r] and Lod with its surrounding
villages), 13 and Beriah and Shema,
who were heads of families of those
living in Aijalon and who drove out
the inhabitants of Gath.
14 Ahio, Shashak, Jeremoth, 15 Zebadiah,
Arad, Eder, 16 Michael, Ishpah and
Joha were the sons of Beriah.
17 Zebadiah, Meshullam, Hizki, Heber,
18 Ishmerai, Izliah and Jobab were
the sons of Elpaal.
19 Jakim, Zicri, Zabdi, 20 Elienai, Zillethai, Eliel, 21 Adaiah, Beraiah and
Shimrath were the sons of Shimei.
22 Ishpan, Eber, Eliel, 23 Abdon, Zicri, Hanan, 24 Hananiah, Elam, Anthothijah, 25 Iphdeiah and Penuel were the
sons of Shashak.
26 Shamsherai, Shehariah, Athaliah,
27 Jaareshiah, Elijah and Zicri were
the sons of Jeroham.
28 All these were heads of families, chiefs
as listed in their genealogy, and they lived
in Jerusalem.
29 Jeiel[d] the father[e] of Gibeon lived in
Gibeon.

8:4 p 2Sa 23:9
8:6 q 1Ch 2:52
8:12 r Ezr 2:33; Ne 6:2

[a] 34 Or *of his brother Shomer: Rohgah* [b] 37 Possibly a variant of *Jether* [c] 3 Or *Gera the father of Ehud* [d] 29 Some Septuagint manuscripts (see also 1 Chron. 9:35); Hebrew does not have *Jeiel.* [e] 29 *Father* may mean *civic leader* or *military leader.*

His wife's name was Maacah, [30]and his firstborn son was Abdon, followed by Zur, Kish, Baal, Ner,[a] Nadab, [31]Gedor, Ahio, Zeker [32]and Mikloth, who was the father of Shimeah. They too lived near their relatives in Jerusalem.

[33]Ner was the father of Kish,[s] Kish the father of Saul[t], and Saul the father of Jonathan, Malki-Shua, Abinadab and Esh-Baal.[bu]

[34]The son of Jonathan:[v]

Merib-Baal,[cw] who was the father of Micah.

[35]The sons of Micah:

Pithon, Melech, Tarea and Ahaz.

[36]Ahaz was the father of Jehoaddah, Jehoaddah was the father of Alemeth, Azmaveth and Zimri, and Zimri was the father of Moza. [37]Moza was the father of Binea; Raphah was his son, Eleasah his son and Azel his son.

[38]Azel had six sons, and these were their names:

Azrikam, Bokeru, Ishmael, Sheariah, Obadiah and Hanan. All these were the sons of Azel.

[39]The sons of his brother Eshek:

Ulam his firstborn, Jeush the second son and Eliphelet the third. [40]The sons of Ulam were brave warriors who could handle the bow. They had many sons and grandsons—150 in all.

All these were the descendants of Benjamin.

9 All Israel was listed in the genealogies recorded in the book of the kings of Israel.

## The People in Jerusalem

The people of Judah were taken captive to Babylon because of their unfaithfulness.[x] [2]Now the first to resettle on their own property in their own towns[y] were some Israelites, priests, Levites and temple servants.[z]

[3]Those from Judah, from Benjamin, and from Ephraim and Manasseh who lived in Jerusalem were:

[4]Uthai son of Ammihud, the son of Omri, the son of Imri, the son of Bani, a descendant of Perez son of Judah.[a]

[5]Of the Shilonites:

Asaiah the firstborn and his sons.

[6]Of the Zerahites:

Jeuel.

The people from Judah numbered 690.

[7]Of the Benjamites:

Sallu son of Meshullam, the son of Hodaviah, the son of Hassenuah; [8]Ibneiah son of Jeroham; Elah son of Uzzi, the son of Micri; and Meshullam son of Shephatiah, the son of Reuel, the son of Ibnijah.

[9]The people from Benjamin, as listed in their genealogy, numbered 956. All these men were heads of their families.

[10]Of the priests:

Jedaiah; Jehoiarib; Jakin;

[11]Azariah son of Hilkiah, the son of Meshullam, the son of Zadok, the son of Meraioth, the son of Ahitub, the official in charge of the house of God;

[12]Adaiah son of Jeroham, the son of Pashhur, the son of Malkijah; and Maasai son of Adiel, the son of Jahzerah, the son of Meshullam, the son of Meshillemith, the son of Immer.

[13]The priests, who were heads of families, numbered 1,760. They were able men, responsible for ministering in the house of God.

[14]Of the Levites:

Shemaiah son of Hasshub, the son of Azrikam, the son of Hashabiah, a Merarite; [15]Bakbakkar, Heresh, Galal and Mattaniah son of Mica, the son of Zicri, the son of Asaph; [16]Obadiah son of Shemaiah, the son of Galal, the son of Jeduthun; and Berekiah son of Asa, the son of Elkanah, who lived in the villages of the Netophathites.

[17]The gatekeepers:[b]

**8:33** s 1Sa 9:1 t 1Sa 14:49 u 2Sa 2:8
**8:34** v 2Sa 9:12 w 2Sa 4:4
**9:1** x 1Ch 5:25
**9:2** y Ezr 2:70 z Ezr 2:43,58; 8:20; Ne 7:60
**9:4** a Ge 46:12
**9:17** b ver 22

[a]30 Some Septuagint manuscripts (see also 1 Chron. 9:36); Hebrew does not have *Ner.* [b]33 Also known as *Ish-Bosheth*
[c]34 Also known as *Mephibosheth*

**9:18** c 1Ch 26:14; Eze 46:1
**9:19** d Jer 35:4
**9:20** e Nu 25:7–13
**9:21** f 1Ch 26:2,14
**9:25** g 2Ki 11:5; 2Ch 23:8
**9:27** h 1Ch 23:30–32
**9:29** i 1Ch 23:29
**9:30** j Ex 30:23–25

Shallum, Akkub, Talmon, Ahiman and their brothers, Shallum their chief 18 being stationed at the King's Gate[c] on the east, up to the present time. These were the gatekeepers belonging to the camp of the Levites. 19 Shallum[d] son of Kore, the son of Ebiasaph, the son of Korah, and his fellow gatekeepers from his family (the Korahites) were responsible for guarding the thresholds of the Tent[a] just as their fathers had been responsible for guarding the entrance to the dwelling of the LORD. 20 In earlier times Phinehas[e] son of Eleazar was in charge of the gatekeepers, and the LORD was with him. 21 Zechariah[f] son of Meshelemiah was the gatekeeper at the entrance to the Tent of Meeting.

22 Altogether, those chosen to be gatekeepers at the thresholds numbered 212. They were registered by genealogy in their villages. The gatekeepers had been assigned to their positions of trust by David and Samuel the seer. 23 They and their descendants were in charge of guarding the gates of the house of the LORD—the house called the Tent. 24 The gatekeepers were on the four sides: east, west, north and south. 25 Their brothers in their villages had to come from time to time and share their duties for seven-day[g] periods. 26 But the four principal gatekeepers, who were Levites, were entrusted with the responsibility for the rooms and treasuries in the house of God. 27 They would spend the night stationed around the house of God,[h] because they had to guard it; and they had charge of the key for opening it each morning.

28 Some of them were in charge of the articles used in the temple service; they counted them when they were brought in and when they were taken out. 29 Others were assigned to take care of the furnishings and all the other articles of the sanctuary,[i] as well as the flour and wine, and the oil, incense and spices. 30 But some[j] of the priests took care of mixing the spices. 31 A Levite named Mattithiah, the firstborn son of Shallum the Korahite, was entrusted with the responsibility for baking the offering bread. 32 Some of their Kohathite brothers were in charge of preparing for every Sabbath the bread set out on the table.[k]

33 Those who were musicians,[l] heads of Levite families, stayed in the rooms of the temple and were exempt from other duties because they were responsible for the work day and night.[m]

34 All these were heads of Levite families, chiefs as listed in their genealogy, and they lived in Jerusalem.

**9:32** k Lev 24:5–8
**9:33** l 1Ch 6:31; 25:1–31 m Ps 134:1
**9:35** n 1Ch 8:29
**9:39** o 1Ch 8:33

## The Genealogy of Saul

35 Jeiel[n] the father[b] of Gibeon lived in Gibeon.

His wife's name was Maacah, 36 and his firstborn son was Abdon, followed by Zur, Kish, Baal, Ner, Nadab, 37 Gedor, Ahio, Zechariah and Mikloth. 38 Mikloth was the father of Shimeam. They too lived near their relatives in Jerusalem.

39 Ner[o] was the father of Kish, Kish the father of Saul, and Saul the father of Jonathan, Malki-Shua, Abinadab and Esh-Baal.[c]

40 The son of Jonathan:

Merib-Baal,[d] who was the father of Micah.

41 The sons of Micah:

Pithon, Melech, Tahrea and Ahaz.[e]

42 Ahaz was the father of Jadah, Jadah[f] was the father of Alemeth, Azmaveth and Zimri, and Zimri was the father of Moza. 43 Moza was the father of Binea; Rephaiah was his son, Eleasah his son and Azel his son.

44 Azel had six sons, and these were their names:

Azrikam, Bokeru, Ishmael, Sheariah, Obadiah and Hanan. These were the sons of Azel.

[a] 19 That is, the temple; also in verses 21 and 23 [b] 35 *Father* may mean *civic leader* or *military leader.* [c] 39 Also known as *Ish-Bosheth* [d] 40 Also known as *Mephibosheth* [e] 41 Vulgate and Syriac (see also Septuagint and 1 Chron. 8:35); Hebrew does not have *and Ahaz.* [f] 42 Some Hebrew manuscripts and Septuagint (see also 1 Chron. 8:36); most Hebrew manuscripts *Jarah, Jarah*

# Inspire leadership FOCUS

## HUMAN RESOURCE MANAGEMENT

Human resource management can be defined as the management of people to achieve individual behavior and performance that will enhance an organization's effectiveness. As leaders in the workplace, church and home, managing people is part of our responsibilities.

Think about the enormous tasks faced by those who returned to Jerusalem after the exile. They had to reestablish homes, workplaces and government. One of the most important tasks facing them was reestablishment of the worship of God. Think about all the management issues that needed to be addressed as you read through 1 Chronicles 9. The priests and Levites mentioned in verses 10–34 were responsible not only for the offering of animal sacrifices but also for many other tasks: guarding entrances to the temple, taking care of the articles used in the temple service, maintaining the temple furnishings, mixing the spices and baking the bread used in offerings, and serving as musicians in the house of the Lord.

We all have gifts given to us by our heavenly Father—gifts that are to be used to build up and encourage the body of Christ. While these gifts are given to us individually, God does not expect us to accomplish the task of building the body individually. He wants all of our individual gifts to work together to accomplish this task.

We need to keep this principle in mind as we lead. Just as a manager working to create a manual uses one employee's strength in research, another employee's strength in writing and another employee's strength in design to create a better manual, so, too, a ministry leader should cultivate one committee member's gift of organization, another member's gift of teaching and another member's gift of hospitality to produce a powerful ministry. So, too, a mother should encourage one child's talent in music and another child's talent in sports to create a well-rounded family.

In our roles as leaders, we must remember that it is our responsibility to equip those whom God has given us to lead. We must unite them so they can work with one purpose. We must mentor and train them so they are ready for service. It takes the united talents and gifts of all the members to achieve the goal.

As a leader, successful human resource management means that as you cultivate the individual talents and gifts of those whom you lead, the contribution of each member will achieve success for the entire body.

—Y. Williams

For the next Inspire note, go to page 542.

### read

1 Chronicles 9:1–34;
1 Corinthians 12.

**See also** the Inspire Note "Leadership: Brick by Brick, Together," and the Women of the Bible Notes "Candace: Secure Leader" and "Lydia: A Model for Women in Business."

### WOMAN of COLOR

Ask God for guidance in developing the gifts, talents and strengths of the people whom he has given you to lead. Take time to determine how individual talents can contribute to the whole, and know that by working together you can achieve more than you could ever dream possible.

## Saul Takes His Life

10 Now the Philistines fought against Israel; the Israelites fled before them, and many fell slain on Mount Gilboa. [2]The Philistines pressed hard after Saul and his sons, and they killed his sons Jonathan, Abinadab and Malki-Shua. [3]The fighting grew fierce around Saul, and when the archers overtook him, they wounded him.

[4]Saul said to his armor-bearer, "Draw your sword and run me through, or these uncircumcised fellows will come and abuse me."

But his armor-bearer was terrified and would not do it; so Saul took his own sword and fell on it. [5]When the armor-bearer saw that Saul was dead, he too fell on his sword and died. [6]So Saul and his three sons died, and all his house died together.

[7]When all the Israelites in the valley saw that the army had fled and that Saul and his sons had died, they abandoned their towns and fled. And the Philistines came and occupied them.

[8]The next day, when the Philistines came to strip the dead, they found Saul and his sons fallen on Mount Gilboa. [9]They stripped him and took his head and his armor, and sent messengers throughout the land of the Philistines to proclaim the news among their idols and their people. [10]They put his armor in the temple of their gods and hung up his head in the temple of Dagon.

[11]When all the inhabitants of Jabesh Gilead heard of everything the Philistines had done to Saul, [12]all their valiant men went and took the bodies of Saul and his sons and brought them to Jabesh. Then they buried their bones under the great tree in Jabesh, and they fasted seven days.

[13]Saul died because he was unfaithful[p] to the LORD; he did not keep[q] the word of the LORD and even consulted a medium[r] for guidance, [14]and did not inquire of the LORD. So the LORD put him to death and turned[s] the kingdom[t] over to David son of Jesse.

## David Becomes King Over Israel

11 All Israel came together to David at Hebron and said, "We are your own flesh and blood. [2]In the past, even while Saul was king, you were the one who led Israel on their military campaigns. And the LORD your God said to you, 'You will shepherd[u] my people Israel, and you will become their ruler.'"

[3]When all the elders of Israel had come to King David at Hebron, he made a compact with them at Hebron before the LORD, and they anointed[v] David king over Israel, as the LORD had promised through Samuel.

## David Conquers Jerusalem

[4]David and all the Israelites marched to Jerusalem (that is, Jebus). The Jebusites[w] who lived there [5]said to David, "You will not get in here." Nevertheless, David captured the fortress of Zion, the City of David.

[6]David had said, "Whoever leads the attack on the Jebusites will become commander-in-chief." Joab[x] son of Zeruiah went up first, and so he received the command.

[7]David then took up residence in the fortress, and so it was called the City of David. [8]He built up the city around it, from the supporting terraces[a] to the surrounding wall, while Joab restored the rest of the city. [9]And David became more and more powerful,[y] because the LORD Almighty was with him.

## David's Mighty Men

[10]These were the chiefs of David's mighty men—they, together with all Israel, gave his kingship strong support to extend it over the whole land, as the LORD had promised—[11]this is the list of David's mighty men:[z]

Jashobeam,[b] a Hacmonite, was chief of the officers[c]; he raised his spear against three hundred men, whom he killed in one encounter.

[12]Next to him was Eleazar son of Dodai the Ahohite, one of the three mighty men. [13]He was with David at Pas Dammim when the Philistines gathered there for battle. At a place where there was a field full of barley, the troops fled from the Philistines. [14]But they took their stand in the middle of the field. They defended it and struck the Philistines down, and the LORD brought about a great victory.

**10:13** p 1Sa 15:23 q 1Sa 13:13 r Lev 19:31; 1Sa 28:7
**10:14** s 1Ch 12:23 t 1Sa 15:28
**11:2** u Ps 78:71
**11:3** v 1Sa 16:1–13
**11:4** w Jdg 1:21; 19:10
**11:6** x 2Sa 8:16
**11:9** y 2Sa 3:1
**11:11** z 2Sa 17:10

[a]8 Or *the Millo* [b]11 Possibly a variant of *Jashob-Baal* [c]11 Or *Thirty*; some Septuagint manuscripts *Three* (see also 2 Samuel 23:8)

11:15 a 1Ch 14:9
11:16 b 2Sa 5:17
11:20 c 1Sa 26:6
11:23 d 1Sa 17:7
11:26 e 2Sa 2:18
11:29 f 2Sa 21:18

[15]Three of the thirty chiefs came down to David to the rock at the cave of Adullam, while a band of Philistines was encamped in the Valley[a] of Rephaim. [16]At that time David was in the stronghold,[b] and the Philistine garrison was at Bethlehem. [17]David longed for water and said, "Oh, that someone would get me a drink of water from the well near the gate of Bethlehem!" [18]So the Three broke through the Philistine lines, drew water from the well near the gate of Bethlehem and carried it back to David. But he refused to drink it; instead, he poured it out before the LORD. [19]"God forbid that I should do this!" he said. "Should I drink the blood of these men who went at the risk of their lives?" Because they risked their lives to bring it back, David would not drink it.

Such were the exploits of the three mighty men.

[20]Abishai[c] the brother of Joab was chief of the Three. He raised his spear against three hundred men, whom he killed, and so he became as famous as the Three. [21]He was doubly honored above the Three and became their commander, even though he was not included among them.

[22]Benaiah son of Jehoiada was a valiant fighter from Kabzeel, who performed great exploits. He struck down two of Moab's best men. He also went down into a pit on a snowy day and killed a lion. [23]And he struck down an Egyptian who was seven and a half feet[a] tall. Although the Egyptian had a spear like a weaver's rod[d] in his hand, Benaiah went against him with a club. He snatched the spear from the Egyptian's hand and killed him with his own spear. [24]Such were the exploits of Benaiah son of Jehoiada; he too was as famous as the three mighty men. [25]He was held in greater honor than any of the Thirty, but he was not included among the Three. And David put him in charge of his bodyguard.

[26]The mighty men were:
Asahel[e] the brother of Joab,
Elhanan son of Dodo from Bethlehem,
[27]Shammoth the Harorite,
Helez the Pelonite,
[28]Ira son of Ikkesh from Tekoa,
Abiezer from Anathoth,
[29]Sibbecai[f] the Hushathite,
Ilai the Ahohite,
[30]Maharai the Netophathite,
Heled son of Baanah the Netophathite,
[31]Ithai son of Ribai from Gibeah in Benjamin,
Benaiah the Pirathonite,
[32]Hurai from the ravines of Gaash,
Abiel the Arbathite,
[33]Azmaveth the Baharumite,
Eliahba the Shaalbonite,
[34]the sons of Hashem the Gizonite,
Jonathan son of Shagee the Hararite,
[35]Ahiam son of Sacar the Hararite,
Eliphal son of Ur,

[a]23 Hebrew *five cubits* (about 2.3 meters)

## The African Presence

### 1 Chronicles 11

Reference is made to the Jebusites, Philistines, Perizzites and Hivites—all of whom were descendants of Ham (see Ge 10:6–19). Because Ham's offspring represent the geographic territories once dominated by Egypt—present-day Egypt, Libya and Sudan and into the area today known as Israel—they can claim a relation to African heritage. Since "heritage" is something "passed down" or "inherited," Canaan (Israel or Palestine) most certainly received or was influenced by Egypt culturally, politically, religiously, etc.

**11:41** g 2Sa 11:6
**12:1** h 1Sa 27:2–6
**12:2** i Jdg 3:15; 20:16

36 Hepher the Mekerathite,
Ahijah the Pelonite,
37 Hezro the Carmelite,
Naarai son of Ezbai,
38 Joel the brother of Nathan,
Mibhar son of Hagri,
39 Zelek the Ammonite,
Naharai the Berothite, the armor-bearer of Joab son of Zeruiah,
40 Ira the Ithrite,
Gareb the Ithrite,
41 Uriah[g] the Hittite,
Zabad son of Ahlai,
42 Adina son of Shiza the Reubenite, who was chief of the Reubenites, and the thirty with him,
43 Hanan son of Maacah,
Joshaphat the Mithnite,
44 Uzzia the Ashterathite,
Shama and Jeiel the sons of Hotham the Aroerite,
45 Jediael son of Shimri,
his brother Joha the Tizite,
46 Eliel the Mahavite,
Jeribai and Joshaviah the sons of Elnaam,
Ithmah the Moabite,
47 Eliel, Obed and Jaasiel the Mezobaite.

## Warriors Join David

12 These were the men who came to David at Ziklag,[h] while he was banished from the presence of Saul son of Kish (they were among the warriors who helped him in battle;
2 they were armed with bows and were able to shoot arrows or to sling stones right-handed or left-handed;[i] they were kinsmen of Saul from the tribe of Benjamin):

3 Ahiezer their chief and Joash the sons of Shemaah the Gibeathite; Jeziel and Pelet the sons of Azmaveth; Beracah, Jehu the Anathothite,
4 and Ishmaiah the Gibeonite, a mighty man among the Thirty, who was a leader of the Thirty; Jeremiah, Jahaziel, Johanan, Jozabad the Gederathite,
5 Eluzai, Jerimoth, Bealiah, Shemariah and Shephatiah the Haruphite;
6 Elkanah, Isshiah, Azarel, Joezer and Jashobeam the Korahites;
7 and Joelah and Zebadiah the sons of Jeroham from Gedor.

8 Some Gadites defected to David at his stronghold in the desert. They were brave warriors, ready for battle and able to handle the shield and spear. Their faces were the faces of lions,[j] and they were as swift as gazelles[k] in the mountains.

9 Ezer was the chief,
Obadiah the second in command, Eliab the third,
10 Mishmannah the fourth, Jeremiah the fifth,
11 Attai the sixth, Eliel the seventh,
12 Johanan the eighth, Elzabad the ninth,
13 Jeremiah the tenth and Macbannai the eleventh.

14 These Gadites were army commanders; the least was a match for a hundred, and the greatest for a thousand.[l]
15 It was they who crossed the Jordan in the first month when it was overflowing all its banks,[m] and they put to flight everyone living in the valleys, to the east and to the west.

16 Other Benjamites and some men from Judah also came to David in his stronghold.
17 David went out to meet them and said to them, "If you have come to me in peace, to help me, I am ready to have you unite with me. But if you have come to betray me to my enemies when my hands are free from violence, may the God of our fathers see it and judge you."

18 Then the Spirit[n] came upon Amasai,[o] chief of the Thirty, and he said:

"We are yours, O David!
We are with you, O son of Jesse!
Success, success to you,
and success to those who help you,
for your God will help you."

So David received them and made them leaders of his raiding bands.

19 Some of the men of Manasseh defected to David when he went with the Philistines to fight against Saul. (He and his men did not help the Philistines because, after consultation, their rulers sent him away. They said, "It will cost us our heads if he deserts to his master Saul.")[p]
20 When David went to Ziklag, these were the men of Manasseh who

**12:8** j 2Sa 17:10 k 2Sa 2:18
**12:14** l Dt 32:30
**12:15** m Jos 3:15
**12:18** n Jdg 6:34 o 2Sa 17:25
**12:19** p 1Sa 29:2–11

**12:23** q 2Sa 2:3–4 r 1Ch 10:14 s 1Sa 16:1
**12:28** t 2Sa 8:17
**12:29** u 2Sa 2:8–9
**12:32** v Est 1:13

defected to him: Adnah, Jozabad, Jediael, Michael, Jozabad, Elihu and Zillethai, leaders of units of a thousand in Manasseh. 21 They helped David against raiding bands, for all of them were brave warriors, and they were commanders in his army. 22 Day after day men came to help David, until he had a great army, like the army of God.[a]

## Others Join David at Hebron

23 These are the numbers of the men armed for battle who came to David at Hebron[q] to turn[r] Saul's kingdom over to him, as the LORD had said:[s]

24 men of Judah, carrying shield and spear—6,800 armed for battle;
25 men of Simeon, warriors ready for battle—7,100;
26 men of Levi—4,600, 27 including Jehoiada, leader of the family of Aaron, with 3,700 men, 28 and Zadok,[t] a brave young warrior, with 22 officers from his family;
29 men of Benjamin, Saul's kinsmen—3,000, most[u] of whom had remained loyal to Saul's house until then;
30 men of Ephraim, brave warriors, famous in their own clans—20,800;
31 men of half the tribe of Manasseh, designated by name to come and make David king—18,000;
32 men of Issachar, who understood the times and knew what Israel should do[v]—200 chiefs, with all their relatives under their command;
33 men of Zebulun, experienced soldiers prepared for battle with every type of weapon, to help David with undivided loyalty—50,000;
34 men of Naphtali—1,000 officers, together with 37,000 men carrying shields and spears;
35 men of Dan, ready for battle—28,600;
36 men of Asher, experienced soldiers prepared for battle—40,000;
37 and from east of the Jordan, men of Reuben, Gad and the half-tribe of Manasseh, armed with every type of weapon—120,000.

38 All these were fighting men who volunteered to serve in the ranks. They came to Hebron fully determined to make David king over all Israel.[w] All the rest of the Israelites were also of one mind to make David king. 39 The men spent three days there with David, eating and drinking, for their families had supplied provisions for them. 40 Also, their neighbors from as far away as Issachar, Zebulun and Naphtali came bringing food on donkeys, camels, mules and oxen. There were plentiful supplies of flour, fig cakes, raisin[x] cakes, wine, oil, cattle and sheep, for there was joy in Israel.

## Bringing Back the Ark

**13** David conferred with each of his officers, the commanders of thousands and commanders of hundreds. 2 He then said to the whole assembly of Israel, "If it seems good to you and if it is the will of the LORD our God, let us send word far and wide to the rest of our brothers throughout the territories of Israel, and also to the priests and Levites who are with them in their towns and pasturelands, to come and join us. 3 Let us bring the ark of our God back to us,[y] for we did not inquire of[b] it[c] during the reign of Saul." 4 The whole assembly agreed to do this, because it seemed right to all the people.

5 So David assembled all the Israelites,[z] from the Shihor River in Egypt to Lebo[d] Hamath, to bring the ark of God from Kiriath Jearim.[a] 6 David and all the Israelites with him went to Baalah[b] of Judah (Kiriath Jearim) to bring up from there the ark of God the LORD, who is enthroned between the cherubim[c]—the ark that is called by the Name.

7 They moved the ark of God from Abinadab's[d] house on a new cart, with Uzzah and Ahio guiding it. 8 David and all the Israelites were celebrating with all their might before God, with songs and with harps, lyres, tambourines, cymbals and trumpets.[e]

9 When they came to the threshing floor of Kidon, Uzzah reached out his hand to steady the ark, because the oxen stumbled. 10 The LORD's anger[f] burned against Uzzah, and he struck him down[g] because he had put his hand on the ark. So he died there before God.

11 Then David was angry because the

**12:38** w 2Sa 5:1–3
**12:40** x 1Sa 25:18
**13:3** y 1Sa 7:1–2
**13:5** z 1Ch 15:3 a 1Sa 6:21; 7:2
**13:6** b Jos 15:9; 2Sa 6:2 c 2Ki 19:15
**13:7** d Nu 4:15; 1Sa 7:1
**13:8** e 2Sa 6:5
**13:10** f 1Ch 15:13,15 g Lev 10:2

[a] 22 Or *a great and mighty army* [b] 3 Or *we neglected* [c] 3 Or *him* [d] 5 Or *to the entrance to*

**13:14** h 1Ch 26:4–5
**14:4** i 1Ch 3:9
**14:9** j 1Ch 11:15
**14:13** k ver 9

LORD's wrath had broken out against Uzzah, and to this day that place is called Perez Uzzah.[a]

12 David was afraid of God that day and asked, "How can I ever bring the ark of God to me?" 13 He did not take the ark to be with him in the City of David. Instead, he took it aside to the house of Obed-Edom the Gittite. 14 The ark of God remained with the family of Obed-Edom in his house for three months, and the LORD blessed his household[h] and everything he had.

## David's House and Family

14 Now Hiram king of Tyre sent messengers to David, along with cedar logs, stonemasons and carpenters to build a palace for him. 2 And David knew that the LORD had established him as king over Israel and that his kingdom had been highly exalted for the sake of his people Israel.

3 In Jerusalem David took more wives and became the father of more sons and daughters. 4 These are the names of the children born to him there:[i] Shammua, Shobab, Nathan, Solomon, 5 Ibhar, Elishua, Elpelet, 6 Nogah, Nepheg, Japhia, 7 Elishama, Beeliada[b] and Eliphelet.

## David Defeats the Philistines

8 When the Philistines heard that David had been anointed king over all Israel, they went up in full force to search for him, but David heard about it and went out to meet them. 9 Now the Philistines had come and raided the Valley[j] of Rephaim; 10 so David inquired of God: "Shall I go and attack the Philistines? Will you hand them over to me?"

The LORD answered him, "Go, I will hand them over to you."

11 So David and his men went up to Baal Perazim, and there he defeated them. He said, "As waters break out, God has broken out against my enemies by my hand." So that place was called Baal Perazim.[c] 12 The Philistines had abandoned their gods there, and David gave orders to burn them in the fire.

13 Once more the Philistines raided the valley;[k] 14 so David inquired of God again, and God answered him, "Do not go straight up, but circle around them and attack them in front of the balsam trees. 15 As soon as you hear the sound of marching in the tops of the balsam trees, move out to battle, because that will mean God has gone out in front of you to strike the Philistine army." 16 So David did as God commanded him, and they struck down the Philistine army, all the way from Gibeon to Gezer.

17 So David's fame[l] spread throughout every land, and the LORD made all the nations fear[m] him.

## The Ark Brought to Jerusalem

15 After David had constructed buildings for himself in the City of David, he prepared a place for the ark of God and pitched[n] a tent for it. 2 Then David said, "No one but the Levites[o] may carry the ark of God, because the LORD chose them to carry the ark of the LORD and to minister before him forever."

3 David assembled all Israel[p] in Jerusalem to bring up the ark of the LORD to the place he had prepared for it. 4 He called together the descendants of Aaron and the Levites:

5 From the descendants of Kohath,
Uriel the leader and 120 relatives;
6 from the descendants of Merari,
Asaiah the leader and 220 relatives;
7 from the descendants of Gershon,[d]
Joel the leader and 130 relatives;
8 from the descendants of Elizaphan,
Shemaiah the leader and 200 relatives;
9 from the descendants of Hebron,
Eliel the leader and 80 relatives;
10 from the descendants of Uzziel,
Amminadab the leader and 112 relatives.

11 Then David summoned Zadok and Abiathar the priests, and Uriel, Asaiah, Joel, Shemaiah, Eliel and Amminadab the Levites. 12 He said to them, "You are the heads of the Levitical families; you and your fellow Levites are to consecrate yourselves and bring up the ark of the LORD, the God of Israel, to the place I have prepared for it. 13 It was because you, the Levites, did not

**14:17** l Jos 6:27 m Dt 2:25
**15:1** n 1Ch 16:1
**15:2** o Nu 4:15; Dt 10:8
**15:3** p 1Ki 8:1; 1Ch 13:5

[a] 11 *Perez Uzzah* means *outbreak against Uzzah.* [b] 7 A variant of *Eliada* [c] 11 *Baal Perazim* means *the lord who breaks out.*
[d] 7 Hebrew *Gershom,* a variant of *Gershon*

bring it up the first time that the LORD our God broke out in anger against us.[q] We did not inquire of him about how to do it in the prescribed way." 14 So the priests and Levites consecrated themselves in order to bring up the ark of the LORD, the God of Israel. 15 And the Levites carried the ark of God with the poles on their shoulders, as Moses had commanded[r] in accordance with the word of the LORD.

16 David told the leaders of the Levites to appoint their brothers as singers to sing joyful songs, accompanied by musical instruments: lyres, harps and cymbals.[s]

17 So the Levites appointed Heman[t] son of Joel; from his brothers, Asaph[u] son of Berekiah; and from their brothers the Merarites,[v] Ethan son of Kushaiah; 18 and with them their brothers next in rank: Zechariah,[a] Jaaziel, Shemiramoth, Jehiel, Unni, Eliab, Benaiah, Maaseiah, Mattithiah, Eliphelehu, Mikneiah, Obed-Edom and Jeiel,[b] the gatekeepers.

19 The musicians Heman, Asaph and Ethan were to sound the bronze cymbals; 20 Zechariah, Aziel, Shemiramoth, Jehiel, Unni, Eliab, Maaseiah and Benaiah were to play the lyres according to *alamoth*,[c] 21 and Mattithiah, Eliphelehu, Mikneiah, Obed-Edom, Jeiel and Azaziah were to play the harps, directing according to *sheminith*.[c] 22 Kenaniah the head Levite was in charge of the singing; that was his responsibility because he was skillful at it.

23 Berekiah and Elkanah were to be doorkeepers for the ark. 24 Shebaniah, Joshaphat, Nethanel, Amasai, Zechariah, Benaiah and Eliezer the priests were to blow trumpets[w] before the ark of God. Obed-Edom and Jehiah were also to be doorkeepers for the ark.

25 So David and the elders of Israel and the commanders of units of a thousand went to bring up the ark[x] of the covenant of the LORD from the house of Obed-Edom, with rejoicing. 26 Because God had helped the Levites who were carrying the ark of the covenant of the LORD, seven bulls and seven rams were sacrificed. 27 Now David was clothed in a robe of fine linen, as were all the Levites who were carrying the ark, and as were the singers, and Kenaniah, who was in charge of the singing of the choirs. David also wore a linen ephod. 28 So all Israel brought up the ark of the covenant of the LORD with shouts, with the sounding of rams' horns and trumpets, and of cymbals, and the playing of lyres and harps.

29 As the ark of the covenant of the LORD was entering the City of David, Michal daughter of Saul watched from a window. And when she saw King David dancing and celebrating, she despised him in her heart.

16 They brought the ark of God and set it inside the tent that David had pitched[y] for it, and they presented burnt offerings and fellowship offerings[d] before God. 2 After David had finished sacrificing the burnt offerings and fellowship offerings, he blessed the people in the name of the LORD. 3 Then he gave a loaf of bread, a cake of dates and a cake of raisins to each Israelite man and woman.

4 He appointed some of the Levites to minister before the ark of the LORD, to make petition, to give thanks, and to praise the LORD, the God of Israel: 5 Asaph was the chief, Zechariah second, then Jeiel, Shemiramoth, Jehiel, Mattithiah, Eliab, Benaiah, Obed-Edom and Jeiel. They were to play the lyres and harps, Asaph was to sound the cymbals, 6 and Benaiah and Jahaziel the priests were to blow the trumpets regularly before the ark of the covenant of God.

## David's Psalm of Thanks

7 That day David first committed to Asaph and his associates this psalm[z] of thanks to the LORD:

8 Give thanks to the LORD, call on his name;
make known among the nations[a] what he has done.
9 Sing to him, sing praise to him;
tell of all his wonderful acts.
10 Glory in his holy name;
let the hearts of those who seek the LORD rejoice.
11 Look to the LORD and his strength;
seek[b] his face always.
12 Remember the wonders he has done,

15:13 q 2Sa 6:3; 1Ch 13:7–10
15:15 r Ex 25:14
15:16 s 1Ch 25:1
15:17 t 1Ch 6:33 u 1Ch 6:39 v 1Ch 6:44
15:24 w ver 28; 1Ch 16:6
15:25 x 1Ch 13:13
16:1 y 1Ch 15:1
16:7 z 2Sa 23:1
16:8 a 2Ki 19:19
16:11 b Ps 24:6

[a] 18 Three Hebrew manuscripts and most Septuagint manuscripts (see also verse 20 and 1 Chron. 16:5); most Hebrew manuscripts *Zechariah son and* or *Zechariah, Ben and* [b] 18 Hebrew; Septuagint (see also verse 21) *Jeiel and Azaziah* [c] 20,21 Probably a musical term [d] 1 Traditionally *peace offerings*; also in verse 2

his miracles,[c] and the judgments he
pronounced,
[13] O descendants of Israel his servant,
O sons of Jacob, his chosen ones.
[14] He is the LORD our God;
his judgments are in all the earth.
[15] He remembers[a] his covenant forever,
the word he commanded, for a
thousand generations,
[16] the covenant[d] he made with Abraham,
the oath he swore to Isaac.
[17] He confirmed it to Jacob[e] as a decree,
to Israel as an everlasting covenant:
[18] "To you I will give the land of Canaan[f]
as the portion you will inherit."
[19] When they were but few in number,[g]
few indeed, and strangers in it,
[20] they[b] wandered from nation to nation,
from one kingdom to another.
[21] He allowed no man to oppress them;
for their sake he rebuked kings:[h]
[22] "Do not touch my anointed ones;
do my prophets no harm."
[23] Sing to the LORD, all the earth;
proclaim his salvation day after day.
[24] Declare his glory among the nations,
his marvelous deeds among all
peoples.
[25] For great is the LORD and most worthy of
praise;
he is to be feared[i] above all gods.
[26] For all the gods of the nations are idols,
but the LORD made the heavens.[j]
[27] Splendor and majesty are before him;
strength and joy in his dwelling place.
[28] Ascribe to the LORD, O families of nations,
ascribe to the LORD glory and
strength,[k]
[29] ascribe to the LORD the glory due his
name.
Bring an offering and come before him;
worship the LORD in the splendor of
his[c] holiness.
[30] Tremble before him, all the earth!
The world is firmly established; it
cannot be moved.
[31] Let the heavens rejoice, let the earth be
glad;[l]
let them say among the nations, "The
LORD reigns![m]"
[32] Let the sea resound, and all that is in it;[n]
let the fields be jubilant, and
everything in them!
[33] Then the trees of the forest will sing,
they will sing for joy before the LORD,
for he comes to judge the earth.
[34] Give thanks to the LORD, for he is good;
his love endures forever.[o]
[35] Cry out, "Save us, O God our Savior;
gather us and deliver us from the
nations,
that we may give thanks to your holy
name,
that we may glory in your praise."
[36] Praise be to the LORD, the God of Israel,[p]
from everlasting to everlasting.

Then all the people said "Amen" and "Praise
the LORD."

[37] David left Asaph and his associates be-
fore the ark of the covenant of the LORD to
minister there regularly, according to each
day's requirements.[q] [38] He also left Obed-
Edom[r] and his sixty-eight associates to
minister with them. Obed-Edom son of Je-
duthun, and also Hosah,[s] were gatekeepers.

[39] David left Zadok the priest and his fel-
low priests before the tabernacle of the LORD
at the high place in Gibeon[t] [40] to present
burnt offerings to the LORD on the altar of
burnt offering regularly, morning and eve-
ning, in accordance with everything writ-
ten in the Law[u] of the LORD, which he had
given Israel. [41] With them were Heman[v] and
Jeduthun and the rest of those chosen and
designated by name to give thanks to the
LORD, "for his love endures forever." [42] He-
man and Jeduthun were responsible for the
sounding of the trumpets and cymbals and
for the playing of the other instruments for
sacred song.[w] The sons of Jeduthun were sta-
tioned at the gate.

[43] Then all the people left, each for his
own home, and David returned home to
bless his family.

**16:12** c Ps 78:43
**16:16** d Ge 17:2; 26:3
**16:17** e Ge 35:9–12
**16:18** f Ge 13:14–17
**16:19** g Ge 34:30
**16:21** h Ge 12:17; 20:3; Ex 7:15–18
**16:25** i Ps 89:7
**16:26** j Lev 19:4
**16:28** k Ps 29:1–2
**16:31** l Isa 49:13
**16:31** m Ps 93:1
**16:32** n Ps 98:7
**16:34** o Ezr 3:11; Ps 136:1–26; Jer 33:11
**16:36** p Dt 27:15; 1Ki 8:15; Ps 72:18–19
**16:37** q 2Ch 8:14
**16:38** r 1Ch 13:13 s 1Ch 26:10
**16:39** t 1Ki 3:4; 2Ch 1:3
**16:40** u Ex 29:38; Nu 28:1–8
**16:41** v 2Ch 5:13
**16:42** w 2Ch 7:6

[a] 15 Some Septuagint manuscripts (see also Psalm 105:8); Hebrew *Remember* [b] 18–20 One Hebrew manuscript, Septuagint and Vulgate (see also Psalm 105:12); most Hebrew manuscripts *inherit, / [19] though you are but few in number, / few indeed, and strangers in it." / [20] They* [c] 29 Or *LORD with the splendor of*

17:4 x 1Ch 28:3
17:7 y 2Sa 6:21
17:10 z Jdg 2:16
17:13 a 2Co 6:18

## God's Promise to David

17 After David was settled in his palace, he said to Nathan the prophet, "Here I am, living in a palace of cedar, while the ark of the covenant of the LORD is under a tent."

2 Nathan replied to David, "Whatever you have in mind, do it, for God is with you."

3 That night the word of God came to Nathan, saying:

4 "Go and tell my servant David, 'This is what the LORD says: You[x] are not the one to build me a house to dwell in. 5 I have not dwelt in a house from the day I brought Israel up out of Egypt to this day. I have moved from one tent site to another, from one dwelling place to another. 6 Wherever I have moved with all the Israelites, did I ever say to any of their leaders[a] whom I commanded to shepherd my people, "Why have you not built me a house of cedar?"'

7 "Now then, tell my servant David, 'This is what the LORD Almighty says: I took you from the pasture and from following the flock, to be ruler[y] over my people Israel. 8 I have been with you wherever you have gone, and I have cut off all your enemies from before you. Now I will make your name like the names of the greatest men of the earth. 9 And I will provide a place for my people Israel and will plant them so that they can have a home of their own and no longer be disturbed. Wicked people will not oppress them anymore, as they did at the beginning 10 and have done ever since the time I appointed leaders[z] over my people Israel. I will also subdue all your enemies.

"'I declare to you that the LORD will build a house for you: 11 When your days are over and you go to be with your fathers, I will raise up your offspring to succeed you, one of your own sons, and I will establish his kingdom. 12 He is the one who will build a house for me, and I will establish his throne forever. 13 I will be his father,[a] and he will be my son.[b] I will never take my love away from him, as I took it away from your predecessor. 14 I will set him over my house and my kingdom forever; his throne[c] will be established forever.[d]'"

15 Nathan reported to David all the words of this entire revelation.

## David's Prayer

16 Then King David went in and sat before the LORD, and he said:

"Who am I, O LORD God, and what is my family, that you have brought me this far? 17 And as if this were not enough in your sight, O God, you have spoken about the future of the house of your servant. You have looked on me as though I were the most exalted of men, O LORD God.

18 "What more can David say to you for honoring your servant? For you know your servant, 19 O LORD. For the sake[e] of your servant and according to your will, you have done this great thing and made known all these great promises.[f]

20 "There is no one like you, O LORD, and there is no God but you,[g] as we have heard with our own ears. 21 And who is like your people Israel—the one nation on earth whose God went out to redeem[h] a people for himself, and to make a name for yourself, and to perform great and awesome wonders by driving out nations from before your people, whom you redeemed from Egypt? 22 You made your people Israel your very own forever,[i] and you, O LORD, have become their God.

23 "And now, LORD, let the promise you have made concerning your servant and his house be established forever. Do as you promised, 24 so that it will be established and that your name will be great forever. Then men will say, 'The LORD Almighty, the God over Israel, is Israel's God!' And the house of your servant David will be established before you.

17:13 b Heb 1:5*
17:14 c 1Ki 2:12 d Jer 33:17
17:19 e Isa 37:35 f 2Sa 7:25
17:20 g Ex 9:14; Isa 44:6
17:21 h Ex 6:6
17:22 i Ex 19:5–6

[a]6 Traditionally *judges*; also in verse 10

25"You, my God, have revealed to your servant that you will build a house for him. So your servant has found courage to pray to you. 26O LORD, you are God! You have promised these good things to your servant. 27Now you have been pleased to bless the house of your servant, that it may continue forever in your sight;[j] for you, O LORD, have blessed it, and it will be blessed forever."

## David's Victories

18 In the course of time, David defeated the Philistines and subdued them, and he took Gath and its surrounding villages from the control of the Philistines.

2David also defeated the Moabites, and they became subject to him and brought tribute.

3Moreover, David fought Hadadezer king of Zobah, as far as Hamath, when he went to establish his control along the Euphrates River. 4David captured a thousand of his chariots, seven thousand charioteers and twenty thousand foot soldiers. He hamstrung all but a hundred of the chariot horses.

5When the Arameans of Damascus[k] came to help Hadadezer king of Zobah, David struck down twenty-two thousand of them. 6He put garrisons in the Aramean kingdom of Damascus, and the Arameans became subject to him and brought tribute. The LORD gave David victory everywhere he went.

7David took the gold shields carried by the officers of Hadadezer and brought them to Jerusalem. 8From Tebah[a] and Cun, towns that belonged to Hadadezer, David took a great quantity of bronze, which Solomon used to make the bronze Sea,[l] the pillars and various bronze articles.

9When Tou king of Hamath heard that David had defeated the entire army of Hadadezer king of Zobah, 10he sent his son Hadoram to King David to greet him and congratulate him on his victory in battle over Hadadezer, who had been at war with Tou. Hadoram brought all kinds of articles of gold and silver and bronze.

11King David dedicated these articles to the LORD, as he had done with the silver and gold he had taken from all these nations: Edom and Moab, the Ammonites and the Philistines, and Amalek.

12Abishai son of Zeruiah struck down eighteen thousand Edomites[m] in the Valley of Salt. 13He put garrisons in Edom, and all the Edomites became subject to David. The LORD gave David victory everywhere he went.

## David's Officials

14David reigned over all Israel,[n] doing what was just and right for all his people. 15Joab[o] son of Zeruiah was over the army; Jehoshaphat son of Ahilud was recorder; 16Zadok[p] son of Ahitub and Ahimelech[b][q] son of Abiathar were priests; Shavsha was secretary; 17Benaiah son of Jehoiada was over the Kerethites and Pelethites;[r] and David's sons were chief officials at the king's side.

## The Battle Against the Ammonites

19 In the course of time, Nahash king of the Ammonites[s] died, and his son succeeded him as king. 2David thought, "I will show kindness to Hanun son of Nahash, because his father showed kindness to me." So David sent a delegation to express his sympathy to Hanun concerning his father.

When David's men came to Hanun in the land of the Ammonites to express sympathy to him, 3the Ammonite nobles said to Hanun, "Do you think David is honoring your father by sending men to you to express sympathy? Haven't his men come to you to explore and spy out[t] the country and overthrow it?" 4So Hanun seized David's men, shaved them, cut off their garments in the middle at the buttocks, and sent them away.

5When someone came and told David about the men, he sent messengers to meet them, for they were greatly humiliated. The king said, "Stay at Jericho till your beards have grown, and then come back."

6When the Ammonites realized that they had become a stench in David's nostrils, Ha-

**17:27** j Ps 21:6
**18:5** k 1Ch 19:6
**18:8** l 1Ki 7:23; 2Ch 4:12,15–16
**18:12** m 1Ki 11:15
**18:14** n 1Ch 11:1
**18:15** o 1Ch 11:6
**18:16** p 2Sa 8:17; q 1Ch 24:6
**18:17** r 2Sa 8:18
**19:1** s Ge 19:38
**19:3** t Nu 21:32

[a]8 Hebrew *Tibhath,* a variant of *Tebah* [b]16 Some Hebrew manuscripts, Vulgate and Syriac (see also 2 Samuel 8:17); most Hebrew manuscripts *Abimelech*

**19:6** u 1Ch 18:3,5,9
**19:7** v Nu 21:30; Jos 13:9,16
**19:11** w 1Sa 26:6

nun and the Ammonites sent a thousand talents[a] of silver to hire chariots and charioteers from Aram Naharaim,[b] Aram Maacah and Zobah.[u] [7]They hired thirty-two thousand chariots and charioteers, as well as the king of Maacah with his troops, who came and camped near Medeba,[v] while the Ammonites were mustered from their towns and moved out for battle.

[8]On hearing this, David sent Joab out with the entire army of fighting men. [9]The Ammonites came out and drew up in battle formation at the entrance to their city, while the kings who had come were by themselves in the open country.

[10]Joab saw that there were battle lines in front of him and behind him; so he selected some of the best troops in Israel and deployed them against the Arameans. [11]He put the rest of the men under the command of Abishai[w] his brother, and they were deployed against the Ammonites. [12]Joab said, "If the Arameans are too strong for me, then you are to rescue me; but if the Ammonites are too strong for you, then I will rescue you. [13]Be strong and let us fight bravely for our people and the cities of our God. The LORD will do what is good in his sight."

[14]Then Joab and the troops with him advanced to fight the Arameans, and they fled before him. [15]When the Ammonites saw that the Arameans were fleeing, they too fled before his brother Abishai and went inside the city. So Joab went back to Jerusalem.

[16]After the Arameans saw that they had been routed by Israel, they sent messengers and had Arameans brought from beyond the River,[c] with Shophach the commander of Hadadezer's army leading them.

[17]When David was told of this, he gathered all Israel and crossed the Jordan; he advanced against them and formed his battle lines opposite them. David formed his lines to meet the Arameans in battle, and they fought against him. [18]But they fled before Israel, and David killed seven thousand of their charioteers and forty thousand of their foot soldiers. He also killed Shophach the commander of their army.

[19]When the vassals of Hadadezer saw that they had been defeated by Israel, they made peace with David and became subject to him.

So the Arameans were not willing to help the Ammonites anymore.

**20:1** x 2Sa 12:26
**20:5** y 1Sa 17:7
**21:1** z 2Ch 18:21

## The Capture of Rabbah

**20** In the spring, at the time when kings go off to war, Joab led out the armed forces. He laid waste the land of the Ammonites and went to Rabbah[x] and besieged it, but David remained in Jerusalem. Joab attacked Rabbah and left it in ruins. [2]David took the crown from the head of their king[d]—its weight was found to be a talent[e] of gold, and it was set with precious stones—and it was placed on David's head. He took a great quantity of plunder from the city [3]and brought out the people who were there, consigning them to labor with saws and with iron picks and axes. David did this to all the Ammonite towns. Then David and his entire army returned to Jerusalem.

## War With the Philistines

[4]In the course of time, war broke out with the Philistines, at Gezer. At that time Sibbecai the Hushathite killed Sippai, one of the descendants of the Rephaites, and the Philistines were subjugated.

[5]In another battle with the Philistines, Elhanan son of Jair killed Lahmi the brother of Goliath the Gittite, who had a spear with a shaft like a weaver's rod.[y]

[6]In still another battle, which took place at Gath, there was a huge man with six fingers on each hand and six toes on each foot—twenty-four in all. He also was descended from Rapha. [7]When he taunted Israel, Jonathan son of Shimea, David's brother, killed him.

[8]These were descendants of Rapha in Gath, and they fell at the hands of David and his men.

## David Numbers the Fighting Men

**21** Satan[z] rose up against Israel and incited David to take a census of Israel. [2]So David said to Joab and the

[a]6 That is, about 37 tons (about 34 metric tons) [b]6 That is, Northwest Mesopotamia [c]16 That is, the Euphrates [d]2 Or *of Milcom,* that is, Molech [e]2 That is, about 75 pounds (about 34 kilograms)

commanders of the troops, "Go and count[a] the Israelites from Beersheba to Dan. Then report back to me so that I may know how many there are."

3 But Joab replied, "May the LORD multiply his troops a hundred times over.[b] My lord the king, are they not all my lord's subjects? Why does my lord want to do this? Why should he bring guilt on Israel?"

4 The king's word, however, overruled Joab; so Joab left and went throughout Israel and then came back to Jerusalem. 5 Joab reported the number of the fighting men to David: In all Israel there were one million one hundred thousand men who could handle a sword, including four hundred and seventy thousand in Judah.

---

Dear God,

*I need you to help me resist temptation.*

*Help me to rely on you for everything,*

*including the resolve to overcome*

*the lure of evil. I love you.*

Amen

1 CHRONICLES 21:1–5

---

6 But Joab did not include Levi and Benjamin in the numbering, because the king's command was repulsive to him. 7 This command was also evil in the sight of God; so he punished Israel.

8 Then David said to God, "I have sinned greatly by doing this. Now, I beg you, take away the guilt of your servant. I have done a very foolish thing."

9 The LORD said to Gad, David's seer,[c] 10 "Go and tell David, 'This is what the LORD says: I am giving you three options. Choose one of them for me to carry out against you.'"

11 So Gad went to David and said to him, "This is what the LORD says: 'Take your choice: 12 three years of famine,[d] three months of being swept away[a] before your enemies, with their swords overtaking you, or three days of the sword of the LORD—days of plague in the land, with the angel of the LORD ravaging every part of Israel.' Now then, decide how I should answer the one who sent me."

13 David said to Gad, "I am in deep distress. Let me fall into the hands of the LORD, for his mercy[e] is very great; but do not let me fall into the hands of men."

14 So the LORD sent a plague on Israel, and seventy thousand men of Israel fell dead.[f] 15 And God sent an angel to destroy Jerusalem. But as the angel was doing so, the LORD saw it and was grieved[g] because of the calamity and said to the angel who was destroying the people, "Enough! Withdraw your hand." The angel of the LORD was then standing at the threshing floor of Araunah[b] the Jebusite.

16 David looked up and saw the angel of the LORD standing between heaven and earth, with a drawn sword in his hand extended over Jerusalem. Then David and the elders, clothed in sackcloth, fell facedown.[h]

17 David said to God, "Was it not I who ordered the fighting men to be counted? I am the one who has sinned and done wrong. These are but sheep.[i] What have they done? O LORD my God, let your hand fall upon me and my family, but do not let this plague remain on your people."

18 Then the angel of the LORD ordered Gad to tell David to go up and build an altar to the LORD on the threshing floor[j] of Araunah the Jebusite. 19 So David went up in obedience to the word that Gad had spoken in the name of the LORD.

20 While Araunah was threshing wheat, he turned and saw the angel; his four sons who were with him hid themselves. 21 Then David approached, and when Araunah looked and saw him, he left the threshing floor and bowed down before David with his face to the ground.

22 David said to him, "Let me have the site of your threshing floor so I can build an altar to the LORD, that the plague on the people may be stopped. Sell it to me at the full price."

**21:2** a 1Ch27:23–24
**21:3** b Dt1:11
**21:9** c 1Sa9:9
**21:12** d Dt32:24
**21:13** e Ps130:4,7
**21:14** f 1Ch27:24
**21:15** g Ge6:6; Ex32:14
**21:16** h Nu14:5
**21:17** i 2Sa7:8; Ps74:1
**21:18** j 2Ch3:1

[a]12 Hebrew; Septuagint and Vulgate (see also 2 Samuel 24:13) *of fleeing* [b]15 Hebrew *Ornan*, a variant of *Araunah*; also in verses 18–28

21:26 k Lev 9:24
21:29 l 1Ki 3:4; 1Ch 16:39
22:1 m 1Ch 21:18–29; 2Ch 3:1
22:2 n 1Ki 9:21
22:3 o ver 14
22:4 p 1Ki 5:6
22:5 q 1Ch 29:1

23 Araunah said to David, "Take it! Let my lord the king do whatever pleases him. Look, I will give the oxen for the burnt offerings, the threshing sledges for the wood, and the wheat for the grain offering. I will give all this."

24 But King David replied to Araunah, "No, I insist on paying the full price. I will not take for the LORD what is yours, or sacrifice a burnt offering that costs me nothing."

25 So David paid Araunah six hundred shekels[a] of gold for the site. 26 David built an altar to the LORD there and sacrificed burnt offerings and fellowship offerings.[b] He called on the LORD, and the LORD answered him with fire[k] from heaven on the altar of burnt offering.

27 Then the LORD spoke to the angel, and he put his sword back into its sheath. 28 At that time, when David saw that the LORD had answered him on the threshing floor of Araunah the Jebusite, he offered sacrifices there. 29 The tabernacle of the LORD, which Moses had made in the desert, and the altar of burnt offering were at that time on the high place at Gibeon.[l] 30 But David could not go before it to inquire of God, because he was afraid of the sword of the angel of the LORD.

22 Then David said, "The house of the LORD God[m] is to be here, and also the altar of burnt offering for Israel."

## Preparations for the Temple

2 So David gave orders to assemble the aliens[n] living in Israel, and from among them he appointed stonecutters to prepare dressed stone for building the house of God. 3 He provided a large amount of iron to make nails for the doors of the gateways and for the fittings, and more bronze than could be weighed.[o] 4 He also provided more cedar logs[p] than could be counted, for the Sidonians and Tyrians had brought large numbers of them to David.

5 David said, "My son Solomon is young[q] and inexperienced, and the house to be built for the LORD should be of great magnificence and fame and splendor in the sight of all the nations. Therefore I will make preparations for it." So David made extensive preparations before his death.

6 Then he called for his son Solomon and charged him to build a house for the LORD, the God of Israel. 7 David said to Solomon: "My son, I had it in my heart[r] to build a house for the Name of the LORD my God. 8 But this word of the LORD came to me: 'You have shed much blood and have fought many wars. You are not to build a house for my Name, because you have shed much blood on the earth in my sight. 9 But you will have a son who will be a man of peace and rest, and I will give him rest from all his enemies on every side. His name will be Solomon,[c] and I will grant Israel peace and quiet during his reign. 10 He is the one who will build a house for my Name.[s] He will be my son,[t] and I will be his father. And I will establish the throne of his kingdom over Israel forever.'

11 "Now, my son, the LORD be with[u] you, and may you have success and build the house of the LORD your God, as he said you would. 12 May the LORD give you discretion and understanding[v] when he puts you in command over Israel, so that you may keep the law of the LORD your God. 13 Then you will have success if you are careful to observe the decrees and laws[w] that the LORD gave Moses for Israel. Be strong and courageous.[x] Do not be afraid or discouraged.

*Daughter,*

*You will find wisdom when you seek me.*

*Your Father God*

1 CHRONICLES 22:12–13

14 "I have taken great pains to provide for the temple of the LORD a hundred thousand talents[d] of gold, a million talents[e] of silver, quantities of bronze and iron too great to be weighed, and wood and stone. And you may add to them. 15 You have many workmen: stonecutters, masons and carpenters,

22:7 r 1Ch 17:2
22:10 s 1Ch 17:12 t 2Sa 7:13
22:11 u ver 16
22:12 v 1Ki 3:9–12
22:13 w 1Ch 28:7 x Jos 1:6–9

[a] 25 That is, about 15 pounds (about 7 kilograms) [b] 26 Traditionally *peace offerings* [c] 9 *Solomon* sounds like and may be derived from the Hebrew for *peace.* [d] 14 That is, about 3,750 tons (about 3,450 metric tons) [e] 14 That is, about 37,500 tons (about 34,500 metric tons)

**22:16** y ver 11
**22:17** z 1Ch 28:1–6
**22:18** a 1Ch 23:25 b 2Sa 7:1
**22:19** c 2Ch 5:7
**23:1** d 1Ki 1:33–39; 1Ch 28:5 e 1Ch 29:28
**23:3** f Nu 4:3–49
**23:4** g 2Ch 19:8
**23:5** h 1Ch 15:16
**23:6** i 2Ch 8:14

as well as men skilled in every kind of work 16 in gold and silver, bronze and iron—craftsmen[y] beyond number. Now begin the work, and the LORD be with you."

17 Then David ordered[z] all the leaders of Israel to help his son Solomon. 18 He said to them, "Is not the LORD your God with you? And has he not granted you rest[a] on every side?[b] For he has handed the inhabitants of the land over to me, and the land is subject to the LORD and to his people. 19 Now devote your heart and soul to seeking the LORD your God.[c] Begin to build the sanctuary of the LORD God, so that you may bring the ark of the covenant of the LORD and the sacred articles belonging to God into the temple that will be built for the Name of the LORD."

## The Levites

23 When David was old and full of years, he made his son Solomon[d] king over Israel.[e]

2 He also gathered together all the leaders of Israel, as well as the priests and Levites. 3 The Levites thirty years old or more were counted, and the total number of men was thirty-eight thousand.[f] 4 David said, "Of these, twenty-four thousand are to supervise the work of the temple of the LORD and six thousand are to be officials and judges.[g] 5 Four thousand are to be gatekeepers and four thousand are to praise the LORD with the musical instruments[h] I have provided for that purpose."

6 David divided[i] the Levites into groups corresponding to the sons of Levi: Gershon, Kohath and Merari.

## Gershonites

7 Belonging to the Gershonites:
Ladan and Shimei.
8 The sons of Ladan:
Jehiel the first, Zetham and Joel—three in all.
9 The sons of Shimei:
Shelomoth, Haziel and Haran—three in all.
These were the heads of the families of Ladan.
10 And the sons of Shimei:
Jahath, Ziza,[a] Jeush and Beriah.
These were the sons of Shimei—four in all.
11 Jahath was the first and Ziza the second, but Jeush and Beriah did not have many sons; so they were counted as one family with one assignment.

## Kohathites

12 The sons of Kohath:[j]
Amram, Izhar, Hebron and Uzziel—four in all.
13 The sons of Amram:[k]
Aaron and Moses.
Aaron was set apart,[l] he and his descendants forever, to consecrate the most holy things, to offer sacrifices before the LORD, to minister before him and to pronounce blessings in his name forever. 14 The sons of Moses the man of God were counted as part of the tribe of Levi.
15 The sons of Moses:
Gershom and Eliezer.
16 The descendants of Gershom:[m]
Shubael was the first.
17 The descendants of Eliezer:
Rehabiah was the first.
Eliezer had no other sons, but the sons of Rehabiah were very numerous.
18 The sons of Izhar:
Shelomith was the first.
19 The sons of Hebron:
Jeriah the first, Amariah the second, Jahaziel the third and Jekameam the fourth.
20 The sons of Uzziel:
Micah the first and Isshiah the second.

## Merarites

21 The sons of Merari:[n]
Mahli and Mushi.
The sons of Mahli:
Eleazar and Kish.
22 Eleazar died without having sons: he had only daughters. Their cousins, the sons of Kish, married them.
23 The sons of Mushi:

**23:12** j Ex 6:18
**23:13** k Ex 6:20; 28:1 l Ex 30:7–10
**23:16** m 1Ch 26:24–28
**23:21** n 1Ch 24:26

[a] 10 One Hebrew manuscript, Septuagint and Vulgate (see also verse 11); most Hebrew manuscripts *Zina*

**23:24**
o Nu 10:17,21

**23:26**
p Nu 4:5,15; Dt 10:8

**23:29**
q Ex 25:30
r Lev 2:4–7; 6:20–23
s Lev 19:35–36; 1Ch 9:29,32

**23:31**
t Lev 23:4; Isa 1:13–14

**23:32**
u Nu 1:53
v Nu 3:6–8,38

**24:1**
w Ex 6:23

**24:2**
x Lev 10:1–2; Nu 3:4

Mahli, Eder and Jerimoth—three
in all.

24 These were the descendants of Levi
by their families—the heads of families
as they were registered under their names
and counted individually, that is, the work-
ers twenty years old or more[o] who served
in the temple of the LORD. 25 For David had
said, "Since the LORD, the God of Israel, has
granted rest to his people and has come to
dwell in Jerusalem forever, 26 the Levites no
longer need to carry the tabernacle or any
of the articles used in its service."[p] 27 Accord-
ing to the last instructions of David, the Le-
vites were counted from those twenty years
old or more.

28 The duty of the Levites was to help Aar-
on's descendants in the service of the temple
of the LORD: to be in charge of the courtyards,
the side rooms, the purification of all sacred
things and the performance of other duties
at the house of God. 29 They were in charge of
the bread set out on the table,[q] the flour for
the grain offerings,[r] the unleavened wafers,
the baking and the mixing, and all measure-
ments of quantity and size.[s] 30 They were
also to stand every morning to thank and
praise the LORD. They were to do the same
in the evening 31 and whenever burnt offer-
ings were presented to the LORD on Sabbaths
and at New Moon festivals and at appointed
feasts.[t] They were to serve before the LORD
regularly in the proper number and in the
way prescribed for them.

32 And so the Levites[u] carried out their
responsibilities for the Tent of Meeting,[v] for
the Holy Place and, under their brothers the
descendants of Aaron, for the service of the
temple of the LORD.

## The Divisions of Priests

24 These were the divisions of the sons
of Aaron:

The sons of Aaron were Nadab, Abihu, El-
eazar and Ithamar.[w] 2 But Nadab and Abihu
died before their father did,[x] and they had
no sons; so Eleazar and Ithamar served as
the priests. 3 With the help of Zadok a de-
scendant of Eleazar and Ahimelech a de-
scendant of Ithamar, David separated them
into divisions for their appointed order of
ministering. 4 A larger number of leaders
were found among Eleazar's descendants
than among Ithamar's, and they were di-
vided accordingly: sixteen heads of families
from Eleazar's descendants and eight heads
of families from Ithamar's descendants.
5 They divided them impartially by drawing
lots,[y] for there were officials of the sanctu-
ary and officials of God among the descen-
dants of both Eleazar and Ithamar.

6 The scribe Shemaiah son of Nethanel, a
Levite, recorded their names in the pres-
ence of the king and of the officials: Zadok
the priest, Ahimelech[z] son of Abiathar
and the heads of families of the priests and
of the Levites—one family being taken
from Eleazar and then one from Ithamar.

7 The first lot fell to Jehoiarib,
the second to Jedaiah,
8 the third to Harim,
the fourth to Seorim,
9 the fifth to Malkijah,
the sixth to Mijamin,
10 the seventh to Hakkoz,
the eighth to Abijah,[a]
11 the ninth to Jeshua,
the tenth to Shecaniah,
12 the eleventh to Eliashib,
the twelfth to Jakim,
13 the thirteenth to Huppah,
the fourteenth to Jeshebeab,
14 the fifteenth to Bilgah,
the sixteenth to Immer,
15 the seventeenth to Hezir,
the eighteenth to Happizzez,
16 the nineteenth to Pethahiah,
the twentieth to Jehezkel,
17 the twenty-first to Jakin,
the twenty-second to Gamul,
18 the twenty-third to Delaiah
and the twenty-fourth to Maaziah.

19 This was their appointed order of
ministering when they entered the temple
of the LORD, according to the regulations
prescribed for them by their forefather
Aaron, as the LORD, the God of Israel, had
commanded him.

## The Rest of the Levites

20 As for the rest of the descendants of Levi:
from the sons of Amram: Shubael;
from the sons of Shubael: Jehdeiah.

**24:5**
y ver 31

**24:6**
z 1Ch 18:16

**24:10**
a Ne 12:4,17; Lk 1:5

**24:21** b 1Ch 23:17
**24:23** c 1Ch 23:19
**24:26** d 1Ch 6:19; 23:21
**24:31** e ver 5
**25:1** f 1Ch 6:39 g 1Ch 6:33 h 1Sa 10:5; 2Ki 3:15 i 1Ch 15:16
**25:3** j 1Ch 16:41–42
**25:6** k 1Ch 15:16 l 1Ch 15:19
**25:8** m 1Ch 26:13
**25:9** n 1Ch 6:39

21 As for Rehabiah,[b] from his sons:
Isshiah was the first.
22 From the Izharites: Shelomoth;
from the sons of Shelomoth: Jahath.
23 The sons of Hebron:[c] Jeriah the first,[a]
Amariah the second, Jahaziel the third and Jekameam the fourth.
24 The son of Uzziel: Micah;
from the sons of Micah: Shamir.
25 The brother of Micah: Isshiah;
from the sons of Isshiah: Zechariah.
26 The sons of Merari:[d] Mahli and Mushi.
The son of Jaaziah: Beno.
27 The sons of Merari:
from Jaaziah: Beno, Shoham, Zaccur and Ibri.
28 From Mahli: Eleazar, who had no sons.
29 From Kish: the son of Kish:
Jerahmeel.
30 And the sons of Mushi: Mahli, Eder and Jerimoth.

These were the Levites, according to their families.
31 They also cast lots,[e] just as their brothers the descendants of Aaron did, in the presence of King David and of Zadok, Ahimelech, and the heads of families of the priests and of the Levites. The families of the oldest brother were treated the same as those of the youngest.

## The Singers

25 David, together with the commanders of the army, set apart some of the sons of Asaph,[f] Heman[g] and Jeduthun for the ministry of prophesying,[h] accompanied by harps, lyres and cymbals.[i] Here is the list of the men who performed this service:

2 From the sons of Asaph:
Zaccur, Joseph, Nethaniah and Asarelah. The sons of Asaph were under the supervision of Asaph, who prophesied under the king's supervision.
3 As for Jeduthun, from his sons:[j]
Gedaliah, Zeri, Jeshaiah, Shimei,[b] Hashabiah and Mattithiah, six in all, under the supervision of their father Jeduthun, who prophesied, using the harp in thanking and praising the LORD.
4 As for Heman, from his sons:
Bukkiah, Mattaniah, Uzziel, Shubael and Jerimoth; Hananiah, Hanani, Eliathah, Giddalti and Romamti-Ezer; Joshbekashah, Mallothi, Hothir and Mahazioth.
5 All these were sons of Heman the king's seer. They were given him through the promises of God to exalt him.[c] God gave Heman fourteen sons and three daughters.

6 All these men were under the supervision of their fathers[k] for the music of the temple of the LORD, with cymbals, lyres and harps, for the ministry at the house of God. Asaph, Jeduthun and Heman[l] were under the supervision of the king.
7 Along with their relatives—all of them trained and skilled in music for the LORD—they numbered 288.
8 Young and old alike, teacher as well as student, cast lots[m] for their duties.

9 The first lot, which was for Asaph,[n] fell to Joseph,
his sons and relatives,[d] 12[e]
the second to Gedaliah,
he and his relatives and sons, 12
10 the third to Zaccur,
his sons and relatives, 12
11 the fourth to Izri,[f]
his sons and relatives, 12
12 the fifth to Nethaniah,
his sons and relatives, 12
13 the sixth to Bukkiah,
his sons and relatives, 12
14 the seventh to Jesarelah,[g]
his sons and relatives, 12
15 the eighth to Jeshaiah,
his sons and relatives, 12
16 the ninth to Mattaniah,
his sons and relatives, 12
17 the tenth to Shimei,
his sons and relatives, 12
18 the eleventh to Azarel,[h]

[a] 23 Two Hebrew manuscripts and some Septuagint manuscripts (see also 1 Chron. 23:19); most Hebrew manuscripts *The sons of Jeriah:* [b] 3 One Hebrew manuscript and some Septuagint manuscripts (see also verse 17); most Hebrew manuscripts do not have *Shimei.* [c] 5 Hebrew *exalt the horn* [d] 9 See Septuagint; Hebrew does not have *his sons and relatives.* [e] 9 See the total in verse 7; Hebrew does not have *twelve.* [f] 11 A variant of *Zeri* [g] 14 A variant of *Asarelah* [h] 18 A variant of *Uzziel*

26:5
o 2Sa 6:10;
1Ch 13:13

his sons and relatives, 12
19 the twelfth to Hashabiah,
his sons and relatives, 12
20 the thirteenth to Shubael,
his sons and relatives, 12
21 the fourteenth to Mattithiah,
his sons and relatives, 12
22 the fifteenth to Jerimoth,
his sons and relatives, 12
23 the sixteenth to Hananiah,
his sons and relatives, 12
24 the seventeenth to Joshbekashah,
his sons and relatives, 12
25 the eighteenth to Hanani,
his sons and relatives, 12
26 the nineteenth to Mallothi,
his sons and relatives, 12
27 the twentieth to Eliathah,
his sons and relatives, 12
28 the twenty-first to Hothir,
his sons and relatives, 12
29 the twenty-second to Giddalti,
his sons and relatives, 12
30 the twenty-third to Mahazioth,
his sons and relatives, 12
31 the twenty-fourth to Romamti-Ezer,
his sons and relatives, 12

## The Gatekeepers

**26** The divisions of the gatekeepers:

From the Korahites: Meshelemiah son
of Kore, one of the sons of Asaph.
2 Meshelemiah had sons:
Zechariah the firstborn,
Jediael the second,
Zebadiah the third,
Jathniel the fourth,
3 Elam the fifth,
Jehohanan the sixth
and Eliehoenai the seventh.
4 Obed-Edom also had sons:
Shemaiah the firstborn,
Jehozabad the second,
Joah the third,
Sacar the fourth,
Nethanel the fifth,
5 Ammiel the sixth,
Issachar the seventh
and Peullethai the eighth.
(For God had blessed Obed-Edom.[o])

6 His son Shemaiah also had sons,
who were leaders in their father's
family because they were very ca-
pable men. 7 The sons of Shemaiah:
Othni, Rephael, Obed and Elzabad;
his relatives Elihu and Semakiah
were also able men. 8 All these were
descendants of Obed-Edom; they
and their sons and their relatives
were capable men with the strength
to do the work—descendants of
Obed-Edom, 62 in all.
9 Meshelemiah had sons and relatives,
who were able men—18 in all.

10 Hosah the Merarite had sons: Shimri
the first (although he was not the
firstborn, his father had appointed
him the first), 11 Hilkiah the second,
Tabaliah the third and Zechariah
the fourth. The sons and relatives
of Hosah were 13 in all.

12 These divisions of the gatekeepers,
through their chief men, had duties for
ministering in the temple of the LORD, just
as their relatives had. 13 Lots[p] were cast for
each gate, according to their families, young
and old alike.

14 The lot for the East Gate fell to Shele-
miah.[a] Then lots were cast for his son
Zechariah, a wise counselor, and the lot for
the North Gate fell to him. 15 The lot for the
South Gate fell to Obed-Edom, and the lot
for the storehouse fell to his sons. 16 The lots
for the West Gate and the Shalleketh Gate on
the upper road fell to Shuppim and Hosah.

Guard was alongside of guard: 17 There
were six Levites a day on the east, four a day
on the north, four a day on the south and
two at a time at the storehouse. 18 As for the
court to the west, there were four at the road
and two at the court itself.

19 These were the divisions of the gate-
keepers who were descendants of Korah
and Merari.

## The Treasurers and Other Officials

20 Their fellow Levites were[b] in charge of
the treasuries of the house of God and the
treasuries for the dedicated things.[q]

26:13
p 1Ch 24:5,31;
25:8

26:20
q 1Ch 28:12

[a] 14 A variant of *Meshelemiah* [b] 20 Septuagint; Hebrew *As for the Levites, Ahijah was*

**26:21** r 1Ch 23:7; 29:8
**26:24** s 1Ch 23:16
**26:25** t 1Ch 23:18
**26:26** u 2Sa 8:11
**26:28** v 1Sa 9:9
**26:29** w 1Ch 23:4
**26:30** x 1Ch 27:17
**26:31** y 1Ch 23:19

21 The descendants of Ladan, who were
Gershonites through Ladan and who were
heads of families belonging to Ladan the
Gershonite,[r] were Jehieli, 22 the sons of
Jehieli, Zetham and his brother Joel. They
were in charge of the treasuries of the tem-
ple of the LORD.
23 From the Amramites, the Izharites, the
Hebronites and the Uzzielites:

24 Shubael,[s] a descendant of Gershom
son of Moses, was the officer in
charge of the treasuries. 25 His rel-
atives through Eliezer: Rehabiah
his son, Jeshaiah his son, Joram his
son, Zicri his son and Shelomith[t] his
son. 26 Shelomith and his relatives
were in charge of all the treasuries
for the things dedicated[u] by King
David, by the heads of families who
were the commanders of thousands
and commanders of hundreds, and
by the other army commanders.
27 Some of the plunder taken in bat-
tle they dedicated for the repair of
the temple of the LORD. 28 And every-
thing dedicated by Samuel the seer[v]
and by Saul son of Kish, Abner son
of Ner and Joab son of Zeruiah, and
all the other dedicated things were
in the care of Shelomith and his rel-
atives.
29 From the Izharites: Kenaniah and his
sons were assigned duties away
from the temple, as officials and
judges[w] over Israel.
30 From the Hebronites: Hashabiah[x] and
his relatives—seventeen hundred
able men—were responsible in
Israel west of the Jordan for all the
work of the LORD and for the king's
service. 31 As for the Hebronites,[y]
Jeriah was their chief according to
the genealogical records of their
families. In the fortieth year of Da-
vid's reign a search was made in the
records, and capable men among
the Hebronites were found at Ja-
zer in Gilead. 32 Jeriah had twenty-
seven hundred relatives, who were
able men and heads of families,
and King David put them in charge
of the Reubenites, the Gadites and
the half-tribe of Manasseh for every
matter pertaining to God and for
the affairs of the king.

## Army Divisions

27 This is the list of the Israelites—
heads of families, commanders of
thousands and commanders of hundreds,
and their officers, who served the king in
all that concerned the army divisions that
were on duty month by month through-
out the year. Each division consisted of
24,000 men.

2 In charge of the first division, for the
first month, was Jashobeam[z] son of
Zabdiel. There were 24,000 men in
his division. 3 He was a descendant of
Perez and chief of all the army officers
for the first month.
4 In charge of the division for the second
month was Dodai[a] the Ahohite; Mik-
loth was the leader of his division.
There were 24,000 men in his divi-
sion.
5 The third army commander, for the third
month, was Benaiah son of Jehoiada
the priest. He was chief and there were
24,000 men in his division. 6 This was
the Benaiah who was a mighty man
among the Thirty and was over the
Thirty. His son Ammizabad was in
charge of his division.
7 The fourth, for the fourth month, was
Asahel[b] the brother of Joab; his son
Zebadiah was his successor. There
were 24,000 men in his division.
8 The fifth, for the fifth month, was the
commander Shamhuth the Izrahite.
There were 24,000 men in his divi-
sion.
9 The sixth, for the sixth month, was Ira[c]
the son of Ikkesh the Tekoite. There
were 24,000 men in his division.
10 The seventh, for the seventh month, was
Helez[d] the Pelonite, an Ephraimite.
There were 24,000 men in his divi-
sion.
11 The eighth, for the eighth month, was
Sibbecai[e] the Hushathite, a Zerahite.
There were 24,000 men in his divi-
sion.

**27:2** z 2Sa 23:8; 1Ch 11:11
**27:4** a 2Sa 23:9
**27:7** b 2Sa 2:18; 1Ch 11:26
**27:9** c 2Sa 23:26; 1Ch 11:28
**27:10** d 2Sa 23:26; 1Ch 11:27
**27:11** e 2Sa 21:18

27:12 f 2Sa 23:27; 1Ch 11:28
27:13 g 2Sa 23:28; 1Ch 11:30
27:14 h 1Ch 11:31
27:17 i 1Ch 26:30
27:23 j Ge 15:5
27:24 k 2Sa 24:15

12 The ninth, for the ninth month, was Abiezer[f] the Anathothite, a Benjamite. There were 24,000 men in his division.
13 The tenth, for the tenth month, was Maharai[g] the Netophathite, a Zerahite. There were 24,000 men in his division.
14 The eleventh, for the eleventh month, was Benaiah[h] the Pirathonite, an Ephraimite. There were 24,000 men in his division.
15 The twelfth, for the twelfth month, was Heldai the Netophathite, from the family of Othniel. There were 24,000 men in his division.

## Officers of the Tribes

16 The officers over the tribes of Israel:

over the Reubenites: Eliezer son of Zicri;
over the Simeonites: Shephatiah son of Maacah;
17 over Levi: Hashabiah[i] son of Kemuel;
over Aaron: Zadok;
18 over Judah: Elihu, a brother of David;
over Issachar: Omri son of Michael;
19 over Zebulun: Ishmaiah son of Obadiah;
over Naphtali: Jerimoth son of Azriel;
20 over the Ephraimites: Hoshea son of Azaziah;
over half the tribe of Manasseh: Joel son of Pedaiah;
21 over the half-tribe of Manasseh in Gilead: Iddo son of Zechariah;
over Benjamin: Jaasiel son of Abner;
22 over Dan: Azarel son of Jeroham.

These were the officers over the tribes of Israel.

23 David did not take the number of the men twenty years old or less, because the LORD had promised to make Israel as numerous as the stars[j] in the sky.
24 Joab son of Zeruiah began to count the men but did not finish. Wrath came on Israel on account of this numbering,[k] and the number was not entered in the book[a] of the annals of King David.

## The King's Overseers

25 Azmaveth son of Adiel was in charge of the royal storehouses.

Jonathan son of Uzziah was in charge of the storehouses in the outlying districts, in the towns, the villages and the watchtowers.

26 Ezri son of Kelub was in charge of the field workers who farmed the land.

27 Shimei the Ramathite was in charge of the vineyards.

Zabdi the Shiphmite was in charge of the produce of the vineyards for the wine vats.

28 Baal-Hanan the Gederite was in charge of the olive and sycamore-fig[l] trees in the western foothills.

Joash was in charge of the supplies of olive oil.

29 Shitrai the Sharonite was in charge of the herds grazing in Sharon.

Shaphat son of Adlai was in charge of the herds in the valleys.

30 Obil the Ishmaelite was in charge of the camels.

Jehdeiah the Meronothite was in charge of the donkeys.

31 Jaziz the Hagrite was in charge of the flocks.

All these were the officials in charge of King David's property.

32 Jonathan, David's uncle, was a counselor, a man of insight and a scribe. Jehiel son of Hacmoni took care of the king's sons.

33 Ahithophel[m] was the king's counselor.

Hushai[n] the Arkite was the king's friend.
34 Ahithophel was succeeded by Jehoiada son of Benaiah and by Abiathar.[o]

Joab[p] was the commander of the royal army.

## David's Plans for the Temple

28 David summoned all the officials[q] of Israel to assemble at Jerusalem: the officers over the tribes, the commanders of the divisions in the service of the king, the commanders of thousands and commanders of hundreds, and the officials in charge of all the property and livestock belonging to the king and his sons, together with the

27:28 l 1Ki 10:27
27:33 m 2Sa 15:12 n 2Sa 15:37
27:34 o 1Ki 1:7 p 1Ch 11:6
28:1 q 1Ch 27:1–31

[a] 24 Septuagint; Hebrew *number*

palace officials, the mighty men and all the brave warriors.

[2]King David rose to his feet and said: "Listen to me, my brothers and my people. I had it in my heart to build a house as a place of rest for the ark of the covenant of the LORD, for the footstool[r] of our God, and I made plans to build it. [3]But God said to me, 'You are not to build a house for my Name,[s] because you are a warrior and have shed blood.'

[4]"Yet the LORD, the God of Israel, chose me from my whole family[t] to be king over Israel forever. He chose Judah[u] as leader, and from the house of Judah he chose my family, and from my father's sons he was pleased to make me king over all Israel. [5]Of all my sons—and the LORD has given me many[v]—he has chosen my son Solomon[w] to sit on the throne of the kingdom of the LORD over Israel. [6]He said to me: 'Solomon your son is the one who will build my house and my courts, for I have chosen him to be my son,[x] and I will be his father. [7]I will establish his kingdom forever if he is unswerving in carrying out my commands and laws,[y] as is being done at this time.'

[8]"So now I charge you in the sight of all Israel and of the assembly of the LORD, and in the hearing of our God: Be careful to follow all the commands of the LORD your God, that you may possess this good land and pass it on as an inheritance to your descendants forever.

[9]"And you, my son Solomon, acknowledge the God of your father, and serve him with wholehearted devotion and with a willing mind, for the LORD searches every heart[z] and understands every motive behind the thoughts. If you seek him, he will be found by you; but if you forsake[a] him, he will reject you forever. [10]Consider now, for the LORD has chosen you to build a temple as a sanctuary. Be strong and do the work."

[11]Then David gave his son Solomon the plans[b] for the portico of the temple, its buildings, its storerooms, its upper parts, its inner rooms and the place of atonement. [12]He gave him the plans of all that the Spirit had put in his mind for the courts of the temple of the LORD and all the surrounding rooms, for the treasuries of the temple of God and for the treasuries for the dedicated things.[c] [13]He gave him instructions for the divisions[d] of the priests and Levites, and for all the work of serving in the temple of the LORD, as well as for all the articles to be used in its service. [14]He designated the weight of gold for all the gold articles to be used in various kinds of service, and the weight of silver for all the silver articles to be used in various kinds of service: [15]the weight of gold for the gold lampstands[e] and their lamps, with the weight for each lampstand and its lamps; and the weight of silver for each silver lampstand and its lamps, according to the use of each lampstand; [16]the weight of gold for each table for consecrated bread; the weight of silver for the silver tables; [17]the weight of pure gold for the forks, sprinkling bowls and pitchers; the weight of gold for each gold dish; the weight of silver for each silver dish; [18]and the weight of the refined gold for the altar of incense.[f] He also gave him the plan for the chariot,[g] that is, the cherubim of gold that spread their wings and shelter[h] the ark of the covenant of the LORD.

[19]"All this," David said, "I have in writing from the hand of the LORD upon me, and he gave me understanding in all the details of the plan."

[20]David also said to Solomon his son, "Be strong and courageous,[i] and do the work. Do not be afraid or discouraged, for the LORD God, my God, is with you. He will not fail you or forsake you until all the work for the service of the temple of the LORD is finished. [21]The divisions of the priests and Levites are ready for all the work on the temple of God, and every willing man skilled[j] in any craft will help you in all the work. The officials and all the people will obey your every command."

## Gifts for Building the Temple

**29** Then King David said to the whole assembly: "My son Solomon, the one whom God has chosen, is young and inexperienced.[k] The task is great, because this palatial structure is not for man but for the LORD God. [2]With all my resources I have provided for the temple of my God—gold for the gold work, silver for the silver, bronze for the bronze, iron for the iron and wood

**28:2** r Ps 132:7
**28:3** s 1Ch 22:8
**28:4** t 1Sa 16:1–13 u Ge 49:10; 1Ch 5:2
**28:5** v 1Ch 3:1 w 1Ch 22:9; 23:1
**28:6** x 2Sa 7:13
**28:7** y 1Ch 22:13
**28:9** z 1Sa 16:7 a 2Ch 15:2
**28:11** b Ex 25:9
**28:12** c 1Ch 26:20
**28:13** d 1Ch 24:1
**28:15** e Ex 25:31
**28:18** f Ex 30:1–10 g Ex 25:18–22 h Ex 25:20
**28:20** i Dt 31:6; 1Ch 22:13
**28:21** j Ex 35:25–36:5
**29:1** k 1Ki 3:7; 1Ch 22:5

**29:2** l Isa 54:11 m 1Ch 22:2–5
**29:4** n 1Ch 22:14
**29:6** o 1Ch 27:1; 28:1
**29:7** p Ne 7:70–71
**29:8** q 1Ch 26:21
**29:9** r 1Ki 8:61; 2Co 9:7
**29:11** s Rev 5:12–13
**29:12** t 2Ch 1:12

for the wood, as well as onyx for the settings, turquoise,[a][l] stones of various colors, and all kinds of fine stone and marble—all of these in large quantities.[m] 3 Besides, in my devotion to the temple of my God I now give my personal treasures of gold and silver for the temple of my God, over and above everything I have provided for this holy temple: 4 three thousand talents[b] of gold (gold of Ophir) and seven thousand talents[c] of refined silver,[n] for the overlaying of the walls of the buildings, 5 for the gold work and the silver work, and for all the work to be done by the craftsmen. Now, who is willing to consecrate himself today to the LORD?"

6 Then the leaders of families, the officers of the tribes of Israel, the commanders of thousands and commanders of hundreds, and the officials[o] in charge of the king's work gave willingly. 7 They[p] gave toward the work on the temple of God five thousand talents[d] and ten thousand darics[e] of gold, ten thousand talents[f] of silver, eighteen thousand talents[g] of bronze and a hundred thousand talents[h] of iron. 8 Any who had precious stones gave them to the treasury of the temple of the LORD in the custody of Jehiel the Gershonite.[q] 9 The people rejoiced at the willing response of their leaders, for they had given freely and wholeheartedly[r] to the LORD. David the king also rejoiced greatly.

## David's Prayer

10 David praised the LORD in the presence of the whole assembly, saying,

"Praise be to you, O LORD,
God of our father Israel,
from everlasting to everlasting.
11 Yours, O LORD, is the greatness and the power
and the glory and the majesty and the splendor,
for everything in heaven and earth is yours.
Yours, O LORD, is the kingdom;
you are exalted as head over all.[s]
12 Wealth and honor[t] come from you;
you are the ruler of all things.
In your hands are strength and power
to exalt and give strength to all.
13 Now, our God, we give you thanks,
and praise your glorious name.

14 "But who am I, and who are my people, that we should be able to give as generously as this? Everything comes from you, and we have given you only what comes from your hand. 15 We are aliens and strangers[u] in your sight, as were all our forefathers. Our days on earth are like a shadow,[v] without hope. 16 O LORD our God, as for all this abundance that we have provided for building you a temple for your Holy Name, it comes from your hand, and all of it belongs to you. 17 I know, my God, that you test the heart and are pleased with integrity. All these things have I given willingly and with honest intent. And now I have seen with joy how willingly your people who are here have given to you.[w] 18 O LORD, God of our fathers Abraham, Isaac and Israel, keep this desire in the hearts of your people forever, and keep their hearts loyal to you. 19 And give my son Solomon the wholehearted devotion[x] to keep your commands, requirements and decrees[y] and to do everything to build the palatial structure for which I have provided."[z]

20 Then David said to the whole assembly, "Praise the LORD your God." So they all praised the LORD, the God of their fathers;

**29:15** u Ps 39:12; Heb 11:13 v Job 14:2
**29:17** w 1Ch 28:9
**29:19** x 1Ch 28:9 y Ps 72:1 z 1Ch 22:14

*My cherished daughter,*

*All good and perfect gifts—indeed, all blessings—come from me. So partake and enjoy, without forgetting to offer back your firstfruits.*

*Your Father–Provider*

1 CHRONICLES 29:14–18

[a] 2 The meaning of the Hebrew for this word is uncertain. [b] 4 That is, about 110 tons (about 100 metric tons) [c] 4 That is, about 260 tons (about 240 metric tons) [d] 7 That is, about 190 tons (about 170 metric tons) [e] 7 That is, about 185 pounds (about 84 kilograms) [f] 7 That is, about 375 tons (about 345 metric tons) [g] 7 That is, about 675 tons (about 610 metric tons) [h] 7 That is, about 3,750 tons (about 3,450 metric tons)

**29:21** a 1Ki 8:62
**29:22** b 1Ch 23:1 c 1Ki 1:33–39

they bowed low and fell prostrate before the LORD and the king.

## Solomon Acknowledged as King

21 The next day they made sacrifices to the LORD and presented burnt offerings to him:[a] a thousand bulls, a thousand rams and a thousand male lambs, together with their drink offerings, and other sacrifices in abundance for all Israel. 22 They ate and drank with great joy[b] in the presence of the LORD that day.

Then they acknowledged Solomon son of David as king a second time, anointing him before the LORD to be ruler and Zadok[c] to be priest. 23 So Solomon sat on the throne of the LORD as king in place of his father David. He prospered and all Israel obeyed him. 24 All the officers and mighty men, as well as all of King David's sons, pledged their submission to King Solomon.

25 The LORD highly exalted Solomon in the sight of all Israel and bestowed on him royal splendor[d] such as no king over Israel ever had before.[e]

## The Death of David

26 David son of Jesse was king[f] over all Israel. 27 He ruled over Israel forty years—seven in Hebron and thirty-three in Jerusalem.[g] 28 He died[h] at a good old age, having enjoyed long life, wealth and honor. His son Solomon succeeded him as king.[i]

29 As for the events of King David's reign, from beginning to end, they are written in the records of Samuel the seer, the records of Nathan the prophet and the records of Gad the seer, 30 together with the details of his reign and power, and the circumstances that surrounded him and Israel and the kingdoms of all the other lands.

**29:25** d 2Ch 1:1,12 e 1Ki 3:13
**29:26** f 1Ch 18:14
**29:27** g 2Sa 5:4–5; 1Ki 2:11
**29:28** h Ge 15:15 i 1Ch 23:1

# 2 Chronicles

## OVERVIEW

The second book of Chronicles continues the account of the legacy of David's kingdom line (recounting only the kings of Judah, not Israel). The book covers the time from Solomon's reign to the Babylonian exile, paralleling many of the same events that are described in 1 and 2 Kings. The focus is again on God's faithfulness to his covenant and the blessings for those who honor God. Unfortunately, the people repeatedly chose to disobey God; consequently, Jerusalem fell, the temple was destroyed and the Israelites were exiled.

The book of 2 Chronicles analyzes the lives of those who followed after God—those who "did what was good and right" versus those who did evil. Women believers must focus on the legacy they will leave when their time on earth is done. Will their children, grandchildren, nieces and nephews see a positive relationship with Jesus Christ or will they suffer from the poor decisions made by the adults in their lives?

## OUTLINE

I. Reign of Solomon (1:1—9:31)
II. The Kingdom Divides (10:1—12:16)
III. Judah's Kings Until the Babylonian Captivity (13:1—36:23)

### SCANNABLE FACTS:

**Author:** Unknown; possibly Ezra

**Time Written:** About 450 B.C.

**Theme to Note:** God is faithful to his covenant

**Notable Women:** The queen of Sheba, Athaliah, Jehosheba, Huldah the prophetess

1:1
a 1Ki 2:12,26
b Ge 39:2
c 1Ch 29:25
1:4
d 2Sa 6:17
1:5
e Ex 38:2
1:8
f 1Ch 28:5
1:10
g Nu 27:17
1:12
h 1Ch 29:25; 2Ch 9:22

## Solomon Asks for Wisdom

**1** Solomon son of David established[a] himself firmly over his kingdom, for the LORD his God was with[b] him and made him exceedingly great.[c]

2 Then Solomon spoke to all Israel—to the commanders of thousands and commanders of hundreds, to the judges and to all the leaders in Israel, the heads of families— 3 and Solomon and the whole assembly went to the high place at Gibeon, for God's Tent of Meeting was there, which Moses the LORD's servant had made in the desert. 4 Now David had brought up the ark of God from Kiriath Jearim to the place he had prepared for it, because he had pitched a tent[d] for it in Jerusalem. 5 But the bronze altar[e] that Bezalel son of Uri, the son of Hur, had made was in Gibeon in front of the tabernacle of the LORD; so Solomon and the assembly inquired of him there. 6 Solomon went up to the bronze altar before the LORD in the Tent of Meeting and offered a thousand burnt offerings on it.

7 That night God appeared to Solomon and said to him, "Ask for whatever you want me to give you."

8 Solomon answered God, "You have shown great kindness to David my father and have made me[f] king in his place. 9 Now, LORD God, let your promise to my father David be confirmed, for you have made me king over a people who are as numerous as the dust of the earth. 10 Give me wisdom and knowledge, that I may lead[g] this people, for who is able to govern this great people of yours?"

11 God said to Solomon, "Since this is your heart's desire and you have not asked for wealth, riches or honor, nor for the death of your enemies, and since you have not asked for a long life but for wisdom and knowledge to govern my people over whom I have made you king, 12 therefore wisdom and knowledge will be given you. And I will also give you wealth, riches and honor, such as no king who was before you ever had and none after you will have.[h]"

13 Then Solomon went to Jerusalem from the high place at Gibeon, from before the Tent of Meeting. And he reigned over Israel.

14 Solomon accumulated chariots[i] and horses; he had fourteen hundred chariots and twelve thousand horses,[a] which he kept in the chariot cities and also with him in Jerusalem. 15 The king made silver and gold as common in Jerusalem as stones, and cedar as plentiful as sycamore-fig trees in the foothills. 16 Solomon's horses were imported from Egypt[b] and from Kue[c]—the royal merchants purchased them from Kue. 17 They imported a chariot from Egypt for six hundred shekels[d] of silver, and a horse for a hundred and fifty.[e] They also exported them to all the kings of the Hittites and of the Arameans.

## Preparations for Building the Temple

**2** Solomon gave orders to build a temple for the Name of the LORD and a royal palace for himself. 2 He conscripted seventy thousand men as carriers and eighty thousand as stonecutters in the hills and thirty-six hundred as foremen over them.[j]

3 Solomon sent this message to Hiram[f] king of Tyre:

"Send me cedar logs[k] as you did for my father David when you sent him cedar to build a palace to live in. 4 Now I am about to build a temple for the Name of the LORD my God and to dedicate it to him for burning fragrant incense[l] before him, for setting out the consecrated bread[m] regularly, and for making burnt offerings every morning and evening and on Sabbaths[n] and New Moons and at the appointed feasts of the LORD our God. This is a lasting ordinance for Israel.

5 "The temple I am going to build will be great, because our God is greater than all other gods.[o] 6 But who is able to build a temple for him, since the heavens, even the highest heavens, cannot contain him?[p] Who then am I to build a temple for him, except as a place to burn sacrifices before him?

1:14
i 1Ki 4:26
2:2
j ver 18
2:3
k 1Ch 14:1
2:4
l Ex 30:7
m Ex 25:30
n Nu 28:9–10
2:5
o 1Ch 16:25
2:6
p 1Ki 8:27

[a] 14 Or *charioteers* [b] 16 Or possibly *Muzur,* a region in Cilicia; also in verse 17 [c] 16 Probably Cilicia [d] 17 That is, about 15 pounds (about 7 kilograms) [e] 17 That is, about 3 3/4 pounds (about 1.7 kilograms) [f] 3 Hebrew *Huram,* a variant of *Hiram;* also in verses 11 and 12

2:7
q 1Ch 22:16

2:11
r 1Ki 10:9; 2Ch 9:8

2:12
s Ps 33:6; 102:25

2:13
t 1Ki 7:13

2:15
u ver 10

7 “Send me, therefore, a man skilled to work in gold and silver, bronze and iron, and in purple, crimson and blue yarn, and experienced in the art of engraving, to work in Judah and Jerusalem with my skilled craftsmen,[q] whom my father David provided.

8 “Send me also cedar, pine and algum[a] logs from Lebanon, for I know that your men are skilled in cutting timber there. My men will work with yours 9 to provide me with plenty of lumber, because the temple I build must be large and magnificent. 10 I will give your servants, the woodsmen who cut the timber, twenty thousand cors[b] of ground wheat, twenty thousand cors of barley, twenty thousand baths[c] of wine and twenty thousand baths of olive oil.”

11 Hiram king of Tyre replied by letter to Solomon:

> “Because the LORD loves[r] his people, he has made you their king.”

12 And Hiram added:

> “Praise be to the LORD, the God of Israel, who made heaven and earth![s] He has given King David a wise son, endowed with intelligence and discernment, who will build a temple for the LORD and a palace for himself.
>
> 13 “I am sending you Huram-Abi,[t] a man of great skill, 14 whose mother was from Dan and whose father was from Tyre. He is trained to work in gold and silver, bronze and iron, stone and wood, and with purple and blue and crimson yarn and fine linen. He is experienced in all kinds of engraving and can execute any design given to him. He will work with your craftsmen and with those of my lord, David your father.
>
> 15 “Now let my lord send his servants the wheat and barley and the olive oil[u] and wine he promised, 16 and we will cut all the logs from Lebanon that you need and will float them in rafts by sea down to Joppa. You can then take them up to Jerusalem.”

2:17
v 1Ch 22:2

3:1
w 1Ch 21:18

3:10
x Ex 25:18

17 Solomon took a census of all the aliens[v] who were in Israel, after the census his father David had taken; and they were found to be 153,600. 18 He assigned 70,000 of them to be carriers and 80,000 to be stonecutters in the hills, with 3,600 foremen over them to keep the people working.

## Solomon Builds the Temple

3 Then Solomon began to build the temple of the LORD in Jerusalem on Mount Moriah, where the LORD had appeared to his father David. It was on the threshing floor of Araunah[d][w] the Jebusite, the place provided by David. 2 He began building on the second day of the second month in the fourth year of his reign.

3 The foundation Solomon laid for building the temple of God was sixty cubits long and twenty cubits wide[e] (using the cubit of the old standard). 4 The portico at the front of the temple was twenty cubits[f] long across the width of the building and twenty cubits[g] high.

He overlaid the inside with pure gold. 5 He paneled the main hall with pine and covered it with fine gold and decorated it with palm tree and chain designs. 6 He adorned the temple with precious stones. And the gold he used was gold of Parvaim. 7 He overlaid the ceiling beams, doorframes, walls and doors of the temple with gold, and he carved cherubim on the walls.

8 He built the Most Holy Place, its length corresponding to the width of the temple—twenty cubits long and twenty cubits wide. He overlaid the inside with six hundred talents[h] of fine gold. 9 The gold nails weighed fifty shekels.[i] He also overlaid the upper parts with gold.

10 In the Most Holy Place he made a pair[x] of sculptured cherubim and overlaid them with gold. 11 The total wingspan of the cherubim was twenty cubits. One wing of the first

[a] 8 Probably a variant of *almug*; possibly juniper [b] 10 That is, probably about 125,000 bushels (about 4,400 kiloliters) [c] 10 That is, probably about 115,000 gallons (about 440 kiloliters) [d] 1 Hebrew *Ornan*, a variant of *Araunah* [e] 3 That is, about 90 feet (about 27 meters) long and 30 feet (about 9 meters) wide [f] 4 That is, about 30 feet (about 9 meters); also in verses 8, 11 and 13 [g] 4 Some Septuagint and Syriac manuscripts; Hebrew *and a hundred and twenty* [h] 8 That is, about 23 tons (about 21 metric tons) [i] 9 That is, about 1 1/4 pounds (about 0.6 kilogram)

cherub was five cubits[a] long and touched the
temple wall, while its other wing, also five
cubits long, touched the wing of the other
cherub. 12 Similarly one wing of the second
cherub was five cubits long and touched the
other temple wall, and its other wing, also
five cubits long, touched the wing of the
first cherub. 13 The wings of these cherubim
extended twenty cubits. They stood on their
feet, facing the main hall.[b]

14 He made the curtain[y] of blue, purple
and crimson yarn and fine linen, with cheru-
bim worked into it.

15 In the front of the temple he made two
pillars,[z] which ⌞together⌟ were thirty-five
cubits[c] long, each with a capital on top mea-
suring five cubits. 16 He made interwoven
chains[d] and put them on top of the pillars.
He also made a hundred pomegranates[a] and
attached them to the chains. 17 He erected
the pillars in the front of the temple, one
to the south and one to the north. The one
to the south he named Jakin[e] and the one to
the north Boaz.[f]

## The Temple's Furnishings

4 He made a bronze altar[b] twenty cubits
long, twenty cubits wide and ten cubits
high.[g] 2 He made the Sea of cast metal, circu-
lar in shape, measuring ten cubits from rim
to rim and five cubits[h] high. It took a line of
thirty cubits[i] to measure around it. 3 Below
the rim, figures of bulls encircled it—ten to
a cubit.[j] The bulls were cast in two rows in
one piece with the Sea.

4 The Sea stood on twelve bulls, three fac-
ing north, three facing west, three facing
south and three facing east. The Sea rested
on top of them, and their hindquarters were
toward the center. 5 It was a handbreadth[k] in
thickness, and its rim was like the rim of a
cup, like a lily blossom. It held three thou-
sand baths.[l]

6 He then made ten basins[c] for washing
and placed five on the south side and five on
the north. In them the things to be used for
the burnt offerings were rinsed, but the Sea
was to be used by the priests for washing.

7 He made ten gold lampstands[d] accord-
ing to the specifications[e] for them and
placed them in the temple, five on the south
side and five on the north.

8 He made ten tables and placed them in
the temple, five on the south side and five
on the north. He also made a hundred gold
sprinkling bowls.

9 He made the courtyard[f] of the priests,
and the large court and the doors for the
court, and overlaid the doors with bronze.
10 He placed the Sea on the south side, at the
southeast corner.

11 He also made the pots and shovels and
sprinkling bowls.

So Huram finished the work he had
undertaken for King Solomon in the temple
of God:

12 the two pillars;
the two bowl-shaped capitals on top of
the pillars;
the two sets of network decorating the
two bowl-shaped capitals on top of
the pillars;
13 the four hundred pomegranates for
the two sets of network (two rows
of pomegranates for each network,
decorating the bowl-shaped capi-
tals on top of the pillars);
14 the stands[g] with their basins;
15 the Sea and the twelve bulls under it;
16 the pots, shovels, meat forks and all
related articles.

All the objects that Huram-Abi[h] made
for King Solomon for the temple of the LORD
were of polished bronze. 17 The king had
them cast in clay molds in the plain of the
Jordan between Succoth and Zarethan.[m]
18 All these things that Solomon made
amounted to so much that the weight of the
bronze was not determined.

19 Solomon also made all the furnishings
that were in God's temple:

the golden altar;
the tables[i] on which was the bread of
the Presence;

**3:14** y Ex 26:31,33; Heb 9:3
**3:15** z 1Ki 7:15
**3:16** a 1Ki 7:20
**4:1** b Ex 27:1–2; 2Ki 16:14
**4:6** c Ex 30:18
**4:7** d Ex 25:31 e Ex 25:40
**4:9** f 1Ki 6:36; 2Ki 21:5
**4:14** g 1Ki 7:27–30
**4:16** h 1Ki 7:13
**4:19** i Ex 25:23,30

[a]11 That is, about 7 1/2 feet (about 2.3 meters); also in verse 15 [b]13 Or *facing inward* [c]15 That is, about 52 feet (about 16 meters) [d]16 Or possibly *made chains in the inner sanctuary*; the meaning of the Hebrew for this phrase is uncertain. [e]17 *Jakin* probably means *he establishes.* [f]17 *Boaz* probably means *in him is strength.* [g]1 That is, about 30 feet (about 9 meters) long and wide, and about 15 feet (about 4.5 meters) high [h]2 That is, about 7 1/2 feet (about 2.3 meters) [i]2 That is, about 45 feet (about 13.5 meters) [j]3 That is, about 1 1/2 feet (about 0.5 meter) [k]5 That is, about 3 inches (about 8 centimeters) [l]5 That is, about 17,500 gallons (about 66 kiloliters) [m]17 Hebrew *Zeredatha,* a variant of *Zarethan*

**4:20** j Ex25:31
**5:1** k 2Sa8:11
**5:2** l 2Sa6:12; 1Ch15:25
**5:10** m Heb9:4 n Dt10:2

[20] the lampstands[j] of pure gold with their lamps, to burn in front of the inner sanctuary as prescribed;
[21] the gold floral work and lamps and tongs (they were solid gold);
[22] the pure gold wick trimmers, sprinkling bowls, dishes and censers; and the gold doors of the temple: the inner doors to the Most Holy Place and the doors of the main hall.

5 When all the work Solomon had done for the temple of the LORD was finished, he brought in the things his father David had dedicated[k]—the silver and gold and all the furnishings—and he placed them in the treasuries of God's temple.

## The Ark Brought to the Temple

[2]Then Solomon summoned to Jerusalem the elders of Israel, all the heads of the tribes and the chiefs of the Israelite families, to bring up the ark[l] of the LORD's covenant from Zion, the City of David. [3]And all the men of Israel came together to the king at the time of the festival in the seventh month.

[4]When all the elders of Israel had arrived, the Levites took up the ark, [5]and they brought up the ark and the Tent of Meeting and all the sacred furnishings in it. The priests, who were Levites, carried them up; [6]and King Solomon and the entire assembly of Israel that had gathered about him were before the ark, sacrificing so many sheep and cattle that they could not be recorded or counted.

[7]The priests then brought the ark of the LORD's covenant to its place in the inner sanctuary of the temple, the Most Holy Place, and put it beneath the wings of the cherubim. [8]The cherubim spread their wings over the place of the ark and covered the ark and its carrying poles. [9]These poles were so long that their ends, extending from the ark, could be seen from in front of the inner sanctuary, but not from outside the Holy Place; and they are still there today. [10]There was nothing in the ark except[m] the two tablets[n] that Moses had placed in it at Horeb, where the LORD made a covenant with the Israelites after they came out of Egypt.

[11]The priests then withdrew from the Holy Place. All the priests who were there had consecrated themselves, regardless of their divisions.[o] [12]All the Levites who were musicians[p]—Asaph, Heman, Jeduthun and their sons and relatives—stood on the east side of the altar, dressed in fine linen and playing cymbals, harps and lyres. They were accompanied by 120 priests sounding trumpets.[q] [13]The trumpeters and singers joined in unison, as with one voice, to give praise and thanks to the LORD. Accompanied by trumpets, cymbals and other instruments, they raised their voices in praise to the LORD and sang:

"He is good;
his love endures forever."[r]

Then the temple of the LORD was filled with a cloud, [14]and the priests could not perform[s] their service because of the cloud, for the glory of the LORD filled the temple of God.

6 Then Solomon said, "The LORD has said that he would dwell in a dark cloud;[t] [2]I have built a magnificent temple for you, a place for you to dwell forever."

[3]While the whole assembly of Israel was standing there, the king turned around and blessed them. [4]Then he said:

"Praise be to the LORD, the God of Israel, who with his hands has fulfilled what he promised with his mouth to my father David. For he said, [5]'Since the day I brought my people out of Egypt, I have not chosen a city in any tribe of Israel to have a temple built for my Name to be there, nor have I chosen anyone to be the leader over my people Israel. [6]But now I have chosen Jerusalem for my Name[u] to be there, and I have chosen David[v] to rule my people Israel.'

[7]"My father David had it in his heart to build a temple for the Name of the LORD, the God of Israel. [8]But the LORD said to my father David, 'Because it was in your heart to build a temple for my Name, you did well to have this in your heart. [9]Nevertheless, you are not the one to build the temple, but your son, who is your own flesh and blood—he is the one who will build the temple for my Name.'

**5:11** o 1Ch24:1
**5:12** p 1Ch25:1 q 1Ch15:24
**5:13** r 1Ch16:34,41; 2Ch7:3
**5:14** s Ex40:35
**6:1** t 1Ki8:12–50
**6:6** u 2Ch12:13 v 1Ch28:4

**6:11** w 2Ch 5:10
**6:14** x Ex 15:11; y Dt 7:9
**6:15** z 1Ch 22:10
**6:16** a 2Sa 7:13,15; 1Ki 2:4; 2Ch 7:18
**6:18** b 2Ch 2:6; Isa 66:1; Ac 7:49
**6:20** c Ps 34:15
**6:20** d Dt 12:11
**6:21** e Isa 43:25; 44:22; Mic 7:18
**6:23** f Isa 3:11
**6:26** g 1Ki 17:1
**6:28** h 2Ch 20:9

10"The LORD has kept the promise
he made. I have succeeded David my
father and now I sit on the throne of
Israel, just as the LORD promised, and
I have built the temple for the Name
of the LORD, the God of Israel. 11 There
I have placed the ark, in which is the
covenant[w] of the LORD that he made
with the people of Israel."

## Solomon's Prayer of Dedication

12 Then Solomon stood before the altar of
the LORD in front of the whole assembly of
Israel and spread out his hands. 13 Now he
had made a bronze platform, five cubits[a]
long, five cubits wide and three cubits[b]
high, and had placed it in the center of the
outer court. He stood on the platform and
then knelt down before the whole assembly
of Israel and spread out his hands toward
heaven. 14 He said:

"O LORD, God of Israel, there is no
God like you[x] in heaven or on earth—
you who keep your covenant of love[y]
with your servants who continue
wholeheartedly in your way. 15 You
have kept your promise to your servant
David my father; with your mouth you
have promised[z] and with your hand
you have fulfilled it—as it is today.

16"Now LORD, God of Israel, keep
for your servant David my father the
promises you made to him when you
said, 'You shall never fail[a] to have a
man to sit before me on the throne of
Israel, if only your sons are careful in
all they do to walk before me accord-
ing to my law, as you have done.' 17 And
now, O LORD, God of Israel, let your
word that you promised your servant
David come true.

18"But will God really dwell on earth
with men? The heavens,[b] even the high-
est heavens, cannot contain you. How
much less this temple I have built!
19 Yet give attention to your servant's
prayer and his plea for mercy, O LORD
my God. Hear the cry and the prayer
that your servant is praying in your
presence. 20 May your eyes[c] be open
toward this temple day and night, this
place of which you said you would put
your Name[d] there. May you hear the
prayer your servant prays toward this
place. 21 Hear the supplications of your
servant and of your people Israel when
they pray toward this place. Hear from
heaven, your dwelling place; and when
you hear, forgive.[e]

22"When a man wrongs his neigh-
bor and is required to take an oath and
he comes and swears the oath before
your altar in this temple, 23 then hear
from heaven and act. Judge between
your servants, repaying[f] the guilty by
bringing down on his own head what
he has done. Declare the innocent not
guilty and so establish his innocence.

24"When your people Israel have
been defeated by an enemy because
they have sinned against you and
when they turn back and confess your
name, praying and making supplica-
tion before you in this temple, 25 then
hear from heaven and forgive the sin
of your people Israel and bring them
back to the land you gave to them and
their fathers.

26"When the heavens are shut up
and there is no rain[g] because your peo-
ple have sinned against you, and when
they pray toward this place and con-
fess your name and turn from their
sin because you have afflicted them,
27 then hear from heaven and forgive
the sin of your servants, your people
Israel. Teach them the right way to
live, and send rain on the land you
gave your people for an inheritance.

28"When famine[h] or plague comes
to the land, or blight or mildew, lo-
custs or grasshoppers, or when en-
emies besiege them in any of their
cities, whatever disaster or disease
may come, 29 and when a prayer or plea
is made by any of your people Israel—
each one aware of his afflictions and
pains, and spreading out his hands to-
ward this temple— 30 then hear from
heaven, your dwelling place. Forgive,
and deal with each man according to

[a]13 That is, about 7 1/2 feet (about 2.3 meters) [b]13 That is, about 4 1/2 feet (about 1.3 meters)

**6:30** i 1Sa 16:7; 1Ch 28:9
**6:33** j 2Ch 7:14
**6:36** k Job 15:14; Jas 3:1; 1Jn 1:8–10
**6:40** l 2Ch 7:15
**6:41** m 1Ch 28:2

all he does, since you know his heart (for you alone know the hearts of men),[i] 31 so that they will fear you and walk in your ways all the time they live in the land you gave our fathers.

32 "As for the foreigner who does not belong to your people Israel but has come from a distant land because of your great name and your mighty hand and your outstretched arm—when he comes and prays toward this temple, 33 then hear from heaven, your dwelling place, and do whatever the foreigner[j] asks of you, so that all the peoples of the earth may know your name and fear you, as do your own people Israel, and may know that this house I have built bears your Name.

34 "When your people go to war against their enemies, wherever you send them, and when they pray to you toward this city you have chosen and the temple I have built for your Name, 35 then hear from heaven their prayer and their plea, and uphold their cause.

36 "When they sin against you—for there is no one who does not sin[k]—and you become angry with them and give them over to the enemy, who takes them captive to a land far away or near; 37 and if they have a change of heart in the land where they are held captive, and repent and plead with you in the land of their captivity and say, 'We have sinned, we have done wrong and acted wickedly'; 38 and if they turn back to you with all their heart and soul in the land of their captivity where they were taken, and pray toward the land you gave their fathers, toward the city you have chosen and toward the temple I have built for your Name; 39 then from heaven, your dwelling place, hear their prayer and their pleas, and uphold their cause. And forgive your people, who have sinned against you.

40 "Now, my God, may your eyes be open and your ears attentive[l] to the prayers offered in this place.

41 "Now arise, O LORD God, and come
to your resting place,[m]

*My own child,*

*My eyes are always on you.*

*Love,*

*The All-Seeing One*

2 CHRONICLES 6:40

you and the ark of your might.
May your priests,[n] O LORD God, be
clothed with salvation,
may your saints rejoice in your
goodness.
42 O LORD God, do not reject your
anointed one.
Remember the great love[o]
promised to David your
servant."

## The Dedication of the Temple

7 When Solomon finished praying, fire[p] came down from heaven and consumed the burnt offering and the sacrifices, and the glory of the LORD filled the temple. 2 The priests could not enter the temple of the LORD because the glory of the LORD filled it. 3 When all the Israelites saw the fire coming down and the glory of the LORD above the temple, they knelt on the pavement with their faces to the ground, and they worshiped and gave thanks to the LORD, saying,

"He is good;
his love endures forever."[q]

4 Then the king and all the people offered sacrifices before the LORD. 5 And King Solomon offered a sacrifice of twenty-two thousand head of cattle and a hundred and twenty thousand sheep and goats. So the king and all the people dedicated the temple of God. 6 The priests took their positions, as did the Levites[r] with the LORD's musical instruments,[s] which King David had made for praising the LORD and which were used when he gave thanks, saying, "His love endures forever." Opposite the Levites, the priests blew their trumpets, and all the Israelites were standing.

**6:41** n Ps 132:16
**6:42** o Ps 89:24,28
**7:1** p Lev 9:24; 1Ki 18:38
**7:3** q 2Ch 5:13
**7:6** r 1Ch 15:16 s 2Ch 5:12

7:8 t Ge15:18
7:9 u Lev23:36
7:12 v Dt12:5
7:14 w 2Ch6:37 x 2Ch6:27
7:15 y 2Ch6:40
7:17 z 1Ki9:4

[7]Solomon consecrated the middle part of the courtyard in front of the temple of the LORD, and there he offered burnt offerings and the fat of the fellowship offerings,[a] because the bronze altar he had made could not hold the burnt offerings, the grain offerings and the fat portions.

[8]So Solomon observed the festival at that time for seven days, and all Israel with him—a vast assembly, people from Lebo[b] Hamath to the Wadi of Egypt.[t] [9]On the eighth day they held an assembly, for they had celebrated the dedication of the altar for seven days and the festival[u] for seven days more. [10]On the twenty-third day of the seventh month he sent the people to their homes, joyful and glad in heart for the good things the LORD had done for David and Solomon and for his people Israel.

## The LORD Appears to Solomon

[11]When Solomon had finished the temple of the LORD and the royal palace, and had succeeded in carrying out all he had in mind to do in the temple of the LORD and in his own palace, [12]the LORD appeared to him at night and said:

"I have heard your prayer and have chosen this place for myself[v] as a temple for sacrifices.

[13]"When I shut up the heavens so that there is no rain, or command locusts to devour the land or send a plague among my people, [14]if my people, who are called by my name, will humble[w] themselves and pray and seek my face and turn from their wicked ways, then will I hear from heaven and will forgive[x] their sin and will heal their land. [15]Now my eyes will be open and my ears attentive to the prayers offered in this place.[y] [16]I have chosen and consecrated this temple so that my Name may be there forever. My eyes and my heart will always be there.

[17]"As for you, if you walk before me[z] as David your father did, and do all I command, and observe my decrees and laws, [18]I will establish your royal throne, as I covenanted with David your father when I said, 'You shall never fail to have a man[a] to rule over Israel.'

[19]"But if you[c] turn away[b] and forsake the decrees and commands I have given you[c] and go off to serve other gods and worship them, [20]then I will uproot[c] Israel from my land, which I have given them, and will reject this temple I have consecrated for my Name. I will make it a byword and an object of ridicule among all peoples. [21]And though this temple is now so imposing, all who pass by will be appalled and say,[d] 'Why has the LORD done such a thing to this land and to this temple?' [22]People will answer, 'Because they have forsaken the LORD, the God of their fathers, who brought them out of Egypt, and have embraced other gods, worshiping and serving them—that is why he brought all this disaster on them.'"

## Solomon's Other Activities

**8** At the end of twenty years, during which Solomon built the temple of the LORD and his own palace, [2]Solomon rebuilt the villages that Hiram[d] had given him, and settled Israelites in them. [3]Solomon then went to Hamath Zobah and captured it. [4]He also built up Tadmor in the desert and all the store cities he had built in Hamath. [5]He rebuilt Upper Beth Horon and Lower Beth Horon as fortified cities, with walls and with gates and bars, [6]as well as Baalath and all his store cities, and all the cities for his chariots and for his horses[e]—whatever he desired to build in Jerusalem, in Lebanon and throughout all the territory he ruled.

[7]All the people left from the Hittites, Amorites, Perizzites, Hivites and Jebusites (these peoples were not Israelites), [8]that is, their descendants remaining in the land, whom the Israelites had not destroyed—these Solomon conscripted for his slave labor force, as it is to this day. [9]But Solomon did not make slaves of the Israelites for his work; they were his fighting men, commanders of

7:18 a 2Ch6:16
7:19 b Dt28:15
7:20 c Dt29:28
7:21 d Dt29:24

[a]7 Traditionally *peace offerings* [b]8 Or *from the entrance to* [c]19 The Hebrew is plural. [d]2 Hebrew *Huram,* a variant of *Hiram*; also in verse 18 [e]6 Or *charioteers*

**8:11** e 1Ki 3:1
**8:13** f Ex 29:38; Nu 28:3 g Ex 23:14
**8:14** h 1Ch 25:1 i Ne 12:24,36
**8:18** j 2Ch 9:9
**9:1** k Mt 12:42; Lk 11:31

his captains, and commanders of his chariots and charioteers. [10]They were also King Solomon's chief officials—two hundred and fifty officials supervising the men.

[11]Solomon brought Pharaoh's daughter[e] up from the City of David to the palace he had built for her, for he said, "My wife must not live in the palace of David king of Israel, because the places the ark of the LORD has entered are holy."

[12]On the altar of the LORD that he had built in front of the portico, Solomon sacrificed burnt offerings to the LORD, [13]according to the daily requirement[f] for offerings commanded by Moses for Sabbaths, New Moons and the three[g] annual feasts—the Feast of Unleavened Bread, the Feast of Weeks and the Feast of Tabernacles. [14]In keeping with the ordinance of his father David, he appointed the divisions of the priests for their duties, and the Levites[h] to lead the praise and to assist the priests according to each day's requirement. He also appointed the gatekeepers by divisions for the various gates, because this was what David the man of God[i] had ordered. [15]They did not deviate from the king's commands to the priests or to the Levites in any matter, including that of the treasuries.

[16]All Solomon's work was carried out, from the day the foundation of the temple of the LORD was laid until its completion. So the temple of the LORD was finished.

[17]Then Solomon went to Ezion Geber and Elath on the coast of Edom. [18]And Hiram sent him ships commanded by his own officers, men who knew the sea. These, with Solomon's men, sailed to Ophir and brought back four hundred and fifty talents[a] of gold,[j] which they delivered to King Solomon.

## The Queen of Sheba Visits Solomon

**9** When the queen of Sheba[k] heard of Solomon's fame, she came to Jerusalem to test him with hard questions. Arriving with a very great caravan—with camels carrying spices, large quantities of gold, and precious stones—she came to Solomon and talked with him about all she had on her mind. [2]Solomon answered all her questions; nothing was too hard for him to explain to her. [3]When the queen of Sheba saw the wisdom of Solomon,[l] as well as the palace he had built, [4]the food on his table, the seating of his officials, the attending servants in their robes, the cupbearers in their robes and the burnt offerings he made at[b] the temple of the LORD, she was overwhelmed.

[5]She said to the king, "The report I heard in my own country about your achievements and your wisdom is true. [6]But I did not believe what they said until I came and saw with my own eyes. Indeed, not even half the greatness of your wisdom was told me; you have far exceeded the report I heard. [7]How happy your men must be! How happy your officials, who continually stand before you and hear your wisdom! [8]Praise be to the LORD your God, who has delighted in you and placed you on his throne[m] as king to rule for the LORD your God. Because of the love of your God for Israel and his desire to uphold them forever, he has made you king[n] over them, to maintain justice and righteousness."

[9]Then she gave the king 120 talents[c] of gold, large quantities of spices, and precious stones. There had never been such spices as those the queen of Sheba gave to King Solomon.

[10](The men of Hiram and the men of Solomon brought gold from Ophir;[o] they also brought algumwood[d] and precious stones. [11]The king used the algumwood to make steps for the temple of the LORD and for the royal palace, and to make harps and lyres for the musicians. Nothing like them had ever been seen in Judah.)

[12]King Solomon gave the queen of Sheba all she desired and asked for; he gave her more than she had brought to him. Then she left and returned with her retinue to her own country.

## Solomon's Splendor

[13]The weight of the gold that Solomon received yearly was 666 talents,[e] [14]not including the revenues brought in by merchants and traders. Also all the kings of Arabia and

**9:3** l 1Ki 5:12
**9:8** m 1Ch 28:5; 29:23 n 2Ch 2:11
**9:10** o 2Ch 8:18

[a]18 That is, about 17 tons (about 16 metric tons) [b]4 Or *the ascent by which he went up to* [c]9 That is, about 4 1/2 tons (about 4 metric tons) [d]10 Probably a variant of *almugwood* [e]13 That is, about 25 tons (about 23 metric tons)

9:22 p 1Ki3:13; 2Ch1:12
9:25 q 1Ki4:26

the governors of the land brought gold and
silver to Solomon.
15 King Solomon made two hundred large
shields of hammered gold; six hundred be-
kas[a] of hammered gold went into each shield.
16 He also made three hundred small shields
of hammered gold, with three hundred be-
kas[b] of gold in each shield. The king put them
in the Palace of the Forest of Lebanon.
17 Then the king made a great throne in-
laid with ivory and overlaid with pure gold.
18 The throne had six steps, and a footstool
of gold was attached to it. On both sides of
the seat were armrests, with a lion standing
beside each of them. 19 Twelve lions stood on
the six steps, one at either end of each step.
Nothing like it had ever been made for any
other kingdom. 20 All King Solomon's gob-
lets were gold, and all the household articles
in the Palace of the Forest of Lebanon were
pure gold. Nothing was made of silver, be-
cause silver was considered of little value in
Solomon's day. 21 The king had a fleet of trad-
ing ships[c] manned by Hiram's[d] men. Once
every three years it returned, carrying gold,
silver and ivory, and apes and baboons.
22 King Solomon was greater in riches
and wisdom than all the other kings of the
earth.[p] 23 All the kings of the earth sought
audience with Solomon to hear the wisdom
God had put in his heart. 24 Year after year,
everyone who came brought a gift—articles
of silver and gold, and robes, weapons and
spices, and horses and mules.
25 Solomon had four thousand stalls for
horses and chariots,[q] and twelve thousand
horses,[e] which he kept in the chariot cities
and also with him in Jerusalem. 26 He ruled[r]
over all the kings from the River[f] to the land
of the Philistines, as far as the border of
Egypt.[s] 27 The king made silver as common
in Jerusalem as stones, and cedar as plen-
tiful as sycamore-fig trees in the foothills.
28 Solomon's horses were imported from
Egypt[g] and from all other countries.

## Solomon's Death

29 As for the other events of Solomon's
reign, from beginning to end, are they not
written in the records of Nathan the prophet,
in the prophecy of Ahijah the Shilonite and
in the visions of Iddo the seer concerning
Jeroboam son of Nebat? 30 Solomon reigned
in Jerusalem over all Israel forty years.
31 Then he rested with his fathers and was
buried in the city of David[t] his father. And
Rehoboam his son succeeded him as king.

## Israel Rebels Against Rehoboam

10 Rehoboam went to Shechem, for
all the Israelites had gone there to
make him king. 2 When Jeroboam son of
Nebat heard this (he was in Egypt, where he
had fled[u] from King Solomon), he returned
from Egypt. 3 So they sent for Jeroboam,
and he and all Israel went to Rehoboam and
said to him: 4 "Your father put a heavy yoke
on us, but now lighten the harsh labor and
the heavy yoke he put on us, and we will
serve you."
5 Rehoboam answered, "Come back to me
in three days." So the people went away.
6 Then King Rehoboam consulted the
elders[v] who had served his father Solomon

9:26 r 1Ki4:21 s Ge15:18–21
9:31 t 1Ki2:10
10:2 u 1Ki11:40
10:6 v Job8:8–9

[a] 15 That is, about 7 1/2 pounds (about 3.5 kilograms) [b] 16 That is, about 3 3/4 pounds (about 1.7 kilograms) [c] 21 Hebrew *of ships that could go to Tarshish* [d] 21 Hebrew *Huram,* a variant of *Hiram* [e] 25 Or *charioteers* [f] 26 That is, the Euphrates [g] 28 Or possibly *Muzur,* a region in Cilicia

## The African Presence

### 2 Chronicles 9

The queen of Sheba—the ancient historian Josephus (*Antiquities,* 8.6.5) called her the "queen of Egypt and Ethiopia"—visited Solomon. Sheba was located in southern Arabia (present-day Yemen), across the Red Sea from present-day Ethiopia.

**10:8** w Pr 13:20
**10:15** x 2Ch 25:16-20 y 1Ki 11:29
**10:16** z 2Sa 20:1

during his lifetime. "How would you advise me to answer these people?" he asked.

7 They replied, "If you will be kind to these people and please them and give them a favorable answer, they will always be your servants."

8 But Rehoboam rejected the advice the elders[w] gave him and consulted the young men who had grown up with him and were serving him. 9 He asked them, "What is your advice? How should we answer these people who say to me, 'Lighten the yoke your father put on us'?"

10 The young men who had grown up with him replied, "Tell the people who have said to you, 'Your father put a heavy yoke on us, but make our yoke lighter'—tell them, 'My little finger is thicker than my father's waist. 11 My father laid on you a heavy yoke; I will make it even heavier. My father scourged you with whips; I will scourge you with scorpions.'"

12 Three days later Jeroboam and all the people returned to Rehoboam, as the king had said, "Come back to me in three days." 13 The king answered them harshly. Rejecting the advice of the elders, 14 he followed the advice of the young men and said, "My father made your yoke heavy; I will make it even heavier. My father scourged you with whips; I will scourge you with scorpions." 15 So the king did not listen to the people, for this turn of events was from God,[x] to fulfill the word the LORD had spoken to Jeroboam son of Nebat through Ahijah the Shilonite.[y]

16 When all Israel saw that the king refused to listen to them, they answered the king:

"What share do we have in David,[z]
  what part in Jesse's son?
To your tents, O Israel!
  Look after your own house, O David!"

So all the Israelites went home. 17 But as for the Israelites who were living in the towns of Judah, Rehoboam still ruled over them.

18 King Rehoboam sent out Adoniram,[a] who was in charge of forced labor, but the Israelites stoned him to death. King Rehoboam, however, managed to get into his chariot and escape to Jerusalem. 19 So Israel has been in rebellion against the house of David to this day.

11 When Rehoboam arrived in Jerusalem,[a] he mustered the house of Judah and Benjamin—a hundred and eighty thousand fighting men—to make war against Israel and to regain the kingdom for Rehoboam.

2 But this word of the LORD came to Shemaiah[b] the man of God: 3 "Say to Rehoboam son of Solomon king of Judah and to all the Israelites in Judah and Benjamin, 4 'This is what the LORD says: Do not go up to fight against your brothers. Go home, every one of you, for this is my doing.'" So they obeyed the words of the LORD and turned back from marching against Jeroboam.

## Rehoboam Fortifies Judah

5 Rehoboam lived in Jerusalem and built up towns for defense in Judah: 6 Bethlehem, Etam, Tekoa, 7 Beth Zur, Soco, Adullam, 8 Gath, Mareshah, Ziph, 9 Adoraim, Lachish, Azekah, 10 Zorah, Aijalon and Hebron. These were fortified cities in Judah and Benjamin. 11 He strengthened their defenses and put commanders in them, with supplies of food, olive oil and wine. 12 He put shields and spears in all the cities, and made them very strong. So Judah and Benjamin were his.

13 The priests and Levites from all their districts throughout Israel sided with him. 14 The Levites[c] even abandoned their pasturelands and property,[d] and came to Judah and Jerusalem because Jeroboam and his sons had rejected them as priests of the LORD. 15 And he appointed[e] his own priests[f] for the high places and for the goat and calf idols he had made. 16 Those from every tribe of Israel[g] who set their hearts on seeking the LORD, the God of Israel, followed the Levites to Jerusalem to offer sacrifices to the LORD, the God of their fathers. 17 They strengthened[h] the kingdom of Judah and supported Rehoboam son of Solomon three years, walking in the ways of David and Solomon during this time.

## Rehoboam's Family

18 Rehoboam married Mahalath, who was the daughter of David's son Jerimoth

**11:1** a 1Ki 12:21
**11:2** b 2Ch 12:5-7,15
**11:14** c Nu 35:2-5 d 2Ch 13:9
**11:15** e 1Ki 13:33 f 1Ki 12:31
**11:16** g 2Ch 15:9
**11:17** h 2Ch 12:1

[a] 18 Hebrew *Hadoram*, a variant of *Adoniram*

and of Abihail, the daughter of Jesse's son Eliab. 19 She bore him sons: Jeush, Shemariah and Zaham. 20 Then he married Maacah daughter of Absalom, who bore him Abijah, Attai, Ziza and Shelomith. 21 Rehoboam loved Maacah daughter of Absalom more than any of his other wives and concubines. In all, he had eighteen wives and sixty concubines, twenty-eight sons and sixty daughters.

22 Rehoboam appointed Abijah[i] son of Maacah to be the chief prince among his brothers, in order to make him king. 23 He acted wisely, dispersing some of his sons throughout the districts of Judah and Benjamin, and to all the fortified cities. He gave them abundant provisions and took many wives for them.

## Shishak Attacks Jerusalem

12 After Rehoboam's position as king was established and he had become strong,[j] he and all Israel[a] with him abandoned the law of the LORD. 2 Because they had been unfaithful to the LORD, Shishak king of Egypt attacked Jerusalem in the fifth year of King Rehoboam. 3 With twelve hundred chariots and sixty thousand horsemen and the innumerable troops of Libyans, Sukkites and Cushites[b][k] that came with him from Egypt, 4 he captured the fortified cities of Judah and came as far as Jerusalem.

5 Then the prophet Shemaiah[l] came to Rehoboam and to the leaders of Judah who had assembled in Jerusalem for fear of Shishak, and he said to them, "This is what the LORD says, 'You have abandoned me; therefore, I now abandon you to Shishak.' "

6 The leaders of Israel and the king humbled themselves and said, "The LORD is just."[m]

7 When the LORD saw that they humbled themselves, this word of the LORD came to Shemaiah: "Since they have humbled themselves, I will not destroy them but will soon give them deliverance.[n] My wrath will not be poured out on Jerusalem through Shishak. 8 They will, however, become subject[o] to him, so that they may learn the difference between serving me and serving the kings of other lands."

9 When Shishak king of Egypt attacked Jerusalem, he carried off the treasures of the temple of the LORD and the treasures of the royal palace. He took everything, including the gold shields[p] Solomon had made. 10 So King Rehoboam made bronze shields to replace them and assigned these to the commanders of the guard on duty at the entrance to the royal palace. 11 Whenever the king went to the LORD's temple, the guards went with him, bearing the shields, and afterward they returned them to the guardroom.

12 Because Rehoboam humbled himself, the LORD's anger turned from him, and he was not totally destroyed. Indeed, there was some good[q] in Judah.

13 King Rehoboam established himself firmly in Jerusalem and continued as king. He was forty-one years old when he became king, and he reigned seventeen years in Jerusalem, the city the LORD had chosen out of all the tribes of Israel in which to put his Name.[r] His mother's name was Naamah; she was an Ammonite. 14 He did evil because he had not set his heart on seeking the LORD.

15 As for the events of Rehoboam's reign,

**11:22** i Dt 21:15-17
**12:1** j 2Ch 11:17
**12:3** k 2Ch 16:8
**12:5** l 2Ch 11:2
**12:6** m Ex 9:27
**12:7** n 1Ki 21:29
**12:8** o Dt 28:48
**12:9** p 2Ch 9:16
**12:12** q 2Ch 19:3
**12:13** r Dt 12:5

[a] 1 That is, Judah, as frequently in 2 Chronicles [b] 3 That is, people from the upper Nile region

### The African Presence

**2 Chronicles 12**

Shishak, king of Egypt, attacked Jerusalem with the Libyans, Sukkites and Cushites—all of whom were of African origin.

**12:15**
s 2Ch 9:29
**13:2**
t 2Ch 11:20
**13:4**
u Jos 18:22
v 1Ch 11:1
**13:5**
w 2Sa 7:13
x Nu 18:19
**13:6**
y 1Ki 11:26
**13:8**
z 1Ki 12:28; 2Ch 11:15
**13:9**
a 2Ch 11:14–15
**13:11**
b 2Ch 2:4

from beginning to end, are they not written in the records of Shemaiah[s] the prophet and of Iddo the seer that deal with genealogies? There was continual warfare between Rehoboam and Jeroboam. [16]Rehoboam rested with his fathers and was buried in the City of David. And Abijah his son succeeded him as king.

## Abijah King of Judah

13 In the eighteenth year of the reign of Jeroboam, Abijah became king of Judah, [2]and he reigned in Jerusalem three years. His mother's name was Maacah,[a] a daughter[b] of Uriel of Gibeah.

There was war between Abijah[t] and Jeroboam. [3]Abijah went into battle with a force of four hundred thousand able fighting men, and Jeroboam drew up a battle line against him with eight hundred thousand able troops.

[4]Abijah stood on Mount Zemaraim,[u] in the hill country of Ephraim, and said, "Jeroboam and all Israel,[v] listen to me! [5]Don't you know that the LORD, the God of Israel, has given the kingship of Israel to David and his descendants forever[w] by a covenant of salt?[x] [6]Yet Jeroboam son of Nebat, an official of Solomon son of David, rebelled[y] against his master. [7]Some worthless scoundrels gathered around him and opposed Rehoboam son of Solomon when he was young and indecisive and not strong enough to resist them.

[8]"And now you plan to resist the kingdom of the LORD, which is in the hands of David's descendants. You are indeed a vast army and have with you the golden calves[z] that Jeroboam made to be your gods. [9]But didn't you drive out the priests of the LORD,[a] the sons of Aaron, and the Levites, and make priests of your own as the peoples of other lands do? Whoever comes to consecrate himself with a young bull and seven rams may become a priest of what are not gods.

[10]"As for us, the LORD is our God, and we have not forsaken him. The priests who serve the LORD are sons of Aaron, and the Levites assist them. [11]Every morning and evening[b] they present burnt offerings and fragrant incense to the LORD. They set out the bread on the ceremonially clean table[c] and light the lamps on the gold lampstand every evening. We are observing the requirements of the LORD our God. But you have forsaken him. [12]God is with us; he is our leader. His priests with their trumpets will sound the battle cry against you.[d] Men of Israel, do not fight against the LORD, the God of your fathers, for you will not succeed."

[13]Now Jeroboam had sent troops around to the rear, so that while he was in front of Judah the ambush was behind them. [14]Judah turned and saw that they were being attacked at both front and rear. Then they cried out[e] to the LORD. The priests blew their trumpets [15]and the men of Judah raised the battle cry. At the sound of their battle cry, God routed Jeroboam and all Israel before Abijah and Judah. [16]The Israelites fled before Judah, and God delivered[f] them into their hands. [17]Abijah and his men inflicted heavy losses on them, so that there were five hundred thousand casualties among Israel's able men. [18]The men of Israel were subdued on that occasion, and the men of Judah were victorious because they relied[g] on the LORD, the God of their fathers.

[19]Abijah pursued Jeroboam and took from him the towns of Bethel, Jeshanah and Ephron, with their surrounding villages. [20]Jeroboam did not regain power during the time of Abijah. And the LORD struck him down and he died.

[21]But Abijah grew in strength. He married fourteen wives and had twenty-two sons and sixteen daughters.

[22]The other events of Abijah's reign, what he did and what he said, are written in the annotations of the prophet Iddo.

14 And Abijah rested with his fathers and was buried in the City of David. Asa his son succeeded him as king, and in his days the country was at peace for ten years.

## Asa King of Judah

[2]Asa did what was good and right in the eyes of the LORD his God. [3]He removed the foreign altars and the high places, smashed

**13:11**
c Lev 24:5–9
**13:12**
d Nu 10:8–9
**13:14**
e 2Ch 14:11
**13:16**
f 2Ch 16:8
**13:18**
g Ps 22:5

[a]2 Most Septuagint manuscripts and Syriac (see also 2 Chron. 11:20 and 1 Kings 15:2); Hebrew *Micaiah* [b]2 Or *granddaughter*

the sacred stones and cut down the Asherah poles.[a][h] [4]He commanded Judah to seek the LORD, the God of their fathers, and to obey his laws and commands. [5]He removed the high places and incense altars[i] in every town in Judah, and the kingdom was at peace under him. [6]He built up the fortified cities of Judah, since the land was at peace. No one was at war with him during those years, for the LORD gave him rest.

[7]"Let us build up these towns," he said to Judah, "and put walls around them, with towers, gates and bars. The land is still ours, because we have sought the LORD our God; we sought him and he has given us rest on every side." So they built and prospered.

[8]Asa had an army of three hundred thousand men from Judah, equipped with large shields and with spears, and two hundred and eighty thousand from Benjamin, armed with small shields and with bows. All these were brave fighting men.

[9]Zerah the Cushite[j] marched out against them with a vast army[b] and three hundred chariots, and came as far as Mareshah.[k] [10]Asa went out to meet him, and they took up battle positions in the Valley of Zephathah near Mareshah.

[11]Then Asa called[l] to the LORD his God and said, "LORD, there is no one like you to help the powerless against the mighty. Help us, O LORD our God, for we rely on you, and in your name[m] we have come against this vast army. O LORD, you are our God; do not let man prevail against you."

[12]The LORD struck down[n] the Cushites before Asa and Judah. The Cushites fled, [13]and Asa and his army pursued them as far as Gerar.[o] Such a great number of Cushites fell that they could not recover; they were crushed before the LORD and his forces. The men of Judah carried off a large amount of plunder. [14]They destroyed all the villages around Gerar, for the terror[p] of the LORD had fallen upon them. They plundered all these villages, since there was much booty there. [15]They also attacked the camps of the herdsmen and carried off droves of sheep and goats and camels. Then they returned to Jerusalem.

## Asa's Reform

**15** The Spirit of God came upon[q] Azariah son of Oded. [2]He went out to meet Asa and said to him, "Listen to me, Asa and all Judah and Benjamin. The LORD is with you[r] when you are with him.[s] If you seek him, he will be found by you, but if you forsake him, he will forsake you. [3]For a long time Israel was without the true God, without a priest to teach[t] and without the law. [4]But in their distress they turned to the LORD, the God of Israel, and sought him,[u] and he was found by them. [5]In those days it was not safe to travel about,[v] for all the inhabitants of the lands were in great turmoil. [6]One nation was being crushed by another and one city by another,[w] because God was troubling them with every kind of distress. [7]But as for you, be strong[x] and do not give up, for your work will be rewarded."

[8]When Asa heard these words and the prophecy of Azariah son of[c] Oded the prophet, he took courage. He removed the detestable idols from the whole land of Judah and Benjamin and from the towns he

**14:3** h Ex 34:13; 1Ki 15:12–14
**14:5** i 2Ch 34:4,7
**14:9** j 2Ch 16:8 k 2Ch 11:8
**14:11** l 2Ch 13:14 m 1Sa 17:45
**14:12** n 2Ch 13:15
**14:13** o Ge 10:19
**14:14** p Ge 35:5
**15:1** q 2Ch 20:14
**15:2** r ver 4,15 s Jas 4:8
**15:3** t Lev 10:11
**15:4** u Dt 4:29
**15:5** v Jdg 5:6
**15:6** w Mt 24:7
**15:7** x Jos 1:7,9

[a]3 That is, symbols of the goddess Asherah; here and elsewhere in 2 Chronicles [b]9 Hebrew *with an army of a thousand thousands* or *with an army of thousands upon thousands* [c]8 Vulgate and Syriac (see also Septuagint and verse 1); Hebrew does not have *Azariah son of.*

## The African Presence

**2 Chronicles 14**

**Zerah, a Cushite, marched out against King Asa of Judah. When Asa called on the Lord, he was given victory over Zerah's army.**

**15:8** y 2Ch 13:19
**15:9** z 2Ch 11:16–17
**15:11** a 2Ch 14:13
**15:13** b Ex 22:20; Dt 13:9–16
**15:16** c Ex 34:13; 2Ch 14:2–5

had captured[y] in the hills of Ephraim. He repaired the altar of the LORD that was in front of the portico of the LORD's temple.

[9]Then he assembled all Judah and Benjamin and the people from Ephraim, Manasseh and Simeon who had settled among them, for large numbers[z] had come over to him from Israel when they saw that the LORD his God was with him.

[10]They assembled at Jerusalem in the third month of the fifteenth year of Asa's reign. [11]At that time they sacrificed to the LORD seven hundred head of cattle and seven thousand sheep and goats from the plunder[a] they had brought back. [12]They entered into a covenant to seek the LORD, the God of their fathers, with all their heart and soul. [13]All who would not seek the LORD, the God of Israel, were to be put to death,[b] whether small or great, man or woman. [14]They took an oath to the LORD with loud acclamation, with shouting and with trumpets and horns. [15]All Judah rejoiced about the oath because they had sworn it wholeheartedly. They sought God eagerly, and he was found by them. So the LORD gave them rest on every side.

[16]King Asa also deposed his grandmother Maacah from her position as queen mother, because she had made a repulsive Asherah pole.[c] Asa cut the pole down, broke it up and burned it in the Kidron Valley. [17]Although he did not remove the high places from Israel, Asa's heart was fully committed ⌞to the LORD⌟ all his life. [18]He brought into the temple of God the silver and gold and the articles that he and his father had dedicated.

[19]There was no more war until the thirty-fifth year of Asa's reign.

*God,*

*I pray for our leaders today. Help them to hear your voice and to move forward in step with your plan. Even when it doesn't appear as though they are complying, help me to remember that you ultimately have every situation completely in hand.*

*Amen*

2 CHRONICLES 15:8–18

**16:1** d Jer 41:9
**16:7** e 1Ki 16:1
**16:8** f 2Ch 12:3
**16:9** g Pr 15:3; Zec 4:10 h 1Sa 13:13

## Asa's Last Years

**16** In the thirty-sixth year of Asa's reign Baasha[d] king of Israel went up against Judah and fortified Ramah to prevent anyone from leaving or entering the territory of Asa king of Judah.

[2]Asa then took the silver and gold out of the treasuries of the LORD's temple and of his own palace and sent it to Ben-Hadad king of Aram, who was ruling in Damascus. [3]"Let there be a treaty between me and you," he said, "as there was between my father and your father. See, I am sending you silver and gold. Now break your treaty with Baasha king of Israel so he will withdraw from me."

[4]Ben-Hadad agreed with King Asa and sent the commanders of his forces against the towns of Israel. They conquered Ijon, Dan, Abel Maim[a] and all the store cities of Naphtali. [5]When Baasha heard this, he stopped building Ramah and abandoned his work. [6]Then King Asa brought all the men of Judah, and they carried away from Ramah the stones and timber Baasha had been using. With them he built up Geba and Mizpah.

[7]At that time Hanani[e] the seer came to Asa king of Judah and said to him: "Because you relied on the king of Aram and not on the LORD your God, the army of the king of Aram has escaped from your hand. [8]Were not the Cushites[b][f] and Libyans a mighty army with great numbers of chariots and horsemen[c]? Yet when you relied on the LORD, he delivered them into your hand. [9]For the eyes[g] of the LORD range throughout the earth to strengthen those whose hearts are fully committed to him. You have done a foolish[h] thing, and from now on you will be at war."

[10]Asa was angry with the seer because of this; he was so enraged that he put him in prison. At the same time Asa brutally oppressed some of the people.

[a]4 Also known as *Abel Beth Maacah* [b]8 That is, people from the upper Nile region [c]8 Or *charioteers*

16:12 i Jer 17:5–6
16:14 j Ge 50:2 k 2Ch 21:19
17:2 l 2Ch 15:8
17:4 m 1Ki 12:28; 2Ch 22:9
17:5 n 2Ch 18:1
17:6 o 2Ch 15:17 p 2Ch 19:3; 20:33
17:7 q 2Ch 15:3
17:8 r 2Ch 19:8
17:9 s Dt 6:4–9
17:10 t Ge 35:5; 2Ch 14:14
17:11 u 2Ch 9:14; 26:8

11 The events of Asa's reign, from beginning to end, are written in the book of the kings of Judah and Israel. 12 In the thirty-ninth year of his reign Asa was afflicted with a disease in his feet. Though his disease was severe, even in his illness he did not seek help from the LORD,[i] but only from the physicians. 13 Then in the forty-first year of his reign Asa died and rested with his fathers. 14 They buried him in the tomb that he had cut out for himself in the City of David. They laid him on a bier covered with spices and various blended perfumes,[j] and they made a huge fire[k] in his honor.

## Jehoshaphat King of Judah

17 Jehoshaphat his son succeeded him as king and strengthened himself against Israel. 2 He stationed troops in all the fortified cities of Judah and put garrisons in Judah and in the towns of Ephraim that his father Asa had captured.[l]

3 The LORD was with Jehoshaphat because in his early years he walked in the ways his father David had followed. He did not consult the Baals 4 but sought[m] the God of his father and followed his commands rather than the practices of Israel. 5 The LORD established the kingdom under his control; and all Judah brought gifts to Jehoshaphat, so that he had great wealth and honor.[n] 6 His heart was devoted[o] to the ways of the LORD; furthermore, he removed the high places[p] and the Asherah poles from Judah.

7 In the third year of his reign he sent his officials Ben-Hail, Obadiah, Zechariah, Nethanel and Micaiah to teach[q] in the towns of Judah. 8 With them were certain Levites[r]—Shemaiah, Nethaniah, Zebadiah, Asahel, Shemiramoth, Jehonathan, Adonijah, Tobijah and Tob-Adonijah—and the priests Elishama and Jehoram. 9 They taught throughout Judah, taking with them the Book of the Law[s] of the LORD; they went around to all the towns of Judah and taught the people.

10 The fear[t] of the LORD fell on all the kingdoms of the lands surrounding Judah, so that they did not make war with Jehoshaphat. 11 Some Philistines brought Jehoshaphat gifts and silver as tribute, and the Arabs[u] brought him flocks: seven thousand seven hundred rams and seven thousand seven hundred goats.

12 Jehoshaphat became more and more powerful; he built forts and store cities in Judah 13 and had large supplies in the towns of Judah. He also kept experienced fighting men in Jerusalem. 14 Their enrollment by families was as follows:

From Judah, commanders of units of 1,000:
Adnah the commander, with 300,000 fighting men;
15 next, Jehohanan the commander, with 280,000;
16 next, Amasiah son of Zicri, who volunteered[v] himself for the service of the LORD, with 200,000.
17 From Benjamin:
Eliada, a valiant soldier, with 200,000 men armed with bows and shields;
18 next, Jehozabad, with 180,000 men armed for battle.

19 These were the men who served the king, besides those he stationed in the fortified cities throughout Judah.

## Micaiah Prophesies Against Ahab

18 Now Jehoshaphat had great wealth and honor,[w] and he allied himself with Ahab by marriage. 2 Some years later he went down to visit Ahab in Samaria. Ahab slaughtered many sheep and cattle for him and the people with him and urged him to attack Ramoth Gilead. 3 Ahab king of Israel asked Jehoshaphat king of Judah, "Will you go with me against Ramoth Gilead?"

Jehoshaphat replied, "I am as you are, and my people as your people; we will join you in the war." 4 But Jehoshaphat also said to the king of Israel, "First seek the counsel of the LORD."

5 So the king of Israel brought together the prophets—four hundred men—and asked them, "Shall we go to war against Ramoth Gilead, or shall I refrain?"

"Go," they answered, "for God will give it into the king's hand."

6 But Jehoshaphat asked, "Is there not a

17:16 v Jdg 5:9; 1Ch 29:9
18:1 w 2Ch 17:5

**18:11** x 2Ch 22:5
**18:13** y Nu 22:18,20,35
**18:16** z Nu 27:17

prophet of the LORD here whom we can inquire of?"

[7]The king of Israel answered Jehoshaphat, "There is still one man through whom we can inquire of the LORD, but I hate him because he never prophesies anything good about me, but always bad. He is Micaiah son of Imlah."

"The king should not say that," Jehoshaphat replied.

[8]So the king of Israel called one of his officials and said, "Bring Micaiah son of Imlah at once."

[9]Dressed in their royal robes, the king of Israel and Jehoshaphat king of Judah were sitting on their thrones at the threshing floor by the entrance to the gate of Samaria, with all the prophets prophesying before them. [10]Now Zedekiah son of Kenaanah had made iron horns, and he declared, "This is what the LORD says: 'With these you will gore the Arameans until they are destroyed.' "

[11]All the other prophets were prophesying the same thing. "Attack Ramoth Gilead[x] and be victorious," they said, "for the LORD will give it into the king's hand."

[12]The messenger who had gone to summon Micaiah said to him, "Look, as one man the other prophets are predicting success for the king. Let your word agree with theirs, and speak favorably."

[13]But Micaiah said, "As surely as the LORD lives, I can tell him only what my God says."[y]

[14]When he arrived, the king asked him, "Micaiah, shall we go to war against Ramoth Gilead, or shall I refrain?"

"Attack and be victorious," he answered, "for they will be given into your hand."

[15]The king said to him, "How many times must I make you swear to tell me nothing but the truth in the name of the LORD?"

[16]Then Micaiah answered, "I saw all Israel scattered on the hills like sheep without a shepherd,[z] and the LORD said, 'These people have no master. Let each one go home in peace.' "

[17]The king of Israel said to Jehoshaphat, "Didn't I tell you that he never prophesies anything good about me, but only bad?"

**18:21** a Job 1:6; Jn 8:44
**18:22** b Job 12:16; Eze 14:9
**18:23** c Jer 20:2; Mk 14:65; Ac 23:2
**18:26** d 2Ch 16:10
**18:31** e 2Ch 13:14

[18]Micaiah continued, "Therefore hear the word of the LORD: I saw the LORD sitting on his throne with all the host of heaven standing on his right and on his left. [19]And the LORD said, 'Who will entice Ahab king of Israel into attacking Ramoth Gilead and going to his death there?'

"One suggested this, and another that. [20]Finally, a spirit came forward, stood before the LORD and said, 'I will entice him.'

" 'By what means?' the LORD asked.

[21]" 'I will go and be a lying spirit[a] in the mouths of all his prophets,' he said.

" 'You will succeed in enticing him,' said the LORD. 'Go and do it.'

[22]"So now the LORD has put a lying spirit in the mouths of these prophets of yours.[b] The LORD has decreed disaster for you."

[23]Then Zedekiah son of Kenaanah went up and slapped[c] Micaiah in the face. "Which way did the spirit from[a] the LORD go when he went from me to speak to you?" he asked.

[24]Micaiah replied, "You will find out on the day you go to hide in an inner room."

[25]The king of Israel then ordered, "Take Micaiah and send him back to Amon the ruler of the city and to Joash the king's son, [26]and say, 'This is what the king says: Put this fellow in prison[d] and give him nothing but bread and water until I return safely.' "

[27]Micaiah declared, "If you ever return safely, the LORD has not spoken through me." Then he added, "Mark my words, all you people!"

## Ahab Killed at Ramoth Gilead

[28]So the king of Israel and Jehoshaphat king of Judah went up to Ramoth Gilead. [29]The king of Israel said to Jehoshaphat, "I will enter the battle in disguise, but you wear your royal robes." So the king of Israel disguised himself and went into battle.

[30]Now the king of Aram had ordered his chariot commanders, "Do not fight with anyone, small or great, except the king of Israel." [31]When the chariot commanders saw Jehoshaphat, they thought, "This is the king of Israel." So they turned to attack him, but Jehoshaphat cried out,[e] and the LORD helped him. God drew them away from him, [32]for when the chariot commanders saw that he

[a]23 Or *Spirit of*

was not the king of Israel, they stopped pursuing him.

33 But someone drew his bow at random and hit the king of Israel between the sections of his armor. The king told the chariot driver, "Wheel around and get me out of the fighting. I've been wounded." 34 All day long the battle raged, and the king of Israel propped himself up in his chariot facing the Arameans until evening. Then at sunset he died.

**19** When Jehoshaphat king of Judah returned safely to his palace in Jerusalem, 2 Jehu the seer, the son of Hanani, went out to meet him and said to the king, "Should you help the wicked and love[a] those who hate the LORD?[f] Because of this, the wrath[g] of the LORD is upon you. 3 There is, however, some good[h] in you, for you have rid the land of the Asherah poles[i] and have set your heart on seeking God."

## Jehoshaphat Appoints Judges

4 Jehoshaphat lived in Jerusalem, and he went out again among the people from Beersheba to the hill country of Ephraim and turned them back to the LORD, the God of their fathers. 5 He appointed judges in the land, in each of the fortified cities of Judah. 6 He told them, "Consider carefully what you do, because you are not judging for man[j] but for the LORD, who is with you whenever you give a verdict. 7 Now let the fear of the LORD be upon you. Judge carefully, for with the LORD our God there is no injustice[k] or partiality[l] or bribery."

8 In Jerusalem also, Jehoshaphat appointed some of the Levites, priests and heads of Israelite families to administer[m] the law of the LORD and to settle disputes. And they lived in Jerusalem. 9 He gave them these orders: "You must serve faithfully and wholeheartedly in the fear of the LORD. 10 In every case that comes before you from your fellow countrymen who live in the cities—whether bloodshed or other concerns of the law, commands, decrees or ordinances—you are to warn them not to sin against the LORD;[n] otherwise his wrath will come on you and your brothers. Do this, and you will not sin.

11 "Amariah the chief priest will be over you in any matter concerning the LORD, and Zebadiah son of Ishmael, the leader of the tribe of Judah, will be over you in any matter concerning the king, and the Levites will serve as officials before you. Act with courage,[o] and may the LORD be with those who do well."

## Jehoshaphat Defeats Moab and Ammon

**20** After this, the Moabites and Ammonites with some of the Meunites[b] came to make war on Jehoshaphat.

2 Some men came and told Jehoshaphat, "A vast army is coming against you from Edom,[c] from the other side of the Sea.[d] It is already in Hazazon Tamar[p]" (that is, En Gedi). 3 Alarmed, Jehoshaphat resolved to inquire of the LORD, and he proclaimed a fast[q] for all Judah. 4 The people of Judah came together to seek help from the LORD; indeed, they came from every town in Judah to seek him.

5 Then Jehoshaphat stood up in the assembly of Judah and Jerusalem at the temple of the LORD in the front of the new courtyard 6 and said:

"O LORD, God of our fathers, are you
not the God who is in heaven?[r] You rule
over all the kingdoms[s] of the nations.
Power and might are in your hand,
and no one can withstand you. 7 O our
God, did you not drive out the inhabitants of this land before your people
Israel and give it forever to the descendants of Abraham your friend?[t] 8 They
have lived in it and have built in it a
sanctuary for your Name, saying, 9 'If
calamity comes upon us, whether the
sword of judgment, or plague or famine, we will stand in your presence before this temple that bears your Name
and will cry out to you in our distress,
and you will hear us and save us.'

10 "But now here are men from Ammon, Moab and Mount Seir, whose
territory you would not allow Israel to
invade when they came from Egypt;[u]
so they turned away from them and

**19:2** f Ps 139:21–22 g 2Ch 32:25
**19:3** h 2Ch 12:12 i 2Ch 17:6
**19:6** j Dt 1:17; 16:18–20; 17:8–13
**19:7** k Ge 18:25 l Dt 10:17
**19:8** m 2Ch 17:8–9
**19:10** n Dt 17:8–13
**19:11** o 1Ch 28:20
**20:2** p Ge 14:7
**20:3** q 2Ch 19:3
**20:6** r Dt 4:39 s 1Ch 29:11–12
**20:7** t Isa 41:8
**20:10** u Nu 20:14–21

[a] 2 Or *and make alliances with* [b] 1 Some Septuagint manuscripts; Hebrew *Ammonites* [c] 2 One Hebrew manuscript; most Hebrew manuscripts, Septuagint and Vulgate *Aram* [d] 2 That is, the Dead Sea

did not destroy them. [11]See how they are repaying us by coming to drive us out of the possession[v] you gave us as an inheritance. [12]O our God, will you not judge them?[w] For we have no power to face this vast army that is attacking us. We do not know what to do, but our eyes are upon you.[x]"

[13]All the men of Judah, with their wives and children and little ones, stood there before the LORD.

[14]Then the Spirit[y] of the LORD came upon Jahaziel son of Zechariah, the son of Benaiah, the son of Jeiel, the son of Mattaniah, a Levite and descendant of Asaph, as he stood in the assembly.

[15]He said: "Listen, King Jehoshaphat and all who live in Judah and Jerusalem! This is what the LORD says to you: 'Do not be afraid or discouraged[z] because of this vast army. For the battle[a] is not yours, but God's. [16]Tomorrow march down against them. They will be climbing up by the Pass of Ziz, and you will find them at the end of the gorge in the Desert of Jeruel. [17]You will not have to fight this battle. Take up your positions; stand firm and see[b] the deliverance the LORD will give you, O Judah and Jerusalem. Do not be afraid; do not be discouraged. Go out to face them tomorrow, and the LORD will be with you.' "

[18]Jehoshaphat bowed with his face to the ground, and all the people of Judah and Jerusalem fell down in worship before the LORD. [19]Then some Levites from the Kohathites and Korahites stood up and praised the LORD, the God of Israel, with a very loud voice.

[20]Early in the morning they left for the Desert of Tekoa. As they set out, Jehoshaphat stood and said, "Listen to me, Judah and people of Jerusalem! Have faith[c] in the LORD your God and you will be upheld; have faith in his prophets and you will be successful." [21]After consulting the people, Jehoshaphat appointed men to sing to the LORD and to praise him for the splendor of his[a] holiness[d] as they went out at the head of the army, saying:

"Give thanks to the Lord,
for his love endures forever."

[22]As they began to sing and praise, the LORD set ambushes[e] against the men of Ammon and Moab and Mount Seir who were invading Judah, and they were defeated. [23]The men of Ammon and Moab rose up against the men from Mount Seir to destroy and annihilate them. After they finished slaughtering the men from Seir, they helped to destroy one another.[f]

[24]When the men of Judah came to the place that overlooks the desert and looked toward the vast army, they saw only dead bodies lying on the ground; no one had escaped. [25]So Jehoshaphat and his men went to carry off their plunder, and they found among them a great amount of equipment and clothing[b] and also articles of value—more than they could take away. There was so much plunder that it took three days to collect it. [26]On the fourth day they assembled in the Valley of Beracah, where they praised the LORD. This is why it is called the Valley of Beracah[c] to this day.

[27]Then, led by Jehoshaphat, all the men of Judah and Jerusalem returned joyfully to Jerusalem, for the LORD had given them cause to rejoice over their enemies. [28]They entered Jerusalem and went to the temple of the LORD with harps and lutes and trumpets.

[29]The fear[g] of God came upon all the kingdoms of the countries when they heard how the LORD had fought against the enemies of Israel. [30]And the kingdom of Jehoshaphat was at peace, for his God had given him rest[h] on every side.

## The End of Jehoshaphat's Reign

[31]So Jehoshaphat reigned over Judah. He was thirty-five years old when he became king of Judah, and he reigned in Jerusalem twenty-five years. His mother's name was Azubah daughter of Shilhi. [32]He walked in the ways of his father Asa and did not stray from them; he did what was right in the eyes of the LORD. [33]The high places,[i] however, were not removed, and the people still had not set their hearts on the God of their fathers.

[34]The other events of Jehoshaphat's reign,

**20:11** v Ps 83:1–12
**20:12** w Jdg 11:27 x Ps 25:15
**20:14** y 2Ch 15:1
**20:15** z 2Ch 32:7 a 1Sa 17:47
**20:17** b Ex 14:13
**20:20** c Isa 7:9
**20:21** d 1Ch 16:29
**20:22** e 2Ch 13:13
**20:23** f Jdg 7:22; 1Sa 14:20
**20:29** g 2Ch 17:10
**20:30** h 2Ch 15:15
**20:33** i 2Ch 17:6; 19:3

[a]21 Or *him with the splendor of* [b]25 Some Hebrew manuscripts and Vulgate; most Hebrew manuscripts *corpses*
[c]26 *Beracah* means *praise.*

**20:34** j 1Ki 16:1
**20:37** k 2Ch 9:21
**21:4** l Jdg 9:5
**21:6** m 1Ki 12:28–30 n 2Ch 18:1
**21:7** o 2Sa 7:13 p 1Ki 11:36
**21:8** q 2Ch 20:22–23

from beginning to end, are written in the annals of Jehu[j] son of Hanani, which are recorded in the book of the kings of Israel.

35 Later, Jehoshaphat king of Judah made an alliance with Ahaziah king of Israel, who was guilty of wickedness. 36 He agreed with him to construct a fleet of trading ships.[a] After these were built at Ezion Geber, 37 Eliezer son of Dodavahu of Mareshah prophesied against Jehoshaphat, saying, "Because you have made an alliance with Ahaziah, the LORD will destroy what you have made." The ships[k] were wrecked and were not able to set sail to trade.[b]

21 Then Jehoshaphat rested with his fathers and was buried with them in the City of David. And Jehoram his son succeeded him as king. 2 Jehoram's brothers, the sons of Jehoshaphat, were Azariah, Jehiel, Zechariah, Azariahu, Michael and Shephatiah. All these were sons of Jehoshaphat king of Israel.[c] 3 Their father had given them many gifts of silver and gold and articles of value, as well as fortified cities in Judah, but he had given the kingdom to Jehoram because he was his firstborn son.

## Jehoram King of Judah

4 When Jehoram established himself firmly over his father's kingdom, he put all his brothers[l] to the sword along with some of the princes of Israel. 5 Jehoram was thirty-two years old when he became king, and he reigned in Jerusalem eight years. 6 He walked in the ways of the kings of Israel,[m] as the house of Ahab had done, for he married a daughter of Ahab.[n] He did evil in the eyes of the LORD. 7 Nevertheless, because of the covenant the LORD had made with David,[o] the LORD was not willing to destroy the house of David. He had promised to maintain a lamp[p] for him and his descendants forever.

8 In the time of Jehoram, Edom[q] rebelled against Judah and set up its own king. 9 So Jehoram went there with his officers and all his chariots. The Edomites surrounded him and his chariot commanders, but he rose up and broke through by night. 10 To this day Edom has been in rebellion against Judah.

Libnah revolted at the same time, because Jehoram had forsaken the LORD, the God of his fathers. 11 He had also built high places on the hills of Judah and had caused the people of Jerusalem to prostitute themselves and had led Judah astray.

12 Jehoram received a letter from Elijah the prophet, which said:

> "This is what the LORD, the God of your father[r] David, says: 'You have not walked in the ways of your father Jehoshaphat or of Asa[s] king of Judah. 13 But you have walked in the ways of the kings of Israel, and you have led Judah and the people of Jerusalem to prostitute themselves, just as the house of Ahab did.[t] You have also murdered your own brothers, members of your father's house, men who were better than you. 14 So now the LORD is about to strike your people, your sons, your wives and everything that is yours, with a heavy blow. 15 You yourself will be very ill with a lingering disease of the bowels, until the disease causes your bowels to come out.' "

16 The LORD aroused against Jehoram the hostility of the Philistines and of the Arabs[u] who lived near the Cushites. 17 They attacked Judah, invaded it and carried off all the goods found in the king's palace, together with his sons and wives. Not a son was left to him except Ahaziah,[d] the youngest.

18 After all this, the LORD afflicted Jehoram with an incurable disease of the bowels. 19 In the course of time, at the end of the second year, his bowels came out because of the disease, and he died in great pain. His people made no fire in his honor,[v] as they had for his fathers.

20 Jehoram was thirty-two years old when he became king, and he reigned in Jerusalem eight years. He passed away, to no one's regret, and was buried[w] in the City of David, but not in the tombs of the kings.

## Ahaziah King of Judah

22 The people of Jerusalem made Ahaziah, Jehoram's youngest son, king in his place, since the raiders,[x] who came with the Arabs into the camp, had

**21:12** r 2Ch 17:3–6 s 2Ch 14:2
**21:13** t 1Ki 16:29–33
**21:16** u 2Ch 17:10–11; 22:1
**21:19** v 2Ch 16:14
**21:20** w 2Ch 24:25; 28:27; Jer 22:18,28
**22:1** x 2Ch 21:16–17

[a] 36 Hebrew *of ships that could go to Tarshish* [b] 37 Hebrew *sail for Tarshish* [c] 2 That is, Judah, as frequently in 2 Chronicles
[d] 17 Hebrew *Jehoahaz,* a variant of *Ahaziah*

killed all the older sons. So Ahaziah son of Jehoram king of Judah began to reign.

2 Ahaziah was twenty-two[a] years old when he became king, and he reigned in Jerusalem one year. His mother's name was Athaliah, a granddaughter of Omri.

3 He too walked in the ways of the house of Ahab,[y] for his mother encouraged him in doing wrong. 4 He did evil in the eyes of the LORD, as the house of Ahab had done, for after his father's death they became his advisers, to his undoing. 5 He also followed their counsel when he went with Joram[b] son of Ahab king of Israel to war against Hazael king of Aram at Ramoth Gilead. The Arameans wounded Joram; 6 so he returned to Jezreel to recover from the wounds they had inflicted on him at Ramoth[c] in his battle with Hazael king of Aram.

Then Ahaziah[d] son of Jehoram king of Judah went down to Jezreel to see Joram son of Ahab because he had been wounded.

7 Through Ahaziah's[z] visit to Joram, God brought about Ahaziah's downfall. When Ahaziah arrived, he went out with Joram to meet Jehu son of Nimshi, whom the LORD had anointed to destroy the house of Ahab. 8 While Jehu was executing judgment on the house of Ahab,[a] he found the princes of Judah and the sons of Ahaziah's relatives, who had been attending Ahaziah, and he killed them. 9 He then went in search of Ahaziah, and his men captured him while he was hiding in Samaria. He was brought to Jehu and put to death. They buried him, for they said, "He was a son of Jehoshaphat, who sought[b] the LORD with all his heart." So there was no one in the house of Ahaziah powerful enough to retain the kingdom.

## Athaliah and Joash

10 When Athaliah the mother of Ahaziah saw that her son was dead, she proceeded to destroy the whole royal family of the house of Judah. 11 But Jehosheba,[e] the daughter of King Jehoram, took Joash son of Ahaziah and stole him away from among the royal princes who were about to be murdered and put him and his nurse in a bedroom. Because Jehosheba,[e] the daughter of King Jehoram and wife of the priest Jehoiada, was Ahaziah's sister, she hid the child from Athaliah so she could not kill him. 12 He remained hidden with them at the temple of God for six years while Athaliah ruled the land.

23 In the seventh year Jehoiada showed his strength. He made a covenant with the commanders of units of a hundred: Azariah son of Jeroham, Ishmael son of Jehohanan, Azariah son of Obed, Maaseiah son of Adaiah, and Elishaphat son of Zicri. 2 They went throughout Judah and gathered the Levites and the heads of Israelite families from all the towns. When they came to Jerusalem, 3 the whole assembly made a covenant with the king at the temple of God.

Jehoiada said to them, "The king's son shall reign, as the LORD promised concerning the descendants of David.[c] 4 Now this is what you are to do: A third of you priests and Levites who are going on duty on the Sabbath are to keep watch at the doors, 5 a third of you at the royal palace and a third at the Foundation Gate, and all the other men are to be in the courtyards of the temple of the LORD. 6 No one is to enter the temple of the LORD except the priests and Levites on duty; they may enter because they are consecrated, but all the other men are to guard what the LORD has assigned to them.[f] 7 The Levites are to station themselves around the king, each man with his weapons in his hand. Anyone who enters the temple must be put to death. Stay close to the king wherever he goes."

8 The Levites and all the men of Judah did just as Jehoiada the priest ordered. Each one took his men—those who were going on duty on the Sabbath and those who were going off duty—for Jehoiada the priest had not released any of the divisions.[d] 9 Then he gave the commanders of units of a hundred the spears and the large and small shields that had belonged to King David and that were in the temple of God. 10 He stationed all the men, each with his weapon in his hand, around the king—near the altar and

**22:3** y 2Ch 21:6
**22:7** z 2Ch 10:15
**22:8** a 2Ki 10:13
**22:9** b 2Ch 17:4
**23:3** c 2Sa 7:12; 1Ki 2:4; 2Ch 6:16; 21:7
**23:8** d 1Ch 24:1

[a] 2 Some Septuagint manuscripts and Syriac (see also 2 Kings 8:26); Hebrew *forty-two* [b] 5 Hebrew *Jehoram,* a variant of *Joram;* also in verses 6 and 7 [c] 6 Hebrew *Ramah,* a variant of *Ramoth* [d] 6 Some Hebrew manuscripts, Septuagint, Vulgate and Syriac (see also 2 Kings 8:29); most Hebrew manuscripts *Azariah* [e] 11 Hebrew *Jehoshabeath,* a variant of *Jehosheba* [f] 6 Or *to observe the LORD's command ⌊not to enter⌋*

# Athaliah

## *An Angry Woman*

Athaliah, at a glance, appears to be nothing short of wicked; she's hard-core, low-down, good for nothing and rotten to the bone. How often, after all, do you hear of a woman murdering her own grandchildren to grasp power—like she did following the deaths of her husband and son, the kings of Judah (see 2Ch 22:10–11)? Growing up in the royal family of the northern kingdom of Israel, Athaliah was the granddaughter of the idolatrous King Omri and the daughter of none other than the notorious King Ahab, who was married to Jezebel. (Though it is uncertain, some believe that Jezebel was Athaliah's mother.) Talk about a generational curse! The makeup of Athaliah's life is nothing short of a counselor's nightmare.

Imagine coming from the family into which she was born. Though her family had power and money, they are remembered for their evil choices and idolatry. Athaliah grew up in a palace steeped in Baal worship. Such a life certainly influenced her later choices. She became a woman who was power-hungry, violent and evil.

Prisons, detention centers and rehabs are full of Athaliahs—angry women who lash out violently at anybody and everybody, trusting no one. Athaliahs believe that anger and violence are the realities of life. After all, that's the way it was with her mama and her mama before her.

Athaliahs tend to deny that their own anger is the problem. They usually blame their problems on something else: "I'm black. I'm poor. I'm fat. I'm ugly. Everybody's always picking on me." Athaliahs tend to see themselves as victims. This thinking ultimately produces the very thing it believes. But the excuse of victimization becomes a prison, trapping them in their own anger. Letting go of their anger at the world is often difficult to do, but letting go is the only way for them to give their burdens to Jesus and let him truly love them. Athaliahs have to evaluate the past, release unhealthy patterns and learn new patterns to live healthy and whole lives as daughters of God.

—E. Walters

### reflection

*What unhealthy patterns from your past do you need to release?*

*Remember that you are God's beautiful daughter—regardless of what kind of earthly family you come from.*

### read

2 Chronicles 21:4—23:21; see also 2 Kings 8:25–27.

See also the Inspire Notes "Rebellion," "Anger: Act or React," "Courage to Heal," "Help for the Addict" and "Self-Control," and the Women of the Bible Notes "Jezebel: A Wicked Queen" and "Jehosheba: Standing Firm."

For the next Women of the Bible note, go to page 528.

# Jehosheba

## *Standing Firm*

Jehosheba was the daughter of King Jehoram, king of Judah, and the savior of the heir to the throne. Jehoram had married Athaliah, a daughter of Ahab (Israel's evil, idolatrous king). After the deaths of Jehoram and his successor, Athaliah's son Ahaziah, Athaliah's lust for power led her to kill off all those of the house of David who were the rightful heirs to the throne. Never mind that these heirs happened to be her own grandsons! Athaliah became one of the most detestable rulers of Judah and the only queen of Judah to rule in her own name.

Jehosheba was likely Athaliah's stepdaughter, the daughter of Jehoram by another wife. She was used by God to rescue her infant nephew Joash. She hid him and his nurse in a bedroom while the other royal princes were murdered (see 2Ch 22:11). And she continued to keep him hidden for six years in the temple of the Lord (see 2Ch 22:12). The temple provided a safe place for Joash and an environment in which he could be prepared for his future as king. During that time Queen Athaliah ruled with a vengeance, never knowing that one of the legitimate heirs to the throne was under her nose the entire time. By rescuing Joash, Jehosheba became an instrument of God in his divine plan to keep his promise that a son of David would always be king.

Today there are many who despise the name of Jesus Christ and will behave as Queen Athaliah in an attempt to destroy God's people. But believers must stand firm and trust God to determine the outcome of our enemy's plans. Whatever God's plans are for us, no amount of adversity can thwart them.

As Christian women we are to encourage one another. Whatever trials we face, we can trust our Lord to hide us in the shadow of his wings and cause our enemies to become our footstools.

—J. Josey

### reflection

*Reflect on the fact that God's plans will not be thwarted.*

*Rejoice in the plan God has for your life.*

### read

2 Chronicles 22:10–12; see also 2 Kings 11:1–3.

See also the Inspire Notes "Confidence," "Fear," "Bumping Into Omnipotence," "Distress" and "God Is Sovereign," and the Women of the Bible Notes "Jael: Just Another Woman on the Lord's Side" and "Athaliah: An Angry Woman."

For the next Women of the Bible note, go to page 583.

the temple, from the south side to the north side of the temple.

11 Jehoiada and his sons brought out the king's son and put the crown on him; they presented him with a copy of the covenant and proclaimed him king. They anointed him and shouted, "Long live the king!"

12 When Athaliah heard the noise of the people running and cheering the king, she went to them at the temple of the LORD. 13 She looked, and there was the king, standing by his pillar at the entrance. The officers and the trumpeters were beside the king, and all the people of the land were rejoicing and blowing trumpets, and singers with musical instruments were leading the praises. Then Athaliah tore her robes and shouted, "Treason! Treason!"

14 Jehoiada the priest sent out the commanders of units of a hundred, who were in charge of the troops, and said to them: "Bring her out between the ranks[a] and put to the sword anyone who follows her." For the priest had said, "Do not put her to death at the temple of the LORD." 15 So they seized her as she reached the entrance of the Horse Gate[e] on the palace grounds, and there they put her to death.

16 Jehoiada then made a covenant that he and the people and the king[b] would be the LORD's people. 17 All the people went to the temple of Baal and tore it down. They smashed the altars and idols and killed[f] Mattan the priest of Baal in front of the altars.

18 Then Jehoiada placed the oversight of the temple of the LORD in the hands of the priests, who were Levites,[g] to whom David had made assignments in the temple,[h] to present the burnt offerings of the LORD as written in the Law of Moses, with rejoicing and singing, as David had ordered. 19 He also stationed doorkeepers[i] at the gates of the LORD's temple so that no one who was in any way unclean might enter.

20 He took with him the commanders of hundreds, the nobles, the rulers of the people and all the people of the land and brought the king down from the temple of the LORD. They went into the palace through the Upper Gate and seated the king on the royal throne, 21 and all the people of the land rejoiced. And the city was quiet, because Athaliah had been slain with the sword.

## Joash Repairs the Temple

**24** Joash was seven years old when he became king, and he reigned in Jerusalem forty years. His mother's name was Zibiah; she was from Beersheba. 2 Joash did what was right in the eyes of the LORD[j] all the years of Jehoiada the priest. 3 Jehoiada chose two wives for him, and he had sons and daughters.

4 Some time later Joash decided to restore the temple of the LORD. 5 He called together the priests and Levites and said to them, "Go to the towns of Judah and collect the money due annually from all Israel, to repair the temple of your God. Do it now." But the Levites did not act at once.

6 Therefore the king summoned Jehoiada the chief priest and said to him, "Why haven't you required the Levites to bring in from Judah and Jerusalem the tax imposed by Moses the servant of the LORD and by the assembly of Israel for the Tent of the Testimony?"[k]

7 Now the sons of that wicked woman Athaliah had broken into the temple of God and had used even its sacred objects for the Baals.

8 At the king's command, a chest was made and placed outside, at the gate of the temple of the LORD. 9 A proclamation was then issued in Judah and Jerusalem that they should bring to the LORD the tax that Moses the servant of God had required of Israel in the desert. 10 All the officials and all the people brought their contributions gladly, dropping them into the chest until it was full. 11 Whenever the chest was brought in by the Levites to the king's officials and they saw that there was a large amount of money, the royal secretary and the officer of the chief priest would come and empty the chest and carry it back to its place. They did this regularly and collected a great amount of money. 12 The king and Jehoiada gave it to the men who carried out the work required for the temple of the LORD. They hired masons and carpenters to restore the LORD's temple, and also workers in iron and bronze to repair the temple.

**23:15** e Ne 3:28; Jer 31:40
**23:17** f Dt 13:6–9
**23:18** g 1Ch 23:28–32 h 1Ch 23:6
**23:19** i 1Ch 9:22
**24:2** j 2Ch 26:5
**24:6** k Ex 30:12–16

[a] 14 Or *out from the precincts* [b] 16 Or *covenant between* ⌊*the LORD*⌋ *and the people and the king that they* (see 2 Kings 11:17)

**24:18** l ver 4 m Ex 34:13; 1Ki 14:23 n Jos 22:20; 2Ch 19:2
**24:19** o Jer 7:25
**24:20** p Jdg 3:10; 1Ch 12:18; 2Ch 20:14 q Nu 14:41 r 2Ch 15:2
**24:21** s Ac 7:58–59 t Ne 9:26 u Mt 23:35
**24:22** v Ge 9:5
**24:23** w 2Ki 12:17–18

13 The men in charge of the work were diligent, and the repairs progressed under them. They rebuilt the temple of God according to its original design and reinforced it. 14 When they had finished, they brought the rest of the money to the king and Jehoiada, and with it were made articles for the LORD's temple: articles for the service and for the burnt offerings, and also dishes and other objects of gold and silver. As long as Jehoiada lived, burnt offerings were presented continually in the temple of the LORD.

15 Now Jehoiada was old and full of years, and he died at the age of a hundred and thirty. 16 He was buried with the kings in the City of David, because of the good he had done in Israel for God and his temple.

## The Wickedness of Joash

17 After the death of Jehoiada, the officials of Judah came and paid homage to the king, and he listened to them. 18 They abandoned[l] the temple of the LORD, the God of their fathers, and worshiped Asherah poles and idols.[m] Because of their guilt, God's anger[n] came upon Judah and Jerusalem. 19 Although the LORD sent prophets to the people to bring them back to him, and though they testified against them, they would not listen.[o]

20 Then the Spirit[p] of God came upon Zechariah son of Jehoiada the priest. He stood before the people and said, "This is what God says: 'Why do you disobey the LORD's commands? You will not prosper.[q] Because you have forsaken the LORD, he has forsaken[r] you.'"

21 But they plotted against him, and by order of the king they stoned[s] him to death[t] in the courtyard of the LORD's temple.[u] 22 King Joash did not remember the kindness Zechariah's father Jehoiada had shown him but killed his son, who said as he lay dying, "May the LORD see this and call you to account."[v]

23 At the turn of the year,[a] the army of Aram marched against Joash; it invaded Judah and Jerusalem and killed all the leaders of the people.[w] They sent all the plunder to their king in Damascus. 24 Although the Aramean army had come with only a few men, the LORD delivered into their hands a much larger army.[x] Because Judah had forsaken the LORD, the God of their fathers, judgment was executed on Joash. 25 When the Arameans withdrew, they left Joash severely wounded. His officials conspired against him for murdering the son of Jehoiada the priest, and they killed him in his bed. So he died and was buried in the City of David, but not in the tombs of the kings.

26 Those who conspired against him were Zabad,[b] son of Shimeath an Ammonite woman, and Jehozabad, son of Shimrith[c][y] a Moabite woman. 27 The account of his sons, the many prophecies about him, and the record of the restoration of the temple of God are written in the annotations on the book of the kings. And Amaziah his son succeeded him as king.

## Amaziah King of Judah

25 Amaziah was twenty-five years old when he became king, and he reigned in Jerusalem twenty-nine years. His mother's name was Jehoaddin[d]; she was from Jerusalem. 2 He did what was right in the eyes of the LORD, but not wholeheartedly.[z] 3 After the kingdom was firmly in his control, he executed the officials who had murdered his father the king. 4 Yet he did not put their sons to death, but acted in accordance with what is written in the Law, in the Book of Moses, where the LORD commanded: "Fathers shall not be put to death for their children, nor children put to death for their fathers; each is to die for his own sins."[e][a]

5 Amaziah called the people of Judah

*Lord,*

*help me never to leave you or turn from your ways. I desire to follow you completely, with an undivided heart. In your Son's name,*

*Amen*

2 CHRONICLES 25:1–2

**24:24** x Lev 26:23–25; Dt 28:25
**24:26** y 2Ki 12:21
**25:2** z ver 14
**25:4** a Dt 24:16

[a] 23 Probably in the spring [b] 26 A variant of *Jozabad* [c] 26 A variant of *Shomer* [d] 1 Hebrew *Jehoaddan,* a variant of *Jehoaddin* [e] 4 Deut. 24:16

together and assigned them according to their families to commanders of thousands and commanders of hundreds for all Judah and Benjamin. He then mustered those twenty years old or more and found that there were three hundred thousand men ready for military service,[b] able to handle the spear and shield. 6He also hired a hundred thousand fighting men from Israel for a hundred talents[a] of silver.

7But a man of God came to him and said, "O king, these troops from Israel must not march with you, for the LORD is not with Israel—not with any of the people of Ephraim. 8Even if you go and fight courageously in battle, God will overthrow you before the enemy, for God has the power to help or to overthrow."[c]

9Amaziah asked the man of God, "But what about the hundred talents I paid for these Israelite troops?"

The man of God replied, "The LORD can give you much more than that."[d]

10So Amaziah dismissed the troops who had come to him from Ephraim and sent them home. They were furious with Judah and left for home in a great rage.

11Amaziah then marshaled his strength and led his army to the Valley of Salt, where he killed ten thousand men of Seir. 12The army of Judah also captured ten thousand men alive, took them to the top of a cliff and threw them down so that all were dashed to pieces.

13Meanwhile the troops that Amaziah had sent back and had not allowed to take part in the war raided Judean towns from Samaria to Beth Horon. They killed three thousand people and carried off great quantities of plunder.

14When Amaziah returned from slaughtering the Edomites, he brought back the gods of the people of Seir. He set them up as his own gods,[e] bowed down to them and burned sacrifices to them. 15The anger of the LORD burned against Amaziah, and he sent a prophet to him, who said, "Why do you consult this people's gods, which could not save[f] their own people from your hand?"

16While he was still speaking, the king said to him, "Have we appointed you an adviser to the king? Stop! Why be struck down?"

So the prophet stopped but said, "I know that God has determined to destroy you, because you have done this and have not listened to my counsel."

17After Amaziah king of Judah consulted his advisers, he sent this challenge to Jehoash[b] son of Jehoahaz, the son of Jehu, king of Israel: "Come, meet me face to face."

18But Jehoash king of Israel replied to Amaziah king of Judah: "A thistle[g] in Lebanon sent a message to a cedar in Lebanon, 'Give your daughter to my son in marriage.' Then a wild beast in Lebanon came along and trampled the thistle underfoot. 19You say to yourself that you have defeated Edom, and now you are arrogant and proud. But stay at home! Why ask for trouble and cause your own downfall and that of Judah also?"

20Amaziah, however, would not listen, for God so worked that he might hand them over to ⌊Jehoash⌋, because they sought the gods of Edom.[h] 21So Jehoash king of Israel attacked. He and Amaziah king of Judah faced each other at Beth Shemesh in Judah. 22Judah was routed by Israel, and every man fled to his home. 23Jehoash king of Israel captured Amaziah king of Judah, the son of Joash, the son of Ahaziah,[c] at Beth Shemesh. Then Jehoash brought him to Jerusalem and broke down the wall of Jerusalem from the Ephraim Gate to the Corner Gate—a section about six hundred feet[d] long. 24He took all the gold and silver and all the articles found in the temple of God that had been in the care of Obed-Edom, together with the palace treasures and the hostages, and returned to Samaria.

25Amaziah son of Joash king of Judah lived for fifteen years after the death of Jehoash son of Jehoahaz king of Israel. 26As for the other events of Amaziah's reign, from beginning to end, are they not written in the book of the kings of Judah and Israel? 27From the time that Amaziah turned away from following the LORD, they conspired against him in Jerusalem and he fled to Lachish, but they sent men after him to

**25:5** b Nu 1:3
**25:8** c 2Ch 14:11; 20:6
**25:9** d Dt 8:18; Pr 10:22
**25:14** e Ex 20:3; 2Ch 28:23
**25:15** f Ps 96:5
**25:18** g Jdg 9:8–15
**25:20** h 1Ki 12:15; 2Ch 22:7

[a]6 That is, about 3 3/4 tons (about 3.4 metric tons); also in verse 9 [b]17 Hebrew *Joash*, a variant of *Jehoash*; also in verses 18, 21, 23 and 25 [c]23 Hebrew *Jehoahaz*, a variant of *Ahaziah* [d]23 Hebrew *four hundred cubits* (about 180 meters)

Lachish and killed him there. 28 He was brought back by horse and was buried with his fathers in the City of Judah.

## Uzziah King of Judah

26 Then all the people of Judah took Uzziah,[a] who was sixteen years old, and made him king in place of his father Amaziah. 2 He was the one who rebuilt Elath and restored it to Judah after Amaziah rested with his fathers.

3 Uzziah was sixteen years old when he became king, and he reigned in Jerusalem fifty-two years. His mother's name was Jecoliah; she was from Jerusalem. 4 He did what was right in the eyes of the LORD, just as his father Amaziah had done. 5 He sought God during the days of Zechariah, who instructed him in the fear[b] of God.[i] As long as he sought the LORD, God gave him success.

*Princess,*

*I am your King. Keep me always on the throne of your life.*

*Your Lord and God*

2 CHRONICLES 26:3–5

6 He went to war against the Philistines[j] and broke down the walls of Gath, Jabneh and Ashdod. He then rebuilt towns near Ashdod and elsewhere among the Philistines. 7 God helped him against the Philistines and against the Arabs[k] who lived in Gur Baal and against the Meunites. 8 The Ammonites[l] brought tribute to Uzziah, and his fame spread as far as the border of Egypt, because he had become very powerful.

9 Uzziah built towers in Jerusalem at the Corner Gate,[m] at the Valley Gate[n] and at the angle of the wall, and he fortified them. 10 He also built towers in the desert and dug many cisterns, because he had much livestock in the foothills and in the plain. He had people working his fields and vineyards in the hills and in the fertile lands, for he loved the soil.

11 Uzziah had a well-trained army, ready to go out by divisions according to their numbers as mustered by Jeiel the secretary and Maaseiah the officer under the direction of Hananiah, one of the royal officials. 12 The total number of family leaders over the fighting men was 2,600. 13 Under their command was an army of 307,500 men trained for war, a powerful force to support the king against his enemies. 14 Uzziah provided shields, spears, helmets, coats of armor, bows and slingstones for the entire army. 15 In Jerusalem he made machines designed by skillful men for use on the towers and on the corner defenses to shoot arrows and hurl large stones. His fame spread far and wide, for he was greatly helped until he became powerful.

16 But after Uzziah became powerful, his pride led to his downfall.[o] He was unfaithful to the LORD his God, and entered the temple of the LORD to burn incense[p] on the altar of incense. 17 Azariah[q] the priest with eighty other courageous priests of the LORD followed him in. 18 They confronted him and said, "It is not right for you, Uzziah, to burn incense to the LORD. That is for the priests,[r] the descendants of Aaron,[s] who have been consecrated to burn incense. Leave the sanctuary, for you have been unfaithful; and you will not be honored by the LORD God."

19 Uzziah, who had a censer in his hand ready to burn incense, became angry. While he was raging at the priests in their presence before the incense altar in the LORD's temple, leprosy[c][t] broke out on his forehead. 20 When Azariah the chief priest and all the other priests looked at him, they saw that he had leprosy on his forehead, so they hurried him out. Indeed, he himself was eager to leave, because the LORD had afflicted him.

21 King Uzziah had leprosy until the day he died. He lived in a separate house[d][u]—leprous, and excluded from the temple of the

**26:5** i 2Ch 24:2; Da 1:17
**26:6** j Isa 14:29
**26:7** k 2Ch 21:16
**26:8** l 2Ch 17:11
**26:9** m 2Ch 25:23 n Ne 3:13
**26:16** o Dt 32:15; 2Ch 25:19 p 2Ki 16:12
**26:17** q 1Ch 6:10
**26:18** r Nu 16:39 s Ex 30:7
**26:19** t 2Ki 5:25–27
**26:21** u Lev 13:46; Nu 5:2

[a]1 Also called *Azariah* [b]5 Many Hebrew manuscripts, Septuagint and Syriac; other Hebrew manuscripts *vision*
[c]19 The Hebrew word was used for various diseases affecting the skin—not necessarily leprosy; also in verses 20, 21 and 23. [d]21 Or *in a house where he was relieved of responsibilities*

26:22 v Isa 1:1
26:23 w Isa 6:1
27:3 x 2Ch 33:14; Ne 3:26
27:6 y 2Ch 26:5
28:2 z Ex 34:17

LORD. Jotham his son had charge of the palace and governed the people of the land.

22The other events of Uzziah's reign, from beginning to end, are recorded by the prophet Isaiah[v] son of Amoz. 23Uzziah[w] rested with his fathers and was buried near them in a field for burial that belonged to the kings, for people said, "He had leprosy." And Jotham his son succeeded him as king.

## Jotham King of Judah

27 Jotham was twenty-five years old when he became king, and he reigned in Jerusalem sixteen years. His mother's name was Jerusha daughter of Zadok. 2He did what was right in the eyes of the LORD, just as his father Uzziah had done, but unlike him he did not enter the temple of the LORD. The people, however, continued their corrupt practices. 3Jotham rebuilt the Upper Gate of the temple of the LORD and did extensive work on the wall at the hill of Ophel.[x] 4He built towns in the Judean hills and forts and towers in the wooded areas.

5Jotham made war on the king of the Ammonites and conquered them. That year the Ammonites paid him a hundred talents[a] of silver, ten thousand cors[b] of wheat and ten thousand cors of barley. The Ammonites brought him the same amount also in the second and third years.

6Jotham grew powerful[y] because he walked steadfastly before the LORD his God.

7The other events in Jotham's reign, including all his wars and the other things he did, are written in the book of the kings of Israel and Judah. 8He was twenty-five years old when he became king, and he reigned in Jerusalem sixteen years. 9Jotham rested with his fathers and was buried in the City of David. And Ahaz his son succeeded him as king.

## Ahaz King of Judah

28 Ahaz was twenty years old when he became king, and he reigned in Jerusalem sixteen years. Unlike David his father, he did not do what was right in the eyes of the LORD. 2He walked in the ways of the kings of Israel and also made cast idols[z] for worshiping the Baals. 3He burned sacrifices in the Valley of Ben Hinnom and sacrificed his sons[a] in the fire, following the detestable ways of the nations the LORD had driven out before the Israelites. 4He offered sacrifices and burned incense at the high places, on the hilltops and under every spreading tree.

5Therefore the LORD his God handed him over to the king of Aram.[b] The Arameans defeated him and took many of his people as prisoners and brought them to Damascus.

He was also given into the hands of the king of Israel, who inflicted heavy casualties on him. 6In one day Pekah[c] son of Remaliah killed a hundred and twenty thousand soldiers in Judah—because Judah had forsaken the LORD, the God of their fathers. 7Zicri, an Ephraimite warrior, killed Maaseiah the king's son, Azrikam the officer in charge of the palace, and Elkanah, second to the king. 8The Israelites took captive from their kinsmen[d] two hundred thousand wives, sons and daughters. They also took a great deal of plunder, which they carried back to Samaria.

9But a prophet of the LORD named Oded was there, and he went out to meet the army when it returned to Samaria. He said to them, "Because the LORD, the God of your fathers, was angry[e] with Judah, he gave them into your hand. But you have slaughtered them in a rage that reaches to heaven.[f] 10And now you intend to make the men and women of Judah and Jerusalem your slaves.[g] But aren't you also guilty of sins against the LORD your God? 11Now listen to me! Send back your fellow countrymen you have taken as prisoners, for the LORD's fierce anger rests on you."

12Then some of the leaders in Ephraim—Azariah son of Jehohanan, Berekiah son of Meshillemoth, Jehizkiah son of Shallum, and Amasa son of Hadlai—confronted those who were arriving from the war. 13"You must not bring those prisoners here," they said, "or we will be guilty before the LORD. Do you intend to add to our sin and guilt? For our guilt is already great, and his fierce anger rests on Israel."

14So the soldiers gave up the prisoners and plunder in the presence of the officials

28:3 a Lev 18:21; 2Ch 33:6
28:5 b Isa 7:1
28:6 c 2Ki 15:25,27
28:8 d 2Ch 11:4
28:9 e Isa 47:6 f Ezr 9:6; Rev 18:5
28:10 g Lev 25:39–46

[a]5 That is, about 3 3/4 tons (about 3.4 metric tons) [b]5 That is, probably about 62,000 bushels (about 2,200 kiloliters)

**28:15** h 2Ki 6:22 i Dt 34:3
**28:16** j 2Ki 16:7
**28:18** k Eze 16:27,57
**28:19** l 2Ch 21:2
**28:20** m 2Ki 16:7
**28:23** n 2Ch 25:14 o Jer 44:17–18
**28:24** p 2Ki 16:18 q 2Ch 29:7
**28:27** r Isa 14:28–32 s 2Ch 24:25

and all the assembly. 15 The men designated by name took the prisoners, and from the plunder they clothed all who were naked. They provided them with clothes and sandals, food and drink,[h] and healing balm. All those who were weak they put on donkeys. So they took them back to their fellow countrymen at Jericho, the City of Palms,[i] and returned to Samaria.

16 At that time King Ahaz sent to the king[a] of Assyria[j] for help. 17 The Edomites had again come and attacked Judah and carried away prisoners, 18 while the Philistines[k] had raided towns in the foothills and in the Negev of Judah. They captured and occupied Beth Shemesh, Aijalon and Gederoth, as well as Soco, Timnah and Gimzo, with their surrounding villages. 19 The LORD had humbled Judah because of Ahaz king of Israel,[b] for he had promoted wickedness in Judah and had been most unfaithful[l] to the LORD. 20 Tiglath-Pileser[c] king of Assyria came to him, but he gave him trouble instead of help.[m] 21 Ahaz took some of the things from the temple of the LORD and from the royal palace and from the princes and presented them to the king of Assyria, but that did not help him.

22 In his time of trouble King Ahaz became even more unfaithful to the LORD. 23 He offered sacrifices to the gods[n] of Damascus, who had defeated him; for he thought, "Since the gods of the kings of Aram have helped them, I will sacrifice to them so they will help me."[o] But they were his downfall and the downfall of all Israel.

24 Ahaz gathered together the furnishings from the temple of God[p] and took them away.[d] He shut the doors[q] of the LORD's temple and set up altars at every street corner in Jerusalem. 25 In every town in Judah he built high places to burn sacrifices to other gods and provoked the LORD, the God of his fathers, to anger.

26 The other events of his reign and all his ways, from beginning to end, are written in the book of the kings of Judah and Israel. 27 Ahaz rested[r] with his fathers and was buried[s] in the city of Jerusalem, but he was not placed in the tombs of the kings of Israel. And Hezekiah his son succeeded him as king.

## Hezekiah Purifies the Temple

29 Hezekiah was twenty-five years old when he became king, and he reigned in Jerusalem twenty-nine years. His mother's name was Abijah daughter of Zechariah. 2 He did what was right in the eyes of the LORD, just as his father David[t] had done.

3 In the first month of the first year of his reign, he opened the doors of the temple of the LORD and repaired[u] them. 4 He brought in the priests and the Levites, assembled them in the square on the east side 5 and said: "Listen to me, Levites! Consecrate[v] yourselves now and consecrate the temple of the LORD, the God of your fathers. Remove all defilement from the sanctuary. 6 Our fathers[w] were unfaithful;[x] they did evil in the eyes of the LORD our God and forsook him. They turned their faces away from the LORD's dwelling place and turned their backs on him. 7 They also shut the doors of the portico and put out the lamps. They did not burn incense or present any burnt offerings at the sanctuary to the God of Israel. 8 Therefore, the anger of the LORD has fallen on Judah and Jerusalem; he has made them an object of dread and horror[y] and scorn,[z] as you can see with your own eyes. 9 This is why our fathers have fallen by the sword and why our sons and daughters and our wives are in captivity.[a] 10 Now I intend to make a covenant[b] with the LORD, the God of Israel, so that his fierce anger will turn away from us. 11 My sons, do not be negligent now, for the LORD has chosen you to stand before him and serve him,[c] to minister before him and to burn incense."

12 Then these Levites set to work:
from the Kohathites,
Mahath son of Amasai and Joel son of Azariah;
from the Merarites,
Kish son of Abdi and Azariah son of Jehallelel;
from the Gershonites,
Joah son of Zimmah and Eden son of Joah;
13 from the descendants of Elizaphan,
Shimri and Jeiel;

**29:2** t 2Ch 34:2
**29:3** u 2Ch 28:24
**29:5** v 2Ch 35:6
**29:6** w Jer 2:27 x Eze 8:16
**29:8** y Dt 28:25; 2Ch 24:18 z Jer 25:9,18
**29:9** a 2Ch 28:5–8,17
**29:10** b 2Ch 23:16
**29:11** c Nu 3:6; 8:6,14

[a]16 One Hebrew manuscript, Septuagint and Vulgate (see also 2 Kings 16:7); most Hebrew manuscripts *kings* [b]19 That is, Judah, as frequently in 2 Chronicles [c]20 Hebrew *Tilgath-Pilneser,* a variant of *Tiglath-Pileser* [d]24 Or *and cut them up*

**29:15** d ver 5; 1Ch 23:28; 2Ch 30:12
**29:19** e 2Ch 28:24
**29:21** f Lev 4:13–14
**29:22** g Lev 4:18
**29:23** h Lev 4:15
**29:24** i Lev 4:26

from the descendants of Asaph,
Zechariah and Mattaniah;
14 from the descendants of Heman,
Jehiel and Shimei;
from the descendants of Jeduthun,
Shemaiah and Uzziel.

15 When they had assembled their brothers and consecrated themselves, they went in to purify[d] the temple of the LORD, as the king had ordered, following the word of the LORD. 16 The priests went into the sanctuary of the LORD to purify it. They brought out to the courtyard of the LORD's temple everything unclean that they found in the temple of the LORD. The Levites took it and carried it out to the Kidron Valley. 17 They began the consecration on the first day of the first month, and by the eighth day of the month they reached the portico of the LORD. For eight more days they consecrated the temple of the LORD itself, finishing on the sixteenth day of the first month.

18 Then they went in to King Hezekiah and reported: "We have purified the entire temple of the LORD, the altar of burnt offering with all its utensils, and the table for setting out the consecrated bread, with all its articles. 19 We have prepared and consecrated all the articles[e] that King Ahaz removed in his unfaithfulness while he was king. They are now in front of the LORD's altar."

20 Early the next morning King Hezekiah gathered the city officials together and went up to the temple of the LORD. 21 They brought seven bulls, seven rams, seven male lambs and seven male goats as a sin offering[f] for the kingdom, for the sanctuary and for Judah. The king commanded the priests, the descendants of Aaron, to offer these on the altar of the LORD. 22 So they slaughtered the bulls, and the priests took the blood and sprinkled it on the altar; next they slaughtered the rams and sprinkled their blood on the altar; then they slaughtered the lambs and sprinkled their blood[g] on the altar. 23 The goats for the sin offering were brought before the king and the assembly, and they laid their hands[h] on them. 24 The priests then slaughtered the goats and presented their blood on the altar for a sin offering to atone[i] for all Israel, because the king had ordered the burnt offering and the sin offering for all Israel.

25 He stationed the Levites in the temple of the LORD with cymbals, harps and lyres in the way prescribed by David[j] and Gad[k] the king's seer and Nathan the prophet; this was commanded by the LORD through his prophets. 26 So the Levites stood ready with David's instruments, and the priests with their trumpets.[l]

27 Hezekiah gave the order to sacrifice the burnt offering on the altar. As the offering began, singing to the LORD began also, accompanied by trumpets and the instruments[m] of David king of Israel. 28 The whole assembly bowed in worship, while the singers sang and the trumpeters played. All this continued until the sacrifice of the burnt offering was completed.

29 When the offerings were finished, the king and everyone present with him knelt down and worshiped.[n] 30 King Hezekiah and his officials ordered the Levites to praise the LORD with the words of David and of Asaph the seer. So they sang praises with gladness and bowed their heads and worshiped.

31 Then Hezekiah said, "You have now dedicated yourselves to the LORD. Come and bring sacrifices and thank offerings to the temple of the LORD." So the assembly brought sacrifices and thank offerings, and all whose hearts were willing[o] brought burnt offerings.

32 The number of burnt offerings the assembly brought was seventy bulls, a hundred rams and two hundred male lambs—all of them for burnt offerings to the LORD. 33 The animals consecrated as sacrifices amounted to six hundred bulls and three thousand sheep and goats. 34 The priests, however, were too few to skin all the burnt offerings; so their kinsmen the Levites helped them until the task was finished and until other priests had been consecrated,[p] for the Levites had been more conscientious in consecrating themselves than the priests had been. 35 There were burnt offerings in abundance, together with the fat[q] of the fellowship offerings[a] and the drink offerings[r] that accompanied the burnt offerings.

**29:25** j 1Ch 25:6; 2Ch 8:14 k 2Sa 24:11
**29:26** l 1Ch 15:24; 23:5
**29:27** m 2Ch 23:18
**29:29** n 2Ch 20:18
**29:31** o Ex 35:22
**29:34** p 2Ch 30:3,15
**29:35** q Lev 3:16 r Nu 15:5–10

[a]35 Traditionally *peace offerings*

So the service of the temple of the LORD was reestablished. 36 Hezekiah and all the people rejoiced at what God had brought about for his people, because it was done so quickly.

## Hezekiah Celebrates the Passover

**30** Hezekiah sent word to all Israel and Judah and also wrote letters to Ephraim and Manasseh, inviting them to come to the temple of the LORD in Jerusalem and celebrate the Passover to the LORD, the God of Israel. 2 The king and his officials and the whole assembly in Jerusalem decided to celebrate[s] the Passover in the second month. 3 They had not been able to celebrate it at the regular time because not enough priests had consecrated[t] themselves and the people had not assembled in Jerusalem. 4 The plan seemed right both to the king and to the whole assembly. 5 They decided to send a proclamation throughout Israel, from Beersheba to Dan,[u] calling the people to come to Jerusalem and celebrate the Passover to the LORD, the God of Israel. It had not been celebrated in large numbers according to what was written.

6 At the king's command, couriers went throughout Israel and Judah with letters from the king and from his officials, which read:

> "People of Israel, return to the LORD, the God of Abraham, Isaac and Israel, that he may return to you who are left, who have escaped from the hand of the kings of Assyria. 7 Do not be like your fathers[v] and brothers, who were unfaithful to the LORD, the God of their fathers, so that he made them an object of horror,[w] as you see. 8 Do not be stiff-necked,[x] as your fathers were; submit to the LORD. Come to the sanctuary, which he has consecrated forever. Serve the LORD your God, so that his fierce anger[y] will turn away from you. 9 If you return[z] to the LORD, then your brothers and your children will be shown compassion by their captors and will come back to this land, for the LORD your God is gracious and compassionate.[a] He will not turn his face from you if you return to him."

10 The couriers went from town to town in Ephraim and Manasseh, as far as Zebulun, but the people scorned and ridiculed[b] them. 11 Nevertheless, some men of Asher, Manasseh and Zebulun humbled themselves and went to Jerusalem. 12 Also in Judah the hand of God was on the people to give them unity of mind to carry out what the king and his officials had ordered, following the word of the LORD.

13 A very large crowd of people assembled in Jerusalem to celebrate the Feast of Unleavened Bread in the second month. 14 They removed the altars[c] in Jerusalem and cleared away the incense altars and threw them into the Kidron Valley.

15 They slaughtered the Passover lamb on the fourteenth day of the second month. The priests and the Levites were ashamed and consecrated[d] themselves and brought burnt offerings to the temple of the LORD. 16 Then they took up their regular positions as prescribed in the Law of Moses the man of God. The priests sprinkled the blood handed to them by the Levites. 17 Since many in the crowd had not consecrated themselves, the Levites had to kill[e] the Passover lambs for all those who were not ceremonially clean and could not consecrate their lambs to the LORD. 18 Although most of the many people who came from Ephraim, Manasseh, Issachar and Zebulun had not purified themselves,[f] yet they ate the Passover, contrary to what was written. But Hezekiah prayed for them, saying, "May the LORD, who is good, pardon everyone 19 who sets his heart on seeking God—the LORD, the God of his fathers—even if he is not clean according to the rules of the sanctuary." 20 And the LORD heard Hezekiah and healed the people.

21 The Israelites who were present in Jerusalem celebrated the Feast of Unleavened Bread[g] for seven days with great rejoicing, while the Levites and priests sang to the LORD every day, accompanied by the LORD's instruments of praise.[a]

22 Hezekiah spoke encouragingly to all

**30:2** s Nu 9:10
**30:3** t 2Ch 29:34
**30:5** u Jdg 20:1
**30:7** v Eze 20:18; w 2Ch 29:8
**30:8** x Ex 32:9; y 2Ch 29:10
**30:9** z Dt 30:2–5; Isa 55:7
**30:9** a Mic 7:18
**30:10** b 2Ch 36:16
**30:14** c 2Ch 28:24
**30:15** d 2Ch 29:34
**30:17** e 2Ch 29:34
**30:18** f Ex 12:43–49
**30:21** g Ex 12:15,17; 13:6

[a] 21 Or *priests praised the LORD every day with resounding instruments belonging to the LORD*

**30:23** h 1Ki 8:65
**30:24** i 2Ch 35:7
**30:27** j Nu 6:23
**31:1** k 2Ki 18:4
**31:2** l 1Ch 24:1; m 1Ch 23:28–32
**31:3** n Nu 28:1—29:40
**31:4** o Nu 18:8; Ne 13:10

the Levites, who showed good understand-
ing of the service of the LORD. For the seven
days they ate their assigned portion and of-
fered fellowship offerings[a] and praised the
LORD, the God of their fathers.
[23]The whole assembly then agreed to cel-
ebrate[h] the festival seven more days; so for
another seven days they celebrated joyfully.
[24]Hezekiah king of Judah provided[i] a thou-
sand bulls and seven thousand sheep and
goats for the assembly, and the officials
provided them with a thousand bulls and
ten thousand sheep and goats. A great num-
ber of priests consecrated themselves. [25]The
entire assembly of Judah rejoiced, along
with the priests and Levites and all who had
assembled from Israel, including the aliens
who had come from Israel and those who
lived in Judah. [26]There was great joy in Je-
rusalem, for since the days of Solomon son
of David king of Israel there had been noth-
ing like this in Jerusalem. [27]The priests and
the Levites stood to bless[j] the people, and
God heard them, for their prayer reached
heaven, his holy dwelling place.

31 When all this had ended, the Israel-
ites who were there went out to the
towns of Judah, smashed the sacred stones
and cut down[k] the Asherah poles. They
destroyed the high places and the altars
throughout Judah and Benjamin and in
Ephraim and Manasseh. After they had de-
stroyed all of them, the Israelites returned to
their own towns and to their own property.

## Contributions for Worship

[2]Hezekiah assigned the priests and Le-
vites to divisions[l]—each of them according
to their duties as priests or Levites—to offer
burnt offerings and fellowship offerings,[a] to
minister, to give thanks and to sing praises
at the gates of the LORD's dwelling.[m] [3]The
king contributed from his own possessions
for the morning and evening burnt offerings
and for the burnt offerings on the Sabbaths,
New Moons and appointed feasts as written
in the Law of the LORD.[n] [4]He ordered the peo-
ple living in Jerusalem to give the portion[o]
due the priests and Levites so they could
devote themselves to the Law of the LORD.
[5]As soon as the order went out, the Israel-
ites generously gave the firstfruits[p] of their
grain, new wine, oil and honey and all that
the fields produced. They brought a great
amount, a tithe of everything. [6]The men of
Israel and Judah who lived in the towns of
Judah also brought a tithe[q] of their herds
and flocks and a tithe of the holy things
dedicated to the LORD their God, and they
piled them in heaps.[r] [7]They began doing
this in the third month and finished in the
seventh month. [8]When Hezekiah and his of-
ficials came and saw the heaps, they praised
the LORD and blessed[s] his people Israel.
[9]Hezekiah asked the priests and Levites
about the heaps; [10]and Azariah the chief
priest, from the family of Zadok, answered,
"Since the people began to bring their con-
tributions to the temple of the LORD, we have
had enough to eat and plenty to spare, be-
cause the LORD has blessed his people, and
this great amount is left over."[t]
[11]Hezekiah gave orders to prepare store-
rooms in the temple of the LORD, and this
was done. [12]Then they faithfully brought in
the contributions, tithes and dedicated gifts.
Conaniah, a Levite, was in charge of these
things, and his brother Shimei was next in
rank. [13]Jehiel, Azaziah, Nahath, Asahel, Jeri-
moth, Jozabad, Eliel, Ismakiah, Mahath and
Benaiah were supervisors under Conaniah
and Shimei his brother, by appointment of
King Hezekiah and Azariah the official in
charge of the temple of God.
[14]Kore son of Imnah the Levite, keeper
of the East Gate, was in charge of the free-
will offerings given to God, distributing the
contributions made to the LORD and also
the consecrated gifts. [15]Eden,[u] Miniamin,
Jeshua, Shemaiah, Amariah and Shecaniah
assisted him faithfully in the towns[v] of
the priests, distributing to their fellow
priests according to their divisions, old and
young alike.
[16]In addition, they distributed to the
males three years old or more whose names
were in the genealogical records—all who
would enter the temple of the LORD to per-
form the daily duties of their various tasks,
according to their responsibilities and
their divisions. [17]And they distributed to
the priests enrolled by their families in the

**31:5** p Ne 13:12
**31:6** q Lev 27:30; r Dt 14:28
**31:8** s Ps 144:13–15
**31:10** t Mal 3:10–12
**31:15** u 2Ch 29:12; v Jos 21:9–19

[a] 22,2 Traditionally *peace offerings*

genealogical records and likewise to the Levites twenty years old or more, according to their responsibilities and their divisions. 18 They included all the little ones, the wives, and the sons and daughters of the whole community listed in these genealogical records. For they were faithful in consecrating themselves.

19 As for the priests, the descendants of Aaron, who lived on the farm lands around their towns or in any other towns,[w] men were designated by name to distribute portions to every male among them and to all who were recorded in the genealogies of the Levites.

20 This is what Hezekiah did throughout Judah, doing what was good and right and faithful[x] before the LORD his God. 21 In everything that he undertook in the service of God's temple and in obedience to the law and the commands, he sought his God and worked wholeheartedly. And so he prospered.[y]

## Sennacherib Threatens Jerusalem

32 After all that Hezekiah had so faithfully done, Sennacherib[z] king of Assyria came and invaded Judah. He laid siege to the fortified cities, thinking to conquer them for himself. 2 When Hezekiah saw that Sennacherib had come and that he intended to make war on Jerusalem, 3 he consulted with his officials and military staff about blocking off the water from the springs outside the city, and they helped him. 4 A large force of men assembled, and they blocked all the springs[a] and the stream that flowed through the land. "Why should the kings[a] of Assyria come and find plenty of water?" they said. 5 Then he worked hard repairing all the broken sections of the wall[b] and building towers on it. He built another wall outside that one and reinforced the supporting terraces[b][c] of the City of David. He also made large numbers of weapons and shields.

6 He appointed military officers over the people and assembled them before him in the square at the city gate and encouraged them with these words: 7 "Be strong and courageous.[d] Do not be afraid or discouraged because of the king of Assyria and the vast army with him, for there is a greater power with us than with him.[e] 8 With him is only the arm of flesh,[f] but with us is the LORD our God to help us and to fight our battles."[g] And the people gained confidence from what Hezekiah the king of Judah said.

9 Later, when Sennacherib king of Assyria and all his forces were laying siege to Lachish, he sent his officers to Jerusalem with this message for Hezekiah king of Judah and for all the people of Judah who were there:

> 10 "This is what Sennacherib king of Assyria says: On what are you basing your confidence, that you remain in Jerusalem under siege? 11 When Hezekiah says, 'The LORD our God will save us from the hand of the king of Assyria,' he is misleading you, to let you die of hunger and thirst. 12 Did not Hezekiah himself remove this god's high places and altars, saying to Judah and Jerusalem, 'You must worship before one altar[h] and burn sacrifices on it'?
>
> 13 "Do you not know what I and my fathers have done to all the peoples of the other lands? Were the gods of those nations ever able to deliver their land from my hand? 14 Who of all the gods of these nations that my fathers destroyed has been able to save his people from me? How then can your god deliver you from my hand? 15 Now do not let Hezekiah deceive you and mislead you like this. Do not believe him, for no god of any nation or kingdom has been able to deliver[i] his people from my hand or the hand of my fathers.[j] How much less will your god deliver you from my hand!"

16 Sennacherib's officers spoke further against the LORD God and against his servant Hezekiah. 17 The king also wrote letters insulting the LORD, the God of Israel, and saying this against him: "Just as the gods[k] of the peoples of the other lands did not rescue their people from my hand, so the god of Hezekiah will not rescue his people from my hand." 18 Then they called out in Hebrew to the people of Jerusalem who were on the

**31:19** w Lev 25:34; Nu 35:2–5
**31:20** x 2Ki 20:3
**31:21** y Dt 29:9
**32:1** z 2Ki 18:13–19; Isa 36:1
**32:4** a 2Ki 20:20
**32:5** b 2Ch 25:23 c 1Ki 9:24
**32:7** d Dt 31:6; 1Ch 22:13
**32:7** e 2Ki 6:16
**32:8** f Jer 17:5 g 2Ch 20:17
**32:12** h 2Ch 31:1
**32:15** i Da 3:15 j Ex 5:2
**32:17** k 2Ki 19:12

[a] 4 Hebrew; Septuagint and Syriac *king* [b] 5 Or *the Millo*

wall, to terrify them and make them afraid in order to capture the city. 19 They spoke about the God of Jerusalem as they did about the gods of the other peoples of the world—the work of men's hands.[l]

20 King Hezekiah and the prophet Isaiah son of Amoz cried out in prayer to heaven about this. 21 And the LORD sent an angel, who annihilated all the fighting men and the leaders and officers in the camp of the Assyrian king. So he withdrew to his own land in disgrace. And when he went into the temple of his god, some of his sons cut him down with the sword.

22 So the LORD saved Hezekiah and the people of Jerusalem from the hand of Sennacherib king of Assyria and from the hand of all others. He took care of them[a] on every side. 23 Many brought offerings to Jerusalem for the LORD and valuable gifts[m] for Hezekiah king of Judah. From then on he was highly regarded by all the nations.

## Hezekiah's Pride, Success and Death

24 In those days Hezekiah became ill and was at the point of death. He prayed to the LORD, who answered him and gave him a miraculous sign. 25 But Hezekiah's heart was proud[n] and he did not respond to the kindness shown him; therefore the LORD's wrath[o] was on him and on Judah and Jerusalem. 26 Then Hezekiah repented[p] of the pride of his heart, as did the people of Jerusalem; therefore the LORD's wrath did not come upon them during the days of Hezekiah.

27 Hezekiah had very great riches and honor, and he made treasuries for his silver and gold and for his precious stones, spices, shields and all kinds of valuables. 28 He also made buildings to store the harvest of grain, new wine and oil; and he made stalls for various kinds of cattle, and pens for the flocks. 29 He built villages and acquired great numbers of flocks and herds, for God had given him very great riches.[q]

30 It was Hezekiah who blocked the upper outlet of the Gihon[r] spring and channeled the water down to the west side of the City of David. He succeeded in everything he undertook. 31 But when envoys were sent by the rulers of Babylon[s] to ask him about the miraculous sign that had occurred in the land, God left him to test[t] him and to know everything that was in his heart.

32 The other events of Hezekiah's reign and his acts of devotion are written in the vision of the prophet Isaiah son of Amoz in the book of the kings of Judah and Israel. 33 Hezekiah rested with his fathers and was buried on the hill where the tombs of David's descendants are. All Judah and the people of Jerusalem honored him when he died. And Manasseh his son succeeded him as king.

## Manasseh King of Judah

33 Manasseh was twelve years old when he became king, and he reigned in Jerusalem fifty-five years. 2 He did evil in the eyes of the LORD, following the detestable[u] practices of the nations the LORD had driven out before the Israelites. 3 He rebuilt the high places his father Hezekiah had demolished; he also erected altars to the Baals and made Asherah poles.[v] He bowed down[w] to all the starry hosts and worshiped them. 4 He built altars in the temple of the LORD, of which the LORD had said, "My Name[x] will remain in Jerusalem forever." 5 In both courts of the temple of the LORD,[y] he built altars to all the starry hosts. 6 He sacrificed his sons[z] in[b] the fire in the Valley of Ben Hinnom, practiced sorcery, divination and witchcraft, and consulted mediums and spiritists. He did much evil in the eyes of the LORD, provoking him to anger.

7 He took the carved image he had made and put it in God's temple, of which God had said to David and to his son Solomon, "In this temple and in Jerusalem, which I have chosen out of all the tribes of Israel, I will put my Name forever. 8 I will not again make the feet of the Israelites leave the land[a] I assigned to your forefathers, if only they will be careful to do everything I commanded them concerning all the laws, decrees and ordinances given through Moses." 9 But Manasseh led Judah and the people of Jerusalem astray, so that they did more evil than the nations the LORD had destroyed before the Israelites.

**32:19** l 2Ki 19:18; Ps 115:4–8
**32:23** m 2Ch 17:5
**32:25** n 2Ch 26:16 o 2Ch 24:18
**32:26** p Jer 26:18–19
**32:29** q 1Ch 29:12
**32:30** r 1Ki 1:33
**32:31** s Isa 39:1 t Dt 8:16
**33:2** u Dt 18:9; 2Ch 28:3
**33:3** v Dt 16:21–22 w 2Ch 31:1
**33:4** x 2Ch 7:16
**33:5** y 2Ch 4:9
**33:6** z Lev 18:21; 2Ch 28:3
**33:8** a 2Sa 7:10

[a] 22 Hebrew; Septuagint and Vulgate *He gave them rest* [b] 6 Or *He made his sons pass through*

10The LORD spoke to Manasseh and his people, but they paid no attention. 11So the LORD brought against them the army commanders of the king of Assyria, who took Manasseh prisoner,[b] put a hook in his nose, bound him with bronze shackles and took him to Babylon. 12In his distress he sought the favor of the LORD his God and humbled[c] himself greatly before the God of his fathers. 13And when he prayed to him, the LORD was moved by his entreaty and listened to his plea; so he brought him back to Jerusalem and to his kingdom. Then Manasseh knew that the LORD is God.

14Afterward he rebuilt the outer wall of the City of David, west of the Gihon[d] spring in the valley, as far as the entrance of the Fish Gate and encircling the hill of Ophel;[e] he also made it much higher. He stationed military commanders in all the fortified cities in Judah.

15He got rid of the foreign gods and removed[f] the image from the temple of the LORD, as well as all the altars he had built on the temple hill and in Jerusalem; and he threw them out of the city. 16Then he restored the altar of the LORD and sacrificed fellowship offerings[*a*] and thank offerings[g] on it, and told Judah to serve the LORD, the God of Israel. 17The people, however, continued to sacrifice at the high places, but only to the LORD their God.

18The other events of Manasseh's reign, including his prayer to his God and the words the seers spoke to him in the name of the LORD, the God of Israel, are written in the annals of the kings of Israel.[*b*] 19His prayer and how God was moved by his entreaty, as well as all his sins and unfaithfulness, and the sites where he built high places and set up Asherah poles and idols before he humbled himself—all are written in the records of the seers.[*c*] 20Manasseh rested with his fathers and was buried[h] in his palace. And Amon his son succeeded him as king.

## Amon King of Judah

21Amon was twenty-two years old when he became king, and he reigned in Jerusalem two years. 22He did evil in the eyes of the LORD, as his father Manasseh had done. Amon worshiped and offered sacrifices to all the idols Manasseh had made. 23But unlike his father Manasseh, he did not humble[i] himself before the LORD; Amon increased his guilt.

24Amon's officials conspired against him and assassinated him in his palace. 25Then the people of the land killed all who had plotted against King Amon, and they made Josiah his son king in his place.

## Josiah's Reforms

**34** Josiah[j] was eight years old when he became king, and he reigned in Jerusalem thirty-one years. 2He did what was right in the eyes of the LORD and walked in the ways of his father David,[k] not turning aside to the right or to the left.

3In the eighth year of his reign, while he was still young, he began to seek the God[l] of his father David. In his twelfth year he began to purge Judah and Jerusalem of high places, Asherah poles, carved idols and cast images. 4Under his direction the altars of the Baals were torn down; he cut to pieces the incense altars that were above them, and smashed the Asherah poles, the idols and the images. These he broke to pieces and scattered over the graves of those who had sacrificed to them.[m] 5He burned[n] the bones of the priests on their altars, and so he purged Judah and Jerusalem. 6In the towns of Manasseh, Ephraim and Simeon, as far as Naphtali, and in the ruins around them, 7he tore down the altars and the Asherah poles and crushed the idols to powder[o] and cut to pieces all the incense altars throughout Israel. Then he went back to Jerusalem.

8In the eighteenth year of Josiah's reign, to purify the land and the temple, he sent Shaphan son of Azaliah and Maaseiah the ruler of the city, with Joah son of Joahaz, the recorder, to repair the temple of the LORD his God.

9They went to Hilkiah[p] the high priest and gave him the money that had been brought into the temple of God, which the Levites who were the doorkeepers had collected from the people of Manasseh,

**33:11** b Dt 28:36
**33:12** c 2Ch 32:26; 1Pe 5:6
**33:14** d 1Ki 1:33 e 2Ch 27:3
**33:15** f ver 3–7
**33:16** g Lev 7:11–18
**33:20** h 2Ki 21:18
**33:23** i ver 12
**34:1** j 1Ch 3:14
**34:2** k 2Ch 29:2
**34:3** l 1Ki 13:2; 2Ch 15:2; 33:17,22
**34:4** m Ex 32:20; Lev 26:30
**34:5** n 1Ki 13:2
**34:7** o 2Ch 31:1
**34:9** p 2Ch 35:8

*a*16 Traditionally *peace offerings* *b*18 That is, Judah, as frequently in 2 Chronicles *c*19 One Hebrew manuscript and Septuagint; most Hebrew manuscripts *of Hozai*

34:11 q 2Ch 33:4–7
34:12 r 2Ki 12:15 s 1Ch 25:1
34:13 t 1Ch 23:4
34:19 u Dt 28:3–68 v Jos 7:6
34:21 w 2Ch 29:8

Ephraim and the entire remnant of Israel and from all the people of Judah and Benjamin and the inhabitants of Jerusalem. 10 Then they entrusted it to the men appointed to supervise the work on the LORD's temple. These men paid the workers who repaired and restored the temple. 11 They also gave money to the carpenters and builders to purchase dressed stone, and timber for joists and beams for the buildings that the kings of Judah had allowed to fall into ruin.[q]

12 The men did the work faithfully.[r] Over them to direct them were Jahath and Obadiah, Levites descended from Merari, and Zechariah and Meshullam, descended from Kohath. The Levites—all who were skilled in playing musical instruments—[s] 13 had charge of the laborers[t] and supervised all the workers from job to job. Some of the Levites were secretaries, scribes and doorkeepers.

## The Book of the Law Found

14 While they were bringing out the money that had been taken into the temple of the LORD, Hilkiah the priest found the Book of the Law of the LORD that had been given through Moses. 15 Hilkiah said to Shaphan the secretary, "I have found the Book of the Law in the temple of the LORD." He gave it to Shaphan.

16 Then Shaphan took the book to the king and reported to him: "Your officials are doing everything that has been committed to them. 17 They have paid out the money that was in the temple of the LORD and have entrusted it to the supervisors and workers." 18 Then Shaphan the secretary informed the king, "Hilkiah the priest has given me a book." And Shaphan read from it in the presence of the king.

19 When the king heard the words of the Law,[u] he tore[v] his robes. 20 He gave these orders to Hilkiah, Ahikam son of Shaphan, Abdon son of Micah,[a] Shaphan the secretary and Asaiah the king's attendant: 21 "Go and inquire of the LORD for me and for the remnant in Israel and Judah about what is written in this book that has been found. Great is the LORD's anger that is poured out[w] on us because our fathers have not kept the word of the LORD; they have not acted in accordance with all that is written in this book."

22 Hilkiah and those the king had sent with him[b] went to speak to the prophetess Huldah, who was the wife of Shallum son of Tokhath,[c] the son of Hasrah,[d] keeper of the wardrobe. She lived in Jerusalem, in the Second District.

23 She said to them, "This is what the LORD, the God of Israel, says: Tell the man who sent you to me, 24 'This is what the LORD says: I am going to bring disaster on this place and its people[x]—all the curses[y] written in the book that has been read in the presence of the king of Judah. 25 Because they have forsaken me[z] and burned incense to other gods and provoked me to anger by all that their hands have made,[e] my anger will be poured out on this place and will not be quenched.' 26 Tell the king of Judah, who sent you to inquire of the LORD, 'This is what the LORD, the God of Israel, says concerning the words you heard: 27 Because your heart was responsive[a] and you humbled yourself before God when you heard what he spoke against this place and its people, and because you humbled yourself before me and tore your robes and wept in my presence, I have heard you, declares the LORD. 28 Now I will gather you to your fathers, and you will be buried in peace. Your eyes will not see all the disaster I am going to bring on this place and on those who live here.'"

So they took her answer back to the king.

29 Then the king called together all the elders of Judah and Jerusalem. 30 He went up to the temple of the LORD[b] with the men of Judah, the people of Jerusalem, the priests and the Levites—all the people from the least to the greatest. He read in their hearing all the words of the Book of the Covenant, which had been found in the temple of the LORD. 31 The king stood by his pillar[c] and renewed the covenant[d] in the presence of the LORD—to follow the LORD and keep his commands, regulations and decrees with all his heart and all his soul, and to obey the words of the covenant written in this book.

32 Then he had everyone in Jerusalem and

34:24 x 2Ch 36:14–20 y Dt 28:15–68
34:25 z 2Ch 33:3–6
34:27 a 2Ch 12:7; 32:26
34:30 b 2Ki 23:2; Ne 8:1–3
34:31 c 2Ki 11:14 d 2Ch 23:16

[a] 20 Also called *Acbor son of Micaiah* [b] 22 One Hebrew manuscript, Vulgate and Syriac; most Hebrew manuscripts do not have *had sent with him.* [c] 22 Also called *Tikvah* [d] 22 Also called *Harhas* [e] 25 Or *by everything they have done*

# Inspire leadership FOCUS

## RESPONSIBLE DECISIONS IN LEADERSHIP

The account in 2 Chronicles 34:14–33 provides a powerful backdrop for women of color in employing the principles of responsible decision making in leadership. God used Huldah, the prophetess, as his instrument to communicate the word of the Lord and to warn the king of God's judgment for the nation's sinful, wayward acts. God's call transcends gender, race, cultural background and human imperfection. God calls women and men to be his vehicles for truth, honesty and justice in a world that has turned away from the Creator. When the appointed delegation came to Huldah, she heeded the word from the Lord, obeyed God's message and interpreted it as she was led.

Throughout Biblical history, God has used women as agents of justice, of goodwill and of the gospel message. God used Huldah to speak and interpret his word of coming disaster for the Hebrew people in the face of their worship of other gods and their ignorance of his teachings. God used Deborah, Rahab, Miriam, Abigail, Esther, Mary (Jesus' mother) and countless others to show courage and strength in decision making, to display exemplary leadership and to speak the truth in love.

In our work in the world, God will place people in our lives from whom we can glean knowledge that will aid our success. We must call upon trusted leaders to assist our work for God's kingdom. Huldah's legacy is one that instructs us to discern carefully, to remain prayerful and to speak the truth of God's justice and mercy.

Women of color face special challenges in the journey through life. Learning the important principles of responsible decision making, delegation and teamwork requires prayerful deliberation, strategic thinking and dialogue with trusted mentors and friends. God has given us the gift of discernment in our decision making, creative thinking for our choices and the ability to seek out allies and colleagues to work with us in the professional arena. Huldah's story illustrates the gift of leadership, responsibility and mentoring. Let us find a message in her story and apply it to our lives.

—M. Newbern-Williams

### read

2 Chronicles 34:14–33; see also Exodus 18:13–26; Joshua 24:15; Psalm 65:4; John 15:16.

**See also** the Women of the Bible Notes "Rahab: Willing to Be Used by God," "Huldah: A Prophetess of God" and "The Revelation 12 Woman: A Woman of Focus."

### WOMAN of COLOR

What kind of women do you seek out for spiritual guidance? Professional guidance? Personal guidance?

For the next Inspire note, go to page 549.

Benjamin pledge themselves to it; the people of Jerusalem did this in accordance with the covenant of God, the God of their fathers.

33 Josiah removed all the detestable idols from all the territory belonging to the Israelites, and he had all who were present in Israel serve the LORD their God. As long as he lived, they did not fail to follow the LORD, the God of their fathers.

## Josiah Celebrates the Passover

**35** Josiah celebrated the Passover[e] to the LORD in Jerusalem, and the Passover lamb was slaughtered on the fourteenth day of the first month. 2 He appointed the priests to their duties and encouraged them in the service of the LORD's temple. 3 He said to the Levites, who instructed[f] all Israel and who had been consecrated to the LORD: "Put the sacred ark in the temple that Solomon son of David king of Israel built. It is not to be carried about on your shoulders. Now serve the LORD your God and his people Israel. 4 Prepare yourselves by families in your divisions,[g] according to the directions written by David king of Israel and by his son Solomon.

5 "Stand in the holy place with a group of Levites for each subdivision of the families of your fellow countrymen, the lay people. 6 Slaughter the Passover lambs, consecrate yourselves[h] and prepare ⌊the lambs⌋ for your fellow countrymen, doing what the LORD commanded through Moses."

7 Josiah provided for all the lay people who were there a total of thirty thousand sheep and goats for the Passover offerings,[i] and also three thousand cattle—all from the king's own possessions.

8 His officials also contributed voluntarily to the people and the priests and Levites. Hilkiah, Zechariah and Jehiel, the administrators of God's temple, gave the priests twenty-six hundred Passover offerings and three hundred cattle. 9 Also Conaniah[j] along with Shemaiah and Nethanel, his brothers, and Hashabiah, Jeiel and Jozabad, the leaders of the Levites, provided five thousand Passover offerings and five hundred head of cattle for the Levites.

10 The service was arranged and the priests stood in their places with the Levites in their divisions as the king had ordered. 11 The Passover lambs were slaughtered,[k] and the priests sprinkled the blood handed to them, while the Levites skinned the animals. 12 They set aside the burnt offerings to give them to the subdivisions of the families of the people to offer to the LORD, as is written in the Book of Moses. They did the same with the cattle. 13 They roasted the Passover animals over the fire as prescribed,[l] and boiled the holy offerings in pots, caldrons and pans and served them quickly to all the people. 14 After this, they made preparations for themselves and for the priests, because the priests, the descendants of Aaron, were sacrificing the burnt offerings and the fat portions until nightfall. So the Levites made preparations for themselves and for the Aaronic priests.

15 The musicians,[m] the descendants of Asaph, were in the places prescribed by David, Asaph, Heman and Jeduthun the king's seer. The gatekeepers at each gate did not need to leave their posts, because their fellow Levites made the preparations for them.

16 So at that time the entire service of the LORD was carried out for the celebration of the Passover and the offering of burnt offerings on the altar of the LORD, as King Josiah had ordered. 17 The Israelites who were present celebrated the Passover at that time and observed the Feast of Unleavened Bread for seven days. 18 The Passover had not been observed like this in Israel since the days of the prophet Samuel; and none of the kings of Israel had ever celebrated such a Passover as did Josiah, with the priests, the Levites and all Judah and Israel who were there with the people of Jerusalem. 19 This Passover was celebrated in the eighteenth year of Josiah's reign.

## The Death of Josiah

20 After all this, when Josiah had set the temple in order, Neco king of Egypt went up to fight at Carchemish[n] on the Euphrates, and Josiah marched out to meet him in battle. 21 But Neco sent messengers to him, saying, "What quarrel is there between you and me, O king of Judah? It is not you I am attacking at this time, but the house with which I am at war. God has told me to hurry;

**35:1** e Ex 12:1–30
**35:3** f 1Ch 23:26; 2Ch 17:7
**35:4** g 1Ch 9:10–13; 2Ch 8:14; Ezr 6:18
**35:6** h 2Ch 29:5,15
**35:7** i 2Ch 30:24
**35:9** j 2Ch 31:12
**35:11** k 2Ch 29:22,34
**35:13** l Ex 12:2–11
**35:15** m 1Ch 25:1; 26:12–19
**35:20** n Isa 10:9; Jer 46:2

so stop opposing God, who is with me, or he will destroy you."

22 Josiah, however, would not turn away from him, but disguised himself to engage him in battle. He would not listen to what Neco had said at God's command but went to fight him on the plain of Megiddo.

23 Archers shot King Josiah, and he told his officers, "Take me away; I am badly wounded." 24 So they took him out of his chariot, put him in the other chariot he had and brought him to Jerusalem, where he died. He was buried in the tombs of his fathers, and all Judah and Jerusalem mourned for him.

25 Jeremiah composed laments for Josiah, and to this day all the men and women singers commemorate Josiah in the laments.[o] These became a tradition in Israel and are written in the Laments.

26 The other events of Josiah's reign and his acts of devotion, according to what is written in the Law of the LORD— 27 all the events, from beginning to end, are written in the book of the kings of Israel and Judah.

**36** 1 And the people of the land took Jehoahaz son of Josiah and made him king in Jerusalem in place of his father.

## Jehoahaz King of Judah

2 Jehoahaz[a] was twenty-three years old when he became king, and he reigned in Jerusalem three months. 3 The king of Egypt dethroned him in Jerusalem and imposed on Judah a levy of a hundred talents[b] of silver and a talent[c] of gold. 4 The king of Egypt made Eliakim, a brother of Jehoahaz, king over Judah and Jerusalem and changed Eliakim's name to Jehoiakim. But Neco took Eliakim's brother Jehoahaz and carried him off to Egypt.

## Jehoiakim King of Judah

5 Jehoiakim[p] was twenty-five years old when he became king, and he reigned in Jerusalem eleven years. He did evil in the eyes of the LORD his God. 6 Nebuchadnezzar king of Babylon attacked him and bound him with bronze shackles to take him to Babylon.[q] 7 Nebuchadnezzar also took to Babylon articles from the temple of the LORD and put them in his temple[d] there.[r]

8 The other events of Jehoiakim's reign, the detestable things he did and all that was found against him, are written in the book of the kings of Israel and Judah. And Jehoiachin his son succeeded him as king.

## Jehoiachin King of Judah

9 Jehoiachin was eighteen[e] years old when he became king, and he reigned in Jerusalem three months and ten days. He did evil in the eyes of the LORD. 10 In the spring, King Nebuchadnezzar sent for him and brought him to Babylon,[s] together with articles of value from the temple of the LORD, and he made Jehoiachin's uncle,[f] Zedekiah, king over Judah and Jerusalem.

## Zedekiah King of Judah

11 Zedekiah[t] was twenty-one years old when he became king, and he reigned in Jerusalem eleven years. 12 He did evil in the eyes of the LORD his God and did not humble[u] himself before Jeremiah the prophet, who spoke the word of the LORD. 13 He also rebelled against King Nebuchadnezzar, who had made him take an oath in God's name. He became stiff-necked[v] and hardened his heart and would not turn to the LORD, the God of Israel. 14 Furthermore, all the leaders of the priests and the people became more and more unfaithful, following all the detestable practices of the nations and defiling the temple of the LORD, which he had consecrated in Jerusalem.

## The Fall of Jerusalem

15 The LORD, the God of their fathers, sent word to them through his messengers again and again,[w] because he had pity on his people and on his dwelling place. 16 But they mocked God's messengers, despised his words and scoffed[x] at his prophets until the wrath[y] of the LORD was aroused against his people and there was no remedy.[z] 17 He brought up against them the king of the Babylonians,[g] who killed their young men with

**35:25** o Jer 22:10,15–16
**36:5** p Jer 26:1; 35:1
**36:6** q 2Ch 33:11
**36:7** r 2Ki 24:13
**36:10** s Jer 22:25; 24:1; 37:1; Eze 17:12
**36:11** t Jer 27:1; 28:1
**36:12** u 2Ch 33:23; Jer 21:3–7
**36:13** v 2Ki 17:14; 2Ch 30:8
**36:15** w Jer 7:13,25; 25:3–4
**36:16** x Pr 1:25; Jer 5:13 y Ezr 5:12; Pr 1:30–31 z 2Ch 30:10

[a]2 Hebrew *Joahaz,* a variant of *Jehoahaz;* also in verse 4 [b]3 That is, about 3 3/4 tons (about 3.4 metric tons) [c]3 That is, about 75 pounds (about 34 kilograms) [d]7 Or *palace* [e]9 One Hebrew manuscript, some Septuagint manuscripts and Syriac (see also 2 Kings 24:8); most Hebrew manuscripts *eight* [f]10 Hebrew *brother,* that is, relative (see 2 Kings 24:17) [g]17 Or *Chaldeans*

**36:19** a 1Ki 9:8–9 b Ps 79:1–3
**36:20** c Jer 27:7
**36:21** d Lev 25:4; 26:34

the sword in the sanctuary, and spared nei-
ther young man nor young woman, old man
or aged. God handed all of them over to Neb-
uchadnezzar. 18 He carried to Babylon all the
articles from the temple of God, both large
and small, and the treasures of the LORD's
temple and the treasures of the king and
his officials. 19 They set fire to God's temple[a]
and broke down the wall of Jerusalem; they
burned all the palaces and destroyed every-
thing of value there.[b]

20 He carried into exile to Babylon the rem-
nant, who escaped from the sword, and they
became servants[c] to him and his sons until
the kingdom of Persia came to power. 21 The
land enjoyed its sabbath rests;[d] all the time
of its desolation it rested, until the seventy
years[e] were completed in fulfillment of the
word of the LORD spoken by Jeremiah.

22 In the first year of Cyrus[f] king of Per-
sia, in order to fulfill the word of the LORD
spoken by Jeremiah, the LORD moved the
heart of Cyrus king of Persia to make a proc-
lamation throughout his realm and to put it
in writing:

23 "This is what Cyrus king of Persia says:

"'The LORD, the God of heaven, has
given me all the kingdoms of the earth
and he has appointed me to build a
temple for him at Jerusalem in Judah.
Anyone of his people among you—
may the LORD his God be with him,
and let him go up.'"

**36:21** e Jer 25:11; 29:10; Da 9:2
**36:22** f Isa 44:28; Jer 25:12; 29:10

# Ezra

## OVERVIEW

After the people of Judah spent 70 years in exile in Babylon, the Babylonians were conquered by the Persians. Soon thereafter, Cyrus, the king of Persia, made a proclamation that the Jewish exiles could return to their land and rebuild the temple. Approximately 42,000 Israelites returned to Judah under Sheshbazzar's leadership (see Ezr 1:8,11; 2:64).

When the people reached their homeland, they worked hard to restore the land and their temple. But they soon had opposition from their neighbors, who sent a letter to Darius, the new king of Persia, appealing to him to end the building project (see Ezr 5). Their plan backfired, however, as Darius decreed that the Jews' enemies were to offer no interference to the reconstruction of the temple. Consequently, the temple was completed and dedicated amidst great joy (see Ezr 6).

Nearly 60 years later, Ezra, a priest and scribe, led an additional group of Jews to return to the land (see Ezr 7–8). The rest of the book contains Ezra's exhortations for the people to maintain complete obedience to God's Word. Through Ezra's encouragement and impassioned leadership, the Israelites experienced a great spiritual revival (Ezr 9–10; see also Ne 8–10).

Every woman who believes in the Lord Jesus Christ will experience opposition in her walk with God. Resistance may come from family members, friends or even other Christians. Reflecting on the success of the Israelites in the face of opposition and persecution reveals how God makes a way to overcome when his people place their complete trust in him.

## OUTLINE

I. The Return Under Sheshbazzar (1:1—2:70)
II. The Restoration of Temple Worship (3:1–13)
III. Opposition to Rebuilding and Completion of the Temple (4:1—6:22)
IV. Ezra's Return to Jerusalem (7:1—8:36)
V. Ezra's Reforms (9:1—10:44)

## SCANNABLE FACTS:

**Author:** Unknown; possibly Ezra

**Time Written:** About 450 B.C.

**Theme to Note:** God's chosen people return home

**Notable Women:** Foreign women married to Israelite men who disobeyed God by intermarrying

## Cyrus Helps the Exiles to Return

1 In the first year of Cyrus king of Persia, in order to fulfill the word of the LORD spoken by Jeremiah,[a] the LORD moved the heart[b] of Cyrus king of Persia to make a proclamation throughout his realm and to put it in writing:

2 "This is what Cyrus king of Persia says:

" 'The LORD, the God of heaven, has given me all the kingdoms of the earth and he has appointed[c] me to build[d] a temple for him at Jerusalem in Judah. 3 Anyone of his people among you—may his God be with him, and let him go up to Jerusalem in Judah and build the temple of the LORD, the God of Israel, the God who is in Jerusalem. 4 And the people of any place where survivors may now be living are to provide him with silver and gold, with goods and livestock, and with freewill offerings for the temple of God in Jerusalem.' "

5 Then the family heads of Judah and Benjamin, and the priests and Levites—everyone whose heart God had moved[e]—prepared to go up and build the house of the LORD in Jerusalem. 6 All their neighbors assisted them with articles of silver and gold, with goods and livestock, and with valuable gifts, in addition to all the freewill offerings. 7 Moreover, King Cyrus brought out the articles belonging to the temple of the LORD, which Nebuchadnezzar had carried away from Jerusalem and had placed in the temple of his god.[a][f] 8 Cyrus king of Persia had them brought by Mithredath the treasurer, who counted them out to Sheshbazzar[g] the prince of Judah.

9 This was the inventory:

| | |
|---|---|
| gold dishes | 30 |
| silver dishes | 1,000 |
| silver pans[b] | 29 |
| 10 gold bowls | 30 |
| matching silver bowls | 410 |
| other articles | 1,000 |

11 In all, there were 5,400 articles of gold and of silver. Sheshbazzar brought all these along when the exiles came up from Babylon to Jerusalem.

## The List of the Exiles Who Returned

2 Now these are the people of the province who came up from the captivity of the exiles,[h] whom Nebuchadnezzar king of Babylon[i] had taken captive to Babylon (they returned to Jerusalem and Judah, each to his own town,[j] 2 in company with Zerubbabel, Jeshua, Nehemiah, Seraiah, Reelaiah, Mordecai, Bilshan, Mispar, Bigvai, Rehum and Baanah):

The list of the men of the people of Israel:

| | |
|---|---|
| 3 the descendants of Parosh | 2,172 |
| 4 of Shephatiah | 372 |
| 5 of Arah | 775 |
| 6 of Pahath-Moab (through the line of Jeshua and Joab) | 2,812 |
| 7 of Elam | 1,254 |
| 8 of Zattu | 945 |
| 9 of Zaccai | 760 |
| 10 of Bani | 642 |
| 11 of Bebai | 623 |
| 12 of Azgad | 1,222 |
| 13 of Adonikam | 666 |
| 14 of Bigvai | 2,056 |
| 15 of Adin | 454 |
| 16 of Ater (through Hezekiah) | 98 |
| 17 of Bezai | 323 |
| 18 of Jorah | 112 |
| 19 of Hashum | 223 |
| 20 of Gibbar | 95 |
| 21 the men of Bethlehem | 123 |
| 22 of Netophah | 56 |
| 23 of Anathoth | 128 |
| 24 of Azmaveth | 42 |
| 25 of Kiriath Jearim,[c] Kephirah and Beeroth | 743 |
| 26 of Ramah[k] and Geba | 621 |
| 27 of Micmash | 122 |
| 28 of Bethel and Ai | 223 |
| 29 of Nebo | 52 |
| 30 of Magbish | 156 |
| 31 of the other Elam | 1,254 |
| 32 of Harim | 320 |

**1:1** a Jer 25:11–12; 29:10–14 b 2Ch 36:22,23
**1:2** c Isa 44:28; 45:13 d Ezr 5:13
**1:5** e ver 1; Php 2:13
**1:7** f 2Ki 24:13; 2Ch 36:7,10; Ezr 5:14; 6:5
**1:8** g Ezr 5:14
**2:1** h 2Ch 36:20; Ne 7:6 i 2Ki 24:16; 25:12 j Ne 7:73
**2:26** k Jos 18:25

[a]7 Or *gods* [b]9 The meaning of the Hebrew for this word is uncertain. [c]25 See Septuagint (see also Neh. 7:29); Hebrew *Kiriath Arim.*

Inspire leadership FOCUS

# FOLLOWING GOD-GIVEN VISIONS

A vision is a mental picture of something—a thought, an image or a concept. Once we have that mental picture, we make it our goal or mission to attain what we've seen. Sometimes God gives women leaders a vision to improve an organization or community, to start a business, or to create something that will improve the lives of those around us. Sometimes we understand our God-given visions clearly and therefore know what our missions in life are; other times we understand them bit by bit. But when God grants us a vision, it stays with us until we act upon it. So how can those of us who have been called to fulfill a certain mission act upon our God-given visions?

Those of us wrestling with the vision God has given us can find help and inspiration in the book of Ezra. Here we see many people envisioning the exiled Israelites returning to a restored Jerusalem and worshiping in the rebuilt temple. The mission then was for the exiles to come together to rebuild the city and God's temple.

When God gives us a vision, he will give us the provision to accomplish what we need to do. Sometimes this provision comes through unlikely sources, such as the king of Persia in Ezra 1. In that instance, God moved the heart of the king in order to help the exiles. In your situation, know that God can move the hearts of those around you. If you need certain resources, watch God deliver them to you—sometimes through unlikely sources. While you should always thank your benefactors for their resources, remember to give the due credit to God as the ultimate provider of all you need.

Our task is to stay committed to the goal and vision. Even when it looks like things will not come to pass, we must constantly revisit the mandate from God. As women leaders, we should always ask God to lead us and give us discernment. We must not forget that it is *God's* vision; we are only the stewards, the caretakers, of his vision.

Don't step ahead of God because you desire something. Wait on God for direction and only move when you're clear God is telling you to move. Then you will accomplish all that God has planned and ordained—and your life, as well as countless other lives, will be blessed.

—K. Washington

## read

Ezra 1; Nehemiah 2; Philippians 1:3–11.

**See also** the Inspire Notes "Write It Down!" "Doing Your Best" and "Be Focused," and the Women of the Bible Note "Mary, the Mother of James and Joses: Sacrificing for Christ."

## WOMAN *of* COLOR

What vision has God given you? Write it down. Pray about the steps you need to take to accomplish this vision.

For the next Inspire note, go to page 565.

| | |
|---|---|
| 33 of Lod, Hadid and Ono | 725 |
| 34 of Jericho[l] | 345 |
| 35 of Senaah | 3,630 |

36 The priests:

| | |
|---|---|
| the descendants of Jedaiah[m] (through the family of Jeshua) | 973 |
| 37 of Immer[n] | 1,052 |
| 38 of Pashhur[o] | 1,247 |
| 39 of Harim[p] | 1,017 |

40 The Levites:

| | |
|---|---|
| the descendants of Jeshua[q] and Kadmiel (through the line of Hodaviah) | 74 |

41 The singers:

| | |
|---|---|
| the descendants of Asaph | 128 |

42 The gatekeepers of the temple:

| | |
|---|---|
| the descendants of Shallum, Ater, Talmon, Akkub, Hatita and Shobai | 139 |

43 The temple servants:[r]

the descendants of
Ziha, Hasupha, Tabbaoth,
44 Keros, Siaha, Padon,
45 Lebanah, Hagabah, Akkub,
46 Hagab, Shalmai, Hanan,
47 Giddel, Gahar, Reaiah,
48 Rezin, Nekoda, Gazzam,
49 Uzza, Paseah, Besai,
50 Asnah, Meunim, Nephusim,
51 Bakbuk, Hakupha, Harhur,
52 Bazluth, Mehida, Harsha,
53 Barkos, Sisera, Temah,
54 Neziah and Hatipha

55 The descendants of the servants of Solomon:

the descendants of
Sotai, Hassophereth, Peruda,
56 Jaala, Darkon, Giddel,
57 Shephatiah, Hattil,
Pokereth-Hazzebaim and Ami

| | |
|---|---|
| 58 The temple servants[s] and the descendants of the servants of Solomon | 392 |

59 The following came up from the
towns of Tel Melah, Tel Harsha, Kerub, Addon and Immer, but they could
not show that their families were
descended from Israel:

| | |
|---|---|
| 60 The descendants of Delaiah, Tobiah and Nekoda | 652 |

61 And from among the priests:

The descendants of
Hobaiah, Hakkoz and Barzillai (a man who had married a daughter of Barzillai the Gileadite[t] and was called by that name).

62 These searched for their family
records, but they could not find them
and so were excluded from the priesthood[u] as unclean.
63 The governor ordered them not to eat any of the most
sacred food[v] until there was a priest
ministering with the Urim and Thummim.[w]

64 The whole company numbered
42,360,
65 besides their 7,337 menservants and maidservants; and they
also had 200 men and women singers.
66 They had 736 horses, 245 mules,
67 435 camels and 6,720 donkeys.

68 When they arrived at the house of the
LORD in Jerusalem, some of the heads of
the families gave freewill offerings toward
the rebuilding of the house of God on its
site.
69 According to their ability they gave
to the treasury for this work 61,000 drachmas[a] of gold, 5,000 minas[b] of silver and 100
priestly garments.

70 The priests, the Levites, the singers, the
gatekeepers and the temple servants settled
in their own towns, along with some of the
other people, and the rest of the Israelites
settled in their towns.[x]

## Rebuilding the Altar

3 When the seventh month came and the
Israelites had settled in their towns,[y]
the people assembled as one man in Jerusalem.
2 Then Jeshua[z] son of Jozadak[a] and
his fellow priests and Zerubbabel son of
Shealtiel[b] and his associates began to build

**2:34** l 1Ki 16:34; 2Ch 28:15
**2:36** m 1Ch 24:7
**2:37** n 1Ch 24:14
**2:38** o 1Ch 9:12
**2:39** p 1Ch 24:8
**2:40** q Ezr 3:9
**2:43** r 1Ch 9:2
**2:58** s 1Ch 9:2
**2:61** t 2Sa 17:27
**2:62** u Nu 3:10; 16:39–40
**2:63** v Lev 2:3,10 w Ex 28:30
**2:70** x 1Ch 9:2; Ne 11:3–4
**3:1** y Ne 7:73
**3:2** z Ezr 2:2 a Hag 1:1 b 1Ch 3:17

[a] 69 That is, about 1,100 pounds (about 500 kilograms) [b] 69 That is, about 3 tons (about 2.9 metric tons)

3:2
c Dt 12:5–6
3:3
d Ezr 4:4
e Nu 28:1–8
3:4
f Ex 23:16; Nu 29:12–38; Ne 8:14–18; Zec 14:16–19
3:5
g Nu 28:3,11,14
h Nu 29:39
3:7
i Ezr 1:2–4; 6:3
3:8
j 1Ch 23:24
3:9
k Ezr 2:40

*Lord,*

*I give myself to you fully. Restore the broken places of my life, and give me the strength to live as a whole person.*

*Amen*

EZRA 3:1–3

the altar of the God of Israel to sacrifice burnt offerings on it, in accordance with what is written in the Law of Moses[c] the man of God. 3 Despite their fear[d] of the peoples around them, they built the altar on its foundation and sacrificed burnt offerings on it to the LORD, both the morning and evening sacrifices.[e] 4 Then in accordance with what is written, they celebrated the Feast of Tabernacles[f] with the required number of burnt offerings prescribed for each day. 5 After that, they presented the regular burnt offerings, the New Moon[g] sacrifices and the sacrifices for all the appointed sacred feasts of the LORD,[h] as well as those brought as freewill offerings to the LORD. 6 On the first day of the seventh month they began to offer burnt offerings to the LORD, though the foundation of the LORD's temple had not yet been laid.

## Rebuilding the Temple

7 Then they gave money to the masons and carpenters, and gave food and drink and oil to the people of Sidon and Tyre, so that they would bring cedar logs by sea from Lebanon to Joppa, as authorized by Cyrus[i] king of Persia.

8 In the second month of the second year after their arrival at the house of God in Jerusalem, Zerubbabel son of Shealtiel, Jeshua son of Jozadak and the rest of their brothers (the priests and the Levites and all who had returned from the captivity to Jerusalem) began the work, appointing Levites twenty[j] years of age and older to supervise the building of the house of the LORD. 9 Jeshua[k] and his sons and brothers and Kadmiel and his sons (descendants of Hodaviah[a]) and the sons of Henadad and their sons and brothers—all Levites—joined together in supervising those working on the house of God.

10 When the builders laid the foundation of the temple of the LORD, the priests in their vestments and with trumpets,[l] and the Levites (the sons of Asaph) with cymbals, took their places to praise[m] the LORD, as prescribed by David[n] king of Israel. 11 With praise and thanksgiving they sang to the LORD:

"He is good;
his love to Israel endures forever."[o]

And all the people gave a great shout[p] of praise to the LORD, because the foundation of the house of the LORD was laid. 12 But many of the older priests and Levites and family heads, who had seen the former temple, wept aloud when they saw the foundation of this temple being laid, while many others shouted for joy. 13 No one could distinguish the sound of the shouts of joy from the sound of weeping, because the people made so much noise. And the sound was heard far away.

## Opposition to the Rebuilding

4 When the enemies of Judah and Benjamin heard that the exiles were building a temple for the LORD, the God of Israel, 2 they came to Zerubbabel and to the heads of the families and said, "Let us help you build because, like you, we seek your God and have been sacrificing to him since the time of Esarhaddon[q] king of Assyria, who brought us here."

3 But Zerubbabel, Jeshua and the rest of the heads of the families of Israel answered, "You have no part with us in building a temple to our God. We alone will build it for the LORD, the God of Israel, as King Cyrus, the king of Persia, commanded us."[r]

4 Then the peoples around them set out to discourage the people of Judah and make them afraid to go on building.[b][s] 5 They hired counselors to work against them and frustrate their plans during the entire reign of Cyrus king of Persia and down to the reign of Darius king of Persia.

3:10
l 1Ch 16:6
m 1Ch 25:1
n 1Ch 6:31
3:11
o 1Ch 16:34,41; 2Ch 7:3
p Ne 12:24
4:2
q 2Ki 17:24
4:3
r Ezr 1:1–4; Ne 2:20
4:4
s Ezr 3:3

[a]9 Hebrew *Yehudah,* probably a variant of *Hodaviah* [b]4 Or *and troubled them as they built*

**4:6** t Est 1:1; Da 9:1
**4:7** u 2Ki 18:26; Da 2:4
**4:10** v ver 17
**4:12** w Ezr 5:3,9
**4:13** x Ezr 7:24

## Later Opposition Under Xerxes and Artaxerxes

6 At the beginning of the reign of Xerxes,[a][t] they lodged an accusation against the people of Judah and Jerusalem.

7 And in the days of Artaxerxes king of Persia, Bishlam, Mithredath, Tabeel and the rest of his associates wrote a letter to Artaxerxes. The letter was written in Aramaic script and in the Aramaic[u] language.[b,c]

8 Rehum the commanding officer and Shimshai the secretary wrote a letter against Jerusalem to Artaxerxes the king as follows:

> 9 Rehum the commanding officer and Shimshai the secretary, together with the rest of their associates—the judges and officials over the men from Tripolis, Persia,[d] Erech and Babylon, the Elamites of Susa, 10 and the other people whom the great and honorable Ashurbanipal[e] deported and settled in the city of Samaria and elsewhere in Trans-Euphrates.[v]

11 (This is a copy of the letter they sent him.)

> To King Artaxerxes,
>
> From your servants, the men of Trans-Euphrates:
>
> 12 The king should know that the Jews who came up to us from you have gone to Jerusalem and are rebuilding that rebellious and wicked city. They are restoring the walls and repairing the foundations.[w]
>
> 13 Furthermore, the king should know that if this city is built and its walls are restored, no more taxes, tribute or duty[x] will be paid, and the royal revenues will suffer. 14 Now since we are under obligation to the palace and it is not proper for us to see the king dishonored, we are sending this message to inform the king, 15 so that a search may be made in the archives of your predecessors. In these records you will find that this city is a rebellious city, troublesome to kings and provinces, a place of rebellion from ancient times. That is why this city was destroyed. 16 We inform the king that if this city is built and its walls are restored, you will be left with nothing in Trans-Euphrates.

17 The king sent this reply:

> To Rehum the commanding officer, Shimshai the secretary and the rest of their associates living in Samaria and elsewhere in Trans-Euphrates:
>
> Greetings.
>
> 18 The letter you sent us has been read and translated in my presence. 19 I issued an order and a search was made, and it was found that this city has a long history of revolt against kings and has been a place of rebellion and sedition. 20 Jerusalem has had powerful kings ruling over the whole of Trans-Euphrates,[y] and taxes, tribute and duty were paid to them. 21 Now issue an order to these men to stop work, so that this city will not be rebuilt until I so order. 22 Be careful not to neglect this matter. Why let this threat grow, to the detriment of the royal interests?

23 As soon as the copy of the letter of King Artaxerxes was read to Rehum and Shimshai the secretary and their associates, they went immediately to the Jews in Jerusalem and compelled them by force to stop.

24 Thus the work on the house of God in Jerusalem came to a standstill until the second year of the reign of Darius king of Persia.

## Tattenai's Letter to Darius

5 Now Haggai[z] the prophet and Zechariah[a] the prophet, a descendant of Iddo, prophesied to the Jews in Judah and Jerusalem in the name of the God of Israel, who was over them. 2 Then Zerubbabel son of Shealtiel and Jeshua[b] son of Jozadak set to work to rebuild the house of God in Jeru-

**4:20** y Ge 15:18–21; Jos 1:4; 1Ki 4:21; Ps 72:8–11
**5:1** z Hag 1:1,3,12 a Zec 1:1
**5:2** b Ezr 3:2

[a]6 Hebrew *Ahasuerus,* a variant of Xerxes' Persian name [b]7 Or *written in Aramaic and translated* [c]7 The text of Ezra 4:8—6:18 is in Aramaic. [d]9 Or *officials, magistrates and governors over the men from* [e]10 Aramaic *Osnappar,* a variant of *Ashurbanipal*

salem. And the prophets of God were with them, helping them.

[3]At that time Tattenai,[c] governor of Trans-Euphrates, and Shethar-Bozenai and their associates went to them and asked, "Who authorized you to rebuild this temple and restore this structure?"[d] [4]They also asked, "What are the names of the men constructing this building?"[a] [5]But the eye of their God[e] was watching over the elders of the Jews, and they were not stopped until a report could go to Darius and his written reply be received.

[6]This is a copy of the letter that Tattenai, governor of Trans-Euphrates, and Shethar-Bozenai and their associates, the officials of Trans-Euphrates, sent to King Darius. [7]The report they sent him read as follows:

To King Darius:

Cordial greetings.

[8]The king should know that we went to the district of Judah, to the temple of the great God. The people are building it with large stones and placing the timbers in the walls. The work is being carried on with diligence and is making rapid progress under their direction.

[9]We questioned the elders and asked them, "Who authorized you to rebuild this temple and restore this structure?" [10]We also asked them their names, so that we could write down the names of their leaders for your information.

[11]This is the answer they gave us:

"We are the servants of the God of heaven and earth, and we are rebuilding the temple[f] that was built many years ago, one that a great king of Israel built and finished. [12]But because our fathers angered[g] the God of heaven, he handed them over to Nebuchadnezzar the Chaldean, king of Babylon, who destroyed this temple and deported the people to Babylon.[h]

[13]"However, in the first year of Cyrus king of Babylon, King Cyrus issued a decree[i] to rebuild this house of God. [14]He even removed from the temple[b] of Babylon the gold and silver articles of the house of God, which Nebuchadnezzar had taken from the temple in Jerusalem and brought to the temple[b] in Babylon.[j]

"Then King Cyrus gave them to a man named Sheshbazzar, whom he had appointed governor, [15]and he told him, 'Take these articles and go and deposit them in the temple in Jerusalem. And rebuild the house of God on its site.' [16]So this Sheshbazzar came and laid the foundations of the house of God[k] in Jerusalem. From that day to the present it has been under construction but is not yet finished."

[17]Now if it pleases the king, let a search be made in the royal archives[l] of Babylon to see if King Cyrus did in fact issue a decree to rebuild this house of God in Jerusalem. Then let the king send us his decision in this matter.

## The Decree of Darius

**6** King Darius then issued an order, and they searched in the archives[m] stored in the treasury at Babylon. [2]A scroll was found in the citadel of Ecbatana in the province of Media, and this was written on it:

Memorandum:

[3]In the first year of King Cyrus, the king issued a decree concerning the temple of God in Jerusalem:

Let the temple be rebuilt as a place to present sacrifices, and let its foundations be laid. It is to be ninety feet[c] high and ninety feet wide, [4]with three courses[n] of large stones and one of timbers. The costs are to be paid by the royal treasury. [5]Also, the gold and silver articles of the house of God, which Nebuchadnezzar took from the temple in Jerusalem and brought to Babylon, are to be returned to their places in the temple in Jerusalem; they are to be deposited in the house of God.[o]

**5:3** c Ezr 6:6 d ver 9; Ezr 1:3
**5:5** e Ezr 7:6,9,28; Ps 33:18
**5:11** f 1Ki 6:1
**5:12** g 2Ch 36:16 h 2Ki 24:1; 25:8,9,11
**5:13** i Ezr 1:1
**5:14** j Ezr 1:7; 6:5
**5:16** k Ezr 3:10; 6:15
**5:17** l Ezr 6:1,2
**6:1** m Ezr 5:17
**6:4** n 1Ki 6:36
**6:5** o Ezr 1:7; 5:14

[a]4 See Septuagint; Aramaic [4]*We told them the names of the men constructing this building.* [b]14 Or *palace* [c]3 Aramaic *sixty cubits* (about 27 meters)

6:6 p Ezr 5:3
6:10 q Ezr 7:23
6:11 r Ezr 7:26; Da 2:5; 3:29
6:12 s Dt 12:5
6:14 t Ezr 5:1 u Ezr 7:1

[6]Now then, Tattenai,[p] governor of Trans-Euphrates, and Shethar-Bozenai and you, their fellow officials of that province, stay away from there. [7]Do not interfere with the work on this temple of God. Let the governor of the Jews and the Jewish elders rebuild this house of God on its site.

[8]Moreover, I hereby decree what you are to do for these elders of the Jews in the construction of this house of God:

The expenses of these men are to be fully paid out of the royal treasury, from the revenues of Trans-Euphrates, so that the work will not stop. [9]Whatever is needed—young bulls, rams, male lambs for burnt offerings to the God of heaven, and wheat, salt, wine and oil, as requested by the priests in Jerusalem—must be given them daily without fail, [10]so that they may offer sacrifices pleasing to the God of heaven and pray for the well-being of the king and his sons.[q]

[11]Furthermore, I decree that if anyone changes this edict, a beam is to be pulled from his house and he is to be lifted up and impaled on it. And for this crime his house is to be made a pile of rubble.[r] [12]May God, who has caused his Name to dwell there,[s] overthrow any king or people who lifts a hand to change this decree or to destroy this temple in Jerusalem.

I Darius have decreed it. Let it be carried out with diligence.

## Completion and Dedication of the Temple

[13]Then, because of the decree King Darius had sent, Tattenai, governor of Trans-Euphrates, and Shethar-Bozenai and their associates carried it out with diligence. [14]So the elders of the Jews continued to build and prosper under the preaching[t] of Haggai the prophet and Zechariah, a descendant of Iddo. They finished building the temple according to the command of the God of Israel and the decrees of Cyrus, Darius and Artaxerxes,[u] kings of Persia. [15]The temple was completed on the third day of the month

*Lord,*

*teach me to follow your will despite opposition from others. I need you to help me stay focused on you and your plans. In the strong name of Jesus,*

*Amen.*

EZRA 6:13–16

Adar, in the sixth year of the reign of King Darius.[v]

[16]Then the people of Israel—the priests, the Levites and the rest of the exiles—celebrated the dedication[w] of the house of God with joy. [17]For the dedication of this house of God they offered[x] a hundred bulls, two hundred rams, four hundred male lambs and, as a sin offering for all Israel, twelve male goats, one for each of the tribes of Israel. [18]And they installed the priests in their divisions[y] and the Levites in their groups for the service of God at Jerusalem, according to what is written in the Book of Moses.[z]

## The Passover

[19]On the fourteenth day of the first month, the exiles celebrated the Passover.[a] [20]The priests and Levites had purified themselves and were all ceremonially clean. The Levites slaughtered the Passover lamb for all the exiles, for their brothers the priests and for themselves. [21]So the Israelites who had returned from the exile ate it, together with all who had separated themselves[b] from the unclean practices of their Gentile neighbors in order to seek the LORD, the God of Israel. [22]For seven days they celebrated with joy the Feast of Unleavened Bread, because the LORD had filled them with joy by changing the attitude[c] of the king of Assyria, so that he assisted them in the work on the house of God, the God of Israel.

## Ezra Comes to Jerusalem

7 After these things, during the reign of Artaxerxes king of Persia, Ezra son of Seraiah, the son of Azariah, the son of

6:15 v Zec 1:1; 4:9
6:16 w 1Ki 8:63; 2Ch 7:5
6:17 x Ezr 8:35
6:18 y 1Ch 23:6; 2Ch 35:4 z Nu 3:6–9; 8:9–11
6:19 a Ex 12:11
6:21 b Ne 9:2
6:22 c Ezr 1:1

Hilkiah, 2the son of Shallum, the son of Zadok, the son of Ahitub, 3the son of Amariah, the son of Azariah, the son of Meraioth, 4the son of Zerahiah, the son of Uzzi, the son of Bukki, 5the son of Abishua, the son of Phinehas, the son of Eleazar, the son of Aaron the chief priest— 6this Ezra came up from Babylon. He was a teacher well versed in the Law of Moses, which the LORD, the God of Israel, had given. The king had granted him everything he asked, for the hand of the LORD his God was on him. 7Some of the Israelites, including priests, Levites, singers, gatekeepers and temple servants, also came up to Jerusalem in the seventh year of King Artaxerxes.[d]

8Ezra arrived in Jerusalem in the fifth month of the seventh year of the king. 9He had begun his journey from Babylon on the first day of the first month, and he arrived in Jerusalem on the first day of the fifth month, for the gracious hand of his God was on him. 10For Ezra had devoted himself to the study and observance of the Law of the LORD, and to teaching its decrees and laws in Israel.

## King Artaxerxes' Letter to Ezra

11This is a copy of the letter King Artaxerxes had given to Ezra the priest and teacher, a man learned in matters concerning the commands and decrees of the LORD for Israel:

12[a]Artaxerxes, king of kings,[e]

To Ezra the priest, a teacher of the Law of the God of heaven:

Greetings.

13Now I decree that any of the Israelites in my kingdom, including priests and Levites, who wish to go to Jerusalem with you, may go. 14You are sent by the king and his seven advisers[f] to inquire about Judah and Jerusalem with regard to the Law of your God, which is in your hand. 15Moreover, you are to take with you the silver and gold that the king and his advisers have freely given to the God of Israel, whose dwelling[g] is in Jerusalem, 16together with all the silver and gold you may obtain from the province of Babylon, as well as the freewill offerings of the people and priests for the temple of their God in Jerusalem. 17With this money be sure to buy bulls, rams and male lambs, together with their grain offerings and drink offerings,[h] and sacrifice[i] them on the altar of the temple of your God in Jerusalem.

18You and your brother Jews may then do whatever seems best with the rest of the silver and gold, in accordance with the will of your God. 19Deliver to the God of Jerusalem all the articles entrusted to you for worship in the temple of your God. 20And anything else needed for the temple of your God that you may have occasion to supply, you may provide from the royal treasury.[j]

21Now I, King Artaxerxes, order all the treasurers of Trans-Euphrates to provide with diligence whatever Ezra the priest, a teacher of the Law of the God of heaven, may ask of you— 22up to a hundred talents[b] of silver, a hundred cors[c] of wheat, a hundred baths[d] of wine, a hundred baths[d] of olive oil, and salt without limit. 23Whatever the God of heaven has prescribed, let it be done with diligence for the temple of the God of heaven. Why should there be wrath against the realm of the king and of his sons?[k] 24You are also to know that you have no authority to impose taxes, tribute or duty on any of the priests, Levites, singers, gatekeepers, temple servants or other workers at this house of God.

25And you, Ezra, in accordance with the wisdom of your God, which you possess, appoint[l] magistrates and judges to administer justice to all the people of Trans-Euphrates—all who know the laws of your God. And you are to teach[m] any who do not know them. 26Whoever does not obey the law of your God and the law of the king must surely be punished by death,

**7:7** d Ezr 8:1
**7:12** e Eze 26:7; Da 2:37
**7:14** f Est 1:14
**7:15** g 2Ch 6:2
**7:17** h Nu 15:5–12 i Dt 12:5–11
**7:20** j Ezr 6:4
**7:23** k Ezr 6:10
**7:25** l Ex 18:21,26; Dt 16:18 m ver 10

[a]12 The text of Ezra 7:12–26 is in Aramaic. [b]22 That is, about 3 3/4 tons (about 3.4 metric tons) [c]22 That is, probably about 600 bushels (about 22 kiloliters) [d]22 That is, probably about 600 gallons (about 2.2 kiloliters)

**7:27**
n Ezr 6:22

banishment, confiscation of property, or imprisonment.

*"I knew we had no aviators . . . and I knew the race needed to be represented, so I thought it my duty to risk my life to learn aviation and encourage flying among men and women of our race."*

—Bessie Coleman,
First African American
Licensed Pilot

27 Praise be to the Lord, the God of our fathers, who has put it into the king's heart[n] to bring honor to the house of the Lord in Jerusalem in this way 28 and who has extended his good favor to me before the king and his advisers and all the king's powerful officials. Because the hand of the Lord my God was on me,[o] I took courage and gathered leading men from Israel to go up with me.

**7:28**
o Ezr 5:5; 9:9

**8:3**
p 1Ch 3:22
q Ezr 2:3

## List of the Family Heads Returning With Ezra

8 These are the family heads and those registered with them who came up with me from Babylon during the reign of King Artaxerxes:

2 of the descendants of Phinehas, Gershom;
of the descendants of Ithamar, Daniel;
of the descendants of David, Hattush
3 of the descendants of Shecaniah;[p]

of the descendants of Parosh,[q] Zechariah, and with him were registered 150 men;
4 of the descendants of Pahath-Moab, Eliehoenai son of Zerahiah, and with him 200 men;
5 of the descendants of Zattu,[a] Shecaniah son of Jahaziel, and with him 300 men;
6 of the descendants of Adin, Ebed son of Jonathan, and with him 50 men;
7 of the descendants of Elam, Jeshaiah son of Athaliah, and with him 70 men;
8 of the descendants of Shephatiah, Zebadiah son of Michael, and with him 80 men;
9 of the descendants of Joab, Obadiah son of Jehiel, and with him 218 men;
10 of the descendants of Bani,[b] Shelomith son of Josiphiah, and with him 160 men;
11 of the descendants of Bebai, Zechariah son of Bebai, and with him 28 men;
12 of the descendants of Azgad, Johanan son of Hakkatan, and with him 110 men;
13 of the descendants of Adonikam, the last ones, whose names were Eliphelet, Jeuel and Shemaiah, and with them 60 men;
14 of the descendants of Bigvai, Uthai and Zaccur, and with them 70 men.

## The Return to Jerusalem

15 I assembled them at the canal that flows toward Ahava,[r] and we camped there three days. When I checked among the people and the priests, I found no Levites[s] there. 16 So I summoned Eliezer, Ariel, Shemaiah, Elnathan, Jarib, Elnathan, Nathan, Zechariah and Meshullam, who were leaders, and Joiarib and Elnathan, who were men of learning, 17 and I sent them to Iddo, the leader in Casiphia. I told them what to say to Iddo and his kinsmen, the temple servants[t] in Casiphia, so that they might bring attendants to us for the house of our God. 18 Because the gracious hand of our God was on us, they brought us Sherebiah, a capable man, from the descendants of Mahli son of Levi, the son of Israel, and Sherebiah's sons and brothers, 18 men; 19 and Hashabiah, together with Jeshaiah from the descendants of Merari, and his brothers and nephews, 20 men. 20 They also brought 220 of the temple servants[u]—a body that David and the officials had established to assist the Levites. All were registered by name.

21 There, by the Ahava Canal,[v] I proclaimed a fast, so that we might humble ourselves before our God and ask him for a safe journey for us and our children, with all our possessions. 22 I was ashamed to ask the king for soldiers[w] and horsemen to protect us from enemies on the road, because we had told the king, "The gracious hand of our God is on everyone who looks to him, but his great anger is against all

**8:15**
r ver 21,31
s Ezr 2:40; 7:7

**8:17**
t Ezr 2:43

**8:20**
u Ezr 2:43

**8:21**
v 2Ch 20:3

**8:22**
w Ezr 7:6,9,28

[a]5 Some Septuagint manuscripts (also 1 Esdras 8:32); Hebrew does not have *Zattu.* [b]10 Some Septuagint manuscripts (also 1 Esdras 8:36); Hebrew does not have *Bani.*

who forsake him.[x]" 23 So we fasted[y] and petitioned our God about this, and he answered our prayer.

24 Then I set apart twelve of the leading priests, together with Sherebiah, Hashabiah and ten of their brothers, 25 and I weighed out[z] to them the offering of silver and gold and the articles that the king, his advisers, his officials and all Israel present there had donated for the house of our God. 26 I weighed out to them 650 talents[a] of silver, silver articles weighing 100 talents,[b] 100 talents[b] of gold, 27 20 bowls of gold valued at 1,000 darics,[c] and two fine articles of polished bronze, as precious as gold.

28 I said to them, "You as well as these articles are consecrated to the LORD.[a] The silver and gold are a freewill offering to the LORD, the God of your fathers. 29 Guard them carefully until you weigh them out in the chambers of the house of the LORD in Jerusalem before the leading priests and the Levites and the family heads of Israel." 30 Then the priests and Levites received the silver and gold and sacred articles that had been weighed out to be taken to the house of our God in Jerusalem.

31 On the twelfth day of the first month we set out from the Ahava Canal to go to Jerusalem. The hand of our God was on us, and he protected us from enemies and bandits along the way. 32 So we arrived in Jerusalem, where we rested three days.[b]

*Woman of color,*

*I specialize in restoring my people.*

*God of All*

EZRA 8:31–32

33 On the fourth day, in the house of our God, we weighed out the silver and gold and the sacred articles into the hands of Meremoth son of Uriah, the priest. Eleazar son of Phinehas was with him, and so were the Levites Jozabad son of Jeshua and Noadiah son of Binnui. 34 Everything was accounted for by number and weight, and the entire weight was recorded at that time.

35 Then the exiles who had returned from captivity sacrificed burnt offerings to the God of Israel: twelve bulls for all Israel, ninety-six rams, seventy-seven male lambs and, as a sin offering, twelve male goats. All this was a burnt offering to the LORD. 36 They also delivered the king's orders[c] to the royal satraps and to the governors of Trans-Euphrates, who then gave assistance to the people and to the house of God.

## Ezra's Prayer About Intermarriage

9 After these things had been done, the leaders came to me and said, "The people of Israel, including the priests and the Levites, have not kept themselves separate[d] from the neighboring peoples with their detestable practices, like those of the Canaanites, Hittites, Perizzites, Jebusites, Ammonites, Moabites, Egyptians and Amorites. 2 They have taken some of their daughters as wives for themselves and their sons, and have mingled the holy race[e] with the peoples around them. And the leaders and officials have led the way in this unfaithfulness."

3 When I heard this, I tore my tunic and cloak, pulled hair from my head and beard and sat down appalled. 4 Then everyone who trembled[f] at the words of the God of Israel gathered around me because of this unfaithfulness of the exiles. And I sat there appalled until the evening sacrifice.

5 Then, at the evening sacrifice, I rose from my self-abasement, with my tunic and cloak torn, and fell on my knees with my hands spread out to the LORD my God 6 and prayed:

"O my God, I am too ashamed and disgraced to lift up my face to you, my God, because our sins are higher than our heads and our guilt has reached to the heavens.[g] 7 From the days of our forefathers until now, our guilt has been great. Because of our sins, we and our kings and our priests have been

**8:22** x 2Ch 15:2
**8:23** y 2Ch 33:13
**8:25** z Ezr 7:15,16
**8:28** a Lev 21:6; 22:2–3
**8:32** b Ne 2:11
**8:36** c Ezr 7:21–24
**9:1** d Ezr 6:21; Ne 9:2
**9:2** e Ex 22:31
**9:4** f Ezr 10:3
**9:6** g 2Ch 28:9; Rev 18:5

[a] 26 That is, about 25 tons (about 22 metric tons) [b] 26 That is, about 3 3/4 tons (about 3.4 metric tons) [c] 27 That is, about 19 pounds (about 8.5 kilograms)

9:7
h Dt28:37

9:8
i Isa22:23
j Ps13:3

9:9
k Ne9:36
l Ezr7:28

9:12
m Dt7:3; 23:6

subjected to the sword and captivity, to pillage and humiliation[h] at the hand of foreign kings, as it is today.

[8]"But now, for a brief moment, the LORD our God has been gracious in leaving us a remnant and giving us a firm place[i] in his sanctuary, and so our God gives light to our eyes[j] and a little relief in our bondage. [9]Though we are slaves,[k] our God has not deserted us in our bondage. He has shown us kindness[l] in the sight of the kings of Persia: He has granted us new life to rebuild the house of our God and repair its ruins, and he has given us a wall of protection in Judah and Jerusalem.

[10]"But now, O our God, what can we say after this? For we have disregarded the commands [11]you gave through your servants the prophets when you said: 'The land you are entering to possess is a land polluted by the corruption of its peoples. By their detestable practices they have filled it with their impurity from one end to the other. [12]Therefore, do not give your daughters in marriage to their sons or take their daughters for your sons. Do not seek a treaty of friendship with them[m] at any time, that you may be strong and eat the good things of the land and leave it to your children as an everlasting inheritance.'

[13]"What has happened to us is a result of our evil deeds and our great guilt, and yet, our God, you have punished us less than our sins have deserved and have given us a remnant like this. [14]Shall we again break your commands and intermarry with the peoples who commit such detestable practices? Would you not be angry enough with us to destroy us,[n] leaving us no remnant[o] or survivor? [15]O LORD, God of Israel, you are righteous! We are left this day as a remnant. Here we are before you in our guilt, though because of it not one of us can stand[p] in your presence."

## The People's Confession of Sin

10 While Ezra was praying and confessing,[q] weeping and throwing himself down before the house of God, a large crowd of Israelites—men, women and children—gathered around him. They too wept bitterly. [2]Then Shecaniah son of Jehiel, one of the descendants of Elam, said to Ezra, "We have been unfaithful[r] to our God by marrying foreign women from the peoples around us. But in spite of this, there is still hope for Israel. [3]Now let us make a covenant[s] before our God to send away[t] all these women and their children, in accordance with the counsel of my lord and of those who fear the commands of our God. Let it be done according

9:14
n Dt9:8
o Dt9:14

9:15
p Ne9:33; Ps130:3

10:1
q 2Ch20:9; Da9:20

10:2
r Ezr9:2; Ne13:27

10:3
s 2Ch34:31
t Dt7:2–3; Ezr9:4

## *The African Presence*

**Ezra 9**

Leaders in the land came to Ezra complaining about the Israelites (including priests and Levites) who had intermarried with the people of the land: the Canaanites, Hittites, Perizzites, Jebusites, Ammonites, Moabites, Egyptians and Amorites. All these peoples, with the possible exception of the Ammonites and Moabites, were descendants of Ham. Because Ham's offspring represent the geographic territories once dominated by Egypt—present-day Egypt, Libya and Sudan and into the area today known as Israel—they can claim a relation to African heritage. Since "heritage" is something "passed down" or "inherited," Canaan (Israel or Palestine) most certainly received or was influenced by Egypt culturally, politically, religiously, etc.

**10:5** u Ne 5:12; 13:25
**10:6** v Dt 9:18
**10:11** w ver 3; Dt 24:1; Mal 2:10–16
**10:14** x 2Ch 29:10; 30:8

to the Law. 4 Rise up; this matter is in your
hands. We will support you, so take courage
and do it."

5 So Ezra rose up and put the leading
priests and Levites and all Israel under oath[u]
to do what had been suggested. And they
took the oath. 6 Then Ezra withdrew from be-
fore the house of God and went to the room
of Jehohanan son of Eliashib. While he was
there, he ate no food and drank no water,[v]
because he continued to mourn over the un-
faithfulness of the exiles.

7 A proclamation was then issued
throughout Judah and Jerusalem for all
the exiles to assemble in Jerusalem. 8 Any-
one who failed to appear within three days
would forfeit all his property, in accordance
with the decision of the officials and elders,
and would himself be expelled from the as-
sembly of the exiles.

9 Within the three days, all the men of
Judah and Benjamin had gathered in Je-
rusalem. And on the twentieth day of the
ninth month, all the people were sitting in
the square before the house of God, greatly
distressed by the occasion and because of
the rain. 10 Then Ezra the priest stood up and
said to them, "You have been unfaithful;
you have married foreign women, adding
to Israel's guilt. 11 Now make confession to
the LORD, the God of your fathers, and do his
will. Separate yourselves from the peoples
around you and from your foreign wives."[w]

12 The whole assembly responded with a
loud voice: "You are right! We must do as
you say. 13 But there are many people here
and it is the rainy season; so we cannot
stand outside. Besides, this matter cannot
be taken care of in a day or two, because we
have sinned greatly in this thing. 14 Let our
officials act for the whole assembly. Then
let everyone in our towns who has married
a foreign woman come at a set time, along
with the elders and judges of each town, un-
til the fierce anger[x] of our God in this matter
is turned away from us." 15 Only Jonathan
son of Asahel and Jahzeiah son of Tikvah,
supported by Meshullam and Shabbethai
the Levite, opposed this.

16 So the exiles did as was proposed. Ezra
the priest selected men who were family
heads, one from each family division, and
all of them designated by name. On the first
day of the tenth month they sat down to in-
vestigate the cases, 17 and by the first day of
the first month they finished dealing with all
the men who had married foreign women.

## Those Guilty of Intermarriage

18 Among the descendants of the priests, the following had married foreign women:

From the descendants of Jeshua[y] son of Jozadak, and his brothers: Maaseiah, Eliezer, Jarib and Gedaliah.
19 (They all gave their hands[z] in pledge to put away their wives, and for their guilt they each presented a ram from the flock as a guilt offering.)[a]

20 From the descendants of Immer:
Hanani and Zebadiah.

21 From the descendants of Harim:
Maaseiah, Elijah, Shemaiah, Jehiel and Uzziah.

22 From the descendants of Pashhur:
Elioenai, Maaseiah, Ishmael, Nethanel, Jozabad and Elasah.

23 Among the Levites:

Jozabad, Shimei, Kelaiah (that is, Kelita), Pethahiah, Judah and Eliezer.

24 From the singers:
Eliashib.

From the gatekeepers:
Shallum, Telem and Uri.

25 And among the other Israelites:

From the descendants of Parosh:[b]
Ramiah, Izziah, Malkijah, Mijamin, Eleazar, Malkijah and Benaiah.

26 From the descendants of Elam:
Mattaniah, Zechariah, Jehiel, Abdi, Jeremoth and Elijah.

27 From the descendants of Zattu:
Elioenai, Eliashib, Mattaniah, Jeremoth, Zabad and Aziza.

28 From the descendants of Bebai:
Jehohanan, Hananiah, Zabbai and Athlai.

29 From the descendants of Bani:
Meshullam, Malluch, Adaiah, Jashub, Sheal and Jeremoth.

**10:18** y Ezr 2:2
**10:19** z 2Ki 10:15 a Lev 5:15; 6:6
**10:25** b Ezr 2:3

[30] From the descendants of Pahath-Moab:
Adna, Kelal, Benaiah, Maaseiah, Mattaniah, Bezalel, Binnui and Manasseh.
[31] From the descendants of Harim:
Eliezer, Ishijah, Malkijah, Shemaiah, Shimeon, [32] Benjamin, Malluch and Shemariah.
[33] From the descendants of Hashum:
Mattenai, Mattattah, Zabad, Eliphelet, Jeremai, Manasseh and Shimei.
[34] From the descendants of Bani:
Maadai, Amram, Uel, [35] Benaiah, Bedeiah, Keluhi, [36] Vaniah, Meremoth, Eliashib, [37] Mattaniah, Mattenai and Jaasu.
[38] From the descendants of Binnui:[a]
Shimei, [39] Shelemiah, Nathan, Adaiah, [40] Macnadebai, Shashai, Sharai, [41] Azarel, Shelemiah, Shemariah, [42] Shallum, Amariah and Joseph.
[43] From the descendants of Nebo:
Jeiel, Mattithiah, Zabad, Zebina, Jaddai, Joel and Benaiah.

[44] All these had married foreign women, and some of them had children by these wives.[b]

[a] 37,38 See Septuagint (also 1 Esdras 9:34); Hebrew *Jaasu* [38] *and Bani and Binnui,* [b] 44 Or *and they sent them away with their children*

# Nehemiah

## OVERVIEW

Nehemiah was a man of action and leadership, and his story is illustrated in this book that bears his name. When Nehemiah received word from his brother, Hanani, that the walls of Jerusalem were broken down and the people were in great danger, he fasted and prayed and requested permission from King Artaxerxes to return to his homeland to help rebuild the wall. The king gave his permission along with supplies, and Nehemiah made the journey to Jerusalem. Despite the opposition of Sanballat and Tobiah, Nehemiah succeeded in leading the rebuilding effort. Later he participated with Ezra in reforms to keep the people from sliding back into idolatry and immorality.

Nehemiah instructed the people to work and be ready for battle if necessary: "Those who carried materials did their work with one hand and held a weapon in the other" (Ne 4:17). In this time of grace, women believers must also recognize and be prepared to face their adversary, the devil. While he seeks to destroy the family and tear up churches, women must pray and fast like Nehemiah did. The prayer of a righteous woman is "powerful and effective" (Jas 5:16).

## OUTLINE

I. Nehemiah's Prayer and Return to Jerusalem to Begin Building (1:1—3:32)
II. Opposition to and Completion of the Wall (4:1—7:73)
III. Revival and Reform Under the Leadership of Ezra and Nehemiah (8:1—13:31)

### SCANNABLE FACTS:

**Author:** Unknown; possibly Ezra

**Time Written:** About 430 B.C.

**Theme to Note:** Prayer and work go hand in hand

**Notable Women:** Women who traveled with their families back to Jerusalem; Shallum's daughters, who helped rebuild the wall (see Ne 3:12)

1:1 a Ne 10:1; Zec 7:1
1:3 b Ne 2:3,13,17
1:5 c Ne 4:14
d Ex 20:6; Da 9:4
1:6 e Da 9:17
1:7 f Dt 28:14–15
1:8 g Lev 26:33
1:9 h Dt 30:4
1:10 i Dt 9:29
1:11 j ver 6

## Nehemiah's Prayer

1 The words of Nehemiah son of Hacaliah:

In the month of Kislev[a] in the twentieth year, while I was in the citadel of Susa, 2Hanani, one of my brothers, came from Judah with some other men, and I questioned them about the Jewish remnant that survived the exile, and also about Jerusalem.

3They said to me, "Those who survived the exile and are back in the province are in great trouble and disgrace. The wall of Jerusalem is broken down, and its gates have been burned with fire.[b]"

4When I heard these things, I sat down and wept. For some days I mourned and fasted and prayed before the God of heaven. 5Then I said:

"O LORD, God of heaven, the great and awesome God,[c] who keeps his covenant of love[d] with those who love him and obey his commands, 6let your ear be attentive and your eyes open to hear the prayer[e] your servant is praying before you day and night for your servants, the people of Israel. I confess the sins we Israelites, including myself and my father's house, have committed against you. 7We have acted very wickedly[f] toward you. We have not obeyed the commands, decrees and laws you gave your servant Moses.

8"Remember the instruction you gave your servant Moses, saying, 'If you are unfaithful, I will scatter[g] you among the nations, 9but if you return to me and obey my commands, then even if your exiled people are at the farthest horizon, I will gather[h] them from there and bring them to the place I have chosen as a dwelling for my Name.'

10"They are your servants and your people, whom you redeemed by your great strength and your mighty hand.[i] 11O Lord, let your ear be attentive[j] to the prayer of this your servant and to the prayer of your servants who delight in revering your name. Give your servant success today by granting him favor in the presence of this man."

I was cupbearer to the king.

*Seeking child.*

*I hear your prayers.*

*Love always,*
*Your Father*

NEHEMIAH 1:4–11

## Artaxerxes Sends Nehemiah to Jerusalem

2 In the month of Nisan in the twentieth year of King Artaxerxes, when wine was brought for him, I took the wine and gave it to the king. I had not been sad in his presence before; 2so the king asked me, "Why does your face look so sad when you are not ill? This can be nothing but sadness of heart."

I was very much afraid, 3but I said to the king, "May the king live forever![k] Why should my face not look sad when the city where my fathers are buried lies in ruins, and its gates have been destroyed by fire?[l]"

4The king said to me, "What is it you want?"

Then I prayed to the God of heaven, 5and I answered the king, "If it pleases the king and if your servant has found favor in his sight, let him send me to the city in Judah where my fathers are buried so that I can rebuild it."

6Then the king[m], with the queen sitting beside him, asked me, "How long will your journey take, and when will you get back?" It pleased the king to send me; so I set a time.

7I also said to him, "If it pleases the king, may I have letters to the governors of Trans-Euphrates,[n] so that they will provide me safe-conduct until I arrive in Judah? 8And may I have a letter to Asaph, keeper of the king's forest, so he will give me timber to

2:3 k Da 2:4
l Ne 1:3
2:6 m Ne 5:14; 13:6
2:7 n Ezr 8:36

**2:8** o Ne 7:2 p ver 18; Ezr 7:6
**2:9** q Ezr 8:22
**2:10** r ver 19; Ne 4:1,7
**2:13** s Ne 3:13 t Ne 1:3
**2:14** u Ne 3:15
**2:17** v Ne 1:3
**2:18** w 2Sa 2:7

make beams for the gates of the citadel[o] by
the temple and for the city wall and for the
residence I will occupy?" And because
the gracious hand of my God was upon me,[p]
the king granted my requests. [9]So I went
to the governors of Trans-Euphrates and
gave them the king's letters. The king
had also sent army officers and cavalry[q]
with me.
[10]When Sanballat[r] the Horonite and
Tobiah the Ammonite official heard about
this, they were very much disturbed that
someone had come to promote the welfare
of the Israelites.

## Nehemiah Inspects Jerusalem's Walls

[11]I went to Jerusalem, and after staying
there three days [12]I set out during the night
with a few men. I had not told anyone what
my God had put in my heart to do for Jerusalem. There were no mounts with me except
the one I was riding on.
[13]By night I went out through the Valley
Gate toward the Jackal[a] Well and the Dung
Gate,[s] examining the walls[t] of Jerusalem,
which had been broken down, and its gates,
which had been destroyed by fire. [14]Then I
moved on toward the Fountain Gate[u] and
the King's Pool, but there was not enough
room for my mount to get through; [15]so I
went up the valley by night, examining the
wall. Finally, I turned back and reentered
through the Valley Gate. [16]The officials did
not know where I had gone or what I was
doing, because as yet I had said nothing to
the Jews or the priests or nobles or officials
or any others who would be doing the work.
[17]Then I said to them, "You see the trouble we are in: Jerusalem lies in ruins, and its
gates have been burned with fire.[v] Come, let
us rebuild the wall of Jerusalem, and we will
no longer be in disgrace." [18]I also told them
about the gracious hand of my God upon
me[w] and what the king had said to me.
They replied, "Let us start rebuilding."
So they began this good work.
[19]But when Sanballat the Horonite,
Tobiah the Ammonite official and Geshem
the Arab heard about it, they mocked and
ridiculed us. "What is this you are doing?"
they asked. "Are you rebelling against the
king?"
[20]I answered them by saying, "The God of
heaven will give us success. We his servants
will start rebuilding, but as for you, you
have no share[x] in Jerusalem or any claim or
historic right to it."

## Builders of the Wall

3 Eliashib the high priest and his fellow
priests went to work and rebuilt the
Sheep Gate.[y] They dedicated it and set its
doors in place, building as far as the Tower
of the Hundred, which they dedicated, and
as far as the Tower of Hananel.[z] [2]The men
of Jericho[a] built the adjoining section, and
Zaccur son of Imri built next to them.

[3]The Fish Gate[b] was rebuilt by the sons
of Hassenaah. They laid its beams and
put its doors and bolts and bars in place.
[4]Meremoth son of Uriah, the son of Hakkoz, repaired the next section. Next to him
Meshullam son of Berekiah, the son of
Meshezabel, made repairs, and next to him
Zadok son of Baana also made repairs. [5]The
next section was repaired by the men of
Tekoa, but their nobles would not put their
shoulders to the work under their supervisors.[b]

[6]The Jeshanah[c] Gate[c] was repaired by
Joiada son of Paseah and Meshullam son
of Besodeiah. They laid its beams and put
its doors and bolts and bars in place. [7]Next
to them, repairs were made by men from
Gibeon[d] and Mizpah—Melatiah of Gibeon
and Jadon of Meronoth—places under
the authority of the governor of Trans-Euphrates. [8]Uzziel son of Harhaiah, one of
the goldsmiths, repaired the next section;
and Hananiah, one of the perfume-makers,
made repairs next to that. They restored[d]
Jerusalem as far as the Broad Wall.[e] [9]Rephaiah son of Hur, ruler of a half-district
of Jerusalem, repaired the next section.
[10]Adjoining this, Jedaiah son of Harumaph
made repairs opposite his house, and Hattush son of Hashabneiah made repairs
next to him. [11]Malkijah son of Harim and
Hasshub son of Pahath-Moab repaired
another section and the Tower of the Ovens.[f]

**2:20** x Ezr 4:3
**3:1** y Ne 12:39 z Jer 31:38
**3:2** a Ne 7:36
**3:3** b Ne 12:39
**3:6** c Ne 12:39
**3:7** d Ne 2:7
**3:8** e Ne 12:38
**3:11** f Ne 12:38

[a]13 Or *Serpent* or *Fig* [b]5 Or *their Lord* or *the governor* [c]6 Or *Old* [d]8 Or *They left out part of*

Inspire leadership FOCUS

# LEADERSHIP: BRICK BY BRICK, TOGETHER

To see a model of godly leadership, read the book of Nehemiah. Nehemiah exhibited organizational and administrative gifts. He was a man who knew how to conceptualize a task, organize the work and workers, and—in spite of obstacles and naysayers—persist until the task was completed.

Someone once asked, "How do you eat an elephant?" The answer is, "One bite at a time." This amusing but thought-provoking riddle leads us to ponder other questions: How do you rebuild a wall? Brick by brick. How do you restore a community? School by school, church by church, home by home, business by business. How do you restore a people? One child, one family, one soul at a time. Always remember that people are more important than the task.

Nehemiah took a holistic approach to the restoration of Jerusalem. While rebuilding the wall was his initial project, he knew that the rebuilding process would not be complete until the people restored their relationship with God. Women of color must also take a holistic approach to restoring our communities. Restoring institutions, our "walls," is a necessary task to make our communities economically viable and financially stable. But restoring institutions is not the only issue. Until the people have restored their relationship with God, the rebuilding process is incomplete—a patchwork solution at best.

As we seek to be equal partners in Nehemiah's "business plan," we must be willing to do our part not only to lay bricks, but also to lay a spiritual foundation for our children, our families and our neighbors. "Let us start rebuilding . . . The God of heaven will give us success" (Ne 2:18,20).

Leadership is an awesome responsibility. Leaders must seek godly counsel (see Pr 15:22), work willingly and energetically with others (see Ezr 3:9), and possess a servant's heart (see Pr 3:27). Let us work together, prayer by prayer, side by side, brick by brick. Nehemiah knew that it would "take a village," the whole village—men and women, sons and daughters (see Ne 3:12)—to get the work done. Let those of us with a mind to work get busy.

—D. Johnson

For the next Inspire note, go to page 595.

## read

Nehemiah 1–2.

See also the Inspire Note "Human Resource Management," and the Women of the Bible Note "Candace: Secure Leader."

## WOMAN of COLOR

What rebuilding project are you working on? How can Nehemiah's example teach you to lead more effectively?

3:13
g Ne 2:13

12 Shallum son of Hallohesh, ruler of a half-district of Jerusalem, repaired the next section with the help of his daughters.

13 The Valley Gate was repaired by Hanun and the residents of Zanoah. They rebuilt it and put its doors and bolts and bars in place. They also repaired five hundred yards[a] of the wall as far as the Dung Gate.[g]

14 The Dung Gate was repaired by Malkijah son of Recab, ruler of the district of Beth Hakkerem. He rebuilt it and put its doors and bolts and bars in place.

15 The Fountain Gate was repaired by Shallun son of Col-Hozeh, ruler of the district of Mizpah. He rebuilt it, roofing it over and putting its doors and bolts and bars in place. He also repaired the wall of the Pool of Siloam,[b] by the King's Garden, as far as the steps going down from the City of David. 16 Beyond him, Nehemiah son of Azbuk, ruler of a half-district of Beth Zur, made repairs up to a point opposite the tombs[c] of David, as far as the artificial pool and the House of the Heroes.

17 Next to him, the repairs were made by the Levites under Rehum son of Bani. Beside him, Hashabiah, ruler of half the district of Keilah, carried out repairs for his district. 18 Next to him, the repairs were made by their countrymen under Binnui[d] son of Henadad, ruler of the other half-district of Keilah. 19 Next to him, Ezer son of Jeshua, ruler of Mizpah, repaired another section, from a point facing the ascent to the armory as far as the angle. 20 Next to him, Baruch son of Zabbai zealously repaired another section, from the angle to the entrance of the house of Eliashib the high priest. 21 Next to him, Meremoth son of Uriah, the son of Hakkoz, repaired another section, from the entrance of Eliashib's house to the end of it.

22 The repairs next to him were made by the priests from the surrounding region. 23 Beyond them, Benjamin and Hasshub made repairs in front of their house; and next to them, Azariah son of Maaseiah, the son of Ananiah, made repairs beside his house. 24 Next to him, Binnui son of Henadad repaired another section, from Azariah's house to the angle and the corner, 25 and Palal son of Uzai worked opposite the angle and the tower projecting from the upper palace near the court of the guard.[h] Next to him, Pedaiah son of Parosh 26 and the temple servants[i] living on the hill of Ophel made repairs up to a point opposite the Water Gate[j] toward the east and the projecting tower. 27 Next to them, the men of Tekoa repaired another section, from the great projecting tower to the wall of Ophel.

28 Above the Horse Gate,[k] the priests made repairs, each in front of his own house. 29 Next to them, Zadok son of Immer made repairs opposite his house. Next to him, Shemaiah son of Shecaniah, the guard at the East Gate, made repairs. 30 Next to him, Hananiah son of Shelemiah, and Hanun, the sixth son of Zalaph, repaired another section. Next to them, Meshullam son of Berekiah made repairs opposite his living quarters. 31 Next to him, Malkijah, one of the goldsmiths, made repairs as far as the house of the temple servants and the merchants, opposite the Inspection Gate, and as far as the room above the corner; 32 and between the room above the corner and the Sheep Gate the goldsmiths and merchants made repairs.

## Opposition to the Rebuilding

4 When Sanballat[l] heard that we were rebuilding the wall, he became angry and was greatly incensed. He ridiculed the Jews, 2 and in the presence of his associates and the army of Samaria, he said, "What are those feeble Jews doing? Will they restore their wall? Will they offer sacrifices? Will they finish in a day? Can they bring the stones back to life from those heaps of rubble—burned as they are?"

3 Tobiah[m] the Ammonite, who was at his side, said, "What they are building—if even a fox climbed up on it, he would break down their wall of stones!"

4 Hear us, O our God, for we are despised.[n]
Turn their insults back on their own heads.
Give them over as plunder in a land of

3:25
h Jer 32:2; 37:21
3:26
i Ne 7:46; 11:21
j Ne 8:1,3,16
3:28
k 2Ki 11:16; 2Ch 23:15; Jer 31:40
4:1
l Ne 2:10
4:3
m Ne 2:10
4:4
n Ps 79:12; 123:3–4

[a] 13 Hebrew *a thousand cubits* (about 450 meters) [b] 15 Hebrew *Shelah*, a variant of *Shiloah*, that is, Siloam [c] 16 Hebrew; Septuagint, some Vulgate manuscripts and Syriac *tomb* [d] 18 Two Hebrew manuscripts and Syriac (see also Septuagint and verse 24); most Hebrew manuscripts *Bavvai*

captivity. 5 Do not cover up their guilt or blot out their sins from your sight,[o] for they have thrown insults in the face of[a] the builders.

6 So we rebuilt the wall till all of it reached half its height, for the people worked with all their heart.

7 But when Sanballat, Tobiah, the Arabs, the Ammonites and the men of Ashdod heard that the repairs to Jerusalem's walls had gone ahead and that the gaps were being closed, they were very angry. 8 They all plotted together to come and fight against Jerusalem and stir up trouble against it. 9 But we prayed to our God and posted a guard day and night to meet this threat.

10 Meanwhile, the people in Judah said, "The strength of the laborers is giving out, and there is so much rubble that we cannot rebuild the wall."

11 Also our enemies said, "Before they know it or see us, we will be right there among them and will kill them and put an end to the work."

12 Then the Jews who lived near them came and told us ten times over, "Wherever you turn, they will attack us."

13 Therefore I stationed some of the people behind the lowest points of the wall at the exposed places, posting them by families, with their swords, spears and bows. 14 After I looked things over, I stood up and said to the nobles, the officials and the rest of the people, "Don't be afraid[p] of them. Remember the Lord, who is great and awesome, and fight[q] for your brothers, your sons and your daughters, your wives and your homes."

15 When our enemies heard that we were aware of their plot and that God had frustrated it,[r] we all returned to the wall, each to his own work.

16 From that day on, half of my men did the work, while the other half were equipped with spears, shields, bows and armor. The officers posted themselves behind all the people of Judah 17 who were building the wall. Those who carried materials did their work with one hand and held a weapon in the other, 18 and each of the builders wore his sword at his side as he worked. But the man who sounded the trumpet stayed with me.

19 Then I said to the nobles, the officials and the rest of the people, "The work is extensive and spread out, and we are widely separated from each other along the wall. 20 Wherever you hear the sound of the trumpet, join us there. Our God will fight[s] for us!"

21 So we continued the work with half the men holding spears, from the first light of dawn till the stars came out. 22 At that time I also said to the people, "Have every man and his helper stay inside Jerusalem at night, so they can serve us as guards by night and workmen by day." 23 Neither I nor my brothers nor my men nor the guards with me took off our clothes; each had his weapon, even when he went for water.[b]

## Nehemiah Helps the Poor

5 Now the men and their wives raised a great outcry against their Jewish brothers. 2 Some were saying, "We and our sons and daughters are numerous; in order for us to eat and stay alive, we must get grain."

3 Others were saying, "We are mortgaging our fields, our vineyards and our homes to get grain during the famine."

4 Still others were saying, "We have had to borrow money to pay the king's tax[t] on our fields and vineyards. 5 Although we are of the same flesh and blood as our countrymen and though our sons are as good as theirs, yet we have to subject our sons and daughters to slavery.[u] Some of our daughters have already been enslaved, but we are powerless, because our fields and our vineyards belong to others."

6 When I heard their outcry and these charges, I was very angry. 7 I pondered them in my mind and then accused the nobles and officials. I told them, "You are exacting usury[v] from your own countrymen!" So I called together a large meeting to deal with them 8 and said: "As far as possible, we have bought[w] back our Jewish brothers who were sold to the Gentiles. Now you are selling your brothers, only for them to be sold back to us!" They kept quiet, because they could find nothing to say.

9 So I continued, "What you are doing is not right. Shouldn't you walk in the fear of

**4:5** o Ps 69:27–28; Jer 18:23
**4:14** p Nu 14:9; Dt 1:29 q 2Sa 10:12
**4:15** r 2Sa 17:14; Job 5:12
**4:20** s Ex 14:14; Dt 1:30; 20:4
**5:4** t Ezr 4:13
**5:5** u Lev 25:39–43,47
**5:7** v Ex 22:25–27; Lev 25:35–37
**5:8** w Lev 25:47

[a] 5 Or *have provoked you to anger before* [b] 23 The meaning of the Hebrew for this clause is uncertain.

**5:12** x Ezr 10:5
**5:13** y Mt 10:14; Ac 18:6
**5:14** z Ne 13:6

our God to avoid the reproach of our Gentile enemies? 10 I and my brothers and my men are also lending the people money and grain. But let the exacting of usury stop! 11 Give back to them immediately their fields, vineyards, olive groves and houses, and also the usury you are charging them—the hundredth part of the money, grain, new wine and oil."

12 "We will give it back," they said. "And we will not demand anything more from them. We will do as you say."

Then I summoned the priests and made the nobles and officials take an oath[x] to do what they had promised. 13 I also shook[y] out the folds of my robe and said, "In this way may God shake out of his house and possessions every man who does not keep this promise. So may such a man be shaken out and emptied!"

At this the whole assembly said, "Amen," and praised the LORD. And the people did as they had promised.

*My daughter,*

*Treat your brothers and sisters as you would like to be treated—not just on occasion, but always.*

*Love,*
*God*

NEHEMIAH 5:1–13

14 Moreover, from the twentieth year of King Artaxerxes,[z] when I was appointed to be their governor in the land of Judah, until his thirty-second year—twelve years—neither I nor my brothers ate the food allotted to the governor. 15 But the earlier governors—those preceding me—placed a heavy burden on the people and took forty shekels[a] of silver from them in addition to food and wine. Their assistants also lorded it over the people. But out of reverence for God I did not act like that. 16 Instead, I devoted myself to the work on this wall. All my men were assembled there for the work; we[b] did not acquire any land.

17 Furthermore, a hundred and fifty Jews and officials ate at my table, as well as those who came to us from the surrounding nations. 18 Each day one ox, six choice sheep and some poultry[a] were prepared for me, and every ten days an abundant supply of wine of all kinds. In spite of all this, I never demanded the food allotted to the governor, because the demands were heavy on these people.

19 Remember[b] me with favor, O my God, for all I have done for these people.

## Further Opposition to the Rebuilding

6 When word came to Sanballat, Tobiah,[c] Geshem[d] the Arab and the rest of our enemies that I had rebuilt the wall and not a gap was left in it—though up to that time I had not set the doors in the gates— 2 Sanballat and Geshem sent me this message: "Come, let us meet together in one of the villages[c] on the plain of Ono.[e]"

But they were scheming to harm me; 3 so I sent messengers to them with this reply: "I am carrying on a great project and cannot go down. Why should the work stop while I leave it and go down to you?" 4 Four times they sent me the same message, and each time I gave them the same answer.

5 Then, the fifth time, Sanballat sent his aide to me with the same message, and in his hand was an unsealed letter 6 in which was written:

> "It is reported among the nations—and Geshem[d][f] says it is true—that you and the Jews are plotting to revolt, and therefore you are building the wall. Moreover, according to these reports you are about to become their king 7 and have even appointed prophets to make this proclamation about you in Jerusalem: 'There is a king in Judah!' Now this report will get back to the king; so come, let us confer together."

**5:18** a 1Ki 4:23
**5:19** b Ne 1:8; 13:14,22,31
**6:1** c Ne 2:10 d Ne 2:19
**6:2** e 1Ch 8:12
**6:6** f Ne 2:19

[a]15 That is, about 1 pound (about 0.5 kilogram) [b]16 Most Hebrew manuscripts; some Hebrew manuscripts, Septuagint, Vulgate and Syriac *I* [c]2 Or *in Kephirim* [d]6 Hebrew *Gashmu*, a variant of *Geshem*

8 I sent him this reply: "Nothing like what you are saying is happening; you are just making it up out of your head."

9 They were all trying to frighten us, thinking, "Their hands will get too weak for the work, and it will not be completed."

⌊But I prayed,⌋ "Now strengthen my hands."

---

*Lord,*

*prepare me to handle the circumstances in my life, whatever they may be. Remove fear and uncertainty from my soul and replace them with confidence and determination.*

*Amen*

NEHEMIAH 6:9

---

10 One day I went to the house of Shemaiah son of Delaiah, the son of Mehetabel, who was shut in at his home. He said, "Let us meet in the house of God, inside the temple, and let us close the temple doors, because men are coming to kill you—by night they are coming to kill you."

11 But I said, "Should a man like me run away? Or should one like me go into the temple to save his life? I will not go!" 12 I realized that God had not sent him, but that he had prophesied against me[g] because Tobiah and Sanballat had hired him. 13 He had been hired to intimidate me so that I would commit a sin by doing this, and then they would give me a bad name to discredit me.

14 Remember Tobiah and Sanballat, O my God, because of what they have done; remember also the prophetess[h] Noadiah and the rest of the prophets[i] who have been trying to intimidate me.

## The Completion of the Wall

15 So the wall was completed on the twenty-fifth of Elul, in fifty-two days. 16 When all our enemies heard about this, all the surrounding nations were afraid and lost their self-confidence, because they realized that this work had been done with the help of our God.

17 Also, in those days the nobles of Judah were sending many letters to Tobiah, and replies from Tobiah kept coming to them. 18 For many in Judah were under oath to him, since he was son-in-law to Shecaniah son of Arah, and his son Jehohanan had married the daughter of Meshullam son of Berekiah. 19 Moreover, they kept reporting to me his good deeds and then telling him what I said. And Tobiah sent letters to intimidate me.

7 After the wall had been rebuilt and I had set the doors in place, the gatekeepers[j] and the singers[k] and the Levites[l] were appointed. 2 I put in charge of Jerusalem my brother Hanani,[m] along with[a] Hananiah[n] the commander of the citadel,[o] because he was a man of integrity and feared God more than most men do. 3 I said to them, "The gates of Jerusalem are not to be opened until the sun is hot. While the gatekeepers are still on duty, have them shut the doors and bar them. Also appoint residents of Jerusalem as guards, some at their posts and some near their own houses."

## The List of the Exiles Who Returned

4 Now the city was large and spacious, but there were few people in it, and the houses had not yet been rebuilt. 5 So my God put it into my heart to assemble the nobles, the officials and the common people for registration by families. I found the genealogical record of those who had been the first to return. This is what I found written there:

> 6 These are the people of the province who came up from the captivity of the exiles[p] whom Nebuchadnezzar king of Babylon had taken captive (they returned to Jerusalem and Judah, each to his own town, 7 in company with Zerubbabel,[q] Jeshua, Nehemiah, Azariah, Raamiah, Nahamani, Mordecai, Bilshan, Mispereth, Bigvai, Nehum and Baanah):

[a]2 Or *Hanani, that is,*

**6:12** g Eze 13:22–23
**6:14** h Eze 13:17–23 i Ne 13:29
**7:1** j Ne 6:1,15 k Ps 68:25 l Ne 8:9
**7:2** m Ne 1:2 n Ne 10:23 o Ne 2:8
**7:6** p Ezr 2:1–70
**7:7** q Ezr 2:2

7:27 r Jos 21:18
7:36 s Ne 3:2

The list of the men of Israel:

8 the descendants of Parosh 2,172
9 of Shephatiah 372
10 of Arah 652
11 of Pahath-Moab (through
the line of Jeshua and Joab) 2,818
12 of Elam 1,254
13 of Zattu 845
14 of Zaccai 760
15 of Binnui 648
16 of Bebai 628
17 of Azgad 2,322
18 of Adonikam 667
19 of Bigvai 2,067
20 of Adin 655
21 of Ater (through Hezekiah) 98
22 of Hashum 328
23 of Bezai 324
24 of Hariph 112
25 of Gibeon 95

26 the men of Bethlehem
and Netophah 188
27 of Anathoth[r] 128
28 of Beth Azmaveth 42
29 of Kiriath Jearim,
Kephirah and Beeroth 743
30 of Ramah and Geba 621
31 of Micmash 122
32 of Bethel and Ai 123
33 of the other Nebo 52
34 of the other Elam 1,254
35 of Harim 320
36 of Jericho[s] 345
37 of Lod, Hadid and Ono 721
38 of Senaah 3,930

39 The priests:

the descendants of Jedaiah
(through the family of Jeshua) 973
40 of Immer 1,052
41 of Pashhur 1,247
42 of Harim 1,017

43 The Levites:

the descendants of Jeshua
(through Kadmiel through
the line of Hodaviah) 74

44 The singers:

the descendants of Asaph 148

45 The gatekeepers:

the descendants of
Shallum, Ater, Talmon,
Akkub, Hatita and Shobai 138

46 The temple servants:

the descendants of
Ziha, Hasupha, Tabbaoth,
47 Keros, Sia, Padon,
48 Lebana, Hagaba, Shalmai,
49 Hanan, Giddel, Gahar,
50 Reaiah, Rezin, Nekoda,
51 Gazzam, Uzza, Paseah,
52 Besai, Meunim, Nephusim,
53 Bakbuk, Hakupha, Harhur,
54 Bazluth, Mehida, Harsha,
55 Barkos, Sisera, Temah,
56 Neziah and Hatipha

57 The descendants of the servants of Solomon:

the descendants of
Sotai, Sophereth, Perida,
58 Jaala, Darkon, Giddel,
59 Shephatiah, Hattil,
Pokereth-Hazzebaim and Amon

60 The temple servants and the
descendants of the servants
of Solomon 392

61 The following came up from the
towns of Tel Melah, Tel Harsha, Ke-
rub, Addon and Immer, but they could
not show that their families were
descended from Israel:

62 the descendants of
Delaiah, Tobiah and Nekoda 642

63 And from among the priests:

the descendants of
Hobaiah, Hakkoz and Barzillai (a man who had married a daughter of Barzillai the Gileadite and was called by that name).

64 These searched for their family
records, but they could not find them
and so were excluded from the priest-
hood as unclean.
65 The governor, there-
fore, ordered them not to eat any of the
most sacred food until there should be

7:65
t Ex 28:30; Ne 8:9

7:73
u Ezr 3:1

8:1
v Ne 3:26
w Dt 28:61; 2Ch 34:15; Ezr 7:6

8:2
x Lev 23:23–25
y Dt 31:11

a priest ministering with the Urim
and Thummim.[t]
66 The whole company numbered
42,360, 67 besides their 7,337 men-
servants and maidservants; and they
also had 245 men and women singers.
68 There were 736 horses, 245 mules,[a]
69 435 camels and 6,720 donkeys.
70 Some of the heads of the families
contributed to the work. The governor
gave to the treasury 1,000 drachmas[b]
of gold, 50 bowls and 530 garments for
priests. 71 Some of the heads of the fam-
ilies gave to the treasury for the work
20,000 drachmas[c] of gold and 2,200
minas[d] of silver. 72 The total given by
the rest of the people was 20,000
drachmas of gold, 2,000 minas[e] of sil-
ver and 67 garments for priests.
73 The priests, the Levites, the gate-
keepers, the singers and the temple
servants, along with certain of the
people and the rest of the Israelites,
settled in their own towns.

## Ezra Reads the Law

When the seventh month came and the
8 Israelites had settled in their towns,[u] 1 all
the people assembled as one man in
the square before the Water Gate.[v] They
told Ezra the scribe to bring out the Book
of the Law of Moses,[w] which the LORD had
commanded for Israel.
2 So on the first day of the seventh month[x]
Ezra the priest brought the Law[y] before the
assembly, which was made up of men and
women and all who were able to understand.
3 He read it aloud from daybreak till noon as
he faced the square before the Water Gate in
the presence of the men, women and others
who could understand. And all the people
listened attentively to the Book of the Law.
4 Ezra the scribe stood on a high wooden
platform built for the occasion. Beside
him on his right stood Mattithiah, Shema,
Anaiah, Uriah, Hilkiah and Maaseiah; and
on his left were Pedaiah, Mishael, Malki-
jah, Hashum, Hashbaddanah, Zechariah
and Meshullam.
5 Ezra opened the book. All the people
could see him because he was standing[z]
above them; and as he opened it, the peo-
ple all stood up. 6 Ezra praised the LORD, the
great God; and all the people lifted their
hands[a] and responded, "Amen! Amen!"
Then they bowed down and worshiped the
LORD with their faces to the ground.
7 The Levites—Jeshua, Bani, Sherebiah,
Jamin, Akkub, Shabbethai, Hodiah, Maase-
iah, Kelita, Azariah, Jozabad, Hanan and
Pelaiah—instructed[b] the people in the Law
while the people were standing there. 8 They
read from the Book of the Law of God, mak-
ing it clear[f] and giving the meaning so that
the people could understand what was be-
ing read.
9 Then Nehemiah the governor, Ezra the
priest and scribe, and the Levites who were
instructing the people said to them all,
"This day is sacred to the LORD your God. Do
not mourn or weep." For all the people had
been weeping as they listened to the words
of the Law.
10 Nehemiah said, "Go and enjoy choice
food and sweet drinks, and send some to
those who have nothing prepared. This day
is sacred to our Lord. Do not grieve, for the
joy of the LORD is your strength."
11 The Levites calmed all the people, say-
ing, "Be still, for this is a sacred day. Do
not grieve."
12 Then all the people went away to eat
and drink, to send portions of food and to
celebrate with great joy, because they now
understood the words that had been made
known to them.
13 On the second day of the month, the
heads of all the families, along with the
priests and the Levites, gathered around
Ezra the scribe to give attention to the words
of the Law. 14 They found written in the Law,
which the LORD had commanded through
Moses, that the Israelites were to live in
booths during the feast of the seventh
month 15 and that they should proclaim this
word and spread it throughout their towns
and in Jerusalem: "Go out into the hill coun-
try and bring back branches from olive and
wild olive trees, and from myrtles, palms

8:5
z Jdg 3:20

8:6
a Ex 4:31; Ezr 9:5; 1Ti 2:8

8:7
b Lev 10:11; 2Ch 17:7

[a] 68 Some Hebrew manuscripts (see also Ezra 2:66); most Hebrew manuscripts do not have this verse. [b] 70 That is, about 19 pounds (about 8.5 kilograms) [c] 71 That is, about 375 pounds (about 170 kilograms); also in verse 72 [d] 71 That is, about 1 1/3 tons (about 1.2 metric tons) [e] 72 That is, about 1 1/4 tons (about 1.1 metric tons) [f] 8 Or *God, translating it*

and shade trees, to make booths"—as it is written.[a]

16So the people went out and brought back branches and built themselves booths on their own roofs, in their courtyards, in the courts of the house of God and in the square by the Water Gate and the one by the Gate of Ephraim.[c] 17The whole company that had returned from exile built booths and lived in them. From the days of Joshua son of Nun until that day, the Israelites had not celebrated[d] it like this. And their joy was very great.

18Day after day, from the first day to the last, Ezra read[e] from the Book of the Law of God. They celebrated the feast for seven days, and on the eighth day, in accordance with the regulation,[f] there was an assembly.

## The Israelites Confess Their Sins

9 On the twenty-fourth day of the same month, the Israelites gathered together, fasting and wearing sackcloth and having dust on their heads.[g] 2Those of Israelite descent had separated themselves from all foreigners.[h] They stood in their places and confessed their sins and the wickedness of their fathers.[i] 3They stood where they were and read from the Book of the Law of the LORD their God for a quarter of the day, and spent another quarter in confession and in worshiping the LORD their God. 4Standing on the stairs were the Levites—Jeshua, Bani, Kadmiel, Shebaniah, Bunni, Sherebiah, Bani and Kenani—who called with loud voices to the LORD their God. 5And the Levites—Jeshua, Kadmiel, Bani, Hashabneiah, Sherebiah, Hodiah, Shebaniah and Pethahiah—said: "Stand up and praise the LORD your God, who is from everlasting to everlasting.[b]"

"Blessed be your glorious name,
and may it be exalted above all blessing and praise. 6You alone are the LORD. You made the heavens,[j] even the highest heavens, and all their starry host, the earth[k] and all that is on it, the seas and all that is in them. You give life to everything, and the multitudes of heaven worship you.

7"You are the LORD God, who chose Abram and brought him out of Ur of the Chaldeans[l] and named him Abraham.[m] 8You found his heart faithful to you, and you made a covenant with him to give to his descendants the land of the Canaanites, Hittites, Amorites, Perizzites, Jebusites and Girgashites.[n] You have kept your promise because you are righteous.[o]

9"You saw the suffering of our forefathers in Egypt; you heard their cry at the Red Sea.[c][p] 10You sent miraculous signs and wonders against Pharaoh, against all his officials and all the people of his land, for you knew how arrogantly the Egyptians treated them. You made a name for yourself, which remains to this day. 11You divided the sea before them,[q] so that they passed through it on dry ground, but you hurled their pursuers into the depths, like a stone into mighty waters.[r] 12By day you led them with a pillar of cloud,[s] and by night with a pillar of fire to give them light on the way they were to take.

13"You came down on Mount Sinai; you spoke to them from heaven. You gave them regulations and laws that are just and right, and decrees and commands that are good.[t] 14You made known to them your holy Sabbath[u] and gave them commands, decrees and laws through your servant Moses. 15In their hunger you gave them bread from heaven[v] and in their thirst you brought them water from the rock;[w] you told them to go in and take possession of the land you had sworn with uplifted hand to give them.[x]

16"But they, our forefathers, became arrogant and stiff-necked, and did not obey your commands. 17They refused to listen and failed to remember the miracles you performed among them. They became stiff-necked and in their rebellion appointed a leader in order to return to their slavery.[y] But you are a forgiving God, gracious and compassionate, slow to anger and abounding

8:16 c 2Ki 14:13; Ne 12:39
8:17 d 2Ch 30:21
8:18 e Dt 31:11 f Lev 23:36,40; Nu 29:35
9:1 g 1Sa 4:12
9:2 h Ne 13:3,30 i Ezr 10:11
9:6 j 2Ki 19:15 k Ge 1:1
9:7 l Ge 11:31 m Ge 17:5
9:8 n Ge 15:18–21 o Ge 15:6
9:9 p Ex 14:10–30
9:11 q Ex 14:21 r Ex 15:4–5,10
9:12 s Ex 13:21
9:13 t Ex 20:1
9:14 u Ex 20:8–11
9:15 v Ex 16:4 w Ex 17:6 x Dt 1:8,21
9:17 y Nu 14:1–4

[a]15 See Lev. 23:37–40. [b]5 Or *God for ever and ever* [c]9 Hebrew *Yam Suph*; that is, Sea of Reeds

in love. Therefore you did not desert them,[z] 18even when they cast for themselves an image of a calf[a] and said, 'This is your god, who brought you up out of Egypt,' or when they committed awful blasphemies.

19"Because of your great compassion you did not abandon them in the desert. By day the pillar of cloud did not cease to guide them on their path, nor the pillar of fire by night to shine on the way they were to take. 20You gave your good Spirit[b] to instruct them. You did not withhold your manna from their mouths, and you gave them water for their thirst. 21For forty years you sustained them in the desert; they lacked nothing,[c] their clothes did not wear out nor did their feet become swollen.

22"You gave them kingdoms and nations, allotting to them even the remotest frontiers. They took over the country of Sihon[a][d] king of Heshbon and the country of Og king of Bashan. 23You made their sons as numerous as the stars in the sky, and you brought them into the land that you told their fathers to enter and possess. 24Their sons went in and took possession of the land. You subdued before them the Canaanites, who lived in the land; you handed the Canaanites over to them, along with their kings and the peoples of the land, to deal with them as they pleased. 25They captured fortified cities and fertile land; they took possession of houses filled with all kinds of good things, wells already dug, vineyards, olive groves and fruit trees in abundance. They ate to the full and were well-nourished;[e] they reveled in your great goodness.[f]

26"But they were disobedient and rebelled against you; they put your law behind their backs.[g] They killed your prophets, who had admonished them in order to turn them back to you; they committed awful blasphemies.[h] 27So you handed them over to their enemies,[i] who oppressed them. But when they were oppressed they cried out to you. From heaven you heard them, and in your great compassion you gave them deliverers, who rescued them from the hand of their enemies.

28"But as soon as they were at rest, they again did what was evil in your sight. Then you abandoned them to the hand of their enemies so that they ruled over them. And when they cried out to you again, you heard from heaven, and in your compassion you delivered them[j] time after time.

29"You warned them to return to your law, but they became arrogant and disobeyed your commands. They sinned against your ordinances, by which a man will live if he obeys them.[k] Stubbornly they turned their backs on you, became stiff-necked and refused to listen.[l] 30For many years you were patient with them. By your Spirit you admonished them through your prophets.[m] Yet they paid no attention, so you handed them over to the neighboring peoples. 31But in your great mercy you did not put an end to them or abandon them, for you are a gracious and merciful God.

32"Now therefore, O our God, the great, mighty and awesome God, who keeps his covenant of love, do not let all this hardship seem trifling in your eyes—the hardship that has come upon us, upon our kings and leaders, upon our priests and prophets, upon our fathers and all your people, from the days of the kings of Assyria until today. 33In all that has happened to us, you have been just;[n] you have acted faithfully, while we did wrong.[o] 34Our kings, our leaders, our priests and our fathers did not follow your law; they did not pay attention to

> *"There will always be curve balls in your life. Teach your children to thrive in that adversity."*
>
> —JEANNE MOUTOUSSAMY-ASHE, PHOTOGRAPHER AND WIDOW OF TENNIS GREAT ARTHUR ASHE

**9:17** z Ps 78:11
**9:18** a Ex 32:4
**9:20** b Nu 11:17; Isa 63:11,14
**9:21** c Dt 2:7
**9:22** d Nu 21:21
**9:25** e Dt 6:10–12 f Dt 32:12–15
**9:26** g 1Ki 14:9 h Jdg 2:12–13
**9:27** i Jdg 2:14
**9:28** j Ps 106:43
**9:29** k Dt 30:16 l Zec 7:11–12
**9:30** m 2Ki 17:13–18
**9:33** n Ge 18:25 o Da 9:7–8,14

[a]22 One Hebrew manuscript and Septuagint; most Hebrew manuscripts *Sihon, that is, the country of the*

**9:35** p Dt28:45–48
**9:36** q Dt28:48; Ezr9:9
**9:37** r Dt28:33

your commands or the warnings you gave them. 35 Even while they were in their kingdom, enjoying your great goodness to them in the spacious and fertile land you gave them, they did not serve you[p] or turn from their evil ways.

36 "But see, we are slaves[q] today, slaves in the land you gave our forefathers so they could eat its fruit and the other good things it produces. 37 Because of our sins, its abundant harvest goes to the kings you have placed over us. They rule over our bodies and our cattle as they please. We are in great distress.[r]

## The Agreement of the People

38 "In view of all this, we are making a binding agreement, putting it in writing, and our leaders, our Levites and our priests are affixing their seals to it."

**10** Those who sealed it were:

Nehemiah the governor, the son of Hacaliah.

Zedekiah, 2 Seraiah, Azariah, Jeremiah,
3 Pashhur, Amariah, Malkijah,
4 Hattush, Shebaniah, Malluch,
5 Harim, Meremoth, Obadiah,
6 Daniel, Ginnethon, Baruch,
7 Meshullam, Abijah, Mijamin,
8 Maaziah, Bilgai and Shemaiah.
These were the priests.

9 The Levites:

Jeshua son of Azaniah, Binnui of the sons of Henadad, Kadmiel,
10 and their associates: Shebaniah,
Hodiah, Kelita, Pelaiah, Hanan,
11 Mica, Rehob, Hashabiah,
12 Zaccur, Sherebiah, Shebaniah,
13 Hodiah, Bani and Beninu.

14 The leaders of the people:

Parosh, Pahath-Moab, Elam, Zattu, Bani,
15 Bunni, Azgad, Bebai,
16 Adonijah, Bigvai, Adin,
17 Ater, Hezekiah, Azzur,
18 Hodiah, Hashum, Bezai,
19 Hariph, Anathoth, Nebai,
20 Magpiash, Meshullam, Hezir,
21 Meshezabel, Zadok, Jaddua,
22 Pelatiah, Hanan, Anaiah,
23 Hoshea, Hananiah, Hasshub,
24 Hallohesh, Pilha, Shobek,
25 Rehum, Hashabnah, Maaseiah,
26 Ahiah, Hanan, Anan,
27 Malluch, Harim and Baanah.

28 "The rest of the people—priests, Levites, gatekeepers, singers, temple servants and all who separated themselves from the neighboring peoples[s] for the sake of the Law of God, together with their wives and all their sons and daughters who are able to understand— 29 all these now join their brothers the nobles, and bind themselves with a curse and an oath to follow the Law of God given through Moses the servant of God and to obey carefully all the commands, regulations and decrees of the LORD our Lord.

30 "We promise not to give our daughters in marriage to the peoples around us or take their daughters for our sons.[t]

31 "When the neighboring peoples bring merchandise or grain to sell on the Sabbath,[u] we will not buy from them on the Sabbath or on any holy day. Every seventh year we will forgo working the land[v] and will cancel all debts.[w]

32 "We assume the responsibility for carrying out the commands to give a third of a shekel[a] each year for the service of the house of our God: 33 for the bread set out on the table;[x] for the regular grain offerings and burnt offerings; for the offerings on the Sabbaths, New Moon festivals and appointed feasts; for the holy offerings; for sin offerings to make atonement for Israel; and for all the duties of the house of our God.

34 "We—the priests, the Levites and the people—have cast lots to determine when each of our families is to

**10:28** s Ne9:2
**10:30** t Ex34:16; Dt7:3
**10:31** u Ne13:16,18 v Ex23:11; Lev25:1–7 w Dt15:1
**10:33** x Lev24:6

[a] 32 That is, about 1/8 ounce (about 4 grams)

10:34
y Ne 13:31
10:35
z Ex 23:19; Nu 18:12
a Dt 26:1–11
10:36
b Ex 13:2; Nu 18:14–16
10:37
c Lev 23:17
d Lev 27:30; Nu 18:21
10:38
e Nu 18:26
10:39
f Dt 12:6; Ne 13:11,12
11:1
g Ne 7:4
h ver 18; Isa 48:2
11:3
i 1Ch 9:2–3; Ezr 2:1

bring to the house of our God at set times each year a contribution of wood[y] to burn on the altar of the LORD our God, as it is written in the Law.

35“We also assume responsibility for bringing to the house of the LORD each year the firstfruits[z] of our crops and of every fruit tree.[a]

36“As it is also written in the Law, we will bring the firstborn[b] of our sons and of our cattle, of our herds and of our flocks to the house of our God, to the priests ministering there.

37“Moreover, we will bring to the storerooms of the house of our God, to the priests, the first of our ground meal, of our ⌊grain⌋ offerings, of the fruit of all our trees and of our new wine and oil.[c] And we will bring a tithe[d] of our crops to the Levites, for it is the Levites who collect the tithes in all the towns where we work. 38A priest descended from Aaron is to accompany the Levites when they receive the tithes, and the Levites are to bring a tenth of the tithes[e] up to the house of our God, to the storerooms of the treasury. 39The people of Israel, including the Levites, are to bring their contributions of grain, new wine and oil to the storerooms where the articles for the sanctuary are kept and where the ministering priests, the gatekeepers and the singers stay.

“We will not neglect the house of our God.”[f]

## The New Residents of Jerusalem

11 Now the leaders of the people settled in Jerusalem, and the rest of the people cast lots to bring one out of every ten to live in Jerusalem,[g] the holy city,[h] while the remaining nine were to stay in their own towns. 2The people commended all the men who volunteered to live in Jerusalem.

3These are the provincial leaders who settled in Jerusalem (now some Israelites, priests, Levites, temple servants and descendants of Solomon’s servants lived in the towns of Judah, each on his own property in the various towns,[i] 4while other people from both Judah and Benjamin lived in Jerusalem):

From the descendants of Judah:

Athaiah son of Uzziah, the son of Zechariah, the son of Amariah, the son of Shephatiah, the son of Mahalalel, a descendant of Perez; 5and Maaseiah son of Baruch, the son of Col-Hozeh, the son of Hazaiah, the son of Adaiah, the son of Joiarib, the son of Zechariah, a descendant of Shelah. 6The descendants of Perez who lived in Jerusalem totaled 468 able men.

7From the descendants of Benjamin:

Sallu son of Meshullam, the son of Joed, the son of Pedaiah, the son of Kolaiah, the son of Maaseiah, the son of Ithiel, the son of Jeshaiah, 8and his followers, Gabbai and Sallai—928 men. 9Joel son of Zicri was their chief officer, and Judah son of Hassenuah was over the Second District of the city.

10From the priests:

Jedaiah; the son of Joiarib; Jakin; 11Seraiah son of Hilkiah, the son of Meshullam, the son of Zadok, the son of Meraioth, the son of Ahitub, supervisor in the house of God, 12and their associates, who carried on work for the temple—822 men; Adaiah son of Jeroham, the son of Pelaliah, the son of Amzi, the son of Zechariah, the son of Pashhur, the son of Malkijah, 13and his associates, who were heads of families—242 men; Amashsai son of Azarel, the son of Ahzai, the son of Meshillemoth, the son of Immer, 14and his[a] associates, who were able men—128. Their chief officer was Zabdiel son of Haggedolim.

15From the Levites:

Shemaiah son of Hasshub, the son of Azrikam, the son of Hashabiah, the son of Bunni; 16Shabbethai and Jozabad, two of the heads of the Levites, who had charge of the outside work of the house of God; 17Mattaniah son

[a]14 Most Septuagint manuscripts; Hebrew *their*

of Mica, the son of Zabdi, the son of Asaph, the director who led in thanksgiving and prayer; Bakbukiah, second among his associates; and Abda son of Shammua, the son of Galal, the son of Jeduthun. 18 The Levites in the holy city totaled 284.

19 The gatekeepers:

Akkub, Talmon and their associates, who kept watch at the gates—172 men.

20 The rest of the Israelites, with the priests and Levites, were in all the towns of Judah, each on his ancestral property.

21 The temple servants[j] lived on the hill of Ophel, and Ziha and Gishpa were in charge of them.

22 The chief officer of the Levites in Jerusalem was Uzzi son of Bani, the son of Hashabiah, the son of Mattaniah,[k] the son of Mica. Uzzi was one of Asaph's descendants, who were the singers responsible for the service of the house of God. 23 The singers[l] were under the king's orders, which regulated their daily activity.

24 Pethahiah son of Meshezabel, one of the descendants of Zerah[m] son of Judah, was the king's agent in all affairs relating to the people.

25 As for the villages with their fields, some of the people of Judah lived in Kiriath Arba[n] and its surrounding settlements, in Dibon and its settlements, in Jekabzeel and its villages, 26 in Jeshua, in Moladah, in Beth Pelet, 27 in Hazar Shual, in Beersheba[o] and its settlements, 28 in Ziklag,[p] in Meconah and its settlements, 29 in En Rimmon, in Zorah, in Jarmuth, 30 Zanoah, Adullam and their villages, in Lachish[q] and its fields, and in Azekah and its settlements. So they were living all the way from Beersheba to the Valley of Hinnom.

31 The descendants of the Benjamites from Geba[r] lived in Micmash,[s] Aija, Bethel and its settlements, 32 in Anathoth,[t] Nob and Ananiah, 33 in Hazor,[u] Ramah and Gittaim, 34 in Hadid, Zeboim[v] and Neballat, 35 in Lod and Ono, and in the Valley of the Craftsmen.

36 Some of the divisions of the Levites of Judah settled in Benjamin.

## Priests and Levites

12 These were the priests[w] and Levites who returned with Zerubbabel son of Shealtiel and with Jeshua:[x]

Seraiah, Jeremiah, Ezra,
2 Amariah, Malluch, Hattush,
3 Shecaniah, Rehum, Meremoth,
4 Iddo, Ginnethon,[a] Abijah,[y]
5 Mijamin,[b] Moadiah, Bilgah,
6 Shemaiah, Joiarib, Jedaiah,
7 Sallu, Amok, Hilkiah and Jedaiah.

These were the leaders of the priests and their associates in the days of Jeshua.

8 The Levites were Jeshua, Binnui, Kadmiel, Sherebiah, Judah, and also Mattaniah,[z] who, together with his associates, was in charge of the songs of thanksgiving. 9 Bakbukiah and Unni, their associates, stood opposite them in the services.

10 Jeshua was the father of Joiakim, Joiakim the father of Eliashib, Eliashib the father of Joiada, 11 Joiada the father of Jonathan, and Jonathan the father of Jaddua.

12 In the days of Joiakim, these were the heads of the priestly families:

of Seraiah's family, Meraiah;
of Jeremiah's, Hananiah;
13 of Ezra's, Meshullam;
of Amariah's, Jehohanan;
14 of Malluch's, Jonathan;
of Shecaniah's,[c] Joseph;
15 of Harim's, Adna;
of Meremoth's,[d] Helkai;
16 of Iddo's, Zechariah;
of Ginnethon's, Meshullam;
17 of Abijah's, Zicri;
of Miniamin's and of Moadiah's, Piltai;
18 of Bilgah's, Shammua;
of Shemaiah's, Jehonathan;
19 of Joiarib's, Mattenai;
of Jedaiah's, Uzzi;
20 of Sallu's, Kallai;
of Amok's, Eber;
21 of Hilkiah's, Hashabiah;
of Jedaiah's, Nethanel.

22 The family heads of the Levites in the

**11:21** j Ne 3:26
**11:22** k 1Ch 9:15
**11:23** l Ne 7:44
**11:24** m Ge 38:30
**11:25** n Jos 14:15
**11:27** o Ge 21:14
**11:28** p 1Sa 27:6
**11:30** q Jos 10:3
**11:31** r Jos 21:17 s 1Sa 13:2
**11:32** t Jos 21:18; Isa 10:30
**11:33** u Jos 11:1
**11:34** v 1Sa 13:18
**12:1** w Ne 10:1–8 x Ezr 2:2
**12:4** y Lk 1:5
**12:8** z Ne 11:17

[a] 4 Many Hebrew manuscripts and Vulgate (see also Neh. 12:16); most Hebrew manuscripts *Ginnethoi* [b] 5 A variant of *Miniamin* [c] 14 Very many Hebrew manuscripts, some Septuagint manuscripts and Syriac (see also Neh. 12:3); most Hebrew manuscripts *Shebaniah's* [d] 15 Some Septuagint manuscripts (see also Neh. 12:3); Hebrew *Meraioth's*

12:27 a 1Ch 25:6 days of Eliashib, Joiada, Johanan and Jad-
dua, as well as those of the priests, were
12:28 b 1Ch 9:16 recorded in the reign of Darius the Persian.
23The family heads among the descendants
of Levi up to the time of Johanan son of
Eliashib were recorded in the book of the
annals. 24And the leaders of the Levites
were Hashabiah, Sherebiah, Jeshua son of
Kadmiel, and their associates, who stood
opposite them to give praise and thanksgiv-
ing, one section responding to the other, as
prescribed by David the man of God.
25Mattaniah, Bakbukiah, Obadiah, Me-
shullam, Talmon and Akkub were gate-
keepers who guarded the storerooms at the
gates. 26They served in the days of Joiakim
son of Jeshua, the son of Jozadak, and in the
days of Nehemiah the governor and of Ezra
the priest and scribe.

## Dedication of the Wall of Jerusalem

27At the dedication of the wall of Jeru-
salem, the Levites were sought out from
where they lived and were brought to Jeru-
salem to celebrate joyfully the dedication
with songs of thanksgiving and with the
music of cymbals, harps and lyres.[a] 28The
singers also were brought together from
the region around Jerusalem—from the
villages of the Netophathites,[b] 29from Beth
Gilgal, and from the area of Geba and Azma-
veth, for the singers had built villages for
themselves around Jerusalem. 30When the
priests and Levites had purified themselves
ceremonially, they purified the people, the
gates and the wall.
31I had the leaders of Judah go up on top[a]

*Lord,*

*Thank you for your infinite blessings.*

*Help me to praise you throughout this day*

*and to always remember your goodness.*

*Amen*

NEHEMIAH 12:27–30

of the wall. I also assigned two large choirs 12:31 c Ne 2:13
to give thanks. One was to proceed on top[b]
of the wall to the right, toward the Dung 12:37 d Ne 2:14; 3:15
Gate.[c] 32Hoshaiah and half the leaders of e Ne 3:26
Judah followed them, 33along with Azariah, 12:38 f Ne 3:11
Ezra, Meshullam, 34Judah, Benjamin, She- g Ne 3:8
maiah, Jeremiah, 35as well as some priests 12:39 h 2Ki 14:13;
with trumpets, and also Zechariah son of Ne 8:16 i Ne 3:6
Jonathan, the son of Shemaiah, the son j Ne 3:3 k Ne 3:1
of Mattaniah, the son of Micaiah, the son 12:44
of Zaccur, the son of Asaph, 36and his asso- l Ne 13:4,13
ciates—Shemaiah, Azarel, Milalai, Gilalai,
Maai, Nethanel, Judah and Hanani—with
musical instruments ⌞prescribed by⌟ David
the man of God. Ezra the scribe led the pro-
cession. 37At the Fountain Gate[d] they contin-
ued directly up the steps of the City of David
on the ascent to the wall and passed above
the house of David to the Water Gate[e] on
the east.
38The second choir proceeded in the
opposite direction. I followed them on top[c]
of the wall, together with half the people—
past the Tower of the Ovens[f] to the Broad
Wall,[g] 39over the Gate of Ephraim,[h] the Jesh-
anah[d] Gate,[i] the Fish Gate,[j] the Tower of
Hananel[k] and the Tower of the Hundred,
as far as the Sheep Gate. At the Gate of the
Guard they stopped.
40The two choirs that gave thanks then
took their places in the house of God; so did
I, together with half the officials, 41as well as
the priests—Eliakim, Maaseiah, Miniamin,
Micaiah, Elioenai, Zechariah and Hananiah
with their trumpets— 42and also Maase-
iah, Shemaiah, Eleazar, Uzzi, Jehohanan,
Malkijah, Elam and Ezer. The choirs sang
under the direction of Jezrahiah. 43And on
that day they offered great sacrifices, rejoic-
ing because God had given them great joy.
The women and children also rejoiced. The
sound of rejoicing in Jerusalem could be
heard far away.
44At that time men were appointed to
be in charge of the storerooms[l] for the con-
tributions, firstfruits and tithes. From the
fields around the towns they were to bring
into the storerooms the portions required
by the Law for the priests and the Levites,
for Judah was pleased with the minister-
ing priests and Levites. 45They performed

[a]31 Or *go alongside* [b]31 Or *proceed alongside* [c]38 Or *them alongside* [d]39 Or *Old*

**12:45** m 1Ch 25:1
**12:47** n Nu 18:21; Dt 18:8
**13:1** o Dt 23:3
**13:2** p Nu 22:3–11 q Nu 23:11; Dt 23:4–5
**13:3** r Ne 9:2
**13:4** s Ne 12:44 t Ne 2:10
**13:5** u Nu 18:21
**13:6** v Ne 5:14
**13:9** w 2Ch 29:5

the service of their God and the service of
purification, as did also the singers and gate-
keepers, according to the commands of Da-
vid[m] and his son Solomon. [46]For long ago, in
the days of David and Asaph, there had been
directors for the singers and for the songs
of praise and thanksgiving to God. [47]So in
the days of Zerubbabel and of Nehemiah, all
Israel contributed the daily portions for the
singers and gatekeepers. They also set aside
the portion for the other Levites, and the
Levites set aside the portion for the descen-
dants of Aaron.[n]

## Nehemiah's Final Reforms

**13** On that day the Book of Moses was
read aloud in the hearing of the peo-
ple and there it was found written that no
Ammonite or Moabite should ever be admit-
ted into the assembly of God,[o] [2]because they
had not met the Israelites with food and
water but had hired Balaam[p] to call a curse
down on them. (Our God, however, turned
the curse into a blessing.)[q] [3]When the peo-
ple heard this law, they excluded from Israel
all who were of foreign descent.[r]

[4]Before this, Eliashib the priest had been
put in charge of the storerooms[s] of the house
of our God. He was closely associated with
Tobiah,[t] [5]and he had provided him with a
large room formerly used to store the grain
offerings and incense and temple articles,
and also the tithes[u] of grain, new wine and
oil prescribed for the Levites, singers and
gatekeepers, as well as the contributions for
the priests.

[6]But while all this was going on, I was not
in Jerusalem, for in the thirty-second year of
Artaxerxes[v] king of Babylon I had returned
to the king. Some time later I asked his per-
mission [7]and came back to Jerusalem. Here
I learned about the evil thing Eliashib had
done in providing Tobiah a room in the
courts of the house of God. [8]I was greatly
displeased and threw all Tobiah's house-
hold goods out of the room. [9]I gave orders to
purify the rooms,[w] and then I put back into
them the equipment of the house of God,
with the grain offerings and the incense.

[10]I also learned that the portions as-
signed to the Levites had not been given to
them, and that all the Levites and singers
responsible for the service had gone back to
their own fields. [11]So I rebuked the officials
and asked them, "Why is the house of God
neglected?"[x] Then I called them together
and stationed them at their posts.

[12]All Judah brought the tithes of grain,
new wine and oil into the storerooms.[y] [13]I
put Shelemiah the priest, Zadok the scribe,
and a Levite named Pedaiah in charge of
the storerooms and made Hanan son of Zac-
cur, the son of Mattaniah, their assistant,
because these men were considered trust-
worthy. They were made responsible for dis-
tributing the supplies to their brothers.[z]

[14]Remember me for this, O my God, and
do not blot out what I have so faithfully done
for the house of my God and its services.

[15]In those days I saw men in Judah tread-
ing winepresses on the Sabbath and bring-
ing in grain and loading it on donkeys,
together with wine, grapes, figs and all other
kinds of loads. And they were bringing all
this into Jerusalem on the Sabbath.[a] There-
fore I warned them against selling food on
that day. [16]Men from Tyre who lived in Jeru-
salem were bringing in fish and all kinds
of merchandise and selling them in Jerusa-
lem on the Sabbath to the people of Judah.
[17]I rebuked the nobles of Judah and said to
them, "What is this wicked thing you are do-
ing—desecrating the Sabbath day? [18]Didn't
your forefathers do the same things, so that
our God brought all this calamity upon us
and upon this city? Now you are stirring up
more wrath against Israel by desecrating
the Sabbath."[b]

[19]When evening shadows fell on the gates
of Jerusalem before the Sabbath,[c] I ordered
the doors to be shut and not opened until the
Sabbath was over. I stationed some of my
own men at the gates so that no load could
be brought in on the Sabbath day. [20]Once or
twice the merchants and sellers of all kinds
of goods spent the night outside Jerusalem.
[21]But I warned them and said, "Why do you
spend the night by the wall? If you do this
again, I will lay hands on you." From that
time on they no longer came on the Sabbath.
[22]Then I commanded the Levites to purify
themselves and go and guard the gates in or-
der to keep the Sabbath day holy.

**13:11** x Ne 10:37–39
**13:12** y Ne 10:37–39; Mal 3:10
**13:13** z Ne 12:44
**13:15** a Ex 20:8–11; Ne 10:31
**13:18** b Jer 17:21–23
**13:19** c Lev 23:32

Remember[d] me for this also, O my God, and show mercy to me according to your great love.

[23]Moreover, in those days I saw men of Judah who had married[e] women from Ashdod, Ammon and Moab. [24]Half of their children spoke the language of Ashdod or the language of one of the other peoples, and did not know how to speak the language of Judah. [25]I rebuked them and called curses down on them. I beat some of the men and pulled out their hair. I made them take an oath in God's name and said: "You are not to give your daughters in marriage to their sons, nor are you to take their daughters in marriage for your sons or for yourselves. [26]Was it not because of marriages like these that Solomon king of Israel sinned? Among the many nations there was no king like him.[f] He was loved by his God,[g] and God made him king over all Israel, but even he was led into sin by foreign women.[h] [27]Must we hear now that you too are doing all this terrible wickedness and are being unfaithful to our God by marrying[i] foreign women?"

[28]One of the sons of Joiada son of Eliashib the high priest was son-in-law to Sanballat the Horonite. And I drove him away from me.

[29]Remember[j] them, O my God, because they defiled the priestly office and the covenant of the priesthood and of the Levites.

[30]So I purified the priests and the Levites of everything foreign,[k] and assigned them duties, each to his own task. [31]I also made provision for contributions of wood[l] at designated times, and for the firstfruits.

Remember[m] me with favor, O my God.

**13:22** d Ne 12:30
**13:23** e Ezr 9:1–2
**13:26** f 1Ki 3:13; 2Ch 1:12 g 2Sa 12:25 h 1Ki 11:3
**13:27** i Ezr 10:2
**13:29** j Ne 6:14
**13:30** k Ne 10:30
**13:31** l Ne 10:34 m ver 14,22; Ge 8:1

# Esther

## OVERVIEW

The book of Esther tells the story of how God directed the events and politics in the court of the Persian king to save the Jews from genocide. The story begins with a lavish feast thrown by King Xerxes during which he called for Queen Vashti to display herself to the crowd. She refused his request and was consequently banished from the king's presence. The king sought a new queen, and Esther was chosen.

Haman, a noble in the king's court, put forth a plan to wipe out all the Jews in the Persian Empire. His wife supported his wickedness (see Est 5:14). Esther was called upon to speak up for her people. After three days of fasting and prayer, she appeared before the king, who accepted her petition. She strategically invited Haman to dinners with the king to expose his evil plot. As a result, Haman himself was put to death, along with his ten sons, while the Jews were given power to protect themselves from their enemies. The Jewish people instituted the festival of Purim to celebrate this event, and it is still celebrated to this day.

Although this male-dominated society gave women little power and authority, God used Esther to redeem his people from their enemies. For those who follow Christ, there is no power on earth that can stop what God has purposed for his people. Women in the body of Christ are part of the "royal priesthood" of God (1Pe 2:9) and set apart for his glory. Learn from Esther how prayer and fasting can change the course of a community.

## OUTLINE

I. Queen Vashti Rejected (1:1–22)

II. Esther Chosen to Replace the Queen (2:1–23)

III. Jewish People Threatened by Haman's Plot (3:1—4:17)

IV. Queen Esther Intercedes for the Jews (5:1–8:17)

V. Jews Delivered From Their Enemies (9:1–32)

VI. Mordecai Promoted (10:1–3)

## SCANNABLE FACTS:

**Author:** Unknown

**Time Written:** Sometime after about 460 B.C., when the events of the book occurred

**Theme to Note:** God takes care of his people

**Notable Women:** Queen Vashti; Esther; Haman's wife, Zeresh (see Est 5:14)

1:1
a Ezr 4:6; Da 9:1
b Est 9:30
c Est 8:9

1:2
d Ne 1:1

1:3
e Est 2:18

1:5
f Est 7:7–8

1:6
g Eze 23:41; Am 6:4

1:7
h Est 2:18

1:10
i Jdg 16:25
j Est 7:9

## Queen Vashti Deposed

1 This is what happened during the time
of Xerxes,[a][a] the Xerxes who ruled over
127 provinces[b] stretching from India to
Cush[b]:[c] 2 At that time King Xerxes reigned
from his royal throne in the citadel of Susa,[d]
3 and in the third year of his reign he gave
a banquet[e] for all his nobles and officials.
The military leaders of Persia and Media,
the princes, and the nobles of the provinces
were present.
4 For a full 180 days he displayed the vast
wealth of his kingdom and the splendor and
glory of his majesty. 5 When these days were
over, the king gave a banquet, lasting seven
days, in the enclosed garden[f] of the king's
palace, for all the people from the least to
the greatest, who were in the citadel of Susa.
6 The garden had hangings of white and blue
linen, fastened with cords of white linen
and purple material to silver rings on mar-
ble pillars. There were couches[g] of gold and
silver on a mosaic pavement of porphyry,
marble, mother-of-pearl and other costly
stones. 7 Wine was served in goblets of gold,
each one different from the other, and the
royal wine was abundant, in keeping with
the king's liberality.[h] 8 By the king's com-
mand each guest was allowed to drink in
his own way, for the king instructed all
the wine stewards to serve each man what
he wished.
9 Queen Vashti also gave a banquet for the
women in the royal palace of King Xerxes.
10 On the seventh day, when King Xerxes
was in high spirits[i] from wine, he com-
manded the seven eunuchs who served
him—Mehuman, Biztha, Harbona,[j] Bigtha,
Abagtha, Zethar and Carcas— 11 to bring
before him Queen Vashti, wearing her royal
crown, in order to display her beauty to the
people and nobles, for she was lovely to look
at. 12 But when the attendants delivered the
king's command, Queen Vashti refused to
come. Then the king became furious and
burned with anger.
13 Since it was customary for the king to
consult experts in matters of law and jus-
tice, he spoke with the wise men who under-
stood the times[k] 14 and were closest to the
king—Carshena, Shethar, Admatha, Tar-
shish, Meres, Marsena and Memucan, the
seven nobles[l] of Persia and Media who had
special access to the king and were highest
in the kingdom.
15 "According to law, what must be done
to Queen Vashti?" he asked. "She has not
obeyed the command of King Xerxes that
the eunuchs have taken to her."
16 Then Memucan replied in the presence
of the king and the nobles, "Queen Vashti
has done wrong, not only against the king
but also against all the nobles and the peo-
ples of all the provinces of King Xerxes.
17 For the queen's conduct will become
known to all the women, and so they will
despise their husbands and say, 'King Xer-
xes commanded Queen Vashti to be brought
before him, but she would not come.' 18 This
very day the Persian and Median women
of the nobility who have heard about the
queen's conduct will respond to all the
king's nobles in the same way. There will be
no end of disrespect and discord.
19 "Therefore, if it pleases the king, let him
issue a royal decree and let it be written in
the laws of Persia and Media, which cannot
be repealed,[m] that Vashti is never again to

1:13
k 1Ch 12:32; Jer 10:7; Da 2:12

1:14
l 2Ki 25:19

1:19
m Est 8:8; Da 6:8,12

[a]1 Hebrew *Ahasuerus,* a variant of Xerxes' Persian name; here and throughout Esther [b]1 That is, the upper Nile region

### The African Presence

**Esther 1**

King Xerxes of Persia ruled from 486 to 465 B.C. His sovereignty extended to North Africa, Northeast Africa, Arabia, Asia, Mesopotamia and India.

# Queen Vashti

## A Woman of Strength

King Xerxes, the ruler of 127 provinces from India to Cush (the upper Nile region, south of Egypt), gave a banquet for all his underlings—probably in an attempt to rally support for an invasion of Greece. He and his royal cabinet and provincial leaders partied for 180 days—six months. This probably meant six months of drinking, telling tall tales and more drinking—plus whatever unmentionable things they could think of doing. An after-party, which also included all the local residents, lasted another seven days.

While the men became drunk at their party, Queen Vashti gave a party for the women. On the seventh day of the after-party, the king sent seven eunuchs to get Queen Vashti. She was told to come to the men's party wearing the royal crown. She was his trophy, and he wanted to show her off.

The eunuchs came to the queen to deliver King Xerxes' message, but she would not come (see Est 1:12). She would not be made to look like a fool to these provincial women to whom she was an example of all that a woman could be. Now, she was not ignorant of the price she would have to pay, but she was willing to challenge the king's drunken foolishness in order to be true to herself. This woman was a strong sister—willing to take a chance for the good that she might be able to do for those who came behind her.

Sometimes we have to step out there and be an example so that those who follow will know what can be done. Strength and wisdom are qualities that each of us needs to rely on God for and encourage in our sisters.

We have but to remember our history: Hatshepsut, the Egyptian queen of the Eighteenth Dynasty; the beautiful warrior queen Makeda; Ann Zingha, the amazon queen of Matamba, West Africa; Sojourner Truth; Harriet Tubman; Mary McLeod Bethune; Marian Anderson; Barbara Jordan; Fannie Lou Hamer; and Rosa Parks, as well as the women you have been blessed to observe.

—M. Allen Bellinger

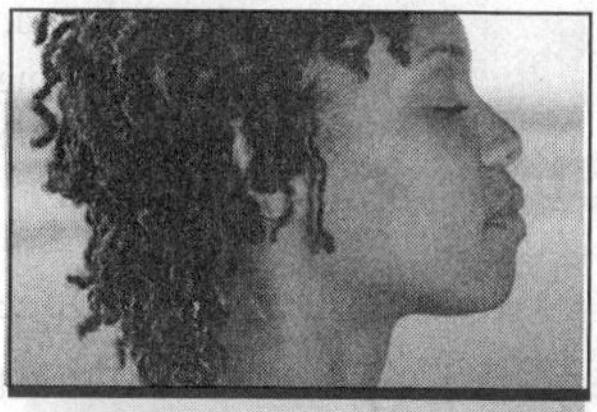

### reflection

*Reflect on the strength and wisdom of women you know.*

*Ask God for strength and wisdom to guide you through this day.*

### read

Esther 1.
See also the Inspire Notes "Influencing Others," "Confidence for Each Day," "Female Ministers and Evangelists" and "Servant-Leadership," and the Women of the Bible Notes "Deborah: An Uncommon Leader," "Huldah: A Prophetess of God," "Esther: More Than a Beauty Queen," "A Virtuous Woman: A Strong Woman, Dependent on God," "Candace: Secure Leader," and "Philip's Daughters: Those Preaching Women."

For the next Women of the Bible note, go to page 586.

**1:22** n Eph 5:22–24
**2:1** o Est 1:19–20; 7:10
**2:5** p Est 3:2
**2:6** q 2Ki 24:6,15; 2Ch 36:10,20
**2:8** r ver 3,15

enter the presence of King Xerxes. Also let the king give her royal position to someone else who is better than she. [20]Then when the king's edict is proclaimed throughout all his vast realm, all the women will respect their husbands, from the least to the greatest."

[21]The king and his nobles were pleased with this advice, so the king did as Memucan proposed. [22]He sent dispatches to all parts of the kingdom, to each province in its own script and to each people in its own language,[n] proclaiming in each people's tongue that every man should be ruler over his own household.

## Esther Made Queen

**2** Later when the anger of King Xerxes had subsided,[o] he remembered Vashti and what she had done and what he had decreed about her. [2]Then the king's personal attendants proposed, "Let a search be made for beautiful young virgins for the king. [3]Let the king appoint commissioners in every province of his realm to bring all these beautiful girls into the harem at the citadel of Susa. Let them be placed under the care of Hegai, the king's eunuch, who is in charge of the women; and let beauty treatments be given to them. [4]Then let the girl who pleases the king be queen instead of Vashti." This advice appealed to the king, and he followed it.

[5]Now there was in the citadel of Susa a Jew of the tribe of Benjamin, named Mordecai son of Jair, the son of Shimei, the son of Kish,[p] [6]who had been carried into exile from Jerusalem by Nebuchadnezzar king of Babylon, among those taken captive with Jehoiachin[a][q] king of Judah. [7]Mordecai had a cousin named Hadassah, whom he had brought up because she had neither father nor mother. This girl, who was also known as Esther, was lovely in form and features, and Mordecai had taken her as his own daughter when her father and mother died.

[8]When the king's order and edict had been proclaimed, many girls were brought to the citadel of Susa[r] and put under the care of Hegai. Esther also was taken to the king's palace and entrusted to Hegai, who had charge of the harem. [9]The girl pleased him and won his favor. Immediately he provided her with her beauty treatments and special food. He assigned to her seven maids selected from the king's palace and moved her and her maids into the best place in the harem.

[10]Esther had not revealed her nationality and family background, because Mordecai had forbidden her to do so.[s] [11]Every day he walked back and forth near the courtyard of the harem to find out how Esther was and what was happening to her.

[12]Before a girl's turn came to go in to King Xerxes, she had to complete twelve months of beauty treatments prescribed for the women, six months with oil of myrrh and six with perfumes and cosmetics. [13]And this is how she would go to the king: Anything she wanted was given her to take with her from the harem to the king's palace. [14]In the evening she would go there and in the morning return to another part of the harem to the care of Shaashgaz, the king's eunuch who was in charge of the concubines. She would not return to the king unless he was pleased with her and summoned her by name.

[15]When the turn came for Esther (the girl Mordecai had adopted, the daughter of his uncle Abihail[t]) to go to the king, she asked for nothing other than what Hegai, the king's eunuch who was in charge of the harem, suggested. And Esther won the favor of everyone who saw her. [16]She was taken to King Xerxes in the royal residence in the tenth month, the month of Tebeth, in the seventh year of his reign.

[17]Now the king was attracted to Esther more than to any of the other women, and she won his favor and approval more than any of the other virgins. So he set a royal crown on her head and made her queen[u] instead of Vashti. [18]And the king gave a great banquet,[v] Esther's banquet, for all his nobles and officials. He proclaimed a holiday throughout the provinces and distributed gifts with royal liberality.[w]

## Mordecai Uncovers a Conspiracy

[19]When the virgins were assembled a second time, Mordecai was sitting at the

**2:10** s ver 20
**2:15** t Est 9:29
**2:17** u Est 1:11
**2:18** v Est 1:3 w Est 1:7

[a] 6 Hebrew *Jeconiah,* a variant of *Jehoiachin*

2:19 x ver 21; Est 3:2
2:20 y ver 10
2:21 z Est 6:2
2:23 a Ps 7:14–16 b Est 6:1; 10:2
3:1 c Nu 24:7
3:5 d Est 5:9
3:6 e Ps 83:4
3:7 f Est 9:24,26

king's gate.[x] 20 But Esther had kept secret her family background and nationality just as Mordecai had told her to do, for she continued to follow Mordecai's instructions as she had done when he was bringing her up.[y]

21 During the time Mordecai was sitting at the king's gate, Bigthana[a] and Teresh, two of the king's officers[z] who guarded the doorway, became angry and conspired to assassinate King Xerxes. 22 But Mordecai found out about the plot and told Queen Esther, who in turn reported it to the king, giving credit to Mordecai. 23 And when the report was investigated and found to be true, the two officials were hanged[a] on a gallows.[b] All this was recorded in the book of the annals[b] in the presence of the king.

## Haman's Plot to Destroy the Jews

**3** After these events, King Xerxes honored Haman son of Hammedatha, the Agagite,[c] elevating him and giving him a seat of honor higher than that of all the other nobles. 2 All the royal officials at the king's gate knelt down and paid honor to Haman, for the king had commanded this concerning him. But Mordecai would not kneel down or pay him honor.

3 Then the royal officials at the king's gate asked Mordecai, "Why do you disobey the king's command?" 4 Day after day they spoke to him but he refused to comply. Therefore they told Haman about it to see whether Mordecai's behavior would be tolerated, for he had told them he was a Jew.

5 When Haman saw that Mordecai would not kneel down or pay him honor, he was enraged.[d] 6 Yet having learned who Mordecai's people were, he scorned the idea of killing only Mordecai. Instead Haman looked for a way to destroy[e] all Mordecai's people, the Jews, throughout the whole kingdom of Xerxes.

7 In the twelfth year of King Xerxes, in the first month, the month of Nisan, they cast the *pur*[f] (that is, the lot) in the presence of Haman to select a day and month. And the lot fell on[c] the twelfth month, the month of Adar.

8 Then Haman said to King Xerxes, "There is a certain people dispersed and scattered among the peoples in all the provinces of your kingdom whose customs[g] are different from those of all other people and who do not obey the king's laws; it is not in the king's best interest to tolerate them.[h] 9 If it pleases the king, let a decree be issued to destroy them, and I will put ten thousand talents[d] of silver into the royal treasury for the men who carry out this business."

10 So the king took his signet ring[i] from his finger and gave it to Haman son of Hammedatha, the Agagite, the enemy of the Jews. 11 "Keep the money," the king said to Haman, "and do with the people as you please."

12 Then on the thirteenth day of the first month the royal secretaries were summoned. They wrote out in the script of each province and in the language of each people all Haman's orders to the king's satraps, the governors of the various provinces and the nobles of the various peoples. These were written in the name of King Xerxes himself and sealed[j] with his own ring. 13 Dispatches were sent by couriers to all the king's provinces with the order to destroy, kill and annihilate all the Jews[k]—young and old, women and little children—on a single day, the thirteenth day of the twelfth month, the month of Adar, and to plunder[l] their goods. 14 A copy of the text of the edict was to be issued as law in every province and made known to the people of every nationality so they would be ready for that day.

15 Spurred on by the king's command, the couriers went out, and the edict was issued in the citadel of Susa. The king and Haman sat down to drink, but the city of Susa was bewildered.[m]

## Mordecai Persuades Esther to Help

**4** When Mordecai learned of all that had been done, he tore his clothes, put on sackcloth and ashes,[n] and went out into the city, wailing loudly and bitterly. 2 But he went only as far as the king's gate, because no one clothed in sackcloth was allowed to enter it. 3 In every province to which the

3:8 g Ac 16:20–21 h Ezr 4:15
3:10 i Ge 41:42; Est 7:6; 8:2
3:12 j 1Ki 21:8; Est 8:8–10
3:13 k Est 8:10–14 l Est 8:11
3:15 m Est 8:15
4:1 n Eze 27:30–31

[a] 21 Hebrew *Bigthan,* a variant of *Bigthana*  [b] 23 Or *were hung* (or *impaled*) *on poles*; similarly elsewhere in Esther
[c] 7 Septuagint; Hebrew does not have *And the lot fell on.*  [d] 9 That is, about 375 tons (about 345 metric tons)

# Esther

## *More Than a Beauty Queen*

The story of Esther reminds women of color that our outward beauty is not the only, or the most important, characteristic we have been blessed to receive. Esther spent 12 months enhancing her physical appearance (see Est 2:12). And she clearly had it going on. She won the favor of King Xerxes over all of the other young ladies who were being pampered and prepared to be queen. She was definitely beautiful.

However, Esther's true worth didn't come from her beauty, and it is not her beauty that has left a lasting impression on Bible readers throughout history. This beauty queen had to make a decision once she heard from her cousin Mordecai about a plan to destroy the Jewish people who lived throughout the empire. She had to approach the king and ask him to stop this plan, to revoke the edict he had been convinced to decree, and to spare her people's lives. She had to be brave to approach the king, so she called for the people to fast; and we remember her famous words: "And if I perish, I perish" (Est 4:16). Esther remembered her people, and she was willing to sacrifice her life to save them.

Esther shows us that we are called to help others, regardless of our position. When we have influence in high places, we should use that influence to help those less fortunate than ourselves. We should use that influence to fight for justice rather than to merely gain a position that makes us look good. Esther reminds us that it's not all about how we look; it's about what we do. While we pour time and money into making sure we look good, let's make sure we *do* good—even when we have to take risks.

—K. Washington

### reflection

*How have you used your influence to help others or help determine the outcome of a situation?*

*Pray for the courage of Esther to do the right thing no matter what the circumstances.*

### read

Esther 2–8.

See also the Inspire Notes "Influencing Others," "Commitment to Community," "Confidence for Each Day," "Vanity," "Female Ministers and Evangelists" and "Servant-Leadership," and the Women of the Bible Notes "Queen Vashti: A Woman of Strength," "A Virtuous Woman: A Strong Woman, Dependent on God," "Candace: Secure Leader" and "Philip's Daughters: Those Preaching Women."

For the next Women of the Bible note, go to page 597.

edict and order of the king came, there was
great mourning among the Jews, with fast-
ing, weeping and wailing. Many lay in sack-
cloth and ashes.
4 When Esther's maids and eunuchs came
and told her about Mordecai, she was in
great distress. She sent clothes for him to
put on instead of his sackcloth, but he would
not accept them. 5 Then Esther summoned
Hathach, one of the king's eunuchs assigned
to attend her, and ordered him to find out
what was troubling Mordecai and why.
6 So Hathach went out to Mordecai in the
open square of the city in front of the king's
gate. 7 Mordecai told him everything that had
happened to him, including the exact amount
of money Haman had promised to pay into
the royal treasury for the destruction of the
Jews.[o] 8 He also gave him a copy of the text of
the edict for their annihilation, which had
been published in Susa, to show to Esther
and explain it to her, and he told him to urge
her to go into the king's presence to beg for
mercy and plead with him for her people.
9 Hathach went back and reported to Es-
ther what Mordecai had said. 10 Then she
instructed him to say to Mordecai, 11 "All the
king's officials and the people of the royal
provinces know that for any man or woman
who approaches the king in the inner court
without being summoned the king has but
one law:[p] that he be put to death. The only
exception to this is for the king to extend the
gold scepter[q] to him and spare his life. But
thirty days have passed since I was called to
go to the king."
12 When Esther's words were reported to
Mordecai, 13 he sent back this answer: "Do
not think that because you are in the king's
house you alone of all the Jews will escape.

*Woman of courage,*

*Stand for truth, remembering*
*always that I stand with you.*

*God*

ESTHER 4:12–14

14 For if you remain silent at this time, relief
and deliverance for the Jews will arise from
another place, but you and your father's
family will perish. And who knows but that
you have come to royal position for such a
time as this?"
15 Then Esther sent this reply to Mordecai:
16 "Go, gather together all the Jews who are
in Susa, and fast for me. Do not eat or drink
for three days, night or day. I and my maids
will fast as you do. When this is done, I will
go to the king, even though it is against the
law. And if I perish, I perish."
17 So Mordecai went away and carried out
all of Esther's instructions.

## Esther's Request to the King

5 On the third day Esther put on her royal
robes[r] and stood in the inner court of
the palace, in front of the king's[s] hall. The
king was sitting on his royal throne in the
hall, facing the entrance. 2 When he saw
Queen Esther standing in the court, he was
pleased with her and held out to her the
gold scepter that was in his hand. So Esther
approached and touched the tip of the scep-
ter.[t]
3 Then the king asked, "What is it, Queen
Esther? What is your request? Even up to
half the kingdom,[u] it will be given you."
4 "If it pleases the king," replied Esther,
"let the king, together with Haman, come to-
day to a banquet I have prepared for him."
5 "Bring Haman at once," the king said,
"so that we may do what Esther asks."
So the king and Haman went to the ban-
quet Esther had prepared. 6 As they were
drinking wine, the king again asked Esther,
"Now what is your petition? It will be given
you. And what is your request? Even up to
half the kingdom, it will be granted."[v]
7 Esther replied, "My petition and my re-
quest is this: 8 If the king regards me with
favor and if it pleases the king to grant my
petition and fulfill my request, let the king
and Haman come tomorrow to the banquet
I will prepare for them. Then I will answer
the king's question."

## Haman's Rage Against Mordecai

9 Haman went out that day happy and in
high spirits. But when he saw Mordecai at

4:7 o Est 3:9
4:11 p Da 2:9 q Est 5:1,2; 8:4
5:1 r Est 4:16 s Est 6:4
5:2 t Est 4:11; 8:4
5:3 u Est 7:2; Mk 6:23
5:6 v Est 7:2

5:10 w Est6:13
5:11 x Est9:7–10,13
5:14 y Est7:9 z Est6:4
6:1 a Da6:18 b Est2:23

the king's gate and observed that he neither rose nor showed fear in his presence, he was filled with rage against Mordecai. 10 Nevertheless, Haman restrained himself and went home.

Calling together his friends and Zeresh,[w] his wife, 11 Haman boasted to them about his vast wealth, his many sons,[x] and all the ways the king had honored him and how he had elevated him above the other nobles and officials. 12 "And that's not all," Haman added. "I'm the only person Queen Esther invited to accompany the king to the banquet she gave. And she has invited me along with the king tomorrow. 13 But all this gives me no satisfaction as long as I see that Jew Mordecai sitting at the king's gate."

14 His wife Zeresh and all his friends said to him, "Have a gallows built, seventy-five feet[a] high,[y] and ask the king in the morning to have Mordecai hanged[z] on it. Then go with the king to the dinner and be happy." This suggestion delighted Haman, and he had the gallows built.

## Mordecai Honored

6 That night the king could not sleep;[a] so he ordered the book of the chronicles,[b] the record of his reign, to be brought in and read to him. 2 It was found recorded there that Mordecai had exposed Bigthana and Teresh, two of the king's officers who guarded the doorway, who had conspired to assassinate King Xerxes.

3 "What honor and recognition has Mordecai received for this?" the king asked.

"Nothing has been done for him," his attendants answered.

4 The king said, "Who is in the court?" Now Haman had just entered the outer court of the palace to speak to the king about hanging Mordecai on the gallows he had erected for him.

5 His attendants answered, "Haman is standing in the court."

"Bring him in," the king ordered.

6 When Haman entered, the king asked him, "What should be done for the man the king delights to honor?"

Now Haman thought to himself, "Who is there that the king would rather honor than me?" 7 So he answered the king, "For the man the king delights to honor, 8 have them bring a royal robe the king has worn and a horse[c] the king has ridden, one with a royal crest placed on its head. 9 Then let the robe and horse be entrusted to one of the king's most noble princes. Let them robe the man the king delights to honor, and lead him on the horse through the city streets, proclaiming before him, 'This is what is done for the man the king delights to honor!'[d]"

10 "Go at once," the king commanded Haman. "Get the robe and the horse and do just as you have suggested for Mordecai the Jew, who sits at the king's gate. Do not neglect anything you have recommended."

11 So Haman got the robe and the horse. He robed Mordecai, and led him on horseback through the city streets, proclaiming before him, "This is what is done for the man the king delights to honor!"

12 Afterward Mordecai returned to the king's gate. But Haman rushed home, with his head covered[e] in grief, 13 and told Zeresh[f] his wife and all his friends everything that had happened to him.

His advisers and his wife Zeresh said to him, "Since Mordecai, before whom your downfall has started, is of Jewish origin, you cannot stand against him—you will surely come to ruin!" 14 While they were still talking with him, the king's eunuchs arrived and hurried Haman away to the banquet[g] Esther had prepared.

## Haman Hanged

7 So the king and Haman went to dine with Queen Esther, 2 and as they were drinking wine on that second day, the king again asked, "Queen Esther, what is your petition? It will be given you. What is your request? Even up to half the kingdom,[h] it will be granted.[i]"

3 Then Queen Esther answered, "If I have found favor with you, O king, and if it pleases your majesty, grant me my life—this is my petition. And spare my people—this is my request. 4 For I and my people have been sold for destruction and slaughter and annihilation.[j] If we had merely been sold as male and female slaves, I would have kept quiet,

6:8 c 1Ki1:33
6:9 d Ge41:43
6:12 e 2Sa15:30
6:13 f Est5:10
6:14 g Est5:8
7:2 h Est5:3 i Est9:12
7:4 j Est3:9

[a] 14 Hebrew *fifty cubits* (about 23 meters)

**7:7** k Est 1:12
**7:8** l Est 1:6
**7:9** m Est 1:10 n Est 5:14 o Ps 7:14–16; Pr 11:5–6
**8:1** p Est 2:7; 7:6

because no such distress would justify disturbing the king.[a]"

[5]King Xerxes asked Queen Esther, "Who is he? Where is the man who has dared to do such a thing?"

[6]Esther said, "The adversary and enemy is this vile Haman."

Then Haman was terrified before the king and queen. [7]The king got up in a rage,[k] left his wine and went out into the palace garden. But Haman, realizing that the king had already decided his fate, stayed behind to beg Queen Esther for his life.

*Heavenly Father,*

*thank you for modern-day Esthers, for those resolute women who are willing to take time out for inner beauty and for development of the spiritual woman.*

*Amen*

ESTHER 7:1–6

[8]Just as the king returned from the palace garden to the banquet hall, Haman was falling on the couch[l] where Esther was reclining.

The king exclaimed, "Will he even molest the queen while she is with me in the house?"

As soon as the word left the king's mouth, they covered Haman's face. [9]Then Harbona,[m] one of the eunuchs attending the king, said, "A gallows seventy-five feet[b] high[n] stands by Haman's house. He had it made for Mordecai, who spoke up to help the king."

The king said, "Hang him on it!"[o] [10]So they hanged Haman on the gallows he had prepared for Mordecai. Then the king's fury subsided.

## The King's Edict in Behalf of the Jews

8 That same day King Xerxes gave Queen Esther the estate of Haman,[p] the enemy of the Jews. And Mordecai came into the presence of the king, for Esther had told how he was related to her. [2]The king took off his signet ring,[q] which he had reclaimed from Haman, and presented it to Mordecai. And Esther appointed him over Haman's estate.

[3]Esther again pleaded with the king, falling at his feet and weeping. She begged him to put an end to the evil plan of Haman the Agagite, which he had devised against the Jews. [4]Then the king extended the gold scepter[r] to Esther and she arose and stood before him.

[5]"If it pleases the king," she said, "and if he regards me with favor and thinks it the right thing to do, and if he is pleased with me, let an order be written overruling the dispatches that Haman son of Hammedatha, the Agagite, devised and wrote to destroy the Jews in all the king's provinces. [6]For how can I bear to see disaster fall on my people? How can I bear to see the destruction of my family?"[s]

[7]King Xerxes replied to Queen Esther and to Mordecai the Jew, "Because Haman attacked the Jews, I have given his estate to Esther, and they have hanged him on the gallows. [8]Now write another decree[t] in the king's name in behalf of the Jews as seems best to you, and seal it with the king's signet ring—for no document written in the king's name and sealed with his ring can be revoked."[u]

[9]At once the royal secretaries were summoned—on the twenty-third day of the third month, the month of Sivan. They wrote out all Mordecai's orders to the Jews, and to the satraps, governors and nobles of the 127 provinces stretching from India to Cush.[c][v] These orders were written in the script of each province and the language of each people and also to the Jews in their own script and language.[w] [10]Mordecai wrote in the name of King Xerxes, sealed the dispatches with the king's signet ring, and sent them by mounted couriers, who rode fast horses especially bred for the king.

[11]The king's edict granted the Jews in every city the right to assemble and protect themselves; to destroy, kill and annihilate any armed force of any nationality or province that might attack them and

**8:2** q Est 3:10
**8:4** r Est 4:11
**8:6** s Est 7:4
**8:8** t Est 3:12–14 u Est 1:19
**8:9** v Est 1:1 w Est 1:22

[a]4 Or *quiet, but the compensation our adversary offers cannot be compared with the loss the king would suffer*
[b]9 Hebrew *fifty cubits* (about 23 meters) [c]9 That is, the upper Nile region

**8:13** x Est 3:14
**8:16** y Ps 97:10–12
**8:17** z Est 9:3
**9:1** a Est 8:12 b Est 3:12–14
**9:2** c Est 8:11,17; Ps 71:13,24

their women and children; and to plunder the property of their enemies. [12]The day appointed for the Jews to do this in all the provinces of King Xerxes was the thirteenth day of the twelfth month, the month of Adar. [13]A copy of the text of the edict was to be issued as law in every province and made known to the people of every nationality so that the Jews would be ready on that day[x] to avenge themselves on their enemies.

[14]The couriers, riding the royal horses, raced out, spurred on by the king's command. And the edict was also issued in the citadel of Susa.

[15]Mordecai left the king's presence wearing royal garments of blue and white, a large crown of gold and a purple robe of fine linen. And the city of Susa held a joyous celebration. [16]For the Jews it was a time of happiness and joy,[y] gladness and honor. [17]In every province and in every city, wherever the edict of the king went, there was joy and gladness among the Jews, with feasting and celebrating. And many people of other nationalities became Jews because fear of the Jews had seized them.[z]

## Triumph of the Jews

9 On the thirteenth day of the twelfth month, the month of Adar,[a] the edict commanded by the king was to be carried out. On this day the enemies of the Jews had hoped to overpower them, but now the tables were turned and the Jews got the upper hand over those who hated them.[b] [2]The Jews assembled in their cities in all the provinces of King Xerxes to attack those seeking their destruction. No one could stand against them,[c] because the people of all the other nationalities were afraid of them. [3]And all

*My child,*

*Focus on me, not on your opposition.*

*Love,*
*Your Way-Maker*

ESTHER 9:1–2

the nobles of the provinces, the satraps, the governors and the king's administrators helped the Jews, because fear of Mordecai had seized them. [4]Mordecai was prominent in the palace; his reputation spread throughout the provinces, and he became more and more powerful.[d]

[5]The Jews struck down all their enemies with the sword, killing and destroying them, and they did what they pleased to those who hated them. [6]In the citadel of Susa, the Jews killed and destroyed five hundred men. [7]They also killed Parshandatha, Dalphon, Aspatha, [8]Poratha, Adalia, Aridatha, [9]Parmashta, Arisai, Aridai and Vaizatha, [10]the ten sons[e] of Haman son of Hammedatha, the enemy of the Jews. But they did not lay their hands on the plunder.[f]

[11]The number of those slain in the citadel of Susa was reported to the king that same day. [12]The king said to Queen Esther, "The Jews have killed and destroyed five hundred men and the ten sons of Haman in the citadel of Susa. What have they done in the rest of the king's provinces? Now what is your petition? It will be given you. What is your request? It will also be granted."[g]

[13]"If it pleases the king," Esther answered, "give the Jews in Susa permission to carry out this day's edict tomorrow also, and let Haman's ten sons be hanged on gallows."

[14]So the king commanded that this be done. An edict was issued in Susa, and they hanged the ten sons of Haman. [15]The Jews in Susa came together on the fourteenth day of the month of Adar, and they put to death in Susa three hundred men, but they did not lay their hands on the plunder.[h]

[16]Meanwhile, the remainder of the Jews who were in the king's provinces also assembled to protect themselves and get relief from their enemies. They killed seventy-five thousand of them but did not lay their hands on the plunder. [17]This happened on the thirteenth day of the month of Adar, and on the fourteenth they rested and made it a day of feasting and joy.

## Purim Celebrated

[18]The Jews in Susa, however, had assembled on the thirteenth and fourteenth, and

**9:4** d 2Sa 3:1; 1Ch 11:9
**9:10** e Est 5:11 f Est 8:11
**9:12** g Est 5:6; 7:2
**9:15** h Est 8:11

**9:19** i ver 22; Ne 8:10,12
**9:22** j Ne 8:12; Ps 30:11–12
**9:24** k Est 3:7
**9:25** l Ps 7:16

then on the fifteenth they rested and made it a day of feasting and joy.

19 That is why rural Jews—those living in villages—observe the fourteenth of the month of Adar as a day of joy and feasting, a day for giving presents to each other.[i]

20 Mordecai recorded these events, and he sent letters to all the Jews throughout the provinces of King Xerxes, near and far, 21 to have them celebrate annually the fourteenth and fifteenth days of the month of Adar 22 as the time when the Jews got relief from their enemies, and as the month when their sorrow was turned into joy and their mourning into a day of celebration.[j] He wrote them to observe the days as days of feasting and joy and giving presents of food to one another and gifts to the poor.

*Lord,*

*Thank you for helping me understand the value of godly achievement and success. Help me to make decisions in the light of your truth and to make the most of every opportunity. Be glorified today in all I do and say.*

*Amen*

ESTHER 9:18–22

23 So the Jews agreed to continue the celebration they had begun, doing what Mordecai had written to them. 24 For Haman son of Hammedatha, the Agagite, the enemy of all the Jews, had plotted against the Jews to destroy them and had cast the *pur*[k] (that is, the lot) for their ruin and destruction. 25 But when the plot came to the king's attention,[a] he issued written orders that the evil scheme Haman had devised against the Jews should come back onto his own head,[l] and that he and his sons should be hanged on the gallows.[m] 26 (Therefore these days were called Purim, from the word *pur.*[n]) Because of everything written in this letter and because of what they had seen and what had happened to them, 27 the Jews took it upon themselves to establish the custom that they and their descendants and all who join them should without fail observe these two days every year, in the way prescribed and at the time appointed. 28 These days should be remembered and observed in every generation by every family, and in every province and in every city. And these days of Purim should never cease to be celebrated by the Jews, nor should the memory of them die out among their descendants.

29 So Queen Esther, daughter of Abihail,[o] along with Mordecai the Jew, wrote with full authority to confirm this second letter concerning Purim. 30 And Mordecai sent letters to all the Jews in the 127 provinces[p] of the kingdom of Xerxes—words of goodwill and assurance— 31 to establish these days of Purim at their designated times, as Mordecai the Jew and Queen Esther had decreed for them, and as they had established for themselves and their descendants in regard to their times of fasting and lamentation.[q] 32 Esther's decree confirmed these regulations about Purim, and it was written down in the records.

## The Greatness of Mordecai

**10** King Xerxes imposed tribute throughout the empire, to its distant shores.[r] 2 And all his acts of power and might, together with a full account of the greatness of Mordecai[s] to which the king had raised him, are they not written in the book of the annals[t] of the kings of Media and Persia? 3 Mordecai the Jew was second in rank[u] to King Xerxes,[v] preeminent among the Jews, and held in high esteem by his many fellow Jews, because he worked for the good of his people and spoke up for the welfare of all the Jews.[w]

**9:25** m Est 7:10
**9:26** n ver 20
**9:29** o Est 2:15
**9:30** p Est 1:1
**9:31** q Est 4:1–3
**10:1** r Ps 72:10; Isa 24:15
**10:2** s Est 8:15; 9:4 t Est 2:23
**10:3** u Ge 41:43 v Ge 41:40 w Ne 2:10

[a] 25 Or *when Esther came before the king*

# Job

## OVERVIEW

The book of Job opens with dialogue between God and Satan concerning Job, a man who lived during the early period of the Old Testament, perhaps in the time of Abraham. Although Job was not a Hebrew, he was a devout follower of God. Satan insisted that Job only served God because God had blessed Job with family and wealth. So God allowed Satan to do anything to prove Job's faithfulness—anything except striking Job himself. As a result, Job suffered the loss of all his livestock and servants, plus the devastation of losing every one of his ten children—all in one day. In all of his pain, Job did not curse God, but still trusted in him.

At another presentation before God, Satan insisted that if Job suffered physically, he would curse God. God gave Satan permission to test Job a second time, but not to take his life. Job was covered with painful sores from the top of his head to the bottom of his feet. Job's wife chided him for his integrity, saying, "Curse God and die!" (Job 2:9). Job refused, however, because he knew that both good and bad can happen to anyone.

Three of Job's friends came and sat with him in silence for seven days and seven nights. Job's friends then asserted that his tragedies were the consequence of some sin against God. Job refused to admit that he had sinned, and he longed for an advocate to stand between him and God to vindicate him for his suffering. God appeared to Job in a storm, asking questions that no one can answer. Afterward Job understood that God is beyond human comprehension. Job's friends were scolded by God for their remarks. But after Job prayed for his friends, the Lord blessed Job even beyond his former wealth. In the end, Job was blessed with ten more children and lived to see their children to the fourth generation.

Jesus Christ is the Advocate for women who put their trust in him. He speaks in their defense before the Father (see 1Jn 2:1) and against the devil, who accuses them day and night (see Rev 12:10). That's something to be thankful for! After reading the book of Job with a discerning heart, you may also want to pray that God will give you a heart of compassion for the suffering.

## OUTLINE

I. Job's First and Second Tests (1:1—2:13)
II. Discourse Between Job and His Friends (3:1—37:24)
III. God Speaks to Job (38:1—41:34)
IV. Job's Blessings (42:1–17)

### SCANNABLE FACTS:

**Author:** Unknown

**Time Written:** Perhaps many years after the time of Job himself, which may have been as early as 2000 B.C.

**Theme to Note:** Suffering is universal, but God doesn't desert his faithful ones

**Notable Woman:** Job's wife

1:1 a Eze 14:14,20; Jas 5:11 b Ge 6:9; 17:1
1:2 c Job 42:13
1:5 d Ge 8:20 e 1Ki 21:10,13
1:7 f 1Pe 5:8

## Prologue

1 In the land of Uz there lived a man whose name was Job.[a] This man was blameless[b] and upright; he feared God and shunned evil. 2 He had seven sons and three daughters,[c] 3 and he owned seven thousand sheep, three thousand camels, five hundred yoke of oxen and five hundred donkeys, and had a large number of servants. He was the greatest man among all the people of the East.

4 His sons used to take turns holding feasts in their homes, and they would invite their three sisters to eat and drink with them. 5 When a period of feasting had run its course, Job would send and have them purified. Early in the morning he would sacrifice a burnt offering[d] for each of them, thinking, "Perhaps my children have sinned and cursed God[e] in their hearts." This was Job's regular custom.

## Job's First Test

6 One day the angels[*a*] came to present themselves before the LORD, and Satan[*b*] also came with them. 7 The LORD said to Satan, "Where have you come from?"

Satan answered the LORD, "From roaming through the earth and going back and forth in it."[f]

8 Then the LORD said to Satan, "Have you considered my servant Job? There is no one on earth like him; he is blameless and upright, a man who fears God and shuns evil."

9 "Does Job fear God for nothing?" Satan replied. 10 "Have you not put a hedge around him and his household and everything he has?[g] You have blessed the work of his hands, so that his flocks and herds are spread throughout the land.[h] 11 But stretch out your hand and strike everything he has,[i] and he will surely curse you to your face."[j]

12 The LORD said to Satan, "Very well, then, everything he has is in your hands, but on the man himself do not lay a finger."

Then Satan went out from the presence of the LORD.

13 One day when Job's sons and daughters were feasting and drinking wine at the oldest brother's house, 14 a messenger came to Job and said, "The oxen were plowing and the donkeys were grazing nearby, 15 and the Sabeans attacked and carried them off. They put the servants to the sword, and I am the only one who has escaped to tell you!"

16 While he was still speaking, another messenger came and said, "The fire of God fell from the sky and burned up the sheep and the servants,[k] and I am the only one who has escaped to tell you!"

17 While he was still speaking, another messenger came and said, "The Chaldeans[l] formed three raiding parties and swept down on your camels and carried them off. They put the servants to the sword, and I am the only one who has escaped to tell you!"

18 While he was still speaking, yet another messenger came and said, "Your sons and daughters were feasting and drinking wine at the oldest brother's house, 19 when suddenly a mighty wind swept in from the desert and struck the four corners of the

1:10 g Ps 34:7 h Job 29:6; Ps 128:1–2
1:11 i Job 19:21 j Job 2:5
1:16 k Lev 10:2; Nu 11:1–3
1:17 l Ge 11:28,31

[a] 6 Hebrew *the sons of God* [b] 6 *Satan* means *accuser.*

## The African Presence

### Job 1:15

The Sabeans were descendants of Cush, who was a son of Ham (see Ge 10:7; 1Ch 1:9). Also called Sheba in Job 6:19; Sheba was in southern Arabia (present-day Yemen), across the Red Sea from present-day Ethiopia. The queen of Sheba was well known for visiting King Solomon (see 1Ki 10:1–13; she is called the "Queen of the South" in Mt 12:42). The Sabeans traded in gold and incense (see Isa 60:6; Jer 6:20) as well as slaves (see Joel 3:8).

1:20
m Ge 37:29
n 1Pe 5:6

house. It collapsed on them and they are
dead, and I am the only one who has es-
caped to tell you!"
20 At this, Job got up and tore his robe[m]
and shaved his head. Then he fell to the
ground in worship[n] 21 and said:

"Naked I came from my mother's womb,
and naked I will depart.[a][o]
The LORD gave and the LORD has taken
away;
may the name of the LORD be praised."[p]

[a] 21 Or *will return there*

1:21
o Ecc 5:15; 1Ti 6:7
p Job 2:10; Eph 5:20; 1Th 5:18

# Inspire

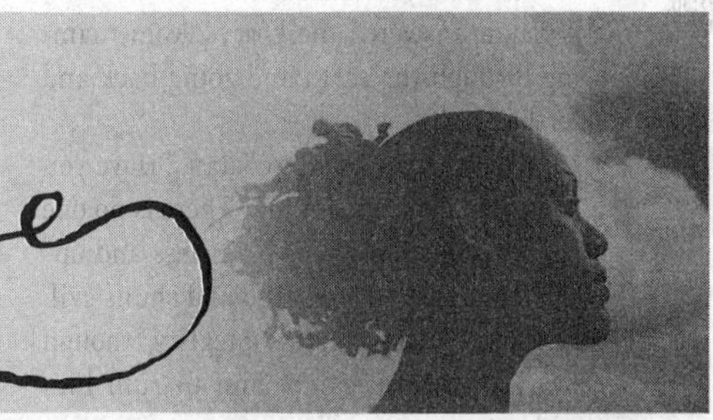

## SUFFERING

The Bible does not give any easy answers to the questions surrounding suffering. However, suffering is assured, and sufferers can be reassured through God's Word. Job was a "blameless and upright" man who feared God and shunned evil (see Job 2:3). Yet even he experienced severe pain and never determined the reason why God allowed him to suffer. Sometimes in our suffering our human instinct leads us to ask, "Why, God?" While we may not receive an answer, we are encouraged to remain patient (see Jas 5:7–8).

How does one remain patient in view of continuous, seemingly endless and meaningless suffering? Being patient in the midst of suffering is a difficult task, but remember that even in suffering the sovereignty of God prevails. Job persevered and was finally restored to health. He was also blessed with more children and more wealth (see Job 42:7–17).

We may not understand the reasons why we suffer, but we can be assured that God is our strength; he can give us supernatural power to endure. God is our help in our time of need. In fact, God knows exactly what we need. He knows our need better than we do, for we don't see the full picture of what we're going through. God feeds our every hunger. God walks beside us night and day through every moment of our journey. Even in our suffering, God is with us.

—A. Gordon

### read

Job 1–2; see also 2 Kings 4:8–37.

See also the Inspire Notes "Courage to Heal," "Distress," "Waiting on God," "The Paradox of Life and Suffering," "Praying for Patience" and "Peace," and the Women of the Bible Notes "Rizpah: A Grieving Mother," "The Shunammite Woman: Our Sister's Grief Is Our Grief," "Job's Wife: She Was Tested Too" and "Hemorrhaging Woman: Faith to Press In."

### WOMAN of COLOR

How does knowing God is sovereign help you handle suffering?

For the next Inspire note, go to page 601.

[22]In all this, Job did not sin by charging God with wrongdoing.[q]

## Job's Second Test

2 On another day the angels[a] came to present themselves before the LORD, and Satan also came with them[r] to present himself before him. [2]And the LORD said to Satan, "Where have you come from?"

Satan answered the LORD, "From roaming through the earth and going back and forth in it."

[3]Then the LORD said to Satan, "Have you considered my servant Job? There is no one on earth like him; he is blameless and upright, a man who fears God and shuns evil. And he still maintains his integrity,[s] though you incited me against him to ruin him without any reason."[t]

[4]"Skin for skin!" Satan replied. "A man will give all he has for his own life. [5]But stretch out your hand and strike his flesh and bones,[u] and he will surely curse you to your face."[v]

[6]The LORD said to Satan, "Very well, then, he is in your hands; but you must spare his life."

[7]So Satan went out from the presence of the LORD and afflicted Job with painful sores from the soles of his feet to the top of his head. [8]Then Job took a piece of broken pottery and scraped himself with it as he sat among the ashes.[w]

[9]His wife said to him, "Are you still holding on to your integrity? Curse God and die!"

[10]He replied, "You are talking like a foolish[b] woman. Shall we accept good from God, and not trouble?"[x]

In all this, Job did not sin in what he said.

## Job's Three Friends

[11]When Job's three friends, Eliphaz the Temanite, Bildad the Shuhite[y] and Zophar the Naamathite, heard about all the troubles that had come upon him, they set out from their homes and met together by agreement to go and sympathize with him and comfort him.[z] [12]When they saw him from a distance, they could hardly recognize him; they began to weep aloud, and they tore their robes and sprinkled dust on their heads.[a] [13]Then they sat on the ground with him for seven days and seven nights.[b] No one said a word to him, because they saw how great his suffering was.

## Job Speaks

3 After this, Job opened his mouth and cursed the day of his birth. [2]He said:

[3]"May the day of my birth perish,
  and the night it was said, 'A boy is
    born!'[c]
[4]That day—may it turn to darkness;
  may God above not care about it;
  may no light shine upon it.
[5]May darkness and deep shadow[c] claim it
    once more;
  may a cloud settle over it;
  may blackness overwhelm its light.
[6]That night—may thick darkness seize it;
  may it not be included among the days
    of the year

1:22 q Job 2:10
2:1 r Job 1:6
2:3 s Job 27:6 t Job 9:17
2:5 u Job 19:20 v Job 1:11
2:8 w Job 42:6; Eze 27:30; Mt 11:21
2:10 x Job 1:21
2:11 y Ge 25:2 z Job 42:11
2:12 a La 2:10; Eze 27:30
2:13 b Ge 50:10
3:3 c Jer 20:14–18

[a]1 Hebrew *the sons of God* [b]10 The Hebrew word rendered *foolish* denotes moral deficiency. [c]5 Or *and the shadow of death*

### *The African Presence*

**Job 2:11**

Eliphaz the Temanite was descended from one of the 12 sons of Ishmael (see Ge 25:13–15), who was born to Abraham by Hagar the Egyptian. Bildad the Shuhite was a descendant of Abraham and Keturah (see Ge 25:2 and the African Presence note on Ge 25:1–2).

# Job's Wife

## She Was Tested Too

There was once a woman who lived in the land of Uz. She had a husband by the name of Job. The Bible says that he was a faithful man. Can we not assume that she was a faithful woman also? They had seven sons and three daughters. They had numerous livestock and a number of servants. Job is described as "the greatest man among all the people of the East" (Job 1:3), so we can assume that Job's wife was the greatest woman.

Then, at the hand of Satan, the test came. It is traditionally called "Job's Test," but it was "Mrs. Job's Test" as well. Their livestock and servants were destroyed, their assets were lost and all ten of their children were killed. The Biblical camera then focuses on Job's grief, giving no attention to Mrs. Job. Indeed, the heavenly wager that had been placed on her husband had destroyed her world too. The pain intensified when her husband was stricken with sores all over his body. We should not be surprised that her faith faltered and she cried out to Job, "Are you still holding on to your integrity? Curse God and die!" (Job 2:9). These are the words that have provoked commentators, past and present, to scorn Mrs. Job. Although Satan surely used her words to tempt Job (compare Job 2:9 with Job 2:5), anyone who has experienced great loss can understand her outburst. She, too, suffered as she watched the one she loved endure such great pain. She also was in mourning, for she also had lost her sons and daughters. It is probable that she suggested death to Job because death is what she wished for herself. She felt that faith and courage were unattainable at that moment. Furthermore, haven't we all said things for which we have had to repent?

Job 42:10–13 tells us that the Lord blessed the latter part of Job's life with double the earthly possessions and ten more children. We can safely assume that the mother of the last ten children was the mother of the first ten. Restoration and reconciliation, then, were Mrs. Job's, just as they were Job's. As we reflect on this beleaguered woman, we can find comfort in the hope of restoration and reconciliation when we endure suffering.

—M. McCollins Flake

### reflection

*Do you need restoration and reconciliation?*

*Reflect on the story of Job's wife to inspire you to keep your faith in God. Share her story with someone you know who needs restoration and reconciliation.*

### read

Job 1:1—2:10; 42:10–13. See also the Inspire Notes "Suffering," "God Is in Control" and "The Paradox of Life and Suffering," and the Women of the Bible Notes "Bathsheba: A Silent Affair," "Rizpah: A Grieving Mother" and "Ezekiel's Wife: On God's Stage."

For the next Women of the Bible note, go to page 736.

**3:11**
d Job 10:18

**3:21**
e Rev 9:6

**3:23**
f La 3:7

**3:24**
g Ps 42:3,4

nor be entered in any of the months.
7 May that night be barren;
may no shout of joy be heard in it.
8 May those who curse days[a] curse that day,
those who are ready to rouse Leviathan.
9 May its morning stars become dark;
may it wait for daylight in vain
and not see the first rays of dawn,
10 for it did not shut the doors of the womb on me
to hide trouble from my eyes.

11 "Why did I not perish at birth,
and die as I came from the womb?[d]
12 Why were there knees to receive me
and breasts that I might be nursed?
13 For now I would be lying down in peace;
I would be asleep and at rest
14 with kings and counselors of the earth,
who built for themselves places now lying in ruins,
15 with rulers who had gold,
who filled their houses with silver.
16 Or why was I not hidden in the ground like a stillborn child,
like an infant who never saw the light of day?
17 There the wicked cease from turmoil,
and there the weary are at rest.
18 Captives also enjoy their ease;
they no longer hear the slave driver's shout.
19 The small and the great are there,
and the slave is freed from his master.

20 "Why is light given to those in misery,
and life to the bitter of soul,
21 to those who long for death that does not come,[e]
who search for it more than for hidden treasure,
22 who are filled with gladness
and rejoice when they reach the grave?
23 Why is life given to a man
whose way is hidden,
whom God has hedged in?[f]
24 For sighing comes to me instead of food;
my groans pour out like water.[g]
25 What I feared has come upon me;
what I dreaded has happened to me.
26 I have no peace, no quietness;
I have no rest, but only turmoil."

## Eliphaz

4 Then Eliphaz the Temanite replied:

2 "If someone ventures a word with you, will you be impatient?
But who can keep from speaking?
3 Think how you have instructed many,
how you have strengthened feeble hands.[h]
4 Your words have supported those who stumbled;
you have strengthened faltering knees.[i]
5 But now trouble comes to you, and you are discouraged;
it strikes[j] you, and you are dismayed.[k]
6 Should not your piety be your confidence[l]
and your blameless[m] ways your hope?

7 "Consider now: Who, being innocent, has ever perished?
Where were the upright ever destroyed?[n]
8 As I have observed, those who plow evil
and those who sow trouble reap it.[o]
9 At the breath of God[p] they are destroyed;
at the blast of his anger they perish.
10 The lions may roar and growl,
yet the teeth of the great lions are broken.[q]
11 The lion perishes for lack of prey,[r]
and the cubs of the lioness are scattered.

12 "A word was secretly brought to me,
my ears caught a whisper[s] of it.
13 Amid disquieting dreams in the night,
when deep sleep falls on men,[t]
14 fear and trembling seized me
and made all my bones shake.
15 A spirit glided past my face,
and the hair on my body stood on end.
16 It stopped,
but I could not tell what it was.
A form stood before my eyes,
and I heard a hushed voice:
17 'Can a mortal be more righteous than God?[u]

**4:3**
h Isa 35:3

**4:4**
i Isa 35:3; Heb 12:12

**4:5**
j Job 19:21
k Job 6:14

**4:6**
l Pr 3:26
m Job 1:1

**4:7**
n Ps 37:25

**4:8**
o Pr 22:8; Hos 10:13; Gal 6:7–8

**4:9**
p Isa 30:33

**4:10**
q Ps 58:6

**4:11**
r Ps 34:10

**4:12**
s Job 26:14

**4:13**
t Job 33:15

**4:17**
u Job 9:2

[a] 8 Or *the sea*

Can a man be more pure than his
Maker?[v]
18 If God places no trust in his servants,
if he charges his angels with error,[w]
19 how much more those who live in houses
of clay,[x]
whose foundations[y] are in the dust,
who are crushed more readily than a
moth!
20 Between dawn and dusk they are broken
to pieces;
unnoticed, they perish forever.[z]
21 Are not the cords of their tent pulled up,
so that they die without wisdom?'[a][a]

5 "Call if you will, but who will answer
you?
To which of the holy ones[b] will you
turn?
2 Resentment kills a fool,
and envy slays the simple.[c]
3 I myself have seen a fool taking root,[d]
but suddenly his house was cursed.
4 His children are far from safety,
crushed in court without a defender.
5 The hungry consume his harvest,
taking it even from among thorns,
and the thirsty pant after his wealth.
6 For hardship does not spring from the
soil,
nor does trouble sprout from the
ground.
7 Yet man is born to trouble
as surely as sparks fly upward.

8 "But if it were I, I would appeal to God;
I would lay my cause before him.
9 He performs wonders that cannot be
fathomed,
miracles that cannot be counted.
10 He bestows rain on the earth;
he sends water upon the countryside.
11 The lowly he sets on high,[e]
and those who mourn are lifted to
safety.
12 He thwarts the plans[f] of the crafty,
so that their hands achieve no success.
13 He catches the wise in their craftiness,
and the schemes of the wily are swept
away.
14 Darkness comes upon them in the
daytime;
at noon they grope as in the night.
15 He saves the needy[g] from the sword in
their mouth;
he saves them from the clutches of the
powerful.
16 So the poor have hope,
and injustice shuts its mouth.[h]

17 "Blessed is the man whom God corrects;
so do not despise the discipline[i] of the
Almighty.[b][j]
18 For he wounds, but he also binds up;
he injures, but his hands also heal.
19 From six calamities he will rescue you;
in seven no harm will befall you.[k]
20 In famine[l] he will ransom you from
death,
and in battle from the stroke of the
sword.
21 You will be protected from the lash of the
tongue,[m]
and need not fear when destruction
comes.
22 You will laugh at destruction and
famine,
and need not fear the beasts of the
earth.[n]
23 For you will have a covenant with the
stones of the field,
and the wild animals will be at peace
with you.[o]
24 You will know that your tent is secure;
you will take stock of your property
and find nothing missing.
25 You will know that your children will be
many,[p]
and your descendants like the grass of
the earth.[q]
26 You will come to the grave in full vigor,
like sheaves gathered in season.

27 "We have examined this, and it is true.
So hear it and apply it to yourself."

## Job

6 Then Job replied:

2 "If only my anguish could be weighed
and all my misery be placed on the
scales![r]
3 It would surely outweigh the sand of the
seas—

**4:17** v Job 35:10
**4:18** w Job 15:15
**4:19** x Job 10:9; y Job 22:16
**4:20** z Job 20:7; Ps 90:5–6
**4:21** a Job 36:12
**5:1** b Job 15:15
**5:2** c Pr 12:16
**5:3** d Jer 12:2
**5:11** e Ps 113:7–8
**5:12** f Ne 4:15; Ps 33:10
**5:15** g Ps 35:10
**5:16** h Ps 107:42
**5:17** i Ps 94:12; j Heb 12:5–11
**5:19** k Ps 34:19; 91:10
**5:20** l Ps 33:19
**5:21** m Ps 31:20
**5:22** n Ps 91:13
**5:23** o Isa 11:6–9
**5:25** p Ps 112:2; q Ps 72:16
**6:2** r Job 31:6

[a]21 Some interpreters end the quotation after verse 17. [b]17 Hebrew *Shaddai*; here and throughout Job

**6:4** s Ps 38:2 t Job 21:20 u Ps 88:15–18
**6:10** v Job 23:12
**6:13** w Job 26:2
**6:15** x Ps 38:11; Jer 15:18
**6:17** y Job 24:19
**6:19** z Ge 25:15

no wonder my words have been
impetuous.
4 The arrows[s] of the Almighty are in me,
my spirit drinks[t] in their poison;
God's terrors are marshaled
against me.[u]
5 Does a wild donkey bray when it has
grass,
or an ox bellow when it has fodder?
6 Is tasteless food eaten without salt,
or is there flavor in the white of an
egg[a]?
7 I refuse to touch it;
such food makes me ill.

8 "Oh, that I might have my request,
that God would grant what I hope
for,
9 that God would be willing to crush me,
to let loose his hand and cut me off!
10 Then I would still have this
consolation—
my joy in unrelenting pain—
that I had not denied the words[v] of the
Holy One.

11 "What strength do I have, that I should
still hope?
What prospects, that I should be
patient?
12 Do I have the strength of stone?
Is my flesh bronze?
13 Do I have any power to help myself,[w]
now that success has been driven
from me?

14 "A despairing man should have the
devotion of his friends,
even though he forsakes the fear of the
Almighty.
15 But my brothers are as undependable as
intermittent streams,[x]
as the streams that overflow
16 when darkened by thawing ice
and swollen with melting snow,
17 but that cease to flow in the dry season,
and in the heat[y] vanish from their
channels.
18 Caravans turn aside from their routes;
they go up into the wasteland and
perish.
19 The caravans of Tema[z] look for water,
the traveling merchants of Sheba look
in hope.
20 They are distressed, because they had
been confident;
they arrive there, only to be
disappointed.[a]
21 Now you too have proved to be of no help;
you see something dreadful and are
afraid.[b]
22 Have I ever said, 'Give something on my
behalf,
pay a ransom for me from your wealth,
23 deliver me from the hand of the enemy,
ransom me from the clutches of the
ruthless'?

24 "Teach me, and I will be quiet;
show me where I have been wrong.
25 How painful are honest words!
But what do your arguments prove?
26 Do you mean to correct what I say,
and treat the words of a despairing
man as wind?[c]
27 You would even cast lots[d] for the
fatherless
and barter away your friend.

28 "But now be so kind as to look at me.
Would I lie to your face?[e]
29 Relent, do not be unjust;
reconsider, for my integrity is at
stake.[b]
30 Is there any wickedness on my lips?
Can my mouth not discern[f] malice?

7 "Does not man have hard service[g] on
earth?
Are not his days like those of a hired
man?[h]
2 Like a slave longing for the evening
shadows,
or a hired man waiting eagerly for his
wages,
3 so I have been allotted months of futility,
and nights of misery have been
assigned to me.
4 When I lie down I think, 'How long before
I get up?'[i]
The night drags on, and I toss till dawn.
5 My body is clothed with worms and
scabs,
my skin is broken and festering.

**6:20** a Jer 14:3
**6:21** b Ps 38:11
**6:26** c Job 8:2
**6:27** d Joel 3:3
**6:28** e Job 27:4
**6:30** f Job 12:11
**7:1** g Job 14:14 h Job 14:6
**7:4** i Dt 28:67

[a]6 The meaning of the Hebrew for this phrase is uncertain. [b]29 Or *my righteousness still stands*

# Inspire leadership FOCUS

## PATIENCE

We live in a "microwave culture." We can prepare a complete meal in minutes. We can research something on the Internet and within seconds have more information than we can possibly read. In a society that moves quickly and delivers results immediately, we've come to expect our entire life to travel at space-shuttle speed. This is especially true of us as women and leaders. With days filled with projects and meetings and overflowing schedules, we expect life to move forward on our timeline.

However, there are times when circumstances, situations or conditions force us to slow down or even stop. There are times when projects and goals are just not happening in our time frame. It's difficult to handle those moments. How can we sit back and wait on the Lord when so much is expected of us—and when we expect so much of ourselves? How can we develop patience when our society doesn't reward patience or see it as a virtue? Yet, in this world that is always in a hurry, God will sometimes make us "slow our roll." He will sometimes put us in holding patterns and make us wait—and we are to be still and stay . . . with patience.

If anyone was ever forced into a holding pattern, it was Job. And adding insult to injury, his "friends" proclaimed that surely Job had sinned to cause such suffering. In response, Job said, "What strength do I have, that I should still hope? What prospects, that I should be patient?" (Job 6:11). Yet the Lord did good things in Job's life through his afflictions, and Job is held up as an example of patience: "You have heard of Job's perseverance and have seen what the Lord finally brought about. The Lord is full of compassion and mercy" (Jas 5:11).

As Christian leaders, developing patience may be challenging, but it is a mandate. God calls us to be still and learn the lessons he has for us. There are many reasons why God will slow us down or even stop us. Maybe he wants to build our faith. Or possibly he knows that as we sit still, we will listen—we will block out all other sounds and hear his voice. And sometimes God is teaching those around us valuable lessons.

Scripture tells us that during waiting moments, God can renew us and restore our strength (see Isa 40:29–31). We learn the lessons of fortitude and perseverance. While challenging, there is always a purpose in our waiting—to learn more, to grow more—and eventually, waiting will allow us to do more. Patience tests our faith, and our faith grows with patience. This is one of the greatest lessons we can learn and teach others in this get-up-and-go world.

—V. Murray

**read**

Job 6; James 1:2–4; 5:7–11.

**See also** the Inspire Notes "Waiting on God" and "Praying for Patience," and the Women of the Bible Notes "Leah: Courage, Resistance and Struggle," "Job's Wife: She Was Tested Too" and "The Canaanite Woman: Persistence Pays Off."

**WOMAN of COLOR**

Reflect on lessons you've learned during your waiting moments. How did those lessons help you to grow? Remember them as you continue to wait on God today.

For the next Inspire note, go to page 620.

**7:6** j Job 9:25 k Job 13:15
**7:7** l Ps 78:39
**7:8** m Job 20:7,9,21
**7:9** n Job 11:8 o 2Sa 12:23
**7:11** p Ps 40:9 q 1Sa 1:10
**7:13** r Job 9:27
**7:16** s Job 10:1
**7:17** t Ps 8:4; 144:3; Heb 2:6
**7:20** u Job 35:6
**7:21** v Job 10:14

6 “My days are swifter than a weaver’s
shuttle,[j]
and they come to an end without
hope.[k]
7 Remember, O God, that my life is but a
breath;[l]
my eyes will never see happiness
again.
8 The eye that now sees me will see me no
longer;
you will look for me, but I will be no
more.[m]
9 As a cloud vanishes and is gone,
so he who goes down to the grave[a][n]
does not return.[o]
10 He will never come to his house again;
his place will know him no more.

11 “Therefore I will not keep silent;[p]
I will speak out in the anguish of my
spirit,
I will complain in the bitterness of my
soul.[q]
12 Am I the sea, or the monster of the deep,
that you put me under guard?
13 When I think my bed will comfort me
and my couch will ease my complaint,[r]
14 even then you frighten me with dreams
and terrify me with visions,
15 so that I prefer strangling and death,
rather than this body of mine.
16 I despise my life;[s] I would not live forever.
Let me alone; my days have no
meaning.

17 “What is man that you make so much of
him,
that you give him so much attention,[t]
18 that you examine him every morning
and test him every moment?
19 Will you never look away from me,
or let me alone even for an instant?
20 If I have sinned, what have I done to you,[u]
O watcher of men?
Why have you made me your target?
Have I become a burden to you?[b]
21 Why do you not pardon my offenses
and forgive my sins?[v]
For I will soon lie down in the dust;
you will search for me, but I will be no
more.”

## Bildad

8 Then Bildad the Shuhite replied:

2 “How long will you say such things?
Your words are a blustering wind.
3 Does God pervert justice?[w]
Does the Almighty pervert what is
right?[x]
4 When your children sinned against him,
he gave them over to the penalty of
their sin.[y]
5 But if you will look to God
and plead with the Almighty,
6 if you are pure and upright,
even now he will rouse himself on your
behalf
and restore you to your rightful place.
7 Your beginnings will seem humble,
so prosperous will your future be.

8 “Ask the former generations[z]
and find out what their fathers
learned,
9 for we were born only yesterday and
know nothing,[a]
and our days on earth are but a
shadow.[b]
10 Will they not instruct you and tell you?
Will they not bring forth words from
their understanding?
11 Can papyrus grow tall where there is no
marsh?
Can reeds thrive without water?
12 While still growing and uncut,
they wither more quickly than grass.
13 Such is the destiny of all who forget God;
so perishes the hope of the godless.[c]
14 What he trusts in is fragile[c];
what he relies on is a spider’s web.[d]
15 He leans on his web,[e] but it gives way;
he clings to it, but it does not hold.
16 He is like a well-watered plant in the
sunshine,
spreading its shoots[f] over the garden;[g]
17 it entwines its roots around a pile of
rocks
and looks for a place among the stones.
18 But when it is torn from its spot,
that place disowns it and says, ‘I never
saw you.’

**8:3** w Ro 3:5 x Ge 18:25
**8:4** y Job 1:19
**8:8** z Dt 4:32; 32:7
**8:9** a Ge 47:9 b 1Ch 29:15
**8:13** c Job 11:20
**8:14** d Isa 59:5
**8:15** e Job 27:18
**8:16** f Ps 80:11 g Ps 37:35

[a]9 Hebrew *Sheol* [b]20 A few manuscripts of the Masoretic Text, an ancient Hebrew scribal tradition and Septuagint; most manuscripts of the Masoretic Text *I have become a burden to myself.* [c]14 The meaning of the Hebrew for this word is uncertain.

**8:21**
h Ps 126:2

**8:22**
i Ps 35:26; 109:29

**9:2**
j Ro 3:20

**9:4**
k 2Ch 13:12

**9:6**
l Isa 2:21; Heb 12:26

19 Surely its life withers away,
and[a] from the soil other plants grow.
20 "Surely God does not reject a blameless man
or strengthen the hands of evildoers.
21 He will yet fill your mouth with laughter
and your lips with shouts of joy.[h]
22 Your enemies will be clothed in shame,[i]
and the tents of the wicked will be no more."

## Job

9 Then Job replied:

2 "Indeed, I know that this is true.
But how can a mortal be righteous before God?[j]
3 Though one wished to dispute with him,
he could not answer him one time out of a thousand.
4 His wisdom is profound, his power is vast.
Who has resisted him and come out unscathed?[k]
5 He moves mountains without their knowing it
and overturns them in his anger.
6 He shakes the earth[l] from its place
and makes its pillars tremble.
7 He speaks to the sun and it does not shine;
he seals off the light of the stars.
8 He alone stretches out the heavens

*Weary One,*

*Remember that I am the Creator of heaven and earth. At my perfect discretion I send both the rain and the sunshine.*

*In love and power,*
*The Almighty*

JOB 9:7–8

and treads on the waves of the sea.
9 He is the Maker of the Bear and Orion,
the Pleiades and the constellations of the south.[m]
10 He performs wonders that cannot be fathomed,
miracles that cannot be counted.
11 When he passes me, I cannot see him;
when he goes by, I cannot perceive him.[n]
12 If he snatches away, who can stop him?[o]
Who can say to him, 'What are you doing?'[p]
13 God does not restrain his anger;
even the cohorts of Rahab[q] cowered at his feet.

14 "How then can I dispute with him?
How can I find words to argue with him?
15 Though I were innocent, I could not answer him;[r]
I could only plead[s] with my Judge for mercy.
16 Even if I summoned him and he responded,
I do not believe he would give me a hearing.
17 He would crush me[t] with a storm
and multiply[u] my wounds for no reason.[v]
18 He would not let me regain my breath
but would overwhelm me with misery.
19 If it is a matter of strength, he is mighty!
And if it is a matter of justice, who will summon him[b]?
20 Even if I were innocent, my mouth would condemn me;
if I were blameless, it would pronounce me guilty.

21 "Although I am blameless,
I have no concern for myself;
I despise my own life.[w]
22 It is all the same; that is why I say,
'He destroys both the blameless and the wicked.'[x]
23 When a scourge brings sudden death,
he mocks the despair of the innocent.
24 When a land falls into the hands of the wicked,[y]

**9:9**
m Ge 1:16

**9:11**
n Job 23:8–9; 35:14

**9:12**
o Job 11:10
p Isa 45:9; Ro 9:20

**9:13**
q Job 26:12; Isa 30:7

**9:15**
r Job 10:15
s Job 8:5

**9:17**
t Job 16:12
u Job 16:14
v Job 2:3

**9:21**
w Job 7:16

**9:22**
x Ecc 9:2,3; Eze 21:3

**9:24**
y Job 10:3

[a]19 Or *Surely all the joy it has / is that* [b]19 See Septuagint; Hebrew *me.*

9:24 z Job 12:6
9:25 a Job 7:6
9:26 b Hab 1:8
9:28 c Job 7:21
9:30 d Jer 2:22
9:32 e Ro 9:20 f Ecc 6:10
9:33 g 1Sa 2:25
9:34 h Ps 39:10
10:1 i 1Ki 19:4 j Job 7:11
10:4 k 1Sa 16:7
10:9 l Ge 2:7
10:15 m Job 9:13
10:16 n Isa 38:13; La 3:10
10:17 o Job 16:8 p Ru 1:21
10:18 q Job 3:11
10:20 r Job 7:16

he blindfolds its judges.[z]
If it is not he, then who is it?

25 "My days are swifter than a runner;[a]
they fly away without a glimpse of joy.
26 They skim past like boats of papyrus,
like eagles swooping down on their prey.[b]
27 If I say, 'I will forget my complaint,
I will change my expression, and smile,'
28 I still dread all my sufferings,
for I know you will not hold me innocent.[c]
29 Since I am already found guilty,
why should I struggle in vain?
30 Even if I washed myself with soap[a]
and my hands with washing soda,[d]
31 you would plunge me into a slime pit
so that even my clothes would detest me.

32 "He is not a man like me that I might answer him,[e]
that we might confront each other in court.[f]
33 If only there were someone to arbitrate between us,[g]
to lay his hand upon us both,
34 someone to remove God's rod from me,[h]
so that his terror would frighten me no more.
35 Then I would speak up without fear of him,
but as it now stands with me, I cannot.

10 "I loathe my very life;[i]
therefore I will give free rein to my complaint
and speak out in the bitterness of my soul.[j]
2 I will say to God: Do not condemn me,
but tell me what charges you have against me.
3 Does it please you to oppress me,
to spurn the work of your hands,
while you smile on the schemes of the wicked?
4 Do you have eyes of flesh?
Do you see as a mortal sees?[k]
5 Are your days like those of a mortal
or your years like those of a man,
6 that you must search out my faults
and probe after my sin—
7 though you know that I am not guilty
and that no one can rescue me from your hand?

8 "Your hands shaped me and made me.
Will you now turn and destroy me?
9 Remember that you molded me like clay.
Will you now turn me to dust again?[l]
10 Did you not pour me out like milk
and curdle me like cheese,
11 clothe me with skin and flesh
and knit me together with bones and sinews?
12 You gave me life and showed me kindness,
and in your providence watched over my spirit.

13 "But this is what you concealed in your heart,
and I know that this was in your mind:
14 If I sinned, you would be watching me
and would not let my offense go unpunished.
15 If I am guilty—woe to me![m]
Even if I am innocent, I cannot lift my head,
for I am full of shame
and drowned in[b] my affliction.
16 If I hold my head high, you stalk me like a lion[n]
and again display your awesome power against me.
17 You bring new witnesses against me[o]
and increase your anger toward me;[p]
your forces come against me wave upon wave.

18 "Why then did you bring me out of the womb?[q]
I wish I had died before any eye saw me.
19 If only I had never come into being,
or had been carried straight from the womb to the grave!
20 Are not my few days almost over?
Turn away from me[r] so I can have a moment's joy
21 before I go to the place of no return,

[a]30 Or *snow* [b]15 Or *and aware of*

11:2
s Job 8:2
11:3
t Job 17:2; 21:3
11:4
u Job 10:7
11:6
v Ezr 9:13
11:7
w Ecc 3:11
11:10
x Job 9:12; Rev 3:7
11:11
y Ps 10:14
11:13
z 1Sa 7:3; Ps 78:8
a Ps 88:9
11:14
b Ps 101:4
c Job 22:23

to the land of gloom and deep shadow,[a]
22 to the land of deepest night,
of deep shadow and disorder,
where even the light is like darkness."

## Zophar

11 Then Zophar the Naamathite replied:

2 "Are all these words to go unanswered?[s]
Is this talker to be vindicated?
3 Will your idle talk reduce men to silence?
Will no one rebuke you when you mock?[t]
4 You say to God, 'My beliefs are flawless
and I am pure[u] in your sight.'
5 Oh, how I wish that God would speak,
that he would open his lips against you
6 and disclose to you the secrets of wisdom,
for true wisdom has two sides.
Know this: God has even forgotten
some of your sin.[v]

7 "Can you fathom[w] the mysteries of God?
Can you probe the limits of the Almighty?
8 They are higher than the heavens—what can you do?
They are deeper than the depths of the grave[b]—what can you know?
9 Their measure is longer than the earth
and wider than the sea.

10 "If he comes along and confines you in prison
and convenes a court, who can oppose him?[x]
11 Surely he recognizes deceitful men;
and when he sees evil, does he not take note?[y]
12 But a witless man can no more become wise
than a wild donkey's colt can be born a man.[c]

13 "Yet if you devote your heart[z] to him
and stretch out your hands to him,[a]
14 if you put away the sin that is in your hand
and allow no evil[b] to dwell in your tent,[c]
15 then you will lift up your face without shame;
you will stand firm and without fear.
16 You will surely forget your trouble,[d]
recalling it only as waters gone by.
17 Life will be brighter than noonday,[e]
and darkness will become like morning.
18 You will be secure, because there is hope;
you will look about you and take your rest[f] in safety.[g]
19 You will lie down, with no one to make you afraid,
and many will court your favor.
20 But the eyes of the wicked will fail,[h]
and escape will elude them;
their hope will become a dying gasp."

## Job

12 Then Job replied:

2 "Doubtless you are the people,
and wisdom will die with you!
3 But I have a mind as well as you;
I am not inferior to you.
Who does not know all these things?[i]

4 "I have become a laughingstock to my friends,
though I called upon God and he answered[j]—
a mere laughingstock, though righteous and blameless![k]
5 Men at ease have contempt for misfortune
as the fate of those whose feet are slipping.
6 The tents of marauders are undisturbed,
and those who provoke God are secure[l]—
those who carry their god in their hands.[d]

7 "But ask the animals, and they will teach you,
or the birds of the air, and they will tell you;
8 or speak to the earth, and it will teach you,
or let the fish of the sea inform you.

11:16
d Isa 65:16
11:17
e Ps 37:6; Isa 58:8,10
11:18
f Ps 3:5
g Lev 26:6; Pr 3:24
11:20
h Dt 28:65
12:3
i Job 13:2
12:4
j Ps 91:15
k Job 6:29
12:6
l Job 9:24

[a]21 Or *and the shadow of death*; also in verse 22 [b]8 Hebrew *than Sheol* [c]12 Or *wild donkey can be born tame*
[d]6 Or *secure / in what God's hand brings them*

12:10 m Ac 17:28
12:11 n Job 34:3
12:12 o Job 32:7,9
12:13 p Job 9:4
12:14 q Job 19:10
12:15 r 1Ki 8:35 s Ge 7:11
12:16 t Job 13:7,9
12:18 u Ps 116:16
12:20 v Job 32:9
12:22 w 1Co 4:5 x Da 2:22
12:23 y Ps 107:38; Isa 9:3
12:25 z Job 5:14

9 Which of all these does not know
that the hand of the LORD has done
this?
10 In his hand is the life of every creature
and the breath of all mankind.[m]
11 Does not the ear test words
as the tongue tastes food?[n]
12 Is not wisdom found among the aged?
Does not long life bring
understanding?[o]

13 "To God belong wisdom and power;[p]
counsel and understanding are his.
14 What he tears down[q] cannot be rebuilt;
the man he imprisons cannot be
released.
15 If he holds back the waters,[r] there is
drought;
if he lets them loose, they devastate
the land.[s]
16 To him belong strength and victory;
both deceived and deceiver are his.[t]
17 He leads counselors away stripped
and makes fools of judges.
18 He takes off the shackles[u] put on by kings
and ties a loincloth[a] around their
waist.
19 He leads priests away stripped
and overthrows men long established.
20 He silences the lips of trusted advisers
and takes away the discernment of
elders.[v]
21 He pours contempt on nobles
and disarms the mighty.
22 He reveals the deep things of darkness[w]
and brings deep shadows into the
light.[x]
23 He makes nations great, and destroys
them;
he enlarges nations,[y] and disperses
them.
24 He deprives the leaders of the earth of
their reason;
he sends them wandering through a
trackless waste.
25 They grope in darkness with no light;[z]
he makes them stagger like
drunkards.

13 "My eyes have seen all this,
my ears have heard and
understood it.
2 What you know, I also know;
I am not inferior to you.[a]
3 But I desire to speak to the Almighty
and to argue my case with God.[b]
4 You, however, smear me with lies;[c]
you are worthless physicians, all of
you!
5 If only you would be altogether silent!
For you, that would be wisdom.[d]
6 Hear now my argument;
listen to the plea of my lips.
7 Will you speak wickedly on God's behalf?
Will you speak deceitfully for him?
8 Will you show him partiality?
Will you argue the case for God?
9 Would it turn out well if he examined
you?
Could you deceive him as you might
deceive men?
10 He would surely rebuke you
if you secretly showed partiality.
11 Would not his splendor[e] terrify you?
Would not the dread of him fall on
you?
12 Your maxims are proverbs of ashes;
your defenses are defenses of clay.

13 "Keep silent and let me speak;
then let come to me what may.
14 Why do I put myself in jeopardy
and take my life in my hands?
15 Though he slay me, yet will I hope in
him;[f]
I will surely[b] defend my ways to his
face.[g]
16 Indeed, this will turn out for my
deliverance,
for no godless man would dare come
before him!
17 Listen carefully to my words;
let your ears take in what I say.
18 Now that I have prepared my case,[h]
I know I will be vindicated.
19 Can anyone bring charges against me?[i]
If so, I will be silent and die.

20 "Only grant me these two things, O God,
and then I will not hide from you:
21 Withdraw your hand far from me,
and stop frightening me with your
terrors.
22 Then summon me and I will answer,[j]

13:2 a Job 12:3
13:3 b Job 23:3–4
13:4 c Ps 119:69; Jer 23:32
13:5 d Pr 17:28
13:11 e Job 31:23
13:15 f Ps 23:4; Pr 14:32 g Job 27:5
13:18 h Job 23:4
13:19 i Isa 50:8
13:22 j Job 14:15

[a]18 Or *shackles of kings / and ties a belt* [b]15 Or *He will surely slay me; I have no hope — / yet I will*

13:24 k Dt 32:20 l Job 19:11; La 2:5
13:25 m Isa 42:3
13:26 n Ps 25:7
13:27 o Job 33:11
14:1 p Ecc 2:23
14:2 q Ps 90:5–6 r Job 8:9
14:3 s Ps 144:3
14:4 t Ps 51:10 u Eph 2:1–3 v Jn 3:6; Ro 5:12
14:6 w Job 7:19

or let me speak, and you reply.
23 How many wrongs and sins have I committed?
Show me my offense and my sin.
24 Why do you hide your face[k]
and consider me your enemy?[l]
25 Will you torment a windblown leaf?
Will you chase after dry chaff?[m]
26 For you write down bitter things against me
and make me inherit the sins of my youth.[n]
27 You fasten my feet in shackles;[o]
you keep close watch on all my paths
by putting marks on the soles of my feet.

28 "So man wastes away like something rotten,
like a garment eaten by moths.

14 "Man born of woman
is of few days and full of trouble.[p]
2 He springs up like a flower and withers away;[q]
like a fleeting shadow,[r] he does not endure.
3 Do you fix your eye on such a one?[s]
Will you bring him[a] before you for judgment?
4 Who can bring what is pure[t] from the impure?[u]
No one![v]
5 Man's days are determined;
you have decreed the number of his months
and have set limits he cannot exceed.
6 So look away from him and let him alone,[w]
till he has put in his time like a hired man.

7 "At least there is hope for a tree:
If it is cut down, it will sprout again,
and its new shoots will not fail.
8 Its roots may grow old in the ground
and its stump die in the soil,
9 yet at the scent of water it will bud
and put forth shoots like a plant.
10 But man dies and is laid low;
he breathes his last and is no more.
11 As water disappears from the sea
or a riverbed becomes parched and dry,
12 so man lies down and does not rise;
till the heavens are no more,[x] men will not awake
or be roused from their sleep.[y]

13 "If only you would hide me in the grave[b]
and conceal me till your anger has passed!
If only you would set me a time
and then remember me!
14 If a man dies, will he live again?
All the days of my hard service
I will wait for my renewal[c] to come.
15 You will call and I will answer you;[z]
you will long for the creature your hands have made.
16 Surely then you will count my steps[a]
but not keep track of my sin.[b]
17 My offenses will be sealed up in a bag;[c]
you will cover over my sin.

18 "But as a mountain erodes and crumbles
and as a rock is moved from its place,
19 as water wears away stones
and torrents wash away the soil,
so you destroy man's hope.
20 You overpower him once for all,
and he is gone;
you change his countenance
and send him away.
21 If his sons are honored, he does not know it;
if they are brought low, he does not see it.[d]
22 He feels but the pain of his own body
and mourns only for himself."

## Eliphaz

15 Then Eliphaz the Temanite replied:
2 "Would a wise man answer with empty notions
or fill his belly with the hot east wind?
3 Would he argue with useless words,

14:12 x Rev 20:11; 21:1 y Ac 3:21
14:15 z Job 13:22
14:16 a Pr 5:21; Jer 32:19 b Job 10:6
14:17 c Dt 32:34
14:21 d Ecc 9:5; Isa 63:16

*"You don't get to choose how you're going to die, or when. You can only decide how you're going to live now."*
—Joan Baez, singer and activist

[a]3 Septuagint, Vulgate and Syriac; Hebrew *me* [b]13 Hebrew *Sheol* [c]14 Or *release*

with speeches that have no value?
4 But you even undermine piety
and hinder devotion to God.
5 Your sin prompts your mouth;
you adopt the tongue of the crafty.
6 Your own mouth condemns you, not
mine;
your own lips testify against you.[e]

7 "Are you the first man ever born?[f]
Were you brought forth before the
hills?[g]
8 Do you listen in on God's council?[h]
Do you limit wisdom to yourself?
9 What do you know that we do not
know?
What insights do you have that we do
not have?[i]
10 The gray-haired and the aged[j] are on our
side,
men even older than your father.
11 Are God's consolations not enough for
you,
words spoken gently to you?
12 Why has your heart carried you away,
and why do your eyes flash,
13 so that you vent your rage against God
and pour out such words from your
mouth?

14 "What is man, that he could be pure,
or one born of woman,[k] that he could
be righteous?[l]
15 If God places no trust in his holy ones,
if even the heavens are not pure in his
eyes,[m]
16 how much less man, who is vile and
corrupt,[n]
who drinks up evil like water![o]

17 "Listen to me and I will explain to you;
let me tell you what I have seen,
18 what wise men have declared,
hiding nothing received from their
fathers[p]
19 (to whom alone the land was given
when no alien passed among them):
20 All his days the wicked man suffers
torment,
the ruthless through all the years
stored up for him.
21 Terrifying sounds fill his ears;
when all seems well, marauders attack
him.[q]
22 He despairs of escaping the darkness;
he is marked for the sword.
23 He wanders about[r]—food for vultures[a];
he knows the day of darkness is at
hand.[s]
24 Distress and anguish fill him with terror;
they overwhelm him, like a king
poised to attack,
25 because he shakes his fist at God
and vaunts himself against the
Almighty,[t]
26 defiantly charging against him
with a thick, strong shield.

27 "Though his face is covered with fat
and his waist bulges with flesh,
28 he will inhabit ruined towns
and houses where no one lives,
houses crumbling to rubble.
29 He will no longer be rich and his wealth
will not endure,
nor will his possessions spread over
the land.
30 He will not escape the darkness;
a flame[u] will wither his shoots,
and the breath of God's mouth will
carry him away.
31 Let him not deceive himself by trusting
what is worthless,[v]
for he will get nothing in return.
32 Before his time he will be paid in full,[w]
and his branches will not flourish.
33 He will be like a vine stripped of its
unripe grapes,
like an olive tree shedding its
blossoms.
34 For the company of the godless will be
barren,
and fire will consume the tents of
those who love bribes.
35 They conceive trouble and give birth to
evil;[x]
their womb fashions deceit."

## Job 16

16 Then Job replied:

2 "I have heard many things like these;
miserable comforters are you all!

[a]23 Or *about, looking for food*

**15:6** e Lk 19:22
**15:7** f Job 38:21 g Ps 90:2; Pr 8:25
**15:8** h Ro 11:34
**15:9** i Job 13:2
**15:10** j Job 32:6–7
**15:14** k Job 14:4 l Pr 20:9; Ecc 7:20
**15:15** m Job 25:5
**15:16** n Ps 14:1 o Job 34:7; Pr 19:28
**15:18** p Job 8:8
**15:21** q 1Th 5:3
**15:23** r Ps 109:10 s Job 18:12
**15:25** t Job 36:9
**15:30** u Job 22:20
**15:31** v Isa 59:4
**15:32** w Job 22:16; Ps 55:23
**15:35** x Ps 7:14; Isa 59:4

16:3
y Job 6:26
16:4
z Ps 22:7; 109:25; La 2:15; Mt 27:39
16:7
a Job 7:3
16:8
b Job 19:20
c Job 10:17
16:9
d Ps 35:16
e Job 13:24
16:10
f Ps 22:13
g La 3:30; Mic 5:1
16:12
h Job 9:17
16:13
i Job 20:24
16:14
j Joel 2:7
16:15
k Ge 37:34
16:18
l Ps 66:18–19
16:19
m Ro 1:9

3 Will your long-winded speeches never
end?
What ails you that you keep on
arguing?[y]
4 I also could speak like you,
if you were in my place;
I could make fine speeches against you
and shake my head[z] at you.
5 But my mouth would encourage you;
comfort from my lips would bring you
relief.

6 "Yet if I speak, my pain is not relieved;
and if I refrain, it does not go away.
7 Surely, O God, you have worn me out;[a]
you have devastated my entire
household.
8 You have bound me—and it has become
a witness;
my gauntness[b] rises up and testifies
against me.[c]
9 God assails me and tears me in his anger
and gnashes his teeth at me;[d]
my opponent fastens on me his
piercing eyes.[e]
10 Men open their mouths[f] to jeer at me;
they strike my cheek[g] in scorn
and unite together against me.
11 God has turned me over to evil men
and thrown me into the clutches of the
wicked.
12 All was well with me, but he
shattered me;
he seized me by the neck and
crushed me.[h]
He has made me his target;
13 his archers surround me.
Without pity, he pierces[i] my kidneys
and spills my gall on the ground.
14 Again and again he bursts upon me;
he rushes at me like a warrior.[j]

15 "I have sewed sackcloth[k] over my skin
and buried my brow in the dust.
16 My face is red with weeping,
deep shadows ring my eyes;
17 yet my hands have been free of violence
and my prayer is pure.

18 "O earth, do not cover my blood;
may my cry never be laid to rest![l]
19 Even now my witness[m] is in heaven;
my advocate is on high.
20 My intercessor is my friend[a]
as my eyes pour out tears to God;
21 on behalf of a man he pleads with God
as a man pleads for his friend.

22 "Only a few years will pass
before I go on the journey of no return.

*My hurting daughter,*

*Whatever you may be facing, don't forget that I am able and willing to bring you through it. Wait on me.*

*Your Gracious "Abba"*

JOB 16:19–21

17 1 My spirit is broken,
my days are cut short,
the grave awaits me.[n]
2 Surely mockers surround me;
my eyes must dwell on their hostility.

3 "Give me, O God, the pledge you
demand.[o]
Who else will put up security for me?
4 You have closed their minds to
understanding;
therefore you will not let them
triumph.
5 If a man denounces his friends for
reward,
the eyes of his children will fail.[p]
6 "God has made me a byword[q] to
everyone,
a man in whose face people spit.
7 My eyes have grown dim with grief;
my whole frame is but a shadow.
8 Upright men are appalled at this;
the innocent are aroused against the
ungodly.
9 Nevertheless, the righteous[r] will hold to
their ways,

17:1
n Ps 88:3–4
17:3
o Ps 119:122
17:5
p Job 11:20
17:6
q Job 30:9
17:9
r Pr 4:18

[a]20 Or *My friends treat me with scorn*

and those with clean hands will grow
stronger.
[10] "But come on, all of you, try again!
I will not find a wise man among you.
[11] My days have passed, my plans are
shattered,
and so are the desires of my heart.[s]
[12] These men turn night into day;
in the face of darkness they say, 'Light
is near.'
[13] If the only home I hope for is the grave,[a][t]
if I spread out my bed in darkness,
[14] if I say to corruption, 'You are my father,'
and to the worm, 'My mother' or 'My
sister,'
[15] where then is my hope?
Who can see any hope for me?
[16] Will it go down to the gates of death[a]?[u]
Will we descend together into the
dust?"

## Bildad

**18** Then Bildad the Shuhite replied:

[2] "When will you end these speeches?
Be sensible, and then we can talk.
[3] Why are we regarded as cattle
and considered stupid in your sight?[v]
[4] You who tear yourself[w] to pieces in your
anger,
is the earth to be abandoned for your
sake?
Or must the rocks be moved from their
place?

[5] "The lamp of the wicked is snuffed out;[x]
the flame of his fire stops burning.
[6] The light in his tent becomes dark;
the lamp beside him goes out.
[7] The vigor of his step is weakened;
his own schemes[y] throw him down.
[8] His feet thrust him into a net[z]
and he wanders into its mesh.
[9] A trap seizes him by the heel;
a snare holds him fast.
[10] A noose is hidden for him on the ground;
a trap lies in his path.
[11] Terrors startle him on every side[a]
and dog his every step.
[12] Calamity is hungry[b] for him;
disaster is ready for him when he falls.
[13] It eats away parts of his skin;
death's firstborn devours his limbs.
[14] He is torn from the security of his tent
and marched off to the king of terrors.
[15] Fire resides[b] in his tent;
burning sulfur is scattered over his
dwelling.
[16] His roots dry up below[c]
and his branches wither above.[d]
[17] The memory of him perishes from the
earth;
he has no name in the land.[e]
[18] He is driven from light into darkness[f]
and is banished from the world.
[19] He has no offspring[g] or descendants[h]
among his people,
no survivor where once he lived.
[20] Men of the west are appalled at his fate;
men of the east are seized with horror.
[21] Surely such is the dwelling of an evil
man;
such is the place of one who knows not
God."[i]

## Job

**19** Then Job replied:

[2] "How long will you torment me
and crush me with words?
[3] Ten times now you have reproached me;
shamelessly you attack me.
[4] If it is true that I have gone astray,
my error remains my concern alone.
[5] If indeed you would exalt yourselves
above me[j]
and use my humiliation against me,
[6] then know that God has wronged me
and drawn his net[k] around me.

[7] "Though I cry, 'I've been wronged!' I get
no response;[l]
though I call for help, there is no
justice.
[8] He has blocked my way so I cannot pass;
he has shrouded my paths in
darkness.[m]
[9] He has stripped me of my honor
and removed the crown from my head.
[10] He tears me down[n] on every side till I am
gone;
he uproots my hope[o] like a tree.

[a]13,16 Hebrew *Sheol* [b]15 Or *Nothing he had remains*

**17:11** s Job 7:6
**17:13** t Job 3:13
**17:16** u Job 3:17–19; Jnh 2:6
**18:3** v Ps 73:22
**18:4** w Job 13:14
**18:5** x Pr 13:9
**18:7** y Job 5:13
**18:8** z Job 22:10; Ps 9:15; 35:7
**18:11** a Job 15:21
**18:12** b Isa 8:21
**18:16** c Isa 5:24; Am 2:9 d Mal 4:1
**18:17** e Ps 34:16; Pr 10:7
**18:18** f Job 5:14
**18:19** g Jer 22:30 h Isa 14:22
**18:21** i 1Th 4:5
**19:5** j Ps 35:26; 38:16
**19:6** k Job 18:8
**19:7** l Job 30:20
**19:8** m Job 30:26
**19:10** n Job 12:14 o Job 7:6

19:11
p Job 16:9
q Job 13:24

19:18
r 2Ki 2:23

19:19
s Ps 55:12–13

19:20
t Ps 102:5

19:22
u Ps 69:26

19:25
v Ps 78:35; Isa 43:14
w Job 16:19

19:26
x Mt 5:8; 1Co 13:12; 1Jn 3:2

11 His anger[p] burns against me;
he counts me among his enemies.[q]
12 His troops advance in force;
they build a siege ramp against me
and encamp around my tent.

13 "He has alienated my brothers from me;
my acquaintances are completely
estranged from me.
14 My kinsmen have gone away;
my friends have forgotten me.
15 My guests and my maidservants count
me a stranger;
they look upon me as an alien.
16 I summon my servant, but he does not
answer,
though I beg him with my own mouth.
17 My breath is offensive to my wife;
I am loathsome to my own brothers.
18 Even the little boys[r] scorn me;
when I appear, they ridicule me.
19 All my intimate friends[s] detest me;
those I love have turned against me.
20 I am nothing but skin and bones;[t]
I have escaped with only the skin of
my teeth.[a]

21 "Have pity on me, my friends, have pity,
for the hand of God has struck me.
22 Why do you pursue me as God does?
Will you never get enough of my
flesh?[u]

23 "Oh, that my words were recorded,
that they were written on a scroll,
24 that they were inscribed with an iron tool
on[b] lead,
or engraved in rock forever!
25 I know that my Redeemer[c][v] lives,[w]
and that in the end he will stand upon
the earth.[d]
26 And after my skin has been destroyed,
yet[e] in[f] my flesh I will see God;[x]
27 I myself will see him
with my own eyes—I, and not
another.
How my heart yearns within me!

28 "If you say, 'How we will hound him,
since the root of the trouble lies in
him,[g]'
29 you should fear the sword yourselves;

*Lord,*

*hear my prayer. Work in my situation. Give me the strength to endure. Above all, let your will be done in my life, now and forever.*

*Amen.*

JOB 19:25–27

for wrath will bring punishment by
the sword,
and then you will know that there is
judgment.[h]"

## Zophar

20 Then Zophar the Naamathite
replied:

2 "My troubled thoughts prompt me to
answer
because I am greatly disturbed.
3 I hear a rebuke[y] that dishonors me,
and my understanding inspires me
to reply.

4 "Surely you know how it has been from of
old,
ever since man[i] was placed on the
earth,
5 that the mirth of the wicked is brief,
the joy of the godless lasts but a
moment.[z]
6 Though his pride reaches to the heavens
and his head touches the clouds,[a]
7 he will perish forever,[b] like his own dung;
those who have seen him will say,
'Where is he?'
8 Like a dream[c] he flies away, no more to be
found,
banished like a vision of the night.[d]
9 The eye that saw him will not see him
again;
his place will look on him no more.[e]
10 His children must make amends to the
poor;
his own hands must give back his
wealth.

20:3
y Job 19:3

20:5
z Ps 37:35–36

20:6
a Isa 14:13–14; Ob 1:3–4

20:7
b Job 4:20

20:8
c Ps 73:20
d Ps 90:5

20:9
e Job 7:8

[a]20 Or *only my gums* [b]24 Or *and* [c]25 Or *defender* [d]25 Or *upon my grave* [e]26 Or *And after I awake, / though this ⌊body⌋ has been destroyed, / then* [f]26 Or */ apart from* [g]28 Many Hebrew manuscripts, Septuagint and Vulgate; most Hebrew manuscripts *me* [h]29 Or */ that you may come to know the Almighty* [i]4 Or *Adam*

**20:11** f Job 13:26
**20:20** g Ecc 5:12–14
**20:24** h Isa 24:18; Am 5:19
**20:25** i Job 18:11 j Job 16:13
**20:26** k Ps 21:9

11 The youthful vigor[f] that fills his bones
will lie with him in the dust.

12 "Though evil is sweet in his mouth
and he hides it under his tongue,
13 though he cannot bear to let it go
and keeps it in his mouth,
14 yet his food will turn sour in his
stomach;
it will become the venom of serpents
within him.
15 He will spit out the riches he swallowed;
God will make his stomach vomit
them up.
16 He will suck the poison of serpents;
the fangs of an adder will kill him.
17 He will not enjoy the streams,
the rivers flowing with honey and
cream.
18 What he toiled for he must give back
uneaten;
he will not enjoy the profit from his
trading.
19 For he has oppressed the poor and left
them destitute;
he has seized houses he did not build.

20 "Surely he will have no respite from his
craving;[g]
he cannot save himself by his treasure.
21 Nothing is left for him to devour;
his prosperity will not endure.
22 In the midst of his plenty, distress will
overtake him;
the full force of misery will come upon
him.
23 When he has filled his belly,
God will vent his burning anger
against him
and rain down his blows upon him.
24 Though he flees[h] from an iron weapon,
a bronze-tipped arrow pierces him.
25 He pulls it out of his back,
the gleaming point out of his liver.
Terrors[i] will come over him;[j]
26 total darkness lies in wait for his
treasures.
A fire unfanned will consume him[k]
and devour what is left in his tent.
27 The heavens will expose his guilt;
the earth will rise up against him.
28 A flood will carry off his house,
rushing waters[a] on the day of God's
wrath.
29 Such is the fate God allots the wicked,
the heritage appointed for them by
God."[l]

## Job 21

21 Then Job replied:

2 "Listen carefully to my words;
let this be the consolation you give me.
3 Bear with me while I speak,
and after I have spoken, mock on.

4 "Is my complaint directed to man?
Why should I not be impatient?
5 Look at me and be astonished;
clap your hand over your mouth.[m]
6 When I think about this, I am terrified;
trembling seizes my body.
7 Why do the wicked live on,
growing old and increasing in power?[n]
8 They see their children established
around them,
their offspring before their eyes.[o]
9 Their homes are safe and free from fear;
the rod of God is not upon them.
10 Their bulls never fail to breed;
their cows calve and do not miscarry.[p]
11 They send forth their children as a flock;
their little ones dance about.
12 They sing to the music of tambourine
and harp;
they make merry to the sound of the
flute.
13 They spend their years in prosperity[q]
and go down to the grave[b] in peace.[c]
14 Yet they say to God, 'Leave us alone![r]
We have no desire to know your ways.
15 Who is the Almighty, that we should
serve him?
What would we gain by praying to
him?'[s]
16 But their prosperity is not in their own
hands,
so I stand aloof from the counsel of the
wicked.

17 "Yet how often is the lamp of the wicked
snuffed out?[t]
How often does calamity come upon
them,

**20:29** l Job 27:13
**21:5** m Jdg 18:19; Job 29:9; 40:4
**21:7** n Ps 73:3; Jer 12:1
**21:8** o Ps 17:14
**21:10** p Ex 23:26
**21:13** q Job 36:11
**21:14** r Job 22:17
**21:15** s Job 34:9
**21:17** t Job 18:5

[a]28 Or *The possessions in his house will be carried off, / washed away* [b]13 Hebrew *Sheol* [c]13 Or *in an instant*

21:18 u Ps 1:4
21:19 v Ex 20:5
21:20 w Isa 51:17 x Jer 25:15; Rev 14:10
21:22 y Isa 40:13–14; Ro 11:34
21:26 z Job 24:20; Ecc 9:2–3
21:28 a Job 8:22
21:30 b Pr 16:4 c Job 20:22,28; 2Pe 2:9
21:33 d Job 3:19

the fate God allots in his anger?
18 How often are they like straw before the
wind,
like chaff[u] swept away by a gale?
19 ⌞It is said,⌟ 'God stores up a man's
punishment for his sons.'[v]
Let him repay the man himself, so that
he will know it!
20 Let his own eyes see his destruction;
let him drink[w] of the wrath of the
Almighty.[a][x]
21 For what does he care about the family he
leaves behind
when his allotted months come to an
end?

22 "Can anyone teach knowledge to God,[y]
since he judges even the highest?
23 One man dies in full vigor,
completely secure and at ease,
24 his body[b] well nourished,
his bones rich with marrow.
25 Another man dies in bitterness of soul,
never having enjoyed anything good.
26 Side by side they lie in the dust,
and worms cover them both.[z]

27 "I know full well what you are thinking,
the schemes by which you would
wrong me.
28 You say, 'Where now is the great man's
house,
the tents where wicked men lived?'[a]
29 Have you never questioned those who
travel?
Have you paid no regard to their
accounts—
30 that the evil man is spared from the day
of calamity,[b]
that he is delivered from[c] the day of
wrath?[c]
31 Who denounces his conduct to his face?
Who repays him for what he has
done?
32 He is carried to the grave,
and watch is kept over his tomb.
33 The soil in the valley is sweet to him;
all men follow after him,
and a countless throng goes[d] before
him.[d]
34 "So how can you console me with your
nonsense?
Nothing is left of your answers but
falsehood!"

## Eliphaz

22 Then Eliphaz the Temanite replied:

2 "Can a man be of benefit to God?[e]
Can even a wise man benefit him?
3 What pleasure would it give the Almighty
if you were righteous?
What would he gain if your ways were
blameless?

4 "Is it for your piety that he rebukes you
and brings charges against you?
5 Is not your wickedness great?
Are not your sins endless?
6 You demanded security[f] from your
brothers for no reason;
you stripped men of their clothing,
leaving them naked.
7 You gave no water to the weary
and you withheld food from the
hungry,
8 though you were a powerful man, owning
land—
an honored man, living on it.
9 And you sent widows away empty-
handed[g]
and broke the strength of the fatherless.
10 That is why snares are all around you,
why sudden peril terrifies you,
11 why it is so dark[h] you cannot see,
and why a flood of water covers you.[i]

12 "Is not God in the heights of heaven?[j]
And see how lofty are the highest
stars!
13 Yet you say, 'What does God know?[k]
Does he judge through such darkness?
14 Thick clouds[l] veil him, so he does not
see us
as he goes about in the vaulted
heavens.'
15 Will you keep to the old path
that evil men have trod?
16 They were carried off before their time,[m]
their foundations washed away by a
flood.[n]

22:2 e Lk 17:10
22:6 f Ex 22:26
22:9 g Job 24:3,21
22:11 h Job 5:14 i Ps 69:1–2
22:12 j Job 11:8
22:13 k Ps 10:11
22:14 l Job 26:9
22:16 m Job 15:32 n Mt 7:26–27

[a]17–20 Verses 17 and 18 may be taken as exclamations and 19 and 20 as declarations. [b]24 The meaning of the Hebrew for this word is uncertain. [c]30 Or *man is reserved for the day of calamity, / that he is brought forth to* [d]33 Or */ as a countless throng went*

**22:19** o Ps 58:10; 107:42
**22:23** p Isa 19:22 q Job 11:14
**22:26** r Job 27:10; Isa 58:14
**22:27** s Isa 58:9
**22:29** t Mt 23:12; 1Pe 5:5
**23:2** u Job 6:3

17 They said to God, 'Leave us alone!
What can the Almighty do to us?'
18 Yet it was he who filled their houses with
good things,
so I stand aloof from the counsel of the
wicked.

19 "The righteous see their ruin and
rejoice;[o]
the innocent mock them, saying,
20 'Surely our foes are destroyed,
and fire devours their wealth.'

21 "Submit to God and be at peace with him;
in this way prosperity will come to
you.
22 Accept instruction from his mouth
and lay up his words in your heart.
23 If you return to the Almighty, you will be
restored:[p]
If you remove wickedness far from
your tent[q]
24 and assign your nuggets to the dust,
your gold of Ophir to the rocks in the
ravines,
25 then the Almighty will be your gold,
the choicest silver for you.
26 Surely then you will find delight in the
Almighty[r]
and will lift up your face to God.
27 You will pray to him,[s] and he will hear
you,
and you will fulfill your vows.
28 What you decide on will be done,
and light will shine on your ways.
29 When men are brought low and you say,
'Lift them up!'
then he will save the downcast.[t]
30 He will deliver even one who is not
innocent,
who will be delivered through the
cleanness of your hands."

## Job

# 23

Then Job replied:

2 "Even today my complaint is bitter;[u]
his hand[a] is heavy in spite of[b] my
groaning.
3 If only I knew where to find him;
if only I could go to his dwelling!
4 I would state my case before him
and fill my mouth with arguments.
5 I would find out what he would
answer me,
and consider what he would say.
6 Would he oppose me with great power?[v]
No, he would not press charges
against me.
7 There an upright man could present his
case before him,[w]
and I would be delivered forever from
my judge.

8 "But if I go to the east, he is not there;
if I go to the west, I do not find him.
9 When he is at work in the north, I do not
see him;
when he turns to the south, I catch no
glimpse of him.
10 But he knows the way that I take;
when he has tested me,[x] I will come
forth as gold.
11 My feet have closely followed his steps;
I have kept to his way without turning
aside.[y]
12 I have not departed from the commands
of his lips;
I have treasured the words of his
mouth more than my daily
bread.[z]

13 "But he stands alone, and who can
oppose him?
He does whatever he pleases.
14 He carries out his decree against me,
and many such plans he still has in
store.[a]
15 That is why I am terrified before him;
when I think of all this, I fear him.
16 God has made my heart faint;
the Almighty has terrified me.
17 Yet I am not silenced by the darkness,[b]
by the thick darkness that covers my
face.

# 24

"Why does the Almighty not set
times for judgment?
Why must those who know him look in
vain for such days?[c]
2 Men move boundary stones;[d]
they pasture flocks they have stolen.
3 They drive away the orphan's donkey
and take the widow's ox in pledge.

**23:6** v Job 9:4
**23:7** w Job 13:3
**23:10** x Ps 139:1–3
**23:11** y Ps 44:18
**23:12** z Jn 4:32,34
**23:14** a 1Th 3:3
**23:17** b Job 19:8
**24:1** c Ac 1:7
**24:2** d Dt 19:14; 27:17

[a]2 Septuagint and Syriac; Hebrew / *the hand on me* [b]2 Or *heavy on me in*

[4] They thrust the needy from the path
and force all the poor of the land into
hiding.[e]
[5] Like wild donkeys in the desert,
the poor go about their labor[f] of
foraging food;
the wasteland provides food for their
children.
[6] They gather fodder in the fields
and glean in the vineyards of the
wicked.
[7] Lacking clothes, they spend the night
naked;
they have nothing to cover themselves
in the cold.[g]
[8] They are drenched by mountain rains
and hug[h] the rocks for lack of shelter.
[9] The fatherless child is snatched from the
breast;
the infant of the poor is seized for a
debt.
[10] Lacking clothes, they go about naked;
they carry the sheaves, but still go
hungry.
[11] They crush olives among the terraces[a];
they tread the winepresses, yet suffer
thirst.
[12] The groans of the dying rise from the
city,
and the souls of the wounded cry out
for help.
But God charges no one with
wrongdoing.[i]

[13] "There are those who rebel against the
light,
who do not know its ways
or stay in its paths.
[14] When daylight is gone, the murderer
rises up
and kills the poor and needy;
in the night he steals forth like a thief.[j]
[15] The eye of the adulterer watches for
dusk;[k]
he thinks, 'No eye will see me,'[l]
and he keeps his face concealed.
[16] In the dark, men break into houses,[m]
but by day they shut themselves in;
they want nothing to do with the light.
[17] For all of them, deep darkness is their
morning[b];
they make friends with the terrors of
darkness.[c]

[18] "Yet they are foam on the surface of the
water;
their portion of the land is cursed,
so that no one goes to the vineyards.
[19] As heat and drought snatch away the
melted snow,[n]
so the grave[d] snatches away those who
have sinned.
[20] The womb forgets them,
the worm feasts on them;
evil men are no longer remembered[o]
but are broken like a tree.
[21] They prey on the barren and childless
woman,
and to the widow show no kindness.[p]
[22] But God drags away the mighty by his
power;
though they become established, they
have no assurance of life.
[23] He may let them rest in a feeling of
security,
but his eyes are on their ways.
[24] For a little while they are exalted, and
then they are gone;[q]
they are brought low and gathered up
like all others;
they are cut off like heads of grain.

[25] "If this is not so, who can prove me false
and reduce my words to nothing?"[r]

## Bildad

25 Then Bildad the Shuhite replied:

[2] "Dominion and awe belong to God;[s]
he establishes order in the heights of
heaven.
[3] Can his forces be numbered?
Upon whom does his light not rise?[t]
[4] How then can a man be righteous before
God?
How can one born of woman be pure?[u]
[5] If even the moon is not bright
and the stars are not pure in his eyes,[v]
[6] how much less man, who is but a
maggot—
a son of man, who is only a worm!"[w]

24:4 e Pr 28:28
24:5 f Ps 104:23
24:7 g Ex 22:27; Job 22:6
24:8 h La 4:5
24:12 i Job 9:23
24:14 j Ps 10:9
24:15 k Pr 7:8–9 l Ps 10:11
24:16 m Ex 22:2
24:19 n Job 6:17
24:20 o Pr 10:7
24:21 p Job 22:9
24:24 q Ps 37:10
24:25 r Job 6:28
25:2 s Job 9:4
25:3 t Jas 1:17
25:4 u Job 4:17
25:5 v Job 15:15
25:6 w Ps 22:6

[a]11 Or *olives between the millstones*; the meaning of the Hebrew for this word is uncertain. [b]17 Or *them, their morning is like the shadow of death* [c]17 Or *of the shadow of death* [d]19 Hebrew *Sheol*

26:6 x Ps 139:8 y Heb 4:13
26:7 z Job 9:8
26:8 a Pr 30:4
26:10 b Job 38:8–11
26:12 c Isa 51:15; Jer 31:35
26:13 d Isa 27:1
27:2 e Job 34:5
27:3 f Job 32:8; 33:4

## Job

**26** Then Job replied:

2 "How you have helped the powerless!
How you have saved the arm that is feeble!
3 What advice you have offered to one without wisdom!
And what great insight you have displayed!
4 Who has helped you utter these words?
And whose spirit spoke from your mouth?

5 "The dead are in deep anguish,
those beneath the waters and all that live in them.
6 Death[a][x] is naked before God;
Destruction[b] lies uncovered.[y]
7 He spreads out the northern ⌞skies⌟[z] over empty space;
he suspends the earth over nothing.
8 He wraps up the waters[a] in his clouds,
yet the clouds do not burst under their weight.
9 He covers the face of the full moon,
spreading his clouds over it.
10 He marks out the horizon on the face of the waters
for a boundary between light and darkness.[b]
11 The pillars of the heavens quake,
aghast at his rebuke.
12 By his power he churned up the sea;[c]
by his wisdom he cut Rahab to pieces.
13 By his breath the skies became fair;
his hand pierced the gliding serpent.[d]
14 And these are but the outer fringe of his works;
how faint the whisper we hear of him!
Who then can understand the thunder of his power?"

**27** And Job continued his discourse:

2 "As surely as God lives, who has denied me justice,[e]
the Almighty, who has made me taste bitterness of soul,
3 as long as I have life within me,
the breath of God[f] in my nostrils,
4 my lips will not speak wickedness,
and my tongue will utter no deceit.
5 I will never admit you are in the right;
till I die, I will not deny my integrity.
6 I will maintain my righteousness and never let go of it;
my conscience will not reproach me as long as I live.[g]

7 "May my enemies be like the wicked,
my adversaries like the unjust!
8 For what hope has the godless when he is cut off,
when God takes away his life?
9 Does God listen to his cry
when distress comes upon him?[h]
10 Will he find delight in the Almighty?[i]
Will he call upon God at all times?

11 "I will teach you about the power of God;
the ways of the Almighty I will not conceal.
12 You have all seen this yourselves.
Why then this meaningless talk?

13 "Here is the fate God allots to the wicked,
the heritage a ruthless man receives from the Almighty:[j]
14 However many his children, their fate is the sword;[k]
his offspring will never have enough to eat.[l]
15 The plague will bury those who survive him,
and their widows will not weep for them.[m]
16 Though he heaps up silver like dust
and clothes like piles of clay,
17 what he lays up the righteous will wear,[n]
and the innocent will divide his silver.
18 The house he builds is like a moth's cocoon,
like a hut made by a watchman.
19 He lies down wealthy, but will do so no more;
when he opens his eyes, all is gone.
20 Terrors overtake him like a flood;[o]
a tempest snatches him away in the night.[p]
21 The east wind carries him off, and he is gone;
it sweeps him out of his place.[q]
22 It hurls itself against him without mercy[r]

27:6 g Job 2:3
27:9 h Job 35:12; Pr 1:28; Isa 1:15; Jer 14:12; Mic 3:4
27:10 i Job 22:26
27:13 j Job 20:29
27:14 k Dt 28:41; Hos 9:13 l Job 20:10
27:15 m Ps 78:64
27:17 n Pr 28:8; Ecc 2:26
27:20 o Job 15:21 p Job 20:8
27:21 q Job 7:10
27:22 r Jer 13:14; Eze 5:11

[a]6 Hebrew *Sheol* [b]6 Hebrew *Abaddon*

as he flees headlong from its power.
23 It claps its hands in derision
and hisses him out of his place.

28 "There is a mine for silver
and a place where gold is refined.
2 Iron is taken from the earth,
and copper is smelted from ore.
3 Man puts an end to the darkness;[s]
he searches the farthest recesses
for ore in the blackest darkness.
4 Far from where people dwell he cuts a shaft,
in places forgotten by the foot of man;
far from men he dangles and sways.
5 The earth, from which food comes,[t]
is transformed below as by fire;
6 sapphires[a] come from its rocks,
and its dust contains nuggets of gold.
7 No bird of prey knows that hidden path,
no falcon's eye has seen it.
8 Proud beasts do not set foot on it,
and no lion prowls there.
9 Man's hand assaults the flinty rock
and lays bare the roots of the mountains.
10 He tunnels through the rock;
his eyes see all its treasures.
11 He searches[b] the sources of the rivers
and brings hidden things to light.

12 "But where can wisdom be found?[u]
Where does understanding dwell?
13 Man does not comprehend its worth;[v]
it cannot be found in the land of the living.
14 The deep says, 'It is not in me';
the sea says, 'It is not with me.'
15 It cannot be bought with the finest gold,
nor can its price be weighed in silver.[w]
16 It cannot be bought with the gold of Ophir,
with precious onyx or sapphires.
17 Neither gold nor crystal can compare with it,
nor can it be had for jewels of gold.
18 Coral and jasper are not worthy of mention;
the price of wisdom is beyond rubies.
19 The topaz of Cush cannot compare with it;
it cannot be bought with pure gold.

20 "Where then does wisdom come from?
Where does understanding dwell?
21 It is hidden from the eyes of every living thing,
concealed even from the birds of the air.
22 Destruction[c] and Death say,
'Only a rumor of it has reached our ears.'
23 God understands the way to it
and he alone knows where it dwells,
24 for he views the ends of the earth
and sees everything under the heavens.[x]
25 When he established the force of the wind
and measured out the waters,[y]
26 when he made a decree for the rain
and a path for the thunderstorm,
27 then he looked at wisdom and appraised it;
he confirmed it and tested it.
28 And he said to man,
'The fear of the Lord—that is wisdom,
and to shun evil is understanding.[z]' "

*Lord,*

*I thank you for, as well as in, my trials and tribulations. Through them I have learned to trust you more. When I'm faced with new challenges, remind me anew of all you have done. In your strong name,*

*Amen*

JOB 28:20–28

29 Job continued his discourse:

2 "How I long for the months gone by,
for the days when God watched over me,
3 when his lamp shone upon my head
and by his light I walked through darkness!
4 Oh, for the days when I was in my prime,

28:3 s Ecc 1:13
28:5 t Ps 104:14
28:12 u Ecc 7:24
28:13 v Pr 3:15
28:15 w Pr 3:13–14; 8:10–11
28:24 x Pr 15:3
28:25 y Ps 135:7
28:28 z Dt 4:6; Pr 1:7

[a]6 Or *lapis lazuli*; also in verse 16 [b]11 Septuagint, Aquila and Vulgate; Hebrew *He dams up* [c]22 Hebrew *Abaddon*

29:4 a Ps25:14
29:6 b Job20:17 c Ps81:16 d Dt32:13
29:9 e Job21:5
29:10 f Ps137:6
29:12 g Job31:17,21 h Ps72:12; Pr21:13
29:14 i Isa59:17; 61:10; Eph6:14
29:15 j Nu10:31
29:16 k Pr29:7
29:17 l Ps3:7
29:18 m Ps30:6
29:19 n Jer17:8
29:20 o Ps18:34 p Ge49:24
29:22 q Dt32:2

when God's intimate friendship
blessed my house,[a]
5 when the Almighty was still with me
and my children were around me,
6 when my path was drenched with cream[b]
and the rock[c] poured out for me
streams of olive oil.[d]

7 "When I went to the gate of the city
and took my seat in the public square,
8 the young men saw me and stepped aside
and the old men rose to their feet;
9 the chief men refrained from speaking
and covered their mouths with their
hands;[e]
10 the voices of the nobles were hushed,
and their tongues stuck to the roof of
their mouths.[f]
11 Whoever heard me spoke well of me,
and those who saw me
commended me,
12 because I rescued the poor who cried for
help,
and the fatherless[g] who had none to
assist him.[h]
13 The man who was dying blessed me;
I made the widow's heart sing.
14 I put on righteousness[i] as my clothing;
justice was my robe and my turban.
15 I was eyes[j] to the blind
and feet to the lame.
16 I was a father to the needy;[k]
I took up the case of the stranger.
17 I broke the fangs of the wicked
and snatched the victims from their
teeth.[l]

18 "I thought, 'I will die in my own house,
my days as numerous as the grains of
sand.[m]
19 My roots will reach to the water,[n]
and the dew will lie all night on my
branches.
20 My glory will remain fresh in me,
the bow[o] ever new in my hand.'[p]

21 "Men listened to me expectantly,
waiting in silence for my counsel.
22 After I had spoken, they spoke no
more;
my words fell gently on their ears.[q]
23 They waited for me as for showers
and drank in my words as the spring
rain.
24 When I smiled at them, they scarcely
believed it;
the light of my face was precious to
them.[a]
25 I chose the way for them and sat as their
chief;
I dwelt as a king among his troops;
I was like one who comforts mourners.

30 "But now they mock me,
men younger than I,
whose fathers I would have disdained
to put with my sheep dogs.
2 Of what use was the strength of their
hands to me,
since their vigor had gone from them?
3 Haggard from want and hunger,
they roamed[b] the parched land
in desolate wastelands at night.
4 In the brush they gathered salt herbs,
and their food[c] was the root of the
broom tree.
5 They were banished from their fellow
men,
shouted at as if they were thieves.
6 They were forced to live in the dry stream
beds,
among the rocks and in holes in the
ground.
7 They brayed among the bushes
and huddled in the undergrowth.
8 A base and nameless brood,
they were driven out of the land.

9 "And now their sons mock me[r] in song;
I have become a byword[s] among them.
10 They detest me and keep their distance;
they do not hesitate to spit in my face.[t]
11 Now that God has unstrung my bow and
afflicted me,
they throw off restraint in my
presence.
12 On my right the tribe[d] attacks;
they lay snares for my feet,[u]
they build their siege ramps
against me.[v]
13 They break up my road;
they succeed in destroying me—
without anyone's helping them.[e]

30:9 r Ps69:11 s Job17:6
30:10 t Nu12:14; Dt25:9; Isa50:6; Mt26:67
30:12 u Ps140:4–5 v Job19:12

[a]24 The meaning of the Hebrew for this clause is uncertain. [b]3 Or *gnawed* [c]4 Or *fuel* [d]12 The meaning of the Hebrew for this word is uncertain. [e]13 Or *me. / 'No one can help him,' ⌊they say⌋.*

30:16 w Ps 42:4
30:22 x Job 27:21 y Job 9:17
30:25 z Ps 35:13–14; Ro 12:15
30:26 a Jer 8:15
30:28 b Ps 42:9
30:29 c Mic 1:8
30:30 d Ps 102:3

14 They advance as through a gaping breach;
amid the ruins they come rolling in.
15 Terrors overwhelm me;
my dignity is driven away as by the wind,
my safety vanishes like a cloud.

16 "And now my life ebbs away;[w]
days of suffering grip me.
17 Night pierces my bones;
my gnawing pains never rest.
18 In his great power ⌊God⌋ becomes like clothing to me[a];
he binds me like the neck of my garment.
19 He throws me into the mud,
and I am reduced to dust and ashes.

20 "I cry out to you, O God, but you do not answer;
I stand up, but you merely look at me.
21 You turn on me ruthlessly;
with the might of your hand you attack me.
22 You snatch me up and drive me before the wind;[x]
you toss me about in the storm.[y]
23 I know you will bring me down to death,
to the place appointed for all the living.

24 "Surely no one lays a hand on a broken man
when he cries for help in his distress.
25 Have I not wept for those in trouble?
Has not my soul grieved for the poor?[z]
26 Yet when I hoped for good, evil came;
when I looked for light, then came darkness.[a]
27 The churning inside me never stops;
days of suffering confront me.
28 I go about blackened,[b] but not by the sun;
I stand up in the assembly and cry for help.
29 I have become a brother of jackals,
a companion of owls.[c]
30 My skin grows black and peels;
my body burns with fever.[d]
31 My harp is tuned to mourning,
and my flute to the sound of wailing.

31:1 e Mt 5:28
31:2 f Job 20:29
31:3 g Job 21:30
31:4 h 2Ch 16:9 i Pr 5:21
31:7 j Job 23:11
31:8 k Lev 26:16
31:9 l Job 24:15
31:10 m Jer 8:10
31:11 n Ge 38:24
31:13 o Dt 24:14–15
31:16 p Job 22:9

31 "I made a covenant with my eyes
not to look lustfully at a girl.[e]
2 For what is man's lot from God above,
his heritage from the Almighty on high?[f]
3 Is it not ruin[g] for the wicked,
disaster for those who do wrong?
4 Does he not see my ways[h]
and count my every step?[i]

5 "If I have walked in falsehood
or my foot has hurried after deceit—
6 let God weigh me in honest scales
and he will know that I am blameless—
7 if my steps have turned from the path,[j]
if my heart has been led by my eyes,
or if my hands have been defiled,
8 then may others eat what I have sown,[k]
and may my crops be uprooted.

9 "If my heart has been enticed[l] by a woman,
or if I have lurked at my neighbor's door,
10 then may my wife grind another man's grain,
and may other men sleep with her.[m]
11 For that would have been shameful,
a sin to be judged.[n]
12 It is a fire that burns to Destruction[b];
it would have uprooted my harvest.

13 "If I have denied justice to my menservants and maidservants
when they had a grievance against me,[o]
14 what will I do when God confronts me?
What will I answer when called to account?
15 Did not he who made me in the womb make them?
Did not the same one form us both within our mothers?

16 "If I have denied the desires of the poor
or let the eyes of the widow[p] grow weary,
17 if I have kept my bread to myself,
not sharing it with the fatherless—
18 but from my youth I reared him as would a father,

[a]18 Hebrew; Septuagint ⌊*God*⌋ *grasps my clothing* [b]12 Hebrew *Abaddon*

# Inspire

## OVERCOMING ABUSE

*The People Could Fly* is an African American folktale written by Virginia Hamilton. The folktale tells of a people with tremendous mystical powers who were captured and taken into slavery, which made them miserable. They eventually forgot that they had the power to fly. One day, an old man named Toby arose and spoke ancient words, long forgotten, to a fallen man. The words "went deep inside the man," revived him, and he "rolled over on the air" and flew. Next Toby spoke the words to a woman who had been whipped with her baby on her back. Toby went from one slave to the next speaking the ancient words, and one by one they rose on the air, leaving behind them the burdens, shame, violence and psyche of a victim. Toby reminded the people of who they were, and that ancient knowledge was the key to their freedom.

Women of color have lived in a world dominated by destructive actions and messages that bind, burden and produce guilt and shame. Most have internalized these disparaging messages and now find themselves laboring in arenas that God never created them to labor in. To internalize the violence is to become its victim. It is to forget that "every human life is a reflection of the divinity." To internalize the abuse is to forget the divine testimony proclaimed about us: "It was very good" (Ge 1:31). To internalize the shame is to forget that God cared enough to shape and make us in our mother's womb (see Job 31:15; Ps 22:9–10). Internalizing the violence causes self-blame and destroys the ability to see ourselves evolving. Internalizing negativity blocks us from realizing our tremendous creative potential that mirrors the divine impulse to beget life.

We have creative potential to bring forth life not only in procreation, but also through our spirit and through our thoughts. We can let go of old destructive patterns that limit the Holy Spirit within us and curb intellectual, psychological and emotional development. As reflections of God, we have the propensity to love, forgive and show patience with ourselves and others. Let us remember.

—N. Bryant

For the next Inspire note, go to page 628.

### read

Job 31:15; see also Genesis 1:27–31; 9:6; Psalm 139:13–16.

**See also** the Inspire Notes "Courage to Heal," "Sexual Abuse," "Suffering," "Distress," "The Paradox of Life and Suffering," "Domestic Violence," "Forgiveness: The Doorway to Healing and Reconciliation" and "Peace," and the Women of the Bible Notes "Hagar: Battered, Beaten and Rejected—but Not Abandoned," "Dinah: An Abused Woman," "The Levite's Concubine: Broken Pieces" and "Tamar: A Violated Woman."

### WOMAN of COLOR

What are you internalizing that causes you to forget who you were created to be?

and from my birth I guided the
widow—
19 if I have seen anyone perishing for lack of
clothing,
or a needy man without a garment,
20 and his heart did not bless me
for warming him with the fleece from
my sheep,
21 if I have raised my hand against the
fatherless,
knowing that I had influence in court,
22 then let my arm fall from the shoulder,
let it be broken off at the joint.[q]
23 For I dreaded destruction from God,
and for fear of his splendor[r] I could not
do such things.

24 "If I have put my trust in gold
or said to pure gold, 'You are my
security,'[s]
25 if I have rejoiced over my great wealth,[t]
the fortune my hands had gained,
26 if I have regarded the sun[u] in its radiance
or the moon moving in splendor,
27 so that my heart was secretly enticed
and my hand offered them a kiss of
homage,
28 then these also would be sins to be
judged,[v]
for I would have been unfaithful to
God on high.

29 "If I have rejoiced at my enemy's
misfortune
or gloated over the trouble that came
to him[w]—
30 I have not allowed my mouth to sin
by invoking a curse against his life—
31 if the men of my household have never
said,
'Who has not had his fill of Job's
meat?'[x]—
32 but no stranger had to spend the night in
the street,
for my door was always open to the
traveler[y]—
33 if I have concealed[z] my sin as men do,[a]
by hiding my guilt in my heart
34 because I so feared the crowd[a]
and so dreaded the contempt of the
clans
that I kept silent and would not go
outside—

35 ("Oh, that I had someone to hear me![b]
I sign now my defense—let the
Almighty answer me;
let my accuser[c] put his indictment in
writing.
36 Surely I would wear it on my shoulder,
I would put it on like a crown.
37 I would give him an account of my every
step;
like a prince[d] I would approach
him.)—

38 "if my land cries out against me
and all its furrows are wet with tears,
39 if I have devoured its yield without
payment[e]
or broken the spirit of its tenants,[f]
40 then let briers[g] come up instead of wheat
and weeds instead of barley."

The words of Job are ended.

## Elihu

32 So these three men stopped answer-
ing Job, because he was righteous in
his own eyes.[h] 2 But Elihu son of Barakel the
Buzite,[i] of the family of Ram, became very
angry with Job for justifying himself rather
than God. 3 He was also angry with the three
friends, because they had found no way to
refute Job, and yet had condemned him.[b]
4 Now Elihu had waited before speaking to
Job because they were older than he. 5 But
when he saw that the three men had nothing
more to say, his anger was aroused.

6 So Elihu son of Barakel the Buzite said:

"I am young in years,
and you are old;[j]
that is why I was fearful,
not daring to tell you what I know.
7 I thought, 'Age should speak;
advanced years should teach wisdom.'
8 But it is the spirit[c] in a man,
the breath of the Almighty, that gives
him understanding.[k]
9 It is not only the old[d] who are wise,[l]
not only the aged who understand
what is right.

**31:22** q Job 38:15
**31:23** r Job 13:11
**31:24** s Mt 6:24; Mk 10:24
**31:25** t Ps 62:10
**31:26** u Eze 8:16
**31:28** v Dt 17:2–7
**31:29** w Pr 17:5
**31:31** x Job 22:7
**31:32** y Ge 19:2–3
**31:33** z Pr 28:13
**31:34** a Ex 23:2
**31:35** b Job 19:7; 30:28 c Job 35:14
**31:37** d Job 1:3; 29:25
**31:39** e 1Ki 21:19 f Jas 5:4
**31:40** g Ge 3:18
**32:1** h Job 33:9
**32:2** i Ge 22:21
**32:6** j Job 15:10
**32:8** k Pr 2:6
**32:9** l 1Co 1:26

[a]33 Or *as Adam did* [b]3 Masoretic Text; an ancient Hebrew scribal tradition *Job, and so had condemned God* [c]8 Or *Spirit*; also in verse 18 [d]9 Or *many*; or *great*

10 "Therefore I say: Listen to me;
I too will tell you what I know.
11 I waited while you spoke,
I listened to your reasoning;
while you were searching for words,
12 I gave you my full attention.
But not one of you has proved Job wrong;
none of you has answered his arguments.
13 Do not say, 'We have found wisdom;[m]
let God refute him, not man.'
14 But Job has not marshaled his words against me,
and I will not answer him with your arguments.

15 "They are dismayed and have no more to say;
words have failed them.
16 Must I wait, now that they are silent,
now that they stand there with no reply?
17 I too will have my say;
I too will tell what I know.
18 For I am full of words,
and the spirit within me compels me;
19 inside I am like bottled-up wine,
like new wineskins ready to burst.
20 I must speak and find relief;
I must open my lips and reply.
21 I will show partiality[n] to no one,[o]
nor will I flatter any man;
22 for if I were skilled in flattery,
my Maker would soon take me away.

33 "But now, Job, listen to my words;
pay attention to everything I say.
2 I am about to open my mouth;
my words are on the tip of my tongue.
3 My words come from an upright heart;
my lips sincerely speak what I know.[p]
4 The Spirit of God has made me;[q]
the breath of the Almighty[r] gives me life.
5 Answer me then, if you can;
prepare yourself and confront me.
6 I am just like you before God;
I too have been taken from clay.
7 No fear of me should alarm you,
nor should my hand be heavy upon you.

8 "But you have said in my hearing—
I heard the very words—
9 'I am pure[s] and without sin;
I am clean and free from guilt.
10 Yet God has found fault with me;
he considers me his enemy.[t]
11 He fastens my feet in shackles;[u]
he keeps close watch on all my paths.'

12 "But I tell you, in this you are not right,
for God is greater than man.
13 Why do you complain to him[v]
that he answers none of man's words[a]?
14 For God does speak[w]—now one way, now another—
though man may not perceive it.
15 In a dream,[x] in a vision of the night,
when deep sleep falls on men
as they slumber in their beds,
16 he may speak[y] in their ears
and terrify them with warnings,
17 to turn man from wrongdoing
and keep him from pride,
18 to preserve his soul from the pit,[b]
his life from perishing by the sword.[c]
19 Or a man may be chastened on a bed of pain
with constant distress in his bones,
20 so that his very being finds food[z] repulsive
and his soul loathes the choicest meal.
21 His flesh wastes away to nothing,
and his bones, once hidden, now stick out.[a]
22 His soul draws near to the pit,[d]
and his life to the messengers of death.[e]

23 "Yet if there is an angel on his side
as a mediator, one out of a thousand,
to tell a man what is right for him,
24 to be gracious to him and say,
'Spare him from going down to the pit[f];
I have found a ransom for him'—
25 then his flesh is renewed like a child's;
it is restored as in the days of his youth.
26 He prays to God and finds favor with him,
he sees God's face and shouts for joy;[b]

**32:13** m Jer 9:23
**32:21** n Lev 19:15 o Mt 22:16
**33:3** p Job 6:28; 27:4; 36:4
**33:4** q Ge 2:7 r Job 27:3
**33:9** s Job 10:7
**33:10** t Job 13:24
**33:11** u Job 13:27
**33:13** v Isa 45:9
**33:14** w Ps 62:11
**33:15** x Job 4:13
**33:16** y Job 36:10,15
**33:20** z Ps 107:18
**33:21** a Job 16:8
**33:26** b Job 22:26

[a]13 Or *that he does not answer for any of his actions* [b]18 Or *preserve him from the grave* [c]18 Or *from crossing the River* [d]22 Or *He draws near to the grave* [e]22 Or *to the dead* [f]24 Or *grave*

33:27 c Lk 15:21 d Ro 6:21
33:28 e Job 22:28
33:29 f Eph 1:11; Php 2:13
33:30 g Ps 56:13
34:3 h Job 12:11
34:7 i Job 15:16
34:10 j Job 8:3
34:11 k Ps 62:12; Mt 16:27

he is restored by God to his righteous state.
27 Then he comes to men and says,
'I sinned, and perverted what was right,[c]
but I did not get what I deserved.[d]
28 He redeemed my soul from going down to the pit,[a]
and I will live to enjoy the light.'[e]

29 "God does all these things to a man[f]—
twice, even three times—
30 to turn back his soul from the pit,[b]
that the light of life[g] may shine on him.
31 "Pay attention, Job, and listen to me;
be silent, and I will speak.
32 If you have anything to say, answer me;
speak up, for I want you to be cleared.
33 But if not, then listen to me;
be silent, and I will teach you wisdom."

34 Then Elihu said:

2 "Hear my words, you wise men;
listen to me, you men of learning.
3 For the ear tests words
as the tongue tastes food.[h]
4 Let us discern for ourselves what is right;
let us learn together what is good.

5 "Job says, 'I am innocent,
but God denies me justice.
6 Although I am right,
I am considered a liar;
although I am guiltless,
his arrow inflicts an incurable wound.'
7 What man is like Job,
who drinks scorn like water?[i]
8 He keeps company with evildoers;
he associates with wicked men.
9 For he says, 'It profits a man nothing
when he tries to please God.'

10 "So listen to me, you men of understanding.
Far be it from God to do evil,
from the Almighty to do wrong.[j]
11 He repays a man for what he has done;[k]
he brings upon him what his conduct deserves.
12 It is unthinkable that God would do wrong,
that the Almighty would pervert justice.[l]
13 Who appointed him over the earth?
Who put him in charge of the whole world?[m]
14 If it were his intention
and he withdrew his spirit[c] and breath,[n]
15 all mankind would perish together
and man would return to the dust.[o]

16 "If you have understanding, hear this;
listen to what I say.
17 Can he who hates justice govern?[p]
Will you condemn the just and mighty One?
18 Is he not the One who says to kings, 'You are worthless,'
and to nobles, 'You are wicked,'[q]
19 who shows no partiality[r] to princes
and does not favor the rich over the poor,
for they are all the work of his hands?
20 They die in an instant, in the middle of the night;[s]
the people are shaken and they pass away;
the mighty are removed without human hand.[t]

21 "His eyes are on the ways of men;
he sees their every step.[u]
22 There is no dark place,[v] no deep shadow,[w]
where evildoers can hide.
23 God has no need to examine men further,
that they should come before him for judgment.
24 Without inquiry he shatters the mighty
and sets up others in their place.[x]
25 Because he takes note of their deeds,
he overthrows them in the night and they are crushed.
26 He punishes them for their wickedness
where everyone can see them,
27 because they turned from following him
and had no regard for any of his ways.[y]
28 They caused the cry of the poor to come before him,
so that he heard the cry of the needy.[z]
29 But if he remains silent, who can condemn him?
If he hides his face, who can see him?

34:12 l Job 8:3
34:13 m Job 38:4,6
34:14 n Ps 104:29
34:15 o Ge 3:19
34:17 p 2Sa 23:3–4
34:18 q Ex 22:28
34:19 r Dt 10:17
34:20 s Ex 12:29 t Job 12:19
34:21 u Job 31:4
34:22 v Ps 139:12 w Am 9:2–3
34:24 x Da 2:21
34:27 y 1Sa 15:11
34:28 z Ex 22:23; Jas 5:4

[a]28 Or *redeemed me from going down to the grave* [b]30 Or *turn back him back from the grave* [c]14 Or *Spirit*

**34:35**
a Job 35:16
**34:36**
b Job 22:15
**35:3**
c Job 9:29–31; 34:9
**35:5**
d Job 22:12
**35:7**
e Pr 9:12
f Job 22:2–3; Lk 17:10
**35:9**
g Ex 2:23
h Job 12:19

Yet he is over man and nation alike,
30 to keep a godless man from ruling,
from laying snares for the people.
31 "Suppose a man says to God,
'I am guilty but will offend no more.
32 Teach me what I cannot see;
if I have done wrong, I will not do so again.'
33 Should God then reward you on your terms,
when you refuse to repent?
You must decide, not I;
so tell me what you know.

34 "Men of understanding declare,
wise men who hear me say to me,
35 'Job speaks without knowledge;[a]
his words lack insight.'
36 Oh, that Job might be tested to the utmost
for answering like a wicked man![b]
37 To his sin he adds rebellion;
scornfully he claps his hands among us
and multiplies his words against God."

# 35

Then Elihu said:

2 "Do you think this is just?
You say, 'I will be cleared by God.[a]'
3 Yet you ask him, 'What profit is it to me,[b]
and what do I gain by not sinning?'[c]

4 "I would like to reply to you
and to your friends with you.
5 Look up at the heavens and see;
gaze at the clouds so high above you.[d]
6 If you sin, how does that affect him?
If your sins are many, what does that do to him?
7 If you are righteous, what do you give to him,
or what does he receive[e] from your hand?[f]
8 Your wickedness affects only a man like yourself,
and your righteousness only the sons of men.

9 "Men cry out[g] under a load of oppression;
they plead for relief from the arm of the powerful.[h]
10 But no one says, 'Where is God my Maker,
who gives songs in the night,[i]
11 who teaches[j] more to us than to[c] the beasts of the earth
and makes us wiser than[d] the birds of the air?'
12 He does not answer[k] when men cry out
because of the arrogance of the wicked.
13 Indeed, God does not listen to their empty plea;
the Almighty pays no attention to it.[l]
14 How much less, then, will he listen
when you say that you do not see him,
that your case is before him
and you must wait for him,
15 and further, that his anger never punishes
and he does not take the least notice of wickedness.[e]
16 So Job opens his mouth with empty talk;
without knowledge he multiplies words."[m]

# 36

Elihu continued:

2 "Bear with me a little longer and I will show you
that there is more to be said in God's behalf.
3 I get my knowledge from afar;
I will ascribe justice to my Maker.
4 Be assured that my words are not false;
one perfect in knowledge is with you.

5 "God is mighty, but does not despise men;
he is mighty, and firm in his purpose.
6 He does not keep the wicked alive
but gives the afflicted their rights.
7 He does not take his eyes off the righteous;[n]
he enthrones them with kings[o]
and exalts them forever.
8 But if men are bound in chains,
held fast by cords of affliction,
9 he tells them what they have done—
that they have sinned arrogantly.
10 He makes them listen[p] to correction

**35:10**
i Ps 42:8; Ac 16:25
**35:11**
j Ps 94:12
**35:12**
k Pr 1:28
**35:13**
l Isa 1:15; Jer 11:11
**35:16**
m Job 34:35,37
**36:7**
n Ps 33:18
o Ps 113:8
**36:10**
p Job 33:16

[a]2 Or *My righteousness is more than God's* [b]3 Or *you* [c]11 Or *teaches us by* [d]11 Or *us wise by* [e]15 Symmachus, Theodotion and Vulgate; the meaning of the Hebrew for this word is uncertain.

36:11 q Isa 1:19
36:12 r Job 15:22
36:16 s Hos 2:14 t Ps 23:5
36:20 u Job 34:20,25
36:21 v Ps 66:18 w Heb 11:25
36:23 x Job 34:13
36:24 y Ps 92:5 z Rev 15:3
36:26 a 1Co 13:12

and commands them to repent of their
evil.
11 If they obey and serve him,[q]
they will spend the rest of their days in
prosperity
and their years in contentment.
12 But if they do not listen,
they will perish by the sword[a][r]
and die without knowledge.

13 "The godless in heart harbor resentment;
even when he fetters them, they do not
cry for help.
14 They die in their youth,
among male prostitutes of the shrines.
15 But those who suffer he delivers in their
suffering;
he speaks to them in their affliction.

16 "He is wooing[s] you from the jaws of
distress
to a spacious place free from
restriction,
to the comfort of your table[t] laden with
choice food.
17 But now you are laden with the judgment
due the wicked;
judgment and justice have taken hold
of you.
18 Be careful that no one entices you by
riches;
do not let a large bribe turn you aside.
19 Would your wealth
or even all your mighty efforts
sustain you so you would not be in
distress?
20 Do not long for the night,[u]
to drag people away from their
homes.[b]
21 Beware of turning to evil,[v]
which you seem to prefer to affliction.[w]

22 "God is exalted in his power.
Who is a teacher like him?
23 Who has prescribed his ways for him,[x]
or said to him, 'You have done wrong'?
24 Remember to extol his work,[y]
which men have praised in song.[z]
25 All mankind has seen it;
men gaze on it from afar.
26 How great is God—beyond our
understanding![a]
The number of his years is past finding
out.[b]
27 "He draws up the drops of water,
which distill as rain to the streams[c];[c]
28 the clouds pour down their moisture
and abundant showers fall on
mankind.
29 Who can understand how he spreads out
the clouds,
how he thunders from his pavilion?
30 See how he scatters
his lightning
about him,
bathing the depths
of the sea.
31 This is the way he
governs[d] the
nations[d]
and provides food in
abundance.[e]
32 He fills his hands with
lightning
and commands it
to strike its
mark.
33 His thunder
announces the
coming storm;
even the cattle make known its
approach.[e]

*"God revealed himself . . . with all the suddenness of a flash of lighting, showing . . . that he pervaded the universe and that there was no place where God was not."*
—SOJOURNER TRUTH, ACTIVIST AND ABOLITIONIST

37 "At this my heart pounds
and leaps from its place.
2 Listen! Listen to the roar of his voice,
to the rumbling that comes from his
mouth.
3 He unleashes his lightning beneath the
whole heaven
and sends it to the ends of the earth.
4 After that comes the sound of his roar;
he thunders with his majestic voice.
When his voice resounds,
he holds nothing back.
5 God's voice thunders in marvelous ways;
he does great things beyond our
understanding.[f]
6 He says to the snow,[g] 'Fall on the earth,'
and to the rain shower, 'Be a mighty
downpour.'
7 So that all men he has made may know
his work,

36:26 b Heb 1:12
36:27 c Ps 147:8
36:31 d Job 37:13 e Ac 14:17
37:5 f Job 5:9
37:6 g Job 38:22

[a] 12 Or *will cross the River* [b] 20 The meaning of the Hebrew for verses 18–20 is uncertain. [c] 27 Or *distill from the mist as rain* [d] 31 Or *nourishes* [e] 33 Or *announces his coming— / the One zealous against evil*

he stops every man from his labor.[a]
[8] The animals take cover;
they remain in their dens.[h]
[9] The tempest comes out from its chamber,
the cold from the driving winds.
[10] The breath of God produces ice,
and the broad waters become frozen.[i]
[11] He loads the clouds with moisture;
he scatters his lightning through them.
[12] At his direction they swirl around
over the face of the whole earth
to do whatever he commands them.[j]
[13] He brings the clouds to punish men,
or to water his earth[b] and show his love.[k]

[14] "Listen to this, Job;
stop and consider God's wonders.
[15] Do you know how God controls the clouds
and makes his lightning flash?
[16] Do you know how the clouds hang poised,
those wonders of him who is perfect in knowledge?[l]
[17] You who swelter in your clothes
when the land lies hushed under the south wind,
[18] can you join him in spreading out the skies,[m]
hard as a mirror of cast bronze?

[19] "Tell us what we should say to him;
we cannot draw up our case because of our darkness.
[20] Should he be told that I want to speak?
Would any man ask to be swallowed up?
[21] Now no one can look at the sun,
bright as it is in the skies
after the wind has swept them clean.
[22] Out of the north he comes in golden splendor;
God comes in awesome majesty.
[23] The Almighty is beyond our reach and exalted in power;[n]
in his justice and great righteousness,
he does not oppress.
[24] Therefore, men revere him,[o]
for does he not have regard for all the wise[p] in heart?[c]"

## The LORD Speaks

**38** Then the LORD answered Job out of the storm.[q] He said:

[2] "Who is this that darkens my counsel
with words without knowledge?
[3] Brace yourself like a man;
I will question you,
and you shall answer me.[r]

[4] "Where were you when I laid the earth's foundation?[s]
Tell me, if you understand.
[5] Who marked off its dimensions? Surely you know!
Who stretched a measuring line across it?
[6] On what were its footings set,
or who laid its cornerstone[t]—
[7] while the morning stars sang together
and all the angels[d] shouted for joy?

[8] "Who shut up the sea behind doors
when it burst forth from the womb,[u]
[9] when I made the clouds its garment
and wrapped it in thick darkness,
[10] when I fixed limits for it
and set its doors and bars in place,[v]
[11] when I said, 'This far you may come and no farther;
here is where your proud waves halt'?[w]

[12] "Have you ever given orders to the morning,
or shown the dawn its place,
[13] that it might take the earth by the edges
and shake the wicked[x] out of it?
[14] The earth takes shape like clay under a seal;
its features stand out like those of a garment.
[15] The wicked are denied their light,
and their upraised arm is broken.[y]

[16] "Have you journeyed to the springs of the sea
or walked in the recesses of the deep?
[17] Have the gates of death been shown to you?

**37:8** h Ps 104:22
**37:10** i Job 38:29–30; Ps 147:17
**37:12** j Ps 148:8
**37:13** k Ex 9:18; 1Ki 18:45; Job 38:27
**37:16** l Job 36:4
**37:18** m Isa 44:24
**37:23** n 1Ti 6:16
**37:24** o Mt 10:28
**37:24** p Mt 11:25
**38:1** q Job 40:6
**38:3** r Job 40:7
**38:4** s Ps 104:5; Pr 8:29
**38:6** t Job 26:7
**38:8** u Ge 1:9–10
**38:10** v Job 26:10
**38:11** w Ps 89:9
**38:13** x Ps 104:35
**38:15** y Ps 10:15

[a]7 Or *I he fills all men with fear by his power* [b]13 Or *to favor them* [c]24 Or *for he does not have regard for any who think they are wise.* [d]7 Hebrew *the sons of God*

**38:23** z Isa 30:30; Eze 13:11 a Ex 9:18; Jos 10:11; Rev 16:21
**38:27** b Ps 104:14
**38:28** c Ps 147:8; Jer 14:22
**38:29** d Ps 147:16–17
**38:31** e Job 9:9; Am 5:8

Have you seen the gates of the shadow
of death[a]?
18 Have you comprehended the vast
expanses of the earth?
Tell me, if you know all this.

19 "What is the way to the abode of light?
And where does darkness reside?
20 Can you take them to their places?
Do you know the paths to their
dwellings?
21 Surely you know, for you were already
born!
You have lived so many years!

22 "Have you entered the storehouses of the
snow
or seen the storehouses of the hail,
23 which I reserve for times of trouble,[z]
for days of war and battle?[a]
24 What is the way to the place where the
lightning is dispersed,
or the place where the east winds are
scattered over the earth?
25 Who cuts a channel for the torrents of
rain,
and a path for the thunderstorm,
26 to water a land where no man lives,
a desert with no one in it,
27 to satisfy a desolate wasteland
and make it sprout with grass?[b]
28 Does the rain have a father?[c]
Who fathers the drops of dew?
29 From whose womb comes the ice?
Who gives birth to the frost from the
heavens[d]
30 when the waters become hard as stone,
when the surface of the deep is
frozen?

31 "Can you bind the beautiful[b] Pleiades?
Can you loose the cords of Orion?[e]
32 Can you bring forth the constellations in
their seasons[c]
or lead out the Bear[d] with its cubs?
33 Do you know the laws of the heavens?
Can you set up ⌊God's[e]⌋ dominion over
the earth?

34 "Can you raise your voice to the clouds
and cover yourself with a flood of
water?
35 Do you send the lightning bolts on their
way?
Do they report to you, 'Here we are'?
36 Who endowed the heart[f] with wisdom
or gave understanding[f] to the mind[f]?
37 Who has the wisdom to count the clouds?
Who can tip over the water jars of the
heavens
38 when the dust becomes hard
and the clods of earth stick together?

39 "Do you hunt the prey for the lioness
and satisfy the hunger of the lions[g]
40 when they crouch in their dens
or lie in wait in a thicket?
41 Who provides food for the raven
when its young cry out to God
and wander about for lack of food?[h]

39 "Do you know when the mountain
goats give birth?
Do you watch when the doe bears her
fawn?
2 Do you count the months till they bear?
Do you know the time they give birth?
3 They crouch down and bring forth their
young;
their labor pains are ended.
4 Their young thrive and grow strong in
the wilds;
they leave and do not return.

5 "Who let the wild donkey go free?
Who untied his ropes?
6 I gave him the wasteland[i] as his home,
the salt flats as his habitat.[j]
7 He laughs at the commotion in the town;
he does not hear a driver's shout.
8 He ranges the hills for his pasture
and searches for any green thing.

9 "Will the wild ox[k] consent to serve you?
Will he stay by your manger at night?
10 Can you hold him to the furrow with a
harness?
Will he till the valleys behind you?
11 Will you rely on him for his great
strength?
Will you leave your heavy work to
him?
12 Can you trust him to bring in your grain
and gather it to your threshing floor?

**38:36** f Job 32:8; Ps 51:6; Ecc 2:26
**38:39** g Ps 104:21
**38:41** h Ps 147:9; Mt 6:26
**39:6** i Job 24:5; Jer 2:24 j Hos 8:9
**39:9** k Nu 23:22; Dt 33:17

[a]17 Or *gates of deep shadows* [b]31 Or *the twinkling*; or *the chains of the* [c]32 Or *the morning star in its season*
[d]32 Or *out Leo* [e]33 Or *his*; or *their* [f]36 The meaning of the Hebrew for this word is uncertain.

Inspire leadership FOCUS

## GOD IS IN CONTROL

Knowing God's purpose for our lives is a gift in and of itself. As we walk through life with the revelation of who we are and why we were created, we can have confidence that the Lord is in control. Job 38 details many ways in which God is mighty and all-knowing. From governing the constellations (see vv. 31–33) to controlling the weather (see vv. 34–38) to providing for the natural order (see vv. 39–41), God has the universe in his hand.

As children of God, we were made in his image. Our divine DNA is connected to the One who has all power in his hands. He placed everything inside of us that we need to continue our divine journey. We never have to doubt that we have been equipped with every resource we need to fulfill God's purpose for our lives (see Eph 1:3–10).

As leaders, we will face challenges and trials in life. Giving up on our hopes, dreams and visions can sometimes be tempting when life doesn't seem to go in the direction we expect. However, we must remember that God's ways are not like ours (see Isa 55:9). While we are often emotionally moved by a glimpse of the momentary situation, our Lord sits on high and sees beyond our circumstance. Understanding our purpose allows us to know that we are victorious in all of our endeavors, no matter what is going on around us. Every obstacle we overcome and every trial we get through is uniquely intertwined into God's destiny for us.

The fact that we were chosen to be leaders—to walk in the purpose and destiny God has given us—means that he has entrusted us with our divine assignments. He knows that we will get through the good and the bad. Job was faced with incredible trials and tribulations (see Job 1–2). No matter what he faced, he knew God was more powerful and had all circumstances under his control (see Job 42:2).

As leaders, we can learn from the example of Job. As we lead in our predestined purpose, we should remain faithful and fearless. We were created by God with greatness in mind. We were created to serve God's people. Lead on, my sisters! Serve on!

—S. Givens

### read

Job 39–40; Psalm 86:8–10; Isaiah 55:8–9.

See also the Inspire Notes "Bumping Into Omnipotence," "God Is Immutable," "God Is Sovereign" and "Omniscience: God Is All-Knowing," and the Women of the Bible Note "Job's Wife: She Was Tested Too."

### WOMAN of COLOR

When you question yourself and your purpose, look to the Bible for strength, and remember whose you are.

For the next Inspire note, go to page 637.

[13] "The wings of the ostrich flap joyfully,
but they cannot compare with the
pinions and feathers of the stork.
[14] She lays her eggs on the ground
and lets them warm in the sand,
[15] unmindful that a foot may crush them,
that some wild animal may trample
them.
[16] She treats her young harshly,[l] as if they
were not hers;
she cares not that her labor was in
vain,
[17] for God did not endow her with wisdom
or give her a share of good sense.
[18] Yet when she spreads her feathers to run,
she laughs at horse and rider.

[19] "Do you give the horse his strength
or clothe his neck with a flowing
mane?
[20] Do you make him leap like a locust,
striking terror with his proud
snorting?
[21] He paws fiercely, rejoicing in his strength,
and charges into the fray.[m]
[22] He laughs at fear, afraid of nothing;
he does not shy away from the sword.
[23] The quiver rattles against his side,
along with the flashing spear and
lance.
[24] In frenzied excitement he eats up the
ground;
he cannot stand still when the trumpet
sounds.
[25] At the blast of the trumpet he snorts,
'Aha!'
He catches the scent of battle from
afar,
the shout of commanders and the
battle cry.

[26] "Does the hawk take flight by your
wisdom
and spread his wings toward the
south?
[27] Does the eagle soar at your command
and build his nest on high?[n]
[28] He dwells on a cliff and stays there at
night;
a rocky crag is his stronghold.
[29] From there he seeks out his food;
his eyes detect it from afar.
[30] His young ones feast on blood,
and where the slain are, there is he."[o]

# 40

[1] The LORD said to Job:[p]

[2] "Will the one who contends with the
Almighty correct him?
Let him who accuses God answer
him!"

[3] Then Job answered the LORD:

[4] "I am unworthy—how can I reply to you?
I put my hand over my mouth.[q]
[5] I spoke once, but I have no answer—
twice, but I will say no more."

[6] Then the LORD spoke to Job out of the
storm:[r]

[7] "Brace yourself like a man;
I will question you,
and you shall answer me.[s]

[8] "Would you discredit my justice?[t]
Would you condemn me to justify
yourself?
[9] Do you have an arm like God's,
and can your voice thunder like his?
[10] Then adorn yourself with glory and
splendor,
and clothe yourself in honor and
majesty.[u]
[11] Unleash the fury of your wrath,
look at every proud man and bring
him low,[v]
[12] look at every proud man and humble
him,[w]
crush the wicked where they stand.
[13] Bury them all in the dust together;
shroud their faces in the grave.
[14] Then I myself will admit to you
that your own right hand can save you.

[15] "Look at the behemoth,[a]
which I made along with you
and which feeds on grass like an ox.
[16] What strength he has in his loins,
what power in the muscles of his belly!
[17] His tail[b] sways like a cedar;
the sinews of his thighs are close-knit.
[18] His bones are tubes of bronze,
his limbs like rods of iron.
[19] He ranks first among the works of God,[x]

**39:16** l La 4:3
**39:21** m Jer 8:6
**39:27** n Ob 1:4
**39:30** o Mt 24:28; Lk 17:37
**40:1** p Job 33:13
**40:4** q Job 29:9
**40:6** r Job 38:1
**40:7** s Job 42:4
**40:8** t Ro 3:3
**40:10** u Ps 93:1; 104:1
**40:11** v Isa 2:11,12,17; Da 4:37
**40:12** w 1Sa 2:7
**40:19** x Job 41:33

[a] 15 Possibly the hippopotamus or the elephant [b] 17 Possibly trunk

40:20
y Ps 104:14
z Ps 104:26

41:1
a Ps 104:26; Isa 27:1

41:2
b Isa 37:29

41:11
c Ro 11:35
d Ex 19:5; Dt 10:14; 1Co 10:26

yet his Maker can approach him with
his sword.
20 The hills bring him their produce,[y]
and all the wild animals play[z] nearby.
21 Under the lotus plants he lies,
hidden among the reeds in the marsh.
22 The lotuses conceal him in their shadow;
the poplars by the stream surround
him.
23 When the river rages, he is not alarmed;
he is secure, though the Jordan should
surge against his mouth.
24 Can anyone capture him by the eyes,[a]
or trap him and pierce his nose?

41 "Can you pull in the leviathan[b][a] with
a fishhook
or tie down his tongue with a rope?
2 Can you put a cord through his nose
or pierce his jaw with a hook?[b]
3 Will he keep begging you for mercy?
Will he speak to you with gentle
words?
4 Will he make an agreement with you
for you to take him as your slave for
life?
5 Can you make a pet of him like a bird
or put him on a leash for your girls?
6 Will traders barter for him?
Will they divide him up among the
merchants?
7 Can you fill his hide with harpoons
or his head with fishing spears?
8 If you lay a hand on him,
you will remember the struggle and
never do it again!
9 Any hope of subduing him is false;
the mere sight of him is overpowering.
10 No one is fierce enough to rouse him.
Who then is able to stand against me?
11 Who has a claim against me that I must
pay?[c]
Everything under heaven belongs
to me.[d]
12 "I will not fail to speak of his limbs,
his strength and his graceful form.
13 Who can strip off his outer coat?
Who would approach him with a
bridle?
14 Who dares open the doors of his mouth,
ringed about with his fearsome teeth?
15 His back has[c] rows of shields
tightly sealed together;
16 each is so close to the next
that no air can pass between.
17 They are joined fast to one another;
they cling together and cannot be
parted.
18 His snorting throws out flashes of light;
his eyes are like the rays of dawn.
19 Firebrands stream from his mouth;
sparks of fire shoot out.
20 Smoke pours from his nostrils
as from a boiling pot over a fire of
reeds.
21 His breath sets coals ablaze,
and flames dart from his mouth.
22 Strength resides in his neck;
dismay goes before him.
23 The folds of his flesh are tightly joined;
they are firm and immovable.
24 His chest is hard as rock,
hard as a lower millstone.
25 When he rises up, the mighty are
terrified;
they retreat before his thrashing.
26 The sword that reaches him has no effect,
nor does the spear or the dart or the
javelin.
27 Iron he treats like straw
and bronze like rotten wood.
28 Arrows do not make him flee;
slingstones are like chaff to him.
29 A club seems to him but a piece of straw;
he laughs at the rattling of the lance.
30 His undersides are jagged potsherds,
leaving a trail in the mud like a
threshing sledge.
31 He makes the depths churn like a boiling
caldron
and stirs up the sea like a pot of
ointment.
32 Behind him he leaves a glistening wake;
one would think the deep had white
hair.
33 Nothing on earth is his equal—
a creature without fear.
34 He looks down on all that are haughty;
he is king over all that are proud."

[a]24 Or *by a water hole* [b]1 Possibly the crocodile [c]15 Or *His pride is his*

**42:2** e Ge 18:14; Mt 19:26
**42:3** f Job 38:2
**42:4** g Job 38:3; 40:7
**42:6** h Job 40:4 i Ezr 9:6
**42:8** j Nu 23:1,29 k Jas 5:15–16; 1Jn 5:16

## Job

**42** Then Job replied to the LORD:

2 "I know that you can do all things;[e]
 no plan of yours can be thwarted.
3 ⌊You asked,⌋ 'Who is this that obscures my
 counsel without knowledge?'[f]
Surely I spoke of things I did not
 understand,
things too wonderful for me to know.

4 ⌊"You said,⌋ 'Listen now, and I will speak;
 I will question you,
 and you shall answer me.'[g]
5 My ears had heard of you
 but now my eyes have seen you.
6 Therefore I despise myself[h]
 and repent in dust and ashes."[i]

### Epilogue

7 After the LORD had said these things to Job, he said to Eliphaz the Temanite, "I am angry with you and your two friends, because you have not spoken of me what is right, as my servant Job has. 8 So now take seven bulls and seven rams[j] and go to my servant Job and sacrifice a burnt offering for yourselves. My servant Job will pray for you, and I will accept his prayer[k] and not deal with you according to your folly. You have not spoken of me what is right, as my servant Job has." 9 So Eliphaz the Temanite, Bildad the Shuhite and Zophar the Naamathite did what the LORD told them; and the LORD accepted Job's prayer.

10 After Job had prayed for his friends, the LORD made him prosperous again[l] and gave him twice as much as he had before. 11 All his brothers and sisters and everyone who had known him before[m] came and ate with him in his house. They comforted and consoled him over all the trouble the LORD had brought upon him, and each one gave him a piece of silver[a] and a gold ring.

12 The LORD blessed the latter part of Job's life more than the first. He had fourteen thousand sheep, six thousand camels, a thousand yoke of oxen and a thousand donkeys. 13 And he also had seven sons and three daughters. 14 The first daughter he named Jemimah, the second Keziah and the third Keren-Happuch. 15 Nowhere in all the land were there found women as beautiful as Job's daughters, and their father granted them an inheritance along with their brothers.

16 After this, Job lived a hundred and forty years; he saw his children and their children to the fourth generation. 17 And so he died, old and full of years.[n]

**42:10** l Ps 14:7
**42:11** m Job 19:13
**42:17** n Ge 25:8

[a] 11 Hebrew *him a kesitah*; a kesitah was a unit of money of unknown weight and value.

# Psalms

## OVERVIEW

The book of Psalms is a compilation of prayer, praise and instruction for personal and corporate expressions between God and his people. Among the five divisions, the psalms lend themselves to a number of themes: thanksgiving, worship, petition, instruction and requests for God's judgment and forgiveness. Also included are Scriptures that direct attention to the Messiah, Jesus Christ.

The emotions of a woman are as diverse as the psalms in this book. As women we find many psalms to relate to, and as Christians we resonate with the psalmists in their portrayals of their relationship with God. Within this book are songs of ecstatic joy, laments of sorrows and expressions of fear, anger and hope. As you read through the book of Psalms, meditate on those Scriptures that most closely relate to your stage of life and growth as a believer.

## OUTLINE

I. Book I (Psalms 1–41)
II. Book II (Psalms 42–72)
III. Book III (Psalms 73–89)
IV. Book IV (Psalms 90–106)
V. Book V (Psalms 107–150)

## SCANNABLE FACTS:

**Authors:** Moses, David, Asaph, the "Sons of Korah" and other named or unnamed authors

**Time Written:** Other than Psalm 90—traditionally ascribed to Moses (around 1440 B.C.)—the psalms were written between the time of David (around 1000 B.C.) and the period following the Babylonian captivity (sometime after 538 B.C.)

**Themes to Note:** Prayer, praise, penance, justice and worship

**Notable Women:** Various types of women are referred to in poetical fashion: a royal bride, a barren woman, etc.

1:1
a Pr 4:14
b Ps 26:4; Jer 15:17

1:2
c Ps 119:16,35
d Jos 1:8

1:3
e Jer 17:8
f Ge 39:3

1:4
g Job 21:18; Isa 17:13

1:6
h Ps 37:18; 2Ti 2:19

# BOOK I

*Psalms 1—41*

## Psalm 1

1 Blessed is the man
who does not walk[a] in the counsel of the wicked
or stand in the way of sinners
or sit[b] in the seat of mockers.
2 But his delight[c] is in the law of the LORD,
and on his law he meditates[d] day and night.
3 He is like a tree planted by streams of water,[e]
which yields its fruit in season
and whose leaf does not wither.
Whatever he does prospers.[f]

*My treasure,*

*Meditate on me throughout this day and every day.*

*The Living Word*

PSALM 1:1–3

4 Not so the wicked!
They are like chaff[g]
that the wind blows away.
5 Therefore the wicked will not stand in the judgment,
nor sinners in the assembly of the righteous.

6 For the LORD watches over[h] the way of the righteous,
but the way of the wicked will perish.

## Psalm 2

1 Why do the nations conspire[a]
and the peoples plot in vain?
2 The kings of the earth take their stand
and the rulers gather together
against the LORD
and against his Anointed[i] One.[b][j]
3 "Let us break their chains," they say,
"and throw off their fetters."

4 The One enthroned in heaven laughs;[k]
the Lord scoffs at them.
5 Then he rebukes them in his anger
and terrifies them in his wrath, saying,
6 "I have installed my King[c]
on Zion, my holy hill."

7 I will proclaim the decree of the LORD:

He said to me, "You are my Son[d];
today I have become your Father.[e][l]
8 Ask of me,
and I will make the nations your inheritance,
the ends of the earth[m] your possession.
9 You will rule them with an iron scepter[f];
you will dash them to pieces[n] like pottery.[o]"

10 Therefore, you kings, be wise;
be warned, you rulers of the earth.
11 Serve the LORD with fear
and rejoice with trembling.
12 Kiss the Son, lest he be angry
and you be destroyed in your way,
for his wrath[p] can flare up in a moment.
Blessed are all who take refuge in him.

## Psalm 3

A psalm of David. When he fled from his son Absalom.[q]

1 O LORD, how many are my foes!
How many rise up against me!
2 Many are saying of me,
"God will not deliver him.[r]" *Selah*[g]

3 But you are a shield[s] around me, O LORD;
you bestow glory on me and lift[h] up my head.[t]
4 To the LORD I cry aloud,
and he answers me from his holy hill. *Selah*

5 I lie down and sleep;[u]
I wake again, because the LORD sustains me.
6 I will not fear[v] the tens of thousands
drawn up against me on every side.

2:2
i Jn 1:41
j Ac 4:25–26*

2:4
k Ps 37:13

2:7
l Ac 13:33*

2:8
m Ps 22:27

2:9
n Ps 89:23
o Rev 2:27*

2:12
p Rev 6:16

3:1
q 2Sa 15:14

3:2
r Ps 71:11

3:3
s Ge 15:1; Ps 28:7
t Ps 27:6

3:5
u Lev 26:6

3:6
v Ps 27:3

[a]1 Hebrew; Septuagint *rage* [b]2 Or *anointed one* [c]6 Or *king* [d]7 Or *son*; also in verse 12 [e]7 Or *have begotten you* [f]9 Or *will break them with a rod of iron* [g]2 A word of uncertain meaning, occurring frequently in the Psalms; possibly a musical term [h]3 Or *LORD, / my Glorious One, who lifts*

**3:7** w Job 16:10
**3:8** x Isa 43:3,11
**4:1** y Ps 17:6
**4:4** z Eph 4:26* a Ps 77:6
**4:5** b Dt 33:19; Ps 37:3
**4:6** c Nu 6:25

*God,*

*Thank you for lifting up my head,*
*for loving me so much and for hearing*
*my prayers. Help me to remember to*
*share your goodness with others.*

*Amen.*

PSALM 3:3–4

7 Arise, O LORD!
Deliver me, O my God!
Strike[w] all my enemies on the jaw;
break the teeth of the wicked.

8 From the LORD comes deliverance.[x]
May your blessing be on your people.
*Selah*

## Psalm 4

For the director of music.
With stringed instruments.
A psalm of David.

1 Answer me when I call to you,
O my righteous God.
Give me relief from my distress;
be merciful to me and hear my prayer.[y]
2 How long, O men, will you turn my glory
into shame[a]?
How long will you love delusions and
seek false gods[b]? *Selah*
3 Know that the LORD has set apart the
godly for himself;
the LORD will hear when I call to him.

4 In your anger do not sin;[z]
when you are on your beds,[a]
search your hearts and be silent.
*Selah*
5 Offer right sacrifices
and trust in the LORD.[b]
6 Many are asking, "Who can show us any
good?"
Let the light of your face shine upon
us,[c] O LORD.
7 You have filled my heart with greater joy[d]
than when their grain and new wine
abound.
8 I will lie down and sleep[e] in peace,
for you alone, O LORD,
make me dwell in safety.[f]

## Psalm 5

For the director of music. For flutes.
A psalm of David.

1 Give ear to my words, O LORD,
consider my sighing.
2 Listen to my cry for help,
my King and my God,
for to you I pray.
3 In the morning, O LORD, you hear my
voice;
in the morning I lay my requests
before you
and wait in expectation.

4 You are not a God who
takes pleasure
in evil;
with you the wicked
cannot dwell.
5 The arrogant[g] cannot
stand in your
presence;
you hate all who do
wrong.
6 You destroy those who
tell lies;[h]
bloodthirsty and
deceitful men
the LORD abhors.

7 But I, by your great mercy,
will come into your house;
in reverence will I bow down
toward your holy temple.
8 Lead me, O LORD, in your righteousness
because of my enemies—
make straight your way before me.

9 Not a word from their mouth can be
trusted;
their heart is filled with destruction.
Their throat is an open grave;
with their tongue they speak deceit.[i]
10 Declare them guilty, O God!
Let their intrigues be their downfall.

**4:7** d Isa 9:3
**4:8** e Ps 3:5 f Lev 25:18
**5:5** g Ps 73:3
**5:6** h Ps 55:23
**5:9** i Ro 3:13*

*"The best and most beautiful things in the world cannot be seen or touched . . . but are felt in the heart."*
—HELEN KELLER, ADVOCATE FOR BLIND AND DEAF PEOPLE

[a]2 Or *you dishonor my Glorious One* [b]2 Or *seek lies*

**5:11** j Ps69:36
**5:12** k Ps32:7
**6:2** l Ps22:14
**6:3** m Jn12:27
**6:5** n Ps30:9; Isa38:18
**6:7** o Ps31:9
**6:8** p Ps119:115
**6:9** q Ps116:1
**7:1** r Ps31:15

Banish them for their many sins,
for they have rebelled against you.

11 But let all who take refuge in you be glad;
let them ever sing for joy.
Spread your protection over them,
that those who love your name[j] may
rejoice in you.
12 For surely, O LORD, you bless the righteous;
you surround them[k] with your favor as
with a shield.

## Psalm 6

For the director of music. With
stringed instruments. According to
*sheminith.*[a] A psalm of David.

1 O LORD, do not rebuke me in your anger
or discipline me in your wrath.
2 Be merciful to me, LORD, for I am faint;
O LORD, heal me, for my bones are in
agony.[l]
3 My soul is in anguish.[m]
How long, O LORD, how long?
4 Turn, O LORD, and deliver me;
save me because of your unfailing love.
5 No one remembers you when he is dead.
Who praises you from the grave[b]?[n]

6 I am worn out from groaning;
all night long I flood my bed with
weeping
and drench my couch with tears.
7 My eyes grow weak[o] with sorrow;
they fail because of all my foes.

8 Away from me,[p] all you who do evil,
for the LORD has heard my weeping.
9 The LORD has heard my cry for mercy;[q]
the LORD accepts my prayer.
10 All my enemies will be ashamed and
dismayed;
they will turn back in sudden disgrace.

## Psalm 7

A *shiggaion*[c] of David, which he
sang to the LORD concerning
Cush, a Benjamite.

1 O LORD my God, I take refuge in you;
save and deliver me from all who
pursue me,[r]
2 or they will tear me like a lion
and rip me to pieces with no one to
rescue me.

3 O LORD my God, if I have done this
and there is guilt on my hands[s]—
4 if I have done evil to him who is at peace
with me
or without cause have robbed my
foe—
5 then let my enemy pursue and
overtake me;
let him trample my life to the ground
and make me sleep in the dust. *Selah*

6 Arise,[t] O LORD, in your anger;
rise up against the rage of my enemies.
Awake,[u] my God; decree justice.
7 Let the assembled peoples gather around
you.
Rule over them from on high;
8 let the LORD judge the peoples.
Judge me, O LORD, according to my
righteousness,[v]
according to my integrity, O Most
High.
9 O righteous God,[w]
who searches minds and hearts,[x]
bring to an end the violence of the wicked
and make the righteous secure.

10 My shield[d] is God Most High,
who saves the upright in heart.[y]
11 God is a righteous judge,
a God who expresses his wrath every
day.
12 If he does not relent,
he[e] will sharpen his sword;[z]
he will bend and string his bow.
13 He has prepared his deadly weapons;
he makes ready his flaming arrows.

14 He who is pregnant with evil
and conceives trouble gives birth[a] to
disillusionment.
15 He who digs a hole and scoops it out
falls into the pit he has made.[b]
16 The trouble he causes recoils on himself;
his violence comes down on his own
head.

17 I will give thanks to the LORD because of
his righteousness

**7:3** s 1Sa24:11; Isa59:3
**7:6** t Ps94:2 u Ps44:23
**7:8** v Ps18:20
**7:9** w Jer11:20 x Rev2:23
**7:10** y Ps125:4
**7:12** z Dt32:41
**7:14** a Isa59:4; Jas1:15
**7:15** b Job4:8

[a] Title: Probably a musical term [b] 5 Hebrew *Sheol* [c] Title: Probably a literary or musical term [d] 10 Or *sovereign*
[e] 12 Or *If a man does not repent, / God*

Inspire

## TRUE JOY

Joy is a deep, inner gladness that comes from a clear conscience. It is not the same as happiness because happiness depends on what happens to you. If you have a bad day, you are not happy. But joy comes from trusting God and believing in God's promises. "Let all who take refuge in [God] be glad; let them ever sing for joy" (Ps 5:11).

Joy is a result of our faith and obedience (see Jn 15:10–11). We can have joy because our hope lies in God, and we know that God is faithful. Joy is not something we can work for; joy is a product of our faith, a fruit of the Holy Spirit (see Gal 5:22). The Bible says the joy of the Lord is our strength (see Ne 8:10).

I have often wondered at the joy expressed in the hearts and minds of our ancestors. These women and men experienced unimaginable suffering, dehumanizing conditions and immobilizing fear—yet they managed to be joyful. The lives of slaves contained little happiness, but there were many times when the joyous cries of Africa's dark children could be heard. There were times when the slaves could momentarily set aside their bondage and freely dance and sing. I'm certain that there were times when heaven itself looked down and wondered at the joy and adulation of God's children. This joy expressed itself most often when the slaves gathered in brush arbors, in fields and in secret places for worship.

Worship is the key to joy, giving honor to the Most High God. Communion with God produces joy—joy like a river—joy, unspeakable joy flooding the soul! The abundance of joy is in direct proportion to the intimacy and steadfastness of the believer's walk with God.

True joy is evident regardless of circumstances. Those who love God rejoice even in the midst of troubles (see Jas 1:2–3). The harshness of this world, especially as it relates to persons of color, has a marked effect on happiness. But God promises a joy that the world can't give and that the world can't take away. Spend time with God and receive your joy! "Rejoice in the Lord and be glad, you righteous; sing, all you who are upright in heart!" (Ps 32:11).

—C. Belt

### read

Psalm 5; see also Nehemiah 8:2–12; James 1:2–4.
**See also** the Inspire Notes "Dance, Sisters, Dance" and "Adopted Through Love," and the Women of the Bible Notes "Michal: A Disappointed Bride" and "Mary of Bethany: The Unforgotten Woman."

### WOMAN of COLOR

Does your communion with God produce joy despite the difficult circumstances of life?

For the next Inspire note, go to page 647.

8:1 c Ps 113:4; 148:13
8:2 d Mt 21:16* e Ps 44:16
8:4 f Job 7:17
8:5 g Ps 21:5; 103:4
8:6 h Heb 2:6–8*

and will sing praise to the name of the
LORD Most High.

## Psalm 8

For the director of music. According to *gittith.*[a] A psalm of David.

1 O LORD, our Lord,
how majestic is your name in all the earth!

You have set your glory
above the heavens.[c]
2 From the lips of children and infants
you have ordained praise[b][d]
because of your enemies,
to silence the foe[e] and the avenger.

3 When I consider your heavens,
the work of your fingers,
the moon and the stars,
which you have set in place,
4 what is man that you are mindful of him,
the son of man that you care for him?[f]
5 You made him a little lower than the heavenly beings[c]
and crowned him with glory and honor.[g]

*Father God,*

*when I think of your awesome creation, I am humbled. Thank you for making me a part of your divine plan. Help me always to act as your daughter, made by your hand.*

*Amen*

PSALM 8:3–5

6 You made him ruler over the works of your hands;
you put everything under his feet:[h]
7 all flocks and herds,
and the beasts of the field,
8 the birds of the air,
and the fish of the sea,
all that swim the paths of the seas.

9 O LORD, our Lord,
how majestic is your name in all the earth![i]

8:9 i ver 1
9:1 j Ps 86:12
9:2 k Ps 5:11 l Ps 83:18
9:6 m Ps 34:16
9:8 n Ps 96:13
9:9 o Ps 32:7
9:10 p Ps 91:14
9:11 q Ps 105:1
9:12 r Ge 9:5

## Psalm 9[d]

For the director of music. To ⌊the tune of⌋ "The Death of the Son." A psalm of David.

1 I will praise you, O LORD, with all my heart;[j]
I will tell of all your wonders.
2 I will be glad and rejoice[k] in you;
I will sing praise to your name,[l] O Most High.

3 My enemies turn back;
they stumble and perish before you.
4 For you have upheld my right and my cause;
you have sat on your throne, judging righteously.
5 You have rebuked the nations and destroyed the wicked;
you have blotted out their name for ever and ever.
6 Endless ruin has overtaken the enemy,
you have uprooted their cities;
even the memory of them[m] has perished.

7 The LORD reigns forever;
he has established his throne for judgment.
8 He will judge the world in righteousness;[n]
he will govern the peoples with justice.
9 The LORD is a refuge for the oppressed,
a stronghold in times of trouble.[o]
10 Those who know your name[p] will trust in you,
for you, LORD, have never forsaken those who seek you.

11 Sing praises to the LORD, enthroned in Zion;
proclaim among the nations what he has done.[q]
12 For he who avenges blood[r] remembers;
he does not ignore the cry of the afflicted.

[a]Title: Probably a musical term [b]2 Or *strength* [c]5 Or *than God* [d]Psalms 9 and 10 may have been originally a single acrostic poem, the stanzas of which begin with the successive letters of the Hebrew alphabet. In the Septuagint they constitute one psalm.

9:14 s Ps 13:5
9:15 t Ps 7:15–16
9:17 u Job 8:13
9:18 v Pr 23:18
10:1 w Ps 22:1,11
10:3 x Ps 94:4

13 O LORD, see how my enemies
persecute me!
Have mercy and lift me up from the
gates of death,
14 that I may declare your praises
in the gates of the Daughter of Zion
and there rejoice in your salvation.[s]
15 The nations have fallen into the pit they
have dug;[t]
their feet are caught in the net they
have hidden.
16 The LORD is known by his justice;
the wicked are ensnared by the work of
their hands. *Higgaion.*[a] *Selah*
17 The wicked return to the grave,[b]
all the nations that forget God.[u]
18 But the needy will not always be
forgotten,
nor the hope[v] of the afflicted ever
perish.

19 Arise, O LORD, let not man triumph;
let the nations be judged in your
presence.
20 Strike them with terror, O LORD;
let the nations know they are but men.
*Selah*

## Psalm 10[c]

1 Why, O LORD, do you stand far off?[w]
Why do you hide yourself in times of
trouble?

2 In his arrogance the wicked man hunts
down the weak,
who are caught in the schemes he
devises.
3 He boasts[x] of the cravings of his heart;
he blesses the greedy and reviles the
LORD.
4 In his pride the wicked does not seek
him;
in all his thoughts there is no room
for God.
5 His ways are always prosperous;
he is haughty and your laws are far
from him;
he sneers at all his enemies.
6 He says to himself, "Nothing will
shake me;
I'll always be happy[y] and never have
trouble."
7 His mouth is full of curses[z] and lies and
threats;
trouble and evil are under his tongue.
8 He lies in wait near the villages;
from ambush he murders the
innocent,
watching in secret for his victims.
9 He lies in wait like a lion in cover;
he lies in wait to catch the helpless;
he catches the helpless and drags them
off in his net.
10 His victims are crushed, they collapse;
they fall under his strength.
11 He says to himself, "God has forgotten;[a]
he covers his face and never sees."

12 Arise, LORD! Lift up your hand,[b] O God.
Do not forget the helpless.[c]
13 Why does the wicked man revile God?
Why does he say to himself,
"He won't call me to account"?
14 But you, O God, do see trouble and grief;
you consider it to take it in hand.
The victim commits himself to you;
you are the helper[d] of the fatherless.
15 Break the arm of the wicked and evil
man;
call him to account for his wickedness
that would not be found out.

16 The LORD is King for ever and ever;[e]
the nations[f] will perish from his land.
17 You hear, O LORD, the desire of the
afflicted;
you encourage them, and you listen to
their cry,
18 defending the fatherless and the
oppressed,[g]
in order that man, who is of the earth,
may terrify no more.

## Psalm 11

For the director of music. Of David.

1 In the LORD I take refuge.
How then can you say to me:
"Flee like a bird to your mountain.
2 For look, the wicked bend their bows;

10:6 y Rev 18:7
10:7 z Ro 3:14*
10:11 a Job 22:13
10:12 b Mic 5:9 c Ps 9:12
10:14 d Ps 68:5
10:16 e Ps 29:10 f Dt 8:20
10:18 g Ps 9:9

[a]16 Or *Meditation*; possibly a musical notation [b]17 Hebrew *Sheol* [c]Psalms 9 and 10 may have been originally a single acrostic poem, the stanzas of which begin with the successive letters of the Hebrew alphabet. In the Septuagint they constitute one psalm.

they set their arrows[h] against the strings
to shoot from the shadows
at the upright in heart.[i]
3 When the foundations[j] are being destroyed,
what can the righteous do[a]?"

4 The LORD is in his holy temple;[k]
the LORD is on his heavenly throne.
He observes the sons of men;
his eyes examine[l] them.
5 The LORD examines the righteous,[m]
but the wicked[b] and those who love violence
his soul hates.[n]
6 On the wicked he will rain
fiery coals and burning sulfur;
a scorching wind will be their lot.

7 For the LORD is righteous,
he loves justice;
upright men will see his face.[o]

## Psalm 12

For the director of music. According to *sheminith.*[c] A psalm of David.

1 Help, LORD, for the godly are no more;[p]
the faithful have vanished from among men.
2 Everyone lies to his neighbor;
their flattering lips speak with deception.

3 May the LORD cut off all flattering lips
and every boastful tongue
4 that says, "We will triumph with our tongues;
we own our lips[d]—who is our master?"

5 "Because of the oppression of the weak
and the groaning of the needy,
I will now arise," says the LORD.
"I will protect them from those who malign them."
6 And the words of the LORD are flawless,[q]
like silver refined in a furnace of clay,
purified seven times.

7 O LORD, you will keep us safe
and protect us from such people forever.
8 The wicked freely strut[r] about
when what is vile is honored among men.

## Psalm 13

For the director of music.
A psalm of David.

1 How long, O LORD? Will you forget me forever?
How long will you hide your face[s] from me?
2 How long must I wrestle with my thoughts[t]
and every day have sorrow in my heart?
How long will my enemy triumph over me?

3 Look on me and answer, O LORD my God.
Give light to my eyes,[u] or I will sleep in death;[v]
4 my enemy will say, "I have overcome him,[w]"
and my foes will rejoice when I fall.

5 But I trust in your unfailing love;
my heart rejoices in your salvation.[x]
6 I will sing to the LORD,
for he has been good to me.

## Psalm 14

For the director of music. Of David.

1 The fool[e] says in his heart,
"There is no God."[y]
They are corrupt, their deeds are vile;
there is no one who does good.

2 The LORD looks down from heaven[z]
on the sons of men
to see if there are any who understand,[a]
any who seek God.
3 All have turned aside,
they have together become corrupt;
there is no one who does good,
not even one.[b]

[a]3 Or *what is the Righteous One doing* [b]5 Or *The LORD, the Righteous One, examines the wicked, /* [c]Title: Probably a musical term [d]4 Or */ our lips are our plowshares* [e]1 The Hebrew words rendered *fool* in Psalms denote one who is morally deficient.

**11:2** h Ps 7:13 i Ps 64:3–4
**11:3** j Ps 82:5
**11:4** k Ps 18:6 l Ps 34:15–16
**11:5** m Ge 22:1 n Ps 5:5
**11:7** o Ps 17:15
**12:1** p Isa 57:1
**12:6** q 2Sa 22:31; Ps 18:30; Pr 30:5
**12:8** r Ps 55:10–11
**13:1** s Job 13:24
**13:2** t Ps 42:4
**13:3** u Ezr 9:8 v Jer 51:39
**13:4** w Ps 25:2
**13:5** x Ps 9:14
**14:1** y Ps 10:4
**14:2** z Ps 33:13 a Ps 92:6
**14:3** b Ro 3:10–12*

14:4 c Isa 64:7
14:6 d Ps 9:9
14:7 e Ps 53:6
15:1 f Ps 24:3–5
15:2 g Eph 4:25
15:3 h Ex 23:1
15:4 i Ac 28:10
15:5 j Ex 22:25 k 2Pe 1:10
16:2 l Ps 73:25
16:3 m Ps 101:6
16:4 n Ps 32:10

4 Will evildoers never learn—
those who devour my people as men eat bread
and who do not call on the LORD?[c]
5 There they are, overwhelmed with dread,
for God is present in the company of the righteous.
6 You evildoers frustrate the plans of the poor,
but the LORD is their refuge.[d]
7 Oh, that salvation for Israel would come out of Zion!
When the LORD restores the fortunes[e] of his people,
let Jacob rejoice and Israel be glad!

## Psalm 15

A psalm of David.

1 LORD, who may dwell in your sanctuary?
Who may live on your holy hill?[f]
2 He whose walk is blameless
and who does what is righteous,
who speaks the truth[g] from his heart
3 and has no slander[h] on his tongue,
who does his neighbor no wrong
and casts no slur on his fellowman,
4 who despises a vile man
but honors[i] those who fear the LORD,
who keeps his oath
even when it hurts,
5 who lends his money without usury[j]
and does not accept a bribe against the innocent.

He who does these things
will never be shaken.[k]

## Psalm 16

A *miktam*[a] of David.

1 Keep me safe, O God,
for in you I take refuge.
2 I said to the LORD, "You are my Lord;
apart from you I have no good thing."[l]
3 As for the saints who are in the land,[m]
they are the glorious ones in whom is all my delight.[b]
4 The sorrows[n] of those will increase

*Child,*

*I am your refuge. Seek me always.*

*Your Loving Father*

PSALM 16:1

who run after other gods.
I will not pour out their libations of blood
or take up their names[o] on my lips.
5 LORD, you have assigned me my portion and my cup;[p]
you have made my lot secure.
6 The boundary lines have fallen for me in pleasant places;
surely I have a delightful inheritance.
7 I will praise the LORD, who counsels me;[q]
even at night my heart instructs me.
8 I have set the LORD always before me.
Because he is at my right hand,
I will not be shaken.
9 Therefore my heart is glad[r] and my tongue rejoices;
my body also will rest secure,
10 because you will not abandon me to the grave,[c]
nor will you let your Holy One[d] see decay.
11 You have made[e] known to me the path of life;[s]
you will fill me with joy in your presence,[t]
with eternal pleasures at your right hand.

## Psalm 17

A prayer of David.

1 Hear, O LORD, my righteous plea;
listen to my cry.
Give ear to my prayer—
it does not rise from deceitful lips.[u]

16:4 o Ex 23:13
16:5 p Ps 23:5
16:7 q Ps 73:24
16:9 r Ps 4:7
16:11 s Mt 7:14 t Ac 2:25–28*
17:1 u Isa 29:13

[a]Title: Probably a literary or musical term [b]3 Or *As for the pagan priests who are in the land / and the nobles in whom all delight, I said:* [c]10 Hebrew *Sheol* [d]10 Or *your faithful one* [e]11 Or *You will make*

2 May my vindication come from you;
may your eyes see what is right.

3 Though you probe my heart and examine me at night,
though you test me, you will find nothing;[v]
I have resolved that my mouth will not sin.
4 As for the deeds of men—
by the word of your lips
I have kept myself
from the ways of the violent.
5 My steps have held to your paths;[w]
my feet have not slipped.

6 I call on you, O God, for you will answer me;
give ear to me[x] and hear my prayer.
7 Show the wonder of your great love,[y]
you who save by your right hand
those who take refuge in you from their foes.
8 Keep me as the apple of your eye;[z]
hide me in the shadow of your wings
9 from the wicked who assail me,
from my mortal enemies who surround me.

10 They close up their callous hearts,[a]
and their mouths speak with arrogance.[b]
11 They have tracked me down, they now surround me,[c]
with eyes alert, to throw me to the ground.
12 They are like a lion[d] hungry for prey,
like a great lion crouching in cover.

13 Rise up, O LORD, confront them, bring them down;
rescue me from the wicked by your sword.
14 O LORD, by your hand save me from such men,
from men of this world whose reward is in this life.

You still the hunger of those you cherish;
their sons have plenty,
and they store up wealth for their children.

15 And I—in righteousness I will see your face;
when I awake, I will be satisfied with seeing your likeness.[e]

## Psalm 18

For the director of music. Of David the servant of the LORD. He sang to the LORD the words of this song when the LORD delivered him from the hand of all his enemies and from the hand of Saul. He said:

1 I love you, O LORD, my strength.

2 The LORD is my rock, my fortress and my deliverer;
my God is my rock, in whom I take refuge.
He is my shield and the horn[a] of my salvation, my stronghold.
3 I call to the LORD, who is worthy of praise,
and I am saved from my enemies.

4 The cords of death[f] entangled me;
the torrents[g] of destruction overwhelmed me.
5 The cords of the grave[b] coiled around me;
the snares of death confronted me.
6 In my distress I called to the LORD;
I cried to my God for help.
From his temple he heard my voice;
my cry came before him, into his ears.

7 The earth trembled and quaked,
and the foundations of the mountains shook;
they trembled because he was angry.
8 Smoke rose from his nostrils;
consuming fire came from his mouth,
burning coals blazed out of it.
9 He parted the heavens and came down;[h]
dark clouds were under his feet.
10 He mounted the cherubim and flew;
he soared on the wings of the wind.[i]
11 He made darkness his covering,[j] his canopy around him—
the dark rain clouds of the sky.
12 Out of the brightness of his presence[k] clouds advanced,
with hailstones and bolts of lightning.
13 The LORD thundered[l] from heaven;

**17:3** v Job 23:10
**17:5** w Ps 44:18
**17:6** x Ps 116:2
**17:7** y Ps 31:21
**17:8** z Dt 32:10
**17:10** a Ps 73:7 b 1Sa 2:3
**17:11** c Ps 88:17
**17:12** d Ps 7:2
**17:15** e Ps 4:6–7; 16:11; 1Jn 3:2
**18:4** f Ps 116:3 g Ps 124:4
**18:9** h Ps 144:5
**18:10** i Ps 104:3
**18:11** j Ps 97:2
**18:12** k Ps 104:2
**18:13** l Ps 29:3

[a]2 *Horn* here symbolizes strength. [b]5 Hebrew *Sheol*

the voice of the Most High resounded.[a]
14 He shot his arrows and scattered ⌞the enemies⌟,
great bolts of lightning and routed them.[m]
15 The valleys of the sea were exposed
and the foundations of the earth laid bare
at your rebuke,[n] O LORD,
at the blast of breath from your nostrils.

16 He reached down from on high and took hold of me;
he drew me out of deep waters.
17 He rescued me from my powerful enemy,
from my foes, who were too strong for me.
18 They confronted me in the day of my disaster,
but the LORD was my support.
19 He brought me out into a spacious place;[o]
he rescued me because he delighted in me.

20 The LORD has dealt with me according to my righteousness;
according to the cleanness of my hands he has rewarded me.
21 For I have kept the ways of the LORD;[p]
I have not done evil by turning from my God.
22 All his laws are before me;
I have not turned away from his decrees.
23 I have been blameless before him
and have kept myself from sin.
24 The LORD has rewarded me according to my righteousness,[q]
according to the cleanness of my hands in his sight.

25 To the faithful you show yourself faithful,
to the blameless you show yourself blameless,
26 to the pure you show yourself pure,
but to the crooked you show yourself shrewd.[r]
27 You save the humble
but bring low those whose eyes are haughty.[s]
28 You, O LORD, keep my lamp burning;
my God turns my darkness into light.[t]
29 With your help I can advance against a troop[b];
with my God I can scale a wall.

30 As for God, his way is perfect;[u]
the word of the LORD is flawless.[v]
He is a shield
for all who take refuge in him.
31 For who is God besides the LORD?[w]
And who is the Rock[x] except our God?
32 It is God who arms me with strength
and makes my way perfect.
33 He makes my feet like the feet of a deer;[y]
he enables me to stand on the heights.[z]
34 He trains my hands for battle;[a]
my arms can bend a bow of bronze.
35 You give me your shield of victory,
and your right hand sustains me;
you stoop down to make me great.
36 You broaden the path beneath me,
so that my ankles do not turn.

37 I pursued my enemies and overtook them;
I did not turn back till they were destroyed.
38 I crushed them so that they could not rise;[b]
they fell beneath my feet.
39 You armed me with strength for battle;
you made my adversaries bow at my feet.
40 You made my enemies turn their backs in flight,
and I destroyed my foes.
41 They cried for help, but there was no one to save them—
to the LORD, but he did not answer.[c]
42 I beat them as fine as dust borne on the wind;
I poured them out like mud in the streets.

43 You have delivered me from the attacks of the people;
you have made me the head of nations;[d]
people I did not know are subject to me.
44 As soon as they hear me, they obey me;
foreigners cringe before me.

**18:14** m Ps 144:6
**18:15** n Ps 76:6; 106:9
**18:19** o Ps 31:8
**18:21** p 2Ch 34:33
**18:24** q 1Sa 26:23
**18:26** r Pr 3:34
**18:27** s Pr 6:17
**18:28** t Job 18:6
**18:30** u Dt 32:4 v Ps 12:6
**18:31** w Dt 32:39; 86:8; Isa 45:5,6,14, 18,21 x Dt 32:31
**18:33** y Hab 3:19 z Dt 32:13
**18:34** a Ps 144:1
**18:38** b Ps 36:12
**18:41** c Pr 1:28
**18:43** d 2Sa 8:1–14

[a]13 Some Hebrew manuscripts and Septuagint (see also 2 Samuel 22:14); most Hebrew manuscripts *resounded, / amid hailstones and bolts of lightning* [b]29 Or *can run through a barricade*

**18:45** e Mic 7:17
**18:47** f Ps 47:3
**18:49** g Ps 108:1 h Ro 15:9*
**18:50** i Ps 144:10
**19:1** j Isa 40:22 k Ro 1:19
**19:2** l Ps 74:16
**19:4** m Ro 10:18*
**19:6** n Ps 113:3
**19:7** o Ps 23:3 p Ps 93:5; 111:7
**19:8** q Ps 119:128

45 They all lose heart;
they come trembling from their strongholds.[e]

46 The LORD lives! Praise be to my Rock!
Exalted be God my Savior!
47 He is the God who avenges me,
who subdues nations[f] under me,
48 who saves me from my enemies.
You exalted me above my foes;
from violent men you rescued me.
49 Therefore I will praise you among the nations, O LORD;
I will sing[g] praises to your name.[h]
50 He gives his king great victories;
he shows unfailing kindness to his anointed,
to David[i] and his descendants forever.

## Psalm 19

For the director of music.
A psalm of David.

1 The heavens[j] declare[k] the glory of God;
the skies proclaim the work of his hands.
2 Day after day they pour forth speech;
night after night they display knowledge.[l]
3 There is no speech or language
where their voice is not heard.[a]
4 Their voice[b] goes out into all the earth,
their words to the ends of the world.[m]

In the heavens he has pitched a tent for the sun,
5 which is like a bridegroom coming forth from his pavilion,
like a champion rejoicing to run his course.
6 It rises at one end of the heavens
and makes its circuit to the other;[n]
nothing is hidden from its heat.

7 The law of the LORD is perfect,
reviving the soul.[o]
The statutes of the LORD are trustworthy,[p]
making wise the simple.
8 The precepts of the LORD are right,[q]
giving joy to the heart.
The commands of the LORD are radiant,
giving light to the eyes.
9 The fear of the LORD is pure,
enduring forever.
The ordinances of the LORD are sure
and altogether righteous.
10 They are more precious than gold,
than much pure gold;
they are sweeter than honey,
than honey from the comb.
11 By them is your servant warned;
in keeping them there is great reward.

12 Who can discern his errors?
Forgive my hidden faults.[r]
13 Keep your servant also from willful sins;
may they not rule over me.
Then will I be blameless,
innocent of great transgression.

14 May the words of my mouth and the meditation of my heart
be pleasing[s] in your sight,
O LORD, my Rock and my Redeemer.

## Psalm 20

For the director of music.
A psalm of David.

1 May the LORD answer you when you are in distress;
may the name of the God of Jacob protect you.[t]
2 May he send you help from the sanctuary
and grant you support from Zion.
3 May he remember all your sacrifices
and accept your burnt offerings. *Selah*
4 May he give you the desire of your heart[u]
and make all your plans succeed.
5 We will shout for joy when you are victorious
and will lift up our banners in the name of our God.
May the LORD grant all your requests.[v]

6 Now I know that the LORD saves his anointed;[w]
he answers him from his holy heaven
with the saving power of his right hand.
7 Some trust in chariots and some in horses,
but we trust in the name of the LORD our God.[x]

**19:12** r Ps 51:2; 90:8
**19:14** s Ps 104:34
**20:1** t Ps 91:14
**20:4** u Ps 21:2; 145:16,19
**20:5** v 1Sa 1:17
**20:6** w Ps 28:8
**20:7** x 2Ch 32:8

[a]3 Or *They have no speech, there are no words; / no sound is heard from them* [b]4 Septuagint, Jerome and Syriac; Hebrew *line*

20:8
y Ps 37:23

21:4
z Ps 133:3

21:6
a 1Ch 17:27

21:8
b Isa 10:10

21:11
c Ps 2:1
d Ps 10:2

8 They are brought to their knees and fall,
but we rise up and stand firm.[y]
9 O LORD, save the king!
Answer[a] us when we call!

## Psalm 21

For the director of music.
A psalm of David.

1 O LORD, the king rejoices in your strength.
How great is his joy in the victories
you give!
2 You have granted him the desire of his
heart
and have not withheld the request of
his lips. *Selah*
3 You welcomed him with rich blessings
and placed a crown of pure gold on
his head.
4 He asked you for life, and you gave it to
him—
length of days, for ever and ever.[z]
5 Through the victories you gave, his glory
is great;
you have bestowed on him splendor
and majesty.
6 Surely you have granted him eternal
blessings
and made him glad with the joy of
your presence.[a]
7 For the king trusts in the LORD;
through the unfailing love of the Most
High
he will not be shaken.
8 Your hand will lay hold[b] on all your
enemies;
your right hand will seize your foes.
9 At the time of your appearing
you will make them like a fiery
furnace.
In his wrath the LORD will swallow
them up,
and his fire will consume them.
10 You will destroy their descendants from
the earth,
their posterity from mankind.
11 Though they plot evil[c] against you
and devise wicked schemes,[d] they
cannot succeed;
12 for you will make them turn their backs
when you aim at them with drawn
bow.
13 Be exalted, O LORD, in your strength;
we will sing and praise your might.

## Psalm 22

For the director of music. To ⌊the
tune of⌋ "The Doe of the Morning."
A psalm of David.

1 My God, my God, why have you forsaken
me?[e]
Why are you so far from saving me,
so far from the words of my groaning?
2 O my God, I cry out by day, but you do not
answer,
by night,[f] and am not silent.
3 Yet you are enthroned as the Holy One;
you are the praise of Israel.[b]
4 In you our fathers put their trust;
they trusted and you delivered them.
5 They cried to you and were saved;
in you they trusted and were not
disappointed.[g]
6 But I am a worm[h] and not a man,
scorned by men[i] and despised by the
people.
7 All who see me mock me;
they hurl insults,[j] shaking their heads:
8 "He trusts in the LORD;
let the LORD rescue him.[k]
Let him deliver him,
since he delights[l] in him."
9 Yet you brought me out of the womb;[m]
you made me trust in you
even at my mother's breast.
10 From birth[n] I was cast upon you;
from my mother's womb you have
been my God.
11 Do not be far from me,
for trouble is near
and there is no one to help.
12 Many bulls[o] surround me;
strong bulls of Bashan encircle me.
13 Roaring lions tearing their prey
open their mouths wide against me.
14 I am poured out like water,
and all my bones are out of joint.

22:1
e Mt 27:46*;
Mk 15:34*

22:2
f Ps 42:3

22:5
g Isa 49:23

22:6
h Job 25:6
i Ps 31:11

22:7
j Mt 27:39,44

22:8
k Ps 91:14
l Mt 27:43

22:9
m Ps 71:6

22:10
n Isa 46:3

22:12
o Ps 68:30

[a]9 Or *save! / O King, answer* [b]3 Or *Yet you are holy, / enthroned on the praises of Israel*

22:14 p Da 5:6
22:15 q Ps 104:29
22:16 r Isa 53:5; Zec 12:10; Jn 19:34
22:17 s Lk 23:35
22:18 t Jn 19:24*
22:20 u Ps 35:17
22:22 v Heb 2:12*
22:23 w Ps 135:19
22:24 x Heb 5:7
22:25 y Ps 35:18

My heart has turned to wax;
it has melted away[p] within me.
15 My strength is dried up like a potsherd,
and my tongue sticks to the roof of my mouth;
you lay me[a] in the dust[q] of death.
16 Dogs have surrounded me;
a band of evil men has encircled me,
they have pierced[b][r] my hands and my feet.
17 I can count all my bones;
people stare[s] and gloat over me.
18 They divide my garments among them
and cast lots[t] for my clothing.

19 But you, O LORD, be not far off;
O my Strength, come quickly to help me.
20 Deliver my life from the sword,
my precious life[u] from the power of the dogs.
21 Rescue me from the mouth of the lions;
save[c] me from the horns of the wild oxen.

22 I will declare your name to my brothers;
in the congregation I will praise you.[v]
23 You who fear the LORD, praise him![w]
All you descendants of Jacob, honor him!
Revere him, all you descendants of Israel!
24 For he has not despised or disdained
the suffering of the afflicted one;
he has not hidden his face from him
but has listened to his cry for help.[x]

25 From you comes the theme of my praise
in the great assembly;[y]
before those who fear you[d] will I fulfill my vows.
26 The poor will eat and be satisfied;
they who seek the LORD will praise him—
may your hearts live forever!
27 All the ends of the earth
will remember and turn to the LORD,
and all the families of the nations
will bow down before him,
28 for dominion belongs to the LORD
and he rules over the nations.

29 All the rich of the earth will feast and worship;
all who go down to the dust will kneel before him—
those who cannot keep themselves alive.
30 Posterity will serve him;
future generations will be told about the Lord.
31 They will proclaim his righteousness
to a people yet unborn[z]—
for he has done it.

## Psalm 23

A psalm of David.

1 The LORD is my shepherd,[a] I shall not be in want.[b]
2 He makes me lie down in green pastures,
he leads me beside quiet waters,[c]
3 he restores my soul.
He guides me in paths of righteousness[d]
for his name's sake.
4 Even though I walk
through the valley of the shadow of death,[e]
I will fear no evil,
for you are with me;[e]
your rod and your staff,
they comfort me.

5 You prepare a table before me
in the presence of my enemies.
You anoint my head with oil;[f]
my cup overflows.
6 Surely goodness and love will follow me
all the days of my life,
and I will dwell in the house of the LORD
forever.

## Psalm 24

Of David. A psalm.

1 The earth is the LORD's, and everything in it,
the world, and all who live in it;
2 for he founded it upon the seas
and established it upon the waters.

3 Who may ascend the hill of the LORD?
Who may stand in his holy place?[g]

22:31 z Ps 78:6
23:1 a Isa 40:11; Jn 10:11 b Php 4:19
23:2 c Eze 34:14; Rev 7:17
23:3 d Ps 5:8
23:4 e Isa 43:2
23:5 f Ps 92:10
24:3 g Ps 15:1

[a]15 Or / *I am laid* [b]16 Some Hebrew manuscripts, Septuagint and Syriac; most Hebrew manuscripts / *like the lion,*
[c]21 Or / *you have heard* [d]25 Hebrew *him* [e]4 Or *through the darkest valley*

24:4 h Job 17:9 i Mt 5:8

4 He who has clean hands[h] and a pure
heart,[i]
who does not lift up his soul to an idol
or swear by what is false.[a]
5 He will receive blessing from the LORD
and vindication from God his Savior.
6 Such is the generation of those who seek
him,
who seek your face,[j] O God of Jacob.[b]
*Selah*

24:6 j Ps 27:8

[a]4 Or *swear falsely* [b]6 Two Hebrew manuscripts and Syriac (see also Septuagint); most Hebrew manuscripts *face, Jacob*

# Inspire

## GRACE AND MERCY

We have historically defined *grace* as God's special gift to us or as the things we do not deserve from God. We think of *mercy* as God's compassion on us—as when God does not bring judgment against us but rather steps in and helps us. We often plead for God to "have mercy on us," for we know that we'd be in bad shape if he gave us exactly what we deserved.

At times, however, it is hard for us to see or feel the presence of God's grace and mercy in our lives because we perceive ourselves as unworthy and assume that what we cannot see or feel does not exist. Maybe we cannot see or feel grace and mercy because, as David says in Psalm 23, it follows us. It is always there behind us, upholding us, supporting us, seeing us through life, death and the darkest valleys. "Surely goodness and love [mercy] will follow me all the days of my life, and I will dwell in the house of the LORD forever" (v. 6).

When we do not feel or see God's grace and mercy, we should remember the words of the psalmist David. We should walk in the assurance that God is forever pouring out mercy and grace upon us. We should praise God for his mercy and grace—even if we cannot see it. Blessed are those who remember that God's grace and mercy are always with them and that they are never alone.

It is reassuring to know that we cannot do anything to prompt or to stop God's grace and mercy; they are both special gifts from God. Our only response should be "thank you" for these blessings. God's grace includes undeserved favor, unexpected acceptance and unconditional love—we receive those every day and should thank God for them each day!

—D. TINSLEY TAYLOR

### read

Psalm 23.

See also the Inspire Note "Forgiveness: God's Extended Mercy," and the Women of the Bible Notes "The Servant Girl: The Truth, the Whole Truth and Nothing but the Truth" and "The Forgiven Adulteress: Caught but Not Condemned."

### WOMAN *of* COLOR

How do you thank God for his grace and mercy?

For the next Inspire note, go to page 650.

**24:7** k Isa 26:2
**25:1** l Ps 86:4
**25:6** m Ps 103:17; Isa 63:7,15
**25:7** n Job 13:26 o Ps 51:1

7 Lift up your heads, O you gates;[k]
be lifted up, you ancient doors,
that the King of glory may come in.
8 Who is this King of glory?
The LORD strong and mighty,
the LORD mighty in battle.
9 Lift up your heads, O you gates;
lift them up, you ancient doors,
that the King of glory may come in.
10 Who is he, this King of glory?
The LORD Almighty—
he is the King of glory. *Selah*

## Psalm 25[a]

Of David.

1 To you, O LORD, I lift up my soul;[l]
2 in you I trust, O my God.
Do not let me be put to shame,
nor let my enemies triumph over me.
3 No one whose hope is in you
will ever be put to shame,
but they will be put to shame
who are treacherous without excuse.

*Woman of color,*

*Put your hope in me and me alone!*

*Your Sustainer*

PSALM 25:1–3

4 Show me your ways, O LORD,
teach me your paths;
5 guide me in your truth and teach me,
for you are God my Savior,
and my hope is in you all day long.
6 Remember, O LORD, your great mercy and
love,[m]
for they are from of old.
7 Remember not the sins of my youth[n]
and my rebellious ways;
according to your love[o] remember me,
for you are good, O LORD.

8 Good and upright is the LORD;
therefore he instructs sinners in his
ways.
9 He guides the humble in what is right
and teaches them his way.
10 All the ways of the LORD are loving and
faithful
for those who keep the demands of his
covenant.[p]
11 For the sake of your name, O LORD,
forgive my iniquity, though it is
great.
12 Who, then, is the man that fears the
LORD?
He will instruct him in the way chosen
for him.
13 He will spend his days in prosperity,
and his descendants will inherit the
land.
14 The LORD confides[q] in those who fear
him;
he makes his covenant known to them.
15 My eyes are ever on the LORD,[r]
for only he will release my feet from
the snare.
16 Turn to me[s] and be gracious to me,
for I am lonely and afflicted.
17 The troubles of my heart have multiplied;
free me from my anguish.
18 Look upon my affliction and my distress[t]
and take away all my sins.
19 See how my enemies[u] have increased
and how fiercely they hate me!
20 Guard my life[v] and rescue me;
let me not be put to shame,
for I take refuge in you.
21 May integrity and uprightness
protect me,
because my hope is in you.

22 Redeem Israel,[w] O God,
from all their troubles!

## Psalm 26

Of David.

1 Vindicate me, O LORD,
for I have led a blameless life;[x]
I have trusted in the LORD
without wavering.[y]
2 Test me, O LORD, and try me,
examine my heart and my mind;
3 for your love is ever before me,
and I walk continually[z] in your truth.

**25:10** p Ps 103:18
**25:14** q Pr 3:32
**25:15** r Ps 141:8
**25:16** s Ps 69:16
**25:18** t 2Sa 16:12
**25:19** u Ps 3:1
**25:20** v Ps 86:2
**25:22** w Ps 130:8
**26:1** x Ps 7:8 y 2Ki 20:3; Heb 10:23
**26:3** z 2Ki 20:3

[a] This psalm is an acrostic poem, the verses of which begin with the successive letters of the Hebrew alphabet.

**26:4** a Ps 1:1
**26:5** b Ps 139:21
**26:6** c Ps 73:13
**26:7** d Ps 9:1
**26:8** e Ps 27:4
**26:9** f Ps 28:3
**26:12** g Ps 27:11; 40:2
**27:1** h Isa 60:19 i Ex 15:2
**27:2** j Ps 14:4
**27:3** k Ps 3:6
**27:4** l Ps 90:17 m Ps 26:8

4 I do not sit[a] with deceitful men,
nor do I consort with hypocrites;
5 I abhor[b] the assembly of evildoers
and refuse to sit with the wicked.
6 I wash my hands in innocence,[c]
and go about your altar, O LORD,
7 proclaiming aloud your praise
and telling of all your wonderful
deeds.[d]
8 I love[e] the house where you live, O LORD,
the place where your glory dwells.

9 Do not take away my soul along with
sinners,
my life with bloodthirsty men,[f]
10 in whose hands are wicked schemes,
whose right hands are full of bribes.
11 But I lead a blameless life;
redeem me and be merciful to me.

12 My feet stand on level ground;[g]
in the great assembly I will praise the
LORD.

## Psalm 27

Of David.

1 The LORD is my light[h] and my
salvation[i]—
whom shall I fear?
The LORD is the stronghold of my life—
of whom shall I be afraid?
2 When evil men advance against me
to devour my flesh,[a]
when my enemies and my foes
attack me,
they will stumble and fall.[j]
3 Though an army besiege me,
my heart will not fear;[k]
though war break out against me,
even then will I be confident.

4 One thing[l] I ask of the LORD,
this is what I seek:
that I may dwell in the house of the LORD
all the days of my life,[m]
to gaze upon the beauty of the LORD
and to seek him in his temple.
5 For in the day of trouble
he will keep me safe in his dwelling;
he will hide me in the shelter of his
tabernacle
and set me high upon a rock.[n]
6 Then my head will be exalted[o]
above the enemies who surround me;
at his tabernacle will I sacrifice with
shouts of joy;
I will sing and make music to the LORD.

7 Hear my voice when I call, O LORD;
be merciful to me and answer me.
8 My heart says of you, "Seek his[b] face!"
Your face, LORD, I will seek.
9 Do not hide your face[p] from me,
do not turn your servant away in anger;
you have been my helper.
Do not reject me or forsake me,
O God my Savior.
10 Though my father and mother
forsake me,
the LORD will receive me.
11 Teach me your way, O LORD;
lead me in a straight path[q]
because of my oppressors.
12 Do not turn me over to the desire of my
foes,
for false witnesses rise up against me,
breathing out violence.

13 I am still confident of this:
I will see the goodness of the LORD
in the land of the living.
14 Wait for the LORD;
be strong and take heart
and wait for the LORD.

## Psalm 28

Of David.

1 To you I call, O LORD my Rock;
do not turn a deaf ear to me.
For if you remain silent,[r]
I will be like those who have gone
down to the pit.[s]
2 Hear my cry for mercy[t]
as I call to you for help,
as I lift up my hands
toward your Most Holy Place.[u]

3 Do not drag me away with the wicked,
with those who do evil,
who speak cordially with their neighbors
but harbor malice in their hearts.[v]
4 Repay them for their deeds

**27:5** n Ps 40:2
**27:6** o Ps 3:3
**27:9** p Ps 69:17
**27:11** q Ps 25:4
**28:1** r Ps 83:1 s Ps 88:4
**28:2** t Ps 138:2 u Ps 5:7
**28:3** v Ps 12:2

[a]2 Or *to slander me* [b]8 Or *To you, O my heart, he has said, "Seek my*

and for their evil work;
repay them for what their hands have done
and bring back upon them what they
deserve.[w]
5 Since they show no regard for the works
of the LORD
and what his hands have done,[x]
he will tear them down
and never build them up again.

6 Praise be to the LORD,
for he has heard my cry for mercy.
7 The LORD is my strength[y] and my shield;
my heart trusts[z] in him, and I am
helped.

28:4 w Rev 18:6
28:5 x Isa 5:12
28:7 y Ps 18:1 z Ps 13:5

Inspire

## CONFIDENCE

Confidence is not always an appreciated or encouraged character trait for women of color. However, a confidence based in Christ should exist in all of us. Our relationship with Christ allows us to be confident in God's ability to do all things.

True confidence begins with faith in God, faith in his Word, and faith in Jesus, our Lord and Savior. God's grace is at work in each Christian to produce the desire and power to do his will. Believing in him, one can truly say, "I can do everything through him who gives me strength" (Php 4:13).

When our confidence is truly rooted in Christ, we can identify with the words of the psalmist David: "The LORD is my light and my salvation—whom shall I fear? The LORD is the stronghold of my life—of whom shall I be afraid? . . . Though an army besiege me, my heart will not fear; though war break out against me, even then will I be confident" (Ps 27:1,3).

The ability to enjoy life and succeed in one's pursuits are gifts from God. When we are brought into a right relationship with God and are submissive to him, he then gives us joy and confidence in what we do. God promises to do great things for those who wait for him (see Ps 27:13–14). Look to him and persevere in hope, confidence and patience. Press on with confidence.

—R. HAYNES

**read**

Psalm 27; Proverbs 3:21–26; Isaiah 30:15–18; 32:17.

See also the Inspire Notes "Fear" and "Confidence for Each Day," and the Women of the Bible Notes "Jael: Just Another Woman on the Lord's Side," "Jehosheba: Standing Firm" and "Mary Magdalene: Setting Her Reputation Straight."

**WOMAN of COLOR**

In whom or in what is your confidence based?

For the next Inspire note, go to page 655.

**28:8** a Ps 20:6
**28:9** b Dt 9:29
**29:1** c 1Ch 16:28
**29:2** d 2Ch 20:21
**29:3** e Job 37:5
**29:6** f Ps 114:4 g Dt 3:9
**29:8** h Nu 13:26
**29:10** i Ps 10:16
**29:11** j Ps 28:8
**30:1** k Ps 25:2

My heart leaps for joy
and I will give thanks to him in song.
8 The LORD is the strength of his people,
a fortress of salvation for his anointed one.[a]
9 Save your people and bless your inheritance;[b]
be their shepherd and carry them forever.

## Psalm 29

A psalm of David.

1 Ascribe to the LORD,[c] O mighty ones,
ascribe to the LORD glory and strength.
2 Ascribe to the LORD the glory due his name;
worship the LORD in the splendor of his[a] holiness.[d]

3 The voice[e] of the LORD is over the waters;
the God of glory thunders,
the LORD thunders over the mighty waters.
4 The voice of the LORD is powerful;
the voice of the LORD is majestic.
5 The voice of the LORD breaks the cedars;
the LORD breaks in pieces the cedars of Lebanon.
6 He makes Lebanon skip[f] like a calf,
Sirion[b][g] like a young wild ox.
7 The voice of the LORD strikes
with flashes of lightning.
8 The voice of the LORD shakes the desert;
the LORD shakes the Desert of Kadesh.[h]
9 The voice of the LORD twists the oaks[c]
and strips the forests bare.
And in his temple all cry, "Glory!"

10 The LORD sits[d] enthroned over the flood;
the LORD is enthroned as King forever.[i]
11 The LORD gives strength to his people;[j]
the LORD blesses his people with peace.

## Psalm 30

A psalm. A song. For the dedication of the temple.[e] Of David.

1 I will exalt you, O LORD,
for you lifted me out of the depths
and did not let my enemies gloat over me.[k]
2 O LORD my God, I called to you for help
and you healed me.
3 O LORD, you brought me up from the grave[f];
you spared me from going down into the pit.[l]

4 Sing to the LORD, you saints of his;
praise his holy name.
5 For his anger[m] lasts only a moment,
but his favor lasts a lifetime;
weeping may remain for a night,
but rejoicing comes in the morning.

6 When I felt secure, I said,
"I will never be shaken."
7 O LORD, when you favored me,
you made my mountain[g] stand firm;
but when you hid your face,[n]
I was dismayed.

8 To you, O LORD, I called;
to the Lord I cried for mercy:
9 "What gain is there in my destruction,[h]
in my going down into the pit?
Will the dust praise you?
Will it proclaim your faithfulness?[o]
10 Hear, O LORD, and be merciful to me;
O LORD, be my help."

11 You turned my wailing into dancing;
you removed my sackcloth and clothed me with joy,
12 that my heart may sing to you and not be silent.
O LORD my God, I will give you thanks forever.

## Psalm 31

For the director of music.
A psalm of David.

1 In you, O LORD, I have taken refuge;
let me never be put to shame;
deliver me in your righteousness.
2 Turn your ear to me,
come quickly to my rescue;
be my rock of refuge,
a strong fortress to save me.
3 Since you are my rock and my fortress,[p]
for the sake of your name[q] lead and guide me.
4 Free me from the trap that is set for me,

**30:3** l Ps 86:13
**30:5** m Ps 103:9
**30:7** n Ps 104:29
**30:9** o Ps 6:5
**31:3** p Ps 18:2 q Ps 23:3

[a]2 Or *LORD with the splendor of* [b]6 That is, Mount Hermon [c]9 Or *LORD makes the deer give birth* [d]10 Or *sat* [e]Title: Or *palace* [f]3 Hebrew *Sheol* [g]7 Or *hill country* [h]9 Or *there if I am silenced*

**31:5** r Lk 23:46
**31:6** s Jnh 2:8

for you are my refuge.
5 Into your hands I commit my spirit;[r]
redeem me, O LORD, the God of truth.

*"I never really look for things. I accept whatever God throws my way. Whichever way God turns my feet, I go."*
—PEARL BAILEY, SINGER

6 I hate those who cling to worthless idols;
I trust in the LORD.[s]
7 I will be glad and rejoice in your love,
for you saw my affliction
and knew the anguish of my soul.
8 You have not handed me over[t] to the enemy
but have set my feet in a spacious place.

**31:8** t Dt 32:30
**31:9** u Ps 6:7
**31:12** v Ps 88:4
**31:13** w Jer 20:3,10 x Mt 27:1
**31:16** y Ps 4:6
**31:17** z Ps 25:2–3

9 Be merciful to me, O LORD, for I am in distress;
my eyes grow weak with sorrow,[u]
my soul and my body with grief.
10 My life is consumed by anguish
and my years by groaning;
my strength fails because of my affliction,[a]
and my bones grow weak.
11 Because of all my enemies,
I am the utter contempt of my neighbors;
I am a dread to my friends—
those who see me on the street flee from me.
12 I am forgotten by them as though I were dead;[v]
I have become like broken pottery.
13 For I hear the slander of many;
there is terror on every side;[w]
they conspire against me
and plot to take my life.[x]

14 But I trust in you, O LORD;
I say, "You are my God."
15 My times are in your hands;
deliver me from my enemies
and from those who pursue me.
16 Let your face shine[y] on your servant;
save me in your unfailing love.
17 Let me not be put to shame,[z] O LORD,
for I have cried out to you;
but let the wicked be put to shame
and lie silent in the grave.[b]
18 Let their lying lips[a] be silenced,
for with pride and contempt
they speak arrogantly[b] against the righteous.

19 How great is your goodness,
which you have stored up for those who fear you,
which you bestow in the sight of men[c]
on those who take refuge in you.
20 In the shelter of your presence you hide[d] them
from the intrigues of men;[e]
in your dwelling you keep them safe
from accusing tongues.

21 Praise be to the LORD,
for he showed his wonderful love[f] to me
when I was in a besieged city.[g]
22 In my alarm[h] I said,
"I am cut off from your sight!"
Yet you heard my cry[i] for mercy
when I called to you for help.

23 Love the LORD, all his saints!
The LORD preserves the faithful,
but the proud he pays back in full.
24 Be strong and take heart,[j]
all you who hope in the LORD.

## Psalm 32

Of David. A *maskil*.[c]

1 Blessed is he
whose transgressions are forgiven,
whose sins are covered.[k]
2 Blessed is the man
whose sin the LORD does not count against him[l]
and in whose spirit is no deceit.[m]

3 When I kept silent,
my bones wasted away
through my groaning all day long.
4 For day and night
your hand was heavy[n] upon me;
my strength was sapped
as in the heat of summer. *Selah*
5 Then I acknowledged my sin to you

**31:18** a Ps 120:2 b Ps 94:4
**31:19** c Isa 64:4
**31:20** d Ps 27:5 e Job 5:21
**31:21** f Ps 17:7 g 1Sa 23:7
**31:22** h Ps 116:11 i La 3:54
**31:24** j Ps 27:14
**32:1** k Ps 85:2
**32:2** l 2Co 5:19 m Jn 1:47
**32:4** n Job 33:7

[a]10 Or *guilt* [b]17 Hebrew *Sheol* [c]Title: Probably a literary or musical term

**32:5**
o Pr 28:13

**32:10**
p Ro 2:9
q Pr 16:20

**32:11**
r Ps 64:10

**33:1**
s Ps 147:1
t Ps 32:11

**33:3**
u Ps 96:1

**33:5**
v Ps 11:7
w Ps 119:64

and did not cover up my iniquity.
I said, "I will confess[o]
my transgressions to the LORD"—
and you forgave
the guilt of my sin. *Selah*

6 Therefore let everyone who is godly pray to you
while you may be found;
surely when the mighty waters rise,
they will not reach him.
7 You are my hiding place;
you will protect me from trouble
and surround me with songs of deliverance. *Selah*

8 I will instruct you and teach you in the way you should go;
I will counsel you and watch over you.
9 Do not be like the horse or the mule,
which have no understanding
but must be controlled by bit and bridle
or they will not come to you.
10 Many are the woes of the wicked,[p]
but the LORD's unfailing love
surrounds the man who trusts[q] in him.

11 Rejoice in the LORD[r] and be glad, you righteous;
sing, all you who are upright in heart!

## Psalm 33

1 Sing joyfully to the LORD, you righteous;
it is fitting[s] for the upright[t] to praise him.
2 Praise the LORD with the harp;
make music to him on the ten-stringed lyre.
3 Sing to him a new song;[u]
play skillfully, and shout for joy.
4 For the word of the LORD is right and true;
he is faithful in all he does.
5 The LORD loves righteousness and justice;[v]
the earth is full of his unfailing love.[w]
6 By the word of the LORD were the heavens made,
their starry host by the breath of his mouth.
7 He gathers the waters of the sea into jars[a];
he puts the deep into storehouses.
8 Let all the earth fear the LORD;
let all the people of the world revere him.
9 For he spoke, and it came to be;
he commanded,[x] and it stood firm.
10 The LORD foils the plans of the nations;[y]
he thwarts the purposes of the peoples.
11 But the plans of the LORD stand firm forever,
the purposes[z] of his heart through all generations.

12 Blessed is the nation whose God is the LORD,
the people he chose[a] for his inheritance.
13 From heaven the LORD looks down
and sees all mankind;[b]
14 from his dwelling place he watches
all who live on earth—
15 he who forms the hearts of all,
who considers everything they do.[c]
16 No king is saved by the size of his army;
no warrior escapes by his great strength.
17 A horse[d] is a vain hope for deliverance;
despite all its great strength it cannot save.
18 But the eyes of the LORD are on those who fear him,
on those whose hope is in his unfailing love,
19 to deliver them from death
and keep them alive in famine.

20 We wait[e] in hope for the LORD;
he is our help and our shield.
21 In him our hearts rejoice,[f]
for we trust in his holy name.
22 May your unfailing love rest upon us, O LORD,
even as we put our hope in you.

## Psalm 34[b]

Of David. When he pretended to be insane before Abimelech, who drove him away, and he left.

1 I will extol the LORD at all times;
his praise will always be on my lips.

**33:9**
x Ge 1:3

**33:10**
y Isa 8:10

**33:11**
z Job 23:13

**33:12**
a Ex 19:5; Dt 7:6

**33:13**
b Job 28:24; Ps 11:4

**33:15**
c Jer 32:19

**33:17**
d Ps 20:7

**33:20**
e Ps 130:6

**33:21**
f Jn 16:22

[a]7 Or *sea as into a heap* [b]This psalm is an acrostic poem, the verses of which begin with the successive letters of the Hebrew alphabet.

34:2 g Jer 9:24
34:3 h Lk 1:46
34:4 i Mt 7:7
34:7 j Da 6:22
34:8 k 1Pe 2:3 l Ps 2:12
34:10 m Ps 84:11
34:12 n 1Pe 3:10
34:14 o Ps 37:27 p Heb 12:14
34:15 q Job 36:7
34:16 r Pr 10:7
34:17 s Ps 145:19
34:18 t Isa 57:15
34:19 u Pr 24:16

2 My soul will boast[g] in the LORD;
let the afflicted hear and rejoice.
3 Glorify the LORD with me;
let us exalt[h] his name together.

4 I sought the LORD,[i] and he answered me;
he delivered me from all my fears.
5 Those who look to him are radiant;
their faces are never covered with shame.
6 This poor man called, and the LORD heard him;
he saved him out of all his troubles.
7 The angel of the LORD[j] encamps around those who fear him,
and he delivers them.

8 Taste and see that the LORD is good;[k]
blessed is the man who takes refuge[l] in him.
9 Fear the LORD, you his saints,
for those who fear him lack nothing.
10 The lions may grow weak and hungry,
but those who seek the LORD lack no good thing.[m]
11 Come, my children, listen to me;
I will teach you the fear of the LORD.
12 Whoever of you loves life[n]
and desires to see many good days,
13 keep your tongue from evil
and your lips from speaking lies.
14 Turn from evil and do good;[o]
seek peace[p] and pursue it.

15 The eyes of the LORD are on the righteous[q]
and his ears are attentive to their cry;
16 the face of the LORD is against those who do evil,
to cut off the memory[r] of them from the earth.

17 The righteous cry out, and the LORD hears[s] them;
he delivers them from all their troubles.
18 The LORD is close to the brokenhearted[t]
and saves those who are crushed in spirit.

19 A righteous man may have many troubles,
but the LORD delivers him from them all;[u]
20 he protects all his bones,
not one of them will be broken.[v]

21 Evil will slay the wicked;[w]
the foes of the righteous will be condemned.
22 The LORD redeems[x] his servants;
no one will be condemned who takes refuge in him.

## Psalm 35

Of David.

1 Contend, O LORD, with those who contend with me;
fight against those who fight against me.
2 Take up shield and buckler;
arise and come to my aid.
3 Brandish spear and javelin[a]
against those who pursue me.
Say to my soul,
"I am your salvation."
4 May those who seek my life
be disgraced[y] and put to shame;
may those who plot my ruin
be turned back in dismay.
5 May they be like chaff[z] before the wind,
with the angel of the LORD driving them away;
6 may their path be dark and slippery,
with the angel of the LORD pursuing them.
7 Since they hid their net for me without cause
and without cause dug a pit for me,
8 may ruin overtake them by surprise—[a]
may the net they hid entangle them,
may they fall into the pit, to their ruin.
9 Then my soul will rejoice in the LORD
and delight in his salvation.
10 My whole being will exclaim,
"Who is like you,[b] O LORD?
You rescue the poor from those too strong for them,
the poor and needy from those who rob them."
11 Ruthless witnesses come forward;
they question me on things I know nothing about.

34:20 v Jn 19:36*
34:21 w Ps 94:23
34:22 x 1Ki 1:29; Ps 71:23
35:4 y Ps 70:2
35:5 z Job 21:18
35:8 a 1Th 5:3
35:10 b Ex 15:11

[a]3 Or *and block the way*

35:12 c Jn 10:32
35:13 d Job 30:25

12 They repay me evil for good[c]
and leave my soul forlorn.
13 Yet when they were ill, I put on sackcloth
and humbled myself with fasting.[d]
When my prayers returned to me
unanswered,
14 I went about mourning
as though for my friend or brother.
I bowed my head in grief
as though weeping for my mother.
15 But when I stumbled, they gathered in
glee;

Inspire

## FEAR

"Why are you so afraid, Mommy?" my then six-year-old daughter, Maisha, asked as she responded to my tightened grip on her hand and my hastened gait. "Don't you know that God made you half woman and half angel?" I stared into the serenity of her light brown eyes that twinkled in the moonlight. Her calm was contagious. Although her assessment of my physical composition was not totally correct, her spiritual insight was right on point: God had made me and God would protect me! My grasp on her small hand loosened as we continued down the long, dark walkway that led from the garage to our apartment's front entrance.

Despite our historic lineage of bravery, courage and seemingly supernatural strength, we women of color have often found ourselves alone and in the dark. Unpredictable events startle us, and worry overwhelms us. Shocked by the electrifying bolt of fear, we become paralyzed and forget that we are God's daughters. I understand the fears of women. Perhaps a sister fears that she will live alone or even die alone. Perhaps she fears that God is angry with her because she has not found a husband to be one with and to be fruitful and multiply with. If she is a single parent, she may be fearful that her paychecks won't meet all of her financial responsibilities. Or if she's married and her relationship is not going well, she fears it will end in divorce.

Whatever our current circumstances may be, we must refuse to, as theologian Howard Thurman writes, "allow the events of our life to make us a prisoner." Instead, we must remember that "our lives offer so much more than our immediate experience discloses to us." We must allow God to deliver us from our fears as we press on to live according to his will.

—M. Dyson

**read**

Psalms 34; 55:1–8,22–23; Isaiah 43:1–7.

See also the Inspire Notes "The Faithfulness of God," "Confidence" and "Confidence for Each Day," and the Women of the Bible Notes "Jehosheba: Standing Firm" and "Hemorrhaging Woman: Faith to Press In."

**WOMAN of COLOR**

What fears do you need to be delivered from?

For the next Inspire note, go to page 658.

**35:15** e Job 30:1,8
**35:16** f La 2:16
**35:17** g Hab 1:13 h Ps 22:20
**35:19** i Ps 38:19; 69:4 j Ps 13:4
**35:21** k Ps 22:13 l Ps 40:15
**35:22** m Ex 3:7 n Ps 10:1; 28:1
**35:23** o Ps 44:23
**35:25** p La 2:16

attackers gathered against me when I
was unaware.
They slandered[e] me without ceasing.
16 Like the ungodly they maliciously
mocked[a];
they gnashed their teeth[f] at me.
17 O Lord, how long[g] will you look on?
Rescue my life from their ravages,
my precious life[h] from these lions.
18 I will give you thanks in the great
assembly;
among throngs of people I will praise
you.

19 Let not those gloat over me
who are my enemies without cause;
let not those who hate me without
reason[i]
maliciously wink the eye.[j]
20 They do not speak peaceably,
but devise false accusations
against those who live quietly in the
land.
21 They gape[k] at me and say, "Aha! Aha!
With our own eyes we have seen it."[l]

22 O LORD, you have seen[m] this; be not silent.
Do not be far[n] from me, O Lord.
23 Awake,[o] and rise to my defense!
Contend for me, my God and Lord.
24 Vindicate me in your righteousness,
O LORD my God;
do not let them gloat over me.
25 Do not let them think, "Aha, just what we
wanted!"
or say, "We have swallowed him up."[p]

26 May all who gloat over my distress
be put to shame and confusion;
may all who exalt themselves over me
be clothed with shame and disgrace.
27 May those who delight in my vindication
shout for joy and gladness;
may they always say, "The LORD be
exalted,
who delights in the well-being of his
servant."
28 My tongue will speak of your
righteousness
and of your praises all day long.

## Psalm 36

For the director of music. Of David
the servant of the LORD.

1 An oracle is within my heart
concerning the sinfulness of the
wicked:[b]
There is no fear of God
before his eyes.[q]
2 For in his own eyes he flatters himself
too much to detect or hate his sin.
3 The words of his mouth are wicked and
deceitful;
he has ceased to be wise and to do
good.[r]
4 Even on his bed he plots evil;[s]
he commits himself to a sinful course[t]
and does not reject what is wrong.

5 Your love, O LORD, reaches to the heavens,
your faithfulness to the skies.
6 Your righteousness is like the mighty
mountains,
your justice like the great deep.[u]
O LORD, you preserve both man and beast.
7 How priceless is your unfailing love!
Both high and low among men
find[c] refuge in the shadow of your wings.
8 They feast on the abundance of your
house;[v]
you give them drink from your river[w]
of delights.
9 For with you is the fountain of life;[x]
in your light we see light.

10 Continue your love to those who know
you,
your righteousness to the upright in
heart.
11 May the foot of the proud not come
against me,
nor the hand of the wicked drive me
away.
12 See how the evildoers lie fallen—
thrown down, not able to rise!

## Psalm 37[d]

Of David.

1 Do not fret because of evil men
or be envious[y] of those who do wrong;[z]

**36:1** q Ro 3:18*
**36:3** r Jer 4:22
**36:4** s Pr 4:16 t Isa 65:2
**36:6** u Ro 11:33
**36:8** v Ps 65:4 w Job 20:17; Rev 22:1
**36:9** x Jer 2:13
**37:1** y Pr 23:17–18 z Ps 73:3

[a]16 Septuagint; Hebrew may mean *ungodly circle of mockers.* [b]1 Or *heart: / Sin proceeds from the wicked.* [c]7 Or *love, O God! / Men find*; or *love! / Both heavenly beings and men / find* [d]This psalm is an acrostic poem, the stanzas of which begin with the successive letters of the Hebrew alphabet.

2 for like the grass they will soon wither,
like green plants they will soon die away.[a]
3 Trust in the LORD and do good;
dwell in the land and enjoy safe pasture.
4 Delight[b] yourself in the LORD
and he will give you the desires of your heart.

5 Commit your way to the LORD;
trust in him[c] and he will do this:
6 He will make your righteousness shine like the dawn,[d]
the justice of your cause like the noonday sun.

7 Be still before the LORD and wait patiently for him;
do not fret when men succeed in their ways,
when they carry out their wicked schemes.

8 Refrain from anger and turn from wrath;
do not fret—it leads only to evil.
9 For evil men will be cut off,
but those who hope in the LORD will inherit the land.
10 A little while, and the wicked will be no more;[e]
though you look for them, they will not be found.
11 But the meek will inherit the land[f]
and enjoy great peace.

12 The wicked plot against the righteous
and gnash their teeth[g] at them;
13 but the Lord laughs at the wicked,
for he knows their day is coming.[h]

14 The wicked draw the sword
and bend the bow
to bring down the poor and needy,
to slay those whose ways are upright.
15 But their swords will pierce their own hearts,
and their bows will be broken.

16 Better the little that the righteous have
than the wealth[i] of many wicked;
17 for the power of the wicked will be broken,[j]
but the LORD upholds the righteous.

18 The days of the blameless are known to the LORD,[k]
and their inheritance will endure forever.
19 In times of disaster they will not wither;
in days of famine they will enjoy plenty.

20 But the wicked will perish:
The LORD's enemies will be like the beauty of the fields,
they will vanish—vanish like smoke.[l]

21 The wicked borrow and do not repay,
but the righteous give generously;[m]
22 those the LORD blesses will inherit the land,
but those he curses[n] will be cut off.

23 If the LORD delights in a man's way,
he makes his steps firm;[o]
24 though he stumble, he will not fall,[p]
for the LORD upholds him with his hand.

25 I was young and now I am old,
yet I have never seen the righteous forsaken
or their children begging bread.
26 They are always generous and lend freely;
their children will be blessed.

27 Turn from evil and do good;[q]
then you will dwell in the land forever.
28 For the LORD loves the just
and will not forsake his faithful ones.

They will be protected forever,
but the offspring of the wicked will be cut off;[r]
29 the righteous will inherit the land
and dwell in it forever.

30 The mouth of the righteous man utters wisdom,
and his tongue speaks what is just.
31 The law of his God is in his heart;
his feet do not slip.

32 The wicked lie in wait[s] for the righteous,
seeking their very lives;
33 but the LORD will not leave them in their power
or let them be condemned when brought to trial.[t]

**37:2** a Ps 90:6
**37:4** b Isa 58:14
**37:5** c Ps 55:22
**37:6** d Job 11:17
**37:10** e Job 7:10
**37:11** f Mt 5:5
**37:12** g Ps 35:16
**37:13** h 1Sa 26:10; Ps 2:4
**37:16** i Pr 15:16
**37:17** j Ps 10:15
**37:18** k Ps 1:6
**37:20** l Ps 102:3
**37:21** m Ps 112:5
**37:22** n Pr 3:33
**37:23** o 1Sa 2:9
**37:24** p Pr 24:16
**37:27** q Ps 34:14
**37:28** r Ps 21:10
**37:32** s Ps 10:8
**37:33** t Ps 109:31; 2Pe 2:9

37:34
u Ps 27:14
v Ps 52:6

37:35
w Job 5:3

37:36
x Job 20:5

37:38
y Ps 1:4

34 Wait for the LORD[u]
and keep his way.
He will exalt you to inherit the land;
when the wicked are cut off, you will
see[v] it.

35 I have seen a wicked and ruthless man
flourishing[w] like a green tree in its
native soil,
36 but he soon passed away and was no more;
though I looked for him, he could not
be found.[x]

37 Consider the blameless, observe the
upright;
there is a future[a] for the man of
peace.
38 But all sinners will be destroyed;
the future[b] of the wicked will be cut
off.[y]

[a]37 Or *there will be posterity* [b]38 Or *posterity*

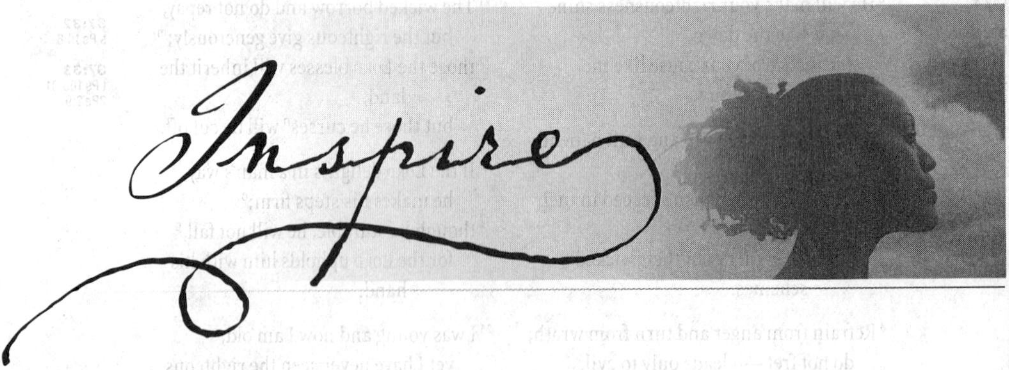


## DATING

Many books, television shows and experts endeavor to reveal the secrets of successful dating. Although the Bible does not specifically discuss dating, general Biblical standards should govern dating relationships. Whether you are considering dating someone or are currently in a relationship, you should consider the following questions:

1. Does your date have a growing relationship with Jesus Christ? The Bible teaches that we should not be unequally yoked with unbelievers (see 2Co 6:14). Not only does this text speak to one's spirituality, but it also speaks to values, lifestyles, goals and worldviews.
2. Are you placing God first in every area of your life? Oftentimes we allow ourselves to become preoccupied with our dating relationships, or lack thereof, due to our need for companionship. This preoccupation can take a toll on our commitment to Christ. We are exhorted to seek God first, and in return we shall receive the desires of our heart (which may be reshaped as we seek him). "Delight yourself in the LORD and he will give you the desires of your heart. Commit your way to the LORD; trust in him" (Ps 37:4–5).

Also, remember that "all that glitters is not gold." We must look past outward appearances and other superficialities in dating relationships and allow God to reveal to us what's in the heart (see 1Sa 16:6–7; Pr 27:19).

—J. THOMPSON

For the next Inspire note, go to page 663.

**read**

Psalm 37:1–6;
Proverbs 27:19.

See also the Inspire Notes "Romance: A Biblical Perspective," "Marriage," "What Is Intimacy?" "Celibacy" and "Love."

**WOMAN *of* COLOR**

How are you placing God first in every area of your life?

37:39 z Ps 3:8 a Ps 9:9
37:40 b 1Ch 5:20 c Isa 31:5
38:1 d Ps 6:1
38:2 e Job 6:4; Ps 32:4
38:4 f Ezr 9:6
38:6 g Ps 35:14
38:9 h Job 3:24
38:10 i Ps 6:7
38:15 j Ps 39:7

39 The salvation[z] of the righteous comes
from the LORD;
he is their stronghold in time of
trouble.[a]
40 The LORD helps[b] them and delivers[c] them;
he delivers them from the wicked and
saves them,
because they take refuge in him.

## Psalm 38

A psalm of David. A petition.

1 O LORD, do not rebuke me in your anger
or discipline me in your wrath.[d]
2 For your arrows[e] have pierced me,
and your hand has come down upon
me.
3 Because of your wrath there is no health
in my body;
my bones have no soundness because
of my sin.
4 My guilt has overwhelmed me
like a burden too heavy to bear.[f]

5 My wounds fester and are loathsome
because of my sinful folly.
6 I am bowed down and brought very low;
all day long I go about mourning.[g]
7 My back is filled with searing pain;
there is no health in my body.
8 I am feeble and utterly crushed;
I groan in anguish of heart.

9 All my longings lie open before you,
O Lord;
my sighing[h] is not hidden from you.
10 My heart pounds, my strength fails me;
even the light has gone from my eyes.[i]
11 My friends and companions avoid me
because of my wounds;
my neighbors stay far away.
12 Those who seek my life set their traps,
those who would harm me talk of my
ruin;
all day long they plot deception.

13 I am like a deaf man, who cannot hear,
like a mute, who cannot open his
mouth;
14 I have become like a man who does not
hear,
whose mouth can offer no reply.
15 I wait[j] for you, O LORD;
you will answer, O Lord my God.
16 For I said, "Do not let them gloat[k]
or exalt themselves over me when my
foot slips."

17 For I am about to fall,
and my pain is ever with me.
18 I confess my iniquity;
I am troubled by my sin.
19 Many are those who are my vigorous
enemies;
those who hate me without reason are
numerous.
20 Those who repay my good with evil[l]
slander me when I pursue what is good.

21 O LORD, do not forsake me;
be not far[m] from me, O my God.
22 Come quickly to help me,
O Lord my Savior.

## Psalm 39

For the director of music. For
Jeduthun. A psalm of David.

1 I said, "I will watch my ways[n]
and keep my tongue from sin;
I will put a muzzle on my mouth
as long as the wicked are in my
presence."
2 But when I was silent[o] and still,
not even saying anything good,
my anguish increased.
3 My heart grew hot within me,
and as I meditated, the fire burned;
then I spoke with my tongue:

4 "Show me, O LORD, my life's end
and the number of my days;
let me know how fleeting is my life.
5 You have made my days a mere
handbreadth;
the span of my years is as nothing
before you.
Each man's life is but a breath. *Selah*
6 Man is a mere phantom as he goes to and
fro:
He bustles about, but only in vain;
he heaps up wealth, not knowing who
will get it.[p]

7 "But now, Lord, what do I look for?
My hope is in you.
8 Save me from all my transgressions;[q]
do not make me the scorn of fools.
9 I was silent; I would not open my mouth,[r]

38:16 k Ps 35:26
38:20 l Ps 35:12
38:21 m Ps 35:22
39:1 n 1Ki 2:4
39:2 o Ps 38:13
39:6 p Lk 12:20
39:8 q Ps 44:13
39:9 r Job 2:10

39:11 s Job 13:28
39:13 t Job 10:21
40:1 u Ps 27:14
40:2 v Ps 69:14 w Ps 27:5
40:3 x Ps 33:3

for you are the one who has done this.
10 Remove your scourge from me;
I am overcome by the blow of your hand.
11 You rebuke and discipline men for their sin;
you consume their wealth like a moth[s]—
each man is but a breath. *Selah*

12 "Hear my prayer, O LORD,
listen to my cry for help;
be not deaf to my weeping.
For I dwell with you as an alien,
a stranger, as all my fathers were.
13 Look away from me, that I may rejoice again
before I depart and am no more."[t]

## Psalm 40

For the director of music.
Of David. A psalm.

1 I waited patiently[u] for the LORD;
he turned to me and heard my cry.
2 He lifted me out of the slimy pit,
out of the mud and mire;[v]
he set my feet on a rock[w]
and gave me a firm place to stand.
3 He put a new song[x] in my mouth,
a hymn of praise to our God.
Many will see and fear
and put their trust in the LORD.

4 Blessed is the man
who makes the LORD his trust,
who does not look to the proud,

*Lord,*

*Thank you for putting a new song in my mouth. I vow always to sing your praises, beginning right now. Accept, I pray, my love and gratitude.*

*Amen*

PSALM 40:1–3

to those who turn aside to false gods.[a]
5 Many, O LORD my God,
are the wonders you have done.
The things you planned for us
no one can recount[y] to you;
were I to speak and tell of them,
they would be too many to declare.

6 Sacrifice and offering you did not desire,[z]
but my ears you have pierced[b,c];
burnt offerings and sin offerings
you did not require.
7 Then I said, "Here I am, I have come—
it is written about me in the scroll.[d]
8 I desire to do your will,[a] O my God;
your law is within my heart."[b]
9 I proclaim righteousness in the great assembly;[c]
I do not seal my lips,
as you know,[d] O LORD.
10 I do not hide your righteousness in my heart;
I speak of your faithfulness[e] and salvation.
I do not conceal your love and your truth
from the great assembly.[f]

11 Do not withhold your mercy from me, O LORD;
may your love and your truth[g] always protect me.
12 For troubles without number surround me;
my sins have overtaken me, and I cannot see.[h]
They are more than the hairs of my head,
and my heart fails[i] within me.

13 Be pleased, O LORD, to save me;
O LORD, come quickly to help me.
14 May all who seek to take my life
be put to shame and confusion;
may all who desire my ruin[j]
be turned back in disgrace.
15 May those who say to me, "Aha! Aha!"
be appalled at their own shame.
16 But may all who seek you
rejoice and be glad in you;
may those who love your salvation always say,
"The LORD be exalted!"[k]

40:5 y Isa 55:8
40:6 z 1Sa 15:22
40:8 a Jn 4:34 b Ps 37:31
40:9 c Ps 22:25 d Ps 119:13
40:10 e Ps 89:1 f Ac 20:20
40:11 g Ps 43:3
40:12 h Ps 38:4 i Ps 73:26
40:14 j Ps 35:4
40:16 k Ps 35:27

[a]4 Or *to falsehood* [b]6 Hebrew; Septuagint *but a body you have prepared for me* (see also Symmachus and Theodotion)
[c]6 Or *opened* [d]7 Or *come / with the scroll written for me*

40:17
l Ps 70:5

41:2
m Ps 37:22
n Ps 27:12

41:5
o Ps 38:12

41:9
p Ps 55:12
q Job 19:19; Jn 13:18*

41:12
r Job 36:7

17 Yet I am poor and needy;
may the Lord think of me.
You are my help and my deliverer;
O my God, do not delay.[l]

## Psalm 41

For the director of music.
A psalm of David.

1 Blessed is he who has regard for the weak;
the LORD delivers him in times of trouble.
2 The LORD will protect him and preserve his life;
he will bless him in the land[m]
and not surrender him to the desire of his foes.[n]
3 The LORD will sustain him on his sickbed
and restore him from his bed of illness.

4 I said, "O LORD, have mercy on me;
heal me, for I have sinned against you."
5 My enemies say of me in malice,
"When will he die and his name perish?[o]"
6 Whenever one comes to see me,
he speaks falsely, while his heart gathers slander;
then he goes out and spreads it abroad.

7 All my enemies whisper together against me;
they imagine the worst for me, saying,
8 "A vile disease has beset him;
he will never get up from the place where he lies."
9 Even my close friend,[p] whom I trusted,
he who shared my bread,
has lifted up his heel against me.[q]
10 But you, O LORD, have mercy on me;
raise me up, that I may repay them.
11 I know that you are pleased with me,
for my enemy does not triumph over me.
12 In my integrity you uphold me
and set me in your presence forever.[r]

41:13
s Ps 106:48

42:2
t Ps 63:1

42:3
u Ps 80:5

42:4
v Isa 30:29

42:5
w La 3:24

42:7
x Ps 88:7

42:8
y Job 35:10

13 Praise be to the LORD, the God of Israel,
from everlasting to everlasting.
Amen and Amen.[s]

# BOOK II

*Psalms 42–72*

## Psalm 42[a]

For the director of music. A *maskil*[b]
of the Sons of Korah.

1 As the deer pants for streams of water,
so my soul pants for you, O God.
2 My soul thirsts[t] for God, for the living God.
When can I go and meet with God?
3 My tears[u] have been my food
day and night,
while men say to me all day long,
"Where is your God?"
4 These things I remember
as I pour out my soul:
how I used to go with the multitude,
leading the procession to the house of God,[v]
with shouts of joy and thanksgiving
among the festive throng.

5 Why are you downcast, O my soul?
Why so disturbed within me?
Put your hope in God,[w]
for I will yet praise him,
my Savior and [6]my God.

My[c] soul is downcast within me;
therefore I will remember you
from the land of the Jordan,
the heights of Hermon—from Mount Mizar.
7 Deep calls to deep
in the roar of your waterfalls;
all your waves and breakers
have swept over me.[x]

8 By day the LORD directs his love,
at night[y] his song is with me—
a prayer to the God of my life.

9 I say to God my Rock,
"Why have you forgotten me?

[a]In many Hebrew manuscripts Psalms 42 and 43 constitute one psalm. [b]Title: Probably a literary or musical term
[c]5,6 A few Hebrew manuscripts, Septuagint and Syriac; most Hebrew manuscripts *praise him for his saving help. /* [6]*O my God, my*

Why must I go about mourning,[z]
oppressed by the enemy?"
10 My bones suffer mortal agony
as my foes taunt me,
saying to me all day long,
"Where is your God?"

11 Why are you downcast, O my soul?
Why so disturbed within me?
Put your hope in God,
for I will yet praise him,
my Savior and my God.

## Psalm 43[a]

1 Vindicate me, O God,
and plead my cause[a] against an ungodly nation;
rescue me from deceitful and wicked men.
2 You are God my stronghold.
Why have you rejected me?
Why must I go about mourning,
oppressed by the enemy?[b]
3 Send forth your light and your truth,
let them guide me;
let them bring me to your holy mountain,
to the place where you dwell.
4 Then will I go to the altar of God,
to God, my joy and my delight.
I will praise you with the harp,
O God, my God.

5 Why are you downcast, O my soul?
Why so disturbed within me?
Put your hope in God,
for I will yet praise him,
my Savior and my God.[c]

## Psalm 44

For the director of music. Of the Sons of Korah. A *maskil*.[b]

1 We have heard with our ears, O God;
our fathers have told us[d]
what you did in their days,
in days long ago.
2 With your hand you drove out the nations
and planted[e] our fathers;
you crushed the peoples
and made our fathers flourish.[f]
3 It was not by their sword[g] that they won the land,
nor did their arm bring them victory;
it was your right hand, your arm,
and the light of your face, for you loved[h] them.

4 You are my King[i] and my God,
who decrees[c] victories for Jacob.
5 Through you we push back our enemies;
through your name we trample our foes.
6 I do not trust in my bow,[j]
my sword does not bring me victory;
7 but you give us victory over our enemies,
you put our adversaries to shame.
8 In God we make our boast[k] all day long,
and we will praise your name forever.
*Selah*

9 But now you have rejected and humbled us;
you no longer go out with our armies.[l]
10 You made us retreat[m] before the enemy,
and our adversaries have plundered us.
11 You gave us up to be devoured like sheep
and have scattered us among the nations.[n]
12 You sold your people for a pittance,[o]
gaining nothing from their sale.

13 You have made us a reproach to our neighbors,
the scorn and derision of those around us.
14 You have made us a byword among the nations;
the peoples shake their heads[p] at us.
15 My disgrace is before me all day long,
and my face is covered with shame
16 at the taunts of those who reproach and revile me,
because of the enemy, who is bent on revenge.

17 All this happened to us,
though we had not forgotten you
or been false to your covenant.
18 Our hearts had not turned[q] back;

**42:9** z Ps 38:6
**43:1** a Ps 26:1
**43:2** b Ps 42:9
**43:5** c Ps 42:6
**44:1** d Ex 12:26; Ps 78:3
**44:2** e Ex 15:17 f Ps 80:9
**44:3** g Jos 24:12 h Dt 7:7–8
**44:4** i Ps 74:12
**44:6** j Ps 33:16
**44:8** k Ps 34:2
**44:9** l Ps 60:1,10
**44:10** m Lev 26:17
**44:11** n Dt 28:64
**44:12** o Isa 52:3; Jer 15:13
**44:14** p Jer 24:9
**44:18** q Job 23:11

[a] In many Hebrew manuscripts Psalms 42 and 43 constitute one psalm. [b] Title: Probably a literary or musical term
[c] 4 Septuagint, Aquila and Syriac; Hebrew *King, O God; / command*

our feet had not strayed from your
path.
19 But you crushed us and made us a haunt
for jackals
and covered us over with deep
darkness.
20 If we had forgotten the name of our God
or spread out our hands to a foreign
god,
21 would not God have discovered it,
since he knows the secrets of the
heart?[r]

44:21
r Ps 139:1–2

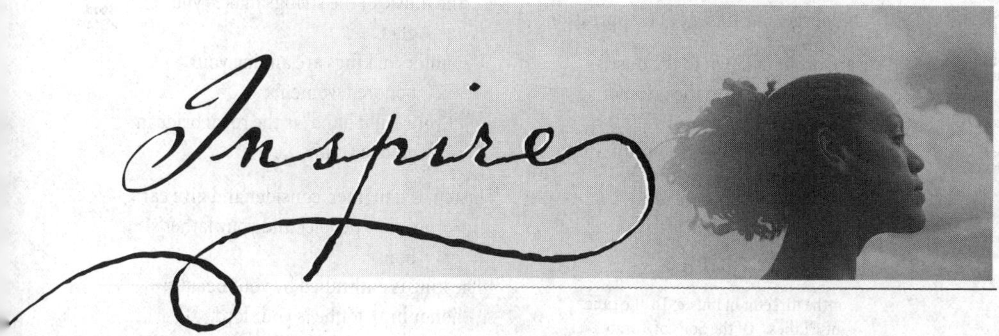


## LONELINESS

Feelings of loneliness are a reality at various times in a woman's life. Such feelings can be frightening and leave us with a sense of abandonment and powerlessness. Even if loneliness is not triggered by a single event, we sometimes become so tired of being tired that the thought of going on any longer is no longer appealing or meaningful. It is at times like these that we feel that no one can possibly understand what we are going through.

The depth of despair that can accompany such feelings becomes fertile ground for destructive thoughts and behaviors. Withdrawal, addiction or possibly even suicidal thinking can become a way of coping. Anything that eases the pain becomes a viable option.

Out of the depths, our soul cries out for God in wordless prayers emanating from holes so deeply hewn by our despair that rescue seems incomprehensible. It is in these moments that we can lament with the psalmist, saying, "As the deer pants for streams of water, so my soul pants for you, O God" (Ps 42:1).

Within these words we understand how a lonely and unsatisfied soul can long so deeply for God, how a lonely soul can feel far away from God because of the circumstances of life. But within this psalm we also find great encouragement. After describing how lonely and desperate he feels in the beginning of the psalm, the writer then finds hope. He asks himself some pertinent questions and reminds himself of the good deeds God has done.

When we are downcast, lonely and without hope, we, too, should ask ourselves pertinent questions and remind ourselves about the God we serve. Then our faith, which is the certainty of things unseen (see Heb 11:1), will invade the void, become our companion in the very midst of the loneliness, and whisper, "Do not fear, for I am with you. Believe in me, for I am here."

—C. Swafford Harris

For the next Inspire note, go to page 684.

### read

Psalm 42.

**See also** the Inspire Notes "The Gift of Aloneness," "Intimacy: Relationships With Other Christians" and "Adopted Through Love," and the Women of the Bible Note "Leah: Courage, Resistance and Struggle."

### WOMAN of COLOR

How do you handle moments of loneliness and despair?

**44:22** s Ro 8:36*
**44:23** t Ps 7:6
**44:24** u Job 13:24
**44:25** v Ps 119:25
**45:2** w Lk 4:22
**45:3** x Isa 9:6
**45:6** y Ps 93:2
**45:7** z Ps 33:5

22 Yet for your sake we face death all day long;
we are considered as sheep to be slaughtered.[s]

23 Awake,[t] O Lord! Why do you sleep?
Rouse yourself! Do not reject us forever.
24 Why do you hide your face[u]
and forget our misery and oppression?

25 We are brought down to the dust;[v]
our bodies cling to the ground.
26 Rise up and help us;
redeem us because of your unfailing love.

## Psalm 45

For the director of music. To ⌊the tune of⌋ "Lilies." Of the Sons of Korah. A *maskil*.[a] A wedding song.

1 My heart is stirred by a noble theme
as I recite my verses for the king;
my tongue is the pen of a skillful writer.

2 You are the most excellent of men
and your lips have been anointed with grace,[w]
since God has blessed you forever.
3 Gird your sword upon your side,
O mighty one;[x]
clothe yourself with splendor and majesty.
4 In your majesty ride forth victoriously
in behalf of truth, humility and righteousness;
let your right hand display awesome deeds.
5 Let your sharp arrows pierce the hearts of the king's enemies;
let the nations fall beneath your feet.
6 Your throne, O God, will last for ever and ever;[y]
a scepter of justice will be the scepter of your kingdom.
7 You love righteousness[z] and hate wickedness;
therefore God, your God, has set you
above your companions
by anointing you with the oil of joy.[a]
8 All your robes are fragrant with myrrh
and aloes and cassia;
from palaces adorned with ivory
the music of the strings makes you glad.
9 Daughters of kings are among your honored women;
at your right hand[b] is the royal bride in gold of Ophir.

10 Listen, O daughter, consider and give ear:
Forget your people[c] and your father's house.
11 The king is enthralled by your beauty;
honor him, for he is your lord.
12 The Daughter of Tyre will come with a gift,[b]
men of wealth will seek your favor.
13 All glorious is the princess within ⌊her chamber⌋;
her gown is interwoven with gold.
14 In embroidered garments she is led to the king;[d]
her virgin companions follow her
and are brought to you.
15 They are led in with joy and gladness;
they enter the palace of the king.

16 Your sons will take the place of your fathers;
you will make them princes
throughout the land.
17 I will perpetuate your memory through all generations;
therefore the nations will praise you
for ever and ever.

> *"Courage is very important. Like a muscle, it is strengthened by use."*
> —Ruth Gordon, actress

## Psalm 46

For the director of music. Of the Sons of Korah. According to *alamoth*.[c] A song.

1 God is our refuge and strength,
an ever-present[e] help in trouble.
2 Therefore we will not fear, though the earth give way
and the mountains fall into the heart of the sea,

**45:7** a Heb 1:8–9*
**45:9** b 1Ki 2:19
**45:10** c Dt 21:13
**45:14** d SS 1:4
**46:1** e Dt 4:7

[a]Title: Probably a literary or musical term [b]12 Or *A Tyrian robe is among the gifts* [c]Title: Probably a musical term

3 though its waters roar[f] and foam
and the mountains quake with their surging. *Selah*
4 There is a river whose streams make glad the city of God,[g]
the holy place where the Most High dwells.
5 God is within her,[h] she will not fall;
God will help her at break of day.
6 Nations[i] are in uproar, kingdoms fall;
he lifts his voice, the earth melts.
7 The LORD Almighty is with us;
the God of Jacob is our fortress.[j] *Selah*

8 Come and see the works of the LORD,[k]
the desolations he has brought on the earth.
9 He makes wars[l] cease to the ends of the earth;
he breaks the bow[m] and shatters the spear,
he burns the shields[a] with fire.[n]
10 "Be still, and know that I am God;
I will be exalted[o] among the nations,
I will be exalted in the earth."

11 The LORD Almighty is with us;
the God of Jacob is our fortress. *Selah*

## Psalm 47

For the director of music. Of the Sons of Korah. A psalm.

1 Clap your hands, all you nations;
shout to God with cries of joy.

*My own princess,*

*I am seated on my lofty throne. From that vantage point, I see all that you go through. You are in my loving gaze and under my constant care.*

*Your King*

PSALM 47:2–4

2 How awesome[p] is the LORD Most High,
the great King over all the earth!
3 He subdued[q] nations under us,
peoples under our feet.
4 He chose our inheritance[r] for us,
the pride of Jacob, whom he loved. *Selah*

5 God has ascended amid shouts of joy,
the LORD amid the sounding of trumpets.
6 Sing praises to God, sing praises;
sing praises to our King, sing praises.

7 For God is the King of all the earth;
sing to him a psalm[b][s] of praise.
8 God reigns[t] over the nations;
God is seated on his holy throne.
9 The nobles of the nations assemble
as the people of the God of Abraham,
for the kings[c] of the earth belong to God;[u]
he is greatly exalted.

## Psalm 48

A song. A psalm of the Sons of Korah.

1 Great is the LORD,[v] and most worthy of praise,
in the city of our God, his holy mountain.[w]
2 It is beautiful[x] in its loftiness,
the joy of the whole earth.
Like the utmost heights of Zaphon[d] is Mount Zion,
the[e] city of the Great King.[y]
3 God is in her citadels;
he has shown himself to be her fortress.

4 When the kings joined forces,
when they advanced together,[z]
5 they saw ⌊her⌋ and were astounded;
they fled in terror.
6 Trembling seized them there,
pain like that of a woman in labor.
7 You destroyed them like ships of Tarshish
shattered by an east wind.[a]

8 As we have heard,
so have we seen
in the city of the LORD Almighty,

**46:3** f Ps 93:3
**46:4** g Ps 48:1,8; Isa 60:14
**46:5** h Isa 12:6
**46:6** i Ps 2:1
**46:7** j Ps 9:9
**46:8** k Ps 66:5
**46:9** l Isa 2:4 m Ps 76:3 n Eze 39:9
**46:10** o Isa 2:11
**47:2** p Dt 7:21
**47:3** q Ps 18:39,47
**47:4** r 1Pe 1:4
**47:7** s Col 3:16
**47:8** t 1Ch 16:31
**47:9** u Ps 89:18
**48:1** v Ps 96:4 w Mic 4:1; Zec 8:3
**48:2** x Ps 50:2 y Mt 5:35
**48:4** z 2Sa 10:1–19
**48:7** a Jer 18:17

[a]9 Or *chariots* [b]7 Or *a maskil* (probably a literary or musical term) [c]9 Or *shields* [d]2 *Zaphon* can refer to a sacred mountain or the direction north. [e]2 Or *earth, / Mount Zion, on the northern side / of the*

48:9 b Ps 26:3
48:10 c Jos 7:9
48:11 d Ps 97:8
48:13 e Ps 78:6
49:3 f Ps 37:30
49:4 g Ps 78:2
49:5 h Ps 23:4
49:8 i Mt 16:26
49:9 j Ps 89:48
49:10 k Ecc 2:16

in the city of our God:
God makes her secure forever. *Selah*

9 Within your temple, O God,
we meditate on your unfailing love.[b]
10 Like your name,[c] O God,
your praise reaches to the ends of the earth;
your right hand is filled with righteousness.
11 Mount Zion rejoices,
the villages of Judah are glad
because of your judgments.[d]

12 Walk about Zion, go around her,
count her towers,
13 consider well her ramparts,
view her citadels,
that you may tell of them to the next generation.[e]
14 For this God is our God for ever and ever;
he will be our guide even to the end.

## Psalm 49

For the director of music. Of the Sons of Korah. A psalm.

1 Hear this, all you peoples;
listen, all who live in this world,
2 both low and high,
rich and poor alike:
3 My mouth will speak words of wisdom;[f]
the utterance from my heart will give understanding.
4 I will turn my ear to a proverb;[g]
with the harp I will expound my riddle:

5 Why should I fear[h] when evil days come,
when wicked deceivers surround me—
6 those who trust in their wealth
and boast of their great riches?
7 No man can redeem the life of another
or give to God a ransom for him—
8 the ransom for a life is costly,
no payment is ever enough—[i]
9 that he should live on[j] forever
and not see decay.

10 For all can see that wise men die;[k]
the foolish and the senseless alike perish
and leave their wealth to others.
11 Their tombs will remain their houses[a] forever,
their dwellings for endless generations,
though they had[b] named lands after themselves.

12 But man, despite his riches, does not endure;
he is[c] like the beasts that perish.

13 This is the fate of those who trust in themselves,
and of their followers, who approve their sayings. *Selah*
14 Like sheep they are destined for the grave,[d]
and death will feed on them.
The upright will rule[l] over them in the morning;
their forms will decay in the grave,[d]
far from their princely mansions.
15 But God will redeem my life[e] from the grave;[m]
he will surely take me to himself. *Selah*

16 Do not be overawed when a man grows rich,
when the splendor of his house increases;
17 for he will take nothing with him when he dies,
his splendor will not descend with him.[n]
18 Though while he lived he counted himself blessed—
and men praise you when you prosper—
19 he will join the generation of his fathers,
who will never see the light[o] ⌊of life⌋.

20 A man who has riches without understanding
is like the beasts that perish.

## Psalm 50

A psalm of Asaph.

1 The Mighty One, God, the LORD,
speaks and summons the earth

49:14 l Da 7:18; Mal 4:3
49:15 m Hos 13:14
49:17 n 1Ti 6:7
49:19 o Job 33:30

[a]11 Septuagint and Syriac; Hebrew *In their thoughts their houses will remain* [b]11 Or / *for they have* [c]12 Hebrew; Septuagint and Syriac read verse 12 the same as verse 20. [d]14 Hebrew *Sheol*; also in verse 15 [e]15 Or *soul*

**50:3** p Ps 97:3; Da 7:10
**50:4** q Dt 4:26
**50:5** r Ex 24:7
**50:6** s Ps 75:7
**50:7** t Ex 20:2
**50:8** u Hos 6:6
**50:14** v Heb 13:15 w Dt 23:21
**50:15** x Ps 22:23
**50:17** y Ne 9:26; Ro 2:21–22
**50:18** z Ro 1:32; 1Ti 5:22
**50:19** a Ps 52:2

from the rising of the sun to the place
where it sets.
2 From Zion, perfect in beauty,
God shines forth.
3 Our God comes and will not be silent;
a fire devours before him,[p]
and around him a tempest rages.
4 He summons the heavens above,
and the earth,[q] that he may judge his
people:
5 "Gather to me my consecrated ones,
who made a covenant[r] with me by
sacrifice."
6 And the heavens proclaim his
righteousness,
for God himself is judge.[s] *Selah*

7 "Hear, O my people, and I will speak,
O Israel, and I will testify against you:
I am God, your God.[t]
8 I do not rebuke you for your sacrifices
or your burnt offerings,[u] which are
ever before me.
9 I have no need of a bull from your stall
or of goats from your pens,
10 for every animal of the forest is mine,
and the cattle on a thousand hills.
11 I know every bird in the mountains,
and the creatures of the field are mine.
12 If I were hungry I would not tell you,
for the world is mine, and all that is
in it.
13 Do I eat the flesh of bulls
or drink the blood of goats?
14 Sacrifice thank offerings[v] to God,
fulfill your vows[w] to the Most High,
15 and call upon me in the day of trouble;
I will deliver you, and you will
honor[x] me."

16 But to the wicked, God says:

"What right have you to recite my laws
or take my covenant on your lips?
17 You hate my instruction
and cast my words behind[y] you.
18 When you see a thief, you join[z] with him;
you throw in your lot with adulterers.
19 You use your mouth for evil
and harness your tongue to deceit.[a]
20 You speak continually against your
brother
and slander your own mother's son.
21 These things you have done and I kept
silent;[b]
you thought I was altogether[a] like you.
But I will rebuke you
and accuse[c] you to your face.

22 "Consider this, you who forget God,[d]
or I will tear you to pieces, with none
to rescue:
23 He who sacrifices thank offerings
honors me,
and he prepares the way
so that I may show him[b] the salvation
of God."

## Psalm 51

For the director of music. A psalm
of David. When the prophet Nathan
came to him after David had
committed adultery with Bathsheba.

1 Have mercy on me, O God,
according to your unfailing love;
according to your great compassion
blot out my transgressions.[e]
2 Wash away all my iniquity
and cleanse[f] me from my sin.

3 For I know my transgressions,
and my sin is always before me.
4 Against you, you only, have I sinned
and done what is evil in your sight,
so that you are proved right when you
speak
and justified when you judge.[g]
5 Surely I was sinful[h] at birth,
sinful from the time my mother
conceived me.
6 Surely you desire truth in the inner
parts[c];
you teach[d] me wisdom in the inmost
place.
7 Cleanse me with hyssop,[i] and I will be
clean;
wash me, and I will be whiter than
snow.[j]
8 Let me hear joy and gladness;
let the bones you have crushed rejoice.
9 Hide your face from my sins[k]
and blot out all my iniquity.

**50:21** b Ecc 8:11 c Ps 90:8
**50:22** d Job 8:13; Ps 9:17
**51:1** e Isa 43:25
**51:2** f Heb 9:14
**51:4** g Ro 3:4*
**51:5** h Job 14:4
**51:7** i Lev 14:4; Heb 9:19 j Isa 1:18
**51:9** k Jer 16:17

[a]21 Or *thought the 'I AM' was* [b]23 Or *and to him who considers his way / I will show* [c]6 The meaning of the Hebrew for this phrase is uncertain. [d]6 Or *you desired . . . ; / you taught*

51:10 l Ac 15:9 m Eze 18:31
51:14 n 2Sa 12:9 o Ps 35:28
51:16 p 1Sa 15:22; Ps 40:6
51:17 q Ps 34:18
51:19 r Ps 4:5
52:2 s Ps 57:4
52:3 t Jer 9:5

10 Create in me a pure heart,[l] O God,
and renew a steadfast spirit
within me.[m]
11 Do not cast me from your presence
or take your Holy Spirit from me.
12 Restore to me the joy of your salvation
and grant me a willing spirit, to
sustain me.

13 Then I will teach transgressors your
ways,
and sinners will turn back to you.
14 Save me from bloodguilt,[n] O God,
the God who saves me,
and my tongue will sing of your
righteousness.[o]
15 O Lord, open my lips,
and my mouth will declare your
praise.
16 You do not delight in sacrifice,[p] or I
would bring it;
you do not take pleasure in burnt
offerings.
17 The sacrifices of God are[a] a broken spirit;
a broken and contrite heart,[q]
O God, you will not despise.

18 In your good pleasure make Zion
prosper;
build up the walls of Jerusalem.
19 Then there will be righteous sacrifices,[r]
whole burnt offerings to delight you;
then bulls will be offered on your altar.

## Psalm 52

For the director of music. A *maskil*[b] of David. When Doeg the Edomite had gone to Saul and told him: "David has gone to the house of Ahimelech."

1 Why do you boast of evil, you mighty
man?
Why do you boast all day long,
you who are a disgrace in the eyes of
God?
2 Your tongue plots destruction;
it is like a sharpened razor,[s]
you who practice deceit.
3 You love evil rather than good,
falsehood[t] rather than speaking the
truth. *Selah*
4 You love every harmful word,
O you deceitful tongue!

5 Surely God will bring you down to
everlasting ruin:
He will snatch you up and tear you
from your tent;
he will uproot[u] you from the land of
the living. *Selah*
6 The righteous will see and fear;
they will laugh[v] at him, saying,
7 "Here now is the man
who did not make God his
stronghold
but trusted in his great wealth[w]
and grew strong by destroying
others!"

8 But I am like an olive tree[x]
flourishing in the house of God;
I trust in God's unfailing love
for ever and ever.
9 I will praise you forever[y] for what you
have done;
in your name I will hope, for your
name is good.[z]
I will praise you in the presence of
your saints.

## Psalm 53

For the director of music. According to *mahalath*.[c] A *maskil*[b] of David.

1 The fool[a] says in his heart,
"There is no God."
They are corrupt, and their ways are vile;
there is no one who does good.

2 God looks down from heaven
on the sons of men
to see if there are any who understand,
any who seek God.
3 Everyone has turned away,
they have together become corrupt;
there is no one who does good,
not even one.

4 Will the evildoers never learn—
those who devour my people as men
eat bread
and who do not call on God?
5 There they were, overwhelmed with
dread,

52:5 u Pr 2:22
52:6 v Job 22:19; Ps 37:34
52:7 w Ps 49:6
52:8 x Jer 11:16
52:9 y Ps 30:12 z Ps 54:6
53:1 a Ro 3:10

[a]17 Or *My sacrifice, O God, is* [b]Title: Probably a literary or musical term [c]Title: Probably a musical term

where there was nothing to dread.[b]
God scattered the bones[c] of those who attacked you;
you put them to shame, for God despised them.

6 Oh, that salvation for Israel would come out of Zion!
When God restores the fortunes of his people,
let Jacob rejoice and Israel be glad!

## Psalm 54

For the director of music. With stringed instruments. A *maskil*[a] of David. When the Ziphites had gone to Saul and said, "Is not David hiding among us?"

1 Save me, O God, by your name;
vindicate me by your might.
2 Hear my prayer, O God;
listen to the words of my mouth.

3 Strangers are attacking me;[d]
ruthless men seek my life—
men without regard for God. *Selah*

4 Surely God is my help;[e]
the Lord is the one who sustains me.

5 Let evil recoil on those who slander me;
in your faithfulness[f] destroy them.
6 I will sacrifice a freewill offering to you;
I will praise your name, O LORD,
for it is good.
7 For he has delivered me from all my troubles,
and my eyes have looked in triumph on my foes.[g]

## Psalm 55

For the director of music. With stringed instruments. A *maskil*[a] of David.

1 Listen to my prayer, O God,
do not ignore my plea;
2 hear me and answer me.
My thoughts trouble me and I am distraught[h]
3 at the voice of the enemy,
at the stares of the wicked;
for they bring down suffering upon me[i]
and revile me in their anger.

4 My heart is in anguish within me;
the terrors[j] of death assail me.
5 Fear and trembling have beset me;
horror has overwhelmed me.
6 I said, "Oh, that I had the wings of a dove!
I would fly away and be at rest—
7 I would flee far away
and stay in the desert; *Selah*
8 I would hurry to my place of shelter,
far from the tempest and storm."

9 Confuse the wicked, O Lord, confound their speech,
for I see violence and strife[k] in the city.
10 Day and night they prowl about on its walls;
malice and abuse are within it.
11 Destructive forces are at work in the city;
threats and lies never leave its streets.
12 If an enemy were insulting me,
I could endure it;
if a foe were raising himself against me,
I could hide from him.
13 But it is you, a man like myself,
my companion, my close friend,[l]
14 with whom I once enjoyed sweet fellowship
as we walked with the throng at the house of God.[m]

15 Let death take my enemies by surprise;
let them go down alive to the grave,[b][n]
for evil finds lodging among them.

16 But I call to God,
and the LORD saves me.
17 Evening, morning and noon
I cry out in distress,
and he hears my voice.
18 He ransoms me unharmed
from the battle waged against me,
even though many oppose me.
19 God, who is enthroned forever,[o]
will hear them and afflict them— *Selah*
men who never change their ways
and have no fear of God.

20 My companion attacks his friends;[p]
he violates his covenant.

**53:5** b Lev 26:17 c Eze 6:5
**54:3** d Ps 86:14
**54:4** e Ps 118:7
**54:5** f Ps 89:49
**54:7** g Ps 59:10
**55:2** h Isa 38:14
**55:3** i 2Sa 16:6–8
**55:4** j Ps 116:3
**55:9** k Jer 6:7
**55:13** l Ps 41:9
**55:14** m Ps 42:4
**55:15** n Nu 16:30,33
**55:19** o Dt 33:27
**55:20** p Ps 7:4

[a]Title: Probably a literary or musical term [b]15 Hebrew *Sheol*

55:21 q Ps 28:3
55:22 r Ps 37:5 s Ps 37:24
55:23 t Ps 5:6 u Job 15:32; Pr 10:27
56:1 v Ps 57:1–3
56:2 w Ps 57:3
56:4 x Ps 118:6
56:6 y Ps 59:3
56:9 z Ro 8:31

21 His speech is smooth as butter,
yet war is in his heart;
his words are more soothing than oil,
yet they are drawn swords.[q]

22 Cast your cares on the LORD
and he will sustain you;[r]
he will never let the righteous fall.[s]
23 But you, O God, will bring down the wicked
into the pit of corruption;
bloodthirsty and deceitful men[t]
will not live out half their days.[u]

But as for me, I trust in you.

## Psalm 56

For the director of music. To ⌊the tune of⌋ "A Dove on Distant Oaks." Of David. A *miktam*.[a] When the Philistines had seized him in Gath.

1 Be merciful to me, O God, for men hotly pursue me;[v]
all day long they press their attack.
2 My slanderers pursue me all day long;[w]
many are attacking me in their pride.

3 When I am afraid,
I will trust in you.
4 In God, whose word I praise,
in God I trust; I will not be afraid.
What can mortal man do to me?[x]

5 All day long they twist my words;
they are always plotting to harm me.
6 They conspire,[y] they lurk,
they watch my steps,
eager to take my life.

7 On no account let them escape;
in your anger, O God, bring down the nations.
8 Record my lament;
list my tears on your scroll[b]—
are they not in your record?

9 Then my enemies will turn back
when I call for help.
By this I will know that God is for me.[z]
10 In God, whose word I praise,
in the LORD, whose word I praise—
11 in God I trust; I will not be afraid.
What can man do to me?

12 I am under vows to you, O God;
I will present my thank offerings to you.
13 For you have delivered me[c] from death[a]
and my feet from stumbling,
that I may walk before God
in the light of life.[d][b]

## Psalm 57

For the director of music. ⌊To the tune of⌋ "Do Not Destroy." Of David. A *miktam*.[a] When he had fled from Saul into the cave.

1 Have mercy on me, O God, have mercy on me,
for in you my soul takes refuge.[c]
I will take refuge in the shadow of your wings[d]
until the disaster has passed.[e]

2 I cry out to God Most High,
to God, who fulfills ⌊his purpose⌋ for me.[f]
3 He sends from heaven and saves me,
rebuking those who hotly pursue me;[g] *Selah*
God sends his love and his faithfulness.

4 I am in the midst of lions;[h]
I lie among ravenous beasts—
men whose teeth are spears and arrows,
whose tongues are sharp swords.[i]

5 Be exalted, O God, above the heavens;
let your glory be over all the earth.[j]

6 They spread a net for my feet—
I was bowed down[k] in distress.
They dug a pit in my path—
but they have fallen into it themselves. *Selah*

7 My heart is steadfast, O God,
my heart is steadfast;[l]
I will sing and make music.
8 Awake, my soul!
Awake, harp and lyre![m]
I will awaken the dawn.

9 I will praise you, O Lord, among the nations;
I will sing of you among the peoples.

56:13 a Ps 116:8 b Job 33:30
57:1 c Ps 2:12 d Ps 17:8 e Isa 26:20
57:2 f Ps 138:8
57:3 g Ps 56:1
57:4 h Ps 35:17 i Pr 30:14
57:5 j Ps 108:5
57:6 k Ps 145:14
57:7 l Ps 108:1
57:8 m Ps 16:9

[a]Title: Probably a literary or musical term [b]8 Or / *put my tears in your wineskin* [c]13 Or *my soul* [d]13 Or *the land of the living*

**57:10** n Ps 36:5
**58:2** o Ps 94:20
**58:6** p Job 4:10

*Precious one,*

*I am merciful. I desire nothing more intensely than to be in relationship with you, my daughter.*

*Your Doting Father*

PSALM 57:9–10

[10] For great is your love, reaching to the
heavens;
your faithfulness reaches to the skies.[n]
[11] Be exalted, O God, above the heavens;
let your glory be over all the earth.

## Psalm 58

For the director of music. ⌊To the tune of⌋ "Do Not Destroy." Of David. A *miktam*.[a]

[1] Do you rulers indeed speak justly?
Do you judge uprightly among men?
[2] No, in your heart you devise injustice,
and your hands mete out violence on
the earth.[o]
[3] Even from birth the wicked go astray;
from the womb they are wayward and
speak lies.
[4] Their venom is like the venom of a snake,
like that of a cobra that has stopped
its ears,
[5] that will not heed the tune of the
charmer,
however skillful the enchanter may be.

[6] Break the teeth in their mouths, O God;
tear out, O LORD, the fangs of the
lions![p]
[7] Let them vanish like water that flows
away;
when they draw the bow, let their
arrows be blunted.
[8] Like a slug melting away as it moves
along,
like a stillborn child,[q] may they not see
the sun.

[9] Before your pots can feel ⌊the heat of⌋ the
thorns—
whether they be green or dry—the
wicked will be swept away.[b r]
[10] The righteous will be glad when they are
avenged,
when they bathe their feet in the blood
of the wicked.[s]
[11] Then men will say,
"Surely the righteous still are rewarded;
surely there is a God who judges the
earth."

## Psalm 59

For the director of music. ⌊To the tune of⌋ "Do Not Destroy." Of David. A *miktam*.[a] When Saul had sent men to watch David's house in order to kill him.

[1] Deliver me from my enemies, O God;[t]
protect me from those who rise up
against me.
[2] Deliver me from evildoers
and save me from bloodthirsty men.[u]

[3] See how they lie in wait for me!
Fierce men conspire[v] against me
for no offense or sin of mine, O LORD.
[4] I have done no wrong, yet they are ready
to attack me.[w]
Arise to help me; look on my plight!
[5] O LORD God Almighty, the God of Israel,
rouse yourself to punish all the
nations;
show no mercy to wicked traitors.[x]
*Selah*

[6] They return at evening,
snarling like dogs,[y]
and prowl about the city.
[7] See what they spew from their mouths—
they spew out swords[z] from their lips,
and they say, "Who can hear us?"[a]
[8] But you, O LORD, laugh at them;[b]
you scoff at all those nations.

[9] O my Strength, I watch for you;
you, O God, are my fortress, [10] my
loving God.

**58:8** q Job 3:16
**58:9** r Pr 10:25
**58:10** s Ps 68:23
**59:1** t Ps 143:9
**59:2** u Ps 139:19
**59:3** v Ps 56:6
**59:4** w Ps 35:19,23
**59:5** x Jer 18:23
**59:6** y ver 14
**59:7** z Ps 57:4 a Ps 10:11
**59:8** b Ps 37:13

[a]Title: Probably a literary or musical term [b]9 The meaning of the Hebrew for this verse is uncertain.

59:11 c Dt 4:9
59:12 d Pr 12:13
59:13 e Ps 104:35
59:16 f Ps 101:1
60:1 g Ps 44:9
60:2 h 2Ch 7:14
60:3 i Ps 71:20

God will go before me
and will let me gloat over those who slander me.
[11] But do not kill them, O Lord our shield,[a]
or my people will forget.[c]
In your might make them wander about,
and bring them down.
[12] For the sins of their mouths,
for the words of their lips,[d]
let them be caught in their pride.
For the curses and lies they utter,
[13] consume them in wrath,
consume them till they are no more.[e]
Then it will be known to the ends of the earth
that God rules over Jacob. *Selah*

[14] They return at evening,
snarling like dogs,
and prowl about the city.
[15] They wander about for food
and howl if not satisfied.
[16] But I will sing of your strength,
in the morning I will sing of your love;[f]
for you are my fortress,
my refuge in times of trouble.

[17] O my Strength, I sing praise to you;
you, O God, are my fortress, my loving God.

## Psalm 60

For the director of music. To ⌊the tune of⌋ "The Lily of the Covenant." A *miktam*[b] of David. For teaching. When he fought Aram Naharaim[c] and Aram Zobah,[d] and when Joab returned and struck down twelve thousand Edomites in the Valley of Salt.

[1] You have rejected us,[g] O God, and burst forth upon us;
you have been angry—now restore us!
[2] You have shaken the land and torn it open;
mend its fractures,[h] for it is quaking.
[3] You have shown your people desperate times;[i]
you have given us wine that makes us stagger.
[4] But for those who fear you, you have raised a banner
to be unfurled against the bow. *Selah*

[5] Save us and help us with your right hand,[j]
that those you love may be delivered.
[6] God has spoken from his sanctuary:
"In triumph I will parcel out Shechem[k]
and measure off the Valley of Succoth.
[7] Gilead is mine, and Manasseh is mine;
Ephraim is my helmet,
Judah[l] my scepter.[m]
[8] Moab is my washbasin,
upon Edom I toss my sandal;
over Philistia I shout in triumph.[n]"

[9] Who will bring me to the fortified city?
Who will lead me to Edom?
[10] Is it not you, O God, you who have rejected us
and no longer go out with our armies?
[11] Give us aid against the enemy,
for the help of man is worthless.[o]
[12] With God we will gain the victory,
and he will trample down our enemies.[p]

## Psalm 61

For the director of music. With stringed instruments. Of David.

[1] Hear my cry, O God;[q]
listen to my prayer.

[2] From the ends of the earth I call to you,
I call as my heart grows faint;
lead me to the rock that is higher than I.
[3] For you have been my refuge,
a strong tower against the foe.[r]

[4] I long to dwell in your tent forever
and take refuge in the shelter of your wings.[s] *Selah*
[5] For you have heard my vows,[t] O God;
you have given me the heritage of those who fear your name.

[6] Increase the days of the king's life,
his years for many generations.
[7] May he be enthroned in God's presence forever;[u]
appoint your love and faithfulness to protect him.

60:5 j Ps 108:6
60:6 k Ge 12:6
60:7 l Dt 33:17 m Ge 49:10
60:8 n 2Sa 8:1
60:11 o Ps 146:3
60:12 p Nu 24:18
61:1 q Ps 64:1
61:3 r Pr 18:10
61:4 s Ps 91:4
61:5 t Ps 56:12
61:7 u Ps 41:12

[a] 11 Or *sovereign* [b] Title: Probably a literary or musical term [c] Title: That is, Arameans of Northwest Mesopotamia [d] Title: That is, Arameans of central Syria

62:1 v Ps 33:20
62:3 w Isa 30:13
62:4 x Ps 28:3
62:8 y 1Sa 1:15; La 2:19
62:9 z Ps 39:5,11 a Isa 40:15
62:12 b Mt 16:27

8 Then will I ever sing praise to your name
and fulfill my vows day after day.

## Psalm 62

For the director of music. For Jeduthun. A psalm of David.

1 My soul finds rest[v] in God alone;
my salvation comes from him.
2 He alone is my rock and my salvation;
he is my fortress, I will never be shaken.

3 How long will you assault a man?
Would all of you throw him down—
this leaning wall,[w] this tottering fence?
4 They fully intend to topple him
from his lofty place;
they take delight in lies.
With their mouths they bless,
but in their hearts they curse.[x] *Selah*

5 Find rest, O my soul, in God alone;
my hope comes from him.
6 He alone is my rock and my salvation;
he is my fortress, I will not be shaken.
7 My salvation and my honor depend on God[a];
he is my mighty rock, my refuge.
8 Trust in him at all times, O people;
pour out your hearts to him,[y]
for God is our refuge. *Selah*

9 Lowborn men are but a breath,[z]
the highborn are but a lie;
if weighed on a balance,[a] they are nothing;
together they are only a breath.
10 Do not trust in extortion
or take pride in stolen goods;
though your riches increase,
do not set your heart on them.

11 One thing God has spoken,
two things have I heard:
that you, O God, are strong,
12 and that you, O Lord, are loving.
Surely you will reward each person
according to what he has done.[b]

## Psalm 63

A psalm of David. When he was in the Desert of Judah.

1 O God, you are my God,
earnestly I seek you;
my soul thirsts for you,[c]
my body longs for you,
in a dry and weary land
where there is no water.

*Thirsting one,*

*Looking for satisfaction? Come to me.*

*The Living Water*

PSALM 63:1

2 I have seen you in the sanctuary[d]
and beheld your power and your glory.
3 Because your love is better than life,
my lips will glorify you.
4 I will praise you as long as I live,[e]
and in your name I will lift up my hands.
5 My soul will be satisfied as with the richest of foods;
with singing lips my mouth will praise you.

6 On my bed I remember you;
I think of you through the watches of the night.[f]
7 Because you are my help,[g]
I sing in the shadow of your wings.
8 My soul clings to you;
your right hand upholds me.

9 They who seek my life will be destroyed;
they will go down to the depths of the earth.[h]
10 They will be given over to the sword
and become food for jackals.

11 But the king will rejoice in God;
all who swear by God's name will praise him,[i]
while the mouths of liars will be silenced.

63:1 c Ps 42:2
63:2 d Ps 27:4
63:4 e Ps 104:33
63:6 f Ps 42:8
63:7 g Ps 27:9
63:9 h Ps 55:15
63:11 i Dt 6:13; Isa 45:23

[a]7 Or / *God Most High is my salvation and my honor*

**64:1** j Ps 140:1
**64:3** k Ps 58:7
**64:5** l Ps 10:11
**64:8** m Pr 18:7
**64:10** n Ps 32:11
**65:2** o Isa 66:23

## Psalm 64

For the director of music.
A psalm of David.

1 Hear me, O God, as I voice my complaint;
protect my life from the threat of the enemy.[j]
2 Hide me from the conspiracy of the wicked,
from that noisy crowd of evildoers.

3 They sharpen their tongues like swords
and aim their words like deadly arrows.[k]
4 They shoot from ambush at the innocent man;
they shoot at him suddenly, without fear.

5 They encourage each other in evil plans,
they talk about hiding their snares;
they say, "Who will see them[a]?"[l]
6 They plot injustice and say,
"We have devised a perfect plan!"
Surely the mind and heart of man are cunning.

7 But God will shoot them with arrows;
suddenly they will be struck down.
8 He will turn their own tongues against them[m]
and bring them to ruin;
all who see them will shake their heads in scorn.

9 All mankind will fear;
they will proclaim the works of God
and ponder what he has done.
10 Let the righteous rejoice in the LORD
and take refuge in him;
let all the upright in heart praise him![n]

## Psalm 65

For the director of music. A psalm of David. A song.

1 Praise awaits[b] you, O God, in Zion;
to you our vows will be fulfilled.
2 O you who hear prayer,
to you all men will come.[o]
3 When we were overwhelmed by sins,
you forgave[c] our transgressions.
4 Blessed are those you choose[p]
and bring near to live in your courts!
We are filled with the good things of your house,[q]
of your holy temple.

5 You answer us with awesome deeds of righteousness,
O God our Savior,
the hope of all the ends of the earth
and of the farthest seas,
6 who formed the mountains by your power,
having armed yourself with strength,[r]
7 who stilled the roaring of the seas,[s]
the roaring of their waves,
and the turmoil of the nations.[t]
8 Those living far away fear your wonders;
where morning dawns and evening fades
you call forth songs of joy.

9 You care for the land and water it;
you enrich it abundantly.
The streams of God are filled with water
to provide the people with grain,[u]
for so you have ordained it.[d]
10 You drench its furrows
and level its ridges;
you soften it with showers
and bless its crops.
11 You crown the year with your bounty,
and your carts overflow with abundance.
12 The grasslands of the desert overflow;
the hills are clothed with gladness.
13 The meadows are covered with flocks
and the valleys are mantled with grain;
they shout for joy and sing.

## Psalm 66

For the director of music.
A song. A psalm.

1 Shout with joy to God, all the earth![v]
2 Sing the glory of his name;
make his praise glorious!
3 Say to God, "How awesome are your deeds![w]
So great is your power

**65:4** p Ps 4:3; 33:12 q Ps 36:8
**65:6** r Ps 93:1
**65:7** s Mt 8:26 t Isa 17:12–13
**65:9** u Ps 46:4
**66:1** v Ps 100:1
**66:3** w Ps 65:5

[a]5 Or *us* [b]1 Or *befits*; the meaning of the Hebrew for this word is uncertain. [c]3 Or *made atonement for* [d]9 Or *for that is how you prepare the land*

66:3 x Ps 18:44
66:6 y Ex 14:22
66:10 z Ps 17:3; Isa 48:10; Zec 13:9; 1Pe 1:6–7
66:11 a La 1:13
66:12 b Isa 51:23 c Isa 43:2
66:13 d Ecc 5:4
66:18 e Jas 4:3
66:19 f Ps 116:1–2

that your enemies cringe[x] before you.
[4] All the earth bows down to you;
they sing praise to you,
they sing praise to your name." *Selah*

[5] Come and see what God has done,
how awesome his works in man's behalf!
[6] He turned the sea into dry land,[y]
they passed through the waters on foot—
come, let us rejoice in him.
[7] He rules forever by his power,
his eyes watch the nations—
let not the rebellious rise up against him. *Selah*

[8] Praise our God, O peoples,
let the sound of his praise be heard;
[9] he has preserved our lives
and kept our feet from slipping.
[10] For you, O God, tested us;
you refined us like silver.[z]
[11] You brought us into prison
and laid burdens[a] on our backs.
[12] You let men ride over our heads;[b]
we went through fire and water,
but you brought us to a place of abundance.[c]

[13] I will come to your temple with burnt offerings
and fulfill my vows[d] to you—
[14] vows my lips promised and my mouth spoke
when I was in trouble.
[15] I will sacrifice fat animals to you
and an offering of rams;
I will offer bulls and goats. *Selah*

[16] Come and listen, all you who fear God;
let me tell you what he has done for me.
[17] I cried out to him with my mouth;
his praise was on my tongue.
[18] If I had cherished sin in my heart,
the Lord would not have listened;[e]
[19] but God has surely listened
and heard my voice[f] in prayer.
[20] Praise be to God,
who has not rejected my prayer
or withheld his love from me!

## Psalm 67

For the director of music.
With stringed instruments.
A psalm. A song.

[1] May God be gracious to us and bless us
and make his face shine upon us,[g] *Selah*
[2] that your ways may be known on earth,
your salvation among all nations.[h]

[3] May the peoples praise you, O God;
may all the peoples praise you.
[4] May the nations be glad and sing for joy,
for you rule the peoples justly
and guide the nations of the earth. *Selah*
[5] May the peoples praise you, O God;
may all the peoples praise you.

[6] Then the land will yield its harvest,[i]
and God, our God, will bless us.
[7] God will bless us,
and all the ends of the earth will fear him.

## Psalm 68

For the director of music. Of David.
A psalm. A song.

[1] May God arise, may his enemies be scattered;
may his foes flee[j] before him.
[2] As smoke[k] is blown away by the wind,
may you blow them away;
as wax melts[l] before the fire,
may the wicked perish before God.
[3] But may the righteous be glad
and rejoice before God;
may they be happy and joyful.

[4] Sing to God, sing praise to his name,
extol him who rides on the clouds[a]—
his name is the LORD—
and rejoice before him.
[5] A father to the fatherless, a defender of widows,
is God in his holy dwelling.
[6] God sets the lonely in families,[b]
he leads forth the prisoners[m] with singing;
but the rebellious live in a sun-scorched land.[n]

67:1 g Nu 6:24–26
67:2 h Tit 2:11
67:6 i Lev 26:4; Ps 85:12; Eze 34:27
68:1 j Nu 10:35
68:2 k Hos 13:3 l Isa 9:18; Mic 1:4
68:6 m Ac 12:6 n Ps 107:34

[a]4 Or / *prepare the way for him who rides through the deserts* [b]6 Or *the desolate in a homeland*

68:7 o Ex 13:21
68:9 p Dt 11:11
68:10 q Ps 74:19
68:14 r Jos 10:10
68:16 s Dt 12:5
68:17 t Dt 33:2
68:18 u Jdg 5:12 v Eph 4:8*

7 When you went out[o] before your people,
O God,
when you marched through the
wasteland, *Selah*
8 the earth shook,
the heavens poured down rain,
before God, the One of Sinai,
before God, the God of Israel.
9 You gave abundant showers,[p] O God;
you refreshed your weary inheritance.
10 Your people settled in it,
and from your bounty, O God, you
provided[q] for the poor.

11 The Lord announced the word,
and great was the company of those
who proclaimed it:
12 "Kings and armies flee in haste;
in the camps men divide the plunder.
13 Even while you sleep among the
campfires,[a]
the wings of ⌊my⌋ dove are sheathed
with silver,
its feathers with shining gold."
14 When the Almighty[b] scattered[r] the kings
in the land,
it was like snow fallen on Zalmon.

15 The mountains of Bashan are majestic
mountains;
rugged are the mountains of Bashan.
16 Why gaze in envy, O rugged mountains,
at the mountain where God chooses[s]
to reign,
where the LORD himself will dwell
forever?
17 The chariots of God are tens of thousands
and thousands of thousands;[t]
the Lord ⌊has come⌋ from Sinai into his
sanctuary.
18 When you ascended on high,
you led captives[u] in your train;
you received gifts from men,[v]
even from[c] the rebellious—
that you,[d] O LORD God, might dwell
there.

19 Praise be to the Lord, to God our Savior,
who daily bears our burdens. *Selah*
20 Our God is a God who saves;
from the Sovereign LORD comes escape
from death.

68:22 w Nu 21:33
68:23 x Ps 58:10 y 1Ki 21:19
68:25 z 1Ch 13:8
68:26 a Isa 48:1
68:27 b 1Sa 9:21
68:29 c Ps 72:10
68:30 d Ps 22:12
68:31 e Isa 45:14
68:33 f Ps 18:10
68:34 g Ps 29:1

21 Surely God will crush the heads of his
enemies,
the hairy crowns of those who go on in
their sins.
22 The Lord says, "I will bring them from
Bashan;
I will bring them from the depths of
the sea,[w]
23 that you may plunge your feet in the
blood of your foes,[x]
while the tongues of your dogs[y] have
their share."

24 Your procession has come into view,
O God,
the procession of my God and King
into the sanctuary.
25 In front are the singers, after them the
musicians;
with them are the maidens playing
tambourines.[z]
26 Praise God in the great congregation;
praise the LORD in the assembly of
Israel.[a]
27 There is the little tribe[b] of Benjamin,
leading them,
there the great throng of Judah's
princes,
and there the princes of Zebulun and
of Naphtali.

28 Summon your power, O God[e];
show us your strength, O God, as you
have done before.
29 Because of your temple at Jerusalem
kings will bring you gifts.[c]
30 Rebuke the beast among the reeds,
the herd of bulls[d] among the calves of
the nations.
Humbled, may it bring bars of silver.
Scatter the nations who delight in war.
31 Envoys will come from Egypt;[e]
Cush[f] will submit herself to God.

32 Sing to God, O kingdoms of the earth,
sing praise to the Lord, *Selah*
33 to him who rides[f] the ancient skies
above,
who thunders with mighty voice.
34 Proclaim the power[g] of God,
whose majesty is over Israel,
whose power is in the skies.

[a]13 Or *saddlebags* [b]14 Hebrew *Shaddai* [c]18 Or *gifts for men, / even* [d]18 Or *they* [e]28 Many Hebrew manuscripts, Septuagint and Syriac; most Hebrew manuscripts *Your God has summoned power for you* [f]31 That is, the upper Nile region

## The African Presence

**Psalm 68:31**

"Cush" is also called "Ethiopia" (that is, Nubia; see the African Presence note on Ex 5:1–5).

35 You are awesome, O God, in your
sanctuary;
the God of Israel gives power and
strength to his people.

Praise be to God!

## Psalm 69

For the director of music. To ⌞the tune of⌟ "Lilies." Of David.

1 Save me, O God,
for the waters have come up to my
neck.
2 I sink in the miry depths,[h]
where there is no foothold.
I have come into the deep waters;
the floods engulf me.
3 I am worn out calling for help;[i]
my throat is parched.
My eyes fail,[j]
looking for my God.
4 Those who hate me without reason[k]
outnumber the hairs of my head;
many are my enemies without cause,[l]
those who seek to destroy me.
I am forced to restore
what I did not steal.
5 You know my folly, O God;
my guilt is not hidden from you.
6 May those who hope in you
not be disgraced because of me,
O Lord, the LORD Almighty;
may those who seek you
not be put to shame because of me,
O God of Israel.
7 For I endure scorn for your sake,
and shame covers my face.
8 I am a stranger to my brothers,
an alien to my own mother's sons;
9 for zeal for your house consumes me,[m]
and the insults of those who insult you
fall on me.
10 When I weep and fast,[n]
I must endure scorn;
11 when I put on sackcloth,
people make sport of me.
12 Those who sit at the gate mock me,
and I am the song of the drunkards.[o]
13 But I pray to you, O LORD,
in the time of your favor;[p]
in your great love, O God,
answer me with your sure salvation.
14 Rescue me from the mire,
do not let me sink;
deliver me from those who hate me,
from the deep waters.[q]
15 Do not let the floodwaters engulf me
or the depths swallow me up[r]
or the pit close its mouth over me.

*Lord,*

*I need you—now, as always.*

*Help me, strengthen me and guide me.*

*Hear my cry. In Jesus' awesome name,*

*Amen.*

PSALM 69:13–15

16 Answer me, O LORD, out of the goodness
of your love;
in your great mercy turn to me.
17 Do not hide your face[s] from your
servant;
answer me quickly, for I am in trouble.
18 Come near and rescue me;
redeem me because of my foes.

**69:2** h Ps 40:2
**69:3** i Ps 6:6 j Ps 119:82; Isa 38:14
**69:4** k Jn 15:25* l Ps 35:19
**69:9** m Jn 2:17*
**69:10** n Ps 35:13
**69:12** o Job 30:9
**69:13** p Isa 49:8
**69:14** q Ps 144:7
**69:15** r Nu 16:33
**69:17** s Ps 27:9

**69:19** t Ps 22:6
**69:20** u Job 16:2 v Isa 63:5
**69:21** w Jn 19:28–30
**69:23** x Ro 11:9–10*
**69:25** y Mt 23:38
**69:26** z Isa 53:4
**69:28** a Ex 32:32–33; Php 4:3
**69:30** b Ps 28:7
**69:31** c Ps 50:9–13
**69:32** d Ps 34:2 e Ps 22:26
**69:34** f Ps 96:11; Isa 44:23
**69:35** g Ps 51:18; Isa 44:26

19 You know how I am scorned,[t] disgraced
and shamed;
all my enemies are before you.
20 Scorn has broken my heart
and has left me helpless;
I looked for sympathy, but there was
none,
for comforters,[u] but I found none.[v]
21 They put gall in my food
and gave me vinegar for my thirst.[w]

22 May the table set before them become a
snare;
may it become retribution and[a] a trap.
23 May their eyes be darkened so they
cannot see,
and their backs be bent forever.[x]
24 Pour out your wrath on them;
let your fierce anger overtake them.
25 May their place be deserted;[y]
let there be no one to dwell in their
tents.
26 For they persecute those you wound
and talk about the pain of those you
hurt.[z]
27 Charge them with crime upon crime;
do not let them share in your salvation.
28 May they be blotted out of the book of
life[a]
and not be listed with the righteous.

29 I am in pain and distress;
may your salvation, O God, protect me.

30 I will praise God's name in song[b]
and glorify him with thanksgiving.
31 This will please the LORD more than
an ox,
more than a bull with its horns and
hoofs.[c]
32 The poor will see and be glad[d]—
you who seek God, may your hearts
live![e]
33 The LORD hears the needy
and does not despise his captive
people.

34 Let heaven and earth praise him,
the seas and all that move in them,[f]
35 for God will save Zion
and rebuild the cities of Judah.[g]
Then people will settle there and
possess it;
36 the children of his servants will
inherit it,
and those who love his name will dwell
there.[h]

## Psalm 70

For the director of music. Of David.
A petition.

1 Hasten, O God, to save me;
O LORD, come quickly to help me.
2 May those who seek my life[i]
be put to shame and confusion;
may all who desire my ruin
be turned back in disgrace.[j]
3 May those who say to me, "Aha! Aha!"
turn back because of their shame.
4 But may all who seek you
rejoice and be glad in you;
may those who love your salvation always
say,
"Let God be exalted!"

5 Yet I am poor and needy;[k]
come quickly to me, O God.
You are my help and my deliverer;
O LORD, do not delay.

## Psalm 71

1 In you, O LORD, I have taken refuge;
let me never be put to shame.[l]
2 Rescue me and deliver me in your
righteousness;
turn your ear[m] to me and save me.
3 Be my rock of refuge,
to which I can always go;
give the command to save me,
for you are my rock and my fortress.
4 Deliver me, O my God, from the hand of
the wicked,[n]
from the grasp of evil and cruel men.

5 For you have been my hope, O Sovereign
LORD,
my confidence[o] since my youth.
6 From birth[p] I have relied on you;
you brought me forth from my
mother's womb.[q]
I will ever praise[r] you.
7 I have become like a portent[s] to many,
but you are my strong refuge.[t]

**69:36** h Ps 102:28
**70:2** i Ps 35:4 j Ps 35:26
**70:5** k Ps 40:17
**71:1** l Ps 25:2–3; 31:1
**71:2** m Ps 17:6
**71:4** n Ps 140:4
**71:5** o Jer 17:7
**71:6** p Ps 22:10 q Isa 46:3 r Ps 34:1
**71:7** s Isa 8:18; 1Co 4:9 t Ps 61:3

[a]22 Or *snare / and their fellowship become*

71:8 u Ps35:28
71:9 v ver 18
71:11 w Ps7:2
71:12 x Ps35:22 y Ps70:1
71:15 z Ps35:28; 40:5
71:16 a Ps106:2
71:17 b Ps26:7
71:19 c Ps57:10 d Ps35:10
71:20 e Ps60:3 f Hos6:2

8 My mouth is filled with your praise,
declaring your splendor[u] all day long.
9 Do not cast me away when I am old;[v]
do not forsake me when my strength
is gone.
10 For my enemies speak against me;
those who wait to kill me conspire
together.
11 They say, "God has forsaken him;
pursue him and seize him,
for no one will rescue[w] him."
12 Be not far[x] from me, O God;
come quickly, O my God, to help[y] me.
13 May my accusers perish in shame;
may those who want to harm me
be covered with scorn and disgrace.

14 But as for me, I will always have hope;
I will praise you more and more.
15 My mouth will tell[z] of your
righteousness,
of your salvation all day long,
though I know not its measure.
16 I will come and proclaim your mighty
acts,[a] O Sovereign LORD;
I will proclaim your righteousness,
yours alone.
17 Since my youth, O God, you have taught
me,
and to this day I declare your
marvelous deeds.[b]
18 Even when I am old and gray,
do not forsake me, O God,
till I declare your power to the next
generation,
your might to all who are to come.

19 Your righteousness reaches to the skies,[c]
O God,
you who have done great things.
Who, O God, is like you?[d]
20 Though you have made me see troubles,[e]
many and bitter,
you will restore[f] my life again;
from the depths of the earth
you will again bring me up.
21 You will increase my honor
and comfort me once again.

22 I will praise you with the harp
for your faithfulness, O my God;
I will sing praise to you with the lyre,
O Holy One of Israel.
23 My lips will shout for joy
when I sing praise to you—
I, whom you have redeemed.[g]
24 My tongue will tell of your righteous acts
all day long,[h]
for those who wanted to harm me
have been put to shame and confusion.

## Psalm 72

Of Solomon.

1 Endow the king with your justice, O God,
the royal son with your righteousness.
2 He will[a] judge your people in
righteousness,[i]
your afflicted ones with justice.
3 The mountains will bring prosperity to
the people,
the hills the fruit of righteousness.
4 He will defend the afflicted among the
people
and save the children of the needy;[j]
he will crush the oppressor.

5 He will endure[b] as long as the sun,
as long as the moon, through all
generations.
6 He will be like rain[k] falling on a mown
field,
like showers watering the earth.
7 In his days the righteous will flourish;
prosperity will abound till the moon is
no more.

8 He will rule from sea to sea
and from the River[c][l] to the ends of the
earth.[d][m]
9 The desert tribes will bow before him
and his enemies will lick the dust.
10 The kings of Tarshish and of distant
shores
will bring tribute to him;
the kings of Sheba and Seba
will present him gifts.[n]
11 All kings will bow down to him
and all nations will serve him.

12 For he will deliver the needy who cry out,
the afflicted who have no one to help.
13 He will take pity on the weak and the
needy

71:23 g Ps103:4
71:24 h Ps35:28
72:2 i Isa9:7
72:4 j Isa11:4
72:6 k Hos6:3
72:8 l Ex23:31 m Zec9:10
72:10 n 2Ch9:24

[a]2 Or *May he*; similarly in verses 3–11 and 17 [b]5 Septuagint; Hebrew *You will be feared* [c]8 That is, the Euphrates
[d]8 Or *the end of the land*

## The African Presence

**Psalm 72:10**
Sheba was located in southern Arabia; Seba, along the eastern African coast.

and save the needy from death.
14 He will rescue them from oppression and
violence,
for precious[o] is their blood in his sight.

15 Long may he live!
May gold from Sheba be given him.
May people ever pray for him
and bless him all day long.
16 Let grain abound throughout the land;
on the tops of the hills may it sway.
Let its fruit flourish like Lebanon;
let it thrive like the grass of the field.
17 May his name endure forever;
may it continue as long as the sun.[p]

All nations will be blessed through him,
and they will call him blessed.[q]

18 Praise be to the LORD God, the God of
Israel,[r]
who alone does marvelous deeds.
19 Praise be to his glorious name forever;
may the whole earth be filled with his
glory.[s]
Amen and Amen.

20 This concludes the prayers of David son
of Jesse.

# BOOK III

*Psalms 73–89*

## Psalm 73

A psalm of Asaph.

1 Surely God is good to Israel,
to those who are pure in heart.

2 But as for me, my feet had almost
slipped;
I had nearly lost my foothold.
3 For I envied[t] the arrogant
when I saw the prosperity of the
wicked.

4 They have no struggles;
their bodies are healthy and strong.[a]
5 They are free[u] from the burdens common
to man;
they are not plagued by human ills.
6 Therefore pride is their necklace;
they clothe themselves with violence.[v]
7 From their callous hearts comes
iniquity[b];
the evil conceits of their minds know
no limits.
8 They scoff, and speak with malice;
in their arrogance[w] they threaten
oppression.
9 Their mouths lay claim to heaven,
and their tongues take possession of
the earth.
10 Therefore their people turn to them
and drink up waters in abundance.[c]
11 They say, "How can God know?
Does the Most High have knowledge?"

12 This is what the wicked are like—
always carefree, they increase in
wealth.

13 Surely in vain[x] have I kept my heart pure;
in vain have I washed my hands in
innocence.[y]
14 All day long I have been plagued;
I have been punished every morning.

15 If I had said, "I will speak thus,"
I would have betrayed your children.

**72:14** o Ps 116:15
**72:17** p Ps 89:36; q Ge 12:3; Lk 1:48
**72:18** r 1Ch 29:10
**72:19** s Nu 14:21; Ne 9:5
**73:3** t Ps 37:1
**73:5** u Job 21:9
**73:6** v Ps 109:18
**73:8** w Jude 16
**73:13** x Job 34:9; y Ps 26:6

[a] 4 With a different word division of the Hebrew; Masoretic Text *struggles at their death; / their bodies are healthy*
[b] 7 Syriac (see also Septuagint); Hebrew *Their eyes bulge with fat* [c] 10 The meaning of the Hebrew for this verse is uncertain.

73:16 z Ecc 8:17
73:17 a Ps 77:13 b Ps 37:38
73:18 c Ps 35:6
73:20 d Job 20:8
73:24 e Ps 48:14 f Ps 32:8
73:25 g Php 3:8
73:26 h Ps 84:2
73:27 i Ps 119:155
73:28 j Heb 10:22
74:1 k Dt 29:20 l Ps 95:7
74:2 m Ps 68:16

16 When I tried to understand[z] all this,
it was oppressive to me
17 till I entered the sanctuary[a] of God;
then I understood their final destiny.[b]
18 Surely you place them on slippery
ground;[c]
you cast them down to ruin.
19 How suddenly are they destroyed,
completely swept away by terrors!
20 As a dream[d] when one awakes,
so when you arise, O Lord,
you will despise them as fantasies.

21 When my heart was grieved
and my spirit embittered,
22 I was senseless and ignorant;
I was a brute beast before you.

23 Yet I am always with you;
you hold me by my right hand.
24 You guide[e] me with your counsel,[f]
and afterward you will take me into
glory.
25 Whom have I in heaven but you?
And earth has nothing I desire besides
you.[g]
26 My flesh and my heart[h] may fail,
but God is the strength of my heart
and my portion forever.

27 Those who are far from you will perish;[i]
you destroy all who are unfaithful to
you.
28 But as for me, it is good to be near God.[j]
I have made the Sovereign LORD my
refuge;
I will tell of all your deeds.

## Psalm 74

A *maskil*[a] of Asaph.

1 Why have you rejected us forever,[k]
O God?
Why does your anger smolder against
the sheep of your pasture?[l]
2 Remember the people you purchased of
old,
the tribe of your inheritance, whom
you redeemed—
Mount Zion, where you dwelt.[m]
3 Turn your steps toward these everlasting
ruins,
all this destruction the enemy has
brought on the sanctuary.

4 Your foes roared[n] in the place where you
met with us;
they set up their standards as signs.
5 They behaved like men wielding axes
to cut through a thicket of trees.[o]
6 They smashed all the carved paneling
with their axes and hatchets.
7 They burned your sanctuary to the
ground;
they defiled the dwelling place of your
Name.
8 They said in their hearts, "We will crush[p]
them completely!"
They burned every place where God
was worshiped in the land.
9 We are given no miraculous signs;
no prophets are left,
and none of us knows how long this
will be.

10 How long will the enemy mock you,
O God?
Will the foe revile your name forever?
11 Why do you hold back your hand, your
right hand?[q]
Take it from the folds of your garment
and destroy them!

12 But you, O God, are my king[r] from of old;
you bring salvation upon the earth.
13 It was you who split open the sea[s] by your
power;
you broke the heads of the monster[t] in
the waters.
14 It was you who crushed the heads of
Leviathan
and gave him as food to the creatures
of the desert.
15 It was you who opened up springs[u] and
streams;
you dried up[v] the ever flowing rivers.
16 The day is yours, and yours also the
night;
you established the sun and moon.
17 It was you who set all the boundaries of
the earth;
you made both summer and winter.[w]

18 Remember how the enemy has mocked
you, O LORD,

74:4 n La 2:7
74:5 o Jer 46:22
74:8 p Ps 83:4
74:11 q La 2:3
74:12 r Ps 44:4
74:13 s Ex 14:21 t Isa 51:9
74:15 u Ex 17:6; Nu 20:11 v Jos 3:13
74:17 w Ge 8:22

[a]Title: Probably a literary or musical term

**74:18** x Ps 39:8
**74:19** y Ps 9:18
**74:20** z Ge 17:7; Ps 106:45
**74:21** a Ps 35:10
**74:23** b Ps 65:7
**75:1** c Ps 145:18
**75:4** d Zec 1:21
**75:7** e Ps 50:6 f 1Sa 2:7; Da 2:21
**75:8** g Pr 23:30

how foolish people[x] have reviled your
name.
19 Do not hand over the life of your dove to
wild beasts;
do not forget the lives of your afflicted[y]
people forever.
20 Have regard for your covenant,[z]
because haunts of violence fill the dark
places of the land.
21 Do not let the oppressed retreat in
disgrace;
may the poor and needy[a] praise your
name.
22 Rise up, O God, and defend your
cause;
remember how fools mock you all day
long.
23 Do not ignore the clamor of your
adversaries,[b]
the uproar of your enemies, which
rises continually.

## Psalm 75

For the director of music. ⌊To the tune of⌋ "Do Not Destroy."
A psalm of Asaph. A song.

1 We give thanks to you, O God,
we give thanks, for your Name is
near;[c]
men tell of your wonderful deeds.
2 You say, "I choose the appointed time;
it is I who judge uprightly.
3 When the earth and all its people
quake,
it is I who hold its pillars firm. *Selah*
4 To the arrogant I say, 'Boast no more,'
and to the wicked, 'Do not lift up your
horns.[d]
5 Do not lift your horns against heaven;
do not speak with outstretched
neck.' "
6 No one from the east or the west
or from the desert can exalt a man.
7 But it is God who judges:[e]
He brings one down, he exalts
another.[f]
8 In the hand of the LORD is a cup
full of foaming wine mixed[g] with
spices;
he pours it out, and all the wicked of the
earth
drink it down to its very dregs.[h]
9 As for me, I will declare this forever;
I will sing praise to the God of Jacob.
10 I will cut off the horns of all the wicked,
but the horns of the righteous will be
lifted up.[i]

## Psalm 76

For the director of music.
With stringed instruments.
A psalm of Asaph. A song.

1 In Judah God is known;
his name is great in Israel.
2 His tent is in Salem,
his dwelling place in Zion.
3 There he broke the flashing arrows,
the shields and the swords, the
weapons of war.[j] *Selah*
4 You are resplendent with light,
more majestic than mountains rich
with game.
5 Valiant men lie plundered,
they sleep their last sleep;
not one of the warriors
can lift his hands.
6 At your rebuke, O God of Jacob,
both horse and chariot[k] lie still.
7 You alone are to be feared.
Who can stand before you when you
are angry?[l]
8 From heaven you pronounced
judgment,
and the land feared[m] and was quiet—
9 when you, O God, rose up to judge,[n]
to save all the afflicted of the land.
*Selah*
10 Surely your wrath against men brings
you praise,
and the survivors of your wrath are
restrained.[a]
11 Make vows to the LORD your God and
fulfill them;
let all the neighboring lands
bring gifts[o] to the One to be feared.
12 He breaks the spirit of rulers;
he is feared by the kings of the earth.

**75:8** h Jer 25:15
**75:10** i Ps 89:17; 148:14
**76:3** j Ps 46:9
**76:6** k Ex 15:1
**76:7** l Na 1:6
**76:8** m 2Ch 20:29–30
**76:9** n Ps 9:8
**76:11** o Ps 68:29

[a]10 Or *Surely the wrath of men brings you praise, / and with the remainder of wrath you arm yourself*

## Psalm 77

For the director of music. For Jeduthun. Of Asaph. A psalm.

1 I cried out to God[p] for help;
I cried out to God to hear me.
2 When I was in distress,[q] I sought the Lord;
at night I stretched out untiring hands
and my soul refused to be comforted.

3 I remembered you, O God, and I groaned;
I mused, and my spirit grew faint.
*Selah*

4 You kept my eyes from closing;
I was too troubled to speak.
5 I thought about the former days,[r]
the years of long ago;
6 I remembered my songs in the night.
My heart mused and my spirit inquired:

7 "Will the Lord reject forever?
Will he never show his favor[s] again?
8 Has his unfailing love vanished forever?
Has his promise failed for all time?
9 Has God forgotten to be merciful?
Has he in anger withheld his compassion?[t]"
*Selah*

10 Then I thought, "To this I will appeal:
the years of the right hand of the Most High."
11 I will remember the deeds of the LORD;
yes, I will remember your miracles of long ago.
12 I will meditate on all your works
and consider all your mighty deeds.

13 Your ways, O God, are holy.
What god is so great as our God?[u]
14 You are the God who performs miracles;
you display your power among the peoples.
15 With your mighty arm you redeemed your people,[v]
the descendants of Jacob and Joseph.
*Selah*

16 The waters[w] saw you, O God,
the waters saw you and writhed;
the very depths were convulsed.
17 The clouds poured down water,
the skies resounded with thunder;
your arrows flashed back and forth.
18 Your thunder was heard in the whirlwind,
your lightning lit up the world;
the earth trembled and quaked.
19 Your path led through the sea,[x]
your way through the mighty waters,
though your footprints were not seen.

20 You led your people[y] like a flock[z]
by the hand of Moses and Aaron.

## Psalm 78

A *maskil*[a] of Asaph.

1 O my people, hear my teaching;[a]
listen to the words of my mouth.
2 I will open my mouth in parables,[b]
I will utter hidden things, things from of old—
3 what we have heard and known,
what our fathers have told us.[c]
4 We will not hide them from their children;
we will tell the next generation
the praiseworthy deeds of the LORD,
his power, and the wonders he has done.
5 He decreed statutes for Jacob[d]
and established the law in Israel,
which he commanded our forefathers
to teach their children,
6 so the next generation would know them,
even the children yet to be born,[e]
and they in turn would tell their children.
7 Then they would put their trust in God
and would not forget his deeds
but would keep his commands.
8 They would not be like their forefathers—
a stubborn[f] and rebellious generation,
whose hearts were not loyal to God,
whose spirits were not faithful to him.

9 The men of Ephraim, though armed with bows,
turned back on the day of battle;
10 they did not keep God's covenant
and refused to live by his law.
11 They forgot what he had done,[g]
the wonders he had shown them.

**77:1** p Ps3:4
**77:2** q Ps50:15; Isa26:9,16
**77:5** r Dt32:7; Ps143:5; Isa51:9
**77:7** s Ps85:1
**77:9** t Isa49:15
**77:13** u Ex15:11
**77:15** v Ex6:6; Dt9:29
**77:16** w Ex14:21,28
**77:19** x Hab3:15
**77:20** y Ex13:21 z Isa63:11
**78:1** a Isa51:4
**78:2** b Mt13:35*
**78:3** c Ps44:1
**78:5** d Ps147:19
**78:6** e Ps102:18
**78:8** f Ex32:9
**78:11** g Ps106:13

[a]Title: Probably a literary or musical term

# Inspire

## PARENTING

Parenting can be frightening, but it is one of the most rewarding experiences God has ordained for humankind. There is no perfect way of, or foolproof formula for, parenting. Some people have a natural instinct for it, while others grow into it through experience. Either way, parenting is an awesome responsibility.

When God formed us in his image, he parented us. He provided everything for the first family, Adam and Eve: light to see, water to drink, vegetation to eat, trees for shade and shelter (see Ge 1:3–29). God frequently stopped by to see how they were doing. On one of these visits he found it necessary to expose their disobedience for going against his instructions (see Ge 3:8–13). God had given them liberty to exercise their free will, with one stipulation: Under no circumstances were they to eat from the tree of the knowledge of good and evil (see Ge 2:16–17). God had guided them in the right direction. They had everything they needed to protect them from the storms of life, but, as is the case with many children, they did not listen. They allowed the serpent to influence their thinking, to deceive them into ignoring God's warning (see Ge 3:1–7). They rebelled against God, but he never stopped loving them—even though it meant exercising "tough love"—and providing for them (see Ge 3:14–24).

God is the ultimate example of a loving parent. Parenting involves praising, advising, reminding, encouraging, nurturing, teaching, training, influencing, nourishing, giving—and disciplining. Parenting for us as Christians entails teaching our children to live godly lives—through our words and by our example. The Bible reminds us of the importance of teaching our children about God (see Ps 78:1–6). Then they, in turn, will teach their children (see Ps 78:6).

At times it's just plain hard to be a parent. But during those difficult phases we are called to walk in faith. Parenting is a full-time, lifelong position that forces us to reflect on God's unconditional love as we attempt to love our children consistently and unconditionally.

—S. Demby

### read

Psalm 78:1–8; see also Deuteronomy 6:1–9; Proverbs 19:18; 22:6,15; Ephesians 6:1–4; Titus 2:1–8; Hebrews 12:4–11.

**See also** the Inspire Notes "A Great Challenge: Teaching Our Children," "Motherhood," "Raising Children: Modeling Discipleship," "Children: A Blessed Heritage From God" and "Nurturing Spiritual Gifts in Our Children," and the Women of the Bible Notes "Jochebed: She Knew It Would Take a Village," "Samson's Mother: The Strength of a Wife and Mother," "Micah's Mother: The Consequences of Ignoring God" and "Mary, the Mother of Jesus: A Model of Motherhood."

### WOMAN of COLOR

How has parenting your children or children in your community helped you reflect on God's unconditional love?

For the next Inspire note, go to page 692.

[12] He did miracles in the sight of their
fathers
in the land of Egypt, in the region of
Zoan.[h]
[13] He divided the sea[i] and led them
through;
he made the water stand firm like a
wall.[j]
[14] He guided them with the cloud by day
and with light from the fire all night.[k]
[15] He split the rocks[l] in the desert
and gave them water as abundant as
the seas;
[16] he brought streams out of a rocky crag
and made water flow down like rivers.
[17] But they continued to sin[m] against him,
rebelling in the desert against the
Most High.
[18] They willfully put God to the test
by demanding the food they craved.
[19] They spoke against God, saying,
"Can God spread a table in the desert?
[20] When he struck the rock, water gushed
out,[n]
and streams flowed abundantly.
But can he also give us food?
Can he supply meat for his people?"
[21] When the LORD heard them, he was very
angry;
his fire broke out[o] against Jacob,
and his wrath rose against Israel,
[22] for they did not believe in God
or trust[p] in his deliverance.
[23] Yet he gave a command to the skies
above
and opened the doors of the heavens;
[24] he rained down manna[q] for the people to
eat,
he gave them the grain of heaven.
[25] Men ate the bread of angels;
he sent them all the food they could
eat.
[26] He let loose the east wind[r] from the
heavens
and led forth the south wind by his
power.
[27] He rained meat down on them like dust,
flying birds like sand on the seashore.
[28] He made them come down inside their
camp,
all around their tents.
[29] They ate till they had more than enough,[s]
for he had given them what they
craved.
[30] But before they turned from the food they
craved,
even while it was still in their mouths,
[31] God's anger rose against them;
he put to death the sturdiest among
them,
cutting down the young men of Israel.
[32] In spite of all this, they kept on sinning;
in spite of his wonders, they did not
believe.
[33] So he ended their days in futility[t]
and their years in terror.
[34] Whenever God slew them, they would
seek[u] him;
they eagerly turned to him again.
[35] They remembered that God was their
Rock,
that God Most High was their
Redeemer.
[36] But then they would flatter him with their
mouths,[v]
lying to him with their tongues;
[37] their hearts were not loyal to him,
they were not faithful to his covenant.
[38] Yet he was merciful;
he forgave[w] their iniquities
and did not destroy them.
Time after time he restrained his anger
and did not stir up his full wrath.
[39] He remembered that they were but flesh,[x]
a passing breeze[y] that does not return.
[40] How often they rebelled against him in
the desert[z]
and grieved him in the wasteland!
[41] Again and again they put God to the
test;
they vexed the Holy One of Israel.
[42] They did not remember his power—
the day he redeemed them from the
oppressor,
[43] the day he displayed his miraculous signs
in Egypt,
his wonders in the region of Zoan.
[44] He turned their rivers to blood;[a]
they could not drink from their
streams.
[45] He sent swarms of flies[b] that devoured
them,
and frogs[c] that devastated them.
[46] He gave their crops to the grasshopper,

**78:12** h Nu 13:22
**78:13** i Ex 14:21 j Ex 15:8
**78:14** k Ex 13:21
**78:15** l Nu 20:11
**78:17** m Heb 3:16
**78:20** n Nu 20:11
**78:21** o Nu 11:1
**78:22** p Heb 3:19
**78:24** q Jn 6:31*
**78:26** r Nu 11:31
**78:29** s Nu 11:20
**78:33** t Nu 14:29,35
**78:34** u Hos 5:15
**78:36** v Eze 33:31
**78:38** w Isa 48:10
**78:39** x Ps 103:14 y Job 7:7
**78:40** z Ps 95:8
**78:44** a Ex 7:20–21
**78:45** b Ex 8:24; Ps 105:31 c Ex 8:2,6

78:47 d Ex 9:23
78:51 e Ex 12:29
78:52 f Ps 77:20
78:53 g Ex 14:28
78:54 h Ps 44:3
78:55 i Ps 44:2
78:57 j Eze 20:27

their produce to the locust.
47 He destroyed their vines with hail[d]
and their sycamore-figs with sleet.
48 He gave over their cattle to the hail,
their livestock to bolts of lightning.
49 He unleashed against them his hot anger,
his wrath, indignation and hostility—
a band of destroying angels.
50 He prepared a path for his anger;
he did not spare them from death
but gave them over to the plague.
51 He struck down all the firstborn of Egypt,[e]
the firstfruits of manhood in the tents of Ham.
52 But he brought his people out like a flock;[f]
he led them like sheep through the desert.
53 He guided them safely, so they were unafraid;
but the sea engulfed[g] their enemies.
54 Thus he brought them to the border of his holy land,
to the hill country his right hand[h] had taken.
55 He drove out nations[i] before them
and allotted their lands to them as an inheritance;
he settled the tribes of Israel in their homes.

56 But they put God to the test
and rebelled against the Most High;
they did not keep his statutes.
57 Like their fathers[j] they were disloyal and faithless,
as unreliable as a faulty bow.
58 They angered him with their high places;
they aroused his jealousy with their idols.
59 When God heard them, he was very angry;
he rejected Israel completely.
60 He abandoned the tabernacle of Shiloh,
the tent he had set up among men.
61 He sent ⌞the ark of⌟ his might into captivity,
his splendor into the hands of the enemy.
62 He gave his people over to the sword;
he was very angry with his inheritance.
63 Fire consumed their young men,
and their maidens had no wedding songs;[k]
64 their priests were put to the sword,[l]
and their widows could not weep.

65 Then the Lord awoke as from sleep,
as a man wakes from the stupor of wine.
66 He beat back his enemies;
he put them to everlasting shame.[m]
67 Then he rejected the tents of Joseph,
he did not choose the tribe of Ephraim;
68 but he chose the tribe of Judah,
Mount Zion,[n] which he loved.
69 He built his sanctuary like the heights,
like the earth that he established forever.
70 He chose David[o] his servant
and took him from the sheep pens;
71 from tending the sheep he brought him
to be the shepherd[p] of his people Jacob,
of Israel his inheritance.
72 And David shepherded them with integrity of heart;[q]
with skillful hands he led them.

78:63 k Jer 7:34
78:64 l 1Sa 22:18
78:66 m 1Sa 5:6
78:68 n Ps 87:2
78:70 o 1Sa 16:1
78:71 p 2Sa 5:2
78:72 q 1Ki 9:4

## The African Presence

**Psalm 78:51**

The "land of Ham" is a poetic description of Egypt. One of Ham's sons was Mizraim. The word *mizraim* means "two Egypts," referring to Upper and Lower Egypt. (See Ps 105:23,27; 106:22 for other associations of "Ham" and "Egypt"; see also the African Presence notes on Ge 10:6–12 and Ge 10:6.)

79:1 r Ps 74:2
79:2 s Jer 7:33
79:5 t Ps 74:10 u Ps 74:1 v Zep 3:8
79:6 w Jer 10:25; 2Th 1:8
79:8 x Isa 64:9
79:9 y Jer 14:7
79:10 z Ps 42:10

## Psalm 79

A psalm of Asaph.

1 O God, the nations have invaded your
inheritance;[r]
they have defiled your holy temple,
they have reduced Jerusalem to
rubble.
2 They have given the dead bodies of your
servants
as food to the birds of the air,
the flesh of your saints to the beasts of
the earth.[s]
3 They have poured out blood like water
all around Jerusalem,
and there is no one to bury the dead.
4 We are objects of reproach to our
neighbors,
of scorn and derision to those
around us.

5 How long,[t] O LORD? Will you be angry[u]
forever?
How long will your jealousy burn like
fire?[v]
6 Pour out your wrath on the nations
that do not acknowledge[w] you,
on the kingdoms
that do not call on your name;
7 for they have devoured Jacob
and destroyed his homeland.
8 Do not hold against us the sins of the
fathers;[x]
may your mercy come quickly to
meet us,
for we are in desperate need.

9 Help us, O God our Savior,
for the glory of your name;
deliver us and forgive our sins
for your name's sake.[y]
10 Why should the nations say,
"Where is their God?"[z]
Before our eyes, make known among the
nations
that you avenge the outpoured blood of
your servants.
11 May the groans of the prisoners come
before you;
by the strength of your arm
preserve those condemned to die.
12 Pay back into the laps[a] of our neighbors
seven times[b]
the reproach they have hurled at you,
O Lord.
13 Then we your people, the sheep of your
pasture,[c]
will praise you forever;
from generation to generation
we will recount your praise.

## Psalm 80

For the director of music. To ⌞the
tune of⌟ "The Lilies of the Covenant."
Of Asaph. A psalm.

1 Hear us, O Shepherd of Israel,
you who lead Joseph like a flock;
you who sit enthroned between the
cherubim, shine forth
2 before Ephraim, Benjamin and
Manasseh.
Awaken your might;
come and save us.

3 Restore[d] us,[e] O God;
make your face shine upon us,
that we may be saved.

4 O LORD God Almighty,
how long will your anger smolder
against the prayers of your people?
5 You have fed them with the bread of
tears;
you have made them drink tears by the
bowlful.[f]
6 You have made us a source of contention
to our neighbors,
and our enemies mock us.

7 Restore us, O God Almighty;
make your face shine upon us,
that we may be saved.

8 You brought a vine out of Egypt;
you drove out the nations and
planted it.
9 You cleared the ground for it,
and it took root and filled the land.
10 The mountains were covered with its
shade,
the mighty cedars with its branches.
11 It sent out its boughs to the Sea,[a]
its shoots as far as the River.[b]

79:12 a Isa 65:6; Jer 32:18 b Ge 4:15
79:13 c Ps 74:1; 95:7
80:3 d La 5:21 e Nu 6:25
80:5 f Ps 42:3

[a]11 Probably the Mediterranean [b]11 That is, the Euphrates

80:14 g Isa 63:15
80:16 h Ps 39:11; 76:6
81:7 i Ex 2:23; Ps 50:15 j Ex 19:19

12 Why have you broken down its walls
so that all who pass by pick its grapes?
13 Boars from the forest ravage it
and the creatures of the field feed on it.
14 Return to us, O God Almighty!
Look down from heaven and see![g]
Watch over this vine,
15 the root your right hand has planted,
the son[a] you have raised up for yourself.

16 Your vine is cut down, it is burned with fire;
at your rebuke[h] your people perish.
17 Let your hand rest on the man at your right hand,
the son of man you have raised up for yourself.
18 Then we will not turn away from you;
revive us, and we will call on your name.

19 Restore us, O LORD God Almighty;
make your face shine upon us,
that we may be saved.

## Psalm 81

For the director of music. According to *gittith*.[b] Of Asaph.

1 Sing for joy to God our strength;
shout aloud to the God of Jacob!
2 Begin the music, strike the tambourine,
play the melodious harp and lyre.

3 Sound the ram's horn at the New Moon,
and when the moon is full, on the day of our Feast;
4 this is a decree for Israel,
an ordinance of the God of Jacob.
5 He established it as a statute for Joseph
when he went out against Egypt,
where we heard a language we did not understand.[c]

6 He says, "I removed the burden from their shoulders;
their hands were set free from the basket.
7 In your distress you called[i] and I rescued you,
I answered[j] you out of a thundercloud;
I tested you at the waters of Meribah.[k]
*Selah*

8 "Hear, O my people,[l] and I will warn you—
if you would but listen to me, O Israel!
9 You shall have no foreign god[m] among you;
you shall not bow down to an alien god.
10 I am the LORD your God,
who brought you up out of Egypt.[n]
Open wide your mouth and I will fill it.

11 "But my people would not listen to me;
Israel would not submit to me.
12 So I gave them over[o] to their stubborn hearts
to follow their own devices.

13 "If my people would but listen to me,[p]
if Israel would follow my ways,
14 how quickly would I subdue their enemies
and turn my hand against their foes!
15 Those who hate the LORD would cringe before him,
and their punishment would last forever.
16 But you would be fed with the finest of wheat;[q]
with honey from the rock I would satisfy you."

## Psalm 82

A psalm of Asaph.

1 God presides in the great assembly;
he gives judgment among the "gods":

2 "How long will you[d] defend the unjust
and show partiality[r] to the wicked?
*Selah*

3 Defend the cause of the weak and fatherless;
maintain the rights of the poor and oppressed.
4 Rescue the weak and needy;
deliver them from the hand of the wicked.

5 "They know nothing, they understand nothing.[s]

81:7 k Ex 17:7
81:8 l Ps 50:7
81:9 m Ex 20:3; Dt 32:12; Isa 43:12
81:10 n Ex 20:2
81:12 o Ac 7:42
81:13 p Dt 5:29; Isa 48:18
81:16 q Dt 32:14
82:2 r Dt 1:17
82:5 s Mic 3:1

[a]15 Or *branch* [b]Title: Probably a musical term [c]5 Or */ and we heard a voice we had not known* [d]2 The Hebrew is plural.

82:5 t Ps 11:3
82:6 u Jn 10:34*
82:7 v Ps 49:12
82:8 w Ps 2:8; Rev 11:15
83:1 x Ps 28:1
83:2 y Ps 2:1 z Ps 81:15
83:6 a 2Ch 20:1
83:11 b Jdg 8:12,21
83:13 c Ps 35:5; Isa 17:13
83:14 d Dt 32:22

They walk about in darkness;
all the foundations[t] of the earth are shaken.

[6] "I said, 'You are "gods";[u]
you are all sons of the Most High.'
[7] But you will die[v] like mere men;
you will fall like every other ruler."

[8] Rise up, O God, judge the earth,
for all the nations are your inheritance.[w]

## Psalm 83

A song. A psalm of Asaph.

[1] O God, do not keep silent;[x]
be not quiet, O God, be not still.
[2] See how your enemies are astir,[y]
how your foes rear their heads.[z]
[3] With cunning they conspire against your people;
they plot against those you cherish.
[4] "Come," they say, "let us destroy them as a nation,
that the name of Israel be remembered no more."

[5] With one mind they plot together;
they form an alliance against you—
[6] the tents of Edom and the Ishmaelites,
of Moab[a] and the Hagrites,
[7] Gebal,[a] Ammon and Amalek,
Philistia, with the people of Tyre.
[8] Even Assyria has joined them
to lend strength to the descendants of Lot. *Selah*

[9] Do to them as you did to Midian,
as you did to Sisera and Jabin at the river Kishon,
[10] who perished at Endor
and became like refuse on the ground.
[11] Make their nobles like Oreb and Zeeb,
all their princes like Zebah and Zalmunna,[b]
[12] who said, "Let us take possession
of the pasturelands of God."

[13] Make them like tumbleweed, O my God,
like chaff[c] before the wind.
[14] As fire consumes the forest
or a flame sets the mountains ablaze,[d]
[15] so pursue them with your tempest
and terrify them with your storm.
[16] Cover their faces with shame
so that men will seek your name,
O LORD.

[17] May they ever be ashamed and dismayed;
may they perish in disgrace.
[18] Let them know that you, whose name is the LORD—
that you alone are the Most High over all the earth.[e]

## Psalm 84

For the director of music. According to *gittith*.[b] Of the Sons of Korah. A psalm.

[1] How lovely is your dwelling place,[f]
O LORD Almighty!
[2] My soul yearns,[g] even faints,
for the courts of the LORD;
my heart and my flesh cry out
for the living God.

[3] Even the sparrow has found a home,
and the swallow a nest for herself,
where she may have her young—
a place near your altar,
O LORD Almighty, my King and my God.
[4] Blessed are those who dwell in your house;
they are ever praising you. *Selah*

[5] Blessed are those whose strength is in you,
who have set their hearts on pilgrimage.
[6] As they pass through the Valley of Baca,
they make it a place of springs;
the autumn rains also cover it with pools.[c]
[7] They go from strength to strength,[h]
till each appears[i] before God in Zion.

[8] Hear my prayer, O LORD God Almighty;
listen to me, O God of Jacob. *Selah*
[9] Look upon our shield,[d] O God;
look with favor on your anointed one.

[10] Better is one day in your courts
than a thousand elsewhere;

83:18 e Ps 59:13
84:1 f Ps 27:4
84:2 g Ps 42:1–2
84:7 h Pr 4:18 i Dt 16:16

[a]7 That is, Byblos [b]Title: Probably a musical term [c]6 Or *blessings* [d]9 Or *sovereign*

I would rather be a doorkeeper in the
house of my God
than dwell in the tents of the wicked.
11 For the LORD God is a sun[j] and shield;[k]
the LORD bestows favor and honor;
no good thing does he withhold[l]
from those whose walk is blameless.

12 O LORD Almighty,
blessed[m] is the man who trusts in you.

## Psalm 85

For the director of music. Of the Sons of Korah. A psalm.

1 You showed favor to your land, O LORD;
you restored the fortunes[n] of Jacob.
2 You forgave the iniquity of your people
and covered all their sins. *Selah*
3 You set aside all your wrath
and turned from your fierce anger.[o]

4 Restore[p] us again, O God our Savior,
and put away your displeasure
toward us.
5 Will you be angry with us forever?[q]
Will you prolong your anger through
all generations?
6 Will you not revive us again,
that your people may rejoice in you?
7 Show us your unfailing love, O LORD,
and grant us your salvation.

8 I will listen to what God the LORD will say;
he promises peace[r] to his people, his
saints—
but let them not return to folly.
9 Surely his salvation[s] is near those who
fear him,
that his glory[t] may dwell in our land.

10 Love and faithfulness meet together;
righteousness[u] and peace kiss each
other.
11 Faithfulness springs forth from the
earth,
and righteousness looks down from
heaven.
12 The LORD will indeed give what is good,[v]
and our land will yield its harvest.
13 Righteousness goes before him
and prepares the way for his steps.

**84:11** j Isa 60:19 k Ge 15:1 l Ps 34:10
**84:12** m Ps 2:12
**85:1** n Jer 30:18; Eze 39:25
**85:3** o Dt 13:17
**85:4** p Ps 80:3,7
**85:5** q Ps 79:5
**85:8** r Zec 9:10
**85:9** s Isa 46:13 t Zec 2:5
**85:10** u Ps 72:2–3; Isa 32:17
**85:12** v Ps 84:11; Jas 1:17

## Psalm 86

A prayer of David.

1 Hear, O LORD, and answer me,
for I am poor and needy.
2 Guard my life, for I am devoted to you.
You are my God; save your servant
who trusts in you.
3 Have mercy[w] on me, O Lord,
for I call to you all day long.
4 Bring joy to your servant,
for to you, O Lord,
I lift[x] up my soul.

5 You are forgiving and good, O Lord,
abounding in love[y] to all who call to
you.
6 Hear my prayer, O LORD;
listen to my cry for mercy.
7 In the day of my trouble I will call to
you,
for you will answer me.

8 Among the gods there is none like you,[z]
O Lord;
no deeds can compare with yours.
9 All the nations you have made
will come and worship[a] before you,
O Lord;
they will bring glory to your name.
10 For you are great and do marvelous
deeds;[b]
you alone[c] are God.

11 Teach me your way,[d] O LORD,
and I will walk in your truth;
give me an undivided heart,
that I may fear your name.
12 I will praise you, O Lord my God, with all
my heart;
I will glorify your name forever.
13 For great is your love toward me;
you have delivered me from the depths
of the grave.[a]

14 The arrogant are attacking me, O God;
a band of ruthless men seeks my
life—
men without regard for you.
15 But you, O Lord, are a compassionate and
gracious God,
slow to anger, abounding in love and
faithfulness.

**86:3** w Ps 57:1
**86:4** x Ps 25:1; 143:8
**86:5** y Ps 145:8; Joel 2:13
**86:8** z Ex 15:11; Dt 3:24; Ps 89:6
**86:9** a Rev 15:4
**86:10** b Ps 72:18 c Dt 6:4; Mk 12:29
**86:11** d Ps 25:5

[a]13 Hebrew *Sheol*

87:2 e Ps78:68
87:3 f Isa60:1
87:6 g Eze13:9
88:3 h Ps107:18,26

16 Turn to me and have mercy on me;
grant your strength to your servant
and save the son of your
maidservant.[a]
17 Give me a sign of your goodness,
that my enemies may see it and be put
to shame,
for you, O LORD, have helped me and
comforted me.

## Psalm 87

Of the Sons of Korah. A psalm.
A song.

1 He has set his foundation on the holy
mountain;
2 the LORD loves the gates of Zion[e]
more than all the dwellings of Jacob.
3 Glorious things are said of you,
O city of God:[f] *Selah*
4 "I will record Rahab[b] and Babylon
among those who acknowledge me—
Philistia too, and Tyre, along with
Cush[c]—
and will say, 'This[d] one was born in
Zion.' "

5 Indeed, of Zion it will be said,
"This one and that one were born in
her,
and the Most High himself will
establish her."
6 The LORD will write in the register[g] of the
peoples:
"This one was born in Zion." *Selah*
7 As they make music they will sing,
"All my fountains are in you."

## Psalm 88

A song. A psalm of the Sons of Korah.
For the director of music. According
to *mahalath leannoth.*[e] A *maskil*[f] of
Heman the Ezrahite.

1 O LORD, the God who saves me,
day and night I cry out before you.
2 May my prayer come before you;
turn your ear to my cry.

3 For my soul is full of trouble
and my life draws near the grave.[g][h]
4 I am counted among those who go down
to the pit;[i]
I am like a man without strength.
5 I am set apart with the dead,
like the slain who lie in the grave,
whom you remember no more,
who are cut off[j] from your care.

6 You have put me in the lowest pit,
in the darkest depths.
7 Your wrath lies heavily upon me;
you have overwhelmed me with all
your waves.[k] *Selah*
8 You have taken from me my closest
friends[l]
and have made me repulsive to
them.
I am confined and cannot escape;
9 my eyes are dim with grief.

I call[m] to you, O Lord, every day;
I spread out my hands[n] to you.
10 Do you show your wonders to the dead?
Do those who are dead rise up and
praise you?[o] *Selah*
11 Is your love declared in the grave,
your faithfulness in Destruction[h]?
12 Are your wonders known in the place of
darkness,
or your righteous deeds in the land of
oblivion?

13 But I cry to you for help, O LORD;
in the morning[p] my prayer comes
before you.
14 Why, O LORD, do you reject me
and hide your face[q] from me?
15 From my youth I have been afflicted and
close to death;
I have suffered your terrors[r] and am in
despair.
16 Your wrath has swept over me;
your terrors have destroyed me.
17 All day long they surround me like a
flood;[s]
they have completely engulfed me.
18 You have taken my companions[t] and
loved ones from me;
the darkness is my closest friend.

88:4 i Ps28:1
88:5 j Isa53:8
88:7 k Ps42:7
88:8 l Job19:13
88:9 m Ps86:3 n Ps143:6
88:10 o Ps6:5
88:13 p Ps5:3
88:14 q Job13:24; Ps13:1
88:15 r Job6:4
88:17 s Ps22:16
88:18 t Job19:13

[a]16 Or *save your faithful son* [b]4 A poetic name for Egypt [c]4 That is, the upper Nile region [d]4 Or *"O Rahab and Babylon, / Philistia, Tyre and Cush, / I will record concerning those who acknowledge me: / 'This* [e]Title: Possibly a tune, "The Suffering of Affliction" [f]Title: Probably a literary or musical term [g]3 Hebrew *Sheol* [h]11 Hebrew *Abaddon*

Inspire

## COPING WITH LIFE'S TASKS

Caregiver, coach, cook, counselor, chaplain, chauffeur, confidant, craftsperson, conflict mediator, companion, consultant, coordinator of special events—these are descriptions to which many women of color can relate. Many of us try to be all things to all people, and we are left with great and high intentions but low energy levels. We often find ourselves crying out because of the trouble we encounter, trying to address every need and every item on our to-do lists. How do we juggle the roles, relationships, requests and life requirements that vie continuously for our attention?

One thing we can do to ease our burden is to covenant with God to be open to anxiety, frustration and irritation. We certainly see many of the psalmists, as here in Psalm 88, expressing their raw emotions about such things to the Lord. These feelings can serve as mentors to our souls; by acknowledging and working through these feelings, obstacles can turn into opportunities for growth, and we can receive the resilience inherent in God's grace.

Women of color with too many things to do can also learn to discern what's important from what is urgent. Immediacy plus ability doesn't equal obligation. Urgent does not mean important. We really don't have to do everything. Instead, we can ask God for wisdom to prioritize our involvement and obligations.

When you are feeling troubled by your to-do list and are wondering how to cope, purpose in your heart to recall previous victories and determine to display godly character toward yourself and others as you scale what is currently the "insurmountable" mountain. Avoid heeding the call of anger, bitterness and resentment; instead, rely on God to give you discernment, energy and the ability to do all he has purposed for you to do—and the wisdom to let the rest go.

—B. Glover-Williams

### read

Psalm 88.

See also the Inspire Notes "Rest," "Responsible Decisions in Leadership," "Seek Wisdom," "Stress Management: Learning to Say 'No.' " "Write It Down!" and "Be Focused," and the Women of the Bible Notes "A Virtuous Woman: A Strong Woman, Dependent on God" and "The 'Chosen Lady': A Woman Worth Imitating."

### WOMAN of COLOR

How do you deal with the multiple tasks you have to complete?

For the next Inspire note, go to page 700.

89:1 u Ps 101:1
89:4 v Lk 1:33
89:5 w Ps 19:1
89:9 x Ps 65:7
89:10 y Ps 87:4
89:12 z Jos 19:22 a Jos 12:1

## Psalm 89

A *maskil*[a] of Ethan the Ezrahite.

1 I will sing[u] of the LORD's great love
forever;
with my mouth I will make your
faithfulness known through all
generations.
2 I will declare that your love stands firm
forever,
that you established your faithfulness
in heaven itself.

3 You said, "I have made a covenant with
my chosen one,
I have sworn to David my servant,
4 'I will establish your line forever
and make your throne firm through all
generations.' "[v] *Selah*

5 The heavens[w] praise your wonders,
O LORD,
your faithfulness too, in the assembly
of the holy ones.
6 For who in the skies above can compare
with the LORD?
Who is like the LORD among the
heavenly beings?
7 In the council of the holy ones God is
greatly feared;
he is more awesome than all who
surround him.
8 O LORD God Almighty, who is like you?
You are mighty, O LORD, and your
faithfulness surrounds you.

9 You rule over the surging sea;
when its waves mount up, you still
them.[x]
10 You crushed Rahab[y] like one of the slain;
with your strong arm you scattered
your enemies.
11 The heavens are yours, and yours also the
earth;
you founded the world and all that is
in it.
12 You created the north and the south;
Tabor[z] and Hermon[a] sing for joy at
your name.
13 Your arm is endued with power;
your hand is strong, your right hand
exalted.
14 Righteousness and justice are the
foundation of your throne;
love and faithfulness go before you.
15 Blessed are those who have learned to
acclaim you,
who walk in the light of your presence,
O LORD.
16 They rejoice in your name all day long;
they exult in your righteousness.
17 For you are their glory and strength,
and by your favor you exalt our horn.[b]
18 Indeed, our shield[c] belongs to the LORD,
our king to the Holy One of Israel.

19 Once you spoke in a vision,
to your faithful people you said:
"I have bestowed strength on a warrior;
I have exalted a young man from
among the people.
20 I have found David my servant;
with my sacred oil I have anointed[b]
him.
21 My hand will sustain him;
surely my arm will strengthen him.
22 No enemy will subject him to tribute;
no wicked man will oppress[c] him.
23 I will crush his foes before him
and strike down his adversaries.[d]
24 My faithful love will be with him,
and through my name his horn[d] will
be exalted.
25 I will set his hand over the sea,
his right hand over the rivers.
26 He will call out to me, 'You are my Father,
my God, the Rock my Savior.'[e]
27 I will also appoint him my firstborn,
the most exalted[f] of the kings of the
earth.
28 I will maintain my love to him forever,
and my covenant with him will never
fail.
29 I will establish his line forever,
his throne as long as the heavens
endure.[g]

30 "If his sons forsake my law
and do not follow my statutes,
31 if they violate my decrees
and fail to keep my commands,
32 I will punish their sin with the rod,
their iniquity with flogging;

89:20 b 1Sa 16:1,12
89:22 c 2Sa 7:10
89:23 d 2Sa 7:9
89:26 e 2Sa 22:47
89:27 f Nu 24:7
89:29 g Dt 11:21; Jer 33:17

[a]Title: Probably a literary or musical term [b]17 *Horn* here symbolizes strong one. [c]18 Or *sovereign* [d]24 *Horn* here symbolizes strength.

**89:33** h 2Sa 7:15
**89:38** i Dt 32:19; 1Ch 28:9
**89:39** j La 5:16
**89:41** k Ps 44:13
**89:46** l Ps 79:5
**89:47** m Job 7:7
**89:48** n Ps 49:9
**89:50** o Ps 69:19

33 but I will not take my love from him,[h]
nor will I ever betray my faithfulness.
34 I will not violate my covenant
or alter what my lips have uttered.
35 Once for all, I have sworn by my holiness—
and I will not lie to David—
36 that his line will continue forever
and his throne endure before me like the sun;
37 it will be established forever like the moon,
the faithful witness in the sky." *Selah*

38 But you have rejected,[i] you have spurned,
you have been very angry with your anointed one.
39 You have renounced the covenant with your servant
and have defiled his crown in the dust.[j]
40 You have broken through all his walls
and reduced his strongholds to ruins.
41 All who pass by have plundered him;
he has become the scorn of his neighbors.[k]
42 You have exalted the right hand of his foes;
you have made all his enemies rejoice.
43 You have turned back the edge of his sword
and have not supported him in battle.
44 You have put an end to his splendor
and cast his throne to the ground.
45 You have cut short the days of his youth;
you have covered him with a mantle of shame. *Selah*

46 How long, O LORD? Will you hide yourself forever?
How long will your wrath burn like fire?
47 Remember how fleeting is my life.[m]
For what futility you have created all men!
48 What man can live and not see death,
or save himself from the power of the grave[a]?[n] *Selah*
49 O Lord, where is your former great love,
which in your faithfulness you swore to David?
50 Remember, Lord, how your servant has[b] been mocked,[o]
how I bear in my heart the taunts of all the nations,
51 the taunts with which your enemies have mocked, O LORD,
with which they have mocked every step of your anointed one.

52 Praise be to the LORD forever!
Amen and Amen.[p]

# BOOK IV

*Psalms 90–106*

## Psalm 90

A prayer of Moses the man of God.

1 Lord, you have been our dwelling place[q]
throughout all generations.
2 Before the mountains were born[r]
or you brought forth the earth and the world,
from everlasting to everlasting you are God.

3 You turn men back to dust,
saying, "Return to dust, O sons of men."
4 For a thousand years in your sight
are like a day that has just gone by,
or like a watch in the night.[s]
5 You sweep men away[t] in the sleep of death;
they are like the new grass of the morning—
6 though in the morning it springs up new,
by evening it is dry and withered.

7 We are consumed by your anger
and terrified by your indignation.
8 You have set our iniquities before you,
our secret sins[u] in the light of your presence.
9 All our days pass away under your wrath;
we finish our years with a moan.
10 The length of our days is seventy years—
or eighty, if we have the strength;
yet their span[c] is but trouble and sorrow,
for they quickly pass, and we fly away.
11 Who knows the power of your anger?
For your wrath is as great as the fear that is due you.

**89:52** p Ps 41:13
**90:1** q Eze 11:16
**90:2** r Pr 8:25
**90:4** s 2Pe 3:8
**90:5** t Isa 40:6
**90:8** u Ps 19:12

[a]48 Hebrew *Sheol* [b]50 Or *your servants have* [c]10 Or *yet the best of them*

**90:12** v Ps 39:4
**90:13** w Dt 32:36
**90:14** x Ps 85:6
**90:16** y Hab 3:2
**90:17** z Isa 26:12
**91:1** a Ps 31:20 b Ps 17:8
**91:2** c Ps 142:5
**91:3** d Ps 124:7

12 Teach us to number our days[v] aright,
that we may gain a heart of wisdom.
13 Relent, O LORD! How long will it be?
Have compassion on your servants.[w]
14 Satisfy us in the morning with your unfailing love,
that we may sing for joy[x] and be glad all our days.
15 Make us glad for as many days as you have afflicted us,
for as many years as we have seen trouble.
16 May your deeds be shown to your servants,
your splendor to their children.[y]
17 May the favor[a] of the Lord our God rest upon us;
establish the work of our hands for us—
yes, establish the work of our hands.[z]

## Psalm 91

1 He who dwells in the shelter[a] of the Most High
will rest in the shadow[b] of the Almighty.[b]
2 I will say[c] of the LORD, "He is my refuge[c]
and my fortress,
my God, in whom I trust."

*Dear child,*

*I am faithful. I keep my promises.*

*Your Heavenly Father*

PSALM 91:1–2

3 Surely he will save you from the fowler's snare[d]
and from the deadly pestilence.
4 He will cover you with his feathers,
and under his wings you will find refuge;
his faithfulness will be your shield and rampart.
5 You will not fear the terror of night,
nor the arrow that flies by day,
6 nor the pestilence that stalks in the darkness,
nor the plague that destroys at midday.
7 A thousand may fall at your side,
ten thousand at your right hand,
but it will not come near you.
8 You will only observe with your eyes
and see the punishment of the wicked.

9 If you make the Most High your dwelling—
even the LORD, who is my refuge—
10 then no harm[e] will befall you,
no disaster will come near your tent.
11 For he will command his angels[f] concerning you
to guard you in all your ways;[g]
12 they will lift you up in their hands,
so that you will not strike your foot against a stone.[h]
13 You will tread upon the lion and the cobra;
you will trample the great lion and the serpent.

14 "Because he loves me," says the LORD, "I will rescue him;
I will protect him, for he acknowledges my name.
15 He will call upon me, and I will answer him;
I will be with him in trouble,
I will deliver him and honor him.[i]
16 With long life will I satisfy him
and show him my salvation."

## Psalm 92

A psalm. A song. For the Sabbath day.

1 It is good to praise the LORD
and make music to your name,[j] O Most High,
2 to proclaim your love in the morning
and your faithfulness at night,
3 to the music of the ten-stringed lyre
and the melody of the harp.[k]

**91:10** e Pr 12:21
**91:11** f Heb 1:14 g Ps 34:7
**91:12** h Mt 4:6*; Lk 4:10–11*
**91:15** i 1Sa 2:30; Ps 50:15
**92:1** j Ps 147:1
**92:3** k Ps 33:2

[a]17 Or *beauty* [b]1 Hebrew *Shaddai* [c]2 Or *He says*

92:5 l Ps 40:5; Ro 11:33
92:6 m Ps 73:22
92:9 n Ps 68:1
92:10 o Ps 89:17; p Ps 23:5
92:11 q Ps 54:7
92:12 r Ps 52:8; Hos 14:6
92:13 s Ps 100:4
93:1 t Ps 97:1; u Ps 104:1; v Ps 65:6; w Ps 96:10
93:2 x Ps 45:6

4 For you make me glad by your deeds,
O LORD;
I sing for joy at the works of your
hands.
5 How great are your works, O LORD,
how profound your thoughts![l]
6 The senseless man[m] does not know,
fools do not understand,
7 that though the wicked spring up like
grass
and all evildoers flourish,
they will be forever destroyed.

8 But you, O LORD, are exalted forever.

9 For surely your enemies, O LORD,
surely your enemies will perish;
all evildoers will be scattered.[n]
10 You have exalted my horn[a][o] like that of a
wild ox;
fine oils[p] have been poured upon me.
11 My eyes have seen the defeat of my
adversaries;
my ears have heard the rout of my
wicked foes.[q]

12 The righteous will flourish like a palm
tree,
they will grow like a cedar of
Lebanon;[r]
13 planted in the house of the LORD,
they will flourish in the courts of our
God.[s]
14 They will still bear fruit in old age,
they will stay fresh and green,
15 proclaiming, "The LORD is upright;
he is my Rock, and there is no
wickedness in him."

## Psalm 93

1 The LORD reigns,[t] he is robed in majesty;[u]
the LORD is robed in majesty
and is armed with strength.[v]
The world is firmly established;
it cannot be moved.[w]
2 Your throne was established long ago;
you are from all eternity.[x]

3 The seas have lifted up, O LORD,
the seas have lifted up their voice;
the seas have lifted up their pounding
waves.
4 Mightier than the thunder[y] of the great
waters,
mightier than the breakers of the sea—
the LORD on high is mighty.

5 Your statutes stand firm;
holiness adorns your house
for endless days, O LORD.

## Psalm 94

1 O LORD, the God who avenges,
O God who avenges, shine forth.
2 Rise up, O Judge[z] of the earth;
pay back to the proud what they
deserve.
3 How long will the wicked, O LORD,
how long will the wicked be jubilant?

4 They pour out arrogant[a] words;
all the evildoers are full of boasting.
5 They crush your people, O LORD;
they oppress your inheritance.
6 They slay the widow and the alien;
they murder the fatherless.
7 They say, "The LORD does not see;[b]
the God of Jacob pays no heed."

8 Take heed, you senseless ones among the
people;
you fools, when will you become wise?
9 Does he who implanted the ear not hear?
Does he who formed the eye not see?[c]
10 Does he who disciplines nations not
punish?
Does he who teaches[d] man lack
knowledge?
11 The LORD knows the thoughts of man;
he knows that they are futile.[e]

12 Blessed is the man you discipline,[f]
O LORD,
the man you teach from your law;
13 you grant him relief from days of trouble,
till a pit is dug for the wicked.
14 For the LORD will not reject his people;[g]
he will never forsake his inheritance.
15 Judgment will again be founded on
righteousness,
and all the upright in heart will
follow it.

16 Who will rise up for me against the
wicked?

93:4 y Ps 65:7
94:2 z Ge 18:25
94:4 a Ps 31:18
94:7 b Ps 10:11
94:9 c Ex 4:11
94:10 d Job 35:11; Isa 28:26
94:11 e 1Co 3:20*
94:12 f Job 5:17; Heb 12:5
94:14 g 1Sa 12:22; Ro 11:2

[a]10 *Horn* here symbolizes strength.

94:17
h Ps 124:2
94:18
i Ps 38:16
94:21
j Pr 17:15,26
94:22
k Ps 59:9
94:23
l Ps 7:16
95:3
m Ps 96:4
95:7
n Ps 79:13
95:8
o Ex 17:7
95:9
p Ps 78:18; 1Co 10:9

Who will take a stand for me against
evildoers?
17 Unless the LORD had given me help,[h]
I would soon have dwelt in the silence
of death.
18 When I said, "My foot is slipping,[i]"
your love, O LORD, supported me.
19 When anxiety was great within me,
your consolation brought joy to my
soul.
20 Can a corrupt throne be allied with
you—
one that brings on misery by its
decrees?
21 They band together against the righteous
and condemn the innocent[j] to death.
22 But the LORD has become my fortress,
and my God the rock in whom I take
refuge.[k]
23 He will repay[l] them for their sins
and destroy them for their wickedness;
the LORD our God will destroy them.

## Psalm 95

1 Come, let us sing for joy to the LORD;
let us shout aloud to the Rock of our
salvation.
2 Let us come before him with
thanksgiving
and extol him with music and song.
3 For the LORD is the great God,
the great King above all gods.[m]
4 In his hand are the depths of the earth,
and the mountain peaks belong to
him.
5 The sea is his, for he made it,
and his hands formed the dry land.
6 Come, let us bow down in worship,
let us kneel before the LORD our Maker;
7 for he is our God
and we are the people of his pasture,[n]
the flock under his care.

Today, if you hear his voice,
8 do not harden your hearts as you did at
Meribah,[a][o]
as you did that day at Massah[b] in the
desert,
9 where your fathers tested[p] and tried me,
though they had seen what I did.
10 For forty years I was angry with that
generation;
I said, "They are a people whose hearts
go astray,
and they have not known my ways."
11 So I declared on oath in my anger,
"They shall never enter my rest."[q]

## Psalm 96

1 Sing to the LORD[r] a new song;
sing to the LORD, all the earth.
2 Sing to the LORD, praise his name;
proclaim his salvation day after day.
3 Declare his glory among the nations,
his marvelous deeds among all
peoples.
4 For great is the LORD and most worthy of
praise;[s]
he is to be feared above all gods.[t]
5 For all the gods of the nations are idols,
but the LORD made the heavens.
6 Splendor and majesty are before him;
strength and glory are in his
sanctuary.
7 Ascribe to the LORD,[u] O families of
nations,
ascribe to the LORD glory and strength.
8 Ascribe to the LORD the glory due his
name;
bring an offering and come into his
courts.
9 Worship the LORD in the splendor of his[c]
holiness;[v]
tremble before him, all the earth.
10 Say among the nations, "The LORD
reigns."
The world is firmly established, it
cannot be moved;
he will judge the peoples with equity.[w]
11 Let the heavens rejoice, let the earth be
glad;
let the sea resound, and all that is in it;
12 let the fields be jubilant, and
everything in them.
Then all the trees of the forest will sing
for joy;
13 they will sing before the LORD, for he
comes,

95:11
q Heb 4:3*
96:1
r 1Ch 16:23
96:4
s Ps 18:3; 145:3
t Ps 95:3
96:7
u Ps 29:1
96:9
v Ps 29:2
96:10
w Ps 67:4

[a] 8 *Meribah* means *quarreling.* [b] 8 *Massah* means *testing.* [c] 9 Or *LORD with the splendor of*

he comes to judge[x] the earth.
He will judge the world in righteousness
and the peoples in his truth.

## Psalm 97

1 The LORD reigns,[y] let the earth be glad;
let the distant shores rejoice.

2 Clouds and thick darkness[z] surround him;
righteousness and justice are the foundation of his throne.[a]
3 Fire goes before him
and consumes[b] his foes on every side.
4 His lightning lights up the world;
the earth sees and trembles.
5 The mountains melt[c] like wax before the LORD,
before the Lord of all the earth.
6 The heavens proclaim his righteousness,
and all the peoples see his glory.

7 All who worship images are put to shame,
those who boast in idols—
worship him,[d] all you gods!

8 Zion hears and rejoices
and the villages of Judah are glad
because of your judgments, O LORD.
9 For you, O LORD, are the Most High over all the earth;[e]
you are exalted[f] far above all gods.

10 Let those who love the LORD hate evil,[g]
for he guards the lives of his faithful ones
and delivers[h] them from the hand of the wicked.[i]
11 Light is shed[j] upon the righteous
and joy on the upright in heart.
12 Rejoice in the LORD, you who are righteous,
and praise his holy name.[k]

## Psalm 98

A psalm.

1 Sing to the LORD a new song,
for he has done marvelous things;
his right hand[l] and his holy arm[m]
have worked salvation for him.
2 The LORD has made his salvation known
and revealed his righteousness to the nations.
3 He has remembered[n] his love
and his faithfulness to the house of Israel;
all the ends of the earth have seen
the salvation of our God.

4 Shout for joy to the LORD, all the earth,
burst into jubilant song with music;
5 make music to the LORD with the harp,
with the harp and the sound of singing,
6 with trumpets[o] and the blast of the ram's horn—
shout for joy before the LORD, the King.

7 Let the sea resound, and everything in it,
the world, and all who live in it.
8 Let the rivers clap their hands,
let the mountains sing together for joy;
9 let them sing before the LORD,
for he comes to judge the earth.
He will judge the world in righteousness
and the peoples with equity.[p]

## Psalm 99

1 The LORD reigns,
let the nations tremble;
he sits enthroned between the cherubim,[q]
let the earth shake.
2 Great is the LORD in Zion;
he is exalted[r] over all the nations.
3 Let them praise your great and awesome name—
he is holy.

4 The King is mighty, he loves justice—
you have established equity;
in Jacob you have done
what is just and right.
5 Exalt the LORD our God
and worship at his footstool;
he is holy.

6 Moses and Aaron were among his priests,
Samuel[s] was among those who called on his name;
they called on the LORD
and he answered[t] them.
7 He spoke to them from the pillar of cloud;[u]
they kept his statutes and the decrees he gave them.

**96:13** x Rev 19:11
**97:1** y Ps 96:10
**97:2** z Ps 18:11 a Ps 89:14
**97:3** b Ps 18:8
**97:5** c Mic 1:4
**97:7** d Heb 1:6
**97:9** e Ps 83:18; 95:3 f Ex 18:11
**97:10** g Ps 34:14; Am 5:15 h Da 3:28 i Ps 37:40
**97:11** j Job 22:28
**97:12** k Ps 30:4
**98:1** l Ex 15:6 m Isa 52:10
**98:3** n Lk 1:54
**98:6** o Nu 10:10
**98:9** p Ps 96:10
**99:1** q Ex 25:22
**99:2** r Ps 97:9
**99:6** s Jer 15:1 t 1Sa 7:9
**99:7** u Ex 33:9

99:8 v Nu 14:20
100:3 w Ps 46:10
100:4 x Ps 116:17
100:5 y Ps 119:90
101:1 z Ps 89:1
101:4 a Pr 11:20
101:5 b Pr 6:17

8 O LORD our God,
you answered them;
you were to Israel[a] a forgiving God,[v]
though you punished their misdeeds.[b]
9 Exalt the LORD our God
and worship at his holy mountain,
for the LORD our God is holy.

## Psalm 100

A psalm. For giving thanks.

1 Shout for joy to the LORD, all the earth.
2 Worship the LORD with gladness;
come before him with joyful songs.
3 Know that the LORD is God.[w]
It is he who made us, and we are his[c];
we are his people, the sheep of his
pasture.
4 Enter his gates with thanksgiving
and his courts with praise;
give thanks to him and praise his
name.[x]
5 For the LORD is good and his love endures
forever;
his faithfulness[y] continues through all
generations.

## Psalm 101

Of David. A psalm.

1 I will sing of your love[z] and justice;
to you, O LORD, I will sing praise.
2 I will be careful to lead a blameless life—
when will you come to me?

I will walk in my house
with blameless heart.
3 I will set before my eyes
no vile thing.

The deeds of faithless men I hate;
they will not cling to me.
4 Men of perverse heart[a] shall be far from
me;
I will have nothing to do with evil.

5 Whoever slanders his neighbor in secret,
him will I put to silence;
whoever has haughty eyes[b] and a proud
heart,
him will I not endure.

6 My eyes will be on the faithful in the
land,
that they may dwell with me;
he whose walk is blameless[c]
will minister to me.

7 No one who practices deceit
will dwell in my house;
no one who speaks falsely
will stand in my presence.

8 Every morning[d] I will put to silence
all the wicked[e] in the land;
I will cut off every evildoer[f]
from the city of the LORD.

## Psalm 102

A prayer of an afflicted man. When
he is faint and pours out his
lament before the LORD.

1 Hear my prayer, O LORD;
let my cry for help come to you.
2 Do not hide your face[g] from me
when I am in distress.
Turn your ear to me;
when I call, answer me quickly.
3 For my days vanish like smoke;[h]
my bones burn like glowing embers.
4 My heart is blighted and withered like
grass;[i]
I forget to eat my food.
5 Because of my loud groaning
I am reduced to skin and bones.
6 I am like a desert owl,[j]
like an owl among the ruins.
7 I lie awake;[k] I have become
like a bird alone on a roof.
8 All day long my enemies taunt me;
those who rail against me use my
name as a curse.
9 For I eat ashes as my food
and mingle my drink with tears[l]
10 because of your great wrath,
for you have taken me up and thrown
me aside.
11 My days are like the evening shadow;
I wither away like grass.

12 But you, O LORD, sit enthroned forever;
your renown endures[m] through all
generations.

101:6 c Ps 119:1
101:8 d Jer 21:12 e Ps 75:10 f Ps 118:10–12
102:2 g Ps 69:17
102:3 h Jas 4:14
102:4 i Ps 37:2
102:6 j Isa 34:11
102:7 k Ps 77:4
102:9 l Ps 42:3
102:12 m Ps 135:13

[a]8 Hebrew *them* [b]8 Or */ an avenger of the wrongs done to them* [c]3 Or *and not we ourselves*

Inspire

## BUMPING INTO OMNIPOTENCE

Have you ever been minding your own business, doing your own thing, when suddenly you ran smack dab into the omnipotence of God? I know this may seem like a strange question, but I've experienced that very thing. As a matter of fact, I've experienced it more than once. Every time I think I have my life figured out, every time I think I can read God's mind or I get the notion that I am the omnipotent one who has the ability to fight my own battles—BAM! I run into the omnipotence of God.

The omnipotence of God? Many of us think women of color are the omnipotent ones—all-powerful; almighty; ruling everything and everybody; able to leap tall buildings of sexism, racism and classism; able to single-handedly raise small children from childhood to healthy adulthood; able to handle all stressful situations with grace and poise, never letting the world see us sweat.

My sisters, let's face it—we are not omnipotent. To be omnipotent means to reign supreme with all (unlimited) authority. That is an attribute that belongs to God and God alone. Our attempts to be omnipotent only lead to emotional and physical breakdowns. We must learn to let God be God. "Know that the LORD is God. It is he who made us, and we are his; we are his people, the sheep of his pasture" (Ps 100:3). We must learn that the creator and sustainer of the universe cares about us and hears our faintest cry. God never loses control, nor does he sleep.

If you feel burdened, overwhelmed or abandoned, and you can't take another unexpected turn in the road, remember God's words found in Jeremiah 29:11: "For I know the plans I have for you . . . plans to prosper you and not to harm you, plans to give you hope and a future."

I have grown weary of bumping into the omnipotence of God and finding that God really does know best, that his ways are not my ways and his thoughts are not my thoughts (see Isa 55:8–9). I now live a life surrendered to God's will. There is nothing that I will encounter that God is not Lord over.

—K. HAYES

For the next Inspire note, go to page 702.

**read**

Psalm 100; see also Psalms 86:8–10; 93:1–5; Jeremiah 32:17–27.

**See also** the Inspire Notes "God Is in Control," "God Is Immutable," "God Is Sovereign" and "Omniscience: God Is All-Knowing," and the Women of the Bible Notes "Samson's Bride: Nothing by Chance," "Jehosheba: Standing Firm" and "Fortune-Telling Slave Girl: A Surprising Testimony to God's Work."

**WOMAN of COLOR**

How does remembering that God is omnipotent help you cope with life?

102:13 n Isa 60:10
102:16 o Isa 60:1–2
102:18 p Ro 15:4 q Ps 22:31
102:21 r Ps 22:22
102:24 s Ps 90:2
102:25 t Heb 1:10–12*
102:26 u Isa 34:4
102:27 v Mal 3:6
102:28 w Ps 69:36

13 You will arise and have compassion[n] on
Zion,
for it is time to show favor to her;
the appointed time has come.
14 For her stones are dear to your servants;
her very dust moves them to pity.
15 The nations will fear the name of the
LORD,
all the kings of the earth will revere
your glory.
16 For the LORD will rebuild Zion
and appear in his glory.[o]
17 He will respond to the prayer of the
destitute;
he will not despise their plea.

18 Let this be written[p] for a future
generation,
that a people not yet created[q] may
praise the LORD:
19 "The LORD looked down from his
sanctuary on high,
from heaven he viewed the earth,
20 to hear the groans of the prisoners
and release those condemned to
death."
21 So the name of the LORD will be declared[r]
in Zion
and his praise in Jerusalem
22 when the peoples and the kingdoms
assemble to worship the LORD.

23 In the course of my life[a] he broke my
strength;
he cut short my days.
24 So I said:
"Do not take me away, O my God, in
the midst of my days;
your years go on[s] through all
generations.
25 In the beginning[t] you laid the
foundations of the earth,
and the heavens are the work of your
hands.
26 They will perish,[u] but you remain;
they will all wear out like a garment.
Like clothing you will change them
and they will be discarded.
27 But you remain the same,[v]
and your years will never end.
28 The children of your servants[w] will live in
your presence;
their descendants will be established
before you."

## Psalm 103

Of David.

1 Praise the LORD, O my soul;[x]
all my inmost being, praise his holy
name.
2 Praise the LORD, O my soul,
and forget not all his benefits—
3 who forgives all your sins
and heals all your diseases,
4 who redeems your life from the pit
and crowns you with love and
compassion,
5 who satisfies your desires with good
things
so that your youth is renewed like the
eagle's.

6 The LORD works righteousness
and justice for all the oppressed.

7 He made known his ways to Moses,
his deeds to the people of Israel:
8 The LORD is compassionate and
gracious,[y]
slow to anger, abounding in love.
9 He will not always accuse,
nor will he harbor his anger forever;[z]
10 he does not treat us as our sins deserve[a]
or repay us according to our
iniquities.
11 For as high as the heavens are above the
earth,
so great is his love for those who fear
him;
12 as far as the east is from the west,
so far has he removed our
transgressions from us.
13 As a father has compassion[b] on his
children,
so the LORD has compassion on those
who fear him;
14 for he knows how we are formed,
he remembers that we are dust.
15 As for man, his days are like grass,
he flourishes like a flower[c] of the field;
16 the wind blows over it and it is gone,
and its place[d] remembers it no more.
17 But from everlasting to everlasting

103:1 x Ps 104:1
103:8 y Ex 34:6
103:9 z Ps 30:5
103:10 a Ezr 9:13
103:13 b Mal 3:17
103:15 c Job 14:2; 1Pe 1:24
103:16 d Job 7:10

[a]23 Or *By his power*

103:18 e Dt7:9

the LORD's love is with those who fear
him,
and his righteousness with their
children's children—
18 with those who keep his covenant
and remember to obey his precepts.[e]

19 The LORD has established his throne in
heaven,
and his kingdom rules[f] over all.
20 Praise the LORD, you his angels,[g]
you mighty ones who do his bidding,
who obey his word.

103:19 f Ps47:2

103:20 g Ps148:2

Inspire

## GOD IS IMMUTABLE

Putting a jigsaw puzzle together reminds us of how God works in our lives. We know that if we find the pieces with the smooth edges, they will form our guide, and we can build the framework of the puzzle. Once we've established the working parameters, we can proceed with certainty that all of the other jumbled parts of the puzzle will fit into place one piece at a time.

Through Jesus Christ, we have our framework for life. No matter how many pieces may seem to be mixed up, as long as we are guided by the smooth edges of God's Spirit, God's Word and Christ's example, our hope is secure. God on the left, God on the right, God above, God beneath, God all around. Our life in God through Christ gives us structure—not confinement, but definition!

The Bible shows us that God has established the foundation and framework for all creation from beginning to end. "In the beginning you laid the foundations of the earth, and the heavens are the work of your hands. They will perish, but you remain . . . You remain the same, and your years will never end" (Ps 102:25–27).

As children of the Most High, we are a part of God's creation and God's plan. The puzzles in life serve to remind us that God has set the framework, and God does not change. God is sure. While we cannot trust our jumbled circumstances, we can trust the promises of the God who is immutable—constant and unchangeable. Build your life within the framework of God's plans, and you will find peace in the midst of life's jigsaw puzzle.

—A. MIDDLETON

### read

Psalm 102; James 1:17.

**See also** the Inspire Notes "God Is in Control," "Bumping Into Omnipotence," "God Is Sovereign" and "Omniscience: God Is All-Knowing," and the Women of the Bible Notes "Tamar: The Link Between Judah and Jesus," "Samson's Bride: Nothing by Chance" and "Fortune-Telling Slave Girl: A Surprising Testimony to God's Work."

### WOMAN of COLOR

How are you living within God's framework for your life?

For the next Inspire note, go to page 709.

**104:2** h Da 7:9 i Isa 40:22
**104:3** j Am 9:6 k Isa 19:1 l Ps 18:10
**104:4** m Heb 1:7*
**104:13** n Ps 147:8
**104:14** o Ge 1:30; Job 28:5

21 Praise the LORD, all his heavenly hosts,
you his servants who do his will.
22 Praise the LORD, all his works
everywhere in his dominion.

Praise the Lord, O my soul.

## Psalm 104

1 Praise the LORD, O my soul.

O Lord my God, you are very great;
you are clothed with splendor and majesty.
2 He wraps[h] himself in light as with a garment;
he stretches out the heavens[i] like a tent
3 and lays the beams[j] of his upper chambers on their waters.
He makes the clouds[k] his chariot
and rides on the wings of the wind.[l]
4 He makes winds his messengers,[a][m]
flames of fire his servants.

5 He set the earth on its foundations;
it can never be moved.
6 You covered it with the deep as with a garment;
the waters stood above the mountains.
7 But at your rebuke the waters fled,
at the sound of your thunder they took to flight;
8 they flowed over the mountains,
they went down into the valleys,
to the place you assigned for them.
9 You set a boundary they cannot cross;
never again will they cover the earth.

10 He makes springs pour water into the ravines;
it flows between the mountains.
11 They give water to all the beasts of the field;
the wild donkeys quench their thirst.
12 The birds of the air nest by the waters;
they sing among the branches.
13 He waters the mountains[n] from his upper chambers;
the earth is satisfied by the fruit of his work.
14 He makes grass grow for the cattle,
and plants for man to cultivate—
bringing forth food[o] from the earth:
15 wine[p] that gladdens the heart of man,
oil to make his face shine,
and bread that sustains his heart.
16 The trees of the LORD are well watered,
the cedars of Lebanon that he planted.
17 There the birds make their nests;
the stork has its home in the pine trees.
18 The high mountains belong to the wild goats;
the crags are a refuge for the coneys.[b]

19 The moon marks off the seasons,[q]
and the sun knows when to go down.
20 You bring darkness,[r] it becomes night,
and all the beasts of the forest prowl.
21 The lions roar for their prey
and seek their food from God.[s]
22 The sun rises, and they steal away;
they return and lie down in their dens.
23 Then man goes out to his work,[t]
to his labor until evening.

24 How many are your works, O LORD!
In wisdom you made[u] them all;
the earth is full of your creatures.
25 There is the sea, vast and spacious,
teeming with creatures beyond number—
living things both large and small.
26 There the ships go to and fro,
and the leviathan,[v] which you formed to frolic there.

27 These all look to you
to give them their food[w] at the proper time.
28 When you give it to them,
they gather it up;
when you open your hand,
they are satisfied with good things.
29 When you hide your face,
they are terrified;
when you take away their breath,
they die and return to the dust.[x]
30 When you send your Spirit,
they are created,
and you renew the face of the earth.

31 May the glory of the LORD endure forever;
may the LORD rejoice in his works[y]—
32 he who looks at the earth, and it trembles,

**104:15** p Jdg 9:13
**104:19** q Ge 1:14
**104:20** r Isa 45:7
**104:21** s Job 38:39
**104:23** t Ge 3:19
**104:24** u Pr 3:19
**104:26** v Job 41:1
**104:27** w Ps 136:25
**104:29** x Job 34:14; Ecc 12:7
**104:31** y Ge 1:31

[a]4 Or *angels* [b]18 That is, the hyrax or rock badger

**104:32** z Ps 144:5
**104:33** a Ps 63:4
**105:4** b Ps 27:8
**105:5** c Ps 77:11
**105:8** d Lk 1:72
**105:9** e Ge 17:2; 22:16–18
**105:11** f Ge 13:15; 15:18
**105:12** g Ge 34:30; Dt 7:7 h Heb 11:9
**105:14** i Ge 35:5 j Ge 12:17–20

who touches the mountains, and they
smoke.[z]

33 I will sing[a] to the LORD all my life;
I will sing praise to my God as long as
I live.
34 May my meditation be pleasing to him,
as I rejoice in the LORD.
35 But may sinners vanish from the earth
and the wicked be no more.

Praise the Lord, O my soul.

Praise the Lord.[a]

## Psalm 105

1 Give thanks to the LORD, call on his name;
make known among the nations what
he has done.
2 Sing to him, sing praise to him;
tell of all his wonderful acts.
3 Glory in his holy name;
let the hearts of those who seek the
LORD rejoice.
4 Look to the LORD and his strength;
seek his face[b] always.
5 Remember the wonders he has done,
his miracles, and the judgments he
pronounced,[c]
6 O descendants of Abraham his servant,
O sons of Jacob, his chosen ones.
7 He is the LORD our God;
his judgments are in all the earth.

8 He remembers his covenant[d] forever,
the word he commanded, for a
thousand generations,
9 the covenant he made with Abraham,[e]
the oath he swore to Isaac.
10 He confirmed it to Jacob as a decree,
to Israel as an everlasting covenant:
11 "To you I will give the land of Canaan[f]
as the portion you will inherit."

12 When they were but few in number,[g]
few indeed, and strangers in it,[h]
13 they wandered from nation to nation,
from one kingdom to another.
14 He allowed no one to oppress[i] them;
for their sake he rebuked kings:[j]
15 "Do not touch my anointed ones;
do my prophets no harm."

16 He called down famine[k] on the land
and destroyed all their supplies of
food;
17 and he sent a man before them—
Joseph, sold as a slave.[l]
18 They bruised his feet with shackles,
his neck was put in irons,
19 till what he foretold came to pass,
till the word of the LORD proved him
true.
20 The king sent and released him,
the ruler of peoples set him free.[m]
21 He made him master of his household,
ruler over all he possessed,
22 to instruct his princes as he pleased
and teach his elders wisdom.

23 Then Israel entered Egypt;[n]
Jacob lived as an alien in the land of
Ham.
24 The LORD made his people very fruitful;
he made them too numerous[o] for their
foes,
25 whose hearts he turned to hate his
people,
to conspire against his servants.
26 He sent Moses[p] his servant,
and Aaron, whom he had chosen.
27 They performed his miraculous signs
among them,
his wonders in the land of Ham.
28 He sent darkness[q] and made the land
dark—
for had they not rebelled against his
words?
29 He turned their waters into blood,
causing their fish to die.[r]
30 Their land teemed with frogs,[s]
which went up into the bedrooms of
their rulers.
31 He spoke, and there came swarms of flies,
and gnats[t] throughout their country.
32 He turned their rain into hail,[u]
with lightning throughout their land;
33 he struck down their vines and fig trees
and shattered the trees of their
country.
34 He spoke, and the locusts came,
grasshoppers without number;
35 they ate up every green thing in their
land,

**105:16** k Lev 26:26; Isa 3:1
**105:17** l Ge 37:28
**105:20** m Ge 41:14
**105:23** n Ge 46:6
**105:24** o Ex 1:7,9
**105:26** p Ex 3:10
**105:28** q Ex 10:22
**105:29** r Ex 7:21
**105:30** s Ex 8:2,6
**105:31** t Ex 8:16–18
**105:32** u Ex 9:22–25

[a]35 Hebrew *Hallelu Yah*; in the Septuagint this line stands at the beginning of Psalm 105.

105:39
v Ex 13:21
105:40
w Ex 16:13
105:41
x 1Co 10:4
105:44
y Jos 13:6–7

ate up the produce of their soil.
36 Then he struck down all the firstborn in
their land,
the firstfruits of all their manhood.
37 He brought out Israel, laden with silver
and gold,
and from among their tribes no one
faltered.
38 Egypt was glad when they left,
because dread of Israel had fallen on
them.
39 He spread out a cloud[v] as a covering,
and a fire to give light at night.
40 They asked, and he brought them quail[w]
and satisfied them with the bread of
heaven.
41 He opened the rock,[x] and water gushed
out;
like a river it flowed in the desert.

42 For he remembered his holy promise
given to his servant Abraham.
43 He brought out his people with rejoicing,
his chosen ones with shouts of joy;
44 he gave them the lands of the nations,[y]
and they fell heir to what others had
toiled for—
45 that they might keep his precepts
and observe his laws.

Praise the Lord.[a]

## Psalm 106

1 Praise the LORD.[b]

Give thanks to the Lord, for he is good;
his love endures forever.
2 Who can proclaim the mighty acts of the
LORD
or fully declare his praise?
3 Blessed are they who maintain justice,
who constantly do what is right.[z]
4 Remember me,[a] O LORD, when you show
favor to your people,
come to my aid when you save them,
5 that I may enjoy the prosperity of your
chosen ones,
that I may share in the joy of your
nation
and join your inheritance in giving
praise.

6 We have sinned,[b] even as our fathers did;
we have done wrong and acted
wickedly.
7 When our fathers were in Egypt,
they gave no thought to your miracles;
they did not remember your many
kindnesses,
and they rebelled by the sea,[c] the Red
Sea.[c]
8 Yet he saved them for his name's sake,[d]
to make his mighty power known.
9 He rebuked[e] the Red Sea, and it dried up;[f]
he led them through[g] the depths as
through a desert.
10 He saved them[h] from the hand of the foe;
from the hand of the enemy he
redeemed them.
11 The waters covered their adversaries;
not one of them survived.
12 Then they believed his promises
and sang his praise.

13 But they soon forgot what he had done
and did not wait for his counsel.
14 In the desert they gave in to their craving;
in the wasteland they put God to the
test.[i]

106:3
z Ps 15:2
106:4
a Ps 119:132
106:6
b Da 9:5
106:7
c Ex 14:11–12
106:8
d Ex 9:16
106:9
e Ps 18:15
f Ex 14:21
g Isa 63:11–14
106:10
h Ex 14:30
106:14
i 1Co 10:9

[a]45 Hebrew *Hallelu Yah* [b]1 Hebrew *Hallelu Yah*; also in verse 48 [c]7 Hebrew *Yam Suph*; that is, Sea of Reeds; also in verses 9 and 22

### The African Presence

**Psalm 105:23–38**

These verses reference Israel's stay in Egypt. (See Ps 78:51; 106:22 for other associations of "Ham" and "Egypt"; see also the African Presence notes on Ge 10:6–12 and Ge 10:6.)

106:15 j Nu 11:31 k Isa 10:16
106:16 l Nu 16:1–3
106:17 m Dt 11:6
106:19 n Ex 32:4
106:20 o Jer 2:11; Ro 1:23
106:21 p Ps 78:11
106:23 q Ex 32:10
106:24 r Dt 8:7 s Heb 3:18–19

15 So he gave them[j] what they asked for,
but sent a wasting disease[k] upon them.

16 In the camp they grew envious[l] of Moses
and of Aaron, who was consecrated to the LORD.
17 The earth opened[m] up and swallowed Dathan;
it buried the company of Abiram.
18 Fire blazed among their followers;
a flame consumed the wicked.

19 At Horeb they made a calf[n]
and worshiped an idol cast from metal.
20 They exchanged their Glory[o]
for an image of a bull, which eats grass.
21 They forgot the God[p] who saved them,
who had done great things in Egypt,
22 miracles in the land of Ham
and awesome deeds by the Red Sea.
23 So he said he would destroy[q] them—
had not Moses, his chosen one,
stood in the breach before him
to keep his wrath from destroying them.

24 Then they despised the pleasant land;[r]
they did not believe[s] his promise.
25 They grumbled in their tents
and did not obey the LORD.
26 So he swore to them with uplifted hand
that he would make them fall in the desert,
27 make their descendants fall among the nations
and scatter them throughout the lands.

28 They yoked themselves to the Baal of Peor
and ate sacrifices offered to lifeless gods;
29 they provoked the LORD to anger by their wicked deeds,
and a plague broke out among them.
30 But Phinehas stood up and intervened,
and the plague was checked.[t]
31 This was credited to him as righteousness
for endless generations to come.

32 By the waters of Meribah[u] they angered the LORD,
and trouble came to Moses because of them;
33 for they rebelled against the Spirit of God,
and rash words came from Moses' lips.[a][v]

34 They did not destroy[w] the peoples
as the LORD had commanded them,
35 but they mingled[x] with the nations
and adopted their customs.
36 They worshiped their idols,[y]
which became a snare to them.
37 They sacrificed their sons
and their daughters to demons.
38 They shed innocent blood,
the blood of their sons[z] and daughters,
whom they sacrificed to the idols of Canaan,
and the land was desecrated by their blood.
39 They defiled themselves[a] by what they did;

106:30 t Nu 25:8
106:32 u Nu 20:2–13
106:33 v Nu 20:8–12
106:34 w Jdg 1:21
106:35 x Jdg 3:5–6
106:36 y Jdg 2:12
106:38 z Nu 35:33
106:39 a Eze 20:18

[a]33 Or *against his spirit, / and rash words came from his lips*

## *The African Presence*

**Psalm 106:22**

The "land of Ham" is a poetic description of Egypt. One of Ham's sons was Mizraim. The word *mizraim* means "two Egypts," referring to Upper and Lower Egypt. (See Ps 78:51; 105:23,27 for other associations of "Ham" and "Egypt"; see also the African Presence notes on Ge 10:6–12 and Ge 10:6.)

106:39 b Lev 17:7; Nu 15:39
106:41 c Jdg 2:14; Ne 9:27
106:44 d Jdg 10:10
106:45 e Jdg 2:18
106:46 f Ezr 9:9; Jer 42:12
106:48 g Ps 41:13
107:2 h Ps 106:10
107:3 i Ps 106:47

by their deeds they prostituted[b]
themselves.
40 Therefore the LORD was angry with his
people
and abhorred his inheritance.
41 He handed them over[c] to the nations,
and their foes ruled over them.
42 Their enemies oppressed them
and subjected them to their power.
43 Many times he delivered them,
but they were bent on rebellion
and they wasted away in their sin.

44 But he took note of their distress
when he heard their cry;[d]
45 for their sake he remembered his
covenant
and out of his great love[e] he relented.
46 He caused them to be pitied[f]
by all who held them captive.

47 Save us, O LORD our God,
and gather us from the nations,
that we may give thanks to your holy
name
and glory in your praise.

48 Praise be to the LORD, the God of Israel,
from everlasting to everlasting.
Let all the people say, "Amen!"[g]
Praise the LORD.

# BOOK V

*Psalms 107–150*

## Psalm 107

1 Give thanks to the LORD, for he is good;
his love endures forever.
2 Let the redeemed[h] of the LORD say this—
those he redeemed from the hand of
the foe,
3 those he gathered[i] from the lands,
from east and west, from north and
south.[a]

4 Some wandered in desert wastelands,
finding no way to a city where they
could settle.
5 They were hungry and thirsty,
and their lives ebbed away.

6 Then they cried out[j] to the LORD in their
trouble,
and he delivered them from their
distress.
7 He led them by a straight way[k]
to a city where they could settle.
8 Let them give thanks to the LORD for his
unfailing love
and his wonderful deeds for men,
9 for he satisfies[l] the thirsty
and fills the hungry with good things.

10 Some sat in darkness[m] and the deepest
gloom,
prisoners suffering in iron chains,[n]
11 for they had rebelled against the words of
God
and despised the counsel of the Most
High.
12 So he subjected them to bitter labor;
they stumbled, and there was no one
to help.[o]
13 Then they cried to the LORD in their
trouble,
and he saved them from their distress.
14 He brought them out of darkness and the
deepest gloom
and broke away their chains.[p]
15 Let them give thanks to the LORD for his
unfailing love
and his wonderful deeds for men,
16 for he breaks down gates of bronze
and cuts through bars of iron.

17 Some became fools through their
rebellious ways
and suffered affliction because of their
iniquities.
18 They loathed all food
and drew near the gates of death.[q]
19 Then they cried to the LORD in their
trouble,
and he saved them from their distress.
20 He sent forth his word[r] and healed them;[s]
he rescued them from the grave.[t]
21 Let them give thanks to the LORD for his
unfailing love
and his wonderful deeds for men.
22 Let them sacrifice thank offerings[u]
and tell of his works[v] with songs of
joy.

107:6 j Ps 50:15
107:7 k Ezr 8:21
107:9 l Lk 1:53
107:10 m Lk 1:79 n Job 36:8
107:12 o Ps 22:11
107:14 p Ac 12:7
107:18 q Job 33:22; Ps 9:13
107:20 r Mt 8:8 s Ps 103:3 t Ps 30:3
107:22 u Lev 7:12 v Ps 9:11; 73:28; 118:17

[a]3 Hebrew *north and the sea*

**107:25** w Jnh 1:4
**107:26** x Ps 22:14
**107:29** y Mt 8:26; z Ps 89:9
**107:32** a Ps 22:22,25
**107:34** b Ge 13:10
**107:38** c Ge 12:2

23 Others went out on the sea in ships;
they were merchants on the mighty waters.
24 They saw the works of the LORD,
his wonderful deeds in the deep.
25 For he spoke and stirred up a tempest[w]
that lifted high the waves.
26 They mounted up to the heavens and went down to the depths;
in their peril their courage melted[x] away.
27 They reeled and staggered like drunken men;
they were at their wits' end.
28 Then they cried out to the LORD in their trouble,
and he brought them out of their distress.
29 He stilled the storm[y] to a whisper;
the waves[z] of the sea were hushed.
30 They were glad when it grew calm,
and he guided them to their desired haven.
31 Let them give thanks to the LORD for his unfailing love
and his wonderful deeds for men.
32 Let them exalt him in the assembly[a] of the people
and praise him in the council of the elders.

33 He turned rivers into a desert,
flowing springs into thirsty ground,
34 and fruitful land into a salt waste,[b]
because of the wickedness of those who lived there.
35 He turned the desert into pools of water
and the parched ground into flowing springs;
36 there he brought the hungry to live,
and they founded a city where they could settle.
37 They sowed fields and planted vineyards
that yielded a fruitful harvest;
38 he blessed them, and their numbers greatly increased,[c]
and he did not let their herds diminish.

39 Then their numbers decreased, and they were humbled
by oppression, calamity and sorrow;
40 he who pours contempt on nobles
made them wander in a trackless waste.
41 But he lifted the needy[d] out of their affliction
and increased their families like flocks.
42 The upright see and rejoice,
but all the wicked shut their mouths.[e]

43 Whoever is wise,[f] let him heed these things
and consider the great love of the LORD.

## Psalm 108

A song. A psalm of David.

1 My heart is steadfast, O God;
I will sing and make music with all my soul.
2 Awake, harp and lyre!
I will awaken the dawn.
3 I will praise you, O LORD, among the nations;
I will sing of you among the peoples.
4 For great is your love, higher than the heavens;
your faithfulness reaches to the skies.
5 Be exalted, O God, above the heavens,
and let your glory be over all the earth.

6 Save us and help us with your right hand,
that those you love may be delivered.
7 God has spoken from his sanctuary:
"In triumph I will parcel out Shechem
and measure off the Valley of Succoth.
8 Gilead is mine, Manasseh is mine;
Ephraim is my helmet,
Judah my scepter.
9 Moab is my washbasin,
upon Edom I toss my sandal;
over Philistia I shout in triumph."

10 Who will bring me to the fortified city?
Who will lead me to Edom?
11 Is it not you, O God, you who have rejected us
and no longer go out with our armies?
12 Give us aid against the enemy,
for the help of man is worthless.
13 With God we will gain the victory,
and he will trample down our enemies.

**107:41** d 1Sa 2:8; Ps 113:7–9
**107:42** e Job 5:16; Ro 3:19
**107:43** f Jer 9:12; Hos 14:9

# Psalm 109

For the director of music.
Of David. A psalm.

1 O God, whom I praise,
do not remain silent,[g]
2 for wicked and deceitful men
have opened their mouths against me;
they have spoken against me with
lying tongues.
3 With words of hatred[h] they surround me;
they attack me without cause.
4 In return for my friendship they
accuse me,

109:1 g Ps83:1
109:3 h Ps69:4

Inspire

## DISTRESS

Psalm 107 covers all the forms of distress that most of us will see in our entire lifetime. This passage of Scripture deals with the distress of those who are lost and wandering; those who are imprisoned by someone or something; those who are sick in the mind or body; those who are being tossed about by some storm of life. But for each trauma, the response is sure: "Then they cried out to the LORD in their trouble, and he saved them from [or "delivered them from" or "brought them out of"] their distress" (vv. 6,13,19,28).

Because we are human, distresses will enter into our lives. But if we allow the Lord into our lives, we will have immediate access to the One who not only cares that we are troubled, but is also powerful enough to bring us out of our troubles. Sometimes we make the mistake of believing that when God brings us out of a situation, it will be resolved to our own satisfaction. We assume that God will agree with the way that we think the dilemma should be settled. Often God does not change the circumstances in order to relieve our problems. Instead he makes a change in us—in the way we view or react to what is going on around us and inside of us.

The peace of God is the answer to many of the things that cause sadness or needless worry. Once you allow God to control your life, you learn to let your problems be handled by the One most capable of solving them. No matter how extreme your situation seems, there is a God who is able to deliver you. Cry out to the Lord in your trouble!

—A. ADAMS-MORRIS

For the next Inspire note, go to page 713.

**read**

Psalm 107; see also Nehemiah 9:1–37.

**See also** the Inspire Notes "Suffering" and "The Paradox of Life and Suffering," and the Women of the Bible Notes "Hannah: What Do You Do When God Says 'No'?" "The Prophet's Widow: God Provides," "The Widow's Offering: Selfless Giving" and "The Persistent Widow: Always Pray."

**WOMAN of COLOR**

Whom are you allowing to handle your problems? Remember that God is more capable of solving them than you are.

but I am a man of prayer.
[5] They repay me evil for good,[i]
and hatred for my friendship.

[6] Appoint[a] an evil man[b] to oppose him;
let an accuser[c][j] stand at his right hand.
[7] When he is tried, let him be found guilty,
and may his prayers condemn[k] him.
[8] May his days be few;
may another take his place[l] of
leadership.
[9] May his children be fatherless
and his wife a widow.[m]
[10] May his children be wandering beggars;
may they be driven[d] from their ruined
homes.
[11] May a creditor seize all he has;
may strangers plunder the fruits of his
labor.[n]
[12] May no one extend kindness to him
or take pity on his fatherless children.
[13] May his descendants be cut off,[o]
their names blotted out[p] from the next
generation.
[14] May the iniquity of his fathers[q] be
remembered before the LORD;
may the sin of his mother never be
blotted out.
[15] May their sins always remain before the
LORD,
that he may cut off the memory[r] of
them from the earth.

[16] For he never thought of doing a kindness,
but hounded to death the poor
and the needy and the brokenhearted.
[17] He loved to pronounce a curse—
may it[e] come on him;[s]
he found no pleasure in blessing—
may it be[f] far from him.
[18] He wore cursing as his garment;
it entered into his body like water,[t]
into his bones like oil.
[19] May it be like a cloak wrapped about him,
like a belt tied forever around him.
[20] May this be the LORD's payment to my
accusers,
to those who speak evil of me.

[21] But you, O Sovereign LORD,
deal well with me for your name's sake;
out of the goodness of your love,
deliver me.
[22] For I am poor and needy,
and my heart is wounded within me.
[23] I fade away like an evening shadow;
I am shaken off like a locust.
[24] My knees give[u] way from fasting;
my body is thin and gaunt.
[25] I am an object of scorn[v] to my accusers;
when they see me, they shake their
heads.[w]

[26] Help me, O LORD my God;
save me in accordance with your love.
[27] Let them know[x] that it is your hand,
that you, O LORD, have done it.
[28] They may curse,[y] but you will bless;
when they attack they will be put to
shame,
but your servant will rejoice.[z]
[29] My accusers will be clothed with disgrace
and wrapped in shame[a] as in a cloak.

[30] With my mouth I will greatly extol the
LORD;
in the great throng I will praise him.
[31] For he stands at the right hand[b] of the
needy one,
to save his life from those who
condemn him.

## Psalm 110

Of David. A psalm.

[1] The LORD says[c] to my Lord:
"Sit at my right hand
until I make your enemies
a footstool for your feet."[d]

[2] The LORD will extend your mighty scepter
from Zion;
you will rule in the midst of your
enemies.
[3] Your troops will be willing
on your day of battle.
Arrayed in holy majesty,[e]
from the womb of the dawn
you will receive the dew of your youth.[g]

[4] The LORD has sworn
and will not change his mind:

**109:5** i Ps 35:12; 38:20
**109:6** j Zec 3:1
**109:7** k Pr 28:9
**109:8** l Ac 1:20*
**109:9** m Ex 22:24
**109:11** n Job 5:5
**109:13** o Ps 37:28 p Pr 10:7
**109:14** q Ex 20:5; Ne 4:5; Jer 18:23
**109:15** r Ps 34:16
**109:17** s Pr 14:14
**109:18** t Nu 5:22
**109:24** u Heb 12:12
**109:25** v Ps 22:6 w Mt 27:39
**109:27** x Job 37:7
**109:28** y 2Sa 16:12 z Isa 65:14
**109:29** a Ps 35:26
**109:31** b Ps 16:8
**110:1** c Mt 22:44*; Mk 12:36*; Lk 20:42*; Ac 2:34* d 1Co 15:25
**110:3** e Jdg 5:2; Ps 96:9

[a]6 Or ⌊*They say:*⌋ *"Appoint* (with quotation marks at the end of verse 19) [b]6 Or *the Evil One* [c]6 Or *let Satan*
[d]10 Septuagint; Hebrew *sought* [e]17 Or *curse, / and it has* [f]17 Or *blessing, / and it is* [g]3 Or */ your young men will come to you like the dew*

"You are a priest forever,
in the order of Melchizedek."
5 The Lord is at your right hand;[f]
he will crush kings[g] on the day of his wrath.[h]
6 He will judge the nations, heaping up the dead
and crushing the rulers of the whole earth.
7 He will drink from a brook beside the way[a];
therefore he will lift up his head.

## Psalm 111[b]

1 Praise the LORD.[c]

I will extol the Lord with all my heart
in the council of the upright and in the assembly.
2 Great are the works[i] of the LORD;
they are pondered by all who delight in them.
3 Glorious and majestic are his deeds,
and his righteousness endures forever.
4 He has caused his wonders to be remembered;
the LORD is gracious and compassionate.
5 He provides food for those who fear him;
he remembers his covenant forever.
6 He has shown his people the power of his works,
giving them the lands of other nations.
7 The works of his hands are faithful and just;
all his precepts are trustworthy.[j]
8 They are steadfast for ever and ever,
done in faithfulness and uprightness.
9 He provided redemption[k] for his people;
he ordained his covenant forever—
holy and awesome is his name.
10 The fear of the LORD is the beginning of wisdom;
all who follow his precepts have good understanding.
To him belongs eternal praise.

## Psalm 112[b]

1 Praise the LORD.[c]

Blessed is the man who fears the Lord,
who finds great delight[l] in his commands.

2 His children will be mighty in the land;
the generation of the upright will be blessed.
3 Wealth and riches are in his house,
and his righteousness endures forever.
4 Even in darkness light dawns for the upright,
for the gracious and compassionate and righteous man.[d]
5 Good will come to him who is generous and lends freely,[m]
who conducts his affairs with justice.
6 Surely he will never be shaken;
a righteous man will be remembered[n] forever.
7 He will have no fear of bad news;
his heart is steadfast,[o] trusting in the LORD.
8 His heart is secure, he will have no fear;
in the end he will look in triumph on his foes.
9 He has scattered abroad his gifts to the poor,[p]
his righteousness endures forever;
his horn[e] will be lifted[q] high in honor.

10 The wicked man will see and be vexed,
he will gnash his teeth[r] and waste away;
the longings of the wicked will come to nothing.

## Psalm 113

1 Praise the LORD.[f]

Praise, O servants of the Lord,
praise the name of the LORD.
2 Let the name of the LORD be praised,
both now and forevermore.[s]
3 From the rising of the sun to the place where it sets,
the name of the LORD is to be praised.

110:5 f Ps 16:8 g Ps 2:12 h Ps 2:5; Ro 2:5
111:2 i Ps 92:5
111:7 j Ps 19:7
111:9 k Lk 1:68
112:1 l Ps 119:14,16, 47,92
112:5 m Ps 37:21,26
112:6 n Pr 10:7
112:7 o Ps 57:7
112:9 p 2Co 9:9* q Ps 75:10
112:10 r Ps 37:12
113:2 s Da 2:20

[a]7 Or / *The One who grants succession will set him in authority* [b]This psalm is an acrostic poem, the lines of which begin with the successive letters of the Hebrew alphabet. [c]1 Hebrew *Hallelu Yah* [d]4 Or / *for* ⌊*the* LORD⌋ *is gracious and compassionate and righteous* [e]9 *Horn* here symbolizes dignity. [f]1 Hebrew *Hallelu Yah*; also in verse 9

4 The LORD is exalted[t] over all the nations,
his glory above the heavens.[u]
5 Who is like the LORD our God,
the One who sits enthroned on high,
6 who stoops down to look[v]
on the heavens and the earth?

7 He raises the poor[w] from the dust
and lifts the needy[x] from the ash heap;
8 he seats them with princes,
with the princes of their people.
9 He settles the barren[y] woman in her home
as a happy mother of children.

Praise the LORD.

## Psalm 114

1 When Israel came out of Egypt,[z]
the house of Jacob from a people of foreign tongue,
2 Judah became God's sanctuary,
Israel his dominion.

3 The sea looked and fled,[a]
the Jordan turned back;
4 the mountains skipped like rams,
the hills like lambs.

5 Why was it, O sea, that you fled,
O Jordan, that you turned back,
6 you mountains, that you skipped like rams,
you hills, like lambs?

7 Tremble, O earth, at the presence of the Lord,
at the presence of the God of Jacob,
8 who turned the rock into a pool,
the hard rock into springs of water.[b]

## Psalm 115

1 Not to us, O LORD, not to us
but to your name be the glory,
because of your love and faithfulness.

2 Why do the nations say,
"Where is their God?"[c]
3 Our God is in heaven;
he does whatever pleases him.[d]
4 But their idols are silver and gold,
made by the hands of men.[e]
5 They have mouths, but cannot speak,
eyes, but they cannot see;
6 they have ears, but cannot hear,
noses, but they cannot smell;
7 they have hands, but cannot feel,
feet, but they cannot walk;
nor can they utter a sound with their throats.
8 Those who make them will be like them,
and so will all who trust in them.

9 O house of Israel, trust in the LORD—
he is their help and shield.
10 O house of Aaron, trust in the LORD—
he is their help and shield.
11 You who fear him, trust in the LORD—
he is their help and shield.

12 The LORD remembers us and will bless us:
He will bless the house of Israel,
he will bless the house of Aaron,
13 he will bless those who fear[f] the LORD—
small and great alike.

14 May the LORD make you increase,
both you and your children.
15 May you be blessed by the LORD,
the Maker of heaven[g] and earth.

16 The highest heavens belong to the LORD,
but the earth he has given to man.
17 It is not the dead[h] who praise the LORD,
those who go down to silence;
18 it is we who extol the LORD,
both now and forevermore.[i]

Praise the LORD.[a]

## Psalm 116

1 I love the LORD,[j] for he heard my voice;
he heard my cry for mercy.
2 Because he turned his ear to me,
I will call on him as long as I live.

3 The cords of death entangled me,
the anguish of the grave[b] came upon me;
I was overcome by trouble and sorrow.
4 Then I called on the name of the LORD:
"O LORD, save me!"

5 The LORD is gracious and righteous;[k]
our God is full of compassion.

**113:4** t Ps 99:2 u Ps 8:1
**113:6** v Ps 11:4; 138:6; Isa 57:15
**113:7** w 1Sa 2:8 x Ps 107:41
**113:9** y 1Sa 2:5
**114:1** z Ex 13:3
**114:3** a Ex 14:21
**114:8** b Ex 17:6; Nu 20:11
**115:2** c Ps 42:3
**115:3** d Ps 135:6
**115:4** e Jer 10:3–5
**115:13** f Ps 128:1,4
**115:15** g Ge 1:1; Ps 96:5
**115:17** h Ps 6:5
**115:18** i Ps 113:2
**116:1** j Ps 18:1
**116:5** k Ezr 9:15; Ps 103:8

[a]18 Hebrew *Hallelu Yah* [b]3 Hebrew *Sheol*

[6] The LORD protects the simplehearted;
when I was in great need, he
saved me.

[7] Be at rest[l] once more, O my soul,
for the LORD has been good[m] to you.

[8] For you, O LORD, have delivered my soul[n]
from death,
my eyes from tears,
my feet from stumbling,
[9] that I may walk before the LORD
in the land of the living.[o]

116:7 l Mt11:29 m Ps13:6
116:8 n Ps56:13
116:9 o Ps27:13

# Inspire

## GOD IS SOVEREIGN

We have an expectation of what we consider "fair." Then we are bewildered when God does not meet our expectation. But God's authority does not operate within the confines of who we think he should be, because God is in control. He is accountable to no one and is supreme in authority, power and rank. When the nations taunted Israel following calamity, saying, "Where is their God?" the psalmist's answer was, "Our God is in heaven; he does whatever pleases him" (Ps 115:2–3).

Many times we desire to serve a God whom we have created in our image. As "modernized" women, we tend to do away with those things that our foremothers taught us about fearing and submitting to God. Instead, some of us have elected to take a loftier road to spiritual enlightenment and self-satisfaction. We think we can reach God on our own. Yet the road that many of us have elected to travel is one that leads us away from the God of the Bible and toward the god of self-service.

Some of us have metaphorical "full plates" that leave little or no room for Christ—especially as the main course. We like our Jesus à la carte! But to be women of God, we must foremost and perpetually recognize that God is not merely an important aspect of life; rather, God *is* life. Since all life comes from him, he retains the ultimate authority over our lives.

God is sovereign. God is the source and authority of, and over, all that exists. God is not simply the object of Sunday morning worship, Wednesday night prayer meeting, daily devotions or Bible study class. God must be Lord of all if he is to be Lord at all.

—A. MIDDLETON

For the next Inspire note, go to page 723.

### read

Psalm 115; Matthew 7:15–23.

See also the Inspire Notes "God Is in Control," "Bumping Into Omnipotence," "God Is Immutable" and "Omniscience: God Is All-Knowing," and the Women of the Bible Notes "Samson's Bride: Nothing by Chance" and "Fortune-Telling Slave Girl: A Surprising Testimony to God's Work."

### WOMAN of COLOR

Is the Lord the main course in your life or just a side dish? How do your actions support your answer?

**116:10** p 2Co4:13*
**116:11** q Ro3:4
**116:14** r Ps22:25
**116:15** s Ps72:14
**116:16** t Ps119:125; 143:12 u Ps86:16
**116:17** v Ps50:14
**116:19** w Ps96:8
**117:1** x Ro15:11*
**118:2** y Ps115:9

10 I believed;[p] therefore[a] I said,
"I am greatly afflicted."
11 And in my dismay I said,
"All men are liars."[q]

12 How can I repay the LORD
for all his goodness to me?
13 I will lift up the cup of salvation
and call on the name of the LORD.
14 I will fulfill my vows[r] to the LORD
in the presence of all his people.

15 Precious in the sight[s] of the LORD
is the death of his saints.
16 O LORD, truly I am your servant;[t]
I am your servant, the son of your
maidservant[b];[u]
you have freed me from my chains.

17 I will sacrifice a thank offering[v] to you
and call on the name of the LORD.
18 I will fulfill my vows to the LORD
in the presence of all his people,
19 in the courts[w] of the house of the
LORD—
in your midst, O Jerusalem.

Praise the Lord.[c]

## Psalm 117

1 Praise the LORD, all you nations;[x]
extol him, all you peoples.
2 For great is his love toward us,
and the faithfulness of the LORD
endures forever.

Praise the Lord.[c]

> *"I grew up like a neglected weed, ignorant of liberty, having no experience of it. Now that I've been free, I know what a dreadful condition slavery is."*
>
> —HARRIET TUBMAN, ABOLITIONIST

## Psalm 118

1 Give thanks to the
LORD, for he is
good;
his love endures
forever.

2 Let Israel say:[y]
"His love endures
forever."
3 Let the house of Aaron
say:
"His love endures
forever."
4 Let those who fear the LORD say:
"His love endures forever."

5 In my anguish[z] I cried to the LORD,
and he answered by setting me free.
6 The LORD is with me;[a] I will not be afraid.
What can man do to me?
7 The LORD is with me; he is my helper.
I will look in triumph on my enemies.

8 It is better to take refuge in the LORD[b]
than to trust in man.
9 It is better to take refuge in the LORD
than to trust in princes.[c]

10 All the nations surrounded me,
but in the name of the LORD I cut
them off.
11 They surrounded me on every side,
but in the name of the LORD I cut
them off.
12 They swarmed around me like bees,[d]
but they died out as quickly as burning
thorns;
in the name of the LORD I cut them off.
13 I was pushed back and about to fall,
but the LORD helped me.
14 The LORD is my strength[e] and my song;
he has become my salvation.

15 Shouts of joy and victory
resound in the tents of the righteous:
"The LORD's right hand has done mighty
things!
16 The LORD's right hand is lifted high;
the LORD's right hand has done mighty
things!"
17 I will not die[f] but live,
and will proclaim[g] what the LORD has
done.
18 The LORD has chastened me severely,
but he has not given me over to death.
19 Open for me the gates of righteousness;
I will enter and give thanks to the
LORD.
20 This is the gate of the LORD
through which the righteous may
enter.[h]
21 I will give you thanks, for you
answered me;
you have become my salvation.

**118:5** z Ps120:1
**118:6** a Heb13:6*
**118:8** b Ps40:4
**118:9** c Ps146:3
**118:12** d Dt1:44
**118:14** e Ex15:2
**118:17** f Hab1:12 g Ps73:28
**118:20** h Rev22:14

[a]10 Or *believed even when* [b]16 Or *servant, your faithful son* [c]19,2 Hebrew *Hallelu Yah*

**118:22** i Mt 21:42; Mk 12:10; Lk 20:17*; Ac 4:11*
**118:26** j Mt 21:9*; Mk 11:9*; Lk 19:38*
**118:27** k 1Pe 2:9
**118:28** l Isa 25:1 m Ex 15:2
**119:1** n Ps 128:1
**119:3** o 1Jn 3:9; 5:18

22 The stone the builders rejected
has become the capstone;[i]
23 the LORD has done this,
and it is marvelous in our eyes.
24 This is the day the LORD has made;
let us rejoice and be glad in it.

25 O LORD, save us;
O LORD, grant us success.
26 Blessed is he who comes[j] in the name of
the LORD.
From the house of the LORD we bless
you.[a]
27 The LORD is God,
and he has made his light shine[k]
upon us.
With boughs in hand, join in the festal
procession
up[b] to the horns of the altar.

28 You are my God, and I will give you
thanks;
you are my God,[l] and I will exalt[m] you.

29 Give thanks to the LORD, for he is good;
his love endures forever.

## Psalm 119[c]

### א Aleph

1 Blessed are they whose ways are blameless,
who walk[n] according to the law of the
LORD.
2 Blessed are they who keep his statutes
and seek him with all their heart.
3 They do nothing wrong;[o]
they walk in his ways.
4 You have laid down precepts
that are to be fully obeyed.
5 Oh, that my ways were steadfast
in obeying your decrees!
6 Then I would not be put to shame
when I consider all your commands.
7 I will praise you with an upright heart
as I learn your righteous laws.
8 I will obey your decrees;
do not utterly forsake me.

### ב Beth

9 How can a young man keep his way pure?
By living according to your word.
10 I seek you with all my heart;[p]
do not let me stray from your
commands.
11 I have hidden your word in my heart[q]
that I might not sin against you.
12 Praise be to you, O LORD;
teach me your decrees.
13 With my lips I recount
all the laws that come from your
mouth.
14 I rejoice in following your statutes
as one rejoices in great riches.
15 I meditate on your precepts[r]
and consider your ways.
16 I delight[s] in your decrees;
I will not neglect your word.

### ג Gimel

17 Do good to your servant, and I will live;
I will obey your word.
18 Open my eyes that I may see
wonderful things in your law.
19 I am a stranger on earth;[t]
do not hide your commands from me.
20 My soul is consumed[u] with longing
for your laws at all times.
21 You rebuke the arrogant, who are cursed
and who stray from your commands.
22 Remove from me scorn[v] and contempt,
for I keep your statutes.
23 Though rulers sit together and
slander me,
your servant will meditate on your
decrees.
24 Your statutes are my delight;
they are my counselors.

### ד Daleth

25 I am laid low in the dust;[w]
preserve my life according to your
word.
26 I recounted my ways and you answered
me;
teach me your decrees.
27 Let me understand the teaching of your
precepts;
then I will meditate on your wonders.[x]
28 My soul is weary with sorrow;[y]
strengthen me according to your word.
29 Keep me from deceitful ways;

**119:10** p 2Ch 15:15
**119:11** q Ps 37:31; Lk 2:19,51
**119:15** r Ps 1:2
**119:16** s Ps 1:2
**119:19** t 1Ch 29:15; Ps 39:12; Heb 11:13
**119:20** u Ps 42:2
**119:22** v Ps 39:8
**119:25** w Ps 44:25
**119:27** x Ps 145:5
**119:28** y Ps 107:26

[a]26 The Hebrew is plural. [b]27 Or *Bind the festal sacrifice with ropes / and take it* [c]This psalm is an acrostic poem; the verses of each stanza begin with the same letter of the Hebrew alphabet.

**119:36** z Lk 12:15
**119:37** a Ps 71:20; Isa 33:15
**119:38** b 2Sa 7:25

be gracious to me through your law.
30 I have chosen the way of truth;
I have set my heart on your laws.
31 I hold fast to your statutes, O LORD;
do not let me be put to shame.
32 I run in the path of your commands,
for you have set my heart free.

### ה He

33 Teach me, O LORD, to follow your decrees;
then I will keep them to the end.
34 Give me understanding, and I will keep your law
and obey it with all my heart.
35 Direct me in the path of your commands,
for there I find delight.
36 Turn my heart toward your statutes
and not toward selfish gain.[z]
37 Turn my eyes away from worthless things;
preserve my life[a] according to your word.[a]
38 Fulfill your promise[b] to your servant,
so that you may be feared.
39 Take away the disgrace I dread,
for your laws are good.
40 How I long for your precepts!
Preserve my life in your righteousness.

### ו Waw

41 May your unfailing love come to me, O LORD,
your salvation according to your promise;
42 then I will answer the one who taunts me,
for I trust in your word.
43 Do not snatch the word of truth from my mouth,
for I have put my hope in your laws.

*Beloved,*

*My love is unfailing. Trust me.*

*Your God*

PSALM 119:41–42

44 I will always obey your law,
for ever and ever.
45 I will walk about in freedom,
for I have sought out your precepts.
46 I will speak of your statutes before kings[c]
and will not be put to shame,
47 for I delight in your commands
because I love them.
48 I lift up my hands to[b] your commands, which I love,
and I meditate on your decrees.

### ז Zayin

49 Remember your word to your servant,
for you have given me hope.
50 My comfort in my suffering is this:
Your promise preserves my life.[d]
51 The arrogant mock me without restraint,
but I do not turn[e] from your law.
52 I remember your ancient laws, O LORD,
and I find comfort in them.
53 Indignation grips me[f] because of the wicked,
who have forsaken your law.
54 Your decrees are the theme of my song
wherever I lodge.
55 In the night I remember[g] your name, O LORD,
and I will keep your law.
56 This has been my practice:
I obey your precepts.

### ח Heth

57 You are my portion,[h] O LORD;
I have promised to obey your words.
58 I have sought your face with all my heart;
be gracious to me according to your promise.
59 I have considered my ways[i]
and have turned my steps to your statutes.
60 I will hasten and not delay
to obey your commands.
61 Though the wicked bind me with ropes,
I will not forget your law.
62 At midnight I rise to give you thanks
for your righteous laws.
63 I am a friend to all who fear you,
to all who follow your precepts.

**119:46** c Mt 10:18; Ac 26:1–2
**119:50** d Ro 15:4
**119:51** e Job 23:11
**119:53** f Ezr 9:3
**119:55** g Ps 63:6
**119:57** h Ps 16:5
**119:59** i Lk 15:17–18

[a]37 Two manuscripts of the Masoretic Text and Dead Sea Scrolls; most manuscripts of the Masoretic Text *life in your way*
[b]48 Or *for*

64 The earth is filled with your love,[j] O LORD;
teach me your decrees.

## ט Teth

65 Do good to your servant
according to your word, O LORD.
66 Teach me knowledge and good judgment,
for I believe in your commands.
67 Before I was afflicted I went astray,[k]
but now I obey your word.
68 You are good,[l] and what you do is good;
teach me your decrees.
69 Though the arrogant have smeared me with lies,[m]
I keep your precepts with all my heart.
70 Their hearts are callous[n] and unfeeling,
but I delight in your law.
71 It was good for me to be afflicted
so that I might learn your decrees.
72 The law from your mouth is more precious to me
than thousands of pieces of silver and gold.[o]

## י Yodh

73 Your hands made me[p] and formed me;
give me understanding to learn your commands.
74 May those who fear you rejoice[q] when they see me,
for I have put my hope in your word.
75 I know, O LORD, that your laws are righteous,
and in faithfulness[r] you have afflicted me.
76 May your unfailing love be my comfort,
according to your promise to your servant.
77 Let your compassion come to me that I may live,
for your law is my delight.
78 May the arrogant be put to shame for wronging me without cause;
but I will meditate on your precepts.
79 May those who fear you turn to me,
those who understand your statutes.
80 May my heart be blameless toward your decrees,
that I may not be put to shame.

## כ Kaph

81 My soul faints[s] with longing for your salvation,
but I have put my hope in your word.
82 My eyes fail,[t] looking for your promise;
I say, "When will you comfort me?"
83 Though I am like a wineskin in the smoke,
I do not forget your decrees.
84 How long[u] must your servant wait?
When will you punish my persecutors?
85 The arrogant dig pitfalls[v] for me,
contrary to your law.
86 All your commands are trustworthy;
help me, for men persecute me without cause.
87 They almost wiped me from the earth,
but I have not forsaken your precepts.
88 Preserve my life according to your love,
and I will obey the statutes of your mouth.

## ל Lamedh

89 Your word, O LORD, is eternal;[w]
it stands firm in the heavens.
90 Your faithfulness continues through all generations;
you established the earth, and it endures.
91 Your laws endure[x] to this day,
for all things serve you.
92 If your law had not been my delight,
I would have perished in my affliction.
93 I will never forget your precepts,
for by them you have preserved my life.
94 Save me, for I am yours;
I have sought out your precepts.
95 The wicked are waiting to destroy me,
but I will ponder your statutes.
96 To all perfection I see a limit;
but your commands are boundless.

## מ Mem

97 Oh, how I love your law!
I meditate[y] on it all day long.
98 Your commands make me wiser[z] than my enemies,
for they are ever with me.
99 I have more insight than all my teachers,
for I meditate on your statutes.

**119:64** j Ps 33:5
**119:67** k Jer 31:18–19; Heb 12:11
**119:68** l Ps 106:1
**119:69** m Job 13:4
**119:70** n Ps 17:10
**119:72** o Ps 19:10; Pr 8:10–11,19
**119:73** p Job 10:8; Ps 138:8
**119:74** q Ps 34:2
**119:75** r Heb 12:5–11
**119:81** s Ps 84:2
**119:82** t Ps 69:3
**119:84** u Ps 39:4; Rev 6:10
**119:85** v Ps 35:7
**119:89** w 1Pe 1:25
**119:91** x Jer 33:25
**119:97** y Ps 1:2
**119:98** z Dt 4:6

**119:100** a Job 32:7–9
**119:101** b Pr 1:15
**119:103** c Ps 19:10
**119:105** d Pr 6:23
**119:106** e Ne 10:29
**119:108** f Hos 14:2; Heb 13:15
**119:110** g Ps 140:5
**119:115** h Ps 6:8; Mt 7:23
**119:116** i Ps 25:2; Ro 5:5

100 I have more understanding than
the elders,
for I obey your precepts.[a]
101 I have kept my feet[b] from every evil path
so that I might obey your word.
102 I have not departed from your laws,
for you yourself have taught me.
103 How sweet are your words to my taste,
sweeter than honey[c] to my mouth!
104 I gain understanding from your
precepts;
therefore I hate every wrong path.

### נ Nun

105 Your word is a lamp to my feet
and a light[d] for my path.
106 I have taken an oath[e] and confirmed it,
that I will follow your righteous laws.
107 I have suffered much;
preserve my life, O LORD, according to
your word.
108 Accept, O LORD, the willing praise of
my mouth,[f]
and teach me your laws.
109 Though I constantly take my life in
my hands,
I will not forget your law.
110 The wicked have set a snare[g] for me,
but I have not strayed from your
precepts.
111 Your statutes are my heritage forever;
they are the joy of my heart.
112 My heart is set on keeping your decrees
to the very end.

### ס Samekh

113 I hate double-minded men,
but I love your law.
114 You are my refuge and my shield;
I have put my hope in your word.
115 Away from me,[h] you evildoers,
that I may keep the commands of my
God!
116 Sustain me according to your promise,
and I will live;
do not let my hopes be dashed.[i]
117 Uphold me, and I will be delivered;
I will always have regard for your
decrees.
118 You reject all who stray from
your decrees,
for their deceitfulness is in vain.
119 All the wicked of the earth you discard
like dross;[j]
therefore I love your statutes.
120 My flesh trembles[k] in fear of you;
I stand in awe of your laws.

### ע Ayin

121 I have done what is righteous and just;
do not leave me to my oppressors.
122 Ensure your servant's well-being;
let not the arrogant oppress me.
123 My eyes fail, looking for your salvation,
looking for your righteous promise.
124 Deal with your servant according to
your love
and teach me your decrees.
125 I am your servant;[l] give me discernment
that I may understand your statutes.
126 It is time for you to act, O LORD;
your law is being broken.
127 Because I love your commands
more than gold,[m] more than pure gold,
128 and because I consider all your
precepts right,
I hate every wrong path.

### פ Pe

129 Your statutes are wonderful;
therefore I obey them.
130 The unfolding of your words gives light;
it gives understanding to the simple.[n]
131 I open my mouth and pant,
longing for your commands.
132 Turn to me and have mercy on me,
as you always do to those who love
your name.
133 Direct my footsteps according to
your word;[o]
let no sin rule[p] over me.
134 Redeem me from the oppression of men,
that I may obey your precepts.
135 Make your face shine[q] upon your servant
and teach me your decrees.
136 Streams of tears[r] flow from my eyes,
for your law is not obeyed.

### צ Tsadhe

137 Righteous are you, O LORD,
and your laws are right.
138 The statutes you have laid down
are righteous;[s]
they are fully trustworthy.

**119:119** j Eze 22:18,19
**119:120** k Hab 3:16
**119:125** l Ps 116:16
**119:127** m Ps 19:10
**119:130** n Ps 19:7
**119:133** o Ps 17:5; p Ps 19:13
**119:135** q Ps 4:6
**119:136** r Jer 9:1,18
**119:138** s Ps 19:7

119:139 t Ps 69:9
119:140 u Ps 12:6
119:142 v Ps 19:7
119:147 w Ps 5:3
119:151 x Ps 145:18
119:152 y Lk 21:33
119:154 z 1Sa 24:15
119:155 a Job 5:4

139 My zeal wears me out,[t]
for my enemies ignore your words.
140 Your promises have been
thoroughly tested,[u]
and your servant loves them.
141 Though I am lowly and despised,
I do not forget your precepts.
142 Your righteousness is everlasting
and your law is true.[v]
143 Trouble and distress have come upon me,
but your commands are my delight.
144 Your statutes are forever right;
give me understanding that I may live.

ק Qoph

145 I call with all my heart; answer me,
O LORD,
and I will obey your decrees.
146 I call out to you; save me
and I will keep your statutes.
147 I rise before dawn[w] and cry for help;
I have put my hope in your word.
148 My eyes stay open through the watches of
the night,
that I may meditate on your promises.
149 Hear my voice in accordance with
your love;
preserve my life, O LORD, according to
your laws.
150 Those who devise wicked schemes
are near,
but they are far from your law.
151 Yet you are near,[x] O LORD,
and all your commands are true.
152 Long ago I learned from your statutes
that you established them to last
forever.[y]

ר Resh

153 Look upon my suffering and deliver me,
for I have not forgotten your law.
154 Defend my cause and redeem me;[z]
preserve my life according to your
promise.
155 Salvation is far from the wicked,
for they do not seek out[a] your decrees.
156 Your compassion is great, O LORD;
preserve my life according to your
laws.
157 Many are the foes who persecute me,
but I have not turned from your
statutes.
158 I look on the faithless with loathing,
for they do not obey your word.
159 See how I love your precepts;
preserve my life, O LORD, according to
your love.
160 All your words are true;
all your righteous laws are eternal.

ש Sin and Shin

161 Rulers persecute me[b] without cause,
but my heart trembles at your word.
162 I rejoice in your promise
like one who finds great spoil.
163 I hate and abhor falsehood
but I love your law.
164 Seven times a day I praise you
for your righteous laws.
165 Great peace[c] have they who love your law,
and nothing can make them stumble.
166 I wait for your salvation,[d] O LORD,
and I follow your commands.
167 I obey your statutes,
for I love them greatly.
168 I obey your precepts and your statutes,
for all my ways are known[e] to you.

ת Taw

169 May my cry come before you, O LORD;
give me understanding according to
your word.
170 May my supplication come before you;
deliver me according to your promise.
171 May my lips overflow with praise,
for you teach me your decrees.
172 May my tongue sing of your word,
for all your commands are righteous.
173 May your hand be ready to help me,
for I have chosen your precepts.
174 I long for your salvation, O LORD,

*Gracious Lord,*

*forgive me all my sins. Cleanse me*

*and restore your joy to me.*

*In my Savior's matchless name,*

*Amen*

PSALM 119:170–176

119:161 b 1Sa 24:11
119:165 c Pr 3:2; Isa 32:17
119:166 d Ge 49:18
119:168 e Pr 5:21

**119:176**
f Isa 53:6
**120:1**
g Jnh 2:2
**120:5**
h Ge 25:13; Jer 49:28
**121:2**
i Ps 115:15; 124:8
**121:5**
j Isa 25:4
**121:6**
k Ps 91:5; Isa 49:10
**121:8**
l Dt 28:6

and your law is my delight.
175 Let me live that I may praise you,
and may your laws sustain me.
176 I have strayed like a lost sheep.[f]
Seek your servant,
for I have not forgotten your
commands.

## Psalm 120

A song of ascents.

1 I call on the LORD in my distress,[g]
and he answers me.
2 Save me, O LORD, from lying lips
and from deceitful tongues.

3 What will he do to you,
and what more besides, O deceitful
tongue?
4 He will punish you with a warrior's sharp
arrows,
with burning coals of the broom tree.

5 Woe to me that I dwell in Meshech,
that I live among the tents of Kedar![h]
6 Too long have I lived
among those who hate peace.
7 I am a man of peace;
but when I speak, they are for war.

## Psalm 121

A song of ascents.

1 I lift up my eyes to the hills—
where does my help come from?
2 My help comes from the LORD,
the Maker of heaven and earth.[i]

3 He will not let your foot slip—
he who watches over you will not
slumber;
4 indeed, he who watches over Israel
will neither slumber nor sleep.

5 The LORD watches over[j] you—
the LORD is your shade at your right
hand;
6 the sun[k] will not harm you by day,
nor the moon by night.

7 The LORD will keep you from all harm—
he will watch over your life;
8 the LORD will watch over your coming and
going
both now and forevermore.[l]

## Psalm 122

A song of ascents. Of David.

1 I rejoiced with those who said to me,
"Let us go to the house of the LORD."
2 Our feet are standing
in your gates, O Jerusalem.

3 Jerusalem is built like a city
that is closely compacted together.
4 That is where the tribes go up,
the tribes of the LORD,
to praise the name of the LORD
according to the statute given to Israel.
5 There the thrones for judgment stand,
the thrones of the house of David.

6 Pray for the peace of Jerusalem:
"May those who love[m] you be secure.
7 May there be peace within your walls
and security within your citadels."
8 For the sake of my brothers and friends,
I will say, "Peace be within you."
9 For the sake of the house of the LORD our
God,
I will seek your prosperity.[n]

## Psalm 123

A song of ascents.

1 I lift up my eyes to you,
to you whose throne[o] is in heaven.
2 As the eyes of slaves look to the hand of
their master,
as the eyes of a maid look to the hand
of her mistress,
so our eyes look to the LORD our God,
till he shows us his mercy.

3 Have mercy on us, O LORD, have mercy
on us,
for we have endured much contempt.
4 We have endured much ridicule from the
proud,
much contempt from the arrogant.

## Psalm 124

A song of ascents. Of David.

1 If the LORD had not been on our side—
let Israel say[p]—
2 if the LORD had not been on our side
when men attacked us,
3 when their anger flared against us,

**122:6**
m Ps 51:18
**122:9**
n Ne 2:10
**123:1**
o Ps 11:4; 121:1; 141:8
**124:1**
p Ps 129:1

124:7 q Ps 91:3; Pr 6:5
124:8 r Ge 1:1; Ps 121:2
125:3 s Pr 22:8; Isa 14:5
125:5 t Pr 2:15 u Ps 128:6
126:1 v Ps 85:1
126:2 w Job 8:21

they would have swallowed us alive;
4 the flood would have engulfed us,
the torrent would have swept over us,
5 the raging waters
would have swept us away.

6 Praise be to the LORD,
who has not let us be torn by their teeth.
7 We have escaped like a bird
out of the fowler's snare;[q]
the snare has been broken,
and we have escaped.
8 Our help is in the name of the LORD,
the Maker of heaven[r] and earth.

## Psalm 125

A song of ascents.

1 Those who trust in the LORD are like Mount Zion,
which cannot be shaken but endures forever.
2 As the mountains surround Jerusalem,
so the LORD surrounds his people
both now and forevermore.

3 The scepter of the wicked will not remain[s]
over the land allotted to the righteous,
for then the righteous might use
their hands to do evil.

4 Do good, O LORD, to those who are good,
to those who are upright in heart.
5 But those who turn to crooked ways[t]
the LORD will banish with the evildoers.

Peace be upon Israel.[u]

## Psalm 126

A song of ascents.

1 When the LORD brought back[v] the captives to[a] Zion,
we were like men who dreamed.[b]
2 Our mouths were filled with laughter,
our tongues with songs of joy.[w]
Then it was said among the nations,
"The LORD has done great things for them."
3 The LORD has done great things for us,
and we are filled with joy.

4 Restore our fortunes,[c] O LORD,
like streams in the Negev.
5 Those who sow in tears
will reap with songs of joy.
6 He who goes out weeping,
carrying seed to sow,
will return with songs of joy,
carrying sheaves with him.

## Psalm 127

A song of ascents. Of Solomon.

1 Unless the LORD builds the house,
its builders labor in vain.
Unless the LORD watches[x] over the city,
the watchmen stand guard in vain.
2 In vain you rise early
and stay up late,
toiling for food[y] to eat—
for he grants sleep to[d] those he loves.
3 Sons are a heritage from the LORD,
children a reward[z] from him.
4 Like arrows in the hands of a warrior
are sons born in one's youth.
5 Blessed is the man
whose quiver is full of them.
They will not be put to shame
when they contend with their enemies[a]
in the gate.

## Psalm 128

A song of ascents.

1 Blessed are all who fear the LORD,
who walk in his ways.[b]
2 You will eat the fruit of your labor;[c]
blessings and prosperity will be yours.
3 Your wife will be like a fruitful vine[d]
within your house;
your sons will be like olive shoots[e]
around your table.
4 Thus is the man blessed
who fears the LORD.

5 May the LORD bless you from Zion[f]
all the days of your life;
may you see the prosperity of Jerusalem,

127:1 x Ps 121:4
127:2 y Ge 3:17
127:3 z Ge 33:5
127:5 a Pr 27:11
128:1 b Ps 119:1–3
128:2 c Isa 3:10
128:3 d Eze 19:10 e Ps 52:8; 144:12
128:5 f Ps 134:3

[a]1 Or *LORD restored the fortunes of* [b]1 Or *men restored to health* [c]4 Or *Bring back our captives* [d]2 Or *eat— / for while they sleep he provides for*

6 and may you live to see your children's
children.[g]

Peace be upon Israel.[h]

## Psalm 129

A song of ascents.

1 They have greatly oppressed me from my
youth—
let Israel say[i]—
2 they have greatly oppressed me from my
youth,
but they have not gained the victory
over me.
3 Plowmen have plowed my back
and made their furrows long.
4 But the LORD is righteous;
he has cut me free from the cords of
the wicked.

5 May all who hate Zion
be turned back in shame.
6 May they be like grass on the roof,
which withers[j] before it can grow;
7 with it the reaper cannot fill his hands,
nor the one who gathers fill his arms.
8 May those who pass by not say,
"The blessing of the LORD be upon you;
we bless you[k] in the name of the LORD."

## Psalm 130

A song of ascents.

1 Out of the depths I cry to you, O LORD;
2 O Lord, hear my voice.
Let your ears be attentive
to my cry for mercy.

3 If you, O LORD, kept a record of sins,
O Lord, who could stand?
4 But with you there is forgiveness;[l]
therefore you are feared.[m]

5 I wait for the LORD,[n] my soul waits,
and in his word[o] I put my hope.
6 My soul waits for the Lord
more than watchmen wait for the
morning,
more than watchmen wait for the
morning.[p]

7 O Israel, put your hope[q] in the LORD,
for with the LORD is unfailing love
and with him is full redemption.
8 He himself will redeem Israel
from all their sins.

## Psalm 131

A song of ascents. Of David.

1 My heart is not proud,[r] O LORD,
my eyes are not haughty;
I do not concern myself with great
matters
or things too wonderful for me.
2 But I have stilled and quieted my
soul;
like a weaned child with its mother,
like a weaned child is my soul[s]
within me.

3 O Israel, put your hope[t] in the LORD
both now and forevermore.

## Psalm 132

A song of ascents.

1 O LORD, remember David
and all the hardships he endured.

2 He swore an oath to the LORD
and made a vow to the Mighty One of
Jacob:[u]
3 "I will not enter my house
or go to my bed—
4 I will allow no sleep to my eyes,
no slumber to my eyelids,
5 till I find a place[v] for the LORD,
a dwelling for the Mighty One of
Jacob."

6 We heard it in Ephrathah,[w]
we came upon it in the fields of
Jaar[a]:[b][x]
7 "Let us go to his dwelling place;[y]
let us worship at his footstool—
8 arise, O LORD,[z] and come to your resting
place,
you and the ark of your might.
9 May your priests be clothed with
righteousness;
may your saints sing for joy."

128:6 g Job 42:16 h Ps 125:5
129:1 i Ps 124:1
129:6 j Ps 37:2
129:8 k Ru 2:4; Ps 118:26
130:4 l Ex 34:7; Jer 33:8 m 1Ki 8:40
130:5 n Isa 8:17 o Ps 119:81
130:6 p Ps 119:147
130:7 q Ps 131:3
131:1 r Ro 12:16
131:2 s Mt 18:3; 1Co 14:20
131:3 t Ps 130:7
132:2 u Ge 49:24
132:5 v Ac 7:46
132:6 w 1Sa 17:12 x 1Sa 7:2
132:7 y Ps 5:7
132:8 z Nu 10:35

[a]6 That is, Kiriath Jearim [b]6 Or *heard of it in Ephrathah, / we found it in the fields of Jaar.* (And no quotes around verses 7–9)

132:11 a Ps 89:3–4,35

10 For the sake of David your servant,
do not reject your anointed one.

11 The LORD swore an oath to David,[a]
a sure oath that he will not revoke:
"One of your own descendants
I will place on your throne—
12 if your sons keep my covenant
and the statutes I teach them,
then their sons will sit
on your throne for ever and ever."

13 For the LORD has chosen Zion,[b]
he has desired it for his dwelling:
14 "This is my resting place for ever and ever;
here I will sit enthroned, for I have desired it—

132:13 b Ps 48:1–2

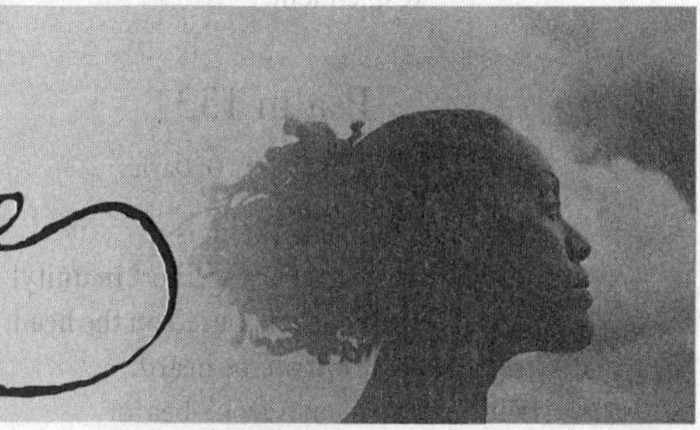

Inspire

## WAITING ON GOD

Women are familiar with waiting. Women of color especially know the attributes of waiting. We wait for the restoration of our homes and the revival of our communities. We wait for an end to racism and the elimination of sexism. We wait for our children to be recognized as young and gifted in a society that suppresses their beauty and talent. We wait for our men to overcome the burden of oppression and self-hatred. We wait for our relationships to be empowered and renewed; and we wait for ourselves to be made whole by the Word of God.

Our waiting should not produce anxiety, irritation, confusion or passive resignation. Our waiting should not lead to jealousy, envy or rage. However, waiting with a God-given patience means moving with God; it means allowing God to have his perfect way in our lives. This patience allows God to regenerate us. Our attitudes while waiting should reflect our anticipation that God will arrive and be victorious. Our souls wait on the Lord and we know—because of his Word and his demonstrated past—that he will show up and show out. We put our hope in God, as the psalmist proclaimed in Psalm 130:5: "I wait for the LORD, my soul waits, and in his word I put my hope."

Woman of color, rejoice in your waiting—because God waits with you, moves for you and has already worked matters out on your behalf!

—C. COOKE

**read**

Psalm 130; Romans 5:1–5; 1 Corinthians 13:4–7; Galatians 5:22–23.

See also the Inspire Notes "Patience," "God Is in Control," "Prayer: The Antidote to Worry" and "Peace," and the Women of the Bible Notes "Sarah: Is Anything Too Hard for God?" "The Persistent Widow: Always Pray" and "Rhoda: Doing Her Duty."

**WOMAN of COLOR**

For what are you waiting on God? How are you waiting?

For the next Inspire note, go to page 738.

132:15 c Ps 147:14
132:17 d Eze 29:21; Lk 1:69
133:1 e Ge 13:8
133:3 f Dt 4:48 g Lev 25:21
134:1 h Ps 135:1–2

15 I will bless her with abundant provisions;
her poor will I satisfy with food.[c]
16 I will clothe her priests with salvation,
and her saints will ever sing for joy.

17 "Here I will make a horn[a] grow[d] for David
and set up a lamp for my anointed one.
18 I will clothe his enemies with shame,
but the crown on his head will be resplendent."

## Psalm 133

A song of ascents. Of David.

1 How good and pleasant it is
when brothers live together[e] in unity!
2 It is like precious oil poured on the head,
running down on the beard,
running down on Aaron's beard,
down upon the collar of his robes.
3 It is as if the dew of Hermon[f]
were falling on Mount Zion.
For there the LORD bestows his blessing,[g]
even life forevermore.

*Father,*

*in the name of Jesus, I make a fresh commitment to you to live in peace. I am letting go of bitterness, hurt and unkindness and asking for your forgiveness and the release of all who have wronged me. Help me to walk in love and peace, to behave toward others in a way that is glorifying to you.*

*Amen*

PSALM 133:1–3

## Psalm 134

A song of ascents.

1 Praise the LORD, all you servants[h] of the LORD
who minister by night in the house of the LORD.
2 Lift up your hands[i] in the sanctuary
and praise the LORD.

3 May the LORD, the Maker of heaven[j] and earth,
bless you from Zion.

## Psalm 135

1 Praise the LORD.[b]

Praise the name of the Lord;
praise him, you servants of the LORD,
2 you who minister in the house of the LORD,
in the courts of the house of our God.

3 Praise the LORD, for the LORD is good;[k]
sing praise to his name, for that is pleasant.[l]
4 For the LORD has chosen Jacob to be his own,
Israel to be his treasured possession.[m]

5 I know that the LORD is great,
that our Lord is greater than all gods.
6 The LORD does whatever pleases him,[n]
in the heavens and on the earth,
in the seas and all their depths.
7 He makes clouds rise from the ends of the earth;
he sends lightning with the rain[o]
and brings out the wind from his storehouses.

8 He struck down the firstborn[p] of Egypt,
the firstborn of men and animals.
9 He sent his signs and wonders into your midst, O Egypt,
against Pharaoh and all his servants.[q]
10 He struck down many[r] nations
and killed mighty kings—
11 Sihon king of the Amorites,
Og king of Bashan
and all the kings of Canaan[s]—
12 and he gave their land as an inheritance,
an inheritance to his people Israel.

13 Your name, O LORD, endures forever,[t]
your renown,[u] O LORD, through all generations.
14 For the LORD will vindicate his people
and have compassion on his servants.[v]

134:2 i 1Ti 2:8
134:3 j Ps 124:8
135:3 k Ps 119:68 l Ps 147:1
135:4 m Ex 19:5; Dt 7:6
135:6 n Ps 115:3
135:7 o Jer 10:13; Zec 10:1
135:8 p Ex 12:12
135:9 q Ps 136:10–15
135:10 r Nu 21:21–25; Ps 136:17–21
135:11 s Jos 12:7–24
135:13 t Ex 3:15 u Ps 102:12
135:14 v Dt 32:36

[a] 17 *Horn* here symbolizes strong one, that is, king. [b] 1 Hebrew *Hallelu Yah*; also in verses 3 and 21

[15] The idols of the nations are silver and
gold,
made by the hands of men.
[16] They have mouths, but cannot speak,
eyes, but they cannot see;
[17] they have ears, but cannot hear,
nor is there breath in their mouths.
[18] Those who make them will be like them,
and so will all who trust in them.

[19] O house of Israel, praise the LORD;
O house of Aaron, praise the LORD;
[20] O house of Levi, praise the LORD;
you who fear him, praise the LORD.
[21] Praise be to the LORD from Zion,[w]
to him who dwells in Jerusalem.

Praise the Lord.

## Psalm 136

[1] Give thanks to the LORD, for he is good.[x]
*His love endures forever.*
[2] Give thanks to the God of gods.[y]
*His love endures forever.*
[3] Give thanks to the Lord of lords:
*His love endures forever.*

[4] to him who alone does great wonders,
*His love endures forever.*
[5] who by his understanding[z] made the
heavens,[a]
*His love endures forever.*
[6] who spread out the earth[b] upon the
waters,
*His love endures forever.*
[7] who made the great lights[c]—
*His love endures forever.*
[8] the sun to govern the day,
*His love endures forever.*
[9] the moon and stars to govern the night;
*His love endures forever.*

[10] to him who struck down the firstborn[d] of
Egypt
*His love endures forever.*
[11] and brought Israel out[e] from among them
*His love endures forever.*
[12] with a mighty hand and outstretched
arm;
*His love endures forever.*

[13] to him who divided the Red Sea[a][f] asunder
*His love endures forever.*
[14] and brought Israel through the midst
of it,
*His love endures forever.*
[15] but swept Pharaoh and his army into the
Red Sea;[g]
*His love endures forever.*

[16] to him who led his people through the
desert,[h]
*His love endures forever.*
[17] who struck down great kings,[i]
*His love endures forever.*
[18] and killed mighty kings—
*His love endures forever.*
[19] Sihon king of the Amorites
*His love endures forever.*
[20] and Og king of Bashan—
*His love endures forever.*
[21] and gave their land[j] as an inheritance,
*His love endures forever.*
[22] an inheritance to his servant Israel;
*His love endures forever.*

[23] to the One who remembered us in our low
estate
*His love endures forever.*
[24] and freed us from our enemies,
*His love endures forever.*
[25] and who gives food[k] to every creature.
*His love endures forever.*

[26] Give thanks to the God of heaven.
*His love endures forever.*

## Psalm 137

[1] By the rivers of Babylon we sat and wept
when we remembered Zion.
[2] There on the poplars
we hung our harps,
[3] for there our captors asked us for songs,
our tormentors demanded songs of
joy;
they said, "Sing us one of the songs of
Zion!"

[4] How can we sing the songs of the LORD
while in a foreign land?
[5] If I forget you, O Jerusalem,
may my right hand forget ⌞its skill⌟.
[6] May my tongue cling to the roof[l] of my
mouth
if I do not remember you,

[a]13 Hebrew *Yam Suph*; that is, Sea of Reeds; also in verse 15

**135:21** w Ps 134:3
**136:1** x Ps 106:1
**136:2** y Dt 10:17
**136:5** z Pr 3:19; Jer 51:15 a Ge 1:1
**136:6** b Jer 10:12
**136:7** c Ge 1:14,16
**136:10** d Ex 12:29; Ps 135:8
**136:11** e Ex 6:6; 12:51
**136:13** f Ex 14:21; Ps 78:13
**136:15** g Ex 14:27
**136:16** h Ex 13:18
**136:17** i Ps 135:9–12
**136:21** j Jos 12:1
**136:25** k Ps 104:27; 145:15
**137:6** l Eze 3:26

**137:7** m Jer 49:7; La 4:21–22
**137:8** n Isa 13:1,19; Jer 25:12,26; Rev 18:6
**138:2** o 1Ki 8:29
**138:4** p Ps 102:15
**138:7** q Ps 23:4
**138:8** r Ps 57:2; Php 1:6 s Job 10:3,8

if I do not consider Jerusalem
my highest joy.

7 Remember, O LORD, what the Edomites[m] did
on the day Jerusalem fell.
"Tear it down," they cried,
"tear it down to its foundations!"

8 O Daughter of Babylon, doomed to destruction,[n]
happy is he who repays you
for what you have done to us—
9 he who seizes your infants
and dashes them against the rocks.

## Psalm 138

Of David.

1 I will praise you, O LORD, with all my heart;
before the "gods" I will sing your praise.
2 I will bow down toward your holy temple[o]
and will praise your name
for your love and your faithfulness,
for you have exalted above all things
your name and your word.
3 When I called, you answered me;
you made me bold and stouthearted.

4 May all the kings of the earth[p] praise you, O LORD,
when they hear the words of your mouth.
5 May they sing of the ways of the LORD,
for the glory of the LORD is great.

6 Though the LORD is on high, he looks upon the lowly,
but the proud he knows from afar.
7 Though I walk[q] in the midst of trouble,
you preserve my life;
you stretch out your hand against the anger of my foes,
with your right hand you save me.
8 The LORD will fulfill ⌊his purpose⌋ for me;
your love, O LORD, endures forever—
do not abandon the works of your hands.[s]

## Psalm 139

For the director of music.
Of David. A psalm.

1 O LORD, you have searched me[t]
and you know[u] me.
2 You know when I sit and when I rise;[v]
you perceive my thoughts[w] from afar.
3 You discern my going out and my lying down;
you are familiar with all my ways.[x]
4 Before a word is on my tongue
you know it completely,[y] O LORD.

5 You hem me in—behind and before;
you have laid your hand upon me.

*Lord,*

*Search me and try me.*
*Let me be open before you.*

*Amen*

PSALM 139:1–5

6 Such knowledge is too wonderful for me,
too lofty[z] for me to attain.

7 Where can I go from your Spirit?
Where can I flee[a] from your presence?
8 If I go up to the heavens,[b] you are there;
if I make my bed[c] in the depths,[a] you are there.
9 If I rise on the wings of the dawn,
if I settle on the far side of the sea,
10 even there your hand will guide me,
your right hand will hold me fast.

11 If I say, "Surely the darkness will hide me
and the light become night around me,"
12 even the darkness will not be dark[d] to you;
the night will shine like the day,
for darkness is as light to you.

13 For you created my inmost being;
you knit me together in my mother's womb.

**139:1** t Ps 17:3 u Jer 12:3
**139:2** v 2Ki 19:27 w Mt 9:4
**139:3** x Job 31:4
**139:4** y Heb 4:13
**139:6** z Job 42:3
**139:7** a Jer 23:24
**139:8** b Am 9:2–3 c Pr 15:11
**139:12** d Job 34:22

[a]8 Hebrew *Sheol*

139:17 e Ps 40:5
139:19 f Isa 11:4 g Ps 119:115
139:20 h Jude 15
139:23 i Job 31:6
139:24 j Ps 5:8
140:2 k Ps 56:6
140:3 l Ps 58:4
140:4 m Ps 71:4

14 I praise you because I am fearfully and
wonderfully made;
your works are wonderful,
I know that full well.
15 My frame was not hidden from you
when I was made in the secret place.
When I was woven together in the depths
of the earth,
16 your eyes saw my unformed body.
All the days ordained for me
were written in your book
before one of them came to be.

17 How precious to[a] me are your thoughts,
O God![e]
How vast is the sum of them!
18 Were I to count them,
they would outnumber the grains of
sand.
When I awake,
I am still with you.

19 If only you would slay the wicked,[f] O God!
Away from me,[g] you bloodthirsty men!
20 They speak of you with evil intent;
your adversaries misuse your name.[h]
21 Do I not hate those who hate you, O LORD,
and abhor those who rise up against
you?
22 I have nothing but hatred for them;
I count them my enemies.

23 Search me,[i] O God, and know my heart;
test me and know my anxious
thoughts.
24 See if there is any offensive way in me,
and lead me[j] in the way everlasting.

## Psalm 140

For the director of music.
A psalm of David.

1 Rescue me, O LORD, from evil men;
protect me from men of violence,
2 who devise evil plans[k] in their hearts
and stir up war every day.
3 They make their tongues as sharp as a
serpent's;
the poison of vipers[l] is on their lips.
*Selah*

4 Keep me, O LORD, from the hands of the
wicked;[m]
protect me from men of violence
who plan to trip my feet.
5 Proud men have hidden a snare for me;
they have spread out the cords of their
net
and have set traps[n] for me along my
path. *Selah*

6 O LORD, I say to you, "You are my God."
Hear, O LORD, my cry for mercy.
7 O Sovereign LORD, my strong deliverer,
who shields my head in the day of
battle—
8 do not grant the wicked their desires,
O LORD;
do not let their plans succeed,
or they will become proud. *Selah*

9 Let the heads of those who surround me
be covered with the trouble their lips
have caused.[o]
10 Let burning coals fall upon them;
may they be thrown into the fire,[p]
into miry pits, never to rise.
11 Let slanderers not be established in the
land;
may disaster hunt down men of
violence.

12 I know that the LORD secures justice for
the poor
and upholds the cause[q] of the needy.
13 Surely the righteous will praise your
name
and the upright will live before you.

## Psalm 141

A psalm of David.

1 O LORD, I call to you; come quickly[r] to me.
Hear my voice when I call to you.
2 May my prayer be set before you like
incense;[s]
may the lifting up of my hands be like
the evening sacrifice.[t]

3 Set a guard over my mouth, O LORD;
keep watch over the door of my lips.
4 Let not my heart be drawn to what is evil,
to take part in wicked deeds
with men who are evildoers;
let me not eat of their delicacies.[u]

140:5 n Ps 31:4
140:9 o Ps 7:16
140:10 p Ps 11:6
140:12 q Ps 9:4
141:1 r Ps 70:5
141:2 s Rev 5:8; 8:3 t Ex 29:39,41
141:4 u Pr 23:6

[a]17 Or *concerning*

141:5 v Pr 9:8
141:8 w Ps 25:15
141:10 x Ps 35:8
142:1 y Ps 30:8
142:3 z Ps 140:5; 143:4,7
142:4 a Ps 31:11
142:5 b Ps 27:13
142:6 c Ps 116:6

5 Let a righteous man[a] strike me—it is a kindness;
let him rebuke me[v]—it is oil on my head.
My head will not refuse it.

Yet my prayer is ever against the deeds of evildoers;
6 their rulers will be thrown down from the cliffs,
and the wicked will learn that my words were well spoken.
7 They will say, "As one plows and breaks up the earth,
so our bones have been scattered at the mouth of the grave.[b]"

8 But my eyes are fixed[w] on you,
O Sovereign LORD;
in you I take refuge—do not give me over to death.
9 Keep me from the snares they have laid for me,
from the traps set by evildoers.
10 Let the wicked fall[x] into their own nets,
while I pass by in safety.

## Psalm 142

A *maskil*[c] of David. When he was in the cave. A prayer.

1 I cry aloud to the LORD;
I lift up my voice to the LORD for mercy.[y]
2 I pour out my complaint before him;
before him I tell my trouble.

3 When my spirit grows faint[z] within me,
it is you who know my way.
In the path where I walk
men have hidden a snare for me.
4 Look to my right and see;
no one is concerned for me.
I have no refuge;
no one cares[a] for my life.

5 I cry to you, O LORD;
I say, "You are my refuge,
my portion in the land of the living."[b]
6 Listen to my cry,
for I am in desperate need;[c]
rescue me from those who pursue me,
for they are too strong for me.
7 Set me free from my prison,
that I may praise your name.

Then the righteous will gather about me
because of your goodness to me.[d]

## Psalm 143

A psalm of David.

1 O LORD, hear my prayer,
listen to my cry for mercy;
in your faithfulness and righteousness
come to my relief.
2 Do not bring your servant into judgment,
for no one living is righteous before you.

3 The enemy pursues me,
he crushes me to the ground;
he makes me dwell in darkness
like those long dead.
4 So my spirit grows faint within me;
my heart within me is dismayed.
5 I remember[e] the days of long ago;
I meditate on all your works
and consider what your hands have done.
6 I spread out my hands[f] to you;
my soul thirsts for you like a parched land. *Selah*

7 Answer me quickly, O LORD;
my spirit fails.
Do not hide your face[g] from me
or I will be like those who go down to the pit.
8 Let the morning bring me word of your unfailing love,
for I have put my trust in you.
Show me the way I should go,
for to you I lift up my soul.[h]
9 Rescue me from my enemies, O LORD,
for I hide myself in you.
10 Teach me to do your will,
for you are my God;
may your good Spirit
lead[i] me on level ground.

11 For your name's sake, O LORD, preserve my life;[j]
in your righteousness, bring me out of trouble.

142:7 d Ps 13:6
143:5 e Ps 77:6
143:6 f Ps 63:1; 88:9
143:7 g Ps 28:1
143:8 h Ps 25:1–2
143:10 i Ne 9:20; Ps 25:4–5
143:11 j Ps 119:25

[a]5 Or *Let the Righteous One* [b]7 Hebrew *Sheol* [c]Title: Probably a literary or musical term

143:12 k Ps 54:5
144:1 l Ps 18:2,34
144:3 m Ps 8:4; Heb 2:6
144:4 n Ps 102:11
144:5 o Ps 18:9 p Ps 104:32
144:6 q Ps 18:14
144:8 r Ps 12:2
144:9 s Ps 33:2–3
144:10 t Ps 18:50
144:12 u Ps 128:3

12 In your unfailing love, silence my
enemies;
destroy all my foes,[k]
for I am your servant.

## Psalm 144

Of David.

1 Praise be to the LORD my Rock,[l]
who trains my hands for war,
my fingers for battle.
2 He is my loving God and my fortress,
my stronghold and my deliverer,
my shield, in whom I take refuge,
who subdues peoples[a] under me.

3 O LORD, what is man[m] that you care for
him,
the son of man that you think of him?
4 Man is like a breath;
his days are like a fleeting shadow.[n]

5 Part your heavens,[o] O LORD, and come
down;
touch the mountains, so that they
smoke.[p]
6 Send forth lightning and scatter ⌊the
enemies⌋;
shoot your arrows[q] and rout them.
7 Reach down your hand from on high;
deliver me and rescue me
from the mighty waters,
from the hands of foreigners
8 whose mouths are full of lies,[r]
whose right hands are deceitful.

9 I will sing a new song to you, O God;
on the ten-stringed lyre[s] I will make
music to you,
10 to the One who gives victory to kings,
who delivers his servant David[t] from
the deadly sword.

11 Deliver me and rescue me
from the hands of foreigners
whose mouths are full of lies,
whose right hands are deceitful.

12 Then our sons in their youth
will be like well-nurtured plants,[u]
and our daughters will be like pillars
carved to adorn a palace.
13 Our barns will be filled
with every kind of provision.
Our sheep will increase by thousands,
by tens of thousands in our fields;
14 our oxen will draw heavy loads.[b]
There will be no breaching of walls,
no going into captivity,
no cry of distress in our streets.
15 Blessed are the people[v] of whom this is
true;
blessed are the people whose God is
the LORD.

## Psalm 145[c]

A psalm of praise. Of David.

1 I will exalt you,[w] my God the King;
I will praise your name for ever and
ever.
2 Every day I will praise you
and extol your name for ever and ever.

3 Great is the LORD and most worthy of
praise;
his greatness no one can fathom.[x]
4 One generation[y] will commend your
works to another;
they will tell of your mighty acts.
5 They will speak of the glorious splendor
of your majesty,
and I will meditate on your wonderful
works.[d]
6 They will tell of the power of your
awesome works,[z]
and I will proclaim[a] your great deeds.
7 They will celebrate your abundant
goodness
and joyfully sing of your
righteousness.

8 The LORD is gracious and
compassionate,[b]
slow to anger and rich in love.

9 The LORD is good to all;
he has compassion on all he has made.
10 All you have made will praise you,[c]
O LORD;
your saints will extol you.

144:15 v Ps 33:12
145:1 w Ps 30:1; 34:1
145:3 x Job 5:9; Ro 11:33
145:4 y Isa 38:19
145:6 z Ps 66:3 a Dt 32:3
145:8 b Ps 86:15
145:10 c Ps 19:1

[a]2 Many manuscripts of the Masoretic Text, Dead Sea Scrolls, Aquila, Jerome and Syriac; most manuscripts of the Masoretic Text *subdues my people* [b]14 Or *our chieftains will be firmly established* [c]This psalm is an acrostic poem, the verses of which (including verse 13b) begin with the successive letters of the Hebrew alphabet. [d]5 Dead Sea Scrolls and Syriac (see also Septuagint); Masoretic Text *On the glorious splendor of your majesty / and on your wonderful works I will meditate*

145:13 d 2Pe 1:11
145:14 e Ps 146:8
145:15 f Ps 104:27
145:18 g Dt 4:7 h Jn 4:24
145:20 i Ps 31:23

11 They will tell of the glory of your
kingdom
and speak of your might,
12 so that all men may know of your mighty
acts
and the glorious splendor of your
kingdom.
13 Your kingdom is an everlasting
kingdom,[d]
and your dominion endures through
all generations.

The Lord is faithful to all his promises
and loving toward all he has made.[a]
14 The Lord upholds all those who fall
and lifts up all[e] who are bowed down.
15 The eyes of all look to you,
and you give them their food[f] at the
proper time.
16 You open your hand
and satisfy the desires of every living
thing.

17 The Lord is righteous in all his ways
and loving toward all he has made.
18 The Lord is near[g] to all who call on him,[h]
to all who call on him in truth.
19 He fulfills the desires of those who fear
him;
he hears their cry and saves them.

*Uncertain child,*

*I am gracious and compassionate.*
*Follow my lead.*

*Your Guide*

PSALM 145:17–19

20 The Lord watches over all who love him,[i]
but all the wicked he will destroy.

21 My mouth will speak in praise of the
Lord.
Let every creature praise his holy
name
for ever and ever.

## Psalm 146

1 Praise the Lord.[b]

Praise the Lord,[j] O my soul.
2 I will praise the Lord all my life;[k]
I will sing praise to my God as long as
I live.

3 Do not put your trust in princes,
in mortal men,[l] who cannot save.
4 When their spirit departs, they return to
the ground;[m]
on that very day their plans come to
nothing.

5 Blessed is he whose help is the God of
Jacob,
whose hope is in the Lord his God,
6 the Maker of heaven and earth,
the sea, and everything in them—
the Lord, who remains faithful forever.
7 He upholds the cause of the oppressed[n]
and gives food to the hungry.[o]
The Lord sets prisoners free,
8 the Lord gives sight to the blind,[p]
the Lord lifts up those who are bowed
down,
the Lord loves the righteous.
9 The Lord watches over the alien
and sustains the fatherless and the
widow,
but he frustrates the ways of the
wicked.

10 The Lord reigns[q] forever,
your God, O Zion, for all generations.

Praise the Lord.

## Psalm 147

1 Praise the Lord.[c]

How good it is to sing praises to our God,
how pleasant[r] and fitting to praise
him![s]

2 The Lord builds up Jerusalem;[t]
he gathers the exiles[u] of Israel.
3 He heals the brokenhearted
and binds up their wounds.
4 He determines the number of the stars[v]

146:1 j Ps 103:1
146:2 k Ps 104:33
146:3 l Isa 2:22
146:4 m Ecc 12:7
146:7 n Ps 103:6 o Ps 107:9
146:8 p Mt 9:30
146:10 q Ex 15:18; Ps 10:16
147:1 r Ps 135:3 s Ps 33:1
147:2 t Ps 102:16 u Dt 30:3
147:4 v Isa 40:26

[a]13 One manuscript of the Masoretic Text, Dead Sea Scrolls and Syriac (see also Septuagint); most manuscripts of the Masoretic Text do not have the last two lines of verse 13. [b]1 Hebrew *Hallelu Yah*; also in verse 10 [c]1 Hebrew *Hallelu Yah*; also in verse 20

147:5 w Ps 48:1 x Isa 40:28
147:6 y Ps 146:8–9
147:8 z Job 38:26 a Ps 104:14
147:9 b Ps 104:27–28
147:10 c Ps 33:16–17
147:14 d Ps 132:15
147:16 e Job 37:6
147:19 f Mal 4:4

and calls them each by name.
5 Great is our Lord[w] and mighty in power;
his understanding has no limit.[x]
6 The LORD sustains the humble[y]
but casts the wicked to the ground.

7 Sing to the LORD with thanksgiving;
make music to our God on the harp.
8 He covers the sky with clouds;
he supplies the earth with rain[z]
and makes grass grow[a] on the hills.
9 He provides food[b] for the cattle
and for the young ravens when they call.
10 His pleasure is not in the strength of the horse,[c]
nor his delight in the legs of a man;
11 the LORD delights in those who fear him,
who put their hope in his unfailing love.

12 Extol the LORD, O Jerusalem;
praise your God, O Zion,
13 for he strengthens the bars of your gates
and blesses your people within you.
14 He grants peace to your borders
and satisfies you[d] with the finest of wheat.

15 He sends his command to the earth;
his word runs swiftly.
16 He spreads the snow[e] like wool
and scatters the frost like ashes.
17 He hurls down his hail like pebbles.
Who can withstand his icy blast?
18 He sends his word and melts them;
he stirs up his breezes, and the waters flow.

19 He has revealed his word to Jacob,
his laws and decrees[f] to Israel.
20 He has done this for no other nation;
they do not know his laws.

Praise the Lord.

## Psalm 148

1 Praise the LORD.[a]

Praise the Lord from the heavens,
praise him in the heights above.
2 Praise him, all his angels,
praise him, all his heavenly hosts.
3 Praise him, sun and moon,
praise him, all you shining stars.
4 Praise him, you highest heavens
and you waters above the skies.[g]
5 Let them praise the name of the LORD,
for he commanded[h] and they were created.
6 He set them in place for ever and ever;
he gave a decree[i] that will never pass away.

7 Praise the LORD from the earth,
you great sea creatures and all ocean depths,
8 lightning and hail, snow and clouds,
stormy winds that do his bidding,[j]
9 you mountains and all hills,[k]
fruit trees and all cedars,
10 wild animals and all cattle,
small creatures and flying birds,
11 kings of the earth and all nations,
you princes and all rulers on earth,
12 young men and maidens,
old men and children.

13 Let them praise the name of the LORD,[l]
for his name alone is exalted;
his splendor is above the earth and the heavens.[m]
14 He has raised up for his people a horn,[b][n]
the praise of all his saints,
of Israel, the people close to his heart.

Praise the Lord.

## Psalm 149

1 Praise the LORD.[c][o]

Sing to the Lord a new song,
his praise in the assembly of the saints.

2 Let Israel rejoice in their Maker;
let the people of Zion be glad in their King.
3 Let them praise his name with dancing
and make music to him with tambourine and harp.[p]
4 For the LORD takes delight[q] in his people;
he crowns the humble with salvation.[r]
5 Let the saints rejoice in this honor
and sing for joy on their beds.[s]

148:4 g Ge 1:7
148:5 h Ge 1:1,6; Ps 33:6,9
148:6 i Ps 89:37; Jer 33:25
148:8 j Ps 147:15–18
148:9 k Isa 44:23
148:13 l Isa 12:4 m Ps 113:4
148:14 n Ps 75:10
149:1 o Ps 33:2
149:3 p Ps 81:2
149:4 q Ps 35:27 r Ps 132:16
149:5 s Job 35:10

[a]1 Hebrew *Hallelu Yah*; also in verse 14 [b]14 *Horn* here symbolizes strong one, that is, king. [c]1 Hebrew *Hallelu Yah*; also in verse 9

149:6 t Heb 4:12; Rev 1:16
149:9 u Ps 148:14

6 May the praise of God be in their mouths
and a double-edged[t] sword in their hands,
7 to inflict vengeance on the nations
and punishment on the peoples,
8 to bind their kings with fetters,
their nobles with shackles of iron,
9 to carry out the sentence written against them.
This is the glory of all his saints.[u]

Praise the Lord.

## Psalm 150

1 Praise the LORD.[a]

Praise God in his sanctuary;
praise him in his mighty heavens.
2 Praise him for his acts of power;[v]
praise him for his surpassing greatness.
3 Praise him with the sounding of the trumpet,
praise him with the harp and lyre,[w]
4 praise him with tambourine and dancing,
praise him with the strings and flute,
5 praise him with the clash of cymbals,[x]
praise him with resounding cymbals.

6 Let everything that has breath praise the LORD.

Praise the Lord.

150:2 v Dt 3:24
150:3 w Ps 149:3
150:5 x 1Ch 15:16

[a]1 Hebrew *Hallelu Yah*; also in verse 6

# Proverbs

## OVERVIEW

Readers of the book of Proverbs are instructed in moral and ethical living rooted in proper relationship with God. The foundation of the book is found in Proverbs 1:7: "The fear of the LORD is the beginning of knowledge." Insights into the nature of humans and God are revealed in Proverbs.

This book describes the behavior and lifestyle of a virtuous woman (see Pr 31:10–31). A careful study of this passage will reveal not only how God encourages positive character traits in every woman believer, but also how he enables each woman through Jesus Christ to experience this fulfilling and purposeful life.

## OUTLINE

I. Prologue: Purpose and Theme (1:1–7)
II. Exhortations to Embrace Wisdom (1:8—9:18)
III. Proverbs of Solomon (10:1—22:16)
IV. Sayings of the Wise (22:17—24:34)
V. More Proverbs of Solomon (25:1—29:27)
VI. Sayings of Agur and King Lemuel (30:1—31:9)
VII. The Ideal Wife (31:10–31)

### SCANNABLE FACTS:

**Authors:** Primarily Solomon, but also Agur, King Lemuel and others

**Time Written:** Most were written during Solomon's reign, 970–930 B.C.

**Theme to Note:** Wisdom is essential to living a fulfilled life

**Notable Woman:** The wife of noble character (see Pr 31)

**1:1** a 1Ki 4:29–34
**1:4** b Pr 8:5 c Pr 8:12
**1:5** d Pr 9:9
**1:6** e Ps 78:2
**1:7** f Job 28:28; Ps 111:10; Ecc 12:13
**1:8** g Pr 4:1 h Pr 6:20
**1:10** i Dt 13:8
**1:12** j Ps 28:1
**1:15** k Ps 119:101 l Ps 1:1
**1:16** m Isa 59:7

## Prologue: Purpose and Theme

1 The proverbs of Solomon[a] son of David,
king of Israel:

2 for attaining wisdom and discipline;
for understanding words of insight;
3 for acquiring a disciplined and prudent
life,
doing what is right and just and fair;
4 for giving prudence to the simple,[b]
knowledge and discretion[c] to the
young—
5 let the wise listen and add to their
learning,[d]
and let the discerning get guidance—
6 for understanding proverbs and
parables,[e]
the sayings and riddles of the wise.

7 The fear of the LORD[f] is the beginning of
knowledge,
but fools[a] despise wisdom and
discipline.

## Exhortations to Embrace Wisdom

### Warning Against Enticement

8 Listen, my son,[g] to your father's
instruction
and do not forsake your mother's
teaching.[h]
9 They will be a garland to grace your head
and a chain to adorn your neck.

10 My son, if sinners entice you,
do not give in[i] to them.
11 If they say, "Come along with us;
let's lie in wait for someone's blood,
let's waylay some harmless soul;
12 let's swallow them alive, like the grave,[b]
and whole, like those who go down to
the pit;[j]
13 we will get all sorts of valuable things
and fill our houses with plunder;
14 throw in your lot with us,
and we will share a common purse"—
15 my son, do not go along with them,
do not set foot[k] on their paths;[l]
16 for their feet rush into sin,
they are swift to shed blood.[m]
17 How useless to spread a net
in full view of all the birds!
18 These men lie in wait for their own blood;
they waylay only themselves!
19 Such is the end of all who go after ill-
gotten gain;
it takes away the lives of those who
get it.

### Warning Against Rejecting Wisdom

20 Wisdom calls aloud in the street,
she raises her voice in the public
squares;
21 at the head of the noisy streets[c] she cries
out,
in the gateways of the city she makes
her speech:

22 "How long will you simple ones[d] love
your simple ways?
How long will mockers delight in
mockery
and fools hate knowledge?
23 If you had responded to my rebuke,
I would have poured out my heart to
you
and made my thoughts known to you.
24 But since you rejected me when I called[n]
and no one gave heed when I stretched
out my hand,
25 since you ignored all my advice
and would not accept my rebuke,
26 I in turn will laugh[o] at your disaster;
I will mock when calamity overtakes
you[p]—
27 when calamity overtakes you like a
storm,
when disaster sweeps over you like a
whirlwind,
when distress and trouble overwhelm
you.

28 "Then they will call to me but I will not
answer;[q]
they will look for me but will not find
me.[r]
29 Since they hated knowledge
and did not choose to fear the LORD,
30 since they would not accept my advice
and spurned my rebuke,[s]

**1:24** n Isa 65:12; 66:4; Jer 7:13; Zec 7:11
**1:26** o Ps 2:4 p Pr 10:24
**1:28** q Isa 1:15; Mic 3:4 r Eze 8:18; Zec 7:13
**1:30** s Ps 81:11

[a]7 The Hebrew words rendered *fool* in Proverbs, and often elsewhere in the Old Testament, denote one who is morally deficient. [b]12 Hebrew *Sheol* [c]21 Hebrew; Septuagint */ on the tops of the walls* [d]22 The Hebrew word rendered *simple* in Proverbs generally denotes one without moral direction and inclined to evil.

# Wisdom Personified

## The Cry of Wisdom

Beginning in Proverbs 1:20, wisdom is portrayed as, and communicated by, a woman. This reveals that there has been, and still can be, an image of femininity that personifies wisdom. This concept in the book of Proverbs calls us to establish the expectation that women will bring to the solution of the world's problems a precious perspective not available from any other source. It calls us to provide a fresh stimulus of challenge and a freeing of dormant powers because wisdom can be and is personified in the women of the world.

Wisdom is not portrayed as the cold, objective, dispassionate scholar. Instead, she cries her message all over town. She has a strange conviction that she cannot repress, and her "scholarship" is so centered on human concerns that she exceeds the bounds of dignity. Because she is in dialogue with people at the market, the courts, the highways and the lofty walls of mass communication, she will not be caught out of touch with human realities and existential concerns. Perhaps because she is a mother as well as a sage, she cannot view that which affects mothers' children with the detachment of a professor. She demands that her insights be implemented, and she is the personification of passionate practicality, as opposed to the almost helpless female.

Wisdom demands application. She insists on being a doer of truth rather than a hearer only. The fact that she must cry out her message seems to suggest that she does not have the power to apply her principles arbitrarily. But she does not hide behind her lack of authority. She goes out and risks her image, choosing rather to have tried and lost than never to have tried at all. Wisdom is not a distant dilettante or pretty patron. She rolls up her sleeves and goes to work. She goes out into the marketplace.

Wisdom must never cease her cry. And we must never cease to expect her to cry out and save us. If we do, we will perish.

—E. Pearson Mitchell

### reflection

*How will you apply wisdom?*

*Live as a wise woman today.*

### read

Proverbs 1:20–33.

**See also** the Inspire Notes "Discernment," "Responsible Decisions in Leadership" and "Seek Wisdom," and the Women of the Bible Notes "Abigail: A Wise Wife" and "The Queen of Sheba: In Search of True Wisdom."

For the next Women of the Bible note, go to page 743.

1:31 t Job 4:8; Isa 3:11; Jer 6:19
1:33 u Ps 25:12
2:4 v Pr 3:14; Mt 13:44
2:6 w 1Ki 3:9,12; Jas 1:5
2:7 x Ps 84:11
2:8 y 1Sa 2:9; Ps 66:9
2:11 z Pr 6:22
2:13 a Jn 3:19
2:14 b Jer 11:15

31 they will eat the fruit of their ways
and be filled with the fruit of their schemes.[t]
32 For the waywardness of the simple will kill them,
and the complacency of fools will destroy them;
33 but whoever listens to me will live in safety[u]
and be at ease, without fear of harm."

## Moral Benefits of Wisdom

2 My son, if you accept my words
and store up my commands within you,
2 turning your ear to wisdom
and applying your heart to understanding,
3 and if you call out for insight
and cry aloud for understanding,
4 and if you look for it as for silver
and search for it as for hidden treasure,[v]
5 then you will understand the fear of the LORD
and find the knowledge of God.
6 For the LORD gives wisdom,[w]
and from his mouth come knowledge and understanding.
7 He holds victory in store for the upright,
he is a shield to those whose walk is blameless,[x]
8 for he guards the course of the just
and protects the way of his faithful ones.[y]

9 Then you will understand what is right and just
and fair—every good path.
10 For wisdom will enter your heart,
and knowledge will be pleasant to your soul.
11 Discretion will protect you,
and understanding will guard you.[z]

12 Wisdom will save you from the ways of wicked men,
from men whose words are perverse,
13 who leave the straight paths
to walk in dark ways,[a]
14 who delight in doing wrong
and rejoice in the perverseness of evil,[b]
15 whose paths are crooked[c]
and who are devious in their ways.

16 It will save you also from the adulteress,
from the wayward wife with her seductive words,
17 who has left the partner of her youth
and ignored the covenant she made before God.[a][d]
18 For her house leads down to death
and her paths to the spirits of the dead.[e]
19 None who go to her return
or attain the paths of life.

20 Thus you will walk in the ways of good men
and keep to the paths of the righteous.
21 For the upright will live in the land,[f]
and the blameless will remain in it;
22 but the wicked will be cut off from the land,
and the unfaithful will be torn from it.

## Further Benefits of Wisdom

3 My son, do not forget my teaching,
but keep my commands in your heart,
2 for they will prolong your life many years
and bring you prosperity.

3 Let love and faithfulness never leave you;
bind them around your neck,
write them on the tablet of your heart.
4 Then you will win favor and a good name
in the sight of God and man.

5 Trust in the LORD[g] with all your heart
and lean not on your own understanding;
6 in all your ways acknowledge him,
and he will make your paths[h] straight.[b]

7 Do not be wise in your own eyes;[i]
fear the LORD and shun evil.[j]
8 This will bring health to your body
and nourishment to your bones.[k]

9 Honor the LORD with your wealth,
with the firstfruits of all your crops;
10 then your barns will be filled[l] to overflowing,
and your vats will brim over with new wine.

2:15 c Ps 125:5
2:17 d Mal 2:14
2:18 e Pr 7:27
2:21 f Ps 37:29
3:5 g Ps 37:3,5
3:6 h 1Ch 28:9
3:7 i Ro 12:16; j Pr 16:6
3:8 k Job 21:24
3:10 l Dt 28:8

[a] 17 Or *covenant of her God* [b] 6 Or *will direct your paths*

# Inspire

## RAISING CHILDREN: MODELING DISCIPLESHIP

Raising children is filled with challenges, victories, joys and sorrows—learning experiences for you and hope for your children. Raising children includes introducing them to God at an early age and persevering through the process of making them disciples.

There are no perfect parents. Yet learning to listen both to God and our children will facilitate the task of transforming our children from parent-controlled youngsters into self-controlled, independent decision makers. Proverbs 3:5–6 reminds us that God guides us perfectly. Whether we need to make important, life-changing decisions or just daily choices, we can trust God to show us the way. In turn, when our children see us leaning and trusting on God for each decision, they will learn to live a God-controlled lifestyle too. From our example, our children will learn to make wise, God-honoring decisions.

The Bible teaches us that children are entitled to be respected for their childlike opinions. Yet God also teaches us to correct unacceptable behavior. Correcting bad behavior promptly will prevent negative patterns from being established. Discipline helps children to understand that their disobedience is not only disobedience of their parents, but disobedience of God as well.

Listening to God, introducing children to Christ as babies, listening actively to our children and offering parental guidance will enable children to make good decisions throughout their lives. Consistent spiritual nurturing will provide a basis for a godly life and will help our children learn to lean on God for understanding.

—F. A. Sourie Johnson

For the next Inspire note, go to page 752.

### read

Proverbs 3:5–6; 22:6; Ephesians 6:1–4; Hebrews 12:7–11.

**See also** the Inspire Notes "A Great Challenge: Teaching Our Children," "Motherhood," "Parenting," "Children: A Blessed Heritage From God" and "Nurturing Spiritual Gifts in Our Children," and the Women of the Bible Notes "Daughter of Jairus: A Testament of Faith," "Herodias and Salome: Evil Choices" and "Mary, the Mother of Jesus: A Model of Motherhood."

### WOMAN of COLOR

How do you lean and depend on God to make all of your decisions? How can your actions be an example for the children in your life?

[11] My son, do not despise the LORD's
discipline
and do not resent his rebuke,
[12] because the LORD disciplines those he
loves,
as a father[a] the son he delights in.[m]

[13] Blessed is the man who finds wisdom,
the man who gains understanding,
[14] for she is more profitable than silver
and yields better returns than gold.[n]
[15] She is more precious than rubies;
nothing you desire can compare with
her.
[16] Long life is in her right hand;
in her left hand are riches and honor.
[17] Her ways are pleasant ways,
and all her paths are peace.
[18] She is a tree of life[o] to those who embrace
her;
those who lay hold of her will be
blessed.

[19] By wisdom the LORD laid the earth's
foundations,[p]
by understanding he set the heavens
in place;
[20] by his knowledge the deeps were
divided,
and the clouds let drop the dew.

[21] My son, preserve sound judgment and
discernment,
do not let them out of your sight;
[22] they will be life for you,
an ornament to grace your neck.[q]
[23] Then you will go on your way in safety,
and your foot will not stumble;
[24] when you lie down,[r] you will not be
afraid;
when you lie down, your sleep will be
sweet.
[25] Have no fear of sudden disaster
or of the ruin that overtakes the
wicked,
[26] for the LORD will be your confidence
and will keep your foot from being
snared.

[27] Do not withhold good from those who
deserve it,
when it is in your power to act.
[28] Do not say to your neighbor,
"Come back later; I'll give it
tomorrow"—
when you now have it with you.[s]
[29] Do not plot harm against your neighbor,
who lives trustfully near you.
[30] Do not accuse a man for no reason—
when he has done you no harm.

[31] Do not envy[t] a violent man
or choose any of his ways,
[32] for the LORD detests a perverse man
but takes the upright into his
confidence.[u]
[33] The LORD's curse[v] is on the house of the
wicked,
but he blesses the home of the
righteous.
[34] He mocks proud mockers
but gives grace to the humble.[w]
[35] The wise inherit honor,
but fools he holds up to shame.

## Wisdom Is Supreme

4 Listen, my sons,[x] to a father's
instruction;
pay attention and gain understanding.
[2] I give you sound learning,
so do not forsake my teaching.
[3] When I was a boy in my father's house,
still tender, and an only child of my
mother,
[4] he taught me and said,
"Lay hold of my words with all your
heart;
keep my commands and you will
live.[y]
[5] Get wisdom, get understanding;
do not forget my words or swerve from
them.
[6] Do not forsake wisdom, and she will
protect you;[z]
love her, and she will watch over you.
[7] Wisdom is supreme; therefore get
wisdom.
Though it cost all you have,[b] get
understanding.
[8] Esteem her, and she will exalt you;
embrace her, and she will honor you.
[9] She will set a garland of grace on your
head

**3:12** m Dt 8:5; Heb 12:5–6*
**3:14** n Job 28:15
**3:18** o Ge 2:9
**3:19** p Ps 104:24
**3:22** q Pr 1:8–9
**3:24** r Ps 3:5
**3:28** s Lev 19:13
**3:31** t Ps 37:1
**3:32** u Ps 25:14
**3:33** v Mal 2:2
**3:34** w Jas 4:6*; 1Pe 5:5*
**4:1** x Pr 1:8
**4:4** y Pr 7:2
**4:6** z 2Th 2:10

[a]12 Hebrew; Septuagint / *and he punishes* [b]7 Or *Whatever else you get*

and present you with a crown of
splendor.[a]"
10 Listen, my son, accept what I say,
and the years of your life will be many.[b]
11 I guide you in the way of wisdom
and lead you along straight paths.
12 When you walk, your steps will not be
hampered;
when you run, you will not stumble.
13 Hold on to instruction, do not let it go;
guard it well, for it is your life.
14 Do not set foot on the path of the wicked
or walk in the way of evil men.[c]
15 Avoid it, do not travel on it;
turn from it and go on your way.
16 For they cannot sleep till they do evil;[d]
they are robbed of slumber till they
make someone fall.
17 They eat the bread of wickedness
and drink the wine of violence.

18 The path of the righteous is like the first
gleam of dawn,
shining ever brighter till the full light
of day.[e]
19 But the way of the wicked is like deep
darkness;[f]
they do not know what makes them
stumble.

20 My son, pay attention to what I say;
listen closely to my words.
21 Do not let them out of your sight,[g]
keep them within your heart;
22 for they are life to those who find them
and health to a man's whole body.[h]
23 Above all else, guard your heart,
for it is the wellspring of life.
24 Put away perversity from your mouth;
keep corrupt talk far from your lips.
25 Let your eyes look straight ahead,
fix your gaze directly before you.
26 Make level[a] paths for your feet[i]
and take only ways that are firm.
27 Do not swerve to the right or the left;[j]
keep your foot from evil.

## Warning Against Adultery

5 My son, pay attention to my wisdom,
listen well to my words of insight,
2 that you may maintain discretion
and your lips may preserve knowledge.
3 For the lips of an adulteress drip honey,
and her speech is smoother than oil;[k]
4 but in the end she is bitter as gall,[l]
sharp as a double-edged sword.
5 Her feet go down to death;
her steps lead straight to the grave.[b][m]
6 She gives no thought to the way of life;
her paths are crooked, but she knows
it not.

7 Now then, my sons, listen to me;
do not turn aside from what I say.
8 Keep to a path far from her,
do not go near the door of her house,
9 lest you give your best strength to others
and your years to one who is cruel,
10 lest strangers feast on your wealth
and your toil enrich another man's
house.
11 At the end of your life you will groan,
when your flesh and body are spent.
12 You will say, "How I hated discipline!
How my heart spurned correction![n]
13 I would not obey my teachers
or listen to my instructors.
14 I have come to the brink of utter ruin
in the midst of the whole assembly."

15 Drink water from your own cistern,
running water from your own well.
16 Should your springs overflow in the
streets,
your streams of water in the public
squares?
17 Let them be yours alone,
never to be shared with strangers.
18 May your fountain be blessed,
and may you rejoice in the wife of your
youth.[o]
19 A loving doe, a graceful deer[p]—
may her breasts satisfy you always,
may you ever be captivated by her
love.
20 Why be captivated, my son, by an
adulteress?
Why embrace the bosom of another
man's wife?
21 For a man's ways are in full view[q] of the
LORD,
and he examines all his paths.[r]

[a]26 Or *Consider the* [b]5 Hebrew *Sheol*

**4:9** a Pr 1:8–9
**4:10** b Pr 3:2
**4:14** c Ps 1:1; Pr 1:15
**4:16** d Ps 36:4
**4:18** e 2Sa 23:4
**4:19** f Job 18:5; Isa 59:9–10; Jn 12:35
**4:21** g Pr 3:21
**4:22** h Pr 3:8; 12:18
**4:26** i Heb 12:13*
**4:27** j Dt 5:32; 28:14
**5:3** k Ps 55:21; Pr 2:16
**5:4** l Ecc 7:26
**5:5** m Pr 7:26–27
**5:12** n Pr 1:29; 12:1
**5:18** o Mal 2:14
**5:19** p SS 2:9; 4:5
**5:21** q Hos 7:2 r Job 31:4; 34:21; Pr 15:3; Jer 16:17; Heb 4:13

5:22 s Ps 9:16
5:23 t Job 4:21; 36:12
6:1 u Pr 11:15
6:4 v Ps 132:4
6:14 w Mic 2:1 x ver 16–19
6:15 y 2Ch 36:16

22 The evil deeds of a wicked man ensnare
him;[s]
the cords of his sin hold him fast.
23 He will die for lack of discipline,[t]
led astray by his own great folly.

## Warnings Against Folly

6 My son, if you have put up security for
your neighbor,
if you have struck hands in pledge[u] for
another,
2 if you have been trapped by what you
said,
ensnared by the words of your mouth,
3 then do this, my son, to free yourself,
since you have fallen into your
neighbor's hands:
Go and humble yourself;
press your plea with your neighbor!
4 Allow no sleep to your eyes,
no slumber to your eyelids.[v]
5 Free yourself, like a gazelle from the hand
of the hunter,
like a bird from the snare of the fowler.

6 Go to the ant, you sluggard;
consider its ways and be wise!
7 It has no commander,
no overseer or ruler,
8 yet it stores its provisions in summer
and gathers its food at harvest.

9 How long will you lie there, you sluggard?
When will you get up from your sleep?
10 A little sleep, a little slumber,
a little folding of the hands to rest—
11 and poverty will come on you like a
bandit
and scarcity like an armed man.[a]

12 A scoundrel and villain,
who goes about with a corrupt mouth,
13 who winks with his eye,
signals with his feet
and motions with his fingers,
14 who plots evil[w] with deceit in his
heart—
he always stirs up dissension.[x]
15 Therefore disaster will overtake him in
an instant;
he will suddenly be destroyed—
without remedy.[y]

16 There are six things the LORD hates,
seven that are detestable to him:
17 haughty eyes,
a lying tongue,[z]
hands that shed innocent blood,[a]
18 a heart that devises wicked
schemes,
feet that are quick to rush into evil,[b]
19 a false witness[c] who pours out lies
and a man who stirs up dissension
among brothers.

## Warning Against Adultery

20 My son, keep your father's commands
and do not forsake your mother's
teaching.
21 Bind them upon your heart forever;
fasten them around your neck.[d]
22 When you walk, they will guide you;
when you sleep, they will watch over
you;
when you awake, they will speak to
you.
23 For these commands are a lamp,
this teaching is a light,[e]
and the corrections of discipline
are the way to life,
24 keeping you from the immoral woman,
from the smooth tongue of the
wayward wife.
25 Do not lust in your heart after her
beauty
or let her captivate you with her eyes,
26 for the prostitute reduces you to a loaf of
bread,
and the adulteress preys upon your
very life.[f]
27 Can a man scoop fire into his lap
without his clothes being burned?
28 Can a man walk on hot coals
without his feet being scorched?
29 So is he who sleeps with another man's
wife;
no one who touches her will go
unpunished.

30 Men do not despise a thief if he steals
to satisfy his hunger when he is
starving.
31 Yet if he is caught, he must pay
sevenfold,[g]

6:17 z Ps 120:2 a Isa 1:15
6:18 b Ge 6:5
6:19 c Ps 27:12
6:21 d Pr 3:3; 7:1–3
6:23 e Ps 19:8
6:26 f Pr 7:22–23; 29:3
6:31 g Ex 22:1–14

[a]11 Or *like a vagrant / and scarcity like a beggar*

6:32 h Pr7:7
7:1 i Pr2:1
7:2 j Pr4:4
7:3 k Dt6:8; Pr3:3
7:7 l Pr6:32
7:9 m Job24:15
7:11 n Pr9:13; 1Ti5:13

though it costs him all the wealth of
his house.
32 But a man who commits adultery lacks
judgment;[h]
whoever does so destroys himself.
33 Blows and disgrace are his lot,
and his shame will never be wiped
away;
34 for jealousy arouses a husband's fury,
and he will show no mercy when he
takes revenge.
35 He will not accept any compensation;
he will refuse the bribe, however great
it is.

## Warning Against the Adulteress

7 My son,[i] keep my words
and store up my commands within
you.
2 Keep my commands and you will live;[j]
guard my teachings as the apple of
your eye.
3 Bind them on your fingers;
write them on the tablet of your heart.[k]
4 Say to wisdom, "You are my sister,"
and call understanding your kinsman;
5 they will keep you from the adulteress,
from the wayward wife with her
seductive words.

6 At the window of my house
I looked out through the lattice.
7 I saw among the simple,
I noticed among the young men,
a youth who lacked judgment.[l]
8 He was going down the street near her
corner,
walking along in the direction of her
house
9 at twilight,[m] as the day was fading,
as the dark of night set in.

10 Then out came a woman to meet him,
dressed like a prostitute and with
crafty intent.
11 (She is loud[n] and defiant,
her feet never stay at home;
12 now in the street, now in the squares,
at every corner she lurks.)
13 She took hold of him and kissed him
and with a brazen face she said:

14 "I have fellowship offerings[a] at home;
today I fulfilled my vows.
15 So I came out to meet you;
I looked for you and have found you!
16 I have covered my bed
with colored linens from Egypt.
17 I have perfumed my bed
with myrrh, aloes and cinnamon.
18 Come, let's drink deep of love till
morning;
let's enjoy ourselves with love!
19 My husband is not at home;
he has gone on a long journey.
20 He took his purse filled with money
and will not be home till full moon."

21 With persuasive words she led him
astray;
she seduced him with her smooth talk.[o]
22 All at once he followed her
like an ox going to the slaughter,
like a deer[b] stepping into a noose[c]
23 till an arrow pierces his liver,
like a bird darting into a snare,
little knowing it will cost him his life.[p]

24 Now then, my sons, listen to me;
pay attention to what I say.
25 Do not let your heart turn to her ways
or stray into her paths.
26 Many are the victims she has brought
down;
her slain are a mighty throng.
27 Her house is a highway to the grave,[d]
leading down to the chambers of
death.[q]

## Wisdom's Call

8 Does not wisdom call out?[r]
Does not understanding raise her
voice?
2 On the heights along the way,
where the paths meet, she takes her
stand;
3 beside the gates leading into the city,
at the entrances, she cries aloud:
4 "To you, O men, I call out;
I raise my voice to all mankind.
5 You who are simple, gain prudence;
you who are foolish, gain
understanding.

7:21 o Pr5:3
7:23 p Ecc9:12
7:27 q Pr2:18; 5:5; 9:18
8:1 r Pr1:20; 9:3

[a]14 Traditionally *peace offerings* [b]22 Syriac (see also Septuagint); Hebrew *fool* [c]22 The meaning of the Hebrew for this line is uncertain. [d]27 Hebrew *Sheol*

# The Adulteress of Proverbs

## The Path to Death

Proverbs 5–7 gives a loud warning about involvement with the adulteress. The adulteress is an immoral woman and an unfaithful wife. She heads down a crooked path that leads to death. Her seductive speech is deceptive and cunning, resulting in an unhealthy, heart-crushing experience.

Her marriage vows are openly broken and disregarded. She has forgotten the covenant words of God. She describes the sex act to lure the man to her bed (see Pr 7:16–18). Her trap is set during the night; she approaches boldly, dressed like a prostitute (see Pr 7:10–15), inviting the man to her house, assuring him of their privacy (see Pr 7:19–20), and while flattering him, she then traps him (see Pr 7:21–23).

The adulteress wants to possess the soul of her victim and take his strength. She causes a wound and brings dishonor to his life (see Pr 6:33). His life is stricken in many ways: his body may become diseased (see Pr 5:11); he may become publicly disgraced (see Pr 5:14); and his soul may be destroyed (see Pr 6:32; 7:27).

Proverbs gives several ways a man can avoid the adulteress: He must pay attention to wisdom (see Pr 5:1), avoid the adulteress's door (see Pr 5:8), keep the law of God in his heart (see Pr 7:1–3), and be ravished always with the sexual love of his wife (see Pr 5:15–19).

The African American woman is seen, at times, as the spiritual strength of the family. When the adulteress taints her life, it is devastating to her marriage and spirit. It poisons the husband-wife relationship, breaking trust, and it eats away at the wife's ability to love. She can lose the ability to fulfill the marriage commitment, be afraid to trust, and avoid openness with her spouse. Sad to say, adultery can lead to divorce, which divides her family and makes trusting another man difficult.

The adulteress is no one to envy, for her path leads to destruction. But Jesus can forgive her sins (see Jn 8:1–11) and create a clean heart within her. She can become a woman devoted to Jesus, and she can receive eternal life, instead of being a woman who leads another life to death. Certainly the Word of God provides a healing balm and guiding light for every woman.

—G. London

### reflection

*How has the Word of God provided a healing balm and guiding light for you?*

*Share your testimony with a woman who needs to hear some good news today.*

### read

Proverbs 5–7.
See also the Inspire Notes "Grace and Mercy," "Adultery," "Temptation" and "Forgiveness: God's Extended Mercy," and the Women of the Bible Notes "Bathsheba: A Silent Affair," "Gomer: An Unfaithful Wife" and "The Forgiven Adulteress: Caught but Not Condemned."

For the next Women of the Bible note, go to page 769.

**8:11** s Job 28:17–19 t Pr 3:13–15
**8:13** u Pr 16:6
**8:14** v Ecc 7:19
**8:15** w Da 2:21; Ro 13:1
**8:17** x 1Sa 2:30; Jn 14:21–24 y Jas 1:5
**8:18** z Pr 3:16 a Mt 6:33
**8:19** b Pr 3:13–14

6 Listen, for I have worthy things to say;
I open my lips to speak what is right.
7 My mouth speaks what is true,
for my lips detest wickedness.
8 All the words of my mouth are just;
none of them is crooked or perverse.
9 To the discerning all of them are right;
they are faultless to those who have knowledge.
10 Choose my instruction instead of silver,
knowledge rather than choice gold,
11 for wisdom is more precious[s] than rubies,
and nothing you desire can compare with her.[t]

12 "I, wisdom, dwell together with prudence;
I possess knowledge and discretion.
13 To fear the LORD is to hate evil;[u]
I hate pride and arrogance,
evil behavior and perverse speech.
14 Counsel and sound judgment are mine;
I have understanding and power.[v]
15 By me kings reign
and rulers[w] make laws that are just;
16 by me princes govern,
and all nobles who rule on earth.[a]
17 I love those who love me,[x]
and those who seek me find me.[y]
18 With me are riches and honor,[z]
enduring wealth and prosperity.[a]
19 My fruit is better than fine gold;
what I yield surpasses choice silver.[b]
20 I walk in the way of righteousness,
along the paths of justice,
21 bestowing wealth on those who love me
and making their treasuries full.

22 "The LORD brought me forth as the first of his works,[b,c]
before his deeds of old;
23 I was appointed[d] from eternity,
from the beginning, before the world began.
24 When there were no oceans, I was given birth,
when there were no springs abounding with water;
25 before the mountains were settled in place,
before the hills, I was given birth,
26 before he made the earth or its fields
or any of the dust of the world.
27 I was there when he set the heavens in place,
when he marked out the horizon on the face of the deep,
28 when he established the clouds above
and fixed securely the fountains of the deep,
29 when he gave the sea its boundary[c]
so the waters would not overstep his command,
and when he marked out the foundations of the earth.[d]
30 Then I was the craftsman at his side.[e]
I was filled with delight day after day,
rejoicing always in his presence,
31 rejoicing in his whole world
and delighting in mankind.[f]

32 "Now then, my sons, listen to me;
blessed are[g] those who keep my ways.
33 Listen to my instruction and be wise;
do not ignore it.
34 Blessed is the man who listens to me,
watching daily at my doors,
waiting at my doorway.
35 For whoever finds me finds life
and receives favor from the LORD.
36 But whoever fails to find me harms himself;
all who hate me love death."

## Invitations of Wisdom and of Folly

9 Wisdom has built[h] her house;
she has hewn out its seven pillars.
2 She has prepared her meat and mixed her wine;
she has also set her table.
3 She has sent out her maids, and she calls[i]
from the highest point of the city.
4 "Let all who are simple come in here!"
she says to those who lack judgment.[j]
5 "Come, eat my food
and drink the wine I have mixed.[k]
6 Leave your simple ways and you will live;
walk in the way of understanding.

**8:29** c Job 38:10 d Job 38:5
**8:30** e Jn 1:1–3
**8:31** f Ps 16:3
**8:32** g Lk 11:28
**9:1** h Eph 2:20–22; 1Pe 2:5
**9:3** i Pr 8:1–3
**9:4** j Pr 6:32
**9:5** k Isa 55:1

[a]16 Many Hebrew manuscripts and Septuagint; most Hebrew manuscripts *and nobles—all righteous rulers* [b]22 Or *way*; or *dominion* [c]22 Or *The LORD possessed me at the beginning of his work*; or *The LORD brought me forth at the beginning of his work* [d]23 Or *fashioned*

9:8
l Ps 141:5

9:9
m Pr 1:5,7

9:10
n Job 28:28; Pr 1:7

9:11
o Pr 3:16

9:13
p Pr 7:11

9:14
q ver 3

9:17
r Pr 20:17

7 "Whoever corrects a mocker invites
insult;
whoever rebukes a wicked man incurs
abuse.
8 Do not rebuke a mocker or he will hate
you;
rebuke a wise man and he will love
you.[l]
9 Instruct a wise man and he will be wiser
still;
teach a righteous man and he will add
to his learning.[m]
10 "The fear of the LORD[n] is the beginning of
wisdom,
and knowledge of the Holy One is
understanding.

*Searching one,*

*Wisdom begins with me.*

*Seek and you will find.*

*The Fount of Wisdom*

PROVERBS 9:10

11 For through me your days will be many,
and years will be added to your life.[o]
12 If you are wise, your wisdom will reward
you;
if you are a mocker, you alone will
suffer."

13 The woman Folly is loud;[p]
she is undisciplined and without
knowledge.
14 She sits at the door of her house,
on a seat at the highest point of the city,[q]
15 calling out to those who pass by,
who go straight on their way.
16 "Let all who are simple come in here!"
she says to those who lack judgment.
17 "Stolen water is sweet;
food eaten in secret is delicious!"[r]
18 But little do they know that the dead are
there,
that her guests are in the depths of the
grave.[a]

## Proverbs of Solomon

10:1
s Pr 15:20

10:4
t Pr 13:4

10:9
u Isa 33:15
v Ps 23:4
w Pr 28:18

10:11
x Ps 37:30

10:12
y 1Pe 4:8

10:13
z Pr 26:3

10 The proverbs of Solomon:

A wise son brings joy to his father,[s]
but a foolish son grief to his mother.

2 Ill-gotten treasures are of no value,
but righteousness delivers from death.

3 The LORD does not let the righteous go
hungry
but he thwarts the craving of the
wicked.

4 Lazy hands make a man poor,
but diligent hands bring wealth.[t]

5 He who gathers crops in summer is a
wise son,
but he who sleeps during harvest is a
disgraceful son.

6 Blessings crown the head of the
righteous,
but violence overwhelms the mouth of
the wicked.[b]

7 The memory of the righteous will be a
blessing,
but the name of the wicked will rot.

8 The wise in heart accept commands,
but a chattering fool comes to ruin.

9 The man of integrity[u] walks securely,[v]
but he who takes crooked paths will be
found out.[w]

10 He who winks maliciously causes grief,
and a chattering fool comes to ruin.

11 The mouth of the righteous is a fountain
of life,[x]
but violence overwhelms the mouth of
the wicked.

12 Hatred stirs up dissension,
but love covers over all wrongs.[y]

13 Wisdom is found on the lips of the
discerning,
but a rod is for the back of him who
lacks judgment.[z]

[a]18 Hebrew *Sheol* [b]6 Or *but the mouth of the wicked conceals violence*; also in verse 11

**10:14** a Pr 18:6,7
**10:19** b Ecc 5:3; Jas 3:2–12
**10:22** c Ge 24:35
**10:23** d Pr 15:21
**10:24** e Ps 145:17–19; Mt 5:6; 1Jn 5:14–15
**10:25** f Ps 15:5

14 Wise men store up knowledge,
but the mouth of a fool invites ruin.[a]

15 The wealth of the rich is their fortified city,
but poverty is the ruin of the poor.

16 The wages of the righteous bring them life,
but the income of the wicked brings them punishment.

17 He who heeds discipline shows the way to life,
but whoever ignores correction leads others astray.

18 He who conceals his hatred has lying lips,
and whoever spreads slander is a fool.

19 When words are many, sin is not absent,
but he who holds his tongue is wise.[b]

20 The tongue of the righteous is choice silver,
but the heart of the wicked is of little value.

21 The lips of the righteous nourish many,
but fools die for lack of judgment.

22 The blessing of the LORD brings wealth,[c]
and he adds no trouble to it.

23 A fool finds pleasure in evil conduct,[d]
but a man of understanding delights in wisdom.

---

*Lord,*

*I desire to be wise. Remind me to seek you in every decision I need to make. I love you.*

*Amen*

PROVERBS 10:23

---

24 What the wicked dreads will overtake him;
what the righteous desire will be granted.[e]

25 When the storm has swept by, the wicked are gone,
but the righteous stand firm[f] forever.

26 As vinegar to the teeth and smoke to the eyes,
so is a sluggard to those who send him.

27 The fear of the LORD adds length to life,[g]
but the years of the wicked are cut short.

28 The prospect of the righteous is joy,
but the hopes of the wicked come to nothing.

29 The way of the LORD is a refuge for the righteous,
but it is the ruin of those who do evil.

30 The righteous will never be uprooted,
but the wicked will not remain in the land.

31 The mouth of the righteous brings forth wisdom,[h]
but a perverse tongue will be cut out.

32 The lips of the righteous know what is fitting,
but the mouth of the wicked only what is perverse.

11 The LORD abhors dishonest scales,[i]
but accurate weights are his delight.

2 When pride comes, then comes disgrace,[j]
but with humility comes wisdom.

3 The integrity of the upright guides them,
but the unfaithful are destroyed by their duplicity.[k]

4 Wealth is worthless in the day of wrath,[l]
but righteousness delivers from death.[m]

5 The righteousness of the blameless makes a straight way for them,
but the wicked are brought down by their own wickedness.

6 The righteousness of the upright delivers them,
but the unfaithful are trapped by evil desires.

7 When a wicked man dies, his hope perishes;
all he expected from his power comes to nothing.[n]

**10:27** g Pr 9:10–11
**10:31** h Ps 37:30
**11:1** i Lev 19:36; Dt 25:13–16
**11:2** j Pr 16:18
**11:3** k Pr 13:6
**11:4** l Eze 7:19; Zep 1:18 m Ge 7:1
**11:7** n Pr 10:28

11:13
o Lev 19:16; Pr 20:19

11:18
p Hos 10:12–13

8 The righteous man is rescued from
trouble,
and it comes on the wicked instead.

9 With his mouth the godless destroys his
neighbor,
but through knowledge the righteous
escape.

10 When the righteous prosper, the city
rejoices;
when the wicked perish, there are
shouts of joy.

11 Through the blessing of the upright a city
is exalted,
but by the mouth of the wicked it is
destroyed.

12 A man who lacks judgment derides his
neighbor,
but a man of understanding holds his
tongue.

13 A gossip betrays a confidence,[o]
but a trustworthy man keeps a secret.

14 For lack of guidance a nation falls,
but many advisers make victory sure.

15 He who puts up security for another will
surely suffer,
but whoever refuses to strike hands in
pledge is safe.

16 A kindhearted woman gains respect,
but ruthless men gain only wealth.

17 A kind man benefits himself,
but a cruel man brings trouble on
himself.

18 The wicked man earns deceptive wages,
but he who sows righteousness reaps a
sure reward.[p]

19 The truly righteous man attains life,
but he who pursues evil goes to his
death.

20 The LORD detests men of perverse heart
but he delights in those whose ways
are blameless.

21 Be sure of this: The wicked will not go
unpunished,
but those who are righteous will go
free.

22 Like a gold ring in a pig's snout
is a beautiful woman who shows no
discretion.

23 The desire of the righteous ends only in
good,
but the hope of the wicked only in
wrath.

24 One man gives freely, yet gains even
more;
another withholds unduly, but comes
to poverty.

25 A generous man will prosper;
he who refreshes others will himself be
refreshed.[q]

26 People curse the man who hoards grain,
but blessing crowns him who is willing
to sell.

27 He who seeks good finds goodwill,
but evil comes to him who searches
for it.[r]

28 Whoever trusts in his riches will fall,[s]
but the righteous will thrive like a
green leaf.[t]

29 He who brings trouble on his family will
inherit only wind,
and the fool will be servant to the wise.

30 The fruit of the righteous is a tree of
life,[u]
and he who wins souls is wise.

31 If the righteous receive their due on
earth,
how much more the ungodly and the
sinner!

12 Whoever loves discipline loves
knowledge,
but he who hates correction is stupid.

2 A good man obtains favor from the LORD,
but the LORD condemns a crafty man.

3 A man cannot be established through
wickedness,
but the righteous cannot be uprooted.[v]

4 A wife of noble character is her husband's
crown,
but a disgraceful wife is like decay in
his bones.[w]

11:25
q Mt 5:7; 2Co 9:6–9

11:27
r Est 7:10; Ps 7:15–16

11:28
s Mk 10:25; 1Ti 6:17
t Ps 1:3; Jer 17:8

11:30
u Jas 5:20

12:3
v Pr 10:25

12:4
w Pr 14:30

> *"O, ye daughters of Africa, awake! Arise! No longer sleep nor slumber, but distinguish yourselves. Show forth to the world that ye are endowed with noble and exalted faculties."*
>
> —MARTHA W. STEWART, LECTURER

**12:6** x Pr 14:3
**12:11** y Pr 28:19
**12:13** z 2Pe 2:9
**12:14** a Pr 13:2 b Isa 3:10–11
**12:16** c Pr 29:11

5 The plans of the righteous are just,
but the advice of the wicked is deceitful.

6 The words of the wicked lie in wait for blood,
but the speech of the upright rescues them.[x]

7 Wicked men are overthrown and are no more,
but the house of the righteous stands firm.

8 A man is praised according to his wisdom,
but men with warped minds are despised.

9 Better to be a nobody and yet have a servant
than pretend to be somebody and have no food.

10 A righteous man cares for the needs of his animal,
but the kindest acts of the wicked are cruel.

11 He who works his land will have abundant food,
but he who chases fantasies lacks judgment.[y]

12 The wicked desire the plunder of evil men,
but the root of the righteous flourishes.

13 An evil man is trapped by his sinful talk,
but a righteous man escapes trouble.[z]

14 From the fruit of his lips a man is filled with good things[a]
as surely as the work of his hands rewards him.[b]

15 The way of a fool seems right to him,
but a wise man listens to advice.

16 A fool shows his annoyance at once,
but a prudent man overlooks an insult.[c]

17 A truthful witness gives honest testimony,
but a false witness tells lies.

18 Reckless words pierce like a sword,[d]
but the tongue of the wise brings healing.

19 Truthful lips endure forever,
but a lying tongue lasts only a moment.

20 There is deceit in the hearts of those who plot evil,
but joy for those who promote peace.

21 No harm befalls the righteous,
but the wicked have their fill of trouble.

22 The LORD detests lying lips,[e]
but he delights in men who are truthful.

23 A prudent man keeps his knowledge to himself,[f]
but the heart of fools blurts out folly.

24 Diligent hands will rule,
but laziness ends in slave labor.

25 An anxious heart weighs a man down,[g]
but a kind word cheers him up.

26 A righteous man is cautious in friendship,[a]
but the way of the wicked leads them astray.

27 The lazy man does not roast[b] his game,
but the diligent man prizes his possessions.

28 In the way of righteousness there is life;
along that path is immortality.

13 A wise son heeds his father's instruction,
but a mocker does not listen to rebuke.

2 From the fruit of his lips a man enjoys good things,[h]
but the unfaithful have a craving for violence.

3 He who guards his lips[i] guards his life,
but he who speaks rashly will come to ruin.

**12:18** d Ps 57:4
**12:22** e Rev 22:15
**12:23** f Pr 13:16
**12:25** g Pr 15:13; Isa 50:4
**13:2** h Pr 12:14
**13:3** i Jas 3:2

[a]26 Or *man is a guide to his neighbor* [b]27 The meaning of the Hebrew for this word is uncertain.

13:6 j Pr 11:3,5
13:7 k 2Co 6:10
13:9 l Job 18:5; Pr 24:20
13:13 m 2Ch 36:16
13:14 n Pr 10:11
13:16 o Pr 12:23
13:17 p Pr 25:13

4 The sluggard craves and gets nothing,
but the desires of the diligent are fully satisfied.

5 The righteous hate what is false,
but the wicked bring shame and disgrace.

6 Righteousness guards the man of integrity,
but wickedness overthrows the sinner.[j]

7 One man pretends to be rich, yet has nothing;
another pretends to be poor, yet has great wealth.[k]

8 A man's riches may ransom his life,
but a poor man hears no threat.

9 The light of the righteous shines brightly,
but the lamp of the wicked is snuffed out.[l]

10 Pride only breeds quarrels,
but wisdom is found in those who take advice.

11 Dishonest money dwindles away,
but he who gathers money little by little makes it grow.

12 Hope deferred makes the heart sick,
but a longing fulfilled is a tree of life.

13 He who scorns instruction will pay for it,[m]
but he who respects a command is rewarded.

14 The teaching of the wise is a fountain of life,[n]
turning a man from the snares of death.

15 Good understanding wins favor,
but the way of the unfaithful is hard.[a]

16 Every prudent man acts out of knowledge,
but a fool exposes his folly.[o]

17 A wicked messenger falls into trouble,
but a trustworthy envoy brings healing.[p]

18 He who ignores discipline comes to poverty and shame,
but whoever heeds correction is honored.[q]

19 A longing fulfilled is sweet to the soul,
but fools detest turning from evil.

20 He who walks with the wise grows wise,
but a companion of fools suffers harm.

21 Misfortune pursues the sinner,
but prosperity is the reward of the righteous.[r]

22 A good man leaves an inheritance for his children's children,
but a sinner's wealth is stored up for the righteous.[s]

23 A poor man's field may produce abundant food,
but injustice sweeps it away.

24 He who spares the rod hates his son,
but he who loves him is careful to discipline him.[t]

25 The righteous eat to their hearts' content,
but the stomach of the wicked goes hungry.[u]

14 The wise woman builds her house,
but with her own hands the foolish one tears hers down.

2 He whose walk is upright fears the LORD,
but he whose ways are devious despises him.

3 A fool's talk brings a rod to his back,
but the lips of the wise protect them.[v]

4 Where there are no oxen, the manger is empty,
but from the strength of an ox comes an abundant harvest.

5 A truthful witness does not deceive,
but a false witness pours out lies.[w]

6 The mocker seeks wisdom and finds none,
but knowledge comes easily to the discerning.

7 Stay away from a foolish man,
for you will not find knowledge on his lips.

13:18 q Pr 15:5,31–32
13:21 r Ps 32:10
13:22 s Job 27:17; Ecc 2:26
13:24 t Pr 19:18; 22:15; 29:15,17
13:25 u Ps 34:10
14:3 v Pr 12:6
14:5 w Pr 6:19; 12:17

[a]15 Or *unfaithful does not endure*

14:12 x Pr 16:25
14:13 y Ecc 2:2
14:14 z Pr 1:31 a Pr 12:14
14:16 b Pr 22:3
14:20 c Pr 19:4,7
14:21 d Ps 41:1

8 The wisdom of the prudent is to give
thought to their ways,
but the folly of fools is deception.

9 Fools mock at making amends for sin,
but goodwill is found among the
upright.

10 Each heart knows its own bitterness,
and no one else can share its joy.

11 The house of the wicked will be
destroyed,
but the tent of the upright will flourish.

12 There is a way that seems right to a man,
but in the end it leads to death.[x]

13 Even in laughter[y] the heart may ache,
and joy may end in grief.

14 The faithless will be fully repaid for their
ways,[z]
and the good man rewarded for his.[a]

15 A simple man believes anything,
but a prudent man gives thought to
his steps.

16 A wise man fears the LORD and shuns
evil,[b]
but a fool is hotheaded and reckless.

17 A quick-tempered man does foolish
things,
and a crafty man is hated.

18 The simple inherit folly,
but the prudent are crowned with
knowledge.

19 Evil men will bow down in the presence
of the good,
and the wicked at the gates of the
righteous.

20 The poor are shunned even by their
neighbors,
but the rich have many friends.[c]

21 He who despises his neighbor sins,
but blessed is he who is kind to the
needy.[d]

22 Do not those who plot evil go astray?
But those who plan what is good find[a]
love and faithfulness.

23 All hard work brings a profit,
but mere talk leads only to poverty.

24 The wealth of the wise is their crown,
but the folly of fools yields folly.

25 A truthful witness saves lives,
but a false witness is deceitful.[e]

26 He who fears the LORD has a secure
fortress,
and for his children it will be a refuge.

27 The fear of the LORD is a fountain of life,
turning a man from the snares of
death.

28 A large population is a king's glory,
but without subjects a prince is
ruined.

29 A patient man has great understanding,
but a quick-tempered man displays
folly.[f]

30 A heart at peace gives life to the body,
but envy rots the bones.[g]

31 He who oppresses the poor shows
contempt for their Maker,[h]
but whoever is kind to the needy
honors God.

32 When calamity comes, the wicked are
brought down,
but even in death the righteous have
a refuge.[i]

33 Wisdom reposes in the heart of the
discerning[j]
and even among fools she lets herself
be known.[b]

34 Righteousness exalts a nation,
but sin is a disgrace to any people.

35 A king delights in a wise servant,
but a shameful servant incurs his
wrath.[k]

15 A gentle answer turns away wrath,[l]
but a harsh word stirs up anger.

2 The tongue of the wise commends
knowledge,
but the mouth of the fool gushes
folly.[m]

14:25 e ver 5
14:29 f Jas 1:19
14:30 g Pr 12:4
14:31 h Pr 17:5
14:32 i 2Ti 4:18
14:33 j Pr 2:6–10
14:35 k Mt 24:45–51
15:1 l Pr 25:15
15:2 m Pr 12:23

[a]22 Or *show* [b]33 Hebrew; Septuagint and Syriac / *but in the heart of fools she is not known*

15:3 n Heb 4:13
15:8 o Isa 1:11; Jer 6:20
15:9 p 1Ti 6:11
15:11 q Job 26:6; Ps 139:8 r 2Ch 6:30
15:12 s Am 5:10
15:13 t Pr 12:25; 17:22
15:16 u Ps 37:16–17; 1Ti 6:6
15:17 v Pr 17:1

3 The eyes of the LORD are everywhere,[n]
keeping watch on the wicked and the good.

4 The tongue that brings healing is a tree of life,
but a deceitful tongue crushes the spirit.

5 A fool spurns his father's discipline,
but whoever heeds correction shows prudence.

6 The house of the righteous contains great treasure,
but the income of the wicked brings them trouble.

7 The lips of the wise spread knowledge;
not so the hearts of fools.

8 The LORD detests the sacrifice of the wicked,[o]
but the prayer of the upright pleases him.

9 The LORD detests the way of the wicked
but he loves those who pursue righteousness.[p]

10 Stern discipline awaits him who leaves the path;
he who hates correction will die.

11 Death and Destruction[a] lie open before the LORD[q]—
how much more the hearts of men![r]

12 A mocker resents correction;[s]
he will not consult the wise.

13 A happy heart makes the face cheerful,
but heartache crushes the spirit.[t]

14 The discerning heart seeks knowledge,
but the mouth of a fool feeds on folly.

15 All the days of the oppressed are wretched,
but the cheerful heart has a continual feast.

16 Better a little with the fear of the LORD
than great wealth with turmoil.[u]

17 Better a meal of vegetables where there is love
than a fattened calf with hatred.[v]

18 A hot-tempered man stirs up dissension,[w]
but a patient man calms a quarrel.

19 The way of the sluggard is blocked with thorns,
but the path of the upright is a highway.

20 A wise son brings joy to his father,[x]
but a foolish man despises his mother.

21 Folly delights a man who lacks judgment,
but a man of understanding keeps a straight course.

22 Plans fail for lack of counsel,
but with many advisers they succeed.

23 A man finds joy in giving an apt reply—
and how good is a timely word![y]

24 The path of life leads upward for the wise
to keep him from going down to the grave.[b]

25 The LORD tears down the proud man's house[z]
but he keeps the widow's boundaries intact.[a]

26 The LORD detests the thoughts of the wicked,
but those of the pure are pleasing to him.

27 A greedy man brings trouble to his family,
but he who hates bribes will live.

28 The heart of the righteous weighs its answers,[b]
but the mouth of the wicked gushes evil.

29 The LORD is far from the wicked
but he hears the prayer of the righteous.[c]

30 A cheerful look brings joy to the heart,
and good news gives health to the bones.

31 He who listens to a life-giving rebuke
will be at home among the wise.

32 He who ignores discipline despises himself,

15:18 w Pr 26:21
15:20 x Pr 10:1
15:23 y Pr 25:11
15:25 z Pr 12:7 a Ps 68:5–6
15:28 b 1Pe 3:15
15:29 c Ps 145:18–19

[a]11 Hebrew *Sheol and Abaddon* [b]24 Hebrew *Sheol*

Inspire leadership FOCUS

## SEEK WISDOM

In our world of fast cars, fast food, busy schedules, countless appointments and instant communication, we must seek wisdom to gain an understanding and purpose for our lives as Christian women who have been blessed with the responsibility of leadership.

Our society looks for earthly wisdom in life coaches, secular how-to books, television and astrology. God has chosen the foolish things of the world to shame the wise, and God has chosen the weak things of the world to shame the strong (see 1Co 1:27). As Christian women, we will encounter many dilemmas in our homes, on our jobs and in our churches that will test our Christian ethics, beliefs and morals. When we possess Biblical wisdom, we hold in our hands the understanding and power to answer life's complex questions without compromising our faith.

How do we obtain godly wisdom? We must ask God (see Jas 1:5). Wisdom begins with the fear of the Lord and an understanding of him (see Pr 15:33). Those who obtain godly wisdom possess a spirit of discernment of what is right and what is wrong according to the Word of God. If we are to be in alignment with God's heart, as God's women we must actively seek wisdom by reading the Word of God and applying it to every aspect of our lives (see Ps 119:97–104).

Our faithful sisters Abigail, Queen Esther and Rahab were moved by the Holy Spirit in acts of faith and wisdom. As we learn from their examples, we cultivate a desire to have the godly wisdom that they had. Gaining wisdom is a gift from the Lord that is freely given to those who ask. And it is a gift that we must use in our lives as leaders who have been chosen by God for our various responsibilities.

—K. Yancy

### read

Proverbs 1–4; 15.

**See also** the Inspire Notes "Discernment," "Responsible Decisions in Leadership" and "Character," and the Women of the Bible Notes "Acsah: A Wise Daughter," "Abigail: A Wise Wife," "The Queen of Sheba: In Search of True Wisdom" and "Wisdom Personified: The Cry of Wisdom."

### WOMAN of COLOR

Take time daily to seek godly wisdom through reading the Word, praying and meditating. Celebrate this gift and become a *WOW Woman*: a Woman of Wisdom, a Woman of the Word and a Woman of Worship!

For the next Inspire note, go to page 775.

15:33
d Pr 1:7

16:3
e Ps 37:5–6

16:5
f Pr 11:20–21

16:6
g Pr 14:16

16:9
h Jer 10:23

16:12
i Pr 25:5

but whoever heeds correction gains
understanding.

33 The fear of the LORD[d] teaches a man
wisdom,[a]
and humility comes before honor.

# 16

To man belong the plans of the
heart,
but from the LORD comes the reply of
the tongue.

2 All a man's ways seem innocent to him,
but motives are weighed by the LORD.

3 Commit to the LORD whatever you do,
and your plans will succeed.[e]

4 The LORD works out everything for his
own ends—
even the wicked for a day of disaster.

5 The LORD detests all the proud of heart.
Be sure of this: They will not go
unpunished.[f]

6 Through love and faithfulness sin is
atoned for;
through the fear of the LORD a man
avoids evil.[g]

7 When a man's ways are pleasing to the
LORD,
he makes even his enemies live at
peace with him.

8 Better a little with righteousness
than much gain with injustice.

9 In his heart a man plans his course,
but the LORD determines his steps.[h]

10 The lips of a king speak as an oracle,
and his mouth should not betray justice.

11 Honest scales and balances are from the
LORD;
all the weights in the bag are of his
making.

12 Kings detest wrongdoing,
for a throne is established through
righteousness.[i]

13 Kings take pleasure in honest lips;
they value a man who speaks the
truth.

14 A king's wrath is a messenger of death,
but a wise man will appease it.

15 When a king's face brightens, it means
life;[j]
his favor is like a rain cloud in spring.

16 How much better to get wisdom than
gold,
to choose understanding rather than
silver![k]

17 The highway of the upright avoids evil;
he who guards his way guards his life.

18 Pride goes before destruction,
a haughty spirit before a fall.[l]

19 Better to be lowly in spirit and among the
oppressed
than to share plunder with the proud.

20 Whoever gives heed to instruction
prospers,
and blessed is he who trusts in the
LORD.[m]

21 The wise in heart are called discerning,
and pleasant words promote
instruction.[b]

22 Understanding is a fountain of life to
those who have it,
but folly brings punishment to fools.

23 A wise man's heart guides his mouth,
and his lips promote
instruction.[c]

24 Pleasant words are a
honeycomb,
sweet to the soul
and healing to
the bones.

25 There is a way that
seems right to
a man,
but in the end
it leads to
death.[n]

26 The laborer's appetite works for him;
his hunger drives him on.

27 A scoundrel plots evil,
and his speech is like a scorching fire.[o]

*"If there be words of kindness or encouragement speak them now. Someone, somewhere is waiting for them."*
—UNKNOWN

16:15
j Job 29:24

16:16
k Pr 8:10,19

16:18
l Pr 11:2

16:20
m Ps 34:8; Jer 17:7

16:25
n Pr 14:12

16:27
o Jas 3:6

[a] 33 Or *Wisdom teaches the fear of the LORD* [b] 21 Or *words make a man persuasive* [c] 23 Or *mouth / and makes his lips persuasive*

16:28 p Pr 17:9
16:29 q Pr 1:10
16:31 r Pr 20:29
17:1 s Pr 15:16,17
17:3 t Pr 27:21 u Ps 26:2
17:5 v Pr 14:31 w Job 31:29
17:9 x Pr 10:12

28 A perverse man stirs up dissension,
and a gossip separates close friends.[p]

29 A violent man entices his neighbor
and leads him down a path that is not good.[q]

30 He who winks with his eye is plotting perversity;
he who purses his lips is bent on evil.

31 Gray hair is a crown of splendor;[r]
it is attained by a righteous life.

32 Better a patient man than a warrior,
a man who controls his temper than one who takes a city.

33 The lot is cast into the lap,
but its every decision is from the LORD.

17 Better a dry crust with peace and quiet
than a house full of feasting,[a] with strife.[s]

2 A wise servant will rule over a disgraceful son,
and will share the inheritance as one of the brothers.

3 The crucible for silver and the furnace for gold,[t]
but the LORD tests the heart.[u]

4 A wicked man listens to evil lips;
a liar pays attention to a malicious tongue.

5 He who mocks the poor shows contempt for their Maker;[v]
whoever gloats over disaster[w] will not go unpunished.

6 Children's children are a crown to the aged,
and parents are the pride of their children.

7 Arrogant[b] lips are unsuited to a fool—
how much worse lying lips to a ruler!

8 A bribe is a charm to the one who gives it;
wherever he turns, he succeeds.

9 He who covers over an offense promotes love,[x]
but whoever repeats the matter separates close friends.[y]

10 A rebuke impresses a man of discernment
more than a hundred lashes a fool.

11 An evil man is bent only on rebellion;
a merciless official will be sent against him.

12 Better to meet a bear robbed of her cubs
than a fool in his folly.

13 If a man pays back evil[z] for good,
evil will never leave his house.

14 Starting a quarrel is like breaching a dam;
so drop the matter before a dispute breaks out.[a]

15 Acquitting the guilty and condemning the innocent—
the LORD detests them both.[b]

16 Of what use is money in the hand of a fool,
since he has no desire to get wisdom?

17 A friend loves at all times,
and a brother is born for adversity.

18 A man lacking in judgment strikes hands in pledge
and puts up security for his neighbor.[c]

19 He who loves a quarrel loves sin;
he who builds a high gate invites destruction.

20 A man of perverse heart does not prosper;
he whose tongue is deceitful falls into trouble.

21 To have a fool for a son brings grief;
there is no joy for the father of a fool.[d]

22 A cheerful heart is good medicine,
but a crushed spirit dries up the bones.[e]

23 A wicked man accepts a bribe[f] in secret
to pervert the course of justice.

24 A discerning man keeps wisdom in view,
but a fool's eyes[g] wander to the ends of the earth.

17:9 y Pr 16:28
17:13 z Ps 109:4–5; Jer 18:20
17:14 a Pr 20:3
17:15 b Ex 23:6–7; Isa 5:23
17:18 c Pr 6:1–5
17:21 d Pr 10:1
17:22 e Ps 22:15
17:23 f Ex 23:8
17:24 g Ecc 2:14

[a]1 Hebrew *sacrifices* [b]7 Or *Eloquent*

17:25 h Pr 10:1
17:26 i Pr 18:5
17:27 j Jas 1:19
17:28 k Job 13:5
18:5 l Lev 19:15
18:7 m Pr 10:14
18:9 n Pr 28:24
18:10 o 2Sa 22:3
18:11 p Pr 10:15

25 A foolish son brings grief to his father
and bitterness to the one who bore him.[h]

26 It is not good to punish an innocent man,[i]
or to flog officials for their integrity.

27 A man of knowledge uses words with restraint,
and a man of understanding is even-tempered.[j]

28 Even a fool is thought wise if he keeps silent,
and discerning if he holds his tongue.[k]

## 18

An unfriendly man pursues selfish ends;
he defies all sound judgment.

2 A fool finds no pleasure in understanding
but delights in airing his own opinions.

3 When wickedness comes, so does contempt,
and with shame comes disgrace.

4 The words of a man's mouth are deep waters,
but the fountain of wisdom is a bubbling brook.

5 It is not good to be partial to the wicked[l]
or to deprive the innocent of justice.

6 A fool's lips bring him strife,
and his mouth invites a beating.

7 A fool's mouth is his undoing,
and his lips are a snare to his soul.[m]

8 The words of a gossip are like choice morsels;
they go down to a man's inmost parts.

9 One who is slack in his work
is brother to one who destroys.[n]

10 The name of the LORD is a strong tower;[o]
the righteous run to it and are safe.

11 The wealth of the rich is their fortified city;[p]
they imagine it an unscalable wall.

12 Before his downfall a man's heart is proud,
but humility comes before honor.

13 He who answers before listening—
that is his folly and his shame.[q]

14 A man's spirit sustains him in sickness,
but a crushed spirit who can bear?

15 The heart of the discerning acquires knowledge;
the ears of the wise seek it out.

16 A gift[r] opens the way for the giver
and ushers him into the presence of the great.

17 The first to present his case seems right,
till another comes forward and questions him.

18 Casting the lot settles disputes[s]
and keeps strong opponents apart.

19 An offended brother is more unyielding than a fortified city,
and disputes are like the barred gates of a citadel.

20 From the fruit of his mouth a man's stomach is filled;
with the harvest from his lips he is satisfied.[t]

21 The tongue has the power of life and death,
and those who love it will eat its fruit.[u]

22 He who finds a wife finds what is good
and receives favor from the LORD.[v]

23 A poor man pleads for mercy,
but a rich man answers harshly.

24 A man of many companions may come to ruin,
but there is a friend who sticks closer than a brother.[w]

## 19

Better a poor man whose walk is blameless
than a fool whose lips are perverse.[x]

2 It is not good to have zeal without knowledge,
nor to be hasty and miss the way.

3 A man's own folly ruins his life,
yet his heart rages against the LORD.

4 Wealth brings many friends,
but a poor man's friend deserts him.[y]

18:13 q Jn 7:51
18:16 r Ge 32:20
18:18 s Pr 16:33
18:20 t Pr 12:14
18:21 u Mt 12:37
18:22 v Pr 19:14
18:24 w Pr 17:17
19:1 x Pr 28:6
19:4 y Pr 14:20

**19:5** z Ex 23:1
**19:6** a Pr 29:26
**19:7** b Ps 38:11
**19:8** c Pr 16:20
**19:9** d ver 5
**19:11** e Pr 16:32
**19:12** f Pr 16:14–15
**19:13** g Pr 21:9
**19:14** h 2Co 12:14

5 A false witness[z] will not go unpunished,
and he who pours out lies will not go free.

6 Many curry favor with a ruler,[a]
and everyone is the friend of a man who gives gifts.

7 A poor man is shunned by all his relatives—
how much more do his friends avoid him!
Though he pursues them with pleading,
they are nowhere to be found.[a][b]

8 He who gets wisdom loves his own soul;
he who cherishes understanding prospers.[c]

9 A false witness will not go unpunished,
and he who pours out lies will perish.[d]

10 It is not fitting for a fool to live in luxury—
how much worse for a slave to rule over princes!

11 A man's wisdom gives him patience;[e]
it is to his glory to overlook an offense.

*God,*

*you know how badly I need patience. Teach me always to wait on you for all things and to demonstrate your love and mercy to others. In Jesus' gracious name,*

*Amen*

PROVERBS 19:11

12 A king's rage is like the roar of a lion,
but his favor is like dew on the grass.[f]

13 A foolish son is his father's ruin,
and a quarrelsome wife is like a constant dripping.[g]

14 Houses and wealth are inherited from parents,[h]
but a prudent wife is from the LORD.

15 Laziness brings on deep sleep,
and the shiftless man goes hungry.[i]

16 He who obeys instructions guards his life,
but he who is contemptuous of his ways will die.[j]

17 He who is kind to the poor lends to the LORD,
and he will reward him for what he has done.[k]

18 Discipline your son, for in that there is hope;
do not be a willing party to his death.[l]

19 A hot-tempered man must pay the penalty;
if you rescue him, you will have to do it again.

20 Listen to advice and accept instruction,
and in the end you will be wise.

21 Many are the plans in a man's heart,
but it is the LORD's purpose that prevails.[m]

22 What a man desires is unfailing love[b];
better to be poor than a liar.

23 The fear of the LORD leads to life:
Then one rests content, untouched by trouble.[n]

24 The sluggard buries his hand in the dish;
he will not even bring it back to his mouth![o]

25 Flog a mocker, and the simple will learn prudence;
rebuke a discerning man, and he will gain knowledge.[p]

26 He who robs his father and drives out his mother[q]
is a son who brings shame and disgrace.

27 Stop listening to instruction, my son,
and you will stray from the words of knowledge.

28 A corrupt witness mocks at justice,
and the mouth of the wicked gulps down evil.[r]

**19:15** i Pr 6:9
**19:16** j Lk 10:28
**19:17** k Mt 10:42
**19:18** l Pr 13:24
**19:21** m Ps 33:11
**19:23** n Pr 12:21
**19:24** o Pr 26:15
**19:25** p Pr 9:9
**19:26** q Pr 28:24
**19:28** r Job 15:16

[a]7 The meaning of the Hebrew for this sentence is uncertain. [b]22 Or *A man's greed is his shame*

29 Penalties are prepared for mockers,
and beatings for the backs of fools.[s]

# 20

Wine is a mocker and beer a brawler;
whoever is led astray by them is not wise.

2 A king's wrath is like the roar of a lion;[t]
he who angers him forfeits his life.[u]

3 It is to a man's honor to avoid strife,
but every fool is quick to quarrel.[v]

4 A sluggard does not plow in season;
so at harvest time he looks but finds nothing.

5 The purposes of a man's heart are deep waters,
but a man of understanding draws them out.

6 Many a man claims to have unfailing love,
but a faithful man who can find?[w]

7 The righteous man leads a blameless life;
blessed are his children after him.[x]

8 When a king sits on his throne to judge,
he winnows out all evil with his eyes.[y]

9 Who can say, "I have kept my heart pure;
I am clean and without sin"?[z]

10 Differing weights and differing measures—
the LORD detests them both.[a]

11 Even a child is known by his actions,
by whether his conduct is pure[b] and right.

12 Ears that hear and eyes that see—
the LORD has made them both.

13 Do not love sleep or you will grow poor;[c]
stay awake and you will have food to spare.

14 "It's no good, it's no good!" says the buyer;
then off he goes and boasts about his purchase.

15 Gold there is, and rubies in abundance,
but lips that speak knowledge are a rare jewel.

16 Take the garment of one who puts up security for a stranger;
hold it in pledge if he does it for a wayward woman.

17 Food gained by fraud tastes sweet to a man,[d]
but he ends up with a mouth full of gravel.

18 Make plans by seeking advice;
if you wage war, obtain guidance.[e]

19 A gossip betrays a confidence;[f]
so avoid a man who talks too much.

20 If a man curses his father or mother,
his lamp will be snuffed out in pitch darkness.[g]

21 An inheritance quickly gained at the beginning
will not be blessed at the end.

22 Do not say, "I'll pay you back for this wrong!"
Wait for the LORD, and he will deliver you.[h]

23 The LORD detests differing weights,
and dishonest scales do not please him.[i]

24 A man's steps are directed by the LORD.
How then can anyone understand his own way?

25 It is a trap for a man to dedicate something rashly
and only later to consider his vows.[j]

26 A wise king winnows out the wicked;
he drives the threshing wheel over them.[k]

27 The lamp of the LORD searches the spirit of a man[a];
it searches out his inmost being.

28 Love and faithfulness keep a king safe;
through love his throne is made secure.

29 The glory of young men is their strength,
gray hair the splendor of the old.[l]

30 Blows and wounds cleanse away evil,
and beatings purge the inmost being.

**19:29** s Pr 26:3
**20:2** t Pr 19:12 u Pr 8:36
**20:3** v Pr 17:14
**20:6** w Ps 12:1
**20:7** x Ps 37:25–26
**20:8** y ver 26
**20:9** z 1Ki 8:46
**20:10** a ver 23
**20:11** b Mt 7:16
**20:13** c Pr 6:11
**20:17** d Pr 9:17
**20:18** e Pr 24:6
**20:19** f Pr 11:13
**20:20** g Job 18:5
**20:22** h Ro 12:19
**20:23** i ver 10
**20:25** j Ecc 5:2,4–5
**20:26** k ver 8
**20:29** l Pr 16:31

[a]27 Or *The spirit of man is the LORD's lamp*

21:2 m Pr 16:2; 24:12; Lk 16:15
21:3 n 1Sa 15:22; Isa 1:11; Mic 6:6–8
21:5 o Pr 10:4
21:11 p Pr 19:25
21:12 q Pr 14:11

21 The king's heart is in the hand of the LORD;
he directs it like a watercourse
wherever he pleases.

2 All a man's ways seem right to him,
but the LORD weighs the heart.[m]

3 To do what is right and just
is more acceptable to the LORD than sacrifice.[n]

4 Haughty eyes and a proud heart,
the lamp of the wicked, are sin!

5 The plans of the diligent lead to profit[o]
as surely as haste leads to poverty.

6 A fortune made by a lying tongue
is a fleeting vapor and a deadly snare.[a]

7 The violence of the wicked will drag them away,
for they refuse to do what is right.

8 The way of the guilty is devious,
but the conduct of the innocent is upright.

9 Better to live on a corner of the roof
than share a house with a quarrelsome wife.

10 The wicked man craves evil;
his neighbor gets no mercy from him.

11 When a mocker is punished, the simple gain wisdom;
when a wise man is instructed, he gets knowledge.[p]

12 The Righteous One[b] takes note of the house of the wicked
and brings the wicked to ruin.[q]

13 If a man shuts his ears to the cry of the poor,
he too will cry out and not be answered.

14 A gift given in secret soothes anger,
and a bribe concealed in the cloak pacifies great wrath.

15 When justice is done, it brings joy to the righteous
but terror to evildoers.

16 A man who strays from the path of understanding
comes to rest in the company of the dead.

17 He who loves pleasure will become poor;
whoever loves wine and oil will never be rich.

18 The wicked become a ransom[r] for the righteous,
and the unfaithful for the upright.

19 Better to live in a desert
than with a quarrelsome and ill-tempered wife.

20 In the house of the wise are stores of choice food and oil,
but a foolish man devours all he has.

21 He who pursues righteousness and love
finds life, prosperity[c] and honor.[s]

*Dear one,*

*Love me. Love yourself,*
*just as I love you.*
*Love all of my children.*

*Your God*

PROVERBS 21:21

22 A wise man attacks the city of the mighty[t]
and pulls down the stronghold in which they trust.

23 He who guards his mouth[u] and his tongue
keeps himself from calamity.[v]

24 The proud and arrogant man—"Mocker" is his name;
he behaves with overweening pride.

25 The sluggard's craving will be the death of him,[w]
because his hands refuse to work.

21:18 r Pr 11:8
21:21 s Mt 5:6
21:22 t Ecc 9:15–16
21:23 u Jas 3:2 v Pr 12:13
21:25 w Pr 13:4

[a]6 Some Hebrew manuscripts, Septuagint and Vulgate; most Hebrew manuscripts *vapor for those who seek death*
[b]12 Or *The righteous man* [c]21 Or *righteousness*

[26] All day long he craves for more,
but the righteous give without sparing.

[27] The sacrifice of the wicked is detestable[x]—
how much more so when brought with evil intent!

[28] A false witness will perish,
and whoever listens to him will be destroyed forever.[a]

[29] A wicked man puts up a bold front,
but an upright man gives thought to his ways.

[30] There is no wisdom,[y] no insight, no plan
that can succeed against the LORD.[z]

[31] The horse is made ready for the day of battle,
but victory rests with the LORD.[a]

22 A good name is more desirable than great riches;
to be esteemed is better than silver or gold.[b]

[2] Rich and poor have this in common:
The LORD is the Maker of them all.

[3] A prudent man sees danger and takes refuge,
but the simple keep going and suffer for it.[c]

[4] Humility and the fear of the LORD
bring wealth and honor and life.

[5] In the paths of the wicked lie thorns and snares,[d]
but he who guards his soul stays far from them.

[6] Train[b] a child in the way he should go,[e]
and when he is old he will not turn from it.

[7] The rich rule over the poor,
and the borrower is servant to the lender.

[8] He who sows wickedness reaps trouble,
and the rod of his fury will be destroyed.

[9] A generous man will himself be blessed,[f]
for he shares his food with the poor.

[10] Drive out the mocker, and out goes strife;
quarrels and insults are ended.

[11] He who loves a pure heart and whose speech is gracious
will have the king for his friend.[g]

[12] The eyes of the LORD keep watch over knowledge,
but he frustrates the words of the unfaithful.

[13] The sluggard says, "There is a lion outside!"[h]
or, "I will be murdered in the streets!"

[14] The mouth of an adulteress is a deep pit;[i]
he who is under the LORD's wrath will fall into it.[j]

[15] Folly is bound up in the heart of a child,
but the rod of discipline will drive it far from him.[k]

[16] He who oppresses the poor to increase his wealth
and he who gives gifts to the rich—
both come to poverty.

## Sayings of the Wise

[17] Pay attention and listen to the sayings of the wise;
apply your heart to what I teach,
[18] for it is pleasing when you keep them in your heart
and have all of them ready on your lips.
[19] So that your trust may be in the LORD,
I teach you today, even you.
[20] Have I not written thirty[c] sayings for you,
sayings of counsel and knowledge,
[21] teaching you true and reliable words,[l]
so that you can give sound answers
to him who sent you?

[22] Do not exploit the poor[m] because they are poor
and do not crush the needy in court,[n]
[23] for the LORD will take up their case[o]
and will plunder those who plunder them.

[24] Do not make friends with a hot-tempered man,

**21:27** x Jer 6:20
**21:30** y Jer 9:23; z Isa 8:10; Ac 5:39
**21:31** a Ps 3:8
**22:1** b Ecc 7:1
**22:3** c Pr 27:12
**22:5** d Pr 15:19
**22:6** e Eph 6:4
**22:9** f 2Co 9:6
**22:11** g Mt 5:8
**22:13** h Pr 26:13
**22:14** i Pr 2:16; 5:3–5; j Ecc 7:26
**22:15** k Pr 13:24
**22:21** l Lk 1:3–4
**22:22** m Zec 7:10; n Mal 3:5
**22:23** o Ps 12:5

[a]28 Or */ but the words of an obedient man will live on* [b]6 Or *Start* [c]20 Or *not formerly written*; or *not written excellent*

22:25 p 1Co 15:33
22:28 q Dt 19:14
23:5 r Pr 27:24

do not associate with one easily
angered,
25 or you may learn his ways
and get yourself ensnared.[p]

26 Do not be a man who strikes hands in
pledge
or puts up security for debts;
27 if you lack the means to pay,
your very bed will be snatched from
under you.

28 Do not move an ancient boundary stone[q]
set up by your forefathers.

29 Do you see a man skilled in his work?
He will serve before kings;
he will not serve before obscure men.

23 When you sit to dine with a ruler,
note well what[a] is before you,
2 and put a knife to your throat
if you are given to gluttony.
3 Do not crave his delicacies,
for that food is deceptive.

4 Do not wear yourself out to get rich;
have the wisdom to show restraint.
5 Cast but a glance at riches, and they are
gone,
for they will surely sprout wings
and fly off to the sky like an eagle.[r]

6 Do not eat the food of a stingy man,
do not crave his delicacies;
7 for he is the kind of man
who is always thinking about the cost.[b]
"Eat and drink," he says to you,
but his heart is not with you.
8 You will vomit up the little you have eaten
and will have wasted your
compliments.

9 Do not speak to a fool,
for he will scorn the wisdom of your
words.[s]

10 Do not move an ancient boundary stone
or encroach on the fields of the
fatherless,
11 for their Defender is strong;
he will take up their case against you.[t]

12 Apply your heart to instruction
and your ears to words of knowledge.

13 Do not withhold discipline from a child;
if you punish him with the rod, he will
not die.
14 Punish him with the rod
and save his soul from death.[c]

15 My son, if your heart is wise,
then my heart will be glad;
16 my inmost being will rejoice
when your lips speak what is right.

17 Do not let your heart envy[u] sinners,
but always be zealous for the fear of
the LORD.
18 There is surely a future hope for you,
and your hope will not be cut off.

19 Listen, my son, and be wise,
and keep your heart on the right path.
20 Do not join those who drink too much
wine[v]
or gorge themselves on meat,
21 for drunkards and gluttons become poor,[w]
and drowsiness clothes them in rags.

23:9 s Pr 9:7; Mt 7:6
23:11 t Pr 22:22–23
23:17 u Ps 37:1
23:20 v Isa 5:11,22
23:21 w Pr 21:17

[a]1 Or *who* [b]7 Or *for as he thinks within himself, / so he is*; or *for as he puts on a feast, / so he is* [c]14 Hebrew *Sheol*

## The African Presence

**Proverbs 22:17—24:34**

This section of the book of Proverbs contains proverbs that are similar to sayings in the Egyptian work "The Instruction of Amenemope." Although the relationship is debated (who copied whom), the similarities are striking and show the interrelatedness of the cultures and the influence each had on the other.

23:22 x Pr 1:8; Eph 6:1–2
23:23 y Pr 4:7
23:24 z ver 15–16; Pr 10:1
23:27 a Pr 22:14
23:28 b Pr 7:11–12; Ecc 7:26
23:30 c Ps 75:8; Isa 5:11; Eph 5:18
24:1 d Ps 37:1; 73:3; Pr 3:31–32; 23:17–18

22 Listen to your father, who gave you life,
and do not despise your mother when she is old.[x]
23 Buy the truth and do not sell it;
get wisdom, discipline and understanding.[y]
24 The father of a righteous man has great joy;
he who has a wise son delights in him.[z]
25 May your father and mother be glad;
may she who gave you birth rejoice!

26 My son, give me your heart
and let your eyes keep to my ways,
27 for a prostitute is a deep pit[a]
and a wayward wife is a narrow well.
28 Like a bandit she lies in wait,[b]
and multiplies the unfaithful among men.

29 Who has woe? Who has sorrow?
Who has strife? Who has complaints?
Who has needless bruises? Who has bloodshot eyes?
30 Those who linger over wine,[c]
who go to sample bowls of mixed wine.
31 Do not gaze at wine when it is red,
when it sparkles in the cup,
when it goes down smoothly!
32 In the end it bites like a snake
and poisons like a viper.
33 Your eyes will see strange sights
and your mind imagine confusing things.
34 You will be like one sleeping on the high seas,
lying on top of the rigging.
35 "They hit me," you will say, "but I'm not hurt!
They beat me, but I don't feel it!
When will I wake up
so I can find another drink?"

24 Do not envy[d] wicked men,
do not desire their company;
2 for their hearts plot violence,
and their lips talk about making trouble.

3 By wisdom a house is built,
and through understanding it is established;
4 through knowledge its rooms are filled
with rare and beautiful treasures.

5 A wise man has great power,
and a man of knowledge increases strength;
6 for waging war you need guidance,
and for victory many advisers.

7 Wisdom is too high for a fool;
in the assembly at the gate he has nothing to say.

8 He who plots evil
will be known as a schemer.
9 The schemes of folly are sin,
and men detest a mocker.

10 If you falter in times of trouble,
how small is your strength!

11 Rescue those being led away to death;
hold back those staggering toward slaughter.[e]
12 If you say, "But we knew nothing about this,"
does not he who weighs[f] the heart perceive it?
Does not he who guards your life know it?
Will he not repay each person
according to what he has done?[g]

13 Eat honey, my son, for it is good;
honey from the comb is sweet to your taste.
14 Know also that wisdom is sweet to your soul;
if you find it, there is a future hope for you,
and your hope will not be cut off.

15 Do not lie in wait like an outlaw against a righteous man's house,
do not raid his dwelling place;
16 for though a righteous man falls seven times, he rises again,
but the wicked are brought down by calamity.[h]

17 Do not gloat[i] when your enemy falls;
when he stumbles, do not let your heart rejoice,[j]
18 or the LORD will see and disapprove
and turn his wrath away from him.

19 Do not fret[k] because of evil men
or be envious of the wicked,
20 for the evil man has no future hope,

24:11 e Ps 82:4; Isa 58:6–7
24:12 f Pr 21:2 g Ro 2:6*
24:16 h Mic 7:8
24:17 i Ob 1:12 j Job 31:29
24:19 k Ps 37:1

and the lamp of the wicked will be
snuffed out.

21 Fear the LORD and the king,[l] my son,
and do not join with the rebellious,
22 for those two will send sudden
destruction upon them,
and who knows what calamities they
can bring?

## Further Sayings of the Wise

23 These also are sayings of the wise:

To show partiality[m] in judging is not
good:
24 Whoever says to the guilty, "You are
innocent"—
peoples will curse him and nations
denounce him.
25 But it will go well with those who convict
the guilty,
and rich blessing will come upon
them.

26 An honest answer
is like a kiss on the lips.

27 Finish your outdoor work
and get your fields ready;
after that, build your house.

28 Do not testify against your neighbor
without cause,[n]
or use your lips to deceive.
29 Do not say, "I'll do to him as he has done
to me;
I'll pay that man back for what he
did."[o]

30 I went past the field of the sluggard,[p]
past the vineyard of the man who lacks
judgment;
31 thorns had come up everywhere,
the ground was covered with weeds,
and the stone wall was in ruins.
32 I applied my heart to what I observed
and learned a lesson from what I saw:
33 A little sleep, a little slumber,
a little folding of the hands to rest[q]—
34 and poverty will come on you like a
bandit
and scarcity like an armed man.[a]

## More Proverbs of Solomon

25 These are more proverbs[r] of Solomon, copied by the men of Hezekiah
king of Judah:[s]

2 It is the glory of God to conceal a
matter;
to search out a matter is the glory of
kings.

3 As the heavens are high and the earth is
deep,
so the hearts of kings are
unsearchable.

4 Remove the dross from the silver,
and out comes material for[b] the
silversmith;
5 remove the wicked from the king's
presence,[t]
and his throne will be established
through righteousness.[u]

6 Do not exalt yourself in the king's
presence,
and do not claim a place among great
men;
7 it is better for him to say to you, "Come
up here,"[v]
than for him to humiliate you before a
nobleman.

What you have seen with your eyes
8 do not bring[c] hastily to court,
for what will you do in the end
if your neighbor puts you to
shame?[w]

9 If you argue your case with a neighbor,
do not betray another man's
confidence,
10 or he who hears it may shame you
and you will never lose your bad
reputation.

11 A word aptly spoken
is like apples of gold in settings of
silver.[x]

12 Like an earring of gold or an ornament of
fine gold
is a wise man's rebuke to a listening
ear.[y]

**24:21** l Ro 13:1–5; 1Pe 2:17
**24:23** m Lev 19:15
**24:28** n Eph 4:25
**24:29** o Pr 20:22; Mt 5:38–41
**24:30** p Pr 6:6–11
**24:33** q Pr 6:10
**25:1** r 1Ki 4:32 s Pr 1:1
**25:5** t Pr 20:8 u Pr 16:12
**25:7** v Lk 14:7–10
**25:8** w Mt 5:25–26
**25:11** x Pr 15:23
**25:12** y Pr 15:31

[a] 34 Or *like a vagrant / and scarcity like a beggar* [b] 4 Or *comes a vessel from* [c] 7,8 Or *nobleman / on whom you had set your eyes. / [8] Do not go*

25:13
z Pr 13:17

25:15
a Ecc 10:4
b Pr 15:1

25:16
c ver 27

25:18
d Ps 57:4; Pr 12:18

25:22
e 2Sa 16:12; Ro 12:20*

25:24
f Pr 21:9

25:25
g Pr 15:30

25:27
h ver 16
i Pr 27:2

13 Like the coolness of snow at harvest time
is a trustworthy messenger to those who send him;
he refreshes the spirit of his masters.[z]

14 Like clouds and wind without rain
is a man who boasts of gifts he does not give.

15 Through patience a ruler can be persuaded,[a]
and a gentle tongue can break a bone.[b]

16 If you find honey, eat just enough—
too much of it, and you will vomit.[c]

17 Seldom set foot in your neighbor's house—
too much of you, and he will hate you.

18 Like a club or a sword or a sharp arrow
is the man who gives false testimony against his neighbor.[d]

19 Like a bad tooth or a lame foot
is reliance on the unfaithful in times of trouble.

20 Like one who takes away a garment on a cold day,
or like vinegar poured on soda,
is one who sings songs to a heavy heart.

21 If your enemy is hungry, give him food to eat;
if he is thirsty, give him water to drink.

22 In doing this, you will heap burning coals on his head,
and the LORD will reward you.[e]

23 As a north wind brings rain,
so a sly tongue brings angry looks.

24 Better to live on a corner of the roof
than share a house with a quarrelsome wife.[f]

25 Like cold water to a weary soul
is good news from a distant land.[g]

26 Like a muddied spring or a polluted well
is a righteous man who gives way to the wicked.

27 It is not good to eat too much honey,[h]
nor is it honorable to seek one's own honor.[i]

28 Like a city whose walls are broken down
is a man who lacks self-control.

26 Like snow in summer or rain[j] in harvest,
honor is not fitting for a fool.

2 Like a fluttering sparrow or a darting swallow,
an undeserved curse does not come to rest.[k]

3 A whip for the horse, a halter for the donkey,[l]
and a rod for the backs of fools!

4 Do not answer a fool according to his folly,
or you will be like him yourself.

5 Answer a fool according to his folly,
or he will be wise in his own eyes.

6 Like cutting off one's feet or drinking violence
is the sending of a message by the hand of a fool.

7 Like a lame man's legs that hang limp
is a proverb in the mouth of a fool.

8 Like tying a stone in a sling
is the giving of honor to a fool.

9 Like a thornbush in a drunkard's hand
is a proverb in the mouth of a fool.

10 Like an archer who wounds at random
is he who hires a fool or any passer-by.

11 As a dog returns to its vomit,[m]
so a fool repeats his folly.[n]

12 Do you see a man wise in his own eyes?[o]
There is more hope for a fool than for him.[p]

13 The sluggard says, "There is a lion in the road,
a fierce lion roaming the streets!"[q]

14 As a door turns on its hinges,
so a sluggard turns on his bed.

15 The sluggard buries his hand in the dish;
he is too lazy to bring it back to his mouth.[r]

16 The sluggard is wiser in his own eyes
than seven men who answer discreetly.

26:1
j 1Sa 12:17

26:2
k Dt 23:5

26:3
l Ps 32:9

26:11
m 2Pe 2:22*
n Ex 8:15

26:12
o Pr 3:7
p Pr 29:20

26:13
q Pr 22:13

26:15
r Pr 19:24

26:20 s Pr 22:10
26:21 t Pr 15:18
26:22 u Pr 18:8
26:25 v Ps 28:3 w Jer 9:4–8
26:27 x Ps 7:15 y Pr 28:10
26:28 z Pr 29:5
27:1 a Lk 12:19–20; Jas 4:13–16
27:2 b Pr 25:27

17 Like one who seizes a dog by the ears
is a passer-by who meddles in a quarrel not his own.

18 Like a madman shooting
firebrands or deadly arrows
19 is a man who deceives his neighbor
and says, "I was only joking!"

20 Without wood a fire goes out;
without gossip a quarrel dies down.[s]

21 As charcoal to embers and as wood to fire,
so is a quarrelsome man for kindling strife.[t]

22 The words of a gossip are like choice morsels;
they go down to a man's inmost parts.[u]

23 Like a coating of glaze[a] over earthenware
are fervent lips with an evil heart.

24 A malicious man disguises himself with his lips,
but in his heart he harbors deceit.
25 Though his speech is charming,[v] do not believe him,
for seven abominations fill his heart.[w]
26 His malice may be concealed by deception,
but his wickedness will be exposed in the assembly.

27 If a man digs a pit,[x] he will fall into it;
if a man rolls a stone, it will roll back on him.[y]

28 A lying tongue hates those it hurts,
and a flattering mouth[z] works ruin.

*"Many people know how to criticize, but few know how to praise."*
—Ethel Waters, singer, dancer and actress

27 Do not boast about tomorrow,
for you do not know what a day may bring forth.[a]
2 Let another praise you, and not your own mouth;
someone else, and not your own lips.[b]

3 Stone is heavy and sand a burden,
but provocation by a fool is heavier than both.
4 Anger is cruel and fury overwhelming,
but who can stand before jealousy?

5 Better is open rebuke
than hidden love.

6 Wounds from a friend can be trusted,
but an enemy multiplies kisses.

7 He who is full loathes honey,
but to the hungry even what is bitter tastes sweet.

8 Like a bird that strays from its nest
is a man who strays from his home.

9 Perfume and incense bring joy to the heart,
and the pleasantness of one's friend springs from his earnest counsel.

10 Do not forsake your friend and the friend of your father,
and do not go to your brother's house when disaster[c] strikes you—
better a neighbor nearby than a brother far away.

11 Be wise, my son, and bring joy to my heart;[d]
then I can answer anyone who treats me with contempt.

12 The prudent see danger and take refuge,
but the simple keep going and suffer for it.

13 Take the garment of one who puts up security for a stranger;
hold it in pledge if he does it for a wayward woman.[e]

14 If a man loudly blesses his neighbor early in the morning,
it will be taken as a curse.

15 A quarrelsome wife is like
a constant dripping on a rainy day;
16 restraining her is like restraining the wind
or grasping oil with the hand.

27:10 c Pr 17:17; 18:24
27:11 d Pr 10:1; 23:15–16
27:13 e Pr 20:16

[a]23 With a different word division of the Hebrew; Masoretic Text *of silver dross*

27:18 f 1Co 9:7 g Lk 19:12–27
27:20 h Hab 2:5 i Ecc 1:8
27:21 j Pr 17:3
28:1 k Lev 26:17; Ps 53:5

17 As iron sharpens iron,
so one man sharpens another.

18 He who tends a fig tree will eat its fruit,[f]
and he who looks after his master will be honored.[g]

19 As water reflects a face,
so a man's heart reflects the man.

20 Death and Destruction[a] are never satisfied,[h]
and neither are the eyes of man.[i]

21 The crucible for silver and the furnace for gold,[j]
but man is tested by the praise he receives.

22 Though you grind a fool in a mortar,
grinding him like grain with a pestle,
you will not remove his folly from him.

23 Be sure you know the condition of your flocks,
give careful attention to your herds;
24 for riches do not endure forever,
and a crown is not secure for all generations.
25 When the hay is removed and new growth appears
and the grass from the hills is gathered in,
26 the lambs will provide you with clothing,
and the goats with the price of a field.
27 You will have plenty of goats' milk
to feed you and your family
and to nourish your servant girls.

28 The wicked man flees though no one pursues,[k]
but the righteous are as bold as a lion.

2 When a country is rebellious, it has many rulers,
but a man of understanding and knowledge maintains order.

3 A ruler[b] who oppresses the poor
is like a driving rain that leaves no crops.

4 Those who forsake the law praise the wicked,
but those who keep the law resist them.

5 Evil men do not understand justice,
but those who seek the LORD understand it fully.

6 Better a poor man whose walk is blameless
than a rich man whose ways are perverse.[l]

7 He who keeps the law is a discerning son,
but a companion of gluttons disgraces his father.[m]

8 He who increases his wealth by exorbitant interest
amasses it for another,[n] who will be kind to the poor.

9 If anyone turns a deaf ear to the law,
even his prayers are detestable.[o]

10 He who leads the upright along an evil path
will fall into his own trap,[p]
but the blameless will receive a good inheritance.

11 A rich man may be wise in his own eyes,
but a poor man who has discernment sees through him.

12 When the righteous triumph, there is great elation;
but when the wicked rise to power, men go into hiding.[q]

13 He who conceals his sins does not prosper,
but whoever confesses and renounces them finds mercy.[r]

14 Blessed is the man who always fears the LORD,
but he who hardens his heart falls into trouble.

15 Like a roaring lion or a charging bear
is a wicked man ruling over a helpless people.

16 A tyrannical ruler lacks judgment,
but he who hates ill-gotten gain will enjoy a long life.

17 A man tormented by the guilt of murder
will be a fugitive[s] till death;
let no one support him.

28:6 l Pr 19:1
28:7 m Pr 23:19–21
28:8 n Pr 13:22
28:9 o Ps 66:18; Pr 15:8
28:10 p Pr 26:27
28:12 q Pr 11:10
28:13 r Ps 32:1–5
28:17 s Ge 9:6

[a]20 Hebrew *Sheol and Abaddon* [b]3 Or *A poor man*

**28:18** t Pr 10:9
**28:19** u Pr 12:11
**28:20** v ver 22; 1Ti 6:9
**28:21** w Pr 18:5 x Eze 13:19
**28:23** y Pr 27:5–6
**28:24** z Pr 18:9
**28:25** a Pr 29:25
**29:1** b 2Ch 36:16; Pr 6:15
**29:3** c Pr 10:1

18 He whose walk is blameless is kept safe,
but he whose ways are perverse will
suddenly fall.[t]

19 He who works his land will have
abundant food,
but the one who chases fantasies will
have his fill of poverty.[u]

20 A faithful man will be richly blessed,
but one eager to get rich will not go
unpunished.[v]

21 To show partiality is not good[w]—
yet a man will do wrong for a piece of
bread.[x]

22 A stingy man is eager to get rich
and is unaware that poverty awaits
him.

23 He who rebukes a man will in the end
gain more favor
than he who has a flattering tongue.[y]

24 He who robs his father or mother
and says, "It's not wrong"—
he is partner to him who destroys.[z]

25 A greedy man stirs up dissension,
but he who trusts in the Lord[a] will
prosper.

26 He who trusts in himself is a fool,
but he who walks in wisdom is kept
safe.

27 He who gives to the poor will lack
nothing,
but he who closes his eyes to them
receives many curses.

28 When the wicked rise to power, people go
into hiding;
but when the wicked perish, the
righteous thrive.

29 A man who remains stiff-necked
after many rebukes
will suddenly be destroyed—without
remedy.[b]

2 When the righteous thrive, the people
rejoice;
when the wicked rule, the people
groan.

3 A man who loves wisdom brings joy to
his father,[c]
but a companion of prostitutes
squanders his wealth.[d]

4 By justice a king gives a country stability,
but one who is greedy for bribes tears
it down.

5 Whoever flatters his neighbor
is spreading a net for his feet.

6 An evil man is snared by his own sin,
but a righteous one can sing and be
glad.

7 The righteous care about justice for the
poor,[e]
but the wicked have no such concern.

8 Mockers stir up a city,
but wise men turn away anger.[f]

9 If a wise man goes to court with a fool,
the fool rages and scoffs, and there is
no peace.

10 Bloodthirsty men hate a man of integrity
and seek to kill the upright.[g]

11 A fool gives full vent to his anger,
but a wise man keeps himself under
control.[h]

12 If a ruler listens to lies,
all his officials become wicked.

13 The poor man and the oppressor have
this in common:
The Lord gives sight to the eyes of both.

14 If a king judges the poor with fairness,
his throne will always be secure.[i]

15 The rod of correction imparts wisdom,
but a child left to himself disgraces his
mother.[j]

16 When the wicked thrive, so does sin,
but the righteous will see their
downfall.[k]

17 Discipline your son, and he will give you
peace;
he will bring delight to your soul.

18 Where there is no revelation, the people
cast off restraint;
but blessed is he who keeps the law.[l]

19 A servant cannot be corrected by mere
words;

**29:3** d Pr 5:8–10; Lk 15:11–32
**29:7** e Job 29:16; Ps 41:1
**29:8** f Pr 11:11
**29:10** g 1Jn 3:12
**29:11** h Pr 12:16
**29:14** i Ps 72:1–5
**29:15** j Pr 13:24
**29:16** k Ps 37:35–36; 91:8
**29:18** l Ps 1:1–2; 119:1–2

29:20
m Pr 26:12
29:23
n Pr 11:2; Isa 66:2; Mt 23:12
29:24
o Lev 5:1
30:4
p Jn 3:13
30:5
q Ps 12:6; 18:30

though he understands, he will not
respond.
[20] Do you see a man who speaks in haste?
There is more hope for a fool than for
him.[m]
[21] If a man pampers his servant from youth,
he will bring grief[a] in the end.
[22] An angry man stirs up dissension,
and a hot-tempered one commits
many sins.
[23] A man's pride brings him low,
but a man of lowly spirit gains honor.[n]
[24] The accomplice of a thief is his own
enemy;
he is put under oath and dare not
testify.[o]
[25] Fear of man will prove to be a snare,
but whoever trusts in the LORD is kept
safe.
[26] Many seek an audience with a ruler,
but it is from the LORD that man gets
justice.
[27] The righteous detest the dishonest;
the wicked detest the upright.

## Sayings of Agur

30 The sayings of Agur son of Jakeh—
an oracle[b]:

This man declared to Ithiel,
to Ithiel and to Ucal:[c]
[2] "I am the most ignorant of men;
I do not have a man's understanding.
[3] I have not learned wisdom,
nor have I knowledge of the Holy One.
[4] Who has gone up[p] to heaven and come
down?
Who has gathered up the wind in the
hollow of his hands?
Who has wrapped up the waters in his
cloak?
Who has established all the ends of
the earth?
What is his name, and the name of his
son?
Tell me if you know!

[5] "Every word of God is flawless;[q]
he is a shield to those who take refuge
in him.
[6] Do not add[r] to his words,
or he will rebuke you and prove you
a liar.

[7] "Two things I ask of you, O LORD;
do not refuse me before I die:
[8] Keep falsehood and lies far from me;
give me neither poverty nor riches,
but give me only my daily bread.[s]
[9] Otherwise, I may have too much and
disown you
and say, 'Who is the LORD?'[t]
Or I may become poor and steal,
and so dishonor the name of my God.

[10] "Do not slander a servant to his master,
or he will curse you, and you will pay
for it.

[11] "There are those who curse their fathers
and do not bless their mothers;[u]
[12] those who are pure in their own eyes[v]
and yet are not cleansed of their filth;
[13] those whose eyes are ever so haughty,[w]
whose glances are so disdainful;
[14] those whose teeth[x] are swords
and whose jaws are set with knives
to devour[y] the poor[z] from the earth,
the needy from among mankind.

[15] "The leech has two daughters.
'Give! Give!' they cry.

"There are three things that are never
satisfied,
four that never say, 'Enough!':
[16] the grave,[d] [a] the barren womb,
land, which is never satisfied with
water,
and fire, which never says, 'Enough!'

[17] "The eye that mocks a father,
that scorns obedience to a mother,
will be pecked out by the ravens of the
valley,
will be eaten by the vultures.

[18] "There are three things that are too
amazing for me,
four that I do not understand:
[19] the way of an eagle in the sky,

30:6
r Dt 4:2; Rev 22:18
30:8
s Mt 6:11
30:9
t Dt 8:10–14; Hos 13:6
30:11
u Pr 20:20
30:12
v Lk 18:11
30:13
w Pr 6:17
30:14
x Job 29:17
y Ps 14:4
z Am 8:4
30:16
a Pr 27:20; Hab 2:5

[a]21 The meaning of the Hebrew for this word is uncertain. [b]1 Or *Jakeh of Massa* [c]1 Masoretic Text; with a different word division of the Hebrew *declared, "I am weary, O God; / I am weary, O God, and faint.* [d]16 Hebrew *Sheol*

30:20 b Pr 5:6
30:22 c Pr 19:10
30:25 d Pr 6:6–8
30:26 e Ps 104:18
30:32 f Job 21:5
31:2 g Isa 49:15
31:3 h Dt 17:17; 1Ki 11:3; Ne 13:26; Pr 5:1–14

the way of a snake on a rock,
the way of a ship on the high seas,
and the way of a man with a maiden.

20 "This is the way of an adulteress:
She eats and wipes her mouth
and says, 'I've done nothing wrong.'[b]

21 "Under three things the earth trembles,
under four it cannot bear up:
22 a servant who becomes king,[c]
a fool who is full of food,
23 an unloved woman who is married,
and a maidservant who displaces her mistress.

24 "Four things on earth are small,
yet they are extremely wise:
25 Ants are creatures of little strength,
yet they store up their food in the summer;[d]
26 coneys[a][e] are creatures of little power,
yet they make their home in the crags;
27 locusts have no king,
yet they advance together in ranks;
28 a lizard can be caught with the hand,
yet it is found in kings' palaces.

29 "There are three things that are stately in their stride,
four that move with stately bearing:
30 a lion, mighty among beasts,
who retreats before nothing;
31 a strutting rooster, a he-goat,
and a king with his army around him.[b]

32 "If you have played the fool and exalted yourself,
or if you have planned evil,
clap your hand over your mouth![f]
33 For as churning the milk produces butter,
and as twisting the nose produces blood,
so stirring up anger produces strife."

## Sayings of King Lemuel

31 The sayings of King Lemuel—an oracle[c] his mother taught him:

2 "O my son, O son of my womb,
O son of my vows,[d][g]
3 do not spend your strength on women,
your vigor on those who ruin kings.[h]

4 "It is not for kings, O Lemuel—
not for kings to drink wine,[i]
not for rulers to crave beer,
5 lest they drink and forget what the law decrees,
and deprive all the oppressed of their rights.
6 Give beer to those who are perishing,
wine to those who are in anguish;
7 let them drink and forget their poverty
and remember their misery no more.

8 "Speak[j] up for those who cannot speak for themselves,
for the rights of all who are destitute.
9 Speak up and judge fairly;
defend the rights of the poor and needy."[k]

## Epilogue: The Wife of Noble Character

10[e] A wife of noble character[l] who can find?[m]
She is worth far more than rubies.
11 Her husband has full confidence in her
and lacks nothing of value.
12 She brings him good, not harm,
all the days of her life.
13 She selects wool and flax
and works with eager hands.
14 She is like the merchant ships,
bringing her food from afar.
15 She gets up while it is still dark;
she provides food for her family
and portions for her servant girls.
16 She considers a field and buys it;
out of her earnings she plants a vineyard.
17 She sets about her work vigorously;
her arms are strong for her tasks.
18 She sees that her trading is profitable,
and her lamp does not go out at night.
19 In her hand she holds the distaff
and grasps the spindle with her fingers.
20 She opens her arms to the poor
and extends her hands to the needy.[n]
21 When it snows, she has no fear for her household;
for all of them are clothed in scarlet.
22 She makes coverings for her bed;

31:4 i Pr 20:1; Ecc 10:16–17; Isa 5:22
31:8 j Job 29:12–17
31:9 k Lev 19:15; Dt 1:16; Isa 1:17; Jer 22:16
31:10 l Ru 3:11; Pr 12:4; 18:22 m Pr 19:14
31:20 n Dt 15:11; Eph 4:28; Heb 13:16

[a]26 That is, the hyrax or rock badger [b]31 Or *king secure against revolt* [c]1 Or *of Lemuel king of Massa, which* [d]2 Or */ the answer to my prayers* [e]10 Verses 10–31 are an acrostic, each verse beginning with a successive letter of the Hebrew alphabet.

# A Virtuous Woman

## A Strong Woman, Dependent on God

While the NIV refers to the woman of Proverbs 31 as a "wife of noble character" (Pr 31:10), many of us have grown up calling her the "virtuous woman" (KJV). The virtuous woman in Proverbs 31 selects wool and flax, works with willing hands, brings her household food, gets up while it is still dark, buys fields, plants vineyards and so on. The word *virtuous* implies strength, and this proverb extols the dignity of women and emphasizes the importance of motherhood and home. A virtuous woman has strength and honor, and she is able to bear up under many crosses and disappointments.

How many of us have held up under corporate America's glass ceiling, sexism in the workplace, racism, unruly children, divorce and single parenthood? A virtuous woman speaks words that are wise and kind. She knows how to temper her words and hold her peace if need be. She takes care of her household, meaning she can make a meal out of nothing or stretch a week's worth of food into four weeks' worth; she can cook and clean with a baby on her hip while helping another child with homework. All of us can see ourselves in this virtuous woman.

But how do we maintain our virtue? How are we able to remain strong? It is through our reverence of God and submission to his will. We must put God above everything in our lives. We must seek him; we must serve him; we must witness to others about him; we must love him with all our hearts, with all our souls and with all our minds. Proverbs 31:30–31 says, "Charm is deceptive, and beauty is fleeting; but a woman who fears the LORD is to be praised. Give her the reward she has earned, and let her works bring her praise at the city gate." We strong women earn our reward by knowing God and seeking to please him and by depending on God for wisdom to care for ourselves and our families.

The Scriptures don't tell us *who* the woman in Proverbs 31 was—only *what* she was. A closer look at the virtuous woman can provide invaluable assistance to women today who are trying desperately to balance their lives and walk in God's will.

—T. BOOKER

For the next Women of the Bible note, go to page 787.

### reflection

*How often do you seek God first before you begin the many tasks you have to do?*

*Begin each task today with a talk with God. Seek God's guidance and wisdom throughout the day.*

### read

Proverbs 31:10–31.

See also the Inspire Notes "Submission," "Coping With Life's Tasks," "Integrity," "Doing Your Best" and "Character," and the Women of the Bible Notes "Acsah: A Wise Daughter," "Abigail: A Wise Wife" and "The 'Chosen Lady': A Woman Worth Imitating."

**31:23**
o Ru 4:1,11; Pr 12:4

**31:26**
p Pr 10:31

she is clothed in fine linen and purple.
23 Her husband is respected at the city gate,
where he takes his seat among the elders[o] of the land.
24 She makes linen garments and sells them,
and supplies the merchants with sashes.
25 She is clothed with strength and dignity;
she can laugh at the days to come.
26 She speaks with wisdom,
and faithful instruction is on her tongue.[p]
27 She watches over the affairs of her household
and does not eat the bread of idleness.
28 Her children arise and call her blessed;
her husband also, and he praises her:
29 "Many women do noble things,
but you surpass them all."
30 Charm is deceptive, and beauty is fleeting;
but a woman who fears the LORD is to be praised.
31 Give her the reward she has earned,
and let her works bring her praise at the city gate.

# Ecclesiastes

## OVERVIEW

The "Teacher" of Ecclesiastes searched for the meaning of life. He found joy, sorrow, pain, success and failure. After the Teacher's search, he determined that knowing God and living according to his precepts are the only comfort for life's challenges.

Women searching for purpose in their lives can find it only through a relationship with Jesus Christ. All wisdom is found in him and is freely given to those who ask God for it (see Jas 1:5).

## OUTLINE

I. Meaninglessness of Life (1:1—2:26)
II. A Time for Everything (3:1–22)
III. The Good and Bad of Life (4:1—6:12)
IV. Wisdom Is Supreme (7:1—12:8)
V. Conclusion of the Matter (12:9–14)

## SCANNABLE FACTS:

**Author:** Probably Solomon

**Time Written:** If written by Solomon, then most likely near the end of his life in 930 B.C.

**Theme to Note:** Life without God lacks meaning

**Notable Woman:** A scheming woman (see Ecc 7:26)

1:1
a ver 12; Ecc 7:27; 12:10
1:2
b Ps 39:5–6; 62:9; 144:4; Ecc 12:8
1:3
c Ecc 2:11,22
1:4
d Ps 104:5; 119:90
1:5
e Ps 19:5–6
1:8
f Pr 27:20
1:9
g Ecc 3:15
1:12
h ver 1
1:13
i Ecc 3:10
1:15
j Ecc 7:13

## Everything Is Meaningless

**1** The words of the Teacher,[a][a] son of
David, king in Jerusalem:

2 "Meaningless! Meaningless!"
says the Teacher.
"Utterly meaningless!
Everything is meaningless."[b]

3 What does man gain from all his labor
at which he toils under the sun?[c]
4 Generations come and generations go,
but the earth remains forever.[d]
5 The sun rises and the sun sets,
and hurries back to where it rises.[e]
6 The wind blows to the south
and turns to the north;
round and round it goes,
ever returning on its course.
7 All streams flow into the sea,
yet the sea is never full.
To the place the streams come from,
there they return again.
8 All things are wearisome,
more than one can say.
The eye never has enough of seeing,[f]
nor the ear its fill of hearing.
9 What has been will be again,
what has been done will be done again;[g]
there is nothing new under the sun.
10 Is there anything of which one can say,
"Look! This is something new"?
It was here already, long ago;
it was here before our time.
11 There is no remembrance of men of old,
and even those who are yet to come
will not be remembered
by those who follow.

## Wisdom Is Meaningless

12 I, the Teacher,[h] was king over Israel in
Jerusalem. 13 I devoted myself to study and
to explore by wisdom all that is done under
heaven. What a heavy burden God has laid
on men![i] 14 I have seen all the things that are
done under the sun; all of them are mean-
ingless, a chasing after the wind.

15 What is twisted cannot be straightened;[j]
what is lacking cannot be counted.

16 I thought to myself, "Look, I have grown
and increased in wisdom more than anyone
who has ruled over Jerusalem before me;[k]
I have experienced much of wisdom and
knowledge." 17 Then I applied myself to the
understanding of wisdom, and also of mad-
ness and folly,[l] but I learned that this, too, is
a chasing after the wind.

18 For with much wisdom comes much
sorrow;
the more knowledge, the more grief.[m]

## Pleasures Are Meaningless

**2** I thought in my heart, "Come now, I will
test you with pleasure to find out what
is good." But that also proved to be mean-
ingless. 2 "Laughter," I said, "is foolish. And
what does pleasure accomplish?" 3 I tried
cheering myself with wine, and embracing
folly—my mind still guiding me with wis-
dom. I wanted to see what was worthwhile
for men to do under heaven during the few
days of their lives.

4 I undertook great projects: I built
houses for myself and planted vineyards.
5 I made gardens and parks and planted all
kinds of fruit trees in them. 6 I made reser-
voirs to water groves of flourishing trees. 7 I
bought male and female slaves and had other
slaves who were born in my house. I also
owned more herds and flocks than anyone in
Jerusalem before me. 8 I amassed silver and
gold[n] for myself, and the treasure of kings
and provinces. I acquired men and women
singers, and a harem[b] as well—the delights
of the heart of man. 9 I became greater by far
than anyone in Jerusalem before me. In all
this my wisdom stayed with me.

10 I denied myself nothing my eyes desired;
I refused my heart no pleasure.
My heart took delight in all my work,
and this was the reward for all my
labor.
11 Yet when I surveyed all that my hands
had done
and what I had toiled to achieve,
everything was meaningless, a chasing
after the wind;[o]
nothing was gained under the sun.[p]

1:16
k 1Ki 3:12
1:17
l Ecc 2:3,12
1:18
m Ecc 12:12
2:8
n 1Ki 9:28; 10:10,14,21
2:11
o Ecc 1:14
p Ecc 1:3

[a]1 Or *leader of the assembly*; also in verses 2 and 12 [b]8 The meaning of the Hebrew for this phrase is uncertain.

**2:12** q Ecc 1:17
**2:14** r Ps 49:10; Ecc 9:3,11–12
**2:18** s Ps 49:10
**2:22** t Ecc 1:3
**2:23** u Job 5:7; 14:1
**2:24** v Ecc 8:15; w Ecc 3:22

## Wisdom and Folly Are Meaningless

12 Then I turned my thoughts to consider
wisdom,
and also madness and folly.[q]
What more can the king's successor do
than what has already been done?
13 I saw that wisdom is better than folly,
just as light is better than darkness.
14 The wise man has eyes in his head,
while the fool walks in the darkness;
but I came to realize
that the same fate overtakes them
both.[r]

15 Then I thought in my heart,

"The fate of the fool will overtake me
also.
What then do I gain by being wise?"
I said in my heart,
"This too is meaningless."
16 For the wise man, like the fool, will not
be long remembered;
in days to come both will be forgotten.
Like the fool, the wise man too must die!

## Toil Is Meaningless

17 So I hated life, because the work that
is done under the sun was grievous to me.
All of it is meaningless, a chasing after the
wind. 18 I hated all the things I had toiled for
under the sun, because I must leave them
to the one who comes after me.[s] 19 And who
knows whether he will be a wise man or a
fool? Yet he will have control over all the
work into which I have poured my effort
and skill under the sun. This too is mean-
ingless. 20 So my heart began to despair over
all my toilsome labor under the sun. 21 For a
man may do his work with wisdom, knowl-
edge and skill, and then he must leave all he
owns to someone who has not worked for it.
This too is meaningless and a great misfor-
tune. 22 What does a man get for all the toil
and anxious striving with which he labors
under the sun?[t] 23 All his days his work is
pain and grief;[u] even at night his mind does
not rest. This too is meaningless.

24 A man can do nothing better than to
eat and drink[v] and find satisfaction in his
work.[w] This too, I see, is from the hand of
God,[x] 25 for without him, who can eat or find
enjoyment? 26 To the man who pleases him,
God gives wisdom, knowledge and happi-
ness, but to the sinner he gives the task of
gathering and storing up wealth[y] to hand it
over to the one who pleases God. This too is
meaningless, a chasing after the wind.

## A Time for Everything

3 There is a time[z] for everything,
and a season for every activity under
heaven:
2 a time to be born and a time to die,
a time to plant and a time to uproot,
3 a time to kill and a time to heal,
a time to tear down and a time to
build,
4 a time to weep and a time to laugh,
a time to mourn and a time to dance,
5 a time to scatter stones and a time to
gather them,
a time to embrace and a time to
refrain,
6 a time to search and a time to give up,
a time to keep and a time to throw
away,
7 a time to tear and a time to mend,
a time to be silent and a time to speak,
8 a time to love and a time to hate,
a time for war and a time for peace.

9 What does the worker gain from his
toil?[a] 10 I have seen the burden God has laid
on men.[b] 11 He has made everything beauti-
ful in its time. He has also set eternity in
the hearts of men; yet they cannot fathom[c]
what God has done from beginning to end.[d]
12 I know that there is nothing better for men
than to be happy and do good while they
live. 13 That everyone may eat and drink, and
find satisfaction in all his toil—this is the
gift of God.[e] 14 I know that everything God
does will endure forever; nothing can be
added to it and nothing taken from it. God
does it so that men will revere him.

15 Whatever is has already been,
and what will be has been before;[f]
and God will call the past to account.[a]

16 And I saw something else under the
sun:

**2:24** x Ecc 3:12–13; 5:17–19
**2:26** y Job 27:17
**3:1** z ver 11,17; Ecc 8:6
**3:9** a Ecc 1:3
**3:10** b Ecc 1:13
**3:11** c Ecc 8:17; d Ro 11:33
**3:13** e Ecc 2:24
**3:15** f Ecc 1:9

[a] 15 Or *God calls back the past*

Inspire

# AGING: FOOTPRINTS ON THE SANDS OF TIME

A popular daytime soap opera introduces each episode with the image of an hourglass, as a voice says, "Like sands through the hourglass, so are the days of our lives." In our lives, the image of an hourglass is a fitting reminder that our days are limited on this earth.

As we age, as we "pass through the hourglass," the meaning and purpose of our lives unfold. Our passing through, our aging, signifies movement from one era to another. Ecclesiastes 3:1 reminds us that "there is a time for everything, and a season for every activity under heaven."

A woman's appearance, health and circumstances change with time. Many women attempt to cope with these changes by clinging to outward beauty, youthful behaviors and past achievements. However, once we realize that we are made in accordance with God's plan and that his plan carries us through change, we come to grips with aging. Women, as well as others who live each day for the Lord, will not only bear fruit while in their youth, but they will also bear fruit in their old age (see Ps 92:12–15).

Sands of time—seconds, minutes, hours, days, weeks, months and years—pass through the hourglass. Yet the passing sands do not merely count the days of our lives and settle into a meaningless heap at the bottom. They also carry footprints that mark the essence of our passing through. Contained therein are imprints of all that we do to contribute to God's creative order—the impressions we make as we touch people's lives and the trails we blaze for others to follow.

The footprints of other faithful pilgrims illuminate, inform and enrich our lives, leaving a legacy of commitment to those things that are true, honest, just and pure. We are, therefore, challenged to do likewise. As we age, let us do so with grace, striving to use our gift of time to honor God and uplift others. Then one day our lives will be counted and remembered as testimonies of love and service, as we make our footprints on the sands of time.

—A. Adams Powell

**read**

Ecclesiastes 3:1–14; see also Psalm 92.

See also the Inspire Notes "Influencing Others," "Commitment to Community" and "Faith," and the Women of the Bible Note "Anna: A Model of Spiritual Devotion."

**WOMAN of COLOR**

What imprint or impression are you making in the sands of time as you pass through this life?

For the next Inspire note, go to page 777.

**3:17** g Ro 2:6–8; 2Th 1:6–7 h ver 1
**3:18** i Ps 73:22
**3:20** j Ge 3:19
**3:21** k Ecc 12:7
**3:22** l Ecc 2:24
**4:1** m Ecc 3:16
**4:3** n Job 3:16; Ecc 6:3
**4:5** o Pr 6:10

In the place of judgment—wickedness
was there,
in the place of justice—wickedness
was there.

17 I thought in my heart,

"God will bring to judgment[g]
both the righteous and the wicked,
for there will be a time for every activity,
a time for every deed."[h]

18 I also thought, "As for men, God tests
them so that they may see that they are like
the animals.[i] 19 Man's fate is like that of the
animals; the same fate awaits them both: As
one dies, so dies the other. All have the same
breath[a]; man has no advantage over the ani-
mal. Everything is meaningless. 20 All go to
the same place; all come from dust, and to
dust all return.[j] 21 Who knows if the spirit of
man rises upward[k] and if the spirit of the an-
imal[b] goes down into the earth?"

22 So I saw that there is nothing better for
a man than to enjoy his work,[l] because that
is his lot. For who can bring him to see what
will happen after him?

## Oppression, Toil, Friendlessness

4 Again I looked and saw all the oppres-
sion[m] that was taking place under
the sun:

I saw the tears of the oppressed—
and they have no comforter;
power was on the side of their
oppressors—
and they have no comforter.
2 And I declared that the dead,
who had already died,
are happier than the living,
who are still alive.
3 But better than both
is he who has not yet been,[n]
who has not seen the evil
that is done under the sun.

4 And I saw that all labor and all achieve-
ment spring from man's envy of his neigh-
bor. This too is meaningless, a chasing after
the wind.

5 The fool folds his hands[o]
and ruins himself.
6 Better one handful with tranquillity
than two handfuls with toil[p]
and chasing after the wind.

7 Again I saw something meaningless un-
der the sun:

8 There was a man all alone;
he had neither son nor brother.
There was no end to his toil,
yet his eyes were not content[q] with his
wealth.
"For whom am I toiling," he asked,
"and why am I depriving myself of
enjoyment?"
This too is meaningless—
a miserable business!

9 Two are better than one,
because they have a good return for
their work:
10 If one falls down,
his friend can help him up.
But pity the man who falls
and has no one to help him up!
11 Also, if two lie down together, they will
keep warm.
But how can one keep warm alone?
12 Though one may be overpowered,
two can defend themselves.
A cord of three strands is not quickly
broken.

## Advancement Is Meaningless

13 Better a poor but wise youth than an old
but foolish king who no longer knows how
to take warning. 14 The youth may have come
from prison to the kingship, or he may have
been born in poverty within his kingdom.
15 I saw that all who lived and walked under
the sun followed the youth, the king's suc-
cessor. 16 There was no end to all the people
who were before them. But those who came
later were not pleased with the successor.
This too is meaningless, a chasing after
the wind.

## Stand in Awe of God

5 Guard your steps when you go to the
house of God. Go near to listen rather
than to offer the sacrifice of fools, who do
not know that they do wrong.

**4:6** p Pr 15:16–17; 16:8
**4:8** q Pr 27:20

[a]19 Or *spirit* [b]21 Or *Who knows the spirit of man, which rises upward, or the spirit of the animal, which*

# Inspire

## FRIENDSHIP

When expounding on three great tenets of Christianity—faith, hope and love—the apostle Paul emphatically pointed out that the greatest of these is love (see 1Co 13:13). During a discussion on love and friendship, Jesus commented that there is no greater love than that of one who lays down his or her life for a friend (see Jn 15:13). So it is apparent that the word *friendship* denotes a most powerful relationship and is not to be taken lightly.

Women need the fellowship and nurturing companionship of other women. Often the term *friend* is used in reference to a mere acquaintance. The words *friend* and *acquaintance* should never be used interchangeably. True friendship is rare and should be valued as such. The bond of friendship is formed out of mutual trust, commitment and unconditional love. Acquaintances are superficial and cannot withstand the tests of a true friend. A person who is wealthy or famous often has many so-called friends. Yet when their resources are depleted, these "friends" typically are not to be found.

True friends will stick closer than a sibling (see Pr 18:24). In trying times, true friends are concerned about your welfare. They applaud your successes and are not jealous or consumed with their own selfish ambition (see 1Co 13:4–5). They love you at all times (see Pr 17:17).

Friendships are built and maintained with effort and by being a true friend yourself. No one should have to travel through life alone. Ecclesiastes 4:9–10 says, "Two are better than one, because they have a good return for their work: If one falls down, his friend can help him up. But pity the man who falls and has no one to help him up!"

Friendship between two women is based on love, loyalty and commitment. A New Testament example of a devoted friendship between two women is seen in the friendship of Elizabeth and Mary (see Lk 1:39–56); in the Old Testament, the mother-in-law/daughter-in-law relationship between Ruth and Naomi blossomed into a lifelong friendship (see Ru 1).

Women of color are encouraged to build lasting friendships that will endure life's challenges.

—A. Howell

### read

Ecclesiastes 4:7–12;
1 Corinthians 13;
Philippians 2:1–5.

See also the Inspire Notes "Intimate Friendships" and "Intimacy: Relationships With Other Christians," and the Women of the Bible Notes "Ruth: A Model of Friendship and Sisterhood," "Naomi: Call Me Bitter" and "Euodia and Syntyche: Women in Conflict."

### WOMAN *of* COLOR

How do you nurture your friendships?

For the next Inspire note, go to page 789.

[2] Do not be quick with your mouth,
do not be hasty in your heart
to utter anything before God.
God is in heaven
and you are on earth,
so let your words be few.[r]
[3] As a dream comes when there are many cares,
so the speech of a fool when there are many words.

[4]When you make a vow to God, do not delay in fulfilling it. He has no pleasure in fools; fulfill your vow. [5]It is better not to vow than to make a vow and not fulfill it.[s] [6]Do not let your mouth lead you into sin. And do not protest to the ⌊temple⌋ messenger, "My vow was a mistake." Why should God be angry at what you say and destroy the work of your hands? [7]Much dreaming and many words are meaningless. Therefore stand in awe of God.[t]

## Riches Are Meaningless

[8]If you see the poor oppressed in a district, and justice and rights denied, do not be surprised at such things; for one official is eyed by a higher one, and over them both are others higher still. [9]The increase from the land is taken by all; the king himself profits from the fields.

[10] Whoever loves money never has money enough;
whoever loves wealth is never satisfied with his income.
This too is meaningless.

[11] As goods increase,
so do those who consume them.
And what benefit are they to the owner
except to feast his eyes on them?

[12] The sleep of a laborer is sweet,
whether he eats little or much,
but the abundance of a rich man
permits him no sleep.

[13]I have seen a grievous evil under the sun:[u]

wealth hoarded to the harm of its owner,
[14] or wealth lost through some misfortune,
so that when he has a son
there is nothing left for him.
[15] Naked a man comes from his mother's womb,
and as he comes, so he departs.[v]
He takes nothing from his labor[w]
that he can carry in his hand.

[16]This too is a grievous evil:

As a man comes, so he departs,
and what does he gain,
since he toils for the wind?[x]
[17] All his days he eats in darkness,
with great frustration, affliction and anger.

[18]Then I realized that it is good and proper for a man to eat and drink, and to find satisfaction in his toilsome labor[y] under the sun during the few days of life God has given him—for this is his lot. [19]Moreover, when God gives any man wealth and possessions, and enables him to enjoy them, to accept his lot and be happy in his work—this is a gift of God.[z] [20]He seldom reflects on the days of his life, because God keeps him occupied with gladness of heart.

6 I have seen another evil under the sun, and it weighs heavily on men: [2]God gives a man wealth, possessions and honor, so that he lacks nothing his heart desires, but God does not enable him to enjoy them,[a] and a stranger enjoys them instead. This is meaningless, a grievous evil.

[3]A man may have a hundred children and live many years; yet no matter how long he lives, if he cannot enjoy his prosperity and does not receive proper burial, I say that a stillborn[b] child is better off than he. [4]It comes without meaning, it departs in darkness, and in darkness its name is shrouded. [5]Though it never saw the sun or knew anything, it has more rest than does that man— [6]even if he lives a thousand years twice over but fails to enjoy his prosperity. Do not all go to the same place?

[7] All man's efforts are for his mouth,
yet his appetite is never satisfied.[c]
[8] What advantage has a wise man
over a fool?[d]
What does a poor man gain
by knowing how to conduct himself
before others?

**5:2** r Pr 10:19
**5:5** s Pr 20:25; Ac 5:4
**5:7** t Ecc 12:13
**5:13** u Ecc 6:1–2
**5:15** v Job 1:21 w Ps 49:17; 1Ti 6:7
**5:16** x Pr 11:29; Ecc 1:3
**5:18** y Ecc 2:10,24
**5:19** z Ecc 2:24; 3:13
**6:2** a Ps 17:14
**6:3** b Job 3:16; Ecc 4:3
**6:7** c Pr 16:26
**6:8** d Ecc 2:15

6:12 e Ps 39:6
7:1 f Pr 22:1
7:3 g Pr 14:13
7:5 h Ps 141:5; Pr 15:31–32

*Lord,*

*help me to enjoy all that you have given me*
*and to take inventory of all that I possess*
*instead of concentrating on what I feel I lack.*

*Amen*

ECCLESIASTES 6:7–9

[9] Better what the eye sees
than the roving of the appetite.
This too is meaningless,
a chasing after the wind.

[10] Whatever exists has already been named,
and what man is has been known;
no man can contend
with one who is stronger than he.
[11] The more the words,
the less the meaning,
and how does that profit anyone?

[12]For who knows what is good for a man in life, during the few and meaningless days he passes through like a shadow?[e] Who can tell him what will happen under the sun after he is gone?

## Wisdom

7 A good name is better than fine
perfume,[f]
and the day of death better than the
day of birth.
[2] It is better to go to a house of mourning
than to go to a house of feasting,
for death is the destiny of every man;
the living should take this to heart.
[3] Sorrow is better than laughter,[g]
because a sad face is good for the
heart.
[4] The heart of the wise is in the house of
mourning,
but the heart of fools is in the house of
pleasure.
[5] It is better to heed a wise man's rebuke[h]
than to listen to the song of fools.
[6] Like the crackling of thorns under the
pot,
so is the laughter[i] of fools.
This too is meaningless.

[7] Extortion turns a wise man into a fool,
and a bribe[j] corrupts the heart.
[8] The end of a matter is better than its
beginning,
and patience[k] is better than pride.
[9] Do not be quickly provoked[l] in your
spirit,
for anger resides in the lap of fools.

[10] Do not say, "Why were the old days better
than these?"
For it is not wise to ask such questions.

[11] Wisdom, like an inheritance, is a good
thing
and benefits those who see the sun.
[12] Wisdom is a shelter
as money is a shelter,
but the advantage of knowledge is this:
that wisdom preserves the life of its
possessor.

[13]Consider what God has done:

Who can straighten
what he has made crooked?[m]
[14] When times are good, be happy;
but when times are bad, consider:
God has made the one
as well as the other.
Therefore, a man cannot discover
anything about his future.

[15]In this meaningless life of mine I have seen both of these:

a righteous man perishing in his
righteousness,
and a wicked man living long in his
wickedness.[n]
[16] Do not be overrighteous,
neither be overwise—
why destroy yourself?
[17] Do not be overwicked,
and do not be a fool—
why die before your time?[o]
[18] It is good to grasp the one
and not let go of the other.
The man who fears God will avoid all
⌞extremes⌟.[a]

7:6 i Ecc 2:2
7:7 j Ex 23:8; Dt 16:19
7:8 k Pr 14:29
7:9 l Pr 14:17; Jas 1:19
7:13 m Ecc 1:15
7:15 n Ecc 8:12–14
7:17 o Ps 55:23

[a]18 Or *will follow them both*

7:19 p Ecc 9:13–18
7:20 q 1Ki 8:46; 2Ch 6:36; Pr 20:9
7:24 r Job 28:12
7:25 s Ecc 1:17
7:26 t Pr 5:3–5

19 Wisdom makes one wise man more
powerful[p]
than ten rulers in a city.
20 There is not a righteous man on earth
who does what is right and never sins.[q]
21 Do not pay attention to every word people
say,
or you may hear your servant cursing
you—
22 for you know in your heart
that many times you yourself have
cursed others.

23 All this I tested by wisdom and I said,

"I am determined to be wise"—
but this was beyond me.
24 Whatever wisdom may be,
it is far off and most profound—
who can discover it?[r]
25 So I turned my mind to understand,
to investigate and to search out
wisdom and the scheme of
things
and to understand the stupidity of
wickedness
and the madness of folly.[s]

26 I find more bitter than death
the woman who is a snare,
whose heart is a trap
and whose hands are chains.
The man who pleases God will escape
her,
but the sinner she will ensnare.[t]

27 "Look," says the Teacher,[a] "this is what
I have discovered:

"Adding one thing to another to discover
the scheme of things—
28 while I was still searching
but not finding—
I found one ⌊upright⌋ man among a
thousand,
but not one ⌊upright⌋ woman among
them all.
29 This only have I found:
God made mankind upright,
but men have gone in search of many
schemes."

8 Who is like the wise man?
Who knows the explanation of things?
Wisdom brightens a man's face
and changes its hard appearance.

## Obey the King

2 Obey the king's command, I say, be-
cause you took an oath before God. 3 Do not
be in a hurry to leave the king's presence.
Do not stand up for a bad cause, for he will
do whatever he pleases. 4 Since a king's word
is supreme, who can say to him, "What are
you doing?"

5 Whoever obeys his command will come
to no harm,
and the wise heart will know the
proper time and procedure.
6 For there is a proper time and procedure
for every matter,[u]
though a man's misery weighs heavily
upon him.

7 Since no man knows the future,
who can tell him what is to come?
8 No man has power over the wind to
contain it[b];
so no one has power over the day of
his death.
As no one is discharged in time of war,
so wickedness will not release those
who practice it.

9 All this I saw, as I applied my mind to
everything done under the sun. There is a
time when a man lords it over others to his
own[c] hurt. 10 Then too, I saw the wicked bur-
ied—those who used to come and go from
the holy place and receive praise[d] in the city
where they did this. This too is meaning-
less.

11 When the sentence for a crime is not
quickly carried out, the hearts of the people
are filled with schemes to do wrong. 12 Al-
though a wicked man commits a hundred
crimes and still lives a long time, I know
that it will go better[v] with God-fearing
men, who are reverent before God. 13 Yet be-
cause the wicked do not fear God, it will not
go well with them, and their days will not
lengthen like a shadow.
14 There is something else meaningless

8:6 u Ecc 3:1
8:12 v Ps 37:11,18–19; Pr 1:32–33; Isa 3:10–11

[a]27 Or *leader of the assembly* [b]8 Or *over his spirit to retain it* [c]9 Or *to their* [d]10 Some Hebrew manuscripts and Septuagint (Aquila); most Hebrew manuscripts *and are forgotten*

that occurs on earth: righteous men who get what the wicked deserve, and wicked men who get what the righteous deserve.[w] This too, I say, is meaningless.[x] 15 So I commend the enjoyment of life, because nothing is better for a man under the sun than to eat and drink and be glad.[y] Then joy will accompany him in his work all the days of the life God has given him under the sun.

16 When I applied my mind to know wisdom and to observe man's labor on earth—his eyes not seeing sleep day or night— 17 then I saw all that God has done. No one can comprehend what goes on under the sun. Despite all his efforts to search it out, man cannot discover its meaning. Even if a wise man claims he knows, he cannot really comprehend it.[z]

## A Common Destiny for All

9 So I reflected on all this and concluded that the righteous and the wise and what they do are in God's hands, but no man knows whether love or hate awaits him.[a] 2 All share a common destiny—the righteous and the wicked, the good and the bad,[a] the clean and the unclean, those who offer sacrifices and those who do not.

As it is with the good man,
so with the sinner;
as it is with those who take oaths,
so with those who are afraid to take them.[b]

3 This is the evil in everything that happens under the sun: The same destiny overtakes all. The hearts of men, moreover, are full of evil and there is madness in their hearts while they live, and afterward they join the dead. 4 Anyone who is among the living has hope[b]—even a live dog is better off than a dead lion!

5 For the living know that they will die,
but the dead know nothing;[c]
they have no further reward,
and even the memory of them is forgotten.[d]
6 Their love, their hate
and their jealousy have long since vanished;
never again will they have a part
in anything that happens under the sun.

7 Go, eat your food with gladness, and drink your wine with a joyful heart,[e] for it is now that God favors what you do. 8 Always be clothed in white, and always anoint your head with oil. 9 Enjoy life with your wife, whom you love, all the days of this meaningless life that God has given you under the sun—all your meaningless days. For this is your lot in life and in your toilsome labor under the sun. 10 Whatever your hand finds to do, do it with all your might, for in the grave,[c] where you are going, there is neither working nor planning nor knowledge nor wisdom.

11 I have seen something else under the sun:

The race is not to the swift
or the battle to the strong,[f]
nor does food come to the wise
or wealth to the brilliant
or favor to the learned;
but time and chance happen to them all.

12 Moreover, no man knows when his hour will come:

As fish are caught in a cruel net,
or birds are taken in a snare,
so men are trapped by evil times[g]
that fall unexpectedly upon them.[h]

## Wisdom Better Than Folly

13 I also saw under the sun this example of wisdom that greatly impressed me: 14 There was once a small city with only a few people in it. And a powerful king came against it, surrounded it and built huge siegeworks against it. 15 Now there lived in that city a man poor but wise, and he saved the city by his wisdom. But nobody remembered that poor man. 16 So I said, "Wisdom is better than strength." But the poor man's wisdom is despised, and his words are no longer heeded.[i]

17 The quiet words of the wise are more to be heeded

**8:14** w Ps 73:14 x Ecc 7:15
**8:15** y Ecc 2:24; 3:12–13; 5:18; 9:7
**8:17** z Ecc 3:11; Ro 11:33
**9:1** a Ecc 10:14
**9:2** b Job 9:22
**9:5** c Job 14:21 d Isa 26:14
**9:7** e Ecc 8:15
**9:11** f Am 2:14–15
**9:12** g Pr 29:6 h Ecc 8:7
**9:16** i Pr 21:22; Ecc 7:19

[a]2 Septuagint (Aquila), Vulgate and Syriac; Hebrew does not have *and the bad.* [b]4 Or *What then is to be chosen? With all who live, there is hope* [c]10 Hebrew *Sheol*

9:18
j ver 16

10:3
k Pr 13:16; 18:2

10:4
l Ecc 8:3
m Pr 25:15

10:7
n Pr 19:10

10:8
o Ps 7:15; Pr 26:27

10:11
p Ps 58:5

10:12
q Pr 10:32
r Pr 10:14

10:14
s Pr 15:2; Ecc 8:7

than the shouts of a ruler of fools.
18 Wisdom[j] is better than weapons of war,
but one sinner destroys much good.

10 As dead flies give perfume a bad smell,
so a little folly outweighs wisdom and honor.
2 The heart of the wise inclines to the right,
but the heart of the fool to the left.
3 Even as he walks along the road,
the fool lacks sense
and shows everyone[k] how stupid he is.
4 If a ruler's anger rises against you,
do not leave your post;[l]
calmness can lay great errors to rest.[m]

5 There is an evil I have seen under the sun,
the sort of error that arises from a ruler:
6 Fools are put in many high positions,
while the rich occupy the low ones.
7 I have seen slaves on horseback,
while princes go on foot like slaves.[n]

8 Whoever digs a pit may fall into it;[o]
whoever breaks through a wall may be bitten by a snake.
9 Whoever quarries stones may be injured by them;
whoever splits logs may be endangered by them.

10 If the ax is dull
and its edge unsharpened,
more strength is needed
but skill will bring success.

11 If a snake bites before it is charmed,
there is no profit for the charmer.[p]

12 Words from a wise man's mouth are gracious,[q]
but a fool is consumed by his own lips.[r]
13 At the beginning his words are folly;
at the end they are wicked madness—
14 and the fool multiplies words.[s]

No one knows what is coming—
who can tell him what will happen after him?

15 A fool's work wearies him;
he does not know the way to town.

16 Woe to you, O land whose king was a servant[a][t]
and whose princes feast in the morning.
17 Blessed are you, O land whose king is of noble birth
and whose princes eat at a proper time—
for strength and not for drunkenness.[u]

18 If a man is lazy, the rafters sag;
if his hands are idle, the house leaks.

19 A feast is made for laughter,
and wine makes life merry,
but money is the answer for everything.

20 Do not revile the king[v] even in your thoughts,
or curse the rich in your bedroom,
because a bird of the air may carry your words,
and a bird on the wing may report what you say.

## Bread Upon the Waters

11 Cast your bread upon the waters,
for after many days you will find it again.[w]
2 Give portions to seven, yes to eight,
for you do not know what disaster may come upon the land.

3 If clouds are full of water,
they pour rain upon the earth.
Whether a tree falls to the south or to the north,
in the place where it falls, there will it lie.
4 Whoever watches the wind will not plant;
whoever looks at the clouds will not reap.

5 As you do not know the path of the wind,[x]
or how the body is formed[b] in a mother's womb,[y]
so you cannot understand the work of God,
the Maker of all things.

6 Sow your seed in the morning,
and at evening let not your hands be idle,
for you do not know which will succeed,

10:16
t Isa 3:4–5,12

10:17
u Pr 31:4

10:20
v Ex 22:28

11:1
w Pr 19:17; Mt 10:42

11:5
x Jn 3:8–10
y Ps 139:14–16

[a]16 Or *king is a child* [b]5 Or *know how life* (or *the spirit*) */ enters the body being formed*

**11:7** z Ecc 7:11
**11:9** a Ecc 12:14
**12:1** b Ecc 11:8

whether this or that,
or whether both will do equally well.

## Remember Your Creator While Young

7 Light is sweet,
and it pleases the eyes to see the sun.[z]
8 However many years a man may live,
let him enjoy them all.
But let him remember the days of darkness,
for they will be many.
Everything to come is meaningless.

9 Be happy, young man, while you are young,
and let your heart give you joy in the days of your youth.
Follow the ways of your heart
and whatever your eyes see,
but know that for all these things
God will bring you to judgment.[a]
10 So then, banish anxiety from your heart
and cast off the troubles of your body,
for youth and vigor are meaningless.

12 Remember[b] your Creator
in the days of your youth,
before the days of trouble come
and the years approach when you will say,
"I find no pleasure in them"—

*My cherished creation,*

*Remember me, your Creator,*
*today and always.*

*God*

ECCLESIASTES 12:1

2 before the sun and the light
and the moon and the stars grow dark,
and the clouds return after the rain;
3 when the keepers of the house tremble,
and the strong men stoop,
when the grinders cease because they are few,
and those looking through the windows grow dim;
4 when the doors to the street are closed
and the sound of grinding fades;
when men rise up at the sound of birds,
but all their songs grow faint;
5 when men are afraid of heights
and of dangers in the streets;
when the almond tree blossoms
and the grasshopper drags himself along
and desire no longer is stirred.
Then man goes to his eternal home[c]
and mourners[d] go about the streets.

6 Remember him—before the silver cord is severed,
or the golden bowl is broken;
before the pitcher is shattered at the spring,
or the wheel broken at the well,
7 and the dust returns[e] to the ground it came from,
and the spirit returns to God[f] who gave it.[g]

8 "Meaningless! Meaningless!" says the Teacher.[a]
"Everything is meaningless!"

## The Conclusion of the Matter

9 Not only was the Teacher wise, but also he imparted knowledge to the people. He pondered and searched out and set in order many proverbs.[h] 10 The Teacher searched to find just the right words, and what he wrote was upright and true.

11 The words of the wise are like goads, their collected sayings like firmly embedded nails—given by one Shepherd. 12 Be warned, my son, of anything in addition to them.

Of making many books there is no end, and much study wearies the body.[i]

13 Now all has been heard;
here is the conclusion of the matter:
Fear God and keep his commandments,[j]
for this is the whole ⌊duty⌋ of man.
14 For God will bring every deed into judgment,
including every hidden thing,[k]
whether it is good or evil.

**12:5** c Job 17:13 d Jer 9:17
**12:7** e Ge 3:19; Job 34:15 f Ecc 3:21 g Zec 12:1
**12:9** h 1Ki 4:32
**12:12** i Ecc 1:18
**12:13** j Dt 10:12
**12:14** k 1Co 4:5

[a]8 Or *the leader of the assembly*; also in verses 9 and 10

# Song of Songs

## OVERVIEW

Love is celebrated in its noblest sense in this book, which records the dialogue between two lovers, the Lover and the Beloved. Their deepening affection for each other is described in poetic language. Besides celebrating love and the sexual desire between a husband and wife, this story also is symbolic of the pure and unconditional love of God and his Son Jesus Christ for the believer.

Under the inspiration of the Holy Spirit, Paul wrote in detail how unconditional love is expressed (see 1Co 13). This *agape* love should be expressed to every person in a woman's life. As you read through the Song of Songs, think about how you can express your love to those around you under the leading of the Holy Spirit.

## OUTLINE

I. The Attraction (1:1—2:7)
II. The Deepening (2:8—3:5)
III. The Wedding (3:6—5:1)
IV. The Absent Husband (5:2—6:3)
V. The Wife's Beauty and the Husband's Attractiveness (6:4—8:4)
VI. The Glory of Love (8:5–14)

## SCANNABLE FACTS:

**Author:** Probably Solomon

**Time Written:** If written by Solomon, then sometime during his reign, 970–930 B.C.

**Theme to Note:** The glory of love

**Notable Women:** "The Beloved" and her "Friends"

1:1 a 1Ki4:32
1:2 b SS4:10
1:4 c Ps45:15
1:8 d SS5:9
1:9 e 2Ch 1:17
1:15 f SS4:1; 5:2,12

1 Solomon's Song of Songs.[a]

*Beloved*[a]

2 Let him kiss me with the kisses of his
mouth—
for your love[b] is more delightful than
wine.
3 Pleasing is the fragrance of your
perfumes;
your name is like perfume poured out.
No wonder the maidens love you!
4 Take me away with you—let us hurry!
Let the king bring me into his
chambers.[c]

*Friends*

We rejoice and delight in you[b];
we will praise your love more than wine.

*Beloved*

How right they are to adore you!

5 Dark am I, yet lovely,
O daughters of Jerusalem,
dark like the tents of Kedar,
like the tent curtains of Solomon.[c]
6 Do not stare at me because I am dark,
because I am darkened by the sun.
My mother's sons were angry with me
and made me take care of the
vineyards;
my own vineyard I have neglected.
7 Tell me, you whom I love, where you
graze your flock
and where you rest your sheep at
midday.
Why should I be like a veiled woman
beside the flocks of your friends?

*Friends*

8 If you do not know, most beautiful of
women,[d]
follow the tracks of the sheep
and graze your young goats
by the tents of the shepherds.

*Lover*

9 I liken you, my darling, to a mare
harnessed to one of the chariots[e] of
Pharaoh.
10 Your cheeks are beautiful with earrings,
your neck with strings of jewels.
11 We will make you earrings of gold,
studded with silver.

*Beloved*

12 While the king was at his table,
my perfume spread its fragrance.
13 My lover is to me a sachet of myrrh
resting between my breasts.
14 My lover is to me a cluster of henna
blossoms
from the vineyards of En Gedi.

*Lover*

15 How beautiful you are, my darling!
Oh, how beautiful!
Your eyes are doves.[f]

[a]Primarily on the basis of the gender of the Hebrew pronouns used, male and female speakers are indicated in the margins by the captions *Lover* and *Beloved* respectively. The words of others are marked *Friends*. In some instances the divisions and their captions are debatable. [b]4 The Hebrew is masculine singular. [c]5 Or *Salma*

## The African Presence

### Song of Songs 1

Some scholars believe the beloved woman refers to the Egyptian wife whom Solomon married (see 1Ki 3:1); others believe she was from Lebanon. The reference in 6:13 indicates she may have been from Shunem, an area in Canaan.

The woman described herself as "black and beautiful" according to the Septuagint, or "dark am I, yet lovely" (1:5, NIV). Her blackness was compared to the tents of Kedar, which were made of black goat hair.

# The Bridegroom and His Bride

## Soul Mates in Life

The Shulammite bride in Song of Songs has been described as many different things. She has been classified as rich, poor, a commoner and a princess. But she was first and foremost a woman in love. She was a woman who endured much to be with the one she loved. The bride spoke of their courtship, remembering how the groom looked and behaved toward her.

The bride spoke of her engagement to her man, of misunderstandings, and of her restless thoughts when separated from him. The length of their separation and her longing for him troubled her sleep—not once, but twice. She longed for her best friend, her banner, her lover and her lord. Even as she went about her daily tasks, her mind was on the love of her life, the man who had swept her off her feet with kind words, gentle strength and tender embraces.

When the bride and bridegroom finally were reunited, it was with a joy reserved for people who have endured misunderstandings, temptations and pain in order to be together. Alternately passionate and shy, the bride built up her husband, loving him with the sweetness of her words and body. While she was jealous of him, she still loved him with all of her being. Her husband was her friend—implying that they were soul mates before they consummated their union.

The relationship between the bride and her husband personifies love in its purest form—a monogamous relationship between a husband and wife who have an abiding respect and a replete and unassuming trust. This same desire is found in the spiritual relationship of knowing Jesus as Lord. We are to love him with the same passion and all-consuming fire, the same jealousy, abiding love and respect with which we would love our spouse. We must come to Jesus, our Bridegroom, with the same unabashed love that he demonstrates daily to Christians, those whom he considers his bride.

—M. Cotton Bohanon

### reflection

*Do you long for Jesus as much as the bride longed for her lover?*

*Fall in love with the Lord all over again today. Think about all he has done for you and all he means to you throughout the day.*

### read

Song of Songs.

See also the Inspire Notes "Let's Talk About Sex," "Romance: A Biblical Perspective," "Marriage," "What Is Intimacy?" and "Love."

For the next Women of the Bible note, go to page 972.

2:6 g SS 8:3
2:7 h SS 3:5; 8:4

*Beloved*

16 How handsome you are, my lover!
Oh, how charming!
And our bed is verdant.

*Lover*

17 The beams of our house are cedars;
our rafters are firs.

*Beloved*[a]

2 I am a rose[b] of Sharon,
a lily of the valleys.

*Lover*

2 Like a lily among thorns
is my darling among the maidens.

*Beloved*

3 Like an apple tree among the trees of the forest
is my lover among the young men.
I delight to sit in his shade,
and his fruit is sweet to my taste.
4 He has taken me to the banquet hall,
and his banner over me is love.
5 Strengthen me with raisins,
refresh me with apples,
for I am faint with love.
6 His left arm is under my head,
and his right arm embraces me.[g]
7 Daughters of Jerusalem, I charge you
by the gazelles and by the does of the field:
Do not arouse or awaken love
until it so desires.[h]

8 Listen! My lover!
Look! Here he comes,
leaping across the mountains,

*Lord,*

*teach me to wait on you for love, and prevent me from rushing any season or passage in my life. Help me to find true satisfaction in you first of all. In Jesus' precious name,*

*Amen*

SONG OF SONGS 2:7

bounding over the hills.
9 My lover is like a gazelle or a young stag.[i]
Look! There he stands behind our wall,
gazing through the windows,
peering through the lattice.
10 My lover spoke and said to me,
"Arise, my darling,
my beautiful one, and come with me.
11 See! The winter is past;
the rains are over and gone.
12 Flowers appear on the earth;
the season of singing has come,
the cooing of doves
is heard in our land.
13 The fig tree forms its early fruit;
the blossoming vines spread their fragrance.
Arise, come, my darling;
my beautiful one, come with me."

*Lover*

14 My dove in the clefts of the rock,
in the hiding places on the mountainside,
show me your face,
let me hear your voice;
for your voice is sweet,
and your face is lovely.[j]
15 Catch for us the foxes,
the little foxes
that ruin the vineyards,
our vineyards that are in bloom.

*Beloved*

16 My lover is mine and I am his;[k]
he browses among the lilies.[l]
17 Until the day breaks
and the shadows flee,
turn, my lover,
and be like a gazelle
or like a young stag[m]
on the rugged hills.[c]

3 All night long on my bed
I looked for the one my heart loves;
I looked for him but did not find him.
2 I will get up now and go about the city,
through its streets and squares;
I will search for the one my heart loves.
So I looked for him but did not find him.
3 The watchmen found me

2:9 i ver 17
2:14 j SS 1:5; 8:13
2:16 k SS 7:10 l SS 6:3
2:17 m ver 9

[a] Or *Lover* [b] 1 Possibly a member of the crocus family [c] 17 Or *the hills of Bether*

3:3
n SS5:7

as they made their rounds in the city.[n]
"Have you seen the one my heart
loves?"
4 Scarcely had I passed them
when I found the one my heart loves.
I held him and would not let him go
till I had brought him to my mother's
house,
to the room of the one who
conceived me.
5 Daughters of Jerusalem, I charge
you[o]
by the gazelles and by the does of the
field:
Do not arouse or awaken love
until it so desires.[p]

3:5
o SS2:7
p SS8:4

Inspire

## ROMANCE: A BIBLICAL PERSPECTIVE

One would probably not think to look in the Bible for a definition of romance, but the deepest exposition on romance in its finest declaration can be found in the Song of Songs. This love poem sets the stage for a modern man and woman's ideal of courtship—an expression of love and promise. The words are so fervent and noble that centuries of Christian Biblical scholars have identified the book as a divine allegory representing the love between Christ and his church.

In the Song of Songs, the depth of devotion possible for lovers is captured by the phrase "the one my heart loves"—repeated four times in 3:1–4. The beloved also declared, "This is my lover, this my friend" (5:16). She expressed intense emotion and commitment. This intensity reaches its pinnacle in 8:6–7: "Love is as strong as death . . . It burns like blazing fire . . . Many waters cannot quench love." This, then, is true romance: affection, friendship, respect and tenderness between the lovers.

Beginning romantic relationships with friendship and respect develops the foundation that leads one to love with one's heart and soul; and that same friendship and respect needs to remain a constant theme throughout the marriage for the love to be sustained.

—K. Smallwood

### read

Song of Songs 1–4; Revelation 21:2.
See also the Inspire Notes "Let's Talk About Sex," "Dating," "Marriage," "What Is Intimacy?" "Celibacy" and "Love," and the Women of the Bible Note "The Bridegroom and His Bride: Soul Mates in Life."

### WOMAN of COLOR

Single woman of color: How can you build romantic relationships based on friendship and respect?

Married woman of color: How do you sustain your marriage through friendship and respect?

For the next Inspire note, go to page 792.

**3:6** q SS 8:5
**4:1** r SS 1:15; 5:12 s SS 6:5
**4:2** t SS 6:6
**4:3** u SS 6:7
**4:4** v SS 7:4
**4:5** w SS 7:3

[6] Who is this coming up from the desert[q]
like a column of smoke,
perfumed with myrrh and incense
made from all the spices of the
merchant?
[7] Look! It is Solomon's carriage,
escorted by sixty warriors,
the noblest of Israel,
[8] all of them wearing the sword,
all experienced in battle,
each with his sword at his side,
prepared for the terrors of the night.
[9] King Solomon made for himself the
carriage;
he made it of wood from Lebanon.
[10] Its posts he made of silver,
its base of gold.
Its seat was upholstered with purple,
its interior lovingly inlaid
by[a] the daughters of Jerusalem.
[11] Come out, you daughters of Zion,
and look at King Solomon wearing the
crown,
the crown with which his mother
crowned him
on the day of his wedding,
the day his heart rejoiced.

*Lover*

4 How beautiful you are, my darling!
Oh, how beautiful!
Your eyes behind your veil are doves.[r]
Your hair is like a flock of goats
descending from Mount Gilead.[s]
[2] Your teeth are like a flock of sheep just
shorn,
coming up from the washing.
Each has its twin;
not one of them is alone.[t]
[3] Your lips are like a scarlet ribbon;
your mouth is lovely.
Your temples behind your veil
are like the halves of a pomegranate.[u]
[4] Your neck is like the tower[v] of David,
built with elegance[b];
on it hang a thousand shields,
all of them shields of warriors.
[5] Your two breasts[w] are like two fawns,
like twin fawns of a gazelle
that browse among the lilies.
[6] Until the day breaks
and the shadows flee,[x]
I will go to the mountain of myrrh
and to the hill of incense.
[7] All beautiful you are, my darling;
there is no flaw in you.
[8] Come with me from Lebanon, my bride,
come with me from Lebanon.
Descend from the crest of Amana,
from the top of Senir,[y] the summit of
Hermon,
from the lions' dens
and the mountain haunts of the
leopards.
[9] You have stolen my heart, my sister, my
bride;
you have stolen my heart
with one glance of your eyes,
with one jewel of your necklace.
[10] How delightful is your love, my sister, my
bride!
How much more pleasing is your love
than wine,
and the fragrance of your perfume
than any spice!
[11] Your lips drop sweetness as the
honeycomb, my bride;
milk and honey are under your tongue.
The fragrance of your garments is like
that of Lebanon.
[12] You are a garden locked up, my sister, my
bride;
you are a spring enclosed, a sealed
fountain.
[13] Your plants are an orchard of
pomegranates
with choice fruits,
with henna and nard,
[14] nard and saffron,
calamus and cinnamon,
with every kind of incense tree,
with myrrh and aloes
and all the finest spices.
[15] You are[c] a garden fountain,
a well of flowing water
streaming down from Lebanon.

*Beloved*

[16] Awake, north wind,
and come, south wind!
Blow on my garden,

**4:6** x SS 2:17
**4:8** y Dt 3:9

[a]10 Or *its inlaid interior a gift of love / from* [b]4 The meaning of the Hebrew for this word is uncertain. [c]15 Or *I am* (spoken by the *Beloved*)

**4:16** z SS 5:1
**5:1** a SS 4:11

*Woman of color,*

*I've created each of my daughters*
*with unique gifts, talents and beauty.*
*Use them all to glorify me.*

*The Master Artist*

SONG OF SONGS 4:15

that its fragrance may spread abroad.
Let my lover come into his garden
and taste its choice fruits.[z]

*Lover*

5 I have come into my garden, my sister, my bride;
I have gathered my myrrh with my spice.
I have eaten my honeycomb and my honey;
I have drunk my wine and my milk.[a]

*Friends*

Eat, O friends, and drink;
drink your fill, O lovers.

*Beloved*

2 I slept but my heart was awake.
Listen! My lover is knocking:
"Open to me, my sister, my darling,
my dove, my flawless one.
My head is drenched with dew,
my hair with the dampness of the night."
3 I have taken off my robe—
must I put it on again?
I have washed my feet—
must I soil them again?
4 My lover thrust his hand through the latch-opening;
my heart began to pound for him.
5 I arose to open for my lover,
and my hands dripped with myrrh,
my fingers with flowing myrrh,
on the handles of the lock.
6 I opened for my lover,
but my lover had left; he was gone.
My heart sank at his departure.[a]
I looked[b] for him but did not find him.
I called him but he did not answer.
7 The watchmen found me
as they made their rounds in the city.[c]
They beat me, they bruised me;
they took away my cloak,
those watchmen of the walls!
8 O daughters of Jerusalem, I charge you—
if you find my lover,
what will you tell him?
Tell him I am faint with love.

*Friends*

9 How is your beloved better than others,
most beautiful of women?[d]
How is your beloved better than others,
that you charge us so?

*Beloved*

10 My lover is radiant and ruddy,
outstanding among ten thousand.
11 His head is purest gold;
his hair is wavy
and black as a raven.
12 His eyes are like doves[e]
by the water streams,
washed in milk,
mounted like jewels.
13 His cheeks are like beds of spice
yielding perfume.
His lips are like lilies
dripping with myrrh.
14 His arms are rods of gold
set with chrysolite.
His body is like polished ivory
decorated with sapphires.[b]
15 His legs are pillars of marble
set on bases of pure gold.
His appearance is like Lebanon,
choice as its cedars.
16 His mouth is sweetness itself;
he is altogether lovely.
This is my lover, this my friend,
O daughters of Jerusalem.

*Friends*

6 Where has your lover gone,
most beautiful of women?[f]
Which way did your lover turn,
that we may look for him with you?

**5:6** b SS 3:1
**5:7** c SS 3:3
**5:9** d SS 1:8
**5:12** e SS 1:15; 4:1
**6:1** f SS 1:8

[a]6 Or *heart had gone out to him when he spoke* [b]14 Or *lapis lazuli*

# Inspire

## MARRIAGE

The marriage relationship is a great picture of the type of intimacy that God intended for all of creation. When two "become one flesh" (Ge 2:24), it signifies that two people, previously unrelated, have become so intimately connected that other human relationships pale in comparison.

The Biblical narrative tells us that before the fall, Adam and Eve enjoyed a close, intimate relationship. There was nothing that they could not share; there was no self-consciousness or face-saving barriers between them. "The man and his wife were both naked, and they felt no shame" (Ge 2:25). This speaks not only of physical nakedness but also of spiritual openness to each other. There were no sinful secrets to taint their relationship.

The first chapters of Genesis portray marriage as God intended it: mutual love and respect between one man and one woman. But soon the serpent led Eve and then Adam into sin, and the marriage relationship suffered. After they sinned, Adam and Eve realized they were naked (see Ge 3:7). They were no longer an innocent, intimate couple; sin had brought a barrier between them.

Before long, men began to take multiple wives in marriage (see Ge 4:19). As a result, the marriage bond was broken as jealousy, anger and strife entered into the relationships (see Ge 29:16—30:24; 1Sa 1:1–8).

Although sin has tainted the marriage relationship, God still longs for men and women to have fulfilling, beautiful, loving relationships in marriage. The entire book of Song of Songs is dedicated to expressing marital love and longing. It portrays a man and a woman who delight in each other to the exclusion of all others (see SS 7:10). This is God's divine plan for men and women: genuine love that is "as strong as death," "like a mighty flame" and so powerful that "rivers cannot wash it away" (SS 8:6–7).

—E. Alexander

For the next Inspire note, go to page 794.

### read

Song of Songs; see also Genesis 2:4–25; Ephesians 5:21–33.

**See also** the Inspire Notes "Let's Talk About Sex," "Dating," "Romance: A Biblical Perspective," "What Is Intimacy?" and "Love," and the Women of the Bible Notes "Rebekah: A Woman of Obsessive Love," "Michal: A Disappointed Bride," "The Bridegroom and His Bride: Soul Mates in Life" and "Sapphira: A Lost Opportunity for Truth."

### WOMAN of COLOR

How do you honor marriage? Do you affirm it and support the married people you know? If you are married, do you respect the power and beauty of your marriage?

:3 SS7:10 SS2:16
:4 ver 10
:5 SS4:1
:6 SS4:2
:7 SS4:3
:11 SS7:12

*Beloved*

2 My lover has gone down to his garden,
to the beds of spices,
to browse in the gardens
and to gather lilies.
3 I am my lover's and my lover is mine;[g]
he browses among the lilies.[h]

*Lover*

4 You are beautiful, my darling, as Tirzah,
lovely as Jerusalem,
majestic as troops with banners.[i]
5 Turn your eyes from me;
they overwhelm me.
Your hair is like a flock of goats
descending from Gilead.[j]
6 Your teeth are like a flock of sheep
coming up from the washing.
Each has its twin,
not one of them is alone.[k]
7 Your temples behind your veil
are like the halves of a pomegranate.[l]
8 Sixty queens there may be,
and eighty concubines,
and virgins beyond number;
9 but my dove, my perfect one, is unique,
the only daughter of her mother,
the favorite of the one who bore her.
The maidens saw her and called her
blessed;
the queens and concubines praised
her.

*Friends*

10 Who is this that appears like the dawn,
fair as the moon, bright as the sun,
majestic as the stars in procession?

*Lover*

11 I went down to the grove of nut trees
to look at the new growth in the valley,
to see if the vines had budded
or the pomegranates were in bloom.[m]
12 Before I realized it,
my desire set me among the royal
chariots of my people.[a]

*Friends*

13 Come back, come back, O Shulammite;
come back, come back, that we may
gaze on you!

*Lover*

Why would you gaze on the Shulammite
as on the dance of Mahanaim?

7 How beautiful your sandaled feet,
O prince's[n] daughter!
Your graceful legs are like jewels,
the work of a craftsman's hands.
2 Your navel is a rounded goblet
that never lacks blended wine.
Your waist is a mound of wheat
encircled by lilies.
3 Your breasts[o] are like two fawns,
twins of a gazelle.
4 Your neck is like an ivory tower.[p]
Your eyes are the pools of Heshbon
by the gate of Bath Rabbim.
Your nose is like the tower of Lebanon
looking toward Damascus.
5 Your head crowns you like Mount
Carmel.[q]
Your hair is like royal tapestry;
the king is held captive by its tresses.
6 How beautiful[r] you are and how pleasing,
O love, with your delights!
7 Your stature is like that of the palm,
and your breasts like clusters of fruit.
8 I said, "I will climb the palm tree;
I will take hold of its fruit."
May your breasts be like the clusters of
the vine,
the fragrance of your breath like
apples,[s]
9 and your mouth like the best wine.

*Beloved*

May the wine go straight to my lover,
flowing gently over lips and teeth.[b]
10 I belong to my lover,
and his desire[t] is for me.[u]
11 Come, my lover, let us go to the
countryside,
let us spend the night in the villages.[c]
12 Let us go early to the vineyards
to see if the vines have budded,
if their blossoms have opened,
and if the pomegranates are in
bloom[v]—
there I will give you my love.
13 The mandrakes[w] send out their
fragrance,
and at our door is every delicacy,

7:1 n Ps 45:13
7:3 o SS 4:5
7:4 p SS 4:4
7:5 q Isa 35:2
7:6 r SS 1:15
7:8 s SS 2:5
7:10 t Ps 45:11 u SS 2:16; 6:3
7:12 v SS 6:11
7:13 w Ge 30:14

[a]12 Or *among the chariots of Amminadab*; or *among the chariots of the people of the prince* [b]9 Septuagint, Aquila, Vulgate and Syriac; Hebrew *lips of sleepers* [c]11 Or *henna bushes*

# Inspire

## WHAT IS INTIMACY?

Many of us long for the true intimacy that we see between the lover and the beloved in Song of Songs. In order t have true intimacy, we must understand what intimacy is and how it is developed.

First, we must understand that if there is no real communication between individuals, there can be no rea intimacy. Sharing all of who we are with another person, even though that may mean risking rejection and perhap even ridicule—is the first step toward intimacy. Another important prerequisite to an intimate relationship wi another person is self-knowledge. Many of us are uncomfortable with, as well as fearful of, getting to know th person behind the face we see in the mirror. Until we come to know ourselves on a deep level, we can never b truly happy with ourselves or in our relationships with others. We must get in touch with who we really are ar face ourselves with all of our flaws, while at the same time acknowledging our strengths and the God-given gif that we bring to a relationship. When we look to another person for our identity instead of understanding o innate God-given identity, we set ourselves up for disappointment and disillusionment. We must realize that o identity comes from seeing ourselves through God's eyes and embracing the Holy Spirit within us.

As we come to know more fully who we are as women of color, we will be better able to engage in relationships. Our strength comes from knowing who we are in God. That knowledge removes the fear of becoming close to another person and allows us to be authentically who we are and honest with those whom God allows into our lives. To reach this level of intimacy, some of us need healing from past relationships. For others, a rebuilding of self-confidence and a renewed sense of womanhood has to occur. But as our relationship with God becomes more intimate, we become more willing not only to risk revealing ourselves to others, but also to trust God for the outcome of those interactions. Our relationship with God will determine our relationships with others. Without the risk that intimacy involves, either with ourselves or with others, we can never be all that God would have us to be.

—B. A. Heard

### read

Song of Songs 5–8.

**See also** the Inspire Notes "Let's Talk About Sex," "Dating," "Romance: A Biblical Perspective" and "Love," and the Women of the Bible Notes "Rebekah: A Woman of Obsessive Love," "Michal: A Disappointed Bride" and "The Bridegroom and His Bride: Soul Mates in Life."

### WOMAN of COLOR

How intimately do you know God and yourself?

For the next Inspire note, go to page 804.

8:3 x SS 2:6
8:4 y SS 2:7; 3:5
8:5 z SS 3:6

both new and old,
that I have stored up for you, my lover.

8 If only you were to me like a brother,
who was nursed at my mother's breasts!
Then, if I found you outside,
I would kiss you,
and no one would despise me.
2 I would lead you
and bring you to my mother's house—
she who has taught me.
I would give you spiced wine to drink,
the nectar of my pomegranates.
3 His left arm is under my head
and his right arm embraces me.[x]
4 Daughters of Jerusalem, I charge you:
Do not arouse or awaken love
until it so desires.[y]

*Friends*

5 Who is this coming up from the desert[z]
leaning on her lover?

*Beloved*

Under the apple tree I roused you;
there your mother conceived you,
there she who was in labor gave you birth.
6 Place me like a seal over your heart,
like a seal on your arm;
for love is as strong as death,
its jealousy[a] unyielding as the grave.[b]
It burns like blazing fire,
like a mighty flame.[c]
7 Many waters cannot quench love;
rivers cannot wash it away.
If one were to give
all the wealth of his house for love,
it[d] would be utterly scorned.[a]

*Friends*

8 We have a young sister,
and her breasts are not yet grown.
What shall we do for our sister
for the day she is spoken for?
9 If she is a wall,
we will build towers of silver on her.
If she is a door,
we will enclose her with panels of cedar.

*Beloved*

10 I am a wall,
and my breasts are like towers.
Thus I have become in his eyes
like one bringing contentment.
11 Solomon had a vineyard[b] in Baal Hamon;
he let out his vineyard to tenants.
Each was to bring for its fruit
a thousand shekels[e][c] of silver.
12 But my own vineyard is mine to give;
the thousand shekels are for you,
O Solomon,
and two hundred[f] are for those who tend its fruit.

*Lover*

13 You who dwell in the gardens
with friends in attendance,
let me hear your voice!

*Beloved*

14 Come away, my lover,
and be like a gazelle
or like a young stag[d]
on the spice-laden mountains.[e]

8:7 a Pr 6:35
8:11 b Ecc 2:4 c Isa 7:23
8:14 d SS 2:9 e SS 2:8,17

[a]6 Or *ardor* [b]6 Hebrew *Sheol* [c]6 Or / *like the very flame of the Lord* [d]7 Or *he* [e]11 That is, about 25 pounds (about 11.5 kilograms); also in verse 12 [f]12 That is, about 5 pounds (about 2.3 kilograms)

# Isaiah

## OVERVIEW

Isaiah wrote about God's disappointment and judgment toward the people of Israel as they broke their covenant made at Mount Sinai. In the midst of these pronouncements of judgment, Isaiah called on the people to repent (see Isa 1–5). After recording his vision of the throne of God and the resulting commission he received (see Isa 6), Isaiah wrote about God's plan to judge the surrounding nations as well. In this book, the first 39 chapters primarily deal with judgment, while the remaining chapters focus on the future restoration and blessings for the entire world.

Every Christian woman should consider how God will judge both the living and the dead. His judgment will be fair and just, according to his divine nature. As believers in Jesus Christ, we will be judged for the things we have done, whether good or bad (see 2Co 5:10). Therefore each believer should take time for a daily examination to make sure that God receives honor and glory for every good work.

## OUTLINE

I. Prophecies of Judgment, Culminating in Isaiah's Commission (1:1—6:13)
II. Various Prophecies, Culminating in Songs of Praise (7:1—12:6)
III. Prophecies of Judgment Against Other Nations (13:1—27:13)
IV. Woe to Israel and Assyria (28:1—33:24)
V. Judgment and Joy (34:1—35:10)
VI. King Hezekiah's Victory Over Assyria (36:1—37:38)
VII. King Hezekiah's Sickness, Healing and Judgment (38:1—39:8)
VIII. Hope and Restoration (40:1—45:25)
IX. The Fall of Babylon (46:1—47:15)
X. Israel's Sin and Future Glory (48:1—66:24)

## SCANNABLE FACTS:

**Author:** Isaiah

**Time Written:** Around 700–680 B.C.

**Theme to Note:** God's restoration of Israel and the world

**Notable Women:** The arrogant "women of Zion" (see Isa 3:16—4:6); Isaiah's wife, referred to as a "prophetess" (see Isa 8:3)

**1:1** a Isa 2:1 b 2Ki 16:1
**1:3** c Jer 9:3,6
**1:4** d Isa 14:20 e Isa 5:19,24
**1:5** f Isa 31:6 g Isa 33:6,24
**1:6** h Ps 38:3
**1:8** i Job 27:18
**1:9** j Ge 19:24; Ro 9:29*
**1:10** k Isa 28:14 l Eze 16:49; Rev 11:8

1 The vision concerning Judah and Jerusalem that Isaiah son of Amoz saw[a] during the reigns of Uzziah, Jotham, Ahaz[b] and Hezekiah, kings of Judah.

## A Rebellious Nation

2 Hear, O heavens! Listen, O earth!
For the LORD has spoken:
"I reared children and brought them up,
but they have rebelled against me.
3 The ox knows his master,
the donkey his owner's manger,
but Israel does not know,[c]
my people do not understand."

4 Ah, sinful nation,
a people loaded with guilt,
a brood of evildoers,[d]
children given to corruption!
They have forsaken the LORD;
they have spurned the Holy One[e] of Israel
and turned their backs on him.

5 Why should you be beaten anymore?
Why do you persist in rebellion?[f]
Your whole head is injured,
your whole heart afflicted.[g]
6 From the sole of your foot to the top of your head
there is no soundness[h]—
only wounds and welts
and open sores,
not cleansed or bandaged
or soothed with oil.

7 Your country is desolate,
your cities burned with fire;
your fields are being stripped by foreigners
right before you,
laid waste as when overthrown by strangers.
8 The Daughter of Zion is left
like a shelter in a vineyard,
like a hut[i] in a field of melons,
like a city under siege.
9 Unless the LORD Almighty
had left us some survivors,
we would have become like Sodom,
we would have been like Gomorrah.[j]

10 Hear the word of the LORD,[k]
you rulers of Sodom;[l]
listen to the law of our God,
you people of Gomorrah!
11 "The multitude of your sacrifices—
what are they to me?" says the LORD.
"I have more than enough of burnt offerings,
of rams and the fat of fattened animals;
I have no pleasure
in the blood of bulls and lambs and goats.[m]
12 When you come to appear before me,
who has asked this of you,[n]
this trampling of my courts?
13 Stop bringing meaningless offerings![o]
Your incense[p] is detestable to me.
New Moons, Sabbaths and convocations[q]—
I cannot bear your evil assemblies.
14 Your New Moon festivals and your appointed feasts[r]
my soul hates.
They have become a burden to me;
I am weary[s] of bearing them.
15 When you spread out your hands in prayer,
I will hide my eyes from you;
even if you offer many prayers,
I will not listen.
Your hands are full of blood;[t]
16 wash and make yourselves clean.
Take your evil deeds
out of my sight!
Stop doing wrong,[u]
17 learn to do right!
Seek justice,
encourage the oppressed.[a]
Defend the cause of the fatherless,[v]
plead the case of the widow.

18 "Come now, let us reason together,"[w]
says the LORD.
"Though your sins are like scarlet,
they shall be as white as snow;[x]
though they are red as crimson,
they shall be like wool.
19 If you are willing and obedient,
you will eat the best from the land;[y]
20 but if you resist and rebel,
you will be devoured by the sword."[z]
For the mouth of the LORD
has spoken.

**1:11** m 1Sa 15:22
**1:12** n Ex 23:17
**1:13** o Isa 66:3 p Jer 7:9 q 1Ch 23:31
**1:14** r Nu 28:11–29:39 s Isa 43:22,24
**1:15** t Isa 59:3
**1:16** u Isa 55:7
**1:17** v Ps 82:3
**1:18** w Isa 43:9,26 x Ps 51:7; Rev 7:14
**1:19** y Dt 30:15–16
**1:20** z Isa 3:25

[a]17 Or / *rebuke the oppressor*

1:21 a Jer 2:20
1:23 b Jer 5:28
1:24 c Isa 35:4
1:25 d Mal 3:3
1:26 e Jer 33:7,11 f Zec 8:3
1:28 g Ps 9:5; 2Th 1:8–9
1:29 h Isa 57:5 i Isa 65:3

21 See how the faithful city
has become a harlot![a]
She once was full of justice;
righteousness used to dwell in her—
but now murderers!
22 Your silver has become dross,
your choice wine is diluted with water.
23 Your rulers are rebels,
companions of thieves;
they all love bribes
and chase after gifts.
They do not defend the cause of the fatherless;
the widow's case does not come before them.[b]
24 Therefore the Lord, the LORD Almighty,
the Mighty One of Israel, declares:
"Ah, I will get relief from my foes
and avenge[c] myself on my enemies.
25 I will turn my hand against you;
I will thoroughly purge away your dross
and remove all your impurities.[d]
26 I will restore your judges as in days of old,[e]
your counselors as at the beginning.
Afterward you will be called
the City of Righteousness,[f]
the Faithful City."

27 Zion will be redeemed with justice,
her penitent ones with righteousness.
28 But rebels and sinners will both be broken,
and those who forsake the LORD will perish.[g]

29 "You will be ashamed because of the sacred oaks[h]
in which you have delighted;
you will be disgraced because of the gardens[i]
that you have chosen.
30 You will be like an oak with fading leaves,
like a garden without water.
31 The mighty man will become tinder
and his work a spark;
both will burn together,
with no one to quench the fire."

## The Mountain of the LORD

2 This is what Isaiah son of Amoz saw concerning Judah and Jerusalem:

2 In the last days

the mountain[j] of the LORD's temple will be established
as chief among the mountains;
it will be raised above the hills,
and all nations will stream to it.

3 Many peoples will come and say,

"Come, let us go up to the mountain of the LORD,
to the house of the God of Jacob.
He will teach us his ways,
so that we may walk in his paths."
The law will go out from Zion,
the word of the LORD from Jerusalem.[k]
4 He will judge between the nations
and will settle disputes for many peoples.
They will beat their swords into plowshares
and their spears into pruning hooks.
Nation will not take up sword against nation,[l]
nor will they train for war anymore.

5 Come, O house of Jacob,[m]
let us walk in the light of the LORD.

## The Day of the LORD

6 You have abandoned[n] your people,
the house of Jacob.
They are full of superstitions from the East;
they practice divination like the Philistines
and clasp hands with pagans.[o]
7 Their land is full of silver and gold;
there is no end to their treasures.
Their land is full of horses;[p]
there is no end to their chariots.
8 Their land is full of idols;
they bow down to the work of their hands,
to what their fingers[q] have made.
9 So man will be brought low
and mankind humbled—
do not forgive them.[a]

2:2 j Mic 4:7
2:3 k Lk 24:47
2:4 l Isa 32:18; Hos 2:18
2:5 m Isa 58:1
2:6 n Dt 31:17 o 2Ki 16:7
2:7 p Dt 17:16
2:8 q Isa 17:8

[a]9 Or *not raise them up*

**2:10** r 2Th 1:9; Rev 6:15–16
**2:11** s Isa 5:15
**2:12** t Isa 24:4,21
**2:13** u Zec 11:2
**2:14** v Isa 30:25
**2:18** w Isa 21:9
**2:19** x Heb 12:26
**2:21** y ver 19
**2:22** z Ps 146:3 a Jas 4:14

10 Go into the rocks,
hide in the ground
from dread of the LORD
and the splendor of his majesty![r]
11 The eyes of the arrogant man will be
humbled
and the pride[s] of men brought low;
the LORD alone will be exalted in that day.

12 The LORD Almighty has a day in store
for all the proud and lofty,
for all that is exalted[t]
(and they will be humbled),
13 for all the cedars of Lebanon, tall and
lofty,
and all the oaks of Bashan,[u]
14 for all the towering mountains
and all the high hills,[v]
15 for every lofty tower
and every fortified wall,
16 for every trading ship[a]
and every stately vessel.
17 The arrogance of man will be brought low
and the pride of men humbled;
the LORD alone will be exalted in that day,
18 and the idols will totally disappear.[w]
19 Men will flee to caves in the rocks
and to holes in the ground
from dread of the LORD
and the splendor of his majesty,
when he rises to shake the earth.[x]
20 In that day men will throw away
to the rodents and bats
their idols of silver and idols of gold,
which they made to worship.
21 They will flee to caverns in the rocks
and to the overhanging crags
from dread of the LORD
and the splendor of his majesty,
when he rises to shake the earth.[y]

22 Stop trusting in man,[z]
who has but a breath in his nostrils.
Of what account is he?[a]

## Judgment on Jerusalem and Judah

3 See now, the Lord,
the LORD Almighty,
is about to take from Jerusalem and
Judah
both supply and support:
all supplies of food[b] and all supplies of
water,
2 the hero and warrior,
the judge and prophet,
the soothsayer and elder,
3 the captain of fifty and man of rank,
the counselor, skilled craftsman and
clever enchanter.

4 I will make boys their officials;
mere children will govern them.[c]
5 People will oppress each other—
man against man, neighbor against
neighbor.[d]
The young will rise up against the old,
the base against the honorable.

6 A man will seize one of his brothers
at his father's home, and say,
"You have a cloak, you be our leader;
take charge of this heap of ruins!"
7 But in that day he will cry out,
"I have no remedy.[e]
I have no food or clothing in my
house;
do not make me the leader of the
people."

8 Jerusalem staggers,
Judah is falling;[f]
their words and deeds are against the
LORD,
defying his glorious presence.
9 The look on their faces testifies against
them;
they parade their sin like Sodom;[g]
they do not hide it.
Woe to them!
They have brought disaster upon
themselves.

10 Tell the righteous it will be well with
them,
for they will enjoy the fruit of their
deeds.
11 Woe to the wicked! Disaster is upon
them!
They will be paid back for what their
hands have done.

12 Youths[h] oppress my people,
women rule over them.

**3:1** b Lev 26:26
**3:4** c Ecc 10:16
**3:5** d Mic 7:2,6
**3:7** e Eze 34:4
**3:8** f Isa 1:7
**3:9** g Ge 13:13
**3:12** h ver 4

[a]16 Hebrew *every ship of Tarshish*

3:12 i Isa 9:16
3:13 j Mic 6:2
3:14 k Jas 2:6
3:18 l Jdg 8:21
3:20 m Ex 39:28
3:24 n Isa 22:12
3:25 o Isa 1:20
3:26 p Jer 14:2 q La 2:10
4:1 r Isa 13:12 s 2Th 3:12

O my people, your guides lead you
astray;[i]
they turn you from the path.
13 The LORD takes his place in court;
he rises to judge[j] the people.
14 The LORD enters into judgment
against the elders and leaders of his
people:
"It is you who have ruined my vineyard;
the plunder[k] from the poor is in your
houses.
15 What do you mean by crushing my
people
and grinding the faces of the poor?"
declares the Lord,
the LORD Almighty.

16 The LORD says,
"The women of Zion are haughty,
walking along with outstretched necks,
flirting with their eyes,
tripping along with mincing steps,
with ornaments jingling on their
ankles.
17 Therefore the Lord will bring sores on the
heads of the women of Zion;
the LORD will make their scalps bald."

18 In that day the Lord will snatch away
their finery: the bangles and headbands
and crescent necklaces,[l] 19 the earrings and
bracelets and veils, 20 the headdresses[m] and
ankle chains and sashes, the perfume bot-
tles and charms, 21 the signet rings and nose
rings, 22 the fine robes and the capes and
cloaks, the purses 23 and mirrors, and the
linen garments and tiaras and shawls.

24 Instead of fragrance there will be a
stench;
instead of a sash, a rope;
instead of well-dressed hair, baldness;[n]
instead of fine clothing, sackcloth;
instead of beauty, branding.
25 Your men will fall by the sword,[o]
your warriors in battle.
26 The gates of Zion will lament and mourn;[p]
destitute, she will sit on the ground.[q]

4 1 In that day seven women
will take hold of one man[r]
and say, "We will eat our own food[s]
and provide our own clothes;
only let us be called by your name.
Take away our disgrace!"

## The Branch of the LORD

2 In that day the Branch of the LORD[t] will
be beautiful and glorious, and the fruit of
the land will be the pride and glory of the
survivors in Israel. 3 Those who are left in
Zion, who remain in Jerusalem, will be
called holy,[u] all who are recorded[v] among
the living in Jerusalem. 4 The Lord will wash
away the filth of the women of Zion; he will
cleanse the bloodstains from Jerusalem by
a spirit[a] of judgment[w] and a spirit[a] of fire.
5 Then the LORD will create over all of Mount
Zion and over those who assemble there a
cloud of smoke by day and a glow of flam-
ing fire by night;[x] over all the glory will be a
canopy. 6 It will be a shelter and shade from
the heat of the day, and a refuge[y] and hiding
place from the storm and rain.

*Sister girl,*

*I am a restorer. Wait on me
and watch me work.*

*Love,
Your Provider*

ISAIAH 4:2–6

## The Song of the Vineyard

5 I will sing for the one I love
a song about his vineyard:[z]
My loved one had a vineyard
on a fertile hillside.
2 He dug it up and cleared it of stones
and planted it with the choicest vines.[a]
He built a watchtower in it
and cut out a winepress as well.
Then he looked for a crop of good grapes,
but it yielded only bad fruit.[b]

3 "Now you dwellers in Jerusalem and men
of Judah,
judge between me and my vineyard.[c]

4:2 t Jer 23:5–6
4:3 u Isa 60:21 v Lk 10:20
4:4 w Isa 28:6
4:5 x Ex 13:21
4:6 y Isa 25:4
5:1 z Ps 80:8–9
5:2 a Jer 2:21 b Lk 13:6
5:3 c Mt 21:40

[a] 4 Or *the Spirit*

**5:4** d Mt 23:37
**5:5** e Ps 80:12 f Lk 21:24
**5:7** g Ps 80:8
**5:8** h Mic 2:2
**5:9** i Isa 22:14
**5:11** j Pr 23:29–30

4 What more could have been done for my vineyard
than I have done for it?[d]
When I looked for good grapes,
why did it yield only bad?
5 Now I will tell you
what I am going to do to my vineyard:
I will take away its hedge,
and it will be destroyed;
I will break down its wall,[e]
and it will be trampled.[f]
6 I will make it a wasteland,
neither pruned nor cultivated,
and briers and thorns will grow there.
I will command the clouds
not to rain on it."

7 The vineyard[g] of the LORD Almighty
is the house of Israel,
and the men of Judah
are the garden of his delight.
And he looked for justice, but saw bloodshed;
for righteousness, but heard cries of distress.

## Woes and Judgments

8 Woe to you who add house to house
and join field to field[h]
till no space is left
and you live alone in the land.

9 The LORD Almighty has declared in my hearing:[i]

"Surely the great houses will become desolate,
the fine mansions left without occupants.
10 A ten-acre[a] vineyard will produce only a bath[b] of wine,
a homer[c] of seed only an ephah[d] of grain."

11 Woe to those who rise early in the morning
to run after their drinks,
who stay up late at night
till they are inflamed with wine.[j]
12 They have harps and lyres at their banquets,
tambourines and flutes and wine,
but they have no regard[k] for the deeds of the LORD,
no respect for the work of his hands.[l]
13 Therefore my people will go into exile
for lack of understanding;
their men of rank will die of hunger
and their masses will be parched with thirst.
14 Therefore the grave[e] enlarges its appetite
and opens its mouth without limit;
into it will descend their nobles and masses
with all their brawlers and revelers.
15 So man will be brought low
and mankind humbled,[m]
the eyes of the arrogant[n] humbled.
16 But the LORD Almighty will be exalted by his justice,
and the holy God will show himself holy[o] by his righteousness.
17 Then sheep will graze as in their own pasture;
lambs will feed[f] among the ruins of the rich.

18 Woe to those who draw sin along with cords of deceit,
and wickedness[p] as with cart ropes,
19 to those who say, "Let God hurry,
let him hasten his work
so we may see it.
Let it approach,
let the plan of the Holy One of Israel come,
so we may know it."[q]

20 Woe to those who call evil good
and good evil,
who put darkness for light
and light for darkness,[r]
who put bitter for sweet
and sweet for bitter.

21 Woe to those who are wise in their own eyes[s]
and clever in their own sight.

22 Woe to those who are heroes at drinking wine
and champions at mixing drinks,
23 who acquit the guilty for a bribe,
but deny justice to the innocent.[t]

**5:12** k Job 34:27 l Ps 28:5; Am 6:5–6
**5:15** m Isa 2:9 n Isa 2:11
**5:16** o Isa 29:23
**5:18** p Isa 59:4–8
**5:19** q Eze 12:22; 2Pe 3:4
**5:20** r Mt 6:22–23
**5:21** s Ro 12:16
**5:23** t Ps 94:21

[a] 10 Hebrew *ten-yoke,* that is, the land plowed by 10 yoke of oxen in one day [b] 10 That is, probably about 6 gallons (about 22 liters) [c] 10 That is, probably about 6 bushels (about 220 liters) [d] 10 That is, probably about 3/5 bushel (about 22 liters) [e] 14 Hebrew *Sheol* [f] 17 Septuagint; Hebrew */ strangers will eat*

24 ob 18:16
25 Ki 22:13 sa 9:12,17,21
26 sa 7:18 t 28:49
27 oel 2:7–8
28 s 7:12
29 er 51:38 sa 10:6 sa 42:22
30 sa 8:22
1 Ki 15:7 n 12:41

24 Therefore, as tongues of fire lick up straw
and as dry grass sinks down in the flames,
so their roots will decay[u]
and their flowers blow away like dust;
for they have rejected the law of the LORD Almighty
and spurned the word of the Holy One of Israel.
25 Therefore the LORD's anger[v] burns against his people;
his hand is raised and he strikes them down.
The mountains shake,
and the dead bodies are like refuse in the streets.

Yet for all this, his anger is not turned away,
his hand is still upraised.[w]

26 He lifts up a banner for the distant nations,
he whistles[x] for those at the ends of the earth.[y]
Here they come,
swiftly and speedily!
27 Not one of them grows tired or stumbles,
not one slumbers or sleeps;
not a belt is loosened at the waist,
not a sandal thong is broken.[z]
28 Their arrows are sharp,
all their bows[a] are strung;
their horses' hoofs seem like flint,
their chariot wheels like a whirlwind.
29 Their roar is like that of the lion,[b]
they roar like young lions;
they growl as they seize[c] their prey
and carry it off with no one to rescue.[d]
30 In that day they will roar over it
like the roaring of the sea.
And if one looks at the land,
he will see darkness and distress;[e]
even the light will be darkened by the clouds.

## Isaiah's Commission

6 In the year that King Uzziah died,[f] I saw the Lord[g] seated on a throne, high and exalted, and the train of his robe filled the temple. 2 Above him were seraphs, each with six wings: With two wings they covered their faces, with two they covered their feet, and with two they were flying. 3 And they were calling to one another:

"Holy, holy, holy is the LORD Almighty;
the whole earth is full of his glory."[h]

4 At the sound of their voices the doorposts and thresholds shook and the temple was filled with smoke.

5 "Woe to me!" I cried. "I am ruined! For I am a man of unclean lips, and I live among a people of unclean lips, and my eyes have seen the King, the LORD Almighty."

6 Then one of the seraphs flew to me with a live coal in his hand, which he had taken with tongs from the altar. 7 With it he touched my mouth and said, "See, this has touched your lips;[i] your guilt is taken away and your sin atoned for."

8 Then I heard the voice of the Lord saying, "Whom shall I send? And who will go for us?"

And I said, "Here am I. Send me!"

9 He said, "Go and tell this people:

" 'Be ever hearing, but never understanding;
be ever seeing, but never perceiving.'[j]
10 Make the heart of this people calloused;[k]
make their ears dull
and close their eyes.[a]
Otherwise they might see with their eyes,
hear with their ears,[l]
understand with their hearts,
and turn and be healed."[m]

11 Then I said, "For how long, O Lord?"
And he answered:
"Until the cities lie ruined
and without inhabitant,
until the houses are left deserted
and the fields ruined and ravaged,
12 until the LORD has sent everyone far away
and the land is utterly forsaken.[n]
13 And though a tenth remains in the land,
it will again be laid waste.
But as the terebinth and oak
leave stumps when they are cut down,
so the holy seed will be the stump in the land."

6:3 h Ps 72:19; Rev 4:8
6:7 i Jer 1:9
6:9 j Mt 13:15*
6:10 k Ps 119:70 l Jer 5:21 m Mk 4:12* Ac 28:26–27*
6:12 n Jer 4:29

[a] 9,10 Hebrew; Septuagint *'You will be ever hearing, but never understanding; / you will be ever seeing, but never perceiving.' / 10 This people's heart has become calloused; / they hardly hear with their ears, / and they have closed their eyes*

7:1 o 2Ki 15:37

## The Sign of Immanuel

7 When Ahaz son of Jotham, the son of
Uzziah, was king of Judah, King Rezin[o]
of Aram and Pekah son of Remaliah king
of Israel marched up to fight against Jerusa-
lem, but they could not overpower it.
2 Now the house of David[p] was told,
"Aram has allied itself with[b] Ephraim";
so the hearts of Ahaz and his people were
shaken, as the trees of the forest are shaken
by the wind.
3 Then the LORD said to Isaiah, "Go out,

7:2 p ver 13

[b]2 Or *has set up camp in*

# Inspire

## GOD IS HOLY

The word *holy* means "unique," "set apart," "unlike all others." The basic idea of holiness is that of distinctiv-ness. It is first applied to God and then, by application, to his people. God is separated from the universe. God i by his very nature, holy. Sin does not exist in God; therefore, God does not deceive. This is an aspect of God that very difficult to grasp. Our own understanding of holiness is limited by our attempts at being holy. Because we often try to remake God in our own image, we cannot grasp the notion that God is distinct from his creation. G is the one and only. In his great vision, Isaiah saw the Lord in his temple (see Isa 6). He saw God's glory and hea the angels declare, "Holy, holy, holy is the LORD Almighty; the whole earth is full of his glory" (Isa 6:3).

Once Isaiah comprehended God's holiness, he understood his own sinfulness. He declared, "Woe me! . . . I am ruined! For I am a man of unclean lips, and I live among a people of unclean lips, and my eyes have seen the King, the LORD Almighty" (Isa 6:5). True worship of God is possible only when we recognize his holiness and awesomeness.

As we look at our communities, witness the senseless violence by and against our children, and labor under the systematic racism of our society, it is important that we know who God is and why we serve him. Isaiah said to the people of Israel, "Do not call conspiracy everything that these people call conspiracy; do not fear what they fear, and do not dread it. The LORD Almighty is the one you are to regard as holy, he is the one you are to fear, he is the one you are to dread" (Isa 8:12–13).

Since the Lord alone is holy, we should not be surprised—or sidetracked—by various scandals, sensationalistic news and dire statistics. Our response to a world gone haywire is to be still and know that he is God (see Ps 46:10).

—C. BELT

### read

Isaiah 6:1–13; 8:11–17; see also Exodus 33:12–23; Leviticus 19:1–2; 1 Peter 1:13–16.

See also the Inspire Notes "The Faithfulness of God" and "God Is a Jealous God."

### WOMAN of COLO

How does reflecting on God's holiness help you cope with all you have to face today?

For the next Inspire note, go to page 829.

you and your son Shear-Jashub,[a] to meet Ahaz at the end of the aqueduct of the Upper Pool, on the road to the Washerman's Field.[q] 4 Say to him, 'Be careful, keep calm[r] and don't be afraid. Do not lose heart because of these two smoldering stubs of firewood—because of the fierce anger[s] of Rezin and Aram and of the son of Remaliah. 5 Aram, Ephraim and Remaliah's son have plotted your ruin, saying, 6 "Let us invade Judah; let us tear it apart and divide it among ourselves, and make the son of Tabeel king over it." 7 Yet this is what the Sovereign LORD says:

" 'It will not take place,
it will not happen,[t]
8 for the head of Aram is Damascus,
and the head of Damascus is only Rezin.
Within sixty-five years
Ephraim will be too shattered[u] to be a people.
9 The head of Ephraim is Samaria,
and the head of Samaria is only Remaliah's son.
If you do not stand firm in your faith,[v]
you will not stand at all.' "

10 Again the LORD spoke to Ahaz, 11 "Ask the LORD your God for a sign, whether in the deepest depths or in the highest heights."

12 But Ahaz said, "I will not ask; I will not put the LORD to the test."

13 Then Isaiah said, "Hear now, you house of David! Is it not enough to try the patience of men? Will you try the patience of my God also? 14 Therefore the Lord himself will give you[b] a sign: The virgin will be with child and will give birth to a son, and[c] will call him Immanuel.[d][w] 15 He will eat curds and honey when he knows enough to reject the wrong and choose the right. 16 But before the boy knows[x] enough to reject the wrong and choose the right, the land of the two kings you dread will be laid waste. 17 The LORD will bring on you and on your people and on the house of your father a time unlike any since Ephraim broke away[y] from Judah—he will bring the king of Assyria.[z]"

18 In that day the LORD will whistle[a] for flies from the distant streams of Egypt and for bees from the land of Assyria. 19 They will all come and settle in the steep ravines and in the crevices in the rocks, on all the thornbushes and at all the water holes. 20 In that day the Lord will use[b] a razor hired from beyond the River[e]—the king of Assyria—to shave your head and the hair of your legs, and to take off your beards also. 21 In that day, a man will keep alive a young cow and two goats. 22 And because of the abundance of the milk they give, he will have curds to eat. All who remain in the land will eat curds and honey. 23 In that day, in every place where there were a thousand vines worth a thousand silver shekels,[f] there will be only briers and thorns.[c] 24 Men will go there with bow and arrow, for the land will be covered with briers and thorns. 25 As for all the hills once cultivated by the hoe, you will no longer go there for fear of the briers and thorns; they will become places where cattle are turned loose and where sheep run.

## Assyria, the LORD's Instrument

8 The LORD said to me, "Take a large scroll and write on it with an ordinary pen: Maher-Shalal-Hash-Baz.[g] 2 And I will call in Uriah[d] the priest and Zechariah son of Jeberekiah as reliable witnesses for me."

3 Then I went to the prophetess, and she conceived and gave birth to a son. And the LORD said to me, "Name him Maher-Shalal-Hash-Baz. 4 Before the boy knows[e] how to say 'My father' or 'My mother,' the wealth of Damascus and the plunder of Samaria will be carried off by the king of Assyria."

5 The LORD spoke to me again:

6 "Because this people has rejected
the gently flowing waters of Shiloah
and rejoices over Rezin
and the son of Remaliah,[f]
7 therefore the Lord is about to bring against them
the mighty floodwaters of the River[e]—
the king of Assyria with all his pomp.
It will overflow all its channels,
run over all its banks

7:3 q 2Ki 18:17
7:4 r Isa 30:15 s Isa 10:24
7:7 t Isa 8:10
7:8 u Isa 17:1–3
7:9 v 2Ch 20:20
7:14 w Isa 8:8,10; Mt 1:23*
7:16 x Isa 8:4
7:17 y 1Ki 12:16 z 2Ch 28:20
7:18 a Isa 5:26
7:20 b Isa 10:15
7:23 c Isa 5:6
8:2 d 2Ki 16:10
8:4 e Isa 7:16
8:6 f Isa 7:1

[a] 3 *Shear-Jashub* means *a remnant will return.* [b] 14 The Hebrew is plural. [c] 14 Masoretic Text; Dead Sea Scrolls *and he* or *and they* [d] 14 *Immanuel* means *God with us.* [e] 20,7 That is, the Euphrates [f] 23 That is, about 25 pounds (about 11.5 kilograms) [g] 1 *Maher-Shalal-Hash-Baz* means *quick to the plunder, swift to the spoil*; also in verse 3.

**8:8**
g Isa 7:14
**8:10**
h Job 5:12
i Isa 7:7
j Ro 8:31
**8:12**
k Isa 7:2
l 1Pe 3:14*
**8:13**
m Nu 20:12
**8:14**
n Eze 11:16
o Lk 2:34; Ro 9:33*; 1Pe 2:8*
**8:15**
p Lk 20:18
**8:18**
q Heb 2:13*

8 and sweep on into Judah, swirling over it,
passing through it and reaching up to the neck.
Its outspread wings will cover the breadth of your land,
O Immanuel[a]!"[g]

9 Raise the war cry,[b] you nations, and be shattered!
Listen, all you distant lands.
Prepare for battle, and be shattered!
Prepare for battle, and be shattered!
10 Devise your strategy, but it will be thwarted;[h]
propose your plan, but it will not stand,[i]
for God is with us.[c][j]

## Fear God

11 The LORD spoke to me with his strong hand upon me, warning me not to follow the way of this people. He said:

12 "Do not call conspiracy[k]
everything that these people call conspiracy[d];
do not fear what they fear,
and do not dread it.[l]
13 The LORD Almighty is the one you are to regard as holy,[m]
he is the one you are to fear,
he is the one you are to dread,
14 and he will be a sanctuary;[n]
but for both houses of Israel he will be
a stone that causes men to stumble
and a rock that makes them fall.[o]
And for the people of Jerusalem he will be
a trap and a snare.
15 Many of them will stumble;[p]
they will fall and be broken,
they will be snared and captured."

16 Bind up the testimony
and seal up the law among my disciples.
17 I will wait for the LORD,
who is hiding his face from the house of Jacob.
I will put my trust in him.

18 Here am I, and the children the LORD has given me.[q] We are signs and symbols in
Israel from the LORD Almighty, who dwells on Mount Zion.
19 When men tell you to consult[r] mediums
and spiritists, who whisper and mutter,
should not a people inquire of their God?
Why consult the dead on behalf of the liv-
ing? 20 To the law[s] and to the testimony! If
they do not speak according to this word,
they have no light[t] of dawn. 21 Distressed and
hungry, they will roam through the land;
when they are famished, they will become
enraged and, looking upward, will curse
their king and their God. 22 Then they will
look toward the earth and see only distress
and darkness and fearful gloom, and they
will be thrust into utter darkness.[u]

## To Us a Child Is Born

9 Nevertheless, there will be no more gloom for those who were in distress. In the past he humbled the land of Zebulun and the land of Naphtali,[v] but in the future he will honor Galilee of the Gentiles, by the way of the sea, along the Jordan—

2 The people walking in darkness
have seen a great light;[w]
on those living in the land of the shadow of death[e]
a light has dawned.[x]
3 You have enlarged the nation
and increased their joy;
they rejoice before you
as people rejoice at the harvest,
as men rejoice
when dividing the plunder.
4 For as in the day of Midian's defeat,
you have shattered
the yoke that burdens them,
the bar across their shoulders,[y]
the rod of their oppressor.[z]
5 Every warrior's boot used in battle
and every garment rolled in blood
will be destined for burning,
will be fuel for the fire.
6 For to us a child is born,[a]
to us a son is given,[b]
and the government[c] will be on his shoulders.
And he will be called
Wonderful Counselor,[f] Mighty God,[d]

**8:19**
r 1Sa 28:8
**8:20**
s Lk 16:29
t Mic 3:6
**8:22**
u Isa 5:30
**9:1**
v 2Ki 15:29
**9:2**
w Eph 5:8
x Mt 4:15–16*
**9:4**
y Isa 10:27
z Isa 14:4
**9:6**
a Lk 2:11
b Jn 3:16
c Mt 28:18
d Isa 10:21

[a]8 *Immanuel* means *God with us.* [b]9 Or *Do your worst* [c]10 Hebrew *Immanuel* [d]12 Or *Do not call for a treaty / every time these people call for a treaty* [e]2 Or *land of darkness* [f]6 Or *Wonderful, Counselor*

**9:7**
e Da 2:44; Lk 1:33
f Isa 11:4
g Isa 37:32
**9:9**
h Isa 46:12
**9:11**
i Isa 7:8
**9:12**
j 2Ch 28:18
**9:13**
k Jer 5:3
**9:14**
l Rev 18:8
**9:16**
m Isa 3:12

Everlasting Father, Prince of Peace.
7 Of the increase of his government and
peace
there will be no end.[e]
He will reign on David's throne
and over his kingdom,
establishing and upholding it
with justice[f] and righteousness
from that time on and forever.
The zeal[g] of the LORD Almighty
will accomplish this.

## The LORD's Anger Against Israel

8 The Lord has sent a message against
Jacob;
it will fall on Israel.
9 All the people will know it—
Ephraim and the inhabitants of
Samaria—
who say with pride
and arrogance[h] of heart,
10 "The bricks have fallen down,
but we will rebuild with dressed
stone;
the fig trees have been felled,
but we will replace them with cedars."
11 But the LORD has strengthened Rezin's[i]
foes against them
and has spurred their enemies on.
12 Arameans from the east and Philistines[j]
from the west
have devoured Israel with open mouth.

Yet for all this, his anger is not turned
away,
his hand is still upraised.

13 But the people have not returned to him
who struck[k] them,
nor have they sought the LORD
Almighty.
14 So the LORD will cut off from Israel both
head and tail,
both palm branch and reed in a single
day;[l]
15 the elders and prominent men are the
head,
the prophets who teach lies are the tail.
16 Those who guide this people mislead
them,
and those who are guided are led
astray.[m]
17 Therefore the Lord will take no pleasure
in the young men,
nor will he pity the fatherless and
widows,
for everyone is ungodly[n] and wicked,
every mouth speaks vileness.

Yet for all this, his anger is not turned
away,
his hand is still upraised.[o]

18 Surely wickedness burns like a fire;[p]
it consumes briers and thorns,
it sets the forest thickets ablaze,
so that it rolls upward in a column of
smoke.
19 By the wrath of the LORD Almighty
the land will be scorched
and the people will be fuel for the fire;
no one will spare his brother.[q]
20 On the right they will devour,
but still be hungry;
on the left they will eat,
but not be satisfied.
Each will feed on the flesh of his own
offspring[a]:
21 Manasseh will feed on Ephraim, and
Ephraim on Manasseh;
together they will turn against
Judah.

Yet for all this, his anger is not turned
away,
his hand is still upraised.[s]

10 Woe to those who make unjust
laws,
to those who issue oppressive
decrees,
2 to deprive the poor of their rights
and withhold justice from the
oppressed of my people,
making widows their prey
and robbing the fatherless.
3 What will you do on the day of
reckoning,[t]
when disaster[u] comes from afar?
To whom will you run for help?[v]
Where will you leave your riches?
4 Nothing will remain but to cringe among
the captives
or fall among the slain.

**9:17**
n Isa 10:6
o Isa 5:25
**9:18**
p Mal 4:1
**9:19**
q Mic 7:2,6
**9:20**
r Isa 49:26
**9:21**
s Isa 5:25
**10:3**
t Job 31:14; Hos 9:7
u Lk 19:44
v Isa 20:6

[a]20 Or *arm*

Yet for all this, his anger is not turned away,[w]
his hand is still upraised.

## God's Judgment on Assyria

5 "Woe to the Assyrian, the rod of my anger,
in whose hand is the club[x] of my wrath!
6 I send him against a godless[y] nation,
I dispatch him against a people who anger me,
to seize loot and snatch plunder,[z]
and to trample them down like mud in the streets.
7 But this is not what he intends,[a]
this is not what he has in mind;
his purpose is to destroy,
to put an end to many nations.
8 'Are not my commanders all kings?' he says.
9 'Has not Calno fared like Carchemish?[b]
Is not Hamath like Arpad,
and Samaria like Damascus?[c]
10 As my hand seized the kingdoms of the idols,[d]
kingdoms whose images excelled those of Jerusalem and Samaria—
11 shall I not deal with Jerusalem and her images
as I dealt with Samaria and her idols?' "

12 When the Lord has finished all his work against Mount Zion[e] and Jerusalem, he will say, "I will punish the king of Assyria for the willful pride of his heart and the haughty look in his eyes. 13 For he says:

" 'By the strength of my hand I have done this,[f]
and by my wisdom, because I have understanding.
I removed the boundaries of nations,
I plundered their treasures;[g]
like a mighty one I subdued[a] their kings.
14 As one reaches into a nest,
so my hand reached for the wealth[h] of the nations;
as men gather abandoned eggs,
so I gathered all the countries;
not one flapped a wing,
or opened its mouth to chirp.' "
15 Does the ax raise itself above him who swings it,
or the saw boast against him who uses it?[i]
As if a rod were to wield him who lifts it up,
or a club brandish him who is not wood!
16 Therefore, the Lord, the LORD Almighty,
will send a wasting disease[j] upon his sturdy warriors;
under his pomp a fire will be kindled
like a blazing flame.
17 The Light of Israel will become a fire,
their Holy One[k] a flame;
in a single day it will burn and consume
his thorns and his briers.
18 The splendor of his forests and fertile fields
it will completely destroy,
as when a sick man wastes away.
19 And the remaining trees of his forests will be so few
that a child could write them down.

## The Remnant of Israel

20 In that day the remnant of Israel,
the survivors of the house of Jacob,
will no longer rely[l] on him
who struck them down
but will truly rely on the LORD,
the Holy One of Israel.
21 A remnant will return,[b] a remnant of Jacob
will return to the Mighty God.
22 Though your people, O Israel, be like the sand by the sea,
only a remnant will return.
Destruction has been decreed,[m]
overwhelming and righteous.
23 The Lord, the LORD Almighty, will carry out
the destruction decreed upon the whole land.[n]

24 Therefore, this is what the Lord, the LORD Almighty, says:

[a] 13 Or / *I subdued the mighty,* [b] 21 Hebrew *shear-jashub*; also in verse 22

10:4 w Isa 5:25
10:5 x Jer 51:20
10:6 y Isa 9:17 z Isa 5:29
10:7 a Ge 50:20
10:9 b 2Ch 35:20 c 2Ki 16:9
10:10 d 2Ki 19:18
10:12 e 2Ki 19:31
10:13 f Isa 37:24; Da 4:30 g Eze 28:4
10:14 h Job 31:25
10:15 i Ro 9:20–21
10:16 j Isa 17:4
10:17 k Isa 37:23
10:20 l 2Ki 16:7
10:22 m Isa 28:22
10:23 n Ro 9:27–28*

**10:24** o Ps 87:5–6
**10:26** p Isa 37:36–38 q Ex 14:16
**10:28** r 1Sa 14:2 s 1Sa 13:2
**10:30** t 1Sa 25:44
**10:32** u 1Sa 21:1
**10:33** v Am 2:9
**11:1** w Rev 5:5 x Isa 4:2

"O my people who live in Zion,[o]
do not be afraid of the Assyrians,
who beat you with a rod
and lift up a club against you, as Egypt did.
25 Very soon my anger against you will end
and my wrath will be directed to their destruction."

26 The LORD Almighty will lash[p] them with a whip,
as when he struck down Midian at the rock of Oreb;
and he will raise his staff over the waters,[q]
as he did in Egypt.
27 In that day their burden will be lifted
from your shoulders,
their yoke from your neck;
the yoke will be broken
because you have grown so fat.[a]

28 They enter Aiath;
they pass through Migron;[r]
they store supplies at Micmash.[s]
29 They go over the pass, and say,
"We will camp overnight at Geba."
Ramah trembles;
Gibeah of Saul flees.
30 Cry out, O Daughter of Gallim![t]
Listen, O Laishah!
Poor Anathoth!
31 Madmenah is in flight;
the people of Gebim take cover.
32 This day they will halt at Nob;[u]
they will shake their fist
at the mount of the Daughter of Zion,
at the hill of Jerusalem.

33 See, the Lord, the LORD Almighty,
will lop off the boughs with great power.
The lofty trees will be felled,
the tall[v] ones will be brought low.
34 He will cut down the forest thickets with an ax;
Lebanon will fall before the Mighty One.

## The Branch From Jesse

**11** A shoot will come up from the stump of Jesse;[w]
from his roots a Branch[x] will bear fruit.
2 The Spirit[y] of the LORD will rest on him—
the Spirit of wisdom and of understanding,
the Spirit of counsel and of power,
the Spirit of knowledge and of the fear of the LORD—
3 and he will delight in the fear of the LORD.
He will not judge by what he sees with his eyes,[z]
or decide by what he hears with his ears;[a]
4 but with righteousness he will judge the needy,
with justice he will give decisions for the poor of the earth.
He will strike[b] the earth with the rod of his mouth;
with the breath[c] of his lips he will slay the wicked.
5 Righteousness will be his belt
and faithfulness the sash around his waist.[d]

6 The wolf will live with the lamb,[e]
the leopard will lie down with the goat,
the calf and the lion and the yearling[b] together;
and a little child will lead them.
7 The cow will feed with the bear,
their young will lie down together,
and the lion will eat straw like the ox.
8 The infant will play near the hole of the cobra,
and the young child put his hand into the viper's nest.
9 They will neither harm nor destroy[f]
on all my holy mountain,
for the earth will be full of the knowledge[g] of the LORD
as the waters cover the sea.

**11:2** y Isa 61:1; Mt 3:16; Jn 1:32–33
**11:3** z Jn 7:24 a Jn 2:25
**11:4** b Mal 4:6 c Job 4:9; 2Th 2:8
**11:5** d Eph 6:14
**11:6** e Isa 65:25
**11:9** f Job 5:23 g Hab 2:14

*Weary soul,*

*I desire to set you free from all oppression!*

*Your God*

ISAIAH 11:1–9

[a]27 Hebrew; Septuagint *broken / from your shoulders* [b]6 Hebrew; Septuagint *lion will feed*

**11:10** h Lk 2:32 i Ro 15:12*
**11:11** j Mic 7:12; Zec 10:10
**11:13** k Jer 3:18; Eze 37:16–17,22
**11:14** l Da 11:41
**11:16** m Isa 19:23 n Ex 14:26–31
**12:2** o Ex 15:2; Ps 118:14

10 In that day the Root of Jesse will stand
as a banner for the peoples; the nations[h] will
rally to him,[i] and his place of rest will be glo-
rious. 11 In that day the Lord will reach out
his hand a second time to reclaim the rem-
nant that is left of his people from Assyria,[j]
from Lower Egypt, from Upper Egypt,[a] from
Cush,[b] from Elam, from Babylonia,[c] from
Hamath and from the islands of the sea.

12 He will raise a banner for the nations
and gather the exiles of Israel;
he will assemble the scattered people of Judah
from the four quarters of the earth.
13 Ephraim's jealousy will vanish,
and Judah's enemies[d] will be cut off;
Ephraim will not be jealous of Judah,
nor Judah hostile toward Ephraim.[k]
14 They will swoop down on the slopes of Philistia to the west;
together they will plunder the people to the east.
They will lay hands on Edom[l] and Moab,
and the Ammonites will be subject to them.
15 The LORD will dry up
the gulf of the Egyptian sea;
with a scorching wind he will sweep his hand
over the Euphrates River.[e]
He will break it up into seven streams
so that men can cross over in sandals.
16 There will be a highway[m] for the remnant of his people
that is left from Assyria,
as there was for Israel
when they came up from Egypt.[n]

## Songs of Praise

**12** In that day you will say:

"I will praise you, O LORD.
Although you were angry with me,
your anger has turned away
and you have comforted me.
2 Surely God is my salvation;
I will trust and not be afraid.
The LORD, the LORD, is my strength and my song;
he has become my salvation.[o]"
3 With joy you will draw water[p]
from the wells of salvation.

4 In that day you will say:

"Give thanks to the LORD, call on his name;[q]
make known among the nations what he has done,
and proclaim that his name is exalted.
5 Sing[r] to the LORD, for he has done glorious things;[s]
let this be known to all the world.
6 Shout aloud and sing for joy, people of Zion,
for great is the Holy One of Israel among you.[t]"

## A Prophecy Against Babylon

**13** An oracle concerning Babylon that Isaiah son of Amoz saw:

2 Raise a banner[u] on a bare hilltop,
shout to them;
beckon to them
to enter the gates of the nobles.
3 I have commanded my holy ones;
I have summoned my warriors[v] to carry out my wrath—
those who rejoice[w] in my triumph.

4 Listen, a noise on the mountains,
like that of a great multitude!
Listen, an uproar among the kingdoms,
like nations massing together!
The LORD Almighty is mustering
an army for war.
5 They come from faraway lands,
from the ends of the heavens[x]—
the LORD and the weapons of his wrath—
to destroy[y] the whole country.

6 Wail, for the day[z] of the LORD is near;
it will come like destruction from the Almighty.[f]
7 Because of this, all hands will go limp,
every man's heart will melt.[a]
8 Terror will seize them,
pain and anguish will grip them;
they will writhe like a woman in labor.
They will look aghast at each other,
their faces aflame.

**12:3** p Jn 4:10,14
**12:4** q Ps 105:1
**12:5** r Ex 15:1 s Ps 98:1
**12:6** t Zep 3:14–17
**13:2** u Jer 51:27
**13:3** v Joel 3:11 w Ps 149:2
**13:5** x Isa 5:26 y Isa 24:1
**13:6** z Joel 1:15
**13:7** a Eze 21:7

[a] 11 Hebrew *from Pathros* [b] 11 That is, the upper Nile region [c] 11 Hebrew *Shinar* [d] 13 Or *hostility* [e] 15 Hebrew *the River*
[f] 6 Hebrew *Shaddai*

13:10 b Isa 5:30 c Eze 32:7; Mt 24:29*; Mk 13:24*
13:12 d Isa 4:1
13:13 e Isa 34:4; 51:6; Hag 2:6
13:14 f Jer 50:16
13:15 g Isa 14:19
13:16 h Ps 137:9
13:19 i Da 4:30 j Ge 19:24

9 See, the day of the LORD is coming
—a cruel day, with wrath and fierce anger—
to make the land desolate
and destroy the sinners within it.
10 The stars of heaven and their constellations
will not show their light.
The rising sun will be darkened[b]
and the moon will not give its light.[c]
11 I will punish the world for its evil,
the wicked for their sins.
I will put an end to the arrogance of the haughty
and will humble the pride of the ruthless.
12 I will make man[d] scarcer than pure gold,
more rare than the gold of Ophir.
13 Therefore I will make the heavens tremble;[e]
and the earth will shake from its place
at the wrath of the LORD Almighty,
in the day of his burning anger.

14 Like a hunted gazelle,
like sheep without a shepherd,
each will return to his own people,
each will flee to his native land.[f]
15 Whoever is captured will be thrust through;
all who are caught will fall by the sword.[g]
16 Their infants[h] will be dashed to pieces
before their eyes;
their houses will be looted and their wives ravished.

17 See, I will stir up against them the Medes,
who do not care for silver
and have no delight in gold.
18 Their bows will strike down the young men;
they will have no mercy on infants
nor will they look with compassion on children.
19 Babylon, the jewel of kingdoms,
the glory[i] of the Babylonians'[a] pride,
will be overthrown by God
like Sodom and Gomorrah.[j]
20 She will never be inhabited
or lived in through all generations;
no Arab will pitch his tent there,
no shepherd will rest his flocks there.
21 But desert creatures will lie there,
jackals will fill her houses;
there the owls will dwell,
and there the wild goats will leap about.
22 Hyenas will howl in her strongholds,
jackals in her luxurious palaces.
Her time is at hand,[k]
and her days will not be prolonged.

13:22 k Jer 51:33
14:1 l Ps 102:13 m Zec 1:17; 2:12 n Eph 2:12–19
14:2 o Isa 60:9 p Isa 49:7,23 q Isa 60:14
14:4 r Hab 2:6
14:6 s Isa 10:14 t Isa 47:6
14:8 u Eze 31:16
14:9 v Eze 32:21

14 The LORD will have compassion[l] on Jacob;
once again he will choose[m] Israel
and will settle them in their own land.
Aliens[n] will join them
and unite with the house of Jacob.
2 Nations will take them
and bring[o] them to their own place.
And the house of Israel will possess the nations[p]
as menservants and maidservants in the LORD's land.
They will make captives of their captors
and rule over their oppressors.[q]

3 On the day the LORD gives you relief from
suffering and turmoil and cruel bondage,
4 you will take up this taunt[r] against the king
of Babylon:

How the oppressor has come to an end!
How his fury[b] has ended!
5 The LORD has broken the rod of the wicked,
the scepter of the rulers,
6 which in anger struck down peoples[s]
with unceasing blows,
and in fury subdued nations
with relentless aggression.[t]
7 All the lands are at rest and at peace;
they break into singing.
8 Even the pine trees[u] and the cedars of Lebanon
exult over you and say,
"Now that you have been laid low,
no woodsman comes to cut us down."
9 The grave[c][v] below is all astir
to meet you at your coming;
it rouses the spirits of the departed to greet you—

[a]19 Or *Chaldeans'* [b]4 Dead Sea Scrolls, Septuagint and Syriac; the meaning of the word in the Masoretic Text is uncertain.
[c]9 Hebrew *Sheol*; also in verses 11 and 15

14:12 w Isa 34:4; Lk 10:18
14:13 x Da 8:10 y Eze 28:2
14:14 z Isa 47:8; 2Th 2:4
14:15 a Mt 11:23
14:17 b Joel 2:3
14:19 c Isa 22:16–18

all those who were leaders in the world;
it makes them rise from their thrones—
all those who were kings over the nations.
10 They will all respond,
they will say to you,
"You also have become weak, as we are;
you have become like us."
11 All your pomp has been brought down to the grave,
along with the noise of your harps;
maggots are spread out beneath you
and worms cover you.

12 How you have fallen[w] from heaven,
O morning star, son of the dawn!
You have been cast down to the earth,
you who once laid low the nations!
13 You said in your heart,
"I will ascend[x] to heaven;
I will raise my throne[y]
above the stars of God;
I will sit enthroned on the mount of assembly,
on the utmost heights of the sacred mountain.[a]
14 I will ascend above the tops of the clouds;
I will make myself like the Most High."[z]
15 But you are brought down to the grave,
to the depths[a] of the pit.

16 Those who see you stare at you,
they ponder your fate:
"Is this the man who shook the earth
and made kingdoms tremble,
17 the man who made the world a desert,[b]
who overthrew its cities
and would not let his captives go home?"

18 All the kings of the nations lie in state,
each in his own tomb.
19 But you are cast out[c] of your tomb
like a rejected branch;
you are covered with the slain,
with those pierced by the sword,
those who descend to the stones of the pit.
Like a corpse trampled underfoot,
20 you will not join them in burial,
for you have destroyed your land
and killed your people.

The offspring[d] of the wicked
will never be mentioned[e] again.
21 Prepare a place to slaughter his sons
for the sins of their forefathers;[f]
they are not to rise to inherit the land
and cover the earth with their cities.

22 "I will rise up against them,"
declares the LORD Almighty.
"I will cut off from Babylon her name and survivors,
her offspring and descendants,[g]"
declares the LORD.
23 "I will turn her into a place for owls[h]
and into swampland;
I will sweep her with the broom of destruction,"
declares the LORD Almighty.

## A Prophecy Against Assyria

24 The LORD Almighty has sworn,

"Surely, as I have planned, so it will be,
and as I have purposed, so it will stand.[i]
25 I will crush the Assyrian[j] in my land;
on my mountains I will trample him down.
His yoke will be taken from my people,
and his burden removed from their shoulders.[k]"

26 This is the plan determined for the whole world;
this is the hand[l] stretched out over all nations.
27 For the LORD Almighty has purposed, and who can thwart him?
His hand is stretched out, and who can turn it back?[m]

## A Prophecy Against the Philistines

28 This oracle came in the year King Ahaz[n] died:

29 Do not rejoice, all you Philistines,[o]
that the rod that struck you is broken;
from the root of that snake will spring up a viper,

14:20 d Job 18:19 e Ps 21:10
14:21 f Ex 20:5
14:22 g Job 18:19
14:23 h Isa 34:11–15; Zep 2:14
14:24 i Ac 4:28
14:25 j Isa 10:5,12 k Isa 10:27
14:26 l Ex 15:12
14:27 m 2Ch 20:6; Isa 43:13; Da 4:35
14:28 n 2Ki 16:20
14:29 o 2Ch 26:6

[a]13 Or *the north*; Hebrew *Zaphon*

its fruit will be a darting, venomous
serpent.
30 The poorest of the poor will find pasture,
and the needy[p] will lie down in safety.
But your root I will destroy by famine;
it will slay your survivors.

31 Wail, O gate! Howl, O city!
Melt away, all you Philistines!
A cloud of smoke comes from the north,[q]
and there is not a straggler in its
ranks.
32 What answer shall be given
to the envoys of that nation?
"The LORD has established Zion,[r]
and in her his afflicted people will find
refuge."

## A Prophecy Against Moab

15 An oracle concerning Moab:

Ar in Moab is ruined,
destroyed in a night!
Kir in Moab is ruined,
destroyed in a night!
2 Dibon goes up to its temple,
to its high places to weep;
Moab wails over Nebo and Medeba.
Every head is shaved[s]
and every beard cut off.
3 In the streets they wear sackcloth;
on the roofs and in the public squares[t]
they all wail,
prostrate with weeping.
4 Heshbon and Elealeh cry out,
their voices are heard all the way to
Jahaz.
Therefore the armed men of Moab cry
out,
and their hearts are faint.

5 My heart cries out over Moab;
her fugitives flee as far as Zoar,
as far as Eglath Shelishiyah.
They go up the way to Luhith,
weeping as they go;
on the road to Horonaim
they lament their destruction.[u]
6 The waters of Nimrim are dried up
and the grass is withered;[v]
the vegetation is gone
and nothing green is left.
7 So the wealth they have acquired[w] and
stored up
they carry away over the Ravine of the
Poplars.
8 Their outcry echoes along the border of
Moab;
their wailing reaches as far as Eglaim,
their lamentation as far as Beer Elim.
9 Dimon's[a] waters are full of blood,
but I will bring still more upon
Dimon[a]—
a lion[x] upon the fugitives of Moab
and upon those who remain in the
land.

16 Send lambs[y] as tribute
to the ruler of the land,
from Sela,[z] across the desert,
to the mount of the Daughter of Zion.
2 Like fluttering birds
pushed from the nest,
so are the women of Moab
at the fords of the Arnon.[a]

3 "Give us counsel,
render a decision.
Make your shadow like night—
at high noon.
Hide the fugitives,
do not betray the refugees.
4 Let the Moabite fugitives stay with you;
be their shelter from the destroyer."

The oppressor[b] will come to an end,
and destruction will cease;
the aggressor will vanish from the
land.
5 In love a throne[c] will be established;
in faithfulness a man will sit on it—
one from the house[b] of David[d]—
one who in judging seeks justice
and speeds the cause of righteousness.

6 We have heard of Moab's pride—
her overweening pride and conceit,
her pride and her insolence—
but her boasts are empty.
7 Therefore the Moabites wail,
they wail together for Moab.
Lament and grieve
for the men[c] of Kir Hareseth.[e]

**14:30** p Isa 3:15
**14:31** q Jer 1:14
**14:32** r Ps 87:2,5
**15:2** s Lev 21:5
**15:3** t Jer 48:38
**15:5** u Jer 48:5
**15:6** v Joel 1:12
**15:7** w Isa 30:6
**15:9** x 2Ki 17:25
**16:1** y 2Ki 3:4 z 2Ki 14:7
**16:2** a Nu 21:13–14
**16:4** b Isa 9:4
**16:5** c Da 7:14; Mic 4:7 d Lk 1:32
**16:7** e 2Ki 3:25

[a]9 Masoretic Text; Dead Sea Scrolls, some Septuagint manuscripts and Vulgate *Dibon* [b]5 Hebrew *tent* [c]7 Or "*raisin cakes,*" a wordplay

[8] The fields of Heshbon wither,
the vines of Sibmah also.
The rulers of the nations
have trampled down the choicest
vines,
which once reached Jazer
and spread toward the desert.
Their shoots spread out
and went as far as the sea.
[9] So I weep,[f] as Jazer weeps,
for the vines of Sibmah.
O Heshbon, O Elealeh,
I drench you with tears!
The shouts of joy over your ripened fruit
and over your harvests[g] have been
stilled.
[10] Joy and gladness are taken away from the
orchards;[h]
no one sings or shouts in the
vineyards;
no one treads out wine at the presses,
for I have put an end to the shouting.
[11] My heart laments for Moab like a harp,
my inmost being[i] for Kir Hareseth.
[12] When Moab appears at her high place,
she only wears herself out;
when she goes to her shrine[j] to pray,
it is to no avail.

[13]This is the word the LORD has already
spoken concerning Moab. [14]But now the
LORD says: "Within three years, as a ser-
vant bound by contract would count them,
Moab's splendor and all her many people
will be despised, and her survivors will be
very few and feeble."[k]

## An Oracle Against Damascus

**17** An oracle concerning Damascus:[l]

"See, Damascus will no longer be a city
but will become a heap of ruins.[m]
[2] The cities of Aroer will be deserted
and left to flocks, which will lie down,
with no one to make them afraid.[n]
[3] The fortified city will disappear from
Ephraim,
and royal power from Damascus;
the remnant of Aram will be
like the glory of the Israelites,"[o]
declares the LORD Almighty.

[4] "In that day the glory of Jacob will fade;
the fat of his body will waste[p] away.
[5] It will be as when a reaper gathers the
standing grain
and harvests[q] the grain with his arm—
as when a man gleans heads of grain
in the Valley of Rephaim.
[6] Yet some gleanings will remain,[r]
as when an olive tree is beaten,
leaving two or three olives on the topmost
branches,
four or five on the fruitful boughs,"
declares the LORD, the God
of Israel.
[7] In that day men will look to their Maker
and turn their eyes to the Holy One[s]
of Israel.
[8] They will not look to the altars,
the work of their hands,
and they will have no regard for the
Asherah poles[a]
and the incense altars their fingers
have made.

[9]In that day their strong cities, which
they left because of the Israelites, will be
like places abandoned to thickets and under-
growth. And all will be desolation.

[10] You have forgotten God your Savior;[t]
you have not remembered the Rock,
your fortress.
Therefore, though you set out the finest
plants
and plant imported vines,
[11] though on the day you set them out, you
make them grow,
and on the morning[u] when you plant
them, you bring them to bud,
yet the harvest will be as nothing
in the day of disease and incurable
pain.[v]
[12] Oh, the raging of many nations—
they rage like the raging sea![w]
Oh, the uproar of the peoples—
they roar like the roaring of great
waters!
[13] Although the peoples roar like the roar of
surging waters,
when he rebukes[x] them they flee far
away,

[a]8 That is, symbols of the goddess Asherah

16:9 f Isa 15:3 g Jer 40:12
16:10 h Isa 24:7–8
16:11 i Isa 63:15
16:12 j Isa 15:2
16:14 k Isa 21:17
17:1 l Jer 49:23 m Am 1:3; Zec 9:1
17:2 n Jer 7:33
17:3 o Isa 7:8,16; 8:4
17:4 p Isa 10:16
17:5 q Jer 51:33
17:6 r Isa 24:13
17:7 s Mic 7:7
17:10 t Ps 68:19
17:11 u Ps 90:6 v Job 4:8
17:12 w Jer 6:23
17:13 x Ps 9:5

17:14
y 2Ki 19:35

18:1
z Isa 20:3–5; Eze 30:4–5,9; Zep 2:12; 3:10

18:2
a ver 7

18:4
b Isa 26:19

driven before the wind like chaff on the
hills,
like tumbleweed before a gale.
[14] In the evening, sudden terror!
Before the morning, they are gone![y]
This is the portion of those who loot us,
the lot of those who plunder us.

## A Prophecy Against Cush

18 Woe to the land of whirring wings[a]
along the rivers of Cush,[b z]
[2] which sends envoys by sea
in papyrus boats over the water.

Go, swift messengers,
to a people tall and smooth-skinned,
to a people feared far and wide,
an aggressive nation of strange speech,
whose land is divided by rivers.[a]

[3] All you people of the world,
you who live on the earth,
when a banner is raised on the
mountains,
you will see it,
and when a trumpet sounds,
you will hear it.
[4] This is what the LORD says to me:
"I will remain quiet and will look on
from my dwelling place,
like shimmering heat in the sunshine,
like a cloud of dew[b] in the heat of
harvest."
[5] For, before the harvest, when the blossom
is gone
and the flower becomes a ripening
grape,
he will cut off the shoots with pruning
knives,
and cut down and take away the
spreading branches.
[6] They will all be left to the mountain birds
of prey
and to the wild animals;[c]
the birds will feed on them all summer,
the wild animals all winter.

[7] At that time gifts will be brought to the
LORD Almighty

from a people tall and smooth-skinned,
from a people feared far and wide,
an aggressive nation of strange speech,
whose land is divided by rivers—

the gifts will be brought to Mount Zion, the
place of the Name of the LORD Almighty.[d]

## A Prophecy About Egypt

19 An oracle[e] concerning Egypt:[f]

See, the LORD rides on a swift cloud[g]
and is coming to Egypt.
The idols of Egypt tremble before him,
and the hearts of the Egyptians melt
within them.

[2] "I will stir up Egyptian against
Egyptian—
brother will fight against brother,[h]
neighbor against neighbor,
city against city,
kingdom against kingdom.[i]
[3] The Egyptians will lose heart,
and I will bring their plans to nothing;

18:6
c Jer 7:33

18:7
d Ps 68:31

19:1
e Jer 43:12
f Ex 12:12
g Ps 18:10; 104:3

19:2
h Jdg 7:22
i 2Ch 20:23

[a]1 Or *of locusts* [b]1 That is, the upper Nile region

## The African Presence

### Isaiah 18:1

"Cush" is also called "Ethiopia" (that is, Nubia). The exact geographic region is disputed; however, most scholars generally agree that the area of Nubia included the middle of the Nile from what is present-day southern Egypt and northern Sudan. In 715 B.C. a Cushite named Shabako gained control of Egypt and founded the Twenty-fifth Dynasty. See also the African Presence note on Exodus 5:1–5.

## The African Presence

**Isaiah 19:1**

See the African Presence note on Genesis 10:6 for more information on Egypt.

they will consult the idols and the spirits
of the dead,
the mediums and the spiritists.[j]
4 I will hand the Egyptians over
to the power of a cruel master,
and a fierce king[k] will rule over them,"
declares the Lord, the LORD Almighty.

5 The waters of the river will dry up,[l]
and the riverbed will be parched and
dry.
6 The canals will stink;
the streams of Egypt will dwindle and
dry up.[m]
The reeds and rushes will wither,
7 also the plants along the Nile,
at the mouth of the river.
Every sown field along the Nile
will become parched, will blow away
and be no more.
8 The fishermen will groan and lament,
all who cast hooks into the Nile;
those who throw nets on the water
will pine away.
9 Those who work with combed flax will
despair,
the weavers of fine linen[n] will lose hope.
10 The workers in cloth will be dejected,
and all the wage earners will be sick
at heart.

11 The officials of Zoan[o] are nothing but
fools;
the wise counselors of Pharaoh give
senseless advice.
How can you say to Pharaoh,
"I am one of the wise men,
a disciple of the ancient kings"?
12 Where are your wise men now?
Let them show you and make known
what the LORD Almighty
has planned against Egypt.
13 The officials of Zoan have become fools,
the leaders of Memphis[a][p] are deceived;
the cornerstones of her peoples
have led Egypt astray.
14 The LORD has poured into them
a spirit of dizziness;
they make Egypt stagger in all that she
does,
as a drunkard staggers around in his
vomit.
15 There is nothing Egypt can do—
head or tail, palm branch or reed.[q]

16 In that day the Egyptians will be like
women. They will shudder with fear at
the uplifted hand[r] that the LORD Almighty
raises against them. 17 And the land of Judah
will bring terror to the Egyptians; everyone
to whom Judah is mentioned will be terri-
fied, because of what the LORD Almighty is
planning against them.
18 In that day five cities in Egypt will
speak the language of Canaan and swear al-
legiance to the LORD Almighty. One of them
will be called the City of Destruction.[b]
19 In that day there will be an altar[s] to
the LORD in the heart of Egypt, and a mon-
ument[t] to the LORD at its border. 20 It will be
a sign and witness to the LORD Almighty in
the land of Egypt. When they cry out to the
LORD because of their oppressors, he will
send them a savior and defender, and he will
rescue[u] them. 21 So the LORD will make him-
self known to the Egyptians, and in that day
they will acknowledge the LORD. They will
worship with sacrifices and grain offerings;
they will make vows to the LORD and keep
them. 22 The LORD will strike Egypt with a

**19:3** j Isa 8:19
**19:4** k Isa 20:4; Jer 46:26; Eze 29:19
**19:5** l Jer 51:36
**19:6** m Eze 30:12
**19:9** n Pr 7:16
**19:11** o Nu 13:22
**19:13** p Jer 2:16
**19:15** q Isa 9:14
**19:16** r Isa 11:15
**19:19** s Jos 22:10 t Ge 28:18
**19:20** u Isa 49:24–26

[a] 13 Hebrew *Noph* [b] 18 Most manuscripts of the Masoretic Text; some manuscripts of the Masoretic Text, Dead Sea Scrolls and Vulgate *City of the Sun* (that is, Heliopolis)

**19:22** v Isa 45:14
**19:23** w Isa 11:16 x Isa 27:13
**19:25** y Ps 100:3 z Isa 29:23; Eph 2:10 a Hos 2:23
**20:1** b 2Ki 18:17
**20:2** c Zec 13:4 d 1Sa 19:24 e Mic 1:8
**20:3** f Isa 8:18
**20:5** g 2Ki 18:21
**21:1** h Zec 9:14
**21:2** i Isa 33:1

plague; he will strike them and heal them. They will turn[v] to the LORD, and he will respond to their pleas and heal them.

23 In that day there will be a highway[w] from Egypt to Assyria. The Assyrians will go to Egypt and the Egyptians to Assyria. The Egyptians and Assyrians will worship[x] together. 24 In that day Israel will be the third, along with Egypt and Assyria, a blessing on the earth. 25 The LORD Almighty will bless them, saying, "Blessed be Egypt my people,[y] Assyria my handiwork,[z] and Israel my inheritance.[a]"

## A Prophecy Against Egypt and Cush

**20** In the year that the supreme commander,[b] sent by Sargon king of Assyria, came to Ashdod and attacked and captured it— 2 at that time the LORD spoke through Isaiah son of Amoz. He said to him, "Take off the sackcloth[c] from your body and the sandals from your feet." And he did so, going around stripped[d] and barefoot.[e]

3 Then the LORD said, "Just as my servant Isaiah has gone stripped and barefoot for three years, as a sign[f] and portent against Egypt and Cush,[a] 4 so the king of Assyria will lead away stripped and barefoot the Egyptian captives and Cushite exiles, young and old, with buttocks bared—to Egypt's shame. 5 Those who trusted in Cush and boasted in Egypt[g] will be afraid and put to shame. 6 In that day the people who live on this coast will say, 'See what has happened to those we relied on, those we fled to for help and deliverance from the king of Assyria! How then can we escape?' "

## A Prophecy Against Babylon

**21** An oracle concerning the Desert by the Sea:

Like whirlwinds sweeping through the
    southland,[h]
  an invader comes from the desert,
  from a land of terror.

2 A dire vision has been shown to me:
  The traitor betrays,[i] the looter takes
    loot.
Elam,[j] attack! Media, lay siege!
  I will bring to an end all the groaning
    she caused.

3 At this my body is racked with pain,
  pangs seize me, like those of a woman
    in labor;
I am staggered by what I hear,
  I am bewildered by what I see.
4 My heart falters,
  fear makes me tremble;
the twilight I longed for
  has become a horror to me.

5 They set the tables,
  they spread the rugs,
  they eat, they drink!
Get up, you officers,
  oil the shields!

6 This is what the Lord says to me:

"Go, post a lookout
  and have him report what he sees.
7 When he sees chariots[k]
  with teams of horses,
riders on donkeys
  or riders on camels,
let him be alert,
  fully alert."

8 And the lookout[b][l] shouted,

"Day after day, my lord, I stand on the
    watchtower;
  every night I stay at my post.
9 Look, here comes a man in a chariot
  with a team of horses.
And he gives back the answer:
  'Babylon[m] has fallen,[n] has fallen!
All the images of its gods[o]
  lie shattered on the ground!' "

10 O my people, crushed on the threshing
    floor,[p]
  I tell you what I have heard
from the LORD Almighty,
  from the God of Israel.

## A Prophecy Against Edom

11 An oracle concerning Dumah[c]:

Someone calls to me from Seir,
  "Watchman, what is left of the night?

**21:2** j Jer 49:34
**21:7** k ver 9
**21:8** l Hab 2:1
**21:9** m Rev 14:8 n Jer 51:8; Rev 18:2 o Isa 46:1; Jer 50:2; 51:44
**21:10** p Jer 51:33

[a] 3 That is, the upper Nile region; also in verse 5 [b] 8 Dead Sea Scrolls and Syriac; Masoretic Text *A lion* [c] 11 *Dumah* means *silence* or *stillness,* a wordplay on *Edom.*

21:16 q Isa 16:14 r Ps 120:5; Isa 60:7
22:1 s Joel 3:2,12,14
22:2 t Isa 32:13

Watchman, what is left of the night?"
12 The watchman replies,
"Morning is coming, but also the night.
If you would ask, then ask;
and come back yet again."

## A Prophecy Against Arabia

13 An oracle concerning Arabia:

You caravans of Dedanites,
who camp in the thickets of Arabia,
14 bring water for the thirsty;
you who live in Tema,
bring food for the fugitives.
15 They flee from the sword,
from the drawn sword,
from the bent bow
and from the heat of battle.

16 This is what the Lord says to me:
"Within one year, as a servant bound by con-
tract[q] would count it, all the pomp of Kedar[r]
will come to an end. 17 The survivors of the
bowmen, the warriors of Kedar, will be few."
The LORD, the God of Israel, has spoken.

## A Prophecy About Jerusalem

22 An oracle concerning the Valley[s] of Vision:

What troubles you now,
that you have all gone up on the roofs,
2 O town full of commotion,
O city of tumult and revelry?[t]
Your slain were not killed by the sword,
nor did they die in battle.
3 All your leaders have fled together;
they have been captured without using the bow.
All you who were caught were taken prisoner together,
having fled while the enemy was still far away.
4 Therefore I said, "Turn away from me;
let me weep bitterly.
Do not try to console me
over the destruction of my people."[u]
5 The Lord, the LORD Almighty, has a day
of tumult and trampling and terror[v]
in the Valley of Vision,
a day of battering down walls
and of crying out to the mountains.
6 Elam takes up the quiver,[w]
with her charioteers and horses;
Kir[x] uncovers the shield.
7 Your choicest valleys are full of chariots,
and horsemen are posted at the city gates;
8 the defenses of Judah are stripped away.

And you looked in that day
to the weapons in the Palace of the Forest;[y]
9 you saw that the City of David
had many breaches in its defenses;
you stored up water
in the Lower Pool.
10 You counted the buildings in Jerusalem
and tore down houses to strengthen the wall.
11 You built a reservoir between the two walls[z]
for the water of the Old Pool,[a]
but you did not look to the One who made it,
or have regard for the One who planned it long ago.

12 The Lord, the LORD Almighty,
called you on that day
to weep and to wail,

22:4 u Jer 9:1
22:5 v La 1:5
22:6 w Jer 49:35 x 2Ki 16:9
22:8 y 1Ki 7:2
22:11 z 2Ki 25:4 a 2Ch 32:4

### The African Presence

**Isaiah 21:13**

According to 2 Chronicles 21:16, Arabs lived near "Cushites," who were also known as Ethiopians or Nubians (see the African Presence notes on Ge 10:6–12 and Ex 5:1–5).

**22:12** b Mic 1:16 c Joel 1:13
**22:13** d Isa 56:12 e 1Co 15:32*
**22:14** f Isa 5:9
**22:15** g 2Ki 18:18; Isa 36:3
**22:16** h Mt 27:60
**22:18** i Isa 17:13
**22:20** j 2Ki 18:18
**22:22** k Rev 3:7 l Job 12:14
**22:23** m Ezr 9:8 n Job 36:7

to tear out your hair[b] and put on
sackcloth.[c]
13 But see, there is joy and revelry,
slaughtering of cattle and killing of sheep,
eating of meat and drinking of wine![d]
"Let us eat and drink," you say,
"for tomorrow we die!"[e]

14 The LORD Almighty has revealed this in my hearing:[f] "Till your dying day this sin will not be atoned for," says the Lord, the LORD Almighty.

15 This is what the Lord, the LORD Almighty, says:

"Go, say to this steward,
to Shebna,[g] who is in charge of the palace:
16 What are you doing here and who gave you permission
to cut out a grave[h] for yourself here,
hewing your grave on the height
and chiseling your resting place in the rock?
17 "Beware, the LORD is about to take firm hold of you
and hurl you away, O you mighty man.
18 He will roll you up tightly like a ball
and throw[i] you into a large country.
There you will die
and there your splendid chariots will remain—
you disgrace to your master's house!
19 I will depose you from your office,
and you will be ousted from your position.

20 "In that day I will summon my servant,
Eliakim[j] son of Hilkiah. 21 I will clothe him with your robe and fasten your sash around him and hand your authority over to him. He will be a father to those who live in Jerusalem and to the house of Judah.
22 I will place on his shoulder the key[k] to the house of David; what he opens no one can shut, and what he shuts no one can open.[l]
23 I will drive him like a peg into a firm place;[m] he will be a seat[a] of honor[n] for the house of his father.
24 All the glory of his family will hang on him: its offspring and offshoots—all its lesser vessels, from the bowls to all the jars.

25 "In that day," declares the LORD Almighty, "the peg[o] driven into the firm place will give way; it will be sheared off and will fall, and the load hanging on it will be cut down." The LORD has spoken.[p]

## A Prophecy About Tyre

23 An oracle concerning Tyre:[q]

Wail, O ships of Tarshish!
For Tyre is destroyed
and left without house or harbor.
From the land of Cyprus[b]
word has come to them.
2 Be silent, you people of the island
and you merchants of Sidon,
whom the seafarers have enriched.
3 On the great waters
came the grain of the Shihor;
the harvest of the Nile[c] was the revenue of Tyre,[r]
and she became the marketplace of the nations.

4 Be ashamed, O Sidon, and you, O fortress of the sea,
for the sea has spoken:
"I have neither been in labor nor given birth;
I have neither reared sons nor brought up daughters."
5 When word comes to Egypt,
they will be in anguish at the report from Tyre.
6 Cross over to Tarshish;
wail, you people of the island.
7 Is this your city of revelry,[s]
the old, old city,
whose feet have taken her
to settle in far-off lands?
8 Who planned this against Tyre,
the bestower of crowns,
whose merchants are princes,
whose traders are renowned in the earth?
9 The LORD Almighty planned it,
to bring low[t] the pride of all glory

**22:25** o ver 23 p Isa 46:11
**23:1** q Jer 47:4; Eze 26,27,28; Zec 9:2–4
**23:3** r Eze 27:3
**23:7** s Isa 22:2; 32:13
**23:9** t Job 40:11

[a]23 Or *throne* [b]1 Hebrew *Kittim* [c]2,3 Masoretic Text; one Dead Sea Scroll *Sidon, / who cross over the sea; / your envoys* [3]*are on the great waters. / The grain of the Shihor, / the harvest of the Nile,*

and to humble all who are renowned[u]
on the earth.

10 Till[a] your land as along the Nile,
O Daughter of Tarshish,
for you no longer have a harbor.
11 The LORD has stretched out his hand over
the sea
and made its kingdoms tremble.
He has given an order concerning
Phoenicia[b]
that her fortresses be destroyed.[v]
12 He said, "No more of your reveling,[w]
O Virgin Daughter of Sidon, now
crushed!

"Up, cross over to Cyprus[c];
even there you will find no rest."
13 Look at the land of the Babylonians,[d]
this people that is now of no account!
The Assyrians[x] have made it
a place for desert creatures;
they raised up their siege towers,
they stripped its fortresses bare
and turned it into a ruin.[y]

14 Wail, you ships of Tarshish;
your fortress is destroyed!

15 At that time Tyre[z] will be forgotten for seventy years, the span of a king's life. But at the end of these seventy years, it will happen to Tyre as in the song of the prostitute:

16 "Take up a harp, walk through the city,
O prostitute forgotten;
play the harp well, sing many a song,
so that you will be remembered."

17 At the end of seventy years, the LORD will deal with Tyre. She will return to her hire as a prostitute[a] and will ply her trade with all the kingdoms on the face of the earth.
18 Yet her profit and her earnings will be set apart for the LORD; they will not be stored up or hoarded. Her profits will go to those who live before the LORD,[b] for abundant food and fine clothes.

## The LORD's Devastation of the Earth

24 See, the LORD is going to lay waste
the earth
and devastate it;
he will ruin its face
and scatter its inhabitants—
2 it will be the same
for priest as for people,[c]
for master as for servant,
for mistress as for maid,
for seller as for buyer,
for borrower as for lender,
for debtor as for creditor.[d]
3 The earth will be completely laid waste
and totally plundered.
The LORD has spoken this word.

4 The earth dries up and withers,
the world languishes and withers,
the exalted of the earth languish.
5 The earth is defiled[e] by its people;
they have disobeyed the laws,
violated the statutes
and broken the everlasting covenant.
6 Therefore a curse consumes the earth;
its people must bear their guilt.
Therefore earth's inhabitants are burned
up,
and very few are left.
7 The new wine dries up and the vine
withers;[f]
all the merrymakers groan.[g]
8 The gaiety of the tambourines is stilled,
the noise[h] of the revelers has stopped,
the joyful harp[i] is silent.[j]
9 No longer do they drink wine with a
song;
the beer is bitter[k] to its drinkers.
10 The ruined city lies desolate;
the entrance to every house is barred.
11 In the streets they cry out for wine;
all joy turns to gloom,
all gaiety is banished from the earth.
12 The city is left in ruins,
its gate is battered to pieces.
13 So will it be on the earth
and among the nations,
as when an olive tree is beaten,[l]
or as when gleanings are left after the
grape harvest.

14 They raise their voices, they shout for joy;
from the west they acclaim the LORD's
majesty.
15 Therefore in the east give glory to the
LORD;

**23:9** u Isa 5:13
**23:11** v Isa 25:2
**23:12** w Rev 18:22
**23:13** x Isa 10:5 y Isa 10:7
**23:15** z Jer 25:22
**23:17** a Eze 16:26; Rev 17:1
**23:18** b Isa 60:5–9

**24:2** c Hos 4:9 d Dt 23:19–20
**24:5** e Ge 3:17; Nu 35:33
**24:7** f Joel 1:10–12 g Isa 16:8–10
**24:8** h Hos 2:11 i Rev 18:22 j Eze 26:13
**24:9** k Isa 5:20
**24:13** l Isa 17:6

[a]10 Dead Sea Scrolls and some Septuagint manuscripts; Masoretic Text *Go through* [b]11 Hebrew *Canaan* [c]12 Hebrew *Kittim* [d]13 Or *Chaldeans*

24:15
m Mal 1:11
24:16
n Jer 5:11
24:17
o Jer 48:43
24:18
p Ge 7:11
q Ps 18:7
24:20
r Isa 19:14
24:21
s Isa 10:12
24:23
t Isa 13:10
u Heb 12:22
v Isa 60:19
25:1
w Ps 98:1
25:2
x Isa 17:1

exalt[m] the name of the LORD, the God
of Israel,
in the islands of the sea.
16 From the ends of the earth we hear
singing:
"Glory to the Righteous One."

But I said, "I waste away, I waste away!
Woe to me!
The treacherous betray!
With treachery the treacherous
betray![n]"
17 Terror and pit and snare[o] await you,
O people of the earth.
18 Whoever flees at the sound of terror
will fall into a pit;
whoever climbs out of the pit
will be caught in a snare.

The floodgates of the heavens[p] are
opened,
the foundations of the earth shake.[q]
19 The earth is broken up,
the earth is split asunder,
the earth is thoroughly shaken.
20 The earth reels like a drunkard,[r]
it sways like a hut in the wind;
so heavy upon it is the guilt of its
rebellion
that it falls—never to rise again.

21 In that day the LORD will punish[s]
the powers in the heavens above
and the kings on the earth below.
22 They will be herded together
like prisoners bound in a dungeon;
they will be shut up in prison
and be punished[a] after many days.
23 The moon will be abashed, the sun[t]
ashamed;
for the LORD Almighty will reign
on Mount Zion[u] and in Jerusalem,
and before its elders, gloriously.[v]

## Praise to the LORD

25 O LORD, you are my God;
I will exalt you and praise your
name,
for in perfect faithfulness
you have done marvelous things,[w]
things planned long ago.
2 You have made the city a heap of rubble,[x]
the fortified town a ruin,
the foreigners' stronghold[y] a city no
more;
it will never be rebuilt.
3 Therefore strong peoples will honor you;
cities of ruthless nations will revere
you.
4 You have been a refuge[z] for the poor,
a refuge for the needy in his distress,
a shelter from the storm
and a shade from the heat.
For the breath of the ruthless
is like a storm driving against a wall
5 and like the heat of the desert.
You silence[a] the uproar of foreigners;
as heat is reduced by the shadow of a
cloud,
so the song of the ruthless is stilled.

*Lord,*

*thank you for being my shelter in times of storm. Help me always to find refuge in you and in you alone. In the strong name of Jesus, who alone can calm life's tempests,*

*Amen.*

ISAIAH 25:4–5

6 On this mountain[b] the LORD Almighty will
prepare
a feast[c] of rich food for all peoples,
a banquet of aged wine—
the best of meats and the finest of
wines.[d]
7 On this mountain he will destroy
the shroud[e] that enfolds all peoples,
the sheet that covers all nations;
8 he will swallow up death[f] forever.
The Sovereign LORD will wipe away the
tears[g]
from all faces;
he will remove the disgrace of his people
from all the earth.
The LORD has spoken.

9 In that day they will say,

25:2
y Isa 13:22
25:4
z Isa 4:6
25:5
a Jer 51:55
25:6
b Isa 2:2
c Mt 8:11; 22:4
d Pr 9:2
25:7
e 2Co 3:15–16
25:8
f Hos 13:14;
1Co 15:54–55*
g Rev 7:17; 21:4

[a] 22 Or *released*

"Surely this is our God;[h]
we trusted in him, and he saved[i] us.
This is the LORD, we trusted in him;
let us rejoice and be glad in his salvation."
10 The hand of the LORD will rest on this mountain;
but Moab will be trampled under him
as straw is trampled down in the manure.
11 They will spread out their hands in it,
as a swimmer spreads out his hands to swim.
God will bring down their pride
despite the cleverness[a] of their hands.
12 He will bring down your high fortified walls
and lay them low;
he will bring them down to the ground,
to the very dust.

## A Song of Praise

26 In that day this song will be sung in the land of Judah:

We have a strong city;
God makes salvation
its walls[j] and ramparts.
2 Open the gates
that the righteous nation may enter,
the nation that keeps faith.
3 You will keep in perfect peace
him whose mind is steadfast,
because he trusts in you.
4 Trust in the LORD forever,
for the LORD, the LORD, is the Rock eternal.
5 He humbles those who dwell on high,
he lays the lofty city low;
he levels it to the ground[k]
and casts it down to the dust.
6 Feet trample it down—
the feet of the oppressed,
the footsteps of the poor.[l]

7 The path of the righteous is level;
O upright One, you make the way of the righteous smooth.
8 Yes, LORD, walking in the way of your laws,[b][m]
we wait for you;
your name and renown
are the desire of our hearts.
9 My soul yearns for you in the night;
in the morning my spirit longs[n] for you.
When your judgments come upon the earth,
the people of the world learn righteousness.
10 Though grace is shown to the wicked,
they do not learn righteousness;
even in a land of uprightness they go on doing evil
and regard[o] not the majesty of the LORD.
11 O LORD, your hand is lifted high,
but they do not see it.
Let them see your zeal for your people
and be put to shame;
let the fire reserved for your enemies
consume them.

12 LORD, you establish peace for us;
all that we have accomplished you have done for us.
13 O LORD, our God, other lords[p] besides you
have ruled over us,
but your name alone do we honor.
14 They are now dead, they live no more;
those departed spirits do not rise.
You punished them and brought them to ruin;
you wiped out all memory of them.
15 You have enlarged the nation, O LORD;
you have enlarged the nation.
You have gained glory for yourself;

---

*Seeker,*

*Do you want peace?*
*Keep your mind focused on me.*

*Always,*
*God*

ISAIAH 26:1–4

---

**25:9** h Isa 40:9
i Ps 20:5; Isa 33:22
**26:1** j Isa 60:18
**26:5** k Isa 25:12
**26:6** l Isa 3:15
**26:8** m Isa 56:1
**26:9** n Isa 55:6
**26:10** o Isa 22:12–13
**26:13** p Isa 2:8; 10:5,11

[a] 11 The meaning of the Hebrew for this word is uncertain. [b] 8 Or *judgments*

you have extended all the borders[q] of
the land.

16 LORD, they came to you in their distress;[r]
when you disciplined them,
they could barely whisper a prayer.[a]
17 As a woman with child and about to give
birth[s]
writhes and cries out in her pain,
so were we in your presence, O LORD.
18 We were with child, we writhed in pain,
but we gave birth to wind.
We have not brought salvation[t] to the
earth;
we have not given birth to people of
the world.

19 But your dead will live;
their bodies will rise.
You who dwell in the dust,
wake up and shout for joy.
Your dew is like the dew of the morning;
the earth will give birth to her dead.[u]
20 Go, my people, enter your rooms
and shut the doors[v] behind you;
hide yourselves for a little while
until his wrath has passed by.[w]
21 See, the LORD is coming[x] out of his
dwelling[y]
to punish the people of the earth for
their sins.
The earth will disclose the blood shed
upon her;
she will conceal her slain no longer.

## Deliverance of Israel

27 In that day,

the LORD will punish with his sword,
his fierce, great and powerful sword,
Leviathan the gliding serpent,
Leviathan the coiling serpent;
he will slay the monster[z] of the sea.

2 In that day—
"Sing about a fruitful vineyard:[a]
3 I, the LORD, watch over it;
I water it continually.
I guard it day and night
so that no one may harm it.
4 I am not angry.
If only there were briers and thorns
confronting me!
I would march against them in battle;
I would set them all on fire.
5 Or else let them come to me for refuge;[b]
let them make peace[c] with me,
yes, let them make peace with me."

6 In days to come Jacob will take root,
Israel will bud and blossom[d]
and fill all the world with fruit.[e]

7 Has ⌊the LORD⌋ struck her
as he struck down those who struck
her?
Has she been killed
as those were killed who killed her?
8 By warfare[b] and exile you contend with
her—
with his fierce blast he drives her out,
as on a day the east wind blows.
9 By this, then, will Jacob's guilt be atoned
for,
and this will be the full fruitage of the
removal of his sin:[f]
When he makes all the altar stones
to be like chalk stones crushed to
pieces,
no Asherah poles[c] or incense altars
will be left standing.
10 The fortified city stands desolate,[g]
an abandoned settlement, forsaken
like the desert;
there the calves graze,
there they lie down;[h]
they strip its branches bare.
11 When its twigs are dry, they are broken
off
and women come and make fires with
them.
For this is a people without
understanding;[i]
so their Maker has no compassion on
them,
and their Creator[j] shows them no
favor.

12 In that day the LORD will thresh from
the flowing Euphrates[d] to the Wadi of Egypt,
and you, O Israelites, will be gathered up
one by one. 13 And in that day a great trum-
pet[k] will sound. Those who were perishing

**26:15** q Isa 33:17
**26:16** r Hos 5:15
**26:17** s Jn 16:21
**26:18** t Ps 17:14
**26:19** u Eze 37:1–14; Da 12:2
**26:20** v Ex 12:23 w Ps 30:5; Isa 54:7–8
**26:21** x Jude 1:14 y Mic 1:3
**27:1** z Ps 74:13
**27:2** a Jer 2:21
**27:5** b Isa 25:4 c Job 22:21
**27:6** d Hos 14:5–6 e Isa 37:31
**27:9** f Ro 11:27*
**27:10** g Isa 32:14 h Isa 17:2
**27:11** i Dt 32:28; Isa 1:3; Jer 8:7 j Dt 32:18; Isa 43:1,7,15; 44:1–2,21,24
**27:13** k Lev 25:9; Mt 24:31

[a]16 The meaning of the Hebrew for this clause is uncertain. [b]8 See Septuagint; the meaning of the Hebrew for this word is uncertain. [c]9 That is, symbols of the goddess Asherah [d]12 Hebrew *River*

28:2 l Isa 30:30; Eze 13:11
28:4 m Hos 9:10
28:5 n Isa 62:3
28:6 o Isa 11:2–4
28:7 p Isa 56:10–12 q Hos 4:11
28:8 r Jer 48:26

in Assyria and those who were exiled in Egypt will come and worship the LORD on the holy mountain in Jerusalem.

## Woe to Ephraim

28 Woe to that wreath, the pride of
Ephraim's drunkards,
to the fading flower, his glorious
beauty,
set on the head of a fertile valley—
to that city, the pride of those laid low
by wine!
2 See, the Lord has one who is powerful
and strong.
Like a hailstorm[l] and a destructive
wind,
like a driving rain and a flooding
downpour,
he will throw it forcefully to the ground.
3 That wreath, the pride of Ephraim's
drunkards,
will be trampled underfoot.
4 That fading flower, his glorious beauty,
set on the head of a fertile valley,
will be like a fig[m] ripe before harvest—
as soon as someone sees it and takes it
in his hand,
he swallows it.

5 In that day the LORD Almighty
will be a glorious crown,[n]
a beautiful wreath
for the remnant of his people.
6 He will be a spirit of justice[o]
to him who sits in judgment,
a source of strength
to those who turn back the battle at
the gate.

7 And these also stagger from wine
and reel[p] from beer:
Priests and prophets stagger from beer
and are befuddled with wine;
they reel from beer,
they stagger when seeing visions,[q]
they stumble when rendering
decisions.
8 All the tables are covered with vomit[r]
and there is not a spot without filth.

9 "Who is it he is trying to teach?
To whom is he explaining his message?
To children weaned[s] from their milk,
to those just taken from the breast?
10 For it is:
Do and do, do and do,
rule on rule, rule on rule[a];
a little here, a little there."
11 Very well then, with foreign lips and
strange tongues
God will speak to this people,[t]
12 to whom he said,
"This is the resting place, let the weary
rest";[u]
and, "This is the place of repose"—
but they would not listen.
13 So then, the word of the LORD to them will
become:
Do and do, do and do,
rule on rule, rule on rule;
a little here, a little there—
so that they will go and fall backward,
be injured and snared and captured.
14 Therefore hear the word of the LORD, you
scoffers
who rule this people in Jerusalem.
15 You boast, "We have entered into a
covenant with death,
with the grave[b] we have made an
agreement.
When an overwhelming scourge
sweeps by,[v]
it cannot touch us,
for we have made a lie our refuge
and falsehood[c] our hiding place.[w]"

16 So this is what the Sovereign LORD says:

"See, I lay a stone in Zion,
a tested stone,[x]
a precious cornerstone for a sure
foundation;
the one who trusts will never be
dismayed.[y]
17 I will make justice[z] the measuring line
and righteousness the plumb line;
hail will sweep away your refuge, the lie,
and water will overflow your hiding
place.
18 Your covenant with death will be
annulled;
your agreement with the grave will not
stand.

28:9 s Ps 131:2
28:11 t 1Co 14:21*
28:12 u Mt 11:28–29
28:15 v ver 2,18 w Isa 29:15
28:16 x Ps 118:22; Mt 21:42; Ac 4:11; Eph 2:20 y Ro 9:33*; 10:11*; 1Pe 2:6*
28:17 z Isa 5:16

[a]10 Hebrew */ sav lasav sav lasav / kav lakav kav lakav* (possibly meaningless sounds; perhaps a mimicking of the prophet's words); also in verse 13 [b]15 Hebrew *Sheol*; also in verse 18 [c]15 Or *false gods*

28:18 a ver 15
28:21 b 1Ch 14:11 c Jos 10:10,12; 1Ch 14:16
28:22 d Isa 10:22 e Isa 10:23

When the overwhelming scourge
sweeps by,[a]
you will be beaten down by it.
19 As often as it comes it will carry you away;
morning after morning, by day and
by night,
it will sweep through."

The understanding of this message
will bring sheer terror.
20 The bed is too short to stretch out on,
the blanket too narrow to wrap around
you.
21 The LORD will rise up as he did at Mount
Perazim,[b]
he will rouse himself as in the Valley of
Gibeon[c]—
to do his work, his strange work,
and perform his task, his alien task.
22 Now stop your mocking,
or your chains will become heavier;
the Lord, the LORD Almighty, has told me
of the destruction decreed[d] against the
whole land.[e]

23 Listen and hear my voice;
pay attention and hear what I say.
24 When a farmer plows for planting, does
he plow continually?
Does he keep on breaking up and
harrowing the soil?
25 When he has leveled the surface,
does he not sow caraway and scatter
cummin?
Does he not plant wheat in its place,[a]
barley in its plot,[a]
and spelt in its field?
26 His God instructs him
and teaches him the right way.

27 Caraway is not threshed with a sledge,
nor is a cartwheel rolled over cummin;
caraway is beaten out with a rod,
and cummin with a stick.
28 Grain must be ground to make bread;
so one does not go on threshing it
forever.
Though he drives the wheels of his
threshing cart over it,
his horses do not grind it.
29 All this also comes from the LORD
Almighty,
wonderful in counsel[f] and magnificent
in wisdom.[g]

## Woe to David's City

29 Woe to you, Ariel, Ariel,[h]
the city where David settled!
Add year to year
and let your cycle of festivals go on.
2 Yet I will besiege Ariel;
she will mourn and lament,[i]
she will be to me like an altar hearth.[b]
3 I will encamp against you all around;
I will encircle[j] you with towers
and set up my siege works against you.
4 Brought low, you will speak from the
ground;
your speech will mumble[k] out of the
dust.
Your voice will come ghostlike from the
earth;
out of the dust your speech will
whisper.

5 But your many enemies will become like
fine dust,
the ruthless hordes like blown chaff.
Suddenly,[l] in an instant,
6 the LORD Almighty will come
with thunder and earthquake and great
noise,
with windstorm and tempest and
flames of a devouring fire.
7 Then the hordes of all the nations that
fight against Ariel,
that attack her and her fortress and
besiege her,
will be as it is with a dream,[m]
with a vision in the night—
8 as when a hungry man dreams that he is
eating,
but he awakens, and his hunger
remains;
as when a thirsty man dreams that he is
drinking,
but he awakens faint, with his thirst
unquenched.
So will it be with the hordes of all the
nations
that fight against Mount Zion.

9 Be stunned and amazed,
blind yourselves and be sightless;

28:29 f Isa 9:6 g Ro 11:33
29:1 h 2Sa 5:9
29:2 i Isa 3:26; La 2:5
29:3 j Lk 19:43–44
29:4 k Isa 8:19
29:5 l Isa 17:14
29:7 m Job 20:8

[a]25 The meaning of the Hebrew for this word is uncertain. [b]2 The Hebrew for *altar hearth* sounds like the Hebrew for *Ariel*.

be drunk, but not from wine,[n]
stagger, but not from beer.
10 The LORD has brought over you a deep sleep:
He has sealed your eyes[o] (the prophets);
he has covered your heads (the seers).

11 For you this whole vision is nothing but words sealed[p] in a scroll. And if you give the scroll to someone who can read, and say to him, "Read this, please," he will answer, "I can't; it is sealed." 12 Or if you give the scroll to someone who cannot read, and say, "Read this, please," he will answer, "I don't know how to read."

13 The Lord says:

"These people come near to me with their mouth
and honor me with their lips,
but their hearts are far from me.[q]
Their worship of me
is made up only of rules taught by men.[a][r]
14 Therefore once more I will astound these people
with wonder upon wonder;[s]
the wisdom of the wise[t] will perish,
the intelligence of the intelligent will vanish.[u]"
15 Woe to those who go to great depths
to hide their plans from the LORD,
who do their work in darkness and think,
"Who sees us?[v] Who will know?"
16 You turn things upside down,
as if the potter were thought to be like the clay!
Shall what is formed say to him who formed it,
"He did not make me"?
Can the pot say of the potter,[w]
"He knows nothing"?

17 In a very short time, will not Lebanon be turned into a fertile field
and the fertile field seem like a forest?[x]
18 In that day the deaf will hear the words of the scroll,
and out of gloom and darkness
the eyes of the blind will see.[y]
19 Once more the humble[z] will rejoice in the LORD;
the needy[a] will rejoice in the Holy One of Israel.
20 The ruthless will vanish,
the mockers will disappear,
and all who have an eye for evil will be cut down—
21 those who with a word make a man out to be guilty,
who ensnare the defender in court[b]
and with false testimony deprive the innocent of justice.

22 Therefore this is what the LORD, who redeemed Abraham, says to the house of Jacob:

"No longer will Jacob be ashamed;
no longer will their faces grow pale.
23 When they see among them their children,
the work of my hands,
they will keep my name holy;
they will acknowledge the holiness of the Holy One of Jacob,
and will stand in awe of the God of Israel.
24 Those who are wayward[c] in spirit will gain understanding;
those who complain will accept instruction."

## Woe to the Obstinate Nation

30 "Woe[d] to the obstinate children,"
declares the LORD,
"to those who carry out plans that are not mine,
forming an alliance, but not by my Spirit,
heaping sin upon sin;
2 who go down to Egypt[e]
without consulting me;
who look for help to Pharaoh's protection,
to Egypt's shade for refuge.
3 But Pharaoh's protection will be to your shame,
Egypt's shade will bring you disgrace.[f]
4 Though they have officials in Zoan[g]
and their envoys have arrived in Hanes,
5 everyone will be put to shame
because of a people[h] useless to them,

**29:9** n Isa 51:21–22
**29:10** o Ps 69:23; Isa 6:9–10; Ro 11:8*
**29:11** p Isa 8:16
**29:13** q Eze 33:31 r Mt 15:8–9*; Mk 7:6–7*
**29:14** s Hab 1:5 t Jer 49:7 u 1Co 1:19*
**29:15** v Ps 94:7
**29:16** w Isa 45:9; Ro 9:20–21*
**29:17** x Isa 32:15
**29:18** y Isa 35:5
**29:19** z Isa 61:1
**29:19** a Jas 2:5
**29:21** b Am 5:10,15
**29:24** c Isa 28:7
**30:1** d Isa 29:15
**30:2** e Isa 31:1
**30:3** f Isa 20:4–5
**30:4** g Isa 19:11
**30:5** h ver 7

[a]13 Hebrew; Septuagint *They worship me in vain; / their teachings are but rules taught by men*

**30:6** i Isa 15:7
**30:9** j Isa 28:15
**30:11** k Job 21:14
**30:13** l Ps 62:3; m Isa 29:5
**30:14** n Ps 2:9; Jer 19:10–11

who bring neither help nor advantage,
but only shame and disgrace."

6 An oracle concerning the animals of the Negev:

Through a land of hardship and distress,
of lions and lionesses,
of adders and darting snakes,
the envoys carry their riches on donkeys' backs,
their treasures[i] on the humps of camels,
to that unprofitable nation,
7 to Egypt, whose help is utterly useless.
Therefore I call her
Rahab the Do-Nothing.

8 Go now, write it on a tablet for them,
inscribe it on a scroll,
that for the days to come
it may be an everlasting witness.
9 These are rebellious people, deceitful[j] children,
children unwilling to listen to the LORD's instruction.
10 They say to the seers,
"See no more visions!"
and to the prophets,
"Give us no more visions of what is right!
Tell us pleasant things,
prophesy illusions.
11 Leave this way,
get off this path,
and stop confronting[k] us
with the Holy One of Israel!"

12 Therefore, this is what the Holy One of Israel says:

"Because you have rejected this message,
relied on oppression
and depended on deceit,
13 this sin will become for you
like a high wall,[l] cracked and bulging,
that collapses suddenly,[m] in an instant.
14 It will break in pieces like pottery,[n]
shattered so mercilessly
that among its pieces not a fragment will be found
for taking coals from a hearth
or scooping water out of a cistern."

15 This is what the Sovereign LORD, the Holy One of Israel, says:

"In repentance and rest is your salvation,
in quietness and trust[o] is your strength,
but you would have none of it.
16 You said, 'No, we will flee on horses.'[p]
Therefore you will flee!
You said, 'We will ride off on swift horses.'
Therefore your pursuers will be swift!
17 A thousand will flee
at the threat of one;
at the threat of five[q]
you will all flee[r] away,
till you are left
like a flagstaff on a mountaintop,
like a banner on a hill."

18 Yet the LORD longs[s] to be gracious to you;
he rises to show you compassion.
For the LORD is a God of justice.[t]
Blessed are all who wait for him!

19 O people of Zion, who live in Jerusalem,
you will weep no more. How gracious he
will be when you cry for help! As soon as he
hears, he will answer you. 20 Although the
Lord gives you the bread[u] of adversity and
the water of affliction, your teachers will
be hidden[v] no more; with your own eyes
you will see them. 21 Whether you turn to
the right or to the left, your ears will hear a
voice behind you, saying, "This is the way;
walk in it." 22 Then you will defile your idols
overlaid with silver and your images cov-
ered with gold; you will throw them away
like a menstrual cloth and say to them,
"Away with you!"

23 He will also send you rain for the seed
you sow in the ground, and the food that
comes from the land will be rich and plen-
tiful. In that day your cattle will graze in
broad meadows.[w] 24 The oxen and donkeys
that work the soil will eat fodder and mash,
spread out with fork and shovel. 25 In the
day of great slaughter, when the towers fall,
streams of water will flow on every high
mountain and every lofty hill. 26 The moon
will shine like the sun,[x] and the sunlight
will be seven times brighter, like the light of
seven full days, when the LORD binds up the

**30:15** o Isa 32:17
**30:16** p Isa 31:1,3
**30:17** q Lev 26:8; Jos 23:10; r Dt 28:25
**30:18** s Isa 42:14; t Isa 5:16
**30:20** u 1Ki 22:27; v Ps 74:9; Am 8:11
**30:23** w Ps 65:13
**30:26** x Isa 60:19–20; Rev 21:23

30:26 y Isa 1:5
30:27 z Isa 59:19
30:28 a Isa 11:4 b Isa 8:8 c 2Ki 19:28; Isa 37:29
30:29 d Ps 42:4
30:31 e Isa 10:5,12
30:32 f Eze 32:10
31:1 g Isa 30:2,5

bruises of his people and heals[y] the wounds
he inflicted.

27 See, the Name[z] of the LORD comes from
afar,
with burning anger and dense clouds
of smoke;
his lips are full of wrath,
and his tongue is a consuming fire.
28 His breath[a] is like a rushing torrent,
rising up to the neck.[b]
He shakes the nations in the sieve of
destruction;
he places in the jaws of the peoples
a bit[c] that leads them astray.
29 And you will sing
as on the night you celebrate a holy
festival;
your hearts will rejoice
as when people go up with flutes
to the mountain[d] of the LORD,
to the Rock of Israel.
30 The LORD will cause men to hear his
majestic voice
and will make them see his arm
coming down
with raging anger and consuming fire,
with cloudburst, thunderstorm and
hail.
31 The voice of the LORD will shatter Assyria;[e]
with his scepter he will strike them
down.
32 Every stroke the LORD lays on them
with his punishing rod
will be to the music of tambourines and
harps,
as he fights them in battle with the
blows of his arm.[f]
33 Topheth has long been prepared;
it has been made ready for the king.
Its fire pit has been made deep and wide,
with an abundance of fire and wood;
the breath of the LORD,
like a stream of burning sulfur,
sets it ablaze.

## Woe to Those Who Rely on Egypt

31 Woe to those who go down to Egypt[g]
for help,
who rely on horses,
who trust in the multitude of their
chariots
and in the great strength of their
horsemen,
but do not look to the Holy One of Israel,
or seek help from the LORD.[h]
2 Yet he too is wise and can bring disaster;
he does not take back his words.[i]
He will rise up against the house of the
wicked,
against those who help evildoers.
3 But the Egyptians are men and not God;[j]
their horses are flesh and not spirit.
When the LORD stretches out his hand,
he who helps will stumble,
he who is helped[k] will fall;
both will perish together.

4 This is what the LORD says to me:

"As a lion[l] growls,
a great lion over his prey—
and though a whole band of shepherds
is called together against him,
he is not frightened by their shouts
or disturbed by their clamor—
so the LORD Almighty will come down[m]
to do battle on Mount Zion and on its
heights.
5 Like birds hovering overhead,
the LORD Almighty will shield[n]
Jerusalem;
he will shield it and deliver it,
he will 'pass over' it and will rescue it."

6 Return to him you have so greatly re-
volted against, O Israelites. 7 For in that day
every one of you will reject the idols of silver
and gold[o] your sinful hands have made.

8 "Assyria[p] will fall by a sword that is not of
man;
a sword, not of mortals, will devour
them.
They will flee before the sword
and their young men will be put to
forced labor.
9 Their stronghold[q] will fall because of
terror;
at sight of the battle standard their
commanders will panic,"
declares the LORD,
whose fire[r] is in Zion,
whose furnace is in Jerusalem.

31:1 h Ps 20:7; Da 9:13
31:2 i Nu 23:19
31:3 j Eze 28:9 k Isa 30:5–7
31:4 l Am 3:8 m Isa 42:13
31:5 n Ps 91:4
31:7 o Isa 2:20
31:8 p Isa 10:12
31:9 q Dt 32:31,37 r Isa 10:17

32:1 s Isa 9:7
32:2 t Isa 4:6

## The Kingdom of Righteousness

32 See, a king will reign in
righteousness
and rulers will rule with justice.[s]
2 Each man will be like a shelter[t] from the
wind
and a refuge from the storm,
like streams of water in the desert
and the shadow of a great rock in a
thirsty land.
3 Then the eyes of those who see will no
longer be closed,[u]

32:3 u Isa 29:18

# Inspire leadership FOCUS

## SPIRITUAL DISCIPLINE

Life, even at its best, demands much of us. Often there are two things we don't have or don't have enough of: spiritual energy (faith) and physical energy. We are living in a fast-moving world, a complex society that absorbs and channels our energies. Only a very few of us can deny a feeling of exhaustion from day to day—that feeling that prompts us to think, *I need to, and I want to, but I can't.*

We need to stop and ask ourselves, *What are we seeking? What are we running from?* We have lost control of ourselves by not seeking some basic foundations on which to build our lives. One way we can lay a foundation is by setting goals and then sticking to those goals. God can help us achieve this. While we work toward our goals, we need to look to the right, to the left and sometimes behind us as we move forward. Can you imagine getting into a car and driving without looking where you're going? What about the risk of not stopping at a red light or not slowing down in a curve? Those rules are for your benefit, just as God's encouragement is for our benefit. His words guide us to reach our goals.

We are in motion not to *be* but to *become.* This is why God tells us, "Whether you turn to the right or to the left, your ears will hear a voice behind you, saying, 'This is the way; walk in it' " (Isa 30:21).

Even though God blesses us, he anticipates our inability to live perfect lives. So he helps us to become disciplined in order to grow spiritually. Then he helps us to make our way along the tightrope of circumstances that we face daily. As we practice discipline, with his help, we grow higher, deeper and wider. As time passes, we are more able to conquer difficulties, and we acquire more of God's power. Without spiritual discipline, a woman cannot grow in faith nor can she experience all of her faculties unfolding and truth descending into her soul. But with spiritual discipline we feel more alive, more genuinely ourselves.

—E. McNair

For the next Inspire note, go to page 847.

### read

Isaiah 30.

**See also** the Inspire Notes "Rest," "Coping With Life's Tasks," "Doing Your Best" and "Faith," and the Women of the Bible Note "A Virtuous Woman: A Strong Woman, Dependent on God."

### WOMAN of COLOR

What spiritual disciplines revive and restore you?

and the ears of those who hear will
listen.
4 The mind of the rash will know and
understand,
and the stammering tongue will be
fluent and clear.
5 No longer will the fool[v] be called noble
nor the scoundrel be highly respected.
6 For the fool speaks folly,
his mind is busy with evil:
He practices ungodliness
and spreads error concerning the
LORD;
the hungry he leaves empty[w]
and from the thirsty he withholds
water.
7 The scoundrel's methods are wicked,[x]
he makes up evil schemes
to destroy the poor with lies,
even when the plea of the needy is just.
8 But the noble man makes noble plans,
and by noble deeds he stands.

## The Women of Jerusalem

9 You women who are so complacent,
rise up and listen[y] to me;
you daughters who feel secure,
hear what I have to say!
10 In little more than a year
you who feel secure will tremble;
the grape harvest will fail,[z]
and the harvest of fruit will not come.
11 Tremble, you complacent women;
shudder, you daughters who feel secure!
Strip off your clothes,[a]
put sackcloth around your waists.
12 Beat your breasts[b] for the pleasant fields,
for the fruitful vines
13 and for the land of my people,
a land overgrown with thorns and
briers—
yes, mourn for all houses of merriment
and for this city of revelry.[c]
14 The fortress[d] will be abandoned,
the noisy city deserted;
citadel and watchtower will become a
wasteland forever,
the delight of donkeys, a pasture for
flocks,
15 till the Spirit[e] is poured upon us from on
high,
and the desert becomes a fertile field,
and the fertile field seems like a forest.[f]
16 Justice will dwell in the desert
and righteousness live in the fertile
field.
17 The fruit of righteousness will be peace;[g]
the effect of righteousness will be
quietness and confidence[h]
forever.
18 My people will live in peaceful dwelling
places,
in secure homes,
in undisturbed places of rest.
19 Though hail[i] flattens the forest[j]
and the city is leveled completely,
20 how blessed you will be,
sowing your seed by every stream,
and letting your cattle and donkeys
range free.[k]

## Distress and Help

33 Woe to you, O destroyer,
you who have not been destroyed!
Woe to you, O traitor,
you who have not been betrayed!
When you stop destroying,
you will be destroyed;[l]
when you stop betraying,
you will be betrayed.[m]

2 O LORD, be gracious to us;
we long for you.
Be our strength every morning,
our salvation[n] in time of distress.
3 At the thunder of your voice, the peoples
flee;
when you rise up, the nations scatter.
4 Your plunder, O nations, is harvested as
by young locusts;
like a swarm of locusts men pounce
on it.

5 The LORD is exalted,[o] for he dwells on
high;
he will fill Zion with justice and
righteousness.
6 He will be the sure foundation for your
times,
a rich store of salvation and wisdom
and knowledge;
the fear[p] of the LORD is the key to this
treasure.[a]

[a]6 Or *is a treasure from him*

**32:5** v 1Sa 25:25
**32:6** w Isa 3:15
**32:7** x Jer 5:26–28
**32:9** y Isa 28:23
**32:10** z Isa 5:5–6
**32:11** a Isa 47:2
**32:12** b Na 2:7
**32:13** c Isa 22:2
**32:14** d Isa 13:22
**32:15** e Joel 2:28
**32:15** f Isa 29:17
**32:17** g Jas 3:18 h Isa 30:15
**32:19** i Isa 30:30 j Zec 11:2
**32:20** k Isa 30:24
**33:1** l Hab 2:8 m Isa 21:2
**33:2** n Isa 25:9
**33:5** o Ps 97:9
**33:6** p Mt 6:33

7 Look, their brave men cry aloud in the streets;
the envoys[q] of peace weep bitterly.
8 The highways are deserted,
no travelers are on the roads.
The treaty is broken,
its witnesses[a] are despised,
no one is respected.
9 The land mourns[b] and wastes away,
Lebanon[r] is ashamed and withers;[s]
Sharon is like the Arabah,
and Bashan and Carmel drop their leaves.

10 "Now will I arise,[t]" says the LORD.
"Now will I be exalted;
now will I be lifted up.
11 You conceive[u] chaff,
you give birth to straw;
your breath is a fire that consumes you.
12 The peoples will be burned as if to lime;
like cut thornbushes they will be set ablaze."

13 You who are far away,[v] hear what I have done;
you who are near, acknowledge my power!
14 The sinners in Zion are terrified;
trembling grips the godless:
"Who of us can dwell with the consuming fire?
Who of us can dwell with everlasting burning?"
15 He who walks righteously
and speaks what is right,[w]
who rejects gain from extortion
and keeps his hand from accepting bribes,
who stops his ears against plots of murder
and shuts his eyes[x] against contemplating evil—
16 this is the man who will dwell on the heights,
whose refuge[y] will be the mountain fortress.
His bread will be supplied,
and water will not fail him.

17 Your eyes will see the king in his beauty
and view a land that stretches afar.[z]
18 In your thoughts you will ponder the former terror:[a]
"Where is that chief officer?
Where is the one who took the revenue?
Where is the officer in charge of the towers?"
19 You will see those arrogant people no more,
those people of an obscure speech,
with their strange, incomprehensible tongue.[b]

20 Look upon Zion, the city of our festivals;
your eyes will see Jerusalem,
a peaceful abode, a tent that will not be moved;[c]
its stakes will never be pulled up,
nor any of its ropes broken.
21 There the LORD will be our Mighty One.
It will be like a place of broad rivers and streams.
No galley with oars will ride them,
no mighty ship will sail them.
22 For the LORD is our judge,
the LORD is our lawgiver,[d]
the LORD is our king;
it is he who will save us.

23 Your rigging hangs loose:
The mast is not held secure,
the sail is not spread.
Then an abundance of spoils will be divided
and even the lame will carry off plunder.
24 No one living in Zion will say, "I am ill";
and the sins of those who dwell there will be forgiven.[e]

## Judgment Against the Nations

34 Come near, you nations, and listen;
pay attention, you peoples!
Let the earth[f] hear, and all that is in it,
the world, and all that comes out of it![g]
2 The LORD is angry with all nations;
his wrath is upon all their armies.
He will totally destroy[c] them,
he will give them over to slaughter.
3 Their slain will be thrown out,

33:7 q 2Ki 18:37
33:9 r Isa 2:13 s Isa 24:4
33:10 t Ps 12:5
33:11 u Ps 7:14; Isa 59:4
33:13 v Ps 49:1
33:15 w Ps 15:2; 24:4 x Ps 119:37
33:16 y Isa 25:4
33:17 z Isa 26:15
33:18 a Isa 17:14
33:19 b Jer 5:15
33:20 c Ps 46:5; 125:1–2
33:22 d Jas 4:12
33:24 e Jer 50:20
34:1 f Ps 49:1 g Dt 32:1

[a]8 Dead Sea Scrolls; Masoretic Text / *the cities* [b]9 Or *dries up* [c]2 The Hebrew term refers to the irrevocable giving over of things or persons to the LORD, often by totally destroying them; also in verse 5.

**34:3** h Joel 2:20
**34:4** i 2Pe 3:10 j Eze 32:7–8 k Joel 2:31; Mt 24:29*; Rev 6:13
**34:5** l Jer 46:10 m Mal 1:4
**34:8** n Isa 63:4
**34:10** o Rev 14:10–11; 19:3
**34:11** p Zep 2:14 q 2Ki 21:13; La 2:8
**34:13** r Isa 13:22; 32:13
**34:14** s Isa 13:22

their dead bodies will send up a
stench;[h]
the mountains will be soaked with
their blood.
4 All the stars of the heavens will be
dissolved[i]
and the sky rolled up[j] like a scroll;
all the starry host will fall[k]
like withered leaves from the vine,
like shriveled figs from the fig tree.

5 My sword[l] has drunk its fill in the
heavens;
see, it descends in judgment on Edom,
the people I have totally destroyed.[m]
6 The sword of the LORD is bathed in blood,
it is covered with fat—
the blood of lambs and goats,
fat from the kidneys of rams.
For the LORD has a sacrifice in Bozrah
and a great slaughter in Edom.
7 And the wild oxen will fall with them,
the bull calves and the great bulls.
Their land will be drenched with blood,
and the dust will be soaked with fat.

8 For the LORD has a day of vengeance,[n]
a year of retribution, to uphold Zion's
cause.
9 Edom's streams will be turned into pitch,
her dust into burning sulfur;
her land will become blazing pitch!
10 It will not be quenched night and day;
its smoke will rise forever.[o]
From generation to generation it will lie
desolate;
no one will ever pass through it again.
11 The desert owl[a][p] and screech owl[a] will
possess it;
the great owl[a] and the raven will nest
there.
God will stretch out over Edom
the measuring line of chaos
and the plumb line[q] of desolation.
12 Her nobles will have nothing there to be
called a kingdom,
all her princes will vanish away.
13 Thorns will overrun her citadels,
nettles and brambles her strongholds.[r]
She will become a haunt for jackals,
a home for owls.
14 Desert creatures will meet with hyenas,[s]
and wild goats will bleat to each other;
there the night creatures will also repose
and find for themselves places of rest.
15 The owl will nest there and lay eggs,
she will hatch them, and care for her
young under the shadow of her
wings;
there also the falcons will gather,
each with its mate.

16 Look in the scroll of the LORD and read:

None of these will be missing,
not one will lack her mate.
For it is his mouth that has given the
order,
and his Spirit will gather them
together.
17 He allots their portions;[t]
his hand distributes them by measure.
They will possess it forever
and dwell there from generation to
generation.

## Joy of the Redeemed

35 The desert and the parched land will
be glad;
the wilderness will rejoice and
blossom.
Like the crocus, 2 it will burst into bloom;
it will rejoice greatly and shout for joy.[u]
The glory of Lebanon[v] will be given to it,
the splendor of Carmel and Sharon;
they will see the glory of the LORD,
the splendor of our God.

3 Strengthen the feeble hands,
steady the knees[w] that give way;
4 say to those with fearful hearts,
"Be strong, do not fear;
your God will come,
he will come with vengeance;
with divine retribution
he will come to save you."

5 Then will the eyes of the blind be opened[x]
and the ears of the deaf[y] unstopped.
6 Then will the lame[z] leap like a deer,
and the mute tongue[a] shout for joy.
Water will gush forth in the wilderness
and streams[b] in the desert.
7 The burning sand will become a pool,
the thirsty ground bubbling springs.

**34:17** t Jer 13:25
**35:2** u Isa 55:12 v Isa 32:15
**35:3** w Job 4:4; Heb 12:12
**35:5** x Mt 11:5; Jn 9:6–7 y Isa 29:18
**35:6** z Mt 15:30; Jn 5:8–9 a Mt 9:32–33 b Isa 41:18; Jn 7:38

[a] 11 The precise identification of these birds is uncertain.

**35:8**
c Mt7:13–14
**35:10**
d Isa51:11; Rev7:17; 21:4
**36:1**
e 2Ch32:1
**36:3**
f Isa22:20–21
**36:6**
g Isa30:2,5
h Eze29:6–7

In the haunts where jackals once lay,
grass and reeds and papyrus will grow.
8 And a highway[c] will be there;
it will be called the Way of Holiness.
The unclean will not journey on it;
it will be for those who walk in that
Way;
wicked fools will not go about on it.[a]
9 No lion will be there,
nor will any ferocious beast get up
on it;
they will not be found there.
But only the redeemed will walk there,
10 and the ransomed of the LORD will
return.
They will enter Zion with singing;
everlasting joy will crown their heads.
Gladness and joy will overtake them,
and sorrow and sighing will flee away.[d]

## Sennacherib Threatens Jerusalem

**36** In the fourteenth year of King Hez-
ekiah's reign, Sennacherib[e] king of
Assyria attacked all the fortified cities of
Judah and captured them. 2 Then the king
of Assyria sent his field commander with
a large army from Lachish to King Hezeki-
ah at Jerusalem. When the commander
stopped at the aqueduct of the Upper Pool,
on the road to the Washerman's Field, 3 Eli-
akim[f] son of Hilkiah the palace administra-
tor, Shebna the secretary, and Joah son of
Asaph the recorder went out to him.

4 The field commander said to them,
"Tell Hezekiah,

"'This is what the great king, the
king of Assyria, says: On what are you
basing this confidence of yours? 5 You
say you have strategy and military
strength—but you speak only empty
words. On whom are you depending,
that you rebel against me? 6 Look
now, you are depending on Egypt,[g]
that splintered reed[h] of a staff, which
pierces a man's hand and wounds him
if he leans on it! Such is Pharaoh king
of Egypt to all who depend on him.
7 And if you say to me, "We are depend-
ing on the LORD our God"—isn't he
the one whose high places and altars
Hezekiah removed,[i] saying to Judah
and Jerusalem, "You must worship be-
fore this altar"?

8 "'Come now, make a bargain with
my master, the king of Assyria: I will
give you two thousand horses—if you
can put riders on them! 9 How then can
you repulse one officer of the least of
my master's officials, even though you
are depending on Egypt for chariots
and horsemen?[j] 10 Furthermore, have
I come to attack and destroy this land
without the LORD? The LORD himself
told me to march against this country
and destroy it.'"

11 Then Eliakim, Shebna and Joah said to
the field commander, "Please speak to your
servants in Aramaic,[k] since we understand
it. Don't speak to us in Hebrew in the hear-
ing of the people on the wall."

12 But the commander replied, "Was it
only to your master and you that my master
sent me to say these things, and not to the
men sitting on the wall—who, like you, will
have to eat their own filth and drink their
own urine?"

13 Then the commander stood and called
out in Hebrew,[l] "Hear the words of the great
king, the king of Assyria! 14 This is what the
king says: Do not let Hezekiah deceive you.
He cannot deliver you! 15 Do not let Hezekiah
persuade you to trust in the LORD when he
says, 'The LORD will surely deliver us; this
city will not be given into the hand of the
king of Assyria.'

16 "Do not listen to Hezekiah. This is what
the king of Assyria says: Make peace with
me and come out to me. Then every one of
you will eat from his own vine and fig tree[m]
and drink water from his own cistern,[n] 17 un-
til I come and take you to a land like your
own—a land of grain and new wine, a land
of bread and vineyards.

18 "Do not let Hezekiah mislead you when
he says, 'The LORD will deliver us.' Has
the god of any nation ever delivered his
land from the hand of the king of Assyria?
19 Where are the gods of Hamath and Arpad?
Where are the gods of Sepharvaim? Have
they rescued Samaria from my hand? 20 Who

**36:7**
i 2Ki18:4
**36:9**
j Isa30:2–5
**36:11**
k Ezr4:7
**36:13**
l 2Ch32:18
**36:16**
m Zec3:10
n Pr5:15

[a] 8 Or */ the simple will not stray from it*

of all the gods[o] of these countries has been able to save his land from me? How then can the LORD deliver Jerusalem from my hand?"

21 But the people remained silent and said nothing in reply, because the king had commanded, "Do not answer him."

22 Then Eliakim son of Hilkiah the palace administrator, Shebna the secretary, and Joah son of Asaph the recorder went to Hezekiah, with their clothes torn, and told him what the field commander had said.

## Jerusalem's Deliverance Foretold

37 When King Hezekiah heard this, he tore his clothes and put on sackcloth and went into the temple of the LORD. 2 He sent Eliakim the palace administrator, Shebna the secretary, and the leading priests, all wearing sackcloth, to the prophet Isaiah son of Amoz. 3 They told him, "This is what Hezekiah says: This day is a day of distress and rebuke and disgrace, as when children come to the point of birth[p] and there is no strength to deliver them. 4 It may be that the LORD your God will hear the words of the field commander, whom his master, the king of Assyria, has sent to ridicule the living God, and that he will rebuke him for the words the LORD your God has heard.[q] Therefore pray for the remnant that still survives."

5 When King Hezekiah's officials came to Isaiah, 6 Isaiah said to them, "Tell your master, 'This is what the LORD says: Do not be afraid[r] of what you have heard—those words with which the underlings of the king of Assyria have blasphemed me. 7 Listen! I am going to put a spirit in him so that when he hears a certain report,[s] he will return to his own country, and there I will have him cut down with the sword.'"

8 When the field commander heard that the king of Assyria had left Lachish, he withdrew and found the king fighting against Libnah.

9 Now Sennacherib received a report[t] that Tirhakah, the Cushite[a] king ⌞of Egypt⌟, was marching out to fight against him. When he heard it, he sent messengers to Hezekiah with this word: 10 "Say to Hezekiah king of Judah: Do not let the god you depend on deceive you when he says, 'Jerusalem will not be handed over to the king of Assyria.'[u] 11 Surely you have heard what the kings of Assyria have done to all the countries, destroying them completely. And will you be delivered?[v] 12 Did the gods of the nations that were destroyed by my forefathers deliver them—the gods of Gozan, Haran,[w] Rezeph and the people of Eden who were in Tel Assar? 13 Where is the king of Hamath, the king of Arpad, the king of the city of Sepharvaim, or of Hena or Ivvah?"

## Hezekiah's Prayer

14 Hezekiah received the letter from the messengers and read it. Then he went up to the temple of the LORD and spread it out before the LORD. 15 And Hezekiah prayed to the LORD: 16 "O LORD Almighty, God of Israel, enthroned between the cherubim, you alone are God[x] over all the kingdoms of the earth. You have made heaven and earth. 17 Give ear, O LORD, and hear; open your eyes, O LORD, and see;[y] listen to all the words Sennacherib has sent to insult the living God.

18 "It is true, O LORD, that the Assyrian kings have laid waste all these peoples and

**36:20** o 1Ki 20:23
**37:3** p Isa 26:18
**37:4** q Isa 36:13,18–20
**37:6** r Isa 7:4
**37:7** s ver 9
**37:9** t ver 7
**37:10** u Isa 36:15
**37:11** v Isa 36:18–20
**37:12** w Ge 11:31
**37:16** x Dt 10:17
**37:17** y Da 9:18

[a] 9 That is, from the upper Nile region

### The African Presence

**Isaiah 37:9**

Sennacherib, king of Assyria, received a report that Tirhakah, the Cushite ruler of Egypt during the Twenty-fifth Dynasty, was marching out to fight against him (see also 2Ki 19:9–13).

**37:18** z 2Ki 15:29
**37:20** a Ps 46:10
**37:22** b Job 16:4
**37:23** c Isa 2:11
**37:24** d Isa 14:8
**37:26** e Ac 2:23

their lands.[z] 19They have thrown their gods
into the fire and destroyed them, for they
were not gods but only wood and stone,
fashioned by human hands. 20Now, O LORD
our God, deliver us from his hand, so that
all kingdoms on earth may know that you
alone, O LORD, are God.[a][a]"

## Sennacherib's Fall

21Then Isaiah son of Amoz sent a mes-
sage to Hezekiah: "This is what the LORD,
the God of Israel, says: Because you have
prayed to me concerning Sennacherib king
of Assyria, 22this is the word the LORD has
spoken against him:

"The Virgin Daughter of Zion
  despises and mocks you.
The Daughter of Jerusalem
  tosses her head[b] as you flee.
23 Who is it you have insulted and
    blasphemed?
  Against whom have you raised your
    voice
and lifted your eyes in pride?[c]
  Against the Holy One of Israel!
24 By your messengers
  you have heaped insults on the Lord.
And you have said,
  'With my many chariots
I have ascended the heights of the
    mountains,
  the utmost heights of Lebanon.[d]
I have cut down its tallest cedars,
  the choicest of its pines.
I have reached its remotest heights,
  the finest of its forests.
25 I have dug wells in foreign lands[b]
  and drunk the water there.
With the soles of my feet
  I have dried up all the streams of
    Egypt.'

26 "Have you not heard?
  Long ago I ordained[e] it.
In days of old I planned it;
  now I have brought it to pass,
that you have turned fortified cities
  into piles of stone.
27 Their people, drained of power,
  are dismayed and put to shame.
They are like plants in the field,
  like tender green shoots,
like grass sprouting on the roof,[f]
  scorched[c] before it grows up.

28 "But I know where you stay
  and when you come and go
  and how you rage against me.
29 Because you rage against me
  and because your insolence[g] has
    reached my ears,
I will put my hook in your nose[h]
  and my bit in your mouth,
and I will make you return
  by the way you came.[i]

30"This will be the sign for you, O Hez-
ekiah:

"This year you will eat what grows by
    itself,
  and the second year what springs from
    that.
But in the third year sow and reap,
  plant vineyards and eat their fruit.
31 Once more a remnant of the house of
    Judah
  will take root below and bear fruit[j]
    above.
32 For out of Jerusalem will come a
    remnant,
  and out of Mount Zion a band of
    survivors.
The zeal[k] of the LORD Almighty
  will accomplish this.

33"Therefore this is what the LORD says
concerning the king of Assyria:

"He will not enter this city
  or shoot an arrow here.
He will not come before it with shield
  or build a siege ramp against it.
34 By the way that he came he will return;
  he will not enter this city,"
    declares the LORD.
35 "I will defend[l] this city and save it,
  for my sake and for the sake of David[m]
    my servant!"

36Then the angel of the LORD went out
and put to death a hundred and eighty-five
thousand men in the Assyrian camp. When

**37:27** f Ps 129:6
**37:29** g Isa 10:12; h Isa 30:28; Eze 38:4; i ver 34
**37:31** j Isa 27:6
**37:32** k Isa 9:7
**37:35** l Isa 38:6; m 2Ki 20:6

[a]20 Dead Sea Scrolls (see also 2 Kings 19:19); Masoretic Text *alone are the LORD* [b]25 Dead Sea Scrolls (see also 2 Kings 19:24); Masoretic Text does not have *in foreign lands.* [c]27 Some manuscripts of the Masoretic Text, Dead Sea Scrolls and some Septuagint manuscripts (see also 2 Kings 19:26); most manuscripts of the Masoretic Text *roof / and terraced fields*

the people got up the next morning—there were all the dead bodies! 37 So Sennacherib king of Assyria broke camp and withdrew. He returned to Nineveh and stayed there.

38 One day, while he was worshiping in the temple of his god Nisroch, his sons Adrammelech and Sharezer cut him down with the sword, and they escaped to the land of Ararat.[n] And Esarhaddon his son succeeded him as king.

## Hezekiah's Illness

**38** In those days Hezekiah became ill and was at the point of death. The prophet Isaiah son of Amoz went to him and said, "This is what the LORD says: Put your house in order,[o] because you are going to die; you will not recover."

2 Hezekiah turned his face to the wall and prayed to the LORD, 3 "Remember, O LORD, how I have walked[p] before you faithfully and with wholehearted devotion and have done what is good in your eyes." And Hezekiah wept bitterly.

4 Then the word of the LORD came to Isaiah: 5 "Go and tell Hezekiah, 'This is what the LORD, the God of your father David, says: I have heard your prayer and seen your tears; I will add fifteen years[q] to your life. 6 And I will deliver you and this city from the hand of the king of Assyria. I will defend[r] this city.

7 " 'This is the LORD's sign[s] to you that the LORD will do what he has promised: 8 I will make the shadow cast by the sun go back the ten steps it has gone down on the stairway of Ahaz.' " So the sunlight went back the ten steps it had gone down.

9 A writing of Hezekiah king of Judah after his illness and recovery:

10 I said, "In the prime of my life[t]
must I go through the gates of death[a]
and be robbed of the rest of my
years?[u]"
11 I said, "I will not again see the LORD,
the LORD, in the land of the living;[v]
no longer will I look on mankind,
or be with those who now dwell in this
world.[b]
12 Like a shepherd's tent my house
has been pulled down and taken
from me.
Like a weaver I have rolled[w] up my life,
and he has cut me off from the loom;[x]
day and night you made an end of me.
13 I waited patiently till dawn,
but like a lion he broke all my bones;[y]
day and night you made an end of me.
14 I cried like a swift or thrush,
I moaned like a mourning dove.[z]
My eyes grew weak as I looked to the
heavens.
I am troubled; O Lord, come to my
aid!"

15 But what can I say?
He has spoken to me, and he himself
has done this.
I will walk humbly[a] all my years
because of this anguish of my soul.[b]
16 Lord, by such things men live;
and my spirit finds life in them too.
You restored me to health
and let me live.
17 Surely it was for my benefit
that I suffered such anguish.
In your love you kept me
from the pit[c] of destruction;
you have put all my sins
behind your back.
18 For the grave[a][d] cannot praise you,
death cannot sing your praise;[e]
those who go down to the pit
cannot hope for your faithfulness.
19 The living, the living—they praise[f] you,
as I am doing today;
fathers tell their children
about your faithfulness.

20 The LORD will save me,
and we will sing with stringed
instruments[g]
all the days of our lives
in the temple[h] of the LORD.

21 Isaiah had said, "Prepare a poultice of figs and apply it to the boil, and he will recover."

22 Hezekiah had asked, "What will be the sign that I will go up to the temple of the LORD?"

**37:38** n Jer 51:27
**38:1** o 2Sa 17:23
**38:3** p Ne 13:14
**38:5** q 2Ki 18:2
**38:6** r Isa 37:35
**38:7** s Isa 7:11,14
**38:10** t Ps 102:24 u Job 17:11
**38:11** v Ps 27:13; 116:9
**38:12** w Heb 1:12 x Job 7:6
**38:13** y Job 10:16
**38:14** z Isa 59:11
**38:15** a 1Ki 21:27 b Job 7:11
**38:17** c Ps 30:3
**38:18** d Ecc 9:10 e Ps 6:5; 88:10–11
**38:19** f Dt 6:7
**38:20** g Ps 33:2 h Ps 116:17–19

[a] 10,18 Hebrew *Sheol* [b] 11 A few Hebrew manuscripts; most Hebrew manuscripts *in the place of cessation*

39:2 i 2Ch 32:31 j 2Ki 18:15
39:6 k Jer 20:5
39:7 l Da 1:1–7
39:8 m 2Ch 32:26
40:1 n Isa 12:1
40:2 o Isa 35:4 p Isa 41:11–13

## Envoys From Babylon

39 At that time Merodach-Baladan
son of Baladan king of Babylon sent
Hezekiah letters and a gift, because he had
heard of his illness and recovery. 2 Hezekiah
received the envoys[i] gladly and showed
them what was in his storehouses—the
silver, the gold,[j] the spices, the fine oil, his
entire armory and everything found among
his treasures. There was nothing in his pal-
ace or in all his kingdom that Hezekiah did
not show them.
3 Then Isaiah the prophet went to King
Hezekiah and asked, "What did those men
say, and where did they come from?"
"From a distant land," Hezekiah replied.
"They came to me from Babylon."
4 The prophet asked, "What did they see
in your palace?"
"They saw everything in my palace,"
Hezekiah said. "There is nothing among my
treasures that I did not show them."
5 Then Isaiah said to Hezekiah, "Hear the
word of the LORD Almighty: 6 The time will
surely come when everything in your pal-
ace, and all that your fathers have stored up
until this day, will be carried off to Babylon.[k]
Nothing will be left, says the LORD. 7 And
some of your descendants, your own flesh
and blood who will be born to you, will be
taken away, and they will become eunuchs
in the palace of the king of Babylon.[l]"
8 "The word of the LORD you have spoken
is good," Hezekiah replied. For he thought,
"There will be peace and security in my life-
time.[m]"

## Comfort for God's People

40 Comfort, comfort[n] my people,
says your God.
2 Speak tenderly[o] to Jerusalem,
and proclaim to her
that her hard service has been completed,[p]
that her sin has been paid for,
that she has received from the LORD's
hand
double for all her sins.

3 A voice of one calling:
"In the desert prepare
the way[q] for the LORD[a];
make straight in the wilderness
a highway for our God.[b r]
4 Every valley shall be raised up,
every mountain and hill made low;
the rough ground shall become level,
the rugged places a plain.
5 And the glory of the LORD will be revealed,
and all mankind together will see it.[s]
For the mouth of the LORD
has spoken."

6 A voice says, "Cry out."
And I said, "What shall I cry?"

"All men are like grass,[t]
and all their glory is like the flowers of
the field.
7 The grass withers and the flowers fall,
because the breath of the LORD blows
on them.
Surely the people are grass.
8 The grass withers and the flowers fall,
but the word[u] of our God stands
forever.[v]"

9 You who bring good tidings[w] to Zion,
go up on a high mountain.
You who bring good tidings to
Jerusalem,[c]
lift up your voice with a shout,
lift it up, do not be afraid;
say to the towns of Judah,
"Here is your God!"
10 See, the Sovereign LORD comes with
power,
and his arm[x] rules for him.
See, his reward[y] is with him,
and his recompense accompanies him.
11 He tends his flock like a shepherd:[z]
He gathers the lambs in his arms
and carries them close to his heart;
he gently leads those that have young.

12 Who has measured the waters in the
hollow of his hand,
or with the breadth of his hand
marked off the heavens?
Who has held the dust of the earth in a
basket,
or weighed the mountains on the
scales

40:3 q Mal 3:1 r Mt 3:3*
40:5 s Isa 52:10; Lk 3:4–6*
40:6 t Job 14:2
40:8 u Isa 55:11 v Mt 5:18; 1Pe 1:24–25*
40:9 w Isa 52:7–10
40:10 x Isa 59:16 y Isa 62:11; Rev 22:12
40:11 z Eze 34:23; Jn 10:11

[a] 3 Or *A voice of one calling in the desert: / "Prepare the way for the LORD* [b] 3 Hebrew; Septuagint *make straight the paths of our God* [c] 9 Or *O Zion, bringer of good tidings, / go up on a high mountain. / O Jerusalem, bringer of good tidings*

**40:13** a 1Co 2:16*
**40:14** b Job 21:22
**40:18** c Isa 46:5 d Ac 17:29
**40:19** e Isa 41:7
**40:21** f Ps 19:1; Ac 14:17 g Ro 1:19
**40:22** h Ps 104:2; Isa 42:5

and the hills in a balance?
13 Who has understood the mind[a] of the
LORD,
or instructed him as his counselor?[a]
14 Whom did the LORD consult to enlighten
him,
and who taught him the right way?
Who was it that taught him knowledge[b]
or showed him the path of
understanding?

15 Surely the nations are like a drop in a
bucket;
they are regarded as dust on the scales;
he weighs the islands as though they
were fine dust.
16 Lebanon is not sufficient for altar fires,
nor its animals enough for burnt
offerings.
17 Before him all the nations are as nothing;
they are regarded by him as worthless
and less than nothing.

18 To whom, then, will you compare God?[c]
What image[d] will you compare him to?
19 As for an idol, a craftsman casts it,
and a goldsmith[e] overlays it with gold
and fashions silver chains for it.
20 A man too poor to present such an
offering
selects wood that
will not rot.
He looks for a skilled
craftsman
to set up an idol that
will not topple.

*"If your faith can't move mountains, it should at least climb them."*

—QUEEN MOTHER MOORE, ACTIVIST

21 Do you not know?
Have you not heard?
Has it not been told[f]
you from the
beginning?
Have you not understood[g] since the
earth was founded?
22 He sits enthroned above the circle of the
earth,
and its people are like grasshoppers.[h]
He stretches out the heavens like a
canopy,
and spreads them out like a tent to
live in.
23 He brings princes to naught
and reduces the rulers of this world to
nothing.[i]
24 No sooner are they planted,
no sooner are they sown,
no sooner do they take root in the
ground,
than he blows on them and they wither,
and a whirlwind sweeps them away
like chaff.

25 "To whom will you compare me?[j]
Or who is my equal?" says the Holy
One.
26 Lift your eyes and look to the heavens:[k]
Who created all these?
He who brings out the starry host[l] one
by one,
and calls them each by name.
Because of his great power and mighty
strength,
not one of them is missing.

27 Why do you say, O Jacob,
and complain, O Israel,
"My way is hidden from the LORD;
my cause is disregarded by my God"?
28 Do you not know?
Have you not heard?
The LORD is the everlasting[m] God,
the Creator of the ends of the earth.
He will not grow tired or weary,
and his understanding no one can
fathom.[n]
29 He gives strength to the weary[o]
and increases the power of the
weak.
30 Even youths grow tired and weary,
and young men stumble and fall;
31 but those who hope in the LORD
will renew their strength.
They will soar on wings like eagles;[p]
they will run and not grow weary,
they will walk and not be faint.

## The Helper of Israel

41 "Be silent[q] before me, you islands!
Let the nations renew their
strength!
Let them come forward and speak;
let us meet together[r] at the place of
judgment.

**40:23** i Job 12:21; Ps 107:40
**40:25** j ver 18
**40:26** k Isa 51:6 l Ps 147:4
**40:28** m Ps 90:2 n Ps 147:5; Ro 11:33
**40:29** o Jer 31:25
**40:31** p Ps 103:5
**41:1** q Zec 2:13 r Isa 34:1

[a]13 Or *Spirit*; or *spirit*

41:2 s Isa 45:1,13
41:4 t Isa 44:6; Rev 1:8,17; 22:13
41:8 u 2Ch 20:7; Jas 2:23
41:10 v Isa 43:2,5
41:11 w Isa 45:24

2 "Who has stirred up one from the east,[s]
calling him in righteousness to his service[a]?
He hands nations over to him
and subdues kings before him.
He turns them to dust with his sword,
to windblown chaff with his bow.
3 He pursues them and moves on unscathed,
by a path his feet have not traveled before.
4 Who has done this and carried it through,
calling forth the generations from the beginning?
I, the LORD—with the first of them
and with the last[t]—I am he."

5 The islands have seen it and fear;
the ends of the earth tremble.
They approach and come forward;
6 each helps the other
and says to his brother, "Be strong!"
7 The craftsman encourages the goldsmith,
and he who smooths with the hammer
spurs on him who strikes the anvil.
He says of the welding, "It is good."
He nails down the idol so it will not topple.

8 "But you, O Israel, my servant,
Jacob, whom I have chosen,
you descendants of Abraham my friend,[u]
9 I took you from the ends of the earth,
from its farthest corners I called you.
I said, 'You are my servant';
I have chosen you and have not rejected you.
10 So do not fear, for I am with you;[v]
do not be dismayed, for I am your God.
I will strengthen you and help you;
I will uphold you with my righteous right hand.

11 "All who rage against you
will surely be ashamed and disgraced;[w]
those who oppose you
will be as nothing and perish.
12 Though you search for your enemies,
you will not find them.
Those who wage war against you
will be as nothing[x] at all.
13 For I am the LORD, your God,
who takes hold of your right hand
and says to you, Do not fear;
I will help you.
14 Do not be afraid, O worm Jacob,
O little Israel,
for I myself will help you," declares the LORD,
your Redeemer, the Holy One of Israel.
15 "See, I will make you into a threshing sledge,[y]
new and sharp, with many teeth.
You will thresh the mountains and crush them,
and reduce the hills to chaff.
16 You will winnow[z] them, the wind will pick them up,
and a gale will blow them away.
But you will rejoice in the LORD
and glory in the Holy One of Israel.

17 "The poor and needy search for water,
but there is none;
their tongues are parched with thirst.
But I the LORD will answer them;
I, the God of Israel, will not forsake them.
18 I will make rivers flow on barren heights,
and springs within the valleys.
I will turn the desert[a] into pools of water,
and the parched ground into springs.[b]
19 I will put in the desert
the cedar and the acacia, the myrtle and the olive.
I will set pines in the wasteland,
the fir and the cypress together,
20 so that people may see and know,
may consider and understand,
that the hand of the LORD has done this,
that the Holy One of Israel has created it.

21 "Present your case," says the LORD.
"Set forth your arguments," says Jacob's King.
22 "Bring in ⌊your idols⌋ to tell us
what is going to happen.[c]
Tell us what the former things were,
so that we may consider them
and know their final outcome.

41:12 x Isa 17:14
41:15 y Mic 4:13
41:16 z Jer 51:2
41:18 a Isa 43:19 b Isa 35:7
41:22 c Isa 45:21

[a] 2 Or / *whom victory meets at every step*

41:23 d Isa 42:9; 44:7–8 e Jer 10:5
41:24 f Isa 44:9; 1Co 8:4 g Ps 115:8
41:25 h ver 2
41:26 i Hab 2:18–19
41:27 j Isa 40:9
41:28 k Isa 63:5
41:29 l ver 24 m Jer 5:13
42:1 n Isa 43:10 o Mt 3:16–17
42:4 p Mt 12:18–21*

Or declare to us the things to come,
23 tell us what the future holds,
so we may know[d] that you are gods.
Do something, whether good or bad,[e]
so that we will be dismayed and filled with fear.
24 But you are less than nothing[f]
and your works are utterly worthless;
he who chooses you is detestable.[g]

25 "I have stirred up one from the north,[h]
and he comes—
one from the rising sun who calls on my name.
He treads on rulers as if they were mortar,
as if he were a potter treading the clay.
26 Who told of this from the beginning, so we could know,
or beforehand, so we could say, 'He was right'?
No one told of this,
no one foretold it,
no one heard any words[i] from you.
27 I was the first to tell Zion, 'Look, here they are!'
I gave to Jerusalem a messenger of good tidings.[j]
28 I look but there is no one[k]—
no one among them to give counsel,
no one to give answer when I ask them.
29 See, they are all false!
Their deeds amount to nothing;[l]
their images are but wind[m] and confusion.

## The Servant of the LORD

42 "Here is my servant, whom I uphold,
my chosen one[n] in whom I delight;
I will put my Spirit[o] on him
and he will bring justice to the nations.
2 He will not shout or cry out,
or raise his voice in the streets.
3 A bruised reed he will not break,
and a smoldering wick he will not snuff out.
In faithfulness he will bring forth justice;
4 he will not falter or be discouraged
till he establishes justice on earth.
In his law the islands will put their hope."[p]

5 This is what God the LORD says—
he who created the heavens and stretched them out,
who spread out the earth and all that comes out of it,
who gives breath[q] to its people,
and life to those who walk on it:
6 "I, the LORD, have called you in righteousness;
I will take hold of your hand.
I will keep you and will make you
to be a covenant[r] for the people
and a light for the Gentiles,[s]
7 to open eyes that are blind,[t]
to free[u] captives from prison
and to release from the dungeon those who sit in darkness.

8 "I am the LORD; that is my name!
I will not give my glory to another[v]
or my praise to idols.
9 See, the former things have taken place,
and new things I declare;
before they spring into being
I announce them to you."

## Song of Praise to the LORD

10 Sing to the LORD a new song,[w]
his praise from the ends of the earth,
you who go down to the sea, and all that is in it,
you islands, and all who live in them.
11 Let the desert and its towns raise their voices;
let the settlements where Kedar lives rejoice.
Let the people of Sela sing for joy;
let them shout from the mountaintops.
12 Let them give glory[x] to the LORD
and proclaim his praise in the islands.
13 The LORD will march out like a mighty[y] man,
like a warrior he will stir up his zeal;
with a shout he will raise the battle cry
and will triumph over his enemies.[z]

14 "For a long time I have kept silent,
I have been quiet and held myself back.
But now, like a woman in childbirth,
I cry out, I gasp and pant.
15 I will lay waste the mountains and hills
and dry up all their vegetation;

42:5 q Ac 17:25
42:6 r Isa 49:8 s Lk 2:32; Ac 13:47
42:7 t Isa 35:5 u Isa 61:1
42:8 v Isa 48:11
42:10 w Ps 33:3; 40:3; 98:1
42:12 x Isa 24:15
42:13 y Isa 9:6 z Isa 66:14

42:16 a Lk 3:5
42:17 b Ps 97:7; Isa 1:29; 44:11; 45:16
42:19 c Isa 43:8
42:22 d Isa 24:18
42:24 e Isa 30:15
42:25 f 2Ki 25:9

I will turn rivers into islands
and dry up the pools.
16 I will lead the blind by ways they have not known,
along unfamiliar paths I will guide them;
I will turn the darkness into light before them
and make the rough places smooth.[a]
These are the things I will do;
I will not forsake them.
17 But those who trust in idols,
who say to images, 'You are our gods,'
will be turned back in utter shame.[b]

## Israel Blind and Deaf

18 "Hear, you deaf;
look, you blind, and see!
19 Who is blind[c] but my servant,
and deaf like the messenger I send?
Who is blind like the one committed to me,
blind like the servant of the LORD?
20 You have seen many things, but have paid no attention;
your ears are open, but you hear nothing."
21 It pleased the LORD
for the sake of his righteousness
to make his law great and glorious.
22 But this is a people plundered and looted,
all of them trapped in pits[d]
or hidden away in prisons.
They have become plunder,
with no one to rescue them;
they have been made loot,
with no one to say, "Send them back."

23 Which of you will listen to this
or pay close attention in time to come?
24 Who handed Jacob over to become loot,
and Israel to the plunderers?
Was it not the LORD,
against whom we have sinned?
For they would not follow[e] his ways;
they did not obey his law.
25 So he poured out on them his burning anger,
the violence of war.
It enveloped them in flames,[f] yet they did not understand;
it consumed them, but they did not take it to heart.[g]

## Israel's Only Savior

43 But now, this is what the LORD says—
he who created you, O Jacob,
he who formed you, O Israel:[h]
"Fear not, for I have redeemed[i] you;
I have summoned you by name;[j] you are mine.
2 When you pass through the waters,
I will be with you;[k]
and when you pass through the rivers,
they will not sweep over you.
When you walk through the fire,
you will not be burned;
the flames will not set you ablaze.[l]
3 For I am the LORD, your God,
the Holy One of Israel, your Savior;
I give Egypt for your ransom,
Cush[a] and Seba in your stead.
4 Since you are precious and honored in my sight,
and because I love you,
I will give men in exchange for you,
and people in exchange for your life.
5 Do not be afraid, for I am with you;
I will bring your children from the east
and gather you from the west.
6 I will say to the north, 'Give them up!'
and to the south, 'Do not hold them back.'
Bring my sons from afar
and my daughters from the ends of the earth—
7 everyone who is called by my name,
whom I created for my glory,
whom I formed and made.[m]"

8 Lead out those who have eyes but are blind,[n]
who have ears but are deaf.[o]
9 All the nations gather together
and the peoples assemble.
Which of them foretold[p] this
and proclaimed to us the former things?
Let them bring in their witnesses to prove they were right,

42:25 g Hos 7:9
43:1 h Isa 44:21 i Isa 44:2,6 j Isa 45:3–4
43:2 k Dt 31:6,8 l Ps 66:12; Da 3:25–27
43:7 m Ps 100:3; Eph 2:10
43:8 n Isa 6:9–10 o Isa 42:20; Eze 12:2
43:9 p Isa 41:26

[a]3 That is, the upper Nile region

so that others may hear and say, "It is true."
[10] "You are my witnesses," declares the LORD,
"and my servant whom I have chosen,
so that you may know and believe me
and understand that I am he.
Before me no god[q] was formed,
nor will there be one after me.
[11] I, even I, am the LORD,
and apart from me there is no savior.[r]
[12] I have revealed and saved and proclaimed—
I, and not some foreign god[s] among you.
You are my witnesses,[t]" declares the LORD, "that I am God.
[13] Yes, and from ancient days[u] I am he.
No one can deliver out of my hand.
When I act, who can reverse it?"[v]

## God's Mercy and Israel's Unfaithfulness

[14] This is what the LORD says—
your Redeemer, the Holy One of Israel:
"For your sake I will send to Babylon
and bring down as fugitives all the Babylonians,[a]
in the ships in which they took pride.
[15] I am the LORD, your Holy One,
Israel's Creator, your King."

[16] This is what the LORD says—
he who made a way through the sea,
a path through the mighty waters,[w]
[17] who drew out the chariots and horses,
the army and reinforcements together,
and they lay there, never to rise again,
extinguished, snuffed out like a wick:
[18] "Forget the former things;
do not dwell on the past.
[19] See, I am doing a new thing![x]
Now it springs up; do you not perceive it?
I am making a way in the desert[y]
and streams in the wasteland.
[20] The wild animals honor me,
the jackals and the owls,
because I provide water[z] in the desert
and streams in the wasteland,
to give drink to my people, my chosen,
[21] the people I formed for myself
that they may proclaim my praise.[a]

[22] "Yet you have not called upon me, O Jacob,
you have not wearied yourselves for me, O Israel.
[23] You have not brought me sheep for burnt offerings,
nor honored me with your sacrifices.[b]
I have not burdened you with grain offerings
nor wearied you with demands for incense.
[24] You have not bought any fragrant calamus for me,
or lavished on me the fat of your sacrifices.
But you have burdened me with your sins
and wearied[c] me with your offenses.[d]

[25] "I, even I, am he who blots out
your transgressions, for my own sake,[e]
and remembers your sins no more.[f]
[26] Review the past for me,
let us argue the matter together;
state the case for your innocence.
[27] Your first father sinned;
your spokesmen rebelled against me.
[28] So I will disgrace the dignitaries of your temple,
and I will consign Jacob to destruction[b]
and Israel to scorn.

## Israel the Chosen

44 "But now listen, O Jacob, my servant,[g]
Israel, whom I have chosen.
[2] This is what the LORD says—
he who made you, who formed you in the womb,
and who will help you:
Do not be afraid, O Jacob, my servant,
Jeshurun,[h] whom I have chosen.
[3] For I will pour water on the thirsty land,
and streams on the dry ground;
I will pour out my Spirit[i] on your offspring,
and my blessing on your descendants.
[4] They will spring up like grass in a meadow,

**43:10** q Isa 44:6,8
**43:11** r Isa 45:21
**43:12** s Dt 32:12; Ps 81:9 t Isa 44:8
**43:13** u Ps 90:2 v Isa 14:27
**43:16** w Ps 77:19; Isa 51:10
**43:19** x 2Co 5:17 y Ex 17:6; Nu 20:11
**43:20** z Isa 48:21
**43:21** a Ps 102:18
**43:23** b Am 5:25
**43:24** c Isa 1:14 d Mal 2:17
**43:25** e Eze 36:22 f Jer 31:34
**44:1** g ver 21; Jer 30:10; 46:27–28
**44:2** h Dt 32:15
**44:3** i Joel 2:28

[a]14 Or *Chaldeans* [b]28 The Hebrew term refers to the irrevocable giving over of things or persons to the LORD, often by totally destroying them.

**44:6** j Isa 41:4; Rev 1:8,17; 22:13
**44:7** k Isa 41:22,26
**44:8** l Isa 43:10 m Dt 4:35; 1Sa 2:2
**44:10** n Jer 10:5
**44:11** o Isa 42:17
**44:12** p Isa 40:19 q Jer 10:3–5
**44:13** r Isa 41:7

like poplar trees by flowing streams.
5 One will say, 'I belong to the LORD';
another will call himself by the name
of Jacob;
still another will write on his hand, 'The
LORD's,'
and will take the name Israel.

## The LORD, Not Idols

6 "This is what the LORD says—
Israel's King and Redeemer, the LORD
Almighty:
I am the first and I am the last;[j]
apart from me there is no God.
7 Who then is like me? Let him proclaim it.
Let him declare and lay out before me
what has happened since I established my
ancient people,
and what is yet to come—
yes, let him foretell[k] what will come.
8 Do not tremble, do not be afraid.
Did I not proclaim this and foretell it
long ago?
You are my witnesses. Is there any God[l]
besides me?
No, there is no other Rock;[m] I know
not one."
9 All who make idols are nothing,
and the things they treasure are
worthless.
Those who would speak up for them are
blind;
they are ignorant, to their own shame.
10 Who shapes a god and casts an idol,
which can profit him nothing?[n]
11 He and his kind will be put to shame;
craftsmen are nothing but men.
Let them all come together and take their
stand;
they will be brought down to terror
and infamy.[o]
12 The blacksmith[p] takes a tool
and works with it in the coals;
he shapes an idol with hammers,
he forges it with the might of his arm.[q]
He gets hungry and loses his strength;
he drinks no water and grows faint.
13 The carpenter[r] measures with a line
and makes an outline with a marker;
he roughs it out with chisels
and marks it with compasses.
He shapes it in the form of man,
of man in all his glory,
that it may dwell in a shrine.
14 He cut down cedars,
or perhaps took a cypress or oak.
He let it grow among the trees of the
forest,
or planted a pine, and the rain made
it grow.
15 It is man's fuel for burning;
some of it he takes and warms
himself,
he kindles a fire and bakes bread.
But he also fashions a god and
worships it;
he makes an idol and bows[s] down to it.
16 Half of the wood he burns in the fire;
over it he prepares his meal,
he roasts his meat and eats his fill.
He also warms himself and says,
"Ah! I am warm; I see the fire."
17 From the rest he makes a god, his idol;
he bows down to it and worships.
He prays[t] to it and says,
"Save me; you are my god."
18 They know nothing, they understand
nothing;
their eyes[u] are plastered over so they
cannot see,
and their minds closed so they cannot
understand.
19 No one stops to think,
no one has the knowledge or
understanding[v] to say,
"Half of it I used for fuel;
I even baked bread over its coals,
I roasted meat and I ate.
Shall I make a detestable[w] thing from
what is left?
Shall I bow down to a block of wood?"
20 He feeds on ashes,[x] a deluded[y] heart
misleads him;
he cannot save himself, or say,
"Is not this thing in my right hand a
lie?"
21 "Remember[z] these things, O Jacob,
for you are my servant, O Israel.
I have made you, you are my servant;
O Israel, I will not forget you.[a]
22 I have swept away your offenses like a
cloud,
your sins like the morning mist.

**44:15** s 2Ch 25:14
**44:17** t 1Ki 18:26
**44:18** u Isa 6:9–10
**44:19** v Isa 45:20 w Dt 27:15
**44:20** x Ps 102:9 y Job 15:31; Ro 1:21–23,28; 2Th 2:11
**44:21** z Isa 46:8 a Isa 49:15

Return to me,
for I have redeemed you."

23 Sing for joy, O heavens, for the LORD has done this;
shout aloud, O earth beneath.
Burst into song, you mountains,
you forests and all your trees,
for the LORD has redeemed Jacob,
he displays his glory[b] in Israel.

## Jerusalem to Be Inhabited

24 "This is what the LORD says—
your Redeemer,[c] who formed you in the womb:

I am the LORD,
who has made all things,
who alone stretched out the heavens,
who spread out the earth by myself,

25 who foils the signs of false prophets
and makes fools of diviners,
who overthrows the learning of the wise[d]
and turns it into nonsense,
26 who carries out the words[e] of his servants
and fulfills the predictions of his messengers,

who says of Jerusalem, 'It shall be inhabited,'
of the towns of Judah, 'They shall be built,'
and of their ruins, 'I will restore them,'
27 who says to the watery deep, 'Be dry,
and I will dry up your streams,'
28 who says of Cyrus,[f] 'He is my shepherd
and will accomplish all that I please;
he will say of Jerusalem, "Let it be rebuilt,"
and of the temple,[g] "Let its foundations be laid." '

45 "This is what the LORD says to his anointed,
to Cyrus, whose right hand I take hold[h] of
to subdue nations before him
and to strip kings of their armor,
to open doors before him
so that gates will not be shut:
2 I will go before you
and will level[i] the mountains[a];
I will break down gates of bronze
and cut through bars of iron.[j]
3 I will give you the treasures of darkness,
riches stored in secret places,
so that you may know that I am the LORD,
the God of Israel, who summons you by name.[k]
4 For the sake of Jacob my servant,
of Israel my chosen,
I summon you by name
and bestow on you a title of honor,
though you do not acknowledge me.
5 I am the LORD, and there is no other;[l]
apart from me there is no God.
I will strengthen you,
though you have not acknowledged me,
6 so that from the rising of the sun
to the place of its setting[m]
men may know there is none besides me.
I am the LORD, and there is no other.
7 I form the light and create darkness,
I bring prosperity and create disaster;[n]
I, the LORD, do all these things.

8 "You heavens above, rain[o] down righteousness;[p]
let the clouds shower it down.
Let the earth open wide,
let salvation spring up,
let righteousness grow with it;
I, the LORD, have created it.

9 "Woe to him who quarrels with his Maker,
to him who is but a potsherd among the potsherds on the ground.
Does the clay say to the potter,[q]
'What are you making?'
Does your work say,
'He has no hands'?
10 Woe to him who says to his father,
'What have you begotten?'
or to his mother,
'What have you brought to birth?'

11 "This is what the LORD says—
the Holy One of Israel, and its Maker:
Concerning things to come,
do you question me about my children,
or give me orders about the work of my hands?

44:23 b Isa 61:3
44:24 c Isa 43:14
44:25 d 1Co 1:27
44:26 e Zec 1:6
44:28 f 2Ch 36:22 g Ezr 1:2–4
45:1 h Isa 41:13
45:2 i Isa 40:4
45:2 j Ps 107:16
45:3 k Ex 33:12
45:5 l Isa 44:8
45:6 m Mal 1:11
45:7 n Am 3:6
45:8 o Ps 72:6 p Ps 85:11
45:9 q Isa 29:16; Ro 9:20–21*

[a]2 Dead Sea Scrolls and Septuagint; the meaning of the word in the Masoretic Text is uncertain.

[12] It is I who made the earth
and created mankind upon it.
My own hands stretched out the heavens;[r]
I marshaled their starry hosts.
[13] I will raise up Cyrus[a][s] in my righteousness:
I will make all his ways straight.
He will rebuild my city
and set my exiles free,
but not for a price or reward,[t]
says the LORD Almighty."

[14] This is what the LORD says:

"The products of Egypt and the merchandise of Cush,[b]
and those tall Sabeans—
they will come over to you
and will be yours;
they will trudge behind you,
coming over to you in chains.[u]
They will bow down before you
and plead with you, saying,
'Surely God is with you,[v] and there is no other;
there is no other god.' "

[15] Truly you are a God who hides himself,
O God and Savior of Israel.
[16] All the makers of idols will be put to shame and disgraced;[w]
they will go off into disgrace together.
[17] But Israel will be saved by the LORD
with an everlasting salvation;[x]
you will never be put to shame or disgraced,
to ages everlasting.

[18] For this is what the LORD says—
he who created the heavens,
he is God;
he who fashioned and made the earth,
he founded it;
he did not create it to be empty,[y]
but formed it to be inhabited[z]—
he says:
"I am the LORD,
and there is no other.[a]
[19] I have not spoken in secret,
from somewhere in a land of darkness;
I have not said to Jacob's descendants,[b]
'Seek me in vain.'
I, the LORD, speak the truth;
I declare what is right.

[20] "Gather together and come;
assemble, you fugitives from the nations.
Ignorant are those who carry[c] about idols of wood,
who pray to gods that cannot save.[d]
[21] Declare what is to be, present it—
let them take counsel together.
Who foretold this long ago,
who declared it from the distant past?
Was it not I, the LORD?
And there is no God apart from me,
a righteous God and a Savior;
there is none but me.

[22] "Turn to me and be saved,
all you ends of the earth;
for I am God, and there is no other.
[23] By myself I have sworn,
my mouth has uttered in all integrity[e]
a word that will not be revoked:
Before me every knee will bow;
by me every tongue will swear.[f]
[24] They will say of me, 'In the LORD alone
are righteousness and strength.' "
All who have raged against him
will come to him and be put to shame.[g]
[25] But in the LORD all the descendants of Israel
will be found righteous and will exult.

*"Now women forget all those things they don't want to remember, and remember everything they don't want to forget. The dream is the truth. Then they act and do things accordingly."*

—ZORA NEALE HURSTON, WRITER AND FOLKLORIST

## Gods of Babylon

46 Bel[h] bows down, Nebo stoops low;
their idols are borne by beasts of burden.[c]
The images that are carried about are burdensome,
a burden for the weary.
[2] They stoop and bow down together;

**45:12** r Ge 2:1; Isa 42:5
**45:13** s Isa 41:2 t Isa 52:3
**45:14** u Isa 14:1–2 v 1Co 14:25
**45:16** w Isa 44:9,11
**45:17** x Isa 26:4
**45:18** y Ge 1:2 z Isa 42:5 a ver 5
**45:19** b Isa 41:8
**45:20** c Jer 10:5 d Isa 46:6–7
**45:23** e Heb 6:13 f Ro 14:11*
**45:24** g Isa 41:11
**46:1** h Isa 21:9; Jer 50:2

[a] 13 Hebrew *him* [b] 14 That is, the upper Nile region [c] 1 Or *are but beasts and cattle*

46:3
i ver 12
46:5
j Isa 40:18,25
46:6
k Isa 40:19
l Isa 44:17
46:7
m Isa 45:20
46:8
n Isa 44:21
46:9
o Isa 45:5,21
46:10
p Isa 45:21
q Ac 5:39
46:12
r ver 3
s Jer 2:5

unable to rescue the burden,
they themselves go off into captivity.

3 "Listen[i] to me, O house of Jacob,
all you who remain of the house of Israel,
you whom I have upheld since you were conceived,
and have carried since your birth.
4 Even to your old age and gray hairs
I am he, I am he who will sustain you.
I have made you and I will carry you;
I will sustain you and I will rescue you.

5 "To whom will you compare me or count me equal?
To whom will you liken me that we may be compared?[j]
6 Some pour out gold from their bags
and weigh out silver on the scales;
they hire a goldsmith[k] to make it into a god,
and they bow down and worship it.[l]
7 They lift it to their shoulders and carry it;
they set it up in its place, and there it stands.
From that spot it cannot move.
Though one cries out to it, it does not answer;
it cannot save[m] him from his troubles.

8 "Remember[n] this, fix it in mind,
take it to heart, you rebels.
9 Remember the former things, those of long ago;
I am God, and there is no other;
I am God, and there is none like me.[o]
10 I make known the end from the beginning,
from ancient times,[p] what is still to come.
I say: My purpose will stand,[q]
and I will do all that I please.
11 From the east I summon a bird of prey;
from a far-off land, a man to fulfill my purpose.
What I have said, that will I bring about;
what I have planned, that will I do.
12 Listen[r] to me, you stubborn-hearted,
you who are far from righteousness.[s]
13 I am bringing my righteousness near,
it is not far away;
and my salvation will not be delayed.
I will grant salvation to Zion,
my splendor[t] to Israel.

## The Fall of Babylon

47 "Go down, sit in the dust,
Virgin Daughter of Babylon;
sit on the ground without a throne,
Daughter of the Babylonians.[a][u]
No more will you be called
tender or delicate.
2 Take millstones[v] and grind flour;
take off your veil.
Lift up your skirts, bare your legs,
and wade through the streams.
3 Your nakedness[w] will be exposed
and your shame uncovered.
I will take vengeance;
I will spare no one."

4 Our Redeemer—the LORD Almighty is his name—
is the Holy One of Israel.

5 "Sit in silence, go into darkness,[x]
Daughter of the Babylonians;
no more will you be called
queen of kingdoms.[y]
6 I was angry with my people
and desecrated my inheritance;
I gave them into your hand,
and you showed them no mercy.
Even on the aged
you laid a very heavy yoke.
7 You said, 'I will continue forever—
the eternal queen!'
But you did not consider these things
or reflect on what might happen.[z]

8 "Now then, listen, you wanton creature,
lounging in your security[a]
and saying to yourself,
'I am, and there is none besides me.[b]
I will never be a widow[c]
or suffer the loss of children.'
9 Both of these will overtake you
in a moment,[d] on a single day:
loss of children and widowhood.
They will come upon you in full measure,
in spite of your many sorceries[e]
and all your potent spells.

46:13
t Isa 44:23
47:1
u Jer 51:33
47:2
v Ex 11:5; Mt 24:41
47:3
w Eze 16:37
47:5
x Isa 13:10
y Isa 13:19
47:7
z Dt 32:29
47:8
a Isa 32:9
b Zep 2:15
c Rev 18:7
47:9
d 1Th 5:3
e Na 3:4

[a]1 Or *Chaldeans*; also in verse 5

47:10
f Ps 52:7
g Isa 29:15

10 You have trusted[f] in your wickedness
and have said, 'No one sees me.'[g]
Your wisdom and knowledge mislead
you
when you say to yourself,
'I am, and there is none besides me.'
11 Disaster will come upon you,
and you will not know how to conjure
it away.
A calamity will fall upon you
that you cannot ward off with a
ransom;

# Inspire

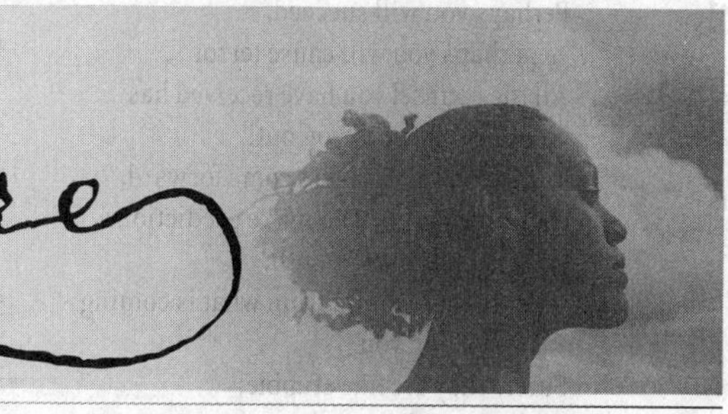

## OMNISCIENCE: GOD IS ALL-KNOWING

God has perfect knowledge of all that transpires in human experience. God does not have to reason or search things out and learn gradually. God's knowledge of the past, present and future is simultaneous and all-encompassing. He learns from no one, he is never surprised and there is no one else like him (see Isa 46:9–10).

It follows, then, that God knows his children completely. He prepares them from the beginning for ministry, marriage, employment or whatever else he has in mind for them. On the basis of this knowledge and in spite of a hostile world, God weaves into the fabric of our lives all the characteristics we need to grow and thrive as women of color. God has equipped us with strength, courage, independence and vigilance.

Woman of color, even though your upbringing may have been characterized by ups and downs, you can be thankful that God in his wisdom knew exactly what you would need and when that need would become apparent. God knows you fully: your past, where you go, what you do, what you think and say, and what you need (see Ps 33:13–15; 139:1–4). God even knows what motivates your heart as a woman (see 1Sa 16:7). His strength is perfect in light of your weakness (see 2Co 12:7–10).

As you grow in understanding God's great wisdom, you gain courage, knowing that you are loved and accepted by God. As you depend on God, you move away from an unhealthy dependence on others.

Thank God for his knowledge—a knowledge "too wonderful" (Ps 139:6) for us to fathom but always available for us to accept.

—B. Whipple

### read

Isaiah 46:5–10; see also Psalm 33:12–19; 139:1–18; Romans 11:33–36.

See also the Inspire Notes "God Is in Control," "Bumping Into Omnipotence," "God Is Immutable" and "God Is Sovereign," and the Women of the Bible Notes "Tamar: The Link Between Judah and Jesus," "Zipporah: Fulfilling Her Purpose" and "Fortune-Telling Slave Girl: A Surprising Testimony to God's Work."

### WOMAN of COLOR

How does reflecting on God's omniscience inspire you?

For the next Inspire note, go to page 861.

**47:11**
h 1Th 5:3
**47:13**
i Isa 57:10
**47:14**
j Na 1:10
**47:15**
k Rev 18:11
**48:1**
l Jer 4:2
**48:2**
m Isa 52:1
n Mic 3:11; Ro 2:17
**48:4**
o Dt 31:27
p Ex 32:9

a catastrophe you cannot foresee
will suddenly[h] come upon you.

12 "Keep on, then, with your magic spells
and with your many sorceries,
which you have labored at since
childhood.
Perhaps you will succeed,
perhaps you will cause terror.
13 All the counsel you have received has
only worn you out![i]
Let your astrologers come forward,
those stargazers who make predictions
month by month,
let them save you from what is coming
upon you.
14 Surely they are like stubble;[j]
the fire will burn them up.
They cannot even save themselves
from the power of the flame.
Here are no coals to warm anyone;
here is no fire to sit by.
15 That is all they can do for you—
these you have labored with
and trafficked[k] with since childhood.
Each of them goes on in his error;
there is not one that can save you.

## Stubborn Israel

48 "Listen to this, O house of Jacob,
you who are called by the name of
Israel
and come from the line of Judah,
you who take oaths in the name of the
LORD
and invoke the God of Israel—
but not in truth[l] or righteousness—
2 you who call yourselves citizens of the
holy city[m]
and rely[n] on the God of Israel—
the LORD Almighty is his name:
3 I foretold the former things long ago,
my mouth announced them and I
made them known;
then suddenly I acted, and they came
to pass.
4 For I knew how stubborn[o] you were;
the sinews of your neck[p] were iron,
your forehead was bronze.
5 Therefore I told you these things long
ago;
before they happened I announced
them to you
so that you could not say,
'My idols did them;
my wooden image and metal god
ordained them.'
6 You have heard these things; look at them
all.
Will you not admit them?

"From now on I will tell you of new
things,
of hidden things unknown to you.
7 They are created now, and not long ago;
you have not heard of them before
today.
So you cannot say,
'Yes, I knew of them.'
8 You have neither heard nor understood;
from of old your ear has not been
open.
Well do I know how treacherous you are;
you were called a rebel[q] from birth.
9 For my own name's sake I delay my
wrath;[r]
for the sake of my praise I hold it back
from you,
so as not to cut you off.
10 See, I have refined you, though not as
silver;
I have tested you in the furnace of
affliction.
11 For my own sake, for my own sake, I do
this.
How can I let myself be defamed?[s]
I will not yield my glory to another.[t]

## Israel Freed

12 "Listen to me, O Jacob,
Israel, whom I have called:
I am he;
I am the first and I am the last.[u]
13 My own hand laid the foundations of the
earth,
and my right hand spread out the
heavens;
when I summon them,
they all stand up together.[v]
14 "Come together, all of you, and listen:
Which of ⌊the idols⌋ has foretold these
things?
The LORD's chosen ally
will carry out his purpose against
Babylon;

**48:8**
q Ps 58:3
**48:9**
r Ps 78:38
**48:11**
s Dt 32:27; Eze 20:9,14, 22,44
t Isa 42:8
**48:12**
u Rev 1:17; 22:13
**48:13**
v Isa 40:26

his arm will be against the
Babylonians.[a]
15 I, even I, have spoken;
yes, I have called[w] him.
I will bring him,
and he will succeed in his mission.

16 "Come near me and listen to this:

"From the first announcement I have not
spoken in secret;[x]
at the time it happens, I am there."
And now the Sovereign LORD has
sent[y] me,
with his Spirit.

17 This is what the LORD says—
your Redeemer, the Holy One[z] of
Israel:
"I am the LORD your God,
who teaches you what is best for you,
who directs you in the way[a] you
should go.
18 If only you had paid attention[b] to my
commands,
your peace[c] would have been like a
river,
your righteousness like the waves of
the sea.
19 Your descendants would have been like
the sand,
your children like its numberless
grains;[d]
their name would never be cut off
nor destroyed from before me."

20 Leave Babylon,
flee[e] from the Babylonians!
Announce this with shouts of joy
and proclaim it.
Send it out to the ends of the earth;
say, "The LORD has redeemed his
servant Jacob."
21 They did not thirst when he led them
through the deserts;
he made water flow for them from the
rock;
he split the rock
and water gushed out.[f]

22 "There is no peace," says the LORD, "for
the wicked."[g]

48:15 w Isa 45:1
48:16 x Isa 45:19 y Zec 2:9,11
48:17 z Isa 43:14 a Ps 32:8
48:18 b Dt 32:29 c Ps 119:165
48:19 d Ge 22:17
48:20 e Jer 50:8
48:21 f Ex 17:6; Nu 20:11
48:22 g Isa 57:21

## The Servant of the LORD

49 Listen to me, you islands;
hear this, you distant nations:
Before I was born[h] the LORD called me;
from my birth he has made mention of
my name.
2 He made my mouth like a sharpened
sword,[i]
in the shadow of his hand he hid me;
he made me into a polished arrow
and concealed me in his quiver.
3 He said to me, "You are my servant,[j]
Israel, in whom I will display my
splendor."
4 But I said, "I have labored to no purpose;
I have spent my strength in vain and
for nothing.
Yet what is due me is in the LORD's hand,
and my reward is with my God."

5 And now the LORD says—
he who formed me in the womb to be
his servant
to bring Jacob back to him
and gather Israel to himself,
for I am honored[k] in the eyes of the LORD
and my God has been my strength—
6 he says:
"It is too small a thing for you to be my
servant
to restore the tribes of Jacob
and bring back those of Israel I have
kept.
I will also make you a light for the
Gentiles,[l]
that you may bring my salvation to the
ends of the earth."[m]

7 This is what the LORD says—
the Redeemer and Holy One of
Israel—
to him who was despised and abhorred
by the nation,
to the servant of rulers:
"Kings[n] will see you and rise up,
princes will see and bow down,
because of the LORD, who is faithful,
the Holy One of Israel, who has chosen
you."

## Restoration of Israel

8 This is what the LORD says:

49:1 h Isa 44:24
49:2 i Rev 1:16
49:3 j Zec 3:8
49:5 k Isa 43:4
49:6 l Lk 2:32 m Ac 13:47*
49:7 n Isa 52:15

[a] 14 Or *Chaldeans*; also in verse 20

**49:8** o Ps 69:13 p 2Co 6:2* q Isa 42:6
**49:9** r Isa 42:7
**49:10** s Ps 121:6; Rev 7:16
**49:11** t Isa 40:4
**49:12** u Isa 43:5–6
**49:13** v Isa 44:23 w Isa 40:1

"In the time of my favor[o] I will answer
you,
and in the day of salvation I will help
you;[p]
I will keep you and will make you
to be a covenant for the people,[q]
to restore the land
and to reassign its desolate
inheritances,
9 to say to the captives,[r] 'Come out,'
and to those in darkness, 'Be free!'

"They will feed beside the roads
and find pasture on every barren hill.
10 They will neither hunger nor thirst,
nor will the desert heat or the sun beat
upon them.[s]
He who has compassion on them will
guide them
and lead them beside springs of water.
11 I will turn all my mountains into roads,
and my highways will be raised up.[t]
12 See, they will come from afar[u]—
some from the north, some from the
west,
some from the region of Aswan.[a]"
13 Shout for joy, O heavens;
rejoice, O earth;
burst into song, O mountains![v]
For the LORD comforts[w] his people
and will have compassion on his
afflicted ones.

14 But Zion said, "The LORD has
forsaken me,
the Lord has forgotten me."
15 "Can a mother forget the baby at her
breast

*My child,*

*You are my own beloved daughter.*
*How could I ever forget you?*

*Father God*

ISAIAH 49:15–16

and have no compassion on the child
she has borne?
Though she may forget,
I will not forget you![x]
16 See, I have engraved[y] you on the palms of
my hands;
your walls are ever before me.
17 Your sons hasten back,
and those who laid you waste depart
from you.
18 Lift up your eyes and look around;
all your sons gather[z] and come to you.
As surely as I live," declares the LORD,
"you will wear[a] them all as ornaments;
you will put them on, like a bride.

19 "Though you were ruined and made
desolate[b]
and your land laid waste,
now you will be too small for your people,[c]
and those who devoured you will be
far away.
20 The children born during your
bereavement
will yet say in your hearing,
'This place is too small for us;
give us more space to live in.'[d]
21 Then you will say in your heart,
'Who bore me these?
I was bereaved and barren;
I was exiled and rejected.
Who brought these up?
I was left all alone,
but these—where have they come
from?' "

22 This is what the Sovereign LORD says:

"See, I will beckon to the Gentiles,
I will lift up my banner to the peoples;
they will bring your sons in their arms
and carry your daughters on their
shoulders.[e]
23 Kings will be your foster fathers,
and their queens your nursing
mothers.[f]
They will bow down before you with their
faces to the ground;
they will lick the dust[g] at your feet.
Then you will know that I am the LORD;[h]
those who hope in me will not be
disappointed."

**49:15** x Isa 44:21
**49:16** y SS 8:6
**49:18** z Isa 60:4 a Isa 52:1
**49:19** b Isa 54:1,3 c Zec 10:10
**49:20** d Isa 54:1–3
**49:22** e Isa 60:4
**49:23** f Isa 60:16 g Ps 72:9 h Mic 7:17

[a]12 Dead Sea Scrolls; Masoretic Text *Sinim*

49:24 i Mt 12:29
49:25 j Isa 25:9
49:26 k Isa 9:20
50:1 l Dt 24:1 m Isa 52:3
50:2 n Nu 11:23 o Ex 14:22; Jos 3:16
50:3 p Rev 6:12

24 Can plunder be taken from warriors,[i]
or captives rescued from the fierce[a]?
25 But this is what the LORD says:

"Yes, captives will be taken from warriors,
and plunder retrieved from the fierce;
I will contend with those who contend with you,
and your children I will save.[j]
26 I will make your oppressors eat[k] their own flesh;
they will be drunk on their own blood, as with wine.
Then all mankind will know
that I, the LORD, am your Savior,
your Redeemer, the Mighty One of Jacob."

## Israel's Sin and the Servant's Obedience

50 This is what the LORD says:

"Where is your mother's certificate of divorce[l]
with which I sent her away?
Or to which of my creditors
did I sell you?
Because of your sins you were sold;[m]
because of your transgressions your mother was sent away.
2 When I came, why was there no one?
When I called, why was there no one to answer?
Was my arm too short[n] to ransom you?
Do I lack the strength to rescue you?
By a mere rebuke I dry up the sea,[o]
I turn rivers into a desert;
their fish rot for lack of water
and die of thirst.
3 I clothe the sky with darkness
and make sackcloth[p] its covering."
4 The Sovereign LORD has given me an instructed tongue,
to know the word that sustains the weary.
He wakens me morning by morning,
wakens my ear to listen like one being taught.
5 The Sovereign LORD has opened my ears,
and I have not been rebellious;[q]
I have not drawn back.
6 I offered my back to those who beat[r] me,
my cheeks to those who pulled out my beard;
I did not hide my face
from mocking and spitting.[s]
7 Because the Sovereign LORD helps me,
I will not be disgraced.
Therefore have I set my face like flint,[t]
and I know I will not be put to shame.
8 He who vindicates me is near.
Who then will bring charges against me?[u]
Let us face each other!
Who is my accuser?
Let him confront me!
9 It is the Sovereign LORD who helps[v] me.
Who is he that will condemn me?
They will all wear out like a garment;
the moths[w] will eat them up.
10 Who among you fears the LORD
and obeys the word of his servant?
Let him who walks in the dark,
who has no light,
trust in the name of the LORD
and rely on his God.
11 But now, all you who light fires
and provide yourselves with flaming torches,
go, walk in the light of your fires
and of the torches you have set ablaze.
This is what you shall receive from my hand:
You will lie down in torment.[x]

## Everlasting Salvation for Zion

51 "Listen to me, you who pursue righteousness
and who seek the LORD:
Look to the rock from which you were cut
and to the quarry from which you were hewn;
2 look to Abraham,[y] your father,
and to Sarah, who gave you birth.
When I called him he was but one,
and I blessed him and made him many.[z]
3 The LORD will surely comfort Zion

50:5 q Mt 26:39; Jn 14:31
50:6 r Lk 22:63 s Mt 26:67
50:7 t Eze 3:8–9
50:8 u Ro 8:32–34
50:9 v Isa 41:10 w Job 13:28
50:11 x Isa 65:13–15
51:2 y Heb 11:11 z Ge 12:2

[a]24 Dead Sea Scrolls, Vulgate and Syriac (see also Septuagint and verse 25); Masoretic Text *righteous*

51:3 a Isa 52:9
51:4 b Isa 2:4 c Isa 42:4,6
51:5 d Isa 46:13
51:6 e Mt 24:35; 2Pe 3:10
51:7 f ver 1 g Ps 37:31 h Ac 5:41
51:9 i Ps 74:13
51:11 j Isa 35:9

and will look with compassion on all
her ruins;[a]
he will make her deserts like Eden,
her wastelands like the garden of the
LORD.
Joy and gladness will be found in her,
thanksgiving and the sound of
singing.

4 "Listen to me, my people;
hear me, my nation:
The law will go out from me;
my justice[b] will become a light to the
nations.[c]
5 My righteousness draws near speedily,
my salvation is on the way,[d]
and my arm will bring justice to the
nations.
The islands will look to me
and wait in hope for my arm.
6 Lift up your eyes to the heavens,
look at the earth beneath;
the heavens will vanish like smoke,[e]
the earth will wear out like a garment
and its inhabitants die like flies.
But my salvation will last forever,
my righteousness will never fail.

7 "Hear me, you who know what is right,[f]
you people who have my law in your
hearts:[g]
Do not fear the reproach of men
or be terrified by their insults.[h]
8 For the moth will eat them up like a
garment;
the worm will devour them like wool.
But my righteousness will last forever,
my salvation through all generations."

9 Awake, awake! Clothe yourself with
strength,
O arm of the LORD;
awake, as in days gone by,
as in generations of old.
Was it not you who cut Rahab to pieces,
who pierced that monster[i] through?
10 Was it not you who dried up the sea,
the waters of the great deep,
who made a road in the depths of the sea
so that the redeemed might cross over?
11 The ransomed[j] of the LORD will return.
They will enter Zion with singing;
everlasting joy will crown their heads.
Gladness and joy will overtake them,
and sorrow and sighing will flee away.[k]

12 "I, even I, am he who comforts you.
Who are you that you fear mortal
men,[l]
the sons of men, who are but grass,[m]
13 that you forget[n] the LORD your Maker,
who stretched out the heavens[o]
and laid the foundations of the earth,
that you live in constant terror every day
because of the wrath of the oppressor,
who is bent on destruction?
For where is the wrath of the oppressor?
14 The cowering prisoners will soon be
set free;
they will not die in their dungeon,
nor will they lack bread.[p]
15 For I am the LORD your God,
who churns up the sea[q] so that its
waves roar—
the LORD Almighty is his name.
16 I have put my words in your mouth[r]
and covered you with the shadow of
my hand—
I who set the heavens in place,
who laid the foundations of the earth,
and who say to Zion, 'You are my
people.' "

## The Cup of the LORD's Wrath

17 Awake, awake![s]
Rise up, O Jerusalem,
you who have drunk from the hand of
the LORD
the cup of his wrath,[t]
you who have drained to its dregs
the goblet that makes men stagger.
18 Of all the sons she bore
there was none to guide her;
of all the sons she reared
there was none to take her by the hand.
19 These double calamities have come upon
you—
who can comfort you?—
ruin and destruction, famine and
sword—
who can[a] console you?
20 Your sons have fainted;
they lie at the head of every street,[u]

51:11 k Rev 7:17
51:12 l Ps 118:6 m 1Pe 1:24
51:13 n Isa 17:10 o Ps 104:2
51:14 p Isa 49:10
51:15 q Jer 31:35
51:16 r Dt 18:18; Isa 59:21
51:17 s Isa 52:1 t Job 21:20
51:20 u Isa 5:25

[a]19 Dead Sea Scrolls, Septuagint, Vulgate and Syriac; Masoretic Text */ how can I*

51:23
v Jer 25:15–17,26,28; 49:12
w Zec 12:2

52:1
x Isa 51:17
y Ne 11:1; Mt 4:5
z Rev 21:27

52:3
a Ps 44:12

52:4
b Ge 46:6

52:5
c Eze 36:20; Ro 2:24*

like antelope caught in a net.
They are filled with the wrath of the LORD
and the rebuke of your God.

21 Therefore hear this, you afflicted one,
made drunk, but not with wine.
22 This is what your Sovereign LORD says,
your God, who defends his people:
"See, I have taken out of your hand
the cup that made you stagger;
from that cup, the goblet of my wrath,
you will never drink again.
23 I will put it into the hands of your tormentors,[v]
who said to you,
'Fall prostrate[w] that we may walk over you.'
And you made your back like the ground,
like a street to be walked over."

52 Awake, awake,[x] O Zion,
clothe yourself with strength.
Put on your garments of splendor,
O Jerusalem, the holy city.[y]
The uncircumcised and defiled
will not enter you again.[z]
2 Shake off your dust;
rise up, sit enthroned, O Jerusalem.
Free yourself from the chains on your neck,
O captive Daughter of Zion.

3 For this is what the LORD says:

"You were sold for nothing,[a]
and without money you will be redeemed."

4 For this is what the Sovereign LORD says:

"At first my people went down to Egypt[b]
to live;
lately, Assyria has oppressed them.

5 "And now what do I have here?" declares the LORD.

"For my people have been taken away for nothing,
and those who rule them mock,[a]"
declares the LORD.
"And all day long
my name is constantly blasphemed.[c]
6 Therefore my people will know my name;
therefore in that day they will know
that it is I who foretold it.
Yes, it is I."

7 How beautiful on the mountains
are the feet of those who bring good news,[d]
who proclaim peace,
who bring good tidings,
who proclaim salvation,
who say to Zion,
"Your God reigns!"[e]
8 Listen! Your watchmen lift up their voices;
together they shout for joy.
When the LORD returns to Zion,
they will see it with their own eyes.
9 Burst into songs of joy together,
you ruins of Jerusalem,
for the LORD has comforted his people,
he has redeemed Jerusalem.[f]
10 The LORD will lay bare his holy arm
in the sight of all the nations,
and all the ends of the earth will see
the salvation[g] of our God.

11 Depart, depart, go out from there!
Touch no unclean thing![h]
Come out from it and be pure,
you who carry the vessels of the LORD.
12 But you will not leave in haste
or go in flight;
for the LORD will go before you,
the God of Israel will be your rear guard.

## The Suffering and Glory of the Servant

13 See, my servant[i] will act wisely[b];
he will be raised and lifted up and highly exalted.[j]
14 Just as there were many who were appalled at him[c]—
his appearance was so disfigured
beyond that of any man
and his form marred beyond human likeness—
15 so will he sprinkle many nations,[d]
and kings will shut their mouths
because of him.
For what they were not told, they will see,

52:7
d Ro 10:15*
e Ps 93:1

52:9
f Isa 48:20

52:10
g Ps 98:2–3; Lk 3:6

52:11
h 2Co 6:17*

52:13
i Isa 42:1
j Php 2:9

[a]5 Dead Sea Scrolls and Vulgate; Masoretic Text *wail* [b]13 Or *will prosper* [c]14 Hebrew *you* [d]15 Hebrew; Septuagint *so will many nations marvel at him*

**52:15**
k Ro 15:21*
**53:1**
l Ro 10:16*
m Jn 12:38*
**53:2**
n Isa 52:14
**53:3**
o Ps 22:6;
Jn 1:10–11
**53:4**
p Mt 8:17*
**53:5**
q Ro 4:25
r 1Pe 2:24–25
**53:7**
s Mk 14:61
**53:8**
t Ac 8:32–33*

and what they have not heard, they
will understand.[k]

53 Who has believed our message[l]
and to whom has the arm of the
LORD been revealed?[m]
2 He grew up before him like a tender
shoot,
and like a root out of dry ground.
He had no beauty or majesty to attract us
to him,
nothing in his appearance[n] that we
should desire him.
3 He was despised and rejected by men,
a man of sorrows, and familiar with
suffering.
Like one from whom men hide their faces
he was despised,[o] and we esteemed
him not.

4 Surely he took up our infirmities
and carried our sorrows,[p]
yet we considered him stricken by God,
smitten by him, and afflicted.
5 But he was pierced for our
transgressions,[q]
he was crushed for our iniquities;
the punishment that brought us peace
was upon him,
and by his wounds we are healed.[r]
6 We all, like sheep, have gone astray,
each of us has turned to his own way;
and the LORD has laid on him
the iniquity of us all.

7 He was oppressed and afflicted,
yet he did not open his mouth;[s]
he was led like a lamb to the slaughter,
and as a sheep before her shearers is
silent,
so he did not open his mouth.
8 By oppression[a] and judgment he was
taken away.
And who can speak of his
descendants?
For he was cut off from the land of the
living;[t]
for the transgression of my people he
was stricken.[b]
9 He was assigned a grave with the wicked,
and with the rich[u] in his death,
though he had done no violence,
nor was any deceit in his mouth.[v]

10 Yet it was the LORD's will[w] to crush him
and cause him to suffer,
and though the LORD makes[c] his life a
guilt offering,
he will see his offspring and prolong his
days,
and the will of the LORD will prosper in
his hand.
11 After the suffering[x] of his soul,
he will see the light ⌊of life⌋[d] and be
satisfied[e];
by his knowledge[f] my righteous servant
will justify[y] many,
and he will bear their iniquities.
12 Therefore I will give him a portion
among the great,[g]
and he will divide the spoils with the
strong,[h]
because he poured out his life unto
death,[z]
and was numbered with the
transgressors.[a]
For he bore the sin of many,
and made intercession for the
transgressors.

## The Future Glory of Zion

54 "Sing, O barren woman,
you who never bore a child;
burst into song, shout for joy,
you who were never in labor;
because more are the children of the
desolate woman
than of her who has a husband,[b]"
says the LORD.
2 "Enlarge the place of your tent,[c]
stretch your tent curtains wide,
do not hold back;
lengthen your cords,
strengthen your stakes.
3 For you will spread out to the right and to
the left;
your descendants will dispossess
nations
and settle in their desolate[d] cities.

**53:9**
u Mt 27:57–60
v 1Pe 2:22*
**53:10**
w Isa 46:10
**53:11**
x Jn 10:14–18
y Ro 5:18–19
**53:12**
z Mt 26:28,38,
39,42
a Lk 22:37*
**54:1**
b Gal 4:27*
**54:2**
c Isa 49:19–20
**54:3**
d Isa 49:19

[a]8 Or *From arrest* [b]8 Or *away. / Yet who of his generation considered / that he was cut off from the land of the living / for the transgression of my people, / to whom the blow was due?* [c]10 Hebrew *though you make* [d]11 Dead Sea Scrolls (see also Septuagint); Masoretic Text does not have *the light ⌊of life⌋*. [e]11 Or (with Masoretic Text) [11]*He will see the result of the suffering of his soul / and be satisfied* [f]11 Or *by knowledge of him* [g]12 Or *many* [h]12 Or *numerous*

54:5 e Jer 3:14 f Isa 48:17
54:6 g Isa 62:4,12
54:7 h Isa 26:20
54:8 i Isa 60:10
54:9 j Isa 12:1
54:10 k Isa 51:6 l Ps 89:34
54:11 m 1Ch 29:2; Rev 21:18
54:13 n Jn 6:45*

4 "Do not be afraid; you will not suffer
shame.
Do not fear disgrace; you will not be
humiliated.
You will forget the shame of your youth
and remember no more the reproach
of your widowhood.
5 For your Maker is your husband[e]—
the LORD Almighty is his name—
the Holy One of Israel is your Redeemer;[f]
he is called the God of all the earth.
6 The LORD will call you back
as if you were a wife deserted[g] and
distressed in spirit—
a wife who married young,
only to be rejected," says your God.
7 "For a brief moment[h] I abandoned you,
but with deep compassion I will bring
you back.
8 In a surge of anger[i]
I hid my face from you for a moment,
but with everlasting kindness
I will have compassion on you,"
says the LORD your Redeemer.
9 "To me this is like the days of Noah,
when I swore that the waters of Noah
would never again cover the
earth.
So now I have sworn not to be angry[j] with
you,
never to rebuke you again.
10 Though the mountains be shaken
and the hills be removed,
yet my unfailing love for you will not be
shaken[k]
nor my covenant[l] of peace be
removed,"
says the LORD, who has compassion
on you.

11 "O afflicted city, lashed by storms and
not comforted,
I will build you with stones of
turquoise,[a][m]
your foundations with sapphires.[b]
12 I will make your battlements of rubies,
your gates of sparkling jewels,
and all your walls of precious stones.
13 All your sons will be taught by the LORD,[n]
and great will be your children's peace.
14 In righteousness you will be established:
Tyranny[o] will be far from you;
you will have nothing to fear.
Terror will be far removed;
it will not come near you.
15 If anyone does attack you, it will not be
my doing;
whoever attacks you will surrender[p]
to you.

16 "See, it is I who created the blacksmith
who fans the coals into flame
and forges a weapon fit for its work.
And it is I who have created the destroyer
to work havoc;
17 no weapon forged against you will
prevail,[q]
and you will refute[r] every tongue that
accuses you.
This is the heritage of the servants of the
LORD,
and this is their vindication from me,"
declares the LORD.

## Invitation to the Thirsty

55 "Come, all you who are thirsty,[s]
come to the waters;
and you who have no money,
come, buy[t] and eat!
Come, buy wine and milk
without money and without cost.
2 Why spend money on what is not bread,
and your labor on what does not
satisfy?
Listen, listen to me, and eat what is good,
and your soul will delight in the
richest of fare.
3 Give ear and come to me;
hear me, that your soul may live.
I will make an everlasting covenant[u] with
you,
my faithful love promised to David.[v]
4 See, I have made him a witness to the
peoples,
a leader and commander[w] of the
peoples.
5 Surely you will summon nations you
know not,
and nations that do not know you will
hasten to you,
because of the LORD your God,
the Holy One of Israel,

54:14 o Isa 9:4
54:15 p Isa 41:11–16
54:17 q Isa 29:8 r Isa 45:24–25
55:1 s Jn 4:14 t Rev 3:18
55:3 u Isa 61:8 v Ac 13:34*
55:4 w Jer 30:9; Eze 34:23–24

[a]11 The meaning of the Hebrew for this word is uncertain. [b]11 Or *lapis lazuli*

for he has endowed you with
splendor."[x]

6 Seek the LORD while he may be found;[y]
call on him while he is near.
7 Let the wicked forsake his way
and the evil man his thoughts.
Let him turn[z] to the LORD, and he will
have mercy on him,
and to our God, for he will freely
pardon.
8 "For my thoughts are not your thoughts,
neither are your ways my ways,"
declares the LORD.
9 "As the heavens are higher than the
earth,[a]
so are my ways higher than your
ways
and my thoughts than your thoughts.
10 As the rain[b] and the snow
come down from heaven,
and do not return to it
without watering the earth
and making it bud and flourish,
so that it yields seed for the sower and
bread for the eater,[c]
11 so is my word that goes out from my
mouth:
It will not return to me empty,
but will accomplish what I desire
and achieve the purpose for which I
sent it.
12 You will go out in joy
and be led forth in peace;[d]
the mountains and hills
will burst into song before you,
and all the trees[e] of the field
will clap their hands.
13 Instead of the thornbush will grow the
pine tree,
and instead of briers the myrtle[f] will
grow.
This will be for the LORD's renown,[g]
for an everlasting sign,
which will not be destroyed."

## Salvation for Others

56 This is what the LORD says:

"Maintain justice
and do what is right,
for my salvation is close at hand
and my righteousness will soon be
revealed.
2 Blessed is the man who does this,
the man who holds it fast,
who keeps the Sabbath[h] without
desecrating it,
and keeps his hand from doing any
evil."

3 Let no foreigner who has bound himself
to the LORD say,
"The LORD will surely exclude me from
his people."
And let not any eunuch[i] complain,
"I am only a dry tree."

4 For this is what the LORD says:

"To the eunuchs who keep my Sabbaths,
who choose what pleases me
and hold fast to my covenant—
5 to them I will give within my temple and
its walls
a memorial and a name
better than sons and daughters;
I will give them an everlasting name
that will not be cut off.[j]
6 And foreigners who bind themselves to
the LORD
to serve[k] him,
to love the name of the LORD,
and to worship him,
all who keep the Sabbath without
desecrating it
and who hold fast to my covenant—
7 these I will bring to my holy mountain
and give them joy in my house of
prayer.
Their burnt offerings and sacrifices[l]
will be accepted on my altar;
for my house will be called
a house of prayer for all nations.[m]"
8 The Sovereign LORD declares—
he who gathers the exiles of Israel:
"I will gather[n] still others to them
besides those already gathered."

## God's Accusation Against the Wicked

9 Come, all you beasts of the field,[o]
come and devour, all you beasts of the
forest!
10 Israel's watchmen are blind,
they all lack knowledge;

55:5 x Isa 60:9
55:6 y Ps 32:6; 2Co 6:1–2
55:7 z Isa 44:22
55:9 a Ps 103:11
55:10 b Isa 30:23 c 2Co 9:10
55:12 d Isa 54:10,13 e 1Ch 16:33
55:13 f Isa 41:19 g Isa 63:12
56:2 h Isa 58:13
56:3 i Ac 8:27
56:5 j Isa 48:19
56:6 k Isa 60:7,10
56:7 l Heb 13:15 m Mt 21:13*
56:8 n Isa 11:12; Jn 10:16
56:9 o Jer 12:9

they are all mute dogs,
they cannot bark;
they lie around and dream,
they love to sleep.
11 They are dogs with mighty appetites;
they never have enough.
They are shepherds who lack
understanding;
they all turn to their own way,
each seeks his own gain.[p]
12 "Come," each one cries, "let me get wine!
Let us drink our fill of beer!
And tomorrow will be like today,
or even far better."[q]

57 The righteous perish,[r]
and no one ponders it in his heart;
devout men are taken away,
and no one understands
that the righteous are taken away
to be spared from evil.
2 Those who walk uprightly[s]
enter into peace;
they find rest as they lie in death.

3 "But you—come here, you sons of a
sorceress,
you offspring of adulterers[t] and
prostitutes!
4 Whom are you mocking?
At whom do you sneer
and stick out your tongue?
Are you not a brood of rebels,
the offspring of liars?
5 You burn with lust among the oaks
and under every spreading tree;[u]
you sacrifice your children in the ravines
and under the overhanging crags.
6 ⌊The idols⌋ among the smooth stones of
the ravines are your portion;
they, they are your lot.
Yes, to them you have poured out drink
offerings[v]
and offered grain offerings.
In the light of these things, should I
relent?
7 You have made your bed on a high and
lofty hill;[w]
there you went up to offer your
sacrifices.
8 Behind your doors and your doorposts
you have put your pagan symbols.
Forsaking me, you uncovered your bed,
you climbed into it and opened it wide;
you made a pact with those whose beds
you love,[x]
and you looked on their nakedness.
9 You went to Molech[a] with olive oil
and increased your perfumes.
You sent your ambassadors[b][y] far away;
you descended to the grave[c] itself!
10 You were wearied by all your ways,
but you would not say, 'It is hopeless.'[z]
You found renewal of your strength,
and so you did not faint.

11 "Whom have you so dreaded and feared
that you have been false to me,
and have neither remembered me
nor pondered this in your hearts?
Is it not because I have long been silent[a]
that you do not fear me?
12 I will expose your righteousness and your
works,
and they will not benefit you.
13 When you cry out for help,
let your collection ⌊of idols⌋ save you!
The wind will carry all of them off,
a mere breath will blow them away.
But the man who makes me his refuge
will inherit the land
and possess my holy mountain."

## Comfort for the Contrite

14 And it will be said:

"Build up, build up, prepare the road!
Remove the obstacles out of the way of
my people."[b]
15 For this is what the high and lofty One
says—
he who lives forever, whose name is
holy:
"I live in a high and holy place,
but also with him who is contrite and
lowly in spirit,[c]
to revive the spirit of the lowly
and to revive the heart of the contrite.[d]
16 I will not accuse forever,
nor will I always be angry,[e]
for then the spirit of man would grow
faint before me—
the breath of man that I have created.

[a]9 Or *to the king* [b]9 Or *idols* [c]9 Hebrew *Sheol*

**56:11** p Mic 3:11
**56:12** q Lk 12:18–19
**57:1** r Ps 12:1
**57:2** s Isa 26:7
**57:3** t Mt 16:4
**57:5** u 2Ki 16:4
**57:6** v Jer 7:18
**57:7** w Eze 16:16
**57:8** x Eze 16:26
**57:9** y Eze 23:16,40
**57:10** z Jer 2:25
**57:11** a Ps 50:21
**57:14** b Jer 18:15
**57:15** c Ps 34:18; 51:17 d Isa 61:1
**57:16** e Ps 85:5; 103:9; Mic 7:18

**57:17** f Isa 1:4
**57:18** g Isa 61:1–3
**57:19** h Heb 13:15 i Eph 2:17 j Ac 2:39
**57:21** k Isa 48:22
**58:2** l Isa 48:1
**58:3** m Mal 3:14
**58:4** n 1Ki 21:9–13
**58:5** o Zec 7:5

17 I was enraged by his sinful greed;
I punished him, and hid my face in anger,
yet he kept on in his willful ways.[f]
18 I have seen his ways, but I will heal him;
I will guide him and restore comfort[g] to him,
19 creating praise on the lips[h] of the mourners in Israel.
Peace, peace,[i] to those far and near,"[j]
says the LORD. "And I will heal them."
20 But the wicked are like the tossing sea,
which cannot rest,
whose waves cast up mire and mud.
21 "There is no peace," says my God, "for the wicked."[k]

## True Fasting

58 "Shout it aloud, do not hold back.
Raise your voice like a trumpet.
Declare to my people their rebellion
and to the house of Jacob their sins.
2 For day after day they seek[l] me out;
they seem eager to know my ways,
as if they were a nation that does what is right
and has not forsaken the commands of its God.
They ask me for just decisions
and seem eager for God to come near them.
3 'Why have we fasted,' they say,
'and you have not seen it?
Why have we humbled ourselves,
and you have not noticed?'[m]

"Yet on the day of your fasting, you do as you please
and exploit all your workers.
4 Your fasting ends in quarreling and strife,[n]
and in striking each other with wicked fists.
You cannot fast as you do today
and expect your voice to be heard on high.
5 Is this the kind of fast[o] I have chosen,
only a day for a man to humble himself?
Is it only for bowing one's head like a reed
and for lying on sackcloth and ashes?
Is that what you call a fast,
a day acceptable to the LORD?

6 "Is not this the kind of fasting I have chosen:
to loose the chains of injustice[p]
and untie the cords of the yoke,
to set the oppressed[q] free
and break every yoke?
7 Is it not to share your food with the hungry
and to provide the poor wanderer with shelter—
when you see the naked, to clothe[r] him,
and not to turn away from your own flesh and blood?[s]
8 Then your light will break forth like the dawn,
and your healing will quickly appear;
then your righteousness[a] will go before you,
and the glory of the LORD will be your rear guard.[t]

*God,*

*I ask you to cleanse my heart and purify my motives. Reveal to me anything within me that fails to reflect your self, and grant me the strength to change those things that are displeasing to you. I desire to be whatever you want me to be. In the name of Jesus, my example,*

*Amen.*

ISAIAH 58:3–8

9 Then you will call, and the LORD will answer;
you will cry for help, and he will say:
Here am I.

"If you do away with the yoke of oppression,
with the pointing finger and malicious talk,[u]

**58:6** p Ne 5:10–11 q Jer 34:9
**58:7** r Job 31:19–20; Mt 25:36 s Ge 29:14
**58:8** t Ex 14:19
**58:9** u Ps 12:2

[a]8 Or *your righteous One*

**58:11** v Jn 4:14
**58:12** w Isa 49:8
**58:13** x Isa 56:2
**58:14** y Dt 32:13; z Isa 1:20
**59:1** a Nu 11:23; Isa 50:2
**59:2** b Isa 1:15; 58:4
**59:3** c Isa 1:15

10 and if you spend yourselves in behalf of the hungry
and satisfy the needs of the oppressed,
then your light will rise in the darkness,
and your night will become like the noonday.
11 The LORD will guide you always;
he will satisfy your needs in a sun-scorched land
and will strengthen your frame.
You will be like a well-watered garden,
like a spring[v] whose waters never fail.
12 Your people will rebuild the ancient ruins[w]
and will raise up the age-old foundations;
you will be called Repairer of Broken Walls,
Restorer of Streets with Dwellings.
13 "If you keep your feet from breaking the Sabbath[x]
and from doing as you please on my holy day,
if you call the Sabbath a delight
and the LORD's holy day honorable,
and if you honor it by not going your own way
and not doing as you please or speaking idle words,
14 then you will find your joy in the LORD,
and I will cause you to ride on the heights[y] of the land
and to feast on the inheritance of your father Jacob."
The mouth of the LORD has spoken.[z]

## Sin, Confession and Redemption

59 Surely the arm of the LORD is not too short[a] to save,
nor his ear too dull to hear.
2 But your iniquities have separated you from your God;
your sins have hidden his face from you,
so that he will not hear.[b]
3 For your hands are stained with blood,[c]
your fingers with guilt.
Your lips have spoken lies,
and your tongue mutters wicked things.
4 No one calls for justice;
no one pleads his case with integrity.
They rely on empty arguments and speak lies;
they conceive trouble and give birth to evil.[d]
5 They hatch the eggs of vipers
and spin a spider's web.[e]
Whoever eats their eggs will die,
and when one is broken, an adder is hatched.
6 Their cobwebs are useless for clothing;
they cannot cover themselves with what they make.[f]
Their deeds are evil deeds,
and acts of violence[g] are in their hands.
7 Their feet rush into sin;
they are swift to shed innocent blood.
Their thoughts are evil thoughts;
ruin and destruction mark their ways.[h]
8 The way of peace they do not know;
there is no justice in their paths.
They have turned them into crooked roads;
no one who walks in them will know peace.

9 So justice is far from us,
and righteousness does not reach us.
We look for light, but all is darkness;[i]
for brightness, but we walk in deep shadows.
10 Like the blind[j] we grope along the wall,
feeling our way like men without eyes.
At midday we stumble[k] as if it were twilight;
among the strong, we are like the dead.
11 We all growl like bears;
we moan mournfully like doves.[l]
We look for justice, but find none;
for deliverance, but it is far away.

12 For our offenses are many in your sight,
and our sins testify against us.
Our offenses are ever with us,
and we acknowledge our iniquities:
13 rebellion and treachery against the LORD,
turning our backs[m] on our God,
fomenting oppression and revolt,
uttering lies our hearts have conceived.
14 So justice is driven back,

**59:4** d Job 15:35; Ps 7:14
**59:5** e Job 8:14
**59:6** f Isa 28:20; g Isa 58:4
**59:7** h Ro 3:15–17*
**59:9** i Isa 5:30
**59:10** j Dt 28:29; k Isa 8:15
**59:11** l Isa 38:14; Eze 7:16
**59:13** m Tit 1:16

and righteousness[n] stands at a distance;
truth has stumbled in the streets,
honesty cannot enter.
15 Truth is nowhere to be found,
and whoever shuns evil becomes a prey.
The LORD looked and was displeased
that there was no justice.
16 He saw that there was no one,
he was appalled that there was no one to intervene;
so his own arm worked salvation[o] for him,
and his own righteousness sustained him.
17 He put on righteousness as his breastplate,[p]
and the helmet[q] of salvation on his head;
he put on the garments of vengeance
and wrapped himself in zeal as in a cloak.
18 According to what they have done,
so will he repay
wrath to his enemies
and retribution to his foes;
he will repay the islands their due.
19 From the west, men will fear the name of the LORD,
and from the rising of the sun,[r] they will revere his glory.
For he will come like a pent-up flood
that the breath of the LORD drives along.[a]

20 "The Redeemer will come to Zion,
to those in Jacob who repent of their sins,"[s]
declares the LORD.

21 "As for me, this is my covenant with
them," says the LORD. "My Spirit, who is on
you, and my words that I have put in your
mouth will not depart from your mouth, or
from the mouths of your children, or from
the mouths of their descendants from this
time on and forever," says the LORD.

## The Glory of Zion

60 "Arise, shine, for your light[t] has come,
and the glory of the LORD rises upon you.
2 See, darkness covers the earth
and thick darkness[u] is over the peoples,
but the LORD rises upon you
and his glory appears over you.
3 Nations will come to your light,
and kings[v] to the brightness of your dawn.

4 "Lift up your eyes and look about you:
All assemble and come to you;
your sons come from afar,
and your daughters are carried on the arm.[w]
5 Then you will look and be radiant,
your heart will throb and swell with joy;
the wealth on the seas will be brought to you,
to you the riches of the nations will come.
6 Herds of camels will cover your land,
young camels of Midian and Ephah.[x]
And all from Sheba[y] will come,
bearing gold and incense
and proclaiming the praise of the LORD.
7 All Kedar's[z] flocks will be gathered to you,
the rams of Nebaioth will serve you;
they will be accepted as offerings on my altar,
and I will adorn my glorious temple.[a]

8 "Who are these that fly along like clouds,
like doves to their nests?
9 Surely the islands look to me;
in the lead are the ships of Tarshish,[b]
bringing your sons from afar,
with their silver and gold,
to the honor of the LORD your God,
the Holy One of Israel,
for he has endowed you with splendor.[b]

10 "Foreigners will rebuild your walls,
and their kings[c] will serve you.
Though in anger I struck you,
in favor I will show you compassion.[d]
11 Your gates will always stand open,

59:14 n Isa 1:21
59:16 o Ps 98:1; Isa 63:5
59:17 p Eph 6:14 q 1Th 5:8
59:19 r Ps 113:3
59:20 s Ro 11:26–27*

60:1 t Eph 5:14
60:2 u Col 1:13
60:3 v Isa 49:23
60:4 w Isa 49:20–22
60:6 x Ge 25:4 y Ps 72:10
60:7 z Ge 25:13 a Hag 2:3,7,9
60:9 b Isa 55:5
60:10 c Isa 49:23; Rev 21:24 d Isa 54:8

[a]19 Or *When the enemy comes in like a flood, / the Spirit of the LORD will put him to flight* [b]9 Or *the trading ships*

# Inspire leadership FOCUS

## INTEGRITY

Integrity is one of the most important traits we should possess as leaders. In Isaiah 59:4 the prophet laments a lack of integrity in the people. Their lack of this important character trait was part of the reason that God judged them. God takes integrity seriously. Possessing integrity is God's plan for our lives. Since God commanded us to have integrity, we should rest in the fact that we can develop this godly character trait, and God will give us the strength to do his will.

The most important sense of integrity relates to one's general character, one's honesty. Having integrity involves having a sense of honor and being incorruptible. However, some people have lost their commitment to be moral—and integrity cannot exist without morality. Integrity and morality often have fallen by the wayside in our society. We seek personal gain by any means possible. If we have to step over, step on, lie to or lie about someone to get our needs and wants met, so be it. Our word no longer means anything. Some of us believe this behavior is permissible because we live in a world where dishonesty is accepted.

As leaders in our churches, communities and families, we sometimes become lackadaisical when it comes to possessing integrity. However, we cannot have integrity halfway. Integrity is one of the most important attributes of moral strength. It is a Biblical quality that is attainable for all of us and is especially important in our roles as leaders.

Sister, are you a woman of integrity? Integrity means you are honest on your job. Integrity means you keep your word. Integrity means you don't spread rumors. Integrity means you are honest in your home. A woman of integrity can be trusted when no one is looking. A woman of integrity honors God.

—T. Ulmer

### read

Isaiah 59; see also 1 Chronicles 29:10–20; Titus 2:1–15.

See also the Inspire Notes "Discernment," "Spiritual Discipline," "Discipline," "Self-Control" and "Character," and the Women of the Bible Notes "A Virtuous Woman: A Strong Woman, Dependent on God," "Sapphira: A Lost Opportunity for Truth" and "The 'Chosen Lady': A Woman Worth Imitating."

### WOMAN of COLOR

God is pleased when we display integrity. In a society in which dishonesty, immorality and corruption are accepted, God wants us to be examples of light in the darkness of this world. How do you display integrity in the various arenas of your life—home, work, church, community?

For the next Inspire note, go to page 883.

**60:11** e Ps 149:8
**60:13** f Isa 35:2 g 1Ch 28:2; Ps 132:7
**60:14** h Isa 49:23; Rev 3:9 i Heb 12:22
**60:16** j Isa 49:23
**60:18** k Isa 26:1
**60:19** l Zec 2:5; Rev 21:23

they will never be shut, day or night,
so that men may bring you the wealth of the nations—
their kings[e] led in triumphal procession.
12 For the nation or kingdom that will not serve you will perish;
it will be utterly ruined.

13 "The glory of Lebanon[f] will come to you,
the pine, the fir and the cypress together,
to adorn the place of my sanctuary;
and I will glorify the place of my feet.[g]
14 The sons of your oppressors will come bowing before you;
all who despise you will bow down[h] at your feet
and will call you the City of the LORD,
Zion[i] of the Holy One of Israel.

15 "Although you have been forsaken and hated,
with no one traveling through,
I will make you the everlasting pride
and the joy of all generations.
16 You will drink the milk of nations
and be nursed[j] at royal breasts.
Then you will know that I, the LORD, am your Savior,
your Redeemer, the Mighty One of Jacob.
17 Instead of bronze I will bring you gold,
and silver in place of iron.
Instead of wood I will bring you bronze,
and iron in place of stones.
I will make peace your governor
and righteousness your ruler.
18 No longer will violence be heard in your land,
nor ruin or destruction within your borders,
but you will call your walls Salvation[k]
and your gates Praise.
19 The sun will no more be your light by day,
nor will the brightness of the moon shine on you,
for the LORD will be your everlasting light,
and your God will be your glory.[l]
20 Your sun will never set again,
and your moon will wane no more;
the LORD will be your everlasting light,
and your days of sorrow will end.
21 Then will all your people be righteous
and they will possess[m] the land forever.
They are the shoot I have planted,
the work of my hands,[n]
for the display of my splendor.
22 The least of you will become a thousand,
the smallest a mighty nation.
I am the LORD;
in its time I will do this swiftly."

## The Year of the LORD's Favor

61 The Spirit of the Sovereign LORD is on me,
because the LORD has anointed me
to preach good news to the poor.[o]
He has sent me to bind up[p] the brokenhearted,
to proclaim freedom for the captives[q]
and release from darkness for the prisoners,[a]
2 to proclaim the year of the LORD's favor[r]
and the day of vengeance[s] of our God,
to comfort[t] all who mourn,
3 and provide for those who grieve in Zion—
to bestow on them a crown of beauty
instead of ashes,
the oil of gladness
instead of mourning,
and a garment of praise
instead of a spirit of despair.
They will be called oaks of righteousness,
a planting of the LORD
for the display of his splendor.[u]

4 They will rebuild the ancient ruins[v]
and restore the places long devastated;
they will renew the ruined cities
that have been devastated for generations.
5 Aliens will shepherd your flocks;
foreigners will work your fields and vineyards.
6 And you will be called priests of the LORD,
you will be named ministers of our God.
You will feed on the wealth of nations,
and in their riches you will boast.

**60:21** m Ps 37:11,22 n Isa 29:23
**61:1** o Mt 11:5 p Isa 57:15 q Isa 42:7
**61:2** r Lk 4:18–19* s Isa 34:8 t Isa 57:18; Mt 5:4
**61:3** u Isa 60:20–21
**61:4** v Isa 49:8; Eze 36:33

[a] 1 Hebrew; Septuagint *the blind*

61:7 w Isa 40:2; Zec 9:12
61:8 x Isa 55:3
61:10 y Isa 49:18; Rev 21:2
61:11 z Ps 85:11
62:2 a Isa 60:3 b ver 4,12
62:3 c Zec 9:16

7 Instead of their shame
my people will receive a double[w] portion,
and instead of disgrace
they will rejoice in their inheritance;
and so they will inherit a double portion in their land,
and everlasting joy will be theirs.

8 "For I, the LORD, love justice;
I hate robbery and iniquity.
In my faithfulness I will reward them
and make an everlasting covenant[x] with them.
9 Their descendants will be known among the nations
and their offspring among the peoples.
All who see them will acknowledge
that they are a people the LORD has blessed."

10 I delight greatly in the LORD;
my soul rejoices in my God.
For he has clothed me with garments of salvation
and arrayed me in a robe of righteousness,
as a bridegroom adorns his head like a priest,
and as a bride[y] adorns herself with her jewels.
11 For as the soil makes the sprout come up
and a garden causes seeds to grow,
so the Sovereign LORD will make
righteousness[z] and praise
spring up before all nations.

## Zion's New Name

62 For Zion's sake I will not keep silent,
for Jerusalem's sake I will not remain quiet,
till her righteousness shines out like the dawn,
her salvation like a blazing torch.
2 The nations[a] will see your righteousness,
and all kings your glory;
you will be called by a new name[b]
that the mouth of the LORD will bestow.
3 You will be a crown[c] of splendor in the LORD's hand,
a royal diadem in the hand of your God.
4 No longer will they call you Deserted,[d]
or name your land Desolate.
But you will be called Hephzibah,[a]
and your land Beulah[b];
for the LORD will take delight in you,
and your land will be married.
5 As a young man marries a maiden,
so will your sons[c] marry you;
as a bridegroom rejoices over his bride,
so will your God rejoice[e] over you.

6 I have posted watchmen[f] on your walls, O Jerusalem;
they will never be silent day or night.
You who call on the LORD,
give yourselves no rest,
7 and give him no rest till he establishes Jerusalem
and makes her the praise of the earth.

8 The LORD has sworn by his right hand
and by his mighty arm:
"Never again will I give your grain[g]
as food for your enemies,
and never again will foreigners drink the new wine
for which you have toiled;
9 but those who harvest it will eat it
and praise the LORD,
and those who gather the grapes will drink it
in the courts of my sanctuary."

10 Pass through, pass through the gates!
Prepare the way for the people.
Build up, build up the highway![h]
Remove the stones.
Raise a banner for the nations.

11 The LORD has made proclamation
to the ends of the earth:
"Say to the Daughter of Zion,[i]
'See, your Savior comes!
See, his reward is with him,
and his recompense accompanies him.'"[j]
12 They will be called[k] the Holy People,
the Redeemed of the LORD;
and you will be called Sought After,
the City No Longer Deserted.

62:4 d Isa 54:6
62:5 e Isa 65:19
62:6 f Isa 52:8; Eze 3:17
62:8 g Dt 28:30–33; Jer 5:17
62:10 h Isa 57:14
62:11 i Zec 9:9; Mt 21:5 j Isa 40:10
62:12 k ver 4

[a]4 *Hephzibah* means *my delight is in her.* [b]4 *Beulah* means *married.* [c]5 Or *Builder*

**63:1** l Am 1:12
**63:3** m Rev 14:20; 19:15
**63:5** n Isa 59:16
**63:6** o Isa 34:3
**63:7** p Isa 54:8; q Ps 51:1
**63:9** r Dt 7:7–8

## God's Day of Vengeance and Redemption

63 Who is this coming from Edom,
from Bozrah,[l] with his garments
stained crimson?
Who is this, robed in splendor,
striding forward in the greatness of his
strength?

"It is I, speaking in righteousness,
mighty to save."

2 Why are your garments red,
like those of one treading the
winepress?

3 "I have trodden the winepress[m] alone;
from the nations no one was with me.
I trampled them in my anger
and trod them down in my wrath;
their blood spattered my garments,
and I stained all my clothing.
4 For the day of vengeance was in my heart,
and the year of my redemption has
come.
5 I looked, but there was no one to help,
I was appalled that no one gave
support;
so my own arm worked salvation for me,
and my own wrath sustained me.[n]
6 I trampled the nations in my anger;
in my wrath I made them drunk
and poured their blood[o] on the
ground."

## Praise and Prayer

7 I will tell of the kindnesses[p] of the LORD,
the deeds for which he is to be praised,
according to all the LORD has done for
us—
yes, the many good things he has done
for the house of Israel,
according to his compassion[q] and
many kindnesses.
8 He said, "Surely they are my people,
sons who will not be false to me";
and so he became their Savior.
9 In all their distress he too was distressed,
and the angel of his presence saved
them.
In his love and mercy he redeemed[r] them;
he lifted them up and carried them
all the days of old.
10 Yet they rebelled[s]
and grieved his Holy Spirit.[t]
So he turned and became their enemy
and he himself fought against them.

11 Then his people recalled[a] the days of old,
the days of Moses and his people—
where is he who brought them through
the sea,[u]
with the shepherd of his flock?
Where is he who set
his Holy Spirit[v] among them,
12 who sent his glorious arm of power
to be at Moses' right hand,
who divided the waters before them,
to gain for himself everlasting renown,
13 who led them through the depths?
Like a horse in open country,
they did not stumble;
14 like cattle that go down to the plain,
they were given rest by the Spirit of
the LORD.
This is how you guided your people
to make for yourself a glorious name.

15 Look down from heaven[w] and see
from your lofty throne, holy and
glorious.
Where are your zeal and your might?
Your tenderness and compassion[x] are
withheld from us.
16 But you are our Father,
though Abraham does not know us
or Israel acknowledge us;
you, O LORD, are our Father,
our Redeemer from of old is your
name.
17 Why, O LORD, do you make us wander
from your ways
and harden our hearts so we do not
revere[y] you?
Return for the sake of your servants,
the tribes that are your inheritance.
18 For a little while your people possessed
your holy place,
but now our enemies have trampled
down your sanctuary.[z]
19 We are yours from of old;
but you have not ruled over them,
they have not been called by your
name.[b]

**63:10** s Ps 78:40; t Ps 51:11; Ac 7:51; Eph 4:30
**63:11** u Ex 14:22,30; v Nu 11:17
**63:15** w Dt 26:15; Ps 80:14; x Jer 31:20; Hos 11:8
**63:17** y Isa 29:13
**63:18** z Ps 74:3–8

[a]11 Or *But may he recall* [b]19 Or *We are like those you have never ruled, / like those never called by your name*

64:1
a Ps 144:5
64:2
b Jer 5:22
64:3
c Ps 65:5
64:4
d 1Co 2:9*
64:6
e Isa 46:12
f Ps 90:5–6
64:8
g Isa 63:16
h Isa 29:16
64:11
i Ps 74:3–7

64 Oh, that you would rend the
heavens[a] and come down,
that the mountains would tremble
before you!
2 As when fire sets twigs ablaze
and causes water to boil,
come down to make your name known to
your enemies
and cause the nations to quake[b] before
you!
3 For when you did awesome[c] things that
we did not expect,
you came down, and the mountains
trembled before you.
4 Since ancient times no one has heard,
no ear has perceived,
no eye has seen any God besides you,
who acts on behalf of those who wait
for him.[d]
5 You come to the help of those who gladly
do right,
who remember your ways.
But when we continued to sin against
them,
you were angry.
How then can we be saved?
6 All of us have become like one who is
unclean,
and all our righteous[e] acts are like
filthy rags;
we all shrivel up like a leaf,[f]
and like the wind our sins sweep us
away.
7 No one calls on your name
or strives to lay hold of you;
for you have hidden your face from us
and made us waste away because of
our sins.
8 Yet, O LORD, you are our Father.[g]
We are the clay, you are the potter;[h]
we are all the work of your hand.
9 Do not be angry beyond measure, O LORD;
do not remember our sins forever.
Oh, look upon us, we pray,
for we are all your people.
10 Your sacred cities have become a desert;
even Zion is a desert, Jerusalem a
desolation.
11 Our holy and glorious temple,[i] where our
fathers praised you,
has been burned with fire,
and all that we treasured lies in ruins.

*Dear one,*

*Allow me to mold you into the woman I have called you to be.*

*The Potter*

ISAIAH 64:8

12 After all this, O LORD, will you hold
yourself back?[j]
Will you keep silent and punish us
beyond measure?

## Judgment and Salvation

65 "I revealed myself to those who did
not ask for me;
I was found by those who did not
seek me.[k]
To a nation that did not call on my name,
I said, 'Here am I, here am I.'
2 All day long I have held out my hands
to an obstinate people,[l]
who walk in ways not good,
pursuing their own imaginations—
3 a people who continually provoke me
to my very face,
offering sacrifices in gardens
and burning incense on altars of brick;
4 who sit among the graves
and spend their nights keeping secret
vigil;
who eat the flesh of pigs,[m]
and whose pots hold broth of unclean
meat;
5 who say, 'Keep away; don't come near me,
for I am too sacred[n] for you!'
Such people are smoke in my nostrils,
a fire that keeps burning all day.
6 "See, it stands written before me:
I will not keep silent[o] but will pay
back[p] in full;
I will pay it back into their laps—
7 both your sins and the sins of your
fathers,"
says the LORD.
"Because they burned sacrifices on the
mountains

64:12
j Isa 42:14
65:1
k Ro 10:20*
65:2
l Ro 10:21*
65:4
m Lev 11:7
65:5
n Mt 9:11;
Lk 18:9–12
65:6
o Ps 50:3
p Jer 16:18

65:7 q Isa 57:7
65:9 r Isa 32:18
65:10 s Isa 35:2
65:11 t Dt 29:24–25
65:12 u Pr 1:24–25 v 2Ch 36:15–16; Jer 7:13
65:13 w Isa 1:19
65:14 x Mt 8:12
65:15 y Zec 8:13

and defied me on the hills,[q]
I will measure into their laps
the full payment for their former
deeds."

8 This is what the LORD says:

"As when juice is still found in a cluster
of grapes
and men say, 'Don't destroy it,
there is yet some good in it,'
so will I do in behalf of my servants;
I will not destroy them all.
9 I will bring forth descendants from
Jacob,
and from Judah those who will possess
my mountains;
my chosen people will inherit them,
and there will my servants live.[r]
10 Sharon[s] will become a pasture for flocks,
and the Valley of Achor a resting place
for herds,
for my people who seek me.

11 "But as for you who forsake[t] the LORD
and forget my holy mountain,
who spread a table for Fortune
and fill bowls of mixed wine for
Destiny,
12 I will destine you for the sword,
and you will all bend down for the
slaughter;
for I called but you did not answer,[u]
I spoke but you did not listen.[v]
You did evil in my sight
and chose what displeases me."

13 Therefore this is what the Sovereign
LORD says:

"My servants will eat,[w]
but you will go hungry;
my servants will drink,
but you will go thirsty;
my servants will rejoice,
but you will be put to shame.
14 My servants will sing
out of the joy of their hearts,
but you will cry out[x]
from anguish of heart
and wail in brokenness of spirit.
15 You will leave your name
to my chosen ones as a curse;[y]
the Sovereign LORD will put you to death,
but to his servants he will give another
name.
16 Whoever invokes a blessing in the land
will do so by the God of truth;[z]
he who takes an oath in the land
will swear by the God of truth.
For the past troubles will be forgotten
and hidden from my eyes.

## New Heavens and a New Earth

17 "Behold, I will create
new heavens and a new earth.[a]
The former things will not be
remembered,[b]
nor will they come to mind.
18 But be glad and rejoice forever
in what I will create,
for I will create Jerusalem to be a delight
and its people a joy.
19 I will rejoice[c] over Jerusalem
and take delight in my people;
the sound of weeping and of crying[d]
will be heard in it no more.

20 "Never again will there be in it
an infant who lives but a few days,
or an old man who does not live out
his years;[e]
he who dies at a hundred
will be thought a mere youth;
he who fails to reach[a] a hundred
will be considered accursed.
21 They will build houses and dwell in
them;
they will plant vineyards and eat their
fruit.
22 No longer will they build houses and
others live in them,
or plant and others eat.
For as the days of a tree,[f]
so will be the days of my people;
my chosen ones will long enjoy
the works of their hands.
23 They will not toil in vain
or bear children doomed to
misfortune;
for they will be a people blessed[g] by the
LORD,
they and their descendants with them.
24 Before they call I will answer;

65:16 z Ps 31:5
65:17 a 2Pe 3:13 b Isa 43:18
65:19 c Isa 35:10; 62:5 d Rev 7:17
65:20 e Ecc 8:13
65:22 f Ps 92:12–14
65:23 g Isa 61:9

[a]20 Or *the sinner who reaches*

while they are still speaking[h] I will
hear.
25 The wolf and the lamb[i] will feed together,
and the lion will eat straw like the ox,
but dust will be the serpent's[j] food.
They will neither harm nor destroy
on all my holy mountain,"
says the LORD.

## Judgment and Hope

66 This is what the LORD says:

"Heaven is my throne,
and the earth is my footstool.[k]
Where is the house you will build for me?
Where will my resting place be?
2 Has not my hand made all these things,[l]
and so they came into being?"
declares the LORD.

"This is the one I esteem:
he who is humble and contrite in
spirit,[m]
and trembles at my word.
3 But whoever sacrifices a bull[n]
is like one who kills a man,
and whoever offers a lamb,
like one who breaks a dog's neck;
whoever makes a grain offering
is like one who presents pig's blood,
and whoever burns memorial incense,
like one who worships an idol.
They have chosen their own ways,
and their souls delight in their
abominations;
4 so I also will choose harsh treatment for
them
and will bring upon them what they
dread.
For when I called, no one answered,[o]
when I spoke, no one listened.
They did evil in my sight
and chose what displeases me."[p]

5 Hear the word of the LORD,
you who tremble at his word:
"Your brothers who hate you,
and exclude you because of my name,
have said,
'Let the LORD be glorified,
that we may see your joy!'
Yet they will be put to shame.[q]
6 Hear that uproar from the city,
hear that noise from the temple!
It is the sound of the LORD
repaying[r] his enemies all they deserve.

7 "Before she goes into labor,
she gives birth;
before the pains come upon her,
she delivers a son.
8 Who has ever heard of such a thing?
Who has ever seen[s] such things?
Can a country be born in a day
or a nation be brought forth in a
moment?
Yet no sooner is Zion in labor
than she gives birth to her children.
9 Do I bring to the moment of birth
and not give delivery?" says the LORD.
"Do I close up the womb
when I bring to delivery?" says your
God.
10 "Rejoice with Jerusalem and be glad for
her,
all you who love[t] her;
rejoice greatly with her,
all you who mourn over her.
11 For you will nurse[u] and be satisfied
at her comforting breasts;
you will drink deeply
and delight in her overflowing
abundance."

12 For this is what the LORD says:

"I will extend peace to her like a river,[v]
and the wealth[w] of nations like a
flooding stream;
you will nurse and be carried[x] on her arm
and dandled on her knees.
13 As a mother comforts her child,
so will I comfort[y] you;
and you will be comforted over
Jerusalem."

14 When you see this, your heart will
rejoice
and you will flourish like grass;
the hand of the LORD will be made known
to his servants,
but his fury will be shown to his foes.
15 See, the LORD is coming with fire,
and his chariots are like a whirlwind;
he will bring down his anger with fury,
and his rebuke with flames of fire.
16 For with fire[z] and with his sword

65:24 h Da 9:20–23
65:25 i Isa 11:6 j Ge 3:14
66:1 k 1Ki 8:27; Mt 5:34–35
66:2 l Ac 7:50* m Isa 57:15
66:3 n Isa 1:11
66:4 o Pr 1:24; Jer 7:13 p Isa 65:12
66:5 q Lk 13:17
66:6 r Isa 65:6
66:8 s Isa 64:4
66:10 t Ps 26:8
66:11 u Isa 60:16
66:12 v Isa 48:18 w Isa 60:5 x Isa 60:4
66:13 y 2Co 1:4
66:16 z Isa 30:30

66:17
a Ps 37:20

66:19
b Eze 27:10

the LORD will execute judgment upon
all men,
and many will be those slain by the
LORD.

17"Those who consecrate and purify
themselves to go into the gardens, following
the one in the midst of[a] those who eat the
flesh of pigs and rats and other abominable
things—they will meet their end[a] together,"
declares the LORD.

18"And I, because of their actions and
their imaginations, am about to come[b] and
gather all nations and tongues, and they
will come and see my glory.

19"I will set a sign among them, and I
will send some of those who survive to the
nations—to Tarshish, to the Libyans[c] and
Lydians[b] (famous as archers), to Tubal and
Greece, and to the distant islands that have
not heard of my fame or seen my glory. They
will proclaim my glory among the nations.
20And they will bring all your brothers,
from all the nations, to my holy mountain
in Jerusalem as an offering to the LORD—on
horses, in chariots and wagons, and on
mules and camels," says the LORD. "They
will bring them, as the Israelites bring their
grain offerings, to the temple of the LORD
in ceremonially clean vessels. 21And I will
select some of them also to be priests[c] and
Levites," says the LORD.

22"As the new heavens and the new earth[d]
that I make will endure before me," declares
the LORD, "so will your name and descen-
dants endure. 23From one New Moon to
another and from one Sabbath to another,
all mankind will come and bow down be-
fore me," says the LORD. 24"And they will go
out and look upon the dead bodies of those
who rebelled against me; their worm will
not die, nor will their fire be quenched,[e] and
they will be loathsome to all mankind."

66:21
c Ex 19:6;
Isa 61:6;
1Pe 2:5,9

66:22
d Isa 65:17;
2Pe 3:13;
Rev 21:1

66:24
e Isa 1:31;
Mk 9:48*

[a]17 Or *gardens behind one of your temples, and* [b]18 The meaning of the Hebrew for this clause is uncertain. [c]19 Some Septuagint manuscripts *Put* (Libyans); Hebrew *Pul*

# Jeremiah

## OVERVIEW

Jeremiah prophesied during the time when the Babylonians were emerging as the new world power. He preached to the people about God's impending judgment. During this dark period in the history of Judah (Israel had been destroyed by the Assyrians nearly a century earlier), Jeremiah offered a glimmer of hope of restoration. He also prophesied God's judgment on the surrounding nations (see Jer 46–51).

Whether a nation is experiencing prosperity or poverty, God still speaks through the Bible. It is during times of suffering that most people are open to hearing what God has to say. Like the prophet Jeremiah, women of today can offer a firm foundation of hope for others if they themselves are well trained in the study of God's Word.

## OUTLINE

I. Jeremiah's Call (1:1–19)
II. Judah's Sin and God's Judgment (2:1—18:23)
III. Jeremiah's Confrontation of Leaders (19:1—29:32)
IV. Promises of Restoration (30:1—33:26)
V. Historical Appendix: Zedekiah, Slaves and Recabites (34:1—35:19)
VI. Jeremiah's Sufferings and Persecutions (36:1—38:28)
VII. Jerusalem's Fall and Its Aftermath (39:1—44:30)
VIII. Historical Appendix: A Message to Baruch (45:1–5)
IX. Prophecies Against the Nations (46:1—51:64)
X. Historical Appendix: The Fall of Jerusalem (52:1–34)

### SCANNABLE FACTS:

**Author:** Jeremiah

**Time Written:** During Jeremiah's ministry, which spanned from about 626 to 586 B.C.

**Theme to Note:** God's judgment and restoration

**Notable Women:** Wives who burned incense to false gods (see Jer 44)

# 1

The words of Jeremiah son of Hilkiah, one of the priests at Anathoth[a] in the territory of Benjamin. 2 The word of the LORD came to him in the thirteenth year of the reign of Josiah son of Amon king of Judah, 3 and through the reign of Jehoiakim son of Josiah king of Judah, down to the fifth month of the eleventh year of Zedekiah[b] son of Josiah king of Judah, when the people of Jerusalem went into exile.

## The Call of Jeremiah

4 The word of the LORD came to me, saying,

5 "Before I formed you in the womb I
knew[a] you,
before you were born[c] I set you apart;
I appointed you as a prophet to the
nations."

6 "Ah, Sovereign LORD," I said, "I do not know how to speak;[d] I am only a child."

7 But the LORD said to me, "Do not say, 'I am only a child.' You must go to everyone I send you to and say whatever I command you. 8 Do not be afraid[e] of them, for I am with you[f] and will rescue you," declares the LORD.

9 Then the LORD reached out his hand and touched[g] my mouth and said to me, "Now, I have put my words in your mouth. 10 See, today I appoint you over nations and kingdoms to uproot and tear down, to destroy and overthrow, to build and to plant."[h]

11 The word of the LORD came to me: "What do you see, Jeremiah?"

"I see the branch of an almond tree," I replied.

*Sister,*

*Don't be afraid of anything.*

*I am with you always.*

*Your Sustainer*

JEREMIAH 1:4–10

12 The LORD said to me, "You have seen correctly, for I am watching[b] to see that my word is fulfilled."

13 The word of the LORD came to me again: "What do you see?"

"I see a boiling pot, tilting away from the north," I answered.

14 The LORD said to me, "From the north disaster will be poured out on all who live in the land. 15 I am about to summon all the peoples of the northern kingdoms," declares the LORD.

"Their kings will come and set up their
thrones
in the entrance of the gates of
Jerusalem;
they will come against all her
surrounding walls
and against all the towns of Judah.
16 I will pronounce my judgments on my
people
because of their wickedness[i] in
forsaking me,[j]
in burning incense to other gods
and in worshiping what their hands
have made.

17 "Get yourself ready! Stand up and say to them whatever I command you. Do not be terrified[k] by them, or I will terrify you before them. 18 Today I have made you a fortified city, an iron pillar and a bronze wall to stand against the whole land—against the kings of Judah, its officials, its priests and the people of the land. 19 They will fight against you but will not overcome you, for I am with you and will rescue[l] you," declares the LORD.

## Israel Forsakes God

# 2

The word of the LORD came to me: 2 "Go and proclaim in the hearing of Jerusalem:

"'I remember the devotion of your
youth,[m]
how as a bride you loved me
and followed me through the desert,[n]
through a land not sown.
3 Israel was holy to the LORD,[o]
the firstfruits of his harvest;

1:1 a Jos 21:18; 1Ch 6:60; Jer 32:7–9
1:3 b Jer 39:2
1:5 c Isa 49:1
1:6 d Ex 4:10
1:8 e Eze 2:6 f Jer 15:20
1:9 g Isa 6:7
1:10 h Jer 18:7–10
1:16 i Dt 28:20 j Jer 17:13
1:17 k Eze 2:6
1:19 l ver 8
2:2 m Eze 16:8–14,60 n Dt 2:7
2:3 o Ex 19:6

[a]5 Or *chose* [b]12 The Hebrew for *watching* sounds like the Hebrew for *almond tree.*

all who devoured her were held guilty,[p]
and disaster overtook them,' "
declares the LORD.

4 Hear the word of the LORD, O house of
Jacob,
all you clans of the house of Israel.

5 This is what the LORD says:

"What fault did your fathers find in me,
that they strayed so far from me?
They followed worthless idols
and became worthless[q] themselves.
6 They did not ask, 'Where is the LORD,
who brought us up out of Egypt
and led us through the barren
wilderness,
through a land of deserts[r] and rifts,[s]
a land of drought and darkness,[a]
a land where no one travels and no one
lives?'
7 I brought you into a fertile land
to eat its fruit and rich produce.[t]
But you came and defiled my land
and made my inheritance
detestable.
8 The priests did not ask,
'Where is the LORD?'
Those who deal with the law did not
know me;
the leaders rebelled against me.
The prophets prophesied by Baal,[u]
following worthless idols.

9 "Therefore I bring charges[v] against you
again,"
declares the LORD.
"And I will bring charges against your
children's children.
10 Cross over to the coasts of Kittim[b] and
look,
send to Kedar[c] and observe closely;
see if there has ever been anything
like this:
11 Has a nation ever changed its gods?
(Yet they are not gods[w] at all.)
But my people have exchanged their[d]
Glory[x]
for worthless idols.
12 Be appalled at this, O heavens,
and shudder with great horror,"
declares the LORD.
13 "My people have committed two sins:
They have forsaken me,
the spring of living water,[y]
and have dug their own cisterns,
broken cisterns that cannot hold water.
14 Is Israel a servant, a slave by birth?
Why then has he become plunder?
15 Lions[z] have roared;
they have growled at him.
They have laid waste his land;
his towns are burned and deserted.
16 Also, the men of Memphis[e] and
Tahpanhes
have shaved the crown of your head.[f]
17 Have you not brought this on yourselves[a]
by forsaking the LORD your God
when he led you in the way?
18 Now why go to Egypt[b]
to drink water from the Shihor[g]?[c]
And why go to Assyria
to drink water from the River[h]?
19 Your wickedness will punish you;
your backsliding will rebuke you.
Consider then and realize
how evil and bitter it is for you

2:3 p Jer 50:7
2:5 q 2Ki 17:15
2:6 r Dt 8:15 s Dt 32:10
2:7 t Nu 13:27
2:8 u Jer 23:13
2:9 v Eze 20:35–36
2:11 w Isa 37:19 x Ps 106:20; Ro 1:23
2:13 y Ps 36:9; Jn 4:14
2:15 z Jer 4:7
2:17 a Jer 4:18
2:18 b Isa 30:2 c Jos 13:3

[a] 6 Or *and the shadow of death* [b] 10 That is, Cyprus and western coastlands [c] 10 The home of Bedouin tribes in the Syro-Arabian desert [d] 11 Masoretic Text; an ancient Hebrew scribal tradition *my* [e] 16 Hebrew *Noph* [f] 16 Or *have cracked your skull* [g] 18 That is, a branch of the Nile [h] 18 That is, the Euphrates

## The African Presence

### Jeremiah 2:10

The people of Kedar were the descendants of Abraham and Hagar the Egyptian (see Ge 25:13). Kedar was the home of Bedouin tribes in the Syro-Arabian desert.

**2:20** d Dt 12:2
**2:21** e Ex 15:17; f Isa 5:4
**2:23** g Pr 30:12; h Jer 7:31
**2:24** i Jer 14:6

when you forsake the LORD your God
and have no awe of me,"
declares the Lord,
the LORD Almighty.

20 "Long ago you broke off your yoke
and tore off your bonds;
you said, 'I will not serve you!'
Indeed, on every high hill
and under every spreading tree[d]
you lay down as a prostitute.
21 I had planted[e] you like a choice vine
of sound and reliable stock.
How then did you turn against me
into a corrupt,[f] wild vine?
22 Although you wash yourself with soda
and use an abundance of soap,
the stain of your guilt is still before
me,"
declares the Sovereign LORD.
23 "How can you say, 'I am not defiled;[g]
I have not run after the Baals'?
See how you behaved in the valley;[h]
consider what you have done.
You are a swift she-camel
running here and there,
24 a wild donkey[i] accustomed to the desert,
sniffing the wind in her craving—
in her heat who can restrain her?
Any males that pursue her need not tire
themselves;
at mating time they will find her.
25 Do not run until your feet are bare
and your throat is dry.
But you said, 'It's no use!
I love foreign gods,
and I must go after them.'

26 "As a thief is disgraced[j] when he is
caught,
so the house of Israel is disgraced—
they, their kings and their officials,
their priests and their prophets.
27 They say to wood, 'You are my father,'
and to stone, 'You gave me birth.'
They have turned their backs to me
and not their faces;
yet when they are in trouble,[k] they say,
'Come and save us!'
28 Where then are the gods[l] you made for
yourselves?
Let them come if they can save you
when you are in trouble!
For you have as many gods
as you have towns,[m] O Judah.

29 "Why do you bring charges against me?
You have all rebelled against me,"
declares the LORD.
30 "In vain I punished your people;
they did not respond to correction.
Your sword has devoured your prophets[n]
like a ravening lion.

31 "You of this generation, consider the
word of the LORD:

"Have I been a desert to Israel
or a land of great darkness?[o]
Why do my people say, 'We are free to
roam;
we will come to you no more'?
32 Does a maiden forget her jewelry,
a bride her wedding ornaments?
Yet my people have forgotten me,
days without number.

**2:26** j Jer 48:27
**2:27** k Isa 26:16
**2:28** l Isa 45:20; m Jer 11:13
**2:30** n Ac 7:52
**2:31** o Isa 45:19

## The African Presence

### Jeremiah 2:18,36

These verses reference the Assyrians—descendants of Cush (see Ge 10:8–11), son of Ham. Because Ham's offspring represent the geographic territories once dominated by Egypt—present-day Egypt, Libya and Sudan and into the area today known as Israel—they can claim a relation to African heritage. Since "heritage" is something "passed down" or "inherited," Canaan (Israel or Palestine) most certainly received or was influenced by Egypt culturally, politically, religiously, etc.

**2:34** p Ex 22:2
**2:36** q Isa 30:2,3,7
**2:37** r 2Sa 13:19
**3:1** s Dt 24:1–4 t Jer 2:20,25; Eze 16:26,29
**3:2** u Jer 2:7
**3:3** v Lev 26:19 w Jer 6:15
**3:5** x Ps 103:9; Isa 57:16

33 How skilled you are at pursuing love!
Even the worst of women can learn
from your ways.
34 On your clothes men find
the lifeblood of the innocent poor,
though you did not catch them
breaking in.[p]
Yet in spite of all this
35 you say, 'I am innocent;
he is not angry with me.'
But I will pass judgment on you
because you say, 'I have not sinned.'
36 Why do you go about so much,
changing your ways?
You will be disappointed by Egypt[q]
as you were by Assyria.
37 You will also leave that place
with your hands on your head,[r]
for the LORD has rejected those you trust;
you will not be helped by them.

3 "If a man divorces[s] his wife
and she leaves him and marries
another man,
should he return to her again?
Would not the land be completely
defiled?
But you have lived as a prostitute with
many lovers[t]—
would you now return to me?"
declares the LORD.
2 "Look up to the barren heights and see.
Is there any place where you have not
been ravished?
By the roadside you sat waiting for lovers,
sat like a nomad[a] in the desert.
You have defiled the land[u]
with your prostitution and
wickedness.
3 Therefore the showers have been
withheld,[v]
and no spring rains have fallen.
Yet you have the brazen look of a
prostitute;
you refuse to blush with shame.[w]
4 Have you not just called to me:
'My Father, my friend from my youth,
5 will you always be angry?[x]
Will your wrath continue forever?'
This is how you talk,
but you do all the evil you can."

## Unfaithful Israel

6 During the reign of King Josiah, the
LORD said to me, "Have you seen what faith-
less Israel has done? She has gone up on
every high hill and under every spreading
tree and has committed adultery there. 7 I
thought that after she had done all this she
would return to me but she did not, and her
unfaithful sister[y] Judah saw it. 8 I gave faith-
less Israel her certificate of divorce and sent
her away because of all her adulteries. Yet I
saw that her unfaithful sister Judah had no
fear;[z] she also went out and committed adul-
tery. 9 Because Israel's immorality mattered
so little to her, she defiled the land and com-
mitted adultery with stone and wood.[a] 10 In
spite of all this, her unfaithful sister Judah
did not return to me with all her heart, but
only in pretense," declares the LORD.

11 The LORD said to me, "Faithless Israel
is more righteous[b] than unfaithful Ju-
dah. 12 Go, proclaim this message toward
the north:

"'Return, faithless Israel,' declares the
LORD,
'I will frown on you no longer,
for I am merciful,' declares the LORD,
'I will not be angry[c] forever.
13 Only acknowledge[d] your guilt—
you have rebelled against the LORD
your God,
you have scattered your favors to foreign
gods[e]
under every spreading tree,[f]
and have not obeyed me,'"
declares the LORD.

14 "Return,[g] faithless people," declares
the LORD, "for I am your husband. I will
choose you—one from a town and two
from a clan—and bring you to Zion. 15 Then
I will give you shepherds[h] after my own
heart, who will lead you with knowledge
and understanding. 16 In those days, when
your numbers have increased greatly in
the land," declares the LORD, "men will no
longer say, 'The ark of the covenant of the
LORD.' It will never enter their minds or be
remembered;[i] it will not be missed, nor will
another one be made. 17 At that time they
will call Jerusalem The Throne of the LORD,

**3:7** y Eze 16:46
**3:8** z Eze 23:11
**3:9** a Jer 2:27
**3:11** b Eze 16:52
**3:12** c Ps 86:15
**3:13** d Dt 30:1–3 e Jer 2:25 f Dt 12:2
**3:14** g Hos 2:19
**3:15** h Ac 20:28
**3:16** i Isa 65:17

[a] 2 Or *an Arab*

3:17 j Isa 60:9 k Jer 11:8
3:18 l Hos 1:11 m Isa 11:13 n Jer 31:8 o Am 9:15
3:19 p Isa 63:16
3:22 q Hos 14:4 r Hos 6:1
3:23 s Ps 3:8
3:25 t Ezr 9:6 u Jer 22:21
4:1 v Jer 3:1,22; Joel 2:12

and all nations will gather in Jerusalem to honor[j] the name of the LORD. No longer will they follow the stubbornness of their evil hearts.[k] 18 In those days the house of Judah will join the house of Israel,[l] and together[m] they will come from a northern[n] land to the land[o] I gave your forefathers as an inheritance.

19 "I myself said,

" 'How gladly would I treat you like sons
and give you a desirable land,
the most beautiful inheritance of any nation.'
I thought you would call me 'Father'[p]
and not turn away from following me.
20 But like a woman unfaithful to her husband,
so you have been unfaithful to me,
O house of Israel,"
declares the LORD.

21 A cry is heard on the barren heights,
the weeping and pleading of the people of Israel,
because they have perverted their ways
and have forgotten the LORD their God.

22 "Return,[q] faithless people;
I will cure[r] you of backsliding."

"Yes, we will come to you,
for you are the LORD our God.
23 Surely the idolatrous commotion on the hills
and mountains is a deception;
surely in the LORD our God
is the salvation[s] of Israel.
24 From our youth shameful gods have consumed
the fruits of our fathers' labor—
their flocks and herds,
their sons and daughters.
25 Let us lie down in our shame,[t]
and let our disgrace cover us.
We have sinned against the LORD our God,
both we and our fathers;
from our youth[u] till this day
we have not obeyed the LORD our God."

4 "If you will return[v], O Israel,
return to me,"
declares the LORD.

"If you put your detestable idols out of my sight
and no longer go astray,
2 and if in a truthful, just and righteous way
you swear,[w] 'As surely as the LORD lives,'
then the nations will be blessed[x] by him
and in him they will glory."

3 This is what the LORD says to the men of Judah and to Jerusalem:

"Break up your unplowed ground[y]
and do not sow among thorns.[z]
4 Circumcise yourselves to the LORD,
circumcise your hearts,[a]
you men of Judah and people of Jerusalem,
or my wrath will break out and burn like fire
because of the evil you have done—
burn with no one to quench it.

## Disaster From the North

5 "Announce in Judah and proclaim in Jerusalem and say:
'Sound the trumpet throughout the land!'
Cry aloud and say:
'Gather together!
Let us flee to the fortified cities!'[b]
6 Raise the signal to go to Zion!
Flee for safety without delay!
For I am bringing disaster from the north,[c]
even terrible destruction."

7 A lion has come out of his lair;
a destroyer of nations has set out.
He has left his place
to lay waste[d] your land.
Your towns will lie in ruins[e]
without inhabitant.
8 So put on sackcloth,[f]
lament and wail,
for the fierce anger of the LORD
has not turned away from us.

9 "In that day," declares the LORD,
"the king and the officials will lose heart,
the priests will be horrified,
and the prophets will be appalled."

4:2 w Dt 10:20; Isa 65:16 x Ge 22:18; Gal 3:8
4:3 y Hos 10:12 z Mk 4:18
4:4 a Dt 10:16; Jer 9:26
4:5 b Jer 8:14
4:6 c Jer 1:13–15
4:7 d Isa 1:7 e Jer 25:9
4:8 f Isa 22:12

**4:10** g 2Th 2:11 h Jer 14:13
**4:11** i Eze 17:10
**4:13** j Isa 5:28
**4:14** k Jas 4:8
**4:17** l 2Ki 25:1,4
**4:18** m Ps 107:17; Isa 50:1 n Jer 2:17 o Jer 2:19
**4:20** p Jer 10:20

10 Then I said, "Ah, Sovereign LORD, how
completely you have deceived[g] this people
and Jerusalem by saying, 'You will have
peace,'[h] when the sword is at our throats."
11 At that time this people and Jerusalem
will be told, "A scorching wind[i] from the bar-
ren heights in the desert blows toward my
people, but not to winnow or cleanse; 12 a
wind too strong for that comes from me.[a]
Now I pronounce my judgments against
them."

13 Look! He advances like the clouds,
his chariots come like a whirlwind,[j]
his horses are swifter than eagles.
Woe to us! We are ruined!
14 O Jerusalem, wash[k] the evil from your heart and be saved.
How long will you harbor wicked thoughts?
15 A voice is announcing from Dan,
proclaiming disaster from the hills of Ephraim.
16 "Tell this to the nations,
proclaim it to Jerusalem:
'A besieging army is coming from a distant land,
raising a war cry against the cities of Judah.
17 They surround[l] her like men guarding a field,
because she has rebelled against me,'"
declares the LORD.
18 "Your own conduct and actions[m]
have brought this upon you.[n]
This is your punishment.
How bitter[o] it is!
How it pierces to the heart!"

19 Oh, my anguish, my anguish!
I writhe in pain.
Oh, the agony of my heart!
My heart pounds within me,
I cannot keep silent.
For I have heard the sound of the trumpet;
I have heard the battle cry.
20 Disaster follows disaster;
the whole land lies in ruins.
In an instant my tents[p] are destroyed,
my shelter in a moment.
21 How long must I see the battle standard
and hear the sound of the trumpet?

22 "My people are fools;
they do not know me.
They are senseless children;
they have no understanding.
They are skilled in doing evil;
they know not how to do good."

23 I looked at the earth,
and it was formless and empty;[q]
and at the heavens,
and their light was gone.
24 I looked at the mountains,
and they were quaking;
all the hills were swaying.
25 I looked, and there were no people;
every bird in the sky had flown away.[r]
26 I looked, and the fruitful land was a desert;
all its towns lay in ruins
before the LORD, before his fierce anger.

27 This is what the LORD says:

"The whole land will be ruined,
though I will not destroy[s] it completely.
28 Therefore the earth will mourn[t]
and the heavens above grow dark,
because I have spoken and will not relent,[u]
I have decided and will not turn back."

29 At the sound of horsemen and archers
every town takes to flight.
Some go into the thickets;
some climb up among the rocks.
All the towns are deserted;
no one lives in them.

30 What are you doing, O devastated one?
Why dress yourself in scarlet
and put on jewels of gold?
Why shade your eyes with paint?[v]
You adorn yourself in vain.
Your lovers despise you;
they seek your life.

31 I hear a cry as of a woman in labor,
a groan as of one bearing her first child—
the cry of the Daughter of Zion gasping for breath,

**4:23** q Ge 1:2
**4:25** r Zep 1:3
**4:27** s Jer 5:10,18; 30:11; 46:28
**4:28** t Hos 4:3 u Nu 23:19
**4:30** v 2Ki 9:30

[a]12 Or *comes at my command*

4:31 w Isa 1:15; La 1:17
5:1 x Eze 22:30 y Ge 18:32
5:2 z Jer 4:2
5:3 a Isa 9:13
5:5 b Mic 3:1,9
5:6 c Hos 13:7
5:7 d Jos 23:7 e Dt 32:21; Gal 4:8
5:8 f Eze 22:11

stretching out her hands[w] and saying,
"Alas! I am fainting;
my life is given over to murderers."

## Not One Is Upright

5 "Go up and down[x] the streets of
Jerusalem,
look around and consider,
search through her squares.
If you can find but one person[y]
who deals honestly and seeks the
truth,
I will forgive this city.
2 Although they say, 'As surely as the LORD
lives,'[z]
still they are swearing falsely."
3 O LORD, do not your eyes look for truth?
You struck[a] them, but they felt no
pain;
you crushed them, but they refused
correction.
They made their faces harder than stone
and refused to repent.
4 I thought, "These are only the poor;
they are foolish,
for they do not know the way of the LORD,
the requirements of their God.
5 So I will go to the leaders[b]
and speak to them;
surely they know the way of the LORD,
the requirements of their God."
But with one accord they too had broken
off the yoke
and torn off the bonds.
6 Therefore a lion from the forest will
attack them,
a wolf from the desert will ravage
them,
a leopard[c] will lie in wait near their towns
to tear to pieces any who venture out,
for their rebellion is great
and their backslidings many.
7 "Why should I forgive you?
Your children have forsaken me
and sworn[d] by gods that are not gods.[e]
I supplied all their needs,
yet they committed adultery
and thronged to the houses of
prostitutes.
8 They are well-fed, lusty stallions,
each neighing for another man's wife.[f]
9 Should I not punish them for this?"[g]
declares the LORD.
"Should I not avenge myself
on such a nation as this?
10 "Go through her vineyards and ravage
them,
but do not destroy them completely.
Strip off her branches,
for these people do not belong to the
LORD.
11 The house of Israel and the house of
Judah
have been utterly unfaithful[h] to me,"
declares the LORD.
12 They have lied about the LORD;
they said, "He will do nothing!
No harm will come to us;
we will never see sword or famine.[i]
13 The prophets are but wind
and the word is not in them;
so let what they say be done to them."

14 Therefore this is what the LORD God Almighty says:

"Because the people have spoken these
words,
I will make my words in your mouth[j]
a fire
and these people the wood it
consumes.
15 O house of Israel," declares the LORD,
"I am bringing a distant nation[k]
against you—
an ancient and enduring nation,
a people whose language you do not
know,
whose speech you do not understand.
16 Their quivers are like an open grave;
all of them are mighty warriors.
17 They will devour[l] your harvests and food,
devour[m] your sons and daughters;
they will devour[n] your flocks and herds,
devour your vines and fig trees.
With the sword they will destroy
the fortified cities in which you trust.

18 "Yet even in those days," declares the
LORD, "I will not destroy you completely.
19 And when the people ask,[o] 'Why has the
LORD our God done all this to us?' you will
tell them, 'As you have forsaken me and
served foreign gods in your own land, so

5:9 g Jer 9:9
5:11 h Jer 3:20
5:12 i Jer 14:13
5:14 j Jer 1:9
5:15 k Dt 28:49; Isa 5:26; Jer 4:16
5:17 l Lev 26:16 m Dt 28:32 n Dt 28:31
5:19 o Dt 29:24–26; 1Ki 9:9

now you will serve foreigners[p] in a land not
your own.'

20 "Announce this to the house of Jacob
and proclaim it in Judah:
21 Hear this, you foolish and senseless
people,
who have eyes[q] but do not see,
who have ears but do not hear:[r]
22 Should you not fear me?" declares the
LORD.
"Should you not tremble in my
presence?
I made the sand a boundary for the sea,
an everlasting barrier it cannot cross.
The waves may roll, but they cannot
prevail;
they may roar, but they cannot cross it.
23 But these people have stubborn and
rebellious hearts;
they have turned aside and gone away.
24 They do not say to themselves,
'Let us fear the LORD our God,
who gives autumn and spring rains in
season,
who assures us of the regular weeks of
harvest.'[s]
25 Your wrongdoings have kept these away;
your sins have deprived you of good.

26 "Among my people are wicked men
who lie in wait like men who snare
birds
and like those who set traps to catch
men.
27 Like cages full of birds,
their houses are full of deceit;
they have become rich and powerful
28 and have grown fat[t] and sleek.
Their evil deeds have no limit;
they do not plead the case of the
fatherless[u] to win it,
they do not defend the rights of the
poor.[v]
29 Should I not punish them for this?"
declares the LORD.
"Should I not avenge myself
on such a nation as this?

30 "A horrible[w] and shocking thing
has happened in the land:
31 The prophets prophesy lies,[x]
the priests rule by their own authority,
and my people love it this way.
But what will you do in the end?

## Jerusalem Under Siege

6 "Flee for safety, people of Benjamin!
Flee from Jerusalem!
Sound the trumpet in Tekoa!
Raise the signal over Beth Hakkerem![y]
For disaster looms out of the north,[z]
even terrible destruction.
2 I will destroy the Daughter of Zion,
so beautiful and delicate.
3 Shepherds with their flocks will come
against her;
they will pitch their tents around[a] her,
each tending his own portion."

4 "Prepare for battle against her!
Arise, let us attack at noon!
But, alas, the daylight is fading,
and the shadows of evening grow long.
5 So arise, let us attack at night
and destroy her fortresses!"

6 This is what the LORD Almighty says:

"Cut down the trees
and build siege ramps against
Jerusalem.
This city must be punished;
it is filled with oppression.
7 As a well pours out its water,
so she pours out her wickedness.
Violence[b] and destruction[c] resound in
her;
her sickness and wounds are ever
before me.
8 Take warning, O Jerusalem,
or I will turn away[d] from you
and make your land desolate
so no one can live in it."

9 This is what the LORD Almighty says:

"Let them glean the remnant of Israel
as thoroughly as a vine;
pass your hand over the branches again,
like one gathering grapes."

10 To whom can I speak and give warning?
Who will listen to me?
Their ears are closed[a][e]
so they cannot hear.

[a]10 Hebrew *uncircumcised*

**5:19** p Dt 28:48
**5:21** q Isa 6:10; Eze 12:2 r Mt 13:15
**5:24** s Ge 8:22
**5:28** t Dt 32:15 u Zec 7:10 v Isa 1:23
**5:30** w Hos 6:10
**5:31** x Eze 13:6; Mic 2:11
**6:1** y Ne 3:14 z Jer 4:6
**6:3** a 2Ki 25:4
**6:7** b Ps 55:9; Eze 7:11,23 c Jer 20:8
**6:8** d Hos 9:12
**6:10** e Ac 7:51

The word[f] of the LORD is offensive to them;
they find no pleasure in it.
11 But I am full of the wrath of the LORD,
and I cannot hold it in.

"Pour it out on the children in the street
and on the young men gathered together;
both husband and wife will be caught in it,
and the old, those weighed down with years.
12 Their houses will be turned over to others,[g]
together with their fields and their wives,[h]
when I stretch out my hand
against those who live in the land,"
declares the LORD.
13 "From the least to the greatest,
all are greedy for gain;[i]
prophets and priests alike,
all practice deceit.[j]
14 They dress the wound of my people
as though it were not serious.
'Peace, peace,' they say,
when there is no peace.[k]
15 Are they ashamed of their loathsome conduct?
No, they have no shame at all;
they do not even know how to blush.[l]
So they will fall among the fallen;
they will be brought down when I punish them,"
says the LORD.

16 This is what the LORD says:

"Stand at the crossroads and look;
ask for the ancient paths,[m]
ask where the good way is, and walk in it,
and you will find rest[n] for your souls.
But you said, 'We will not walk in it.'
17 I appointed watchmen over you and said,
'Listen to the sound of the trumpet!'
But you said, 'We will not listen.'
18 Therefore hear, O nations;
observe, O witnesses,
what will happen to them.
19 Hear, O earth:
I am bringing disaster on this people,
the fruit of their schemes,[o]
because they have not listened to my words
and have rejected my law.
20 What do I care about incense from Sheba
or sweet calamus from a distant land?
Your burnt offerings are not acceptable;[p]
your sacrifices[q] do not please me."[r]

21 Therefore this is what the LORD says:

"I will put obstacles before this people.
Fathers and sons alike will stumble over them;
neighbors and friends will perish."

22 This is what the LORD says:

"Look, an army is coming
from the land of the north;
a great nation is being stirred up
from the ends of the earth.
23 They are armed with bow and spear;
they are cruel and show no mercy.
They sound like the roaring sea
as they ride on their horses;
they come like men in battle formation
to attack you, O Daughter of Zion."

24 We have heard reports about them,
and our hands hang limp.
Anguish has gripped us,
pain like that of a woman in labor.[s]
25 Do not go out to the fields
or walk on the roads,
for the enemy has a sword,
and there is terror on every side.
26 O my people, put on sackcloth[t]
and roll in ashes;[u]
mourn with bitter wailing
as for an only son,[v]
for suddenly the destroyer
will come upon us.

27 "I have made you a tester of metals
and my people the ore,
that you may observe
and test their ways.
28 They are all hardened rebels,
going about to slander.
They are bronze and iron;[w]
they all act corruptly.
29 The bellows blow fiercely
to burn away the lead with fire,
but the refining goes on in vain;
the wicked are not purged out.
30 They are called rejected silver,
because the LORD has rejected them."

**6:10** f Jer 20:8
**6:12** g Dt 28:30 h Jer 8:10
**6:13** i Isa 56:11 j Jer 8:10
**6:14** k Jer 8:11; Eze 13:10
**6:15** l Jer 3:3
**6:16** m Jer 18:15 n Mt 11:29
**6:19** o Pr 1:31
**6:20** p Am 5:22 q Mic 6:7–8 r Isa 1:11
**6:24** s Jer 4:31; 50:41–43
**6:26** t Jer 4:8 u Jer 25:34 v Zec 12:10
**6:28** w Eze 22:18

## False Religion Worthless

7 This is the word that came to Jeremiah from the LORD: [2]"Stand at the gate of the LORD's house and there proclaim this message:

" 'Hear the word of the LORD, all you people of Judah who come through these gates to worship the LORD. [3]This is what the LORD Almighty, the God of Israel, says: Reform your ways[x] and your actions, and I will let you live in this place. [4]Do not trust in deceptive[y] words and say, "This is the temple of the LORD, the temple of the LORD, the temple of the LORD!" [5]If you really change your ways and your actions and deal with each other justly,[z] [6]if you do not oppress the alien, the fatherless or the widow and do not shed innocent blood in this place, and if you do not follow other gods[a] to your own harm, [7]then I will let you live in this place, in the land I gave your forefathers for ever and ever. [8]But look, you are trusting in deceptive words that are worthless.

[9]" 'Will you steal and murder, commit adultery and perjury,[a] burn incense to Baal and follow other gods[b] you have not known, [10]and then come and stand before me in this house,[c] which bears my Name, and say, "We are safe"—safe to do all these detestable things? [11]Has this house, which bears my Name, become a den of robbers[d] to you? But I have been watching! declares the LORD.

[12]" 'Go now to the place in Shiloh[e] where I first made a dwelling for my Name, and see what I did[f] to it because of the wickedness of my people Israel. [13]While you were doing all these things, declares the LORD, I spoke to you again and again, but you did not listen;[g] I called you, but you did not answer. [14]Therefore, what I did to Shiloh I will now do to the house that bears my Name, the temple you trust in, the place I gave to you and your fathers. [15]I will thrust you from my presence, just as I did all your brothers, the people of Ephraim.'[h]

[16]"So do not pray for this people nor offer any plea[i] or petition for them; do not plead with me, for I will not listen to you. [17]Do you not see what they are doing in the towns of Judah and in the streets of Jerusalem? [18]The children gather wood, the fathers light the fire, and the women knead the dough and make cakes of bread for the Queen of Heaven. They pour out drink offerings to other gods to provoke me to anger. [19]But am I the one they are provoking? declares the LORD. Are they not rather harming themselves, to their own shame?

[20]" 'Therefore this is what the Sovereign LORD says: My anger and my wrath will be poured out on this place, on man and beast, on the trees of the field and on the fruit of the ground, and it will burn and not be quenched.

[21]" 'This is what the LORD Almighty, the God of Israel, says: Go ahead, add your burnt offerings to your other sacrifices[j] and eat[k] the meat yourselves! [22]For when I brought your forefathers out of Egypt and spoke to them, I did not just give them commands about burnt offerings and sacrifices,[l] [23]but I gave them this command: Obey me, and I will be your God and you will be my people.[m] Walk in all the ways I command you, that it may go well with you. [24]But they did not listen or pay attention; instead, they followed the stubborn inclinations of their evil hearts. They went backward and not forward. [25]From the time your forefathers left Egypt until now, day after day, again and again I sent you my servants the prophets. [26]But they did not listen to me or pay attention. They were stiff-necked and did more evil than their forefathers.'[n]

[27]"When you tell[o] them all this, they will not listen to you; when you call to them, they will not answer. [28]Therefore say to them, 'This is the nation that has not obeyed the LORD its God or responded to correction. Truth has perished; it has vanished from their lips. [29]Cut off[p] your hair and throw it away; take up a lament on the barren heights, for the LORD has rejected and abandoned this generation that is under his wrath.

## The Valley of Slaughter

[30]" 'The people of Judah have done evil in my eyes, declares the LORD. They have set up their detestable idols[q] in the house that bears my Name and have defiled it. [31]They have built the high places of Topheth[r] in the

[a]9 Or *and swear by false gods*

**7:3** x Jer 18:11; 26:13
**7:4** y Mic 3:11
**7:5** z Jer 22:3
**7:6** a Dt 8:19
**7:9** b Ex 20:3
**7:10** c Jer 32:34; Eze 23:38–39
**7:11** d Mt 21:13*
**7:12** e Jos 18:1 f 1Sa 4:10–11,22
**7:13** g Isa 65:12
**7:15** h Ps 78:67
**7:16** i Ex 32:10
**7:21** j Isa 1:11; Am 5:21–22 k Hos 8:13
**7:22** l 1Sa 15:22; Ps 51:16; Hos 6:6
**7:23** m Lev 26:12
**7:26** n Jer 16:12
**7:27** o Eze 2:7
**7:29** p Job 1:20
**7:30** q Eze 7:20–22
**7:31** r 2Ki 23:10

**7:32**
s Jer 19:6
t Jer 19:11

**7:34**
u Isa 24:8
v Rev 18:23

**8:3**
w Job 3:22; Rev 9:6

Valley of Ben Hinnom to burn their sons
and daughters in the fire—something I did
not command, nor did it enter my mind.
32 So beware, the days are coming, declares
the LORD, when people will no longer call it
Topheth or the Valley of Ben Hinnom, but
the Valley of Slaughter,[s] for they will bury[t]
the dead in Topheth until there is no more
room. 33 Then the carcasses of this people
will become food for the birds of the air and
the beasts of the earth, and there will be no
one to frighten them away. 34 I will bring an
end to the sounds[u] of joy and gladness and
to the voices of bride and bridegroom[v] in the
towns of Judah and the streets of Jerusalem,
for the land will become desolate.

8 "'At that time, declares the LORD, the
bones of the kings and officials of Ju-
dah, the bones of the priests and prophets,
and the bones of the people of Jerusalem
will be removed from their graves. 2 They
will be exposed to the sun and the moon and
all the stars of the heavens, which they have
loved and served and which they have fol-
lowed and consulted and worshiped. They
will not be gathered up or buried, but will be
like refuse lying on the ground. 3 Wherever
I banish them, all the survivors of this evil
nation will prefer death to life,[w] declares the
LORD Almighty.'

## Sin and Punishment

4 "Say to them, 'This is what the LORD says:

"'When men fall down, do they not get up?
When a man turns away, does he not return?
5 Why then have these people turned away?
Why does Jerusalem always turn away?
They cling to deceit;
they refuse to return.
6 I have listened attentively,
but they do not say what is right.
No one repents of his wickedness,
saying, "What have I done?"
Each pursues his own course
like a horse charging into battle.
7 Even the stork in the sky
knows her appointed seasons,
and the dove, the swift and the thrush
observe the time of their migration.
But my people do not know[x]
the requirements of the LORD.

8 "'How can you say, "We are wise,
for we have the law[y] of the LORD,"
when actually the lying pen of the scribes
has handled it falsely?
9 The wise will be put to shame;
they will be dismayed and trapped.
Since they have rejected the word of the LORD,
what kind of wisdom do they have?
10 Therefore I will give their wives to other men
and their fields to new owners.
From the least to the greatest,
all are greedy for gain;[z]
prophets and priests alike,
all practice deceit.
11 They dress the wound of my people
as though it were not serious.
"Peace, peace," they say,
when there is no peace.[a]
12 Are they ashamed of their loathsome conduct?
No, they have no shame[b] at all;
they do not even know how to blush.
So they will fall among the fallen;
they will be brought down when they are punished,
says the LORD.

13 "'I will take away their harvest,
declares the LORD.
There will be no grapes on the vine.[c]
There will be no figs on the tree,
and their leaves will wither.[d]
What I have given them
will be taken from them.[a]'"

14 "Why are we sitting here?
Gather together!
Let us flee to the fortified cities[e]
and perish there!
For the LORD our God has doomed us to perish
and given us poisoned water[f] to drink,
because we have sinned[g] against him.
15 We hoped for peace

**8:7**
x Isa 1:3; Jer 5:4–5

**8:8**
y Ro 2:17

**8:10**
z Isa 56:11

**8:11**
a Jer 6:14

**8:12**
b Jer 3:3

**8:13**
c Joel 1:7
d Mt 21:19

**8:14**
e Jer 4:5
f Jer 9:15
g Jer 14:7,20

[a] 13 The meaning of the Hebrew for this sentence is uncertain.

8:15 h Jer 14:19
8:16 i Jer 4:15
8:17 j Ps 58:5
8:22 k Ge 37:25
9:1 l Isa 22:4
9:2 m Jer 5:7–8
9:3 n Ps 64:3

but no good has come,
for a time of healing
but there was only terror.[h]
16 The snorting of the enemy's horses
is heard from Dan;[i]
at the neighing of their stallions
the whole land trembles.
They have come to devour
the land and everything in it,
the city and all who live there."
17 "See, I will send venomous snakes among
you,
vipers that cannot be charmed,[j]
and they will bite you,"
declares the LORD.

18 O my Comforter[a] in sorrow,
my heart is faint within me.
19 Listen to the cry of my people
from a land far away:
"Is the LORD not in Zion?
Is her King no longer there?"

"Why have they provoked me to anger
with their images,
with their worthless foreign idols?"

20 "The harvest is past,
the summer has ended,
and we are not saved."
21 Since my people are crushed, I am
crushed;
I mourn, and horror grips me.
22 Is there no balm in Gilead?[k]
Is there no physician there?
Why then is there no healing
for the wound of my people?

9 [1]Oh, that my head were a spring of
water
and my eyes a fountain of tears!
I would weep day and night
for the slain of my people.[l]
2 Oh, that I had in the desert
a lodging place for travelers,
so that I might leave my people
and go away from them;
for they are all adulterers,[m]
a crowd of unfaithful people.

3 "They make ready their tongue
like a bow, to shoot lies;[n]
it is not by truth
that they triumph[b] in the land.
They go from one sin to another;
they do not acknowledge me,"
declares the LORD.
4 "Beware of your friends;
do not trust your brothers.[o]
For every brother is a deceiver,[c]
and every friend a slanderer.
5 Friend deceives friend,
and no one speaks the truth.
They have taught their tongues to lie;
they weary themselves with sinning.
6 You[d] live in the midst of deception;[p]
in their deceit they refuse to
acknowledge me,"
declares the LORD.

7 Therefore this is what the LORD Almighty
says:

"See, I will refine[q] and test them,
for what else can I do
because of the sin of my people?
8 Their tongue is a deadly arrow;
it speaks with deceit.
With his mouth each speaks cordially to
his neighbor,
but in his heart he sets a trap for him.
9 Should I not punish them for this?"
declares the LORD.
"Should I not avenge[r] myself
on such a nation as this?"

10 I will weep and wail for the mountains
and take up a lament concerning the
desert pastures.
They are desolate and untraveled,
and the lowing of cattle is not heard.
The birds of the air[s] have fled
and the animals are gone.
11 "I will make Jerusalem a heap of ruins,
a haunt of jackals;[t]
and I will lay waste the towns of Judah
so no one can live there."[u]

12 What man is wise enough to under-
stand this? Who has been instructed by the
LORD and can explain it? Why has the land
been ruined and laid waste like a desert that
no one can cross?
13 The LORD said, "It is because they have

9:4 o Mic 7:5–6
9:6 p Jer 5:27
9:7 q Isa 1:25
9:9 r Jer 5:9,29
9:10 s Jer 4:25; Hos 4:3
9:11 t Isa 34:13 u Isa 25:2

[a]18 The meaning of the Hebrew for this word is uncertain. [b]3 Or *lies; / they are not valiant for truth* [c]4 Or *a deceiving Jacob* [d]6 That is, Jeremiah (the Hebrew is singular)

Inspire

# THE PARADOX OF LIFE AND SUFFERING

Suffering covers a wide spectrum of circumstances. A woman's life is inextricably tied to suffering, making it impossible to live without the experience. Someone else's suffering may not be the same as yours, but you share a common bond through the mutual feelings suffering produces. Suffering may often be characterized as an experience of desolation—an emptiness, a barrenness, an aloneness. Suffering may take the form of an experience of separation from God, from other people and even from engagement in living. Suffering is often an experience of desperation—a longing for life as we once knew it—often accompanied by the acknowledgment and understanding that life will, in fact, never be quite the same. Suffering, even in its lesser degrees, could be termed "life-threatening." It threatens our souls, our minds and our hearts. The resulting disappointment and disillusionment can poison our thoughts and feelings, threatening our ability to live an abundant life.

The Lord gave the prophet Jeremiah the ability to envision the great suffering of his people when they would be conquered and taken captive to Babylon (see Jer 8:18–22). African slaves in America experienced untold suffering. Victims of domestic violence endure tragic and often silent suffering. People wrestling with addictions suffer. And Jesus suffered. Suffering is inescapable, yet even in our worst anguish we can embrace the sure knowledge that the sovereignty of God prevails. God is able to instill meaning into our most bitter pain. When Jeremiah cried out in his pain on behalf of his people, he still addressed God as "my Comforter in sorrow" (Jer 8:18).

When we suffer, we tend to become disheartened as we search for understanding. We question and cry out in despair, only to discover a self we may not want to recognize—an angry, hateful, vengeful self, but a true self nonetheless. In addition, we are likely to encounter a weak, humbled, needy, dependent, longing aspect of our self. All the while, in and through our suffering, we discover a self who understands, perhaps for the first time, that without God there is no life.

Faith is the thread that maintains the balance between our life as a whole and our suffering. In our suffering, faith becomes the hinge to the door of life, the vein that carries life to our soul. Our affliction comes as a test of our profession of faith in God through Christ Jesus. And with it comes a unique opportunity for us to glorify God.

—L. Wooden

For the next Inspire note, go to page 893.

## read

Jeremiah 8:13–22; see also Job 1:6–22; 2 Corinthians 4:7–18; 12:1–10; James 1:2–12; 1 Peter 5:6–11.

See also the Inspire Notes "Courage to Heal," "Suffering," "Distress," "Waiting on God," "Praying for Patience" and "Peace," and the Women of the Bible Notes "Rizpah: A Grieving Mother," "The Shunammite Woman: Our Sister's Grief Is Our Grief," "Job's Wife: She Was Tested Too" and "Ezekiel's Wife: On God's Stage."

## WOMAN of COLOR

How do you handle suffering?

9:15 v Jer 8:14
9:16 w Lev 26:33 x Dt 28:64 y Eze 5:2 z Jer 44:27
9:17 a Ecc 12:5; Am 5:16
9:18 b Jer 14:17
9:22 c Jer 8:2
9:23 d Ecc 9:11

forsaken my law, which I set before them;
they have not obeyed me or followed my law.
14 Instead, they have followed the stubborn-
ness of their hearts; they have followed the
Baals, as their fathers taught them." 15 There-
fore, this is what the LORD Almighty, the God
of Israel, says: "See, I will make this people
eat bitter food and drink poisoned water.[v]
16 I will scatter them among nations[w] that
neither they nor their fathers have known,[x]
and I will pursue them with the sword[y] until
I have destroyed them."[z]

17 This is what the LORD Almighty says:

"Consider now! Call for the wailing
women[a] to come;
send for the most skillful of them.
18 Let them come quickly
and wail over us
till our eyes overflow with tears
and water streams from our eyelids.[b]
19 The sound of wailing is heard from Zion:
'How ruined we are!
How great is our shame!
We must leave our land
because our houses are in ruins.' "

20 Now, O women, hear the word of the
LORD;
open your ears to the words of his
mouth.
Teach your daughters how to wail;
teach one another a lament.
21 Death has climbed in through our
windows
and has entered our fortresses;
it has cut off the children from the streets
and the young men from the public
squares.

22 Say, "This is what the LORD declares:

" 'The dead bodies of men will lie
like refuse[c] on the open field,
like cut grain behind the reaper,
with no one to gather them.' "

23 This is what the LORD says:

"Let not the wise man boast of his
wisdom[d]
or the strong man boast of his strength
or the rich man boast of his riches,
24 but let him who boasts boast[e] about this:
that he understands and knows me,
that I am the LORD,[f] who exercises
kindness,[g]
justice and righteousness on earth,
for in these I delight,"
declares the LORD.

9:24 e 1Co 1:31* f 2Co 10:17* g Ps 51:1; Mic 7:18
9:25 h Ro 2:8–9
9:26 i Jer 25:23 j Lev 26:41; Ro 2:28
10:2 k Lev 20:23
10:3 l Isa 40:19
10:4 m Isa 41:7
10:5 n 1Co 12:2

*God,*

*please help me to do what you have called me to do. Help me not to look to others for approval, but to seek ever to please you. I need your help day by day in this area.*

*Amen*

JEREMIAH 9:23–24

25 "The days are coming," declares the
LORD, "when I will punish all who are cir-
cumcised only in the flesh[h]— 26 Egypt, Ju-
dah, Edom, Ammon, Moab and all who live
in the desert in distant places.[a][i] For all these
nations are really uncircumcised, and even
the whole house of Israel is uncircumcised
in heart.[j]"

## God and Idols

10 Hear what the LORD says to you, O
house of Israel. 2 This is what the
LORD says:

"Do not learn the ways of the nations[k]
or be terrified by signs in the sky,
though the nations are terrified by
them.
3 For the customs of the peoples are
worthless;
they cut a tree out of the forest,
and a craftsman[l] shapes it with his
chisel.
4 They adorn it with silver and gold;
they fasten it with hammer and nails
so it will not totter.[m]
5 Like a scarecrow in a melon patch,
their idols cannot speak;[n]
they must be carried

[a]26 Or *desert and who clip the hair by their foreheads*

10:5
o Ps 115:5,7
p Isa 41:24; 46:7
10:9
q Ps 115:4
10:11
r Ps 96:5; Isa 2:18
10:12
s Ge 1:1,8;
Isa 40:22
10:13
t Ps 135:7

because they cannot walk.[o]
Do not fear them;
they can do no harm
nor can they do any good."[p]

[6] No one is like you, O LORD;
you are great,
and your name is mighty in power.
[7] Who should not revere you,
O King of the nations?
This is your due.
Among all the wise men of the nations
and in all their kingdoms,
there is no one like you.
[8] They are all senseless and foolish;
they are taught by worthless wooden idols.
[9] Hammered silver is brought from Tarshish
and gold from Uphaz.
What the craftsman and goldsmith have made[q]
is then dressed in blue and purple—
all made by skilled workers.
[10] But the LORD is the true God;
he is the living God, the eternal King.
When he is angry, the earth trembles;
the nations cannot endure his wrath.

[11] "Tell them this: 'These gods, who did
not make the heavens and the earth, will
perish[r] from the earth and from under
the heavens.'"[a]

[12] But God made the earth by his power;
he founded the world by his wisdom
and stretched out the heavens[s] by his understanding.
[13] When he thunders, the waters in the heavens roar;
he makes clouds rise from the ends of the earth.
He sends lightning with the rain[t]
and brings out the wind from his storehouses.

[14] Everyone is senseless and without knowledge;
every goldsmith is shamed by his idols.
His images are a fraud;
they have no breath in them.
[15] They are worthless, the objects of mockery;
when their judgment comes, they will perish.
[16] He who is the Portion[u] of Jacob is not like these,
for he is the Maker of all things,
including Israel, the tribe of his inheritance—
the LORD Almighty is his name.

## Coming Destruction

[17] Gather up your belongings[v] to leave the land,
you who live under siege.
[18] For this is what the LORD says:
"At this time I will hurl[w] out
those who live in this land;
I will bring distress on them
so that they may be captured."
[19] Woe to me because of my injury!
My wound is incurable!
Yet I said to myself,
"This is my sickness, and I must endure[x] it."
[20] My tent[y] is destroyed;
all its ropes are snapped.
My sons are gone from me and are no more;
no one is left now to pitch my tent
or to set up my shelter.
[21] The shepherds are senseless
and do not inquire of the LORD;
so they do not prosper
and all their flock is scattered.[z]
[22] Listen! The report is coming—
a great commotion from the land of the north!
It will make the towns of Judah desolate,
a haunt of jackals.[a]

## Jeremiah's Prayer

[23] I know, O LORD, that a man's life is not his own;
it is not for man to direct his steps.
[24] Correct me, LORD, but only with justice—
not in your anger,[b]
lest you reduce me to nothing.
[25] Pour out your wrath on the nations
that do not acknowledge you,

10:16
u Dt 32:9
10:17
v Eze 12:3–12
10:18
w 1Sa 25:29
10:19
x Mic 7:9
10:20
y Jer 4:20
10:21
z Jer 23:2
10:22
a Jer 9:11
10:24
b Ps 6:1

[a]11 The text of this verse is in Aramaic.

on the peoples who do not call on your
name.
For they have devoured[c] Jacob;
they have devoured him completely
and destroyed his homeland.[d]

## The Covenant Is Broken

11 This is the word that came to Jeremiah from the LORD: 2“Listen to the terms of this covenant and tell them to the people of Judah and to those who live in Jerusalem. 3Tell them that this is what the LORD, the God of Israel, says: ‘Cursed[e] is the man who does not obey the terms of this covenant— 4the terms I commanded your forefathers when I brought them out of Egypt, out of the iron-smelting furnace.[f]’ I said, ‘Obey[g] me and do everything I command you, and you will be my people,[h] and I will be your God. 5Then I will fulfill the oath I swore[i] to your forefathers, to give them a land flowing with milk and honey’—the land you possess today.”

I answered, “Amen, LORD.”

6The LORD said to me, “Proclaim all these words in the towns of Judah and in the streets of Jerusalem: ‘Listen to the terms of this covenant and follow[j] them. 7From the time I brought your forefathers up from Egypt until today, I warned them again and again, saying, “Obey me.” 8But they did not listen or pay attention; instead, they followed the stubbornness of their evil hearts. So I brought on them all the curses of the covenant I had commanded them to follow but that they did not keep.’”

9Then the LORD said to me, “There is a conspiracy[k] among the people of Judah and those who live in Jerusalem. 10They have returned to the sins of their forefathers, who refused to listen to my words. They have followed other gods[l] to serve them. Both the house of Israel and the house of Judah have broken the covenant I made with their forefathers. 11Therefore this is what the LORD says: ‘I will bring on them a disaster they cannot escape. Although they cry[m] out to me, I will not listen to them. 12The towns of Judah and the people of Jerusalem will go and cry out to the gods to whom they burn incense, but they will not help them at all when disaster[n] strikes. 13You have as many gods as you have towns, O Judah; and the altars you have set up to burn incense to that shameful god Baal are as many as the streets of Jerusalem.’

14“Do not pray[o] for this people nor offer any plea or petition for them, because I will not listen when they call to me in the time of their distress.

15 “What is my beloved doing in my temple
as she works out her evil schemes with
many?
Can consecrated meat avert ⌞your
punishment⌟?
When you engage in your wickedness,
then you rejoice.[a]”

16 The LORD called you a thriving olive tree
with fruit beautiful in form.
But with the roar of a mighty storm
he will set it on fire,[p]
and its branches will be broken.

17The LORD Almighty, who planted[q] you, has decreed disaster for you, because the house of Israel and the house of Judah have done evil and provoked me to anger by burning incense to Baal.

## Plot Against Jeremiah

18Because the LORD revealed their plot to me, I knew it, for at that time he showed me what they were doing. 19I had been like a gentle lamb led to the slaughter; I did not realize that they had plotted against me, saying,

“Let us destroy the tree and its fruit;
let us cut him off from the land of the
living,
that his name be remembered[r] no
more.”
20 But, O LORD Almighty, you who judge
righteously
and test the heart and mind,[s]
let me see your vengeance upon them,
for to you I have committed my cause.

21“Therefore this is what the LORD says about the men of Anathoth who are seeking your life[t] and saying, ‘Do not prophesy in the name of the LORD or you will die by our hands’— 22therefore this is what the LORD

**10:25** c Jer 8:16 d Ps 79:6–7
**11:3** e Dt 27:26
**11:4** f Dt 4:20 g Ex 24:8 h Jer 7:23
**11:5** i Dt 7:12
**11:6** j Dt 15:5; Ro 2:13; Jas 1:22
**11:9** k Eze 22:25
**11:10** l Jdg 2:12–13
**11:11** m Jer 14:12
**11:12** n Dt 32:37
**11:14** o Ex 32:10
**11:16** p Jer 21:14
**11:17** q Isa 5:2
**11:19** r Ps 83:4
**11:20** s Ps 7:9
**11:21** t Jer 12:6

[a]15 Or *Could consecrated meat avert your punishment? / Then you would rejoice*

**11:22** u Jer 18:21
**11:23** v Jer 23:12
**12:1** w Jer 5:27–28
**12:2** x Jer 11:17
**12:3** y Ps 139:1–4; Jer 11:20
**12:4** z Joel 1:10–12
**12:6** a Pr 26:24–25; Jer 9:4

Almighty says: 'I will punish them. Their
young men[u] will die by the sword, their sons
and daughters by famine. 23 Not even a rem-
nant will be left to them, because I will bring
disaster on the men of Anathoth in the year
of their punishment.[v]'"

## Jeremiah's Complaint

12 You are always righteous, O LORD,
when I bring a case before you.
Yet I would speak with you about your
justice:
Why does the way of the wicked
prosper?[w]
Why do all the faithless live at ease?
2 You have planted[x] them, and they have
taken root;
they grow and bear fruit.
You are always on their lips
but far from their hearts.
3 Yet you know me, O LORD;
you see me and test[y] my thoughts
about you.
Drag them off like sheep to be butchered!
Set them apart for the day of slaughter!
4 How long will the land lie parched[a]
and the grass in every field be
withered?[z]
Because those who live in it are wicked,
the animals and birds have perished.
Moreover, the people are saying,
"He will not see what happens to us."

## God's Answer

5 "If you have raced with men on foot
and they have worn you out,
how can you compete with horses?
If you stumble in safe country,[b]
how will you manage in the thickets
by[c] the Jordan?
6 Your brothers, your own family—
even they have betrayed you;
they have raised a loud cry against
you.[a]
Do not trust them,
though they speak well of you.
7 "I will forsake my house,
abandon my inheritance;
I will give the one I love
into the hands of her enemies.
8 My inheritance has become to me
like a lion in the forest.
She roars at me;
therefore I hate her.[b]
9 Has not my inheritance become to me
like a speckled bird of prey
that other birds of prey surround and
attack?
Go and gather all the wild beasts;
bring them to devour.[c]
10 Many shepherds will ruin my vineyard
and trample down my field;
they will turn my pleasant field
into a desolate wasteland.[d]
11 It will be made a wasteland,
parched and desolate before me;[e]
the whole land will be laid waste
because there is no one who cares.
12 Over all the barren heights in the desert
destroyers will swarm,
for the sword of the LORD will devour
from one end of the land to the other;
no one will be safe.
13 They will sow wheat but reap thorns;
they will wear themselves out but gain
nothing.[f]
So bear the shame of your harvest
because of the LORD's fierce anger."

14 This is what the LORD says: "As for all my
wicked neighbors who seize the inheritance
I gave my people Israel, I will uproot[g] them
from their lands and I will uproot the house
of Judah from among them. 15 But after I up-
root them, I will again have compassion and
will bring[h] each of them back to his own in-
heritance and his own country. 16 And if they
learn well the ways of my people and swear
by my name, saying, 'As surely as the LORD
lives'[i]—even as they once taught my people
to swear by Baal—then they will be estab-
lished among my people. 17 But if any nation
does not listen, I will completely uproot and
destroy[j] it," declares the LORD.

## A Linen Belt

13 This is what the LORD said to me:
"Go and buy a linen belt and put it
around your waist, but do not let it touch wa-
ter." 2 So I bought a belt, as the LORD directed,
and put it around my waist.

**12:8** b Hos 9:15
**12:9** c Isa 56:9
**12:10** d Isa 5:1–7
**12:11** e Isa 42:25
**12:13** f Lev 26:20; Dt 28:38; Mic 6:15
**12:14** g Zec 2:7–9
**12:15** h Am 9:14–15
**12:16** i Jer 4:2
**12:17** j Isa 60:12

[a] 4 Or *land mourn* [b] 5 Or *If you put your trust in a land of safety* [c] 5 Or *the flooding of*

**13:5** k Ex 40:16
**13:9** l Lev 26:19
**13:10** m Jer 11:8; 16:12 n Jer 9:14
**13:11** o Jer 32:20; 33:9 p Ex 19:5–6
**13:13** q Isa 51:17; 63:6
**13:14** r Jer 16:5

3 Then the word of the LORD came to me
a second time: 4 "Take the belt you bought
and are wearing around your waist, and go
now to Perath[a] and hide it there in a crevice
in the rocks." 5 So I went and hid it at Perath,
as the LORD told me.[k]
6 Many days later the LORD said to me, "Go
now to Perath and get the belt I told you to
hide there." 7 So I went to Perath and dug up
the belt and took it from the place where I
had hidden it, but now it was ruined and
completely useless.
8 Then the word of the LORD came to me:
9 "This is what the LORD says: 'In the same
way I will ruin the pride of Judah and the
great pride[l] of Jerusalem. 10 These wicked
people, who refuse to listen to my words,
who follow the stubbornness of their
hearts[m] and go after other gods[n] to serve
and worship them, will be like this belt—
completely useless! 11 For as a belt is bound
around a man's waist, so I bound the whole
house of Israel and the whole house of Judah
to me,' declares the LORD, 'to be my people
for my renown[o] and praise and honor.[p] But
they have not listened.'

## Wineskins

12 "Say to them: 'This is what the LORD, the
God of Israel, says: Every wineskin should
be filled with wine.' And if they say to you,
'Don't we know that every wineskin should
be filled with wine?' 13 then tell them, 'This
is what the LORD says: I am going to fill with
drunkenness[q] all who live in this land, in-
cluding the kings who sit on David's throne,
the priests, the prophets and all those liv-
ing in Jerusalem. 14 I will smash them one
against the other, fathers and sons alike,
declares the LORD. I will allow no pity or
mercy or compassion[r] to keep me from de-
stroying them.'"

## Threat of Captivity

15 Hear and pay attention,
do not be arrogant,
for the LORD has spoken.
16 Give glory to the LORD your God
before he brings the darkness,
before your feet stumble
on the darkening hills.
You hope for light,
but he will turn it to thick darkness
and change it to deep gloom.[s]
17 But if you do not listen,
I will weep in secret
because of your pride;
my eyes will weep bitterly,
overflowing with tears,[t]
because the LORD's flock will be taken
captive.[u]

18 Say to the king and to the queen mother,
"Come down from your thrones,
for your glorious crowns
will fall from your heads."
19 The cities in the Negev will be shut up,
and there will be no one to open them.
All Judah[v] will be carried into exile,
carried completely away.

20 Lift up your eyes and see
those who are coming from the
north.[w]
Where is the flock that was entrusted to
you,
the sheep of which you boasted?
21 What will you say when ⌞the LORD⌟ sets
over you
those you cultivated as your special
allies?
Will not pain grip you
like that of a woman in labor?
22 And if you ask yourself,
"Why has this happened to me?"—
it is because of your many sins[x]
that your skirts have been torn off
and your body mistreated.[y]
23 Can the Ethiopian[b] change his skin
or the leopard its spots?
Neither can you do good
who are accustomed to doing evil.

24 "I will scatter you like chaff
driven by the desert wind.
25 This is your lot,
the portion[z] I have decreed for you,"
declares the LORD,
"because you have forgotten me
and trusted in false gods.
26 I will pull up your skirts over your face
that your shame may be seen[a]—
27 your adulteries and lustful neighings,

**13:16** s Isa 59:9
**13:17** t Jer 9:1 u Jer 14:18
**13:19** v Jer 20:4
**13:20** w Jer 6:22
**13:22** x Jer 16:10–12 y Eze 16:37; Na 3:5–6
**13:25** z Job 20:29
**13:26** a La 1:8

[a]4 Or possibly *the Euphrates*; also in verses 5–7 [b]23 Hebrew *Cushite* (probably a person from the upper Nile region)

your shameless prostitution![b]
I have seen your detestable acts
on the hills and in the fields.
Woe to you, O Jerusalem!
How long will you be unclean?"

## Drought, Famine, Sword

14 This is the word of the LORD to Jeremiah concerning the drought:

2 "Judah mourns,[c]
her cities languish;
they wail for the land,
and a cry goes up from Jerusalem.
3 The nobles send their servants for water;
they go to the cisterns
but find no water.[d]
They return with their jars unfilled;
dismayed and despairing,
they cover their heads.[e]
4 The ground is cracked
because there is no rain in the land;
the farmers are dismayed
and cover their heads.
5 Even the doe in the field
deserts her newborn fawn
because there is no grass.[f]
6 Wild donkeys stand on the barren heights[g]
and pant like jackals;
their eyesight fails
for lack of pasture."

7 Although our sins testify against us,
O LORD, do something for the sake of
your name.
For our backsliding is great;
we have sinned against you.
8 O Hope[h] of Israel,
its Savior in times of distress,
why are you like a stranger in the land,
like a traveler who stays only a night?
9 Why are you like a man taken by
surprise,
like a warrior powerless to save?
You are among us, O LORD,
and we bear your name;
do not forsake us!

10 This is what the LORD says about this people:

"They greatly love to wander;
they do not restrain their feet.[i]
So the LORD does not accept them;
he will now remember their
wickedness
and punish them for their sins."[j]

11 Then the LORD said to me, "Do not
pray[k] for the well-being of this people. 12 Al-
though they fast, I will not listen to their
cry;[l] though they offer burnt offerings[m] and
grain offerings, I will not accept[n] them. In-
stead, I will destroy them with the sword,
famine and plague."

13 But I said, "Ah, Sovereign LORD, the
prophets keep telling them, 'You will not see
the sword or suffer famine.[o] Indeed, I will
give you lasting peace in this place.' "

14 Then the LORD said to me, "The proph-
ets are prophesying lies in my name. I have
not sent them or appointed them or spoken
to them. They are prophesying to you false
visions, divinations, idolatries[a] and the de-
lusions of their own minds. 15 Therefore, this
is what the LORD says about the prophets
who are prophesying in my name: I did not
send them, yet they are saying, 'No sword
or famine will touch this land.' Those same
prophets will perish by sword and famine.[p]
16 And the people they are prophesying to
will be thrown out into the streets of Jerusa-
lem because of the famine and sword. There
will be no one to bury them or their wives,
their sons or their daughters. I will pour out
on them the calamity they deserve.

17 "Speak this word to them:

" 'Let my eyes overflow with tears[q]
night and day without ceasing;
for my virgin daughter—my people—
has suffered a grievous wound,
a crushing blow.
18 If I go into the country,
I see those slain by the sword;
if I go into the city,
I see the ravages of famine.[r]
Both prophet and priest
have gone to a land they know not.' "

19 Have you rejected Judah completely?
Do you despise Zion?
Why have you afflicted us
so that we cannot be healed?[s]
We hoped for peace

[a]14 Or *visions, worthless divinations*

**13:27** b Jer 2:20
**14:2** c Isa 3:26; Jer 8:21
**14:3** d 2Ki 18:31 e 2Sa 15:30
**14:5** f Isa 15:6
**14:6** g Jer 2:24
**14:8** h Jer 17:13
**14:10** i Jer 2:25 j Hos 8:13
**14:11** k Ex 32:10
**14:12** l Isa 1:15 m Jer 7:21 n Jer 6:20
**14:13** o Jer 5:12
**14:15** p Jer 5:12–13
**14:17** q Jer 9:1
**14:18** r Eze 7:15
**14:19** s Jer 30:12–13

**14:19** t Jer 8:15
**14:21** u Jer 3:17
**15:1** v Ex 32:11 w 1Sa 7:9 x Jer 7:16; Eze 14:14,20
**15:3** y Lev 26:16 z Dt 28:26
**15:4** a Dt 28:25 b 2Ki 23:26–27
**15:5** c Isa 51:19
**15:6** d Jer 6:19; 7:24

but no good has come,
for a time of healing
but there is only terror.[t]
20 O LORD, we acknowledge our wickedness
and the guilt of our fathers;
we have indeed sinned against you.
21 For the sake of your name do not
despise us;
do not dishonor your glorious throne.[u]
Remember your covenant with us
and do not break it.
22 Do any of the worthless idols of the
nations bring rain?
Do the skies themselves send down
showers?
No, it is you, O LORD our God.
Therefore our hope is in you,
for you are the one who does all this.

15 Then the LORD said to me: "Even if
Moses[v] and Samuel[w] were to stand
before me, my heart would not go out to this
people.[x] Send them away from my presence!
Let them go! 2 And if they ask you, 'Where
shall we go?' tell them, 'This is what the
LORD says:

" 'Those destined for death, to death;
those for the sword, to the sword;
those for starvation, to starvation;
those for captivity, to captivity.'

3 "I will send four kinds of destroyers[y]
against them," declares the LORD, "the sword
to kill and the dogs to drag away and the
birds[z] of the air and the beasts of the earth
to devour and destroy. 4 I will make them
abhorrent to all the kingdoms of the earth[a]
because of what Manasseh[b] son of Hezekiah
king of Judah did in Jerusalem.

5 "Who will have pity[c] on you,
O Jerusalem?
Who will mourn for you?
Who will stop to ask how you are?
6 You have rejected[d] me," declares the LORD.
"You keep on backsliding.
So I will lay hands on you and destroy
you;
I can no longer show compassion.
7 I will winnow them with a winnowing
fork
at the city gates of the land.
I will bring bereavement and destruction
on my people,[e]
for they have not changed their ways.
8 I will make their widows more numerous
than the sand of the sea.
At midday I will bring a destroyer
against the mothers of their young
men;
suddenly I will bring down on them
anguish and terror.
9 The mother of seven will grow faint[f]
and breathe her last.
Her sun will set while it is still day;
she will be disgraced and humiliated.
I will put the survivors to the sword
before their enemies,"
declares the LORD.

10 Alas, my mother, that you gave me birth,[g]
a man with whom the whole land
strives and contends!
I have neither lent nor borrowed,
yet everyone curses me.

11 The LORD said,

"Surely I will deliver you for a good
purpose;
surely I will make your enemies plead
with you
in times of disaster and times of
distress.

12 "Can a man break iron—
iron from the north—or bronze?
13 Your wealth and your treasures
I will give as plunder, without charge,[h]
because of all your sins
throughout your country.
14 I will enslave you to your enemies
in[a] a land you do not know,[i]
for my anger will kindle a fire[j]
that will burn against you."

15 You understand, O LORD;
remember me and care for me.
Avenge me on my persecutors.[k]
You are long-suffering—do not take me
away;
think of how I suffer reproach for your
sake.[l]
16 When your words came, I ate[m] them;

**15:7** e Jer 18:21
**15:9** f 1Sa 2:5
**15:10** g Job 3:1
**15:13** h Ps 44:12
**15:14** i Jer 16:13 j Dt 32:22
**15:15** k Jer 12:3 l Ps 69:7–9
**15:16** m Eze 3:3

[a]14 Some Hebrew manuscripts, Septuagint and Syriac (see also Jer. 17:4); most Hebrew manuscripts *I will cause your enemies to bring you / into*

**15:17** n Ps 1:1; 26:4–5; Jer 16:8
**15:18** o Jer 30:15
**15:20** p Jer 20:11
**16:4** q Ps 83:10 r Jer 15:3; 34:20

they were my joy and my heart's
delight,
for I bear your name,
O LORD God Almighty.
17 I never sat[n] in the company of revelers,
never made merry with them;
I sat alone because your hand was on me
and you had filled me with
indignation.
18 Why is my pain unending
and my wound grievous and
incurable?[o]
Will you be to me like a deceptive brook,
like a spring that fails?

19 Therefore this is what the LORD says:

"If you repent, I will restore you
that you may serve me;
if you utter worthy, not worthless, words,
you will be my spokesman.
Let this people turn to you,
but you must not turn to them.
20 I will make you a wall to this people,
a fortified wall of bronze;
they will fight against you
but will not overcome you,
for I am with you
to rescue and save you,"[p]
declares the LORD.
21 "I will save you from the hands of the
wicked
and redeem you from the grasp of the
cruel."

## Day of Disaster

**16** Then the word of the LORD came to me: 2 "You must not marry and have sons or daughters in this place." 3 For this is what the LORD says about the sons and daughters born in this land and about the women who are their mothers and the men who are their fathers: 4 "They will die of deadly diseases. They will not be mourned or buried but will be like refuse lying on the ground.[q] They will perish by sword and famine, and their dead bodies will become food for the birds of the air and the beasts of the earth."[r]

5 For this is what the LORD says: "Do not enter a house where there is a funeral meal; do not go to mourn or show sympathy, because I have withdrawn my blessing, my love and my pity from this people," declares the LORD. 6 "Both high and low will die in this land. They will not be buried or mourned, and no one will cut himself or shave[s] his head for them. 7 No one will offer food to comfort those who mourn for the dead—not even for a father or a mother—nor will anyone give them a drink to console them.

8 "And do not enter a house where there is feasting and sit down to eat and drink. 9 For this is what the LORD Almighty, the God of Israel, says: Before your eyes and in your days I will bring an end to the sounds[t] of joy and gladness and to the voices of bride and bridegroom in this place.[u]

10 "When you tell these people all this and they ask you, 'Why has the LORD decreed such a great disaster against us? What wrong have we done? What sin have we committed against the LORD our God?'[v] 11 then say to them, 'It is because your fathers forsook me,' declares the LORD, 'and followed other gods and served and worshiped them. They forsook me and did not keep my law.[w] 12 But you have behaved more wickedly than your fathers.[x] See how each of you is following the stubbornness of his evil heart[y] instead of obeying me. 13 So I will throw you out of this land into a land neither you nor your fathers have known,[z] and there you will serve other gods day and night, for I will show you no favor.'

14 "However, the days are coming," declares the LORD, "when men will no longer say, 'As surely as the LORD lives, who brought the Israelites up out of Egypt,'[a] 15 but they will say, 'As surely as the LORD lives, who brought the Israelites up out of the land of the north and out of all the countries where he had banished them.' For I will restore[b] them to the land I gave their forefathers.

16 "But now I will send for many fishermen," declares the LORD, "and they will catch them.[c] After that I will send for many hunters, and they will hunt them down on every mountain and hill and from the crevices of the rocks. 17 My eyes are on all their ways; they are not hidden from me, nor is their sin concealed from my eyes. 18 I will repay them double for their wickedness and their sin, because they have defiled my land with the lifeless forms of their vile

**16:6** s Jer 41:5; 47:5
**16:9** t Hos 2:11 u Rev 18:23
**16:10** v Dt 29:24; Jer 5:19
**16:11** w Jer 22:9
**16:12** x Jer 7:26 y Jer 13:10
**16:13** z Dt 28:36
**16:14** a Jer 23:7–8
**16:15** b Jer 24:6
**16:16** c Am 4:2; Hab 1:14–15

16:20
d Isa 37:19; Jer 2:11

17:1
e Job 19:24
f Pr 3:3; 2Co 3:3

17:4
g Jer 15:14

17:5
h Isa 30:1–3

17:6
i Dt 29:23

images and have filled my inheritance with their detestable idols."

19 O LORD, my strength and my fortress,
my refuge in time of distress,
to you the nations will come
from the ends of the earth and say,
"Our fathers possessed nothing but false gods,
worthless idols that did them no good.
20 Do men make their own gods?
Yes, but they are not gods!"[d]
21 "Therefore I will teach them—
this time I will teach them
my power and might.
Then they will know
that my name is the LORD.

17 "Judah's sin is engraved with an iron tool,[e]
inscribed with a flint point,
on the tablets of their hearts[f]
and on the horns of their altars.
2 Even their children remember
their altars and Asherah poles[a]
beside the spreading trees
and on the high hills.
3 My mountain in the land
and your[b] wealth and all your treasures
I will give away as plunder,
together with your high places,
because of sin throughout your country.
4 Through your own fault you will lose
the inheritance I gave you.
I will enslave you to your enemies
in a land you do not know,
for you have kindled my anger,
and it will burn[g] forever."

5 This is what the LORD says:

"Cursed is the one who trusts in man,[h]
who depends on flesh for his strength
and whose heart turns away from the LORD.
6 He will be like a bush in the wastelands;
he will not see prosperity when it comes.
He will dwell in the parched places of the desert,
in a salt[i] land where no one lives.

7 "But blessed is the man who trusts[j] in the LORD,
whose confidence is in him.
8 He will be like a tree planted by the water
that sends out its roots by the stream.
It does not fear when heat comes;
its leaves are always green.
It has no worries in a year of drought
and never fails to bear fruit."[k]

9 The heart is deceitful above all things
and beyond cure.
Who can understand it?
10 "I the LORD search the heart[l]
and examine the mind,[m]
to reward[n] a man according to his conduct,
according to what his deeds deserve."[o]

11 Like a partridge that hatches eggs it did not lay
is the man who gains riches by unjust means.
When his life is half gone, they will desert him,
and in the end he will prove to be a fool.

12 A glorious throne, exalted from the beginning,
is the place of our sanctuary.
13 O LORD, the hope[p] of Israel,
all who forsake[q] you will be put to shame.
Those who turn away from you will be written in the dust
because they have forsaken the LORD,
the spring of living water.

14 Heal me, O LORD, and I will be healed;
save me and I will be saved,
for you are the one I praise.[r]
15 They keep saying to me,
"Where is the word of the LORD?
Let it now be fulfilled!"[s]
16 I have not run away from being your shepherd;
you know I have not desired the day of despair.
What passes my lips is open before you.

17:7
j Ps 34:8; Pr 16:20

17:8
k Ps 1:3

17:10
l 1Sa 16:7
m Jer 20:12; Ro 8:27
n Jer 32:19
o Ro 2:6

17:13
p Jer 14:8
q Isa 1:28

17:14
r Ps 109:1

17:15
s Isa 5:19

[a] 2 That is, symbols of the goddess Asherah [b] 2,3 Or *hills / 3 and the mountains of the land. / Your*

17:17 t Jer 16:19

17 Do not be a terror to me;
you are my refuge[t] in the day of disaster.
18 Let my persecutors be put to shame,
but keep me from shame;
let them be terrified,
but keep me from terror.
Bring on them the day of disaster;
destroy them with double destruction.[u]

17:18 u Ps 35:1–8

Inspire

## STRESS MANAGEMENT: LEARNING TO SAY "NO"

One of the greatest combinations of blessings and burdens that women of color carry is the legacy of not being able to say "no." We are socialized to take care of our families, our friends, our communities and everyone else but ourselves. Sometimes this is a result of a desire for acceptance. Sometimes we feel that we are the only ones who can meet the needs of our family and friends. Either way, we end up feeling stressed as we try to do everything. Adding to our anxiety is the thought that while we are meeting everyone else's needs, our own needs will not be met. To top it off, we are often consumed with guilt at the thought of putting our needs before someone else's. However, for the sake of sanity, sometimes that is just what we need to do.

Alleviating stress begins with learning to say "no" and recognizing our strengths and limitations. By taking time out to revive ourselves—spiritually, mentally, emotionally and physically—we are actually doing our loved ones a favor, because once our needs are met, we are better equipped to attend to the needs of others. When we are tired, it is hard to fulfill Jesus' instruction to let our light shine before others (see Mt 5:16).

We have to learn that sometimes "no" is the right and healthy answer. Although it will not be easy, we must learn to say it. Self-deception, pride and independence can prevent self-awareness and discernment; we need to rely on God to search our minds and our conduct (see Jer 17:9–10).

Having been programmed to say "yes" all our lives, saying "no" will feel uncomfortable at first. However, as you practice saying it and offering alternatives to the demands on your time and resources, saying "no" will become easier. Others will be taken aback at first, but you will feel better and, ultimately, serve them better. Once a woman acknowledges her dependence on God and submits to his will for her life, stress will decrease.

—J. Anderson-Blair

For the next Inspire note, go to page 1016.

### read

Jeremiah 17:5–10; see also Psalm 139:23–24.

See also the Inspire Notes "Rest," "Responsible Decisions in Leadership," "Coping With Life's Tasks," "Seek Wisdom," "Write It Down!" and "Be Focused," and the Women of the Bible Notes "A Virtuous Woman: A Strong Woman, Dependent on God" and "The 'Chosen Lady': A Woman Worth Imitating."

### WOMAN of COLOR

How easy is it for you to say "no"?

## Keeping the Sabbath Holy

19 This is what the LORD said to me: "Go and stand at the gate of the people, through which the kings of Judah go in and out; stand also at all the other gates of Jerusalem. 20 Say to them, 'Hear the word of the LORD, O kings of Judah and all people of Judah and everyone living in Jerusalem who come through these gates. 21 This is what the LORD says: Be careful not to carry a load on the Sabbath[v] day or bring it through the gates of Jerusalem. 22 Do not bring a load out of your houses or do any work on the Sabbath, but keep the Sabbath day holy, as I commanded your forefathers.[w] 23 Yet they did not listen or pay attention;[x] they were stiff-necked and would not listen or respond to discipline. 24 But if you are careful to obey me, declares the LORD, and bring no load through the gates of this city on the Sabbath, but keep the Sabbath day holy by not doing any work on it, 25 then kings who sit on David's throne[y] will come through the gates of this city with their officials. They and their officials will come riding in chariots and on horses, accompanied by the men of Judah and those living in Jerusalem, and this city will be inhabited forever. 26 People will come from the towns of Judah and the villages around Jerusalem, from the territory of Benjamin and the western foothills, from the hill country and the Negev,[z] bringing burnt offerings and sacrifices, grain offerings, incense and thank offerings to the house of the LORD. 27 But if you do not obey me to keep the Sabbath day holy by not carrying any load as you come through the gates of Jerusalem on the Sabbath day, then I will kindle an unquenchable fire in the gates of Jerusalem that will consume her fortresses.'"[a]

## At the Potter's House

**18** This is the word that came to Jeremiah from the LORD: 2 "Go down to the potter's house, and there I will give you my message." 3 So I went down to the potter's house, and I saw him working at the wheel. 4 But the pot he was shaping from the clay was marred in his hands; so the potter formed it into another pot, shaping it as seemed best to him.

5 Then the word of the LORD came to me: 6 "O house of Israel, can I not do with you as this potter does?" declares the LORD. "Like clay[b] in the hand of the potter, so are you in my hand, O house of Israel. 7 If at any time I announce that a nation or kingdom is to be uprooted,[c] torn down and destroyed, 8 and if that nation I warned repents of its evil, then I will relent[d] and not inflict on it the disaster I had planned. 9 And if at another time I announce that a nation or kingdom is to be built up and planted, 10 and if it does evil[e] in my sight and does not obey me, then I will reconsider the good I had intended to do for it.

11 "Now therefore say to the people of Judah and those living in Jerusalem, 'This is what the LORD says: Look! I am preparing a disaster for you and devising a plan against you. So turn[f] from your evil ways, each one of you, and reform your ways and your actions.' 12 But they will reply, 'It's no use.[g] We will continue with our own plans; each of us will follow the stubbornness of his evil heart.'"

13 Therefore this is what the LORD says:

"Inquire among the nations:
  Who has ever heard anything like this?
A most horrible[h] thing has been done
  by Virgin Israel.
14 Does the snow of Lebanon
  ever vanish from its rocky slopes?
Do its cool waters from distant sources
  ever cease to flow?[a]
15 Yet my people have forgotten me;
  they burn incense to worthless idols,
which made them stumble in their ways
  and in the ancient paths.[i]
They made them walk in bypaths
  and on roads not built up.
16 Their land will be laid waste,
  an object of lasting scorn;
all who pass by will be appalled
  and will shake their heads.
17 Like a wind[j] from the east,
  I will scatter them before their
    enemies;
I will show them my back and not my
    face[k]
  in the day of their disaster."

**17:21** v Nu 15:32–36; Ne 13:15–21
**17:22** w Ex 20:8
**17:23** x Jer 7:26
**17:25** y Jer 22:2,4
**17:26** z Zec 7:7
**17:27** a 2Ki 25:9

**18:6** b Isa 45:9; Ro 9:20–21
**18:7** c Jer 1:10
**18:8** d Jer 26:13; Jnh 3:8–10
**18:10** e Eze 33:18
**18:11** f 2Ki 17:13
**18:12** g Isa 57:10; Jer 2:25
**18:13** h Jer 5:30
**18:15** i Jer 6:16
**18:17** j Jer 13:24; k Jer 2:27

[a] 14 The meaning of the Hebrew for this sentence is uncertain.

**18:18**
l Jer 11:19
m Mal 2:7
**18:20**
n Ps 35:7
**18:21**
o Ps 109:9
**19:2**
p Jos 15:8
**19:3**
q Jer 17:20
r 1Sa 3:11
**19:4**
s Isa 65:11

18 They said, "Come, let's make plans[l] against Jeremiah; for the teaching of the law by the priest[m] will not be lost, nor will counsel from the wise, nor the word from the prophets. So come, let's attack him with our tongues and pay no attention to anything he says."

19 Listen to me, O LORD;
hear what my accusers are saying!
20 Should good be repaid with evil?
Yet they have dug a pit[n] for me.
Remember that I stood before you
and spoke in their behalf
to turn your wrath away from them.
21 So give their children over to famine;
hand them over to the power of the
sword.
Let their wives be made childless and
widows;[o]
let their men be put to death,
their young men slain by the sword in
battle.
22 Let a cry be heard from their houses
when you suddenly bring invaders
against them,
for they have dug a pit to capture me
and have hidden snares for my feet.
23 But you know, O LORD,
all their plots to kill me.
Do not forgive their crimes
or blot out their sins from your sight.
Let them be overthrown before you;
deal with them in the time of your anger.

**19** This is what the LORD says: "Go and buy a clay jar from a potter. Take along some of the elders of the people and of the priests 2 and go out to the Valley of Ben Hinnom,[p] near the entrance of the Potsherd Gate. There proclaim the words I tell you, 3 and say, 'Hear the word of the LORD, O kings[q] of Judah and people of Jerusalem. This is what the LORD Almighty, the God of Israel, says: Listen! I am going to bring a disaster on this place that will make the ears of everyone who hears of it tingle.[r] 4 For they have forsaken[s] me and made this a place of foreign gods; they have burned sacrifices in it to gods that neither they nor their fathers nor the kings of Judah ever knew, and they have filled this place with the blood of the innocent.[t] 5 They have built the high places of Baal to burn their sons[u] in the fire as offerings to Baal—something I did not command or mention, nor did it enter my mind. 6 So beware, the days are coming, declares the LORD, when people will no longer call this place Topheth or the Valley of Ben Hinnom,[v] but the Valley of Slaughter.

7 " 'In this place I will ruin[a] the plans of Judah and Jerusalem. I will make them fall by the sword before their enemies, at the hands of those who seek their lives, and I will give their carcasses[w] as food to the birds of the air and the beasts of the earth. 8 I will devastate this city and make it an object of scorn;[x] all who pass by will be appalled and will scoff because of all its wounds. 9 I will make them eat[y] the flesh of their sons and daughters, and they will eat one another's flesh during the stress of the siege imposed on them by the enemies who seek their lives.'

10 "Then break the jar while those who go with you are watching, 11 and say to them, 'This is what the LORD Almighty says: I will smash[z] this nation and this city just as this potter's jar is smashed and cannot be repaired. They will bury[a] the dead in Topheth until there is no more room. 12 This is what I will do to this place and to those who live here, declares the LORD. I will make this city like Topheth. 13 The houses in Jerusalem and those of the kings of Judah will be defiled like this place, Topheth—all the houses where they burned incense on the roofs to all the starry hosts and poured out drink offerings to other gods.' "

14 Jeremiah then returned from Topheth, where the LORD had sent him to prophesy, and stood in the court[b] of the LORD's temple and said to all the people, 15 "This is what the LORD Almighty, the God of Israel, says: 'Listen! I am going to bring on this city and the villages around it every disaster I pronounced against them, because they were stiff-necked[c] and would not listen to my words.' "

## Jeremiah and Pashhur

**20** When the priest Pashhur son of Immer,[d] the chief officer in the temple of the LORD, heard Jeremiah prophesying

**19:4**
t 2Ki 21:16
**19:5**
u Lev 18:21
**19:6**
v Jos 15:8
**19:7**
w Jer 16:4
**19:8**
x Jer 18:16
**19:9**
y Dt 28:49–57; La 4:10
**19:11**
z Ps 2:9; Isa 30:14
a Jer 7:32
**19:14**
b 2Ch 20:5
**19:15**
c Jer 7:26; 17:23
**20:1**
d 1Ch 24:14

[a] 7 The Hebrew for *ruin* sounds like the Hebrew for *jar* (see verses 1 and 10).

these things, [2]he had Jeremiah the prophet
beaten and put in the stocks at the Upper
Gate of Benjamin at the LORD's temple. [3]The
next day, when Pashhur released him from
the stocks, Jeremiah said to him, "The
LORD's name for you is not Pashhur, but Ma-
gor-Missabib.[a] [4]For this is what the LORD
says: 'I will make you a terror to yourself
and to all your friends; with your own eyes[e]
you will see them fall by the sword of their
enemies. I will hand all Judah over to the
king of Babylon, who will carry them away
to Babylon or put them to the sword. [5]I will
hand over to their enemies all the wealth of
this city—all its products, all its valuables
and all the treasures of the kings of Judah.
They will take it away[f] as plunder and carry
it off to Babylon. [6]And you, Pashhur, and all
who live in your house will go into exile to
Babylon. There you will die and be buried,
you and all your friends to whom you have
prophesied[g] lies.'"

## Jeremiah's Complaint

[7] O LORD, you deceived[b] me, and I was
deceived[b];
you overpowered me and prevailed.
I am ridiculed all day long;
everyone mocks me.
[8] Whenever I speak, I cry out
proclaiming violence and
destruction.[h]
So the word of the LORD has brought me
insult and reproach all day long.
[9] But if I say, "I will not mention him
or speak any more in his name,"
his word is in my heart like a fire,[i]
a fire shut up in my bones.
I am weary of holding it in;[j]
indeed, I cannot.
[10] I hear many whispering,
"Terror on every side!
Report him! Let's report him!"
All my friends
are waiting for me to slip,[k] saying,
"Perhaps he will be deceived;
then we will prevail over him
and take our revenge on him."
[11] But the LORD is with me like a mighty
warrior;
so my persecutors[l] will stumble and
not prevail.[m]
They will fail and be thoroughly
disgraced;
their dishonor will never be forgotten.
[12] O LORD Almighty, you who examine the
righteous
and probe the heart and mind,[n]
let me see your vengeance upon them,
for to you I have committed[o] my cause.
[13] Sing to the LORD!
Give praise to the LORD!
He rescues the life of the needy
from the hands of the wicked.
[14] Cursed be the day I was born![p]
May the day my mother bore me not
be blessed!
[15] Cursed be the man who brought my
father the news,
who made him very glad, saying,
"A child is born to you—a son!"
[16] May that man be like the towns[q]
the LORD overthrew without pity.
May he hear wailing in the morning,
a battle cry at noon.
[17] For he did not kill me in the womb,[r]
with my mother as my grave,
her womb enlarged forever.
[18] Why did I ever come out of the womb
to see trouble and sorrow
and to end my days in shame?

## God Rejects Zedekiah's Request

21 The word came to Jeremiah from
the LORD when King Zedekiah[s] sent
to him Pashhur son of Malkijah and the
priest Zephaniah[t] son of Maaseiah. They
said: [2]"Inquire now of the LORD for us be-
cause Nebuchadnezzar[c] king of Babylon is
attacking us. Perhaps the LORD will perform
wonders for us as in times past so that he
will withdraw from us."
[3]But Jeremiah answered them, "Tell
Zedekiah, [4]'This is what the LORD, the God of
Israel, says: I am about to turn against you
the weapons of war that are in your hands,
which you are using to fight the king of Bab-
ylon and the Babylonians[d] who are outside
the wall besieging you. And I will gather

**20:4** e Jer 29:21
**20:5** f 2Ki 20:17
**20:6** g Jer 14:15
**20:8** h Jer 6:7
**20:9** i Ps 39:3; j Job 32:18–20; Ac 4:20
**20:10** k Lk 11:53–54
**20:11** l Jer 17:18; m Jer 15:20
**20:12** n Jer 17:10; o Jer 11:20
**20:14** p Job 3:3; Jer 15:10
**20:16** q Ge 19:25
**20:17** r Job 10:18–19
**21:1** s 2Ki 24:18; t 2Ki 25:18

[a]3 *Magor-Missabib* means *terror on every side.* [b]7 Or *persuaded* [c]2 Hebrew *Nebuchadrezzar,* of which *Nebuchadnezzar* is a variant; here and often in Jeremiah and Ezekiel [d]4 Or *Chaldeans*; also in verse 9

them inside this city. 5 I myself will fight against you with an outstretched hand and a mighty arm in anger and fury and great wrath. 6 I will strike down those who live in this city—both men and animals—and they will die of a terrible plague.[u] 7 After that, declares the LORD, I will hand over Zedekiah[v] king of Judah, his officials and the people in this city who survive the plague, sword and famine, to Nebuchadnezzar king of Babylon[w] and to their enemies who seek their lives. He will put them to the sword; he will show them no mercy or pity or compassion.'[x]

8 "Furthermore, tell the people, 'This is what the LORD says: See, I am setting before you the way of life and the way of death. 9 Whoever stays in this city will die by the sword, famine or plague.[y] But whoever goes out and surrenders to the Babylonians who are besieging you will live; he will escape with his life.[z] 10 I have determined to do this city harm[a] and not good, declares the LORD. It will be given into the hands[b] of the king of Babylon, and he will destroy it with fire.'[c]

11 "Moreover, say to the royal house of Judah, 'Hear the word of the LORD; 12 O house of David, this is what the LORD says:

" 'Administer justice every morning;
rescue from the hand of his oppressor
the one who has been robbed,
or my wrath will break out and burn
like fire
because of the evil you have done—
burn with no one to quench it.
13 I am against[d] you, ⌊Jerusalem,⌋
you who live above this valley
on the rocky plateau,
declares the LORD—
you who say, "Who can come against us?
Who can enter our refuge?"[e]
14 I will punish you as your deeds[f] deserve,
declares the LORD.
I will kindle a fire[g] in your forests
that will consume everything around
you.' "

## Judgment Against Evil Kings

22 This is what the LORD says: "Go down to the palace of the king of Judah and proclaim this message there: 2 'Hear the word of the LORD, O king of Judah, you who sit on David's throne—you, your officials and your people who come through these gates. 3 This is what the LORD says: Do what is just and right. Rescue from the hand of his oppressor[h] the one who has been robbed. Do no wrong or violence to the alien, the fatherless or the widow, and do not shed innocent blood in this place. 4 For if you are careful to carry out these commands, then kings[i] who sit on David's throne will come through the gates of this palace, riding in chariots and on horses, accompanied by their officials and their people. 5 But if you do not obey[j] these commands, declares the LORD, I swear[k] by myself that this palace will become a ruin.' "

6 For this is what the LORD says about the palace of the king of Judah:

"Though you are like Gilead to me,
like the summit of Lebanon,
I will surely make you like a desert,
like towns not inhabited.
7 I will send destroyers against you,
each man with his weapons,
and they will cut[l] up your fine cedar beams
and throw them into the fire.

8 "People from many nations will pass by this city and will ask one another, 'Why has the LORD done such a thing to this great city?'[m] 9 And the answer will be: 'Because they have forsaken the covenant of the LORD their God and have worshiped and served other gods.'[n] "

10 Do not weep for the dead ⌊king⌋ or mourn
his loss;
rather, weep bitterly for him who is
exiled,
because he will never return
nor see his native land again.

11 For this is what the LORD says about Shallum[a][o] son of Josiah, who succeeded his father as king of Judah but has gone from this place: "He will never return. 12 He will die in the place where they have led him captive; he will not see this land again."

13 "Woe to him who builds[p] his palace by
unrighteousness,

[a]11 Also called *Jehoahaz*

**21:6** u Jer 14:12
**21:7** v Jer 52:9 w Jer 37:17; 39:5 x 2Ch 36:17
**21:9** y Jer 14:12 z Jer 38:2,17; 39:18; 45:5
**21:10** a Jer 44:11,27 b Jer 38:2–3 c Jer 52:13
**21:13** d Eze 13:8 e Jer 49:4
**21:14** f Isa 3:10–11 g 2Ch 36:19

**22:3** h Jer 21:12
**22:4** i Jer 17:25
**22:5** j Jer 17:27 k Heb 6:13
**22:7** l Isa 10:34
**22:8** m Dt 29:25–26; 1Ki 9:8–9
**22:9** n 2Ki 22:17
**22:11** o 2Ki 23:31
**22:13** p Mic 3:10; Hab 2:9

**22:13** q Jas 5:4
**22:14** r Isa 5:8–9
**22:15** s Isa 3:10
**22:16** t Ps 72:1–4,12–13
**22:19** u Jer 36:30
**22:21** v Jer 3:25

his upper rooms by injustice,
making his countrymen work for nothing,
not paying[q] them for their labor.
14 He says, 'I will build myself a great palace[r]
with spacious upper rooms.'
So he makes large windows in it,
panels it with cedar
and decorates it in red.

15 "Does it make you a king
to have more and more cedar?
Did not your father have food and drink?
He did what was right and just,
so all went well[s] with him.
16 He defended the cause of the poor and needy,[t]
and so all went well.
Is that not what it means to know me?"
declares the LORD.
17 "But your eyes and your heart
are set only on dishonest gain,
on shedding innocent blood
and on oppression and extortion."

18 Therefore this is what the LORD says about
Jehoiakim son of Josiah king of Judah:

"They will not mourn for him:
'Alas, my brother! Alas, my sister!'
They will not mourn for him:
'Alas, my master! Alas, his splendor!'
19 He will have the burial of a donkey—
dragged away and thrown[u]
outside the gates of Jerusalem."

20 "Go up to Lebanon and cry out,
let your voice be heard in Bashan,
cry out from Abarim,
for all your allies are crushed.
21 I warned you when you felt secure,
but you said, 'I will not listen!'
This has been your way from your youth;[v]
you have not obeyed me.
22 The wind will drive all your shepherds away,
and your allies will go into exile.
Then you will be ashamed and disgraced
because of all your wickedness.
23 You who live in 'Lebanon,'[a]
who are nestled in cedar buildings,
how you will groan when pangs come upon you,
pain[w] like that of a woman in labor!

24 "As surely as I live," declares the LORD,
"even if you, Jehoiachin[b] son of Jehoiakim
king of Judah, were a signet ring on my right
hand, I would still pull you off. 25 I will hand
you over[x] to those who seek your life, those
you fear—to Nebuchadnezzar king of Bab-
ylon and to the Babylonians.[c] 26 I will hurl[y]
you and the mother who gave you birth into
another country, where neither of you was
born, and there you both will die. 27 You will
never come back to the land you long to re-
turn to."

28 Is this man Jehoiachin a despised, broken pot,[z]
an object no one wants?
Why will he and his children be hurled out,
cast into a land they do not know?
29 O land,[a] land, land,
hear the word of the LORD!
30 This is what the LORD says:
"Record this man as if childless,[b]
a man who will not prosper in his lifetime,
for none of his offspring will prosper,
none will sit on the throne of David
or rule anymore in Judah."

## The Righteous Branch

23 "Woe to the shepherds[c] who are de-
stroying and scattering the sheep
of my pasture!" declares the LORD. 2 There-
fore this is what the LORD, the God of Israel,
says to the shepherds who tend my people:
"Because you have scattered my flock and
driven them away and have not bestowed
care on them, I will bestow punishment on
you for the evil you have done," declares the
LORD. 3 "I myself will gather the remnant[d]
of my flock out of all the countries where I
have driven them and will bring them back
to their pasture, where they will be fruitful
and increase in number. 4 I will place shep-
herds[e] over them who will tend them, and
they will no longer be afraid[f] or terrified,
nor will any be missing," declares the LORD.

**22:23** w Jer 4:31
**22:25** x Jer 34:20
**22:26** y 2Ki 24:8; 2Ch 36:10
**22:28** z Ps 31:12; Jer 48:38; Hos 8:8
**22:29** a Jer 6:19
**22:30** b 1Ch 3:18; Mt 1:12
**23:1** c Jer 10:21
**23:3** d Jer 32:37
**23:4** e Jer 3:15; Eze 34:23 f Jer 30:10

[a] 23 That is, the palace in Jerusalem (see 1 Kings 7:2) [b] 24 Hebrew *Coniah,* a variant of *Jehoiachin*; also in verse 28
[c] 25 Or *Chaldeans*

**23:5** g Isa 4:2 h Isa 9:7 i Isa 11:1; Zec 6:12
**23:6** j Jer 33:16 k 1Co 1:30
**23:7** l Jer 16:14
**23:10** m Jer 9:10
**23:11** n Jer 6:13; Zep 3:4
**23:12** o Jer 13:16 p Jer 11:23

5 "The days are coming," declares the LORD,
"when I will raise up to David[a] a
righteous Branch,[g]
a King who will reign[h] wisely
and do what is just and right[i] in the
land.
6 In his days Judah will be saved
and Israel will live in safety.
This is the name[j] by which he will be
called:
The LORD Our Righteousness.[k]

7 "So then, the days are coming," declares
the LORD, "when people will no longer say,
'As surely as the LORD lives, who brought
the Israelites up out of Egypt,'[l] 8 but they will
say, 'As surely as the LORD lives, who brought
the descendants of Israel up out of the land
of the north and out of all the countries
where he had banished them.' Then they
will live in their own land."

## Lying Prophets

9 Concerning the prophets:

My heart is broken within me;
all my bones tremble.
I am like a drunken man,
like a man overcome by wine,
because of the LORD
and his holy words.
10 The land is full of adulterers;
because of the curse[b] the land lies
parched[c]
and the pastures[m] in the desert are
withered.
The ⌞prophets⌟ follow an evil course
and use their power unjustly.

11 "Both prophet and priest are godless;[n]
even in my temple I find their
wickedness,"
declares the LORD.
12 "Therefore their path will become
slippery;[o]
they will be banished to darkness
and there they will fall.
I will bring disaster on them
in the year they are punished,[p]"
declares the LORD.

13 "Among the prophets of Samaria
I saw this repulsive thing:
They prophesied by Baal
and led my people Israel astray.
14 And among the prophets of Jerusalem
I have seen something horrible:
They commit adultery and live a lie.[q]
They strengthen the hands of evildoers,
so that no one turns from his
wickedness.
They are all like Sodom to me;
the people of Jerusalem are like
Gomorrah."

15 Therefore, this is what the LORD Al-
mighty says concerning the prophets:

"I will make them eat bitter food
and drink poisoned water,
because from the prophets of Jerusalem
ungodliness has spread throughout
the land."

16 This is what the LORD Almighty says:

"Do not listen to what the prophets are
prophesying to you;
they fill you with false hopes.
They speak visions[r] from their own
minds,
not from the mouth of the LORD.
17 They keep saying to those who
despise me,
'The LORD says: You will have peace.'
And to all who follow the stubbornness of
their hearts
they say, 'No harm[s] will come to you.'
18 But which of them has stood in the
council of the LORD
to see or to hear his word?
Who has listened and heard his word?
19 See, the storm[t] of the LORD
will burst out in wrath,
a whirlwind swirling down
on the heads of the wicked.
20 The anger of the LORD will not turn back
until he fully accomplishes
the purposes of his heart.
In days to come
you will understand it clearly.
21 I did not send[u] these prophets,
yet they have run with their message;
I did not speak to them,
yet they have prophesied.
22 But if they had stood in my council,

**23:14** q Jer 29:23
**23:16** r Jer 14:14
**23:17** s Jer 5:12; Mic 3:11
**23:19** t Jer 25:32; 30:23
**23:21** u Jer 14:14

[a] 5 Or *up from David's line* [b] 10 Or *because of these things* [c] 10 Or *land mourns*

they would have proclaimed my words
to my people
and would have turned them from their
evil ways
and from their evil deeds.

23 "Am I only a God nearby,"[v]
declares the LORD,
"and not a God far away?
24 Can anyone hide in secret places
so that I cannot see him?"
declares the LORD.
"Do not I fill heaven and earth?"[w]
declares the LORD.

25 "I have heard what the prophets say who prophesy lies[x] in my name. They say, 'I had a dream! I had a dream!' 26 How long will this continue in the hearts of these lying prophets, who prophesy the delusions of their own minds? 27 They think the dreams they tell one another will make my people forget my name, just as their fathers forgot[y] my name through Baal worship. 28 Let the prophet who has a dream tell his dream, but let the one who has my word speak it faithfully. For what has straw to do with grain?" declares the LORD. 29 "Is not my word like fire," declares the LORD, "and like a hammer that breaks a rock in pieces?

30 "Therefore," declares the LORD, "I am against the prophets[z] who steal from one another words supposedly from me. 31 Yes," declares the LORD, "I am against the prophets who wag their own tongues and yet declare, 'The LORD declares.' 32 Indeed, I am against those who prophesy false dreams," declares the LORD. "They tell them and lead my people astray with their reckless lies, yet I did not send or appoint them. They do not benefit these people in the least," declares the LORD.

## False Oracles and False Prophets

33 "When these people, or a prophet or a priest, ask you, 'What is the oracle[a][a] of the LORD?' say to them, 'What oracle?[b] I will forsake[b] you, declares the LORD.' 34 If a prophet or a priest or anyone else claims, 'This is the oracle[c] of the LORD,' I will punish that man and his household. 35 This is what each of you keeps on saying to his friend or relative: 'What is the LORD's answer?'[d] or 'What has the LORD spoken?' 36 But you must not mention 'the oracle of the LORD' again, because every man's own word becomes his oracle and so you distort the words of the living God, the LORD Almighty, our God. 37 This is what you keep saying to a prophet: 'What is the LORD's answer to you?' or 'What has the LORD spoken?' 38 Although you claim, 'This is the oracle of the LORD,' this is what the LORD says: You used the words, 'This is the oracle of the LORD,' even though I told you that you must not claim, 'This is the oracle of the LORD.' 39 Therefore, I will surely forget you and cast you out of my presence along with the city I gave to you and your fathers. 40 I will bring upon you everlasting disgrace[e]—everlasting shame that will not be forgotten."

## Two Baskets of Figs

24 After Jehoiachin[c][f] son of Jehoiakim king of Judah and the officials, the craftsmen and the artisans of Judah were carried into exile from Jerusalem to Babylon by Nebuchadnezzar king of Babylon, the LORD showed me two baskets of figs[g] placed in front of the temple of the LORD. 2 One basket had very good figs, like those that ripen early; the other basket had very poor figs, so bad they could not be eaten.

3 Then the LORD asked me, "What do you see,[h] Jeremiah?"

"Figs," I answered. "The good ones are very good, but the poor ones are so bad they cannot be eaten."

4 Then the word of the LORD came to me: 5 "This is what the LORD, the God of Israel, says: 'Like these good figs, I regard as good the exiles from Judah, whom I sent away from this place to the land of the Babylonians.[d] 6 My eyes will watch over them for their good, and I will bring them back[i] to this land. I will build[j] them up and not tear them down; I will plant them and not uproot them. 7 I will give them a heart to know me, that I am the LORD. They will be my people,[k] and I will be their God, for they will return[l] to me with all their heart.

**23:23** v Ps 139:1–10
**23:24** w 1Ki 8:27
**23:25** x Jer 14:14
**23:27** y Jdg 3:7
**23:30** z Dt 18:20
**23:33** a Mal 1:1 b ver 39
**23:34** c La 2:14
**23:35** d Jer 33:3
**23:40** e Jer 20:11
**24:1** f 2Ch 36:9; Jer 29:2 g Am 8:1–2
**24:3** h Jer 1:11
**24:6** i Jer 29:10 j Jer 33:7; 42:10
**24:7** k Jer 31:33; Heb 8:10 l Jer 32:40

[a]33 Or *burden* (see Septuagint and Vulgate) [b]33 Hebrew; Septuagint and Vulgate *'You are the burden.* (The Hebrew for *oracle* and *burden* is the same.) [c]1 Hebrew *Jeconiah,* a variant of *Jehoiachin* [d]5 Or *Chaldeans*

**24:8** m Jer 29:17

**24:9** n Jer 15:4; 34:17 o 1Ki 9:7 p Jer 29:18

**25:1** q 2Ki 24:2; Jer 36:1

**25:3** r Jer 1:2

**25:9** s Jer 1:15 t Jer 27:6 u Jer 18:16

[8]"'But like the poor[m] figs, which are so bad they cannot be eaten,' says the LORD, 'so will I deal with Zedekiah king of Judah, his officials and the survivors from Jerusalem, whether they remain in this land or live in Egypt. [9]I will make them abhorrent[n] and an offense to all the kingdoms of the earth, a reproach and a byword,[o] an object of ridicule and cursing,[p] wherever I banish them. [10]I will send the sword, famine and plague against them until they are destroyed from the land I gave to them and their fathers.'"

## Seventy Years of Captivity

**25** The word came to Jeremiah concerning all the people of Judah in the fourth year of Jehoiakim[q] son of Josiah king of Judah, which was the first year of Nebuchadnezzar king of Babylon. [2]So Jeremiah the prophet said to all the people of Judah and to all those living in Jerusalem: [3]For twenty-three years—from the thirteenth year of Josiah[r] son of Amon king of Judah until this very day—the word of the LORD has come to me and I have spoken to you again and again, but you have not listened.

[4]And though the LORD has sent all his servants the prophets to you again and again, you have not listened or paid any attention. [5]They said, "Turn now, each of you, from your evil ways and your evil practices, and you can stay in the land the LORD gave to you and your fathers for ever and ever. [6]Do not follow other gods to serve and worship them; do not provoke me to anger with what your hands have made. Then I will not harm you."

[7]"But you did not listen to me," declares the LORD, "and you have provoked me with what your hands have made, and you have brought harm to yourselves."

[8]Therefore the LORD Almighty says this: "Because you have not listened to my words, [9]I will summon all the peoples of the north[s] and my servant[t] Nebuchadnezzar king of Babylon," declares the LORD, "and I will bring them against this land and its inhabitants and against all the surrounding nations. I will completely destroy[a] them and make them an object of horror and scorn,[u] and an everlasting ruin. [10]I will banish from them the sounds of joy and gladness, the voices of bride and bridegroom, the sound of millstones and the light of the lamp.[v] [11]This whole country will become a desolate wasteland, and these nations will serve the king of Babylon seventy years.

[12]"But when the seventy years are fulfilled, I will punish the king of Babylon and his nation, the land of the Babylonians,[b] for their guilt," declares the LORD, "and will make it desolate forever. [13]I will bring upon that land all the things I have spoken against it, all that are written in this book and prophesied by Jeremiah against all the nations. [14]They themselves will be enslaved by many nations[w] and great kings; I will repay[x] them according to their deeds and the work of their hands."

## The Cup of God's Wrath

[15]This is what the LORD, the God of Israel, said to me: "Take from my hand this cup[y] filled with the wine of my wrath and make all the nations to whom I send you drink it. [16]When they drink it, they will stagger and go mad because of the sword I will send among them."

[17]So I took the cup from the LORD's hand and made all the nations to whom he sent[z] me drink it: [18]Jerusalem and the towns of Judah, its kings and officials, to make them a ruin and an object of horror and scorn and cursing,[a] as they are today; [19]Pharaoh king of Egypt, his attendants, his officials and all his people, [20]and all the foreign people there; all the kings of Uz; all the kings of the Philistines (those of Ashkelon, Gaza, Ekron, and the people left at Ashdod); [21]Edom, Moab and Ammon;[b] [22]all the kings of Tyre and Sidon; the kings of the coastlands across the sea; [23]Dedan, Tema, Buz and all who are in distant places[c];[c] [24]all the kings of Arabia and all the kings of the foreign people who live in the desert; [25]all the kings of Zimri, Elam and Media; [26]and all the kings of the north,[d] near and far, one after the other—all the kingdoms on the face of the earth. And after all of them, the king of Sheshach[d] will drink it too.

**25:10** v Rev 18:22–23

**25:14** w Jer 50:9; 51:27–28 x Jer 51:6

**25:15** y Isa 51:17; Ps 75:8

**25:17** z Jer 1:10

**25:18** a Jer 24:9

**25:21** b Jer 49:1

**25:23** c Jer 9:26

**25:26** d Jer 50:3,9

[a]9 The Hebrew term refers to the irrevocable giving over of things or persons to the LORD, often by totally destroying them.
[b]12 Or *Chaldeans* [c]23 Or *who clip the hair by their foreheads* [d]26 *Sheshach* is a cryptogram for Babylon.

## The African Presence

**Jeremiah 25:24**
According to 2 Chronicles 21:16, Arabs lived near "Cushites," who were also known as Ethiopians or Nubians (see the African Presence note on Ge 10:6–12).

27"Then tell them, 'This is what the LORD
Almighty, the God of Israel, says: Drink, get
drunk[e] and vomit, and fall to rise no more
because of the sword[f] I will send among
you.' 28But if they refuse to take the cup
from your hand and drink, tell them, 'This
is what the LORD Almighty says: You must
drink it! 29See, I am beginning to bring disaster on the city that bears my Name, and
will you indeed go unpunished? You will
not go unpunished, for I am calling down
a sword upon all who live on the earth, declares the LORD Almighty.'

30"Now prophesy all these words against
them and say to them:

"'The LORD will roar[g] from on high;
he will thunder from his holy
dwelling
and roar mightily against his land.
He will shout like those who tread the
grapes,
shout against all who live on the earth.
31 The tumult will resound to the ends of
the earth,
for the LORD will bring charges[h] against
the nations;
he will bring judgment on all mankind
and put the wicked to the sword,'"
declares the LORD.

32This is what the LORD Almighty says:

"Look! Disaster is spreading
from nation to nation;[i]
a mighty storm[j] is rising
from the ends of the earth."

33At that time those slain[k] by the LORD will
be everywhere—from one end of the earth
to the other. They will not be mourned or
gathered[l] up or buried,[m] but will be like refuse lying on the ground.

34 Weep and wail, you shepherds;
roll[n] in the dust, you leaders of the
flock.
For your time to be slaughtered[o] has
come;
you will fall and be shattered like fine
pottery.
35 The shepherds will have nowhere to flee,
the leaders of the flock no place to
escape.
36 Hear the cry of the shepherds,
the wailing of the leaders of the flock,
for the LORD is destroying their
pasture.
37 The peaceful meadows will be laid waste
because of the fierce anger of the LORD.
38 Like a lion[p] he will leave his lair,
and their land will become desolate
because of the sword[a] of the oppressor
and because of the LORD's fierce anger.

### Jeremiah Threatened With Death

26 Early in the reign of Jehoiakim[q] son
of Josiah king of Judah, this word
came from the LORD: 2"This is what the
LORD says: Stand in the courtyard[r] of the
LORD's house and speak to all the people of
the towns of Judah who come to worship
in the house of the LORD. Tell[s] them everything I command you; do not omit[t] a word.
3Perhaps they will listen and each will turn
from his evil way. Then I will relent[u] and not
bring on them the disaster I was planning
because of the evil they have done. 4Say to
them, 'This is what the LORD says: If you do
not listen[v] to me and follow my law, which I
have set before you, 5and if you do not listen

**25:27** e Hab 2:16 f Eze 21:4
**25:30** g Isa 16:10; 42:13
**25:31** h Hos 4:1
**25:32** i Isa 34:2 j Jer 23:19
**25:33** k Isa 66:16 l Jer 16:4 m Ps 79:3
**25:34** n Jer 6:26 o Isa 34:6
**25:38** p Jer 4:7
**26:1** q 2Ki 23:36
**26:2** r Jer 19:14 s Jer 1:17; Ac 20:27 t Dt 4:2
**26:3** u Jer 18:8
**26:4** v Lev 26:14

[a]38 Some Hebrew manuscripts and Septuagint (see also Jer. 46:16 and 50:16); most Hebrew manuscripts *anger*

**26:5** w Jer 25:4
**26:9** x Jer 9:11
**26:11** y Jer 38:4; Mt 26:66
**26:13** z Jer 7:5; Joel 2:12–14
**26:14** a Jer 38:5
**26:16** b Ac 5:34–39; 23:29

to the words of my servants the prophets,
whom I have sent to you again and again
(though you have not listened[w]), [6]then I will
make this house like Shiloh and this city an
object of cursing among all the nations of
the earth.' "

[7]The priests, the prophets and all the peo-
ple heard Jeremiah speak these words in the
house of the LORD. [8]But as soon as Jeremiah
finished telling all the people everything
the LORD had commanded him to say, the
priests, the prophets and all the people
seized him and said, "You must die! [9]Why
do you prophesy in the LORD's name that this
house will be like Shiloh and this city will
be desolate and deserted?"[x] And all the peo-
ple crowded around Jeremiah in the house
of the LORD.

[10]When the officials of Judah heard
about these things, they went up from the
royal palace to the house of the LORD and
took their places at the entrance of the New
Gate of the LORD's house. [11]Then the priests
and the prophets said to the officials and
all the people, "This man should be sen-
tenced to death[y] because he has prophesied
against this city. You have heard it with your
own ears!"

[12]Then Jeremiah said to all the officials
and all the people: "The LORD sent me to
prophesy against this house and this city all
the things you have heard. [13]Now reform[z]
your ways and your actions and obey the
LORD your God. Then the LORD will relent and
not bring the disaster he has pronounced
against you. [14]As for me, I am in your
hands;[a] do with me whatever you think is
good and right. [15]Be assured, however, that
if you put me to death, you will bring the
guilt of innocent blood on yourselves and
on this city and on those who live in it, for in
truth the LORD has sent me to you to speak
all these words in your hearing."

[16]Then the officials and all the people
said to the priests and the prophets, "This
man should not be sentenced to death![b] He
has spoken to us in the name of the LORD
our God."

[17]Some of the elders of the land stepped
forward and said to the entire assembly of
people, [18]"Micah[c] of Moresheth prophesied
in the days of Hezekiah king of Judah. He
told all the people of Judah, 'This is what the
LORD Almighty says:

" 'Zion will be plowed like a field,
Jerusalem will become a heap of
rubble,
the temple hill[d] a mound overgrown
with thickets.'[a]

[19]"Did Hezekiah king of Judah or anyone
else in Judah put him to death? Did not
Hezekiah[e] fear the LORD and seek his fa-
vor? And did not the LORD relent, so that he
did not bring the disaster he pronounced
against them? We are about to bring a terri-
ble disaster on ourselves!"

[20](Now Uriah son of Shemaiah from Kir-
iath Jearim[f] was another man who prophe-
sied in the name of the LORD; he prophesied
the same things against this city and this
land as Jeremiah did. [21]When King Jehoia-
kim and all his officers and officials heard
his words, the king sought to put him to
death. But Uriah heard of it and fled[g] in fear
to Egypt. [22]King Jehoiakim, however, sent
Elnathan[h] son of Acbor to Egypt, along with
some other men. [23]They brought Uriah out
of Egypt and took him to King Jehoiakim,
who had him struck down with a sword and
his body thrown into the burial place of the
common people.)

[24]Furthermore, Ahikam[i] son of Sha-
phan supported Jeremiah, and so he was
not handed over to the people to be put to
death.

## Judah to Serve Nebuchadnezzar

**27** Early in the reign of Zedekiah[b] son
of Josiah king of Judah, this word
came to Jeremiah from the LORD: [2]This is
what the LORD said to me: "Make a yoke[j]
out of straps and crossbars and put it on
your neck. [3]Then send word to the kings
of Edom, Moab, Ammon, Tyre and Sidon
through the envoys who have come to Je-
rusalem to Zedekiah king of Judah. [4]Give
them a message for their masters and say,
'This is what the LORD Almighty, the God
of Israel, says: "Tell this to your masters:

**26:18** c Mic 1:1 d Zec 8:3
**26:19** e 2Ch 32:24–26
**26:20** f Jos 9:17
**26:21** g Mt 10:23
**26:22** h Jer 36:12,25
**26:24** i 2Ki 22:12
**27:2** j Jer 28:10,13

[a]18 Micah 3:12 [b]1 A few Hebrew manuscripts and Syriac (see also Jer. 27:3, 12 and 28:1); most Hebrew manuscripts *Jehoiakim* (Most Septuagint manuscripts do not have this verse.)

**27:5**
k Ps 115:16

**27:6**
l Jer 25:9
m Eze 29:18–20
n Jer 28:14

**27:7**
o Jer 25:12

**27:9**
p Dt 18:11

**27:10**
q Jer 23:25

**27:11**
r Jer 21:9

**27:13**
s Eze 18:31

**27:14**
t Jer 14:14

**27:15**
u Jer 6:15

**27:16**
v 2Ch 36:7,10; Jer 28:3; Da 1:2

5 With my great power and outstretched arm I made the earth and its people and the animals that are on it, and I give[k] it to anyone I please. 6 Now I will hand all your countries over to my servant[l] Nebuchadnezzar[m] king of Babylon; I will make even the wild animals subject to him.[n] 7 All nations will serve him and his son and his grandson until the time[o] for his land comes; then many nations and great kings will subjugate him.

8 " ' "If, however, any nation or kingdom will not serve Nebuchadnezzar king of Babylon or bow its neck under his yoke, I will punish that nation with the sword, famine and plague, declares the LORD, until I destroy it by his hand. 9 So do not listen to your prophets, your diviners, your interpreters of dreams, your mediums[p] or your sorcerers who tell you, 'You will not serve the king of Babylon.' 10 They prophesy lies[q] to you that will only serve to remove you far from your lands; I will banish you and you will perish. 11 But if any nation will bow its neck under the yoke[r] of the king of Babylon and serve him, I will let that nation remain in its own land to till it and to live there, declares the LORD." ' "

12 I gave the same message to Zedekiah king of Judah. I said, "Bow your neck under the yoke of the king of Babylon; serve him and his people, and you will live. 13 Why will you and your people die[s] by the sword, famine and plague with which the LORD has threatened any nation that will not serve the king of Babylon? 14 Do not listen to the words of the prophets who say to you, 'You will not serve the king of Babylon,' for they are prophesying lies[t] to you. 15 'I have not sent them,' declares the LORD. 'They are prophesying lies in my name. Therefore, I will banish you and you will perish,[u] both you and the prophets who prophesy to you.' "

16 Then I said to the priests and all these people, "This is what the LORD says: Do not listen to the prophets who say, 'Very soon now the articles[v] from the LORD's house will be brought back from Babylon.' They are prophesying lies to you. 17 Do not listen to them. Serve the king of Babylon, and you will live. Why should this city become a ruin? 18 If they are prophets and have the word of the LORD, let them plead with the LORD Almighty that the furnishings remaining in the house of the LORD and in the palace of the king of Judah and in Jerusalem not be taken to Babylon. 19 For this is what the LORD Almighty says about the pillars, the Sea,[w] the movable stands and the other furnishings[x] that are left in this city, 20 which Nebuchadnezzar king of Babylon did not take away when he carried[y] Jehoiachin[a] son of Jehoiakim king of Judah into exile from Jerusalem to Babylon, along with all the nobles of Judah and Jerusalem— 21 yes, this is what the LORD Almighty, the God of Israel, says about the things that are left in the house of the LORD and in the palace of the king of Judah and in Jerusalem: 22 'They will be taken to Babylon and there they will remain until the day I come for them,' declares the LORD. 'Then I will bring[z] them back and restore them to this place.' "

**27:19**
w 2Ki 25:13
x Jer 52:17–23

**27:20**
y Jer 24:1

**27:22**
z Ezr 1:7; 7:19

**28:1**
a Jer 27:1,3

**28:2**
b Jer 27:12

**28:3**
c 2Ki 24:13

**28:4**
d Jer 22:24–27

## The False Prophet Hananiah

28 In the fifth month of that same year, the fourth year, early in the reign of Zedekiah[a] king of Judah, the prophet Hananiah son of Azzur, who was from Gibeon, said to me in the house of the LORD in the presence of the priests and all the people: 2 "This is what the LORD Almighty, the God of Israel, says: 'I will break the yoke[b] of the king of Babylon. 3 Within two years I will bring back to this place all the articles[c] of the LORD's house that Nebuchadnezzar king of Babylon removed from here and took to Babylon. 4 I will also bring back to this place Jehoiachin[a][d] son of Jehoiakim king of Judah and all the other exiles from Judah who went to Babylon,' declares the LORD, 'for I will break the yoke of the king of Babylon.' "

5 Then the prophet Jeremiah replied to the prophet Hananiah before the priests and all the people who were standing in the house of the LORD. 6 He said, "Amen! May the LORD do so! May the LORD fulfill the words you have prophesied by bringing the articles of the LORD's house and all the exiles back to this place from Babylon. 7 Nevertheless, listen to what I have to say in your hearing and in the hearing of all the people: 8 From early times the prophets who preceded you and me have

[a] 20,4 Hebrew *Jeconiah,* a variant of *Jehoiachin*

**28:9** e Dt 18:22
**28:10** f Jer 27:2
**28:14** g Dt 28:48 h Jer 27:6
**28:15** i Eze 13:6
**28:16** j Dt 13:5; Jer 29:32

prophesied war, disaster and plague against many countries and great kingdoms. [9]But the prophet who prophesies peace will be recognized as one truly sent by the LORD only if his prediction comes true.[e]"

[10]Then the prophet Hananiah took the yoke[f] off the neck of the prophet Jeremiah and broke it, [11]and he said before all the people, "This is what the LORD says: 'In the same way will I break the yoke of Nebuchadnezzar king of Babylon off the neck of all the nations within two years.'" At this, the prophet Jeremiah went on his way.

[12]Shortly after the prophet Hananiah had broken the yoke off the neck of the prophet Jeremiah, the word of the LORD came to Jeremiah: [13]"Go and tell Hananiah, 'This is what the LORD says: You have broken a wooden yoke, but in its place you will get a yoke of iron. [14]This is what the LORD Almighty, the God of Israel, says: I will put an iron yoke[g] on the necks of all these nations to make them serve Nebuchadnezzar king of Babylon, and they will serve him. I will even give him control over the wild animals.[h]'"

*Follower,*

*I hear the prayers of the righteous.*
*Keep on seeking me. I won't be hiding.*
*In fact, I will myself to be found.*

*The God Who Will Be Found*

JEREMIAH 29:12–14

[15]Then the prophet Jeremiah said to Hananiah the prophet, "Listen, Hananiah! The LORD has not sent you, yet you have persuaded this nation to trust in lies.[i] [16]Therefore, this is what the LORD says: 'I am about to remove you from the face of the earth. This very year you are going to die, because you have preached rebellion[j] against the LORD.'"

[17]In the seventh month of that same year, Hananiah the prophet died.

## A Letter to the Exiles

**29** This is the text of the letter that the prophet Jeremiah sent from Jerusalem to the surviving elders among the exiles and to the priests, the prophets and all the other people Nebuchadnezzar had carried into exile from Jerusalem to Babylon. [2](This was after King Jehoiachin[a][k] and the queen mother, the court officials and the leaders of Judah and Jerusalem, the craftsmen and the artisans had gone into exile from Jerusalem.) [3]He entrusted the letter to Elasah son of Shaphan and to Gemariah son of Hilkiah, whom Zedekiah king of Judah sent to King Nebuchadnezzar in Babylon. It said:

[4]This is what the LORD Almighty, the God of Israel, says to all those I carried[l] into exile from Jerusalem to Babylon: [5]"Build houses and settle down; plant gardens and eat what they produce. [6]Marry and have sons and daughters; find wives for your sons and give your daughters in marriage, so that they too may have sons and daughters. Increase in number there; do not decrease. [7]Also, seek the peace and prosperity of the city to which I have carried you into exile. Pray[m] to the LORD for it, because if it prospers, you too will prosper." [8]Yes, this is what the LORD Almighty, the God of Israel, says: "Do not let the prophets and diviners among you deceive you. Do not listen to the dreams you encourage them to have. [9]They are prophesying lies[n] to you in my name. I have not sent them," declares the LORD.

[10]This is what the Lord says: "When seventy years[o] are completed for Babylon, I will come to you and fulfill my gracious promise to bring you back[p] to this place. [11]For I know the plans I have for you," declares the Lord, "plans to prosper you and not to harm you, plans to give you hope and a future. [12]Then you will call upon me and come and pray to me, and I will

**29:2** k 2Ki 24:12; Jer 22:24–28
**29:4** l Jer 24:5
**29:7** m Ezr 6:10; 1Ti 2:1–2
**29:9** n Jer 14:14
**29:10** o 2Ch 36:21; Jer 25:12; Da 9:2 p Jer 21:22

[a]2 Hebrew *Jeconiah*, a variant of *Jehoiachin*

**29:12** q Ps 145:19
**29:13** r Jer 24:7
**29:17** s Jer 24:8–10
**29:18** t Dt 28:25; Jer 42:18
**29:19** u Jer 25:4

listen[q] to you. [13]You will seek me and
find me when you seek me with all
your heart.[r] [14]I will be found by you,"
declares the Lord, "and will bring you
back from captivity.[a] I will gather you
from all the nations and places where I
have banished you," declares the Lord,
"and will bring you back to the place
from which I carried you into exile."
[15]You may say, "The Lord has raised
up prophets for us in Babylon," [16]but
this is what the Lord says about the
king who sits on David's throne and
all the people who remain in this city,
your countrymen who did not go with
you into exile— [17]yes, this is what
the Lord Almighty says: "I will send
the sword, famine and plague against
them and I will make them like poor
figs[s] that are so bad they cannot be
eaten. [18]I will pursue them with the
sword, famine and plague and will
make them abhorrent to all the king-
doms of the earth and an object of curs-
ing and horror,[t] of scorn and reproach,
among all the nations where I drive
them. [19]For they have not listened to
my words," declares the Lord, "words
that I sent to them again and again by
my servants the prophets.[u] And you ex-
iles have not listened either," declares
the Lord.
[20]Therefore, hear the word of the
Lord, all you exiles whom I have sent
away from Jerusalem to Babylon.
[21]This is what the Lord Almighty, the
God of Israel, says about Ahab son of
Kolaiah and Zedekiah son of Maase-
iah, who are prophesying lies to you
in my name: "I will hand them over to
Nebuchadnezzar king of Babylon, and
he will put them to death before your
very eyes. [22]Because of them, all the ex-
iles from Judah who are in Babylon will
use this curse: 'The Lord treat you like
Zedekiah and Ahab, whom the king
of Babylon burned in the fire.' [23]For
they have done outrageous things in
Israel; they have committed adultery
with their neighbors' wives and in my
name have spoken lies, which I did not
tell them to do. I know it and am a wit-
ness to it," declares the Lord.

## Message to Shemaiah

[24]Tell Shemaiah the Nehelamite, [25]"This
is what the LORD Almighty, the God of Israel,
says: You sent letters in your own name to
all the people in Jerusalem, to Zephaniah[v]
son of Maaseiah the priest, and to all the
other priests. You said to Zephaniah, [26]'The
LORD has appointed you priest in place of
Jehoiada to be in charge of the house of the
LORD; you should put any madman who acts
like a prophet into the stocks[w] and neck-
irons. [27]So why have you not reprimanded
Jeremiah from Anathoth, who poses as a
prophet among you? [28]He has sent this mes-
sage to us in Babylon: It will be a long time.
Therefore build[x] houses and settle down;
plant gardens and eat what they produce.'"
[29]Zephaniah the priest, however, read the
letter to Jeremiah the prophet. [30]Then the
word of the LORD came to Jeremiah: [31]"Send
this message to all the exiles: 'This is what
the LORD says about Shemaiah the Nehela-
mite: Because Shemaiah has prophesied to
you, even though I did not send[y] him, and
has led you to believe a lie, [32]this is what the
LORD says: I will surely punish Shemaiah
the Nehelamite and his descendants. He
will have no one left among this people, nor
will he see the good things I will do for my
people, declares the LORD, because he has
preached rebellion[z] against me.'"

## Restoration of Israel

30 This is the word that came to
Jeremiah from the LORD: [2]"This is
what the LORD, the God of Israel, says: 'Write
in a book all the words I have spoken to you.
[3]The days are coming,' declares the LORD,
'when I will bring my people Israel and Ju-
dah back from captivity[b] and restore them
to the land I gave their forefathers to pos-
sess,' says the LORD."
[4]These are the words the LORD spoke con-
cerning Israel and Judah: [5]"This is what the
LORD says:

"'Cries of fear are heard—
terror, not peace.

**29:25** v 2Ki 25:18
**29:26** w Jer 20:2
**29:28** x ver 5
**29:31** y Jer 14:14; 28:15
**29:32** z Jer 28:16

[a]14 Or *will restore your fortunes* [b]3 Or *will restore the fortunes of my people Israel and Judah*

6 Ask and see:
Can a man bear children?
Then why do I see every strong man
with his hands on his stomach like a woman in labor,[a]
every face turned deathly pale?
7 How awful that day[b] will be!
None will be like it.
It will be a time of trouble for Jacob,
but he will be saved out of it.

8 " 'In that day,' declares the LORD Almighty,
'I will break the yoke off their necks
and will tear off their bonds;
no longer will foreigners enslave them.
9 Instead, they will serve the LORD their God
and David[c] their king,[d]
whom I will raise up for them.

10 " 'So do not fear,[e] O Jacob my servant;[f]
do not be dismayed, O Israel,'
declares the LORD.
'I will surely save you out of a distant place,
your descendants from the land of their exile.
Jacob will again have peace and security,
and no one will make him afraid.
11 I am with you and will save you,'
declares the LORD.
'Though I completely destroy all the nations
among which I scatter you,
I will not completely destroy[g] you.
I will discipline[h] you but only with justice;
I will not let you go entirely unpunished.'

12 "This is what the LORD says:

" 'Your wound is incurable,
your injury beyond healing.
13 There is no one to plead your cause,
no remedy for your sore,
no healing for you.
14 All your allies[i] have forgotten you;
they care nothing for you.
I have struck you as an enemy would
and punished you as would the cruel,
because your guilt is so great
and your sins[j] so many.
15 Why do you cry out over your wound,
your pain that has no cure?
Because of your great guilt and many sins
I have done these things to you.

16 " 'But all who devour[k] you will be devoured;
all your enemies will go into exile.
Those who plunder you will be plundered;
all who make spoil of you I will despoil.
17 But I will restore you to health
and heal your wounds,'
declares the LORD,
'because you are called an outcast,
Zion for whom no one cares.'

18 "This is what the LORD says:

" 'I will restore the fortunes[l] of Jacob's tents
and have compassion[m] on his dwellings;
the city will be rebuilt on her ruins,
and the palace will stand in its proper place.
19 From them will come songs of thanksgiving
and the sound of rejoicing.
I will add to their numbers,
and they will not be decreased;
I will bring them honor,
and they will not be disdained.
20 Their children will be as in days of old,
and their community will be established[n] before me;
I will punish all who oppress them.
21 Their leader will be one of their own;
their ruler will arise from among them.
I will bring him near[o] and he will come close to me,
for who is he who will devote himself
to be close to me?'
declares the LORD.
22 " 'So you will be my people,
and I will be your God.' "

23 See, the storm[p] of the LORD
will burst out in wrath,
a driving wind swirling down
on the heads of the wicked.

**30:6** a Jer 4:31
**30:7** b Joel 2:11
**30:9** c Isa 55:3–4; Lk 1:69; Ac 2:30; 13:23 d Eze 34:23–24; 37:24; Hos 3:5
**30:10** e Isa 43:5 f Isa 44:2
**30:11** g Jer 4:27; 46:28 h Jer 10:24
**30:14** i La 1:2
**30:14** j Jer 5:6
**30:16** k Isa 33:1; Jer 10:25
**30:18** l Jer 31:23 m Ps 102:13
**30:20** n Isa 54:14
**30:21** o Nu 16:5
**30:23** p Jer 23:19

24 The fierce anger of the LORD will not turn
back
until he fully accomplishes
the purposes of his heart.
In days to come
you will understand this.

31 "At that time," declares the LORD, "I
will be the God[q] of all the clans of
Israel, and they will be my people."

2 This is what the LORD says:

"The people who survive the sword
will find favor[r] in the desert;
I will come to give rest to Israel."

3 The LORD appeared to us in the past,[a]
saying:

"I have loved you with an everlasting love;
I have drawn[s] you with loving-
kindness.
4 I will build you up again
and you will be rebuilt, O Virgin Israel.
Again you will take up your tambourines
and go out to dance with the joyful.[t]
5 Again you will plant vineyards
on the hills of Samaria;
the farmers will plant them
and enjoy their fruit.[u]
6 There will be a day when watchmen cry
out
on the hills of Ephraim,
'Come, let us go up to Zion,
to the LORD our God.'"[v]

7 This is what the LORD says:

"Sing with joy for Jacob;
shout for the foremost[w] of the nations.
Make your praises heard, and say,
'O LORD, save your people,
the remnant of Israel.'
8 See, I will bring them from the land of the
north[x]
and gather them from the ends of the
earth.
Among them will be the blind[y] and the
lame,
expectant mothers and women in
labor;
a great throng will return.
9 They will come with weeping;
they will pray as I bring them back.
I will lead them beside streams of water
on a level[z] path where they will not
stumble,
because I am Israel's father,
and Ephraim is my firstborn son.

10 "Hear the word of the LORD, O nations;
proclaim it in distant coastlands:
'He who scattered Israel will gather them
and will watch over his flock like a
shepherd.'[a]
11 For the LORD will ransom Jacob
and redeem[b] them from the hand of
those stronger than they.
12 They will come and shout for joy on the
heights[c] of Zion;
they will rejoice in the bounty of the
LORD—
the grain, the new wine and the oil,
the young of the flocks and herds.
They will be like a well-watered garden,
and they will sorrow no more.
13 Then maidens will dance and be glad,
young men and old as well.
I will turn their mourning into gladness;
I will give them comfort and joy[d]
instead of sorrow.
14 I will satisfy the priests with abundance,
and my people will be filled with my
bounty,"
declares the LORD.

15 This is what the LORD says:

"A voice is heard in Ramah,[e]
mourning and great weeping,
Rachel weeping for her children
and refusing to be comforted,
because her children are no more."[f]

16 This is what the LORD says:

"Restrain your voice from weeping
and your eyes from tears,
for your work will be rewarded,"
declares the LORD.
"They will return[g] from the land of the
enemy.
17 So there is hope for your future,"
declares the LORD.
"Your children will return to their own
land.

**31:1** q Jer 30:22
**31:2** r Nu 14:20
**31:3** s Hos 11:4
**31:4** t Jer 30:19
**31:5** u Isa 65:21; Am 9:14
**31:6** v Isa 2:3; Mic 4:2
**31:7** w Dt 28:13
**31:8** x Jer 3:18; 23:8 y Isa 42:16
**31:9** z Isa 49:11
**31:10** a Isa 40:11
**31:11** b Isa 44:23; 48:20
**31:12** c Eze 17:23
**31:13** d Isa 51:11
**31:15** e Jos 18:25 f Mt 2:17–18*
**31:16** g Eze 11:17

[a]3 Or *LORD has appeared to us from afar*

[18] "I have surely heard Ephraim's moaning:
'You disciplined[h] me like an unruly calf,
and I have been disciplined.
Restore me, and I will return,
because you are the LORD my God.
[19] After I strayed,
I repented;
after I came to understand,
I beat my breast.
I was ashamed and humiliated
because I bore the disgrace of my youth.'
[20] Is not Ephraim my dear son,
the child in whom I delight?
Though I often speak against him,
I still remember[i] him.
Therefore my heart yearns for him;
I have great compassion[j] for him,"
declares the LORD.

[21] "Set up road signs;
put up guideposts.
Take note of the highway,[k]
the road that you take.
Return, O Virgin Israel,
return to your towns.
[22] How long will you wander,
O unfaithful daughter?
The LORD will create a new thing on earth—
a woman will surround[a] a man."

[23] This is what the LORD Almighty, the
God of Israel, says: "When I bring them
back from captivity,[b] the people in the land
of Judah and in its towns will once again
use these words: 'The LORD bless you, O righ-
teous dwelling,[l] O sacred mountain.'[m] [24] Peo-
ple will live together in Judah and all its
towns—farmers and those who move about
with their flocks. [25] I will refresh the weary
and satisfy the faint."

[26] At this I awoke and looked around. My
sleep had been pleasant to me.

[27] "The days are coming," declares the
LORD, "when I will plant[n] the house of Israel
and the house of Judah with the offspring of
men and of animals. [28] Just as I watched over
them to uproot and tear down, and to over-
throw, destroy and bring disaster,[o] so I will
watch over them to build and to plant,"[p] de-
clares the LORD. [29] "In those days people will
no longer say,

'The fathers have eaten sour grapes,
and the children's teeth are set on edge.'[q]

[30] Instead, everyone will die for his own sin;
whoever eats sour grapes—his own teeth
will be set on edge.

[31] "The time is coming," declares the LORD,
"when I will make a new covenant[r]
with the house of Israel
and with the house of Judah.
[32] It will not be like the covenant
I made with their forefathers
when I took them by the hand
to lead them out of Egypt,
because they broke my covenant,
though I was a husband to[c] them,[d]"
declares the LORD.
[33] "This is the covenant I will make with the house of Israel
after that time," declares the LORD.
"I will put my law in their minds
and write it on their hearts.
I will be their God,
and they will be my people.[s]
[34] No longer will a man teach his neighbor,
or a man his brother, saying, 'Know the LORD,'
because they will all know[t] me,
from the least of them to the greatest,"
declares the LORD.
"For I will forgive[u] their wickedness
and will remember their sins[v] no more."

[35] This is what the LORD says,

he who appoints the sun
to shine by day,
who decrees the moon and stars
to shine by night,[w]
who stirs up the sea
so that its waves roar—
the LORD Almighty is his name:[x]
[36] "Only if these decrees[y] vanish from my sight,"
declares the LORD,

**31:18** h Job 5:17
**31:20** i Hos 4:4; 11:8 j Isa 63:15
**31:21** k Jer 50:5
**31:23** l Isa 1:26 m Zec 8:3
**31:27** n Eze 36:9–11; Hos 2:23
**31:28** o Jer 44:27
**31:28** p Jer 1:10
**31:29** q Eze 18:2
**31:31** r Jer 32:40; Heb 8:8–12*
**31:33** s Jer 24:7
**31:34** t Jn 6:45 u Isa 54:13 v Mic 7:19; Heb 10:17*
**31:35** w Ge 1:16 x Jer 10:16
**31:36** y Jer 33:20–26

[a]22 Or *will go about ⌊seeking⌋*; or *will protect* [b]23 Or *I restore their fortunes* [c]32 Hebrew; Septuagint and Syriac */ and I turned away from* [d]32 Or *was their master*

"will the descendants of Israel ever cease
to be a nation before me."

37 This is what the LORD says:

"Only if the heavens above can be
measured[z]
and the foundations of the earth below
be searched out
will I reject all the descendants of
Israel
because of all they have done,"
declares the LORD.

38 "The days are coming," declares the
LORD, "when this city will be rebuilt for
me from the Tower of Hananel[a] to the Cor-
ner Gate. 39 The measuring line will stretch
from there straight to the hill of Gareb and
then turn to Goah. 40 The whole valley where
dead bodies and ashes are thrown, and all
the terraces out to the Kidron Valley on the
east as far as the corner of the Horse Gate,
will be holy[b] to the LORD. The city will never
again be uprooted or demolished."

## Jeremiah Buys a Field

32 This is the word that came to
Jeremiah from the LORD in the tenth[c]
year of Zedekiah king of Judah, which was
the eighteenth year of Nebuchadnezzar.
2 The army of the king of Babylon was then
besieging Jerusalem, and Jeremiah the
prophet was confined in the courtyard of
the guard[d] in the royal palace of Judah.
3 Now Zedekiah king of Judah had im-
prisoned him there, saying, "Why do you
prophesy as you do? You say, 'This is what
the LORD says: I am about to hand this city
over to the king of Babylon, and he will cap-
ture[e] it. 4 Zedekiah king of Judah will not es-
cape[f] out of the hands of the Babylonians[a]
but will certainly be handed over to the king
of Babylon, and will speak with him face to
face and see him with his own eyes. 5 He will
take Zedekiah to Babylon, where he will
remain until I deal with him, declares the
LORD. If you fight against the Babylonians,
you will not succeed.'"
6 Jeremiah said, "The word of the LORD
came to me: 7 Hanamel son of Shallum your
uncle is going to come to you and say, 'Buy
my field at Anathoth, because as nearest rel-
ative it is your right and duty[g] to buy it.'
8 "Then, just as the LORD had said, my
cousin Hanamel came to me in the court-
yard of the guard and said, 'Buy my field
at Anathoth in the territory of Benjamin.
Since it is your right to redeem it and pos-
sess it, buy it for yourself.'
"I knew that this was the word of the
LORD; 9 so I bought the field at Anathoth from
my cousin Hanamel and weighed out for
him seventeen shekels[b] of silver.[h] 10 I signed
and sealed the deed, had it witnessed, and
weighed out the silver on the scales. 11 I took
the deed of purchase—the sealed copy con-
taining the terms and conditions, as well as
the unsealed copy— 12 and I gave this deed
to Baruch[i] son of Neriah, the son of Mahse-
iah, in the presence of my cousin Hanamel
and of the witnesses who had signed the
deed and of all the Jews sitting in the court-
yard of the guard.
13 "In their presence I gave Baruch these
instructions: 14 'This is what the LORD Al-
mighty, the God of Israel, says: Take these
documents, both the sealed and unsealed
copies of the deed of purchase, and put them
in a clay jar so they will last a long time.
15 For this is what the LORD Almighty, the
God of Israel, says: Houses, fields and vine-
yards will again be bought in this land.'
16 "After I had given the deed of pur-
chase to Baruch son of Neriah, I prayed to
the LORD:

17 "Ah, Sovereign LORD, you have made
the heavens and the earth by your great
power and outstretched arm.[j] Nothing
is too hard for you. 18 You show love to
thousands but bring the punishment
for the fathers' sins into the laps of
their children[k] after them. O great and
powerful God, whose name is the LORD
Almighty,[l] 19 great are your purposes
and mighty are your deeds.[m] Your
eyes are open to all the ways of men;[n]
you reward everyone according to his
conduct and as his deeds deserve.[o]
20 You performed miraculous signs
and wonders in Egypt[p] and have con-
tinued them to this day, both in Israel

**31:37** z Jer 33:22
**31:38** a Ne 3:1
**31:40** b Joel 3:17
**32:1** c 2Ki 25:1
**32:2** d Ne 3:25
**32:3** e Jer 34:2–3
**32:4** f Jer 38:18,23; 39:5–7
**32:7** g Lev 25:24–25; Ru 4:3–4
**32:9** h Ge 23:16
**32:12** i Jer 36:4
**32:17** j 2Ki 19:15
**32:18** k Ex 20:5 l Jer 10:16
**32:19** m Isa 28:29 n Jer 16:17 o Jer 17:10
**32:20** p Ex 9:16

[a]4 Or *Chaldeans*; also in verses 5, 24, 25, 28, 29 and 43 [b]9 That is, about 7 ounces (about 200 grams)

and among all mankind, and have gained the renown that is still yours. 21 You brought your people Israel out of Egypt with signs and wonders, by a mighty hand[q] and an outstretched arm and with great terror. 22 You gave them this land you had sworn to give their forefathers, a land flowing with milk and honey.[r] 23 They came in and took possession of it, but they did not obey you or follow your law;[s] they did not do what you commanded them to do. So you brought all this disaster upon them.

24 "See how the siege ramps are built up to take the city. Because of the sword, famine and plague, the city will be handed over to the Babylonians who are attacking it. What you said has happened, as you now see. 25 And though the city will be handed over to the Babylonians, you, O Sovereign LORD, say to me, 'Buy the field with silver and have the transaction witnessed.' "

26 Then the word of the LORD came to Jeremiah: 27 "I am the LORD, the God of all mankind.[t] Is anything too hard for me? 28 Therefore, this is what the LORD says: I am about to hand this city over to the Babylonians and to Nebuchadnezzar king of Babylon, who will capture it. 29 The Babylonians who are attacking this city will come in and set it on fire; they will burn it down,[u] along with the houses[v] where the people provoked me to anger by burning incense on the roofs to Baal and by pouring out drink offerings to other gods.

30 "The people of Israel and Judah have done nothing but evil in my sight from their youth; indeed, the people of Israel have done nothing but provoke me with what their hands have made, declares the LORD. 31 From the day it was built until now, this city has so aroused my anger and wrath that I must remove it from my sight. 32 The people of Israel and Judah have provoked me by all the evil[w] they have done—they, their kings and officials, their priests and prophets, the men of Judah and the people of Jerusalem. 33 They turned their backs[x] to me and not their faces; though I taught them again and again, they would not listen or respond to discipline. 34 They set up their abominable idols in the house that bears my Name and defiled it. 35 They built high places for Baal in the Valley of Ben Hinnom to sacrifice their sons and daughters[a] to Molech,[y] though I never commanded, nor did it enter my mind,[z] that they should do such a detestable thing and so make Judah sin.

36 "You are saying about this city, 'By the sword, famine and plague it will be handed over to the king of Babylon'; but this is what the LORD, the God of Israel, says: 37 I will surely gather[a] them from all the lands where I banish them in my furious anger and great wrath; I will bring them back to this place and let them live in safety.[b] 38 They will be my people,[c] and I will be their God. 39 I will give them singleness of heart and action, so that they will always fear me for their own good and the good of their children after them. 40 I will make an everlasting covenant[d] with them: I will never stop doing good to them, and I will inspire them to fear me, so that they will never turn away from me. 41 I will rejoice in doing them good[e] and will assuredly plant[f] them in this land with all my heart and soul.

42 "This is what the LORD says: As I have brought all this great calamity on this people, so I will give them all the prosperity I have promised[g] them. 43 Once more fields will be bought[h] in this land of which you say, 'It is a desolate waste, without men or animals, for it has been handed over to the Babylonians.' 44 Fields will be bought for silver, and deeds will be signed, sealed and witnessed in the territory of Benjamin, in the villages around Jerusalem, in the towns of Judah and in the towns of the hill country, of the western foothills and of the Negev,[i] because I will restore their fortunes,[b] declares the LORD."

## Promise of Restoration

33 While Jeremiah was still confined in the courtyard of the guard, the word of the LORD came to him a second time: 2 "This is what the LORD says, he who made the earth, the LORD who formed it

[a]35 Or *to make their sons and daughters pass through ⌊the fire⌋*  [b]44 Or *will bring them back from captivity*

**32:21** q Ex 6:6; Da 9:15
**32:22** r Ex 3:8
**32:23** s Jer 11:8
**32:27** t Nu 16:22
**32:29** u Jer 21:10; 52:13 v Jer 19:13
**32:32** w Da 9:8
**32:33** x Jer 2:27
**32:35** y Lev 18:21 z Jer 19:5
**32:37** a Jer 23:3,6 b Dt 30:3
**32:38** c 2Co 6:16*
**32:40** d Isa 55:3
**32:41** e Dt 30:9 f Am 9:15
**32:42** g Jer 31:28
**32:43** h ver 15
**32:44** i Jer 17:26

**33:2** j Ex 15:3
**33:3** k Jer 29:12
**33:7** l Jer 32:44
**33:8** m Heb 9:13–14

*My child,*

*Listen to my Word and follow it wholeheartedly.*

*The Author of Truth*

JEREMIAH 33:1–3

and established it—the LORD is his name:[j]
3'Call[k] to me and I will answer you and tell
you great and unsearchable things you do
not know.' 4For this is what the LORD, the
God of Israel, says about the houses in this
city and the royal palaces of Judah that have
been torn down to be used against the siege
ramps and the sword 5in the fight with the
Babylonians[a]: 'They will be filled with the
dead bodies of the men I will slay in my an-
ger and wrath. I will hide my face from this
city because of all its wickedness.
6" 'Nevertheless, I will bring health and
healing to it; I will heal my people and will
let them enjoy abundant peace and security.
7I will bring Judah[l] and Israel back from
captivity[b] and will rebuild them as they
were before. 8I will cleanse[m] them from all
the sin they have committed against me and
will forgive all their sins of rebellion against
me. 9Then this city will bring me renown,
joy, praise and honor before all nations on
earth that hear of all the good things I do

*Lord,*

*have mercy on me and on my people.*
*We have not always listened to you.*
*Forgive us, heal us and make*
*us whole. In Jesus' name,*

*Amen*

JEREMIAH 33:6–9

for it; and they will be in awe and will trem-
ble at the abundant prosperity and peace I
provide for it.'
10"This is what the LORD says: 'You say
about this place, "It is a desolate waste, with-
out men or animals."[n] Yet in the towns of
Judah and the streets of Jerusalem that are
deserted, inhabited by neither men nor an-
imals, there will be heard once more 11the
sounds of joy and gladness, the voices of
bride and bridegroom, and the voices of
those who bring thank offerings[o] to the
house of the LORD, saying,

"Give thanks to the LORD Almighty,
for the LORD is good;
his love endures forever."[p]

For I will restore the fortunes of the land as
they were before,' says the LORD.
12"This is what the LORD Almighty says:
'In this place, desolate and without men or
animals—in all its towns there will again
be pastures for shepherds to rest their
flocks.[q] 13In the towns of the hill country,
of the western foothills and of the Negev,[r]
in the territory of Benjamin, in the villages
around Jerusalem and in the towns of Ju-
dah, flocks will again pass under the hand[s]
of the one who counts them,' says the LORD.
14" 'The days are coming,' declares the
LORD, 'when I will fulfill the gracious prom-
ise I made to the house of Israel and to the
house of Judah.

15" 'In those days and at that time
I will make a righteous Branch[t] sprout
from David's line;
he will do what is just and right in the
land.
16In those days Judah will be saved
and Jerusalem will live in safety.
This is the name by which it[c] will be called:
The LORD Our Righteousness.'

17For this is what the LORD says: 'David will
never fail[u] to have a man to sit on the throne
of the house of Israel, 18nor will the priests,
who are Levites, ever fail to have a man to
stand before me continually to offer burnt
offerings, to burn grain offerings and to pre-
sent sacrifices.' "
19The word of the LORD came to Jeremiah:

**33:10** n Jer 32:43
**33:11** o Lev 7:12 p 2Ch 5:13
**33:12** q Isa 65:10
**33:13** r Jer 17:26 s Lev 27:32
**33:15** t Isa 4:2
**33:17** u 2Sa 7:13; 1Ki 2:4

[a]5 Or *Chaldeans* [b]7 Or *will restore the fortunes of Judah and Israel* [c]16 Or *he*

20“This is what the LORD says: ‘If you can break my covenant with the day and my covenant with the night, so that day and night no longer come at their appointed time, 21then my covenant with David my servant—and my covenant with the Levites who are priests ministering before me—can be broken and David will no longer have a descendant to reign on his throne. 22I will make the descendants of David my servant and the Levites who minister before me as countless[v] as the stars of the sky and as measureless as the sand on the seashore.’ ”

23The word of the LORD came to Jeremiah: 24“Have you not noticed that these people are saying, ‘The LORD has rejected the two kingdoms[a] he chose’? So they despise my people and no longer regard them as a nation. 25This is what the LORD says: ‘If I have not established my covenant with day and night[w] and the fixed laws of heaven and earth,[x] 26then I will reject[y] the descendants of Jacob and David my servant and will not choose one of his sons to rule over the descendants of Abraham, Isaac and Jacob. For I will restore their fortunes[b] and have compassion on them.’ ”

## Warning to Zedekiah

34 While Nebuchadnezzar king of Babylon and all his army and all the kingdoms and peoples in the empire he ruled were fighting against Jerusalem[z] and all its surrounding towns, this word came to Jeremiah from the LORD: 2“This is what the LORD, the God of Israel, says: Go to Zedekiah king of Judah and tell him, ‘This is what the LORD says: I am about to hand this city over to the king of Babylon, and he will burn it down.[a] 3You will not escape from his grasp but will surely be captured and handed over[b] to him. You will see the king of Babylon with your own eyes, and he will speak with you face to face. And you will go to Babylon.

4“ ‘Yet hear the promise of the LORD, O Zedekiah king of Judah. This is what the LORD says concerning you: You will not die by the sword; 5you will die peacefully. As people made a funeral fire[c] in honor of your fathers, the former kings who preceded you, so they will make a fire in your honor and lament, “Alas,[d] O master!” I myself make this promise, declares the LORD.’ ”

6Then Jeremiah the prophet told all this to Zedekiah king of Judah, in Jerusalem, 7while the army of the king of Babylon was fighting against Jerusalem and the other cities of Judah that were still holding out—Lachish and Azekah.[e] These were the only fortified cities left in Judah.

## Freedom for Slaves

8The word came to Jeremiah from the LORD after King Zedekiah had made a covenant with all the people in Jerusalem to proclaim freedom[f] for the slaves. 9Everyone was to free his Hebrew slaves, both male and female; no one was to hold a fellow Jew in bondage.[g] 10So all the officials and people who entered into this covenant agreed that they would free their male and female slaves and no longer hold them in bondage. They agreed, and set them free. 11But afterward they changed their minds and took back the slaves they had freed and enslaved them again.

12Then the word of the LORD came to Jeremiah: 13“This is what the LORD, the God of Israel, says: I made a covenant with your forefathers when I brought them out of Egypt, out of the land of slavery. I said, 14‘Every seventh year each of you must free any fellow Hebrew who has sold himself to you. After he has served you six years, you must let him go free.’[c][h] Your fathers, however, did not listen to me or pay attention[i] to me. 15Recently you repented and did what is right in my sight: Each of you proclaimed freedom to his countrymen. You even made a covenant before me in the house that bears my Name.[j] 16But now you have turned around and profaned[k] my name; each of you has taken back the male and female slaves you had set free to go where they wished. You have forced them to become your slaves again.

17“Therefore, this is what the LORD says: You have not obeyed me; you have not proclaimed freedom for your fellow countrymen. So I now proclaim ‘freedom’ for you,[l] declares the LORD—‘freedom’ to fall by the sword, plague and famine. I will make you

**33:22** v Ge 15:5
**33:25** w Jer 31:35–36 x Ps 74:16–17
**33:26** y Jer 31:37
**34:1** z 2Ki 25:1; Jer 39:1
**34:2** a Jer 32:29
**34:3** b Jer 32:4
**34:5** c 2Ch 16:14
**34:5** d Jer 22:18
**34:7** e 2Ch 11:9
**34:8** f Ex 21:2
**34:9** g Lev 25:39–46
**34:14** h Ex 21:2 i Dt 15:12
**34:15** j Jer 7:10–11
**34:16** k Ex 20:7; Lev 19:12
**34:17** l Mt 7:2

[a]24 Or *families* [b]26 Or *will bring them back from captivity* [c]14 Deut. 15:12

abhorrent to all the kingdoms of the earth.[m] [18]The men who have violated my covenant and have not fulfilled the terms of the covenant they made before me, I will treat like the calf they cut in two and then walked between its pieces.[n] [19]The leaders of Judah and Jerusalem, the court officials, the priests and all the people of the land who walked between the pieces of the calf, [20]I will hand over to their enemies who seek their lives. Their dead bodies will become food for the birds of the air and the beasts of the earth.[o]

[21]"I will hand Zedekiah king of Judah and his officials over to their enemies who seek their lives, to the army of the king of Babylon, which has withdrawn[p] from you. [22]I am going to give the order, declares the LORD, and I will bring them back to this city. They will fight against it, take it and burn it down. And I will lay waste the towns of Judah so no one can live there."

## The Recabites

35 This is the word that came to Jeremiah from the LORD during the reign of Jehoiakim son of Josiah king of Judah: [2]"Go to the Recabite[q] family and invite them to come to one of the side rooms[r] of the house of the LORD and give them wine to drink."

[3]So I went to get Jaazaniah son of Jeremiah, the son of Habazziniah, and his brothers and all his sons—the whole family of the Recabites. [4]I brought them into the house of the LORD, into the room of the sons of Hanan son of Igdaliah the man of God. It was next to the room of the officials, which was over that of Maaseiah son of Shallum[s] the doorkeeper. [5]Then I set bowls full of wine and some cups before the men of the Recabite family and said to them, "Drink some wine."

[6]But they replied, "We do not drink wine, because our forefather Jonadab[t] son of Recab gave us this command: 'Neither you nor your descendants must ever drink wine. [7]Also you must never build houses, sow seed or plant vineyards; you must never have any of these things, but must always live in tents. Then you will live a long time in the land[u] where you are nomads.' [8]We have obeyed everything our forefather Jonadab son of Recab commanded us. Neither we nor our wives nor our sons and daughters have ever drunk wine [9]or built houses to live in or had vineyards, fields or crops. [10]We have lived in tents and have fully obeyed everything our forefather Jonadab commanded us. [11]But when Nebuchadnezzar king of Babylon invaded this land, we said, 'Come, we must go to Jerusalem to escape the Babylonian[a] and Aramean armies.' So we have remained in Jerusalem."

[12]Then the word of the LORD came to Jeremiah, saying: [13]"This is what the LORD Almighty, the God of Israel, says: Go and tell the men of Judah and the people of Jerusalem, 'Will you not learn a lesson[v] and obey my words?' declares the LORD. [14]'Jonadab son of Recab ordered his sons not to drink wine and this command has been kept. To this day they do not drink wine, because they obey their forefather's command. But I have spoken to you again and again,[w] yet you have not obeyed me. [15]Again and again I sent all my servants the prophets to you. They said, "Each of you must turn from your wicked ways and reform[x] your actions; do not follow other gods to serve them. Then you will live in the land I have given to you and your fathers." But you have not paid attention or listened to me. [16]The descendants of Jonadab son of Recab have carried out the command their forefather gave them, but these people have not obeyed me.'

[17]"Therefore, this is what the LORD God Almighty, the God of Israel, says: 'Listen! I am going to bring on Judah and on everyone living in Jerusalem every disaster I pronounced against them. I spoke to them, but they did not listen;[y] I called to them, but they did not answer.'"[z]

[18]Then Jeremiah said to the family of the Recabites, "This is what the LORD Almighty, the God of Israel, says: 'You have obeyed the command of your forefather Jonadab and have followed all his instructions and have done everything he ordered.' [19]Therefore, this is what the LORD Almighty, the God of Israel, says: 'Jonadab son of Recab will never fail to have a man to serve[a] me.'"

[a]11 Or *Chaldean*

**34:17** m Dt28:25,64
**34:18** n Ge15:10
**34:20** o Jer7:33; 19:7
**34:21** p Jer37:5
**35:2** q 2Ki10:15; 1Ch2:55 r 1Ki6:5
**35:4** s 1Ch9:19
**35:6** t 2Ki10:15
**35:7** u Ex20:12; Eph6:2–3
**35:13** v Jer32:33
**35:14** w Jer7:13
**35:15** x Jer18:11
**35:17** y Pr1:24 z Isa65:12; 66:4; Jer7:13
**35:19** a Jer15:19

**36:2** b Jer 30:2 c Jer 25:3
**36:3** d ver 7 e Mk 4:12 f Jer 26:3; Jnh 3:8; Ac 3:19 g Jer 18:8
**36:4** h Jer 32:12 i ver 18 j Eze 2:9
**36:10** k Jer 26:10
**36:12** l Jer 26:22

## Jehoiakim Burns Jeremiah's Scroll

**36** In the fourth year of Jehoiakim son of Josiah king of Judah, this word came to Jeremiah from the LORD: 2"Take a scroll[b] and write on it all the words I have spoken to you concerning Israel, Judah and all the other nations from the time I began speaking to you in the reign of Josiah[c] till now. 3Perhaps[d] when the people of Judah hear[e] about every disaster I plan to inflict on them, each of them will turn[f] from his wicked way; then I will forgive[g] their wickedness and their sin."

4So Jeremiah called Baruch[h] son of Neriah, and while Jeremiah dictated[i] all the words the LORD had spoken to him, Baruch wrote them on the scroll.[j] 5Then Jeremiah told Baruch, "I am restricted; I cannot go to the LORD's temple. 6So you go to the house of the LORD on a day of fasting and read to the people from the scroll the words of the LORD that you wrote as I dictated. Read them to all the people of Judah who come in from their towns. 7Perhaps they will bring their petition before the LORD, and each will turn from his wicked ways, for the anger and wrath pronounced against this people by the LORD are great."

8Baruch son of Neriah did everything Jeremiah the prophet told him to do; at the LORD's temple he read the words of the LORD from the scroll. 9In the ninth month of the fifth year of Jehoiakim son of Josiah king of Judah, a time of fasting before the LORD was proclaimed for all the people in Jerusalem and those who had come from the towns of Judah. 10From the room of Gemariah son of Shaphan the secretary, which was in the upper courtyard at the entrance of the New Gate[k] of the temple, Baruch read to all the people at the LORD's temple the words of Jeremiah from the scroll.

11When Micaiah son of Gemariah, the son of Shaphan, heard all the words of the LORD from the scroll, 12he went down to the secretary's room in the royal palace, where all the officials were sitting: Elishama the secretary, Delaiah son of Shemaiah, Elnathan[l] son of Acbor, Gemariah son of Shaphan, Zedekiah son of Hananiah, and all the other officials. 13After Micaiah told them everything he had heard Baruch read to the people from the scroll, 14all the officials sent Jehudi son of Nethaniah, the son of Shelemiah, the son of Cushi, to say to Baruch, "Bring the scroll from which you have read to the people and come." So Baruch son of Neriah went to them with the scroll in his hand. 15They said to him, "Sit down, please, and read it to us."

So Baruch read it to them. 16When they heard all these words, they looked at each other in fear and said to Baruch, "We must report all these words to the king." 17Then they asked Baruch, "Tell us, how did you come to write all this? Did Jeremiah dictate it?"

18"Yes," Baruch replied, "he dictated[m] all these words to me, and I wrote them in ink on the scroll."

19Then the officials said to Baruch, "You and Jeremiah, go and hide. Don't let anyone know where you are."

20After they put the scroll in the room of Elishama the secretary, they went to the king in the courtyard and reported everything to him. 21The king sent Jehudi to get the scroll, and Jehudi brought it from the room of Elishama the secretary and read it to the king and all the officials standing beside him. 22It was the ninth month and the king was sitting in the winter apartment,[n] with a fire burning in the firepot in front of him. 23Whenever Jehudi had read three or four columns of the scroll, the king cut them off with a scribe's knife and threw them into the firepot, until the entire scroll was burned in the fire. 24The king and all his attendants who heard all these words showed no fear, nor did they tear their clothes.[o] 25Even though Elnathan, Delaiah and Gemariah urged the king not to burn the scroll, he would not listen to them. 26Instead, the king commanded Jerahmeel, a son of the king, Seraiah son of Azriel and Shelemiah son of Abdeel to arrest Baruch the scribe and Jeremiah the prophet. But the LORD had hidden them.

27After the king burned the scroll containing the words that Baruch had written at Jeremiah's dictation,[p] the word of the LORD came to Jeremiah: 28"Take another scroll and write on it all the words that were

**36:18** m ver 4
**36:22** n Am 3:15
**36:24** o 2Ki 22:11; Isa 37:1
**36:27** p ver 4

**36:29** q Isa 30:10
**36:30** r Jer 22:19
**36:32** s ver 4
**37:1** t 2Ki 24:17 u 2Ch 36:10; Jer 22:24
**37:2** v 2Ch 36:12,14
**37:3** w Jer 29:25; 52:24 x Jer 21:1–2
**37:4** y ver 15
**37:5** z Eze 17:15 a 2Ki 24:7

on the first scroll, which Jehoiakim king of
Judah burned up. 29 Also tell Jehoiakim king
of Judah, 'This is what the LORD says: You
burned that scroll and said, "Why did you
write on it that the king of Babylon would
certainly come and destroy this land and
cut off both men and animals from it?"[q]
30 Therefore, this is what the LORD says about
Jehoiakim king of Judah: He will have no
one to sit on the throne of David; his body
will be thrown out[r] and exposed to the heat
by day and the frost by night. 31 I will punish
him and his children and his attendants for
their wickedness; I will bring on them and
those living in Jerusalem and the people of
Judah every disaster I pronounced against
them, because they have not listened.' "

32 So Jeremiah took another scroll and
gave it to the scribe Baruch son of Neriah,
and as Jeremiah dictated,[s] Baruch wrote on
it all the words of the scroll that Jehoiakim
king of Judah had burned in the fire. And
many similar words were added to them.

## Jeremiah in Prison

37 Zedekiah[t] son of Josiah was made
king of Judah by Nebuchadnezzar
king of Babylon; he reigned in place of Jehoi-
achin[a][u] son of Jehoiakim. 2 Neither he nor
his attendants nor the people of the land
paid any attention[v] to the words the LORD
had spoken through Jeremiah the prophet.

3 King Zedekiah, however, sent Jehucal
son of Shelemiah with the priest Zephaniah[w]
son of Maaseiah to Jeremiah the prophet
with this message: "Please pray[x] to the LORD
our God for us."

4 Now Jeremiah was free to come and
go among the people, for he had not yet
been put in prison.[y] 5 Pharaoh's army had
marched out of Egypt,[z] and when the Bab-
ylonians[b] who were besieging Jerusalem
heard the report about them, they withdrew
from Jerusalem.[a]

6 Then the word of the LORD came to
Jeremiah the prophet: 7 "This is what the
LORD, the God of Israel, says: Tell the king
of Judah, who sent you to inquire of me,
'Pharaoh's army, which has marched out to
support you, will go back to its own land, to
Egypt. 8 Then the Babylonians will return
and attack this city; they will capture it and
burn[b] it down.'

9 "This is what the LORD says: Do not
deceive yourselves, thinking, 'The Bab-
ylonians will surely leave us.' They will
not! 10 Even if you were to defeat the entire
Babylonian[c] army that is attacking you
and only wounded men were left in their
tents, they would come out and burn this
city down."

11 After the Babylonian army had with-
drawn from Jerusalem because of Phar-
aoh's army, 12 Jeremiah started to leave the
city to go to the territory of Benjamin to get
his share of the property among the people
there. 13 But when he reached the Benjamin
Gate, the captain of the guard, whose name
was Irijah son of Shelemiah, the son of
Hananiah, arrested him and said, "You are
deserting to the Babylonians!"

14 "That's not true!" Jeremiah said. "I
am not deserting to the Babylonians." But
Irijah would not listen to him; instead, he
arrested[c] Jeremiah and brought him to the
officials. 15 They were angry with Jeremiah
and had him beaten and imprisoned in the
house of Jonathan the secretary, which they
had made into a prison.

16 Jeremiah was put into a vaulted cell in
a dungeon, where he remained a long time.
17 Then King Zedekiah sent for him and had
him brought to the palace, where he asked
him privately, "Is there any word from
the LORD?"

"Yes," Jeremiah replied, "you will be
handed over to the king of Babylon."

18 Then Jeremiah said to King Zedekiah,
"What crime have I committed against you
or your officials or this people, that you have
put me in prison? 19 Where are your prophets
who prophesied to you, 'The king of Babylon
will not attack you or this land'? 20 But now,
my lord the king, please listen. Let me bring
my petition before you: Do not send me
back to the house of Jonathan the secretary,
or I will die there."

21 King Zedekiah then gave orders for
Jeremiah to be placed in the courtyard of
the guard and given bread from the street

**37:8** b Jer 34:22
**37:14** c Jer 40:4

[a]1 Hebrew *Coniah,* a variant of *Jehoiachin* [b]5 Or *Chaldeans;* also in verses 8, 9, 13 and 14 [c]10 Or *Chaldean;* also in verse 11

of the bakers each day until all the bread[d] in the city was gone.[e] So Jeremiah remained in the courtyard of the guard.[f]

## Jeremiah Thrown Into a Cistern

38 Shephatiah son of Mattan, Gedaliah son of Pashhur, Jehucal[a][g] son of Shelemiah, and Pashhur son of Malkijah heard what Jeremiah was telling all the people when he said, 2"This is what the LORD says: 'Whoever stays in this city will die by the sword, famine or plague, but whoever goes over to the Babylonians[b] will live. He will escape with his life; he will live.'[h] 3And this is what the LORD says: 'This city will certainly be handed over to the army of the king of Babylon, who will capture it.' "[i]

4Then the officials said to the king, "This man should be put to death.[j] He is discouraging the soldiers who are left in this city, as well as all the people, by the things he is saying to them. This man is not seeking the good of these people but their ruin."

5"He is in your hands," King Zedekiah answered. "The king can do nothing to oppose you."

6So they took Jeremiah and put him into the cistern of Malkijah, the king's son, which was in the courtyard of the guard.[k] They lowered Jeremiah by ropes into the cistern; it had no water in it, only mud, and Jeremiah sank down into the mud.

7But Ebed-Melech,[l] a Cushite,[c] an official[d] in the royal palace, heard that they had put Jeremiah into the cistern. While the king was sitting in the Benjamin Gate, 8Ebed-Melech went out of the palace and said to him, 9"My lord the king, these men have acted wickedly in all they have done to Jeremiah the prophet. They have thrown him into a cistern, where he will starve to death when there is no longer any bread[m] in the city."

10Then the king commanded Ebed-Melech the Cushite, "Take thirty men from here with you and lift Jeremiah the prophet out of the cistern before he dies."

11So Ebed-Melech took the men with him and went to a room under the treasury in the palace. He took some old rags and worn-out clothes from there and let them down with ropes to Jeremiah in the cistern. 12Ebed-Melech the Cushite said to Jeremiah, "Put these old rags and worn-out clothes under your arms to pad the ropes." Jeremiah did so, 13and they pulled him up with the ropes and lifted him out of the cistern. And Jeremiah remained in the courtyard of the guard.[n]

## Zedekiah Questions Jeremiah Again

14Then King Zedekiah sent for Jeremiah the prophet and had him brought to the third entrance to the temple of the LORD. "I am going to ask you something," the king said to Jeremiah. "Do not hide anything from me."

15Jeremiah said to Zedekiah, "If I give you an answer, will you not kill me? Even if I did give you counsel, you would not listen to me."

16But King Zedekiah swore this oath secretly[o] to Jeremiah: "As surely as the LORD lives, who has given us breath,[p] I will neither kill you nor hand you over to those who are seeking your life."

17Then Jeremiah said to Zedekiah, "This

**37:21** d Jer 38:9 e Jer 52:6 f Jer 32:2; 38:6,13,28
**38:1** g Jer 37:3
**38:2** h Jer 21:9
**38:3** i Jer 21:4,10; 32:3
**38:4** j Jer 26:11
**38:6** k Jer 37:21
**38:7** l Jer 39:16
**38:9** m Jer 37:21
**38:13** n Jer 37:21
**38:16** o Jer 37:17 p Isa 57:16

[a]1 Hebrew *Jucal*, a variant of *Jehucal* [b]2 Or *Chaldeans*; also in verses 18, 19 and 23 [c]7 Probably from the upper Nile region [d]7 Or *a eunuch*

### The African Presence

**Jeremiah 38:7–13**

Ebed-Melech, a Cushite, rescued Jeremiah from the pit. God promised him deliverance when the Babylonians invaded the land.

is what the LORD God Almighty, the God of Israel, says: 'If you surrender to the officers of the king of Babylon, your life will be spared and this city will not be burned down; you and your family will live.[q] [18]But if you will not surrender to the officers of the king of Babylon, this city will be handed over[r] to the Babylonians and they will burn it down; you yourself will not escape[s] from their hands.' "

[19]King Zedekiah said to Jeremiah, "I am afraid[t] of the Jews who have gone over to the Babylonians, for the Babylonians may hand me over to them and they will mistreat me."

[20]"They will not hand you over," Jeremiah replied. "Obey[u] the LORD by doing what I tell you. Then it will go well with you, and your life will be spared. [21]But if you refuse to surrender, this is what the LORD has revealed to me: [22]All the women[v] left in the palace of the king of Judah will be brought out to the officials of the king of Babylon. Those women will say to you:

" 'They misled you and overcame you—
those trusted friends of yours.
Your feet are sunk in the mud;
your friends have deserted you.'

[23]"All your wives and children will be brought out to the Babylonians. You yourself will not escape from their hands but will be captured[w] by the king of Babylon; and this city will[a] be burned down."

[24]Then Zedekiah said to Jeremiah, "Do not let anyone know about this conversation, or you may die. [25]If the officials hear that I talked with you, and they come to you and say, 'Tell us what you said to the king and what the king said to you; do not hide it from us or we will kill you,' [26]then tell them, 'I was pleading with the king not to send me back to Jonathan's house[x] to die there.' "

[27]All the officials did come to Jeremiah and question him, and he told them everything the king had ordered him to say. So they said no more to him, for no one had heard his conversation with the king.

[28]And Jeremiah remained in the courtyard of the guard[y] until the day Jerusalem was captured.

## The Fall of Jerusalem

**39** This is how Jerusalem was taken: [1]In the ninth year of Zedekiah king of Judah, in the tenth month, Nebuchadnezzar king of Babylon marched against Jerusalem with his whole army and laid siege[z] to it. [2]And on the ninth day of the fourth month of Zedekiah's eleventh year, the city wall was broken through. [3]Then all the officials of the king of Babylon came and took seats in the Middle Gate: Nergal-Sharezer of Samgar, Nebo-Sarsekim[b] a chief officer, Nergal-Sharezer a high official and all the other officials of the king of Babylon. [4]When Zedekiah king of Judah and all the soldiers saw them, they fled; they left the city at night by way of the king's garden, through the gate between the two walls, and headed toward the Arabah.[c]

[5]But the Babylonian[d] army pursued them and overtook Zedekiah[a] in the plains of Jericho. They captured him and took him to Nebuchadnezzar king of Babylon at Riblah[b] in the land of Hamath, where he pronounced sentence on him. [6]There at Riblah the king of Babylon slaughtered the sons of Zedekiah before his eyes and also killed all the nobles of Judah. [7]Then he put out Zedekiah's eyes[c] and bound him with bronze shackles to take him to Babylon.[d]

[8]The Babylonians[e] set fire[e] to the royal palace and the houses of the people and broke down the walls of Jerusalem. [9]Nebuzaradan commander of the imperial guard carried into exile to Babylon the people who remained in the city, along with those who had gone over to him, and the rest of the people. [10]But Nebuzaradan the commander of the guard left behind in the land of Judah some of the poor people, who owned nothing; and at that time he gave them vineyards and fields.

[11]Now Nebuchadnezzar king of Babylon had given these orders about Jeremiah through Nebuzaradan commander of the imperial guard: [12]"Take him and look after him; don't harm him but do for him whatever he asks." [13]So Nebuzaradan the commander of the guard, Nebushazban a chief officer, Nergal-Sharezer a high official

**38:17** q 2Ki 24:12
**38:18** r Jer 34:3 s Jer 32:4
**38:19** t Isa 51:12
**38:20** u Jer 11:4
**38:22** v Jer 6:12
**38:23** w Jer 41:10
**38:26** x Jer 37:15
**38:28** y Jer 37:21; 39:14
**39:1** z 2Ki 25:1
**39:5** a Jer 32:4 b 2Ki 23:33
**39:7** c Eze 12:13 d Jer 32:5
**39:8** e Jer 38:18

[a]23 Or *and you will cause this city to* [b]3 Or *Nergal-Sharezer, Samgar-Nebo, Sarsekim* [c]4 Or *the Jordan Valley*
[d]5 Or *Chaldean* [e]8 Or *Chaldeans*

**39:14** f Jer 38:28
**39:16** g Jer 38:7; h Da 9:12
**39:18** i Jer 45:5; j Jer 21:9
**40:2** k Jer 50:7
**40:3** l Da 9:11
**40:4** m Jer 39:11–12
**40:5** n Jer 39:14
**40:6** o Jdg 20:1

and all the other officers of the king of Babylon 14 sent and had Jeremiah taken out of the courtyard of the guard.[f] They turned him over to Gedaliah son of Ahikam, the son of Shaphan, to take him back to his home. So he remained among his own people.

15 While Jeremiah had been confined in the courtyard of the guard, the word of the LORD came to him: 16 "Go and tell Ebed-Melech[g] the Cushite, 'This is what the LORD Almighty, the God of Israel, says: I am about to fulfill my words against this city through disaster,[h] not prosperity. At that time they will be fulfilled before your eyes. 17 But I will rescue you on that day, declares the LORD; you will not be handed over to those you fear. 18 I will save you; you will not fall by the sword[i] but will escape with your life,[j] because you trust in me, declares the LORD.' "

## Jeremiah Freed

**40** The word came to Jeremiah from the LORD after Nebuzaradan commander of the imperial guard had released him at Ramah. He had found Jeremiah bound in chains among all the captives from Jerusalem and Judah who were being carried into exile to Babylon. 2 When the commander of the guard found Jeremiah, he said to him, "The LORD your God decreed this disaster for this place.[k] 3 And now the LORD has brought it about; he has done just as he said he would. All this happened because you people sinned[l] against the LORD and did not obey him. 4 But today I am freeing you from the chains on your wrists. Come with me to Babylon, if you like, and I will look after you; but if you do not want to, then don't come. Look, the whole country lies before you; go wherever you please."[m] 5 However, before Jeremiah turned to go,[a] Nebuzaradan added, "Go back to Gedaliah son of Ahikam, the son of Shaphan, whom the king of Babylon has appointed over the towns of Judah, and live with him among the people, or go anywhere else you please."[n]

Then the commander gave him provisions and a present and let him go. 6 So Jeremiah went to Gedaliah son of Ahikam at Mizpah[o] and stayed with him among the people who were left behind in the land.

## Gedaliah Assassinated

7 When all the army officers and their men who were still in the open country heard that the king of Babylon had appointed Gedaliah son of Ahikam as governor over the land and had put him in charge of the men, women and children who were the poorest[p] in the land and who had not been carried into exile to Babylon, 8 they came to Gedaliah at Mizpah—Ishmael[q] son of Nethaniah, Johanan and Jonathan the sons of Kareah, Seraiah son of Tanhumeth, the sons of Ephai the Netophathite, and Jaazaniah[b] the son of the Maacathite, and their men. 9 Gedaliah son of Ahikam, the son of Shaphan, took an oath to reassure them and their men. "Do not be afraid to serve[r] the Babylonians,[c]" he said. "Settle down in the land and serve the king of Babylon, and it will go well with you.[s] 10 I myself will stay at Mizpah to represent you before the Babylonians who come to us, but you are to harvest the wine, summer fruit and oil, and put them in your storage jars, and live in the towns you have taken over."

11 When all the Jews in Moab, Ammon, Edom and all the other countries heard that the king of Babylon had left a remnant in Judah and had appointed Gedaliah son of Ahikam, the son of Shaphan, as governor over them, 12 they all came back to the land of Judah, to Gedaliah at Mizpah, from all the countries where they had been scattered.[t] And they harvested an abundance of wine and summer fruit.

13 Johanan son of Kareah and all the army officers still in the open country came to Gedaliah at Mizpah 14 and said to him, "Don't you know that Baalis king of the Ammonites[u] has sent Ishmael son of Nethaniah to take your life?" But Gedaliah son of Ahikam did not believe them.

15 Then Johanan son of Kareah said privately to Gedaliah in Mizpah, "Let me go and kill Ishmael son of Nethaniah, and no one will know it. Why should he take your life and cause all the Jews who are gathered around you to be scattered and the remnant of Judah to perish?"

16 But Gedaliah son of Ahikam said to Johanan son of Kareah, "Don't do such a

**40:7** p Jer 39:10
**40:8** q Jer 41:1,2
**40:9** r Jer 27:11; s Jer 38:20
**40:12** t Jer 43:5
**40:14** u Jer 41:10

[a] 5 Or *Jeremiah answered* [b] 8 Hebrew *Jezaniah,* a variant of *Jaazaniah* [c] 9 Or *Chaldeans;* also in verse 10

thing! What you are saying about Ishmael is not true."

# 41

In the seventh month Ishmael[v] son of Nethaniah, the son of Elishama, who was of royal blood and had been one of the king's officers, came with ten men to Gedaliah son of Ahikam at Mizpah. While they were eating together there, 2 Ishmael son of Nethaniah and the ten men who were with him got up and struck down Gedaliah son of Ahikam, the son of Shaphan, with the sword, killing the one whom the king of Babylon had appointed[w] as governor over the land. 3 Ishmael also killed all the Jews who were with Gedaliah at Mizpah, as well as the Babylonian[a] soldiers who were there.

4 The day after Gedaliah's assassination, before anyone knew about it, 5 eighty men who had shaved off their beards,[x] torn their clothes and cut themselves came from Shechem, Shiloh and Samaria,[y] bringing grain offerings and incense with them to the house of the LORD.[z] 6 Ishmael son of Nethaniah went out from Mizpah to meet them, weeping as he went. When he met them, he said, "Come to Gedaliah son of Ahikam." 7 When they went into the city, Ishmael son of Nethaniah and the men who were with him slaughtered them and threw them into a cistern. 8 But ten of them said to Ishmael, "Don't kill us! We have wheat and barley, oil and honey, hidden in a field." So he let them alone and did not kill them with the others. 9 Now the cistern where he threw all the bodies of the men he had killed along with Gedaliah was the one King Asa[a] had made as part of his defense against Baasha king of Israel. Ishmael son of Nethaniah filled it with the dead.

10 Ishmael made captives of all the rest of the people who were in Mizpah—the king's daughters along with all the others who were left there, over whom Nebuzaradan commander of the imperial guard had appointed Gedaliah son of Ahikam. Ishmael son of Nethaniah took them captive and set out to cross over to the Ammonites.[b]

11 When Johanan[c] son of Kareah and all the army officers who were with him heard about all the crimes Ishmael son of Nethaniah had committed, 12 they took all their men and went to fight Ishmael son of Nethaniah. They caught up with him near the great pool[d] in Gibeon. 13 When all the people Ishmael had with him saw Johanan son of Kareah and the army officers who were with him, they were glad. 14 All the people Ishmael had taken captive at Mizpah turned and went over to Johanan son of Kareah. 15 But Ishmael son of Nethaniah and eight of his men escaped from Johanan and fled to the Ammonites.

## Flight to Egypt

16 Then Johanan son of Kareah and all the army officers who were with him led away all the survivors from Mizpah whom he had recovered from Ishmael son of Nethaniah after he had assassinated Gedaliah son of Ahikam: the soldiers, women, children and court officials he had brought from Gibeon. 17 And they went on, stopping at Geruth Kimham[e] near Bethlehem on their way to Egypt 18 to escape the Babylonians.[b] They were afraid of them because Ishmael son of Nethaniah had killed Gedaliah[f] son of Ahikam, whom the king of Babylon had appointed as governor over the land.

# 42

Then all the army officers, including Johanan[g] son of Kareah and Jezaniah[c] son of Hoshaiah, and all the people from the least to the greatest approached 2 Jeremiah the prophet and said to him, "Please hear our petition and pray to the LORD your God for this entire remnant. For as you now see, though we were once many, now only a few are left. 3 Pray that the LORD your God will tell us where we should go and what we should do."

4 "I have heard you," replied Jeremiah the prophet. "I will certainly pray to the LORD your God as you have requested; I will tell you everything the LORD says and will keep nothing back from you."[h]

5 Then they said to Jeremiah, "May the LORD be a true and faithful witness[i] against us if we do not act in accordance with everything the LORD your God sends you to tell us. 6 Whether it is favorable or unfavorable, we will obey the LORD our God, to whom we are sending you, so that it will go well[j] with us, for we will obey the LORD our God."

**41:1** v Jer 40:8
**41:2** w Jer 40:5
**41:5** x Lev 19:27 y 1Ki 16:24 z 2Ki 25:9
**41:9** a 1Ki 15:22; 2Ch 16:6
**41:10** b Jer 40:14
**41:11** c Jer 40:8
**41:12** d 2Sa 2:13
**41:17** e 2Sa 19:37
**41:18** f Jer 40:5
**42:1** g Jer 40:13; 41:11
**42:4** h 1Ki 22:14; 1Sa 3:17
**42:5** i Ge 31:50
**42:6** j Dt 6:3; Jer 7:23

[a] 3 Or *Chaldean* [b] 18 Or *Chaldeans* [c] 1 Hebrew; Septuagint (see also 43:2) *Azariah*

**42:10**
k Jer 24:6
l Jer 31:28

**42:11**
m Isa 43:5
n Ro 8:31

**42:12**
o Ps 106:44–46

**42:13**
p Jer 44:16

**42:17**
q Jer 44:13

**42:18**
r Jer 7:20
s Jer 29:18

**42:19**
t Dt 17:16

7Ten days later the word of the LORD came
to Jeremiah. 8So he called together Johanan
son of Kareah and all the army officers who
were with him and all the people from the
least to the greatest. 9He said to them, "This
is what the LORD, the God of Israel, to whom
you sent me to present your petition, says:
10'If you stay in this land, I will build[k] you
up and not tear you down; I will plant[l] you
and not uproot you, for I am grieved over
the disaster I have inflicted on you. 11Do not
be afraid of the king of Babylon, whom you
now fear. Do not be afraid of him, declares
the LORD, for I am with you and will save[m]
you and deliver you from his hands.[n] 12I
will show you compassion so that he will
have compassion on you and restore you to
your land.'[o]

13"However, if you say, 'We will not stay
in this land,' and so disobey[p] the LORD your
God, 14and if you say, 'No, we will go and live
in Egypt, where we will not see war or hear
the trumpet or be hungry for bread,' 15then
hear the word of the LORD, O remnant of Ju-
dah. This is what the LORD Almighty, the
God of Israel, says: 'If you are determined
to go to Egypt and you do go to settle there,
16then the sword you fear will overtake you
there, and the famine you dread will follow
you into Egypt, and there you will die. 17In-
deed, all who are determined to go to Egypt
to settle there will die by the sword, famine
and plague;[q] not one of them will survive
or escape the disaster I will bring on them.'
18This is what the LORD Almighty, the God of
Israel, says: 'As my anger and wrath[r] have
been poured out on those who lived in Jeru-
salem, so will my wrath be poured out on
you when you go to Egypt. You will be an
object of cursing and horror,[s] of condemna-
tion and reproach; you will never see this
place again.'

19"O remnant of Judah, the LORD has told
you, 'Do not go to Egypt.'[t] Be sure of this: I
warn you today 20that you made a fatal mis-
take[a] when you sent me to the LORD your
God and said, 'Pray to the LORD our God for
us; tell us everything he says and we will do
it.' 21I have told you today, but you still have
not obeyed the LORD your God in all he sent
me to tell you. 22So now, be sure of this: You
will die by the sword, famine and plague in
the place where you want to go to settle."

43 When Jeremiah finished telling the
people all the words of the LORD
their God—everything the LORD had sent
him to tell them— 2Azariah son of Hosha-
iah and Johanan[u] son of Kareah and all the
arrogant men said to Jeremiah, "You are
lying! The LORD our God has not sent you
to say, 'You must not go to Egypt to settle
there.' 3But Baruch son of Neriah is inciting
you against us to hand us over to the Babylo-
nians,[b] so they may kill us or carry us into
exile to Babylon."

4So Johanan son of Kareah and all the
army officers and all the people disobeyed
the LORD's command to stay in the land of
Judah. 5Instead, Johanan son of Kareah and
all the army officers led away all the rem-
nant of Judah who had come back to live
in the land of Judah from all the nations
where they had been scattered.[v] 6They also
led away all the men, women and children
and the king's daughters whom Nebuzara-
dan commander of the imperial guard had
left with Gedaliah son of Ahikam, the son of
Shaphan, and Jeremiah the prophet and Bar-
uch son of Neriah. 7So they entered Egypt
in disobedience to the LORD and went as far
as Tahpanhes.[w]

8In Tahpanhes the word of the LORD came
to Jeremiah: 9"While the Jews are watching,
take some large stones with you and bury
them in clay in the brick pavement at the
entrance to Pharaoh's palace in Tahpanhes.
10Then say to them, 'This is what the LORD
Almighty, the God of Israel, says: I will send
for my servant[x] Nebuchadnezzar king of
Babylon, and I will set his throne over these
stones I have buried here; he will spread his
royal canopy above them. 11He will come and
attack Egypt,[y] bringing death to those des-
tined for death, captivity to those destined
for captivity, and the sword to those des-
tined for the sword.[z] 12He[c] will set fire to the
temples of the gods[a] of Egypt; he will burn
their temples and take their gods captive. As
a shepherd wraps his garment around him,
so will he wrap Egypt around himself and
depart from there unscathed. 13There in the
temple of the sun[d] in Egypt he will demolish

**43:2**
u Jer 42:1

**43:5**
v Jer 40:12

**43:7**
w Jer 44:1

**43:10**
x Jer 25:9; 27:6

**43:11**
y Jer 46:13–26
z Jer 15:2; 44:13

**43:12**
a Jer 46:25

[a]20 Or *you erred in your hearts* [b]3 Or *Chaldeans* [c]12 Or *I* [d]13 Or *in Heliopolis*

**44:1** b Jer 43:7,8 c Isa 19:13 d Jer 46:14
**44:2** e Jer 9:11; 34:22
**44:3** f Dt 13:6–11 g Dt 32:17; Jer 19:4
**44:4** h Jer 7:25; 25:4; 26:5
**44:8** i Jer 25:6–7 j Jer 42:18
**44:11** k Jer 21:10; Am 9:4

the sacred pillars and will burn down the temples of the gods of Egypt.’ ”

## Disaster Because of Idolatry

44 This word came to Jeremiah concerning all the Jews living in Lower Egypt—in Migdol, Tahpanhes[b] and Memphis[a][c]—and in Upper Egypt[b]:[d] 2“This is what the LORD Almighty, the God of Israel, says: You saw the great disaster I brought on Jerusalem and on all the towns of Judah. Today they lie deserted and in ruins[e] 3because of the evil they have done. They provoked me to anger by burning incense and by worshiping other gods[f] that neither they nor you nor your fathers[g] ever knew. 4Again and again I sent my servants the prophets,[h] who said, ‘Do not do this detestable thing that I hate!’ 5But they did not listen or pay attention; they did not turn from their wickedness or stop burning incense to other gods. 6Therefore, my fierce anger was poured out; it raged against the towns of Judah and the streets of Jerusalem and made them the desolate ruins they are today.

7“Now this is what the LORD God Almighty, the God of Israel, says: Why bring such great disaster on yourselves by cutting off from Judah the men and women, the children and infants, and so leave yourselves without a remnant? 8Why provoke me to anger with what your hands have made,[i] burning incense to other gods in Egypt, where you have come to live? You will destroy yourselves and make yourselves an object of cursing and reproach[j] among all the nations on earth. 9Have you forgotten the wickedness committed by your fathers and by the kings and queens of Judah and the wickedness committed by you and your wives in the land of Judah and the streets of Jerusalem? 10To this day they have not humbled themselves or shown reverence, nor have they followed my law and the decrees I set before you and your fathers.

11“Therefore, this is what the LORD Almighty, the God of Israel, says: I am determined to bring disaster[k] on you and to destroy all Judah. 12I will take away the remnant of Judah who were determined to go to Egypt to settle there. They will all perish in Egypt; they will fall by the sword or die from famine. From the least to the greatest, they will die by sword or famine. They will become an object of cursing and horror, of condemnation and reproach.[l] 13I will punish those who live in Egypt with the sword, famine and plague, as I punished Jerusalem. 14None of the remnant of Judah who have gone to live in Egypt will escape or survive to return to the land of Judah, to which they long to return and live; none will return except a few fugitives.”[m]

15Then all the men who knew that their wives were burning incense to other gods, along with all the women who were present—a large assembly—and all the people living in Lower and Upper Egypt,[c] said to Jeremiah, 16“We will not listen to the message you have spoken to us in the name of the LORD! 17We will certainly do everything we said we would:[n] We will burn incense to the Queen of Heaven[o] and will pour out drink offerings to her just as we and our fathers, our kings and our officials did in the towns of Judah and in the streets of Jerusalem. At that time we had plenty of food and were well off and suffered no harm. 18But ever since we stopped burning incense to the Queen of Heaven and pouring out drink offerings to her, we have had nothing and have been perishing by sword and famine.”

19The women added, “When we burned incense to the Queen of Heaven[p] and poured out drink offerings to her, did not our husbands know that we were making cakes like her image and pouring out drink offerings to her?”

20Then Jeremiah said to all the people, both men and women, who were answering him, 21“Did not the LORD remember and think about the incense burned in the towns of Judah and the streets of Jerusalem by you and your fathers, your kings and your officials and the people of the land? 22When the LORD could no longer endure your wicked actions and the detestable things you did, your land became an object of cursing[q] and a desolate waste without inhabitants, as it is today. 23Because you have burned incense and have sinned against the LORD and have not obeyed him or followed his law or his

**44:12** l Jer 42:15–18
**44:14** m ver 28; Jer 22:24–27
**44:17** n Dt 23:23 o Jer 7:18
**44:19** p Jer 7:18
**44:22** q Jer 25:18

[a]1 Hebrew *Noph* [b]1 Hebrew *in Pathros* [c]15 Hebrew *in Egypt and Pathros*

**44:23** r Da 9:11–12
**44:24** s ver 15 t Jer 43:7
**44:26** u Ge 22:16
**44:27** v Jer 31:28
**44:28** w ver 13–14
**44:30** x Jer 46:26; Eze 30:21 y Jer 39:5
**45:1** z Jer 36:4,18,32

decrees or his stipulations, this disaster has
come upon you, as you now see."[r]
24 Then Jeremiah said to all the people,
including the women,[s] "Hear the word of
the LORD, all you people of Judah in Egypt.[t]
25 This is what the LORD Almighty, the God of
Israel, says: You and your wives have shown
by your actions what you promised when
you said, 'We will certainly carry out the
vows we made to burn incense and pour out
drink offerings to the Queen of Heaven.'
"Go ahead then, do what you promised!
Keep your vows! 26 But hear the word of the
LORD, all Jews living in Egypt: 'I swear[u] by
my great name,' says the LORD, 'that no one
from Judah living anywhere in Egypt will
ever again invoke my name or swear, "As
surely as the Sovereign LORD lives." 27 For I
am watching over them for harm,[v] not for
good; the Jews in Egypt will perish by sword
and famine until they are all destroyed.
28 Those who escape the sword and return
to the land of Judah from Egypt will be very
few.[w] Then the whole remnant of Judah who
came to live in Egypt will know whose word
will stand—mine or theirs.
29 " 'This will be the sign to you that I will
punish you in this place,' declares the LORD,
'so that you will know that my threats of
harm against you will surely stand.' 30 This
is what the LORD says: 'I am going to hand
Pharaoh[x] Hophra king of Egypt over to his
enemies who seek his life, just as I handed
Zedekiah king of Judah over to Nebuchad-
nezzar king of Babylon, the enemy who was
seeking his life.' "[y]

## A Message to Baruch

45 This is what Jeremiah the prophet
told Baruch[z] son of Neriah in the
fourth year of Jehoiakim son of Josiah
king of Judah, after Baruch had written on
a scroll the words Jeremiah was then dic-
tating: 2 "This is what the LORD, the God of
Israel, says to you, Baruch: 3 You said, 'Woe
to me! The LORD has added sorrow to my
pain; I am worn out with groaning and find
no rest.' "
4 ⌞The LORD said,⌟ "Say this to him: 'This is
what the LORD says: I will overthrow what I
have built and uproot what I have planted,
throughout the land.[a] 5 Should you then seek
great things for yourself? Seek them not. For
I will bring disaster on all people, declares
the LORD, but wherever you go I will let you
escape with your life.' "[b]

## A Message About Egypt

46 This is the word of the LORD that
came to Jeremiah the prophet con-
cerning the nations:[c]

2 Concerning Egypt:

This is the message against the army of
Pharaoh Neco[d] king of Egypt, which was
defeated at Carchemish[e] on the Euphrates
River by Nebuchadnezzar king of Babylon
in the fourth year of Jehoiakim son of Josiah
king of Judah:

3 "Prepare your shields,[f] both large and
small,
and march out for battle!
4 Harness the horses,
mount the steeds!
Take your positions
with helmets on!
Polish your spears,
put on your armor!
5 What do I see?
They are terrified,
they are retreating,
their warriors are defeated.
They flee in haste
without looking back,
and there is terror[g] on every side,"
declares the LORD.
6 "The swift cannot flee
nor the strong escape.
In the north by the River Euphrates
they stumble and fall.[h]

7 "Who is this that rises like the Nile,
like rivers of surging waters?[i]
8 Egypt rises like the Nile,
like rivers of surging waters.
She says, 'I will rise and cover the earth;
I will destroy cities and their people.'
9 Charge, O horses!
Drive furiously, O charioteers!
March on, O warriors—
men of Cush[a] and Put who carry
shields,

**45:4** a Isa 5:5–7
**45:5** b Jer 21:9; 38:2; 39:18
**46:1** c Jer 25:15–38
**46:2** d 2Ki 23:29 e 2Ch 35:20
**46:3** f Jer 51:11–12
**46:5** g Jer 49:29
**46:6** h Da 11:19
**46:7** i Jer 47:2

[a]9 That is, the upper Nile region

**46:9** j Isa 66:19
**46:10** k Joel 1:15 l Zep 1:7
**46:11** m Jer 8:22 n Isa 47:1
**46:13** o Isa 19:1
**46:16** p Lev 26:37
**46:18** q Jer 48:15

men of Lydia[j] who draw the bow.
10 But that day[k] belongs to the Lord, the
LORD Almighty—
a day of vengeance, for vengeance on
his foes.
The sword will devour till it is satisfied,
till it has quenched its thirst with
blood.
For the Lord, the LORD Almighty, will
offer sacrifice[l]
in the land of the north by the River
Euphrates.

11 "Go up to Gilead and get balm,[m]
O Virgin[n] Daughter of Egypt.
But you multiply remedies in vain;
there is no healing for you.
12 The nations will hear of your shame;
your cries will fill the earth.
One warrior will stumble over another;
both will fall down together."

13 This is the message the LORD spoke to
Jeremiah the prophet about the coming
of Nebuchadnezzar king of Babylon to at-
tack Egypt:[o]

14 "Announce this in Egypt, and proclaim it
in Migdol;
proclaim it also in Memphis[a] and
Tahpanhes:
'Take your positions and get ready,
for the sword devours those around
you.'
15 Why will your warriors be laid low?
They cannot stand, for the LORD will
push them down.
16 They will stumble[p] repeatedly;
they will fall over each other.
They will say, 'Get up, let us go back
to our own people and our native
lands,
away from the sword of the oppressor.'
17 There they will exclaim,
'Pharaoh king of Egypt is only a loud
noise;
he has missed his opportunity.'
18 "As surely as I live," declares the King,[q]
whose name is the LORD Almighty,
"one will come who is like Tabor among
the mountains,
like Carmel by the sea.

19 Pack your belongings for exile,[r]
you who live in Egypt,
for Memphis will be laid waste
and lie in ruins without inhabitant.

20 "Egypt is a beautiful heifer,
but a gadfly is coming
against her from the north.
21 The mercenaries in her ranks
are like fattened calves.
They too will turn and flee together,
they will not stand their ground,
for the day[s] of disaster is coming upon
them,
the time for them to be punished.
22 Egypt will hiss like a fleeing serpent
as the enemy advances in force;
they will come against her with axes,
like men who cut down trees.
23 They will chop down her forest,"
declares the LORD,
"dense though it be.
They are more numerous than locusts,
they cannot be counted.
24 The Daughter of Egypt will be put to
shame,
handed over to the people of the
north.[t]"

25 The LORD Almighty, the God of Israel,
says: "I am about to bring punishment
on Amon god of Thebes,[b][u] on Pharaoh, on
Egypt and her gods[v] and her kings, and on
those who rely on Pharaoh. 26 I will hand
them over to those who seek their lives,
to Nebuchadnezzar king[w] of Babylon and
his officers. Later, however, Egypt will be
inhabited[x] as in times past," declares the
LORD.

27 "Do not fear,[y] O Jacob my servant;
do not be dismayed, O Israel.
I will surely save you out of a distant
place,
your descendants from the land of
their exile.
Jacob will again have peace and security,
and no one will make him afraid.
28 Do not fear, O Jacob my servant,
for I am with you," declares the LORD.
"Though I completely destroy[z] all the
nations

**46:19** r Isa 20:4
**46:21** s Ps 37:13
**46:24** t Jer 1:15
**46:25** u Eze 30:14 v Jer 43:12
**46:26** w Eze 32:11 x Eze 29:11–16
**46:27** y Isa 41:13; 43:5
**46:28** z Jer 4:27

[a] 14 Hebrew *Noph*; also in verse 19 [b] 25 Hebrew *No*

47:1 a Am 1:6; Zec 9:5–7
47:2 b Isa 8:7
47:4 c Ge 10:14
47:5 d Mic 1:16 e Jer 25:20
47:6 f Jer 12:12

among which I scatter you,
I will not completely destroy you.
I will discipline you but only with justice;
I will not let you go entirely
unpunished."

## A Message About the Philistines

47 This is the word of the LORD that came to Jeremiah the prophet concerning the Philistines before Pharaoh attacked Gaza:[a]

2 This is what the LORD says:

"See how the waters are rising in the
north;[b]
they will become an overflowing
torrent.
They will overflow the land and
everything in it,
the towns and those who live in them.
The people will cry out;
all who dwell in the land will wail
3 at the sound of the hoofs of galloping
steeds,
at the noise of enemy chariots
and the rumble of their wheels.
Fathers will not turn to help their
children;
their hands will hang limp.
4 For the day has come
to destroy all the Philistines
and to cut off all survivors
who could help Tyre and Sidon.
The LORD is about to destroy the
Philistines,[c]
the remnant from the coasts of
Caphtor.[a]
5 Gaza will shave[d] her head in mourning;
Ashkelon[e] will be silenced.
O remnant on the plain,
how long will you cut yourselves?

6 " 'Ah, sword[f] of the LORD,' ⌊you cry,⌋
'how long till you rest?
Return to your scabbard;
cease and be still.'
7 But how can it rest
when the LORD has commanded it,
when he has ordered it
to attack Ashkelon and the coast?"

## A Message About Moab

48 Concerning Moab:

This is what the LORD Almighty, the God of Israel, says:

"Woe to Nebo, for it will be ruined.
Kiriathaim[g] will be disgraced and
captured;
the stronghold[b] will be disgraced and
shattered.
2 Moab will be praised[h] no more;
in Heshbon[c] men will plot her
downfall:
'Come, let us put an end to that nation.'
You too, O Madmen,[d] will be silenced;
the sword will pursue you.
3 Listen to the cries from Horonaim,
cries of great havoc and destruction.
4 Moab will be broken;
her little ones will cry out.[e]
5 They go up the way to Luhith,[i]
weeping bitterly as they go;
on the road down to Horonaim
anguished cries over the destruction
are heard.
6 Flee! Run for your lives;
become like a bush[f] in the desert.
7 Since you trust in your deeds and riches,
you too will be taken captive,
and Chemosh[j] will go into exile,
together with his priests and officials.
8 The destroyer will come against every
town,
and not a town will escape.
The valley will be ruined
and the plateau destroyed,
because the LORD has spoken.
9 Put salt on Moab,
for she will be laid waste[g];
her towns will become desolate,
with no one to live in them.

10 "A curse on him who is lax in doing the
LORD's work!
A curse on him who keeps his sword
from bloodshed![k]

11 "Moab has been at rest from youth,
like wine left on its dregs,[l]
not poured from one jar to another—

48:1 g Nu 32:37
48:2 h Isa 16:14
48:5 i Isa 15:5
48:7 j Nu 21:29
48:10 k 1Ki 20:42
48:11 l Zep 1:12

[a]4 That is, Crete [b]1 Or */ Misgab* [c]2 The Hebrew for *Heshbon* sounds like the Hebrew for *plot.* [d]2 The name of the Moabite town Madmen sounds like the Hebrew for *be silenced.* [e]4 Hebrew; Septuagint */ proclaim it to Zoar* [f]6 Or *like Aroer* [g]9 Or *Give wings to Moab, / for she will fly away*

she has not gone into exile.
So she tastes as she did,
and her aroma is unchanged.
12 But days are coming,"
declares the LORD,
"when I will send men who pour from jars,
and they will pour her out;
they will empty her jars
and smash her jugs.
13 Then Moab will be ashamed of Chemosh,
as the house of Israel was ashamed
when they trusted in Bethel.

14 "How can you say, 'We are warriors,
men valiant in battle'?
15 Moab will be destroyed and her towns invaded;
her finest young men will go down in the slaughter,[m]"
declares the King,[n] whose name is the LORD Almighty.
16 "The fall of Moab is at hand;
her calamity will come quickly.
17 Mourn for her, all who live around her,
all who know her fame;
say, 'How broken is the mighty scepter,
how broken the glorious staff!'

18 "Come down from your glory
and sit on the parched ground,[o]
O inhabitants of the Daughter of Dibon,
for he who destroys Moab
will come up against you
and ruin your fortified cities.
19 Stand by the road and watch,
you who live in Aroer.[p]
Ask the man fleeing and the woman escaping,
ask them, 'What has happened?'
20 Moab is disgraced, for she is shattered.
Wail and cry out!
Announce by the Arnon[q]
that Moab is destroyed.
21 Judgment has come to the plateau—
to Holon, Jahzah and Mephaath,[r]
22 to Dibon, Nebo and Beth Diblathaim,
23 to Kiriathaim, Beth Gamul and Beth Meon,
24 to Kerioth[s] and Bozrah—
to all the towns of Moab, far and near.
25 Moab's horn[a][t] is cut off;
her arm is broken,"
declares the LORD.

26 "Make her drunk,[u]
for she has defied the LORD.
Let Moab wallow in her vomit;
let her be an object of ridicule.
27 Was not Israel the object of your ridicule?[v]
Was she caught among thieves,
that you shake your head in scorn
whenever you speak of her?
28 Abandon your towns and dwell among the rocks,
you who live in Moab.
Be like a dove that makes its nest
at the mouth of a cave.

29 "We have heard of Moab's pride[w]—
her overweening pride and conceit,
her pride and arrogance
and the haughtiness of her heart.
30 I know her insolence but it is futile,"
declares the LORD,
"and her boasts accomplish nothing.
31 Therefore I wail[x] over Moab,
for all Moab I cry out,
I moan for the men of Kir Hareseth.
32 I weep for you, as Jazer weeps,
O vines of Sibmah.
Your branches spread as far as the sea;
they reached as far as the sea of Jazer.
The destroyer has fallen
on your ripened fruit and grapes.
33 Joy and gladness are gone
from the orchards and fields of Moab.
I have stopped the flow of wine from the presses;
no one treads them with shouts of joy.[y]
Although there are shouts,
they are not shouts of joy.

34 "The sound of their cry rises
from Heshbon to Elealeh and Jahaz,[z]
from Zoar as far as Horonaim[a] and Eglath Shelishiyah,
for even the waters of Nimrim are dried up.[b]
35 In Moab I will put an end
to those who make offerings on the high places[c]

[a]25 *Horn* here symbolizes strength.

**48:15** m Jer 50:27 n Jer 46:18
**48:18** o Isa 47:1
**48:19** p Dt 2:36
**48:20** q Nu 21:13
**48:21** r Jos 13:18
**48:24** s Am 2:2
**48:25** t Ps 75:10
**48:26** u Jer 25:16,27
**48:27** v Jer 2:26
**48:29** w Isa 16:6
**48:31** x Isa 15:5–8
**48:33** y Joel 1:12
**48:34** z Isa 15:4 a Isa 15:5 b Isa 15:6
**48:35** c Isa 15:2; 16:12

48:36 d Isa 15:7
48:37 e Isa 15:2
48:38 f Jer 22:28
48:40 g Isa 8:8
48:41 h Isa 21:3
48:43 i Isa 24:17
48:45 j Nu 21:21,26–28 k Nu 24:17

and burn incense to their gods,"
declares the LORD.
36 "So my heart laments for Moab like a flute;
it laments like a flute for the men of Kir Hareseth.
The wealth they acquired[d] is gone.
37 Every head is shaved[e]
and every beard cut off;
every hand is slashed
and every waist is covered with sackcloth.
38 On all the roofs in Moab
and in the public squares
there is nothing but mourning,
for I have broken Moab
like a jar[f] that no one wants,"
declares the LORD.
39 "How shattered she is! How they wail!
How Moab turns her back in shame!
Moab has become an object of ridicule,
an object of horror to all those around her."

40 This is what the LORD says:

"Look! An eagle is swooping down,
spreading its wings[g] over Moab.
41 Kerioth[a] will be captured
and the strongholds taken.
In that day the hearts of Moab's warriors
will be like the heart of a woman in labor.[h]
42 Moab will be destroyed as a nation
because she defied the LORD.
43 Terror and pit and snare[i] await you,
O people of Moab,"
declares the LORD.
44 "Whoever flees from the terror
will fall into a pit,
whoever climbs out of the pit
will be caught in a snare;
for I will bring upon Moab
the year of her punishment,"
declares the LORD.

45 "In the shadow of Heshbon
the fugitives stand helpless,
for a fire has gone out from Heshbon,
a blaze from the midst of Sihon;[j]
it burns the foreheads of Moab,
the skulls[k] of the noisy boasters.
46 Woe to you, O Moab![l]
The people of Chemosh are destroyed;
your sons are taken into exile
and your daughters into captivity.

47 "Yet I will restore[m] the fortunes of Moab
in days to come,"
declares the LORD.

Here ends the judgment on Moab.

## A Message About Ammon

49 Concerning the Ammonites:[n]

This is what the LORD says:

"Has Israel no sons?
Has she no heirs?
Why then has Molech[b] taken possession of Gad?
Why do his people live in its towns?
2 But the days are coming,"
declares the LORD,
"when I will sound the battle cry[o]
against Rabbah of the Ammonites;
it will become a mound of ruins,
and its surrounding villages will be set on fire.
Then Israel will drive out
those who drove her out,[p]"
says the LORD.
3 "Wail, O Heshbon, for Ai is destroyed!
Cry out, O inhabitants of Rabbah!
Put on sackcloth and mourn;
rush here and there inside the walls,
for Molech will go into exile,[q]
together with his priests and officials.
4 Why do you boast of your valleys,
boast of your valleys so fruitful?
O unfaithful daughter,
you trust in your riches and say,
'Who will attack me?'
5 I will bring terror on you
from all those around you,"
declares the Lord,
the LORD Almighty.
"Every one of you will be driven away,
and no one will gather the fugitives.

6 "Yet afterward, I will restore[r] the
fortunes of the Ammonites,"
declares the LORD.

48:46 l Nu 21:29
48:47 m Jer 49:6,39
49:1 n Am 1:13; Zep 2:8–9
49:2 o Jer 4:19 p Eze 21:28–32; 25:2–11
49:3 q Jer 48:7
49:6 r ver 39; Jer 48:47

[a]41 Or *The cities* [b]1 Or *their king*; Hebrew *malcam*; also in verse 3

**49:7** s Eze 25:12
**49:12** t Jer 25:28–29
**49:13** u Ge 22:16; v Isa 34:6
**49:16** w Job 39:27; Am 9:2

## A Message About Edom

7 Concerning Edom:[s]

This is what the LORD Almighty says:

"Is there no longer wisdom in Teman?
Has counsel perished from the prudent?
Has their wisdom decayed?
8 Turn and flee, hide in deep caves,
you who live in Dedan,
for I will bring disaster on Esau
at the time I punish him.
9 If grape pickers came to you,
would they not leave a few grapes?
If thieves came during the night,
would they not steal only as much as they wanted?
10 But I will strip Esau bare;
I will uncover his hiding places,
so that he cannot conceal himself.
His children, relatives and neighbors will perish,
and he will be no more.
11 Leave your orphans; I will protect their lives.
Your widows too can trust in me."

12 This is what the LORD says: "If those who
do not deserve to drink the cup must drink
it, why should you go unpunished?[t] You will
not go unpunished, but must drink it.
13 I swear[u] by myself," declares the LORD, "that
Bozrah[v] will become a ruin and an object of
horror, of reproach and of cursing; and all
its towns will be in ruins forever."

14 I have heard a message from the LORD:
An envoy was sent to the nations to say,
"Assemble yourselves to attack it!
Rise up for battle!"

15 "Now I will make you small among the nations,
despised among men.
16 The terror you inspire
and the pride of your heart have deceived you,
you who live in the clefts of the rocks,
who occupy the heights of the hill.
Though you build your nest[w] as high as the eagle's,
from there I will bring you down,"
declares the LORD.
17 "Edom will become an object of horror;
all who pass by will be appalled and will scoff
because of all its wounds.[x]
18 As Sodom and Gomorrah[y] were overthrown,
along with their neighboring towns,"
says the LORD,
"so no one will live there;
no man will dwell in it.

19 "Like a lion coming up from Jordan's thickets[z]
to a rich pastureland,
I will chase Edom from its land in an instant.
Who is the chosen one I will appoint for this?
Who is like me and who can challenge me?[a]
And what shepherd can stand against me?"
20 Therefore, hear what the LORD has planned against Edom,
what he has purposed against those who live in Teman:
The young of the flock[b] will be dragged away;
he will completely destroy[c] their pasture because of them.
21 At the sound of their fall the earth will tremble;
their cry[d] will resound to the Red Sea.[a]
22 Look! An eagle will soar and swoop down,
spreading its wings over Bozrah.
In that day the hearts of Edom's warriors
will be like the heart of a woman in labor.[e]

## A Message About Damascus

23 Concerning Damascus:

"Hamath[f] and Arpad are dismayed,
for they have heard bad news.
They are disheartened,
troubled like[b] the restless sea.[g]
24 Damascus has become feeble,
she has turned to flee
and panic has gripped her;

**49:17** x Jer 50:13
**49:18** y Ge 19:24; Dt 29:23
**49:19** z Jer 12:5; a Jer 50:44
**49:20** b Jer 50:45; c Mal 1:3–4
**49:21** d Jer 50:46
**49:22** e Jer 48:40–41
**49:23** f Isa 10:9; g Isa 57:20

[a] 21 Hebrew *Yam Suph*; that is, Sea of Reeds [b] 23 Hebrew *on* or *by*

49:26 h Jer 50:30
49:27 i Am 1:4 j 1Ki 15:18
49:29 k Jer 6:25; 46:5
49:31 l Eze 38:11
49:32 m Jer 9:26
49:33 n Jer 10:22

anguish and pain have seized her,
pain like that of a woman in labor.
25 Why has the city of renown not been abandoned,
the town in which I delight?
26 Surely, her young men will fall in the streets;
all her soldiers will be silenced[h] in that day,"
declares the LORD Almighty.
27 "I will set fire[i] to the walls of Damascus;
it will consume the fortresses of Ben-Hadad.[j]"

## A Message About Kedar and Hazor

28 Concerning Kedar and the kingdoms of Hazor, which Nebuchadnezzar king of Babylon attacked:

This is what the LORD says:

"Arise, and attack Kedar
and destroy the people of the East.
29 Their tents and their flocks will be taken;
their shelters will be carried off
with all their goods and camels.
Men will shout to them,
'Terror[k] on every side!'

30 "Flee quickly away!
Stay in deep caves, you who live in Hazor,"
declares the LORD.
"Nebuchadnezzar king of Babylon has plotted against you;
he has devised a plan against you.

31 "Arise and attack a nation at ease,
which lives in confidence,"
declares the LORD,
"a nation that has neither gates nor bars;[l]
its people live alone.
32 Their camels will become plunder,
and their large herds will be booty.
I will scatter to the winds those who are in distant places[a][m]
and will bring disaster on them from every side,"
declares the LORD.
33 "Hazor will become a haunt of jackals,
a desolate[n] place forever.
No one will live there;
no man will dwell in it."

## A Message About Elam

34 This is the word of the LORD that came to Jeremiah the prophet concerning Elam, early in the reign of Zedekiah king of Judah:

35 This is what the LORD Almighty says:

"See, I will break the bow[o] of Elam,
the mainstay of their might.
36 I will bring against Elam the four winds
from the four quarters of the heavens;
I will scatter them to the four winds,
and there will not be a nation
where Elam's exiles do not go.
37 I will shatter Elam before their foes,
before those who seek their lives;
I will bring disaster upon them,
even my fierce anger,"
declares the LORD.
"I will pursue them with the sword[p]
until I have made an end of them.
38 I will set my throne in Elam
and destroy her king and officials,"
declares the LORD.

39 "Yet I will restore[q] the fortunes of Elam
in days to come,"
declares the LORD.

## A Message About Babylon

50 This is the word the LORD spoke through Jeremiah the prophet concerning Babylon[r] and the land of the Babylonians[b]:

2 "Announce and proclaim among the nations,
lift up a banner and proclaim it;
keep nothing back, but say,
'Babylon will be captured;
Bel[s] will be put to shame,
Marduk filled with terror.
Her images will be put to shame
and her idols filled with terror.'
3 A nation from the north will attack her
and lay waste her land.
No one will live in it;
both men and animals will flee away.

49:35 o Isa 22:6
49:37 p Jer 9:16
49:39 q Jer 48:47
50:1 r Ge 10:10; Isa 13:1
50:2 s Isa 46:1

[a] 32 Or *who clip the hair by their foreheads* [b] 1 Or *Chaldeans*; also in verses 8, 25, 35 and 45

**50:4**
t Hos 1:11
u Ezr 3:12; Jer 31:9
v Hos 3:5

**50:6**
w Isa 53:6
x Jer 3:6

**50:8**
y Isa 48:20; Jer 51:6; Rev 18:4

**50:11**
z Isa 47:6

4 "In those days, at that time,"
declares the LORD,
"the people of Israel and the people of Judah together[t]
will go in tears[u] to seek[v] the LORD their God.
5 They will ask the way to Zion
and turn their faces toward it.
They will come and bind themselves to the LORD
in an everlasting covenant
that will not be forgotten.

6 "My people have been lost sheep;[w]
their shepherds have led them astray
and caused them to roam on the mountains.
They wandered over mountain and hill[x]
and forgot their own resting place.
7 Whoever found them devoured them;
their enemies said, 'We are not guilty,
for they sinned against the LORD, their true pasture,
the LORD, the hope of their fathers.'
8 "Flee[y] out of Babylon;
leave the land of the Babylonians,
and be like the goats that lead the flock.
9 For I will stir up and bring against Babylon
an alliance of great nations from the land of the north.
They will take up their positions against her,
and from the north she will be captured.
Their arrows will be like skilled warriors
who do not return empty-handed.
10 So Babylonia[a] will be plundered;
all who plunder her will have their fill,"
declares the LORD.

11 "Because you rejoice and are glad,
you who pillage my inheritance,[z]
because you frolic like a heifer threshing grain
and neigh like stallions,
12 your mother will be greatly ashamed;
she who gave you birth will be disgraced.
She will be the least of the nations—
a wilderness, a dry land, a desert.
13 Because of the LORD's anger she will not be inhabited
but will be completely desolate.
All who pass Babylon will be horrified and scoff
because of all her wounds.[a]

14 "Take up your positions around Babylon,
all you who draw the bow.
Shoot at her! Spare no arrows,
for she has sinned against the LORD.
15 Shout[b] against her on every side!
She surrenders, her towers fall,
her walls[c] are torn down.
Since this is the vengeance of the LORD,
take vengeance on her;
do to her as she has done to others.
16 Cut off from Babylon the sower,
and the reaper with his sickle at harvest.
Because of the sword of the oppressor
let everyone return to his own people,
let everyone flee to his own land.

17 "Israel is a scattered flock
that lions[d] have chased away.
The first to devour him
was the king[e] of Assyria;
the last to crush his bones
was Nebuchadnezzar[f] king of Babylon."

18 Therefore this is what the LORD Almighty, the God of Israel, says:

"I will punish the king of Babylon and his land
as I punished the king of Assyria.
19 But I will bring Israel back to his own pasture
and he will graze on Carmel and Bashan;
his appetite will be satisfied
on the hills[g] of Ephraim and Gilead.
20 In those days, at that time,"
declares the LORD,
"search will be made for Israel's guilt,
but there will be none,
and for the sins of Judah,
but none will be found,
for I will forgive[h] the remnant[i] I spare.

**50:13**
a Jer 49:17

**50:15**
b Jer 51:14
c Jer 51:44,58

**50:17**
d Jer 2:15
e 2Ki 17:6
f 2Ki 24:10,14

**50:19**
g Jer 33:12

**50:20**
h Jer 31:34
i Isa 1:9

[a]10 Or *Chaldea*

[21] "Attack the land of Merathaim
and those who live in Pekod.[j]
Pursue, kill and completely destroy[a]
them,"
declares the LORD.
"Do everything I have commanded
you.
[22] The noise[k] of battle is in the land,
the noise of great destruction!
[23] How broken and shattered
is the hammer of the whole earth!
How desolate is Babylon
among the nations!
[24] I set a trap[l] for you, O Babylon,
and you were caught before you
knew it;
you were found and captured[m]
because you opposed the LORD.
[25] The LORD has opened his arsenal
and brought out the weapons[n] of his
wrath,
for the Sovereign LORD Almighty has work
to do
in the land of the Babylonians.
[26] Come against her from afar.
Break open her granaries;
pile her up like heaps of grain.
Completely destroy her
and leave her no remnant.
[27] Kill all her young bulls;
let them go down to the slaughter!
Woe to them! For their day has
come,
the time for them to be punished.
[28] Listen to the fugitives and refugees from
Babylon
declaring in Zion[o]
how the LORD our God has taken
vengeance,
vengeance for his temple.

[29] "Summon archers against Babylon,
all those who draw the bow.
Encamp all around her;
let no one escape.
Repay[p] her for her deeds;[q]
do to her as she has done.
For she has defied the LORD,
the Holy One of Israel.
[30] Therefore, her young men[r] will fall in the
streets;
all her soldiers will be silenced in that
day,"
declares the LORD.
[31] "See, I am against you, O arrogant one,"
declares the Lord, the LORD Almighty,
"for your day has come,
the time for you to be punished.
[32] The arrogant one will stumble and fall
and no one will help her up;
I will kindle a fire[s] in her towns
that will consume all who are around
her."

[33] This is what the LORD Almighty says:

"The people of Israel are oppressed,
and the people of Judah as well.
All their captors hold them fast,
refusing to let them go.
[34] Yet their Redeemer is strong;
the LORD Almighty is his name.
He will vigorously defend their cause
so that he may bring rest to their land,
but unrest to those who live in
Babylon.

[35] "A sword against the Babylonians!"
declares the LORD—
"against those who live in Babylon
and against her officials and wise men!
[36] A sword against her false prophets!
They will become fools.
A sword against her warriors!
They will be filled with terror.
[37] A sword against her horses and chariots
and all the foreigners in her ranks!
They will become women.[t]
A sword against her treasures!
They will be plundered.
[38] A drought on[b] her waters!
They will dry[u] up.
For it is a land of idols,
idols that will go mad with terror.

[39] "So desert creatures and hyenas will live
there,
and there the owl will dwell.
It will never again be inhabited
or lived in from generation to
generation.[v]
[40] As God overthrew Sodom and
Gomorrah[w]

**50:21** j Eze 23:23
**50:22** k Jer 51:54
**50:24** l Da 5:30–31 m Jer 51:31
**50:25** n Isa 13:5
**50:28** o Jer 51:10
**50:29** p Rev 18:6 q Jer 51:56
**50:30** r Jer 49:26
**50:32** s Jer 21:14; 49:27
**50:37** t Jer 51:30; Na 3:13
**50:38** u Jer 51:36
**50:39** v Isa 13:19–22
**50:40** w Ge 19:24

[a] 21 The Hebrew term refers to the irrevocable giving over of things or persons to the LORD, often by totally destroying them; also in verse 26. [b] 38 Or *A sword against*

**50:41**
x Jer 6:22

**50:42**
y Isa 13:18
z Isa 5:30
a Jer 6:23

**50:44**
b Job 41:10; Jer 49:19

**50:45**
c Isa 14:24; Jer 51:11

along with their neighboring towns,"
declares the LORD,
"so no one will live there;
no man will dwell in it.

41 "Look! An army is coming from the north;[x]
a great nation and many kings
are being stirred up from the ends of the earth.
42 They are armed with bows and spears;
they are cruel and without mercy.[y]
They sound like the roaring sea[z]
as they ride on their horses;
they come like men in battle formation
to attack you, O Daughter of Babylon.[a]
43 The king of Babylon has heard reports about them,
and his hands hang limp.
Anguish has gripped him,
pain like that of a woman in labor.
44 Like a lion coming up from Jordan's thickets
to a rich pastureland,
I will chase Babylon from its land in an instant.
Who is the chosen one I will appoint for this?
Who is like me and who can challenge me?[b]
And what shepherd can stand against me?"
45 Therefore, hear what the LORD has planned against Babylon,
what he has purposed[c] against the land of the Babylonians:
The young of the flock will be dragged away;
he will completely destroy their pasture because of them.
46 At the sound of Babylon's capture the earth will tremble;
its cry will resound among the nations.

51 This is what the LORD says:

"See, I will stir up the spirit of a destroyer
against Babylon and the people of Leb Kamai.[a]
2 I will send foreigners to Babylon
to winnow[d] her and to devastate her land;
they will oppose her on every side
in the day of her disaster.
3 Let not the archer string his bow,
nor let him put on his armor.
Do not spare her young men;
completely destroy[b] her army.
4 They will fall down slain in Babylon,[c]
fatally wounded in her streets.[e]
5 For Israel and Judah have not been forsaken
by their God, the LORD Almighty,
though their land[d] is full of guilt
before the Holy One of Israel.

6 "Flee[f] from Babylon!
Run for your lives!
Do not be destroyed because of her sins.[g]
It is time for the LORD's vengeance;[h]
he will pay[i] her what she deserves.
7 Babylon was a gold cup[j] in the LORD's hand;
she made the whole earth drunk.
The nations drank her wine;
therefore they have now gone mad.
8 Babylon will suddenly fall[k] and be broken.
Wail over her!
Get balm for her pain;
perhaps she can be healed.

9 " 'We would have healed Babylon,
but she cannot be healed;
let us leave[l] her and each go to his own land,
for her judgment[m] reaches to the skies,
it rises as high as the clouds.'

10 " 'The LORD has vindicated us;
come, let us tell in Zion
what the LORD our God has done.'[n]

11 "Sharpen the arrows,
take up the shields![o]
The LORD has stirred up the kings of the Medes,
because his purpose is to destroy Babylon.
The LORD will take vengeance,
vengeance for his temple.[p]

**51:2**
d Jer 15:7

**51:4**
e Jer 49:26; 50:30

**51:6**
f Jer 50:8
g Rev 18:4
h Jer 50:15
i Jer 25:14

**51:7**
j Jer 25:15–16; Rev 14:8–10; 17:4

**51:8**
k Isa 21:9; Rev 14:8

**51:9**
l Isa 13:14; Jer 50:16
m Rev 18:4–5

**51:10**
n Jer 50:28

**51:11**
o Jer 46:4
p Jer 50:28

[a]1 *Leb Kamai* is a cryptogram for Chaldea, that is, Babylonia. [b]3 The Hebrew term refers to the irrevocable giving over of things or persons to the LORD, often by totally destroying them. [c]4 Or *Chaldea* [d]5 Or */ and the land ⌊of the Babylonians⌋*

51:13 q Rev 17:1,15
51:14 r Na 3:15
51:15 s Ge 1:1
51:16 t Ps 135:7
51:20 u Isa 10:5

12 Lift up a banner against the walls of Babylon!
Reinforce the guard,
station the watchmen,
prepare an ambush!
The LORD will carry out his purpose,
his decree against the people of Babylon.
13 You who live by many waters[q]
and are rich in treasures,
your end has come,
the time for you to be cut off.
14 The LORD Almighty has sworn by himself:
I will surely fill you with men, as with a swarm of locusts,[r]
and they will shout in triumph over you.

15 "He made the earth by his power;
he founded the world by his wisdom
and stretched[s] out the heavens by his understanding.
16 When he thunders, the waters in the heavens roar;
he makes clouds rise from the ends of the earth.
He sends lightning with the rain
and brings out the wind from his storehouses.[t]

17 "Every man is senseless and without knowledge;
every goldsmith is shamed by his idols.
His images are a fraud;
they have no breath in them.
18 They are worthless, the objects of mockery;
when their judgment comes, they will perish.
19 He who is the Portion of Jacob is not like these,
for he is the Maker of all things,
including the tribe of his inheritance—
the LORD Almighty is his name.

20 "You are my war club,[u]
my weapon for battle—
with you I shatter nations,
with you I destroy kingdoms,
21 with you I shatter horse and rider,
with you I shatter chariot and driver,
22 with you I shatter man and woman,
with you I shatter old man and youth,
with you I shatter young man and maiden,[v]
23 with you I shatter shepherd and flock,
with you I shatter farmer and oxen,
with you I shatter governors and officials.

24 "Before your eyes I will repay[w] Babylon
and all who live in Babylonia[a] for all the
wrong they have done in Zion," declares the
LORD.

25 "I am against you, O destroying mountain,
you who destroy the whole earth,"
declares the LORD.
"I will stretch out my hand against you,
roll you off the cliffs,
and make you a burned-out mountain.[x]
26 No rock will be taken from you for a cornerstone,
nor any stone for a foundation,
for you will be desolate forever,"
declares the LORD.

27 "Lift up a banner[y] in the land!
Blow the trumpet among the nations!
Prepare the nations for battle against her;
summon against her these kingdoms:
Ararat, Minni and Ashkenaz.
Appoint a commander against her;
send up horses like a swarm of locusts.
28 Prepare the nations for battle against her—
the kings of the Medes,[z]
their governors and all their officials,
and all the countries they rule.
29 The land trembles and writhes,
for the LORD's purposes against Babylon stand—
to lay waste the land of Babylon
so that no one will live there.
30 Babylon's warriors[a] have stopped fighting;
they remain in their strongholds.
Their strength is exhausted;
they have become like women.
Her dwellings are set on fire;
the bars[b] of her gates are broken.

51:22 v 2Ch 36:17; Isa 13:17–18
51:24 w Jer 50:15
51:25 x Zec 4:7
51:27 y Isa 13:2
51:28 z ver 11
51:30 a Jer 50:36 b La 2:9; Na 3:13

[a]24 Or *Chaldea*; also in verse 35

51:33 c Isa 21:10 d Isa 17:5; Hos 6:11
51:34 e Jer 50:17
51:36 f Jer 50:38
51:37 g Rev 18:2

31 One courier follows another
and messenger follows messenger
to announce to the king of Babylon
that his entire city is captured,
32 the river crossings seized,
the marshes set on fire,
and the soldiers terrified."

33 This is what the LORD Almighty, the God of Israel, says:

"The Daughter of Babylon is like a threshing floor[c]
at the time it is trampled;
the time to harvest[d] her will soon come."

34 "Nebuchadnezzar[e] king of Babylon has devoured us,
he has thrown us into confusion,
he has made us an empty jar.
Like a serpent he has swallowed us
and filled his stomach with our delicacies,
and then has spewed us out.
35 May the violence done to our flesh[a] be upon Babylon,"
say the inhabitants of Zion.
"May our blood be on those who live in Babylonia,"
says Jerusalem.

36 Therefore, this is what the LORD says:

"See, I will defend your cause
and avenge you;
I will dry up[f] her sea
and make her springs dry.
37 Babylon will be a heap of ruins,
a haunt[g] of jackals,
an object of horror and scorn,
a place where no one lives.
38 Her people all roar like young lions,
they growl like lion cubs.
39 But while they are aroused,
I will set out a feast for them
and make them drunk,
so that they shout with laughter—
then sleep forever and not awake,"
declares the LORD.
40 "I will bring them down
like lambs to the slaughter,
like rams and goats.

41 "How Sheshach[b][h] will be captured,
the boast of the whole earth seized!
What a horror Babylon will be
among the nations!
42 The sea will rise over Babylon;
its roaring waves[i] will cover her.
43 Her towns will be desolate,
a dry and desert land,
a land where no one lives,
through which no man travels.
44 I will punish Bel[j] in Babylon
and make him spew out what he has swallowed.
The nations will no longer stream to him.
And the wall[k] of Babylon will fall.

45 "Come out[l] of her, my people!
Run[m] for your lives!
Run from the fierce anger of the LORD.
46 Do not lose heart or be afraid
when rumors[n] are heard in the land;
one rumor comes this year, another the next,
rumors of violence in the land
and of ruler against ruler.
47 For the time will surely come
when I will punish the idols[o] of Babylon;
her whole land will be disgraced
and her slain will all lie fallen within her.
48 Then heaven and earth and all that is in them
will shout[p] for joy over Babylon,
for out of the north
destroyers will attack her,"
declares the LORD.

49 "Babylon must fall because of Israel's slain,
just as the slain in all the earth
have fallen because of Babylon.[q]
50 You who have escaped the sword,
leave and do not linger!
Remember the LORD in a distant land,
and think on Jerusalem."

51 "We are disgraced,[r]
for we have been insulted
and shame covers our faces,
because foreigners have entered
the holy places of the LORD's house."

51:41 h Jer 25:26
51:42 i Isa 8:7
51:44 j Isa 46:1 k ver 58
51:45 l Rev 18:4 m ver 6; Jer 50:8
51:46 n 2Ki 19:7
51:47 o ver 52
51:48 p Isa 44:23
51:49 q Jer 50:29
51:51 r Ps 44:13–16

[a]35 Or *done to us and to our children* [b]41 *Sheshach* is a cryptogram for Babylon.

**51:53** s Isa 14:13–14 t Jer 49:16
**51:54** u Jer 50:22
**51:56** v ver 6; Ps 94:1–2
**51:57** w Ps 76:5 x Jer 46:18; 48:15
**51:58** y Hab 2:13
**51:59** z Jer 28:1
**51:60** a Jer 30:2
**51:62** b Jer 50:13,39

52 "But days are coming," declares the LORD,
"when I will punish her idols,
and throughout her land
the wounded will groan.
53 Even if Babylon reaches the sky[s]
and fortifies her lofty stronghold,
I will send destroyers[t] against her,"
declares the LORD.

54 "The sound of a cry comes from Babylon,
the sound of great destruction[u]
from the land of the Babylonians.[a]
55 The LORD will destroy Babylon;
he will silence her noisy din.
Waves ⌞of enemies⌟ will rage like great waters;
the roar of their voices will resound.
56 A destroyer will come against Babylon;
her warriors will be captured,
and their bows will be broken.
For the LORD is a God of retribution;
he will repay[v] in full.
57 I will make her officials and wise men drunk,
her governors, officers and warriors as well;
they will sleep[w] forever and not awake,"
declares the King,[x] whose name is the LORD Almighty.

58 This is what the LORD Almighty says:

"Babylon's thick wall will be leveled
and her high gates set on fire;
the peoples exhaust themselves for nothing,
the nations' labor is only fuel for the flames."[y]

59 This is the message Jeremiah gave to the staff officer Seraiah son of Neriah, the son of Mahseiah, when he went to Babylon with Zedekiah king of Judah in the fourth[z] year of his reign. 60 Jeremiah had written on a scroll[a] about all the disasters that would come upon Babylon—all that had been recorded concerning Babylon. 61 He said to Seraiah, "When you get to Babylon, see that you read all these words aloud. 62 Then say, 'O LORD, you have said you will destroy this place, so that neither man nor animal will live in it; it will be desolate[b] forever.' 63 When you finish reading this scroll, tie a stone to it and throw it into the Euphrates. 64 Then say, 'So will Babylon sink to rise no more because of the disaster I will bring upon her. And her people[c] will fall.' "

The words of Jeremiah end here.

## The Fall of Jerusalem

52 Zedekiah[d] was twenty-one years old when he became king, and he reigned in Jerusalem eleven years. His mother's name was Hamutal daughter of Jeremiah; she was from Libnah. 2 He did evil in the eyes of the LORD, just as Jehoiakim had done. 3 It was because of the LORD's anger that all this happened to Jerusalem and Judah,[e] and in the end he thrust them from his presence.

Now Zedekiah rebelled against the king of Babylon.

4 So in the ninth year of Zedekiah's reign, on the tenth[f] day of the tenth month, Nebuchadnezzar king of Babylon marched against Jerusalem[g] with his whole army. They camped outside the city and built siege works all around it. 5 The city was kept under siege until the eleventh year of King Zedekiah.

6 By the ninth day of the fourth month the famine in the city had become so severe that there was no food for the people to eat. 7 Then the city wall was broken through, and the whole army fled. They left the city at night through the gate between the two walls near the king's garden, though the Babylonians[b] were surrounding the city. They fled toward the Arabah,[c] 8 but the Babylonian[d] army pursued King Zedekiah and overtook him in the plains of Jericho. All his soldiers were separated from him and scattered, 9 and he was captured.[h]

He was taken to the king of Babylon at Riblah in the land of Hamath, where he pronounced sentence on him. 10 There at Riblah the king of Babylon slaughtered the sons of Zedekiah before his eyes; he also killed all the officials of Judah. 11 Then he put out Zedekiah's eyes, bound him with bronze shackles and took him to Babylon, where he put him in prison till the day of his death.[i]

12 On the tenth day of the fifth month, in

**51:64** c ver 58
**52:1** d 2Ki 24:17
**52:3** e Isa 3:1
**52:4** f Zec 8:19 g 2Ki 25:1–7; Jer 39:1
**52:9** h Jer 32:4
**52:11** i Eze 12:13

[a]54 Or *Chaldeans* [b]7 Or *Chaldeans*; also in verse 17 [c]7 Or *the Jordan Valley* [d]8 Or *Chaldean*; also in verse 14

**52:12** j Jer 39:9
**52:13** k 2Ch 36:19
**52:17** l 1Ki 7:15 m 1Ki 7:27–37 n Jer 27:19–22
**52:19** o 1Ki 7:50
**52:20** p 1Ki 7:47
**52:21** q 1Ki 7:15

the nineteenth year of Nebuchadnezzar king of Babylon, Nebuzaradan[j] commander of the imperial guard, who served the king of Babylon, came to Jerusalem. [13]He set fire[k] to the temple of the LORD, the royal palace and all the houses of Jerusalem. Every important building he burned down. [14]The whole Babylonian army under the commander of the imperial guard broke down all the walls around Jerusalem. [15]Nebuzaradan the commander of the guard carried into exile some of the poorest people and those who remained in the city, along with the rest of the craftsmen[a] and those who had gone over to the king of Babylon. [16]But Nebuzaradan left behind the rest of the poorest people of the land to work the vineyards and fields.

[17]The Babylonians broke up the bronze pillars,[l] the movable stands[m] and the bronze Sea that were at the temple of the LORD and they carried all the bronze to Babylon.[n] [18]They also took away the pots, shovels, wick trimmers, sprinkling bowls, dishes and all the bronze articles used in the temple service. [19]The commander of the imperial guard took away the basins, censers,[o] sprinkling bowls, pots, lampstands, dishes and bowls used for drink offerings—all that were made of pure gold or silver.

[20]The bronze from the two pillars, the Sea and the twelve bronze bulls under it, and the movable stands, which King Solomon had made for the temple of the LORD, was more than could be weighed.[p] [21]Each of the pillars was eighteen cubits high and twelve cubits in circumference[b]; each was four fingers thick, and hollow.[q] [22]The bronze capital on top of the one pillar was five cubits[c] high and was decorated with a network and pomegranates of bronze all around. The other pillar, with its pomegranates, was similar. [23]There were ninety-six pomegranates on the sides; the total number of pomegranates[r] above the surrounding network was a hundred.

**52:23** r 1Ki 7:20
**52:24** s 2Ki 25:18 t Jer 21:1; 37:3
**52:28** u 2Ki 24:14–16
**52:33** v 2Sa 9:7
**52:34** w 2Sa 9:10

[24]The commander of the guard took as prisoners Seraiah[s] the chief priest, Zephaniah[t] the priest next in rank and the three doorkeepers. [25]Of those still in the city, he took the officer in charge of the fighting men, and seven royal advisers. He also took the secretary who was chief officer in charge of conscripting the people of the land and sixty of his men who were found in the city. [26]Nebuzaradan the commander took them all and brought them to the king of Babylon at Riblah. [27]There at Riblah, in the land of Hamath, the king had them executed.

So Judah went into captivity, away from her land. [28]This is the number of the people Nebuchadnezzar carried into exile:[u]

in the seventh year, 3,023 Jews;
[29]in Nebuchadnezzar's eighteenth year,
832 people from Jerusalem;
[30]in his twenty-third year,
745 Jews taken into exile by Nebuzaradan the commander of the imperial guard.
There were 4,600 people in all.

## Jehoiachin Released

[31]In the thirty-seventh year of the exile of Jehoiachin king of Judah, in the year Evil-Merodach[d] became king of Babylon, he released Jehoiachin king of Judah and freed him from prison on the twenty-fifth day of the twelfth month. [32]He spoke kindly to him and gave him a seat of honor higher than those of the other kings who were with him in Babylon. [33]So Jehoiachin put aside his prison clothes and for the rest of his life ate regularly at the king's table.[v] [34]Day by day the king of Babylon gave Jehoiachin a regular allowance[w] as long as he lived, till the day of his death.

[a]15 Or *populace* [b]21 That is, about 27 feet (about 8.1 meters) high and 18 feet (about 5.4 meters) in circumference
[c]22 That is, about 7 1/2 feet (about 2.3 meters) [d]31 Also called *Amel-Marduk*

# Lamentations

## OVERVIEW

The book of Lamentations records the grief of the author (likely the prophet Jeremiah) over the destruction of Jerusalem. He lamented the people's punishment and relied on God's mercy for their restoration.

At the end of the world, there won't be enough oceans to hold all the tears shed over humanity's sin and the resulting consequences. In this book, Jeremiah cried out because of his people's refusal to serve only the true God. Yet how many tears do women believers in Jesus Christ shed for those who are lost? As you read through Lamentations, ask God to give you a heart for those people around you who don't know Christ.

## OUTLINE

I. Lord, Look at Our Condition (1:1–22)
II. Lord, Your People Have Sinned (2:1–22)
III. Lord, You Are Faithful (3:1–66)
IV. Lord, Your Punishment Is Severe (4:1–22)
V. Lord, Please Remember Us (5:1–22)

### SCANNABLE FACTS:

**Author:** Anonymous, but probably Jeremiah

**Time Written:** Most likely soon after the fall of Jerusalem in 586 B.C.

**Theme to Note:** God's judgment brings pain and suffering

**Notable Women:** Women who have suffered tragedy and grief

1:1 a Isa 47:8 b Isa 3:26
1:3 c Jer 13:19
1:4 d Joel 1:8–13
1:5 e Jer 52:28–30
1:6 f Jer 13:18

1[a] How deserted lies the city,
once so full of people!
How like a widow[a] is she,
who once was great among the nations!
She who was queen among the provinces
has now become a slave.[b]

2 Bitterly she weeps at night,
tears are upon her cheeks.
Among all her lovers
there is none to comfort her.
All her friends have betrayed her;
they have become her enemies.

*My fragile flower,*

*I see the glistening moisture of your tears.*
*Allow me to use them to help you grow.*

*Your Master Gardener*

LAMENTATIONS 1:1–2

3 After affliction and harsh labor,
Judah has gone into exile.[c]
She dwells among the nations;
she finds no resting place.
All who pursue her have overtaken her
in the midst of her distress.

4 The roads to Zion mourn,
for no one comes to her appointed
feasts.
All her gateways are desolate,
her priests groan,
her maidens grieve,
and she is in bitter anguish.[d]

5 Her foes have become her masters;
her enemies are at ease.
The LORD has brought her grief
because of her many sins.
Her children have gone into exile,[e]
captive before the foe.

6 All the splendor has departed
from the Daughter of Zion.[f]
Her princes are like deer
that find no pasture;
in weakness they have fled
before the pursuer.

7 In the days of her affliction and
wandering
Jerusalem remembers all the treasures
that were hers in days of old.
When her people fell into enemy hands,
there was no one to help her.[g]
Her enemies looked at her
and laughed at her destruction.

8 Jerusalem has sinned greatly
and so has become unclean.
All who honored her despise her,
for they have seen her nakedness;[h]
she herself groans
and turns away.

9 Her filthiness clung to her skirts;
she did not consider her future.[i]
Her fall was astounding;
there was none to comfort her.
"Look, O LORD, on my affliction,
for the enemy has triumphed."

10 The enemy laid hands
on all her treasures;[j]
she saw pagan nations
enter her sanctuary[k]—
those you had forbidden[l]
to enter your assembly.

11 All her people groan
as they search for bread;[m]
they barter their treasures for food
to keep themselves alive.
"Look, O LORD, and consider,
for I am despised."

12 "Is it nothing to you, all you who pass
by?[n]
Look around and see.
Is any suffering like my suffering
that was inflicted on me,
that the LORD brought on me
in the day of his fierce anger?[o]

13 "From on high he sent fire,
sent it down into my bones.
He spread a net for my feet
and turned me back.

1:7 g Jer 37:7
1:8 h Jer 13:22,26
1:9 i Dt 32:28–29; Isa 47:7
1:10 j Isa 64:11 k Jer 51:51 l Dt 23:3
1:11 m Jer 52:6
1:12 n Jer 18:16 o Jer 30:24

[a] This chapter is an acrostic poem, the verses of which begin with the successive letters of the Hebrew alphabet.

**1:13** p Jer 44:6
**1:14** q Dt 28:48
**1:15** r Isa 41:2
**1:16** s La 2:11,18 t Jer 13:17
**1:17** u Jer 4:31
**1:18** v 1Sa 12:14
**1:19** w La 2:20
**1:20** x Jer 4:19 y La 2:11 z Eze 7:15

He made me desolate,[p]
faint all the day long.

14 "My sins have been bound into a yoke[a];[q]
by his hands they were woven
together.
They have come upon my neck
and the Lord has sapped my strength.
He has handed me over
to those I cannot withstand.

15 "The Lord has rejected
all the warriors in my midst;
he has summoned an army[r] against me
to[b] crush my young men.
In his winepress the Lord has trampled
the Virgin Daughter of Judah.

16 "This is why I weep
and my eyes overflow with tears.[s]
No one is near to comfort me,
no one to restore my spirit.
My children are destitute
because the enemy has prevailed."[t]

17 Zion stretches out her hands,[u]
but there is no one to comfort her.
The LORD has decreed for Jacob
that his neighbors become his foes;
Jerusalem has become
an unclean thing among them.

18 "The LORD is righteous,
yet I rebelled[v] against his command.
Listen, all you peoples;
look upon my suffering.
My young men and maidens
have gone into exile.

19 "I called to my allies
but they betrayed me.
My priests and my elders
perished[w] in the city
while they searched for food
to keep themselves alive.

20 "See, O LORD, how distressed[x] I am!
I am in torment[y] within,
and in my heart I am disturbed,
for I have been most rebellious.
Outside, the sword bereaves;
inside, there is only death.[z]

**1:21** a La 2:15 b Jer 30:16
**2:1** c Ps 99:5
**2:2** d Ps 89:39–40 e Isa 25:12
**2:3** f Ps 74:11
**2:4** g La 3:12–13 h Eze 24:16,25

21 "People have heard my groaning,
but there is no one to comfort me.
All my enemies have heard of my
distress;
they rejoice[a] at what you have done.
May you bring the day[b] you have
announced
so they may become like me.

22 "Let all their wickedness come before
you;
deal with them
as you have dealt with me
because of all my sins.
My groans are many
and my heart is faint."

2 [c] How the Lord has covered the
Daughter of Zion
with the cloud of his anger[d]!
He has hurled down the splendor of Israel
from heaven to earth;
he has not remembered his footstool[c]
in the day of his anger.

2 Without pity the Lord has swallowed up
all the dwellings of Jacob;
in his wrath he has torn down
the strongholds[d] of the Daughter of
Judah.
He has brought her kingdom and its
princes
down to the ground[e] in dishonor.

3 In fierce anger he has cut off
every horn[e] of Israel.
He has withdrawn his right hand[f]
at the approach of the enemy.
He has burned in Jacob like a flaming fire
that consumes everything around it.

4 Like an enemy he has strung his bow;[g]
his right hand is ready.
Like a foe he has slain
all who were pleasing to the eye;[h]
he has poured out his wrath like fire
on the tent of the Daughter of Zion.

5 The Lord is like an enemy;
he has swallowed up Israel.
He has swallowed up all her palaces

[a]14 Most Hebrew manuscripts; Septuagint *He kept watch over my sins* [b]15 Or *has set a time for me / when he will* [c]This chapter is an acrostic poem, the verses of which begin with the successive letters of the Hebrew alphabet. [d]1 Or *How the Lord in his anger / has treated the Daughter of Zion with contempt* [e]3 Or */ all the strength*; or *every king*; *horn* here symbolizes strength.

and destroyed her strongholds.
He has multiplied mourning and lamentation
for the Daughter of Judah.[i]

6 He has laid waste his dwelling like a garden;
he has destroyed his place of meeting.[j]
The LORD has made Zion forget
her appointed feasts and her Sabbaths;[k]
in his fierce anger he has spurned
both king and priest.

7 The Lord has rejected his altar
and abandoned his sanctuary.
He has handed over to the enemy
the walls of her palaces;[l]
they have raised a shout in the house of the LORD
as on the day of an appointed feast.

8 The LORD determined to tear down
the wall around the Daughter of Zion.
He stretched out a measuring line[m]
and did not withhold his hand from destroying.
He made ramparts and walls lament;
together they wasted away.

9 Her gates have sunk into the ground;
their bars he has broken and destroyed.
Her king and her princes are exiled[n]
among the nations,
the law is no more,
and her prophets no longer find
visions from the LORD.

10 The elders of the Daughter of Zion
sit on the ground in silence;
they have sprinkled dust on their heads[o]
and put on sackcloth.[p]
The young women of Jerusalem
have bowed their heads to the ground.[q]

11 My eyes fail from weeping,[r]
I am in torment within,
my heart is poured out[s] on the ground
because my people are destroyed,
because children and infants faint
in the streets of the city.

12 They say to their mothers,
"Where is bread and wine?"
as they faint like wounded men
in the streets of the city,
as their lives ebb away
in their mothers' arms.

13 What can I say for you?
With what can I compare you,
O Daughter of Jerusalem?
To what can I liken you,
that I may comfort you,
O Virgin Daughter of Zion?
Your wound is as deep as the sea.[t]
Who can heal you?

14 The visions of your prophets
were false and worthless;
they did not expose your sin
to ward off your captivity.
The oracles they gave you
were false and misleading.

15 All who pass your way
clap their hands at you;[u]
they scoff and shake their heads
at the Daughter of Jerusalem:
"Is this the city that was called
the perfection of beauty,
the joy of the whole earth?"[v]

16 All your enemies open their mouths
wide against you;[w]
they scoff and gnash their teeth
and say, "We have swallowed her up.
This is the day we have waited for;
we have lived to see it."

17 The LORD has done what he planned;
he has fulfilled his word,
which he decreed long ago.[x]
He has overthrown you without pity,
he has let the enemy gloat over you,
he has exalted the horn[a] of your foes.

18 The hearts of the people
cry out to the Lord.
O wall of the Daughter of Zion,
let your tears[y] flow like a river
day and night;
give yourself no relief,
your eyes no rest.

19 Arise, cry out in the night,
as the watches of the night begin;
pour out your heart[z] like water

[a]17 *Horn* here symbolizes strength.

**2:5** i Jer 9:17–20
**2:6** j Jer 52:13 k Zep 3:18
**2:7** l Jer 33:4–5
**2:8** m 2Ki 21:13; Isa 34:11
**2:9** n Dt 28:36
**2:10** o Job 2:12 p Isa 15:3 q Job 2:13; Isa 3:26
**2:11** r La 3:48–51 s Ps 22:14
**2:13** t La 1:12
**2:15** u Eze 25:6 v Ps 48:2
**2:16** w Ps 56:2; La 3:46
**2:17** x Dt 28:15–45
**2:18** y La 1:16
**2:19** z Ps 62:8

in the presence of the Lord.
Lift up your hands to him
for the lives of your children,
who faint[a] from hunger
at the head of every street.

20 "Look, O LORD, and consider:
Whom have you ever treated like this?
Should women eat their offspring,[b]
the children they have cared for?
Should priest and prophet be killed
in the sanctuary of the Lord?

21 "Young and old lie together
in the dust of the streets;
my young men and maidens
have fallen by the sword.[c]
You have slain them in the day of your
anger;
you have slaughtered them without
pity.

22 "As you summon to a feast day,
so you summoned against me terrors[d]
on every side.
In the day of the LORD's anger
no one escaped or survived;
those I cared for and reared,
my enemy has destroyed."

3[a] I am the man who has seen affliction
by the rod of his wrath.
2 He has driven me away and made me walk
in darkness rather than light;
3 indeed, he has turned his hand
against me
again and again, all day long.

4 He has made my skin and my flesh grow
old
and has broken my bones.[e]
5 He has besieged me and surrounded me
with bitterness and hardship.
6 He has made me dwell in darkness
like those long dead.[f]

7 He has walled me in so I cannot escape;
he has weighed me down with chains.
8 Even when I call out or cry for help,
he shuts out my prayer.[g]
9 He has barred my way with blocks of
stone;
he has made my paths crooked.

10 Like a bear lying in wait,
like a lion in hiding,
11 he dragged me from the path and
mangled[h] me
and left me without help.
12 He drew his bow
and made me the target[i] for his
arrows.

13 He pierced my heart
with arrows from his quiver.
14 I became the laughingstock[j] of all my
people;
they mock me in song[k] all day long.
15 He has filled me with bitter herbs
and sated me with gall.[l]

16 He has broken my teeth with gravel;[m]
he has trampled me in the dust.
17 I have been deprived of peace;
I have forgotten what prosperity is.
18 So I say, "My splendor is gone
and all that I had hoped from the
LORD."

19 I remember my affliction and my
wandering,
the bitterness and the gall.
20 I well remember them,
and my soul is downcast within me.
21 Yet this I call to mind
and therefore I have hope:

22 Because of the LORD's great love we are
not consumed,
for his compassions never fail.[n]
23 They are new every morning;
great is your faithfulness.
24 I say to myself, "The LORD is my portion;
therefore I will wait for him."

25 The LORD is good to those whose hope is
in him,
to the one who seeks him;
26 it is good to wait quietly
for the salvation of the LORD.[o]
27 It is good for a man to bear the yoke
while he is young.

28 Let him sit alone in silence,[p]
for the LORD has laid it on him.
29 Let him bury his face in the dust—
there may yet be hope.

[a]This chapter is an acrostic poem; the verses of each stanza begin with the successive letters of the Hebrew alphabet, and the verses within each stanza begin with the same letter.

**2:19** a Isa 51:20
**2:20** b Jer 19:9
**2:21** c 2Ch 36:17
**2:22** d Ps 31:13
**3:4** e Ps 51:8; Isa 38:13
**3:6** f Ps 88:5–6
**3:8** g Job 30:20
**3:11** h Hos 6:1
**3:12** i Job 7:20
**3:14** j Jer 20:7 k Job 30:9
**3:15** l Jer 9:15
**3:16** m Pr 20:17
**3:22** n Mal 3:6
**3:26** o Ps 37:7
**3:28** p Jer 15:17

**3:30** q Isa 50:6
**3:31** r Ps 94:14
**3:33** s Eze 33:11
**3:36** t Hab 1:13
**3:37** u Ps 33:9–11
**3:38** v Job 2:10
**3:39** w Mic 7:9
**3:40** x Ps 119:59
**3:42** y Da 9:5
**3:44** z ver 8

*My God,*

*as I awake in the morning, I acknowledge that you have given me one more day. You are faithful. Your mercies, so long-standing and dependable, are renewed with each sunrise. Thank you!*

*Amen*

LAMENTATIONS 3:22–24

30 Let him offer his cheek to one who would
strike him,[q]
and let him be filled with disgrace.
31 For men are not cast off
by the Lord forever.[r]
32 Though he brings grief, he will show
compassion,
so great is his unfailing love.
33 For he does not willingly bring affliction
or grief to the children of men.[s]

34 To crush underfoot
all prisoners in the land,
35 to deny a man his rights
before the Most High,
36 to deprive a man of justice—
would not the Lord see such things?[t]
37 Who can speak and have it happen
if the Lord has not decreed it?[u]
38 Is it not from the mouth of the Most High
that both calamities and good things
come?[v]
39 Why should any living man complain
when punished for his sins?[w]

40 Let us examine our ways and test them,
and let us return to the LORD.[x]
41 Let us lift up our hearts and our hands
to God in heaven, and say:
42 "We have sinned and rebelled[y]
and you have not forgiven.

43 "You have covered yourself with anger
and pursued us;
you have slain without pity.
44 You have covered yourself with a cloud
so that no prayer[z] can get through.
45 You have made us scum[a] and refuse
among the nations.

46 "All our enemies have opened their
mouths
wide against us.[b]
47 We have suffered terror and pitfalls,
ruin and destruction.[c]"
48 Streams of tears flow from my eyes
because my people are destroyed.

49 My eyes will flow unceasingly,
without relief,[d]
50 until the LORD looks down
from heaven and sees.[e]
51 What I see brings grief to my soul
because of all the women of my city.

52 Those who were my enemies without
cause
hunted me like a bird.[f]
53 They tried to end my life in a pit[g]
and threw stones at me;
54 the waters closed over my head,[h]
and I thought I was about to be cut off.

55 I called on your name, O LORD,
from the depths of the pit.[i]
56 You heard my plea: "Do not close your
ears
to my cry for relief."
57 You came near when I called you,
and you said, "Do not fear."[j]

58 O Lord, you took up my case;
you redeemed my life.
59 You have seen, O LORD, the wrong done
to me.
Uphold my cause!
60 You have seen the depth of their
vengeance,
all their plots against me.[k]

61 O LORD, you have heard their insults,
all their plots against me—
62 what my enemies whisper and mutter
against me all day long.
63 Look at them! Sitting or standing,
they mock me in their songs.

64 Pay them back what they deserve, O LORD,
for what their hands have done.[l]
65 Put a veil over their hearts,[m]
and may your curse be on them!
66 Pursue them in anger and destroy them
from under the heavens of the LORD.

**3:45** a 1Co 4:13
**3:46** b La 2:16
**3:47** c Isa 24:17–18
**3:49** d Jer 14:17
**3:50** e Isa 63:15
**3:52** f Ps 35:7
**3:53** g Jer 37:16
**3:54** h Ps 69:2
**3:55** i Jnh 2:2
**3:57** j Isa 41:10
**3:60** k Jer 11:20
**3:64** l Ps 28:4
**3:65** m Isa 6:10

**4:4** n La 2:11,12
**4:6** o Ge 19:25
**4:8** p Ps 102:3–5
**4:10** q Dt 28:53–57; La 2:20
**4:11** r Dt 32:22; Jer 7:20

# 4

[a] How the gold has lost its luster,
the fine gold become dull!
The sacred gems are scattered
at the head of every street.

2 How the precious sons of Zion,
once worth their weight in gold,
are now considered as pots of clay,
the work of a potter's hands!

3 Even jackals offer their breasts
to nurse their young,
but my people have become heartless
like ostriches in the desert.

4 Because of thirst the infant's tongue
sticks to the roof of its mouth;
the children beg for bread,
but no one gives it to them.[n]

5 Those who once ate delicacies
are destitute in the streets.
Those nurtured in purple
now lie on ash heaps.

6 The punishment of my people
is greater than that of Sodom,[o]
which was overthrown in a moment
without a hand turned to help her.

7 Their princes were brighter than snow
and whiter than milk,
their bodies more ruddy than rubies,
their appearance like sapphires.[b]

8 But now they are blacker than soot;
they are not recognized in the streets.
Their skin has shriveled on their bones;[p]
it has become as dry as a stick.

9 Those killed by the sword are better off
than those who die of famine;
racked with hunger, they waste away
for lack of food from the field.

10 With their own hands compassionate
women
have cooked their own children,[q]
who became their food
when my people were destroyed.

11 The LORD has given full vent to his wrath;
he has poured out his fierce anger.
He kindled a fire in Zion
that consumed her foundations.[r]

12 The kings of the earth did not believe,
nor did any of the world's people,
that enemies and foes could enter
the gates of Jerusalem.

13 But it happened because of the sins of her
prophets
and the iniquities of her priests,[s]
who shed within her
the blood of the righteous.

14 Now they grope through the streets
like men who are blind.
They are so defiled with blood[t]
that no one dares to touch their
garments.

15 "Go away! You are unclean!" men cry to
them.
"Away! Away! Don't touch us!"
When they flee and wander about,
people among the nations say,
"They can stay here no longer."[u]

16 The LORD himself has scattered them;
he no longer watches over them.
The priests are shown no honor,
the elders no favor.

17 Moreover, our eyes failed,
looking in vain for help;
from our towers we watched
for a nation[v] that could not save us.

18 Men stalked us at every step,
so we could not walk in our streets.
Our end was near, our days were
numbered,
for our end had come.[w]

19 Our pursuers were swifter
than eagles in the sky;
they chased us over the mountains
and lay in wait for us in the desert.

20 The LORD's anointed,[x] our very life breath,
was caught in their traps.
We thought that under his shadow
we would live among the nations.

21 Rejoice and be glad, O Daughter of Edom,
you who live in the land of Uz.
But to you also the cup will be passed;
you will be drunk and stripped naked.

**4:13** s Jer 6:13; Eze 22:28
**4:14** t Jer 2:34; 19:4
**4:15** u Lev 13:46
**4:17** v Jer 37:7
**4:18** w Eze 7:2–12
**4:20** x 2Sa 19:21

[a] This chapter is an acrostic poem, the verses of which begin with the successive letters of the Hebrew alphabet. [b] 7 Or *lapis lazuli*

4:22 y Isa 40:2
5:1 z Ps 44:13–16
5:3 a Jer 15:8
5:5 b Ne 9:37
5:7 c Jer 14:20
5:8 d Zec 11:6

22 O Daughter of Zion, your punishment
will end;[y]
he will not prolong your exile.
But, O Daughter of Edom, he will punish
your sin
and expose your wickedness.

5 Remember, O LORD, what has happened
to us;
look, and see our disgrace.[z]
2 Our inheritance has been turned over to
aliens,
our homes to foreigners.
3 We have become orphans and fatherless,
our mothers like widows.[a]
4 We must buy the water we drink;
our wood can be had only at a price.
5 Those who pursue us are at our heels;
we are weary[b] and find no rest.
6 We submitted to Egypt and Assyria
to get enough bread.
7 Our fathers sinned and are no more,
and we bear their punishment.[c]
8 Slaves rule over us,
and there is none to free us from their
hands.[d]
9 We get our bread at the risk of our lives
because of the sword in the desert.
10 Our skin is hot as an oven,
feverish from hunger.
11 Women have been ravished[e] in Zion,
and virgins in the towns of Judah.
12 Princes have been hung up by their
hands;
elders are shown no respect.
13 Young men toil at the millstones;
boys stagger under loads of wood.
14 The elders are gone from the city gate;
the young men have stopped their
music.[f]
15 Joy is gone from our hearts;
our dancing has turned to mourning.
16 The crown[g] has fallen from our head.
Woe to us, for we have sinned!
17 Because of this our hearts[h] are faint,
because of these things our eyes grow
dim
18 for Mount Zion, which lies desolate,
with jackals prowling over it.
19 You, O LORD, reign forever;
your throne endures[i] from generation
to generation.
20 Why do you always forget us?[j]
Why do you forsake us so long?
21 Restore us to yourself, O LORD, that we
may return;
renew our days as of old
22 unless you have utterly rejected us
and are angry with us beyond
measure.

5:11 e Zec 14:2
5:14 f Jer 7:34
5:16 g Ps 89:39
5:17 h Isa 1:5
5:19 i Ps 45:6
5:20 j Ps 13:1

## The African Presence

### Lamentations 5:6

According to Genesis 10:8–12, Nimrod (a son of Cush) traveled throughout Assyria, as well as Babylon, Erech, Akkad and Calneh. Throughout ancient history, Assyria maintained a long and impressive rule. Nineveh, the capital city built by Nimrod, was defeated during the battle of 612 B.C. when Babylon and Persia joined forces. In 605 B.C. Babylon defeated Egypt, which gave it an undisputed domination of the Fertile Crescent, the territory from Egypt to the Persian Gulf.

# Ezekiel

## OVERVIEW

Ezekiel was called to be "a watchman for the house of Israel" (Eze 3:17). Already exiled to Babylon in the deportation of 597 B.C., he prophesied the siege and destruction of Jerusalem in 588–586 B.C. In a vision the Lord took Ezekiel, who was himself a priest, into the temple so that he could see the secret worship of idols by Judah's leaders; and he was informed by God that Jerusalem would be destroyed because of idol worship (see Eze 8–9). Then Ezekiel witnessed the departure of the glory of God from the temple (see Eze 10).

In his book, Ezekiel chided the false prophets—both male and female (see Eze 13:17–23). He announced God's judgment on the surrounding nations of Ammon, Moab, Edom, Philistia, Tyre, Sidon and Egypt. Also in this book, we read that Ezekiel suffered when the "delight of [his] eyes"—his wife—died and he was instructed to not mourn her death as a sign of God's impending judgment (see Eze 24:15–24).

Despite the coming judgment through King Nebuchadnezzar of Babylon, there was hope for Israel. God would restore her, as the dry bones received life in Ezekiel's vision recorded in chapter 37. Furthermore, a new temple would be constructed according to the pattern shown to him (see Eze 40–48).

Every now and then the church needs a revival to awaken "dry bones" to new life in Christ Jesus. What areas of your life need a refreshing renewal? Through a relationship with Jesus Christ, God provides living water that will never run dry (see Jn 7:37–39).

## OUTLINE

I. Ezekiel's Call and Commission (1:1—3:27)

II. Judgment on Judah and Jerusalem (4:1—24:27)

III. Judgment on the Surrounding Nations (25:1—32:32)

IV. Restoration for Israel (33:1—48:35)

## SCANNABLE FACTS:

**Author:** Ezekiel

**Time Written:** 593–571 B.C.

**Theme to Note:** Hope and restoration for the exiles

**Notable Women:** Ezekiel's wife, women who prophesied falsely

## The Living Creatures and the Glory of the LORD

1 In the[a] thirtieth year, in the fourth month on the fifth day, while I was among the exiles by the Kebar River, the heavens were opened[a] and I saw visions of God.

[2]On the fifth of the month—it was the fifth year of the exile of King Jehoiachin—[3]the word of the LORD came to Ezekiel the priest, the son of Buzi,[b] by the Kebar River in the land of the Babylonians.[c] There the hand of the LORD was upon him.[b]

[4]I looked, and I saw a windstorm coming out of the north—an immense cloud with flashing lightning and surrounded by brilliant light. The center of the fire looked like glowing metal, [5]and in the fire was what looked like four living creatures.[c] In appearance their form was that of a man, [6]but each of them had four faces and four wings. [7]Their legs were straight; their feet were like those of a calf and gleamed like burnished bronze.[d] [8]Under their wings on their four sides they had the hands of a man.[e] All four of them had faces and wings, [9]and their wings touched one another. Each one went straight ahead; they did not turn as they moved.

[10]Their faces looked like this: Each of the four had the face of a man, and on the right side each had the face of a lion, and on the left the face of an ox; each also had the face of an eagle.[f] [11]Such were their faces. Their wings[g] were spread out upward; each had two wings, one touching the wing of another creature on either side, and two wings covering its body. [12]Each one went straight ahead. Wherever the spirit would go, they would go, without turning as they went. [13]The appearance of the living creatures was like burning coals of fire or like torches. Fire moved back and forth among the creatures; it was bright, and lightning[h] flashed out of it. [14]The creatures sped back and forth like flashes of lightning.

[15]As I looked at the living creatures, I saw a wheel on the ground beside each creature with its four faces. [16]This was the appearance and structure of the wheels: They sparkled like chrysolite,[i] and all four looked alike. Each appeared to be made like a wheel intersecting a wheel. [17]As they moved, they would go in any one of the four directions the creatures faced; the wheels did not turn about[d] as the creatures went. [18]Their rims were high and awesome, and all four rims were full of eyes[j] all around.

[19]When the living creatures moved, the wheels beside them moved; and when the living creatures rose from the ground, the wheels also rose. [20]Wherever the spirit would go, they would go,[k] and the wheels would rise along with them, because the spirit of the living creatures was in the wheels. [21]When the creatures moved, they also moved; when the creatures stood still, they also stood still; and when the creatures rose from the ground, the wheels rose along with them, because the spirit of the living creatures was in the wheels.[l]

[22]Spread out above the heads of the living creatures was what looked like an expanse,[m] sparkling like ice, and awesome. [23]Under the expanse their wings were stretched out one toward the other, and each had two wings covering its body. [24]When the creatures moved, I heard the sound of their wings, like the roar of rushing waters, like the voice[n] of the Almighty,[e] like the tumult of an army. When they stood still, they lowered their wings.

[25]Then there came a voice from above the expanse over their heads as they stood with lowered wings. [26]Above the expanse over their heads was what looked like a throne of sapphire,[f][o] and high above on the throne was a figure like that of a man. [27]I saw that from what appeared to be his waist up he looked like glowing metal, as if full of fire, and that from there down he looked like fire; and brilliant light surrounded him.[p] [28]Like the appearance of a rainbow[q] in the clouds on a rainy day, so was the radiance around him.[r]

This was the appearance of the likeness of the glory of the LORD. When I saw it, I fell facedown, and I heard the voice of one speaking.

[a]1 Or ⌊*my*⌋ [b]3 Or *Ezekiel son of Buzi the priest* [c]3 Or *Chaldeans* [d]17 Or *aside* [e]24 Hebrew *Shaddai* [f]26 Or *lapis lazuli*

**1:1** a Mt3:16; Ac7:56
**1:3** b 2Ki3:15
**1:5** c Rev4:6
**1:7** d Rev1:15
**1:8** e Eze10:8
**1:10** f Rev4:7
**1:11** g Isa6:2
**1:13** h Rev4:5
**1:16** i Eze10:9–11
**1:18** j Eze10:12; Rev4:6
**1:20** k ver12
**1:21** l Eze10:17
**1:22** m Eze10:1
**1:24** n Eze10:5; 43:2; Rev1:15
**1:26** o Ex24:10
**1:27** p Eze8:2
**1:28** q Rev10:1 r Rev4:2

## Ezekiel's Call

**2** He said to me, "Son of man, stand[s] up on your feet and I will speak to you." 2 As he spoke, the Spirit came into me and raised me[t] to my feet, and I heard him speaking to me.

3 He said: "Son of man, I am sending you to the Israelites, to a rebellious nation that has rebelled against me; they and their fathers have been in revolt against me to this very day.[u] 4 The people to whom I am sending you are obstinate and stubborn.[v] Say to them, 'This is what the Sovereign LORD says.' 5 And whether they listen or fail to listen[w]—for they are a rebellious house[x]—they will know that a prophet has been among them.[y] 6 And you, son of man, do not be afraid of them or their words. Do not be afraid, though briers and thorns[z] are all around you and you live among scorpions. Do not be afraid of what they say or terrified by them, though they are a rebellious house. 7 You must speak my words to them, whether they listen or fail to listen, for they are rebellious.[a] 8 But you, son of man, listen to what I say to you. Do not rebel like that rebellious house; open your mouth and eat[b] what I give you."

*Woman of color,*

*I am everywhere. Don't be afraid of anyone,*

*and don't forget to reverence my name.*

*The Omnipresent One*

EZEKIEL 2:6

9 Then I looked, and I saw a hand[c] stretched out to me. In it was a scroll, 10 which he unrolled before me. On both sides of it were written words of lament and mourning and woe.

**3** And he said to me, "Son of man, eat what is before you, eat this scroll; then go and speak to the house of Israel." 2 So I opened my mouth, and he gave me the scroll to eat.

3 Then he said to me, "Son of man, eat this scroll I am giving you and fill your stomach with it." So I ate[d] it, and it tasted as sweet as honey[e] in my mouth.

4 He then said to me: "Son of man, go now to the house of Israel and speak my words to them. 5 You are not being sent to a people of obscure speech and difficult language, but to the house of Israel— 6 not to many peoples of obscure speech and difficult language, whose words you cannot understand. Surely if I had sent you to them, they would have listened to you. 7 But the house of Israel is not willing to listen to you because they are not willing to listen to me, for the whole house of Israel is hardened and obstinate. 8 But I will make you as unyielding and hardened as they are. 9 I will make your forehead like the hardest stone, harder than flint. Do not be afraid of them or terrified by them, though they are a rebellious house."

10 And he said to me, "Son of man, listen carefully and take to heart all the words I speak to you. 11 Go now to your countrymen in exile and speak to them. Say to them, 'This is what the Sovereign LORD says,' whether they listen or fail to listen."

12 Then the Spirit lifted me up,[f] and I heard behind me a loud rumbling sound—May the glory of the LORD be praised in his dwelling place!— 13 the sound of the wings of the living creatures brushing against each other and the sound of the wheels beside them, a loud rumbling sound. 14 The Spirit then lifted me up and took me away, and I went in bitterness and in the anger of my spirit, with the strong hand of the LORD upon me. 15 I came to the exiles who lived at Tel Abib near the Kebar River. And there, where they were living, I sat among them for seven days—overwhelmed.

## Warning to Israel

16 At the end of seven days the word of the LORD came to me: 17 "Son of man, I have made you a watchman[g] for the house of Israel; so hear the word I speak and give them warning from me. 18 When I say to a wicked man, 'You will surely die,' and you do not warn him or speak out to dissuade him from his evil ways in order to save his life, that wicked man will die

**2:1** s Da 10:11
**2:2** t Eze 3:24
**2:3** u Jer 3:25; Eze 20:8–24
**2:4** v Eze 3:7
**2:5** w Eze 3:11 x Eze 3:27 y Eze 33:33
**2:6** z Mic 7:4
**2:7** a Jer 1:7
**2:8** b Rev 10:9
**2:9** c Eze 8:3
**3:3** d Jer 15:16 e Ps 19:10; Rev 10:9–10
**3:12** f Eze 8:3
**3:17** g Isa 52:8

for[a] his sin, and I will hold you accountable for his blood. [19]But if you do warn the wicked man and he does not turn from his wickedness or from his evil ways, he will die for his sin; but you will have saved yourself.[h]

[20]"Again, when a righteous man turns from his righteousness and does evil, and I put a stumbling block before him, he will die. Since you did not warn him, he will die for his sin. The righteous things he did will not be remembered, and I will hold you accountable for his blood.[i] [21]But if you do warn the righteous man not to sin and he does not sin, he will surely live because he took warning, and you will have saved yourself."

[22]The hand of the LORD was upon me there, and he said to me, "Get up and go[j] out to the plain, and there I will speak to you." [23]So I got up and went out to the plain. And the glory of the LORD was standing there, like the glory I had seen by the Kebar River,[k] and I fell facedown.

[24]Then the Spirit came into me and raised me[l] to my feet. He spoke to me and said: "Go, shut yourself inside your house. [25]And you, son of man, they will tie with ropes; you will be bound so that you cannot go out among the people.[m] [26]I will make your tongue stick to the roof of your mouth so that you will be silent and unable to rebuke them, though they are a rebellious house.[n] [27]But when I speak to you, I will open your mouth and you shall say to them, 'This is what the Sovereign LORD says.' Whoever will listen let him listen, and whoever will refuse let him refuse; for they are a rebellious house.[o]

## Siege of Jerusalem Symbolized

4 "Now, son of man, take a clay tablet, put it in front of you and draw the city of Jerusalem on it. [2]Then lay siege to it: Erect siege works against it, build a ramp up to it, set up camps against it and put battering rams around it. [3]Then take an iron pan, place it as an iron wall between you and the city and turn your face toward it. It will be under siege, and you shall besiege it. This will be a sign[p] to the house of Israel.

[4]"Then lie on your left side and put the sin of the house of Israel upon yourself.[b] You are to bear their sin for the number of days you lie on your side. [5]I have assigned you the same number of days as the years of their sin. So for 390 days you will bear the sin of the house of Israel.

[6]"After you have finished this, lie down again, this time on your right side, and bear the sin of the house of Judah. I have assigned you 40 days, a day for each year. [7]Turn your face toward the siege of Jerusalem and with bared arm prophesy against her. [8]I will tie you up with ropes so that you cannot turn from one side to the other until you have finished the days of your siege.[q]

[9]"Take wheat and barley, beans and lentils, millet and spelt; put them in a storage jar and use them to make bread for yourself. You are to eat it during the 390 days you lie on your side. [10]Weigh out twenty shekels[c] of food to eat each day and eat it at set times. [11]Also measure out a sixth of a hin[d] of water and drink it at set times. [12]Eat the food as you would a barley cake; bake it in the sight of the people, using human excrement for fuel." [13]The LORD said, "In this way the people of Israel will eat defiled food among the nations where I will drive them."[r]

[14]Then I said, "Not so, Sovereign LORD! I have never defiled myself. From my youth until now I have never eaten anything found dead or torn by wild animals. No unclean meat has ever entered my mouth."

[15]"Very well," he said, "I will let you bake your bread over cow manure instead of human excrement."

[16]He then said to me: "Son of man, I will cut off the supply of food in Jerusalem. The people will eat rationed food in anxiety and drink rationed water in despair,[s] [17]for food and water will be scarce. They will be appalled at the sight of each other and will waste away because of[e] their sin.[t]

5 "Now, son of man, take a sharp sword and use it as a barber's razor to shave[u] your head and your beard.[v] Then take a set of scales and divide up the hair. [2]When the days of your siege come to an end, burn a third of the hair with fire inside the city. Take a third and strike it with the sword all

**3:19** h Ac 20:26
**3:20** i Eze 18:24
**3:22** j Ac 9:6
**3:23** k Eze 1:1
**3:24** l Eze 2:2
**3:25** m Eze 4:8
**3:26** n Eze 24:27
**3:27** o Eze 24:27; 33:22
**4:3** p Eze 12:3–6
**4:8** q Eze 3:25
**4:13** r Hos 9:3
**4:16** s ver 10–11; Lev 26:26; Isa 3:1; Eze 12:19
**4:17** t Lev 26:39; Eze 24:23
**5:1** u Eze 44:20 v Lev 21:5

[a]18 Or *in*; also in verses 19 and 20 [b]4 Or *your side* [c]10 That is, about 8 ounces (about 0.2 kilogram) [d]11 That is, about 2/3 quart (about 0.6 liter) [e]17 Or *away in*

**5:6** w Zec 7:11
**5:7** x Eze 16:47
**5:9** y Da 9:12
**5:10** z Lev 26:29; a Eze 12:14; Zec 2:6
**5:12** b Eze 12:14
**5:14** c Ne 2:17

around the city. And scatter a third to the wind. For I will pursue them with drawn sword. 3 But take a few strands of hair and tuck them away in the folds of your garment. 4 Again, take a few of these and throw them into the fire and burn them up. A fire will spread from there to the whole house of Israel.

5 "This is what the Sovereign LORD says: This is Jerusalem, which I have set in the center of the nations, with countries all around her. 6 Yet in her wickedness she has rebelled against my laws and decrees more than the nations and countries around her. She has rejected my laws and has not followed my decrees.[w]

7 "Therefore this is what the Sovereign LORD says: You have been more unruly than the nations around you and have not followed my decrees or kept my laws. You have not even[a] conformed to the standards of the nations around you.[x]

8 "Therefore this is what the Sovereign LORD says: I myself am against you, Jerusalem, and I will inflict punishment on you in the sight of the nations. 9 Because of all your detestable idols, I will do to you what I have never done before and will never do again.[y] 10 Therefore in your midst fathers will eat their children, and children will eat their fathers.[z] I will inflict punishment on you and will scatter all your survivors to the winds.[a] 11 Therefore as surely as I live, declares the Sovereign LORD, because you have defiled my sanctuary with all your vile images and detestable practices, I myself will withdraw my favor; I will not look on you with pity or spare you. 12 A third of your people will die of the plague or perish by famine inside you; a third will fall by the sword outside your walls; and a third I will scatter to the winds and pursue with drawn sword.[b]

13 "Then my anger will cease and my wrath against them will subside, and I will be avenged. And when I have spent my wrath upon them, they will know that I the LORD have spoken in my zeal.

14 "I will make you a ruin and a reproach among the nations around you, in the sight of all who pass by.[c] 15 You will be a reproach and a taunt, a warning and an object of horror to the nations around you when I inflict punishment on you in anger and in wrath and with stinging rebuke. I the LORD have spoken.[d] 16 When I shoot at you with my deadly and destructive arrows of famine, I will shoot to destroy you. I will bring more and more famine upon you and cut off your supply of food.[e] 17 I will send famine and wild beasts against you, and they will leave you childless. Plague and bloodshed[f] will sweep through you, and I will bring the sword against you. I the LORD have spoken.[g]"

## A Prophecy Against the Mountains of Israel

6 The word of the LORD came to me: 2 "Son of man, set your face against the mountains[h] of Israel; prophesy against them 3 and say: 'O mountains of Israel, hear the word of the Sovereign LORD. This is what the Sovereign LORD says to the mountains and hills, to the ravines and valleys: I am about to bring a sword against you, and I will destroy your high places.[i] 4 Your altars will be demolished and your incense altars will be smashed; and I will slay your people in front of your idols. 5 I will lay the dead bodies of the Israelites in front of their idols, and I will scatter your bones[j] around your altars. 6 Wherever you live, the towns will be laid waste and the high places demolished, so that your altars will be laid waste and devastated, your idols[k] smashed and ruined, your incense altars broken down, and what you have made wiped out. 7 Your people will fall slain among you, and you will know that I am the LORD.

8 " 'But I will spare some, for some of you will escape[l] the sword when you are scattered among the lands and nations.[m] 9 Then in the nations where they have been carried captive, those who escape will remember me—how I have been grieved[n] by their adulterous hearts, which have turned away from me, and by their eyes, which have lusted after their idols. They will loathe themselves for the evil they have done and for all their detestable practices.[o] 10 And they will know that I am the LORD; I did not threaten in vain to bring this calamity on them.

11 " 'This is what the Sovereign LORD says:

**5:15** d Eze 25:17
**5:16** e Dt 32:24
**5:17** f Eze 38:22; g Eze 14:21
**6:2** h Eze 36:1
**6:3** i Lev 26:30
**6:5** j Jer 8:1–2
**6:6** k Zec 13:2
**6:8** l Jer 44:28; m Eze 14:22
**6:9** n Ps 78:40; Isa 7:13; o Eze 20:43

[a]7 Most Hebrew manuscripts; some Hebrew manuscripts and Syriac *You have*

Strike your hands together and stamp your feet and cry out "Alas!" because of all the wicked and detestable practices of the house of Israel, for they will fall by the sword, famine and plague.[p] [12]He that is far away will die of the plague, and he that is near will fall by the sword, and he that survives and is spared will die of famine. So will I spend my wrath upon them.[q] [13]And they will know that I am the LORD, when their people lie slain among their idols around their altars, on every high hill and on all the mountaintops, under every spreading tree and every leafy oak[r]—places where they offered fragrant incense to all their idols.[s] [14]And I will stretch out my hand against them and make the land a desolate waste from the desert to Diblah[a]—wherever they live. Then they will know that I am the LORD.' "

## The End Has Come

7 The word of the LORD came to me: [2]"Son of man, this is what the Sovereign LORD says to the land of Israel: The end![t] The end has come upon the four corners of the land. [3]The end is now upon you and I will unleash my anger against you. I will judge you according to your conduct and repay you for all your detestable practices. [4]I will not look on you with pity[u] or spare you; I will surely repay you for your conduct and the detestable practices among you. Then you will know that I am the LORD.

[5]"This is what the Sovereign LORD says: Disaster![v] An unheard-of[b] disaster is coming. [6]The end has come! The end has come! It has roused itself against you. It has come! [7]Doom has come upon you—you who dwell in the land. The time has come, the day is near; there is panic, not joy, upon the mountains. [8]I am about to pour out my wrath on you and spend my anger against you; I will judge you according to your conduct and repay you for all your detestable practices.[w] [9]I will not look on you with pity or spare you; I will repay you in accordance with your conduct and the detestable practices among you. Then you will know that it is I the LORD who strikes the blow.

[10]"The day is here! It has come! Doom has burst forth, the rod[x] has budded, arrogance has blossomed! [11]Violence has grown into[c] a rod to punish wickedness; none of the people will be left, none of that crowd—no wealth, nothing of value.[y] [12]The time has come, the day has arrived. Let not the buyer rejoice nor the seller grieve, for wrath is upon the whole crowd. [13]The seller will not recover the land he has sold as long as both of them live, for the vision concerning the whole crowd will not be reversed. Because of their sins, not one of them will preserve his life. [14]Though they blow the trumpet and get everything ready, no one will go into battle, for my wrath is upon the whole crowd.

[15]"Outside is the sword, inside are plague and famine; those in the country will die by the sword, and those in the city will be devoured by famine and plague.[z] [16]All who survive and escape will be in the mountains, moaning like doves of the valleys, each because of his sins.[a] [17]Every hand will go limp, and every knee will become as weak as water. [18]They will put on sackcloth and be clothed with terror. Their faces will be covered with shame and their heads will be shaved.[b] [19]They will throw their silver into the streets, and their gold will be an unclean thing. Their silver and gold will not be able to save them in the day of the LORD's wrath.[c] They will not satisfy their hunger or fill their stomachs with it, for it has made them stumble into sin.[d] [20]They were proud of their beautiful jewelry and used it to make their detestable idols and vile images. Therefore I will turn these into an unclean thing for them. [21]I will hand it all over as plunder to foreigners and as loot to the wicked of the earth, and they will defile it. [22]I will turn my face away from them, and they will desecrate my treasured place; robbers will enter it and desecrate it.

[23]"Prepare chains, because the land is full of bloodshed[e] and the city is full of violence. [24]I will bring the most wicked of the nations to take possession of their houses; I will put an end to the pride of the mighty, and their sanctuaries[f] will be desecrated. [25]When terror comes, they will seek peace, but there will be none. [26]Calamity upon calamity[g]

**6:11** p Eze 5:12; 21:14,17
**6:12** q Eze 5:12
**6:13** r Isa 57:5; s Jer 2:20; Hos 4:13
**7:2** t Am 8:2,10
**7:4** u Eze 5:11
**7:5** v 2Ki 21:12
**7:8** w Eze 20:8,21
**7:10** x Isa 10:5
**7:11** y Jer 16:6
**7:15** z Dt 32:25
**7:16** a Eze 6:8
**7:18** b Isa 15:2–3; Am 8:10
**7:19** c Zep 1:7,18; d Pr 11:4
**7:23** e 2Ki 21:16
**7:24** f Eze 24:21
**7:26** g Jer 4:20

[a]14 Most Hebrew manuscripts; a few Hebrew manuscripts *Riblah* [b]5 Most Hebrew manuscripts; some Hebrew manuscripts and Syriac *Disaster after* [c]11 Or *The violent one has become*

7:27 h Eze 26:16
8:1 i Eze 14:1
8:2 j Eze 1:4,26–27
8:3 k Eze 11:1
8:4 l Eze 1:28

will come, and rumor upon rumor. They will try to get a vision from the prophet; the teaching of the law by the priest will be lost, as will the counsel of the elders. 27 The king will mourn, the prince will be clothed with despair,[h] and the hands of the people of the land will tremble. I will deal with them according to their conduct, and by their own standards I will judge them. Then they will know that I am the LORD."

## Idolatry in the Temple

8 In the sixth year, in the sixth month on the fifth day, while I was sitting in my house and the elders[i] of Judah were sitting before me, the hand of the Sovereign LORD came upon me there. 2 I looked, and I saw a figure like that of a man.[a] From what appeared to be his waist down he was like fire, and from there up his appearance was as bright as glowing metal.[j] 3 He stretched out what looked like a hand and took me by the hair of my head. The Spirit lifted me up[k] between earth and heaven and in visions of God he took me to Jerusalem, to the entrance to the north gate of the inner court, where the idol that provokes to jealousy stood. 4 And there before me was the glory[l] of the God of Israel, as in the vision I had seen in the plain.

5 Then he said to me, "Son of man, look toward the north." So I looked, and in the entrance north of the gate of the altar I saw this idol of jealousy.

6 And he said to me, "Son of man, do you see what they are doing—the utterly detestable things the house of Israel is doing here, things that will drive me far from my sanctuary? But you will see things that are even more detestable."

7 Then he brought me to the entrance to the court. I looked, and I saw a hole in the wall. 8 He said to me, "Son of man, now dig into the wall." So I dug into the wall and saw a doorway there.

9 And he said to me, "Go in and see the wicked and detestable things they are doing here." 10 So I went in and looked, and I saw portrayed all over the walls all kinds of crawling things and detestable animals and all the idols of the house of Israel. 11 In front of them stood seventy elders of the house of Israel, and Jaazaniah son of Shaphan was standing among them. Each had a censer in his hand, and a fragrant cloud of incense was rising.

12 He said to me, "Son of man, have you seen what the elders of the house of Israel are doing in the darkness, each at the shrine of his own idol? They say, 'The LORD does not see[m] us; the LORD has forsaken the land.'" 13 Again, he said, "You will see them doing things that are even more detestable."

14 Then he brought me to the entrance to the north gate of the house of the LORD, and I saw women sitting there, mourning for Tammuz. 15 He said to me, "Do you see this, son of man? You will see things that are even more detestable than this."

16 He then brought me into the inner court of the house of the LORD, and there at the entrance to the temple, between the portico and the altar, were about twenty-five men. With their backs toward the temple of the LORD and their faces toward the east, they were bowing down to the sun in the east.[n]

17 He said to me, "Have you seen this, son of man? Is it a trivial matter for the house of Judah to do the detestable things they are doing here? Must they also fill the land with violence[o] and continually provoke me to anger? Look at them putting the branch to their nose! 18 Therefore I will deal with them in anger; I will not look on them with pity or spare them. Although they shout in my ears, I will not listen[p] to them."

## Idolaters Killed

9 Then I heard him call out in a loud voice, "Bring the guards of the city here, each with a weapon in his hand." 2 And I saw six men coming from the direction of the upper gate, which faces north, each with a deadly weapon in his hand. With them was a man clothed in linen who had a writing kit at his side. They came in and stood beside the bronze altar.

3 Now the glory[q] of the God of Israel went up from above the cherubim,[r] where it had been, and moved to the threshold of the temple. Then the LORD called to the man clothed in linen who had the writing kit at his side

8:12 m Eze 9:9
8:16 n Dt 4:19; Jer 2:27
8:17 o Eze 9:9
8:18 p Isa 1:15; Jer 11:11; Mic 3:4; Zec 7:13
9:3 q Eze 10:4 r Eze 11:22

[a]2 Or *saw a fiery figure*

4 and said to him, "Go throughout the city of Jerusalem and put a mark[s] on the foreheads of those who grieve and lament[t] over all the detestable things that are done in it.[u]"

5 As I listened, he said to the others, "Follow him through the city and kill, without showing pity or compassion. 6 Slaughter old men, young men and maidens, women and children, but do not touch anyone who has the mark. Begin at my sanctuary." So they began with the elders who were in front of the temple.[v]

7 Then he said to them, "Defile the temple and fill the courts with the slain. Go!" So they went out and began killing throughout the city. 8 While they were killing and I was left alone, I fell facedown, crying out, "Ah, Sovereign LORD! Are you going to destroy the entire remnant of Israel in this outpouring of your wrath on Jerusalem?[w]"

9 He answered me, "The sin of the house of Israel and Judah is exceedingly great; the land is full of bloodshed and the city is full of injustice. They say, 'The LORD has forsaken the land; the LORD does not see.'[x] 10 So I will not look on them with pity[y] or spare them, but I will bring down on their own heads what they have done.[z]"

11 Then the man in linen with the writing kit at his side brought back word, saying, "I have done as you commanded."

## The Glory Departs From the Temple

**10** I looked, and I saw the likeness of a throne of sapphire[a] above the expanse[a] that was over the heads of the cherubim. 2 The LORD said to the man clothed in linen, "Go in among the wheels beneath the cherubim. Fill[b] your hands with burning coals from among the cherubim and scatter them over the city." And as I watched, he went in.

3 Now the cherubim were standing on the south side of the temple when the man went in, and a cloud filled the inner court. 4 Then the glory of the LORD[c] rose from above the cherubim and moved to the threshold of the temple. The cloud filled the temple, and the court was full of the radiance of the glory of the LORD. 5 The sound of the wings of the cherubim could be heard as far away as the outer court, like the voice[d] of God Almighty[b] when he speaks.

6 When the LORD commanded the man in linen, "Take fire from among the wheels, from among the cherubim," the man went in and stood beside a wheel. 7 Then one of the cherubim reached out his hand to the fire that was among them. He took up some of it and put it into the hands of the man in linen, who took it and went out. 8 (Under the wings of the cherubim could be seen what looked like the hands of a man.)

9 I looked, and I saw beside the cherubim four wheels, one beside each of the cherubim; the wheels sparkled like chrysolite.[e] 10 As for their appearance, the four of them looked alike; each was like a wheel intersecting a wheel. 11 As they moved, they would go in any one of the four directions the cherubim faced; the wheels did not turn about[c] as the cherubim went. The cherubim went in whatever direction the head faced, without turning as they went. 12 Their entire bodies, including their backs, their hands and their wings, were completely full of eyes, as were their four wheels. 13 I heard the wheels being called "the whirling wheels." 14 Each of the cherubim had four faces:[f] One face was that of a cherub, the second the face of a man, the third the face of a lion, and the fourth the face of an eagle.[g]

15 Then the cherubim rose upward. These were the living creatures[h] I had seen by the Kebar River. 16 When the cherubim moved, the wheels beside them moved; and when the cherubim spread their wings to rise from the ground, the wheels did not leave their side. 17 When the cherubim stood still, they also stood still; and when the cherubim rose, they rose with them, because the spirit of the living creatures was in them.[i]

18 Then the glory of the LORD departed from over the threshold of the temple and stopped above the cherubim. 19 While I watched, the cherubim spread their wings and rose from the ground, and as they went, the wheels went with them.[j] They stopped at the entrance to the east gate of the LORD's house, and the glory of the God of Israel was above them.

**9:4** s Ex 12:7; Rev 7:3; 9:4 t Ps 119:136 u Ps 119:53
**9:6** v 2Ch 36:17; Jer 25:29
**9:8** w Eze 11:13
**9:9** x Eze 8:12
**9:10** y Eze 7:4; 8:18 z Eze 11:21
**10:1** a Eze 1:22
**10:2** b Rev 8:5
**10:4** c Eze 1:28; 9:3
**10:5** d Eze 1:24
**10:9** e Eze 1:15–16
**10:14** f Eze 1:6 g Eze 1:10
**10:15** h Eze 1:3,5
**10:17** i Eze 1:20–21
**10:19** j Eze 11:1,22

[a]1 Or *lapis lazuli* [b]5 Hebrew *El-Shaddai* [c]11 Or *aside*

20 These were the living creatures I had seen beneath the God of Israel by the Kebar River, and I realized that they were cherubim. 21 Each had four faces and four wings,[k] and under their wings was what looked like the hands of a man. 22 Their faces had the same appearance as those I had seen by the Kebar River. Each one went straight ahead.

## Judgment on Israel's Leaders

11 Then the Spirit lifted me up and brought me to the gate of the house of the LORD that faces east. There at the entrance to the gate were twenty-five men, and I saw among them Jaazaniah son of Azzur and Pelatiah son of Benaiah, leaders of the people. 2 The LORD said to me, "Son of man, these are the men who are plotting evil and giving wicked advice in this city. 3 They say, 'Will it not soon be time to build houses?[a] This city is a cooking pot,[l] and we are the meat.' 4 Therefore prophesy against them; prophesy, son of man."

5 Then the Spirit of the LORD came upon me, and he told me to say: "This is what the LORD says: That is what you are saying, O house of Israel, but I know what is going through your mind. 6 You have killed many people in this city and filled its streets with the dead.[m]

7 "Therefore this is what the Sovereign LORD says: The bodies you have thrown there are the meat and this city is the pot, but I will drive you out of it.[n] 8 You fear the sword, and the sword is what I will bring against you, declares the Sovereign LORD. 9 I will drive you out of the city and hand you over to foreigners and inflict punishment on you.[o] 10 You will fall by the sword, and I will execute judgment on you at the borders of Israel.[p] Then you will know that I am the LORD. 11 This city will not be a pot for you, nor will you be the meat in it; I will execute judgment on you at the borders of Israel. 12 And you will know that I am the LORD, for you have not followed my decrees or kept my laws but have conformed to the standards of the nations around you.[q]"

13 Now as I was prophesying, Pelatiah son of Benaiah died. Then I fell facedown and cried out in a loud voice, "Ah, Sovereign LORD! Will you completely destroy the remnant of Israel?[r]"

14 The word of the LORD came to me: 15 "Son of man, your brothers—your brothers who are your blood relatives[b] and the whole house of Israel—are those of whom the people of Jerusalem have said, 'They are[c] far away from the LORD; this land was given to us as our possession.'

## Promised Return of Israel

16 "Therefore say: 'This is what the Sovereign LORD says: Although I sent them far away among the nations and scattered them among the countries, yet for a little while I have been a sanctuary[s] for them in the countries where they have gone.'

17 "Therefore say: 'This is what the Sovereign LORD says: I will gather you from the nations and bring you back from the countries where you have been scattered, and I will give you back the land of Israel again.'[t]

18 "They will return to it and remove all its vile images and detestable idols.[u] 19 I will give them an undivided heart[v] and put a new spirit in them; I will remove from them their heart of stone and give them a heart of flesh.[w] 20 Then they will follow my decrees and be careful to keep my laws.[x] They will be my people, and I will be their God.[y] 21 But as for those whose hearts are devoted to their vile images and detestable idols, I will bring down on their own heads what they have done, declares the Sovereign LORD.[z]"

22 Then the cherubim, with the wheels beside them, spread their wings, and the glory of the God of Israel was above them.[a] 23 The glory[b] of the LORD went up from within the city and stopped above the mountain[c] east of it. 24 The Spirit lifted me up and brought me to the exiles in Babylonia[d] in the vision given by the Spirit of God.

Then the vision I had seen went up from me, 25 and I told the exiles everything the LORD had shown me.

## The Exile Symbolized

12 The word of the LORD came to me: 2 "Son of man, you are living among a rebellious people. They have eyes to see

10:21 k Eze 1:6
11:3 l Jer 1:13; Eze 24:3
11:6 m Eze 7:23
11:7 n Eze 24:3–13; Mic 3:2–3
11:9 o Eze 5:8
11:10 p 2Ki 14:25
11:12 q Eze 8:10
11:13 r Eze 9:8
11:16 s Isa 8:14
11:17 t Jer 24:5–6
11:18 u Eze 37:23
11:19 v Jer 32:39; w Eze 18:31; 36:26
11:20 x Ps 105:45; y Eze 14:11
11:21 z Eze 9:10
11:22 a Eze 10:19
11:23 b Eze 8:4; c Zec 14:4

[a] 3 Or *This is not the time to build houses.* [b] 15 Or *are in exile with you* (see Septuagint and Syriac) [c] 15 Or *those to whom the people of Jerusalem have said, 'Stay* [d] 24 Or *Chaldea*

**12:2** d Mt 13:15
**12:6** e Isa 8:18; Eze 4:3; 24:24
**12:9** f Eze 17:12; 24:19

but do not see and ears to hear but do not hear, for they are a rebellious people.[d]

3"Therefore, son of man, pack your belongings for exile and in the daytime, as they watch, set out and go from where you are to another place. Perhaps they will understand, though they are a rebellious house. 4During the daytime, while they watch, bring out your belongings packed for exile. Then in the evening, while they are watching, go out like those who go into exile. 5While they watch, dig through the wall and take your belongings out through it. 6Put them on your shoulder as they are watching and carry them out at dusk. Cover your face so that you cannot see the land, for I have made you a sign[e] to the house of Israel."

7So I did as I was commanded. During the day I brought out my things packed for exile. Then in the evening I dug through the wall with my hands. I took my belongings out at dusk, carrying them on my shoulders while they watched.

8In the morning the word of the LORD came to me: 9"Son of man, did not that rebellious house of Israel ask you, 'What are you doing?'[f]

10"Say to them, 'This is what the Sovereign LORD says: This oracle concerns the prince in Jerusalem and the whole house of Israel who are there.' 11Say to them, 'I am a sign to you.'

"As I have done, so it will be done to them. They will go into exile as captives.

12"The prince among them will put his things on his shoulder at dusk[g] and leave, and a hole will be dug in the wall for him to go through. He will cover his face so that he cannot see the land. 13I will spread my net for him, and he will be caught in my snare; I will bring him to Babylonia, the land of the Chaldeans, but he will not see it, and there he will die.[h] 14I will scatter to the winds all those around him—his staff and all his troops—and I will pursue them with drawn sword.[i]

15"They will know that I am the LORD, when I disperse them among the nations and scatter them through the countries. 16But I will spare a few of them from the sword, famine and plague, so that in the nations where they go they may acknowledge all their detestable practices. Then they will know that I am the LORD."

17The word of the LORD came to me: 18"Son of man, tremble as you eat your food,[j] and shudder in fear as you drink your water. 19Say to the people of the land: 'This is what the Sovereign LORD says about those living in Jerusalem and in the land of Israel: They will eat their food in anxiety and drink their water in despair, for their land will be stripped of everything[k] in it because of the violence of all who live there. 20The

**12:12** g Jer 39:4
**12:13** h Jer 52:11
**12:14** i 2Ki 25:5; Eze 5:10,12
**12:18** j Eze 4:16
**12:19** k Zec 7:14

## The African Presence

### Ezekiel 12:13

Chaldeans were the inhabitants of the southern regions of Mesopotamia. They established the Neo-Babylonian Empire (626–539 B.C.). In many Biblical passages, the word "Chaldeans" is used as a synonym for "Babylonians" (see also Eze 23:14–15,23). Their language was similar to Galla, the scientific and religious language of the Cushites. The Galla or Oromo are/were Nubian tribes in what is now Abyssinia, Ethiopia. They refer to themselves and their language as Oromo; their language is likely a dialect of an ancient Cushite language.

The Babylonian language is a dialect of the Akkadian language. Akkadian is a Semite language that belongs to the Afro-Asiatic language family. It is possible that the African influence of the Akkadian language can be traced through the Akkadian word "Babilu" ("Babylon"), which broken down means "gate" (*babu*) and "god" (*ilu*).

**12:22** l Eze 11:3; Am 6:3; 2Pe 3:4
**12:23** m Joel 2:1; Zep 1:14
**12:24** n Eze 13:23
**13:5** o Eze 22:30
**13:6** p Eze 22:28

inhabited towns will be laid waste and the land will be desolate. Then you will know that I am the LORD.' "

21 The word of the LORD came to me: 22 "Son of man, what is this proverb you have in the land of Israel: 'The days go by and every vision comes to nothing'?[l] 23 Say to them, 'This is what the Sovereign LORD says: I am going to put an end to this proverb, and they will no longer quote it in Israel.' Say to them, 'The days are near when every vision will be fulfilled.[m] 24 For there will be no more false visions or flattering divinations[n] among the people of Israel. 25 But I the LORD will speak what I will, and it shall be fulfilled without delay. For in your days, you rebellious house, I will fulfill whatever I say, declares the Sovereign LORD.' "

26 The word of the LORD came to me: 27 "Son of man, the house of Israel is saying, 'The vision he sees is for many years from now, and he prophesies about the distant future.'

28 "Therefore say to them, 'This is what the Sovereign LORD says: None of my words will be delayed any longer; whatever I say will be fulfilled, declares the Sovereign LORD.' "

## False Prophets Condemned

13 The word of the LORD came to me: 2 "Son of man, prophesy against the prophets of Israel who are now prophesying. Say to those who prophesy out of their own imagination: 'Hear the word of the LORD! 3 This is what the Sovereign LORD says: Woe to the foolish[a] prophets who follow their own spirit and have seen nothing! 4 Your prophets, O Israel, are like jackals among ruins. 5 You have not gone up to the breaks in the wall to repair[o] it for the house of Israel so that it will stand firm in the battle on the day of the LORD. 6 Their visions are false and their divinations a lie. They say, "The LORD declares," when the LORD has not sent them; yet they expect their words to be fulfilled.[p] 7 Have you not seen false visions and uttered lying divinations when you say, "The LORD declares," though I have not spoken?

8 " 'Therefore this is what the Sovereign LORD says: Because of your false words and lying visions, I am against you, declares the Sovereign LORD. 9 My hand will be against the prophets who see false visions and utter lying divinations. They will not belong to the council of my people or be listed in the records of the house of Israel, nor will they enter the land of Israel. Then you will know that I am the Sovereign LORD.

10 " 'Because they lead my people astray, saying, "Peace," when there is no peace, and because, when a flimsy wall is built, they cover it with whitewash,[q] 11 therefore tell those who cover it with whitewash that it is going to fall. Rain will come in torrents, and I will send hailstones hurtling down, and violent winds will burst forth.[r] 12 When the wall collapses, will people not ask you, "Where is the whitewash you covered it with?"

13 " 'Therefore this is what the Sovereign LORD says: In my wrath I will unleash a violent wind, and in my anger hailstones and torrents of rain will fall with destructive fury.[s] 14 I will tear down the wall you have covered with whitewash and will level it to the ground so that its foundation will be laid bare. When it[b] falls, you will be destroyed in it; and you will know that I am the LORD. 15 So I will spend my wrath against the wall and against those who covered it with whitewash. I will say to you, "The wall is gone and so are those who whitewashed it, 16 those prophets of Israel who prophesied to Jerusalem and saw visions of peace for her when there was no peace, declares the Sovereign LORD.[t]" '

17 "Now, son of man, set your face against the daughters of your people who prophesy out of their own imagination. Prophesy against them[u] 18 and say, 'This is what the Sovereign LORD says: Woe to the women who sew magic charms on all their wrists and make veils of various lengths for their heads in order to ensnare people. Will you ensnare the lives of my people but preserve your own? 19 You have profaned me among my people for a few handfuls of barley and scraps of bread. By lying to my people, who listen to lies, you have killed those who should not have died and have spared those who should not live.[v]

20 " 'Therefore this is what the Sovereign LORD says: I am against your magic charms with which you ensnare people like birds

**13:10** q Eze 22:28
**13:11** r Eze 38:22
**13:13** s Isa 30:30
**13:16** t Isa 57:21
**13:17** u ver 2
**13:19** v Pr 28:21

[a]3 Or *wicked* [b]14 Or *the city*

**13:22** w Jer 23:14
**13:23** x ver 6; Eze 12:24 y Mic 3:6
**14:1** z Eze 8:1; 20:1
**14:3** a Eze 7:19
**14:5** b Zec 11:8
**14:6** c Isa 2:20
**14:8** d Eze 15:7 e Eze 5:15
**14:9** f Jer 4:10

and I will tear them from your arms; I will set free the people that you ensnare like birds. 21 I will tear off your veils and save my people from your hands, and they will no longer fall prey to your power. Then you will know that I am the LORD. 22 Because you disheartened the righteous with your lies, when I had brought them no grief, and because you encouraged the wicked not to turn from their evil ways and so save their lives,[w] 23 therefore you will no longer see false visions or practice divination.[x] I will save my people from your hands. And then you will know that I am the LORD.[y]' "

## Idolaters Condemned

14 Some of the elders of Israel came to me and sat down in front of me.[z] 2 Then the word of the LORD came to me: 3 "Son of man, these men have set up idols in their hearts and put wicked stumbling blocks[a] before their faces. Should I let them inquire of me at all? 4 Therefore speak to them and tell them, 'This is what the Sovereign LORD says: When any Israelite sets up idols in his heart and puts a wicked stumbling block before his face and then goes to a prophet, I the LORD will answer him myself in keeping with his great idolatry. 5 I will do this to recapture the hearts of the people of Israel, who have all deserted[b] me for their idols.'

6 "Therefore say to the house of Israel, 'This is what the Sovereign LORD says: Repent! Turn from your idols and renounce all your detestable practices![c]

7 " 'When any Israelite or any alien living in Israel separates himself from me and sets up idols in his heart and puts a wicked stumbling block before his face and then goes to a prophet to inquire of me, I the LORD will answer him myself. 8 I will set my face against[d] that man and make him an example and a byword.[e] I will cut him off from my people. Then you will know that I am the LORD.

9 " 'And if the prophet is enticed[f] to utter a prophecy, I the LORD have enticed that prophet, and I will stretch out my hand against him and destroy him from among my people Israel. 10 They will bear their guilt—the prophet will be as guilty as the one who consults him. 11 Then the people of Israel will no longer stray from me, nor will they defile themselves anymore with all their sins. They will be my people, and I will be their God, declares the Sovereign LORD.[g]' "

## Judgment Inescapable

12 The word of the LORD came to me: 13 "Son of man, if a country sins against me by being unfaithful and I stretch out my hand against it to cut off its food supply[h] and send famine upon it and kill its men and their animals, 14 even if these three men—Noah, Daniel[a] and Job—were in it, they could save only themselves by their righteousness,[i] declares the Sovereign LORD.

15 "Or if I send wild beasts[j] through that country and they leave it childless and it becomes desolate so that no one can pass through it because of the beasts, 16 as surely as I live, declares the Sovereign LORD, even if these three men were in it, they could not save their own sons or daughters. They alone would be saved, but the land would be desolate.

17 "Or if I bring a sword[k] against that country and say, 'Let the sword pass throughout the land,' and I kill its men and their animals,[l] 18 as surely as I live, declares the Sovereign LORD, even if these three men were in it, they could not save their own sons or daughters. They alone would be saved.

19 "Or if I send a plague into that land and pour out my wrath upon it through bloodshed, killing its men and their animals,[m] 20 as surely as I live, declares the Sovereign LORD, even if Noah, Daniel and Job were in it, they could save neither son nor daughter. They would save only themselves by their righteousness.

21 "For this is what the Sovereign LORD says: How much worse will it be when I send against Jerusalem my four dreadful judgments—sword and famine and wild beasts and plague—to kill its men and their animals![n] 22 Yet there will be some survivors—sons and daughters who will be brought out of it. They will come to you, and when you see their conduct and their actions, you will be consoled regarding the disaster I have

**14:11** g Eze 11:19–20
**14:13** h Lev 26:26
**14:14** i Jer 15:1
**14:15** j Eze 5:17
**14:17** k Eze 5:12; 21:3–4 l Eze 25:13
**14:19** m Eze 38:22
**14:21** n Eze 5:17

[a]14 Or *Danel*; the Hebrew spelling may suggest a person other than the prophet Daniel; also in verse 20.

brought upon Jerusalem—every disaster I have brought upon it. 23 You will be consoled when you see their conduct and their actions, for you will know that I have done nothing in it without cause, declares the Sovereign LORD.[o]"

## Jerusalem, A Useless Vine

**15** The word of the LORD came to me: 2 "Son of man, how is the wood of a vine[p] better than that of a branch on any of the trees in the forest? 3 Is wood ever taken from it to make anything useful? Do they make pegs from it to hang things on? 4 And after it is thrown on the fire as fuel and the fire burns both ends and chars the middle, is it then useful for anything?[q] 5 If it was not useful for anything when it was whole, how much less can it be made into something useful when the fire has burned it and it is charred?

6 "Therefore this is what the Sovereign LORD says: As I have given the wood of the vine among the trees of the forest as fuel for the fire, so will I treat the people living in Jerusalem. 7 I will set my face against[r] them. Although they have come out of the fire, the fire will yet consume them. And when I set my face against them, you will know that I am the LORD.[s] 8 I will make the land desolate because they have been unfaithful, declares the Sovereign LORD."

## An Allegory of Unfaithful Jerusalem

**16** The word of the LORD came to me: 2 "Son of man, confront Jerusalem with her detestable practices[t] 3 and say, 'This is what the Sovereign LORD says to Jerusalem: Your ancestry and birth were in the land of the Canaanites; your father was an Amorite and your mother a Hittite. 4 On the day you were born[u] your cord was not cut, nor were you washed with water to make you clean, nor were you rubbed with salt or wrapped in cloths. 5 No one looked on you with pity or had compassion enough to do any of these things for you. Rather, you were thrown out into the open field, for on the day you were born you were despised.

6 " 'Then I passed by and saw you kicking about in your blood, and as you lay there in your blood I said to you, "Live!"[a] 7 I made you grow like a plant of the field. You grew up and developed and became the most beautiful of jewels.[b] Your breasts were formed and your hair grew, you who were naked and bare.[v]

8 " 'Later I passed by, and when I looked at you and saw that you were old enough for love, I spread the corner of my garment[w] over you and covered your nakedness. I gave you my solemn oath and entered into a covenant with you, declares the Sovereign LORD, and you became mine.[x]

> *My child,*
>
> *I have always loved you, and I will continue forever to cherish you as my own.*
>
> *Your Lord and Father*
>
> EZEKIEL 16:8

9 " 'I bathed[c] you with water and washed the blood from you and put ointments on you. 10 I clothed you with an embroidered dress and put leather sandals on you. I dressed you in fine linen and covered you with costly garments. 11 I adorned you with jewelry:[y] I put bracelets on your arms and a necklace around your neck, 12 and I put a ring on your nose,[z] earrings on your ears and a beautiful crown on your head. 13 So you were adorned with gold and silver; your clothes were of fine linen and costly fabric and embroidered cloth. Your food was fine flour, honey and olive oil.[a] You became very beautiful and rose to be a queen.[b] 14 And your fame spread among the nations on account of your beauty,[c] because the splendor I had given you made your beauty perfect, declares the Sovereign LORD.

15 " 'But you trusted in your beauty and

**14:23** o Jer 22:8–9
**15:2** p Hos 10:1
**15:4** q Jn 15:6
**15:7** r Eze 14:8; s Isa 24:18
**16:2** t Eze 20:4; 22:2
**16:4** u Hos 2:3
**16:7** v Ex 1:7
**16:8** w Ru 3:9; x Jer 2:2
**16:11** y Eze 23:40
**16:12** z Isa 3:21
**16:13** a 1Sa 10:1; b Dt 32:13–14
**16:14** c La 2:15

[a] 6 A few Hebrew manuscripts, Septuagint and Syriac; most Hebrew manuscripts *"Live!" And as you lay there in your blood I said to you, "Live!"* [b] 7 Or *became mature* [c] 9 Or *I had bathed*

**16:15** d Isa 57:8; Jer 2:20
**16:19** e Hos 2:8
**16:20** f Ps 106:37–38
**16:22** g Jer 2:2 h ver 6
**16:24** i Isa 57:7
**16:25** j Pr 9:14
**16:26** k Eze 8:17
**16:27** l 2Ch 28:18
**16:28** m 2Ki 16:7
**16:30** n Jer 3:3

used your fame to become a prostitute. You lavished your favors on anyone who passed by and your beauty became his.[a][d] 16 You took some of your garments to make gaudy high places, where you carried on your prostitution. Such things should not happen, nor should they ever occur. 17 You also took the fine jewelry I gave you, the jewelry made of my gold and silver, and you made for yourself male idols and engaged in prostitution with them. 18 And you took your embroidered clothes to put on them, and you offered my oil and incense before them. 19 Also the food I provided for you—the fine flour, olive oil and honey I gave you to eat—you offered as fragrant incense before them. That is what happened, declares the Sovereign LORD.[e]

20 "'And you took your sons and daughters whom you bore to me and sacrificed them as food to the idols. Was your prostitution not enough?[f] 21 You slaughtered my children and sacrificed them[b] to the idols. 22 In all your detestable practices and your prostitution you did not remember the days of your youth,[g] when you were naked and bare, kicking about in your blood.[h]

23 "'Woe! Woe to you, declares the Sovereign LORD. In addition to all your other wickedness, 24 you built a mound for yourself and made a lofty shrine[i] in every public square. 25 At the head of every street you built your lofty shrines and degraded your beauty, offering your body with increasing promiscuity to anyone who passed by.[j] 26 You engaged in prostitution with the Egyptians, your lustful neighbors, and provoked[k] me to anger with your increasing promiscuity. 27 So I stretched out my hand against you and reduced your territory; I gave you over to the greed of your enemies, the daughters of the Philistines,[l] who were shocked by your lewd conduct. 28 You engaged in prostitution with the Assyrians[m] too, because you were insatiable; and even after that, you still were not satisfied. 29 Then you increased your promiscuity to include Babylonia,[c] a land of merchants, but even with this you were not satisfied.

30 "'How weak-willed you are, declares the Sovereign LORD, when you do all these things, acting like a brazen prostitute![n] 31 When you built your mounds at the head of every street and made your lofty shrines in every public square, you were unlike a prostitute, because you scorned payment.

32 "'You adulterous wife! You prefer strangers to your own husband! 33 Every prostitute receives a fee, but you give gifts to all your lovers, bribing them to come to you from everywhere for your illicit favors.[o] 34 So in your prostitution you are the opposite of others; no one runs after you for your favors. You are the very opposite, for you give payment and none is given to you.

35 "'Therefore, you prostitute, hear the word of the LORD! 36 This is what the Sovereign LORD says: Because you poured out your wealth[d] and exposed your nakedness in your promiscuity with your lovers, and because of all your detestable idols, and because you gave them your children's blood,[p] 37 therefore I am going to gather all your lovers, with whom you found pleasure, those you loved as well as those you hated. I will gather them against you from all around and will strip you in front of them, and they will see all your nakedness. 38 I will sentence you to the punishment of women who commit adultery and who shed blood;[q] I will bring upon you the blood vengeance of my wrath and jealous anger. 39 Then I will hand you over to your lovers, and they will tear down your mounds and destroy your lofty shrines. They will strip you of your clothes and take your fine jewelry and leave you naked and bare.[r] 40 They will bring a mob against you, who will stone you and hack you to pieces with their swords. 41 They will burn down your houses and inflict punishment on you in the sight of many women. I will put a stop[s] to your prostitution, and you will no longer pay your lovers. 42 Then my wrath against you will subside and my jealous anger will turn away from you; I will be calm and no longer angry.[t]

43 "'Because you did not remember[u] the days of your youth but enraged me with all these things, I will surely bring down[v] on your head what you have done, declares the Sovereign LORD. Did you not add lewdness to all your other detestable practices?[w]

44 "'Everyone who quotes proverbs will

**16:33** o Hos 8:9–10
**16:36** p Jer 19:5
**16:38** q Eze 23:45
**16:39** r Eze 23:26
**16:41** s Eze 23:27,48
**16:42** t Eze 5:13
**16:43** u Ps 78:42 v Eze 22:31 w ver 22; Eze 11:21

[a] 15 Most Hebrew manuscripts; one Hebrew manuscript (see some Septuagint manuscripts) *by. Such a thing should not happen* [b] 21 Or *and made them pass through ⌊the fire⌋* [c] 29 Or *Chaldea* [d] 36 Or *lust*

quote this proverb about you: "Like mother, like daughter." 45 You are a true daughter of your mother, who despised her husband and her children; and you are a true sister of your sisters, who despised their husbands and their children. Your mother was a Hittite and your father an Amorite. 46 Your older sister was Samaria, who lived to the north of you with her daughters; and your younger sister, who lived to the south of you with her daughters, was Sodom. 47 You not only walked in their ways and copied their detestable practices, but in all your ways you soon became more depraved than they.[x] 48 As surely as I live, declares the Sovereign LORD, your sister Sodom and her daughters never did what you and your daughters have done.[y]

49 " 'Now this was the sin of your sister Sodom:[z] She and her daughters were arrogant, overfed and unconcerned; they did not help the poor and needy. 50 They were haughty and did detestable things before me. Therefore I did away with them as you have seen. 51 Samaria did not commit half the sins you did. You have done more detestable things than they, and have made your sisters seem righteous by all these things you have done.[a] 52 Bear your disgrace, for you have furnished some justification for your sisters. Because your sins were more vile than theirs, they appear more righteous than you. So then, be ashamed and bear your disgrace, for you have made your sisters appear righteous.

53 " 'However, I will restore the fortunes of Sodom and her daughters and of Samaria and her daughters, and your fortunes along with them, 54 so that you may bear your disgrace[b] and be ashamed of all you have done in giving them comfort. 55 And your sisters, Sodom with her daughters and Samaria with her daughters, will return to what they were before; and you and your daughters will return to what you were before. 56 You would not even mention your sister Sodom in the day of your pride, 57 before your wickedness was uncovered. Even so, you are now scorned by the daughters of Edom[a][c] and all her neighbors and the daughters of the Philistines—all those around you who despise you. 58 You will bear the consequences of your lewdness and your detestable practices, declares the LORD.[d]

59 " 'This is what the Sovereign LORD says: I will deal with you as you deserve, because you have despised my oath by breaking the covenant. 60 Yet I will remember the covenant I made with you in the days of your youth, and I will establish an everlasting covenant[e] with you. 61 Then you will remember your ways and be ashamed when you receive your sisters, both those who are older than you and those who are younger. I will give them to you as daughters, but not on the basis of my covenant with you. 62 So I will establish my covenant with you, and you will know that I am the LORD.[f] 63 Then, when I make atonement for you for all you have done, you will remember and be ashamed and never again open your mouth[g] because of your humiliation, declares the Sovereign LORD.' "

## Two Eagles and a Vine

17 The word of the LORD came to me: 2 "Son of man, set forth an allegory and tell the house of Israel a parable.[h] 3 Say to them, 'This is what the Sovereign LORD says: A great eagle with powerful wings, long feathers and full plumage of varied colors came to Lebanon.[i] Taking hold of the top of a cedar, 4 he broke off its topmost shoot and carried it away to a land of merchants, where he planted it in a city of traders.

5 " 'He took some of the seed of your land and put it in fertile soil. He planted it like a willow by abundant water,[j] 6 and it sprouted and became a low, spreading vine. Its branches turned toward him, but its roots remained under it. So it became a vine and produced branches and put out leafy boughs.

7 " 'But there was another great eagle with powerful wings and full plumage. The vine now sent out its roots toward him from the plot where it was planted and stretched out its branches to him for water. 8 It had been planted in good soil by abundant water so that it would produce branches, bear fruit and become a splendid vine.'

9 "Say to them, 'This is what the Sovereign LORD says: Will it thrive? Will it not be

**16:47** x 2Ki 21:9; Eze 5:7
**16:48** y Mt 10:15; 11:23–24
**16:49** z Ge 13:13
**16:51** a Jer 3:8–11
**16:54** b Eze 14:22
**16:57** c 2Ki 16:6
**16:58** d Eze 23:49
**16:60** e Jer 32:40
**16:62** f Eze 20:37,43–44
**16:63** g Ro 3:19
**17:2** h Eze 20:49
**17:3** i Jer 22:23
**17:5** j Dt 8:7–9; Isa 44:4

[a]57 Many Hebrew manuscripts and Syriac; most Hebrew manuscripts, Septuagint and Vulgate *Aram*

uprooted and stripped of its fruit so that
it withers? All its new growth will wither.
It will not take a strong arm or many peo-
ple to pull it up by the roots. 10 Even if it[k]
is transplanted, will it thrive? Will it not
wither completely when the east wind
strikes it—wither away in the plot where
it grew?' "

11 Then the word of the LORD came to me:
12 "Say to this rebellious house, 'Do you
not know what these things mean?[l]' Say to
them: 'The king of Babylon went to Jerusa-
lem and carried off her king and her nobles,
bringing them back with him to Babylon.
13 Then he took a member of the royal family
and made a treaty with him, putting him
under oath.[m] He also carried away the lead-
ing men of the land, 14 so that the kingdom
would be brought low,[n] unable to rise again,
surviving only by keeping his treaty. 15 But
the king rebelled against him by sending
his envoys to Egypt to get horses and a large
army. Will he succeed? Will he who does
such things escape? Will he break the treaty
and yet escape?

16 " 'As surely as I live, declares the Sover-
eign LORD, he shall die[o] in Babylon, in the
land of the king who put him on the throne,
whose oath he despised and whose treaty
he broke. 17 Pharaoh[p] with his mighty army
and great horde will be of no help to him in
war, when ramps are built and siege works
erected to destroy many lives.[q] 18 He despised
the oath by breaking the covenant. Because
he had given his hand in pledge[r] and yet did
all these things, he shall not escape.

19 " 'Therefore this is what the Sovereign
LORD says: As surely as I live, I will bring
down on his head my oath that he despised
and my covenant that he broke. 20 I will
spread my net[s] for him, and he will be
caught in my snare. I will bring him to Bab-
ylon and execute judgment[t] upon him there
because he was unfaithful to me. 21 All his
fleeing troops will fall by the sword,[u] and
the survivors will be scattered to the winds.
Then you will know that I the LORD have spo-
ken.

22 " 'This is what the Sovereign LORD says:
I myself will take a shoot from the very top
of a cedar and plant it; I will break off a ten-
der sprig from its topmost shoots and plant
it on a high and lofty mountain.[v] 23 On the
mountain heights of Israel I will plant it; it
will produce branches and bear fruit and be-
come a splendid cedar. Birds of every kind
will nest in it; they will find shelter in the
shade of its branches. 24 All the trees of the
field[w] will know that I the LORD bring down
the tall tree and make the low tree grow tall.
I dry up the green tree and make the dry
tree flourish.

" 'I the LORD have spoken, and I will
do it.' "

## The Soul Who Sins Will Die

18 The word of the LORD came to me:
2 "What do you people mean by quot-
ing this proverb about the land of Israel:

" 'The fathers eat sour grapes,
and the children's teeth are set on
edge'?[x]

3 "As surely as I live, declares the Sover-
eign LORD, you will no longer quote this prov-
erb in Israel. 4 For every living soul belongs
to me, the father as well as the son—both
alike belong to me. The soul who sins is the
one who will die.[y]

5 "Suppose there is a righteous man
who does what is just and right.
6 He does not eat at the mountain[z] shrines
or look to the idols of the house of
Israel.
He does not defile his neighbor's wife
or lie with a woman during her period.
7 He does not oppress[a] anyone,
but returns what he took in pledge[b] for
a loan.
He does not commit robbery
but gives his food to the hungry
and provides clothing for the naked.
8 He does not lend at usury
or take excessive interest.[a][c]
He withholds his hand from doing
wrong
and judges fairly[d] between man and
man.
9 He follows my decrees
and faithfully keeps my laws.
That man is righteous;

**17:10** k Hos 13:15
**17:12** l Eze 12:9
**17:13** m 2Ch 36:13
**17:14** n Eze 29:14
**17:16** o Eze 12:13
**17:17** p Jer 37:7 q Eze 29:6–7
**17:18** r 1Ch 29:24
**17:20** s Eze 12:13 t Eze 20:36
**17:21** u Eze 12:14
**17:22** v Jer 23:5
**17:24** w Ps 96:12
**18:2** x Jer 31:29
**18:4** y Ro 6:23
**18:6** z Eze 22:9
**18:7** a Ex 22:21 b Dt 24:12
**18:8** c Ex 22:25; Lev 25:35–37; Dt 23:19–20 d Zec 8:16

[a]8 Or *take interest*; similarly in verses 13 and 17

**18:9** e Am 5:4
**18:12** f Am 4:1 g Isa 59:6–7; Eze 8:6,17
**18:19** h Ex 20:5

he will surely live,[e]
declares the Sovereign LORD.

10“Suppose he has a violent son, who
sheds blood or does any of these other
things[a] 11(though the father has done none
of them):

“He eats at the mountain shrines.
He defiles his neighbor’s wife.
12 He oppresses the poor[f] and needy.
He commits robbery.
He does not return what he took in pledge.
He looks to the idols.
He does detestable things.[g]
13 He lends at usury and takes excessive
interest.

Will such a man live? He will not! Because
he has done all these detestable things, he
will surely be put to death and his blood will
be on his own head.

14“But suppose this son has a son who sees
all the sins his father commits, and though
he sees them, he does not do such things:

15 “He does not eat at the mountain shrines
or look to the idols of the house of
Israel.
He does not defile his neighbor’s wife.
16 He does not oppress anyone
or require a pledge for a loan.
He does not commit robbery
but gives his food to the hungry
and provides clothing for the naked.
17 He withholds his hand from sin[b]
and takes no usury or excessive
interest.
He keeps my laws and follows my decrees.

He will not die for his father’s sin; he will
surely live. 18But his father will die for his
own sin, because he practiced extortion,
robbed his brother and did what was wrong
among his people.

19“Yet you ask, ‘Why does the son not
share the guilt of his father?’ Since the son
has done what is just and right and has been
careful to keep all my decrees, he will surely
live.[h] 20The soul who sins is the one who will
die. The son will not share the guilt of the fa-
ther, nor will the father share the guilt of the
son. The righteousness of the righteous man
will be credited to him, and the wickedness
of the wicked will be charged against him.[i]

21“But if a wicked man turns away from
all the sins he has committed and keeps
all my decrees and does what is just and
right, he will surely live; he will not die.[j]
22None of the offenses he has committed
will be remembered against him. Because
of the righteous things he has done, he will
live.[k] 23Do I take any pleasure in the death
of the wicked? declares the Sovereign LORD.
Rather, am I not pleased when they turn
from their ways and live?[l]

24“But if a righteous man turns from his
righteousness and commits sin and does
the same detestable things the wicked man
does, will he live? None of the righteous
things he has done will be remembered. Be-
cause of the unfaithfulness he is guilty of
and because of the sins he has committed,
he will die.[m]

25“Yet you say, ‘The way of the Lord is not
just.’ Hear, O house of Israel: Is my way un-
just?[n] Is it not your ways that are unjust? 26If
a righteous man turns from his righteous-
ness and commits sin, he will die for it; be-
cause of the sin he has committed he will
die. 27But if a wicked man turns away from
the wickedness he has committed and does
what is just and right, he will save his life.
28Because he considers all the offenses he
has committed and turns away from them,
he will surely live; he will not die. 29Yet the
house of Israel says, ‘The way of the Lord
is not just.’ Are my ways unjust, O house of
Israel? Is it not your ways that are unjust?

30“Therefore, O house
of Israel, I will judge
you, each one according
to his ways, declares the
Sovereign LORD. Repent!
Turn away from all your
offenses; then sin will
not be your downfall.[o]
31Rid yourselves of all the
offenses you have com-
mitted, and get a new
heart and a new spirit.
Why will you die, O house of Israel?[p] 32For I
take no pleasure in the death of anyone, de-
clares the Sovereign LORD. Repent and live!

> *“Why hate when you can spend your time doing other things.”*
>
> —MIRIAM MAKEBA, FOLKSINGER

**18:20** i Dt 24:16; Isa 3:11; Ro 2:9
**18:21** j Eze 33:12,19
**18:22** k Ps 18:20–24
**18:23** l Eze 33:11
**18:24** m Eze 3:20
**18:25** n Eze 33:17
**18:30** o Eze 7:3
**18:31** p Eze 11:19; 36:26

[a]10 Or *things to a brother* [b]17 Septuagint (see also verse 8); Hebrew *from the poor*

**19:4** q 2Ki 23:33–34; 2Ch 36:4
**19:8** r 2Ki 24:2
**19:9** s 2Ch 36:6
**19:11** t Eze 31:3

## A Lament for Israel's Princes

19 "Take up a lament concerning the princes of Israel 2and say:

"'What a lioness was your mother
among the lions!
She lay down among the young lions
and reared her cubs.
3 She brought up one of her cubs,
and he became a strong lion.
He learned to tear the prey
and he devoured men.
4 The nations heard about him,
and he was trapped in their pit.
They led him with hooks
to the land of Egypt.[q]

5 "'When she saw her hope unfulfilled,
her expectation gone,
she took another of her cubs
and made him a strong lion.
6 He prowled among the lions,
for he was now a strong lion.
He learned to tear the prey
and he devoured men.
7 He broke down[a] their strongholds
and devastated their towns.
The land and all who were in it
were terrified by his roaring.
8 Then the nations[r] came against him,
those from regions round about.
They spread their net for him,
and he was trapped in their pit.
9 With hooks they pulled him into a cage
and brought him to the king of
Babylon.[s]
They put him in prison,
so his roar was heard no longer
on the mountains of Israel.

10 "'Your mother was like a vine in your
vineyard[b]
planted by the water;
it was fruitful and full of branches
because of abundant water.
11 Its branches were strong,
fit for a ruler's scepter.
It towered high
above the thick foliage,
conspicuous for its height
and for its many branches.[t]
12 But it was uprooted[u] in fury
and thrown to the ground.
The east wind made it shrivel,
it was stripped of its fruit;
its strong branches withered
and fire consumed them.[v]
13 Now it is planted in the desert,
in a dry and thirsty land.
14 Fire spread from one of its main[c]
branches
and consumed its fruit.
No strong branch is left on it
fit for a ruler's scepter.'[w]

This is a lament and is to be used as a lament."

## Rebellious Israel

20 In the seventh year, in the fifth
month on the tenth day, some of the
elders of Israel came to inquire of the LORD,
and they sat down in front of me.[x]
2Then the word of the LORD came to me:
3"Son of man, speak to the elders of Israel
and say to them, 'This is what the Sovereign
LORD says: Have you come to inquire[y] of me?
As surely as I live, I will not let you inquire
of me, declares the Sovereign LORD.'
4"Will you judge them? Will you judge
them, son of man? Then confront them with
the detestable practices of their fathers[z]
5and say to them: 'This is what the Sovereign
LORD says: On the day I chose Israel, I swore
with uplifted hand to the descendants of the
house of Jacob and revealed myself to them
in Egypt. With uplifted hand I said to them,
"I am the LORD your God.[a]" 6On that day I
swore to them that I would bring them out
of Egypt into a land I had searched out for
them, a land flowing with milk and honey,[b]
the most beautiful of all lands.[c] 7And I said
to them, "Each of you, get rid of the vile
images you have set your eyes on, and do
not defile yourselves with the idols of Egypt.
I am the LORD your God.[d]"
8"'But they rebelled against me and
would not listen to me; they did not get rid
of the vile images they had set their eyes on,
nor did they forsake the idols of Egypt.[e] So I
said I would pour out my wrath on them and
spend my anger against them in Egypt. 9But

**19:12** u Eze 17:10; v Hos 13:15
**19:14** w Eze 15:4
**20:1** x Eze 8:1
**20:3** y Eze 14:3
**20:4** z Eze 16:2; 22:2
**20:5** a Ex 6:7
**20:6** b Ex 3:8; Jer 32:22; c Dt 8:7; Ps 48:2
**20:7** d Dt 29:18
**20:8** e Eze 7:8

[a] 7 Targum (see Septuagint); Hebrew *He knew* [b] 10 Two Hebrew manuscripts; most Hebrew manuscripts *your blood*
[c] 14 Or *from under its*

for the sake of my name I did what would keep it from being profaned in the eyes of the nations they lived among and in whose sight I had revealed myself to the Israelites by bringing them out of Egypt.[f] 10Therefore I led them out of Egypt and brought them into the desert. 11I gave them my decrees and made known to them my laws, for the man who obeys them will live by them.[g] 12Also I gave them my Sabbaths as a sign between us, so they would know that I the LORD made them holy.

13"'Yet the people of Israel rebelled[h] against me in the desert. They did not follow my decrees but rejected my laws—although the man who obeys them will live by them—and they utterly desecrated my Sabbaths. So I said I would pour out my wrath on them and destroy them in the desert. 14But for the sake of my name I did what would keep it from being profaned in the eyes of the nations in whose sight I had brought them out. 15Also with uplifted hand I swore to them in the desert that I would not bring them into the land I had given them—a land flowing with milk and honey, most beautiful of all lands[i]— 16because they rejected my laws and did not follow my decrees and desecrated my Sabbaths. For their hearts were devoted to their idols.[j] 17Yet I looked on them with pity and did not destroy them or put an end to them in the desert. 18I said to their children in the desert, "Do not follow the statutes of your fathers or keep their laws or defile yourselves with their idols. 19I am the LORD your God; follow my decrees and be careful to keep my laws.[k] 20Keep my Sabbaths holy, that they may be a sign between us. Then you will know that I am the LORD your God."

21"'But the children rebelled against me: They did not follow my decrees, they were not careful to keep my laws—although the man who obeys them will live by them—and they desecrated my Sabbaths. So I said I would pour out my wrath on them and spend my anger against them in the desert. 22But I withheld[l] my hand, and for the sake of my name I did what would keep it from being profaned in the eyes of the nations in whose sight I had brought them out. 23Also with uplifted hand I swore to them in the desert that I would disperse them among the nations and scatter[m] them through the countries, 24because they had not obeyed my laws but had rejected my decrees and desecrated my Sabbaths, and their eyes ⌊lusted⌋ after[n] their fathers' idols. 25I also gave them over[o] to statutes that were not good and laws they could not live by; 26I let them become defiled through their gifts—the sacrifice of every firstborn[a]—that I might fill them with horror so they would know that I am the LORD.'

27"Therefore, son of man, speak to the people of Israel and say to them, 'This is what the Sovereign LORD says: In this also your fathers blasphemed[p] me by forsaking me: 28When I brought them into the land I had sworn to give them and they saw any high hill or any leafy tree, there they offered their sacrifices, made offerings that provoked me to anger, presented their fragrant incense and poured out their drink offerings.[q] 29Then I said to them: What is this high place you go to?'" (It is called Bamah[b] to this day.)

## Judgment and Restoration

30"Therefore say to the house of Israel: 'This is what the Sovereign LORD says: Will you defile yourselves the way your fathers did and lust after their vile images?[r] 31When you offer your gifts—the sacrifice of your sons[s] in[c] the fire—you continue to defile yourselves with all your idols to this day. Am I to let you inquire of me, O house of Israel? As surely as I live, declares the Sovereign LORD, I will not let you inquire of me.[t]

32"'You say, "We want to be like the nations, like the peoples of the world, who serve wood and stone." But what you have in mind will never happen. 33As surely as I live, declares the Sovereign LORD, I will rule over you with a mighty hand and an outstretched arm and with outpoured wrath.[u] 34I will bring you from the nations and gather you from the countries where you have been scattered—with a mighty hand and an outstretched arm and with outpoured wrath.[v]

[a]26 Or *—making every firstborn pass through ⌊the fire⌋* [b]29 *Bamah* means *high place.* [c]31 Or *—making your sons pass through*

**20:9** f Eze 36:22
**20:11** g Lev 18:5
**20:13** h Ps 78:40
**20:15** i Ps 95:11
**20:16** j Am 5:26
**20:19** k Dt 5:32–33
**20:22** l Ps 78:38
**20:23** m Lev 26:33; Dt 28:64
**20:24** n Eze 6:9
**20:25** o Ps 81:12
**20:27** p Ro 2:24
**20:28** q Eze 6:13
**20:30** r Jer 16:12
**20:31** s Eze 16:20 t Ps 106:37–39
**20:33** u Jer 21:5
**20:34** v Jer 44:6

**20:37** w Lev 27:32; Jer 33:13
**20:38** x Eze 34:17–22
**20:39** y Isa 1:13
**20:40** z Isa 60:7; a Isa 56:7
**20:42** b Eze 34:13
**20:43** c Eze 16:61; Hos 5:15
**20:44** d Eze 36:22; e Eze 24:24
**20:46** f Eze 21:2

35 I will bring you into the desert of the nations and there, face to face, I will execute judgment upon you. 36 As I judged your fathers in the desert of the land of Egypt, so I will judge you, declares the Sovereign LORD. 37 I will take note of you as you pass under my rod,[w] and I will bring you into the bond of the covenant. 38 I will purge[x] you of those who revolt and rebel against me. Although I will bring them out of the land where they are living, yet they will not enter the land of Israel. Then you will know that I am the LORD.

39 "'As for you, O house of Israel, this is what the Sovereign LORD says: Go and serve your idols, every one of you! But afterward you will surely listen to me and no longer profane my holy name with your gifts and idols.[y] 40 For on my holy mountain, the high mountain of Israel, declares the Sovereign LORD, there in the land the entire house of Israel will serve me, and there I will accept them. There I will require your offerings[z] and your choice gifts,[a] along with all your holy sacrifices.[a] 41 I will accept you as fragrant incense when I bring you out from the nations and gather you from the countries where you have been scattered, and I will show myself holy among you in the sight of the nations. 42 Then you will know that I am the LORD, when I bring you into the land of Israel,[b] the land I had sworn with uplifted hand to give to your fathers. 43 There you will remember your conduct and all the actions by which you have defiled yourselves, and you will loathe yourselves for all the evil you have done.[c] 44 You will know that I am the LORD, when I deal with you for my name's sake[d] and not according to your evil ways and your corrupt practices, O house of Israel, declares the Sovereign LORD.[e]'"

## Prophecy Against the South

45 The word of the LORD came to me: 46 "Son of man, set your face toward the south; preach against the south and prophesy against[f] the forest of the southland. 47 Say to the southern forest: 'Hear the word of the LORD. This is what the Sovereign LORD says: I am about to set fire to you, and it will consume all your trees, both green and dry. The blazing flame will not be quenched, and every face from south to north will be scorched by it.[g] 48 Everyone will see that I the LORD have kindled it; it will not be quenched.[h]'"

*Lord,*

*reveal to me all the ways that I have displeased you. Show my heart what righteousness and holiness look like, so that I may glorify you in every aspect of my life. Where and when I have stumbled, forgive me, I pray. Convict me when I am headed down the wrong path. In the name of Jesus, my guide,*

*Amen*

EZEKIEL 20:39–44

49 Then I said, "Ah, Sovereign LORD! They are saying of me, 'Isn't he just telling parables?'"

## Babylon, God's Sword of Judgment

21 The word of the LORD came to me: 2 "Son of man, set your face against Jerusalem and preach against the sanctuary. Prophesy against[i] the land of Israel 3 and say to her: 'This is what the LORD says: I am against you. I will draw my sword from its scabbard and cut off from you both the righteous and the wicked. 4 Because I am going to cut off the righteous and the wicked, my sword will be unsheathed against everyone from south to north.[j] 5 Then all people will know that I the LORD have drawn my sword from its scabbard; it will not return again.'

6 "Therefore groan, son of man! Groan before them with broken heart and bitter grief.[k] 7 And when they ask you, 'Why are you groaning?' you shall say, 'Because of the news that is coming. Every heart will melt and every hand go limp;[l] every spirit will become faint and every knee become as weak as water.' It is coming! It will surely take place, declares the Sovereign LORD."

**20:47** g Jer 21:14
**20:48** h Jer 7:20
**21:2** i Eze 20:46
**21:4** j Eze 20:47
**21:6** k Isa 22:4
**21:7** l Eze 7:17

[a] 40 Or *and the gifts of your firstfruits*

8 The word of the LORD came to me: 9 "Son
of man, prophesy and say, 'This is what the
Lord says:

" 'A sword, a sword,
sharpened and polished—
10 sharpened for the slaughter,[m]
polished to flash like lightning!

" 'Shall we rejoice in the scepter of my
son ⌊Judah⌋? The sword despises every
such stick.

11 " 'The sword is appointed to be polished,
to be grasped with the hand;
it is sharpened and polished,
made ready for the hand of the slayer.
12 Cry out and wail, son of man,
for it is against my people;
it is against all the princes of Israel.
They are thrown to the sword
along with my people.
Therefore beat your breast.[n]

13 " 'Testing will surely come. And what
if the scepter ⌊of Judah⌋, which the sword
despises, does not continue? declares the
Sovereign LORD.'

14 "So then, son of man, prophesy
and strike your hands[o] together.
Let the sword strike twice,
even three times.
It is a sword for slaughter—
a sword for great slaughter,
closing in on them from every side.
15 So that hearts may melt
and the fallen be many,
I have stationed the sword for slaughter[a]
at all their gates.
Oh! It is made to flash like lightning,
it is grasped for slaughter.
16 O sword, slash to the right,
then to the left,
wherever your blade is turned.
17 I too will strike my hands[p] together,
and my wrath will subside.
I the LORD have spoken."

18 The word of the LORD came to me: 19 "Son
of man, mark out two roads for the sword of
the king of Babylon to take, both starting
from the same country. Make a signpost
where the road branches off to the city.
20 Mark out one road for the sword to come
against Rabbah of the Ammonites[q] and
another against Judah and fortified Jerusa-
lem. 21 For the king of Babylon will stop at
the fork in the road, at the junction of the
two roads, to seek an omen: He will cast
lots[r] with arrows, he will consult his idols,
he will examine the liver.[s] 22 Into his right
hand will come the lot for Jerusalem, where
he is to set up battering rams, to give the
command to slaughter, to sound the battle
cry, to set battering rams against the gates,
to build a ramp and to erect siege works.[t]
23 It will seem like a false omen to those who
have sworn allegiance to him, but he will
remind them of their guilt and take them
captive.

24 "Therefore this is what the Sover-
eign LORD says: 'Because you people have
brought to mind your guilt by your open re-
bellion, revealing your sins in all that you
do—because you have done this, you will
be taken captive.

25 " 'O profane and wicked prince of
Israel, whose day has come, whose time of
punishment has reached its climax, 26 this
is what the Sovereign LORD says: Take off
the turban, remove the crown.[u] It will not
be as it was: The lowly will be exalted and
the exalted will be brought low. 27 A ruin! A
ruin! I will make it a ruin! It will not be re-
stored until he comes to whom it rightfully
belongs; to him I will give it.'[v]

28 "And you, son of man, prophesy and
say, 'This is what the Sovereign LORD says
about the Ammonites and their insults:

" 'A sword, a sword,
drawn for the slaughter,
polished to consume
and to flash like lightning!
29 Despite false visions concerning you
and lying divinations about you,
it will be laid on the necks
of the wicked who are to be slain,
whose day has come,
whose time of punishment has reached
its climax.[w]
30 Return the sword to its scabbard.[x]
In the place where you were created,
in the land of your ancestry,

21:10 m Isa 34:5–6
21:12 n Jer 31:19
21:14 o Nu 24:10
21:17 p Eze 22:13
21:20 q Jer 49:2; Am 1:14
21:21 r Pr 16:33 s Nu 23:23
21:22 t Eze 4:2
21:26 u Jer 13:18
21:27 v Ps 2:6; Eze 37:24
21:29 w Eze 22:28
21:30 x Jer 47:6

[a] 15 Septuagint; the meaning of the Hebrew for this word is uncertain.

**21:31**
y Eze 22:20–21
**21:32**
z Eze 25:10
**22:2**
a Na 3:1
**22:4**
b 2Ki 21:16
**22:6**
c Isa 1:23
**22:7**
d Dt 27:16
e Ex 22:21–22
**22:10**
f Lev 18:8,19
**22:11**
g Lev 18:15

I will judge you.
31 I will pour out my wrath upon you
and breathe out my fiery anger[y]
against you;
I will hand you over to brutal men,
men skilled in destruction.
32 You will be fuel for the fire,
your blood will be shed in your land,
you will be remembered[z] no more;
for I the LORD have spoken.' "

## Jerusalem's Sins

22 The word of the LORD came to me:
2"Son of man, will you judge her?
Will you judge this city of bloodshed?[a]
Then confront her with all her detestable
practices 3and say: 'This is what the Sover-
eign LORD says: O city that brings on herself
doom by shedding blood in her midst and
defiles herself by making idols, 4you have be-
come guilty because of the blood you have
shed[b] and have become defiled by the idols
you have made. You have brought your days
to a close, and the end of your years has
come. Therefore I will make you an object of
scorn to the nations and a laughingstock to
all the countries. 5Those who are near and
those who are far away will mock you, O in-
famous city, full of turmoil.
6" 'See how each of the princes of Israel
who are in you uses his power to shed
blood.[c] 7In you they have treated father
and mother with contempt;[d] in you they
have oppressed the alien and mistreated
the fatherless and the widow.[e] 8You have
despised my holy things and desecrated my
Sabbaths. 9In you are slanderous men bent
on shedding blood; in you are those who eat
at the mountain shrines and commit lewd
acts. 10In you are those who dishonor their
fathers' bed; in you are those who violate
women during their period, when they are
ceremonially unclean.[f] 11In you one man
commits a detestable offense with his neigh-
bor's wife, another shamefully defiles his
daughter-in-law,[g] and another violates his
sister, his own father's daughter. 12In you
men accept bribes to shed blood; you take
usury and excessive interest[*a*] and make un-
just gain from your neighbors by extortion.
And you have forgotten me, declares the Sov-
ereign LORD.
13" 'I will surely strike my hands together
at the unjust gain you have made and at
the blood you have shed in your midst.
14Will your courage endure or your hands
be strong in the day I deal with you? I the
LORD have spoken, and I will do it.[h] 15I will
disperse you among the nations and scatter[i]
you through the countries; and I will put an
end to your uncleanness.[j] 16When you have
been defiled[*b*] in the eyes of the nations, you
will know that I am the LORD.' "
17Then the word of the LORD came to me:
18"Son of man, the house of Israel has be-
come dross[k] to me; all of them are the cop-
per, tin, iron and lead left inside a furnace.
They are but the dross of silver.[l] 19Therefore
this is what the Sovereign LORD says: 'Be-
cause you have all become dross, I will gather
you into Jerusalem. 20As men gather silver,
copper, iron, lead and tin into a furnace to
melt it with a fiery blast, so will I gather you
in my anger and my wrath and put you inside
the city and melt you. 21I will gather you and
I will blow on you with my fiery wrath, and
you will be melted inside her. 22As silver is
melted in a furnace, so you will be melted in-
side her, and you will know that I the LORD
have poured out my wrath upon you.' "[m]
23Again the word of the LORD came to me:
24"Son of man, say to the land, 'You are a
land that has had no rain or showers[*c*] in the
day of wrath.' 25There is a conspiracy of her
princes[*d*] within her like a roaring lion tear-
ing its prey; they devour people,[n] take trea-
sures and precious things and make many
widows within her. 26Her priests do violence
to my law and profane my holy things;
they do not distinguish between the holy
and the common; they teach that there is
no difference between the unclean and the
clean;[o] and they shut their eyes to the keep-
ing of my Sabbaths, so that I am profaned
among them. 27Her officials within her are
like wolves tearing their prey; they shed
blood and kill people to make unjust gain.[p]
28Her prophets whitewash these deeds for
them by false visions and lying divinations.
They say, 'This is what the Sovereign LORD

**22:14**
h Eze 21:7
**22:15**
i Dt 4:27
j Eze 23:27
**22:18**
k Isa 1:22
l Jer 6:28–30
**22:22**
m Eze 20:8,33
**22:25**
n Hos 6:9
**22:26**
o Lev 10:10
**22:27**
p Isa 1:23

[a]12 Or *usury and interest* [b]16 Or *When I have allotted you your inheritance* [c]24 Septuagint; Hebrew *has not been cleansed or rained on* [d]25 Septuagint; Hebrew *prophets*

22:28 q Eze 13:2,6–7
22:29 r Ex 23:9
22:30 s Eze 13:5 t Ps 106:23; Jer 5:1
22:31 u Eze 9:10
23:5 v Hos 8:9
23:7 w Hos 5:3
23:8 x Ex 32:4
23:10 y Eze 16:36
23:11 z Jer 3:8–11
23:12 a 2Ki 16:7–15

says'—when the LORD has not spoken.[q] [29]The people of the land practice extortion and commit robbery; they oppress the poor and needy and mistreat the alien,[r] denying them justice.

[30]"I looked for a man among them who would build up the wall[s] and stand before me in the gap on behalf of the land so I would not have to destroy it, but I found none.[t] [31]So I will pour out my wrath on them and consume them with my fiery anger, bringing down on their own heads all they have done, declares the Sovereign LORD.[u]"

## Two Adulterous Sisters

23 The word of the LORD came to me: [2]"Son of man, there were two women, daughters of the same mother. [3]They became prostitutes in Egypt, engaging in prostitution from their youth. In that land their breasts were fondled and their virgin bosoms caressed. [4]The older was named Oholah, and her sister was Oholibah. They were mine and gave birth to sons and daughters. Oholah is Samaria, and Oholibah is Jerusalem.

[5]"Oholah engaged in prostitution while she was still mine; and she lusted after her lovers, the Assyrians—warriors[v] [6]clothed in blue, governors and commanders, all of them handsome young men, and mounted horsemen. [7]She gave herself as a prostitute to all the elite of the Assyrians and defiled herself with all the idols of everyone she lusted after.[w] [8]She did not give up the prostitution she began in Egypt,[x] when during her youth men slept with her, caressed her virgin bosom and poured out their lust upon her.

[9]"Therefore I handed her over to her lovers, the Assyrians, for whom she lusted. [10]They stripped her naked, took away her sons and daughters and killed her with the sword. She became a byword among women, and punishment was inflicted on her.[y]

[11]"Her sister Oholibah saw this, yet in her lust and prostitution she was more depraved than her sister.[z] [12]She too lusted after the Assyrians—governors and commanders, warriors in full dress, mounted horsemen, all handsome young men.[a] [13]I saw that she too defiled herself; both of them went the same way.

[14]"But she carried her prostitution still further. She saw men portrayed on a wall,[b] figures of Chaldeans[a] portrayed in red, [15]with belts around their waists and flowing turbans on their heads; all of them looked like Babylonian chariot officers, natives of Chaldea.[b] [16]As soon as she saw them, she lusted after them and sent messengers to them in Chaldea. [17]Then the Babylonians came to her, to the bed of love, and in their lust they defiled her. After she had been defiled by them, she turned away from them in disgust. [18]When she carried on her prostitution openly and exposed her nakedness, I turned away[c] from her in disgust, just as I had turned away from her sister. [19]Yet she became more and more promiscuous as she recalled the days of her youth, when she was a prostitute in Egypt. [20]There she lusted after her lovers, whose genitals were like those of donkeys and whose emission was like that of horses. [21]So you longed for the lewdness of your youth, when in Egypt your bosom was caressed and your young breasts fondled.[c]

[22]"Therefore, Oholibah, this is what the Sovereign LORD says: I will stir up your lovers against you, those you turned away from in disgust, and I will bring them against you from every side[d]— [23]the Babylonians and all the Chaldeans, the men of Pekod[e] and Shoa and Koa, and all the Assyrians with them, handsome young men, all of them governors and commanders, chariot officers and men of high rank, all mounted on horses. [24]They will come against you with weapons,[d] chariots and wagons and with a throng of people; they will take up positions against you on every side with large and small shields and with helmets. I will turn you over to them for punishment,[f] and they will punish you according to their standards. [25]I will direct my jealous anger against you, and they will deal with you in fury. They will cut off your noses and your ears, and those of you who are left will fall by the sword. They will take away your sons and daughters,[g] and those of you who are left will be consumed by fire.

23:14 b Eze 8:10
23:18 c Jer 6:8
23:22 d Eze 16:37
23:23 e Jer 50:21
23:24 f Jer 39:5–6
23:25 g ver 47

[a]14 Or *Babylonians* [b]15 Or *Babylonia*; also in verse 16 [c]21 Syriac (see also verse 3); Hebrew *caressed because of your young breasts* [d]24 The meaning of the Hebrew for this word is uncertain.

26 "They will also strip you of your clothes and take your fine jewelry.[h] 27 So I will put a stop[i] to the lewdness and prostitution you began in Egypt. You will not look on these things with longing or remember Egypt anymore.

28 "For this is what the Sovereign LORD says: I am about to hand you over to those you hate, to those you turned away from in disgust. 29 They will deal with you in hatred and take away everything you have worked for. They will leave you naked and bare, and the shame of your prostitution will be exposed. Your lewdness and promiscuity 30 have brought this upon you, because you lusted after the nations and defiled yourself with their idols.[j] 31 You have gone the way of your sister; so I will put her cup into your hand.

32 "This is what the Sovereign LORD says:

"You will drink your sister's cup,
  a cup large and deep;
it will bring scorn and derision,
  for it holds so much.[k]
33 You will be filled with drunkenness and
    sorrow,
  the cup of ruin and desolation,
  the cup of your sister Samaria.
34 You will drink it[l] and drain it dry;
  you will dash it to pieces
  and tear your breasts.

I have spoken, declares the Sovereign LORD.

35 "Therefore this is what the Sovereign LORD says: Since you have forgotten[m] me and thrust me behind your back,[n] you must bear the consequences of your lewdness and prostitution."

36 The LORD said to me: "Son of man, will you judge Oholah and Oholibah? Then confront them with their detestable practices,[o] 37 for they have committed adultery and blood is on their hands. They committed adultery with their idols; they even sacrificed their children, whom they bore to me,[a] as food for them. 38 They have also done this to me: At that same time they defiled my sanctuary and desecrated my Sabbaths. 39 On the very day they sacrificed their children to their idols, they entered my sanctuary and desecrated it. That is what they did in my house.

40 "They even sent messengers for men who came from far away, and when they arrived you bathed yourself for them, painted your eyes[p] and put on your jewelry.[q] 41 You sat on an elegant couch,[r] with a table spread before it on which you had placed the incense and oil that belonged to me.

42 "The noise of a carefree crowd was around her; Sabeans[b] were brought from the desert along with men from the rabble, and they put bracelets on the arms of the woman and her sister and beautiful crowns on their heads. 43 Then I said about the one worn out by adultery, 'Now let them use her as a prostitute, for that is all she is.' 44 And they slept with her. As men sleep with a prostitute, so they slept with those lewd women, Oholah and Oholibah. 45 But righteous men will sentence them to the punishment of women who commit adultery and shed blood, because they are adulterous and blood is on their hands.[s]

46 "This is what the Sovereign LORD says: Bring a mob against them and give them over to terror and plunder. 47 The mob will stone them and cut them down with their swords; they will kill their sons and daughters and burn[t] down their houses.[u]

48 "So I will put an end to lewdness in the land, that all women may take warning and not imitate you.[v] 49 You will suffer the penalty for your lewdness and bear the consequences of your sins of idolatry. Then you will know that I am the Sovereign LORD."

## The Cooking Pot

24 In the ninth year, in the tenth month on the tenth day, the word of the LORD came to me: 2 "Son of man, record this date, this very date, because the king of Babylon has laid siege to Jerusalem this very day.[w] 3 Tell this rebellious house a parable[x] and say to them: 'This is what the Sovereign LORD says:

" 'Put on the cooking pot;[y] put it on
  and pour water into it.
4 Put into it the pieces of meat,
  all the choice pieces—the leg and the
    shoulder.

**23:26** h Eze 16:39
**23:27** i Eze 16:41
**23:30** j Eze 6:9
**23:32** k Isa 51:17; Jer 25:15
**23:34** l Isa 51:17
**23:35** m Jer 3:21 n 1Ki 14:9
**23:36** o Isa 58:1
**23:40** p 2Ki 9:30 q Jer 4:30
**23:41** r Est 1:6; Am 6:4
**23:45** s Eze 16:38
**23:47** t 2Ch 36:19 u Eze 16:40-41
**23:48** v 2Pe 2:6
**24:2** w 2Ki 25:1; Jer 39:1; 52:4
**24:3** x Eze 17:2 y Jer 1:13; Eze 11:3

[a] 37 Or *even made the children they bore to me pass through ⌊the fire⌋* [b] 42 Or *drunkards*

24:6
z Eze 22:2
24:7
a Lev 17:13
24:11
b Eze 22:15
24:13
c Jer 6:28–30
24:14
d Eze 36:19

Fill it with the best of these bones;
5 take the pick of the flock.
Pile wood beneath it for the bones;
bring it to a boil
and cook the bones in it.

6 " 'For this is what the Sovereign LORD says:

" 'Woe to the city of bloodshed,[z]
to the pot now encrusted,
whose deposit will not go away!
Empty it piece by piece
without casting lots for them.

7 " 'For the blood she shed is in her midst:
She poured it on the bare rock;
she did not pour it on the ground,
where the dust would cover it.[a]
8 To stir up wrath and take revenge
I put her blood on the bare rock,
so that it would not be covered.

9 " 'Therefore this is what the Sovereign LORD
says:

" 'Woe to the city of bloodshed!
I, too, will pile the wood high.
10 So heap on the wood
and kindle the fire.
Cook the meat well,
mixing in the spices;
and let the bones be charred.
11 Then set the empty pot on the coals
till it becomes hot and its copper glows
so its impurities may be melted
and its deposit burned away.[b]
12 It has frustrated all efforts;
its heavy deposit has not been
removed,
not even by fire.

13 " 'Now your impurity is lewdness. Be-
cause I tried to cleanse you but you would
not be cleansed from your impurity, you
will not be clean again until my wrath
against you has subsided.[c]

14 " 'I the LORD have spoken. The time has
come for me to act. I will not hold back; I will
not have pity, nor will I relent. You will be
judged according to your conduct and your
actions,[d] declares the Sovereign LORD.' "

## Ezekiel's Wife Dies

15 The word of the LORD came to me:
16 "Son of man, with one blow I am about
to take away from you the delight of your
eyes. Yet do not lament or weep or shed any
tears.[e] 17 Groan quietly; do not mourn for the
dead. Keep your turban fastened and your
sandals on your feet; do not cover the lower
part of your face or eat the customary food
⌊of mourners⌋."
18 So I spoke to the people in the morning,
and in the evening my wife died. The next
morning I did as I had been commanded.
19 Then the people asked me, "Won't
you tell us what these things have to do
with us?"
20 So I said to them, "The word of the LORD
came to me: 21 Say to the house of Israel, 'This
is what the Sovereign LORD says: I am about
to desecrate my sanctuary—the stronghold
in which you take pride, the delight of your
eyes, the object of your affection. The sons
and daughters you left behind will fall by
the sword.[g] 22 And you will do as I have done.
You will not cover the lower part of your face
or eat the customary food ⌊of mourners⌋.[h]
23 You will keep your turbans on your heads
and your sandals on your feet. You will not
mourn or weep but will waste away because
of[a] your sins and groan among yourselves.[i]
24 Ezekiel will be a sign[j] to you; you will do
just as he has done. When this happens, you
will know that I am the Sovereign LORD.'
25 "And you, son of man, on the day I take
away their stronghold, their joy and glory,
the delight of their eyes, their heart's desire,
and their sons and daughters as well— 26 on
that day a fugitive will come to tell you
the news. 27 At that time your mouth will
be opened; you will speak with him and
will no longer be silent. So you will be a
sign to them, and they will know that I am
the LORD.[k]"

## A Prophecy Against Ammon

25 The word of the LORD came to me:
2 "Son of man, set your face against
the Ammonites[l] and prophesy against
them.[m] 3 Say to them, 'Hear the word of the
Sovereign LORD. This is what the Sovereign
LORD says: Because you said "Aha![n]" over

24:16
e Jer 13:17
24:19
f Eze 12:9
24:21
g Eze 23:47
24:22
h Jer 16:7
24:23
i Ps 78:64
24:24
j Eze 4:3
24:27
k Eze 3:26
25:2
l Zep 2:8–9
m Jer 49:1–6
25:3
n Eze 26:2

[a] 23 Or *away in*

# Ezekiel's Wife

## On God's Stage

Ezekiel and his wife were among a group of Israelites who had been exiled to Babylon. Once there, the Lord called Ezekiel, a priest, to prophesy to his fellow exiles. Ezekiel was forewarned of his wife's death, but he was compelled by God not to mourn or do the normal ceremonial things associated with grieving (see Eze 24:15–17). The death of his wife was to be a sign to the people of the impending fall of Jerusalem.

Ezekiel's wife is unnamed, but we may assume that she was a godly woman. God called her the "delight" of Ezekiel's eyes (Eze 24:16). It is obvious that to Ezekiel, she was beloved. Ezekiel is one of the most dramatic prophets in the Scriptures. His ministry was one of acting out the word of the Lord to the people. It appears that Ezekiel's wife was accustomed to having her life portrayed as if on stage. Furthermore, since Ezekiel occasionally met with the elders of the people in his house (see Eze 8:1; 14:1; 20:1), we can assume that his wife was a hospitable hostess. Because of the dramatic demonstrations Ezekiel enacted before the people to communicate God's message, his wife surely must have had a keen sense of God herself. From one moment to the next, Ezekiel was caught up in unusual behavior. Much of his book is prophetic, poetic and symbolic; therefore, we might assume that Ezekiel's wife experienced firsthand the actions and poetry of love.

Ezekiel was told that his grief following his wife's sudden death was to be experienced in silence. This was because God wanted to demonstrate to Israel that what they had loved would be destroyed, and, because of their sins, they would waste away in remorse rather than mourn in a healthy way (see Eze 24:23). Ezekiel and his wife were used by God to demonstrate the heartbreak of disobedience.

We often do not know what role we are playing on this stage of life. God has a purpose for all that is done in our lives. Yet because we are often not the *main* character, we feel obscure. The story of Ezekiel's wife speaks to those of us who maintain our place of love but never see its impact during our lifetime. Ezekiel's wife died to promote God's truth that we must love the Lord and obey the Lord no matter what the circumstances.

—D. L. Shumake JaPhia

### reflection

*Determine to play your role in life faithfully and well.*

*You never know how God is using you to touch someone else.*

*Reflect on one thing you will do faithfully and well today.*

### read

Ezekiel 24.

**See also** the Inspire Notes "Suffering," "The Paradox of Life and Suffering," "Commitment to God" and "Bon Voyage: The Courage to Say Good-bye," and the Women of the Bible Notes "Rizpah: A Grieving Mother," "The Shunammite Woman: Our Sister's Grief Is Our Grief" and "Job's Wife: She Was Tested Too."

For the next Women of the Bible note, go to page 1023.

my sanctuary when it was desecrated and over the land of Israel when it was laid waste and over the people of Judah when they went into exile, 4therefore I am going to give you to the people of the East as a possession. They will set up their camps and pitch their tents among you; they will eat your fruit and drink your milk. 5I will turn Rabbah[o] into a pasture for camels and Ammon into a resting place for sheep.[p] Then you will know that I am the LORD. 6For this is what the Sovereign LORD says: Because you have clapped your hands and stamped your feet, rejoicing with all the malice of your heart against the land of Israel,[q] 7therefore I will stretch out my hand against you and give you as plunder to the nations. I will cut you off from the nations and exterminate you from the countries. I will destroy you, and you will know that I am the LORD.' "

## A Prophecy Against Moab

8"This is what the Sovereign LORD says: 'Because Moab[r] and Seir said, "Look, the house of Judah has become like all the other nations," 9therefore I will expose the flank of Moab, beginning at its frontier towns—Beth Jeshimoth[s], Baal Meon and Kiriathaim—the glory of that land. 10I will give Moab along with the Ammonites to the people of the East as a possession, so that the Ammonites will not be remembered[t] among the nations; 11and I will inflict punishment on Moab. Then they will know that I am the LORD.' "

## A Prophecy Against Edom

12"This is what the Sovereign LORD says: 'Because Edom[u] took revenge on the house of Judah and became very guilty by doing so, 13therefore this is what the Sovereign LORD says: I will stretch out my hand against Edom and kill its men and their animals. I will lay it waste, and from Teman to Dedan[v] they will fall by the sword. 14I will take vengeance on Edom by the hand of my people Israel, and they will deal with Edom in accordance with my anger and my wrath; they will know my vengeance, declares the Sovereign LORD.' "

## A Prophecy Against Philistia

15"This is what the Sovereign LORD says: 'Because the Philistines[w] acted in vengeance and took revenge with malice in their hearts, and with ancient hostility sought to destroy Judah, 16therefore this is what the Sovereign LORD says: I am about to stretch out my hand against the Philistines,[x] and I will cut off the Kerethites[y] and destroy those remaining along the coast. 17I will carry out great vengeance on them and punish them in my wrath. Then they will know that I am the LORD, when I take vengeance on them.' "

## A Prophecy Against Tyre

**26** In the eleventh year, on the first day of the month, the word of the LORD came to me: 2"Son of man, because Tyre[z] has said of Jerusalem, 'Aha![a] The gate to the nations is broken, and its doors have swung open to me; now that she lies in ruins I will prosper,' 3therefore this is what the Sovereign LORD says: I am against you, O Tyre, and I will bring many nations against you, like the sea[b] casting up its waves. 4They will destroy the walls of Tyre[c] and pull down her towers; I will scrape away her rubble and make her a bare rock. 5Out in the sea[d] she will become a place to spread fishnets, for I have spoken, declares the Sovereign LORD. She will become plunder[e] for the nations, 6and her settlements on the mainland will be ravaged by the sword. Then they will know that I am the LORD.

7"For this is what the Sovereign LORD says: From the north I am going to bring against Tyre Nebuchadnezzar[a] king of Babylon, king of kings,[f] with horses and chariots, with horsemen and a great army. 8He will ravage your settlements on the mainland with the sword; he will set up siege works against you, build a ramp[g] up to your walls and raise his shields against you. 9He will direct the blows of his battering rams against your walls and demolish your towers with his weapons. 10His horses will be so many that they will cover you with dust. Your walls will tremble at the noise of the war horses, wagons and chariots[h] when he enters your gates as men

[a]7 Hebrew *Nebuchadrezzar,* of which *Nebuchadnezzar* is a variant; here and often in Ezekiel and Jeremiah

**25:5** o Eze 21:20 p Isa 17:2
**25:6** q Zep 2:8
**25:8** r Jer 48:1; Am 2:1
**25:9** s Nu 33:49
**25:10** t Eze 21:32
**25:12** u 2Ch 28:17
**25:13** v Jer 25:23
**25:15** w 2Ch 28:18
**25:16** x Jer 47:1–7 y 1Sa 30:14; Zep 2:4–5
**26:2** z Isa 23 a Eze 25:3
**26:3** b Jer 50:42
**26:4** c Am 1:10
**26:5** d Eze 27:32 e Eze 29:19
**26:7** f Ezr 7:12; Da 2:37
**26:8** g Eze 21:22
**26:10** h Jer 4:13

**26:11** i Jer 43:13
**26:13** j Isa 14:11 k Rev 18:22
**26:15** l Jer 49:21
**26:17** m Eze 27:32

enter a city whose walls have been broken
through. 11 The hoofs of his horses will trample all your streets; he will kill your people
with the sword, and your strong pillars[i] will
fall to the ground. 12 They will plunder your
wealth and loot your merchandise; they will
break down your walls and demolish your
fine houses and throw your stones, timber
and rubble into the sea. 13 I will put an end
to your noisy songs, and the music of your
harps[j] will be heard no more.[k] 14 I will make
you a bare rock, and you will become a place
to spread fishnets. You will never be rebuilt,
for I the LORD have spoken, declares the Sovereign LORD.

15 "This is what the Sovereign LORD says to
Tyre: Will not the coastlands tremble[l] at the
sound of your fall, when the wounded groan
and the slaughter takes place in you? 16 Then
all the princes of the coast will step down
from their thrones and lay aside their robes
and take off their embroidered garments.
Clothed with terror, they will sit on the
ground, trembling every moment, appalled
at you. 17 Then they will take up a lament[m]
concerning you and say to you:

"'How you are destroyed, O city of
renown,
peopled by men of the sea!
You were a power on the seas,
you and your citizens;
you put your terror
on all who lived there.
18 Now the coastlands tremble
on the day of your fall;
the islands in the sea
are terrified at your collapse.'

19 "This is what the Sovereign LORD says:
When I make you a desolate city, like cities
no longer inhabited, and when I bring the
ocean depths over you and its vast waters
cover you, 20 then I will bring you down with
those who go down to the pit, to the people
of long ago. I will make you dwell in the
earth below, as in ancient ruins, with those
who go down to the pit, and you will not return or take your place[a] in the land of the living. 21 I will bring you to a horrible end and
you will be no more. You will be sought, but
you will never again be found, declares the
Sovereign LORD."[n]

## A Lament for Tyre

27 The word of the LORD came to me:
2 "Son of man, take up a lament concerning Tyre. 3 Say to Tyre, situated at the
gateway to the sea, merchant of peoples on
many coasts, 'This is what the Sovereign
LORD says:

"'You say, O Tyre,
"I am perfect in beauty."[o]
4 Your domain was on the high seas;
your builders brought your beauty to
perfection.
5 They made all your timbers
of pine trees from Senir[b];[p]
they took a cedar from Lebanon
to make a mast for you.
6 Of oaks[q] from Bashan
they made your oars;
of cypress wood[c] from the coasts of
Cyprus[d]
they made your deck, inlaid with ivory.
7 Fine embroidered linen from Egypt was
your sail
and served as your banner;
your awnings were of blue and purple
from the coasts of Elishah.
8 Men of Sidon and Arvad were your
oarsmen;
your skilled men, O Tyre, were aboard
as your seamen.[r]
9 Veteran craftsmen of Gebal[e][s] were on
board
as shipwrights to caulk your seams.
All the ships of the sea and their
sailors
came alongside to trade for your
wares.

10 "'Men of Persia, Lydia and Put[t]
served as soldiers in your army.
They hung their shields and helmets on
your walls,
bringing you splendor.
11 Men of Arvad and Helech
manned your walls on every side;
men of Gammad
were in your towers.

**26:21** n Eze 27:36; 28:19
**27:3** o Eze 28:2
**27:5** p Dt 3:9
**27:6** q Zec 11:2
**27:8** r 1Ki 9:27
**27:9** s 1Ki 5:18
**27:10** t Eze 30:5

[a]20 Septuagint; Hebrew *return, and I will give glory* [b]5 That is, Hermon [c]6 Targum; the Masoretic Text has a different division of the consonants. [d]6 Hebrew *Kittim* [e]9 That is, Byblos

## The African Presence

**Ezekiel 27:10**

**Put was the third son of Ham (see Ge 10:6). The land of Put has been identified as present-day Libya, located in North Africa. (See also Eze 30:5; 38:5.)**

They hung their shields around your
walls;
they brought your beauty to
perfection.

12 "'Tarshish did business with you be-
cause of your great wealth of goods; they
exchanged silver, iron, tin and lead for your
merchandise.
13 "'Greece, Tubal and Meshech[u] traded
with you; they exchanged slaves[v] and arti-
cles of bronze for your wares.
14 "'Men of Beth Togarmah[w] exchanged
work horses, war horses and mules for your
merchandise.
15 "'The men of Rhodes[a][x] traded with you,
and many coastlands were your customers;
they paid you with ivory[y] tusks and ebony.
16 "'Aram[b] did business with you because
of your many products; they exchanged tur-
quoise,[z] purple fabric, embroidered work,
fine linen, coral and rubies for your mer-
chandise.
17 "'Judah and Israel traded with you; they
exchanged wheat from Minnith[a] and confec-
tions,[c] honey, oil and balm for your wares.
18 "'Damascus,[b] because of your many
products and great wealth of goods, did
business with you in wine from Helbon and
wool from Zahar.
19 "'Danites and Greeks from Uzal bought
your merchandise; they exchanged wrought
iron, cassia and calamus for your wares.
20 "'Dedan traded in saddle blankets with
you.
21 "'Arabia and all the princes of Kedar[c]
were your customers; they did business
with you in lambs, rams and goats.
22 "'The merchants of Sheba[d] and Raa-
mah traded with you; for your merchandise
they exchanged the finest of all kinds of
spices and precious stones, and gold.
23 "'Haran,[e] Canneh and Eden and mer-
chants of Sheba, Asshur and Kilmad traded
with you.
24 In your marketplace they traded
with you beautiful garments, blue fabric,
embroidered work and multicolored rugs
with cords twisted and tightly knotted.
25 "'The ships of Tarshish[f] serve
as carriers for your wares.
You are filled with heavy cargo
in the heart of the sea.
26 Your oarsmen take you
out to the high seas.
But the east wind[g] will break you to pieces
in the heart of the sea.
27 Your wealth,[h] merchandise and wares,
your mariners, seamen and
shipwrights,
your merchants and all your soldiers,
and everyone else on board
will sink into the heart of the sea
on the day of your shipwreck.
28 The shorelands will quake[i]
when your seamen cry out.
29 All who handle the oars
will abandon their ships;
the mariners and all the seamen
will stand on the shore.
30 They will raise their voice
and cry bitterly over you;
they will sprinkle dust on their heads
and roll[j] in ashes.[k]
31 They will shave their heads because of you
and will put on sackcloth.
They will weep over you with anguish
of soul

**27:13** u Ge 10:2 v Rev 18:13
**27:14** w Eze 38:6
**27:15** x Ge 10:7 y Rev 18:12
**27:16** z Eze 28:13
**27:17** a Jdg 11:33
**27:18** b Eze 47:16–18
**27:21** c Isa 60:7
**27:22** d Ge 10:7,28; 1Ki 10:1–2; Isa 60:6
**27:23** e 2Ki 19:12
**27:25** f Isa 2:16
**27:26** g Ps 48:7
**27:27** h Pr 11:4
**27:28** i Eze 26:15
**27:30** j Jer 6:26 k Rev 18:18–19

[a]15 Septuagint; Hebrew *Dedan* [b]16 Most Hebrew manuscripts; some Hebrew manuscripts and Syriac *Edom* [c]17 The meaning of the Hebrew for this word is uncertain.

and with bitter mourning.
32 As they wail and mourn over you,
they will take up a lament[l] concerning you:
"Who was ever silenced like Tyre,
surrounded by the sea?"
33 When your merchandise went out on the seas,
you satisfied many nations;
with your great wealth and your wares
you enriched the kings of the earth.
34 Now you are shattered by the sea
in the depths of the waters;
your wares and all your company
have gone down with you.[m]
35 All who live in the coastlands[n]
are appalled at you;
their kings shudder with horror
and their faces are distorted with fear.
36 The merchants among the nations hiss at you;[o]
you have come to a horrible end
and will be no more.[p]' "

## A Prophecy Against the King of Tyre

28 The word of the LORD came to me: 2"Son of man, say to the ruler of Tyre, 'This is what the Sovereign LORD says:

" 'In the pride of your heart
you say, "I am a god;
I sit on the throne of a god
in the heart of the seas."
But you are a man and not a god,
though you think you are as wise as a god.
3 Are you wiser than Daniel[a]?
Is no secret hidden from you?
4 By your wisdom and understanding
you have gained wealth for yourself
and amassed gold and silver
in your treasuries.
5 By your great skill in trading
you have increased your wealth,
and because of your wealth
your heart has grown proud.

6" 'Therefore this is what the Sovereign LORD says:

" 'Because you think you are wise,
as wise as a god,
7 I am going to bring foreigners against you,
the most ruthless of nations;[q]
they will draw their swords against your beauty and wisdom
and pierce your shining splendor.
8 They will bring you down to the pit,
and you will die a violent death
in the heart of the seas.
9 Will you then say, "I am a god,"
in the presence of those who kill you?
You will be but a man, not a god,
in the hands of those who slay you.
10 You will die the death of the uncircumcised[r]
at the hands of foreigners.

I have spoken, declares the Sovereign LORD.' "

11 The word of the LORD came to me: 12"Son of man, take up a lament concerning the king of Tyre and say to him: 'This is what the Sovereign LORD says:

" 'You were the model of perfection,
full of wisdom and perfect in beauty.[s]
13 You were in Eden,
the garden of God;[t]
every precious stone adorned you:
ruby, topaz and emerald,
chrysolite, onyx and jasper,
sapphire,[b] turquoise and beryl.[c]
Your settings and mountings[d] were made of gold;
on the day you were created they were prepared.
14 You were anointed as a guardian cherub,[u]
for so I ordained you.
You were on the holy mount of God;
you walked among the fiery stones.
15 You were blameless in your ways
from the day you were created
till wickedness was found in you.
16 Through your widespread trade
you were filled with violence,
and you sinned.
So I drove you in disgrace from the mount of God,
and I expelled you, O guardian cherub,

**27:32** l Eze 26:17
**27:34** m Zec 9:4
**27:35** n Eze 26:15
**27:36** o Jer 18:16 p Eze 26:21
**28:7** q Eze 30:11; 31:12; 32:12
**28:10** r Eze 31:18
**28:12** s Eze 27:2–4
**28:13** t Eze 31:8–9
**28:14** u Ex 25:17–20

[a] 3 Or *Danel*; the Hebrew spelling may suggest a person other than the prophet Daniel. [b] 13 Or *lapis lazuli* [c] 13 The precise identification of some of these precious stones is uncertain. [d] 13 The meaning of the Hebrew for this phrase is uncertain.

28:19 v Eze 26:21; 27:36
28:21 w Eze 6:2
28:23 x Eze 38:22
28:24 y Nu 33:55; Jos 23:13
28:25 z Isa 11:12 a Eze 20:41
28:26 b Jer 23:6 c Am 9:14–15

from among the fiery stones.
17 Your heart became proud
on account of your beauty,
and you corrupted your wisdom
because of your splendor.
So I threw you to the earth;
I made a spectacle of you before kings.
18 By your many sins and dishonest trade
you have desecrated your sanctuaries.
So I made a fire come out from you,
and it consumed you,
and I reduced you to ashes on the ground
in the sight of all who were watching.
19 All the nations who knew you
are appalled at you;
you have come to a horrible end
and will be no more.[v]' "

## A Prophecy Against Sidon

20 The word of the LORD came to me:
21 "Son of man, set your face against[w] Sidon;
prophesy against her 22 and say: 'This is
what the Sovereign LORD says:

" 'I am against you, O Sidon,
and I will gain glory within you.
They will know that I am the LORD,
when I inflict punishment on her
and show myself holy within her.
23 I will send a plague upon her
and make blood flow in her streets.
The slain will fall within her,
with the sword against her on every
side.
Then they will know that I am the LORD.[x]

24 " 'No longer will the people of Israel
have malicious neighbors who are painful
briers and sharp thorns.[y] Then they will
know that I am the Sovereign LORD.

25 " 'This is what the Sovereign LORD says:
When I gather the people of Israel from the
nations where they have been scattered,[z] I
will show myself holy[a] among them in the
sight of the nations. Then they will live in
their own land, which I gave to my servant
Jacob. 26 They will live there in safety[b] and
will build houses and plant vineyards; they
will live in safety when I inflict punishment
on all their neighbors who maligned them.
Then they will know that I am the LORD
their God.[c]' "

## A Prophecy Against Egypt

29 In the tenth year, in the tenth month
on the twelfth day, the word of the
LORD came to me: 2 "Son of man, set your face
against Pharaoh king of Egypt and prophesy
against him and against all Egypt.[d] 3 Speak
to him and say: 'This is what the Sovereign
LORD says:

" 'I am against you, Pharaoh king of
Egypt,
you great monster[e] lying among your
streams.
You say, "The Nile is mine;
I made it for myself."
4 But I will put hooks in your jaws
and make the fish of your streams
stick to your scales.
I will pull you out from among your
streams,
with all the fish sticking to your
scales.[f]
5 I will leave you in the desert,
you and all the fish of your streams.
You will fall on the open field
and not be gathered or picked up.
I will give you as food
to the beasts of the earth and the birds
of the air.[g]

6 Then all who live in Egypt will know that I
am the LORD.

" 'You have been a staff of reed for the
house of Israel. 7 When they grasped you
with their hands, you splintered and you
tore open their shoulders; when they
leaned on you, you broke and their backs
were wrenched.[a][h]

8 " 'Therefore this is what the Sovereign
LORD says: I will bring a sword against
you and kill your men and their animals.[i]
9 Egypt will become a desolate wasteland.
Then they will know that I am the LORD.

" 'Because you said, "The Nile is mine; I
made it," 10 therefore I am against you and
against your streams, and I will make the
land of Egypt a ruin and a desolate waste
from Migdol to Aswan, as far as the border
of Cush.[b] 11 No foot of man or animal will
pass through it; no one will live there for
forty years.[j] 12 I will make the land of Egypt

29:2 d Isa 19:1–17; Jer 46:2
29:3 e Isa 27:1; Eze 32:2
29:4 f Eze 38:4
29:5 g Jer 7:33; 34:20
29:7 h Eze 17:15–17
29:8 i Eze 14:17
29:11 j Eze 32:13

[a] 7 Syriac (see also Septuagint and Vulgate); Hebrew *and you caused their backs to stand* [b] 10 That is, the upper Nile region

## The African Presence

**Ezekiel 29:10**

"Cush" is also called "Ethiopia" (that is, Nubia; see also chs. 30; 38). The exact geographic region of ancient Cush is disputed; however, most scholars generally agree that the area of Nubia included the middle of the Nile from what is present-day southern Egypt and northern Sudan (see the African Presence note on Ex 5:1–5). The conquest of Cush through Babylon was described by Ezekiel.

**29:12** k Eze 30:7,23,26
**29:16** l Isa 36:4,6 m Isa 30:2
**29:18** n Jer 27:6; Eze 26:7–8

desolate among devastated lands, and her cities will lie desolate forty years among ruined cities. And I will disperse the Egyptians among the nations and scatter them through the countries.[k]

13“ ‘Yet this is what the Sovereign LORD says: At the end of forty years I will gather the Egyptians from the nations where they were scattered. 14I will bring them back from captivity and return them to Upper Egypt,[a] the land of their ancestry. There they will be a lowly kingdom. 15It will be the lowliest of kingdoms and will never again exalt itself above the other nations. I will make it so weak that it will never again rule over the nations. 16Egypt will no longer be a source of confidence[l] for the people of Israel but will be a reminder of their sin in turning to her for help. Then they will know that I am the Sovereign LORD.[m]’ ”

17In the twenty-seventh year, in the first month on the first day, the word of the LORD came to me: 18“Son of man, Nebuchadnezzar[n] king of Babylon drove his army in a hard campaign against Tyre; every head was rubbed bare and every shoulder made raw. Yet he and his army got no reward from the campaign he led against Tyre. 19Therefore this is what the Sovereign LORD says: I am going to give Egypt to Nebuchadnezzar king of Babylon, and he will carry off its wealth. He will loot and plunder the land as pay for his army. 20I have given him Egypt as a reward for his efforts because he and his army did it for me, declares the Sovereign LORD.[o]

21“On that day I will make a horn[b][p] grow for the house of Israel, and I will open your mouth among them. Then they will know that I am the LORD.[q]”

### A Lament for Egypt

**30** The word of the LORD came to me: 2“Son of man, prophesy and say: ‘This is what the Sovereign LORD says:

“ ‘Wail[r] and say,
“Alas for that day!”
3 For the day is near,[s]
the day of the LORD[t] is near—
a day of clouds,
a time of doom for the nations.
4 A sword will come against Egypt,
and anguish will come upon Cush.[c]
When the slain fall in Egypt,
her wealth will be carried away
and her foundations torn down.[u]

5Cush and Put, Lydia and all Arabia, Libya[d] and the people[v] of the covenant land will fall by the sword along with Egypt.

6“ ‘This is what the LORD says:

“ ‘The allies of Egypt will fall
and her proud strength will fail.
From Migdol to Aswan
they will fall by the sword within her,
declares the Sovereign LORD.
7“ ‘They will be desolate
among desolate lands,

**29:20** o Jer 25:9
**29:21** p Ps 132:17 q Eze 24:27
**30:2** r Isa 13:6
**30:3** s Joel 2:1,11 t Eze 7:12,19
**30:4** u Eze 29:19
**30:5** v Jer 25:20

[a]14 Hebrew *to Pathros* [b]21 *Horn* here symbolizes strength. [c]4 That is, the upper Nile region; also in verses 5 and 9 [d]5 Hebrew *Cub*

**30:7** w Eze 29:12
**30:9** x Isa 18:1–2 y Eze 32:9–10
**30:10** z Eze 29:19
**30:11** a Eze 28:7
**30:13** b Zec 10:11
**30:14** c Eze 29:14 d Ps 78:12,43

and their cities will lie
among ruined cities.[w]
8 Then they will know that I am the LORD,
when I set fire to Egypt
and all her helpers are crushed.

9 "'On that day messengers will go out from me in ships to frighten Cush[x] out of her complacency. Anguish will take hold of them on the day of Egypt's doom, for it is sure to come.[y]

10 "'This is what the Sovereign LORD says:

"'I will put an end to the hordes of Egypt
by the hand of Nebuchadnezzar king
of Babylon.[z]
11 He and his army—the most ruthless of
nations[a]—
will be brought in to destroy the land.
They will draw their swords against Egypt
and fill the land with the slain.
12 I will dry up the streams of the Nile
and sell the land to evil men;
by the hand of foreigners
I will lay waste the land and
everything in it.
I the LORD have spoken.

13 "'This is what the Sovereign LORD says:

"'I will destroy the idols
and put an end to the images in
Memphis.[a]
No longer will there be a prince in Egypt,[b]
and I will spread fear throughout the
land.
14 I will lay[c] waste Upper Egypt,[b]
set fire to Zoan[d]
and inflict punishment on Thebes.[c]
15 I will pour out my wrath on Pelusium,[d]
the stronghold of Egypt,
and cut off the hordes of Thebes.
16 I will set fire to Egypt;
Pelusium will writhe in agony.
Thebes will be taken by storm;
Memphis will be in constant distress.
17 The young men of Heliopolis[e] and
Bubastis[f]
will fall by the sword,
and the cities themselves will go into
captivity.
18 Dark will be the day at Tahpanhes
when I break the yoke of Egypt;
there her proud strength will come to
an end.
She will be covered with clouds,
and her villages will go into captivity.[e]
19 So I will inflict punishment on Egypt,
and they will know that I am the
LORD.'"

20 In the eleventh year, in the first month on the seventh day, the word of the LORD came to me: 21 "Son of man, I have broken the arm of Pharaoh king of Egypt. It has not been bound up for healing[f] or put in a splint so as to become strong enough to hold a sword. 22 Therefore this is what the Sovereign LORD says: I am against Pharaoh king of Egypt. I will break both his arms, the good arm as well as the broken one, and make the sword fall from his hand. 23 I will disperse the Egyptians among the nations and scatter them through the countries.[g] 24 I will strengthen[h] the arms of the king of Babylon and put my sword[i] in his hand, but I will break the arms of Pharaoh, and he will groan before him like a mortally wounded man. 25 I will strengthen the arms of the king of Babylon, but the arms of Pharaoh will fall limp. Then they will know that I am the LORD, when I put my sword into the hand of the king of Babylon and he brandishes it against Egypt. 26 I will disperse the Egyptians among the nations and scatter them through the countries. Then they will know that I am the LORD.[j]"

## A Cedar in Lebanon

31 In the eleventh year, in the third month on the first day, the word of the LORD came to me: 2 "Son of man, say to Pharaoh king of Egypt and to his hordes:

"'Who can be compared with you in
majesty?
3 Consider Assyria, once a cedar in
Lebanon,
with beautiful branches
overshadowing the forest;
it towered on high,
its top above the thick foliage.[k]

**30:18** e ver 3
**30:21** f Jer 46:11
**30:23** g Eze 29:12
**30:24** h Zec 10:6,12 i Zep 2:12
**30:26** j Eze 29:12
**31:3** k Isa 10:34

[a]13 Hebrew *Noph*; also in verse 16 [b]14 Hebrew *waste Pathros* [c]14 Hebrew *No*; also in verses 15 and 16
[d]15 Hebrew *Sin*; also in verse 16 [e]17 Hebrew *Awen* (or *On*) [f]17 Hebrew *Pi Beseth*

4 The waters nourished it,
deep springs made it grow tall;
their streams flowed
all around its base
and sent their channels
to all the trees of the field.
5 So it towered higher
than all the trees of the field;
its boughs increased
and its branches grew long,
spreading because of abundant
waters.
6 All the birds of the air
nested in its boughs,
all the beasts of the field
gave birth under its branches;
all the great nations
lived in its shade.[l]
7 It was majestic in beauty,
with its spreading boughs,
for its roots went down
to abundant waters.
8 The cedars in the garden of God
could not rival it,
nor could the pine trees
equal its boughs,
nor could the plane trees
compare with its branches—
no tree in the garden of God
could match its beauty.[m]
9 I made it beautiful
with abundant branches,
the envy of all the trees of Eden
in the garden of God.

10 " 'Therefore this is what the Sovereign
LORD says: Because it towered on high, lift-
ing its top above the thick foliage, and be-
cause it was proud of its height, 11 I handed
it over to the ruler of the nations, for him to
deal with according to its wickedness. I cast
it aside,[n] 12 and the most ruthless of foreign
nations[o] cut it down and left it. Its boughs
fell on the mountains and in all the valleys;[p]
its branches lay broken in all the ravines of
the land. All the nations of the earth came
out from under its shade and left it. 13 All
the birds of the air settled on the fallen tree,
and all the beasts of the field were among its
branches.[q] 14 Therefore no other trees by the
waters are ever to tower proudly on high,
lifting their tops above the thick foliage.
No other trees so well-watered are ever to
reach such a height; they are all destined for
death, for the earth below, among mortal
men, with those who go down to the pit.

15 " 'This is what the Sovereign LORD says:
On the day it was brought down to the grave[a]
I covered the deep springs with mourning
for it; I held back its streams, and its abun-
dant waters were restrained. Because of it
I clothed Lebanon with gloom, and all the
trees of the field withered away. 16 I made the
nations tremble[r] at the sound of its fall when
I brought it down to the grave with those
who go down to the pit. Then all the trees[s]
of Eden, the choicest and best of Lebanon,
all the trees that were well-watered, were
consoled[t] in the earth below.[u] 17 Those who
lived in its shade, its allies among the na-
tions, had also gone down to the grave with
it, joining those killed by the sword.

18 " 'Which of the trees of Eden can be
compared with you in splendor and majesty?
Yet you, too, will be brought down with the
trees of Eden to the earth below; you will lie
among the uncircumcised,[v] with those
killed by the sword.

" 'This is Pharaoh and all his hordes, de-
clares the Sovereign LORD.' "

## A Lament for Pharaoh

32 In the twelfth year, in the twelfth
month on the first day, the word of
the LORD came to me: 2 "Son of man, take
up a lament[w] concerning Pharaoh king of
Egypt and say to him:

" 'You are like a lion among the nations;
you are like a monster in the seas
thrashing about in your streams,
churning the water with your feet
and muddying the streams.

3 " 'This is what the Sovereign LORD says:

" 'With a great throng of people
I will cast my net over you,
and they will haul you up in my net.[x]
4 I will throw you on the land
and hurl you on the open field.
I will let all the birds of the air settle on
you

[a]15 Hebrew *Sheol*; also in verses 16 and 17

**31:6** l Eze 17:23
**31:8** m Ge 2:8–9
**31:11** n Da 5:20
**31:12** o Eze 28:7 p Eze 32:5; 35:8
**31:13** q Isa 18:6; Eze 32:4
**31:16** r Eze 26:15 s Isa 14:8 t Eze 32:31 u Isa 14:15
**31:18** v Eze 32:19,21
**32:2** w Eze 27:2
**32:3** x Eze 12:13

- 32:7 y Isa 13:10; Joel 2:2,31; 3:15
- 32:10 z Eze 26:16
- 32:11 a Jer 46:26
- 32:12 b Eze 28:7
- 32:13 c Eze 29:8,11

and all the beasts of the earth gorge
themselves on you.
5 I will spread your flesh on the mountains
and fill the valleys with your remains.
6 I will drench the land with your flowing
blood
all the way to the mountains,
and the ravines will be filled with your
flesh.
7 When I snuff you out, I will cover the
heavens
and darken their stars;
I will cover the sun with a cloud,
and the moon will not give its light.[y]
8 All the shining lights in the heavens
I will darken over you;
I will bring darkness over your land,
declares the Sovereign LORD.
9 I will trouble the hearts of many peoples
when I bring about your destruction
among the nations,
among[a] lands you have not known.
10 I will cause many peoples to be appalled
at you,
and their kings will shudder with
horror because of you
when I brandish my sword before
them.
On the day of your downfall
each of them will tremble
every moment for his life.[z]

11 " 'For this is what the Sovereign LORD
says:

" 'The sword of the king of Babylon[a]
will come against you.
12 I will cause your hordes to fall
by the swords of mighty men—
the most ruthless of all nations.[b]
They will shatter the pride of Egypt,
and all her hordes will be overthrown.
13 I will destroy all her cattle
from beside abundant waters
no longer to be stirred by the foot of man
or muddied by the hoofs of cattle.[c]
14 Then I will let her waters settle
and make her streams flow like oil,
declares the Sovereign LORD.
15 When I make Egypt desolate
and strip the land of everything in it,
when I strike down all who live there,
then they will know that I am the
LORD.[d]'

16 "This is the lament[e] they will chant for
her. The daughters of the nations will chant
it; for Egypt and all her hordes they will
chant it, declares the Sovereign LORD."

17 In the twelfth year, on the fifteenth day
of the month, the word of the LORD came to
me: 18 "Son of man, wail for the hordes of
Egypt and consign to the earth below both
her and the daughters of mighty nations,
with those who go down to the pit.[f] 19 Say to
them, 'Are you more favored than others?
Go down and be laid among the uncircum-
cised.'[g] 20 They will fall among those killed
by the sword. The sword is drawn; let her
be dragged off with all her hordes. 21 From
within the grave[b][h] the mighty leaders will
say of Egypt and her allies, 'They have come
down and they lie with the uncircumcised,
with those killed by the sword.'

22 "Assyria is there with her whole army;
she is surrounded by the graves of all her
slain, all who have fallen by the sword.
23 Their graves are in the depths of the pit[i]
and her army lies around her grave. All who
had spread terror in the land of the living
are slain, fallen by the sword.

24 "Elam is there, with all her hordes
around her grave. All of them are slain,
fallen by the sword.[j] All who had spread
terror in the land of the living went down
uncircumcised to the earth below. They
bear their shame with those who go down
to the pit. 25 A bed is made for her among the
slain, with all her hordes around her grave.
All of them are uncircumcised, killed by the
sword. Because their terror had spread in
the land of the living, they bear their shame
with those who go down to the pit; they are
laid among the slain.

26 "Meshech and Tubal[k] are there, with all
their hordes around their graves. All of them
are uncircumcised, killed by the sword be-
cause they spread their terror in the land of
the living. 27 Do they not lie with the other
uncircumcised warriors who have fallen,
who went down to the grave with their weap-
ons of war, whose swords were placed under
their heads? The punishment for their sins

- 32:15 d Ex 7:5; Eze 6:7
- 32:16 e 2Ch 35:25
- 32:18 f Eze 31:14,16
- 32:19 g Eze 28:10; 31:18
- 32:21 h Isa 14:9
- 32:23 i Isa 14:15
- 32:24 j Jer 49:37
- 32:26 k Eze 27:13

[a] 9 Hebrew; Septuagint *bring you into captivity among the nations, / to* [b] 21 Hebrew *Sheol*; also in verse 27

**32:29**
l Isa 34:5–15
m Eze 25:12–14
**32:30**
n Eze 38:6; 39:2
**32:31**
o Eze 31:16
**33:2**
p Eze 3:11
**33:4**
q Eze 18:13; Ac 18:6

rested on their bones, though the terror of these warriors had stalked through the land of the living.

28“You too, O Pharaoh, will be broken and will lie among the uncircumcised, with those killed by the sword.

29“Edom[l] is there, her kings and all her princes; despite their power, they are laid with those killed by the sword. They lie with the uncircumcised, with those who go down to the pit.[m]

30“All the princes of the north[n] and all the Sidonians are there; they went down with the slain in disgrace despite the terror caused by their power. They lie uncircumcised with those killed by the sword and bear their shame with those who go down to the pit.

31“Pharaoh—he and all his army—will see them and he will be consoled[o] for all his hordes that were killed by the sword, declares the Sovereign LORD. 32Although I had him spread terror in the land of the living, Pharaoh and all his hordes will be laid among the uncircumcised, with those killed by the sword, declares the Sovereign LORD.”

## Ezekiel a Watchman

33 The word of the LORD came to me: 2“Son of man, speak to your countrymen and say to them: ‘When I bring the sword against a land, and the people of the land choose one of their men and make him their watchman,[p] 3and he sees the sword coming against the land and blows the trumpet to warn the people, 4then if anyone hears the trumpet but does not take warning and the sword comes and takes his life, his blood will be on his own head.[q] 5Since he heard the sound of the trumpet but did not take warning, his blood will be on his own head. If he had taken warning, he would have saved himself. 6But if the watchman sees the sword coming and does not blow the trumpet to warn the people and the sword comes and takes the life of one of them, that man will be taken away because of his sin, but I will hold the watchman accountable for his blood.’

7“Son of man, I have made you a watchman for the house of Israel; so hear the word I speak and give them warning from me.[r] 8When I say to the wicked, ‘O wicked man, you will surely die,’ and you do not speak out to dissuade him from his ways, that wicked man will die for[a] his sin, and I will hold you accountable for his blood. 9But if you do warn the wicked man to turn from his ways and he does not do so, he will die for his sin, but you will have saved yourself.

10“Son of man, say to the house of Israel, ‘This is what you are saying: “Our offenses and sins weigh us down, and we are wasting away[s] because of[b] them. How then can we live?”’ 11Say to them, ‘As surely as I live, declares the Sovereign LORD, I take no pleasure in the death of the wicked, but rather that they turn from their ways and live.[t] Turn! Turn from your evil ways! Why will you die, O house of Israel?’

*God,*

*help me to recognize that misfortune is only temporary, that from it and through it I can be drawn closer to you. Bring into my life those who need an encouraging word or a word of testimony during their own trials.*

*Amen*

EZEKIEL 33:10–11

12“Therefore, son of man, say to your countrymen, ‘The righteousness of the righteous man will not save him when he disobeys, and the wickedness of the wicked man will not cause him to fall when he turns from it. The righteous man, if he sins, will not be allowed to live because of his former righteousness.’[u] 13If I tell the righteous man that he will surely live, but then he trusts in his righteousness and does evil, none of the righteous things he has done will be remembered; he will die for the evil he has done.[v] 14And if I say to the wicked man, ‘You will surely die,’ but he then turns away from his sin and does what is just[w] and right— 15if

**33:7**
r Eze 3:17
**33:10**
s Eze 24:23
**33:11**
t Eze 18:32; 2Pe 3:9
**33:12**
u 2Ch 7:14; Eze 3:20
**33:13**
v Eze 18:24
**33:14**
w Eze 18:27

[a]8 Or *in*; also in verse 9 [b]10 Or *away in*

he gives back what he took in pledge for a
loan, returns what he has stolen,[x] follows
the decrees that give life, and does no evil,
he will surely live; he will not die.[y] 16None
of the sins he has committed will be remem-
bered against him. He has done what is just
and right; he will surely live.[z]

17"Yet your countrymen say, 'The way of
the Lord is not just.' But it is their way that is
not just. 18If a righteous man turns from his
righteousness and does evil, he will die for
it.[a] 19And if a wicked man turns away from
his wickedness and does what is just and
right, he will live by doing so. 20Yet, O house
of Israel, you say, 'The way of the Lord is not
just.' But I will judge each of you according
to his own ways."

## Jerusalem's Fall Explained

21In the twelfth year of our exile, in the
tenth month on the fifth day, a man who
had escaped from Jerusalem came to me
and said, "The city has fallen![b]" 22Now the
evening before the man arrived, the hand of
the LORD was upon me,[c] and he opened my
mouth before the man came to me in the
morning. So my mouth was opened and I
was no longer silent.[d]

23Then the word of the LORD came to me:
24"Son of man, the people living in those
ruins in the land of Israel are saying, 'Abra-
ham was only one man, yet he possessed the
land. But we are many; surely the land has
been given to us as our possession.'[e] 25There-
fore say to them, 'This is what the Sover-
eign LORD says: Since you eat meat with the
blood[f] still in it and look to your idols and
shed blood, should you then possess the
land?[g] 26You rely on your sword, you do de-
testable things, and each of you defiles his
neighbor's wife. Should you then possess
the land?'

27"Say this to them: 'This is what the Sov-
ereign LORD says: As surely as I live, those
who are left in the ruins will fall by the
sword, those out in the country I will give
to the wild animals to be devoured, and
those in strongholds and caves will die of
a plague.[h] 28I will make the land a desolate
waste, and her proud strength will come
to an end, and the mountains of Israel will
become desolate so that no one will cross
them. 29Then they will know that I am the
LORD, when I have made the land a desolate
waste because of all the detestable things
they have done.'

30"As for you, son of man, your country-
men are talking together about you by the
walls and at the doors of the houses, saying
to each other, 'Come and hear the message
that has come from the LORD.' 31My people
come to you, as they usually do, and sit be-
fore you to listen to your words, but they
do not put them into practice. With their
mouths they express devotion, but their
hearts are greedy for unjust gain.[i] 32Indeed,
to them you are nothing more than one who
sings love songs with a beautiful voice and
plays an instrument well, for they hear your
words but do not put them into practice.

33"When all this comes true—and it
surely will—then they will know that a
prophet has been among them.[j]"

## Shepherds and Sheep

34 The word of the LORD came to me:
2"Son of man, prophesy against
the shepherds of Israel; prophesy and say
to them: 'This is what the Sovereign LORD
says: Woe to the shepherds of Israel who
only take care of themselves! Should not
shepherds take care of the flock?[k] 3You eat
the curds, clothe yourselves with the wool
and slaughter the choice animals, but you
do not take care of the flock.[l] 4You have not
strengthened the weak or healed the sick or
bound up the injured. You have not brought
back the strays or searched for the lost. You
have ruled them harshly and brutally.[m] 5So
they were scattered because there was no
shepherd, and when they were scattered
they became food for all the wild animals.
6My sheep wandered over all the mountains
and on every high hill. They were scattered
over the whole earth, and no one searched
or looked for them.

7"'Therefore, you shepherds, hear the
word of the LORD: 8As surely as I live, de-
clares the Sovereign LORD, because my
flock lacks a shepherd and so has been plun-
dered and has become food for all the wild
animals, and because my shepherds did
not search for my flock but cared for them-
selves rather than for my flock, 9therefore,

**33:15** x Lev 6:2–5 y Eze 20:11
**33:16** z Eze 18:22
**33:18** a Eze 18:26
**33:21** b 2Ki 25:4,10
**33:22** c Eze 1:3 d Eze 24:27
**33:24** e Isa 51:2; Ac 7:5
**33:25** f Dt 12:16 g Eze 22:6,27
**33:27** h 1Sa 13:6
**33:31** i Ps 78:36–37; Isa 29:13
**33:33** j 1Sa 3:20
**34:2** k Jer 23:1; Jn 10:11
**34:3** l Isa 56:11; Eze 22:27; Zec 11:16
**34:4** m Zec 11:15–17

**34:10** n Jer 21:13 o 1Sa 2:29–30
**34:12** p Eze 30:3
**34:14** q Ps 23:2
**34:16** r Isa 10:16; Lk 5:32
**34:17** s Mt 25:32–33
**34:21** t Dt 33:17

O shepherds, hear the word of the LORD:
10 This is what the Sovereign LORD says: I am
against[n] the shepherds and will hold them
accountable for my flock. I will remove them
from tending the flock so that the shepherds
can no longer feed themselves. I will rescue
my flock from their mouths, and it will no
longer be food for them.[o]
11 "'For this is what the Sovereign LORD
says: I myself will search for my sheep and
look after them. 12 As a shepherd looks after
his scattered flock when he is with them,
so will I look after my sheep. I will rescue
them from all the places where they were
scattered on a day of clouds and darkness.[p]
13 I will bring them out from the nations and
gather them from the countries, and I will
bring them into their own land. I will pas-
ture them on the mountains of Israel, in
the ravines and in all the settlements in the
land. 14 I will tend them in a good pasture,
and the mountain heights of Israel will be
their grazing land. There they will lie down
in good grazing land, and there they will
feed in a rich pasture[q] on the mountains
of Israel. 15 I myself will tend my sheep and
have them lie down, declares the Sovereign
LORD. 16 I will search for the lost and bring
back the strays. I will bind up the injured
and strengthen the weak, but the sleek and
the strong I will destroy. I will shepherd the
flock with justice.[r]
17 "'As for you, my flock, this is what the
Sovereign LORD says: I will judge between
one sheep and another, and between rams
and goats.[s] 18 Is it not enough for you to feed
on the good pasture? Must you also trample
the rest of your pasture with your feet? Is
it not enough for you to drink clear water?
Must you also muddy the rest with your
feet? 19 Must my flock feed on what you have
trampled and drink what you have muddied
with your feet?
20 "'Therefore this is what the Sovereign
LORD says to them: See, I myself will judge
between the fat sheep and the lean sheep.
21 Because you shove with flank and shoul-
der, butting all the weak sheep with your
horns[t] until you have driven them away,
22 I will save my flock, and they will no lon-
ger be plundered. I will judge between one
sheep and another. 23 I will place over them
one shepherd, my servant David, and he will
tend[u] them; he will tend them and be their
shepherd. 24 I the LORD will be their God,
and my servant David will be prince among
them. I the LORD have spoken.
25 "'I will make a covenant of peace with
them and rid the land of wild beasts so that
they may live in the desert and sleep in the
forests in safety.[v] 26 I will bless them and
the places surrounding my hill.[a] I will send
down showers in season; there will be show-
ers of blessing. 27 The trees of the field will
yield their fruit and the ground will yield
its crops; the people will be secure in their
land. They will know that I am the LORD,
when I break the bars of their yoke and
rescue them from the hands of those who
enslaved them. 28 They will no longer be plun-
dered by the nations, nor will wild animals
devour them. They will live in safety, and no
one will make them afraid.[w] 29 I will provide
for them a land renowned for its crops, and
they will no longer be victims of famine[x] in
the land or bear the scorn[y] of the nations.
30 Then they will know that I, the LORD their
God, am with them and that they, the house
of Israel, are my people, declares the Sover-
eign LORD. 31 You my sheep, the sheep of my
pasture,[z] are people, and I am your God, de-
clares the Sovereign LORD.'"

## A Prophecy Against Edom

35 The word of the LORD came to me:
2 "Son of man, set your face against
Mount Seir; prophesy against it 3 and say:
'This is what the Sovereign LORD says: I am
against you, Mount Seir, and I will stretch
out my hand[a] against you and make you a
desolate waste. 4 I will turn your towns into
ruins and you will be desolate. Then you
will know that I am the LORD.
5 "'Because you harbored an ancient
hostility and delivered the Israelites over
to the sword at the time of their calamity,
the time their punishment reached its cli-
max,[b] 6 therefore as surely as I live, declares
the Sovereign LORD, I will give you over to
bloodshed and it will pursue you. Since you
did not hate bloodshed, bloodshed will pur-
sue you. 7 I will make Mount Seir a desolate

**34:23** u Isa 40:11
**34:25** v Isa 11:6–9; Hos 2:18
**34:28** w Jer 30:10
**34:29** x Eze 36:29 y Eze 36:6
**34:31** z Ps 100:3
**35:3** a Jer 6:12
**35:5** b Eze 21:29

[a]26 Or *I will make them and the places surrounding my hill a blessing*

waste and cut off from it all who come and
go. 8I will fill your mountains with the slain;
those killed by the sword will fall on your
hills and in your valleys and in all your ra-
vines. 9I will make you desolate forever;
your towns will not be inhabited. Then you
will know that I am the LORD.[c]
10" 'Because you have said, "These two
nations and countries will be ours and we
will take possession of them," even though
I the LORD was there, 11therefore as surely
as I live, declares the Sovereign LORD, I will
treat you in accordance with the anger and
jealousy you showed in your hatred of them
and I will make myself known among them
when I judge you.[d] 12Then you will know
that I the LORD have heard all the contempt-
ible things you have said against the moun-
tains of Israel. You said, "They have been
laid waste and have been given over to us
to devour." 13You boasted against me and
spoke against me without restraint, and I
heard it. 14This is what the Sovereign LORD
says: While the whole earth rejoices, I will
make you desolate.[e] 15Because you rejoiced
when the inheritance of the house of Israel
became desolate, that is how I will treat you.
You will be desolate, O Mount Seir, you and
all of Edom.[f] Then they will know that I am
the LORD.' "

## A Prophecy to the Mountains of Israel

36 "Son of man, prophesy to the moun-
tains of Israel and say, 'O mountains
of Israel, hear the word of the LORD. 2This is
what the Sovereign LORD says: The enemy
said of you, "Aha![g] The ancient heights
have become our possession.[h]" ' 3Therefore
prophesy and say, 'This is what the Sover-
eign LORD says: Because they ravaged and
hounded you from every side so that you be-
came the possession of the rest of the nations
and the object of people's malicious talk and
slander, 4therefore, O mountains of Israel,
hear the word of the Sovereign LORD: This is
what the Sovereign LORD says to the moun-
tains and hills, to the ravines and valleys,
to the desolate ruins and the deserted towns
that have been plundered and ridiculed by
the rest of the nations around you[i]— 5this
is what the Sovereign LORD says: In my burn-
ing zeal I have spoken against the rest of the
nations, and against all Edom, for with glee
and with malice in their hearts they made
my land their own possession so that they
might plunder its pastureland.'[j] 6Therefore
prophesy concerning the land of Israel
and say to the mountains and hills, to the
ravines and valleys: 'This is what the Sover-
eign LORD says: I speak in my jealous wrath
because you have suffered the scorn of the
nations.[k] 7Therefore this is what the Sover-
eign LORD says: I swear with uplifted hand
that the nations around you will also suf-
fer scorn.
8" 'But you, O mountains of Israel, will
produce branches and fruit for my people
Israel, for they will soon come home. 9I
am concerned for you and will look on you
with favor; you will be plowed and sown,
10and I will multiply the number of people
upon you, even the whole house of Israel.
The towns will be inhabited and the ruins
rebuilt.[l] 11I will increase the number of men
and animals upon you, and they will be
fruitful and become numerous. I will settle
people on you as in the past and will make
you prosper more than before. Then you
will know that I am the LORD. 12I will cause
people, my people Israel, to walk upon you.
They will possess you, and you will be their
inheritance; you will never again deprive
them of their children.
13" 'This is what the Sovereign LORD says:
Because people say to you, "You devour
men[m] and deprive your nation of its chil-
dren," 14therefore you will no longer devour
men or make your nation childless, declares
the Sovereign LORD. 15No longer will I make
you hear the taunts of the nations, and no
longer will you suffer the scorn of the peo-
ples or cause your nation to fall, declares the
Sovereign LORD.[n]' "
16Again the word of the LORD came to me:
17"Son of man, when the people of Israel
were living in their own land, they defiled
it by their conduct and their actions. Their
conduct was like a woman's monthly un-
cleanness in my sight. 18So I poured out
my wrath on them because they had shed
blood in the land and because they had
defiled it with their idols. 19I dispersed
them among the nations, and they were

**35:9** c Jer 49:13
**35:11** d Ps 9:16; Mt 7:2
**35:14** e Jer 51:48
**35:15** f Jer 50:11–13
**36:2** g Eze 25:3 h Eze 35:10
**36:4** i Ps 79:4; Eze 34:28
**36:5** j Eze 35:10,15
**36:6** k Ps 123:3–4; Eze 34:29
**36:10** l ver 33
**36:13** m Nu 13:32
**36:15** n Eze 34:29

**36:19** o Eze 39:24
**36:20** p Ro 2:24; q Isa 52:5
**36:21** r Ps 74:18
**36:23** s Eze 20:41
**36:24** t Eze 34:13; 37:21
**36:25** u Heb 10:22; v Zec 13:2
**36:26** w Eze 11:19
**36:28** x Eze 37:14,27
**36:29** y Eze 34:29
**36:30** z Eze 34:27
**36:31** a Eze 20:43

scattered through the countries; I judged them according to their conduct and their actions.[o] 20 And wherever they went among the nations they profaned[p] my holy name, for it was said of them, 'These are the LORD's people, and yet they had to leave his land.'[q] 21 I had concern for my holy name, which the house of Israel profaned among the nations where they had gone.[r]

22 "Therefore say to the house of Israel, 'This is what the Sovereign LORD says: It is not for your sake, O house of Israel, that I am going to do these things, but for the sake of my holy name, which you have profaned among the nations where you have gone. 23 I will show the holiness of my great name, which has been profaned among the nations, the name you have profaned among them. Then the nations will know that I am the LORD, declares the Sovereign LORD, when I show myself holy[s] through you before their eyes.

24 " 'For I will take you out of the nations; I will gather you from all the countries and bring you back into your own land.[t] 25 I will sprinkle[u] clean water on you, and you will be clean; I will cleanse you from all your impurities and from all your idols.[v] 26 I will give you a new heart and put a new spirit in you; I will remove from you your heart of stone and give you a heart of flesh.[w] 27 And I will put my Spirit in you and move you to follow my decrees and be careful to keep my laws. 28 You will live in the land I gave your forefathers; you will be my people, and I will be your God.[x] 29 I will save you from all your uncleanness. I will call for the grain and make it plentiful and will not bring famine[y] upon you. 30 I will increase the fruit of the trees and the crops of the field, so that you will no longer suffer disgrace among the nations because of famine.[z] 31 Then you will remember your evil ways and wicked deeds, and you will loathe yourselves for your sins and detestable practices.[a] 32 I want you to know that I am not doing this for your sake, declares the Sovereign LORD. Be ashamed and disgraced for your conduct, O house of Israel!

33 " 'This is what the Sovereign LORD says: On the day I cleanse you from all your sins, I will resettle your towns, and the ruins will be rebuilt. 34 The desolate land will be cultivated instead of lying desolate in the sight of all who pass through it. 35 They will say, "This land that was laid waste has become like the garden of Eden;[b] the cities that were lying in ruins, desolate and destroyed, are now fortified and inhabited."[c] 36 Then the nations around you that remain will know that I the LORD have rebuilt what was destroyed and have replanted what was desolate. I the LORD have spoken, and I will do it.'[d]

37 "This is what the Sovereign LORD says: Once again I will yield to the plea of the house of Israel and do this for them: I will make their people as numerous as sheep, 38 as numerous as the flocks for offerings at Jerusalem during her appointed feasts. So will the ruined cities be filled with flocks of people. Then they will know that I am the LORD."

## The Valley of Dry Bones

37 The hand of the LORD was upon me,[e] and he brought me out by the Spirit[f] of the LORD and set me in the middle of a valley; it was full of bones. 2 He led me back and forth among them, and I saw a great many bones on the floor of the valley, bones that were very dry. 3 He asked me, "Son of man, can these bones live?"

I said, "O Sovereign LORD, you alone know.[g]"

4 Then he said to me, "Prophesy to these bones and say to them, 'Dry bones, hear the word of the LORD! 5 This is what the Sovereign LORD says to these bones: I will make breath[a] enter you, and you will come to life.[h] 6 I will attach tendons to you and make flesh come upon you and cover you with skin; I will put breath in you, and you will come to life. Then you will know that I am the LORD.[i]' "

7 So I prophesied as I was commanded. And as I was prophesying, there was a noise, a rattling sound, and the bones came together, bone to bone. 8 I looked, and tendons and flesh appeared on them and skin covered them, but there was no breath in them.

**36:35** b Joel 2:3; c Isa 51:3
**36:36** d Eze 22:14; 37:14
**37:1** e Eze 1:3; 8:3; f Eze 11:24
**37:3** g Dt 32:39; 1Sa 2:6
**37:5** h Ps 104:29–30
**37:6** i Joel 2:27; 3:17

[a]5 The Hebrew for this word can also mean *wind* or *spirit* (see verses 6–14).

**37:9** j Ps 104:30
**37:10** k Rev 11:11
**37:12** l Isa 26:19; Hos 13:14
**37:14** m Eze 36:27–28,36
**37:16** n Nu 17:2–3; 2Ch 15:9
**37:18** o Eze 24:19
**37:21** p Eze 36:24; 39:27

9Then he said to me, "Prophesy to the
breath;[j] prophesy, son of man, and say to it,
'This is what the Sovereign LORD says: Come
from the four winds, O breath, and breathe
into these slain, that they may live.' " 10So
I prophesied as he commanded me, and
breath entered them; they came to life and
stood up on their feet—a vast army.[k]

11Then he said to me: "Son of man, these
bones are the whole house of Israel. They
say, 'Our bones are dried up and our hope is
gone; we are cut off.' 12Therefore prophesy
and say to them: 'This is what the Sovereign
LORD says: O my people, I am going to open
your graves and bring you up from them;
I will bring you back to the land of Israel.[l]
13Then you, my people, will know that I am
the LORD, when I open your graves and bring
you up from them. 14I will put my Spirit in
you and you will live, and I will settle you
in your own land. Then you will know that
I the LORD have spoken, and I have done it,
declares the LORD.[m]' "

## One Nation Under One King

15The word of the LORD came to me: 16"Son
of man, take a stick of wood and write on
it, 'Belonging to Judah and the Israelites
associated with him.[n]' Then take another
stick of wood, and write on it, 'Ephraim's
stick, belonging to Joseph and all the house
of Israel associated with him.' 17Join them
together into one stick so that they will become one in your hand.

18"When your countrymen ask you,
'Won't you tell us what you mean by this?'[o]
19say to them, 'This is what the Sovereign
LORD says: I am going to take the stick of
Joseph—which is in Ephraim's hand—and
of the Israelite tribes associated with him,
and join it to Judah's stick, making them a
single stick of wood, and they will become
one in my hand.' 20Hold before their eyes
the sticks you have written on 21and say
to them, 'This is what the Sovereign LORD
says: I will take the Israelites out of the nations where they have gone. I will gather
them from all around and bring them back
into their own land.[p] 22I will make them
one nation in the land, on the mountains
of Israel. There will be one king over all
of them and they will never again be two
nations or be divided into two kingdoms.[q]
23They will no longer defile[r] themselves
with their idols and vile images or with
any of their offenses, for I will save them
from all their sinful backsliding,[a] and I will
cleanse them. They will be my people, and I
will be their God.[s]

24" 'My servant David will be king over
them, and they will all have one shepherd.[t]
They will follow my laws and be careful to
keep my decrees. 25They will live in the land
I gave to my servant Jacob, the land where
your fathers lived. They and their children
and their children's children will live there
forever, and David my servant will be their
prince forever. 26I will make a covenant of
peace[u] with them; it will be an everlasting
covenant. I will establish them and increase
their numbers, and I will put my sanctuary
among them forever. 27My dwelling place[v]
will be with them; I will be their God, and
they will be my people.[w] 28Then the nations will know that I the LORD make Israel
holy,[x] when my sanctuary is among them
forever.' "

*My daughter,*

*I have made a covenant with you,*
*and I'll always keep my part of the*
*deal. Will you keep your part?*

*God*

EZEKIEL 37:24–28

## A Prophecy Against Gog

38 The word of the LORD came to me:
2"Son of man, set your face against
Gog, of the land of Magog, the chief prince
of[b] Meshech and Tubal;[y] prophesy against
him 3and say: 'This is what the Sovereign
LORD says: I am against you, O Gog, chief
prince of[c] Meshech and Tubal. 4I will turn

**37:22** q Jer 3:18
**37:23** r Eze 36:25 s Eze 36:28
**37:24** t Isa 40:11; Eze 34:23
**37:26** u Isa 55:3
**37:27** v Jn 1:14 w 2Co 6:16*
**37:28** x Eze 20:12
**38:2** y Rev 20:8

[a]23 Many Hebrew manuscripts (see also Septuagint); most Hebrew manuscripts *all their dwelling places where they sinned*
[b]2 Or *the prince of Rosh,* [c]3 Or *Gog, prince of Rosh,*

**38:6** z Ge 10:2; a Eze 27:14
**38:9** b Isa 28:2
**38:11** c Jer 49:31
**38:13** d Eze 27:22
**38:15** e Eze 39:2

you around, put hooks in your jaws and bring you out with your whole army—your horses, your horsemen fully armed, and a great horde with large and small shields, all of them brandishing their swords. 5 Persia, Cush[a] and Put will be with them, all with shields and helmets, 6 also Gomer[z] with all its troops, and Beth Togarmah[a] from the far north with all its troops—the many nations with you.

7 " 'Get ready; be prepared, you and all the hordes gathered about you, and take command of them. 8 After many days you will be called to arms. In future years you will invade a land that has recovered from war, whose people were gathered from many nations to the mountains of Israel, which had long been desolate. They had been brought out from the nations, and now all of them live in safety. 9 You and all your troops and the many nations with you will go up, advancing like a storm;[b] you will be like a cloud covering the land.

10 " 'This is what the Sovereign LORD says: On that day thoughts will come into your mind and you will devise an evil scheme. 11 You will say, "I will invade a land of unwalled villages; I will attack a peaceful and unsuspecting people—all of them living without walls and without gates and bars.[c] 12 I will plunder and loot and turn my hand against the resettled ruins and the people gathered from the nations, rich in livestock and goods, living at the center of the land." 13 Sheba[d] and Dedan and the merchants of Tarshish and all her villages[b] will say to you, "Have you come to plunder? Have you gathered your hordes to loot, to carry off silver and gold, to take away livestock and goods and to seize much plunder?" '

14 "Therefore, son of man, prophesy and say to Gog: 'This is what the Sovereign LORD says: In that day, when my people Israel are living in safety, will you not take notice of it? 15 You will come from your place in the far north, you and many nations with you, all of them riding on horses, a great horde, a mighty army.[e] 16 You will advance against my people Israel like a cloud that covers the land. In days to come, O Gog, I will bring you against my land, so that the nations may know me when I show myself holy through you before their eyes.

17 " 'This is what the Sovereign LORD says: Are you not the one I spoke of in former days by my servants the prophets of Israel? At that time they prophesied for years that I would bring you against them. 18 This is what will happen in that day: When Gog attacks the land of Israel, my hot anger will be aroused, declares the Sovereign LORD. 19 In my zeal and fiery wrath I declare that at that time there shall be a great earthquake in the land of Israel.[f] 20 The fish of the sea, the birds of the air, the beasts of the field, every creature that moves along the ground, and all the people on the face of the earth will tremble at my presence. The mountains will be overturned, the cliffs will crumble and every wall will fall to the ground.[g] 21 I will summon a sword[h] against Gog on all my mountains, declares the Sovereign LORD. Every man's sword will be against his brother.[i] 22 I will execute judgment[j] upon him with plague and bloodshed; I will pour down torrents of rain, hailstones[k] and burning sulfur on him and on his troops and on the many nations with him. 23 And so I will show my greatness and my holiness, and I will make myself known in the sight of many nations. Then they will know that I am the LORD.'

**39** "Son of man, prophesy against Gog and say: 'This is what the Sovereign LORD says: I am against you, O Gog, chief prince of[c] Meshech and Tubal.[l] 2 I will turn you around and drag you along. I will bring you from the far north and send you against the mountains of Israel. 3 Then I will strike your bow[m] from your left hand and make your arrows drop from your right hand. 4 On the mountains of Israel you will fall, you and all your troops and the nations with you. I will give you as food to all kinds of carrion birds and to the wild animals.[n] 5 You will fall in the open field, for I have spoken, declares the Sovereign LORD. 6 I will send fire[o] on Magog and on those who live in safety in the coastlands, and they will know that I am the LORD.

7 " 'I will make known my holy name among my people Israel. I will no longer let my holy name be profaned, and the nations

**38:19** f Hag 2:6,21
**38:20** g Hos 4:3
**38:21** h Eze 14:17; i 1Sa 14:20
**38:22** j Isa 66:16; Jer 25:31; k Rev 16:21
**39:1** l Eze 38:2,3
**39:3** m Hos 1:5
**39:4** n Eze 33:27
**39:6** o Am 1:4

[a] 5 That is, the upper Nile region [b] 13 Or *her strong lions* [c] 1 Or *Gog, prince of Rosh,*

**39:7** p Eze 36:16,23
**39:9** q Ps 46:9
**39:10** r Isa 14:2
**39:13** s Eze 28:22
**39:17** t Rev 19:17
**39:18** u Ps 22:12

will know that I the LORD am the Holy One in Israel.[p] 8 It is coming! It will surely take place, declares the Sovereign LORD. This is the day I have spoken of.

9 "'Then those who live in the towns of Israel will go out and use the weapons for fuel and burn them up—the small and large shields, the bows and arrows, the war clubs and spears. For seven years they will use them for fuel.[q] 10 They will not need to gather wood from the fields or cut it from the forests, because they will use the weapons for fuel. And they will plunder those who plundered them and loot those who looted them, declares the Sovereign LORD.[r]

11 "'On that day I will give Gog a burial place in Israel, in the valley of those who travel east toward[a] the Sea.[b] It will block the way of travelers, because Gog and all his hordes will be buried there. So it will be called the Valley of Hamon Gog.[c]

12 "'For seven months the house of Israel will be burying them in order to cleanse the land. 13 All the people of the land will bury them, and the day I am glorified[s] will be a memorable day for them, declares the Sovereign LORD.

14 "'Men will be regularly employed to cleanse the land. Some will go throughout the land and, in addition to them, others will bury those that remain on the ground. At the end of the seven months they will begin their search. 15 As they go through the land and one of them sees a human bone, he will set up a marker beside it until the gravediggers have buried it in the Valley of Hamon Gog. 16 (Also a town called Hamonah[d] will be there.) And so they will cleanse the land.'

17 "Son of man, this is what the Sovereign LORD says: Call out to every kind of bird[t] and all the wild animals: 'Assemble and come together from all around to the sacrifice I am preparing for you, the great sacrifice on the mountains of Israel. There you will eat flesh and drink blood. 18 You will eat the flesh of mighty men and drink the blood of the princes of the earth as if they were rams and lambs, goats and bulls—all of them fattened animals from Bashan.[u] 19 At the sacrifice I am preparing for you, you will eat fat till you are glutted and drink blood till you are drunk. 20 At my table you will eat your fill of horses and riders, mighty men and soldiers of every kind,' declares the Sovereign LORD.[v]

21 "I will display my glory among the nations, and all the nations will see the punishment I inflict and the hand I lay upon them.[w] 22 From that day forward the house of Israel will know that I am the LORD their God. 23 And the nations will know that the people of Israel went into exile for their sin, because they were unfaithful to me. So I hid my face from them and handed them over to their enemies, and they all fell by the sword.[x] 24 I dealt with them according to their uncleanness and their offenses, and I hid my face from them.[y]

25 "Therefore this is what the Sovereign LORD says: I will now bring Jacob back from captivity[e][z] and will have compassion[a] on all the people of Israel, and I will be zealous for my holy name. 26 They will forget their shame and all the unfaithfulness they showed toward me when they lived in safety in their land with no one to make them afraid.[b] 27 When I have brought them back from the nations and have gathered them from the countries of their enemies, I will show myself holy through them in the sight of many nations.[c] 28 Then they will know that I am the LORD their God, for though I sent them into exile among the nations, I will gather them to their own land, not leaving any behind. 29 I will no longer hide my face from them, for I will pour out my Spirit[d] on the house of Israel, declares the Sovereign LORD."

## The New Temple Area

**40** In the twenty-fifth year of our exile, at the beginning of the year, on the tenth of the month, in the fourteenth year after the fall of the city—on that very day the hand of the LORD was upon me[e] and he took me there. 2 In visions[f] of God he took me to the land of Israel and set me on a very high mountain,[g] on whose south side were some buildings that looked like a city. 3 He

**39:20** v Rev 19:17–18
**39:21** w Eze 38:16
**39:23** x Isa 59:2
**39:24** y Eze 36:19
**39:25** z Eze 34:13 a Jer 30:18
**39:26** b Isa 17:2; Eze 34:28
**39:27** c Eze 36:23–24; 38:16
**39:29** d Joel 2:28; Ac 2:17
**40:1** e Eze 1:3
**40:2** f Da 7:1,7 g Rev 21:10

[a] 11 Or *of* [b] 11 That is, the Dead Sea [c] 11 *Hamon Gog* means *hordes of Gog.* [d] 16 *Hamonah* means *horde.* [e] 25 Or *now restore the fortunes of Jacob*

**40:3** h Eze 1:7; Da 10:6 i Eze 47:3; Rev 11:1; 21:15
**40:4** j Eze 44:5
**40:5** k Eze 42:20
**40:7** l ver 36

took me there, and I saw a man whose appearance was like bronze;[h] he was standing in the gateway with a linen cord and a measuring rod[i] in his hand. 4The man said to me, "Son of man, look with your eyes and hear with your ears and pay attention to everything I am going to show you, for that is why you have been brought here. Tell the house of Israel everything you see.[j]"

## The East Gate to the Outer Court

5I saw a wall completely surrounding the temple area. The length of the measuring rod in the man's hand was six long cubits, each of which was a cubit[a] and a handbreadth.[b] He measured[k] the wall; it was one measuring rod thick and one rod high.

6Then he went to the gate facing east. He climbed its steps and measured the threshold of the gate; it was one rod deep.[c] 7The alcoves[l] for the guards were one rod long and one rod wide, and the projecting walls between the alcoves were five cubits thick. And the threshold of the gate next to the portico facing the temple was one rod deep.

8Then he measured the portico of the gateway; 9it[d] was eight cubits deep and its jambs were two cubits thick. The portico of the gateway faced the temple.

10Inside the east gate were three alcoves on each side; the three had the same measurements, and the faces of the projecting walls on each side had the same measurements. 11Then he measured the width of the entrance to the gateway; it was ten cubits and its length was thirteen cubits. 12In front of each alcove was a wall one cubit high, and the alcoves were six cubits square. 13Then he measured the gateway from the top of the rear wall of one alcove to the top of the opposite one; the distance was twenty-five cubits from one parapet opening to the opposite one. 14He measured along the faces of the projecting walls all around the inside of the gateway—sixty cubits. The measurement was up to the portico[e] facing the courtyard.[f] 15The distance from the entrance of the gateway to the far end of its portico was fifty cubits. 16The alcoves and the projecting walls inside the gateway were surmounted by narrow parapet openings all around, as was the portico; the openings all around faced inward. The faces of the projecting walls were decorated with palm trees.

## The Outer Court

17Then he brought me into the outer court.[m] There I saw some rooms and a pavement that had been constructed all around the court; there were thirty rooms along the pavement. 18It abutted the sides of the gateways and was as wide as they were long; this was the lower pavement. 19Then he measured the distance from the inside of the lower gateway to the outside of the inner court; it was a hundred cubits on the east side as well as on the north.

## The North Gate

20Then he measured the length and width of the gate facing north, leading into the outer court. 21Its alcoves—three on each side—its projecting walls and its portico had the same measurements as those of the first gateway. It was fifty cubits long and twenty-five cubits wide. 22Its openings, its portico[n] and its palm tree decorations had the same measurements as those of the gate facing east. Seven steps led up to it, with its portico opposite them. 23There was a gate to the inner court facing the north gate, just as there was on the east. He measured from one gate to the opposite one; it was a hundred cubits.

## The South Gate

24Then he led me to the south side and I saw a gate facing south. He measured its jambs and its portico, and they had the same measurements as the others. 25The gateway and its portico had narrow openings all around, like the openings of the others. It was fifty cubits long and twenty-five cubits wide. 26Seven steps led up to it, with its portico opposite them; it had palm tree decorations on the faces of the projecting walls on each side.[o] 27The inner court also

**40:17** m Rev 11:2
**40:22** n ver 49
**40:26** o ver 22

[a]5 The common cubit was about 1 1/2 feet (about 0.5 meter). [b]5 That is, about 3 inches (about 8 centimeters) [c]6 Septuagint; Hebrew *deep, the first threshold, one rod deep* [d]8,9 Many Hebrew manuscripts, Septuagint, Vulgate and Syriac; most Hebrew manuscripts *gateway facing the temple; it was one rod deep. 9Then he measured the portico of the gateway; it* [e]14 Septuagint; Hebrew *projecting wall* [f]14 The meaning of the Hebrew for this verse is uncertain.

**40:30** p ver 21
**40:35** q Eze 44:4
**40:38** r 2Ch 4:6; Eze 42:13
**40:39** s Lev 4:3,28 t Lev 7:1

had a gate facing south, and he measured from this gate to the outer gate on the south side; it was a hundred cubits.

## Gates to the Inner Court

[28]Then he brought me into the inner court through the south gate, and he measured the south gate; it had the same measurements as the others. [29]Its alcoves, its projecting walls and its portico had the same measurements as the others. The gateway and its portico had openings all around. It was fifty cubits long and twenty-five cubits wide. [30](The porticoes[p] of the gateways around the inner court were twenty-five cubits wide and five cubits deep.) [31]Its portico faced the outer court; palm trees decorated its jambs, and eight steps led up to it.

[32]Then he brought me to the inner court on the east side, and he measured the gateway; it had the same measurements as the others. [33]Its alcoves, its projecting walls and its portico had the same measurements as the others. The gateway and its portico had openings all around. It was fifty cubits long and twenty-five cubits wide. [34]Its portico faced the outer court; palm trees decorated the jambs on either side, and eight steps led up to it.

[35]Then he brought me to the north gate[q] and measured it. It had the same measurements as the others, [36]as did its alcoves, its projecting walls and its portico, and it had openings all around. It was fifty cubits long and twenty-five cubits wide. [37]Its portico[a] faced the outer court; palm trees decorated the jambs on either side, and eight steps led up to it.

## The Rooms for Preparing Sacrifices

[38]A room with a doorway was by the portico in each of the inner gateways, where the burnt offerings[r] were washed. [39]In the portico of the gateway were two tables on each side, on which the burnt offerings, sin offerings[s] and guilt offerings[t] were slaughtered. [40]By the outside wall of the portico of the gateway, near the steps at the entrance to the north gateway were two tables, and on the other side of the steps were two tables. [41]So there were four tables on one side of the gateway and four on the other—eight tables in all—on which the sacrifices were slaughtered. [42]There were also four tables of dressed stone for the burnt offerings, each a cubit and a half long, a cubit and a half wide and a cubit high. On them were placed the utensils for slaughtering the burnt offerings and the other sacrifices. [43]And double-pronged hooks, each a handbreadth long, were attached to the wall all around. The tables were for the flesh of the offerings.

## Rooms for the Priests

[44]Outside the inner gate, within the inner court, were two rooms, one[b] at the side of the north gate and facing south, and another at the side of the south[c] gate and facing north. [45]He said to me, "The room facing south is for the priests who have charge of the temple,[u] [46]and the room facing north is for the priests who have charge of the altar.[v] These are the sons of Zadok,[w] who are the only Levites who may draw near to the LORD to minister before him.[x]"

[47]Then he measured the court: It was square—a hundred cubits long and a hundred cubits wide. And the altar was in front of the temple.

## The Temple

[48]He brought me to the portico of the temple and measured the jambs of the portico; they were five cubits wide on either side. The width of the entrance was fourteen cubits and its projecting walls were[d] three cubits wide on either side. [49]The portico[y] was twenty cubits wide, and twelve[e] cubits from front to back. It was reached by a flight of stairs,[f] and there were pillars on each side of the jambs.

# 41

Then the man brought me to the outer sanctuary and measured the jambs; the width of the jambs was six cubits[g] on each side.[h] [2]The entrance was ten cubits wide, and the projecting walls on each side of it were five cubits wide. He also measured

**40:45** u 1Ch 9:23
**40:46** v Nu 18:5 w 1Ki 2:35 x Eze 43:19; 44:15
**40:49** y 1Ki 6:3

[a]37 Septuagint (see also verses 31 and 34); Hebrew *jambs* [b]44 Septuagint; Hebrew *were rooms for singers, which were* [c]44 Septuagint; Hebrew *east* [d]48 Septuagint; Hebrew *entrance was* [e]49 Septuagint; Hebrew *eleven* [f]49 Hebrew; Septuagint *Ten steps led up to it* [g]1 The common cubit was about 1 1/2 feet (about 0.5 meter). [h]1 One Hebrew manuscript and Septuagint; most Hebrew manuscripts *side, the width of the tent*

41:2 z 2Ch 3:3
41:4 a 1Ki 6:20 b Heb 9:3–8
41:6 c 1Ki 6:5
41:7 d 1Ki 6:8
41:14 e Eze 40:47

the outer sanctuary; it was forty cubits long
and twenty cubits wide.[z]
3 Then he went into the inner sanctuary
and measured the jambs of the entrance;
each was two cubits wide. The entrance was
six cubits wide, and the projecting walls on
each side of it were seven cubits wide. 4 And
he measured the length of the inner sanctu-
ary; it was twenty cubits, and its width was
twenty cubits across the end of the outer
sanctuary.[a] He said to me, "This is the Most
Holy Place.[b]"
5 Then he measured the wall of the temple;
it was six cubits thick, and each side room
around the temple was four cubits wide.
6 The side rooms were on three levels, one
above another, thirty on each level. There
were ledges all around the wall of the tem-
ple to serve as supports for the side rooms,
so that the supports were not inserted into
the wall of the temple.[c] 7 The side rooms all
around the temple were wider at each suc-
cessive level. The structure surrounding the
temple was built in ascending stages, so that
the rooms widened as one went upward. A
stairway[d] went up from the lowest floor to
the top floor through the middle floor.
8 I saw that the temple had a raised base
all around it, forming the foundation of
the side rooms. It was the length of the
rod, six long cubits. 9 The outer wall of the
side rooms was five cubits thick. The open
area between the side rooms of the temple
10 and the ⌊priests'⌋ rooms was twenty cubits
wide all around the temple. 11 There were
entrances to the side rooms from the open
area, one on the north and another on the
south; and the base adjoining the open area
was five cubits wide all around.
12 The building facing the temple court-
yard on the west side was seventy cubits
wide. The wall of the building was five cu-
bits thick all around, and its length was
ninety cubits.
13 Then he measured the temple; it was a
hundred cubits long, and the temple court-
yard and the building with its walls were
also a hundred cubits long. 14 The width of
the temple courtyard on the east, including
the front of the temple, was a hundred cu-
bits.[e]
15 Then he measured the length of the
building facing the courtyard at the rear of
the temple, including its galleries on each
side; it was a hundred cubits.
The outer sanctuary, the inner sanc-
tuary and the portico facing the court,
16 as well as the thresholds and the narrow
windows and galleries around the three of
them—everything beyond and including
the threshold was covered with wood. The
floor, the wall up to the windows, and the
windows were covered.[f] 17 In the space above
the outside of the entrance to the inner sanc-
tuary and on the walls at regular intervals
all around the inner and outer sanctuary
18 were carved cherubim and palm trees.[g]
Palm trees alternated with cherubim. Each
cherub had two faces: 19 the face of a man to-
ward the palm tree on one side and the face
of a lion toward the palm tree on the other.
They were carved all around the whole tem-
ple.[h] 20 From the floor to the area above the
entrance, cherubim and palm trees were
carved on the wall of the outer sanctuary.
21 The outer sanctuary[i] had a rectangular
doorframe, and the one at the front of the
Most Holy Place was similar. 22 There was
a wooden altar[j] three cubits high and two
cubits square[a]; its corners, its base[b] and
its sides were of wood. The man said to me,
"This is the table[k] that is before the LORD."
23 Both the outer sanctuary[l] and the Most
Holy Place had double doors.[m] 24 Each door
had two leaves—two hinged leaves for each
door. 25 And on the doors of the outer sanc-
tuary were carved cherubim and palm trees
like those carved on the walls, and there
was a wooden overhang on the front of the
portico. 26 On the sidewalls of the portico
were narrow windows with palm trees
carved on each side. The side rooms of the
temple also had overhangs.[n]

## Rooms for the Priests

42 Then the man led me northward
into the outer court and brought
me to the rooms opposite the temple court-
yard[o] and opposite the outer wall on the
north side. 2 The building whose door faced
north was a hundred cubits[c] long and fifty
cubits wide. 3 Both in the section twenty cu-

41:16 f ver 25–26; 1Ki 6:15; Eze 42:3
41:18 g 1Ki 6:29; 7:36
41:19 h Eze 10:14
41:21 i ver 1
41:22 j Ex 30:1 k Eze 44:16; Mal 1:7,12
41:23 l ver 1 m 1Ki 6:32
41:26 n ver 15–16; Eze 40:16
42:1 o Eze 41:12–14

[a] 22 Septuagint; Hebrew *long* [b] 22 Septuagint; Hebrew *length* [c] 2 The common cubit was about 1 1/2 feet (about 0.5 meter).

42:3
p Eze 41:16
42:9
q Eze 44:5; 46:19
42:13
r Lev 10:17; 6:25
s Lev 6:29
42:14
t Eze 44:19
u Ex 29:9

bits from the inner court and in the section
opposite the pavement of the outer court,
gallery faced gallery at the three levels.[p] 4In
front of the rooms was an inner passageway
ten cubits wide and a hundred cubits[a] long.
Their doors were on the north. 5Now the up-
per rooms were narrower, for the galleries
took more space from them than from the
rooms on the lower and middle floors of the
building. 6The rooms on the third floor had
no pillars, as the courts had; so they were
smaller in floor space than those on the
lower and middle floors. 7There was an outer
wall parallel to the rooms and the outer
court; it extended in front of the rooms for
fifty cubits. 8While the row of rooms on the
side next to the outer court was fifty cubits
long, the row on the side nearest the sanctu-
ary was a hundred cubits long. 9The lower
rooms had an entrance[q] on the east side as
one enters them from the outer court.

10On the south side[b] along the length of
the wall of the outer court, adjoining the
temple courtyard and opposite the outer
wall, were rooms 11with a passageway in
front of them. These were like the rooms
on the north; they had the same length and
width, with similar exits and dimensions.
Similar to the doorways on the north 12were
the doorways of the rooms on the south.
There was a doorway at the beginning of
the passageway that was parallel to the cor-
responding wall extending eastward, by
which one enters the rooms.

13Then he said to me, "The north and
south rooms facing the temple courtyard
are the priests' rooms, where the priests
who approach the LORD will eat the most
holy offerings. There they will put the most
holy offerings—the grain offerings, the sin
offerings[r] and the guilt offerings—for the
place is holy.[s] 14Once the priests enter the
holy precincts, they are not to go into
the outer court until they leave behind the
garments[t] in which they minister, for these
are holy. They are to put on other clothes be-
fore they go near the places that are for
the people.[u]"

15When he had finished measuring what
was inside the temple area, he led me out
by the east gate and measured the area all
around: 16He measured the east side with
the measuring rod; it was five hundred cu-
bits.[c] 17He measured the north side; it was
five hundred cubits[d] by the measuring rod.
18He measured the south side; it was five hun-
dred cubits by the measuring rod. 19Then he
turned to the west side and measured; it was
five hundred cubits by the measuring rod.
20So he measured[v] the area on all four sides.
It had a wall around it, five hundred cubits
long and five hundred cubits wide,[w] to sepa-
rate the holy from the common.

## The Glory Returns to the Temple

43 Then the man brought me to the
gate facing east,[x] 2and I saw the
glory of the God of Israel coming from
the east. His voice was like the roar of rush-
ing waters,[y] and the land was radiant with
his glory.[z] 3The vision I saw was like the vi-
sion I had seen when he[e] came to destroy the
city and like the visions I had seen by the
Kebar River, and I fell facedown. 4The glory
of the LORD entered the temple through the
gate facing east.[a] 5Then the Spirit lifted me
up[b] and brought me into the inner court,
and the glory of the LORD filled the temple.

*Sister friend,*

*I want to be present and instrumental in your life. Please let me in.*

*Your God*

EZEKIEL 43:1–5

6While the man was standing beside me,
I heard someone speaking to me from inside
the temple. 7He said: "Son of man, this is the
place of my throne and the place for the soles
of my feet. This is where I will live among
the Israelites forever. The house of Israel
will never again defile my holy name—
neither they nor their kings—by their

42:20
v Eze 40:5
w Eze 45:2
43:1
x Eze 10:19; 46:1
43:2
y Rev 1:15
z Eze 11:23; Rev 18:1
43:4
a Eze 10:19
43:5
b Eze 8:3

[a]4 Septuagint and Syriac; Hebrew *and one cubit* [b]10 Septuagint; Hebrew *Eastward* [c]16 See Septuagint of verse 17; Hebrew *rods*; also in verses 18 and 19. [d]17 Septuagint; Hebrew *rods* [e]3 Some Hebrew manuscripts and Vulgate; most Hebrew manuscripts *I*

**43:7** c Lev 26:30
**43:11** d Eze 44:5
**43:12** e Eze 40:2
**43:17** f Ex 20:26
**43:18** g Lev 1:5,11

prostitution[a] and the lifeless idols[b] of their kings at their high places.[c] 8When they placed their threshold next to my threshold and their doorposts beside my doorposts, with only a wall between me and them, they defiled my holy name by their detestable practices. So I destroyed them in my anger. 9Now let them put away from me their prostitution and the lifeless idols of their kings, and I will live among them forever.

10"Son of man, describe the temple to the people of Israel, that they may be ashamed of their sins. Let them consider the plan, 11and if they are ashamed of all they have done, make known to them the design of the temple—its arrangement, its exits and entrances—its whole design and all its regulations[c] and laws. Write these down before them so that they may be faithful to its design and follow all its regulations.[d]

12"This is the law of the temple: All the surrounding area[e] on top of the mountain will be most holy. Such is the law of the temple.

## The Altar

13"These are the measurements of the altar in long cubits, that cubit being a cubit[d] and a handbreadth[e]: Its gutter is a cubit deep and a cubit wide, with a rim of one span[f] around the edge. And this is the height of the altar: 14From the gutter on the ground up to the lower ledge it is two cubits high and a cubit wide, and from the smaller ledge up to the larger ledge it is four cubits high and a cubit wide. 15The altar hearth is four cubits high, and four horns project upward from the hearth. 16The altar hearth is square, twelve cubits long and twelve cubits wide. 17The upper ledge also is square, fourteen cubits long and fourteen cubits wide, with a rim of half a cubit and a gutter of a cubit all around. The steps[f] of the altar face east."

18Then he said to me, "Son of man, this is what the Sovereign LORD says: These will be the regulations for sacrificing burnt offerings and sprinkling blood[g] upon the altar when it is built: 19You are to give a young bull[h] as a sin offering to the priests, who are Levites, of the family of Zadok,[i] who come near to minister before me, declares the Sovereign LORD. 20You are to take some of its blood and put it on the four horns of the altar and on the four corners of the upper ledge and all around the rim, and so purify the altar and make atonement for it. 21You are to take the bull for the sin offering and burn it in the designated part of the temple area outside the sanctuary.[j]

22"On the second day you are to offer a male goat without defect for a sin offering, and the altar is to be purified as it was purified with the bull. 23When you have finished purifying it, you are to offer a young bull and a ram from the flock, both without defect. 24You are to offer them before the LORD, and the priests are to sprinkle salt[k] on them and sacrifice them as a burnt offering to the LORD.

25"For seven days[l] you are to provide a male goat daily for a sin offering; you are also to provide a young bull and a ram from the flock, both without defect. 26For seven days they are to make atonement for the altar and cleanse it; thus they will dedicate it. 27At the end of these days, from the eighth day[m] on, the priests are to present your burnt offerings and fellowship offerings[g] on the altar. Then I will accept you, declares the Sovereign LORD."

## The Prince, the Levites, the Priests

**44** Then the man brought me back to the outer gate of the sanctuary, the one facing east, and it was shut. 2The LORD said to me, "This gate is to remain shut. It must not be opened; no one may enter through it.[n] It is to remain shut because the LORD, the God of Israel, has entered through it. 3The prince himself is the only one who may sit inside the gateway to eat in the presence of the LORD. He is to enter by way of the portico of the gateway and go out the same way.[o]"

4Then the man brought me by way of the north gate to the front of the temple. I

**43:19** h Eze 45:18–19 i Eze 44:15
**43:21** j Ex 29:14; Heb 13:11
**43:24** k Lev 2:13
**43:25** l Lev 8:33
**43:27** m Lev 9:1
**44:2** n Eze 43:4–5
**44:3** o Eze 46:2,8

[a]7 Or *their spiritual adultery*; also in verse 9 [b]7 Or *the corpses*; also in verse 9 [c]11 Some Hebrew manuscripts and Septuagint; most Hebrew manuscripts *regulations and its whole design* [d]13 The common cubit was about 1 1/2 feet (about 0.5 meter). [e]13 That is, about 3 inches (about 8 centimeters) [f]13 That is, about 9 inches (about 22 centimeters) [g]27 Traditionally *peace offerings*

44:4 p Eze 1:28; 3:23
44:5 q Eze 40:4
44:6 r Eze 3:9
44:7 s Lev 26:41 t Lev 22:25
44:10 u 2Ki 23:8
44:11 v 2Ch 29:34 w Nu 16:9
44:13 x Nu 18:3
44:14 y Nu 18:4
44:15 z Eze 40:46

looked and saw the glory of the LORD filling the temple of the LORD, and I fell facedown.[p]

5 The LORD said to me, "Son of man, look carefully, listen closely and give attention to everything I tell you concerning all the regulations regarding the temple of the LORD. Give attention to the entrance of the temple and all the exits of the sanctuary.[q] 6 Say to the rebellious house[r] of Israel, 'This is what the Sovereign LORD says: Enough of your detestable practices, O house of Israel! 7 In addition to all your other detestable practices, you brought foreigners uncircumcised in heart[s] and flesh into my sanctuary, desecrating my temple while you offered me food, fat and blood, and you broke my covenant.[t] 8 Instead of carrying out your duty in regard to my holy things, you put others in charge of my sanctuary. 9 This is what the Sovereign LORD says: No foreigner uncircumcised in heart and flesh is to enter my sanctuary, not even the foreigners who live among the Israelites.

10 " 'The Levites who went far from me when Israel went astray[u] and who wandered from me after their idols must bear the consequences of their sin. 11 They may serve in my sanctuary, having charge of the gates of the temple and serving in it; they may slaughter the burnt offerings[v] and sacrifices for the people and stand before the people and serve them.[w] 12 But because they served them in the presence of their idols and made the house of Israel fall into sin, therefore I have sworn with uplifted hand that they must bear the consequences of their sin, declares the Sovereign LORD. 13 They are not to come near to serve me as priests or come near any of my holy things or my most holy offerings; they must bear the shame of their detestable practices.[x] 14 Yet I will put them in charge of the duties of the temple and all the work that is to be done in it.[y]

15 " 'But the priests, who are Levites and descendants of Zadok and who faithfully carried out the duties of my sanctuary when the Israelites went astray from me, are to come near to minister before me; they are to stand before me to offer sacrifices of fat and blood, declares the Sovereign LORD.[z] 16 They alone are to enter my sanctuary; they alone are to come near my table to minister before me and perform my service.

17 " 'When they enter the gates of the inner court, they are to wear linen clothes; they must not wear any woolen garment while ministering at the gates of the inner court or inside the temple. 18 They are to wear linen turbans[a] on their heads and linen undergarments around their waists. They must not wear anything that makes them perspire. 19 When they go out into the outer court where the people are, they are to take off the clothes they have been ministering in and are to leave them in the sacred rooms, and put on other clothes, so that they do not consecrate[b] the people by means of their garments.[c]

20 " 'They must not shave their heads or let their hair grow long, but they are to keep the hair of their heads trimmed.[d] 21 No priest is to drink wine when he enters the inner court.[e] 22 They must not marry widows or divorced women; they may marry only virgins of Israelite descent or widows of priests.[f] 23 They are to teach my people the difference between the holy and the common and show them how to distinguish between the unclean and the clean.[g]

24 " 'In any dispute, the priests are to serve as judges[h] and decide it according to my ordinances. They are to keep my laws and my decrees for all my appointed feasts, and they are to keep my Sabbaths holy.

25 " 'A priest must not defile himself by going near a dead person; however, if the dead person was his father or mother, son or daughter, brother or unmarried sister, then he may defile himself. 26 After he is cleansed, he must wait seven days. 27 On the day he goes into the inner court of the sanctuary to minister in the sanctuary, he is to offer a sin offering for himself, declares the Sovereign LORD.

28 " 'I am to be the only inheritance[i] the priests have. You are to give them no possession in Israel; I will be their possession. 29 They will eat the grain offerings, the sin offerings and the guilt offerings; and everything in Israel devoted[a] to the LORD[j] will belong to them.[k] 30 The best of all the firstfruits and of all your special gifts will belong to

44:18 a Ex 28:39
44:19 b Eze 46:20 c Eze 42:14
44:20 d Lev 21:5
44:21 e Lev 10:9
44:22 f Lev 21:7
44:23 g Mal 2:7
44:24 h Dt 17:8–9
44:28 i Nu 18:20
44:29 j Lev 27:21 k Nu 18:9,14

[a] 29 The Hebrew term refers to the irrevocable giving over of things or persons to the LORD.

45:1
l Eze 47:21–22
m Eze 48:8–9,29

45:4
n Eze 48:10–11

45:5
o Eze 48:13

45:6
p Eze 48:15–18

45:7
q Eze 48:21

45:8
r Eze 46:18

45:9
s Jer 22:3

45:10
t Lev 19:36

the priests. You are to give them the first por-
tion of your ground meal so that a blessing
may rest on your household. 31 The priests
must not eat anything, bird or animal,
found dead or torn by wild animals.

## Division of the Land

45 "'When you allot the land as an
inheritance,[l] you are to present to
the LORD a portion of the land as a sacred
district, 25,000 cubits long and 20,000[a] cu-
bits wide; the entire area will be holy.[m] 2 Of
this, a section 500 cubits square is to be for
the sanctuary, with 50 cubits around it for
open land. 3 In the sacred district, measure
off a section 25,000 cubits[b] long and 10,000
cubits[c] wide. In it will be the sanctuary, the
Most Holy Place. 4 It will be the sacred por-
tion of the land for the priests, who minis-
ter in the sanctuary and who draw near to
minister before the LORD. It will be a place
for their houses as well as a holy place for
the sanctuary.[n] 5 An area 25,000 cubits long
and 10,000 cubits wide will belong to the Le-
vites, who serve in the temple, as their pos-
session for towns to live in.[d][o]

6 "'You are to give the city as its property
an area 5,000 cubits wide and 25,000 cubits
long, adjoining the sacred portion; it will be-
long to the whole house of Israel.[p]

7 "'The prince will have the land border-
ing each side of the area formed by the sa-
cred district and the property of the city. It
will extend westward from the west side and
eastward from the east side, running length-
wise from the western to the eastern border
parallel to one of the tribal portions.[q] 8 This
land will be his possession in Israel. And my
princes will no longer oppress my people
but will allow the house of Israel to possess
the land according to their tribes.[r]

9 "'This is what the Sovereign LORD says:
You have gone far enough, O princes of
Israel! Give up your violence and oppres-
sion and do what is just and right.[s] Stop
dispossessing my people, declares the Sover-
eign LORD. 10 You are to use accurate scales,
an accurate ephah[e][t] and an accurate bath.[f]
11 The ephah and the bath are to be the same
size, the bath containing a tenth of a homer[g]
and the ephah a tenth of a homer; the ho-
mer is to be the standard measure for both.
12 The shekel[h] is to consist of twenty gerahs.[u]
Twenty shekels plus twenty-five shekels plus
fifteen shekels equal one mina.[i]

## Offerings and Holy Days

13 "'This is the special gift you are to of-
fer: a sixth of an ephah from each homer
of wheat and a sixth of an ephah from each
homer of barley. 14 The prescribed portion
of oil, measured by the bath, is a tenth of
a bath from each cor (which consists of
ten baths or one homer, for ten baths are
equivalent to a homer). 15 Also one sheep is
to be taken from every flock of two hundred
from the well-watered pastures of Israel.
These will be used for the grain offerings,
burnt offerings[v] and fellowship offerings[j]
to make atonement for the people, declares
the Sovereign LORD. 16 All the people of the
land will participate in this special gift for
the use of the prince in Israel. 17 It will be
the duty of the prince to provide the burnt
offerings, grain offerings and drink offer-
ings at the festivals, the New Moons and the
Sabbaths—at all the appointed feasts of the
house of Israel. He will provide the sin offer-
ings, grain offerings, burnt offerings and
fellowship offerings to make atonement for
the house of Israel.

18 "'This is what the Sovereign LORD says:
In the first month on the first day you are to
take a young bull without defect and purify
the sanctuary. 19 The priest is to take some
of the blood of the sin offering and put it
on the doorposts of the temple, on the four
corners of the upper ledge of the altar[w] and
on the gateposts of the inner court. 20 You
are to do the same on the seventh day of the
month for anyone who sins unintentionally[x]
or through ignorance; so you are to make
atonement for the temple.

21 "'In the first month on the fourteenth
day you are to observe the Passover,[y] a feast
lasting seven days, during which you shall

45:12
u Ex 30:13; Lev 27:25; Nu 3:47

45:15
v Lev 1:4

45:19
w Eze 43:20

45:20
x Lev 4:27

45:21
y Ex 12:11; Lev 23:5–6

[a] 1 Septuagint (see also verses 3 and 5 and 48:9); Hebrew *10,000* [b] 3 That is, about 7 miles (about 12 kilometers) [c] 3 That is, about 3 miles (about 5 kilometers) [d] 5 Septuagint; Hebrew *temple; they will have as their possession 20 rooms* [e] 10 An ephah was a dry measure. [f] 10 A bath was a liquid measure. [g] 11 A homer was a dry measure. [h] 12 A shekel weighed about 2/5 ounce (about 11.5 grams). [i] 12 That is, 60 shekels; the common mina was 50 shekels. [j] 15 Traditionally *peace offerings*; also in verse 17

eat bread made without yeast. 22 On that day the prince is to provide a bull as a sin offering for himself and for all the people of the land.[z] 23 Every day during the seven days of the Feast he is to provide seven bulls and seven rams without defect as a burnt offering to the LORD, and a male goat for a sin offering.[a] 24 He is to provide as a grain offering an ephah for each bull and an ephah for each ram, along with a hin[a] of oil for each ephah.

25 "'During the seven days of the Feast, which begins in the seventh month on the fifteenth day, he is to make the same provision for sin offerings, burnt offerings, grain offerings and oil.[b]

# 46

"'This is what the Sovereign LORD says: The gate of the inner court facing east is to be shut on the six working days, but on the Sabbath day and on the day of the New Moon it is to be opened. 2 The prince is to enter from the outside through the portico[c] of the gateway and stand by the gatepost. The priests are to sacrifice his burnt offering and his fellowship offerings.[b] He is to worship at the threshold of the gateway and then go out, but the gate will not be shut until evening.[d] 3 On the Sabbaths and New Moons the people of the land are to worship in the presence of the LORD at the entrance to that gateway.[e] 4 The burnt offering the prince brings to the LORD on the Sabbath day is to be six male lambs and a ram, all without defect. 5 The grain offering given with the ram is to be an ephah,[c] and the grain offering with the lambs is to be as much as he pleases, along with a hin[a] of oil for each ephah.[f] 6 On the day of the New Moon[g] he is to offer a young bull, six lambs and a ram, all without defect. 7 He is to provide as a grain offering one ephah with the bull, one ephah with the ram, and with the lambs as much as he wants to give, along with a hin of oil with each ephah. 8 When the prince enters, he is to go in through the portico[h] of the gateway, and he is to come out the same way.[i]

9 "'When the people of the land come before the LORD at the appointed feasts,[j] whoever enters by the north gate to worship is to go out the south gate; and whoever enters by the south gate is to go out the north gate. No one is to return through the gate by which he entered, but each is to go out the opposite gate. 10 The prince is to be among them, going in when they go in and going out when they go out.

11 "'At the festivals and the appointed feasts, the grain offering is to be an ephah with a bull, an ephah with a ram, and with the lambs as much as one pleases, along with a hin of oil for each ephah.[k] 12 When the prince provides[l] a freewill offering to the LORD—whether a burnt offering or fellowship offerings—the gate facing east is to be opened for him. He shall offer his burnt offering or his fellowship offerings as he does on the Sabbath day. Then he shall go out, and after he has gone out, the gate will be shut.[m]

13 "'Every day you are to provide a year-old lamb without defect for a burnt offering to the LORD; morning by morning you shall provide it.[n] 14 You are also to provide with it morning by morning a grain offering, consisting of a sixth of an ephah with a third of a hin of oil to moisten the flour. The presenting of this grain offering to the LORD is a lasting ordinance. 15 So the lamb and the grain offering and the oil shall be provided morning by morning for a regular[o] burnt offering.[p]

16 "'This is what the Sovereign LORD says: If the prince makes a gift from his inheritance to one of his sons, it will also belong to his descendants; it is to be their property by inheritance. 17 If, however, he makes a gift from his inheritance to one of his servants, the servant may keep it until the year of freedom;[q] then it will revert to the prince. His inheritance belongs to his sons only; it is theirs. 18 The prince must not take any of the inheritance[r] of the people, driving them off their property. He is to give his sons their inheritance out of his own property, so that none of my people will be separated from his property.'"

19 Then the man brought me through the entrance at the side of the gate to the sacred rooms facing north, which belonged to the priests, and showed me a place at the western end. 20 He said to me, "This is the place where the priests will cook the guilt offering

**45:22** z Lev 4:14
**45:23** a Nu 28:16–25
**45:25** b Lev 23:34–43; Nu 29:12–38
**46:2** c ver 8; d ver 12; Eze 44:3
**46:3** e Lk 1:10
**46:5** f ver 11; Eze 45:24
**46:6** g ver 1
**46:8** h ver 2; i Eze 44:3
**46:9** j Ex 23:14
**46:11** k ver 5
**46:12** l Eze 45:17; m ver 2
**46:13** n Ex 29:38; Nu 28:3
**46:15** o Ex 29:42; p Nu 28:5–6
**46:17** q Lev 25:10
**46:18** r Eze 45:8; Mic 2:1–2

[a] 24,5 That is, probably about 4 quarts (about 4 liters) [b] 2 Traditionally *peace offerings*; also in verse 12 [c] 5 That is, probably about 3/5 bushel (about 22 liters)

and the sin offering and bake the grain offering, to avoid bringing them into the outer court and consecrating the people."

21 He then brought me to the outer court and led me around to its four corners, and I saw in each corner another court. 22 In the four corners of the outer court were enclosed[a] courts, forty cubits long and thirty cubits wide; each of the courts in the four corners was the same size. 23 Around the inside of each of the four courts was a ledge of stone, with places for fire built all around under the ledge. 24 He said to me, "These are the kitchens where those who minister at the temple will cook the sacrifices of the people."

## The River From the Temple

47 The man brought me back to the entrance of the temple, and I saw water coming out from under the threshold of the temple toward the east (for the temple faced east). The water was coming down from under the south side of the temple, south of the altar.[s] 2 He then brought me out through the north gate and led me around the outside to the outer gate facing east, and the water was flowing from the south side.

3 As the man went eastward with a measuring line[t] in his hand, he measured off a thousand cubits[b] and then led me through water that was ankle-deep. 4 He measured off another thousand cubits and led me through water that was knee-deep. He measured off another thousand and led me through water that was up to the waist. 5 He measured off another thousand, but now it was a river that I could not cross, because the water had risen and was deep enough to swim in—a river that no one could cross. 6 He asked me, "Son of man, do you see this?"

Then he led me back to the bank of the river. 7 When I arrived there, I saw a great number of trees on each side of the river.[u] 8 He said to me, "This water flows toward the eastern region and goes down into the Arabah,[c][v] where it enters the Sea.[d] When it empties into the Sea,[d] the water there becomes fresh. 9 Swarms of living creatures will live wherever the river flows. There will be large numbers of fish, because this water flows there and makes the salt water fresh; so where the river flows everything will live. 10 Fishermen will stand along the shore; from En Gedi to En Eglaim there will be places for spreading nets.[w] The fish will be of many kinds—like the fish of the Great Sea.[e] 11 But the swamps and marshes will not become fresh; they will be left for salt. 12 Fruit trees of all kinds will grow on both banks of the river.[x] Their leaves will not wither, nor will their fruit[y] fail. Every month they will bear, because the water from the sanctuary flows to them. Their fruit will serve for food and their leaves for healing.[z]"

## The Boundaries of the Land

13 This is what the Sovereign LORD says: "These are the boundaries[a] by which you are to divide the land for an inheritance among the twelve tribes of Israel, with two portions for Joseph.[b] 14 You are to divide it equally among them. Because I swore with uplifted hand to give it to your forefathers, this land will become your inheritance.[c]

15 "This is to be the boundary of the land:

"On the north side it will run from the Great Sea by the Hethlon road[d] past Lebo[f] Hamath to Zedad, 16 Berothah[g] and Sibraim (which lies on the border between Damascus and Hamath), as far as Hazer Hatticon, which is on the border of Hauran. 17 The boundary will extend from the sea to Hazar Enan,[h] along the northern border of Damascus, with the border of Hamath to the north. This will be the north boundary.[e]

18 "On the east side the boundary will run between Hauran and Damascus, along the Jordan between Gilead and the land of Israel, to the eastern sea and as far as Tamar.[i] This will be the east boundary.

19 "On the south side it will run from Tamar as far as the waters of Meribah Kadesh,[f] then along the Wadi ⌊of Egypt⌋

47:1 s Joel 3:18; Rev 22:1
47:3 t Eze 40:3
47:7 u Rev 22:2
47:8 v Dt 3:17; Jos 3:16
47:10 w Eze 26:5
47:12 x ver 7; Rev 22:2 y Ps 1:3 z Jer 17:8
47:13 a Nu 34:2–12 b Ge 48:5
47:14 c Eze 20:5–6
47:15 d Eze 48:1
47:17 e Eze 48:1
47:19 f Dt 32:51

[a] 22 The meaning of the Hebrew for this word is uncertain. [b] 3 That is, about 1,500 feet (about 450 meters) [c] 8 Or *the Jordan Valley* [d] 8 That is, the Dead Sea [e] 10 That is, the Mediterranean; also in verses 15, 19 and 20 [f] 15 Or *past the entrance to* [g] 15,16 See Septuagint and Ezekiel 48:1; Hebrew *road to go into Zedad, 16 Hamath, Berothah* [h] 17 Hebrew *Enon,* a variant of *Enan* [i] 18 Septuagint and Syriac; Hebrew *Israel. You will measure to the eastern sea*

to the Great Sea.[g] This will be the
south boundary.
20"On the west side, the Great Sea will be the
boundary to a point opposite Lebo[a] Ha-
math. This will be the west boundary.

21"You are to distribute this land among
yourselves according to the tribes of Israel.
22You are to allot it as an inheritance for
yourselves and for the aliens who have set-
tled among you and who have children. You
are to consider them as native-born Israel-
ites; along with you they are to be allotted
an inheritance among the tribes of Israel.[h]
23In whatever tribe the alien settles, there
you are to give him his inheritance," de-
clares the Sovereign LORD.

## The Division of the Land

48 "These are the tribes, listed by
name: At the northern frontier, Dan
will have one portion; it will follow the Heth-
lon road[i] to Lebo[b] Hamath; Hazar Enan and
the northern border of Damascus next to
Hamath will be part of its border from the
east side to the west side.
2"Asher[j] will have one portion; it will bor-
der the territory of Dan from east to west.
3"Naphtali[k] will have one portion; it will
border the territory of Asher from east to
west.
4"Manasseh[l] will have one portion; it will
border the territory of Naphtali from east
to west.
5"Ephraim[m] will have one portion; it will
border the territory of Manasseh from east
to west.
6"Reuben[n] will have one portion; it will
border the territory of Ephraim from east
to west.
7"Judah[o] will have one portion; it will
border the territory of Reuben from east
to west.
8"Bordering the territory of Judah from
east to west will be the portion you are to pre-
sent as a special gift. It will be 25,000 cubits[c]
wide, and its length from east to west will
equal one of the tribal portions; the sanctu-
ary will be in the center of it.
9"The special portion you are to offer
to the LORD will be 25,000 cubits long and
10,000 cubits[d] wide. 10This will be the sa-
cred portion for the priests. It will be 25,000
cubits long on the north side, 10,000 cubits
wide on the west side, 10,000 cubits wide
on the east side and 25,000 cubits long on
the south side. In the center of it will be the
sanctuary of the LORD.[p] 11This will be for
the consecrated priests, the Zadokites, who
were faithful in serving me and did not go
astray as the Levites did when the Israelites
went astray.[q] 12It will be a special gift to
them from the sacred portion of the land, a
most holy portion, bordering the territory
of the Levites.
13"Alongside the territory of the priests,
the Levites will have an allotment 25,000
cubits long and 10,000 cubits wide. Its total
length will be 25,000 cubits and its width
10,000 cubits. 14They must not sell or ex-
change any of it. This is the best of the land
and must not pass into other hands, because
it is holy to the LORD.[r]
15"The remaining area, 5,000 cubits wide
and 25,000 cubits long, will be for the com-
mon use of the city, for houses and for pas-
tureland. The city will be in the center of it
16and will have these measurements: the
north side 4,500 cubits, the south side 4,500
cubits, the east side 4,500 cubits, and the
west side 4,500 cubits.[s] 17The pastureland for
the city will be 250 cubits on the north, 250
cubits on the south, 250 cubits on the east,
and 250 cubits on the west. 18What remains
of the area, bordering on the sacred portion
and running the length of it, will be 10,000
cubits on the east side and 10,000 cubits on
the west side. Its produce will supply food
for the workers of the city. 19The workers
from the city who farm it will come from all
the tribes of Israel. 20The entire portion will
be a square, 25,000 cubits on each side. As a
special gift you will set aside the sacred por-
tion, along with the property of the city.
21"What remains on both sides of the
area formed by the sacred portion and the
city property will belong to the prince. It
will extend eastward from the 25,000 cubits
of the sacred portion to the eastern border,
and westward from the 25,000 cubits to the
western border. Both these areas running

**47:19** g Eze 48:28
**47:22** h Eph 3:6; Col 3:11
**48:1** i Eze 47:15–17
**48:2** j Jos 19:24–31
**48:3** k Jos 19:32–39
**48:4** l Jos 17:1–11
**48:5** m Jos 16:5–9
**48:6** n Jos 13:15–21
**48:7** o Jos 15:1–63
**48:10** p Eze 45:3–4
**48:11** q Eze 44:15
**48:14** r Lev 25:34; 27:10,28
**48:16** s Rev 21:16

[a]20 Or *opposite the entrance to* [b]1 Or *to the entrance to* [c]8 That is, about 7 miles (about 12 kilometers) [d]9 That is, about 3 miles (about 5 kilometers)

**48:21** t ver 8,10; Eze 45:7
**48:23** u Jos 18:11–28
**48:24** v Jos 19:1–9
**48:25** w Jos 19:17–23
**48:26** x Jos 19:10–16
**48:27** y Jos 13:24–28
**48:28** z Eze 47:19

the length of the tribal portions will belong to the prince, and the sacred portion with the temple sanctuary will be in the center of them.[t] 22 So the property of the Levites and the property of the city will lie in the center of the area that belongs to the prince. The area belonging to the prince will lie between the border of Judah and the border of Benjamin.

23 "As for the rest of the tribes: Benjamin[u] will have one portion; it will extend from the east side to the west side.

24 "Simeon[v] will have one portion; it will border the territory of Benjamin from east to west.

25 "Issachar[w] will have one portion; it will border the territory of Simeon from east to west.

26 "Zebulun[x] will have one portion; it will border the territory of Issachar from east to west.

27 "Gad[y] will have one portion; it will border the territory of Zebulun from east to west.

28 "The southern boundary of Gad will run south from Tamar to the waters of Meribah Kadesh, then along the Wadi ⌞of Egypt⌟ to the Great Sea.[a][z]

29 "This is the land you are to allot as an inheritance to the tribes of Israel, and these will be their portions," declares the Sovereign LORD.

## The Gates of the City

30 "These will be the exits of the city: Beginning on the north side, which is 4,500 cubits long, 31 the gates of the city will be named after the tribes of Israel. The three gates on the north side will be the gate of Reuben, the gate of Judah and the gate of Levi.

32 "On the east side, which is 4,500 cubits long, will be three gates: the gate of Joseph, the gate of Benjamin and the gate of Dan.

33 "On the south side, which measures 4,500 cubits, will be three gates: the gate of Simeon, the gate of Issachar and the gate of Zebulun.

34 "On the west side, which is 4,500 cubits long, will be three gates: the gate of Gad, the gate of Asher and the gate of Naphtali.

35 "The distance all around will be 18,000 cubits.

"And the name of the city from that time on will be:

THE LORD IS THERE.[a]"

**48:35** a Jer 3:17; 33:16; Joel 3:21; Zec 2:10; Rev 21:3

[a]28 That is, the Mediterranean

# Daniel

## OVERVIEW

The book of Daniel gives an account of some of those who were exiled from Judah during the Babylonian captivity. This has long been a favorite book of believers because it records God's miraculous intervention of his faithful people in the midst of a kingdom hostile to God. The book details the refusal of Daniel and his friends Shadrach, Meshach and Abednego to defile themselves with the king's food. Shadrach, Meshach and Abednego also risked death in a fiery furnace rather than bow to an idol. Later in the book, Daniel's persistence in praying to God every day is highlighted. He continues to worship God in the face of persecution and threats—even the threat of being thrown into a den of lions. Daniel's visions concerning the future of his own people and the Gentile nations conclude this famous book of the Bible.

"Persecuted, but not abandoned; struck down, but not destroyed"—this is what the apostle Paul wrote about those who put their trust in Christ (2Co 4:9). As Daniel and his fellow exiles faced many dangers and struggles, so do the followers of Jesus Christ. The hope for today's Christian woman is not to be found in this world, but in the "author and perfecter of our faith," the Lord Jesus (Heb 12:2).

## OUTLINE

I. Daniel and His Friends in Babylon (1:1–21)
II. Daniel Interprets Nebuchadnezzar's Dream (2:1–49)
III. Refusal to Worship an Idol (3:1–30)
IV. Nebuchadnezzar's Dream and Madness (4:1–37)
V. The Writing on the Wall (5:1–31)
VI. Daniel in the Lions' Den (6:1–28)
VII. Daniel's Dreams and Visions (7:1—12:13)

## SCANNABLE FACTS:

**Author:** Daniel

**Time Written:** Around 530 B.C.

**Theme to Note:** God is faithful to those who love him

**Notable Woman:** The Babylonian queen (see Da 5:10–12)

## Daniel's Training in Babylon

1 In the third year of the reign of Jehoiakim king of Judah, Nebuchadnezzar[a] king of Babylon came to Jerusalem and besieged it.[b] [2]And the Lord delivered Jehoiakim king of Judah into his hand, along with some of the articles from the temple of God. These he carried off to the temple of his god in Babylonia[a] and put in the treasure house of his god.[c]

[3]Then the king ordered Ashpenaz, chief of his court officials, to bring in some of the Israelites from the royal family and the nobility[d]— [4]young men without any physical defect, handsome, showing aptitude for every kind of learning, well informed, quick to understand, and qualified to serve in the king's palace. He was to teach them the language and literature of the Babylonians.[b] [5]The king assigned them a daily amount of food and wine from the king's table. They were to be trained for three years, and after that they were to enter the king's service.[e]

[6]Among these were some from Judah: Daniel, Hananiah, Mishael and Azariah. [7]The chief official gave them new names: to Daniel, the name Belteshazzar;[f] to Hananiah, Shadrach; to Mishael, Meshach; and to Azariah, Abednego.

[8]But Daniel resolved not to defile[g] himself with the royal food and wine, and he asked the chief official for permission not to defile himself this way. [9]Now God had caused the official to show favor[h] and sympathy to Daniel, [10]but the official told Daniel, "I am afraid of my lord the king, who has assigned your[c] food and drink. Why should he see you looking worse than the other young men your age? The king would then have my head because of you."

[11]Daniel then said to the guard whom the chief official had appointed over Daniel, Hananiah, Mishael and Azariah, [12]"Please test your servants for ten days: Give us nothing but vegetables to eat and water to drink. [13]Then compare our appearance with that of the young men who eat the royal food, and treat your servants in accordance with what you see." [14]So he agreed to this and tested them for ten days.

[15]At the end of the ten days they looked healthier and better nourished than any of the young men who ate the royal food. [16]So the guard took away their choice food and the wine they were to drink and gave them vegetables instead.

[17]To these four young men God gave knowledge and understanding of all kinds of literature and learning. And Daniel could understand visions and dreams of all kinds.[i]

[18]At the end of the time set by the king to bring them in, the chief official presented them to Nebuchadnezzar. [19]The king talked with them, and he found none equal to Daniel, Hananiah, Mishael and Azariah; so they entered the king's service.[j] [20]In every matter of wisdom and understanding about which the king questioned them, he found them ten times better than all the magicians and enchanters in his whole kingdom.

[21]And Daniel remained there until the first year of King Cyrus.[k]

## Nebuchadnezzar's Dream

2 In the second year of his reign, Nebuchadnezzar had dreams;[l] his mind was troubled[m] and he could not sleep.[n] [2]So the king summoned the magicians,[o] enchanters, sorcerers[p] and astrologers[d] to tell him what he had dreamed. When they came in and stood before the king, [3]he said to them, "I have had a dream that troubles me and I want to know what it means.[e]"

[4]Then the astrologers answered the king in Aramaic,[f] "O king, live forever! Tell your servants the dream, and we will interpret it."

[5]The king replied to the astrologers, "This is what I have firmly decided: If you do not tell me what my dream was and interpret it, I will have you cut into pieces and your houses turned into piles of rubble.[q] [6]But if you tell me the dream and explain it, you will receive from me gifts and rewards and great honor.[r] So tell me the dream and interpret it for me."

[7]Once more they replied, "Let the king tell his servants the dream, and we will interpret it."

**1:1** a 2Ki 24:1 b 2Ch 36:6
**1:2** c Jer 27:19–20; Zec 5:5–11
**1:3** d Isa 39:7
**1:5** e ver 19
**1:7** f Da 4:8; 5:12
**1:8** g Eze 4:13–14
**1:9** h Pr 16:7
**1:17** i Da 2:19,30
**1:19** j Ge 41:46
**1:21** k Da 6:28; 10:1
**2:1** l Da 4:5 m Ge 41:8 n Est 6:1
**2:2** o Ge 41:8 p Ex 7:11
**2:5** q Ezr 6:11; Da 3:29
**2:6** r Da 5:7,16

[a]2 Hebrew *Shinar* [b]4 Or *Chaldeans* [c]10 The Hebrew for *your* and *you* in this verse is plural. [d]2 Or *Chaldeans*; also in verses 4, 5 and 10 [e]3 Or *was* [f]4 The text from here through chapter 7 is in Aramaic.

8 Then the king answered, "I am certain that you are trying to gain time, because you realize that this is what I have firmly decided: 9 If you do not tell me the dream, there is just one penalty[s] for you. You have conspired to tell me misleading and wicked things, hoping the situation will change. So then, tell me the dream, and I will know that you can interpret it for me."

*"The future belongs to those who see possibilities before they are obvious."*

—Unknown

10 The astrologers answered the king, "There is not a man on earth who can do what the king asks! No king, however great and mighty, has ever asked such a thing of any magician or enchanter or astrologer.[t] 11 What the king asks is too difficult. No one can reveal it to the king except the gods, and they do not live among men."

12 This made the king so angry and furious that he ordered the execution of all the wise men of Babylon. 13 So the decree was issued to put the wise men to death, and men were sent to look for Daniel and his friends to put them to death.[u]

14 When Arioch, the commander of the king's guard, had gone out to put to death the wise men of Babylon, Daniel spoke to him with wisdom and tact. 15 He asked the king's officer, "Why did the king issue such a harsh decree?" Arioch then explained the matter to Daniel. 16 At this, Daniel went in to the king and asked for time, so that he might interpret the dream for him.

17 Then Daniel returned to his house and explained the matter to his friends Hananiah, Mishael and Azariah. 18 He urged them to plead for mercy[v] from the God of heaven concerning this mystery,[w] so that he and his friends might not be executed with the rest of the wise men of Babylon. 19 During the night the mystery was revealed to Daniel in a vision.[x] Then Daniel praised the God of heaven 20 and said:

"Praise be to the name of God for ever
and ever;[y]
wisdom and power[z] are his.
21 He changes times and seasons;
he sets up kings and deposes them.
He gives wisdom[a] to the wise
and knowledge to the discerning.
22 He reveals deep and hidden things;[b]
he knows what lies in darkness,[c]
and light[d] dwells with him.
23 I thank and praise you, O God of my
fathers:
You have given me wisdom[e] and
power,
you have made known to me what we
asked of you,
you have made known to us the dream
of the king."

## Daniel Interprets the Dream

24 Then Daniel went to Arioch, whom the king had appointed to execute the wise men of Babylon, and said to him, "Do not execute the wise men of Babylon. Take me to the king, and I will interpret his dream for him."

25 Arioch took Daniel to the king at once and said, "I have found a man among the exiles from Judah[f] who can tell the king what his dream means."

26 The king asked Daniel (also called Belteshazzar), "Are you able to tell me what I saw in my dream and interpret it?"

27 Daniel replied, "No wise man, enchanter, magician or diviner can explain to the king the mystery he has asked about,[g] 28 but there is a God in heaven who reveals mysteries.[h] He has shown King Nebuchadnezzar what will happen in days to come. Your dream and the visions that passed through your mind[i] as you lay on your bed are these:

29 "As you were lying there, O king, your mind turned to things to come, and the revealer of mysteries showed you what is going to happen. 30 As for me, this mystery has been revealed to me, not because I have greater wisdom than other living men, but so that you, O king, may know the interpretation and that you may understand what went through your mind.

31 "You looked, O king, and there before you stood a large statue—an enormous, dazzling statue,[j] awesome in appearance. 32 The head of the statue was made of pure gold, its chest and arms of silver, its belly and thighs of bronze, 33 its legs of iron, its feet

**2:9** s Est 4:11
**2:10** t ver 27
**2:13** u Da 1:20
**2:18** v Isa 37:4; w Jer 33:3
**2:19** x Job 33:15
**2:20** y Ps 113:2; z Jer 32:19
**2:21** a Jas 1:5
**2:22** b Job 12:22; Da 5:11; c Ps 139:11–12; d Isa 45:7
**2:23** e Da 1:17
**2:25** f Da 1:6
**2:27** g ver 10
**2:28** h Ge 40:8; i Da 4:5
**2:31** j Hab 1:7

**2:34** k Zec 4:6 l Da 8:25
**2:35** m Ps 37:10 n Isa 2:3
**2:37** o Jer 27:7
**2:38** p Da 4:21–22
**2:40** q Da 7:7,23
**2:44** r Ps 2:9 s Da 4:34; Mic 4:7,13

partly of iron and partly of baked clay.
34 While you were watching, a rock was cut
out, but not by human hands.[k] It struck the
statue on its feet of iron and clay and smashed
them.[l] 35 Then the iron, the clay, the bronze,
the silver and the gold were broken to pieces
at the same time and became like chaff on a
threshing floor in the summer. The wind
swept them away[m] without leaving a trace.
But the rock that struck the statue became a
huge mountain[n] and filled the whole earth.
36 "This was the dream, and now we will
interpret it to the king. 37 You, O king, are
the king of kings. The God of heaven has
given you dominion[o] and power and might
and glory; 38 in your hands he has placed
mankind and the beasts of the field and the
birds of the air. Wherever they live, he has
made you ruler over them all.[p] You are that
head of gold.
39 "After you, another kingdom will rise,
inferior to yours. Next, a third kingdom,
one of bronze, will rule over the whole
earth. 40 Finally, there will be a fourth king-
dom, strong as iron—for iron breaks and
smashes everything—and as iron breaks
things to pieces, so it will crush and break
all the others.[q] 41 Just as you saw that the
feet and toes were partly of baked clay and
partly of iron, so this will be a divided king-
dom; yet it will have some of the strength
of iron in it, even as you saw iron mixed
with clay. 42 As the toes were partly iron and
partly clay, so this kingdom will be partly
strong and partly brittle. 43 And just as you
saw the iron mixed with baked clay, so the
people will be a mixture and will not remain
united, any more than iron mixes with clay.
44 "In the time of those kings, the God of
heaven will set up a kingdom that will never
be destroyed, nor will it be left to another
people. It will crush[r] all those kingdoms
and bring them to an end, but it will itself
endure forever.[s] 45 This is the meaning of the
vision of the rock cut out of a mountain, but
not by human hands—a rock that broke the
iron, the bronze, the clay, the silver and the
gold to pieces.

"The great God has shown the king what
will take place in the future. The dream is
true and the interpretation is trustworthy."

46 Then King Nebuchadnezzar fell pros-
trate[t] before Daniel and paid him honor and
ordered that an offering[u] and incense be
presented to him. 47 The king said to Daniel,
"Surely your God is the God of gods[v] and the
Lord of kings and a revealer of mysteries,
for you were able to reveal this mystery."
48 Then the king placed Daniel in a high
position and lavished many gifts on him. He
made him ruler over the entire province of
Babylon and placed him in charge of all its
wise men.[w] 49 Moreover, at Daniel's request
the king appointed Shadrach, Meshach and
Abednego administrators over the province
of Babylon, while Daniel himself remained
at the royal court.

## The Image of Gold and the Fiery Furnace

3 King Nebuchadnezzar made an image[x]
of gold, ninety feet high and nine feet[a]
wide, and set it up on the plain of Dura in
the province of Babylon. 2 He then sum-
moned the satraps, prefects, governors, ad-
visers, treasurers, judges, magistrates and
all the other provincial officials[y] to come to
the dedication of the image he had set up.
3 So the satraps, prefects, governors, advis-
ers, treasurers, judges, magistrates and all
the other provincial officials assembled for
the dedication of the image that King Nebu-
chadnezzar had set up, and they stood be-
fore it.
4 Then the herald loudly proclaimed,
"This is what you are commanded to do,
O peoples, nations and men of every lan-
guage:[z] 5 As soon as you hear the sound of
the horn, flute, zither, lyre, harp, pipes and
all kinds of music, you must fall down and
worship the image of gold that King Nebu-
chadnezzar has set up.[a] 6 Whoever does not
fall down and worship will immediately be
thrown into a blazing furnace."[b]
7 Therefore, as soon as they heard the
sound of the horn, flute, zither, lyre, harp
and all kinds of music, all the peoples, na-
tions and men of every language fell down
and worshiped the image of gold that King
Nebuchadnezzar had set up.
8 At this time some astrologers[b] came
forward and denounced the Jews. 9 They

**2:46** t Ac 10:25 u Ac 14:13
**2:47** v Da 11:36
**2:48** w ver 6
**3:1** x Isa 46:6; Hab 2:19
**3:2** y ver 27
**3:4** z Da 4:1; 6:25
**3:5** a ver 10,15
**3:6** b Jer 29:22

[a] 1 Aramaic *sixty cubits high and six cubits wide* (about 27 meters high and 2.7 meters wide) [b] 8 Or *Chaldeans*

**3:9** c Da 5:10
**3:10** d ver 4–6
**3:12** e Da 2:49
**3:13** f Da 2:12
**3:14** g Isa 46:1; Jer 50:2
**3:15** h Isa 36:18–20
**3:17** i Ps 27:1–2

said to King Nebuchadnezzar, "O king, live forever![c] 10You have issued a decree, O king, that everyone who hears the sound of the horn, flute, zither, lyre, harp, pipes and all kinds of music must fall down and worship the image of gold,[d] 11and that whoever does not fall down and worship will be thrown into a blazing furnace. 12But there are some Jews whom you have set over the affairs of the province of Babylon—Shadrach, Meshach and Abednego[e]—who pay no attention to you, O king. They neither serve your gods nor worship the image of gold you have set up."

13Furious[f] with rage, Nebuchadnezzar summoned Shadrach, Meshach and Abednego. So these men were brought before the king, 14and Nebuchadnezzar said to them, "Is it true, Shadrach, Meshach and Abednego, that you do not serve my gods[g] or worship the image of gold I have set up? 15Now when you hear the sound of the horn, flute, zither, lyre, harp, pipes and all kinds of music, if you are ready to fall down and worship the image I made, very good. But if you do not worship it, you will be thrown immediately into a blazing furnace. Then what god[h] will be able to rescue you from my hand?"

16Shadrach, Meshach and Abednego replied to the king, "O Nebuchadnezzar, we do not need to defend ourselves before you in this matter. 17If we are thrown into the blazing furnace, the God we serve is able to save[i] us from it, and he will rescue us from your hand, O king. 18But even if he does not, we want you to know, O king, that we will

*Lord,*

*help me to stand for you no matter what opposition I may face. Grant me the faith of Shadrach, Meshach and Abednego. Help me trust that you are able and willing to bring me out of any fiery furnace. In Jesus' name,*

*Amen*

DANIEL 3:13–18

not serve your gods or worship the image of gold you have set up.[j]"

19Then Nebuchadnezzar was furious with Shadrach, Meshach and Abednego, and his attitude toward them changed. He ordered the furnace heated seven times hotter than usual 20and commanded some of the strongest soldiers in his army to tie up Shadrach, Meshach and Abednego and throw them into the blazing furnace. 21So these men, wearing their robes, trousers, turbans and other clothes, were bound and thrown into the blazing furnace. 22The king's command was so urgent and the furnace so hot that the flames of the fire killed the soldiers who took up Shadrach, Meshach and Abednego, 23and these three men, firmly tied, fell into the blazing furnace.

24Then King Nebuchadnezzar leaped to his feet in amazement and asked his advisers, "Weren't there three men that we tied up and threw into the fire?"

They replied, "Certainly, O king."

25He said, "Look! I see four men walking around in the fire, unbound and unharmed, and the fourth looks like a son of the gods."

26Nebuchadnezzar then approached the opening of the blazing furnace and shouted, "Shadrach, Meshach and Abednego, servants of the Most High God,[k] come out! Come here!"

So Shadrach, Meshach and Abednego came out of the fire, 27and the satraps, prefects, governors and royal advisers crowded around them.[l] They saw that the fire had not harmed their bodies, nor was a hair of their heads singed; their robes were not scorched, and there was no smell of fire on them.

28Then Nebuchadnezzar said, "Praise be to the God of Shadrach, Meshach and Abednego, who has sent his angel[m] and rescued his servants! They trusted in him and defied the king's command and were willing to give up their lives rather than serve or worship any god except their own God. 29Therefore I decree[n] that the people of any nation or language who say anything against the God of Shadrach, Meshach and Abednego be cut into pieces and their houses be turned into piles of rubble, for no other god can save[o] in this way."

30Then the king promoted Shadrach,

**3:18** j ver 28
**3:26** k Da 4:2,34
**3:27** l Heb 11:32–34
**3:28** m Ps 34:7; Da 6:22
**3:29** n Da 6:26 o Da 6:27

Meshach and Abednego in the province of
Babylon.[p]

## Nebuchadnezzar's Dream of a Tree

4 King Nebuchadnezzar,

To the peoples, nations and men
of every language, who live in all the
world:

May you prosper greatly![q]

2 It is my pleasure to tell you about
the miraculous signs and wonders that
the Most High God[r] has performed
for me.

3 How great are his signs,
how mighty his wonders![s]
His kingdom is an eternal kingdom;
his dominion endures[t] from
generation to generation.

4 I, Nebuchadnezzar, was at home in
my palace, contented and prosperous.
5 I had a dream[u] that made me afraid.
As I was lying in my bed, the images
and visions that passed through my
mind[v] terrified me. 6 So I commanded
that all the wise men of Babylon be
brought before me to interpret the
dream for me. 7 When the magicians,
enchanters, astrologers[a] and diviners[w]
came, I told them the dream, but they
could not interpret it for me. 8 Finally,
Daniel came into my presence and I
told him the dream. (He is called Belte-
shazzar,[x] after the name of my god, and
the spirit of the holy gods is in him.)

9 I said, "Belteshazzar, chief[y] of the
magicians, I know that the spirit of
the holy gods[z] is in you, and no mys-
tery is too difficult for you. Here is
my dream; interpret it for me. 10 These
are the visions I saw while lying in
my bed: I looked, and there before
me stood a tree in the middle of the
land. Its height was enormous.[a] 11 The
tree grew large and strong and its top
touched the sky; it was visible to the
ends of the earth. 12 Its leaves were
beautiful, its fruit abundant, and on
it was food for all. Under it the beasts
of the field found shelter, and the birds
of the air lived in its branches; from it
every creature was fed.

13 "In the visions I saw while lying
in my bed, I looked, and there before
me was a messenger,[b] a holy one,[b] com-
ing down from heaven. 14 He called in a
loud voice: 'Cut down the tree and trim
off its branches; strip off its leaves and
scatter its fruit. Let the animals flee
from under it and the birds from its
branches.[c] 15 But let the stump and its
roots, bound with iron and bronze,
remain in the ground, in the grass of
the field.

"'Let him be drenched with the
dew of heaven, and let him live with
the animals among the plants of the
earth. 16 Let his mind be changed from
that of a man and let him be given the
mind of an animal, till seven times[c]
pass by for him.

17 "'The decision is announced by
messengers, the holy ones declare the
verdict, so that the living may know
that the Most High[d] is sovereign[e] over
the kingdoms of men and gives them
to anyone he wishes and sets over
them the lowliest of men.'

18 "This is the dream that I, King
Nebuchadnezzar, had. Now, Belteshaz-
zar, tell me what it means, for none of
the wise men in my kingdom can inter-
pret it for me.[f] But you can,[g] because
the spirit of the holy gods is in you."[h]

## Daniel Interprets the Dream

19 Then Daniel (also called Belte-
shazzar) was greatly perplexed for a
time, and his thoughts terrified[i] him.
So the king said, "Belteshazzar, do not
let the dream or its meaning alarm
you."

Belteshazzar answered, "My lord,
if only the dream applied to your en-
emies and its meaning to your adver-
saries! 20 The tree you saw, which grew
large and strong, with its top touching
the sky, visible to the whole earth,
21 with beautiful leaves and abundant

**3:30** p Da 2:49
**4:1** q Da 6:25
**4:2** r Da 3:26
**4:3** s Da 6:27 t Da 2:44
**4:5** u Da 2:1 v Da 2:28
**4:7** w Da 2:2
**4:8** x Da 1:7
**4:9** y Da 2:48 z Da 5:11–12
**4:10** a Eze 31:3–4
**4:13** b ver 23
**4:14** c Eze 31:12; Mt 3:10
**4:17** d ver 2,25 e Da 5:18–21
**4:18** f Ge 41:8; Da 5:8,15 g Ge 41:15 h ver 7–9
**4:19** i Da 7:15,28

[a]7 Or *Chaldeans* [b]13 Or *watchman*; also in verses 17 and 23 [c]16 Or *years*; also in verses 23, 25 and 32

**4:22** j Jer 27:7
**4:24** k Job 40:12
**4:25** l ver 17; m Jer 27:5; Da 5:21
**4:27** n Isa 55:6–7; o 1Ki 21:29; Ps 41:3; Eze 18:22
**4:30** p Da 5:20

fruit, providing food for all, giving
shelter to the beasts of the field, and
having nesting places in its branches
for the birds of the air— 22you, O king,
are that tree! You have become great
and strong; your greatness has grown
until it reaches the sky, and your do-
minion extends to distant parts of
the earth.[j]

23"You, O king, saw a messenger, a
holy one, coming down from heaven
and saying, 'Cut down the tree and de-
stroy it, but leave the stump, bound
with iron and bronze, in the grass of
the field, while its roots remain in the
ground. Let him be drenched with
the dew of heaven; let him live like the
wild animals, until seven times pass
by for him.'

24"This is the interpretation, O king,
and this is the decree[k] the Most High
has issued against my lord the king:
25You will be driven away from people
and will live with the wild animals;
you will eat grass like cattle and be
drenched with the dew of heaven.
Seven times will pass by for you until
you acknowledge that the Most High[l]
is sovereign over the kingdoms of men
and gives them to anyone he wishes.[m]
26The command to leave the stump of
the tree with its roots means that your
kingdom will be restored to you when
you acknowledge that Heaven rules.
27Therefore, O king, be pleased to ac-
cept my advice: Renounce your sins by
doing what is right, and your wicked-
ness by being kind to the oppressed.[n]
It may be that then your prosperity
will continue.[o]"

## The Dream Is Fulfilled

28All this happened to King Nebu-
chadnezzar. 29Twelve months later,
as the king was walking on the roof
of the royal palace of Babylon, 30he
said, "Is not this the great Babylon I
have built as the royal residence, by
my mighty power and for the glory of
my majesty?"[p]

31The words were still on his lips
when a voice came from heaven, "This
is what is decreed for you, King
Nebuchadnezzar: Your royal authority
has been taken from you. 32You will
be driven away from people and will
live with the wild animals; you will eat
grass like cattle. Seven times will pass
by for you until you acknowledge that
the Most High is sovereign over the
kingdoms of men and gives them to
anyone he wishes."

33Immediately what had been said
about Nebuchadnezzar was fulfilled.
He was driven away from people and
ate grass like cattle. His body was
drenched with the dew of heaven un-
til his hair grew like the feathers of
an eagle and his nails like the claws of
a bird.[q]

34At the end of that time, I, Nebu-
chadnezzar, raised my eyes toward
heaven, and my sanity was restored.
Then I praised the Most High; I hon-
ored and glorified him who lives
forever.[r]

His dominion is an eternal dominion;
his kingdom endures from generation
to generation.[s]
35 All the peoples of the earth
are regarded as nothing.[t]
He does as he pleases[u]
with the powers of heaven
and the peoples of the earth.
No one can hold back his hand
or say to him: "What have you done?"[v]

36At the same time that my sanity
was restored, my honor and splendor
were returned to me for the glory of
my kingdom. My advisers and nobles
sought me out, and I was restored to
my throne and became even greater
than before. 37Now I, Nebuchadnez-
zar, praise and exalt and glorify the
King of heaven, because everything he
does is right and all his ways are just.[w]
And those who walk in pride he is able
to humble.

## The Writing on the Wall

5 King Belshazzar gave a great banquet
for a thousand of his nobles and drank
wine with them. 2While Belshazzar was

**4:33** q Da 5:20–21
**4:34** r Da 12:7; s Lk 1:33
**4:35** t Isa 40:17; u Ps 115:3; 135:6; v Isa 45:9; Ro 9:20
**4:37** w Ps 33:4–5

5:2 x Jer 52:19 y Da 1:2
5:4 z Rev 9:20
5:7 a Da 4:6–7
5:10 b Da 3:9
5:11 c Da 2:47–48
5:12 d Da 1:7 e Da 6:3

drinking his wine, he gave orders to bring in the gold and silver goblets[x] that Nebuchadnezzar his father[a] had taken from the temple in Jerusalem, so that the king and his nobles, his wives and his concubines might drink from them.[y] [3]So they brought in the gold goblets that had been taken from the temple of God in Jerusalem, and the king and his nobles, his wives and his concubines drank from them. [4]As they drank the wine, they praised the gods of gold and silver, of bronze, iron, wood and stone.[z]

[5]Suddenly the fingers of a human hand appeared and wrote on the plaster of the wall, near the lampstand in the royal palace. The king watched the hand as it wrote. [6]His face turned pale and he was so frightened that his knees knocked together and his legs gave way.

[7]The king called out for the enchanters, astrologers[b] and diviners to be brought and said to these wise[a] men of Babylon, "Whoever reads this writing and tells me what it means will be clothed in purple and have a gold chain placed around his neck, and he will be made the third highest ruler in the kingdom."

[8]Then all the king's wise men came in, but they could not read the writing or tell the king what it meant. [9]So King Belshazzar became even more terrified and his face grew more pale. His nobles were baffled.

[10]The queen,[c] hearing the voices of the king and his nobles, came into the banquet hall. "O king, live forever!"[b] she said. "Don't be alarmed! Don't look so pale! [11]There is a man in your kingdom who has the spirit of the holy gods in him. In the time of your father he was found to have insight and intelligence and wisdom like that of the gods. King Nebuchadnezzar your father—your father the king, I say—appointed him chief of the magicians, enchanters, astrologers and diviners.[c] [12]This man Daniel, whom the king called Belteshazzar,[d] was found to have a keen mind and knowledge and understanding, and also the ability to interpret dreams, explain riddles and solve difficult problems.[e] Call for Daniel, and he will tell you what the writing means."

[13]So Daniel was brought before the king, and the king said to him, "Are you Daniel, one of the exiles my father the king brought from Judah?[f] [14]I have heard that the spirit of the gods is in you and that you have insight, intelligence and outstanding wisdom. [15]The wise men and enchanters were brought before me to read this writing and tell me what it means, but they could not explain it. [16]Now I have heard that you are able to give interpretations and to solve difficult problems. If you can read this writing and tell me what it means, you will be clothed in purple and have a gold chain placed around your neck, and you will be made the third highest ruler in the kingdom."

[17]Then Daniel answered the king, "You may keep your gifts for yourself and give your rewards to someone else. Nevertheless, I will read the writing for the king and tell him what it means.

[18]"O king, the Most High God gave your father Nebuchadnezzar sovereignty and greatness and glory and splendor.[g] [19]Because of the high position he gave him, all the peoples and nations and men of every language dreaded and feared him. Those the king wanted to put to death, he put to death;[h] those he wanted to spare, he spared; those he wanted to promote, he promoted; and those he wanted to humble, he humbled. [20]But when his heart became arrogant and hardened with pride,[i] he was deposed from his royal throne and stripped of his glory. [21]He was driven away from people and given the mind of an animal; he lived with the wild donkeys and ate grass like cattle; and his body was drenched with the dew of heaven, until he acknowledged that the Most High God is sovereign over the kingdoms of men and sets over them anyone he wishes.[j]

[22]"But you his son,[d] O Belshazzar, have not humbled yourself, though you knew all this. [23]Instead, you have set yourself up against the Lord of heaven. You had the goblets from his temple brought to you, and you and your nobles, your wives and your concubines drank wine from them. You praised the gods of silver and gold, of bronze, iron,

5:13 f Da 6:13
5:18 g Jer 27:7; Da 2:37–38
5:19 h Da 2:12–13
5:20 i Da 4:30
5:21 j Da 4:16–17,35

[a]2 Or *ancestor*; or *predecessor*; also in verses 11, 13 and 18 [b]7 Or *Chaldeans*; also in verse 11 [c]10 Or *queen mother*
[d]22 Or *descendant*; or *successor*

**5:23** k Ps 115:4–8; Hab 2:19 l Jer 10:23
**5:26** m Isa 13:6
**5:27** n Ps 62:9
**5:28** o Da 6:28
**5:30** p Jer 51:31
**5:31** q Da 6:1; 9:1
**6:2** r Da 2:48–49
**6:3** s Est 10:3; Da 5:12–14

wood and stone, which cannot see or hear
or understand.[k] But you did not honor the
God who holds in his hand your life and all
your ways.[l] 24 Therefore he sent the hand
that wrote the inscription.
25 "This is the inscription that was
written:

MENE, MENE, TEKEL, PARSIN[a]

26 "This is what these words mean:

*Mene*[b]: God has numbered the days
of your reign and brought it to
an end.[m]
27 *Tekel*[c]: You have been weighed on
the scales and found wanting.[n]
28 *Peres*[d]: Your kingdom is divided
and given to the Medes and
Persians."[o]

> *"The secret of being a saint is being a saint in secret."*
> —MARY MCLEOD BETHUNE, EDUCATOR

29 Then at Belshazzar's
command, Daniel was
clothed in purple, a gold
chain was placed around
his neck, and he was pro-
claimed the third highest
ruler in the kingdom.
30 That very night
Belshazzar, king of the
Babylonians,[e] was slain,[p]
31 and Darius[q] the Mede took over the king-
dom, at the age of sixty-two.

## Daniel in the Den of Lions

6 It pleased Darius to appoint 120 sa-
traps to rule throughout the kingdom,
2 with three administrators over them, one
of whom was Daniel.[r] The satraps were
made accountable to them so that the king
might not suffer loss. 3 Now Daniel so distin-
guished himself among the administrators
and the satraps by his exceptional qualities
that the king planned to set him over the
whole kingdom.[s] 4 At this, the administra-
tors and the satraps tried to find grounds
for charges against Daniel in his conduct of
government affairs, but they were unable
to do so. They could find no corruption in
him, because he was trustworthy and nei-
ther corrupt nor negligent. 5 Finally these
men said, "We will never find any basis
for charges against this man Daniel un-
less it has something to do with the law of
his God."
6 So the administrators and the satraps
went as a group to the king and said:
"O King Darius, live forever![t] 7 The royal
administrators, prefects, satraps, advisers
and governors[u] have all agreed that the
king should issue an edict and enforce the
decree that anyone who prays to any god or
man during the next thirty days, except to
you, O king, shall be thrown into the lions'
den.[v] 8 Now, O king, issue the decree and put
it in writing so that it cannot be altered—in
accordance with the laws of the Medes and
Persians, which cannot be repealed."[w] 9 So
King Darius put the decree in writing.
10 Now when Daniel learned that the de-
cree had been published, he went home
to his upstairs room where the windows
opened toward Jerusalem. Three times a
day he got down on his knees[x] and prayed,
giving thanks to his God, just as he had
done before. 11 Then these men went as a
group and found Daniel praying and asking
God for help. 12 So they went to the king and
spoke to him about his royal decree: "Did
you not publish a decree that during the
next thirty days anyone who prays to any
god or man except to you, O king, would be
thrown into the lions' den?"
The king answered, "The decree stands
—in accordance with the laws of the Medes
and Persians, which cannot be repealed."[y]
13 Then they said to the king, "Daniel,
who is one of the exiles from Judah, pays
no attention[z] to you, O king, or to the de-
cree you put in writing. He still prays three
times a day." 14 When the king heard this, he
was greatly distressed;[a] he was determined
to rescue Daniel and made every effort until
sundown to save him.
15 Then the men went as a group to the
king and said to him, "Remember, O king,
that according to the law of the Medes and
Persians no decree or edict that the king is-
sues can be changed."
16 So the king gave the order, and they
brought Daniel and threw him into the
lions' den. The king said to Daniel, "May

**6:6** t Ne 2:3
**6:7** u Da 3:2 v Ps 59:3; Da 3:6
**6:8** w Est 1:19
**6:10** x Ps 95:6
**6:12** y Da 3:8–12
**6:13** z Est 3:8
**6:14** a Mk 6:26

[a] 25 Aramaic *UPARSIN* (that is, *AND PARSIN*) [b] 26 *Mene* can mean *numbered* or *mina* (a unit of money). [c] 27 *Tekel* can mean *weighed* or *shekel.* [d] 28 *Peres* (the singular of *Parsin*) can mean *divided* or *Persia* or *a half mina* or *a half shekel.* [e] 30 Or *Chaldeans*

**6:17** b Mt 27:66
**6:18** c 2Sa 12:17 d Est 6:1
**6:20** e Da 3:17
**6:22** f Da 3:28 g Heb 11:33 h 2Ti 4:17
**6:23** i Da 3:27
**6:24** j Dt 24:16; 2Ki 14:6
**6:25** k Da 4:1
**6:26** l Da 3:29 m Da 2:44
**6:27** n Da 4:3

your God, whom you serve continually, rescue you!"
17 A stone was brought and placed over
the mouth of the den, and the king sealed[b]
it with his own signet ring and with the
rings of his nobles, so that Daniel's situation might not be changed.
18 Then the king
returned to his palace and spent the night
without eating[c] and without any entertainment being brought to him. And he could
not sleep.[d]
19 At the first light of dawn, the king got
up and hurried to the lions' den.
20 When he
came near the den, he called to Daniel in
an anguished voice, "Daniel, servant of the
living God, has your God, whom you serve
continually, been able to rescue you from
the lions?"[e]
21 Daniel answered, "O king, live forever!
22 My God sent his angel,[f] and he shut the
mouths of the lions.[g] They have not hurt me,
because I was found innocent in his sight.[h]
Nor have I ever done any wrong before you,
O king."
23 The king was overjoyed and gave orders
to lift Daniel out of the den. And when Daniel was lifted from the den, no wound[i] was
found on him, because he had trusted in
his God.
24 At the king's command, the men who
had falsely accused Daniel were brought in
and thrown into the lions' den, along with
their wives and children.[j] And before they
reached the floor of the den, the lions overpowered them and crushed all their bones.
25 Then King Darius wrote to all the peoples, nations and men of every language
throughout the land:

"May you prosper greatly![k]

26 "I issue a decree that in every part
of my kingdom people must fear and
reverence the God of Daniel.[l]

"For he is the living God
and he endures forever;
his kingdom will not be destroyed,
his dominion will never end.[m]
27 He rescues and he saves;
he performs signs and wonders[n]
in the heavens and on the earth.
He has rescued Daniel
from the power of the lions."

28 So Daniel prospered during the reign of
Darius and the reign of Cyrus[a][o] the Persian.

*Woman of color,*

*You can trust me because I never change.*

*Your God*

DANIEL 6:25–27

## Daniel's Dream of Four Beasts

**6:28** o Da 1:21
**7:1** p Da 1:17
**7:3** q Rev 13:1
**7:5** r Da 2:39
**7:7** s Da 2:40 t Rev 12:3

7 In the first year of Belshazzar king of
Babylon, Daniel had a dream, and visions passed through his mind[p] as he was
lying on his bed. He wrote down the substance of his dream.
2 Daniel said: "In my vision at night I
looked, and there before me were the four
winds of heaven churning up the great sea.
3 Four great beasts,[q] each different from the
others, came up out of the sea.
4 "The first was like a lion, and it had
the wings of an eagle. I watched until its
wings were torn off and it was lifted from
the ground so that it stood on two feet like a
man, and the heart of a man was given to it.
5 "And there before me was a second
beast, which looked like a bear. It was raised
up on one of its sides, and it had three ribs in
its mouth between its teeth. It was told, 'Get
up and eat your fill of flesh!'[r]
6 "After that, I looked, and there before
me was another beast, one that looked like
a leopard. And on its back it had four wings
like those of a bird. This beast had four
heads, and it was given authority to rule.
7 "After that, in my vision at night I looked,
and there before me was a fourth beast—
terrifying and frightening and very powerful. It had large iron[s] teeth; it crushed and
devoured its victims and trampled underfoot whatever was left. It was different from
all the former beasts, and it had ten horns.[t]
8 "While I was thinking about the horns,

[a]28 Or *Darius, that is, the reign of Cyrus*

**7:8**
u Da 8:9
v Rev 13:5–6

**7:9**
w Rev 1:14
x Eze 1:15

**7:10**
y Ps 50:3
z Rev 5:11
a Rev 20:11–15

**7:11**
b Rev 19:20

**7:13**
c Mt 8:20*;
Rev 1:13*
d Rev 1:7

**7:14**
e Ps 72:11
f Heb 12:28

**7:18**
g Isa 60:12–14;
Rev 2:26

there before me was another horn, a little[u] one, which came up among them; and three of the first horns were uprooted before it. This horn had eyes like the eyes of a man and a mouth that spoke boastfully.[v]

9 "As I looked,

"thrones were set in place,
  and the Ancient of Days took his seat.
His clothing was as white as snow;
  the hair of his head was white like
    wool.[w]
His throne was flaming with fire,
  and its wheels[x] were all ablaze.
10 A river of fire[y] was flowing,
  coming out from before him.[z]
Thousands upon thousands attended him;
  ten thousand times ten thousand
    stood before him.
The court was seated,
  and the books[a] were opened.

11 "Then I continued to watch because of the boastful words the horn was speaking. I kept looking until the beast was slain and its body destroyed and thrown into the blazing fire.[b] 12 (The other beasts had been stripped of their authority, but were allowed to live for a period of time.)

13 "In my vision at night I looked, and there before me was one like a son of man,[c] coming with the clouds of heaven.[d] He approached the Ancient of Days and was led into his presence. 14 He was given authority, glory and sovereign power; all peoples, nations and men of every language worshiped him.[e] His dominion is an everlasting dominion that will not pass away, and his kingdom is one that will never be destroyed.[f]

## The Interpretation of the Dream

15 "I, Daniel, was troubled in spirit, and the visions that passed through my mind disturbed me. 16 I approached one of those standing there and asked him the true meaning of all this.

"So he told me and gave me the interpretation of these things: 17 'The four great beasts are four kingdoms that will rise from the earth. 18 But the saints of the Most High will receive the kingdom and will possess it forever—yes, for ever and ever.'[g]

19 "Then I wanted to know the true meaning of the fourth beast, which was different from all the others and most terrifying, with its iron teeth and bronze claws—the beast that crushed and devoured its victims and trampled underfoot whatever was left. 20 I also wanted to know about the ten horns on its head and about the other horn that came up, before which three of them fell—the horn that looked more imposing than the others and that had eyes and a mouth that spoke boastfully. 21 As I watched, this horn was waging war against the saints and defeating them,[h] 22 until the Ancient of Days came and pronounced judgment in favor of the saints of the Most High, and the time came when they possessed the kingdom.

23 "He gave me this explanation: 'The fourth beast is a fourth kingdom that will appear on earth. It will be different from all the other kingdoms and will devour the whole earth, trampling it down and crushing it. 24 The ten horns[i] are ten kings who will come from this kingdom. After them another king will arise, different from the earlier ones; he will subdue three kings. 25 He will speak against the Most High and oppress his saints and try to change the set times[j] and the laws. The saints will be handed over to him for a time, times and half a time.[a]

26 " 'But the court will sit, and his power will be taken away and completely destroyed forever. 27 Then the sovereignty, power and greatness of the kingdoms under the whole heaven will be handed over to the saints, the people of the Most High. His kingdom will be an everlasting[k] kingdom, and all rulers will worship and obey him.'

28 "This is the end of the matter. I, Daniel, was deeply troubled by my thoughts, and my face turned pale, but I kept the matter to myself."

## Daniel's Vision of a Ram and a Goat

8 In the third year of King Belshazzar's reign, I, Daniel, had a vision, after the one that had already appeared to me. 2 In my vision I saw myself in the citadel of Susa in the province of Elam; in the vision I was

**7:21**
h Rev 13:7

**7:24**
i Rev 17:12

**7:25**
j Da 2:21

**7:27**
k Lk 1:33;
Rev 11:15

[a] 25 Or *for a year, two years and half a year*

**8:3** l Da 10:5
**8:8** m 2Ch 26:16–21 n Da 7:2
**8:9** o Da 11:16
**8:10** p Rev 12:4
**8:11** q Da 11:36–37 r Da 11:31; 12:11
**8:13** s Da 4:23 t Da 12:6

beside the Ulai Canal. 3 I looked up,[l] and
there before me was a ram with two horns,
standing beside the canal, and the horns
were long. One of the horns was longer than
the other but grew up later. 4 I watched the
ram as he charged toward the west and the
north and the south. No animal could stand
against him, and none could rescue from
his power. He did as he pleased and became
great.

5 As I was thinking about this, suddenly
a goat with a prominent horn between his
eyes came from the west, crossing the whole
earth without touching the ground. 6 He
came toward the two-horned ram I had
seen standing beside the canal and charged
at him in great rage. 7 I saw him attack the
ram furiously, striking the ram and shatter-
ing his two horns. The ram was powerless to
stand against him; the goat knocked him to
the ground and trampled on him, and none
could rescue the ram from his power. 8 The
goat became very great, but at the height of
his power his large horn was broken off,[m]
and in its place four prominent horns grew
up toward the four winds of heaven.[n]

9 Out of one of them came another horn,
which started small but grew in power to
the south and to the east and toward the
Beautiful Land.[o] 10 It grew until it reached
the host of the heavens, and it threw some of
the starry host down to the earth[p] and tram-
pled on them. 11 It set itself up to be as great
as the Prince of the host;[q] it took away the
daily sacrifice from him, and the place of his
sanctuary was brought low.[r] 12 Because of re-
bellion, the host ⌊of the saints⌋[a] and the daily
sacrifice were given over to it. It prospered
in everything it did, and truth was thrown
to the ground.

13 Then I heard a holy one[s] speaking, and
another holy one said to him, "How long
will it take for the vision to be fulfilled[t]—
the vision concerning the daily sacrifice,
the rebellion that causes desolation, and the
surrender of the sanctuary and of the host
that will be trampled underfoot?"

14 He said to me, "It will take 2,300 eve-
nings and mornings; then the sanctuary
will be reconsecrated."

## The Interpretation of the Vision

15 While I, Daniel, was watching the vi-
sion and trying to understand it, there be-
fore me stood one who looked like a man.
16 And I heard a man's voice from the Ulai
calling, "Gabriel,[u] tell this man the mean-
ing of the vision."

17 As he came near the place where I
was standing, I was terrified and fell pros-
trate.[v] "Son of man," he said to me, "under-
stand that the vision concerns the time of
the end."

18 While he was speaking to me, I was in
a deep sleep, with my face to the ground.[w]
Then he touched me and raised me to my
feet.[x]

19 He said: "I am going to tell you what will
happen later in the time of wrath, because
the vision concerns the appointed time of
the end.[b][y] 20 The two-horned ram that you
saw represents the kings of Media and Per-
sia. 21 The shaggy goat is the king of Greece,
and the large horn between his eyes is the
first king. 22 The four horns that replaced the
one that was broken off represent four king-
doms that will emerge from his nation but
will not have the same power.

23 "In the latter part of their reign, when
rebels have become completely wicked, a
stern-faced king, a master of intrigue, will
arise. 24 He will become very strong, but not
by his own power. He will cause astounding
devastation and will succeed in whatever
he does. He will destroy the mighty men
and the holy people.[z] 25 He will cause deceit
to prosper, and he will consider himself
superior. When they feel secure, he will de-
stroy many and take his stand against the
Prince of princes. Yet he will be destroyed,
but not by human power.[a]

26 "The vision of the evenings and morn-
ings that has been given you is true,[b] but
seal up the vision, for it concerns the dis-
tant future."[c]

27 I, Daniel, was exhausted and lay ill for
several days. Then I got up and went about
the king's business. I was appalled by the vi-
sion; it was beyond understanding.

**8:16** u Lk 1:19
**8:17** v Eze 1:28; Rev 1:17
**8:18** w Da 10:9 x Eze 2:2
**8:19** y Hab 2:3
**8:24** z Da 11:36
**8:25** a Da 2:34
**8:26** b Da 10:1 c Da 10:14

[a] 12 Or *rebellion, the armies* [b] 19 Or *because the end will be at the appointed time*

9:2 d 2Ch 36:21
9:3 e Jer 29:12
9:4 f Dt 7:9
9:5 g Ps 106:6
9:6 h 2Ch 36:16
9:9 i Ne 9:17
9:10 j 2Ki 17:13–15
9:11 k Isa 1:4–6
9:12 l Zec 1:6

## Daniel's Prayer

9 In the first year of Darius son of Xerxes[a] (a Mede by descent), who was made ruler over the Babylonian[b] kingdom— 2 in the first year of his reign, I, Daniel, understood from the Scriptures, according to the word of the LORD given to Jeremiah the prophet, that the desolation of Jerusalem would last seventy[d] years. 3 So I turned to the Lord God and pleaded with him in prayer and petition, in fasting, and in sackcloth and ashes.[e]

4 I prayed to the LORD my God and confessed:

"O Lord, the great and awesome God, who keeps his covenant of love[f] with all who love him and obey his commands, 5 we have sinned and done wrong.[g] We have been wicked and have rebelled; we have turned away from your commands and laws. 6 We have not listened to your servants the prophets,[h] who spoke in your name to our kings, our princes and our fathers, and to all the people of the land.

7 "Lord, you are righteous, but this day we are covered with shame—the men of Judah and people of Jerusalem and all Israel, both near and far, in all the countries where you have scattered us because of our unfaithfulness to you. 8 O LORD, we and our kings, our princes and our fathers are covered with shame because we have sinned against you. 9 The Lord our God is merciful and forgiving, even though we have rebelled against him;[i] 10 we have not obeyed the LORD our God or kept the laws he gave us through his servants the prophets.[j] 11 All Israel has transgressed your law and turned away, refusing to obey you.

"Therefore the curses and sworn judgments written in the Law of Moses, the servant of God, have been poured out on us, because we have sinned[k] against you. 12 You have fulfilled[l] the words spoken against us and against our rulers by bringing upon us great disaster. Under the whole heaven nothing has ever been done like what has been done to Jerusalem.[m] 13 Just as it is written in the Law of Moses, all this disaster has come upon us, yet we have not sought the favor of the LORD our God by turning from our sins and giving attention to your truth.[n] 14 The LORD did not hesitate to bring the disaster upon us, for the LORD our God is righteous in everything he does; yet we have not obeyed him.

15 "Now, O Lord our God, who brought your people out of Egypt with a mighty hand[o] and who made for yourself a name[p] that endures to this day, we have sinned, we have done wrong. 16 O Lord, in keeping with all your righteous acts,[q] turn away your anger and your wrath from Jerusalem, your city, your holy hill. Our sins and the iniquities of our fathers have made Jerusalem and your people an object of scorn to all those around us.

17 "Now, our God, hear the prayers and petitions of your servant. For your sake, O Lord, look with favor[r] on your desolate sanctuary. 18 Give ear, O God, and hear; open your eyes and see the desolation of the city that bears your Name.[s] We do not make requests of you because we are righteous, but because of your great mercy. 19 O Lord, listen! O Lord, forgive! O Lord, hear and act! For your sake, O my God, do not delay, because your city and your people bear your Name."

## The Seventy "Sevens"

20 While I was speaking and praying, confessing my sin and the sin of my people Israel and making my request to the LORD my God for his holy hill— 21 while I was still in prayer, Gabriel,[t] the man I had seen in the earlier vision, came to me in swift flight about the time of the evening sacrifice. 22 He instructed me and said to me, "Daniel, I have now come to give you insight and understanding. 23 As soon as you began to pray, an answer was given, which I have come to tell you, for you are highly esteemed. There-

9:12 m Eze 5:9
9:13 n Isa 9:13; Jer 2:30
9:15 o Jer 32:21 p Ne 9:10
9:16 q Ps 31:1
9:17 r Nu 6:24–26
9:18 s Isa 37:17
9:21 t Da 8:16

[a]1 Hebrew *Ahasuerus* [b]1 Or *Chaldean*

**9:23** u Mt 24:15
**9:26** v Isa 53:8
**9:27** w Isa 10:22
**10:1** x Da 1:7; y Da 8:26
**10:5** z Jer 10:9
**10:6** a Rev 19:12; b Rev 1:15

fore, consider the message and understand the vision:[u]

24“Seventy ‘sevens’[a] are decreed for your people and your holy city to finish[b] transgression, to put an end to sin, to atone for wickedness, to bring in everlasting righteousness, to seal up vision and prophecy and to anoint the most holy.[c]

25“Know and understand this: From the issuing of the decree[d] to restore and rebuild Jerusalem until the Anointed One,[e] the ruler, comes, there will be seven ‘sevens,’ and sixty-two ‘sevens.’ It will be rebuilt with streets and a trench, but in times of trouble. 26After the sixty-two ‘sevens,’ the Anointed One will be cut off[v] and will have nothing.[f] The people of the ruler who will come will destroy the city and the sanctuary. The end will come like a flood: War will continue until the end, and desolations have been decreed. 27He will confirm a covenant with many for one ‘seven.’[g] In the middle of the ‘seven’[g] he will put an end to sacrifice and offering. And on a wing ⌞of the temple⌟ he will set up an abomination that causes desolation, until the end that is decreed[w] is poured out on him.[h]”[i]

## Daniel’s Vision of a Man

**10** In the third year of Cyrus king of Persia, a revelation was given to Daniel (who was called Belteshazzar).[x] Its message was true[y] and it concerned a great war.[j] The understanding of the message came to him in a vision.

2At that time I, Daniel, mourned for three weeks. 3I ate no choice food; no meat or wine touched my lips; and I used no lotions at all until the three weeks were over.

4On the twenty-fourth day of the first month, as I was standing on the bank of the great river, the Tigris, 5I looked up and there before me was a man dressed in linen, with a belt of the finest gold[z] around his waist. 6His body was like chrysolite, his face like lightning, his eyes like flaming torches,[a] his arms and legs like the gleam of burnished bronze,[b] and his voice like the sound of a multitude.

7I, Daniel, was the only one who saw the vision; the men with me did not see it, but such terror overwhelmed them that they fled and hid themselves. 8So I was left alone,[c] gazing at this great vision; I had no strength left, my face turned deathly pale and I was helpless. 9Then I heard him speaking, and as I listened to him, I fell into a deep sleep, my face to the ground.

10A hand touched me[d] and set me trembling on my hands and knees. 11He said, “Daniel, you who are highly esteemed,[e] consider carefully the words I am about to speak to you, and stand up, for I have now been sent to you.” And when he said this to me, I stood up trembling.

12Then he continued, “Do not be afraid, Daniel. Since the first day that you set your mind to gain understanding and to humble[f] yourself before your God, your words were heard, and I have come in response to them.[g] 13But the prince of the Persian kingdom resisted me twenty-one days. Then Michael,[h] one of the chief princes, came to help me, because I was detained there with the king of Persia. 14Now I have come to explain to you what will happen to your people in the future, for the vision concerns a time yet to come.[i]”

15While he was saying this to me, I bowed with my face toward the ground and was speechless.[j] 16Then one who looked like a man[k] touched my lips, and I opened my mouth and began to speak.[k] I said to the one standing before me, “I am overcome with anguish because of the vision, my lord, and I am helpless. 17How can I, your servant, talk with you, my lord? My strength is gone and I can hardly breathe.”

18Again the one who looked like a man touched me and gave me strength. 19“Do not be afraid, O man highly esteemed,” he said. “Peace![l] Be strong now; be strong.”

When he spoke to me, I was strengthened and said, “Speak, my lord, since you have given me strength.”

20So he said, “Do you know why I have come to you? Soon I will return to fight

**10:8** c Ge 32:24
**10:10** d Jer 1:9
**10:11** e Da 9:23
**10:12** f Da 9:3; g Da 9:20
**10:13** h ver 21; Da 12:1; Jude 1:9
**10:14** i Da 2:28; 8:26
**10:15** j Eze 24:27
**10:16** k Jer 1:9; Da 8:15–18
**10:19** l Jdg 6:23

[a]24 Or *‘weeks’*; also in verses 25 and 26 [b]24 Or *restrain* [c]24 Or *Most Holy Place*; or *most holy One* [d]25 Or *word* [e]25 Or *an anointed one*; also in verse 26 [f]26 Or *off and will have no one*; or *off, but not for himself* [g]27 Or *‘week’* [h]27 Or *it* [i]27 Or *And one who causes desolation will come upon the pinnacle of the abominable ⌞temple⌟, until the end that is decreed is poured out on the desolated ⌞city⌟* [j]1 Or *true and burdensome* [k]16 Most manuscripts of the Masoretic Text; one manuscript of the Masoretic Text, Dead Sea Scrolls and Septuagint *Then something that looked like a man’s hand*

10:20 m Da 8:21; 11:2

against the prince of Persia, and when I go,
the prince of Greece[m] will come; 21 but first I
will tell you what is written in the Book of
Truth. (No one supports me against them
except Michael,[n] your prince. 11 1 And
in the first year of Darius[o] the
Mede, I took my stand to support and protect him.)

10:21 n ver 13

11:1 o Da 5:31

Inspire leadership FOCUS

## PRAYING FOR PATIENCE

It is not uncommon for leaders to scurry through life, juggling the kids, laundry, dinner, work, husband, school and ministry. As women, we are masters at multitasking, but when an unexpected trial is thrown into this balancing act, everything can fall apart without the right perspective.

Trials signal the need to pray for patience. But have you ever been encouraged *not* to pray for patience? Some people believe that if you pray for patience, then God will make you wait, seemingly for a lifetime, for something your heart desires. What folly! Patience goes far beyond waiting. It is a precious spiritual commodity—an expression of love to our husbands, children, family and the body of Christ (see 1Co 13:4). Patience is the pathway to becoming a mature, complete woman of God, not lacking anything (see Jas 1:4).

As leaders, we must refresh our perspective about the trials of life to effectively minister to our sisters in Christ. All trials—even the "flaming arrows of the evil one" (Eph 6:16)—can be used by God to test our faith and to produce a loving, patient woman. Let's not give the devil credit; instead, let's give the credit to God. Trials deliver patience as a gift. When Daniel prayed to God and mourned for three weeks, he was cultivating patience and trust in God (see Da 10:2). Daniel's prayer was answered with a vision from heaven. God used the enemy, who was fighting against Daniel's prayers, to teach Daniel to continue in prayer and to not give up praying (see Da 10:12–14).

When we see trials as a gift, we can then change our mindset—counting every trial, no matter how large or small, as joyous, because the final product is a complete woman (see Jas 1:2–4).

Shall we dare pray for patience? Absolutely! Seek after it. Embrace it. Condition and massage it. God wants us to be complete women of God.

—M. Robinson

For the next Inspire note, go to page 1047.

**read**

Daniel 10; Galatians 5:22–23; Colossians 1:3–14.

**See also** the Inspire Notes "Patience" and "Waiting on God," and the Women of the Bible Notes "Hannah: What Do You Do When God Says 'No'?" "Job's Wife: She Was Tested Too" and "The Canaanite Woman: Persistence Pays Off."

**WOMAN of COLOR**

Pray for patience. Ask God to remove any fear associated with this prayer and to reveal any areas of anxiety in your life.

## The Kings of the South and the North

2"Now then, I tell you the truth: Three more kings will appear in Persia, and then a fourth, who will be far richer than all the others. When he has gained power by his wealth, he will stir up everyone against the kingdom of Greece. 3Then a mighty king will appear, who will rule with great power and do as he pleases.[p] 4After he has appeared, his empire will be broken up and parceled out toward the four winds of heaven.[q] It will not go to his descendants, nor will it have the power he exercised, because his empire will be uprooted and given to others.

5"The king of the South will become strong, but one of his commanders will become even stronger than he and will rule his own kingdom with great power. 6After some years, they will become allies. The daughter of the king of the South will go to the king of the North to make an alliance, but she will not retain her power, and he and his power[a] will not last. In those days she will be handed over, together with her royal escort and her father[b] and the one who supported her.

7"One from her family line will arise to take her place. He will attack the forces of the king of the North and enter his fortress; he will fight against them and be victorious. 8He will also seize their gods,[r] their metal images and their valuable articles of silver and gold and carry them off to Egypt.[s] For some years he will leave the king of the North alone. 9Then the king of the North will invade the realm of the king of the South but will retreat to his own country. 10His sons will prepare for war and assemble a great army, which will sweep on like an irresistible flood[t] and carry the battle as far as his fortress.

11"Then the king of the South will march out in a rage and fight against the king of the North, who will raise a large army, but it will be defeated. 12When the army is carried off, the king of the South will be filled with pride and will slaughter many thousands, yet he will not remain triumphant. 13For the king of the North will muster another army, larger than the first; and after several years, he will advance with a huge army fully equipped.

14"In those times many will rise against the king of the South. The violent men among your own people will rebel in fulfillment of the vision, but without success. 15Then the king of the North will come and build up siege ramps[u] and will capture a fortified city. The forces of the South will be powerless to resist; even their best troops will not have the strength to stand. 16The invader will do as he pleases; no one will be able to stand against him.[v] He will establish himself in the Beautiful Land and will have the power to destroy it. 17He will determine to come with the might of his entire kingdom and will make an alliance with the king of the South. And he will give him a daughter in marriage in order to overthrow the kingdom, but his plans[c] will not succeed or help him. 18Then he will turn his attention to the coastlands[w] and will take many of them, but a commander will put an end to his insolence and will turn his insolence back upon him.[x] 19After this, he will turn back toward the fortresses of his own country but will stumble and fall,[y] to be seen no more.

20"His successor will send out a tax collector to maintain the royal splendor.[z] In a few years, however, he will be destroyed, yet not in anger or in battle.

21"He will be succeeded by a contemptible person who has not been given the honor of royalty. He will invade the kingdom when its people feel secure, and he will seize it through intrigue. 22Then an overwhelming army will be swept away before him; both it and a prince of the covenant will be destroyed.[a] 23After coming to an agreement with him, he will act deceitfully,[b] and with only a few people he will rise to power. 24When the richest provinces feel secure, he will invade them and will achieve what neither his fathers nor his forefathers did. He will distribute plunder, loot and wealth among his followers. He will plot the overthrow of fortresses—but only for a time.

25"With a large army he will stir up his strength and courage against the king of the South. The king of the South will wage war

1:3 Da 8:4,21
1:4 Da 8:22
1:8 Isa 37:19; 6:1–2 Jer 43:12
1:10 Isa 8:8; er 46:8; Da 9:26

11:15 u Eze 4:2
11:16 v Jos 1:5; Da 8:7
11:18 w Isa 66:19 x Hos 12:14
11:19 y Ps 27:2
11:20 z Isa 60:17
11:22 a Da 8:10–11
11:23 b Da 8:25

[a]6 Or *offspring* [b]6 Or *child* (see Vulgate and Syriac) [c]17 Or *but she*

with a large and very powerful army, but he will not be able to stand because of the plots devised against him. 26Those who eat from the king's provisions will try to destroy him; his army will be swept away, and many will fall in battle. 27The two kings, with their hearts bent on evil,[c] will sit at the same table and lie to each other, but to no avail, because an end will still come at the appointed time.[d] 28The king of the North will return to his own country with great wealth, but his heart will be set against the holy covenant. He will take action against it and then return to his own country.

29"At the appointed time he will invade the South again, but this time the outcome will be different from what it was before. 30Ships of the western coastlands[a][e] will oppose him, and he will lose heart. Then he will turn back and vent his fury against the holy covenant. He will return and show favor to those who forsake the holy covenant.

31"His armed forces will rise up to desecrate the temple fortress and will abolish the daily sacrifice. Then they will set up the abomination that causes desolation.[f] 32With flattery he will corrupt those who have violated the covenant, but the people who know their God will firmly resist[g] him.

33"Those who are wise will instruct many, though for a time they will fall by the sword or be burned or captured or plundered.[h] 34When they fall, they will receive a little help, and many who are not sincere[i] will join them. 35Some of the wise will stumble, so that they may be refined,[j] purified and made spotless until the time of the end, for it will still come at the appointed time.

## The King Who Exalts Himself

36"The king will do as he pleases. He will exalt and magnify himself above every god and will say unheard-of things[k] against the God of gods. He will be successful until the time of wrath is completed, for what has been determined must take place. 37He will show no regard for the gods of his fathers or for the one desired by women, nor will he regard any god, but will exalt himself above them all. 38Instead of them, he will honor a god of fortresses; a god unknown to his fathers he will honor with gold and silver, with precious stones and costly gifts. 39He will attack the mightiest fortresses with the help of a foreign god and will greatly honor those who acknowledge him. He will make them rulers over many people and will distribute the land at a price.[b]

40"At the time of the end the king of the South will engage him in battle, and the king of the North will storm[l] out against him with chariots and cavalry and a great fleet of ships. He will invade many countries and sweep through them like a flood. 41He will also invade the Beautiful Land. Many countries will fall, but Edom, Moab[m] and the leaders of Ammon will be delivered from his hand. 42He will extend his power over many countries; Egypt will not escape. 43He will gain control of the treasures of gold and silver and all the riches of Egypt, with the Libyans[n] and Nubians in submission. 44But reports from the east and the north will alarm him, and he will set out in a great rage to destroy and annihilate many. 45He will pitch his royal tents between the seas at[c] the beautiful holy mountain. Yet he will come to his end, and no one will help him.

## The End Times

12 "At that time Michael,[o] the great prince who protects your people, will arise. There will be a time of distress[p] such as has not happened from the beginning of nations until then. But at that time your people—everyone whose name is found written in the book—will be delivered.[q] 2Multitudes who sleep in the dust of the earth will awake: some to everlasting life, others to shame and everlasting contempt.[r] 3Those who are wise[d][s] will shine like the brightness of the heavens, and those who lead many to righteousness, like the stars for ever and ever. 4But you, Daniel, close up and seal the words of the scroll until the time of the end.[t] Many will go here and there to increase knowledge."

5Then I, Daniel, looked, and there before me stood two others, one on this bank of the river and one on the opposite bank.[u] 6One of them said to the man clothed in linen, who

**11:27** c Ps 64:6 d Hab 2:3
**11:30** e Ge 10:4
**11:31** f Da 8:11–13; Mt 24:15*
**11:32** g Mic 5:7–9
**11:33** h Mt 24:9; Jn 16:2; Heb 11:32–38
**11:34** i Mt 7:15; Ro 16:18
**11:35** j Da 12:10; Zec 13:9; Jn 15:2
**11:36** k Rev 13:5–6
**11:40** l Isa 5:28
**11:41** m Jer 48:47
**11:43** n 2Ch 12:3; Na 3:9
**12:1** o Da 10:13 p Rev 16:18 q Jer 30:7
**12:2** r Mt 25:46
**12:3** s Da 11:33
**12:4** t Rev 22:10
**12:5** u Da 10:4

[a] 30 Hebrew *of Kittim* [b] 39 Or *land for a reward* [c] 45 Or *the sea and* [d] 3 Or *who impart wisdom*

was above the waters of the river, "How long
will it be before these astonishing things
are fulfilled?"
7 The man clothed in linen, who was
above the waters of the river, lifted his right
hand and his left hand toward heaven, and
I heard him swear by him who lives forever,
saying, "It will be for a time, times and half
a time.[a][v] When the power of the holy people
has been finally broken, all these things will
be completed.[w]"
8 I heard, but I did not understand. So I
asked, "My lord, what will the outcome of
all this be?"
9 He replied, "Go your way, Daniel, be-
cause the words are closed up and sealed
until the time of the end. 10 Many will be
purified, made spotless and refined, but the
wicked will continue to be wicked.[x] None of
the wicked will understand, but those who
are wise will understand.
11 "From the time that the daily sacrifice is
abolished and the abomination that causes
desolation is set up, there will be 1,290
days. 12 Blessed is the one who waits[y] for and
reaches the end of the 1,335 days.
13 "As for you, go your way till the end.
You will rest, and then at the end of the days
you will rise to receive your allotted inheri-
tance.[z]"

**12:7**
v Da 7:25
w Lk 21:24

**12:10**
x Isa 32:7

**12:12**
y Isa 30:18

**12:13**
z Rev 14:13

[a] 7 Or *a year, two years and half a year*

# Hosea

## OVERVIEW

Hosea was chosen by God to warn the people of Israel to abandon their idolatry, faithlessness to God and other indulgent practices. Hosea challenged the people to obey the covenant their ancestors swore to obey under Moses at Mount Sinai.

God directed Hosea to marry Gomer, an adulterous woman, and he suffered for her wandering ways. God used Hosea's experience as an object lesson of how the people of Israel sinned against God; yet the Lord was continually willing to forgive—if the people would repent of their sinfulness.

Everyone has sinned against God and needs his forgiveness and reconciliation. As women believers in Jesus Christ, there must be an openness to forgive others as Christ has forgiven us. Reflect on how Hosea offered his wife mercy, just as God grants mercy to us.

## OUTLINE

I. The Unfaithful Wife and the Faithful Husband (1:1—3:5)

II. Israel's Unfaithfulness (4:1—5:15)

III. Israel's Punishment (6:1—10:15)

IV. The Lord's Faithful Love (11:1—13:16)

V. Israel's Repentance Will Bring Blessing (14:1–9)

## SCANNABLE FACTS:

**Author:** Hosea

**Time Written:** About 715 B.C.

**Theme to Note:** Israel's idolatry and God's desire for reconciliation

**Notable Woman:** Gomer, wife of Hosea

**1:1** a 2Ki 13:13
**1:2** b Hos 3:1 c Dt 31:16; Hos 5:3
**1:4** d 2Ki 10:1–14
**1:6** e Hos 2:4
**1:7** f Zec 4:6
**1:10** g Ro 9:26*
**1:11** h Isa 11:12,13 i Eze 37:15–28
**2:2** j Isa 50:1

1 The word of the LORD that came to Ho-
sea son of Beeri during the reigns of
Uzziah, Jotham, Ahaz and Hezekiah, kings
of Judah, and during the reign of Jeroboam[a]
son of Jehoash[a] king of Israel:

## Hosea's Wife and Children

2 When the LORD began to speak through
Hosea, the LORD said to him, "Go, take to
yourself an adulterous[b] wife and children
of unfaithfulness, because the land is guilty
of the vilest adultery[c] in departing from the
LORD." 3 So he married Gomer daughter of
Diblaim, and she conceived and bore him
a son.
4 Then the LORD said to Hosea, "Call him
Jezreel,[d] because I will soon punish the
house of Jehu for the massacre at Jezreel,
and I will put an end to the kingdom of
Israel. 5 In that day I will break Israel's bow
in the Valley of Jezreel."
6 Gomer conceived again and gave birth
to a daughter. Then the LORD said to Hosea,
"Call her Lo-Ruhamah,[b] for I will no lon-
ger show love to the house of Israel,[e] that I
should at all forgive them. 7 Yet I will show
love to the house of Judah; and I will save
them—not by bow, sword or battle, or by
horses and horsemen, but by the LORD their
God.[f]"
8 After she had weaned Lo-Ruhamah, Go-
mer had another son. 9 Then the LORD said,
"Call him Lo-Ammi,[c] for you are not my
people, and I am not your God.
10 "Yet the Israelites will be like the sand
on the seashore, which cannot be measured
or counted. In the place where it was said to
them, 'You are not my people,' they will be
called 'sons of the living God.'[g] 11 The peo-
ple of Judah and the people of Israel will be
reunited,[h] and they will appoint one leader
and will come up out of the land,[i] for great
will be the day of Jezreel.

2 "Say of your brothers, 'My people,' and
of your sisters, 'My loved one.'

## Israel Punished and Restored

2 "Rebuke your mother,[j] rebuke her,
for she is not my wife,
and I am not her husband.
Let her remove the adulterous look from
her face
and the unfaithfulness from between
her breasts.
3 Otherwise I will strip her naked
and make her as bare as on the day she
was born;[k]
I will make her like a desert,
turn her into a parched land,
and slay her with thirst.
4 I will not show my love to her children,
because they are the children of
adultery.
5 Their mother has been unfaithful
and has conceived them in disgrace.
She said, 'I will go after my lovers,
who give me my food and my water,
my wool and my linen, my oil and my
drink.'[l]
6 Therefore I will block her path with
thornbushes;
I will wall her in so that she cannot
find her way.[m]
7 She will chase after her lovers but not
catch them;
she will look for them but not find
them.
Then she will say,
'I will go back to my husband as at
first,
for then I was better off[n] than now.'
8 She has not acknowledged[o] that I was the
one
who gave her the grain, the new wine
and oil,
who lavished on her the silver and gold—
which they used for Baal.

9 "Therefore I will take away my grain[p]
when it ripens,
and my new wine[q] when it is ready.
I will take back my wool and my linen,
intended to cover her nakedness.
10 So now I will expose her lewdness
before the eyes of her lovers;
no one will take her out of my hands.[r]
11 I will stop all her celebrations:
her yearly festivals, her New Moons,
her Sabbath days—all her appointed
feasts.[s]
12 I will ruin her vines and her fig trees,
which she said were her pay from her
lovers;
I will make them a thicket,[t]

**2:3** k Eze 16:4,22
**2:5** l Jer 44:17–18
**2:6** m La 3:9
**2:7** n Eze 16:8
**2:8** o Isa 1:3
**2:9** p Hos 8:7 q Hos 9:2
**2:10** r Eze 16:37
**2:11** s Isa 1:14; Am 8:10
**2:12** t Isa 5:6

[a]1 Hebrew *Joash,* a variant of *Jehoash* [b]6 *Lo-Ruhamah* means *not loved.* [c]9 *Lo-Ammi* means *not my people.*

# Gomer

## *An Unfaithful Wife*

On the surface the story of Gomer is filled with pain and disappointment, yet her story does shed light on God's forgiveness. Gomer is used to show us how much God loves us, cares for us and is willing to forgive us.

Gomer was the wife of the prophet Hosea. God instructed Hosea to marry Gomer, an adulterous woman (see Hos 1:2). Gomer's behavior is used throughout the prophetic book of Hosea as symbolic of Israel. Just as Gomer was an unfaithful wife, Israel had been unfaithful to God.

Hosea and Gomer had children, and their babies were named according to God's directives. They, too, were used to show what God would do to his unfaithful people: *Jezreel* means "God scatters" and refers to punishment; *Lo-Ruhamah* means "not loved"; and *Lo-Ammi* means "not my people."

Although Gomer was guilty of being unfaithful during her marriage, God instructed Hosea to reconcile with his wife. Hosea was told to show love to his wife, just as the Lord loved the Israelites even though they were unfaithful. So Hosea obediently purchased his unfaithful wife from slavery (see Hos 3:1–3).

While the story of Israel was a cycle of obedience and disobedience, and it was filled with the blessings and curses of God, we can't help but read the prophets and think of God's grace and love. It is clear that God loved Israel and loves us. However, we, just as the Israelites did, break God's heart time and time again. While we often have to live with the consequences of our bad decisions, we can find joy and hope in reconciliation with God, who is ready and willing to receive us when we repent. God wants to be in relationship with us. God wants to love us—it's evident in the gift of Christ.

Yes, unfaithful ones, we have a chance to be reconciled to our faithful God, our true lover.

—K. Washington

### reflection

*Have you repented for your unfaithfulness?*

*God is ready and willing to be reconciled with you. Share this good news with another sister today!*

### read

Hosea 1–3.

**See also** the Inspire Notes "Grace and Mercy," "Adultery" and "Forgiveness: God's Extended Mercy," and the Women of the Bible Notes "The Adulteress of Proverbs: The Path to Death" and "The Forgiven Adulteress: Caught but Not Condemned."

For the next Women of the Bible note, go to page 1137.

and wild animals will devour them.
13 I will punish her for the days
she burned incense to the Baals;
she decked herself with rings and jewelry,
and went after her lovers,
but me she forgot,[u]"
declares the LORD.

14 "Therefore I am now going to allure her;
I will lead her into the desert
and speak tenderly to her.
15 There I will give her back her vineyards,
and will make the Valley of Achor[a][v] a
door of hope.
There she will sing[b] as in the days of her
youth,[w]
as in the day she came up out of
Egypt.

16 "In that day," declares the LORD,
"you will call me 'my husband';
you will no longer call me 'my
master.[c]'
17 I will remove the names of the Baals from
her lips;[x]
no longer will their names be invoked.
18 In that day I will make a covenant for
them
with the beasts of the field and the
birds of the air
and the creatures that move along the
ground.[y]
Bow and sword and battle
I will abolish from the land,
so that all may lie down in safety.[z]
19 I will betroth you to me forever;
I will betroth you in[d] righteousness
and justice,
in[e] love and compassion.
20 I will betroth you in faithfulness,
and you will acknowledge[a] the LORD.

21 "In that day I will respond,"
declares the LORD—
"I will respond[b] to the skies,
and they will respond to the earth;
22 and the earth will respond to the grain,
the new wine and oil,
and they will respond to Jezreel.[f]
23 I will plant[c] her for myself in the land;
I will show my love to the one I called
'Not my loved one.[g][d]'
I will say to those called 'Not my people,[h]'
'You are my people';[e]
and they will say, 'You are my God.[f]'"

## Hosea's Reconciliation With His Wife

3 The LORD said to me, "Go, show your
love to your wife again, though she is
loved by another and is an adulteress.[g] Love
her as the LORD loves the Israelites, though
they turn to other gods and love the sacred
raisin cakes.[h]"
2 So I bought her for fifteen shekels[i] of sil-
ver and about a homer and a lethek[j] of bar-
ley. 3 Then I told her, "You are to live with[k]
me many days; you must not be a prostitute
or be intimate with any man, and I will live
with[k] you."
4 For the Israelites will live many days
without king or prince,[i] without sacrifice[j]
or sacred stones, without ephod or idol.[k] 5 Af-
terward the Israelites will return and seek
the LORD their God and David their king.
They will come trembling to the LORD and to
his blessings in the last days.[l]

[a]15 *Achor* means *trouble.* [b]15 Or *respond* [c]16 Hebrew *baal* [d]19 Or *with*; also in verse 20 [e]19 Or *with* [f]22 *Jezreel* means *God plants.* [g]23 Hebrew *Lo-Ruhamah* [h]23 Hebrew *Lo-Ammi* [i]2 That is, about 6 ounces (about 170 grams) [j]2 That is, probably about 10 bushels (about 330 liters) [k]3 Or *wait for*

2:13 u Hos 4:6
2:15 v Jos 7:24,26 w Jer 2:2
2:17 x Ex 23:13; Ps 16:4
2:18 y Job 5:22 z Eze 34:25
2:20 a Jer 31:34
2:21 b Zec 8:12
2:23 c Jer 31:27 d Hos 1:6 e Hos 1:10 f Ro 9:25*
3:1 g Hos 1:2 h 2Sa 6:19
3:4 i Hos 13:11 j Hos 2:11 k Jdg 17:5–6
3:5 l Jer 50:4–5

## The African Presence

### Hosea 2:15

Egypt is located in North Africa. For more on Egypt, see the African Presence note on Genesis 10:6.

4:2 m Hos 7:1
4:3 n Zep 1:3
4:4 o Dt 17:12
4:5 p Hos 2:2
4:6 q Hos 2:13 r Hos 8:1,12
4:7 s Hos 10:1,6; 13:6
4:9 t Isa 24:2 u Jer 5:31; Hos 9:9,15
4:10 v Lev 26:26; Mic 6:14 w Hos 7:14

## The Charge Against Israel

4 Hear the word of the LORD, you
Israelites,
because the LORD has a charge to bring
against you who live in the land:
"There is no faithfulness, no love,
no acknowledgment of God in the
land.
2 There is only cursing,[a] lying and murder,
stealing[m] and adultery;
they break all bounds,
and bloodshed follows bloodshed.
3 Because of this the land mourns,[b]
and all who live in it waste away;
the beasts of the field and the birds of
the air
and the fish of the sea are dying.[n]
4 "But let no man bring a charge,
let no man accuse another,
for your people are like those
who bring charges against a priest.[o]
5 You stumble day and night,
and the prophets stumble with you.
So I will destroy your mother[p]—
6 my people are destroyed from lack of
knowledge.[q]

"Because you have rejected knowledge,
I also reject you as my priests;
because you have ignored the law[r] of your
God,
I also will ignore your children.
7 The more the priests increased,
the more they sinned against me;
they exchanged[c] their[d] Glory for
something disgraceful.[s]
8 They feed on the sins of my people
and relish their wickedness.
9 And it will be: Like people, like priests.[t]
I will punish both of them for their ways
and repay them for their deeds.[u]

10 "They will eat but not have enough;[v]
they will engage in prostitution but not
increase,
because they have deserted[w] the LORD
to give themselves 11 to prostitution,
to old wine and new,
which take away the understanding
12 of my people.
They consult a wooden idol[x]
and are answered by a stick of wood.
A spirit of prostitution leads them astray;
they are unfaithful to their God.
13 They sacrifice on the mountaintops
and burn offerings on the hills,
under oak, poplar and terebinth,
where the shade is pleasant.
Therefore your daughters turn to
prostitution
and your daughters-in-law to
adultery.[y]

14 "I will not punish your daughters
when they turn to prostitution,
nor your daughters-in-law
when they commit adultery,
because the men themselves consort with
harlots
and sacrifice with shrine prostitutes—
a people without understanding will
come to ruin!

15 "Though you commit
adultery,
O Israel,
let not Judah
become guilty.

"Do not go to Gilgal;[z]
do not go up to Beth
Aven.[e]
And do not swear, 'As
surely as the LORD lives!'
16 The Israelites are stubborn,
like a stubborn heifer.
How then can the LORD pasture them
like lambs in a meadow?
17 Ephraim is joined to idols;
leave him alone!
18 Even when their drinks are gone,
they continue their prostitution;
their rulers dearly love shameful ways.
19 A whirlwind[a] will sweep them away,
and their sacrifices will bring them
shame.

*"I was afraid, because I was ignorant."*
—TAWANA BRAWLEY,
CRIME SUSPECT

4:12 x Jer 2:27
4:13 y Hos 2:13
4:15 z Hos 9:15; 12:11
4:19 a Hos 12:1

## Judgment Against Israel

5 "Hear this, you priests!
Pay attention, you Israelites!
Listen, O royal house!

[a]2 That is, to pronounce a curse upon [b]3 Or *dries up* [c]7 Syriac and an ancient Hebrew scribal tradition; Masoretic Text *I will exchange* [d]7 Masoretic Text; an ancient Hebrew scribal tradition *my* [e]15 *Beth Aven* means *house of wickedness* (a name for Bethel, which means *house of God*).

5:1 b Hos 6:9
5:4 c Hos 4:11
5:6 d Mic 6:6–7
5:7 e Hos 6:7 f Hos 2:11–12
5:8 g Isa 10:29
5:9 h Isa 46:10
5:10 i Dt 19:14
5:11 j Mic 6:16
5:13 k Hos 7:11
5:14 l Mic 5:8
5:15 m Jer 2:27
6:1 n Hos 5:14 o Dt 32:39
6:3 p Joel 2:23

This judgment is against you:
You have been a snare[b] at Mizpah,
a net spread out on Tabor.
2 The rebels are deep in slaughter.
I will discipline all of them.
3 I know all about Ephraim;
Israel is not hidden from me.
Ephraim, you have now turned to prostitution;
Israel is corrupt.

4 "Their deeds do not permit them
to return to their God.
A spirit of prostitution[c] is in their heart;
they do not acknowledge the LORD.
5 Israel's arrogance testifies against them;
the Israelites, even Ephraim, stumble in their sin;
Judah also stumbles with them.
6 When they go with their flocks and herds
to seek the LORD,[d]
they will not find him;
he has withdrawn himself from them.
7 They are unfaithful[e] to the LORD;
they give birth to illegitimate children.
Now their New Moon festivals
will devour[f] them and their fields.

8 "Sound the trumpet in Gibeah,
the horn in Ramah.[g]
Raise the battle cry in Beth Aven[a];
lead on, O Benjamin.
9 Ephraim will be laid waste
on the day of reckoning.
Among the tribes of Israel
I proclaim what is certain.[h]
10 Judah's leaders are like those
who move boundary stones.[i]
I will pour out my wrath on them
like a flood of water.
11 Ephraim is oppressed,
trampled in judgment,
intent on pursuing idols.[b][j]
12 I am like a moth to Ephraim,
like rot to the people of Judah.

13 "When Ephraim saw his sickness,
and Judah his sores,
then Ephraim turned to Assyria,[k]
and sent to the great king for help.
But he is not able to cure you,
not able to heal your sores.
14 For I will be like a lion to Ephraim,
like a great lion to Judah.
I will tear them to pieces and go away;
I will carry them off, with no one to rescue them.[l]
15 Then I will go back to my place
until they admit their guilt.
And they will seek my face;
in their misery[m] they will earnestly seek me."

## Israel Unrepentant

6 "Come, let us return to the LORD.
He has torn us to pieces[n]
but he will heal us;
he has injured us
but he will bind up our wounds.[o]
2 After two days he will revive us;
on the third day he will restore us,
that we may live in his presence.
3 Let us acknowledge the LORD;
let us press on to acknowledge him.
As surely as the sun rises,
he will appear;
he will come to us like the winter rains,[p]
like the spring rains that water the earth."

[a] 8 *Beth Aven* means *house of wickedness* (a name for Bethel, which means *house of God*). [b] 11 The meaning of the Hebrew for this word is uncertain.

### The African Presence

**Hosea 5:13**

The Assyrians were descendants of Cush (see Ge 10:8–11), son of Ham. For more on the Assyrians, see the African Presence note on Jeremiah 2:18,36.

4 "What can I do with you, Ephraim?[q]
What can I do with you, Judah?
Your love is like the morning mist,
like the early dew that disappears.
5 Therefore I cut you in pieces with my prophets,
I killed you with the words of my mouth;
my judgments flashed like lightning upon you.
6 For I desire mercy, not sacrifice,[r]
and acknowledgment of God rather than burnt offerings.
7 Like Adam,[a] they have broken the covenant—
they were unfaithful[s] to me there.
8 Gilead is a city of wicked men,
stained with footprints of blood.
9 As marauders lie in ambush for a man,
so do bands of priests;
they murder on the road to Shechem,
committing shameful crimes.
10 I have seen a horrible[t] thing
in the house of Israel.
There Ephraim is given to prostitution
and Israel is defiled.

11 "Also for you, Judah,
a harvest[u] is appointed.

"Whenever I would restore the fortunes of my people,

# 7

1 whenever I would heal Israel,
the sins of Ephraim are exposed
and the crimes of Samaria revealed.[v]
They practice deceit,
thieves break into houses,[w]
bandits rob in the streets;
2 but they do not realize
that I remember all their evil deeds.
Their sins engulf them;[x]
they are always before me.

3 "They delight the king with their wickedness,
the princes with their lies.[y]
4 They are all adulterers,[z]
burning like an oven
whose fire the baker need not stir
from the kneading of the dough till it rises.
5 On the day of the festival of our king
the princes become inflamed with wine,[a]
and he joins hands with the mockers.
6 Their hearts are like an oven;
they approach him with intrigue.
Their passion smolders all night;
in the morning it blazes like a flaming fire.
7 All of them are hot as an oven;
they devour their rulers.
All their kings fall,
and none of them calls on me.

8 "Ephraim mixes[b] with the nations;
Ephraim is a flat cake not turned over.
9 Foreigners sap his strength,[c]
but he does not realize it.
His hair is sprinkled with gray,
but he does not notice.
10 Israel's arrogance testifies against him,[d]
but despite all this
he does not return to the LORD his God
or search[e] for him.

11 "Ephraim is like a dove,[f]
easily deceived and senseless—
now calling to Egypt,
now turning to Assyria.
12 When they go, I will throw my net[g] over them;
I will pull them down like birds of the air.
When I hear them flocking together,
I will catch them.
13 Woe to them,
because they have strayed from me!
Destruction to them,
because they have rebelled against me!
I long to redeem them
but they speak lies against me.
14 They do not cry out to me from their hearts[h]
but wail upon their beds.
They gather together[b] for grain and new wine
but turn away from me.
15 I trained them and strengthened them,
but they plot evil[i] against me.
16 They do not turn to the Most High;
they are like a faulty bow.
Their leaders will fall by the sword

**6:4** q Hos 11:8
**6:6** r Isa 1:11; Mt 9:13*
**6:7** s Hos 5:7
**6:10** t Jer 5:30
**6:11** u Joel 3:13
**7:1** v Hos 6:4 w Hos 4:2
**7:2** x Jer 2:19
**7:3** y Mic 7:3
**7:4** z Jer 9:2
**7:5** a Isa 28:1,7
**7:8** b Ps 106:35
**7:9** c Hos 8:7
**7:10** d Hos 5:5 e Isa 9:13
**7:11** f Hos 11:11
**7:12** g Eze 12:13
**7:14** h Jer 3:10
**7:15** i Na 1:9,11

[a] 7 Or *As at Adam*; or *Like men* [b] 14 Most Hebrew manuscripts; some Hebrew manuscripts and Septuagint *They slash themselves*

7:16 j Hos 9:3
8:1 k Jer 4:13 l Hos 4:6
8:5 m Jer 13:27
8:7 n Pr 22:8
8:8 o Jer 51:34
8:10 p Eze 16:37
8:11 q Hos 10:1

because of their insolent words.
For this they will be ridiculed
in the land of Egypt.[j]

## Israel to Reap the Whirlwind

8 "Put the trumpet to your lips!
An eagle[k] is over the house of the LORD
because the people have broken my covenant
and rebelled against my law.[l]
2 Israel cries out to me,
'O our God, we acknowledge you!'
3 But Israel has rejected what is good;
an enemy will pursue him.
4 They set up kings without my consent;
they choose princes without my approval.
With their silver and gold
they make idols for themselves
to their own destruction.
5 Throw out your calf-idol, O Samaria!
My anger burns against them.
How long will they be incapable of purity?[m]
6 They are from Israel!
This calf—a craftsman has made it;
it is not God.
It will be broken in pieces,
that calf of Samaria.

7 "They sow the wind
and reap the whirlwind.[n]
The stalk has no head;
it will produce no flour.
Were it to yield grain,
foreigners would swallow it up.
8 Israel is swallowed up;[o]
now she is among the nations
like a worthless thing.
9 For they have gone up to Assyria
like a wild donkey wandering alone.
Ephraim has sold herself to lovers.
10 Although they have sold themselves
among the nations,
I will now gather them together.[p]
They will begin to waste away
under the oppression of the mighty king.

11 "Though Ephraim built many altars for sin offerings,
these have become altars for sinning.[q]
12 I wrote for them the many things of my law,
but they regarded them as something alien.
13 They offer sacrifices given to me
and they eat the meat,
but the LORD is not pleased with them.
Now he will remember[r] their wickedness
and punish their sins:
They will return to Egypt.
14 Israel has forgotten his Maker
and built palaces;
Judah has fortified many towns.
But I will send fire upon their cities
that will consume their fortresses."[s]

## Punishment for Israel

9 Do not rejoice, O Israel;
do not be jubilant[t] like the other nations.
For you have been unfaithful to your God;
you love the wages of a prostitute
at every threshing floor.
2 Threshing floors and winepresses will not feed the people;
the new wine[u] will fail them.
3 They will not remain in the LORD's land;
Ephraim will return to Egypt[v]
and eat unclean[a] food in Assyria.[w]
4 They will not pour out wine offerings to the LORD,
nor will their sacrifices please him.
Such sacrifices will be to them like the bread of mourners;
all who eat them will be unclean.[x]
This food will be for themselves;
it will not come into the temple of the LORD.

5 What will you do[y] on the day of your appointed feasts,
on the festival days of the LORD?
6 Even if they escape from destruction,
Egypt will gather them,
and Memphis will bury them.
Their treasures of silver will be taken over by briers,
and thorns will overrun their tents.
7 The days of punishment[z] are coming,
the days of reckoning are at hand.

8:13 r Hos 7:2
8:14 s Jer 17:27
9:1 t Isa 22:12–13
9:2 u Hos 2:9
9:3 v Hos 8:13 w Eze 4:13
9:4 x Hag 2:13–14
9:5 y Isa 10:3; Jer 5:31
9:7 z Isa 34:8; Jer 10:15

[a]3 That is, ceremonially unclean

## The African Presence

### Hosea 9:6

The city of Memphis was located in Lower (northern) Egypt on the west bank of the Nile River about 400 miles south of the Mediterranean coast. Hosea foretold a return to Memphis by Israelites.

9:7 a Eze 14:9–10
9:9 b Hos 5:8
9:10 c Nu 25:1–5; Ps 106:28–29
9:11 d Hos 4:7
9:12 e Dt 31:17
9:14 f Lk 23:29
9:15 g Hos 7:2 h Isa 1:23
9:16 i Hos 5:11 j Hos 8:7
9:17 k Hos 4:10
10:1 l Hos 8:11
10:2 m 1Ki 18:21 n Hos 13:16
10:4 o Am 5:7

Let Israel know this.
Because your sins are so many
and your hostility so great,
the prophet is considered a fool,[a]
the inspired man a maniac.
8 The prophet, along with my God,
is the watchman over Ephraim,[a]
yet snares await him on all his paths,
and hostility in the house of his God.
9 They have sunk deep into corruption,
as in the days of Gibeah.[b]
God will remember their wickedness
and punish them for their sins.

10 "When I found Israel,
it was like finding grapes in the desert;
when I saw your fathers,
it was like seeing the early fruit on the fig tree.
But when they came to Baal Peor,[c]
they consecrated themselves to that shameful idol
and became as vile as the thing they loved.
11 Ephraim's glory will fly away like a bird[d]—
no birth, no pregnancy, no conception.
12 Even if they rear children,
I will bereave them of every one.
Woe to them
when I turn away from them![e]
13 I have seen Ephraim, like Tyre,
planted in a pleasant place.
But Ephraim will bring out
their children to the slayer."

14 Give them, O LORD—
what will you give them?
Give them wombs that miscarry
and breasts that are dry.[f]
15 "Because of all their wickedness in Gilgal,
I hated them there.
Because of their sinful deeds,[g]
I will drive them out of my house.
I will no longer love them;
all their leaders are rebellious.[h]
16 Ephraim[i] is blighted,
their root is withered,
they yield no fruit.[j]
Even if they bear children,
I will slay their cherished offspring."
17 My God will reject them
because they have not obeyed[k] him;
they will be wanderers among the nations.

10 Israel was a spreading vine;
he brought forth fruit for himself.
As his fruit increased,
he built more altars;
as his land prospered,
he adorned his sacred stones.[l]
2 Their heart is deceitful,[m]
and now they must bear their guilt.[n]
The LORD will demolish their altars
and destroy their sacred stones.

3 Then they will say, "We have no king
because we did not revere the LORD.
But even if we had a king,
what could he do for us?"
4 They make many promises,
take false oaths
and make agreements;[o]
therefore lawsuits spring up

[a]8 Or *The prophet is the watchman over Ephraim, / the people of my God*

like poisonous weeds in a plowed field.
5 The people who live in Samaria fear
for the calf-idol of Beth Aven.[a]
Its people will mourn over it,
and so will its idolatrous priests,
those who had rejoiced over its splendor,
because it is taken from them into
exile.[p]
6 It will be carried to Assyria[q]
as tribute for the great king.
Ephraim will be disgraced;[r]
Israel will be ashamed of its wooden
idols.[b]
7 Samaria and its king will float away[s]
like a twig on the surface of the
waters.
8 The high places of wickedness[c][t] will be
destroyed—
it is the sin of Israel.
Thorns and thistles will grow up
and cover their altars.
Then they will say to the mountains,
"Cover us!"
and to the hills, "Fall on us!"[u]

9 "Since the days of Gibeah, you have
sinned, O Israel,
and there you have remained.[d]
Did not war overtake
the evildoers in Gibeah?
10 When I please, I will punish[v] them;
nations will be gathered against them
to put them in bonds for their double
sin.
11 Ephraim is a trained heifer
that loves to thresh;
so I will put a yoke
on her fair neck.
I will drive Ephraim,
Judah must plow,
and Jacob must break up the ground.
12 Sow for yourselves righteousness,
reap the fruit of unfailing love,
and break up your unplowed ground;[w]
for it is time to seek[x] the LORD,
until he comes
and showers righteousness on you.
13 But you have planted wickedness,
you have reaped evil,[y]
you have eaten the fruit of deception.
Because you have depended on your own
strength
and on your many warriors,
14 the roar of battle will rise against your
people,
so that all your fortresses will be
devastated[z]—
as Shalman devastated Beth Arbel on the
day of battle,
when mothers were dashed to the
ground with their children.[a]
15 Thus will it happen to you, O Bethel,
because your wickedness is great.
When that day dawns,
the king of Israel will be completely
destroyed.

## God's Love for Israel

11 "When Israel was a child, I loved
him,
and out of Egypt I called my son.[b]
2 But the more I[e] called Israel,
the further they went from me.[f]
They sacrificed to the Baals
and they burned incense to images.
3 It was I who taught Ephraim to walk,
taking them by the arms;[c]
but they did not realize
it was I who healed them.
4 I led them with cords of human kindness,
with ties of love;
I lifted the yoke[d] from their neck
and bent down to feed[e] them.

5 "Will they not return to Egypt[f]
and will not Assyria rule over them
because they refuse to repent?
6 Swords[g] will flash in their cities,
will destroy the bars of their gates
and put an end to their plans.
7 My people are determined to turn
from me.
Even if they call to the Most High,
he will by no means exalt them.

8 "How can I give you up, Ephraim?
How can I hand you over, Israel?
How can I treat you like Admah?
How can I make you like Zeboiim?[h]
My heart is changed within me;
all my compassion is aroused.

**10:5** p Hos 8:5
**10:6** q Hos 11:5 r Hos 4:7
**10:7** s Hos 13:11
**10:8** t 1Ki 12:28–30 u Lk 23:30*; Rev 6:16
**10:10** v Eze 5:13
**10:12** w Jer 4:3 x Hos 12:6
**10:13** y Job 4:8; Gal 6:7–8
**10:14** z Isa 17:3 a Hos 13:16
**11:1** b Hos 12:9,13; Mt 2:15*
**11:3** c Dt 1:31
**11:4** d Lev 26:13 e Ps 78:25
**11:5** f Hos 7:16
**11:6** g Hos 13:16
**11:8** h Ge 14:8

[a]5 *Beth Aven* means *house of wickedness* (a name for Bethel, which means *house of God*). [b]6 Or *its counsel* [c]8 Hebrew *aven,* a reference to Beth Aven (a derogatory name for Bethel) [d]9 Or *there a stand was taken* [e]2 Some Septuagint manuscripts; Hebrew *they* [f]2 Septuagint; Hebrew *them*

9 I will not carry out my fierce anger,
nor will I turn and devastate Ephraim.
For I am God, and not man—
the Holy One among you.
I will not come in wrath.[a]

*Child,*

*I love you and am wholly committed to you.*

*Your Faithful Father*

HOSEA 11:8–9

10 They will follow the LORD;
he will roar like a lion.
When he roars,
his children will come trembling from the west.[i]
11 They will come trembling
like birds from Egypt,
like doves from Assyria.
I will settle them in their homes,"[j]
declares the LORD.

## Israel's Sin

12 Ephraim has surrounded me with lies,[k]
the house of Israel with deceit.
And Judah is unruly against God,
even against the faithful Holy One.

12 1 Ephraim feeds on the wind;
he pursues the east wind all day
and multiplies lies and violence.
He makes a treaty with Assyria
and sends olive oil to Egypt.
2 The LORD has a charge[l] to bring against Judah;
he will punish Jacob[b] according to his ways
and repay him according to his deeds.
3 In the womb he grasped his brother's heel;[m]
as a man he struggled[n] with God.
4 He struggled with the angel and overcame him;
he wept and begged for his favor.
He found him at Bethel
and talked with him there—
5 the LORD God Almighty,
the LORD is his name[o] of renown!
6 But you must return to your God;
maintain love and justice,
and wait for your God always.

7 The merchant uses dishonest scales;[p]
he loves to defraud.
8 Ephraim boasts,
"I am very rich; I have become wealthy.[q]
With all my wealth they will not find in me
any iniquity or sin."

9 "I am the LORD your God,
⌊who brought you⌋ out of[c] Egypt;[r]
I will make you live in tents again,
as in the days of your appointed feasts.
10 I spoke to the prophets,
gave them many visions
and told parables[s] through them."[t]

11 Is Gilead wicked?
Its people are worthless!
Do they sacrifice bulls in Gilgal?
Their altars will be like piles of stones
on a plowed field.
12 Jacob fled to the country of Aram[d];[u]
Israel served to get a wife,
and to pay for her he tended sheep.
13 The LORD used a prophet to bring Israel
up from Egypt,
by a prophet he cared for him.
14 But Ephraim has bitterly provoked him to anger;
his Lord will leave upon him the guilt of his bloodshed[v]
and will repay him for his contempt.[w]

## The LORD's Anger Against Israel

13 When Ephraim spoke, men trembled;
he was exalted in Israel.
But he became guilty of Baal worship and died.
2 Now they sin more and more;
they make idols for themselves from their silver,
cleverly fashioned images,

[a]9 Or *come against any city* [b]2 *Jacob* means *he grasps the heel* (figuratively, *he deceives*). [c]9 Or *God / ever since you were in* [d]12 That is, Northwest Mesopotamia

**11:10** i Hos 6:1–3
**11:11** j Eze 28:26
**11:12** k Hos 4:2
**12:2** l Mic 6:2
**12:3** m Ge 25:26 n Ge 32:24–29
**12:5** o Ex 3:15
**12:7** p Am 8:5
**12:8** q Rev 3:17
**12:9** r Lev 23:43
**12:10** s Eze 20:49 t 2Ki 17:13
**12:12** u Ge 28:5
**12:14** v Eze 18:13 w Da 11:18

all of them the work of craftsmen.
It is said of these people,
"They offer human sacrifice
and kiss[a] the calf-idols."
[3] Therefore they will be like the morning
mist,
like the early dew that disappears,[x]
like chaff swirling from a threshing
floor,[y]
like smoke escaping through a
window.

[4] "But I am the LORD your God,
⌊who brought you⌋ out of[b] Egypt.[z]
You shall acknowledge no God but me,
no Savior[a] except me.
[5] I cared for you in the desert,
in the land of burning heat.
[6] When I fed them, they were satisfied;
when they were satisfied, they became
proud;
then they forgot me.[b]
[7] So I will come upon them like a lion,
like a leopard I will lurk by the path.
[8] Like a bear robbed of her cubs,[c]
I will attack them and rip them open.
Like a lion I will devour them;
a wild animal will tear them apart.[d]

[9] "You are destroyed, O Israel,
because you are against me, against
your helper.
[10] Where is your king, that he may save
you?
Where are your rulers in all your
towns,
of whom you said,
'Give me a king and princes'?[e]
[11] So in my anger I gave you a king,
and in my wrath I took him away.[f]
[12] The guilt of Ephraim is stored up,
his sins are kept on record.[g]
[13] Pains as of a woman in childbirth[h] come
to him,
but he is a child without wisdom;
when the time arrives,
he does not come to the opening of the
womb.

[14] "I will ransom them from the power of
the grave[c];[i]
I will redeem them from death.
Where, O death, are your plagues?
Where, O grave,[c] is your destruction?[j]

"I will have no compassion,
15 even though he thrives[k] among his
brothers.
An east wind[l] from the LORD will come,
blowing in from the desert;
his spring will fail
and his well dry up.
His storehouse will be plundered[m]
of all its treasures.
[16] The people of Samaria must bear their
guilt,[n]
because they have rebelled against
their God.
They will fall by the sword;
their little ones will be dashed[o] to the
ground,
their pregnant women[p] ripped open."

## Repentance to Bring Blessing

14 Return, O Israel, to the LORD your
God.
Your sins have been your downfall!
[2] Take words with you
and return to the LORD.
Say to him:
"Forgive all our sins
and receive us graciously,[q]
that we may offer the fruit of our lips.[d][r]

*Lord,*

*forgive me for backsliding, for failing to do the things I know I should have done. Restore and renew me. Guide me in a forward direction. In Jesus' name,*

*Amen*

HOSEA 14:1–2

[3] Assyria cannot save us;
we will not mount war-horses.
We will never again say 'Our gods'[s]
to what our own hands have made,

13:3 x Hos 6:4 y Da 2:35
13:4 z Hos 12:9 a Isa 43:11
13:6 b Dt 32:12–15; Hos 2:13
13:8 c 2Sa 17:8 d Ps 50:22
13:10 e Hos 8:4
13:11 f 1Ki 14:10
13:12 g Dt 32:34
13:13 h Mic 4:9–10
13:14 i Eze 37:12–13
13:14 j 1Co 15:55*
13:15 k Hos 10:1 l Eze 19:12 m Jer 20:5
13:16 n Hos 10:2 o Hos 10:14 p 2Ki 15:16
14:2 q Mic 7:18–19 r Heb 13:15
14:3 s Hos 8:6

[a]2 Or *"Men who sacrifice / kiss* [b]4 Or *God / ever since you were in* [c]14 Hebrew *Sheol* [d]2 Or *offer our lips as sacrifices of bulls*

14:3 t Ps 10:14
14:4 u Zep 3:17
14:5 v Isa 35:2
14:6 w SS 4:11
14:7 x Ps 91:1–4

for in you the fatherless[t] find
compassion."

4 "I will heal their waywardness
and love them freely,[u]
for my anger has turned away from
them.
5 I will be like the dew to Israel;
he will blossom like a lily.
Like a cedar of Lebanon[v]
he will send down his roots;
6 his young shoots will grow.
His splendor will be like an olive tree,
his fragrance like a cedar of
Lebanon.[w]
7 Men will dwell again in his shade.[x]
He will flourish like the grain.
He will blossom like a vine,
and his fame will be like the wine from
Lebanon.[y]
8 O Ephraim, what more have I[a] to do with
idols?
I will answer him and care for him.
I am like a green pine tree;
your fruitfulness comes from me."

9 Who is wise? He will realize these things.
Who is discerning? He will understand
them.[z]
The ways of the LORD are right;
the righteous walk[a] in them,
but the rebellious stumble in them.

14:7 y Eze 17:23
14:9 z Pr 10:29; Isa 1:28
a Isa 26:7

[a]8 Or *What more has Ephraim*

# Joel

## OVERVIEW

Joel used the description of a locust invasion to portray the devastation to come against the land of Judah if the people did not repent. Joel described how God would give signs in heaven and earth of his impending condemnation of the people's sin.

Later, Joel told the people that judgment would be followed by restoration. He said that God would "pour out [his] Spirit on all people" (Joel 2:28) to accomplish his purposes.

If the people of Judah were to avoid God's judgment, they had to repent from their sins. Even today we must cultivate a repentant heart so that we will be sensitive to the Spirit's leading in our lives. This means turning away from sin and beginning to do what is right. For every woman who makes a decision to accept Jesus Christ's sacrifice for her sins, repentance is the first step toward living a full life.

## OUTLINE

I. The Plague of Locusts (1:1—2:27)
II. The Day of the Lord (2:28—3:21)

### SCANNABLE FACTS:

**Author:** Joel

**Time Written:** Unknown

**Theme to Note:** The day of the Lord will arrive

**Notable Women:** Women who receive God's Spirit

1 The word of the LORD that came[a] to Joel son of Pethuel.

## An Invasion of Locusts

2 Hear this,[b] you elders;
listen, all who live in the land.
Has anything like this ever happened in your days
or in the days of your forefathers?[c]
3 Tell it to your children,
and let your children tell it to their children,
and their children to the next generation.
4 What the locust swarm has left
the great locusts have eaten;
what the great locusts have left
the young locusts have eaten;
what the young locusts have left
other locusts[a] have eaten.[d]

5 Wake up, you drunkards, and weep!
Wail, all you drinkers of wine;[e]
wail because of the new wine,
for it has been snatched from your lips.
6 A nation has invaded my land,
powerful and without number;
it has the teeth[f] of a lion,
the fangs of a lioness.
7 It has laid waste[g] my vines
and ruined my fig trees.
It has stripped off their bark
and thrown it away,
leaving their branches white.

8 Mourn like a virgin[b] in sackcloth[h]
grieving for the husband[c] of her youth.
9 Grain offerings and drink offerings
are cut off from the house of the LORD.
The priests are in mourning,
those who minister before the LORD.
10 The fields are ruined,
the ground is dried up[d];[i]
the grain is destroyed,
the new wine is dried up,
the oil fails.
11 Despair, you farmers,
wail, you vine growers;
grieve for the wheat and the barley,
because the harvest of the field is destroyed.[j]
12 The vine is dried up
and the fig tree is withered;
the pomegranate, the palm and the apple tree—
all the trees of the field—are dried up.
Surely the joy of mankind
is withered away.

## A Call to Repentance

13 Put on sackcloth,[k] O priests, and mourn;
wail, you who minister before the altar.
Come, spend the night in sackcloth,
you who minister before my God;
for the grain offerings and drink offerings
are withheld from the house of your God.
14 Declare a holy fast;[l]
call a sacred assembly.
Summon the elders
and all who live in the land
to the house of the LORD your God,
and cry out to the LORD.

15 Alas for that[m] day!
For the day of the LORD[n] is near;
it will come like destruction from the Almighty.[e]

16 Has not the food been cut off
before our very eyes—
joy and gladness
from the house of our God?[o]
17 The seeds are shriveled
beneath the clods.[f][p]
The storehouses are in ruins,
the granaries have been broken down,
for the grain has dried up.
18 How the cattle moan!
The herds mill about
because they have no pasture;
even the flocks of sheep are suffering.

19 To you, O LORD, I call,[q]
for fire has devoured the open pastures[r]
and flames have burned up all the trees of the field.
20 Even the wild animals pant for you;[s]
the streams of water have dried up[t]

**1:1** a Jer 1:2
**1:2** b Hos 5:1 c Joel 2:2
**1:4** d Dt 28:39; Na 3:15
**1:5** e Joel 3:3
**1:6** f Rev 9:8
**1:7** g Isa 5:6
**1:8** h Isa 22:12
**1:10** i Isa 24:4
**1:11** j Isa 17:11
**1:13** k Jer 4:8
**1:14** l 2Ch 20:3
**1:15** m Jer 30:7 n Joel 2:1,11,31
**1:16** o Dt 12:7
**1:17** p Isa 17:10–11
**1:19** q Ps 50:15 r Jer 9:10
**1:20** s Ps 104:21 t 1Ki 17:7

[a] 4 The precise meaning of the four Hebrew words used here for locusts is uncertain. [b] 8 Or *young woman* [c] 8 Or *betrothed*
[d] 10 Or *ground mourns* [e] 15 Hebrew *Shaddai* [f] 17 The meaning of the Hebrew for this word is uncertain.

2:1
u Zep 1:14–16

2:2
v Am 5:18
w Joel 1:6

2:3
x Ps 105:34–35

2:4
y Rev 9:7

2:5
z Rev 9:9

*God,*

*help me to rely on you more fully. Use my trials and tribulations to make me trust you more and more. In Jesus' dependable name,*

*Amen*

JOEL 1:19–20

and fire has devoured the open
pastures.

## An Army of Locusts

2 Blow the trumpet in Zion;
sound the alarm on my holy hill.
Let all who live in the land tremble,
for the day of the LORD[u] is coming.
It is close at hand—
2 a day of darkness[v] and gloom,
a day of clouds and blackness.
Like dawn spreading across the
mountains
a large and mighty army[w] comes,
such as never was of old
nor ever will be in ages to come.
3 Before them fire devours,
behind them a flame blazes.
Before them the land is like the garden
of Eden,
behind them, a desert waste[x]—
nothing escapes them.
4 They have the appearance of horses;[y]
they gallop along like cavalry.
5 With a noise like that of chariots[z]
they leap over the mountaintops,
like a crackling fire consuming stubble,
like a mighty army drawn up for
battle.
6 At the sight of them, nations are in
anguish;
every face turns pale.
7 They charge like warriors;
they scale walls like soldiers.
They all march in line,
not swerving from their course.
8 They do not jostle each other;
each marches straight ahead.
They plunge through defenses
without breaking ranks.
9 They rush upon the city;
they run along the wall.
They climb into the houses;
like thieves they enter through the
windows.[a]
10 Before them the earth shakes,[b]
the sky trembles,
the sun and moon are darkened,
and the stars no longer shine.
11 The LORD thunders
at the head of his army;
his forces are beyond number,
and mighty are those who obey his
command.
The day of the LORD is great;
it is dreadful.
Who can endure it?

## Rend Your Heart

12 "Even now," declares the LORD,
"return[c] to me with all your heart,
with fasting and weeping and
mourning."

2:9
a Jer 9:21

2:10
b Ps 18:7

2:12
c Hos 12:6

## *The African Presence*

**Joel 2:3**

**Though some Biblical scholars believe the Garden of Eden was located in the Mesopotamian area, recent discoveries lead others to conclude that the geography referred to more easily fits descriptions of the area of East Africa. The earliest remains of humankind were found in Tanzania. For more on Eden, see the African Presence notes on Genesis 2:8 and 2:10–14.**

**2:13**
d Job 1:20
e Ex 34:6

**2:14**
f Hag 2:19
g Joel 1:13

**2:15**
h Nu 10:2

**2:17**
i Eze 8:16
j Ps 44:13
k Ps 42:3

**2:18**
l Zec 1:14

**2:19**
m Eze 34:29

**2:20**
n Jer 1:14–15

13 Rend your heart
and not your garments.[d]
Return to the LORD your God,
for he is gracious and compassionate,
slow to anger and abounding in love,[e]
and he relents from sending calamity.
14 Who knows? He may turn and have pity
and leave behind a blessing[f]—
grain offerings and drink offerings[g]
for the LORD your God.

15 Blow the trumpet[h] in Zion,
declare a holy fast,
call a sacred assembly.
16 Gather the people,
consecrate the assembly;
bring together the elders,
gather the children,
those nursing at the breast.
Let the bridegroom leave his room
and the bride her chamber.
17 Let the priests, who minister before the LORD,
weep between the temple porch and the altar.[i]
Let them say, "Spare your people, O LORD.
Do not make your inheritance an object of scorn,[j]
a byword among the nations.
Why should they say among the peoples,
'Where is their God?[k]' "

## The LORD's Answer

18 Then the LORD will be jealous[l] for his land
and take pity on his people.

19 The LORD will reply[a] to them:

"I am sending you grain, new wine and oil,
enough to satisfy you fully;
never again will I make you
an object of scorn[m] to the nations.

20 "I will drive the northern army[n] far from you,
pushing it into a parched and barren land,
with its front columns going into the eastern sea[b]
and those in the rear into the western sea.[c]
And its stench[o] will go up;
its smell will rise."

Surely he has done great things.[d]
21 Be not afraid, O land;
be glad and rejoice.
Surely the LORD has done great things.
22 Be not afraid, O wild animals,
for the open pastures are becoming green.[p]
The trees are bearing their fruit;
the fig tree and the vine yield their riches.
23 Be glad, O people of Zion,
rejoice[q] in the LORD your God,
for he has given you
the autumn rains in righteousness.[e]
He sends you abundant showers,
both autumn and spring rains, as before.
24 The threshing floors will be filled with grain;
the vats will overflow[r] with new wine and oil.

25 "I will repay you for the years the locusts have eaten—
the great locust and the young locust,
the other locusts and the locust swarm[f]—
my great army that I sent among you.
26 You will have plenty to eat, until you are full,[s]
and you will praise the name of the LORD your God,
who has worked wonders[t] for you;
never again will my people be shamed.
27 Then you will know that I am in Israel,
that I am the LORD[u] your God,
and that there is no other;
never again will my people be shamed.

## The Day of the LORD

28 "And afterward,
I will pour out my Spirit[v] on all people.
Your sons and daughters will prophesy,
your old men will dream dreams,
your young men will see visions.
29 Even on my servants,[w] both men and women,
I will pour out my Spirit in those days.

**2:20**
o Isa 34:3

**2:22**
p Ps 65:12

**2:23**
q Isa 41:16; Hab 3:18

**2:24**
r Mal 3:10

**2:26**
s Lev 26:5
t Isa 25:1

**2:27**
u Joel 3:17

**2:28**
v Eze 39:29

**2:29**
w 1Co 12:13; Gal 3:28

[a] 18,19 Or *LORD was jealous . . . / and took pity . . . / [19] The LORD replied* [b] 20 That is, the Dead Sea [c] 20 That is, the Mediterranean [d] 20 Or *rise. / Surely it has done great things."* [e] 23 Or */ the teacher for righteousness:* [f] 25 The precise meaning of the four Hebrew words used here for locusts is uncertain.

2:30
x Lk 21:11
y Mk 13:24–25

2:31
z Mal 4:1,5

2:32
a Ro 10:13*
b Isa 46:13
c Mic 4:7; Ro 9:27

3:2
d Eze 36:5

30 I will show wonders in the heavens[x]
and on the earth,[y]
blood and fire and billows of smoke.
31 The sun will be turned to darkness
and the moon to blood
before the coming of the great and
dreadful day of the LORD.[z]
32 And everyone who calls
on the name of the LORD will be saved;[a]
for on Mount Zion[b] and in Jerusalem
there will be deliverance,
as the LORD has said,
among the survivors[c]
whom the LORD calls.

## The Nations Judged

3 "In those days and at that time,
when I restore the fortunes of Judah
and Jerusalem,
2 I will gather all nations
and bring them down to the Valley of
Jehoshaphat.[a]
There I will enter into judgment[d] against
them
concerning my inheritance, my people
Israel,
for they scattered my people among the
nations
and divided up my land.
3 They cast lots for my people
and traded boys for prostitutes;
they sold girls for wine
that they might drink.

4 "Now what have you against me, O Tyre
and Sidon and all you regions of Philistia?
Are you repaying me for something I have
done? If you are paying me back, I will
swiftly and speedily return on your own
heads what you have done. 5 For you took
my silver and my gold and carried off my
finest treasures to your temples.[e] 6 You sold
the people of Judah and Jerusalem to the
Greeks, that you might send them far from
their homeland.
7 "See, I am going to rouse them out of the
places to which you sold them,[f] and I will
return on your own heads what you have
done. 8 I will sell your sons and daughters to
the people of Judah, and they will sell them
to the Sabeans, a nation far away." The LORD
has spoken.

9 Proclaim this among the nations:
Prepare for war!
Rouse the warriors!
Let all the fighting men draw near and
attack.
10 Beat your plowshares into swords
and your pruning hooks[g] into spears.
Let the weakling[h] say,
"I am strong!"
11 Come quickly, all you nations from every
side,
and assemble there.

Bring down your warriors,[i] O LORD!

12 "Let the nations be roused;
let them advance into the Valley of
Jehoshaphat,
for there I will sit
to judge[j] all the nations on every side.
13 Swing the sickle,
for the harvest[k] is ripe.
Come, trample the grapes,
for the winepress[l] is full
and the vats overflow—
so great is their wickedness!"

14 Multitudes, multitudes
in the valley of decision!
For the day of the LORD[m] is near

3:5
e 2Ch 21:16–17

3:7
f Isa 43:5–6;
Jer 23:8

3:10
g Isa 2:4; Mic 4:3
h Zec 12:8

3:11
i Isa 13:3

3:12
j Isa 2:4

3:13
k Rev 14:15–19
l Rev 14:20

3:14
m Joel 1:15

[a] 2 *Jehoshaphat* means *the LORD judges*; also in verse 12.

**The African Presence**

**Joel 3:8**

For a discussion of the Sabeans, see the African Presence note on Job 1:15.

3:16 n Am 1:2

in the valley of decision.
15 The sun and moon will be darkened,
and the stars no longer shine.
16 The LORD will roar from Zion
and thunder from Jerusalem;[n]
the earth and the sky will tremble.
But the LORD will be a refuge for his
people,
a stronghold for the people of Israel.

## Blessings for God's People

17 "Then you will know that I, the LORD your
God,
dwell in Zion, my holy hill.
Jerusalem will be holy;
never again will foreigners invade her.

18 "In that day the mountains will drip new
wine,
and the hills will flow with milk;
all the ravines of Judah will run with
water.[o]
A fountain will flow out of the LORD's
house
and will water the valley of acacias.[a]
19 But Egypt will be desolate,
Edom a desert waste,
because of violence done to the people of
Judah,
in whose land they shed innocent
blood.
20 Judah will be inhabited forever[p]
and Jerusalem through all generations.
21 Their bloodguilt, which I have not
pardoned,
I will pardon."

The LORD dwells in Zion!

3:18 o Isa 30:25

3:20 p Am 9:15

## The African Presence

**Joel 3:19**

Egypt is located in North Africa. For more on Egypt, see the African Presence note on Genesis 10:6.

[a] 18 Or *Valley of Shittim*

# Amos

## OVERVIEW

The book of Amos contains warnings of judgments against Israel and the surrounding nations. Why was God angry with his people? Amos pointed out the people's religious hypocrisy and legal injustice: They had become lazy, self-centered and indulgent; those who were rich were exploiting the poor and defenseless. Amos warned that God's judgment would come as swarming locusts, devouring fire and the sword, but he then concluded with a promise of future restoration when the people repented.

At its earliest conception, the church of Jesus Christ was filled with generosity and mercy toward the poor. Acts 4:32–35 notes that the early Christians took care of the needy among them. As members of Christ's body, women believers of today continue in their giving to the unfortunate. As you read through the book of Amos, reflect on the things that bother God the most; ask God to give you a heart that will move you to make a difference in the world around you.

## OUTLINE

I. The Basis of God's Judgment on Israel's Neighbors (1:1—2:5)
II. The Basis of God's Judgment on Israel (2:6—6:14)
III. The Nature of God's Judgment on Israel (7:1—9:10)
IV. The Promise of Israel's Restoration (9:11–15)

## SCANNABLE FACTS:

**Author:** Amos

**Time Written:** About 750 B.C.

**Theme to Note:** God will judge the sin of exploiting others

**Notable Women:** Israelite women who oppressed the poor (see Am 4:1)

1:1 a 2Sa 14:2 b Zec 14:5
1:2 c Joel 3:16
1:3 d Isa 8:4
1:4 e 2Ki 6:24
1:5 f Jer 51:30
1:6 g Ob 1:11
1:8 h Eze 25:16 i Zep 2:4–7

1 The words of Amos, one of the shepherds of Tekoa[a]—what he saw concerning Israel two years before the earthquake,[b] when Uzziah was king of Judah and Jeroboam son of Jehoash[a] was king of Israel.

2 He said:

"The LORD roars from Zion
and thunders from Jerusalem;[c]
the pastures of the shepherds dry up,[b]
and the top of Carmel withers."

## Judgment on Israel's Neighbors

3 This is what the LORD says:

"For three sins of Damascus,[d]
even for four, I will not turn back ⌊my wrath⌋.
Because she threshed Gilead
with sledges having iron teeth,
4 I will send fire upon the house of Hazael
that will consume the fortresses of Ben-Hadad.[e]
5 I will break down the gate[f] of Damascus;
I will destroy the king who is in[c] the Valley of Aven[d]
and the one who holds the scepter in Beth Eden.
The people of Aram will go into exile to Kir,"
says the LORD.

6 This is what the LORD says:

"For three sins of Gaza,
even for four, I will not turn back ⌊my wrath⌋.
Because she took captive whole communities
and sold them to Edom,[g]
7 I will send fire upon the walls of Gaza
that will consume her fortresses.
8 I will destroy the king[e] of Ashdod
and the one who holds the scepter in Ashkelon.
I will turn my hand against Ekron,
till the last of the Philistines[h] is dead,"
says the Sovereign LORD.[i]

9 This is what the LORD says:

"For three sins of Tyre,[j]
even for four, I will not turn back ⌊my wrath⌋.
Because she sold whole communities of captives to Edom,
disregarding a treaty of brotherhood,
10 I will send fire upon the walls of Tyre
that will consume her fortresses.[k]"

11 This is what the LORD says:

"For three sins of Edom,[l]
even for four, I will not turn back ⌊my wrath⌋.
Because he pursued his brother with a sword,
stifling all compassion,[f]
because his anger raged continually
and his fury flamed unchecked,
12 I will send fire upon Teman[m]
that will consume the fortresses of Bozrah."

13 This is what the LORD says:

"For three sins of Ammon,[n]
even for four, I will not turn back ⌊my wrath⌋.
Because he ripped open the pregnant women of Gilead
in order to extend his borders,
14 I will set fire to the walls of Rabbah[o]
that will consume her fortresses
amid war cries on the day of battle,
amid violent winds on a stormy day.
15 Her king[g] will go into exile,
he and his officials together,"
says the LORD.

2 This is what the LORD says:

"For three sins of Moab,
even for four, I will not turn back ⌊my wrath⌋.
Because he burned, as if to lime,
the bones of Edom's king,
2 I will send fire upon Moab
that will consume the fortresses of Kerioth.[h]
Moab will go down in great tumult
amid war cries and the blast of the trumpet.
3 I will destroy her ruler[p]

1:9 j Isa 23:1–18
1:10 k Zec 9:1–4
1:11 l Jer 49:7–22
1:12 m Ob 1:9–10
1:13 n Jer 49:1–6
1:14 o Dt 3:11
2:3 p Ps 2:10

[a]1 Hebrew *Joash*, a variant of *Jehoash* [b]2 Or *shepherds mourn* [c]5 Or *the inhabitants of* [d]5 *Aven* means *wickedness.* [e]8 Or *inhabitants* [f]11 Or *sword / and destroyed his allies* [g]15 Or */ Molech*; Hebrew *malcam* [h]2 Or *of her cities*

2:3 q Isa 40:23
2:4 r 2Ki 17:19 s Jer 6:19
2:5 t Jer 17:27; Hos 8:14
2:7 u Am 5:11–12
2:8 v Ex 22:26

and kill all her officials with him,"[q]
says the LORD.

[4]This is what the LORD says:

"For three sins of Judah,[r]
even for four, I will not turn back ⌊my wrath⌋.
Because they have rejected the law[s] of the LORD
and have not kept his decrees,
because they have been led astray by false gods,[a]
the gods[b] their ancestors followed,
[5] I will send fire upon Judah
that will consume the fortresses of Jerusalem.[t]"

## Judgment on Israel

[6]This is what the LORD says:

"For three sins of Israel,
even for four, I will not turn back ⌊my wrath⌋.
They sell the righteous for silver,
and the needy for a pair of sandals.
[7] They trample on the heads of the poor
as upon the dust of the ground
and deny justice to the oppressed.
Father and son use the same girl
and so profane my holy name.[u]
[8] They lie down beside every altar
on garments taken in pledge.[v]
In the house of their god
they drink wine taken as fines.

[9] "I destroyed the Amorite[w] before them,
though he was tall as the cedars
and strong as the oaks.
I destroyed his fruit above
and his roots below.

[10] "I brought you up out of Egypt,[x]
and I led you forty years in the desert[y]
to give you the land of the Amorites.
[11] I also raised up prophets[z] from among your sons
and Nazirites from among your young men.
Is this not true, people of Israel?"
declares the LORD.
[12] "But you made the Nazirites drink wine
and commanded the prophets not to prophesy.[a]

[13] "Now then, I will crush you
as a cart crushes when loaded with grain.
[14] The swift will not escape,
the strong will not muster their strength,
and the warrior will not save his life.[b]
[15] The archer[c] will not stand his ground,
the fleet-footed soldier will not get away,
and the horseman will not save his life.
[16] Even the bravest warriors
will flee naked on that day,"
declares the LORD.

2:9 w Nu 21:23–26
2:10 x Ex 20:2 y Dt 2:7
2:11 z Jer 7:25
2:12 a Isa 30:10; Jer 11:21; Mic 2:6
2:14 b Ps 33:16
2:15 c Eze 39:3

[a]4 Or *by lies* [b]4 Or *lies*

## The African Presence

### Amos 2:9–10

The Amorites were descendants of Ham through Canaan. They were described as tall people, strong as oak trees. Because Ham's offspring represent the geographic territories once dominated by Egypt—present-day Egypt, Libya and Sudan and into the area today known as Israel—they can claim a relation to African heritage. Since "heritage" is something "passed down" or "inherited," Canaan (Israel or Palestine) most certainly received or was influenced by Egypt culturally, politically, religiously, etc.

3:2 d Dt 7:6 e Jer 14:10
3:6 f Isa 14:24–27
3:7 g Ge 18:17; Jn 15:15
3:8 h Jer 20:9; Ac 4:20
3:9 i Am 4:1

## Witnesses Summoned Against Israel

3 Hear this word the LORD has spoken against you, O people of Israel—against the whole family I brought up out of Egypt:

2 "You only have I chosen[d]
of all the families of the earth;
therefore I will punish you
for all your sins.[e]"

3 Do two walk together
unless they have agreed to do so?
4 Does a lion roar in the thicket
when he has no prey?
Does he growl in his den
when he has caught nothing?
5 Does a bird fall into a trap on the ground
where no snare has been set?
Does a trap spring up from the earth
when there is nothing to catch?
6 When a trumpet sounds in a city,
do not the people tremble?
When disaster comes to a city,
has not the LORD caused it?[f]

7 Surely the Sovereign LORD does nothing
without revealing his plan[g]
to his servants the prophets.
8 The lion has roared—
who will not fear?
The Sovereign LORD has spoken—
who can but prophesy?[h]

9 Proclaim to the fortresses of Ashdod
and to the fortresses of Egypt:
"Assemble yourselves on the mountains
of Samaria;[i]
see the great unrest within her
and the oppression among her people."

10 "They do not know how to do right,"
declares the LORD,
"who hoard plunder[j] and loot in their
fortresses."[k]

11 Therefore this is what the Sovereign LORD says:

"An enemy will overrun the land;
he will pull down your strongholds
and plunder your fortresses."

12 This is what the LORD says:

"As a shepherd saves from the lion's[l]
mouth
only two leg bones or a piece of an ear,
so will the Israelites be saved,
those who sit in Samaria
on the edge of their beds
and in Damascus on their couches.[a]"

13 "Hear this and testify[m] against the house of Jacob," declares the Lord, the LORD God Almighty.

14 "On the day I punish Israel for her sins,
I will destroy the altars of Bethel;
the horns of the altar will be cut off
and fall to the ground.
15 I will tear down the winter house[n]
along with the summer house;[o]
the houses adorned with ivory[p] will be
destroyed
and the mansions will be demolished,"
declares the LORD.

## Israel Has Not Returned to God

4 Hear this word, you cows of Bashan[q]
on Mount Samaria,
you women who oppress the poor and
crush the needy

[a]12 The meaning of the Hebrew for this line is uncertain.

3:10 j Hab 2:8 k Zep 1:9
3:12 l 1Sa 17:34
3:13 m Eze 2:7
3:15 n Jer 36:22 o Jdg 3:20 p 1Ki 22:39
4:1 q Ps 22:12

### The African Presence

**Amos 3:9**

Egypt is located in North Africa. For more on Egypt, see the African Presence note on Genesis 10:6.

4:2 r Am 6:8
4:4 s Nu 28:3
4:5 t Lev 7:13 u Lev 22:18–21
4:6 v Jer 5:3; Hag 2:17
4:7 w Dt 11:17
4:9 x Dt 28:22
4:10 y Ex 9:3

and say to your husbands, "Bring us
some drinks!"
2 The Sovereign LORD has sworn by his
holiness:
"The time will surely come
when you will be taken away[r] with hooks,
the last of you with fishhooks.
3 You will each go straight out
through breaks in the wall,
and you will be cast out toward
Harmon,[a]"
declares the LORD.

4 "Go to Bethel and sin;
go to Gilgal and sin yet more.
Bring your sacrifices every morning,[s]
your tithes every three years.[b]
5 Burn leavened bread[t] as a thank offering
and brag about your freewill
offerings[u]—
boast about them, you Israelites,
for this is what you love to do,"
declares the Sovereign LORD.

6 "I gave you empty stomachs[c] in every city
and lack of bread in every town,
yet you have not returned to me,"
declares the LORD.[v]

7 "I also withheld rain from you
when the harvest was still three
months away.
I sent rain on one town,
but withheld it from another.[w]
One field had rain;
another had none and dried up.
8 People staggered from town to town for
water
but did not get enough to drink,
yet you have not returned to me,"
declares the LORD.

9 "Many times I struck your gardens and
vineyards,
I struck them with blight and mildew.[x]
Locusts devoured your fig and olive
trees,
yet you have not returned to me,"
declares the LORD.

10 "I sent plagues[y] among you
as I did to Egypt.
I killed your young men with the sword,
along with your captured horses.
I filled your nostrils with the stench of
your camps,
yet you have not returned to me,"
declares the LORD.

11 "I overthrew some of you
as I[d] overthrew Sodom and
Gomorrah.[z]
You were like a burning stick snatched
from the fire,
yet you have not returned to me,"
declares the LORD.

12 "Therefore this is what I will do to you,
Israel,
and because I will do this to you,
prepare to meet your God, O Israel."

13 He who forms the mountains,
creates the wind,
and reveals his thoughts[a] to man,
he who turns dawn to darkness,
and treads the high places of the
earth[b]—
the LORD God Almighty is his name.

## A Lament and Call to Repentance

5 Hear this word, O house of Israel, this
lament I take up concerning you:

2 "Fallen is Virgin Israel,
never to rise again,
deserted in her own land,
with no one to lift her up.[c]"

3 This is what the Sovereign LORD says:

"The city that marches out a thousand
strong for Israel
will have only a hundred left;
the town that marches out a hundred
strong
will have only ten left."

4 This is what the LORD says to the house
of Israel:

"Seek me and live;[d]
5 do not seek Bethel,
do not go to Gilgal,[e]
do not journey to Beersheba.[f]
For Gilgal will surely go into exile,

4:11 z Jer 23:14
4:13 a Da 2:28 b Mic 1:3
5:2 c Am 8:14
5:4 d Isa 55:3
5:5 e Am 4:4 f Am 8:14

[a]3 Masoretic Text; with a different word division of the Hebrew (see Septuagint) *out, O mountain of oppression* [b]4 Or *tithes on the third day* [c]6 Hebrew *you cleanness of teeth* [d]11 Hebrew *God*

# Inspire

## PURPOSEFUL GIVING

The inequity of wealth distribution in the United States is often reflected within our faith communities. The relatively recent phenomenon that some have labeled "prosperity teaching" suggests that if you're not wealthy (defined as the acquisition of material goods), then your faith must be deficient.

While the Scriptures do state that God will bless the godly in all sorts of ways, the Bible's overarching emphasis is placed on relationship building and compassion for one another rather than on self-serving goals—which in some cases can even be considered idolatry. For example, God issued a strong warning through the prophet Amos to Israelite women who oppressed the poor (see Am 4:1–3).

When we focus on personal prosperity as a sign of God's providence, we forget that Jesus requires us to care for those who are incapable of caring for themselves (see Lk 14:12–14). Fulfilling this requirement is often difficult, but not impossible. Honoring the commitment sometimes requires that we rethink our understanding and application of tithing and stewardship, which might direct us away from "blind" giving.

If the Holy Spirit is working in a woman's life, his presence will be evident by her generous heart. When a woman realizes she has been blessed with God's grace and mercy, she will give her time, energy and financial resources.

Ultimately, we are accountable for contributing to kingdom building. Do our contributions make a difference in the communities in which we worship? Are we involved with ministries that meet the needs of the community they serve? It's time to make a difference in someone else's life.

How blessed we are when we realize that everything we have belongs to God and has been loaned to us to share with others. Let us therefore handle money in a manner that reflects the liberty found in our relationship with Jesus the Christ. Giving to others will bring a woman abundant joy!

—A. Stewart Sims

### read

Amos 4:1–3; Luke 14:12–14; 21:1–4; 2 Corinthians 8:1–15.

**See also** the Inspire Notes "Commitment to Community" and "Sacrificial Living," and the Women of the Bible Notes "The Widow's Offering: Selfless Giving," "Mary, the Mother of James and Joses: Sacrificing for Christ" and "Claudia: A Sincere Supporter."

### WOMAN *of* COLOR

How are you giving purposefully?

For the next Inspire note, go to page 1081.

**5:7** g Am 6:12
**5:8** h Job 9:9; i Am 4:13
**5:10** j Isa 29:21; k 1Ki 22:8
**5:11** l Mic 6:15
**5:12** m Am 2:6–7

and Bethel will be reduced to
nothing.[a]"
6 Seek the LORD and live,
or he will sweep through the house of
Joseph like a fire;
it will devour,
and Bethel will have no one to
quench it.

7 You who turn justice into bitterness[g]
and cast righteousness to the ground
8 (he who made the Pleiades and Orion,[h]
who turns blackness into dawn
and darkens day into night,
who calls for the waters of the sea
and pours them out over the face of the
land—
the LORD is his name[i]—
9 he flashes destruction on the stronghold
and brings the fortified city to ruin),
10 you hate the one who reproves in court[j]
and despise him who tells the truth.[k]

11 You trample on the poor
and force him to give you grain.
Therefore, though you have built stone
mansions,
you will not live in them;
though you have planted lush vineyards,
you will not drink their wine.[l]
12 For I know how many are your offenses
and how great your sins.

You oppress the righteous and take bribes
and you deprive the poor of justice in
the courts.[m]
13 Therefore the prudent man keeps quiet in
such times,
for the times are evil.

---

*Woman of color,*

*Never forget that success comes from me.*

*Don't worship my gifts; worship me.*

*God*

AMOS 5:14

---

14 Seek good, not evil,
that you may live.
Then the LORD God Almighty will be with
you,
just as you say he is.
15 Hate evil,[n] love good;
maintain justice in the courts.
Perhaps the LORD God Almighty will have
mercy[o]
on the remnant of Joseph.

16 Therefore this is what the Lord, the
LORD God Almighty, says:

"There will be wailing in all the streets
and cries of anguish in every public
square.
The farmers will be summoned to weep
and the mourners to wail.
17 There will be wailing in all the vineyards,
for I will pass through your midst,"
says the LORD.

## The Day of the LORD

18 Woe to you who long
for the day of the LORD!
Why do you long for the day of the LORD?
That day will be darkness, not light.[p]
19 It will be as though a man fled from a lion
only to meet a bear,
as though he entered his house
and rested his hand on the wall
only to have a snake bite him.[q]
20 Will not the day of the LORD be darkness,
not light—
pitch-dark, without a ray of
brightness?

21 "I hate, I despise your religious feasts;[r]
I cannot stand your assemblies.[s]
22 Even though you bring me burnt
offerings and grain offerings,
I will not accept them.
Though you bring choice fellowship
offerings,[b]
I will have no regard for them.[tu]
23 Away with the noise of your songs!
I will not listen to the music of your
harps.
24 But let justice roll on like a river,
righteousness like a never-failing
stream![v]

**5:15** n Ro 12:9; o Joel 2:14
**5:18** p Isa 5:19,30
**5:19** q Jer 48:44
**5:21** r Lev 26:31; s Isa 1:11–16
**5:22** t Mic 6:6–7; u Isa 66:3
**5:24** v Mic 6:8

[a]5 Or *grief*; or *wickedness*; Hebrew *aven,* a reference to Beth Aven (a derogatory name for Bethel) [b]22 Traditionally *peace offerings*

5:27
w Ac 7:42–43*

6:1
x Lk 6:24
y Isa 32:9–11

6:2
z Na 3:8

6:3
a Am 9:10

6:4
b Eze 34:2–3; Am 3:12

6:6
c Am 2:8

25 “Did you bring me sacrifices and offerings
forty years in the desert, O house of
Israel?
26 You have lifted up the shrine of your king,
the pedestal of your idols,
the star of your god[a]—
which you made for yourselves.
27 Therefore I will send you into exile
beyond Damascus,”
says the LORD, whose name is God
Almighty.[w]

## Woe to the Complacent

6 Woe to you[x] who are complacent in Zion,
and to you who feel secure on Mount
Samaria,
you notable men of the foremost nation,
to whom the people of Israel come![y]
2 Go to Calneh and look at it;
go from there to great Hamath,
and then go down to Gath in Philistia.
Are they better off than[z] your two
kingdoms?
Is their land larger than yours?
3 You put off the evil day
and bring near a reign of terror.[a]
4 You lie on beds inlaid with ivory
and lounge on your couches.
You dine on choice lambs
and fattened calves.[b]
5 You strum away on your harps like David
and improvise on musical
instruments.
6 You drink wine[c] by the bowlful
and use the finest lotions,
but you do not grieve over the ruin of
Joseph.
7 Therefore you will be among the first to
go into exile;
your feasting and lounging will end.

## The LORD Abhors the Pride of Israel

8 The Sovereign LORD has sworn by him-
self—the LORD God Almighty declares:

“I abhor the pride of Jacob
and detest his fortresses;
I will deliver up the city
and everything in it.”

9 If ten[d] men are left in one house, they too
will die. 10 And if a relative who is to burn the
bodies comes to carry them out of the house
and asks anyone still hiding there, “Is any-
one with you?” and he says, “No,” then he
will say, “Hush![e] We must not mention the
name of the LORD.”

11 For the LORD has given the command,
and he will smash the great house[f] into
pieces
and the small house into bits.[g]

12 Do horses run on the rocky crags?
Does one plow there with oxen?
But you have turned justice into poison[h]
and the fruit of righteousness into
bitterness[i]—
13 you who rejoice in the conquest of Lo
Debar[b]
and say, “Did we not take Karnaim[c] by
our own strength?”

14 For the LORD God Almighty declares,
“I will stir up a nation[j] against you,
O house of Israel,

6:9
d Am 5:3

6:10
e Am 8:3

6:11
f Am 3:15
g Isa 55:11

6:12
h Hos 10:4
i Am 5:7

6:14
j Jer 5:15

[a]26 Or *lifted up Sakkuth your king / and Kaiwan your idols, / your star-gods*; Septuagint *lifted up the shrine of Molech / and the star of your god Rephan, / their idols* [b]13 *Lo Debar* means *nothing.* [c]13 *Karnaim* means *horns*; *horn* here symbolizes strength.

## The African Presence

**Amos 6:2**

The ancestry of the Philistines is traced to Ham’s son Mizraim (see Ge 10:6,13; see also the African Presence note on Ge 10:6). They occupied the coastland of Canaan. For more on the Philistines, see the African Presence note on 1 Samuel 17.

**7:1** k Joel 1:4
**7:2** l Eze 11:13
**7:3** m Dt 32:36
**7:4** n Isa 66:16
**7:5** o ver 1–2
**7:8** p Am 8:2 q 2Ki 21:13
**7:9** r 2Ki 15:9; Hos 10:8
**7:10** s 2Ki 14:23

that will oppress you all the way
from Lebo[a] Hamath to the valley of the
Arabah."

## Locusts, Fire and a Plumb Line

7 This is what the Sovereign LORD showed me: He was preparing swarms of locusts[k] after the king's share had been harvested and just as the second crop was coming up. 2 When they had stripped the land clean, I cried out, "Sovereign LORD, forgive! How can Jacob survive? He is so small![l]"

3 So the LORD relented.[m]

"This will not happen," the LORD said.

4 This is what the Sovereign LORD showed me: The Sovereign LORD was calling for judgment by fire;[n] it dried up the great deep and devoured the land. 5 Then I cried out, "Sovereign LORD, I beg you, stop! How can Jacob survive? He is so small![o]"

6 So the LORD relented.

"This will not happen either," the Sovereign LORD said.

7 This is what he showed me: The Lord was standing by a wall that had been built true to plumb, with a plumb line in his hand. 8 And the LORD asked me, "What do you see, Amos?[p]"

"A plumb line,[q]" I replied.

Then the Lord said, "Look, I am setting a plumb line among my people Israel; I will spare them no longer.

9 "The high places of Isaac will be destroyed
and the sanctuaries of Israel will be
ruined;
with my sword I will rise against the
house of Jeroboam.[r]"

## Amos and Amaziah

10 Then Amaziah the priest of Bethel sent a message to Jeroboam[s] king of Israel: "Amos is raising a conspiracy against you in the very heart of Israel. The land cannot bear all his words. 11 For this is what Amos is saying:

"'Jeroboam will die by the sword,
and Israel will surely go into exile,
away from their native land.'"

12 Then Amaziah said to Amos, "Get out, you seer! Go back to the land of Judah. Earn your bread there and do your prophesying there. 13 Don't prophesy anymore at Bethel, because this is the king's sanctuary and the temple of the kingdom.[t]"

14 Amos answered Amaziah, "I was neither a prophet[u] nor a prophet's son, but I was a shepherd, and I also took care of sycamore-fig trees. 15 But the LORD took me from tending the flock and said to me, 'Go, prophesy to my people Israel.'[v] 16 Now then, hear the word of the LORD. You say,

"'Do not prophesy against Israel,
and stop preaching against the house
of Isaac.'

17 "Therefore this is what the LORD says:

"'Your wife will become a prostitute[w] in
the city,
and your sons and daughters will fall
by the sword.
Your land will be measured and
divided up,
and you yourself will die in a pagan[b]
country.
And Israel will certainly go into exile,
away from their native land.'"

## A Basket of Ripe Fruit

8 This is what the Sovereign LORD showed me: a basket of ripe fruit. 2 "What do you see, Amos?[x]" he asked.

"A basket of ripe fruit," I answered.

Then the LORD said to me, "The time is ripe for my people Israel; I will spare them no longer.[y]

3 "In that day," declares the Sovereign LORD, "the songs in the temple will turn to wailing.[c] Many, many bodies—flung everywhere! Silence![z]"

4 Hear this, you who trample the needy
and do away with the poor[a] of the
land,[b]

5 saying,

"When will the New Moon be over
that we may sell grain,
and the Sabbath be ended
that we may market wheat?"—

**7:13** t Am 2:12
**7:14** u 2Ki 2:5
**7:15** v Eze 2:3–4
**7:17** w Hos 4:13
**8:2** x Am 7:8 y Eze 7:2–9
**8:3** z Am 6:10
**8:4** a Pr 30:14 b Ps 14:4

[a]14 Or *from the entrance to* [b]17 Hebrew *an unclean* [c]3 Or *"the temple singers will wail*

skimping the measure,
boosting the price
and cheating with dishonest scales,[c]
6 buying the poor with silver
and the needy for a pair of sandals,
selling even the sweepings with the
wheat.[d]

7 The LORD has sworn by the Pride of Ja-
cob: "I will never forget[e] anything they have
done.

8 "Will not the land tremble for this,
and all who live in it mourn?
The whole land will rise like the Nile;
it will be stirred up and then sink
like the river of Egypt.[f]

9 "In that day," declares the Sovereign
LORD,

"I will make the sun go down at noon
and darken the earth in broad
daylight.[g]
10 I will turn your religious feasts into
mourning
and all your singing into weeping.
I will make all of you wear sackcloth
and shave your heads.
I will make that time like mourning for
an only son
and the end of it like a bitter day.[h]

11 "The days are coming," declares the
Sovereign LORD,
"when I will send a famine through
the land—
not a famine of food or a thirst for water,
but a famine of hearing the words of
the LORD.[i]
12 Men will stagger from sea to sea
and wander from north to east,
searching for the word of the LORD,
but they will not find it.

13 "In that day

"the lovely young women and strong
young men
will faint because of thirst.[j]
14 They who swear by the shame[a] of
Samaria,
or say, 'As surely as your god lives,
O Dan,'
or, 'As surely as the god[b] of Beersheba[k]
lives'—
they will fall,
never to rise again."

## Israel to Be Destroyed

9 I saw the Lord standing by the altar,
and he said:

"Strike the tops of the pillars
so that the thresholds shake.
Bring them down on the heads[l] of all the
people;
those who are left I will kill with the
sword.
Not one will get away,
none will escape.
2 Though they dig down to the depths of
the grave,[c]
from there my hand will take them.
Though they climb up to the heavens,[m]
from there I will bring them down.
3 Though they hide themselves on the top
of Carmel,
there I will hunt them down and seize
them.
Though they hide from me at the bottom
of the sea,
there I will command the serpent to
bite them.[n]
4 Though they are driven into exile by their
enemies,
there I will command the sword[o] to
slay them.
I will fix my eyes upon them
for evil and not for good."

5 The Lord, the LORD Almighty,
he who touches the earth and it
melts,
and all who live in it mourn—
the whole land rises like the Nile,
then sinks like the river of Egypt[p]—
6 he who builds his lofty palace[d] in the
heavens
and sets its foundation[e] on the
earth,
who calls for the waters of the sea
and pours them out over the face of the
land—
the LORD is his name.[q]

8:5 c Ne 13:15–16; Mic 6:10–11
8:6 d Am 2:6
8:7 e Hos 8:13
8:8 f Am 9:5
8:9 g Job 5:14; Jer 15:9; Mic 3:6
8:10 h Eze 7:18
8:11 i 1Sa 3:1; 2Ch 15:3
8:13 j Hos 2:3
8:14 k Am 5:5
9:1 l Ps 68:21
9:2 m Jer 51:53
9:3 n Jer 16:16–17
9:4 o Lev 26:33
9:5 p Am 8:8
9:6 q Ps 104:1–3,5–6,13; Am 5:8

[a]14 Or *by Ashima*; or *by the idol* [b]14 Or *power* [c]2 Hebrew *to Sheol* [d]6 The meaning of the Hebrew for this phrase is uncertain. [e]6 The meaning of the Hebrew for this word is uncertain.

## The African Presence

**Amos 9:7**

Cush is also called "Ethiopia" (that is, Nubia). The exact geographic region is disputed; however, most scholars generally agree that the area of Nubia included the middle of the Nile from what is present-day southern Egypt and northern Sudan. For more on Cush, see the African Presence note on Exodus 5:1–5.

9:7 r Dt 2:23
9:9 s Isa 30:28
9:10 t Am 6:3
9:11 u Ps 80:12
9:12 v Ac 15:16–17*

7 "Are not you Israelites
the same to me as the Cushites[a]?"
declares the LORD.
"Did I not bring Israel up from Egypt,
the Philistines from Caphtor[b r]
and the Arameans from Kir?
8 "Surely the eyes of the Sovereign LORD
are on the sinful kingdom.
I will destroy it
from the face of the earth—
yet I will not totally destroy
the house of Jacob,"
declares the LORD.
9 "For I will give the command,
and I will shake the house of Israel
among all the nations
as grain is shaken in a sieve,[s]
and not a pebble will reach the ground.
10 All the sinners among my people
will die by the sword,
all those who say,
'Disaster will not overtake or meet us.'[t]

### Israel's Restoration

11 "In that day I will restore
David's fallen tent.
I will repair its broken places,
restore its ruins,
and build it as it used to be,[u]
12 so that they may possess the remnant of Edom
and all the nations that bear my name,[c]"
declares the LORD,
who will do these things.[v]

13 "The days are coming," declares the LORD,
"when the reaper will be overtaken by the plowman[w]
and the planter by the one treading grapes.
New wine will drip from the mountains
and flow from all the hills.[x]
14 I will bring back my exiled[d] people Israel;
they will rebuild the ruined cities[y] and live in them.
They will plant vineyards and drink their wine;
they will make gardens and eat their fruit.
15 I will plant[z] Israel in their own land,
never again to be uprooted
from the land I have given them,"
says the LORD your God.[a]

9:13 w Lev 26:5 x Joel 3:18
9:14 y Isa 61:4
9:15 z Isa 60:21 a Eze 34:25–28

*Lord,*

*have mercy on me. Forgive my sins and teach me to follow you unquestioningly and wholeheartedly. Help me also to forgive myself and to always seek your face. In the name of Jesus, my Redeemer,*

*Amen*

AMOS 9:11–12

[a]7 That is, people from the upper Nile region [b]7 That is, Crete [c]12 Hebrew; Septuagint *so that the remnant of men / and all the nations that bear my name may seek ⌞the Lord⌟* [d]14 Or *will restore the fortunes of my*

# Obadiah

## OVERVIEW

Obadiah is the shortest book in the Old Testament. It contains prophecies about the destruction of Edom as judgment for their relentless opposition to the ancestors of Jacob (the nation of Israel). Edom's people were arrogant because they assumed that their location in the mountains would protect them from defeat. However, history shows that invaders soon began forcing the Edomites out of their mountain fortresses, and as a result of the Romans' destruction of Jerusalem in A.D. 70, the nation totally disappeared.

Christian women living today cannot afford to put their trust in missile defense systems or any human invention. The only dependable shelter from the storms of life is in knowing the Lord Jesus Christ. In him there is peace in the midst of chaos, love in times of dissension and joy in the center of sadness. Learn to meditate and trust in God's Word for knowledge and wisdom before the time of trouble.

## OUTLINE

I. Edom's Judgment Declared (1–9)
II. Reasons for Judgment (10–14)
III. The Day of the Lord (15–16)
IV. Israel's Deliverance Foretold (17–21)

### SCANNABLE FACTS:

**Author:** Obadiah

**Time Written:** Unknown, but probably between 605 and 586 B.C.

**Theme to Note:** God will repay those who persecute his people

**Notable Women:** There are no women mentioned in this book

1
a Jer 49:7–22; Eze 25:12–14
b Jer 6:4–5

3
c Isa 16:6

4
d Job 20:6

8
e Job 5:12; Isa 29:14

10
f Joel 3:19
g Am 1:11–12

1 The vision of Obadiah.

This is what the Sovereign LORD says about Edom[a]—

We have heard a message from the LORD:
An envoy was sent to the nations to say,
"Rise, and let us go against her for battle"[b]—

2 "See, I will make you small among the nations;
you will be utterly despised.
3 The pride[c] of your heart has deceived you,
you who live in the clefts of the rocks[a]
and make your home on the heights,
you who say to yourself,
'Who can bring me down to the ground?'
4 Though you soar like the eagle
and make your nest among the stars,
from there I will bring you down,"
declares the LORD.[d]
5 "If thieves came to you,
if robbers in the night—
Oh, what a disaster awaits you—
would they not steal only as much as they wanted?
If grape pickers came to you,
would they not leave a few grapes?
6 But how Esau will be ransacked,
his hidden treasures pillaged!
7 All your allies will force you to the border;
your friends will deceive and overpower you;
those who eat your bread will set a trap for you,[b]
but you will not detect it.

8 "In that day," declares the LORD,
"will I not destroy[e] the wise men of Edom,
men of understanding in the mountains of Esau?
9 Your warriors, O Teman, will be terrified,
and everyone in Esau's mountains
will be cut down in the slaughter.
10 Because of the violence[f] against your brother Jacob,[g]
you will be covered with shame;
you will be destroyed forever.
11 On the day you stood aloof
while strangers carried off his wealth
and foreigners entered his gates
and cast lots for Jerusalem,
you were like one of them.
12 You should not look down on your brother
in the day of his misfortune,
nor rejoice[h] over the people of Judah
in the day of their destruction,
nor boast so much
in the day of their trouble.[i]
13 You should not march through the gates of my people
in the day of their disaster,
nor look down on them in their calamity
in the day of their disaster,
nor seize their wealth
in the day of their disaster.
14 You should not wait at the crossroads
to cut down their fugitives,
nor hand over their survivors
in the day of their trouble.

15 "The day of the LORD is near[j]
for all nations.
As you have done, it will be done to you;
your deeds[k] will return upon your own head.

*Child,*

*I am the Judge.*
*Leave everything in my hands.*

*Love,*
*God*

OBADIAH 15

16 Just as you drank on my holy hill,
so all the nations will drink continually;
they will drink and drink
and be as if they had never been.
17 But on Mount Zion will be deliverance;[l]

12
h Eze 35:15
i Mic 4:11

15
j Eze 30:3
k Hab 2:8.

17
l Am 9:11–15

[a]3 Or *of Sela* [b]7 The meaning of the Hebrew for this clause is uncertain.

it will be holy,
and the house of Jacob
will possess its inheritance.
18 The house of Jacob will be a fire
and the house of Joseph a flame;
the house of Esau will be stubble,
and they will set it on fire and
consume it.
There will be no survivors
from the house of Esau."
The LORD has spoken.
19 People from the Negev will occupy
the mountains of Esau,
and people from the foothills will possess
the land of the Philistines.
They will occupy the fields of Ephraim
and Samaria,
and Benjamin will possess Gilead.
20 This company of Israelite exiles who are
in Canaan
will possess ⌞the land⌟ as far as
Zarephath;[m]
the exiles from Jerusalem who are in
Sepharad
will possess the towns of the Negev.[n]
21 Deliverers will go up on[a] Mount Zion
to govern the mountains of Esau.
And the kingdom will be the LORD's.[o]

20
m 1Ki 17:9–10
n Jer 33:13

21
o Rev 11:15

## The African Presence

**Obadiah 19**

For more on the Philistines, see the African Presence note on 1 Samuel 17.

[a]21 Or *from*

# Jonah

## OVERVIEW

God commissioned Jonah to warn the residents of the great Assyrian city of Nineveh of their impending judgment. Perhaps Jonah was aware of Amos and Hosea's prediction that the northern tribes of Israel were destined for capture by another kingdom, presumably Assyria. If so, Jonah may have hoped that God's judgment of Nineveh would spare his own country. He therefore chose to disobey God's command. Instead of going to Nineveh, he boarded a ship heading in the other direction—to Tarshish, likely in southern Spain.

God did not allow his servant to run away. He disrupted the ship's journey with a terrible storm. Jonah knew the cause of the storm and told the sailors to throw him overboard. Once he was in the water, the storm ceased. The story continues with the famous account of a great fish swallowing Jonah and then spitting him out on the shore. Jonah gave the Lord thanks and praise, and God again instructed him to go and warn the people of Nineveh. As a result of Jonah's prophecies, the Ninevites repented and avoided God's judgment—provoking Jonah's anger at the Lord's compassion.

"Where can I go from your Spirit? Where can I flee from your presence?" asked the psalmist (Ps 139:7). Some people chuckle about Jonah's false assumption that he could run from God, but many women believers attempt to run from him every day. They run from prayer and meditating on the Bible because they fear God's wrath and judgment. But as in the case of Jonah—and the Ninevites—God is everywhere all the time, and he longs for reconciliation with his daughters.

## OUTLINE

I. The Prophet's Flight (1:1–17)
II. The Prophet's Prayer (2:1–10)
III. The Prophet's Preaching (3:1–10)
IV. The Prophet's Despondency (4:1–11)

### SCANNABLE FACTS:

**Author:** Jonah

**Time Written:** Probably about 750 B.C.

**Theme to Note:** God is a God of second chances

**Notable Women:** There are no women mentioned in this book

1:1 a Mt12:39–41
1:3 b Ps139:7
1:4 c Ps107:23–26
1:6 d Ps107:28
1:7 e Jos7:10–18; 1Sa14:42
1:9 f Ps146:6

## Jonah Flees From the LORD

1 The word of the LORD came to Jonah[a]
son of Amittai: 2“Go to the great city of
Nineveh and preach against it, because its
wickedness has come up before me.”
3But Jonah ran[b] away from the LORD
and headed for Tarshish. He went down
to Joppa, where he found a ship bound for
that port. After paying the fare, he went
aboard and sailed for Tarshish to flee from
the LORD.
4Then the LORD sent a great wind on the
sea, and such a violent storm arose that the
ship threatened to break up.[c] 5All the sailors
were afraid and each cried out to his own
god. And they threw the cargo into the sea
to lighten the ship.
But Jonah had gone below deck, where
he lay down and fell into a deep sleep. 6The
captain went to him and said, “How can you
sleep? Get up and call on your god! Maybe
he will take notice of us, and we will not
perish.”[d]
7Then the sailors said to each other,
“Come, let us cast lots to find out who is re-
sponsible for this calamity.”[e] They cast lots
and the lot fell on Jonah.
8So they asked him, “Tell us, who is re-
sponsible for making all this trouble for us?
What do you do? Where do you come from?
What is your country? From what people
are you?”
9He answered, “I am a Hebrew and I wor-
ship the LORD, the God of heaven, who made
the sea and the land.[f]”
10This terrified them and they asked,
“What have you done?” (They knew he was
running away from the LORD, because he
had already told them so.)
11The sea was getting rougher and
rougher. So they asked him, “What should
we do to you to make the sea calm down
for us?”
12“Pick me up and throw me into the sea,”
he replied, “and it will become calm. I know
that it is my fault that this great storm has
come upon you.”
13Instead, the men did their best to row
back to land. But they could not, for the sea
grew even wilder than before. 14Then they
cried to the LORD, “O LORD, please do not let
us die for taking this man’s life. Do not hold
us accountable for killing an innocent man,
for you, O LORD, have done as you pleased.”
15Then they took Jonah and threw him over-
board, and the raging sea grew calm.[g] 16At
this the men greatly feared the LORD, and
they offered a sacrifice to the LORD and made
vows to him.
17But the LORD provided a great fish to
swallow Jonah,[h] and Jonah was inside the
fish three days and three nights.

1:15 g Lk8:24
1:17 h Mt12:40

## Jonah’s Prayer

2 From inside the fish Jonah prayed to the
LORD his God. 2He said:

“In my distress I called to the LORD,
and he answered me.
From the depths of the grave[a] I called
for help,
and you listened to my cry.
3 You hurled me into the deep,
into the very heart of the seas,

[a]2 Hebrew *Sheol*

## The African Presence

**Jonah 1:1**

According to Genesis 10:8–11, Nimrod, a son of Cush, built the city of Nineveh. During the time of Jonah, the nation of Assyria was in a state of decline. However, the nation recovered and in 722 B.C. defeated the northern kingdom of Israel, carrying off 27,000 Israelites. In 612 B.C. Nineveh was defeated during a fierce battle when Babylon and Persia joined forces.

**2:3** i Ps 42:7
**2:4** j Ps 31:22
**2:5** k Ps 69:1–2
**2:7** l Ps 77:11–12; m Ps 18:6
**2:9** n Ps 50:14,23; o Ps 3:8

and the currents swirled about me;
all your waves and breakers
swept over me.[i]
4 I said, 'I have been banished
from your sight;[j]
yet I will look again
toward your holy temple.'
5 The engulfing waters threatened me,[a]
the deep surrounded me;
seaweed was wrapped around my
head.[k]
6 To the roots of the mountains I sank
down;
the earth beneath barred me in
forever.
But you brought my life up from the pit,
O LORD my God.

7 "When my life was ebbing away,
I remembered[l] you, LORD,
and my prayer rose to you,
to your holy temple.[m]

8 "Those who cling to worthless idols
forfeit the grace that could be theirs.
9 But I, with a song of thanksgiving,
will sacrifice[n] to you.
What I have vowed I will make good.
Salvation[o] comes from the LORD."

10 And the Lord commanded the fish, and it vomited Jonah onto dry land.

## Jonah Goes to Nineveh

3 Then the word of the LORD came to Jonah a second time: 2 "Go to the great city of Nineveh and proclaim to it the message I give you."

3 Jonah obeyed the word of the LORD and went to Nineveh. Now Nineveh was a very important city—a visit required three days. 4 On the first day, Jonah started into the city. He proclaimed: "Forty more days and Nineveh will be overturned." 5 The Ninevites believed God. They declared a fast, and all of them, from the greatest to the least, put on sackcloth.

6 When the news reached the king of Nineveh, he rose from his throne, took off his royal robes, covered himself with sackcloth and sat down in the dust. 7 Then he issued a proclamation in Nineveh:

"By the decree of the king and his nobles:

Do not let any man or beast, herd or flock, taste anything; do not let them eat or drink.[p] 8 But let man and beast be covered with sackcloth. Let everyone call[q] urgently on God. Let them give up their evil ways and their violence. 9 Who knows?[r] God may yet relent and with compassion turn[s] from his fierce anger so that we will not perish."

10 When God saw what they did and how they turned from their evil ways, he had compassion[t] and did not bring upon them the destruction[u] he had threatened.

## Jonah's Anger at the LORD's Compassion

4 But Jonah was greatly displeased and became angry. 2 He prayed to the LORD, "O LORD, is this not what I said when I was still at home? That is why I was so quick to flee to Tarshish. I knew that you are a gracious and compassionate God, slow to anger and abounding in love,[v] a God who relents from sending calamity.[w] 3 Now, O LORD, take away my life, for it is better for me to die than to live."

4 But the LORD replied, "Have you any right to be angry?"

*Dear God,*

*you know there are some people with whom I don't want to share your mercy and grace. Teach me that your love is for everyone—those I like, those I don't like, people I agree with and admire, and those I think are despicable. Teach me to share your love with* everyone *through my words and deeds. In Jesus' gracious name,*

*Amen*

JONAH 4:1–4

**3:7** p 2Ch 20:3
**3:8** q Jnh 1:6
**3:9** r 2Sa 12:22; s Joel 2:14
**3:10** t Am 7:6; u Jer 18:8
**4:2** v Ps 86:5,15; w Joel 2:13

[a]5 Or *waters were at my throat*

[5]Jonah went out and sat down at a place
east of the city. There he made himself a
shelter, sat in its shade and waited to see
what would happen to the city. [6]Then the
LORD God provided a vine and made it grow
up over Jonah to give shade for his head to
ease his discomfort, and Jonah was very
happy about the vine. [7]But at dawn the next
day God provided a worm, which chewed
the vine so that it withered. [8]When the sun
rose, God provided a scorching east wind,
and the sun blazed on Jonah's head so that
he grew faint. He wanted to die, and said, "It
would be better for me to die than to live."
[9]But God said to Jonah, "Do you have a
right to be angry about the vine?"

"I do," he said. "I am angry enough to
die."

[10]But the LORD said, "You have been con-
cerned about this vine, though you did
not tend it or make it grow. It sprang up
overnight and died overnight. [11]But Nine-
veh[x] has more than a hundred and twenty
thousand people who cannot tell their right
hand from their left, and many cattle as
well. Should I not be concerned about that
great city?"

*My devoted child,*

*I am loving and compassionate.*

*Follow my example.*

*Your Merciful God*

JONAH 4:1–11

**4:11**
x Jnh 1:2; 3:2

# Micah

## OVERVIEW

Micah prophesied against Samaria (the capital of the northern kingdom of Israel) and Jerusalem (the capital of the southern kingdom of Judah) for coveting fields and houses, defrauding helpless women and children, being dishonest in business practices, using false scales and bribing judges.

Micah also condemned the people's reliance on false prophets. Micah had the difficult job of delivering an unpopular message of God's judgment. However, he was also able to assure the people that the Lord promised a restoration at the appointed time.

How can today's Christian woman recognize a false prophet? The same way the banks recognize a counterfeit bill: by fully understanding what a real one looks like. By daily study of God's Word, women can recognize false teachers or prophets when their words are in contrast to what the Bible teaches. Learn from Micah what false prophets say to people living outside the will of God.

## OUTLINE

I. Predictions of Judgment (1:1—3:12)
II. Promises of Restoration (4:1—5:15)
III. Punishment and Mercy Reaffirmed (6:1—7:20)

## SCANNABLE FACTS:

**Author:** Micah

**Time Written:** Between 750 and 686 B.C.

**Theme to Note:** God will judge false prophets and leaders

**Notable Women:** There are no women mentioned in this book

1:1 a Jer 26:18
1:2 b Ps 50:7 c Ps 11:4
1:3 d Am 4:13
1:4 e Na 1:5
1:5 f Am 8:14
1:6 g Am 5:11 h Eze 13:14
1:7 i Dt 9:21
1:9 j 2Ki 18:13
1:11 k Eze 23:29
1:12 l Jer 14:19

1 The word of the LORD that came to Micah of Moresheth[a] during the reigns of Jotham, Ahaz and Hezekiah, kings of Judah—the vision he saw concerning Samaria and Jerusalem.

2 Hear, O peoples, all of you,[b]
listen, O earth and all who are in it,
that the Sovereign LORD may witness against you,
the Lord from his holy temple.[c]

## Judgment Against Samaria and Jerusalem

3 Look! The LORD is coming from his dwelling place;
he comes down and treads the high places of the earth.[d]
4 The mountains melt beneath him
and the valleys split apart,[e]
like wax before the fire,
like water rushing down a slope.
5 All this is because of Jacob's transgression,
because of the sins of the house of Israel.
What is Jacob's transgression?
Is it not Samaria?[f]
What is Judah's high place?
Is it not Jerusalem?

6 "Therefore I will make Samaria a heap of rubble,
a place for planting vineyards.
I will pour her stones[g] into the valley
and lay bare her foundations.[h]
7 All her idols will be broken to pieces;
all her temple gifts will be burned with fire;
I will destroy all her images.[i]
Since she gathered her gifts from the wages of prostitutes,
as the wages of prostitutes they will again be used."

## Weeping and Mourning

8 Because of this I will weep and wail;
I will go about barefoot and naked.
I will howl like a jackal
and moan like an owl.
9 For her wound is incurable;
it has come to Judah.[j]
It[a] has reached the very gate of my people,
even to Jerusalem itself.
10 Tell it not in Gath[b];
weep not at all.[c]
In Beth Ophrah[d]
roll in the dust.
11 Pass on in nakedness[k] and shame,
you who live in Shaphir.[e]
Those who live in Zaanan[f]
will not come out.
Beth Ezel is in mourning;
its protection is taken from you.
12 Those who live in Maroth[g] writhe in pain,
waiting for relief,[l]
because disaster has come from the LORD,
even to the gate of Jerusalem.
13 You who live in Lachish,[h]
harness the team to the chariot.
You were the beginning of sin
to the Daughter of Zion,
for the transgressions of Israel

[a]9 Or *He* [b]10 *Gath* sounds like the Hebrew for *tell.* [c]10 Hebrew; Septuagint may suggest *not in Acco.* The Hebrew for *in Acco* sounds like the Hebrew for *weep.* [d]10 *Beth Ophrah* means *house of dust.* [e]11 *Shaphir* means *pleasant.* [f]11 *Zaanan* sounds like the Hebrew for *come out.* [g]12 *Maroth* sounds like the Hebrew for *bitter.* [h]13 *Lachish* sounds like the Hebrew for *team.*

## The African Presence

### Micah 1:10,14

Gath was one of the principal cities of Philistia. The ancestry of the Philistines can be traced to Ham's son Mizraim (see Ge 10:6,13). For more on the Philistines, see the African Presence note on 1 Samuel 17.

**1:14** m 2Ki 16:8 n Jos 15:44 o Jer 15:18
**1:15** p Jos 15:44 q Jos 12:15
**2:2** r Isa 5:8
**2:3** s Jer 18:11; Am 3:1–2 t Isa 2:12
**2:6** u Am 2:12
**2:7** v Ps 15:2

were found in you.
14 Therefore you will give parting gifts[m]
to Moresheth Gath.
The town of Aczib[a][n] will prove deceptive[o]
to the kings of Israel.
15 I will bring a conqueror against you
who live in Mareshah.[b][p]
He who is the glory of Israel
will come to Adullam.[q]
16 Shave your heads in mourning
for the children in whom you delight;
make yourselves as bald as the vulture,
for they will go from you into exile.

## Man's Plans and God's

2 Woe to those who plan iniquity,
to those who plot evil on their beds!
At morning's light they carry it out
because it is in their power to do it.
2 They covet fields[r] and seize them,
and houses, and take them.
They defraud a man of his home,
a fellowman of his inheritance.

3 Therefore, the LORD says:

"I am planning disaster[s] against this
people,
from which you cannot save yourselves.
You will no longer walk proudly,[t]
for it will be a time of calamity.
4 In that day men will ridicule you;
they will taunt you with this mournful
song:
'We are utterly ruined;
my people's possession is divided up.
He takes it from me!
He assigns our fields to traitors.' "
5 Therefore you will have no one in the
assembly of the LORD
to divide the land by lot.

## False Prophets

6 "Do not prophesy," their prophets say.
"Do not prophesy about these things;
disgrace will not overtake us.[u]"
7 Should it be said, O house of Jacob:
"Is the Spirit of the LORD angry?
Does he do such things?"

"Do not my words do good
to him whose ways are upright?[v]
8 Lately my people have risen up
like an enemy.
You strip off the rich robe
from those who pass by without a care,
like men returning from battle.
9 You drive the women of my people
from their pleasant homes.[w]
You take away my blessing
from their children forever.
10 Get up, go away!
For this is not your resting place,[x]
because it is defiled,
it is ruined, beyond all remedy.
11 If a liar and deceiver comes and says,
'I will prophesy for you plenty of wine
and beer,'
he would be just the prophet for this
people!

## Deliverance Promised

12 "I will surely gather all of you, O Jacob;
I will surely bring together the
remnant[y] of Israel.
I will bring them together like sheep in
a pen,
like a flock in its pasture;
the place will throng with people.
13 One who breaks open the way will go up
before[z] them;
they will break through the gate and
go out.
Their king will pass through before them,
the LORD at their head."

## Leaders and Prophets Rebuked

3 Then I said,

"Listen, you leaders[a] of Jacob,
you rulers of the house of Israel.
Should you not know justice,
2 you who hate good and love evil;
who tear the skin from my people
and the flesh from their bones;[b]
3 who eat my people's flesh,[c]
strip off their skin
and break their bones in pieces;[d]
who chop them up like meat for the pan,
like flesh for the pot?"

4 Then they will cry out to the LORD,
but he will not answer them.[e]

**2:9** w Jer 10:20
**2:10** x Dt 12:9
**2:12** y Mic 4:7
**2:13** z Isa 52:12
**3:1** a Jer 5:5
**3:2** b Eze 22:27
**3:3** c Ps 14:4 d Zep 3:3
**3:4** e Ps 18:41; Isa 1:15

[a]14 *Aczib* means *deception.* [b]15 *Mareshah* sounds like the Hebrew for *conqueror.*

**3:5** f Isa 3:12
**3:6** g Isa 8:19–22
**3:7** h Mic 7:16
**3:8** i Isa 58:1
**3:10** j Jer 22:13 k Eze 22:27
**3:11** l Isa 1:23; Jer 6:13
**3:12** m Jer 26:18

At that time he will hide his face from
them
because of the evil they have done.
5 This is what the LORD says:
"As for the prophets
who lead my people astray,[f]
if one feeds them,
they proclaim 'peace';
if he does not,
they prepare to wage war against him.
6 Therefore night will come over you,
without visions,
and darkness, without divination.[g]
The sun will set for the prophets,
and the day will go dark for them.
7 The seers will be ashamed[h]
and the diviners disgraced.
They will all cover their faces
because there is no answer from God."
8 But as for me, I am filled with power,
with the Spirit of the LORD,
and with justice and might,
to declare to Jacob his transgression,
to Israel his sin.[i]
9 Hear this, you leaders of the house of
Jacob,
you rulers of the house of Israel,
who despise justice
and distort all that is right;
10 who build[j] Zion with bloodshed,
and Jerusalem with wickedness.[k]
11 Her leaders judge for a bribe,
her priests teach for a price,
and her prophets tell fortunes for
money.[l]
Yet they lean upon the LORD and say,
"Is not the LORD among us?
No disaster will come upon us."
12 Therefore because of you,
Zion will be plowed like a field,
Jerusalem will become a heap of rubble,[m]
the temple hill a mound overgrown
with thickets.

## The Mountain of the LORD

4 In the last days
the mountain of the LORD's temple will be
established
as chief among the mountains;
it will be raised above the hills,
and peoples will stream to it.
2 Many nations will come and say,
"Come, let us go up to the mountain of
the LORD,[n]
to the house of the God of Jacob.
He will teach us his ways,
so that we may walk in his paths."
The law will go out from Zion,
the word of the LORD from Jerusalem.
3 He will judge between many peoples
and will settle disputes for strong
nations far and wide.
They will beat their swords into
plowshares
and their spears into pruning hooks.[o]
Nation will not take up sword against
nation,
nor will they train for war anymore.[p]
4 Every man will sit under his own vine
and under his own fig tree,[q]
and no one will make them afraid,
for the LORD Almighty has spoken.[r]
5 All the nations may walk
in the name of their gods;[s]
we will walk in the name of the LORD
our God for ever and ever.[t]

## The LORD's Plan

6 "In that day," declares the LORD,
"I will gather the lame;
I will assemble the exiles
and those I have brought to grief.[u]
7 I will make the lame a remnant,
those driven away a strong nation.
The LORD will rule over them in Mount
Zion
from that day and forever.[v]
8 As for you, O watchtower of the flock,
O stronghold[a] of the Daughter of
Zion,
the former dominion will be restored to
you;
kingship will come to the Daughter of
Jerusalem."
9 Why do you now cry aloud—
have you no king?[w]
Has your counselor perished,

**4:2** n Jer 31:6
**4:3** o Joel 3:10 p Isa 2:4
**4:4** q 1Ki 4:25 r Zec 3:10
**4:5** s 2Ki 17:29 t Zec 10:12
**4:6** u Eze 34:13,16
**4:7** v Rev 11:15
**4:9** w Jer 8:19

[a]8 Or *hill*

4:9 x Jer 30:6
4:12 y Isa 55:8
4:13 z Da 2:44
5:1 a La 3:30

that pain seizes you like that of a
woman in labor?[x]
10 Writhe in agony, O Daughter of Zion,
like a woman in labor,
for now you must leave the city
to camp in the open field.
You will go to Babylon;
there you will be rescued.
There the LORD will redeem you
out of the hand of your enemies.

11 But now many nations
are gathered against you.
They say, "Let her be defiled,
let our eyes gloat over Zion!"
12 But they do not know
the thoughts of the LORD;
they do not understand his plan,[y]
he who gathers them like sheaves to
the threshing floor.

13 "Rise and thresh, O Daughter of Zion,
for I will give you horns of iron;
I will give you hoofs of bronze
and you will break to pieces many
nations."[z]

You will devote their ill-gotten gains to
the LORD,
their wealth to the Lord of all the
earth.

## A Promised Ruler From Bethlehem

5 Marshal your troops, O city of troops,[a]
for a siege is laid against us.
They will strike Israel's ruler
on the cheek[a] with a rod.

2 "But you, Bethlehem[b] Ephrathah,
though you are small among the clans[b]
of Judah,
out of you will come for me
one who will be ruler over Israel,
whose origins[c] are from of old,
from ancient times.[d]"[c]

3 Therefore Israel will be abandoned
until the time when she who is in labor
gives birth
and the rest of his brothers return
to join the Israelites.

4 He will stand and shepherd his flock[d]
in the strength of the LORD,
in the majesty of the name of the LORD
his God.
And they will live securely, for then his
greatness
will reach to the ends of the earth.
5 And he will be their peace.[e]

## Deliverance and Destruction

When the Assyrian invades our land
and marches through our fortresses,
we will raise against him seven
shepherds,
even eight leaders of men.
6 They will rule[e] the land of Assyria with
the sword,
the land of Nimrod[f] with drawn sword.[f]
He will deliver us from the Assyrian
when he invades our land
and marches into our borders.[g]

7 The remnant[h] of Jacob will be
in the midst of many peoples
like dew from the LORD,

5:2 b Jn 7:42 c Mt 2:6*
5:4 d Isa 40:11; Eze 34:11–15,23
5:5 e Isa 9:6
5:6 f Ge 10:8 g Na 2:11–13
5:7 h Mic 2:12

[a]1 Or *Strengthen your walls, O walled city* [b]2 Or *rulers* [c]2 Hebrew *goings out* [d]2 Or *from days of eternity* [e]6 Or *crush*
[f]6 Or *Nimrod in its gates*

### The African Presence

**Micah 5:5–6**

According to Genesis 10, Nimrod (a son of Cush) built many cities in Babylon and Assyria. For more on the Assyrians, see the African Presence note on Jeremiah 2:18,36. Also see the African Presence notes on Genesis 10.

**5:8** i Mic 4:13 j Hos 5:14
**5:9** k Ps 10:12
**5:10** l Hos 14:3; Zec 9:10
**5:11** m Am 5:9
**5:12** n Isa 2:6
**5:13** o Zec 13:2
**5:15** p Isa 65:12

like showers on the grass,
which do not wait for man
or linger for mankind.
8 The remnant of Jacob will be among the nations,
in the midst of many peoples,
like a lion among the beasts of the forest,
like a young lion among flocks of sheep,
which mauls and mangles[i] as it goes,
and no one can rescue.[j]
9 Your hand will be lifted up[k] in triumph over your enemies,
and all your foes will be destroyed.

10 "In that day," declares the LORD,
"I will destroy your horses from among you
and demolish your chariots.[l]
11 I will destroy the cities of your land
and tear down all your strongholds.[m]
12 I will destroy your witchcraft
and you will no longer cast spells.[n]
13 I will destroy your carved images
and your sacred stones from among you;
you will no longer bow down
to the work of your hands.[o]
14 I will uproot from among you your Asherah poles[a]
and demolish your cities.
15 I will take vengeance[p] in anger and wrath
upon the nations that have not obeyed me."

## The LORD's Case Against Israel

6 Listen to what the LORD says:

"Stand up, plead your case before the mountains;
let the hills hear what you have to say.
2 Hear, O mountains, the LORD's accusation;[q]
listen, you everlasting foundations of the earth.
For the LORD has a case against his people;
he is lodging a charge against Israel.

3 "My people, what have I done to you?
How have I burdened[r] you?
Answer me.
4 I brought you up out of Egypt
and redeemed you from the land of slavery.
I sent Moses to lead you,
also Aaron[s] and Miriam.[t]
5 My people, remember
what Balak[u] king of Moab counseled
and what Balaam son of Beor answered.
Remember ⌊your journey⌋ from Shittim[v] to Gilgal,[w]
that you may know the righteous acts of the LORD."

6 With what shall I come before the LORD
and bow down before the exalted God?
Shall I come before him with burnt offerings,
with calves a year old?
7 Will the LORD be pleased with thousands of rams,
with ten thousand rivers of oil?[x]
Shall I offer my firstborn for my transgression,
the fruit of my body for the sin of my soul?[y]
8 He has showed you, O man, what is good.
And what does the LORD require of you?

**6:2** q Hos 12:2
**6:3** r Jer 2:5
**6:4** s Ps 77:20 t Ex 15:20
**6:5** u Nu 22:5–6 v Nu 25:1 w Jos 5:9–10
**6:7** x Ps 50:8–10 y 2Ki 16:3

[a] 14 That is, symbols of the goddess Asherah

## The African Presence

**Micah 6:4**

The history of Egypt can be traced as far back as 10,000 B.C. For more on Egypt, see the African Presence note on Genesis 10:6.

6:8
z Dt 10:12–13; Hos 6:6
6:10
a Am 3:10
6:11
b Hos 12:7
6:12
c Jer 9:3
6:15
d Am 5:11
6:16
e 1Ki 16:25

*Sister,*

*Act justly, love mercy and walk humbly with me. That's all I require.*

*Love always,*
*God*

MICAH 6:6–8

To act justly and to love mercy
and to walk humbly with your God.[z]

## Israel's Guilt and Punishment

9 Listen! The LORD is calling to the city—
and to fear your name is wisdom—
"Heed the rod and the One who
appointed it.[a]
10 Am I still to forget, O wicked house,
your ill-gotten treasures
and the short ephah,[b] which is
accursed?[a]
11 Shall I acquit a man with dishonest
scales,[b]
with a bag of false weights?
12 Her rich men are violent;
her people are liars
and their tongues speak deceitfully.[c]
13 Therefore, I have begun to destroy you,
to ruin you because of your sins.
14 You will eat but not be satisfied;
your stomach will still be empty.[c]
You will store up but save nothing,
because what you save I will give to the
sword.
15 You will plant but not harvest;
you will press olives but not use the oil
on yourselves,
you will crush grapes but not drink
the wine.[d]
16 You have observed the statutes of Omri[e]
and all the practices of Ahab's house,
and you have followed their
traditions.
Therefore I will give you over to ruin
and your people to derision;
you will bear the scorn of the
nations.[d]"

## Israel's Misery

7 What misery is mine!
I am like one who gathers summer
fruit
at the gleaning of the vineyard;
there is no cluster of grapes to eat,
none of the early figs that I crave.
2 The godly have been swept from the
land;[f]
not one upright man remains.
All men lie in wait to shed blood;
each hunts his brother with a net.[g]
3 Both hands are skilled in doing evil;
the ruler demands gifts,
the judge accepts bribes,
the powerful dictate what they
desire—
they all conspire together.
4 The best of them is like a brier,[h]
the most upright worse than a thorn
hedge.
The day of your watchmen has come,
the day God visits you.
Now is the time of their confusion.[i]
5 Do not trust a neighbor;
put no confidence in a friend.[j]
Even with her who lies in your embrace
be careful of your words.
6 For a son dishonors his father,
a daughter rises up against her mother,
a daughter-in-law against her mother-
in-law—
a man's enemies are the members of
his own household.[k]

7 But as for me, I watch in hope for the
LORD,
I wait for God my Savior;
my God will hear me.

## Israel Will Rise

8 Do not gloat over me,[l] my enemy!
Though I have fallen, I will rise.
Though I sit in darkness,
the LORD will be my light.[m]
9 Because I have sinned against him,
I will bear the LORD's wrath,[n]
until he pleads my case

7:2
f Ps 12:1
g Jer 5:26
7:4
h Eze 2:6
i Hos 9:7
7:5
j Jer 9:4
7:6
k Mt 10:35–36*
7:8
l Pr 24:17
m Isa 9:2
7:9
n La 3:39–40

[a]9 The meaning of the Hebrew for this line is uncertain. [b]10 An ephah was a dry measure. [c]14 The meaning of the Hebrew for this word is uncertain. [d]16 Septuagint; Hebrew *scorn due my people*

**7:10** o Isa 51:23
**7:12** p Isa 19:23–25
**7:14** q Mic 5:4; r Jer 50:19
**7:15** s Ex 3:20
**7:16** t Isa 26:11

and establishes my right.
He will bring me out into the light;
I will see his righteousness.
10 Then my enemy will see it
and will be covered with shame,
she who said to me,
"Where is the LORD your God?"
My eyes will see her downfall;[o]
even now she will be trampled
underfoot
like mire in the streets.

11 The day for building your walls will
come,
the day for extending your boundaries.
12 In that day people will come to you
from Assyria and the cities of Egypt,
even from Egypt to the Euphrates
and from sea to sea
and from mountain to mountain.[p]
13 The earth will become desolate because
of its inhabitants,
as the result of their deeds.

## Prayer and Praise

14 Shepherd[q] your people with your staff,
the flock of your inheritance,
which lives by itself in a forest,
in fertile pasturelands.[a]
Let them feed in Bashan and Gilead[r]
as in days long ago.

15 "As in the days when you came out of
Egypt,
I will show them my wonders.[s]"

16 Nations will see and be ashamed,[t]
deprived of all their power.
They will lay their hands on their mouths
and their ears will become deaf.
17 They will lick dust like a snake,
like creatures that crawl on the
ground.
They will come trembling out of their
dens;
they will turn in fear[u] to the LORD our
God
and will be afraid of you.
18 Who is a God like you,
who pardons sin[v] and forgives the
transgression
of the remnant of his inheritance?[w]
You do not stay angry forever
but delight to show mercy.
19 You will again have compassion on us;
you will tread our sins underfoot
and hurl all our iniquities[x] into the
depths of the sea.
20 You will be true to Jacob,
and show mercy to Abraham,
as you pledged on oath to our fathers[y]
in days long ago.

*Lord,*

*thank you for the righteousness that has been accredited to me through Christ's sacrifice. Help me to live my life as a continuous offering of thanksgiving for your gift. In Jesus' wonderful name,*

*Amen*

MICAH 7:18–20

**7:17** u Isa 49:23
**7:18** v Isa 43:25; w Ex 34:9
**7:19** x Isa 43:25
**7:20** y Lk 1:72

[a]14 Or *in the middle of Carmel*

# Nahum

## OVERVIEW

The book of Nahum details God's displeasure with Assyria, the dominant world power at that time, represented by its capital city of Nineveh. The people of Assyria used their power for torture, enslavement and the destruction of other nations. Nahum affirmed the majesty and power of God, who would carry out his judgment against the wicked nation of Assyria. Nahum prophesied about the nature of the devastation to be carried out and pointed out the reasons why God was decreeing and implementing his judgment.

Are we as women believers of this age aware of the things that displease God? Or do we continue in the same direction as the rest of the world, with no concern for our rebellious ways? As you read through the book of Nahum, pray for God's discernment regarding how to take the lead in living a pure life that goes against the flow of unrighteousness around you.

## OUTLINE

I. Announcement of Judgment (1:1–15)
II. Description of Judgment (2:1–13)
III. Reasons for Judgment (3:1–19)

### SCANNABLE FACTS:

**Author:** Nahum

**Time Written:** Likely written shortly before the fall of Nineveh in 612 B.C.

**Theme to Note:** God's judgment

**Notable Woman:** Nineveh is compared to a harlot

# 1

An oracle concerning Nineveh.[a] The book of the vision of Nahum the Elkoshite.

## The LORD's Anger Against Nineveh

2 The LORD is a jealous[b] and avenging
God;
the LORD takes vengeance and is filled
with wrath.
The LORD takes vengeance on his foes
and maintains his wrath against his
enemies.
3 The LORD is slow to anger[c] and great in
power;
the LORD will not leave the guilty
unpunished.
His way is in the whirlwind and the
storm,
and clouds[d] are the dust of his feet.
4 He rebukes the sea and dries it up;
he makes all the rivers run dry.
Bashan and Carmel[e] wither
and the blossoms of Lebanon fade.
5 The mountains quake before him
and the hills melt away.[f]
The earth trembles at his presence,
the world and all who live in it.
6 Who can withstand his indignation?
Who can endure his fierce anger?
His wrath is poured out like fire;[g]
the rocks are shattered before him.

7 The LORD is good,[h]
a refuge in times of trouble.
He cares for those who trust in him,
8 but with an overwhelming flood
he will make an end of ⌊Nineveh⌋;
he will pursue his foes into darkness.

9 Whatever they plot against the LORD
he[a] will bring to an end;
trouble will not come a second time.
10 They will be entangled among thorns[i]
and drunk from their wine;
they will be consumed like dry
stubble.[b][j]
11 From you, ⌊O Nineveh,⌋ has one come forth
who plots evil against the LORD
and counsels wickedness.

12 This is what the LORD says:

"Although they have allies and are
numerous,
they will be cut off and pass away.
Although I have afflicted you, ⌊O Judah,⌋
I will afflict you no more.
13 Now I will break their yoke from your
neck
and tear your shackles away."

14 The LORD has given a command
concerning you, ⌊Nineveh⌋:
"You will have no descendants to bear
your name.
I will destroy the carved images[k] and
cast idols
that are in the temple of your gods.
I will prepare your grave,
for you are vile."

15 Look, there on the mountains,
the feet of one who brings good news,[l]
who proclaims peace!
Celebrate your festivals,[m] O Judah,
and fulfill your vows.
No more will the wicked invade you;
they will be completely destroyed.

*Lord,*

*help me to remember to rejoice in you always. You are my strength and the source of all my confidence.*

*Amen*

NAHUM 1:15

## Nineveh to Fall

# 2

An attacker[n] advances against you,
⌊Nineveh⌋.
Guard the fortress,
watch the road,
brace yourselves,
marshal all your strength!

2 The LORD will restore[o] the splendor of
Jacob
like the splendor of Israel,
though destroyers have laid them waste
and have ruined their vines.

1:1 a Jnh 1:2; Zep 2:13
1:2 b Ex 20:5
1:3 c Ne 9:17 d Ps 104:3
1:4 e Isa 33:9
1:5 f Mic 1:4
1:6 g Jer 10:10
1:7 h Jer 33:11
1:10 i 2Sa 23:6 j Mal 4:1
1:14 k Mic 5:13
1:15 l Ro 10:15 m Lev 23:2–4
2:1 n Jer 51:20
2:2 o Eze 37:23

[a] 9 Or *What do you foes plot against the LORD? / He* [b] 10 The meaning of the Hebrew for this verse is uncertain.

2:3 p Eze 23:14–15
2:4 q Jer 4:13
2:5 r Jer 46:12
2:7 s Isa 59:11
2:11 t Isa 5:29

3 The shields of his soldiers are red;
the warriors are clad in scarlet.[p]
The metal on the chariots flashes
on the day they are made ready;
the spears of pine are brandished.[a]
4 The chariots[q] storm through the streets,
rushing back and forth through the squares.
They look like flaming torches;
they dart about like lightning.

5 He summons his picked troops,
yet they stumble[r] on their way.
They dash to the city wall;
the protective shield is put in place.
6 The river gates are thrown open
and the palace collapses.
7 It is decreed[b] that ⌞the city⌟
be exiled and carried away.
Its slave girls moan[s] like doves
and beat upon their breasts.
8 Nineveh is like a pool,
and its water is draining away.
"Stop! Stop!" they cry,
but no one turns back.
9 Plunder the silver!
Plunder the gold!
The supply is endless,
the wealth from all its treasures!
10 She is pillaged, plundered, stripped!
Hearts melt, knees give way,
bodies tremble, every face grows pale.

11 Where now is the lions' den,[t]
the place where they fed their young,
where the lion and lioness went,
and the cubs, with nothing to fear?
12 The lion killed enough for his cubs
and strangled the prey for his mate,
filling his lairs with the kill
and his dens with the prey.

13 "I am against[u] you,"
declares the LORD Almighty.
"I will burn up your chariots in smoke,[v]
and the sword will devour your young lions.
I will leave you no prey on the earth.
The voices of your messengers
will no longer be heard."

## Woe to Nineveh

3 Woe to the city of blood,
full of lies,
full of plunder,
never without victims!
2 The crack of whips,
the clatter of wheels,
galloping horses
and jolting chariots!
3 Charging cavalry,
flashing swords
and glittering spears!
Many casualties,
piles of dead,
bodies without number,
people stumbling over the corpses[w]—
4 all because of the wanton lust of a harlot,
alluring, the mistress of sorceries,[x]
who enslaved nations by her prostitution[y]
and peoples by her witchcraft.
5 "I am against[z] you," declares the LORD Almighty.
"I will lift your skirts over your face.
I will show the nations your nakedness[a]
and the kingdoms your shame.
6 I will pelt you with filth,
I will treat you with contempt[b]

2:13 u Na 3:5 v Ps 46:9
3:3 w Isa 34:3
3:4 x Isa 47:9 y Isa 23:17
3:5 z Na 2:13 a Isa 47:3
3:6 b Jer 51:37

[a] 3 Hebrew; Septuagint and Syriac / *the horsemen rush to and fro* [b] 7 The meaning of the Hebrew for this word is uncertain.

### The African Presence

**Nahum 3:8**

Thebes was located on both sides of the Nile River in Egypt. Its name in Hebrew, *No Amon*, means "city of (the god) Amun."

## The African Presence

### Nahum 3:9

"Cush" is also called "Ethiopia" (that is, Nubia). The exact geographic region is disputed; however, most scholars generally agree that the area of Nubia included the middle of the Nile from what is present-day southern Egypt and northern Sudan. For more on Cush, see the African Presence note on Exodus 5:1–5.

Libya and Put are synonyms. Put was the third son of Ham (see Ge 10:6). The Libyans were frequently associated with the Egyptians and Cushites, as they were located near each other in North Africa.

and make you a spectacle.[c]
7 All who see you will flee from you and
say,
'Nineveh is in ruins—who will mourn
for her?'[d]
Where can I find anyone to comfort[e]
you?"

8 Are you better than Thebes,[a][f]
situated on the Nile,
with water around her?
The river was her defense,
the waters her wall.
9 Cush[b] and Egypt were her boundless
strength;
Put[g] and Libya were among her allies.
10 Yet she was taken captive[h]
and went into exile.
Her infants were dashed[i] to pieces
at the head of every street.
Lots were cast for her nobles,
and all her great men were put in
chains.
11 You too will become drunk;
you will go into hiding
and seek refuge from the enemy.

12 All your fortresses are like fig trees
with their first ripe fruit;
when they are shaken,
the figs fall into the mouth of the
eater.
13 Look at your troops—
they are all women![j]
The gates of your land
are wide open to your enemies;
fire has consumed their bars.

14 Draw water for the siege,
strengthen your defenses![k]
Work the clay,
tread the mortar,
repair the brickwork!
15 There the fire will devour you;
the sword will cut you down
and, like grasshoppers, consume you.
Multiply like grasshoppers,
multiply like locusts![l]
16 You have increased the number of your
merchants
till they are more than the stars of the
sky,
but like locusts they strip the land
and then fly away.
17 Your guards are like locusts,
your officials like swarms of locusts
that settle in the walls on a cold
day—
but when the sun appears they fly
away,
and no one knows where.

18 O king of Assyria, your shepherds[c]
slumber;[m]
your nobles lie down to rest.
Your people are scattered[n] on the
mountains
with no one to gather them.

**3:6** c Isa 14:16
**3:7** d Jer 15:5 e Isa 51:19
**3:8** f Jer 46:25
**3:9** g Eze 27:10
**3:10** h Isa 20:4 i Isa 13:16; Hos 13:16
**3:13** j Jer 50:37
**3:14** k Na 2:1
**3:15** l Joel 1:4
**3:18** m Ps 76:5–6 n 1Ki 22:17

[a] 8 Hebrew *No Amon* [b] 9 That is, the upper Nile region [c] 18 Or *rulers*

19 Nothing can heal your wound;
your injury is fatal.
Everyone who hears the news about you
claps his hands[o] at your fall,
for who has not felt
your endless cruelty?

3:19 o La 2:15

## The African Presence

### Nahum 3:18

The Assyrians were descendants of Cush (see Ge 10:8–11), son of Ham. For more on the Assyrians, see the African Presence note on Jeremiah 2:18,36.

# Habakkuk

## OVERVIEW

The book of Habakkuk records a conversation between the prophet Habakkuk and God in which God responds to age-old questions about why he appears to allow evil to go unpunished.

In answer to Habakkuk's first complaint, regarding Judah's injustice, God said that the Babylonians would attack the nation. That prompted Habakkuk's second complaint: How could a just God use the evil Babylonians to punish a people more righteous than themselves? God replied that the Babylonians would also be punished and that he would reward the faith of righteous people.

The book ends with Habakkuk's praise for God in spite of the suffering of his people. Habakkuk learned to rest in God's sovereignty and wait for his working.

We see injustice everywhere, including in our homes, in the church and in the workplace. Only by faith can a woman believer persevere in the face of suffering. Living by faith requires the daily study of God's Word and a commitment to pray. Faith helps the believer to be patient and wait for God's timing. Learn from Habakkuk how to praise God in advance of his deliverance, for "without faith it is impossible to please God" (Heb 11:6).

## OUTLINE

I. Habakkuk's First Complaint (1:1–4)
II. God's Answer (1:5–11)
III. Habakkuk's Second Complaint (1:12—2:1)
IV. God's Answer (2:2–20)
V. Habakkuk's Prayer and Praise (3:1–19)

### SCANNABLE FACTS:

**Author:** Habakkuk

**Time Written:** Around 605 B.C.

**Theme to Note:** God makes sense even when the world around us doesn't seem to

**Notable Women:** There are no women mentioned in this book

1:1 a Na 1:1
1:2 b Ps 13:1–2
1:3 c Jer 20:8
1:4 d Ps 119:126 e Isa 5:20
1:5 f Ac 13:41*
1:6 g 2Ki 24:2
1:7 h Jer 39:5–9
1:9 i Hab 2:5
1:10 j 2Ch 36:6
1:11 k Jer 4:11–12
1:12 l Isa 10:6
1:15 m Jer 16:16

1 The oracle[a] that Habakkuk the prophet received.

## Habakkuk's Complaint

2 How long, O LORD, must I call for help,
but you do not listen?[b]
Or cry out to you, "Violence!"
but you do not save?
3 Why do you make me look at injustice?
Why do you tolerate wrong?
Destruction and violence[c] are before me;
there is strife, and conflict abounds.
4 Therefore the law[d] is paralyzed,
and justice never prevails.
The wicked hem in the righteous,
so that justice is perverted.[e]

## The LORD's Answer

5 "Look at the nations and watch—
and be utterly amazed.
For I am going to do something in your days
that you would not believe,
even if you were told.[f]
6 I am raising up the Babylonians,[a][g]
that ruthless and impetuous people,
who sweep across the whole earth
to seize dwelling places not their own.
7 They are a feared and dreaded people;[h]
they are a law to themselves
and promote their own honor.
8 Their horses are swifter than leopards,
fiercer than wolves at dusk.
Their cavalry gallops headlong;
their horsemen come from afar.
They fly like a vulture swooping to devour;
9 they all come bent on violence.
Their hordes[b] advance like a desert wind
and gather prisoners[i] like sand.
10 They deride kings
and scoff at rulers.[j]
They laugh at all fortified cities;
they build earthen ramps and capture them.
11 Then they sweep past like the wind[k] and go on—
guilty men, whose own strength is their god."

## Habakkuk's Second Complaint

12 O LORD, are you not from everlasting?
My God, my Holy One, we will not die.
O LORD, you have appointed[l] them to execute judgment;
O Rock, you have ordained them to punish.
13 Your eyes are too pure to look on evil;
you cannot tolerate wrong.
Why then do you tolerate the treacherous?
Why are you silent while the wicked
swallow up those more righteous than themselves?
14 You have made men like fish in the sea,
like sea creatures that have no ruler.
15 The wicked foe pulls all of them up with hooks,
he catches them in his net,[m]
he gathers them up in his dragnet;
and so he rejoices and is glad.
16 Therefore he sacrifices to his net
and burns incense to his dragnet,
for by his net he lives in luxury

[a]6 Or *Chaldeans* [b]9 The meaning of the Hebrew for this word is uncertain.

## *The African Presence*

### Habakkuk 1:6

The Babylonians were a powerful people who replaced Assyria as the dominant power of the time. This area is the same area in which Abraham lived prior to his departure to Haran and Canaan. For more on the Babylonians, also called Chaldeans, see the African Presence note on Ezekiel 12:13.

and enjoys the choicest food.
17 Is he to keep on emptying his net,
destroying nations without mercy?[n]

2 I will stand at my watch[o]
and station myself on the ramparts;
I will look to see what he will say to me,
and what answer I am to give to this
complaint.[a]

## The LORD's Answer

2 Then the LORD replied:

"Write[p] down the revelation
and make it plain on tablets
so that a herald[b] may run with it.
3 For the revelation awaits an appointed
time;
it speaks of the end[q]
and will not prove false.
Though it linger, wait for it;
it[c] will certainly come and will not
delay.[r]

4 "See, he is puffed up;
his desires are not upright—
but the righteous will live by his
faith[d][s]—
5 indeed, wine[t] betrays him;
he is arrogant and never at rest.
Because he is as greedy as the grave[e]
and like death is never satisfied,
he gathers to himself all the nations
and takes captive all the peoples.

6 "Will not all of them taunt him with ridi-
cule and scorn, saying,

" 'Woe to him who piles up stolen goods
and makes himself wealthy by
extortion!
How long must this go on?'
7 Will not your debtors[f] suddenly arise?
Will they not wake up and make you
tremble?
Then you will become their victim.[u]
8 Because you have plundered many
nations,
the peoples who are left will plunder
you.[v]
For you have shed man's blood;
you have destroyed lands and cities
and everyone in them.

9 "Woe to him who builds his realm by
unjust gain
to set his nest on high,
to escape the clutches of ruin!
10 You have plotted the ruin[w] of many
peoples,
shaming your own house and
forfeiting your life.
11 The stones[x] of the wall will cry out,
and the beams of the woodwork will
echo it.

12 "Woe to him who builds a city with
bloodshed[y]
and establishes a town by crime!
13 Has not the LORD Almighty determined
that the people's labor is only fuel for
the fire,[z]
that the nations exhaust themselves
for nothing?
14 For the earth will be filled with the
knowledge of the glory of the
LORD,
as the waters cover the sea.[a]

15 "Woe to him who gives drink to his
neighbors,
pouring it from the wineskin till they
are drunk,
so that he can gaze on their naked
bodies.
16 You will be filled with shame instead of
glory.
Now it is your turn! Drink and be
exposed[g][b]
The cup from the LORD's right hand is
coming around to you,
and disgrace will cover your glory.
17 The violence[c] you have done to Lebanon
will overwhelm you,
and your destruction of animals will
terrify you.
For you have shed man's blood;[d]
you have destroyed lands and cities
and everyone in them.

18 "Of what value is an idol, since a man has
carved it?
Or an image that teaches lies?

1:17 n Isa 14:6
2:1 o Isa 21:8
2:2 p Rev 1:19
2:3 q Da 8:17 r Eze 12:25
2:4 s Ro 1:17*; Gal 3:11*; Heb 10:37–38*
2:5 t Pr 20:1
2:7 u Pr 29:1
2:8 v Isa 33:1
2:10 w Jer 26:19
2:11 x Jos 24:27; Lk 19:40
2:12 y Mic 3:10
2:13 z Isa 50:11
2:14 a Isa 11:9
2:16 b La 4:21
2:17 c Jer 51:35 d ver 8

[a]1 Or *and what to answer when I am rebuked* [b]2 Or *so that whoever reads it* [c]3 Or *Though he linger, wait for him; / he* [d]4 Or *faithfulness* [e]5 Hebrew *Sheol* [f]7 Or *creditors* [g]16 Masoretic Text; Dead Sea Scrolls, Aquila, Vulgate and Syriac (see also Septuagint) *and stagger*

# Inspire leadership FOCUS

## WRITE IT DOWN!

As women of great vision and purpose, we carry an enormous amount of responsibility. We have many dreams and goals that we desire to accomplish, and therefore we need to make the most of each day. With so many priorities pulling us in different directions, how can we, as leaders in our homes and communities, best utilize our time on a daily basis to fulfill our destiny? The answer: proper planning.

As God reveals to us ideas and plans for our lives, we need to record the ideas and write down the plans in detail. God said to the Old Testament prophet and leader Habakkuk: "Write down the revelation and make it plain on tablets so that a herald may run with it" (Hab 2:2). It is important for us as today's leaders to write out our visions, so we can map out a strategy for success. Just as we would not embark on a long road trip without a map or directions, we cannot possibly consider going through life without a blueprint.

Planning lays the foundation for better organization, allowing us to maximize each day's potential. Planning helps us to focus on what is really important and gives us clarity to put less emphasis on things that are insignificant.

It's been said that "most people don't plan to fail, they simply fail to plan." Unpreparedness, or poor planning, causes disorganization and lack of focus. We then become frustrated and disappointed that our lives are not moving forward. When there are so many others depending on us, we cannot afford to waste precious time. God's desire is that we make the most of our time and fulfill the purposes that he has set for us.

Leader, is your plan set on paper? An effective plan involves writing out a clear vision statement for your life—a declaration of the role(s) you are called to play and how you will execute your responsibilities. Writing a vision statement energizes leaders and provides daily direction.

—K. Hill

### read

Habakkuk 2.

See also the Inspire Notes "Responsible Decisions in Leadership," "Following God-Given Visions," "Seek Wisdom," "Doing Your Best" and "Be Focused," and the Women of the Bible Notes "A Virtuous Woman: A Strong Woman, Dependent on God" and "The 'Chosen Lady': A Woman Worth Imitating."

### WOMAN of COLOR

Schedule quiet time to map out a plan to accomplish your dreams. Write out a detailed vision statement that clearly dictates how you will execute your goals; then set timelines to realize them. Be specific. Then trust God and step out with faith, boldness and a courageous confidence to achieve your goals.

For the next Inspire note, go to page 1111.

**2:18** e Ps 115:4–5
**2:19** f 1Ki 18:27
**3:2** g Ps 119:120 h Isa 54:8
**3:3** i Ps 48:10
**3:7** j Jdg 7:24–25 k Ex 15:14
**3:8** l Ps 68:17

For he who makes it trusts in his own
creation;
he makes idols that cannot speak.[e]
19 Woe to him who says to wood, 'Come to
life!'
Or to lifeless stone, 'Wake up!'[f]
Can it give guidance?
It is covered with gold and silver;
there is no breath in it.
20 But the LORD is in his holy temple;
let all the earth be silent before him."

## Habakkuk's Prayer

3 A prayer of Habakkuk the prophet.
On *shigionoth.*[a]

2 LORD, I have heard of your fame;
I stand in awe[g] of your deeds, O LORD.
Renew them in our day,
in our time make them known;
in wrath remember mercy.[h]

3 God came from Teman,
the Holy One from Mount Paran.
*Selah*[b]

His glory covered the heavens
and his praise filled the earth.[i]
4 His splendor was like the sunrise;
rays flashed from his hand,
where his power was hidden.
5 Plague went before him;
pestilence followed his steps.
6 He stood, and shook the earth;
he looked, and made the nations
tremble.
The ancient mountains crumbled
and the age-old hills collapsed.
His ways are eternal.
7 I saw the tents of Cushan in distress,
the dwellings of Midian[j] in anguish.[k]

8 Were you angry with the rivers,
O LORD?
Was your wrath against the streams?
Did you rage against the sea
when you rode with your horses
and your victorious chariots?[l]
9 You uncovered your bow,
you called for many arrows. *Selah*
You split the earth with rivers;
10 the mountains saw you and writhed.
Torrents of water swept by;
the deep roared
and lifted its waves on high.

11 Sun and moon stood still in the
heavens
at the glint of your flying arrows,[m]
at the lightning of your flashing spear.
12 In wrath you strode through the earth
and in anger you threshed[n] the
nations.
13 You came out to deliver your people,
to save your anointed one.
You crushed[o] the leader of the land of
wickedness,
you stripped him from head to foot.
*Selah*
14 With his own spear you pierced his head
when his warriors stormed out to
scatter us,[p]
gloating as though about to devour
the wretched who were in hiding.
15 You trampled the sea with your horses,
churning the great waters.

16 I heard and my heart pounded,
my lips quivered at the sound;
decay crept into my bones,
and my legs trembled.
Yet I will wait patiently for the day of
calamity
to come on the nation invading us.
17 Though the fig tree does not bud
and there are no grapes on the vines,
though the olive crop fails

**3:11** m Ps 18:14
**3:12** n Isa 41:15
**3:13** o Ps 110:6
**3:14** p Jdg 7:22

*Lord,*

*you have led me on a journey through challenges, questions and answers. Help me to understand what you are doing in my life, to be content in you, knowing that you will keep me—because I want to be sheltered by you. I love you.*

*Amen*

HABAKKUK 3:17–19

[a]1 Probably a literary or musical term [b]3 A word of uncertain meaning; possibly a musical term; also in verses 9 and 13

3:17
q Jer 5:17

and the fields produce no food,
though there are no sheep in the pen
and no cattle in the stalls,[q]
18 yet I will rejoice in the LORD,
I will be joyful in God my Savior.

19 The Sovereign LORD is my strength;[r]
he makes my feet like the feet of a deer,
he enables me to go on the heights.[s]

For the director of music. On my stringed instruments.

3:19
r Dt 33:29
s 2Sa 22:34; Ps 18:33

# Zephaniah

## OVERVIEW

Zephaniah recognized that God's judgment would begin with Judah but would ultimately become worldwide. He gave specific prophecies against Philistia, Moab, Ammon, Cush and Assyria. As with most of the prophets, Zephaniah ended his pronouncements of doom by pointing to the future restoration of God's people.

There is always hope for restoration when a woman puts her trust in Jesus Christ for the forgiveness of sins. While God doesn't always remove the consequences of sin, he does provide healing and renewal when there is true repentance. As you read through this book, look for how God brings a future hope to his people of yesterday and today.

## OUTLINE

I. The Day of the Lord Is Near (1:1—2:3)
II. God's Judgment Against Other Nations (2:4–15)
III. God's Judgment Against Jerusalem (3:1–8)
IV. Promise of Future Blessing (3:9–20)

## SCANNABLE FACTS:

**Author:** Zephaniah

**Time Written:** During the reign of King Josiah (640–609 B.C.)

**Theme to Note:** The great day of the Lord is coming

**Notable Women:** There are no women mentioned in this book

1:1 a 2Ki 22:1
1:4 b Mic 5:13 c Hos 10:5
1:6 d Isa 1:4 e Hos 7:7
1:7 f Hab 2:20; Zec 2:13 g Jer 46:10
1:8 h Isa 24:21

1 The word of the LORD that came to Zephaniah son of Cushi, the son of Gedaliah, the son of Amariah, the son of Hezekiah, during the reign of Josiah[a] son of Amon king of Judah:

## Warning of Coming Destruction

2 "I will sweep away everything
from the face of the earth,"
declares the LORD.
3 "I will sweep away both men and animals;
I will sweep away the birds of the air
and the fish of the sea.
The wicked will have only heaps of rubble[a]
when I cut off man from the face of the earth,"
declares the LORD.

## Against Judah

4 "I will stretch out my hand against Judah
and against all who live in Jerusalem.
I will cut off from this place every remnant of Baal,[b]
the names of the pagan and the idolatrous priests[c]—
5 those who bow down on the roofs
to worship the starry host,
those who bow down and swear by the LORD
and who also swear by Molech,[b]
6 those who turn back from following[d] the LORD
and neither seek the LORD nor inquire[e] of him.
7 Be silent[f] before the Sovereign LORD,
for the day of the LORD is near.
The LORD has prepared a sacrifice;[g]
he has consecrated those he has invited.
8 On the day of the LORD's sacrifice
I will punish[h] the princes
and the king's sons
and all those clad
in foreign clothes.
9 On that day I will punish
all who avoid stepping on the threshold,[c]
who fill the temple of their gods
with violence and deceit.

10 "On that day," declares the LORD,
"a cry will go up from the Fish Gate,[i]
wailing from the New Quarter,
and a loud crash from the hills.
11 Wail, you who live in the market district[d];
all your merchants will be wiped out,
all who trade with[e] silver will be ruined.
12 At that time I will search Jerusalem with lamps
and punish those who are complacent,
who are like wine left on its dregs,[j]
who think, 'The LORD will do nothing,[k]
either good or bad.'
13 Their wealth will be plundered,
their houses demolished.
They will build houses
but not live in them;
they will plant vineyards
but not drink the wine.[l]

## The Great Day of the LORD

14 "The great day of the LORD is near—
near and coming quickly.
Listen! The cry on the day of the LORD will be bitter,
the shouting of the warrior there.
15 That day will be a day of wrath,
a day of distress and anguish,
a day of trouble and ruin,
a day of darkness and gloom,
a day of clouds and blackness,[m]
16 a day of trumpet and battle cry[n]
against the fortified cities
and against the corner towers.
17 I will bring distress on the people
and they will walk like blind men,
because they have sinned against the LORD.
Their blood will be poured out[o] like dust
and their entrails like filth.
18 Neither their silver nor their gold
will be able to save them
on the day of the LORD's wrath.
In the fire of his jealousy
the whole world will be consumed,[p]

1:10 i 2Ch 33:14
1:12 j Jer 48:11 k Eze 8:12
1:13 l Am 5:11
1:15 m Isa 22:5
1:16 n Jer 4:19
1:17 o Ps 79:3
1:18 p ver 2–3; Zep 3:8

[a]3 The meaning of the Hebrew for this line is uncertain. [b]5 Hebrew *Malcam,* that is, Milcom [c]9 See 1 Samuel 5:5. [d]11 Or *the Mortar* [e]11 Or *in*

for he will make a sudden end
of all who live in the earth."

2 Gather together,[q] gather together,
O shameful[r] nation,
2 before the appointed time arrives
and that day sweeps on like chaff,[s]
before the fierce anger of the LORD comes
upon you,
before the day of the LORD's wrath
comes upon you.
3 Seek[t] the LORD, all you humble of the
land,
you who do what he commands.
Seek righteousness, seek humility;[u]
perhaps you will be sheltered
on the day of the LORD's anger.

## Against Philistia

4 Gaza[v] will be abandoned
and Ashkelon left in ruins.
At midday Ashdod will be emptied
and Ekron uprooted.
5 Woe to you who live by the sea,
O Kerethite people;
the word of the LORD is against you,[w]
O Canaan, land of the Philistines.

"I will destroy you,
and none will be left."[x]

6 The land by the sea, where the Kerethites[a]
dwell,
will be a place for shepherds and sheep
pens.
7 It will belong to the remnant of the house
of Judah;
there they will find pasture.
In the evening they will lie down
in the houses of Ashkelon.
The LORD their God will care for
them;
he will restore their fortunes.[b]

## Against Moab and Ammon

8 "I have heard the insults of Moab
and the taunts of the Ammonites,
who insulted[y] my people
and made threats against their land.
9 Therefore, as surely as I live,"
declares the LORD Almighty, the God
of Israel,
"surely Moab[z] will become like
Sodom,[a]
the Ammonites like Gomorrah—
a place of weeds and salt pits,
a wasteland forever.
The remnant of my people will plunder[b]
them;
the survivors of my nation will inherit
their land."
10 This is what they will get in return for
their pride,
for insulting and mocking the people
of the LORD Almighty.
11 The LORD will be awesome[c] to them
when he destroys all the gods[d] of the
land.

2:1 q Joel 1:14 r Jer 3:3
2:2 s Isa 17:13
2:3 t Am 5:6 u Am 5:14–15
2:4 v Am 1:6,7–8; Zec 9:5–7
2:5 w Am 3:1 x Isa 14:30
2:8 y Eze 25:3
2:9 z Isa 15:1–16:14 a Dt 29:23 b Isa 11:14
2:11 c Joel 2:11 d Zep 1:4

[a]6 The meaning of the Hebrew for this word is uncertain. [b]7 Or *will bring back their captives*

## The African Presence

### Zephaniah 2:4–7

Gaza, Ashkelon, Ashdod and Ekron were Philistine cities located west of Judah. The ancestry of the Philistines can be traced to Ham's son Mizraim (see Ge 10:6,13). They occupied the coastland of Canaan. Because Ham's offspring represent the geographic territories once dominated by Egypt—present-day Egypt, Libya and Sudan and into the area today known as Israel—they can claim a relation to African heritage. Since "heritage" is something "passed down" or "inherited," Canaan (Israel or Palestine) most certainly received or was influenced by Egypt culturally, politically, religiously, etc.

## The African Presence

### Zephaniah 2:12

Cush is also called "Ethiopia" (that is, Nubia). The exact geographic region is disputed; however, most scholars generally agree that the area of Nubia included the middle of the Nile from what is present-day southern Egypt and northern Sudan. For more on Cush, see the African Presence note on Exodus 5:1–5.

2:11 e Zep 3:9
2:13 f Na 1:1
2:15 g Isa 47:8

The nations on every shore will worship him,[e]
every one in its own land.

### Against Cush

12 "You too, O Cushites,[a]
will be slain by my sword."

### Against Assyria

13 He will stretch out his hand against the north
and destroy Assyria,
leaving Nineveh[f] utterly desolate
and dry as the desert.
14 Flocks and herds will lie down there,
creatures of every kind.
The desert owl and the screech owl
will roost on her columns.
Their calls will echo through the windows,
rubble will be in the doorways,
the beams of cedar will be exposed.
15 This is the carefree city
that lived in safety.[g]
She said to herself,
"I am, and there is none besides me."
What a ruin she has become,
a lair for wild beasts!
All who pass by her scoff
and shake their fists.

### The Future of Jerusalem

3 Woe to the city of oppressors,[h]
rebellious and defiled!
2 She obeys[i] no one,
she accepts no correction.
She does not trust in the LORD,
she does not draw near[j] to her God.
3 Her officials are roaring lions,
her rulers are evening wolves,
who leave nothing for the morning.
4 Her prophets are arrogant;
they are treacherous men.
Her priests profane the sanctuary
and do violence to the law.[k]
5 The LORD within her is righteous;
he does no wrong.[l]
Morning by morning he dispenses his justice,
and every new day he does not fail,
yet the unrighteous know no shame.

3:1 h Jer 6:6
3:2 i Jer 22:21 j Ps 73:28
3:4 k Eze 22:26
3:5 l Dt 32:4

[a] 12 That is, people from the upper Nile region

## The African Presence

### Zephaniah 2:13–15

The Assyrians were descendants of Cush (see Ge 10:8–11), son of Ham. For more on the Assyrians, see the African Presence note on Jeremiah 2:18,36.

[6] "I have cut off nations;
their strongholds are demolished.
I have left their streets deserted,
with no one passing through.
Their cities are destroyed;
no one will be left—no one at all.
[7] I said to the city,
'Surely you will fear me
and accept correction!'
Then her dwelling would not be cut off,
nor all my punishments come upon
her.
But they were still eager
to act corruptly[m] in all they did.
[8] Therefore wait[n] for me," declares the
LORD,
"for the day I will stand up to testify.[a]
I have decided to assemble the
nations,[o]
to gather the kingdoms
and to pour out my wrath on them—
all my fierce anger.
The whole world will be consumed[p]
by the fire of my jealous anger.

[9] "Then will I purify the lips of the
peoples,
that all of them may call on the name
of the LORD
and serve[q] him shoulder to shoulder.
[10] From beyond the rivers of Cush[b][r]
my worshipers, my scattered people,
will bring me offerings.
[11] On that day you will not be put to shame
for all the wrongs you have done to me,
because I will remove from this city
those who rejoice in their pride.
Never again will you be haughty
on my holy hill.
[12] But I will leave within you
the meek[s] and humble,
who trust in the name of the LORD.
[13] The remnant[t] of Israel will do no
wrong;
they will speak no lies,[u]
nor will deceit be found in their
mouths.
They will eat and lie down
and no one will make them afraid."

[14] Sing, O Daughter of Zion;
shout aloud, O Israel!
Be glad and rejoice with all your heart,
O Daughter of Jerusalem!
[15] The LORD has taken away your
punishment,
he has turned back your enemy.
The LORD, the King of Israel, is with
you;[v]
never again will you fear any harm.
[16] On that day they will say to Jerusalem,
"Do not fear, O Zion;
do not let your hands hang limp.[w]
[17] The LORD your God is with you,
he is mighty to save.
He will take great delight[x] in you,
he will quiet you with his love,
he will rejoice over you with singing."

[18] "The sorrows for the appointed feasts
I will remove from you;
they are a burden and a reproach to
you.[c]
[19] At that time I will deal
with all who oppressed you;
I will rescue the lame

3:7 m Hos 9:9
3:8 n Ps 27:14 o Joel 3:2 p Zep 1:18
3:9 q Isa 19:18
3:10 r Ps 68:31
3:12 s Isa 14:32
3:13 t Mic 4:7 u Rev 14:5
3:15 v Eze 37:26–28
3:16 w Isa 35:3–4; Heb 12:12
3:17 x Isa 62:4

[a]8 Septuagint and Syriac; Hebrew *will rise up to plunder* [b]10 That is, the upper Nile region [c]18 Or *"I will gather you who mourn for the appointed feasts; / your reproach is a burden to you*

## The African Presence

### Zephaniah 3:10

Zephaniah made this reference to Cush in his prophecies of restoration. This Scripture indicates the presence of Jews beyond Cush; Jews were in the continent of Africa before their return to the land where God planted them.

**3:19**
y Eze 34:16; Mic 4:6

**3:20**
z Eze 37:12
a Isa 56:5

and gather those who have been
scattered.[y]
I will give them praise and honor
in every land where they were put to
shame.
20 At that time I will gather you;
at that time I will bring[z] you home.
I will give you honor[a] and praise
among all the peoples of the earth
when I restore your fortunes[a]
before your very eyes,"
says the LORD.

*Daughter,*

*I can turn your prayer requests into praise reports. Watch me.*

*"Abba"*

ZEPHANIAH 3:17–20

[a]20 Or *I bring back your captives*

# Haggai

## OVERVIEW

The exiles had returned to their land, and yet they were not prospering. Haggai encouraged the people to take care of God's business first—that is, rebuilding the temple. However, after the temple was completed, the older generation of Israelites were troubled (see Hag 2:3). They remembered the former temple, so they were disappointed over the smaller size and diminished grandeur of this new temple. However, God promised that this new temple would be better than the former one because his glory would fill it (see Hag 2:7–9) in the person of the Messiah, Jesus Christ.

When Solomon dedicated the first temple, no priest could perform his duties because the glory of the Lord filled the temple (see 1Ki 8:11). Our bodies are the temple of the Holy Spirit (see 1Co 6:19), and this sacred place (see 1Co 3:17) must be taken care of or it will experience a decline. Reflect on the inner condition of your temple. Does it bring glory to God?

## OUTLINE

I. The Call to Rebuild the Temple (1:1–11)
II. Fulfilling the Call (1:12–15)
III. The Promise of the New Temple's Glory (2:1–9)
IV. The Promise of Blessing (2:10–23)

## SCANNABLE FACTS:

**Author:** Haggai

**Time Written:** 520 B.C.

**Theme to Note:** The glory of this temple will be great because of the presence of the Messiah

**Notable Women:** There are no women mentioned in this book

1:1
a Ezr 4:24
b Ezr 5:3

1:4
c ver 9

1:6
d Zec 8:10

1:8
e Ps 132:13–14

1:10
f Dt 28:23

## A Call to Build the House of the LORD

1 In the second year of King Darius,[a] on
the first day of the sixth month, the
word of the LORD came through the prophet
Haggai to Zerubbabel son of Shealtiel,
governor[b] of Judah, and to Joshua[a] son of
Jehozadak, the high priest:
2This is what the LORD Almighty says:
"These people say, 'The time has not yet
come for the LORD's house to be built.'"
3Then the word of the LORD came
through the prophet Haggai: 4"Is it a time
for you yourselves to be living in your paneled houses, while this house remains a
ruin?[c]"
5Now this is what the LORD Almighty
says: "Give careful thought to your ways.
6You have planted much, but have harvested
little. You eat, but never have enough. You
drink, but never have your fill. You put on
clothes, but are not warm. You earn wages,[d]
only to put them in a purse with holes
in it."
7This is what the LORD Almighty says:
"Give careful thought to your ways. 8Go up
into the mountains and bring down timber
and build the house, so that I may take pleasure[e] in it and be honored," says the LORD.
9"You expected much, but see, it turned out
to be little. What you brought home, I blew
away. Why?" declares the LORD Almighty.
"Because of my house, which remains a
ruin, while each of you is busy with his own
house. 10Therefore, because of you the heavens have withheld their dew and the earth
its crops.[f] 11I called for a drought on the
fields and the mountains, on the grain, the
new wine, the oil and whatever the ground
produces, on men and cattle, and on the labor of your hands.[g]"
12Then Zerubbabel son of Shealtiel,
Joshua son of Jehozadak, the high priest,
and the whole remnant of the people obeyed
the voice of the LORD their God and the message of the prophet Haggai, because the
LORD their God had sent him. And the people feared the LORD.
13Then Haggai, the LORD's messenger,
gave this message of the LORD to the people: "I am with[h] you," declares the LORD.
14So the LORD stirred up the spirit of Zerubbabel[i] son of Shealtiel, governor of Judah,
and the spirit of Joshua son of Jehozadak,
the high priest, and the spirit of the whole
remnant of the people. They came and
began to work on the house of the LORD Almighty, their God, 15on the twenty-fourth
day of the sixth month in the second year
of King Darius.

[a]1 A variant of *Jeshua*; here and elsewhere in Haggai

*Woman of color,*

*Do the work that honors me;*

*I will take care of the rest.*

*Your Provider*

HAGGAI 1:1–11

1:11
g Hag 2:17

1:13
h Ro 8:31

1:14
i Ezr 5:2

## *The African Presence*

### Haggai 1:1

King Darius of Persia gave the Jews permission to return to their land. Darius ruled over the land of Mesopotamia, a land known as "the land between the rivers." Asshur, the ancient capital of Assyria, was located on the Tigris River; Babylon, the capital of Babylonia, on the Euphrates River. For more on Mesopotamia, see the African Presence note on Genesis 2:8.

2:3 j Ezr 3:12
2:4 k Zec 8:9
2:5 l Ex 29:46 m Ne 9:20; Isa 63:11
2:6 n Heb 12:26*
2:7 o Isa 60:7
2:11 p Lev 10:10–11
2:12 q Mt 23:19

## The Promised Glory of the New House

2 On the twenty-first day of the seventh month, the word of the LORD came through the prophet Haggai: [2]"Speak to Zerubbabel son of Shealtiel, governor of Judah, to Joshua son of Jehozadak, the high priest, and to the remnant of the people. Ask them, [3]'Who of you is left who saw this house[j] in its former glory? How does it look to you now? Does it not seem to you like nothing? [4]But now be strong, O Zerubbabel,' declares the LORD. 'Be strong,[k] O Joshua son of Jehozadak, the high priest. Be strong, all you people of the land,' declares the LORD, 'and work. For I am with you,' declares the LORD Almighty. [5]'This is what I covenanted with you when you came out of Egypt.[l] And my Spirit[m] remains among you. Do not fear.'

[6]"This is what the LORD Almighty says: 'In a little while I will once more shake the heavens and the earth,[n] the sea and the dry land. [7]I will shake all nations, and the desired of all nations will come, and I will fill this house[o] with glory,' says the LORD Almighty. [8]'The silver is mine and the gold is mine,' declares the LORD Almighty. [9]'The glory of this present house will be greater than the glory of the former house,' says the LORD Almighty. 'And in this place I will grant peace,' declares the LORD Almighty."

## Blessings for a Defiled People

[10]On the twenty-fourth day of the ninth month, in the second year of Darius, the word of the LORD came to the prophet Haggai: [11]"This is what the LORD Almighty says: 'Ask the priests[p] what the law says: [12]If a person carries consecrated meat in the fold of his garment, and that fold touches some bread or stew, some wine, oil or other food, does it become consecrated?[q]' "

The priests answered, "No."

[13]Then Haggai said, "If a person defiled by contact with a dead body touches one of these things, does it become defiled?"

"Yes," the priests replied, "it becomes defiled."

[14]Then Haggai said, " 'So it is with this people and this nation in my sight,' declares the LORD. 'Whatever they do and whatever they offer there is defiled.

[15]" 'Now give careful thought[r] to this from this day on[a]—consider how things were before one stone was laid on another in the LORD's temple.[s] [16]When anyone came to a heap of twenty measures, there were only ten. When anyone went to a wine vat to draw fifty measures, there were only twenty.[t] [17]I struck all the work of your hands with blight,[u] mildew and hail, yet you did not turn to me,' declares the LORD. [18]'From this day on, from this twenty-fourth day of the ninth month, give careful thought to the day when the foundation[v] of the LORD's temple was laid. Give careful thought: [19]Is there yet any seed left in the barn? Until now, the vine and the fig tree, the pomegranate and the olive tree have not borne fruit.

" 'From this day on I will bless you.' "

## Zerubbabel the LORD's Signet Ring

[20]The word of the LORD came to Haggai a second time on the twenty-fourth day of the month: [21]"Tell Zerubbabel governor of Judah that I will shake the heavens and the earth. [22]I will overturn royal thrones and shatter the power of the foreign kingdoms.[w] I will overthrow chariots[x] and their drivers; horses and their riders will fall, each by the sword of his brother.

[23]" 'On that day,' declares the LORD Almighty, 'I will take you, my servant Zerubbabel son of Shealtiel,' declares the LORD, 'and I will make you like my signet ring, for I have chosen you,' declares the LORD Almighty."

2:15 r Hag 1:5 s Ezr 4:24
2:16 t Hag 1:6
2:17 u Dt 28:22
2:18 v Zec 8:9
2:22 w Da 2:44 x Mic 5:10

[a]15 Or *to the days past*

# Zechariah

## OVERVIEW

Zechariah began his prophetic ministry in 520 B.C., the same year that Haggai delivered his prophetic messages. A large group of Israelites had returned from the land of their captivity about 17 years earlier and had immediately begun rebuilding the temple at Jerusalem, but no work had been done for the past 10 years. Because of Haggai and Zechariah's prophecies, the people once again focused on rebuilding the temple. Through Zechariah's ongoing ministry, which lasted for many years, they were also encouraged about the wonderful future that God had planned for them. Zechariah's prophecies tell of God's plan to extend his blessings beyond Israel to the entire world.

Zechariah's fellow Israelites had become discouraged about rebuilding the temple. Even for women who trust in God, there are times of dejection; however, God is still faithful to his word, as he was to the people in Zechariah's day. Meditate on the prophet's instruction: "'Return to me,' declares the LORD Almighty" (Zec 1:3). Make sure that your heart is completely submitted to him during times of difficulty.

## OUTLINE

I. God's Call for Judah to Return to Him (1:1–6)
II. Eight Symbolic Visions (1:7—6:8)
III. The Crowning of Joshua (6:9–15)
IV. Fasting and the Future (7:1—8:23)
V. The Coming of the Messianic King (9:1—10:12)
VI. The Rejection of the Messianic Shepherd-King (11:1–17)
VII. The Deliverance and Conversion of Israel (12:1—13:9)
VIII. The Coming of the Messiah's Kingdom (14:1–21)

### SCANNABLE FACTS:

**Author:** Zechariah

**Time Written:** Around 520–480 B.C.

**Theme to Note:** The hope of a future Messiah

**Notable Woman:** The vision of the woman in a basket

**1:1**
a Ezr 4:24
b Ne 12:4
**1:3**
c Mal 3:7; Jas 4:8
**1:4**
d 2Ch 36:15
e Jer 6:17
**1:6**
f La 2:17
**1:8**
g Rev 6:4
h Zec 6:2–7

## A Call to Return to the LORD

1 In the eighth month of the second year of Darius,[a] the word of the LORD came to the prophet Zechariah son of Berekiah, the son of Iddo:[b]

2 "The LORD was very angry with your forefathers. 3 Therefore tell the people: This is what the LORD Almighty says: 'Return to me,' declares the LORD Almighty, 'and I will return to you,'[c] says the LORD Almighty. 4 Do not be like your forefathers,[d] to whom the earlier prophets proclaimed: This is what the LORD Almighty says: 'Turn from your evil ways and your evil practices.' But they would not listen or pay attention to me,[e] declares the LORD. 5 Where are your forefathers now? And the prophets, do they live forever? 6 But did not my words and my decrees, which I commanded my servants the prophets, overtake your forefathers?

*Daughter,*

*Come back to me. I wait with open arms to welcome you home.*

*Your Yearning Father*

ZECHARIAH 1:2–3

"Then they repented and said, 'The LORD Almighty has done to us what our ways and practices deserve,[f] just as he determined to do.'"

## The Man Among the Myrtle Trees

7 On the twenty-fourth day of the eleventh month, the month of Shebat, in the second year of Darius, the word of the LORD came to the prophet Zechariah son of Berekiah, the son of Iddo.

8 During the night I had a vision—and there before me was a man riding a red[g] horse! He was standing among the myrtle trees in a ravine. Behind him were red, brown and white horses.[h]

9 I asked, "What are these, my lord?"

The angel who was talking with me answered, "I will show you what they are."

10 Then the man standing among the myrtle trees explained, "They are the ones the LORD has sent to go throughout the earth."

11 And they reported to the angel of the LORD, who was standing among the myrtle trees, "We have gone throughout the earth and found the whole world at rest and in peace."[i]

12 Then the angel of the LORD said, "LORD Almighty, how long will you withhold mercy from Jerusalem and from the towns of Judah, which you have been angry with these seventy years?" 13 So the LORD spoke kind and comforting words to the angel who talked with me.[j]

14 Then the angel who was speaking to me said, "Proclaim this word: This is what the LORD Almighty says: 'I am very jealous[k] for Jerusalem and Zion, 15 but I am very angry with the nations that feel secure. I was only a little angry, but they added to the calamity.'[l]

16 "Therefore, this is what the LORD says: 'I will return to Jerusalem with mercy, and there my house will be rebuilt. And the measuring line[m] will be stretched out over Jerusalem,' declares the LORD Almighty.

17 "Proclaim further: This is what the LORD Almighty says: 'My towns will again overflow with prosperity, and the LORD will again comfort[n] Zion and choose Jerusalem.'"[o]

## Four Horns and Four Craftsmen

18 Then I looked up—and there before me were four horns! 19 I asked the angel who was speaking to me, "What are these?"

He answered me, "These are the horns that scattered Judah, Israel and Jerusalem."

20 Then the LORD showed me four craftsmen. 21 I asked, "What are these coming to do?"

He answered, "These are the horns that scattered Judah so that no one could raise his head, but the craftsmen have come to terrify them and throw down these horns of the nations who lifted up their horns against the land of Judah to scatter its people."[p]

**1:11**
i Isa 14:7
**1:13**
j Zec 4:1
**1:14**
k Zec 8:2
**1:15**
l Am 1:11
**1:16**
m Zec 2:1–2
**1:17**
n Isa 51:3
o Zec 2:12
**1:21**
p Ps 75:10

2:2 q Rev 21:15
2:4 r Eze 38:11
2:5 s Isa 26:1
2:6 t Eze 17:21
2:8 u Dt 32:10
2:9 v Zec 4:9
2:12 w Zec 1:17
2:13 x Hab 2:20

## A Man With a Measuring Line

**2** Then I looked up—and there before me was a man with a measuring line in his hand! 2I asked, "Where are you going?"

He answered me, "To measure Jerusalem, to find out how wide and how long it is."[q]

3Then the angel who was speaking to me left, and another angel came to meet him 4and said to him: "Run, tell that young man, 'Jerusalem will be a city without walls[r] because of the great number of men and livestock in it. 5And I myself will be a wall[s] of fire around it,' declares the LORD, 'and I will be its glory within.'

6"Come! Come! Flee from the land of the north," declares the LORD, "for I have scattered you to the four winds of heaven,"[t] declares the LORD.

7"Come, O Zion! Escape, you who live in the Daughter of Babylon!" 8For this is what the LORD Almighty says: "After he has honored me and has sent me against the nations that have plundered you—for whoever touches you touches the apple of his eye[u]— 9I will surely raise my hand against them so that their slaves will plunder them.[a] Then you will know that the LORD Almighty has sent me.[v]

10"Shout and be glad, O Daughter of Zion. For I am coming, and I will live among you," declares the LORD. 11"Many nations will be joined with the LORD in that day and will become my people. I will live among you and you will know that the LORD Almighty has sent me to you. 12The LORD will inherit Judah as his portion in the holy land and will again choose[w] Jerusalem. 13Be still[x] before the LORD, all mankind, because he has roused himself from his holy dwelling."

## Clean Garments for the High Priest

**3** Then he showed me Joshua[b] the high priest standing before the angel of the LORD, and Satan[c][y] standing at his right side to accuse him. 2The LORD said to Satan, "The LORD rebuke you,[z] Satan! The LORD, who has chosen Jerusalem, rebuke you! Is not this man a burning stick snatched from the fire?"[a]

3Now Joshua was dressed in filthy clothes as he stood before the angel. 4The angel said to those who were standing before him, "Take off his filthy clothes."

Then he said to Joshua, "See, I have taken away your sin, and I will put rich garments on you."

5Then I said, "Put a clean turban on his head." So they put a clean turban on his head and clothed him, while the angel of the LORD stood by.

6The angel of the LORD gave this charge to Joshua: 7"This is what the LORD Almighty says: 'If you will walk in my ways and keep my requirements, then you will govern my house[b] and have charge of my courts, and I will give you a place among these standing here.

8" 'Listen, O high priest Joshua and your associates seated before you, who are men symbolic[c] of things to come: I am going to bring my servant, the Branch. 9See, the stone I have set in front of Joshua! There are seven eyes[d] on that one stone,[d] and I will engrave an inscription on it,' says the LORD

3:1 y Ps 109:6
3:2 z Jude 1:9; a Jude 1:23
3:7 b Dt 17:8–11; Eze 44:15–16
3:8 c Eze 12:11
3:9 d Isa 28:16

[a]8,9 Or *says after . . . eye: 9 "I . . . plunder them."* [b]1 A variant of *Jeshua*; here and elsewhere in Zechariah [c]1 *Satan* means *accuser.* [d]9 Or *facets*

## The African Presence

### Zechariah 2:7

Some cities in Babylonia were built by Nimrod, son of Cush. For more on Nimrod, see the African Presence note on Genesis 10.

Almighty, 'and I will remove the sin of this
land in a single day.
10"'In that day each of you will invite his
neighbor to sit under his vine and fig tree,[e]'
declares the LORD Almighty."

## The Gold Lampstand and the Two Olive Trees

4 Then the angel who talked with me
returned and wakened[f] me, as a man
is wakened from his sleep. 2He asked me,
"What do you see?"
I answered, "I see a solid gold lampstand
with a bowl at the top and seven lights[g] on
it, with seven channels to the lights. 3Also
there are two olive trees[h] by it, one on the
right of the bowl and the other on its left."
4I asked the angel who talked with me,
"What are these, my lord?"
5He answered, "Do you not know what
these are?"
"No, my lord," I replied.
6So he said to me, "This is the word of
the LORD to Zerubbabel: 'Not by might nor
by power, but by my Spirit,'[i] says the LORD
Almighty.
7"What[a] are you, O mighty mountain?
Before Zerubbabel you will become level
ground.[j] Then he will bring out the cap-
stone[k] to shouts of 'God bless it! God bless
it!'"
8Then the word of the LORD came to me:
9"The hands of Zerubbabel have laid the
foundation[l] of this temple; his hands will
also complete it.[m] Then you will know that
the LORD Almighty has sent me[n] to you.
10"Who despises the day of small things?[o]
Men will rejoice when they see the plumb
line in the hand of Zerubbabel.
"(These seven are the eyes of the LORD,
which range throughout the earth.)"
11Then I asked the angel, "What are these
two olive trees[p] on the right and the left of
the lampstand?"
12Again I asked him, "What are these two
olive branches beside the two gold pipes
that pour out golden oil?"
13He replied, "Do you not know what
these are?"
"No, my lord," I said.

3:10 e Mic 4:4
4:1 f Da 8:18
4:2 g Rev 4:5
4:3 h Rev 11:4
4:6 i Hos 1:7
4:7 j Jer 51:25 k Ps 118:22
4:9 l Ezr 3:11 m Ezr 6:15 n Zec 2:9
4:10 o Hag 2:3
4:11 p ver 3

14So he said, "These are the two who are
anointed to[b] serve the Lord of all the earth."

## The Flying Scroll

5 I looked again—and there before me
was a flying scroll!
2He asked me, "What do you see?"
I answered, "I see a flying scroll, thirty
feet long and fifteen feet wide.[c]"
3And he said to me, "This is the curse[q]
that is going out over the whole land; for
according to what it says on one side, ev-
ery thief will be banished, and according
to what it says on the other, everyone who
swears falsely will be banished. 4The LORD
Almighty declares, 'I will send it out, and
it will enter the house of the thief and the
house of him who swears falsely by my
name. It will remain in his house and de-
stroy it, both its timbers and its stones.'[r]"

## The Woman in a Basket

5Then the angel who was speaking to me
came forward and said to me, "Look up and
see what this is that is appearing."
6I asked, "What is it?"
He replied, "It is a measuring basket.[d]"
And he added, "This is the iniquity[e] of the
people throughout the land."
7Then the cover of lead was raised, and
there in the basket sat a woman! 8He said,
"This is wickedness," and he pushed her
back into the basket and pushed the lead
cover down over its mouth.[s]
9Then I looked up—and there before
me were two women, with the wind in
their wings! They had wings like those of a
stork, and they lifted up the basket between
heaven and earth.
10"Where are they taking the basket?" I
asked the angel who was speaking to me.
11He replied, "To the country of Babylo-
nia[f][t] to build a house[u] for it. When it is ready,
the basket will be set there in its place."

## Four Chariots

6 I looked up again—and there before
me were four chariots coming out from
between two mountains—mountains of
bronze! 2The first chariot had red horses,

5:3 q Mal 3:9
5:4 r Lev 14:34–45; Mal 3:5
5:8 s Mic 6:11
5:11 t Ge 10:10 u Jer 29:5,28

[a]7 Or *Who* [b]14 Or *two who bring oil and* [c]2 Hebrew *twenty cubits long and ten cubits wide* (about 9 meters long and 4.5 meters wide) [d]6 Hebrew *an ephah*; also in verses 7–11 [e]6 Or *appearance* [f]11 Hebrew *Shinar*

6:2
v Rev 6:5
6:5
w Eze 37:9; Mt 24:31; Rev 7:1
6:10
x Jer 28:6
6:11
y Ezr 3:2
6:12
z Zec 3:8
a Zec 4:6–9
6:13
b Ps 110:4
6:15
c Isa 60:10
d Zec 3:7
7:1
e Ne 1:1

the second black,[v] 3 the third white, and the
fourth dappled—all of them powerful. 4 I
asked the angel who was speaking to me,
"What are these, my lord?"
5 The angel answered me, "These are the
four spirits[a][w] of heaven, going out from stand-
ing in the presence of the Lord of the whole
world. 6 The one with the black horses is going
toward the north country, the one with the
white horses toward the west,[b] and the one
with the dappled horses toward the south."
7 When the powerful horses went out, they
were straining to go throughout the earth.
And he said, "Go throughout the earth!" So
they went throughout the earth.
8 Then he called to me, "Look, those go-
ing toward the north country have given my
Spirit[c] rest in the land of the north."

## A Crown for Joshua

9 The word of the LORD came to me:
10 "Take ⌊silver and gold⌋ from the exiles
Heldai, Tobijah and Jedaiah, who have ar-
rived from Babylon.[x] Go the same day to
the house of Josiah son of Zephaniah. 11 Take
the silver and gold and make a crown, and
set it on the head of the high priest, Joshua
son of Jehozadak.[y] 12 Tell him this is what the
LORD Almighty says: 'Here is the man whose
name is the Branch,[z] and he will branch
out from his place and build the temple of
the LORD.[a] 13 It is he who will build the tem-
ple of the LORD, and he will be clothed with
majesty and will sit and rule on his throne.
And he will be a priest[b] on his throne. And
there will be harmony between the two.'
14 The crown will be given to Heldai,[d] Tobi-
jah, Jedaiah and Hen[e] son of Zephaniah as a
memorial in the temple of the LORD. 15 Those
who are far away will come and help to build
the temple of the LORD,[c] and you will know
that the LORD Almighty has sent me to you.
This will happen if you diligently obey[d] the
LORD your God."

## Justice and Mercy, Not Fasting

7 In the fourth year of King Darius, the
word of the LORD came to Zechariah
on the fourth day of the ninth month, the
month of Kislev.[e] 2 The people of Bethel had
sent Sharezer and Regem-Melech, together
with their men, to entreat the LORD 3 by ask-
ing the priests of the house of the LORD Al-
mighty and the prophets, "Should I mourn
and fast in the fifth[f] month, as I have done
for so many years?"
4 Then the word of the LORD Almighty
came to me: 5 "Ask all the people of the land
and the priests, 'When you fasted[g] and
mourned in the fifth and seventh months
for the past seventy years, was it really for
me that you fasted? 6 And when you were
eating and drinking, were you not just feast-
ing for yourselves? 7 Are these not the words
the LORD proclaimed through the earlier
prophets when Jerusalem and its surround-
ing towns were at rest[h] and prosperous, and
the Negev and the western foothills were
settled?' "
8 And the word of the LORD came again to
Zechariah: 9 "This is what the LORD Almighty
says: 'Administer true justice;[i] show mercy
and compassion to one another. 10 Do not op-
press the widow or the fatherless, the alien
or the poor. In your hearts do not think evil
of each other.'

*Sister,*

*Always show mercy and compassion to all of my children.*

*Love,*
*Your Lord and God*

ZECHARIAH 7:8–10

11 "But they refused to pay attention;
stubbornly they turned their backs and
stopped up their ears.[j] 12 They made their
hearts as hard as flint and would not listen
to the law or to the words that the LORD Al-
mighty had sent by his Spirit through the
earlier prophets.[k] So the LORD Almighty was
very angry.

7:3
f Zec 8:19
7:5
g Isa 58:5
7:7
h Jer 22:21
7:9
i Zec 8:16
7:11
j Jer 11:10
7:12
k Ne 9:29

[a]5 Or *winds* [b]6 Or *horses after them* [c]8 Or *spirit* [d]14 Syriac; Hebrew *Helem* [e]14 Or *and the gracious one, the*

7:13 l Isa 1:15
7:14 m Jer 44:6
8:4 n Isa 65:20
8:5 o Jer 30:20
8:6 p Ps 118:23
8:7 q Isa 11:11
8:8 r Zec 2:11
8:9 s Ezr 5:1 t Hag 2:4
8:12 u Joel 2:22

13" 'When I called, they did not listen; so
when they called, I would not listen,'[l] says
the LORD Almighty. 14'I scattered them with
a whirlwind among all the nations, where
they were strangers. The land was left so
desolate behind them that no one could
come or go. This is how they made the pleas-
ant land desolate.[m]' "

## The LORD Promises to Bless Jerusalem

8 Again the word of the LORD Almighty
came to me. 2This is what the LORD Al-
mighty says: "I am very jealous for Zion; I
am burning with jealousy for her."
3This is what the LORD says: "I will return
to Zion and dwell in Jerusalem. Then Jeru-
salem will be called the City of Truth, and
the mountain of the LORD Almighty will be
called the Holy Mountain."
4This is what the LORD Almighty says:
"Once again men and women of ripe old
age will sit in the streets of Jerusalem,[n] each
with cane in hand because of his age. 5The
city streets will be filled with boys and girls
playing there.[o]"
6This is what the LORD Almighty says: "It
may seem marvelous to the remnant of this
people at that time,[p] but will it seem marvel-
ous to me?" declares the LORD Almighty.
7This is what the LORD Almighty says: "I
will save my people from the countries of
the east and the west.[q] 8I will bring them
back to live in Jerusalem; they will be my
people,[r] and I will be faithful and righteous
to them as their God."
9This is what the LORD Almighty says:
"You who now hear these words spoken
by the prophets[s] who were there when the
foundation was laid for the house of the
LORD Almighty, let your hands be strong[t] so
that the temple may be built. 10Before that
time there were no wages for man or beast.
No one could go about his business safely
because of his enemy, for I had turned ev-
ery man against his neighbor. 11But now
I will not deal with the remnant of this
people as I did in the past," declares the
LORD Almighty.
12"The seed will grow well, the vine will
yield its fruit,[u] the ground will produce its
crops, and the heavens will drop their dew.
I will give all these things as an inheritance
to the remnant of this people. 13As you have
been an object of cursing[v] among the na-
tions, O Judah and Israel, so will I save you,
and you will be a blessing. Do not be afraid,
but let your hands be strong."
14This is what the LORD Almighty says:
"Just as I had determined to bring disaster
upon you and showed no pity when your fa-
thers angered me," says the LORD Almighty,
15"so now I have determined to do good[w]
again to Jerusalem and Judah. Do not be
afraid. 16These are the things you are to do:
Speak the truth[x] to each other, and render
true and sound judgment in your courts;[y]
17do not plot evil[z] against your neighbor,
and do not love to swear falsely. I hate all
this," declares the LORD.
18Again the word of the LORD Almighty
came to me. 19This is what the LORD Al-
mighty says: "The fasts of the fourth, fifth,
seventh and tenth[a] months will become
joyful and glad occasions and happy festi-
vals for Judah. Therefore love truth[b] and
peace."
20This is what the LORD Almighty says:
"Many peoples and the inhabitants of many
cities will yet come, 21and the inhabitants of
one city will go to another and say, 'Let us go
at once to entreat the LORD and seek the LORD
Almighty. I myself am going.' 22And many
peoples and powerful nations will come to
Jerusalem to seek the LORD Almighty and to
entreat him."
23This is what the LORD Almighty says:
"In those days ten men from all languages
and nations will take firm hold of one Jew
by the hem of his robe and say, 'Let us go
with you, because we have heard that God
is with you.' "[c]

## Judgment on Israel's Enemies

An Oracle

9 The word of the LORD is against the
land of Hadrach
and will rest upon Damascus—
for the eyes of men and all the tribes of
Israel
are on the LORD—[a]

8:13 v Jer 42:18
8:15 w Jer 29:11
8:16 x Eph 4:25 y Zec 7:9
8:17 z Pr 3:29
8:19 a Jer 52:4 b ver 16
8:23 c 1Co 14:25

[a]1 Or *Damascus. / For the eye of the LORD is on all mankind, / as well as on the tribes of Israel,*

**9:2** d Jer 49:23 e Eze 28:1–19
**9:4** f Isa 23:1
**9:9** g Isa 9:6–7; Zep 3:14–15 h Mt 21:5*; Jn 12:15*

2 and upon Hamath[d] too, which borders
on it,
and upon Tyre[e] and Sidon, though
they are very skillful.
3 Tyre has built herself a stronghold;
she has heaped up silver like dust,
and gold like the dirt of the streets.
4 But the Lord will take away her
possessions
and destroy her power on the sea,
and she will be consumed by fire.[f]
5 Ashkelon will see it and fear;
Gaza will writhe in agony,
and Ekron too, for her hope will
wither.
Gaza will lose her king
and Ashkelon will be deserted.
6 Foreigners will occupy Ashdod,
and I will cut off the pride of the
Philistines.
7 I will take the blood from their mouths,
the forbidden food from between their
teeth.
Those who are left will belong to our God
and become leaders in Judah,
and Ekron will be like the Jebusites.
8 But I will defend my house
against marauding forces.
Never again will an oppressor overrun
my people,
for now I am keeping watch.

## The Coming of Zion's King

9 Rejoice greatly, O Daughter of Zion!
Shout, Daughter of Jerusalem!
See, your king[a] comes to you,
righteous and having salvation,[g]
gentle and riding on a donkey,
on a colt, the foal of a donkey.[h]
10 I will take away the chariots from
Ephraim
and the war-horses from Jerusalem,
and the battle bow will be broken.[i]
He will proclaim peace to the nations.
His rule will extend from sea to sea
and from the River[b] to the ends of the
earth.[c]
11 As for you, because of the blood of my
covenant[j] with you,
I will free your prisoners from the
waterless pit.
12 Return to your fortress, O prisoners of
hope;
even now I announce that I will restore
twice as much to you.
13 I will bend Judah as I bend my bow
and fill it with Ephraim.
I will rouse your sons, O Zion,
against your sons, O Greece,[k]
and make you like a warrior's sword.

## The LORD Will Appear

14 Then the LORD will appear over them;
his arrow will flash like lightning.[l]
The Sovereign LORD will sound the
trumpet;
he will march in the storms[m] of the
south,
15 and the LORD Almighty will shield[n]
them.
They will destroy
and overcome with slingstones.
They will drink and roar as with wine;
they will be full like a bowl

**9:10** i Hos 1:7
**9:11** j Ex 24:8
**9:13** k Joel 3:6
**9:14** l Ps 18:14 m Isa 21:1
**9:15** n Isa 37:35

[a]9 Or *King* [b]10 That is, the Euphrates [c]10 Or *the end of the land*

## *The African Presence*

**Zechariah 9:5–6**

Ashkelon, Gaza and Ekron were three of the five major Philistine cities. The ancestry of the Philistines can be traced to Ham's son Mizraim (see Ge 10:6,13; see also the African Presence note on Ge 10:6). They occupied the coastland of Canaan. For more on the Philistines, see the African Presence note on 1 Samuel 17.

9:15 o Ex 27:2
9:16 p Jer 31:11
10:2 q Eze 21:21 r Eze 34:5; Hos 3:4
10:3 s Jer 25:34
10:5 t 2Sa 22:43 u Hag 2:22

used for sprinkling[a] the corners[o] of
the altar.
16 The LORD their God will save them on that
day
as the flock of his people.
They will sparkle in his land
like jewels in a crown.[p]
17 How attractive and beautiful they will be!
Grain will make the young men thrive,
and new wine the young women.

## The LORD Will Care for Judah

10 Ask the LORD for rain in the
springtime;
it is the Lord who makes the storm
clouds.
He gives showers of rain to men,
and plants of the field to everyone.
2 The idols[q] speak deceit,
diviners see visions that lie;
they tell dreams that are false,
they give comfort in vain.
Therefore the people wander like sheep
oppressed for lack of a shepherd.[r]

3 "My anger burns against the shepherds,
and I will punish the leaders;[s]
for the LORD Almighty will care
for his flock, the house of Judah,
and make them like a proud horse in
battle.
4 From Judah will come the cornerstone,
from him the tent peg,
from him the battle bow,
from him every ruler.
5 Together they[b] will be like mighty men
trampling the muddy streets in battle.[t]
Because the LORD is with them,
they will fight and overthrow the
horsemen.[u]

[a]15 Or *bowl, / like* [b]4,5 Or *ruler, all of them together. / [5] They*

6 "I will strengthen the house of Judah
and save the house of Joseph.
I will restore them
because I have compassion on them.
They will be as though
I had not rejected them,
for I am the LORD their God
and I will answer[v] them.
7 The Ephraimites will become like mighty
men,
and their hearts will be glad as with
wine.
Their children will see it and be joyful;
their hearts will rejoice in the Lord.
8 I will signal[w] for them
and gather them in.
Surely I will redeem them;
they will be as numerous[x] as before.
9 Though I scatter them among the
peoples,
yet in distant lands they will
remember me.
They and their children will survive,
and they will return.
10 I will bring them back from Egypt
and gather them from Assyria.[y]
I will bring them to Gilead and Lebanon,
and there will not be room enough for
them.
11 They will pass through the sea of trouble;
the surging sea will be subdued
and all the depths of the Nile will
dry up.[z]
Assyria's pride will be brought down
and Egypt's scepter[a] will pass away.
12 I will strengthen them in the LORD
and in his name they will walk,[b]"
declares the Lord.

10:6 v Zec 13:9
10:8 w Isa 5:26 x Eze 36:11
10:10 y Isa 11:11
10:11 z Isa 19:5–7 a Eze 30:13
10:12 b Mic 4:5

## The African Presence

### Zechariah 10:10–11

The Assyrians were descendants of Cush (see Ge 10:8–11), son of Ham. For more on the Assyrians, see the African Presence note on Jeremiah 2:18,36.

11 Open your doors, O Lebanon,[c]
so that fire may devour your cedars!
2 Wail, O pine tree, for the cedar has fallen;
the stately trees are ruined!
Wail, oaks of Bashan;
the dense forest[d] has been cut down!
3 Listen to the wail of the shepherds;
their rich pastures are destroyed!
Listen to the roar of the lions;
the lush thicket of the Jordan is ruined!

## Two Shepherds

4 This is what the LORD my God says: "Pasture the flock marked for slaughter. 5 Their buyers slaughter them and go unpunished. Those who sell them say, 'Praise the LORD, I am rich!' Their own shepherds do not spare them.[e] 6 For I will no longer have pity on the people of the land," declares the LORD. "I will hand everyone over to his neighbor and his king. They will oppress the land, and I will not rescue them from their hands."[f]

7 So I pastured the flock marked for slaughter, particularly the oppressed of the flock. Then I took two staffs and called one Favor and the other Union, and I pastured the flock. 8 In one month I got rid of the three shepherds.

The flock detested me, and I grew weary of them 9 and said, "I will not be your shepherd. Let the dying die, and the perishing perish.[g] Let those who are left eat one another's flesh."

10 Then I took my staff called Favor and broke it, revoking[h] the covenant I had made with all the nations. 11 It was revoked on that day, and so the afflicted of the flock who were watching me knew it was the word of the LORD.

12 I told them, "If you think it best, give me my pay; but if not, keep it." So they paid me thirty pieces of silver.[i]

13 And the LORD said to me, "Throw it to the potter"—the handsome price at which they priced me! So I took the thirty pieces of silver and threw them into the house of the LORD to the potter.[j]

14 Then I broke my second staff called Union, breaking the brotherhood between Judah and Israel.

15 Then the LORD said to me, "Take again the equipment of a foolish shepherd. 16 For I am going to raise up a shepherd over the land who will not care for the lost, or seek the young, or heal the injured, or feed the healthy, but will eat the meat of the choice sheep, tearing off their hoofs.

17 "Woe to the worthless shepherd,
who deserts the flock!
May the sword strike his arm and his
right eye!
May his arm be completely withered,
his right eye totally blinded!"[k]

## Jerusalem's Enemies to Be Destroyed

### An Oracle

12 This is the word of the LORD concerning Israel. The LORD, who stretches out the heavens, who lays the foundation of the earth, and who forms the spirit of man[l] within him, declares: 2 "I am going to make Jerusalem a cup that sends all the surrounding peoples reeling.[m] Judah[n] will be besieged as well as Jerusalem. 3 On that day, when all the nations[o] of the earth are gathered against her, I will make Jerusalem an immovable rock for all the nations. All who try to move it will injure themselves. 4 On that day I will strike every horse with panic and its rider with madness," declares the LORD. "I will keep a watchful eye over the house of Judah, but I will blind all the horses of the nations. 5 Then the leaders of Judah will say in their hearts, 'The people of Jerusalem are strong, because the LORD Almighty is their God.'

6 "On that day I will make the leaders of Judah like a firepot in a woodpile, like a flaming torch among sheaves. They will consume[p] right and left all the surrounding peoples, but Jerusalem will remain intact in her place.

7 "The LORD will save the dwellings of Judah first, so that the honor of the house of David and of Jerusalem's inhabitants may not be greater than that of Judah. 8 On that day the LORD will shield[q] those who live in Jerusalem, so that the feeblest among them will be like David, and the house of David will be like God, like the Angel of the LORD going before them. 9 On that day I will set out to destroy all the nations that attack Jerusalem.

**11:1** c Eze 31:3
**11:2** d Isa 32:19
**11:5** e Jer 50:7
**11:6** f Mic 5:8
**11:9** g Jer 15:2
**11:10** h Jer 14:21
**11:12** i Ex 21:32; Mt 26:15
**11:13** j Mt 27:9–10*
**11:17** k Jer 23:1
**12:1** l Isa 57:16
**12:2** m Isa 51:23 n Zec 14:14
**12:3** o Zec 14:2
**12:6** p Ob 1:18
**12:8** q Zec 9:15

**12:10** r Isa 44:3; Eze 39:29; Joel 2:28–29 s Jn 19:34,37* Rev 1:7
**12:11** t 2Ki 23:29
**13:1** u Ps 51:2
**13:2** v Jer 23:14–15
**13:3** w Dt 18:20
**13:4** x Mt 3:4
**13:5** y Am 7:14
**13:7** z Jer 47:6 a Isa 40:11

## Mourning for the One They Pierced

10 "And I will pour out on the house of
David and the inhabitants of Jerusalem a
spirit[a] of grace and supplication.[r] They will
look on[b] me, the one they have pierced,[s] and
they will mourn for him as one mourns for
an only child, and grieve bitterly for him
as one grieves for a firstborn son. 11 On that
day the weeping in Jerusalem will be great,
like the weeping of Hadad Rimmon in the
plain of Megiddo.[t] 12 The land will mourn,
each clan by itself, with their wives by themselves:
the clan of the house of David and
their wives, the clan of the house of Nathan
and their wives, 13 the clan of the house of
Levi and their wives, the clan of Shimei and
their wives, 14 and all the rest of the clans
and their wives.

## Cleansing From Sin

13 "On that day a fountain will be
opened to the house of David and
the inhabitants of Jerusalem, to cleanse[u]
them from sin and impurity.

2 "On that day, I will banish the names
of the idols from the land, and they will be
remembered no more," declares the LORD
Almighty. "I will remove both the prophets[v]
and the spirit of impurity from the land.
3 And if anyone still prophesies, his father
and mother, to whom he was born, will say
to him, 'You must die, because you have told
lies in the LORD's name.' When he prophesies,
his own parents will stab him.[w]

4 "On that day every prophet will be
ashamed of his prophetic vision. He will
not put on a prophet's garment[x] of hair in
order to deceive. 5 He will say, 'I am not a
prophet. I am a farmer; the land has been
my livelihood since my youth.[c]'[y] 6 If someone
asks him, 'What are these wounds on
your body[d]?' he will answer, 'The wounds I
was given at the house of my friends.'

## The Shepherd Struck, the Sheep Scattered

7 "Awake, O sword,[z] against my shepherd,[a]
against the man who is close to me!"
declares the Lord Almighty.
"Strike the shepherd,
and the sheep will be scattered,[b]
and I will turn my hand against the
little ones.
8 In the whole land," declares the LORD,
"two-thirds will be struck down and
perish;
yet one-third will be left in it.
9 This third I will bring into the fire;
I will refine them like silver[c]
and test them like gold.
They will call on my name
and I will answer them;
I will say, 'They are my people,'[d]
and they will say, 'The Lord is our
God.'"

*God,*

*I need you to grasp my hand and lead me through this refining fire. You promise to hear me when I pray, so I'm trusting you to work this thing out. I desire to come forth as pure gold, polished and radiant. I pledge to always give you the glory and honor, for you are my God.*

*Amen*

ZECARIAH 13:8–9

## The LORD Comes and Reigns

14 A day of the LORD[e] is coming when
your plunder will be divided among
you.

2 I will gather all the nations to Jerusalem
to fight against it; the city will be captured,
the houses ransacked, and the women
raped. Half of the city will go into exile, but
the rest of the people will not be taken from
the city.

3 Then the LORD will go out and fight
against those nations, as he fights in the
day of battle. 4 On that day his feet will stand
on the Mount of Olives,[f] east of Jerusalem,
and the Mount of Olives will be split in two
from east to west, forming a great valley,
with half of the mountain moving north

**13:7** b Mt 26:31*
**13:9** c 1Pe 1:6–7 d Jer 30:22
**14:1** e Mal 4:1
**14:4** f Eze 11:23

[a] 10 Or *the Spirit* [b] 10 Or *to* [c] 5 Or *farmer; a man sold me in my youth* [d] 6 Or *wounds between your hands*

14:5 g Am 1:1
14:7 h Isa 30:26
14:8 i Eze 47:1–12; Rev 22:1–2
14:9 j Rev 11:15
14:10 k Am 9:11 l Zec 12:6
14:12 m Dt 28:22

and half moving south. 5 You will flee by
my mountain valley, for it will extend to
Azel. You will flee as you fled from the earth-
quake[a][g] in the days of Uzziah king of Judah.
Then the LORD my God will come, and all the
holy ones with him.
6 On that day there will be no light, no
cold or frost. 7 It will be a unique day, with-
out daytime or nighttime—a day known to
the LORD. When evening comes, there will
be light.[h]
8 On that day living water[i] will flow out
from Jerusalem, half to the eastern sea[b]
and half to the western sea,[c] in summer and
in winter.
9 The LORD will be king over the whole
earth.[j] On that day there will be one LORD,
and his name the only name.
10 The whole land, from Geba to Rimmon,
south of Jerusalem, will become like the
Arabah. But Jerusalem will be raised up[k]
and remain in its place,[l] from the Benjamin
Gate to the site of the First Gate, to the Cor-
ner Gate, and from the Tower of Hananel to
the royal winepresses. 11 It will be inhabited;
never again will it be destroyed. Jerusalem
will be secure.
12 This is the plague with which the LORD
will strike all the nations that fought against
Jerusalem: Their flesh will rot while they are
still standing on their feet, their eyes will rot
in their sockets, and their tongues will rot
in their mouths.[m] 13 On that day men will be
stricken by the LORD with great panic. Each
man will seize the hand of another, and they
will attack each other.[n] 14 Judah too will fight
at Jerusalem. The wealth of all the surround-
ing nations will be collected—great quan-
tities of gold and silver and clothing. 15 A
similar plague[o] will strike the horses and
mules, the camels and donkeys, and all the
animals in those camps.
16 Then the survivors from all the na-
tions that have attacked Jerusalem will go
up year after year to worship the King, the
LORD Almighty, and to celebrate the Feast
of Tabernacles.[p] 17 If any of the peoples
of the earth do not go up to Jerusalem to
worship the King, the LORD Almighty, they
will have no rain.[q] 18 If the Egyptian people
do not go up and take part, they will have
no rain. The LORD[d] will bring on them the
plague he inflicts on the nations that do not
go up to celebrate the Feast of Tabernacles.[r]
19 This will be the punishment of Egypt and
the punishment of all the nations that do
not go up to celebrate the Feast of Taberna-
cles.
20 On that day HOLY TO THE LORD will be in-
scribed on the bells of the horses, and the
cooking pots in the LORD's house will be like
the sacred bowls in front of the altar. 21 Every
pot in Jerusalem and Judah will be holy[s] to
the LORD Almighty, and all who come to sac-
rifice will take some of the pots and cook in
them. And on that day[t] there will no longer
be a Canaanite[e] in the house of the LORD
Almighty.

14:13 n Zec 11:6
14:15 o ver 12
14:16 p Isa 60:6–9
14:17 q Am 4:7
14:18 r ver 12
14:21 s 1Co 10:31 t Ne 8:10

## The African Presence

**Zechariah 14:18–19**

For more on Egypt, see the African Presence note on Genesis 10:6.

[a] 5 Or 5 *My mountain valley will be blocked and will extend to Azel. It will be blocked as it was blocked because of the earthquake* [b] 8 That is, the Dead Sea [c] 8 That is, the Mediterranean [d] 18 Or *part, then the LORD* [e] 21 Or *merchant*

# Malachi

## OVERVIEW

Malachi was the last of God's messengers for 400 years, until John the Baptist announced the arrival of the "Lamb of God, who takes away the sin of the world" (Jn 1:29). The people of Israel had been back in their land for more than 100 years since the Babylonian exile. Their worship and sacrifices had become empty and meaningless, for the people had broken faith with both God and each other (see Mal 2:7–16). Malachi scolded the nation for their apostasy, promised God's blessing to the obedient and predicted the coming of God's messenger (see Mal 3:1)—fulfilled in John the Baptist.

A woman's service to God will become a monotonous routine if she allows impurity to rule her heart. A sinful lifestyle erodes spiritual vitality. Examine the book of Malachi to understand why God would not accept the people's sacrifices. Reflect on your service to God. Does it come from a dedicated heart?

## OUTLINE

I. Affirming God's Love for Israel (1:1–5)
II. Condemning the People's Unfaithfulness (1:6—2:16)
III. Proclaiming the Day of God's Judgment (2:17—3:5)
IV. Reproving the Neglect of Tithes and Offerings (3:6–18)
V. Announcing the Coming of the Lord (4:1–6)

### SCANNABLE FACTS:

**Author:** Malachi

**Time Written:** Around 430 B.C.

**Theme to Note:** God's judgment and promise

**Notable Women:** Women divorced by their husbands

1 An oracle:[a] The word of the LORD to Israel through Malachi.[a]

## Jacob Loved, Esau Hated

2 "I have loved you," says the LORD.

"But you ask, 'How have you loved us?'

"Was not Esau Jacob's brother?" the LORD says. "Yet I have loved Jacob,[b] 3 but Esau I have hated, and I have turned his mountains into a wasteland and left his inheritance to the desert jackals."

4 Edom may say, "Though we have been crushed, we will rebuild the ruins."

But this is what the LORD Almighty says: "They may build, but I will demolish. They will be called the Wicked Land, a people always under the wrath of the LORD. 5 You will see it with your own eyes and say, 'Great[c] is the LORD—even beyond the borders of Israel!'

## Blemished Sacrifices

6 "A son honors his father, and a servant his master. If I am a father, where is the honor due me? If I am a master, where is the respect due me?" says the LORD Almighty. "It is you, O priests, who show contempt for my name.

"But you ask, 'How have we shown contempt for your name?'

7 "You place defiled food[d] on my altar.

"But you ask, 'How have we defiled you?'

"By saying that the LORD's table is contemptible. 8 When you bring blind animals for sacrifice, is that not wrong? When you sacrifice crippled or diseased animals,[e] is that not wrong? Try offering them to your governor! Would he be pleased with you? Would he accept you?" says the LORD Almighty.

9 "Now implore God to be gracious to us. With such offerings from your hands, will he accept you?"—says the LORD Almighty.

10 "Oh, that one of you would shut the temple doors, so that you would not light useless fires on my altar! I am not pleased[f] with you," says the LORD Almighty, "and I will accept no offering[g] from your hands. 11 My name will be great among the nations, from the rising to the setting of the sun. In every place incense[h] and pure offerings will be brought to my name, because my name will be great among the nations," says the LORD Almighty.

12 "But you profane it by saying of the Lord's table, 'It is defiled,' and of its food,[i] 'It is contemptible.' 13 And you say, 'What a burden!'[j] and you sniff at it contemptuously," says the LORD Almighty.

"When you bring injured, crippled or diseased animals and offer them as sacrifices, should I accept them from your hands?" says the LORD. 14 "Cursed is the cheat who has an acceptable male in his flock and vows to give it, but then sacrifices a blemished animal[k] to the Lord. For I am a great king," says the LORD Almighty, "and my name is to be feared among the nations.

[a]1 *Malachi* means *my messenger.*

**1:1** a Na 1:1
**1:2** b Ro 9:13*
**1:5** c Ps 35:27
**1:7** d ver 12; Lev 21:6
**1:8** e Lev 22:22
**1:10** f Hos 5:6 g Isa 1:11–14; Jer 14:12
**1:11** h Isa 60:6–7; Rev 8:3
**1:12** i ver 7
**1:13** j Isa 43:22–24
**1:14** k Lev 22:18–21

## The African Presence

### Malachi 1:6–14

The Lord admonished the Jews for their false worship at the temple. When the temple of Israel was rebuilt, the construction, as well as the design of furniture, essentially followed the pattern of the first temple. Probably the articles of furniture were remade according to the instructions that God had given Moses when he was on Mount Sinai (see Ex 25:9). It is likely that much of the design and workmanship employed by the Israelites was influenced by their stay in Egypt before the exodus.

## Admonition for the Priests

2 "And now this admonition is for you, O priests. [2]If you do not listen, and if you do not set your heart to honor my name," says the LORD Almighty, "I will send a curse upon you, and I will curse your blessings. Yes, I have already cursed them, because you have not set your heart to honor me.

[3]"Because of you I will rebuke[a] your descendants[b]; I will spread on your faces the offal[l] from your festival sacrifices, and you will be carried off with it. [4]And you will know that I have sent you this admonition so that my covenant with Levi may continue," says the LORD Almighty. [5]"My covenant was with him, a covenant of life and peace,[m] and I gave them to him; this called for reverence and he revered me and stood in awe of my name. [6]True instruction was in his mouth and nothing false was found on his lips. He walked with me in peace and uprightness, and turned many from sin.[n]

[7]"For the lips of a priest ought to preserve knowledge, and from his mouth men should seek instruction—because he is the messenger of the LORD Almighty. [8]But you have turned from the way and by your teaching have caused many to stumble;[o] you have violated the covenant with Levi," says the LORD Almighty. [9]"So I have caused you to be despised and humiliated before all the people, because you have not followed my ways but have shown partiality in matters of the law."

## Judah Unfaithful

[10]Have we not all one Father[c]?[p] Did not one God create us? Why do we profane the covenant[q] of our fathers by breaking faith with one another?

[11]Judah has broken faith. A detestable thing has been committed in Israel and in Jerusalem: Judah has desecrated the sanctuary the LORD loves, by marrying the daughter of a foreign god. [12]As for the man who does this, whoever he may be, may the LORD cut him off from the tents of Jacob[d]—even though he brings offerings[r] to the LORD Almighty.

[13]Another thing you do: You flood the LORD's altar with tears. You weep and wail because he no longer pays attention to your offerings or accepts them with pleasure from your hands. [14]You ask, "Why?" It is because the LORD is acting as the witness between you and the wife of your youth,[s] because you have broken faith with her, though she is your partner, the wife of your marriage covenant.

[15]Has not ⌊the LORD⌋ made them one?[t] In flesh and spirit they are his. And why one? Because he was seeking godly offspring.[e] So guard yourself in your spirit, and do not break faith with the wife of your youth.

[16]"I hate divorce,[u]" says the LORD God of Israel, "and I hate a man's covering himself[f] with violence as well as with his garment," says the LORD Almighty.

So guard yourself in your spirit, and do not break faith.

## The Day of Judgment

[17]You have wearied[v] the LORD with your words.

"How have we wearied him?" you ask.

By saying, "All who do evil are good in the eyes of the LORD, and he is pleased with them" or "Where is the God of justice?"

3 "See, I will send my messenger, who will prepare the way before me.[w] Then suddenly the Lord you are seeking will come to his temple; the messenger of the covenant, whom you desire, will come," says the LORD Almighty.

[2]But who can endure[x] the day of his coming? Who can stand when he appears? For he will be like a refiner's fire[y] or a launderer's soap. [3]He will sit as a refiner and purifier of silver; he will purify[z] the Levites and refine them like gold and silver. Then the LORD will have men who will bring offerings in righteousness, [4]and the offerings[a] of Judah and Jerusalem will be acceptable to the LORD, as in days gone by, as in former years.

[5]"So I will come near to you for judgment. I will be quick to testify against sorcerers, adulterers and perjurers, against those who defraud laborers of their wages,[b] who oppress the widows and the fatherless, and deprive aliens of justice, but do not fear me," says the LORD Almighty.

**2:3** l Ex 29:14
**2:5** m Nu 25:12
**2:6** n Jer 23:22
**2:8** o Jer 18:15
**2:10** p 1Co 8:6; q Ex 19:5
**2:12** r Mal 1:10
**2:14** s Pr 5:18
**2:15** t Mt 19:4–6
**2:16** u Dt 24:1; Mt 5:31–32
**2:17** v Isa 43:24
**3:1** w Mt 11:10*; Mk 1:2*; Lk 7:27*
**3:2** x Rev 6:17; y Mt 3:10–12
**3:3** z Isa 1:25
**3:4** a Mal 1:11
**3:5** b Lev 19:13

[a]3 Or *cut off* (see Septuagint) [b]3 Or *will blight your grain* [c]10 Or *father* [d]12 Or *[12]May the LORD cut off from the tents of Jacob anyone who gives testimony in behalf of the man who does this* [e]15 Or *[15]But the one ⌊who is our father⌋ did not do this, not as long as life remained in him. And what was he seeking? An offspring from God* [f]16 Or *his wife*

# Inspire

## DOMESTIC VIOLENCE

" 'I hate a man's covering himself with violence as well as with his garment,' says the Lord Almighty" (Mal 2:16). Through the prophet Malachi, the Lord denounced the men of Israel for "breaking faith" with their wives. And God was reminding the people that judgment was in store for those who hurt the vulnerable of society (see Mal 3:5).

Today, many women endure violence in their closest relationships, but love should never require a woman to endure violence of any kind—physical, sexual, psychological or economic. Such abuse is a sin and is absolutely incompatible with love as God intends it. Violent relationships break God's commandments—and his heart. Furthermore, we know that the Holy Spirit neither produces nor condones abuse; in contrast, love and gentleness are the fruit of living by the Spirit (see Gal 5:22–25).

Our great God of the universe loves his children, and he becomes angry when they are hurt. God wants his children to love him and each other: "Love the Lord your God with all your heart . . . 'Love your neighbor as yourself.' There is no commandment greater than these" (Mk 12:30–31).

Too often women of color overlook the requirement included in this second commandment: We must love ourselves. Our culture does not always embrace us, and we are sent messages not to love ourselves. Furthermore, we sometimes fail to understand what love does and does not require, particularly in terms of our intimate relationships. We cannot love another in the way God desires if we do not love, respect and protect ourselves first.

Woman of color, you are valuable to God. His sacrifice for you demonstrates that indisputable fact. No matter what you have been told, what you have experienced, what mistakes you may have made, God loves you and wants you to love yourself and be loved by others. He wants you to take good care of your life and to protect yourself. No one has the right to demean or brutalize you. No earthly promise can supersede God's commands. If you are in a relationship that threatens your mental, emotional, spiritual or physical health (your soul or your temple), seek guidance and strength from the Spirit to bring your life into accordance with God's will that all of his children "enjoy good health" (3Jn 2). Get help. Consult with trained professionals to assist you in protecting yourself from abuse and adopting a lifestyle that will bring you into compliance with God's command to love yourself. If you know a sister who needs help learning to love herself, seek guidance in helping her to embrace God's love. We *are* our sisters' keepers, and we need to remind each other of God's commandment to love him above all and our neighbors *as* (to the same degree that) we love ourselves.

—L. Ammons

For the next Inspire note, go to page 1120.

### read

Malachi 2:10–16;
Mark 12:28–34;
Galatians 5:13–26.

**See also** the Inspire Notes "Courage to Heal," "Suffering," "Overcoming Abuse," "Distress" and "The Paradox of Life and Suffering."

### WOMAN of COLOR

Do you need to learn to love yourself? Allow God's Spirit to guide you toward a life of love and wholeness.

3:6 c Nu 23:19; Jas 1:17
3:7 d Ac 7:51 e Zec 1:3
3:8 f Ne 13:10–12
3:12 g Isa 61:9 h Isa 62:4
3:13 i Mal 2:17
3:14 j Isa 58:3
3:15 k Jer 7:10

## Robbing God

6 "I the LORD do not change.[c] So you, O descendants of Jacob, are not destroyed. 7 Ever since the time of your forefathers you have turned away[d] from my decrees and have not kept them. Return to me, and I will return to you,"[e] says the LORD Almighty.

"But you ask, 'How are we to return?'

8 "Will a man rob God? Yet you rob me.

"But you ask, 'How do we rob you?'

"In tithes[f] and offerings. 9 You are under a curse—the whole nation of you—because you are robbing me. 10 Bring the whole tithe into the storehouse, that there may be food in my house. Test me in this," says the LORD Almighty, "and see if I will not throw open the floodgates of heaven and pour out so much blessing that you will not have room enough for it. 11 I will prevent pests from devouring your crops, and the vines in your fields will not cast their fruit," says the LORD Almighty. 12 "Then all the nations will call you blessed,[g] for yours will be a delightful land,"[h] says the LORD Almighty.

13 "You have said harsh things[i] against me," says the LORD.

"Yet you ask, 'What have we said against you?'

14 "You have said, 'It is futile to serve God. What did we gain by carrying out his requirements and going about like mourners[j] before the LORD Almighty? 15 But now we call the arrogant blessed. Certainly the evildoers[k] prosper, and even those who challenge God escape.' "

*My God,*

*search me and reveal to me those deeds and areas of my life in which I have robbed you. Show me how to honor you with my gifts and resources. Help me to be a blessing to others, even as you continue to bless me.*

*Amen*

MALACHI 3:8–10

*Child,*

*See to it that you don't rob me. I am your provider.*

*God*

MALACHI 3:6–12

16 Then those who feared the LORD talked with each other, and the LORD listened and heard.[l] A scroll[m] of remembrance was written in his presence concerning those who feared the LORD and honored his name.

17 "They will be mine," says the LORD Almighty, "in the day when I make up my treasured possession.[a][n] I will spare[o] them, just as in compassion a man spares his son who serves him. 18 And you will again see the distinction between the righteous[p] and the wicked, between those who serve God and those who do not.

## The Day of the LORD

4 "Surely the day is coming;[q] it will burn like a furnace. All the arrogant and every evildoer will be stubble, and that day that is coming will set them on fire," says the LORD Almighty. "Not a root or a branch will be left to them. 2 But for you who revere my name, the sun of righteousness[r] will rise with healing in its wings. And you will go out and leap like calves released from the stall. 3 Then you will trample down the wicked; they will be ashes under the soles of your feet on the day when I do these things," says the LORD Almighty.

4 "Remember the law of my servant Moses, the decrees and laws I gave him at Horeb for all Israel.

5 "See, I will send you the prophet Elijah[s] before that great and dreadful day of the LORD comes. 6 He will turn the hearts of the fathers to their children, and the hearts of the children to their fathers; or else I will come and strike the land with a curse."

3:16 l Ps 34:15 m Ps 56:8
3:17 n Dt 7:6 o Ps 103:13
3:18 p Ge 18:25
4:1 q Joel 2:31
4:2 r Lk 1:78; Eph 5:14
4:5 s Mt 11:14; Lk 1:17

[a] 17 Or *Almighty, "my treasured possession, in the day when I act*

# New Testament

# Matthew

## OVERVIEW

The Gospel of Matthew introduces us to Jesus as the legitimate heir to the throne of David. Through this book, we experience the life, death and resurrection of Christ—the fulfillment of God's promise of salvation.

Throughout Matthew's Gospel, the Messiah interacts with several women of his time. Jesus entered the world as a human through Mary, the young woman God chose to carry the Christ-child (see Mt 1). Mary was instrumental in God's plan throughout Jesus' earthly ministry. Mary Magdalene and a third woman by the name of Mary were the first to find the empty tomb, see the risen Christ and spread the news of his resurrection (see Mt 28).

Jesus still interacts with women today, regardless of our backgrounds, positions or ages. He longs for every mother, sister, daughter, aunt, cousin and friend to know him as Lord and Savior. As you read through the Gospel of Matthew, reflect on how Jesus responded to the women he encountered during his earthly ministry. Let his words and actions draw you closer to him and his mission.

# OUTLINE

I. The Introduction of the King (1:1—4:25)
II. The Platform of the King (5:1—7:29)
III. The Credentials of the King (8:1—11:30)
IV. The Opposition to the King (12:1—16:4)
V. The Preparation of the King's Disciples (16:5—20:34)
VI. The Presentation, Rejection and Crucifixion of the King (21:1—27:66)
VII. The Resurrection and Commission of the King (28:1–20)

## SCANNABLE FACTS:

**Author:** Matthew

**Time Written:** Sometime between A.D. 50 and 80

**Theme to Note:** Jesus as the promised Messiah

**Notable Women:** Mary, the mother of Jesus; a Canaanite woman; Mary Magdalene; Pilate's wife; Mary, the mother of James and Joses

**1:1** a Isa 11:1; Ro 1:3 b Ge 22:18
**1:2** c Ge 25:26 d Ge 29:35
**1:3** e Ge 38:27–30
**1:6** f 1Sa 16:1 g 2Sa 12:24

## The Genealogy of Jesus

1 A record of the genealogy of Jesus Christ the son of David,[a] the son of Abraham:[b]

2 Abraham was the father of Isaac,
Isaac the father of Jacob,[c]
Jacob the father of Judah and his brothers,[d]
3 Judah the father of Perez and Zerah, whose mother was Tamar,[e]
Perez the father of Hezron,
Hezron the father of Ram,
4 Ram the father of Amminadab,
Amminadab the father of Nahshon,
Nahshon the father of Salmon,
5 Salmon the father of Boaz, whose mother was Rahab,
Boaz the father of Obed, whose mother was Ruth,
Obed the father of Jesse,
6 and Jesse the father of King David.[f]

David was the father of Solomon, whose mother had been Uriah's wife,[g]
7 Solomon the father of Rehoboam,
Rehoboam the father of Abijah,
Abijah the father of Asa,
8 Asa the father of Jehoshaphat,
Jehoshaphat the father of Jehoram,
Jehoram the father of Uzziah,
9 Uzziah the father of Jotham,
Jotham the father of Ahaz,
Ahaz the father of Hezekiah,
10 Hezekiah the father of Manasseh,[h]
Manasseh the father of Amon,
Amon the father of Josiah,
11 and Josiah the father of Jeconiah[a] and his brothers at the time of the exile to Babylon.[i]

12 After the exile to Babylon:
Jeconiah was the father of Shealtiel,[j]
Shealtiel the father of Zerubbabel,
13 Zerubbabel the father of Abiud,
Abiud the father of Eliakim,
Eliakim the father of Azor,
14 Azor the father of Zadok,
Zadok the father of Akim,
Akim the father of Eliud,
15 Eliud the father of Eleazar,
Eleazar the father of Matthan,
Matthan the father of Jacob,
16 and Jacob the father of Joseph, the husband of Mary, of whom was born Jesus, who is called Christ.

17 Thus there were fourteen generations in all from Abraham to David, fourteen from David to the exile to Babylon, and fourteen from the exile to the Christ.[b]

## The Birth of Jesus Christ

18 This is how the birth of Jesus Christ came about: His mother Mary was pledged to be married to Joseph, but before they came together, she was found to be with

**1:10** h 2Ki 20:21
**1:11** i 2Ki 24:14–16; Jer 27:20; Da 1:1,2
**1:12** j 1Ch 3:17

[a] 11 That is, Jehoiachin; also in verse 12 [b] 17 Or *Messiah.* "The Christ" (Greek) and "the Messiah" (Hebrew) both mean "the Anointed One."

### The African Presence

**Matthew 1:6**

Uriah was a Hittite. Hittites were descendants of Ham's son Canaan (see Ge 10:6,15). Because Ham's offspring represent the geographic territories once dominated by Egypt—present-day Egypt, Libya and Sudan and into the area today known as Israel—they can claim a relation to African heritage. Since "heritage" is something "passed down" or "inherited," Canaan (Israel or Palestine) most certainly received or was influenced by Egypt culturally, politically, religiously, etc.

## The African Presence

**Matthew 1:12,17**

According to Genesis 10, Nimrod (a son of Cush) built many cities in Babylonia and Assyria.
For more on Nimrod, see the African Presence note on Genesis 10.

**1:18** k Lk 1:35
**1:19** l Dt 24:1
**1:21** m Lk 1:31 n Lk 2:11; Ac 13:23,28
**1:23** o Isa 7:14
**2:1** p Lk 2:4–7
**2:2** q Jer 23:5; Jn 1:49 r Nu 24:17

child through the Holy Spirit.[k] 19 Because
Joseph her husband was a righteous man
and did not want to expose her to public
disgrace, he had in mind to divorce[l] her
quietly.
20 But after he had considered this, an an-
gel of the Lord appeared to him in a dream
and said, "Joseph son of David, do not be
afraid to take Mary home as your wife, be-
cause what is conceived in her is from the
Holy Spirit. 21 She will give birth to a son,
and you are to give him the name Jesus,[a m]
because he will save his people from
their sins."[n]
22 All this took place to fulfill what the Lord
had said through the prophet: 23 "The virgin
will be with child and will give birth to a
son, and they will call him Immanuel"[b o]—
which means, "God with us."
24 When Joseph woke up, he did what the
angel of the Lord had commanded him and
took Mary home as his wife. 25 But he had no
union with her until she gave birth to a son.
And he gave him the name Jesus.

### The Visit of the Magi

2 After Jesus was born in Bethlehem in
Judea,[p] during the time of King Herod,
Magi[c] from the east came to Jerusalem
2 and asked, "Where is the one who has
been born king of the Jews?[q] We saw his
star[r] in the east[d] and have come to worship
him."
3 When King Herod heard this he was dis-
turbed, and all Jerusalem with him. 4 When
he had called together all the people's chief
priests and teachers of the law, he asked
them where the Christ[e] was to be born. 5 "In
Bethlehem[s] in Judea," they replied, "for this
is what the prophet has written:

6 " 'But you, Bethlehem, in the land of
Judah,
are by no means least among the rulers
of Judah;
for out of you will come a ruler
who will be the shepherd of my people
Israel.'[f]"

7 Then Herod called the Magi secretly
and found out from them the exact time
the star had appeared. 8 He sent them to
Bethlehem and said, "Go and make a care-
ful search for the child. As soon as you find
him, report to me, so that I too may go and
worship him."
9 After they had heard the king, they went
on their way, and the star they had seen in
the east[g] went ahead of them until it stopped
over the place where the child was. 10 When
they saw the star, they were overjoyed. 11 On
coming to the house, they saw the child with
his mother Mary, and they bowed down and
worshiped him.[t] Then they opened their
treasures and presented him with gifts[u] of
gold and of incense and of myrrh. 12 And hav-
ing been warned[v] in a dream not to go back
to Herod, they returned to their country by
another route.

### The Escape to Egypt

13 When they had gone, an angel of the
Lord appeared to Joseph in a dream. "Get
up," he said, "take the child and his mother
and escape to Egypt. Stay there until I tell
you, for Herod is going to search for the
child to kill him."

**2:5** s Jn 7:42
**2:11** t Isa 60:3 u Ps 72:10
**2:12** v Heb 11:7

[a]21 *Jesus* is the Greek form of *Joshua,* which means *the Lord saves.* [b]23 Isaiah 7:14 [c]1 Traditionally *Wise Men*
[d]2 Or *star when it rose* [e]4 Or *Messiah* [f]6 Micah 5:2 [g]9 Or *seen when it rose*

## The African Presence

**Matthew 2:13**

Egyptians trace their heritage to Mizraim, one of Ham's sons. The word *mizraim* means "two Egypts," referring to Upper and Lower Egypt. For more on Egypt, see the African Presence note on Genesis 10:6.

**2:15** w Ex 4:22,23; Hos 11:1
**2:18** x Jer 31:15
**2:22** y ver 12,13,19 z Lk 2:39
**2:23** a Lk 1:26 b Mk 1:24

14 So he got up, took the child and his
mother during the night and left for Egypt,
15 where he stayed until the death of Herod.
And so was fulfilled what the Lord had said
through the prophet: "Out of Egypt I called
my son."[a][w]
16 When Herod realized that he had been
outwitted by the Magi, he was furious, and
he gave orders to kill all the boys in Bethle-
hem and its vicinity who were two years old
and under, in accordance with the time he
had learned from the Magi. 17 Then what was
said through the prophet Jeremiah was ful-
filled:

18 "A voice is heard in Ramah,
weeping and great mourning,
Rachel weeping for her children
and refusing to be comforted,
because they are no more."[b][x]

### The Return to Nazareth

19 After Herod died, an angel of the Lord
appeared in a dream to Joseph in Egypt
20 and said, "Get up, take the child and his
mother and go to the land of Israel, for those
who were trying to take the child's life are
dead."
21 So he got up, took the child and his
mother and went to the land of Israel. 22 But
when he heard that Archelaus was reigning
in Judea in place of his father Herod, he was
afraid to go there. Having been warned in a
dream,[y] he withdrew to the district of Gali-
lee,[z] 23 and he went and lived in a town called
Nazareth.[a] So was fulfilled what was said
through the prophets: "He will be called
a Nazarene."[b]

### John the Baptist Prepares the Way

3 In those days John the Baptist[c] came,
preaching in the Desert of Judea 2 and
saying, "Repent, for the kingdom of heaven[d]
is near." 3 This is he who was spoken of
through the prophet Isaiah:

"A voice of one calling in the desert,
'Prepare the way for the Lord,
make straight paths for him.' "[c][e]

4 John's clothes were made of camel's hair,
and he had a leather belt around his waist.[f]
His food was locusts[g] and wild honey. 5 Peo-
ple went out to him from Jerusalem and all
Judea and the whole region of the Jordan.
6 Confessing their sins, they were baptized
by him in the Jordan River.
7 But when he saw many of the Pharisees
and Sadducees coming to where he was
baptizing, he said to them: "You brood of
vipers![h] Who warned you to flee from the
coming wrath?[i] 8 Produce fruit in keeping
with repentance.[j] 9 And do not think you can
say to yourselves, 'We have Abraham as our
father.' I tell you that out of these stones God
can raise up children for Abraham. 10 The ax
is already at the root of the trees, and every
tree that does not produce good fruit will be
cut down and thrown into the fire.[k]
11 "I baptize you with[d] water for repen-
tance. But after me will come one who is
more powerful than I, whose sandals I am
not fit to carry. He will baptize you with the
Holy Spirit and with fire.[l] 12 His winnowing
fork is in his hand, and he will clear his
threshing floor, gathering his wheat into
the barn and burning up the chaff with
unquenchable fire."[m]

**3:1** c Lk 3:2–19
**3:2** d Da 2:44; Mt 4:17
**3:3** e Isa 40:3; Lk 1:76; Jn 1:23
**3:4** f 2Ki 1:8 g Lev 11:22
**3:7** h Mt 12:34; 23:33 i Ro 1:18; 1Th 1:10
**3:8** j Ac 26:20
**3:10** k Mt 7:19
**3:11** l Isa 4:4
**3:12** m Mt 13:30

[a] 15 Hosea 11:1 [b] 18 Jer. 31:15 [c] 3 Isaiah 40:3 [d] 11 Or *in*

**3:16** n Isa 11:2
**3:17** o Ps 2:7 p Mt 12:18; Lk 9:35
**4:2** q 1Ki 19:8
**4:3** r 1Th 3:5
**4:4** s Dt 8:3
**4:5** t Ne 11:1; Mt 27:53
**4:6** u Ps 91:11,12
**4:7** v Dt 6:16
**4:10** w Dt 6:13
**4:11** x Lk 22:43

## The Baptism of Jesus

13 Then Jesus came from Galilee to the Jordan to be baptized by John. 14 But John tried to deter him, saying, "I need to be baptized by you, and do you come to me?"

15 Jesus replied, "Let it be so now; it is proper for us to do this to fulfill all righteousness." Then John consented.

16 As soon as Jesus was baptized, he went up out of the water. At that moment heaven was opened, and he saw the Spirit of God[n] descending like a dove and lighting on him. 17 And a voice from heaven said, "This is my Son,[o] whom I love; with him I am well pleased."[p]

## The Temptation of Jesus

4 Then Jesus was led by the Spirit into the desert to be tempted by the devil. 2 After fasting forty days and forty nights,[q] he was hungry. 3 The tempter[r] came to him and said, "If you are the Son of God, tell these stones to become bread."

4 Jesus answered, "It is written: 'Man does not live on bread alone, but on every word that comes from the mouth of God.'[a]"[s]

5 Then the devil took him to the holy city[t] and had him stand on the highest point of the temple. 6 "If you are the Son of God," he said, "throw yourself down. For it is written:

"'He will command his angels
concerning you,
and they will lift you up in their hands,
so that you will not strike your foot
against a stone.'[b]"[u]

7 Jesus answered him, "It is also written: 'Do not put the Lord your God to the test.'[c]"[v]

8 Again, the devil took him to a very high mountain and showed him all the kingdoms of the world and their splendor. 9 "All this I will give you," he said, "if you will bow down and worship me."

10 Jesus said to him, "Away from me, Satan! For it is written: 'Worship the Lord your God, and serve him only.'[d]"[w]

11 Then the devil left him, and angels came and attended him.[x]

## Jesus Begins to Preach

12 When Jesus heard that John had been put in prison, he returned to Galilee. 13 Leaving Nazareth, he went and lived in Capernaum, which was by the lake in the area of Zebulun and Naphtali— 14 to fulfill what was said through the prophet Isaiah:

15 "Land of Zebulun and land of Naphtali,
the way to the sea, along the Jordan,
Galilee of the Gentiles—
16 the people living in darkness
have seen a great light;
on those living in the land of the shadow
of death
a light has dawned."[e][y]

17 From that time on Jesus began to preach, "Repent, for the kingdom of heaven[z] is near."

## The Calling of the First Disciples

18 As Jesus was walking beside the Sea of Galilee, he saw two brothers, Simon called Peter and his brother Andrew. They were casting a net into the lake, for they were fishermen. 19 "Come, follow me,"[a] Jesus said, "and I will make you fishers of men." 20 At once they left their nets and followed him.

21 Going on from there, he saw two other brothers, James son of Zebedee and his brother John. They were in a boat with their father Zebedee, preparing their nets. Jesus called them, 22 and immediately they left the boat and their father and followed him.

## Jesus Heals the Sick

23 Jesus went throughout Galilee,[b] teaching in their synagogues,[c] preaching the good news[d] of the kingdom, and healing every disease and sickness among the people. 24 News about him spread all over Syria,[e] and people brought to him all who were ill with various diseases, those suffering severe pain, the demon-possessed,[f] those having seizures, and the paralyzed, and he healed them. 25 Large crowds from Galilee, the Decapolis,[f] Jerusalem, Judea and the region across the Jordan followed him.[g]

**4:16** y Isa 9:1,2
**4:17** z Mt 3:2
**4:19** a Mk 10:21,28,52
**4:23** b Mk 1:39; Lk 4:15,44 c Mt 9:35; Mk 1:21 d Mk 1:14
**4:24** e Lk 2:2 f Mk 1:32
**4:25** g Mk 3:7,8

[a] 4 Deut. 8:3 [b] 6 Psalm 91:11,12 [c] 7 Deut. 6:16 [d] 10 Deut. 6:13 [e] 16 Isaiah 9:1,2 [f] 25 That is, the Ten Cities

## The Beatitudes

5 Now when he saw the crowds, he went
up on a mountainside and sat down.
His disciples came to him, 2and he began to
teach them, saying:

3 "Blessed are the poor in spirit,
for theirs is the kingdom of heaven.
4 Blessed are those who mourn,
for they will be comforted.[h]
5 Blessed are the meek,

5:4
h Isa 61:2,3

Inspire

## EVANGELISM: GONE FISHIN'

I was reminded of the importance of evangelism as the girls from my mentoring group planned a fishing trip. We talked about asking some of the elders and senior citizens of our congregation to teach us to fish. When I thought about this trip, I was reminded of Jesus' words to his first disciples: "I will make you fishers of men" (Mt 4:19). It was then that I realized we could tie in this fishing trip with a lesson on spreading the gospel.

We decided to ask those trailblazers to share with us some tricks of the trade, but we also asked them to share Biblical stories as well as their own testimonies. We talked about how Jesus chose fishermen as some of his disciples. We talked about the net that initially came up empty but that, once given over to the Master's direction, began to tear from the abundance of the catch (see Lk 5:4–7).

Today, as then, the harvest is plentiful. And still the laborers are few. Could this be the case because we have not availed ourselves of the resources lying, unused, at our own backdoors? When was the last time you went fishing for Christ? When was the last time you took a young person along with you and shared your testimony with him or her? Remember: If you give one woman a fish, you supply her with a meal, but if you teach her to fish, you equip her for life—both practically and spiritually.

Are you waiting to take some time off—vacation time, spare time? Or are you willing to fish for Christ on a regular basis—in the pond nearest you, in your neighborhood creek? Remember that there is peace by the river. So go on, take your gear; pick up a couple of other would-be anglers; head for the creek, the river or wherever; then cast your nets and see whether you find your net breaking due to the weight of the catch. May Christ find you, at his return, out on the shores, "gone fishin'."

—L. Melton-Dolberry

For the next Inspire note, go to page 1122.

### read

Matthew 4:18–22; 28:16–20; Mark 1:14–20; Luke 5:1–11; 10:1–2.

**See also** the Inspire Notes "Influencing Others," "Commitment to Community" and "Confessing Salvation," and the Women of the Bible Notes "Candace: Secure Leader," "Lydia: A Model for Women in Business" and "Priscilla: An Open-Door Policy."

### WOMAN of COLOR

How are you fishing for Christ? With whom have you shared your testimony lately?

5:5 i Ps37:11
5:6 j Isa55:1,2
5:8 k Heb12:14
5:9 l Ro8:14
5:10 m 1Pe3:14
5:11 n 1Pe4:14
5:12 o Ac7:52
5:13 p Mk9:50; Lk14:34,35
5:15 q Mk4:21; Lk8:16
5:18 r Lk16:17
5:19 s Jas2:10

for they will inherit the earth.[i]
6 Blessed are those who hunger and thirst
for righteousness,
for they will be filled.[j]
7 Blessed are the merciful,
for they will be shown mercy.
8 Blessed are the pure in heart,
for they will see God.[k]
9 Blessed are the peacemakers,
for they will be called sons of God.[l]
10 Blessed are those who are persecuted
because of righteousness,[m]
for theirs is the kingdom of heaven.

11 "Blessed are you when people insult you,[n] persecute you and falsely say all kinds of evil against you because of me. 12 Rejoice and be glad, because great is your reward in heaven, for in the same way they persecuted the prophets who were before you.[o]

## Salt and Light

13 "You are the salt of the earth. But if the salt loses its saltiness, how can it be made salty again? It is no longer good for anything, except to be thrown out and trampled by men.[p]

14 "You are the light of the world. A city on a hill cannot be hidden. 15 Neither do people light a lamp and put it under a bowl. Instead they put it on its stand, and it gives light to everyone in the house.[q] 16 In the same way, let your light shine before men, that they may see your good deeds and praise your Father in heaven.

## The Fulfillment of the Law

17 "Do not think that I have come to abolish the Law or the Prophets; I have not come to abolish them but to fulfill them. 18 I tell you the truth, until heaven and earth disappear, not the smallest letter, not the least stroke of a pen, will by any means disappear from the Law until everything is accomplished.[r] 19 Anyone who breaks one of the least of these commandments[s] and teaches others to do the same will be called least in the kingdom of heaven, but whoever practices and teaches these commands will be called great in the kingdom of heaven. 20 For I tell you that unless your righteousness surpasses that of the Pharisees and the teachers of the law, you will certainly not enter the kingdom of heaven.

5:21 t Ex20:13
5:22 u 1Jn3:15
5:27 v Ex20:14; Dt5:18
5:28 w Pr6:25
5:29 x Mk9:42–47
5:31 y Dt24:1–4
5:32 z Lk16:18

## Murder

21 "You have heard that it was said to the people long ago, 'Do not murder,[a][t] and anyone who murders will be subject to judgment.' 22 But I tell you that anyone who is angry with his brother[b] will be subject to judgment.[u] Again, anyone who says to his brother, 'Raca,[c]' is answerable to the Sanhedrin. But anyone who says, 'You fool!' will be in danger of the fire of hell.

23 "Therefore, if you are offering your gift at the altar and there remember that your brother has something against you, 24 leave your gift there in front of the altar. First go and be reconciled to your brother; then come and offer your gift.

25 "Settle matters quickly with your adversary who is taking you to court. Do it while you are still with him on the way, or he may hand you over to the judge, and the judge may hand you over to the officer, and you may be thrown into prison. 26 I tell you the truth, you will not get out until you have paid the last penny.[d]

## Adultery

27 "You have heard that it was said, 'Do not commit adultery.'[e][v] 28 But I tell you that anyone who looks at a woman lustfully has already committed adultery with her in his heart.[w] 29 If your right eye causes you to sin,[x] gouge it out and throw it away. It is better for you to lose one part of your body than for your whole body to be thrown into hell. 30 And if your right hand causes you to sin, cut it off and throw it away. It is better for you to lose one part of your body than for your whole body to go into hell.

## Divorce

31 "It has been said, 'Anyone who divorces his wife must give her a certificate of divorce.'[f][y] 32 But I tell you that anyone who divorces his wife, except for marital unfaithfulness, causes her to become an adulteress, and anyone who marries the divorced woman commits adultery.[z]

[a]21 Exodus 20:13 [b]22 Some manuscripts *brother without cause* [c]22 An Aramaic term of contempt [d]26 Greek *kodrantes* [e]27 Exodus 20:14 [f]31 Deut. 24:1

5:33
a Lev 19:12
b Nu 30:2; Mt 23:16–22

## Oaths

33 "Again, you have heard that it was said
to the people long ago, 'Do not break your
oath,[a] but keep the oaths you have made to
the Lord.'[b] 34 But I tell you, Do not swear at
all:[c] either by heaven, for it is God's throne;[d]
35 or by the earth, for it is his footstool; or
by Jerusalem, for it is the city of the Great
King.[e] 36 And do not swear by your head,
for you cannot make even one hair white or

5:34
c Jas 5:12
d Isa 66:1

5:35
e Ps 48:2

Inspire

## GOODNESS

In my church the children often sing "This little light of mine, I'm gonna let it shine, let it shine, let it shine, let it shine!" The lyrics of this song are inspired by Scripture: "Let your light shine before men, that they may see your good deeds and praise your Father in heaven" (Mt 5:16).

In the early church, as Christians served others God's good purposes were revealed and the body of Christ was built up (see Eph 4:11–13). Today, goodness still expresses itself in good works. It is manifested whenever we do good to our neighbors, shelter the homeless or help the helpless. Goodness expresses itself when we go out of our way for another, not expecting anything in return. First Timothy 6:17–19 commands Christians to put their hope in God, not in wealth, and to be rich in good works, generous and willing to share. It is by these actions that we lay up for ourselves a treasure in heaven.

Every Christian woman has a responsibility to follow these commands. But goodness can be cultivated only when we walk with the Lord. Psalm 23:6 tells us that when we allow the Lord to be our "shepherd," goodness and love will follow us all the days of our lives and we will remain in his presence forever.

This goodness is to be shared with others. You are a light and a beacon to others (see Mt 5:14–16). How will people see your light unless you show them? When was the last time you reached out and helped another sister or brother? We live in a world in which we are taught to look out for number one, to take care of our own and to let others fend for themselves. But God calls us to a higher standard: We are to maintain good works, to show a pattern of good works and to be zealous for good works. Many people will only see the goodness of God as they witness that goodness in others. As a fruit of the Spirit, goodness is a natural result of love, joy, peace, patience and kindness at work in a woman's life (see Gal 5:22–23).

—C. Belt

For the next Inspire note, go to page 1124.

### read

Matthew 5:13–16;
Galatians 5:16–25;
Ephesians 5:1–20;
2 Peter 1:3–11.

**See also** the Inspire Notes "Discernment" and "Sacrificial Living," and the Women of the Bible Note "Claudia: A Sincere Supporter."

### WOMAN of COLOR

How are you showing goodness to others?

**5:38** f Ex 21:24; Lev 24:20; Dt 19:21
**5:39** g Lk 6:29; 1Co 6:7
**5:42** h Lk 6:30
**5:43** i Lev 19:18 j Dt 23:6
**5:44** k Lk 6:27,28; Ac 7:60
**5:48** l Lev 19:2
**6:5** m Mk 11:25

black. [37]Simply let your 'Yes' be 'Yes,' and
your 'No,' 'No'; anything beyond this comes
from the evil one.

## An Eye for an Eye

[38]"You have heard that it was said, 'Eye for
eye, and tooth for tooth.'[a f] [39]But I tell you, Do
not resist an evil person. If someone strikes
you on the right cheek, turn to him the other
also.[g] [40]And if someone wants to sue you and
take your tunic, let him have your cloak as
well. [41]If someone forces you to go one mile,
go with him two miles. [42]Give to the one who
asks you, and do not turn away from the one
who wants to borrow from you.[h]

## Love for Enemies

[43]"You have heard that it was said, 'Love
your neighbor[b i] and hate your enemy.'[j] [44]But
I tell you: Love your enemies[c] and pray for
those who persecute you,[k] [45]that you may be
sons of your Father in heaven. He causes his
sun to rise on the evil and the good, and sends
rain on the righteous and the unrighteous.
[46]If you love those who love you, what reward
will you get? Are not even the tax collectors
doing that? [47]And if you greet only your
brothers, what are you doing more than oth-
ers? Do not even pagans do that? [48]Be perfect,
therefore, as your heavenly Father is perfect.[l]

## Giving to the Needy

6 "Be careful not to do your 'acts of righ-
teousness' before men, to be seen by
them. If you do, you will have no reward
from your Father in heaven.

[2]"So when you give to the needy, do not
announce it with trumpets, as the hypo-
crites do in the synagogues and on the
streets, to be honored by men. I tell you the
truth, they have received their reward in
full. [3]But when you give to the needy, do not
let your left hand know what your right
hand is doing, [4]so that your giving may be
in secret. Then your Father, who sees what
is done in secret, will reward you.

## Prayer

[5]"And when you pray, do not be like the
hypocrites, for they love to pray standing[m] in
the synagogues and on the street corners to
be seen by men. I tell you the truth, they have
received their reward in full. [6]But when you
pray, go into your room, close the door and
pray to your Father,[n] who is unseen. Then
your Father, who sees what is done in secret,
will reward you. [7]And when you pray, do not
keep on babbling like pagans, for they think
they will be heard because of their many
words.[o] [8]Do not be like them, for your Father
knows what you need before you ask him.

[9]"This, then, is how you should pray:

"'Our Father in heaven,
hallowed be your name,
[10]your kingdom come,
your will be done[p]
on earth as it is in heaven.
[11]Give us today our daily bread.[q]
[12]Forgive us our debts,
as we also have forgiven our debtors.[r]
[13]And lead us not into temptation,
but deliver us from the evil one.'[d]

[14]For if you forgive men when they sin
against you, your heavenly Father will also
forgive you.[s] [15]But if you do not forgive men
their sins, your Father will not forgive your
sins.[t]

## Fasting

[16]"When you fast, do not look somber[u] as
the hypocrites do, for they disfigure their
faces to show men they are fasting. I tell you
the truth, they have received their reward
in full. [17]But when you fast, put oil on your
head and wash your face, [18]so that it will not
be obvious to men that you are fasting, but
only to your Father, who is unseen; and your
Father, who sees what is done in secret, will
reward you.[v]

## Treasures in Heaven

[19]"Do not store up for yourselves trea-
sures on earth,[w] where moth and rust de-
stroy, and where thieves break in and steal.
[20]But store up for yourselves treasures in
heaven,[x] where moth and rust do not de-
stroy, and where thieves do not break in
and steal. [21]For where your treasure is, there
your heart will be also.

**6:6** n 2Ki 4:33
**6:7** o 1Ki 18:26–29
**6:10** p Mt 26:39
**6:11** q Pr 30:8
**6:12** r Mt 18:21–35
**6:14** s Mk 11:25,26; Col 3:13
**6:15** t Mt 18:35
**6:16** u Isa 58:5
**6:18** v ver 4,6
**6:19** w Heb 13:5
**6:20** x Mt 19:21; Lk 12:33; 1Ti 6:19

[a]38 Exodus 21:24; Lev. 24:20; Deut. 19:21 [b]43 Lev. 19:18 [c]44 Some late manuscripts *enemies, bless those who curse you, do good to those who hate you* [d]13 Or *from evil*; some late manuscripts *one, / for yours is the kingdom and the power and the glory forever. Amen.*

Inspire

## FORGIVENESS: THE DOORWAY TO HEALING AND RECONCILIATION

One of life's greatest challenges is finding within ourselves the willingness to forgive someone who has hurt us. Offenses range from the uncomfortable to the unbearable. Sometimes the pain can be extreme. Yet when someone asks you for forgiveness, you have an obligation as a Christian to grant it. Forgiveness of others' offenses against us is a prerequisite for God's forgiveness of our offenses against him (see Mt 6:14–15; Jas 2:13).

God showed the world the ultimate act of forgiveness when he allowed his Son, Jesus Christ, to die for our sins. In this gift we also witness an amazing display of love, the primary ingredient of forgiveness. When love seems absent because we are overwhelmed by negative feelings, we can remember that we are to forgive by faith, which is not necessarily accompanied by feelings. Even if we don't feel love for those who have wronged us, we can trust God to help us.

We are called to remember that we, in ourselves, embody the gift of forgiveness. This gift flowed to us from God at Calvary! It was given to us as human beings before we even asked for it. Romans 5:10 says, "When we were God's enemies, we were reconciled to him through the death of his Son." Just as God, in Christ, forgave us before we even knew to ask for forgiveness, so we are called to forgive others before we are asked. In many cases those who have wronged us will never ask for, or deserve, our forgiveness. However, if we wish for both ourselves and our "debtors" (Mt 6:12) to be healed from the hurt, we will give the gift that not only makes individual healing possible but also allows for a possible reconciliation of relationships.

To forgive is not easy, but it is possible. Be willing to let go of grudges and resentments over past hurts, to pray for the offender, to surrender the pain to God and thus to serve as a channel for God's grace. Most important, forgiveness is the doorway to reconciliation. If we desire to live reconciled lives—at peace with God and creation—we will share this gift as often as necessary. Giving it away sets us free to be healed and made whole! A forgiving spirit blesses both ourselves and others.

—C. Belt

**read**

Matthew 6:12–15; 18:21–35; Mark 11:25; Ephesians 4:31–32.

**See also** the Inspire Notes "Sexual Abuse," "Overcoming Abuse," "Grace and Mercy" and "Forgiveness: God's Extended Mercy," and the Women of the Bible Notes "Bathsheba: A Silent Affair," "The Forgiven Adulteress: Caught but Not Condemned" and "Euodia and Syntyche: Women in Conflict."

**WOMAN of COLOR**

Who do you need God's help to forgive?

For the next Inspire note, go to page 1141.

**6:24** y Lk 16:13
**6:25** z Lk 12:11,22; Php 4:6; 1Pe 5:7
**6:26** a Ps 147:9
**6:27** b Ps 39:5
**6:29** c 1Ki 10:4–7
**6:30** d Mt 8:26
**6:33** e Mt 19:29; Mk 10:29–30
**7:1** f 1Co 4:5
**7:2** g Mk 4:24

22 "The eye is the lamp of the body. If your eyes are good, your whole body will be full of light. 23 But if your eyes are bad, your whole body will be full of darkness. If then the light within you is darkness, how great is that darkness!

24 "No one can serve two masters. Either he will hate the one and love the other, or he will be devoted to the one and despise the other. You cannot serve both God and Money.[y]

## Do Not Worry

25 "Therefore I tell you, do not worry[z] about your life, what you will eat or drink; or about your body, what you will wear. Is not life more important than food, and the body more important than clothes? 26 Look at the birds of the air; they do not sow or reap or store away in barns, and yet your heavenly Father feeds them.[a] Are you not much more valuable than they? 27 Who of you by worrying can add a single hour to his life[a]?[b]

28 "And why do you worry about clothes? See how the lilies of the field grow. They do not labor or spin. 29 Yet I tell you that not even Solomon in all his splendor[c] was dressed like one of these. 30 If that is how God clothes the grass of the field, which is here today and tomorrow is thrown into the fire, will he not much more clothe you, O you of little faith?[d] 31 So do not worry, saying, 'What shall we eat?' or 'What shall we drink?' or 'What shall we wear?' 32 For the pagans run after all these things, and your heavenly Father knows that you need them. 33 But seek first his kingdom and his righteousness, and all these things will be given to you as well.[e] 34 Therefore do not worry about tomorrow, for tomorrow will worry about itself. Each day has enough trouble of its own.

## Judging Others

7 "Do not judge, or you too will be judged.[f] 2 For in the same way you judge others, you will be judged, and with the measure you use, it will be measured to you.[g]

3 "Why do you look at the speck of sawdust in your brother's eye and pay no attention to the plank in your own eye? 4 How can you say to your brother, 'Let me take the speck out of your eye,' when all the time there is a plank in your own eye? 5 You hypocrite, first take the plank out of your own eye, and then you will see clearly to remove the speck from your brother's eye.

6 "Do not give dogs what is sacred; do not throw your pearls to pigs. If you do, they may trample them under their feet, and then turn and tear you to pieces.

## Ask, Seek, Knock

7 "Ask and it will be given to you;[h] seek and you will find; knock and the door will be opened to you. 8 For everyone who asks receives; he who seeks finds;[i] and to him who knocks, the door will be opened.

9 "Which of you, if his son asks for bread, will give him a stone? 10 Or if he asks for a fish, will give him a snake? 11 If you, then, though you are evil, know how to give good gifts to your children, how much more will your Father in heaven give good gifts to those who ask him! 12 So in everything, do to others what you would have them do to you,[j] for this sums up the Law and the Prophets.[k]

## The Narrow and Wide Gates

13 "Enter through the narrow gate.[l] For wide is the gate and broad is the road that leads to destruction, and many enter through it. 14 But small is the gate and narrow the road that leads to life, and only a few find it.

## A Tree and Its Fruit

15 "Watch out for false prophets.[m] They come to you in sheep's clothing, but inwardly they are ferocious wolves.[n] 16 By their fruit you will recognize them.[o] Do people pick grapes from thornbushes, or figs from thistles? 17 Likewise every good tree bears good fruit, but a bad tree bears bad fruit. 18 A good tree cannot bear bad fruit, and a bad tree cannot bear good fruit. 19 Every tree that does not bear good fruit is cut down and thrown into the fire. 20 Thus, by their fruit you will recognize them.

21 "Not everyone who says to me, 'Lord, Lord,'[p] will enter the kingdom of heaven, but only he who does the will of my Father who is in heaven.[q] 22 Many will say to me on

**7:7** h Mk 11:24; Jn 15:7,16; 16:23,24; 1Jn 3:22; 5:14,15
**7:8** i Jer 29:12,13
**7:12** j Lk 6:31; k Ro 13:8–10; Gal 5:14
**7:13** l Lk 13:24
**7:15** m Mk 13:22; 2Pe 2:1; 1Jn 4:1; n Ac 20:29
**7:16** o Lk 6:44
**7:21** p Mt 25:11; q Jas 1:22

[a]27 Or *single cubit to his height*

**7:23**
r Ps 6:8; Lk 13:25–27

**7:28**
s Mt 13:53
t Mk 1:22; 6:2; Lk 4:32

**8:4**
u Mk 5:43
v Lev 14:2–32

that day, 'Lord, Lord, did we not prophesy in your name, and in your name drive out demons and perform many miracles?' [23]Then I will tell them plainly, 'I never knew you. Away from me, you evildoers!'[r]

## The Wise and Foolish Builders

[24]"Therefore everyone who hears these words of mine and puts them into practice is like a wise man who built his house on the rock. [25]The rain came down, the streams rose, and the winds blew and beat against that house; yet it did not fall, because it had its foundation on the rock. [26]But everyone who hears these words of mine and does not put them into practice is like a foolish man who built his house on sand. [27]The rain came down, the streams rose, and the winds blew and beat against that house, and it fell with a great crash."

[28]When Jesus had finished saying these things,[s] the crowds were amazed at his teaching,[t] [29]because he taught as one who had authority, and not as their teachers of the law.

## The Man With Leprosy

**8** When he came down from the mountainside, large crowds followed him. [2]A man with leprosy[a] came and knelt before him and said, "Lord, if you are willing, you can make me clean."

[3]Jesus reached out his hand and touched the man. "I am willing," he said. "Be clean!" Immediately he was cured[b] of his leprosy. [4]Then Jesus said to him, "See that you don't tell anyone.[u] But go, show yourself to the priest and offer the gift Moses commanded,[v] as a testimony to them."

## The Faith of the Centurion

[5]When Jesus had entered Capernaum, a centurion came to him, asking for help. [6]"Lord," he said, "my servant lies at home paralyzed and in terrible suffering."

[7]Jesus said to him, "I will go and heal him."

[8]The centurion replied, "Lord, I do not deserve to have you come under my roof. But just say the word, and my servant will be healed. [9]For I myself am a man under authority, with soldiers under me. I tell this one, 'Go,' and he goes; and that one, 'Come,' and he comes. I say to my servant, 'Do this,' and he does it."

[10]When Jesus heard this, he was astonished and said to those following him, "I tell you the truth, I have not found anyone in Israel with such great faith. [11]I say to you that many will come from the east and the west,[w] and will take their places at the feast with Abraham, Isaac and Jacob in the kingdom of heaven.[x] [12]But the subjects of the kingdom will be thrown outside, into the darkness, where there will be weeping and gnashing of teeth."[y]

[13]Then Jesus said to the centurion, "Go! It will be done just as you believed it would." And his servant was healed at that very hour.

*Sister,*

*I alone have the power to do the impossible.*
*Stay close to me.*

*God*

MATTHEW 8:5–13

## Jesus Heals Many

[14]When Jesus came into Peter's house, he saw Peter's mother-in-law lying in bed with a fever. [15]He touched her hand and the fever left her, and she got up and began to wait on him.

[16]When evening came, many who were demon-possessed were brought to him, and he drove out the spirits with a word and healed all the sick. [17]This was to fulfill what was spoken through the prophet Isaiah:

"He took up our infirmities
and carried our diseases."[c][z]

## The Cost of Following Jesus

[18]When Jesus saw the crowd around him, he gave orders to cross to the other side of

**8:11**
w Isa 49:12; 59:19; Mal 1:11
x Lk 13:29

**8:12**
y Mt 13:42,50; 22:13; 24:51; 25:30; Lk 13:28

**8:17**
z Isa 53:4

[a]2 The Greek word was used for various diseases affecting the skin—not necessarily leprosy. [b]3 Greek *made clean*
[c]17 Isaiah 53:4

the lake.[a] [19]Then a teacher of the law came to him and said, "Teacher, I will follow you wherever you go."

[20]Jesus replied, "Foxes have holes and birds of the air have nests, but the Son of Man has no place to lay his head."

[21]Another disciple said to him, "Lord, first let me go and bury my father."

[22]But Jesus told him, "Follow me, and let the dead bury their own dead."

## Jesus Calms the Storm

[23]Then he got into the boat and his disciples followed him. [24]Without warning, a furious storm came up on the lake, so that the waves swept over the boat. But Jesus was sleeping. [25]The disciples went and woke him, saying, "Lord, save us! We're going to drown!"

[26]He replied, "You of little faith, why are you so afraid?" Then he got up and rebuked the winds and the waves, and it was completely calm.[b]

[27]The men were amazed and asked, "What kind of man is this? Even the winds and the waves obey him!"

## The Healing of Two Demon-possessed Men

[28]When he arrived at the other side in the region of the Gadarenes,[a] two demon-possessed men coming from the tombs met him. They were so violent that no one could pass that way. [29]"What do you want with us,[c] Son of God?" they shouted. "Have you come here to torture us before the appointed time?"

[30]Some distance from them a large herd of pigs was feeding. [31]The demons begged Jesus, "If you drive us out, send us into the herd of pigs."

[32]He said to them, "Go!" So they came out and went into the pigs, and the whole herd rushed down the steep bank into the lake and died in the water. [33]Those tending the pigs ran off, went into the town and reported all this, including what had happened to the demon-possessed men. [34]Then the whole town went out to meet Jesus. And when they saw him, they pleaded with him to leave their region.[d]

**8:18** a Mk4:35
**8:26** b Ps65:7; 89:9; 107:29
**8:29** c Jdg11:12; 2Sa16:10; Mk1:24; Jn2:4
**8:34** d Lk5:8; Ac16:39

## Jesus Heals a Paralytic

9 Jesus stepped into a boat, crossed over and came to his own town.[e] [2]Some men brought to him a paralytic, lying on a mat. When Jesus saw their faith, he said to the paralytic, "Take heart, son; your sins are forgiven."

[3]At this, some of the teachers of the law said to themselves, "This fellow is blaspheming!"

[4]Knowing their thoughts,[f] Jesus said, "Why do you entertain evil thoughts in your hearts? [5]Which is easier: to say, 'Your sins are forgiven,' or to say, 'Get up and walk'? [6]But so that you may know that the Son of Man has authority on earth to forgive sins . . ." Then he said to the paralytic, "Get up, take your mat and go home." [7]And the man got up and went home. [8]When the crowd saw this, they were filled with awe; and they praised God,[g] who had given such authority to men.

## The Calling of Matthew

[9]As Jesus went on from there, he saw a man named Matthew sitting at the tax collector's booth. "Follow me," he told him, and Matthew got up and followed him.

[10]While Jesus was having dinner at Matthew's house, many tax collectors and "sinners" came and ate with him and his disciples. [11]When the Pharisees saw this, they asked his disciples, "Why does your teacher eat with tax collectors and 'sinners'?"[h]

[12]On hearing this, Jesus said, "It is not the healthy who need a doctor, but the sick. [13]But go and learn what this means: 'I desire mercy, not sacrifice.'[b][i] For I have not come to call the righteous, but sinners."[j]

## Jesus Questioned About Fasting

[14]Then John's disciples came and asked him, "How is it that we and the Pharisees fast,[k] but your disciples do not fast?"

[15]Jesus answered, "How can the guests of the bridegroom mourn while he is with them?[l] The time will come when the bridegroom will be taken from them; then they will fast.[m]

[16]"No one sews a patch of unshrunk cloth

**9:1** e Mt4:13
**9:4** f Mt12:25; Lk6:8; 9:47; 11:17
**9:8** g Mt5:16; Ac4:21
**9:11** h Mt11:19
**9:13** i Hos6:6; Mt12:7 j 1Ti1:15
**9:14** k Lk18:12
**9:15** l Jn3:29 m Ac13:2,3

[a]28 Some manuscripts *Gergesenes*; others *Gerasenes* [b]13 Hosea 6:6

**9:20** n Mt14:36
**9:22** o Lk7:50; 17:19; 18:42 p Mt15:28
**9:23** q 2Ch35:25
**9:24** r Ac20:10 s Jn11:11–14
**9:27** t Mt15:22; Mk10:47

on an old garment, for the patch will pull away from the garment, making the tear worse. 17Neither do men pour new wine into old wineskins. If they do, the skins will burst, the wine will run out and the wineskins will be ruined. No, they pour new wine into new wineskins, and both are preserved."

## A Dead Girl and a Sick Woman

18While he was saying this, a ruler came and knelt before him and said, "My daughter has just died. But come and put your hand on her, and she will live." 19Jesus got up and went with him, and so did his disciples.

20Just then a woman who had been subject to bleeding for twelve years came up behind him and touched the edge of his cloak.[n] 21She said to herself, "If I only touch his cloak, I will be healed."

22Jesus turned and saw her. "Take heart, daughter," he said, "your faith has healed you."[o] And the woman was healed from that moment.[p]

23When Jesus entered the ruler's house and saw the flute players and the noisy crowd,[q] 24he said, "Go away. The girl is not dead[r] but asleep."[s] But they laughed at him. 25After the crowd had been put outside, he went in and took the girl by the hand, and she got up. 26News of this spread through all that region.

> *"The doctors told me I would never walk, but my mother told me I would—so I believed my mother."*
>
> —WILMA RUDOLPH, FIRST AMERICAN WOMAN TO WIN THREE OLYMPIC GOLD MEDALS IN TRACK AND FIELD

## Jesus Heals the Blind and Mute

27As Jesus went on from there, two blind men followed him, calling out, "Have mercy on us, Son of David!"[t]

28When he had gone indoors, the blind men came to him, and he asked them, "Do you believe that I am able to do this?"

"Yes, Lord," they replied.

29Then he touched their eyes and said, "According to your faith will it be done to you"; 30and their sight was restored. Jesus warned them sternly, "See that no one knows about this."[u] 31But they went out and spread the news about him all over that region.[v]

32While they were going out, a man who was demon-possessed and could not talk[w] was brought to Jesus. 33And when the demon was driven out, the man who had been mute spoke. The crowd was amazed and said, "Nothing like this has ever been seen in Israel."

34But the Pharisees said, "It is by the prince of demons that he drives out demons."[x]

## The Workers Are Few

35Jesus went through all the towns and villages, teaching in their synagogues, preaching the good news of the kingdom and healing every disease and sickness. 36When he saw the crowds, he had compassion on them, because they were harassed and helpless, like sheep without a shepherd. 37Then he said to his disciples, "The harvest is plentiful but the workers are few.[y] 38Ask the Lord of the harvest, therefore, to send out workers into his harvest field."

## Jesus Sends Out the Twelve

**10** He called his twelve disciples to him and gave them authority to drive out evil[a] spirits[z] and to heal every disease and sickness.

2These are the names of the twelve apostles: first, Simon (who is called Peter) and his brother Andrew; James son of Zebedee, and his brother John; 3Philip and Bartholomew; Thomas and Matthew the tax collector; James son of Alphaeus, and Thaddaeus; 4Simon the Zealot and Judas Iscariot, who betrayed him.[a]

5These twelve Jesus sent out with the following instructions: "Do not go among the Gentiles or enter any town of the Samaritans.[b] 6Go rather to the lost sheep of Israel.[c] 7As you go, preach this message: 'The kingdom of heaven[d] is near.' 8Heal the sick, raise the dead, cleanse those who have leprosy,[b] drive out demons. Freely you have received, freely give. 9Do not take along any gold or silver or copper in your belts; 10take no bag for the journey, or extra tu-

**9:30** u Mt8:4
**9:31** v Mk7:36
**9:32** w Mt12:22–24
**9:34** x Mt12:24; Lk11:15
**9:37** y Lk10:2
**10:1** z Mk3:13–15
**10:4** a Jn13:2,26,27
**10:5** b Lk9:52
**10:6** c Mt15:24
**10:7** d Mt3:2

[a]1 Greek *unclean* [b]8 The Greek word was used for various diseases affecting the skin—not necessarily leprosy.

10:10
e 1Ti 5:18
10:14
f Ac 13:51
10:15
g Mt 11:22,24
10:16
h Lk 10:3
i Ro 16:19
10:17
j Mk 13:9
10:21
k Mic 7:6
10:24
l Lk 6:40; Jn 13:16; 15:20
10:25
m Mk 3:22
10:26
n Mk 4:22; Lk 8:17
10:28
o Heb 10:31

nic, or sandals or a staff; for the worker is worth his keep.[e]

11 "Whatever town or village you enter, search for some worthy person there and stay at his house until you leave. 12 As you enter the home, give it your greeting. 13 If the home is deserving, let your peace rest on it; if it is not, let your peace return to you. 14 If anyone will not welcome you or listen to your words, shake the dust off your feet[f] when you leave that home or town. 15 I tell you the truth, it will be more bearable for Sodom and Gomorrah on the day of judgment than for that town.[g] 16 I am sending you out like sheep among wolves.[h] Therefore be as shrewd as snakes and as innocent as doves.[i]

17 "Be on your guard against men; they will hand you over to the local councils and flog you in their synagogues.[j] 18 On my account you will be brought before governors and kings as witnesses to them and to the Gentiles. 19 But when they arrest you, do not worry about what to say or how to say it. At that time you will be given what to say, 20 for it will not be you speaking, but the Spirit of your Father speaking through you.

21 "Brother will betray brother to death, and a father his child; children will rebel against their parents[k] and have them put to death. 22 All men will hate you because of me, but he who stands firm to the end will be saved. 23 When you are persecuted in one place, flee to another. I tell you the truth, you will not finish going through the cities of Israel before the Son of Man comes.

24 "A student is not above his teacher, nor a servant above his master.[l] 25 It is enough for the student to be like his teacher, and the servant like his master. If the head of the house has been called Beelzebub,[a][m] how much more the members of his household!

26 "So do not be afraid of them. There is nothing concealed that will not be disclosed, or hidden that will not be made known.[n] 27 What I tell you in the dark, speak in the daylight; what is whispered in your ear, proclaim from the roofs. 28 Do not be afraid of those who kill the body but cannot kill the soul. Rather, be afraid of the One[o] who can destroy both soul and body in hell. 29 Are not two sparrows sold for a penny[b]? Yet not one of them will fall to the ground apart from the will of your Father. 30 And even the very hairs of your head are all numbered.[p] 31 So don't be afraid; you are worth more than many sparrows.

32 "Whoever acknowledges me before men,[q] I will also acknowledge him before my Father in heaven. 33 But whoever disowns me before men, I will disown him before my Father in heaven.

34 "Do not suppose that I have come to bring peace to the earth. I did not come to bring peace, but a sword. 35 For I have come to turn

"'a man against his father,
a daughter against her mother,
a daughter-in-law against her mother-in-law—
36 a man's enemies will be the members of his own household.'[c][r]

37 "Anyone who loves his father or mother more than me is not worthy of me; anyone who loves his son or daughter more than me is not worthy of me;[s] 38 and anyone who does not take his cross and follow me is not worthy of me. 39 Whoever finds his life will lose it, and whoever loses his life for my sake will find it.[t]

*"The Lord who told me to take care of my people meant me to do it just as long as I live, and so I do what he told me."*
—HARRIET TUBMAN, ABOLITIONIST

40 "He who receives you receives me,[u] and he who receives me receives the one who sent me.[v] 41 Anyone who receives a prophet because he is a prophet will receive a prophet's reward, and anyone who receives a righteous man because he is a righteous man will receive a righteous man's reward. 42 And if anyone gives even a cup of cold water to one of these little ones because he is my disciple, I tell you the truth, he will certainly not lose his reward."[w]

## Jesus and John the Baptist

11 After Jesus had finished instructing his twelve disciples, he went on from there to teach and preach in the towns of Galilee.[d]

10:30
p Lk 21:18; Ac 27:34
10:32
q Ro 10:9
10:36
r Mic 7:6
10:37
s Lk 14:26
10:39
t Jn 12:25
10:40
u Gal 4:14
v Lk 9:48; Jn 12:44
10:42
w Mt 25:40; Heb 6:10

[a] 25 Greek *Beezeboul* or *Beelzeboul* [b] 29 Greek *an assarion* [c] 36 Micah 7:6 [d] 1 Greek *in their towns*

**11:2** x Mt 14:3
**11:5** y Isa 35:4–6; 61:1; Lk 4:18,19
**11:7** z Mt 3:1
**11:9** a Lk 1:76
**11:10** b Mal 3:1; Mk 1:2
**11:14** c Mal 4:5; Lk 1:17
**11:15** d Mt 13:9,43

2 When John heard in prison[x] what Christ was doing, he sent his disciples 3 to ask him, "Are you the one who was to come, or should we expect someone else?"

4 Jesus replied, "Go back and report to John what you hear and see: 5 The blind receive sight, the lame walk, those who have leprosy[a] are cured, the deaf hear, the dead are raised, and the good news is preached to the poor.[y] 6 Blessed is the man who does not fall away on account of me."

7 As John's[z] disciples were leaving, Jesus began to speak to the crowd about John: "What did you go out into the desert to see? A reed swayed by the wind? 8 If not, what did you go out to see? A man dressed in fine clothes? No, those who wear fine clothes are in kings' palaces. 9 Then what did you go out to see? A prophet?[a] Yes, I tell you, and more than a prophet. 10 This is the one about whom it is written:

> " 'I will send my messenger ahead of you,
> who will prepare your way before you.'[b][b]

11 I tell you the truth: Among those born of women there has not risen anyone greater than John the Baptist; yet he who is least in the kingdom of heaven is greater than he. 12 From the days of John the Baptist until now, the kingdom of heaven has been forcefully advancing, and forceful men lay hold of it. 13 For all the Prophets and the Law prophesied until John. 14 And if you are willing to accept it, he is the Elijah who was to come.[c] 15 He who has ears, let him hear.[d]

> *"It's not the load that breaks you down, it's the way you carry it."*
> —Lena Horne, singer and actress

16 "To what can I compare this generation? They are like children sitting in the marketplaces and calling out to others:

> 17 " 'We played the flute for you,
> and you did not dance;
> we sang a dirge,
> and you did not mourn.'

18 For John came neither eating nor drinking, and they say, 'He has a demon.' 19 The Son of Man came eating and drinking, and they say, 'Here is a glutton and a drunkard, a friend of tax collectors and "sinners." '[e] But wisdom is proved right by her actions."

## Woe on Unrepentant Cities

20 Then Jesus began to denounce the cities in which most of his miracles had been performed, because they did not repent. 21 "Woe to you, Korazin! Woe to you, Bethsaida! If the miracles that were performed in you had been performed in Tyre and Sidon, they would have repented long ago in sackcloth and ashes.[f] 22 But I tell you, it will be more bearable for Tyre and Sidon on the day of judgment than for you.[g] 23 And you, Capernaum, will you be lifted up to the skies? No, you will go down to the depths.[c][h] If the miracles that were performed in you had been performed in Sodom, it would have remained to this day. 24 But I tell you that it will be more bearable for Sodom on the day of judgment than for you."[i]

## Rest for the Weary

25 At that time Jesus said, "I praise you, Father, Lord of heaven and earth, because you have hidden these things from the wise and learned, and revealed them to little children. 26 Yes, Father, for this was your good pleasure.

27 "All things have been committed to me[j] by my Father.[k] No one knows the Son except the Father, and no one knows the Father except the Son and those to whom the Son chooses to reveal him.

28 "Come to me,[l] all you who are weary and burdened, and I will give you rest. 29 Take my yoke upon you and learn from me,[m] for I am gentle and humble in heart, and you will find rest for your souls.[n] 30 For my yoke is easy and my burden is light."

## Lord of the Sabbath

12 At that time Jesus went through the grainfields on the Sabbath. His disciples were hungry and began to pick some heads of grain[o] and eat them. 2 When the Pharisees saw this, they said to him, "Look!

**11:19** e Mt 9:11
**11:21** f Jnh 3:5–9
**11:22** g ver 24; Mt 10:15
**11:23** h Isa 14:13–15
**11:24** i Mt 10:15
**11:27** j Mt 28:18 k Jn 3:35
**11:28** l Jn 7:37
**11:29** m Jn 13:15; Php 2:5; 1Pe 2:21; 1Jn 2:6 n Jer 6:16
**12:1** o Dt 23:25

[a] 5 The Greek word was used for various diseases affecting the skin—not necessarily leprosy. [b] 10 Mal. 3:1 [c] 23 Greek *Hades*

12:2 p ver 10; Lk 13:14; 14:3; Jn 5:10; 9:16
12:3 q 1Sa 21:6
12:5 r Nu 28:9,10
12:7 s Hos 6:6
12:10 t Lk 13:14
12:14 u Mk 3:6; Jn 11:53
12:18 v Mt 3:17

Your disciples are doing what is unlawful on the Sabbath."[p]

3 He answered, "Haven't you read what David did when he and his companions were hungry?[q] 4 He entered the house of God, and he and his companions ate the consecrated bread—which was not lawful for them to do, but only for the priests. 5 Or haven't you read in the Law that on the Sabbath the priests in the temple desecrate the day[r] and yet are innocent? 6 I tell you that one[a] greater than the temple is here. 7 If you had known what these words mean, 'I desire mercy, not sacrifice,'[b][s] you would not have condemned the innocent. 8 For the Son of Man is Lord of the Sabbath."

9 Going on from that place, he went into their synagogue, 10 and a man with a shriveled hand was there. Looking for a reason to accuse Jesus, they asked him, "Is it lawful to heal on the Sabbath?"[t]

11 He said to them, "If any of you has a sheep and it falls into a pit on the Sabbath, will you not take hold of it and lift it out? 12 How much more valuable is a man than a sheep! Therefore it is lawful to do good on the Sabbath."

13 Then he said to the man, "Stretch out your hand." So he stretched it out and it was completely restored, just as sound as the other. 14 But the Pharisees went out and plotted how they might kill Jesus.[u]

## God's Chosen Servant

15 Aware of this, Jesus withdrew from that place. Many followed him, and he healed all their sick, 16 warning them not to tell who he was. 17 This was to fulfill what was spoken through the prophet Isaiah:

18 "Here is my servant whom I have chosen,
the one I love, in whom I delight;[v]
I will put my Spirit on him,
and he will proclaim justice to the nations.
19 He will not quarrel or cry out;
no one will hear his voice in the streets.
20 A bruised reed he will not break,
and a smoldering wick he will not snuff out,
till he leads justice to victory.
21 In his name the nations will put their hope."[c]

*Lord Jesus,*

*I fall before you with outstretched arms.*
*I offer you my broken life and my sinful nature, believing that you have died for me. I accept your full pardon and ask you to wash me and fill me with your Spirit. In your precious name,*

*Amen*

MATTHEW 12:18–21

## Jesus and Beelzebub

22 Then they brought him a demon-possessed man who was blind and mute, and Jesus healed him, so that he could both talk and see.[w] 23 All the people were astonished and said, "Could this be the Son of David?"

24 But when the Pharisees heard this, they said, "It is only by Beelzebub,[d] the prince of demons, that this fellow drives out demons."[x]

25 Jesus knew their thoughts[y] and said to them, "Every kingdom divided against itself will be ruined, and every city or household divided against itself will not stand. 26 If Satan drives out Satan, he is divided against himself. How then can his kingdom stand? 27 And if I drive out demons by Beelzebub, by whom do your people[z] drive them out? So then, they will be your judges. 28 But if I drive out demons by the Spirit of God, then the kingdom of God has come upon you.

29 "Or again, how can anyone enter a strong man's house and carry off his possessions unless he first ties up the strong man? Then he can rob his house.

30 "He who is not with me is against me, and he who does not gather with me scatters. 31 And so I tell you, every sin and blasphemy will be forgiven men, but the

12:22 w Mt 9:32–33
12:24 x Mt 9:34
12:25 y Mt 9:4
12:27 z Ac 19:13

[a] 6 Or *something*; also in verses 41 and 42 [b] 7 Hosea 6:6 [c] 21 Isaiah 42:1–4 [d] 24 Greek *Beezeboul* or *Beelzeboul*; also in verse 27

**12:31** a Lk 12:10
**12:33** b Mt 7:16,17
**12:34** c Mt 3:7; 23:33 d Lk 6:45
**12:38** e Mt 16:1; Mk 8:11,12; Jn 2:18; 1Co 1:22
**12:39** f Mt 16:4
**12:40** g Jnh 1:17
**12:41** h Jnh 3:5
**12:42** i 1Ki 10:1; 2Ch 9:1

blasphemy against the Spirit will not be forgiven.[a] [32]Anyone who speaks a word against the Son of Man will be forgiven, but anyone who speaks against the Holy Spirit will not be forgiven, either in this age or in the age to come.

[33]"Make a tree good and its fruit will be good, or make a tree bad and its fruit will be bad, for a tree is recognized by its fruit.[b] [34]You brood of vipers,[c] how can you who are evil say anything good? For out of the overflow of the heart the mouth speaks.[d] [35]The good man brings good things out of the good stored up in him, and the evil man brings evil things out of the evil stored up in him. [36]But I tell you that men will have to give account on the day of judgment for every careless word they have spoken. [37]For by your words you will be acquitted, and by your words you will be condemned."

## The Sign of Jonah

[38]Then some of the Pharisees and teachers of the law said to him, "Teacher, we want to see a miraculous sign from you."[e]

[39]He answered, "A wicked and adulterous generation asks for a miraculous sign! But none will be given it except the sign of the prophet Jonah.[f] [40]For as Jonah was three days and three nights in the belly of a huge fish,[g] so the Son of Man will be three days and three nights in the heart of the earth. [41]The men of Nineveh will stand up at the judgment with this generation and condemn it; for they repented at the preaching of Jonah,[h] and now one[a] greater than Jonah is here. [42]The Queen of the South will rise at the judgment with this generation and condemn it; for she came[i] from the ends of the earth to listen to Solomon's wisdom, and now one greater than Solomon is here.

[43]"When an evil[b] spirit comes out of a man, it goes through arid places seeking rest and does not find it. [44]Then it says, 'I will return to the house I left.' When it arrives, it finds the house unoccupied, swept clean and put in order. [45]Then it goes and takes with it seven other spirits more wicked than itself, and they go in and live there. And the final condition of that man is worse than the first.[j] That is how it will be with this wicked generation."

## Jesus' Mother and Brothers

[46]While Jesus was still talking to the crowd, his mother and brothers[k] stood outside, wanting to speak to him. [47]Someone told him, "Your mother and brothers are standing outside, wanting to speak to you."[c]

[48]He replied to him, "Who is my mother, and who are my brothers?" [49]Pointing to his disciples, he said, "Here are my mother and my brothers. [50]For whoever does the will of my Father in heaven is my brother and sister and mother."

## The Parable of the Sower

**13** That same day Jesus went out of the house and sat by the lake. [2]Such large crowds gathered around him that he got into a boat[l] and sat in it, while all the people stood on the shore. [3]Then he told them many things in parables, saying: "A farmer went out to sow his seed. [4]As he was scattering the seed, some fell along the path, and the birds came and ate it up. [5]Some fell on rocky places, where it did not have much soil. It sprang up quickly, because the soil was shallow. [6]But when the sun came up, the plants were scorched, and they withered because they had no root. [7]Other seed fell among thorns, which grew up and choked the plants. [8]Still other seed fell on good soil, where it produced a crop—a hundred,[m] sixty or thirty times what was sown. [9]He who has ears, let him hear."[n]

[10]The disciples came to him and asked, "Why do you speak to the people in parables?"

[11]He replied, "The knowledge of the secrets of the kingdom of heaven has been given to you,[o] but not to them. [12]Whoever has will be given more, and he will have an abundance. Whoever does not have, even what he has will be taken from him.[p] [13]This is why I speak to them in parables:

"Though seeing, they do not see;
though hearing, they do not hear or
understand.

**12:45** j 2Pe 2:20
**12:46** k Mt 13:55; Jn 2:12; 7:3,5; Ac 1:14; 1Co 9:5; Gal 1:19
**13:2** l Lk 5:3
**13:8** m Ge 26:12
**13:9** n Mt 11:15
**13:11** o 1Co 2:10,14; 1Jn 2:20,27
**13:12** p Mt 25:29; Lk 19:26

[a]41 Or *something*; also in verse 42 [b]43 Greek *unclean* [c]47 Some manuscripts do not have verse 47.

**13:15** q Isa 6:9,10; Jn 12:40; Ac 28:26,27
**13:16** r Mt 16:17
**13:17** s Heb 11:13; 1Pe 1:10–12
**13:19** t Mt 4:23
**13:21** u Mt 11:6
**13:22** v Mt 19:23; 1Ti 6:9,10,17

14 In them is fulfilled the prophecy of Isaiah:

"'You will be ever hearing but never
understanding;
you will be ever seeing but never
perceiving.
15 For this people's heart has become
calloused;
they hardly hear with their ears,
and they have closed their eyes.
Otherwise they might see with their eyes,
hear with their ears,
understand with their hearts
and turn, and I would heal them.'[a][q]

16 But blessed are your eyes because they see,
and your ears because they hear.[r] 17 For I tell
you the truth, many prophets and righteous
men longed to see what you see[s] but did not
see it, and to hear what you hear but did not
hear it.
18 "Listen then to what the parable of the
sower means: 19 When anyone hears the mes-
sage about the kingdom[t] and does not un-
derstand it, the evil one comes and snatches
away what was sown in his heart. This is the
seed sown along the path. 20 The one who re-
ceived the seed that fell on rocky places is
the man who hears the word and at once re-
ceives it with joy. 21 But since he has no root,
he lasts only a short time. When trouble or
persecution comes because of the word, he
quickly falls away.[u] 22 The one who received
the seed that fell among the thorns is the
man who hears the word, but the worries
of this life and the deceitfulness of wealth[v]
choke it, making it unfruitful. 23 But the one
who received the seed that fell on good soil
is the man who hears the word and under-
stands it. He produces a crop, yielding a hun-
dred, sixty or thirty times what was sown."

## The Parable of the Weeds

24 Jesus told them another parable: "The
kingdom of heaven is like a man who sowed
good seed in his field. 25 But while everyone
was sleeping, his enemy came and sowed
weeds among the wheat, and went away.
26 When the wheat sprouted and formed
heads, then the weeds also appeared.
27 "The owner's servants came to him
and said, 'Sir, didn't you sow good seed
in your field? Where then did the weeds
come from?'
28 "'An enemy did this,' he replied.
"The servants asked him, 'Do you want
us to go and pull them up?'
29 "'No,' he answered, 'because while you
are pulling the weeds, you may root up the
wheat with them. 30 Let both grow together
until the harvest. At that time I will tell the
harvesters: First collect the weeds and tie
them in bundles to be burned; then gather
the wheat and bring it into my barn.'"[w]

## The Parables of the Mustard Seed and the Yeast

31 He told them another parable: "The
kingdom of heaven is like a mustard seed,
which a man took and planted in his field.
32 Though it is the smallest of all your seeds,
yet when it grows, it is the largest of garden
plants and becomes a tree, so that the birds
of the air come and perch in its branches."[x]
33 He told them still another parable:
"The kingdom of heaven is like yeast that
a woman took and mixed into a large
amount[b] of flour[y] until it worked all through
the dough."
34 Jesus spoke all these things to the crowd
in parables; he did not say anything to them
without using a parable.[z] 35 So was fulfilled
what was spoken through the prophet:

"I will open my mouth in parables,
I will utter things hidden since the
creation of the world."[c][a]

## The Parable of the Weeds Explained

36 Then he left the crowd and went into
the house. His disciples came to him and
said, "Explain to us the parable of the weeds
in the field."
37 He answered, "The one who sowed the
good seed is the Son of Man. 38 The field is
the world, and the good seed stands for the
sons of the kingdom. The weeds are the sons
of the evil one,[b] 39 and the enemy who sows
them is the devil. The harvest is the end of
the age,[c] and the harvesters are angels.
40 "As the weeds are pulled up and
burned in the fire, so it will be at the end

**13:30** w Mt 3:12
**13:32** x Ps 104:12; Eze 17:23; Da 4:12
**13:33** y Ge 18:6
**13:34** z Mk 4:33
**13:35** a Ps 78:2; 1Co 2:7
**13:38** b Jn 8:44,45
**13:39** c Mt 24:3

[a] 15 Isaiah 6:9,10 [b] 33 Greek *three satas* (probably about 1/2 bushel or 22 liters) [c] 35 Psalm 78:2

of the age. 41 The Son of Man will send out his angels, and they will weed out of his kingdom everything that causes sin and all who do evil. 42 They will throw them into the fiery furnace, where there will be weeping and gnashing of teeth.[d] 43 Then the righteous will shine like the sun[e] in the kingdom of their Father. He who has ears, let him hear.

## The Parables of the Hidden Treasure and the Pearl

44 "The kingdom of heaven is like treasure hidden in a field. When a man found it, he hid it again, and then in his joy went and sold all he had and bought that field.[f]

45 "Again, the kingdom of heaven is like a merchant looking for fine pearls. 46 When he found one of great value, he went away and sold everything he had and bought it.

## The Parable of the Net

47 "Once again, the kingdom of heaven is like a net that was let down into the lake and caught all kinds[g] of fish. 48 When it was full, the fishermen pulled it up on the shore. Then they sat down and collected the good fish in baskets, but threw the bad away. 49 This is how it will be at the end of the age. The angels will come and separate the wicked from the righteous[h] 50 and throw them into the fiery furnace, where there will be weeping and gnashing of teeth.

51 "Have you understood all these things?" Jesus asked.

"Yes," they replied.

52 He said to them, "Therefore every teacher of the law who has been instructed about the kingdom of heaven is like the owner of a house who brings out of his storeroom new treasures as well as old."

## A Prophet Without Honor

53 When Jesus had finished these parables,[i] he moved on from there. 54 Coming to his hometown, he began teaching the people in their synagogue,[j] and they were amazed.[k] "Where did this man get this wisdom and these miraculous powers?" they asked. 55 "Isn't this the carpenter's son?[l] Isn't his mother's[m] name Mary, and aren't his brothers James, Joseph, Simon and Judas? 56 Aren't all his sisters with us? Where then did this man get all these things?" 57 And they took offense at him.

But Jesus said to them, "Only in his hometown and in his own house is a prophet without honor."[n]

58 And he did not do many miracles there because of their lack of faith.

## John the Baptist Beheaded

14 At that time Herod[o] the tetrarch heard the reports about Jesus,[p] 2 and he said to his attendants, "This is John the Baptist; he has risen from the dead! That is why miraculous powers are at work in him."

3 Now Herod had arrested John and bound him and put him in prison because of Herodias, his brother Philip's wife,[q] 4 for John had been saying to him: "It is not lawful for you to have her."[r] 5 Herod wanted to kill John, but he was afraid of the people, because they considered him a prophet.

6 On Herod's birthday the daughter of Herodias danced for them and pleased Herod so much 7 that he promised with an oath to give her whatever she asked. 8 Prompted by her mother, she said, "Give me here on a platter the head of John the Baptist." 9 The king was distressed, but because of his oaths and his dinner guests, he ordered that her request be granted 10 and had John beheaded in the prison. 11 His head was brought in on a platter and given to the girl, who carried it to her mother. 12 John's disciples came and took his body and buried it. Then they went and told Jesus.

## Jesus Feeds the Five Thousand

13 When Jesus heard what had happened, he withdrew by boat privately to a solitary place. Hearing of this, the crowds followed him on foot from the towns. 14 When Jesus landed and saw a large crowd, he had compassion on them[s] and healed their sick.

15 As evening approached, the disciples came to him and said, "This is a remote place, and it's already getting late. Send the crowds away, so they can go to the villages and buy themselves some food."

16 Jesus replied, "They do not need to go away. You give them something to eat."

**13:42** d ver 50; Mt 8:12
**13:43** e Da 12:3
**13:44** f Isa 55:1; Php 3:7,8
**13:47** g Mt 22:10
**13:49** h Mt 25:32
**13:53** i Mt 7:28
**13:54** j Mt 4:23 k Mt 7:28
**13:55** l Jn 6:42 m Mt 12:46
**13:57** n Jn 4:44
**14:1** o Mk 8:15; Ac 4:27 p Lk 9:7-9
**14:3** q Lk 3:19,20
**14:4** r Lev 18:16; 20:21
**14:14** s Mt 9:36

**14:17** t Mt16:9
**14:19** u 1Sa9:13; Lk24:30
**14:26** v Lk24:37
**14:27** w Mt9:2 x Mt17:7; 28:10; Rev1:17
**14:31** y Mt6:30
**14:33** z Ps2:7

17“We have here only five loaves[t] of bread and two fish,” they answered.

18“Bring them here to me,” he said. 19And he directed the people to sit down on the grass. Taking the five loaves and the two fish and looking up to heaven, he gave thanks and broke the loaves.[u] Then he gave them to the disciples, and the disciples gave them to the people. 20They all ate and were satisfied, and the disciples picked up twelve basketfuls of broken pieces that were left over. 21The number of those who ate was about five thousand men, besides women and children.

## Jesus Walks on the Water

22Immediately Jesus made the disciples get into the boat and go on ahead of him to the other side, while he dismissed the crowd. 23After he had dismissed them, he went up on a mountainside by himself to pray. When evening came, he was there alone, 24but the boat was already a considerable distance[a] from land, buffeted by the waves because the wind was against it.

25During the fourth watch of the night Jesus went out to them, walking on the lake. 26When the disciples saw him walking on the lake, they were terrified. “It’s a ghost,”[v] they said, and cried out in fear.

27But Jesus immediately said to them: “Take courage![w] It is I. Don’t be afraid.”[x]

28“Lord, if it’s you,” Peter replied, “tell me to come to you on the water.”

29“Come,” he said.

Then Peter got down out of the boat, walked on the water and came toward Jesus. 30But when he saw the wind, he was afraid and, beginning to sink, cried out, “Lord, save me!”

31Immediately Jesus reached out his hand and caught him. “You of little faith,”[y] he said, “why did you doubt?”

32And when they climbed into the boat, the wind died down. 33Then those who were in the boat worshiped him, saying, “Truly you are the Son of God.”[z]

34When they had crossed over, they landed at Gennesaret. 35And when the men of that place recognized Jesus, they sent word to all the surrounding country. People brought all their sick to him 36and begged him to let the sick just touch the edge of his cloak,[a] and all who touched him were healed.

## Clean and Unclean

**15** Then some Pharisees and teachers of the law came to Jesus from Jerusalem and asked, 2“Why do your disciples break the tradition of the elders? They don’t wash their hands before they eat!”[b]

3Jesus replied, “And why do you break the command of God for the sake of your tradition? 4For God said, ‘Honor your father and mother’[b][c] and ‘Anyone who curses his father or mother must be put to death.’[c][d] 5But you say that if a man says to his father or mother, ‘Whatever help you might otherwise have received from me is a gift devoted to God,’ 6he is not to ‘honor his father[d]’ with it. Thus you nullify the word of God for the sake of your tradition. 7You hypocrites! Isaiah was right when he prophesied about you:

8“ ‘These people honor me with their lips,
but their hearts are far from me.
9They worship me in vain;
their teachings are but rules taught by
men.[e]’[e][f]”

10Jesus called the crowd to him and said, “Listen and understand. 11What goes into a man’s mouth does not make him ‘unclean,’[g] but what comes out of his mouth, that is what makes him ‘unclean.’ ”

12Then the disciples came to him and asked, “Do you know that the Pharisees were offended when they heard this?”

13He replied, “Every plant that my heavenly Father has not planted[h] will be pulled up by the roots. 14Leave them; they are blind guides.[f][i] If a blind man leads a blind man, both will fall into a pit.”[j]

15Peter said, “Explain the parable to us.”[k]

16“Are you still so dull?”[l] Jesus asked them. 17“Don’t you see that whatever enters the mouth goes into the stomach and then out of the body? 18But the things that come out of the mouth come from the heart,[m] and these make a man ‘unclean.’ 19For out of the

**14:36** a Mt9:20
**15:2** b Lk11:38
**15:4** c Ex20:12; Dt5:16 d Lev20:9
**15:9** e Col2:20–22 f Isa29:13
**15:11** g Ac10:14,15
**15:13** h Isa60:21
**15:14** i Mt23:16,24 j Lk6:39
**15:15** k Mt13:36
**15:16** l Mt16:9
**15:18** m Mt12:34; Jas3:6

[a]24 Greek *many stadia* [b]4 Exodus 20:12; Deut. 5:16 [c]4 Exodus 21:17; Lev. 20:9 [d]6 Some manuscripts *father or his mother* [e]9 Isaiah 29:13 [f]14 Some manuscripts *guides of the blind*

heart come evil thoughts, murder, adultery, sexual immorality, theft, false testimony, slander.[n] 20 These are what make a man 'unclean'; but eating with unwashed hands does not make him 'unclean.' "

## The Faith of the Canaanite Woman

21 Leaving that place, Jesus withdrew to the region of Tyre and Sidon. 22 A Canaanite woman from that vicinity came to him, crying out, "Lord, Son of David,[o] have mercy on me! My daughter is suffering terribly from demon-possession."[p]

23 Jesus did not answer a word. So his disciples came to him and urged him, "Send her away, for she keeps crying out after us."

24 He answered, "I was sent only to the lost sheep of Israel."[q]

25 The woman came and knelt before him.[r] "Lord, help me!" she said.

26 He replied, "It is not right to take the children's bread and toss it to their dogs."

27 "Yes, Lord," she said, "but even the dogs eat the crumbs that fall from their masters' table."

28 Then Jesus answered, "Woman, you have great faith![s] Your request is granted." And her daughter was healed from that very hour.

## Jesus Feeds the Four Thousand

29 Jesus left there and went along the Sea of Galilee. Then he went up on a mountainside and sat down. 30 Great crowds came to him, bringing the lame, the blind, the crippled, the mute and many others, and laid them at his feet; and he healed them.[t] 31 The people were amazed when they saw the mute speaking, the crippled made well, the lame walking and the blind seeing. And they praised the God of Israel.[u]

32 Jesus called his disciples to him and said, "I have compassion for these people;[v] they have already been with me three days and have nothing to eat. I do not want to send them away hungry, or they may collapse on the way."

33 His disciples answered, "Where could we get enough bread in this remote place to feed such a crowd?"

34 "How many loaves do you have?" Jesus asked.

"Seven," they replied, "and a few small fish."

35 He told the crowd to sit down on the ground. 36 Then he took the seven loaves and the fish, and when he had given thanks, he broke them[w] and gave them to the disciples, and they in turn to the people. 37 They all ate and were satisfied. Afterward the disciples picked up seven basketfuls of broken pieces that were left over.[x] 38 The number of those who ate was four thousand, besides women and children. 39 After Jesus had sent the crowd away, he got into the boat and went to the vicinity of Magadan.

## The Demand for a Sign

16 The Pharisees and Sadducees came to Jesus and tested him by asking him to show them a sign from heaven.[y]

2 He replied,[a] "When evening comes, you say, 'It will be fair weather, for the sky is red,' 3 and in the morning, 'Today it will be stormy, for the sky is red and overcast.' You know how to interpret the appearance of the sky, but you cannot interpret the signs of the times.[z] 4 A wicked and adulterous generation looks for a miraculous sign, but none will be given it except the sign of Jonah."[a] Jesus then left them and went away.

## The Yeast of the Pharisees and Sadducees

5 When they went across the lake, the disciples forgot to take bread. 6 "Be careful," Jesus said to them. "Be on your guard against the yeast of the Pharisees and Sadducees."[b]

7 They discussed this among themselves and said, "It is because we didn't bring any bread."

8 Aware of their discussion, Jesus asked, "You of little faith,[c] why are you talking among yourselves about having no bread? 9 Do you still not understand? Don't you remember the five loaves for the five thousand, and how many basketfuls you gathered?[d] 10 Or the seven loaves for the four thousand, and how many basketfuls you gathered?[e] 11 How is it you don't understand that I was not talking to you about bread?

**15:19** n Gal 5:19–21
**15:22** o Mt 9:27; p Mt 4:24
**15:24** q Mt 10:6,23
**15:25** r Mt 8:2
**15:28** s Mt 9:22
**15:30** t Mt 4:23
**15:31** u Mt 9:8
**15:32** v Mt 9:36
**15:36** w Mt 14:19
**15:37** x Mt 16:10
**16:1** y Mt 12:38
**16:3** z Lk 12:54–56
**16:4** a Mt 12:39
**16:6** b Lk 12:1
**16:8** c Mt 6:30
**16:9** d Mt 14:17–21
**16:10** e Mt 15:34–38

[a] 2 Some early manuscripts do not have the rest of verse 2 and all of verse 3.

# The Canaanite Woman

## Persistence Pays Off

When the worst of our troubles attack us, as wise women we know whom to go to for help. Our sister, the Canaanite woman, knew where to go and whom to see. She knew what Jesus could do. Can you imagine what she was like? A small woman, nothing notable, just hot and tired, lines of worry deeply etched in her face. She got to Jesus, and the disciples had the nerve to try to send her away because she was bothering them! The disciples didn't recognize that this woman was on a mission. To her, it didn't matter if Jesus was trying to rest or if the disciples didn't want her there. She had made up her mind. She wasn't leaving.

When the Canaanite woman faced Jesus (see both Mt 15:21–28 and Mk 7:24–30), Jesus responded to her request in a seemingly negative manner. He questioned her and tested her faith. But Jesus' seemingly harsh words did not deter the woman from her goal. When we are worried and scared for our children, we don't tolerate obstacles put in our way. This woman persisted. She was determined and pressed her case with Jesus. In effect, she said to him, "I know that God sent you first to the Jews, not to us Gentiles. But look at me. You are my last hope, and you know it. Can you really turn me away? Can you really let my child continue to suffer?" Sisters, have you been there?

The Canaanite woman persisted. Jesus heard her. He was impressed with her persistence and faith. Her faith was so great that she was able to withstand any obstacles. She placed her trust soundly in Christ. Like her, we cannot give up, turn around or turn away. Like her, we must have strong faith in Jesus.

—M. Allen Bellinger

### reflection

*Do you feel like giving up? Persist! Don't be discouraged, no matter what others say.*

*Continue to seek God and take your burdens to him.*

### read

Matthew 15:21–28; Mark 7:24–30.

See also the Inspire Notes "Motherhood," "Confidence," "Faith" and "Be Focused," and the Women of the Bible Note "The Shunammite Woman: Our Sister's Grief Is Our Grief."

For the next Women of the Bible note, go to page 1150.

**16:14** f Mt 14:2 g Mk 6:15; Jn 1:21
**16:16** h Jn 11:27
**16:17** i 1Co 15:50; Gal 1:16
**16:18** j Jn 1:42
**16:19** k Mt 18:18; Jn 20:23
**16:21** l Lk 17:25 m Mk 9:31
**16:24** n Mt 10:38; Lk 14:27

But be on your guard against the yeast of the Pharisees and Sadducees." 12Then they understood that he was not telling them to guard against the yeast used in bread, but against the teaching of the Pharisees and Sadducees.

## Peter's Confession of Christ

13When Jesus came to the region of Caesarea Philippi, he asked his disciples, "Who do people say the Son of Man is?"

14They replied, "Some say John the Baptist;[f] others say Elijah; and still others, Jeremiah or one of the prophets."[g]

15"But what about you?" he asked. "Who do you say I am?"

16Simon Peter answered, "You are the Christ,[a] the Son of the living God."[h]

17Jesus replied, "Blessed are you, Simon son of Jonah, for this was not revealed to you by man,[i] but by my Father in heaven. 18And I tell you that you are Peter,[b][j] and on this rock I will build my church, and the gates of Hades[c] will not overcome it.[d] 19I will give you the keys of the kingdom of heaven; whatever you bind on earth will be[e] bound in heaven, and whatever you loose on earth will be[e] loosed in heaven."[k] 20Then he warned his disciples not to tell anyone that he was the Christ.

## Jesus Predicts His Death

21From that time on Jesus began to explain to his disciples that he must go to Jerusalem and suffer many things[l] at the hands of the elders, chief priests and teachers of the law, and that he must be killed and on the third day be raised to life.[m]

22Peter took him aside and began to rebuke him. "Never, Lord!" he said. "This shall never happen to you!"

23Jesus turned and said to Peter, "Get behind me, Satan! You are a stumbling block to me; you do not have in mind the things of God, but the things of men."

24Then Jesus said to his disciples, "If anyone would come after me, he must deny himself and take up his cross and follow me.[n] 25For whoever wants to save his life[f] will lose it, but whoever loses his life for me will find it. 26What good will it be for a man if he gains the whole world, yet forfeits his soul? Or what can a man give in exchange for his soul? 27For the Son of Man is going to come in his Father's glory with his angels, and then he will reward each person according to what he has done.[o] 28I tell you the truth, some who are standing here will not taste death before they see the Son of Man coming in his kingdom."

## The Transfiguration

17 After six days Jesus took with him Peter, James and John the brother of James, and led them up a high mountain by themselves. 2There he was transfigured before them. His face shone like the sun, and his clothes became as white as the light. 3Just then there appeared before them Moses and Elijah, talking with Jesus.

4Peter said to Jesus, "Lord, it is good for us to be here. If you wish, I will put up three shelters—one for you, one for Moses and one for Elijah."

5While he was still speaking, a bright cloud enveloped them, and a voice from the cloud said, "This is my Son, whom I love; with him I am well pleased.[p] Listen to him!"[q]

6When the disciples heard this, they fell facedown to the ground, terrified. 7But Jesus came and touched them. "Get up," he said. "Don't be afraid."[r] 8When they looked up, they saw no one except Jesus.

9As they were coming down the mountain, Jesus instructed them, "Don't tell anyone what you have seen, until the Son of Man has been raised from the dead."[s]

10The disciples asked him, "Why then do the teachers of the law say that Elijah must come first?"

11Jesus replied, "To be sure, Elijah comes and will restore all things.[t] 12But I tell you, Elijah has already come,[u] and they did not recognize him, but have done to him everything they wished.[v] In the same way the Son of Man is going to suffer[w] at their hands." 13Then the disciples understood that he was talking to them about John the Baptist.

**16:27** o Ro 2:6; 2Co 5:10; Rev 22:12
**17:5** p Mt 3:17; 2Pe 1:17 q Ac 3:22,23
**17:7** r Mt 14:27
**17:9** s Mt 16:21
**17:11** t Mal 4:6; Lk 1:16,17
**17:12** u Mt 11:14 v Mt 14:3,10 w Mt 16:21

[a]16 Or *Messiah*; also in verse 20 [b]18 *Peter* means *rock.* [c]18 Or *hell* [d]18 Or *not prove stronger than it* [e]19 Or *have been* [f]25 The Greek word means either *life* or *soul*; also in verse 26.

**17:20** x Mt 21:21 y Mk 11:23; Lk 17:6 z 1Co 13:2
**17:24** a Ex 30:13
**17:25** b Mt 22:17–21; Ro 13:7
**17:27** c Jn 6:61

## The Healing of a Boy With a Demon

[14]When they came to the crowd, a man approached Jesus and knelt before him. [15]"Lord, have mercy on my son," he said. "He has seizures and is suffering greatly. He often falls into the fire or into the water. [16]I brought him to your disciples, but they could not heal him."

[17]"O unbelieving and perverse generation," Jesus replied, "how long shall I stay with you? How long shall I put up with you? Bring the boy here to me." [18]Jesus rebuked the demon, and it came out of the boy, and he was healed from that moment.

[19]Then the disciples came to Jesus in private and asked, "Why couldn't we drive it out?"

[20]He replied, "Because you have so little faith. I tell you the truth, if you have faith[x] as small as a mustard seed,[y] you can say to this mountain, 'Move from here to there' and it will move.[z] Nothing will be impossible for you.[a]"

[22]When they came together in Galilee, he said to them, "The Son of Man is going to be betrayed into the hands of men. [23]They will kill him, and on the third day he will be raised to life." And the disciples were filled with grief.

## The Temple Tax

[24]After Jesus and his disciples arrived in Capernaum, the collectors of the two-drachma tax[a] came to Peter and asked, "Doesn't your teacher pay the temple tax[b]?"

[25]"Yes, he does," he replied.

When Peter came into the house, Jesus was the first to speak. "What do you think, Simon?" he asked. "From whom do the kings of the earth collect duty and taxes[b]—from their own sons or from others?"

[26]"From others," Peter answered.

"Then the sons are exempt," Jesus said to him. [27]"But so that we may not offend[c] them, go to the lake and throw out your line. Take the first fish you catch; open its mouth and you will find a four-drachma coin. Take it and give it to them for my tax and yours."

**18:3** d Mt 19:14; 1Pe 2:2
**18:6** e Lk 17:2
**18:7** f Lk 17:1
**18:8** g Mt 5:29; Mk 9:43,45
**18:9** h Mt 5:29
**18:10** i Ps 34:7

## The Greatest in the Kingdom of Heaven

**18** At that time the disciples came to Jesus and asked, "Who is the greatest in the kingdom of heaven?"

[2]He called a little child and had him stand among them. [3]And he said: "I tell you the truth, unless you change and become like little children,[d] you will never enter the kingdom of heaven. [4]Therefore, whoever humbles himself like this child is the greatest in the kingdom of heaven.

[5]"And whoever welcomes a little child like this in my name welcomes me. [6]But if anyone causes one of these little ones who believe in me to sin, it would be better for him to have a large millstone hung around his neck and to be drowned in the depths of the sea.[e]

[7]"Woe to the world because of the things that cause people to sin! Such things must come, but woe to the man through whom they come![f] [8]If your hand or your foot causes you to sin,[g] cut it off and throw it away. It is better for you to enter life maimed or crippled than to have two hands or two feet and be thrown into eternal fire. [9]And if your eye causes you to sin,[h] gouge it out and throw it away. It is better for you to enter life with one eye than to have two eyes and be thrown into the fire of hell.

> *"Disabilities can sometimes be definitions. You can think of yourself in terms of what you can't do and never realize the possibilities of what you can do."*
> —BONNIE ST. JOHN, ATHLETE AND SCHOLAR

## The Parable of the Lost Sheep

[10]"See that you do not look down on one of these little ones. For I tell you that their angels[i] in heaven always see the face of my Father in heaven.[c]

[12]"What do you think? If a man owns a hundred sheep, and one of them wanders away, will he not leave the ninety-nine on the hills and go to look for the one that wandered off? [13]And if he finds it, I tell you the truth, he is happier about that one sheep than about the ninety-nine that did not

[a]20 Some manuscripts *you.* [21]*But this kind does not go out except by prayer and fasting.* [b]24 Greek *the two drachmas*
[c]10 Some manuscripts *heaven.* [11]*The Son of Man came to save what was lost.*

**18:15** j Lev 19:17; Lk 17:3; Jas 5:19,20
**18:16** k Dt 19:15; Jn 8:17; 2Co 13:1; Heb 10:28
**18:18** l Mt 16:19; Jn 20:23
**18:21** m Lk 17:4
**18:22** n Ge 4:24
**18:23** o Mt 25:19
**18:25** p Lk 7:42; q 2Ki 4:1; Ne 5:5,8
**18:26** r Mt 8:2

wander off. [14]In the same way your Father in heaven is not willing that any of these little ones should be lost.

## A Brother Who Sins Against You

[15]"If your brother sins against you,[a] go and show him his fault,[j] just between the two of you. If he listens to you, you have won your brother over. [16]But if he will not listen, take one or two others along, so that 'every matter may be established by the testimony of two or three witnesses.'[b][k] [17]If he refuses to listen to them, tell it to the church; and if he refuses to listen even to the church, treat him as you would a pagan or a tax collector.

[18]"I tell you the truth, whatever you bind on earth will be[c] bound in heaven, and whatever you loose on earth will be[c] loosed in heaven.[l]

[19]"Again, I tell you that if two of you on earth agree about anything you ask for, it will be done for you by my Father in heaven. [20]For where two or three come together in my name, there am I with them."

## The Parable of the Unmerciful Servant

[21]Then Peter came to Jesus and asked, "Lord, how many times shall I forgive my brother when he sins against me? Up to seven times?"[m]

[22]Jesus answered, "I tell you, not seven times, but seventy-seven times.[d][n]

[23]"Therefore, the kingdom of heaven is like a king who wanted to settle accounts[o] with his servants. [24]As he began the settlement, a man who owed him ten thousand talents[e] was brought to him. [25]Since he was not able to pay,[p] the master ordered that he and his wife and his children and all that he had be sold[q] to repay the debt.

[26]"The servant fell on his knees before him.[r] 'Be patient with me,' he begged, 'and I will pay back everything.' [27]The servant's master took pity on him, canceled the debt and let him go.

[28]"But when that servant went out, he found one of his fellow servants who owed him a hundred denarii.[f] He grabbed him and began to choke him. 'Pay back what you owe me!' he demanded.

[29]"His fellow servant fell to his knees and begged him, 'Be patient with me, and I will pay you back.'

[30]"But he refused. Instead, he went off and had the man thrown into prison until he could pay the debt. [31]When the other servants saw what had happened, they were greatly distressed and went and told their master everything that had happened.

[32]"Then the master called the servant in. 'You wicked servant,' he said, 'I canceled all that debt of yours because you begged me to. [33]Shouldn't you have had mercy on your fellow servant just as I had on you?' [34]In anger his master turned him over to the jailers to be tortured, until he should pay back all he owed.

[35]"This is how my heavenly Father will treat each of you unless you forgive your brother from your heart."[s]

## Divorce

**19** When Jesus had finished saying these things, he left Galilee and went into the region of Judea to the other side of the Jordan. [2]Large crowds followed him, and he healed them[t] there.

[3]Some Pharisees came to him to test him. They asked, "Is it lawful for a man to divorce his wife[u] for any and every reason?"

[4]"Haven't you read," he replied, "that at the beginning the Creator 'made them male and female,'[g][v] [5]and said, 'For this reason a man will leave his father and mother and be united to his wife, and the two will become one flesh'[h]?[w] [6]So they are no longer two, but one. Therefore what God has joined together, let man not separate."

[7]"Why then," they asked, "did Moses command that a man give his wife a certificate of divorce and send her away?"[x]

[8]Jesus replied, "Moses permitted you to divorce your wives because your hearts were hard. But it was not this way from the beginning. [9]I tell you that anyone who divorces his wife, except for marital unfaithfulness, and marries another woman commits adultery."[y]

[10]The disciples said to him, "If this is the situation between a husband and wife, it is better not to marry."

**18:35** s Mt 6:14
**19:2** t Mt 4:23
**19:3** u Mt 5:31
**19:4** v Ge 1:27; 5:2
**19:5** w Ge 2:24; 1Co 6:16; Eph 5:31
**19:7** x Dt 24:1–4
**19:9** y Mt 5:32; Lk 16:18

[a]15 Some manuscripts do not have *against you.* [b]16 Deut. 19:15 [c]18 Or *have been* [d]22 Or *seventy times seven* [e]24 That is, millions of dollars [f]28 That is, a few dollars [g]4 Gen. 1:27 [h]5 Gen. 2:24

# Inspire

## ADULTERY

Scripture is clear on the purpose of marriage: God provided the first woman as a suitable helper for Adam (see Ge 2:18), ordaining marriage and blessing it: "Be fruitful and increase in number; fill the earth and subdue it" (Ge 1:28). To preserve the fidelity of marriage, God gave Israel the seventh commandment: "You shall not commit adultery" (Ex 20:14). And Jesus affirmed the sanctity of marriage when he told the Pharisees that a man and woman are joined as one when they marry (see Mt 19:5).

God intends for husbands and wives to be faithful to each other. However, infidelity has been and continues to be a major threat to the three-way covenant relationship between husband, wife and God. *Adultery* is commonly defined as sexual intercourse between a married individual and a person who is not his or her spouse. But many people believe that a type of adultery can also be committed in marriages when one partner is consumed by someone or something other than their spouse—when the person puts another task or person (other than God) before the marriage. Some also consider infidelity to include situations in which a partner fails to be faithful to the marriage vows to love, support and help his or her spouse.

The good news of the gospel of Christ is that those who are unfaithful can repent and receive God's forgiveness. Accepting that forgiveness includes abandoning the sinful pattern that caused the marital trouble in the first place. God says to us—just as Jesus charged the woman caught in adultery—"Go now and leave your life of sin" (Jn 8:11).

Believers are to practice faithfulness both to God and to those with whom they have a personal relationship. God uses the faithfulness between a woman and her husband to demonstrate his faithfulness to his followers. Adultery will inevitably destroy the relationship God wants to have with the children he loves.

—J. Webster

### read

Matthew 19:4–6; see also Deuteronomy 22:22; Matthew 5:27–28; John 8:1–11; Romans 13:8–10.

See also the Inspire Notes "Grace and Mercy," "Marriage," "Forgiveness: God's Extended Mercy" and "Temptation," and the Women of the Bible Notes "The Adulteress of Proverbs: The Path to Death" "Gomer: An Unfaithful Wife" and "The Forgiven Adulteress: Caught but Not Condemned."

### WOMAN of COLOR

Are you allowing anyone or anything else to take God's place in your life? If you are married, are you allowing anyone or anything else to take your husband's place? Be faithful in all of your relationships.

For the next Inspire note, go to page 1152.

**19:11** z Mt 13:11; 1Co 7:7–9,17
**19:14** a Mt 18:3; 1Pe 2:2
**19:16** b Mt 25:46 c Lk 10:25
**19:18** d Jas 2:11
**19:19** e Lev 19:18
**19:21** f Lk 12:33; Ac 2:45; 4:34–35 g Mt 6:20
**19:23** h Mt 13:22

11 Jesus replied, "Not everyone can accept this word, but only those to whom it has been given.[z] 12 For some are eunuchs because they were born that way; others were made that way by men; and others have renounced marriage[a] because of the kingdom of heaven. The one who can accept this should accept it."

## The Little Children and Jesus

13 Then little children were brought to Jesus for him to place his hands on them and pray for them. But the disciples rebuked those who brought them.

14 Jesus said, "Let the little children come to me, and do not hinder them, for the kingdom of heaven belongs to such as these."[a] 15 When he had placed his hands on them, he went on from there.

## The Rich Young Man

16 Now a man came up to Jesus and asked, "Teacher, what good thing must I do to get eternal life[b]?"[c]

17 "Why do you ask me about what is good?" Jesus replied. "There is only One who is good. If you want to enter life, obey the commandments."

18 "Which ones?" the man inquired.

Jesus replied, "'Do not murder, do not commit adultery,[d] do not steal, do not give false testimony, 19 honor your father and mother,'[b] and 'love your neighbor as yourself.'[c]"[e]

20 "All these I have kept," the young man said. "What do I still lack?"

21 Jesus answered, "If you want to be perfect, go, sell your possessions and give to the poor,[f] and you will have treasure in heaven.[g] Then come, follow me."

22 When the young man heard this, he went away sad, because he had great wealth.

23 Then Jesus said to his disciples, "I tell you the truth, it is hard for a rich man[h] to enter the kingdom of heaven. 24 Again I tell you, it is easier for a camel to go through the eye of a needle than for a rich man to enter the kingdom of God."

25 When the disciples heard this, they were greatly astonished and asked, "Who then can be saved?"

26 Jesus looked at them and said, "With man this is impossible, but with God all things are possible."[i]

27 Peter answered him, "We have left everything to follow you! What then will there be for us?"

28 Jesus said to them, "I tell you the truth, at the renewal of all things, when the Son of Man sits on his glorious throne, you who have followed me will also sit on twelve thrones, judging the twelve tribes of Israel.[j] 29 And everyone who has left houses or brothers or sisters or father or mother[d] or children or fields for my sake will receive a hundred times as much and will inherit eternal life. 30 But many who are first will be last, and many who are last will be first.[k]

## The Parable of the Workers in the Vineyard

**20** "For the kingdom of heaven is like[l] a landowner who went out early in the morning to hire men to work in his vineyard. 2 He agreed to pay them a denarius for the day and sent them into his vineyard.

3 "About the third hour he went out and saw others standing in the marketplace doing nothing. 4 He told them, 'You also go and work in my vineyard, and I will pay you whatever is right.' 5 So they went.

"He went out again about the sixth hour and the ninth hour and did the same thing. 6 About the eleventh hour he went out and found still others standing around. He asked them, 'Why have you been standing here all day long doing nothing?'

7 "'Because no one has hired us,' they answered.

"He said to them, 'You also go and work in my vineyard.'

8 "When evening came,[m] the owner of the vineyard said to his foreman, 'Call the workers and pay them their wages, beginning with the last ones hired and going on to the first.'

9 "The workers who were hired about the eleventh hour came and each received a denarius. 10 So when those came who were hired first, they expected to receive more. But each one of them also received a denarius. 11 When they received it, they began to

**19:26** i Ge 18:14; Job 42:2; Jer 32:17; Zec 8:6
**19:28** j Lk 22:28–30; Rev 3:21
**19:30** k Mt 20:16; Lk 13:30
**20:1** l Mt 13:24
**20:8** m Lev 19:13

[a]12 Or *have made themselves eunuchs* [b]19 Exodus 20:12–16; Deut. 5:16–20 [c]19 Lev. 19:18 [d]29 Some manuscripts *mother or wife*

**20:12** n Jnh 4:8; Jas 1:11
**20:15** o Dt 15:9; Mk 7:22
**20:16** p Mt 19:30
**20:18** q Mt 16:21
**20:19** r Mt 16:21 s Ac 2:23
**20:20** t Mt 4:21
**20:21** u Mt 19:28
**20:22** v Mt 26:39,42; Lk 22:42; Jn 18:11
**20:23** w Ac 12:2; Rev 1:9

grumble against the landowner. 12"These men who were hired last worked only one hour,' they said, 'and you have made them equal to us who have borne the burden of the work and the heat[n] of the day.'

13"But he answered one of them, 'Friend, I am not being unfair to you. Didn't you agree to work for a denarius? 14Take your pay and go. I want to give the man who was hired last the same as I gave you. 15Don't I have the right to do what I want with my own money? Or are you envious because I am generous?'[o]

16"So the last will be first, and the first will be last."[p]

## Jesus Again Predicts His Death

17Now as Jesus was going up to Jerusalem, he took the twelve disciples aside and said to them, 18"We are going up to Jerusalem, and the Son of Man will be betrayed to the chief priests and the teachers of the law.[q] They will condemn him to death 19and will turn him over to the Gentiles to be mocked and flogged[r] and crucified.[s] On the third day he will be raised to life!"

## A Mother's Request

20Then the mother of Zebedee's sons[t] came to Jesus with her sons and, kneeling down, asked a favor of him.

21"What is it you want?" he asked.

She said, "Grant that one of these two sons of mine may sit at your right and the other at your left in your kingdom."[u]

22"You don't know what you are asking," Jesus said to them. "Can you drink the cup[v] I am going to drink?"

"We can," they answered.

23Jesus said to them, "You will indeed drink from my cup,[w] but to sit at my right or left is not for me to grant. These places belong to those for whom they have been prepared by my Father."

24When the ten heard about this, they were indignant with the two brothers. 25Jesus called them together and said, "You know that the rulers of the Gentiles lord it over them, and their high officials exercise authority over them. 26Not so with you. Instead, whoever wants to become great among you must be your servant,[x] 27and whoever wants to be first must be your slave— 28just as the Son of Man did not come to be served, but to serve,[y] and to give his life as a ransom[z] for many."

## Two Blind Men Receive Sight

29As Jesus and his disciples were leaving Jericho, a large crowd followed him. 30Two blind men were sitting by the roadside, and when they heard that Jesus was going by, they shouted, "Lord, Son of David,[a] have mercy on us!"

31The crowd rebuked them and told them to be quiet, but they shouted all the louder, "Lord, Son of David, have mercy on us!"

32Jesus stopped and called them. "What do you want me to do for you?" he asked.

33"Lord," they answered, "we want our sight."

34Jesus had compassion on them and touched their eyes. Immediately they received their sight and followed him.

## The Triumphal Entry

21 As they approached Jerusalem and came to Bethphage on the Mount of Olives, Jesus sent two disciples, 2saying to them, "Go to the village ahead of you, and at once you will find a donkey tied there, with her colt by her. Untie them and bring them to me. 3If anyone says anything to you, tell him that the Lord needs them, and he will send them right away."

4This took place to fulfill what was spoken through the prophet:

5"Say to the Daughter of Zion,
'See, your king comes to you,
gentle and riding on a donkey,
on a colt, the foal of a donkey.' "[a][b]

6The disciples went and did as Jesus had instructed them. 7They brought the donkey and the colt, placed their cloaks on them, and Jesus sat on them. 8A very large crowd spread their cloaks on the road, while others cut branches from the trees and spread them on the road. 9The crowds that went ahead of him and those that followed shouted,

"Hosanna[b] to the Son of David!"

**20:26** x Mt 23:11; Mk 9:35
**20:28** y Jn 13:13–16; Php 2:7 z Mt 26:28; 1Ti 2:6; Tit 2:14; Heb 9:28
**20:30** a Mt 9:27
**21:5** b Isa 62:11; Zec 9:9

*a*5 Zech. 9:9 *b*9 A Hebrew expression meaning "Save!" which became an exclamation of praise; also in verse 15

**21:9** c Ps 118:26
**21:11** d Jn 6:14; 7:40
**21:13** e Isa 56:7 f Jer 7:11
**21:16** g Ps 8:2
**21:21** h Mt 17:20; Lk 17:6; Jas 1:6
**21:22** i Mt 7:7

"Blessed is he who comes in the name of
the Lord!"[a][c]
"Hosanna[b] in the highest!"

10 When Jesus entered Jerusalem, the whole city was stirred and asked, "Who is this?"

11 The crowds answered, "This is Jesus, the prophet[d] from Nazareth in Galilee."

## Jesus at the Temple

12 Jesus entered the temple area and drove out all who were buying and selling there. He overturned the tables of the money changers and the benches of those selling doves. 13 "It is written," he said to them, " 'My house will be called a house of prayer,'[c][e] but you are making it a 'den of robbers.'[d]"[f]

14 The blind and the lame came to him at the temple, and he healed them. 15 But when the chief priests and the teachers of the law saw the wonderful things he did and the children shouting in the temple area, "Hosanna to the Son of David," they were indignant.

16 "Do you hear what these children are saying?" they asked him.

"Yes," replied Jesus, "have you never read,

" 'From the lips of children and infants
you have ordained praise'[e]?"[g]

17 And he left them and went out of the city to Bethany, where he spent the night.

## The Fig Tree Withers

18 Early in the morning, as he was on his way back to the city, he was hungry. 19 Seeing a fig tree by the road, he went up to it but found nothing on it except leaves. Then he said to it, "May you never bear fruit again!" Immediately the tree withered.

20 When the disciples saw this, they were amazed. "How did the fig tree wither so quickly?" they asked.

21 Jesus replied, "I tell you the truth, if you have faith and do not doubt,[h] not only can you do what was done to the fig tree, but also you can say to this mountain, 'Go, throw yourself into the sea,' and it will be done. 22 If you believe, you will receive whatever you ask for[i] in prayer."

**21:23** j Ac 4:7
**21:26** k Mk 6:20
**21:28** l ver 33
**21:31** m Lk 7:29 n Lk 7:50
**21:32** o Mt 3:1-12 p Lk 3:12,13
**21:33** q Ps 80:8

## The Authority of Jesus Questioned

23 Jesus entered the temple courts, and, while he was teaching, the chief priests and the elders of the people came to him. "By what authority[j] are you doing these things?" they asked. "And who gave you this authority?"

24 Jesus replied, "I will also ask you one question. If you answer me, I will tell you by what authority I am doing these things. 25 John's baptism—where did it come from? Was it from heaven, or from men?"

They discussed it among themselves and said, "If we say, 'From heaven,' he will ask, 'Then why didn't you believe him?' 26 But if we say, 'From men'—we are afraid of the people, for they all hold that John was a prophet."[k]

27 So they answered Jesus, "We don't know."

Then he said, "Neither will I tell you by what authority I am doing these things.

## The Parable of the Two Sons

28 "What do you think? There was a man who had two sons. He went to the first and said, 'Son, go and work today in the vineyard.'[l]

29 " 'I will not,' he answered, but later he changed his mind and went.

30 "Then the father went to the other son and said the same thing. He answered, 'I will, sir,' but he did not go.

31 "Which of the two did what his father wanted?"

"The first," they answered.

Jesus said to them, "I tell you the truth, the tax collectors[m] and the prostitutes[n] are entering the kingdom of God ahead of you. 32 For John came to you to show you the way of righteousness,[o] and you did not believe him, but the tax collectors[p] and the prostitutes did. And even after you saw this, you did not repent and believe him.

## The Parable of the Tenants

33 "Listen to another parable: There was a landowner who planted[q] a vineyard. He put a wall around it, dug a winepress in it

[a] 9 Psalm 118:26 [b] 9 A Hebrew expression meaning "Save!" which became an exclamation of praise; also in verse 15
[c] 13 Isaiah 56:7 [d] 13 Jer. 7:11 [e] 16 Psalm 8:2

21:33
r Isa 5:1–7
s Mt 25:14,15
21:35
t 2Ch 24:21;
Mt 23:34,37;
Heb 11:36,37
21:38
u Heb 1:2
v Ps 2:8
21:41
w Ac 13:46;
18:6; 28:28
21:42
x Ps 118:22,23;
Ac 4:11
21:43
y Mt 8:12
21:46
z ver 11,26
22:2
a Mt 13:24
22:3
b Mt 21:34

and built a watchtower.[r] Then he rented the
vineyard to some farmers and went away
on a journey.[s] 34When the harvest time ap-
proached, he sent his servants to the tenants
to collect his fruit.
35"The tenants seized his servants; they
beat one, killed another, and stoned a third.[t]
36Then he sent other servants to them, more
than the first time, and the tenants treated
them the same way. 37Last of all, he sent his
son to them. 'They will respect my son,'
he said.
38"But when the tenants saw the son, they
said to each other, 'This is the heir.[u] Come,
let's kill him and take his inheritance.'[v] 39So
they took him and threw him out of the vine-
yard and killed him.
40"Therefore, when the owner of the
vineyard comes, what will he do to those
tenants?"
41"He will bring those wretches to a
wretched end," they replied, "and he will rent
the vineyard to other tenants,[w] who will give
him his share of the crop at harvest time."
42Jesus said to them, "Have you never
read in the Scriptures:

" 'The stone the builders rejected
has become the capstone[a];
the Lord has done this,
and it is marvelous in our eyes'[b]?[x]

43"Therefore I tell you that the kingdom
of God will be taken away from you[y] and
given to a people who will produce its fruit.
44He who falls on this stone will be bro-
ken to pieces, but he on whom it falls will
be crushed."[c]
45When the chief priests and the Phari-
sees heard Jesus' parables, they knew he
was talking about them. 46They looked for
a way to arrest him, but they were afraid of
the crowd because the people held that he
was a prophet.[z]

## The Parable of the Wedding Banquet

22 Jesus spoke to them again in par-
ables, saying: 2"The kingdom of
heaven is like[a] a king who prepared a wed-
ding banquet for his son. 3He sent his ser-
vants[b] to those who had been invited to the
banquet to tell them to come, but they re-
fused to come.
4"Then he sent some more servants[c] and
said, 'Tell those who have been invited that
I have prepared my dinner: My oxen and
fattened cattle have been butchered, and ev-
erything is ready. Come to the wedding ban-
quet.'
5"But they paid no attention and went
off—one to his field, another to his business.
6The rest seized his servants, mistreated
them and killed them. 7The king was en-
raged. He sent his army and destroyed those
murderers[d] and burned their city.
8"Then he said to his servants, 'The wed-
ding banquet is ready, but those I invited
did not deserve to come. 9Go to the street
corners and invite to the banquet anyone
you find.' 10So the servants went out into
the streets and gathered all the people they
could find, both good and bad, and the wed-
ding hall was filled with guests.
11"But when the king came in to see the
guests, he noticed a man there who was not
wearing wedding clothes. 12'Friend,'[e] he
asked, 'how did you get in here without wed-
ding clothes?' The man was speechless.
13"Then the king told the attendants, 'Tie
him hand and foot, and throw him outside,
into the darkness, where there will be weep-
ing and gnashing of teeth.'[f]
14"For many are invited, but few are cho-
sen."

## Paying Taxes to Caesar

15Then the Pharisees went out and laid
plans to trap him in his words. 16They sent
their disciples to him along with the Hero-
dians.[g] "Teacher," they said, "we know you
are a man of integrity and that you teach the
way of God in accordance with the truth.
You aren't swayed by men, because you pay
no attention to who they are. 17Tell us then,
what is your opinion? Is it right to pay taxes[h]
to Caesar or not?"
18But Jesus, knowing their evil intent,
said, "You hypocrites, why are you trying
to trap me? 19Show me the coin used for pay-
ing the tax." They brought him a denarius,
20and he asked them, "Whose portrait is
this? And whose inscription?"

22:4
c Mt 21:36
22:7
d Lk 19:27
22:12
e Mt 20:13; 26:50
22:13
f Mt 8:12
22:16
g Mk 3:6
22:17
h Mt 17:25

[a]42 Or *cornerstone* [b]42 Psalm 118:22,23 [c]44 Some manuscripts do not have verse 44.

21"Caesar's," they replied.

Then he said to them, "Give to Caesar what is Caesar's,[i] and to God what is God's."

22When they heard this, they were amazed. So they left him and went away.

## Marriage at the Resurrection

23That same day the Sadducees, who say there is no resurrection,[j] came to him with a question. 24"Teacher," they said, "Moses told us that if a man dies without having children, his brother must marry the widow and have children for him.[k] 25Now there were seven brothers among us. The first one married and died, and since he had no children, he left his wife to his brother. 26The same thing happened to the second and third brother, right on down to the seventh. 27Finally, the woman died. 28Now then, at the resurrection, whose wife will she be of the seven, since all of them were married to her?"

29Jesus replied, "You are in error because you do not know the Scriptures[l] or the power of God. 30At the resurrection people will neither marry nor be given in marriage; they will be like the angels in heaven. 31But about the resurrection of the dead—have you not read what God said to you, 32'I am the God of Abraham, the God of Isaac, and the God of Jacob'[a]?[m] He is not the God of the dead but of the living."

33When the crowds heard this, they were astonished at his teaching.[n]

## The Greatest Commandment

34Hearing that Jesus had silenced the Sadducees, the Pharisees got together. 35One of them, an expert in the law,[o] tested him with this question: 36"Teacher, which is the greatest commandment in the Law?"

37Jesus replied: "'Love the Lord your God with all your heart and with all your soul and with all your mind.'[b][p] 38This is the first and greatest commandment. 39And the second is like it: 'Love your neighbor as yourself.'[c][q] 40All the Law and the Prophets hang on these two commandments."[r]

## Whose Son Is the Christ?

41While the Pharisees were gathered together, Jesus asked them, 42"What do you think about the Christ[d]? Whose son is he?"

"The son of David," they replied.

43He said to them, "How is it then that David, speaking by the Spirit, calls him 'Lord'? For he says,

44 "'The Lord said to my Lord:
"Sit at my right hand
until I put your enemies
under your feet."'[e][s]

45If then David calls him 'Lord,' how can he be his son?" 46No one could say a word in reply, and from that day on no one dared to ask him any more questions.[t]

## Seven Woes

23 Then Jesus said to the crowds and to his disciples: 2"The teachers of the law and the Pharisees sit in Moses' seat. 3So you must obey them and do everything they tell you. But do not do what they do, for they do not practice what they preach. 4They tie up heavy loads and put them on men's shoulders, but they themselves are not willing to lift a finger to move them.[u]

5"Everything they do is done for men to see:[v] They make their phylacteries[f][w] wide and the tassels on their garments long; 6they love the place of honor at banquets and the most important seats in the synagogues;[x] 7they love to be greeted in the marketplaces and to have men call them 'Rabbi.'

8"But you are not to be called 'Rabbi,' for you have only one Master and you are all brothers. 9And do not call anyone on earth 'father,' for you have one Father, and he is in heaven. 10Nor are you to be called 'teacher,' for you have one Teacher, the Christ.[d] 11The greatest among you will be your servant.[y] 12For whoever exalts himself will be humbled, and whoever humbles himself will be exalted.[z]

13"Woe to you, teachers of the law and Pharisees, you hypocrites! You shut the kingdom of heaven in men's faces. You your-

**22:21** i Ro 13:7
**22:23** j Ac 23:8
**22:24** k Dt 25:5,6
**22:29** l Jn 20:9
**22:32** m Ex 3:6; Ac 7:32
**22:33** n Mt 7:28
**22:35** o Lk 7:30; 10:25; 11:45
**22:37** p Dt 6:5
**22:39** q Lev 19:18; Mt 19:19
**22:40** r Mt 7:12
**22:44** s Ps 110:1; Ac 2:34,35; Heb 1:13; 10:13
**22:46** t Mk 12:34
**23:4** u Lk 11:46
**23:5** v Mt 6:1,2,5,16 w Dt 6:8
**23:6** x Lk 11:43
**23:11** y Mt 20:26
**23:12** z Lk 14:11

[a]32 Exodus 3:6 [b]37 Deut. 6:5 [c]39 Lev. 19:18 [d]42,10 Or *Messiah* [e]44 Psalm 110:1 [f]5 That is, boxes containing Scripture verses, worn on forehead and arm

**23:13** a Lk11:52
**23:16** b ver24 c Mt5:33–35
**23:17** d Ex30:29
**23:19** e Ex29:37
**23:22** f Mt5:34
**23:23** g Lk11:42
**23:25** h Mk7:4 i Lk11:39
**23:27** j Lk11:44
**23:29** k Lk11:47,48

selves do not enter, nor will you let those en-
ter who are trying to.[a][a]
15“Woe to you, teachers of the law and
Pharisees, you hypocrites! You travel over
land and sea to win a single convert, and
when he becomes one, you make him twice
as much a son of hell as you are.
16“Woe to you, blind guides![b] You say, ‘If
anyone swears by the temple, it means noth-
ing; but if anyone swears by the gold of the
temple, he is bound by his oath.’[c] 17You blind
fools! Which is greater: the gold, or the tem-
ple that makes the gold sacred?[d] 18You also
say, ‘If anyone swears by the altar, it means
nothing; but if anyone swears by the gift on
it, he is bound by his oath.’ 19You blind men!
Which is greater: the gift, or the altar that
makes the gift sacred?[e] 20Therefore, he who
swears by the altar swears by it and by every-
thing on it. 21And he who swears by the tem-
ple swears by it and by the one who dwells in
it. 22And he who swears by heaven swears by
God’s throne and by the one who sits on it.[f]
23“Woe to you, teachers of the law and Phar-
isees, you hypocrites! You give a tenth of your
spices—mint, dill and cummin. But you
have neglected the more important matters
of the law—justice, mercy and faithfulness.[g]
You should have practiced the latter, without
neglecting the former. 24You blind guides!
You strain out a gnat but swallow a camel.
25“Woe to you, teachers of the law and
Pharisees, you hypocrites! You clean the
outside of the cup and dish,[h] but inside
they are full of greed and self-indulgence.[i]
26Blind Pharisee! First clean the inside of
the cup and dish, and then the outside also
will be clean.
27“Woe to you, teachers of the law and
Pharisees, you hypocrites! You are like
whitewashed tombs,[j] which look beautiful
on the outside but on the inside are full of
dead men’s bones and everything unclean.
28In the same way, on the outside you appear
to people as righteous but on the inside you
are full of hypocrisy and wickedness.
29“Woe to you, teachers of the law and
Pharisees, you hypocrites! You build tombs
for the prophets[k] and decorate the graves of
the righteous. 30And you say, ‘If we had lived
in the days of our forefathers, we would
not have taken part with them in shedding
the blood of the prophets.’ 31So you testify
against yourselves that you are the descen-
dants of those who murdered the prophets.[l]
32Fill up, then, the measure of the sin of
your forefathers!
33“You snakes! You brood of vipers![m]
How will you escape being condemned to
hell? 34Therefore I am sending you prophets
and wise men and teachers. Some of them
you will kill and crucify;[n] others you will
flog in your synagogues[o] and pursue from
town to town. 35And so upon you will come
all the righteous blood that has been shed
on earth, from the blood of righteous Abel[p]
to the blood of Zechariah son of Berekiah,
whom you murdered between the temple
and the altar.[q] 36I tell you the truth, all this
will come upon this generation.
37“O Jerusalem, Jerusalem, you who kill
the prophets and stone those sent to you,[r]
how often I have longed to gather your chil-
dren together, as a hen gathers her chicks
under her wings, but you were not willing.
38Look, your house is left to you desolate.
39For I tell you, you will not see me again un-
til you say, ‘Blessed is he who comes in the
name of the Lord.’[b]”[s]

## Signs of the End of the Age

**24** Jesus left the temple and was walk-
ing away when his disciples came
up to him to call his attention to its build-
ings. 2“Do you see all these things?” he
asked. “I tell you the truth, not one stone
here will be left on another;[t] every one will
be thrown down.”
3As Jesus was sitting on the Mount of
Olives, the disciples came to him privately.
“Tell us,” they said, “when will this happen,
and what will be the sign of your coming
and of the end of the age?”
4Jesus answered: “Watch out that no one
deceives you. 5For many will come in my
name, claiming, ‘I am the Christ,[c]’ and will
deceive many.[u] 6You will hear of wars and
rumors of wars, but see to it that you are not
alarmed. Such things must happen, but the
end is still to come. 7Nation will rise against

**23:31** l Ac7:51–52
**23:33** m Mt3:7
**23:34** n Lk11:49 o Mt10:17
**23:35** p Ge4:8 q 2Ch24:21
**23:37** r 2Ch24:21
**23:39** s Ps118:26; Mt21:9
**24:2** t Lk19:44
**24:5** u ver11,23,24

[a]13 Some manuscripts *to.* [14]*Woe to you, teachers of the law and Pharisees, you hypocrites! You devour widows’ houses and for a show make lengthy prayers. Therefore you will be punished more severely.* [b]39 Psalm 118:26 [c]5 Or *Messiah*; also in verse 23

nation, and kingdom against kingdom.[v] There will be famines and earthquakes in various places. 8 All these are the beginning of birth pains.

9 "Then you will be handed over to be persecuted[w] and put to death,[x] and you will be hated by all nations because of me. 10 At that time many will turn away from the faith and will betray and hate each other, 11 and many false prophets will appear and deceive many people. 12 Because of the increase of wickedness, the love of most will grow cold, 13 but he who stands firm to the end will be saved.[y] 14 And this gospel of the kingdom will be preached in the whole world[z] as a testimony to all nations, and then the end will come.

15 "So when you see standing in the holy place 'the abomination that causes desolation,'[a][a] spoken of through the prophet Daniel—let the reader understand— 16 then let those who are in Judea flee to the mountains. 17 Let no one on the roof of his house go down to take anything out of the house. 18 Let no one in the field go back to get his cloak. 19 How dreadful it will be in those days for pregnant women and nursing mothers![b] 20 Pray that your flight will not take place in winter or on the Sabbath. 21 For then there will be great distress, unequaled from the beginning of the world until now—and never to be equaled again.[c] 22 If those days had not been cut short, no one would survive, but for the sake of the elect those days will be shortened. 23 At that time if anyone says to you, 'Look, here is the Christ!' or, 'There he is!' do not believe it.[d] 24 For false Christs and false prophets will appear and perform great signs and miracles[e] to deceive even the elect—if that were possible. 25 See, I have told you ahead of time.

26 "So if anyone tells you, 'There he is, out in the desert,' do not go out; or, 'Here he is, in the inner rooms,' do not believe it. 27 For as lightning[f] that comes from the east is visible even in the west, so will be the coming of the Son of Man. 28 Wherever there is a carcass, there the vultures will gather.[g]

29 "Immediately after the distress of those days

"'the sun will be darkened,
and the moon will not give its light;
the stars will fall from the sky,
and the heavenly bodies will be shaken.'[b][h]

30 "At that time the sign of the Son of Man will appear in the sky, and all the nations of the earth will mourn. They will see the Son of Man coming on the clouds of the sky,[i] with power and great glory. 31 And he will send his angels with a loud trumpet call,[j] and they will gather his elect from the four winds, from one end of the heavens to the other.

32 "Now learn this lesson from the fig tree: As soon as its twigs get tender and its leaves come out, you know that summer is near. 33 Even so, when you see all these things, you know that it[c] is near, right at the door.[k] 34 I tell you the truth, this generation[d] will certainly not pass away until all these things have happened.[l] 35 Heaven and earth will pass away, but my words will never pass away.

## The Day and Hour Unknown

36 "No one knows about that day or hour, not even the angels in heaven, nor the Son,[e] but only the Father.[m] 37 As it was in the days of Noah,[n] so it will be at the coming of the Son of Man. 38 For in the days before the flood, people were eating and drinking, marrying and giving in marriage, up to the day Noah entered the ark; 39 and they knew nothing about what would happen until the flood came and took them all away. That is how it will be at the coming of the Son of Man. 40 Two men will be in the field; one will be taken and the other left.[o] 41 Two women will be grinding with a hand mill; one will be taken and the other left.

42 "Therefore keep watch, because you do not know on what day your Lord will come.[p] 43 But understand this: If the owner of the house had known at what time of night the thief was coming,[q] he would have kept watch and would not have let his house be broken into. 44 So you also must be ready, because the Son of Man will come at an hour when you do not expect him.

45 "Who then is the faithful and wise ser-

**24:7** v Isa 19:2
**24:9** w Mt 10:17; x Jn 16:2
**24:13** y Mt 10:22
**24:14** z Ro 10:18; Col 1:6,23; Rev 3:10; 16:14
**24:15** a Da 9:27; 12:11
**24:19** b Lk 23:29
**24:21** c Joel 2:2
**24:23** d Lk 17:23; 21:8
**24:24** e 2Th 2:9–11
**24:27** f Lk 17:24
**24:28** g Lk 17:37
**24:29** h Eze 32:7; Joel 2:10,31
**24:30** i Da 7:13; Rev 1:7
**24:31** j Isa 27:13; 1Co 15:52
**24:33** k Jas 5:9
**24:34** l Mt 16:28
**24:36** m Ac 1:7
**24:37** n Ge 6:5
**24:40** o Lk 17:34
**24:42** p Mt 25:13
**24:43** q Lk 12:39

[a] 15 Daniel 9:27; 11:31; 12:11 [b] 29 Isaiah 13:10; 34:4 [c] 33 Or *he* [d] 34 Or *race* [e] 36 Some manuscripts do not have *nor the Son.*

**24:45** r Mt 25:21,23
**24:46** s Rev 16:15
**24:47** t Mt 25:21,23
**24:51** u Mt 8:12
**25:1** v Mt 13:24; w Rev 19:7
**25:5** x 1Th 5:6
**25:13** y Mt 24:42,44

vant,[r] whom the master has put in charge of
the servants in his household to give them
their food at the proper time? 46 It will be
good for that servant whose master finds
him doing so when he returns.[s] 47 I tell you
the truth, he will put him in charge of all
his possessions.[t] 48 But suppose that servant
is wicked and says to himself, 'My master
is staying away a long time,' 49 and he then
begins to beat his fellow servants and to
eat and drink with drunkards. 50 The mas-
ter of that servant will come on a day when
he does not expect him and at an hour he
is not aware of. 51 He will cut him to pieces
and assign him a place with the hypocrites,
where there will be weeping and gnashing
of teeth.[u]

## The Parable of the Ten Virgins

25 "At that time the kingdom of
heaven will be like[v] ten virgins who
took their lamps and went out to meet the
bridegroom.[w] 2 Five of them were foolish
and five were wise. 3 The foolish ones took
their lamps but did not take any oil with
them. 4 The wise, however, took oil in jars
along with their lamps. 5 The bridegroom
was a long time in coming, and they all be-
came drowsy and fell asleep.[x]

6 "At midnight the cry rang out: 'Here's
the bridegroom! Come out to meet him!'

7 "Then all the virgins woke up and
trimmed their lamps. 8 The foolish ones said
to the wise, 'Give us some of your oil; our
lamps are going out.'

9 " 'No,' they replied, 'there may not be
enough for both us and you. Instead, go to
those who sell oil and buy some for your-
selves.'

10 "But while they were on their way to buy
the oil, the bridegroom arrived. The virgins
who were ready went in with him to the wed-
ding banquet. And the door was shut.

11 "Later the others also came. 'Sir! Sir!'
they said. 'Open the door for us!'

12 "But he replied, 'I tell you the truth, I
don't know you.'

13 "Therefore keep watch, because you do
not know the day or the hour.[y]

**25:14** z Mt 21:33; Lk 19:12
**25:15** a Mt 18:24,25
**25:19** b Mt 18:23
**25:21** c Mt 24:45,47
**25:23** d ver 21

## The Parable of the Talents

14 "Again, it will be like a man going on
a journey,[z] who called his servants and
entrusted his property to them. 15 To one he
gave five talents[a] of money, to another two
talents, and to another one talent, each ac-
cording to his ability.[a] Then he went on his
journey. 16 The man who had received the
five talents went at once and put his money
to work and gained five more. 17 So also, the
one with the two talents gained two more.
18 But the man who had received the one tal-
ent went off, dug a hole in the ground and
hid his master's money.

19 "After a long time the master of those
servants returned and settled accounts with
them.[b] 20 The man who had received the five
talents brought the other five. 'Master,' he
said, 'you entrusted me with five talents.
See, I have gained five more.'

21 "His master replied, 'Well done, good
and faithful servant! You have been faithful
with a few things; I will put you in charge
of many things.[c] Come and share your mas-
ter's happiness!'

22 "The man with the two talents also
came. 'Master,' he said, 'you entrusted me
with two talents; see, I have gained two
more.'

23 "His master replied, 'Well done, good
and faithful servant! You have been faithful
with a few things; I will put you in charge
of many things.[d] Come and share your mas-
ter's happiness!'

24 "Then the man who had received the
one talent came. 'Master,' he said, 'I knew
that you are a hard man, harvesting where
you have not sown and gathering where you
have not scattered seed. 25 So I was afraid
and went out and hid your talent in the
ground. See, here is what belongs to you.'

26 "His master replied, 'You wicked, lazy
servant! So you knew that I harvest where I
have not sown and gather where I have not
scattered seed? 27 Well then, you should have
put my money on deposit with the bankers,
so that when I returned I would have re-
ceived it back with interest.

28 " 'Take the talent from him and give it
to the one who has the ten talents. 29 For ev-
eryone who has will be given more, and he

[a]15 A talent was worth more than a thousand dollars.

# Wise and Foolish Virgins

## Preparing for Christ

Many who read the parable of the ten virgins in Matthew 25 wonder how it can fit with the notion of Jesus Christ as the compassionate, merciful Savior. After all, was it not Jesus himself who, when asked by Peter how many times he had to forgive those who wronged him, gave the answer of 77 times? Didn't Paul plead with us to be kind, compassionate and forgiving of each other? Isn't one of the most tender and moving passages in the New Testament the one in which Paul requested Philemon to take Onesimus back and not punish him (see Phm 8–21)? Think of the parables about the Good Samaritan, who took care of an enemy (see Lk 10:25–37), and the servant who was punished because he showed no mercy when he himself had received mercy (see Lk 20:9–16). The Bible is so full of examples of mercy that it seems that the five foolish virgins got a raw deal.

The five foolish virgins, like the five wise virgins, knew exactly what they needed to do. The precise time of the anticipated wedding procession wasn't announced, but the customs of the day told them how to be prepared: "Bring your lamps. Bring the oil. Trim the wicks. See that you're ready." For whatever reason, the foolish virgins chose not to do so. The five wise virgins, on the other hand, were obedient to do what was required—and therefore they were prepared when the time arrived.

This teaches us several things. First, perhaps we should not question instructions, suggestions and directions we are given—even if they seem mundane, trivial, boring or "beneath" our creativity, uniqueness and specialness. Sometimes we just don't know the full picture and should trust instructions given by God.

Second, obedience is better than sacrifice. How badly will it hurt us to follow the instructions? We should remember to compare the consequences of obedience and disobedience *before* we act.

This parable tells us to be ready because we don't know when Christ will call us. Just because he didn't come today doesn't mean he's not coming tonight or tomorrow. Therefore, we must be obedient, consistent and committed to the glory and honor of God. We cannot be found unprepared like the five foolish virgins.

—A. Bouie

### reflection

*How good are you at listening to instructions from God? From others?*

*Pray for wisdom to weigh the cost of obedience and disobedience before acting.*

### read

Matthew 24:42—25:13; 1 Thessalonians 5:1–6. See also the Inspire Notes "Discernment," "Submission" and "Faith."

For the next Women of the Bible note, go to page 1157.

will have an abundance. Whoever does not
have, even what he has will be taken from
him.[e] 30And throw that worthless servant
outside, into the darkness, where there will
be weeping and gnashing of teeth.'[f]

### The Sheep and the Goats

31"When the Son of Man comes[g] in his
glory, and all the angels with him, he will
sit on his throne[h] in heavenly glory. 32All the
nations will be gathered before him, and he
will separate the people one from another
as a shepherd separates the sheep from the
goats.[i] 33He will put the sheep on his right
and the goats on his left.

34"Then the King will say to those on his
right, 'Come, you who are blessed by my Fa-
ther; take your inheritance, the kingdom[j]
prepared for you since the creation of the
world.[k] 35For I was hungry and you gave me
something to eat, I was thirsty and you gave
me something to drink, I was a stranger and
you invited me in,[l] 36I needed clothes and
you clothed me,[m] I was sick and you looked
after me, I was in prison and you came to
visit me.'[n]

37"Then the righteous will answer him,
'Lord, when did we see you hungry and feed
you, or thirsty and give you something to
drink? 38When did we see you a stranger
and invite you in, or needing clothes and
clothe you? 39When did we see you sick or in
prison and go to visit you?'

40"The King will reply, 'I tell you the
truth, whatever you did for one of the least
of these brothers of mine, you did for me.'[o]

41"Then he will say to those on his left,
'Depart from me,[p] you who are cursed, into
the eternal fire[q] prepared for the devil and
his angels.[r] 42For I was hungry and you gave
me nothing to eat, I was thirsty and you
gave me nothing to drink, 43I was a stranger
and you did not invite me in, I needed clothes
and you did not clothe me, I was sick and in
prison and you did not look after me.'

44"They also will answer, 'Lord, when did
we see you hungry or thirsty or a stranger or
needing clothes or sick or in prison, and did
not help you?'

45"He will reply, 'I tell you the truth,
whatever you did not do for one of the least
of these, you did not do for me.'[s]

46"Then they will go away to eternal pun-
ishment, but the righteous to eternal life."[t]

### The Plot Against Jesus

26 When Jesus had finished saying
all these things,[u] he said to his dis-
ciples, 2"As you know, the Passover[v] is two
days away—and the Son of Man will be
handed over to be crucified."

3Then the chief priests and the elders of
the people assembled[w] in the palace of the
high priest, whose name was Caiaphas,[x]
4and they plotted to arrest Jesus in some
sly way and kill him. 5"But not during the
Feast," they said, "or there may be a riot
among the people."

### Jesus Anointed at Bethany

6While Jesus was in Bethany[y] in the
home of a man known as Simon the Leper,
7a woman came to him with an alabaster
jar of very expensive perfume, which she
poured on his head as he was reclining at
the table.

8When the disciples saw this, they were
indignant. "Why this waste?" they asked.
9"This perfume could have been sold at
a high price and the money given to the
poor."

10Aware of this, Jesus said to them, "Why
are you bothering this woman? She has
done a beautiful thing to me. 11The poor you
will always have with you,[z] but you will not
always have me. 12When she poured this per-
fume on my body, she did it to prepare me
for burial. 13I tell you the truth, wherever
this gospel is preached throughout the
world, what she has done will also be told,
in memory of her."

### Judas Agrees to Betray Jesus

14Then one of the Twelve—the one
called Judas Iscariot—went to the chief
priests 15and asked, "What are you will-
ing to give me if I hand him over to you?"
So they counted out for him thirty silver
coins.[a] 16From then on Judas watched for an
opportunity to hand him over.

### The Lord's Supper

17On the first day of the Feast of Unleav-
ened Bread,[b] the disciples came to Jesus and

**25:29** e Mt 13:12
**25:30** f Mt 8:12
**25:31** g Mt 16:27 h Mt 19:28
**25:32** i Eze 34:17,20
**25:34** j 1Co 15:50 k Rev 13:8
**25:35** l Isa 58:7; Eze 18:7; Heb 13:2
**25:36** m Jas 2:15,16 n 2Ti 1:16
**25:40** o Pr 19:17; Mt 10:40,42
**25:41** p Mt 7:23 q Mk 9:43,48; Jude 7 r 2Pe 2:4
**25:45** s Pr 14:31
**25:46** t Da 12:2; Jn 5:29
**26:1** u Mt 7:28
**26:2** v Jn 13:1
**26:3** w Ps 2:2 x Jn 11:47–53
**26:6** y Mt 21:17
**26:11** z Dt 15:11
**26:15** a Zec 11:12
**26:17** b Ex 12:18–20

asked, "Where do you want us to make prep-
arations for you to eat the Passover?"
18 He replied, "Go into the city to a certain
man and tell him, 'The Teacher says: My
appointed time is near. I am going to cele-
brate the Passover with my disciples at your
house.'" 19 So the disciples did as Jesus had
directed them and prepared the Passover.
20 When evening came, Jesus was reclin-
ing at the table with the Twelve. 21 And while
they were eating, he said, "I tell you the
truth, one of you will betray me."

Inspire leadership FOCUS

## DOING YOUR BEST

As women who have the added responsibility of leadership, we must strive for excellence every day. To strive for excellence means to give our best effort to every job, situation and experience. Excellence has often been defined incorrectly. *The American Heritage College Dictionary* tells us *excellent* means "exceptionally good of its kind." Excellent does not mean "perfect."

In order to accomplish tasks with excellence we must be organized, have well-thought-out plans and be committed to completing tasks in spite of struggles or challenges. As leaders, we must lift our heads and do everything with a spirit of excellence.

The Lord gives us examples of how to perform to the best of our abilities. In Matthew 25:14–30, the parable of the talents, two of the three servants were rewarded when they put their talents to good use. The servant who simply buried his talent in the ground, however, angered his master. By not doing his best, not only was the servant denied a reward, but he lost the one talent he had.

As wise leaders, we must put our gifts and abilities to good use so the windows of greater opportunity will be opened on our behalf. We cannot forfeit our rewards because of fear or laziness. Putting our best foot forward sets the stage for attaining the next level and achieving success far beyond our imaginations. By taking care of business, God will trust us to handle even more. By faith, we must apply our God-given talents and abilities to serve and lead each and every day.

—V. Lowe

### read

Matthew 25:14–30; Luke 19:12–27; Colossians 3:17.

**See also** the Inspire Notes "Following God-Given Visions" and "Spiritual Discipline," and the Women of the Bible Notes "Phoebe: A Faithful Messenger" and "The 'Chosen Lady': A Woman Worth Imitating."

### WOMAN of COLOR

Are you applying a spirit of excellence to every area of your life? Are you utilizing your resources, knowledge and relationships to their fullest potential? If not, develop a list of your talents and create a personal action plan that will put your talents to good use.

For the next Inspire note, go to page 1163.

22 They were very sad and began to say to him one after the other, "Surely not I, Lord?"

23 Jesus replied, "The one who has dipped his hand into the bowl with me will betray me.[c] 24 The Son of Man will go just as it is written about him.[d] But woe to that man who betrays the Son of Man! It would be better for him if he had not been born."

25 Then Judas, the one who would betray him, said, "Surely not I, Rabbi?"

Jesus answered, "Yes, it is you."[a]

26 While they were eating, Jesus took bread, gave thanks and broke it,[e] and gave it to his disciples, saying, "Take and eat; this is my body."

27 Then he took the cup, gave thanks and offered it to them, saying, "Drink from it, all of you. 28 This is my blood of the[b] covenant,[f] which is poured out for many for the forgiveness of sins.[g] 29 I tell you, I will not drink of this fruit of the vine from now on until that day when I drink it anew with you in my Father's kingdom."

30 When they had sung a hymn, they went out to the Mount of Olives.[h]

## Jesus Predicts Peter's Denial

31 Then Jesus told them, "This very night you will all fall away on account of me, for it is written:

"'I will strike the shepherd,
and the sheep of the flock will be scattered.'[c][i]

32 But after I have risen, I will go ahead of you into Galilee."[j]

33 Peter replied, "Even if all fall away on account of you, I never will."

34 "I tell you the truth," Jesus answered, "this very night, before the rooster crows, you will disown me three times."[k]

35 But Peter declared, "Even if I have to die with you,[l] I will never disown you." And all the other disciples said the same.

## Gethsemane

36 Then Jesus went with his disciples to a place called Gethsemane, and he said to them, "Sit here while I go over there and pray." 37 He took Peter and the two sons of Zebedee[m] along with him, and he began to be sorrowful and troubled. 38 Then he said to them, "My soul is overwhelmed with sorrow[n] to the point of death. Stay here and keep watch with me."

39 Going a little farther, he fell with his face to the ground and prayed, "My Father, if it is possible, may this cup[o] be taken from me. Yet not as I will, but as you will."[p]

40 Then he returned to his disciples and found them sleeping. "Could you men not keep watch with me[q] for one hour?" he asked Peter. 41 "Watch and pray so that you will not fall into temptation. The spirit is willing, but the body is weak."

42 He went away a second time and prayed, "My Father, if it is not possible for this cup to be taken away unless I drink it, may your will be done."

43 When he came back, he again found them sleeping, because their eyes were heavy. 44 So he left them and went away once more and prayed the third time, saying the same thing.

45 Then he returned to the disciples and said to them, "Are you still sleeping and resting? Look, the hour is near, and the Son of Man is betrayed into the hands of sinners. 46 Rise, let us go! Here comes my betrayer!"

## Jesus Arrested

47 While he was still speaking, Judas, one of the Twelve, arrived. With him was a large crowd armed with swords and clubs, sent from the chief priests and the elders of the people. 48 Now the betrayer had arranged a signal with them: "The one I kiss is the man; arrest him." 49 Going at once to Jesus, Judas said, "Greetings, Rabbi!"[r] and kissed him.

50 Jesus replied, "Friend,[s] do what you came for."[d]

Then the men stepped forward, seized Jesus and arrested him. 51 With that, one of Jesus' companions reached for his sword, drew it out and struck the servant of the high priest, cutting off his ear.[t]

52 "Put your sword back in its place," Jesus said to him, "for all who draw the sword will die by the sword.[u] 53 Do you think I cannot call on my Father, and he will at once put at my disposal more than twelve legions

**26:23** c Jn 13:18
**26:24** d Isa 53; Mk 9:12; Lk 24:25–27,46; Ac 17:2,3
**26:26** e 1Co 10:16
**26:28** f Heb 9:20 g Mt 20:28
**26:30** h Mk 14:26
**26:31** i Zec 13:7; Jn 16:32
**26:32** j Mt 28:7,10,16
**26:34** k Jn 13:38
**26:35** l Jn 13:37
**26:37** m Mt 4:21
**26:38** n Jn 12:27
**26:39** o Mt 20:22 p Jn 6:38
**26:40** q ver 38
**26:49** r ver 25
**26:50** s Mt 20:13; 22:12
**26:51** t Jn 18:10
**26:52** u Ge 9:6; Rev 13:10

[a] 25 Or *"You yourself have said it"* [b] 28 Some manuscripts *the new* [c] 31 Zech. 13:7 [d] 50 Or *"Friend, why have you come?"*

**26:53** v 2Ki 6:17; Da 7:10
**26:54** w ver 24
**26:58** x Jn 18:15
**26:60** y Ps 27:12; 35:11; Ac 6:13 z Dt 19:15
**26:63** a Mt 27:12,14 b Lev 5:1
**26:64** c Ps 110:1 d Da 7:13
**26:66** e Lev 24:16; Jn 19:7
**26:67** f Mt 27:30
**26:68** g Lk 22:63–65

of angels?[v] 54 But how then would the Scriptures be fulfilled[w] that say it must happen in this way?"

55 At that time Jesus said to the crowd, "Am I leading a rebellion, that you have come out with swords and clubs to capture me? Every day I sat in the temple courts teaching, and you did not arrest me. 56 But this has all taken place that the writings of the prophets might be fulfilled." Then all the disciples deserted him and fled.

## Before the Sanhedrin

57 Those who had arrested Jesus took him to Caiaphas, the high priest, where the teachers of the law and the elders had assembled. 58 But Peter followed him at a distance, right up to the courtyard of the high priest.[x] He entered and sat down with the guards to see the outcome.

59 The chief priests and the whole Sanhedrin were looking for false evidence against Jesus so that they could put him to death. 60 But they did not find any, though many false witnesses[y] came forward.

Finally two[z] came forward 61 and declared, "This fellow said, 'I am able to destroy the temple of God and rebuild it in three days.'"

62 Then the high priest stood up and said to Jesus, "Are you not going to answer? What is this testimony that these men are bringing against you?" 63 But Jesus remained silent.[a]

The high priest said to him, "I charge you under oath[b] by the living God: Tell us if you are the Christ,[a] the Son of God."

64 "Yes, it is as you say," Jesus replied. "But I say to all of you: In the future you will see the Son of Man sitting at the right hand of the Mighty One[c] and coming on the clouds of heaven."[d]

65 Then the high priest tore his clothes and said, "He has spoken blasphemy! Why do we need any more witnesses? Look, now you have heard the blasphemy. 66 What do you think?"

"He is worthy of death,"[e] they answered.

67 Then they spit in his face and struck him with their fists.[f] Others slapped him 68 and said, "Prophesy to us, Christ. Who hit you?"[g]

## Peter Disowns Jesus

69 Now Peter was sitting out in the courtyard, and a servant girl came to him. "You also were with Jesus of Galilee," she said.

70 But he denied it before them all. "I don't know what you're talking about," he said.

71 Then he went out to the gateway, where another girl saw him and said to the people there, "This fellow was with Jesus of Nazareth."

72 He denied it again, with an oath: "I don't know the man!"

73 After a little while, those standing there went up to Peter and said, "Surely you are one of them, for your accent gives you away."

74 Then he began to call down curses on himself and he swore to them, "I don't know the man!"

Immediately a rooster crowed. 75 Then Peter remembered the word Jesus had spoken: "Before the rooster crows, you will disown me three times."[h] And he went outside and wept bitterly.

## Judas Hangs Himself

27 Early in the morning, all the chief priests and the elders of the people came to the decision to put Jesus to death.[i] 2 They bound him, led him away and handed him over[j] to Pilate, the governor.[k]

3 When Judas, who had betrayed him, saw that Jesus was condemned, he was seized with remorse and returned the thirty silver coins[l] to the chief priests and the elders. 4 "I have sinned," he said, "for I have betrayed innocent blood."

"What is that to us?" they replied. "That's your responsibility."[m]

5 So Judas threw the money into the temple and left. Then he went away and hanged himself.[n]

6 The chief priests picked up the coins and said, "It is against the law to put this into the treasury, since it is blood money." 7 So they decided to use the money to buy the potter's field as a burial place for foreigners. 8 That is why it has been called the Field of Blood[o] to this day. 9 Then what was spoken by Jeremiah the prophet was fulfilled: "They took the thirty silver coins, the price set on

**26:75** h ver 34; Jn 13:38
**27:1** i Mk 15:1; Lk 22:66
**27:2** j Mt 20:19 k Ac 3:13
**27:3** l Mt 26:14,15
**27:4** m ver 24
**27:5** n Ac 1:18
**27:8** o Ac 1:19

[a] 63 Or *Messiah*; also in verse 68

**27:12** p Mt26:63; Jn19:9
**27:13** q Mt26:62
**27:15** r Jn18:39
**27:19** s ver24
**27:20** t Ac3:14

him by the people of Israel, 10 and they used them to buy the potter's field, as the Lord commanded me."[a]

## Jesus Before Pilate

11 Meanwhile Jesus stood before the governor, and the governor asked him, "Are you the king of the Jews?"

"Yes, it is as you say," Jesus replied.

12 When he was accused by the chief priests and the elders, he gave no answer.[p] 13 Then Pilate asked him, "Don't you hear the testimony they are bringing against you?"[q] 14 But Jesus made no reply, not even to a single charge—to the great amazement of the governor.

15 Now it was the governor's custom at the Feast to release a prisoner[r] chosen by the crowd. 16 At that time they had a notorious prisoner, called Barabbas. 17 So when the crowd had gathered, Pilate asked them, "Which one do you want me to release to you: Barabbas, or Jesus who is called Christ?" 18 For he knew it was out of envy that they had handed Jesus over to him.

19 While Pilate was sitting on the judge's seat, his wife sent him this message: "Don't have anything to do with that innocent[s] man, for I have suffered a great deal today in a dream because of him."

20 But the chief priests and the elders persuaded the crowd to ask for Barabbas and to have Jesus executed.[t]

21 "Which of the two do you want me to release to you?" asked the governor.

"Barabbas," they answered.

22 "What shall I do, then, with Jesus who is called Christ?" Pilate asked.

They all answered, "Crucify him!"

23 "Why? What crime has he committed?" asked Pilate.

But they shouted all the louder, "Crucify him!"

24 When Pilate saw that he was getting nowhere, but that instead an uproar[u] was starting, he took water and washed his hands in front of the crowd. "I am innocent of this man's blood,"[v] he said. "It is your responsibility!"

25 All the people answered, "Let his blood be on us and on our children!"[w]

26 Then he released Barabbas to them. But he had Jesus flogged,[x] and handed him over to be crucified.

## The Soldiers Mock Jesus

27 Then the governor's soldiers took Jesus into the Praetorium and gathered the whole company of soldiers around him. 28 They stripped him and put a scarlet robe on him, 29 and then twisted together a crown of thorns and set it on his head. They put a staff in his right hand and knelt in front of him and mocked him. "Hail, king of the Jews!" they said.[y] 30 They spit on him, and took the staff and struck him on the head again and again.[z] 31 After they had mocked him, they took off the robe and put his own clothes on him. Then they led him away to crucify him.[a]

## The Crucifixion

32 As they were going out,[b] they met a man from Cyrene, named Simon, and they forced him to carry the cross.[c] 33 They came to a place called Golgotha (which means The Place of the Skull).[d] 34 There they offered Jesus wine to drink, mixed with gall;[e] but

**27:24** u Mt26:5 v Dt21:6–8
**27:25** w Jos2:19; Ac5:28
**27:26** x Isa53:5
**27:29** y Isa53:3
**27:30** z Mt26:67
**27:31** a Isa53:7
**27:32** b Heb13:12 c Mk15:21
**27:33** d Jn19:17
**27:34** e Ps69:21

[a]10 See Zech. 11:12,13; Jer. 19:1–13; 32:6–9.

### *The African Presence*

**Matthew 27:32**

Simon of Cyrene was from an area located on the northern coast of Africa. Cyrene was the chief city in Libya and North Africa.

**27:35** f Ps 22:18
**27:36** g ver 54
**27:39** h Ps 22:7; 109:25
**27:40** i Mt 26:61; Jn 2:19
**27:42** j Jn 1:49
**27:43** k Ps 22:8
**27:46** l Ps 22:1
**27:48** m Ps 69:21
**27:51** n Ex 26:31–33
**27:54** o ver 36

after tasting it, he refused to drink it.
35When they had crucified him, they divided
up his clothes by casting lots.[a,f] 36And sitting
down, they kept watch[g] over him there.
37Above his head they placed the written
charge against him: THIS IS JESUS, THE KING OF
THE JEWS. 38Two robbers were crucified with
him, one on his right and one on his left.
39Those who passed by hurled insults at him,
shaking their heads[h] 40and saying, "You who
are going to destroy the temple and build it
in three days,[i] save yourself! Come down
from the cross, if you are the Son of God!"
41In the same way the chief priests, the
teachers of the law and the elders mocked
him. 42"He saved others," they said, "but he
can't save himself! He's the King of Israel![j]
Let him come down now from the cross, and
we will believe in him. 43He trusts in God.
Let God rescue him[k] now if he wants him,
for he said, 'I am the Son of God.' " 44In the
same way the robbers who were crucified
with him also heaped insults on him.

## The Death of Jesus

45From the sixth hour until the ninth hour
darkness came over all the land. 46About the
ninth hour Jesus cried out in a loud voice,
*"Eloi, Eloi,*[b] *lama sabachthani?"*—which
means, "My God, my God, why have you
forsaken me?"[c,l]
47When some of those standing there
heard this, they said, "He's calling Elijah."
48Immediately one of them ran and got a
sponge. He filled it with wine vinegar,[m] put
it on a stick, and offered it to Jesus to drink.
49The rest said, "Now leave him alone. Let's
see if Elijah comes to save him."
50And when Jesus had cried out again in a
loud voice, he gave up his spirit.
51At that moment the curtain of the tem-
ple[n] was torn in two from top to bottom. The
earth shook and the rocks split. 52The tombs
broke open and the bodies of many holy
people who had died were raised to life.
53They came out of the tombs, and after
Jesus' resurrection they went into the holy
city and appeared to many people.
54When the centurion and those with
him who were guarding[o] Jesus saw the
earthquake and all that had happened, they
were terrified, and exclaimed, "Surely he
was the Son[d] of God!"
55Many women were there, watching
from a distance. They had followed Jesus
from Galilee to care for his needs.[p] 56Among
them were Mary Magdalene, Mary the
mother of James and Joses, and the mother
of Zebedee's sons.

## The Burial of Jesus

57As evening approached, there came a
rich man from Arimathea, named Joseph,
who had himself become a disciple of Jesus.
58Going to Pilate, he asked for Jesus' body,
and Pilate ordered that it be given to him.
59Joseph took the body, wrapped it in a clean
linen cloth, 60and placed it in his own new
tomb[q] that he had cut out of the rock. He
rolled a big stone in front of the entrance to
the tomb and went away. 61Mary Magdalene
and the other Mary were sitting there oppo-
site the tomb.

## The Guard at the Tomb

62The next day, the one after Preparation
Day, the chief priests and the Pharisees went
to Pilate. 63"Sir," they said, "we remember
that while he was still alive that deceiver
said, 'After three days I will rise again.'[r]
64So give the order for the tomb to be made
secure until the third day. Otherwise, his
disciples may come and steal the body and
tell the people that he has been raised from
the dead. This last deception will be worse
than the first."
65"Take a guard," Pilate answered. "Go,
make the tomb as secure as you know how."
66So they went and made the tomb secure
by putting a seal[s] on the stone and posting
the guard.

## The Resurrection

28 After the Sabbath, at dawn on the
first day of the week, Mary Mag-
dalene and the other Mary[t] went to look at
the tomb.
2There was a violent earthquake, for an
angel of the Lord came down from heaven
and, going to the tomb, rolled back the stone

**27:55** p Lk 8:2,3
**27:60** q Mk 16:4
**27:63** r Mt 16:21
**27:66** s Da 6:17
**28:1** t Mt 27:56

[a]35 A few late manuscripts *lots that the word spoken by the prophet might be fulfilled: "They divided my garments among themselves and cast lots for my clothing"* (Psalm 22:18) [b]46 Some manuscripts *Eli, Eli* [c]46 Psalm 22:1 [d]54 Or *a son*

# Mary Magdalene

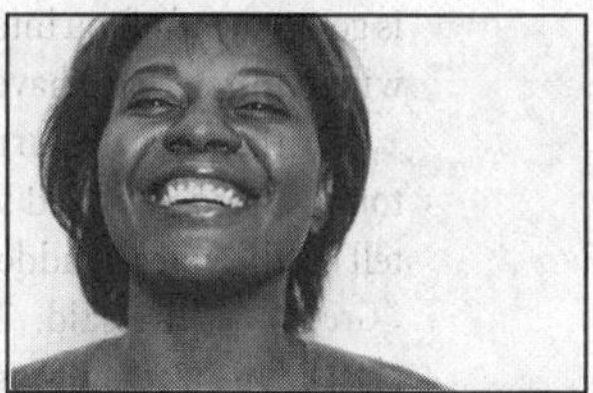

## Setting Her Reputation Straight

Mary Magdalene is specifically mentioned 14 times in the Gospels. On nine occasions she is in the company of other women, and the fact that she is usually named first suggests that she more than likely played a leadership role among Jesus' female followers.

All four Gospels note that Mary was among the witnesses of Christ's resurrection. And depending on which Gospel you are reading, either Jesus or an angel commissioned her to go and tell the disciples that he had risen from the dead. This commissioning to "go and tell" is an affirmation for contemporary women; Jesus was and is intentionally gender-inclusive, establishing the place of women in the proclamation of the gospel through Mary.

But who was this woman before her encounters with Christ? Some have said she was a prostitute. If Mary was indeed a prostitute, to have omitted this important fact from her title is contrary to the way in which Biblical writers typically reported the stories in the Scriptures. A case in point is Rahab, an Old Testament woman (see Jos 2:1–22; 6:22–25) who is listed in the New Testament among the faithful servants, yet she never escaped the stigma of the title "prostitute" (Heb 11:31; Jas 2:25).

More important than the fact that Mary Magdalene is presumed to have been a prostitute is the condition from which Jesus liberated her: She had been possessed with seven demons, a fact mentioned in both Mark 16:9 and Luke 8:2. Old Testament scholar Renita Weems, in *Just a Sister Away* (San Diego: LuraMedia, 1988), ventures to name those seven demons—using names that collectively describe mental, emotional and spiritual conditions that women of all ages have struggled with. They are depression, fear, low self-esteem, doubt, procrastination, bitterness and self-pity. We could add to this list: jealousy, guilt, envy, discord, idolatry and an unforgiving spirit.

But the Great Physician touched Mary Magdalene and made her whole. She became a leader among women, a proclaimer of the gospel to the apostles, an evangelist to the marginalized and a servant in God's kingdom.

For all women, Mary Magdalene is a model of a wounded person who was healed and made whole by the love of Christ, and called and commissioned by him to serve in his kingdom.

—K. Worrill Johnson

For the next Women of the Bible note, go to page 1168.

### reflection

*What issues do you struggle with?*

*Take them to Jesus; ask for God's guidance and wisdom to bring about your healing.*

### read

Matthew 28:1–10;
Mark 15:40—16:11;
Luke 8:1–3; 24:1–11;
John 20:1–18.

**See also** the Inspire Notes "Courage to Heal," "Confidence," "Female Ministers and Evangelists," "Servant-Leadership" and "Women in Preaching Ministries," and the Women of the Bible Notes "Deborah: An Uncommon Leader," "Huldah: A Prophetess of God," "Queen Vashti: A Woman of Strength" and "Philip's Daughters: Those Preaching Women."

**28:3** u Da 10:6
**28:6** v Mt 16:21
**28:7** w Mt 26:32
**28:10** x Ro 8:29; Heb 2:11–13,17

and sat on it. 3His appearance was like light-
ning, and his clothes were white as snow.[u]
4The guards were so afraid of him that they
shook and became like dead men.

5The angel said to the women, "Do not be
afraid, for I know that you are looking for
Jesus, who was crucified. 6He is not here; he
has risen, just as he said.[v] Come and see the
place where he lay. 7Then go quickly and tell
his disciples: 'He has risen from the dead and
is going ahead of you into Galilee.[w] There you
will see him.' Now I have told you."

8So the women hurried away from the
tomb, afraid yet filled with joy, and ran to
tell his disciples. 9Suddenly Jesus met them.
"Greetings," he said. They came to him,
clasped his feet and worshiped him. 10Then
Jesus said to them, "Do not be afraid. Go
and tell my brothers[x] to go to Galilee; there
they will see me."

## The Guards' Report

11While the women were on their way,
some of the guards went into the city and
reported to the chief priests everything
that had happened. 12When the chief priests
had met with the elders and devised a plan,
they gave the soldiers a large sum of money,
13telling them, "You are to say, 'His disciples
came during the night and stole him away
while we were asleep.' 14If this report gets to
the governor, we will satisfy him and keep
you out of trouble." 15So the soldiers took
the money and did as they were instructed.
And this story has been widely circulated
among the Jews to this very day.

## The Great Commission

16Then the eleven disciples went to Gal-
ilee, to the mountain where Jesus had told
them to go.[y] 17When they saw him, they wor-
shiped him; but some doubted. 18Then Jesus
came to them and said, "All authority in
heaven and on earth has been given to me.[z]
19Therefore go and make disciples of all na-
tions,[a] baptizing them in[a] the name of the
Father and of the Son and of the Holy Spirit,
20and teaching[b] them to obey everything I
have commanded you. And surely I am with
you always, to the very end of the age."

**28:16** y ver 7,10; Mt 26:32
**28:18** z Da 7:13,14; Php 2:9,10
**28:19** a Mk 16:15,16
**28:20** b Ac 2:42

[a]19 Or *into*; see Acts 8:16; 19:5; Romans 6:3; 1 Cor. 1:13; 10:2 and Gal. 3:27.

# Mark

## OVERVIEW

The Gospel of Mark displays intense action that allows for only a brief introduction of Jesus before it immediately becomes immersed in Jesus' work as a servant of God. Throughout the book, Mark used a Greek word that is translated "immediately," "at once," "without delay," "quickly" or "just then"—demonstrating that Jesus followed his mission from God with purposefulness and without hesitation.

Mark's Gospel showcases stories of women who placed their faith in Jesus' healing power. We read about the woman who touched Jesus' cloak for her healing (see Mk 5) and the Gentile woman who challenged Jesus so that her daughter could receive healing (see Mk 7). The faith of these unnamed women should serve as models for women today. Regardless of our circumstances, positions or names, we should never stop believing that Jesus heals, restores and saves.

As you read of Jesus' purposeful mission and his followers' faith, reflect on your own response to the mission of Christ—and then be about God's business!

## OUTLINE

I. The Servant's Preparation (1:1–13)
II. The Servant's Work in and Around Galilee (1:14—9:50)
III. The Servant's Work in Judea and Perea (10:1–52)
IV. The Servant's Redeeming Work in Jerusalem (11:1—16:20)

### SCANNABLE FACTS:

**Author:** John Mark

**Time Written:** Sometime between A.D. 50 and 70

**Theme to Note:** Jesus, as God's servant, takes action for the kingdom

**Notable Women:** Mary, the mother of Jesus; Jairus's daughter; Herodias; Salome; the Syrophoenician woman

## John the Baptist Prepares the Way

1 The beginning of the gospel about Jesus Christ, the Son of God.[a]

2 It is written in Isaiah the prophet:

"I will send my messenger ahead of you,
who will prepare your way"[b][a]—
3 "a voice of one calling in the desert,
'Prepare the way for the Lord,
make straight paths for him.'"[c][b]

4 And so John came, baptizing in the desert region and preaching a baptism of repentance for the forgiveness of sins. 5 The whole Judean countryside and all the people of Jerusalem went out to him. Confessing their sins, they were baptized by him in the Jordan River. 6 John wore clothing made of camel's hair, with a leather belt around his waist, and he ate locusts and wild honey. 7 And this was his message: "After me will come one more powerful than I, the thongs of whose sandals I am not worthy to stoop down and untie.[c] 8 I baptize you with[d] water, but he will baptize you with the Holy Spirit."[d]

## The Baptism and Temptation of Jesus

9 At that time Jesus came from Nazareth in Galilee and was baptized by John in the Jordan. 10 As Jesus was coming up out of the water, he saw heaven being torn open and the Spirit descending on him like a dove.[e] 11 And a voice came from heaven: "You are my Son,[f] whom I love; with you I am well pleased."

12 At once the Spirit sent him out into the desert, 13 and he was in the desert forty days, being tempted by Satan. He was with the wild animals, and angels attended him.

## The Calling of the First Disciples

14 After John was put in prison, Jesus went into Galilee, proclaiming the good news of God.[g] 15 "The time has come,"[h] he said. "The kingdom of God is near. Repent and believe the good news!"[i]

16 As Jesus walked beside the Sea of Galilee, he saw Simon and his brother Andrew casting a net into the lake, for they were fishermen. 17 "Come, follow me," Jesus said, "and I will make you fishers of men." 18 At once they left their nets and followed him.

19 When he had gone a little farther, he saw James son of Zebedee and his brother John in a boat, preparing their nets. 20 Without delay he called them, and they left their father Zebedee in the boat with the hired men and followed him.

## Jesus Drives Out an Evil Spirit

21 They went to Capernaum, and when the Sabbath came, Jesus went into the synagogue and began to teach. 22 The people were amazed at his teaching, because he taught them as one who had authority, not as the teachers of the law.[j] 23 Just then a man in their synagogue who was possessed by an evil[e] spirit cried out, 24 "What do you want with us,[k] Jesus of Nazareth? Have you come to destroy us? I know who you are—the Holy One of God!"

25 "Be quiet!" said Jesus sternly. "Come out of him!" 26 The evil spirit shook the man violently and came out of him with a shriek.

27 The people were all so amazed[l] that they asked each other, "What is this? A new teaching—and with authority! He even gives orders to evil spirits and they obey him." 28 News about him spread quickly over the whole region of Galilee.

## Jesus Heals Many

29 As soon as they left the synagogue,[m] they went with James and John to the home of Simon and Andrew. 30 Simon's mother-in-law was in bed with a fever, and they told Jesus about her. 31 So he went to her, took her hand and helped her up. The fever left her and she began to wait on them.

32 That evening after sunset the people brought to Jesus all the sick and demon-possessed.[n] 33 The whole town gathered at the door, 34 and Jesus healed many who had various diseases.[o] He also drove out many demons, but he would not let the demons speak because they knew who he was.[p]

**1:2** a Mal 3:1; Mt 11:10; Lk 7:27
**1:3** b Isa 40:3
**1:7** c Ac 13:25
**1:8** d Isa 44:3
**1:10** e Jn 1:32
**1:11** f Mt 3:17
**1:14** g Mt 4:23
**1:15** h Gal 4:4; Eph 1:10 i Ac 20:21
**1:22** j Mt 7:28,29
**1:24** k Mt 8:29
**1:27** l Mk 10:24,32
**1:29** m ver 21,23
**1:32** n Mt 4:24
**1:34** o Mt 4:23 p Mk 3:12; Ac 16:17,18

[a]1 Some manuscripts do not have *the Son of God.* [b]2 Mal. 3:1 [c]3 Isaiah 40:3 [d]8 Or *in* [e]23 Greek *unclean*; also in verses 26 and 27

## Jesus Prays in a Solitary Place

[35]Very early in the morning, while it was still dark, Jesus got up, left the house and went off to a solitary place, where he prayed. [36]Simon and his companions went to look for him, [37]and when they found him, they exclaimed: "Everyone is looking for you!"

[38]Jesus replied, "Let us go somewhere else—to the nearby villages—so I can preach there also. That is why I have come."[q] [39]So he traveled throughout Galilee, preaching in their synagogues[r] and driving out demons.[s]

> *"The most lonely place in the world is the human heart when love is absent."*
>
> —SADIE ALEXANDER, FIRST AFRICAN AMERICAN FEMALE TO RECEIVE A DOCTORATE IN ECONOMICS

## A Man With Leprosy

[40]A man with leprosy[a] came to him and begged him on his knees,[t] "If you are willing, you can make me clean."

[41]Filled with compassion, Jesus reached out his hand and touched the man. "I am willing," he said. "Be clean!" [42]Immediately the leprosy left him and he was cured.

[43]Jesus sent him away at once with a strong warning: [44]"See that you don't tell this to anyone.[u] But go, show yourself to the priest[v] and offer the sacrifices that Moses commanded for your cleansing,[w] as a testimony to them." [45]Instead he went out and began to talk freely, spreading the news. As a result, Jesus could no longer enter a town openly but stayed outside in lonely places.[x] Yet the people still came to him from everywhere.[y]

## Jesus Heals a Paralytic

2 A few days later, when Jesus again entered Capernaum, the people heard that he had come home. [2]So many[z] gathered that there was no room left, not even outside the door, and he preached the word to them. [3]Some men came, bringing to him a paralytic,[a] carried by four of them. [4]Since they could not get him to Jesus because of the crowd, they made an opening in the roof above Jesus and, after digging through it, lowered the mat the paralyzed man was lying on. [5]When Jesus saw their faith, he said to the paralytic, "Son, your sins are forgiven."

[6]Now some teachers of the law were sitting there, thinking to themselves, [7]"Why does this fellow talk like that? He's blaspheming! Who can forgive sins but God alone?"[b]

[8]Immediately Jesus knew in his spirit that this was what they were thinking in their hearts, and he said to them, "Why are you thinking these things? [9]Which is easier: to say to the paralytic, 'Your sins are forgiven,' or to say, 'Get up, take your mat and walk'? [10]But that you may know that the Son of Man has authority on earth to forgive sins . . ." He said to the paralytic, [11]"I tell you, get up, take your mat and go home." [12]He got up, took his mat and walked out in full view of them all. This amazed everyone and they praised God,[c] saying, "We have never seen anything like this!"[d]

## The Calling of Levi

[13]Once again Jesus went out beside the lake. A large crowd came to him,[e] and he began to teach them. [14]As he walked along, he saw Levi son of Alphaeus sitting at the tax collector's booth. "Follow me," Jesus told him, and Levi got up and followed him.

[15]While Jesus was having dinner at Levi's house, many tax collectors and "sinners" were eating with him and his disciples, for there were many who followed him. [16]When the teachers of the law who were Pharisees[f] saw him eating with the "sinners" and tax collectors, they asked his disciples: "Why does he eat with tax collectors and 'sinners'?"[g]

[17]On hearing this, Jesus said to them, "It is not the healthy who need a doctor, but the sick. I have not come to call the righteous, but sinners."[h]

## Jesus Questioned About Fasting

[18]Now John's disciples and the Pharisees were fasting. Some people came and asked Jesus, "How is it that John's disciples and the disciples of the Pharisees are fasting, but yours are not?"

[19]Jesus answered, "How can the guests of the bridegroom fast while he is with them?

**1:38** q Isa 61:1
**1:39** r Mt 4:23; s Mt 4:24
**1:40** t Mk 10:17
**1:44** u Mt 8:4; v Lev 13:49; w Lev 14:1–32
**1:45** x Lk 5:15,16; y Mk 2:13; Lk 5:17; Jn 6:2
**2:2** z ver 13; Mk 1:45
**2:3** a Mt 4:24
**2:7** b Isa 43:25
**2:12** c Mt 9:8; d Mt 9:33
**2:13** e Mk 1:45
**2:16** f Ac 23:9; g Mt 9:11
**2:17** h Lk 19:10; 1Ti 1:15

[a]40 The Greek word was used for various diseases affecting the skin—not necessarily leprosy.

2:20
i Lk 17:22

They cannot, so long as they have him with
them. [20]But the time will come when the
bridegroom will be taken from them,[i] and
on that day they will fast.
[21]"No one sews a patch of unshrunk cloth
on an old garment. If he does, the new piece
will pull away from the old, making the
tear worse. [22]And no one pours new wine
into old wineskins. If he does, the wine will
burst the skins, and both the wine and the
wineskins will be ruined. No, he pours new
wine into new wineskins."

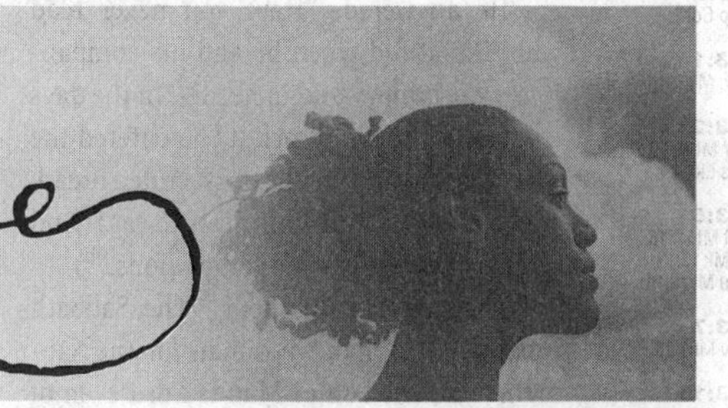

Inspire

## THE GIFT OF ALONENESS

Single women sometimes struggle with being alone. Some hate living alone, going out alone and coming home from work and eating alone. Before Eve was created, God said, "It is not good for the man to be alone" (Ge 2:18). That statement would surely apply to the woman as well as to Adam. But the reality is that some of us *are* alone. We're single, and we're living a life of aloneness.

But while singles may be alone, we don't have to be lonely. Loneliness is an attitude, a state mind. People can be lonely even in a crowd or at a party. It's not necessarily a lack of company that makes a person lonely. Loneliness is a decision; we can choose whether or not to be lonely. When we're lonely, it may mean that we have not yet learned to enjoy our own company. We have not yet realized the gift of aloneness.

Everyone—single or married—needs time to be alone. Aloneness is an investment in oneself. It's a time to recharge one's emotional and spiritual batteries, to think and pray, to gain insight or find a solution to a pressing problem, to rest after a battle or a long day, to find grace to deal with life and all of its challenges, to hear from God.

Jesus took full advantage of his singleness and moments of aloneness or solitude. Mark 1:35 says, "Very early in the morning, while it was still dark, Jesus got up, left the house and went off to a solitary place, where he prayed."

It is when we are alone and still that God can speak to us most profoundly. Didn't he tell the psalmist, "Be still, and know that I am God" (Ps 46:10)? We all need moments of aloneness to hear from God, reflect, meditate and recreate.

Embrace your time of singleness as a special time of aloneness with God, not as a time of loneliness.

—C. Hale

For the next Inspire note, go to page 1177.

**read**

Mark 1:35; see also Genesis 2:18; Psalm 46:10.

See also the Inspire Notes "Single Mothers," "Loneliness," "Single Parenting" and "Singleness: A Stage in Life," and the Women of the Bible Note "Rachel: Taking Care of Business."

**WOMAN of COLOR**

What will you do today to honor and cherish your aloneness with God?

**2:23** j Dt23:25
**2:24** k Mt12:2
**2:26** l 2Sa8:17 m Lev24:5–9 n 1Sa21:1–6
**2:27** o Ex23:12; Dt5:14 p Col2:16
**3:1** q Mk1:21
**3:2** r Mt12:10 s Lk14:1
**3:6** t Mt22:16; Mk12:13 u Mt12:14
**3:7** v Mt4:25
**3:10** w Mt4:23 x Mt9:20

## Lord of the Sabbath

[23]One Sabbath Jesus was going through
the grainfields, and as his disciples walked
along, they began to pick some heads of
grain.[j] [24]The Pharisees said to him, "Look,
why are they doing what is unlawful on
the Sabbath?"[k]

[25]He answered, "Have you never read
what David did when he and his compan-
ions were hungry and in need? [26]In the days
of Abiathar the high priest,[l] he entered the
house of God and ate the consecrated bread,
which is lawful only for priests to eat.[m] And
he also gave some to his companions."[n]

[27]Then he said to them, "The Sabbath
was made for man,[o] not man for the Sab-
bath.[p] [28]So the Son of Man is Lord even of
the Sabbath."

3 Another time he went into the syna-
gogue,[q] and a man with a shriveled
hand was there. [2]Some of them were looking
for a reason to accuse Jesus, so they watched
him closely[r] to see if he would heal him on
the Sabbath.[s] [3]Jesus said to the man with
the shriveled hand, "Stand up in front of ev-
eryone."

[4]Then Jesus asked them, "Which is law-
ful on the Sabbath: to do good or to do evil,
to save life or to kill?" But they remained
silent.

[5]He looked around at them in anger and,
deeply distressed at their stubborn hearts,
said to the man, "Stretch out your hand." He
stretched it out, and his hand was completely
restored. [6]Then the Pharisees went out and
began to plot with the Herodians[t] how they
might kill Jesus.[u]

## Crowds Follow Jesus

[7]Jesus withdrew with his disciples to
the lake, and a large crowd from Galilee
followed.[v] [8]When they heard all he was do-
ing, many people came to him from Judea,
Jerusalem, Idumea, and the regions across
the Jordan and around Tyre and Sidon.
[9]Because of the crowd he told his disciples
to have a small boat ready for him, to keep
the people from crowding him. [10]For he had
healed many,[w] so that those with diseases
were pushing forward to touch him.[x]
[11]Whenever the evil[a] spirits saw him, they
fell down before him and cried out, "You are
the Son of God."[y] [12]But he gave them strict
orders not to tell who he was.[z]

## The Appointing of the Twelve Apostles

[13]Jesus went up on a mountainside and
called to him those he wanted, and they
came to him.[a] [14]He appointed twelve—des-
ignating them apostles[b]—that they might
be with him and that he might send them
out to preach [15]and to have authority to
drive out demons. [16]These are the twelve
he appointed: Simon (to whom he gave
the name Peter);[b] [17]James son of Zebedee
and his brother John (to them he gave the
name Boanerges, which means Sons of
Thunder); [18]Andrew, Philip, Bartholomew,
Matthew, Thomas, James son of Alphaeus,
Thaddaeus, Simon the Zealot [19]and Judas
Iscariot, who betrayed him.

## Jesus and Beelzebub

[20]Then Jesus entered a house, and again a
crowd gathered, so that he and his disciples
were not even able to eat.[c] [21]When his family
heard about this, they went to take charge of
him, for they said, "He is out of his mind."[d]

[22]And the teachers of the law who came
down from Jerusalem said, "He is possessed
by Beelzebub[c]![e] By the prince of demons he
is driving out demons."[f]

[23]So Jesus called them and spoke to them
in parables:[g] "How can Satan drive out Sa-
tan? [24]If a kingdom is divided against itself,
that kingdom cannot stand. [25]If a house is
divided against itself, that house cannot
stand. [26]And if Satan opposes himself and is
divided, he cannot stand; his end has come.
[27]In fact, no one can enter a strong man's
house and carry off his possessions unless
he first ties up the strong man. Then he can
rob his house.[h] [28]I tell you the truth, all the
sins and blasphemies of men will be forgiven
them. [29]But whoever blasphemes against
the Holy Spirit will never be forgiven; he is
guilty of an eternal sin."

[30]He said this because they were saying,
"He has an evil spirit."

**3:11** y Mk1:23,24
**3:12** z Mk1:24,25,34
**3:13** a Mt5:1
**3:16** b Jn1:42
**3:20** c Mk6:31
**3:21** d Jn10:20; Ac26:24
**3:22** e Mt10:25; Jn7:20; 8:48,52; 10:20 f Mt9:34
**3:23** g Mk4:2
**3:27** h Isa49:24,25

[a]11 Greek *unclean*; also in verse 30 [b]14 Some manuscripts do not have *designating them apostles.* [c]22 Greek *Beezeboul* or *Beelzeboul*

## Jesus' Mother and Brothers

31Then Jesus' mother and brothers arrived. Standing outside, they sent someone in to call him. 32A crowd was sitting around him, and they told him, "Your mother and brothers are outside looking for you."

33"Who are my mother and my brothers?" he asked.

34Then he looked at those seated in a circle around him and said, "Here are my mother and my brothers! 35Whoever does God's will is my brother and sister and mother."

*Daughter,*

*You are an indispensable part of my loving family. Act like it!*

*Your Devoted Father*

MARK 3:31–35

## The Parable of the Sower

4 Again Jesus began to teach by the lake.[i] The crowd that gathered around him was so large that he got into a boat and sat in it out on the lake, while all the people were along the shore at the water's edge. 2He taught them many things by parables,[j] and in his teaching said: 3"Listen! A farmer went out to sow his seed. 4As he was scattering the seed, some fell along the path, and the birds came and ate it up. 5Some fell on rocky places, where it did not have much soil. It sprang up quickly, because the soil was shallow. 6But when the sun came up, the plants were scorched, and they withered because they had no root. 7Other seed fell among thorns, which grew up and choked the plants, so that they did not bear grain. 8Still other seed fell on good soil. It came up, grew and produced a crop, multiplying thirty, sixty, or even a hundred times."[k]

9Then Jesus said, "He who has ears to hear, let him hear."[l]

10When he was alone, the Twelve and the others around him asked him about the parables. 11He told them, "The secret of the kingdom of God has been given to you. But to those on the outside[m] everything is said in parables 12so that,

"'they may be ever seeing but never
perceiving,
and ever hearing but never
understanding;
otherwise they might turn and be
forgiven!'[a]"[n]

13Then Jesus said to them, "Don't you understand this parable? How then will you understand any parable? 14The farmer sows the word. 15Some people are like seed along the path, where the word is sown. As soon as they hear it, Satan comes and takes away the word that was sown in them. 16Others, like seed sown on rocky places, hear the word and at once receive it with joy. 17But since they have no root, they last only a short time. When trouble or persecution comes because of the word, they quickly fall away. 18Still others, like seed sown among thorns, hear the word; 19but the worries of this life, the deceitfulness of wealth and the desires for other things come in and choke the word, making it unfruitful. 20Others, like seed sown on good soil, hear the word, accept it, and produce a crop—thirty, sixty or even a hundred times what was sown."

## A Lamp on a Stand

21He said to them, "Do you bring in a lamp to put it under a bowl or a bed? Instead, don't you put it on its stand?[o] 22For whatever is hidden is meant to be disclosed, and whatever is concealed is meant to be brought out into the open.[p] 23If anyone has ears to hear, let him hear."[q]

24"Consider carefully what you hear," he continued. "With the measure you use, it will be measured to you—and even more.[r] 25Whoever has will be given more; whoever does not have, even what he has will be taken from him."[s]

**4:1** i Mk 2:13; 3:7
**4:2** j Mk 3:23
**4:8** k Jn 15:5; Col 1:6
**4:9** l Mt 11:15
**4:11** m 1Co 5:12,13; Col 4:5; 1Th 4:12; 1Ti 3:7
**4:12** n Isa 6:9,10
**4:21** o Mt 5:15
**4:22** p Mt 10:26; Lk 8:17
**4:23** q Mt 11:15
**4:24** r Mt 7:2; Lk 6:38
**4:25** s Mt 13:12; 25:29

[a] 12 Isaiah 6:9,10

**4:26** t Mt13:24
**4:29** u Rev14:15
**4:30** v Mt13:24
**4:33** w Jn16:12
**4:34** x Jn16:25
**4:36** y ver1; Mk3:9; 5:2,21; 6:32,45
**4:40** z Mt14:31; Mk16:14

## The Parable of the Growing Seed

26He also said, "This is what the kingdom of God is like.[t] A man scatters seed on the ground. 27Night and day, whether he sleeps or gets up, the seed sprouts and grows, though he does not know how. 28All by itself the soil produces grain—first the stalk, then the head, then the full kernel in the head. 29As soon as the grain is ripe, he puts the sickle to it, because the harvest has come."[u]

## The Parable of the Mustard Seed

30Again he said, "What shall we say the kingdom of God is like,[v] or what parable shall we use to describe it? 31It is like a mustard seed, which is the smallest seed you plant in the ground. 32Yet when planted, it grows and becomes the largest of all garden plants, with such big branches that the birds of the air can perch in its shade."

33With many similar parables Jesus spoke the word to them, as much as they could understand.[w] 34He did not say anything to them without using a parable.[x] But when he was alone with his own disciples, he explained everything.

## Jesus Calms the Storm

35That day when evening came, he said to his disciples, "Let us go over to the other side." 36Leaving the crowd behind, they took him along, just as he was, in the boat.[y] There were also other boats with him. 37A furious squall came up, and the waves broke over the boat, so that it was nearly swamped. 38Jesus was in the stern, sleeping on a cushion. The disciples woke him and said to him, "Teacher, don't you care if we drown?"

39He got up, rebuked the wind and said to the waves, "Quiet! Be still!" Then the wind died down and it was completely calm.

40He said to his disciples, "Why are you so afraid? Do you still have no faith?"[z]

41They were terrified and asked each other, "Who is this? Even the wind and the waves obey him!"

## The Healing of a Demon-possessed Man

5 They went across the lake to the region of the Gerasenes.[a] 2When Jesus got out of the boat,[a] a man with an evil[b] spirit[b] came from the tombs to meet him. 3This man lived in the tombs, and no one could bind him any more, not even with a chain. 4For he had often been chained hand and foot, but he tore the chains apart and broke the irons on his feet. No one was strong enough to subdue him. 5Night and day among the tombs and in the hills he would cry out and cut himself with stones.

6When he saw Jesus from a distance, he ran and fell on his knees in front of him. 7He shouted at the top of his voice, "What do you want with me,[c] Jesus, Son of the Most High God?[d] Swear to God that you won't torture me!" 8For Jesus had said to him, "Come out of this man, you evil spirit!"

9Then Jesus asked him, "What is your name?"

"My name is Legion,"[e] he replied, "for we are many." 10And he begged Jesus again and again not to send them out of the area.

11A large herd of pigs was feeding on the nearby hillside. 12The demons begged Jesus, "Send us among the pigs; allow us to go into them." 13He gave them permission, and the evil spirits came out and went into the pigs. The herd, about two thousand in number, rushed down the steep bank into the lake and were drowned.

14Those tending the pigs ran off and reported this in the town and countryside, and the people went out to see what had happened. 15When they came to Jesus, they saw the man who had been possessed by the legion[f] of demons,[g] sitting there, dressed and in his right mind; and they were afraid. 16Those who had seen it told the people what had happened to the demon-possessed man—and told about the pigs as well. 17Then the people began to plead with Jesus to leave their region.

18As Jesus was getting into the boat, the man who had been demon-possessed begged to go with him. 19Jesus did not let him, but said, "Go home to your family and tell them how much the Lord has done for

**5:2** a Mk4:1 b Mk1:23
**5:7** c Mt8:29 d Mt4:3; Ac16:17; Heb7:1
**5:9** e ver15
**5:15** f ver9 g ver16,18; Mt4:24

[a]1 Some manuscripts *Gadarenes*; other manuscripts *Gergesenes* [b]2 Greek *unclean*; also in verses 8 and 13

5:20 h Mt4:25; Mk7:31
5:21 i Mt9:1
5:22 j Lk13:14; Ac13:15; 18:8,17
5:23 k Mk6:5; 7:32; 8:23
5:25 l Lev15:25–30
5:29 m ver34
5:30 n Lk5:17
5:34 o Mt9:22
5:35 p ver22

you, and how he has had mercy on you." [20]So the man went away and began to tell in the Decapolis[a][h] how much Jesus had done for him. And all the people were amazed.

## A Dead Girl and a Sick Woman

[21]When Jesus had again crossed over by boat to the other side of the lake,[i] a large crowd gathered around him while he was by the lake. [22]Then one of the synagogue rulers,[j] named Jairus, came there. Seeing Jesus, he fell at his feet [23]and pleaded earnestly with him, "My little daughter is dying. Please come and put your hands on[k] her so that she will be healed and live." [24]So Jesus went with him.

A large crowd followed and pressed around him. [25]And a woman was there who had been subject to bleeding[l] for twelve years. [26]She had suffered a great deal under the care of many doctors and had spent all she had, yet instead of getting better she grew worse. [27]When she heard about Jesus, she came up behind him in the crowd and touched his cloak, [28]because she thought, "If I just touch his clothes, I will be healed." [29]Immediately her bleeding stopped and she felt in her body that she was freed from her suffering.[m]

[30]At once Jesus realized that power[n] had gone out from him. He turned around in the crowd and asked, "Who touched my clothes?"

[31]"You see the people crowding against you," his disciples answered, "and yet you can ask, 'Who touched me?' "

[32]But Jesus kept looking around to see who had done it. [33]Then the woman, knowing what had happened to her, came and fell at his feet and, trembling with fear, told him the whole truth. [34]He said to her, "Daughter, your faith has healed you.[o] Go in peace and be freed from your suffering."

[35]While Jesus was still speaking, some men came from the house of Jairus, the synagogue ruler.[p] "Your daughter is dead," they said. "Why bother the teacher any more?"

[36]Ignoring what they said, Jesus told the synagogue ruler, "Don't be afraid; just believe."

[37]He did not let anyone follow him except Peter, James and John the brother of James. [38]When they came to the home of the synagogue ruler, Jesus saw a commotion, with people crying and wailing loudly. [39]He went in and said to them, "Why all this commotion and wailing? The child is not dead but asleep." [40]But they laughed at him.

After he put them all out, he took the child's father and mother and the disciples who were with him, and went in where the child was. [41]He took her by the hand and said to her, "*Talitha koum!*" (which means, "Little girl, I say to you, get up!").[q] [42]Immediately the girl stood up and walked around (she was twelve years old). At this they were completely astonished. [43]He gave strict orders not to let anyone know about this,[r] and told them to give her something to eat.

## A Prophet Without Honor

**6** Jesus left there and went to his hometown, accompanied by his disciples. [2]When the Sabbath came, he began to teach in the synagogue,[s] and many who heard him were amazed.

"Where did this man get these things?" they asked. "What's this wisdom that has been given him, that he even does miracles! [3]Isn't this the carpenter? Isn't this Mary's son and the brother of James, Joseph,[b] Judas and Simon?[t] Aren't his sisters here with us?" And they took offense at him.[u]

[4]Jesus said to them, "Only in his hometown, among his relatives and in his own house is a prophet without honor."[v] [5]He could not do any miracles there, except lay his hands on[w] a few sick people and heal them. [6]And he was amazed at their lack of faith.

## Jesus Sends Out the Twelve

Then Jesus went around teaching from village to village.[x] [7]Calling the Twelve to him,[y] he sent them out two by two and gave them authority over evil[c] spirits.[z]

[8]These were his instructions: "Take nothing for the journey except a staff—no bread, no bag, no money in your belts. [9]Wear sandals but not an extra tunic. [10]Whenever you enter a house, stay there until you leave

5:41 q Ac9:40
5:43 r Mt8:4
6:2 s Mt4:23
6:3 t Mt12:46 u Mt11:6
6:4 v Jn4:44
6:5 w Mk5:23
6:6 x Mt9:35; Lk13:22
6:7 y Mk3:13 z Mt10:1

[a]20 That is, the Ten Cities [b]3 Greek *Joses*, a variant of *Joseph* [c]7 Greek *unclean*

# Daughter of Jairus

## A Testament of Faith

A Christian mother, father, grandmother, grandfather, guardian or relative will spend a child's lifetime—from infancy to adulthood—embracing the phrase "Just believe."

These adults, concerned for their beloved children's lives, often find themselves going in prayer to Jesus, the miraculous Master Healer. These adults know that drugs, peer pressure, alcohol, gangs, suicide, depression, low self-esteem, violence, etc. have killed off the innocent or sickened the sons and daughters given to them by God. These believers know that if anyone can rescue their precious children from the deadly ills of society, Jesus certainly can.

We learn in Mark 5:21–24,35–43 that Jairus's pleading for his daughter to Jesus made a difference. Jairus loved his daughter and lifted her name up to Jesus. This caring and loving father continued to believe and have patience when Jesus stopped on the way to Jairus's house. During this stop, Jairus's servants arrived and told him that his daughter was dead. As soon as Jesus heard these words, he gave Jairus the encouragement he needed: "Don't be afraid; just believe" (Mk 5:36).

When Jesus arrived at Jairus's house, people were weeping because the girl was dead. Jesus instructed them to stop weeping, for she was only sleeping (see Mk 5:39). After he removed the doubters and unbelievers from the room, he took the little girl's hand and said, " '*Talitha koum!*' (which means, 'Little girl, I say to you, get up!')" (Mk 5:41). Immediately, she rose from the grips of death.

I am certain every adult child who has experienced drugs, alcohol, suicidal thoughts or other deadly temptations can thank God for their parents' desperate prayers to a heavenly Healer and Redeemer who called them to rise above the things that wanted to destroy them. Now they, too, can thank God for Jesus. So parents, pray and plead, plead and pray, and believe that your child—and those around you—will "get up" as Jairus's daughter did.

—D. Moore-James

For the next Women of the Bible note, go to page 1170.

### reflection

*What do you need to "just believe" Jesus for?*

*Seek his guidance and act in faith.*

### read

Mark 5:21–43; see also Matthew 9:18–26; Luke 8:41–56.

See also the Inspire Notes "A Great Challenge: Teaching Our Children," "Motherhood," "Parenting," "Raising Children: Modeling Discipleship," "Children: A Blessed Heritage From God," "Prayer: A God-Given Promise," "Prayer: The Antidote to Worry," "Nurturing Spiritual Gifts in Our Children" and "Prayer."

6:11 a Mt 10:14
6:12 b Lk 9:6
6:13 c Jas 5:14
6:15 d Mt 21:11; e Mt 16:14; Mk 8:28
6:18 f Lev 18:16; 20:21
6:20 g Mt 21:26
6:21 h Est 1:3; 2:18; i Lk 3:1
6:23 j Est 5:3,6; 7:2

that town. 11 And if any place will not welcome you or listen to you, shake the dust off your feet[a] when you leave, as a testimony against them."

12 They went out and preached that people should repent.[b] 13 They drove out many demons and anointed many sick people with oil[c] and healed them.

## John the Baptist Beheaded

14 King Herod heard about this, for Jesus' name had become well known. Some were saying,[a] "John the Baptist has been raised from the dead, and that is why miraculous powers are at work in him."

15 Others said, "He is Elijah."

And still others claimed, "He is a prophet,[d] like one of the prophets of long ago."[e]

16 But when Herod heard this, he said, "John, the man I beheaded, has been raised from the dead!"

17 For Herod himself had given orders to have John arrested, and he had him bound and put in prison. He did this because of Herodias, his brother Philip's wife, whom he had married. 18 For John had been saying to Herod, "It is not lawful for you to have your brother's wife."[f] 19 So Herodias nursed a grudge against John and wanted to kill him. But she was not able to, 20 because Herod feared John and protected him, knowing him to be a righteous and holy man.[g] When Herod heard John, he was greatly puzzled[b]; yet he liked to listen to him.

21 Finally the opportune time came. On his birthday Herod gave a banquet[h] for his high officials and military commanders and the leading men of Galilee.[i] 22 When the daughter of Herodias came in and danced, she pleased Herod and his dinner guests.

The king said to the girl, "Ask me for anything you want, and I'll give it to you." 23 And he promised her with an oath, "Whatever you ask I will give you, up to half my kingdom."[j]

24 She went out and said to her mother, "What shall I ask for?"

"The head of John the Baptist," she answered.

25 At once the girl hurried in to the king with the request: "I want you to give me right now the head of John the Baptist on a platter."

26 The king was greatly distressed, but because of his oaths and his dinner guests, he did not want to refuse her. 27 So he immediately sent an executioner with orders to bring John's head. The man went, beheaded John in the prison, 28 and brought back his head on a platter. He presented it to the girl, and she gave it to her mother. 29 On hearing of this, John's disciples came and took his body and laid it in a tomb.

## Jesus Feeds the Five Thousand

30 The apostles[k] gathered around Jesus and reported to him all they had done and taught.[l] 31 Then, because so many people were coming and going that they did not even have a chance to eat,[m] he said to them, "Come with me by yourselves to a quiet place and get some rest."

32 So they went away by themselves in a boat[n] to a solitary place. 33 But many who saw them leaving recognized them and ran on foot from all the towns and got there ahead of them. 34 When Jesus landed and saw a large crowd, he had compassion on them, because they were like sheep without a shepherd.[o] So he began teaching them many things.

35 By this time it was late in the day, so his disciples came to him. "This is a remote place," they said, "and it's already very late. 36 Send the people away so they can go to the surrounding countryside and villages and buy themselves something to eat."

37 But he answered, "You give them something to eat."[p]

They said to him, "That would take eight months of a man's wages[c]! Are we to go and spend that much on bread and give it to them to eat?"

38 "How many loaves do you have?" he asked. "Go and see."

When they found out, they said, "Five—and two fish."[q]

39 Then Jesus directed them to have all the people sit down in groups on the green grass. 40 So they sat down in groups of

6:30 k Lk 9:10; Ac 1:2,26; l Lk 9:10
6:31 m Mk 3:20
6:32 n ver 45; Mk 4:36
6:34 o Mt 9:36
6:37 p 2Ki 4:42–44
6:38 q Mt 15:34; Mk 8:5

[a]14 Some early manuscripts *He was saying* [b]20 Some early manuscripts *he did many things* [c]37 Greek *take two hundred denarii*

# Herodias and Salome

## Evil Choices

Herodias was a woman out of control. She was politically astute, ambitious, cunning, greedy and would stop at nothing to get what she wanted. Initially married to Herod Philip, the ruler over the Traconitis and Iturea territories, she eventually left him and married his brother Herod Antipas, who was the ruler over Galilee and Perea and was more powerful than Philip. John the Baptist spoke against this marriage (see Mk 6:18), and it infuriated her. Herodias became angry to the point of wanting to kill John. King Herod was in awe of John and realized that the people revered him, so he was afraid to have John killed.

King Herod had a birthday celebration during which the daughter of Herodias (we know from the Jewish historian Josephus that her name was Salome) danced—quite sensuously, no doubt—for him and his guests. He became so intoxicated with her dancing that he agreed to give her anything she asked for, up to half his kingdom (see Mk 6:22–23). Herodias saw this as an opportunity to get what she wanted—a chance to have John the Baptist killed. Salome's request caused Herod great sorrow, but he honored his word. As she requested, John's head was delivered on a platter.

The mother-daughter relationship among African Americans can be godly and productive or ungodly and destructive. A daughter's relationship with her mother is the foundation upon which she learns to relate to others. She should be taught to appreciate her beauty, to be honest and to practice godliness in her life. The life of an African American mother may, at times, bring unpleasant and disappointing occurrences. But it is important for a mother to heed the voice of God, which may come through the Scriptures or through other people led by God. Through the Word she can receive correction and direction for every area of life, as well as repentance and forgiveness.

Words are powerful! Words can bring life or death. A mother should speak words of godly instruction into her daughter's life. Words of manipulation, deceit and seduction only bring devastation and death.

—G. London

### reflection

*What relationships with other women in your life have been godly and productive? Which ones have not been so?*

*How can you make your future relationships with sisters godly and productive?*

### read

Mark 6:14–29; see also Matthew 14:1–12; Luke 3:19–20.

See also the Inspire Notes "Rebellion," "A Great Challenge: Teaching Our Children," "Influencing Others," "Motherhood," "Parenting," "Raising Children: Modeling Discipleship," "Children: A Blessed Heritage From God" and "Nurturing Spiritual Gifts in Our Children."

For the next Women of the Bible note, go to page 1182.

6:41 r Mt 14:19
6:45 s ver 32 t Mt 11:21
6:50 u Mt 14:27
6:51 v ver 32
6:52 w Mk 8:17–21
6:53 x Jn 6:24,25
6:56 y Mt 9:20

hundreds and fifties. 41 Taking the five
loaves and the two fish and looking up
to heaven, he gave thanks and broke the
loaves.[r] Then he gave them to his disciples
to set before the people. He also divided the
two fish among them all. 42 They all ate and
were satisfied, 43 and the disciples picked up
twelve basketfuls of broken pieces of bread
and fish. 44 The number of the men who had
eaten was five thousand.

## Jesus Walks on the Water

45 Immediately Jesus made his disciples
get into the boat[s] and go on ahead of him to
Bethsaida,[t] while he dismissed the crowd.
46 After leaving them, he went up on a mountainside to pray.

47 When evening came, the boat was in
the middle of the lake, and he was alone on
land. 48 He saw the disciples straining at the
oars, because the wind was against them.
About the fourth watch of the night he went
out to them, walking on the lake. He was
about to pass by them, 49 but when they saw
him walking on the lake, they thought he
was a ghost. They cried out, 50 because they
all saw him and were terrified.

Immediately he spoke to them and said,
"Take courage! It is I. Don't be afraid."[u]
51 Then he climbed into the boat[v] with
them, and the wind died down. They were
completely amazed, 52 for they had not understood about the loaves; their hearts
were hardened.[w]

53 When they had crossed over, they
landed at Gennesaret and anchored there.[x]
54 As soon as they got out of the boat, people
recognized Jesus. 55 They ran throughout
that whole region and carried the sick on
mats to wherever they heard he was. 56 And
wherever he went—into villages, towns or
countryside—they placed the sick in the
marketplaces. They begged him to let them
touch even the edge of his cloak,[y] and all
who touched him were healed.

## Clean and Unclean

7 The Pharisees and some of the teachers
of the law who had come from Jerusalem gathered around Jesus and 2 saw some
of his disciples eating food with hands that
were "unclean,"[z] that is, unwashed. 3 (The
Pharisees and all the Jews do not eat unless
they give their hands a ceremonial washing, holding to the tradition of the elders.[a]
4 When they come from the marketplace
they do not eat unless they wash. And they
observe many other traditions, such as the
washing of cups, pitchers and kettles.[a])[b]

5 So the Pharisees and teachers of the
law asked Jesus, "Why don't your disciples
live according to the tradition of the elders[c] instead of eating their food with 'unclean' hands?"

6 He replied, "Isaiah was right when
he prophesied about you hypocrites; as it
is written:

> " 'These people honor me with their lips,
> but their hearts are far from me.
> 7 They worship me in vain;
> their teachings are but rules taught by men.'[b][d]

8 You have let go of the commands of God and
are holding on to the traditions of men."

9 And he said to them: "You have a fine
way of setting aside the commands of God
in order to observe[c] your own traditions!
10 For Moses said, 'Honor your father and
your mother,'[d][e] and, 'Anyone who curses
his father or mother must be put to death.'[e][f]
11 But you say[g] that if a man says to his father or mother: 'Whatever help you might
otherwise have received from me is Corban'
(that is, a gift devoted to God), 12 then you
no longer let him do anything for his father
or mother. 13 Thus you nullify the word of
God by your tradition that you have handed
down. And you do many things like that."

14 Again Jesus called the crowd to him
and said, "Listen to me, everyone, and understand this. 15 Nothing outside a man
can make him 'unclean' by going into him.
Rather, it is what comes out of a man that
makes him 'unclean.'[f]"

17 After he had left the crowd and entered the house, his disciples asked him[h]
about this parable. 18 "Are you so dull?" he
asked. "Don't you see that nothing that enters a man from the outside can make him

7:2 z Ac 10:14,28
7:3 a ver 5,8,9,13
7:4 b Mt 23:25
7:5 c ver 3; Gal 1:14
7:7 d Isa 29:13
7:10 e Ex 20:12; Dt 5:16 f Ex 21:17; Lev 20:9
7:11 g Mt 23:16,18
7:17 h Mk 9:28

[a]4 Some early manuscripts *pitchers, kettles and dining couches* [b]6,7 Isaiah 29:13 [c]9 Some manuscripts *set up*
[d]10 Exodus 20:12; Deut. 5:16 [e]10 Exodus 21:17; Lev. 20:9 [f]15 Some early manuscripts *'unclean.'* 16 *If anyone has ears to hear, let him hear.*

'unclean'? 19For it doesn't go into his heart but into his stomach, and then out of his body." (In saying this, Jesus declared all foods[i] "clean.")[j]

20He went on: "What comes out of a man is what makes him 'unclean.' 21For from within, out of men's hearts, come evil thoughts, sexual immorality, theft, murder, adultery, 22greed,[k] malice, deceit, lewdness, envy, slander, arrogance and folly. 23All these evils come from inside and make a man 'unclean.'"

## The Faith of a Syrophoenician Woman

24Jesus left that place and went to the vicinity of Tyre.[a][l] He entered a house and did not want anyone to know it; yet he could not keep his presence secret. 25In fact, as soon as she heard about him, a woman whose little daughter was possessed by an evil[b] spirit came and fell at his feet. 26The woman was a Greek, born in Syrian Phoenicia. She begged Jesus to drive the demon out of her daughter.

27"First let the children eat all they want," he told her, "for it is not right to take the children's bread and toss it to their dogs."

28"Yes, Lord," she replied, "but even the dogs under the table eat the children's crumbs."

29Then he told her, "For such a reply, you may go; the demon has left your daughter."

30She went home and found her child lying on the bed, and the demon gone.

## The Healing of a Deaf and Mute Man

31Then Jesus left the vicinity of Tyre[m] and went through Sidon, down to the Sea of Galilee[n] and into the region of the Decapolis.[c][o] 32There some people brought to him a man who was deaf and could hardly talk,[p] and they begged him to place his hand on[q] the man.

33After he took him aside, away from the crowd, Jesus put his fingers into the man's ears. Then he spit[r] and touched the man's tongue. 34He looked up to heaven[s] and with a deep sigh[t] said to him, *"Ephphatha!"* (which means, "Be opened!"). 35At this, the man's ears were opened, his tongue was loosened and he began to speak plainly.[u]

36Jesus commanded them not to tell anyone.[v] But the more he did so, the more they kept talking about it. 37People were overwhelmed with amazement. "He has done everything well," they said. "He even makes the deaf hear and the mute speak."

## Jesus Feeds the Four Thousand

8 During those days another large crowd gathered. Since they had nothing to eat, Jesus called his disciples to him and said, 2"I have compassion for these people;[w] they have already been with me three days and have nothing to eat. 3If I send them home hungry, they will collapse on the way, because some of them have come a long distance."

4His disciples answered, "But where in this remote place can anyone get enough bread to feed them?"

5"How many loaves do you have?" Jesus asked.

"Seven," they replied.

6He told the crowd to sit down on the ground. When he had taken the seven loaves and given thanks, he broke them and gave them to his disciples to set before the people, and they did so. 7They had a few small fish as well; he gave thanks for them also and

---

*Mighty God,*

*I believe that you can do all things. I need your help right now with a particular situation. You already know all about it. Guide me in the way I should go. Help me not to be afraid to follow your direction and to believe in you more strongly than I believe in the inevitability of the "facts." In your Son's blessed name,*

*Amen*

MARK 8:1–10

---

**7:19** i Ro 14:1–12; Col 2:16 j Ac 10:15
**7:22** k Mt 20:15
**7:24** l Mt 11:21
**7:31** m ver 24; Mt 11:21 n Mt 4:18 o Mt 4:25; Mk 5:20
**7:32** p Mt 9:32; Lk 11:14 q Mk 5:23
**7:33** r Mk 8:23
**7:34** s Mk 6:41; Jn 11:41 t Mk 8:12
**7:35** u Isa 35:5,6
**7:36** v Mt 8:4
**8:2** w Mt 9:36

[a]24 Many early manuscripts *Tyre and Sidon* [b]25 Greek *unclean* [c]31 That is, the Ten Cities

told the disciples to distribute them.[x] 8The people ate and were satisfied. Afterward the disciples picked up seven basketfuls of broken pieces that were left over.[y] 9About four thousand men were present. And having sent them away, 10he got into the boat with his disciples and went to the region of Dalmanutha.

11The Pharisees came and began to question Jesus. To test him, they asked him for a sign from heaven.[z] 12He sighed deeply[a] and said, "Why does this generation ask for a miraculous sign? I tell you the truth, no sign will be given to it." 13Then he left them, got back into the boat and crossed to the other side.

## The Yeast of the Pharisees and Herod

14The disciples had forgotten to bring bread, except for one loaf they had with them in the boat. 15"Be careful," Jesus warned them. "Watch out for the yeast of the Pharisees[b] and that of Herod."[c]

16They discussed this with one another and said, "It is because we have no bread."

17Aware of their discussion, Jesus asked them: "Why are you talking about having no bread? Do you still not see or understand? Are your hearts hardened?[d] 18Do you have eyes but fail to see, and ears but fail to hear? And don't you remember? 19When I broke the five loaves for the five thousand, how many basketfuls of pieces did you pick up?"

"Twelve,"[e] they replied.

20"And when I broke the seven loaves for the four thousand, how many basketfuls of pieces did you pick up?"

They answered, "Seven."[f]

21He said to them, "Do you still not understand?"[g]

## The Healing of a Blind Man at Bethsaida

22They came to Bethsaida,[h] and some people brought a blind man and begged Jesus to touch him. 23He took the blind man by the hand and led him outside the village. When he had spit[i] on the man's eyes and put his hands on[j] him, Jesus asked, "Do you see anything?"

24He looked up and said, "I see people; they look like trees walking around."

25Once more Jesus put his hands on the man's eyes. Then his eyes were opened, his sight was restored, and he saw everything clearly. 26Jesus sent him home, saying, "Don't go into the village.[a]"

## Peter's Confession of Christ

27Jesus and his disciples went on to the villages around Caesarea Philippi. On the way he asked them, "Who do people say I am?"

28They replied, "Some say John the Baptist; others say Elijah; and still others, one of the prophets."

29"But what about you?" he asked. "Who do you say I am?"

Peter answered, "You are the Christ.[b]"[k]

30Jesus warned them not to tell anyone about him.

## Jesus Predicts His Death

31He then began to teach them that the Son of Man must suffer many things[l] and be rejected by the elders, chief priests and teachers of the law, and that he must be killed and after three days rise again. 32He spoke plainly[m] about this, and Peter took him aside and began to rebuke him.

33But when Jesus turned and looked at his disciples, he rebuked Peter. "Get behind me, Satan!"[n] he said. "You do not have in mind the things of God, but the things of men."

34Then he called the crowd to him along with his disciples and said: "If anyone would come after me, he must deny himself and take up his cross and follow me.[o] 35For whoever wants to save his life[c] will lose it, but whoever loses his life for me and for the gospel will save it.[p] 36What good is it for a man to gain the whole world, yet forfeit his soul? 37Or what can a man give in exchange for his soul? 38If anyone is ashamed of me and my words in this adulterous and sinful generation, the Son of Man[q] will be ashamed of him[r] when he comes in his Father's glory with the holy angels."

**8:7** x Mt 14:19
**8:8** y ver 20
**8:11** z Mt 12:38
**8:12** a Mk 7:34
**8:15** b Lk 12:1 c Mt 14:1; Mk 12:13
**8:17** d Mk 6:52
**8:19** e Mt 14:20; Mk 6:41–44; Lk 9:17; Jn 6:13
**8:20** f ver 6–9; Mt 15:37
**8:21** g Mk 6:52
**8:22** h Mt 11:21
**8:23** i Mk 7:33
**8:23** j Mk 5:23
**8:29** k Jn 6:69; 11:27
**8:31** l Mt 16:21
**8:32** m Jn 18:20
**8:33** n Mt 4:10
**8:34** o Mt 10:38; Lk 14:27
**8:35** p Jn 12:25
**8:38** q Mt 8:20 r Mt 10:33; Lk 12:9

[a]26 Some manuscripts *Don't go and tell anyone in the village* [b]29 Or *Messiah.* "The Christ" (Greek) and "the Messiah" (Hebrew) both mean "the Anointed One." [c]35 The Greek word means either *life* or *soul*; also in verse 36.

9:1 s Mt 24:30
9:3 t Mt 28:3
9:5 u Mt 23:7
9:9 v Mk 8:30
9:12 w Mt 16:21 x Lk 23:11
9:13 y Mt 11:14

**9** And he said to them, "I tell you the truth, some who are standing here will not taste death before they see the kingdom of God come with power."[s]

## The Transfiguration

2 After six days Jesus took Peter, James and John with him and led them up a high mountain, where they were all alone. There he was transfigured before them. 3 His clothes became dazzling white,[t] whiter than anyone in the world could bleach them. 4 And there appeared before them Elijah and Moses, who were talking with Jesus.

5 Peter said to Jesus, "Rabbi,[u] it is good for us to be here. Let us put up three shelters—one for you, one for Moses and one for Elijah." 6 (He did not know what to say, they were so frightened.)

7 Then a cloud appeared and enveloped them, and a voice came from the cloud: "This is my Son, whom I love. Listen to him!"

8 Suddenly, when they looked around, they no longer saw anyone with them except Jesus.

9 As they were coming down the mountain, Jesus gave them orders not to tell anyone[v] what they had seen until the Son of Man had risen from the dead. 10 They kept the matter to themselves, discussing what "rising from the dead" meant.

11 And they asked him, "Why do the teachers of the law say that Elijah must come first?"

12 Jesus replied, "To be sure, Elijah does come first, and restores all things. Why then is it written that the Son of Man must suffer much[w] and be rejected?[x] 13 But I tell you, Elijah has come,[y] and they have done to him everything they wished, just as it is written about him."

## The Healing of a Boy With an Evil Spirit

14 When they came to the other disciples, they saw a large crowd around them and the teachers of the law arguing with them. 15 As soon as all the people saw Jesus, they were overwhelmed with wonder and ran to greet him.

16 "What are you arguing with them about?" he asked.

17 A man in the crowd answered, "Teacher, I brought you my son, who is possessed by a spirit that has robbed him of speech. 18 Whenever it seizes him, it throws him to the ground. He foams at the mouth, gnashes his teeth and becomes rigid. I asked your disciples to drive out the spirit, but they could not."

19 "O unbelieving generation," Jesus replied, "how long shall I stay with you? How long shall I put up with you? Bring the boy to me."

20 So they brought him. When the spirit saw Jesus, it immediately threw the boy into a convulsion. He fell to the ground and rolled around, foaming at the mouth.[z]

21 Jesus asked the boy's father, "How long has he been like this?"

"From childhood," he answered. 22 "It has often thrown him into fire or water to kill him. But if you can do anything, take pity on us and help us."

23 "'If you can'?" said Jesus. "Everything is possible for him who believes."[a]

24 Immediately the boy's father exclaimed, "I do believe; help me overcome my unbelief!"

25 When Jesus saw that a crowd was running to the scene,[b] he rebuked the evil[a] spirit. "You deaf and mute spirit," he said, "I command you, come out of him and never enter him again."

26 The spirit shrieked, convulsed him violently and came out. The boy looked so much like a corpse that many said, "He's dead." 27 But Jesus took him by the hand and lifted him to his feet, and he stood up.

28 After Jesus had gone indoors, his disciples asked him privately,[c] "Why couldn't we drive it out?"

29 He replied, "This kind can come out only by prayer.[b]"

30 They left that place and passed through Galilee. Jesus did not want anyone to know where they were, 31 because he was teaching his disciples. He said to them, "The Son of Man is going to be betrayed into the hands of men. They will kill him,[d] and after three days[e] he will rise." 32 But they did not under-

9:20 z Mk 1:26
9:23 a Mk 11:23; Jn 11:40
9:25 b ver 15
9:28 c Mk 7:17
9:31 d ver 12 e Mt 16:21

[a] 25 Greek *unclean* [b] 29 Some manuscripts *prayer and fasting*

stand what he meant[f] and were afraid to ask him about it.

## Who Is the Greatest?

33 They came to Capernaum. When he was in the house, he asked them, "What were you arguing about on the road?" 34 But they kept quiet because on the way they had argued about who was the greatest.[g]

35 Sitting down, Jesus called the Twelve and said, "If anyone wants to be first, he must be the very last, and the servant of all."[h]

36 He took a little child and had him stand among them. Taking him in his arms,[i] he said to them, 37 "Whoever welcomes one of these little children in my name welcomes me; and whoever welcomes me does not welcome me but the one who sent me."[j]

## Whoever Is Not Against Us Is for Us

38 "Teacher," said John, "we saw a man driving out demons in your name and we told him to stop, because he was not one of us."[k]

39 "Do not stop him," Jesus said. "No one who does a miracle in my name can in the next moment say anything bad about me, 40 for whoever is not against us is for us.[l] 41 I tell you the truth, anyone who gives you a cup of water in my name because you belong to Christ will certainly not lose his reward.[m]

## Causing to Sin

42 "And if anyone causes one of these little ones who believe in me to sin, it would be better for him to be thrown into the sea with a large millstone tied around his neck.[n] 43 If your hand causes you to sin,[o] cut it off. It is better for you to enter life maimed than with two hands to go into hell,[p] where the fire never goes out.[a] 45 And if your foot causes you to sin, cut it off. It is better for you to enter life crippled than to have two feet and be thrown into hell.[b] 47 And if your eye causes you to sin,[q] pluck it out. It is better for you to enter the kingdom of God with one eye than to have two eyes and be thrown into hell, 48 where

"'their worm does not die,
and the fire is not quenched.'[c][r]

49 Everyone will be salted[s] with fire.

50 "Salt is good, but if it loses its saltiness, how can you make it salty again?[t] Have salt in yourselves,[u] and be at peace with each other."[v]

## Divorce

10 Jesus then left that place and went into the region of Judea and across the Jordan.[w] Again crowds of people came to him, and as was his custom, he taught them.

2 Some Pharisees came and tested him by asking, "Is it lawful for a man to divorce his wife?"

3 "What did Moses command you?" he replied.

4 They said, "Moses permitted a man to write a certificate of divorce and send her away."[x]

5 "It was because your hearts were hard that Moses wrote you this law," Jesus replied. 6 "But at the beginning of creation God 'made them male and female.'[d][y] 7 'For this reason a man will leave his father and mother and be united to his wife,[e] 8 and the two will become one flesh.'[f][z] So they are no longer two, but one. 9 Therefore what God has joined together, let man not separate."

10 When they were in the house again, the disciples asked Jesus about this. 11 He answered, "Anyone who divorces his wife and marries another woman commits adultery against her.[a] 12 And if she divorces her husband and marries another man, she commits adultery."

## The Little Children and Jesus

13 People were bringing little children to Jesus to have him touch them, but the disciples rebuked them. 14 When Jesus saw this, he was indignant. He said to them, "Let the little children come to me, and do not hinder them, for the kingdom of God belongs to such as these. 15 I tell you the truth, anyone who will not receive the kingdom of God like a little child will never enter it."[b] 16 And

**9:32** f Lk 2:50; 9:45; 18:34; Jn 12:16
**9:34** g Lk 22:24
**9:35** h Mt 20:26; Mk 10:43; Lk 22:26
**9:36** i Mk 10:16
**9:37** j Mt 10:40
**9:38** k Nu 11:27–29
**9:40** l Mt 12:30
**9:41** m Mt 10:42
**9:42** n Lk 17:2
**9:43** o Mt 5:29 p Mt 5:30
**9:47** q Mt 5:29
**9:48** r Isa 66:24
**9:49** s Lev 2:13
**9:50** t Mt 5:13; Lk 14:34,35 u Col 4:6 v Ro 12:18; 2Co 13:11
**10:1** w Jn 10:40
**10:4** x Dt 24:1–4
**10:6** y Ge 1:27; 5:2
**10:8** z Ge 2:24
**10:11** a Mt 5:32; Lk 16:18
**10:15** b Mt 18:3

[a] 43 Some manuscripts *out,* [44] *where / " 'their worm does not die, / and the fire is not quenched.'* [b] 45 Some manuscripts *hell,* [46] *where / " 'their worm does not die, / and the fire is not quenched.'* [c] 48 Isaiah 66:24 [d] 6 Gen. 1:27 [e] 7 Some early manuscripts do not have *and be united to his wife.* [f] 8 Gen. 2:24

**10:17** c Mk1:40 d Lk10:25
**10:19** e Ex20:12–16
**10:21** f Mt6:20; Lk12:33
**10:27** g Mt19:26
**10:30** h Mt6:33
**10:31** i Mt19:30

he took the children in his arms, put his hands on them and blessed them.

## The Rich Young Man

17 As Jesus started on his way, a man ran up to him and fell on his knees[c] before him. "Good teacher," he asked, "what must I do to inherit eternal life?"[d]

18 "Why do you call me good?" Jesus answered. "No one is good—except God alone. 19 You know the commandments: 'Do not murder, do not commit adultery, do not steal, do not give false testimony, do not defraud, honor your father and mother.'[a]"[e]

20 "Teacher," he declared, "all these I have kept since I was a boy."

21 Jesus looked at him and loved him. "One thing you lack," he said. "Go, sell everything you have and give to the poor, and you will have treasure in heaven.[f] Then come, follow me."

22 At this the man's face fell. He went away sad, because he had great wealth.

23 Jesus looked around and said to his disciples, "How hard it is for the rich to enter the kingdom of God!"

24 The disciples were amazed at his words. But Jesus said again, "Children, how hard it is[b] to enter the kingdom of God! 25 It is easier for a camel to go through the eye of a needle than for a rich man to enter the kingdom of God."

26 The disciples were even more amazed, and said to each other, "Who then can be saved?"

27 Jesus looked at them and said, "With man this is impossible, but not with God; all things are possible with God."[g]

28 Peter said to him, "We have left everything to follow you!"

29 "I tell you the truth," Jesus replied, "no one who has left home or brothers or sisters or mother or father or children or fields for me and the gospel 30 will fail to receive a hundred times as much[h] in this present age (homes, brothers, sisters, mothers, children and fields—and with them, persecutions) and in the age to come, eternal life. 31 But many who are first will be last, and the last first."[i]

## Jesus Again Predicts His Death

32 They were on their way up to Jerusalem, with Jesus leading the way, and the disciples were astonished, while those who followed were afraid. Again he took the Twelve aside and told them what was going to happen to him. 33 "We are going up to Jerusalem," he said, "and the Son of Man will be betrayed to the chief priests and teachers of the law. They will condemn him to death and will hand him over to the Gentiles, 34 who will mock him and spit on him, flog him[j] and kill him. Three days later he will rise."

## The Request of James and John

35 Then James and John, the sons of Zebedee, came to him. "Teacher," they said, "we want you to do for us whatever we ask."

36 "What do you want me to do for you?" he asked.

37 They replied, "Let one of us sit at your right and the other at your left in your glory."[k]

38 "You don't know what you are asking," Jesus said. "Can you drink the cup[l] I drink or be baptized with the baptism I am baptized with?"[m]

39 "We can," they answered.

Jesus said to them, "You will drink the cup I drink and be baptized with the baptism I am baptized with,[n] 40 but to sit at my right or left is not for me to grant. These places belong to those for whom they have been prepared."

41 When the ten heard about this, they became indignant with James and John. 42 Jesus called them together and said, "You know that those who are regarded as rulers of the Gentiles lord it over them, and their high officials exercise authority over them. 43 Not so with you. Instead, whoever wants to become great among you must be your servant,[o] 44 and whoever wants to be first must be slave of all. 45 For even the Son of Man did not come to be served, but to serve,[p] and to give his life as a ransom for many."

## Blind Bartimaeus Receives His Sight

46 Then they came to Jericho. As Jesus and his disciples, together with a large

**10:34** j Mt16:21
**10:37** k Mt19:28
**10:38** l Mt20:22 m Lk12:50
**10:39** n Ac12:2; Rev1:9
**10:43** o Mk9:35
**10:45** p Mt20:28

[a] 19 Exodus 20:12–16; Deut. 5:16–20 [b] 24 Some manuscripts *is for those who trust in riches*

# Inspire

## CHILDREN: A BLESSED HERITAGE FROM GOD

"Children should be seen and not heard" is an old saying that some have used to imply that children are insignificant—they may be cute to look at, but they don't have anything meaningful to say. This perception is absolutely contrary to the way God views little ones. Children, as the psalmist pointed out so long ago, are indeed important, a "heritage" and "reward" from the Lord (Ps 127:3).

Few, if any, of us would deny that children are a blessing from God. Jesus taught his disciples, in fact, that to welcome a child is to welcome him (see Mk 9:37) and that to be like a child is the key to conversion (see Mk 10:15). The Bible teaches that children are significant, and teachings about God are important for their daily lives (see Dt 6:6–7). During Jesus' earthly ministry, mothers brought their little ones to him for a physical blessing, and he gladly took them in his arms and did so (see Mk 9:36–37; 10:13–16). Jesus also warned people not to harm children, especially by causing them to sin (see Mt 18:5–6). Paul added that parents must be careful not to exasperate their children (see Eph 6:4).

Children have traditionally been valued in the African American culture as well as in other cultures. To assure our children's rightful place in society and in the kingdom of God, parents are to introduce them to Jesus. We must prepare our children to fulfill God's call, encourage them to follow wisdom, teach them to make wise choices and instruct them to obey their parents in the Lord.

Unfortunately, destructive criticism, stereotyping, unrealistic expectations and dysfunctional environments can destroy the relationship between parents and children. To build and maintain meaningful relationships with their sons and daughters, parents must provide a loving environment filled with encouragement and spoken love. In such an atmosphere our children are free to thrive and then, in turn, to "build" strong, godly sons and daughters for generations to come.

—G. London

### read

Mark 10:13–16; see also Deuteronomy 6:1–25; Psalm 127:1–5; Matthew 18:1–10; Mark 9:33–37.

**See also** the Inspire Notes "A Great Challenge: Teaching Our Children," "Motherhood," "Parenting," "Raising Children: Modeling Discipleship" and "Nurturing Spiritual Gifts in Our Children," and the Women of the Bible Notes "Daughter of Jairus: A Testament of Faith" and "Mary, the Mother of Jesus: A Model of Motherhood."

### WOMAN *of* COLOR

How do you treat your children or children in your community?

For the next Inspire note, go to page 1179.

> *"Our aim should be service, not success."*
> —Barbara Smith, former model turned restaurateur and entertainer

crowd, were leaving the city, a blind man,
Bartimaeus (that is, the Son of Timaeus),
was sitting by the roadside begging. 47 When
he heard that it was Jesus
of Nazareth,[q] he began to
shout, "Jesus, Son of Da-
vid,[r] have mercy on me!"
48 Many rebuked him
and told him to be quiet,
but he shouted all the
more, "Son of David, have
mercy on me!"
49 Jesus stopped and
said, "Call him."
So they called to the
blind man, "Cheer up! On
your feet! He's calling you." 50 Throwing his
cloak aside, he jumped to his feet and came
to Jesus.
51 "What do you want me to do for you?"
Jesus asked him.
The blind man said, "Rabbi,[s] I want to
see."
52 "Go," said Jesus, "your faith has healed
you."[t] Immediately he received his sight and
followed Jesus along the road.

## The Triumphal Entry

11 As they approached Jerusalem and
came to Bethphage and Bethany[u] at
the Mount of Olives,[v] Jesus sent two of his
disciples, 2 saying to them, "Go to the village
ahead of you, and just as you enter it, you
will find a colt tied there, which no one has
ever ridden. Untie it and bring it here. 3 If
anyone asks you, 'Why are you doing this?'
tell him, 'The Lord needs it and will send it
back here shortly.' "
4 They went and found a colt outside in the
street, tied at a doorway.[w] As they untied it,
5 some people standing there asked, "What
are you doing, untying that colt?" 6 They an-
swered as Jesus had told them to, and the
people let them go. 7 When they brought the
colt to Jesus and threw their cloaks over it,
he sat on it. 8 Many people spread their cloaks
on the road, while others spread branches
they had cut in the fields. 9 Those who went
ahead and those who followed shouted,

"Hosanna![a]"

"Blessed is he who comes in the name of
the Lord!"[b][x]

10 "Blessed is the coming kingdom of our
father David!"

"Hosanna in the highest!"

11 Jesus entered Jerusalem and went to the
temple. He looked around at everything,
but since it was already late, he went out to
Bethany with the Twelve.[y]

## Jesus Clears the Temple

12 The next day as they were leaving
Bethany, Jesus was hungry. 13 Seeing in the
distance a fig tree in leaf, he went to find out
if it had any fruit. When he reached it, he
found nothing but leaves, because it was not
the season for figs. 14 Then he said to the tree,
"May no one ever eat fruit from you again."
And his disciples heard him say it.
15 On reaching Jerusalem, Jesus entered
the temple area and began driving out those
who were buying and selling there. He over-
turned the tables of the money changers and
the benches of those selling doves, 16 and
would not allow anyone to carry merchan-
dise through the temple courts. 17 And as he
taught them, he said, "Is it not written:

" 'My house will be called
a house of prayer for all nations'[c]?[z]
But you have made it 'a den of robbers.'[d]"[a]

18 The chief priests and the teachers of the
law heard this and began looking for a way
to kill him, for they feared him,[b] because the
whole crowd was amazed at his teaching.[c]
19 When evening came, they[e] went out of
the city.[d]

## The Withered Fig Tree

20 In the morning, as they went along,
they saw the fig tree withered from the
roots. 21 Peter remembered and said to
Jesus, "Rabbi,[e] look! The fig tree you cursed
has withered!"
22 "Have[f] faith in God," Jesus answered.
23 "I tell you the truth, if anyone says to
this mountain, 'Go, throw yourself into the
sea,' and does not doubt in his heart but
believes that what he says will happen, it

**10:47** q Mk 1:24; r Mt 9:27
**10:51** s Mt 23:7
**10:52** t Mt 9:22
**11:1** u Mt 21:17; v Mt 21:1
**11:4** w Mk 14:16
**11:9** x Ps 118:25,26; Mt 23:39
**11:11** y Mt 21:12,17
**11:17** z Isa 56:7; a Jer 7:11
**11:18** b Mt 21:46; Mk 12:12; Lk 20:19; c Mt 7:28
**11:19** d Lk 21:37
**11:21** e Mt 23:7

[a] 9 A Hebrew expression meaning "Save!" which became an exclamation of praise; also in verse 10 [b] 9 Psalm 118:25,26 [c] 17 Isaiah 56:7 [d] 17 Jer. 7:11 [e] 19 Some early manuscripts *he* [f] 22 Some early manuscripts *If you have*

# Inspire

## PRAYER: A GOD-GIVEN PROMISE

"Therefore I tell you, whatever you ask for in prayer, believe that you have received it, and it will be yours" (Mk 11:24). These words from the Gospel of Mark can leave us breathless. God promises to hear and answer our prayers whenever we pray in faith. What a remarkable gift from God! However, if we were to take this verse out of the context of the rest of the New Testament, it might appear that we have been given carte blanche for our every desire. God's promises are never "stand-alone" texts. They are always an intrinsic part of our God-given relationship with Jesus Christ.

The promise that God will answer our prayers is not offered to us to satisfy our own selfish whims, to destroy others or to arbitrarily manipulate our own or others' lives. God will not compromise the integrity of his Word in order to respond in the affirmative to our every desire. Our prayers are to be in harmony with the Word. Sometimes God's answers may be unclear or different from those we may have expected or wanted. At other times the manifestation of the answer may be delayed. God's possible answers include yes, no and wait.

Matthew 6 records Jesus' teachings about prayer—including what we have come to call "The Lord's Prayer." Jesus emphasized that we should not worry; God is more than able to care for our material and physical needs. When believers pray with faith and sincerity, God often does more than we expect or even imagine. He answers our prayers liberally and generously.

God's prayer promises are part of his plan to redeem all of creation through the life, death and resurrection of Jesus Christ. We are expected to pray based upon a knowledge of, and belief in, God's truth as revealed to us in Christ, the living Word, and in the Bible, God's written Word. We are to come to God in faith, believing that he is faithful to hear and answer our prayers as his story continues to be revealed in us.

—M. W. Bullock

### read

Mark 11:20–26; see also Matthew 6:5–15,25–34; Luke 11:1–13; John 14:12–14; James 5:13–18; Jude 20.

See also the Inspire Notes "Prayer: The Antidote to Worry," "God's Promises: Always 'Yes' and 'Amen,'" "Prayer" and "Faith," and the Women of the Bible Notes "Hannah: What Do You Do When God Says 'No'?" "Daughter of Jarius: A Testament of Faith," "The Persistent Widow: Always Pray" and "Rhoda: Doing Her Duty."

### WOMAN of COLOR

How is your prayer life? Do you pray with faith that God will answer you?

For the next Inspire note, go to page 1218.

11:23 f Mt21:21
11:24 g Mt7:7
11:25 h Mt6:14
12:1 i Isa5:1–7

will be done for him.[f] 24 Therefore I tell you,
whatever you ask for in prayer, believe that
you have received it, and it will be yours.[g]
25 And when you stand praying, if you hold
anything against anyone, forgive him, so
that your Father in heaven may forgive you
your sins.[a][h]

## The Authority of Jesus Questioned

27 They arrived again in Jerusalem, and
while Jesus was walking in the temple
courts, the chief priests, the teachers of
the law and the elders came to him. 28 "By
what authority are you doing these things?"
they asked. "And who gave you authority to
do this?"

29 Jesus replied, "I will ask you one ques-
tion. Answer me, and I will tell you by what
authority I am doing these things. 30 John's
baptism—was it from heaven, or from
men? Tell me!"

31 They discussed it among themselves
and said, "If we say, 'From heaven,' he will
ask, 'Then why didn't you believe him?'
32 But if we say, 'From men'..." (They feared
the people, for everyone held that John
really was a prophet.)

33 So they answered Jesus, "We don't
know."

Jesus said, "Neither will I tell you by what
authority I am doing these things."

## The Parable of the Tenants

12 He then began to speak to them in
parables: "A man planted a vine-
yard.[i] He put a wall around it, dug a pit for
the winepress and built a watchtower. Then
he rented the vineyard to some farmers and
went away on a journey. 2 At harvest time he
sent a servant to the tenants to collect from
them some of the fruit of the vineyard. 3 But
they seized him, beat him and sent him
away empty-handed. 4 Then he sent another
servant to them; they struck this man on
the head and treated him shamefully. 5 He
sent still another, and that one they killed.
He sent many others; some of them they
beat, others they killed.

6 "He had one left to send, a son, whom he
loved. He sent him last of all,[j] saying, 'They
will respect my son.'

7 "But the tenants said to one another,
'This is the heir. Come, let's kill him, and
the inheritance will be ours.' 8 So they took
him and killed him, and threw him out of
the vineyard.

9 "What then will the owner of the vine-
yard do? He will come and kill those tenants
and give the vineyard to others. 10 Haven't
you read this scripture:

> "'The stone the builders rejected
> has become the capstone[b];[k]
> 11 the Lord has done this,
> and it is marvelous in our eyes'[c]?"[l]

12 Then they looked for a way to arrest him
because they knew he had spoken the para-
ble against them. But they were afraid of the
crowd;[m] so they left him and went away.[n]

## Paying Taxes to Caesar

13 Later they sent some of the Pharisees
and Herodians[o] to Jesus to catch him in
his words. 14 They came to him and said,
"Teacher, we know you are a man of integ-
rity. You aren't swayed by men, because you
pay no attention to who they are; but you
teach the way of God in accordance with
the truth. Is it right to pay taxes to Caesar or
not? 15 Should we pay or shouldn't we?"

But Jesus knew their hypocrisy. "Why
are you trying to trap me?" he asked. "Bring
me a denarius and let me look at it." 16 They
brought the coin, and he asked them, "Whose
portrait is this? And whose inscription?"

"Caesar's," they replied.

17 Then Jesus said to them, "Give to Caesar
what is Caesar's and to God what is God's."[p]

And they were amazed at him.

## Marriage at the Resurrection

18 Then the Sadducees, who say there is no
resurrection,[q] came to him with a question.
19 "Teacher," they said, "Moses wrote for us
that if a man's brother dies and leaves a wife
but no children, the man must marry the
widow and have children for his brother.[r]
20 Now there were seven brothers. The first
one married and died without leaving any

12:6 j Heb1:1–3
12:10 k Ac4:11
12:11 l Ps118:22,23
12:12 m Mk11:18 n Mt22:22
12:13 o Mt22:16; Mk3:6
12:17 p Ro13:7
12:18 q Ac23:8
12:19 r Dt25:5

[a]25 Some manuscripts *sins.* *26 But if you do not forgive, neither will your Father who is in heaven forgive your sins.*
[b]10 Or *cornerstone* [c]11 Psalm 118:22,23

children. [21]The second one married the widow, but he also died, leaving no child. It was the same with the third. [22]In fact, none of the seven left any children. Last of all, the woman died too. [23]At the resurrection[a] whose wife will she be, since the seven were married to her?"

[24]Jesus replied, "Are you not in error because you do not know the Scriptures or the power of God? [25]When the dead rise, they will neither marry nor be given in marriage; they will be like the angels in heaven.[s] [26]Now about the dead rising—have you not read in the book of Moses, in the account of the bush, how God said to him, 'I am the God of Abraham, the God of Isaac, and the God of Jacob'[b]?[t] [27]He is not the God of the dead, but of the living. You are badly mistaken!"

## The Greatest Commandment

[28]One of the teachers of the law[u] came and heard them debating. Noticing that Jesus had given them a good answer, he asked him, "Of all the commandments, which is the most important?"

[29]"The most important one," answered Jesus, "is this: 'Hear, O Israel, the Lord our God, the Lord is one.[c] [30]Love the Lord your God with all your heart and with all your soul and with all your mind and with all your strength.'[d][v] [31]The second is this: 'Love your neighbor as yourself.'[e][w] There is no commandment greater than these."

[32]"Well said, teacher," the man replied. "You are right in saying that God is one and there is no other but him.[x] [33]To love him with all your heart, with all your understanding and with all your strength, and to love your neighbor as yourself is more important than all burnt offerings and sacrifices."[y]

[34]When Jesus saw that he had answered wisely, he said to him, "You are not far from the kingdom of God." And from then on no one dared ask him any more questions.[z]

## Whose Son Is the Christ?

[35]While Jesus was teaching in the temple courts,[a] he asked, "How is it that the teachers of the law say that the Christ[f] is the son of David?[b] [36]David himself, speaking by the Holy Spirit, declared:

"'The Lord said to my Lord:
"Sit at my right hand
until I put your enemies
under your feet."'[g][c]

[37]David himself calls him 'Lord.' How then can he be his son?"

The large crowd[d] listened to him with delight.

[38]As he taught, Jesus said, "Watch out for the teachers of the law. They like to walk around in flowing robes and be greeted in the marketplaces, [39]and have the most important seats in the synagogues and the places of honor at banquets.[e] [40]They devour widows' houses and for a show make lengthy prayers. Such men will be punished most severely."

## The Widow's Offering

[41]Jesus sat down opposite the place where the offerings were put[f] and watched the crowd putting their money into the temple treasury. Many rich people threw in large amounts. [42]But a poor widow came and put in two very small copper coins,[h] worth only a fraction of a penny.[i]

[43]Calling his disciples to him, Jesus said, "I tell you the truth, this poor widow has put more into the treasury than all the others. [44]They all gave out of their wealth; but she, out of her poverty, put in everything—all she had to live on."[g]

## Signs of the End of the Age

13 As he was leaving the temple, one of his disciples said to him, "Look, Teacher! What massive stones! What magnificent buildings!"

[2]"Do you see all these great buildings?" replied Jesus. "Not one stone here will be left on another; every one will be thrown down."[h]

[3]As Jesus was sitting on the Mount of Olives opposite the temple, Peter, James, John and Andrew asked him privately, [4]"Tell us, when will these things happen? And what will be the sign that they are all about to be fulfilled?"

[5]Jesus said to them: "Watch out that no one deceives you.[i] [6]Many will come in my

**12:25** s 1Co 15:42, 49,52
**12:26** t Ex 3:6
**12:28** u Lk 10:25–28; 20:39
**12:30** v Dt 6:4,5
**12:31** w Lev 19:18
**12:32** x Dt 4:35,39; Isa 45:6,14; 46:9
**12:33** y 1Sa 15:22; Hos 6:6; Mic 6:6–8
**12:34** z Mt 22:46
**12:35** a Mt 26:55; b Mt 9:27
**12:36** c Ps 110:1
**12:37** d Jn 12:9
**12:39** e Lk 11:43
**12:41** f 2Ki 12:9; Jn 8:20
**12:44** g 2Co 8:12
**13:2** h Lk 19:44
**13:5** i Eph 5:6

[a]23 Some manuscripts *resurrection, when men rise from the dead,* [b]26 Exodus 3:6 [c]29 Or *the Lord our God is one Lord*
[d]30 Deut. 6:4,5 [e]31 Lev. 19:18 [f]35 Or *Messiah* [g]36 Psalm 110:1 [h]42 Greek *two lepta* [i]42 Greek *kodrantes*

# The Widow's Offering

## Selfless Giving

Jesus sat down in the temple and watched the multitude of people bring their monetary gifts to one of the 13 trumpet-shaped treasury boxes (see Mk 12:41). Many of the people were wealthy and gave large sums of money. Some gave according to tradition, calculated to the penny by the laws of tithing. One by one they dropped their offerings into the treasury boxes. Quietly, Jesus watched them give funds they did not need for survival.

Jesus noticed a poor widow approach one of the treasury boxes. One could imagine her as an older woman, slightly bent from age. Her head may have been covered with an old cloth, and she probably wore a torn, faded dress. Her fragile, withered hand may have been pressed against her breast, clutching her gift as she walked slowly toward the treasury box. Yet it was not her appearance that drew Jesus' attention. It was her willingness to be obedient to God to the point of giving everything she had. This poor widow dropped two copper coins into the box. These coins were the smallest coins in circulation at that time. But these coins were all she had.

In Jesus' eyes, this woman's gift was greater than all the other gifts combined because her gift constituted all she had. The spirit in which her gift was given made it priceless, for this poor woman had given from her heart. She had given her last in gratitude to God. Jesus was touched by her giving spirit and remarked to his disciples how great her sacrifice was in comparison to the others.

Like the multitude, many of us may give in abundance for self-glorification. Yet Jesus desires that we give of ourselves—our time, talent and money. Jesus calls us to reach beyond the comfortable and give sacrificially. Jesus calls us to be willing to give even our last penny in gratitude to God.

—T. Wade

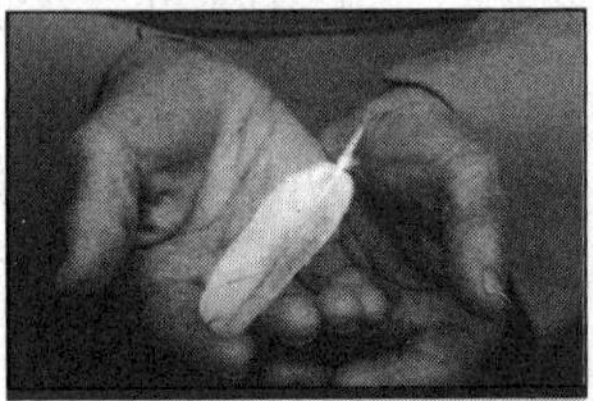

### reflection

*What is your sacrificial gift to God?*

*Give it joyously to the benefit of God's kingdom.*

### read

Mark 12:41–44; Luke 21:1–4.

See also the Inspire Notes "Distress," "Purposeful Giving," "Sacrificial Living" and "Faith," and the Women of the Bible Notes "The Prophet's Widow: God Provides" and "Wise and Foolish Virgins: Preparing for Christ."

For the next Women of the Bible note, go to page 1187.

**13:9** j Mt 10:17
**13:11** k Mt 10:19,20; Lk 12:11,12
**13:12** l Mic 7:6; Mt 10:21
**13:13** m Jn 15:21 n Mt 10:22
**13:14** o Da 9:27; 11:31; 12:11
**13:19** p Da 9:26
**13:21** q Lk 17:23
**13:22** r Mt 7:15 s Jn 4:48
**13:23** t 2Pe 3:17

name, claiming, 'I am he,' and will deceive
many. 7 When you hear of wars and rumors
of wars, do not be alarmed. Such things
must happen, but the end is still to come.
8 Nation will rise against nation, and king-
dom against kingdom. There will be earth-
quakes in various places, and famines.
These are the beginning of birth pains.

9 "You must be on your guard. You will
be handed over to the local councils and
flogged in the synagogues.[j] On account of
me you will stand before governors and
kings as witnesses to them. 10 And the gos-
pel must first be preached to all nations.
11 Whenever you are arrested and brought to
trial, do not worry beforehand about what
to say. Just say whatever is given you at the
time, for it is not you speaking, but the Holy
Spirit.[k]

12 "Brother will betray brother to death,
and a father his child. Children will rebel
against their parents and have them put to
death.[l] 13 All men will hate you because of
me,[m] but he who stands firm to the end will
be saved.[n]

14 "When you see 'the abomination that
causes desolation'[a][o] standing where it[b]
does not belong—let the reader under-
stand—then let those who are in Judea flee
to the mountains. 15 Let no one on the roof
of his house go down or enter the house to
take anything out. 16 Let no one in the field
go back to get his cloak. 17 How dreadful it
will be in those days for pregnant women
and nursing mothers! 18 Pray that this will
not take place in winter, 19 because those
will be days of distress unequaled from the
beginning, when God created the world, un-
til now—and never to be equaled again.[p]
20 If the Lord had not cut short those days,
no one would survive. But for the sake of the
elect, whom he has chosen, he has shortened
them. 21 At that time if anyone says to you,
'Look, here is the Christ[c]!' or, 'Look, there
he is!' do not believe it.[q] 22 For false Christs
and false prophets[r] will appear and perform
signs and miracles[s] to deceive the elect—if
that were possible. 23 So be on your guard;[t] I
have told you everything ahead of time.

24 "But in those days, following that dis-
tress,

" 'the sun will be darkened,
and the moon will not give its light;
25 the stars will fall from the sky,
and the heavenly bodies will be
shaken.'[d][u]

26 "At that time men will see the Son of
Man coming in clouds[v] with great power
and glory. 27 And he will send his angels
and gather his elect from the four winds,
from the ends of the earth to the ends of the
heavens.[w]

28 "Now learn this lesson from the fig tree:
As soon as its twigs get tender and its leaves
come out, you know that summer is near.
29 Even so, when you see these things hap-
pening, you know that it is near, right at the
door. 30 I tell you the truth, this generation[e]
will certainly not pass away until all these
things have happened.[x] 31 Heaven and earth
will pass away, but my words will never
pass away.[y]

## The Day and Hour Unknown

32 "No one knows about that day or hour,
not even the angels in heaven, nor the Son,
but only the Father.[z] 33 Be on guard! Be
alert[f]![a] You do not know when that time
will come. 34 It's like a man going away: He
leaves his house and puts his servants[b] in
charge, each with his assigned task, and
tells the one at the door to keep watch.

35 "Therefore keep watch because you do
not know when the owner of the house will
come back—whether in the evening, or at
midnight, or when the rooster crows, or at
dawn. 36 If he comes suddenly, do not let him
find you sleeping. 37 What I say to you, I say
to everyone: 'Watch!' "

## Jesus Anointed at Bethany

14 Now the Passover[c] and the Feast of
Unleavened Bread were only two
days away, and the chief priests and the
teachers of the law were looking for some
sly way to arrest Jesus and kill him.[d] 2 "But
not during the Feast," they said, "or the peo-
ple may riot."

3 While he was in Bethany,[e] reclining at
the table in the home of a man known as
Simon the Leper, a woman came with an

**13:25** u Isa 34:4
**13:26** v Da 7:13; Mt 16:27; Rev 1:7
**13:27** w Zec 2:6
**13:30** x Mk 9:1
**13:31** y Mt 5:18
**13:32** z Ac 1:7
**13:33** a 1Th 5:6
**13:34** b Mt 25:14
**14:1** c Jn 11:55; 13:1 d Mt 12:14
**14:3** e Mt 21:17

[a] 14 Daniel 9:27; 11:31; 12:11 [b] 14 Or *he*; also in verse 29 [c] 21 Or *Messiah* [d] 25 Isaiah 13:10; 34:4 [e] 30 Or *race*
[f] 33 Some manuscripts *alert and pray*

**14:3** f Lk7:37–39
**14:7** g Dt15:11
**14:8** h Jn19:40
**14:12** i Ex12:1–11; 1Co5:7

alabaster jar of very expensive perfume,
made of pure nard. She broke the jar and
poured the perfume on his head.[f]
4Some of those present were saying
indignantly to one another, "Why this
waste of perfume? 5It could have been sold
for more than a year's wages[a] and the money
given to the poor." And they rebuked her
harshly.
6"Leave her alone," said Jesus. "Why are
you bothering her? She has done a beautiful
thing to me. 7The poor you will always have
with you, and you can help them any time
you want.[g] But you will not always have me.
8She did what she could. She poured per-
fume on my body beforehand to prepare for
my burial.[h] 9I tell you the truth, wherever
the gospel is preached throughout the
world, what she has done will also be told,
in memory of her."
10Then Judas Iscariot, one of the Twelve,
went to the chief priests to betray Jesus to
them. 11They were delighted to hear this and
promised to give him money. So he watched
for an opportunity to hand him over.

## The Lord's Supper

12On the first day of the Feast of Unleav-
ened Bread, when it was customary to sac-
rifice the Passover lamb,[i] Jesus' disciples
asked him, "Where do you want us to go and
make preparations for you to eat the Pass-
over?"
13So he sent two of his disciples, telling
them, "Go into the city, and a man carry-
ing a jar of water will meet you. Follow
him. 14Say to the owner of the house he en-
ters, 'The Teacher asks: Where is my guest
room, where I may eat the Passover with my
disciples?' 15He will show you a large upper
room, furnished and ready. Make prepara-
tions for us there."
16The disciples left, went into the city and
found things just as Jesus had told them. So
they prepared the Passover.
17When evening came, Jesus arrived with
the Twelve. 18While they were reclining at
the table eating, he said, "I tell you the truth,
one of you will betray me—one who is eat-
ing with me."
19They were saddened, and one by one
they said to him, "Surely not I?"
20"It is one of the Twelve," he replied,
"one who dips bread into the bowl with me.
21The Son of Man will go just as it is written
about him. But woe to that man who betrays
the Son of Man! It would be better for him if
he had not been born."
22While they were eating, Jesus took
bread, gave thanks and broke it,[j] and gave
it to his disciples, saying, "Take it; this is
my body."
23Then he took the cup, gave thanks
and offered it to them, and they all drank
from it.[k]
24"This is my blood of the[b] covenant,
which is poured out for many," he said
to them. 25"I tell you the truth, I will not
drink again of the fruit of the vine until that
day when I drink it anew in the kingdom
of God."
26When they had sung a hymn, they went
out to the Mount of Olives.[l]

## Jesus Predicts Peter's Denial

27"You will all fall away," Jesus told them,
"for it is written:

"'I will strike the shepherd,
and the sheep will be scattered.'[c][m]

28But after I have risen, I will go ahead of
you into Galilee."[n]
29Peter declared, "Even if all fall away, I
will not."
30"I tell you the truth," Jesus answered,
"today—yes, tonight—before the rooster
crows twice[d] you yourself will disown me
three times."[o]
31But Peter insisted emphatically, "Even
if I have to die with you, I will never disown
you." And all the others said the same.

## Gethsemane

32They went to a place called Gethsemane,
and Jesus said to his disciples, "Sit here
while I pray." 33He took Peter, James and
John along with him, and he began to be
deeply distressed and troubled. 34"My soul
is overwhelmed with sorrow to the point

**14:22** j Mt14:19
**14:23** k 1Co10:16
**14:26** l Mt21:1
**14:27** m Zec13:7
**14:28** n Mk16:7
**14:30** o ver 66–72; Lk22:34; Jn13:38

[a]5 Greek *than three hundred denarii* [b]24 Some manuscripts *the new* [c]27 Zech. 13:7 [d]30 Some early manuscripts do not have *twice.*

of death,"[p] he said to them. "Stay here and keep watch."

35 Going a little farther, he fell to the ground and prayed that if possible the hour[q] might pass from him. 36 "*Abba*,[a] Father,"[r] he said, "everything is possible for you. Take this cup from me. Yet not what I will, but what you will."[s]

37 Then he returned to his disciples and found them sleeping. "Simon," he said to Peter, "are you asleep? Could you not keep watch for one hour? 38 Watch and pray so that you will not fall into temptation.[t] The spirit is willing, but the body is weak."[u]

39 Once more he went away and prayed the same thing. 40 When he came back, he again found them sleeping, because their eyes were heavy. They did not know what to say to him.

41 Returning the third time, he said to them, "Are you still sleeping and resting? Enough! The hour[v] has come. Look, the Son of Man is betrayed into the hands of sinners. 42 Rise! Let us go! Here comes my betrayer!"

## Jesus Arrested

43 Just as he was speaking, Judas, one of the Twelve, appeared. With him was a crowd armed with swords and clubs, sent from the chief priests, the teachers of the law, and the elders.

44 Now the betrayer had arranged a signal with them: "The one I kiss is the man; arrest him and lead him away under guard." 45 Going at once to Jesus, Judas said, "Rabbi!"[w] and kissed him. 46 The men seized Jesus and arrested him. 47 Then one of those standing near drew his sword and struck the servant of the high priest, cutting off his ear.

48 "Am I leading a rebellion," said Jesus, "that you have come out with swords and clubs to capture me? 49 Every day I was with you, teaching in the temple courts, and you did not arrest me. But the Scriptures must be fulfilled."[x] 50 Then everyone deserted him and fled.[y]

51 A young man, wearing nothing but a linen garment, was following Jesus. When they seized him, 52 he fled naked, leaving his garment behind.

## Before the Sanhedrin

53 They took Jesus to the high priest, and all the chief priests, elders and teachers of the law came together. 54 Peter followed him at a distance, right into the courtyard of the high priest.[z] There he sat with the guards and warmed himself at the fire.[a]

55 The chief priests and the whole Sanhedrin[b] were looking for evidence against Jesus so that they could put him to death, but they did not find any. 56 Many testified falsely against him, but their statements did not agree.

57 Then some stood up and gave this false testimony against him: 58 "We heard him say, 'I will destroy this man-made temple and in three days will build another,[c] not made by man.'" 59 Yet even then their testimony did not agree.

60 Then the high priest stood up before them and asked Jesus, "Are you not going to answer? What is this testimony that these men are bringing against you?" 61 But Jesus remained silent and gave no answer.[d]

Again the high priest asked him, "Are you the Christ,[b] the Son of the Blessed One?"

62 "I am," said Jesus. "And you will see the Son of Man sitting at the right hand of the Mighty One and coming on the clouds of heaven."

63 The high priest tore his clothes.[e] "Why do we need any more witnesses?" he asked. 64 "You have heard the blasphemy. What do you think?"

They all condemned him as worthy of death.[f] 65 Then some began to spit at him; they blindfolded him, struck him with their fists, and said, "Prophesy!" And the guards took him and beat him.

## Peter Disowns Jesus

66 While Peter was below in the courtyard,[g] one of the servant girls of the high priest came by. 67 When she saw Peter warming himself,[h] she looked closely at him.

"You also were with that Nazarene, Jesus,"[i] she said.

68 But he denied it. "I don't know or understand what you're talking about," he said, and went out into the entryway.[c]

69 When the servant girl saw him there,

**14:34** p Jn 12:27
**14:35** q ver 41
**14:36** r Ro 8:15; Gal 4:6 s Mt 26:39
**14:38** t Mt 6:13 u Ro 7:22,23
**14:41** v ver 35
**14:45** w Mt 23:7
**14:49** x Isa 53:7–12
**14:50** y ver 27
**14:54** z Mt 26:3 a Jn 18:18
**14:55** b Mt 5:22
**14:58** c Mk 15:29; Jn 2:19
**14:61** d Isa 53:7
**14:63** e Nu 14:6; Ac 14:14
**14:64** f Lev 24:16
**14:66** g ver 54
**14:67** h ver 54 i Mk 1:24

[a] 36 Aramaic for *Father* [b] 61 Or *Messiah* [c] 68 Some early manuscripts *entryway and the rooster crowed*

**14:70** j ver 30,68,72 k Ac 2:7
**14:72** l ver 30,68
**15:1** m Mt 27:1; Lk 22:66 n Mt 5:22

she said again to those standing around,
"This fellow is one of them." 70 Again he de-
nied it.[j]

After a little while, those standing near
said to Peter, "Surely you are one of them,
for you are a Galilean."[k]

71 He began to call down curses on him-
self, and he swore to them, "I don't know
this man you're talking about."

72 Immediately the rooster crowed the
second time.[a] Then Peter remembered the
word Jesus had spoken to him: "Before
the rooster crows twice[b] you will disown
me three times."[l] And he broke down
and wept.

## Jesus Before Pilate

15 Very early in the morning, the chief
priests, with the elders, the teach-
ers of the law[m] and the whole Sanhedrin,[n]
reached a decision. They bound Jesus, led
him away and handed him over to Pilate.

2 "Are you the king of the Jews?" asked
Pilate.

"Yes, it is as you say," Jesus replied.

3 The chief priests accused him of many
things. 4 So again Pilate asked him, "Aren't
you going to answer? See how many things
they are accusing you of."

5 But Jesus still made no reply, and Pilate
was amazed.

6 Now it was the custom at the Feast to re-
lease a prisoner whom the people requested.
7 A man called Barabbas was in prison with
the insurrectionists who had committed
murder in the uprising. 8 The crowd came
up and asked Pilate to do for them what he
usually did.

9 "Do you want me to release to you the
king of the Jews?" asked Pilate, 10 knowing
it was out of envy that the chief priests had
handed Jesus over to him. 11 But the chief
priests stirred up the crowd to have Pilate
release Barabbas[o] instead.

12 "What shall I do, then, with the one
you call the king of the Jews?" Pilate
asked them.

13 "Crucify him!" they shouted.

14 "Why? What crime has he committed?"
asked Pilate.

But they shouted all the louder, "Crucify
him!"

15 Wanting to satisfy the crowd, Pilate
released Barabbas to them. He had Jesus
flogged, and handed him over to be cruci-
fied.

## The Soldiers Mock Jesus

16 The soldiers led Jesus away into the
palace (that is, the Praetorium) and called
together the whole company of soldiers.
17 They put a purple robe on him, then
twisted together a crown of thorns and set it
on him. 18 And they began to call out to him,
"Hail, king of the Jews!" 19 Again and again
they struck him on the head with a staff and
spit on him. Falling on their knees, they
paid homage to him. 20 And when they had
mocked him, they took off the purple robe
and put his own clothes on him. Then they
led him out to crucify him.

## The Crucifixion

21 A certain man from Cyrene,[p] Simon,
the father of Alexander and Rufus,[q] was
passing by on his way in from the country,
and they forced him to carry the cross.[r]
22 They brought Jesus to the place called

**15:11** o Ac 3:14
**15:21** p Mt 27:32 q Ro 16:13 r Lk 23:26

[a] 72 Some early manuscripts do not have *the second time.* [b] 72 Some early manuscripts do not have *twice.*

## The African Presence

**Mark 15:21**

Simon of Cyrene was from an area located on the northern coast of Africa. Cyrene was the chief city in Libya and North Africa.

# The Servant Girl

## The Truth, the Whole Truth and Nothing but the Truth

Throughout most of his time with Jesus, Simon Peter showed himself strong, brave, loyal and faithful. He vowed never to deny Jesus, even under the most strenuous circumstances (see Mk 14:29–31). But who was he really? What hidden truth did Jesus know about Peter? Little did Peter know that an unnamed servant girl would reveal a side of him that not even he knew existed.

While warming himself by a fire in the courtyard of the high priest after the arrest of Jesus, Peter was approached by this servant girl. "You also were with that Nazarene, Jesus," she said (Mk 14:67). It was then that Peter first denied any association with Jesus.

A second time the girl accused Peter, and again he denied his relationship to Jesus. Jesus was in the process of being interrogated and beaten, and Peter surely feared for his own life. The servant girl and those with her accused Peter again. This time he called down curses on himself if he was lying and swore that he did not know Jesus. In his first two denials, Peter denied being identified *with* Jesus. In his third denial, he denied *Jesus himself.*

While Peter had three opportunities to speak the truth, he allowed a spirit of fear and self-preservation to control him. But by lying to the girl and those around her, he was really lying to himself. But he couldn't lie to God. God used both Peter and the servant girl to illustrate to us that even those who profess to love Jesus—even those who follow him and promise to give up their lives for him—can fall into the trap of fear and hopelessness if they do not fully place their trust in him.

Consider how often we lie to others and to ourselves in the midst of unpleasant situations (or keep silent when we know we should speak). How often do we deny God, compromising our trust, loyalty and strength of character in an effort to alleviate the pain or discomfort of a given situation? By God's grace Peter was forgiven (see Lk 24:34; Jn 21:15–19), and the same grace allows us to be forgiven too. Let's remember that when we learn to tell the truth, the whole truth and nothing but the truth—no matter the circumstances—that God is better able to use us for his glory.

—M. Cotton Bohanon

### reflection

*Whom has God used to show you the truth about yourself?*

*Thank God for his grace and mercy.*

*Show grace and mercy to others today.*

### read

Mark 14:66–72; see also Matthew 26:69–75; Luke 22:54–62; John 18:15–18,25–27.

See also the Inspire Notes "Grace and Mercy" and "Forgiveness: God's Extended Mercy" and the Women of the Bible Note "Sapphira: A Lost Opportunity for Truth."

For the next Women of the Bible note, go to page 1189.

Golgotha (which means The Place of the Skull). 23 Then they offered him wine mixed with myrrh, but he did not take it. 24 And they crucified him. Dividing up his clothes, they cast lots[s] to see what each would get.

25 It was the third hour when they crucified him. 26 The written notice of the charge against him read: THE KING OF THE JEWS. 27 They crucified two robbers with him, one on his right and one on his left.[a] 29 Those who passed by hurled insults at him, shaking their heads[t] and saying, "So! You who are going to destroy the temple and build it in three days,[u] 30 come down from the cross and save yourself!"

31 In the same way the chief priests and the teachers of the law mocked him[v] among themselves. "He saved others," they said, "but he can't save himself! 32 Let this Christ,[b] this King of Israel, come down now from the cross, that we may see and believe." Those crucified with him also heaped insults on him.

## The Death of Jesus

33 At the sixth hour darkness came over the whole land until the ninth hour. 34 And at the ninth hour Jesus cried out in a loud voice, *"Eloi, Eloi, lama sabachthani?"*— which means, "My God, my God, why have you forsaken me?"[c][w]

35 When some of those standing near heard this, they said, "Listen, he's calling Elijah."

36 One man ran, filled a sponge with wine vinegar,[x] put it on a stick, and offered it to Jesus to drink. "Now leave him alone. Let's see if Elijah comes to take him down," he said.

37 With a loud cry, Jesus breathed his last.[y]

38 The curtain of the temple was torn in two from top to bottom. 39 And when the centurion, who stood there in front of Jesus, heard his cry and[d] saw how he died, he said, "Surely this man was the Son[e] of God!"

40 Some women were watching from a distance.[z] Among them were Mary Magdalene, Mary the mother of James the younger and of Joses, and Salome.[a] 41 In Galilee these women had followed him and cared for his needs. Many other women who had come up with him to Jerusalem were also there.[b]

## The Burial of Jesus

42 It was Preparation Day (that is, the day before the Sabbath).[c] So as evening approached, 43 Joseph of Arimathea, a prominent member of the Council, who was himself waiting for the kingdom of God,[d] went boldly to Pilate and asked for Jesus' body. 44 Pilate was surprised to hear that he was already dead. Summoning the centurion, he asked him if Jesus had already died. 45 When he learned from the centurion[e] that it was so, he gave the body to Joseph. 46 So Joseph bought some linen cloth, took down the body, wrapped it in the linen, and placed it in a tomb cut out of rock. Then he rolled a stone against the entrance of the tomb. 47 Mary Magdalene and Mary the mother of Joses saw where he was laid.

## The Resurrection

16 When the Sabbath was over, Mary Magdalene, Mary the mother of James, and Salome bought spices[f] so that they might go to anoint Jesus' body. 2 Very early on the first day of the week, just after sunrise, they were on their way to the tomb 3 and they asked each other, "Who will roll the stone away from the entrance of the tomb?"[g]

4 But when they looked up, they saw that the stone, which was very large, had been rolled away. 5 As they entered the tomb, they saw a young man dressed in a white robe[h] sitting on the right side, and they were alarmed.

6 "Don't be alarmed," he said. "You are looking for Jesus the Nazarene,[i] who was crucified. He has risen! He is not here. See the place where they laid him. 7 But go, tell his disciples and Peter, 'He is going ahead of you into Galilee. There you will see him, just as he told you.' "[j]

8 Trembling and bewildered, the women went out and fled from the tomb. They said nothing to anyone, because they were afraid.

**15:24** s Ps 22:18
**15:29** t Ps 22:7; u Mk 14:58; Jn 2:19
**15:31** v Ps 22:7
**15:34** w Ps 22:1
**15:36** x Ps 69:21
**15:37** y Jn 19:30
**15:40** z Ps 38:11
**15:40** a Mk 16:1; Jn 19:25
**15:41** b Lk 8:2,3
**15:42** c Mt 27:62
**15:43** d Lk 2:25,38
**15:45** e ver 39
**16:1** f Lk 23:56; Jn 19:39,40
**16:3** g Mk 15:46
**16:5** h Jn 20:12
**16:6** i Mk 1:24
**16:7** j Mk 14:28

[a] 27 Some manuscripts *left,* [28] *and the scripture was fulfilled which says, "He was counted with the lawless ones"* (Isaiah 53:12) [b] 32 Or *Messiah* [c] 34 Psalm 22:1 [d] 39 Some manuscripts do not have *heard his cry and* [e] 39 Or *a son*

# Mary, the Mother of James and Joses

## Sacrificing for Christ

Scripture does not tell us much about the woman whom Matthew twice referred to as "the other Mary" (Mt 27:61; 28:1). We do know that she was the mother of James (not James the apostle) and Joses (see Mt 27:56; Mk 15:40). Evidently her sons became well known in the early church.

Mary was likely a woman of some means, as Scripture tells us that she was one of the women who had followed Jesus and "cared for his needs" (Mk 15:41). Mary probably had significant resources, since she was able to leave her home and travel with Jesus, ministering to the physical needs of Jesus and his disciples. Mary, having followed Jesus during much of his ministry, was a witness to his death on the cross and was among the first to bring spices to the tomb of her Lord (see Mk 15:40; 16:1). Having sacrificed her wealth for the service of Jesus, Mary did not have any regrets and continued to serve him even when all hope looked lost. God honored Mary in a special way: She was among the women who were the first to receive the news that Jesus had risen from the dead (see Mk 16:1–7).

Mary was probably among those in the upper room awaiting the arrival of the promised Holy Spirit on the day of Pentecost, when 3,000 members were added to the church (see Ac 1:4–5,14; 2:1–4,41). At a time when women were not given much consideration or prominence, Mary counted the cost of serving Jesus and determined that, whatever she had to forsake, it was worth the sacrifice.

Mary is an example of a liberated woman, yet she knew that Jesus Christ alone was her liberator. Therefore, she had no need to make demands of anyone for her equality. She knew all too well that God is impartial; he is merciful and full of grace and exalts whom he will. Mary is an excellent example of one who receives the rewards that faith brings. Through her we know that every deed that we do for God counts.

—J. Josey

For the next Women of the Bible note, go to page 1195.

### reflection

*Reflect on Mary's commitment to Christ.*

*How committed are you to following the way of Christ?*

### read

Mark 15:40—16:8; see also Matthew 27:55—28:10; Luke 24:1–10.

**See also** the Inspire Notes "Following God-Given Visions," "Confidence," "Purposeful Giving," "Sacrificial Living" and "Commitment to God," and the Women of the Bible Notes "The Widow's Offering: Selfless Giving" and "Claudia: A Sincere Supporter."

**16:9** k Jn 20:11–18
**16:11** l Lk 24:11
**16:12** m Lk 24:13–32

[The earliest manuscripts and some
other ancient witnesses do not have
Mark 16:9–20.]

9 When Jesus rose early on the first day
of the week, he appeared first to Mary Mag-
dalene,[k] out of whom he had driven seven
demons. 10 She went and told those who had
been with him and who were mourning and
weeping. 11 When they heard that Jesus was
alive and that she had seen him, they did not
believe it.[l]

12 Afterward Jesus appeared in a different
form to two of them while they were walk-
ing in the country.[m] 13 These returned and
reported it to the rest; but they did not be-
lieve them either.

14 Later Jesus appeared to the Eleven as
they were eating; he rebuked them for their
lack of faith and their stubborn refusal to
believe those who had seen him after he
had risen.[n]

15 He said to them, "Go into all the world
and preach the good news to all creation.[o]
16 Whoever believes and is baptized will be
saved, but whoever does not believe will
be condemned.[p] 17 And these signs will
accompany those who believe: In my name
they will drive out demons;[q] they will speak
in new tongues;[r] 18 they will pick up snakes
with their hands; and when they drink
deadly poison, it will not hurt them at all;
they will place their hands on sick people,
and they will get well."

19 After the Lord Jesus had spoken to
them, he was taken up into heaven[s] and he
sat at the right hand of God.[t] 20 Then the disci-
ples went out and preached everywhere, and
the Lord worked with them and confirmed
his word by the signs that accompanied it.

**16:14** n Lk 24:36–43
**16:15** o Mt 28:18–20
**16:16** p Ac 16:31
**16:17** q Lk 10:17 r Ac 2:4
**16:19** s Lk 24:50,51 t Ps 110:1

# Luke

## OVERVIEW

Luke used the personal stories of those who were closely associated with Jesus to share details of Jesus' birth, ministry, death and resurrection. Luke's Gospel, much more than any other, records wonderful stories related to Jesus' birth and childhood—stories highlighting Zechariah and Elizabeth, John the Baptist, Mary and Joseph, the shepherds and angels, and Simeon and Anna (see Lk 1–2).

Luke's Gospel tells of many women who were affected by the ministry of Jesus: a widow whose son Jesus raised from the dead (see Lk 7:11–17), a sinful woman who anointed Jesus with expensive perfume (see Lk 7:36–50), a woman suffering from severe hemorrhaging (see Lk 8:43–48), Jairus's daughter (see Lk 8:40–42,49–56), Jesus' friends Martha and Mary (see Lk 10:38–42), a crippled woman healed on the Sabbath (see Lk 13:10–17), and a widow who gave all the money she had to live on as an offering at the temple (see Lk 21:1–4).

The details of Luke's Gospel have led many to believe in Christ. Use the accounts of those who first experienced him to renew your commitment and belief in the Savior.

## OUTLINE

I. Foretelling the Births of John the Baptist and Jesus (1:1–56)
II. The Birth of John the Baptist (1:57–80)
III. The Birth and Childhood of Jesus (2:1–52)
IV. Jesus' Preparation for Ministry (3:1—4:13)
V. Jesus' Ministry in Galilee (4:14—9:50)
VI. Jesus' Ministry in Judea (9:51—13:21)
VII. Jesus' Ministry in and Around Perea (13:22—19:27)
VIII. Jesus' Final Days in Jerusalem (19:28—23:25)
IX. Jesus' Crucifixion, Death, Resurrection and Ascension (23:26—24:53)

## SCANNABLE FACTS:

**Author:** Luke

**Time Written:** Probably around A.D. 60

**Theme to Note:** Jesus Christ is the promised Redeemer for the entire world

**Notable Women:** Mary, the mother of Jesus; Elizabeth; Anna the prophetess; Martha and Mary

## Introduction

1 Many have undertaken to draw up an account of the things that have been fulfilled[a] among us, 2 just as they were handed down to us by those who from the first[a] were eyewitnesses[b] and servants of the word. 3 Therefore, since I myself have carefully investigated everything from the beginning, it seemed good also to me to write an orderly account[c] for you, most excellent Theophilus,[d] 4 so that you may know the certainty of the things you have been taught.

## The Birth of John the Baptist Foretold

5 In the time of Herod king of Judea[e] there was a priest named Zechariah, who belonged to the priestly division of Abijah;[f] his wife Elizabeth was also a descendant of Aaron. 6 Both of them were upright in the sight of God, observing all the Lord's commandments and regulations blamelessly.[g] 7 But they had no children, because Elizabeth was barren; and they were both well along in years.

8 Once when Zechariah's division was on duty and he was serving as priest before God,[h] 9 he was chosen by lot, according to the custom of the priesthood, to go into the temple of the Lord and burn incense.[i] 10 And when the time for the burning of incense came, all the assembled worshipers were praying outside.[j]

11 Then an angel of the Lord appeared to him, standing at the right side of the altar of incense. 12 When Zechariah saw him, he was startled and was gripped with fear. 13 But the angel said to him: "Do not be afraid, Zechariah; your prayer has been heard. Your wife Elizabeth will bear you a son, and you are to give him the name John.[k] 14 He will be a joy and delight to you, and many will rejoice because of his birth, 15 for he will be great in the sight of the Lord. He is never to take wine or other fermented drink,[l] and he will be filled with the Holy Spirit even from birth.[b][m] 16 Many of the people of Israel will he bring back to the Lord their God. 17 And he will go on before the Lord, in the spirit and power of Elijah,[n] to turn the hearts of the fathers to their children and the disobedient to the wisdom of the righteous—to make ready a people prepared for the Lord."

18 Zechariah asked the angel, "How can I be sure of this? I am an old man and my wife is well along in years."[o]

19 The angel answered, "I am Gabriel.[p] I stand in the presence of God, and I have been sent to speak to you and to tell you this good news. 20 And now you will be silent and not able to speak until the day this happens, because you did not believe my words, which will come true at their proper time."

21 Meanwhile, the people were waiting for Zechariah and wondering why he stayed so long in the temple. 22 When he came out, he could not speak to them. They realized he had seen a vision in the temple, for he kept making signs[q] to them but remained unable to speak.

23 When his time of service was completed, he returned home. 24 After this his wife Elizabeth became pregnant and for five months remained in seclusion. 25 "The Lord has done this for me," she said. "In these days he has shown his favor and taken away my disgrace[r] among the people."

## The Birth of Jesus Foretold

26 In the sixth month, God sent the angel Gabriel to Nazareth, a town in Galilee, 27 to a virgin pledged to be married to a man named Joseph,[s] a descendant of David. The virgin's name was Mary. 28 The angel went to her and said, "Greetings, you who are highly favored! The Lord is with you."

29 Mary was greatly troubled at his words and wondered what kind of greeting this might be. 30 But the angel said to her, "Do not be afraid, Mary, you have found favor with God. 31 You will be with child and give birth to a son, and you are to give him the name Jesus.[t] 32 He will be great and will be called the Son of the Most High.[u] The Lord God will give him the throne of his father David, 33 and he will reign over the house of Jacob forever; his kingdom will never end."[v]

34 "How will this be," Mary asked the angel, "since I am a virgin?"

35 The angel answered, "The Holy Spirit will come upon you, and the power of the

[a]1 Or *been surely believed* [b]15 Or *from his mother's womb*

**1:2** a Jn 15:27 b Heb 2:3; 2Pe 1:16
**1:3** c Ac 11:4 d Ac 1:1
**1:5** e Mt 2:1 f 1Ch 24:10
**1:6** g Ge 7:1
**1:8** h 1Ch 24:19; 2Ch 8:14
**1:9** i Ex 30:7,8
**1:10** j Lev 16:17
**1:13** k ver 60,63
**1:15** l Nu 6:3; Jdg 13:4; Lk 7:33 m Jer 1:5
**1:17** n Mt 11:14
**1:18** o Ge 17:17
**1:19** p Da 8:16; 9:21
**1:22** q ver 62
**1:25** r Ge 30:23; Isa 4:1
**1:27** s Mt 1:16,18,20
**1:31** t Lk 2:21
**1:32** u Mk 5:7
**1:33** v Da 2:44; 7:14,27

**1:35** w ver 32,76 x Mt 4:3
**1:37** y Mt 19:26
**1:39** z ver 65
**1:42** a Jdg 5:24
**1:46** b Ps 34:2,3
**1:48** c Ps 138:6 d Lk 11:27
**1:49** e Ps 71:19
**1:50** f Ps 103:17
**1:51** g Ps 98:1

Most High[w] will overshadow you. So the
holy one to be born will be called[a] the Son of
God.[x] 36 Even Elizabeth your relative is going
to have a child in her old age, and she who
was said to be barren is in her sixth month.
37 For nothing is impossible with God."[y]
38 "I am the Lord's servant," Mary answered. "May it be to me as you have said."
Then the angel left her.

## Mary Visits Elizabeth

39 At that time Mary got ready and hurried to a town in the hill country of Judea,[z]
40 where she entered Zechariah's home and
greeted Elizabeth. 41 When Elizabeth heard
Mary's greeting, the baby leaped in her
womb, and Elizabeth was filled with the
Holy Spirit. 42 In a loud voice she exclaimed:
"Blessed are you among women,[a] and
blessed is the child you will bear! 43 But why
am I so favored, that the mother of my Lord
should come to me? 44 As soon as the sound
of your greeting reached my ears, the baby
in my womb leaped for joy. 45 Blessed is she
who has believed that what the Lord has
said to her will be accomplished!"

## Mary's Song

46 And Mary said:

"My soul glorifies the Lord[b]
47 and my spirit rejoices in God my
Savior,
48 for he has been mindful
of the humble state of his servant.[c]
From now on all generations will call me
blessed,[d]
49 for the Mighty One has done great
things[e] for me—
holy is his name.
50 His mercy extends to those who fear him,
from generation to generation.[f]
51 He has performed mighty deeds with his
arm;[g]
he has scattered those who are proud
in their inmost thoughts.
52 He has brought down rulers from their
thrones
but has lifted up the humble.
53 He has filled the hungry with good things
but has sent the rich away empty.
54 He has helped his servant Israel,
remembering to be merciful[h]
55 to Abraham and his descendants[i] forever,
even as he said to our fathers."

56 Mary stayed with Elizabeth for about
three months and then returned home.

## The Birth of John the Baptist

57 When it was time for Elizabeth to have
her baby, she gave birth to a son. 58 Her neighbors and relatives heard that the Lord had
shown her great mercy, and they shared
her joy.

59 On the eighth day they came to circumcise[j] the child, and they were going to name
him after his father Zechariah, 60 but his
mother spoke up and said, "No! He is to be
called John."

61 They said to her, "There is no one among
your relatives who has that name."

62 Then they made signs[k] to his father,
to find out what he would like to name the
child. 63 He asked for a writing tablet, and
to everyone's astonishment he wrote, "His
name is John." 64 Immediately his mouth
was opened and his tongue was loosed,
and he began to speak, praising God. 65 The
neighbors were all filled with awe, and
throughout the hill country of Judea people
were talking about all these things. 66 Everyone who heard this wondered about it, asking, "What then is this child going to be?"
For the Lord's hand was with him.[l]

## Zechariah's Song

67 His father Zechariah was filled with the
Holy Spirit and prophesied:[m]

68 "Praise be to the Lord, the God of Israel,
because he has come and has
redeemed his people.[n]
69 He has raised up a horn[b][o] of salvation
for us
in the house of his servant David
70 (as he said through his holy prophets of
long ago),[p]
71 salvation from our enemies
and from the hand of all who
hate us—
72 to show mercy to our fathers
and to remember his holy covenant,

**1:54** h Ps 98:3
**1:55** i Ge 17:19; Ps 132:11; Gal 3:16
**1:59** j Ge 17:12; Lev 12:3
**1:62** k ver 22
**1:66** l Ge 39:2; Ac 11:21
**1:67** m Joel 2:28
**1:68** n Ps 111:9; Lk 7:16
**1:69** o Ps 18:2; 132:17
**1:70** p Jer 23:5

[a]35 Or *So the child to be born will be called holy,* [b]69 *Horn* here symbolizes strength.

# Mary, the Mother of Jesus

## A Model of Motherhood

She is described as "highly favored" (Lk 1:28) and "blessed" (Lk 1:42,45,48). But what makes Mary, the chosen mother of Jesus, worthy of such an honor? What makes Mary a model for motherhood?

Mary was obedient to God's will. Upon hearing the news that she would carry a child, she asked the angel how it was possible for her—a virgin—to have a baby. The angel proceeded to tell Mary that nothing was impossible with God. Mary's response was: "I am the Lord's servant . . . May it be to me as you have said" (Lk 1:38). Obedient women do not always have to have the plan laid out in black and white for them before they are willing to follow it. Mary trusted God; if this was God's plan, then she was ready to follow it.

Mary was humble. In the Magnificat, her song of praise, Mary rejoiced because God had chosen her to be his servant to deliver Jesus into the world; she did not boast in all she had and why she was the perfect candidate for such an honor. She praised God for choosing her; she didn't list her qualifications but recognized that it was God's grace and mercy that had chosen her for such an honor. The spotlight was not on her; it was placed on the Giver of every good gift—God (see Lk 1:46–55).

Mary was observant. Jesus was not an ordinary child. When Mary and Joseph followed the law of God and presented Jesus in the temple, Simeon and Anna prophesied about the child. Mary and Joseph marveled at their words (see Lk 2:33). Mary no doubt was remembering the promises already made to her about her special child. Scripture also records that, after Jesus stayed behind at the temple as a 12-year-old child, "his mother treasured all these things in her heart" (Lk 2:51).

Mothers of today are smart to pay attention to their children, to observe what they say and what they do. They should also remember that God has plans for their children, and it is their obligation as parents to bring their children up knowing God and the plans he has for his creation.

—K. Washington

For the next Women of the Bible note, go to page 1198.

### reflection

*How are you like Mary?*

*Pray for a spirit that is humble, observant and obedient to God's will.*

### read

Luke 1:26—2:52; see also Matthew 1:16–25; John 2:1–11; 19:25–27; Acts 1:14.

See also the Inspire Notes "A Great Challenge: Teaching Our Children," "Influencing Others," "Motherhood," "Submission," "Parenting," "Raising Children: Modeling Discipleship," "Children: A Blessed Heritage From God," "Nurturing Spiritual Gifts in Our Children" and "Humility."

**1:74** q Heb 9:14
**1:75** r Eph 4:24
**1:76** s Mt 11:9 t Mal 3:1
**1:77** u Mk 1:4
**1:79** v Isa 9:2; Mt 4:16
**1:80** w Lk 2:40,52
**2:1** x Lk 3:1
**2:9** y Lk 1:11; Ac 5:19

73 the oath he swore to our father
Abraham:
74 to rescue us from the hand of our enemies,
and to enable us to serve him[q] without
fear
75 in holiness and righteousness[r] before
him all our days.

76 And you, my child, will be called a
prophet[s] of the Most High;
for you will go on before the Lord to
prepare the way for him,[t]
77 to give his people the knowledge of
salvation
through the forgiveness of their sins,[u]
78 because of the tender mercy of our God,
by which the rising sun will come to us
from heaven
79 to shine on those living in darkness
and in the shadow of death,[v]
to guide our feet into the path of peace."

80 And the child grew and became strong in spirit;[w] and he lived in the desert until he appeared publicly to Israel.

## The Birth of Jesus

2 In those days Caesar Augustus[x] issued a decree that a census should be taken of the entire Roman world. 2 (This was the first census that took place while Quirinius was governor of Syria.) 3 And everyone went to his own town to register.

4 So Joseph also went up from the town of Nazareth in Galilee to Judea, to Bethlehem the town of David, because he belonged to the house and line of David. 5 He went there to register with Mary, who was pledged to be married to him and was expecting a child. 6 While they were there, the time came for the baby to be born, 7 and she gave birth to her firstborn, a son. She wrapped him in cloths and placed him in a manger, because there was no room for them in the inn.

## The Shepherds and the Angels

8 And there were shepherds living out in the fields nearby, keeping watch over their flocks at night. 9 An angel[y] of the Lord appeared to them, and the glory of the Lord shone around them, and they were terrified. 10 But the angel said to them, "Do not be afraid.[z] I bring you good news of great joy that will be for all the people. 11 Today in the town of David a Savior has been born to you; he is Christ[a][a] the Lord. 12 This will be a sign[b] to you: You will find a baby wrapped in cloths and lying in a manger."

13 Suddenly a great company of the heavenly host appeared with the angel, praising God and saying,

14 "Glory to God in the highest,
and on earth peace[c] to men on whom
his favor rests."

15 When the angels had left them and gone into heaven, the shepherds said to one another, "Let's go to Bethlehem and see this thing that has happened, which the Lord has told us about."

16 So they hurried off and found Mary and Joseph, and the baby, who was lying in the manger. 17 When they had seen him, they spread the word concerning what had been told them about this child, 18 and all who heard it were amazed at what the shepherds said to them. 19 But Mary treasured up all these things and pondered them in her heart.[d] 20 The shepherds returned, glorifying and praising God for all the things they had heard and seen, which were just as they had been told.

## Jesus Presented in the Temple

21 On the eighth day, when it was time to circumcise him,[e] he was named Jesus, the name the angel had given him before he had been conceived.[f]

22 When the time of their purification according to the Law of Moses had been completed, Joseph and Mary took him to Jerusalem to present him to the Lord 23 (as it is written in the Law of the Lord, "Every firstborn male is to be consecrated to the Lord"[b]),[g] 24 and to offer a sacrifice in keeping with what is said in the Law of the Lord: "a pair of doves or two young pigeons."[c]

25 Now there was a man in Jerusalem called Simeon, who was righteous and devout. He was waiting for the consolation of Israel,[h] and the Holy Spirit was upon

**2:10** z Mt 14:27
**2:11** a Mt 1:16; 16:16,20; Ac 2:36
**2:12** b 1Sa 2:34
**2:14** c Ro 5:1
**2:19** d ver 51
**2:21** e Lk 1:59 f Lk 1:31
**2:23** g Ex 13:2,12,15
**2:25** h ver 38

[a] 11 Or *Messiah.* "The Christ" (Greek) and "the Messiah" (Hebrew) both mean "the Anointed One"; also in verse 26.
[b] 23 Exodus 13:2,12 [c] 24 Lev. 12:8

**2:29** i ver 26
**2:30** j Isa 52:10
**2:32** k Isa 42:6; 49:6; Ac 13:47
**2:34** l Mt 21:44; 1Co 1:23; 2Co 2:16; 1Pe 2:7,8
**2:37** m 1Ti 5:5
**2:38** n ver 25
**2:40** o ver 52; Lk 1:80
**2:41** p Ex 23:15; Dt 16:1–8

him. 26 It had been revealed to him by the Holy Spirit that he would not die before he had seen the Lord's Christ. 27 Moved by the Spirit, he went into the temple courts. When the parents brought in the child Jesus to do for him what the custom of the Law required, 28 Simeon took him in his arms and praised God, saying:

29 "Sovereign Lord, as you have promised,[i]
you now dismiss[a] your servant in
peace.
30 For my eyes have seen your salvation,[j]
31 which you have prepared in the sight
of all people,
32 a light for revelation to the Gentiles
and for glory to your people Israel."[k]

33 The child's father and mother marveled at what was said about him. 34 Then Simeon blessed them and said to Mary, his mother: "This child is destined to cause the falling[l] and rising of many in Israel, and to be a sign that will be spoken against, 35 so that the thoughts of many hearts will be revealed. And a sword will pierce your own soul too."

36 There was also a prophetess, Anna, the daughter of Phanuel, of the tribe of Asher. She was very old; she had lived with her husband seven years after her marriage, 37 and then was a widow until she was eighty-four.[b] She never left the temple but worshiped night and day, fasting and praying.[m] 38 Coming up to them at that very moment, she gave thanks to God and spoke about the child to all who were looking forward to the redemption of Jerusalem.[n]

39 When Joseph and Mary had done everything required by the Law of the Lord, they returned to Galilee to their own town of Nazareth. 40 And the child grew and became strong; he was filled with wisdom, and the grace of God was upon him.[o]

## The Boy Jesus at the Temple

41 Every year his parents went to Jerusalem for the Feast of the Passover.[p] 42 When he was twelve years old, they went up to the Feast, according to the custom. 43 After the Feast was over, while his parents were returning home, the boy Jesus stayed behind in Jerusalem, but they were unaware of it. 44 Thinking he was in their company, they traveled on for a day. Then they began looking for him among their relatives and friends. 45 When they did not find him, they went back to Jerusalem to look for him. 46 After three days they found him in the temple courts, sitting among the teachers, listening to them and asking them questions. 47 Everyone who heard him was amazed at his understanding and his answers. 48 When his parents saw him, they were astonished. His mother said to him, "Son, why have you treated us like this? Your father and I have been anxiously searching for you."

49 "Why were you searching for me?" he asked. "Didn't you know I had to be in my Father's house?"[q] 50 But they did not understand what he was saying to them.

51 Then he went down to Nazareth with them and was obedient to them. But his mother treasured all these things in her heart.[r] 52 And Jesus grew in wisdom and stature, and in favor with God and men.[s]

## John the Baptist Prepares the Way

3 In the fifteenth year of the reign of Tiberius Caesar—when Pontius Pilate was governor of Judea, Herod tetrarch of Galilee, his brother Philip tetrarch of Iturea and Traconitis, and Lysanias tetrarch of Abilene— 2 during the high priesthood of Annas and Caiaphas,[t] the word of God came to John son of Zechariah in the desert. 3 He went into all the country around the Jordan, preaching a baptism of repentance for the forgiveness of sins. 4 As is written in the book of the words of Isaiah the prophet:

"A voice of one calling in the desert,
'Prepare the way for the Lord,
make straight paths for him.
5 Every valley shall be filled in,
every mountain and hill made low.
The crooked roads shall become straight,
the rough ways smooth.
6 And all mankind will see God's
salvation.'"[c][u]

7 John said to the crowds coming out to be baptized by him, "You brood of vipers! Who warned you to flee from the coming wrath?

**2:49** q Jn 2:16
**2:51** r ver 19
**2:52** s ver 40
**3:2** t Jn 18:13; Ac 4:6
**3:6** u Ps 98:2; Isa 52:10; Lk 2:30

[a]29 Or *promised, / now dismiss* [b]37 Or *widow for eighty-four years* [c]6 Isaiah 40:3–5

# Anna

## A Model of Spiritual Devotion

Anna was a prophetess. She was a woman through whom God spoke. When she spoke, those in the temple listened. She was a Messianic watcher and a leader. She represents God calling women to be prophetic leaders. She was so respected that her attestation of Jesus was highly regarded, alongside that of an angel and a righteous man (see Lk 2:9–12,25–32,38).

Anna is a model of spiritual devotion. She kept vigil in the temple—fasting, praying and offering thanksgiving. According to Luke 19:45–46, Jesus said that the temple should be a house of prayer, and that is what Anna did there; she prayed.

This devout woman did not allow her circumstances to stop her from worshiping God and waiting for God's promised Messiah. She became a widow after only seven years of marriage, yet she used her situation as an opportunity to devote herself, even until her old age, to interceding for others and setting an example as a worshiper for many to come (see Lk 2:36–37).

Anna was a forerunner to the apostles, who were commissioned to witness to the entire world beginning in Jerusalem (compare Lk 2:38 and Ac 1:8). She joyously told people who the baby Jesus was and what he would do for people. Anna represents hopeful expectation. She is a model who shows women today how to live righteous and godly lives in anticipation of what God will do.

—P. TURNER WILLIAMSON

### reflection

*How can you be more devout in your service to God and others?*

*Use Anna as an example.*

### read

Luke 2:36–38; see also Isaiah 9:6–7.

See also the Inspire Notes "Aging: Footprints on the Sands of Time," "Female Ministers and Evangelists," "Servant-Leadership" and "Women in Preaching Ministries," and the Women of the Bible Notes "Deborah: An Uncommon Leader," "Huldah: A Prophetess of God," "Mary Magdalene: Setting Her Reputation Straight" and "Philip's Daughters: Those Preaching Women."

For the next Women of the Bible note, go to page 1202.

3:8 v Jn 8:33,39
3:10 w Ac 2:37
3:12 x Lk 7:29
3:13 y Lk 19:8
3:14 z Ex 23:1; Lev 19:11
3:17 a Isa 30:24 b Mt 13:30
3:20 c Mt 14:3,4; Mk 6:17–18
3:21 d Mt 14:23; Lk 5:16; 9:18,28
3:22 e Ac 10:38

8 Produce fruit in keeping with repentance.
And do not begin to say to yourselves, 'We
have Abraham as our father.'[v] For I tell you
that out of these stones God can raise up
children for Abraham. 9 The ax is already at
the root of the trees, and every tree that does
not produce good fruit will be cut down and
thrown into the fire."

10 "What should we do then?"[w] the crowd
asked.

11 John answered, "The man with two
tunics should share with him who has
none, and the one who has food should do
the same."

12 Tax collectors also came to be bap-
tized.[x] "Teacher," they asked, "what should
we do?"

13 "Don't collect any more than you are re-
quired to,"[y] he told them.

14 Then some soldiers asked him, "And
what should we do?"

He replied, "Don't extort money and
don't accuse people falsely[z]—be content
with your pay."

15 The people were waiting expectantly
and were all wondering in their hearts if
John might possibly be the Christ.[a] 16 John
answered them all, "I baptize you with[b] wa-
ter. But one more powerful than I will come,
the thongs of whose sandals I am not wor-
thy to untie. He will baptize you with the
Holy Spirit and with fire. 17 His winnowing
fork[a] is in his hand to clear his threshing
floor and to gather the wheat into his barn,
but he will burn up the chaff with unquench-
able fire."[b] 18 And with many other words
John exhorted the people and preached the
good news to them.

19 But when John rebuked Herod the te-
trarch because of Herodias, his brother's
wife, and all the other evil things he had
done, 20 Herod added this to them all: He
locked John up in prison.[c]

## The Baptism and Genealogy of Jesus

21 When all the people were being bap-
tized, Jesus was baptized too. And as he was
praying,[d] heaven was opened 22 and the Holy
Spirit descended on him[e] in bodily form
like a dove. And a voice came from heaven:
"You are my Son, whom I love; with you I
am well pleased."

23 Now Jesus himself was about thirty
years old when he began his ministry.[f] He
was the son, so it was thought, of Joseph,

the son of Heli, 24 the son of Matthat,
the son of Levi, the son of Melki,
the son of Jannai, the son of Joseph,
25 the son of Mattathias, the son of Amos,
the son of Nahum, the son of Esli,
the son of Naggai, 26 the son of Maath,
the son of Mattathias, the son of Semein,
the son of Josech, the son of Joda,
27 the son of Joanan, the son of Rhesa,
the son of Zerubbabel,[g] the son of Shealtiel,
the son of Neri, 28 the son of Melki,
the son of Addi, the son of Cosam,
the son of Elmadam, the son of Er,
29 the son of Joshua, the son of Eliezer,
the son of Jorim, the son of Matthat,
the son of Levi, 30 the son of Simeon,
the son of Judah, the son of Joseph,
the son of Jonam, the son of Eliakim,
31 the son of Melea, the son of Menna,
the son of Mattatha, the son of Nathan,[h]
the son of David, 32 the son of Jesse,
the son of Obed, the son of Boaz,
the son of Salmon,[c] the son of Nahshon,
33 the son of Amminadab, the son of Ram,[d]
the son of Hezron, the son of Perez,[i]
the son of Judah, 34 the son of Jacob,
the son of Isaac, the son of Abraham,
the son of Terah, the son of Nahor,[j]
35 the son of Serug, the son of Reu,
the son of Peleg, the son of Eber,
the son of Shelah, 36 the son of Cainan,
the son of Arphaxad,[k] the son of Shem,
the son of Noah, the son of Lamech,
37 the son of Methuselah, the son of Enoch,
the son of Jared, the son of Mahalalel,
the son of Kenan, 38 the son of Enosh,
the son of Seth, the son of Adam,
the son of God.

3:23 f Mt 4:17; Ac 1:1
3:27 g Mt 1:12
3:31 h 2Sa 5:14; 1Ch 3:5
3:33 i Ru 4:18–22; 1Ch 2:10–12
3:34 j Ge 11:24,26
3:36 k Ge 11:12

[a] 15 Or *Messiah* [b] 16 Or *in* [c] 32 Some early manuscripts *Sala* [d] 33 Some manuscripts *Amminadab, the son of Admin, the son of Arni*; other manuscripts vary widely.

## The African Presence

**Luke 3:37**

For a discussion on the origins of humankind, see the African Presence notes on Genesis 2:8 and 2:10–14.

## The Temptation of Jesus

4 Jesus, full of the Holy Spirit,[l] returned from the Jordan and was led by the Spirit[m] in the desert, [2]where for forty days[n] he was tempted by the devil. He ate nothing during those days, and at the end of them he was hungry.

[3]The devil said to him, "If you are the Son of God, tell this stone to become bread."

[4]Jesus answered, "It is written: 'Man does not live on bread alone.'[a]"[o]

[5]The devil led him up to a high place and showed him in an instant all the kingdoms of the world. [6]And he said to him, "I will give you all their authority and splendor, for it has been given to me,[p] and I can give it to anyone I want to. [7]So if you worship me, it will all be yours."

[8]Jesus answered, "It is written: 'Worship the Lord your God and serve him only.'[b]"[q]

[9]The devil led him to Jerusalem and had him stand on the highest point of the temple. "If you are the Son of God," he said, "throw yourself down from here. [10]For it is written:

"'He will command his angels
concerning you
to guard you carefully;
[11] they will lift you up in their hands,
so that you will not strike your foot
against a stone.'[c]"[r]

[12]Jesus answered, "It says: 'Do not put the Lord your God to the test.'[d]"[s]

[13]When the devil had finished all this tempting,[t] he left him until an opportune time.

## Jesus Rejected at Nazareth

[14]Jesus returned to Galilee[u] in the power of the Spirit, and news about him spread through the whole countryside. [15]He taught in their synagogues, and everyone praised him.

[16]He went to Nazareth, where he had been brought up, and on the Sabbath day he went into the synagogue,[v] as was his custom. And he stood up to read. [17]The scroll of the prophet Isaiah was handed to him. Unrolling it, he found the place where it is written:

[18] "The Spirit of the Lord is on me,
because he has anointed me
to preach good news to the poor.
He has sent me to proclaim freedom for
the prisoners
and recovery of sight for the blind,
to release the oppressed,
[19] to proclaim the year of the Lord's
favor."[e][w]

[20]Then he rolled up the scroll, gave it back to the attendant and sat down.[x] The eyes of everyone in the synagogue were fastened on him, [21]and he began by saying to them, "Today this scripture is fulfilled in your hearing."

[22]All spoke well of him and were amazed at the gracious words that came from his lips. "Isn't this Joseph's son?" they asked.[y]

[23]Jesus said to them, "Surely you will quote this proverb to me: 'Physician, heal yourself! Do here in your hometown what we have heard that you did in Capernaum.'"

[24]"I tell you the truth," he continued, "no prophet is accepted in his hometown.[z] [25]I assure you that there were many widows

**4:1** l ver 14,18 m Lk 2:27
**4:2** n Ex 34:28
**4:4** o Dt 8:3
**4:6** p Jn 12:31
**4:8** q Dt 6:13
**4:11** r Ps 91:11,12
**4:12** s Dt 6:16
**4:13** t Heb 4:15
**4:14** u Mt 4:12
**4:16** v Mt 13:54
**4:19** w Isa 61:1,2
**4:20** x ver 17
**4:22** y Mt 13:54,55; Jn 6:42
**4:24** z Mt 13:57; Jn 4:44

[a]4 Deut. 8:3 [b]8 Deut. 6:13 [c]11 Psalm 91:11,12 [d]12 Deut. 6:16 [e]19 Isaiah 61:1,2

in Israel in Elijah's time, when the sky was shut for three and a half years and there was a severe famine throughout the land.[a] 26 Yet Elijah was not sent to any of them, but to a widow in Zarephath in the region of Sidon.[b] 27 And there were many in Israel with leprosy[a] in the time of Elisha the prophet, yet not one of them was cleansed—only Naaman the Syrian."[c]

28 All the people in the synagogue were furious when they heard this. 29 They got up, drove him out of the town,[d] and took him to the brow of the hill on which the town was built, in order to throw him down the cliff. 30 But he walked right through the crowd and went on his way.[e]

## Jesus Drives Out an Evil Spirit

31 Then he went down to Capernaum,[f] a town in Galilee, and on the Sabbath began to teach the people. 32 They were amazed at his teaching,[g] because his message had authority.

33 In the synagogue there was a man possessed by a demon, an evil[b] spirit. He cried out at the top of his voice, 34 "Ha! What do you want with us, Jesus of Nazareth? Have you come to destroy us? I know who you are—the Holy One of God!"[h]

35 "Be quiet!" Jesus said sternly.[i] "Come out of him!" Then the demon threw the man down before them all and came out without injuring him.

36 All the people were amazed and said to each other, "What is this teaching? With authority[j] and power he gives orders to evil spirits and they come out!" 37 And the news about him spread throughout the surrounding area.[k]

## Jesus Heals Many

38 Jesus left the synagogue and went to the home of Simon. Now Simon's mother-in-law was suffering from a high fever, and they asked Jesus to help her. 39 So he bent over her and rebuked[l] the fever, and it left her. She got up at once and began to wait on them.

40 When the sun was setting, the people brought to Jesus all who had various kinds of sickness, and laying his hands on each one,[m] he healed them.[n] 41 Moreover, demons came out of many people, shouting, "You are the Son of God!"[o] But he rebuked them and would not allow them to speak,[p] because they knew he was the Christ.[c]

42 At daybreak Jesus went out to a solitary place. The people were looking for him and when they came to where he was, they tried to keep him from leaving them. 43 But he said, "I must preach the good news of the kingdom of God to the other towns also, because that is why I was sent." 44 And he kept on preaching in the synagogues of Judea.[d]

## The Calling of the First Disciples

5 One day as Jesus was standing by the Lake of Gennesaret,[e] with the people crowding around him and listening to the word of God, 2 he saw at the water's edge two boats, left there by the fishermen, who were washing their nets. 3 He got into one of the boats, the one belonging to Simon, and asked him to put out a little from shore. Then he sat down and taught the people from the boat.[q]

4 When he had finished speaking, he said to Simon, "Put out into deep water, and let down[f] the nets for a catch."[r]

5 Simon answered, "Master,[s] we've worked hard all night and haven't caught anything. But because you say so, I will let down the nets."

6 When they had done so, they caught such a large number of fish that their nets began to break. 7 So they signaled their partners in the other boat to come and help them, and they came and filled both boats so full that they began to sink.

8 When Simon Peter saw this, he fell at Jesus' knees and said, "Go away from me, Lord; I am a sinful man!" 9 For he and all his companions were astonished at the catch of fish they had taken, 10 and so were James and John, the sons of Zebedee, Simon's partners.

Then Jesus said to Simon, "Don't be afraid;[t] from now on you will catch men." 11 So they pulled their boats up on shore, left everything and followed him.[u]

**4:25** a 1Ki18:1; Jas5:17,18
**4:26** b 1Ki17:8–16
**4:27** c 2Ki5:1–14
**4:29** d Nu15:35; Ac7:58
**4:30** e Jn8:59; 10:39
**4:31** f Mt4:13
**4:32** g Mt7:28
**4:34** h ver41
**4:35** i ver39,41; Mt8:26
**4:36** j ver32
**4:37** k ver14
**4:39** l ver35,41
**4:40** m Mk5:23 n Mt4:23
**4:41** o Mt4:3 p Mt8:4
**5:3** q Mt13:2
**5:4** r Jn21:6
**5:5** s Lk8:24,45; 9:33,49; 17:13
**5:10** t Mt14:27
**5:11** u ver28

[a]27 The Greek word was used for various diseases affecting the skin—not necessarily leprosy. [b]33 Greek *unclean*; also in verse 36 [c]41 Or *Messiah* [d]44 Or *the land of the Jews*; some manuscripts *Galilee* [e]1 That is, Sea of Galilee
[f]4 The Greek verb is plural.

# Peter's Mother-in-Law

## From Suffering to Service

The healing of Peter's mother-in-law by Jesus is recorded in all three of the Synoptic Gospels: Matthew, Mark and Luke. Peter's mother-in-law was confined and afflicted with a great fever. The affliction must have been very painful because others sought Jesus on her behalf (see Lk 4:38). Jesus bent over and took her by the hand (see Mk 1:31), and she was healed and immediately rose to minister to them. As a form of gratitude, she served the needs of the Lord and those with him. Her gratitude not only said thank you, but it humbled her for service.

Jesus understood the value of a mother to a family. He also valued women even though society considered them inferior. Each recorded account of Jesus healing a woman speaks to the unique way a woman's life can encounter Jesus. The Scriptures assure African American women of three things:

1. Jesus can *touch us* and bring healing to any area of our lives on a continuous basis (see Mt 8:14–15; Lk 4:40; 8:53–55). His touch allows us to feel and experience something other than pain.

2. Jesus can *lift us up* and bring healing to the many painful areas of our lives (see Mk 1:31). We can be elevated emotionally (see Mt 11:28–29), spiritually (see 2Pe 1:3) and physically (see Ro 12:1–2).

3. Jesus can *speak to our lives* and bring complete healing (see Mt 8:16; Lk 4:39; 13:10–13). His words can change us.

Jesus is the only one who can free the African American woman from the pains of life that may have confined her to a certain position or mind-set. Once Jesus touches her life, he brings healing and raises her to a position of servanthood. Then she can serve the needs of others in both her deeds and words. Her gratitude can be seen as she strengthens and encourages other believers by serving them.

—G. London

### reflection

*Reflect on ways Jesus has touched you, lifted you up and spoken to you.*

*Give God thanks by serving others.*

### read

Luke 4:38–39; see also Matthew 8:14–15; Mark 1:29–31.

See also the Inspire Notes "Courage to Heal," "Motherhood," "Suffering," "Servant-Leadership" and "Faith," and the Women of the Bible Notes "The Canaanite Woman: Persistence Pays Off" and "The Persistent Widow: Always Pray."

For the next Women of the Bible note, go to page 1210.

5:12 v Mt 8:2
5:14 w Lev 14:2–32
5:15 x Mt 9:26
5:16 y Mt 14:23; Lk 3:21
5:17 z Mt 15:1; Lk 2:46 a Mk 5:30; Lk 6:19
5:20 b Lk 7:48,49
5:21 c Isa 43:25

## The Man With Leprosy

12 While Jesus was in one of the towns, a man came along who was covered with leprosy.[a][v] When he saw Jesus, he fell with his face to the ground and begged him, "Lord, if you are willing, you can make me clean."

13 Jesus reached out his hand and touched the man. "I am willing," he said. "Be clean!" And immediately the leprosy left him.

14 Then Jesus ordered him, "Don't tell anyone, but go, show yourself to the priest and offer the sacrifices that Moses commanded[w] for your cleansing, as a testimony to them."

15 Yet the news about him spread all the more,[x] so that crowds of people came to hear him and to be healed of their sicknesses. 16 But Jesus often withdrew to lonely places and prayed.[y]

## Jesus Heals a Paralytic

17 One day as he was teaching, Pharisees and teachers of the law,[z] who had come from every village of Galilee and from Judea and Jerusalem, were sitting there. And the power of the Lord was present for him to heal the sick.[a] 18 Some men came carrying a paralytic on a mat and tried to take him into the house to lay him before Jesus. 19 When they could not find a way to do this because of the crowd, they went up on the roof and lowered him on his mat through the tiles into the middle of the crowd, right in front of Jesus.

20 When Jesus saw their faith, he said, "Friend, your sins are forgiven."[b]

21 The Pharisees and the teachers of the law began thinking to themselves, "Who is this fellow who speaks blasphemy? Who can forgive sins but God alone?"[c]

22 Jesus knew what they were thinking and asked, "Why are you thinking these things in your hearts? 23 Which is easier: to say, 'Your sins are forgiven,' or to say, 'Get up and walk'? 24 But that you may know that the Son of Man has authority on earth to forgive sins . . ." He said to the paralyzed man, "I tell you, get up, take your mat and go home." 25 Immediately he stood up in front of them, took what he had been lying on and went home praising God. 26 Everyone was amazed and gave praise to God. They were

*My hurting loved one,*

*I want you to be whole.*

*Pick up your mat and walk.*

*Your Healer*

LUKE 5:17–26

filled with awe and said, "We have seen remarkable things today."

## The Calling of Levi

27 After this, Jesus went out and saw a tax collector by the name of Levi sitting at his tax booth. "Follow me," Jesus said to him, 28 and Levi got up, left everything and followed him.[d]

29 Then Levi held a great banquet for Jesus at his house, and a large crowd of tax collectors[e] and others were eating with them. 30 But the Pharisees and the teachers of the law who belonged to their sect[f] complained to his disciples, "Why do you eat and drink with tax collectors and 'sinners'?"

31 Jesus answered them, "It is not the healthy who need a doctor, but the sick. 32 I have not come to call the righteous, but sinners to repentance."

## Jesus Questioned About Fasting

33 They said to him, "John's disciples[g] often fast and pray, and so do the disciples of the Pharisees, but yours go on eating and drinking."

34 Jesus answered, "Can you make the guests of the bridegroom fast while he is with them? 35 But the time will come when the bridegroom will be taken from them;[h] in those days they will fast."

36 He told them this parable: "No one tears a patch from a new garment and sews it on an old one. If he does, he will have torn the new garment, and the patch from the new will not match the old. 37 And no one pours new wine into old wineskins. If he does, the new wine will burst the skins, the wine will

5:28 d ver 11
5:29 e Lk 15:1
5:30 f Ac 23:9
5:33 g Lk 7:18
5:35 h Lk 17:22

[a]12 The Greek word was used for various diseases affecting the skin—not necessarily leprosy.

**6:1** i Dt23:25
**6:3** j 1Sa21:6
**6:4** k Lev24:5,9
**6:6** l ver 1
**6:8** m Mt9:4
**6:13** n Mk6:30

run out and the wineskins will be ruined. 38 No, new wine must be poured into new wineskins. 39 And no one after drinking old wine wants the new, for he says, 'The old is better.' "

## Lord of the Sabbath

6 One Sabbath Jesus was going through the grainfields, and his disciples began to pick some heads of grain, rub them in their hands and eat the kernels.[i] 2 Some of the Pharisees asked, "Why are you doing what is unlawful on the Sabbath?"

3 Jesus answered them, "Have you never read what David did when he and his companions were hungry?[j] 4 He entered the house of God, and taking the consecrated bread, he ate what is lawful only for priests to eat.[k] And he also gave some to his companions." 5 Then Jesus said to them, "The Son of Man is Lord of the Sabbath."

6 On another Sabbath[l] he went into the synagogue and was teaching, and a man was there whose right hand was shriveled. 7 The Pharisees and the teachers of the law were looking for a reason to accuse Jesus, so they watched him closely to see if he would heal on the Sabbath. 8 But Jesus knew what they were thinking[m] and said to the man with the shriveled hand, "Get up and stand in front of everyone." So he got up and stood there.

9 Then Jesus said to them, "I ask you, which is lawful on the Sabbath: to do good or to do evil, to save life or to destroy it?"

10 He looked around at them all, and then said to the man, "Stretch out your hand." He did so, and his hand was completely restored. 11 But they were furious and began to discuss with one another what they might do to Jesus.

## The Twelve Apostles

12 One of those days Jesus went out to a mountainside to pray, and spent the night praying to God. 13 When morning came, he called his disciples to him and chose twelve of them, whom he also designated apostles:[n] 14 Simon (whom he named Peter), his brother Andrew, James, John, Philip, Bartholomew, 15 Matthew, Thomas, James son of Alphaeus, Simon who was called the Zealot, 16 Judas son of James, and Judas Iscariot, who became a traitor.

## Blessings and Woes

17 He went down with them and stood on a level place. A large crowd of his disciples was there and a great number of people from all over Judea, from Jerusalem, and from the coast of Tyre and Sidon,[o] 18 who had come to hear him and to be healed of their diseases. Those troubled by evil[a] spirits were cured, 19 and the people all tried to touch him, because power was coming from him and healing them all.[p]

20 Looking at his disciples, he said:

"Blessed are you who are poor,
 for yours is the kingdom of God.
21 Blessed are you who hunger now,
 for you will be satisfied.
Blessed are you who weep now,
 for you will laugh.[q]
22 Blessed are you when men hate you,
 when they exclude you[r] and insult you
 and reject your name as evil,
 because of the Son of Man.

23 "Rejoice in that day and leap for joy, because great is your reward in heaven. For that is how their fathers treated the prophets.

24 "But woe to you who are rich,[s]
 for you have already received your comfort.[t]
25 Woe to you who are well fed now,
 for you will go hungry.[u]
Woe to you who laugh now,
 for you will mourn and weep.[v]
26 Woe to you when all men speak well of you,
 for that is how their fathers treated the false prophets.

## Love for Enemies

27 "But I tell you who hear me: Love your enemies, do good to those who hate you,[w] 28 bless those who curse you, pray for those who mistreat you. 29 If someone strikes you on one cheek, turn to him the other also. If someone takes your cloak, do not stop him

**6:17** o Mt4:25; Mk3:7,8
**6:19** p Mt14:36; Lk5:17
**6:21** q Isa61:2,3
**6:22** r Jn9:22; 16:2
**6:24** s Jas5:1 t Lk16:25
**6:25** u Isa65:13 v Pr14:13
**6:27** w ver 35; Mt5:44; Ro12:20

[a] 18 Greek *unclean*

from taking your tunic. 30 Give to everyone who asks you, and if anyone takes what belongs to you, do not demand it back.[x] 31 Do to others as you would have them do to you.[y]

32 "If you love those who love you, what credit is that to you?[z] Even 'sinners' love those who love them. 33 And if you do good to those who are good to you, what credit is that to you? Even 'sinners' do that. 34 And if you lend to those from whom you expect repayment, what credit is that to you?[a] Even 'sinners' lend to 'sinners,' expecting to be repaid in full. 35 But love your enemies, do good to them, and lend to them without expecting to get anything back. Then your reward will be great, and you will be sons of the Most High, because he is kind to the ungrateful and wicked. 36 Be merciful, just as your Father is merciful.

## Judging Others

37 "Do not judge, and you will not be judged.[b] Do not condemn, and you will not be condemned. Forgive, and you will be forgiven. 38 Give, and it will be given to you. A good measure, pressed down, shaken together and running over, will be poured into your lap. For with the measure you use, it will be measured to you."[c]

39 He also told them this parable: "Can a blind man lead a blind man? Will they not both fall into a pit?[d] 40 A student is not above his teacher, but everyone who is fully trained will be like his teacher.[e]

41 "Why do you look at the speck of sawdust in your brother's eye and pay no attention to the plank in your own eye? 42 How can you say to your brother, 'Brother, let me take the speck out of your eye,' when you yourself fail to see the plank in your own eye? You hypocrite, first take the plank out of your eye, and then you will see clearly to remove the speck from your brother's eye.

## A Tree and Its Fruit

43 "No good tree bears bad fruit, nor does a bad tree bear good fruit. 44 Each tree is recognized by its own fruit.[f] People do not pick figs from thornbushes, or grapes from briers. 45 The good man brings good things out of the good stored up in his heart, and the evil man brings evil things out of the evil stored up in his heart. For out of the overflow of his heart his mouth speaks.[g]

## The Wise and Foolish Builders

46 "Why do you call me, 'Lord, Lord,' and do not do what I say?[h] 47 I will show you what he is like who comes to me and hears my words and puts them into practice.[i] 48 He is like a man building a house, who dug down deep and laid the foundation on rock. When a flood came, the torrent struck that house but could not shake it, because it was well built. 49 But the one who hears my words and does not put them into practice is like a man who built a house on the ground without a foundation. The moment the torrent struck that house, it collapsed and its destruction was complete."

## The Faith of the Centurion

7 When Jesus had finished saying all this[j] in the hearing of the people, he entered Capernaum. 2 There a centurion's servant, whom his master valued highly, was sick and about to die. 3 The centurion heard of Jesus and sent some elders of the Jews to him, asking him to come and heal his servant. 4 When they came to Jesus, they pleaded earnestly with him, "This man deserves to have you do this, 5 because he loves our nation and has built our synagogue." 6 So Jesus went with them.

He was not far from the house when the centurion sent friends to say to him: "Lord, don't trouble yourself, for I do not deserve to have you come under my roof. 7 That is why I did not even consider myself worthy to come to you. But say the word, and my servant will be healed. 8 For I myself am a man under authority, with soldiers under me. I tell this one, 'Go,' and he goes; and that one, 'Come,' and he comes. I say to my servant, 'Do this,' and he does it."

9 When Jesus heard this, he was amazed at him, and turning to the crowd following him, he said, "I tell you, I have not found such great faith even in Israel." 10 Then the men who had been sent returned to the house and found the servant well.

**6:30** x Dt15:7,8,10; Pr21:26
**6:31** y Mt7:12
**6:32** z Mt5:46
**6:34** a Mt5:42
**6:37** b Mt7:1
**6:38** c Mk4:24
**6:39** d Mt15:14
**6:40** e Mt10:24; Jn13:16
**6:44** f Mt12:33
**6:45** g Mt12:34,35; Mk7:20
**6:46** h Mal1:6; Mt7:21
**6:47** i Jas1:22–25
**7:1** j Mt7:28

**7:13** k ver 19; Lk 10:1; 13:15; 17:5; 22:61; 24:34; Jn 11:2
**7:14** l Lk 8:54; Jn 11:43; Ac 9:40
**7:16** m Lk 1:65 n Mt 9:8 o Mt 21:11 p Lk 1:68
**7:17** q Mt 9:26
**7:21** r Mt 4:23
**7:22** s Isa 29:18,19; 35:5,6; 61:1,2; Lk 4:18

## Jesus Raises a Widow's Son

11 Soon afterward, Jesus went to a town called Nain, and his disciples and a large crowd went along with him. 12 As he approached the town gate, a dead person was being carried out—the only son of his mother, and she was a widow. And a large crowd from the town was with her. 13 When the Lord[k] saw her, his heart went out to her and he said, "Don't cry."

14 Then he went up and touched the coffin, and those carrying it stood still. He said, "Young man, I say to you, get up!"[l] 15 The dead man sat up and began to talk, and Jesus gave him back to his mother.

16 They were all filled with awe[m] and praised God.[n] "A great prophet[o] has appeared among us," they said. "God has come to help his people."[p] 17 This news about Jesus spread throughout Judea[a] and the surrounding country.[q]

## Jesus and John the Baptist

18 John's disciples told him about all these things. Calling two of them, 19 he sent them to the Lord to ask, "Are you the one who was to come, or should we expect someone else?"

20 When the men came to Jesus, they said, "John the Baptist sent us to you to ask, 'Are you the one who was to come, or should we expect someone else?'"

21 At that very time Jesus cured many who had diseases, sicknesses[r] and evil spirits, and gave sight to many who were blind. 22 So he replied to the messengers, "Go back and report to John what you have seen and heard: The blind receive sight, the lame walk, those who have leprosy[b] are cured, the deaf hear, the dead are raised, and the good news is preached to the poor.[s] 23 Blessed is the man who does not fall away on account of me."

24 After John's messengers left, Jesus began to speak to the crowd about John: "What did you go out into the desert to see? A reed swayed by the wind? 25 If not, what did you go out to see? A man dressed in fine clothes? No, those who wear expensive clothes and indulge in luxury are in palaces. 26 But what did you go out to see? A prophet? Yes, I tell you, and more than a prophet. 27 This is the one about whom it is written:

> "'I will send my messenger ahead of you,
> who will prepare your way before you.'[c][t]

28 I tell you, among those born of women there is no one greater than John; yet the one who is least in the kingdom of God is greater than he."

29 (All the people, even the tax collectors, when they heard Jesus' words, acknowledged that God's way was right, because they had been baptized by John.[u] 30 But the Pharisees and experts in the law[v] rejected God's purpose for themselves, because they had not been baptized by John.)

31 "To what, then, can I compare the people of this generation? What are they like? 32 They are like children sitting in the marketplace and calling out to each other:

> "'We played the flute for you,
> and you did not dance;
> we sang a dirge,
> and you did not cry.'

33 For John the Baptist came neither eating bread nor drinking wine,[w] and you say, 'He has a demon.' 34 The Son of Man came eating and drinking, and you say, 'Here is a glutton and a drunkard, a friend of tax collectors and "sinners."'[x] 35 But wisdom is proved right by all her children."

## Jesus Anointed by a Sinful Woman

36 Now one of the Pharisees invited Jesus to have dinner with him, so he went to the Pharisee's house and reclined at the table. 37 When a woman who had lived a sinful life in that town learned that Jesus was eating at the Pharisee's house, she brought an alabaster jar of perfume, 38 and as she stood behind him at his feet weeping, she began to wet his feet with her tears. Then she wiped them with her hair, kissed them and poured perfume on them.

39 When the Pharisee who had invited him saw this, he said to himself, "If this

**7:27** t Mal 3:1; Mt 11:10; Mk 1:2
**7:29** u Mt 21:32; Lk 3:12
**7:30** v Mt 22:35
**7:33** w Lk 1:15
**7:34** x Lk 5:29,30; 15:1,2

[a] 17 Or *the land of the Jews* [b] 22 The Greek word was used for various diseases affecting the skin—not necessarily leprosy.
[c] 27 Mal. 3:1

man were a prophet,[y] he would know who is touching him and what kind of woman she is—that she is a sinner."

[40]Jesus answered him, "Simon, I have something to tell you."

"Tell me, teacher," he said.

[41]"Two men owed money to a certain moneylender. One owed him five hundred denarii,[a] and the other fifty. [42]Neither of them had the money to pay him back, so he canceled the debts of both. Now which of them will love him more?"

[43]Simon replied, "I suppose the one who had the bigger debt canceled."

"You have judged correctly," Jesus said.

[44]Then he turned toward the woman and said to Simon, "Do you see this woman? I came into your house. You did not give me any water for my feet,[z] but she wet my feet with her tears and wiped them with her hair. [45]You did not give me a kiss, but this woman, from the time I entered, has not stopped kissing my feet. [46]You did not put oil on my head,[a] but she has poured perfume on my feet. [47]Therefore, I tell you, her many sins have been forgiven—for she loved much. But he who has been forgiven little loves little."

[48]Then Jesus said to her, "Your sins are forgiven."[b]

[49]The other guests began to say among themselves, "Who is this who even forgives sins?"

[50]Jesus said to the woman, "Your faith has saved you;[c] go in peace."

## The Parable of the Sower

**8** After this, Jesus traveled about from one town and village to another, proclaiming the good news of the kingdom of God.[d] The Twelve were with him, [2]and also some women who had been cured of evil spirits and diseases: Mary (called Magdalene)[e] from whom seven demons had come out; [3]Joanna the wife of Cuza, the manager of Herod's[f] household; Susanna; and many others. These women were helping to support them out of their own means.

[4]While a large crowd was gathering and people were coming to Jesus from town after town, he told this parable: [5]"A farmer went out to sow his seed. As he was scattering the seed, some fell along the path; it was trampled on, and the birds of the air ate it up. [6]Some fell on rock, and when it came up, the plants withered because they had no moisture. [7]Other seed fell among thorns, which grew up with it and choked the plants. [8]Still other seed fell on good soil. It came up and yielded a crop, a hundred times more than was sown."

When he said this, he called out, "He who has ears to hear, let him hear."[g]

[9]His disciples asked him what this parable meant. [10]He said, "The knowledge of the secrets of the kingdom of God has been given to you, but to others I speak in parables, so that,

"'though seeing, they may not see;
though hearing, they may not
understand.'[b][h]

[11]"This is the meaning of the parable: The seed is the word of God. [12]Those along the path are the ones who hear, and then the devil comes and takes away the word from their hearts, so that they may not believe and be saved. [13]Those on the rock are the ones who receive the word with joy when they hear it, but they have no root. They believe for a while, but in the time of testing they fall away. [14]The seed that fell among thorns stands for those who hear, but as they go on their way they are choked by life's worries, riches and pleasures, and they do not mature. [15]But the seed on good soil stands for those with a noble and good heart, who hear the word, retain it, and by persevering produce a crop.

## A Lamp on a Stand

[16]"No one lights a lamp and hides it in a jar or puts it under a bed. Instead, he puts it on a stand, so that those who come in can see the light.[i] [17]For there is nothing hidden that will not be disclosed, and nothing concealed that will not be known or brought out into the open.[j] [18]Therefore consider carefully how you listen. Whoever has will be given more; whoever does not have, even what he thinks he has will be taken from him."[k]

**7:39** y ver 16
**7:44** z Ge 18:4; 19:2; 43:24; Jdg 19:21; 1Ti 5:10
**7:46** a Ps 23:5; Ecc 9:8
**7:48** b Mt 9:2
**7:50** c Mt 9:22; Mk 5:34; Lk 8:48
**8:1** d Mt 4:23
**8:2** e Mt 27:55,56
**8:3** f Mt 14:1
**8:8** g Mt 11:15
**8:10** h Isa 6:9; Mt 13:13,14
**8:16** i Mt 5:15; Mk 4:21; Lk 11:33
**8:17** j Mt 10:26; Mk 4:22; Lk 12:2
**8:18** k Mt 13:12; 25:29; Lk 19:26

[a]41 A denarius was a coin worth about a day's wages. [b]10 Isaiah 6:9

8:21
l Lk 11:28

8:24
m Lk 5:5
n Lk 4:35,39,41

8:28
o Mt 8:29
p Mk 5:7

## Jesus' Mother and Brothers

19Now Jesus' mother and brothers came to see him, but they were not able to get near him because of the crowd. 20Someone told him, "Your mother and brothers are standing outside, wanting to see you."

21He replied, "My mother and brothers are those who hear God's word and put it into practice."[l]

## Jesus Calms the Storm

22One day Jesus said to his disciples, "Let's go over to the other side of the lake." So they got into a boat and set out. 23As they sailed, he fell asleep. A squall came down on the lake, so that the boat was being swamped, and they were in great danger.

24The disciples went and woke him, saying, "Master, Master,[m] we're going to drown!"

He got up and rebuked[n] the wind and the raging waters; the storm subsided, and all was calm. 25"Where is your faith?" he asked his disciples.

In fear and amazement they asked one another, "Who is this? He commands even the winds and the water, and they obey him."

## The Healing of a Demon-possessed Man

26They sailed to the region of the Gerasenes,[a] which is across the lake from Galilee. 27When Jesus stepped ashore, he was met by a demon-possessed man from the town. For a long time this man had not worn clothes or lived in a house, but had lived in the tombs. 28When he saw Jesus, he cried out and fell at his feet, shouting at the top of his voice, "What do you want with me,[o] Jesus, Son of the Most High God?[p] I beg you, don't torture me!" 29For Jesus had commanded the evil[b] spirit to come out of the man. Many times it had seized him, and though he was chained hand and foot and kept under guard, he had broken his chains and had been driven by the demon into solitary places.

30Jesus asked him, "What is your name?"

"Legion," he replied, because many demons had gone into him. 31And they begged him repeatedly not to order them to go into the Abyss.[q]

32A large herd of pigs was feeding there on the hillside. The demons begged Jesus to let them go into them, and he gave them permission. 33When the demons came out of the man, they went into the pigs, and the herd rushed down the steep bank into the lake[r] and was drowned.

34When those tending the pigs saw what had happened, they ran off and reported this in the town and countryside, 35and the people went out to see what had happened. When they came to Jesus, they found the man from whom the demons had gone out, sitting at Jesus' feet,[s] dressed and in his right mind; and they were afraid. 36Those who had seen it told the people how the demon-possessed[t] man had been cured. 37Then all the people of the region of the Gerasenes asked Jesus to leave them,[u] because they were overcome with fear. So he got into the boat and left.

38The man from whom the demons had gone out begged to go with him, but Jesus sent him away, saying, 39"Return home and tell how much God has done for you." So the man went away and told all over town how much Jesus had done for him.

## A Dead Girl and a Sick Woman

40Now when Jesus returned, a crowd welcomed him, for they were all expecting him. 41Then a man named Jairus, a ruler of the synagogue,[v] came and fell at Jesus' feet, pleading with him to come to his house 42because his only daughter, a girl of about twelve, was dying.

As Jesus was on his way, the crowds almost crushed him. 43And a woman was there who had been subject to bleeding for twelve years,[c] but no one could heal her. 44She came up behind him and touched the edge of his cloak, and immediately her bleeding stopped.

45"Who touched me?" Jesus asked.

When they all denied it, Peter said, "Master,[w] the people are crowding and pressing against you."

46But Jesus said, "Someone touched me;

8:31
q Rev 9:1,2,11; 11:7; 17:8; 20:1,3

8:33
r ver 22,23

8:35
s Lk 10:39

8:36
t Mt 4:24

8:37
u Ac 16:39

8:41
v ver 49; Mk 5:22

8:45
w Lk 5:5

[a]26 Some manuscripts *Gadarenes*; other manuscripts *Gergesenes*; also in verse 37 [b]29 Greek *unclean* [c]43 Many manuscripts *years, and she had spent all she had on doctors*

I know that power has gone out from me."[x]

47 Then the woman, seeing that she could not go unnoticed, came trembling and fell at his feet. In the presence of all the people, she told why she had touched him and how she had been instantly healed. 48 Then he said to her, "Daughter, your faith has healed you.[y] Go in peace."

49 While Jesus was still speaking, someone came from the house of Jairus, the synagogue ruler.[z] "Your daughter is dead," he said. "Don't bother the teacher any more."

50 Hearing this, Jesus said to Jairus, "Don't be afraid; just believe, and she will be healed."

51 When he arrived at the house of Jairus, he did not let anyone go in with him except Peter, John and James, and the child's father and mother. 52 Meanwhile, all the people were wailing and mourning[a] for her. "Stop wailing," Jesus said. "She is not dead but asleep."[b]

53 They laughed at him, knowing that she was dead. 54 But he took her by the hand and said, "My child, get up!"[c] 55 Her spirit returned, and at once she stood up. Then Jesus told them to give her something to eat. 56 Her parents were astonished, but he ordered them not to tell anyone what had happened.[d]

## Jesus Sends Out the Twelve

9 When Jesus had called the Twelve together, he gave them power and authority to drive out all demons[e] and to cure diseases, 2 and he sent them out to preach the kingdom of God and to heal the sick. 3 He told them: "Take nothing for the journey—no staff, no bag, no bread, no money, no extra tunic.[f] 4 Whatever house you enter, stay there until you leave that town. 5 If people do not welcome you, shake the dust off your feet when you leave their town, as a testimony against them."[g] 6 So they set out and went from village to village, preaching the gospel and healing people everywhere.

7 Now Herod[h] the tetrarch heard about all that was going on. And he was perplexed, because some were saying that John had been raised from the dead,[i] 8 others that Elijah had appeared, and still others that one of the prophets of long ago had come back to life. 9 But Herod said, "I beheaded John. Who, then, is this I hear such things about?" And he tried to see him.[j]

## Jesus Feeds the Five Thousand

10 When the apostles[k] returned, they reported to Jesus what they had done. Then he took them with him and they withdrew by themselves to a town called Bethsaida,[l] 11 but the crowds learned about it and followed him. He welcomed them and spoke to them about the kingdom of God, and healed those who needed healing.

12 Late in the afternoon the Twelve came to him and said, "Send the crowd away so they can go to the surrounding villages and countryside and find food and lodging, because we are in a remote place here."

13 He replied, "You give them something to eat."

They answered, "We have only five loaves of bread and two fish—unless we go and buy food for all this crowd." 14 (About five thousand men were there.)

But he said to his disciples, "Have them sit down in groups of about fifty each." 15 The disciples did so, and everybody sat down. 16 Taking the five loaves and the two fish and looking up to heaven, he gave thanks and broke them. Then he gave them to the disciples to set before the people. 17 They all ate and were satisfied, and the disciples picked up twelve basketfuls of broken pieces that were left over.

## Peter's Confession of Christ

18 Once when Jesus was praying in private and his disciples were with him, he asked them, "Who do the crowds say I am?"

19 They replied, "Some say John the Baptist; others say Elijah; and still others, that one of the prophets of long ago has come back to life."[m]

20 "But what about you?" he asked. "Who do you say I am?"

Peter answered, "The Christ[a] of God."[n]

21 Jesus strictly warned them not to tell this to anyone.[o] 22 And he said, "The Son of Man must suffer many things[p] and be

**8:46** x Lk5:17; 6:19
**8:48** y Mt9:22
**8:49** z ver41
**8:52** a Lk23:27; b Jn11:11,13
**8:54** c Lk7:14
**8:56** d Mt8:4
**9:1** e Mt10:1
**9:3** f Lk10:4; 22:35
**9:5** g Mt10:14
**9:7** h Mt14:1; i ver19
**9:9** j Lk23:8
**9:10** k Mk6:30; l Mt11:21
**9:19** m ver7,8
**9:20** n Jn6:66–69
**9:21** o Mt16:20; Mk8:30
**9:22** p Mt16:21

[a] 20 Or *Messiah*

# Hemorrhaging Woman

## *Faith to Press In*

After returning from a trip that took him across the Sea of Galilee, Jesus was surrounded by crowds of people waiting to be healed and to hear him teach. There was a woman in the crowd who had been subject to bleeding for 12 years (see Lk 8:43). Over the years, she had exhausted all of her resources on doctors and medicines, trying to find a cure for her illness, only to be left poor, depressed and sicker than before (see Mk 5:26). She was now considered an untouchable; she was banned from society because she was believed to be "unclean" (see Lev 15:25–30).

When she heard about the man who could heal with just a touch, she believed that he could heal her too. She knew that if she could make it through the crowd and get close enough to touch even the edge of his clothing, she would be made whole. It was her faith in Jesus that gave her the hope that she could be well again. It was her faith in Jesus that made her brave enough to join the crowd, even though she was unclean. When she was able to touch Jesus' cloak, she realized immediately that she had been made well. But, afraid that she might be punished for violating the law of uncleanness, she said nothing.

But Jesus knew who she was and what had happened to him when she touched him, for power had been released from his body at the moment she touched him. He also knew that she needed to overcome her fears and to testify about what had happened to her. He wanted others to know that through faith she was healed and made clean. And he wanted her to know that her faith had healed not only her body, but her soul as well.

—A. Davis

### reflection

*In what area of your life do you need faith to be healed?*

*Use this woman's story to help you press your way to your healing.*

### read

Luke 8:43–48; see also Leviticus 15:25–31; Matthew 9:20–22; Mark 5:25–34.

See also the Inspire Notes "Courage to Heal," "Suffering," "Fear" and "Faith," and the Women of the Bible Notes "The Canaanite Woman: Persistence Pays Off" and "The Persistent Widow: Always Pray."

For the next Women of the Bible note, go to page 1226.

rejected by the elders, chief priests and teachers of the law, and he must be killed and on the third day be raised to life."

[23]Then he said to them all: "If anyone would come after me, he must deny himself and take up his cross daily and follow me.[q] [24]For whoever wants to save his life will lose it, but whoever loses his life for me will save it. [25]What good is it for a man to gain the whole world, and yet lose or forfeit his very self? [26]If anyone is ashamed of me and my words, the Son of Man will be ashamed of him[r] when he comes in his glory and in the glory of the Father and of the holy angels. [27]I tell you the truth, some who are standing here will not taste death before they see the kingdom of God."

## The Transfiguration

[28]About eight days after Jesus said this, he took Peter, John and James with him and went up onto a mountain to pray.[s] [29]As he was praying, the appearance of his face changed, and his clothes became as bright as a flash of lightning. [30]Two men, Moses and Elijah, [31]appeared in glorious splendor, talking with Jesus. They spoke about his departure,[t] which he was about to bring to fulfillment at Jerusalem. [32]Peter and his companions were very sleepy,[u] but when they became fully awake, they saw his glory and the two men standing with him. [33]As the men were leaving Jesus, Peter said to him, "Master,[v] it is good for us to be here. Let us put up three shelters—one for you, one for Moses and one for Elijah." (He did not know what he was saying.)

[34]While he was speaking, a cloud appeared and enveloped them, and they were afraid as they entered the cloud. [35]A voice came from the cloud, saying, "This is my Son, whom I have chosen; listen to him."[w] [36]When the voice had spoken, they found that Jesus was alone. The disciples kept this to themselves, and told no one at that time what they had seen.[x]

## The Healing of a Boy With an Evil Spirit

[37]The next day, when they came down from the mountain, a large crowd met him. [38]A man in the crowd called out, "Teacher, I beg you to look at my son, for he is my only child. [39]A spirit seizes him and he suddenly screams; it throws him into convulsions so that he foams at the mouth. It scarcely ever leaves him and is destroying him. [40]I begged your disciples to drive it out, but they could not."

[41]"O unbelieving and perverse generation," Jesus replied, "how long shall I stay with you and put up with you? Bring your son here."

[42]Even while the boy was coming, the demon threw him to the ground in a convulsion. But Jesus rebuked the evil[a] spirit, healed the boy and gave him back to his father. [43]And they were all amazed at the greatness of God.

While everyone was marveling at all that Jesus did, he said to his disciples, [44]"Listen carefully to what I am about to tell you: The Son of Man is going to be betrayed into the hands of men."[y] [45]But they did not understand what this meant. It was hidden from them, so that they did not grasp it,[z] and they were afraid to ask him about it.

## Who Will Be the Greatest?

[46]An argument started among the disciples as to which of them would be the greatest. [47]Jesus, knowing their thoughts,[a] took a little child and had him stand beside him. [48]Then he said to them, "Whoever welcomes this little child in my name welcomes me; and whoever welcomes me welcomes the one who sent me.[b] For he who is least among you all—he is the greatest."

[49]"Master," said John, "we saw a man driving out demons in your name and we tried to stop him, because he is not one of us."

[50]"Do not stop him," Jesus said, "for whoever is not against you is for you."[c]

## Samaritan Opposition

[51]As the time approached for him to be taken up to heaven,[d] Jesus resolutely set out for Jerusalem.[e] [52]And he sent messengers on ahead, who went into a Samaritan[f] village to get things ready for him; [53]but the people there did not welcome him, because he was heading for Jerusalem. [54]When the

[a]42 Greek *unclean*

**9:23** q Mt 10:38; Lk 14:27
**9:26** r Mt 10:33; Lk 12:9; 2Ti 2:12
**9:28** s Lk 3:21
**9:31** t 2Pe 1:15
**9:32** u Mt 26:43
**9:33** v Lk 5:5
**9:35** w Mt 3:17
**9:36** x Mt 17:9
**9:44** y ver 22
**9:45** z Mk 9:32
**9:47** a Mt 9:4
**9:48** b Mt 10:40
**9:50** c Mt 12:30; Lk 11:23
**9:51** d Mk 16:19 e Lk 13:22; 17:11; 18:31; 19:28
**9:52** f Mt 10:5

## The African Presence

**Luke 9:52**

The exact origin of the Samaritans is difficult to ascertain.

On the one hand, some scholars identify the Samaritans with the inhabitants of Samaria in the northern kingdom. This school of thought maintains that Samaritans claimed direct descent from the surviving northern tribes of Ephraim and Manasseh, the tribes associated with Joseph's sons born to his Egyptian wife, Asenath.

On the other hand, Biblical accounts of the Samaritan presence in Israel characterized by 2 Kings 17:24, and extrabiblical attestation by the Jewish historian Josephus (*Antiquities*, 9.14.3), claim that the Samaritans belonged to outside ethnic groups. After Sargon of Assyria destroyed Samaria (721 B.C.), he deported many of the Israelites and brought in people from other conquered nations.

Conflict arose between Samaritans and Jews upon the return of Jewish exiles to the region and the subsequent rebuilding of the temple and Jerusalem's walls (see Ezr 4:4–5,24). A major source of conflict between Jews and Samaritans was the issue of Jerusalem versus Mount Gerizim as the major site of worship.

In the New Testament, Jesus rebuked the disciples for wanting to destroy the Samaritans (see Lk 9:52–56) and later instructed the disciples to proclaim the gospel in Samaria (see Ac 1:8).

**9:54** g 2Ki 1:10,12
**9:57** h ver 51
**9:58** i Mt 8:20
**9:61** j 1Ki 19:20

disciples James and John saw this, they asked, "Lord, do you want us to call fire down from heaven to destroy them[a]?"[g] [55]But Jesus turned and rebuked them, [56]and[b] they went to another village.

### The Cost of Following Jesus

[57]As they were walking along the road,[h] a man said to him, "I will follow you wherever you go."

[58]Jesus replied, "Foxes have holes and birds of the air have nests, but the Son of Man[i] has no place to lay his head."

[59]He said to another man, "Follow me."

But the man replied, "Lord, first let me go and bury my father."

[60]Jesus said to him, "Let the dead bury their own dead, but you go and proclaim the kingdom of God."

[61]Still another said, "I will follow you, Lord; but first let me go back and say good-by to my family."[j]

[62]Jesus replied, "No one who puts his hand to the plow and looks back is fit for service in the kingdom of God."

### Jesus Sends Out the Seventy-two

**10** After this the Lord[k] appointed seventy-two[c] others[l] and sent them two by two[m] ahead of him to every town and place where he was about to go.[n] [2]He told them, "The harvest is plentiful, but the workers are few. Ask the Lord of the harvest, therefore, to send out workers into his harvest field.[o] [3]Go! I am sending you out like lambs among wolves.[p] [4]Do not take a purse or bag or sandals; and do not greet anyone on the road.

[5]"When you enter a house, first say, 'Peace to this house.' [6]If a man of peace is there, your peace will rest on him; if not, it will return to you. [7]Stay in that house, eating and drinking whatever they give you,

**10:1** k Lk 7:13 l Lk 9:1,2,51,52 m Mk 6:7 n Mt 10:1
**10:2** o Mt 9:37,38; Jn 4:35
**10:3** p Mt 10:16

[a]54 Some manuscripts *them, even as Elijah did* [b]55,56 Some manuscripts *them. And he said, "You do not know what kind of spirit you are of, for the Son of Man did not come to destroy men's lives, but to save them."* [56]*And* [c]1 Some manuscripts *seventy*; also in verse 17

for the worker deserves his wages.[q] Do not move around from house to house.

8“When you enter a town and are welcomed, eat what is set before you. 9Heal the sick who are there and tell them, ‘The kingdom of God[r] is near you.’ 10But when you enter a town and are not welcomed, go into its streets and say, 11‘Even the dust of your town that sticks to our feet we wipe off against you.[s] Yet be sure of this: The kingdom of God is near.’ 12I tell you, it will be more bearable on that day for Sodom[t] than for that town.

13“Woe to you, Korazin! Woe to you, Bethsaida! For if the miracles that were performed in you had been performed in Tyre and Sidon, they would have repented long ago, sitting in sackcloth and ashes. 14But it will be more bearable for Tyre and Sidon at the judgment than for you. 15And you, Capernaum, will you be lifted up to the skies? No, you will go down to the depths.[a]

16“He who listens to you listens to me; he who rejects you rejects me; but he who rejects me rejects him who sent me.”[u]

17The seventy-two returned with joy and said, “Lord, even the demons submit to us in your name.”

18He replied, “I saw Satan fall like lightning from heaven.[v] 19I have given you authority to trample on snakes[w] and scorpions and to overcome all the power of the enemy; nothing will harm you. 20However, do not rejoice that the spirits submit to you, but rejoice that your names are written in heaven.”[x]

21At that time Jesus, full of joy through the Holy Spirit, said, “I praise you, Father, Lord of heaven and earth, because you have hidden these things from the wise and learned, and revealed them to little children. Yes, Father, for this was your good pleasure.

22“All things have been committed to me by my Father. No one knows who the Son is except the Father, and no one knows who the Father is except the Son and those to whom the Son chooses to reveal him.”

23Then he turned to his disciples and said privately, “Blessed are the eyes that see what you see. 24For I tell you that many prophets and kings wanted to see what you see but did not see it, and to hear what you hear but did not hear it.”

## The Parable of the Good Samaritan

25On one occasion an expert in the law stood up to test Jesus. “Teacher,” he asked, “what must I do to inherit eternal life?”[y]

26“What is written in the Law?” he replied. “How do you read it?”

27He answered: “ ‘Love the Lord your God with all your heart and with all your soul and with all your strength and with all your mind’[b];[z] and, ‘Love your neighbor as yourself.’[c]”[a]

28“You have answered correctly,” Jesus replied. “Do this and you will live.”[b]

29But he wanted to justify himself,[c] so he asked Jesus, “And who is my neighbor?”

30In reply Jesus said: “A man was going down from Jerusalem to Jericho, when he fell into the hands of robbers. They stripped him of his clothes, beat him and went away, leaving him half dead. 31A priest happened to be going down the same road, and when he saw the man, he passed by on the other side. 32So too, a Levite, when he came to the place and saw him, passed by on the other side. 33But a Samaritan, as he traveled, came where the man was; and when he saw him, he took pity on him. 34He went to him and bandaged his wounds, pouring on oil and wine. Then he put the man on his own donkey, took him to an inn and took care of him. 35The next day he took out two silver coins[d] and gave them to the innkeeper. ‘Look after him,’ he said, ‘and when I return, I will reimburse you for any extra expense you may have.’

36“Which of these three do you think was a neighbor to the man who fell into the hands of robbers?”

37The expert in the law replied, “The one who had mercy on him.”

Jesus told him, “Go and do likewise.”

## At the Home of Martha and Mary

38As Jesus and his disciples were on their way, he came to a village where a woman named Martha opened her home to him.

[a]15 Greek *Hades* [b]27 Deut. 6:5 [c]27 Lev. 19:18 [d]35 Greek *two denarii*

**10:7** q Mt 10:10; 1Co 9:14; 1Ti 5:18
**10:9** r Mt 3:2; 10:7
**10:11** s Mt 10:14; Mk 6:11
**10:12** t Mt 10:15
**10:16** u Mt 10:40; Jn 13:20
**10:18** v Rev 9:1
**10:19** w Mk 16:18
**10:20** x Ex 32:32; Ps 69:28; Da 12:1; Php 4:3; Heb 12:23; Rev 13:8; 20:12; 21:27
**10:25** y Mt 19:16
**10:27** z Dt 6:5; a Lev 19:18
**10:28** b Lev 18:5
**10:29** c Lk 16:15

**10:39** d Lk8:35
**10:41** e Mt6:25–34
**10:42** f Ps27:4
**11:1** g Lk3:21
**11:4** h Mt18:35; Mk11:25
**11:8** i Lk18:1–6
**11:9** j Mt7:7

39 She had a sister called Mary, who sat at the
Lord's feet[d] listening to what he said. 40 But
Martha was distracted by all the prepara-
tions that had to be made. She came to him
and asked, "Lord, don't you care that my sis-
ter has left me to do the work by myself? Tell
her to help me!"

41 "Martha, Martha," the Lord answered,
"you are worried[e] and upset about many
things, 42 but only one thing is needed.[a][f]
Mary has chosen what is better, and it will
not be taken away from her."

## Jesus' Teaching on Prayer

11 One day Jesus was praying[g] in a cer-
tain place. When he finished, one of
his disciples said to him, "Lord, teach us to
pray, just as John taught his disciples."

2 He said to them, "When you pray, say:

"'Father,[b]
hallowed be your name,
your kingdom come.[c]
3 Give us each day our daily bread.
4 Forgive us our sins,
for we also forgive everyone who sins
against us.[d][h]
And lead us not into temptation.[e]'"

5 Then he said to them, "Suppose one of
you has a friend, and he goes to him at mid-
night and says, 'Friend, lend me three loaves
of bread, 6 because a friend of mine on a jour-
ney has come to me, and I have nothing to
set before him.'

7 "Then the one inside answers, 'Don't
bother me. The door is already locked, and
my children are with me in bed. I can't
get up and give you anything.' 8 I tell you,
though he will not get up and give him the
bread because he is his friend, yet because
of the man's boldness[f] he will get up and
give him as much as he needs.[i]

9 "So I say to you: Ask and it will be given
to you;[j] seek and you will find; knock and
the door will be opened to you. 10 For every-
one who asks receives; he who seeks finds;
and to him who knocks, the door will
be opened.

11 "Which of you fathers, if your son asks
for[g] a fish, will give him a snake instead? 12 Or
if he asks for an egg, will give him a scorpion?
13 If you then, though you are evil, know how
to give good gifts to your children, how
much more will your Father in heaven give
the Holy Spirit to those who ask him!"

## Jesus and Beelzebub

14 Jesus was driving out a demon that was
mute. When the demon left, the man who
had been mute spoke, and the crowd was
amazed.[k] 15 But some of them said, "By Beel-
zebub,[h] the prince of demons, he is driving
out demons."[l] 16 Others tested him by asking
for a sign from heaven.[m]

17 Jesus knew their thoughts and said to
them: "Any kingdom divided against itself
will be ruined, and a house divided against
itself will fall. 18 If Satan[n] is divided against
himself, how can his kingdom stand? I
say this because you claim that I drive out
demons by Beelzebub. 19 Now if I drive out
demons by Beelzebub, by whom do your
followers drive them out? So then, they will
be your judges. 20 But if I drive out demons
by the finger of God,[o] then the kingdom of
God[p] has come to you.

21 "When a strong man, fully armed,
guards his own house, his possessions are
safe. 22 But when someone stronger attacks
and overpowers him, he takes away the ar-
mor in which the man trusted and divides
up the spoils.

23 "He who is not with me is against me,
and he who does not gather with me, scat-
ters.[q]

24 "When an evil[i] spirit comes out of a
man, it goes through arid places seeking
rest and does not find it. Then it says, 'I will
return to the house I left.' 25 When it arrives,
it finds the house swept clean and put in
order. 26 Then it goes and takes seven other
spirits more wicked than itself, and they go
in and live there. And the final condition of
that man is worse than the first."[r]

27 As Jesus was saying these things, a
woman in the crowd called out, "Blessed is
the mother who gave you birth and nursed
you."[s]

**11:14** k Mt9:32,33
**11:15** l Mt9:34
**11:16** m Mt12:38
**11:18** n Mt4:10
**11:20** o Ex8:19 p Mt3:2
**11:23** q Mt12:30; Lk9:50
**11:26** r 2Pe2:20
**11:27** s Lk23:29

[a] 42 Some manuscripts *but few things are needed—or only one* [b] 2 Some manuscripts *Our Father in heaven* [c] 2 Some manuscripts *come. May your will be done on earth as it is in heaven.* [d] 4 Greek *everyone who is indebted to us* [e] 4 Some manuscripts *temptation but deliver us from the evil one* [f] 8 Or *persistence* [g] 11 Some manuscripts *for bread, will give him a stone; or if he asks for* [h] 15 Greek *Beezeboul* or *Beelzeboul*; also in verses 18 and 19 [i] 24 Greek *unclean*

11:28 t Lk8:21
11:29 u Mt12:38
11:31 v 1Ki10:1
11:32 w Jnh3:5
11:33 x Mt5:15; Mk4:21; Lk8:16

[28]He replied, "Blessed rather are those
who hear the word of God and obey it."[t]

## The Sign of Jonah

[29]As the crowds increased, Jesus said,
"This is a wicked generation. It asks for a
miraculous sign,[u] but none will be given it
except the sign of Jonah. [30]For as Jonah was
a sign to the Ninevites, so also will the Son
of Man be to this generation. [31]The Queen of
the South will rise at the judgment with the
men of this generation and condemn them;
for she came from the ends of the earth to
listen to Solomon's wisdom,[v] and now one[a]
greater than Solomon is here. [32]The men of
Nineveh will stand up at the judgment with
this generation and condemn it; for they
repented at the preaching of Jonah,[w] and
now one greater than Jonah is here.

## The Lamp of the Body

[33]"No one lights a lamp and puts it in a
place where it will be hidden, or under a
bowl. Instead he puts it on its stand, so that
those who come in may see the light.[x] [34]Your
eye is the lamp of your body. When your
eyes are good, your whole body also is full
of light. But when they are bad, your body
also is full of darkness. [35]See to it, then, that
the light within you is not darkness. [36]There-
fore, if your whole body is full of light, and
no part of it dark, it will be completely
lighted, as when the light of a lamp shines
on you."

## Six Woes

[37]When Jesus had finished speaking, a
Pharisee invited him to eat with him; so he
went in and reclined at the table. [38]But the
Pharisee, noticing that Jesus did not first
wash before the meal,[y] was surprised.
[39]Then the Lord said to him, "Now then,
you Pharisees clean the outside of the cup
and dish, but inside you are full of greed and
wickedness.[z] [40]You foolish people! Did not
the one who made the outside make the in-
side also? [41]But give what is inside ⌊the dish⌋[b]
to the poor,[a] and everything will be clean
for you.
[42]"Woe to you Pharisees, because you
give God a tenth[b] of your mint, rue and all
other kinds of garden herbs, but you neglect
justice and the love of God. You should have
practiced the latter without leaving the for-
mer undone.[c]
[43]"Woe to you Pharisees, because you love
the most important seats in the synagogues
and greetings in the marketplaces.[d]
[44]"Woe to you, because you are like un-
marked graves,[e] which men walk over with-
out knowing it."
[45]One of the experts in the law answered
him, "Teacher, when you say these things,
you insult us also."
[46]Jesus replied, "And you experts in the
law, woe to you, because you load people
down with burdens they can hardly carry,
and you yourselves will not lift one finger to
help them.[f]
[47]"Woe to you, because you build tombs
for the prophets, and it was your forefa-
thers who killed them. [48]So you testify that
you approve of what your forefathers did;
they killed the prophets, and you build
their tombs. [49]Because of this, God in his
wisdom[g] said, 'I will send them prophets

11:38 y Mk7:3,4
11:39 z Mt23:25,26
11:41 a Lk12:33
11:42 b Lk18:12 c Mt23:23
11:43 d Mt23:6,7; Mk12:38–39
11:44 e Mt23:27
11:46 f Mt23:4
11:49 g 1Co1:24,30

[a]31 Or *something*; also in verse 32 [b]41 Or *what you have*

## *The African Presence*

**Luke 11:31**

"The Queen of the South" is a reference to the queen of Sheba (see the African Presence notes on 1Ki 10:1–13 and 2Ch 9). Sheba was in southern Arabia, in present-day Yemen, across the Red Sea from present-day Ethiopia.

**11:49** h Mt 23:34
**11:51** i Ge 4:8 j 2Ch 24:20,21
**11:52** k Mt 23:13
**11:54** l Mk 12:13
**12:1** m Mt 16:6,11,12; Mk 8:15
**12:2** n Mk 4:22; Lk 8:17
**12:4** o Jn 15:14,15
**12:5** p Heb 10:31
**12:7** q Mt 10:30 r Mt 12:12

and apostles, some of whom they will kill and others they will persecute.'[h] 50 Therefore this generation will be held responsible for the blood of all the prophets that has been shed since the beginning of the world, 51 from the blood of Abel[i] to the blood of Zechariah,[j] who was killed between the altar and the sanctuary. Yes, I tell you, this generation will be held responsible for it all.

52 "Woe to you experts in the law, because you have taken away the key to knowledge. You yourselves have not entered, and you have hindered those who were entering."[k]

53 When Jesus left there, the Pharisees and the teachers of the law began to oppose him fiercely and to besiege him with questions, 54 waiting to catch him in something he might say.[l]

## Warnings and Encouragements

12 Meanwhile, when a crowd of many thousands had gathered, so that they were trampling on one another, Jesus began to speak first to his disciples, saying: "Be on your guard against the yeast of the Pharisees, which is hypocrisy.[m] 2 There is nothing concealed that will not be disclosed, or hidden that will not be made known.[n] 3 What you have said in the dark will be heard in the daylight, and what you have whispered in the ear in the inner rooms will be proclaimed from the roofs.

4 "I tell you, my friends,[o] do not be afraid of those who kill the body and after that can do no more. 5 But I will show you whom you should fear: Fear him who, after the killing of the body, has power to throw you into hell. Yes, I tell you, fear him.[p] 6 Are not five sparrows sold for two pennies[a]? Yet not one of them is forgotten by God. 7 Indeed, the very hairs of your head are all numbered.[q] Don't be afraid; you are worth more than many sparrows.[r]

8 "I tell you, whoever acknowledges me before men, the Son of Man will also acknowledge him before the angels of God. 9 But he who disowns me before men will be disowned before the angels of God. 10 And everyone who speaks a word against the Son of Man will be forgiven, but anyone who blasphemes against the Holy Spirit will not be forgiven.[s]

11 "When you are brought before synagogues, rulers and authorities, do not worry about how you will defend yourselves or what you will say,[t] 12 for the Holy Spirit will teach you at that time what you should say."[u]

## The Parable of the Rich Fool

13 Someone in the crowd said to him, "Teacher, tell my brother to divide the inheritance with me."

14 Jesus replied, "Man, who appointed me a judge or an arbiter between you?" 15 Then he said to them, "Watch out! Be on your guard against all kinds of greed; a man's life does not consist in the abundance of his possessions."

16 And he told them this parable: "The ground of a certain rich man produced a good crop. 17 He thought to himself, 'What shall I do? I have no place to store my crops.'

18 "Then he said, 'This is what I'll do. I will tear down my barns and build bigger ones, and there I will store all my grain and my goods. 19 And I'll say to myself, "You have plenty of good things laid up for many years. Take life easy; eat, drink and be merry."'

20 "But God said to him, 'You fool![v] This very night your life will be demanded from you.[w] Then who will get what you have prepared for yourself?'[x]

21 "This is how it will be with anyone who stores up things for himself but is not rich toward God."[y]

## Do Not Worry

22 Then Jesus said to his disciples: "Therefore I tell you, do not worry about your life, what you will eat; or about your body, what you will wear. 23 Life is more than food, and the body more than clothes. 24 Consider the ravens: They do not sow or reap, they have no storeroom or barn; yet God feeds them.[z] And how much more valuable you are than birds! 25 Who of you by worrying can add a single hour to his life[b]? 26 Since you cannot do this very little thing, why do you worry about the rest?

**12:10** s Mt 12:31,32; Mk 3:28–29; 1Jn 5:16
**12:11** t Mt 10:17,19; Mk 13:11
**12:12** u Mt 10:20
**12:20** v Jer 17:11 w Job 27:8 x Ps 39:6
**12:21** y ver 33
**12:24** z Job 38:41

[a] 6 Greek *two assaria* [b] 25 Or *single cubit to his height*

27“Consider how the lilies grow. They do not labor or spin. Yet I tell you, not even Solomon in all his splendor[a] was dressed like one of these. 28If that is how God clothes the grass of the field, which is here today, and tomorrow is thrown into the fire, how much more will he clothe you, O you of little faith![b] 29And do not set your heart on what you will eat or drink; do not worry about it. 30For the pagan world runs after all such things, and your Father knows that you need them.[c] 31But seek his kingdom, and these things will be given to you as well.

32“Do not be afraid,[d] little flock, for your Father has been pleased to give you the kingdom. 33Sell your possessions and give to the poor.[e] Provide purses for yourselves that will not wear out, a treasure in heaven[f] that will not be exhausted, where no thief comes near and no moth destroys. 34For where your treasure is, there your heart will be also.[g]

## Watchfulness

35“Be dressed ready for service and keep your lamps burning, 36like men waiting for their master to return from a wedding banquet, so that when he comes and knocks they can immediately open the door for him. 37It will be good for those servants whose master finds them watching when he comes.[h] I tell you the truth, he will dress himself to serve, will have them recline at the table and will come and wait on them. 38It will be good for those servants whose master finds them ready, even if he comes in the second or third watch of the night. 39But understand this: If the owner of the house had known at what hour the thief[i] was coming, he would not have let his house be broken into. 40You also must be ready,[j] because the Son of Man will come at an hour when you do not expect him.”

41Peter asked, “Lord, are you telling this parable to us, or to everyone?”

42The Lord[k] answered, “Who then is the faithful and wise manager, whom the master puts in charge of his servants to give them their food allowance at the proper time? 43It will be good for that servant whom the master finds doing so when he returns. 44I tell you the truth, he will put him in charge of all his possessions. 45But suppose the servant says to himself, ‘My master is taking a long time in coming,’ and he then begins to beat the menservants and maidservants and to eat and drink and get drunk. 46The master of that servant will come on a day when he does not expect him and at an hour he is not aware of. He will cut him to pieces and assign him a place with the unbelievers.

47“That servant who knows his master’s will and does not get ready or does not do what his master wants will be beaten with many blows.[l] 48But the one who does not know and does things deserving punishment will be beaten with few blows.[m] From everyone who has been given much, much will be demanded; and from the one who has been entrusted with much, much more will be asked.

## Not Peace but Division

49“I have come to bring fire on the earth, and how I wish it were already kindled! 50But I have a baptism[n] to undergo, and how distressed I am until it is completed! 51Do you think I came to bring peace on earth? No, I tell you, but division. 52From now on there will be five in one family divided against each other, three against two and two against three. 53They will be divided, father against son and son against father, mother against daughter and daughter against mother, mother-in-law against daughter-in-law and daughter-in-law against mother-in-law.”[o]

## Interpreting the Times

54He said to the crowd: “When you see a cloud rising in the west, immediately you say, ‘It’s going to rain,’ and it does.[p] 55And when the south wind blows, you say, ‘It’s going to be hot,’ and it is. 56Hypocrites! You know how to interpret the appearance of the earth and the sky. How is it that you don’t know how to interpret this present time?[q]

57“Why don’t you judge for yourselves what is right? 58As you are going with your adversary to the magistrate, try hard to be reconciled to him on the way, or he may drag you off to the judge, and the judge turn you over to the officer, and the officer throw

12:27 a 1Ki10:4–7
12:28 b Mt6:30
12:30 c Mt6:8
12:32 d Mt14:27
12:33 e Mt19:21 f Mt6:20
12:34 g Mt6:21
12:37 h Mt24:42,46
12:39 i Mt6:19; 1Th5:2; 2Pe3:10; Rev3:3; 16:15
12:40 j Mk13:33; Lk21:36
12:42 k Lk7:13
12:47 l Dt25:2
12:48 m Lev5:17; Nu15:27–30
12:50 n Mk10:38
12:53 o Mic7:6; Mt10:21
12:54 p Mt16:2
12:56 q Mt16:3

# Inspire

## PRAYER: THE ANTIDOTE TO WORRY

As powerful, promising, productive, passionate women, we are not to settle down in the valley and under the shadow of worry. Jesus reminds us not to worry about what we will eat or drink or how we will be clothed, meet our financial obligations or manage our health issues (see Lk 12:22–31). Since we are, after all, of infinitely greater value than the birds, more precious to God than the flowers—all of which God cares for—we do not need to worry.

Worrying can lead to spiritual paralysis, the feeling that nothing can solve our problems—not even prayer. Anxiety can damage our health, disrupt our productivity, alter our perception and ultimately reduce our ability to trust totally in God.

What is the solution to worrying? We can counteract our natural tendency to worry by creating an action plan that both begins and continues with generous doses of prayer. God does not ignore those who depend on him. Prayer is a prelude to promises that develop into provisions (see Ps 18:1–6). God has never promised to give us all we want. But he has pledged to provide all we need (see Php 4:19).

Begin to seek God for all of your provisions by following this plan: (1) Stop focusing on your concerns and start concentrating on prayer (see Ps 37:1–7). (2) With prayer, petition and thanksgiving, let your requests be made known to God (see Php 4:6). (3) Examine your circumstances and, in doing so, learn the secret of contentment. The situation is seldom as bad as you suspect—especially when you put it into perspective (see Php 4:10–13). (4) Recall accounts of how other Christian women have found favor with God through prayer, and remember how God has answered your own prayers in the past. (5) Be open to hearing from God about things you can do to help resolve your dilemma—which may include changing your environment or your mind or simply resolving to wait.

Study God's Word, apply the "prayer plan" listed above and remember that God will take care of you throughout every day, every experience, every change and every challenge. He is your all-sufficient Provider!

—N. Peete

### read

Luke 12:22–34; see also Psalm 37:1–40; Philippians 4:4–19. See also the Inspire Notes "Prayer: A God-Given Promise," "God's Promises: Always 'Yes' and 'Amen,'" "Prayer" and "Faith," and the Women of the Bible Notes "Hannah: What Do You Do When God Says 'No'?" "Daughter of Jarius: A Testament of Faith," "The Persistent Widow: Always Pray" and "Rhoda: Doing Her Duty."

### WOMAN of COLOR

About what do you need to stop worrying and start praying?

For the next Inspire note, go to page 1220.

12:58 r Mt 5:25
12:59 s Mk 12:42
13:1 t Mt 27:2
13:2 u Jn 9:2,3
13:4 v Jn 9:7,11
13:6 w Isa 5:2; Mt 21:19
13:7 x Mt 3:10
13:10 y Mt 4:23
13:11 z ver 16
13:13 a Mk 5:23
13:14 b Lk 14:3 c Mk 5:22 d Ex 20:9
13:15 e Lk 14:5

you into prison.[r] 59 I tell you, you will not get
out until you have paid the last penny.[a]"[s]

## Repent or Perish

13 Now there were some present at that
time who told Jesus about the Gali-
leans whose blood Pilate[t] had mixed with
their sacrifices. 2 Jesus answered, "Do you
think that these Galileans were worse sin-
ners than all the other Galileans because
they suffered this way?[u] 3 I tell you, no! But
unless you repent, you too will all perish.
4 Or those eighteen who died when the tower
in Siloam[v] fell on them—do you think they
were more guilty than all the others living
in Jerusalem? 5 I tell you, no! But unless you
repent, you too will all perish."

6 Then he told this parable: "A man had
a fig tree, planted in his vineyard, and he
went to look for fruit on it, but did not find
any.[w] 7 So he said to the man who took care
of the vineyard, 'For three years now I've
been coming to look for fruit on this fig tree
and haven't found any. Cut it down![x] Why
should it use up the soil?'

8 "'Sir,' the man replied, 'leave it alone for
one more year, and I'll dig around it and fer-
tilize it. 9 If it bears fruit next year, fine! If
not, then cut it down.'"

## A Crippled Woman Healed on the Sabbath

10 On a Sabbath Jesus was teaching in
one of the synagogues,[y] 11 and a woman
was there who had been crippled by a spirit
for eighteen years.[z] She was bent over and
could not straighten up at all. 12 When Jesus
saw her, he called her forward and said to
her, "Woman, you are set free from your
infirmity." 13 Then he put his hands on her,[a]
and immediately she straightened up and
praised God.

14 Indignant because Jesus had healed on
the Sabbath,[b] the synagogue ruler[c] said to
the people, "There are six days for work.[d] So
come and be healed on those days, not on
the Sabbath."

15 The Lord answered him, "You hypo-
crites! Doesn't each of you on the Sabbath
untie his ox or donkey from the stall and
lead it out to give it water?[e] 16 Then should
not this woman, a daughter of Abraham,[f]
whom Satan[g] has kept bound for eighteen
long years, be set free on the Sabbath day
from what bound her?"

17 When he said this, all his opponents
were humiliated, but the people were
delighted with all the wonderful things he
was doing.

## The Parables of the Mustard Seed and the Yeast

18 Then Jesus asked, "What is the king-
dom of God like? What shall I compare it to?
19 It is like a mustard seed, which a man took
and planted in his garden. It grew and be-
came a tree, and the birds of the air perched
in its branches."

20 Again he asked, "What shall I compare
the kingdom of God to? 21 It is like yeast
that a woman took and mixed into a large
amount[b] of flour until it worked all through
the dough."

## The Narrow Door

22 Then Jesus went through the towns and
villages, teaching as he made his way to Je-
rusalem.[h] 23 Someone asked him, "Lord, are
only a few people going to be saved?"

He said to them, 24 "Make every effort to
enter through the narrow door,[i] because
many, I tell you, will try to enter and will
not be able to. 25 Once the owner of the house
gets up and closes the door, you will stand
outside knocking and pleading, 'Sir, open
the door for us.'

"But he will answer, 'I don't know you or
where you come from.'[j]

26 "Then you will say, 'We ate and drank
with you, and you taught in our streets.'

27 "But he will reply, 'I don't know you or
where you come from. Away from me, all
you evildoers!'[k]

28 "There will be weeping there, and
gnashing of teeth,[l] when you see Abraham,
Isaac and Jacob and all the prophets in the
kingdom of God, but you yourselves thrown
out. 29 People will come from east and west[m]
and north and south, and will take their
places at the feast in the kingdom of God.
30 Indeed there are those who are last who
will be first, and first who will be last."[n]

13:16 f Lk 19:9 g Mt 4:10
13:22 h Lk 9:51
13:24 i Mt 7:13
13:25 j Mt 7:23; 25:10–12
13:27 k Mt 7:23; 25:41
13:28 l Mt 8:12
13:29 m Mt 8:11
13:30 n Mt 19:30

[a]59 Greek *lepton* [b]21 Greek *three satas* (probably about 1/2 bushel or 22 liters)

## Jesus' Sorrow for Jerusalem

31At that time some Pharisees came to
Jesus and said to him, "Leave this place and
go somewhere else. Herod wants to kill you."
32He replied, "Go tell that fox, 'I will drive
out demons and heal people today and to-
morrow, and on the third day I will reach my
goal.'o 33In any case, I must keep going today
and tomorrow and the next day—for surely
no prophetp can die outside Jerusalem!
34"O Jerusalem, Jerusalem, you who kill
the prophets and stone those sent to you,

13:32 o Heb 2:10
13:33 p Mt 21:11

Inspire

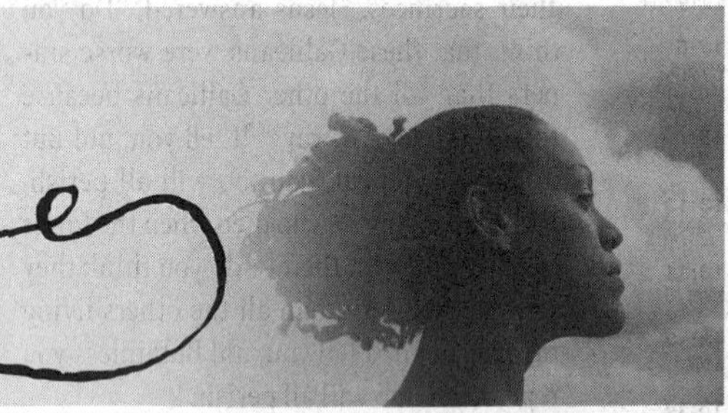

## VANITY

The Bible mentions many women of great beauty, such as Sarah, Rebekah, Rachel, Abigail, Bathsheba and Esther. As Christian women, our appearance should be a complement to our inner spirit—never a detraction from or hindrance to the kingdom of God. We should be concerned more about our inner beauty than about our outer attractiveness. Real beauty entails far more than just an appealing face. It stems from and reflects a Christlike spirit that personifies God's love.

In our vanity we would do well to remember the crippled woman in Luke 13:10–17, that patient saint who carried around her visible affliction for 18 long years. She hadn't always been bent and crooked. She had once stood straight and tall and may well have been elegant and balanced. Her body in that earlier life had not fought against her, and her eyes could gaze straight up into the heavens. But she—like so many women today—was eventually humbled in her body, forced to find other perspectives on which to focus. We have been falsely led to believe that our identity is tied directly to what we look like. But Jesus tells us that the presentation of our lives is what honors the gifts that have been given to us.

Vanity is a product of our will. As women, we must choose whether the center of our affections will be self or God. In our vanity we can misunderstand God's gifts to us. Sadly, we all too easily make them into idols and worship them. They, in turn, separate us from our godly potential, from each other and from God. We are gifted not by the mere appearance of our face and body, but by the love of God who created us, the forgiveness of Christ Jesus who liberates us and the presence of the Holy Spirit who sustains us.

—D. Tinsley Taylor

For the next Inspire note, go to page 1244.

### read

Luke 13:10–17; see also Ephesians 3:14–19; 1 Peter 3:1–6.

**See also** the Inspire Notes "The Creation of Woman," "Aging: Footprints in the Sands of Time" and "The Image of God and the Beauty of the Heart."

### WOMAN of COLOR

Are you ever tempted to place more importance on your outer beauty than your inner beauty? How can you keep your mind focused on what is truly important?

13:34
q Mt 23:37
13:35
r Ps 118:26; Mt 21:9; Lk 19:38
14:3
s Mt 22:35
t Mt 12:2
14:5
u Lk 13:15
14:11
v Mt 23:12; Lk 18:14
14:13
w ver 21
14:14
x Ac 24:15

how often I have longed to gather your chil-
dren together, as a hen gathers her chicks
under her wings,[q] but you were not willing!
35 Look, your house is left to you desolate. I
tell you, you will not see me again until you
say, 'Blessed is he who comes in the name of
the Lord.'[a]"[r]

## Jesus at a Pharisee's House

14 One Sabbath, when Jesus went to eat
in the house of a prominent Phari-
see, he was being carefully watched. 2 There
in front of him was a man suffering from
dropsy. 3 Jesus asked the Pharisees and ex-
perts in the law,[s] "Is it lawful to heal on the
Sabbath or not?"[t] 4 But they remained silent.
So taking hold of the man, he healed him
and sent him away.
5 Then he asked them, "If one of you has a
son[b] or an ox that falls into a well on the Sab-
bath day, will you not immediately pull him
out?"[u] 6 And they had nothing to say.
7 When he noticed how the guests picked
the places of honor at the table, he told them
this parable: 8 "When someone invites you
to a wedding feast, do not take the place
of honor, for a person more distinguished
than you may have been invited. 9 If so, the
host who invited both of you will come and
say to you, 'Give this man your seat.' Then,
humiliated, you will have to take the least
important place. 10 But when you are invited,
take the lowest place, so that when your host
comes, he will say to you, 'Friend, move up
to a better place.' Then you will be honored
in the presence of all your fellow guests.
11 For everyone who exalts himself will be
humbled, and he who humbles himself will
be exalted."[v]
12 Then Jesus said to his host, "When you
give a luncheon or dinner, do not invite your
friends, your brothers or relatives, or your
rich neighbors; if you do, they may invite
you back and so you will be repaid. 13 But
when you give a banquet, invite the poor,
the crippled, the lame, the blind,[w] 14 and you
will be blessed. Although they cannot repay
you, you will be repaid at the resurrection of
the righteous."[x]

## The Parable of the Great Banquet

15 When one of those at the table with him
heard this, he said to Jesus, "Blessed is the
man who will eat at the feast[y] in the king-
dom of God."
16 Jesus replied: "A certain man was pre-
paring a great banquet and invited many
guests. 17 At the time of the banquet he sent
his servant to tell those who had been invited,
'Come, for everything is now ready.'
18 "But they all alike began to make
excuses. The first said, 'I have just bought
a field, and I must go and see it. Please ex-
cuse me.'
19 "Another said, 'I have just bought five
yoke of oxen, and I'm on my way to try them
out. Please excuse me.'
20 "Still another said, 'I just got married,
so I can't come.'
21 "The servant came back and reported
this to his master. Then the owner of the
house became angry and ordered his ser-
vant, 'Go out quickly into the streets and
alleys of the town and bring in the poor, the
crippled, the blind and the lame.'[z]
22 " 'Sir,' the servant said, 'what you
ordered has been done, but there is still
room.'
23 "Then the master told his servant, 'Go
out to the roads and country lanes and make
them come in, so that my house will be full.
24 I tell you, not one of those men who were
invited will get a taste of my banquet.' "[a]

## The Cost of Being a Disciple

25 Large crowds were traveling with Jesus,
and turning to them he said: 26 "If anyone
comes to me and does not hate his father
and mother, his wife and children, his broth-
ers and sisters—yes, even his own life—he
cannot be my disciple.[b] 27 And anyone who
does not carry his cross and follow me can-
not be my disciple.[c]
28 "Suppose one of you wants to build
a tower. Will he not first sit down and esti-
mate the cost to see if he has enough money
to complete it? 29 For if he lays the foundation
and is not able to finish it, everyone who sees
it will ridicule him, 30 saying, 'This fellow be-
gan to build and was not able to finish.'

14:15
y Rev 19:9
14:21
z ver 13
14:24
a Mt 21:43; Ac 13:46
14:26
b Mt 10:37
14:27
c Mt 10:38; Lk 9:23

[a] 35 Psalm 118:26 [b] 5 Some manuscripts *donkey*

**14:33** d Php 3:7,8
**14:34** e Mk 9:50
**14:35** f Mt 5:13; g Mt 11:15
**15:1** h Lk 5:29
**15:2** i Mt 9:11
**15:7** j ver 10

31"Or suppose a king is about to go to war against another king. Will he not first sit down and consider whether he is able with ten thousand men to oppose the one coming against him with twenty thousand? 32If he is not able, he will send a delegation while the other is still a long way off and will ask for terms of peace. 33In the same way, any of you who does not give up everything he has cannot be my disciple.[d]

34"Salt is good, but if it loses its saltiness, how can it be made salty again?[e] 35It is fit neither for the soil nor for the manure pile; it is thrown out.[f]

"He who has ears to hear, let him hear."[g]

## The Parable of the Lost Sheep

15 Now the tax collectors[h] and "sinners" were all gathering around to hear him. 2But the Pharisees and the teachers of the law muttered, "This man welcomes sinners and eats with them."[i]

3Then Jesus told them this parable: 4"Suppose one of you has a hundred sheep and loses one of them. Does he not leave the ninety-nine in the open country and go after the lost sheep until he finds it? 5And when he finds it, he joyfully puts it on his shoulders 6and goes home. Then he calls his friends and neighbors together and says, 'Rejoice with me; I have found my lost sheep.' 7I tell you that in the same way there will be more rejoicing in heaven over one sinner who repents than over ninety-nine righteous persons who do not need to repent.[j]

> *"Two things everybody's got to do for themselves: They've got to trust God, and they've got to find out about living for themselves."*
>
> —ZORA NEALE HURSTON, WRITER AND FOLKLORIST

## The Parable of the Lost Coin

8"Or suppose a woman has ten silver coins[a] and loses one. Does she not light a lamp, sweep the house and search carefully until she finds it? 9And when she finds it, she calls her friends and neighbors together and says, 'Rejoice with me; I have found my lost coin.' 10In the same way, I tell you, there is rejoicing in the presence of the angels of God over one sinner who repents."[k]

> *Lord,*
>
> *thank you for grace. Thank you for your plan of salvation and for loving me unconditionally. Help me to reflect that love and grace to others, so that they in turn may long to know you.*
>
> *Amen.*
>
> LUKE 15:3–7

## The Parable of the Lost Son

11Jesus continued: "There was a man who had two sons.[l] 12The younger one said to his father, 'Father, give me my share of the estate.'[m] So he divided his property[n] between them.

13"Not long after that, the younger son got together all he had, set off for a distant country and there squandered his wealth in wild living. 14After he had spent everything, there was a severe famine in that whole country, and he began to be in need. 15So he went and hired himself out to a citizen of that country, who sent him to his fields to feed pigs. 16He longed to fill his stomach with the pods that the pigs were eating, but no one gave him anything.

17"When he came to his senses, he said, 'How many of my father's hired men have food to spare, and here I am starving to death! 18I will set out and go back to my father and say to him: Father, I have sinned against heaven and against you. 19I am no longer worthy to be called your son; make me like one of your hired men.' 20So he got up and went to his father.

"But while he was still a long way off, his father saw him and was filled with compassion for him; he ran to his son, threw his arms around him and kissed him.[o]

21"The son said to him, 'Father, I have sinned against heaven and against you.[p]

**15:10** k ver 7
**15:11** l Mt 21:28
**15:12** m Dt 21:17; n ver 30
**15:20** o Ge 45:14,15; 46:29; Ac 20:37
**15:21** p Ps 51:4

[a]8 Greek *ten drachmas,* each worth about a day's wages

15:22 q Zec 3:4; Rev 6:11 r Ge 41:42
15:24 s Eph 2:1,5; 5:14; 1Ti 5:6 t ver 32
15:30 u ver 12,13 v Pr 29:3
15:32 w ver 24
16:1 x Lk 15:13,30

I am no longer worthy to be called your
son.[a]'
[22]"But the father said to his servants,
'Quick! Bring the best robe[q] and put it on
him. Put a ring on his finger[r] and sandals
on his feet. [23]Bring the fattened calf and kill
it. Let's have a feast and celebrate. [24]For this
son of mine was dead and is alive again;[s] he
was lost and is found.' So they began to cel-
ebrate.[t]
[25]"Meanwhile, the older son was in the
field. When he came near the house, he
heard music and dancing. [26]So he called
one of the servants and asked him what
was going on. [27]'Your brother has come,'
he replied, 'and your father has killed the
fattened calf because he has him back safe
and sound.'
[28]"The older brother became angry and
refused to go in. So his father went out and
pleaded with him. [29]But he answered his fa-
ther, 'Look! All these years I've been slaving
for you and never disobeyed your orders.
Yet you never gave me even a young goat so I
could celebrate with my friends. [30]But when
this son of yours who has squandered your
property[u] with prostitutes[v] comes home,
you kill the fattened calf for him!'
[31]"'My son,' the father said, 'you are
always with me, and everything I have is
yours. [32]But we had to celebrate and be glad,
because this brother of yours was dead and
is alive again; he was lost and is found.'"[w]

## The Parable of the Shrewd Manager

**16** Jesus told his disciples: "There was
a rich man whose manager was
accused of wasting his possessions.[x] [2]So
he called him in and asked him, 'What is
this I hear about you? Give an account of
your management, because you cannot be
manager any longer.'
[3]"The manager said to himself, 'What
shall I do now? My master is taking away
my job. I'm not strong enough to dig, and
I'm ashamed to beg— [4]I know what I'll do
so that, when I lose my job here, people will
welcome me into their houses.'
[5]"So he called in each one of his master's
debtors. He asked the first, 'How much do
you owe my master?'
[6]"'Eight hundred gallons[b] of olive oil,' he
replied.
"The manager told him, 'Take your bill,
sit down quickly, and make it four hun-
dred.'
[7]"Then he asked the second, 'And how
much do you owe?'
"'A thousand bushels[c] of wheat,' he re-
plied.
"He told him, 'Take your bill and make it
eight hundred.'
[8]"The master commended the dishonest
manager because he had acted shrewdly. For
the people of this world are more shrewd in
dealing with their own kind than are the
people of the light.[y] [9]I tell you, use worldly
wealth to gain friends for yourselves, so that
when it is gone, you will be welcomed into
eternal dwellings.[z]
[10]"Whoever can be trusted with very
little can also be trusted with much,[a] and
whoever is dishonest with very little will
also be dishonest with much. [11]So if you
have not been trustworthy in handling
worldly wealth, who will trust you with true
riches? [12]And if you have not been trust-
worthy with someone else's property, who
will give you property of your own?
[13]"No servant can serve two masters. Ei-
ther he will hate the one and love the other,
or he will be devoted to the one and despise
the other. You cannot serve both God and
Money."[b]
[14]The Pharisees, who loved money, heard
all this and were sneering at Jesus.[c] [15]He said
to them, "You are the ones who justify your-
selves[d] in the eyes of men, but God knows
your hearts.[e] What is highly valued among
men is detestable in God's sight.

## Additional Teachings

[16]"The Law and the Prophets were pro-
claimed until John.[f] Since that time, the
good news of the kingdom of God is being
preached,[g] and everyone is forcing his way
into it. [17]It is easier for heaven and earth to
disappear than for the least stroke of a pen
to drop out of the Law.[h]

16:8 y Jn 12:36; Eph 5:8; 1Th 5:5
16:9 z Mt 19:21
16:10 a Mt 25:21,23
16:13 b Mt 6:24
16:14 c Lk 23:35
16:15 d Lk 10:29 e 1Sa 16:7
16:16 f Mt 11:12,13 g Mt 4:23
16:17 h Mt 5:18

[a]21 Some early manuscripts *son. Make me like one of your hired men.* [b]6 Greek *one hundred batous* (probably about 3 kiloliters) [c]7 Greek *one hundred korous* (probably about 35 kiloliters)

16:18 i Mt 5:31,32; Mk 10:11; 1Co 7:10,11
16:20 j Ac 3:2
16:25 k Lk 6:21,24,25
16:29 l Jn 5:45–47; Ac 15:21 m Lk 4:17

18“Anyone who divorces his wife and marries another woman commits adultery, and the man who marries a divorced woman commits adultery.[i]

## The Rich Man and Lazarus

19“There was a rich man who was dressed in purple and fine linen and lived in luxury every day. 20At his gate was laid a beggar[j] named Lazarus, covered with sores 21and longing to eat what fell from the rich man’s table. Even the dogs came and licked his sores.

22“The time came when the beggar died and the angels carried him to Abraham’s side. The rich man also died and was buried. 23In hell,[a] where he was in torment, he looked up and saw Abraham far away, with Lazarus by his side. 24So he called to him, ‘Father Abraham, have pity on me and send Lazarus to dip the tip of his finger in water and cool my tongue, because I am in agony in this fire.’

25“But Abraham replied, ‘Son, remember that in your lifetime you received your good things, while Lazarus received bad things, but now he is comforted here and you are in agony.[k] 26And besides all this, between us and you a great chasm has been fixed, so that those who want to go from here to you cannot, nor can anyone cross over from there to us.’

27“He answered, ‘Then I beg you, father, send Lazarus to my father’s house, 28for I have five brothers. Let him warn them, so that they will not also come to this place of torment.’

29“Abraham replied, ‘They have Moses[l] and the Prophets;[m] let them listen to them.’

30“ ‘No, father Abraham,’ he said, ‘but if someone from the dead goes to them, they will repent.’

31“He said to him, ‘If they do not listen to Moses and the Prophets, they will not be convinced even if someone rises from the dead.’ ”

## Sin, Faith, Duty

17 Jesus said to his disciples: “Things that cause people to sin are bound to come, but woe to that person through whom they come.[n] 2It would be better for him to be thrown into the sea with a millstone tied around his neck than for him to cause one of these little ones to sin. 3So watch yourselves.

“If your brother sins, rebuke him,[o] and if he repents, forgive him. 4If he sins against you seven times in a day, and seven times comes back to you and says, ‘I repent,’ forgive him.”[p]

5The apostles[q] said to the Lord, “Increase our faith!”

6He replied, “If you have faith as small as a mustard seed,[r] you can say to this mulberry tree, ‘Be uprooted and planted in the sea,’ and it will obey you.

7“Suppose one of you had a servant plowing or looking after the sheep. Would he say to the servant when he comes in from the field, ‘Come along now and sit down to eat’? 8Would he not rather say, ‘Prepare my supper, get yourself ready and wait on me[s] while I eat and drink; after that you may eat and drink’? 9Would he thank the servant because he did what he was told to do? 10So you also, when you have done everything you were told to do, should say, ‘We are unworthy servants; we have only done our duty.’ ”

## Ten Healed of Leprosy

11Now on his way to Jerusalem,[t] Jesus traveled along the border between Samaria and Galilee.[u] 12As he was going into a village, ten men who had leprosy[b] met him. They stood at a distance[v] 13and called out in a loud voice, “Jesus, Master, have pity on us!”

14When he saw them, he said, “Go, show yourselves to the priests.”[w] And as they went, they were cleansed.

15One of them, when he saw he was healed, came back, praising God[x] in a loud voice. 16He threw himself at Jesus’ feet and thanked him—and he was a Samaritan.[y]

17Jesus asked, “Were not all ten cleansed? Where are the other nine? 18Was no one found to return and give praise to God except this foreigner?” 19Then he said to him, “Rise and go; your faith has made you well.”[z]

17:1 n Mt 18:7
17:3 o Mt 18:15
17:4 p Mt 18:21,22
17:5 q Mk 6:30
17:6 r Mt 17:20
17:8 s Lk 12:37
17:11 t Lk 9:51 u Jn 4:3,4
17:12 v Lev 13:45,46
17:14 w Mt 8:4
17:15 x Mt 9:8
17:16 y Mt 10:5
17:19 z Mt 9:22

[a]23 Greek *Hades* [b]12 The Greek word was used for various diseases affecting the skin—not necessarily leprosy.

## The Coming of the Kingdom of God

[20]Once, having been asked by the Pharisees when the kingdom of God would come, Jesus replied, "The kingdom of God does not come with your careful observation, [21]nor will people say, 'Here it is,' or 'There it is,'[a] because the kingdom of God is within[a] you."

[22]Then he said to his disciples, "The time is coming when you will long to see one of the days of the Son of Man, but you will not see it.[b] [23]Men will tell you, 'There he is!' or 'Here he is!' Do not go running off after them.[c] [24]For the Son of Man in his day[b] will be like the lightning,[d] which flashes and lights up the sky from one end to the other. [25]But first he must suffer many things and be rejected[e] by this generation.

[26]"Just as it was in the days of Noah,[f] so also will it be in the days of the Son of Man. [27]People were eating, drinking, marrying and being given in marriage up to the day Noah entered the ark. Then the flood came and destroyed them all.

[28]"It was the same in the days of Lot. People were eating and drinking, buying and selling, planting and building. [29]But the day Lot left Sodom, fire and sulfur rained down from heaven and destroyed them all.

[30]"It will be just like this on the day the Son of Man is revealed.[g] [31]On that day no one who is on the roof of his house, with his goods inside, should go down to get them. Likewise, no one in the field should go back for anything.[h] [32]Remember Lot's wife![i] [33]Whoever tries to keep his life will lose it, and whoever loses his life will preserve it. [34]I tell you, on that night two people will be in one bed; one will be taken and the other left. [35]Two women will be grinding grain together; one will be taken and the other left.[c]"[j]

[37]"Where, Lord?" they asked.

He replied, "Where there is a dead body, there the vultures will gather."[k]

**17:21** a ver 23
**17:22** b Mt 9:15
**17:23** c Mt 24:23; Mk 13:21; Lk 21:8
**17:24** d Mt 24:27
**17:25** e Lk 9:22
**17:26** f Ge 7:6–24
**17:30** g 2Th 1:7
**17:31** h Mt 24:17,18; Mk 13:15–16
**17:32** i Ge 19:26
**17:35** j Mt 24:41
**17:37** k Mt 24:28

## The Parable of the Persistent Widow

**18** Then Jesus told his disciples a parable to show them that they should always pray and not give up.[l] [2]He said: "In a certain town there was a judge who neither feared God nor cared about men. [3]And there was a widow in that town who kept coming to him with the plea, 'Grant me justice against my adversary.'

[4]"For some time he refused. But finally he said to himself, 'Even though I don't fear God or care about men, [5]yet because this widow keeps bothering me, I will see that she gets justice, so that she won't eventually wear me out with her coming!'"[m]

[6]And the Lord said, "Listen to what the unjust judge says. [7]And will not God bring about justice for his chosen ones, who cry out[n] to him day and night? Will he keep putting them off? [8]I tell you, he will see that they get justice, and quickly. However, when the Son of Man comes, will he find faith on the earth?"

## The Parable of the Pharisee and the Tax Collector

[9]To some who were confident of their own righteousness[o] and looked down on everybody else, Jesus told this parable: [10]"Two men went up to the temple to pray, one a Pharisee and the other a tax collector. [11]The Pharisee stood up[p] and prayed about[d] himself: 'God, I thank you that I am not like other men—robbers, evildoers, adulterers—or even like this tax collector. [12]I fast[q] twice a week and give a tenth[r] of all I get.'

[13]"But the tax collector stood at a distance. He would not even look up to heaven, but beat his breast[s] and said, 'God, have mercy on me, a sinner.'

[14]"I tell you that this man, rather than the other, went home justified before God. For everyone who exalts himself will be humbled, and he who humbles himself will be exalted."[t]

## The Little Children and Jesus

[15]People were also bringing babies to Jesus to have him touch them. When the

**18:1** l Lk 11:5–8
**18:5** m Lk 11:8
**18:7** n Rev 6:10
**18:9** o Lk 16:15
**18:11** p Mk 11:25
**18:12** q Mt 9:14 r Lk 11:42
**18:13** s Lk 23:48
**18:14** t Mt 23:12; Lk 14:11

[a]21 Or *among* [b]24 Some manuscripts do not have *in his day.* [c]35 Some manuscripts *left.* [36]*Two men will be in the field; one will be taken and the other left.* [d]11 Or *to*

# The Persistent Widow

## Always Pray

The parable of the persistent widow reminds us to keep knocking at God's door until we receive an answer. Jesus told this parable to show his followers "that they should always pray and not give up" (Lk 18:1). While the widow in the parable received what she needed from an earthly, unjust judge because she kept asking him to grant her justice, we know that our heavenly Judge is much more just and loving and willing to meet our every need and many of our desires than any earthly judge.

We are to "pray continually" (1Th 5:17). No matter what we are going through or what we need, we must be determined to obtain what we need. Persistence is a virtue. With one thing on our minds, and being very, very persistent, we must do what our widow sister did: wait until our change comes.

When you are in dire need of something, you don't care how far you have to go to get it, how much it's going to cost or what you have to sacrifice in order to get it. A deeply felt need will have you crawling, taking risks and using any means necessary to get it met. In spite of who this widow was, what she was, where she was, she had a need. And she knew where to go to get it met. So if there's anything you need from Jesus, go to him, look to him. He can be found.

This woman was able to persist because she was doing so based on faith. If no one else knows, certainly African American women know what it's like to be persistent. Our widow sister lets us know that if we pray long and hard enough, God will give us wings as an eagle and feet that won't become weary (see Isa 40:31). "At the proper time we will reap a harvest if we do not give up" (Gal 6:9).

—J. Wharton

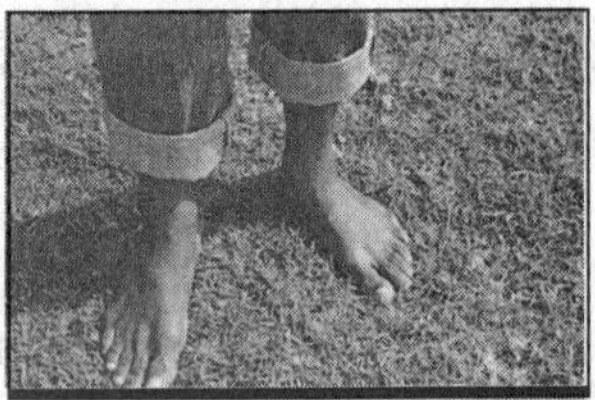

### reflection

*Reflect on something you have consistently prayed about.*

*How has God answered your prayers?*

*Look for his work in your life.*

*Be persistent and keep the faith.*

### read

Luke 18:1–8.

See also the Inspire Notes "Distress," "Waiting on God," "Prayer: A God-Given Promise," "Prayer: The Antidote to Worry," "Peace" and "Prayer," and the Women of the Bible Notes "Hannah: What Do You Do When God Says 'No'?" and "The Canaanite Woman: Persistence Pays Off."

For the next Women of the Bible note, go to page 1251.

18:17
u Mt18:3
18:18
v Lk10:25
18:20
w Ex20:12–16; Dt5:16–20; Ro13:9
18:22
x Mt6:20
18:24
y Pr11:28
18:27
z Mt19:26
18:30
a Mt12:32
18:31
b Lk9:51
c Ps22
18:32
d Lk23:1

disciples saw this, they rebuked them. 16 But
Jesus called the children to him and said,
"Let the little children come to me, and do
not hinder them, for the kingdom of God be-
longs to such as these. 17 I tell you the truth,
anyone who will not receive the kingdom of
God like a little child[u] will never enter it."

## The Rich Ruler

18 A certain ruler asked him, "Good
teacher, what must I do to inherit eternal
life?"[v]

19 "Why do you call me good?" Jesus
answered. "No one is good—except God
alone. 20 You know the commandments:
'Do not commit adultery, do not murder, do
not steal, do not give false testimony, honor
your father and mother.'[a]"[w]

21 "All these I have kept since I was a boy,"
he said.

22 When Jesus heard this, he said to him,
"You still lack one thing. Sell everything
you have and give to the poor, and you will
have treasure in heaven.[x] Then come, fol-
low me."

23 When he heard this, he became very
sad, because he was a man of great wealth.
24 Jesus looked at him and said, "How hard
it is for the rich to enter the kingdom of
God![y] 25 Indeed, it is easier for a camel to go
through the eye of a needle than for a rich
man to enter the kingdom of God."

26 Those who heard this asked, "Who then
can be saved?"

27 Jesus replied, "What is impossible with
men is possible with God."[z]

28 Peter said to him, "We have left all we
had to follow you!"

29 "I tell you the truth," Jesus said to them,
"no one who has left home or wife or broth-
ers or parents or children for the sake of the
kingdom of God 30 will fail to receive many
times as much in this age and, in the age to
come,[a] eternal life."

## Jesus Again Predicts His Death

31 Jesus took the Twelve aside and told
them, "We are going up to Jerusalem,[b] and
everything that is written by the prophets[c]
about the Son of Man will be fulfilled. 32 He
will be handed over to the Gentiles.[d] They
will mock him, insult him, spit on him, flog
him[e] and kill him. 33 On the third day he will
rise again."

34 The disciples did not understand any
of this. Its meaning was hidden from them,
and they did not know what he was talk-
ing about.[f]

## A Blind Beggar Receives His Sight

35 As Jesus approached Jericho, a blind
man was sitting by the roadside begging.
36 When he heard the crowd going by, he
asked what was happening. 37 They told him,
"Jesus of Nazareth is passing by."

38 He called out, "Jesus, Son of David,[g]
have mercy on me!"

39 Those who led the way rebuked him and
told him to be quiet, but he shouted all the
more, "Son of David, have mercy on me!"

40 Jesus stopped and ordered the man
to be brought to him. When he came near,
Jesus asked him, 41 "What do you want me
to do for you?"

"Lord, I want to see," he replied.

42 Jesus said to him, "Receive your sight;
your faith has healed you."[h] 43 Immediately
he received his sight and followed Jesus,
praising God. When all the people saw it,
they also praised God.[i]

## Zacchaeus the Tax Collector

19 Jesus entered Jericho[j] and was pass-
ing through. 2 A man was there by
the name of Zacchaeus; he was a chief tax
collector and was wealthy. 3 He wanted to
see who Jesus was, but being a short man he
could not, because of the crowd. 4 So he ran
ahead and climbed a sycamore-fig[k] tree to
see him, since Jesus was coming that way.

5 When Jesus reached the spot, he looked
up and said to him, "Zacchaeus, come down
immediately. I must stay at your house
today." 6 So he came down at once and wel-
comed him gladly.

7 All the people saw this and began to
mutter, "He has gone to be the guest of a 'sin-
ner.'"[l]

8 But Zacchaeus stood up and said to the
Lord,[m] "Look, Lord! Here and now I give
half of my possessions to the poor, and if

18:32
e Mt16:21
18:34
f Mk9:32; Lk9:45
18:38
g Mt9:27
18:42
h Mt9:22
18:43
i Mt9:8
19:1
j Lk18:35
19:4
k 1Ki10:27; 1Ch27:28
19:7
l Mt9:11
19:8
m Lk7:13

[a] 20 Exodus 20:12–16; Deut. 5:16–20

**19:8** n Ex22:1; Lev6:4,5; Nu5:7; 2Sa12:6
**19:9** o Lk3:8; 13:16; Ro4:16; Gal3:7
**19:11** p Ac1:6
**19:17** q Lk16:10
**19:21** r Mt25:24
**19:22** s 2Sa1:16; Job15:6 t Mt25:26

I have cheated anybody out of anything, I
will pay back four times the amount."[n]
9 Jesus said to him, "Today salvation has
come to this house, because this man, too,
is a son of Abraham.[o] 10 For the Son of Man
came to seek and to save what was lost."

## The Parable of the Ten Minas

11 While they were listening to this, he
went on to tell them a parable, because he
was near Jerusalem and the people thought
that the kingdom of God was going to ap-
pear at once.[p] 12 He said: "A man of noble
birth went to a distant country to have him-
self appointed king and then to return. 13 So
he called ten of his servants and gave them
ten minas.[a] 'Put this money to work,' he
said, 'until I come back.'
14 "But his subjects hated him and sent a
delegation after him to say, 'We don't want
this man to be our king.'
15 "He was made king, however, and re-
turned home. Then he sent for the servants
to whom he had given the money, in order to
find out what they had gained with it.
16 "The first one came and said, 'Sir, your
mina has earned ten more.'
17 " 'Well done, my good servant!' his mas-
ter replied. 'Because you have been trust-
worthy in a very small matter, take charge
of ten cities.'[q]
18 "The second came and said, 'Sir, your
mina has earned five more.'
19 "His master answered, 'You take charge
of five cities.'
20 "Then another servant came and said,
'Sir, here is your mina; I have kept it laid
away in a piece of cloth. 21 I was afraid of you,
because you are a hard man. You take out
what you did not put in and reap what you
did not sow.'[r]
22 "His master replied, 'I will judge you by
your own words,[s] you wicked servant! You
knew, did you, that I am a hard man, taking
out what I did not put in, and reaping what I
did not sow?[t] 23 Why then didn't you put my
money on deposit, so that when I came back,
I could have collected it with interest?'
24 "Then he said to those standing by,
'Take his mina away from him and give it to
the one who has ten minas.'
25 " 'Sir,' they said, 'he already has ten!'
26 "He replied, 'I tell you that to everyone
who has, more will be given, but as for the
one who has nothing, even what he has
will be taken away.[u] 27 But those enemies of
mine who did not want me to be king over
them—bring them here and kill them in
front of me.' "

## The Triumphal Entry

28 After Jesus had said this, he went on
ahead, going up to Jerusalem.[v] 29 As he ap-
proached Bethphage and Bethany at the hill
called the Mount of Olives,[w] he sent two of
his disciples, saying to them, 30 "Go to the
village ahead of you, and as you enter it, you
will find a colt tied there, which no one has
ever ridden. Untie it and bring it here. 31 If
anyone asks you, 'Why are you untying it?'
tell him, 'The Lord needs it.' "
32 Those who were sent ahead went and
found it just as he had told them. 33 As they
were untying the colt, its owners asked
them, "Why are you untying the colt?"
34 They replied, "The Lord needs it."
35 They brought it to Jesus, threw their
cloaks on the colt and put Jesus on it. 36 As
he went along, people spread their cloaks[x]
on the road.
37 When he came near the place where the
road goes down the Mount of Olives, the
whole crowd of disciples began joyfully to
praise God in loud voices for all the miracles
they had seen:

38 "Blessed is the king who comes in the
name of the Lord!"[b][y]

"Peace in heaven and glory in the
highest!"[z]

39 Some of the Pharisees in the crowd said
to Jesus, "Teacher, rebuke your disciples!"[a]
40 "I tell you," he replied, "if they keep
quiet, the stones will cry out."[b]
41 As he approached Jerusalem and saw
the city, he wept over it[c] 42 and said, "If you,
even you, had only known on this day what
would bring you peace—but now it is hid-
den from your eyes. 43 The days will come
upon you when your enemies will build
an embankment against you and encircle

**19:26** u Mt13:12; 25:29; Lk8:18
**19:28** v Mk10:32
**19:29** w Mt21:1
**19:36** x 2Ki9:13
**19:38** y Ps118:26; Lk13:35 z Lk2:14
**19:39** a Mt21:15,16
**19:40** b Hab2:11
**19:41** c Lk13:34,35

[a] 13 A mina was about three months' wages. [b] 38 Psalm 118:26

you and hem you in on every side.[d] 44 They will dash you to the ground, you and the children within your walls. They will not leave one stone on another,[e] because you did not recognize the time of God's coming[f] to you."

## Jesus at the Temple

45 Then he entered the temple area and began driving out those who were selling. 46 "It is written," he said to them, " 'My house will be a house of prayer'[a];[g] but you have made it 'a den of robbers.'[b]"[h]

47 Every day he was teaching at the temple.[i] But the chief priests, the teachers of the law and the leaders among the people were trying to kill him.[j] 48 Yet they could not find any way to do it, because all the people hung on his words.

## The Authority of Jesus Questioned

20 One day as he was teaching the people in the temple courts[k] and preaching the gospel,[l] the chief priests and the teachers of the law, together with the elders, came up to him. 2 "Tell us by what authority you are doing these things," they said. "Who gave you this authority?"[m]

3 He replied, "I will also ask you a question. Tell me, 4 John's baptism—was it from heaven, or from men?"

5 They discussed it among themselves and said, "If we say, 'From heaven,' he will ask, 'Why didn't you believe him?' 6 But if we say, 'From men,' all the people will stone us, because they are persuaded that John was a prophet."

7 So they answered, "We don't know where it was from."

8 Jesus said, "Neither will I tell you by what authority I am doing these things."

## The Parable of the Tenants

9 He went on to tell the people this parable: "A man planted a vineyard, rented it to some farmers and went away for a long time. 10 At harvest time he sent a servant to the tenants so they would give him some of the fruit of the vineyard. But the tenants beat him and sent him away empty-handed. 11 He sent another servant, but that one also they beat and treated shamefully and sent away empty-handed. 12 He sent still a third, and they wounded him and threw him out.

13 "Then the owner of the vineyard said, 'What shall I do? I will send my son, whom I love; perhaps they will respect him.'

14 "But when the tenants saw him, they talked the matter over. 'This is the heir,' they said. 'Let's kill him, and the inheritance will be ours.' 15 So they threw him out of the vineyard and killed him.

"What then will the owner of the vineyard do to them? 16 He will come and kill those tenants[n] and give the vineyard to others."

When the people heard this, they said, "May this never be!"

17 Jesus looked directly at them and asked, "Then what is the meaning of that which is written:

" 'The stone the builders rejected
has become the capstone[c]'[d]?[o]

18 Everyone who falls on that stone will be broken to pieces, but he on whom it falls will be crushed."

19 The teachers of the law and the chief priests looked for a way to arrest him[p] immediately, because they knew he had spoken this parable against them. But they were afraid of the people.

## Paying Taxes to Caesar

20 Keeping a close watch on him, they sent spies, who pretended to be honest. They hoped to catch Jesus in something he said[q] so that they might hand him over to the power and authority of the governor.[r] 21 So the spies questioned him: "Teacher, we know that you speak and teach what is right, and that you do not show partiality but teach the way of God in accordance with the truth.[s] 22 Is it right for us to pay taxes to Caesar or not?"

23 He saw through their duplicity and said to them, 24 "Show me a denarius. Whose portrait and inscription are on it?"

25 "Caesar's," they replied.

He said to them, "Then give to Caesar

**19:43** d Isa 29:3; Jer 6:6; Eze 4:2; Lk 21:20
**19:44** e Mt 24:2; Mk 13:2; Lk 21:6 f 1Pe 2:12
**19:46** g Isa 56:7 h Jer 7:11
**19:47** i Mt 26:55 j Mk 11:18
**20:1** k Mt 26:55 l Lk 8:1
**20:2** m Ac 4:7; 7:27
**20:16** n Lk 19:27
**20:17** o Ps 118:22
**20:19** p Lk 19:47
**20:20** q Mt 12:10 r Mt 27:2
**20:21** s Jn 3:2

[a]46 Isaiah 56:7 [b]46 Jer. 7:11 [c]17 Or *cornerstone* [d]17 Psalm 118:22

20:25 t Lk 23:2; Ro 13:7
20:27 u Ac 23:8
20:28 v Dt 25:5
20:35 w Mt 12:32
20:36 x Jn 1:12; 1Jn 3:1–2
20:37 y Ex 3:6
20:40 z Mt 22:46; Mk 12:34
20:43 a Ps 110:1

what is Caesar's,[t] and to God what is
God's."
26They were unable to trap him in what
he had said there in public. And astonished
by his answer, they became silent.

## The Resurrection and Marriage

27Some of the Sadducees, who say there
is no resurrection,[u] came to Jesus with a
question. 28"Teacher," they said, "Moses
wrote for us that if a man's brother dies and
leaves a wife but no children, the man must
marry the widow and have children for his
brother.[v] 29Now there were seven brothers.
The first one married a woman and died
childless. 30The second 31and then the third
married her, and in the same way the seven
died, leaving no children. 32Finally, the
woman died too. 33Now then, at the resurrec-
tion whose wife will she be, since the seven
were married to her?"
34Jesus replied, "The people of this age
marry and are given in marriage. 35But those
who are considered worthy of taking part
in that age[w] and in the resurrection from
the dead will neither marry nor be given
in marriage, 36and they can no longer die;
for they are like the angels. They are God's
children,[x] since they are children of the res-
urrection. 37But in the account of the bush,
even Moses showed that the dead rise, for he
calls the Lord 'the God of Abraham, and the
God of Isaac, and the God of Jacob.'[a][y] 38He is
not the God of the dead, but of the living, for
to him all are alive."
39Some of the teachers of the law
responded, "Well said, teacher!" 40And no
one dared to ask him any more questions.[z]

## Whose Son Is the Christ?

41Then Jesus said to them, "How is it that
they say the Christ[b] is the Son of David? 42Da-
vid himself declares in the Book of Psalms:

"'The Lord said to my Lord:
"Sit at my right hand
43 until I make your enemies
a footstool for your feet." '[c][a]

44David calls him 'Lord.' How then can he be
his son?"
45While all the people were listening,
Jesus said to his disciples, 46"Beware of the
teachers of the law. They like to walk around
in flowing robes and love to be greeted in
the marketplaces and have the most impor-
tant seats in the synagogues and the places
of honor at banquets.[b] 47They devour wid-
ows' houses and for a show make lengthy
prayers. Such men will be punished most
severely."

20:46 b Lk 11:43
21:1 c Mt 27:6
21:4 d 2Co 8:12
21:6 e Lk 19:44
21:8 f Lk 17:23
21:10 g 2Ch 15:6
21:13 h Php 1:12

## The Widow's Offering

21 As he looked up, Jesus saw the rich
putting their gifts into the temple
treasury.[c] 2He also saw a poor widow put
in two very small copper coins.[d] 3"I tell you
the truth," he said, "this poor widow has put
in more than all the others. 4All these peo-
ple gave their gifts out of their wealth; but
she out of her poverty put in all she had to
live on."[d]

## Signs of the End of the Age

5Some of his disciples were remarking
about how the temple was adorned with
beautiful stones and with gifts dedicated
to God. But Jesus said, 6"As for what you see
here, the time will come when not one stone
will be left on another;[e] every one of them
will be thrown down."
7"Teacher," they asked, "when will these
things happen? And what will be the sign
that they are about to take place?"
8He replied: "Watch out that you are not
deceived. For many will come in my name,
claiming, 'I am he,' and, 'The time is near.'
Do not follow them.[f] 9When you hear of
wars and revolutions, do not be frightened.
These things must happen first, but the end
will not come right away."
10Then he said to them: "Nation will rise
against nation, and kingdom against king-
dom.[g] 11There will be great earthquakes,
famines and pestilences in various places,
and fearful events and great signs from
heaven.
12"But before all this, they will lay hands
on you and persecute you. They will deliver
you to synagogues and prisons, and you will
be brought before kings and governors, and
all on account of my name. 13This will re-
sult in your being witnesses to them.[h] 14But

[a] 37 Exodus 3:6 [b] 41 Or *Messiah* [c] 43 Psalm 110:1 [d] 2 Greek *two lepta*

make up your mind not to worry before-
hand how you will defend yourselves.[i] 15 For
I will give you[j] words and wisdom that none
of your adversaries will be able to resist or
contradict. 16 You will be betrayed even by
parents, brothers, relatives and friends,[k]
and they will put some of you to death. 17 All
men will hate you because of me. 18 But not a
hair of your head will perish.[l] 19 By standing
firm you will gain life.
20 "When you see Jerusalem being
surrounded by armies,[m] you will know that
its desolation is near. 21 Then let those who
are in Judea flee to the mountains, let those
in the city get out, and let those in the coun-
try not enter the city.[n] 22 For this is the time
of punishment[o] in fulfillment of all that has
been written. 23 How dreadful it will be in
those days for pregnant women and nursing
mothers! There will be great distress in the
land and wrath against this people. 24 They
will fall by the sword and will be taken as
prisoners to all the nations. Jerusalem will
be trampled[p] on by the Gentiles until the
times of the Gentiles are fulfilled.
25 "There will be signs in the sun, moon
and stars. On the earth, nations will be in an-
guish and perplexity at the roaring and toss-
ing of the sea.[q] 26 Men will faint from terror,
apprehensive of what is coming on the world,
for the heavenly bodies will be shaken. 27 At
that time they will see the Son of Man com-
ing in a cloud[r] with power and great glory.
28 When these things begin to take place,
stand up and lift up your heads, because
your redemption is drawing near."[s]
29 He told them this parable: "Look at the
fig tree and all the trees. 30 When they sprout
leaves, you can see for yourselves and know
that summer is near. 31 Even so, when you
see these things happening, you know that
the kingdom of God[t] is near.
32 "I tell you the truth, this generation[a]
will certainly not pass away until all these
things have happened. 33 Heaven and earth
will pass away, but my words will never
pass away.
34 "Be careful, or your hearts will be
weighed down with dissipation, drunken-
ness and the anxieties of life,[u] and that day
will close on you unexpectedly[v] like a trap.
35 For it will come upon all those who live on
the face of the whole earth. 36 Be always on
the watch, and pray that you may be able
to escape all that is about to happen, and
that you may be able to stand before the Son
of Man."
37 Each day Jesus was teaching at the tem-
ple, and each evening he went out[w] to spend
the night on the hill called the Mount of Ol-
ives, 38 and all the people came early in the
morning to hear him at the temple.

## Judas Agrees to Betray Jesus

22 Now the Feast of Unleavened Bread,
called the Passover, was approach-
ing, 2 and the chief priests and the teachers
of the law were looking for some way to
get rid of Jesus,[x] for they were afraid of the
people. 3 Then Satan[y] entered Judas, called
Iscariot, one of the Twelve. 4 And Judas went
to the chief priests and the officers of the
temple guard and discussed with them how
he might betray Jesus. 5 They were delighted
and agreed to give him money.[z] 6 He con-
sented, and watched for an opportunity to
hand Jesus over to them when no crowd was
present.

## The Last Supper

7 Then came the day of Unleavened Bread
on which the Passover lamb had to be sac-
rificed. 8 Jesus sent Peter and John,[a] saying,
"Go and make preparations for us to eat
the Passover."
9 "Where do you want us to prepare for
it?" they asked.
10 He replied, "As you enter the city, a man
carrying a jar of water will meet you. Follow
him to the house that he enters, 11 and say to
the owner of the house, 'The Teacher asks:
Where is the guest room, where I may eat
the Passover with my disciples?' 12 He will
show you a large upper room, all furnished.
Make preparations there."
13 They left and found things just as Jesus
had told them. So they prepared the Pass-
over.
14 When the hour came, Jesus and his
apostles reclined at the table.[b] 15 And he said
to them, "I have eagerly desired to eat this
Passover with you before I suffer. 16 For I tell

**21:14** i Lk 12:11
**21:15** j Lk 12:12
**21:16** k Lk 12:52,53
**21:18** l Mt 10:30
**21:20** m Lk 19:43
**21:21** n Lk 17:31
**21:22** o Isa 63:4; Da 9:24–27
**21:24** p Isa 63:18; Da 8:13; Rev 11:2
**21:25** q 2Pe 3:10,12
**21:27** r Rev 1:7
**21:28** s Lk 18:7
**21:31** t Mt 3:2
**21:34** u Mk 4:19 v 1Th 5:2–7
**21:37** w Mk 11:19
**22:2** x Mt 12:14
**22:3** y Jn 13:2
**22:5** z Zec 11:12
**22:8** a Ac 3:1,11
**22:14** b Mt 26:20; Mk 14:17,18

[a] 32 Or *race*

**22:16** c Lk 14:15; Rev 19:9
**22:22** d Ac 2:23; 4:28
**22:24** e Mk 9:34; Lk 9:46
**22:26** f 1Pe 5:5 g Lk 9:48
**22:27** h Mt 20:28; Lk 12:37
**22:29** i 2Ti 2:12
**22:30** j Mt 19:28
**22:31** k Am 9:9
**22:32** l Jn 17:9,15 m Jn 21:15–17

you, I will not eat it again until it finds fulfillment in the kingdom of God."[c]

17 After taking the cup, he gave thanks and said, "Take this and divide it among you. 18 For I tell you I will not drink again of the fruit of the vine until the kingdom of God comes."

19 And he took bread, gave thanks and broke it, and gave it to them, saying, "This is my body given for you; do this in remembrance of me."

20 In the same way, after the supper he took the cup, saying, "This cup is the new covenant in my blood, which is poured out for you. 21 But the hand of him who is going to betray me is with mine on the table. 22 The Son of Man will go as it has been decreed,[d] but woe to that man who betrays him." 23 They began to question among themselves which of them it might be who would do this.

24 Also a dispute arose among them as to which of them was considered to be greatest.[e] 25 Jesus said to them, "The kings of the Gentiles lord it over them; and those who exercise authority over them call themselves Benefactors. 26 But you are not to be like that. Instead, the greatest among you should be like the youngest,[f] and the one who rules like the one who serves.[g] 27 For who is greater, the one who is at the table or the one who serves? Is it not the one who is at the table? But I am among you as one who serves.[h] 28 You are those who have stood by me in my trials. 29 And I confer on you a kingdom,[i] just as my Father conferred one on me, 30 so that you may eat and drink at my table in my kingdom and sit on thrones, judging the twelve tribes of Israel.[j]

31 "Simon, Simon, Satan has asked to sift you[a] as wheat.[k] 32 But I have prayed for you,[l] Simon, that your faith may not fail. And when you have turned back, strengthen your brothers."[m]

33 But he replied, "Lord, I am ready to go with you to prison and to death."

34 Jesus answered, "I tell you, Peter, before the rooster crows today, you will deny three times that you know me."

35 Then Jesus asked them, "When I sent you without purse, bag or sandals,[n] did you lack anything?"

"Nothing," they answered.

36 He said to them, "But now if you have a purse, take it, and also a bag; and if you don't have a sword, sell your cloak and buy one. 37 It is written: 'And he was numbered with the transgressors'[b];[o] and I tell you that this must be fulfilled in me. Yes, what is written about me is reaching its fulfillment."

38 The disciples said, "See, Lord, here are two swords."

"That is enough," he replied.

## Jesus Prays on the Mount of Olives

39 Jesus went out as usual[p] to the Mount of Olives, and his disciples followed him. 40 On reaching the place, he said to them, "Pray that you will not fall into temptation."[q] 41 He withdrew about a stone's throw beyond them, knelt down and prayed, 42 "Father, if you are willing, take this cup from me; yet not my will, but yours be done." 43 An angel from heaven appeared to him and strengthened him.[r] 44 And being in anguish, he prayed more earnestly, and his sweat was like drops of blood falling to the ground.[c]

*Lord God,*

*teach me to pray as Jesus prayed: "Not my will, but yours be done." Teach me to desire what you desire and to follow your directives. I know and trust that you are with me and will provide for my every need.*

*Amen*

LUKE 22:39–42

45 When he rose from prayer and went back to the disciples, he found them asleep, exhausted from sorrow. 46 "Why are you sleeping?" he asked them. "Get up and pray so that you will not fall into temptation."[s]

**22:35** n Mt 10:9,10; Lk 9:3; 10:4
**22:37** o Isa 53:12
**22:39** p Lk 21:37
**22:40** q Mt 6:13
**22:43** r Mt 4:11
**22:46** s ver 40

[a] 31 The Greek is plural. [b] 37 Isaiah 53:12 [c] 44 Some early manuscripts do not have verses 43 and 44.

22:49 t ver 38
22:52 u ver 4
22:53 v Jn 12:27
22:54 w Mt 26:57; Mk 14:53 x Mt 26:58; Mk 14:54; Jn 18:15
22:61 y Lk 7:13 z ver 34

## Jesus Arrested

47 While he was still speaking a crowd
came up, and the man who was called Ju-
das, one of the Twelve, was leading them.
He approached Jesus to kiss him, 48 but Jesus
asked him, "Judas, are you betraying the
Son of Man with a kiss?"
49 When Jesus' followers saw what was go-
ing to happen, they said, "Lord, should we
strike with our swords?"[t] 50 And one of them
struck the servant of the high priest, cutting
off his right ear.
51 But Jesus answered, "No more of this!"
And he touched the man's ear and healed
him.
52 Then Jesus said to the chief priests,
the officers of the temple guard,[u] and the el-
ders, who had come for him, "Am I leading
a rebellion, that you have come with swords
and clubs? 53 Every day I was with you in the
temple courts, and you did not lay a hand
on me. But this is your hour[v]—when dark-
ness reigns."

## Peter Disowns Jesus

54 Then seizing him, they led him away
and took him into the house of the high
priest.[w] Peter followed at a distance.[x] 55 But
when they had kindled a fire in the middle
of the courtyard and had sat down together,
Peter sat down with them. 56 A servant girl
saw him seated there in the firelight. She
looked closely at him and said, "This man
was with him."
57 But he denied it. "Woman, I don't know
him," he said.
58 A little later someone else saw him and
said, "You also are one of them."
"Man, I am not!" Peter replied.
59 About an hour later another asserted,
"Certainly this fellow was with him, for he
is a Galilean."
60 Peter replied, "Man, I don't know what
you're talking about!" Just as he was speak-
ing, the rooster crowed. 61 The Lord[y] turned
and looked straight at Peter. Then Peter re-
membered the word the Lord had spoken to
him: "Before the rooster crows today, you
will disown me three times."[z] 62 And he went
outside and wept bitterly.

## The Guards Mock Jesus

63 The men who were guarding Jesus
began mocking and beating him. 64 They
blindfolded him and demanded, "Prophesy!
Who hit you?" 65 And they said many other
insulting things to him.

## Jesus Before Pilate and Herod

66 At daybreak the council of the elders of
the people, both the chief priests and teach-
ers of the law, met together,[a] and Jesus was
led before them. 67 "If you are the Christ,[a]"
they said, "tell us."
Jesus answered, "If I tell you, you will not
believe me, 68 and if I asked you, you would
not answer. 69 But from now on, the Son of
Man will be seated at the right hand of the
mighty God."
70 They all asked, "Are you then the Son
of God?"
He replied, "You are right in saying
I am."[b]
71 Then they said, "Why do we need any
more testimony? We have heard it from his
own lips."

23 Then the whole assembly rose and
led him off to Pilate.[c] 2 And they be-
gan to accuse him, saying, "We have found
this man subverting our nation. He opposes
payment of taxes to Caesar[d] and claims to
be Christ,[b] a king."[e]
3 So Pilate asked Jesus, "Are you the king
of the Jews?"
"Yes, it is as you say," Jesus replied.
4 Then Pilate announced to the chief
priests and the crowd, "I find no basis for a
charge against this man."
5 But they insisted, "He stirs up the people
all over Judea[c] by his teaching. He started in
Galilee and has come all the way here."
6 On hearing this, Pilate asked if the man
was a Galilean. 7 When he learned that Jesus
was under Herod's jurisdiction, he sent him
to Herod,[f] who was also in Jerusalem at
that time.
8 When Herod saw Jesus, he was greatly
pleased, because for a long time he had
been wanting to see him.[g] From what he
had heard about him, he hoped to see him
perform some miracle. 9 He plied him with
many questions, but Jesus gave him no

22:66 a Mt 27:1; Mk 15:1
22:70 b Mt 27:11; Lk 23:3
23:1 c Mt 27:2; Mk 15:1; Jn 18:28
23:2 d Lk 20:22 e Jn 19:12
23:7 f Mt 14:1; Lk 3:1
23:8 g Lk 9:9

[a]67 Or *Messiah* [b]2 Or *Messiah*; also in verses 35 and 39 [c]5 Or *over the land of the Jews*

**23:11** h Mk 15:17–19; Jn 19:2,3
**23:12** i Ac 4:27
**23:14** j ver 4
**23:16** k Mt 27:26; Jn 19:1
**23:18** l Ac 3:13,14

answer. 10 The chief priests and the teachers
of the law were standing there, vehemently
accusing him. 11 Then Herod and his soldiers
ridiculed and mocked him. Dressing him in
an elegant robe,[h] they sent him back to Pi-
late. 12 That day Herod and Pilate became
friends[i]—before this they had been ene-
mies.

13 Pilate called together the chief priests,
the rulers and the people, 14 and said to them,
"You brought me this man as one who was
inciting the people to rebellion. I have exam-
ined him in your presence and have found
no basis for your charges against him.[j] 15 Nei-
ther has Herod, for he sent him back to us;
as you can see, he has done nothing to de-
serve death. 16 Therefore, I will punish him[k]
and then release him.[a]"

18 With one voice they cried out, "Away
with this man! Release Barabbas to us!"[l]
19 (Barabbas had been thrown into prison
for an insurrection in the city, and for mur-
der.)

20 Wanting to release Jesus, Pilate ap-
pealed to them again. 21 But they kept shout-
ing, "Crucify him! Crucify him!"

22 For the third time he spoke to them:
"Why? What crime has this man commit-
ted? I have found in him no grounds for the
death penalty. Therefore I will have him
punished and then release him."

23 But with loud shouts they insistently
demanded that he be crucified, and their
shouts prevailed. 24 So Pilate decided to
grant their demand. 25 He released the man
who had been thrown into prison for insur-
rection and murder, the one they asked for,
and surrendered Jesus to their will.

## The Crucifixion

26 As they led him away, they seized Si-
mon from Cyrene,[m] who was on his way
in from the country, and put the cross on
him and made him carry it behind Jesus.[n]
27 A large number of people followed him, in-
cluding women who mourned and wailed[o]
for him. 28 Jesus turned and said to them,
"Daughters of Jerusalem, do not weep for
me; weep for yourselves and for your chil-
dren. 29 For the time will come when you
will say, 'Blessed are the barren women, the
wombs that never bore and the breasts that
never nursed!'[p] 30 Then

> " 'they will say to the mountains, "Fall
> on us!"
> and to the hills, "Cover us!" '[b][q]

31 For if men do these things when the tree is
green, what will happen when it is dry?"[r]

32 Two other men, both criminals, were
also led out with him to be executed.[s]
33 When they came to the place called the
Skull, there they crucified him, along with
the criminals—one on his right, the other
on his left. 34 Jesus said, "Father, forgive
them, for they do not know what they are
doing."[c] And they divided up his clothes by
casting lots.[t]

35 The people stood watching, and the
rulers even sneered at him.[u] They said, "He
saved others; let him save himself if he is the
Christ of God, the Chosen One."

36 The soldiers also came up and mocked
him. They offered him wine vinegar[v]
37 and said, "If you are the king of the Jews,
save yourself."

38 There was a written notice above him,
which read: THIS IS THE KING OF THE JEWS.

**23:26** m Mt 27:32 n Jn 19:17
**23:27** o Lk 8:52
**23:29** p Mt 24:19
**23:30** q Isa 2:19; Hos 10:8; Rev 6:16
**23:31** r Eze 20:47
**23:32** s Mt 27:38
**23:34** t Ps 22:18
**23:35** u Ps 22:17
**23:36** v Mt 27:48

[a] 16 Some manuscripts *him."* *17 Now he was obliged to release one man to them at the Feast.* [b] 30 Hosea 10:8 [c] 34 Some early manuscripts do not have this sentence.

## *The African Presence*

**Luke 23:26**

See the African Presence note on Mark 15:21 for information on Cyrene.

39One of the criminals who hung there hurled insults at him: "Aren't you the Christ? Save yourself and us!"[w]

40But the other criminal rebuked him. "Don't you fear God," he said, "since you are under the same sentence? 41We are punished justly, for we are getting what our deeds deserve. But this man has done nothing wrong."

42Then he said, "Jesus, remember me when you come into your kingdom.[a]"

43Jesus answered him, "I tell you the truth, today you will be with me in paradise."[x]

## Jesus' Death

44It was now about the sixth hour, and darkness came over the whole land until the ninth hour, 45for the sun stopped shining. And the curtain of the temple was torn in two. 46Jesus called out with a loud voice,[y] "Father, into your hands I commit my spirit."[z] When he had said this, he breathed his last.[a]

47The centurion, seeing what had happened, praised God and said, "Surely this was a righteous man." 48When all the people who had gathered to witness this sight saw what took place, they beat their breasts and went away. 49But all those who knew him, including the women who had followed him from Galilee,[b] stood at a distance,[c] watching these things.

## Jesus' Burial

50Now there was a man named Joseph, a member of the Council, a good and upright man, 51who had not consented to their decision and action. He came from the Judean town of Arimathea and he was waiting for the kingdom of God.[d] 52Going to Pilate, he asked for Jesus' body. 53Then he took it down, wrapped it in linen cloth and placed it in a tomb cut in the rock, one in which no one had yet been laid. 54It was Preparation Day,[e] and the Sabbath was about to begin.

55The women who had come with Jesus from Galilee followed Joseph and saw the tomb and how his body was laid in it. 56Then they went home and prepared spices and perfumes.[f] But they rested on the Sabbath in obedience to the commandment.[g]

## The Resurrection

24 On the first day of the week, very early in the morning, the women took the spices they had prepared[h] and went to the tomb. 2They found the stone rolled away from the tomb, 3but when they entered, they did not find the body of the Lord Jesus. 4While they were wondering about this, suddenly two men in clothes that gleamed like lightning[i] stood beside them. 5In their fright the women bowed down with their faces to the ground, but the men said to them, "Why do you look for the living among the dead? 6He is not here; he has risen! Remember how he told you, while he was still with you in Galilee:[j] 7'The Son of Man must be delivered into the hands of sinful men, be crucified and on the third day be raised again.'" 8Then they remembered his words.[k]

9When they came back from the tomb, they told all these things to the Eleven and to all the others. 10It was Mary Magdalene, Joanna, Mary the mother of James, and the others with them[l] who told this to the apostles. 11But they did not believe the women, because their words seemed to them like nonsense. 12Peter, however, got up and ran to the tomb. Bending over, he saw the strips of linen lying by themselves,[m] and he went away, wondering to himself what had happened.

## On the Road to Emmaus

13Now that same day two of them were going to a village called Emmaus, about seven miles[b] from Jerusalem.[n] 14They were talking with each other about everything that had happened. 15As they talked and discussed these things with each other, Jesus himself came up and walked along with them; 16but they were kept from recognizing him.[o]

17He asked them, "What are you discussing together as you walk along?"

They stood still, their faces downcast. 18One of them, named Cleopas,[p] asked him, "Are you only a visitor to Jerusalem and do

**23:39** w ver 35,37
**23:43** x 2Co 12:3,4; Rev 2:7
**23:46** y Mt 27:50 z Ps 31:5; 1Pe 2:23 a Jn 19:30
**23:49** b Lk 8:2 c Ps 38:11
**23:51** d Lk 2:25,38
**23:54** e Mt 27:62
**23:56** f Mk 16:1 g Ex 20:10
**24:1** h Lk 23:56
**24:4** i Jn 20:12
**24:6** j Mt 17:22,23; Mk 9:30–31
**24:8** k Jn 2:22
**24:10** l Lk 8:1–3
**24:12** m Jn 20:3–7
**24:13** n Mk 16:12
**24:16** o Jn 20:14; 21:4
**24:18** p Jn 19:25

[a]42 Some manuscripts *come with your kingly power* [b]13 Greek *sixty stadia* (about 11 kilometers)

not know the things that have happened
there in these days?"
19"What things?" he asked.
"About Jesus of Nazareth," they replied.
"He was a prophet,[q] powerful in word and
deed before God and all the people. 20The
chief priests and our rulers handed him
over to be sentenced to death, and they cru-
cified him; 21but we had hoped that he was
the one who was going to redeem Israel.[r]
And what is more, it is the third day since
all this took place. 22In addition, some of
our women amazed us. They went to the
tomb early this morning 23but didn't find
his body. They came and told us that they
had seen a vision of angels, who said he was
alive. 24Then some of our companions went
to the tomb and found it just as the women
had said, but him they did not see."
25He said to them, "How foolish you are,
and how slow of heart to believe all that the
prophets have spoken! 26Did not the Christ[a]
have to suffer these things and then enter
his glory?"[s] 27And beginning with Moses[t]
and all the Prophets,[u] he explained to them
what was said in all the Scriptures concern-
ing himself.
28As they approached the village to which
they were going, Jesus acted as if he were go-
ing farther. 29But they urged him strongly,
"Stay with us, for it is nearly evening; the
day is almost over." So he went in to stay
with them.
30When he was at the table with them, he
took bread, gave thanks, broke it[v] and be-
gan to give it to them. 31Then their eyes were
opened and they recognized him, and he
disappeared from their sight. 32They asked
each other, "Were not our hearts burning
within us while he talked with us on the
road and opened the Scriptures to us?"
33They got up and returned at once to Je-
rusalem. There they found the Eleven and
those with them, assembled together 34and
saying, "It is true! The Lord has risen
and has appeared to Simon."[w] 35Then the
two told what had happened on the way, and
how Jesus was recognized by them when he
broke the bread.

## Jesus Appears to the Disciples

36While they were still talking about this,
Jesus himself stood among them and said to
them, "Peace be with you."[x]
37They were startled and frightened,
thinking they saw a ghost.[y] 38He said to
them, "Why are you troubled, and why do
doubts rise in your minds? 39Look at my
hands and my feet. It is I myself! Touch me
and see; a ghost does not have flesh and
bones, as you see I have."
40When he had said this, he showed them
his hands and feet. 41And while they still
did not believe it because of joy and amaze-
ment, he asked them, "Do you have any-
thing here to eat?" 42They gave him a piece
of broiled fish, 43and he took it and ate it in
their presence.[z]
44He said to them, "This is what I told
you while I was still with you: Everything
must be fulfilled[a] that is written about
me in the Law of Moses, the Prophets and
the Psalms."
45Then he opened their minds so they
could understand the Scriptures. 46He told
them, "This is what is written: The Christ
will suffer and rise from the dead on the
third day, 47and repentance and forgiveness
of sins will be preached in his name[b] to all
nations,[c] beginning at Jerusalem. 48You are
witnesses[d] of these things. 49I am going to
send you what my Father has promised;[e] but
stay in the city until you have been clothed
with power from on high."

## The Ascension

50When he had led them out to the
vicinity of Bethany, he lifted up his hands
and blessed them. 51While he was blessing
them, he left them and was taken up into
heaven. 52Then they worshiped him and re-
turned to Jerusalem with great joy. 53And
they stayed continually at the temple,[f] prais-
ing God.

**24:19** q Mt 21:11
**24:21** r Lk 1:68
**24:26** s 1Pe 1:11
**24:27** t Ge 3:15; Nu 21:9; Dt 18:15 u Isa 7:14; 9:6; Eze 34:23
**24:30** v Mt 14:19
**24:34** w 1Co 15:5
**24:36** x Jn 20:19,21,26
**24:37** y Mk 6:49
**24:43** z Ac 10:41
**24:44** a Mt 16:21; Lk 18:31–33
**24:47** b Ac 5:31; 13:38 c Mt 28:19
**24:48** d Ac 1:8
**24:49** e Ac 1:4
**24:53** f Ac 2:46

[a]26 Or *Messiah*; also in verse 46

# John

## OVERVIEW

The Gospel of John begins with a prologue (see Jn 1:1–18) in which Jesus is introduced as the “Word” who became “flesh” (see Jn 1:14). John wrote that the Word existed before time and throughout eternity and came to our dark world so that many would have eternal life. Through the skillful use of seven selected miracles, or “signs,” John demonstrated the impact of Jesus’ ministry until the crucifixion.

While it was taboo for Jews to have any dealings with the despised Samaritans, and Jewish men typically avoided public encounters with women, Jesus crossed traditional boundaries to reveal himself as the Messiah to a Samaritan woman (see Jn 4). She was not considered a virtuous woman, but Jesus looked beyond her sinfulness and saw her need for a Savior. Through this woman’s testimony, many Samaritans came to believe in Jesus Christ. John’s Gospel also recounts how Jesus restored a woman who was caught in adultery (see Jn 8:1–11).

Many women feel that they have to “get right” before they can come to Jesus. However, the stories of the women in John’s Gospel remind us of Jesus’ ability to forgive our sins and give us all we need to live satisfied, fulfilled lives. Our responsibility then becomes to share what he has done for us so others might know him.

## OUTLINE

I. Prologue: The Word Became Flesh (1:1–18)
II. Jesus' Ministry to the World (1:19—12:50)
III. Jesus' Ministry to His Disciples (13:1—17:26)
IV. Jesus' Suffering, Death and Resurrection (18:1—20:31)
V. Epilogue: Jesus' Recommissioning of His Disciples (21:1–25)

### SCANNABLE FACTS:

**Author:** John

**Time Written:** Probably between A.D. 85 and 90

**Theme to Note:** Jesus Christ is the Son of God

**Notable Women:** A Samaritan woman; a woman caught in adultery; Lazarus's sisters, Mary and Martha; Mary Magdalene

## The Word Became Flesh

1 In the beginning was the Word, and the
Word was with God,[a] and the Word was
God. 2 He was with God in the beginning.
3 Through him all things were made; with-
out him nothing was made that has been
made.[b] 4 In him was life,[c] and that life was
the light of men. 5 The light shines in the
darkness, but the darkness has not under-
stood[a] it.[d]
6 There came a man who was sent from
God; his name was John.[e] 7 He came as a
witness to testify concerning that light, so
that through him all men might believe. 8 He
himself was not the light; he came only as
a witness to the light. 9 The true light[f] that
gives light to every man[g] was coming into
the world.[b]
10 He was in the world, and though the
world was made through him,[h] the world
did not recognize him. 11 He came to that
which was his own, but his own did not re-
ceive him. 12 Yet to all who received him, to
those who believed in his name, he gave the
right to become children of God[i]— 13 chil-
dren born not of natural descent,[c] nor of hu-
man decision or a husband's will, but born
of God.[j]
14 The Word became flesh[k] and made his
dwelling among us. We have seen his glory,
the glory of the One and Only,[d] who came
from the Father, full of grace and truth.
15 John testifies concerning him. He cries
out, saying, "This was he of whom I said,
'He who comes after me has surpassed me
because he was before me.' "[l] 16 From the
fullness[m] of his grace we have all received
one blessing after another. 17 For the law was
given through Moses; grace and truth came
through Jesus Christ. 18 No one has ever seen
God,[n] but God the One and Only,[d,e][o] who is
at the Father's side, has made him known.

## John the Baptist Denies Being the Christ

19 Now this was John's testimony when
the Jews of Jerusalem sent priests and Le-
vites to ask him who he was. 20 He did not
fail to confess, but confessed freely, "I am
not the Christ.[f]"[p]
21 They asked him, "Then who are you?
Are you Elijah?"[q]
He said, "I am not."
"Are you the Prophet?"[r]
He answered, "No."
22 Finally they said, "Who are you? Give
us an answer to take back to those who sent
us. What do you say about yourself?"
23 John replied in the words of Isaiah
the prophet, "I am the voice of one calling
in the desert, 'Make straight the way for
the Lord.' "[g][s]
24 Now some Pharisees who had been sent
25 questioned him, "Why then do you baptize

1:1 a 1Jn 1:2
1:3 b Col 1:16
1:4 c Jn 5:26
1:5 d Jn 3:19
1:6 e Mt 3:1
1:9 f 1Jn 2:8; g Isa 49:6
1:10 h Heb 1:2
1:12 i Gal 3:26
1:13 j Jn 3:6; 1Pe 1:23
1:14 k Gal 4:4; 1Ti 3:16
1:15 l Mt 3:11
1:16 m Col 1:19
1:18 n Ex 33:20; Jn 6:46; o 1Jn 4:9
1:20 p Lk 3:15,16
1:21 q Mt 11:14; r Dt 18:15
1:23 s Isa 40:3

[a]5 Or *darkness, and the darkness has not overcome* [b]9 Or *This was the true light that gives light to every man who comes into the world* [c]13 Greek *of bloods* [d]14,18 Or *the Only Begotten* [e]18 Some manuscripts *but the only* (or *only begotten*) *Son* [f]20 Or *Messiah.* "The Christ" (Greek) and "the Messiah" (Hebrew) both mean "the Anointed One"; also in verse 25. [g]23 Isaiah 40:3

## *The African Presence*

### John 1

The Holy Land in the Middle East was influenced by the African presence because of its proximity to North Africa. The apostle John was born in the land today known as Israel, and he later settled in Ephesus in Asia Minor.

In New Testament times, the entire Mediterranean world derived much of its knowledge from Africa, specifically from Alexandria, which was built by Alexander the Great and located in Egypt. The library at Alexandria held 700,000 books and scrolls. The city was known for being a center of culture and learning.

1:28 t Jn 3:26
1:29 u Isa 53:7; 1Pe 1:19
1:30 v ver 15,27
1:32 w Mt 3:16; Mk 1:10
1:33 x Mt 3:11
1:34 y ver 49
1:36 z ver 29

if you are not the Christ, nor Elijah, nor the Prophet?"

26"I baptize with[a] water," John replied, "but among you stands one you do not know. 27He is the one who comes after me, the thongs of whose sandals I am not worthy to untie."

28This all happened at Bethany on the other side of the Jordan,[t] where John was baptizing.

## Jesus the Lamb of God

29The next day John saw Jesus coming toward him and said, "Look, the Lamb of God,[u] who takes away the sin of the world! 30This is the one I meant when I said, 'A man who comes after me has surpassed me because he was before me.'[v] 31I myself did not know him, but the reason I came baptizing with water was that he might be revealed to Israel."

32Then John gave this testimony: "I saw the Spirit come down from heaven as a dove and remain on him.[w] 33I would not have known him, except that the one who sent me to baptize with water told me, 'The man on whom you see the Spirit come down and remain is he who will baptize with the Holy Spirit.'[x] 34I have seen and I testify that this is the Son of God."[y]

## Jesus' First Disciples

35The next day John was there again with two of his disciples. 36When he saw Jesus passing by, he said, "Look, the Lamb of God!"[z]

37When the two disciples heard him say this, they followed Jesus. 38Turning around, Jesus saw them following and asked, "What do you want?"

They said, "Rabbi" (which means Teacher), "where are you staying?"

39"Come," he replied, "and you will see."

So they went and saw where he was staying, and spent that day with him. It was about the tenth hour.

40Andrew, Simon Peter's brother, was one of the two who heard what John had said and who had followed Jesus. 41The first thing Andrew did was to find his brother Simon and tell him, "We have found the Messiah" (that is, the Christ).[a] 42And he brought him to Jesus.

Jesus looked at him and said, "You are Simon son of John. You will be called Cephas" (which, when translated, is Peter[b]).[b]

## Jesus Calls Philip and Nathanael

43The next day Jesus decided to leave for Galilee. Finding Philip,[c] he said to him, "Follow me."

44Philip, like Andrew and Peter, was from the town of Bethsaida.[d] 45Philip found Nathanael[e] and told him, "We have found the one Moses wrote about in the Law,[f] and about whom the prophets also wrote—Jesus of Nazareth,[g] the son of Joseph."

46"Nazareth! Can anything good come from there?"[h] Nathanael asked.

"Come and see," said Philip.

47When Jesus saw Nathanael approaching, he said of him, "Here is a true Israelite,[i] in whom there is nothing false."

48"How do you know me?" Nathanael asked.

Jesus answered, "I saw you while you were still under the fig tree before Philip called you."

49Then Nathanael declared, "Rabbi, you are the Son of God; you are the King of Israel."[j]

50Jesus said, "You believe[c] because I told you I saw you under the fig tree. You shall see greater things than that." 51He then added, "I tell you[d] the truth, you[d] shall see heaven open, and the angels of God ascending and descending[k] on the Son of Man."

## Jesus Changes Water to Wine

2 On the third day a wedding took place at Cana in Galilee.[l] Jesus' mother was there, 2and Jesus and his disciples had also been invited to the wedding. 3When the wine was gone, Jesus' mother said to him, "They have no more wine."

4"Dear woman,[m] why do you involve me?" Jesus replied. "My time[n] has not yet come."

5His mother said to the servants, "Do whatever he tells you."

6Nearby stood six stone water jars,

1:41 a Jn 4:25
1:42 b Mt 16:18
1:43 c Mt 10:3; Jn 14:8,9
1:44 d Jn 12:21
1:45 e Jn 21:2 f Lk 24:27 g Mt 2:23
1:46 h Jn 7:41,42,52
1:47 i Ro 9:4,6
1:49 j Jn 12:13
1:51 k Ge 28:12
2:1 l Jn 4:46
2:4 m Jn 19:26 n Jn 7:6

[a]26 Or *in*; also in verses 31 and 33 [b]42 Both *Cephas* (Aramaic) and *Peter* (Greek) mean *rock.* [c]50 Or *Do you believe . . . ?*
[d]51 The Greek is plural.

**2:6** o Mk7:3,4; Jn3:25
**2:9** p Jn4:46
**2:11** q Jn1:14
**2:12** r Mt12:46
**2:13** s Dt16:1–6
**2:16** t Lk2:49
**2:17** u Ps69:9
**2:18** v Mt12:38
**2:19** w Mt26:61; 27:40; Mk14:58

the kind used by the Jews for ceremonial washing,[o] each holding from twenty to thirty gallons.[a]

7Jesus said to the servants, "Fill the jars with water"; so they filled them to the brim.

8Then he told them, "Now draw some out and take it to the master of the banquet."

They did so, 9and the master of the banquet tasted the water that had been turned into wine.[p] He did not realize where it had come from, though the servants who had drawn the water knew. Then he called the bridegroom aside 10and said, "Everyone brings out the choice wine first and then the cheaper wine after the guests have had too much to drink; but you have saved the best till now."

11This, the first of his miraculous signs, Jesus performed at Cana in Galilee. He thus revealed his glory,[q] and his disciples put their faith in him.

## Jesus Clears the Temple

12After this he went down to Capernaum with his mother and brothers[r] and his disciples. There they stayed for a few days.

13When it was almost time for the Jewish Passover, Jesus went up to Jerusalem.[s] 14In the temple courts he found men selling cattle, sheep and doves, and others sitting at tables exchanging money. 15So he made a whip out of cords, and drove all from the temple area, both sheep and cattle; he scattered the coins of the money changers and overturned their tables. 16To those who sold doves he said, "Get these out of here! How dare you turn my Father's house[t] into a market!"

17His disciples remembered that it is written: "Zeal for your house will consume me."[b][u]

18Then the Jews demanded of him, "What miraculous sign can you show us to prove your authority to do all this?"[v]

19Jesus answered them, "Destroy this temple, and I will raise it again in three days."[w]

20The Jews replied, "It has taken forty-six years to build this temple, and you are going to raise it in three days?" 21But the temple he had spoken of was his body.[x] 22After he was raised from the dead, his disciples recalled what he had said.[y] Then they believed the Scripture and the words that Jesus had spoken.

23Now while he was in Jerusalem at the Passover Feast, many people saw the miraculous signs he was doing and believed in his name.[c] 24But Jesus would not entrust himself to them, for he knew all men. 25He did not need man's testimony about man, for he knew what was in a man.[z]

## Jesus Teaches Nicodemus

3 Now there was a man of the Pharisees named Nicodemus, a member of the Jewish ruling council. 2He came to Jesus at night and said, "Rabbi, we know you are a teacher who has come from God. For no one could perform the miraculous signs[a] you are doing if God were not with him."[b]

3In reply Jesus declared, "I tell you the truth, no one can see the kingdom of God unless he is born again.[d]"

4"How can a man be born when he is old?" Nicodemus asked. "Surely he cannot enter a second time into his mother's womb to be born!"

5Jesus answered, "I tell you the truth, no one can enter the kingdom of God unless he is born of water and the Spirit. 6Flesh gives birth to flesh, but the Spirit[e] gives birth to spirit. 7You should not be surprised at my saying, 'You[f] must be born again.' 8The wind blows wherever it pleases. You hear its sound, but you cannot tell where it comes from or where it is going. So it is with everyone born of the Spirit."

9"How can this be?" Nicodemus asked.

10"You are Israel's teacher," said Jesus, "and do you not understand these things? 11I tell you the truth, we speak of what we know,[c] and we testify to what we have seen, but still you people do not accept our testimony. 12I have spoken to you of earthly things and you do not believe; how then will you believe if I speak of heavenly things? 13No one has ever gone into heaven[d] except the one who came from heaven[e]—the Son of Man.[g] 14Just as Moses lifted up the snake

**2:21** x 1Co6:19
**2:22** y Lk24:5–8
**2:25** z Jn6:61,64
**3:2** a Jn9:16,33 b Ac2:22; 10:38
**3:11** c Jn7:16,17
**3:13** d Pr30:4; Ac2:34; Eph4:8–10 e Jn6:38,42

[a]6 Greek *two to three metretes* (probably about 75 to 115 liters) [b]17 Psalm 69:9 [c]23 Or *and believed in him* [d]3 Or *born from above*; also in verse 7 [e]6 Or *but spirit* [f]7 The Greek is plural. [g]13 Some manuscripts *Man, who is in heaven*

in the desert,[f] so the Son of Man must be lifted up,[g] 15that everyone who believes in him may have eternal life.[a]

16"For God so loved[h] the world that he gave his one and only Son,[b] that whoever believes in him shall not perish but have eternal life. 17For God did not send his Son into the world to condemn the world, but to save the world through him.[i] 18Whoever believes in him is not condemned,[j] but whoever does not believe stands condemned already because he has not believed in the name of God's one and only Son.[c] 19This is the verdict: Light[k] has come into the world, but men loved darkness instead of light because their deeds were evil. 20Everyone who does evil hates the light, and will not come into the light for fear that his deeds will be exposed.[l] 21But whoever lives by the truth comes into the light, so that it may be seen plainly that what he has done has been done through God."[d]

## John the Baptist's Testimony About Jesus

22After this, Jesus and his disciples went out into the Judean countryside, where he spent some time with them, and baptized.[m] 23Now John also was baptizing at Aenon near Salim, because there was plenty of water, and people were constantly coming to be baptized. 24(This was before John was put in prison.) 25An argument developed between some of John's disciples and a certain Jew[e] over the matter of ceremonial washing. 26They came to John and said to him, "Rabbi, that man who was with you on the other side of the Jordan—the one you testified[n] about—well, he is baptizing, and everyone is going to him."

27To this John replied, "A man can receive only what is given him from heaven. 28You yourselves can testify that I said, 'I am not the Christ[f] but am sent ahead of him.'[o] 29The bride belongs to the bridegroom. The friend who attends the bridegroom waits and listens for him, and is full of joy when he hears the bridegroom's voice. That joy is mine, and it is now complete.[p] 30He must become greater; I must become less.

31"The one who comes from above is above all; the one who is from the earth belongs to the earth, and speaks as one from the earth.[q] The one who comes from heaven is above all. 32He testifies to what he has seen and heard, but no one accepts his testimony.[r] 33The man who has accepted it has certified that God is truthful. 34For the one whom God has sent speaks the words of God, for God[g] gives the Spirit without limit. 35The Father loves the Son and has placed everything in his hands.[s] 36Whoever believes in the Son has eternal life, but whoever rejects the Son will not see life, for God's wrath remains on him."[h]

## Jesus Talks With a Samaritan Woman

4 The Pharisees heard that Jesus was gaining and baptizing more disciples than John,[t] 2although in fact it was not Jesus who baptized, but his disciples. 3When the Lord learned of this, he left Judea[u] and went back once more to Galilee.

4Now he had to go through Samaria. 5So he came to a town in Samaria called Sychar, near the plot of ground Jacob had given to his son Joseph.[v] 6Jacob's well was there, and Jesus, tired as he was from the journey, sat down by the well. It was about the sixth hour.

7When a Samaritan woman came to draw water, Jesus said to her, "Will you give me a drink?" 8(His disciples had gone into the town[w] to buy food.)

9The Samaritan woman said to him, "You are a Jew and I am a Samaritan[x] woman. How can you ask me for a drink?" (For Jews do not associate with Samaritans.[i])

10Jesus answered her, "If you knew the gift of God and who it is that asks you for a drink, you would have asked him and he would have given you living water."[y]

11"Sir," the woman said, "you have nothing to draw with and the well is deep. Where can you get this living water? 12Are you greater than our father Jacob, who gave us the well and drank from it himself, as did also his sons and his flocks and herds?"

13Jesus answered, "Everyone who drinks this water will be thirsty again, 14but

**3:14** f Nu 21:8,9
**3:14** g Jn 8:28
**3:16** h Ro 5:8; 1Jn 4:9,10
**3:17** i Jn 12:47; 1Jn 4:14
**3:18** j Jn 5:24
**3:19** k Jn 1:4
**3:20** l Eph 5:11,13
**3:22** m Jn 4:2
**3:26** n Jn 1:7
**3:28** o Jn 1:20,23
**3:29** p Jn 16:24
**3:31** q Jn 8:23
**3:32** r ver 11
**3:35** s Mt 28:18; Jn 5:20,22; 17:2
**4:1** t Jn 3:22,26
**4:3** u Jn 3:22
**4:5** v Ge 33:19; 48:22; Jos 24:32
**4:8** w ver 5,39
**4:9** x Lk 9:52,53
**4:10** y Isa 44:3

[a]15 Or *believes may have eternal life in him* [b]16 Or *his only begotten Son* [c]18 Or *God's only begotten Son* [d]21 Some interpreters end the quotation after verse 15. [e]25 Some manuscripts *and certain Jews* [f]28 Or *Messiah* [g]34 Greek *he* [h]36 Some interpreters end the quotation after verse 30. [i]9 Or *do not use dishes Samaritans have used*

whoever drinks the water I give him will never thirst.[z] Indeed, the water I give him will become in him a spring of water[a] welling up to eternal life."

15 The woman said to him, "Sir, give me this water so that I won't get thirsty[b] and have to keep coming here to draw water."

16 He told her, "Go, call your husband and come back."

17 "I have no husband," she replied.

Jesus said to her, "You are right when you say you have no husband. 18 The fact is, you have had five husbands, and the man you now have is not your husband. What you have just said is quite true."

19 "Sir," the woman said, "I can see that you are a prophet. 20 Our fathers worshiped on this mountain, but you Jews claim that the place where we must worship is in Jerusalem."

21 Jesus declared, "Believe me, woman, a time is coming when you will worship the Father neither on this mountain nor in Jerusalem.[c] 22 You Samaritans worship what you do not know;[d] we worship what we do know, for salvation is from the Jews.[e] 23 Yet a time is coming and has now come[f] when the true worshipers will worship the Father in spirit[g] and truth, for they are the kind of worshipers the Father seeks. 24 God is spirit,[h] and his worshipers must worship in spirit and in truth."

25 The woman said, "I know that Messiah" (called Christ)[i] "is coming. When he comes, he will explain everything to us."

26 Then Jesus declared, "I who speak to you am he."[j]

## The Disciples Rejoin Jesus

27 Just then his disciples returned[k] and were surprised to find him talking with a woman. But no one asked, "What do you want?" or "Why are you talking with her?"

28 Then, leaving her water jar, the woman went back to the town and said to the people, 29 "Come, see a man who told me everything I ever did.[l] Could this be the Christ[a]?"[m] 30 They came out of the town and made their way toward him.

31 Meanwhile his disciples urged him, "Rabbi, eat something."

32 But he said to them, "I have food to eat that you know nothing about."

33 Then his disciples said to each other, "Could someone have brought him food?"

34 "My food," said Jesus, "is to do the will[n] of him who sent me and to finish his work. 35 Do you not say, 'Four months more and then the harvest'? I tell you, open your eyes and look at the fields! They are ripe for harvest.[o] 36 Even now the reaper draws his wages, even now he harvests[p] the crop for eternal life, so that the sower and the reaper may be glad together. 37 Thus the saying 'One sows and another reaps'[q] is true. 38 I sent you to reap what you have not worked for. Others have done the hard work, and you have reaped the benefits of their labor."

## Many Samaritans Believe

39 Many of the Samaritans from that town believed in him because of the woman's testimony, "He told me everything I ever did."[r] 40 So when the Samaritans came to him, they urged him to stay with them, and he stayed two days. 41 And because of his words many more became believers.

42 They said to the woman, "We no longer believe just because of what you said; now we have heard for ourselves, and we know that this man really is the Savior of the world."[s]

[a]29 Or *Messiah*

**4:14** z Jn 6:35 a Jn 7:38
**4:15** b Jn 6:34
**4:21** c Mal 1:11; 1Ti 2:8
**4:22** d 2Ki 17:28–41 e Isa 2:3; Ro 9:4,5
**4:23** f Jn 5:25 g Php 3:3
**4:24** h Php 3:3
**4:25** i Mt 1:16
**4:26** j Jn 8:24
**4:27** k ver 8
**4:29** l ver 17,18 m Jn 7:26,31
**4:34** n Jn 6:38; 17:4; 19:30
**4:35** o Mt 9:37; Lk 10:2
**4:36** p Ro 1:13
**4:37** q Job 31:8
**4:39** r ver 29
**4:42** s 1Jn 4:14

### *The African Presence*

**John 4**

For information on Samaritans, see the African Presence note on Luke 9:52.

Inspire

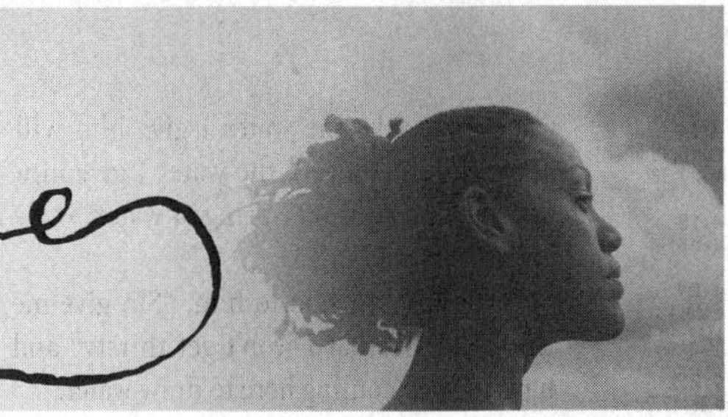

## FEMALE MINISTERS AND EVANGELISTS

My first encounter with a female evangelist took place on the day I was born. Throughout my growing up years, my mother, though not an ordained minister, zealously taught me the Scriptures and thoroughly educated me about the love of God expressed through Jesus Christ. Her testimony kept me from straying from the truth and was influential in my own call to ministry.

Despite some people's opinions, Jesus implicitly affirmed the place of women in ministry, as well as the ministry of female evangelists. This was evident in his interaction with the Samaritan woman at the well (see Jn 4:1–39), who, despite her disreputable past and sordid reputation, was instrumental in evangelizing her entire town. She did not use fancy words or profound theological statements but simply invited them, saying, "Come, see a man who told me everything I ever did. Could this be the Christ?" (Jn 4:29).

Women of color today can take a cue from this Samaritan sister, as well as from the first-century women who first shared the news of Christ's resurrection (see Mt 28:5–10; Jn 20:18). We are to tell what we know of Christ—regardless of what others might think of us or our message. When we've had an encounter with Christ, we'll want to run and tell others all that he has said and done. We will want to bring others to Christ. We will want to share the Good News with everyone—through our actions as well as our words.

Even as our world continues to devalue human beings, we are called to remain willing to step forward and declare that "Jesus saves" to the utmost. Among the many other aspects of our salvation, Jesus saves us from domestic violence, racism, sexism, poverty, low self-esteem, brokenheartedness, loneliness and drug addiction. Jesus saves and liberates us to live as daughters of the Most High God.

—C. Belt

### read

John 4:1–42; see also Matthew 28:1–10; John 20:1–18; Acts 18:1–3,18–28.

**See also** the Inspire Notes "A Great Challenge: Teaching Our Children," "Evangelism: Gone Fishin'," "Women in Preaching Ministries" and "Women in Teaching Ministries," and the Women of the Bible Notes "Huldah: A Prophetess of God," "Queen Vashti: A Woman of Strength," "Mary Magdalene: Setting Her Reputation Straight" and "Priscilla: An Open-Door Policy."

### WOMAN *of* COLOR

With whom have you shared Jesus—through words and actions—lately?

For the next Inspire note, go to page 1261.

## Jesus Heals the Official's Son

43 After the two days he left for Galilee.
44 (Now Jesus himself had pointed out that a
prophet has no honor in his own country.)[t]
45 When he arrived in Galilee, the Galileans
welcomed him. They had seen all that he had
done in Jerusalem at the Passover Feast,[u] for
they also had been there.

46 Once more he visited Cana in Galilee,
where he had turned the water into wine.[v]
And there was a certain royal official whose
son lay sick at Capernaum. 47 When this man
heard that Jesus had arrived in Galilee from
Judea,[w] he went to him and begged him to
come and heal his son, who was close to
death.

48 "Unless you people see miraculous
signs and wonders,"[x] Jesus told him, "you
will never believe."

49 The royal official said, "Sir, come down
before my child dies."

50 Jesus replied, "You may go. Your son
will live."

The man took Jesus at his word and
departed. 51 While he was still on the way,
his servants met him with the news that
his boy was living. 52 When he inquired as to
the time when his son got better, they said
to him, "The fever left him yesterday at the
seventh hour."

53 Then the father realized that this was
the exact time at which Jesus had said to
him, "Your son will live." So he and all his
household[y] believed.

54 This was the second miraculous sign
that Jesus performed, having come from Ju-
dea to Galilee.

## The Healing at the Pool

5 Some time later, Jesus went up to Jeru-
salem for a feast of the Jews. 2 Now there
is in Jerusalem near the Sheep Gate[z] a pool,
which in Aramaic is called Bethesda[a] and
which is surrounded by five covered colon-
nades. 3 Here a great number of disabled
people used to lie—the blind, the lame, the
paralyzed.[b] 5 One who was there had been an
invalid for thirty-eight years. 6 When Jesus
saw him lying there and learned that he had
been in this condition for a long time, he
asked him, "Do you want to get well?"

7 "Sir," the invalid replied, "I have no one
to help me into the pool when the water is
stirred. While I am trying to get in, some-
one else goes down ahead of me."

8 Then Jesus said to him, "Get up! Pick up
your mat and walk."[a] 9 At once the man was
cured; he picked up his mat and walked.

The day on which this took place was a
Sabbath,[b] 10 and so the Jews said to the man
who had been healed, "It is the Sabbath; the
law forbids you to carry your mat."[c]

11 But he replied, "The man who made
me well said to me, 'Pick up your mat and
walk.'"

12 So they asked him, "Who is this fellow
who told you to pick it up and walk?"

13 The man who was healed had no idea
who it was, for Jesus had slipped away into
the crowd that was there.

14 Later Jesus found him at the temple and
said to him, "See, you are well again. Stop
sinning[d] or something worse may happen to
you." 15 The man went away and told the Jews
that it was Jesus who had made him well.

## Life Through the Son

16 So, because Jesus was doing these
things on the Sabbath, the Jews persecuted
him. 17 Jesus said to them, "My Father is al-
ways at his work to this very day, and I, too,
am working." 18 For this reason the Jews
tried all the harder to kill him;[e] not only was
he breaking the Sabbath, but he was even
calling God his own Father, making himself
equal with God.[f]

19 Jesus gave them this answer: "I tell you
the truth, the Son can do nothing by him-
self;[g] he can do only what he sees his Father
doing, because whatever the Father does
the Son also does. 20 For the Father loves the
Son[h] and shows him all he does. Yes, to your
amazement he will show him even greater
things than these. 21 For just as the Father
raises the dead and gives them life, even
so the Son gives life[i] to whom he is pleased
to give it. 22 Moreover, the Father judges
no one, but has entrusted all judgment to
the Son,[j] 23 that all may honor the Son just

**4:44** t Mt13:57
**4:45** u Jn2:23
**4:46** v Jn2:1–11
**4:47** w ver3,54
**4:48** x Da4:2,3
**4:53** y Ac11:14
**5:2** z Ne3:1; 12:39

**5:8** a Mt9:5,6; Mk2:11; Lk5:24
**5:9** b Jn9:14
**5:10** c Ne13:15–22; Jer17:21; Mt12:2
**5:14** d Jn8:11
**5:18** e Jn7:1 f Jn10:30,33
**5:19** g Jn8:28
**5:20** h Jn3:35
**5:21** i Jn11:25
**5:22** j Ac10:42; 17:31

[a]2 Some manuscripts *Bethzatha*; other manuscripts *Bethsaida* [b]3 Some less important manuscripts *paralyzed—and they waited for the moving of the waters. 4From time to time an angel of the Lord would come down and stir up the waters. The first one into the pool after each such disturbance would be cured of whatever disease he had.*

as they honor the Father. He who does not
honor the Son does not honor the Father,
who sent him.[k]
24“I tell you the truth, whoever hears my
word and believes him who sent me has
eternal life and will not be condemned;[l] he
has crossed over from death to life.[m] 25I tell
you the truth, a time is coming and has now
come when the dead will hear the voice of
the Son of God and those who hear will live.
26For as the Father has life in himself, so he
has granted the Son to have life in himself.
27And he has given him authority to judge[n]
because he is the Son of Man.
28“Do not be amazed at this, for a time
is coming when all who are in their graves
will hear his voice 29and come out—those
who have done good will rise to live, and
those who have done evil will rise to be
condemned.[o] 30By myself I can do nothing;
I judge only as I hear, and my judgment is
just, for I seek not to please myself but him
who sent me.

## Testimonies About Jesus

31“If I testify about myself, my testimony
is not valid.[p] 32There is another who testifies
in my favor, and I know that his testimony
about me is valid.
33“You have sent to John and he has testi-
fied to the truth. 34Not that I accept human
testimony; but I mention it that you may be
saved. 35John was a lamp that burned and
gave light, and you chose for a time to enjoy
his light.
36“I have testimony weightier than that of
John. For the very work that the Father has
given me to finish, and which I am doing,
testifies that the Father has sent me.[q] 37And
the Father who sent me has himself testi-
fied concerning me.[r] You have never heard
his voice nor seen his form, 38nor does his
word dwell in you, for you do not believe
the one he sent. 39You diligently study[a] the
Scriptures because you think that by them
you possess eternal life. These are the Scrip-
tures that testify about me,[s] 40yet you refuse
to come to me to have life.
41“I do not accept praise from men, 42but
I know you. I know that you do not have the
love of God in your hearts. 43I have come in
my Father’s name, and you do not accept
me; but if someone else comes in his own
name, you will accept him. 44How can you be-
lieve if you accept praise from one another,
yet make no effort to obtain the praise that
comes from the only God[b]?[t]
45“But do not think I will accuse you be-
fore the Father. Your accuser is Moses,[u] on
whom your hopes are set.[v] 46If you believed
Moses, you would believe me, for he wrote
about me.[w] 47But since you do not believe
what he wrote, how are you going to believe
what I say?”[x]

## Jesus Feeds the Five Thousand

6 Some time after this, Jesus crossed to
the far shore of the Sea of Galilee (that
is, the Sea of Tiberias), 2and a great crowd
of people followed him because they saw the
miraculous signs[y] he had performed on the
sick. 3Then Jesus went up on a mountain-
side and sat down with his disciples. 4The
Jewish Passover Feast[z] was near.
5When Jesus looked up and saw a great
crowd coming toward him, he said to
Philip,[a] “Where shall we buy bread for these
people to eat?” 6He asked this only to test
him, for he already had in mind what he was
going to do.
7Philip answered him, “Eight months’
wages[c] would not buy enough bread for each
one to have a bite!”
8Another of his disciples, Andrew, Si-
mon Peter’s brother,[b] spoke up, 9“Here is a
boy with five small barley loaves and two
small fish, but how far will they go among
so many?”[c]
10Jesus said, “Have the people sit down.”
There was plenty of grass in that place, and
the men sat down, about five thousand of
them. 11Jesus then took the loaves, gave
thanks, and distributed to those who were
seated as much as they wanted. He did the
same with the fish.
12When they had all had enough to eat, he
said to his disciples, “Gather the pieces that
are left over. Let nothing be wasted.” 13So
they gathered them and filled twelve bas-
kets with the pieces of the five barley loaves
left over by those who had eaten.
14After the people saw the miraculous

**5:23** k 1Jn 2:23
**5:24** l Jn 3:18; m 1Jn 3:14
**5:27** n ver 22
**5:29** o Da 12:2; Mt 25:46
**5:31** p Jn 8:14
**5:36** q Jn 10:25
**5:37** r Jn 8:18
**5:39** s Lk 24:27,44
**5:44** t Ro 2:29
**5:45** u Jn 9:28; v Ro 2:17
**5:46** w Lk 24:27,44
**5:47** x Lk 16:29,31
**6:2** y Jn 2:11
**6:4** z Jn 2:13
**6:5** a Jn 1:43
**6:8** b Jn 1:40
**6:9** c 2Ki 4:43

[a] 39 Or *Study diligently* (the imperative) [b] 44 Some early manuscripts *the Only One* [c] 7 Greek *two hundred denarii*

**6:14** d Dt 18:15,18; Mt 11:3
**6:15** e Jn 18:36 f Mt 14:23
**6:22** g ver 2
**6:23** h ver 11
**6:26** i ver 24

sign that Jesus did, they began to say, "Surely this is the Prophet who is to come into the world."[d] 15 Jesus, knowing that they intended to come and make him king[e] by force, withdrew again to a mountain by himself.[f]

*Skeptical one,*

*I can still perform miracles. Watch me.*

*God*

JOHN 6:1–13

## Jesus Walks on the Water

16 When evening came, his disciples went down to the lake, 17 where they got into a boat and set off across the lake for Capernaum. By now it was dark, and Jesus had not yet joined them. 18 A strong wind was blowing and the waters grew rough. 19 When they had rowed three or three and a half miles,[a] they saw Jesus approaching the boat, walking on the water; and they were terrified. 20 But he said to them, "It is I; don't be afraid." 21 Then they were willing to take him into the boat, and immediately the boat reached the shore where they were heading.

22 The next day the crowd that had stayed on the opposite shore of the lake[g] realized that only one boat had been there, and that Jesus had not entered it with his disciples, but that they had gone away alone. 23 Then some boats from Tiberias landed near the place where the people had eaten the bread after the Lord had given thanks.[h] 24 Once the crowd realized that neither Jesus nor his disciples were there, they got into the boats and went to Capernaum in search of Jesus.

## Jesus the Bread of Life

25 When they found him on the other side of the lake, they asked him, "Rabbi, when did you get here?"

26 Jesus answered, "I tell you the truth, you are looking for me,[i] not because you saw miraculous signs but because you ate the loaves and had your fill. 27 Do not work for food that spoils, but for food that endures[j] to eternal life,[k] which the Son of Man will give you. On him God the Father has placed his seal of approval."

28 Then they asked him, "What must we do to do the works God requires?"

29 Jesus answered, "The work of God is this: to believe[l] in the one he has sent."

30 So they asked him, "What miraculous sign then will you give that we may see it and believe you?[m] What will you do? 31 Our forefathers ate the manna[n] in the desert; as it is written: 'He gave them bread from heaven to eat.'[b]"[o]

32 Jesus said to them, "I tell you the truth, it is not Moses who has given you the bread from heaven, but it is my Father who gives you the true bread from heaven. 33 For the bread of God is he who comes down from heaven and gives life to the world."

34 "Sir," they said, "from now on give us this bread."[p]

35 Then Jesus declared, "I am the bread of life.[q] He who comes to me will never go hungry, and he who believes in me will never be thirsty. 36 But as I told you, you have seen me and still you do not believe. 37 All that the Father gives me will come to me, and whoever comes to me I will never drive away. 38 For I have come down from heaven not to do my will but to do the will of him who sent me. 39 And this is the will of him who sent me, that I shall lose none of all that he has given me,[r] but raise them up at the last day. 40 For my Father's will is that everyone who looks to the Son and believes in him shall have eternal life, and I will raise him up at the last day."

41 At this the Jews began to grumble about him because he said, "I am the bread that came down from heaven." 42 They said, "Is this not Jesus, the son of Joseph,[s] whose father and mother we know? How can he now say, 'I came down from heaven'?"

43 "Stop grumbling among yourselves," Jesus answered. 44 "No one can come to me unless the Father who sent me draws him, and I will raise him up at the last day. 45 It is written in the Prophets: 'They will all be taught by God.'[c][t] Everyone who listens to

**6:27** j Isa 55:2 k Jn 4:14
**6:29** l 1Jn 3:23
**6:30** m Mt 12:38
**6:31** n Nu 11:7–9 o Ex 16:4,15; Ne 9:15; Ps 78:24
**6:34** p Jn 4:15
**6:35** q ver 48,51
**6:39** r Jn 10:28; 17:12; 18:9
**6:42** s Lk 4:22
**6:45** t Isa 54:13; Jer 31:33,34; Heb 8:10,11

[a]19 Greek *rowed twenty-five or thirty stadia* (about 5 or 6 kilometers) [b]31 Exodus 16:4; Neh. 9:15; Psalm 78:24,25
[c]45 Isaiah 54:13

6:46 u Jn 1:18
6:48 v ver 35,51
6:49 w ver 31,58
6:52 x Jn 9:16; 10:19
6:56 y 1Jn 3:24; 4:15
6:58 z ver 49–51
6:60 a ver 66
6:62 b Jn 3:13
6:63 c 2Co 3:6
6:64 d Jn 2:25

the Father and learns from him comes to me. 46 No one has seen the Father except the one who is from God;[u] only he has seen the Father. 47 I tell you the truth, he who believes has everlasting life. 48 I am the bread of life.[v] 49 Your forefathers ate the manna in the desert, yet they died.[w] 50 But here is the bread that comes down from heaven, which a man may eat and not die. 51 I am the living bread that came down from heaven. If anyone eats of this bread, he will live forever. This bread is my flesh, which I will give for the life of the world."

52 Then the Jews began to argue sharply among themselves,[x] "How can this man give us his flesh to eat?"

53 Jesus said to them, "I tell you the truth, unless you eat the flesh of the Son of Man and drink his blood, you have no life in you. 54 Whoever eats my flesh and drinks my blood has eternal life, and I will raise him up at the last day. 55 For my flesh is real food and my blood is real drink. 56 Whoever eats my flesh and drinks my blood remains in me, and I in him.[y] 57 Just as the living Father sent me and I live because of the Father, so the one who feeds on me will live because of me. 58 This is the bread that came down from heaven. Your forefathers ate manna and died, but he who feeds on this bread will live forever."[z] 59 He said this while teaching in the synagogue in Capernaum.

## Many Disciples Desert Jesus

60 On hearing it, many of his disciples[a] said, "This is a hard teaching. Who can accept it?"

61 Aware that his disciples were grumbling about this, Jesus said to them, "Does this offend you? 62 What if you see the Son of Man ascend to where he was before![b] 63 The Spirit gives life;[c] the flesh counts for nothing. The words I have spoken to you are spirit[a] and they are life. 64 Yet there are some of you who do not believe." For Jesus had known[d] from the beginning which of them did not believe and who would betray him. 65 He went on to say, "This is why I told you that no one can come to me unless the Father has enabled him."

66 From this time many of his disciples[e] turned back and no longer followed him.

67 "You do not want to leave too, do you?" Jesus asked the Twelve.

68 Simon Peter answered him, "Lord, to whom shall we go? You have the words of eternal life. 69 We believe and know that you are the Holy One of God."

70 Then Jesus replied, "Have I not chosen you, the Twelve? Yet one of you is a devil!"[f] 71 (He meant Judas, the son of Simon Iscariot, who, though one of the Twelve, was later to betray him.)

## Jesus Goes to the Feast of Tabernacles

7 After this, Jesus went around in Galilee, purposely staying away from Judea because the Jews there were waiting to take his life.[g] 2 But when the Jewish Feast of Tabernacles[h] was near, 3 Jesus' brothers[i] said to him, "You ought to leave here and go to Judea, so that your disciples may see the miracles you do. 4 No one who wants to become a public figure acts in secret. Since you are doing these things, show yourself to the world." 5 For even his own brothers did not believe in him.[j]

6 Therefore Jesus told them, "The right time for me has not yet come; for you any time is right. 7 The world cannot hate you, but it hates me because I testify that what it does is evil.[k] 8 You go to the Feast. I am not yet[b] going up to this Feast, because for me the right time has not yet come." 9 Having said this, he stayed in Galilee.

10 However, after his brothers had left for the Feast, he went also, not publicly, but in secret. 11 Now at the Feast the Jews were watching for him[l] and asking, "Where is that man?"

12 Among the crowds there was widespread whispering about him. Some said, "He is a good man."

Others replied, "No, he deceives the people."[m] 13 But no one would say anything publicly about him for fear of the Jews.[n]

## Jesus Teaches at the Feast

14 Not until halfway through the Feast did Jesus go up to the temple courts and begin

6:66 e ver 60
6:70 f Jn 13:27
7:1 g Jn 5:18
7:2 h Lev 23:34
7:3 i Mt 12:46
7:5 j Mk 3:21
7:7 k Jn 3:19,20
7:11 l Jn 11:56
7:12 m ver 40,43
7:13 n Jn 9:22; 12:42; 19:38

[a] 63 Or *Spirit* [b] 8 Some early manuscripts do not have *yet.*

to teach. [15]The Jews were amazed and asked, "How did this man get such learning without having studied?"

[16]Jesus answered, "My teaching is not my own. It comes from him who sent me. [17]If anyone chooses to do God's will, he will find out whether my teaching comes from God or whether I speak on my own. [18]He who speaks on his own does so to gain honor for himself,[o] but he who works for the honor of the one who sent him is a man of truth; there is nothing false about him. [19]Has not Moses given you the law?[p] Yet not one of you keeps the law. Why are you trying to kill me?"

[20]"You are demon-possessed,"[q] the crowd answered. "Who is trying to kill you?"

[21]Jesus said to them, "I did one miracle, and you are all astonished. [22]Yet, because Moses gave you circumcision (though actually it did not come from Moses, but from the patriarchs),[r] you circumcise a child on the Sabbath. [23]Now if a child can be circumcised on the Sabbath so that the law of Moses may not be broken, why are you angry with me for healing the whole man on the Sabbath? [24]Stop judging by mere appearances, and make a right judgment."[s]

## Is Jesus the Christ?

[25]At that point some of the people of Jerusalem began to ask, "Isn't this the man they are trying to kill? [26]Here he is, speaking publicly, and they are not saying a word to him. Have the authorities really concluded that he is the Christ[a]? [27]But we know where this man is from;[t] when the Christ comes, no one will know where he is from."

[28]Then Jesus, still teaching in the temple courts, cried out, "Yes, you know me, and you know where I am from. I am not here on my own, but he who sent me is true. You do not know him, [29]but I know him[u] because I am from him and he sent me."

[30]At this they tried to seize him, but no one laid a hand on him, because his time had not yet come. [31]Still, many in the crowd put their faith in him.[v] They said, "When the Christ comes, will he do more miraculous signs than this man?"

[32]The Pharisees heard the crowd whispering such things about him. Then the chief priests and the Pharisees sent temple guards to arrest him.

[33]Jesus said, "I am with you for only a short time,[w] and then I go to the one who sent me. [34]You will look for me, but you will not find me; and where I am, you cannot come."[x]

[35]The Jews said to one another, "Where does this man intend to go that we cannot find him? Will he go where our people live scattered[y] among the Greeks, and teach the Greeks? [36]What did he mean when he said, 'You will look for me, but you will not find me,' and 'Where I am, you cannot come'?"

[37]On the last and greatest day of the Feast, Jesus stood and said in a loud voice, "If anyone is thirsty, let him come to me and drink.[z] [38]Whoever believes in me, as[b] the Scripture has said, streams of living water will flow from within him." [39]By this he meant the Spirit,[a] whom those who believed in him were later to receive. Up to that time the Spirit had not been given, since Jesus had not yet been glorified.[b]

[40]On hearing his words, some of the people said, "Surely this man is the Prophet."

[41]Others said, "He is the Christ."

Still others asked, "How can the Christ come from Galilee?[c] [42]Does not the Scripture say that the Christ will come from David's family[c] and from Bethlehem,[d] the town where David lived?" [43]Thus the people were divided[e] because of Jesus. [44]Some wanted to seize him, but no one laid a hand on him.[f]

## Unbelief of the Jewish Leaders

[45]Finally the temple guards went back to the chief priests and Pharisees, who asked them, "Why didn't you bring him in?"

[46]"No one ever spoke the way this man does," the guards declared.

[47]"You mean he has deceived you also?" the Pharisees retorted. [48]"Has any of the rulers or of the Pharisees believed in him?[g] [49]No! But this mob that knows nothing of the law—there is a curse on them."

[50]Nicodemus, who had gone to Jesus earlier and who was one of their own number, asked, [51]"Does our law condemn

**7:18** o Jn 5:41; 8:50,54
**7:19** p Jn 1:17
**7:20** q Jn 8:48; 10:20
**7:22** r Ge 17:10–14
**7:24** s Jn 8:15
**7:27** t Mt 13:55
**7:29** u Mt 11:27
**7:31** v Jn 8:30
**7:33** w Jn 13:33; 16:16
**7:34** x Jn 8:21; 13:33
**7:35** y Jas 1:1
**7:37** z Isa 55:1
**7:39** a Joel 2:28 b Jn 12:23
**7:41** c Jn 1:46
**7:42** d Mic 5:2; Mt 2:5,6; Lk 2:4
**7:43** e Jn 9:16; 10:19
**7:44** f ver 30
**7:48** g Jn 12:42

[a]26 Or *Messiah*; also in verses 27, 31, 41 and 42 [b]37,38 Or */ If anyone is thirsty, let him come to me. / And let him drink, [38]who believes in me. / As* [c]42 Greek *seed*

anyone without first hearing him to find out what he is doing?"

52 They replied, "Are you from Galilee, too? Look into it, and you will find that a prophet[a] does not come out of Galilee."

---

[The earliest manuscripts and many other ancient witnesses do not have John 7:53—8:11.]

53 Then each went to his own home.

8 But Jesus went to the Mount of Olives. 2 At dawn he appeared again in the temple courts, where all the people gathered around him, and he sat down to teach them. 3 The teachers of the law and the Pharisees brought in a woman caught in adultery. They made her stand before the group 4 and said to Jesus, "Teacher, this woman was caught in the act of adultery. 5 In the Law Moses commanded us to stone such women.[h] Now what do you say?" 6 They were using this question as a trap, in order to have a basis for accusing him.

But Jesus bent down and started to write on the ground with his finger. 7 When they kept on questioning him, he straightened up and said to them, "If any one of you is without sin, let him be the first to throw a stone[i] at her."[j] 8 Again he stooped down and wrote on the ground.

9 At this, those who heard began to go away one at a time, the older ones first, until only Jesus was left, with the woman still standing there. 10 Jesus straightened up and asked her, "Woman, where are they? Has no one condemned you?"

11 "No one, sir," she said.

"Then neither do I condemn you,"[k] Jesus declared. "Go now and leave your life of sin."[l]

---

## The Validity of Jesus' Testimony

12 When Jesus spoke again to the people, he said, "I am the light of the world.[m] Whoever follows me will never walk in darkness, but will have the light of life."

13 The Pharisees challenged him, "Here you are, appearing as your own witness; your testimony is not valid."[n]

14 Jesus answered, "Even if I testify on my own behalf, my testimony is valid, for I know where I came from and where I am going. But you have no idea where I come from[o] or where I am going. 15 You judge by human standards;[p] I pass judgment on no one.[q] 16 But if I do judge, my decisions are right, because I am not alone. I stand with the Father, who sent me. 17 In your own Law it is written that the testimony of two men is valid.[r] 18 I am one who testifies for myself; my other witness is the Father, who sent me."[s]

19 Then they asked him, "Where is your father?"

"You do not know me or my Father,"[t] Jesus replied. "If you knew me, you would know my Father also." 20 He spoke these words while teaching in the temple area near the place where the offerings were put.[u] Yet no one seized him, because his time had not yet come.

21 Once more Jesus said to them, "I am going away, and you will look for me, and you will die in your sin. Where I go, you cannot come."[v]

22 This made the Jews ask, "Will he kill himself? Is that why he says, 'Where I go, you cannot come'?"

23 But he continued, "You are from below; I am from above. You are of this world; I am not of this world.[w] 24 I told you that you would die in your sins; if you do not believe that I am ⌞the one I claim to be⌟,[b] you will indeed die in your sins."

25 "Who are you?" they asked.

"Just what I have been claiming all along," Jesus replied. 26 "I have much to say in judgment of you. But he who sent me is reliable,[x] and what I have heard from him I tell the world."[y]

27 They did not understand that he was telling them about his Father. 28 So Jesus said, "When you have lifted up the Son of Man,[z] then you will know that I am ⌞the one I claim to be⌟ and that I do nothing on my own but speak just what the Father has taught me. 29 The one who sent me is with

[a]52 Two early manuscripts *the Prophet* [b]24 Or *I am he*; also in verse 28

**8:5** h Lev 20:10; Dt 22:22
**8:7** i Dt 17:7 j Ro 2:1,22
**8:11** k Jn 3:17 l Jn 5:14
**8:12** m Jn 1:4
**8:13** n Jn 5:31
**8:14** o Jn 7:28; 9:29
**8:15** p Jn 7:24 q Jn 3:17
**8:17** r Mt 18:16
**8:18** s Jn 5:37
**8:19** t Jn 16:3
**8:20** u Mk 12:41
**8:21** v Jn 7:34
**8:23** w Jn 3:31
**8:26** x Jn 7:28 y Jn 3:32; 15:15
**8:28** z Jn 12:32

# The Forgiven Adulteress

## Caught but Not Condemned

She was caught. She was dragged before the men of the community. She was accused. She waited to be stoned—to be destroyed by anything they decided to throw at her. Had she loved him? Had he told her it would be all right, that he would fix everything, that he loved her? But when the witnesses burst in on them, he apparently didn't protest, didn't defend her and conveniently escaped prosecution. He left her to face her accusers alone. There was nothing she could say that they were willing to hear. The community let him escape, but she would be stoned to death (see Jn 8:3–5).

The guys may have laughed behind their hands when they saw him, but he had his life. On the other hand, all her friends and acquaintances pulled away. After all, she might be after their man. Can't you hear them—her sisters—their words pouring acid into the wound of her shame? There was no one to stand by her side in her defense. Oh, the pain of being the one caught—exposed for the world to see.

You may have tried drugs and were out there for a while. Finally, enough was enough, but now your family doesn't trust you and has trouble believing in you. Your destructive relationships almost cost you your life—black eyes and swollen lips, hospital visits and the inability to hold a job. You are always hiding, afraid and ashamed. You think everyone knows your business and thinks you're unworthy. So, too, our sister must have felt belittled, judged by the self-righteous and found guilty. But out of the crowd, at the point of her deepest fear and need, stepped Jesus!

God is willing to forgive when you repent and turn to him, writing in the dust of your broken life and challenging the finger-pointers to check out the four fingers pointing back at them!

We might be caught, but Jesus does not condemn us! He forgives us! Jesus paid the price for the adulteress and for all of us. Jesus challenges each of us to make new choices; his grace provides both hope for the future and power to leave our sin in the past.

—M. Allen Bellinger

### reflection

*Remember that Jesus does not condemn you as he calls you to leave behind your sin; neither should you condemn yourself or others.*

*With whom can you share this good news today?*

### read

John 7:53—8:11; see also Exodus 20:14; Leviticus 20:10.

See also the Inspire Notes "Grace and Mercy," "Domestic Violence," "Adultery," "Help for the Addict" and "Forgiveness: God's Extended Mercy," and the Women of the Bible Notes "The Adulteress of Proverbs: The Path to Death," "Bathsheba: A Silent Affair" and "Gomer: An Unfaithful Wife."

For the next Women of the Bible note, go to page 1257.

**8:29** a Jn 4:34
**8:30** b Jn 7:31
**8:33** c Mt 3:9
**8:34** d Ro 6:16; 2Pe 2:19
**8:35** e Gal 4:30
**8:38** f Jn 5:19,30
**8:39** g Ro 9:7; Gal 3:7
**8:40** h ver 26
**8:41** i Isa 63:16; 64:8
**8:42** j 1Jn 5:1 k Jn 7:28
**8:44** l 1Jn 3:8

me; he has not left me alone, for I always do what pleases him."[a] [30]Even as he spoke, many put their faith in him.[b]

## The Children of Abraham

[31]To the Jews who had believed him, Jesus said, "If you hold to my teaching, you are really my disciples. [32]Then you will know the truth, and the truth will set you free."

[33]They answered him, "We are Abraham's descendants[a][c] and have never been slaves of anyone. How can you say that we shall be set free?"

[34]Jesus replied, "I tell you the truth, everyone who sins is a slave to sin.[d] [35]Now a slave has no permanent place in the family, but a son belongs to it forever.[e] [36]So if the Son sets you free, you will be free indeed. [37]I know you are Abraham's descendants. Yet you are ready to kill me, because you have no room for my word. [38]I am telling you what I have seen in the Father's presence,[f] and you do what you have heard from your father.[b]"

[39]"Abraham is our father," they answered.

"If you were Abraham's children,"[g] said Jesus, "then you would[c] do the things Abraham did. [40]As it is, you are determined to kill me, a man who has told you the truth that I heard from God.[h] Abraham did not do such things. [41]You are doing the things your own father does."

"We are not illegitimate children," they protested. "The only Father we have is God himself."[i]

## The Children of the Devil

[42]Jesus said to them, "If God were your Father, you would love me,[j] for I came from God and now am here. I have not come on my own;[k] but he sent me. [43]Why is my language not clear to you? Because you are unable to hear what I say. [44]You belong to your father, the devil,[l] and you want to carry out your father's desire. He was a murderer from the beginning, not holding to the truth, for there is no truth in him. When he lies, he speaks his native language, for he is a liar and the father of lies. [45]Yet because I tell the truth, you do not believe me! [46]Can any of you prove me guilty of sin? If I am telling the truth, why don't you believe me? [47]He who belongs to God hears what God says. The reason you do not hear is that you do not belong to God."

## The Claims of Jesus About Himself

[48]The Jews answered him, "Aren't we right in saying that you are a Samaritan and demon-possessed?"[m]

[49]"I am not possessed by a demon," said Jesus, "but I honor my Father and you dishonor me. [50]I am not seeking glory for myself;[n] but there is one who seeks it, and he is the judge. [51]I tell you the truth, if anyone keeps my word, he will never see death."

[52]At this the Jews exclaimed, "Now we know that you are demon-possessed! Abraham died and so did the prophets, yet you say that if anyone keeps your word, he will never taste death. [53]Are you greater than our father Abraham? He died, and so did the prophets. Who do you think you are?"

[54]Jesus replied, "If I glorify myself, my glory means nothing. My Father, whom you claim as your God, is the one who glorifies me. [55]Though you do not know him, I know him.[o] If I said I did not, I would be a liar like you, but I do know him and keep his word. [56]Your father Abraham rejoiced at the thought of seeing my day; he saw it[p] and was glad."

[57]"You are not yet fifty years old," the Jews said to him, "and you have seen Abraham!"

[58]"I tell you the truth," Jesus answered, "before Abraham was born,[q] I am!" [59]At this, they picked up stones to stone him,[r] but Jesus hid himself, slipping away from the temple grounds.

## Jesus Heals a Man Born Blind

**9** As he went along, he saw a man blind from birth. [2]His disciples asked him, "Rabbi, who sinned,[s] this man or his parents, that he was born blind?"

[3]"Neither this man nor his parents sinned," said Jesus, "but this happened so that the work of God might be displayed in his life.[t] [4]As long as it is day,[u] we must do the

**8:48** m Jn 7:20
**8:50** n Jn 5:41
**8:55** o Jn 7:28,29
**8:56** p Heb 11:13
**8:58** q Jn 17:5,24
**8:59** r Jn 10:31; 11:8
**9:2** s ver 34
**9:3** t Jn 11:4
**9:4** u Jn 11:9; 12:35

[a]33 Greek *seed*; also in verse 37 [b]38 Or *presence. Therefore do what you have heard from the Father.* [c]39 Some early manuscripts *"If you are Abraham's children," said Jesus, "then*

work of him who sent me. Night is coming, when no one can work. 5 While I am in the world, I am the light of the world."[v]

6 Having said this, he spit[w] on the ground, made some mud with the saliva, and put it on the man's eyes. 7 "Go," he told him, "wash in the Pool of Siloam" (this word means Sent). So the man went and washed, and came home seeing.

8 His neighbors and those who had formerly seen him begging asked, "Isn't this the same man who used to sit and beg?" 9 Some claimed that he was.

Others said, "No, he only looks like him."

But he himself insisted, "I am the man."

10 "How then were your eyes opened?" they demanded.

11 He replied, "The man they call Jesus made some mud and put it on my eyes. He told me to go to Siloam and wash. So I went and washed, and then I could see."[x]

12 "Where is this man?" they asked him.

"I don't know," he said.

## The Pharisees Investigate the Healing

13 They brought to the Pharisees the man who had been blind. 14 Now the day on which Jesus had made the mud and opened the man's eyes was a Sabbath.[y] 15 Therefore the Pharisees also asked him how he had received his sight. "He put mud on my eyes," the man replied, "and I washed, and now I see."

16 Some of the Pharisees said, "This man is not from God, for he does not keep the Sabbath."

But others asked, "How can a sinner do such miraculous signs?" So they were divided.[z]

17 Finally they turned again to the blind man, "What have you to say about him? It was your eyes he opened."

The man replied, "He is a prophet."[a]

18 The Jews still did not believe that he had been blind and had received his sight until they sent for the man's parents. 19 "Is this your son?" they asked. "Is this the one you say was born blind? How is it that now he can see?"

20 "We know he is our son," the parents answered, "and we know he was born blind. 21 But how he can see now, or who opened his eyes, we don't know. Ask him. He is of age; he will speak for himself." 22 His parents said this because they were afraid of the Jews,[b] for already the Jews had decided that anyone who acknowledged that Jesus was the Christ[a] would be put out of the synagogue.[c] 23 That was why his parents said, "He is of age; ask him."

24 A second time they summoned the man who had been blind. "Give glory to God,[b]"[d] they said. "We know this man is a sinner."[e]

25 He replied, "Whether he is a sinner or not, I don't know. One thing I do know. I was blind but now I see!"

26 Then they asked him, "What did he do to you? How did he open your eyes?"

27 He answered, "I have told you already and you did not listen. Why do you want to hear it again? Do you want to become his disciples, too?"

28 Then they hurled insults at him and said, "You are this fellow's disciple! We are disciples of Moses![f] 29 We know that God spoke to Moses, but as for this fellow, we don't even know where he comes from."

30 The man answered, "Now that is remarkable! You don't know where he comes from, yet he opened my eyes. 31 We know that God does not listen to sinners. He listens to the godly man who does his will.[g] 32 Nobody has ever heard of opening the eyes of a man born blind. 33 If this man were not from God,[h] he could do nothing."

34 To this they replied, "You were steeped in sin at birth;[i] how dare you lecture us!" And they threw him out.

## Spiritual Blindness

35 Jesus heard that they had thrown him out, and when he found him, he said, "Do you believe in the Son of Man?"

36 "Who is he, sir?" the man asked. "Tell me so that I may believe in him."

37 Jesus said, "You have now seen him; in fact, he is the one speaking with you."[j]

38 Then the man said, "Lord, I believe," and he worshiped him.

39 Jesus said, "For judgment[k] I have come

[a] 22 Or *Messiah* [b] 24 A solemn charge to tell the truth (see Joshua 7:19)

**9:5** v Jn 8:12; 12:46
**9:6** w Mk 7:33; 8:23
**9:11** x ver 7
**9:14** y Jn 5:9
**9:16** z Jn 7:43; 10:19
**9:17** a Mt 21:11
**9:22** b Jn 7:13 c Jn 12:42
**9:24** d Jos 7:19 e ver 16
**9:28** f Jn 5:45
**9:31** g Ps 34:15,16; 66:18; Pr 15:29; Isa 1:15
**9:33** h ver 16
**9:34** i ver 2
**9:37** j Jn 4:26
**9:39** k Jn 5:22

into this world, so that the blind will see and those who see will become blind."[l]

40 Some Pharisees who were with him heard him say this and asked, "What? Are we blind too?"[m]

41 Jesus said, "If you were blind, you would not be guilty of sin; but now that you claim you can see, your guilt remains.[n]

## The Shepherd and His Flock

**10** "I tell you the truth, the man who does not enter the sheep pen by the gate, but climbs in by some other way, is a thief and a robber. 2 The man who enters by the gate is the shepherd of his sheep. 3 The watchman opens the gate for him, and the sheep listen to his voice. He calls his own sheep by name and leads them out. 4 When he has brought out all his own, he goes on ahead of them, and his sheep follow him because they know his voice. 5 But they will never follow a stranger; in fact, they will run away from him because they do not recognize a stranger's voice." 6 Jesus used this figure of speech, but they did not understand what he was telling them.

7 Therefore Jesus said again, "I tell you the truth, I am the gate for the sheep. 8 All who ever came before me were thieves and robbers, but the sheep did not listen to them. 9 I am the gate; whoever enters through me will be saved.[a] He will come in and go out, and find pasture. 10 The thief comes only to steal and kill and destroy; I have come that they may have life, and have it to the full.

11 "I am the good shepherd.[o] The good shepherd lays down his life for the sheep. 12 The hired hand is not the shepherd who owns the sheep. So when he sees the wolf coming, he abandons the sheep and runs away. Then the wolf attacks the flock and scatters it. 13 The man runs away because he is a hired hand and cares nothing for the sheep.

14 "I am the good shepherd; I know my sheep and my sheep know me— 15 just as the Father knows me and I know the Father[p]—and I lay down my life for the sheep. 16 I have other sheep[q] that are not of this sheep pen. I must bring them also. They too will listen to my voice, and there shall be one flock[r] and one shepherd. 17 The reason my Father loves me is that I lay down my life—only to take it up again. 18 No one takes it from me, but I lay it down of my own accord. I have authority to lay it down and authority to take it up again. This command I received from my Father."[s]

19 At these words the Jews were again divided.[t] 20 Many of them said, "He is demon-possessed and raving mad. Why listen to him?"

21 But others said, "These are not the sayings of a man possessed by a demon. Can a demon open the eyes of the blind?"[u]

## The Unbelief of the Jews

22 Then came the Feast of Dedication[b] at Jerusalem. It was winter, 23 and Jesus was in the temple area walking in Solomon's Colonnade.[v] 24 The Jews gathered around him, saying, "How long will you keep us in suspense? If you are the Christ,[c] tell us plainly."

25 Jesus answered, "I did tell you, but you do not believe. The miracles I do in my Father's name speak for me,[w] 26 but you do not believe because you are not my sheep.[x] 27 My sheep listen to my voice; I know them,[y] and they follow me.[z] 28 I give them eternal life, and they shall never perish; no one can snatch them out of my hand. 29 My Father, who has given them to me, is greater than all[d]; no one can snatch them out of my Father's hand. 30 I and the Father are one."[a]

31 Again the Jews picked up stones to stone him,[b] 32 but Jesus said to them, "I have shown you many great miracles from the Father. For which of these do you stone me?"

33 "We are not stoning you for any of these," replied the Jews, "but for blasphemy, because you, a mere man, claim to be God."[c]

34 Jesus answered them, "Is it not written in your Law, 'I have said you are gods'[e]?[d] 35 If he called them 'gods,' to whom the word of God came—and the Scripture cannot be broken— 36 what about the one whom the Father set apart as his very own and sent into the world?[e] Why then do you accuse me of blasphemy because I said, 'I am God's Son'?[f] 37 Do not believe me unless I do what my Father does.[g] 38 But if I do it, even though

**9:39** l Mt 13:13
**9:40** m Ro 2:19
**9:41** n Jn 15:22,24
**10:11** o Isa 40:11; Eze 34:11–16,23; Heb 13:20; 1Pe 5:4
**10:15** p Mt 11:27
**10:16** q Isa 56:8 r Eph 2:11–19
**10:18** s Jn 15:10
**10:19** t Jn 7:43
**10:21** u Ex 4:11; Jn 9:32,33
**10:23** v Ac 3:11; 5:12
**10:25** w Jn 5:36
**10:26** x Jn 8:47
**10:27** y ver 14 z ver 4
**10:30** a Jn 17:21–23
**10:31** b Jn 8:59
**10:33** c Jn 5:18
**10:34** d Ps 82:6
**10:36** e Jn 3:17 f Jn 5:17,18
**10:37** g Jn 15:24

[a] 9 Or *kept safe* [b] 22 That is, Hanukkah [c] 24 Or *Messiah* [d] 29 Many early manuscripts *What my Father has given me is greater than all* [e] 34 Psalm 82:6

you do not believe me, believe the miracles, that you may know and understand that the Father is in me, and I in the Father."[h] 39 Again they tried to seize him,[i] but he escaped their grasp.[j]

40 Then Jesus went back across the Jordan[k] to the place where John had been baptizing in the early days. Here he stayed 41 and many people came to him. They said, "Though John never performed a miraculous sign, all that John said about this man was true." 42 And in that place many believed in Jesus.

## The Death of Lazarus

11 Now a man named Lazarus was sick. He was from Bethany, the village of Mary and her sister Martha.[l] 2 This Mary, whose brother Lazarus now lay sick, was the same one who poured perfume on the Lord and wiped his feet with her hair.[m] 3 So the sisters sent word to Jesus, "Lord, the one you love is sick."

4 When he heard this, Jesus said, "This sickness will not end in death. No, it is for God's glory[n] so that God's Son may be glorified through it." 5 Jesus loved Martha and her sister and Lazarus. 6 Yet when he heard that Lazarus was sick, he stayed where he was two more days.

7 Then he said to his disciples, "Let us go back to Judea."

8 "But Rabbi," they said, "a short while ago the Jews tried to stone you,[o] and yet you are going back there?"

9 Jesus answered, "Are there not twelve hours of daylight? A man who walks by day will not stumble, for he sees by this world's light.[p] 10 It is when he walks by night that he stumbles, for he has no light."

11 After he had said this, he went on to tell them, "Our friend Lazarus has fallen asleep;[q] but I am going there to wake him up."

12 His disciples replied, "Lord, if he sleeps, he will get better." 13 Jesus had been speaking of his death, but his disciples thought he meant natural sleep.[r]

14 So then he told them plainly, "Lazarus is dead, 15 and for your sake I am glad I was not there, so that you may believe. But let us go to him."

16 Then Thomas (called Didymus) said to the rest of the disciples, "Let us also go, that we may die with him."

## Jesus Comforts the Sisters

17 On his arrival, Jesus found that Lazarus had already been in the tomb for four days. 18 Bethany was less than two miles[a] from Jerusalem, 19 and many Jews had come to Martha and Mary to comfort them in the loss of their brother.[s] 20 When Martha heard that Jesus was coming, she went out to meet him, but Mary stayed at home.

21 "Lord," Martha said to Jesus, "if you had been here, my brother would not have died. 22 But I know that even now God will give you whatever you ask."[t]

23 Jesus said to her, "Your brother will rise again."

24 Martha answered, "I know he will rise again in the resurrection[u] at the last day."

25 Jesus said to her, "I am the resurrection and the life.[v] He who believes in me will live, even though he dies; 26 and whoever lives and believes in me will never die. Do you believe this?"

27 "Yes, Lord," she told him, "I believe that you are the Christ,[b] the Son of God,[w] who was to come into the world."[x]

28 And after she had said this, she went back and called her sister Mary aside. "The Teacher[y] is here," she said, "and is asking for you." 29 When Mary heard this, she got up quickly and went to him. 30 Now Jesus had not yet entered the village, but was still at the place where Martha had met him. 31 When the Jews who had been with Mary in the house, comforting her,[z] noticed how quickly she got up and went out, they followed her, supposing she was going to the tomb to mourn there.

32 When Mary reached the place where Jesus was and saw him, she fell at his feet and said, "Lord, if you had been here, my brother would not have died."[a]

33 When Jesus saw her weeping, and the Jews who had come along with her also weeping, he was deeply moved in spirit and troubled.[b] 34 "Where have you laid him?" he asked.

"Come and see, Lord," they replied.

**10:38** h Jn 14:10,11,20; 17:21
**10:39** i Jn 7:30 j Jn 8:59
**10:40** k Jn 1:28
**11:1** l Lk 10:38
**11:2** m Jn 12:3
**11:4** n ver 40; Jn 9:3
**11:8** o Jn 10:31
**11:9** p Jn 9:4
**11:11** q Ac 7:60
**11:13** r Mt 9:24
**11:19** s Job 2:11
**11:22** t Jn 9:31
**11:24** u Jn 5:28,29
**11:25** v Jn 1:4
**11:27** w Mt 16:16 x Jn 6:14
**11:28** y Mt 26:18; Jn 13:13
**11:31** z ver 19
**11:32** a ver 21
**11:33** b Jn 12:27

[a] 18 Greek *fifteen stadia* (about 3 kilometers) [b] 27 Or *Messiah*

**11:35** c Lk 19:41
**11:37** d Jn 9:6,7
**11:38** e Mt 27:60
**11:40** f ver 23–25 g ver 4
**11:42** h Jn 12:30
**11:44** i Jn 19:40 j Jn 20:7
**11:45** k Jn 2:23
**11:47** l Mt 26:3
**11:49** m Mt 26:3 n Jn 18:13,14

[35]Jesus wept.[c]

[36]Then the Jews said, "See how he loved him!"

[37]But some of them said, "Could not he who opened the eyes of the blind man[d] have kept this man from dying?"

## Jesus Raises Lazarus From the Dead

[38]Jesus, once more deeply moved, came to the tomb. It was a cave with a stone laid across the entrance.[e] [39]"Take away the stone," he said.

"But, Lord," said Martha, the sister of the dead man, "by this time there is a bad odor, for he has been there four days."

[40]Then Jesus said, "Did I not tell you that if you believed,[f] you would see the glory of God?"[g]

[41]So they took away the stone. Then Jesus looked up and said, "Father, I thank you that you have heard me. [42]I knew that you always hear me, but I said this for the benefit of the people standing here,[h] that they may believe that you sent me."

[43]When he had said this, Jesus called in a loud voice, "Lazarus, come out!" [44]The dead man came out, his hands and feet wrapped with strips of linen,[i] and a cloth around his face.[j]

Jesus said to them, "Take off the grave clothes and let him go."

## The Plot to Kill Jesus

[45]Therefore many of the Jews who had come to visit Mary, and had seen what Jesus did,[k] put their faith in him. [46]But some of them went to the Pharisees and told them what Jesus had done. [47]Then the chief priests and the Pharisees called a meeting[l] of the Sanhedrin.

"What are we accomplishing?" they asked. "Here is this man performing many miraculous signs. [48]If we let him go on like this, everyone will believe in him, and then the Romans will come and take away both our place[a] and our nation."

[49]Then one of them, named Caiaphas,[m] who was high priest that year,[n] spoke up, "You know nothing at all! [50]You do not realize that it is better for you that one man die for the people than that the whole nation perish."[o]

[51]He did not say this on his own, but as high priest that year he prophesied that Jesus would die for the Jewish nation, [52]and not only for that nation but also for the scattered children of God, to bring them together and make them one.[p] [53]So from that day on they plotted to take his life.

[54]Therefore Jesus no longer moved about publicly among the Jews.[q] Instead he withdrew to a region near the desert, to a village called Ephraim, where he stayed with his disciples.

[55]When it was almost time for the Jewish Passover,[r] many went up from the country to Jerusalem for their ceremonial cleansing[s] before the Passover. [56]They kept looking for Jesus,[t] and as they stood in the temple area they asked one another, "What do you think? Isn't he coming to the Feast at all?" [57]But the chief priests and Pharisees had given orders that if anyone found out where Jesus was, he should report it so that they might arrest him.

## Jesus Anointed at Bethany

**12** Six days before the Passover,[u] Jesus arrived at Bethany, where Lazarus lived, whom Jesus had raised from the dead. [2]Here a dinner was given in Jesus' honor. Martha served,[v] while Lazarus was among those reclining at the table with him. [3]Then Mary took about a pint[b] of pure nard, an expensive perfume; she poured it on Jesus' feet and wiped his feet with her hair.[w] And the house was filled with the fragrance of the perfume.

[4]But one of his disciples, Judas Iscariot, who was later to betray him, objected, [5]"Why wasn't this perfume sold and the money given to the poor? It was worth a year's wages.[c]" [6]He did not say this because he cared about the poor but because he was a thief; as keeper of the money bag,[x] he used to help himself to what was put into it.

[7]"Leave her alone," Jesus replied. "⌞It was intended⌟ that she should save this perfume for the day of my burial.[y] [8]You will always have the poor among you, but you will not always have me."

**11:50** o Jn 18:14
**11:52** p Isa 49:6; Jn 10:16
**11:54** q Jn 7:1
**11:55** r Mk 14:1 s 2Ch 30:17,18
**11:56** t Jn 7:11
**12:1** u Jn 11:55
**12:2** v Lk 10:38–42
**12:3** w Jn 11:2
**12:6** x Jn 13:29
**12:7** y Jn 19:40

[a]48 Or *temple* [b]3 Greek *a litra* (probably about 0.5 liter) [c]5 Greek *three hundred denarii*

# Mary and Martha

## Grieving Sisters

It is sometimes difficult to believe that death could happen to a sister, brother or someone significant to us. Death, we think, always happens to someone else and at some other time. But all too often death does happen to us and our loved ones at the most unexpected times. We then begin to realize that the loss of a loved one touches every one of us.

One of the most remarkable and memorable stories in the Bible about family members dealing with death is found in John 11:1–44. It is the story of sisters Mary and Martha and their brother Lazarus. Clearly Jesus had spent some "quality time" with these siblings in Bethany, a town near Jerusalem (see Mk 11:1,11; Lk 10:38–42). When Mary and Martha sent word to Jesus that their brother was sick, they referred to Lazarus as "the one you love" (Jn 11:3).

The powerful lesson in this story is that Mary and Martha became overcomers because they were willing to cast their burdens upon Jesus, which is why they sent for him when Lazarus was dying. When Lazarus died, Jesus comforted them. But he also demonstrated his power to them by raising Lazarus from the dead. It was a miracle that these two sisters had to experience in order to realize the true glory and compassion of Christ (see Jn 11:4,35–36,40).

When you are faced with the difficulty of loss through death or through other means, cast your cares on Jesus. He cares enough to carry your burdens and carry you through your difficult times. Allow him to receive glory from your situation, just as he did from Mary and Martha's.

—D. Moore-James

### reflection

*When you have been burdened with the loss of a loved one or when you have been through a challenging situation, to whom have you turned for comfort? What did you receive?*

*Remember to cast your cares on Christ.*

### read

John 11:1–44; 1 Peter 5:7.

See also the Inspire Notes "Suffering," "True Joy," "The Paradox of Life and Suffering" and "Peace," and the Women of the Bible Notes "The Shunammite Woman: Our Sister's Grief Is Our Grief," "Job's Wife: She Was Tested Too" and "Mary of Bethany: The Unforgotten Woman."

For the next Women of the Bible note, go to page 1259.

**12:9** z Jn 11:43,44
**12:11** a ver 17,18; Jn 11:45
**12:13** b Ps 118:25,26
**12:15** c Zec 9:9
**12:16** d Jn 7:39
**12:18** e ver 11

9 Meanwhile a large crowd of Jews found out that Jesus was there and came, not only because of him but also to see Lazarus, whom he had raised from the dead.[z] 10 So the chief priests made plans to kill Lazarus as well, 11 for on account of him[a] many of the Jews were going over to Jesus and putting their faith in him.

## The Triumphal Entry

12 The next day the great crowd that had come for the Feast heard that Jesus was on his way to Jerusalem. 13 They took palm branches and went out to meet him, shouting,

"Hosanna![a]"

"Blessed is he who comes in the name of
the Lord!"[b][b]

"Blessed is the King of Israel!"

14 Jesus found a young donkey and sat upon it, as it is written,

15 "Do not be afraid, O Daughter of Zion;
see, your king is coming,
seated on a donkey's colt."[c][c]

16 At first his disciples did not understand all this. Only after Jesus was glorified[d] did they realize that these things had been written about him and that they had done these things to him.

17 Now the crowd that was with him when he called Lazarus from the tomb and raised him from the dead continued to spread the word. 18 Many people, because they had heard that he had given this miraculous sign,[e] went out to meet him. 19 So the Pharisees said to one another, "See, this is getting us nowhere. Look how the whole world has gone after him!"

## Jesus Predicts His Death

20 Now there were some Greeks among those who went up to worship at the Feast. 21 They came to Philip, who was from Bethsaida in Galilee, with a request. "Sir," they said, "we would like to see Jesus." 22 Philip went to tell Andrew; Andrew and Philip in turn told Jesus.

23 Jesus replied, "The hour has come for the Son of Man to be glorified.[f] 24 I tell you the truth, unless a kernel of wheat falls to the ground and dies,[g] it remains only a single seed. But if it dies, it produces many seeds. 25 The man who loves his life will lose it, while the man who hates his life in this world will keep it[h] for eternal life. 26 Whoever serves me must follow me; and where I am, my servant also will be.[i] My Father will honor the one who serves me.

27 "Now my heart is troubled,[j] and what shall I say? 'Father, save me from this hour'? No, it was for this very reason I came to this hour. 28 Father, glorify your name!"

Then a voice came from heaven,[k] "I have glorified it, and will glorify it again." 29 The crowd that was there and heard it said it had thundered; others said an angel had spoken to him.

30 Jesus said, "This voice was for your benefit,[l] not mine. 31 Now is the time for judgment on this world;[m] now the prince of this world[n] will be driven out. 32 But I, when I am lifted up from the earth,[o] will draw all men to myself." 33 He said this to show the kind of death he was going to die.[p]

34 The crowd spoke up, "We have heard from the Law that the Christ[d] will remain forever,[q] so how can you say, 'The Son of Man must be lifted up'? Who is this 'Son of Man'?"

35 Then Jesus told them, "You are going to have the light just a little while longer. Walk while you have the light,[r] before darkness overtakes you. The man who walks in the dark does not know where he is going. 36 Put your trust in the light while you have it, so that you may become sons of light."[s] When he had finished speaking, Jesus left and hid himself from them.[t]

## The Jews Continue in Their Unbelief

37 Even after Jesus had done all these miraculous signs in their presence, they still would not believe in him. 38 This was to fulfill the word of Isaiah the prophet:

"Lord, who has believed our message
and to whom has the arm of the Lord
been revealed?"[e][u]

**12:23** f Jn 13:32
**12:24** g 1Co 15:36
**12:25** h Mt 10:39
**12:26** i Jn 14:3
**12:27** j Mt 26:38,39
**12:28** k Mt 3:17
**12:30** l Jn 11:42
**12:31** m Jn 16:11 n Jn 14:30; Eph 2:2
**12:32** o Jn 3:14
**12:33** p Jn 18:32
**12:34** q Ps 110:4; Eze 37:25
**12:35** r Eph 5:8
**12:36** s Lk 16:8 t Jn 8:59
**12:38** u Isa 53:1

[a] 13 A Hebrew expression meaning "Save!" which became an exclamation of praise [b] 13 Psalm 118:25,26 [c] 15 Zech. 9:9
[d] 34 Or *Messiah* [e] 38 Isaiah 53:1

# Mary of Bethany

## The Unforgotten Woman

Overwhelmed by the cares of the world, African American women are frequently caring for children, elderly parents or even their extended families. Mary of Bethany is an example to be followed concerning priorities. She is portrayed as a disciple and a worshiper. As we will see, Jesus commended her actions by declaring that she knew what to choose and that she would not be forgotten.

Mary was often overshadowed by her siblings, Martha and Lazarus—especially by her sister. These sisters represent a duality found within all of us. Sometimes, we see some of Mary's attributes in our lives; at other times, some of Martha's. It is not a matter of good or bad, but rather good and better, concerning our decisions. There are choices and priorities, and hopefully we will make the better choice in a particular situation. We read in Luke 10:38–42 that Jesus affirmed Mary for making the better choice. There would always be tables to set and meals to prepare, but how many opportunities would there be to spend time with the Lord in one's own home?

Seated at the feet of Jesus, Mary was a true disciple. For the first-century Jew, this position symbolized a level of higher education, which was not the norm for women.

Another aspect of Mary's character is that of a worshiper. In John 12:1–3, Mary used costly perfume to anoint Jesus. Jesus said that her action would not be forgotten (see Mt 26:10–13). After being taught by Jesus, Mary seemed to somehow understand that Jesus had to endure the suffering of the cross. Her act of anointing Jesus symbolized his preparation for burial (see Jn 12:7–8). Could she have had a deeper understanding than her male counterparts? As both a disciple and a worshiper, Mary appears to have had the insight or intuition that Jesus would not always be with them. She seized the day and enjoyed being in his presence.

—A. Aubry

### reflection

*How do you seize the day by enjoying God's presence?*

*Walk in his presence throughout this day.*

### read

John 12:1–8; see also Matthew 26:6–13; Mark 14:1–9; Luke 10:38–42.

See also the Inspire Notes "True Joy," "Sacrificial Living" and "Commitment to God," and the Women of the Bible Note "Mary and Martha: Grieving Sisters."

For the next Women of the Bible note, go to page 1282.

**12:40** v Isa 6:10; Mt 13:13,15
**12:41** w Isa 6:1–4
**12:42** x Jn 7:13 y Jn 9:22
**12:43** z Jn 5:44
**12:44** a Mt 10:40
**12:45** b Jn 14:9
**12:46** c Jn 3:19
**12:47** d Jn 3:17
**12:49** e Jn 14:31
**13:1** f Jn 16:28
**13:3** g Jn 8:42

[39]For this reason they could not believe, because, as Isaiah says elsewhere:

> [40]"He has blinded their eyes
> and deadened their hearts,
> so they can neither see with their eyes,
> nor understand with their hearts,
> nor turn—and I would heal them."[a][v]

[41]Isaiah said this because he saw Jesus' glory[w] and spoke about him.

[42]Yet at the same time many even among the leaders believed in him. But because of the Pharisees[x] they would not confess their faith for fear they would be put out of the synagogue;[y] [43]for they loved praise from men more than praise from God.[z]

[44]Then Jesus cried out, "When a man believes in me, he does not believe in me only, but in the one who sent me.[a] [45]When he looks at me, he sees the one who sent me.[b] [46]I have come into the world as a light,[c] so that no one who believes in me should stay in darkness.

[47]"As for the person who hears my words but does not keep them, I do not judge him. For I did not come to judge the world, but to save it.[d] [48]There is a judge for the one who rejects me and does not accept my words; that very word which I spoke will condemn him at the last day. [49]For I did not speak of my own accord, but the Father who sent me commanded me[e] what to say and how to say it. [50]I know that his command leads to eternal life. So whatever I say is just what the Father has told me to say."

## Jesus Washes His Disciples' Feet

**13** It was just before the Passover Feast. Jesus knew that the time had come for him to leave this world and go to the Father.[f] Having loved his own who were in the world, he now showed them the full extent of his love.[b]

[2]The evening meal was being served, and the devil had already prompted Judas Iscariot, son of Simon, to betray Jesus. [3]Jesus knew that the Father had put all things under his power, and that he had come from God[g] and was returning to God; [4]so he got up from the meal, took off his outer clothing, and wrapped a towel around his waist. [5]After that, he poured water into a basin and began to wash his disciples' feet, drying them with the towel that was wrapped around him.

[6]He came to Simon Peter, who said to him, "Lord, are you going to wash my feet?"

[7]Jesus replied, "You do not realize now what I am doing, but later you will understand."

[8]"No," said Peter, "you shall never wash my feet."

Jesus answered, "Unless I wash you, you have no part with me."

[9]"Then, Lord," Simon Peter replied, "not just my feet but my hands and my head as well!"

[10]Jesus answered, "A person who has had a bath needs only to wash his feet; his whole body is clean. And you are clean,[h] though not every one of you." [11]For he knew who was going to betray him, and that was why he said not every one was clean.

[12]When he had finished washing their feet, he put on his clothes and returned to his place. "Do you understand what I have done for you?" he asked them. [13]"You call me 'Teacher' and 'Lord,'[i] and rightly so, for that is what I am. [14]Now that I, your Lord and Teacher, have washed your feet, you also should wash one another's feet. [15]I have set you an example that you should do as I have done for you. [16]I tell you the truth, no servant is greater than his master,[j] nor is a messenger greater than the one who sent him. [17]Now that you know these things, you will be blessed if you do them.[k]

## Jesus Predicts His Betrayal

[18]"I am not referring to all of you; I know those I have chosen. But this is to fulfill the scripture: 'He who shares my bread has lifted up his heel against me.'[c][l]

[19]"I am telling you now before it happens, so that when it does happen you will believe[m] that I am He. [20]I tell you the truth, whoever accepts anyone I send accepts me; and whoever accepts me accepts the one who sent me."[n]

[21]After he had said this, Jesus was troubled in spirit and testified, "I tell you the truth, one of you is going to betray me."

**13:10** h Jn 15:3
**13:13** i Php 2:11
**13:16** j Mt 10:24
**13:17** k Jas 1:25
**13:18** l Ps 41:9
**13:19** m Jn 14:29; 16:4
**13:20** n Mt 10:40; Lk 10:16

[a]40 Isaiah 6:10 [b]1 Or *he loved them to the last* [c]18 Psalm 41:9

# Inspire Leadership Focus

## SERVANT-LEADERSHIP

**In order to become an effective servant-leader, we must first understand what it means to become a servant-follower. A servant-follower is one who is willing to lay aside all personal plans and desires in order to obediently carry out the wishes and commands of the leader.**

In a culture in which women are in full pursuit of liberation, only a woman who has been liberated by Christ (see Gal 3:26–29) can effectively fulfill the role of a servant-follower and ultimately a servant-leader. God's love and the knowledge of his Word set women free from feelings of oppression, inferiority and insecurity. Through Christ we are liberated to become his joyful servants.

Once we've been liberated to serve, we must understand that God has not called us to be shy, passive servant-followers, but his ultimate plan is for us to blossom into mature servant-leaders who will carry out his will on earth regardless of our race or gender.

Jesus prepared the disciples to become servant-leaders with the simple demonstration of washing their feet (see Jn 13:5). Peter, the fiery disciple, couldn't understand why his master would stoop to the lowly task of washing a roomful of dirty feet. He proclaimed to Jesus, "You shall never wash my feet" (Jn 13:8). It is evident that Peter's definition of a leader was someone who never got his hands dirty and was to be served by his followers. But Jesus taught him, by example, that a real leader is called to serve others, even if it means cleaning up after a dinner meeting, using your own money to meet the budget or . . . washing a roomful of dirty feet.

The challenges of a servant-leader can be great, but we are not called to become the servants of fear, but the servants of faith—willing to say yes to God's call. As Jesus washed the feet of his disciples, he ended the lesson by saying, "Now that you know these things, you will be blessed if you do them" (see Jn 13:17).

—T. McFadden-Solomon

### read

John 13:1–17; see also Mark 10:35–45; 1 Corinthians 3:5–7. See also the Inspire Notes "Submission," "Responsible Decisions in Leadership," "Confidence," "Fear," "Sacrificial Living" and "Humility," and the Women of the Bible Notes "Deborah: An Uncommon Leader," "Anna: A Model of Spiritual Devotion," "Peter's Mother-in-Law: From Suffering to Service" and "Phoebe: A Faithful Messenger."

### WOMAN of COLOR

Reflect on how you follow Christ's servant-leader model in your daily life. How humble are you? Do you do the "dirty" work? Ask God to search your heart and reveal to you areas in which you need to be more like Christ.

For the next Inspire note, go to page 1264.

**13:23** o Jn 19:26; 20:2; 21:7,20
**13:27** p Lk 22:3
**13:29** q Jn 12:6
**13:31** r Jn 14:13; 1Pe 4:11
**13:34** s 1Jn 2:7–11 t Lev 19:18; 1Pe 1:22
**13:35** u 1Jn 4:20
**13:36** v Jn 21:18,19; 2Pe 1:14

22 His disciples stared at one another, at a loss to know which of them he meant. 23 One of them, the disciple whom Jesus loved,[o] was reclining next to him. 24 Simon Peter motioned to this disciple and said, "Ask him which one he means."

25 Leaning back against Jesus, he asked him, "Lord, who is it?"

26 Jesus answered, "It is the one to whom I will give this piece of bread when I have dipped it in the dish." Then, dipping the piece of bread, he gave it to Judas Iscariot, son of Simon. 27 As soon as Judas took the bread, Satan entered into him.[p]

"What you are about to do, do quickly," Jesus told him, 28 but no one at the meal understood why Jesus said this to him. 29 Since Judas had charge of the money,[q] some thought Jesus was telling him to buy what was needed for the Feast, or to give something to the poor. 30 As soon as Judas had taken the bread, he went out. And it was night.

## Jesus Predicts Peter's Denial

31 When he was gone, Jesus said, "Now is the Son of Man glorified and God is glorified in him.[r] 32 If God is glorified in him,[a] God will glorify the Son in himself, and will glorify him at once.

33 "My children, I will be with you only a little longer. You will look for me, and just as I told the Jews, so I tell you now: Where I am going, you cannot come.

34 "A new command[s] I give you: Love one another.[t] As I have loved you, so you must love one another. 35 By this all men will know that you are my disciples, if you love one another."[u]

36 Simon Peter asked him, "Lord, where are you going?"

Jesus replied, "Where I am going, you cannot follow now, but you will follow later."[v]

37 Peter asked, "Lord, why can't I follow you now? I will lay down my life for you."

38 Then Jesus answered, "Will you really lay down your life for me? I tell you the truth, before the rooster crows, you will disown me three times!

## Jesus Comforts His Disciples

14 "Do not let your hearts be troubled. Trust in God[b]; trust also in me. 2 In my Father's house are many rooms; if it were not so, I would have told you. I am going there[w] to prepare a place for you. 3 And if I go and prepare a place for you, I will come back and take you to be with me that you also may be where I am.[x] 4 You know the way to the place where I am going."

## Jesus the Way to the Father

5 Thomas said to him, "Lord, we don't know where you are going, so how can we know the way?"

6 Jesus answered, "I am the way[y] and the truth and the life. No one comes to the Father except through me. 7 If you really knew me, you would know[c] my Father as well. From now on, you do know him and have seen him."

8 Philip said, "Lord, show us the Father and that will be enough for us."

9 Jesus answered: "Don't you know me, Philip, even after I have been among you such a long time? Anyone who has seen me has seen the Father.[z] How can you say, 'Show us the Father'? 10 Don't you believe that I am in the Father, and that the Father is in me?[a] The words I say to you are not just my own. Rather, it is the Father, living in me, who is doing his work. 11 Believe me when I say that I am in the Father and the Father is in me; or at least believe on the evidence of the miracles themselves.[b] 12 I tell you the truth, anyone who has faith in me will do what I have been doing. He will do even greater things than these, because I am going to the Father. 13 And I will do whatever you ask in my name, so that the Son may bring glory to the Father. 14 You may ask me for anything in my name, and I will do it.

## Jesus Promises the Holy Spirit

15 "If you love me, you will obey what I command.[c] 16 And I will ask the Father, and he will give you another Counselor[d] to be with you forever— 17 the Spirit of truth.[e] The world cannot accept him,[f] because it neither sees him nor knows him. But you know him,

**14:2** w Jn 13:33,36
**14:3** x Jn 12:26
**14:6** y Jn 10:9
**14:9** z Jn 12:45
**14:10** a Jn 10:38
**14:11** b Jn 10:38
**14:15** c Jn 15:10; 1Jn 5:3
**14:16** d Jn 15:26
**14:17** e Jn 16:13; 1Jn 4:6 f 1Co 2:14

[a] 32 Many early manuscripts do not have *If God is glorified in him.* [b] 1 Or *You trust in God* [c] 7 Some early manuscripts *If you really have known me, you will know*

for he lives with you and will be[a] in you. 18I will not leave you as orphans; I will come to you.[g] 19Before long, the world will not see me anymore, but you will see me.[h] Because I live, you also will live. 20On that day you will realize that I am in my Father,[i] and you are in me, and I am in you. 21Whoever has my commands and obeys them, he is the one who loves me. He who loves me will be loved by my Father, and I too will love him and show myself to him."

22Then Judas (not Judas Iscariot) said, "But, Lord, why do you intend to show yourself to us and not to the world?"

23Jesus replied, "If anyone loves me, he will obey my teaching. My Father will love him, and we will come to him and make our home with him. 24He who does not love me will not obey my teaching. These words you hear are not my own; they belong to the Father who sent me.

25"All this I have spoken while still with you. 26But the Counselor,[j] the Holy Spirit, whom the Father will send in my name, will teach you all things[k] and will remind you of everything I have said to you. 27Peace I leave with you; my peace I give you.[l] I do not give to you as the world gives. Do not let your hearts be troubled and do not be afraid.

28"You heard me say, 'I am going away and I am coming back to you.'[m] If you loved me, you would be glad that I am going to the Father, for the Father is greater than I. 29I have told you now before it happens, so that when it does happen you will believe.[n] 30I will not speak with you much longer, for the prince of this world[o] is coming. He has no hold on me, 31but the world must learn that I love the Father and that I do exactly what my Father has commanded me.[p]

"Come now; let us leave.

## The Vine and the Branches

15 "I am the true vine,[q] and my Father is the gardener. 2He cuts off every branch in me that bears no fruit, while every branch that does bear fruit he prunes[b] so that it will be even more fruitful. 3You are already clean because of the word I have spoken to you.[r] 4Remain in me, and I will remain in you. No branch can bear fruit by itself; it must remain in the vine. Neither can you bear fruit unless you remain in me.

5"I am the vine; you are the branches. If a man remains in me and I in him, he will bear much fruit; apart from me you can do nothing. 6If anyone does not remain in me, he is like a branch that is thrown away and withers; such branches are picked up, thrown into the fire and burned. 7If you remain in me and my words remain in you, ask whatever you wish, and it will be given you. 8This is to my Father's glory, that you bear much fruit, showing yourselves to be my disciples.[s]

9"As the Father has loved me, so have I loved you. Now remain in my love. 10If you obey my commands,[t] you will remain in my love, just as I have obeyed my Father's commands and remain in his love. 11I have told you this so that my joy may be in you and that your joy may be complete. 12My command is this: Love each other as I have loved you.[u] 13Greater love has no one than this, that he lay down his life for his friends.[v] 14You are my friends if you do what I command.[w] 15I no longer call you servants, because a servant does not know his master's business. Instead, I have called you friends, for everything that I learned from my Father I have made known to you. 16You did not choose me, but I chose you and appointed you[x] to go and bear fruit—fruit that will last. Then the Father will give you whatever you ask in my name. 17This is my command: Love each other.

## The World Hates the Disciples

18"If the world hates you,[y] keep in mind that it hated me first. 19If you belonged to the world, it would love you as its own. As it is, you do not belong to the world, but I have chosen you out of the world. That is why the world hates you.[z] 20Remember the words I spoke to you: 'No servant is greater than his master.'[c] If they persecuted me, they will persecute you also. If they obeyed my teaching, they will obey yours also. 21They will treat you this way because of my name, for they do not know the One who sent me. 22If I had not come and spoken to them, they would not be guilty of sin. Now, however,

**14:18** g ver 3,28
**14:19** h Jn 16:16
**14:20** i Jn 10:38
**14:26** j Jn 15:26 k 1Jn 2:20,27
**14:27** l Php 4:7; Col 3:15
**14:28** m ver 2–4,18
**14:29** n Jn 13:19
**14:30** o Jn 12:31
**14:31** p Jn 10:18
**15:1** q Isa 5:1–7
**15:3** r Jn 13:10; Eph 5:26
**15:8** s Jn 8:31
**15:10** t Jn 14:15
**15:12** u Jn 13:34
**15:13** v Jn 10:11; Ro 5:7,8
**15:14** w Mt 12:50
**15:16** x Jn 13:18
**15:18** y 1Jn 3:13
**15:19** z Jn 17:14

[a]17 Some early manuscripts *and is* [b]2 The Greek for *prunes* also means *cleans.* [c]20 John 13:16

# Inspire

## PEACE

Most people in today's world are searching for peace. Some think peace comes when we are free of financial cares; when we have good jobs or are doing well in our entrepreneurial endeavors; when we can point to large, comfortable places to call home; when we enjoy the company of significant others; or when we are in charge of our lives. Others attempt to escape to a place of peace by smoking, drinking, using drugs, having sex or wielding power.

We may indeed achieve a "high" from the things we believe bring us peace. When the rush of that high is gone, though, we are desperate for its return. We repeat the cycle, become depressed and talk ourselves into being comfortable and content with the habits we have formed. We shrug and say to ourselves, "This is life."

But this is *not* the fulfilled life God has in mind for us. God yearns for each of us to learn that true and lasting peace does not come about through worldly possessions or pleasures. To find true peace we must go to its source.

Jesus said, "Peace I leave with you; my peace I give you. I do not give to you as the world gives. Do not let your hearts be troubled and do not be afraid" (Jn 14:27). Learning God's Word and relying upon God will bring real and lasting peace. Applying God's Word helps us to place all worldly necessities and pleasures in their proper places.

Living by God's Word teaches us that, although in this world we will have trials, tribulations and disappointments (as well as pleasures, successes and happiness), we can have peace in any situation. Why? Because the peace given to us in our Lord and Savior Jesus Christ is the basis of our contentment in whatever circumstances we find ourselves (see Php 4:10–13). This is a peace that takes us far beyond our human ability to comprehend or explain. The secret of overcoming anxiety (the absence of peace) is to constantly rejoice in the Lord and to pray, giving thanks for everything he continues to do for us. When we come to acknowledge and accept that God is taking care of our affairs, we can allow the peace of God to fill our lives.

—C. Richards

### read

John 14:1–27; 16:17–33; Galatians 5:22–23; Philippians 4:4–13; Colossians 3:12–17.

See also the Inspire Notes "Suffering," "Overcoming Abuse," "Confidence," "Fear," "Waiting on God" and "The Paradox of Life and Suffering," and the Women of the Bible Notes "Hannah: What Do You Do When God Says 'No'?" "The Persistent Widow: Always Pray" and "Rhoda: Doing Her Duty."

### WOMAN of COLOR

To what degree are you experiencing peace in your life? What or who is the source of your peace?

For the next Inspire note, go to page 1266.

15:22 a Jn 9:41
15:25 b Ps 35:19; 69:4
15:26 c Jn 14:17 d 1Jn 5:7
15:27 e Lk 24:48
16:1 f Mt 11:6
16:2 g Jn 9:22 h Ac 26:9,10
16:3 i Jn 15:21
16:4 j Jn 13:19
16:5 k Jn 7:33
16:7 l Jn 14:16,26
16:10 m Ac 3:14
16:13 n Jn 14:17 o Jn 14:26

they have no excuse for their sin.[a] 23 He who hates me hates my Father as well. 24 If I had not done among them what no one else did, they would not be guilty of sin. But now they have seen these miracles, and yet they have hated both me and my Father. 25 But this is to fulfill what is written in their Law: 'They hated me without reason.'[a][b]

26 "When the Counselor comes, whom I will send to you from the Father, the Spirit of truth[c] who goes out from the Father, he will testify about me.[d] 27 And you also must testify,[e] for you have been with me from the beginning.

16 "All this I have told you so that you will not go astray.[f] 2 They will put you out of the synagogue;[g] in fact, a time is coming when anyone who kills you will think he is offering a service to God.[h] 3 They will do such things because they have not known the Father or me.[i] 4 I have told you this, so that when the time comes you will remember[j] that I warned you. I did not tell you this at first because I was with you.

## The Work of the Holy Spirit

5 "Now I am going to him who sent me,[k] yet none of you asks me, 'Where are you going?' 6 Because I have said these things, you are filled with grief. 7 But I tell you the truth: It is for your good that I am going away. Unless I go away, the Counselor[l] will not come to you; but if I go, I will send him to you. 8 When he comes, he will convict the world of guilt[b] in regard to sin and righteousness and judgment: 9 in regard to sin, because men do not believe in me; 10 in regard to righteousness,[m] because I am going to the Father, where you can see me no longer; 11 and in regard to judgment, because the prince of this world now stands condemned.

12 "I have much more to say to you, more than you can now bear. 13 But when he, the Spirit of truth,[n] comes, he will guide you into all truth.[o] He will not speak on his own; he will speak only what he hears, and he will tell you what is yet to come. 14 He will bring glory to me by taking from what is mine and making it known to you. 15 All that belongs to the Father is mine. That is why I said the Spirit will take from what is mine and make it known to you.

16 "In a little while you will see me no more, and then after a little while you will see me."[p]

*God,*

*help me yield to your indwelling Spirit. Help me to welcome every situation in my life as a growth opportunity. Teach me how to show loving-kindness to all those with whom I come in contact. In Jesus' name,*

*Amen*

JOHN 16:5–16

## The Disciples' Grief Will Turn to Joy

17 Some of his disciples said to one another, "What does he mean by saying, 'In a little while you will see me no more, and then after a little while you will see me,' and 'Because I am going to the Father'?" 18 They kept asking, "What does he mean by 'a little while'? We don't understand what he is saying."

19 Jesus saw that they wanted to ask him about this, so he said to them, "Are you asking one another what I meant when I said, 'In a little while you will see me no more, and then after a little while you will see me'? 20 I tell you the truth, you will weep and mourn while the world rejoices. You will grieve, but your grief will turn to joy.[q] 21 A woman giving birth to a child has pain[r] because her time has come; but when her baby is born she forgets the anguish because of her joy that a child is born into the world. 22 So with you: Now is your time of grief, but I will see you again and you will rejoice, and no one will take away your joy. 23 In that day you will no longer ask me anything. I tell you the truth, my Father will give you whatever you ask in my name.[s] 24 Until now you have not asked for anything in my

16:16 p Jn 14:18–24
16:20 q Jn 20:20
16:21 r 1Th 5:3
16:23 s Mt 7:7; Jn 15:16

[a]25 Psalms 35:19; 69:4 [b]8 Or *will expose the guilt of the world*

Inspire

## SACRIFICIAL LIVING

"Be strong and take heart and wait for the LORD" (Ps 27:14). Sometimes I believe I can almost hear the souls of women of color crying out, "How long, Lord, must we wait?" We have already waited for countless years for full access to the opportunities and benefits our nation has to offer. We have sacrificed our desires and needs for the good of the whole, and still we are in many ways disenfranchised.

However, the Word instructs us that the "system" into which we are to seek inclusion is the kingdom of God. No earthly government or culture can begin to compare to that realm.

Even though we, by earthly standards, have sacrificed a great deal and are still being asked to sacrifice more, the benefits we forgo could never compare to the sacrifice of Christ Jesus. Just as Jesus laid down his life for us, we are called to lay down our lives for others (see Jn 15:13), offering up our lives completely and wholeheartedly, according to God's will. We would do well to keep in the forefront of our minds that we serve God when we serve God's people.

Women of color have a unique opportunity to illustrate to the rest of Christ's body, as well as to the unsaved world around us, the godly principle of denying ourselves and living for Christ and others (see Mk 8:34–37; Jn 15:12–17). This is the legacy of our ancestors, a legacy not of worldly riches but of sacrifice, service and love for Jesus and for his church. We are called to remove ourselves from the standards of success set by the world and to look instead to the Word of God for our validation (see Jn 13:12–17; Ro 12:1–2). While we grapple with the sacrificial tasks of helping the oppressed (even when we ourselves are suffering oppression), fighting for justice and serving our fellow sisters and brothers, we are to work as though we are working for Jesus, as indeed we are (see Col 3:22–24). The beauty is this: While we are laboring, Jesus is at our side, helping us carry our loads.

—A. MANUEL

**read**

John 15:9–17; see also John 13:1–17; Romans 12:1–2,9–21; 1 John 3:11–24.

See also the Inspire Notes "Purposeful Giving" and "Goodness," and the Women of the Bible Notes "The Widow's Offering: Selfless Giving," "Mary, The Mother of James and Joses: Sacrificing for Christ" and "Claudia: A Sincere Supporter."

**WOMAN of COLOR**

How are you serving others?

For the next Inspire note, go to page 1269.

**16:24**
t Jn 15:11
**16:25**
u Mt 13:34; Jn 10:6
**16:27**
v Jn 14:21,23
**16:28**
w Jn 13:3
**16:32**
x Mt 26:31
**16:33**
y Jn 14:27
z Ro 8:37
**17:1**
a Jn 12:23
**17:2**
b Da 7:14
**17:4**
c Jn 13:31
d Jn 4:34
**17:5**
e Php 2:6
**17:6**
f Jn 6:37,39

name. Ask and you will receive, and your
joy will be complete.[t]
25“Though I have been speaking figura-
tively,[u] a time is coming when I will no lon-
ger use this kind of language but will tell
you plainly about my Father. 26In that day
you will ask in my name. I am not saying
that I will ask the Father on your behalf.
27No, the Father himself loves you because
you have loved me[v] and have believed that
I came from God. 28I came from the Father
and entered the world; now I am leaving the
world and going back to the Father.”[w]
29Then Jesus' disciples said, “Now you
are speaking clearly and without figures of
speech. 30Now we can see that you know all
things and that you do not even need to have
anyone ask you questions. This makes us be-
lieve that you came from God.”
31“You believe at last!”[a] Jesus answered.
32“But a time is coming, and has come,
when you will be scattered,[x] each to his own
home. You will leave me all alone. Yet I am
not alone, for my Father is with me.
33“I have told you these things, so that in
me you may have peace.[y] In this world you
will have trouble. But take heart! I have over-
come[z] the world.”

## Jesus Prays for Himself

17 After Jesus said this, he looked to-
ward heaven and prayed:

“Father, the time has come. Glorify
your Son, that your Son may glorify
you.[a] 2For you granted him authority
over all people that he might give eter-
nal life to all those you have given
him.[b] 3Now this is eternal life: that
they may know you, the only true God,
and Jesus Christ, whom you have sent.
4I have brought you glory[c] on earth
by completing the work you gave me
to do.[d] 5And now, Father, glorify me
in your presence with the glory I had
with you[e] before the world began.

## Jesus Prays for His Disciples

6“I have revealed you[b] to those
whom you gave me[f] out of the world.
They were yours; you gave them to
me and they have obeyed your word.
7Now they know that everything you
have given me comes from you. 8For
I gave them the words you gave me
and they accepted them. They knew
with certainty that I came from you,[g]
and they believed that you sent me. 9I
pray for them. I am not praying for the
world, but for those you have given me,
for they are yours. 10All I have is yours,
and all you have is mine.[h] And glory
has come to me through them. 11I will
remain in the world no longer, but
they are still in the world,[i] and I am
coming to you.[j] Holy Father, protect
them by the power of your name—the
name you gave me—so that they may
be one as we are one. 12While I was
with them, I protected them and kept
them safe by that name you gave me.
None has been lost except the one
doomed to destruction[k] so that Scrip-
ture would be fulfilled.
13“I am coming to you now, but
I say these things while I am still in
the world, so that they may have the
full measure of my joy within them.
14I have given them your word and
the world has hated them, for they
are not of the world any more than I
am of the world.[l] 15My prayer is not
that you take them out of the world
but that you protect them from the
evil one. 16They are not of the world,
even as I am not of it. 17Sanctify[c] them
by the truth; your word is truth. 18As
you sent me into the world, I have sent
them into the world.[m] 19For them I
sanctify myself, that they too may be
truly sanctified.

## Jesus Prays for All Believers

20“My prayer is not for them alone. I
pray also for those who will believe in
me through their message, 21that all of
them may be one, Father, just as you
are in me and I am in you.[n] May they
also be in us so that the world may be-
lieve that you have sent me. 22I have
given them the glory that you gave

**17:8**
g Jn 16:27
**17:10**
h Jn 16:15
**17:11**
i Jn 13:1
j Jn 7:33
**17:12**
k Jn 6:70
**17:14**
l Jn 8:23
**17:18**
m Jn 20:21
**17:21**
n Jn 10:38

[a]31 Or *“Do you now believe?”* [b]6 Greek *your name*; also in verse 26 [c]17 Greek *hagiazo (set apart for sacred use* or *make holy)*; also in verse 19

**17:22** o Jn 14:20
**17:24** p Jn 12:26 q ver 5
**17:25** r Jn 15:21 s Jn 7:29; 16:27
**17:26** t ver 6 u Jn 15:9
**18:1** v 2Sa 15:23
**18:2** w Lk 21:37; 22:39
**18:3** x Ac 1:16
**18:7** y ver 4
**18:9** z Jn 17:12

me, that they may be one as we are
one:[o] 23I in them and you in me. May
they be brought to complete unity to
let the world know that you sent me
and have loved them even as you have
loved me.
24"Father, I want those you have
given me to be with me where I am,[p]
and to see my glory, the glory you have
given me because you loved me before
the creation of the world.[q]
25"Righteous Father, though the
world does not know you,[r] I know you,
and they know that you have sent me.[s]
26I have made you known to them,[t]
and will continue to make you known
in order that the love you have for me
may be in them[u] and that I myself may
be in them."

## Jesus Arrested

18 When he had finished praying, Jesus
left with his disciples and crossed
the Kidron Valley.[v] On the other side there
was an olive grove, and he and his disciples
went into it.
2Now Judas, who betrayed him, knew the
place, because Jesus had often met there
with his disciples.[w] 3So Judas came to the
grove, guiding[x] a detachment of soldiers
and some officials from the chief priests
and Pharisees. They were carrying torches,
lanterns and weapons.
4Jesus, knowing all that was going to
happen to him, went out and asked them,
"Who is it you want?"
5"Jesus of Nazareth," they replied.
"I am he," Jesus said. (And Judas the trai-
tor was standing there with them.) 6When
Jesus said, "I am he," they drew back and
fell to the ground.
7Again he asked them, "Who is it you
want?"[y]
And they said, "Jesus of Nazareth."
8"I told you that I am he," Jesus answered.
"If you are looking for me, then let these
men go." 9This happened so that the words
he had spoken would be fulfilled: "I have
not lost one of those you gave me."[a][z]
10Then Simon Peter, who had a sword,
drew it and struck the high priest's servant,
cutting off his right ear. (The servant's
name was Malchus.)
11Jesus commanded Peter, "Put your
sword away! Shall I not drink the cup[a] the
Father has given me?"

## Jesus Taken to Annas

12Then the detachment of soldiers with
its commander and the Jewish officials
arrested Jesus. They bound him 13and
brought him first to Annas, who was the
father-in-law of Caiaphas, the high priest
that year. 14Caiaphas was the one who had
advised the Jews that it would be good if one
man died for the people.[b]

## Peter's First Denial

15Simon Peter and another disciple were
following Jesus. Because this disciple was
known to the high priest, he went with Jesus
into the high priest's courtyard,[c] 16but Peter
had to wait outside at the door. The other
disciple, who was known to the high priest,
came back, spoke to the girl on duty there
and brought Peter in.
17"You are not one of his disciples, are
you?" the girl at the door asked Peter.
He replied, "I am not."
18It was cold, and the servants and offi-
cials stood around a fire[d] they had made to
keep warm. Peter also was standing with
them, warming himself.[e]

## The High Priest Questions Jesus

19Meanwhile, the high priest questioned
Jesus about his disciples and his teaching.
20"I have spoken openly to the world,"
Jesus replied. "I always taught in syna-
gogues or at the temple,[f] where all the Jews
come together. I said nothing in secret.[g]
21Why question me? Ask those who heard
me. Surely they know what I said."
22When Jesus said this, one of the offi-
cials nearby struck him in the face.[h] "Is
this the way you answer the high priest?"
he demanded.
23"If I said something wrong," Jesus re-
plied, "testify as to what is wrong. But if I
spoke the truth, why did you strike me?"[i]
24Then Annas sent him, still bound, to Caia-
phas the high priest.[b]

**18:11** a Mt 20:22
**18:14** b Jn 11:49–51
**18:15** c Mt 26:58; Mk 14:54; Lk 22:54
**18:18** d Jn 21:9 e Mk 14:54,67
**18:20** f Mt 26:55 g Jn 7:26
**18:22** h Jn 19:3
**18:23** i Ac 23:2–5

[a]9 John 6:39 [b]24 Or *(Now Annas had sent him, still bound, to Caiaphas the high priest.)*

18:25 j ver 18

## Peter's Second and Third Denials

25 As Simon Peter stood warming himself,[j]
he was asked, "You are not one of his disci-
ples, are you?"
He denied it, saying, "I am not."
26 One of the high priest's servants, a rela-
tive of the man whose ear Peter had cut off,
challenged him, "Didn't I see you with him
in the olive grove?" 27 Again Peter denied it,
and at that moment a rooster began to crow.[k]

18:27 k Jn 13:38

*Inspire*

## INTIMACY: RELATIONSHIPS WITH OTHER CHRISTIANS

The most fitting definition of intimacy is, perhaps, "the genuine, open and free communication of one heart to another." The word *intimacy* does not appear in Scripture, yet it is evident from many passages that God is interested in the kind of genuine relationship that intimacy denotes. He desires it in his relationship with his people as well as in the personal connections of individuals with family, friends and other Christians. True intimacy always involves a spiritual dimension, although this degree of understanding and compatibility sometimes eludes even our most treasured relationships. Without it, however, a relationship is compromised.

Intimacy is an essential, sustaining element of our lives. Newborn babies crave intimate contact as much as they desire milk. Without such closeness, in fact, they cannot thrive or, ultimately, even survive. Every human heart yearns for the opportunity to "know fully, even as [we are] fully known" (1Co 13:12) because this is how we were created. When human or spiritual intimacy is missing, we are incomplete and attempt to fill that void with people, things or activities that are less than satisfying.

While we cannot be intimate with a host of people, there is a level of closeness or communion that Christians can enjoy with each other based upon our common heritage and faith. This kind of intimate love is not superficial but comes from the heart (see 1Pe 1:22). Jesus desires that all members of the church share in this kind of closeness, a fellowship that allows a watching world to see a different way of relating to one another. His prayer was that we would be one, knitted together in love, just as he and the Father are one (see Jn 17:20–23). On the eve of his death, Jesus prayed on our behalf: "May they be brought to complete unity to let the world know that you sent me and have loved them even as you have loved me" (Jn 17:23). Why not pledge right now to live as Jesus desired and prayed?

—E. Alexander

For the next Inspire note, go to page 1278.

### read

John 17:6–26; see also John 11:17–36; 1 Corinthians 13:1–13.

See also the Inspire Notes "Intimate Friendships," "Loneliness," "Friendship" and "What Is Intimacy?" and the Women of the Bible Notes "Naomi: Call Me Bitter" and "Ruth: A Model of Friendship and Sisterhood."

### WOMAN of COLOR

With whom are you intimate—or have you erected barriers to prevent such closeness?

## Jesus Before Pilate

28 Then the Jews led Jesus from Caiaphas to the palace of the Roman governor.[l] By now it was early morning, and to avoid ceremonial uncleanness the Jews did not enter the palace; they wanted to be able to eat the Passover.[m] 29 So Pilate came out to them and asked, "What charges are you bringing against this man?"

30 "If he were not a criminal," they replied, "we would not have handed him over to you."

31 Pilate said, "Take him yourselves and judge him by your own law."

"But we have no right to execute anyone," the Jews objected. 32 This happened so that the words Jesus had spoken indicating the kind of death he was going to die[n] would be fulfilled.

33 Pilate then went back inside the palace,[o] summoned Jesus and asked him, "Are you the king of the Jews?"[p]

34 "Is that your own idea," Jesus asked, "or did others talk to you about me?"

35 "Am I a Jew?" Pilate replied. "It was your people and your chief priests who handed you over to me. What is it you have done?"

36 Jesus said, "My kingdom is not of this world. If it were, my servants would fight to prevent my arrest by the Jews.[q] But now my kingdom is from another place."[r]

37 "You are a king, then!" said Pilate.

Jesus answered, "You are right in saying I am a king. In fact, for this reason I was born, and for this I came into the world, to testify to the truth. Everyone on the side of truth listens to me."[s]

38 "What is truth?" Pilate asked. With this he went out again to the Jews and said, "I find no basis for a charge against him.[t] 39 But it is your custom for me to release to you one prisoner at the time of the Passover. Do you want me to release 'the king of the Jews'?"

40 They shouted back, "No, not him! Give us Barabbas!" Now Barabbas had taken part in a rebellion.[u]

## Jesus Sentenced to Be Crucified

**19** Then Pilate took Jesus and had him flogged.[v] 2 The soldiers twisted together a crown of thorns and put it on his head. They clothed him in a purple robe 3 and went up to him again and again, saying, "Hail, king of the Jews!" And they struck him in the face.

4 Once more Pilate came out and said to the Jews, "Look, I am bringing him out[w] to you to let you know that I find no basis for a charge against him."[x] 5 When Jesus came out wearing the crown of thorns and the purple robe, Pilate said to them, "Here is the man!"

6 As soon as the chief priests and their officials saw him, they shouted, "Crucify! Crucify!"

But Pilate answered, "You take him and crucify him.[y] As for me, I find no basis for a charge against him."

7 The Jews insisted, "We have a law, and according to that law he must die,[z] because he claimed to be the Son of God."[a]

8 When Pilate heard this, he was even more afraid, 9 and he went back inside the palace. "Where do you come from?" he asked Jesus, but Jesus gave him no answer. 10 "Do you refuse to speak to me?" Pilate said. "Don't you realize I have power either to free you or to crucify you?"

11 Jesus answered, "You would have no power over me if it were not given to you from above. Therefore the one who handed me over to you[b] is guilty of a greater sin."

12 From then on, Pilate tried to set Jesus free, but the Jews kept shouting, "If you let this man go, you are no friend of Caesar. Anyone who claims to be a king[c] opposes Caesar."

13 When Pilate heard this, he brought Jesus out and sat down on the judge's seat at a place known as the Stone Pavement (which in Aramaic is Gabbatha). 14 It was the day of Preparation[d] of Passover Week, about the sixth hour.[e]

"Here is your king,"[f] Pilate said to the Jews.

15 But they shouted, "Take him away! Take him away! Crucify him!"

"Shall I crucify your king?" Pilate asked.

"We have no king but Caesar," the chief priests answered.

16 Finally Pilate handed him over to them to be crucified.[g]

**18:28** l Mt27:2; Mk15:1; Lk23:1 m Jn11:55
**18:32** n Mt20:19; Jn12:32,33
**18:33** o Jn19:9 p Lk23:3
**18:36** q Mt26:53 r Jn6:15
**18:37** s Jn8:47; 1Jn4:6
**18:38** t Lk23:4; Jn19:4,6
**18:40** u Ac3:14
**19:1** v Mt27:26
**19:4** w Jn18:38 x ver6
**19:6** y Ac3:13
**19:7** z Lev24:16 a Mt26:63–66; Jn5:18; 10:33
**19:11** b Jn18:28–30
**19:12** c Lk23:2
**19:14** d Mt27:62 e Mk15:25 f ver19,21
**19:16** g Mt27:26; Mk15:15; Lk23:25

## The Crucifixion

So the soldiers took charge of Jesus. [17]Carrying his own cross,[h] he went out to the place of the Skull[i] (which in Aramaic is called Golgotha). [18]Here they crucified him, and with him two others—one on each side and Jesus in the middle.

[19]Pilate had a notice prepared and fastened to the cross. It read: JESUS OF NAZARETH, THE KING OF THE JEWS. [20]Many of the Jews read this sign, for the place where Jesus was crucified was near the city, and the sign was written in Aramaic, Latin and Greek. [21]The chief priests of the Jews protested to Pilate, "Do not write 'The King of the Jews,' but that this man claimed to be king of the Jews."[j]

[22]Pilate answered, "What I have written, I have written."

[23]When the soldiers crucified Jesus, they took his clothes, dividing them into four shares, one for each of them, with the undergarment remaining. This garment was seamless, woven in one piece from top to bottom.

[24]"Let's not tear it," they said to one another. "Let's decide by lot who will get it."

This happened that the scripture might be fulfilled which said,

> "They divided my garments among them
> and cast lots for my clothing."[a][k]

So this is what the soldiers did.

[25]Near the cross[l] of Jesus stood his mother, his mother's sister, Mary the wife of Clopas, and Mary Magdalene.[m] [26]When Jesus saw his mother there, and the disciple whom he loved[n] standing nearby, he said to his mother, "Dear woman, here is your son," [27]and to the disciple, "Here is your mother." From that time on, this disciple took her into his home.

## The Death of Jesus

[28]Later, knowing that all was now completed,[o] and so that the Scripture would be fulfilled, Jesus said, "I am thirsty." [29]A jar of wine vinegar[p] was there, so they soaked a sponge in it, put the sponge on a stalk of the hyssop plant, and lifted it to Jesus' lips. [30]When he had received the drink, Jesus said, "It is finished."[q] With that, he bowed his head and gave up his spirit.

[31]Now it was the day of Preparation, and the next day was to be a special Sabbath. Because the Jews did not want the bodies left on the crosses[r] during the Sabbath, they asked Pilate to have the legs broken and the bodies taken down. [32]The soldiers therefore came and broke the legs of the first man who had been crucified with Jesus, and then those of the other. [33]But when they came to Jesus and found that he was already dead, they did not break his legs. [34]Instead, one of the soldiers pierced Jesus' side with a spear, bringing a sudden flow of blood and water.[s] [35]The man who saw it has given testimony, and his testimony is true.[t] He knows that he tells the truth, and he testifies so that you also may believe. [36]These things happened so that the scripture would be fulfilled: "Not one of his bones will be broken,"[b][u] [37]and, as another scripture says, "They will look on the one they have pierced."[c][v]

## The Burial of Jesus

[38]Later, Joseph of Arimathea asked Pilate for the body of Jesus. Now Joseph was a disciple of Jesus, but secretly because he feared the Jews. With Pilate's permission, he came and took the body away. [39]He was accompanied by Nicodemus,[w] the man who earlier had visited Jesus at night. Nicodemus brought a mixture of myrrh and aloes, about seventy-five pounds.[d] [40]Taking Jesus' body, the two of them wrapped it, with the spices, in strips of linen.[x] This was in accordance with Jewish burial customs.[y] [41]At the place where Jesus was crucified, there was a garden, and in the garden a new tomb, in which no one had ever been laid. [42]Because it was the Jewish day of Preparation[z] and since the tomb was nearby, they laid Jesus there.

## The Empty Tomb

20 Early on the first day of the week, while it was still dark, Mary Magdalene went to the tomb and saw that the stone had been removed from the entrance.[a] [2]So she came running to Simon Peter and the

**19:17** h Lk 23:26 i Lk 23:33
**19:21** j ver 14
**19:24** k Ps 22:18
**19:25** l Mt 27:55,56; Mk 15:40,41; Lk 23:49 m Lk 24:18
**19:26** n Jn 13:23
**19:28** o Jn 13:1
**19:29** p Ps 69:21
**19:30** q Jn 17:4
**19:31** r Dt 21:23
**19:34** s 1Jn 5:6,8
**19:35** t Jn 15:27
**19:36** u Ex 12:46; Nu 9:12; Ps 34:20
**19:37** v Zec 12:10
**19:39** w Jn 3:1
**19:40** x Lk 24:12 y Mt 26:12
**19:42** z ver 14,31
**20:1** a Mt 27:60,66

[a]24 Psalm 22:18 [b]36 Exodus 12:46; Num. 9:12; Psalm 34:20 [c]37 Zech. 12:10 [d]39 Greek *a hundred litrai* (about 34 kilograms)

20:2 b Jn 13:23
20:3 c Lk 24:12
20:5 d Jn 19:40
20:12 e Mk 16:5
20:14 f Mk 16:9 g Jn 21:4
20:17 h Mt 28:10 i Jn 7:33
20:18 j Lk 24:10,22,23

other disciple, the one Jesus loved,[b] and
said, "They have taken the Lord out of the
tomb, and we don't know where they have
put him!"
3 So Peter and the other disciple started
for the tomb.[c] 4 Both were running, but the
other disciple outran Peter and reached the
tomb first. 5 He bent over and looked in at
the strips of linen[d] lying there but did not
go in. 6 Then Simon Peter, who was behind
him, arrived and went into the tomb. He saw
the strips of linen lying there, 7 as well as the
burial cloth that had been around Jesus'
head. The cloth was folded up by itself, sep-
arate from the linen. 8 Finally the other dis-
ciple, who had reached the tomb first, also
went inside. He saw and believed. 9 (They
still did not understand from Scripture that
Jesus had to rise from the dead.)

## Jesus Appears to Mary Magdalene

10 Then the disciples went back to their
homes, 11 but Mary stood outside the tomb
crying. As she wept, she bent over to look
into the tomb 12 and saw two angels in
white,[e] seated where Jesus' body had been,
one at the head and the other at the foot.
13 They asked her, "Woman, why are
you crying?"
"They have taken my Lord away," she
said, "and I don't know where they have put
him." 14 At this, she turned around and saw
Jesus standing there,[f] but she did not realize
that it was Jesus.[g]
15 "Woman," he said, "why are you cry-
ing? Who is it you are looking for?"
Thinking he was the gardener, she
said, "Sir, if you have carried him away,
tell me where you have put him, and I will
get him."
16 Jesus said to her, "Mary."
She turned toward him and cried out
in Aramaic, "Rabboni!" (which means
Teacher).
17 Jesus said, "Do not hold on to me, for
I have not yet returned to the Father. Go in-
stead to my brothers[h] and tell them, 'I am
returning to my Father[i] and your Father, to
my God and your God.'"
18 Mary Magdalene went to the disciples[j]
with the news: "I have seen the Lord!" And
she told them that he had said these things
to her.

## Jesus Appears to His Disciples

19 On the evening of that first day of the
week, when the disciples were together,
with the doors locked for fear of the Jews,
Jesus came and stood among them and said,
"Peace be with you!"[k] 20 After he said this,
he showed them his hands and side. The
disciples were overjoyed[l] when they saw
the Lord.
21 Again Jesus said, "Peace be with you!
As the Father has sent me, I am sending
you."[m] 22 And with that he breathed on them
and said, "Receive the Holy Spirit. 23 If you
forgive anyone his sins, they are forgiven;
if you do not forgive them, they are not
forgiven."[n]

## Jesus Appears to Thomas

24 Now Thomas[o] (called Didymus), one of
the Twelve, was not with the disciples when
Jesus came. 25 So the other disciples told
him, "We have seen the Lord!"
But he said to them, "Unless I see the nail
marks in his hands and put my finger where
the nails were, and put my hand into his
side,[p] I will not believe it."
26 A week later his disciples were in the
house again, and Thomas was with them.
Though the doors were locked, Jesus came
and stood among them and said, "Peace
be with you!" 27 Then he said to Thomas,
"Put your finger here; see my hands. Reach
out your hand and put it into my side. Stop
doubting and believe."[q]
28 Thomas said to him, "My Lord and my
God!"
29 Then Jesus told him, "Because you
have seen me, you have believed; blessed
are those who have not seen and yet have
believed."[r]
30 Jesus did many other miraculous signs
in the presence of his disciples, which are
not recorded in this book.[s] 31 But these are
written that you may[a] believe[t] that Jesus is
the Christ, the Son of God, and that by be-
lieving you may have life in his name.

20:19 k Lk 24:36–39
20:20 l Jn 16:20,22
20:21 m Mt 28:19; Jn 17:18
20:23 n Mt 16:19; 18:18
20:24 o Jn 11:16
20:25 p ver 20
20:27 q Lk 24:40
20:29 r 1Pe 1:8
20:30 s Jn 21:25
20:31 t Jn 3:15

[a] 31 Some manuscripts *may continue to*

## Jesus and the Miraculous Catch of Fish

**21** Afterward Jesus appeared again to his disciples,[u] by the Sea of Tiberias.[a][v] It happened this way: 2 Simon Peter, Thomas (called Didymus), Nathanael[w] from Cana in Galilee, the sons of Zebedee,[x] and two other disciples were together. 3 "I'm going out to fish," Simon Peter told them, and they said, "We'll go with you." So they went out and got into the boat, but that night they caught nothing.[y]

4 Early in the morning, Jesus stood on the shore, but the disciples did not realize that it was Jesus.[z]

5 He called out to them, "Friends, haven't you any fish?"

"No," they answered.

6 He said, "Throw your net on the right side of the boat and you will find some." When they did, they were unable to haul the net in because of the large number of fish.[a]

7 Then the disciple whom Jesus loved[b] said to Peter, "It is the Lord!" As soon as Simon Peter heard him say, "It is the Lord," he wrapped his outer garment around him (for he had taken it off) and jumped into the water. 8 The other disciples followed in the boat, towing the net full of fish, for they were not far from shore, about a hundred yards.[b] 9 When they landed, they saw a fire of burning coals there with fish on it, and some bread.

10 Jesus said to them, "Bring some of the fish you have just caught."

11 Simon Peter climbed aboard and dragged the net ashore. It was full of large fish, 153, but even with so many the net was not torn. 12 Jesus said to them, "Come and have breakfast." None of the disciples dared ask him, "Who are you?" They knew it was the Lord. 13 Jesus came, took the bread and gave it to them, and did the same with the fish. 14 This was now the third time Jesus appeared to his disciples[c] after he was raised from the dead.

## Jesus Reinstates Peter

15 When they had finished eating, Jesus said to Simon Peter, "Simon son of John, do you truly love me more than these?"

"Yes, Lord," he said, "you know that I love you."[d]

Jesus said, "Feed my lambs."

16 Again Jesus said, "Simon son of John, do you truly love me?"

He answered, "Yes, Lord, you know that I love you."

Jesus said, "Take care of my sheep."[e]

17 The third time he said to him, "Simon son of John, do you love me?"

Peter was hurt because Jesus asked him the third time, "Do you love me?" He said, "Lord, you know all things;[f] you know that I love you."

Jesus said, "Feed my sheep. 18 I tell you the truth, when you were younger you dressed yourself and went where you wanted; but when you are old you will stretch out your hands, and someone else will dress you and lead you where you do not want to go." 19 Jesus said this to indicate the kind of death by which Peter would glorify God.[g] Then he said to him, "Follow me!"

20 Peter turned and saw that the disciple whom Jesus loved was following them. (This was the one who had leaned back against Jesus at the supper and had said, "Lord, who is going to betray you?")[h] 21 When Peter saw him, he asked, "Lord, what about him?"

22 Jesus answered, "If I want him to remain alive until I return,[i] what is that to you? You must follow me." 23 Because of this, the rumor spread among the brothers[j] that this disciple would not die. But Jesus did not say that he would not die; he only said, "If I want him to remain alive until I return, what is that to you?"

24 This is the disciple who testifies to these things and who wrote them down. We know that his testimony is true.[k]

25 Jesus did many other things as well.[l] If every one of them were written down, I suppose that even the whole world would not have room for the books that would be written.

*"The most lonely place in the world is the human heart when love is absent."*

—Sadie Alexander, first African American female to receive a doctorate in economics

**21:1** u Jn 20:19,26 v Jn 6:1
**21:2** w Jn 1:45 x Mt 4:21
**21:3** y Lk 5:5
**21:4** z Jn 20:14
**21:6** a Lk 5:4–7
**21:7** b Jn 13:23
**21:14** c Jn 20:19,26
**21:15** d Mt 26:33,35
**21:16** e Ac 20:28; 1Pe 5:2,3
**21:17** f Jn 16:30
**21:19** g 2Pe 1:14
**21:20** h Jn 13:25
**21:22** i Mt 16:27
**21:23** j Ac 1:16
**21:24** k Jn 19:35
**21:25** l Jn 20:30

[a] 1 That is, Sea of Galilee [b] 8 Greek *about two hundred cubits* (about 90 meters)

# Acts

## OVERVIEW

The book of Acts is a continuation of Luke's account of the ministry of Jesus that Luke began in his Gospel. This book demonstrates how the early church grew in its faith after the ascension of Jesus. The day of Pentecost was a pivotal moment for the early believers as they were filled with the Holy Spirit. On that day 3,000 people believed in Jesus Christ, and the church was born. Filled with the Holy Spirit, the church was then equipped to fulfill the mandate in Acts 1:8—to be Christ's witnesses "in Jerusalem, and in all Judea and Samaria, and to the ends of the earth" (a virtual outline of the book of Acts).

In the book of Acts, women played a significant role in church building and fellowship. Women, including Mary the mother of Jesus, joined the disciples in constant prayer (see Ac 1:14). Sapphira and her husband, Ananias, paid the consequences for deception and false generosity (see Ac 5). Dorcas was raised from the dead (see Ac 9:36–43). Lydia provided a home for the apostles (see Ac 16). And Priscilla and her husband, Aquila, compassionately shared the complete gospel message with Apollos (see Ac 18). The book of Acts also refers to Philip's daughters as women who prophesied (see Ac 21:8–9).

Just as women helped build the early church, Christian women today are called to use their gifts, talents and resources to draw others to Christ and to encourage fellow believers.

## OUTLINE

I. The Commissioning and Equipping of the Disciples (1:1—2:13)
II. The Witness in Jerusalem (2:14—7:60)
III. The Witness in Judea and Samaria (8:1—9:43)
IV. The Witness to the Ends of the Earth (10:1—28:31)

### SCANNABLE FACTS:

**Author:** Luke

**Time Written:** Probably around A.D. 63

**Theme to Note:** The power of the Holy Spirit

**Notable Women:** Sapphira, Dorcas, Lydia, Priscilla, Philip's daughters

## Jesus Taken Up Into Heaven

1 In my former book,[a] Theophilus, I wrote about all that Jesus began to do and to teach 2until the day he was taken up to heaven, after giving instructions[b] through the Holy Spirit to the apostles he had chosen. 3After his suffering, he showed himself to these men and gave many convincing proofs that he was alive. He appeared to them[c] over a period of forty days and spoke about the kingdom of God. 4On one occasion, while he was eating with them, he gave them this command: "Do not leave Jerusalem, but wait for the gift my Father promised, which you have heard me speak about.[d] 5For John baptized with[a] water, but in a few days you will be baptized with the Holy Spirit."

6So when they met together, they asked him, "Lord, are you at this time going to restore the kingdom to Israel?"

7He said to them: "It is not for you to know the times or dates the Father has set by his own authority.[e] 8But you will receive power when the Holy Spirit comes on you;[f] and you will be my witnesses[g] in Jerusalem, and in all Judea and Samaria, and to the ends of the earth."

9After he said this, he was taken up[h] before their very eyes, and a cloud hid him from their sight.

10They were looking intently up into the sky as he was going, when suddenly two men dressed in white[i] stood beside them. 11"Men of Galilee," they said, "why do you stand here looking into the sky? This same Jesus, who has been taken from you into heaven, will come back in the same way you have seen him go into heaven."

## Matthias Chosen to Replace Judas

12Then they returned to Jerusalem from the hill called the Mount of Olives, a Sabbath day's walk[b] from the city. 13When they arrived, they went upstairs to the room[j] where they were staying. Those present were Peter, John, James and Andrew; Philip and Thomas, Bartholomew and Matthew; James son of Alphaeus and Simon the Zealot, and Judas son of James.[k] 14They all joined together constantly in prayer, along with the women[l] and Mary the mother of Jesus, and with his brothers.

15In those days Peter stood up among the believers[c] (a group numbering about a hundred and twenty) 16and said, "Brothers, the Scripture had to be fulfilled which the Holy Spirit spoke long ago through the mouth of David concerning Judas, who served as guide for those who arrested Jesus— 17he was one of our number[m] and shared in this ministry."[n]

18(With the reward[o] he got for his wickedness, Judas bought a field;[p] there he fell headlong, his body burst open and all his intestines spilled out. 19Everyone in Jerusalem heard about this, so they called that field in their language Akeldama, that is, Field of Blood.)

20"For," said Peter, "it is written in the book of Psalms,

"'May his place be deserted;
let there be no one to dwell in it,'[d][q]

and,

"'May another take his place of
leadership.'[e][r]

21Therefore it is necessary to choose one of the men who have been with us the whole time the Lord Jesus went in and out among us, 22beginning from John's baptism to the time when Jesus was taken up from us. For one of these must become a witness with us of his resurrection."

23So they proposed two men: Joseph called Barsabbas (also known as Justus) and Matthias. 24Then they prayed, "Lord, you know everyone's heart.[s] Show us which of these two you have chosen 25to take over this apostolic ministry, which Judas left to go where he belongs." 26Then they cast lots, and the lot fell to Matthias; so he was added to the eleven apostles.

## The Holy Spirit Comes at Pentecost

2 When the day of Pentecost[t] came, they were all together in one place. 2Suddenly a sound like the blowing of a violent wind came from heaven and filled the

**1:1** a Lk 1:1–4
**1:2** b Mt 28:19,20
**1:3** c Mt 28:17
**1:4** d Lk 24:49; Jn 14:16
**1:7** e Mt 24:36
**1:8** f Ac 2:1–4 g Lk 24:48
**1:9** h ver 2
**1:10** i Jn 20:12
**1:13** j Ac 9:37; 20:8 k Lk 6:14–16
**1:14** l Lk 23:49,55
**1:17** m Jn 6:70,71 n ver 25
**1:18** o Mt 26:14,15 p Mt 27:3–10
**1:20** q Ps 69:25 r Ps 109:8
**1:24** s 1Sa 16:7; Jer 17:10; Rev 2:23
**2:1** t Lev 23:15,16

a5 Or *in* b12 That is, about 3/4 mile (about 1,100 meters) c15 Greek *brothers* d20 Psalm 69:25 e20 Psalm 109:8

**2:2** u Ac 4:31
**2:4** v Mk 16:17; 1Co 12:10
**2:7** w Ac 1:11
**2:9** x Ac 16:6
**2:15** y 1Th 5:7

whole house where they were sitting.[u] 3They
saw what seemed to be tongues of fire that
separated and came to rest on each of them.
4All of them were filled with the Holy Spirit
and began to speak in other tongues[a][v] as the
Spirit enabled them.
5Now there were staying in Jerusalem
God-fearing Jews from every nation under
heaven. 6When they heard this sound, a
crowd came together in bewilderment, be-
cause each one heard them speaking in his
own language. 7Utterly amazed, they asked:
"Are not all these men who are speaking
Galileans?[w] 8Then how is it that each of us
hears them in his own native language?
9Parthians, Medes and Elamites; residents
of Mesopotamia, Judea and Cappadocia,
Pontus and Asia,[x] 10Phrygia and Pamphylia,
Egypt and the parts of Libya near Cyrene;
visitors from Rome 11(both Jews and con-
verts to Judaism); Cretans and Arabs—we
hear them declaring the wonders of God
in our own tongues!" 12Amazed and per-
plexed, they asked one another, "What does
this mean?"
13Some, however, made fun of them and
said, "They have had too much wine.[b]"

## Peter Addresses the Crowd

14Then Peter stood up with the Eleven,
raised his voice and addressed the crowd:
"Fellow Jews and all of you who live in Je-
rusalem, let me explain this to you; listen
carefully to what I say. 15These men are not
drunk, as you suppose. It's only nine in the
morning![y] 16No, this is what was spoken by
the prophet Joel:

17" 'In the last days, God says,
I will pour out my Spirit on all people.
Your sons and daughters will prophesy,
your young men will see visions,
your old men will dream dreams.
18 Even on my servants, both men and
women,
I will pour out my Spirit in those days,
and they will prophesy.[z]
19 I will show wonders in the heaven above
and signs on the earth below,
blood and fire and billows of smoke.
20 The sun will be turned to darkness
and the moon to blood[a]
before the coming of the great and
glorious day of the Lord.
21 And everyone who calls
on the name of the Lord will be saved.'[c][b]

22"Men of Israel, listen to this: Jesus of
Nazareth was a man accredited by God
to you by miracles, wonders and signs,[c]
which God did among you through him,[d]
as you yourselves know. 23This man was
handed over to you by God's set purpose
and foreknowledge;[e] and you, with the
help of wicked men,[d] put him to death by
nailing him to the cross. 24But God raised
him from the dead,[f] freeing him from the
agony of death, because it was impossible
for death to keep its hold on him. 25David
said about him:

" 'I saw the Lord always before me.
Because he is at my right hand,
I will not be shaken.
26 Therefore my heart is glad and my tongue
rejoices;

**2:18** z Ac 21:9–12
**2:20** a Mt 24:29
**2:21** b Ro 10:13
**2:22** c Jn 4:48; Ac 10:38 d Jn 3:2
**2:23** e Lk 22:22; Ac 3:18
**2:24** f 2Co 4:14; Eph 1:20; Col 2:12; Heb 13:20

[a]4 Or *languages*; also in verse 11 [b]13 Or *sweet wine* [c]21 Joel 2:28–32 [d]23 Or *of those not having the law* (that is, Gentiles)

## The African Presence

**Acts 2:5–11**

The Jews of the Diaspora in Jerusalem for the festival of Pentecost included Jews from Egypt and parts of Libya near Cyrene. Luke did not directly mention Jews from Ethiopia; however, those who believed and were baptized (v. 41) included a reference to "all who are far off" (v. 39).

# Inspire

## WOMEN IN PREACHING MINISTRIES

Ever since Mary Magdalene returned in jubilation from the empty tomb (see Jn 20:1–18), women have continued to serve as proclaimers of the Good News of Jesus Christ. The Scriptures provide numerous examples—in both the Old and New Testaments—of women who engaged in prophetic roles. Women throughout Biblical history and beyond have held leadership roles, served heroically in God's cause, preached, sang out their faith and prophesied. Deborah, Miriam, Huldah, Esther, Jesus' mother Mary, Mary Magdalene, Anna, Priscilla, Philip's daughters and many others provide the Biblical witness that God does indeed use women to stand up and declare with boldness, "Thus says the Lord!"

The apostle Paul encouraged women to exercise their gift of prophecy, and he taught them how to do so appropriately according to the accepted custom of the day, in the public assembly of the church (see 1Co 11:3–5). For centuries dauntless women have braved all kinds of hardship to declare the Word in the world's far-flung corners. Even today, however, some church members have never been exposed to women in ministry.

In explaining to the crowd what was happening on the day of Pentecost, Peter quoted the prophet Joel: "In the last days, God says, I will pour out my Spirit on all people. Your sons and daughters will prophesy" (Ac 2:17). God is powerfully using women today to bring the Word in due season. As more and more women continue to answer that call, communities are transformed, churches are revived and women are empowered. Trailblazers like Sojourner Truth, Jarena Lee, Amanda Berry Smith and Julia Foote were God's preaching women long before it was considered acceptable for women to serve in this role. God is still calling and using women to proclaim his Word. Indeed, he has called each of us to declare his name in just such a time as this!

—C. Woods

### read

Acts 1:12–14; 2:1–21; see also John 20:1–18; 1 Corinthians 11:2–16.

See also the Inspire Notes "Influencing Others," "Evangelism: Gone Fishin' " and "Female Ministers and Evangelists," and the Women of the Bible Notes "Deborah: An Uncommon Leader," "Huldah: A Prophetess of God," "Anna: A Model of Spiritual Devotion" and "Philip's Daughters: Those Preaching Women."

### WOMAN of COLOR

What women have been instrumental in your spiritual growth? Thank God for them and pray for their strength in the Lord.

For the next Inspire note, go to page 1305.

**2:29** g Ac 13:36
**2:30** h 2Sa 7:12; Ps 132:11
**2:32** i ver 24 j Ac 1:8
**2:33** k Ac 10:45
**2:35** l Ps 110:1
**2:37** m Lk 3:10,12,14
**2:38** n Lk 24:47; Ac 3:19
**2:39** o Eph 2:13

my body also will live in hope,
27 because you will not abandon me to the
grave,
nor will you let your Holy One see
decay.
28 You have made known to me the paths of
life;
you will fill me with joy in your
presence.'[a]

29“Brothers, I can tell you confidently that
the patriarch David died and was buried,[g]
and his tomb is here to this day. 30But he was
a prophet and knew that God had promised
him on oath that he would place one of his
descendants on his throne.[h] 31Seeing what
was ahead, he spoke of the resurrection of
the Christ,[b] that he was not abandoned to
the grave, nor did his body see decay. 32God
has raised this Jesus to life,[i] and we are all
witnesses[j] of the fact. 33Exalted to the right
hand of God, he has received from the Father
the promised Holy Spirit and has poured
out[k] what you now see and hear. 34For David
did not ascend to heaven, and yet he said,

“ 'The Lord said to my Lord:
“Sit at my right hand
35 until I make your enemies
a footstool for your feet.” '[c][l]

36“Therefore let all Israel be assured of
this: God has made this Jesus, whom you
crucified, both Lord and Christ.”

37When the people heard this, they
were cut to the heart and said to Peter and
the other apostles, “Brothers, what shall
we do?”[m]

38Peter replied, “Repent and be baptized,
every one of you, in the name of Jesus Christ
for the forgiveness of your sins.[n] And you
will receive the gift of the Holy Spirit. 39The
promise is for you and your children and for
all who are far off[o]—for all whom the Lord
our God will call.”

40With many other words he warned
them; and he pleaded with them, “Save
yourselves from this corrupt generation.”
41Those who accepted his message were bap-
tized, and about three thousand were added
to their number that day.

## The Fellowship of the Believers

42They devoted themselves to the apos-
tles' teaching and to the fellowship, to the
breaking of bread and to prayer. 43Everyone
was filled with awe, and many wonders and
miraculous signs were done by the apostles.
44All the believers were together and had
everything in common.[p] 45Selling their pos-
sessions and goods, they gave to anyone as
he had need. 46Every day they continued to
meet together in the temple courts. They
broke bread[q] in their homes and ate together
with glad and sincere hearts, 47praising God
and enjoying the favor of all the people. And
the Lord added to their number[r] daily those
who were being saved.

## Peter Heals the Crippled Beggar

3 One day Peter and John were going up
to the temple at the time of prayer—at
three in the afternoon.[s] 2Now a man crip-
pled from birth[t] was being carried to the
temple gate called Beautiful, where he was
put every day to beg from those going into
the temple courts. 3When he saw Peter
and John about to enter, he asked them for
money. 4Peter looked straight at him, as did
John. Then Peter said, “Look at us!” 5So the
man gave them his attention, expecting to
get something from them.

6Then Peter said, “Silver or gold I do
not have, but what I have I give you. In the
name of Jesus Christ of
Nazareth,[u] walk.” 7Tak-
ing him by the right
hand, he helped him up,
and instantly the man's
feet and ankles became
strong. 8He jumped to his
feet and began to walk.
Then he went with them
into the temple courts,
walking and jumping,
and praising God. 9When
all the people[v] saw him walking and prais-
ing God, 10they recognized him as the same
man who used to sit begging at the temple
gate called Beautiful, and they were filled
with wonder and amazement at what had
happened to him.

*“As soon as healing takes place, go out and heal somebody else.”*
—MAYA ANGELOU, POET AND WRITER

**2:44** p Ac 4:32
**2:46** q Ac 20:7
**2:47** r Ac 5:14
**3:1** s Ps 55:17
**3:2** t Ac 14:8
**3:6** u Ac 4:10
**3:9** v Ac 4:16,21

[a]28 Psalm 16:8–11 [b]31 Or *Messiah.* “The Christ” (Greek) and “the Messiah” (Hebrew) both mean “the Anointed One”; also in verse 36. [c]35 Psalm 110:1

**3:11** w Jn 10:23; Ac 5:12
**3:13** x Ac 5:30 y Mt 27:2
**3:14** z Mk 1:24; Ac 4:27 a Ac 7:52
**3:15** b Ac 2:24
**3:17** c Lk 23:34 d Ac 13:27
**3:18** e Ac 26:22,23
**3:19** f Ac 2:38
**3:21** g Ac 1:11 h Mt 17:11 i Lk 1:70
**3:22** j Dt 18:15,18; Ac 7:37
**3:25** k Ac 2:39 l Ro 9:4,5
**3:26** m Ac 13:46

## Peter Speaks to the Onlookers

11 While the beggar held on to Peter and John, all the people were astonished and came running to them in the place called Solomon's Colonnade.[w] 12 When Peter saw this, he said to them: "Men of Israel, why does this surprise you? Why do you stare at us as if by our own power or godliness we had made this man walk? 13 The God of Abraham, Isaac and Jacob, the God of our fathers,[x] has glorified his servant Jesus. You handed him over to be killed, and you disowned him before Pilate,[y] though he had decided to let him go. 14 You disowned the Holy[z] and Righteous One[a] and asked that a murderer be released to you. 15 You killed the author of life, but God raised him from the dead.[b] We are witnesses of this. 16 By faith in the name of Jesus, this man whom you see and know was made strong. It is Jesus' name and the faith that comes through him that has given this complete healing to him, as you can all see.

17 "Now, brothers, I know that you acted in ignorance,[c] as did your leaders.[d] 18 But this is how God fulfilled what he had foretold through all the prophets, saying that his Christ[a] would suffer.[e] 19 Repent, then, and turn to God, so that your sins may be wiped out,[f] that times of refreshing may come from the Lord, 20 and that he may send the Christ, who has been appointed for you—even Jesus. 21 He must remain in heaven[g] until the time comes for God to restore everything,[h] as he promised long ago through his holy prophets.[i] 22 For Moses said, 'The Lord your God will raise up for you a prophet like me from among your own people; you must listen to everything he tells you.[j] 23 Anyone who does not listen to him will be completely cut off from among his people.'[b]

24 "Indeed, all the prophets from Samuel on, as many as have spoken, have foretold these days. 25 And you are heirs[k] of the prophets and of the covenant[l] God made with your fathers. He said to Abraham, 'Through your offspring all peoples on earth will be blessed.'[c] 26 When God raised up his servant, he sent him first[m] to you to bless you by turning each of you from your wicked ways."

## Peter and John Before the Sanhedrin

4 The priests and the captain of the temple guard[n] and the Sadducees came up to Peter and John while they were speaking to the people. 2 They were greatly disturbed because the apostles were teaching the people and proclaiming in Jesus the resurrection of the dead. 3 They seized Peter and John, and because it was evening, they put them in jail[o] until the next day. 4 But many who heard the message believed, and the number of men grew to about five thousand.

5 The next day the rulers, elders and teachers of the law met in Jerusalem. 6 Annas the high priest was there, and so were Caiaphas,[p] John, Alexander and the other men of the high priest's family. 7 They had Peter and John brought before them and began to question them: "By what power or what name did you do this?"

8 Then Peter, filled with the Holy Spirit, said to them: "Rulers and elders of the people![q] 9 If we are being called to account today for an act of kindness shown to a cripple and are asked how he was healed, 10 then know this, you and all the people of Israel: It is by the name of Jesus Christ of Nazareth, whom you crucified but whom God raised from the dead, that this man stands before you healed. 11 He is

> " 'the stone you builders rejected,
> which has become the capstone.'[d][e][r]

12 Salvation is found in no one else, for there is no other name under heaven given to men by which we must be saved."[s]

13 When they saw the courage of Peter and John and realized that they were unschooled, ordinary men,[t] they were astonished and they took note that these men had been with Jesus. 14 But since they could see the man who had been healed standing there with them, there was nothing they could say. 15 So they ordered them to withdraw from the Sanhedrin and then conferred together. 16 "What are we going to do with these men?"[u] they asked. "Everybody living in Jerusalem knows they have done an outstanding miracle,[v] and we cannot

**4:1** n Lk 22:4
**4:3** o Ac 5:18
**4:6** p Mt 26:3; Lk 3:2
**4:8** q Lk 23:13
**4:11** r Ps 118:22; Mt 21:42
**4:12** s Mt 1:21; Ac 10:43; 1Ti 2:5
**4:13** t Mt 11:25
**4:16** u Jn 11:47 v Ac 3:6–10

[a]18 Or *Messiah*; also in verse 20 [b]23 Deut. 18:15,18,19 [c]25 Gen. 22:18; 26:4 [d]11 Or *cornerstone* [e]11 Psalm 118:22

deny it. [17]But to stop this thing from spreading any further among the people, we must warn these men to speak no longer to anyone in this name."

[18]Then they called them in again and commanded them not to speak or teach at all in the name of Jesus.[w] [19]But Peter and John replied, "Judge for yourselves whether it is right in God's sight to obey you rather than God.[x] [20]For we cannot help speaking about what we have seen and heard."

[21]After further threats they let them go. They could not decide how to punish them, because all the people[y] were praising God for what had happened. [22]For the man who was miraculously healed was over forty years old.

## The Believers' Prayer

[23]On their release, Peter and John went back to their own people and reported all that the chief priests and elders had said to them. [24]When they heard this, they raised their voices together in prayer to God. "Sovereign Lord," they said, "you made the heaven and the earth and the sea, and everything in them. [25]You spoke by the Holy Spirit through the mouth of your servant, our father David:

"'Why do the nations rage
    and the peoples plot in vain?
[26]The kings of the earth take their stand
    and the rulers gather together
against the Lord
    and against his Anointed One.'[a][b][z]

[27]Indeed Herod and Pontius Pilate met together with the Gentiles and the people[c] of Israel in this city to conspire against your holy servant Jesus, whom you anointed. [28]They did what your power and will had decided beforehand should happen.[a] [29]Now, Lord, consider their threats and enable your servants to speak your word with great boldness.[b] [30]Stretch out your hand to heal and perform miraculous signs and wonders through the name of your holy servant Jesus."[c]

[31]After they prayed, the place where they were meeting was shaken.[d] And they were all filled with the Holy Spirit and spoke the word of God boldly.

## The Believers Share Their Possessions

[32]All the believers were one in heart and mind. No one claimed that any of his possessions was his own, but they shared everything they had.[e] [33]With great power the apostles continued to testify to the resurrection of the Lord Jesus, and much grace was upon them all. [34]There were no needy persons among them. For from time to time those who owned lands or houses sold them,[f] brought the money from the sales [35]and put it at the apostles' feet,[g] and it was distributed to anyone as he had need.[h]

[36]Joseph, a Levite from Cyprus, whom the apostles called Barnabas (which means Son of Encouragement), [37]sold a field he owned and brought the money and put it at the apostles' feet.[i]

## Ananias and Sapphira

**5** Now a man named Ananias, together with his wife Sapphira, also sold a piece of property. [2]With his wife's full knowledge he kept back part of the money for himself, but brought the rest and put it at the apostles' feet.

[3]Then Peter said, "Ananias, how is it that Satan has so filled your heart that you have lied to the Holy Spirit[j] and have kept for yourself some of the money you received for the land? [4]Didn't it belong to you before it was sold? And after it was sold, wasn't the money at your disposal? What made you think of doing such a thing? You have not lied to men but to God."

[5]When Ananias heard this, he fell down and died.[k] And great fear[l] seized all who heard what had happened. [6]Then the young men came forward, wrapped up his body,[m] and carried him out and buried him.

[7]About three hours later his wife came in, not knowing what had happened. [8]Peter asked her, "Tell me, is this the price you and Ananias got for the land?"

"Yes," she said, "that is the price."

[9]Peter said to her, "How could you agree to test the Spirit of the Lord?[n] Look! The feet of the men who buried your husband are at the door, and they will carry you out also."

[10]At that moment she fell down at his feet

**4:18** w Ac 5:40
**4:19** x Ac 5:29
**4:21** y Ac 5:26
**4:26** z Ps 2:1,2
**4:28** a Ac 2:23
**4:29** b ver 13,31
**4:30** c ver 27
**4:31** d Ac 2:2
**4:32** e Ac 2:44
**4:34** f Ac 2:45
**4:35** g ver 37; Ac 5:2 h Ac 2:45
**4:37** i ver 35; Ac 5:2
**5:3** j ver 9
**5:5** k ver 10 l ver 11
**5:6** m Jn 19:40
**5:9** n ver 3

[a]26 That is, Christ or Messiah [b]26 Psalm 2:1,2 [c]27 The Greek is plural.

# Sapphira

## A Lost Opportunity for Truth

In the early days of the church, individual believers occasionally sold property and voluntarily brought the proceeds to the apostles to be distributed to those in need (see Ac 4:34–37). During this time, selfishness, a longing for recognition, and deceit entered into the hearts of Sapphira and her husband, Ananias. This couple sold a piece of property and then decided to keep part of the money for themselves and give part of it to the church (see 5:1–2). That would have been fine, but they wanted the apostles and the other believers to think that they were giving *all* of the money. This couple agreed to lie to the church. In doing so, they ultimately lied to God.

When Sapphira's husband approached the apostles with the money, the Holy Spirit exposed his heart to the apostle Peter. As a result of his evil intent, Ananias died immediately. Three hours later Sapphira arrived, not knowing about her husband's death. God led Peter to question Sapphira, giving her an opportunity to speak truthfully. But Sapphira chose to perpetuate the lie. And, like her husband, this resulted in her immediate death. Sapphira placed more confidence in her husband's evil plan than in God. What could have been a blessing to the church turned into a disaster.

The deaths of Sapphira and her husband shocked the church. God showed them all that he will not tolerate dishonesty in relationships. A woman's relationship with God and her husband should be based on integrity and commitment. She is to respect her husband and agree to godly decisions. She is not told to submit to ungodly or wicked schemes, especially ones that would cause her to be untruthful. It is important for her to keep the marriage covenant—something ordained by God. More important, she is always to keep her covenant with God, never willingly putting herself in a position to break that covenant. If by chance she finds herself faced with an ungodly decision made by her spouse, she should speak the truth in love so they can grow together spiritually.

—G. London

### reflection

*How has not telling the entire truth hurt you in the past?*

*Seek to live life truthfully—before God, others and yourself.*

### read

Acts 4:32—5:11; Ephesians 4:14–15,25.

See also the Inspire Notes "Submission," "Marriage," "Integrity," "Self-Control" and "Character," and the Women of the Bible Notes "Delilah: Strength That Builds or Destroys," "The Bridegroom and His Bride: Soul Mates in Life" and "The Servant Girl: The Truth, the Whole Truth and Nothing but the Truth."

For the next Women of the Bible note, go to page 1289.

5:10 o ver5
5:11 p ver5
5:12 q Ac3:11
5:13 r Ac2:47; 4:21
5:15 s Ac19:12
5:17 t Ac4:1
5:20 u Jn6:63,68

and died.[o] Then the young men came in and, finding her dead, carried her out and buried her beside her husband. 11 Great fear[p] seized the whole church and all who heard about these events.

## The Apostles Heal Many

12 The apostles performed many miraculous signs and wonders among the people. And all the believers used to meet together in Solomon's Colonnade.[q] 13 No one else dared join them, even though they were highly regarded by the people.[r] 14 Nevertheless, more and more men and women believed in the Lord and were added to their number. 15 As a result, people brought the sick into the streets and laid them on beds and mats so that at least Peter's shadow might fall on some of them as he passed by.[s] 16 Crowds gathered also from the towns around Jerusalem, bringing their sick and those tormented by evil[a] spirits, and all of them were healed.

*Believer,*

*Share my gospel through your actions. I'd like nothing better than for all my children to hear and "see" the Good News.*

*With love,*
*Father God*

ACTS 5:12–16

## The Apostles Persecuted

17 Then the high priest and all his associates, who were members of the party of the Sadducees,[t] were filled with jealousy. 18 They arrested the apostles and put them in the public jail. 19 But during the night an angel of the Lord opened the doors of the jail and brought them out. 20 "Go, stand in the temple courts," he said, "and tell the people the full message of this new life."[u]

21 At daybreak they entered the temple courts, as they had been told, and began to teach the people.

When the high priest and his associates[v] arrived, they called together the Sanhedrin—the full assembly of the elders of Israel—and sent to the jail for the apostles. 22 But on arriving at the jail, the officers did not find them there. So they went back and reported, 23 "We found the jail securely locked, with the guards standing at the doors; but when we opened them, we found no one inside." 24 On hearing this report, the captain of the temple guard and the chief priests[w] were puzzled, wondering what would come of this.

25 Then someone came and said, "Look! The men you put in jail are standing in the temple courts teaching the people." 26 At that, the captain went with his officers and brought the apostles. They did not use force, because they feared that the people would stone them.

27 Having brought the apostles, they made them appear before the Sanhedrin to be questioned by the high priest. 28 "We gave you strict orders not to teach in this name,"[x] he said. "Yet you have filled Jerusalem with your teaching and are determined to make us guilty of this man's blood."[y]

29 Peter and the other apostles replied: "We must obey God rather than men![z] 30 The God of our fathers[a] raised Jesus from the dead—whom you had killed by hanging him on a tree.[b] 31 God exalted him to his own right hand as Prince and Savior that he might give repentance and forgiveness of sins to Israel. 32 We are witnesses of these things, and so is the Holy Spirit,[c] whom God has given to those who obey him."

33 When they heard this, they were furious[d] and wanted to put them to death. 34 But a Pharisee named Gamaliel, a teacher of the law, who was honored by all the people, stood up in the Sanhedrin and ordered that the men be put outside for a little while. 35 Then he addressed them: "Men of Israel, consider carefully what you intend to do to these men. 36 Some time ago Theudas appeared, claiming to be somebody, and about four hundred men rallied to him. He was killed, all his followers were dispersed, and

5:21 v Ac4:5,6
5:24 w Ac4:1
5:28 x Ac4:18 y Mt23:35; Ac2:23,36; 3:14,15; 7:52
5:29 z Ac4:19
5:30 a Ac3:13 b Ac10:39; Gal3:13
5:32 c Jn15:26
5:33 d Ac2:37; 7:54

[a] 16 Greek *unclean*

**5:40**
e Mt 10:17
**5:42**
f Ac 2:46
**6:1**
g Ac 9:29
h Ac 4:35
**6:5**
i Ac 8:5–40; 21:8
**6:6**
j Ac 1:24
k Ac 9:17; 1Ti 4:14
**6:7**
l Ac 12:24; 19:20

it all came to nothing. 37After him, Judas the
Galilean appeared in the days of the census
and led a band of people in revolt. He too was
killed, and all his followers were scattered.
38Therefore, in the present case I advise you:
Leave these men alone! Let them go! For if
their purpose or activity is of human origin,
it will fail. 39But if it is from God, you will
not be able to stop these men; you will only
find yourselves fighting against God."
40His speech persuaded them. They called
the apostles in and had them flogged.[e] Then
they ordered them not to speak in the name
of Jesus, and let them go.
41The apostles left the Sanhedrin, rejoic-
ing because they had been counted worthy
of suffering disgrace for the Name. 42Day
after day, in the temple courts[f] and from
house to house, they never stopped teaching
and proclaiming the good news that Jesus is
the Christ.[a]

## The Choosing of the Seven

6 In those days when the number of
disciples was increasing, the Grecian
Jews[g] among them complained against the
Hebraic Jews because their widows were be-
ing overlooked in the daily distribution of
food.[h] 2So the Twelve gathered all the disci-
ples together and said, "It would not be right
for us to neglect the ministry of the word of
God in order to wait on tables. 3Brothers,
choose seven men from among you who are
known to be full of the Spirit and wisdom.
We will turn this responsibility over to
them 4and will give our attention to prayer
and the ministry of the word."
5This proposal pleased the whole group.
They chose Stephen, a man full of faith and
of the Holy Spirit; also Philip,[i] Procorus,
Nicanor, Timon, Parmenas, and Nicolas
from Antioch, a convert to Judaism. 6They
presented these men to the apostles, who
prayed[j] and laid their hands on them.[k]
7So the word of God spread.[l] The number
of disciples in Jerusalem increased rapidly,
and a large number of priests became obedi-
ent to the faith.

## Stephen Seized

8Now Stephen, a man full of God's grace
and power, did great wonders and miracu-
lous signs among the people. 9Opposition
arose, however, from members of the Syna-
gogue of the Freedmen (as it was called)—
Jews of Cyrene and Alexandria as well as the
provinces of Cilicia and Asia. These men be-
gan to argue with Stephen, 10but they could
not stand up against his wisdom or the
Spirit by whom he spoke.
11Then they secretly persuaded some
men to say, "We have heard Stephen speak
words of blasphemy against Moses and
against God."
12So they stirred up the people and the el-
ders and the teachers of the law. They seized
Stephen and brought him before the Sanhe-
drin. 13They produced false witnesses, who
testified, "This fellow never stops speaking
against this holy place and against the law.
14For we have heard him say that this Jesus of
Nazareth will destroy this place and change
the customs Moses handed down to us."
15All who were sitting in the Sanhedrin
looked intently at Stephen, and they saw
that his face was like the face of an angel.

## Stephen's Speech to the Sanhedrin

7 Then the high priest asked him, "Are
these charges true?"
2To this he replied: "Brothers and fa-
thers,[m] listen to me! The God of glory ap-
peared to our father Abraham while he was
still in Mesopotamia, before he lived in Ha-
ran. 3'Leave your country and your people,'
God said, 'and go to the land I will show
you.'[b][n]
4"So he left the land of the Chaldeans
and settled in Haran. After the death of
his father, God sent him to this land where
you are now living.[o] 5He gave him no inher-
itance here, not even a foot of ground. But
God promised him that he and his descen-
dants after him would possess the land,[p]
even though at that time Abraham had no
child. 6God spoke to him in this way: 'Your
descendants will be strangers in a country
not their own, and they will be enslaved and
mistreated four hundred years. 7But I will
punish the nation they serve as slaves,' God
said, 'and afterward they will come out of
that country and worship me in this place.'[c][q]

**7:2**
m Ac 22:1
**7:3**
n Ge 12:1
**7:4**
o Ge 12:5
**7:5**
p Ge 12:7
**7:7**
q Ex 3:12

[a]42 Or *Messiah* [b]3 Gen. 12:1 [c]7 Gen. 15:13,14

8 Then he gave Abraham the covenant of circumcision.[r] And Abraham became the father of Isaac and circumcised him eight days after his birth.[s] Later Isaac became the father of Jacob,[t] and Jacob became the father of the twelve patriarchs.[u]

9 "Because the patriarchs were jealous of Joseph,[v] they sold him as a slave into Egypt.[w] But God was with him[x] 10 and rescued him from all his troubles. He gave Joseph wisdom and enabled him to gain the goodwill of Pharaoh king of Egypt; so he made him ruler over Egypt and all his palace.

11 "Then a famine struck all Egypt and Canaan, bringing great suffering, and our fathers could not find food.[y] 12 When Jacob heard that there was grain in Egypt, he sent our fathers on their first visit.[z] 13 On their second visit, Joseph told his brothers who he was,[a] and Pharaoh learned about Joseph's family. 14 After this, Joseph sent for his father Jacob and his whole family,[b] seventy-five in all.[c] 15 Then Jacob went down to Egypt, where he and our fathers died.[d] 16 Their bodies were brought back to Shechem and placed in the tomb that Abraham had bought from the sons of Hamor at Shechem for a certain sum of money.[e]

17 "As the time drew near for God to fulfill his promise to Abraham, the number of our people in Egypt greatly increased.[f] 18 Then another king, who knew nothing about Joseph, became ruler of Egypt. 19 He dealt treacherously with our people and oppressed our forefathers by forcing them to throw out their newborn babies so that they would die.[g]

20 "At that time Moses was born, and he was no ordinary child.[a] For three months he was cared for in his father's house. 21 When he was placed outside, Pharaoh's daughter took him and brought him up as her own son. 22 Moses was educated in all the wisdom of the Egyptians and was powerful in speech and action.

23 "When Moses was forty years old, he decided to visit his fellow Israelites. 24 He saw one of them being mistreated by an Egyptian, so he went to his defense and avenged him by killing the Egyptian. 25 Moses thought that his own people would realize that God was using him to rescue them, but they did not. 26 The next day Moses came upon two Israelites who were fighting. He tried to reconcile them by saying, 'Men, you are brothers; why do you want to hurt each other?'

27 "But the man who was mistreating the other pushed Moses aside and said, 'Who made you ruler and judge over us? 28 Do you want to kill me as you killed the Egyptian yesterday?'[b] 29 When Moses heard this, he fled to Midian, where he settled as a foreigner and had two sons.[h]

30 "After forty years had passed, an angel appeared to Moses in the flames of a burning bush in the desert near Mount Sinai. 31 When he saw this, he was amazed at the sight. As he went over to look more closely, he heard the Lord's voice: 32 'I am the God of your fathers, the God of Abraham, Isaac and Jacob.'[c] Moses trembled with fear and did not dare to look.

33 "Then the Lord said to him, 'Take off your sandals; the place where you are standing is holy ground.[i] 34 I have indeed seen the oppression of my people in Egypt. I have heard their groaning and have come down to set them free. Now come, I will send you back to Egypt.'[d][j]

35 "This is the same Moses whom they had rejected with the words, 'Who made you ruler and judge?' He was sent to be their ruler and deliverer by God himself, through the angel who appeared to him in the bush. 36 He led them out of Egypt[k] and did wonders and miraculous signs in Egypt, at the Red Sea[e] and for forty years in the desert.

37 "This is that Moses who told the Israelites, 'God will send you a prophet like me from your own people.'[f][l] 38 He was in the assembly in the desert, with the angel who spoke to him on Mount Sinai, and with our fathers; and he received living words to pass on to us.[m]

39 "But our fathers refused to obey him. Instead, they rejected him and in their hearts turned back to Egypt. 40 They told Aaron, 'Make us gods who will go before us. As for this fellow Moses who led us out of Egypt—

[a]20 Or *was fair in the sight of God* [b]28 Exodus 2:14 [c]32 Exodus 3:6 [d]34 Exodus 3:5,7,8,10 [e]36 That is, Sea of Reeds [f]37 Deut. 18:15

**7:8** r Ge 17:9–14; s Ge 21:2–4; t Ge 25:26; u Ge 29:31–35
**7:9** v Ge 37:4,11; w Ge 37:28; x Ge 39:2,21,23
**7:11** y Ge 41:54
**7:12** z Ge 42:1,2
**7:13** a Ge 45:1–4
**7:14** b Ge 45:9,10; c Ge 46:26,27; Dt 10:22
**7:15** d Ge 46:5–7; Ex 1:6
**7:16** e Ge 23:16–20; 33:18,19; Jos 24:32
**7:17** f Ex 1:7
**7:19** g Ex 1:10–22
**7:29** h Ex 2:11–15
**7:33** i Ex 3:5
**7:34** j Ex 3:7–10
**7:36** k Ex 12:41
**7:37** l Dt 18:15,18
**7:38** m Ro 3:2

**7:40** n Ex32:1,23
**7:41** o Ex32:4–6
**7:43** p Am5:25–27
**7:44** q Ex25:8,9,40
**7:45** r Jos3:14–17; Ps44:2
**7:46** s 2Sa7:8–16
**7:48** t 1Ki8:27
**7:49** u Mt5:34,35
**7:50** v Isa66:1,2

we don't know what has happened to him!'[a][n] 41 That was the time they made an idol in the form of a calf. They brought sacrifices to it and held a celebration in honor of what their hands had made.[o] 42 But God turned away and gave them over to the worship of the heavenly bodies. This agrees with what is written in the book of the prophets:

"'Did you bring me sacrifices and
offerings
forty years in the desert, O house of
Israel?
43 You have lifted up the shrine of Molech
and the star of your god Rephan,
the idols you made to worship.
Therefore I will send you into exile'[b][p]
beyond Babylon.

44 "Our forefathers had the tabernacle of the Testimony with them in the desert. It had been made as God directed Moses, according to the pattern he had seen.[q] 45 Having received the tabernacle, our fathers under Joshua brought it with them when they took the land from the nations God drove out before them.[r] It remained in the land until the time of David, 46 who enjoyed God's favor and asked that he might provide a dwelling place for the God of Jacob.[c][s] 47 But it was Solomon who built the house for him.

48 "However, the Most High does not live in houses made by men.[t] As the prophet says:

49 "'Heaven is my throne,
and the earth is my footstool.[u]
What kind of house will you build for me?
says the Lord.
Or where will my resting place be?
50 Has not my hand made all these
things?'[d][v]

51 "You stiff-necked people, with uncircumcised hearts[w] and ears! You are just like your fathers: You always resist the Holy Spirit! 52 Was there ever a prophet your fathers did not persecute?[x] They even killed those who predicted the coming of the Righteous One. And now you have betrayed and murdered him[y]— 53 you who have received the law that was put into effect through angels[z] but have not obeyed it."

## The Stoning of Stephen

54 When they heard this, they were furious[a] and gnashed their teeth at him. 55 But Stephen, full of the Holy Spirit, looked up to heaven and saw the glory of God, and Jesus standing at the right hand of God. 56 "Look," he said, "I see heaven open[b] and the Son of Man standing at the right hand of God."

57 At this they covered their ears and, yelling at the top of their voices, they all rushed at him, 58 dragged him out of the city[c] and began to stone him.[d] Meanwhile, the witnesses laid their clothes at the feet of a young man named Saul.

59 While they were stoning him, Stephen prayed, "Lord Jesus, receive my spirit." 60 Then he fell on his knees[e] and cried out, "Lord, do not hold this sin against them." When he had said this, he fell asleep.

**8** And Saul[f] was there, giving approval to his death.

## The Church Persecuted and Scattered

On that day a great persecution broke out against the church at Jerusalem, and all except the apostles were scattered[g] throughout Judea and Samaria. 2 Godly men buried Stephen and mourned deeply for him. 3 But

**7:51** w Lev26:41
**7:52** x 2Ch36:16 y Ac3:14
**7:53** z Gal3:19
**7:54** a Ac5:33
**7:56** b Mt3:16
**7:58** c Lk4:29 d Lev24:14,16; Dt13:9
**7:60** e Ac9:40
**8:1** f Ac7:58 g Ac11:19

[a] 40 Exodus 32:1 [b] 43 Amos 5:25–27 [c] 46 Some early manuscripts *the house of Jacob* [d] 50 Isaiah 66:1,2

### The African Presence

**Acts 8:1**

For information on Samaritans, see the African Presence note on Luke 9:52.

Saul[h] began to destroy the church.[i] Going from house to house, he dragged off men and women and put them in prison.

## Philip in Samaria

4 Those who had been scattered preached the word wherever they went. 5 Philip[j] went down to a city in Samaria and proclaimed the Christ[a] there. 6 When the crowds heard Philip and saw the miraculous signs he did, they all paid close attention to what he said. 7 With shrieks, evil[b] spirits came out of many, and many paralytics and cripples were healed. 8 So there was great joy in that city.

## Simon the Sorcerer

9 Now for some time a man named Simon had practiced sorcery[k] in the city and amazed all the people of Samaria. He boasted that he was someone great,[l] 10 and all the people, both high and low, gave him their attention and exclaimed, "This man is the divine power known as the Great Power." 11 They followed him because he had amazed them for a long time with his magic. 12 But when they believed Philip as he preached the good news of the kingdom of God[m] and the name of Jesus Christ, they were baptized, both men and women. 13 Simon himself believed and was baptized. And he followed Philip everywhere, astonished by the great signs and miracles[n] he saw.

14 When the apostles in Jerusalem heard that Samaria had accepted the word of God, they sent Peter and John to them. 15 When they arrived, they prayed for them that they might receive the Holy Spirit,[o] 16 because the Holy Spirit had not yet come upon any of them;[p] they had simply been baptized into[c] the name of the Lord Jesus.[q] 17 Then Peter and John placed their hands on them,[r] and they received the Holy Spirit.

18 When Simon saw that the Spirit was given at the laying on of the apostles' hands, he offered them money 19 and said, "Give me also this ability so that everyone on whom I lay my hands may receive the Holy Spirit."

20 Peter answered: "May your money perish with you, because you thought you could buy the gift of God with money![s] 21 You have no part or share in this ministry, because your heart is not right before God. 22 Repent of this wickedness and pray to the Lord. Perhaps he will forgive you for having such a thought in your heart. 23 For I see that you are full of bitterness and captive to sin."

24 Then Simon answered, "Pray to the Lord for me so that nothing you have said may happen to me."

25 When they had testified and proclaimed the word of the Lord, Peter and John returned to Jerusalem, preaching the gospel in many Samaritan villages.

## Philip and the Ethiopian

26 Now an angel[t] of the Lord said to Philip, "Go south to the road—the desert road—that goes down from Jerusalem to Gaza." 27 So he started out, and on his way he met an Ethiopian[d] eunuch, an important official in charge of all the treasury of Candace, queen of the Ethiopians. This man had gone to Jerusalem to worship,[u] 28 and on his way home was sitting in his chariot reading the book of Isaiah the prophet. 29 The Spirit told Philip, "Go to that chariot and stay near it."

30 Then Philip ran up to the chariot and heard the man reading Isaiah the prophet. "Do you understand what you are reading?" Philip asked.

31 "How can I," he said, "unless someone explains it to me?" So he invited Philip to come up and sit with him.

32 The eunuch was reading this passage of Scripture:

"He was led like a sheep to the slaughter,
and as a lamb before the shearer is silent,
so he did not open his mouth.
33 In his humiliation he was deprived of justice.
Who can speak of his descendants?
For his life was taken from the earth."[e][v]

34 The eunuch asked Philip, "Tell me, please, who is the prophet talking about, himself or someone else?" 35 Then Philip began with that very passage of Scripture[w] and told him the good news about Jesus.

36 As they traveled along the road, they

[a]5 Or *Messiah* [b]7 Greek *unclean* [c]16 Or *in* [d]27 That is, from the upper Nile region [e]33 Isaiah 53:7,8

**8:3** h Ac 7:58 i 1Co 15:9; Gal 1:13,23; Php 3:6; 1Ti 1:13
**8:5** j Ac 6:5
**8:9** k Ac 13:6 l Ac 5:36
**8:12** m Ac 1:3
**8:13** n Ac 19:11
**8:15** o Ac 2:38
**8:16** p Ac 19:2 q Mt 28:19
**8:17** r Ac 6:6
**8:20** s 2Ki 5:16; Mt 10:8; Ac 2:38
**8:26** t Ac 5:19
**8:27** u Jn 12:20
**8:33** v Isa 53:7,8
**8:35** w Lk 24:27; Ac 18:28

## The African Presence

**Acts 8:26–38**

"Ethiopia" is also called "Cush" (that is, Nubia). The exact geographic region is disputed; however, most scholars generally agree that the area of Nubia included the middle of the Nile from what is present-day southern Egypt and northern Sudan. For more on Cush, see the African Presence note on Exodus 5:1–5.

This Ethiopian eunuch was either a full-fledged proselyte or a Gentile God-fearer (a non-Jew who believed in one God, worshiped in the synagogue and respected the moral and ethical teachings of the Jews but who did not embrace all of the Jewish customs, such as the rite of circumcision). Either way, he was the first Gentile mentioned in the book of Acts to become a believer. The conversion of the Ethiopian eunuch is a fulfillment of the promise to "all who are far off" (Ac 2:39). Cush, or Ethiopia, is often referred to by ancient writers as the ends of the known world or a place "far away." This Ethiopian's interest in Judaism, including possessing a copy of a scroll of the book of Isaiah, might reflect the presence of exiled Jewish communities as far away as Ethiopia.

During the Assyrian and (later) Babylonian conquests, Jews emigrated to Egypt and Libya, among other places. Intermarriages occurred, but under the reforms of Ezra and Nehemiah, the Jews were pressured to divorce their foreign spouses (see Ezr 9:1–2; 10:9–15; Ne 13:23–27).

came to some water and the eunuch said,
"Look, here is water. Why shouldn't I be bap-
tized?"[a][x] 38And he gave orders to stop the
chariot. Then both Philip and the eunuch
went down into the water and Philip bap-
tized him. 39When they came up out of the
water, the Spirit of the Lord suddenly took
Philip away,[y] and the eunuch did not see
him again, but went on his way rejoicing.
40Philip, however, appeared at Azotus and
traveled about, preaching the gospel in all
the towns until he reached Caesarea.

### Saul's Conversion

9 Meanwhile, Saul was still breathing out
murderous threats against the Lord's
disciples.[z] He went to the high priest 2and
asked him for letters to the synagogues in
Damascus, so that if he found any there
who belonged to the Way,[a] whether men or
women, he might take them as prisoners
to Jerusalem. 3As he neared Damascus on
his journey, suddenly a light from heaven
flashed around him.[b] 4He fell to the ground
and heard a voice say to him, "Saul, Saul,
why do you persecute me?"

5"Who are you, Lord?" Saul asked.

"I am Jesus, whom you are persecuting,"
he replied. 6"Now get up and go into the city,
and you will be told what you must do."

7The men traveling with Saul stood there
speechless; they heard the sound but did not
see anyone. 8Saul got up from the ground,
but when he opened his eyes he could see
nothing. So they led him by the hand into
Damascus. 9For three days he was blind,
and did not eat or drink anything.

10In Damascus there was a disciple
named Ananias. The Lord called to him in
a vision, "Ananias!"

"Yes, Lord," he answered.

11The Lord told him, "Go to the house
of Judas on Straight Street and ask for a
man from Tarsus[c] named Saul, for he is

**8:36** x Ac 10:47
**8:39** y 1Ki 18:12; 2Ki 2:16; Eze 3:12,14
**9:1** z Ac 8:3
**9:2** a Ac 19:9,23
**9:3** b 1Co 15:8
**9:11** c Ac 21:39; 22:3

[a]36 Some late manuscripts *baptized?" 37Philip said, "If you believe with all your heart, you may." The eunuch answered, "I believe that Jesus Christ is the Son of God."*

# Candace

## Secure Leader

Just as "Pharaoh" was a reference to the king of Egypt, "Candace" was the title given to the queen of Ethiopia (see Ac 8:27). This queen was perhaps a successor to the queen of Sheba (see 1Ki 10:1). As a ruler in Ethiopia (not the area known as modern Ethiopia, but an area in what is now southern Egypt and northern Sudan), Candace led one of the oldest African nations.

A eunuch, the finance chairman of Candace's treasury and obviously a person who was attracted to Judaism, had gone to Jerusalem to worship. As he was returning home, he sat in his chariot, reading and trying to understand the writings of the prophet Isaiah. Philip, a Christian believer led by the Spirit of God, came along and explained to him the Scriptures and the good news about Jesus.

The fact that this man was allowed to go to Jerusalem to worship speaks volumes about Candace's leadership. The eunuch's understanding of the Scriptures was paramount to his ability to manage the financial affairs of the queen. With greater understanding, he could put his Lord, his life and his job in the proper perspective. The queen benefited from the spirituality of her finance chairman. Believing in God enabled him to deal fairly with others and thus enhance the integrity of her kingdom. As a result of this faith, the eunuch could be long-suffering and kind to those he met. It is quite possible that his strong faith and beliefs were qualities the queen recognized and applauded. She possibly looked beyond his managerial capabilities to his heart, and she found a man compassionate and loving. She sought and found an individual whom she could trust because he worked to please God first and others second.

Candace was confident in who she was, so she did not feel threatened by the eunuch's service to someone else. Because of her confidence, it's likely safe to say that many in the area of ancient Ethiopia and beyond know Christ today. Imagine what would have happened if she had not been a confident leader; she may have tried to suppress her treasurer. The story then would have turned out much differently.

—J. Chambers

### reflection

*How can you incorporate characteristics of Candace's secure leadership into your life?*

*Remember that when you are secure, you have no need to hurt others.*

### read

Acts 8:26–39.
See also the Inspire Notes "Human Resource Management," "Leadership: Brick by Brick, Together," "Confidence," "Confidence for Each Day," "Evangelism: Gone Fishin'" and "Servant-Leadership," and the Women of the Bible Notes "Deborah: An Uncommon Leader," "Esther: More Than a Beauty Queen" and "A Virtuous Woman: A Strong Woman, Dependent on God."

For the next Women of the Bible note, go to page 1295.

**9:14** d ver 2,21
**9:15** e Ac 13:2; Ro 1:1 f Ro 11:13; Gal 2:7,8 g Ac 25:22,23; 26:1
**9:16** h Ac 20:23; 21:11; 2Co 11:23–27
**9:19** i Ac 26:20
**9:21** j Ac 8:3
**9:22** k Ac 18:5,28
**9:26** l Ac 22:17
**9:27** m Ac 4:36

praying. [12]In a vision he has seen a man
named Ananias come and place his hands
on him to restore his sight."

[13]"Lord," Ananias answered, "I have
heard many reports about this man and
all the harm he has done to your saints in
Jerusalem. [14]And he has come here with
authority from the chief priests[d] to arrest all
who call on your name."

[15]But the Lord said to Ananias, "Go! This
man is my chosen instrument[e] to carry
my name before the Gentiles[f] and their
kings[g] and before the people of Israel. [16]I
will show him how much he must suffer for
my name."[h]

[17]Then Ananias went to the house and
entered it. Placing his hands on Saul, he
said, "Brother Saul, the Lord—Jesus, who
appeared to you on the road as you were
coming here—has sent me so that you may
see again and be filled with the Holy Spirit."
[18]Immediately, something like scales fell
from Saul's eyes, and he could see again. He
got up and was baptized, [19]and after taking
some food, he regained his strength.

## Saul in Damascus and Jerusalem

Saul spent several days with the disciples
in Damascus.[i] [20]At once he began to preach in
the synagogues that Jesus is the Son of God.
[21]All those who heard him were astonished
and asked, "Isn't he the man who raised
havoc in Jerusalem among those who call
on this name?[j] And hasn't he come here to
take them as prisoners to the chief priests?"
[22]Yet Saul grew more and more powerful
and baffled the Jews living in Damascus by
proving that Jesus is the Christ.[a][k]

[23]After many days had gone by, the Jews
conspired to kill him, [24]but Saul learned of
their plan. Day and night they kept close
watch on the city gates in order to kill him.
[25]But his followers took him by night and
lowered him in a basket through an opening in the wall.

[26]When he came to Jerusalem,[l] he tried to
join the disciples, but they were all afraid of
him, not believing that he really was a disciple. [27]But Barnabas[m] took him and brought
him to the apostles. He told them how Saul
on his journey had seen the Lord and that
the Lord had spoken to him, and how in Damascus he had preached fearlessly in the
name of Jesus.[n] [28]So Saul stayed with them
and moved about freely in Jerusalem, speaking boldly in the name of the Lord. [29]He
talked and debated with the Grecian Jews,[o]
but they tried to kill him. [30]When the brothers learned of this, they took him down to
Caesarea and sent him off to Tarsus.

[31]Then the church throughout Judea, Galilee and Samaria[p] enjoyed a time of peace.
It was strengthened; and encouraged by the
Holy Spirit, it grew in numbers, living in the
fear of the Lord.

## Aeneas and Dorcas

[32]As Peter traveled about the country, he
went to visit the saints in Lydda. [33]There
he found a man named Aeneas, a paralytic
who had been bedridden for eight years.
[34]"Aeneas," Peter said to him, "Jesus Christ
heals you.[q] Get up and take care of your
mat." Immediately Aeneas got up. [35]All
those who lived in Lydda and Sharon[r] saw
him and turned to the Lord.[s]

[36]In Joppa there was a disciple named Tabitha (which, when translated, is Dorcas[b]),
who was always doing good[t] and helping the
poor. [37]About that time she became sick and
died, and her body was washed and placed
in an upstairs room.[u] [38]Lydda was near
Joppa; so when the disciples[v] heard that Peter was in Lydda, they sent two men to him
and urged him, "Please come at once!"

[39]Peter went with them, and when he arrived he was taken upstairs to the room. All
the widows[w] stood around him, crying and
showing him the robes and other clothing
that Dorcas had made while she was still
with them.

[40]Peter sent them all out of the room;[x]
then he got down on his knees[y] and prayed.
Turning toward the dead woman, he said,
"Tabitha, get up." She opened her eyes, and
seeing Peter she sat up. [41]He took her by
the hand and helped her to her feet. Then
he called the believers and the widows and
presented her to them alive. [42]This became
known all over Joppa, and many people believed in the Lord. [43]Peter stayed in Joppa
for some time with a tanner named Simon.[z]

**9:27** n ver 20,22
**9:29** o Ac 6:1
**9:31** p Ac 8:1
**9:34** q Ac 3:6,16
**9:35** r 1Ch 5:16 s Ac 11:21
**9:36** t 1Ti 2:10
**9:37** u Ac 1:13
**9:38** v Ac 11:26
**9:39** w Ac 6:1
**9:40** x Mt 9:25 y Ac 7:60
**9:43** z Ac 10:6

[a]22 Or *Messiah* [b]36 Both *Tabitha* (Aramaic) and *Dorcas* (Greek) mean *gazelle*.

## Cornelius Calls for Peter

10 At Caesarea there was a man named Cornelius, a centurion in what was known as the Italian Regiment. 2He and all his family were devout and God-fearing;[a] he gave generously to those in need and prayed to God regularly. 3One day at about three in the afternoon[b] he had a vision. He distinctly saw an angel of God, who came to him and said, "Cornelius!"

4Cornelius stared at him in fear. "What is it, Lord?" he asked.

The angel answered, "Your prayers and gifts to the poor have come up as a memorial offering before God.[c] 5Now send men to Joppa to bring back a man named Simon who is called Peter. 6He is staying with Simon the tanner,[d] whose house is by the sea."

7When the angel who spoke to him had gone, Cornelius called two of his servants and a devout soldier who was one of his attendants. 8He told them everything that had happened and sent them to Joppa.

## Peter's Vision

9About noon the following day as they were on their journey and approaching the city, Peter went up on the roof to pray. 10He became hungry and wanted something to eat, and while the meal was being prepared, he fell into a trance. 11He saw heaven opened and something like a large sheet being let down to earth by its four corners. 12It contained all kinds of four-footed animals, as well as reptiles of the earth and birds of the air. 13Then a voice told him, "Get up, Peter. Kill and eat."

14"Surely not, Lord!" Peter replied. "I have never eaten anything impure or unclean."[e]

15The voice spoke to him a second time, "Do not call anything impure that God has made clean."[f]

16This happened three times, and immediately the sheet was taken back to heaven.

17While Peter was wondering about the meaning of the vision, the men sent by Cornelius found out where Simon's house was and stopped at the gate. 18They called out, asking if Simon who was known as Peter was staying there.

19While Peter was still thinking about the vision, the Spirit said to him, "Simon, three[a] men are looking for you. 20So get up and go downstairs. Do not hesitate to go with them, for I have sent them."[g]

21Peter went down and said to the men, "I'm the one you're looking for. Why have you come?"

22The men replied, "We have come from Cornelius the centurion. He is a righteous and God-fearing man, who is respected by all the Jewish people. A holy angel told him to have you come to his house so that he could hear what you have to say." 23Then Peter invited the men into the house to be his guests.

## Peter at Cornelius's House

The next day Peter started out with them, and some of the brothers from Joppa went along.[h] 24The following day he arrived in Caesarea. Cornelius was expecting them and had called together his relatives and close friends. 25As Peter entered the house, Cornelius met him and fell at his feet in reverence. 26But Peter made him get up. "Stand up," he said, "I am only a man myself."[i]

27Talking with him, Peter went inside and found a large gathering of people. 28He said to them: "You are well aware that it is against our law for a Jew to associate with a Gentile or visit him.[j] But God has shown me that I should not call any man impure or unclean.[k] 29So when I was sent for, I came without raising any objection. May I ask why you sent for me?"

30Cornelius answered: "Four days ago I was in my house praying at this hour, at three in the afternoon. Suddenly a man in shining clothes stood before me 31and said, 'Cornelius, God has heard your prayer and remembered your gifts to the poor. 32Send to Joppa for Simon who is called Peter. He is a guest in the home of Simon the tanner, who lives by the sea.' 33So I sent for you immediately, and it was good of you to come. Now we are all here in the presence of God to listen to everything the Lord has commanded you to tell us."

[a]19 One early manuscript *two*; other manuscripts do not have the number.

**10:2** a ver 22,35
**10:3** b Ac 3:1
**10:4** c Rev 8:4
**10:6** d Ac 9:43
**10:14** e Dt 14:3–20; Eze 4:14
**10:15** f Mt 15:11; Ro 14:14,17,20; 1Co 10:25; 1Ti 4:3,4; Tit 1:15
**10:20** g Ac 15:7–9
**10:23** h Ac 11:12
**10:26** i Rev 19:10
**10:28** j Jn 4:9; 18:28; Ac 11:3 k Ac 15:8,9

**10:34** l Dt 10:17; Ro 2:11; Eph 6:9; Col 3:25; 1Pe 1:17
**10:35** m Ac 15:9
**10:36** n Mt 28:18
**10:38** o Jn 3:2
**10:39** p Ac 5:30
**10:40** q Ac 2:24
**10:41** r Jn 14:17,22
**10:42** s Jn 5:22; 1Pe 4:5
**10:43** t Isa 53:11
**10:45** u ver 23
**10:47** v Ac 8:36; w Ac 11:17
**10:48** x Ac 2:38

34 Then Peter began to speak: "I now realize how true it is that God does not show favoritism[l] 35 but accepts men from every nation who fear him and do what is right.[m] 36 You know the message God sent to the people of Israel, telling the good news of peace through Jesus Christ, who is Lord of all.[n] 37 You know what has happened throughout Judea, beginning in Galilee after the baptism that John preached— 38 how God anointed Jesus of Nazareth with the Holy Spirit and power, and how he went around doing good and healing all who were under the power of the devil, because God was with him.[o]

39 "We are witnesses of everything he did in the country of the Jews and in Jerusalem. They killed him by hanging him on a tree,[p] 40 but God raised him from the dead[q] on the third day and caused him to be seen. 41 He was not seen by all the people,[r] but by witnesses whom God had already chosen—by us who ate and drank with him after he rose from the dead. 42 He commanded us to preach to the people and to testify that he is the one whom God appointed as judge of the living and the dead.[s] 43 All the prophets testify about him[t] that everyone who believes in him receives forgiveness of sins through his name."

44 While Peter was still speaking these words, the Holy Spirit came on all who heard the message. 45 The circumcised believers who had come with Peter[u] were astonished that the gift of the Holy Spirit had been poured out even on the Gentiles. 46 For they heard them speaking in tongues[a] and praising God.

Then Peter said, 47 "Can anyone keep these people from being baptized with water?[v] They have received the Holy Spirit just as we have."[w] 48 So he ordered that they be baptized in the name of Jesus Christ.[x] Then they asked Peter to stay with them for a few days.

## Peter Explains His Actions

11 The apostles and the brothers throughout Judea heard that the Gentiles also had received the word of God. 2 So when Peter went up to Jerusalem, the circumcised believers[y] criticized him 3 and said, "You went into the house of uncircumcised men and ate with them."[z]

4 Peter began and explained everything to them precisely as it had happened: 5 "I was in the city of Joppa praying, and in a trance I saw a vision.[a] I saw something like a large sheet being let down from heaven by its four corners, and it came down to where I was. 6 I looked into it and saw four-footed animals of the earth, wild beasts, reptiles, and birds of the air. 7 Then I heard a voice telling me, 'Get up, Peter. Kill and eat.'

8 "I replied, 'Surely not, Lord! Nothing impure or unclean has ever entered my mouth.'

9 "The voice spoke from heaven a second time, 'Do not call anything impure that God has made clean.' 10 This happened three times, and then it was all pulled up to heaven again.

11 "Right then three men who had been sent to me from Caesarea stopped at the house where I was staying. 12 The Spirit told[b] me to have no hesitation about going with them.[c] These six brothers also went with me, and we entered the man's house. 13 He told us how he had seen an angel appear in his house and say, 'Send to Joppa for Simon who is called Peter. 14 He will bring you a message through which you and all your household will be saved.'

15 "As I began to speak, the Holy Spirit came on them as he had come on us at the beginning.[d] 16 Then I remembered what the Lord had said: 'John baptized with[b] water, but you will be baptized with the Holy Spirit.'[e] 17 So if God gave them the same gift as he gave us,[f] who believed in the Lord Jesus Christ, who was I to think that I could oppose God?"

18 When they heard this, they had no further objections and praised God, saying, "So then, God has granted even the Gentiles repentance unto life."

## The Church in Antioch

19 Now those who had been scattered by the persecution in connection with Stephen[g] traveled as far as Phoenicia, Cyprus and Antioch, telling the message only to

**11:2** y Ac 10:45
**11:3** z Ac 10:25,28; Gal 2:12
**11:5** a Ac 10:9–32
**11:12** b Ac 8:29; c Ac 15:9
**11:15** d Ac 2:4
**11:16** e Mk 1:8; Ac 1:5
**11:17** f Ac 10:45,47
**11:19** g Ac 8:1,4

[a] 46 Or *other languages* [b] 16 Or *in*

Jews. 20Some of them, however, men from Cyprus[h] and Cyrene, went to Antioch and began to speak to Greeks also, telling them the good news about the Lord Jesus. 21The Lord's hand was with them,[i] and a great number of people believed and turned to the Lord.[j]

*Dear God,*

*I know that, though he was mocked and scorned for my sins, Jesus refused to return evil for evil. Help me be more honorable than those who would spitefully use me. Increase my desire and capacity for self-control. Help me resist the temptation to get even. Instead, help me in your strength to overcome evil by doing good, following the example of your sinless Son, Jesus Christ.*

*Amen*

ACTS 11:19–21

22News of this reached the ears of the church at Jerusalem, and they sent Barnabas to Antioch. 23When he arrived and saw the evidence of the grace of God,[k] he was glad and encouraged them all to remain true to the Lord with all their hearts. 24He was a good man, full of the Holy Spirit and faith, and a great number of people were brought to the Lord.[l]

25Then Barnabas went to Tarsus[m] to look for Saul, 26and when he found him, he brought him to Antioch. So for a whole year Barnabas and Saul met with the church and taught great numbers of people. The disciples were called Christians first at Antioch.

27During this time some prophets[n] came down from Jerusalem to Antioch. 28One of them, named Agabus,[o] stood up and through the Spirit predicted that a severe famine would spread over the entire Roman world. (This happened during the reign of Claudius.) 29The disciples, each according to his ability, decided to provide help[p] for the brothers living in Judea. 30This they did, sending their gift to the elders by Barnabas and Saul.[q]

## Peter's Miraculous Escape From Prison

12 It was about this time that King Herod arrested some who belonged to the church, intending to persecute them. 2He had James, the brother of John,[r] put to death with the sword. 3When he saw that this pleased the Jews, he proceeded to seize Peter also. This happened during the Feast of Unleavened Bread.[s] 4After arresting him, he put him in prison, handing him over to be guarded by four squads of four soldiers each. Herod intended to bring him out for public trial after the Passover.

5So Peter was kept in prison, but the church was earnestly praying to God for him.

6The night before Herod was to bring him to trial, Peter was sleeping between two soldiers, bound with two chains, and sentries stood guard at the entrance. 7Suddenly an angel[t] of the Lord appeared and a light shone in the cell. He struck Peter on the side and woke him up. "Quick, get up!" he said, and the chains fell off Peter's wrists.

8Then the angel said to him, "Put on your clothes and sandals." And Peter did so. "Wrap your cloak around you and follow me," the angel told him. 9Peter followed him out of the prison, but he had no idea that what the angel was doing was really happening; he thought he was seeing a vision. 10They passed the first and second guards and came to the iron gate leading to the city. It opened for them by itself,[u] and they went through it. When they had walked the length of one street, suddenly the angel left him.

11Then Peter came to himself and said, "Now I know without a doubt that the Lord sent his angel and rescued me[v] from Herod's clutches and from everything the Jewish people were anticipating."

12When this had dawned on him, he went to the house of Mary the mother of John, also called Mark,[w] where many people had gathered and were praying.[x] 13Peter knocked at the outer entrance, and a servant girl named

**11:20** h Ac 4:36
**11:21** i Lk 1:66 j Ac 2:47
**11:23** k Ac 13:43
**11:24** l ver 21; Ac 5:14
**11:25** m Ac 9:11
**11:27** n 1Co 12:28,29
**11:28** o Ac 21:10
**11:29** p Ro 15:26
**11:30** q Ac 12:25
**12:2** r Mt 4:21
**12:3** s Ex 12:15; 23:15
**12:7** t Ac 5:19
**12:10** u Ac 16:26
**12:11** v Da 3:28; 6:22
**12:12** w Ac 15:37,39 x ver 5

Rhoda came to answer the door. 14When she
recognized Peter's voice, she was so over-
joyed she ran back without opening it and
exclaimed, "Peter is at the door!"
15"You're out of your mind," they told her.
When she kept insisting that it was so, they
said, "It must be his angel."[y]
16But Peter kept on knocking, and when
they opened the door and saw him, they
were astonished. 17Peter motioned with his
hand[z] for them to be quiet and described
how the Lord had brought him out of
prison. "Tell James and the brothers about
this," he said, and then he left for another
place.
18In the morning, there was no small
commotion among the soldiers as to what
had become of Peter. 19After Herod had a
thorough search made for him and did not
find him, he cross-examined the guards
and ordered that they be executed.[a]

## Herod's Death

Then Herod went from Judea to Caesa-
rea and stayed there a while. 20He had been
quarreling with the people of Tyre and Si-
don; they now joined together and sought
an audience with him. Having secured the
support of Blastus, a trusted personal ser-
vant of the king, they asked for peace, be-
cause they depended on the king's country
for their food supply.[b]
21On the appointed day Herod, wearing
his royal robes, sat on his throne and deliv-
ered a public address to the people. 22They
shouted, "This is the voice of a god, not of
a man." 23Immediately, because Herod did
not give praise to God, an angel of the Lord
struck him down,[c] and he was eaten by
worms and died.
24But the word of God continued to in-
crease and spread.[d]
25When Barnabas and Saul had finished
their mission,[e] they returned from[a] Jeru-
salem, taking with them John, also called
Mark.

## Barnabas and Saul Sent Off

13 In the church at Antioch there were
prophets and teachers: Barnabas,[f]
Simeon called Niger, Lucius of Cyrene,
Manaen (who had been brought up with
Herod the tetrarch) and Saul. 2While they
were worshiping the Lord and fasting, the
Holy Spirit said, "Set apart for me Barnabas
and Saul for the work[g] to which I have called
them." 3So after they had fasted and prayed,
they placed their hands on them[h] and sent
them off.

## On Cyprus

4The two of them, sent on their way by
the Holy Spirit, went down to Seleucia and
sailed from there to Cyprus.[i] 5When they ar-
rived at Salamis, they proclaimed the word
of God in the Jewish synagogues. John was
with them as their helper.
6They traveled through the whole island
until they came to Paphos. There they met
a Jewish sorcerer[j] and false prophet named
Bar-Jesus, 7who was an attendant of the pro-
consul, Sergius Paulus. The proconsul, an
intelligent man, sent for Barnabas and Saul
because he wanted to hear the word of God.
8But Elymas the sorcerer[k] (for that is what
his name means) opposed them and tried

[a]25 Some manuscripts *to*

**12:15** y Mt 18:10
**12:17** z Ac 13:16; 19:33; 21:40
**12:19** a Ac 16:27
**12:20** b 1Ki 5:9,11; Eze 27:17
**12:23** c 2Sa 24:16,17
**12:24** d Ac 6:7; 19:20
**12:25** e Ac 11:30
**13:1** f Ac 11:22–26
**13:2** g Ac 14:26
**13:3** h Ac 6:6
**13:4** i Ac 4:36
**13:6** j Ac 8:9
**13:8** k Ac 8:9

## *The African Presence*

### Acts 13:1

The church at Antioch began to embrace Gentile believers. Among its leaders were Simeon, called Niger (*Niger* is Latin for "black"), and Lucius from Cyrene (the capital city of Libya on the northern coast of Africa).

# Rhoda

## *Doing Her Duty*

Rhoda was a servant girl in the household of Mary the mother of John Mark. It was in Mary's home that the believers gathered to pray for the release of Peter. That night Rhoda was doing her duty. She could have been complaining about being a servant and not being able to participate in the prayer meeting. She could have been preoccupied with her own thoughts and not attending to her task. She could have even wandered off to her own devices—for after all, although a group was assembled, their eyes were probably closed!

But Rhoda was doing her duty. She was listening for sounds beyond the door so she could warn those gathered of impending danger. The group's prayer was for Peter's safety, for he had again been taken to prison for his courageous preaching.

During the prayer session, Rhoda heard a knock at the door (see Ac 12:13). She recognized Peter's voice and immediately told those praying that their prayers had been answered. Those praying did not believe her (see Ac 12:15). They told her that the knocking must have been done by Peter's angel. But Rhoda never doubted that it was Peter's voice that she heard. She knew that God had heard and answered their prayers.

We can follow Rhoda's example of simple, childlike faith. In the face of others' disbelief, we can stand strong and keep believing. God will answer our prayers in his own way. We must be prepared and ready to receive his answer.

—E. Watson

### reflection

*How are you preparing to receive God's answer to your prayers?*

### read

Acts 12:1–19.

See also the Inspire Notes "Waiting on God," "Prayer: A God-Given Promise," "Prayer: The Antidote to Worry," "Peace" and "Prayer," and the Women of the Bible Notes "Hannah: What Do You Do When God Says 'No'?" and "The Persistent Widow: Always Pray."

For the next Women of the Bible note, go to page 1301.

**13:8** l Ac6:7
**13:9** m Ac4:8
**13:10** n Mt13:38
**13:11** o 1Sa5:6,7
**13:14** p Ac14:19,21 q Ac16:13
**13:17** r Dt7:6–8
**13:18** s Dt1:31
**13:19** t Jos19:51
**13:20** u Jdg2:16 v 1Sa3:19,20
**13:21** w 1Sa8:5,19
**13:22** x 1Sa15:23,26 y Ps89:20 z 1Sa13:14
**13:23** a Mt1:21

to turn the proconsul from the faith.[l] 9 Then Saul, who was also called Paul, filled with the Holy Spirit,[m] looked straight at Elymas and said, 10 "You are a child of the devil[n] and an enemy of everything that is right! You are full of all kinds of deceit and trickery. Will you never stop perverting the right ways of the Lord? 11 Now the hand of the Lord is against you.[o] You are going to be blind, and for a time you will be unable to see the light of the sun."

Immediately mist and darkness came over him, and he groped about, seeking someone to lead him by the hand. 12 When the proconsul saw what had happened, he believed, for he was amazed at the teaching about the Lord.

## In Pisidian Antioch

13 From Paphos, Paul and his companions sailed to Perga in Pamphylia, where John left them to return to Jerusalem. 14 From Perga they went on to Pisidian Antioch.[p] On the Sabbath[q] they entered the synagogue and sat down. 15 After the reading from the Law and the Prophets, the synagogue rulers sent word to them, saying, "Brothers, if you have a message of encouragement for the people, please speak."

16 Standing up, Paul motioned with his hand and said: "Men of Israel and you Gentiles who worship God, listen to me! 17 The God of the people of Israel chose our fathers; he made the people prosper during their stay in Egypt, with mighty power he led them out of that country,[r] 18 he endured their conduct[a][s] for about forty years in the desert, 19 he overthrew seven nations in Canaan and gave their land to his people[t] as their inheritance. 20 All this took about 450 years.

"After this, God gave them judges[u] until the time of Samuel the prophet.[v] 21 Then the people asked for a king,[w] and he gave them Saul son of Kish, of the tribe of Benjamin, who ruled forty years. 22 After removing Saul,[x] he made David their king.[y] He testified concerning him: 'I have found David son of Jesse a man after my own heart;[z] he will do everything I want him to do.'

23 "From this man's descendants God has brought to Israel the Savior Jesus,[a] as he promised. 24 Before the coming of Jesus, John preached repentance and baptism to all the people of Israel. 25 As John was completing his work, he said: 'Who do you think I am? I am not that one. No, but he is coming after me, whose sandals I am not worthy to untie.'[b]

26 "Brothers, children of Abraham, and you God-fearing Gentiles, it is to us that this message of salvation has been sent. 27 The people of Jerusalem and their rulers did not recognize Jesus,[c] yet in condemning him they fulfilled the words of the prophets that are read every Sabbath. 28 Though they found no proper ground for a death sentence, they asked Pilate to have him executed.[d] 29 When they had carried out all that was written about him,[e] they took him down from the tree and laid him in a tomb. 30 But God raised him from the dead, 31 and for many days he was seen by those who had traveled with him from Galilee to Jerusalem.[f] They are now his witnesses to our people.

32 "We tell you the good news: What God promised our fathers[g] 33 he has fulfilled for us, their children, by raising up Jesus. As it is written in the second Psalm:

"'You are my Son;
today I have become your Father.'[b][c]

34 The fact that God raised him from the dead, never to decay, is stated in these words:

"'I will give you the holy and sure
blessings promised to David.'[d][h]

35 So it is stated elsewhere:

"'You will not let your Holy One see
decay.'[e][i]

36 "For when David had served God's purpose in his own generation, he fell asleep; he was buried with his fathers[j] and his body decayed. 37 But the one whom God raised from the dead did not see decay.

38 "Therefore, my brothers, I want you to know that through Jesus the forgiveness of sins is proclaimed to you.[k] 39 Through him everyone who believes is justified from everything you could not be justified from by the law of Moses.[l] 40 Take care that what the prophets have said does not happen to you:

**13:25** b Mt3:11
**13:27** c Ac3:17
**13:28** d Mt27:20–25
**13:29** e Lk18:31
**13:31** f Mt28:16
**13:32** g Ro4:13
**13:34** h Isa55:3
**13:35** i Ps16:10
**13:36** j Ac2:29
**13:38** k Lk24:47
**13:39** l Ro3:28

[a] 18 Some manuscripts *and cared for them* [b] 33 Or *have begotten you* [c] 33 Psalm 2:7 [d] 34 Isaiah 55:3 [e] 35 Psalm 16:10

41 "'Look, you scoffers,
wonder and perish,
for I am going to do something in your
days
that you would never believe,
even if someone told you.'[a]"[m]

42 As Paul and Barnabas were leaving
the synagogue, the people invited them
to speak further about these things on the
next Sabbath. 43 When the congregation was
dismissed, many of the Jews and devout
converts to Judaism followed Paul and Bar-
nabas, who talked with them and urged
them to continue in the grace of God.[n]

44 On the next Sabbath almost the whole
city gathered to hear the word of the Lord.
45 When the Jews saw the crowds, they were
filled with jealousy and talked abusively
against what Paul was saying.

46 Then Paul and Barnabas answered
them boldly: "We had to speak the word of
God to you first.[o] Since you reject it and do
not consider yourselves worthy of eternal
life, we now turn to the Gentiles.[p] 47 For this
is what the Lord has commanded us:

"'I have made you[b] a light for the Gentiles,[q]
that you[b] may bring salvation to the
ends of the earth.'[c]"[r]

48 When the Gentiles heard this, they were
glad and honored the word of the Lord; and
all who were appointed for eternal life be-
lieved.

49 The word of the Lord spread through
the whole region. 50 But the Jews incited the
God-fearing women of high standing and
the leading men of the city. They stirred up
persecution against Paul and Barnabas, and
expelled them from their region. 51 So they
shook the dust from their feet[s] in protest
against them and went to Iconium. 52 And
the disciples were filled with joy and with
the Holy Spirit.

## In Iconium

14 At Iconium Paul and Barnabas went
as usual into the Jewish synagogue.
There they spoke so effectively that a great
number of Jews and Gentiles believed. 2 But
the Jews who refused to believe stirred up
the Gentiles and poisoned their minds
against the brothers. 3 So Paul and Barna-
bas spent considerable time there, speaking
boldly for the Lord, who confirmed the mes-
sage of his grace by enabling them to do mi-
raculous signs and wonders.[t] 4 The people of
the city were divided; some sided with the
Jews, others with the apostles. 5 There was
a plot afoot among the Gentiles and Jews,
together with their leaders, to mistreat
them and stone them. 6 But they found out
about it and fled to the Lycaonian cities of
Lystra and Derbe and to the surrounding
country, 7 where they continued to preach
the good news.

## In Lystra and Derbe

8 In Lystra there sat a man crippled in
his feet, who was lame from birth and had
never walked. 9 He listened to Paul as he was
speaking. Paul looked directly at him, saw
that he had faith to be healed 10 and called
out, "Stand up on your feet!" At that, the
man jumped up and began to walk.

11 When the crowd saw what Paul had
done, they shouted in the Lycaonian lan-
guage, "The gods have come down to us
in human form!"[u] 12 Barnabas they called
Zeus, and Paul they called Hermes because
he was the chief speaker. 13 The priest of
Zeus, whose temple was just outside the
city, brought bulls and wreaths to the city
gates because he and the crowd wanted to
offer sacrifices to them.

14 But when the apostles Barnabas and
Paul heard of this, they tore their clothes
and rushed out into the crowd, shouting:
15 "Men, why are you doing this? We too are
only men,[v] human like you. We are bring-
ing you good news, telling you to turn from
these worthless things[w] to the living God,
who made heaven and earth and sea and
everything in them.[x] 16 In the past, he let[y]
all nations go their own way.[z] 17 Yet he has
not left himself without testimony:[a] He has
shown kindness by giving you rain from
heaven and crops in their seasons;[b] he pro-
vides you with plenty of food and fills your
hearts with joy." 18 Even with these words,
they had difficulty keeping the crowd from
sacrificing to them.

**13:41** m Hab 1:5
**13:43** n Ac 11:23
**13:46** o Ac 3:26; p Ac 18:6; 28:28
**13:47** q Lk 2:32; r Isa 49:6
**13:51** s Mt 10:14; Ac 18:6
**14:3** t Jn 4:48; Heb 2:4
**14:11** u Ac 8:10; 28:6
**14:15** v Ac 10:26; Jas 5:17; w 1Sa 12:21; x Ps 146:6; Rev 14:7
**14:16** y Ac 17:30; z Ps 81:12
**14:17** a Ro 1:20; b Dt 11:14; Job 5:10; Ps 65:10

[a] 41 Hab. 1:5 [b] 47 The Greek is singular. [c] 47 Isaiah 49:6

**14:19** c Ac 13:45 d 2Co 11:25; 2Ti 3:11
**14:22** e 2Ti 3:12
**14:26** f Ac 13:1,3
**14:27** g Ac 15:4,12; 21:19 h 1Co 16:9; 2Co 2:12; Col 4:3
**15:1** i Gal 2:12 j ver 5; Gal 5:2,3
**15:2** k Gal 2:2
**15:3** l Ac 14:27

19 Then some Jews[c] came from Antioch and Iconium and won the crowd over. They stoned Paul[d] and dragged him outside the city, thinking he was dead. 20 But after the disciples had gathered around him, he got up and went back into the city. The next day he and Barnabas left for Derbe.

## The Return to Antioch in Syria

21 They preached the good news in that city and won a large number of disciples. Then they returned to Lystra, Iconium and Antioch, 22 strengthening the disciples and encouraging them to remain true to the faith. "We must go through many hardships[e] to enter the kingdom of God," they said. 23 Paul and Barnabas appointed elders[a] for them in each church and, with prayer and fasting, committed them to the Lord, in whom they had put their trust. 24 After going through Pisidia, they came into Pamphylia, 25 and when they had preached the word in Perga, they went down to Attalia.

26 From Attalia they sailed back to Antioch, where they had been committed to the grace of God for the work they had now completed.[f] 27 On arriving there, they gathered the church together and reported all that God had done through them[g] and how he had opened the door[h] of faith to the Gentiles. 28 And they stayed there a long time with the disciples.

## The Council at Jerusalem

**15** Some men[i] came down from Judea to Antioch and were teaching the brothers: "Unless you are circumcised,[j] according to the custom taught by Moses, you cannot be saved." 2 This brought Paul and Barnabas into sharp dispute and debate with them. So Paul and Barnabas were appointed, along with some other believers, to go up to Jerusalem[k] to see the apostles and elders about this question. 3 The church sent them on their way, and as they traveled through Phoenicia and Samaria, they told how the Gentiles had been converted.[l] This news made all the brothers very glad. 4 When they came to Jerusalem, they were welcomed by the church and the apostles and elders, to whom they reported everything God had done through them.[m]

5 Then some of the believers who belonged to the party of the Pharisees stood up and said, "The Gentiles must be circumcised and required to obey the law of Moses."

6 The apostles and elders met to consider this question. 7 After much discussion, Peter got up and addressed them: "Brothers, you know that some time ago God made a choice among you that the Gentiles might hear from my lips the message of the gospel and believe. 8 God, who knows the heart, showed that he accepted them by giving the Holy Spirit to them,[n] just as he did to us. 9 He made no distinction between us and them,[o] for he purified their hearts by faith. 10 Now then, why do you try to test God by putting on the necks of the disciples a yoke[p] that neither we nor our fathers have been able to bear? 11 No! We believe it is through the grace[q] of our Lord Jesus that we are saved, just as they are."

12 The whole assembly became silent as they listened to Barnabas and Paul telling about the miraculous signs and wonders God had done among the Gentiles through them.[r] 13 When they finished, James[s] spoke up: "Brothers, listen to me. 14 Simon[b] has described to us how God at first showed his concern by taking from the Gentiles a people for himself. 15 The words of the prophets are in agreement with this, as it is written:

16 " 'After this I will return
and rebuild David's fallen tent.
Its ruins I will rebuild,
and I will restore it,
17 that the remnant of men may seek the Lord,
and all the Gentiles who bear my name,
says the Lord, who does these things'[c][t]
18 that have been known for ages.[d]

19 "It is my judgment, therefore, that we should not make it difficult for the Gentiles who are turning to God. 20 Instead we should write to them, telling them to abstain from food polluted by idols,[u] from sexual immorality, from the meat of strangled

**15:4** m ver 12; Ac 14:27
**15:8** n Ac 10:44,47
**15:9** o Ac 10:28,34
**15:10** p Mt 23:4; Gal 5:1
**15:11** q Ro 3:24; Eph 2:5–8
**15:12** r Ac 14:27
**15:13** s Ac 12:17
**15:17** t Am 9:11,12
**15:20** u 1Co 10:14–28

[a] 23 Or *Barnabas ordained elders*; or *Barnabas had elders elected* [b] 14 Greek *Simeon,* a variant of *Simon*; that is, Peter
[c] 17 Amos 9:11,12 [d] 17,18 Some manuscripts *things'— / 18 known to the Lord for ages is his work*

animals and from blood.[v] 21 For Moses has been preached in every city from the earliest times and is read in the synagogues on every Sabbath."

## The Council's Letter to Gentile Believers

22 Then the apostles and elders, with the whole church, decided to choose some of their own men and send them to Antioch with Paul and Barnabas. They chose Judas (called Barsabbas) and Silas, two men who were leaders among the brothers. 23 With them they sent the following letter:

> The apostles and elders, your brothers,
>
> To the Gentile believers in Antioch, Syria and Cilicia:
>
> Greetings.
>
> 24 We have heard that some went out from us without our authorization and disturbed you, troubling your minds by what they said.[w] 25 So we all agreed to choose some men and send them to you with our dear friends Barnabas and Paul— 26 men who have risked their lives[x] for the name of our Lord Jesus Christ. 27 Therefore we are sending Judas and Silas to confirm by word of mouth what we are writing. 28 It seemed good to the Holy Spirit and to us not to burden you with anything beyond the following requirements: 29 You are to abstain from food sacrificed to idols, from blood, from the meat of strangled animals and from sexual immorality.[y] You will do well to avoid these things.
>
> Farewell.

30 The men were sent off and went down to Antioch, where they gathered the church together and delivered the letter. 31 The people read it and were glad for its encouraging message. 32 Judas and Silas, who themselves were prophets, said much to encourage and strengthen the brothers. 33 After spending some time there, they were sent off by the brothers with the blessing of peace[z] to return to those who had sent them.[a] 35 But Paul and Barnabas remained in Antioch, where they and many others taught and preached the word of the Lord.

## Disagreement Between Paul and Barnabas

36 Some time later Paul said to Barnabas, "Let us go back and visit the brothers in all the towns[a] where we preached the word of the Lord and see how they are doing." 37 Barnabas wanted to take John, also called Mark,[b] with them, 38 but Paul did not think it wise to take him, because he had deserted them[c] in Pamphylia and had not continued with them in the work. 39 They had such a sharp disagreement that they parted company. Barnabas took Mark and sailed for Cyprus, 40 but Paul chose Silas and left, commended by the brothers to the grace of the Lord. 41 He went through Syria and Cilicia, strengthening the churches.[d]

## Timothy Joins Paul and Silas

16 He came to Derbe and then to Lystra,[e] where a disciple named Timothy[f] lived, whose mother was a Jewess and a believer, but whose father was a Greek. 2 The brothers at Lystra and Iconium spoke well of him. 3 Paul wanted to take him along on the journey, so he circumcised him because of the Jews who lived in that area, for they all knew that his father was a Greek.[g] 4 As they traveled from town to town, they delivered the decisions reached by the apostles and elders[h] in Jerusalem for the people to obey.[i] 5 So the churches were strengthened in the faith and grew daily in numbers.

## Paul's Vision of the Man of Macedonia

6 Paul and his companions traveled throughout the region of Phrygia[j] and Galatia, having been kept by the Holy Spirit from preaching the word in the province of Asia. 7 When they came to the border of Mysia, they tried to enter Bithynia, but the Spirit of Jesus would not allow them to. 8 So they passed by Mysia and went down to Troas.[k] 9 During the night Paul had a vision[l] of a

[a]33 Some manuscripts *them,* [34]*but Silas decided to remain there*

**15:20** v Ge9:4
**15:24** w ver 1
**15:26** x Ac14:19
**15:29** y ver 20; Ac21:25
**15:33** z 1Co16:11
**15:36** a Ac13:4,13,14,51; 14:1,6,24,25
**15:37** b Ac12:12
**15:38** c Ac13:13
**15:41** d Ac16:5
**16:1** e Ac14:6 f Ac19:22; Ro16:21; 1Co4:17; 2Ti1:2,5,6
**16:3** g Gal2:3
**16:4** h Ac11:30 i Ac15:28,29
**16:6** j Ac18:23
**16:8** k 2Co2:12; 2Ti4:13
**16:9** l Ac9:10

**16:12** m Php 1:1
**16:13** n Ac 13:14
**16:14** o Lk 24:45
**16:16** p 1Sa 28:3,7
**16:17** q Mk 5:7
**16:19** r Ac 19:25,26 s Jas 2:6
**16:20** t Ac 17:6

man of Macedonia standing and begging
him, "Come over to Macedonia and help
us." 10After Paul had seen the vision, we got
ready at once to leave for Macedonia, con-
cluding that God had called us to preach the
gospel to them.

## Lydia's Conversion in Philippi

11From Troas we put out to sea and sailed
straight for Samothrace, and the next day
on to Neapolis. 12From there we traveled to
Philippi,[m] a Roman colony and the leading
city of that district of Macedonia. And we
stayed there several days.

13On the Sabbath[n] we went outside the city
gate to the river, where we expected to find
a place of prayer. We sat down and began
to speak to the women who had gathered
there. 14One of those listening was a woman
named Lydia, a dealer in purple cloth from
the city of Thyatira, who was a worshiper of
God. The Lord opened her heart[o] to respond
to Paul's message. 15When she and the mem-
bers of her household were baptized, she
invited us to her home. "If you consider me
a believer in the Lord," she said, "come and
stay at my house." And she persuaded us.

## Paul and Silas in Prison

16Once when we were going to the place of
prayer, we were met by a slave girl who had a
spirit[p] by which she predicted the future. She
earned a great deal of money for her owners
by fortune-telling. 17This girl followed Paul
and the rest of us, shouting, "These men are
servants of the Most High God,[q] who are
telling you the way to be saved." 18She kept
this up for many days. Finally Paul became
so troubled that he turned around and said
to the spirit, "In the name of Jesus Christ I
command you to come out of her!" At that
moment the spirit left her.

19When the owners of the slave girl re-
alized that their hope of making money[r]
was gone, they seized Paul and Silas and
dragged[s] them into the marketplace to face
the authorities. 20They brought them before
the magistrates and said, "These men are
Jews, and are throwing our city into an up-
roar[t] 21by advocating customs unlawful for
us Romans to accept or practice."

22The crowd joined in the attack against
Paul and Silas, and the magistrates ordered
them to be stripped and beaten.[u] 23After they
had been severely flogged, they were thrown
into prison, and the jailer was commanded
to guard them carefully. 24Upon receiving
such orders, he put them in the inner cell
and fastened their feet in the stocks.[v]

25About midnight Paul and Silas were
praying and singing hymns[w] to God, and
the other prisoners were listening to them.
26Suddenly there was such a violent earth-
quake that the foundations of the prison
were shaken.[x] At once all the prison doors
flew open,[y] and everybody's chains came
loose.[z] 27The jailer woke up, and when he
saw the prison doors open, he drew his
sword and was about to kill himself because
he thought the prisoners had escaped. 28But
Paul shouted, "Don't harm yourself! We are
all here!"

29The jailer called for lights, rushed in
and fell trembling before Paul and Silas.
30He then brought them out and asked,
"Sirs, what must I do to be saved?"[a]

31They replied, "Believe in the Lord
Jesus, and you will be saved—you and your
household." 32Then they spoke the word of
the Lord to him and to all the others in his
house. 33At that hour of the night[b] the jailer
took them and washed their wounds; then
immediately he and all his family were bap-
tized. 34The jailer brought them into his
house and set a meal before them; he was
filled with joy because he had come to be-
lieve in God—he and his whole family.

35When it was daylight, the magistrates
sent their officers to the jailer with the or-
der: "Release those men." 36The jailer[c] told
Paul, "The magistrates have ordered that
you and Silas be released. Now you can
leave. Go in peace."

37But Paul said to the officers: "They beat
us publicly without a trial, even though
we are Roman citizens,[d] and threw us into
prison. And now do they want to get rid of
us quietly? No! Let them come themselves
and escort us out."

38The officers reported this to the mag-
istrates, and when they heard that Paul
and Silas were Roman citizens, they were
alarmed. 39They came to appease them and
escorted them from the prison, requesting

**16:22** u 2Co 11:25; 1Th 2:2
**16:24** v Jer 20:2,3
**16:25** w Eph 5:19
**16:26** x Ac 4:31 y Ac 12:10 z Ac 12:7
**16:30** a Ac 2:37
**16:33** b ver 25
**16:36** c ver 23,27
**16:37** d Ac 22:25–29

# Lydia

## *A Model for Women in Business*

Lydia was a fascinating woman. A successful businesswoman, she traded in dye and dyed goods. Purple cloth was her specialty—a color of fabric that few could afford. She probably had a love for texture and design, and her creative side was balanced with a good sense for business.

Lydia was not only a successful and noted businesswoman, she was also a worshiper of God. On the Sabbath, Lydia was with a group of women by the bank of the river. When she heard Paul's message about Christ, she became a believer and was baptized (see Ac 16:13–15).

Lydia was also a woman of great influence. Her entire household was baptized after she opened her heart to Paul's message. She also felt compelled to invite Paul and his companions into her home. Lydia obviously impressed Paul and the others with her strong leadership. They accepted her invitation to stay with her.

Lydia receives only brief recognition in the book of Acts, yet she symbolizes the importance of strong and capable women in the church's earliest history. She was the first recorded Gentile convert in Europe, one of the first known Christian businesswomen and one of the first believers to open her home for Christian service. She took care of her business as well as God's business.

Women were converts to Christ from the start. From the beginning of church history, women publicly declared themselves followers of Jesus. Even while the disciples were in hiding, it was to women that the risen Christ was first revealed. Women were the ones who searched out the men to bring them the good news of Jesus' resurrection, and women like Lydia helped to support the spread of the Good News.

—R. Walker

### reflection

*What are you doing to help share the Good News of Christ with others?*

### read

Acts 16:6–15,40.

**See also** the Inspire Notes "Commitment to Community" and "Evangelism: Gone Fishin'," and the Women of the Bible Notes "Deborah: An Uncommon Leader" and "A Virtuous Woman: A Strong Woman, Dependent on God."

For the next Women of the Bible note, go to page 1303.

**16:39** e Mt8:34
**16:40** f ver14
**17:1** g 1Th1:1
**17:2** h Ac9:20 i Ac13:14
**17:3** j Lk24:26 k Ac18:28
**17:4** l Ac15:22
**17:5** m Ro16:21
**17:6** n Ac16:19 o Ac16:20
**17:7** p Lk23:2
**17:10** q Ac20:4
**17:11** r Lk16:29; Jn5:39

them to leave the city.[e] 40 After Paul and Silas came out of the prison, they went to Lydia's house,[f] where they met with the brothers and encouraged them. Then they left.

## In Thessalonica

17 When they had passed through Amphipolis and Apollonia, they came to Thessalonica,[g] where there was a Jewish synagogue. 2 As his custom was, Paul went into the synagogue,[h] and on three Sabbath[i] days he reasoned with them from the Scriptures, 3 explaining and proving that the Christ[a] had to suffer[j] and rise from the dead. "This Jesus I am proclaiming to you is the Christ,[a]"[k] he said. 4 Some of the Jews were persuaded and joined Paul and Silas,[l] as did a large number of God-fearing Greeks and not a few prominent women.

5 But the Jews were jealous; so they rounded up some bad characters from the marketplace, formed a mob and started a riot in the city. They rushed to Jason's[m] house in search of Paul and Silas in order to bring them out to the crowd.[b] 6 But when they did not find them, they dragged[n] Jason and some other brothers before the city officials, shouting: "These men who have caused trouble all over the world have now come here,[o] 7 and Jason has welcomed them into his house. They are all defying Caesar's decrees, saying that there is another king, one called Jesus."[p] 8 When they heard this, the crowd and the city officials were thrown into turmoil. 9 Then they made Jason and the others post bond and let them go.

## In Berea

10 As soon as it was night, the brothers sent Paul and Silas away to Berea.[q] On arriving there, they went to the Jewish synagogue. 11 Now the Bereans were of more noble character than the Thessalonians, for they received the message with great eagerness and examined the Scriptures[r] every day to see if what Paul said was true. 12 Many of the Jews believed, as did also a number of prominent Greek women and many Greek men.

13 When the Jews in Thessalonica learned that Paul was preaching the word of God at Berea, they went there too, agitating the crowds and stirring them up. 14 The brothers immediately sent Paul to the coast, but Silas and Timothy[s] stayed at Berea. 15 The men who escorted Paul brought him to Athens[t] and then left with instructions for Silas and Timothy to join him as soon as possible.[u]

## In Athens

16 While Paul was waiting for them in Athens, he was greatly distressed to see that the city was full of idols. 17 So he reasoned in the synagogue with the Jews and the God-fearing Greeks, as well as in the marketplace day by day with those who happened to be there. 18 A group of Epicurean and Stoic philosophers began to dispute with him. Some of them asked, "What is this babbler trying to say?" Others remarked, "He seems to be advocating foreign gods." They said this because Paul was preaching the good news about Jesus and the resurrection.[v] 19 Then they took him and brought him to a meeting of the Areopagus, where they said to him, "May we know what this new teaching is that you are presenting? 20 You are bringing some strange ideas to our ears, and we want to know what they mean." 21 (All the Athenians and the foreigners who lived there spent their time doing nothing but talking about and listening to the latest ideas.)

22 Paul then stood up in the meeting of the Areopagus and said: "Men of Athens! I see that in every way you are very religious. 23 For as I walked around and looked carefully at your objects of worship, I even found an altar with this inscription: TO AN UNKNOWN GOD. Now what you worship as something unknown I am going to proclaim to you.

24 "The God who made the world and everything in it[w] is the Lord of heaven and earth[x] and does not live in temples built by hands.[y] 25 And he is not served by human hands, as if he needed anything, because he himself gives all men life and breath and everything else.[z] 26 From one man he made every nation of men, that they should inhabit the whole earth; and he determined the times set for them and the exact places where they should live.[a] 27 God did this so that men would seek him and perhaps reach out for him and find him, though he is not far from

**17:14** s Ac16:1
**17:15** t ver16,21,22 u Ac18:5
**17:18** v Ac4:2
**17:24** w Ac14:15 x Mt11:25 y Ac7:48
**17:25** z Isa42:5
**17:26** a Dt32:8

[a]3 Or *Messiah* [b]5 Or *the assembly of the people*

# Fortune-Telling Slave Girl

## A Surprising Testimony to God's Work

Fortune-telling was a common practice in the Greek and Roman cultures in New Testament times. Divination, the attempt to foretell the unknown and predict the future, and many superstitious practices were common. In the Jewish culture these practices were punishable by death (see Lev 20:27; Dt 18:10–12). Those who practiced fortune-telling were astrologers, charmers, false prophets and sorcerers.

A young slave girl possessed with a spirit of divination approached Paul and Silas one day when they went to preach at Philippi (see Ac 16:16). The demonic spirit gave her the power to predict the future. The spirit spoke the truth mockingly. Her masters profited from her unfortunate condition by using her for their own gain.

She followed Paul and Silas for several days, yelling that these men were servants of the Most High God and were showing the people the way of salvation (see Ac 16:17). Being grieved in his spirit, Paul took spiritual authority over the unclean spirit and commanded it to leave the young girl. In the name of Jesus, the girl was freed. Her owners were angry when they realized that any chance of making more money from the slave girl was gone. As a result, Paul and Silas were taken before the magistrates, beaten, imprisoned and carefully watched by the prison guard. Through prayer and singing, the miraculous occurred. An earthquake shook the prison doors open, and the prisoners' chains came loose. Grateful that the prisoners did not escape and that he was stopped from committing suicide by Paul, the guard—along with his entire family—was saved and baptized.

This is the only time the book of Acts mentions the fortune-telling slave girl. Her testimony, however, will stand forever, proving that God can bring glory out of the most unfair, abusive and harsh situations. In today's society, divination is subtly camouflaged as entertainment. The commercials and infomercials are creative enough to raise a woman's curiosity. The most important areas of life are targeted: love, sex and work. Women of color must be careful not to fall prey to demonic spirits. We must trust in the true God for our future because his voice is truth.

—G. London

### reflection

*Whose voice do you listen to regarding plans for your future?*

### read

Acts 16:16–40.
**See also** the Inspire Notes "Bumping Into Omnipotence," "God Is Immutable," "God Is Sovereign" and "Omniscience: God Is All-Knowing."

For the next Women of the Bible note, go to page 1310.

each one of us.[b] 28 ‘For in him we live and move and have our being.’ As some of your own poets have said, ‘We are his offspring.’

29 “Therefore since we are God’s offspring, we should not think that the divine being is like gold or silver or stone—an image made by man’s design and skill.[c] 30 In the past God overlooked[d] such ignorance, but now he commands all people everywhere to repent.[e] 31 For he has set a day when he will judge the world with justice by the man he has appointed.[f] He has given proof of this to all men by raising him from the dead.”[g]

32 When they heard about the resurrection of the dead, some of them sneered, but others said, “We want to hear you again on this subject.” 33 At that, Paul left the Council. 34 A few men became followers of Paul and believed. Among them was Dionysius, a member of the Areopagus,[h] also a woman named Damaris, and a number of others.

## In Corinth

18 After this, Paul left Athens[i] and went to Corinth. 2 There he met a Jew named Aquila, a native of Pontus, who had recently come from Italy with his wife Priscilla,[j] because Claudius had ordered all the Jews to leave Rome. Paul went to see them, 3 and because he was a tentmaker as they were, he stayed and worked with them.[k] 4 Every Sabbath he reasoned in the synagogue, trying to persuade Jews and Greeks.

5 When Silas and Timothy came from Macedonia,[l] Paul devoted himself exclusively to preaching, testifying to the Jews that Jesus was the Christ.[a][m] 6 But when the Jews opposed Paul and became abusive, he shook out his clothes in protest and said to them, “Your blood be on your own heads![n] I am clear of my responsibility.[o] From now on I will go to the Gentiles.”[p]

7 Then Paul left the synagogue and went next door to the house of Titius Justus, a worshiper of God. 8 Crispus,[q] the synagogue ruler, and his entire household believed in the Lord; and many of the Corinthians who heard him believed and were baptized.

9 One night the Lord spoke to Paul in a vision: “Do not be afraid; keep on speaking, do not be silent. 10 For I am with you, and no one is going to attack and harm you, because I have many people in this city.” 11 So Paul stayed for a year and a half, teaching them the word of God.

12 While Gallio was proconsul of Achaia, the Jews made a united attack on Paul and brought him into court. 13 “This man,” they charged, “is persuading the people to worship God in ways contrary to the law.”

14 Just as Paul was about to speak, Gallio said to the Jews, “If you Jews were making a complaint about some misdemeanor or serious crime, it would be reasonable for me to listen to you. 15 But since it involves questions about words and names and your own law—settle the matter yourselves. I will not be a judge of such things.” 16 So he had them ejected from the court. 17 Then they all turned on Sosthenes[r] the synagogue ruler and beat him in front of the court. But Gallio showed no concern whatever.

## Priscilla, Aquila and Apollos

18 Paul stayed on in Corinth for some time. Then he left the brothers and sailed for Syria, accompanied by Priscilla and Aquila. Before he sailed, he had his hair cut off at Cenchrea[s] because of a vow he had taken.[t] 19 They arrived at Ephesus, where Paul left Priscilla and Aquila. He himself went into the synagogue and reasoned with the Jews. 20 When they asked him to spend more time with them, he declined. 21 But as he left, he promised, “I will come back if it is God’s will.”[u] Then he set sail from Ephesus. 22 When he landed at Caesarea, he went up and greeted the church and then went down to Antioch.[v]

23 After spending some time in Antioch, Paul set out from there and traveled from place to place throughout the region of Galatia and Phrygia, strengthening all the disciples.

24 Meanwhile a Jew named Apollos,[w] a native of Alexandria, came to Ephesus. He was a learned man, with a thorough knowledge of the Scriptures. 25 He had been instructed in the way of the Lord, and he spoke with great fervor[b] and taught about Jesus accurately, though he knew only the baptism of John.[x] 26 He began to speak boldly in the

**17:27** b Ac 14:17
**17:29** c Isa 40:18–20
**17:30** d Ac 14:16; Ro 3:25 e Lk 24:47; Tit 2:11,12
**17:31** f Ac 10:42 g Ac 2:24
**17:34** h ver 19,22
**18:1** i Ac 17:15
**18:2** j Ro 16:3; 1Co 16:19; 2Ti 4:19
**18:3** k Ac 20:34; 1Co 4:12
**18:5** l Ac 17:14,15 m ver 28; Ac 17:3
**18:6** n 2Sa 1:16 o Ac 20:26 p Ac 13:46
**18:8** q 1Co 1:14
**18:17** r 1Co 1:1
**18:18** s Ro 16:1 t Nu 6:2,5,18; Ac 21:24
**18:21** u 1Co 4:19
**18:22** v Ac 11:19
**18:24** w 1Co 1:12; 3:5,6,22; 4:6; Tit 3:13
**18:25** x Ac 19:3

[a] 5 Or *Messiah;* also in verse 28 [b] 25 Or *with fervor in the Spirit*

# Inspire

## WOMEN IN TEACHING MINISTRIES

Teaching is identified in the New Testament as one of the spiritual gifts (see Ro 12:7; 1Co 12:28; Eph 4:11). The purpose of this gift is "to prepare God's people for works of service, so that the body of Christ may be built up . . . and become mature" (Eph 4:12–13). The teacher is by nature a nurturer and developer, one who is called to train, model and mold others from infancy to maturity.

The role of the teacher (especially of children) has long been a socially acceptable place for women, particularly in the church. This function is considered the natural outgrowth of what a woman is "supposed to do." Many faithful women have taught and nurtured young people, who have in turn gone on to become powerful deliverers of God's Word; many devoted women have planted and nurtured seeds that have grown into sturdy plants in God's kingdom.

In the book of Acts a Jew named Apollos, a man who was knowledgeable in the Old Testament Scriptures and spoke boldly from his limited knowledge of Christ, was taught by a woman named Priscilla and her husband Aquila (see Ac 18:24–28). Numerous Bible scholars have conjectured that Priscilla was probably the main teacher because her name is listed first in the husband-wife pairing in a number of instances (see Ac 18:18,19,26; Ro 16:3; 2Ti 4:19)—an unusual practice in that day. Priscilla's gift of teaching was both evident and acknowledged.

Furthermore, the apostle Paul encouraged older women to teach younger women (see Tit 2:3–5). In 2 Timothy 1:3–5 he applauded Timothy's grandmother Lois and his mother Eunice for nurturing Timothy in the faith. Some of the earliest memories for many Christians of church and of the love of God involve the loving sister who helped form their eager little minds in Sunday school.

Thank God for the teaching ministry of these anointed women! Thank God that these women accepted their calling and were faithful in sharing God's Word through teaching. Pray that the flame of their love and dedication may continue to burn brightly for future generations.

—C. Woods

### read

Acts 18:1–4,18–28; Romans 12:3–8; 1 Corinthians 12:12–30; Ephesians 4:1–16; Titus 2:1–5.

See also the Inspire Notes "A Great Challenge: Teaching Our Children," "Influencing Others," "Evangelism: Gone Fishin' " and "Female Ministers and Evangelists," and the Women of the Bible Notes "Anna: A Model of Spiritual Devotion," "Philip's Daughters: Those Preaching Women" and "Priscilla: An Open-Door Policy."

### WOMAN of COLOR

What female teachers have helped to shape your faith? How can you model their examples?

For the next Inspire note, go to page 1323.

## The African Presence

**Acts 18:24**

Apollos came from Alexandria, a city built by Alexander the Great on the Nile delta on the northern coast of Africa. For more on Alexandria, see the African Presence note on John 1.

**18:28** y ver 5
**19:6** z Ac 6:6; 8:17 a Ac 2:4 b Ac 10:46
**19:8** c Ac 1:3; 28:23
**19:9** d Ac 9:2

synagogue. When Priscilla and Aquila heard him, they invited him to their home and explained to him the way of God more adequately.

27 When Apollos wanted to go to Achaia, the brothers encouraged him and wrote to the disciples there to welcome him. On arriving, he was a great help to those who by grace had believed. 28 For he vigorously refuted the Jews in public debate, proving from the Scriptures that Jesus was the Christ.[y]

### Paul in Ephesus

19 While Apollos was at Corinth, Paul took the road through the interior and arrived at Ephesus. There he found some disciples 2 and asked them, "Did you receive the Holy Spirit when[a] you believed?"

They answered, "No, we have not even heard that there is a Holy Spirit."

3 So Paul asked, "Then what baptism did you receive?"

"John's baptism," they replied.

4 Paul said, "John's baptism was a baptism of repentance. He told the people to believe in the one coming after him, that is, in Jesus." 5 On hearing this, they were baptized into[b] the name of the Lord Jesus. 6 When Paul placed his hands on them,[z] the Holy Spirit came on them,[a] and they spoke in tongues[c][b] and prophesied. 7 There were about twelve men in all.

8 Paul entered the synagogue and spoke boldly there for three months, arguing persuasively about the kingdom of God.[c] 9 But some of them became obstinate; they refused to believe and publicly maligned the Way.[d] So Paul left them. He took the disciples with him and had discussions daily in the lecture hall of Tyrannus. 10 This went on for two years,[e] so that all the Jews and Greeks who lived in the province of Asia heard the word of the Lord.

11 God did extraordinary miracles through Paul, 12 so that even handkerchiefs and aprons that had touched him were taken to the sick, and their illnesses were cured[f] and the evil spirits left them.

13 Some Jews who went around driving out evil spirits[g] tried to invoke the name of the Lord Jesus over those who were demon-possessed. They would say, "In the name of Jesus, whom Paul preaches, I command you to come out." 14 Seven sons of Sceva, a Jewish chief priest, were doing this. 15 ⌞One day,⌟ the evil spirit answered them, "Jesus I know, and I know about Paul, but who are you?" 16 Then the man who had the evil spirit jumped on them and overpowered them all. He gave them such a beating that they ran out of the house naked and bleeding.

17 When this became known to the Jews and Greeks living in Ephesus, they were all seized with fear,[h] and the name of the Lord Jesus was held in high honor. 18 Many of those who believed now came and openly confessed their evil deeds. 19 A number who had practiced sorcery brought their scrolls together and burned them publicly. When they calculated the value of the scrolls, the total came to fifty thousand drachmas.[d] 20 In this way the word of the Lord spread widely and grew in power.[i]

21 After all this had happened, Paul decided to go to Jerusalem,[j] passing through Macedonia and Achaia. "After I have been there," he said, "I must visit Rome also."[k] 22 He sent two of his helpers,[l] Timothy and

**19:10** e Ac 20:31
**19:12** f Ac 5:15
**19:13** g Mt 12:27
**19:17** h Ac 5:5,11
**19:20** i Ac 6:7; 12:24
**19:21** j Ro 15:25 k Ro 15:24,28
**19:22** l Ac 13:5

[a] 2 Or *after* [b] 5 Or *in* [c] 6 Or *other languages* [d] 19 A drachma was a silver coin worth about a day's wages.

Erastus,[m] to Macedonia, while he stayed in the province of Asia a little longer.

## The Riot in Ephesus

23 About that time there arose a great disturbance about the Way. 24 A silversmith named Demetrius, who made silver shrines of Artemis, brought in no little business for the craftsmen. 25 He called them together, along with the workmen in related trades, and said: "Men, you know we receive a good income from this business. 26 And you see and hear how this fellow Paul has convinced and led astray large numbers of people here in Ephesus and in practically the whole province of Asia. He says that man-made gods are no gods at all.[n] 27 There is danger not only that our trade will lose its good name, but also that the temple of the great goddess Artemis will be discredited, and the goddess herself, who is worshiped throughout the province of Asia and the world, will be robbed of her divine majesty."

28 When they heard this, they were furious and began shouting: "Great is Artemis of the Ephesians!" 29 Soon the whole city was in an uproar. The people seized Gaius and Aristarchus,[o] Paul's traveling companions from Macedonia, and rushed as one man into the theater. 30 Paul wanted to appear before the crowd, but the disciples would not let him. 31 Even some of the officials of the province, friends of Paul, sent him a message begging him not to venture into the theater.

32 The assembly was in confusion: Some were shouting one thing, some another. Most of the people did not even know why they were there. 33 The Jews pushed Alexander to the front, and some of the crowd shouted instructions to him. He motioned[p] for silence in order to make a defense before the people. 34 But when they realized he was a Jew, they all shouted in unison for about two hours: "Great is Artemis of the Ephesians!"

35 The city clerk quieted the crowd and said: "Men of Ephesus, doesn't all the world know that the city of Ephesus is the guardian of the temple of the great Artemis and of her image, which fell from heaven? 36 Therefore, since these facts are undeniable, you ought to be quiet and not do anything rash. 37 You have brought these men here, though they have neither robbed temples[q] nor blasphemed our goddess. 38 If, then, Demetrius and his fellow craftsmen have a grievance against anybody, the courts are open and there are proconsuls. They can press charges. 39 If there is anything further you want to bring up, it must be settled in a legal assembly. 40 As it is, we are in danger of being charged with rioting because of today's events. In that case we would not be able to account for this commotion, since there is no reason for it." 41 After he had said this, he dismissed the assembly.

## Through Macedonia and Greece

20 When the uproar had ended, Paul sent for the disciples and, after encouraging them, said good-by and set out for Macedonia. 2 He traveled through that area, speaking many words of encouragement to the people, and finally arrived in Greece, 3 where he stayed three months. Because the Jews made a plot against him[r] just as he was about to sail for Syria, he decided to go back through Macedonia. 4 He was accompanied by Sopater son of Pyrrhus from Berea, Aristarchus[s] and Secundus from Thessalonica, Gaius from Derbe, Timothy[t] also, and Tychicus[u] and Trophimus[v] from the province of Asia. 5 These men went on ahead and waited for us at Troas. 6 But we sailed from Philippi after the Feast of Unleavened Bread, and five days later joined the others at Troas,[w] where we stayed seven days.

## Eutychus Raised From the Dead at Troas

7 On the first day of the week[x] we came together to break bread. Paul spoke to the people and, because he intended to leave the next day, kept on talking until midnight. 8 There were many lamps in the upstairs room[y] where we were meeting. 9 Seated in a window was a young man named Eutychus, who was sinking into a deep sleep as Paul talked on and on. When he was sound asleep, he fell to the ground from the third story and was picked up dead. 10 Paul went down, threw himself on the young man[z] and put his arms around him. "Don't be alarmed," he said. "He's alive!"[a] 11 Then he

**19:22** m Ro 16:23; 2Ti 4:20
**19:26** n Ps 115:4; Isa 44:10–20; Jer 10:3–5
**19:29** o Ac 20:4; 27:2; Col 4:10; Phm 24
**19:33** p Ac 12:17
**19:37** q Ro 2:22
**20:3** r Ac 9:23,24
**20:4** s Ac 19:29 t Ac 16:1 u Eph 6:21; Col 4:7; Tit 3:12 v Ac 21:29; 2Ti 4:20
**20:6** w Ac 16:8
**20:7** x 1Co 16:2; Rev 1:10
**20:8** y Ac 1:13
**20:10** z 1Ki 17:21 a Mt 9:23,24

**20:16** b Ac 19:21 c Ac 2:1
**20:18** d Ac 18:19–21; 19:1–41
**20:20** e ver 27
**20:21** f Ac 18:5 g Ac 2:38
**20:24** h Ac 21:13 i Gal 1:1
**20:26** j Ac 18:6
**20:27** k ver 20

went upstairs again and broke bread and
ate. After talking until daylight, he left.
12 The people took the young man home alive
and were greatly comforted.

## Paul's Farewell to the Ephesian Elders

13 We went on ahead to the ship and sailed
for Assos, where we were going to take Paul
aboard. He had made this arrangement be-
cause he was going there on foot. 14 When he
met us at Assos, we took him aboard and
went on to Mitylene. 15 The next day we set
sail from there and arrived off Kios. The day
after that we crossed over to Samos, and on
the following day arrived at Miletus. 16 Paul
had decided to sail past Ephesus to avoid
spending time in the province of Asia, for
he was in a hurry to reach Jerusalem,[b] if pos-
sible, by the day of Pentecost.[c]
17 From Miletus, Paul sent to Ephesus
for the elders of the church. 18 When they
arrived, he said to them: "You know how I
lived the whole time I was with you,[d] from
the first day I came into the province of Asia.
19 I served the Lord with great humility and
with tears, although I was severely tested
by the plots of the Jews. 20 You know that I
have not hesitated to preach anything[e] that
would be helpful to you but have taught you
publicly and from house to house. 21 I have
declared to both Jews[f] and Greeks that they
must turn to God in repentance[g] and have
faith in our Lord Jesus.
22 "And now, compelled by the Spirit, I am
going to Jerusalem, not knowing what will
happen to me there. 23 I only know that in ev-
ery city the Holy Spirit warns me that prison
and hardships are facing me. 24 However,
I consider my life worth nothing to me,[h] if
only I may finish the race and complete the
task the Lord Jesus has given me[i]—the task
of testifying to the gospel of God's grace.
25 "Now I know that none of you among
whom I have gone about preaching the
kingdom will ever see me again. 26 There-
fore, I declare to you today that I am inno-
cent of the blood of all men.[j] 27 For I have
not hesitated to proclaim to you the whole
will of God.[k] 28 Keep watch over yourselves
and all the flock of which the Holy Spirit
has made you overseers.[a][l] Be shepherds of
the church of God,[b] which he bought with
his own blood. 29 I know that after I leave,
savage wolves will come in among you and
will not spare the flock. 30 Even from your
own number men will arise and distort the
truth in order to draw away disciples after
them. 31 So be on your guard! Remember
that for three years[m] I never stopped warn-
ing each of you night and day with tears.
32 "Now I commit you to God and to the
word of his grace, which can build you
up and give you an inheritance[n] among
all those who are sanctified.[o] 33 I have not
coveted anyone's silver or gold or clothing.[p]
34 You yourselves know that these hands of
mine have supplied my own needs and the
needs of my companions.[q] 35 In everything I
did, I showed you that by this kind of hard
work we must help the weak, remembering
the words the Lord Jesus himself said: 'It is
more blessed to give than to receive.'"
36 When he had said this, he knelt down
with all of them and prayed.[r] 37 They all
wept as they embraced him and kissed him.
38 What grieved them most was his statement
that they would never see his face again.[s]
Then they accompanied him to the ship.

## On to Jerusalem

21 After we had torn ourselves away
from them, we put out to sea and
sailed straight to Cos. The next day we went
to Rhodes and from there to Patara. 2 We
found a ship crossing over to Phoenicia,
went on board and set sail. 3 After sighting
Cyprus and passing to the south of it, we
sailed on to Syria. We landed at Tyre, where
our ship was to unload its cargo. 4 Finding
the disciples there, we stayed with them
seven days. Through the Spirit[t] they urged
Paul not to go on to Jerusalem. 5 But when
our time was up, we left and continued on
our way. All the disciples and their wives
and children accompanied us out of the city,
and there on the beach we knelt to pray.[u] 6 Af-
ter saying good-by to each other, we went
aboard the ship, and they returned home.
7 We continued our voyage from Tyre and
landed at Ptolemais, where we greeted the
brothers and stayed with them for a day.

**20:28** l 1Pe 5:2
**20:31** m Ac 19:10
**20:32** n Col 1:12; 3:24; 1Pe 1:4 o Ac 26:18
**20:33** p 1Co 9:12; 2Co 12:14–17
**20:34** q Ac 18:3
**20:36** r Ac 21:5
**20:38** s ver 25
**21:4** t Ac 20:23
**21:5** u Ac 20:36

[a] 28 Traditionally *bishops* [b] 28 Many manuscripts *of the Lord*

**21:8** v Ac 6:5; w Eph 4:11; 2Ti 4:5
**21:10** x Ac 11:28
**21:13** y Ac 20:24
**21:17** z Ac 15:4
**21:19** a Ac 1:17
**21:20** b Ac 22:3; Ro 10:2; Gal 1:14
**21:21** c 1Co 7:18,19
**21:23** d Ac 18:18

8 Leaving the next day, we reached Caesarea and stayed at the house of Philip[v] the evangelist,[w] one of the Seven. 9 He had four unmarried daughters who prophesied.

10 After we had been there a number of days, a prophet named Agabus[x] came down from Judea. 11 Coming over to us, he took Paul's belt, tied his own hands and feet with it and said, "The Holy Spirit says, 'In this way the Jews of Jerusalem will bind the owner of this belt and will hand him over to the Gentiles.' "

12 When we heard this, we and the people there pleaded with Paul not to go up to Jerusalem. 13 Then Paul answered, "Why are you weeping and breaking my heart? I am ready not only to be bound, but also to die[y] in Jerusalem for the name of the Lord Jesus." 14 When he would not be dissuaded, we gave up and said, "The Lord's will be done."

15 After this, we got ready and went up to Jerusalem. 16 Some of the disciples from Caesarea accompanied us and brought us to the home of Mnason, where we were to stay. He was a man from Cyprus and one of the early disciples.

## Paul's Arrival at Jerusalem

17 When we arrived at Jerusalem, the brothers received us warmly.[z] 18 The next day Paul and the rest of us went to see James, and all the elders were present. 19 Paul greeted them and reported in detail what God had done among the Gentiles through his ministry.[a]

20 When they heard this, they praised God. Then they said to Paul: "You see, brother, how many thousands of Jews have believed, and all of them are zealous[b] for the law. 21 They have been informed that you teach all the Jews who live among the Gentiles to turn away from Moses, telling them not to circumcise their children[c] or live according to our customs. 22 What shall we do? They will certainly hear that you have come, 23 so do what we tell you. There are four men with us who have made a vow.[d] 24 Take these men, join in their purification rites and pay their expenses, so that they can have their heads shaved. Then everybody will know there is no truth in these reports about you, but that you yourself are living in obedience to the law. 25 As for the Gentile believers, we have written to them our decision that they should abstain from food sacrificed to idols, from blood, from the meat of strangled animals and from sexual immorality."[e]

26 The next day Paul took the men and purified himself along with them. Then he went to the temple to give notice of the date when the days of purification would end and the offering would be made for each of them.[f]

## Paul Arrested

27 When the seven days were nearly over, some Jews from the province of Asia saw Paul at the temple. They stirred up the whole crowd and seized him,[g] 28 shouting, "Men of Israel, help us! This is the man who teaches all men everywhere against our people and our law and this place. And besides, he has brought Greeks into the temple area and defiled this holy place."[h] 29 (They had previously seen Trophimus[i] the Ephesian in the city with Paul and assumed that Paul had brought him into the temple area.)

30 The whole city was aroused, and the people came running from all directions. Seizing Paul,[j] they dragged him from the temple, and immediately the gates were shut. 31 While they were trying to kill him, news reached the commander of the Roman troops that the whole city of Jerusalem was in an uproar. 32 He at once took some officers and soldiers and ran down to the crowd. When the rioters saw the commander and his soldiers, they stopped beating Paul.[k]

33 The commander came up and arrested him and ordered him to be bound[l] with two chains.[m] Then he asked who he was and what he had done. 34 Some in the crowd shouted one thing and some another, and since the commander could not get at the truth because of the uproar, he ordered that Paul be taken into the barracks. 35 When Paul reached the steps, the violence of the mob was so great he had to be carried by the soldiers. 36 The crowd that followed kept shouting, "Away with him!"[n]

## Paul Speaks to the Crowd

37 As the soldiers were about to take Paul into the barracks, he asked the commander, "May I say something to you?"

**21:25** e Ac 15:20,29
**21:26** f Nu 6:13–20
**21:27** g Ac 24:18
**21:28** h Ac 24:5,6
**21:29** i Ac 20:4
**21:30** j Ac 26:21
**21:32** k Ac 23:27
**21:33** l ver 11; m Ac 20:23
**21:36** n Lk 23:18; Ac 22:22

# Philip's Daughters

## Those Preaching Women

In the world of the Bible, women were often mentioned in passing, if at all. Yet their gifts and contributions to the life of the community and the work of the ministry often shine through like a candle in a dark room. Such is the case with the daughters of Philip. Acts 21:9 makes a cursory reference to these women. As a matter of fact, one could read this chapter and completely overlook the significance of these women's ministries.

Philip had four daughters (no mention is made of his wife). They were women of high moral character who apparently had chosen to be single and celibate. They were preaching women—women who spoke inspired utterances from God. And they were appreciated for more than their prophetic gifts. A couple of centuries later, the church historian Eusebius wrote that Philip's daughters were recognized as authorities on persons and events of the early church. In fact, Philip and his daughters may well have been key information sources for Luke, the author of the Gospel of Luke and the book of Acts. Yet they lived in a culture that typically denied the personhood and presence of women.

Historical as well as contemporary African American women have faced a similar situation. Too often our contributions have been overlooked in the light of the achievements of African American men. Yet the powerful public preaching of women such as Jarena Lee, Florence Spearing Randolph and Vashti McKenzie continue to break through. As a community of believers, we must work together as women and men of God in the spread of the gospel. Supportive of the gifts that we each bring to the task, we are to model inclusion, thereby advancing God's kingdom.

Whether you are called by God to preach the gospel from the pulpit or to serve faithfully in the pew, as a woman, you continue to play a significant role in the church, in society and in the advancement of God's kingdom. We cannot allow culture, tradition, denomination or gender to hinder us from that which God has called and anointed us to do. Black women: Preach on!

—A. E. Crawford

### reflection

*What has God called you to do today?*

*Do it faithfully!*

### read

Acts 21:8–9; see also Joel 2:28–29; Matthew 19:10–12; 1 Corinthians 7:32–35.

See also the Inspire Notes "Confidence," "Confidence for Each Day," "Female Ministers and Evangelists," "Servant-Leadership," "Women in Preaching Ministries," "Women in Teaching Ministries" and "Celibacy," and the Women of the Bible Notes "Deborah: An Uncommon Leader," "Huldah: A Prophetess of God," "Queen Vashti: A Woman of Strength" and "A Virtuous Woman: A Strong Woman, Dependent on God."

For the next Women of the Bible note, go to page 1341.

## The African Presence

**Acts 21:38**
The Roman official who arrested Paul during a conflict between the Jews and Paul outside the temple mistook Paul for an Egyptian leader of a revolt against Rome. It was not until Paul spoke Greek to the official that he recognized Paul as a Hellenistic Jew.

"Do you speak Greek?" he replied.
38"Aren't you the Egyptian who started a
revolt and led four thousand terrorists out
into the desert some time ago?"[o]
39Paul answered, "I am a Jew, from Tar-
sus[p] in Cilicia, a citizen of no ordinary city.
Please let me speak to the people."
40Having received the commander's
permission, Paul stood on the steps and
motioned[q] to the crowd. When they were
all silent, he said to them in Aramaic[a]:

22 1"Brothers and fathers,[r] listen now
to my defense."
2When they heard him speak to them in
Aramaic, they became very quiet.
Then Paul said: 3"I am a Jew,[s] born in
Tarsus of Cilicia, but brought up in this city.
Under Gamaliel I was thoroughly trained
in the law of our fathers[t] and was just as
zealous[u] for God as any of you are today.
4I persecuted[v] the followers of this Way to
their death, arresting both men and women
and throwing them into prison, 5as also the
high priest and all the Council[w] can testify.
I even obtained letters from them to their
brothers in Damascus,[x] and went there to
bring these people as prisoners to Jerusalem
to be punished.
6"About noon as I came near Damascus,
suddenly a bright light from heaven flashed
around me. 7I fell to the ground and heard
a voice say to me, 'Saul! Saul! Why do you
persecute me?'
8"'Who are you, Lord?' I asked.
"'I am Jesus of Nazareth, whom you are
persecuting,' he replied. 9My companions
saw the light, but they did not understand
the voice[y] of him who was speaking to me.
10"'What shall I do, Lord?' I asked.
"'Get up,' the Lord said, 'and go into
Damascus. There you will be told all that
you have been assigned to do.' 11My com-
panions led me by the hand into Damas-
cus, because the brilliance of the light had
blinded me.
12"A man named Ananias came to see
me.[z] He was a devout observer of the law and
highly respected by all the Jews living there.
13He stood beside me and said, 'Brother
Saul, receive your sight!' And at that very
moment I was able to see him.
14"Then he said: 'The God of our fathers[a]
has chosen you to know his will and to see
the Righteous One and to hear words from
his mouth. 15You will be his witness to all
men of what you have seen and heard. 16And
now what are you waiting for? Get up, be
baptized[b] and wash your sins away,[c] calling
on his name.'
17"When I returned to Jerusalem and was
praying at the temple, I fell into a trance[d]
18and saw the Lord speaking. 'Quick!' he
said to me. 'Leave Jerusalem immediately,
because they will not accept your testimony
about me.'
19"'Lord,' I replied, 'these men know
that I went from one synagogue to another
to imprison[e] and beat[f] those who believe in
you. 20And when the blood of your martyr[b]
Stephen was shed, I stood there giving my
approval and guarding the clothes of those
who were killing him.'[g]
21"Then the Lord said to me, 'Go; I will
send you far away to the Gentiles.'"[h]

### Paul the Roman Citizen

22The crowd listened to Paul until he
said this. Then they raised their voices and

**21:38** o Ac 5:36
**21:39** p Ac 9:11
**21:40** q Ac 12:17
**22:1** r Ac 7:2
**22:3** s Ac 21:39 t Ac 26:5 u Ac 21:20
**22:4** v Ac 8:3
**22:5** w Lk 22:66 x Ac 9:2
**22:9** y Ac 9:7
**22:12** z Ac 9:17
**22:14** a Ac 3:13
**22:16** b Ac 2:38 c Heb 10:22
**22:17** d Ac 10:10
**22:19** e ver 4; Ac 8:3 f Mt 10:17
**22:20** g Ac 8:1
**22:21** h Ac 9:15

[a]40 Or possibly *Hebrew*; also in 22:2 [b]20 Or *witness*

**22:22**
i Ac 21:36
j Ac 25:24

**22:23**
k 2Sa 16:13

**22:25**
l Ac 16:37

**22:30**
m Ac 23:28

**23:1**
n Ac 22:30
o Ac 24:16; 2Co 1:12; 2Ti 1:3

**23:2**
p Jn 18:22

*Woman of color,*

*Remember, I can change anyone's life!*

*God*

ACTS 22:1–21

shouted, "Rid the earth of him![i] He's not fit to live!"[j]

23 As they were shouting and throwing off their cloaks and flinging dust into the air,[k] 24 the commander ordered Paul to be taken into the barracks. He directed that he be flogged and questioned in order to find out why the people were shouting at him like this. 25 As they stretched him out to flog him, Paul said to the centurion standing there, "Is it legal for you to flog a Roman citizen who hasn't even been found guilty?"[l]

26 When the centurion heard this, he went to the commander and reported it. "What are you going to do?" he asked. "This man is a Roman citizen."

27 The commander went to Paul and asked, "Tell me, are you a Roman citizen?"

"Yes, I am," he answered.

28 Then the commander said, "I had to pay a big price for my citizenship."

"But I was born a citizen," Paul replied.

29 Those who were about to question him withdrew immediately. The commander himself was alarmed when he realized that he had put Paul, a Roman citizen, in chains.

## Before the Sanhedrin

30 The next day, since the commander wanted to find out exactly why Paul was being accused by the Jews,[m] he released him and ordered the chief priests and all the Sanhedrin to assemble. Then he brought Paul and had him stand before them.

23 Paul looked straight at the Sanhedrin[n] and said, "My brothers, I have fulfilled my duty to God in all good conscience[o] to this day." 2 At this the high priest Ananias ordered those standing near Paul to strike him on the mouth.[p] 3 Then Paul said to him, "God will strike you, you whitewashed wall! You sit there to judge me according to the law, yet you yourself violate the law by commanding that I be struck!"[q]

4 Those who were standing near Paul said, "You dare to insult God's high priest?"

5 Paul replied, "Brothers, I did not realize that he was the high priest; for it is written: 'Do not speak evil about the ruler of your people.'[a]"[r]

6 Then Paul, knowing that some of them were Sadducees and the others Pharisees, called out in the Sanhedrin, "My brothers,[s] I am a Pharisee,[t] the son of a Pharisee. I stand on trial because of my hope in the resurrection of the dead." 7 When he said this, a dispute broke out between the Pharisees and the Sadducees, and the assembly was divided. 8 (The Sadducees say that there is no resurrection,[u] and that there are neither angels nor spirits, but the Pharisees acknowledge them all.)

9 There was a great uproar, and some of the teachers of the law who were Pharisees stood up and argued vigorously. "We find nothing wrong with this man," they said. "What if a spirit or an angel has spoken to him?"[v] 10 The dispute became so violent that the commander was afraid Paul would be torn to pieces by them. He ordered the troops to go down and take him away from them by force and bring him into the barracks.

11 The following night the Lord stood near Paul and said, "Take courage![w] As you have testified about me in Jerusalem, so you must also testify in Rome."[x]

## The Plot to Kill Paul

12 The next morning the Jews formed a conspiracy and bound themselves with an oath not to eat or drink until they had killed Paul. 13 More than forty men were involved in this plot. 14 They went to the chief priests and elders and said, "We have taken a solemn oath not to eat anything until we have killed Paul. 15 Now then, you and the Sanhedrin[y] petition the commander to bring him before you on the pretext of wanting more accurate information about his case. We are ready to kill him before he gets here."

16 But when the son of Paul's sister heard

**23:3**
q Dt 25:1,2; Jn 7:51

**23:5**
r Ex 22:28

**23:6**
s Ac 22:5
t Ac 26:5; Php 3:5

**23:8**
u Mt 22:23

**23:9**
v Ac 22:7,17,18

**23:11**
w Ac 18:9
x Ac 19:21

**23:15**
y Ac 22:30

[a] 5 Exodus 22:28

**23:20**
z ver 14,15

*Lord,*

*I can't even imagine resisting the urge to react immediately to painful things people say and do to me. My human response stems from my deep-seated desire to inflict still greater pain on my attackers. Help me to demonstrate the wisdom that is pure, peaceable, gentle, merciful and sincere, to keep in mind how you've treated me when I've done wrong. In Jesus' name,*

*Amen*

ACTS 23:12–15

of this plot, he went into the barracks and told Paul.

17Then Paul called one of the centurions and said, "Take this young man to the commander; he has something to tell him." 18So he took him to the commander.

The centurion said, "Paul, the prisoner, sent for me and asked me to bring this young man to you because he has something to tell you."

19The commander took the young man by the hand, drew him aside and asked, "What is it you want to tell me?"

20He said: "The Jews have agreed to ask you to bring Paul before the Sanhedrin tomorrow on the pretext of wanting more accurate information about him.[z] 21Don't give in to them, because more than forty of them are waiting in ambush for him. They have taken an oath not to eat or drink until they have killed him. They are ready now, waiting for your consent to their request."

22The commander dismissed the young man and cautioned him, "Don't tell anyone that you have reported this to me."

## Paul Transferred to Caesarea

23Then he called two of his centurions and ordered them, "Get ready a detachment of two hundred soldiers, seventy horsemen and two hundred spearmen[a] to go to Caesarea at nine tonight.[a] 24Provide mounts for Paul so that he may be taken safely to Governor Felix."[b]

25He wrote a letter as follows:

26Claudius Lysias,

To His Excellency,[c] Governor Felix:

Greetings.[d]

27This man was seized by the Jews and they were about to kill him, but I came with my troops and rescued him,[e] for I had learned that he is a Roman citizen. 28I wanted to know why they were accusing him, so I brought him to their Sanhedrin.[f] 29I found that the accusation had to do with questions about their law,[g] but there was no charge against him[h] that deserved death or imprisonment. 30When I was informed[i] of a plot to be carried out against the man, I sent him to you at once. I also ordered his accusers[j] to present to you their case against him.

31So the soldiers, carrying out their orders, took Paul with them during the night and brought him as far as Antipatris. 32The next day they let the cavalry go on with him, while they returned to the barracks. 33When the cavalry[k] arrived in Caesarea, they delivered the letter to the governor[l] and handed Paul over to him. 34The governor read the letter and asked what province he was from. Learning that he was from Cilicia,[m] 35he said, "I will hear your case when your accusers[n] get here." Then he ordered that Paul be kept under guard[o] in Herod's palace.

## The Trial Before Felix

**24** Five days later the high priest Ananias[p] went down to Caesarea with some of the elders and a lawyer named Tertullus, and they brought their charges[q] against Paul before the governor. 2When Paul was called in, Tertullus presented his case before Felix: "We have enjoyed a long period of peace under you, and your foresight has brought about reforms in this

**23:23**
a ver 33

**23:24**
b Ac 24:1–3,10

**23:26**
c Ac 24:3
d Ac 15:23

**23:27**
e Ac 21:33

**23:28**
f Ac 22:30

**23:29**
g Ac 18:15; 25:19
h Ac 26:31

**23:30**
i ver 20,21
j Ac 24:19

**23:33**
k ver 23,24
l ver 26

**23:34**
m Ac 21:39

**23:35**
n Ac 25:16
o Ac 24:27

**24:1**
p Ac 23:2
q Ac 23:30,35

[a]23 The meaning of the Greek for this word is uncertain.

nation. [3]Everywhere and in every way, most excellent[r] Felix, we acknowledge this with profound gratitude. [4]But in order not to weary you further, I would request that you be kind enough to hear us briefly.

[5]"We have found this man to be a troublemaker, stirring up riots[s] among the Jews all over the world. He is a ringleader of the Nazarene sect [6]and even tried to desecrate the temple;[t] so we seized him. [8]By[a] examining him yourself you will be able to learn the truth about all these charges we are bringing against him."

[9]The Jews joined in the accusation, asserting that these things were true.

[10]When the governor[u] motioned for him to speak, Paul replied: "I know that for a number of years you have been a judge over this nation; so I gladly make my defense. [11]You can easily verify that no more than twelve days[v] ago I went up to Jerusalem to worship. [12]My accusers did not find me arguing with anyone at the temple,[w] or stirring up a crowd in the synagogues or anywhere else in the city. [13]And they cannot prove to you the charges they are now making against me. [14]However, I admit that I worship the God of our fathers as a follower of the Way,[x] which they call a sect. I believe everything that agrees with the Law and that is written in the Prophets,[y] [15]and I have the same hope in God as these men, that there will be a resurrection of both the righteous and the wicked. [16]So I strive always to keep my conscience clear[z] before God and man.

[17]"After an absence of several years, I came to Jerusalem to bring my people gifts for the poor[a] and to present offerings. [18]I was ceremonially clean[b] when they found me in the temple courts doing this. There was no crowd with me, nor was I involved in any disturbance. [19]But there are some Jews from the province of Asia, who ought to be here before you and bring charges if they have anything against me.[c] [20]Or these who are here should state what crime they found in me when I stood before the Sanhedrin— [21]unless it was this one thing I shouted as I stood in their presence: 'It is concerning the resurrection of the dead that I am on trial before you today.' "[d]

[22]Then Felix, who was well acquainted with the Way, adjourned the proceedings. "When Lysias the commander comes," he said, "I will decide your case." [23]He ordered the centurion to keep Paul under guard but to give him some freedom[e] and permit his friends to take care of his needs.[f]

[24]Several days later Felix came with his wife Drusilla, who was a Jewess. He sent for Paul and listened to him as he spoke about faith in Christ Jesus. [25]As Paul discoursed on righteousness, self-control and the judgment to come, Felix was afraid and said, "That's enough for now! You may leave. When I find it convenient, I will send for you." [26]At the same time he was hoping that Paul would offer him a bribe, so he sent for him frequently and talked with him.

[27]When two years had passed, Felix was succeeded by Porcius Festus, but because Felix wanted to grant a favor to the Jews,[g] he left Paul in prison.

## The Trial Before Festus

25 Three days after arriving in the province, Festus went up from Caesarea to Jerusalem, [2]where the chief priests and Jewish leaders appeared before him and presented the charges against Paul.[h] [3]They urgently requested Festus, as a favor to them, to have Paul transferred to Jerusalem, for they were preparing an ambush to kill him along the way. [4]Festus answered, "Paul is being held at Caesarea, and I myself am going there soon. [5]Let some of your leaders come with me and press charges against the man there, if he has done anything wrong."

[6]After spending eight or ten days with them, he went down to Caesarea, and the next day he convened the court and ordered that Paul be brought before him. [7]When Paul appeared, the Jews who had come down from Jerusalem stood around him, bringing many serious charges against him,[i] which they could not prove.[j]

[8]Then Paul made his defense: "I have done nothing wrong against the law of the Jews or against the temple[k] or against Caesar."

[9]Festus, wishing to do the Jews a favor,[l] said to Paul, "Are you willing to go up to Je-

**24:3** r Ac 23:26
**24:5** s Ac 16:20; 17:6
**24:6** t Ac 21:28
**24:10** u Ac 23:24
**24:11** v Ac 21:27
**24:12** w Ac 25:8
**24:14** x Ac 9:2 y Ac 26:6,22
**24:16** z Ac 23:1
**24:17** a Ac 11:29,30; 2Co 8:1–4; Gal 2:10
**24:18** b Ac 21:26
**24:19** c Ac 23:30
**24:21** d Ac 23:6
**24:23** e Ac 28:16 f Ac 27:3
**24:27** g Ac 12:3
**25:2** h ver 15; Ac 24:1
**25:7** i Ac 24:5,6 j Ac 24:13
**25:8** k Ac 6:13; 28:17
**25:9** l Ac 24:27

[a]6–8 Some manuscripts *him and wanted to judge him according to our law.* [7]*But the commander, Lysias, came and with the use of much force snatched him from our hands* [8]*and ordered his accusers to come before you. By*

**25:9** m ver 20
**25:11** n Ac 26:32; 28:19
**25:14** o Ac 24:27
**25:15** p ver 2
**25:16** q ver 4,5
**25:17** r ver 6,10
**25:19** s Ac 18:15; 23:29
**25:21** t ver 11,12
**25:22** u Ac 9:15

rusalem and stand trial before me there on these charges?"[m]

10 Paul answered: "I am now standing before Caesar's court, where I ought to be tried. I have not done any wrong to the Jews, as you yourself know very well. 11 If, however, I am guilty of doing anything deserving death, I do not refuse to die. But if the charges brought against me by these Jews are not true, no one has the right to hand me over to them. I appeal to Caesar!"[n]

12 After Festus had conferred with his council, he declared: "You have appealed to Caesar. To Caesar you will go!"

## Festus Consults King Agrippa

13 A few days later King Agrippa and Bernice arrived at Caesarea to pay their respects to Festus. 14 Since they were spending many days there, Festus discussed Paul's case with the king. He said: "There is a man here whom Felix left as a prisoner.[o] 15 When I went to Jerusalem, the chief priests and elders of the Jews brought charges against him[p] and asked that he be condemned.

16 "I told them that it is not the Roman custom to hand over any man before he has faced his accusers and has had an opportunity to defend himself against their charges.[q] 17 When they came here with me, I did not delay the case, but convened the court the next day and ordered the man to be brought in.[r] 18 When his accusers got up to speak, they did not charge him with any of the crimes I had expected. 19 Instead, they had some points of dispute[s] with him about their own religion and about a dead man named Jesus who Paul claimed was alive. 20 I was at a loss how to investigate such matters; so I asked if he would be willing to go to Jerusalem and stand trial there on these charges. 21 When Paul made his appeal to be held over for the Emperor's decision, I ordered him held until I could send him to Caesar."[t]

22 Then Agrippa said to Festus, "I would like to hear this man myself."

He replied, "Tomorrow you will hear him."[u]

## Paul Before Agrippa

23 The next day Agrippa and Bernice came with great pomp and entered the audience room with the high ranking officers and the leading men of the city. At the command of Festus, Paul was brought in. 24 Festus said: "King Agrippa, and all who are present with us, you see this man! The whole Jewish community[v] has petitioned me about him in Jerusalem and here in Caesarea, shouting that he ought not to live any longer.[w] 25 I found he had done nothing deserving of death,[x] but because he made his appeal to the Emperor I decided to send him to Rome. 26 But I have nothing definite to write to His Majesty about him. Therefore I have brought him before all of you, and especially before you, King Agrippa, so that as a result of this investigation I may have something to write. 27 For I think it is unreasonable to send on a prisoner without specifying the charges against him."

**26** Then Agrippa said to Paul, "You have permission to speak for yourself."[y]

So Paul motioned with his hand and began his defense: 2 "King Agrippa, I consider myself fortunate to stand before you today as I make my defense against all the accusations of the Jews, 3 and especially so because you are well acquainted with all the Jewish customs and controversies. Therefore, I beg you to listen to me patiently.

4 "The Jews all know the way I have lived ever since I was a child,[z] from the beginning of my life in my own country, and also in Jerusalem. 5 They have known me for a long time[a] and can testify, if they are willing, that according to the strictest sect of our religion, I lived as a Pharisee.[b] 6 And now it is because of my hope[c] in what God has promised our fathers[d] that I am on trial today. 7 This is the promise our twelve tribes[e] are hoping to see fulfilled as they earnestly serve God day and night.[f] O king, it is because of this hope that the Jews are accusing me. 8 Why should any of you consider it incredible that God raises the dead?

9 "I too was convinced[g] that I ought to do all that was possible to oppose[h] the name of Jesus of Nazareth. 10 And that is just what I did in Jerusalem. On the authority of the chief priests I put many of the saints in prison,[i] and when they were put to death, I cast my vote against them. 11 Many a time I

**25:24** v ver 2,3,7 w Ac 22:22
**25:25** x Ac 23:9
**26:1** y Ac 9:15
**26:4** z Gal 1:13,14
**26:5** a Ac 22:3 b Ac 23:6
**26:6** c Ac 23:6 d Ac 13:32
**26:7** e Jas 1:1 f 1Th 3:10; 1Ti 5:5
**26:9** g 1Ti 1:13 h Jn 16:2
**26:10** i Ac 8:3

went from one synagogue to another to have them punished, and I tried to force them to blaspheme. In my obsession against them, I even went to foreign cities to persecute them.

12"On one of these journeys I was going to Damascus with the authority and commission of the chief priests. 13About noon, O king, as I was on the road, I saw a light from heaven, brighter than the sun, blazing around me and my companions. 14We all fell to the ground, and I heard a voice saying to me in Aramaic,[a] 'Saul, Saul, why do you persecute me? It is hard for you to kick against the goads.'

15"Then I asked, 'Who are you, Lord?'

" 'I am Jesus, whom you are persecuting,' the Lord replied. 16'Now get up and stand on your feet.[j] I have appeared to you to appoint you as a servant and as a witness of what you have seen of me and what I will show you.[k] 17I will rescue you from your own people and from the Gentiles. I am sending you to them 18to open their eyes[l] and turn them from darkness to light,[m] and from the power of Satan to God, so that they may receive forgiveness of sins and a place among those who are sanctified by faith in me.'

*"People may doubt what you say, but they will always believe what you do."*

—Nannie Helen Burroughs,
educator and civil rights activist

19"So then, King Agrippa, I was not disobedient to the vision from heaven. 20First to those in Damascus,[n] then to those in Jerusalem[o] and in all Judea, and to the Gentiles also, I preached that they should repent and turn to God and prove their repentance by their deeds.[p] 21That is why the Jews seized me[q] in the temple courts and tried to kill me. 22But I have had God's help to this very day, and so I stand here and testify to small and great alike. I am saying nothing beyond what the prophets and Moses said would happen[r]— 23that the Christ[b] would suffer and, as the first to rise from the dead,[s] would proclaim light to his own people and to the Gentiles."[t]

24At this point Festus interrupted Paul's defense. "You are out of your mind,[u] Paul!" he shouted. "Your great learning is driving you insane."

25"I am not insane, most excellent[v] Festus," Paul replied. "What I am saying is true and reasonable. 26The king is familiar with these things, and I can speak freely to him. I am convinced that none of this has escaped his notice, because it was not done in a corner. 27King Agrippa, do you believe the prophets? I know you do."

28Then Agrippa said to Paul, "Do you think that in such a short time you can persuade me to be a Christian?"

29Paul replied, "Short time or long—I pray God that not only you but all who are listening to me today may become what I am, except for these chains."

30The king rose, and with him the governor and Bernice[w] and those sitting with them. 31They left the room, and while talking with one another, they said, "This man is not doing anything that deserves death or imprisonment."

32Agrippa said to Festus, "This man could have been set free if he had not appealed to Caesar."[x]

## Paul Sails for Rome

27 When it was decided that we would sail for Italy,[y] Paul and some other prisoners were handed over to a centurion named Julius, who belonged to the Imperial Regiment. 2We boarded a ship from Adramyttium about to sail for ports along the coast of the province of Asia, and we put out to sea. Aristarchus,[z] a Macedonian from Thessalonica, was with us.

3The next day we landed at Sidon; and Julius, in kindness to Paul, allowed him to go to his friends so they might provide for his needs.[a] 4From there we put out to sea again and passed to the lee of Cyprus because the winds were against us. 5When we had sailed across the open sea off the coast of Cilicia and Pamphylia, we landed at Myra in Lycia. 6There the centurion found an Alexandrian ship[b] sailing for Italy and put us on board. 7We made slow headway for many days and had difficulty arriving off Cnidus. When the

**26:16** j Eze 2:1 k Ac 22:14,15
**26:18** l Isa 35:5 m Isa 42:7,16; Eph 5:8; Col 1:13; 1Pe 2:9
**26:20** n Ac 9:19–25 o Ac 9:26–29 p Mt 3:8
**26:21** q Ac 21:27,30
**26:22** r Lk 24:27,44; Ac 24:14
**26:23** s 1Co 15:20,23; Col 1:18; Rev 1:5 t Lk 2:32
**26:24** u Jn 10:20
**26:25** v Ac 23:26
**26:30** w Ac 25:23
**26:32** x Ac 25:11
**27:1** y Ac 25:12,25
**27:2** z Ac 19:29
**27:3** a Ac 24:23
**27:6** b Ac 28:11

[a]14 Or *Hebrew* [b]23 Or *Messiah*

wind did not allow us to hold our course, we sailed to the lee of Crete, opposite Salmone. 8 We moved along the coast with difficulty and came to a place called Fair Havens, near the town of Lasea.

9 Much time had been lost, and sailing had already become dangerous because by now it was after the Fast.[a][c] So Paul warned them, 10 "Men, I can see that our voyage is going to be disastrous and bring great loss to ship and cargo, and to our own lives also." 11 But the centurion, instead of listening to what Paul said, followed the advice of the pilot and of the owner of the ship. 12 Since the harbor was unsuitable to winter in, the majority decided that we should sail on, hoping to reach Phoenix and winter there. This was a harbor in Crete, facing both southwest and northwest.

## The Storm

13 When a gentle south wind began to blow, they thought they had obtained what they wanted; so they weighed anchor and sailed along the shore of Crete. 14 Before very long, a wind of hurricane force,[d] called the "northeaster," swept down from the island. 15 The ship was caught by the storm and could not head into the wind; so we gave way to it and were driven along. 16 As we passed to the lee of a small island called Cauda, we were hardly able to make the lifeboat secure. 17 When the men had hoisted it aboard, they passed ropes under the ship itself to hold it together. Fearing that they would run aground on the sandbars of Syrtis, they lowered the sea anchor and let the ship be driven along. 18 We took such a violent battering from the storm that the next day they began to throw the cargo overboard.[e] 19 On the third day, they threw the ship's tackle overboard with their own hands. 20 When neither sun nor stars appeared for many days and the storm continued raging, we finally gave up all hope of being saved.

21 After the men had gone a long time without food, Paul stood up before them and said: "Men, you should have taken my advice[f] not to sail from Crete;[g] then you would have spared yourselves this damage and loss. 22 But now I urge you to keep up your courage,[h] because not one of you will be lost; only the ship will be destroyed. 23 Last night an angel[i] of the God whose I am and whom I serve[j] stood beside me[k] 24 and said, 'Do not be afraid, Paul. You must stand trial before Caesar;[l] and God has graciously given you the lives of all who sail with you.'[m] 25 So keep up your courage,[n] men, for I have faith in God that it will happen just as he told me.[o] 26 Nevertheless, we must run aground on some island."[p]

## The Shipwreck

27 On the fourteenth night we were still being driven across the Adriatic[b] Sea, when about midnight the sailors sensed they were approaching land. 28 They took soundings and found that the water was a hundred and twenty feet[c] deep. A short time later they took soundings again and found it was ninety feet[d] deep. 29 Fearing that we would be dashed against the rocks, they dropped four anchors from the stern and prayed for daylight. 30 In an attempt to escape from the ship, the sailors let the lifeboat[q] down into the sea, pretending they were going to lower some anchors from the bow. 31 Then Paul said to the centurion and the soldiers, "Unless these men stay with the ship, you cannot be saved." 32 So the soldiers cut the ropes that held the lifeboat and let it fall away.

33 Just before dawn Paul urged them all to eat. "For the last fourteen days," he said, "you have been in constant suspense and have gone without food—you haven't eaten anything. 34 Now I urge you to take some food. You need it to survive. Not one of you will lose a single hair from his head."[r] 35 After he said this, he took some bread and gave thanks to God in front of them all. Then he broke it and began to eat. 36 They were all encouraged[s] and ate some food themselves. 37 Altogether there were 276 of us on board. 38 When they had eaten as much as they wanted, they lightened the ship by throwing the grain into the sea.[t]

39 When daylight came, they did not recognize the land, but they saw a bay with a sandy beach,[u] where they decided to run the

**27:9** c Lev 23:27–29
**27:14** d Mk 4:37
**27:18** e Jnh 1:5
**27:21** f ver 10 g ver 7
**27:22** h ver 25,36
**27:23** i Ac 5:19 j Ro 1:9 k Ac 23:11
**27:24** l Ac 23:11 m ver 44
**27:25** n ver 22,36 o Ro 4:20,21
**27:26** p Ac 28:1
**27:30** q ver 16
**27:34** r Mt 10:30
**27:36** s ver 22,25
**27:38** t ver 18
**27:39** u Ac 28:1

[a]9 That is, the Day of Atonement (Yom Kippur) [b]27 In ancient times the name referred to an area extending well south of Italy. [c]28 Greek *twenty orguias* (about 37 meters) [d]28 Greek *fifteen orguias* (about 27 meters)

ship aground if they could. 40 Cutting loose the anchors,[v] they left them in the sea and at the same time untied the ropes that held the rudders. Then they hoisted the foresail to the wind and made for the beach. 41 But the ship struck a sandbar and ran aground. The bow stuck fast and would not move, and the stern was broken to pieces by the pounding of the surf.[w]

42 The soldiers planned to kill the prisoners to prevent any of them from swimming away and escaping. 43 But the centurion wanted to spare Paul's life[x] and kept them from carrying out their plan. He ordered those who could swim to jump overboard first and get to land. 44 The rest were to get there on planks or on pieces of the ship. In this way everyone reached land in safety.[y]

## Ashore on Malta

28 Once safely on shore, we found out that the island[z] was called Malta. 2 The islanders showed us unusual kindness. They built a fire and welcomed us all because it was raining and cold. 3 Paul gathered a pile of brushwood and, as he put it on the fire, a viper, driven out by the heat, fastened itself on his hand. 4 When the islanders saw the snake hanging from his hand, they said to each other, "This man must be a murderer; for though he escaped from the sea, Justice has not allowed him to live."[a] 5 But Paul shook the snake off into the fire and suffered no ill effects.[b] 6 The people expected him to swell up or suddenly fall dead, but after waiting a long time and seeing nothing unusual happen to him, they changed their minds and said he was a god.[c]

7 There was an estate nearby that belonged to Publius, the chief official of the island. He welcomed us to his home and for three days entertained us hospitably. 8 His father was sick in bed, suffering from fever and dysentery. Paul went in to see him and, after prayer,[d] placed his hands on him and healed him. 9 When this had happened, the rest of the sick on the island came and were cured. 10 They honored us in many ways and when we were ready to sail, they furnished us with the supplies we needed.

## Arrival at Rome

11 After three months we put out to sea in a ship that had wintered in the island. It was an Alexandrian ship[e] with the figurehead of the twin gods Castor and Pollux. 12 We put in at Syracuse and stayed there three days. 13 From there we set sail and arrived at Rhegium. The next day the south wind came up, and on the following day we reached Puteoli. 14 There we found some brothers[f] who invited us to spend a week with them. And so we came to Rome. 15 The brothers there had heard that we were coming, and they traveled as far as the Forum of Appius and the Three Taverns to meet us. At the sight of these men Paul thanked God and was encouraged. 16 When we got to Rome, Paul was allowed to live by himself, with a soldier to guard him.[g]

## Paul Preaches at Rome Under Guard

17 Three days later he called together the leaders of the Jews. When they had assembled, Paul said to them: "My brothers, although I have done nothing against our people[h] or against the customs of our ancestors,[i] I was arrested in Jerusalem and handed over to the Romans. 18 They examined me[j] and wanted to release me, because I was not guilty of any crime deserving death. 19 But when the Jews objected, I was compelled to appeal to Caesar[k]—not that I had any charge to bring against my own people. 20 For this reason I have asked to see you and talk with you. It is because of the hope of Israel[l] that I am bound with this chain."

21 They replied, "We have not received any letters from Judea concerning you, and none of the brothers who have come from there has reported or said anything bad about you. 22 But we want to hear what your views are, for we know that people everywhere are talking against this sect."[m]

23 They arranged to meet Paul on a certain day, and came in even larger numbers to the place where he was staying. From morning till evening he explained and declared to them the kingdom of God[n] and tried to convince them about Jesus[o] from the Law of Moses and from the Prophets. 24 Some were convinced by what he said, but others would

**27:40** v ver 29
**27:41** w 2Co 11:25
**27:43** x ver 3
**27:44** y ver 22,31
**28:1** z Ac 27:26,39
**28:4** a Lk 13:2,4
**28:5** b Lk 10:19
**28:6** c Ac 14:11
**28:8** d Jas 5:14,15
**28:11** e Ac 27:6
**28:14** f Ac 1:16
**28:16** g Ac 24:23; 27:3
**28:17** h Ac 25:8; i Ac 6:14
**28:18** j Ac 22:24
**28:19** k Ac 25:11
**28:20** l Ac 26:6,7
**28:22** m Ac 24:5,14
**28:23** n Ac 19:8; o Ac 17:3

not believe.[p] 25They disagreed among them-
selves and began to leave after Paul had
made this final statement: "The Holy Spirit
spoke the truth to your forefathers when he
said through Isaiah the prophet:

26" 'Go to this people and say,
"You will be ever hearing but never
understanding;
you will be ever seeing but never
perceiving."
27For this people's heart has become
calloused;
they hardly hear with their ears,
and they have closed their eyes.
Otherwise they might see with their eyes,
hear with their ears,
understand with their hearts
and turn, and I would heal them.'[a][q]

28"Therefore I want you to know that
God's salvation has been sent to the Gen-
tiles,[r] and they will listen!"[b]
30For two whole years Paul stayed there
in his own rented house and welcomed all
who came to see him. 31Boldly and without
hindrance he preached the kingdom of God
and taught about the Lord Jesus Christ.

**28:24** p Ac 14:4
**28:27** q Isa 6:9,10
**28:28** r Ac 13:46

[a]27 Isaiah 6:9,10 [b]28 Some manuscripts *listen!"* [29]*After he said this, the Jews left, arguing vigorously among themselves.*

# Romans

## OVERVIEW

The book of Romans offers the most systematic and extensive presentation of the gospel of all the books of the New Testament. The apostle Paul wrote that all people—both Jew and Gentile—are sinful and fall short of God's glory (see Ro 3). He explained that the only remedy is receiving God's righteousness through faith in Jesus Christ and belief in his atoning work. In the last section of his letter, starting with chapter 12, Paul shared practical applications of how the believer should respond to this gift of salvation.

Paul made a point of singling out women believers who were integral to his ministry. In chapter 16, he listed Phoebe, Priscilla, Mary, Tryphena, Tryphosa, Persis, Rufus's mother, Julia and Nereus's sister as women who worked hard to share Christ with others and build the church.

As you read this important treatise regarding our most wonderful salvation, think about the women who were instrumental in helping to build your faith. Remember to share with others, so they might better understand the work of Christ and the new life they can experience in him.

## OUTLINE

I. Introduction (1:1–15)
II. The Theme: Righteousness From God (1:16–17)
III. No One Is Righteous (1:18—3:20)
IV. Righteousness Through Faith in Christ Alone (3:21—8:39)
V. God's Plan for the Jewish People (9:1—11:36)
VI. Practicing Righteousness (12:1—15:13)
VII. Paul's Plans and Greetings (15:14—16:27)

### SCANNABLE FACTS:

**Author:** Paul

**Time Written:** A.D. 57

**Theme to Note:** God's gift of righteousness through faith in Christ

**Notable Women:** Phoebe, Priscilla

1:1 a Ac 9:15
1:2 b Gal 3:8
1:5 c Ac 9:15; d Ac 6:7
1:7 e 1Co 1:3
1:10 f Ro 15:32

1 Paul, a servant of Christ Jesus, called to be an apostle and set apart[a] for the gospel of God— [2]the gospel he promised beforehand through his prophets in the Holy Scriptures[b] [3]regarding his Son, who as to his human nature was a descendant of David, [4]and who through the Spirit[a] of holiness was declared with power to be the Son of God[b] by his resurrection from the dead: Jesus Christ our Lord. [5]Through him and for his name's sake, we received grace and apostleship to call people from among all the Gentiles[c] to the obedience that comes from faith.[d] [6]And you also are among those who are called to belong to Jesus Christ.

[7]To all in Rome who are loved by God and called to be saints:

Grace and peace to you from God our Father and from the Lord Jesus Christ.[e]

## Paul's Longing to Visit Rome

[8]First, I thank my God through Jesus Christ for all of you, because your faith is being reported all over the world. [9]God, whom I serve with my whole heart in preaching the gospel of his Son, is my witness how constantly I remember you [10]in my prayers at all times; and I pray that now at last by God's will the way may be opened for me to come to you.[f]

[11]I long to see you so that I may impart to you some spiritual gift to make you strong— [12]that is, that you and I may be mutually encouraged by each other's faith. [13]I do not want you to be unaware, brothers, that I planned many times to come to you (but have been prevented from doing so until now) in order that I might have a harvest among you, just as I have had among the other Gentiles.

[14]I am obligated both to Greeks and non-Greeks, both to the wise and the foolish. [15]That is why I am so eager to preach the gospel also to you who are at Rome.

[16]I am not ashamed of the gospel, because it is the power of God[g] for the salvation of everyone who believes: first for the Jew, then for the Gentile. [17]For in the gospel a righteousness from God is revealed,[h] a righteousness that is by faith from first to last,[c] just as it is written: "The righteous will live by faith."[d i]

## God's Wrath Against Mankind

[18]The wrath of God[j] is being revealed from heaven against all the godlessness and wickedness of men who suppress the truth by their wickedness, [19]since what may be known about God is plain to them, because God has made it plain to them.[k] [20]For since the creation of the world God's invisible qualities—his eternal power and divine nature—have been clearly seen, being understood from what has been made,[l] so that men are without excuse.

[21]For although they knew God, they neither glorified him as God nor gave thanks to him, but their thinking became futile and their foolish hearts were darkened.[m] [22]Although they claimed to be wise, they became fools [23]and exchanged the glory of

1:16 g 1Co 1:18
1:17 h Ro 3:21; i Gal 3:11
1:18 j Eph 5:6
1:19 k Ac 14:17
1:20 l Ps 19:1–6
1:21 m Jer 2:5; Eph 4:17,18

[a]4 Or *who as to his spirit* [b]4 Or *was appointed to be the Son of God with power* [c]17 Or *is from faith to faith* [d]17 Hab. 2:4

## The African Presence

**Romans 1**

While there are no specific references to the African presence within the book of Romans, the gospel preached by Paul was influenced by people of North Africa and the Middle East (a historical and cultural subregion of Africa-Eurasia, traditionally held to be countries or regions in Southwest Asia together with Egypt). However, during the time of the New Testament, racial identification did not have the significance that it has today.

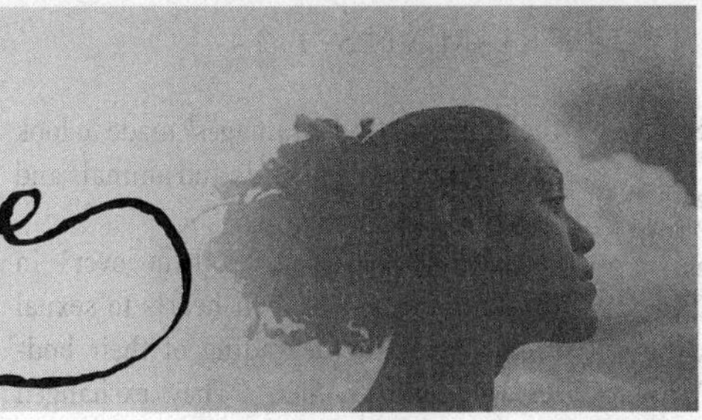

# Inspire

## NURTURING SPIRITUAL GIFTS IN OUR CHILDREN

Children are a gift from God, but sometimes we receive this priceless gift and, for one reason or another, try to return it! God is faithful, and he promises never to ask us to bear more than we are able. Furthermore, every child is spiritually gifted in one way or another; from the foundations of the world God ordained this to be so. If we nurture those gifts through prayer, faith and godly associations, our children will grow up to become the men and women God has purposed them to be. As a single mother of five teenagers, I often ask the Lord to help me raise my youngsters for his glory.

God provides role models in the Bible, through the lives of both Jesus and ordinary people, for nurturing spiritual gifts in others. There is a powerful principle at work here: *impartation*, the idea of communicating the knowledge and actual experience of something. Paul speaks of it in Romans 1:11: "I long to see you so that I may impart to you some spiritual gift to make you strong."

In Matthew 19:13–15 Jesus laid his hands on children and prayed for them. And in 2 Timothy 1:5 Paul speaks to Timothy, his young protégé and spiritual son, about the "sincere faith" in Christ that was modeled throughout Timothy's impressionable years by his grandmother Lois and his mother Eunice. As a result of these women's sincere faith, Timothy grew up to be a wonderful servant of the Lord. Paul, a godly associate and mentor, had earlier laid hands on Timothy, imparting the apostolic spirit Timothy would need to lead the church at Ephesus. Paul stirred up the gift that was already present in Timothy (see 2Ti 1:6).

God instructs us through these examples to "lay hands" on our own children—not hands of violence, but hands guided by God's love to impart some spiritual gift. As we ask God to raise our children to glorify him, we are wise to meditate on the examples of Jesus, Lois, Eunice and Paul. Model for your children, as well as those entrusted to your spiritual direction, undying faith in our heavenly Father, provide them with godly associations and lay hands on them in prayer.

—J. Scott

### read

Romans 1:8–13; see also Matthew 19:13–15; 1 Timothy 4:12–14; 2 Timothy 1:1–7.

**See also** the Inspire Notes "A Great Challenge: Teaching Our Children," "Motherhood," "Parenting," "Raising Children: Modeling Discipleship" and "Children: A Blessed Heritage From God," and the Women of the Bible Notes "Daughter of Jairus: A Testament of Faith" and "Mary, the Mother of Jesus: A Model of Motherhood."

### WOMAN *of* COLOR

What are you imparting to your children or to the children in your extended family or community?

For the next Inspire note, go to page 1329.

the immortal God for images[n] made to look
like mortal man and birds and animals and
reptiles.
24 Therefore God gave them over[o] in
the sinful desires of their hearts to sexual
impurity for the degrading of their bod-
ies with one another. 25 They exchanged
the truth of God for a lie,[p] and worshiped
and served created things[q] rather than the
Creator—who is forever praised. Amen.
26 Because of this, God gave them over
to shameful lusts. Even their women ex-
changed natural relations for unnatural
ones.[r] 27 In the same way the men also aban-
doned natural relations with women and
were inflamed with lust for one another.
Men committed indecent acts with other
men, and received in themselves the due
penalty for their perversion.[s]
28 Furthermore, since they did not think
it worthwhile to retain the knowledge of
God, he gave them over to a depraved mind,
to do what ought not to be done. 29 They
have become filled with every kind of wick-
edness, evil, greed and depravity. They are
full of envy, murder, strife, deceit and mal-
ice. They are gossips, 30 slanderers, God-
haters, insolent, arrogant and boastful; they
invent ways of doing evil; they disobey their
parents;[t] 31 they are senseless, faithless,
heartless, ruthless. 32 Although they know
God's righteous decree that those who do
such things deserve death,[u] they not only
continue to do these very things but also ap-
prove of those who practice them.

## God's Righteous Judgment

2 You, therefore, have no excuse,[v] you
who pass judgment on someone else,
for at whatever point you judge the other,
you are condemning yourself, because you
who pass judgment do the same things.[w]
2 Now we know that God's judgment against
those who do such things is based on truth.
3 So when you, a mere man, pass judgment
on them and yet do the same things, do you
think you will escape God's judgment? 4 Or
do you show contempt for the riches[x] of
his kindness, tolerance[y] and patience,[z] not
realizing that God's kindness leads you to-
ward repentance?[a]

**1:23** n Ps 106:20
**1:24** o Eph 4:19
**1:25** p Isa 44:20; q Jer 10:14
**1:26** r Lev 18:22,23
**1:27** s Lev 18:22
**1:30** t 2Ti 3:2
**1:32** u Ro 6:23
**2:1** v Ro 1:20; w 2Sa 12:5-7; Mt 7:1,2
**2:4** x Eph 1:7,18; y Ro 3:25; z Ex 34:6; a 2Pe 3:9

5 But because of your stubbornness and
your unrepentant heart, you are storing up
wrath against yourself for the day of God's
wrath, when his righteous judgment will
be revealed. 6 God "will give to each person
according to what he has done."[a][b] 7 To those
who by persistence in doing good seek glory,
honor and immortality, he will give eternal
life. 8 But for those who are self-seeking and
who reject the truth and follow evil,[c] there
will be wrath and anger. 9 There will be trou-
ble and distress for every human being who
does evil: first for the Jew, then for the Gen-
tile; 10 but glory, honor and peace for every-
one who does good: first for the Jew, then for
the Gentile.[d] 11 For God does not show favor-
itism.[e]
12 All who sin apart from the law will also
perish apart from the law, and all who sin
under the law[f] will be judged by the law.
13 For it is not those who hear the law who
are righteous in God's sight, but it is those
who obey[g] the law who will be declared
righteous. 14 (Indeed, when Gentiles, who
do not have the law, do by nature things re-
quired by the law, they are a law for them-
selves, even though they do not have the
law, 15 since they show that the requirements
of the law are written on their hearts, their
consciences also bearing witness, and their
thoughts now accusing, now even defend-
ing them.) 16 This will take place on the day
when God will judge men's secrets through
Jesus Christ,[h] as my gospel declares.

## The Jews and the Law

17 Now you, if you call yourself a Jew; if
you rely on the law and brag about your rela-
tionship to God;[i] 18 if you know his will and
approve of what is superior because you are
instructed by the law; 19 if you are convinced
that you are a guide for the blind, a light for
those who are in the dark, 20 an instructor of
the foolish, a teacher of infants, because you
have in the law the embodiment of knowl-
edge and truth— 21 you, then, who teach
others, do you not teach yourself? You who
preach against stealing, do you steal?[j] 22 You
who say that people should not commit
adultery, do you commit adultery? You who
abhor idols, do you rob temples? 23 You who

**2:6** b Ps 62:12
**2:8** c 2Th 2:12
**2:10** d ver 9
**2:11** e Ac 10:34
**2:12** f 1Co 9:20,21
**2:13** g Jas 1:22,23,25
**2:16** h Ac 10:42
**2:17** i Mic 3:11
**2:21** j Mt 23:3,4

[a] 6 Psalm 62:12; Prov. 24:12

brag about the law,[k] do you dishonor God by breaking the law? 24 As it is written: "God's name is blasphemed among the Gentiles because of you."[a][l]

25 Circumcision has value if you observe the law,[m] but if you break the law, you have become as though you had not been circumcised. 26 If those who are not circumcised keep the law's requirements,[n] will they not be regarded as though they were circumcised? 27 The one who is not circumcised physically and yet obeys the law will condemn you[o] who, even though you have the[b] written code and circumcision, are a lawbreaker.

28 A man is not a Jew if he is only one outwardly,[p] nor is circumcision merely outward and physical.[q] 29 No, a man is a Jew if he is one inwardly; and circumcision is circumcision of the heart, by the Spirit, not by the written code. Such a man's praise is not from men, but from God.[r]

## God's Faithfulness

3 What advantage, then, is there in being a Jew, or what value is there in circumcision? 2 Much in every way! First of all, they have been entrusted with the very words of God.[s]

3 What if some did not have faith?[t] Will their lack of faith nullify God's faithfulness? 4 Not at all! Let God be true, and every man a liar. As it is written:

"So that you may be proved right when
you speak
and prevail when you judge."[c][u]

5 But if our unrighteousness brings out God's righteousness more clearly, what shall we say? That God is unjust in bringing his wrath on us? (I am using a human argument.)[v] 6 Certainly not! If that were so, how could God judge the world?[w] 7 Someone might argue, "If my falsehood enhances God's truthfulness and so increases his glory, why am I still condemned as a sinner?" 8 Why not say—as we are being slanderously reported as saying and as some claim that we say—"Let us do evil that good may result"? Their condemnation is deserved.

## No One Is Righteous

9 What shall we conclude then? Are we any better[d]? Not at all! We have already made the charge that Jews and Gentiles alike are all under sin.[x] 10 As it is written:

"There is no one righteous, not even
one;
11 there is no one who understands,
no one who seeks God.
12 All have turned away,
they have together become worthless;
there is no one who does good,
not even one."[e]
13 "Their throats are open graves;
their tongues practice deceit."[f][y]
"The poison of vipers is on their lips."[g]
14 "Their mouths are full of cursing and
bitterness."[h][z]
15 "Their feet are swift to shed blood;
16 ruin and misery mark their ways,
17 and the way of peace they do not know."[i]
18 "There is no fear of God before their
eyes."[j][a]

19 Now we know that whatever the law says,[b] it says to those who are under the law, so that every mouth may be silenced and the whole world held accountable to God. 20 Therefore no one will be declared righteous in his sight by observing the law;[c] rather, through the law we become conscious of sin.[d]

## Righteousness Through Faith

21 But now a righteousness from God,[e] apart from law, has been made known, to which the Law and the Prophets testify. 22 This righteousness from God comes through faith in Jesus Christ to all who believe. There is no difference,[f] 23 for all have sinned and fall short of the glory of God, 24 and are justified freely by his grace[g] through the redemption that came by Christ Jesus. 25 God presented him as a sacrifice of atonement,[k] through faith in his blood.[h] He did this to demonstrate his justice, because in his forbearance he had left the sins committed beforehand unpunished— 26 he did it to demonstrate his justice at the present

**2:23** k ver 17
**2:24** l Isa 52:5
**2:25** m Gal 5:3
**2:26** n Ro 8:4
**2:27** o Mt 12:41,42
**2:28** p Jn 8:39; q Gal 6:15
**2:29** r 2Co 10:18
**3:2** s Dt 4:8; Ps 147:19
**3:3** t Heb 4:2
**3:4** u Ps 51:4
**3:5** v Gal 3:15
**3:6** w Ge 18:25
**3:9** x Gal 3:22
**3:13** y Ps 5:9
**3:14** z Ps 10:7
**3:18** a Ps 36:1
**3:19** b Jn 10:34
**3:20** c Ac 13:39; Gal 2:16; d Ro 7:7
**3:21** e Ro 1:17
**3:22** f Ro 10:12; Gal 3:28
**3:24** g Ro 4:16
**3:25** h Heb 9:12,14

[a]24 Isaiah 52:5; Ezek. 36:22 [b]27 Or *who, by means of a* [c]4 Psalm 51:4 [d]9 Or *worse* [e]12 Psalms 14:1–3; 53:1–3; Eccles. 7:20 [f]13 Psalm 5:9 [g]13 Psalm 140:3 [h]14 Psalm 10:7 [i]17 Isaiah 59:7,8 [j]18 Psalm 36:1 [k]25 Or *as the one who would turn aside his wrath, taking away sin*

time, so as to be just and the one who justifies those who have faith in Jesus.

27 Where, then, is boasting?[i] It is excluded. On what principle? On that of observing the law? No, but on that of faith. 28 For we maintain that a man is justified by faith apart from observing the law. 29 Is God the God of Jews only? Is he not the God of Gentiles too? Yes, of Gentiles too, 30 since there is only one God, who will justify the circumcised by faith and the uncircumcised through that same faith.[j] 31 Do we, then, nullify the law by this faith? Not at all! Rather, we uphold the law.

## Abraham Justified by Faith

4 What then shall we say that Abraham, our forefather, discovered in this matter? 2 If, in fact, Abraham was justified by works, he had something to boast about—but not before God. 3 What does the Scripture say? "Abraham believed God, and it was credited to him as righteousness."[a][k]

4 Now when a man works, his wages are not credited to him as a gift,[l] but as an obligation. 5 However, to the man who does not work but trusts God who justifies the wicked, his faith is credited as righteousness. 6 David says the same thing when he speaks of the blessedness of the man to whom God credits righteousness apart from works:

7 "Blessed are they
whose transgressions are forgiven,
whose sins are covered.
8 Blessed is the man
whose sin the Lord will never count
against him."[b]

9 Is this blessedness only for the circumcised, or also for the uncircumcised? We have been saying that Abraham's faith was credited to him as righteousness. 10 Under what circumstances was it credited? Was it after he was circumcised, or before? It was not after, but before! 11 And he received the sign of circumcision, a seal of the righteousness that he had by faith while he was still uncircumcised.[m] So then, he is the father[n] of all who believe but have not been circumcised, in order that righteousness might be credited to them. 12 And he is also the father of the circumcised who not only are circumcised but who also walk in the footsteps of the faith that our father Abraham had before he was circumcised.

13 It was not through law that Abraham and his offspring received the promise that he would be heir of the world,[o] but through the righteousness that comes by faith. 14 For if those who live by law are heirs, faith has no value and the promise is worthless,[p] 15 because law brings wrath.[q] And where there is no law there is no transgression.[r]

16 Therefore, the promise comes by faith, so that it may be by grace[s] and may be guaranteed to all Abraham's offspring—not only to those who are of the law but also to those who are of the faith of Abraham. He is the father of us all. 17 As it is written: "I have made you a father of many nations."[c][t] He is our father in the sight of God, in whom he believed—the God who gives life to the dead and calls things that are not[u] as though they were.

18 Against all hope, Abraham in hope believed and so became the father of many nations, just as it had been said to him, "So shall your offspring be."[d][v] 19 Without weakening in his faith, he faced the fact that his body was as good as dead[w]—since he was about a hundred years old[x]—and that Sarah's womb was also dead. 20 Yet he did not waver through unbelief regarding the promise of God, but was strengthened in his faith and gave glory to God, 21 being fully persuaded that God had power to do what he had promised.[y] 22 This is why "it was credited to him as righteousness." 23 The words "it was credited to him" were written not for him alone, 24 but also for us,[z] to whom God will credit righteousness—for us who believe in him who raised Jesus our Lord from the dead.[a] 25 He was delivered over to death for our sins and was raised to life for our justification.

## Peace and Joy

5 Therefore, since we have been justified through faith, we[e] have peace with God through our Lord Jesus Christ, 2 through whom we have gained access[b] by faith into

**3:27** i Ro 2:17,23; 1Co 1:29–31
**3:30** j Gal 3:8
**4:3** k Ge 15:6; Gal 3:6; Jas 2:23
**4:4** l Ro 11:6
**4:11** m Ge 17:10,11 n Lk 19:9
**4:13** o Ge 17:4–6
**4:14** p Gal 3:18
**4:15** q Gal 3:10 r Ro 3:20
**4:16** s Ro 3:24
**4:17** t Ge 17:5 u 1Co 1:28
**4:18** v Ge 15:5
**4:19** w Heb 11:11,12 x Ge 17:17
**4:21** y Heb 11:19
**4:24** z Ro 15:4 a Ac 2:24
**5:2** b Eph 2:18

[a] 3 Gen. 15:6; also in verse 22 [b] 8 Psalm 32:1,2 [c] 17 Gen. 17:5 [d] 18 Gen. 15:5 [e] 1 Or *let us*

5:2 c 1Co 15:1
5:3 d Jas 1:2,3
5:6 e Ro 4:25
5:8 f Jn 15:13
5:9 g Ro 3:25
5:10 h Ro 11:28 i 2Co 5:18,19
5:12 j 1Co 15:21,22 k Ge 2:17
5:13 l Ro 4:15
5:14 m 1Co 15:22,45
5:15 n Ac 15:11

this grace in which we now stand.[c] And
we[a] rejoice in the hope of the glory of God.
3Not only so, but we[a] also rejoice in our suf-
ferings, because we know that suffering
produces perseverance;[d] 4perseverance,
character; and character, hope. 5And hope
does not disappoint us, because God has
poured out his love into our hearts by the
Holy Spirit, whom he has given us.
6You see, at just the right time, when
we were still powerless, Christ died for the
ungodly.[e] 7Very rarely will anyone die for
a righteous man, though for a good man
someone might possibly dare to die. 8But
God demonstrates his own love for us in
this: While we were still sinners, Christ
died for us.[f]
9Since we have now been justified by his
blood,[g] how much more shall we be saved
from God's wrath through him! 10For if,
when we were God's enemies,[h] we were rec-
onciled[i] to him through the death of his Son,
how much more, having been reconciled,
shall we be saved through his life! 11Not only
is this so, but we also rejoice in God through
our Lord Jesus Christ, through whom we
have now received reconciliation.

## Death Through Adam, Life Through Christ

12Therefore, just as sin entered the world
through one man,[j] and death through sin,[k]
and in this way death came to all men, be-
cause all sinned— 13for before the law was
given, sin was in the world. But sin is not
taken into account when there is no law.[l]
14Nevertheless, death reigned from the time
of Adam to the time of Moses, even over
those who did not sin by breaking a com-
mand, as did Adam, who was a pattern of
the one to come.[m]
15But the gift is not like the trespass. For
if the many died by the trespass of the one
man, how much more did God's grace and
the gift that came by the grace of the one
man, Jesus Christ,[n] overflow to the many!
16Again, the gift of God is not like the result
of the one man's sin: The judgment followed
one sin and brought condemnation, but the
gift followed many trespasses and brought
justification. 17For if, by the trespass of
the one man, death reigned through that
one man, how much more will those who
receive God's abundant provision of grace
and of the gift of righteousness reign in life
through the one man, Jesus Christ.
18Consequently, just as the result of one
trespass was condemnation for all men, so
also the result of one act of righteousness
was justification[o] that brings life for all men.
19For just as through the disobedience of the
one man the many were made sinners, so
also through the obedience of the one man
the many will be made righteous.
20The law was added so that the trespass
might increase.[p] But where sin increased,
grace increased all the more,[q] 21so that, just
as sin reigned in death, so also grace might
reign through righteousness to bring eter-
nal life through Jesus Christ our Lord.

## Dead to Sin, Alive in Christ

6 What shall we say, then? Shall we go on
sinning so that grace may increase?[r]
2By no means! We died to sin;[s] how can we
live in it any longer? 3Or don't you know that
all of us who were baptized into Christ Jesus
were baptized into his death? 4We were
therefore buried with him through baptism
into death in order that, just as Christ was
raised from the dead[t] through the glory of
the Father, we too may live a new life.[u]
5If we have been united with him like this
in his death, we will certainly also be united
with him in his resurrection. 6For we know
that our old self was crucified with him[v] so
that the body of sin[w] might be done away
with,[b] that we should no longer be slaves
to sin— 7because anyone who has died has
been freed from sin.
8Now if we died with Christ, we believe
that we will also live with him. 9For we know
that since Christ was raised from the dead,
he cannot die again; death no longer has
mastery over him.[x] 10The death he died, he
died to sin once for all; but the life he lives,
he lives to God.
11In the same way, count yourselves
dead to sin but alive to God in Christ Jesus.
12Therefore do not let sin reign in your mor-
tal body so that you obey its evil desires.
13Do not offer the parts of your body to sin,

5:18 o Ro 4:25
5:20 p Gal 3:19 q 1Ti 1:13,14
6:1 r Ro 3:5,8
6:2 s Col 3:3,5; 1Pe 2:24
6:4 t Col 2:12 u Gal 6:15; Col 3:10
6:6 v Gal 2:20 w Ro 7:24
6:9 x Rev 1:18

[a]2,3 Or *let us* [b]6 Or *be rendered powerless*

**6:13** y Ro 7:5 z Ro 12:1
**6:14** a Gal 5:18 b Ro 3:24
**6:16** c Jn 8:34; 2Pe 2:19
**6:17** d 2Ti 1:13
**6:18** e Ro 8:2
**6:19** f Ro 3:5
**6:21** g ver 23
**6:23** h Ro 5:12; Gal 6:7,8
**7:2** i 1Co 7:39

as instruments of wickedness,[y] but rather offer yourselves to God, as those who have been brought from death to life; and offer the parts of your body to him as instruments of righteousness.[z] 14For sin shall not be your master, because you are not under law,[a] but under grace.[b]

## Slaves to Righteousness

15What then? Shall we sin because we are not under law but under grace? By no means! 16Don't you know that when you offer yourselves to someone to obey him as slaves, you are slaves to the one whom you obey—whether you are slaves to sin,[c] which leads to death, or to obedience, which leads to righteousness? 17But thanks be to God that, though you used to be slaves to sin, you wholeheartedly obeyed the form of teaching[d] to which you were entrusted. 18You have been set free from sin[e] and have become slaves to righteousness.

19I put this in human terms[f] because you are weak in your natural selves. Just as you used to offer the parts of your body in slavery to impurity and to ever-increasing wickedness, so now offer them in slavery to righteousness leading to holiness. 20When you were slaves to sin, you were free from the control of righteousness. 21What benefit did you reap at that time from the things you are now ashamed of? Those things result in death![g] 22But now that you have been set free from sin and have become slaves to God, the benefit you reap leads to holiness, and the result is eternal life. 23For the wages of sin is death,[h] but the gift of God is eternal life in[a] Christ Jesus our Lord.

## An Illustration From Marriage

7 Do you not know, brothers—for I am speaking to men who know the law—that the law has authority over a man only as long as he lives? 2For example, by law a married woman is bound to her husband as long as he is alive, but if her husband dies, she is released from the law of marriage.[i] 3So then, if she marries another man while her husband is still alive, she is called an adulteress. But if her husband dies, she is released from that law and is not an adulteress, even though she marries another man.

4So, my brothers, you also died to the law[j] through the body of Christ,[k] that you might belong to another, to him who was raised from the dead, in order that we might bear fruit to God. 5For when we were controlled by the sinful nature,[b] the sinful passions aroused by the law were at work in our bodies,[l] so that we bore fruit for death. 6But now, by dying to what once bound us, we have been released from the law so that we serve in the new way of the Spirit, and not in the old way of the written code.[m]

## Struggling With Sin

7What shall we say, then? Is the law sin? Certainly not! Indeed I would not have known what sin was except through the law.[n] For I would not have known what coveting really was if the law had not said, "Do not covet."[c][o] 8But sin, seizing the opportunity afforded by the commandment, produced in me every kind of covetous desire. For apart from law, sin is dead.[p] 9Once I was alive apart from law; but when the commandment came, sin sprang to life and I died. 10I found that the very commandment that was intended to bring life[q] actually brought death. 11For sin, seizing the opportunity afforded by the commandment, deceived me, and through the commandment put me to death. 12So then, the law is holy, and the commandment is holy, righteous and good.[r]

13Did that which is good, then, become death to me? By no means! But in order that sin might be recognized as sin, it produced death in me through what was good, so that through the commandment sin might become utterly sinful.

14We know that the law is spiritual; but I am unspiritual, sold[s] as a slave to sin. 15I do not understand what I do. For what I want to do I do not do, but what I hate I do.[t] 16And if I do what I do not want to do, I agree that the law is good. 17As it is, it is no longer I myself who do it, but it is sin living in me. 18I know that nothing good lives in me, that is, in my sinful nature.[d] For I have the desire to do what is good, but I cannot carry it out. 19For what I do is not the good I want to do;

**7:4** j Gal 2:19 k Col 1:22
**7:5** l Ro 6:13
**7:6** m Ro 2:29
**7:7** n Ro 3:20 o Ex 20:17; Dt 5:21
**7:8** p Ro 4:15; 1Co 15:56
**7:10** q Lev 18:5
**7:12** r 1Ti 1:8
**7:14** s 2Ki 17:17
**7:15** t Gal 5:17

[a]23 Or *through* [b]5 Or *the flesh*; also in verse 25 [c]7 Exodus 20:17; Deut. 5:21 [d]18 Or *my flesh*

# Inspire

## HELP FOR THE ADDICT

It is both inspirational and comforting when women of color call to mind the experiences of their sisters in meeting the crushing challenges of life. From the slave traders' auction blocks to the concrete corridors of inner cities, African American women have forged the tradition of the strong black woman that helps them lay claim to human dignity. Other women in oppressed cultures around the world have, in a similar manner, exercised great strength to become who they are.

Yet there are times when women of color succumb to life's relentless pressures and fall victim to the destructive disorders of addiction—addiction to alcohol and other drugs, to food, shopping, abusive relationships and other habits that damage their health and disrupt their lives. The desire for relief or pleasure or the felt need to escape life typically underlies an addiction, but the reality is that unforeseen and painful consequences almost invariably follow.

Addicts become powerless puppets controlled by their addictions, no longer able to exercise the ability to reason. Whatever the addict has become dependent upon becomes her undisputed priority in life. When this happens she finds herself scalded by shame and remorse, filled with the constantly escalating fear of losing the dignity that has made her a strong black woman. She does not understand why she continues to do what she is doing and cannot admit her powerlessness; she has always been, after all, resourceful and capable. She has survived all along because of her refusal to accept that she is powerless. To admit helplessness now would be to lose her dignity—and her very life.

Then one day she stumbles upon Romans 7:14–25. It is then that she begins to understand what every truly strong woman of color already knows: An admission of personal powerlessness goes hand in hand with a willingness to rely on the One who has all power. From this moment on she becomes open to God for direction in how to obtain the physical, emotional and spiritual help she needs for a dignified recovery.

The Lord wants the addicted woman to confront reality and to honestly face herself, others and God (see Isa 59:12)—and to be healed of the pain that drove her to seek escape in the first place (see Isa 61:1–3).

—L. Jones Hood

For the next Inspire note, go to page 1332.

### read

Romans 7:7–25; see also Isaiah 61:1–3; Luke 4:14–21; 2 Corinthians 12:7–10; 13:4.

See also the Inspire Notes "The Faithfulness of God," "Courage to Heal" and "Adopted Through Love," and the Women of the Bible Notes "Athaliah: An Angry Woman" and "The Forgiven Adulteress: Caught but Not Condemned."

### WOMAN of COLOR

Have you been set free from your addictions? If not, turn to God for help and guidance. If you have been liberated, how can you help a sister who still struggles with this issue?

**7:22** u Eph 3:16 v Ps 1:2
**7:23** w Gal 5:17
**7:24** x Ro 6:6
**8:2** y 1Co 15:45 z Ro 6:18
**8:3** a Ac 13:39; Heb 7:18
**8:5** b Gal 5:22–25
**8:6** c Gal 6:8
**8:7** d Jas 4:4
**8:9** e 1Co 6:19; Gal 4:6

no, the evil I do not want to do—this I keep
on doing. 20 Now if I do what I do not want
to do, it is no longer I who do it, but it is sin
living in me that does it.
21 So I find this law at work: When I want
to do good, evil is right there with me. 22 For
in my inner being[u] I delight in God's law;[v]
23 but I see another law at work in the mem-
bers of my body, waging war[w] against the
law of my mind and making me a prisoner
of the law of sin at work within my members.
24 What a wretched man I am! Who will res-
cue me from this body of death?[x] 25 Thanks
be to God—through Jesus Christ our Lord!

So then, I myself in my mind am a slave
to God's law, but in the sinful nature a slave
to the law of sin.

## Life Through the Spirit

8 Therefore, there is now no condemna-
tion for those who are in Christ Jesus,[a]
2 because through Christ Jesus the law of the
Spirit of life[y] set me free[z] from the law of sin
and death. 3 For what the law was powerless[a]
to do in that it was weakened by the sinful
nature,[b] God did by sending his own Son
in the likeness of sinful man to be a sin of-
fering.[c] And so he condemned sin in sinful
man,[d] 4 in order that the righteous require-
ments of the law might be fully met in us,
who do not live according to the sinful na-
ture but according to the Spirit.
5 Those who live according to the sinful
nature have their minds set on what that
nature desires; but those who live in accor-
dance with the Spirit have their minds set
on what the Spirit desires.[b] 6 The mind of
sinful man[e] is death, but the mind con-
trolled by the Spirit is life[c] and peace; 7 the
sinful mind[f] is hostile to God.[d] It does not
submit to God's law, nor can it do so. 8 Those
controlled by the sinful nature cannot
please God.
9 You, however, are controlled not by the
sinful nature but by the Spirit, if the Spirit
of God lives in you.[e] And if anyone does not
have the Spirit of Christ, he does not belong
to Christ. 10 But if Christ is in you, your body
is dead because of sin, yet your spirit is alive
because of righteousness. 11 And if the Spirit
of him who raised Jesus from the dead[f] is
living in you, he who raised Christ from the
dead will also give life to your mortal bodies
through his Spirit, who lives in you.
12 Therefore, brothers, we have an obliga-
tion—but it is not to the sinful nature, to
live according to it. 13 For if you live accord-
ing to the sinful nature, you will die; but if
by the Spirit you put to death the misdeeds
of the body, you will live,[g] 14 because those
who are led by the Spirit of God[h] are sons of
God. 15 For you did not receive a spirit that
makes you a slave again to fear,[i] but you re-
ceived the Spirit of sonship.[g] And by him we
cry, "*Abba*,[h] Father." 16 The Spirit himself
testifies with our spirit that we are God's
children. 17 Now if we are children, then we
are heirs—heirs of God and co-heirs with
Christ, if indeed we share in his sufferings
in order that we may also share in his glory.

## Future Glory

18 I consider that our present sufferings
are not worth comparing with the glory that
will be revealed in us.[j] 19 The creation waits
in eager expectation for the sons of God to
be revealed. 20 For the creation was subjected
to frustration, not by its own choice, but by
the will of the one who subjected it,[k] in hope
21 that[i] the creation itself will be liberated
from its bondage to decay[l] and brought
into the glorious freedom of the children
of God.
22 We know that the whole creation has
been groaning as in the pains of childbirth
right up to the present time. 23 Not only so,
but we ourselves, who have the firstfruits
of the Spirit, groan[m] inwardly as we wait
eagerly for our adoption as sons, the re-
demption of our bodies. 24 For in this hope
we were saved. But hope that is seen is no
hope at all. Who hopes for what he already
has? 25 But if we hope for what we do not yet
have, we wait for it patiently.
26 In the same way, the Spirit helps us in
our weakness. We do not know what we
ought to pray for, but the Spirit himself
intercedes for us with groans that words
cannot express. 27 And he who searches our
hearts[n] knows the mind of the Spirit, be-

**8:11** f Ac 2:24
**8:13** g Gal 6:8
**8:14** h Gal 5:18
**8:15** i 2Ti 1:7; Heb 2:15
**8:18** j 2Co 4:17
**8:20** k Ge 3:17–19
**8:21** l Ac 3:21
**8:23** m 2Co 5:2,4
**8:27** n Rev 2:23

[a]1 Some later manuscripts *Jesus, who do not live according to the sinful nature but according to the Spirit,* [b]3 Or *the flesh*; also in verses 4, 5, 8, 9, 12 and 13 [c]3 Or *man, for sin* [d]3 Or *in the flesh* [e]6 Or *mind set on the flesh* [f]7 Or *the mind set on the flesh* [g]15 Or *adoption* [h]15 Aramaic for *Father* [i]20,21 Or *subjected it in hope.* [21]*For*

cause the Spirit intercedes for the saints in accordance with God's will.

## More Than Conquerors

28 And we know that in all things God works for the good of those who love him,[a] who[b] have been called according to his purpose. 29 For those God foreknew he also predestined to be conformed to the likeness of his Son,[o] that he might be the firstborn among many brothers. 30 And those he predestined,[p] he also called; those he called, he also justified;[q] those he justified, he also glorified.

*Sister,*

*I do work all things for your good.*

*Love me and watch it happen.*

*The Master Architect*

ROMANS 8:28

31 What, then, shall we say in response to this? If God is for us, who can be against us?[r] 32 He who did not spare his own Son,[s] but gave him up for us all—how will he not also, along with him, graciously give us all things? 33 Who will bring any charge[t] against those whom God has chosen? It is God who justifies. 34 Who is he that condemns? Christ Jesus, who died—more than that, who was raised to life—is at the right hand of God and is also interceding for us.[u] 35 Who shall separate us from the love of Christ? Shall trouble or hardship or persecution or famine or nakedness or danger or sword? 36 As it is written:

"For your sake we face death all day long;
we are considered as sheep to be slaughtered."[c][v]

37 No, in all these things we are more than conquerors[w] through him who loved us. 38 For I am convinced that neither death nor life, neither angels nor demons,[d] neither the present nor the future, nor any powers,[x] 39 neither height nor depth, nor anything else in all creation, will be able to separate us from the love of God that is in Christ Jesus our Lord.

## God's Sovereign Choice

9 I speak the truth in Christ—I am not lying,[y] my conscience confirms it in the Holy Spirit— 2 I have great sorrow and unceasing anguish in my heart. 3 For I could wish that I myself[z] were cursed and cut off from Christ for the sake of my brothers, those of my own race, 4 the people of Israel. Theirs is the adoption as sons; theirs the divine glory, the covenants,[a] the receiving of the law,[b] the temple worship[c] and the promises. 5 Theirs are the patriarchs, and from them is traced the human ancestry of Christ, who is God over all,[d] forever praised![e] Amen.

6 It is not as though God's word had failed. For not all who are descended from Israel are Israel.[e] 7 Nor because they are his descendants are they all Abraham's children. On the contrary, "It is through Isaac that your offspring will be reckoned."[f] 8 In other words, it is not the natural children who are God's children, but it is the children of the promise who are regarded as Abraham's offspring. 9 For this was how the promise was stated: "At the appointed time I will return, and Sarah will have a son."[g][f]

10 Not only that, but Rebekah's children had one and the same father, our father Isaac.[g] 11 Yet, before the twins were born or had done anything good or bad—in order that God's purpose in election might stand: 12 not by works but by him who calls—she was told, "The older will serve the younger."[h][h] 13 Just as it is written: "Jacob I loved, but Esau I hated."[i][i]

14 What then shall we say? Is God unjust? Not at all! 15 For he says to Moses,

"I will have mercy on whom I have mercy,
and I will have compassion on whom I have compassion."[j][j]

8:29 o Php3:21
8:30 p Eph1:5,11 q 1Co6:11
8:31 r Ps118:6
8:32 s Jn3:16; Ro4:25; 5:8
8:33 t Isa50:8,9
8:34 u Heb7:25; 9:24; 1Jn2:1
8:36 v Ps44:22; 2Co4:11
8:37 w 1Co15:57
8:38 x Eph1:21
9:1 y 1Ti2:7
9:3 z Ex32:32
9:4 a Ac3:25 b Ps147:19 c Heb9:1
9:5 d Jn1:1
9:6 e Gal6:16
9:9 f Ge18:10,14
9:10 g Ge25:21
9:12 h Ge25:23
9:13 i Mal1:2,3
9:15 j Ex33:19

[a] 28 Some manuscripts *And we know that all things work together for good to those who love God* [b] 28 Or *works together with those who love him to bring about what is good—with those who* [c] 36 Psalm 44:22 [d] 38 Or *nor heavenly rulers* [e] 5 Or *Christ, who is over all. God be forever praised!* Or *Christ. God who is over all be forever praised!* [f] 7 Gen. 21:12 [g] 9 Gen. 18:10,14 [h] 12 Gen. 25:23 [i] 13 Mal. 1:2,3 [j] 15 Exodus 33:19

9:17
k Ex 9:16

[16]It does not, therefore, depend on man's de-
sire or effort, but on God's mercy. [17]For the
Scripture says to Pharaoh: "I raised you up
for this very purpose, that I might display
my power in you and that my name might
be proclaimed in all the earth."[a k] [18]There-
fore God has mercy on whom he wants to
have mercy, and he hardens whom he wants
to harden.
[19]One of you will say to me: "Then why
does God still blame us? For who resists
his will?" [20]But who are you, O man, to talk

[a]17 Exodus 9:16

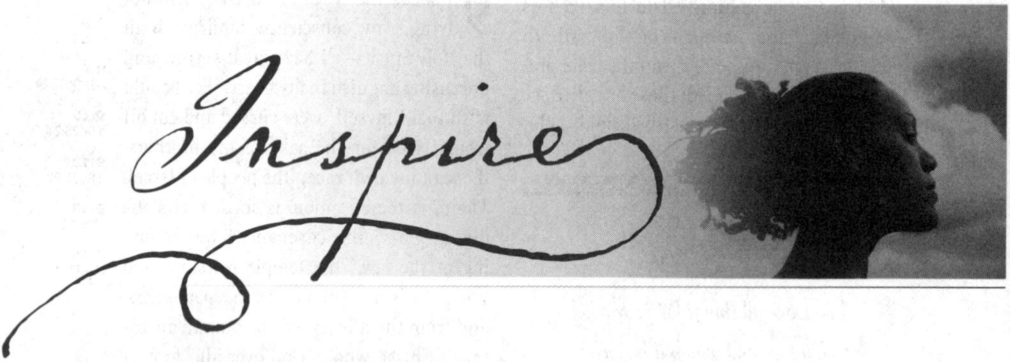


## ADOPTED THROUGH LOVE

At the age of 50, I became a mother through adoption. My 18-month-old great-nephew came to live with me, and I was suddenly a single mother. The adoption process reminded me of what God did for us through Jesus Christ. As Christians we are spiritually adopted by God because he loves us.

God speaks to us through our love for one another, no matter how we came into the "family." God's love makes us part of his family regardless of our external situation. God's love through Jesus draws us close and reminds us: "I wanted you. I love you."

As God's children we are called to constantly remember: "For God so loved the world that he gave his one and only Son, that whoever believes in him shall not perish but have eternal life" (Jn 3:16).

In Romans 8:15, Paul reminds us that, as children of God, we have received not a spirit of bondage but God's Spirit of "sonship"—in our case, "daughtership." In other words, though we willingly serve Jesus and others who populate our world, we are in one important sense no longer servants. Paul says in this verse that we've been emancipated for all time from slavery to fear. Because of God's love, the Spirit of God dwells richly in each of us. We have been reborn by the Spirit and have entered into a relationship with God that only a child and parent can share (see Ro 9:8). God's desire to have a family into whom he could pour his holiness, his righteousness and his love was realized fully when Jesus came to earth and sacrificed himself for our sins.

It is important for us to fully understand that what God has is ours. Good parents take care of their children. We have become a part of the family of God through adoption because God wanted us—and still does. Rejoice! You have been adopted!

—V. Fisher

For the next Inspire note, go to page 1335.

### read

Romans 9:1–9; see also John 1:10–13; Romans 8:12–17; Ephesians 1:3–14; 3:14–21.

See also the Inspire Notes "Peace" and "Love."

### WOMAN of COLOR

How does remembering that you are adopted by God help you to cope with life's ups and downs?

**9:20** l Isa 29:16
**9:23** m Ro 8:30
**9:24** n Ro 3:29
**9:25** o Hos 2:23
**9:26** p Hos 1:10
**9:27** q Ro 11:5
**9:28** r Isa 10:22,23
**9:29** s Isa 13:19
**9:31** t Ro 10:2,3 u Gal 5:4

back to God? "Shall what is formed say to
him who formed it, 'Why did you make me
like this?' "[a][l] [21]Does not the potter have the
right to make out of the same lump of clay
some pottery for noble purposes and some
for common use?

[22]What if God, choosing to show his wrath
and make his power known, bore with great
patience the objects of his wrath—prepared
for destruction? [23]What if he did this to
make the riches of his glory known to the
objects of his mercy, whom he prepared in
advance for glory[m]— [24]even us, whom he
also called, not only from the Jews but also
from the Gentiles?[n] [25]As he says in Hosea:

"I will call them 'my people' who are not
my people;
and I will call her 'my loved one' who
is not my loved one,"[b][o]

[26]and,

"It will happen that in the very place
where it was said to them,
'You are not my people,'
they will be called 'sons of the living
God.' "[c][p]

[27]Isaiah cries out concerning Israel:

"Though the number of the Israelites be
like the sand by the sea,
only the remnant will be saved.[q]
[28]For the Lord will carry out
his sentence on earth with speed and
finality."[d][r]

[29]It is just as Isaiah said previously:

"Unless the Lord Almighty
had left us descendants,
we would have become like Sodom,
we would have been like Gomorrah."[e][s]

## Israel's Unbelief

[30]What then shall we say? That the Gen-
tiles, who did not pursue righteousness,
have obtained it, a righteousness that is by
faith; [31]but Israel, who pursued a law of righ-
teousness,[t] has not attained it.[u] [32]Why not?
Because they pursued it not by faith but as
if it were by works. They stumbled over the
"stumbling stone." [33]As it is written:

"See, I lay in Zion a stone that causes men
to stumble
and a rock that makes them fall,
and the one who trusts in him will never
be put to shame."[f][v]

10 Brothers, my heart's desire and
prayer to God for the Israelites is
that they may be saved. [2]For I can testify
about them that they are zealous[w] for God,
but their zeal is not based on knowledge.
[3]Since they did not know the righteousness
that comes from God and sought to estab-
lish their own, they did not submit to God's
righteousness.[x] [4]Christ is the end of the law[y]
so that there may be righteousness for every-
one who believes.

[5]Moses describes in this way the righ-
teousness that is by the law: "The man who
does these things will live by them."[g][z] [6]But
the righteousness that is by faith says: "Do
not say in your heart, 'Who will ascend into
heaven?'[h]" (that is, to bring Christ down)
[7]"or 'Who will descend into the deep?'[i]"
(that is, to bring Christ up from the dead).
[8]But what does it say? "The word is near
you; it is in your mouth and in your heart,"[j][a]
that is, the word of faith we are proclaim-
ing: [9]That if you confess[b] with your mouth,
"Jesus is Lord," and believe in your heart
that God raised him from the dead, you
will be saved. [10]For it is with your heart
that you believe and are justified, and it is
with your mouth that you confess and are
saved. [11]As the Scripture says, "Anyone who
trusts in him will never be put to shame."[k][c]
[12]For there is no difference between Jew and
Gentile[d]—the same Lord is Lord of all and
richly blesses all who call on him, [13]for, "Ev-
eryone who calls on the name of the Lord[e]
will be saved."[l][f]

[14]How, then, can they call on the one
they have not believed in? And how can
they believe in the one of whom they have
not heard? And how can they hear without
someone preaching to them? [15]And how can
they preach unless they are sent? As it is
written, "How beautiful are the feet of those
who bring good news!"[m][g]

[16]But not all the Israelites accepted the
good news. For Isaiah says, "Lord, who has

**9:33** v Isa 28:16
**10:2** w Ac 21:20
**10:3** x Ro 1:17
**10:4** y Gal 3:24
**10:5** z Ne 9:29
**10:8** a Dt 30:14
**10:9** b Mt 10:32
**10:11** c Isa 28:16
**10:12** d Ro 3:22,29
**10:13** e Ac 2:21 f Joel 2:32
**10:15** g Isa 52:7

[a]20 Isaiah 29:16; 45:9 [b]25 Hosea 2:23 [c]26 Hosea 1:10 [d]28 Isaiah 10:22,23 [e]29 Isaiah 1:9 [f]33 Isaiah 8:14; 28:16
[g]5 Lev. 18:5 [h]6 Deut. 30:12 [i]7 Deut. 30:13 [j]8 Deut. 30:14 [k]11 Isaiah 28:16 [l]13 Joel 2:32 [m]15 Isaiah 52:7

believed our message?"[a][h] 17 Consequently, faith comes from hearing the message, and the message is heard through the word of Christ. 18 But I ask: Did they not hear? Of course they did:

"Their voice has gone out into all the
 earth,
 their words to the ends of the world."[b][i]

19 Again I ask: Did Israel not understand? First, Moses says,

"I will make you envious[j] by those who
 are not a nation;
 I will make you angry by a nation that
 has no understanding."[c]

20 And Isaiah boldly says,

"I was found by those who did not seek me;
 I revealed myself to those who did not
 ask for me."[d][k]

21 But concerning Israel he says,

"All day long I have held out my hands
 to a disobedient and obstinate
 people."[e][l]

## The Remnant of Israel

**11** I ask then: Did God reject his people? By no means![m] I am an Israelite myself, a descendant of Abraham,[n] from the tribe of Benjamin.[o] 2 God did not reject his people, whom he foreknew.[p] Don't you know what the Scripture says in the passage about Elijah—how he appealed to God against Israel: 3 "Lord, they have killed your prophets and torn down your altars; I am the only one left, and they are trying to kill me"[f]?[q] 4 And what was God's answer to him? "I have reserved for myself seven thousand who have not bowed the knee to Baal."[g][r] 5 So too, at the present time there is a remnant[s] chosen by grace. 6 And if by grace, then it is no longer by works;[t] if it were, grace would no longer be grace.[h]

7 What then? What Israel sought so earnestly it did not obtain,[u] but the elect did. The others were hardened,[v] 8 as it is written:

"God gave them a spirit of stupor,
 eyes so that they could not see
 and ears so that they could not hear,
 to this very day."[i][w]

9 And David says:

"May their table become a snare and a
 trap,
 a stumbling block and a retribution
 for them.
10 May their eyes be darkened so they
 cannot see,
 and their backs be bent forever."[j][x]

## Ingrafted Branches

11 Again I ask: Did they stumble so as to fall beyond recovery? Not at all! Rather, because of their transgression, salvation has come to the Gentiles[y] to make Israel envious. 12 But if their transgression means riches for the world, and their loss means riches for the Gentiles, how much greater riches will their fullness bring!

13 I am talking to you Gentiles. Inasmuch as I am the apostle to the Gentiles,[z] I make much of my ministry 14 in the hope that I may somehow arouse my own people to envy and save some of them. 15 For if their rejection is the reconciliation of the world, what will their acceptance be but life from the dead?[a] 16 If the part of the dough offered as firstfruits is holy, then the whole batch is holy; if the root is holy, so are the branches.

17 If some of the branches have been broken off,[b] and you, though a wild olive shoot, have been grafted in among the others[c] and now share in the nourishing sap from the olive root, 18 do not boast over those branches. If you do, consider this: You do not support the root, but the root supports you. 19 You will say then, "Branches were broken off so that I could be grafted in." 20 Granted. But they were broken off because of unbelief, and you stand by faith.[d] Do not be arrogant,[e] but be afraid. 21 For if God did not spare the natural branches, he will not spare you either.

22 Consider therefore the kindness and sternness of God: sternness to those who fell, but kindness to you, provided that you continue[f] in his kindness. Otherwise, you also will be cut off.[g] 23 And if they do not

**10:16** h Isa53:1
**10:18** i Ps19:4
**10:19** j Ro11:11,14
**10:20** k Isa65:1
**10:21** l Isa65:2
**11:1** m 1Sa12:22; n 2Co11:22; o Php3:5
**11:2** p Ro8:29
**11:3** q 1Ki19:10,14
**11:4** r 1Ki19:18
**11:5** s Ro9:27
**11:6** t Ro4:4
**11:7** u Ro9:31; v Ro9:18
**11:8** w Dt29:4; Isa29:10
**11:10** x Ps69:22,23
**11:11** y Ac13:46
**11:13** z Ac9:15
**11:15** a Lk15:24,32
**11:17** b Jer11:16; c Eph2:11–13
**11:20** d 1Co10:12; e Ro12:16
**11:22** f 1Co15:2; Heb3:6; g Jn15:2

[a] 16 Isaiah 53:1 [b] 18 Psalm 19:4 [c] 19 Deut. 32:21 [d] 20 Isaiah 65:1 [e] 21 Isaiah 65:2 [f] 3 1 Kings 19:10,14 [g] 4 1 Kings 19:18 [h] 6 Some manuscripts *be grace. But if by works, then it is no longer grace; if it were, work would no longer be work.* [i] 8 Deut. 29:4; Isaiah 29:10 [j] 10 Psalm 69:22,23

## CONFESSING SALVATION

Biblical salvation may best be described as "God's deliverance." *Salvation* is the noun form of the word *saved.* But what are we, as Christians, saved from, and what does salvation mean to us personally? For many of us, being saved and having salvation simply mean that we are born again; we have been baptized and are now able to sit at God's table with fellow believers, partake of Holy Communion and announce to the world, "I've been saved." But is that all salvation means? Is that all that Jesus has done for us?

The reality for the believer is that salvation is all-encompassing. The word *salvation*, as well as the powerful reality behind it, is synonymous with our healing, our preservation, our protection, our welfare, our deliverance, our health, our help. God, in his infinite wisdom, power and mercy, knew that we needed to be saved from sickness, calamity, bondage and, ultimately, eternal death and damnation. Christ came and saved us from everything that is ungodly, everything that is not like himself. This is our salvation. The very name *Jesus*, the Greek form of the Hebrew name Joshua, means "the LORD saves" (see Mt 1:21 and NIV text note). Jesus Christ embodies our salvation, and through our relationship with him we reap the benefit of an abundant and full life (see Jn 10:10).

How can we obtain this great salvation? We must not only believe that Jesus saves us but be willing to confess that belief with our mouths. We are called to proclaim and acknowledge Christ before others, so that he can *confess us*—commend and recommend us—before his Father in heaven (see Mt 10:32–33; Ro 10:9–13). Being a silent Christian, just like being silently saved, is impossible. We must confess—and the time is now. The reality is that one day soon *every* knee, *every* individual, whether saved or unsaved, will bow and *every* tongue will confess that Jesus is Lord (see Php 2:9–11).

—C. BYRD

### read

Romans 10:1–21; see also Matthew 7:13–23; 10:32–39.

**See also** the Inspire Notes "Evangelism: Gone Fishin'," "Female Ministers and Evangelists," "Prayer" and "Faith," and the Women of the Bible Notes "Mary Magdalene: Setting Her Reputation Straight" and "Priscilla: An Open-Door Policy."

### WOMAN of COLOR

Do you believe in your heart that Jesus is Lord? If so, accept and receive his free gift of salvation and freely confess his name. If not, discuss your questions or reservations with a believer you trust.

For the next Inspire note, go to page 1337.

**11:23** h 2Co 3:16
**11:25** i Lk 21:24
**11:27** j Isa 27:9
**11:28** k Dt 7:8
**11:32** l Ro 3:9
**11:33** m Ps 92:5
**11:34** n Isa 40:13,14; Job 36:22
**11:36** o 1Co 8:6; Col 1:16

persist in unbelief, they will be grafted
in, for God is able to graft them in again.[h]
24 After all, if you were cut out of an olive
tree that is wild by nature, and contrary to
nature were grafted into a cultivated olive
tree, how much more readily will these, the
natural branches, be grafted into their own
olive tree!

## All Israel Will Be Saved

25 I do not want you to be ignorant of this
mystery, brothers, so that you may not be
conceited: Israel has experienced a harden-
ing in part until the full number of the Gen-
tiles has come in.[i] 26 And so all Israel will be
saved, as it is written:

"The deliverer will come from Zion;
he will turn godlessness away from
Jacob.
27 And this is[a] my covenant with them
when I take away their sins."[b][j]

28 As far as the gospel is concerned, they
are enemies on your account; but as far as
election is concerned, they are loved on ac-
count of the patriarchs,[k] 29 for God's gifts
and his call are irrevocable. 30 Just as you
who were at one time disobedient to God
have now received mercy as a result of
their disobedience, 31 so they too have now
become disobedient in order that they too
may now[c] receive mercy as a result of God's
mercy to you. 32 For God has bound all men
over to disobedience[l] so that he may have
mercy on them all.

## Doxology

33 Oh, the depth of the riches of the wisdom
and[d] knowledge of God![m]
How unsearchable his judgments,
and his paths beyond tracing out!
34 "Who has known the mind of the Lord?
Or who has been his counselor?"[e][n]
35 "Who has ever given to God,
that God should repay him?"[f]
36 For from him and through him and to
him are all things.[o]
To him be the glory forever! Amen.

## Living Sacrifices

12 Therefore, I urge you, brothers, in
view of God's mercy, to offer your
bodies as living sacrifices,[p] holy and pleas-
ing to God—this is your spiritual[g] act of
worship. 2 Do not conform[q] any longer to the
pattern of this world, but be transformed
by the renewing of your mind.[r] Then you
will be able to test and approve what God's
will is—his good, pleasing and perfect will.

3 For by the grace given me[s] I say to every
one of you: Do not think of yourself more
highly than you ought, but rather think
of yourself with sober judgment, in accor-
dance with the measure of faith God has
given you. 4 Just as each of us has one body
with many members, and these members
do not all have the same function,[t] 5 so in
Christ we who are many form one body, and
each member belongs to all the others. 6 We
have different gifts,[u] according to the grace
given us. If a man's gift is prophesying, let
him use it in proportion to his[h] faith. 7 If it
is serving, let him serve; if it is teaching, let
him teach; 8 if it is encouraging, let him en-
courage;[v] if it is contributing to the needs
of others, let him give generously;[w] if it is
leadership, let him govern diligently; if it is
showing mercy, let him do it cheerfully.

## Love

9 Love must be sincere. Hate what is
evil; cling to what is good. 10 Be devoted
to one another in brotherly love. Honor
one another above yourselves.[x] 11 Never be
lacking in zeal, but keep your spiritual fer-
vor, serving the Lord. 12 Be joyful in hope,
patient in affliction,[y] faithful in prayer.
13 Share with God's people who are in need.
Practice hospitality.

14 Bless those who persecute you;[z] bless
and do not curse. 15 Rejoice with those who re-
joice; mourn with those who mourn. 16 Live
in harmony with one another.[a] Do not be
proud, but be willing to associate with peo-
ple of low position.[i] Do not be conceited.

17 Do not repay anyone evil for evil. Be
careful to do what is right in the eyes of
everybody.[b] 18 If it is possible, as far as it

**12:1** p Ro 6:13,16,19
**12:2** q 1Pe 1:14 r Eph 4:23
**12:3** s Ro 15:15; Eph 4:7
**12:4** t 1Co 12:12–14; Eph 4:16
**12:6** u 1Co 12:4,8–10
**12:8** v Ac 15:32 w 2Co 9:5–13
**12:10** x Php 2:3
**12:12** y Heb 10:32,36
**12:14** z Mt 5:44
**12:16** a Ro 15:5
**12:17** b 2Co 8:21

[a]27 Or *will be* [b]27 Isaiah 59:20,21; 27:9; Jer. 31:33,34 [c]31 Some manuscripts do not have *now.* [d]33 Or *riches and the wisdom and the* [e]34 Isaiah 40:13 [f]35 Job 41:11 [g]1 Or *reasonable* [h]6 Or *in agreement with the* [i]16 Or *willing to do menial work*

Inspire

## COMMITMENT TO GOD

Romans 12:1–2 describes the kind of commitment God desires and deserves from us. Our lives are to be totally committed to God—a commitment that focuses completely on his will for our lives. This means that our first priority is always to be pleasing God. The implication of such commitment is that we no longer belong to the world or to ourselves; our free will is to be consumed by the Father's will. Every aspect of our lives is to be submitted to God's control. In this way we become "living sacrifices."

Paul suggests that a God-focused commitment is only reasonable for a believer, not simply because of God's priceless gifts of grace and mercy through Jesus Christ but also because of the social and spiritual benefits we gain thereby. Turning our lives over to God brings about a renewing of our minds and a spiritual separation from the world and its destructive forces. A renewed mind defines and refines our reactions to life situations, shifts our perspective on right and wrong and enhances our expectation to live a peaceful life. Spiritual separation from the world gives us complete freedom to be what God wants us to be, without concern for the world's opinion. This kind of separation keeps us from fearing aloneness because we know God will never leave us alone. This kind of commitment views marriage as a vow not only to our spouses, but also to God. This kind of devotion works hard in the church and community because of our relationship to God, not our position or prestige.

As living sacrifices, our lives belong to God, yet his reward becomes ours. Truly committed Christians experience the full joy of a daily walk with a God who is totally committed to us, as demonstrated in his plan of salvation through Christ.

Commitment builds faith and develops strong character. It is a lifetime venture requiring time, work and determination (see Mt 16:24). Commitment requires action, and it cannot be separated from responsibility. When we are truly devoted to Christ, we are committed to seeing his kingdom find fulfillment here on earth!

—B. Whitaker

### read

Romans 12:1–2; see also Matthew 16:21–26; Luke 9:57–62; 14:25–35.

**See also** the Inspire Notes "God Is a Jealous God," "Commitment to Community," "Submission" and "Faith," and the Women of the Bible Notes "Lot's Wife: Why Look Back?" "Sarah: Is Anything Too Hard for God?" "The Woman of Thebez: Protector of Her People," "Mary of Bethany: The Unforgotten Woman" and "Claudia: A Sincere Supporter."

### WOMAN of COLOR

How committed are you to God's will for your life?

For the next Inspire note, go to page 1351.

**12:20** c Mt5:44
**13:1** d 1Pe2:13,14 e Da2:21
**13:3** f 1Pe2:14
**13:4** g 1Th4:6
**13:7** h Mt22:17,21
**13:9** i Ex20:13–15,17

depends on you, live at peace with everyone.
19 Do not take revenge, my friends, but leave
room for God's wrath, for it is written: "It is
mine to avenge; I will repay,"[a] says the Lord.
20 On the contrary:

"If your enemy is hungry, feed him;
if he is thirsty, give him something to
drink.
In doing this, you will heap burning coals
on his head."[b][c]

21 Do not be overcome by evil, but overcome
evil with good.

## Submission to the Authorities

13 Everyone must submit himself to
the governing authorities,[d] for there
is no authority except that which God has
established.[e] The authorities that exist have
been established by God. 2 Consequently, he
who rebels against the authority is rebelling
against what God has instituted, and those
who do so will bring judgment on them-
selves. 3 For rulers hold no terror for those
who do right, but for those who do wrong.
Do you want to be free from fear of the one in
authority? Then do what is right and he will
commend you.[f] 4 For he is God's servant to do
you good. But if you do wrong, be afraid, for
he does not bear the sword for nothing. He
is God's servant, an agent of wrath to bring
punishment on the wrongdoer.[g] 5 Therefore,
it is necessary to submit to the authorities,
not only because of possible punishment
but also because of conscience.

6 This is also why you pay taxes, for the au-
thorities are God's servants, who give their
full time to governing. 7 Give everyone what
you owe him: If you owe taxes, pay taxes;[h]
if revenue, then revenue; if respect, then re-
spect; if honor, then honor.

## Love, for the Day Is Near

8 Let no debt remain outstanding, except
the continuing debt to love one another, for
he who loves his fellowman has fulfilled the
law. 9 The commandments, "Do not commit
adultery," "Do not murder," "Do not steal,"
"Do not covet,"[c][i] and whatever other com-
mandment there may be, are summed up in
this one rule: "Love your neighbor as your-
self."[d] 10 Love does no harm to its neighbor.
Therefore love is the fulfillment of the law.

11 And do this, understanding the present
time. The hour has come[j] for you to wake up
from your slumber, because our salvation
is nearer now than when we first believed.
12 The night is nearly over; the day is almost
here. So let us put aside the deeds of dark-
ness[k] and put on the armor of light. 13 Let
us behave decently, as in the daytime, not
in orgies and drunkenness, not in sexual
immorality and debauchery, not in dissen-
sion and jealousy. 14 Rather, clothe your-
selves with the Lord Jesus Christ,[l] and do
not think about how to gratify the desires of
the sinful nature.[e]

**13:11** j 1Co7:29–31
**13:12** k Eph5:11
**13:14** l Gal3:27; Eph4:24

*Lord,*

*I need your help. I need you to convict me each time I want to follow my sinful nature. Remind me instead to follow your Spirit on the only path that will bring peace, love and joy. Following my own desires dead-ends in short-term gratification. Help me to seek your more excellent way.*

*Amen*

ROMANS 13:11–14

## The Weak and the Strong

14 Accept him whose faith is weak, with-
out passing judgment on disputable
matters. 2 One man's faith allows him to eat
everything, but another man, whose faith is
weak, eats only vegetables. 3 The man who
eats everything must not look down on him
who does not, and the man who does not
eat everything must not condemn the man
who does, for God has accepted him. 4 Who
are you to judge someone else's servant?
To his own master he stands or falls. And
he will stand, for the Lord is able to make
him stand.

5 One man considers one day more sacred

[a]19 Deut. 32:35 [b]20 Prov. 25:21,22 [c]9 Exodus 20:13–15,17; Deut. 5:17–19,21 [d]9 Lev. 19:18 [e]14 Or *the flesh*

**14:5** m Gal 4:10
**14:6** n 1Co 10:30,31; 1Ti 4:3,4
**14:7** o Gal 2:20
**14:8** p Php 1:20
**14:9** q 2Co 5:15
**14:10** r 2Co 5:10
**14:11** s Isa 45:23
**14:12** t Mt 12:36; 1Pe 4:5
**14:14** u 1Co 8:7
**14:15** v 1Co 8:11
**14:17** w 1Co 8:8 x Ro 15:13
**14:18** y 2Co 8:21
**14:19** z Ro 12:18
**14:20** a ver 15 b 1Co 8:9–12

than another;[m] another man considers every day alike. Each one should be fully convinced in his own mind. 6 He who regards one day as special, does so to the Lord. He who eats meat, eats to the Lord, for he gives thanks to God;[n] and he who abstains, does so to the Lord and gives thanks to God. 7 For none of us lives to himself alone[o] and none of us dies to himself alone. 8 If we live, we live to the Lord; and if we die, we die to the Lord. So, whether we live or die, we belong to the Lord.[p]

9 For this very reason, Christ died and returned to life so that he might be the Lord of both the dead and the living.[q] 10 You, then, why do you judge your brother? Or why do you look down on your brother? For we will all stand before God's judgment seat.[r] 11 It is written:

"'As surely as I live,' says the Lord,
'every knee will bow before me;
every tongue will confess to God.'"[a][s]

12 So then, each of us will give an account of himself to God.[t]

13 Therefore let us stop passing judgment on one another. Instead, make up your mind not to put any stumbling block or obstacle in your brother's way. 14 As one who is in the Lord Jesus, I am fully convinced that no food[b] is unclean in itself. But if anyone regards something as unclean, then for him it is unclean.[u] 15 If your brother is distressed because of what you eat, you are no longer acting in love. Do not by your eating destroy your brother for whom Christ died.[v] 16 Do not allow what you consider good to be spoken of as evil. 17 For the kingdom of God is not a matter of eating and drinking,[w] but of righteousness, peace and joy in the Holy Spirit,[x] 18 because anyone who serves Christ in this way is pleasing to God and approved by men.[y]

19 Let us therefore make every effort to do what leads to peace[z] and to mutual edification. 20 Do not destroy the work of God for the sake of food.[a] All food is clean, but it is wrong for a man to eat anything that causes someone else to stumble.[b] 21 It is better not to eat meat or drink wine or to do anything else that will cause your brother to fall.

22 So whatever you believe about these things keep between yourself and God. Blessed is the man who does not condemn[c] himself by what he approves. 23 But the man who has doubts is condemned if he eats, because his eating is not from faith; and everything that does not come from faith is sin.

**15** We who are strong ought to bear with the failings of the weak[d] and not to please ourselves. 2 Each of us should please his neighbor for his good,[e] to build him up.[f] 3 For even Christ did not please himself but, as it is written: "The insults of those who insult you have fallen on me."[c][g] 4 For everything that was written in the past was written to teach us, so that through endurance and the encouragement of the Scriptures we might have hope.

5 May the God who gives endurance and encouragement give you a spirit of unity among yourselves as you follow Christ Jesus, 6 so that with one heart and mouth you may glorify the God and Father of our Lord Jesus Christ.

7 Accept one another,[h] then, just as Christ accepted you, in order to bring praise to God. 8 For I tell you that Christ has become a servant of the Jews[d][i] on behalf of God's truth, to confirm the promises[j] made to the patriarchs 9 so that the Gentiles may glorify God for his mercy, as it is written:

"Therefore I will praise you among the
Gentiles;
I will sing hymns to your name."[e][k]

10 Again, it says,

"Rejoice, O Gentiles, with his people."[f][l]

11 And again,

"Praise the Lord, all you Gentiles,
and sing praises to him, all you
peoples."[g][m]

12 And again, Isaiah says,

"The Root of Jesse[n] will spring up,
one who will arise to rule over the
nations;
the Gentiles will hope in him."[h]

13 May the God of hope fill you with all joy and peace as you trust in him, so that you

**14:22** c 1Jn 3:21
**15:1** d Ro 14:1; Gal 6:1,2
**15:2** e 1Co 10:33 f Ro 14:19
**15:3** g Ps 69:9
**15:7** h Ro 14:1
**15:8** i Mt 15:24; Ac 3:25,26 j 2Co 1:20
**15:9** k Ps 18:49
**15:10** l Dt 32:43
**15:11** m Ps 117:1
**15:12** n Rev 5:5

[a] 11 Isaiah 45:23 [b] 14 Or *that nothing* [c] 3 Psalm 69:9 [d] 8 Greek *circumcision* [e] 9 2 Samuel 22:50; Psalm 18:49
[f] 10 Deut. 32:43 [g] 11 Psalm 117:1 [h] 12 Isaiah 11:10

may overflow with hope by the power of the Holy Spirit.

## Paul the Minister to the Gentiles

[14]I myself am convinced, my brothers, that you yourselves are full of goodness, complete in knowledge and competent to instruct one another. [15]I have written you quite boldly on some points, as if to remind you of them again, because of the grace God gave me [16]to be a minister of Christ Jesus to the Gentiles[o] with the priestly duty of proclaiming the gospel of God, so that the Gentiles might become an offering acceptable to God, sanctified by the Holy Spirit.

[17]Therefore I glory in Christ Jesus in my service to God. [18]I will not venture to speak of anything except what Christ has accomplished through me in leading the Gentiles[p] to obey God by what I have said and done— [19]by the power of signs and miracles,[q] through the power of the Spirit. So from Jerusalem all the way around to Illyricum, I have fully proclaimed the gospel of Christ. [20]It has always been my ambition to preach the gospel where Christ was not known, so that I would not be building on someone else's foundation.[r] [21]Rather, as it is written:

"Those who were not told about him will
see,
and those who have not heard will
understand."[a][s]

[22]This is why I have often been hindered from coming to you.[t]

## Paul's Plan to Visit Rome

[23]But now that there is no more place for me to work in these regions, and since I have been longing for many years to see you,[u] [24]I plan to do so when I go to Spain. I hope to visit you while passing through and to have you assist me on my journey there, after I have enjoyed your company for a while. [25]Now, however, I am on my way to Jerusalem[v] in the service[w] of the saints there. [26]For Macedonia and Achaia were pleased to make a contribution for the poor among the saints in Jerusalem. [27]They were pleased to do it, and indeed they owe it to them. For if the Gentiles have shared in the Jews' spiritual blessings, they owe it to the Jews to share with them their material blessings.[x] [28]So after I have completed this task and have made sure that they have received this fruit, I will go to Spain and visit you on the way. [29]I know that when I come to you, I will come in the full measure of the blessing of Christ.

[30]I urge you, brothers, by our Lord Jesus Christ and by the love of the Spirit, to join me in my struggle by praying to God for me.[y] [31]Pray that I may be rescued from the unbelievers in Judea and that my service in Jerusalem may be acceptable to the saints there, [32]so that by God's will[z] I may come to you[a] with joy and together with you be refreshed. [33]The God of peace[b] be with you all. Amen.

## Personal Greetings

16 I commend to you our sister Phoebe, a servant[b] of the church in Cenchrea.[c] [2]I ask you to receive her in the Lord[d] in a way worthy of the saints and to give her any help she may need from you, for she has been a great help to many people, including me.

[3]Greet Priscilla[c] and Aquila,[e] my fellow workers in Christ Jesus. [4]They risked their lives for me. Not only I but all the churches of the Gentiles are grateful to them.

[5]Greet also the church that meets at their house.[f]

Greet my dear friend Epenetus, who was the first convert[g] to Christ in the province of Asia.

[6]Greet Mary, who worked very hard for you.

[7]Greet Andronicus and Junias, my relatives who have been in prison with me. They are outstanding among the apostles, and they were in Christ before I was.

[8]Greet Ampliatus, whom I love in the Lord.

[9]Greet Urbanus, our fellow worker in Christ, and my dear friend Stachys.

[10]Greet Apelles, tested and approved in Christ.

**15:16** o Ac 9:15
**15:18** p Ac 21:19; Ro 1:5
**15:19** q Ac 19:11
**15:20** r 2Co 10:15,16
**15:21** s Isa 52:15
**15:22** t Ro 1:13
**15:23** u Ac 19:21; Ro 1:10,11
**15:25** v Ac 19:21 w Ac 24:17
**15:27** x 1Co 9:11
**15:30** y 2Co 1:11; Col 4:12
**15:32** z Ac 18:21 a Ro 1:10,13
**15:33** b Ro 16:20; 2Co 13:11; Php 4:9
**16:1** c Ac 18:18
**16:2** d Php 2:29
**16:3** e Ac 18:2
**16:5** f 1Co 16:19; Col 4:15 g 1Co 16:15

[a]21 Isaiah 52:15 [b]1 Or *deaconess* [c]3 Greek *Prisca*, a variant of *Priscilla*

# Phoebe

## A Faithful Messenger

Phoebe, like other women in both the early church and the church today, sacrificed countless hours for the advancement of God's kingdom through her various church ministries (see Ro 16:1–2). She remained focused on the goal of spreading the Good News and accomplished this task against insurmountable odds. Driven by her deep sense of desire, purpose, faith and commitment, Phoebe traveled many miles in order to deliver the apostle Paul's letter to the Christians at Rome. This letter was important, for its contents would become the bridge to understanding God's plan for future Christians. Phoebe's steadfast motivation touched the hearts of countless people who otherwise may not have been receptive to the gospel. Without this diligent and faithful servant, we might not have the book of Romans from which to read and garner spiritual insight.

Phoebe goes virtually unnoticed in the Biblical text, and many servants of Christ today—especially women of color—go unnoticed too. However, Phoebe's work was very important. In Romans 16:1, Paul called her a "servant of the church in Cenchrea." Used in this way, the word "servant" probably refers to the position of woman deacon, or deaconess (see NIV text note on Ro 16:1). She served those who were receiving the message of salvation, and she carried that message to others. While our work may be trying at times, we must focus on the outcome. Others will be blessed in ways we cannot foresee. It is natural to want recognition and affirmation for our work; however, we must not lose focus when we are not acknowledged. Our true Rewarder sees our hard work and knows what we do. Phoebe serves as an example of a faithful servant who is empowered by God to serve.

Woman of color, work as a servant to God; glorify God through all your tasks, and he will remember you as a faithful servant. He will receive the glory, and you and others will be blessed.

—K. DAVIS

### reflection

*How can you adopt an attitude as a servant of God in all you do today?*

### read

Romans 16:1–2.

**See also** the Inspire Notes "Commitment to Community," "Submission," "Female Ministers and Evangelists," "Servant-Leadership" and "Commitment to God," and the Women of the Bible Notes "Deborah: An Uncommon Leader," "Huldah: A Prophetess of God," "Queen Vashti: A Woman of Strength," "A Virtuous Woman: A Strong Woman, Dependent on God" and "Philip's Daughters: Those Preaching Women."

For the next Women of the Bible note, go to page 1362.

**16:16**
h 1Co 16:20; 2Co 13:12

**16:17**
i 2Th 3:6,14

Greet those who belong to the household
of Aristobulus.
11 Greet Herodion, my relative.
Greet those in the household of Narcissus
who are in the Lord.
12 Greet Tryphena and Tryphosa, those
women who work hard in the Lord.
Greet my dear friend Persis, another
woman who has worked very hard in
the Lord.
13 Greet Rufus, chosen in the Lord, and
his mother, who has been a mother to
me, too.
14 Greet Asyncritus, Phlegon, Hermes,
Patrobas, Hermas and the brothers
with them.
15 Greet Philologus, Julia, Nereus and his
sister, and Olympas and all the saints
with them.
16 Greet one another with a holy kiss.[h]
All the churches of Christ send greet-
ings.

17 I urge you, brothers, to watch out for
those who cause divisions and put obstacles
in your way that are contrary to the teaching
you have learned. Keep away from them.[i]
18 For such people are not serving our Lord
Christ, but their own appetites.[j] By smooth
talk and flattery they deceive[k] the minds of
naive people. 19 Everyone has heard[l] about
your obedience, so I am full of joy over you;
but I want you to be wise about what is good,
and innocent about what is evil.[m]

20 The God of peace[n] will soon crush Sa-
tan under your feet.

The grace of our Lord Jesus be with you.

21 Timothy,[o] my fellow worker, sends his
greetings to you, as do Lucius,[p] Jason[q] and
Sosipater, my relatives.

22 I, Tertius, who wrote down this letter,
greet you in the Lord.

23 Gaius, whose hospitality I and the whole
church here enjoy, sends you his greetings.

Erastus, who is the city's director of pub-
lic works, and our brother Quartus send you
their greetings.[a]

25 Now to him who is able to establish
you by my gospel and the proclamation of
Jesus Christ, according to the revelation of
the mystery hidden for long ages past, 26 but
now revealed and made known through the
prophetic writings by the command of the
eternal God, so that all nations might believe
and obey him— 27 to the only wise God be
glory forever through Jesus Christ! Amen.

**16:18**
j Php 3:19
k Col 2:4

**16:19**
l Ro 1:8
m Mt 10:16

**16:20**
n Ro 15:33

**16:21**
o Ac 16:1
p Ac 13:1
q Ac 17:5

[a] 23 Some manuscripts *their greetings.* [24] *May the grace of our Lord Jesus Christ be with all of you. Amen.*

# 1 Corinthians

## OVERVIEW

During his second missionary journey, the apostle Paul established a church in Corinth, a thriving city known for its commerce, temples dedicated to idolatrous religions, and rampant sexual immorality. Prior to writing 1 Corinthians, Paul had received some disturbing reports about a myriad of issues facing the believers in Corinth: factions in the church (see 1Co 1); an incestuous relationship (see 1Co 5); believers taking their disputes to courts composed of unbelievers (see 1Co 6); marital concerns (see 1Co 7); idolatry (see 1Co 8–10); abuses in worship (see 1Co 11); and money (see 1Co 16). Basically, the Corinthian church was heavily influenced by its environment.

Paul addressed these situations and gave the Corinthian believers insights for living godly lives and taking a stand against the evil practices of their culture. Today's Christians should also check their behavior. Are you influencing the world or being influenced by it?

As you read 1 Corinthians, focus on the love of God manifested through Christ. Allow this model of love to guide your actions with believers and unbelievers.

## OUTLINE

I. Introduction (1:1–9)
II. Divisions in the Church (1:10—4:21)
III. Sexual and Ethical Issues (5:1—6:20)
IV. Instruction on Marriage (7:1–40)
V. Instruction on Questionable Practices (8:1—10:33)
VI. Instruction on Public Worship (11:1—14:40)
VII. Instruction on the Resurrection (15:1–58)
VIII. Personal Matters (16:1–24)

## SCANNABLE FACTS:

**Author:** Paul

**Time Written:** A.D. 54 or 55

**Theme to Note:** Living out the Christian faith in a sinful world

**Notable Women:** Chloe, Priscilla

1 Paul, called to be an apostle[a] of Christ
Jesus by the will of God,[b] and our
brother Sosthenes,

[2]To the church of God in Corinth, to those
sanctified in Christ Jesus and called[c] to be
holy, together with all those everywhere
who call on the name of our Lord Jesus
Christ—their Lord and ours:

[3]Grace and peace to you from God our Fa-
ther and the Lord Jesus Christ.[d]

## Thanksgiving

[4]I always thank God for you[e] because of
his grace given you in Christ Jesus. [5]For
in him you have been enriched in every
way—in all your speaking and in all your
knowledge— [6]because our testimony[f] about
Christ was confirmed in you. [7]Therefore you
do not lack any spiritual gift as you eagerly
wait for our Lord Jesus Christ to be re-
vealed.[g] [8]He will keep you strong to the end,
so that you will be blameless on the day of
our Lord Jesus Christ. [9]God, who has called
you into fellowship with his Son Jesus Christ
our Lord, is faithful.[h]

## Divisions in the Church

[10]I appeal to you, brothers, in the name of
our Lord Jesus Christ, that all of you agree
with one another so that there may be no
divisions among you and that you may be
perfectly united in mind and thought. [11]My
brothers, some from Chloe's household have
informed me that there are quarrels among
you. [12]What I mean is this: One of you says,
"I follow Paul"; another, "I follow Apollos";
another, "I follow Cephas[a]"; still another, "I
follow Christ."

[13]Is Christ divided? Was Paul crucified
for you? Were you baptized into[b] the name
of Paul? [14]I am thankful that I did not bap-
tize any of you except Crispus[i] and Gaius,[j]
[15]so no one can say that you were baptized
into my name. [16](Yes, I also baptized the
household of Stephanas;[k] beyond that, I
don't remember if I baptized anyone else.)
[17]For Christ did not send me to baptize, but
to preach the gospel—not with words of
human wisdom, lest the cross of Christ be
emptied of its power.

**1:1** a Ro 1:1 b 2Co 1:1
**1:2** c Ro 1:7
**1:3** d Ro 1:7
**1:4** e Ro 1:8
**1:6** f Rev 1:2
**1:7** g Php 3:20; 2Pe 3:12
**1:9** h Isa 49:7
**1:14** i Ac 18:8; Ro 16:23 j Ac 19:29
**1:16** k 1Co 16:15

## Christ the Wisdom and Power of God

[18]For the message of the cross is foolish-
ness to those who are perishing, but to us
who are being saved it is the power of God.[l]
[19]For it is written:

"I will destroy the wisdom of the wise;
the intelligence of the intelligent I will
frustrate."[c][m]

[20]Where is the wise man? Where is the
scholar? Where is the philosopher of this
age? Has not God made foolish[n] the wisdom
of the world? [21]For since in the wisdom of
God the world through its wisdom did not
know him, God was pleased through the fool-
ishness of what was preached to save those
who believe. [22]Jews demand miraculous
signs[o] and Greeks look for wisdom, [23]but we
preach Christ crucified: a stumbling block[p]
to Jews and foolishness[q] to Gentiles, [24]but to
those whom God has called, both Jews and
Greeks, Christ the power of God and the wis-
dom of God.[r] [25]For the foolishness of God is
wiser than man's wisdom, and the weakness
of God is stronger than man's strength.

[26]Brothers, think of what you were when
you were called. Not many of you were wise
by human standards; not many were influ-
ential; not many were of noble birth. [27]But
God chose[s] the foolish things of the world to
shame the wise; God chose the weak things
of the world to shame the strong. [28]He chose
the lowly things of this world and the de-
spised things—and the things that are
not—to nullify the things that are, [29]so that
no one may boast before him.[t] [30]It is because
of him that you are in Christ Jesus, who has
become for us wisdom from God—that is,
our righteousness, holiness and redemp-
tion.[u] [31]Therefore, as it is written: "Let him
who boasts boast in the Lord."[d][v]

2 When I came to you, brothers, I did not
come with eloquence or superior wis-
dom[w] as I proclaimed to you the testimony
about God.[e] [2]For I resolved to know nothing
while I was with you except Jesus Christ and
him crucified.[x] [3]I came to you in weakness
and fear, and with much trembling. [4]My
message and my preaching were not with

**1:18** l Ro 1:16
**1:19** m Isa 29:14
**1:20** n Ro 1:22
**1:22** o Mt 12:38
**1:23** p Gal 5:11 q 1Co 2:14
**1:24** r Col 2:3
**1:27** s Jas 2:5
**1:29** t Eph 2:9
**1:30** u Eph 1:7,14
**1:31** v Jer 9:23,24
**2:1** w 1Co 1:17
**2:2** x Gal 6:14

[a]12 That is, Peter [b]13 Or *in*; also in verse 15 [c]19 Isaiah 29:14 [d]31 Jer. 9:24 [e]1 Some manuscripts *as I proclaimed to you God's mystery*

**2:4** y Ro 15:19
**2:5** z 2Co 4:7
**2:6** a 1Co 1:20
**2:9** b Isa 64:4
**2:11** c Pr 20:27
**2:12** d Ro 8:15

*Humble friend,*
*Keep me as the center of your life.*
*Love always,*
*God*

1 CORINTHIANS 1:31

wise and persuasive words, but with a dem-
onstration of the Spirit's power,[y] 5so that
your faith might not rest on men's wisdom,
but on God's power.[z]

## Wisdom From the Spirit

6We do, however, speak a message of
wisdom among the mature, but not the wis-
dom of this age[a] or of the rulers of this age,
who are coming to nothing. 7No, we speak
of God's secret wisdom, a wisdom that has
been hidden and that God destined for our
glory before time began. 8None of the rulers
of this age understood it, for if they had,
they would not have crucified the Lord of
glory. 9However, as it is written:

"No eye has seen,
no ear has heard,
no mind has conceived
what God has
prepared for
those who love
him"[a][b]—

10but God has revealed it
to us by his Spirit.
The Spirit searches
all things, even the deep
things of God. 11For who
among men knows the thoughts of a man
except the man's spirit[c] within him? In the
same way no one knows the thoughts of God
except the Spirit of God. 12We have not re-
ceived the spirit[d] of the world but the Spirit
who is from God, that we may understand
what God has freely given us. 13This is what
we speak, not in words taught us by human

> *"There is more pleasure in loving, than in being loved."*
> —JEANNE MOUTOUSSAMY-ASHE, PHOTOGRAPHER AND WIDOW OF TENNIS GREAT ARTHUR ASHE

wisdom but in words taught by the Spirit,
expressing spiritual truths in spiritual
words.[b] 14The man without the Spirit does
not accept the things that come from the
Spirit of God, for they are foolishness[e] to
him, and he cannot understand them, be-
cause they are spiritually discerned. 15The
spiritual man makes judgments about all
things, but he himself is not subject to any
man's judgment:

16"For who has known the mind of the
Lord
that he may instruct him?"[c]

But we have the mind of Christ.[f]

## On Divisions in the Church

3 Brothers, I could not address you as
spiritual[g] but as worldly[h]—mere in-
fants[i] in Christ. 2I gave you milk, not solid
food,[j] for you were not yet ready for it. In-
deed, you are still not ready. 3You are still
worldly. For since there is jealousy and quar-
reling[k] among you, are you not worldly? Are
you not acting like mere men? 4For when
one says, "I follow Paul," and another, "I fol-
low Apollos," are you not mere men?
5What, after all, is Apollos? And what
is Paul? Only servants, through whom you
came to believe—as the Lord has assigned
to each his task. 6I planted the seed,[l] Apol-
los watered it, but God made it grow. 7So
neither he who plants nor he who waters is
anything, but only God, who makes things
grow. 8The man who plants and the man
who waters have one purpose, and each will
be rewarded according to his own labor.
9For we are God's fellow workers;[m] you are
God's field, God's building.[n]
10By the grace God has given me,[o] I laid
a foundation as an expert builder, and
someone else is building on it. But each
one should be careful how he builds. 11For
no one can lay any foundation other than
the one already laid, which is Jesus Christ.[p]
12If any man builds on this foundation us-
ing gold, silver, costly stones, wood, hay or
straw, 13his work will be shown for what it
is, because the Day[q] will bring it to light. It
will be revealed with fire, and the fire will
test the quality of each man's work. 14If what

**2:14** e 1Co 1:18
**2:16** f Jn 15:15
**3:1** g 1Co 2:15 h 1Co 2:14 i Heb 5:13
**3:2** j Heb 5:12–14; 1Pe 2:2
**3:3** k Gal 5:20
**3:6** l Ac 18:4–11
**3:9** m 2Co 6:1 n Eph 2:20–22
**3:10** o Ro 12:3
**3:11** p Eph 2:20
**3:13** q 2Th 1:7–10

[a]9 Isaiah 64:4 [b]13 Or *Spirit, interpreting spiritual truths to spiritual men* [c]16 Isaiah 40:13

## The African Presence

**1 Corinthians 3:5**

Apollos was born in Alexandria (see Ac 18:24), which was located on the northern coast of Africa. As an African Jew, he was versed not only in Jewish Scripture but also in African culture. He was a powerful believer who grew even more in his faith under the tutelage of Aquila and Pricilla. For more on Alexandria, see the African Presence note on John 1.

he has built survives, he will receive his re-
ward. 15 If it is burned up, he will suffer loss;
he himself will be saved, but only as one es-
caping through the flames.[r]
16 Don't you know that you yourselves are
God's temple[s] and that God's Spirit lives in
you? 17 If anyone destroys God's temple, God
will destroy him; for God's temple is sacred,
and you are that temple.
18 Do not deceive yourselves. If any one
of you thinks he is wise by the standards of
this age, he should become a "fool" so that
he may become wise. 19 For the wisdom of
this world is foolishness in God's sight. As
it is written: "He catches the wise in their
craftiness"[a];[t] 20 and again, "The Lord knows
that the thoughts of the wise are futile."[b][u]
21 So then, no more boasting about men! All
things are yours,[v] 22 whether Paul or Apollos
or Cephas[c] or the world or life or death or the
present or the future—all are yours, 23 and
you are of Christ,[w] and Christ is of God.

### Apostles of Christ

4 So then, men ought to regard us as ser-
vants of Christ and as those entrusted
with the secret things of God. 2 Now it is
required that those who have been given
a trust must prove faithful. 3 I care very lit-
tle if I am judged by you or by any human
court; indeed, I do not even judge myself.
4 My conscience is clear, but that does not
make me innocent.[x] It is the Lord who
judges me. 5 Therefore judge nothing[y] be-
fore the appointed time; wait till the Lord
comes. He will bring to light what is hidden
in darkness and will expose the motives of
men's hearts. At that time each will receive
his praise from God.[z]
6 Now, brothers, I have applied these
things to myself and Apollos for your bene-
fit, so that you may learn from us the mean-
ing of the saying, "Do not go beyond what is
written." Then you will not take pride in one
man over against another.[a] 7 For who makes
you different from anyone else? What do
you have that you did not receive? And if you
did receive it, why do you boast as though
you did not?
8 Already you have all you want! Already
you have become rich![b] You have become
kings—and that without us! How I wish
that you really had become kings so that we
might be kings with you! 9 For it seems to
me that God has put us apostles on display

*God,*

*I ask you to purify my heart daily. I pray that you will give me the wisdom and discernment to function as an effective leader of your people. Whether I am in a position of leadership in the home, in a business, in a church or elsewhere, I pray for your guidance and your wisdom.*

*Amen*

1 CORINTHIANS 4:1–2

**3:15** r Jude 23
**3:16** s 2Co 6:16
**3:19** t Job 5:13
**3:20** u Ps 94:11
**3:21** v Ro 8:32
**3:23** w 2Co 10:7; Gal 3:29
**4:4** x Ro 2:13
**4:5** y Ro 2:1
**4:5** z Ro 2:29
**4:6** a 1Co 1:12
**4:8** b Rev 3:17,18

[a] 19 Job 5:13 [b] 20 Psalm 94:11 [c] 22 That is, Peter

at the end of the procession, like men condemned to die in the arena. We have been made a spectacle[c] to the whole universe, to angels as well as to men. 10 We are fools for Christ,[d] but you are so wise in Christ! We are weak, but you are strong! You are honored, we are dishonored! 11 To this very hour we go hungry and thirsty, we are in rags, we are brutally treated, we are homeless.[e] 12 We work hard with our own hands.[f] When we are cursed, we bless; when we are persecuted, we endure it; 13 when we are slandered, we answer kindly. Up to this moment we have become the scum of the earth, the refuse of the world.

14 I am not writing this to shame you, but to warn you, as my dear children.[g] 15 Even though you have ten thousand guardians in Christ, you do not have many fathers, for in Christ Jesus I became your father through the gospel. 16 Therefore I urge you to imitate me.[h] 17 For this reason I am sending to you Timothy, my son whom I love, who is faithful in the Lord. He will remind you of my way of life in Christ Jesus, which agrees with what I teach everywhere in every church.[i]

18 Some of you have become arrogant, as if I were not coming to you. 19 But I will come to you very soon,[j] if the Lord is willing, and then I will find out not only how these arrogant people are talking, but what power they have. 20 For the kingdom of God is not a matter of talk but of power. 21 What do you prefer? Shall I come to you with a whip,[k] or in love and with a gentle spirit?

## Expel the Immoral Brother!

5 It is actually reported that there is sexual immorality among you, and of a kind that does not occur even among pagans: A man has his father's wife.[l] 2 And you are proud! Shouldn't you rather have been filled with grief[m] and have put out of your fellowship the man who did this? 3 Even though I am not physically present, I am with you in spirit.[n] And I have already passed judgment on the one who did this, just as if I were present. 4 When you are assembled in the name of our Lord Jesus and I am with you in spirit, and the power of our Lord Jesus is present, 5 hand this man over[o] to Satan, so that the sinful nature[a] may be destroyed and his spirit saved on the day of the Lord.

6 Your boasting is not good. Don't you know that a little yeast works through the whole batch of dough?[p] 7 Get rid of the old yeast that you may be a new batch without yeast—as you really are. For Christ, our Passover lamb, has been sacrificed.[q] 8 Therefore let us keep the Festival, not with the old yeast, the yeast of malice and wickedness, but with bread without yeast,[r] the bread of sincerity and truth.

9 I have written you in my letter not to associate[s] with sexually immoral people— 10 not at all meaning the people of this world[t] who are immoral, or the greedy and swindlers, or idolaters. In that case you would have to leave this world. 11 But now I am writing you that you must not associate with anyone who calls himself a brother but is sexually immoral or greedy, an idolater or a slanderer, a drunkard or a swindler. With such a man do not even eat.

12 What business is it of mine to judge those outside[u] the church? Are you not to judge those inside?[v] 13 God will judge those outside. "Expel the wicked man from among you."[b][w]

## Lawsuits Among Believers

6 If any of you has a dispute with another, dare he take it before the ungodly for judgment instead of before the saints? 2 Do you not know that the saints will judge the world?[x] And if you are to judge the world, are you not competent to judge trivial cases? 3 Do you not know that we will judge angels? How much more the things of this life! 4 Therefore, if you have disputes about such matters, appoint as judges even men of little account in the church![c] 5 I say this to shame you. Is it possible that there is nobody among you wise enough to judge a dispute between believers? 6 But instead, one brother goes to law against another—and this in front of unbelievers!

7 The very fact that you have lawsuits among you means you have been completely

**4:9** c Heb 10:33
**4:10** d Ac 17:18
**4:11** e Ro 8:35
**4:12** f Ac 18:3
**4:14** g 1Th 2:11
**4:16** h 1Th 1:6
**4:17** i 1Co 7:17
**4:19** j 2Co 1:15,16
**4:21** k 2Co 1:23; 13:2,10
**5:1** l Lev 18:8
**5:2** m 2Co 7:7–11
**5:3** n Col 2:5
**5:5** o 1Ti 1:20
**5:6** p Gal 5:9
**5:7** q 1Pe 1:19
**5:8** r Dt 16:3
**5:9** s Eph 5:11
**5:10** t 1Co 10:27
**5:12** u Mk 4:11; v 1Co 6:1–4
**5:13** w Dt 13:5
**6:2** x Mt 19:28

[a] 5 Or *that his body;* or *that the flesh* [b] 13 Deut. 17:7; 19:19; 21:21; 22:21,24; 24:7 [c] 4 Or *matters, do you appoint as judges men of little account in the church?*

6:7
y Mt 5:39,40
6:8
z 1Th 4:6
6:9
a Gal 5:21
6:12
b 1Co 10:23
6:15
c Ro 12:5
6:16
d Ge 2:24; Mt 19:5; Eph 5:31
6:17
e Jn 17:21–23
6:18
f Heb 13:4
g Ro 6:12
6:19
h Ro 14:7,8
6:20
i 1Pe 1:18,19; Rev 5:9
7:1
j ver 8,26

defeated already. Why not rather be
wronged? Why not rather be cheated?[y] [8]In-
stead, you yourselves cheat and do wrong,
and you do this to your brothers.[z]

[9]Do you not know that the wicked will
not inherit the kingdom of God?[a] Do not be
deceived: Neither the sexually immoral nor
idolaters nor adulterers nor male prostitutes
nor homosexual offenders [10]nor thieves nor
the greedy nor drunkards nor slanderers
nor swindlers will inherit the kingdom of
God. [11]And that is what some of you were.
But you were washed, you were sanctified,
you were justified in the name of the Lord
Jesus Christ and by the Spirit of our God.

## Sexual Immorality

[12]"Everything is permissible for me"—
but not everything is beneficial.[b] "Every-
thing is permissible for me"—but I will not
be mastered by anything. [13]"Food for the
stomach and the stomach for food"—but
God will destroy them both. The body is
not meant for sexual immorality, but for
the Lord, and the Lord for the body. [14]By his
power God raised the Lord from the dead,
and he will raise us also. [15]Do you not know
that your bodies are members of Christ
himself?[c] Shall I then take the members of
Christ and unite them with a prostitute?
Never! [16]Do you not know that he who unites
himself with a prostitute is one with her in
body? For it is said, "The two will become
one flesh."[a][d] [17]But he who unites himself
with the Lord is one with him in spirit.[e]

[18]Flee from sexual immorality.[f] All other
sins a man commits are outside his body,
but he who sins sexually sins against his
own body.[g] [19]Do you not know that your body
is a temple of the Holy Spirit, who is in you,
whom you have received from God? You are
not your own;[h] [20]you were bought at a price.[i]
Therefore honor God with your body.

## Marriage

7 Now for the matters you wrote about: It
is good for a man not to marry.[b][j] [2]But
since there is so much immorality, each man
should have his own wife, and each woman
her own husband. [3]The husband should ful-
fill his marital duty to his wife, and likewise
the wife to her husband. [4]The wife's body
does not belong to her alone but also to her
husband. In the same way, the husband's
body does not belong to him alone but also
to his wife. [5]Do not deprive each other ex-
cept by mutual consent and for a time,[k] so
that you may devote yourselves to prayer.
Then come together again so that Satan
will not tempt you because of your lack of
self-control. [6]I say this as a concession, not
as a command.[l] [7]I wish that all men were as
I am.[m] But each man has his own gift from
God; one has this gift, another has that.[n]

[8]Now to the unmarried and the widows
I say: It is good for them to stay unmarried,
as I am.[o] [9]But if they cannot control them-
selves, they should marry,[p] for it is better to
marry than to burn with passion.

[10]To the married I give this command
(not I, but the Lord): A wife must not sepa-
rate from her husband.[q] [11]But if she does,
she must remain unmarried or else be recon-
ciled to her husband. And a husband must
not divorce his wife.

[12]To the rest I say this (I, not the Lord): If
any brother has a wife who is not a believer
and she is willing to live with him, he must
not divorce her. [13]And if a woman has a hus-
band who is not a believer and he is willing
to live with her, she must not divorce him.
[14]For the unbelieving husband has been
sanctified through his wife, and the unbe-
lieving wife has been sanctified through
her believing husband. Otherwise your
children would be unclean, but as it is, they
are holy.[r]

[15]But if the unbeliever leaves, let him do
so. A believing man or woman is not bound
in such circumstances; God has called us
to live in peace.[s] [16]How do you know, wife,
whether you will save your husband?[t] Or,
how do you know, husband, whether you
will save your wife?

[17]Nevertheless, each one should retain
the place in life that the Lord assigned to
him and to which God has called him. This
is the rule I lay down in all the churches.[u]
[18]Was a man already circumcised when he
was called? He should not become uncir-
cumcised. Was a man uncircumcised when
he was called? He should not be circumcised.[v]

7:5
k Ex 19:15; 1Sa 21:4,5
7:6
l 2Co 8:8
7:7
m 1Co 9:5
n 1Co 12:4,11
7:8
o ver 1,26
7:9
p 1Ti 5:14
7:10
q Mal 2:14–16; Mt 5:32; 19:3–9; Mk 10:11; Lk 16:18
7:14
r Mal 2:15
7:15
s Ro 14:19
7:16
t 1Pe 3:1
7:17
u 1Co 4:17
7:18
v Ac 15:1,2

[a]16 Gen. 2:24 [b]1 Or "*It is good for a man not to have sexual relations with a woman.*"

19 Circumcision is nothing and uncircumcision is nothing.[w] Keeping God's commands is what counts. 20 Each one should remain in the situation which he was in when God called him. 21 Were you a slave when you were called? Don't let it trouble you—although if you can gain your freedom, do so. 22 For he who was a slave when he was called by the Lord is the Lord's freedman;[x] similarly, he who was a free man when he was called is Christ's slave.[y] 23 You were bought at a price;[z] do not become slaves of men. 24 Brothers, each man, as responsible to God, should remain in the situation God called him to.

25 Now about virgins: I have no command from the Lord, but I give a judgment as one who by the Lord's mercy[a] is trustworthy. 26 Because of the present crisis, I think that it is good for you to remain as you are.[b] 27 Are you married? Do not seek a divorce. Are you unmarried? Do not look for a wife. 28 But if you do marry, you have not sinned; and if a virgin marries, she has not sinned. But those who marry will face many troubles in this life, and I want to spare you this.

29 What I mean, brothers, is that the time is short.[c] From now on those who have wives should live as if they had none; 30 those who mourn, as if they did not; those who are happy, as if they were not; those who buy something, as if it were not theirs to keep; 31 those who use the things of the world, as if not engrossed in them. For this world in its present form is passing away.[d]

32 I would like you to be free from concern. An unmarried man is concerned about the Lord's affairs[e]—how he can please the Lord. 33 But a married man is concerned about the affairs of this world—how he can please his wife— 34 and his interests are divided. An unmarried woman or virgin is concerned about the Lord's affairs: Her aim is to be devoted to the Lord in both body and spirit. But a married woman is concerned about the affairs of this world—how she can please her husband. 35 I am saying this for your own good, not to restrict you, but that you may live in a right way in undivided devotion to the Lord.

36 If anyone thinks he is acting improperly toward the virgin he is engaged to, and if she is getting along in years and he feels he ought to marry, he should do as he wants. He is not sinning. They should get married. 37 But the man who has settled the matter in his own mind, who is under no compulsion but has control over his own will, and who has made up his mind not to marry the virgin—this man also does the right thing. 38 So then, he who marries the virgin does right, but he who does not marry her does even better.[a]

39 A woman is bound to her husband as long as he lives.[f] But if her husband dies, she is free to marry anyone she wishes, but he must belong to the Lord.[g] 40 In my judgment, she is happier if she stays as she is—and I think that I too have the Spirit of God.

## Food Sacrificed to Idols

8 Now about food sacrificed to idols:[h] We know that we all possess knowledge.[b] Knowledge puffs up, but love builds up. 2 The man who thinks he knows something does not yet know as he ought to know.[i] 3 But the man who loves God is known by God.[j]

4 So then, about eating food sacrificed to idols: We know that an idol is nothing at all in the world and that there is no God but one.[k] 5 For even if there are so-called gods, whether in heaven or on earth (as indeed there are many "gods" and many "lords"), 6 yet for us there is but one God, the Father,[l] from whom all things came[m] and for whom we live; and there is but one Lord, Jesus Christ, through whom all things came and through whom we live.

7 But not everyone knows this. Some people are still so accustomed to idols that when they eat such food they think of it as having been sacrificed to an idol, and since their conscience is weak,[n] it is defiled. 8 But food does not bring us near to God;[o] we are no worse if we do not eat, and no better if we do.

**7:19** w Gal 5:6
**7:22** x Jn 8:32,36 y Eph 6:6
**7:23** z 1Co 6:20
**7:25** a 1Ti 1:13,16
**7:26** b ver 1,8
**7:29** c Ro 13:11,12
**7:31** d 1Jn 2:17
**7:32** e 1Ti 5:5
**7:39** f Ro 7:2,3 g 2Co 6:14
**8:1** h Ac 15:20
**8:2** i 1Co 13:8,9,12; 1Ti 6:4
**8:3** j Gal 4:9
**8:4** k Dt 6:4
**8:6** l Mal 2:10 m Ro 11:36
**8:7** n Ro 14:14
**8:8** o Ro 14:17

[a] 36–38 Or *36 If anyone thinks he is not treating his daughter properly, and if she is getting along in years, and he feels she ought to marry, he should do as he wants. He is not sinning. He should let her get married. 37 But the man who has settled the matter in his own mind, who is under no compulsion but has control over his own will, and who has made up his mind to keep the virgin unmarried—this man also does the right thing. 38 So then, he who gives his virgin in marriage does right, but he who does not give her in marriage does even better.* [b] 1 Or *"We all possess knowledge," as you say*

8:9 p Gal 5:13

[9]Be careful, however, that the exercise of
your freedom does not become a stumbling
block[p] to the weak. [10]For if anyone with a
weak conscience sees you who have this
knowledge eating in an idol's temple, won't
he be emboldened to eat what has been sac-
rificed to idols? [11]So this weak brother, for
whom Christ died, is destroyed[q] by your
knowledge. [12]When you sin against your
brothers in this way and wound their weak

8:11 q Ro 14:15,20

# Inspire

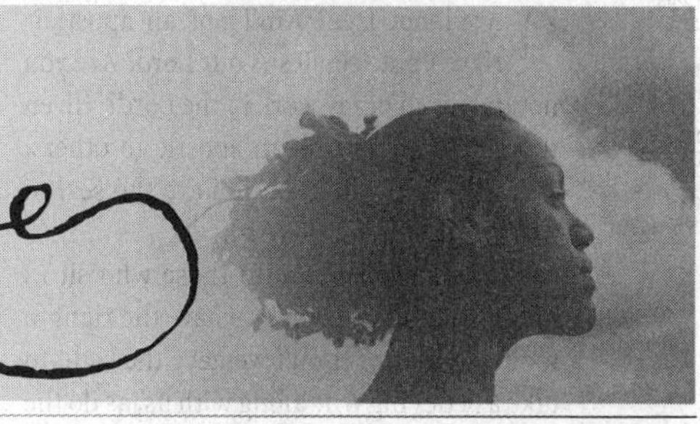

## CELIBACY

Celibacy may be seen as dedication of one's life to God's service; today it is also viewed as the act of maintaining sexual purity while single. For some women celibacy becomes a lifelong vow that frees them to give themselves fully and completely to the Lord and his church (see 1Co 7:32–35). It is a vow to be wholeheartedly and without distraction "concerned about the Lord's affairs . . . devoted to the Lord in both body and spirit" (1Co 7:34). The apostle Paul was celibate, but as the Word clearly states and demonstrates, the gift of celibacy is not given to everyone (see 1Co 7:7–9); God himself, after all, has ordained the institution of marriage (see Ge 1:27–28; 2:18,24). However, celibacy—either for life or during a season of singleness—can lead to a deeper faith and a closer relationship with God.

Instead of looking for security, fulfillment and pleasure in tangible but temporary possessions, relationships and activities, God wants us to experience his love and to lean on him, not just as Father and Savior but also as our "soul mate," our first love, our best friend and most sought-after comforter. He may call us into a marital relationship to illustrate for us and through us the eternal relationship between ourselves and our Savior (see Eph 5:31–32), or he may call us to a single-minded, wholehearted focus on him through singleness and celibacy (see Mt 19:10–12). Through either calling God points us to eternal union with himself, an end for which he is preparing all of us.

Whether married or single, we are called to be imitators of God (see Eph 5:1–3) and to keep our bodies pure as the temples of God's Spirit (see 1Co 6:18–20). Through Christ's redeeming blood and intercession, we receive the grace we need to resist temptation and to lead a life that is pleasing to God (see Heb 4:14–16).

—C. Richards

For the next Inspire note, go to page 1357.

### read

1 Corinthians 7:1–40; see also Jeremiah 16:1–2; Matthew 19:1–12; Luke 2:36–38; 1 Corinthians 6:12–20; Ephesians 5:1–3.

See also the Inspire Notes "Dating," "Romance: A Biblical Perspective," "What Is Intimacy?" and "Singleness: A Stage in Life," and the Women of the Bible Note "Philip's Daughters: Those Preaching Women."

### WOMAN of COLOR

To whom or to what do you turn for security, fulfillment and/or pleasure?

**8:13** r Ro 14:21
**9:1** s 2Co 12:12 t 1Co 3:6
**9:7** u Dt 20:6
**9:9** v Dt 25:4; 1Ti 5:18
**9:11** w Ro 15:27
**9:12** x 2Co 11:7–12
**9:13** y Lev 6:16,26

conscience, you sin against Christ. [13]Therefore, if what I eat causes my brother to fall into sin, I will never eat meat again, so that I will not cause him to fall.[r]

## The Rights of an Apostle

**9** Am I not free? Am I not an apostle?[s] Have I not seen Jesus our Lord? Are you not the result of my work in the Lord?[t] [2]Even though I may not be an apostle to others, surely I am to you! For you are the seal of my apostleship in the Lord.

[3]This is my defense to those who sit in judgment on me. [4]Don't we have the right to food and drink? [5]Don't we have the right to take a believing wife along with us, as do the other apostles and the Lord's brothers and Cephas[a]? [6]Or is it only I and Barnabas who must work for a living?

> *"The roots of happiness grow best in the soil of service."*
> —RUTH B. LOVE, EDUCATOR

[7]Who serves as a soldier at his own expense? Who plants a vineyard[u] and does not eat of its grapes? Who tends a flock and does not drink of the milk? [8]Do I say this merely from a human point of view? Doesn't the Law say the same thing? [9]For it is written in the Law of Moses: "Do not muzzle an ox while it is treading out the grain."[b][v] Is it about oxen that God is concerned? [10]Surely he says this for us, doesn't he? Yes, this was written for us, because when the plowman plows and the thresher threshes, they ought to do so in the hope of sharing in the harvest. [11]If we have sown spiritual seed among you, is it too much if we reap a material harvest from you?[w] [12]If others have this right of support from you, shouldn't we have it all the more?

But we did not use this right. On the contrary, we put up with anything rather than hinder[x] the gospel of Christ. [13]Don't you know that those who work in the temple get their food from the temple, and those who serve at the altar share in what is offered on the altar?[y] [14]In the same way, the Lord has commanded that those who preach the gospel should receive their living from the gospel.

[15]But I have not used any of these rights.[z] And I am not writing this in the hope that you will do such things for me. I would rather die than have anyone deprive me of this boast.[a] [16]Yet when I preach the gospel, I cannot boast, for I am compelled to preach.[b] Woe to me if I do not preach the gospel! [17]If I preach voluntarily, I have a reward;[c] if not voluntarily, I am simply discharging the trust committed to me.[d] [18]What then is my reward? Just this: that in preaching the gospel I may offer it free of charge, and so not make use of my rights in preaching it.

[19]Though I am free and belong to no man, I make myself a slave to everyone,[e] to win as many as possible.[f] [20]To the Jews I became like a Jew, to win the Jews.[g] To those under the law I became like one under the law (though I myself am not under the law), so as to win those under the law. [21]To those not having the law I became like one not having the law[h] (though I am not free from God's law but am under Christ's law), so as to win those not having the law. [22]To the weak I became weak, to win the weak. I have become all things to all men so that by all possible means I might save some. [23]I do all this for the sake of the gospel, that I may share in its blessings.

[24]Do you not know that in a race all the runners run, but only one gets the prize? Run[i] in such a way as to get the prize. [25]Everyone who competes in the games goes into strict training. They do it to get a crown that will not last; but we do it to get a crown that will last forever. [26]Therefore I do not run like a man running aimlessly; I do not fight like a man beating the air. [27]No, I beat my body[j] and make it my slave so that after I have preached to others, I myself will not be disqualified for the prize.

## Warnings From Israel's History

**10** For I do not want you to be ignorant of the fact, brothers, that our forefathers were all under the cloud[k] and that they all passed through the sea.[l] [2]They were all baptized into Moses in the cloud and in the sea. [3]They all ate the same spiritual food [4]and drank the same spiritual drink; for they drank from the spiritual rock[m] that ac-

**9:15** z Ac 18:3 a 2Co 11:9,10
**9:16** b Ro 1:14
**9:17** c 1Co 3:8,14 d Gal 2:7; Col 1:25
**9:19** e Gal 5:13 f Mt 18:15
**9:20** g Ac 16:3
**9:21** h Ro 2:12,14
**9:24** i 2Ti 4:7
**9:27** j Ro 8:13
**10:1** k Ex 13:21 l Ex 14:22,29
**10:4** m Ex 17:6

[a]5 That is, Peter [b]9 Deut. 25:4

companied them, and that rock was Christ. 5Nevertheless, God was not pleased with most of them; their bodies were scattered over the desert.[n]

6Now these things occurred as examples[a] to keep us from setting our hearts on evil things as they did. 7Do not be idolaters, as some of them were; as it is written: "The people sat down to eat and drink and got up to indulge in pagan revelry."[b] 8We should not commit sexual immorality, as some of them did—and in one day twenty-three thousand of them died. 9We should not test the Lord, as some of them did—and were killed by snakes.[o] 10And do not grumble, as some of them did—and were killed by the destroying angel.[p]

11These things happened to them as examples and were written down as warnings for us, on whom the fulfillment of the ages has come. 12So, if you think you are standing firm,[q] be careful that you don't fall! 13No temptation has seized you except what is common to man. And God is faithful; he will not let you be tempted beyond what you can bear.[r] But when you are tempted, he will also provide a way out so that you can stand up under it.

## Idol Feasts and the Lord's Supper

14Therefore, my dear friends, flee from idolatry. 15I speak to sensible people; judge for yourselves what I say. 16Is not the cup of thanksgiving for which we give thanks a participation in the blood of Christ? And is not the bread that we break a participation in the body of Christ?[s] 17Because there is one loaf, we, who are many, are one body,[t] for we all partake of the one loaf.

18Consider the people of Israel: Do not those who eat the sacrifices participate in the altar? 19Do I mean then that a sacrifice offered to an idol is anything, or that an idol is anything? 20No, but the sacrifices of pagans are offered to demons,[u] not to God, and I do not want you to be participants with demons. 21You cannot drink the cup of the Lord and the cup of demons too; you cannot have a part in both the Lord's table and the table of demons.[v] 22Are we trying to arouse the Lord's jealousy?[w] Are we stronger than he?

## The Believer's Freedom

23"Everything is permissible"—but not everything is beneficial.[x] "Everything is permissible"—but not everything is constructive. 24Nobody should seek his own good, but the good of others.[y]

25Eat anything sold in the meat market without raising questions of conscience, 26for, "The earth is the Lord's, and everything in it."[c][z]

27If some unbeliever invites you to a meal and you want to go, eat whatever is put before you[a] without raising questions of conscience. 28But if anyone says to you, "This has been offered in sacrifice," then do not eat it, both for the sake of the man who told you and for conscience' sake[d]— 29the other man's conscience, I mean, not yours. For why should my freedom[b] be judged by another's conscience? 30If I take part in the meal with thankfulness, why am I denounced because of something I thank God for?[c]

31So whether you eat or drink or whatever you do, do it all for the glory of God.[d] 32Do not cause anyone to stumble, whether Jews, Greeks or the church of God[e]— 33even as I try to please everybody in every way.[f] For I am not seeking my own good but the good of many, so that they may be saved.

11 1Follow my example, as I follow the example of Christ.

## Propriety in Worship

2I praise you for remembering me in everything[g] and for holding to the teachings,[e] just as I passed them on to you.

3Now I want you to realize that the head of every man is Christ, and the head of the woman is man,[h] and the head of Christ is God. 4Every man who prays or prophesies with his head covered dishonors his head. 5And every woman who prays or prophesies[i] with her head uncovered dishonors her head—it is just as though her head were shaved.[j] 6If a woman does not cover her head, she should have her hair cut off; and if

10:5 n Nu14:29
10:9 o Nu21:5,6
10:10 p Ex12:23
10:12 q Ro11:20
10:13 r 2Pe2:9
10:16 s Mt26:26–28
10:17 t 1Co12:27
10:20 u Dt32:17; Ps106:37
10:21 v 2Co6:15,16
10:22 w Dt32:16,21
10:23 x 1Co6:12
10:24 y Ro15:1,2
10:26 z Ps24:1
10:27 a Lk10:7
10:29 b Ro14:16
10:30 c Ro14:6
10:31 d Col3:17; 1Pe4:11
10:32 e Ac20:28
10:33 f Ro15:2
11:2 g 1Co4:17
11:3 h Eph5:23
11:5 i Ac21:9 j Dt21:12

[a]6 Or *types*; also in verse 11 [b]7 Exodus 32:6 [c]26 Psalm 24:1 [d]28 Some manuscripts *conscience' sake, for "the earth is the Lord's and everything in it"* [e]2 Or *traditions*

11:7 k Ge 1:26
11:8 l Ge 2:21–23
11:9 m Ge 2:18
11:16 n 1Co 7:17
11:17 o ver 2,22
11:18 p 1Co 1:10–12
11:19 q 1Jn 2:19
11:21 r Jude 12
11:22 s 1Co 10:32 t Jas 2:6
11:23 u 1Co 15:3

it is a disgrace for a woman to have her hair cut or shaved off, she should cover her head. 7 A man ought not to cover his head,[a] since he is the image[k] and glory of God; but the woman is the glory of man. 8 For man did not come from woman, but woman from man;[l] 9 neither was man created for woman, but woman for man.[m] 10 For this reason, and because of the angels, the woman ought to have a sign of authority on her head.

11 In the Lord, however, woman is not independent of man, nor is man independent of woman. 12 For as woman came from man, so also man is born of woman. But everything comes from God. 13 Judge for yourselves: Is it proper for a woman to pray to God with her head uncovered? 14 Does not the very nature of things teach you that if a man has long hair, it is a disgrace to him, 15 but that if a woman has long hair, it is her glory? For long hair is given to her as a covering. 16 If anyone wants to be contentious about this, we have no other practice—nor do the churches of God.[n]

## The Lord's Supper

17 In the following directives I have no praise for you,[o] for your meetings do more harm than good. 18 In the first place, I hear that when you come together as a church, there are divisions[p] among you, and to some extent I believe it. 19 No doubt there have to be differences among you to show which of you have God's approval.[q] 20 When you come together, it is not the Lord's Supper you eat, 21 for as you eat, each of you goes ahead without waiting for anybody else.[r] One remains hungry, another gets drunk. 22 Don't you have homes to eat and drink in? Or do you despise the church of God[s] and humiliate those who have nothing?[t] What shall I say to you? Shall I praise you for this? Certainly not!

23 For I received from the Lord what I also passed on to you:[u] The Lord Jesus, on the night he was betrayed, took bread, 24 and when he had given thanks, he broke it and said, "This is my body, which is for you; do this in remembrance of me." 25 In the same way, after supper he took the cup, saying, "This cup is the new covenant[v] in my blood; do this, whenever you drink it, in remembrance of me." 26 For whenever you eat this bread and drink this cup, you proclaim the Lord's death until he comes.

*Lord,*

*help me to commune with you daily. Keep in the forefront of my mind your great sacrifice for me, and help me to live a life of love in thanksgiving for your great love.*

*Amen*

1 CORINTHIANS 11:23–26

27 Therefore, whoever eats the bread or drinks the cup of the Lord in an unworthy manner will be guilty of sinning against the body and blood of the Lord. 28 A man ought to examine himself[w] before he eats of the bread and drinks of the cup. 29 For anyone who eats and drinks without recognizing the body of the Lord eats and drinks judgment on himself. 30 That is why many among you are weak and sick, and a number of you have fallen asleep. 31 But if we judged ourselves, we would not come under judgment. 32 When we are judged by the Lord, we are being disciplined[x] so that we will not be condemned with the world.

33 So then, my brothers, when you come together to eat, wait for each other. 34 If anyone is hungry, he should eat at home, so that when you meet together it may not result in judgment.

And when I come[y] I will give further directions.

## Spiritual Gifts

12 Now about spiritual gifts,[z] brothers, I do not want you to be ignorant. 2 You know that when you were pagans,[a] somehow or other you were influenced and

11:25 v Lk 22:20
11:28 w 2Co 13:5
11:32 x Ps 94:12
11:34 y 1Co 4:19
12:1 z Ro 1:11; 1Co 14:1,37
12:2 a Eph 2:11,12

[a] 4–7 Or *4 Every man who prays or prophesies with long hair dishonors his head. 5 And every woman who prays or prophesies with no covering of hair on her head dishonors her head—she is just like one of the "shorn women." 6 If a woman has no covering, let her be for now with short hair, but since it is a disgrace for a woman to have her hair shorn or shaved, she should grow it again. 7 A man ought not to have long hair*

**12:2** b Ps 115:5; 1Th 1:9
**12:3** c 1Jn 4:2,3
**12:4** d Ro 12:4–8
**12:8** e 1Co 2:6 f 2Co 8:7
**12:10** g Gal 3:5 h 1Jn 4:1
**12:13** i Gal 3:28; Col 3:11
**12:18** j ver 28

led astray to mute idols.[b] 3Therefore I tell you that no one who is speaking by the Spirit of God says, "Jesus be cursed," and no one can say, "Jesus is Lord," except by the Holy Spirit.[c]

4There are different kinds of gifts, but the same Spirit.[d] 5There are different kinds of service, but the same Lord. 6There are different kinds of working, but the same God works all of them in all men.

7Now to each one the manifestation of the Spirit is given for the common good. 8To one there is given through the Spirit the message of wisdom,[e] to another the message of knowledge[f] by means of the same Spirit, 9to another faith by the same Spirit, to another gifts of healing by that one Spirit, 10to another miraculous powers,[g] to another prophecy, to another distinguishing between spirits,[h] to another speaking in different kinds of tongues,[a] and to still another the interpretation of tongues.[a] 11All these are the work of one and the same Spirit, and he gives them to each one, just as he determines.

## One Body, Many Parts

12The body is a unit, though it is made up of many parts; and though all its parts are many, they form one body. So it is with Christ. 13For we were all baptized by[b] one Spirit into one body—whether Jews or Greeks, slave or free[i]—and we were all given the one Spirit to drink.

14Now the body is not made up of one part but of many. 15If the foot should say, "Because I am not a hand, I do not belong to the body," it would not for that reason cease to be part of the body. 16And if the ear should say, "Because I am not an eye, I do not belong to the body," it would not for that reason cease to be part of the body. 17If the whole body were an eye, where would the sense of hearing be? If the whole body were an ear, where would the sense of smell be? 18But in fact God has arranged[j] the parts in the body, every one of them, just as he wanted them to be. 19If they were all one part, where would the body be? 20As it is, there are many parts, but one body.

21The eye cannot say to the hand, "I don't need you!" And the head cannot say to the feet, "I don't need you!" 22On the contrary, those parts of the body that seem to be weaker are indispensable, 23and the parts that we think are less honorable we treat with special honor. And the parts that are unpresentable are treated with special modesty, 24while our presentable parts need no special treatment. But God has combined the members of the body and has given greater honor to the parts that lacked it, 25so that there should be no division in the body, but that its parts should have equal concern for each other. 26If one part suffers, every part suffers with it; if one part is honored, every part rejoices with it.

27Now you are the body of Christ,[k] and each one of you is a part of it.[l] 28And in the church God has appointed first of all apostles,[m] second prophets, third teachers, then workers of miracles, also those having gifts of healing,[n] those able to help others, those with gifts of administration,[o] and those speaking in different kinds of tongues.[p] 29Are all apostles? Are all prophets? Are all teachers? Do all work miracles? 30Do all have gifts of healing? Do all speak in tongues[c]? Do all interpret? 31But eagerly desire[d][q] the greater gifts.

## Love

And now I will show you the most excellent way.

13 If I speak in the tongues[e] of men and of angels, but have not love, I am only a resounding gong or a clanging cymbal. 2If I have the gift of prophecy and can fathom all mysteries[r] and all knowledge, and if I have a faith that can move mountains, but have not love, I am nothing. 3If I give all I possess to the poor[s] and surrender my body to the flames,[f] but have not love, I gain nothing.

4Love is patient, love is kind. It does not envy, it does not boast, it is not proud. 5It is not rude, it is not self-seeking,[t] it is not easily angered, it keeps no record of wrongs. 6Love does not delight in evil but rejoices with the truth.[u] 7It always protects, always trusts, always hopes, always perseveres.

**12:27** k Eph 1:23; 4:12; Col 1:18,24 l Ro 12:5
**12:28** m Eph 4:11 n ver 9 o Ro 12:6–8 p ver 10
**12:31** q 1Co 14:1,39
**13:2** r 1Co 14:2
**13:3** s Mt 6:2
**13:5** t 1Co 10:24
**13:6** u 2Jn 4

[a]10 Or *languages*; also in verse 28 [b]13 Or *with*; or *in* [c]30 Or *other languages* [d]31 Or *But you are eagerly desiring*
[e]1 Or *languages* [f]3 Some early manuscripts *body that I may boast*

**13:9** v 1Co 8:2
**13:10** w Php 3:12
**13:12** x 2Co 5:7; 1Jn 3:2 y 1Co 8:3
**14:1** z 1Co 12:31
**14:2** a 1Co 13:2
**14:5** b Nu 11:29
**14:6** c ver 26
**14:8** d Nu 10:9

8 Love never fails. But where there are prophecies, they will cease; where there are tongues, they will be stilled; where there is knowledge, it will pass away. 9 For we know in part[v] and we prophesy in part, 10 but when perfection comes,[w] the imperfect disappears. 11 When I was a child, I talked like a child, I thought like a child, I reasoned like a child. When I became a man, I put childish ways behind me. 12 Now we see but a poor reflection as in a mirror; then we shall see face to face.[x] Now I know in part; then I shall know fully, even as I am fully known.[y]

13 And now these three remain: faith, hope and love. But the greatest of these is love.

## Gifts of Prophecy and Tongues

14 Follow the way of love and eagerly desire[z] spiritual gifts, especially the gift of prophecy. 2 For anyone who speaks in a tongue[a] does not speak to men but to God. Indeed, no one understands him; he utters mysteries[a] with his spirit.[b] 3 But everyone who prophesies speaks to men for their strengthening, encouragement and comfort. 4 He who speaks in a tongue edifies himself, but he who prophesies edifies the church. 5 I would like every one of you to speak in tongues,[c] but I would rather have you prophesy.[b] He who prophesies is greater than one who speaks in tongues,[c] unless he interprets, so that the church may be edified.

6 Now, brothers, if I come to you and speak in tongues, what good will I be to you, unless I bring you some revelation[c] or knowledge or prophecy or word of instruction? 7 Even in the case of lifeless things that make sounds, such as the flute or harp, how will anyone know what tune is being played unless there is a distinction in the notes? 8 Again, if the trumpet does not sound a clear call, who will get ready for battle?[d] 9 So it is with you. Unless you speak intelligible words with your tongue, how will anyone know what you are saying? You will just be speaking into the air. 10 Undoubtedly there are all sorts of languages in the world, yet none of them is without meaning. 11 If then I do not grasp the meaning of what someone is saying, I am a foreigner to the speaker, and he is a foreigner to me. 12 So it is with you. Since you are eager to have spiritual gifts, try to excel in gifts that build up the church.

13 For this reason anyone who speaks in a tongue should pray that he may interpret what he says. 14 For if I pray in a tongue, my spirit prays, but my mind is unfruitful. 15 So what shall I do? I will pray with my spirit, but I will also pray with my mind; I will sing[e] with my spirit, but I will also sing with my mind. 16 If you are praising God with your spirit, how can one who finds himself among those who do not understand[d] say "Amen"[f] to your thanksgiving,[g] since he does not know what you are saying? 17 You may be giving thanks well enough, but the other man is not edified.

18 I thank God that I speak in tongues more than all of you. 19 But in the church I would rather speak five intelligible words to instruct others than ten thousand words in a tongue.

20 Brothers, stop thinking like children.[h] In regard to evil be infants,[i] but in your thinking be adults. 21 In the Law[j] it is written:

"Through men of strange tongues
and through the lips of foreigners
I will speak to this people,
but even then they will not listen
to me,"[e][k]
says the Lord.

22 Tongues, then, are a sign, not for believers but for unbelievers; prophecy, however, is for believers, not for unbelievers. 23 So if the whole church comes together and everyone speaks in tongues, and some who do not understand[f] or some unbelievers come in, will they not say that you are out of your mind?[l] 24 But if an unbeliever or someone who does not understand[g] comes in while everybody is prophesying, he will be convinced by all that he is a sinner and will be judged by all, 25 and the secrets of his heart will be laid bare. So he will fall down and worship God, exclaiming, "God is really among you!"[m]

**14:15** e Eph 5:19; Col 3:16
**14:16** f 1Ch 16:36 g 1Co 11:24
**14:20** h Eph 4:14; Heb 5:12,13; 1Pe 2:2 i Ro 16:19
**14:21** j Jn 10:34 k Isa 28:11,12
**14:23** l Ac 2:13
**14:25** m Isa 45:14; Zec 8:23

[a] 2 Or *another language*; also in verses 4, 13, 14, 19, 26 and 27 [b] 2 Or *by the Spirit* [c] 5 Or *other languages*; also in verses 6, 18, 22, 23 and 39 [d] 16 Or *among the inquirers* [e] 21 Isaiah 28:11,12 [f] 23 Or *some inquirers* [g] 24 Or *or some inquirer*

# Inspire

## LOVE

In her song "What's Love Got To Do With It?" Tina Turner raised a question about the validity of the emotion we call love. Some may interpret her lyrics to imply that love is something we can do without; some Christians, unfortunately, feel the same way. For many, love is simply an emotion. But the Bible speaks of another kind of love—not an emotion at all, but an act of the will whereby we align our wills with God's will and do right by one another, regardless of how we feel. This type of love, Biblical love, is not envious, proud, self-centered or rude, and it refuses to keep score. Instead, it is patient and slow to anger, kind and gentle to all, unselfish and giving, truthful and honest, hopeful and encouraging. This love is enduring—so much so that it is without end (see 1Co 13:4–8).

The Greek language, the original language of the New Testament, speaks of three different kinds of love: (1) *eros* (a common word in Greek culture but not used in the New Testament), which refers to the love between a man and woman, encompassing all aspects of sexual desire; (2) *phileo*, which relates to friendship, parental or family love; and (3) *agape*, which was originally a very general word for love conveying fondness, but which the writers of the New Testament infused with new meaning—that of selfless, unconditional love. This latter word (*agape*) defines and is defined by God's love. God calls us to have *agape* love for one another. Paul called this unselfish, loyal, benevolent love for others "the greatest" of Christian virtues, more important and enduring than spiritual gifts (see 1Co 13:13).

This kind of love, in fact, confirms our Christianity. Jesus asserted, "By this all men will know that you are my disciples, if you love one another" (Jn 13:35); and the apostle John warned, "If anyone says, 'I love God,' yet hates his brother, he is a liar. For anyone who does not love his brother, whom he has seen, cannot love God, whom he has not seen" (1Jn 4:20).

As we look at the challenges facing our communities, it is imperative for us to understand that love is the only power that will save us. God's love can look at a seemingly hopeless situation and see hope; it can stand in the midst of hatred and poverty and speak a word of deliverance; it can transform our minds and our communities. The fruit of the Spirit is love—against such there is no law (see Gal 5:22–23).

—C. Belt

For the next Inspire note, go to page 1360.

### read

1 Corinthians 13:1–13; see also Leviticus 19:9–18; Mark 12:28–31; John 13:1–17,31–35; 1 John 3:11–24; 4:7–21.

See also the Inspire Notes "Commitment to Community," "True Joy" and "What Is Intimacy?" and the Women of the Bible Notes "Rebekah: A Woman of Obsessive Love" and "The Bridegroom and His Bride: Soul Mates in Life."

### WOMAN of COLOR

How do your actions exemplify God's unconditional love?

**14:26** n 1Co 12:7–10
**14:29** o 1Co 12:10
**14:34** p 1Ti 2:11,12
**14:37** q 2Co 10:7 r 1Jn 4:6
**14:39** s 1Co 12:31
**14:40** t ver 33

## Orderly Worship

26 What then shall we say, brothers? When you come together, everyone[n] has a hymn, or a word of instruction, a revelation, a tongue or an interpretation. All of these must be done for the strengthening of the church. 27 If anyone speaks in a tongue, two—or at the most three—should speak, one at a time, and someone must interpret. 28 If there is no interpreter, the speaker should keep quiet in the church and speak to himself and God.

29 Two or three prophets should speak, and the others should weigh carefully what is said.[o] 30 And if a revelation comes to someone who is sitting down, the first speaker should stop. 31 For you can all prophesy in turn so that everyone may be instructed and encouraged. 32 The spirits of prophets are subject to the control of prophets. 33 For God is not a God of disorder but of peace.

As in all the congregations of the saints, 34 women should remain silent in the churches. They are not allowed to speak, but must be in submission,[p] as the Law says. 35 If they want to inquire about something, they should ask their own husbands at home; for it is disgraceful for a woman to speak in the church.

36 Did the word of God originate with you? Or are you the only people it has reached? 37 If anybody thinks he is a prophet[q] or spiritually gifted, let him acknowledge that what I am writing to you is the Lord's command.[r] 38 If he ignores this, he himself will be ignored.[a]

39 Therefore, my brothers, be eager[s] to prophesy, and do not forbid speaking in tongues. 40 But everything should be done in a fitting and orderly[t] way.

## The Resurrection of Christ

15 Now, brothers, I want to remind you of the gospel I preached to you, which you received and on which you have taken your stand. 2 By this gospel you are saved, if you hold firmly to the word I preached to you. Otherwise, you have believed in vain.

3 For what I received I passed on to you as of first importance[b]: that Christ died for our sins[u] according to the Scriptures,[v] 4 that he was buried, that he was raised on the third day according to the Scriptures,[w] 5 and that he appeared to Peter,[c][x] and then to the Twelve. 6 After that, he appeared to more than five hundred of the brothers at the same time, most of whom are still living, though some have fallen asleep. 7 Then he appeared to James, then to all the apostles,[y] 8 and last of all he appeared to me also,[z] as to one abnormally born.

9 For I am the least of the apostles[a] and do not even deserve to be called an apostle, because I persecuted[b] the church of God. 10 But by the grace of God I am what I am, and his grace to me was not without effect. No, I worked harder than all of them[c]—yet not I, but the grace of God that was with me.[d] 11 Whether, then, it was I or they, this is what we preach, and this is what you believed.

## The Resurrection of the Dead

12 But if it is preached that Christ has been raised from the dead, how can some of you say that there is no resurrection of the dead? 13 If there is no resurrection of the dead, then not even Christ has been raised. 14 And if Christ has not been raised, our preaching is useless and so is your faith. 15 More than that, we are then found to be false witnesses about God, for we have testified about God that he raised Christ from the dead.[e] But he did not raise him if in fact the dead are not raised. 16 For if the dead are not raised, then Christ has not been raised either. 17 And if Christ has not been raised, your faith is futile; you are still in your sins. 18 Then those also who have fallen asleep in Christ are lost. 19 If only for this life we have hope in Christ, we are to be pitied more than all men.

20 But Christ has indeed been raised from the dead,[f] the firstfruits[g] of those who have fallen asleep. 21 For since death came through a man,[h] the resurrection of the dead comes also through a man. 22 For as in Adam all die, so in Christ all will be made alive. 23 But each in his own turn: Christ, the firstfruits; then, when he comes, those who belong to him. 24 Then the end will come, when he hands over the kingdom[i] to God the Father after he has destroyed all dominion,

**15:3** u Isa 53:5; 1Pe 2:24 v Lk 24:27; Ac 26:22,23
**15:4** w Ac 2:25,30,31
**15:5** x Lk 24:34
**15:7** y Ac 1:3,4
**15:8** z Ac 9:3–6,17
**15:9** a Eph 3:8 b Ac 8:3
**15:10** c 2Co 11:23 d Php 2:13
**15:15** e Ac 2:24
**15:20** f 1Pe 1:3 g Ac 26:23
**15:21** h Ro 5:12
**15:24** i Da 7:14,27

[a] 38 Some manuscripts *If he is ignorant of this, let him be ignorant* [b] 3 Or *you at the first* [c] 5 Greek *Cephas*

authority and power. 25 For he must reign until he has put all his enemies under his feet. 26 The last enemy to be destroyed is death.[j] 27 For he "has put everything under his feet."[a][k] Now when it says that "everything" has been put under him, it is clear that this does not include God himself, who put everything under Christ. 28 When he has done this, then the Son himself will be made subject to him who put everything under him,[l] so that God may be all in all.[m]

29 Now if there is no resurrection, what will those do who are baptized for the dead? If the dead are not raised at all, why are people baptized for them? 30 And as for us, why do we endanger ourselves every hour?[n] 31 I die every day—I mean that, brothers—just as surely as I glory over you in Christ Jesus our Lord. 32 If I fought wild beasts[o] in Ephesus for merely human reasons, what have I gained? If the dead are not raised,

"Let us eat and drink,
for tomorrow we die."[b][p]

33 Do not be misled: "Bad company corrupts good character." 34 Come back to your senses as you ought, and stop sinning; for there are some who are ignorant of God—I say this to your shame.

## The Resurrection Body

35 But someone may ask, "How are the dead raised? With what kind of body will they come?"[q] 36 How foolish! What you sow does not come to life unless it dies.[r] 37 When you sow, you do not plant the body that will be, but just a seed, perhaps of wheat or of something else. 38 But God gives it a body as he has determined, and to each kind of seed he gives its own body. 39 All flesh is not the same: Men have one kind of flesh, animals have another, birds another and fish another. 40 There are also heavenly bodies and there are earthly bodies; but the splendor of the heavenly bodies is one kind, and the splendor of the earthly bodies is another. 41 The sun has one kind of splendor, the moon another and the stars another; and star differs from star in splendor.

42 So will it be[s] with the resurrection of the dead. The body that is sown is perishable, it is raised imperishable; 43 it is sown in dishonor, it is raised in glory;[t] it is sown in weakness, it is raised in power; 44 it is sown a natural body, it is raised a spiritual body.

If there is a natural body, there is also a spiritual body. 45 So it is written: "The first man Adam became a living being"[c];[u] the last Adam,[v] a life-giving spirit. 46 The spiritual did not come first, but the natural, and after that the spiritual. 47 The first man was of the dust of the earth,[w] the second man from heaven. 48 As was the earthly man, so are those who are of the earth; and as is the man from heaven, so also are those who are of heaven. 49 And just as we have borne the likeness of the earthly man,[x] so shall we[d] bear the likeness of the man from heaven.[y]

50 I declare to you, brothers, that flesh and blood cannot inherit the kingdom of God, nor does the perishable inherit the imperishable. 51 Listen, I tell you a mystery: We will not all sleep, but we will all be changed— 52 in a flash, in the twinkling of an eye, at the last trumpet. For the trumpet will sound,[z] the dead will be raised imperishable, and we will be changed. 53 For the perishable must clothe itself with the imperishable,[a] and the mortal with immortality. 54 When the perishable has been clothed with the imperishable, and the mortal with immortality, then the saying that is written will come true: "Death has been swallowed up in victory."[e][b]

55 "Where, O death, is your victory?
Where, O death, is your sting?"[f][c]

56 The sting of death is sin, and the power of sin is the law.[d] 57 But thanks be to God! He gives us the victory through our Lord Jesus Christ.

58 Therefore, my dear brothers, stand firm. Let nothing move you. Always give yourselves fully to the work of the Lord, because you know that your labor in the Lord is not in vain.

## The Collection for God's People

16 Now about the collection[e] for God's people:[f] Do what I told the Galatian churches to do. 2 On the first day of every

15:26 j Rev 20:14
15:27 k Ps 8:6
15:28 l Php 3:21; m 1Co 3:23
15:30 n 2Co 11:26
15:32 o 2Co 1:8; p Lk 12:19
15:35 q Eze 37:3
15:36 r Jn 12:24
15:42 s Mt 13:43
15:43 t Php 3:21
15:45 u Ge 2:7; v Ro 5:14
15:47 w Ge 3:19
15:49 x Ge 5:3; y Ro 8:29
15:52 z Mt 24:31
15:53 a 2Co 5:2,4
15:54 b Isa 25:8
15:55 c Hos 13:14
15:56 d Ro 4:15
16:1 e Ac 24:17; f Ac 9:13

[a] 27 Psalm 8:6 [b] 32 Isaiah 22:13 [c] 45 Gen. 2:7 [d] 49 Some early manuscripts *so let us* [e] 54 Isaiah 25:8
[f] 55 Hosea 13:14

# Inspire

## GRIEVING A MISCARRIAGE OR STILLBORN CHILD

Grief is something each of us will experience at some time in our lives. Grief is universal, a God-given method by which humans cope with pain. It is a normal and healthy response to the loss of a significant person, including that of a child. If you are called upon to endure this excruciatingly painful experience, you will inevitably face the emptiness and the difficult task of moving on. This period will include acknowledging the reality and enormity of the loss, admitting the pain and adjusting to a life bereft of the beautiful newborn you had anticipated. You may face questions from well-meaning friends or acquaintances: "Where is the new baby?" "What did you have—a boy or a girl?"

The grief over a miscarriage or the death of a stillborn child is compounded because of the unexpectedness of it. It is untimely and sudden. Daily you will deal with feelings of unfinished business, guilt, failure and shame. For parents, the death of a child is one of life's most devastating losses.

This experience should bring the parents closer to one another in an effort to cope with their loss. However, that is not always the case. Some couples watch their marriages flounder as they blame each other or themselves. That's why couples dealing with the loss of a child need to rely heavily on their relationship with God.

Your relationship with Jesus will give you support, meaning and hope. Through a daily encounter with Christ, you will find his comfort and peace. Yes, you may experience prolonged periods of shock, numbness, denial, crying, restlessness, loneliness, depression, anger and insomnia. However, daily prayer, singing, Scripture reading and fellowship with empathetic believers will ease the grieving process.

As you begin to recognize the stages of grief, you will learn how to walk within, and grow through, the experience. For parents, that it is no easy task. Such grief slams into our lives without warning, and we receive it reluctantly. Grief can be conquered only when it is faced honestly, with divine support and the care of other human beings. Thank God for the widely available sources of help from family members, friends, fellow believers, ministers, counselors and physicians. After what may seem to be interminable days of hopelessness, you will learn to live with the memory of your loss. This experience will ultimately help you mature and equip you to better reach out to others. In the meantime, reach out your hand daily to God, and trust that Jesus has overcome death. "Death has been swallowed up in victory" (1Co 15:54).

—C. Love

### read

1 Corinthians 15:12–59; see also 2 Samuel 12:13–23; Psalm 23:1–6; 119:28; Isaiah 53:3–4; 1 Thessalonians 4:13–18; Revelation 21:1–4.

See also the Inspire Notes "Courage to Heal," "Suffering," "The Paradox of Life and Suffering" and "Bon Voyage: The Courage to Say Good-bye," and the Women of the Bible Notes "Rizpah: A Grieving Mother" and "The Shunammite Woman: Our Sister's Grief Is Our Grief."

### WOMAN *of* COLOR

Reflect on a time God comforted you during a period of grief; then share your testimony with a sister who needs to hear what God has done for you.

For the next Inspire note, go to page 1366.

week,[g] each one of you should set aside a
sum of money in keeping with his income,
saving it up, so that when I come no collec-
tions will have to be made. 3Then, when I ar-
rive, I will give letters of introduction to the
men you approve and send them with your
gift to Jerusalem. 4If it seems advisable for
me to go also, they will accompany me.

## Personal Requests

5After I go through Macedonia, I will
come to you—for I will be going through
Macedonia. 6Perhaps I will stay with you
awhile, or even spend the winter, so that you
can help me on my journey, wherever I go. 7I
do not want to see you now and make only
a passing visit; I hope to spend some time
with you, if the Lord permits.[h] 8But I will
stay on at Ephesus until Pentecost, 9because
a great door for effective work has opened to
me, and there are many who oppose me.

10If Timothy[i] comes, see to it that he has
nothing to fear while he is with you, for he
is carrying on the work of the Lord,[j] just as
I am. 11No one, then, should refuse to accept
him.[k] Send him on his way in peace[l] so that
he may return to me. I am expecting him
along with the brothers.

12Now about our brother Apollos: I
strongly urged him to go to you with the
brothers. He was quite unwilling to go now,
but he will go when he has the opportunity.

13Be on your guard; stand firm[m] in the
faith; be men of courage; be strong.[n] 14Do
everything in love.

15You know that the household of Steph-
anas were the first converts in Achaia, and
they have devoted themselves to the service
of the saints. I urge you, brothers, 16to sub-
mit to such as these and to everyone who
joins in the work, and labors at it. 17I was
glad when Stephanas, Fortunatus and Acha-
icus arrived, because they have supplied
what was lacking from you.[o] 18For they re-
freshed my spirit and yours also. Such men
deserve recognition.[p]

## Final Greetings

19The churches in the province of Asia
send you greetings. Aquila and Priscilla[a]
greet you warmly in the Lord, and so does
the church that meets at their house.[q] 20All
the brothers here send you greetings. Greet
one another with a holy kiss.

21I, Paul, write this greeting in my own
hand.

22If anyone does not love the Lord[r]—a
curse be on him. Come, O Lord[b]!

23The grace of the Lord Jesus be with
you.[s]

24My love to all of you in Christ Jesus.
Amen.[c]

**16:2** g Ac 20:7
**16:7** h Ac 18:21
**16:10** i Ac 16:1 j 1Co 15:58
**16:11** k 1Ti 4:12 l Ac 15:33
**16:13** m Php 1:27 n Eph 6:10
**16:17** o 2Co 11:9
**16:18** p Php 2:29
**16:19** q Ro 16:5
**16:22** r Eph 6:24
**16:23** s Ro 16:20

[a]19 Greek *Prisca*, a variant of *Priscilla* [b]22 In Aramaic the expression *Come, O Lord* is *Marana tha.* [c]24 Some manuscripts do not have *Amen.*

# Priscilla

## An Open-Door Policy

Priscilla was a bold and courageous woman who met the apostle Paul in Corinth. Like Paul, Priscilla and her husband, Aquila, were tentmakers. Priscilla and Aquila opened their home to Paul, and they became partners with him both in business and in the ministry of the gospel (see Ac 18:1–3). Priscilla wore a familiar crown to women of color: She was not afraid to speak and stand up for what she believed in. Without ever elevating herself above others, she faithfully took her instructions from the Lord and served others; the gospel was taken further because of her.

Priscilla was loyal and devoted. Priscilla and Aquila labored for the gospel as a team. Their names are always mentioned together when they are referred to in the New Testament (see Ac 18:2,18–19,26; Ro 16:3; 1Co 16:19; 2Ti 4:19). What is even more unusual is that Priscilla is generally mentioned first—a hint that she may have played a more active role in ministry than did her husband.

When Paul left Corinth, he took Priscilla and Aquila with him. He left the couple at Ephesus to lay the groundwork for what would become one of the most important churches of the New Testament period (see Ac 18:18–21). During that time Apollos, who would become an influential preacher and leader in the church (see 1Co 1:12; 3:1–7), humbled himself and sat at Priscilla and Aquila's feet to receive instruction (see Ac 18:24–28). Apollos knew and taught only John the Baptist's baptism. Priscilla could have found fault in him, but instead she helped him. She and her husband invited Apollos to their home and compassionately shared the complete gospel message with him. Apollos may not have been able to understand that Jesus was the Savior and then convince his fellow Jews of this truth if it had not been for Priscilla.

Just like so many women who are full of love, wisdom and courage, Priscilla remained a witness and a student of the gospel. She worked side by side with her husband, spreading the Word while also managing her business, church and home.

—W. JOHNSON

### reflection

*How does Priscilla inspire you to be a student of the Word and to use your gifts and your home in Christ's service?*

### read

1 Corinthians 16:19; see also Acts 18; Romans 16:3–5.

**See also** the Inspire Notes "Commitment to Community," "Submission," "Evangelism: Gone Fishin'," "Female Ministers and Evangelists," "Servant-Leadership" and "Women in Teaching Ministries," and the Women of the Bible Notes "Deborah: An Uncommon Leader," "Huldah: A Prophetess of God," and "Philip's Daughters: Those Preaching Women."

For the next Women of the Bible note, go to page 1400.

# 2 Corinthians

## OVERVIEW

Paul wrote the book of 2 Corinthians not long after writing his first letter to the church at Corinth. In his second letter Paul gave thanks for the repentance of the church members. He also responded to his critics and addressed a variety of other topics. Some of Paul's teachings include the following: an admonition to remember that believers are like unimpressive jars of clay that nevertheless contain great treasures (see 2Co 4), the importance of not being intimately connected with unbelievers (see 2Co 6:14—7:1), and the need for believers to give generously (see 2Co 8–9). Paul also addressed his sufferings (see 2Co 6:3–13; 11:16–33) and his vision (see 2Co 12:1–10).

Paul's letter reminds Christians that we are called to represent Christ in all of our dealings. Just as Paul requested of the Corinthians, Christians today should forgive each other and live in reconciliation because of Christ. As you read the second letter to the Corinthian church, focus on how Christ has reconciled you to God, and use this model to live in harmony with all of God's children.

## OUTLINE

I. Reflections on Paul's Relationship With the Corinthians (1:1—3:6)
II. The Glory of the Gospel (3:7—5:21)
III. A Call for Holiness and Reconciliation (6:1—7:16)
IV. Appeal for Generosity in Giving (8:1—9:15)
V. Paul's Defense of His Apostleship (10:1—13:14)

## SCANNABLE FACTS:

**Author:** Paul

**Time Written:** A.D. 55

**Theme to Note:** God's strength in our weakness

**Notable Women:** There are no women mentioned in this book

1 Paul, an apostle of Christ Jesus by the will of God,[a] and Timothy our brother,

To the church of God in Corinth, together with all the saints throughout Achaia:

2 Grace and peace to you from God our Father and the Lord Jesus Christ.[b]

## The God of All Comfort

3 Praise be to the God and Father of our Lord Jesus Christ,[c] the Father of compassion and the God of all comfort, 4 who comforts us in all our troubles, so that we can comfort those in any trouble with the comfort we ourselves have received from God. 5 For just as the sufferings of Christ flow over into our lives,[d] so also through Christ our comfort overflows. 6 If we are distressed, it is for your comfort and salvation;[e] if we are comforted, it is for your comfort, which produces in you patient endurance of the same sufferings we suffer. 7 And our hope for you is firm, because we know that just as you share in our sufferings, so also you share in our comfort.

8 We do not want you to be uninformed, brothers, about the hardships we suffered[f] in the province of Asia. We were under great pressure, far beyond our ability to endure, so that we despaired even of life. 9 Indeed, in our hearts we felt the sentence of death. But this happened that we might not rely on ourselves but on God, who raises the dead. 10 He has delivered us from such a deadly peril, and he will deliver us. On him we have set our hope that he will continue to deliver us, 11 as you help us by your prayers.[g] Then many will give thanks[h] on our[a] behalf for the gracious favor granted us in answer to the prayers of many.

## Paul's Change of Plans

12 Now this is our boast: Our conscience testifies that we have conducted ourselves in the world, and especially in our relations with you, in the holiness and sincerity that are from God. We have done so not according to worldly wisdom but according to God's grace. 13 For we do not write you anything you cannot read or understand. And I hope that, 14 as you have understood us in part, you will come to understand fully that you can boast of us just as we will boast of you in the day of the Lord Jesus.

15 Because I was confident of this, I planned to visit you first so that you might benefit twice.[i] 16 I planned to visit you on my way[j] to Macedonia and to come back to you from Macedonia, and then to have you send me on my way to Judea. 17 When I planned this, did I do it lightly? Or do I make my plans in a worldly manner[k] so that in the same breath I say, "Yes, yes" and "No, no"?

18 But as surely as God is faithful, our message to you is not "Yes" and "No." 19 For the Son of God, Jesus Christ, who was preached among you by me and Silas[b] and Timothy, was not "Yes" and "No," but in him it has always[l] been "Yes." 20 For no matter how many promises[m] God has made, they are "Yes" in Christ. And so through him the "Amen" is spoken by us to the glory of God. 21 Now it is

1:1 a Col 1:1
1:2 b Ro 1:7
1:3 c Eph 1:3; 1Pe 1:3
1:5 d 2Co 4:10
1:6 e 2Co 4:15
1:8 f 1Co 15:32
1:11 g Ro 15:30; Php 1:19 h 2Co 4:15
1:15 i Ro 1:11,13
1:16 j 1Co 16:5–7
1:17 k 2Co 10:2,3
1:19 l Heb 13:8
1:20 m Ro 15:8

[a]11 Many manuscripts *your* [b]19 Greek *Silvanus*, a variant of *Silas*

## *The African Presence*

### 2 Corinthians 1

While there are no specific references to the African presence within the book of 2 Corinthians, the gospel preached by Paul was influenced by people of North Africa and the Middle East (a historical and cultural subregion of Africa-Eurasia, traditionally held to be countries or regions in Southwest Asia together with Egypt). However, during the time of the New Testament, racial identification did not have the significance that it has today.

1:21 n 1Jn2:20,27
1:23 o 1Co4:21; 2Co2:1,3
1:24 p 1Pe5:3

God who makes both us and you stand firm
in Christ. He anointed[n] us, 22 set his seal of
ownership on us, and put his Spirit in our
hearts as a deposit, guaranteeing what is
to come.
23 I call God as my witness that it was in order
to spare you[o] that I did not return to Corinth.
24 Not that we lord it over[p] your faith,
but we work with you for your joy, because it
is by faith you stand firm.[q]

# 2

1 So I made
up my mind that I would not make
another painful visit to you. 2 For if I grieve
you, who is left to make me glad but you
whom I have grieved? 3 I wrote as I did so
that when I came I should not be distressed[r]
by those who ought to make me rejoice. I

1:24 q Ro11:20; 1Co15:1
2:3 r 2Co12:21

Inspire

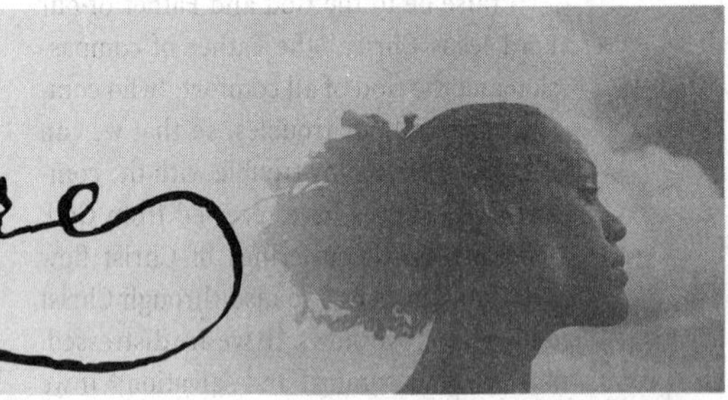

## GOD'S PROMISES: ALWAYS "YES" AND "AMEN"

**God's promises are always fulfilled in Christ ("Yes") and should inspire our heartfelt "Amen" (see 2Co 1:20). "Yes" assures us that his promises will surely come to realization, while "Amen" expresses our sure knowledge that each promise is complete in him. In other words, God's promises are a present reality from the moment they are made. For our part, we are called to believe them without question.**

For example, God promised Mary that she would become a mother. Mary initially questioned God's promise through the angel Gabriel because she could not fathom how a virgin could give birth. Her skepticism and natural reservations were grounded in fact, but God required Mary to submit to his promise rather than to rely on human logic. Mary submitted herself to God in faith, saying, "I am the Lord's servant . . . May it be to me as you have said" (Lk 1:38).

Mary became a spiritual vessel for bringing Jesus into the world. In this way her submission to God's promises resulted in fulfillment of the promises, both for her and for all of humanity. Women today are still to heed the call of the Lord, to submit themselves as vessels to showcase to the world God's Word, life and presence. As long as God's promises are "Yes" and "Amen"—truth and completion, reality and fulfillment—women are to look to him in faith, seek his will for their lives, humble themselves, pray and cease from doing evil. When we do these things, we have so much good to bring forth!

—M. V. Stephens

### read

2 Corinthians 1:12–22; see also Luke 1:26–38; Romans 4:18–25; Hebrews 11:1–40.

**See also** the Inspire Notes "Prayer: A God-Given Promise," "Prayer: The Antidote to Worry" and "Prayer," and the Women of the Bible Note "Mary, the Mother of Jesus: A Model of Motherhood."

### WOMAN of COLOR

How much faith do you have in the promises of God?

For the next Inspire note, go to page 1370.

2:4 s 2Co 7:8,12
2:5 t 1Co 5:1,2
2:6 u 1Co 5:4,5
2:7 v Gal 6:1
2:9 w 2Co 10:6
2:12 x Ac 16:8
2:13 y 2Co 7:5 z 2Co 7:6,13

*My faithful God,*

*help me to remember today that you are the original Promise Keeper and that in Christ all of your promises are fulfilled; indeed, in him they are yes and*

*Amen*

2 CORINTHIANS 1:18–20

had confidence in all of you, that you would all share my joy. 4For I wrote you[s] out of great distress and anguish of heart and with many tears, not to grieve you but to let you know the depth of my love for you.

## Forgiveness for the Sinner

5If anyone has caused grief,[t] he has not so much grieved me as he has grieved all of you, to some extent—not to put it too severely. 6The punishment[u] inflicted on him by the majority is sufficient for him. 7Now instead, you ought to forgive and comfort him,[v] so that he will not be overwhelmed by excessive sorrow. 8I urge you, therefore, to reaffirm your love for him. 9The reason I wrote you was to see if you would stand the test and be obedient in everything.[w] 10If you forgive anyone, I also forgive him. And what I have forgiven—if there was anything to forgive—I have forgiven in the sight of Christ for your sake, 11in order that Satan might not outwit us. For we are not unaware of his schemes.

## Ministers of the New Covenant

12Now when I went to Troas[x] to preach the gospel of Christ and found that the Lord had opened a door for me, 13I still had no peace of mind,[y] because I did not find my brother Titus[z] there. So I said good-by to them and went on to Macedonia.

14But thanks be to God, who always leads us in triumphal procession in Christ and through us spreads everywhere the fragrance of the knowledge of him. 15For we are to God the aroma of Christ among those who are being saved and those who are perishing. 16To the one we are the smell of death;[a] to the other, the fragrance of life. And who is equal to such a task? 17Unlike so many, we do not peddle the word of God for profit. On the contrary, in Christ we speak before God with sincerity, like men sent from God.[b]

3 Are we beginning to commend ourselves[c] again? Or do we need, like some people, letters of recommendation[d] to you or from you? 2You yourselves are our letter, written on our hearts, known and read by everybody.[e] 3You show that you are a letter from Christ, the result of our ministry, written not with ink but with the Spirit of the living God, not on tablets of stone but on tablets of human hearts.[f]

4Such confidence as this is ours through Christ before God. 5Not that we are competent in ourselves to claim anything for ourselves, but our competence comes from God.[g] 6He has made us competent as ministers of a new covenant—not of the letter but of the Spirit; for the letter kills, but the Spirit gives life.[h]

## The Glory of the New Covenant

7Now if the ministry that brought death, which was engraved in letters on stone, came with glory, so that the Israelites could not look steadily at the face of Moses because of its glory,[i] fading though it was, 8will not the ministry of the Spirit be even more glorious? 9If the ministry that condemns men is glorious, how much more glorious is the ministry that brings righteousness![j] 10For what was glorious has no glory now in comparison with the surpassing glory. 11And if what was fading away came with glory, how much greater is the glory of that which lasts!

12Therefore, since we have such a hope, we are very bold. 13We are not like Moses, who would put a veil over his face to keep the Israelites from gazing at it while the radiance was fading away. 14But their minds were made dull, for to this day the same veil remains when the old covenant is read. It has not been removed, because only in Christ is it taken away. 15Even to this day when Moses is read, a veil covers their hearts. 16But whenever anyone turns to the Lord,[k] the veil is taken away. 17Now

2:16 a Lk 2:34
2:17 b 2Co 1:12
3:1 c 2Co 5:12 d Ac 18:27
3:2 e 1Co 9:2
3:3 f Eze 11:19
3:5 g 1Co 15:10
3:6 h Jn 6:63
3:7 i Ex 34:29–35
3:9 j Ro 1:17
3:16 k Ro 11:23

> *"The most rewarding freedom is freedom of the mind."*
>
> —Amy Jacques-Garvey, Nationalist Leader

the Lord is the Spirit, and where the Spirit of the Lord is, there is freedom. 18 And we, who with unveiled faces all reflect[a][l] the Lord's glory,[m] are being transformed into his likeness[n] with ever-increasing glory, which comes from the Lord, who is the Spirit.

## Treasures in Jars of Clay

**4** Therefore, since through God's mercy[o] we have this ministry, we do not lose heart. 2 Rather, we have renounced secret and shameful ways; we do not use deception, nor do we distort the word of God.[p] On the contrary, by setting forth the truth plainly we commend ourselves to every man's conscience in the sight of God. 3 And even if our gospel is veiled, it is veiled to those who are perishing.[q] 4 The god of this age has blinded the minds of unbelievers, so that they cannot see the light of the gospel of the glory of Christ, who is the image of God. 5 For we do not preach ourselves, but Jesus Christ as Lord, and ourselves as your servants for Jesus' sake. 6 For God, who said, "Let light shine out of darkness,"[b][r] made his light shine in our hearts[s] to give us the light of the knowledge of the glory of God in the face of Christ.

7 But we have this treasure in jars of clay to show that this all-surpassing power is from God[t] and not from us. 8 We are hard pressed on every side,[u] but not crushed; perplexed, but not in despair; 9 persecuted, but not abandoned; struck down, but not destroyed.[v] 10 We always carry around in our body the death of Jesus, so that the life of Jesus may also be revealed in our body. 11 For we who are alive are always being given over to death for Jesus' sake, so that his life may be revealed in our mortal body. 12 So then, death is at work in us, but life is at work in you.

13 It is written: "I believed; therefore I have spoken."[c][w] With that same spirit of faith we also believe and therefore speak, 14 because we know that the one who raised the Lord Jesus from the dead will also raise us with Jesus and present us with you in his presence. 15 All this is for your benefit, so that the grace that is reaching more and more people may cause thanksgiving to overflow to the glory of God.

16 Therefore we do not lose heart. Though outwardly we are wasting away, yet inwardly[x] we are being renewed[y] day by day. 17 For our light and momentary troubles are achieving for us an eternal glory that far outweighs them all.[z] 18 So we fix our eyes not on what is seen, but on what is unseen.[a] For what is seen is temporary, but what is unseen is eternal.

## Our Heavenly Dwelling

**5** Now we know that if the earthly tent we live in is destroyed, we have a building from God, an eternal house in heaven, not built by human hands. 2 Meanwhile we groan,[b] longing to be clothed with our heavenly dwelling, 3 because when we are clothed, we will not be found naked. 4 For while we are in this tent, we groan and are burdened, because we do not wish to be unclothed but to be clothed with our heavenly dwelling,[c] so that what is mortal may be swallowed up by life. 5 Now it is God who has made us for this very purpose and has given us the Spirit as a deposit, guaranteeing what is to come.[d]

---

*Dear God,*

*you alone are the giver, sustainer and provider of life. Thank you for the infinite blessings you have showered upon me. Whether I have few or many worldly goods, I have nothing if I don't have you. Lord, help me and everyone else in my faith community to achieve an attitude of victory and to vanquish thoughts of failure and defeat.*

*Amen*

2 CORINTHIANS 4:7–9

---

**3:18** l 1Co 13:12; m 2Co 4:4,6; n Ro 8:29
**4:1** o 1Co 7:25
**4:2** p 2Co 2:17
**4:3** q 1Co 1:18
**4:6** r Ge 1:3; s 2Pe 1:19
**4:7** t 1Co 2:5
**4:8** u 2Co 7:5
**4:9** v Ps 37:24
**4:13** w Ps 116:10
**4:16** x Ro 7:22; y Col 3:10
**4:17** z Ro 8:18
**4:18** a Ro 8:24; Heb 11:1
**5:2** b Ro 8:23
**5:4** c 1Co 15:53,54
**5:5** d Ro 8:23

[a] 18 Or *contemplate* [b] 6 Gen. 1:3 [c] 13 Psalm 116:10

5:10
e Ro 14:10; Eph 6:8
5:11
f Heb 10:31
g 2Co 4:2
5:12
h 2Co 3:1
i 2Co 1:14
5:13
j 2Co 11:1,16,17
5:17
k Rev 21:4,5
5:18
l Ro 5:10
5:20
m 2Co 6:1; Eph 6:20
5:21
n 1Pe 2:22,24; 1Jn 3:5
6:1
o 1Co 3:9; 2Co 5:20

6Therefore we are always confident and
know that as long as we are at home in the
body we are away from the Lord. 7We live by
faith, not by sight. 8We are confident, I say,
and would prefer to be away from the body
and at home with the Lord. 9So we make it
our goal to please him, whether we are at
home in the body or away from it. 10For we
must all appear before the judgment seat of
Christ, that each one may receive what is
due him[e] for the things done while in the
body, whether good or bad.

## The Ministry of Reconciliation

11Since, then, we know what it is to fear
the Lord,[f] we try to persuade men. What we
are is plain to God, and I hope it is also plain
to your conscience.[g] 12We are not trying to
commend ourselves to you again,[h] but are
giving you an opportunity to take pride in
us,[i] so that you can answer those who take
pride in what is seen rather than in what is
in the heart. 13If we are out of our mind,[j] it is
for the sake of God; if we are in our right
mind, it is for you. 14For Christ's love com-
pels us, because we are convinced that one
died for all, and therefore all died. 15And
he died for all, that those who live should no
longer live for themselves but for him who
died for them and was raised again.

16So from now on we regard no one from
a worldly point of view. Though we once
regarded Christ in this way, we do so no
longer. 17Therefore, if anyone is in Christ,
he is a new creation; the old has gone, the
new has come![k] 18All this is from God, who
reconciled us to himself through Christ[l] and
gave us the ministry of reconciliation: 19that
God was reconciling the world to himself
in Christ, not counting men's sins against
them. And he has committed to us the mes-
sage of reconciliation. 20We are therefore
Christ's ambassadors,[m] as though God were
making his appeal through us. We implore
you on Christ's behalf: Be reconciled to God.
21God made him who had no sin[n] to be sin[a]
for us, so that in him we might become the
righteousness of God.

6 As God's fellow workers[o] we urge you
not to receive God's grace in vain. 2For
he says,

"In the time of my favor I heard you,
and in the day of salvation I helped
you."[b][p]

I tell you, now is the time of God's favor, now
is the day of salvation.

*Honored one,*

*You have been made right*
*with me through Christ.*

*Your Savior God*

2 CORINTHIANS 6:1–2

## Paul's Hardships

3We put no stumbling block in anyone's
path,[q] so that our ministry will not be
discredited. 4Rather, as servants of God we
commend ourselves in every way: in great
endurance; in troubles, hardships and
distresses; 5in beatings, imprisonments[r]
and riots; in hard work, sleepless nights
and hunger; 6in purity, understanding,
patience and kindness; in the Holy Spirit
and in sincere love; 7in truthful speech and
in the power of God; with weapons of righ-
teousness[s] in the right hand and in the left;
8through glory and dishonor, bad report
and good report; genuine, yet regarded
as impostors; 9known, yet regarded as un-
known; dying, and yet we live on;[t] beaten,
and yet not killed; 10sorrowful, yet always re-
joicing; poor, yet making many rich; having
nothing, and yet possessing everything.

11We have spoken freely to you, Corinthi-
ans, and opened wide our hearts to you.[u]
12We are not withholding our affection from
you, but you are withholding yours from us.
13As a fair exchange—I speak as to my chil-
dren—open wide your hearts also.

## Do Not Be Yoked With Unbelievers

14Do not be yoked together[v] with unbe-
lievers. For what do righteousness and

6:2
p Isa 49:8
6:3
q 1Co 9:12
6:5
r 2Co 11:23–25
6:7
s 2Co 10:4; Eph 6:10–18
6:9
t 2Co 1:8–10; 4:10,11
6:11
u 2Co 7:3
6:14
v 1Co 5:9,10

[a]21 Or *be a sin offering* [b]2 Isaiah 49:8

# Inspire

## BON VOYAGE: THE COURAGE TO SAY GOOD-BYE

The tumor was malignant. They'd given my young nephew three months, and it had already been two. Larry wasn't running anymore. He used to play practical jokes on the nurses, who regularly had a hard time finding him, but no more. He was struggling to breathe and to eat. My nephew was struggling to live. He had long since repented of his sins and given his life to the Lord. "I'm going to live, Aunt Sandra!" he assured me. "I'm going to beat this thing. God's gonna heal me. Nothing's too hard for God—nothing! Not even this!"

But that wasn't God's plan for Larry. By early May he was no longer eating or talking, and breathing had become his biggest challenge. He was on a morphine drip and no longer responded to our questions. We had shared many secrets in the last two months. I'd spent time with him almost daily. I loved him, but now it was time to let him go. He was suffering, struggling to stay here for our sakes. And like many families, we wanted him to hang on. But the Holy Spirit nudged my heart, asking, "Why? Why should he stay on this side?" By then everyone else had gone home. So I kissed him and gave him permission to go. "We'll be fine, Sweetie," I assured him as bravely as I could. "Don't stay here for us. Jesus has something better for you on the other side, and we'll see you there. I'll miss you so much." Then I climbed into bed with him and began to sing him a song, just as I'd done when the kids were young. I turned my face to the window, so he wouldn't see my tears. When I turned back, he was easing out. I caught him just in time to reassure him one last time: "Babe, Babe. I love you." He squeezed my hand, took four good breaths. *Four.* And then he stepped over.

God gives us the courage to trust him even in the face of death (see Ps 23:4)—courage to believe that he is too wise to make a mistake and too good to do wrong. May God continually remind us that this world is not our final home. We're only to pitch a tent here, not to build a homestead (see 2Co 5:1). And when it's our time, we, too, will hear a song and cross over.

—L. Melton-Dolberry

### read

2 Corinthians 5:1–10; see also Psalm 23:1–6; 1 Corinthians 15:50–58; 2 Corinthians 1:3–7; 4:13–18; 1 Thessalonians 4:13–18; Revelation 21:1–4.

See also the Inspire Notes "Courage to Heal," "Suffering," "Fear," "The Paradox of Life and Suffering" and "Grieving a Miscarriage or Stillborn Child," and the Women of the Bible Notes "Rizpah: A Grieving Mother" and "The Shunammite Woman: Our Sister's Grief Is Our Grief."

### WOMAN of COLOR

Who needs your help today to grieve a loss or to say good-bye to a loved one?

For the next Inspire note, go to page 1373.

6:14
w Eph 5:7,11

6:16
x 1Co 3:16

6:17
y Rev 18:4
z Isa 52:11

7:3
a 2Co 6:11,12

7:5
b 2Co 2:13
c 2Co 4:8
d Dt 32:25

7:6
e 2Co 2:13

7:8
f 2Co 2:2,4

wickedness have in common? Or what fellowship can light have with darkness?[w] [15]What harmony is there between Christ and Belial[a]? What does a believer have in common with an unbeliever? [16]What agreement is there between the temple of God and idols? For we are the temple[x] of the living God. As God has said: "I will live with them and walk among them, and I will be their God, and they will be my people."[b]

[17] "Therefore come out from them[y]
and be separate,
says the Lord.
Touch no unclean thing,
and I will receive you."[c][z]
[18] "I will be a Father to you,
and you will be my sons and
daughters,
says the Lord Almighty."[d]

7 Since we have these promises, dear friends, let us purify ourselves from everything that contaminates body and spirit, perfecting holiness out of reverence for God.

## Paul's Joy

[2]Make room for us in your hearts. We have wronged no one, we have corrupted no one, we have exploited no one. [3]I do not say this to condemn you; I have said before that you have such a place in our hearts[a] that we would live or die with you. [4]I have great confidence in you; I take great pride in you. I am greatly encouraged; in all our troubles my joy knows no bounds.

[5]For when we came into Macedonia,[b] this body of ours had no rest, but we were harassed at every turn[c]—conflicts on the outside, fears within.[d] [6]But God, who comforts the downcast, comforted us by the coming of Titus,[e] [7]and not only by his coming but also by the comfort you had given him. He told us about your longing for me, your deep sorrow, your ardent concern for me, so that my joy was greater than ever.

[8]Even if I caused you sorrow by my letter,[f] I do not regret it. Though I did regret it—I see that my letter hurt you, but only for a little while— [9]yet now I am happy, not because you were made sorry, but because your sorrow led you to repentance. For you became sorrowful as God intended and so were not harmed in any way by us. [10]Godly sorrow brings repentance that leads to salvation and leaves no regret, but worldly sorrow brings death. [11]See what this godly sorrow has produced in you: what earnestness, what eagerness to clear yourselves, what indignation, what alarm, what longing, what concern, what readiness to see justice done. At every point you have proved yourselves to be innocent in this matter. [12]So even though I wrote to you,[g] it was not on account of the one who did the wrong or of the injured party, but rather that before God you could see for yourselves how devoted to us you are. [13]By all this we are encouraged.

In addition to our own encouragement, we were especially delighted to see how happy Titus[h] was, because his spirit has been refreshed by all of you. [14]I had boasted to him about you, and you have not embarrassed me. But just as everything we said to you was true, so our boasting about you to Titus has proved to be true as well. [15]And his affection for you is all the greater when he remembers that you were all obedient,[i] receiving him with fear and trembling.[j] [16]I am glad I can have complete confidence in you.

## Generosity Encouraged

8 And now, brothers, we want you to know about the grace that God has given the Macedonian[k] churches. [2]Out of the most severe trial, their overflowing joy and their extreme poverty welled up in rich generosity. [3]For I testify that they gave as much as they were able,[l] and even beyond their ability. Entirely on their own, [4]they urgently pleaded with us for the privilege of sharing in this service[m] to the saints. [5]And they did not do as we expected, but they gave themselves first to the Lord and then to us in keeping with God's will. [6]So we urged[n] Titus, since he had earlier made a beginning, to bring also to completion this act of grace on your part. [7]But just as you excel in everything[o]—in faith, in speech, in knowledge,[p] in complete earnestness and in your love for us[e]—see that you also excel in this grace of giving.

7:12
g ver 8

7:13
h ver 6

7:15
i 2Co 2:9
j Php 2:12

8:1
k Ac 16:9

8:3
l 1Co 16:2

8:4
m Ac 24:17

8:6
n ver 17; 2Co 12:18

8:7
o 2Co 9:8
p 1Co 1:5

[a]15 Greek *Beliar,* a variant of *Belial* [b]16 Lev. 26:12; Jer. 32:38; Ezek. 37:27 [c]17 Isaiah 52:11; Ezek. 20:34,41
[d]18 2 Samuel 7:14; 7:8 [e]7 Some manuscripts *in our love for you*

8 I am not commanding you,[q] but I want to test the sincerity of your love by comparing it with the earnestness of others. 9 For you know the grace of our Lord Jesus Christ,[r] that though he was rich, yet for your sakes he became poor,[s] so that you through his poverty might become rich.

10 And here is my advice[t] about what is best for you in this matter: Last year you were the first not only to give but also to have the desire to do so.[u] 11 Now finish the work, so that your eager willingness to do it may be matched by your completion of it, according to your means. 12 For if the willingness is there, the gift is acceptable according to what one has,[v] not according to what he does not have.

13 Our desire is not that others might be relieved while you are hard pressed, but that there might be equality. 14 At the present time your plenty will supply what they need, so that in turn their plenty will supply what you need. Then there will be equality, 15 as it is written: "He who gathered much did not have too much, and he who gathered little did not have too little."[a][w]

## Titus Sent to Corinth

16 I thank God, who put into the heart of Titus the same concern I have for you. 17 For Titus not only welcomed our appeal, but he is coming to you with much enthusiasm and on his own initiative.[x] 18 And we are sending along with him the brother[y] who is praised by all the churches for his service to the gospel. 19 What is more, he was chosen by the churches to accompany us[z] as we carry the offering, which we administer in order to honor the Lord himself and to show our eagerness to help. 20 We want to avoid any criticism of the way we administer this liberal gift. 21 For we are taking pains to do what is right, not only in the eyes of the Lord but also in the eyes of men.[a]

22 In addition, we are sending with them our brother who has often proved to us in many ways that he is zealous, and now even more so because of his great confidence in you. 23 As for Titus, he is my partner and fellow worker[b] among you; as for our brothers, they are representatives of the churches and an honor to Christ. 24 Therefore show these men the proof of your love and the reason for our pride in you,[c] so that the churches can see it.

9 There is no need for me to write to you about this service to the saints. 2 For I know your eagerness to help, and I have been boasting about it to the Macedonians, telling them that since last year[d] you in Achaia were ready to give; and your enthusiasm has stirred most of them to action. 3 But I am sending the brothers in order that our boasting about you in this matter should not prove hollow, but that you may be ready, as I said you would be.[e] 4 For if any Macedonians come with me and find you unprepared, we—not to say anything about you—would be ashamed of having been so confident. 5 So I thought it necessary to urge the brothers to visit you in advance and finish the arrangements for the generous gift you had promised. Then it will be ready as a generous gift,[f] not as one grudgingly given.

## Sowing Generously

6 Remember this: Whoever sows sparingly will also reap sparingly, and whoever sows generously will also reap generously. 7 Each man should give what he has decided in his heart to give,[g] not reluctantly or under compulsion, for God loves a cheerful giver.[h] 8 And God is able to make all grace abound to you, so that in all things at all times, having all that you need, you will abound in every good work. 9 As it is written:

"He has scattered abroad his gifts to the
poor;
his righteousness endures forever."[b][i]

10 Now he who supplies seed to the sower and bread for food[j] will also supply and increase your store of seed and will enlarge the harvest of your righteousness.[k] 11 You will be made rich in every way so that you can be generous on every occasion, and through us your generosity will result in thanksgiving to God.

12 This service that you perform is not only supplying the needs[l] of God's people but is also overflowing in many expressions of thanks to God. 13 Because of the service

**8:8** q 1Co 7:6
**8:9** r 2Co 13:14 s Php 2:6–8
**8:10** t 1Co 7:25,40 u 2Co 9:2
**8:12** v Mk 12:43,44
**8:15** w Ex 16:18
**8:17** x ver 6
**8:18** y 2Co 12:18
**8:19** z 1Co 16:3,4
**8:21** a Ro 12:17
**8:23** b Php 2:25
**8:24** c 2Co 9:2
**9:2** d 2Co 8:10
**9:3** e 1Co 16:2
**9:5** f Php 4:17
**9:7** g 2Co 8:12 h Ro 12:8
**9:9** i Ps 112:9
**9:10** j Isa 55:10 k Hos 10:12
**9:12** l 2Co 8:14

[a]15 Exodus 16:18 [b]9 Psalm 112:9

# Inspire leadership FOCUS

## HUMILITY

Sometimes everyday pressures can pull us, as leaders, away from living a truly humble life. Before we know it, we're impatient with the grocer, snappy with our children or rude to a clumsy waiter. We don't mean any harm; sometimes we just lose our focus. We become so self-absorbed and self-centered that we quickly go from representing Jesus and his kingdom to representing ourselves. Too much self-interest leads to either self-justification or self-abasement, neither of which portrays humility. Yet God has made it simple for us to get our focus back. Sometimes all it takes is a memory and a model.

Whenever we stop to remember what is ours in Christ—consolation, mercy and unconditional love—we are quickly prompted to respond with worship and gratitude to our Savior. Worship focuses our thoughts on the character and mercies of God; gratitude reminds us we belong to him. We can trust him with our needs, rights and concerns.

Jesus Christ is trustworthy because he loved us enough to set aside his divine rights and privileges to become one of us. He became poor for our sake (see 2Co 8:9). In our leadership roles, it is not easy to lay aside our interests; to do so calls for an adjustment in our attitude and our approach toward people. It makes us intentionally remember Jesus' sacrifice for each person we meet. Christ died for the belligerent bellboy as well as our best friend; Christ died for our coworkers as well as for our family members. True humility calls us to direct our attention outside ourselves and requires that we consider each human encounter as an opportunity to serve rather than a chance to be served.

We belong to the Lord Jesus Christ, who showers us with love and affection, mercy and compassion. He also laid aside his rights as God in order to serve us with the ultimate sacrifice: death on the cross for our sins. When we consider his example and remember his compassion, we realize we don't have time for pettiness, rudeness, arrogance, low self-esteem or self-criticism. No matter how busy or distracted we become, we must refocus on what is important: a humble walk with God. Since Jesus put aside his privileges for our interests, as leaders we must do the same for others.

—A. Elmore

### read

2 Corinthians 8:1–15; see also John 13:1–17; Philippians 2:1–11.

**See also** the Inspire Notes "Goodness," "Servant-Leadership," "Be Focused" and "Character," and the Women of the Bible Note "Mary, the Mother of Jesus: A Model of Motherhood."

### WOMAN of COLOR

Each day set aside two 5–10 minute sessions (separate from your regular devotions or quiet time) to realign your focus. Use this time to worship and thank your Savior. Finish by asking the Holy Spirit to infuse you with his love for each person you encounter that day, especially the difficult ones.

For the next Inspire note, go to page 1384.

**9:13** m Mt 9:8
**9:15** n Ro 5:15,16
**10:1** o Gal 5:2
**10:2** p 1Co 4:21; 2Co 13:2,10
**10:4** q 1Co 2:5 r Jer 1:10
**10:7** s Jn 7:24 t 1Co 14:37
**10:8** u 2Co 13:10
**10:10** v 1Co 2:3; Gal 4:13,14 w 1Co 1:17

by which you have proved yourselves, men will praise God[m] for the obedience that accompanies your confession of the gospel of Christ, and for your generosity in sharing with them and with everyone else. 14 And in their prayers for you their hearts will go out to you, because of the surpassing grace God has given you. 15 Thanks be to God for his indescribable gift![n]

## Paul's Defense of His Ministry

**10** By the meekness and gentleness of Christ, I appeal to you—I, Paul,[o] who am "timid" when face to face with you, but "bold" when away! 2 I beg you that when I come I may not have to be as bold[p] as I expect to be toward some people who think that we live by the standards of this world. 3 For though we live in the world, we do not wage war as the world does. 4 The weapons we fight with are not the weapons of the world. On the contrary, they have divine power[q] to demolish strongholds.[r] 5 We demolish arguments and every pretension that sets itself up against the knowledge of God, and we take captive every thought to make it obedient to Christ. 6 And we will be ready to punish every act of disobedience, once your obedience is complete.

> *"In life, if you have a purpose in which you can believe, there's no end to the amount of things you can accomplish."*
> —MARIAN ANDERSON, OPERA SINGER

7 You are looking only on the surface of things.[a][s] If anyone is confident that he belongs to Christ,[t] he should consider again that we belong to Christ just as much as he. 8 For even if I boast somewhat freely about the authority the Lord gave us for building you up rather than pulling you down,[u] I will not be ashamed of it. 9 I do not want to seem to be trying to frighten you with my letters. 10 For some say, "His letters are weighty and forceful, but in person he is unimpressive[v] and his speaking amounts to nothing."[w] 11 Such people should realize that what we are in our letters when we are absent, we will be in our actions when we are present.

12 We do not dare to classify or compare ourselves with some who commend themselves. When they measure themselves by themselves and compare themselves with themselves, they are not wise. 13 We, however, will not boast beyond proper limits, but will confine our boasting to the field God has assigned to us,[x] a field that reaches even to you. 14 We are not going too far in our boasting, as would be the case if we had not come to you, for we did get as far as you with the gospel of Christ. 15 Neither do we go beyond our limits by boasting of work done by others.[b][y] Our hope is that, as your faith continues to grow, our area of activity among you will greatly expand, 16 so that we can preach the gospel in the regions beyond you. For we do not want to boast about work already done in another man's territory. 17 But, "Let him who boasts boast in the Lord."[c][z] 18 For it is not the one who commends himself who is approved, but the one whom the Lord commends.[a]

## Paul and the False Apostles

**11** I hope you will put up with a little of my foolishness;[b] but you are already doing that. 2 I am jealous for you with a godly jealousy. I promised you to one husband,[c] to Christ, so that I might present you as a pure virgin to him. 3 But I am afraid that just as Eve was deceived by the serpent's cunning,[d] your minds may somehow be led astray from your sincere and pure devotion to Christ. 4 For if someone comes to you and preaches a Jesus other than the Jesus we preached, or if you receive a different spirit from the one you received, or a different gospel[e] from the one you accepted, you put up with it easily enough. 5 But I do not think I am in the least inferior to those "super-apostles." 6 I may not be a trained speaker,[f] but I do have knowledge.[g] We have made this perfectly clear to you in every way.

7 Was it a sin for me to lower myself in order to elevate you by preaching the gospel of God to you free of charge? 8 I robbed other

**10:13** x ver 15,16
**10:15** y Ro 15:20
**10:17** z Jer 9:24; 1Co 1:31
**10:18** a Ro 2:29
**11:1** b 2Co 5:13
**11:2** c Hos 2:19
**11:3** d Ge 3:1–6,13
**11:4** e Gal 1:6–9
**11:6** f 1Co 1:17 g Eph 3:4

[a]7 Or *Look at the obvious facts* [b]13–15 Or 13 *We, however, will not boast about things that cannot be measured, but we will boast according to the standard of measurement that the God of measure has assigned us—a measurement that relates even to you.* 14 *. . .* 15 *Neither do we boast about things that cannot be measured in regard to the work done by others.*
[c]17 Jer. 9:24

**11:10** h Ro 9:1 i 1Co 9:15
**11:13** j 2Pe 2:1 k Rev 2:2
**11:15** l Php 3:19
**11:17** m 1Co 7:12,25
**11:19** n 1Co 4:10
**11:22** o Ro 9:4
**11:23** p 1Co 15:10
**11:24** q Dt 25:3
**11:25** r Ac 16:22 s Ac 14:19

churches by receiving support from them so as to serve you. 9And when I was with you and needed something, I was not a burden to anyone, for the brothers who came from Macedonia supplied what I needed. I have kept myself from being a burden to you in any way, and will continue to do so. 10As surely as the truth of Christ is in me,[h] nobody in the regions of Achaia will stop this boasting[i] of mine. 11Why? Because I do not love you? God knows I do! 12And I will keep on doing what I am doing in order to cut the ground from under those who want an opportunity to be considered equal with us in the things they boast about.

13For such men are false apostles,[j] deceitful workmen, masquerading as apostles of Christ.[k] 14And no wonder, for Satan himself masquerades as an angel of light. 15It is not surprising, then, if his servants masquerade as servants of righteousness. Their end will be what their actions deserve.[l]

## Paul Boasts About His Sufferings

16I repeat: Let no one take me for a fool. But if you do, then receive me just as you would a fool, so that I may do a little boasting. 17In this self-confident boasting I am not talking as the Lord would,[m] but as a fool. 18Since many are boasting in the way the world does, I too will boast. 19You gladly put up with fools since you are so wise![n] 20In fact, you even put up with anyone who enslaves you or exploits you or takes advantage of you or pushes himself forward or slaps you in the face. 21To my shame I admit that we were too weak for that!

What anyone else dares to boast about—I am speaking as a fool—I also dare to boast about. 22Are they Hebrews? So am I. Are they Israelites? So am I.[o] Are they Abraham's descendants? So am I. 23Are they servants of Christ? (I am out of my mind to talk like this.) I am more. I have worked much harder,[p] been in prison more frequently, been flogged more severely, and been exposed to death again and again. 24Five times I received from the Jews the forty lashes[q] minus one. 25Three times I was beaten with rods,[r] once I was stoned,[s] three times I was shipwrecked, I spent a night and a day in the open sea, 26I have been constantly on the move. I have been in danger from rivers, in danger from bandits, in danger from my own countrymen, in danger from Gentiles; in danger in the city,[t] in danger in the country, in danger at sea; and in danger from false brothers. 27I have labored and toiled and have often gone without sleep; I have known hunger and thirst and have often gone without food;[u] I have been cold and naked. 28Besides everything else, I face daily the pressure of my concern for all the churches. 29Who is weak, and I do not feel weak? Who is led into sin, and I do not inwardly burn?

30If I must boast, I will boast of the things that show my weakness.[v] 31The God and Father of the Lord Jesus, who is to be praised forever, knows that I am not lying. 32In Damascus the governor under King Aretas had the city of the Damascenes guarded in order to arrest me.[w] 33But I was lowered in a basket from a window in the wall and slipped through his hands.

## Paul's Vision and His Thorn

**12** I must go on boasting. Although there is nothing to be gained, I will go on to visions and revelations from the Lord. 2I know a man in Christ who fourteen years ago was caught up to the third heaven.[x] Whether it was in the body or out of the body I do not know—God knows. 3And I know that this man—whether in the body or apart from the body I do not know, but God knows— 4was caught up to paradise.[y] He heard inexpressible things, things that man is not permitted to tell. 5I will boast about a man like that, but I will not boast about myself, except about my weaknesses. 6Even if I should choose to boast, I would not be a fool,[z] because I would be speaking the truth. But I refrain, so no one will think more of me than is warranted by what I do or say.

7To keep me from becoming conceited because of these surpassingly great revelations, there was given me a thorn in my flesh, a messenger of Satan, to torment me. 8Three times I pleaded with the Lord to take it away from me.[a] 9But he said to me, "My grace is sufficient for you, for my power[b] is made perfect in weakness." Therefore I will boast all the more gladly about my

**11:26** t Ac 21:31
**11:27** u 1Co 4:11,12
**11:30** v 1Co 2:3
**11:32** w Ac 9:24
**12:2** x Eph 4:10
**12:4** y Lk 23:43; Rev 2:7
**12:6** z 2Co 11:16
**12:8** a Mt 26:39,44
**12:9** b Php 4:13

weaknesses, so that Christ's power may
rest on me. [10]That is why, for Christ's sake,
I delight in weaknesses, in insults, in hard-
ships,[c] in persecutions, in difficulties. For
when I am weak, then I am strong.

## Paul's Concern for the Corinthians

[11]I have made a fool of myself, but
you drove me to it. I ought to have been
commended by you, for I am not in the
least inferior to the "super-apostles,"[d] even
though I am nothing. [12]The things that
mark an apostle—signs, wonders and mir-
acles—were done among you with great
perseverance. [13]How were you inferior to
the other churches, except that I was never a
burden to you?[e] Forgive me this wrong![f]
[14]Now I am ready to visit you for the third
time,[g] and I will not be a burden to you, be-
cause what I want is not your possessions
but you. After all, children should not have
to save up for their parents,[h] but parents for
their children. [15]So I will very gladly spend
for you everything I have and expend myself
as well.[i] If I love you more, will you love me
less? [16]Be that as it may, I have not been a
burden to you. Yet, crafty fellow that I am,
I caught you by trickery! [17]Did I exploit you
through any of the men I sent you? [18]I urged[j]
Titus to go to you and I sent our brother[k]
with him. Titus did not exploit you, did he?
Did we not act in the same spirit and follow
the same course?
[19]Have you been thinking all along that
we have been defending ourselves to you?
We have been speaking in the sight of God[l]
as those in Christ; and everything we do,
dear friends, is for your strengthening. [20]For
I am afraid that when I come I may not find
you as I want you to be, and you may not find
me as you want me to be. I fear that there
may be quarreling,[m] jealousy, outbursts of
anger, factions, slander, gossip, arrogance
and disorder. [21]I am afraid that when I come
again my God will humble me before you,
and I will be grieved over many who have
sinned earlier[n] and have not repented of
the impurity, sexual sin and debauchery in
which they have indulged.

## Final Warnings

13 This will be my third visit to you.[o]
"Every matter must be estab-
lished by the testimony of two or three
witnesses."[ap] [2]I already gave you a warning
when I was with you the second time. I now
repeat it while absent: On my return I will
not spare[q] those who sinned earlier or any
of the others, [3]since you are demanding
proof that Christ is speaking through me.[r]
He is not weak in dealing with you, but is
powerful among you. [4]For to be sure, he was
crucified in weakness,[s] yet he lives by God's
power.[t] Likewise, we are weak in him, yet by
God's power we will live with him to serve
you.
[5]Examine yourselves[u] to see whether you
are in the faith; test yourselves. Do you not
realize that Christ Jesus is in you—unless,
of course, you fail the test? [6]And I trust that
you will discover that we have not failed the
test. [7]Now we pray to God that you will not
do anything wrong. Not that people will see
that we have stood the test but that you will
do what is right even though we may seem
to have failed. [8]For we cannot do anything
against the truth, but only for the truth. [9]We
are glad whenever we are weak but you are
strong; and our prayer is for your perfec-
tion. [10]This is why I write these things when
I am absent, that when I come I may not
have to be harsh in my use of authority—
the authority the Lord gave me for building
you up, not for tearing you down.[v]

## Final Greetings

[11]Finally, brothers, good-by. Aim for per-
fection, listen to my appeal, be of one mind,
live in peace. And the God of love and peace[w]
will be with you.
[12]Greet one another with a holy kiss.[x]
[13]All the saints send their greetings.[y]
[14]May the grace of the Lord Jesus Christ,
and the love of God, and the fellowship of
the Holy Spirit[z] be with you all.

**12:10** c 2Co 6:4
**12:11** d 2Co 11:5
**12:13** e 1Co 9:12,18 f 2Co 11:7
**12:14** g 2Co 13:1 h 1Co 4:14,15
**12:15** i Php 2:17
**12:18** j 2Co 8:6,16 k 2Co 8:18
**12:19** l Ro 9:1
**12:20** m 1Co 1:11
**12:21** n 2Co 13:2
**13:1** o 2Co 12:14 p Mt 18:16
**13:2** q 2Co 1:23
**13:3** r Mt 10:20; 1Co 5:4
**13:4** s Php 2:7,8; 1Pe 3:18 t Ro 1:4; 6:4
**13:5** u 1Co 11:28
**13:10** v 2Co 10:8
**13:11** w Ro 15:33; Eph 6:23
**13:12** x Ro 16:16
**13:13** y Php 4:22
**13:14** z Php 2:1

[a]1 Deut. 19:15

# Galatians

## OVERVIEW

Paul wrote this letter to the churches he founded in the Roman province of Galatia. Because many of the new Christians had been influenced by Judaizers, who taught that Christians needed to believe in Christ *and* follow Jewish customs, Paul wrote this letter to set the record straight: Salvation comes through faith in Christ alone.

Some of the notions set forth by the Judaizers are still in place today. If you ask people on the street how to get to heaven, most will exclaim, "Be a good person and do good!" Believers should know that we are not justified by good works; we are saved from sin through our belief in Jesus. Our faith in Christ alone makes us right with God. In response to God's gift of grace through Christ, we serve others through good works.

Women can often get caught up in doing good and pleasing others. We must first make sure we have accepted Christ and are relying on him for justification; then we can live out our lives faithfully serving others because of what he has done for us. Allow the words in the book of Galatians to guide you to live according to God's Spirit.

## OUTLINE

I. Greeting and Denunciation (1:1–10)
II. Paul's Authentic Gospel (1:11—2:21)
III. Justification by Faith (3:1—4:31)
IV. Christian Behavior Under Grace (5:1—6:18)

### SCANNABLE FACTS:

**Author:** Paul

**Time Written:** Around A.D. 50

**Theme to Note:** Believers are justified by faith in Christ alone

**Notable Women:** The slave woman (Hagar) and the free woman (Sarah)

1:1 a Ac 2:24
1:2 b Php 4:21 c 1Co 16:1
1:4 d Mt 20:28; Ro 4:25
1:7 e Ac 15:24
1:8 f Ro 9:3
1:10 g Ro 2:29; 1Th 2:4
1:11 h 1Co 15:1

1 Paul, an apostle—sent not from men nor by man, but by Jesus Christ and God the Father, who raised him from the dead[a]— [2]and all the brothers with me,[b]

To the churches in Galatia:[c]

[3]Grace and peace to you from God our Father and the Lord Jesus Christ, [4]who gave himself for our sins[d] to rescue us from the present evil age, according to the will of our God and Father, [5]to whom be glory for ever and ever. Amen.

## No Other Gospel

[6]I am astonished that you are so quickly deserting the one who called you by the grace of Christ and are turning to a different gospel— [7]which is really no gospel at all. Evidently some people are throwing you into confusion[e] and are trying to pervert the gospel of Christ. [8]But even if we or an angel from heaven should preach a gospel other than the one we preached to you, let him be eternally condemned![f] [9]As we have already said, so now I say again: If anybody is preaching to you a gospel other than what you accepted, let him be eternally condemned!

[10]Am I now trying to win the approval of men, or of God? Or am I trying to please men?[g] If I were still trying to please men, I would not be a servant of Christ.

## Paul Called by God

[11]I want you to know, brothers,[h] that the gospel I preached is not something that man made up. [12]I did not receive it from any man, nor was I taught it; rather, I received it by revelation from Jesus Christ.

[13]For you have heard of my previous way of life in Judaism, how intensely I persecuted the church of God and tried to destroy it.[i] [14]I was advancing in Judaism beyond many Jews of my own age and was extremely zealous for the traditions of my fathers.[j] [15]But when God, who set me apart from birth[a][k] and called me by his grace, was pleased [16]to reveal his Son in me so that I might preach him among the Gentiles, I did not consult any man,[l] [17]nor did I go up to Jerusalem to see those who were apostles before I was, but I went immediately into Arabia and later returned to Damascus.

[18]Then after three years, I went up to Jerusalem[m] to get acquainted with Peter[b] and stayed with him fifteen days. [19]I saw none of

1:13 i Ac 8:3
1:14 j Mt 15:2
1:15 k Isa 49:1,5
1:16 l Mt 16:17
1:18 m Ac 9:26,27

*My God,*

*thank you for creating me with a purpose, and grant me the desire and resolve to fulfill that purpose. To that end, I surrender myself to you. I acknowledge that the road ahead will be difficult, but you alone know the godly desires of my heart and can enable me to see them fulfilled in my life. Continue, I pray, to lead and guide me, and I'll give all the glory to you. In Jesus' name,*

*Amen.*

GALATIANS 1:15–24

[a]15 Or *from my mother's womb* [b]18 Greek *Cephas*

## *The African Presence*

### Galatians 1:17

Paul mentioned Arabia as the place where he spent time after visiting Jerusalem and before returning to Damascus. He also referred to Arabia as the location of Mount Sinai (see Gal 4:25). Arabia is located south of the land of Israel, between Africa and the Persian Gulf.

the other apostles—only James, the Lord's brother. 20 I assure you before God that what I am writing you is no lie.[n] 21 Later I went to Syria and Cilicia. 22 I was personally unknown to the churches of Judea[o] that are in Christ. 23 They only heard the report: "The man who formerly persecuted us is now preaching the faith he once tried to destroy." 24 And they praised God because of me.

## Paul Accepted by the Apostles

2 Fourteen years later I went up again to Jerusalem,[p] this time with Barnabas. I took Titus along also. 2 I went in response to a revelation and set before them the gospel that I preach among the Gentiles. But I did this privately to those who seemed to be leaders, for fear that I was running or had run my race[q] in vain. 3 Yet not even Titus, who was with me, was compelled to be circumcised, even though he was a Greek.[r] 4 ⌞This matter arose⌟ because some false brothers[s] had infiltrated our ranks to spy on the freedom[t] we have in Christ Jesus and to make us slaves. 5 We did not give in to them for a moment, so that the truth of the gospel[u] might remain with you.

6 As for those who seemed to be important[v]—whatever they were makes no difference to me; God does not judge by external appearance[w]—those men added nothing to my message. 7 On the contrary, they saw that I had been entrusted with the task[x] of preaching the gospel to the Gentiles,[a] just as Peter had been to the Jews.[b] 8 For God, who was at work in the ministry of Peter as an apostle to the Jews, was also at work in my ministry as an apostle to the Gentiles. 9 James, Peter[c] and John, those reputed to be pillars, gave me and Barnabas the right hand of fellowship when they recognized the grace given to me.[y] They agreed that we should go to the Gentiles, and they to the Jews. 10 All they asked was that we should continue to remember the poor,[z] the very thing I was eager to do.

## Paul Opposes Peter

11 When Peter came to Antioch, I opposed him to his face, because he was clearly in the wrong. 12 Before certain men came from James, he used to eat with the Gentiles.[a] But when they arrived, he began to draw back and separate himself from the Gentiles because he was afraid of those who belonged to the circumcision group. 13 The other Jews joined him in his hypocrisy, so that by their hypocrisy even Barnabas was led astray.

14 When I saw that they were not acting in line with the truth of the gospel,[b] I said to Peter in front of them all, "You are a Jew, yet you live like a Gentile and not like a Jew. How is it, then, that you force Gentiles to follow Jewish customs?

15 "We who are Jews by birth and not 'Gentile sinners' 16 know that a man is not justified by observing the law, but by faith in Jesus Christ.[c] So we, too, have put our faith in Christ Jesus that we may be justified by faith in Christ and not by observing the law, because by observing the law no one will be justified.

17 "If, while we seek to be justified in Christ, it becomes evident that we ourselves are sinners, does that mean that Christ promotes sin? Absolutely not! 18 If I rebuild what I destroyed, I prove that I am a lawbreaker. 19 For through the law I died to the law so that I might live for God.[d] 20 I have been crucified with Christ and I no longer live, but Christ lives in me. The life I live in the body, I live by faith in the Son of God, who loved me and gave himself for me. 21 I do not set aside the grace of God, for if righteousness could be gained through the law, Christ died for nothing!"[d]

## Faith or Observance of the Law

3 You foolish Galatians! Who has bewitched you?[e] Before your very eyes Jesus Christ was clearly portrayed as crucified. 2 I would like to learn just one thing from you: Did you receive the Spirit by observing the law, or by believing what you heard?[f] 3 Are you so foolish? After beginning with the Spirit, are you now trying to attain your goal by human effort? 4 Have you suffered so much for nothing—if it really was for nothing? 5 Does God give you his Spirit and work miracles among you because you

**1:20** n Ro 9:1
**1:22** o 1Th 2:14
**2:1** p Ac 15:2
**2:2** q Php 2:16
**2:3** r Ac 16:3
**2:4** s 2Co 11:26 t Ac 15:1
**2:5** u ver 14
**2:6** v Gal 6:3 w Ac 10:34
**2:7** x 1Th 2:4
**2:9** y Ro 12:3
**2:10** z Ac 24:17
**2:12** a Ac 11:3
**2:14** b ver 5
**2:16** c Ac 13:39; Ro 9:30
**2:19** d 2Co 5:15
**3:1** e Gal 5:7
**3:2** f Ro 10:17

[a]7 Greek *uncircumcised* [b]7 Greek *circumcised*; also in verses 8 and 9 [c]9 Greek *Cephas*; also in verses 11 and 14
[d]21 Some interpreters end the quotation after verse 14.

3:6 g Ge 15:6; Ro 4:3
3:8 h Ge 12:3
3:10 i Dt 27:26
3:11 j Hab 2:4; Gal 2:16; Heb 10:38
3:12 k Lev 18:5; Ro 10:5
3:13 l Dt 21:23
3:14 m Ro 4:9,16 n Ac 2:33
3:17 o Ex 12:40
3:18 p Ro 4:14

observe the law, or because you believe what you heard?

[6]Consider Abraham: "He believed God, and it was credited to him as righteousness."[a][g] [7]Understand, then, that those who believe are children of Abraham. [8]The Scripture foresaw that God would justify the Gentiles by faith, and announced the gospel in advance to Abraham: "All nations will be blessed through you."[b][h] [9]So those who have faith are blessed along with Abraham, the man of faith.

[10]All who rely on observing the law are under a curse, for it is written: "Cursed is everyone who does not continue to do everything written in the Book of the Law."[c][i] [11]Clearly no one is justified before God by the law, because, "The righteous will live by faith."[d][j] [12]The law is not based on faith; on the contrary, "The man who does these things will live by them."[e][k] [13]Christ redeemed us from the curse of the law by becoming a curse for us, for it is written: "Cursed is everyone who is hung on a tree."[f][l] [14]He redeemed us in order that the blessing given to Abraham might come to the Gentiles through Christ Jesus,[m] so that by faith we might receive the promise of the Spirit.[n]

## The Law and the Promise

[15]Brothers, let me take an example from everyday life. Just as no one can set aside or add to a human covenant that has been duly established, so it is in this case. [16]The promises were spoken to Abraham and to his seed. The Scripture does not say "and to seeds," meaning many people, but "and to your seed,"[g] meaning one person, who is Christ. [17]What I mean is this: The law, introduced 430 years[o] later, does not set aside the covenant previously established by God and thus do away with the promise. [18]For if the inheritance depends on the law, then it no longer depends on a promise;[p] but God in his grace gave it to Abraham through a promise.

[19]What, then, was the purpose of the law? It was added because of transgressions until the Seed to whom the promise referred had come. The law was put into effect through angels[q] by a mediator. [20]A mediator,[r] however, does not represent just one party; but God is one.

[21]Is the law, therefore, opposed to the promises of God? Absolutely not! For if a law had been given that could impart life, then righteousness would certainly have come by the law. [22]But the Scripture declares that the whole world is a prisoner of sin,[s] so that what was promised, being given through faith in Jesus Christ, might be given to those who believe.

[23]Before this faith came, we were held prisoners by the law, locked up until faith should be revealed. [24]So the law was put in charge to lead us to Christ[h] that we might be justified by faith. [25]Now that faith has come, we are no longer under the supervision of the law.

## Sons of God

[26]You are all sons of God[t] through faith in Christ Jesus, [27]for all of you who were baptized into Christ[u] have clothed yourselves with Christ.[v] [28]There is neither Jew nor Greek, slave nor free, male nor female, for you are all one in Christ Jesus.[w] [29]If you belong to Christ, then you are Abraham's seed, and heirs according to the promise.

*My darling daughter,*

*You are my heir.*

*Live every day in that knowledge.*

*All my love,*
*Your Doting Father*

GALATIANS 3:26–29

**4** What I am saying is that as long as the heir is a child, he is no different from a slave, although he owns the whole estate. [2]He is subject to guardians and trustees until the time set by his father. [3]So also, when we were children, we were in slavery under the basic principles of the world.[x] [4]But when

3:19 q Ac 7:53
3:20 r Heb 8:6
3:22 s Ro 11:32
3:26 t Ro 8:14
3:27 u Ro 6:3 v Ro 13:14
3:28 w Eph 2:14,15
4:3 x Col 2:8,20

[a]6 Gen. 15:6 [b]8 Gen. 12:3; 18:18; 22:18 [c]10 Deut. 27:26 [d]11 Hab. 2:4 [e]12 Lev. 18:5 [f]13 Deut. 21:23
[g]16 Gen. 12:7; 13:15; 24:7 [h]24 Or *charge until Christ came*

**4:4** y Lk 2:27
**4:5** z Jn 1:12
**4:6** a Ro 5:5
**4:7** b Ro 8:17
**4:8** c Eph 2:12; 1Th 4:5
**4:9** d 1Co 8:3; e Col 2:20
**4:10** f Ro 14:5
**4:11** g 1Th 3:5
**4:13** h 1Co 2:3

the time had fully come, God sent his Son, born of a woman, born under law,[y] 5 to redeem those under law, that we might receive the full rights[z] of sons. 6 Because you are sons, God sent the Spirit of his Son into our hearts,[a] the Spirit who calls out, *"Abba,*[a] Father." 7 So you are no longer a slave, but a son; and since you are a son, God has made you also an heir.[b]

## Paul's Concern for the Galatians

8 Formerly, when you did not know God,[c] you were slaves to those who by nature are not gods. 9 But now that you know God—or rather are known by God[d]—how is it that you are turning back to those weak and miserable principles? Do you wish to be enslaved by them all over again?[e] 10 You are observing special days and months and seasons and years![f] 11 I fear for you, that somehow I have wasted my efforts on you.[g]

12 I plead with you, brothers, become like me, for I became like you. You have done me no wrong. 13 As you know, it was because of an illness[h] that I first preached the gospel to you. 14 Even though my illness was a trial to you, you did not treat me with contempt or scorn. Instead, you welcomed me as if I were an angel of God, as if I were Christ Jesus himself. 15 What has happened to all your joy? I can testify that, if you could have done so, you would have torn out your eyes and given them to me. 16 Have I now become your enemy by telling you the truth?

17 Those people are zealous to win you over, but for no good. What they want is to alienate you ⌞from us⌟, so that you may be zealous for them. 18 It is fine to be zealous, provided the purpose is good, and to be so always and not just when I am with you. 19 My dear children,[i] for whom I am again in the pains of childbirth until Christ is formed in you,[j] 20 how I wish I could be with you now and change my tone, because I am perplexed about you!

## Hagar and Sarah

21 Tell me, you who want to be under the law, are you not aware of what the law says? 22 For it is written that Abraham had two sons, one by the slave woman and the other by the free woman.[k] 23 His son by the slave woman was born in the ordinary way;[l] but his son by the free woman was born as the result of a promise.[m]

24 These things may be taken figuratively, for the women represent two covenants. One covenant is from Mount Sinai and bears children who are to be slaves: This is Hagar. 25 Now Hagar stands for Mount Sinai in Arabia and corresponds to the present city of Jerusalem, because she is in slavery with her children. 26 But the Jerusalem that is above[n] is free, and she is our mother. 27 For it is written:

"Be glad, O barren woman,
who bears no children;
break forth and cry aloud,
you who have no labor pains;
because more are the children of the
desolate woman
than of her who has a husband."[b][o]

28 Now you, brothers, like Isaac, are children of promise. 29 At that time the son born in the ordinary way persecuted the son born

**4:19** i 1Co 4:15; j Eph 4:13
**4:22** k Ge 21:2
**4:23** l Ro 9:7,8; m Heb 11:11
**4:26** n Heb 12:22
**4:27** o Isa 54:1

[a]6 Aramaic for *Father* [b]27 Isaiah 54:1

## The African Presence

**Galatians 4:25**

Paul earlier mentioned Arabia as the place where he spent time after visiting Jerusalem and before returning to Damascus (Gal 1:17). Here he refers to Arabia as the location of Mount Sinai. Arabia is located south of the land of Israel, between Africa and the Persian Gulf.

by the power of the Spirit.[p] It is the same now. [30]But what does the Scripture say? "Get rid of the slave woman and her son, for the slave woman's son will never share in the inheritance with the free woman's son."[a][q] [31]Therefore, brothers, we are not children of the slave woman, but of the free woman.

## Freedom in Christ

**5** It is for freedom that Christ has set us free. Stand firm, then, and do not let yourselves be burdened again by a yoke of slavery.

[2]Mark my words! I, Paul, tell you that if you let yourselves be circumcised,[r] Christ will be of no value to you at all. [3]Again I declare to every man who lets himself be circumcised that he is obligated to obey the whole law.[s] [4]You who are trying to be justified by law have been alienated from Christ; you have fallen away from grace.[t] [5]But by faith we eagerly await through the Spirit the righteousness for which we hope.[u] [6]For in Christ Jesus neither circumcision nor uncircumcision has any value. The only thing that counts is faith expressing itself through love.

[7]You were running a good race. Who cut in on you and kept you from obeying the truth? [8]That kind of persuasion does not come from the one who calls you. [9]"A little yeast works through the whole batch of dough."[v] [10]I am confident[w] in the Lord that you will take no other view. The one who is throwing you into confusion[x] will pay the penalty, whoever he may be. [11]Brothers, if I am still preaching circumcision, why am I still being persecuted?[y] In that case the offense of the cross has been abolished. [12]As for those agitators, I wish they would go the whole way and emasculate themselves!

[13]You, my brothers, were called to be free. But do not use your freedom to indulge the sinful nature[b];[z] rather, serve one another[a] in love. [14]The entire law is summed up in a single command: "Love your neighbor as yourself."[c] [15]If you keep on biting and devouring each other, watch out or you will be destroyed by each other.

## Life by the Spirit

[16]So I say, live by the Spirit, and you will not gratify the desires of the sinful nature. [17]For the sinful nature desires what is contrary to the Spirit, and the Spirit what is contrary to the sinful nature. They are in conflict with each other, so that you do not do what you want.[b] [18]But if you are led by the Spirit, you are not under law.

[19]The acts of the sinful nature are obvious: sexual immorality, impurity and debauchery; [20]idolatry and witchcraft; hatred, discord, jealousy, fits of rage, selfish ambition, dissensions, factions [21]and envy; drunkenness, orgies, and the like. I warn you, as I did before, that those who live like this will not inherit the kingdom of God.

[22]But the fruit[c] of the Spirit is love,[d] joy, peace, patience, kindness, goodness, faithfulness, [23]gentleness and self-control. Against such things there is no law. [24]Those who belong to Christ Jesus have crucified the sinful nature[e] with its passions and desires. [25]Since we live by the Spirit, let us keep in step with the Spirit. [26]Let us not become conceited,[f] provoking and envying each other.

## Doing Good to All

**6** Brothers, if someone is caught in a sin, you who are spiritual[g] should restore him gently. But watch yourself, or you also may be tempted. [2]Carry each other's burdens, and in this way you will fulfill the law of Christ. [3]If anyone thinks he is something[h] when he is nothing, he deceives himself. [4]Each one should test his own actions. Then he can take pride in himself, without comparing himself to somebody else, [5]for each one should carry his own load.

[6]Anyone who receives instruction in the word must share all good things with his instructor.[i]

[7]Do not be deceived:[j] God cannot be mocked. A man reaps what he sows. [8]The one who sows to please his sinful nature, from that nature[d] will reap destruction;[k] the one who sows to please the Spirit, from the Spirit will reap eternal life. [9]Let us not be-

**4:29** p Ge 21:9
**4:30** q Ge 21:10
**5:2** r Ac 15:1
**5:3** s Gal 3:10
**5:4** t Heb 12:15
**5:5** u Ro 8:23,24
**5:9** v 1Co 5:6
**5:10** w 2Co 2:3; x Gal 1:7
**5:11** y Gal 6:12
**5:13** z 1Co 8:9; 1Pe 2:16; a 1Co 9:19
**5:17** b Ro 7:15–23
**5:22** c Eph 5:9; d Col 3:12–15
**5:24** e Ro 6:6
**5:26** f Php 2:3
**6:1** g 1Co 2:15
**6:3** h Ro 12:3
**6:6** i 1Co 9:11,14
**6:7** j 1Co 6:9
**6:8** k Job 4:8

[a]30 Gen. 21:10 [b]13 Or *the flesh*; also in verses 16, 17, 19 and 24 [c]14 Lev. 19:18 [d]8 Or *his flesh, from the flesh*

6:9
l 1Co 15:58
6:10
m Eph 2:19

come weary in doing good,[l] for at the proper
time we will reap a harvest if we do not give
up. 10 Therefore, as we have opportunity, let
us do good to all people, especially to those
who belong to the family[m] of believers.

## Not Circumcision but a New Creation

11 See what large letters I use as I write to
you with my own hand!
12 Those who want to make a good impres-

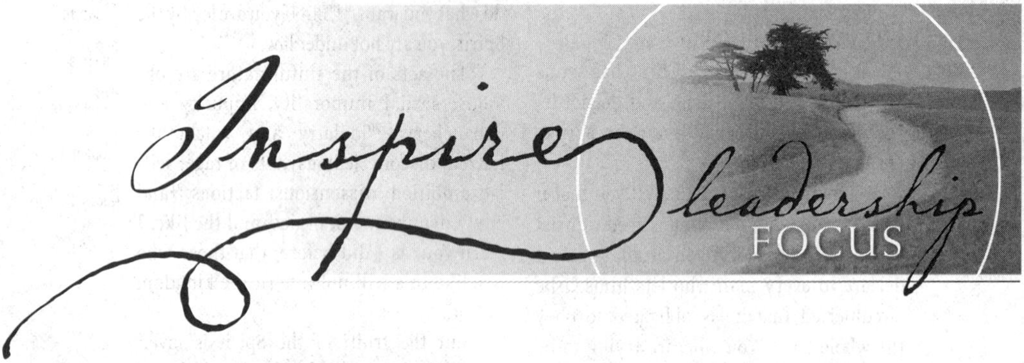


## DISCIPLINE

**Have you ever seen an overweight runner win a marathon or a flabby boxer outlast her opponent? The thought is almost absurd that any athlete without a lean, muscle-strapped body could compete successfully.**

Interesting, isn't it, that the apostle Paul, when describing the benefits of discipline, chose athletes as examples—specifically, a runner and a fighter (see 1Co 9:24–27). Both sports demand the discipline of rigorous daily exercise along with well-balanced diets.

Daily exercise . . . well-balanced diets. Today's grab-as-you-dash lifestyles render the area of physical health as perhaps the most challenging in our lives as women, and especially as leaders, when there are so many people depending on us. Yet, if we are to model the gospel so that it is attractive to those whom we are trying to win to Christ, we have no choice but to examine how well we take care of our physical selves.

The word *discipline* comes from the root of the word *disciple.* At the core of its meaning is self-control. A disciple is one who exercises self-control, a fruit of the Spirit (see Gal 5:22–23).

Being healthy and feeling vibrant, energetic and attractive may allow us to live longer and serve God more effectively. And it gives us the added benefit of feeling well. That's what discipline is all about!

Taking the time to be fit and eating to be lean for life are daily goals for every prize-winner. However, those are not the only areas of our lives into which we, as leaders, should bring discipline. To be spiritually fit means that we must have the discipline to set aside time every day to exercise spiritually. By studying the Word, praying and meditating, we will become spiritually healthy, spiritually strong women.

Enjoy the fruit that blossoms from the disciplined life.

—L. Tolbert

### read

Galatians 5:16; Philippians 3:12–21.

**See also the Inspire Notes "Spiritual Discipline," "Integrity," "Write it Down!" "Self-Control," "Be Focused" and "Character."**

### WOMAN of COLOR

Take a brisk walk today for at least 10 minutes. If need be, decide on a nutritious diet plan to shed extra pounds. And be sure that you also make time to read, study, meditate and pray.

For the next Inspire note, go to page 1393.

sion outwardly are trying to compel you to be circumcised. The only reason they do this is to avoid being persecuted[n] for the cross of Christ. 13 Not even those who are circumcised obey the law, yet they want you to be circumcised that they may boast about your flesh. 14 May I never boast except in the cross of our Lord Jesus Christ, through which[a] the world has been crucified to me, and I to the world.[o] 15 Neither circumcision nor uncircumcision means anything; what counts is a new creation.[p] 16 Peace and mercy to all who follow this rule, even to the Israel of God.

17 Finally, let no one cause me trouble, for I bear on my body the marks of Jesus.

18 The grace of our Lord Jesus Christ be with your spirit, brothers. Amen.

**6:12** n Gal 5:11
**6:14** o Ro 6:2,6
**6:15** p 2Co 5:17

[a] 14 Or *whom*

# Ephesians

## OVERVIEW

The book of Ephesians was written by Paul to believers living in and around Ephesus. At the time Paul wrote this letter, Ephesus was an important trading post, a city famous for its wealth, commerce and religion.

This letter focuses on God's marvelous plans for his church and for every member of it, and it emphasizes the fact that a spirit of unity is essential for the body of Christ. With Jesus as the Head of the church, all believers should submit to one another in marriage, family and work relationships. On the spiritual battlefields, women who follow Christ should be adequately prepared by putting on the full armor of God (see Eph 6:10–18).

As you read Ephesians, focus on the practical advice Paul gave to help Christians serve as a light in a world of darkness.

## OUTLINE

I. Praise for Spiritual Blessings (1:1—2:10)
II. Praise for Oneness of Christ's Body (2:11—4:16)
III. Acceptable Behavior for the Body of Christ (4:17—6:24)

### SCANNABLE FACTS:

**Author:** Paul

**Time Written:** Around A.D. 60

**Theme to Note:** Make every effort to keep unity in the church

**Notable Women:** Wives, in relation to their husbands

**1:1** a 2Co 1:1
**1:3** b 2Co 1:3
**1:5** c Ro 8:29,30
**1:6** d Mt 3:17
**1:9** e Ro 16:25
**1:11** f Eph 3:11

1 Paul, an apostle of Christ Jesus by the
will of God,[a]

To the saints in Ephesus,[a] the faithful[b] in
Christ Jesus:

[2]Grace and peace to you from God our Fa-
ther and the Lord Jesus Christ.

## Spiritual Blessings in Christ

[3]Praise be to the God and Father of our
Lord Jesus Christ,[b] who has blessed us in
the heavenly realms with every spiritual
blessing in Christ. [4]For he chose us in him be-
fore the creation of the world to be holy and
blameless in his sight. In love [5]he[c] predes-
tined[c] us to be adopted as his sons through
Jesus Christ, in accordance with his plea-
sure and will— [6]to the praise of his glorious
grace, which he has freely given us in the
One he loves.[d] [7]In him we have redemption
through his blood, the forgiveness of sins,
in accordance with the riches of God's grace
[8]that he lavished on us with all wisdom and
understanding. [9]And he[d] made known to
us the mystery[e] of his will according to his
good pleasure, which he purposed in Christ,
[10]to be put into effect when the times will
have reached their fulfillment—to bring all
things in heaven and on earth together un-
der one head, even Christ.

[11]In him we were also chosen,[e] having
been predestined according to the plan of
him who works out everything in conformity
with the purpose[f] of his will, [12]in order that
we, who were the first to hope in Christ,
might be for the praise of his glory. [13]And
you also were included in Christ when you
heard the word of truth, the gospel of your
salvation. Having believed, you were
marked in him with a seal,[g] the promised
Holy Spirit, [14]who is a deposit guaranteeing
our inheritance until the redemption of
those who are God's possession—to the
praise of his glory.

## Thanksgiving and Prayer

[15]For this reason, ever since I heard about
your faith in the Lord Jesus and your love
for all the saints,[h] [16]I have not stopped giv-
ing thanks for you, remembering you in
my prayers. [17]I keep asking that the God of
our Lord Jesus Christ, the glorious Father,[i]
may give you the Spirit[f] of wisdom[j] and
revelation, so that you may know him bet-
ter. [18]I pray also that the eyes of your heart
may be enlightened in order that you may
know the hope to which he has called you,
the riches of his glorious inheritance in the

**1:13** g Eph 4:30
**1:15** h Col 1:4
**1:17** i Jn 20:17
j Col 1:9

*Believer,*

*I've given you resurrection power. How will you value and utilize so great a gift?*

*The Ultimate Giver*

EPHESIANS 1:18–21

[a]1 Some early manuscripts do not have *in Ephesus.* [b]1 Or *believers who are* [c]4,5 Or *sight in love.* [5]*He* [d]8,9 Or *us. With all wisdom and understanding,* [9]*he* [e]11 Or *were made heirs* [f]17 Or *a spirit*

## The African Presence

### Ephesians 1

While there are no specific references to the African presence within the book of Ephesians, the gospel preached by Paul was influenced by people of North Africa and the Middle East (a historical and cultural subregion of Africa-Eurasia, traditionally held to be countries or regions in Southwest Asia together with Egypt). However, during the time of the New Testament, racial identification did not have the significance that it has today.

saints, 19and his incomparably great power
for us who believe. That power is like the
working of his mighty strength, 20which he
exerted in Christ when he raised him from
the dead[k] and seated him at his right hand
in the heavenly realms, 21far above all rule
and authority, power and dominion, and
every title[l] that can be given, not only in
the present age but also in the one to come.
22And God placed all things under his feet
and appointed him to be head[m] over every-
thing for the church, 23which is his body,
the fullness of him who fills everything in
every way.

## Made Alive in Christ

2 As for you, you were dead in your trans-
gressions and sins,[n] 2in which you used
to live when you followed the ways of this
world and of the ruler of the kingdom of the
air,[o] the spirit who is now at work in those
who are disobedient.[p] 3All of us also lived
among them at one time, gratifying the crav-
ings of our sinful nature[a][q] and following its
desires and thoughts. Like the rest, we were
by nature objects of wrath. 4But because
of his great love for us, God, who is rich
in mercy, 5made us alive with Christ even
when we were dead in transgressions[r]—it
is by grace you have been saved. 6And God
raised us up with Christ and seated us with
him[s] in the heavenly realms in Christ Jesus,
7in order that in the coming ages he might
show the incomparable riches of his grace,
expressed in his kindness[t] to us in Christ
Jesus. 8For it is by grace you have been
saved, through faith—and this not from
yourselves, it is the gift of God— 9not by
works, so that no one can boast. 10For we are
God's workmanship, created in Christ Jesus
to do good works, which God prepared in ad-
vance for us to do.

## One in Christ

11Therefore, remember that formerly you
who are Gentiles by birth and called "uncir-
cumcised" by those who call themselves
"the circumcision" (that done in the body
by the hands of men)[u]— 12remember that
at that time you were separate from Christ,
excluded from citizenship in Israel and for-
eigners to the covenants of the promise,
without hope and without God in the world.
13But now in Christ Jesus you who once were
far away have been brought near[v] through
the blood of Christ.

14For he himself is our peace, who has
made the two one and has destroyed the
barrier, the dividing wall of hostility, 15by
abolishing in his flesh[w] the law with its com-
mandments and regulations. His purpose
was to create in himself one new man out
of the two, thus making peace, 16and in this
one body to reconcile both of them to God
through the cross, by which he put to death
their hostility. 17He came and preached
peace to you who were far away and peace
to those who were near.[x] 18For through him
we both have access to the Father by one
Spirit.[y]

19Consequently, you are no longer for-
eigners and aliens, but fellow citizens[z] with
God's people and members of God's house-
hold,[a] 20built on the foundation[b] of the apos-
tles and prophets, with Christ Jesus himself
as the chief cornerstone. 21In him the whole
building is joined together and rises to be-
come a holy temple[c] in the Lord. 22And in
him you too are being built together to be-
come a dwelling in which God lives by his
Spirit.

*God,*

*you know I feel alienated sometimes. Help me to release all my hurt feelings and fear. Help me to remember that no matter how others treat me, I belong to you and your family.*

*Amen*

EPHESIANS 2:19–22

## Paul the Preacher to the Gentiles

3 For this reason I, Paul, the prisoner[d]
of Christ Jesus for the sake of you Gen-
tiles—

2Surely you have heard about the admin-
istration of God's grace that was given to me

1:20 k Ac 2:24
1:21 l Php 2:9,10
1:22 m Eph 4:15
2:1 n Col 2:13
2:2 o Eph 6:12 p Eph 5:6
2:3 q Gal 5:16
2:5 r ver 1
2:6 s Eph 1:20
2:7 t Tit 3:4
2:11 u Col 2:11
2:13 v Ac 2:39
2:15 w Col 1:21,22
2:17 x Isa 57:19
2:18 y 1Co 12:13
2:19 z Php 3:20 a Gal 6:10
2:20 b Mt 16:18
2:21 c 1Co 3:16,17
3:1 d Ac 23:18

[a]3 Or *our flesh*

for you, 3that is, the mystery[e] made known
to me by revelation,[f] as I have already writ-
ten briefly. 4In reading this, then, you will
be able to understand my insight into the
mystery of Christ, 5which was not made
known to men in other generations as it has
now been revealed by the Spirit to God's
holy apostles and prophets.[g] 6This mys-
tery is that through the gospel the Gentiles
are heirs[h] together with Israel, members
together of one body, and sharers together
in the promise in Christ Jesus.

7I became a servant of this gospel by the
gift of God's grace given me through the
working of his power. 8Although I am less
than the least of all God's people,[i] this grace
was given me: to preach to the Gentiles the
unsearchable riches of Christ, 9and to make
plain to everyone the administration of
this mystery, which for ages past was kept
hidden in God, who created all things. 10His
intent was that now, through the church, the
manifold wisdom of God[j] should be made
known[k] to the rulers and authorities in the
heavenly realms, 11according to his eternal
purpose which he accomplished in Christ
Jesus our Lord. 12In him and through faith
in him we may approach God[l] with freedom
and confidence.[m] 13I ask you, therefore, not
to be discouraged because of my sufferings
for you, which are your glory.

## A Prayer for the Ephesians

14For this reason I kneel[n] before the Fa-
ther, 15from whom his whole family[a] in
heaven and on earth derives its name. 16I
pray that out of his glorious riches he may
strengthen you with power[o] through his
Spirit in your inner being,[p] 17so that Christ
may dwell in your hearts through faith. And
I pray that you, being rooted and established
in love, 18may have power, together with all
the saints, to grasp how wide and long and
high and deep is the love of Christ, 19and to
know this love that surpasses knowledge—
that you may be filled to the measure of all
the fullness of God.[q]

20Now to him who is able[r] to do immea-
surably more than all we ask or imagine, ac-
cording to his power that is at work within
us, 21to him be glory in the church and in
Christ Jesus throughout all generations, for
ever and ever! Amen.[s]

## Unity in the Body of Christ

4 As a prisoner for the Lord, then, I urge
you to live a life worthy[t] of the calling
you have received. 2Be completely humble
and gentle; be patient, bearing with one
another in love.[u] 3Make every effort to keep
the unity[v] of the Spirit through the bond of
peace. 4There is one body and one Spirit—
just as you were called to one hope when you
were called— 5one Lord, one faith, one bap-
tism; 6one God and Father of all, who is over
all and through all and in all.[w]

7But to each one of us grace has been
given as Christ apportioned it. 8This is why
it[b] says:

"When he ascended on high,
he led captives in his train
and gave gifts to men."[c][x]

9(What does "he ascended" mean except
that he also descended to the lower, earthly
regions[d]? 10He who descended is the very
one who ascended higher than all the heav-
ens, in order to fill the whole universe.) 11It
was he who gave some to be apostles,[y] some
to be prophets, some to be evangelists, and
some to be pastors and teachers, 12to pre-
pare God's people for works of service, so
that the body of Christ[z] may be built up 13un-
til we all reach unity in the faith and in the
knowledge of the Son of God and become
mature, attaining to the whole measure of
the fullness of Christ.

14Then we will no longer be infants,[a]
tossed back and forth by the waves, and
blown here and there by every wind of teach-
ing and by the cunning and craftiness of
men in their deceitful scheming. 15Instead,
speaking the truth in love, we will in all
things grow up into him who is the Head,[b]
that is, Christ. 16From him the whole body,
joined and held together by every support-
ing ligament, grows and builds itself up in
love, as each part does its work.

## Living as Children of Light

17So I tell you this, and insist on it in the
Lord, that you must no longer live as the

**3:3** e Ro 16:25 f 1Co 2:10
**3:5** g Ro 16:26
**3:6** h Gal 3:29
**3:8** i 1Co 15:9
**3:10** j 1Co 2:7 k 1Pe 1:12
**3:12** l Eph 2:18 m Heb 4:16
**3:14** n Php 2:10
**3:16** o Col 1:11 p Ro 7:22
**3:19** q Eph 1:23
**3:20** r Ro 16:25
**3:21** s Ro 11:36
**4:1** t Col 1:10
**4:2** u Eph 1:4
**4:3** v Col 3:14
**4:6** w Ro 11:36
**4:8** x Ps 68:18
**4:11** y 1Co 12:28
**4:12** z 1Co 12:27
**4:14** a 1Co 14:20
**4:15** b Eph 1:22

[a]15 Or *whom all fatherhood* [b]8 Or *God* [c]8 Psalm 68:18 [d]9 Or *the depths of the earth*

**4:17** c Ro 1:21
**4:19** d 1Ti 4:2
**4:23** e Col 3:10
**4:24** f Ro 6:4
**4:25** g Zec 8:16 h Ro 12:5
**4:28** i Ac 20:35 j Lk 3:11
**4:30** k 1Th 5:19
**4:31** l Col 3:8
**5:1** m Lk 6:36
**5:2** n 2Co 2:15

Gentiles do, in the futility of their thinking.[c] [18]They are darkened in their understanding and separated from the life of God because of the ignorance that is in them due to the hardening of their hearts. [19]Having lost all sensitivity,[d] they have given themselves over to sensuality so as to indulge in every kind of impurity, with a continual lust for more.

[20]You, however, did not come to know Christ that way. [21]Surely you heard of him and were taught in him in accordance with the truth that is in Jesus. [22]You were taught, with regard to your former way of life, to put off your old self, which is being corrupted by its deceitful desires; [23]to be made new in the attitude of your minds;[e] [24]and to put on the new self,[f] created to be like God in true righteousness and holiness.

[25]Therefore each of you must put off falsehood and speak truthfully[g] to his neighbor, for we are all members of one body.[h] [26]"In your anger do not sin"[a]: Do not let the sun go down while you are still angry, [27]and do not give the devil a foothold. [28]He who has been stealing must steal no longer, but must work,[i] doing something useful with his own hands, that he may have something to share with those in need.[j]

[29]Do not let any unwholesome talk come out of your mouths, but only what is helpful for building others up according to their needs, that it may benefit those who listen. [30]And do not grieve the Holy Spirit of God,[k] with whom you were sealed for the day of redemption. [31]Get rid of all bitterness, rage and anger, brawling and slander, along with every form of malice.[l] [32]Be kind and compassionate to one another, forgiving each other, just as in Christ God forgave you.

**5** Be imitators of God,[m] therefore, as dearly loved children [2]and live a life of love, just as Christ loved us and gave himself up for us as a fragrant offering and sacrifice to God.[n]

[3]But among you there must not be even a hint of sexual immorality, or of any kind of impurity, or of greed, because these are improper for God's holy people. [4]Nor should there be obscenity, foolish talk or coarse joking, which are out of place, but rather thanksgiving. [5]For of this you can be sure: No immoral, impure or greedy person—such a man is an idolater[o]—has any inheritance in the kingdom of Christ and of God.[b][p] [6]Let no one deceive you with empty words, for because of such things God's wrath[q] comes on those who are disobedient. [7]Therefore do not be partners with them.

[8]For you were once darkness, but now you are light in the Lord. Live as children of light[r] [9](for the fruit[s] of the light consists in all goodness, righteousness and truth) [10]and find out what pleases the Lord. [11]Have nothing to do with the fruitless deeds of darkness, but rather expose them. [12]For it is shameful even to mention what the disobedient do in secret. [13]But everything exposed by the light becomes visible, [14]for it is light that makes everything visible. This is why it is said:

"Wake up, O sleeper,
  rise from the dead,
and Christ will shine on you."[t]

[15]Be very careful, then, how you live—not as unwise but as wise, [16]making the most of every opportunity,[u] because the days are evil. [17]Therefore do not be foolish, but understand what the Lord's will is.[v] [18]Do not get drunk on wine,[w] which leads to debauchery. Instead, be filled with the Spirit. [19]Speak to one another with psalms, hymns and spiritual songs.[x] Sing and make music in your heart to the Lord, [20]always giving thanks to God the Father for everything, in the name of our Lord Jesus Christ.

> *"You lose a lot of time hating people."*
> —Marian Anderson, opera singer

[21]Submit to one another out of reverence for Christ.

## Wives and Husbands

[22]Wives, submit to your husbands as to the Lord.[y] [23]For the husband is the head of the wife as Christ is the head of the church,[z] his body, of which he is the Savior. [24]Now as the church submits to Christ, so also wives should submit to their husbands in everything.

**5:5** o Col 3:5 p 1Co 6:9
**5:6** q Ro 1:18
**5:8** r Lk 16:8
**5:9** s Gal 5:22
**5:14** t Isa 60:1
**5:16** u Col 4:5
**5:17** v Ro 12:2; 1Th 4:3
**5:18** w Pr 20:1
**5:19** x Ac 16:25
**5:22** y Eph 6:5
**5:23** z 1Co 11:3

[a]26 Psalm 4:4 [b]5 Or *kingdom of the Christ and God*

5:25 a Col 3:19
5:27 b Col 1:22
5:31 c Mt 19:5
6:1 d Col 3:20
6:4 e Col 3:21 f Ge 18:19
6:5 g 1Ti 6:1 h Col 3:22

25 Husbands, love your wives,[a] just as Christ loved the church and gave himself up for her 26 to make her holy, cleansing[a] her by the washing with water through the word, 27 and to present her to himself as a radiant church, without stain or wrinkle or any other blemish, but holy and blameless.[b] 28 In this same way, husbands ought to love their wives as their own bodies. He who loves his wife loves himself. 29 After all, no one ever hated his own body, but he feeds and cares for it, just as Christ does the church— 30 for we are members of his body. 31 "For this reason a man will leave his father and mother and be united to his wife, and the two will become one flesh."[bc] 32 This is a profound mystery—but I am talking about Christ and the church. 33 However, each one of you also must love his wife as he loves himself, and the wife must respect her husband.

## Children and Parents

6 Children, obey your parents in the Lord, for this is right.[d] 2 "Honor your father and mother"—which is the first commandment with a promise— 3 "that it may go well with you and that you may enjoy long life on the earth."[c]

4 Fathers, do not exasperate your children;[e] instead, bring them up in the training and instruction of the Lord.[f]

## Slaves and Masters

5 Slaves, obey your earthly masters with respect[g] and fear, and with sincerity of heart,[h] just as you would obey Christ. 6 Obey them not only to win their favor when their eye is on you, but like slaves of Christ, doing the will of God from your heart. 7 Serve wholeheartedly, as if you were serving the Lord, not men, 8 because you know that the Lord will reward everyone for whatever good he does, whether he is slave or free.

9 And masters, treat your slaves in the same way. Do not threaten them, since you know that he who is both their Master and yours is in heaven, and there is no favoritism with him.

## The Armor of God

10 Finally, be strong in the Lord and in his mighty power. 11 Put on the full armor of God so that you can take your stand against the devil's schemes. 12 For our struggle is not against flesh and blood, but against the rulers, against the authorities, against the powers[i] of this dark world and against the spiritual forces of evil in the heavenly realms. 13 Therefore put on the full armor of God, so that when the day of evil comes, you may be able to stand your ground, and after you have done everything, to stand. 14 Stand firm then, with the belt of truth buckled around your waist,[j] with the breastplate of righteousness in place,[k] 15 and with your feet fitted with the readiness that comes from the gospel of peace.[l] 16 In addition to all this, take up the shield of faith, with which you can extinguish all the flaming arrows of the evil one. 17 Take the helmet of salvation and the sword of the Spirit, which is the word of God.[m] 18 And pray in the Spirit on all occasions[n] with all kinds of prayers and requests. With this in mind, be alert and always keep on praying for all the saints.

19 Pray also for me, that whenever I open my mouth, words may be given me so that I will fearlessly[o] make known the mystery of the gospel, 20 for which I am an ambassador[p] in chains. Pray that I may declare it fearlessly, as I should.

## Final Greetings

21 Tychicus,[q] the dear brother and faithful servant in the Lord, will tell you everything, so that you also may know how I am and what I am doing. 22 I am sending him to you for this very purpose, that you may know how we are, and that he may encourage you.

23 Peace[r] to the brothers, and love with faith from God the Father and the Lord Jesus Christ. 24 Grace to all who love our Lord Jesus Christ with an undying love.

6:12 i Ro 8:38
6:14 j Isa 11:5 k Isa 59:17
6:15 l Isa 52:7
6:17 m Heb 4:12
6:18 n Lk 18:1
6:19 o 2Co 3:12
6:20 p 2Co 5:20
6:21 q Ac 20:4
6:23 r 1Pe 5:14

[a]26 Or *having cleansed* [b]31 Gen. 2:24 [c]3 Deut. 5:16

# Inspire

## SINGLE PARENTING

From the very beginning, God ordained that adult men and women would be responsible for raising their young. Adults are to care for, teach, feed and nurture their children until they can function in their environment independently and without the immediate assistance of adults. Ephesians 6:1–4 gives parents, as well as children, a model to follow.

Raising children is not an easy task, but God instructs us to pursue it with kindness. While contemporary parenting styles may differ from those of Bible times, the fact still remains that parenting is a daunting responsibility. Even in two-parent households, issues surrounding child rearing often arise and become points of contention between parents.

In single-parent families, however, the responsibilities of parenting take on an added dimension. The single parent can often become overwhelmed, and the grim statistics about our children don't ease our anxiety. The news media reports gloom and doom about the situation of the child of color and about his/her future—especially when it comes to young men. We must refuse to accept such a grim prognosis for our children. After all, we know from Scripture that "nothing is impossible with God" (Lk 1:37). So pray and rely completely on him. Insist on a drug-free, smoke-free, violence-free, loving home for your children to grow up in. Keep your expectations high without being unrealistic. Whenever choices about college are discussed, the conversation is best centered on *which* college to attend, not *if* he or she will attend.

Life as a single parent will have its fair share of challenges. You might have to pinch pennies, sacrifice—and cry. You may not always be able to buy your children everything that they want—or that you want for them—but remember that God will always provide for your needs. Learn to take at face value the Word of God available on the pages of Scripture; apply it directly, literally and realistically to your life. You'll learn invaluable life lessons and be grateful to God for teaching them to you.

Hold tightly to great expectations for your children, while seeing to it as best you can that the needs in your own life are met. In fact, *expect* them to be met.

—S. Ford Robinson

For the next Inspire note, go to page 1398.

### read

Read Ephesians 6:1–4; see also Genesis 21:8–21; 1 Kings 17:7–16; 2 Kings 4:1–7; Philippians 4:4–19.

See also the Inspire Notes "A Great Challenge: Teaching Our Children," "Single Mothers," "Motherhood," "Parenting," "Raising Children: Modeling Discipleship" and "Children: A Blessed Heritage From God," and the Women of the Bible Notes "Hagar: Battered, Beaten and Rejected—but Not Abandoned" and "The Prophet's Widow: God Provides."

### WOMAN *of* COLOR

How can you help a single parent today? If you are a single parent, share your testimony with another woman in your situation.

# Philippians

## OVERVIEW

This letter begins with Paul offering thanks to God for the church at Philippi and sharing words of encouragement with them. He wanted the believers to continue the work of Christ despite his imprisonment and their suffering (see Php 1:12–30). Using Jesus as an example of humility (see Php 2:1–11), Paul urged the believers to press on toward the prize that God offers to those who are faithful to him (see Php 3:12–16). He wanted them to rejoice in the Lord always and to remember that God supplied all their needs (see Php 4:4,19).

Paul also dealt with a dispute in the church, pleading with Euodia and Syntyche—women believers and Paul's fellow laborers in the gospel—to "agree with each other in the Lord" (see Php 4:2–3).

The teachings in this letter can encourage women believers—especially those who are enduring suffering. The book of Philippians tells us to rejoice in the midst of our circumstances because of our relationship with Jesus. Remembering him places everything in perspective and gives us hope as we continue on our journey.

## OUTLINE

I. Paul's Thanksgiving and Prayer (1:1–11)
II. Progression of the Gospel Despite Paul's Imprisonment (1:12–30)
III. Plea for Humility by Following Christ's Example (2:1–18)
IV. Genuine Faithfulness of Timothy and Epaphroditus (2:19–30)
V. Pressing Toward the Goal (3:1—4:9)
VI. Thankfulness for Gifts Sent to Paul (4:10–23)

### SCANNABLE FACTS:

**Author:** Paul

**Time Written:** Around A.D. 61

**Theme to Note:** Rejoice in the Lord always

**Notable Women:** Euodia and Syntyche

1:1 a Ac 16:1
1:4 b Ro 1:10
1:5 c Ac 2:42; d Ac 16:12–40
1:7 e 2Pe 1:13
1:8 f Ro 1:9
1:9 g 1Th 3:12
1:10 h 1Co 1:8

1 Paul and Timothy,[a] servants of Christ Jesus,

To all the saints in Christ Jesus at Philippi, together with the overseers[a] and deacons:

2 Grace and peace to you from God our Father and the Lord Jesus Christ.

## Thanksgiving and Prayer

3 I thank my God every time I remember you. 4 In all my prayers for all of you, I always pray[b] with joy 5 because of your partnership[c] in the gospel from the first day[d] until now, 6 being confident of this, that he who began a good work in you will carry it on to completion until the day of Christ Jesus.

7 It is right[e] for me to feel this way about all of you, since I have you in my heart; for whether I am in chains or defending and confirming the gospel, all of you share in God's grace with me. 8 God can testify[f] how I long for all of you with the affection of Christ Jesus.

9 And this is my prayer: that your love[g] may abound more and more in knowledge and depth of insight, 10 so that you may be able to discern what is best and may be pure and blameless until the day of Christ,[h] 11 filled with the fruit of righteousness that comes through Jesus Christ—to the glory and praise of God.

## Paul's Chains Advance the Gospel

12 Now I want you to know, brothers, that what has happened to me has really served to advance the gospel. 13 As a result, it has become clear throughout the whole palace guard[b] and to everyone else that I am in chains for Christ. 14 Because of my chains, most of the brothers in the Lord have been encouraged to speak the word of God more courageously and fearlessly.

15 It is true that some preach Christ out of envy and rivalry, but others out of goodwill. 16 The latter do so in love, knowing that I am put here for the defense of the gospel. 17 The former preach Christ out of selfish ambition,[i] not sincerely, supposing that they can stir up trouble for me while I am in chains.[c] 18 But what does it matter? The important thing is that in every way, whether from false motives or true, Christ is preached. And because of this I rejoice.

Yes, and I will continue to rejoice, 19 for I know that through your prayers[j] and the help given by the Spirit of Jesus Christ, what has happened to me will turn out for my deliverance.[d] 20 I eagerly expect[k] and hope that I will in no way be ashamed, but will have sufficient courage so that now as always Christ will be exalted in my body, whether by life or by death. 21 For to me, to live is Christ and to die is gain. 22 If I am to go on living in the body, this will mean fruitful labor for me. Yet what shall I choose? I do not know! 23 I am torn between the two: I desire to depart[l] and be with Christ,[m] which is better by far; 24 but it is more necessary for you that I remain in the body. 25 Convinced of this, I know that I will remain, and I will

1:17 i Php 2:3
1:19 j 2Co 1:11
1:20 k Ro 8:19
1:23 l 2Ti 4:6; m 2Co 5:8

[a]1 Traditionally *bishops* [b]13 Or *whole palace* [c]16,17 Some late manuscripts have verses 16 and 17 in reverse order. [d]19 Or *salvation*

## The African Presence

### Philippians 1

While there are no specific references to the African presence within the book of Philippians, the gospel preached by Paul was influenced by people of North Africa and the Middle East (a historical and cultural subregion of Africa-Eurasia, traditionally held to be countries or regions in Southwest Asia together with Egypt). However, during the time of the New Testament, racial identification did not have the significance that it has today.

continue with all of you for your progress and joy in the faith, 26 so that through my being with you again your joy in Christ Jesus will overflow on account of me.

27 Whatever happens, conduct yourselves in a manner worthy[n] of the gospel of Christ. Then, whether I come and see you or only hear about you in my absence, I will know that you stand firm in one spirit, contending as one man for the faith of the gospel 28 without being frightened in any way by those who oppose you. This is a sign to them that they will be destroyed, but that you will be saved—and that by God. 29 For it has been granted to you[o] on behalf of Christ not only to believe on him, but also to suffer for him, 30 since you are going through the same struggle[p] you saw[q] I had, and now hear that I still have.

## Imitating Christ's Humility

2 If you have any encouragement from being united with Christ, if any comfort from his love, if any fellowship with the Spirit,[r] if any tenderness and compassion,[s] 2 then make my joy complete[t] by being like-minded, having the same love, being one in spirit and purpose. 3 Do nothing out of selfish ambition or vain conceit,[u] but in humility consider others better than yourselves.[v] 4 Each of you should look not only to your own interests, but also to the interests of others.

5 Your attitude should be the same as that of Christ Jesus:[w]

6 Who, being in very nature[a] God,
did not consider equality with God
something to be grasped,
7 but made himself nothing,
taking the very nature[b] of a servant,
being made in human likeness.[x]
8 And being found in appearance as a man,
he humbled himself
and became obedient to death[y]—
even death on a cross!
9 Therefore God exalted him[z] to the highest place
and gave him the name that is above every name,[a]
10 that at the name of Jesus every knee should bow,
in heaven and on earth and under the earth,
11 and every tongue confess that Jesus Christ is Lord,[b]
to the glory of God the Father.

## Shining as Stars

12 Therefore, my dear friends, as you have always obeyed—not only in my presence, but now much more in my absence—continue to work out your salvation with fear and trembling, 13 for it is God who works in you to will and to act according to his good purpose.

14 Do everything without complaining or arguing, 15 so that you may become blameless and pure, children of God[c] without fault in a crooked and depraved generation, in which you shine like stars in the universe 16 as you hold out[c] the word of life—in order that I may boast on the day of Christ that I did not run or labor for nothing. 17 But even if I am being poured out like a drink offering[d] on the sacrifice[e] and service coming from your faith, I am glad and rejoice with all of you. 18 So you too should be glad and rejoice with me.

## Timothy and Epaphroditus

19 I hope in the Lord Jesus to send Timothy to you soon, that I also may be cheered when I receive news about you. 20 I have no one else like him, who takes a genuine interest in your welfare. 21 For everyone looks out for his own interests,[f] not those of Jesus Christ. 22 But you know that Timothy has proved himself, because as a son with his father he has served with me in the work of the gospel. 23 I hope, therefore, to send him as soon as I see how things go with me. 24 And I am confident[g] in the Lord that I myself will come soon.

25 But I think it is necessary to send back to you Epaphroditus, my brother, fellow worker and fellow soldier,[h] who is also your messenger, whom you sent to take care of my needs.[i] 26 For he longs for all of you and is distressed because you heard he was ill. 27 Indeed he was ill, and almost died. But God had mercy on him, and not on him only but also on me, to spare me sorrow upon

[a] 6 Or *in the form of* [b] 7 Or *the form* [c] 16 Or *hold on to*

**1:27** n Eph 4:1
**1:29** o Mt 5:11,12
**1:30** p 1Th 2:2 q Ac 16:19–40
**2:1** r 2Co 13:14 s Col 3:12
**2:2** t Jn 3:29
**2:3** u Gal 5:26 v Ro 12:10
**2:5** w Mt 11:29
**2:7** x Jn 1:14
**2:8** y Mt 26:39; Heb 5:8
**2:9** z Ac 2:33; Heb 2:9 a Eph 1:20,21
**2:11** b Jn 13:13
**2:15** c Mt 5:45,48; Eph 5:1
**2:17** d 2Ti 4:6 e Ro 15:16
**2:21** f 1Co 10:24
**2:24** g Php 1:25
**2:25** h Phm 2 i Php 4:18

2:29 j 1Co 16:18
2:30 k 1Co 16:17

sorrow. 28 Therefore I am all the more eager
to send him, so that when you see him again
you may be glad and I may have less anxi-
ety. 29 Welcome him in the Lord with great
joy, and honor men like him,[j] 30 because he
almost died for the work of Christ, risking
his life to make up for the help you could not
give me.[k]

## No Confidence in the Flesh

3 Finally, my brothers, rejoice in the
Lord! It is no trouble for me to write
the same things to you again, and it is a safe-
guard for you.
2 Watch out for those dogs, those men
who do evil, those mutilators of the flesh.
3 For it is we who are the circumcision,[l] we

3:3 l Gal 6:15

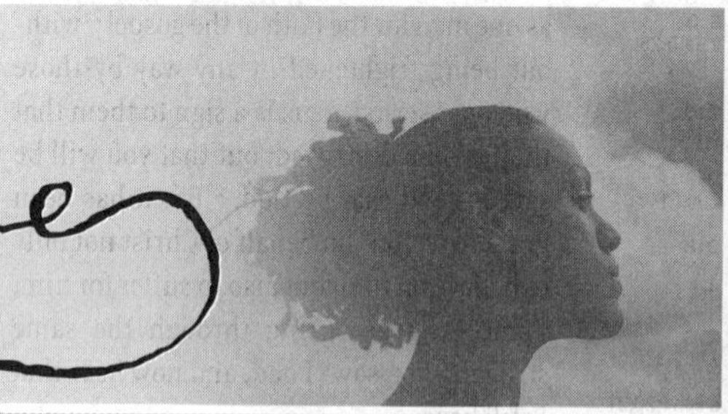

Inspire

## GENTLENESS

Gentleness begins with genuine humility. The basic idea of the word *gentleness* is "great power, held in control." Being gentle is all about knowing one's power—and knowing when and how to use it. Gentleness is not weakness; it is strength directed toward God and expressed in action through service to others.

Jesus is our example of gentleness. He is the one "who, being in very nature God, did not consider equality with God something to be grasped, but made himself nothing, taking the very nature of a servant, being made in human likeness. And being found in appearance as a man, he humbled himself and became obedient to death—even death on a cross!" (Php 2:6–8).

Gentleness demonstrates great strength of character because people who are gentle are often laughed at. Jesus courageously cut through long-standing social practices by refusing to ignore little children and society's outcasts, even though his disciples wanted him to. He welcomed and included in his circle of interest those whom the religious establishment of his day rejected: women, tax collectors and "sinners." To walk in gentleness means to do what Jesus did: to use our power to lift up, to encourage and to uphold someone else.

African American women do wield great power, in spite of our often lowly status in this world. Through Jesus Christ we have been given the power to bind and loose—and to gain heavenly approval for the good we do here on earth (see Mt 16:19). What would it look like if African American women began to walk in the gentleness of Jesus Christ, binding the power of the enemy in our communities, over our children and in our homes, and then loosing others, releasing them to reach their full potential in Jesus Christ?

—C. Belt

For the next Inspire note, go to page 1407.

**read**

Philippians 2:1–11; see also Matthew 11:28–30; Galatians 5:22–23; Ephesians 4:1–3; 1 Timothy 6:11; 1 Peter 3:1–16.

**See also** the Inspire Notes "Submission," "Goodness," "Servant-Leadership," "Humility" and "Character."

**WOMAN of COLOR**

How do you walk in gentleness?

who worship by the Spirit of God, who glory in Christ Jesus, and who put no confidence in the flesh— [4]though I myself have reasons for such confidence.

If anyone else thinks he has reasons to put confidence in the flesh, I have more: [5]circumcised on the eighth day, of the people of Israel,[m] of the tribe of Benjamin,[n] a Hebrew of Hebrews; in regard to the law, a Pharisee; [6]as for zeal, persecuting the church; as for legalistic righteousness, faultless.

[7]But whatever was to my profit I now consider loss[o] for the sake of Christ. [8]What is more, I consider everything a loss compared to the surpassing greatness of knowing[p] Christ Jesus my Lord, for whose sake I have lost all things. I consider them rubbish, that I may gain Christ [9]and be found in him, not having a righteousness of my own that comes from the law, but that which is through faith in Christ—the righteousness that comes from God and is by faith. [10]I want to know Christ and the power of his resurrection and the fellowship of sharing in his sufferings,[q] becoming like him in his death,[r] [11]and so, somehow, to attain to the resurrection from the dead.

## Pressing on Toward the Goal

[12]Not that I have already obtained all this, or have already been made perfect, but I press on to take hold[s] of that for which Christ Jesus took hold of me. [13]Brothers, I do not consider myself yet to have taken hold of it. But one thing I do: Forgetting what is behind[t] and straining toward what is ahead, [14]I press on[u] toward the goal to win the prize for which God has called me heavenward in Christ Jesus.

[15]All of us who are mature[v] should take such a view of things.[w] And if on some point you think differently, that too God will make clear to you. [16]Only let us live up to what we have already attained.

[17]Join with others in following my example,[x] brothers, and take note of those who live according to the pattern we gave you. [18]For, as I have often told you before and now say again even with tears, many live as enemies of the cross of Christ. [19]Their destiny is destruction, their god is their stomach, and their glory is in their shame. Their mind is on earthly things.[y] [20]But our citizenship is in heaven.[z] And we eagerly await a Savior from there, the Lord Jesus Christ,[a] [21]who, by the power[b] that enables him to bring everything under his control, will transform our lowly bodies[c] so that they will be like his glorious body.

4 Therefore, my brothers, you whom I love and long for,[d] my joy and crown, that is how you should stand firm in the Lord, dear friends!

## Exhortations

[2]I plead with Euodia and I plead with Syntyche to agree with each other[e] in the Lord. [3]Yes, and I ask you, loyal yokefellow,[a] help these women who have contended at my side in the cause of the gospel, along with Clement and the rest of my fellow workers, whose names are in the book of life.

[4]Rejoice in the Lord always. I will say it again: Rejoice! [5]Let your gentleness be evident to all. The Lord is near. [6]Do not be anxious about anything,[f] but in everything, by prayer and petition, with thanksgiving, present your requests to God. [7]And the peace of God,[g] which transcends all understanding, will guard your hearts and your minds in Christ Jesus.

[8]Finally, brothers, whatever is true, whatever is noble, whatever is right, whatever is pure, whatever is lovely, whatever is admirable—if anything is excellent or praiseworthy—think about such things. [9]Whatever you have learned or received or heard from me, or seen in me—put it into practice. And the God of peace[h] will be with you.

## Thanks for Their Gifts

[10]I rejoice greatly in the Lord that at last you have renewed your concern for me. Indeed, you have been concerned, but you had no opportunity to show it. [11]I am not saying this because I am in need, for I have learned to be content[i] whatever the circumstances. [12]I know what it is to be in need, and I know what it is to have plenty. I have learned the secret of being content in any and every situation, whether well fed or hungry,[j] whether living in plenty or in

**3:5** m 2Co 11:22 n Ro 11:1
**3:7** o Mt 13:44
**3:8** p Eph 4:13
**3:10** q Ro 8:17 r Ro 6:3–5
**3:12** s 1Ti 6:12
**3:13** t Lk 9:62
**3:14** u Heb 6:1
**3:15** v 1Co 2:6 w Gal 5:10
**3:17** x 1Pe 5:3
**3:19** y Ro 8:5,6
**3:20** z Col 3:1 a 1Co 1:7
**3:21** b Eph 1:19 c 1Co 15:43–53
**4:1** d Php 1:8
**4:2** e Php 2:2
**4:6** f Mt 6:25–34
**4:7** g Jn 14:27; Col 3:15
**4:9** h Ro 15:33
**4:11** i 1Ti 6:6,8
**4:12** j 1Co 4:11

[a]3 Or *loyal Syzygus*

# Euodia and Syntyche

## Women in Conflict

The apostle Paul held Euodia and Syntyche in high esteem. He glowingly referred to them as "women who have contended at my side in the cause of the gospel" (Php 4:3). However, we find Paul addressing the conduct of these two women in his letter to the Philippians—a letter meant to be read to the church publicly no less! Euodia and Syntyche were feuding about some matter that could ultimately have disrupted the life of the church. Therefore, Paul asked the saints in general and an unnamed third person in particular—Paul's "loyal yokefellow" (Php 4:3; see the NIV text note)—to work at bringing about reconciliation between these two women.

Euodia and Syntyche were truly an asset to Paul's ministry. They contributed greatly to the local church, which is why Paul was adamant about bringing wholeness and healing to this situation. If left unchecked, this conflict could have caused harm to both him and the church. When there is division in the household of faith, the work of the church is hindered. Whatever the issue was between Euodia and Syntyche, Paul wanted to put it to rest, and he wanted the other believers to assist in making that happen.

As women of color and of faith, we must focus on important matters and not dwell on minor issues. The time we waste arguing about insignificant matters could be better used doing something to advance the work of the Lord.

Instead of feuding, Paul encourages the saints to rejoice and be gentle with one another (see Php 4:4–5). How can we attract others to the church if we are at odds with each other? They see enough of that outside the church. While we may not always agree with one another, we can strive to compromise. Things do not always have to go our way. We must remember that everyone is someone important to Christ. When we understand this, we will respect each other.

When we are rejoicing in the Lord, we will find ways to encourage someone else. We will consider the other person's well-being just as we would our own. Strife and division are tools of our adversary, so we must continue to focus on our goal: to glorify God and help others live fulfilled lives in Christ.

—D. J. Belt Stroman

### reflection

*Is there a woman of faith you need to reconcile with or others you need to help reconcile?*

*Pray for guidance in your situation.*

### read

Philippians 2:1–11; 4:2–9.

**See also** the Inspire Notes "Intimate Friendships," "Submission," "Forgiveness: The Doorway to Healing and Reconciliation" and "Forgiveness: God's Extended Mercy," and the Women of the Bible Note "Ruth: A Model of Friendship and Sisterhood."

For the next Women of the Bible note, go to page 1433.

4:15 k 2Co 11:8,9
4:18 l Php 2:25

want. 13 I can do everything through him
who gives me strength.
14 Yet it was good of you to share in my
troubles. 15 Moreover, as you Philippians
know, in the early days of your acquain-
tance with the gospel, when I set out from
Macedonia, not one church shared with
me in the matter of giving and receiving,
except you only;[k] 16 for even when I was in
Thessalonica, you sent me aid again and
again when I was in need. 17 Not that I am
looking for a gift, but I am looking for what
may be credited to your account. 18 I have
received full payment and even more; I am
amply supplied, now that I have received
from Epaphroditus[l] the gifts you sent. They
are a fragrant offering, an acceptable sac-
rifice, pleasing to God. 19 And my God will
meet all your needs[m] according to his glori-
ous riches in Christ Jesus.
20 To our God and Father[n] be glory for ever
and ever. Amen.

## Final Greetings

21 Greet all the saints in Christ Jesus.
The brothers who are with me[o] send greet-
ings. 22 All the saints send you greetings,
especially those who belong to Caesar's
household.
23 The grace of the Lord Jesus Christ be
with your spirit. Amen.[a]

4:19 m Ps 23:1
4:20 n Gal 1:4
4:21 o Gal 1:2

[a] 23 Some manuscripts do not have *Amen*.

# Colossians

## OVERVIEW

Paul wrote to the church in the city of Colosse after hearing about the believers' struggles with teachings that were inconsistent with the gospel of Jesus Christ. The letter to the Colossians focuses on the supremacy of Christ over all ideologies and philosophies. Believers are encouraged to live as true examples of Christ by rejecting a worldly lifestyle and living a holy life in their households and workplaces.

The command to "set your hearts on things above, where Christ is seated at the right hand of God" (Col 3:1) is a principle that many women struggle with. As women, we are often tempted to put our desires and dreams on the throne of our hearts instead of on the throne of God. As you read through Colossians, reflect on what dominates your time and attention. Is your heart set on Jesus or the world?

## OUTLINE

I. Introduction (1:1–14)
II. The Superiority of Christ (1:15—2:23)
III. The Believer's Response to Christ's Superiority (3:1—4:6)
IV. Conclusion (4:7–18)

### SCANNABLE FACTS:

**Author:** Paul

**Time Written:** Around A.D. 60

**Theme to Note:** Jesus is supreme over everything

**Notable Women:** Wives, in relation to their husbands; Nympha (see Col 4:15)

1:2 a Ro 1:7
1:4 b Eph 1:15
1:5 c 1Th 5:8; d 1Pe 1:4
1:7 e Phm 23
1:8 f Ro 15:30
1:9 g Eph 1:15
1:10 h Eph 4:1
1:11 i Eph 3:16

1 Paul, an apostle of Christ Jesus by the
will of God, and Timothy our brother,

2 To the holy and faithful[a] brothers in
Christ at Colosse:

Grace and peace to you from God our
Father.[b][a]

## Thanksgiving and Prayer

3 We always thank God, the Father of our
Lord Jesus Christ, when we pray for you, 4 be-
cause we have heard of your faith in Christ
Jesus and of the love you have for all the
saints[b]— 5 the faith and love that spring
from the hope[c] that is stored up for you in
heaven[d] and that you have already heard
about in the word of truth, the gospel 6 that
has come to you. All over the world this gos-
pel is bearing fruit and growing, just as it
has been doing among you since the day you
heard it and understood God's grace in all
its truth. 7 You learned it from Epaphras,[e]
our dear fellow servant, who is a faithful
minister of Christ on our[c] behalf, 8 and who
also told us of your love in the Spirit.[f]

9 For this reason, since the day we heard
about you,[g] we have not stopped praying
for you and asking God to fill you with the
knowledge of his will through all spiritual
wisdom and understanding. 10 And we pray
this in order that you may live a life wor-
thy[h] of the Lord and may please him in ev-
ery way: bearing fruit in every good work,
growing in the knowledge of God, 11 being
strengthened with all power[i] according to
his glorious might so that you may have
great endurance and patience,[j] and joyfully
12 giving thanks to the Father,[k] who has qual-
ified you[d] to share in the inheritance of the
saints in the kingdom of light. 13 For he has
rescued us from the dominion of darkness
and brought us into the kingdom[l] of the Son
he loves, 14 in whom we have redemption,[e]
the forgiveness of sins.[m]

## The Supremacy of Christ

15 He is the image[n] of the invisible God,
the firstborn over all creation. 16 For by
him all things were created: things in
heaven and on earth, visible and invisible,
whether thrones or powers or rulers or au-
thorities;[o] all things were created by him
and for him. 17 He is before all things, and
in him all things hold together. 18 And he is
the head of the body, the church; he is the
beginning and the firstborn from among
the dead,[p] so that in everything he might
have the supremacy. 19 For God was pleased
to have all his fullness[q] dwell in him, 20 and
through him to reconcile[r] to himself all
things, whether things on earth or things
in heaven, by making peace through his
blood,[s] shed on the cross.

21 Once you were alienated from God and
were enemies in your minds because of[f]
your evil behavior. 22 But now he has recon-
ciled you by Christ's physical body through
death to present you holy in his sight, with-
out blemish and free from accusation[t]— 23 if
you continue in your faith, established[u] and

1:11 j Eph 4:2
1:12 k Eph 5:20
1:13 l Eph 6:12; 2Pe 1:11
1:14 m Eph 1:7
1:15 n 2Co 4:4
1:16 o Eph 1:20,21
1:18 p Rev 1:5
1:19 q Jn 1:16
1:20 r 2Co 5:18; s Eph 2:13
1:22 t Eph 5:27
1:23 u Eph 3:17

[a]2 Or *believing* [b]2 Some manuscripts *Father and the Lord Jesus Christ* [c]7 Some manuscripts *your* [d]12 Some manuscripts *us* [e]14 A few late manuscripts *redemption through his blood* [f]21 Or *minds, as shown by*

## The African Presence

### Colossians 1

While there are no specific references to the African presence within the book of Colossians, the gospel preached by Paul was influenced by people of North Africa and the Middle East (a historical and cultural subregion of Africa-Eurasia, traditionally held to be countries or regions in Southwest Asia together with Egypt). However, during the time of the New Testament, racial identification did not have the significance that it has today.

firm, not moved from the hope held out in the gospel. This is the gospel that you heard and that has been proclaimed to every creature under heaven,[v] and of which I, Paul, have become a servant.

## Paul's Labor for the Church

[24]Now I rejoice in what was suffered for you, and I fill up in my flesh what is still lacking in regard to Christ's afflictions,[w] for the sake of his body, which is the church. [25]I have become its servant by the commission God gave me[x] to present to you the word of God in its fullness— [26]the mystery that has been kept hidden for ages and generations, but is now disclosed to the saints. [27]To them God has chosen to make known among the Gentiles the glorious riches of this mystery, which is Christ in you, the hope of glory.

[28]We proclaim him, admonishing[y] and teaching everyone with all wisdom, so that we may present everyone perfect in Christ. [29]To this end I labor,[z] struggling[a] with all his energy, which so powerfully works in me.[b]

**2** I want you to know how much I am struggling[c] for you and for those at Laodicea, and for all who have not met me personally. [2]My purpose is that they may be encouraged in heart and united in love, so that they may have the full riches of complete understanding, in order that they may know the mystery of God, namely, Christ, [3]in whom are hidden all the treasures of wisdom and knowledge.[d] [4]I tell you this so that no one may deceive you by fine-sounding arguments. [5]For though I am absent from you in body, I am present with you in spirit[e] and delight to see how orderly[f] you are and how firm[g] your faith in Christ is.

## Freedom From Human Regulations Through Life With Christ

[6]So then, just as you received Christ Jesus as Lord, continue to live in him, [7]rooted and built up in him, strengthened in the faith as you were taught, and overflowing with thankfulness.

[8]See to it that no one takes you captive through hollow and deceptive philosophy, which depends on human tradition and the basic principles of this world[h] rather than on Christ.

[9]For in Christ all the fullness of the Deity lives in bodily form, [10]and you have been given fullness in Christ, who is the head over every power and authority. [11]In him you were also circumcised,[i] in the putting off of the sinful nature,[a] not with a circumcision done by the hands of men but with the circumcision done by Christ, [12]having been buried with him in baptism and raised with him through your faith in the power of God, who raised him from the dead.[j]

[13]When you were dead in your sins and in the uncircumcision of your sinful nature,[b] God made you[c] alive with Christ. He forgave us all our sins, [14]having canceled the written code, with its regulations,[k] that was against us and that stood opposed to us; he took it away, nailing it to the cross. [15]And having disarmed the powers and authorities,[l] he made a public spectacle of them, triumphing over them by the cross.[d]

[16]Therefore do not let anyone judge you[m] by what you eat or drink, or with regard to a religious festival,[n] a New Moon celebration or a Sabbath day. [17]These are a shadow of the things that were to come;[o] the reality, however, is found in Christ. [18]Do not let anyone who delights in false humility and the worship of angels disqualify you for the prize. Such a person goes into great detail about what he has seen, and his unspiritual mind puffs him up with idle notions. [19]He has lost connection with the Head, from whom the whole body, supported and held together by its ligaments and sinews, grows as God causes it to grow.[p]

[20]Since you died with Christ to the basic principles of this world,[q] why, as though you still belonged to it, do you submit to its rules: [21]"Do not handle! Do not taste! Do not touch!"? [22]These are all destined to perish[r] with use, because they are based on human commands and teachings.[s] [23]Such regulations indeed have an appearance of wisdom, with their self-imposed worship, their false humility and their harsh treatment of the body, but they lack any value in restraining sensual indulgence.

**1:23** v Ro 10:18
**1:24** w 2Co 1:5
**1:25** x Eph 3:2
**1:28** y Col 3:16
**1:29** z 1Co 15:10 a Col 2:1 b Eph 1:19
**2:1** c Col 1:29
**2:3** d Ro 11:33
**2:5** e 1Th 2:17 f 1Co 14:40 g 1Pe 5:9
**2:8** h Gal 4:3
**2:11** i Ro 2:29
**2:12** j Ac 2:24
**2:14** k Eph 2:15
**2:15** l Eph 6:12
**2:16** m Ro 14:3,4 n Ro 14:5
**2:17** o Heb 8:5
**2:19** p Eph 4:16
**2:20** q Gal 4:3,9
**2:22** r 1Co 6:13 s Mt 15:9; Tit 1:14

[a]11 Or *the flesh* [b]13 Or *your flesh* [c]13 Some manuscripts *us* [d]15 Or *them in him*

**3:3** t Ro 6:2
**3:4** u 1Jn 3:2
**3:5** v Eph 5:3; w Eph 5:5
**3:8** x Eph 4:22; y Eph 4:29
**3:9** z Eph 4:22,25
**3:10** a Ro 12:2; Eph 4:23
**3:11** b Gal 3:28; c Eph 1:23
**3:12** d Php 2:3; e Gal 5:22,23
**3:13** f Eph 4:32
**3:14** g Eph 4:3
**3:16** h Eph 5:19
**3:17** i 1Co 10:31

## Rules for Holy Living

3 Since, then, you have been raised with Christ, set your hearts on things above, where Christ is seated at the right hand of God. 2Set your minds on things above, not on earthly things. 3For you died,[t] and your life is now hidden with Christ in God. 4When Christ, who is your[a] life, appears, then you also will appear with him in glory.[u]

5Put to death, therefore, whatever belongs to your earthly nature: sexual immorality, impurity, lust, evil desires and greed,[v] which is idolatry.[w] 6Because of these, the wrath of God is coming.[b] 7You used to walk in these ways, in the life you once lived. 8But now you must rid yourselves[x] of all such things as these: anger, rage, malice, slander, and filthy language from your lips.[y] 9Do not lie to each other,[z] since you have taken off your old self with its practices 10and have put on the new self, which is being renewed[a] in knowledge in the image of its Creator. 11Here there is no Greek or Jew, circumcised or uncircumcised, barbarian, Scythian, slave or free,[b] but Christ is all,[c] and is in all.

12Therefore, as God's chosen people, holy and dearly loved, clothe yourselves with compassion, kindness, humility,[d] gentleness and patience.[e] 13Bear with each other and forgive whatever grievances you may have against one another. Forgive as the Lord forgave you.[f] 14And over all these virtues put on love, which binds them all together in perfect unity.[g]

15Let the peace of Christ rule in your hearts, since as members of one body you were called to peace. And be thankful. 16Let the word of Christ dwell in you richly as you teach and admonish one another with all wisdom, and as you sing psalms, hymns and spiritual songs with gratitude in your hearts to God.[h] 17And whatever you do,[i] whether in word or deed, do it all in the name of the Lord Jesus, giving thanks to God the Father through him.

## Rules for Christian Households

18Wives, submit to your husbands, as is fitting in the Lord.

19Husbands, love your wives and do not be harsh with them.

20Children, obey your parents in everything, for this pleases the Lord.

21Fathers, do not embitter your children, or they will become discouraged.

22Slaves, obey your earthly masters in everything; and do it, not only when their eye is on you and to win their favor, but with sincerity of heart and reverence for the Lord. 23Whatever you do, work at it with all your heart, as working for the Lord, not for men, 24since you know that you will receive an inheritance from the Lord as a reward. It is the Lord Christ you are serving. 25Anyone who does wrong will be repaid for his wrong, and there is no favoritism.[j]

4 Masters, provide your slaves with what is right and fair, because you know that you also have a Master in heaven.

## Further Instructions

2Devote yourselves to prayer, being watchful and thankful. 3And pray for us, too, that God may open a door for our message, so that we may proclaim the mystery of Christ, for which I am in chains.[k] 4Pray that I may proclaim it clearly, as I should. 5Be wise[l] in the way you act toward outsiders; make the most of every opportunity.[m] 6Let your conversation be always full of grace, seasoned with salt,[n] so that you may know how to answer everyone.[o]

*Woman of color,*

*Keep your conversations clean.*

*You represent me to a watching world.*

*God*

COLOSSIANS 4:5–6

## Final Greetings

7Tychicus will tell you all the news about me. He is a dear brother, a faithful minister and fellow servant in the Lord. 8I am sending him to you for the express purpose that

**3:25** j Ac 10:34
**4:3** k Eph 6:19,20
**4:5** l Eph 5:15; m Eph 5:16
**4:6** n Mk 9:50; o 1Pe 3:15

[a]4 Some manuscripts *our* [b]6 Some early manuscripts *coming on those who are disobedient*

4:9 p Phm 10

you may know about our[a] circumstances
and that he may encourage your hearts.
9 He is coming with Onesimus,[p] our faith-
ful and dear brother, who is one of you.
They will tell you everything that is hap-
pening here.

10 My fellow prisoner Aristarchus sends
you his greetings, as does Mark, the cousin
of Barnabas.[q] (You have received instruc-
tions about him; if he comes to you, welcome
him.) 11 Jesus, who is called Justus, also sends
greetings. These are the only Jews among

4:10 q Ac 4:36

[a]8 Some manuscripts *that he may know about your*

*Inspire*

## THE IMAGE OF GOD AND THE BEAUTY OF THE HEART

One of the most important lessons a child can learn is that God created humankind in his own image (see Ge 1:26–27; 9:6). Therefore, each and every one of us is divinely and uniquely beautiful. This description does not pertain to the physical image but rather to the spiritual and moral components of who we are. We are, among many other functions, healers, prophets, teachers and lovers. Therefore, when we are assured of God's love for us, we can embrace a positive self-image early in life. Such an affirmative concept of self can give us strength in the depths of life's valleys and humility during the joy of our mountaintop experiences.

In today's world many women of color awake each morning confronting the demons associated with our society's images and definitions of beauty. Beauty has been quietly empowered within institutions and relationships to suggest who is "in" and who is "out," who is worthwhile and who is not, who will bask in the limelight and who will wait in the shadows. In disobedience to God's Word, which teaches us that beauty is of the heart and the good actions that flow from it, we too often allow our self-image to become entangled with the materialistic, commercial representation of beauty (see 1Pe 3:3–4).

For women of color, reclaiming the power of self-image is one of the first steps to entering a truly loving relationship with God. We owe it to God, to ourselves and to others to awake each and every day to rediscover our true self—renewed "in the image of its Creator" (Col 3:10)—reclaim our positive self-image and teach our children that real beauty is all about heart and action (see Col 3:1–17). Allow no one to negatively influence your image of God or your image of your self.

—I. Carruthers

For the next Inspire note, go to page 1414.

### read

Colossians 3:1–17; see also Genesis 1:26–27, 9:6; Ephesians 4:17–24; 1 Peter 3:1–4.

**See also** the Inspire Notes "The Creation of Woman" and "Vanity," and the Women of the Bible Note "Eve: The First African Woman."

### WOMAN of COLOR

How does remembering and embracing the fact that you are made in God's image help you love yourself more?

**4:12** r Ro 15:30
**4:14** s 2Ti 4:11 t 2Ti 4:10
**4:15** u Ro 16:5

my fellow workers for the kingdom of God,
and they have proved a comfort to me.
12Epaphras, who is one of you and a servant
of Christ Jesus, sends greetings. He is always
wrestling in prayer for you,[r] that you may
stand firm in all the will of God, mature and
fully assured. 13I vouch for him that he is
working hard for you and for those at Laodi-
cea and Hierapolis. 14Our dear friend Luke,[s]
the doctor, and Demas[t] send greetings. 15Give
my greetings to the brothers at Laodicea,
and to Nympha and the church in her house.[u]
16After this letter has been read to you,
see that it is also read in the church of the La-
odiceans and that you in turn read the letter
from Laodicea.
17Tell Archippus:[v] "See to it that you
complete the work you have received in the
Lord."
18I, Paul, write this greeting in my own
hand.[w] Remember[x] my chains. Grace be
with you.[y]

**4:17** v Phm 2
**4:18** w 1Co 16:21 x Heb 13:3 y Heb 13:25

# 1 Thessalonians

## OVERVIEW

The church at Thessalonica was formed during Paul's second missionary journey. Paul's initial visit was cut short when he had to be secretly smuggled out of the city because some jealous Jews had instigated a riot in order to turn the local officials against him (see Ac 17:1–10). Timothy got word to Paul about the accomplishments of the Thessalonian church in spite of their suffering for the gospel. Paul's letter to the Thessalonians was intended to encourage Christian character, promote patience under suffering and give comfort to those who had lost loved ones in death. Paul explained how dead believers will rise first and those still alive "will be caught up together with them in the clouds to meet the Lord" (1Th 4:17). He also admonished the believers to maintain sexual purity (see 1Th 4:1–8) and to be productive and earn a living in order to avoid disgracing the people of God (see 1Th 4:11–12).

Someone once wrote that "character is who you are when no one is looking." As women believers in Jesus, our inner convictions are most noticeable to those around us. As you read through 1 Thessalonians, check to make sure that your life is an exemplary "letter" to your family and friends (see 2Co 3:1–3).

## OUTLINE

I. Thanksgiving for the Thessalonians' Faith (1:1–10)
II. Paul's Work in Thessalonica (2:1–16)
III. Paul's Longing to See the Thessalonians (2:17—3:13)
IV. Living to Please God (4:1–12)
V. The Return of Christ (4:13—5:11)
VI. Final Instructions and Blessing (5:12–28)

### SCANNABLE FACTS:

**Author:** Paul

**Time Written:** Around A.D. 51

**Theme to Note:** Facing the future with hope

**Notable Women:** There are no women mentioned in this book

1:2
a Ro 1:8
1:6
b 1Co 4:16

1 Paul, Silas[a] and Timothy,

To the church of the Thessalonians in God the Father and the Lord Jesus Christ:

Grace and peace to you.[b]

## Thanksgiving for the Thessalonians' Faith

2We always thank God for all of you,[a] mentioning you in our prayers. 3We continually remember before our God and Father your work produced by faith, your labor prompted by love, and your endurance inspired by hope in our Lord Jesus Christ.

*Blessed one,*

*Always give thanks.*

*I am always blessing you.*

*Love,*

*Your Sovereign God*

1 THESSALONIANS 1:2–3

4For we know, brothers loved by God, that he has chosen you, 5because our gospel came to you not simply with words, but also with power, with the Holy Spirit and with deep conviction. You know how we lived among you for your sake. 6You became imitators of us[b] and of the Lord; in spite of severe suffering, you welcomed the message with the joy given by the Holy Spirit. 7And so you became a model to all the believers in Macedonia and Achaia. 8The Lord's message rang out from you not only in Macedonia and Achaia—your faith in God has become known everywhere.[c] Therefore we do not need to say anything about it, 9for they themselves report what kind of reception you gave us. They tell how you turned to God from idols[d] to serve the living and true God, 10and to wait for his Son from heaven, whom he raised from the dead[e]—Jesus, who rescues us from the coming wrath.[f]

## Paul's Ministry in Thessalonica

2 You know, brothers, that our visit to you[g] was not a failure. 2We had previously suffered[h] and been insulted in Philippi, as you know, but with the help of our God we dared to tell you his gospel in spite of strong opposition. 3For the appeal we make does not spring from error or impure motives, nor are we trying to trick you. 4On the contrary, we speak as men approved by God to be entrusted with the gospel. We are not trying to please men[i] but God, who tests our hearts. 5You know we never used flattery, nor did we put on a mask to cover up greed—God is our witness.[j] 6We were not looking for praise from men, not from you or anyone else.

As apostles[k] of Christ we could have been a burden to you, 7but we were gentle among you, like a mother caring for her little children. 8We loved you so much that we were

1:8
c Ro 1:8; 10:18
1:9
d 1Co 12:2
1:10
e Ac 2:24
f Ro 5:9
2:1
g 1Th 1:5,9
2:2
h Ac 16:22; Php 1:30
2:4
i Gal 1:10
2:5
j Ro 1:9
2:6
k 1Co 9:1,2

[a]1 Greek *Silvanus,* a variant of *Silas* [b]1 Some early manuscripts *you from God our Father and the Lord Jesus Christ*

## *The African Presence*

### 1 Thessalonians 1

While there are no specific references to the African presence within the book of 1 Thessalonians, the gospel preached by Paul was influenced by people of North Africa and the Middle East (a historical and cultural subregion of Africa-Eurasia, traditionally held to be countries or regions in Southwest Asia together with Egypt). However, during the time of the New Testament, racial identification did not have the significance that it has today.

*Lord,*

*I sometimes strive to fit in with everyone else. I struggle to keep up and look good. But what I really need to do is concentrate on pleasing you. Help me to get my need for approval filled by you.*

*Amen*

1 THESSALONIANS 2:4–6

delighted to share with you not only the gospel of God but our lives as well,[l] because you had become so dear to us. 9 Surely you remember, brothers, our toil and hardship; we worked night and day in order not to be a burden to anyone[m] while we preached the gospel of God to you.

10 You are witnesses,[n] and so is God, of how holy, righteous and blameless we were among you who believed. 11 For you know that we dealt with each of you as a father deals with his own children, 12 encouraging, comforting and urging you to live lives worthy of God, who calls you into his kingdom and glory.

13 And we also thank God continually[o] because, when you received the word of God, which you heard from us, you accepted it not as the word of men, but as it actually is, the word of God, which is at work in you who believe. 14 For you, brothers, became imitators of God's churches in Judea, which are in Christ Jesus: You suffered from your own countrymen[p] the same things those churches suffered from the Jews, 15 who killed the Lord Jesus[q] and the prophets and also drove us out. They displease God and are hostile to all men 16 in their effort to keep us from speaking to the Gentiles[r] so that they may be saved. In this way they always heap up their sins to the limit.[s] The wrath of God has come upon them at last.[a]

## Paul's Longing to See the Thessalonians

17 But, brothers, when we were torn away from you for a short time (in person, not in thought),[t] out of our intense longing we made every effort to see you.[u] 18 For we wanted to come to you—certainly I, Paul, did, again and again—but Satan stopped us.[v] 19 For what is our hope, our joy, or the crown in which we will glory[w] in the presence of our Lord Jesus when he comes? Is it not you? 20 Indeed, you are our glory and joy.

3 So when we could stand it no longer,[x] we thought it best to be left by ourselves in Athens.[y] 2 We sent Timothy, who is our brother and God's fellow worker[b] in spreading the gospel of Christ, to strengthen and encourage you in your faith, 3 so that no one would be unsettled by these trials. You know quite well that we were destined for them.[z] 4 In fact, when we were with you, we kept telling you that we would be persecuted. And it turned out that way, as you well know. 5 For this reason, when I could stand it no longer, I sent to find out about your faith. I was afraid that in some way the tempter might have tempted you and our efforts might have been useless.[a]

## Timothy's Encouraging Report

6 But Timothy has just now come to us from you and has brought good news about your faith and love. He has told us that you always have pleasant memories of us and that you long to see us, just as we also long to see you. 7 Therefore, brothers, in all our distress and persecution we were encouraged about you because of your faith. 8 For now we really live, since you are standing firm in the Lord. 9 How can we thank God enough for you[b] in return for all the joy we have in the presence of our God because of you? 10 Night and day we pray[c] most earnestly that we may see you again and supply what is lacking in your faith.

11 Now may our God and Father himself and our Lord Jesus clear the way for us to come to you. 12 May the Lord make your love increase and overflow for each other[d] and for everyone else, just as ours does for you. 13 May he strengthen your hearts so that you will be blameless[e] and holy in the presence of our God and Father when our Lord Jesus comes with all his holy ones.

**2:8** l 2Co 12:15
**2:9** m 2Th 3:8
**2:10** n 1Th 1:5
**2:13** o 1Th 1:2
**2:14** p Ac 17:5
**2:15** q Ac 2:23
**2:16** r Ac 13:45,50 s Mt 23:32
**2:17** t 1Co 5:3 u 1Th 3:10
**2:18** v Ro 1:13
**2:19** w 2Co 1:14
**3:1** x ver 5 y Ac 17:15
**3:3** z Ac 9:16
**3:5** a Gal 2:2
**3:9** b 1Th 1:2
**3:10** c 2Ti 1:3
**3:12** d 1Th 4:9,10
**3:13** e 1Co 1:8

[a] 16 Or *them fully* [b] 2 Some manuscripts *brother and fellow worker;* other manuscripts *brother and God's servant*

**4:3** f 1Co 6:18
**4:5** g Ro 1:26; h Eph 4:17
**4:6** i Heb 13:4
**4:7** j Lev 11:44
**4:8** k Ro 5:5
**4:9** l 1Th 5:1
**4:10** m 1Th 1:7; n 1Th 3:12
**4:11** o Eph 4:28; 2Th 3:10–12
**4:13** p Eph 2:12
**4:16** q Mt 24:31; r 1Co 15:23

## Living to Please God

4 Finally, brothers, we instructed you how to live in order to please God, as in fact you are living. Now we ask you and urge you in the Lord Jesus to do this more and more. 2 For you know what instructions we gave you by the authority of the Lord Jesus.

3 It is God's will that you should be sanctified: that you should avoid sexual immorality;[f] 4 that each of you should learn to control his own body[a] in a way that is holy and honorable, 5 not in passionate lust[g] like the heathen,[h] who do not know God; 6 and that in this matter no one should wrong his brother or take advantage of him. The Lord will punish men for all such sins,[i] as we have already told you and warned you. 7 For God did not call us to be impure, but to live a holy life.[j] 8 Therefore, he who rejects this instruction does not reject man but God, who gives you his Holy Spirit.[k]

9 Now about brotherly love we do not need to write to you,[l] for you yourselves have been taught by God to love each other. 10 And in fact, you do love all the brothers throughout Macedonia.[m] Yet we urge you, brothers, to do so more and more.[n]

11 Make it your ambition to lead a quiet life, to mind your own business and to work with your hands,[o] just as we told you, 12 so that your daily life may win the respect of outsiders and so that you will not be dependent on anybody.

## The Coming of the Lord

13 Brothers, we do not want you to be ignorant about those who fall asleep, or to grieve like the rest of men, who have no hope.[p] 14 We believe that Jesus died and rose again and so we believe that God will bring with Jesus those who have fallen asleep in him. 15 According to the Lord's own word, we tell you that we who are still alive, who are left till the coming of the Lord, will certainly not precede those who have fallen asleep. 16 For the Lord himself will come down from heaven, with a loud command, with the voice of the archangel and with the trumpet call of God,[q] and the dead in Christ will rise first.[r] 17 After that, we who are still alive and are left[s] will be caught up together with them in the clouds[t] to meet the Lord in the air. And so we will be with the Lord forever. 18 Therefore encourage each other with these words.

**4:17** s 1Co 15:52; t Ac 1:9
**5:1** u 1Th 4:9
**5:2** v 2Pe 3:10
**5:8** w Eph 6:14
**5:9** x 2Th 2:13,14
**5:14** y 2Th 3:6,7,11
**5:15** z Gal 6:10; Eph 4:32

5 Now, brothers, about times and dates we do not need to write to you,[u] 2 for you know very well that the day of the Lord will come like a thief in the night.[v] 3 While people are saying, "Peace and safety," destruction will come on them suddenly, as labor pains on a pregnant woman, and they will not escape.

4 But you, brothers, are not in darkness so that this day should surprise you like a thief. 5 You are all sons of the light and sons of the day. We do not belong to the night or to the darkness. 6 So then, let us not be like others, who are asleep, but let us be alert and self-controlled. 7 For those who sleep, sleep at night, and those who get drunk, get drunk at night. 8 But since we belong to the day, let us be self-controlled, putting on faith and love as a breastplate,[w] and the hope of salvation as a helmet. 9 For God did not appoint us to suffer wrath but to receive salvation through our Lord Jesus Christ.[x] 10 He died for us so that, whether we are awake or asleep, we may live together with him. 11 Therefore encourage one another and build each other up, just as in fact you are doing.

> *"Surround yourself only with people who are going to lift you higher."*
> —Oprah Winfrey, entertainer

## Final Instructions

12 Now we ask you, brothers, to respect those who work hard among you, who are over you in the Lord and who admonish you. 13 Hold them in the highest regard in love because of their work. Live in peace with each other. 14 And we urge you, brothers, warn those who are idle,[y] encourage the timid, help the weak, be patient with everyone. 15 Make sure that nobody pays back wrong for wrong, but always try to be kind to each other[z] and to everyone else.

[a]4 Or *learn to live with his own wife*; or *learn to acquire a wife*

# Inspire

## PRAYER

Prayer is the opportunity God provides us to become intimately acquainted with him. In our conversations with God, through prayer, we develop a personal relationship with him. Prayer is the greatest power on Earth. It is communication between the heart of a person and the heart of God. This personal contact with God's living presence is a privilege granted to all human beings. Prayer allows us to embrace hope in seemingly hopeless situations and empowers us with strength to see and seek the possible in the apparently impossible.

Prayer is our expression of dependence upon God as well as our affirmation of God's promises to us. The sincerity and potency of our prayer is often indicated by our acknowledgment of a willingness to change. We become openly vulnerable as we bow before the mysterious, awesome presence of the indwelling Spirit of God and listen as God speaks quietly—or sometimes boisterously—to the center of our souls.

In 1 Thessalonians 5:17 we are called to pray "continually," to carry on an open-ended conversation with our Maker (sometimes rambling, sometimes urgent, sometimes expressed in short snippets) as we go about the course of our day. The transition to this new "style" of living may leave us confused or overawed. Sincere prayer may well cause us in our perceived insignificance to tremble before the greatness of an omnipotent, omniscient God. Yet we have continuously before us the assurance that God is not only willing but also able; God always knows best, and he hears and answers our prayers.

Oftentimes we utter ardent requests and become discouraged when God's timing does not coincide with our own and his ways do not surrender to the "demands" we make on the basis of our meager understanding. At these moments we do well to follow the familiar advice to "let go and let God." It is always better to wait on God's timing than to attempt to force a solution. When God is directing a situation, we don't have to force circumstances; they flow. Prayer is not intended to be a means of manipulating God; it is the method he has ordained by which we are to seek his strength, direction and will.

There is absolutely no limitation in God. So pray! Prayer is the springboard of all good and the source of all prosperity. May your life be filled with unspeakable joy, fortified by the peace that surpasses all understanding as you relinquish what you are for what God would have you be. "Not my will, Lord, but yours be done!"

—C. Archibald

For the next Inspire note, go to page 1423.

### read

1 Thessalonians 5:16–18; see also Psalm 37:1–7; Luke 11:1–13; 22:39–42; Philippians 4:4–7.

**See also** the Inspire Notes "Prayer: A God-Given Promise," "Prayer: The Antidote to Worry," "God's Promises: Always 'Yes' and 'Amen' " and "Faith," and the Women of the Bible Notes "Hannah: What Do You Do When God Says 'No'?" "Daughter of Jarius: A Testament of Faith," "The Persistent Widow: Always Pray" and "Rhoda: Doing Her Duty."

### WOMAN of COLOR

How often and sincerely do you pray? Do you see prayer as an open-ended conversation with your Maker? Communicate with God continually!

16 Be joyful always; 17 pray continually;
18 give thanks in all circumstances, for this
is God's will for you in Christ Jesus.
19 Do not put out the Spirit's fire;[a] 20 do not
treat prophecies with contempt. 21 Test ev-
erything. Hold on to the good. 22 Avoid every
kind of evil.
23 May God himself, the God of peace,
sanctify you through and through. May
your whole spirit, soul and body be kept
blameless at the coming of our Lord Jesus
Christ. 24 The one who calls you is faithful[b]
and he will do it.

25 Brothers, pray for us. 26 Greet all the
brothers with a holy kiss. 27 I charge you be-
fore the Lord to have this letter read to all
the brothers.[c]
28 The grace of our Lord Jesus Christ be
with you.

**5:19** a Eph 4:30

**5:24** b 1Co 1:9

**5:27** c Col 4:16

# 2 Thessalonians

## OVERVIEW

Paul's second letter to the Thessalonians likely was written only a few months after he wrote his first letter. Apparently, some believers had misunderstood Paul in the first letter and were not working because they thought the Lord's return was imminent. Paul admonished them, saying, "If a man will not work, he shall not eat" (2Th 3:10).

Paul's letter gives women believers today the same encouragement that he gave the church at Thessalonica: Stand firm on the teachings of God's Word. This means that we must continue to "fulfill every good purpose" (2Th 1:11) because Jesus could return at any given moment. Look to 2 Thessalonians to help you stay focused on doing God's work, regardless of what others around you may be doing.

## OUTLINE

I. Greetings, Thanksgiving and Prayer (1:1–12)
II. The Return of Jesus (2:1–17)
III. A Call to Prayer (3:1–5)
IV. Warnings Against Idleness (3:6–18)

### SCANNABLE FACTS:

**Author:** Paul

**Time Written:** Around A.D. 51 or 52

**Theme to Note:** Stand firm in the faith

**Notable Women:** There are no women mentioned in this book

**1:1** a 1Th 1:1
**1:3** b 1Th 3:12
**1:4** c 1Th 2:14
**1:5** d Php 1:28
**1:7** e 1Th 4:16; Jude 14
**1:8** f Ro 2:8
**1:9** g Php 3:19
**1:11** h ver 5 i 1Th 1:3
**2:1** j Mk 13:27; 1Th 4:15–17
**2:3** k Eph 5:6–8 l Da 7:25
**2:4** m 1Co 8:5 n Isa 14:13,14

1 Paul, Silas[a] and Timothy,[a]

To the church of the Thessalonians in God our Father and the Lord Jesus Christ:

[2]Grace and peace to you from God the Father and the Lord Jesus Christ.

## Thanksgiving and Prayer

[3]We ought always to thank God for you, brothers, and rightly so, because your faith is growing more and more, and the love every one of you has for each other is increasing.[b] [4]Therefore, among God's churches we boast about your perseverance and faith in all the persecutions and trials you are enduring.[c]

[5]All this is evidence[d] that God's judgment is right, and as a result you will be counted worthy of the kingdom of God, for which you are suffering. [6]God is just: He will pay back trouble to those who trouble you [7]and give relief to you who are troubled, and to us as well. This will happen when the Lord Jesus is revealed from heaven in blazing fire with his powerful angels.[e] [8]He will punish those who do not know God and do not obey the gospel of our Lord Jesus.[f] [9]They will be punished with everlasting destruction[g] and shut out from the presence of the Lord and from the majesty of his power [10]on the day he comes to be glorified in his holy people and to be marveled at among all those who have believed. This includes you, because you believed our testimony to you.

[11]With this in mind, we constantly pray for you, that our God may count you worthy[h] of his calling, and that by his power he may fulfill every good purpose of yours and every act prompted by your faith.[i] [12]We pray this so that the name of our Lord Jesus may be glorified in you, and you in him, according to the grace of our God and the Lord Jesus Christ.[b]

## The Man of Lawlessness

2 Concerning the coming of our Lord Jesus Christ and our being gathered to him,[j] we ask you, brothers, [2]not to become easily unsettled or alarmed by some prophecy, report or letter supposed to have come from us, saying that the day of the Lord has already come. [3]Don't let anyone deceive you[k] in any way, for ⌞that day will not come⌟ until the rebellion occurs and the man of lawlessness[c] is revealed,[l] the man doomed to destruction. [4]He will oppose and will exalt himself over everything that is called God[m] or is worshiped, so that he sets himself up in God's temple, proclaiming himself to be God.[n]

[5]Don't you remember that when I was with you I used to tell you these things? [6]And now you know what is holding him back, so that he may be revealed at the proper time. [7]For the secret power of lawlessness is already at work; but the one who now holds it back will continue to do so till he is taken out of the way. [8]And then the lawless one will be revealed, whom the Lord Jesus will overthrow with the breath of his mouth and destroy by the splendor of his

[a]1 Greek *Silvanus*, a variant of *Silas* [b]12 Or *God and Lord, Jesus Christ* [c]3 Some manuscripts *sin*

## *The African Presence*

### 2 Thessalonians 1

While there are no specific references to the African presence within the book of 2 Thessalonians, the gospel preached by Paul was influenced by people of North Africa and the Middle East (a historical and cultural subregion of Africa-Eurasia, traditionally held to be countries or regions in Southwest Asia together with Egypt). However, during the time of the New Testament, racial identification did not have the significance that it has today.

**2:9** o Jn 4:48
**2:12** p Ro 1:32
**2:13** q Eph 1:4 r 1Pe 1:2
**2:15** s 1Co 16:13 t 1Co 11:2

coming. [9]The coming of the lawless one will
be in accordance with the work of Satan dis-
played in all kinds of counterfeit miracles,
signs and wonders,[o] [10]and in every sort of
evil that deceives those who are perishing.
They perish because they refused to love the
truth and so be saved. [11]For this reason God
sends them a powerful delusion so that they
will believe the lie [12]and so that all will be
condemned who have not believed the truth
but have delighted in wickedness.[p]

*Sister,*

*Hold on to the truth.*

*Love,*
*The God of All Truth*

2 THESSALONIANS 2:9–10

## Stand Firm

[13]But we ought always to thank God for
you, brothers loved by the Lord, because
from the beginning God chose you[a][q] to be
saved through the sanctifying work of the
Spirit[r] and through belief in the truth. [14]He
called you to this through our gospel, that
you might share in the glory of our Lord
Jesus Christ. [15]So then, brothers, stand firm[s]
and hold to the teachings[b] we passed on to
you,[t] whether by word of mouth or by letter.
[16]May our Lord Jesus Christ himself
and God our Father, who loved us and by
his grace gave us eternal encouragement
and good hope, [17]encourage your hearts
and strengthen you in every good deed and
word.

## Request for Prayer

3 Finally, brothers, pray for us that the
message of the Lord may spread rapidly
and be honored, just as it was with you.
[2]And pray that we may be delivered from
wicked and evil men,[u] for not everyone
has faith. [3]But the Lord is faithful,[v] and he
will strengthen and protect you from the
evil one. [4]We have confidence in the Lord
that you are doing and will continue to do
the things we command. [5]May the Lord
direct your hearts[w] into God's love and
Christ's perseverance.

## Warning Against Idleness

[6]In the name of the Lord Jesus Christ,
we command you, brothers, to keep away
from every brother who is idle and does not
live according to the teaching[c] you received
from us. [7]For you yourselves know how you
ought to follow our example. We were not
idle when we were with you, [8]nor did we
eat anyone's food without paying for it. On
the contrary, we worked[x] night and day, la-
boring and toiling so that we would not be
a burden to any of you. [9]We did this, not be-
cause we do not have the right to such help,[y]
but in order to make ourselves a model for
you to follow. [10]For even when we were with
you, we gave you this rule: "If a man will not
work,[z] he shall not eat."
[11]We hear that some among you are idle.
They are not busy; they are busybodies.[a]
[12]Such people we command and urge in the
Lord Jesus Christ to settle down and earn
the bread they eat.[b] [13]And as for you, broth-
ers, never tire of doing what is right.[c]
[14]If anyone does not obey our instruction
in this letter, take special note of him. Do
not associate with him, in order that he may
feel ashamed. [15]Yet do not regard him as an
enemy, but warn him as a brother.

## Final Greetings

[16]Now may the Lord of peace[d] himself
give you peace at all times and in every way.
The Lord be with all of you.
[17]I, Paul, write this greeting in my own
hand,[e] which is the distinguishing mark in
all my letters. This is how I write.
[18]The grace of our Lord Jesus Christ be
with you all.[f]

**3:2** u Ro 15:31
**3:3** v 1Co 1:9
**3:5** w 1Ch 29:18
**3:8** x Ac 18:3
**3:9** y 1Co 9:4–14
**3:10** z 1Th 4:11
**3:11** a 1Ti 5:13
**3:12** b 1Th 4:11
**3:13** c Gal 6:9
**3:16** d Ro 15:33
**3:17** e 1Co 16:21
**3:18** f Ro 16:20

[a]13 Some manuscripts *because God chose you as his firstfruits* [b]15 Or *traditions* [c]6 Or *tradition*

# 1 Timothy

## OVERVIEW

The apostle Paul had left Timothy, his young assistant, to lead the church at Ephesus. As a loving spiritual father and mentor, Paul considered Timothy his "true son in the faith" (1Ti 1:2); therefore, his first letter to Timothy is filled with instructions and exhortations for Timothy's personal growth as well as for the church. Timothy was encouraged to confront false teachers and conduct proper public worship. Paul also gave instructions for the elders and deacons in the church, as well as for widows and slaves.

In order for Timothy to be a "good minister of Christ Jesus" (1Ti 4:6), he was encouraged to avoid godless myths and set an example for others in speech, in living, in love, in faith and in purity (see 1Ti 4). Paul wanted Timothy to treat both older and younger people with respect (see 1Ti 5:1–2) and to flee the love of money (see 1Ti 6:10–11).

Just as Timothy in his youth was to be an example for others, the charge is the same for women believers. Do your conversations, appearance and lifestyle bring glory to God or do these things serve as distractions? Study how Paul was training Timothy for leadership in the church, and pray for God's guidance in how you present yourself before him and others.

## OUTLINE



### SCANNABLE FACTS:

**Author:** Paul

**Time Written:** Around A.D. 64

**Theme to Note:** Godliness with contentment is great gain

**Notable Women:** Deacons' wives, widows

**1:1** a Col 1:27
**1:2** b Ac 16:1
**1:3** c Gal 1:6,7
**1:4** d Tit 1:14
**1:5** e 2Ti 2:22
**1:8** f Ro 7:12
**1:10** g 2Ti 4:3; Tit 1:9
**1:11** h Gal 2:7

1 Paul, an apostle of Christ Jesus by the
command of God our Savior and of
Christ Jesus our hope,[a]

2To Timothy[b] my true son in the faith:

Grace, mercy and peace from God the Fa-
ther and Christ Jesus our Lord.

## Warning Against False Teachers of the Law

3As I urged you when I went into Macedo-
nia, stay there in Ephesus so that you may
command certain men not to teach false
doctrines[c] any longer 4nor to devote them-
selves to myths[d] and endless genealogies.
These promote controversies rather than
God's work—which is by faith. 5The goal of
this command is love, which comes from a
pure heart[e] and a good conscience and a sin-
cere faith. 6Some have wandered away from
these and turned to meaningless talk. 7They
want to be teachers of the law, but they do
not know what they are talking about or
what they so confidently affirm.

8We know that the law is good[f] if one uses
it properly. 9We also know that law[a] is made
not for the righteous but for lawbreakers and
rebels, the ungodly and sinful, the unholy
and irreligious; for those who kill their fa-
thers or mothers, for murderers, 10for adul-
terers and perverts, for slave traders and
liars and perjurers—and for whatever else
is contrary to the sound doctrine[g] 11that con-
forms to the glorious gospel of the blessed
God, which he entrusted to me.[h]

## The Lord's Grace to Paul

12I thank Christ Jesus our Lord, who
has given me strength, that he considered
me faithful, appointing me to his service.
13Even though I was once a blasphemer and
a persecutor[i] and a violent man, I was shown
mercy because I acted in ignorance and un-
belief. 14The grace of our Lord was poured
out on me abundantly, along with the faith
and love that are in Christ Jesus.

15Here is a trustworthy saying[j] that de-
serves full acceptance: Christ Jesus came
into the world to save sinners—of whom
I am the worst. 16But for that very reason I
was shown mercy so that in me, the worst
of sinners, Christ Jesus might display his
unlimited patience as an example for those
who would believe on him and receive eter-
nal life. 17Now to the King eternal, immor-
tal, invisible, the only God, be honor and
glory for ever and ever. Amen.

18Timothy, my son, I give you this instruc-
tion in keeping with the prophecies once
made about you,[k] so that by following them
you may fight the good fight,[l] 19holding on
to faith and a good conscience. Some have
rejected these and so have shipwrecked
their faith. 20Among them are Hymenaeus[m]
and Alexander,[n] whom I have handed over
to Satan to be taught not to blaspheme.

## Instructions on Worship

2 I urge, then, first of all, that requests,
prayers, intercession and thanksgiving
be made for everyone— 2for kings and all
those in authority,[o] that we may live peace-

**1:13** i Ac 8:3
**1:15** j 2Ti 2:11
**1:18** k 1Ti 4:14 l 2Ti 2:3
**1:20** m 2Ti 2:17 n 2Ti 4:14
**2:2** o Ezr 6:10; Ro 13:1

[a]9 Or *that the law*

## *The African Presence*

### 1 Timothy 1

While there are no specific references to the African presence within the book of 1 Timothy, the gospel preached by Paul was influenced by people of North Africa and the Middle East (a historical and cultural subregion of Africa-Eurasia, traditionally held to be countries or regions in Southwest Asia together with Egypt). However, during the time of the New Testament, racial identification did not have the significance that it has today.

2:4 p 2Ti 2:25
2:5 q Gal 3:20
2:6 r 1Co 1:6

ful and quiet lives in all godliness and ho-
liness. [3]This is good, and pleases God our
Savior, [4]who wants all men to be saved and
to come to a knowledge of the truth.[p] [5]For
there is one God and one mediator[q] between
God and men, the man Christ Jesus, [6]who
gave himself as a ransom for all men—the
testimony[r] given in its proper time. [7]And
for this purpose I was appointed a herald
and an apostle—I am telling the truth, I am
not lying—and a teacher of the true faith to
the Gentiles.

Inspire

## CONFIDENCE FOR EACH DAY

We are leaders wearing many hats, juggling numerous responsibilities and walking in our purpose. We can get through each day, complete every task, finish all our projects with confidence because we are doing what God has called us to do.

However, no matter how self-assured we are, sometimes we find ourselves feeling uncertain. Doubt can come in many forms: A change in a situation can make us question if we are walking in our purpose. A comment made by another can make us wonder if we're doing the right thing. Or worse, a tragedy can overcome us and make us doubt everything we believe—even question our faith.

Life can sometimes overwhelm us, but no matter what is going on, we can have confidence in knowing that "God has our back." Even before the world began, God knew all of the tragedies and triumphs that we would face. While we were in our mother's womb, God was aware of every hurt that would come our way; and he is more than capable to bring us healing. We don't have to look at circumstances; we don't have to believe the things we see. Our trust can be placed totally in the Lord, recognizing by faith that he knows all that he's planned for us. In 1 Timothy 1:12, Paul reminds his readers it is God who has given him his strength to accomplish his tasks. God gave Paul his assignment, and then God gave Paul what he needed.

No matter what our assignment might be, in God, we can stand strong and have confidence that the things he's told us to do and the promises he's made will come forth. This is, after all, what our faith is all about.

—V. Murray

For the next Inspire note, go to page 1427.

### read

1 Timothy 1:12–20; see also Psalm 146; Proverbs 3:5–6.

**See also** the Inspire Notes "Confidence" and "Fear," and the Women of the Bible Notes "Queen Vashti: A Woman of Strength," "Esther: More Than a Beauty Queen," "Candace: Secure Leader" and "Philip's Daughters: Those Preaching Women."

### WOMAN of COLOR

How has God brought you through your storms? Share your testimony with someone who needs confidence today.

8 I want men everywhere to lift up holy hands[s] in prayer, without anger or disputing.

9 I also want women to dress modestly, with decency and propriety, not with braided hair or gold or pearls or expensive clothes,[t] 10 but with good deeds, appropriate for women who profess to worship God.

11 A woman should learn in quietness and full submission. 12 I do not permit a woman to teach or to have authority over a man; she must be silent. 13 For Adam was formed first, then Eve.[u] 14 And Adam was not the one deceived; it was the woman who was deceived and became a sinner.[v] 15 But women[a] will be saved[b] through childbearing—if they continue in faith, love and holiness with propriety.

## Overseers and Deacons

3 Here is a trustworthy saying: If anyone sets his heart on being an overseer,[c] he desires a noble task. 2 Now the overseer must be above reproach,[w] the husband of but one wife, temperate, self-controlled, respectable, hospitable, able to teach,[x] 3 not given to drunkenness, not violent but gentle, not quarrelsome, not a lover of money. 4 He must manage his own family well and see that his children obey him with proper respect.[y] 5 (If anyone does not know how to manage his own family, how can he take care of God's church?) 6 He must not be a recent convert, or he may become conceited[z] and fall under the same judgment as the devil. 7 He must also have a good reputation with outsiders, so that he will not fall into disgrace and into the devil's trap.[a]

8 Deacons, likewise, are to be men worthy of respect, sincere, not indulging in much wine, and not pursuing dishonest gain. 9 They must keep hold of the deep truths of the faith with a clear conscience.[b] 10 They must first be tested; and then if there is nothing against them, let them serve as deacons.

11 In the same way, their wives[d] are to be women worthy of respect, not malicious talkers[c] but temperate and trustworthy in everything.

12 A deacon must be the husband of but one wife and must manage his children and his household well. 13 Those who have served well gain an excellent standing and great assurance in their faith in Christ Jesus.

14 Although I hope to come to you soon, I am writing you these instructions so that, 15 if I am delayed, you will know how people ought to conduct themselves in God's household, which is the church[d] of the living God, the pillar and foundation of the truth. 16 Beyond all question, the mystery of godliness is great:

He[e] appeared in a body,[f][e]
 was vindicated by the Spirit,
was seen by angels,
 was preached among the nations,
was believed on in the world,
 was taken up in glory.

## Instructions to Timothy

4 The Spirit[f] clearly says that in later times some will abandon the faith and follow deceiving spirits and things taught by demons. 2 Such teachings come through hypocritical liars, whose consciences have been seared as with a hot iron.[g] 3 They forbid people to marry and order them to abstain from certain foods, which God created[h] to be received with thanksgiving[i] by those who believe and who know the truth. 4 For everything God created is good, and nothing is to be rejected if it is received with thanksgiving, 5 because it is consecrated by the word of God and prayer.

6 If you point these things out to the brothers, you will be a good minister of Christ Jesus, brought up in the truths of the faith[j] and of the good teaching that you have followed. 7 Have nothing to do with godless myths and old wives' tales; rather, train yourself to be godly. 8 For physical training is of some value, but godliness has value for all things,[k] holding promise for both the present life and the life to come.

9 This is a trustworthy saying that deserves full acceptance 10 (and for this we labor and strive), that we have put our hope in the living God, who is the Savior of all men, and especially of those who believe.

**2:8** s Ps 134:2
**2:9** t 1Pe 3:3
**2:13** u 1Co 11:8
**2:14** v Ge 3:1–6,13; 2Co 11:3
**3:2** w Tit 1:6–8 x 2Ti 2:24
**3:4** y Tit 1:6
**3:6** z 1Ti 6:4
**3:7** a 2Ti 2:26
**3:9** b 1Ti 1:19
**3:11** c Tit 2:3
**3:15** d ver 5
**3:16** e Jn 1:14
**4:1** f Jn 16:13
**4:2** g Eph 4:19
**4:3** h Ge 1:29 i Ro 14:6
**4:6** j 1Ti 1:10
**4:8** k 1Ti 6:6

[a] 15 Greek *she* [b] 15 Or *restored* [c] 1 Traditionally *bishop*; also in verse 2 [d] 11 Or *way, deaconesses* [e] 16 Some manuscripts *God* [f] 16 Or *in the flesh*

**4:12**
l Tit 2:7
m 1Ti 1:14

**4:14**
n 1Ti 1:18

**5:1**
o Lev 19:32

**5:4**
p Eph 6:1,2

**5:5**
q Lk 2:37

11 Command and teach these things. 12 Don't let anyone look down on you because you are young, but set an example[l] for the believers in speech, in life, in love, in faith[m] and in purity. 13 Until I come, devote yourself to the public reading of Scripture, to preaching and to teaching. 14 Do not neglect your gift, which was given you through a prophetic message[n] when the body of elders laid their hands on you.

*Responsible daughter.*

*Set an example; study my Word; use your gifts.*

*The God and Father of All*

1 TIMOTHY 4:11–14

*Lord,*

*give me boldness to do what you have called me to do. Help me to be thankful for and to love all people, including—and even especially—those who challenge me or disrespect me. Help me to be an example to others. In Jesus' name,*

*Amen*

1 TIMOTHY 4:11–14

15 Be diligent in these matters; give yourself wholly to them, so that everyone may see your progress. 16 Watch your life and doctrine closely. Persevere in them, because if you do, you will save both yourself and your hearers.

## Advice About Widows, Elders and Slaves

5 Do not rebuke an older man harshly,[o] but exhort him as if he were your father. Treat younger men as brothers, 2 older women as mothers, and younger women as sisters, with absolute purity.

3 Give proper recognition to those widows who are really in need. 4 But if a widow has children or grandchildren, these should learn first of all to put their religion into practice by caring for their own family and so repaying their parents and grandparents,[p] for this is pleasing to God. 5 The widow who is really in need and left all alone puts her hope in God and continues night and day to pray[q] and to ask God for help. 6 But the widow who lives for pleasure is dead even while she lives. 7 Give the people these instructions,[r] too, so that no one may be open to blame. 8 If anyone does not provide for his relatives, and especially for his immediate family, he has denied[s] the faith and is worse than an unbeliever.

9 No widow may be put on the list of widows unless she is over sixty, has been faithful to her husband,[a] 10 and is well known for her good deeds, such as bringing up children, showing hospitality, washing the feet[t] of the saints, helping those in trouble and devoting herself to all kinds of good deeds.

11 As for younger widows, do not put them on such a list. For when their sensual desires overcome their dedication to Christ, they want to marry. 12 Thus they bring judgment on themselves, because they have broken their first pledge. 13 Besides, they get into the habit of being idle and going about from house to house. And not only do they become idlers, but also gossips and busybodies,[u] saying things they ought not to. 14 So I counsel younger widows to marry,[v] to have children, to manage their homes and to give the enemy no opportunity for slander. 15 Some have in fact already turned away to follow Satan.

16 If any woman who is a believer has widows in her family, she should help them and not let the church be burdened with them, so that the church can help those widows who are really in need.[w]

17 The elders who direct the affairs of the

**5:7**
r 1Ti 4:11

**5:8**
s Tit 1:16

**5:10**
t Lk 7:44

**5:13**
u 2Th 3:11

**5:14**
v 1Co 7:9

**5:16**
w ver 3–5

[a] 9 Or *has had but one husband*

church well are worthy of double honor, especially those whose work is preaching and teaching. 18 For the Scripture says, "Do not muzzle the ox while it is treading out the grain,"[a][x] and "The worker deserves his wages."[b][y] 19 Do not entertain an accusation against an elder unless it is brought by two or three witnesses. 20 Those who sin are to be rebuked[z] publicly, so that the others may take warning.

21 I charge you, in the sight of God and Christ Jesus[a] and the elect angels, to keep these instructions without partiality, and to do nothing out of favoritism.

22 Do not be hasty in the laying on of hands, and do not share in the sins of others. Keep yourself pure.

23 Stop drinking only water, and use a little wine because of your stomach and your frequent illnesses.

24 The sins of some men are obvious, reaching the place of judgment ahead of them; the sins of others trail behind them. 25 In the same way, good deeds are obvious, and even those that are not cannot be hidden.

6 All who are under the yoke of slavery should consider their masters worthy of full respect,[b] so that God's name and our teaching may not be slandered.[c] 2 Those who have believing masters are not to show less respect for them because they are brothers. Instead, they are to serve them even better, because those who benefit from their service are believers, and dear to them. These are the things you are to teach and urge on them.[d]

## Love of Money

3 If anyone teaches false doctrines and does not agree to the sound instruction of our Lord Jesus Christ and to godly teaching, 4 he is conceited and understands nothing. He has an unhealthy interest in controversies and quarrels about words that result in envy, strife, malicious talk, evil suspicions 5 and constant friction between men of corrupt mind, who have been robbed of the truth and who think that godliness is a means to financial gain.

6 But godliness with contentment[e] is great gain. 7 For we brought nothing into the world, and we can take nothing out of it.[f] 8 But if we have food and clothing, we will be content with that. 9 People who want to get rich fall into temptation and a trap and into many foolish and harmful desires that plunge men into ruin and destruction. 10 For the love of money is a root of all kinds of evil. Some people, eager for money, have wandered from the faith and pierced themselves with many griefs.

## Paul's Charge to Timothy

11 But you, man of God, flee from all this, and pursue righteousness, godliness, faith, love, endurance and gentleness. 12 Fight the good fight[g] of the faith. Take hold of the eternal life to which you were called when you made your good confession in the presence of many witnesses. 13 In the sight of God, who gives life to everything, and of Christ Jesus, who while testifying before Pontius Pilate[h] made the good confession, I charge you[i] 14 to keep this command without spot or blame until the appearing of our Lord Jesus Christ, 15 which God will bring about in his own time—God, the blessed and only Ruler,[j] the King of kings and Lord of lords, 16 who alone is immortal and who lives in unapproachable light, whom no one has seen or can see. To him be honor and might forever. Amen.

17 Command those who are rich in this present world not to be arrogant nor to put their hope in wealth,[k] which is so uncertain, but to put their hope in God, who richly provides us with everything for our enjoyment.[l] 18 Command them to do good, to be rich in good deeds, and to be generous and willing to share. 19 In this way they will lay up treasure for themselves as a firm foundation for the coming age, so that they may take hold of the life that is truly life.

20 Timothy, guard what has been entrusted[m] to your care. Turn away from godless chatter and the opposing ideas of what is falsely called knowledge, 21 which some have professed and in so doing have wandered from the faith.[n]

Grace be with you.

5:18 x 1Co 9:7–9 y Lev 19:13; Dt 24:14,15; Mt 10:10
5:20 z Tit 1:13
5:21 a 1Ti 6:13
6:1 b Tit 2:9; 1Pe 2:18 c Tit 2:5,8
6:2 d 1Ti 4:11
6:6 e Heb 13:5
6:7 f Job 1:21
6:12 g 1Ti 1:18
6:13 h Jn 18:33–37 i 1Ti 5:21
6:15 j 1Ti 1:17
6:17 k Lk 12:20,21 l Ac 14:17
6:20 m 2Ti 1:12,14
6:21 n 2Ti 2:18

[a] 18 Deut. 25:4 [b] 18 Luke 10:7

# Inspire

## SINGLENESS: A STAGE IN LIFE

For many women, being single is sometimes viewed as a "thorn in the flesh"—ranging from a nettling irritant to an overwhelming frustration and disappointment. Some women become restless during this season of their lives and, as a result, find themselves in relationships that are unproductive and unhealthful emotionally, spiritually, psychologically and sometimes physically. But the Bible clearly teaches us that we are to be content in whatever situation we find ourselves (see 1Ti 6:6). This is the key to a successful single life. Contentment means being satisfied with the way things are until God chooses to change them. The Bible teaches us three essential truths that will help us find contentment.

First, the single woman can find rest in knowing that God created her for companionship. In Genesis 2:18 God said, "It is not good for the man to be alone. I will make a helper suitable for him." Adam experienced singleness in the Garden of Eden, but God decided when that period of his life should end.

Second, the single woman can find contentment in recognizing that God has a specific purpose for this stage in her life. Ecclesiastes 3:1 teaches us that there is a season for everything. The responsibility of the single woman is to discover God's purpose for her life during this stage (see 1Co 7:32–34).

Finally, the single woman is to view this passage of life as a period of preparation. In Genesis 2:18 we read that God had to "make" a mate for Adam. Singleness is a period during which we can fully give ourselves over to God's transforming power. We can use the time to prepare ourselves spiritually, financially and physically for whatever God has planned for our future.

For some sisters, singleness is a permanent state; for others, it is temporary. Regardless of whether you have never been married, are widowed, separated or divorced, the key to a successful, fulfilling single life is learning to be satisfied with where you are now, knowing that God is working out and through the details of every life passage for your ultimate good (see Ro 8:28).

—J. Thompson

For the next Inspire note, go to page 1438.

### read

1 Timothy 6:6; **see also** Matthew 6:25–34; 1 Corinthians 7:1–9,25–35; Philippians 4:4–13.

**See also** the Inspire Notes "Single Mothers," "Loneliness," "The Gift of Aloneness" and "Single Parenting," and the Women of the Bible Note "Rachel: Taking Care of Business."

### WOMAN of COLOR

How content are you with your current season of life?

# 2 Timothy

## OVERVIEW

Second Timothy contains Paul's last words to Timothy, his faithful son in the Lord. Paul knew that his time on earth was coming to an end (see 2Ti 4:6–7), and he wanted to make sure that the church would cling to the faith and teachings of Jesus Christ.

Paul reminded Timothy of his spiritual heritage through his grandmother Lois and his mother Eunice (see 2Ti 1:5). Paul also encouraged Timothy that God had given him "a spirit of power, of love and of self-discipline" rather than a spirit of fear (see 2Ti 1:7).

Using the examples of a soldier, athlete and farmer, Paul exhorted Timothy to faithfulness in his walk with Christ (see 2Ti 2:1–7). In writing to Timothy, Paul also challenged all the future generations of ministers to "preach the Word; be prepared in season and out of season" (2Ti 4:2)—as fallen people resist the truth of God's Word.

Discipline is the underlining momentum for every successful woman. Without it, failure is just around the corner. This is certainly true in our spiritual lives. The disciplines of daily prayer, Bible study and living as true servants of God will encourage every believer to take the necessary measures to grow in spiritual development.

## OUTLINE

I. Encouragement to Be Faithful (1:1—2:26)
II. Warning About the Last Days (3:1–9)
III. Paul's Final Charge to Timothy (3:10—4:8)
IV. Personal Remarks (4:9–22)

### SCANNABLE FACTS:

**Author:** Paul

**Time Written:** Around A.D. 67

**Theme to Note:** Fight the good fight, finish the race, keep the faith

**Notable Women:** Lois and Eunice

1:1 a 2Co 1:1
1:2 b 1Ti 1:2
1:3 c Ro 1:8
1:4 d 2Ti 4:9
1:5 e 1Ti 1:5 f Ac 16:1
1:6 g 1Ti 4:14
1:7 h Ro 8:15
1:8 i Eph 3:1

1 Paul, an apostle of Christ Jesus by the
will of God,[a] according to the promise
of life that is in Christ Jesus,

2 To Timothy, my dear son:[b]

Grace, mercy and peace from God the Fa-
ther and Christ Jesus our Lord.

## Encouragement to Be Faithful

3 I thank God,[c] whom I serve, as my fore-
fathers did, with a clear conscience, as night
and day I constantly remember you in my
prayers. 4 Recalling your tears, I long to see
you,[d] so that I may be filled with joy. 5 I have
been reminded of your sincere faith,[e] which
first lived in your grandmother Lois and in
your mother Eunice[f] and, I am persuaded,
now lives in you also. 6 For this reason I re-
mind you to fan into flame the gift of God,
which is in you through the laying on of my
hands.[g] 7 For God did not give us a spirit of
timidity,[h] but a spirit of power, of love and
of self-discipline.

8 So do not be ashamed to testify about
our Lord, or ashamed of me his prisoner.[i]
But join with me in suffering for the gospel,

*My child,*

*Live rightly, knowing that I will help you.*

*"Abba"*

2 TIMOTHY 1:6–7

by the power of God, 9 who has saved us and
called us to a holy life—not because of any-
thing we have done but because of his own
purpose and grace. This grace was given us
in Christ Jesus before the beginning of time,
10 but it has now been revealed through the
appearing of our Savior, Christ Jesus, who
has destroyed death and has brought life
and immortality to light through the gos-
pel. 11 And of this gospel I was appointed a
herald and an apostle and a teacher.[j] 12 That
is why I am suffering as I am. Yet I am not
ashamed, because I know whom I have be-
lieved, and am convinced that he is able
to guard[k] what I have entrusted to him for
that day.

13 What you heard from me, keep[l] as the
pattern of sound teaching, with faith and
love in Christ Jesus.[m] 14 Guard the good
deposit that was entrusted to you—guard
it with the help of the Holy Spirit who lives
in us.

15 You know that everyone in the province
of Asia has deserted me, including Phygelus
and Hermogenes.

16 May the Lord show mercy to the house-
hold of Onesiphorus, because he often
refreshed me and was not ashamed of my
chains. 17 On the contrary, when he was in
Rome, he searched hard for me until he
found me. 18 May the Lord grant that he will
find mercy from the Lord on that day! You
know very well in how many ways he helped
me in Ephesus.

2 You then, my son, be strong[n] in the
grace that is in Christ Jesus. 2 And the
things you have heard me say in the pres-

1:11 j 1Ti 2:7
1:12 k 1Ti 6:20
1:13 l Tit 1:9 m 1Ti 1:14
2:1 n Eph 6:10

## The African Presence

### 2 Timothy 1

While there are no specific references to the African presence within the book of 2 Timothy, the gospel preached by Paul was influenced by people of North Africa and the Middle East (a historical and cultural subregion of Africa-Eurasia, traditionally held to be countries or regions in Southwest Asia together with Egypt). However, during the time of the New Testament, racial identification did not have the significance that it has today.

ence of many witnesses entrust to reliable men who will also be qualified to teach others. [3]Endure hardship with us like a good soldier[o] of Christ Jesus. [4]No one serving as a soldier gets involved in civilian affairs—he wants to please his commanding officer. [5]Similarly, if anyone competes as an athlete, he does not receive the victor's crown[p] unless he competes according to the rules. [6]The hardworking farmer should be the first to receive a share of the crops. [7]Reflect on what I am saying, for the Lord will give you insight into all this.

[8]Remember Jesus Christ, raised from the dead, descended from David. This is my gospel,[q] [9]for which I am suffering even to the point of being chained like a criminal. But God's word is not chained. [10]Therefore I endure everything for the sake of the elect, that they too may obtain the salvation that is in Christ Jesus, with eternal glory.

[11]Here is a trustworthy saying:

If we died with him,
  we will also live with him;
[12]if we endure,
  we will also reign with him.
If we disown him,
  he will also disown us;[r]
[13]if we are faithless,
  he will remain faithful,[s]
  for he cannot disown himself.

## A Workman Approved by God

[14]Keep reminding them of these things. Warn them before God against quarreling about words; it is of no value, and only ruins those who listen. [15]Do your best to present yourself to God as one approved, a workman who does not need to be ashamed and who correctly handles the word of truth. [16]Avoid godless chatter, because those who indulge in it will become more and more ungodly. [17]Their teaching will spread like gangrene. Among them are Hymenaeus[t] and Philetus, [18]who have wandered away from the truth. They say that the resurrection has already taken place, and they destroy the faith of some. [19]Nevertheless, God's solid foundation stands firm, sealed with this inscription: "The Lord knows those who are his,"[a][u] and, "Everyone who confesses the name of the Lord must turn away from wickedness."

[20]In a large house there are articles not only of gold and silver, but also of wood and clay; some are for noble purposes and some for ignoble.[v] [21]If a man cleanses himself from the latter, he will be an instrument for noble purposes, made holy, useful to the Master and prepared to do any good work.[w]

[22]Flee the evil desires of youth, and pursue righteousness, faith, love and peace, along with those who call on the Lord out of a pure heart.[x] [23]Don't have anything to do with foolish and stupid arguments, because you know they produce quarrels. [24]And the Lord's servant must not quarrel; instead, he must be kind to everyone, able to teach, not resentful. [25]Those who oppose him he must gently instruct, in the hope that God will grant them repentance leading them to a knowledge of the truth, [26]and that they will come to their senses and escape from the trap of the devil,[y] who has taken them captive to do his will.

> *"It is not so much what we know as how well we use what we know."*
> —Ernesta Procope, CEO of E.G. Bowman Company

## Godlessness in the Last Days

**3** But mark this: There will be terrible times in the last days.[z] [2]People will be lovers of themselves, lovers of money, boastful, proud, abusive, disobedient to their parents,[a] ungrateful, unholy, [3]without love, unforgiving, slanderous, without self-control, brutal, not lovers of the good, [4]treacherous, rash, conceited, lovers of pleasure rather than lovers of God— [5]having a form of godliness but denying its power. Have nothing to do with them.

[6]They are the kind who worm their way into homes and gain control over weak-willed women, who are loaded down with sins and are swayed by all kinds of evil desires, [7]always learning but never able to

[a]19 Num. 16:5 (see Septuagint)

**2:3** o 1Ti 1:18
**2:5** p 1Co 9:25
**2:8** q Ro 2:16
**2:12** r Mt 10:33
**2:13** s Nu 23:19; Ro 3:3
**2:17** t 1Ti 1:20
**2:19** u Jn 10:14
**2:20** v Ro 9:21
**2:21** w 2Ti 3:17
**2:22** x 1Ti 1:5
**2:26** y 1Ti 3:7
**3:1** z 1Ti 4:1
**3:2** a Ro 1:30

3:8 b Ex7:11 c 1Ti6:5
3:9 d Ex7:12
3:10 e 1Ti4:6
3:13 f 2Ti2:16
3:14 g 2Ti1:13
3:15 h Jn5:39
3:16 i 2Pe1:20,21
3:17 j 1Ti6:11 k 2Ti2:21
4:1 l Ac10:42 m 1Ti5:21
4:2 n 1Ti4:13

acknowledge the truth. 8 Just as Jannes and Jambres opposed Moses,[b] so also these men oppose the truth—men of depraved minds,[c] who, as far as the faith is concerned, are rejected. 9 But they will not get very far because, as in the case of those men,[d] their folly will be clear to everyone.

## Paul's Charge to Timothy

10 You, however, know all about my teaching,[e] my way of life, my purpose, faith, patience, love, endurance, 11 persecutions, sufferings—what kinds of things happened to me in Antioch, Iconium and Lystra, the persecutions I endured. Yet the Lord rescued me from all of them. 12 In fact, everyone who wants to live a godly life in Christ Jesus will be persecuted, 13 while evil men and impostors will go from bad to worse,[f] deceiving and being deceived. 14 But as for you, continue in what you have learned and have become convinced of, because you know those from whom you learned it,[g] 15 and how from infancy you have known the holy Scriptures,[h] which are able to make you wise for salvation through faith in Christ Jesus. 16 All Scripture is God-breathed[i] and is useful for teaching, rebuking, correcting and training in righteousness, 17 so that the man of God[j] may be thoroughly equipped for every good work.[k]

*Lord,*

*help me to rejoice at all times. Thank you for the sweetness of your presence during my darkest hours, and for memories that inspire hope and abiding joy.*

*Amen*

2 TIMOTHY 3:10–12

4 In the presence of God and of Christ Jesus, who will judge the living and the dead,[l] and in view of his appearing and his kingdom, I give you this charge:[m] 2 Preach[n] the Word; be prepared in season and out of season; correct, rebuke[o] and encourage—with great patience and careful instruction. 3 For the time will come when men will not put up with sound doctrine.[p] Instead, to suit their own desires, they will gather around them a great number of teachers to say what their itching ears want to hear. 4 They will turn their ears away from the truth and turn aside to myths. 5 But you, keep your head in all situations, endure hardship, do the work of an evangelist,[q] discharge all the duties of your ministry.

6 For I am already being poured out like a drink offering,[r] and the time has come for my departure.[s] 7 I have fought the good fight, I have finished the race, I have kept the faith. 8 Now there is in store for me the crown of righteousness, which the Lord, the righteous Judge, will award to me on that day[t]—and not only to me, but also to all who have longed for his appearing.

## Personal Remarks

9 Do your best to come to me quickly, 10 for Demas,[u] because he loved this world, has deserted me and has gone to Thessalonica. Crescens has gone to Galatia, and Titus to Dalmatia. 11 Only Luke[v] is with me.[w] Get Mark and bring him with you, because he is helpful to me in my ministry. 12 I sent Tychicus to Ephesus. 13 When you come, bring the cloak that I left with Carpus at Troas, and my scrolls, especially the parchments.

14 Alexander[x] the metalworker did me a great deal of harm. The Lord will repay him for what he has done. 15 You too should be on your guard against him, because he strongly opposed our message.

16 At my first defense, no one came to my support, but everyone deserted me. May it not be held against them.[y] 17 But the Lord stood at my side and gave me strength, so that through me the message might be fully proclaimed and all the Gentiles might hear it. And I was delivered from the lion's mouth. 18 The Lord will rescue me from every evil attack[z] and will bring me safely to his heavenly kingdom. To him be glory for ever and ever. Amen.[a]

4:2 o 1Ti5:20; Tit1:13
4:3 p 1Ti1:10
4:5 q Ac21:8
4:6 r Php2:17 s Php1:23
4:8 t 2Ti1:12
4:10 u Col4:14
4:11 v Col4:14 w 2Ti1:15
4:14 x Ac19:33
4:16 y Ac7:60
4:18 z Ps121:7 a Ro11:36

# Claudia

## A Sincere Supporter

One story that was told to me when I was child has meant more to me as an adult than when I first heard it. That story focused on a woman who had three daughters. Each daughter was considered a valuable member of society: a prominent physician, a leading criminal attorney and a renowned vocalist. Life provided its challenges to each daughter. There were times when they doubted themselves, their abilities to handle situations and their understanding of what their system taught. Yet these women had a praying mother, grandmother, aunt, niece or daughter who was always available to offer encouragement or who never stopped praying.

Everyone needs a cheering squad and a support base. As women of color, we can appreciate the value of stored prayers and those who keep the faith in our stead. Claudia was such an ambassador to young Timothy and Paul (see 2Ti 4:21).

We don't know much about Claudia, but she is mentioned by Paul as a member of Paul's circle of supporters. She must have been the type of person who supported her leader despite what others thought. She was an encourager, nurturer and strong supporter. I believe that the reason Claudia was so supportive is that she did not put her total trust in the messenger, but in the message. Faith was the key to her maintaining a positive base and supportive spirit. She understood the message of Christ; she knew him and what he had done for her and what he promised to do for all believers. Therefore, she was able to support others who were ambassadors for Christ.

Claudia could have been our great-grandmother, grandmother or mother who prevailed through many tribulations and whose travails continue. Despite it all, our Claudias continue to look toward the hills for their help (see Ps 121). That's how they are able to be supportive prayer warriors.

—B. Kitt

### reflection

*Reflect on the women who have constantly prayed for you and served as your support base.*

*How can you be a support to other women?*

### read

2 Timothy 4:21; see also John 17:20–23.

**See also** the Inspire Notes "Purposeful Giving," "Sacrificial Living" and "Commitment to God," and the Women of the Bible Notes "The Widow's Offering: Selfless Giving" and "Mary, the Mother of James and Joses: Sacrificing for Christ."

For the next Women of the Bible note, go to page 1491.

## Final Greetings

19 Greet Priscilla[a] and Aquila and the
household of Onesiphorus. 20 Erastus[b]
stayed in Corinth, and I left Trophimus
sick in Miletus. 21 Do your best to get here
before winter. Eubulus greets you, and
so do Pudens, Linus, Claudia and all the
brothers.

22 The Lord be with your spirit.[c] Grace be
with you.

**4:20**
b Ac 19:22

**4:22**
c Gal 6:18

[a] 19 Greek *Prisca*, a variant of *Priscilla*

# Titus

## OVERVIEW

The apostle Paul had left Titus in Crete, an island in the Mediterranean Sea, to oversee the church there (see Tit 1:5). The culture in Crete encouraged lying, gluttony and monetary greed, so Paul wrote to exhort the believers in the Cretan church to live blameless lives. In his letter, Paul reminded Titus of his responsibility to identify and install reliable leadership (see Tit 1:5–9). Paul also wanted sound doctrine to be taught and for the various groups of people in the church to apply that doctrine through appropriate behavior. Paul appealed to the grace of God as the motivation for holy living (see Tit 2:11–14; 3:3–8).

The precious gift of experience can be passed from one woman to another, as illustrated in Titus 2:3–5. As women believers learn how to love their husbands and care for their children, they have the unique perspective to teach new wives and mothers. Whether married, unmarried, with or without children—every woman can use her wisdom to help the next generation.

## OUTLINE

I. Instructions for Titus (1:1–16)
II. Instructions for Specific Groups (2:1–15)
III. Instructions for Believers in General (3:1–11)
IV. Final Remarks (3:12–15)

### SCANNABLE FACTS:

**Author:** Paul

**Time Written:** Around A.D. 64

**Theme to Note:** Believers should devote themselves to doing what is good

**Notable Women:** Older women and younger women

1:2 a 2Ti1:1
1:3 b 2Ti1:10
1:4 c 2Co2:13
1:6 d 1Ti3:2
1:7 e 1Co4:1
1:8 f 1Ti3:2
1:9 g 1Ti1:10
1:10 h 1Ti1:6

1 Paul, a servant of God and an apostle of
Jesus Christ for the faith of God's elect
and the knowledge of the truth that leads
to godliness— 2 a faith and knowledge rest-
ing on the hope of eternal life,[a] which God,
who does not lie, promised before the begin-
ning of time, 3 and at his appointed season
he brought his word to light[b] through the
preaching entrusted to me by the command
of God our Savior,

4 To Titus,[c] my true son in our common
faith:

Grace and peace from God the Father and
Christ Jesus our Savior.

## Titus's Task on Crete

5 The reason I left you in Crete was that
you might straighten out what was left un-
finished and appoint[a] elders in every town,
as I directed you. 6 An elder must be blame-
less,[d] the husband of but one wife, a man
whose children believe and are not open
to the charge of being wild and disobedi-
ent. 7 Since an overseer[b] is entrusted with
God's work,[e] he must be blameless—not
overbearing, not quick-tempered, not given
to drunkenness, not violent, not pursuing
dishonest gain. 8 Rather he must be hospita-
ble,[f] one who loves what is good, who is self-
controlled, upright, holy and disciplined.
9 He must hold firmly to the trustworthy
message as it has been taught, so that he can
encourage others by sound doctrine[g] and re-
fute those who oppose it.

10 For there are many rebellious people,
mere talkers[h] and deceivers, especially
those of the circumcision group. 11 They
must be silenced, because they are ruining
whole households by teaching things they
ought not to teach—and that for the sake
of dishonest gain. 12 Even one of their own
prophets[i] has said, "Cretans are always liars,
evil brutes, lazy gluttons." 13 This testimony
is true. Therefore, rebuke them sharply, so
that they will be sound in the faith[j] 14 and
will pay no attention to Jewish myths[k] or to
the commands of those who reject the truth.
15 To the pure, all things are pure, but to
those who are corrupted and do not believe,
nothing is pure. In fact, both their minds
and consciences are corrupted. 16 They claim
to know God, but by their actions they deny
him.[l] They are detestable, disobedient and
unfit for doing anything good.

## What Must Be Taught to Various Groups

2 You must teach what is in accord with
sound doctrine. 2 Teach the older men
to be temperate, worthy of respect, self-
controlled, and sound in faith,[m] in love and
in endurance.

3 Likewise, teach the older women to be
reverent in the way they live, not to be slan-
derers or addicted to much wine, but to
teach what is good. 4 Then they can train the
younger women to love their husbands and
children, 5 to be self-controlled and pure, to
be busy at home, to be kind, and to be sub-
ject to their husbands,[n] so that no one will
malign the word of God.

6 Similarly, encourage the young men to
be self-controlled. 7 In everything set them

1:12 i Ac17:28
1:13 j Tit2:2
1:14 k 1Ti1:4
1:16 l 1Jn2:4
2:2 m Tit1:13
2:5 n Eph5:22

[a]5 Or *ordain* [b]7 Traditionally *bishop*

## *The African Presence*

### Titus 1:5

Crete is an island from which the Philistines came to settle in the land of Canaan. The ancestry of the Philistines can be traced to Ham's son Mizraim (see Ge 10:6,13; see also the African Presence note on Ge 10:6). The Philistines occupied the coastland of Canaan. For more on the Philistines, see the African Presence note on 1 Samuel 17.

# Inspire

## SELF-CONTROL

When a woman chooses to control her thoughts, feelings and actions rather than allowing them to master her, she is exercising self-control (see Tit 2:3–5). Being "self-controlled" (mentioned four times in Titus 2) is a personal discipline that allows us to say no to ungodly enticements and yes to God's will for our lives (see Tit 2:11–12). This fruit of the Spirit (see Gal 5:22–23) is what helps us decide to stay home and prepare for the next day when we'd rather be out partying; it's what gives us the strength to say no to activities that are unhealthy for us and to say yes to the good gifts God has for us.

Self-control allows us to be obedient to God even when the world is telling us to do our own thing. It gives us the strength to keep our mouths shut when appropriate and to keep our attitudes in check, to take a stand for Jesus even when we must stand alone. Self-control is necessary if we are to stay focused and be successful in life. God gives us this character trait as we listen to the Holy Spirit and allow him to guide our lives. Paul said, "Live by the Spirit, and you will not gratify the desires of the sinful nature" (Gal 5:16). In the final analysis, the essence of self-control lies in relinquishing our own limited control and yielding ourselves fully to God's enabling Spirit. True self-control means allowing God to control us!

In order to exercise God-control, sisters need to study God's Word and allow it to sink into and permeate their hearts. When we live lives characterized by self-control, we acknowledge that God has a plan for us, and we tell the world that we have chosen to honor God's purpose. Submission to God's will is both liberating and filled with many, often unexpected, blessings. So give up your own control and live a God-controlled life, submitting to his will. That's true self-control.

—K. Belt

For the next Inspire note, go to page 1449

### read

Titus 2:1–15; see also Psalm 19:12–14; Proverbs 25:28; 29:11; Galatians 5:16–26; 1 Peter 5:6–9; 2 Peter 1:3–9.

**See also** the Inspire Notes "Anger: Act or React," "Spiritual Discipline," "Integrity" and "Discipline," and the Women of the Bible Notes "Lot's Wife: Why Look Back?" "Athaliah: An Angry Woman" and "Sapphira: A Lost Opportunity for Truth."

### WOMAN of COLOR

Who or what do you allow to control your life?

2:7 o 1Ti4:12
2:9 p Eph6:5
2:10 q Mt5:16
2:12 r 2Ti3:12
3:2 s Eph4:31; 2Ti2:24

an example[o] by doing what is good. In your
teaching show integrity, seriousness [8]and
soundness of speech that cannot be con-
demned, so that those who oppose you may
be ashamed because they have nothing bad
to say about us.

[9]Teach slaves to be subject to their mas-
ters in everything,[p] to try to please them,
not to talk back to them, [10]and not to steal
from them, but to show that they can be
fully trusted, so that in every way they will
make the teaching about God our Savior at-
tractive.[q]

[11]For the grace of God that brings salva-
tion has appeared to all men. [12]It teaches
us to say "No" to ungodliness and worldly
passions, and to live self-controlled, upright
and godly lives[r] in this present age, [13]while
we wait for the blessed hope—the glorious
appearing of our great God and Savior,
Jesus Christ, [14]who gave himself for us to re-
deem us from all wickedness and to purify
for himself a people that are his very own,
eager to do what is good.

[15]These, then, are the things you should
teach. Encourage and rebuke with all au-
thority. Do not let anyone despise you.

## Doing What Is Good

3 Remind the people to be subject to rul-
ers and authorities, to be obedient, to
be ready to do whatever is good, [2]to slander
no one,[s] to be peaceable and considerate,
and to show true humility toward all men.

[3]At one time we too were foolish, disobe-
dient, deceived and enslaved by all kinds
of passions and pleasures. We lived in mal-
ice and envy, being hated and hating one
another. [4]But when the kindness and love
of God our Savior appeared,[t] [5]he saved us,
not because of righteous things we had
done, but because of his mercy. He saved us
through the washing of rebirth and renewal
by the Holy Spirit, [6]whom he poured out
on us generously through Jesus Christ our
Savior, [7]so that, having been justified by
his grace, we might become heirs having
the hope[u] of eternal life. [8]This is a trustwor-
thy saying.[v] And I want you to stress these
things, so that those who have trusted in
God may be careful to devote themselves to
doing what is good.[w] These things are excel-
lent and profitable for everyone.

[9]But avoid foolish controversies and
genealogies and arguments and quarrels[x]
about the law, because these are unprofit-
able and useless. [10]Warn a divisive person
once, and then warn him a second time.
After that, have nothing to do with him.
[11]You may be sure that such a man is warped
and sinful; he is self-condemned.

## Final Remarks

[12]As soon as I send Artemas or Tychicus[y]
to you, do your best to come to me at Nicop-
olis, because I have decided to winter there.
[13]Do everything you can to help Zenas the
lawyer and Apollos[z] on their way and see
that they have everything they need. [14]Our
people must learn to devote themselves to
doing what is good,[a] in order that they may
provide for daily necessities and not live un-
productive lives.

[15]Everyone with me sends you greetings.
Greet those who love us in the faith.

Grace be with you all.[b]

3:4 t Tit2:11
3:7 u Ro8:24
3:8 v 1Ti1:15 w Tit2:14
3:9 x 1Ti1:4
3:12 y Ac20:4
3:13 z Ac18:24
3:14 a ver8
3:15 b Col4:18

# Philemon

## OVERVIEW

In this brief letter the apostle Paul warmly greeted Philemon, whom Paul likely had led to Christ (see Phm 19), as a dear friend and fellow worker in the Lord (see Phm 1). Philemon owned a slave named Onesimus, who had run away, a crime punishable by death under Roman law. Onesimus had apparently stolen money from Philemon as well (see Phm 18). But Onesimus met Paul and became a believer (see Phm 10), and he now was willing to return to his master.

Paul wrote to Philemon using great skill and persuasive power to convince Philemon to treat Onesimus with kindness. Paul appealed to Philemon to treat Onesimus as a brother in the Lord—with the same care he would give Paul.

Society often separates people according to their race, gender or socioeconomic status. However, "there is neither Jew nor Greek, slave nor free, male nor female, for you are all one in Christ Jesus" (Gal 3:28). As you read through Philemon, recognize how Paul dealt with a challenging situation in a manner that brought honor to God.

## OUTLINE

I. Paul's Greetings (1–3)
II. Paul's Appreciation of Philemon (4–7)
III. Paul's Plea for Onesimus (8–21)
IV. Paul's Closing (22–25)

### SCANNABLE FACTS:

**Author:** Paul

**Time Written:** Around A.D. 60

**Theme to Note:** Forgive on the basis of love

**Notable Woman:** Apphia (probably Philemon's wife)

1 a Eph 3:1 b Php 2:25
2 c Col 4:17 d Php 2:25 e Ro 16:5
5 f Col 1:4

1 Paul, a prisoner[a] of Christ Jesus, and
Timothy our brother,

To Philemon our dear friend and fellow
worker,[b] 2 to Apphia our sister, to Archip-
pus[c] our fellow soldier[d] and to the church
that meets in your home:[e]

3 Grace to you and peace from God our Fa-
ther and the Lord Jesus Christ.

## Thanksgiving and Prayer

4 I always thank my God as I remember
you in my prayers, 5 because I hear about
your faith in the Lord Jesus and your love
for all the saints.[f] 6 I pray that you may be ac-
tive in sharing your faith, so that you will
have a full understanding of every good
thing we have in Christ. 7 Your love has given
me great joy and encouragement, because
you, brother, have refreshed the hearts of
the saints.

## Paul's Plea for Onesimus

8 Therefore, although in Christ I could be
bold and order you to do what you ought to
do, 9 yet I appeal to you on the basis of love.
I then, as Paul—an old man and now also a
prisoner of Christ Jesus— 10 I appeal to you
for my son Onesimus,[a] who became my son
while I was in chains. 11 Formerly he was use-
less to you, but now he has become useful
both to you and to me.
12 I am sending him—who is my very
heart—back to you. 13 I would have liked
to keep him with me so that he could take
your place in helping me while I am in
chains for the gospel. 14 But I did not want to
do anything without your consent, so that
any favor you do will be spontaneous and
not forced.[g] 15 Perhaps the reason he was
separated from you for a little while was that
you might have him back for good— 16 no
longer as a slave, but better than a slave, as
a dear brother.[h] He is very dear to me but
even dearer to you, both as a man and as a
brother in the Lord.

14 g 2Co 9:7
16 h 1Ti 6:2
17 i 2Co 8:23

*God,*

*help me to honor everyone around me as*
*your unique and cherished creation. Grant*
*that my thoughts, words and actions may*
*ever reflect your love. In Jesus' name,*

*Amen*

PHILEMON 10–16

17 So if you consider me a partner,[i] wel-
come him as you would welcome me. 18 If
he has done you any wrong or owes you
anything, charge it to me. 19 I, Paul, am
writing this with my own hand. I will pay
it back—not to mention that you owe me
your very self. 20 I do wish, brother, that
I may have some benefit from you in the
Lord; refresh my heart in Christ. 21 Con-

[a] 10 *Onesimus* means *useful.*

## *The African Presence*

**Philemon 1**

While there are no specific references to the African presence within the book of Philemon, the gospel preached by Paul was influenced by people of North Africa and the Middle East (a historical and cultural subregion of Africa-Eurasia, traditionally held to be countries or regions in Southwest Asia together with Egypt). However, during the time of the New Testament, racial identification did not have the significance that it has today.

22 j Php 1:25 k 2Co 1:11

fident of your obedience, I write to you,
knowing that you will do even more than
I ask.
22 And one thing more: Prepare a guest
room for me, because I hope to be[j] restored
to you in answer to your prayers.[k]

23 Epaphras,[l] my fellow prisoner in Christ
Jesus, sends you greetings. 24 And so do
Mark,[m] Aristarchus, Demas and Luke, my
fellow workers.
25 The grace of the Lord Jesus Christ be
with your spirit.

23 l Col 1:7
24 m Ac 12:12

# Hebrews

## OVERVIEW

The book of Hebrews emphasizes that Jesus Christ, the mediator of the new covenant, is far superior to the old covenant. The book asserts that Jesus is also higher than the angels (see Heb 1–2), Moses and Joshua (see Heb 3:1—4:13), and the highly respected Old Testament priesthood and sacrificial system (see Heb 4:14—10:18). At one point the writer used Melchizedek, the ancient priest-king of Salem (that is, Jerusalem), to show that Jesus Christ fulfilled God's plan to have the priesthood and kingship reside in his own Son (see Heb 7).

In view of Christ's superiority, the recipients of this letter—primarily Jewish converts to Christianity—were charged to resist the temptation to fall back into Judaism. Those who rejected Jesus and his atoning sacrifice had no hope for forgiveness for their sins. To bolster the readers' confidence, the writer listed those who had accomplished mighty works through faith in God in spite of their great afflictions (see Heb 11). The writer presented a roll call of the faithful, including the actions of several obedient women on this roll—Sarah and Rahab are called by name.

Many women make great sacrifices for the good of their family. Christ's sacrifice on the cross was for every single person born on earth. His death and resurrection give life to all men and women who accept him as Lord and Savior. As you read the book of Hebrews, reflect on what makes Jesus' sacrifice supreme—a sacrifice to which no other can compare.

## OUTLINE

I. Introduction: A Superior, New Revelation (1:1–4)
II. Jesus Christ Is Superior to Angels (1:5—2:18)
III. Jesus Christ Is Superior to Moses and Joshua (3:1—4:13)
IV. Jesus Christ Is Superior to the Priesthood and Sacrificial System (4:14—10:18)
V. A Call to Faithful Endurance (10:19—12:29)
VI. Final Exhortations (13:1–25)

## SCANNABLE FACTS:

**Author:** Unknown

**Time Written:** Sometime before the destruction of the temple in Jerusalem in A.D. 70

**Theme to Note:** Without faith it is impossible to please God

**Notable Women:** The women of faith recalled in Hebrews 11

1:1 a Nu 12:6,8
1:3 b Jn 1:14
1:4 c Php 2:9,10
1:5 d Ps 2:7
1:6 e Dt 32:43 (LXX and DSS); Ps 97:7
1:7 f Ps 104:4

## The Son Superior to Angels

1 In the past God spoke to our forefathers through the prophets at many times and in various ways,[a] 2 but in these last days he has spoken to us by his Son, whom he appointed heir of all things, and through whom he made the universe. 3 The Son is the radiance of God's glory[b] and the exact representation of his being, sustaining all things by his powerful word. After he had provided purification for sins, he sat down at the right hand of the Majesty in heaven. 4 So he became as much superior to the angels as the name he has inherited is superior to theirs.[c]

*Favored one,*

*I sent Jesus my Son to redeem the world.*
*You can rest in his cleansing.*

*God*

HEBREWS 1:1–4

5 For to which of the angels did God ever say,

"You are my Son;
today I have become your Father*[a]*"*[b]*?[d]

Or again,

"I will be his Father,
and he will be my Son"*[c]*?

6 And again, when God brings his firstborn into the world, he says,

"Let all God's angels worship him."*[d]*[e]

7 In speaking of the angels he says,

"He makes his angels winds,
his servants flames of fire."*[e]*[f]

8 But about the Son he says,

"Your throne, O God, will last for ever and ever,
and righteousness will be the scepter of your kingdom.
9 You have loved righteousness and hated wickedness;
therefore God, your God, has set you above your companions
by anointing you with the oil[g] of joy."*[f]*

10 He also says,

"In the beginning, O Lord, you laid the foundations of the earth,
and the heavens are the work of your hands.
11 They will perish, but you remain;
they will all wear out like a garment.[h]
12 You will roll them up like a robe;
like a garment they will be changed.
But you remain the same,
and your years will never end."*[g]*

13 To which of the angels did God ever say,

"Sit at my right hand
until I make your enemies
a footstool for your feet"*[h]*?[i]

14 Are not all angels ministering spirits[j] sent to serve those who will inherit salvation?

## Warning to Pay Attention

2 We must pay more careful attention, therefore, to what we have heard, so that we do not drift away. 2 For if the message spoken by angels[k] was binding, and every violation and disobedience received its just punishment, 3 how shall we escape if we ignore such a great salvation?[l] This salvation, which was first announced by the Lord, was confirmed to us by those who heard him.[m] 4 God also testified to it by signs, wonders and various miracles, and gifts of the Holy Spirit[n] distributed according to his will.[o]

## Jesus Made Like His Brothers

5 It is not to angels that he has subjected the world to come, about which we are speaking. 6 But there is a place where someone has testified:

"What is man that you are mindful of him,
the son of man that you care for him?

1:9 g Isa 61:1,3
1:11 h Isa 34:4
1:13 i Ps 110:1
1:14 j Ps 103:20
2:2 k Ac 7:53
2:3 l Heb 10:29 m Lk 1:2
2:4 n 1Co 12:4 o Eph 1:5

*a*5 Or *have begotten you* *b*5 Psalm 2:7 *c*5 2 Samuel 7:14; 1 Chron. 17:13 *d*6 Deut. 32:43 (see Dead Sea Scrolls and Septuagint) *e*7 Psalm 104:4 *f*9 Psalm 45:6,7 *g*12 Psalm 102:25–27 *h*13 Psalm 110:1

**2:8** p Ps 8:4–6; 1Co 15:25
**2:9** q Ac 2:33 r Php 2:7–9 s Jn 3:16
**2:10** t Ro 11:36
**2:11** u Jn 20:17
**2:12** v Ps 22:22
**2:13** w Isa 8:18
**2:14** x Jn 1:14 y 1Co 15:54–57 z 1Jn 3:8
**2:17** a Php 2:7 b Heb 4:14,15
**2:18** c Heb 4:15
**3:1** d Heb 2:11

7 You made him a little[a] lower than the
angels;
you crowned him with glory and honor
8 and put everything under his feet."[b][p]

In putting everything under him, God left nothing that is not subject to him. Yet at present we do not see everything subject to him. 9 But we see Jesus, who was made a little lower than the angels, now crowned with glory and honor[q] because he suffered death,[r] so that by the grace of God he might taste death for everyone.[s]

10 In bringing many sons to glory, it was fitting that God, for whom and through whom everything exists,[t] should make the author of their salvation perfect through suffering. 11 Both the one who makes men holy and those who are made holy are of the same family. So Jesus is not ashamed to call them brothers.[u] 12 He says,

"I will declare your name to my brothers;
in the presence of the congregation I
will sing your praises."[c][v]

13 And again,

"I will put my trust in him."[d]

And again he says,

"Here am I, and the children God has
given me."[e][w]

14 Since the children have flesh and blood, he too shared in their humanity[x] so that by his death he might destroy[y] him who holds the power of death—that is, the devil[z]— 15 and free those who all their lives were held in slavery by their fear of death. 16 For surely it is not angels he helps, but Abraham's descendants. 17 For this reason he had to be made like his brothers[a] in every way, in order that he might become a merciful and faithful high priest[b] in service to God, and that he might make atonement for[f] the sins of the people. 18 Because he himself suffered when he was tempted, he is able to help those who are being tempted.[c]

## Jesus Greater Than Moses

3 Therefore, holy brothers,[d] who share in the heavenly calling, fix your thoughts on Jesus, the apostle and high priest whom we confess. 2 He was faithful to the one who appointed him, just as Moses was faithful in all God's house. 3 Jesus has been found worthy of greater honor than Moses, just as the builder of a house has greater honor than the house itself. 4 For every house is built by someone, but God is the builder of everything. 5 Moses was faithful as a servant[e] in all God's house,[f] testifying to what would be said in the future. 6 But Christ is faithful as a son[g] over God's house. And we are his house,[h] if we hold on to our courage and the hope[i] of which we boast.

## Warning Against Unbelief

7 So, as the Holy Spirit says:

"Today, if you hear his voice,
8 do not harden your hearts
as you did in the rebellion,
during the time of testing in the
desert,
9 where your fathers tested and tried me
and for forty years saw what I did.
10 That is why I was angry with that
generation,
and I said, 'Their hearts are always
going astray,
and they have not known my ways.'
11 So I declared on oath in my anger,
'They shall never enter my rest.' "[g]

12 See to it, brothers, that none of you has a sinful, unbelieving heart that turns away from the living God. 13 But encourage one another daily, as long as it is called Today, so that none of you may be hardened by sin's deceitfulness. 14 We have come to share in Christ if we hold firmly[k] till the end the confidence we had at first. 15 As has just been said:

"Today, if you hear his voice,
do not harden your hearts
as you did in the rebellion."[h][l]

16 Who were they who heard and rebelled? Were they not all those Moses led out of Egypt?[m] 17 And with whom was he angry for forty years? Was it not with those who sinned, whose bodies fell in the desert?[n] 18 And to whom did God swear that they would never enter his rest[o] if not to those

**3:5** e Ex 14:31 f Nu 12:7
**3:6** g Heb 1:2 h 1Co 3:16 i Ro 5:2
**3:11** j Heb 4:3,5
**3:14** k ver 6
**3:15** l ver 7,8
**3:16** m Nu 14:2
**3:17** n Ps 106:26
**3:18** o Nu 14:20–23

[a]7 Or *him for a little while*; also in verse 9 [b]8 Psalm 8:4–6 [c]12 Psalm 22:22 [d]13 Isaiah 8:17 [e]13 Isaiah 8:18
[f]17 Or *and that he might turn aside God's wrath, taking away* [g]11 Psalm 95:7–11 [h]15 Psalm 95:7,8

## The African Presence

**Hebrews 3:16**

Egypt is located in North Africa. For more on Egypt, see the African Presence note on Genesis 10:6.

who disobeyed[a]? 19So we see that they were not able to enter, because of their unbelief.

### A Sabbath-Rest for the People of God

4 Therefore, since the promise of entering his rest still stands, let us be careful that none of you be found to have fallen short of it.[p] 2For we also have had the gospel preached to us, just as they did; but the message they heard was of no value to them, because those who heard did not combine it with faith.[b] 3Now we who have believed enter that rest, just as God has said,

"So I declared on oath in my anger,
'They shall never enter my rest.' "[c][q]

And yet his work has been finished since the creation of the world. 4For somewhere he has spoken about the seventh day in these words: "And on the seventh day God rested from all his work."[d][r] 5And again in the passage above he says, "They shall never enter my rest."

6It still remains that some will enter that rest, and those who formerly had the gospel preached to them did not go in, because of their disobedience.[s] 7Therefore God again set a certain day, calling it Today, when a long time later he spoke through David, as was said before:

"Today, if you hear his voice,
do not harden your hearts."[e][t]

8For if Joshua had given them rest, God would not have spoken later about another day. 9There remains, then, a Sabbath-rest for the people of God; 10for anyone who enters God's rest also rests from his own work, just as God did from his.[u] 11Let us, therefore, make every effort to enter that rest, so that no one will fall by following their example of disobedience.[v]

12For the word of God is living and active.[w] Sharper than any double-edged sword,[x] it penetrates even to dividing soul and spirit, joints and marrow; it judges the thoughts and attitudes of the heart.[y] 13Nothing in all creation is hidden from God's sight.[z] Everything is uncovered and laid bare before the eyes of him to whom we must give account.

### Jesus the Great High Priest

14Therefore, since we have a great high priest who has gone through the heavens,[f] Jesus the Son of God, let us hold firmly to the faith we profess.[a] 15For we do not have a high priest who is unable to sympathize with our weaknesses, but we have one who has been tempted in every way, just as we are—yet was without sin.[b] 16Let us then approach the throne of grace with confidence, so that we may receive mercy and find grace to help us in our time of need.

5 Every high priest is selected from among men and is appointed to represent them in matters related to God, to offer gifts and sacrifices[c] for sins. 2He is able to deal gently with those who are ignorant and are going astray, since he himself is subject to weakness.[d] 3This is why he has to offer sacrifices for his own sins, as well as for the sins of the people.

4No one takes this honor upon himself; he must be called by God, just as Aaron was.[e] 5So Christ also did not take upon himself the glory[f] of becoming a high priest. But God said to him,

**4:1** p Heb 12:15
**4:3** q Ps 95:11
**4:4** r Ex 20:11
**4:6** s Heb 3:18
**4:7** t Ps 95:7,8
**4:10** u ver 4
**4:11** v Heb 3:18
**4:12** w Jer 23:29 x Eph 6:17 y 1Co 14:24,25
**4:13** z Ps 33:13–15
**4:14** a Heb 3:1
**4:15** b 2Co 5:21
**5:1** c Heb 8:3
**5:2** d Heb 7:28
**5:4** e Ex 28:1
**5:5** f Jn 8:54

[a]18 Or *disbelieved* [b]2 Many manuscripts *because they did not share in the faith of those who obeyed* [c]3 Psalm 95:11; also in verse 5 [d]4 Gen. 2:2 [e]7 Psalm 95:7,8 [f]14 Or *gone into heaven*

# Inspire

## ABANDONMENT

One of the issues women face is the fear of abandonment. Perhaps our childhoods were clouded by the reality of a father we never knew or a mother we felt never really wanted us. For others the anxiety trigger may be the dissolution of a marriage, the betrayal of a friend or the unexpected death of a loved one. Regardless of its genesis, each experience we construe as desertion can leave us doubting our self-worth.

But there is hope! We can take comfort in knowing that God understands and cares. The Bible teaches that our heavenly high priest, who himself experienced the full scope of human despair, cannot help but be touched by our weaknesses (see Heb 4:14–16). During God's time on earth in the person of Jesus Christ, he, too, struggled with issues of abandonment. Jesus' own followers deserted him in his darkest hour (see Mt 26:55–56,69–75), and he was betrayed to death by one of his own disciples (see Mt 26:14–16,47–50). In addition, during the times he needed his Father the most—at Gethsemane and Golgotha—Jesus cried out in the depths of mortal anguish, "My soul is overwhelmed with sorrow to the point of death . . . My Father, if it is possible, may this cup be taken from me" (Mt 26:38–39) and "My God, my God, why have you forsaken me?" (Mt 27:46; See also Heb 5:7).

Situations will occur that cause us to feel as though God has forsaken us. But, as Jesus Christ arose from the dead in victory, we, too, can rise from the grip of despair and experience victory over our feelings of rejection. As a first step, we need to relieve ourselves of guilt and an inappropriate sense of responsibility over circumstances that were, at least to some extent, beyond our control. Whether it was the husband who walked out on us or the father who never showed up in the first place, we must accept the reality that the situation was not our fault. We've been fearfully and wonderfully made (see Ps 139:14), created in the image of God and thus intrinsically worthy of love and attention.

Second, we are invited to find comfort in God's love. The Bible reminds us that, even when the unthinkable happens, even when our parents forsake us, God cares (see Ps 27:10). God loves us so much that he sacrificed his Son, Jesus, so that we might have eternal life (see Jn 3:16).

Finally, we can cling to God's promise that he will never leave us nor forsake us (see Heb 13:5).

—J. Thompson

### read

Hebrews 4:14–16; see also Psalm 22:1–31; 27:1–14; Matthew 26:14–16,31–56,69–75; Romans 8:31–39; Hebrews 13:5. See also the Women of the Bible Notes "Hagar: Battered, Beaten and Rejected—but Not Abandoned," "Tamar: The Link Between Judah and Jesus" and "Naomi: Call Me Bitter."

### WOMAN of COLOR

How have you dealt with issues of abandonment and aloneness?

For the next Inspire note, go to page 1457.

## The African Presence

**Hebrews 5**

Abraham paid tithes to Melchizedek, a king-priest (see Ge 14:17–20). He was the king of Salem (that is, Jerusalem)—a land occupied by Canaanites. Because Ham's offspring represent the geographic territories once dominated by Egypt—present-day Egypt, Libya and Sudan and into the area today known as Israel—they can claim a relation to African heritage. Since "heritage" is something "passed down" or "inherited," Canaan (Israel or Palestine) most certainly received or was influenced by Egypt culturally, politically, religiously, etc.

"You are my Son;
today I have become your Father."[a][b][g]

[6]And he says in another place,

"You are a priest forever,
in the order of Melchizedek."[c][h]

[7]During the days of Jesus' life on earth, he offered up prayers and petitions with loud cries and tears[i] to the one who could save him from death, and he was heard because of his reverent submission.[j] [8]Although he was a son, he learned obedience from what he suffered[k] [9]and, once made perfect, he became the source of eternal salvation for all who obey him [10]and was designated by God to be high priest[l] in the order of Melchizedek.

### Warning Against Falling Away

[11]We have much to say about this, but it is hard to explain because you are slow to learn. [12]In fact, though by this time you ought to be teachers, you need someone to teach you the elementary truths of God's word all over again. You need milk, not solid food![m] [13]Anyone who lives on milk, being still an infant, is not acquainted with the teaching about righteousness. [14]But solid food is for the mature,[n] who by constant use have trained themselves to distinguish good from evil.

**6** Therefore let us leave[o] the elementary teachings[p] about Christ and go on to maturity, not laying again the foundation of repentance from acts that lead to death,[d][q] and of faith in God, [2]instruction about baptisms, the laying on of hands, the resurrection of the dead, and eternal judgment. [3]And God permitting,[r] we will do so.

[4]It is impossible for those who have once been enlightened,[s] who have tasted the heavenly gift,[t] who have shared in the Holy Spirit,[u] [5]who have tasted the goodness of the word of God and the powers of the coming age, [6]if they fall away, to be brought back to repentance, because[e] to their loss they are crucifying the Son of God all over again and subjecting him to public disgrace.

[7]Land that drinks in the rain often falling on it and that produces a crop useful to those for whom it is farmed receives the blessing of God. [8]But land that produces thorns and thistles is worthless and is in danger of being cursed. In the end it will be burned.

[9]Even though we speak like this, dear friends, we are confident of better things in your case—things that accompany salvation. [10]God is not unjust; he will not forget your work and the love you have shown him as you have helped his people and continue to help them.[v] [11]We want each of you to show this same diligence to the very end, in order to make your hope[w] sure. [12]We do not want you to become lazy, but to imitate those who through faith and patience inherit what has been promised.

**5:5** g Ps 2:7
**5:6** h Ps 110:4
**5:7** i Mt 27:46,50 j Mk 14:36
**5:8** k Php 2:8
**5:10** l ver 5
**5:12** m 1Co 3:2
**5:14** n 1Co 2:6
**6:1** o Php 3:12–14 p Heb 5:12
**6:1** q Heb 9:14
**6:3** r Ac 18:21
**6:4** s Heb 10:32 t Eph 2:8 u Gal 3:2
**6:10** v Mt 10:40,42; 1Th 1:3
**6:11** w Heb 3:6

[a]5 Or *have begotten you* [b]5 Psalm 2:7 [c]6 Psalm 110:4 [d]1 Or *from useless rituals* [e]6 Or *repentance while*

## The Certainty of God's Promise

13 When God made his promise to Abraham, since there was no one greater for him to swear by, he swore by himself,[x] 14 saying, "I will surely bless you and give you many descendants."[a] 15 And so after waiting patiently, Abraham received what was promised.

16 Men swear by someone greater than themselves, and the oath confirms what is said and puts an end to all argument.[y] 17 Because God wanted to make the unchanging nature of his purpose very clear to the heirs of what was promised,[z] he confirmed it with an oath. 18 God did this so that, by two unchangeable things in which it is impossible for God to lie, we who have fled to take hold of the hope offered to us may be greatly encouraged. 19 We have this hope as an anchor for the soul, firm and secure. It enters the inner sanctuary behind the curtain, 20 where Jesus, who went before us, has entered on our behalf.[a] He has become a high priest forever, in the order of Melchizedek.[b]

## Melchizedek the Priest

7 This Melchizedek was king of Salem and priest of God Most High. He met Abraham returning from the defeat of the kings and blessed him,[c] 2 and Abraham gave him a tenth of everything. First, his name means "king of righteousness"; then also, "king of Salem" means "king of peace." 3 Without father or mother, without genealogy, without beginning of days or end of life, like the Son of God he remains a priest forever.

4 Just think how great he was: Even the patriarch Abraham gave him a tenth of the plunder![d] 5 Now the law requires the descendants of Levi who become priests to collect a tenth from the people[e]—that is, their brothers—even though their brothers are descended from Abraham. 6 This man, however, did not trace his descent from Levi, yet he collected a tenth from Abraham and blessed him who had the promises.[f] 7 And without doubt the lesser person is blessed by the greater. 8 In the one case, the tenth is collected by men who die; but in the other case, by him who is declared to be living.[g] 9 One might even say that Levi, who collects the tenth, paid the tenth through Abraham, 10 because when Melchizedek met Abraham, Levi was still in the body of his ancestor.

## Jesus Like Melchizedek

11 If perfection could have been attained through the Levitical priesthood (for on the basis of it the law was given to the people),[h] why was there still need for another priest to come—one in the order of Melchizedek, not in the order of Aaron? 12 For when there is a change of the priesthood, there must also be a change of the law. 13 He of whom these things are said belonged to a different tribe,[i] and no one from that tribe has ever served at the altar. 14 For it is clear that our Lord descended from Judah,[j] and in regard to that tribe Moses said nothing about priests. 15 And what we have said is even more clear if another priest like Melchizedek appears, 16 one who has become a priest not on the basis of a regulation as to his ancestry but on

[a]14 Gen. 22:17

**6:13** x Ge 22:16; Lk 1:73
**6:16** y Ex 22:11
**6:17** z Heb 11:9
**6:20** a Heb 4:14 b Heb 5:6
**7:1** c Ge 14:18–20
**7:4** d Ge 14:20
**7:5** e Nu 18:21,26
**7:6** f Ro 4:13
**7:8** g Heb 5:6; 6:20
**7:11** h ver 18,19; Heb 8:7
**7:13** i ver 11
**7:14** j Isa 11:1

## *The African Presence*

### Hebrews 6:13–14

Abraham was from Ur, located in Mesopotamia. He lived around 2100 B.C. The traditional location of Ur is about 322 kilometers (200 miles) southeast of Baghdad and about 16 kilometers (10 miles) west of the Euphrates River. For more on Mesopotamia, see the African Presence note on Genesis 2:8.

the basis of the power of an indestructible life. 17 For it is declared:

> "You are a priest forever,
> in the order of Melchizedek."[a][k]

18 The former regulation is set aside because it was weak and useless[l] 19 (for the law made nothing perfect),[m] and a better hope is introduced, by which we draw near to God.[n]

20 And it was not without an oath! Others became priests without any oath, 21 but he became a priest with an oath when God said to him:

> "The Lord has sworn
> and will not change his mind:
> 'You are a priest forever.' "[a][o]

22 Because of this oath, Jesus has become the guarantee of a better covenant.

23 Now there have been many of those priests, since death prevented them from continuing in office; 24 but because Jesus lives forever, he has a permanent priesthood. 25 Therefore he is able to save completely[b] those who come to God through him, because he always lives to intercede for them.[p]

26 Such a high priest meets our need—one who is holy, blameless, pure, set apart from sinners, exalted above the heavens.[q] 27 Unlike the other high priests, he does not need to offer sacrifices[r] day after day, first for his own sins, and then for the sins of the people. He sacrificed for their sins once for all when he offered himself. 28 For the law appoints as high priests men who are weak;[s] but the oath, which came after the law, appointed the Son, who has been made perfect[t] forever.

## The High Priest of a New Covenant

8 The point of what we are saying is this: We do have such a high priest, who sat down at the right hand of the throne of the Majesty in heaven, 2 and who serves in the sanctuary, the true tabernacle[u] set up by the Lord, not by man.

3 Every high priest is appointed to offer both gifts and sacrifices,[v] and so it was necessary for this one also to have something to offer. 4 If he were on earth, he would not be a priest, for there are already men who offer the gifts prescribed by the law. 5 They serve at a sanctuary that is a copy[w] and shadow[x] of what is in heaven. This is why Moses was warned when he was about to build the tabernacle: "See to it that you make everything according to the pattern shown you on the mountain."[c][y] 6 But the ministry Jesus has received is as superior to theirs as the covenant of which he is mediator is superior to the old one, and it is founded on better promises.

7 For if there had been nothing wrong with that first covenant, no place would have been sought for another.[z] 8 But God found fault with the people and said[d]:

> "The time is coming, declares the Lord,
> when I will make a new covenant
> with the house of Israel
> and with the house of Judah.
> 9 It will not be like the covenant
> I made with their forefathers
> when I took them by the hand
> to lead them out of Egypt,
> because they did not remain faithful to
> my covenant,
> and I turned away from them,
> declares the Lord.
> 10 This is the covenant I will make with the
> house of Israel
> after that time, declares the Lord.
> I will put my laws in their minds

*My covenant bearer,*

*I am a God of mercy.*

*Spread mercy in my gracious Name.*

*Love,*
*Your Lord*

HEBREWS 8:10–12

**7:17** k Ps 110:4
**7:18** l Ro 8:3
**7:19** m Ro 3:20; n Heb 4:16
**7:21** o Ps 110:4
**7:25** p Ro 8:34
**7:26** q Heb 4:14
**7:27** r Heb 5:1
**7:28** s Heb 5:2; t Heb 2:10
**8:2** u Heb 9:11,24
**8:3** v Heb 5:1
**8:5** w Heb 9:23; x Col 2:17; y Ex 25:40
**8:7** z Heb 7:11,18

[a] 17,21 Psalm 110:4 [b] 25 Or *forever* [c] 5 Exodus 25:40 [d] 8 Some manuscripts may be translated *fault and said to the people.*

and write them on their hearts.[a]
I will be their God,
and they will be my people.
11 No longer will a man teach his neighbor,
or a man his brother, saying, 'Know
the Lord,'
because they will all know me,[b]
from the least of them to the greatest.
12 For I will forgive their wickedness
and will remember their sins no
more.[c]"[a]

13 By calling this covenant "new," he has made the first one obsolete;[d] and what is obsolete and aging will soon disappear.

## Worship in the Earthly Tabernacle

9 Now the first covenant had regulations for worship and also an earthly sanctuary.[e] 2 A tabernacle was set up. In its first room were the lampstand, the table[f] and the consecrated bread; this was called the Holy Place. 3 Behind the second curtain was a room called the Most Holy Place,[g] 4 which had the golden altar of incense[h] and the gold-covered ark of the covenant.[i] This ark contained the gold jar of manna,[j] Aaron's staff that had budded, and the stone tablets of the covenant. 5 Above the ark were the cherubim of the Glory, overshadowing the atonement cover.[b] But we cannot discuss these things in detail now.

6 When everything had been arranged like this, the priests entered regularly[k] into the outer room to carry on their ministry. 7 But only the high priest entered the inner room, and that only once a year, and never without blood, which he offered for himself[l] and for the sins the people had committed in ignorance. 8 The Holy Spirit was showing by this that the way[m] into the Most Holy Place had not yet been disclosed as long as the first tabernacle was still standing. 9 This is an illustration for the present time, indicating that the gifts and sacrifices being offered were not able to clear the conscience of the worshiper. 10 They are only a matter of food and drink[n] and various ceremonial washings—external regulations applying until the time of the new order.

## The Blood of Christ

11 When Christ came as high priest of the good things that are already here,[c][o] he went through the greater and more perfect tabernacle[p] that is not man-made, that is to say, not a part of this creation. 12 He did not enter by means of the blood of goats and calves; but he entered the Most Holy Place once for all by his own blood, having obtained eternal redemption. 13 The blood of goats and bulls and the ashes of a heifer sprinkled on those who are ceremonially unclean sanctify them so that they are outwardly clean. 14 How much more, then, will the blood of Christ, who through the eternal Spirit offered himself unblemished to God, cleanse our consciences from acts that lead to death,[d] so that we may serve the living God!

15 For this reason Christ is the mediator of a new covenant, that those who are called may receive the promised eternal inheritance—now that he has died as a ransom to set them free from the sins committed under the first covenant.

16 In the case of a will,[e] it is necessary to prove the death of the one who made it, 17 because a will is in force only when somebody has died; it never takes effect while the one who made it is living. 18 This is why even the first covenant was not put into effect without blood.[q] 19 When Moses had proclaimed every commandment of the law to all the people, he took the blood of calves, together with water, scarlet wool and branches of hyssop, and sprinkled the scroll and all the people. 20 He said, "This is the blood of the covenant, which God has commanded you to keep."[f][r] 21 In the same way, he sprinkled with the blood both the tabernacle and everything used in its ceremonies. 22 In fact, the law requires that nearly everything be cleansed with blood,[s] and without the shedding of blood there is no forgiveness.[t]

23 It was necessary, then, for the copies[u] of the heavenly things to be purified with these sacrifices, but the heavenly things themselves with better sacrifices than these. 24 For Christ did not enter a man-made sanctuary that was only a copy of the true one;[v] he

**8:10** a Heb 10:16
**8:11** b Isa 54:13; Jn 6:45
**8:12** c Heb 10:17
**8:13** d 2Co 5:17
**9:1** e Ex 25:8
**9:2** f Ex 25:23–29
**9:3** g Ex 26:31–33
**9:4** h Ex 30:1–5; i Ex 25:10–22; j Ex 16:32,33
**9:6** k Nu 28:3
**9:7** l Heb 5:2,3
**9:8** m Jn 14:6; Heb 10:19,20
**9:10** n Col 2:16
**9:11** o Heb 10:1; p Heb 8:2
**9:18** q Ex 24:6–8
**9:20** r Ex 24:8; Mt 26:28
**9:22** s Lev 8:15; t Lev 17:11
**9:23** u Heb 8:5
**9:24** v Heb 8:2

[a] 12 Jer. 31:31–34 [b] 5 Traditionally *the mercy seat* [c] 11 Some early manuscripts *are to come* [d] 14 Or *from useless rituals*
[e] 16 Same Greek word as *covenant*; also in verse 17 [f] 20 Exodus 24:8

**9:25** w ver 7,8
**9:26** x Heb 7:27
**9:27** y Ge 3:19; z 2Co 5:10
**9:28** a 1Pe 2:24
**10:1** b Heb 9:11
**10:3** c Heb 9:7
**10:5** d 1Pe 2:24
**10:7** e Jer 36:2; f Ps 40:6–8
**10:10** g 1Pe 2:24

entered heaven itself, now to appear for us in God's presence. 25 Nor did he enter heaven to offer himself again and again, the way the high priest enters the Most Holy Place every year with blood that is not his own.[w] 26 Then Christ would have had to suffer many times since the creation of the world. But now he has appeared once for all[x] at the end of the ages to do away with sin by the sacrifice of himself. 27 Just as man is destined to die once,[y] and after that to face judgment,[z] 28 so Christ was sacrificed once to take away the sins of many people; and he will appear a second time, not to bear sin,[a] but to bring salvation to those who are waiting for him.

## Christ's Sacrifice Once for All

**10** The law is only a shadow of the good things[b] that are coming—not the realities themselves. For this reason it can never, by the same sacrifices repeated endlessly year after year, make perfect those who draw near to worship. 2 If it could, would they not have stopped being offered? For the worshipers would have been cleansed once for all, and would no longer have felt guilty for their sins. 3 But those sacrifices are an annual reminder of sins,[c] 4 because it is impossible for the blood of bulls and goats to take away sins.

5 Therefore, when Christ came into the world, he said:

"Sacrifice and offering you did not desire,
but a body you prepared for me;[d]
6 with burnt offerings and sin offerings
you were not pleased.
7 Then I said, 'Here I am—it is written
about me in the scroll[e]—
I have come to do your will, O God.' "[a][f]

8 First he said, "Sacrifices and offerings, burnt offerings and sin offerings you did not desire, nor were you pleased with them" (although the law required them to be made). 9 Then he said, "Here I am, I have come to do your will." He sets aside the first to establish the second. 10 And by that will, we have been made holy through the sacrifice of the body[g] of Jesus Christ once for all.

11 Day after day every priest stands and performs his religious duties; again and again he offers the same sacrifices, which can never take away sins.[h] 12 But when this priest had offered for all time one sacrifice for sins, he sat down at the right hand of God. 13 Since that time he waits for his enemies to be made his footstool, 14 because by one sacrifice he has made perfect[i] forever those who are being made holy.

15 The Holy Spirit also testifies to us about this. First he says:

16 "This is the covenant I will make with them
after that time, says the Lord.
I will put my laws in their hearts,
and I will write them on their minds."[b][j]

17 Then he adds:

"Their sins and lawless acts
I will remember no more."[c][k]

18 And where these have been forgiven, there is no longer any sacrifice for sin.

## A Call to Persevere

19 Therefore, brothers, since we have confidence to enter the Most Holy Place[l] by the blood of Jesus, 20 by a new and living way opened for us through the curtain,[m] that is, his body, 21 and since we have a great priest over the house of God, 22 let us draw near to God with a sincere heart in full assurance of faith, having our hearts sprinkled to cleanse us from a guilty conscience[n] and having our bodies washed with pure water. 23 Let us hold unswervingly to the hope we profess, for he who promised is faithful.[o] 24 And let us consider how we may spur one another on toward love and good deeds. 25 Let us not give up meeting together,[p] as some are in the habit of doing, but let us encourage one another—and all the more as you see the Day approaching.

26 If we deliberately keep on sinning[q] after we have received the knowledge of the truth, no sacrifice for sins is left, 27 but only a fearful expectation of judgment and of raging fire[r] that will consume the enemies of God. 28 Anyone who rejected the law of Moses died without mercy on the testimony of two or three witnesses.[s] 29 How much more

**10:11** h ver 1,4
**10:14** i ver 1
**10:16** j Jer 31:33
**10:17** k Heb 8:12
**10:19** l Eph 2:18
**10:20** m Heb 9:3
**10:22** n Eze 36:25
**10:23** o 1Co 1:9
**10:25** p Ac 2:42
**10:26** q Nu 15:30; 2Pe 2:20
**10:27** r Isa 26:11
**10:28** s Heb 2:2

[a] 7 Psalm 40:6–8 (see Septuagint) [b] 16 Jer. 31:33 [c] 17 Jer. 31:34

10:29 t Heb 6:6 u Eph 4:30
10:30 v Dt 32:35 w Dt 32:36
10:32 x Heb 6:4 y Php 1:29,30
10:33 z 1Co 4:9 a Php 4:14
10:38 b Ro 1:17; Gal 3:11

severely do you think a man deserves to be
punished who has trampled the Son of God
under foot,[t] who has treated as an unholy
thing the blood of the covenant that sancti-
fied him, and who has insulted the Spirit[u]
of grace? 30 For we know him who said, "It
is mine to avenge; I will repay,"[a][v] and again,
"The Lord will judge his people."[b][w] 31 It is a
dreadful thing to fall into the hands of the
living God.

32 Remember those earlier days after you
had received the light,[x] when you stood your
ground in a great contest in the face of suf-
fering.[y] 33 Sometimes you were publicly ex-
posed to insult and persecution;[z] at other
times you stood side by side with those who
were so treated.[a] 34 You sympathized with
those in prison and joyfully accepted the
confiscation of your property, because you
knew that you yourselves had better and
lasting possessions.

35 So do not throw away your confidence;
it will be richly rewarded. 36 You need to per-
severe so that when you have done the will
of God, you will receive what he has prom-
ised. 37 For in just a very little while,

"He who is coming will come and will
not delay.
38 But my righteous one[c] will live by
faith.[b]
And if he shrinks back,
I will not be pleased with him."[d]

*Lord,*

*I thank you for your sustaining presence, even when I face difficult times. Thank you for wiping away the tears the world around me ignores. Accept my gratitude for your immeasurable and incomparable friendship. I am indeed blessed to know that you are with me.*

*Amen*

HEBREWS 10:32–36

39 But we are not of those who shrink back
and are destroyed, but of those who believe
and are saved.

## By Faith

11 Now faith is being sure of what we
hope for and certain of what we do
not see.[c] 2 This is what the ancients were
commended for.[d]

3 By faith we understand that the uni-
verse was formed at God's command,[e] so
that what is seen was not made out of what
was visible.

4 By faith Abel offered God a better
sacrifice than Cain did. By faith he was
commended as a righteous man, when God
spoke well of his offerings.[f] And by faith he
still speaks, even though he is dead.

5 By faith Enoch was taken from this
life, so that he did not experience death; he
could not be found, because God had taken
him away.[g] For before he was taken, he was
commended as one who pleased God. 6 And
without faith it is impossible to please God,
because anyone who comes to him must
believe that he exists and that he rewards
those who earnestly seek him.

7 By faith Noah, when warned about
things not yet seen, in holy fear built an
ark[h] to save his family. By his faith he con-
demned the world and became heir of the
righteousness that comes by faith.

8 By faith Abraham, when called to go to
a place he would later receive as his inheri-
tance, obeyed and went,[i] even though he did
not know where he was going. 9 By faith he
made his home in the promised land like
a stranger in a foreign country; he lived
in tents,[j] as did Isaac and Jacob, who were
heirs with him of the same promise.[k] 10 For
he was looking forward to the city[l] with
foundations, whose architect and builder
is God.

11 By faith Abraham, even though he was
past age—and Sarah herself was barren[m]—
was enabled to become a father because he[e]
considered him faithful who had made the
promise. 12 And so from this one man, and
he as good as dead,[n] came descendants as
numerous as the stars in the sky and as
countless as the sand on the seashore.

11:1 c 2Co 4:18
11:2 d ver 4,39
11:3 e Ge 1
11:4 f Ge 4:4; 1Jn 3:12
11:5 g Ge 5:21–24
11:7 h Ge 6:13–22
11:8 i Ge 12:1–4; Ac 7:2–4
11:9 j Ge 12:8 k Heb 6:17
11:10 l Heb 12:22
11:11 m Ge 17:17–19; 18:11–14
11:12 n Ro 4:19

[a]30 Deut. 32:35 [b]30 Deut. 32:36; Psalm 135:14 [c]38 One early manuscript *But the righteous* [d]38 Hab. 2:3,4
[e]11 Or *By faith even Sarah, who was past age, was enabled to bear children because she*

## The African Presence

**Hebrews 11:8–19**

Abraham was from Ur, located in Mesopotamia. He lived around 2100 B.C. The traditional location of Ur is about 322 kilometers (200 miles) southeast of Baghdad and about 16 kilometers (10 miles) west of the Euphrates River. For more on Mesopotamia, see the African Presence note on Genesis 2:8.

13 All these people were still living by faith when they died. They did not receive the things promised; they only saw them and welcomed them from a distance. And they admitted that they were aliens and strangers on earth.[o] 14 People who say such things show that they are looking for a country of their own. 15 If they had been thinking of the country they had left, they would have had opportunity to return. 16 Instead, they were longing for a better country—a heavenly one. Therefore God is not ashamed to be called their God,[p] for he has prepared a city for them.

17 By faith Abraham, when God tested him, offered Isaac as a sacrifice.[q] He who had received the promises was about to sacrifice his one and only son, 18 even though God had said to him, "It is through Isaac that your offspring[a] will be reckoned."[b][r] 19 Abraham reasoned that God could raise the dead, and figuratively speaking, he did receive Isaac back from death.

20 By faith Isaac blessed Jacob and Esau in regard to their future.

21 By faith Jacob, when he was dying, blessed each of Joseph's sons, and worshiped as he leaned on the top of his staff.

22 By faith Joseph, when his end was near, spoke about the exodus of the Israelites from Egypt and gave instructions about his bones.[s]

23 By faith Moses' parents hid him for three months after he was born,[t] because they saw he was no ordinary child, and they were not afraid of the king's edict.[u]

24 By faith Moses, when he had grown up, refused to be known as the son of Pharaoh's daughter.[v] 25 He chose to be mistreated along with the people of God rather than to enjoy the pleasures of sin for a short time. 26 He regarded disgrace[w] for the sake of Christ as of greater value than the treasures of Egypt, because he was looking ahead to his reward. 27 By faith he left Egypt,[x] not fearing the king's anger; he persevered because he saw him who is invisible. 28 By faith he kept the Passover and the sprinkling of blood, so that the destroyer of the firstborn would not touch the firstborn of Israel.[y]

29 By faith the people passed through the Red Sea[c] as on dry land; but when the Egyptians tried to do so, they were drowned.[z]

30 By faith the walls of Jericho fell, after the people had marched around them for seven days.

31 By faith the prostitute Rahab, because she welcomed the spies, was not killed with those who were disobedient.[d][a]

32 And what more shall I say? I do not have time to tell about Gideon, Barak, Samson, Jephthah, David, Samuel and the prophets, 33 who through faith conquered kingdoms,[b] administered justice, and gained what was promised; who shut the mouths of lions,[c] 34 quenched the fury of the flames, and escaped the edge of the sword; whose weakness was turned to strength; and who became powerful in battle and routed foreign armies.[d] 35 Women received back their dead, raised to life again.[e] Others were tortured and refused to be released, so that they might gain a better resurrection. 36 Some faced jeers and flogging,[f] while still others

**11:13** o Ge 23:4
**11:16** p Ex 3:6,15
**11:17** q Ge 22:1–10
**11:18** r Ge 21:12
**11:22** s Ge 50:24,25
**11:23** t Ex 2:2; u Ex 1:16,22
**11:24** v Ex 2:10,11
**11:26** w Heb 13:13
**11:27** x Ex 12:50,51
**11:28** y Ex 12:21–23
**11:29** z Ex 14:21–31
**11:31** a Jos 6:22–25
**11:33** b 2Sa 7:11; c Da 6:22
**11:34** d Jdg 15:8
**11:35** e 1Ki 17:22,23
**11:36** f Jer 20:2

[a] 18 Greek *seed* [b] 18 Gen. 21:12 [c] 29 That is, Sea of Reeds [d] 31 Or *unbelieving*

# Inspire

## FAITH

The author of Hebrews provides us with a concise and inspiring definition of Christian faith: "Faith is being sure of what we hope for and certain of what we do not see" (Heb 11:1). Faith at its essence is a present act oriented toward a future hope. Faith is intangible, but it manifests itself in tangible results. We are told frankly that "without faith it is impossible to please God" (Heb 11:6). God is the only one worthy of our faith; only the fool says in his heart, "There is no God" (Ps 14:1).

God has given each believer a measure of faith (see Ro 12:3), but this degree or portion of faith can remain stagnate or it can grow. Do nothing with faith, and even that which you have will eventually degenerate to nothing. However, if faith is exercised, it will, like muscles—exercised and stretched, often through pain—grow and become strong. In a world fraught with anxiety brought on by challenges, expectations, conflicts, problems, and fears, faith is essential for our spiritual and even physical survival. We must position ourselves to strengthen our faith by constantly saturating our consciousness with the Word of God until it penetrates and fills every hollow place in our souls (see Heb 4:12).

"With God all things are possible" (Mt 19:26). The author of Hebrews lists numerous past heroes and heroines who did and endured unimaginable things because they lived by faith (see Heb 11:4–38). The writer picturesquely labels this group "a great cloud of witnesses" (Heb 12:1). A brief review of the outworking of their faith confirms that their lives pleased God and that God would reward them for diligently seeking him (see Heb 11:6), although the completion of that reward was yet in their future—in Christ (see Heb 11:39–40).

We must add to this cloud of witnesses God's ebony children—Harriet Tubman, Sojourner Truth, Mary McLeod Bethune, Ida B. Wells, Rosa Parks, Fannie Lou Hamer, along with millions of unsung heroines who operated in faith. Still today, God honors those who honor him.

—C. Archibald

### read

Hebrews 11:1–40; see also Matthew 19:26; Mark 11:20–25; Romans 4:1–25; Hebrews 10:32–39.

See also the Inspire Notes "The Faithfulness of God," "God's Righteousness," "Spiritual Discipline," "Confidence" and "Confidence for Each Day," and the Women of the Bible Notes "Jochebed: She Knew It Would Take a Village," "Rahab: Willing to Be Used by God," "Wise and Foolish Virgins: Preparing for Christ," "Peter's Mother-in-Law: From Suffering to Service" and "The Revelation 12 Woman: A Woman of Focus."

### WOMAN of COLOR

Who would you add to your "cloud of witnesses"? Thank God for blessing you with real-life examples of women operating in faith. Seek to be a witness to someone else.

For the next Inspire note, go to page 1459.

were chained and put in prison. 37They were stoned[a]; they were sawed in two; they were put to death by the sword. They went about in sheepskins and goatskins,[g] destitute, persecuted and mistreated— 38the world was not worthy of them. They wandered in deserts and mountains, and in caves[h] and holes in the ground.

39These were all commended for their faith, yet none of them received what had been promised. 40God had planned something better for us so that only together with us would they be made perfect.

## God Disciplines His Sons

12 Therefore, since we are surrounded by such a great cloud of witnesses, let us throw off everything that hinders and the sin that so easily entangles, and let us run[i] with perseverance the race marked out for us. 2Let us fix our eyes on Jesus, the author and perfecter of our faith, who for the joy set before him endured the cross,[j] scorning its shame, and sat down at the right hand of the throne of God. 3Consider him who endured such opposition from sinful men, so that you will not grow weary[k] and lose heart.

> *"I'm no martyr. I just had a hard day at work. My feet were hurting, and I was too tired to give up my seat."*
>
> —Rosa Parks,
> mother of the civil rights movement

4In your struggle against sin, you have not yet resisted to the point of shedding your blood. 5And you have forgotten that word of encouragement that addresses you as sons:

"My son, do not make light of the Lord's
discipline,
and do not lose heart when he rebukes
you,
6 because the Lord disciplines those he
loves,[l]
and he punishes everyone he accepts
as a son."[b]

7Endure hardship as discipline; God is treating you as sons.[m] For what son is not disciplined by his father? 8If you are not disciplined (and everyone undergoes discipline),[n] then you are illegitimate children and not true sons. 9Moreover, we have all had human fathers who disciplined us and we respected them for it. How much more should we submit to the Father of our spirits[o] and live![p] 10Our fathers disciplined us for a little while as they thought best; but God disciplines us for our good, that we may share in his holiness. 11No discipline seems pleasant at the time, but painful. Later on, however, it produces a harvest of righteousness and peace[q] for those who have been trained by it.

12Therefore, strengthen your feeble arms and weak knees. 13"Make level paths for your feet,"[c][r] so that the lame may not be disabled, but rather healed.[s]

## Warning Against Refusing God

14Make every effort to live in peace with all men and to be holy; without holiness no one will see the Lord.[t] 15See to it that no one misses the grace of God[u] and that no bitter root grows up to cause trouble and defile many. 16See that no one is sexually immoral, or is godless like Esau, who for a single meal sold his inheritance rights as the oldest son.[v] 17Afterward, as you know, when he wanted to inherit this blessing, he was rejected. He could bring about no change of mind, though he sought the blessing with tears.[w]

18You have not come to a mountain that can be touched and that is burning with fire; to darkness, gloom and storm;[x] 19to a trumpet blast or to such a voice speaking words that those who heard it begged that no further word be spoken to them,[y] 20because they could not bear what was commanded: "If even an animal touches the mountain, it must be stoned."[d][z] 21The sight was so terrifying that Moses said, "I am trembling with fear."[e]

22But you have come to Mount Zion, to the heavenly Jerusalem,[a] the city of the living God. You have come to thousands upon thousands of angels in joyful assembly, 23to the church of the firstborn, whose names

**11:37** g 2Ki 1:8
**11:38** h 1Ki 18:4
**12:1** i 1Co 9:24
**12:2** j Php 2:8,9
**12:3** k Gal 6:9
**12:6** l Ps 94:12
**12:7** m Dt 8:5
**12:8** n 1Pe 5:9
**12:9** o Nu 16:22 p Isa 38:16
**12:11** q Jas 3:17,18
**12:13** r Pr 4:26 s Gal 6:1
**12:14** t Mt 5:8
**12:15** u Gal 5:4
**12:16** v Ge 25:29–34
**12:17** w Ge 27:30–40
**12:18** x Dt 4:11
**12:19** y Ex 20:19
**12:20** z Ex 19:12,13
**12:22** a Gal 4:26

[a]37 Some early manuscripts *stoned; they were put to the test;* [b]6 Prov. 3:11,12 [c]13 Prov. 4:26 [d]20 Exodus 19:12,13
[e]21 Deut. 9:19

# Inspire leadership FOCUS

## BE FOCUSED

Hebrews 12:1 reinforces the fact that life is like a marathon. It's a long journey that requires perseverance and training. And just as a marathon runner stays focused on the finish line, we as leaders must keep our eyes on the goal to accomplish all that God has for us. We can do this by first setting appropriate goals that are in line with God's purpose for our lives and by having a well-thought-out plan that can help us stay focused.

However, as leaders we sometimes find ourselves sidetracked from our purpose. Distractions are the enemy's trick to hinder us from accomplishing what God wants us to do. Diversions can masquerade in many forms. Past failures, hurts and disappointments can keep us from staying focused. A lack of self-confidence, having doubts and being worried are other tricks in his arsenal. Sometimes we may not proceed in our calling at all because of a lack of discipline, a tendency to procrastinate or an inability to become organized.

But as deceptive as those tricks are, the enemy has no boundaries in how far he will go to ensnare us. Temptation will come in any form, and it is our job as leaders to recognize the traps and to not fall. It is true that God is gracious and will help us get back up if we fall, but the point is that the enemy very rarely uses new tricks. He will continue to put the same stumbling blocks in our path just to take our focus away from our God-given purpose. He wants us to be entangled in sin so that we cannot stay focused. The key to avoiding this and staying on point is to identify our stumbling blocks and determine the root causes of our failures. Once we do that, we can take action. Sometimes this will mean changing friends, changing environments or changing our mind-set. We must do whatever is necessary to maintain our focus on the race that God has marked out for us.

—K. Moore

### read

Hebrews 12:1–13.

**See also** the Inspire Notes "Following God-Given Visions," "Coping With Life's Tasks, "Stress Management: Learning to Say 'No' " and "Discipline," and the Women of the Bible Notes "Zelophehad's Daughters: Seeking an Inheritance," "Jael: Just Another Woman on the Lord's Side" and "The Canaanite Woman: Persistence Pays Off."

### WOMAN of COLOR

Are there stumbling blocks in your life that are hindering your progress? Are there temptations in your life that are causing you to sin? Pray for wisdom and clarity. Ask the Lord to reveal these areas to you, and then ask him to lead you to the solutions that will allow you to maintain your focus on the things that are important to him.

For the next Inspire note, go to page 1464.

12:23
b Php 3:12
12:25
c Heb 2:2,3
12:26
d Ex 19:18
e Hag 2:6
12:29
f Dt 4:24
13:1
g Ro 12:10
13:2
h Ge 18:1–33
13:3
i Col 4:18
13:4
j 1Co 6:9
13:5
k Php 4:11
13:7
l ver 17,24
m Heb 6:12

are written in heaven. You have come to God, the judge of all men, to the spirits of righteous men made perfect,[b] [24]to Jesus the mediator of a new covenant, and to the sprinkled blood that speaks a better word than the blood of Abel.

[25]See to it that you do not refuse him who speaks. If they did not escape when they refused him who warned them on earth, how much less will we, if we turn away from him who warns us from heaven?[c] [26]At that time his voice shook the earth,[d] but now he has promised, "Once more I will shake not only the earth but also the heavens."[a][e] [27]The words "once more" indicate the removing of what can be shaken—that is, created things—so that what cannot be shaken may remain.

[28]Therefore, since we are receiving a kingdom that cannot be shaken, let us be thankful, and so worship God acceptably with reverence and awe, [29]for our "God is a consuming fire."[b][f]

## Concluding Exhortations

13 Keep on loving each other as brothers.[g] [2]Do not forget to entertain strangers, for by so doing some people have entertained angels without knowing it.[h] [3]Remember those in prison[i] as if you were their fellow prisoners, and those who are mistreated as if you yourselves were suffering.

[4]Marriage should be honored by all, and the marriage bed kept pure, for God will judge the adulterer and all the sexually immoral.[j] [5]Keep your lives free from the love of money and be content with what you have,[k] because God has said,

> "Never will I leave you;
> never will I forsake you."[c]

[6]So we say with confidence,

> "The Lord is my helper; I will not be afraid.
> What can man do to me?"[d]

[7]Remember your leaders,[l] who spoke the word of God to you. Consider the outcome of their way of life and imitate[m] their faith. [8]Jesus Christ is the same yesterday and today and forever.

[9]Do not be carried away by all kinds of strange teachings.[n] It is good for our hearts to be strengthened by grace, not by ceremonial foods, which are of no value to those who eat them. [10]We have an altar from which those who minister at the tabernacle have no right to eat.[o]

[11]The high priest carries the blood of animals into the Most Holy Place as a sin offering, but the bodies are burned outside the camp.[p] [12]And so Jesus also suffered outside the city gate to make the people holy through his own blood. [13]Let us, then, go to him outside the camp, bearing the disgrace he bore. [14]For here we do not have an enduring city, but we are looking for the city that is to come.[q]

[15]Through Jesus, therefore, let us continually offer to God a sacrifice of praise—the fruit of lips[r] that confess his name. [16]And do not forget to do good and to share with others, for with such sacrifices God is pleased.

[17]Obey your leaders and submit to their authority. They keep watch over you as men who must give an account. Obey them so that their work will be a joy, not a burden, for that would be of no advantage to you.

[18]Pray for us.[s] We are sure that we have a clear conscience and desire to live honorably in every way. [19]I particularly urge you to pray so that I may be restored to you soon.[t]

[20]May the God of peace,[u] who through the blood of the eternal covenant[v] brought back from the dead our Lord Jesus, that great Shepherd of the sheep, [21]equip you with everything good for doing his will, and may he work in us[w] what is pleasing to him, through Jesus Christ, to whom be glory for ever and ever. Amen.

[22]Brothers, I urge you to bear with my word of exhortation, for I have written you only a short letter.[x]

[23]I want you to know that our brother Timothy has been released. If he arrives soon, I will come with him to see you.

[24]Greet all your leaders[y] and all God's people. Those from Italy send you their greetings.

[25]Grace be with you all.

13:9
n Eph 4:14
13:10
o 1Co 9:13
13:11
p Ex 29:14
13:14
q Php 3:20
13:15
r Hos 14:2
13:18
s 1Th 5:25
13:19
t Phm 22
13:20
u Ro 15:33
v Zec 9:11
13:21
w Php 2:13
13:22
x 1Pe 5:12
13:24
y ver 7,17

[a]26 Haggai 2:6 [b]29 Deut. 4:24 [c]5 Deut. 31:6 [d]6 Psalm 118:6,7

# James

## OVERVIEW

James, the half brother of Jesus, was regarded as a leader in the Jerusalem church. He became concerned about the spiritual condition of his fellow Jewish Christians scattered over a wide area (see Jas 1:1). Many were facing persecution from the Jewish community, as well as from the broader society. In a fatherly style James encouraged believers to ask God for wisdom when they face the trials of this life (see Jas 1:2–8). He instructed believers to not show favoritism (see Jas 2:1–13), to tame their tongues (see Jas 3:1–12), and to know the difference between worldly and divine wisdom (see Jas 3:13–18). James warned rich oppressors of their coming judgment (see Jas 5:1–6) and encouraged those who were suffering to be patient and persist in prayer (see Jas 5:7–18).

"Faith without deeds is dead" (Jas 2:26) is a principle many women follow in the church. The church needs every member to have a sincere faith *and* to contribute acts of service. As you read through the book of James, take note of the different ways you can help in your local church and community. Live out your faith through your actions.

## OUTLINE

I. Trials and Temptations (1:1–18)
II. Listening and Doing (1:19–27)
III. Favoritism Forbidden (2:1–13)
IV. Faith and Deeds (2:14–26)
V. Taming the Tongue (3:1–12)
VI. Two Kinds of Wisdom (3:13–18)
VII. Warning Against Worldliness (4:1–17)
VIII. Warning to Rich Oppressors (5:1–6)
IX. Patience and Prayer (5:7–20)

### SCANNABLE FACTS:

**Author:** James

**Time Written:** Possibly the first book of the New Testament penned, James was written sometime before A.D. 50

**Theme to Note:** A faith that works

**Notable Woman:** Rahab, who demonstrated her faith by her deeds (see Jas 2:25)

1 James,[a] a servant of God[b] and of the Lord Jesus Christ,

To the twelve tribes scattered[c] among the nations:

Greetings.

## Trials and Temptations

2 Consider it pure joy, my brothers, whenever you face trials of many kinds, 3 because you know that the testing of your faith develops perseverance. 4 Perseverance must finish its work so that you may be mature and complete, not lacking anything. 5 If any of you lacks wisdom, he should ask God,[d] who gives generously to all without finding fault, and it will be given to him. 6 But when he asks, he must believe and not doubt,[e] because he who doubts is like a wave of the sea, blown and tossed by the wind. 7 That man should not think he will receive anything from the Lord; 8 he is a double-minded man, unstable in all he does.

9 The brother in humble circumstances ought to take pride in his high position. 10 But the one who is rich should take pride in his low position, because he will pass away like a wild flower.[f] 11 For the sun rises with scorching heat and withers the plant; its blossom falls and its beauty is destroyed. In the same way, the rich man will fade away even while he goes about his business.

12 Blessed is the man who perseveres under trial, because when he has stood the test, he will receive the crown of life that God has promised to those who love him.

13 When tempted, no one should say, "God is tempting me." For God cannot be tempted by evil, nor does he tempt anyone; 14 but each one is tempted when, by his own evil desire, he is dragged away and enticed. 15 Then, after desire has conceived, it gives birth to sin;[g] and sin, when it is full-grown, gives birth to death.

16 Don't be deceived, my dear brothers. 17 Every good and perfect gift is from above, coming down from the Father of the heavenly lights, who does not change like shifting shadows. 18 He chose to give us birth[h] through the word of truth, that we might be a kind of firstfruits[i] of all he created.

## Listening and Doing

19 My dear brothers, take note of this: Everyone should be quick to listen, slow to speak[j] and slow to become angry, 20 for man's anger does not bring about the righteous life that God desires. 21 Therefore, get rid of all moral filth and the evil that is so prevalent and humbly accept the word planted in you, which can save you.

22 Do not merely listen to the word, and so deceive yourselves. Do what it says. 23 Anyone who listens to the word but does not do what it says is like a man who looks at his face in a mirror 24 and, after looking at himself, goes away and immediately forgets what he looks like. 25 But the man who looks intently into the perfect law that gives freedom,[k] and continues to do this, not forgetting what he has heard, but doing it—he will be blessed in what he does.[l]

26 If anyone considers himself religious

**1:1** a Ac 15:13 b Tit 1:1 c Jn 7:35
**1:5** d 1Ki 3:9,10; Pr 2:3–6
**1:6** e Mk 11:24
**1:10** f 1Co 7:31
**1:15** g Job 15:35; Ps 7:14
**1:18** h Jn 1:13 i Rev 14:4
**1:19** j Pr 10:19
**1:25** k Jas 2:12 l Jn 13:17

## The African Presence

### James 1

While there are no specific references to the African presence within the book of James, the early church was influenced by people of North Africa and the Middle East (a historical and cultural subregion of Africa-Eurasia, traditionally held to be countries or regions in Southwest Asia together with Egypt). However, during the time of the New Testament, racial identification did not have the significance that it has today.

1:27 m Mt25:36

and yet does not keep a tight rein on his
tongue, he deceives himself and his religion
is worthless. 27 Religion that God our Father
accepts as pure and faultless is this: to look
after[m] orphans and widows in their distress
and to keep oneself from being polluted by
the world.

## Favoritism Forbidden

2:1 n 1Co2:8

2 My brothers, as believers in our glo-
rious[n] Lord Jesus Christ, don't show
favoritism. 2 Suppose a man comes into
your meeting wearing a gold ring and fine
clothes, and a poor man in shabby clothes
also comes in. 3 If you show special atten-

Inspire

## TEMPTATION

Life is full of temptation! Every woman will struggle with the lure of evil throughout the course of her life. Temptation is an enticement to sin. Yet the example of Jesus Christ and the instruction of the Word of God demonstrate how we can overcome these allurements. The Bible clearly teaches that God himself does not tempt us. Rather, the temptations we experience arise from two sources: our own evil desire (see Jas 1:13–15) and Satan, the devil (see Ge 3:1–5; 1Co 7:5). God permits us to undergo temptation to teach us obedience, trust and loyalty to him. Since Jesus was tempted as we are, we can "approach the throne of grace with confidence, so that we may receive mercy and find grace to help us in our time of need" (Heb 4:15–16).

Although being a Christian does not exempt us from experiencing temptation, God does promise not to allow us to be tempted beyond what we can bear. Instead, he graciously provides a way of escape (see 1Co 10:13). What is one way of escape when we are tempted? Jesus is our model. He shows us that arming ourselves with and employing the Word of God is an effective means of overcoming temptation. When Satan tempted Jesus in the desert, Jesus countered each temptation with Scripture (see Mt 4:1–11). Furthermore, the psalmist reminds us, "[God's] word is a lamp to my feet and a light for my path" (Ps 119:105). When we submit ourselves to God through obedience and knowledge of his Word, we find strength to resist the devil. The beautiful promise of God is that when we do resist, Satan will flee (see Jas 4:7).

—J. Thompson

### read

James 1:2–18; see also Matthew 4:1–11; 1 Corinthians 10:1–13; Hebrews 4:12–16; James 4:1–10; 1 Peter 5:6–10.

**See also** the Inspire Notes "Let's Talk About Sex," "Adultery" and "Help for the Addict," and the Women of the Bible Notes "Lot's Wife: Why Look Back?" and "Delilah: Strength That Builds or Destroys."

### WOMAN *of* COLOR

What temptation do you need God's help to resist?

For the next Inspire note, go to page 1473.

**2:5** o Lk 12:21
**2:6** p 1Co 11:22
**2:8** q Lev 19:18
**2:10** r Mt 5:19
**2:11** s Ex 20:13
**2:12** t Jas 1:25
**2:14** u Mt 7:26
**2:16** v 1Jn 3:17,18
**2:18** w Jas 3:13
**2:19** x Dt 6:4

tion to the man wearing fine clothes and say, "Here's a good seat for you," but say to the poor man, "You stand there" or "Sit on the floor by my feet," 4 have you not discriminated among yourselves and become judges with evil thoughts?

5 Listen, my dear brothers: Has not God chosen those who are poor in the eyes of the world to be rich in faith[o] and to inherit the kingdom he promised those who love him? 6 But you have insulted the poor.[p] Is it not the rich who are exploiting you? Are they not the ones who are dragging you into court? 7 Are they not the ones who are slandering the noble name of him to whom you belong?

8 If you really keep the royal law found in Scripture, "Love your neighbor as yourself,"[a][q] you are doing right. 9 But if you show favoritism, you sin and are convicted by the law as lawbreakers. 10 For whoever keeps the whole law and yet stumbles at just one point is guilty of breaking all of it.[r] 11 For he who said, "Do not commit adultery,"[b] also said, "Do not murder."[c][s] If you do not commit adultery but do commit murder, you have become a lawbreaker.

12 Speak and act as those who are going to be judged by the law that gives freedom,[t] 13 because judgment without mercy will be shown to anyone who has not been merciful. Mercy triumphs over judgment!

## Faith and Deeds

14 What good is it, my brothers, if a man claims to have faith but has no deeds?[u] Can such faith save him? 15 Suppose a brother or sister is without clothes and daily food. 16 If one of you says to him, "Go, I wish you well; keep warm and well fed," but does nothing about his physical needs, what good is it?[v] 17 In the same way, faith by itself, if it is not accompanied by action, is dead.

18 But someone will say, "You have faith; I have deeds."

Show me your faith without deeds, and I will show you my faith by what I do.[w] 19 You believe that there is one God.[x] Good! Even the demons believe that—and shudder.

20 You foolish man, do you want evidence that faith without deeds is useless[d]? 21 Was not our ancestor Abraham considered righteous for what he did when he offered his son Isaac on the altar?[y] 22 You see that his faith and his actions were working together,[z] and his faith was made complete by what he did. 23 And the scripture was fulfilled that says, "Abraham believed God, and it was credited to him as righteousness,"[e][a] and he was called God's friend.[b] 24 You see that a person is justified by what he does and not by faith alone.

25 In the same way, was not even Rahab the prostitute considered righteous for what she did when she gave lodging to the spies and sent them off in a different direction?[c] 26 As the body without the spirit is dead, so faith without deeds is dead.

## Taming the Tongue

3 Not many of you should presume to be teachers, my brothers, because you know that we who teach will be judged more strictly. 2 We all stumble[d] in many ways. If anyone is never at fault in what he says, he is a perfect man,[e] able to keep his whole body in check.

3 When we put bits into the mouths of horses to make them obey us, we can turn the whole animal.[f] 4 Or take ships as an example. Although they are so large and are

*Lord,*

*help me to combat my inclination to get riled up and snap at my brother or sister. I know that I am not wrestling against flesh and blood but against spiritual powers and principalities. Help me to let your Spirit guide me in everything I say and do, today and every day. Teach me to call on you first for everything I need.*

*Amen*

JAMES 3:3–6

**2:21** y Ge 22:9,12
**2:22** z Heb 11:17
**2:23** a Ge 15:6; Ro 4:3 b 2Ch 20:7; Isa 41:8
**2:25** c Heb 11:31
**3:2** d 1Ki 8:46 e Mt 12:37
**3:3** f Ps 32:9

[a]8 Lev. 19:18 [b]11 Exodus 20:14; Deut. 5:18 [c]11 Exodus 20:13; Deut. 5:17 [d]20 Some early manuscripts *dead*
[e]23 Gen. 15:6

3:5 g Ps 12:3,4
3:6 h Pr 16:27; i Mt 15:11,18,19
3:8 j Ps 140:3
3:9 k Ge 1:26,27
3:13 l Jas 2:18
3:17 m Ro 12:9
3:18 n Pr 11:18
4:1 o Ro 7:23

driven by strong winds, they are steered by a very small rudder wherever the pilot wants to go. 5 Likewise the tongue is a small part of the body, but it makes great boasts.[g] Consider what a great forest is set on fire by a small spark. 6 The tongue also is a fire,[h] a world of evil among the parts of the body. It corrupts the whole person,[i] sets the whole course of his life on fire, and is itself set on fire by hell.

7 All kinds of animals, birds, reptiles and creatures of the sea are being tamed and have been tamed by man, 8 but no man can tame the tongue. It is a restless evil, full of deadly poison.[j]

9 With the tongue we praise our Lord and Father, and with it we curse men, who have been made in God's likeness.[k] 10 Out of the same mouth come praise and cursing. My brothers, this should not be. 11 Can both fresh water and salt[a] water flow from the same spring? 12 My brothers, can a fig tree bear olives, or a grapevine bear figs? Neither can a salt spring produce fresh water.

## Two Kinds of Wisdom

13 Who is wise and understanding among you? Let him show it[l] by his good life, by deeds done in the humility that comes from wisdom. 14 But if you harbor bitter envy and selfish ambition in your hearts, do not boast about it or deny the truth. 15 Such "wisdom" does not come down from heaven but is earthly, unspiritual, of the devil. 16 For where you have envy and selfish ambition, there you find disorder and every evil practice.

17 But the wisdom that comes from heaven is first of all pure; then peace-loving, considerate, submissive, full of mercy and good fruit, impartial and sincere.[m] 18 Peacemakers who sow in peace raise a harvest of righteousness.[n]

## Submit Yourselves to God

4 What causes fights and quarrels among you? Don't they come from your desires that battle[o] within you? 2 You want something but don't get it. You kill and covet, but you cannot have what you want. You quarrel and fight. You do not have, because you do not ask God. 3 When you ask, you do not receive, because you ask with wrong motives, that you may spend what you get on your pleasures.

4 You adulterous people, don't you know that friendship with the world is hatred toward God?[p] Anyone who chooses to be a friend of the world becomes an enemy of God.[q] 5 Or do you think Scripture says without reason that the spirit he caused to live in us envies intensely?[b] 6 But he gives us more grace. That is why Scripture says:

"God opposes the proud
but gives grace to the humble."[c][r]

7 Submit yourselves, then, to God. Resist the devil,[s] and he will flee from you. 8 Come near to God and he will come near to you. Wash your hands,[t] you sinners, and purify your hearts, you double-minded.[u] 9 Grieve, mourn and wail. Change your laughter to mourning and your joy to gloom. 10 Humble yourselves before the Lord, and he will lift you up.

11 Brothers, do not slander one another.[v] Anyone who speaks against his brother or judges him speaks against the law and judges it. When you judge the law, you are not keeping it, but sitting in judgment on it. 12 There is only one Lawgiver and Judge, the one who is able to save and destroy.[w] But you—who are you to judge your neighbor?[x]

## Boasting About Tomorrow

13 Now listen, you who say, "Today or tomorrow we will go to this or that city, spend a year there, carry on business and make money."[y] 14 Why, you do not even know what will happen tomorrow. What is your life? You are a mist that appears for a little while and then vanishes.[z] 15 Instead, you ought to say, "If it is the Lord's will,[a] we will live and do this or that." 16 As it is, you boast and brag. All such boasting is evil.[b] 17 Anyone, then, who knows the good he ought to do and doesn't do it, sins.[c]

4:4 p 1Jn 2:15; q Jn 15:19
4:6 r Pr 3:34
4:7 s 1Pe 5:6–9
4:8 t Isa 1:16; u Jas 1:8
4:11 v 1Pe 2:1
4:12 w Mt 10:28; x Ro 14:4
4:13 y Pr 27:1
4:14 z Job 7:7
4:15 a Ac 18:21
4:16 b 1Co 5:6
4:17 c Lk 12:47; Jn 9:41

[a] 11 Greek *bitter* (see also verse 14) [b] 5 Or *that God jealously longs for the spirit that he made to live in us*; or *that the Spirit he caused to live in us longs jealously* [c] 6 Prov. 3:34

**5:1** d Lk 6:24
**5:2** e Job 13:28; Mt 6:19,20
**5:4** f Lev 19:13 g Dt 24:15
**5:7** h Dt 11:14
**5:9** i Jas 4:11 j Mt 24:33
**5:10** k Mt 5:12
**5:11** l Job 42:10,12–17
**5:12** m Mt 5:34–37

## Warning to Rich Oppressors

5 Now listen, you rich people,[d] weep and wail because of the misery that is coming upon you. 2 Your wealth has rotted, and moths have eaten your clothes.[e] 3 Your gold and silver are corroded. Their corrosion will testify against you and eat your flesh like fire. You have hoarded wealth in the last days. 4 Look! The wages you failed to pay the workmen[f] who mowed your fields are crying out against you. The cries[g] of the harvesters have reached the ears of the Lord Almighty. 5 You have lived on earth in luxury and self-indulgence. You have fattened yourselves in the day of slaughter.[a] 6 You have condemned and murdered innocent men, who were not opposing you.

## Patience in Suffering

7 Be patient, then, brothers, until the Lord's coming. See how the farmer waits for the land to yield its valuable crop and how patient he is for the autumn and spring rains.[h] 8 You too, be patient and stand firm, because the Lord's coming is near. 9 Don't grumble against each other, brothers,[i] or you will be judged. The Judge is standing at the door![j]

10 Brothers, as an example of patience in the face of suffering, take the prophets[k] who spoke in the name of the Lord. 11 As you know, we consider blessed those who have persevered. You have heard of Job's perseverance and have seen what the Lord finally brought about.[l] The Lord is full of compassion and mercy.

12 Above all, my brothers, do not swear—not by heaven or by earth or by anything else. Let your "Yes" be yes, and your "No," no, or you will be condemned.[m]

## The Prayer of Faith

13 Is any one of you in trouble? He should pray. Is anyone happy? Let him sing songs of praise. 14 Is any one of you sick? He should call the elders of the church to pray over him and anoint him with oil[n] in the name of the Lord. 15 And the prayer offered in faith will make the sick person well; the Lord will raise him up. If he has sinned, he will be forgiven. 16 Therefore confess your sins to each other and pray for each other so that you may be healed. The prayer of a righteous man is powerful and effective.

17 Elijah was a man just like us.[o] He prayed earnestly that it would not rain, and it did not rain on the land for three and a half years.[p] 18 Again he prayed, and the heavens gave rain, and the earth produced its crops.[q]

19 My brothers, if one of you should wander from the truth and someone should bring him back,[r] 20 remember this: Whoever turns a sinner from the error of his way will save[s] him from death and cover over a multitude of sins.[t]

**5:14** n Mk 6:13
**5:17** o Ac 14:15 p 1Ki 17:1; Lk 4:25
**5:18** q 1Ki 18:41–45
**5:19** r Mt 18:15
**5:20** s Ro 11:14 t 1Pe 4:8

*Weary soul,*

*You have struggled for a long time.*
*The battle seems overwhelming.*
*Don't give up! I am compassionate;*
*I see what you are going through.*

*Your Faithful Lord*

JAMES 5:10–11

[a] 5 Or *yourselves as in a day of feasting*

# 1 Peter

## OVERVIEW

Peter began his first letter with a strong affirmation of the inheritance each believer possesses in Christ Jesus. It cannot perish, spoil or fade; it is "kept in heaven" (1Pe 1:4). With this in mind, believers should be holy (see 1Pe 1:15), "crave pure spiritual milk" for growth (1Pe 2:2), and submit to authorities (see 1Pe 2:13–25). Peter encouraged wives to submit to their husbands, and husbands to be considerate of their wives and treat them with respect (see 1Pe 3:1–7). Peter gave believers guidance on how to live in an environment of persecution. The elders were admonished to take care of their flock, and the young men were to submit to their leaders (see 1Pe 5:1–5).

An inheritance left by a relative can be a wonderful gift. Yet in the midst of suffering, the eternal heritage of Jesus Christ gives every believer renewed hope and strength in him. As you read through the book of 1 Peter, meditate on the fact that "the eyes of the Lord are on the righteous and his ears are attentive to their prayer" (1Pe 3:12). How can this truth revitalize your joy in Christ?

## OUTLINE

I. Opening Greetings (1:1–2)
II. Praise for Hope and Salvation (1:3–12)
III. Call to Holiness (1:13—2:3)
IV. Applications of Holiness (2:4—5:11)
V. Final Greetings (5:12–14)

## SCANNABLE FACTS:

**Author:** Peter

**Time Written:** The early A.D. 60s, before Peter was martyred in A.D. 67 or 68

**Theme to Note:** Be holy as God is holy

**Notable Women:** Wives

1:2 a 2Th 2:13
1:3 b Jas 1:18 c 1Co 15:20
1:5 d Jn 10:28
1:6 e Jas 1:2
1:7 f Jas 1:3
1:8 g Jn 20:29
1:9 h Ro 6:22

1 Peter, an apostle of Jesus Christ,

To God's elect, strangers in the world, scattered throughout Pontus, Galatia, Cappadocia, Asia and Bithynia, [2]who have been chosen according to the foreknowledge of God the Father, through the sanctifying work of the Spirit,[a] for obedience to Jesus Christ and sprinkling by his blood:

Grace and peace be yours in abundance.

## Praise to God for a Living Hope

[3]Praise be to the God and Father of our Lord Jesus Christ! In his great mercy[b] he has given us new birth into a living hope through the resurrection of Jesus Christ from the dead,[c] [4]and into an inheritance that can never perish, spoil or fade—kept in heaven for you, [5]who through faith are shielded by God's power[d] until the coming of the salvation that is ready to be revealed in the last time. [6]In this you greatly rejoice, though now for a little while you may have had to suffer grief in all kinds of trials.[e] [7]These have come so that your faith—of greater worth than gold, which perishes even though refined by fire—may be proved genuine[f] and may result in praise, glory and honor when Jesus Christ is revealed. [8]Though you have not seen him, you love him; and even though you do not see him now, you believe in him[g] and are filled with an inexpressible and glorious joy, [9]for you are receiving the goal of your faith, the salvation of your souls.[h]

[10]Concerning this salvation, the prophets, who spoke of the grace that was to come to you, searched intently and with the greatest care, [11]trying to find out the time and circumstances to which the Spirit of Christ[i] in them was pointing when he predicted the sufferings of Christ and the glories that would follow. [12]It was revealed to them that they were not serving themselves but you, when they spoke of the things that have now been told you by those who have preached the gospel to you by the Holy Spirit sent from heaven. Even angels long to look into these things.

*My God,*

*cleanse my heart and soul so that nothing may come between us. Restore me to wholeness, I pray. I want to think in a new way about myself and my worth. Help me to let go of exhausting baggage. Grant me freedom and joy.*

*Amen*

1 PETER 1:3–9

## Be Holy

[13]Therefore, prepare your minds for action; be self-controlled; set your hope fully on the grace to be given you when Jesus Christ is revealed. [14]As obedient children, do not conform[j] to the evil desires you had when you lived in ignorance. [15]But just as he

1:11 i 2Pe 1:21
1:14 j Ro 12:2

## *The African Presence*

### 1 Peter 1

While there are no specific references to the African presence within the book of 1 Peter, the early church was influenced by people of North Africa and the Middle East (a historical and cultural subregion of Africa-Eurasia, traditionally held to be countries or regions in Southwest Asia together with Egypt). However, during the time of the New Testament, racial identification did not have the significance that it has today.

who called you is holy, so be holy in all you do;[k] 16 for it is written: "Be holy, because I am holy."[a][l]

17 Since you call on a Father who judges each man's work impartially, live your lives as strangers here in reverent fear.[m] 18 For you know that it was not with perishable things such as silver or gold that you were redeemed[n] from the empty way of life handed down to you from your forefathers, 19 but with the precious blood of Christ, a lamb without blemish or defect. 20 He was chosen before the creation of the world, but was revealed in these last times for your sake. 21 Through him you believe in God, who raised him from the dead and glorified him, and so your faith and hope are in God.

22 Now that you have purified yourselves by obeying the truth so that you have sincere love for your brothers, love one another deeply,[o] from the heart.[b] 23 For you have been born again,[p] not of perishable seed, but of imperishable, through the living and enduring word of God. 24 For,

> "All men are like grass,
>   and all their glory is like the flowers of the field;
> the grass withers and the flowers fall,
> 25 but the word of the Lord stands forever."[c][q]

And this is the word that was preached to you.

2 Therefore, rid yourselves of all malice and all deceit, hypocrisy, envy, and slander of every kind. 2 Like newborn babies, crave pure spiritual milk,[r] so that by it you may grow up in your salvation, 3 now that you have tasted that the Lord is good.[s]

## The Living Stone and a Chosen People

4 As you come to him, the living Stone—rejected by men but chosen by God and precious to him— 5 you also, like living stones, are being built into a spiritual house to be a holy priesthood, offering spiritual sacrifices acceptable to God through Jesus Christ.[t] 6 For in Scripture it says:

> "See, I lay a stone in Zion,
>   a chosen and precious cornerstone,
> and the one who trusts in him
>   will never be put to shame."[d][u]

7 Now to you who believe, this stone is precious. But to those who do not believe,

> "The stone the builders rejected
>   has become the capstone,"[e][f][v]

8 and,

> "A stone that causes men to stumble
>   and a rock that makes them fall."[g][w]

They stumble because they disobey the message—which is also what they were destined for.[x]

9 But you are a chosen people,[y] a royal priesthood, a holy nation, a people belonging to God, that you may declare the praises of him who called you out of darkness into his wonderful light.[z] 10 Once you were not a people, but now you are the people of God;[a] once you had not received mercy, but now you have received mercy.

> *"We are positively a unique people, breathtaking people. Anything we do, we do big! Despite attempts to stereotype us, we are crazy, individual, and uncorralable people."*
>
> —LEONTYNE PRICE, OPERA SINGER

11 Dear friends, I urge you, as aliens and strangers in the world, to abstain from sinful desires, which war against your soul.[b] 12 Live such good lives among the pagans that, though they accuse you of doing wrong, they may see your good deeds[c] and glorify God[d] on the day he visits us.

## Submission to Rulers and Masters

13 Submit yourselves for the Lord's sake to every authority[e] instituted among men: whether to the king, as the supreme authority, 14 or to governors, who are sent by him to punish those who do wrong[f] and to commend those who do right.[g] 15 For it is God's will that by doing good you should silence the ignorant talk of foolish men. 16 Live as free men, but do not use your freedom as

1:15 k 2Co 7:1
1:16 l Lev 11:44,45
1:17 m Heb 12:28
1:18 n 1Co 6:20
1:22 o Heb 13:1
1:23 p Jn 1:13
1:25 q Isa 40:6–8
2:2 r 1Co 3:2
2:3 s Heb 6:5
2:5 t Php 4:18
2:6 u Isa 28:16
2:7 v Ps 118:22
2:8 w Isa 8:14; x Ro 9:22
2:9 y Dt 10:15; z Ac 26:18
2:10 a Hos 1:9,10
2:11 b Jas 4:1
2:12 c Php 2:15; d Mt 5:16
2:13 e Ro 13:1
2:14 f Ro 13:4; g Ro 13:3

[a] 16 Lev. 11:44,45; 19:2 [b] 22 Some early manuscripts *from a pure heart* [c] 25 Isaiah 40:6–8 [d] 6 Isaiah 28:16
[e] 7 Or *cornerstone* [f] 7 Psalm 118:22 [g] 8 Isaiah 8:14

**2:17** h Ro 12:10
**2:18** i Eph 6:5
**2:21** j Mt 16:24
**2:22** k Isa 53:9
**2:23** l Isa 53:7
**2:24** m Heb 9:28 n Isa 53:5
**2:25** o Isa 53:6
**3:3** p 1Ti 2:9
**3:5** q 1Ti 5:5
**3:6** r Ge 18:12

a cover-up for evil; live as servants of God. 17 Show proper respect to everyone: Love the brotherhood of believers,[h] fear God, honor the king.

18 Slaves, submit yourselves to your masters with all respect,[i] not only to those who are good and considerate, but also to those who are harsh. 19 For it is commendable if a man bears up under the pain of unjust suffering because he is conscious of God. 20 But how is it to your credit if you receive a beating for doing wrong and endure it? But if you suffer for doing good and you endure it, this is commendable before God. 21 To this you were called, because Christ suffered for you, leaving you an example,[j] that you should follow in his steps.

22 "He committed no sin,
and no deceit was found in his mouth."[a][k]

23 When they hurled their insults at him, he did not retaliate; when he suffered, he made no threats.[l] Instead, he entrusted himself to him who judges justly. 24 He himself bore our sins[m] in his body on the tree, so that we might die to sins and live for righteousness; by his wounds you have been healed.[n] 25 For you were like sheep going astray,[o] but now you have returned to the Shepherd and Overseer of your souls.

## Wives and Husbands

3 Wives, in the same way be submissive to your husbands so that, if any of them do not believe the word, they may be won over without words by the behavior of their wives, 2 when they see the purity and reverence of your lives. 3 Your beauty should not come from outward adornment, such as braided hair and the wearing of gold jewelry and fine clothes.[p] 4 Instead, it should be that of your inner self, the unfading beauty of a gentle and quiet spirit, which is of great worth in God's sight. 5 For this is the way the holy women of the past who put their hope in God[q] used to make themselves beautiful. They were submissive to their own husbands, 6 like Sarah, who obeyed Abraham and called him her master.[r] You are her daughters if you do what is right and do not give way to fear.

7 Husbands, in the same way be considerate as you live with your wives, and treat them with respect as the weaker partner and as heirs with you of the gracious gift of life, so that nothing will hinder your prayers.

## Suffering for Doing Good

8 Finally, all of you, live in harmony with one another; be sympathetic, love as brothers, be compassionate and humble. 9 Do not repay evil with evil[s] or insult with insult, but with blessing, because to this you were called so that you may inherit a blessing.[t] 10 For,

"Whoever would love life
and see good days
must keep his tongue from evil
and his lips from deceitful speech.
11 He must turn from evil and do good;
he must seek peace and pursue it.
12 For the eyes of the Lord are on the righteous
and his ears are attentive to their prayer,
but the face of the Lord is against those who do evil."[b][u]

13 Who is going to harm you if you are eager to do good?[v] 14 But even if you should suffer for what is right, you are blessed.[w] "Do not fear what they fear[c]; do not be frightened."[d] 15 But in your hearts set apart Christ as Lord. Always be prepared to give an answer[x] to everyone who asks you to give the reason for the hope that you have. But do this with gentleness and respect, 16 keeping a clear conscience,[y] so that those who speak maliciously against your good behavior in

*Protected one,*

*Your hope should be in Christ.*
*Is it? Exclusively?*

*Your Lord*

1 PETER 3:15

**3:9** s Ro 12:17 t Heb 6:14
**3:12** u Ps 34:12–16
**3:13** v Pr 16:7
**3:14** w 1Pe 2:19,20
**3:15** x Col 4:6
**3:16** y Heb 13:18

[a] 22 Isaiah 53:9 [b] 12 Psalm 34:12–16 [c] 14 Or *not fear their threats* [d] 14 Isaiah 8:12

3:16 z 1Pe 2:12,15
3:18 a 1Pe 2:21

Christ may be ashamed of their slander.[z] 17 It
is better, if it is God's will, to suffer for doing
good than for doing evil. 18 For Christ died
for sins[a] once for all, the righteous for the un-
righteous, to bring you to God. He was put
to death in the body[b] but made alive by the
Spirit, 19 through whom[a] also he went and
preached to the spirits in prison 20 who dis-
obeyed long ago when God waited patiently
in the days of Noah while the ark was being

3:18 b Col 1:22

[a]18,19 Or *alive in the spirit,* [19]*through which*

## Inspire leadership FOCUS

# CHARACTER

As leaders, we are always watched, often critiqued. Whether we agree with or approve of others assessing us, this is a fact we must accept in our leadership roles. It is our character—our actions, thoughts, motives—that people are evaluating. Are we above reproach?

Of all the things that the Lord counts as precious, our character leads the list (see 1Pe 3:4). This truth alone should inspire us to emulate the character of Christ. In fact, our character is so precious to the Lord that when it pleases him, he showcases it. Remember Job (see Job 1:8; 2:3)?

In his teachings, Jesus clearly underscored the importance of character. For instance, in Matthew 5:11 we are told that we are blessed when people insult us and falsely say all kinds of evil against us because of Christ. Why are we blessed in this situation? Because if we are falsely accused, it means that despite the best attempts, our accusers—including the devil—cannot find anything against us that we have done or that we have not already confessed in true repentance. We have to guard our character, paying attention to our actions and words so that this is always the case.

Character does not mean perfection, but it does mean striving for perfection by the power of the Holy Spirit. It has often been said that character is defined by who we are when no one is looking. For us as Christian leaders, character is better defined by who we are because we know the Lord is always looking!

—L. Miller Autry

For the next Inspire note, go to page 1484.

## read

1 Peter 3:1–7.

**See also** the Inspire Notes "Seek Wisdom," "Integrity," "Humility" and "Gentleness," and the Women of the Bible Notes "Deborah: An Uncommon Leader," "Abigail: A Wise Wife," "The Virtuous Woman: A Strong Woman, Dependent on God" and "The 'Chosen Lady': A Woman Worth Imitating."

## WOMAN of COLOR

We move ahead in life on our strengths, not our weaknesses. Make a list of your character strengths and decide what you can do to build on them. Also assess any weaknesses so that as a Christian woman who is a leader, no one will be able to accuse you of anything.

built.[c] In it only a few people, eight in all, were saved[d] through water, [21]and this water symbolizes baptism that now saves you[e] also—not the removal of dirt from the body but the pledge[a] of a good conscience toward God. It saves you by the resurrection of Jesus Christ,[f] [22]who has gone into heaven and is at God's right hand—with angels, authorities and powers in submission to him.[g]

## Living for God

4 Therefore, since Christ suffered in his body, arm yourselves also with the same attitude, because he who has suffered in his body is done with sin. [2]As a result, he does not live the rest of his earthly life for evil human desires, but rather for the will of God. [3]For you have spent enough time in the past[h] doing what pagans choose to do—living in debauchery, lust, drunkenness, orgies, carousing and detestable idolatry. [4]They think it strange that you do not plunge with them into the same flood of dissipation, and they heap abuse on you. [5]But they will have to give account to him who is ready to judge the living and the dead.[i] [6]For this is the reason the gospel was preached even to those who are now dead,[j] so that they might be judged according to men in regard to the body, but live according to God in regard to the spirit.

[7]The end of all things is near.[k] Therefore be clear minded and self-controlled so that you can pray. [8]Above all, love each other deeply, because love covers over a multitude of sins.[l] [9]Offer hospitality to one another without grumbling. [10]Each one should use whatever gift he has received to serve others,[m] faithfully administering God's grace in its various forms. [11]If anyone speaks, he should do it as one speaking the very words of God. If anyone serves, he should do it with the strength God provides, so that in all things God may be praised through Jesus Christ. To him be the glory and the power for ever and ever. Amen.

## Suffering for Being a Christian

[12]Dear friends, do not be surprised at the painful trial you are suffering, as though something strange were happening to you. [13]But rejoice that you participate in the sufferings of Christ, so that you may be overjoyed when his glory is revealed.[n] [14]If you are insulted because of the name of Christ, you are blessed, for the Spirit of glory and of God rests on you. [15]If you suffer, it should not be as a murderer or thief or any other kind of criminal, or even as a meddler. [16]However, if you suffer as a Christian, do not be ashamed, but praise God that you bear that name.[o] [17]For it is time for judgment to begin with the family of God; and if it begins with us, what will the outcome be for those who do not obey the gospel of God? [18]And,

"If it is hard for the righteous to be saved,
what will become of the ungodly and
the sinner?"[b][p]

[19]So then, those who suffer according to God's will should commit themselves to their faithful Creator and continue to do good.

## To Elders and Young Men

5 To the elders among you, I appeal as a fellow elder, a witness[q] of Christ's sufferings and one who also will share in the glory to be revealed:[r] [2]Be shepherds of God's flock that is under your care, serving as overseers—not because you must, but because you are willing, as God wants you to be; not greedy for money,[s] but eager to serve; [3]not lording it over[t] those entrusted to you, but being examples to the flock. [4]And when the Chief Shepherd appears, you will receive the crown of glory that will never fade away.

[5]Young men, in the same way be submissive to those who are older. All of you, clothe yourselves with humility toward one another, because,

"God opposes the proud
but gives grace to the humble."[c][u]

[6]Humble yourselves, therefore, under God's mighty hand, that he may lift you up in due time.[v] [7]Cast all your anxiety on him because he cares for you.

[8]Be self-controlled and alert. Your en-

**3:20** c Ge 6:3,5,13,14 d Heb 11:7
**3:21** e Tit 3:5 f 1Pe 1:3
**3:22** g Ro 8:38
**4:3** h Eph 2:2
**4:5** i Ac 10:42; 2Ti 4:1
**4:6** j 1Pe 3:19
**4:7** k Ro 13:11
**4:8** l Pr 10:12
**4:10** m Ro 12:6,7
**4:13** n Ro 8:17
**4:16** o Ac 5:41
**4:18** p Lk 23:31
**5:1** q Lk 24:48 r Rev 1:9
**5:2** s 1Ti 3:3
**5:3** t Eze 34:4
**5:5** u Jas 4:6
**5:6** v Jas 4:10

[a]21 Or *response* [b]18 Prov. 11:31 [c]5 Prov. 3:34

5:9 w Ac 14:22
5:10 x 2Th 2:17
5:12 y Heb 13:22

emy the devil prowls around like a roaring lion looking for someone to devour. 9 Resist him, standing firm in the faith, because you know that your brothers throughout the world are undergoing the same kind of sufferings.[w]

10 And the God of all grace, who called you to his eternal glory in Christ, after you have suffered a little while, will himself restore you and make you strong,[x] firm and steadfast. 11 To him be the power for ever and ever. Amen.

## Final Greetings

12 With the help of Silas,[a] whom I regard as a faithful brother, I have written to you briefly,[y] encouraging you and testifying that this is the true grace of God. Stand fast in it.

13 She who is in Babylon, chosen together with you, sends you her greetings, and so does my son Mark.[z] 14 Greet one another with a kiss of love.[a]

Peace[b] to all of you who are in Christ.

*Lord,*

*I'm casting all of my cares on you because I know you care for me. I need to hear from you today and every day. Lord, speak to me and I will follow your voice. I am ready to receive your direction, your wisdom and your Word, and I pledge in turn to obey you in Jesus' name.*

*Amen*

1 PETER 5:6–11

5:13 z Ac 12:12
5:14 a Ro 16:16 b Eph 6:23

[a]12 Greek *Silvanus*, a variant of *Silas*

# 2 Peter

## OVERVIEW

In his second letter, Peter tackled his concern regarding false teaching that was infiltrating the church. Peter urged believers to add virtues to their faith, all of which would empower their Christian walk (see 2Pe 1:5–9). He warned of greedy false teachers who would "secretly introduce destructive heresies" (see 2Pe 2:1) in order to exploit believers. Peter wrote that believers should anticipate the coming of those who would scoff at the idea of Christ's return, remembering that "the Lord is not slow in keeping his promise, as some understand slowness. He is patient with you, not wanting anyone to perish" (2Pe 3:9).

Broken promises have caused many women to despair of trusting anyone. No matter how many people lie, God does not lie (see 1Sa 15:29; Tit 1:2); and we can be assured that "the day of the Lord will come like a thief" (2Pe 3:10). Knowing this truth, women believers should live "holy and godly lives" (2Pe 3:11), trusting in God to keep his word. As you read through 2 Peter, ask the Holy Spirit to help you live in preparedness of Christ's return.

## OUTLINE

I. Divine Confidence (1:1–21)
II. Warning Against False Teachers (2:1–22)
III. The Certainty of Christ's Return (3:1–18)

### SCANNABLE FACTS:

**Author:** Peter

**Time Written:** Near the end of Peter's life, probably between A.D. 65 and 68

**Theme to Note:** Make your calling and election sure

**Notable Women:** There are no women mentioned in this book

1:1
a Ro1:1
b Tit2:13

1:3
c 1Pe1:5
d 1Th2:12

1:4
e 2Co7:1

1 Simon Peter, a servant[a] and apostle of Jesus Christ,

To those who through the righteousness of our God and Savior Jesus Christ[b] have received a faith as precious as ours:

2 Grace and peace be yours in abundance through the knowledge of God and of Jesus our Lord.

## Making One's Calling and Election Sure

3 His divine power[c] has given us everything we need for life and godliness through our knowledge of him who called us[d] by his own glory and goodness. 4 Through these he has given us his very great and precious promises,[e] so that through them you may participate in the divine nature and escape the corruption in the world caused by evil desires.

5 For this very reason, make every effort to add to your faith goodness; and to goodness, knowledge; 6 and to knowledge, self-control; and to self-control, perseverance; and to perseverance, godliness; 7 and to godliness, brotherly kindness; and to brotherly kindness, love. 8 For if you possess these qualities in increasing measure, they will keep you from being ineffective and unproductive[f] in your knowledge of our Lord Jesus Christ. 9 But if anyone does not have them, he is nearsighted and blind, and has forgotten that he has been cleansed from his past sins.[g]

10 Therefore, my brothers, be all the more eager to make your calling and election sure. For if you do these things, you will never fall, 11 and you will receive a rich welcome into the eternal kingdom of our Lord and Savior Jesus Christ.

## Prophecy of Scripture

12 So I will always remind you of these things,[h] even though you know them and are firmly established in the truth you now have. 13 I think it is right to refresh your memory as long as I live in the tent of this body,[i] 14 because I know that I will soon put it aside,[j] as our Lord Jesus Christ has made clear to me.[k] 15 And I will make every effort to see that after my departure you will always be able to remember these things.

16 We did not follow cleverly invented stories when we told you about the power and coming of our Lord Jesus Christ, but we were eyewitnesses of his majesty.[l] 17 For he received honor and glory from God the Father when the voice came to him from the Majestic Glory, saying, "This is my Son,

1:8
f Jn15:2

1:9
g Eph5:26

1:12
h 1Jn2:21

1:13
i 2Co5:1,4

1:14
j 2Ti4:6
k Jn21:18,19

1:16
l Mt17:1–8

*Laborer,*

*I give you everything you need to live a godly life. Are you making use of my tools?*

*Love,*
*Your Maker*

2 PETER 1:3–8

## The African Presence

### 2 Peter 1

While there are no specific references to the African presence within the book of 2 Peter, the early church was influenced by people of North Africa and the Middle East (a historical and cultural subregion of Africa-Eurasia, traditionally held to be countries or regions in Southwest Asia together with Egypt). However, during the time of the New Testament, racial identification did not have the significance that it has today.

whom I love; with him I am well pleased."[a][m] 18 We ourselves heard this voice that came from heaven when we were with him on the sacred mountain.

19 And we have the word of the prophets made more certain, and you will do well to pay attention to it, as to a light[n] shining in a dark place, until the day dawns and the morning star[o] rises in your hearts. 20 Above all, you must understand that no prophecy of Scripture came about by the prophet's own interpretation. 21 For prophecy never had its origin in the will of man, but men spoke from God[p] as they were carried along by the Holy Spirit.[q]

## False Teachers and Their Destruction

2 But there were also false prophets among the people, just as there will be false teachers among you. They will secretly introduce destructive heresies, even denying the sovereign Lord[r] who bought them—bringing swift destruction on themselves. 2 Many will follow their shameful ways and will bring the way of truth into disrepute. 3 In their greed these teachers will exploit you[s] with stories they have made up. Their condemnation has long been hanging over them, and their destruction has not been sleeping.

4 For if God did not spare angels when they sinned, but sent them to hell,[b] putting them into gloomy dungeons[c] to be held for judgment;[t] 5 if he did not spare the ancient world when he brought the flood on its ungodly people, but protected Noah, a preacher of righteousness, and seven others;[u] 6 if he condemned the cities of Sodom and Gomorrah by burning them to ashes,[v] and made them an example of what is going to happen to the ungodly; 7 and if he rescued Lot,[w] a righteous man, who was distressed by the filthy lives of lawless men 8 (for that righteous man, living among them day after day, was tormented in his righteous soul by the lawless deeds he saw and heard)— 9 if this is so, then the Lord knows how to rescue godly men from trials and to hold the unrighteous for the day of judgment, while continuing their punishment.[d] 10 This is especially true of those who follow the corrupt desire of the sinful nature[e] and despise authority.

Bold and arrogant, these men are not afraid to slander celestial beings;[x] 11 yet even angels, although they are stronger and more powerful, do not bring slanderous accusations against such beings in the presence of the Lord.[y] 12 But these men blaspheme in matters they do not understand. They are like brute beasts, creatures of instinct, born only to be caught and destroyed, and like beasts they too will perish.[z]

13 They will be paid back with harm for the harm they have done. Their idea of pleasure is to carouse in broad daylight.[a] They are blots and blemishes, reveling in their pleasures while they feast with you.[f][b] 14 With eyes full of adultery, they never stop sinning; they seduce the unstable; they are experts in greed—an accursed brood! 15 They have left the straight way and wandered off to follow the way of Balaam[c] son of Beor, who loved the wages of wickedness. 16 But he was rebuked for his wrongdoing by a donkey—a beast without speech—who spoke with a man's voice and restrained the prophet's madness.

17 These men are springs without water[d] and mists driven by a storm. Blackest darkness is reserved for them. 18 For they mouth empty, boastful words[e] and, by appealing to the lustful desires of sinful human nature, they entice people who are just escaping from those who live in error. 19 They promise them freedom, while they themselves are slaves of depravity—for a man is a slave to whatever has mastered him.[f] 20 If they have escaped the corruption of the world by knowing[g] our Lord and Savior Jesus Christ and are again entangled in it and overcome, they are worse off at the end than they were at the beginning.[h] 21 It would have been better for them not to have known the way of righteousness, than to have known it and then to turn their backs on the sacred command that was passed on to them. 22 Of them the proverbs are true: "A dog returns to its vomit,"[g][i] and, "A sow that is washed goes back to her wallowing in the mud."

**1:17** m Mt 3:17
**1:19** n Ps 119:105; o Rev 22:16
**1:21** p 2Ti 3:16; q Ac 1:16
**2:1** r Jude 4
**2:3** s 2Co 2:17
**2:4** t Jude 6; Rev 20:1,2
**2:5** u 1Pe 3:20
**2:6** v Ge 19:24,25
**2:7** w Ge 19:16
**2:10** x Jude 8
**2:11** y Jude 9
**2:12** z Jude 10
**2:13** a Ro 13:13; b 1Co 11:20,21
**2:15** c Nu 22:4–20
**2:17** d Jude 12
**2:18** e Jude 16
**2:19** f Ro 6:16
**2:20** g 2Pe 1:2; h Mt 12:45
**2:22** i Pr 26:11

[a] 17 Matt. 17:5; Mark 9:7; Luke 9:35 [b] 4 Greek *Tartarus* [c] 4 Some manuscripts *into chains of darkness* [d] 9 Or *unrighteous for punishment until the day of judgment* [e] 10 Or *the flesh* [f] 13 Some manuscripts *in their love feasts* [g] 22 Prov. 26:11

3:1 j 2Pe 1:13
3:3 k 2Pe 2:10
3:4 l Eze 12:22
3:5 m Ge 1:6,9 n Ps 24:2
3:7 o ver 10,12
3:8 p Ps 90:4
3:9 q Heb 10:37
3:10 r Mt 24:35
3:12 s 1Co 1:7

## The Day of the Lord

3 Dear friends, this is now my second letter to you. I have written both of them as reminders[j] to stimulate you to wholesome thinking. 2 I want you to recall the words spoken in the past by the holy prophets and the command given by our Lord and Savior through your apostles.

3 First of all, you must understand that in the last days scoffers will come, scoffing and following their own evil desires.[k] 4 They will say, "Where is this 'coming' he promised?[l] Ever since our fathers died, everything goes on as it has since the beginning of creation." 5 But they deliberately forget that long ago by God's word[m] the heavens existed and the earth was formed out of water and by water.[n] 6 By these waters also the world of that time was deluged and destroyed. 7 By the same word the present heavens and earth are reserved for fire,[o] being kept for the day of judgment and destruction of ungodly men.

8 But do not forget this one thing, dear friends: With the Lord a day is like a thousand years, and a thousand years are like a day.[p] 9 The Lord is not slow in keeping his promise,[q] as some understand slowness. He is patient with you, not wanting anyone to perish, but everyone to come to repentance.

10 But the day of the Lord will come like a thief. The heavens will disappear with a roar; the elements will be destroyed by fire, and the earth and everything in it will be laid bare.[a][r]

11 Since everything will be destroyed in this way, what kind of people ought you to be? You ought to live holy and godly lives 12 as you look forward[s] to the day of God and speed its coming.[b] That day will bring about the destruction of the heavens by fire, and the elements will melt in the heat. 13 But in

*Lord,*

*I leave my cares with you this day, knowing that you can and will handle them. I rest in the confidence that you care about me and will bless me with the things that I need, today and each day. Help me to live a godly and holy life as I wait on you for all things. In Jesus' loving name,*

*Amen*

2 PETER 3:11–13

keeping with his promise we are looking forward to a new heaven and a new earth,[t] the home of righteousness.

14 So then, dear friends, since you are looking forward to this, make every effort to be found spotless, blameless and at peace with him. 15 Bear in mind that our Lord's patience means salvation, just as our dear brother Paul also wrote you with the wisdom that God gave him.[u] 16 He writes the same way in all his letters, speaking in them of these matters. His letters contain some things that are hard to understand, which ignorant and unstable[v] people distort, as they do the other Scriptures, to their own destruction.

17 Therefore, dear friends, since you already know this, be on your guard so that you may not be carried away by the error of lawless men and fall from your secure position.[w] 18 But grow in the grace and knowledge of our Lord and Savior Jesus Christ. To him be glory both now and forever! Amen.

3:13 t Isa 65:17; 66:22; Rev 21:1
3:15 u Eph 3:3
3:16 v 2Pe 2:14
3:17 w Rev 2:5

[a] 10 Some manuscripts *be burned up* [b] 12 Or *as you wait eagerly for the day of God to come*

# 1 John

## OVERVIEW

John's first letter emphasizes the certainty of Jesus Christ as "the Word of life"—the one who is life and reveals life (see 1Jn 1:1–4). It also affirms the reality of sin and declares God's remedy through the atoning sacrifice of Christ (see 1Jn 1:8—2:2). John encouraged believers to obey the will of God and resist the pleasures of this fleeting world (see 1Jn 2:15–17).

John mentioned both "the antichrist [who] is coming"—the great enemy of God and his people who will appear before Christ's return—and "many antichrists [who] have come" (1Jn 2:18)—those who deny that Jesus Christ is the Son of God come in the flesh (see 1Jn 2:22; 4:1–3). By reminding believers of God's great love, John challenged his readers to demonstrate the sincerity of their faith by loving one another (see 1Jn 3:11—5:5). John's challenge also applies to us today.

The entire Old Testament law is summarized in two commandments: Love God and love others (see Mt 22:34–40; Gal 5:14). Although many people don't struggle with loving God, loving his people is a completely different matter. First John makes it adamantly clear that it is impossible to love God and hate your brother or sister (see 1Jn 4:19–21). Women believers who understand that "God is love" (1Jn 4:16) can readily receive and give that love as they grow in their relationship with Jesus Christ.

## OUTLINE

I. The Reality of Christ's Incarnation (1:1–4)
II. Living in the Light (1:5—2:17)
III. Warning Against Antichrists (2:18–27)
IV. Loving God and Loving Others (2:28—4:21)
V. Obedience Brings Assurance (5:1–21)

## SCANNABLE FACTS:

**Author:** John

**Time Written:** Between A.D. 85 and 95

**Theme to Note:** Love as God has loved you

**Notable Women:** There are no women mentioned in this book

1:1 a Jn 1:14 b Jn 20:27
1:2 c Jn 1:1–4
1:5 d 1Jn 3:11
1:6 e 2Co 6:14

## The Word of Life

**1** That which was from the beginning, which we have heard, which we have seen with our eyes,[a] which we have looked at and our hands have touched[b]—this we proclaim concerning the Word of life. 2The life appeared;[c] we have seen it and testify to it, and we proclaim to you the eternal life, which was with the Father and has appeared to us. 3We proclaim to you what we have seen and heard, so that you also may have fellowship with us. And our fellowship is with the Father and with his Son, Jesus Christ. 4We write this to make our*[a]* joy complete.

## Walking in the Light

5This is the message we have heard[d] from him and declare to you: God is light; in him there is no darkness at all. 6If we claim to have fellowship with him yet walk in the darkness,[e] we lie and do not live by the truth. 7But if we walk in the light, as he is in the light, we have fellowship with one another, and the blood of Jesus, his Son, purifies us from all*[b]* sin.[f]

8If we claim to be without sin,[g] we deceive ourselves and the truth is not in us.[h] 9If we confess our sins, he is faithful and just and will forgive us our sins and purify us from all unrighteousness. 10If we claim we have not sinned, we make him out to be a liar[i] and his word has no place in our lives.

**2** My dear children, I write this to you so that you will not sin. But if anybody does sin, we have one who speaks to the Father in our defense[j]—Jesus Christ, the Righteous One. 2He is the atoning sacrifice for our sins,[k] and not only for ours but also for*[c]* the sins of the whole world.

3We know that we have come to know him if we obey his commands. 4The man who says, "I know him," but does not do what he commands is a liar, and the truth is not in him.[l] 5But if anyone obeys his word,[m] God's love*[d]* is truly made complete in him.[n] This is how we know we are in him: 6Whoever claims to live in him must walk as Jesus did.[o]

7Dear friends, I am not writing you a new command but an old one, which you have had since the beginning.[p] This old command is the message you have heard. 8Yet I am writing you a new command; its truth is seen in him and you, because the darkness is passing and the true light[q] is already shining.

9Anyone who claims to be in the light

1:7 f Heb 9:14
1:8 g Jas 3:2 h 1Jn 2:4
1:10 i 1Jn 5:10
2:1 j Ro 8:34; Heb 7:25
2:2 k Ro 3:25
2:4 l 1Jn 1:6,8
2:5 m Jn 14:21,23 n 1Jn 4:12
2:6 o 1Pe 2:21
2:7 p 2Jn 5,6
2:8 q Jn 1:9

*Child of the day.*

*Walk in my light and reflect it.*

*It's dark out there, and the world needs to see.*

*Your Source*

1 JOHN 1:5–7

[a]4 Some manuscripts *your* [b]7 Or *every* [c]2 Or *He is the one who turns aside God's wrath, taking away our sins, and not only ours but also* [d]5 Or *word, love for God*

### The African Presence

**1 John 1**

While there are no specific references to the African presence within the book of 1 John, the early church was influenced by people of North Africa and the Middle East (a historical and cultural subregion of Africa-Eurasia, traditionally held to be countries or regions in Southwest Asia together with Egypt). However, during the time of the New Testament, racial identification did not have the significance that it has today.

# Inspire

## FORGIVENESS: GOD'S EXTENDED MERCY

As humans, we all have sinned and fallen short of the glory of God (see Ro 3:23). As sinners, we are victims of the consequences of sin! But we have the Good News: Through God's grace and gift of Jesus Christ, we can receive forgiveness for our sins. "If we claim to be without sin, we deceive ourselves and the truth is not in us. If we confess our sins, he is faithful and just and will forgive us our sins and purify us from all unrighteousness" (1Jn 1:8–9). God's forgiveness is complete, everlasting and always available (see Ps 103:1–18).

In the world of business, a debt is defined as a financial obligation, something one is bound to pay. Some medium of exchange or currency is needed to erase the debt. In the realm of human sinfulness, we also have a debt to pay. We are liable for our sin. The payment is eternal punishment! However, Jesus provided the "currency" through his blood and paid our debt of sin, leaving those who trust him debt-free.

What joy it is to know that God willingly and gladly releases us from the debt of sin and restores our fellowship with him. It is a debt we could never repay or eradicate. Although the gift of forgiveness is free for us, it cost Jesus his own precious blood (see Ro 5:12–19). But despite Jesus' great price for our forgiveness, God unconditionally bestowed it upon us. As children of God we continually need pardoning. But to our benefit, there is always an ample supply of forgiveness flowing through the love of the Father because of Jesus' sacrifice. God's forgiveness is not automatically given. We must humble ourselves before him, confess our sins and cease sinning.

Because we were "sinful at birth" (Ps 51:5), our greatest need is for forgiveness. God forgives our sins, removes them completely, and remembers them no more (see Ps 103:11–12; Jer 31:33–34). Thanks be to God that Jesus Christ has met this need and has restored our fellowship with our heavenly Father! Let us live in the joy of forgiveness and extend this same forgiveness to our brothers and sisters who have sinned against us.

—D. P. Mannes

### read

1 John 1:8—2:2; see also Psalm 51:1–17; 103:1–18.

**See also** the Inspire Notes "Grace and Mercy" and "Forgiveness: The Doorway to Healing and Reconciliation," and the Women of the Bible Notes "Bathsheba: A Silent Affair," "The Adulteress of Proverbs: The Path to Death," "Gomer: An Unfaithful Wife" and "The Forgiven Adulteress: Caught but Not Condemned."

### WOMAN of COLOR

What sin do you need to confess? To whom do you need to extend forgiveness? Allow God's example to help you.

but hates his brother is still in the darkness. 10 Whoever loves his brother lives in the light,[r] and there is nothing in him[a] to make him stumble. 11 But whoever hates his brother is in the darkness and walks around in the darkness; he does not know where he is going, because the darkness has blinded him.

12 I write to you, dear children,
because your sins have been forgiven
on account of his name.
13 I write to you, fathers,
because you have known him who is
from the beginning.
I write to you, young men,
because you have overcome the evil
one.
I write to you, dear children,
because you have known the Father.
14 I write to you, fathers,
because you have known him who is
from the beginning.
I write to you, young men,
because you are strong,[s]
and the word of God lives in you,[t]
and you have overcome the evil one.

## Do Not Love the World

15 Do not love the world or anything in the world.[u] If anyone loves the world, the love of the Father is not in him. 16 For everything in the world—the cravings of sinful man, the lust of his eyes[v] and the boasting of what he has and does—comes not from the Father but from the world. 17 The world and its desires pass away,[w] but the man who does the will of God lives forever.

## Warning Against Antichrists

18 Dear children, this is the last hour; and as you have heard that the antichrist is coming,[x] even now many antichrists have come. This is how we know it is the last hour. 19 They went out from us, but they did not really belong to us. For if they had belonged to us, they would have remained with us; but their going showed that none of them belonged to us.[y]

20 But you have an anointing[z] from the Holy One, and all of you know the truth.[b] 21 I do not write to you because you do not know the truth, but because you do know it[a] and because no lie comes from the truth. 22 Who is the liar? It is the man who denies that Jesus is the Christ. Such a man is the antichrist—he denies the Father and the Son. 23 No one who denies the Son has the Father; whoever acknowledges the Son has the Father also.

24 See that what you have heard from the beginning remains in you. If it does, you also will remain in the Son and in the Father.[b] 25 And this is what he promised us—even eternal life.

26 I am writing these things to you about those who are trying to lead you astray. 27 As for you, the anointing you received from him remains in you, and you do not need anyone to teach you. But as his anointing teaches you about all things and as that anointing is real, not counterfeit—just as it has taught you, remain in him.

## Children of God

28 And now, dear children, continue in him, so that when he appears[c] we may be confident[d] and unashamed before him at his coming.

29 If you know that he is righteous,[e] you know that everyone who does what is right has been born of him.

3 How great is the love the Father has lavished on us, that we should be called children of God![f] And that is what we are! The reason the world does not know us is that it did not know him.[g] 2 Dear friends, now we are children of God, and what we will be has not yet been made known. But we know that when he appears,[c] we shall be like him,[h] for we shall see him as he is. 3 Everyone who has this hope in him purifies himself, just as he is pure.

4 Everyone who sins breaks the law; in fact, sin is lawlessness.[i] 5 But you know that he appeared so that he might take away our sins. And in him is no sin.[j] 6 No one who lives in him keeps on sinning. No one who continues to sin has either seen him or known him.

7 Dear children, do not let anyone lead you astray.[k] He who does what is right is

**2:10** r 1Jn 3:14
**2:14** s Eph 6:10; t Jn 5:38
**2:15** u Ro 12:2
**2:16** v Pr 27:20
**2:17** w 1Co 7:31
**2:18** x 1Jn 4:3
**2:19** y 1Co 11:19
**2:20** z 2Co 1:21
**2:21** a 2Pe 1:12
**2:24** b Jn 14:23
**2:28** c 1Jn 3:2; d 1Jn 4:17
**2:29** e 1Jn 3:7
**3:1** f Jn 1:12; g Jn 16:3
**3:2** h Ro 8:29; 2Pe 1:4
**3:4** i 1Jn 5:17
**3:5** j 2Co 5:21
**3:7** k 1Jn 2:26

[a]10 Or *it* [b]20 Some manuscripts *and you know all things* [c]2 Or *when it is made known*

**3:8** l Jn 8:44
**3:9** m 1Jn 5:18
**3:11** n 1Jn 1:5 o Jn 13:34,35
**3:15** p Mt 5:21,22 q Gal 5:20,21
**3:17** r Dt 15:7,8 s 1Jn 4:20
**3:18** t Ro 12:9
**3:22** u Mt 7:7
**3:23** v Jn 13:34

righteous, just as he is righteous. 8He who does what is sinful is of the devil,[l] because the devil has been sinning from the beginning. The reason the Son of God appeared was to destroy the devil's work. 9No one who is born of God will continue to sin,[m] because God's seed remains in him; he cannot go on sinning, because he has been born of God. 10This is how we know who the children of God are and who the children of the devil are: Anyone who does not do what is right is not a child of God; nor is anyone who does not love his brother.

## Love One Another

11This is the message you heard[n] from the beginning: We should love one another.[o] 12Do not be like Cain, who belonged to the evil one and murdered his brother. And why did he murder him? Because his own actions were evil and his brother's were righteous. 13Do not be surprised, my brothers, if the world hates you. 14We know that we have passed from death to life, because we love our brothers. Anyone who does not love remains in death. 15Anyone who hates his brother is a murderer,[p] and you know that no murderer has eternal life in him.[q]

16This is how we know what love is: Jesus Christ laid down his life for us. And we ought to lay down our lives for our brothers. 17If anyone has material possessions and sees his brother in need but has no pity on him,[r] how can the love of God be in him?[s] 18Dear children, let us not love with words or tongue but with actions and in truth.[t] 19This then is how we know that we belong to the truth, and how we set our hearts at rest in his presence 20whenever our hearts condemn us. For God is greater than our hearts, and he knows everything.

21Dear friends, if our hearts do not condemn us, we have confidence before God 22and receive from him anything we ask,[u] because we obey his commands and do what pleases him. 23And this is his command: to believe in the name of his Son, Jesus Christ, and to love one another as he commanded us.[v] 24Those who obey his commands live in him, and he in them. And this is how we know that he lives in us: We know it by the Spirit he gave us.

## Test the Spirits

4 Dear friends, do not believe every spirit, but test the spirits to see whether they are from God, because many false prophets have gone out into the world.[w] 2This is how you can recognize the Spirit of God: Every spirit that acknowledges that Jesus Christ has come in the flesh is from God,[x] 3but every spirit that does not acknowledge Jesus is not from God. This is the spirit of the antichrist,[y] which you have heard is coming and even now is already in the world.

4You, dear children, are from God and have overcome them, because the one who is in you is greater than the one who is in the world. 5They are from the world[z] and therefore speak from the viewpoint of the world, and the world listens to them. 6We are from God, and whoever knows God listens to us; but whoever is not from God does not listen to us.[a] This is how we recognize the Spirit[a] of truth and the spirit of falsehood.

## God's Love and Ours

7Dear friends, let us love one another,[b] for love comes from God. Everyone who loves has been born of God and knows God. 8Whoever does not love does not know God, because God is love. 9This is how God showed his love among us: He sent his one and only Son[b] into the world that we might live through him.[c] 10This is love: not that we loved God, but that he loved us[d] and sent his Son as an atoning sacrifice for[c] our sins.[e] 11Dear friends, since God so loved us, we also ought to love one another. 12No one has ever seen God;[f] but if we love one another, God lives in us and his love is made complete in us.[g]

13We know that we live in him and he in us, because he has given us of his Spirit. 14And we have seen and testify that the Father has sent his Son to be the Savior of the world. 15If anyone acknowledges that Jesus is the Son of God,[h] God lives in him and he in God. 16And so we know and rely on the love God has for us.

God is love.[i] Whoever lives in love lives

**4:1** w 2Pe 2:1
**4:2** x 1Co 12:3
**4:3** y 2Jn 7
**4:5** z Jn 15:19
**4:6** a Jn 8:47
**4:7** b 1Jn 3:11
**4:9** c Jn 3:16,17; 1Jn 5:11
**4:10** d Ro 5:8,10 e 1Jn 2:2
**4:12** f Jn 1:18 g 1Jn 2:5
**4:15** h Ro 10:9
**4:16** i ver 8

[a] 6 Or *spirit* [b] 9 Or *his only begotten Son* [c] 10 Or *as the one who would turn aside his wrath, taking away*

**4:18** j Ro 8:15
**4:20** k 1Jn 2:4
**5:1** l 1Jn 2:22 m 1Jn 2:23 n Jn 8:42
**5:3** o Jn 14:15
**5:6** p Jn 19:34

in God, and God in him. [17]In this way, love is made complete among us so that we will have confidence on the day of judgment, because in this world we are like him. [18]There is no fear in love. But perfect love drives out fear,[j] because fear has to do with punishment. The one who fears is not made perfect in love.

[19]We love because he first loved us. [20]If anyone says, "I love God," yet hates his brother, he is a liar.[k] For anyone who does not love his brother, whom he has seen, cannot love God, whom he has not seen. [21]And he has given us this command: Whoever loves God must also love his brother.

## Faith in the Son of God

**5** Everyone who believes that Jesus is the Christ[l] is born of God,[m] and everyone who loves the father loves his child as well.[n] [2]This is how we know that we love the children of God: by loving God and carrying out his commands. [3]This is love for God: to obey his commands.[o] And his commands are not burdensome, [4]for everyone born of God overcomes the world. This is the victory that has overcome the world, even our faith. [5]Who is it that overcomes the world? Only he who believes that Jesus is the Son of God.

[6]This is the one who came by water and blood[p]—Jesus Christ. He did not come by water only, but by water and blood. And it is the Spirit who testifies, because the Spirit is the truth. [7]For there are three that testify: [8]the[a] Spirit, the water and the blood; and the three are in agreement. [9]We accept man's testimony, but God's testimony is greater because it is the testimony of God,[q] which he has given about his Son. [10]Anyone who believes in the Son of God has this testimony in his heart.[r] Anyone who does not believe God has made him out to be a liar,[s] because he has not believed the testimony God has given about his Son. [11]And this is the testimony: God has given us eternal life, and this life is in his Son. [12]He who has the Son has life; he who does not have the Son of God does not have life.[t]

Lord God,

*I ask that your will be done in my life. Help me to recognize your will and then pursue it with all of my heart. I thank you and praise you.*

Amen

1 JOHN 5:1–5

## Concluding Remarks

[13]I write these things to you who believe in the name of the Son of God so that you may know that you have eternal life. [14]This is the confidence[u] we have in approaching God: that if we ask anything according to his will, he hears us. [15]And if we know that he hears us—whatever we ask—we know that we have what we asked of him.

[16]If anyone sees his brother commit a sin that does not lead to death, he should pray and God will give him life.[v] I refer to those whose sin does not lead to death. There is a sin that leads to death.[w] I am not saying that he should pray about that. [17]All wrongdoing is sin,[x] and there is sin that does not lead to death.

[18]We know that anyone born of God does not continue to sin; the one who was born of God keeps him safe, and the evil one cannot harm him. [19]We know that we are children of God, and that the whole world is under the control of the evil one. [20]We know also that the Son of God has come and has given us understanding,[y] so that we may know him who is true.[z] And we are in him who is true—even in his Son Jesus Christ. He is the true God and eternal life.

[21]Dear children, keep yourselves from idols.[a]

**5:9** q Mt 3:16,17; Jn 8:17,18
**5:10** r Ro 8:16 s Jn 3:33
**5:12** t Jn 3:15,16,36
**5:14** u 1Jn 3:21
**5:16** v Jas 5:15 w Heb 6:4–6
**5:17** x 1Jn 3:4
**5:20** y Lk 24:45 z Jn 17:3
**5:21** a 1Co 10:14

[a]7,8 Late manuscripts of the Vulgate *testify in heaven: the Father, the Word and the Holy Spirit, and these three are one.* [8]*And there are three that testify on earth: the* (not found in any Greek manuscript before the fourteenth century)

# 2 John

## OVERVIEW

As he did in his first letter, John wrote exhortations for believers to love each other and watch out for deceptive teaching. The "apostle of love" realized that unless followers of Christ practiced love toward God and others, their faith would be hollow. He was so passionate about believers being like Jesus Christ that he instructed them not to provide support or hospitality for traveling ministers whose teachings were not consistent with what they had heard in the beginning of their faith walk (see 2Jn 9–11).

Second John was addressed to "the chosen lady and her children" (2Jn 1). The identity of this lady is unknown. Some believe this letter is addressed to an unnamed Christian woman and her children, while others have suggested that this is a symbolic reference to a particular church and its members.

Believers in the Lord Jesus Christ demonstrate their love for God by obeying his commands. As women of God, we are not merely to obey when it is "convenient," but rather to live a lifestyle of obedience. As you read the short book of 2 John, ask the Holy Spirit to reveal to you any areas of disobedience in your life, so that you may fully express your love to God.

## OUTLINE

I. Introduction (1–3)
II. Commendation (4)
III. Warning (5–11)
IV. Conclusion (12–13)

### SCANNABLE FACTS:

**Author:** John

**Time Written:** Between A.D. 85 and 95

**Theme to Note:** Love one another but avoid false teachers

**Notable Woman:** The chosen lady

**1**
a 3Jn 1
b Jn 8:32
**4**
c 3Jn 3,4
**5**
d 1Jn 3:11
**6**
e 1Jn 2:5

1 The elder,[a]

To the chosen lady and her children, whom I love in the truth—and not I only, but also all who know the truth[b]— 2 because of the truth, which lives in us and will be with us forever:

3 Grace, mercy and peace from God the Father and from Jesus Christ, the Father's Son, will be with us in truth and love.

4 It has given me great joy to find some of your children walking in the truth,[c] just as the Father commanded us. 5 And now, dear lady, I am not writing you a new command but one we have had from the beginning.[d] I ask that we love one another. 6 And this is love:[e] that we walk in obedience to his commands. As you have heard from the beginning, his command is that you walk in love.

7 Many deceivers, who do not acknowledge Jesus Christ as coming in the flesh, have gone out into the world.[f] Any such person is the deceiver and the antichrist. 8 Watch out that you do not lose what you have worked for, but that you may be rewarded fully. 9 Anyone who runs ahead and does not continue in the teaching of Christ does not have God; whoever continues in the teaching has both the Father and the Son.[g] 10 If anyone comes to you and does not bring this teaching, do not take him into your house or welcome him.[h] 11 Anyone who welcomes him shares in his wicked work.

12 I have much to write to you, but I do not want to use paper and ink. Instead, I hope to visit you and talk with you face to face,[i] so that our joy may be complete.

13 The children of your chosen sister send their greetings.

**7**
f 1Jn 4:1
**9**
g 1Jn 2:23
**10**
h Ro 16:17
**12**
i 3Jn 13,14

## *The African Presence*

### 2 John 1

While there are no specific references to the African presence within the book of 2 John, the early church was influenced by people of North Africa and the Middle East (a historical and cultural subregion of Africa-Eurasia, traditionally held to be countries or regions in Southwest Asia together with Egypt). However, during the time of the New Testament, racial identification did not have the significance that it has today.

# The "Chosen Lady"

## A Woman Worth Imitating

There is some debate whether the "chosen lady" of 2 John is a literal or figurative woman. Taken literally, the epistle is written to a particular woman and her children. Taken figuratively, it refers to a local church and its members. Whether a local church or one special woman, the "chosen lady" is to be emulated. This priceless narrative exemplifies what it means to live, love, walk and serve in the spirit of truth. The recipient of this letter enjoyed saintly character and distinguished privilege.

John commended the chosen lady for her virtue and the religious education of her children, and he exhorted her to remain in the doctrine of Christ, to preserve the truth and to carefully avoid the delusions of false teachers. John also commends her and her children for remaining faithful to the truth of the gospel, and he urged them to obey the command to love one another. "As you have heard from the beginning, his command is that you walk in love" (2Jn 6).

At this time in the history of the early church, there were many dangerous false teachers who twisted the truth. John encouraged the woman not to take in perpetrators; instead, she was to practice the great commandment of Christian love and charity while being aware of deceivers. As Jesus said, this woman was to be as shrewd as a snake and as innocent as a dove (see Mt 10:16).

Others loved this lady too, not for her rank but for her holiness. She was not only a chosen one, but also a choice one—a woman of refinement and good manners. She was also honest and treated people with integrity. We are to emulate this chosen lady. Whether or not we are actual leaders in our church, we need to be women of virtue to build our church and communities from the inside out. We are the church, so it is imperative that we are included as role models.

—P. George

### reflection

*How are you walking in love?*

*Follow the chosen lady's example today.*

### read

2 John.

**See also** the Inspire Notes "Submission," "Coping With Life's Tasks," "Integrity," "Doing Your Best" and "Character," and the Women of the Bible Notes "Acsah: A Wise Daughter," "Abigail: A Wise Wife" and "A Virtuous Woman: A Strong Woman, Dependent on God."

For the next Women of the Bible note, go to page 1511.

# 3 John

## OVERVIEW

The third letter of John is addressed to Gaius, who was a beloved Christian brother. John expressed his appreciation for the way Gaius showed hospitality to the traveling ministers sent out by John (see 3Jn 5–8). Then John reproved a church leader named Diotrephes for the arrogant way he treated these same servants of the Lord. Diotrephes not only refused to welcome the missionaries, but he also excommunicated those who did receive them (see 3Jn 9–10). John's letter ends with a commendation of Demetrius (see 3Jn 12).

There are many people like Diotrephes who don't show the proper respect and love for others in the body of Christ. However, a wise woman will recognize her value in the church and do her best to extend love to others. As you read through the book of 3 John, meditate on the words "do not imitate what is evil but what is good" (3Jn 11).

## OUTLINE

I. Introduction (1–2)
II. Commendation of Gaius (3–8)
III. Condemnation of Diotrephes (9–10)
IV. Exhortation to Gaius (11)
V. Commendation of Demetrius (12)
VI. Conclusion (13–14)

## SCANNABLE FACTS:

**Author:** John

**Time Written:** Between A.D. 85 and 95

**Theme to Note:** Walking in the truth

**Notable Women:** There are no women mentioned in this book

1 a 2Jn 1
3 b 2Jn 4
4 c 1Co 4:15
5 d Ro 12:13

1The elder,[a]

To my dear friend Gaius, whom I love in the truth.

2Dear friend, I pray that you may enjoy good health and that all may go well with you, even as your soul is getting along well. 3It gave me great joy to have some brothers come and tell about your faithfulness to the truth and how you continue to walk in the truth.[b] 4I have no greater joy than to hear that my children[c] are walking in the truth.

*Woman of color,*

*I desire for you to enjoy good health and a productive and fulfilling life.*

*Your Creator*

3 JOHN 2

5Dear friend, you are faithful in what you are doing for the brothers, even though they are strangers to you.[d] 6They have told the church about your love. You will do well to send them on their way in a manner worthy of God. 7It was for the sake of the Name that they went out, receiving no help from the pagans.[e] 8We ought therefore to show hospitality to such men so that we may work together for the truth.

9I wrote to the church, but Diotrephes, who loves to be first, will have nothing to do with us. 10So if I come, I will call attention to what he is doing, gossiping maliciously about us. Not satisfied with that, he refuses to welcome the brothers. He also stops those who want to do so and puts them out of the church.

11Dear friend, do not imitate what is evil but what is good.[f] Anyone who does what is good is from God. Anyone who does what is evil has not seen God. 12Demetrius is well spoken of by everyone[g]—and even by the truth itself. We also speak well of him, and you know that our testimony is true.[h]

13I have much to write you, but I do not want to do so with pen and ink. 14I hope to see you soon, and we will talk face to face.

Peace to you. The friends here send their greetings. Greet the friends there by name.

7 e Ac 20:33,35
11 f Ps 37:27
12 g 1Ti 3:7
h Jn 21:24

## The African Presence

### 3 John 1

While there are no specific references to the African presence within the book of 3 John, the early church was influenced by people of North Africa and the Middle East (a historical and cultural subregion of Africa-Eurasia, traditionally held to be countries or regions in Southwest Asia together with Egypt). However, during the time of the New Testament, racial identification did not have the significance that it has today.

# Jude

## OVERVIEW

Although Jude originally intended to write about the doctrine of salvation, he felt compelled instead to deal with heresy that was infiltrating the church (see Jude 3–4). He warned that just as God, in the past, judged those who tried to justify immoral behavior, he would do so again. Jude cited the examples of the unbelieving Israelites in the time of Moses, the fallen angels, and the people of Sodom and Gomorrah. After encouraging his readers to keep themselves in the love of God, he ended the letter by assuring believers that God is able to keep them from falling.

Like Jude's readers, women believers today live in the difficult end times (see Jude 18) and are called to persevere. The hope of every Christian is this: God is "able to keep you from falling and to present you before his glorious presence without fault and with great joy" (Jude 24).

## OUTLINE

I. Greeting (1–2)
II. Occasion for the Letter (3–4)
III. Warnings Against False Teachers (5–16)
IV. A Call to Persevere (17–25)

### SCANNABLE FACTS:

**Author:** Jude

**Time Written:** Probably around A.D. 65

**Theme to Note:** Contend for the faith

**Notable Women:** There are no women mentioned in this book

1 a Ac 1:13
3 b Tit 1:4
4 c Gal 2:4 d 2Pe 2:1
6 e 2Pe 2:4,9
8 f 2Pe 2:10
9 g Da 10:13,21

1 Jude,[a] a servant of Jesus Christ and a
brother of James,

To those who have been called, who
are loved by God the Father and kept by[a]
Jesus Christ:

2 Mercy, peace and love be yours in abun-
dance.

## The Sin and Doom of Godless Men

3 Dear friends, although I was very eager
to write to you about the salvation we share,[b]
I felt I had to write and urge you to contend
for the faith that was once for all entrusted
to the saints. 4 For certain men whose con-
demnation was written about[b] long ago have
secretly slipped in among you.[c] They are
godless men, who change the grace of our
God into a license for immorality and deny
Jesus Christ our only Sovereign and Lord.[d]
5 Though you already know all this, I
want to remind you that the Lord[c] delivered
his people out of Egypt, but later destroyed
those who did not believe. 6 And the angels
who did not keep their positions of authority
but abandoned their own home—these he
has kept in darkness, bound with everlast-
ing chains for judgment on the great Day.[e]
7 In a similar way, Sodom and Gomorrah and
the surrounding towns gave themselves up
to sexual immorality and perversion. They
serve as an example of those who suffer the
punishment of eternal fire.
8 In the very same way, these dreamers
pollute their own bodies, reject authority
and slander celestial beings.[f] 9 But even the
archangel Michael,[g] when he was disputing
with the devil about the body of Moses, did
not dare to bring a slanderous accusation
against him, but said, "The Lord rebuke
you!" 10 Yet these men speak abusively
against whatever they do not understand;
and what things they do understand by in-
stinct, like unreasoning animals—these
are the very things that destroy them.[h]
11 Woe to them! They have taken the way
of Cain; they have rushed for profit into Ba-
laam's error; they have been destroyed in
Korah's rebellion.[i]
12 These men are blemishes at your love
feasts, eating with you without the slightest
qualm—shepherds who feed only them-
selves. They are clouds without rain, blown
along by the wind;[j] autumn trees, without
fruit and uprooted[k]—twice dead. 13 They
are wild waves of the sea,[l] foaming up their
shame;[m] wandering stars, for whom black-
est darkness has been reserved forever.
14 Enoch,[n] the seventh from Adam, proph-
esied about these men: "See, the Lord is
coming with thousands upon thousands of
his holy ones[o] 15 to judge everyone, and to
convict all the ungodly of all the ungodly
acts they have done in the ungodly way,
and of all the harsh words ungodly sinners
have spoken against him." 16 These men are
grumblers and faultfinders; they follow
their own evil desires; they boast[p] about
themselves and flatter others for their own
advantage.

## A Call to Persevere

17 But, dear friends, remember what the
apostles of our Lord Jesus Christ foretold.[q]
18 They said to you, "In the last times[r] there
will be scoffers who will follow their own
ungodly desires." 19 These are the men who

10 h 2Pe 2:12
11 i Nu 16:1–3, 31–35
12 j Eph 4:14 k Mt 15:13
13 l Isa 57:20 m Php 3:19
14 n Ge 5:18,21–24 o Dt 33:2
16 p 2Pe 2:18
17 q 2Pe 3:2
18 r 1Ti 4:1

[a]1 Or *for*; or *in* [b]4 Or *men who were marked out for condemnation* [c]5 Some early manuscripts *Jesus*

*The African Presence*

**Jude 5**

Egypt is located in North Africa. For more on Egypt, see the African Presence note on Genesis 10:6.

The African Presence

**Jude 14**

Regarding Adam and the first humans, see the African Presence notes on Genesis 2:8 and Genesis 2:10–14.

20 s Col 2:7
21 t Tit 2:13; 2Pe 3:12
23 u Am 4:11; Zec 3:2–5
24 v Col 1:22

divide you, who follow mere natural instincts and do not have the Spirit.
20But you, dear friends, build yourselves
up[s] in your most holy faith and pray in the
Holy Spirit. 21Keep yourselves in God's love
as you wait[t] for the mercy of our Lord Jesus
Christ to bring you to eternal life.
22Be merciful to those who doubt;
23snatch others from the fire and save
them;[u] to others show mercy, mixed with
fear—hating even the clothing stained by
corrupted flesh.

## Doxology

24To him who is able to keep you from
falling and to present you before his glorious presence without fault[v] and with great
joy— 25to the only God our Savior be glory,
majesty, power and authority, through Jesus
Christ our Lord, before all ages, now and forevermore! Amen.[w]

25 w Ro 11:36

Stumbling one,

*I am able to keep you from falling.*

*Grasp my hand and trust me.*

Love,
God

JUDE 24–25

# Revelation

## OVERVIEW

John wrote this last book of the Bible while he was exiled on the island of Patmos (see Rev 1:9). He opened this letter by describing the incredible way in which he received this revelation from the Lord. After John recorded the letters from the risen Christ to the seven churches, he was invited to heaven and given a vision of the majesty of God and his attendants.

In John's vision he saw in the "right hand of him who sat on the throne" a scroll sealed with seven seals (Rev 5:1), and only the Lamb could break the seals. As each seal is opened, another judgment follows. The seven trumpet judgments come next, followed by the seven bowl judgments for those who remain on the earth. Chapter 19 records the return of Christ as Warrior-King, with Jesus and the armies of heaven following him, riding on white horses. Then Satan is seized and bound for a thousand years. Following his release, Satan leads another revolt, which results in his doom to the lake of fire, along with all those who rejected Jesus Christ.

In his vision John saw a new heaven and a new earth, with the new Jerusalem as the glorious home of the righteous. The book of Revelation ends with an invitation to everyone to come and drink from the fountain that gives life (see Rev 22:17).

There are dark and perilous days ahead for those who reject Jesus as Lord. Yet there is an eternal life without tears, death, mourning or pain for those who put their trust in him (see Rev 21:4). Will you put your faith in him? With prayer and discernment, read through the book of Revelation with your eternal destination in mind.

## OUTLINE

I. The Risen Christ and the Seven Churches (1:1—3:22)
II. The Throne in Heaven (4:1—5:14)
III. The Seven Seals (6:1—7:17)
IV. The Seven Trumpets (8:1—11:19)
V. The Saints Versus the Serpent (12:1—14:20)
VI. The Seven Bowls (15:1—16:21)
VII. The Fall of Babylon (17:1—19:5)
VIII. The Return of Christ (19:6–21)
IX. Satan Defeated and the Dead Judged (20:1–15)
X. The New Jerusalem (21:1—22:5)
XI. Jesus Is Coming Soon (22:6–21)

## SCANNABLE FACTS:

**Author:** John

**Time Written:** Around A.D. 95

**Theme to Note:** Jesus Christ is coming back

**Notable Women:** The woman pursued by the dragon (see Rev 12), the great prostitute (see Rev 17–18), the bride of the Lamb (see Rev 19:7–8; 21:2,9)

## Prologue

**1** The revelation of Jesus Christ, which God gave him to show his servants what must soon take place. He made it known by sending his angel[a] to his servant John, [2]who testifies to everything he saw—that is, the word of God and the testimony of Jesus Christ.[b] [3]Blessed is the one who reads the words of this prophecy, and blessed are those who hear it and take to heart what is written in it,[c] because the time is near.

## Greetings and Doxology

[4]John,

To the seven churches in the province of Asia:

Grace and peace to you from him who is, and who was, and who is to come, and from the seven spirits[a] before his throne, [5]and from Jesus Christ, who is the faithful witness, the firstborn from the dead,[d] and the ruler of the kings of the earth.

To him who loves us and has freed us from our sins by his blood, [6]and has made us to be a kingdom and priests to serve his God and Father—to him be glory and power for ever and ever! Amen.

[7] Look, he is coming with the clouds,
and every eye will see him,
even those who pierced him;
and all the peoples of the earth will
mourn[e] because of him.
So shall it be! Amen.

[8]"I am the Alpha and the Omega," says the Lord God, "who is, and who was, and who is to come, the Almighty."[f]

## One Like a Son of Man

[9]I, John, your brother and companion in the suffering and kingdom and patient endurance[g] that are ours in Jesus, was on the island of Patmos because of the word of God and the testimony of Jesus. [10]On the Lord's Day I was in the Spirit, and I heard behind me a loud voice like a trumpet,[h] [11]which said: "Write on a scroll what you see and send it to the seven churches: to Ephesus, Smyrna, Pergamum, Thyatira, Sardis, Philadelphia and Laodicea."

[12]I turned around to see the voice that was speaking to me. And when I turned I saw seven golden lampstands,[i] [13]and among the lampstands was someone "like a son of man,"[b][j] dressed in a robe reaching down to his feet and with a golden sash around his chest.[k] [14]His head and hair were white like wool, as white as snow, and his eyes were like blazing fire.[l] [15]His feet were like bronze glowing in a furnace,[m] and his voice was like the sound of rushing waters.[n] [16]In his right hand he held seven stars,[o] and out of his mouth came a sharp double-edged sword.[p] His face was like the sun shining in all its brilliance.

[17]When I saw him, I fell at his feet[q] as though dead. Then he placed his right hand on me and said: "Do not be afraid. I am the First and the Last.[r] [18]I am the Living One; I was dead,[s] and behold I am alive for ever and ever! And I hold the keys of death and Hades.[t]

[19]"Write, therefore, what you have seen, what is now and what will take place later. [20]The mystery of the seven stars that you saw in my right hand and of the seven golden lampstands is this: The seven stars are the angels[c] of the seven churches, and the seven lampstands are the seven churches.

## To the Church in Ephesus

**2** "To the angel[d] of the church in Ephesus write:

These are the words of him who holds the seven stars in his right hand[u] and walks among the seven golden lampstands:[v] [2]I know your deeds,[w] your hard work and your perseverance. I know that you cannot tolerate wicked men, that you have tested[x] those who claim to be apostles but are not, and have found them false.[y] [3]You have persevered and have endured hardships for my name, and have not grown weary.

[4]Yet I hold this against you: You have forsaken your first love. [5]Remember the height from which you have fallen! Repent and do the things you

**1:1** a Rev 22:16
**1:2** b 1Co 1:6
**1:3** c Lk 11:28
**1:5** d Col 1:18
**1:7** e Zec 12:10
**1:8** f Rev 4:8
**1:9** g 2Ti 2:12
**1:10** h Rev 4:1
**1:12** i Ex 25:31–40
**1:13** j Eze 1:26; Da 7:13 k Da 10:5
**1:14** l Da 7:9; 10:6
**1:15** m Da 10:6 n Eze 43:2
**1:16** o Rev 2:1 p Heb 4:12
**1:17** q Da 8:17,18 r Isa 41:4
**1:18** s Ro 6:9 t Rev 20:1
**2:1** u Rev 1:16 v Rev 1:12,13
**2:2** w Rev 3:1,8,15 x 1Jn 4:1 y 2Co 11:13

[a]4 Or *the sevenfold Spirit* [b]13 Daniel 7:13 [c]20 Or *messengers* [d]1 Or *messenger*; also in verses 8, 12 and 18

**2:7**
z Mt 11:15; Rev 3:6,13,22
a Ge 2:9; Rev 22:2,14,19

**2:8**
b Rev 1:17

**2:9**
c Jas 2:5
d Rev 3:9

**2:10**
e Da 1:12,14

**2:11**
f Rev 21:8

*Lord,*

*I acknowledge my tendency to put other people and other desires before you. Forgive me, I pray. Help me to remember that you are my one true love. Help me to keep you ever before me, front and center, as my highest priority. I desire to seek you first, knowing that you will take care of all else. In Jesus' precious name,*

*Amen*

REVELATION 2:4–5

did at first. If you do not repent, I will
come to you and remove your lamp-
stand from its place. 6But you have this
in your favor: You hate the practices of
the Nicolaitans, which I also hate.
7He who has an ear, let him hear[z]
what the Spirit says to the churches.
To him who overcomes, I will give the
right to eat from the tree of life,[a] which
is in the paradise of God.

## To the Church in Smyrna

8"To the angel of the church in Smyrna
write:

These are the words of him who is
the First and the Last,[b] who died and
came to life again. 9I know your afflic-
tions and your poverty—yet you are
rich![c] I know the slander of those who
say they are Jews and are not,[d] but are a
synagogue of Satan. 10Do not be afraid
of what you are about to suffer. I tell
you, the devil will put some of you in
prison to test you, and you will suffer
persecution for ten days.[e] Be faithful,
even to the point of death, and I will
give you the crown of life.
11He who has an ear, let him hear
what the Spirit says to the churches.
He who overcomes will not be hurt at
all by the second death.[f]

## To the Church in Pergamum

12"To the angel of the church in Pergamum
write:

These are the words of him who
has the sharp, double-edged sword.[g]
13I know where you live—where Satan
has his throne. Yet you remain true to
my name. You did not renounce your
faith in me,[h] even in the days of An-
tipas, my faithful witness, who was
put to death in your city—where Sa-
tan lives.
14Nevertheless, I have a few things
against you: You have people there
who hold to the teaching of Balaam,[i]
who taught Balak to entice the Isra-
elites to sin by eating food sacrificed
to idols and by committing sexual
immorality. 15Likewise you also have
those who hold to the teaching of the
Nicolaitans. 16Repent therefore! Other-
wise, I will soon come to you and will
fight against them with the sword of
my mouth.[j]
17He who has an ear, let him hear
what the Spirit says to the churches. To
him who overcomes, I will give some
of the hidden manna. I will also give
him a white stone with a new name
written on it, known only to him who
receives it.[k]

## To the Church in Thyatira

18"To the angel of the church in Thyatira
write:

These are the words of the Son of
God, whose eyes are like blazing fire
and whose feet are like burnished
bronze.[l] 19I know your deeds, your
love and faith, your service and perse-
verance, and that you are now doing
more than you did at first.
20Nevertheless, I have this against
you: You tolerate that woman Jeze-
bel,[m] who calls herself a prophetess.
By her teaching she misleads my ser-
vants into sexual immorality and the
eating of food sacrificed to idols. 21I
have given her time to repent of her
immorality, but she is unwilling.[n] 22So
I will cast her on a bed of suffering,

**2:12**
g Rev 1:16

**2:13**
h Rev 14:12

**2:14**
i 2Pe 2:15

**2:16**
j 2Th 2:8; Rev 1:16

**2:17**
k Rev 19:12

**2:18**
l Rev 1:14,15

**2:20**
m 1Ki 16:31; 21:25; 2Ki 9:7

**2:21**
n Rev 9:20

**2:23** o Jer 11:20; Ac 1:24; Ro 8:27
**2:24** p Ac 15:28
**2:27** q Isa 30:14
**3:1** r Rev 1:4 s Rev 1:16 t Rev 2:2
**3:3** u 2Pe 3:10
**3:4** v Jude 23 w Rev 6:11

and I will make those who commit adultery with her suffer intensely, unless they repent of her ways. 23 I will strike her children dead. Then all the churches will know that I am he who searches hearts and minds,[o] and I will repay each of you according to your deeds. 24 Now I say to the rest of you in Thyatira, to you who do not hold to her teaching and have not learned Satan's so-called deep secrets (I will not impose any other burden on you):[p] 25 Only hold on to what you have until I come.

26 To him who overcomes and does my will to the end, I will give authority over the nations—

27 'He will rule them with an iron
    scepter;
  he will dash them to pieces
    like pottery'[a][q]—

just as I have received authority from my Father. 28 I will also give him the morning star. 29 He who has an ear, let him hear what the Spirit says to the churches.

## To the Church in Sardis

3 "To the angel[b] of the church in Sardis write:

These are the words of him who holds the seven spirits[c][r] of God and the seven stars.[s] I know your deeds;[t] you have a reputation of being alive, but you are dead. 2 Wake up! Strengthen what remains and is about to die, for I have not found your deeds complete in the sight of my God. 3 Remember, therefore, what you have received and heard; obey it, and repent. But if you do not wake up, I will come like a thief,[u] and you will not know at what time I will come to you.

4 Yet you have a few people in Sardis who have not soiled their clothes.[v] They will walk with me, dressed in white,[w] for they are worthy. 5 He who overcomes will, like them, be dressed in white. I will never blot out his name from the book of life, but will acknowledge his name before my Father and his angels. 6 He who has an ear, let him hear[x] what the Spirit says to the churches.

## To the Church in Philadelphia

7 "To the angel of the church in Philadelphia write:

These are the words of him who is holy and true,[y] who holds the key of David.[z] What he opens no one can shut, and what he shuts no one can open. 8 I know your deeds. See, I have placed before you an open door that no one can shut. I know that you have little strength, yet you have kept my word and have not denied my name. 9 I will make those who are of the synagogue of Satan,[a] who claim to be Jews though they are not, but are liars—I will make them come and fall down at your feet[b] and acknowledge that I have loved you. 10 Since you have kept my command to endure patiently, I will also keep you[c] from the hour of trial that is going to come upon the whole world to test those who live on the earth.[d]

11 I am coming soon. Hold on to what you have,[e] so that no one will take your crown.[f] 12 Him who overcomes I will make a pillar[g] in the temple of my God. Never again will he leave it. I will write on him the name of my God[h] and the name of the city of my God, the new Jerusalem, which is coming down out of heaven from my God; and I will also write on him my new name. 13 He who has an ear, let him hear what the Spirit says to the churches.

## To the Church in Laodicea

14 "To the angel of the church in Laodicea write:

These are the words of the Amen, the faithful and true witness, the ruler of God's creation.[i] 15 I know your deeds, that you are neither cold nor hot. I wish you were either one or the other! 16 So, because you are lukewarm—

**3:6** x Rev 2:7
**3:7** y 1Jn 5:20 z Isa 22:22
**3:9** a Rev 2:9 b Isa 49:23
**3:10** c 2Pe 2:9 d Rev 6:10
**3:11** e Rev 2:25 f Rev 2:10
**3:12** g Gal 2:9 h Rev 22:4
**3:14** i Col 1:16,18

[a] 27 Psalm 2:9 [b] 1 Or *messenger*; also in verses 7 and 14 [c] 1 Or *the sevenfold Spirit*

3:17
j Hos 12:8; 1Co 4:8

3:19
k Heb 12:5,6

3:20
l Lk 12:36

3:21
m Mt 19:28

3:22
n Rev 2:7

4:1
o Rev 1:10
p Rev 11:12
q Rev 1:19

4:2
r Rev 1:10
s Isa 6:1

4:4
t Rev 11:16

4:5
u Rev 8:5
v Zec 4:2
w Rev 1:4

4:6
x Rev 15:2

neither hot nor cold—I am about to spit you out of my mouth. [17]You say, 'I am rich; I have acquired wealth and do not need a thing.'[j] But you do not realize that you are wretched, pitiful, poor, blind and naked. [18]I counsel you to buy from me gold refined in the fire, so you can become rich; and white clothes to wear, so you can cover your shameful nakedness; and salve to put on your eyes, so you can see.

[19]Those whom I love I rebuke and discipline.[k] So be earnest, and repent. [20]Here I am! I stand at the door and knock. If anyone hears my voice and opens the door,[l] I will come in and eat with him, and he with me.

[21]To him who overcomes, I will give the right to sit with me on my throne,[m] just as I overcame and sat down with my Father on his throne. [22]He who has an ear, let him hear[n] what the Spirit says to the churches."

## The Throne in Heaven

**4** After this I looked, and there before me was a door standing open in heaven. And the voice I had first heard speaking to me like a trumpet[o] said, "Come up here,[p] and I will show you what must take place after this."[q] [2]At once I was in the Spirit,[r] and there before me was a throne in heaven[s] with someone sitting on it. [3]And the one who sat there had the appearance of jasper and carnelian. A rainbow, resembling an emerald, encircled the throne. [4]Surrounding the throne were twenty-four other thrones, and seated on them were twenty-four elders.[t] They were dressed in white and had crowns of gold on their heads. [5]From the throne came flashes of lightning, rumblings and peals of thunder.[u] Before the throne, seven lamps[v] were blazing. These are the seven spirits[a][w] of God. [6]Also before the throne there was what looked like a sea of glass,[x] clear as crystal.

In the center, around the throne, were four living creatures, and they were covered with eyes, in front and in back. [7]The first living creature was like a lion, the second was like an ox, the third had a face like a man, the fourth was like a flying eagle.[y] [8]Each of the four living creatures had six wings[z] and was covered with eyes all around, even under his wings. Day and night they never stop saying:

> "Holy, holy, holy
> is the Lord God Almighty,[a]
> who was, and is, and is to come."[b]

[9]Whenever the living creatures give glory, honor and thanks to him who sits on the throne and who lives for ever and ever, [10]the twenty-four elders fall down before him[c] who sits on the throne, and worship him who lives for ever and ever. They lay their crowns before the throne and say:

> [11] "You are worthy, our Lord and God,
> to receive glory and honor and power,[d]
> for you created all things,
> and by your will they were created
> and have their being."

## The Scroll and the Lamb

**5** Then I saw in the right hand of him who sat on the throne a scroll with writing on both sides[e] and sealed with seven seals. [2]And I saw a mighty angel proclaiming in a loud voice, "Who is worthy to break the seals and open the scroll?" [3]But no one in heaven or on earth or under the earth could open the scroll or even look inside it. [4]I wept and wept because no one was found who was worthy to open the scroll or look inside. [5]Then one of the elders said to me, "Do not weep! See, the Lion[f] of the tribe of Judah, the

4:7
y Eze 1:10

4:8
z Isa 6:2
a Rev 1:8
b Rev 1:4

4:10
c Rev 5:8,14

4:11
d Rev 5:12

5:1
e Eze 2:9,10

5:5
f Ge 49:9

*Recipient of grace,*

*Jesus is the only worthy one; it is for that reason I gave him up for you.*

*With my love,*
*God, the Giver*

REVELATION 5:1–5

[a]5 Or *the sevenfold Spirit*

Root of David, has triumphed. He is able to open the scroll and its seven seals."

6 Then I saw a Lamb, looking as if it had been slain, standing in the center of the throne, encircled by the four living creatures and the elders. He had seven horns and seven eyes, which are the seven spirits[a] of God sent out into all the earth. 7 He came and took the scroll from the right hand of him who sat on the throne. 8 And when he had taken it, the four living creatures and the twenty-four elders fell down before the Lamb. Each one had a harp[g] and they were holding golden bowls full of incense, which are the prayers of the saints. 9 And they sang a new song:[h]

"You are worthy to take the scroll
and to open its seals,
because you were slain,
and with your blood you purchased[i]
men for God
from every tribe and language and
people and nation.
10 You have made them to be a kingdom and
priests to serve our God,
and they will reign on the earth."

11 Then I looked and heard the voice of many angels, numbering thousands upon thousands, and ten thousand times ten thousand.[j] They encircled the throne and the living creatures and the elders. 12 In a loud voice they sang:

"Worthy is the Lamb, who was slain,
to receive power and wealth and wisdom
and strength
and honor and glory and praise!"

13 Then I heard every creature in heaven and on earth and under the earth[k] and on the sea, and all that is in them, singing:

"To him who sits on the throne and to
the Lamb
be praise and honor and glory and power,
for ever and ever!"

14 The four living creatures said, "Amen," and the elders fell down and worshiped.[l]

5:8 g Rev 14:2
5:9 h Ps 40:3 i 1Co 6:20
5:11 j Da 7:10
5:13 k Php 2:10
5:14 l Rev 4:10

## The Seals

6 I watched as the Lamb opened the first of the seven seals. Then I heard one of the four living creatures say in a voice like thunder, "Come!" 2 I looked, and there before me was a white horse![m] Its rider held a bow, and he was given a crown,[n] and he rode out as a conqueror bent on conquest.

3 When the Lamb opened the second seal, I heard the second living creature[o] say, "Come!" 4 Then another horse came out, a fiery red one. Its rider was given power to take peace from the earth and to make men slay each other. To him was given a large sword.

5 When the Lamb opened the third seal, I heard the third living creature[p] say, "Come!" I looked, and there before me was a black horse! Its rider was holding a pair of scales in his hand. 6 Then I heard what sounded like a voice among the four living creatures, saying, "A quart[b] of wheat for a day's wages,[c] and three quarts of barley for a day's wages,[c] and do not damage[q] the oil and the wine!"

7 When the Lamb opened the fourth seal, I heard the voice of the fourth living creature[r] say, "Come!" 8 I looked, and there before me was a pale horse![s] Its rider was named Death, and Hades was following close behind him. They were given power over a fourth of the earth to kill by sword, famine and plague, and by the wild beasts of the earth.

9 When he opened the fifth seal, I saw under the altar the souls of those who had been slain[t] because of the word of God and the testimony they had maintained. 10 They called out in a loud voice, "How long,[u] Sovereign Lord, holy and true,[v] until you judge the inhabitants of the earth and avenge our blood?" 11 Then each of them was given a white robe, and they were told to wait a little longer, until the number of their fellow servants and brothers who were to be killed as they had been was completed.[w]

12 I watched as he opened the sixth seal. There was a great earthquake.[x] The sun turned black[y] like sackcloth made of goat hair, the whole moon turned blood red, 13 and the stars in the sky fell to earth,[z] as late figs drop from a fig tree when shaken

6:2 m Rev 19:11 n Zec 6:11
6:3 o Rev 4:7
6:5 p Rev 4:7
6:6 q Rev 9:4
6:7 r Rev 4:7
6:8 s Zec 6:3
6:9 t Rev 20:4
6:10 u Zec 1:12 v Rev 3:7
6:11 w Heb 11:40
6:12 x Rev 16:18 y Mt 24:29
6:13 z Rev 8:10

[a] 6 Or *the sevenfold Spirit* [b] 6 Greek *a choinix* (probably about a liter) [c] 6 Greek *a denarius*

**6:14** a Jer 4:24
**6:17** b Zep 1:14,15; Rev 16:14 c Ps 76:7
**7:3** d Rev 6:6 e Rev 22:4
**7:4** f Rev 9:16 g Rev 14:1,3
**7:9** h Rev 5:9

by a strong wind. 14 The sky receded like a scroll, rolling up, and every mountain and island was removed from its place.[a]

15 Then the kings of the earth, the princes, the generals, the rich, the mighty, and every slave and every free man hid in caves and among the rocks of the mountains. 16 They called to the mountains and the rocks, "Fall on us and hide us from the face of him who sits on the throne and from the wrath of the Lamb! 17 For the great day[b] of their wrath has come, and who can stand?"[c]

## 144,000 Sealed

7 After this I saw four angels standing at the four corners of the earth, holding back the four winds of the earth to prevent any wind from blowing on the land or on the sea or on any tree. 2 Then I saw another angel coming up from the east, having the seal of the living God. He called out in a loud voice to the four angels who had been given power to harm the land and the sea: 3 "Do not harm[d] the land or the sea or the trees until we put a seal on the foreheads[e] of the servants of our God." 4 Then I heard the number[f] of those who were sealed: 144,000[g] from all the tribes of Israel.

5 From the tribe of Judah 12,000 were sealed,
from the tribe of Reuben 12,000,
from the tribe of Gad 12,000,
6 from the tribe of Asher 12,000,
from the tribe of Naphtali 12,000,
from the tribe of Manasseh 12,000,
7 from the tribe of Simeon 12,000,
from the tribe of Levi 12,000,
from the tribe of Issachar 12,000,
8 from the tribe of Zebulun 12,000,
from the tribe of Joseph 12,000,
from the tribe of Benjamin 12,000.

## The Great Multitude in White Robes

9 After this I looked and there before me was a great multitude that no one could count, from every nation, tribe, people and language,[h] standing before the throne and in front of the Lamb. They were wearing white robes and were holding palm branches in their hands. 10 And they cried out in a loud voice:

"Salvation belongs to our God,[i]
who sits on the throne,
and to the Lamb."

11 All the angels were standing around the throne and around the elders and the four living creatures.[j] They fell down on their faces before the throne and worshiped God, 12 saying:

"Amen!
Praise and glory
and wisdom and thanks and honor
and power and strength
be to our God for ever and ever.
Amen!"[k]

13 Then one of the elders asked me, "These in white robes—who are they, and where did they come from?"

14 I answered, "Sir, you know."

And he said, "These are they who have come out of the great tribulation; they have washed their robes and made them white in the blood of the Lamb.[l] 15 Therefore,

"they are before the throne of God
and serve him day and night in his temple;
and he who sits on the throne will spread his tent over them.[m]
16 Never again will they hunger;
never again will they thirst.
The sun will not beat upon them,
nor any scorching heat.[n]
17 For the Lamb at the center of the throne will be their shepherd;[o]
he will lead them to springs of living water.
And God will wipe away every tear from their eyes."[p]

## The Seventh Seal and the Golden Censer

8 When he opened the seventh seal,[q] there was silence in heaven for about half an hour.

2 And I saw the seven angels who stand before God, and to them were given seven trumpets.

3 Another angel, who had a golden censer, came and stood at the altar. He was given much incense to offer, with the prayers of all the saints,[r] on the golden altar[s] before the

**7:10** i Ps 3:8; Rev 12:10; 19:1
**7:11** j Rev 4:6
**7:12** k Rev 5:12–14
**7:14** l Heb 9:14; 1Jn 1:7
**7:15** m Rev 21:3
**7:16** n Isa 49:10
**7:17** o Ps 23:1; Jn 10:11 p Isa 25:8; Rev 21:4
**8:1** q Rev 6:1
**8:3** r Rev 5:8 s Ex 30:1–6

**8:4** t Ps 141:2
**8:7** u Eze 38:22 v Rev 9:4
**8:8** w Jer 51:25 x Rev 16:3
**8:10** y Isa 14:12; Rev 9:1 z Rev 16:4
**8:11** a Jer 9:15; 23:15
**8:13** b Rev 14:6; 19:17 c Rev 9:12; 11:14
**9:1** d Rev 8:10 e Lk 8:31
**9:3** f ver 5,10

throne. [4]The smoke of the incense, together with the prayers of the saints, went up before God[t] from the angel's hand. [5]Then the angel took the censer, filled it with fire from the altar, and hurled it on the earth; and there came peals of thunder, rumblings, flashes of lightning and an earthquake.

## The Trumpets

[6]Then the seven angels who had the seven trumpets prepared to sound them.

[7]The first angel sounded his trumpet, and there came hail and fire[u] mixed with blood, and it was hurled down upon the earth. A third of the earth was burned up, a third of the trees were burned up, and all the green grass was burned up.[v]

[8]The second angel sounded his trumpet, and something like a huge mountain,[w] all ablaze, was thrown into the sea. A third of the sea turned into blood,[x] [9]a third of the living creatures in the sea died, and a third of the ships were destroyed.

[10]The third angel sounded his trumpet, and a great star, blazing like a torch, fell from the sky[y] on a third of the rivers and on the springs of water[z]— [11]the name of the star is Wormwood.[a] A third of the waters turned bitter, and many people died from the waters that had become bitter.[a]

[12]The fourth angel sounded his trumpet, and a third of the sun was struck, a third of the moon, and a third of the stars, so that a third of them turned dark. A third of the day was without light, and also a third of the night.

[13]As I watched, I heard an eagle that was flying in midair[b] call out in a loud voice: "Woe! Woe! Woe[c] to the inhabitants of the earth, because of the trumpet blasts about to be sounded by the other three angels!"

9 The fifth angel sounded his trumpet, and I saw a star that had fallen from the sky to the earth.[d] The star was given the key to the shaft of the Abyss.[e] [2]When he opened the Abyss, smoke rose from it like the smoke from a gigantic furnace. The sun and sky were darkened by the smoke from the Abyss. [3]And out of the smoke locusts came down upon the earth and were given power like that of scorpions[f] of the earth. [4]They were told not to harm[g] the grass of the earth or any plant or tree,[h] but only those people who did not have the seal of God on their foreheads. [5]They were not given power to kill them, but only to torture them for five months.[i] And the agony they suffered was like that of the sting of a scorpion when it strikes a man. [6]During those days men will seek death, but will not find it; they will long to die, but death will elude them.[j]

[7]The locusts looked like horses prepared for battle. On their heads they wore something like crowns of gold, and their faces resembled human faces. [8]Their hair was like women's hair, and their teeth were like lions' teeth.[k] [9]They had breastplates like breastplates of iron, and the sound of their wings was like the thundering of many horses and chariots rushing into battle.[l] [10]They had tails and stings like scorpions, and in their tails they had power to torment people for five months. [11]They had as king over them the angel of the Abyss,[m] whose name in Hebrew is Abaddon, and in Greek, Apollyon.[b]

[12]The first woe is past; two other woes are yet to come.[n]

[13]The sixth angel sounded his trumpet, and I heard a voice coming from the horns[c] of the golden altar that is before God. [14]It said to the sixth angel who had the trumpet, "Release the four angels who are bound at the great river Euphrates."[o] [15]And the four angels who had been kept ready for this very hour and day and month and year were released to kill a third of mankind. [16]The number of the mounted troops was two hundred million. I heard their number.[p]

[17]The horses and riders I saw in my vision looked like this: Their breastplates were fiery red, dark blue, and yellow as sulfur. The heads of the horses resembled the heads of lions, and out of their mouths came fire, smoke and sulfur. [18]A third of mankind was killed by the three plagues of fire, smoke and sulfur that came out of their mouths. [19]The power of the horses was in their mouths and in their tails; for their tails were like snakes, having heads with which they inflict injury.

[20]The rest of mankind that were not killed by these plagues still did not repent of the work of their hands; they did not stop

**9:4** g Rev 6:6 h Rev 8:7
**9:5** i ver 10
**9:6** j Jer 8:3
**9:8** k Joel 1:6
**9:9** l Joel 2:5
**9:11** m ver 1,2
**9:12** n Rev 8:13
**9:14** o Rev 16:12
**9:16** p Rev 7:4

[a]11 That is, Bitterness [b]11 *Abaddon* and *Apollyon* mean *Destroyer.* [c]13 That is, projections

9:20 q 1Co 10:20 r Ps 115:4–7
10:1 s Mt 17:2
10:4 t Da 8:26
10:5 u Da 12:7
10:6 v Rev 4:11 w Rev 16:17
10:8 x ver 4

worshiping demons,[q] and idols of gold, silver, bronze, stone and wood—idols that cannot see or hear or walk.[r] [21]Nor did they repent of their murders, their magic arts, their sexual immorality or their thefts.

## The Angel and the Little Scroll

10 Then I saw another mighty angel coming down from heaven. He was robed in a cloud, with a rainbow above his head; his face was like the sun,[s] and his legs were like fiery pillars. [2]He was holding a little scroll, which lay open in his hand. He planted his right foot on the sea and his left foot on the land, [3]and he gave a loud shout like the roar of a lion. When he shouted, the voices of the seven thunders spoke. [4]And when the seven thunders spoke, I was about to write; but I heard a voice from heaven say, "Seal up what the seven thunders have said and do not write it down."[t]

[5]Then the angel I had seen standing on the sea and on the land raised his right hand to heaven.[u] [6]And he swore by him who lives for ever and ever, who created the heavens and all that is in them, the earth and all that is in it, and the sea and all that is in it,[v] and said, "There will be no more delay![w] [7]But in the days when the seventh angel is about to sound his trumpet, the mystery of God will be accomplished, just as he announced to his servants the prophets."

[8]Then the voice that I had heard from heaven[x] spoke to me once more: "Go, take the scroll that lies open in the hand of the angel who is standing on the sea and on the land."

[9]So I went to the angel and asked him to give me the little scroll. He said to me, "Take it and eat it. It will turn your stomach

*Seeker,*

*Meditate upon my Word and internalize its truth. It will keep you on the right path.*

*Your Guide*

REVELATION 10:8–11

sour, but in your mouth it will be as sweet as honey."[y] [10]I took the little scroll from the angel's hand and ate it. It tasted as sweet as honey in my mouth, but when I had eaten it, my stomach turned sour. [11]Then I was told, "You must prophesy again about many peoples, nations, languages and kings."

## The Two Witnesses

11 I was given a reed like a measuring rod[z] and was told, "Go and measure the temple of God and the altar, and count the worshipers there. [2]But exclude the outer court;[a] do not measure it, because it has been given to the Gentiles.[b] They will trample on the holy city for 42 months.[c] [3]And I will give power to my two witnesses, and they will prophesy for 1,260 days, clothed in sackcloth." [4]These are the two olive trees[d] and the two lampstands that stand before the Lord of the earth. [5]If anyone tries to harm them, fire comes from their mouths and devours their enemies.[e] This is how anyone who wants to harm them must die.[f] [6]These men have power to shut up the sky so that it will not rain during the time they are prophesying; and they have power to turn the waters into blood and to strike the earth with every kind of plague as often as they want.

[7]Now when they have finished their testimony, the beast that comes up from the Abyss will attack them,[g] and overpower and kill them. [8]Their bodies will lie in the street of the great city, which is figuratively called Sodom and Egypt, where also their Lord was crucified. [9]For three and a half days men from every people, tribe, language and nation will gaze on their bodies and refuse them burial. [10]The inhabitants of the earth will gloat over them and will celebrate by sending each other gifts,[h] because these two prophets had tormented those who live on the earth.

[11]But after the three and a half days a breath of life from God entered them,[i] and they stood on their feet, and terror struck those who saw them. [12]Then they heard a loud voice from heaven saying to them, "Come up here." And they went up to heaven in a cloud,[j] while their enemies looked on.

[13]At that very hour there was a severe

10:9 y Jer 15:16; Eze 2:8–3:3
11:1 z Eze 40:3; Rev 21:15
11:2 a Eze 40:17,20 b Lk 21:24 c Rev 13:5
11:4 d Ps 52:8; Jer 11:16; Zec 4:3,11
11:5 e 2Ki 1:10 f Nu 16:29,35
11:7 g Da 7:21
11:10 h Est 9:19,22
11:11 i Eze 37:5,9,10,14
11:12 j Ac 1:9

11:13 k Rev 6:12
11:15 l Rev 12:10 m Da 2:44
11:16 n Rev 4:4
11:17 o Rev 19:6
11:18 p Rev 19:5
11:19 q Rev 15:5,8 r Rev 16:21

earthquake[k] and a tenth of the city collapsed. Seven thousand people were killed in the earthquake, and the survivors were terrified and gave glory to the God of heaven.
14 The second woe has passed; the third woe is coming soon.

## The Seventh Trumpet

15 The seventh angel sounded his trumpet, and there were loud voices in heaven, which said:

"The kingdom of the world has become
the kingdom of our Lord and of
his Christ,[l]
and he will reign for ever and ever."[m]

16 And the twenty-four elders,[n] who were seated on their thrones before God, fell on their faces and worshiped God, 17 saying:

"We give thanks to you, Lord God
Almighty,
the One who is and who was,
because you have taken your great power
and have begun to reign.[o]
18 The nations were angry;
and your wrath has come.
The time has come for judging the dead,
and for rewarding your servants the
prophets
and your saints and those who reverence
your name,
both small and great[p]—
and for destroying those who destroy the
earth."

19 Then God's temple[q] in heaven was opened, and within his temple was seen the ark of his covenant. And there came flashes of lightning, rumblings, peals of thunder, an earthquake and a great hailstorm.[r]

## The Woman and the Dragon

**12** A great and wondrous sign appeared in heaven: a woman clothed with the sun, with the moon under her feet and a crown of twelve stars on her head. 2 She was pregnant and cried out in pain as she was about to give birth. 3 Then another sign appeared in heaven: an enormous red dragon with seven heads and ten horns[s] and seven crowns on his heads. 4 His tail swept a third of the stars out of the sky and flung them to the earth.[t] The dragon stood in front of the woman who was about to give birth, so that he might devour her child the moment it was born. 5 She gave birth to a son, a male child, who will rule all the nations with an iron scepter. And her child was snatched up to God and to his throne. 6 The woman fled into the desert to a place prepared for her by God, where she might be taken care of for 1,260 days.

7 And there was war in heaven. Michael and his angels fought against the dragon, and the dragon and his angels fought back. 8 But he was not strong enough, and they lost their place in heaven. 9 The great dragon was hurled down—that ancient serpent[u] called the devil, or Satan, who leads the whole world astray.[v] He was hurled to the earth,[w] and his angels with him.

10 Then I heard a loud voice in heaven[x] say:

"Now have come the salvation and the
power and the kingdom of our
God,
and the authority of his Christ.
For the accuser of our brothers,[y]
who accuses them before our God day
and night,
has been hurled down.

12:3 s Rev 13:1
12:4 t Da 8:10
12:9 u Ge 3:1–7 v Rev 20:3,8,10 w Jn 12:31
12:10 x Rev 11:15 y Job 1:9–11; Zec 3:1

### *The African Presence*

**Revelation 11:8**

Egypt is located in North Africa. For more on Egypt, see the African Presence note on Genesis 10:6.

11 They overcame him
by the blood of the Lamb
and by the word of their testimony;
they did not love their lives so much
as to shrink from death.[z]
12 Therefore rejoice, you heavens[a]
and you who dwell in them!
But woe to the earth and the sea,[b]
because the devil has gone down to you!
He is filled with fury,
because he knows that his time is
short."

13 When the dragon saw that he had been hurled to the earth, he pursued the woman who had given birth to the male child.[c] 14 The woman was given the two wings of a great eagle,[d] so that she might fly to the place prepared for her in the desert, where she would be taken care of for a time, times and half a time,[e] out of the serpent's reach. 15 Then from his mouth the serpent spewed water like a river, to overtake the woman and sweep her away with the torrent. 16 But the earth helped the woman by opening its mouth and swallowing the river that the dragon had spewed out of his mouth. 17 Then the dragon was enraged at the woman and went off to make war[f] against the rest of her offspring[g]—those who obey God's commandments[h] and hold to the testimony of Jesus.

13 1 And the dragon[a] stood on the shore of the sea.

## The Beast out of the Sea

And I saw a beast coming out of the sea.[i] He had ten horns and seven heads, with ten crowns on his horns, and on each head a blasphemous name. 2 The beast I saw resembled a leopard, but had feet like those of a bear and a mouth like that of a lion. The dragon gave the beast his power and his throne and great authority.[j] 3 One of the heads of the beast seemed to have had a fatal wound, but the fatal wound had been healed. The whole world was astonished[k] and followed the beast. 4 Men worshiped the dragon because he had given authority to the beast, and they also worshiped the beast and asked, "Who is like the beast? Who can make war against him?"

5 The beast was given a mouth to utter proud words and blasphemies[l] and to exercise his authority for forty-two months.[m] 6 He opened his mouth to blaspheme God, and to slander his name and his dwelling place and those who live in heaven. 7 He was given power to make war[n] against the saints and to conquer them. And he was given authority over every tribe, people, language and nation. 8 All inhabitants of the earth will worship the beast—all whose names have not been written in the book of life[o] belonging to the Lamb that was slain from the creation of the world.[b]

9 He who has an ear, let him hear.[p]

10 If anyone is to go into captivity,
into captivity he will go.
If anyone is to be killed[c] with the sword,
with the sword he will be killed.

This calls for patient endurance and faithfulness on the part of the saints.[q]

## The Beast out of the Earth

11 Then I saw another beast, coming out of the earth. He had two horns like a lamb, but he spoke like a dragon. 12 He exercised all the authority of the first beast on his behalf, and made the earth and its inhabitants worship the first beast, whose fatal wound had been healed. 13 And he performed great and miraculous signs,[r] even causing fire to come down from heaven to earth in full view of men. 14 Because of the signs[s] he was given power to do on behalf of the first beast, he deceived[t] the inhabitants of the earth. He ordered them to set up an image in honor of the beast who was wounded by the sword and yet lived. 15 He was given power to give breath to the image of the first beast, so that it could speak and cause all who refused to worship the image to be killed. 16 He also forced everyone, small and great, rich and poor, free and slave, to receive a mark on his right hand or on his forehead, 17 so that no one could buy or sell unless he had the mark, which is the name of the beast or the number of his name.[u]

18 This calls for wisdom.[v] If anyone has insight, let him calculate the number of the

**12:11** z Lk 14:26
**12:12** a Ps 96:11; Rev 18:20 b Rev 10:6
**12:13** c ver 5
**12:14** d Ex 19:4 e Da 7:25
**12:17** f Rev 11:7 g Ge 3:15 h Rev 14:12
**13:1** i Da 7:1–6
**13:2** j Rev
**13:3** k Rev 17:8
**13:5** l Da 7:8,11,20,25 m Rev 11:2
**13:7** n Rev 11:7
**13:8** o Rev 3:5
**13:9** p Rev 2:7
**13:10** q Rev 14:12
**13:13** r Mt 24:24
**13:14** s 2Th 2:9,10 t Rev 12:9
**13:17** u Rev 14:11
**13:18** v Rev 17:9

[a]1 Some late manuscripts *And I* [b]8 Or *written from the creation of the world in the book of life belonging to the Lamb that was slain* [c]10 Some manuscripts *anyone kills*

women OF THE Bible

# The Revelation 12 Woman

## A Woman of Focus

Picture this woman. She was pregnant and seemingly alone and in pain as she anticipated the birth of her child. Suddenly, her worst enemy appeared. His breath was on her. He waited to devour the baby as soon as it appeared. How he hated her! He could have easily killed them both immediately. But no, he wanted her to see her child die.

In extreme peril, the woman delivered the boy. Before the enemy could snatch him, the child was swept up to God. Still weak from the birth experience, the woman rose to her feet and ran. With unstable hips and wobbly legs, she ran for her life.

She spoke to no one. She never pleaded with the enemy nor did she call for help. She ran, even without her baby, to the place God had prepared. And the devil followed.

Michael and the angels fought the enemy, and he was hurled from heaven. Still he tried to kill the woman. But God gave the woman the wings of an eagle to speed her escape. Then the serpent sprayed out water from his mouth, but the earth swallowed the flood, allowing the woman another escape. At this point, the devil, defeated and still hating the woman, dedicated his life to killing her earthbound seed.

Who was this woman? We do not know for sure, but she is obviously symbolic and her attributes are instructive. She was strong, courageous—clearly a soldier. The woman had been given specific instruction. She understood what she was to do. Once on her mission, she executed it without question or complaint. Her circumstances and her feelings were irrelevant. Help came from unexpected places. Her success depended on her staying in action—no matter what. Timing was everything.

The Revelation 12 woman was a woman of focus. Self-sacrifice was just the beginning of the contribution she made to life. She gave all she had; the enemy couldn't stop her, and heaven and earth moved on her behalf. She knew her help was in God, and his plans were fulfilled.

—V. Hartsfield

### reflection

*How focused are you on carrying out the mission of God?*

*Use this woman's strength and determination to encourage you as you run your race.*

### read

Revelation 12; see also 1 Corinthians 9:24–25; Hebrews 12:1–3.

**See also** the Inspire Notes "Responsible Decisions in Leadership," "Confidence," "Faith" and "Be Focused," and the Women of the Bible Notes "Rahab: Willing to Be Used by God" and "Jael: Just Another Woman on the Lord's Side."

beast, for it is man's number. His number is 666.

## The Lamb and the 144,000

14 Then I looked, and there before me was the Lamb,[w] standing on Mount Zion, and with him 144,000 who had his name and his Father's name written on their foreheads. 2And I heard a sound from heaven like the roar of rushing waters[x] and like a loud peal of thunder. The sound I heard was like that of harpists playing their harps.[y] 3And they sang a new song[z] before the throne and before the four living creatures and the elders. No one could learn the song except the 144,000 who had been redeemed from the earth. 4These are those who did not defile themselves with women, for they kept themselves pure.[a] They follow the Lamb wherever he goes. They were purchased from among men[b] and offered as firstfruits to God and the Lamb. 5No lie was found in their mouths;[c] they are blameless.

## The Three Angels

6Then I saw another angel flying in midair, and he had the eternal gospel to proclaim to those who live on the earth—to every nation, tribe, language and people. 7He said in a loud voice, "Fear God and give him glory, because the hour of his judgment has come. Worship him who made the heavens, the earth, the sea and the springs of water."

8A second angel followed and said, "Fallen! Fallen is Babylon the Great,[d] which made all the nations drink the maddening wine of her adulteries."

9A third angel followed them and said in a loud voice: "If anyone worships the beast and his image[e] and receives his mark on the forehead or on the hand, 10he, too, will drink of the wine of God's fury,[f] which has been poured full strength into the cup of his wrath.[g] He will be tormented with burning sulfur in the presence of the holy angels and of the Lamb. 11And the smoke of their torment rises for ever and ever.[h] There is no rest day or night for those who worship the beast and his image, or for anyone who receives the mark of his name." 12This calls for patient endurance on the part of the saints[i] who obey God's commandments and remain faithful to Jesus.

13Then I heard a voice from heaven say, "Write: Blessed are the dead who die in the Lord[j] from now on."

"Yes," says the Spirit, "they will rest from their labor, for their deeds will follow them."

## The Harvest of the Earth

14I looked, and there before me was a white cloud, and seated on the cloud was one "like a son of man"[a] with a crown[k] of gold on his head and a sharp sickle in his hand. 15Then another angel came out of the temple and called in a loud voice to him who was sitting on the cloud, "Take your sickle[l] and reap, because the time to reap has come, for the harvest[m] of the earth is ripe." 16So he who was seated on the cloud swung his sickle over the earth, and the earth was harvested.

17Another angel came out of the temple in heaven, and he too had a sharp sickle. 18Still another angel, who had charge of the fire, came from the altar and called in a

**14:1** w Rev 5:6
**14:2** x Rev 1:15 y Rev 5:8
**14:3** z Rev 5:9
**14:4** a Rev 3:4 b Rev 5:9
**14:5** c Ps 32:2; Zep 3:13
**14:8** d Isa 21:9; Jer 51:8
**14:9** e Rev 13:14
**14:10** f Isa 51:17 g Rev 18:6
**14:11** h Isa 34:10
**14:12** i Rev 13:10
**14:13** j 1Co 15:18; 1Th 4:16
**14:14** k Rev 6:2
**14:15** l Joel 3:13 m Jer 51:33

[a] 14 Daniel 7:13

*The African Presence*

**Revelation 14:8**

According to Genesis 10, Nimrod (a son of Cush) built many cities in Babylonia and Assyria. For more on Nimrod, see the African Presence note on Genesis 10.

loud voice to him who had the sharp sickle, "Take your sharp sickle and gather the clusters of grapes from the earth's vine, because its grapes are ripe." 19 The angel swung his sickle on the earth, gathered its grapes and threw them into the great winepress of God's wrath.[n] 20 They were trampled in the winepress outside the city,[o] and blood flowed out of the press, rising as high as the horses' bridles for a distance of 1,600 stadia.[a]

## Seven Angels With Seven Plagues

**15** I saw in heaven another great and marvelous sign:[p] seven angels with the seven last plagues—last, because with them God's wrath is completed. 2 And I saw what looked like a sea of glass[q] mixed with fire and, standing beside the sea, those who had been victorious over the beast and his image[r] and over the number of his name. They held harps given them by God 3 and sang the song of Moses the servant of God and the song of the Lamb:

"Great and marvelous are your deeds,[s]
  Lord God Almighty.
Just and true are your ways,
  King of the ages.
4 Who will not fear you, O Lord,[t]
  and bring glory to your name?
For you alone are holy.
All nations will come
  and worship before you,
for your righteous acts have been
    revealed."

5 After this I looked and in heaven the temple, that is, the tabernacle of the Testimony,[u] was opened. 6 Out of the temple came the seven angels with the seven plagues.[v] They were dressed in clean, shining linen and wore golden sashes around their chests. 7 Then one of the four living creatures[w] gave to the seven angels seven golden bowls filled with the wrath of God, who lives for ever and ever. 8 And the temple was filled with smoke from the glory of God and from his power, and no one could enter the temple[x] until the seven plagues of the seven angels were completed.

**14:19** n Rev 19:15
**14:20** o Heb 13:12
**15:1** p Rev 12:1,3
**15:2** q Rev 4:6 r Rev 13:14
**15:3** s Ps 111:2
**15:4** t Jer 10:7
**15:5** u Nu 1:50
**15:6** v ver 1
**15:7** w Rev 4:6
**15:8** x Ex 40:34,35

## The Seven Bowls of God's Wrath

**16** Then I heard a loud voice from the temple saying to the seven angels,[y] "Go, pour out the seven bowls of God's wrath on the earth."

2 The first angel went and poured out his bowl on the land,[z] and ugly and painful sores broke out on the people who had the mark of the beast and worshiped his image.

3 The second angel poured out his bowl on the sea, and it turned into blood like that of a dead man, and every living thing in the sea died.[a]

4 The third angel poured out his bowl on the rivers and springs of water, and they became blood.[b] 5 Then I heard the angel in charge of the waters say:

"You are just in these judgments,
  you who are and who were, the Holy
    One,
  because you have so judged;
6 for they have shed the blood of your
    saints and prophets,
  and you have given them blood to
    drink[c] as they deserve."

7 And I heard the altar respond:

"Yes, Lord God Almighty,
  true and just are your judgments."[d]

8 The fourth angel poured out his bowl on the sun, and the sun was given power to scorch people with fire. 9 They were seared by the intense heat and they cursed the name of God, who had control over these plagues, but they refused to repent and glorify him.[e]

10 The fifth angel poured out his bowl on the throne of the beast,[f] and his kingdom was plunged into darkness. Men gnawed their tongues in agony 11 and cursed[g] the God of heaven because of their pains and their sores, but they refused to repent of what they had done.

12 The sixth angel poured out his bowl on the great river Euphrates,[h] and its water was dried up to prepare the way for the kings from the East.[i] 13 Then I saw three evil[b] spirits that looked like frogs; they came out of the mouth of the dragon,[j] out of the mouth

**16:1** y Rev 15:1
**16:2** z Rev 8:7
**16:3** a Ex 7:17–21
**16:4** b Ex 7:17–21
**16:6** c Isa 49:26
**16:7** d Rev 15:3
**16:9** e Rev 11:13
**16:10** f Rev 13:2
**16:11** g ver 9,21
**16:12** h Rev 9:14 i Isa 41:2
**16:13** j Rev 12:3

[a] 20 That is, about 180 miles (about 300 kilometers) [b] 13 Greek *unclean*

16:14 k 1Ti 4:1 l Rev 17:14
16:17 m Rev 21:6
16:18 n Da 12:1
16:19 o Rev 18:5 p Rev 14:10
16:20 q Rev 6:14
16:21 r Ex 9:23–25
17:1 s Rev 16:19 t Rev 19:2 u Jer 51:13
17:3 v Rev 12:6,14
17:4 w Jer 51:7

of the beast and out of the mouth of the false prophet. 14They are spirits of demons[k] performing miraculous signs, and they go out to the kings of the whole world, to gather them for the battle[l] on the great day of God Almighty.

15"Behold, I come like a thief! Blessed is he who stays awake and keeps his clothes with him, so that he may not go naked and be shamefully exposed."

16Then they gathered the kings together to the place that in Hebrew is called Armageddon.

17The seventh angel poured out his bowl into the air, and out of the temple came a loud voice from the throne, saying, "It is done!"[m] 18Then there came flashes of lightning, rumblings, peals of thunder and a severe earthquake. No earthquake like it has ever occurred since man has been on earth,[n] so tremendous was the quake. 19The great city split into three parts, and the cities of the nations collapsed. God remembered[o] Babylon the Great and gave her the cup filled with the wine of the fury of his wrath.[p] 20Every island fled away and the mountains could not be found.[q] 21From the sky huge hailstones of about a hundred pounds each fell upon men. And they cursed God on account of the plague of hail,[r] because the plague was so terrible.

## The Woman on the Beast

17 One of the seven angels who had the seven bowls came and said to me, "Come, I will show you the punishment[s] of the great prostitute,[t] who sits on many waters.[u] 2With her the kings of the earth committed adultery and the inhabitants of the earth were intoxicated with the wine of her adulteries."

3Then the angel carried me away in the Spirit into a desert.[v] There I saw a woman sitting on a scarlet beast that was covered with blasphemous names and had seven heads and ten horns. 4The woman was dressed in purple and scarlet, and was glittering with gold, precious stones and pearls. She held a golden cup[w] in her hand, filled with abominable things and the filth of her adulteries. 5This title was written on her forehead:

MYSTERY
BABYLON THE GREAT
THE MOTHER OF PROSTITUTES
AND OF THE ABOMINATIONS OF THE EARTH.

6I saw that the woman was drunk with the blood of the saints, the blood of those who bore testimony to Jesus.

When I saw her, I was greatly astonished. 7Then the angel said to me: "Why are you astonished? I will explain to you the mystery of the woman and of the beast she rides, which has the seven heads and ten horns. 8The beast, which you saw, once was, now is not, and will come up out of the Abyss and go to his destruction.[x] The inhabitants of the earth whose names have not been written in the book of life from the creation of the world will be astonished[y] when they see the beast, because he once was, now is not, and yet will come.

9"This calls for a mind with wisdom.[z] The seven heads are seven hills on which the woman sits. 10They are also seven kings. Five have fallen, one is, the other has not yet come; but when he does come, he must remain for a little while. 11The beast who once was, and now is not,[a] is an eighth king. He belongs to the seven and is going to his destruction.

12"The ten horns you saw are ten kings who have not yet received a kingdom, but who for one hour will receive authority as kings along with the beast. 13They have one purpose and will give their power and authority to the beast. 14They will make war[b] against the Lamb, but the Lamb will overcome them because he is Lord of lords and King of kings[c]—and with him will be his called, chosen and faithful followers."

15Then the angel said to me, "The waters you saw, where the prostitute sits, are peoples, multitudes, nations and languages. 16The beast and the ten horns you saw will hate the prostitute. They will bring her to ruin and leave her naked;[d] they will eat her flesh and burn her with fire.[e] 17For God has put it into their hearts to accomplish his purpose by agreeing to give the beast their power to rule, until God's words are fulfilled.[f] 18The woman you saw is the great city[g] that rules over the kings of the earth."

17:8 x Rev 13:10 y Rev 13:3
17:9 z Rev 13:18
17:11 a ver 8
17:14 b Rev 16:14 c 1Ti 6:15
17:16 d Eze 16:37,39 e Rev 18:8
17:17 f Rev 10:7
17:18 g Rev 16:19

## The Fall of Babylon

18 After this I saw another angel[h] coming down from heaven. He had great authority, and the earth was illuminated by his splendor.[i] 2 With a mighty voice he shouted:

"Fallen! Fallen is Babylon the Great!
She has become a home for demons
and a haunt for every evil[a] spirit,
a haunt for every unclean and
detestable bird.[j]
3 For all the nations have drunk
the maddening wine of her adulteries.[k]
The kings of the earth committed
adultery with her,
and the merchants of the earth grew
rich from her excessive
luxuries."

4 Then I heard another voice from heaven say:

"Come out of her, my people,[l]
so that you will not share in her sins,
so that you will not receive any of her
plagues;
5 for her sins are piled up to heaven,[m]
and God has remembered her crimes.
6 Give back to her as she has given;
pay her back[n] double for what she has
done.
Mix her a double portion from her
own cup.
7 Give her as much torture and grief
as the glory and luxury she gave
herself.[o]
In her heart she boasts,
'I sit as queen; I am not a widow,
and I will never mourn.'[p]
8 Therefore in one day her plagues will
overtake her:
death, mourning and famine.
She will be consumed by fire,[q]
for mighty is the Lord God who judges
her.

9 "When the kings of the earth who committed adultery with her and shared her luxury see the smoke of her burning,[r] they will weep and mourn over her. 10 Terrified at her torment, they will stand far off and cry:

" 'Woe! Woe, O great city,
O Babylon, city of power!
In one hour your doom has come!'

11 "The merchants[s] of the earth will weep and mourn over her because no one buys their cargoes any more— 12 cargoes of gold, silver, precious stones and pearls; fine linen, purple, silk and scarlet cloth; every sort of citron wood, and articles of every kind made of ivory, costly wood, bronze, iron and marble;[t] 13 cargoes of cinnamon and spice, of incense, myrrh and frankincense, of wine and olive oil, of fine flour and wheat; cattle and sheep; horses and carriages; and bodies and souls of men.[u]

14 "They will say, 'The fruit you longed for is gone from you. All your riches and splendor have vanished, never to be recovered.' 15 The merchants who sold these things and gained their wealth from her will stand far off, terrified at her torment. They will weep and mourn 16 and cry out:

" 'Woe! Woe, O great city,
dressed in fine linen, purple and
scarlet,
and glittering with gold, precious
stones and pearls![v]
17 In one hour such great wealth has been
brought to ruin!'

"Every sea captain, and all who travel by ship, the sailors, and all who earn their living from the sea,[w] will stand far off. 18 When they see the smoke of her burning, they will exclaim, 'Was there ever a city like this great city?'[x] 19 They will throw dust on their heads,[y] and with weeping and mourning cry out:

" 'Woe! Woe, O great city,
where all who had ships on the sea
became rich through her wealth!
In one hour she has been brought to ruin!
20 Rejoice over her, O heaven![z]
Rejoice, saints and apostles and
prophets!
God has judged her for the way she
treated you.' "

21 Then a mighty angel picked up a boulder the size of a large millstone and threw it into the sea,[a] and said:

[a]2 Greek *unclean*

**18:1** h Rev 17:1 i Eze 43:2
**18:2** j Isa 13:21,22; Jer 50:39
**18:3** k Rev 14:8
**18:4** l Jer 50:8; 2Co 6:17
**18:5** m Jer 51:9
**18:6** n Ps 137:8; Jer 50:15,29
**18:7** o Eze 28:2–8 p Zep 2:15
**18:8** q Rev 17:16
**18:9** r Rev 19:3

**18:11** s Eze 27:27
**18:12** t Rev 17:4
**18:13** u Eze 27:13
**18:16** v Rev 17:4
**18:17** w Eze 27:28–30
**18:18** x Rev 13:4
**18:19** y Jos 7:6
**18:20** z Jer 51:48
**18:21** a Jer 51:63

**18:22**
b Eze 26:13
c Jer 25:10

**18:23**
d Jer 7:34; 16:9
e Isa 23:8

**18:24**
f Rev 17:6

**19:1**
g Rev 11:15
h Rev 7:10
i Rev 4:11

**19:3**
j Isa 34:10; Rev 14:11

**19:4**
k Rev 4:4
l Rev 4:6

"With such violence
the great city of Babylon will be
thrown down,
never to be found again.
22 The music of harpists and musicians,
flute players and trumpeters,
will never be heard in you again.[b]
No workman of any trade
will ever be found in you again.
The sound of a millstone
will never be heard in you again.[c]
23 The light of a lamp
will never shine in you again.
The voice of bridegroom and bride
will never be heard in you
again.[d]
Your merchants were the world's great
men.[e]
By your magic spell all the nations
were led astray.
24 In her was found the blood of prophets
and of the saints,[f]
and of all who have been killed on the
earth."

## Hallelujah!

19 After this I heard what sounded
like the roar of a great multitude[g] in
heaven shouting:

"Hallelujah!
Salvation[h] and glory and power[i] belong to
our God,
2 for true and just are his judgments.
He has condemned the great prostitute
who corrupted the earth by her
adulteries.
He has avenged on her the blood of his
servants."

3 And again they shouted:

"Hallelujah!
The smoke from her goes up for ever and
ever."[j]

4 The twenty-four elders[k] and the four
living creatures[l] fell down and worshiped
God, who was seated on the throne. And
they cried:

"Amen, Hallelujah!"

5 Then a voice came from the throne,
saying:

"Praise our God,
all you his servants,[m]
you who fear him,
both small and great!"

6 Then I heard what sounded like a great
multitude,[n] like the roar of rushing waters
and like loud peals of thunder, shouting:

"Hallelujah!
For our Lord God Almighty reigns.
7 Let us rejoice and be glad
and give him glory!
For the wedding of the Lamb[o] has come,
and his bride[p] has made herself ready.
8 Fine linen, bright and clean,
was given her to wear."
(Fine linen stands for the righteous acts of
the saints.)

*Great God,*

*I look forward to the wedding
supper of the Lamb when all God's
people will rejoice. Hallelujah!*

*Amen*

REVELATION 19:6–8

9 Then the angel said to me, "Write:
'Blessed are those who are invited to the
wedding supper of the Lamb!'"[q] And he
added, "These are the true words of God."
10 At this I fell at his feet to worship him.
But he said to me, "Do not do it! I am a fel-
low servant with you and with your brothers
who hold to the testimony of Jesus. Worship
God![r] For the testimony of Jesus is the spirit
of prophecy."

## The Rider on the White Horse

11 I saw heaven standing open and there
before me was a white horse, whose rider[s]
is called Faithful and True.[t] With justice
he judges and makes war. 12 His eyes are
like blazing fire,[u] and on his head are many
crowns.[v] He has a name written on him that
no one knows but he himself. 13 He is dressed
in a robe dipped in blood,[w] and his name is
the Word of God. 14 The armies of heaven

**19:5**
m Ps 134:1

**19:6**
n Rev 11:15

**19:7**
o Mt 22:2; Eph 5:32
p Rev 21:2,9

**19:9**
q Lk 14:15

**19:10**
r Rev 22:9

**19:11**
s Rev 6:2
t Rev 3:14

**19:12**
u Rev 1:14
v Rev 6:2

**19:13**
w Isa 63:2,3

**19:15** x Isa 11:4
**19:17** y Eze 39:17
**19:18** z Eze 39:18–20
**19:19** a Rev 16:14,16
**19:20** b Rev 13:12 c Da 7:11
**20:1** d Rev 1:18
**20:2** e 2Pe 2:4
**20:3** f Da 6:17 g Rev 12:9
**20:4** h Da 7:9 i Rev 6:9

were following him, riding on white horses
and dressed in fine linen, white and clean.
15 Out of his mouth comes a sharp sword
with which to strike down[x] the nations. "He
will rule them with an iron scepter."[a] He
treads the winepress of the fury of the wrath
of God Almighty. 16 On his robe and on his
thigh he has this name written:

KING OF KINGS AND LORD OF LORDS.

17 And I saw an angel standing in the sun,
who cried in a loud voice to all the birds fly-
ing in midair, "Come,[y] gather together for
the great supper of God, 18 so that you may
eat the flesh of kings, generals, and mighty
men, of horses and their riders, and the
flesh of all people,[z] free and slave, small
and great."
19 Then I saw the beast and the kings of the
earth[a] and their armies gathered together
to make war against the rider on the horse
and his army. 20 But the beast was captured,
and with him the false prophet who had
performed the miraculous signs on his be-
half.[b] With these signs he had deluded those
who had received the mark of the beast and
worshiped his image. The two of them were
thrown alive into the fiery lake[c] of burning
sulfur. 21 The rest of them were killed with
the sword that came out of the mouth of the
rider on the horse, and all the birds gorged
themselves on their flesh.

## The Thousand Years

20 And I saw an angel coming down
out of heaven, having the key[d] to
the Abyss and holding in his hand a great
chain. 2 He seized the dragon, that ancient
serpent, who is the devil, or Satan, and
bound him for a thousand years.[e] 3 He threw
him into the Abyss, and locked and sealed[f]
it over him, to keep him from deceiving the
nations[g] anymore until the thousand years
were ended. After that, he must be set free
for a short time.
4 I saw thrones[h] on which were seated
those who had been given authority to
judge. And I saw the souls of those who had
been beheaded[i] because of their testimony
for Jesus and because of the word of God.
They had not worshiped the beast or his im-
age and had not received his mark on their
foreheads or their hands.[j] They came to life
and reigned with Christ a thousand years.
5 (The rest of the dead did not come to life
until the thousand years were ended.) This
is the first resurrection. 6 Blessed and holy
are those who have part in the first resurrec-
tion. The second death[k] has no power over
them, but they will be priests of God and of
Christ and will reign with him for a thou-
sand years.

## Satan's Doom

7 When the thousand years are over, Satan
will be released from his prison 8 and will go
out to deceive the nations in the four corners
of the earth—Gog and Magog[l]—to gather
them for battle. In number they are like the
sand on the seashore. 9 They marched across
the breadth of the earth and surrounded[m]
the camp of God's people, the city he loves.
But fire came down from heaven and de-
voured them. 10 And the devil, who deceived
them, was thrown into the lake of burning
sulfur, where the beast and the false prophet
had been thrown. They will be tormented
day and night for ever and ever.

## The Dead Are Judged

11 Then I saw a great white throne and
him who was seated on it. Earth and sky fled
from his presence, and there was no place for
them. 12 And I saw the dead, great and small,
standing before the throne, and books were
opened. Another book was opened, which
is the book of life. The dead were judged ac-
cording to what they had done[n] as recorded
in the books. 13 The sea gave up the dead that
were in it, and death and Hades gave up the
dead that were in them, and each person
was judged according to what he had done.
14 Then death[o] and Hades were thrown into
the lake of fire. The lake of fire is the second
death. 15 If anyone's name was not found
written in the book of life, he was thrown
into the lake of fire.

## The New Jerusalem

21 Then I saw a new heaven and a new
earth,[p] for the first heaven and the
first earth had passed away, and there was

**20:4** j Rev 13:16
**20:6** k Rev 2:11
**20:8** l Eze 38:2
**20:9** m Eze 38:9,16
**20:12** n Mt 16:27
**20:14** o 1Co 15:26
**21:1** p 2Pe 3:13

[a] 15 Psalm 2:9

no longer any sea. [2]I saw the Holy City, the new Jerusalem, coming down out of heaven from God,[q] prepared as a bride beautifully dressed for her husband. [3]And I heard a loud voice from the throne saying, "Now the dwelling of God is with men, and he will live with them. They will be his people, and God himself will be with them and be their God. [4]He will wipe every tear from their eyes. There will be no more death[r] or mourning or crying or pain,[s] for the old order of things has passed away."

*"Let a new earth rise. Let another world be born. Let a bloody peace be written in the sky. Let a second generation full of courage issue forth. Let a people loving freedom come to growth."*

—MARGARET WALKER, WRITER AND LECTURER

[5]He who was seated on the throne[t] said, "I am making everything new!" Then he said, "Write this down, for these words are trustworthy and true."[u]

[6]He said to me: "It is done.[v] I am the Alpha and the Omega,[w] the Beginning and the End. To him who is thirsty I will give to drink without cost from the spring of the water of life.[x] [7]He who overcomes will inherit all this, and I will be his God and he will be my son. [8]But the cowardly, the unbelieving, the vile, the murderers, the sexually immoral, those who practice magic arts, the idolaters and all liars—their place will be in the fiery lake of burning sulfur. This is the second death."

[9]One of the seven angels who had the seven bowls full of the seven last plagues[y] came and said to me, "Come, I will show you the bride, the wife of the Lamb." [10]And he carried me away in the Spirit[z] to a mountain great and high, and showed me the Holy City, Jerusalem, coming down out of heaven from God. [11]It shone with the glory of God,[a] and its brilliance was like that of a very precious jewel, like a jasper, clear as crystal. [12]It had a great, high wall with twelve gates, and with twelve angels at the gates. On the gates were written the names of the twelve tribes of Israel.[b] [13]There were three gates on the east, three on the north, three on the south and three on the west. [14]The wall of the city had twelve foundations, and on them were the names of the twelve apostles of the Lamb.

[15]The angel who talked with me had a measuring rod of gold to measure the city, its gates and its walls. [16]The city was laid out like a square, as long as it was wide. He measured the city with the rod and found it to be 12,000 stadia[a] in length, and as wide and high as it is long. [17]He measured its wall and it was 144 cubits[b] thick,[c] by man's measurement, which the angel was using. [18]The wall was made of jasper, and the city of pure gold, as pure as glass. [19]The foundations of the city walls were decorated with every kind of precious stone.[c] The first foundation was jasper, the second sapphire, the third chalcedony, the fourth emerald, [20]the fifth sardonyx, the sixth carnelian, the seventh chrysolite, the eighth beryl, the ninth topaz, the tenth chrysoprase, the eleventh jacinth, and the twelfth amethyst.[d] [21]The twelve gates were twelve pearls, each gate made of a single pearl. The great street of the city was of pure gold, like transparent glass.

[22]I did not see a temple[d] in the city, because the Lord God Almighty and the Lamb are its temple. [23]The city does not need the sun or the moon to shine on it, for the glory of God gives it light,[e] and the Lamb is its lamp. [24]The nations will walk by its light, and the kings of the earth will bring their splendor into it.[f] [25]On no day will its gates ever be shut,[g] for there will be no night there.[h] [26]The glory and honor of the nations will be brought into it. [27]Nothing impure will ever enter it, nor will anyone who does what is shameful or deceitful,[i] but only those whose names are written in the Lamb's book of life.

## The River of Life

22 Then the angel showed me the river of the water of life, as clear as crystal, flowing[j] from the throne of God and of the Lamb [2]down the middle of the great street of the city. On each side of the river stood the tree of life,[k] bearing twelve crops of fruit, yielding its fruit every month. And

**21:2** q Heb 11:10; Rev 3:12
**21:4** r 1Co 15:26 s Isa 35:10
**21:5** t Rev 4:9; 20:11 u Rev 19:9
**21:6** v Rev 16:17 w Rev 1:8 x Jn 4:10
**21:9** y Rev 15:1,6,7
**21:10** z Rev 1:10
**21:11** a Rev 22:5
**21:12** b Eze 48:30–34
**21:19** c Isa 54:11,12
**21:22** d Jn 4:21,23
**21:23** e Isa 24:23; 60:19,20
**21:24** f Isa 60:3,5
**21:25** g Isa 60:11 h Zec 14:7; Rev 22:5
**21:27** i Isa 52:1; Rev 22:14,15
**22:1** j Eze 47:1
**22:2** k Rev 2:7

[a]16 That is, about 1,400 miles (about 2,200 kilometers) [b]17 That is, about 200 feet (about 65 meters) [c]17 Or *high*
[d]20 The precise identification of some of these precious stones is uncertain.

22:2 l Eze 47:12
22:3 m Zec 14:11
22:4 n Mt 5:8
22:5 o Rev 21:23
22:6 p Rev 1:1
22:7 q Rev 1:3
22:8 r Rev 19:10
22:9 s Rev 19:10
22:10 t Da 8:26
22:11 u Eze 3:27
22:12 v Isa 40:10

the leaves of the tree are for the healing of the nations.[l] [3]No longer will there be any curse.[m] The throne of God and of the Lamb will be in the city, and his servants will serve him. [4]They will see his face,[n] and his name will be on their foreheads. [5]There will be no more night. They will not need the light of a lamp or the light of the sun, for the Lord God will give them light.[o] And they will reign for ever and ever.

[6]The angel said to me,[p] "These words are trustworthy and true. The Lord, the God of the spirits of the prophets, sent his angel to show his servants the things that must soon take place."

## Jesus Is Coming

[7]"Behold, I am coming soon! Blessed[q] is he who keeps the words of the prophecy in this book."

[8]I, John, am the one who heard and saw these things. And when I had heard and seen them, I fell down to worship at the feet[r] of the angel who had been showing them to me. [9]But he said to me, "Do not do it! I am a fellow servant with you and with your brothers the prophets and of all who keep the words of this book. Worship God!"[s]

[10]Then he told me, "Do not seal up[t] the words of the prophecy of this book, because the time is near. [11]Let him who does wrong continue to do wrong; let him who is vile continue to be vile; let him who does right continue to do right; and let him who is holy continue to be holy."[u]

[12]"Behold, I am coming soon! My reward is with me,[v] and I will give to everyone according to what he has done. [13]I am the Alpha and the Omega, the First and the Last, the Beginning and the End.

[14]"Blessed are those who wash their robes, that they may have the right to the

*Believer,*

*I am the Alpha and the Omega.*
*Everything—everything—begins*
*with me and ends with me.*

*The Great "I AM"*

REVELATION 22:13

tree of life and may go through the gates into the city. [15]Outside[w] are the dogs,[x] those who practice magic arts, the sexually immoral, the murderers, the idolaters and everyone who loves and practices falsehood.

[16]"I, Jesus,[y] have sent my angel to give you[a] this testimony for the churches. I am the Root[z] and the Offspring of David, and the bright Morning Star."

[17]The Spirit and the bride say, "Come!" And let him who hears say, "Come!" Whoever is thirsty, let him come; and whoever wishes, let him take the free gift of the water of life.

[18]I warn everyone who hears the words of the prophecy of this book: If anyone adds anything to them,[a] God will add to him the plagues described in this book. [19]And if anyone takes words away from this book of prophecy, God will take away from him his share in the tree of life and in the holy city, which are described in this book.

[20]He who testifies to these things says, "Yes, I am coming soon."

Amen. Come, Lord Jesus.

[21]The grace of the Lord Jesus be with God's people.[b] Amen.

22:15 w Gal 5:19–21 x Php 3:2
22:16 y Rev 1:1 z Rev 5:5
22:18 a Dt 4:2; Pr 30:6
22:21 b Ro 16:20

[a]16 The Greek is plural.

| | BIBLICAL UNIT | APPROXIMATE AMERICAN EQUIVALENT | APPROXIMATE METRIC EQUIVALENT |
|---|---|---|---|
| **WEIGHTS** | talent (60 minas) | 75 pounds | 34 kilograms |
| | mina (50 shekels) | 1 1/4 pounds | 0.6 kilogram |
| | shekel (2 bekas) | 2/5 ounce | 11.5 grams |
| | pim (2/3 shekel) | 1/3 ounce | 7.6 grams |
| | beka (10 gerahs) | 1/5 ounce | 5.5 grams |
| | gerah | 1/50 ounce | 0.6 gram |
| **LENGTH** | cubit | 18 inches | 0.5 meter |
| | span | 9 inches | 23 centimeters |
| | handbreadth | 3 inches | 8 centimeters |
| **CAPACITY** | | | |
| Dry Measure | cor [homer] (10 ephahs) | 6 bushels | 220 liters |
| | lethek (5 ephahs) | 3 bushels | 110 liters |
| | ephah (10 omers) | 3/5 bushel | 22 liters |
| | seah (1/3 ephah) | 7 quarts | 7.3 liters |
| | omer (1/10 ephah) | 2 quarts | 2 liters |
| | cab (1/18 ephah) | 1 quart | 1 liter |
| Liquid Measure | bath (1 ephah) | 6 gallons | 22 liters |
| | hin (1/6 bath) | 4 quarts | 4 liters |
| | log (1/72 bath) | 1/3 quart | 0.3 liter |

The figures of the table are calculated on the basis of a shekel equaling 11.5 grams, a cubit equaling 18 inches and an ephah equaling 22 liters. The quart referred to is either a dry quart (slightly larger than a liter) or a liquid quart (slightly smaller than a liter), whichever is applicable. The ton referred to in the footnotes is the American ton of 2,000 pounds. Since most readers are more familiar with dry measures being given in weight rather than capacity (bushel, quart), dry measures have been converted in the footnotes to approximate weights.

This table is based upon the best available information, but it is not intended to be mathematically precise; like the measurement equivalents in the footnotes, it merely gives approximate amounts and distances. Weights and measures differed somewhat at various times and places in the ancient world. There is uncertainty particularly about the ephah and the bath; further discoveries may shed more light on these units of capacity.

The NIV Concordance, created by Edward W. Goodrick and John R. Kohlenberger III, has been developed specifically for use with the New International Version. Like all concordances, it is a special index which contains an alphabetical listing of words used in the Bible text. By looking up key words, readers can find verses and passages for which they remember a word or two but not their location.

This concordance contains 2,000 word entries, with some 13,000 Scripture references. Each word entry is followed by the Scripture references in which that particular word is found, as well as by a brief excerpt from the surrounding context. The first letter of the entry word is italicized to conserve space and to allow for a longer context excerpt. Variant spellings due to number and tense and compound forms follow the entry in parentheses, and direct the reader to check other forms of that word in locating a passage.

This concordance contains a number of "block entries," which highlight some of the key events and characteristics in the lives of certain Bible figures. The descriptive phrases replace the brief context surrounding each occurrence of the name. In those instances where more than one Bible character has the same name, that name is placed under one block entry, and each person is given a number (1), (2), etc. Insignificant names are not included.

Word or block entries marked with an asterisk (*) list every verse in the Bible in which the word appears.

This concordance is a valuable tool for Bible study. While one of its key purposes is to help the reader find forgotten references to verses, it can also be used to do word studies and to locate and trace biblical themes. Be sure to use this concordance as more than just a verse finder. Whenever you look up a verse, aim to discover the intended meaning of the verse in context. Give special attention to the flow of thought from the beginning of the passage to the end.

### AARON

Priesthood of (Ex 28:1; Nu 17; Heb 5:1-4; 7), garments (Ex 28; 39), consecration (Ex 29), ordination (Lev 8).

Spokesman for Moses (Ex 4:14-16, 27-31; 7:1-2). Supported Moses' hands in battle (Ex 17:8-13). Built golden calf (Ex 32; Dt 9:20). Talked against Moses (Nu 12). Priesthood opposed (Nu 16); staff budded (Nu 17). Forbidden to enter land (Nu 20:1-12). Death (Nu 20:22-29; 33:38-39).

### ABANDON

| | | |
|---|---|---|
| Dt | 4:31 | he will not *a* or destroy you |
| 1Ti | 4:1 | in later times some will *a* the faith |

### ABBA

| | | |
|---|---|---|
| Ro | 8:15 | And by him we cry, "*A*, Father." |
| Gal | 4:6 | the Spirit who calls out, "*A*, Father." |

### ABEL

Second son of Adam (Ge 4:2). Offered proper sacrifice (Ge 4:4; Heb 11:4). Murdered by Cain (Ge 4:8; Mt 23:35; Lk 11:51; 1Jn 3:12).

### ABHORS

| | | |
|---|---|---|
| Pr | 11:1 | The LORD *a* dishonest scales, |

### ABIGAIL

Wife of Nabal (1Sa 25:30); pled for his life with David (1Sa 25:14-35). Became David's wife (1Sa 25:36-42).

### ABIJAH

Son of Rehoboam; king of Judah (1Ki 14:31-15:8; 2Ch 12:16-14:1).

### ABILITY (ABLE)

| | | |
|---|---|---|
| Ezr | 2:69 | According to their *a* they gave |
| 2Co | 1:8 | far beyond our *a* to endure, |
| | 8:3 | were able, and even beyond their *a*. |

### ABIMELECH

1. King of Gerar who took Abraham's wife Sarah, believing her to be his sister (Ge 20). Later made a covenant with Abraham (Ge 21:22-33).
2. King of Gerar who took Isaac's wife Rebekah, believing her to be his sister (Ge 26:1-11). Later made a covenant with Isaac (Ge 26:12-31).

### ABLE (ABILITY ENABLE ENABLED ENABLES)

| | | |
|---|---|---|
| Eze | 7:19 | and gold will not be *a* to save them |
| Da | 3:17 | the God we serve is *a* to save us |
| Ro | 8:39 | will be *a* to separate us |
| | 14:4 | for the Lord is *a* to make him stand |
| | 16:25 | to him who is *a* to establish you |
| 2Co | 9:8 | God is *a* to make all grace abound |
| Eph | 3:20 | him who is *a* to do immeasurably |

2Ti 1:12 and am convinced that he is *a*
3:15 which are *a* to make you wise
Heb 7:25 he is *a* to save completely
Jude :24 To him who is *a* to keep you
Rev 5:5 He is *a* to open the scroll

**ABOLISH**
Mt 5:17 that I have come to *a* the Law

**ABOMINATION**
Da 11:31 set up the *a* that causes desolation.

**ABOUND (ABOUNDING)**
2Co 9:8 able to make all grace *a* to you,
Php 1:9 that your love may *a* more

**ABOUNDING (ABOUND)**
Ex 34:6 slow to anger, *a* in love
Ps 86:5 *a* in love to all who call to you.

**ABRAHAM**
Covenant relation with the LORD (Ge 12:1-3; 13:14-17; 15; 17; 22:15-18; Ex 2:24; Ne 9:8; Ps 105; Mic 7:20; Lk 1:68-75; Ro 4; Heb 6:13-15).

Called from Ur, via Haran, to Canaan (Ge 12:1; Ac 7:2-4; Heb 11:8-10). Moved to Egypt, nearly lost Sarah to Pharoah (Ge 12:10-20). Divided the land with Lot (Ge 13). Saved Lot from four kings (Ge 14:1-16); blessed by Melchizedek (Ge 14:17-20; Heb 7:1-20). Declared righteous by faith (Ge 15:6; Ro 4:3; Gal 3:6-9). Fathered Ishmael by Hagar (Ge 16).

Name changed from Abram (Ge 17:5; Ne 9:7). Circumcised (Ge 17; Ro 4:9-12). Entertained three visitors (Ge 18); promised a son by Sarah (Ge 18:9-15; 17:16) Moved to Gerar; nearly lost Sarah to Abimelech (Ge 20). Fathered Isaac by Sarah (Ge 21:1-7; Ac 7:8; Heb 11:11-12); sent away Hagar and Ishmael (Ge 21:8-21; Gal 4:22-30). Tested by offering Isaac (Ge 22; Heb 11:17-19; Jas 2:21-24). Sarah died; bought field of Ephron for burial (Ge 23). Secured wife for Isaac (Ge 24). Death (Ge 25:7-11).

**ABSALOM**
Son of David by Maacah (2Sa 3:3; 1Ch 3:2). Killed Amnon for rape of his sister Tamar; banished by David (2Sa 13). Returned to Jerusalem; received by David (2Sa 14). Rebelled against David; seized kingdom (2Sa 15-17). Killed (2Sa 18).

**ABSTAIN (ABSTAINS)**
1Pe 2:11 to *a* from sinful desires,

**ABSTAINS* (ABSTAIN)**
Ro 14:6 thanks to God; and he who *a*,

**ABUNDANCE (ABUNDANT)**
Lk 12:15 consist in the *a* of his possessions."
Jude :2 peace and love be yours in *a*.

**ABUNDANT (ABUNDANCE)**
Dt 28:11 will grant you *a* prosperity—
Ps 145:7 will celebrate your *a* goodness
Pr 28:19 works his land will have *a* food,
Ro 5:17 who receive God's *a* provision

**ACCEPT (ACCEPTED ACCEPTS)**
Ex 23:8 "Do not *a* a bribe,
Pr 10:8 The wise in heart *a* commands,
19:20 Listen to advice and *a* instruction,
Ro 15:7 *A* one another, then, just
Jas 1:21 humbly *a* the word planted in you,

**ACCEPTED (ACCEPT)**
Lk 4:24 "no prophet is *a* in his hometown.

**ACCEPTS (ACCEPT)**
Ps 6:9 the LORD *a* my prayer.
Jn 13:20 whoever *a* anyone I send *a* me;

**ACCOMPANY**
Mk 16:17 these signs will *a* those who believe
Heb 6:9 your case—things that *a* salvation.

**ACCOMPLISH**
Isa 55:11 but will *a* what I desire

**ACCORD**
Nu 24:13 not do anything of my own *a*,
Jn 10:18 but I lay it down of my own *a*.
12:49 For I did not speak of my own *a*,

**ACCOUNT (ACCOUNTABLE)**
Mt 12:36 to give *a* on the day of judgment
Ro 14:12 each of us will give an *a* of himself
Heb 4:13 of him to whom we must give *a*.

**ACCOUNTABLE (ACCOUNT)**
Eze 33:6 but I will hold the watchman *a*
Ro 3:19 and the whole world held *a* to God.

**ACCUSATION (ACCUSE)**
1Ti 5:19 Do not entertain an *a*

**ACCUSATIONS (ACCUSE)**
2Pe 2:11 do not bring slanderous *a*

**ACCUSE (ACCUSATION ACCUSATIONS)**
Pr 3:30 Do not *a* a man for no reason—
Lk 3:14 and don't *a* people falsely—

**ACHAN***
Sin at Jericho caused defeat at Ai; stoned (Jos 7; 22:20; 1Ch 2:7).

**ACHE***
Pr 14:13 Even in laughter the heart may *a*,

**ACKNOWLEDGE**
Mt 10:32 *a* him before my Father in heaven.
1Jn 4:3 spirit that does not *a* Jesus is not

**ACQUIT**
Ex 23:7 to death, for I will not *a* the guilty.

**ACTION (ACTIONS ACTIVE ACTS)**
Jas 2:17 if it is not accompanied by *a*,
1Pe 1:13 minds for *a;* be self-controlled;

**ACTIONS (ACTION)**
Mt 11:19 wisdom is proved right by her *a*."
Gal 6:4 Each one should test his own *a*.
Tit 1:16 but by their *a* they deny him.

**ACTIVE (ACTION)**
Heb 4:12 For the word of God is living and *a*

**ACTS (ACTION)**
Ps 145:12 all men may know of your mighty *a*
Ps 150:2 Praise him for his *a* of power;
Isa 64:6 all our righteous *a* are like filthy
Mt 6:1 not to do your '*a* of righteousness'

**ADAM**
First man (Ge 1:26-2:25; Ro 5:14; 1Ti 2:13). Sin of (Ge 3; Hos 6:7; Ro 5:12-21). Children of (Ge 4:1-5:5). Death of (Ge 5:5; Ro 5:12-21; 1Co 15:22).

**ADD**
Dt 12:32 do not *a* to it or take away from it.
Pr 30:6 Do not *a* to his words,
Lk 12:25 by worrying can *a* a single hour
Rev 22:18 God will *a* to him the plagues

**ADMIRABLE***
Php 4:8 whatever is lovely, whatever is *a*—

**ADMONISH**
Col 3:16 and *a* one another with all wisdom,

**ADOPTED (ADOPTION)**
Eph 1:5 In love he predestined us to be *a*

**ADOPTION (ADOPTED)**
Ro 8:23 as we wait eagerly for our *a* as sons,

**ADORE***
SS 1:4 How right they are to *a* you!

**ADORNMENT* (ADORNS)**
1Pe 3:3 should not come from outward *a*,

**ADORNS (ADORNMENT)**
Ps 93:5 holiness *a* your house

**ADULTERY**
Ex 20:14 "You shall not commit *a*.
Mt 5:27 that it was said, 'Do not commit *a*.'
5:28 lustfully has already committed *a*
5:32 the divorced woman commits *a*.
15:19 murder, *a*, sexual immorality, theft

**ADULTS***
1Co 14:20 but in your thinking be *a*.

**ADVANCED**
Job 32:7 *a* years should teach wisdom.'

**ADVANTAGE**
Ex 22:22 "Do not take *a* of a widow
Dt 24:14 Do not take *a* of a hired man who is
1Th 4:6 should wrong his brother or take *a*

**ADVERSITY**
Pr 17:17 and a brother is born for *a*.

**ADVICE**
1Ki 12:8 rejected the *a* the elders
12:14 he followed the *a* of the young men
Pr 12:5 but the *a* of the wicked is deceitful.
12:15 but a wise man listens to *a*.
19:20 Listen to *a* and accept instruction,
20:18 Make plans by seeking *a;*

**AFFLICTION**
Ro 12:12 patient in *a*, faithful in prayer.

**AFRAID (FEAR)**
Ge 26:24 Do not be *a*, for I am with you;
Ex 3:6 because he was *a* to look at God.

Ps 27:1 of whom shall I be *a?*
56:3 When I am *a,* / I will trust in you.
Pr 3:24 lie down, you will not be *a;*
Jer 1:8 Do not be *a* of them, for I am
Mt 8:26 You of little faith, why are you so *a*
10:28 be *a* of the One who can destroy
10:31 So don't be *a;* you are worth more
Mk 5:36 "Don't be *a;* just believe."
Jn 14:27 hearts be troubled and do not be *a.*
Heb 13:6 Lord is my helper; I will not be *a.*

**AGED**
Job 12:12 Is not wisdom found among the *a?*
Pr 17:6 children are a crown to the *a,*

**AGREE**
Mt 18:19 on earth *a* about anything you ask
Ro 7:16 want to do, I *a* that the law is good.
Php 4:2 with Syntyche to *a* with each other

**AHAB**
Son of Omri; king of Israel (1Ki 16:28-22:40), husband of Jezebel (1Ki 16:31). Promoted Baal worship (1Ki 16:31-33); opposed by Elijah (1Ki 17:1; 18; 21), a prophet (1Ki 20:35-43), Micaiah (1Ki 22:1-28). Defeated Ben-Hadad (1Ki 20). Killed for failing to kill Ben-Hadad and for murder of Naboth (1Ki 20:35-21:40).

**AHAZ**
Son of Jotham; king of Judah, (2Ki 16; 2Ch 28; Isa 7).

**AHAZIAH**
1. Son of Ahab; king of Israel (1Ki 22:51-2Ki 1:18; 2Ch 20:35-37).
2. Son of Jehoram; king of Judah (2Ki 8:25-29; 9:14-29), also called Jehoahaz (2Ch 21:17-22:9; 25:23).

**AIM**
1Co 7:34 Her *a* is to be devoted to the Lord
2Co 13:11 *A* for perfection, listen

**AIR**
Mt 8:20 and birds of the *a* have nests,
1Co 9:26 not fight like a man beating the *a.*
Eph 2:2 of the ruler of the kingdom of the *a,*
1Th 4:17 clouds to meet the Lord in the *a.*

**ALABASTER**
Mt 26:7 came to him with an *a* jar

**ALERT**
Jos 8:4 All of you be on the *a.*
Mk 13:33 Be *a!* You do not know
Eph 6:18 be *a* and always keep on praying
1Th 5:6 but let us be *a* and self-controlled.

**ALIEN (ALIENATED)**
Ex 22:21 "Do not mistreat an *a*

**ALIENATED (ALIEN)**
Gal 5:4 by law have been *a* from Christ;

**ALIVE (LIVE)**
Ac 1:3 convincing proofs that he was *a.*
Ro 6:11 but *a* to God in Christ Jesus.
1Co 15:22 so in Christ all will be made *a.*

**ALMIGHTY (MIGHT)**
Ge 17:1 "I am God *A;* walk before me
Job 11:7 Can you probe the limits of the *A?*
33:4 the breath of the *A* gives me life.
Ps 91:1 will rest in the shadow of the *A.*
Isa 6:3 "Holy, holy, holy is the LORD *A;*

**ALTAR**
Ge 22:9 his son Isaac and laid him on the *a,*
Ex 27:1 "Build an *a* of acacia wood,
1Ki 18:30 and he repaired the *a* of the LORD
2Ch 4:1 made a bronze *a* twenty cubits
4:19 the golden *a;* the tables

**ALWAYS**
Ps 16:8 I have set the LORD *a* before me.
51:3 and my sin is *a* before me.
Mt 26:11 The poor you will *a* have with you,
28:20 And surely I will be with you *a,*
1Co 13:7 *a* protects, *a* trusts, *a* hopes, *a*
Php 4:4 Rejoice in the Lord *a.*
1Pe 3:15 *A* be prepared to give an answer

**AMAZIAH**
Son of Joash; king of Judah (2Ki 14; 2Ch 25).

**AMBASSADORS**
2Co 5:20 We are therefore Christ's *a,*

**AMBITION**
Ro 15:20 It has always been my *a*

1Th 4:11 Make it your *a* to lead a quiet life,

**AMON**
Son of Manasseh; king of Judah (2Ki 21:18-26; 1Ch 3:14; 2Ch 33:21-25).

**ANANIAS**
1. Husband of Sapphira; died for lying to God (Ac 5:1-11).
2. Disciple who baptized Saul (Ac 9:10-19).
3. High priest at Paul's arrest (Ac 22:30-24:1).

**ANCHOR**
Heb 6:19 We have this hope as an *a*

**ANCIENT**
Da 7:9 and the *A* of Days took his seat.

**ANDREW***
Apostle; brother of Simon Peter (Mt 4:18; 10:2; Mk 1:16-18, 29; 3:18; 13:3; Lk 6:14; Jn 1:35-44; 6:8-9; 12:22; Ac 1:13).

**ANGEL (ANGELS ARCHANGEL)**
Ps 34:7 The *a* of the LORD encamps
Ac 6:15 his face was like the face of an *a*.
2Co 11:14 Satan himself masquerades as an *a*
Gal 1:8 or an *a* from heaven should preach

**ANGELS (ANGEL)**
Ps 91:11 command his *a* concerning you
Mt 18:10 For I tell you that their *a*
25:41 prepared for the devil and his *a*.
Lk 20:36 for they are like the *a*.
1Co 6:3 you not know that we will judge *a*?
Heb 1:4 as much superior to the *a*
1:14 Are not all *a* ministering spirits
2:7 made him a little lower than the *a;*
13:2 some people have entertained *a*
1Pe 1:12 Even *a* long to look
2Pe 2:4 For if God did not spare *a*

**ANGER (ANGERED ANGRY)**
Ex 32:10 alone so that my *a* may burn
34:6 slow to *a*, abounding in love
Dt 29:28 In furious *a* and in great wrath
2Ki 22:13 Great is the LORD 's *a* that burns
Ps 30:5 For his *a* lasts only a moment,
Pr 15:1 but a harsh word stirs up *a*.
29:11 A fool gives full vent to his *a*,

**ANGERED (ANGER)**
Pr 22:24 do not associate with one easily *a*,
1Co 13:5 it is not easily *a*, it keeps no record

**ANGRY (ANGER)**
Ps 2:12 Kiss the Son, lest he be *a*
Pr 29:22 An *a* man stirs up dissension,
Jas 1:19 slow to speak and slow to become *a*

**ANGUISH**
Ps 118:5 In my *a* I cried to the LORD,

**ANOINT**
Ps 23:5 You *a* my head with oil;
Jas 5:14 and *a* him with oil in the name

**ANT***
Pr 6:6 Go to the *a*, you sluggard;

**ANTICHRIST**
1Jn 2:18 have heard that the *a* is coming,
2Jn :7 person is the deceiver and the *a*.

**ANTIOCH**
Ac 11:26 were called Christians first at *A*.

**ANXIETY (ANXIOUS)**
1Pe 5:7 Cast all your *a* on him

**ANXIOUS (ANXIETY)**
Pr 12:25 An *a* heart weighs a man down,
Php 4:6 Do not be *a* about anything,

**APOLLOS***
Christian from Alexandria, learned in the Scriptures; instructed by Aquila and Priscilla (Ac 18:24-28). Ministered at Corinth (Ac 19:1; 1Co 1:12; 3; Tit 3:13).

**APOSTLES**
See also Andrew, Bartholomew, James, John, Judas, Matthew, Nathanael, Paul, Peter, Philip, Simon, Thaddaeus, Thomas.
Mk 3:14 twelve—designating them *a*—
Ac 1:26 so he was added to the eleven *a*.
2:43 signs were done by the *a*.
1Co 12:28 God has appointed first of all *a*,
15:9 For I am the least of the *a*
2Co 11:13 masquerading as *a* of Christ.
Eph 2:20 built on the foundation of the *a*

**APPEAR (APPEARANCE APPEARING)**

Mk 13:22 false prophets will *a* and perform
2Co 5:10 we must all *a* before the judgment
Col 3:4 also will *a* with him in glory.
Heb 9:24 now to *a* for us in God's presence.
9:28 and he will *a* a second time,

**APPEARANCE (APPEAR)**

1Sa 16:7 Man looks at the outward *a*,
Gal 2:6 God does not judge by external *a*—

**APPEARING (APPEAR)**

2Ti 4:8 to all who have longed for his *a*.
Tit 2:13 the glorious *a* of our great God

**APPLY**

Pr 22:17 *a* your heart to what I teach,
23:12 *A* your heart to instruction

**APPROACH**

Eph 3:12 in him we may *a* God with freedom
Heb 4:16 Let us then *a* the throne of grace

**APPROVED**

2Ti 2:15 to present yourself to God as one *a*,

**AQUILA***

Husband of Priscilla; co-worker with Paul, instructor of Apollos (Ac 18; Ro 16:3; 1Co 16:19; 2Ti 4:19).

**ARARAT**

Ge 8:4 came to rest on the mountains of *A*.

**ARCHANGEL* (ANGEL)**

1Th 4:16 with the voice of the *a*
Jude :9 *a* Michael, when he was disputing

**ARCHITECT***

Heb 11:10 whose *a* and builder is God.

**ARK**

Ge 6:14 So make yourself an *a*
Dt 10:5 put the tablets in the *a* I had made,
2Ch 35:3 "Put the sacred *a* in the temple that
Heb 9:4 This *a* contained the gold jar

**ARM (ARMY)**

Nu 11:23 "Is the LORD's *a* too short?
1Pe 4:1 *a* yourselves also with the same

**ARMAGEDDON***

Rev 16:16 that in Hebrew is called *A*.

**ARMOR (ARMY)**

1Ki 20:11 on his *a* should not boast like one
Eph 6:11 Put on the full *a* of God
6:13 Therefore put on the full *a* of God,

**ARMS (ARMY)**

Dt 33:27 underneath are the everlasting *a*.
Ps 18:32 It is God who *a* me with strength
Pr 31:20 She opens her *a* to the poor
Isa 40:11 He gathers the lambs in his *a*
Mk 10:16 And he took the children in his *a*,

**ARMY (ARM ARMOR ARMS)**

Ps 33:16 No king is saved by the size of his *a*
Rev 19:19 the rider on the horse and his *a*.

**AROMA**

2Co 2:15 For we are to God the *a* of Christ

**ARRAYED***

Ps 110:3 *A* in holy majesty,
Isa 61:10 and *a* me in a robe of righteousness

**ARROGANT**

Ro 11:20 Do not be *a*, but be afraid.

**ARROWS**

Eph 6:16 you can extinguish all the flaming *a*

**ASA**

King of Judah (1Ki 15:8-24; 1Ch 3:10; 2Ch 14-16).

**ASCENDED**

Eph 4:8 "When he *a* on high,

**ASCRIBE**

1Ch 16:28 *a* to the LORD glory and strength,
Job 36:3 I will *a* justice to my Maker.
Ps 29:2 *A* to the LORD the glory due his

**ASHAMED (SHAME)**

Lk 9:26 If anyone is *a* of me and my words,
Ro 1:16 I am not *a* of the gospel,
2Ti 1:8 So do not be *a* to testify about our
2:15 who does not need to be *a*

**ASSIGNED**

Mk 13:34 with his *a* task, and tells the one
1Co 3:5 as the Lord has *a* to each his task.
7:17 place in life that the Lord *a* to him

**ASSOCIATE**

Pr 22:24 do not *a* with one easily angered,

Ro 12:16 but be willing to *a* with people
1Co 5:11 am writing you that you must not *a*
2Th 3:14 Do not *a* with him,

**ASSURANCE**
Heb 10:22 with a sincere heart in full *a* of faith

**ASTRAY**
Pr 10:17 ignores correction leads others *a*.
Isa 53:6 We all, like sheep, have gone *a*,
Jer 50:6 their shepherds have led them *a*
Jn 16:1 you so that you will not go *a*.
1Pe 2:25 For you were like sheep going *a*,
1Jn 3:7 do not let anyone lead you *a*.

**ATHALIAH**
Evil queen of Judah (2Ki 11; 2Ch 23).

**ATHLETE***
2Ti 2:5 if anyone competes as an *a*,

**ATONEMENT**
Ex 25:17 "Make an *a* cover of pure gold—
30:10 Once a year Aaron shall make *a*
Lev 17:11 it is the blood that makes *a*
23:27 this seventh month is the Day of *A*.
Nu 25:13 and made *a* for the Israelites."
Ro 3:25 presented him as a sacrifice of *a*,
Heb 2:17 that he might make *a* for the sins

**ATTENTION**
Pr 4:1 pay *a* and gain understanding.
Pr 5:1 My son, pay *a* to my wisdom,
22:17 Pay *a* and listen to the sayings
Tit 1:14 and will pay no *a* to Jewish myths

**ATTITUDE (ATTITUDES)**
Eph 4:23 new in the *a* of your minds;
Php 2:5 Your *a* should be the same
1Pe 4:1 yourselves also with the same *a*,

**ATTITUDES (ATTITUDE)**
Heb 4:12 it judges the thoughts and *a*

**ATTRACTIVE**
Tit 2:10 teaching about God our Savior *a*.

**AUTHORITIES (AUTHORITY)**
Ro 13:5 it is necessary to submit to the *a*,
13:6 for the *a* are God's servants,
Tit 3:1 people to be subject to rulers and *a*,
1Pe 3:22 *a* and powers in submission to him.

**AUTHORITY (AUTHORITIES)**
Mt 7:29 because he taught as one who had *a*
9:6 the Son of Man has *a* on earth
28:18 "All *a* in heaven and on earth has
Ro 13:1 for there is no *a* except that which
13:2 rebels against the *a* is rebelling
1Co 11:10 to have a sign of *a* on her head.
1Ti 2:2 for kings and all those in *a*,
1Ti 2:12 to teach or to have *a* over a man;
Heb 13:17 your leaders and submit to their *a*.

**AVENGE (VENGEANCE)**
Dt 32:35 It is mine to *a;* I will repay.

**AVOID**
Pr 20:3 It is to a man's honor to *a* strife,
20:19 so *a* a man who talks too much.
1Th 4:3 you should *a* sexual immorality;
5:22 *A* every kind of evil.
2Ti 2:16 *A* godless chatter, because those
Tit 3:9 But *a* foolish controversies

**AWAKE**
Ps 17:15 when I *a*, I will be satisfied

**AWE (AWESOME)**
Job 25:2 "Dominion and *a* belong to God;
Ps 119:120 I stand in *a* of your laws.
Ecc 5:7 Therefore stand in *a* of God.
Isa 29:23 will stand in *a* of the God of Israel.
Jer 33:9 they will be in *a* and will tremble
Hab 3:2 I stand in *a* of your deeds,
Mal 2:5 and stood in *a* of my name.
Mt 9:8 they were filled with *a;*
Lk 7:16 They were all filled with *a*
Ac 2:43 Everyone was filled with *a*,
Heb 12:28 acceptably with reverence and *a*,

**AWESOME (AWE)**
Ge 28:17 and said, "How *a* is this place!
Ex 15:11 *a* in glory,
Dt 7:21 is among you, is a great and *a* God.
10:17 the great God, mighty and *a*,
28:58 revere this glorious and *a* name—
Jdg 13:6 like an angel of God, very *a*.
Ne 1:5 of heaven, the great and *a* God,
9:32 the great, mighty and *a* God,
Job 10:16 again display your *a* power
37:22 God comes in *a* majesty.
Ps 45:4 let your right hand display *a* deeds.
47:2 How *a* is the LORD Most High,
66:5 how *a* his works in man's behalf!
68:35 You are *a*, O God,
89:7 he is more *a* than all who surround
99:3 praise your great and *a* name—
111:9 holy and *a* is his name.
145:6 of the power of your *a* works,
Da 9:4 "O Lord, the great and *a* God,

**BAAL**
1Ki 18:25 Elijah said to the prophets of *B*,

**BAASHA**
King of Israel (1Ki 15:16-16:7; 2Ch 16:1-6).

**BABIES (BABY)**
Lk 18:15 also bringing *b* to Jesus
1Pe 2:2 Like newborn *b*, crave pure

**BABY (BABIES)**
Isa 49:15 "Can a mother forget the *b*
Lk 1:44 the *b* in my womb leaped for joy.
2:12 You will find a *b* wrapped in strips
Jn 16:21 but when her *b* is born she forgets

**BABYLON**
Ps 137:1 By the rivers of *B* we sat and wept

**BACKSLIDING**
Jer 3:22 I will cure you of *b*."
14:7 For our *b* is great;
Eze 37:23 them from all their sinful *b*,

**BALAAM**
Prophet who attempted to curse Israel (Nu 22-24; Dt 23:4-5; 2Pe 2:15; Jude 11). Killed (Nu 31:8; Jos 13:22).

**BALM**
Jer 8:22 Is there no *b* in Gilead?

**BANISH**
Jer 25:10 I will *b* from them the sounds of joy

**BANQUET**
SS 2:4 He has taken me to the *b* hall,
Lk 14:13 when you give a *b*, invite the poor,

**BAPTIZE (BAPTIZED)**
Mt 3:11 He will *b* you with the Holy Spirit
Mk 1:8 he will *b* you with the Holy Spirit."
1Co 1:17 For Christ did not send me to *b*,

**BAPTIZED (BAPTIZE)**
Mt 3:6 they were *b* by him in the Jordan
Mk 1:9 and was *b* by John in the Jordan.
10:38 or be *b* with the baptism I am
16:16 believes and is *b* will be saved,
Jn 4:2 in fact it was not Jesus who *b*,
Ac 1:5 but in a few days you will be *b*

**BARABBAS**
Mt 27:26 Then he released *B* to them.

**BARBS***
Nu 33:55 allow to remain will become *b*

**BARE**
Heb 4:13 and laid *b* before the eyes of him

**BARNABAS***
Disciple, originally Joseph (Ac 4:36), prophet (Ac 13:1), apostle (Ac 14:14). Brought Paul to apostles (Ac 9:27), Antioch (Ac 11:22-29; Gal 2:1-13), on the first missionary journey (Ac 13-14). Together at Jerusalem Council, they separated over John Mark (Ac 15). Later co-workers (1Co 9:6; Col 4:10).

**BARREN**
Ps 113:9 He settles the *b* woman

**BARTHOLOMEW***
Apostle (Mt 10:3; Mk 3:18; Lk 6:14; Ac 1:13). Possibly also known as Nathanael (Jn 1:45-49; 21:2).

**BATH**
Jn 13:10 person who has had a *b* needs only

**BATHSHEBA**
Wife of Uriah who committed adultery with and became wife of David (2Sa 11), mother of Solomon (2Sa 12:24; 1Ki 1-2; 1Ch 3:5).

**BATTLE**
2Ch 20:15 For the *b* is not yours, but God's.

Ps 24:8 the LORD mighty in *b*.
Ecc 9:11 or the *b* to the strong,

**BEAR (BEARING BIRTH BIRTHRIGHT BORN FIRSTBORN NEWBORN)**
Ge 4:13 punishment is more than I can *b*.
Ps 38:4 like a burden too heavy to *b*.
Isa 53:11 and he will *b* their iniquities.
Da 7:5 beast, which looked like a *b*.
Mt 7:18 A good tree cannot *b* bad fruit,
Jn 15:2 branch that does *b* fruit he prunes
15:16 and appointed you to go and *b* fruit—
Ro 15:1 ought to *b* with the failings
1Co 10:13 tempted beyond what you can *b*.
Col 3:13 *B* with each other and forgive

**BEARING (BEAR)**
Eph 4:2 *b* with one another in love.
Col 1:10 *b* fruit in every good work,

**BEAST**
Rev 13:18 him calculate the number of the *b*,

**BEAT (BEATING)**
Isa 2:4 They will *b* their swords
Joel 3:10 *B* your plowshares into swords
1Co 9:27 I *b* my body and make it my slave

**BEATING (BEAT)**
1Co 9:26 I do not fight like a man *b* the air.

1Pe 2:20 if you receive a *b* for doing wrong

**BEAUTIFUL (BEAUTY)**
Ge 6:2 that the daughters of men were *b*,
12:11 "I know what a *b* woman you are.
12:14 saw that she was a very *b* woman.
24:16 The girl was very *b*, a virgin;
26:7 of Rebekah, because she is *b*."
29:17 Rachel was lovely in form, and *b*.
Job 38:31 "Can you bind the *b* Pleiades?
Pr 11:22 is a *b* woman who shows no
Ecc 3:11 He has made everything *b*
Isa 4:2 of the LORD will be *b*
52:7 How *b* on the mountains
Eze 20:6 and honey, the most *b* of all lands.
Zec 9:17 How attractive and *b* they will be!
Mt 23:27 which look *b* on the outside
26:10 She has done a *b* thing to me.
Ro 10:15 "How *b* are the feet
1Pe 3:5 in God used to make themselves *b*.

**BEAUTY (BEAUTIFUL)**
Ps 27:4 to gaze upon the *b* of the LORD
45:11 The king is enthralled by your *b*;
Pr 31:30 is deceptive, and *b* is fleeting;
Isa 33:17 Your eyes will see the king in his *b*
53:2 He had no *b* or majesty
61:3 to bestow on them a crown of *b*
Eze 28:12 full of wisdom and perfect in *b*.
1Pe 3:4 the unfading *b* of a gentle

**BED**
Heb 13:4 and the marriage *b* kept pure,

**BEELZEBUB**
Lk 11:15 "By *B*, the prince of demons,

**BEER**
Pr 20:1 Wine is a mocker and *b* a brawler;

**BEERSHEBA**
Jdg 20:1 all the Israelites from Dan to *B*

**BEGINNING**
Ge 1:1 In the *b* God created the heavens
Ps 102:25 In the *b* you laid the foundations
111:10 of the LORD is the *b* of wisdom;
Pr 1:7 of the LORD is the *b* of knowledge
Jn 1:1 In the *b* was the Word,
1Jn 1:1 That which was from the *b*,
Rev 21:6 and the Omega, the *B* and the End.

**BEHAVE**
Ro 13:13 Let us *b* decently, as in the daytime

**BELIEVE (BELIEVED BELIEVER BELIEVERS BELIEVES BELIEVING)**
Mt 18:6 one of these little ones who *b* in me
21:22 If you *b*, you will receive whatever
Mk 1:15 Repent and *b* the good news!"

Mk 9:24 “I do *b;* help me overcome my
16:17 signs will accompany those who *b:*
Lk 8:50 just *b,* and she will be healed.”
24:25 to *b* all that the prophets have
Jn 1:7 that through him all men might *b.*
3:18 does not *b* stands condemned
6:29 to *b* in the one he has sent.”
10:38 you do not *b* me, *b* the miracles,
11:27 “I *b* that you are the Christ,
14:11 *B* me when I say that I am
16:30 This makes us *b* that you came
16:31 “You *b* at last!” Jesus answered.
17:21 that the world may *b* that you have
20:27 Stop doubting and *b.*”
20:31 written that you may *b* that Jesus is
Ac 16:31 They replied, “*B* in the Lord Jesus,
24:14 I *b* everything that agrees
Ro 3:22 faith in Jesus Christ to all who *b.*
4:11 he is the father of all who *b*
10:9 *b* in your heart that God raised him
10:14 And how can they *b* in the one
16:26 so that all nations might *b*
1Th 4:14 We *b* that Jesus died and rose again
2Th 2:11 delusion so that they will *b* the lie
1Ti 4:10 and especially of those who *b.*
Tit 1:6 a man whose children *b*
Heb 11:6 comes to him must *b* that he exists
Jas 2:19 Even the demons *b* that—
1Jn 4:1 Dear friends, do not *b* every spirit,

**BELIEVED (BELIEVE)**

Ge 15:6 Abram *b* the LORD, and he
Jnh 3:5 The Ninevites *b* God.
Jn 1:12 to those who *b* in his name,
2:22 Then they *b* the Scripture
3:18 because he has not *b* in the name
20:8 He saw and *b.*
20:29 who have not seen and yet have *b.*”
Ac 13:48 were appointed for eternal life *b.*
Ro 4:3 Scripture say? “Abraham *b* God,
10:14 call on the one they have not *b* in?
1Co 15:2 Otherwise, you have *b* in vain.
Gal 3:6 Consider Abraham: “He *b* God,
2Ti 1:12 because I know whom I have *b,*
Jas 2:23 that says, “Abraham *b* God,

**BELIEVER (BELIEVE)**

1Co 7:12 brother has a wife who is not a *b*
2Co 6:15 What does a *b* have in common

**BELIEVERS (BELIEVE)**

Ac 4:32 All the *b* were one in heart
5:12 And all the *b* used to meet together
1Co 6:5 to judge a dispute between *b?*
1Ti 4:12 set an example for the *b* in speech,
1Pe 2:17 Love the brotherhood of *b,*

**BELIEVES (BELIEVE)**

Pr 14:15 A simple man *b* anything,
Mk 9:23 is possible for him who *b.*”
11:23 *b* that what he says will happen,
16:16 Whoever *b* and is baptized will be
Jn 3:16 that whoever *b* in him shall not
3:36 Whoever *b* in the Son has eternal
5:24 *b* him who sent me has eternal life
6:35 and he who *b* in me will never be
6:40 and *b* in him shall have eternal life,
6:47 he who *b* has everlasting life.
7:38 Whoever *b* in me, as the Scripture
11:26 and *b* in me will never die.
Ro 1:16 for the salvation of everyone who *b*
10:4 righteousness for everyone who *b.*
1Jn 5:1 Everyone who *b* that Jesus is
5:5 Only he who *b* that Jesus is the Son

**BELIEVING (BELIEVE)**

Jn 20:31 and that by *b* you may have life

**BELONG (BELONGS)**

Dt 29:29 The secret things *b*
Job 25:2 “Dominion and awe *b* to God;
Ps 47:9 for the kings of the earth *b* to God;

Ps 95:4 and the mountain peaks *b* to him.
Jn 8:44 You *b* to your father, the devil,
15:19 As it is, you do not *b* to the world,
Ro 1:6 called to *b* to Jesus Christ.
7:4 that you might *b* to another,
14:8 we live or die, we *b* to the Lord.
Gal 5:24 Those who *b* to Christ Jesus have
1Th 5:8 But since we *b* to the day, let us be

**BELONGS (BELONG)**
Job 41:11 Everything under heaven *b* to me.
Ps 111:10 To him *b* eternal praise.
Eze 18:4 For every living soul *b* to me,
Jn 8:47 He who *b* to God hears what God
Ro 12:5 each member *b* to all the others.

**BELOVED (LOVE)**
Dt 33:12 "Let the *b* of the LORD rest secure

**BELT**
Isa 11:5 Righteousness will be his *b*
Eph 6:14 with the *b* of truth buckled

**BENEFIT (BENEFITS)**
Ro 6:22 the *b* you reap leads to holiness,
2Co 4:15 All this is for your *b*,

**BENEFITS (BENEFIT)**
Ps 103:2 and forget not all his *b*.
Jn 4:38 you have reaped the *b* of their labor

**BENJAMIN**
Twelfth son of Jacob by Rachel (Ge 35:16-24; 46:19-21; 1Ch 2:2). Jacob refused to send him to Egypt, but relented (Ge 42-45).

**BEREANS***
Ac 17:11 the *B* were of more noble character

**BESTOWS**
Ps 84:11 the LORD *b* favor and honor;

**BETHLEHEM**
Mt 2:1 After Jesus was born in *B* in Judea,

**BETRAY**
Pr 25:9 do not *b* another man's confidence,

**BIND (BINDS)**
Dt 6:8 and *b* them on your foreheads.
Pr 6:21 *B* them upon your heart forever;
Isa 61:1 me to *b* up the brokenhearted,
Mt 16:19 whatever you *b* on earth will be

**BINDS (BIND)**
Ps 147:3 and *b* up their wounds.
Isa 30:26 when the LORD *b* up the bruises

**BIRDS**
Mt 8:20 and *b* of the air have nests,

**BIRTH (BEAR)**
Ps 58:3 Even from *b* the wicked go astray;
Mt 1:18 This is how the *b* of Jesus Christ
1Pe 1:3 great mercy he has given us new *b*

**BIRTHRIGHT (BEAR)**
Ge 25:34 So Esau despised his *b*.

**BLAMELESS**
Ge 17:1 walk before me and be *b*.
Job 1:1 This man was *b* and upright;
Ps 84:11 from those whose walk is *b*.
119:1 Blessed are they whose ways are *b*,
Pr 19:1 Better a poor man whose walk is *b*
1Co 1:8 so that you will be *b* on the day
Eph 5:27 any other blemish, but holy and *b*.
Php 2:15 so that you may become *b* and pure
1Th 3:13 hearts so that you will be *b*
5:23 and body be kept *b* at the coming
Tit 1:6 An elder must be *b*, the husband of
Heb 7:26 *b*, pure, set apart from sinners,
2Pe 3:14 effort to be found spotless, *b*

**BLASPHEMES**
Mk 3:29 whoever *b* against the Holy Spirit

**BLEMISH**
1Pe 1:19 a lamb without *b* or defect.

**BLESS (BLESSED BLESSING BLESSINGS)**
Ge 12:3 I will *b* those who *b* you,
Ro 12:14 Bless those who persecute you; *b*

**BLESSED (BLESS)**
Ge 1:22 God *b* them and said, "Be fruitful
2:3 And God *b* the seventh day
22:18 nations on earth will be *b*,
Ps 1:1 *B* is the man
2:12 *B* are all who take refuge in him.

Ps 33:12 *B* is the nation whose God is
41:1 *B* is he who has regard for the weak
84:5 *B* are those whose strength is
106:3 *B* are they who maintain justice,
112:1 *B* is the man who fears the LORD,
118:26 *B* is he who comes in the name
Pr 29:18 but *b* is he who keeps the law.
31:28 Her children arise and call her *b;*
Mt 5:3 saying: "*B* are the poor in spirit,
5:4 *B* are those who mourn,
5:5 *B* are the meek,
5:6 *B* are those who hunger
5:7 *B* are the merciful,
5:8 *B* are the pure in heart,
5:9 *B* are the peacemakers,
5:10 *B* are those who are persecuted
5:11 "*B* are you when people insult you,
Lk 1:48 on all generations will call me *b,*
Jn 12:13 "*B* is he who comes in the name
Ac 20:35 'It is more *b* to give than to receive
Tit 2:13 while we wait for the *b* hope—
Jas 1:12 *B* is the man who perseveres
Rev 1:3 *B* is the one who reads the words
22:14 "*B* are those who wash their robes,

**BLESSING (BLESS)**

Eze 34:26 there will be showers of *b.*

**BLESSINGS (BLESS)**

Pr 10:6 *B* crown the head of the righteous,

**BLIND**

Mt 15:14 a *b* man leads a *b* man, both will fall
23:16 "Woe to you, *b* guides! You say,
Jn 9:25 I was *b* but now I see!"

**BLOOD**

Ge 9:6 "Whoever sheds the *b* of man,
Ex 12:13 and when I see the *b,* I will pass
24:8 "This is the *b* of the covenant that
Lev 17:11 For the life of a creature is in the *b,*
Ps 72:14 for precious is their *b* in his sight.
Pr 6:17 hands that shed innocent *b,*
Mt 26:28 This is my *b* of the covenant,
Ro 3:25 of atonement, through faith in his *b*
5:9 have now been justified by his *b,*
1Co 11:25 cup is the new covenant in my *b;*
Eph 1:7 we have redemption through his *b,*
2:13 near through the *b* of Christ.
Col 1:20 by making peace through his *b,*
Heb 9:12 once for all by his own *b,*
9:22 of *b* there is no forgiveness.
1Pe 1:19 but with the precious *b* of Christ,
1Jn 1:7 and the *b* of Jesus, his Son,
Rev 1:5 has freed us from our sins by his *b,*
5:9 with your *b* you purchased men
7:14 white in the *b* of the Lamb.
12:11 him by the *b* of the Lamb

**BLOT (BLOTS)**

Ex 32:32 then *b* me out of the book you have
Ps 51:1 *b* out my transgressions.
Rev 3:5 I will never *b* out his name

**BLOTS (BLOT)**

Isa 43:25 "I, even I, am he who *b* out

**BLOWN**

Eph 4:14 and *b* here and there by every wind
Jas 1:6 doubts is like a wave of the sea, *b*

**BOAST**

1Ki 20:11 armor should not *b* like one who
Ps 34:2 My soul will *b* in the LORD;
44:8 In God we make our *b* all day long,
Pr 27:1 Do not *b* about tomorrow,
1Co 1:31 Let him who boasts *b* in the Lord."
Gal 6:14 May I never *b* except in the cross
Eph 2:9 not by works, so that no one can *b.*

**BOAZ**

Wealthy Bethlehemite who showed favor to Ruth (Ru 2), married her (Ru 4). Ancestor of David (Ru 4:18-22; 1Ch 2:12-15), Jesus (Mt 1:5-16; Lk 3:23-32).

**BODIES (BODY)**
Ro 12:1 to offer your *b* as living sacrifices,
1Co 6:15 not know that your *b* are members
Eph 5:28 to love their wives as their own *b*.

**BODY (BODIES)**
Zec 13:6 What are these wounds on your *b*?'
Mt 10:28 afraid of those who kill the *b*
26:26 saying, "Take and eat; this is my *b*
26:41 spirit is willing, but the *b* is weak."
Jn 13:10 wash his feet; his whole *b* is clean.
Ro 6:13 Do not offer the parts of your *b*
12:4 us has one *b* with many members,
1Co 6:19 not know that your *b* is a temple
11:24 "This is my *b*, which is for you;
12:12 The *b* is a unit, though it is made up
Eph 5:30 for we are members of his *b*.

**BOLD (BOLDNESS)**
Ps 138:3 you made me *b* and stouthearted.
Pr 21:29 A wicked man puts up a *b* front,
28:1 but the righteous are as *b* as a lion.

**BOLDNESS* (BOLD)**
Ac 4:29 to speak your word with great *b*.

**BONDAGE**
Ezr 9:9 God has not deserted us in our *b*.

**BOOK (BOOKS)**
Jos 1:8 Do not let this *B* of the Law depart
Ne 8:8 They read from the *B* of the Law
Jn 20:30 which are not recorded in this *b*.
Php 4:3 whose names are in the *b* of life.
Rev 21:27 written in the Lamb's *b* of life.

**BOOKS (BOOK)**
Ecc 12:12 Of making many *b* there is no end,

**BORN (BEAR)**
Isa 9:6 For to us a child is *b*,
Jn 3:7 at my saying, 'You must be *b* again
1Pe 1:23 For you have been *b* again,
1Jn 4:7 Everyone who loves has been *b*
5:1 believes that Jesus is the Christ is *b*

**BORROWER**
Pr 22:7 and the *b* is servant to the lender.

**BOUGHT**
Ac 20:28 which he *b* with his own blood.
1Co 6:20 You are not your own; you were *b*
7:23 You were *b* at a price; do not
2Pe 2:1 the sovereign Lord who *b* them—

**BOW**
Ps 95:6 Come, let us *b* down in worship,
Isa 45:23 Before me every knee will *b*;
Ro 14:11 'every knee will *b* before me;
Php 2:10 name of Jesus every knee should *b*,

**BRANCH (BRANCHES)**
Isa 4:2 In that day the *B* of the LORD will
Jer 33:15 I will make a righteous *B* sprout

**BRANCHES (BRANCH)**
Jn 15:5 "I am the vine; you are the *b*.

**BRAVE**
2Sa 2:7 Now then, be strong and *b*,

**BREAD**
Dt 8:3 that man does not live on *b* alone
Pr 30:8 but give me only my daily *b*.
Ecc 11:1 Cast your *b* upon the waters,
Isa 55:2 Why spend money on what is not *b*
Mt 4:4 'Man does not live on *b* alone,
6:11 Give us today our daily *b*.
Jn 6:35 Jesus declared, "I am the *b* of life.
21:13 took the *b* and gave it to them,
1Co 11:23 took *b*, and when he had given

**BREAK (BREAKING BROKEN)**
Nu 30:2 he must not *b* his word
Jdg 2:1 'I will never *b* my covenant
Isa 42:3 A bruised reed he will not *b*,
Mt 12:20 A bruised reed he will not *b*,

**BREAKING (BREAK)**
Jas 2:10 at just one point is guilty of *b* all

**BREASTPIECE (BREASTPLATE)**
Ex 28:15 Fashion a *b* for making decisions—

**BREASTPLATE* (BREASTPIECE)**
Isa 59:17 He put on righteousness as his *b*,
Eph 6:14 with the *b* of righteousness in place
1Th 5:8 putting on faith and love as a *b*,

**BREATHED (GOD-BREATHED)**
Ge 2:7 *b* into his nostrils the breath of life,
Jn 20:22 And with that he *b* on them

**BREEDS***
Pr 13:10 Pride only *b* quarrels,

**BRIBE**
Ex 23:8 "Do not accept a *b*,
Pr 6:35 will refuse the *b*, however great it

**BRIDE**
Rev 19:7 and his *b* has made herself ready,

**BRIGHTER (BRIGHTNESS)**
Pr 4:18 shining ever *b* till the full light

**BRIGHTNESS (BRIGHTER)**
2Sa 22:13 Out of the *b* of his presence
Da 12:3 who are wise will shine like the *b*

**BROAD**
Mt 7:13 and *b* is the road that leads

**BROKEN (BREAK)**
Ps 51:17 The sacrifices of God are a *b* spirit;
Ecc 4:12 of three strands is not quickly *b*.
Jn 10:35 and the Scripture cannot be *b*—

**BROKENHEARTED* (HEART)**
Ps 34:18 The LORD is close to the *b*
109:16 and the needy and the *b*.
147:3 He heals the *b*
Isa 61:1 He has sent me to bind up the *b*,

**BROTHER (BROTHER'S BROTHERS)**
Pr 17:17 and a *b* is born for adversity.
18:24 a friend who sticks closer than a *b*.
27:10 neighbor nearby than a *b* far away.
Mt 5:24 and be reconciled to your *b*;
18:15 "If your *b* sins against you,
Mk 3:35 Whoever does God's will is my *b*
Lk 17:3 "If your *b* sins, rebuke him,
1Co 8:13 if what I eat causes my *b* to fall
1Jn 2:10 Whoever loves his *b* lives
4:21 loves God must also love his *b*.

**BROTHER'S (BROTHER)**
Ge 4:9 "Am I my *b* keeper?" The LORD

**BROTHERS (BROTHER)**
Ps 133:1 is when *b* live together in unity!
Pr 6:19 who stirs up dissension among *b*.
Mt 25:40 one of the least of these *b* of mine,
Mk 10:29 or *b* or sisters or mother or father
Heb 13:1 Keep on loving each other as *b*.
1Pe 3:8 be sympathetic, love as *b*,
1Jn 3:14 death to life, because we love our *b*.

**BUILD (BUILDING BUILDS BUILT)**
Mt 16:18 and on this rock I will *b* my church,
Ac 20:32 which can *b* you up and give you
1Co 14:12 excel in gifts that *b* up the church.
1Th 5:11 one another and *b* each other up,

**BUILDING (BUILD)**
1Co 3:9 you are God's field, God's *b*.
2Co 10:8 us for *b* you up rather
Eph 4:29 helpful for *b* others up according

**BUILDS (BUILD)**
Ps 127:1 Unless the LORD *b* the house,
1Co 3:10 one should be careful how he *b*.
8:1 Knowledge puffs up, but love *b* up.

**BUILT (BUILD)**
Mt 7:24 is like a wise man who *b* his house
Eph 2:20 *b* on the foundation of the apostles
4:12 the body of Christ may be *b* up

**BURDEN (BURDENED BURDENS)**

Ps 38:4 like a *b* too heavy to bear.
Mt 11:30 my yoke is easy and my *b* is light."

**BURDENED (BURDEN)**

Gal 5:1 do not let yourselves be *b* again

**BURDENS (BURDEN)**

Ps 68:19 who daily bears our *b.*
Gal 6:2 Carry each other's *b,*

**BURIED**

Ro 6:4 *b* with him through baptism
1Co 15:4 that he was *b,* that he was raised

**BURNING**

Lev 6:9 the fire must be kept *b* on the altar.
Ro 12:20 you will heap *b* coals on his head."

**BUSINESS**

Da 8:27 and went about the king's *b.*
1Th 4:11 to mind your own *b* and to work

**BUSY**

1Ki 20:40 While your servant was *b* here
2Th 3:11 They are not *b;* they are
Tit 2:5 to be *b* at home, to be kind,

**CAESAR**

Mt 22:21 "Give to *C* what is Caesar's,

**CAIN**

Firstborn of Adam (Ge 4:1), murdered brother Abel (Ge 4:1-16; 1Jn 3:12).

**CALEB**

Judahite who spied out Canaan (Nu 13:6); allowed to enter land because of faith (Nu 13:30-14:38; Dt 1:36). Possessed Hebron (Jos 14:6-15:19).

**CALF**

Ex 32:4 into an idol cast in the shape of a *c,*
Lk 15:23 Bring the fattened *c* and kill it.

**CALL (CALLED CALLING CALLS)**

Ps 105:1 to the LORD, *c* on his name;
145:18 near to all who *c* on him,
Pr 31:28 children arise and *c* her blessed;
Isa 5:20 Woe to those who *c* evil good
55:6 *c* on him while he is near.
65:24 Before they *c* I will answer;
Jer 33:3 '*C* to me and I will answer you
Mt 9:13 come to *c* the righteous,
Ro 10:12 and richly blesses all who *c* on him,
11:29 gifts and his *c* are irrevocable.
1Th 4:7 For God did not *c* us to be impure,

**CALLED (CALL)**

1Sa 3:5 and said, "Here I am; you *c* me."
2Ch 7:14 if my people, who are *c*
Ps 34:6 This poor man *c,* and the LORD
Mt 21:13 " 'My house will be *c* a house
Ro 8:30 And those he predestined, he also *c*
1Co 7:15 God has *c* us to live in peace.
Gal 5:13 You, my brothers, were *c* to be free
1Pe 2:9 of him who *c* you out of darkness

**CALLING (CALL)**

Jn 1:23 I am the voice of one *c* in the desert
Ac 22:16 wash your sins away, *c* on his name
Eph 4:1 worthy of the *c* you have received.
2Pe 1:10 all the more eager to make your *c*

**CALLS (CALL)**

Joel 2:32 And everyone who *c*
Jn 10:3 He *c* his own sheep by name
Ro 10:13 "Everyone who *c* on the name

**CAMEL**

Mt 19:24 it is easier for a *c* to go
23:24 strain out a gnat but swallow a *c.*

**CANAAN**

1Ch 16:18 "To you I will give the land of *C*

**CANCELED**

Lk 7:42 so he *c* the debts of both.
Col 2:14 having *c* the written code,

**CAPITAL**

Dt 21:22 guilty of a *c* offense is put to death

**CAPSTONE (STONE)**

Ps 118:22 has become the *c;*
1Pe 2:7 has become the *c,*"

**CARE (CAREFUL CARES CARING)**

Ps 8:4 the son of man that you *c* for him?

Pr 29:7 The righteous *c* about justice
Lk 10:34 him to an inn and took *c* of him.
Jn 21:16 Jesus said, "Take *c* of my sheep."
Heb 2:6 the son of man that you *c* for him?
1Pe 5:2 of God's flock that is under your *c*,

**CAREFUL (CARE)**
Ex 23:13 "Be *c* to do everything I have said
Dt 6:3 be *c* to obey so that it may go well
Jos 23:6 be *c* to obey all that is written
23:11 be very *c* to love the LORD your
Pr 13:24 he who loves him is *c*
Mt 6:1 "Be *c* not to do your 'acts
Ro 12:17 Be *c* to do what is right in the eyes
1Co 3:10 each one should be *c* how he builds
8:9 Be *c*, however, that the exercise
Eph 5:15 Be very *c*, then, how you live—

**CARELESS**
Mt 12:36 for every *c* word they have spoken.

**CARES (CARE)**
Ps 55:22 Cast your *c* on the LORD
Na 1:7 He *c* for those who trust in him,
Eph 5:29 but he feeds and *c* for it, just
1Pe 5:7 on him because he *c* for you.

**CARING* (CARE)**
1Th 2:7 like a mother *c* for her little
1Ti 5:4 practice by *c* for their own family

**CARRIED (CARRY)**
Ex 19:4 and how I *c* you on eagles' wings
Isa 53:4 and *c* our sorrows,
Heb 13:9 Do not be *c* away by all kinds
2Pe 1:21 as they were *c* along by the Holy

**CARRIES (CARRY)**
Dt 32:11 and *c* them on its pinions.
Isa 40:11 and *c* them close to his heart;

**CARRY (CARRIED CARRIES)**
Lk 14:27 anyone who does not *c* his cross
Gal 6:2 *C* each other's burdens,
6:5 for each one should *c* his own load.

**CAST**
Ps 22:18 and *c* lots for my clothing.
55:22 *C* your cares on the LORD
Ecc 11:1 *C* your bread upon the waters,
Jn 19:24 and *c* lots for my clothing."
1Pe 5:7 *C* all your anxiety on him

**CATCH (CAUGHT)**
Lk 5:10 from now on you will *c* men."

**CATTLE**
Ps 50:10 and the *c* on a thousand hills.

**CAUGHT (CATCH)**
1Th 4:17 and are left will be *c* up together

**CAUSE (CAUSES)**
Pr 24:28 against your neighbor without *c*,
Ecc 8:3 Do not stand up for a bad *c*,
Mt 18:7 of the things that *c* people to sin!
Ro 14:21 else that will *c* your brother
1Co 10:32 Do not *c* anyone to stumble,

**CAUSES (CAUSE)**
Isa 8:14 a stone that *c* men to stumble
Mt 18:6 if anyone *c* one of these little ones

**CAUTIOUS***
Pr 12:26 A righteous man is *c* in friendship,

**CEASE**
Ps 46:9 He makes wars *c* to the ends

**CENSER**
Lev 16:12 is to take a *c* full of burning coals

**CENTURION**
Mt 8:5 had entered Capernaum, a *c* came

**CERTAIN (CERTAINTY)**
2Pe 1:19 word of the prophets made more *c*,

**CERTAINTY* (CERTAIN)**
Lk 1:4 so that you may know the *c*
Jn 17:8 They knew with *c* that I came

**CHAFF**
Ps 1:4 They are like *c*

**CHAINED**
2Ti 2:9 But God's word is not *c*.

**CHAMPION**
Ps 19:5 like a *c* rejoicing to run his course.

**CHANGE (CHANGED)**
1Sa 15:29 of Israel does not lie or *c* his mind;
Ps 110:4 and will not *c* his mind:
Jer 7:5 If you really *c* your ways
Mal 3:6 "I the LORD do not *c*.
Mt 18:3 unless you *c* and become like little
Heb 7:21 and will not *c* his mind:
Jas 1:17 who does not *c* like shifting

**CHANGED (CHANGE)**
1Co 15:51 but we will all be *c*—in a flash,

**CHARACTER**
Ru 3:11 that you are a woman of noble *c*.
Pr 31:10 A wife of noble *c* who can find?
Ro 5:4 perseverance, *c*; and *c*, hope.
1Co 15:33 "Bad company corrupts good *c*."

**CHARGE**
Ro 8:33 Who will bring any *c*
2Co 11:7 the gospel of God to you free of *c*?
2Ti 4:1 I give you this *c*: Preach the Word;

**CHARIOTS**
2Ki 6:17 and *c* of fire all around Elisha.
Ps 20:7 Some trust in *c* and some in horses,

**CHARM**
Pr 31:30 *C* is deceptive, and beauty is

**CHASES**
Pr 12:11 he who *c* fantasies lacks judgment.

**CHATTER* (CHATTERING)**
1Ti 6:20 Turn away from godless *c*
2Ti 2:16 Avoid godless *c*, because those

**CHATTERING* (CHATTER)**
Pr 10:8 but a *c* fool comes to ruin.
10:10 and a *c* fool comes to ruin.

**CHEAT* (CHEATED)**
Mal 1:14 "Cursed is the *c* who has
1Co 6:8 you yourselves *c* and do wrong,

**CHEATED (CHEAT)**
Lk 19:8 if I have *c* anybody out of anything,
1Co 6:7 Why not rather be *c*? Instead,

**CHEEK**
Mt 5:39 someone strikes you on the right *c*,

**CHEERFUL* (CHEERS)**
Pr 15:13 A happy heart makes the face *c*,
15:15 but the *c* heart has a continual feast
15:30 A *c* look brings joy to the heart,
17:22 A *c* heart is good medicine,
2Co 9:7 for God loves a *c* giver.

**CHEERS (CHEERFUL)**
Pr 12:25 but a kind word *c* him up.

**CHILD (CHILDISH CHILDREN)**
Pr 20:11 Even a *c* is known by his actions,
22:6 Train a *c* in the way he should go,
22:15 Folly is bound up in the heart of a *c*
23:13 not withhold discipline from a *c*;
29:15 *c* left to himself disgraces his mother.
Isa 7:14 The virgin will be with *c*
9:6 For to us a *c* is born,
11:6 and a little *c* will lead them.
66:13 As a mother comforts her *c*,
Mt 1:23 "The virgin will be with *c*
18:2 He called a little *c* and had him
Lk 1:42 and blessed is the *c* you will bear!
1:80 And the *c* grew and became strong
1Co 13:11 When I was a *c*, I talked like a *c*,
1Jn 5:1 who loves the father loves his *c*

**CHILDISH* (CHILD)**
1Co 13:11 When I became a man, I put *c* ways

**CHILDREN (CHILD)**
Dt 4:9 Teach them to your *c*
11:19 them to your *c*, talking about them
Ps 8:2 From the lips of *c* and infants
Pr 17:6 Children's *c* are a crown
31:28 Her *c* arise and call her blessed;
Mt 7:11 how to give good gifts to your *c*,
11:25 and revealed them to little *c*.
18:3 you change and become like little *c*
19:14 "Let the little *c* come to me,

Mt 21:16 " 'From the lips of *c* and infants
Mk 9:37 one of these little *c* in my name
10:14 "Let the little *c* come to me,
10:16 And he took the *c* in his arms,
13:12 *C* will rebel against their parents
Lk 10:21 and revealed them to little *c*.
18:16 "Let the little *c* come to me,
Ro 8:16 with our spirit that we are God's *c*.
2Co 12:14 parents, but parents for their *c*.
Eph 6:1 *C*, obey your parents in the Lord,
6:4 do not exasperate your *c*; instead,
Col 3:20 *C*, obey your parents in everything,
3:21 Fathers, do not embitter your *c*,
1Ti 3:4 and see that his *c* obey him
3:12 and must manage his *c* and his
5:10 bringing up *c*, showing hospitality,
1Jn 3:1 that we should be called *c* of God!

## CHOOSE (CHOOSES CHOSE CHOSEN)

Dt 30:19 Now *c* life, so that you
Jos 24:15 then *c* for yourselves this day
Pr 8:10 *C* my instruction instead of silver,
16:16 to *c* understanding rather
Jn 15:16 You did not *c* me, but I chose you

## CHOOSES (CHOOSE)

Jn 7:17 If anyone *c* to do God's will,

## CHOSE (CHOOSE)

Ge 13:11 So Lot *c* for himself the whole plain
Ps 33:12 the people he *c* for his inheritance.
Jn 15:16 but I *c* you and appointed you to go
1Co 1:27 But God *c* the foolish things
Eph 1:4 he *c* us in him before the creation
2Th 2:13 from the beginning God *c* you

## CHOSEN (CHOOSE)

Isa 41:8 Jacob, whom I have *c*,
Mt 22:14 For many are invited, but few are *c*
Lk 10:42 Mary has *c* what is better,
23:35 the Christ of God, the *C* One."
Jn 15:19 but I have *c* you out of the world.
1Pe 1:20 He was *c* before the creation
2:9 But you are a *c* people, a royal

## CHRIST (CHRIST'S CHRISTIAN CHRISTS)

Mt 1:16 was born Jesus, who is called *C*.
16:16 Peter answered, "You are the *C*,
22:42 "What do you think about the *C*?
Jn 1:41 found the Messiah" (that is, the *C*).
20:31 you may believe that Jesus is the *C*,
Ac 2:36 you crucified, both Lord and *C*."
5:42 the good news that Jesus is the *C*.
9:22 by proving that Jesus is the *C*.
17:3 proving that the *C* had to suffer
18:28 the Scriptures that Jesus was the *C*.
26:23 that the *C* would suffer and,
Ro 3:22 comes through faith in Jesus *C*
5:6 we were still powerless, *C* died
5:8 While we were still sinners, *C* died
5:17 life through the one man, Jesus *C*.
6:4 as *C* was raised from the dead
8:1 for those who are in *C* Jesus,
8:9 Spirit of *C*, he does not belong to *C*.
8:35 us from the love of *C*?
10:4 *C* is the end of the law
14:9 *C* died and returned to life
15:3 For even *C* did not please himself
1Co 1:23 but we preach *C* crucified:
2:2 except Jesus *C* and him crucified.
3:11 one already laid, which is Jesus *C*.
5:7 For *C*, our Passover lamb,
8:6 and there is but one Lord, Jesus *C*,
10:4 them, and that rock was *C*.
11:1 as I follow the example of *C*.
11:3 the head of every man is *C*,
12:27 Now you are the body of *C*,

1Co 15:3 that *C* died for our sins according
15:14 And if *C* has not been raised,
15:22 so in *C* all will be made alive.
15:57 victory through our Lord Jesus *C*.
2Co 3:3 show that you are a letter from *C*,
4:5 not preach ourselves, but Jesus *C*
5:10 before the judgment seat of *C*,
5:17 Therefore, if anyone is in *C*,
11:2 you to one husband, to *C*,
Gal 2:20 I have been crucified with *C*
3:13 *C* redeemed us from the curse
6:14 in the cross of our Lord Jesus *C*,
Eph 1:3 with every spiritual blessing in *C*.
3:8 the unsearchable riches of *C*,
4:13 measure of the fullness of *C*.
5:2 as *C* loved us and gave himself up
5:23 as *C* is the head of the church,
5:25 just as *C* loved the church
Php 1:21 to live is *C* and to die is gain.
1:27 worthy of the gospel of *C*.
4:19 to his glorious riches in *C* Jesus.
Col 1:27 which is *C* in you, the hope of glory
1:28 may present everyone perfect in *C*.
2:6 as you received *C* Jesus as Lord,
Col 2:17 the reality, however, is found in *C*.
3:15 Let the peace of *C* rule
2Th 2:1 the coming of our Lord Jesus *C*
1Ti 1:15 *C* Jesus came into the world
2:5 the man *C* Jesus, who gave himself
2Ti 2:3 us like a good soldier of *C* Jesus.
3:15 salvation through faith in *C* Jesus.
Tit 2:13 our great God and Savior, Jesus *C*,
Heb 3:14 to share in *C* if we hold firmly
9:14 more, then, will the blood of *C*,
9:15 For this reason *C* is the mediator
9:28 so *C* was sacrificed once
10:10 of the body of Jesus *C* once for all.
13:8 Jesus *C* is the same yesterday
1Pe 1:19 but with the precious blood of *C*,
2:21 because *C* suffered for you,
3:18 For *C* died for sins once for all,
4:14 insulted because of the name of *C*,
1Jn 2:22 man who denies that Jesus is the *C*.
3:16 Jesus *C* laid down his life for us.
5:1 believes that Jesus is the *C* is born
Rev 20:4 reigned with *C* a thousand years.

**CHRIST'S (CHRIST)**
2Co 5:14 For *C* love compels us,
5:20 We are therefore *C* ambassadors,
12:9 so that *C* power may rest on me.

**CHRISTIAN (CHRIST)**
1Pe 4:16 as a *C*, do not be ashamed,

**CHRISTS (CHRIST)**
Mt 24:24 For false *C* and false prophets will

**CHURCH**
Mt 16:18 and on this rock I will build my *c*,
18:17 if he refuses to listen even to the *c*,
Ac 20:28 Be shepherds of the *c* of God,
1Co 5:12 of mine to judge those outside the *c*
14:4 but he who prophesies edifies the *c*.
14:12 to excel in gifts that build up the *c*.
14:26 done for the strengthening of the *c*.
Eph 5:23 as Christ is the head of the *c*,
Col 1:24 the sake of his body, which is the *c*.

**CIRCUMCISED**
Ge 17:10 Every male among you shall be *c*.

**CIRCUMSTANCES**
Php 4:11 to be content whatever the *c*.
1Th 5:18 continually; give thanks in all *c*,

**CITIZENS (CITIZENSHIP)**
Eph 2:19 but fellow *c* with God's people

**CITIZENSHIP (CITIZENS)**
Php 3:20 But our *c* is in heaven.

**CITY**
Mt 5:14 A *c* on a hill cannot be hidden.
Heb 13:14 here we do not have an enduring *c*,

**CIVILIAN***
2Ti 2:4 a soldier gets involved in *c* affairs—

**CLAIM (CLAIMS)**
Pr 25:6 do not *c* a place among great men;
1Jn 1:6 If we *c* to have fellowship
1:8 If we *c* to be without sin, we
1:10 If we *c* we have not sinned,

**CLAIMS (CLAIM)**
Jas 2:14 if a man *c* to have faith
1Jn 2:6 Whoever *c* to live in him must walk
2:9 Anyone who *c* to be in the light

**CLAP**
Ps 47:1 *C* your hands, all you nations;
Isa 55:12 will *c* their hands.

**CLAY**
Isa 45:9 Does the *c* say to the potter,
64:8 We are the *c*, you are the potter;
Jer 18:6 "Like *c* in the hand of the potter,
La 4:2 are now considered as pots of *c*,
Da 2:33 partly of iron and partly of baked *c*.
Ro 9:21 of the same lump of *c* some pottery
2Co 4:7 we have this treasure in jars of *c*
2Ti 2:20 and *c*; some are for noble purposes

**CLEAN**
Lev 16:30 you will be *c* from all your sins.
Ps 24:4 He who has *c* hands and a pure
Mt 12:44 the house unoccupied, swept *c*
23:25 You *c* the outside of the cup
Mk 7:19 Jesus declared all foods "*c*.")
Jn 13:10 to wash his feet; his whole body is *c*
15:3 are already *c* because of the word
Ac 10:15 impure that God has made *c*."
Ro 14:20 All food is *c*, but it is wrong

**CLING (CLINGS)**
Ro 12:9 Hate what is evil; *c* to what is good.

**CLINGS (CLING)**
Ps 63:8 My soul *c* to you;

**CLOAK**
2Ki 4:29 "Tuck your *c* into your belt,

**CLOSE (CLOSER)**
Ps 34:18 LORD is *c* to the brokenhearted
Isa 40:11 and carries them *c* to his heart;
Jer 30:21 himself to be *c* to me?'

**CLOSER (CLOSE)**
Ex 3:5 "Do not come any *c*," God said.
Pr 18:24 there is a friend who sticks *c*

**CLOTHE (CLOTHED CLOTHES CLOTHING)**
Ps 45:3 *c* yourself with splendor
Isa 52:1 *c* yourself with strength.
Ro 13:14 *c* yourselves with the Lord Jesus
Col 3:12 *c* yourselves with compassion,
1Pe 5:5 *c* yourselves with humility

**CLOTHED (CLOTHE)**
Ps 30:11 removed my sackcloth and *c* me
Pr 31:25 She is *c* with strength and dignity;
Lk 24:49 until you have been *c* with power

**CLOTHES (CLOTHE)**
Mt 6:25 the body more important than *c*?
6:28 "And why do you worry about *c*?
Jn 11:44 Take off the grave *c* and let him go

**CLOTHING (CLOTHE)**
Dt 22:5 A woman must not wear men's *c*,
Mt 7:15 They come to you in sheep's *c*,

**CLOUD (CLOUDS)**
Ex 13:21 them in a pillar of *c* to guide them
Isa 19:1 See, the LORD rides on a swift *c*
Lk 21:27 of Man coming in a *c* with power
Heb 12:1 by such a great *c* of witnesses,

**CLOUDS (CLOUD)**
Ps 104:3 He makes the *c* his chariot
Da 7:13 coming with the *c* of heaven.
Mk 13:26 coming in *c* with great power
1Th 4:17 with them in the *c* to meet the Lord

**CO-HEIRS* (INHERIT)**
Ro 8:17 heirs of God and *c* with Christ,

**COALS**
Pr 25:22 you will heap burning *c* on his head
Ro 12:20 you will heap burning *c* on his head

**COLD**
Pr 25:25 Like *c* water to a weary soul
Mt 10:42 if anyone gives even a cup of *c* water
24:12 the love of most will grow *c,*

**COMFORT (COMFORTED COMFORTS)**
Ps 23:4 rod and your staff, they *c* me.
119:52 and I find *c* in them.
119:76 May your unfailing love be my *c,*
Zec 1:17 and the LORD will again *c* Zion
1Co 14:3 encouragement and *c.*
2Co 1:4 so that we can *c* those
2:7 you ought to forgive and *c* him,

**COMFORTED (COMFORT)**
Mt 5:4 for they will be *c.*

**COMFORTS* (COMFORT)**
Job 29:25 I was like one who *c* mourners.
Isa 49:13 For the LORD *c* his people
51:12 "I, even I, am he who *c* you.
66:13 As a mother *c* her child,
2Co 1:4 who *c* us in all our troubles,
7:6 But God, who *c* the downcast,

**COMMAND (COMMANDED COMMANDING COMMANDMENT COMMANDMENTS COMMANDS)**
Ex 7:2 You are to say everything I *c* you,
Nu 24:13 to go beyond the *c* of the LORD—
Dt 4:2 Do not add to what I *c* you
30:16 For I *c* you today to love
32:46 so that you may *c* your children
Ps 91:11 For he will *c* his angels concerning
Pr 13:13 but he who respects a *c* is rewarded
Ecc 8:2 Obey the king's *c,* I say,
Joel 2:11 mighty are those who obey his *c.*
Jn 14:15 love me, you will obey what I *c.*
15:12 My *c* is this: Love each other
1Co 14:37 writing to you is the Lord's *c.*
Gal 5:14 law is summed up in a single *c:*
1Ti 1:5 goal of this *c* is love, which comes
Heb 11:3 universe was formed at God's *c,*
1Jn 3:23 this is his *c:* to believe in the name
2Jn :6 his *c* is that you walk in love.

**COMMANDED (COMMAND)**
Ps 33:9 he *c,* and it stood firm.
148:5 for he *c* and they were created.
Mt 28:20 to obey everything I have *c* you.
1Co 9:14 Lord has *c* that those who preach
1Jn 3:23 and to love one another as he *c* us.

**COMMANDING (COMMAND)**
2Ti 2:4 he wants to please his *c* officer.

**COMMANDMENT (COMMAND)**
Jos 22:5 But be very careful to keep the *c*
Mt 22:38 This is the first and greatest *c.*
Jn 13:34 "A new *c* I give you: Love one
Ro 7:12 and the *c* is holy, righteous
Eph 6:2 which is the first *c* with a promise

**COMMANDMENTS (COMMAND)**
Ex 20:6 who love me and keep my *c.*
34:28 of the covenant—the Ten *C.*
Ecc 12:13 Fear God and keep his *c,*
Mt 5:19 one of the least of these *c*
22:40 the Prophets hang on these two *c.*"

**COMMANDS (COMMAND)**
Dt 7:9 those who love him and keep his *c.*
11:27 the blessing if you obey the *c*
Ps 112:1 who finds great delight in his *c.*
119:47 for I delight in your *c*

| | | |
|---|---|---|
| Ps | 119:86 | All your *c* are trustworthy; |
| | 119:98 | Your *c* make me wiser |
| | 119:127 | Because I love your *c* |
| | 119:143 | but your *c* are my delight. |
| | 119:172 | for all your *c* are righteous. |
| Pr | 3:1 | but keep my *c* in your heart, |
| | 6:23 | For these *c* are a lamp, |
| | 10:8 | The wise in heart accept *c*, |
| Da | 9:4 | all who love him and obey his *c*, |
| Mt | 5:19 | teaches these *c* will be called great |
| Jn | 14:21 | Whoever has my *c* and obeys them, |
| Ac | 17:30 | but now he *c* all people everywhere |
| 1Co | 7:19 | Keeping God's *c* is what counts. |
| 1Jn | 5:3 | And his *c* are not burdensome, |
| | 5:3 | This is love for God: to obey his *c*. |

**COMMEND (COMMENDED COMMENDS)**

| | | |
|---|---|---|
| Ecc | 8:15 | So I *c* the enjoyment of life, |
| Ro | 13:3 | do what is right and he will *c* you. |
| 1Pe | 2:14 | and to *c* those who do right. |

**COMMENDED (COMMEND)**

| | | |
|---|---|---|
| Heb | 11:39 | These were all *c* for their faith, |

**COMMENDS (COMMEND)**

| | | |
|---|---|---|
| 2Co | 10:18 | not the one who *c* himself who is |

**COMMIT (COMMITS COMMITTED)**

| | | |
|---|---|---|
| Ex | 20:14 | "You shall not *c* adultery. |
| Ps | 37:5 | *C* your way to the LORD; |
| Mt | 5:27 | that it was said, 'Do not *c* adultery.' |
| Lk | 23:46 | into your hands I *c* my spirit." |
| Ac | 20:32 | I *c* you to God and to the word |
| 1Co | 10:8 | We should not *c* sexual immorality, |
| 1Pe | 4:19 | to God's will should *c* themselves |

**COMMITS (COMMIT)**

| | | |
|---|---|---|
| Pr | 6:32 | man who *c* adultery lacks |
| | 29:22 | a hot-tempered one *c* many sins. |
| Mt | 19:9 | marries another woman *c* adultery |

**COMMITTED (COMMIT)**

| | | |
|---|---|---|
| Nu | 5:7 | and must confess the sin he has *c*. |
| 1Ki | 8:61 | But your hearts must be fully *c* |
| 2Ch | 16:9 | those whose hearts are fully *c* |
| Mt | 5:28 | lustfully has already *c* adultery |
| 2Co | 5:19 | And he has *c* to us the message |
| 1Pe | 2:22 | "He *c* no sin, |

**COMMON**

| | | |
|---|---|---|
| Pr | 22:2 | Rich and poor have this in *c*: |
| 1Co | 10:13 | has seized you except what is *c* |
| 2Co | 6:14 | and wickedness have in *c*? |

**COMPANION (COMPANIONS)**

| | | |
|---|---|---|
| Pr | 13:20 | but a *c* of fools suffers harm. |
| | 28:7 | a *c* of gluttons disgraces his father. |
| | 29:3 | *c* of prostitutes squanders his |

**COMPANIONS (COMPANION)**

| | | |
|---|---|---|
| Pr | 18:24 | A man of many *c* may come to ruin |

**COMPANY**

| | | |
|---|---|---|
| Pr | 24:1 | do not desire their *c*; |
| Jer | 15:17 | I never sat in the *c* of revelers, |
| 1Co | 15:33 | "Bad *c* corrupts good character." |

**COMPARED (COMPARING)**

| | | |
|---|---|---|
| Eze | 31:2 | Who can be *c* with you in majesty? |
| Php | 3:8 | I consider everything a loss *c* |

**COMPARING* (COMPARED)**

| | | |
|---|---|---|
| Ro | 8:18 | present sufferings are not worth *c* |
| 2Co | 8:8 | the sincerity of your love by *c* it |
| Gal | 6:4 | without *c* himself to somebody else |

**COMPASSION (COMPASSIONATE COMPASSIONS)**

| | | |
|---|---|---|
| Ex | 33:19 | I will have *c* on whom I will have *c*. |
| Ne | 9:19 | of your great *c* you did not |
| | 9:28 | in your *c* you delivered them time |
| Ps | 51:1 | according to your great *c* |
| | 103:4 | and crowns you with love and *c*. |
| | 103:13 | As a father has *c* on his children, |

| | | |
|---|---|---|
| Ps | 145:9 | he has *c* on all he has made. |
| Isa | 49:13 | and will have *c* on his afflicted ones |
| | 49:15 | and have no *c* on the child she has |
| Hos | 2:19 | in love and *c*. |
| | 11:8 | all my *c* is aroused. |
| Jnh | 3:9 | with *c* turn from his fierce anger |
| Mt | 9:36 | When he saw the crowds, he had *c* |
| Mk | 8:2 | "I have *c* for these people; |
| Ro | 9:15 | and I will have *c* on whom I have *c* |
| Col | 3:12 | clothe yourselves with *c*, kindness, |
| Jas | 5:11 | The Lord is full of *c* and mercy. |

**COMPASSIONATE (COMPASSION)**

| | | |
|---|---|---|
| Ne | 9:17 | gracious and *c*, slow to anger |
| Ps | 103:8 | The LORD is *c* and gracious, |
| | 112:4 | the gracious and *c* and righteous |
| Eph | 4:32 | Be kind and *c* to one another, |
| 1Pe | 3:8 | love as brothers, be *c* and humble. |

**COMPASSIONS* (COMPASSION)**

| | | |
|---|---|---|
| La | 3:22 | for his *c* never fail. |

**COMPELLED (COMPELS)**

| | | |
|---|---|---|
| Ac | 20:22 | "And now, *c* by the Spirit, |
| 1Co | 9:16 | I cannot boast, for I am *c* to preach. |

**COMPELS (COMPELLED)**

| | | |
|---|---|---|
| 2Co | 5:14 | For Christ's love *c* us, because we |

**COMPETENCE* (COMPETENT)**

| | | |
|---|---|---|
| 2Co | 3:5 | but our *c* comes from God. |

**COMPETENT* (COMPETENCE)**

| | | |
|---|---|---|
| Ro | 15:14 | and *c* to instruct one another. |
| 1Co | 6:2 | are you not *c* to judge trivial cases? |
| 2Co | 3:5 | Not that we are *c* in ourselves |
| | 3:6 | He has made us *c* as ministers |

**COMPETES***

| | | |
|---|---|---|
| 1Co | 9:25 | Everyone who *c* in the games goes |
| 2Ti | 2:5 | Similarly, if anyone *c* as an athlete, |
| | 2:5 | unless he *c* according to the rules. |

**COMPLACENT**

| | | |
|---|---|---|
| Am | 6:1 | Woe to you who are *c* in Zion, |

**COMPLAINING***

| | | |
|---|---|---|
| Php | 2:14 | Do everything without *c* or arguing |

**COMPLETE**

| | | |
|---|---|---|
| Jn | 15:11 | and that your joy may be *c*. |
| | 16:24 | will receive, and your joy will be *c*. |
| | 17:23 | May they be brought to *c* unity |
| Ac | 20:24 | *c* the task the Lord Jesus has given |
| Php | 2:2 | then make my joy *c* |
| Col | 4:17 | to it that you *c* the work you have |
| Jas | 1:4 | so that you may be mature and *c*, |
| | 2:22 | his faith was made *c* by what he did |

**CONCEAL (CONCEALED CONCEALS)**

| | | |
|---|---|---|
| Ps | 40:10 | I do not *c* your love and your truth |
| Pr | 25:2 | It is the glory of God to *c* a matter; |

**CONCEALED (CONCEAL)**

| | | |
|---|---|---|
| Jer | 16:17 | nor is their sin *c* from my eyes. |
| Mt | 10:26 | There is nothing *c* that will not be |
| Mk | 4:22 | and whatever is *c* is meant |

**CONCEALS (CONCEAL)**

| | | |
|---|---|---|
| Pr | 28:13 | He who *c* his sins does not prosper, |

**CONCEITED**

| | | |
|---|---|---|
| Ro | 12:16 | Do not be *c*. |
| Gal | 5:26 | Let us not become *c*, provoking |
| 1Ti | 6:4 | he is *c* and understands nothing. |

**CONCEIVED**

| | | |
|---|---|---|
| Mt | 1:20 | what is *c* in her is from the Holy |
| 1Co | 2:9 | no mind has *c* |

**CONCERN (CONCERNED)**

| | | |
|---|---|---|
| Eze | 36:21 | I had *c* for my holy name, which |
| 1Co | 7:32 | I would like you to be free from *c*. |
| | 12:25 | that its parts should have equal *c* |
| 2Co | 11:28 | of my *c* for all the churches. |

**CONCERNED (CONCERN)**

| | | |
|---|---|---|
| Jnh | 4:10 | "You have been *c* about this vine, |
| 1Co | 7:32 | An unmarried man is *c* about |

**CONDEMN (CONDEMNATION CONDEMNED CONDEMNING CONDEMNS)**

Job 40:8 Would you *c* me to justify yourself?
Isa 50:9 Who is he that will *c* me?
Lk 6:37 Do not *c*, and you will not be
Jn 3:17 Son into the world to *c* the world,
12:48 very word which I spoke will *c* him
Ro 2:27 yet obeys the law will *c* you who,
1Jn 3:20 presence whenever our hearts *c* us.

**CONDEMNATION (CONDEMN)**

Ro 5:18 of one trespass was *c* for all men,
8:1 there is now no *c* for those who are

**CONDEMNED (CONDEMN)**

Ps 34:22 no one will be *c* who takes refuge
Mt 12:37 and by your words you will be *c*."
23:33 How will you escape being *c* to hell
Jn 3:18 Whoever believes in him is not *c*,
5:24 has eternal life and will not be *c*;
16:11 prince of this world now stands *c*.
Ro 14:23 But the man who has doubts is *c*
1Co 11:32 disciplined so that we will not be *c*
Heb 11:7 By his faith he *c* the world

**CONDEMNING (CONDEMN)**

Pr 17:15 the guilty and *c* the innocent—
Ro 2:1 judge the other, you are *c* yourself,

**CONDEMNS (CONDEMN)**

Ro 8:34 Who is he that *c*? Christ Jesus,
2Co 3:9 the ministry that *c* men is glorious,

**CONDUCT**

Pr 10:23 A fool finds pleasure in evil *c*,
20:11 by whether his *c* is pure and right.
21:8 but the *c* of the innocent is upright.
Ecc 6:8 how to *c* himself before others?
Jer 4:18 "Your own *c* and actions
17:10 to reward a man according to his *c*,
Eze 7:3 I will judge you according to your *c*
Php 1:27 *c* yourselves in a manner worthy
1Ti 3:15 to *c* themselves in God's household

**CONFESS (CONFESSION)**

Lev 16:21 and *c* over it all the wickedness
26:40 " 'But if they will *c* their sins
Nu 5:7 must *c* the sin he has committed.
Ps 38:18 I *c* my iniquity;
Ro 10:9 That if you *c* with your mouth,
Php 2:11 every tongue *c* that Jesus Christ is
Jas 5:16 Therefore *c* your sins to each other
1Jn 1:9 If we *c* our sins, he is faithful

**CONFESSION (CONFESS)**

Ezr 10:11 Now make *c* to the LORD,
2Co 9:13 obedience that accompanies your *c*

**CONFIDENCE**

Ps 71:5 my *c* since my youth.
Pr 3:26 for the LORD will be your *c*
11:13 A gossip betrays a *c*,
25:9 do not betray another man's *c*,
31:11 Her husband has full *c* in her
Isa 32:17 will be quietness and *c* forever.
Jer 17:7 whose *c* is in him.
Php 3:3 and who put no *c* in the flesh—
Heb 3:14 till the end the *c* we had at first.
4:16 the throne of grace with *c*,
10:19 since we have *c* to enter the Most
10:35 So do not throw away your *c*;
1Jn 5:14 This is the *c* we have

**CONFORM* (CONFORMED)**

Ro 12:2 Do not *c* any longer to the pattern
1Pe 1:14 do not *c* to the evil desires you had

**CONFORMED (CONFORM)**

Ro 8:29 predestined to be *c* to the likeness

**CONQUERORS**

Ro 8:37 than *c* through him who loved us.

**CONSCIENCE (CONSCIENCES)**

Ro 13:5 punishment but also because of *c*.

1Co 8:7 since their *c* is weak, it is defiled.
8:12 in this way and wound their weak *c*
10:25 without raising questions of *c*,
10:29 freedom be judged by another's *c*?
Heb 10:22 to cleanse us from a guilty *c*
1Pe 3:16 and respect, keeping a clear *c*,

**CONSCIENCES* (CONSCIENCE)**
Ro 2:15 their *c* also bearing witness,
1Ti 4:2 whose *c* have been seared
Tit 1:15 their minds and *c* are corrupted.
Heb 9:14 cleanse our *c* from acts that lead

**CONSCIOUS***
Ro 3:20 through the law we become *c* of sin
1Pe 2:19 of unjust suffering because he is *c*

**CONSECRATE (CONSECRATED)**
Ex 13:2 "*C* to me every firstborn male.
Lev 20:7 " '*C* yourselves and be holy,

**CONSECRATED (CONSECRATE)**
Ex 29:43 and the place will be *c* by my glory.
1Ti 4:5 because it is *c* by the word of God

**CONSIDER (CONSIDERATE CONSIDERED CONSIDERS)**
1Sa 12:24 *c* what great things he has done
Job 37:14 stop and *c* God's wonders.
Ps 8:3 When I *c* your heavens,
107:43 and *c* the great love of the LORD.
143:5 and *c* what your hands have done.
Lk 12:24 *C* the ravens: They do not sow
12:27 about the rest? "*C* how the lilies
Php 2:3 but in humility *c* others better
3:8 I *c* everything a loss compared
Heb 10:24 And let us *c* how we may spur one
Jas 1:2 *C* it pure joy, my brothers,

**CONSIDERATE* (CONSIDER)**
Tit 3:2 to be peaceable and *c*,
Jas 3:17 then peace-loving, *c*, submissive,
1Pe 2:18 only to those who are good and *c*,
3:7 in the same way be *c* as you live

**CONSIDERED (CONSIDER)**
Job 1:8 "Have you *c* my servant Job?
2:3 "Have you *c* my servant Job?
Ps 44:22 we are *c* as sheep to be slaughtered.
Isa 53:4 yet we *c* him stricken by God,
Ro 8:36 we are *c* as sheep to be slaughtered

**CONSIDERS (CONSIDER)**
Pr 31:16 She *c* a field and buys it;
Ro 14:5 One man *c* one day more sacred
Jas 1:26 If anyone *c* himself religious

**CONSIST**
Lk 12:15 a man's life does not *c*

**CONSOLATION**
Ps 94:19 your *c* brought joy to my soul.

**CONSTRUCTIVE***
1Co 10:23 but not everything is *c*.

**CONSUME (CONSUMING)**
Jn 2:17 "Zeal for your house will *c* me."

**CONSUMING (CONSUME)**
Dt 4:24 For the LORD your God is a *c* fire,
Heb 12:29 and awe, for our "God is a *c* fire."

**CONTAIN**
1Ki 8:27 the highest heaven, cannot *c* you.
2Pe 3:16 His letters *c* some things that are

**CONTAMINATES***
2Co 7:1 from everything that *c* body

**CONTEMPT**
Pr 14:31 He who oppresses the poor shows *c*
17:5 He who mocks the poor shows *c*
18:3 When wickedness comes, so does *c*
Da 12:2 others to shame and everlasting *c*.
Ro 2:4 Or do you show *c* for the riches
Gal 4:14 you did not treat me with *c*
1Th 5:20 do not treat prophecies with *c*.

**CONTEND (CONTENDING)**
Jude :3 you to *c* for the faith that was once

**CONTENDING* (CONTEND)**

Php 1:27 *c* as one man for the faith

**CONTENT (CONTENTMENT)**

Pr 13:25 The righteous eat to their hearts' *c*,
Php 4:11 to be *c* whatever the circumstances
4:12 I have learned the secret of being *c*
1Ti 6:8 and clothing, we will be *c* with that.
Heb 13:5 and be *c* with what you have,

**CONTENTMENT (CONTENT)**

1Ti 6:6 But godliness with *c* is great gain.

**CONTINUAL (CONTINUE)**

Pr 15:15 but the cheerful heart has a *c* feast.

**CONTINUE (CONTINUAL)**

Php 2:12 *c* to work out your salvation
2Ti 3:14 *c* in what you have learned
1Jn 5:18 born of God does not *c* to sin;
Rev 22:11 and let him who is holy *c* to be holy
22:11 let him who does right *c* to do right;

**CONTRITE***

Ps 51:17 a broken and *c* heart,
Isa 57:15 also with him who is *c* and lowly
57:15 and to revive the heart of the *c*.
66:2 he who is humble and *c* in spirit,

**CONTROL (CONTROLLED SELF-CONTROL SELF-CONTROLLED)**

Pr 29:11 a wise man keeps himself under *c*.
1Co 7:9 But if they cannot *c* themselves,
7:37 but has *c* over his own will,
1Th 4:4 you should learn to *c* his own body

**CONTROLLED (CONTROL)**

Ps 32:9 but must be *c* by bit and bridle
Ro 8:6 but the mind *c* by the Spirit is life
8:8 Those *c* by the sinful nature cannot

**CONTROVERSIES**

Tit 3:9 But avoid foolish *c* and genealogies

**CONVERSATION**

Col 4:6 Let your *c* be always full of grace,

**CONVERT**

1Ti 3:6 He must not be a recent *c*,

**CONVICT**

Jn 16:8 he will *c* the world of guilt in regard

**CONVINCED (CONVINCING)**

Ro 8:38 For I am *c* that neither death
2Ti 1:12 and am *c* that he is able
3:14 have learned and have become *c*

**CONVINCING* (CONVINCED)**

Ac 1:3 and gave many *c* proofs that he was

**CORNELIUS***

Roman to whom Peter preached; first Gentile Christian (Ac 10).

**CORNERSTONE (STONE)**

Isa 28:16 a precious *c* for a sure foundation;
Eph 2:20 Christ Jesus himself as the chief *c*.
1Pe 2:6 a chosen and precious *c*,

**CORRECT (CORRECTING CORRECTION CORRECTS)**

2Ti 4:2 *c*, rebuke and encourage—

**CORRECTING* (CORRECT)**

2Ti 3:16 *c* and training in righteousness,

**CORRECTION (CORRECT)**

Pr 10:17 whoever ignores *c* leads others
12:1 but he who hates *c* is stupid.
15:5 whoever heeds *c* shows prudence.
15:10 he who hates *c* will die.
29:15 The rod of *c* imparts wisdom,

**CORRECTS* (CORRECT)**

Job 5:17 "Blessed is the man whom God *c*;
Pr 9:7 Whoever *c* a mocker invites insult;

**CORRUPT (CORRUPTS)**

Ge 6:11 Now the earth was *c* in God's sight

**CORRUPTS* (CORRUPT)**

Ecc 7:7 and a bribe *c* the heart.
1Co 15:33 "Bad company *c* good character."
Jas 3:6 It *c* the whole person, sets

**COST**
Pr 4:7 Though it *c* all you have, get
Isa 55:1 milk without money and without *c*.
Rev 21:6 to drink without *c* from the spring

**COUNSEL (COUNSELOR)**
1Ki 22:5 "First seek the *c* of the LORD."
Pr 15:22 Plans fail for lack of *c*,
Rev 3:18 I *c* you to buy from me gold refined

**COUNSELOR (COUNSEL)**
Isa 9:6 Wonderful *C*, Mighty God,
Jn 14:16 he will give you another *C* to be
14:26 But the *C*, the Holy Spirit,

**COUNT (COUNTING COUNTS)**
Ro 4:8 whose sin the Lord will never *c*
6:11 *c* yourselves dead to sin

**COUNTING (COUNT)**
2Co 5:19 not *c* men's sins against them.

**COUNTRY**
Jn 4:44 prophet has no honor in his own *c*.)

**COUNTS (COUNT)**
Jn 6:63 The Spirit gives life; the flesh *c*
1Co 7:19 God's commands is what *c*.
Gal 5:6 only thing that *c* is faith expressing

**COURAGE (COURAGEOUS)**
Ac 23:11 "Take *c*! As you have testified
1Co 16:13 stand firm in the faith; be men of *c*;

**COURAGEOUS (COURAGE)**
Dt 31:6 Be strong and *c*.
Jos 1:6 and *c*, because you will lead these

**COURSE**
Ps 19:5 a champion rejoicing to run his *c*.
Pr 15:21 of understanding keeps a straight *c*.

**COURTS**
Ps 84:10 Better is one day in your *c*
100:4 and his *c* with praise;

**COVENANT (COVENANTS)**
Ge 9:9 "I now establish my *c* with you
Ex 19:5 if you obey me fully and keep my *c*,
1Ch 16:15 He remembers his *c* forever,
Job 31:1 "I made a *c* with my eyes
Jer 31:31 "when I will make a new *c*
1Co 11:25 "This cup is the new *c* in my blood;
Gal 4:24 One *c* is from Mount Sinai
Heb 9:15 Christ is the mediator of a new *c*,

**COVENANTS (COVENANT)**
Ro 9:4 theirs the divine glory, the *c*,
Gal 4:24 for the women represent two *c*.

**COVER (COVER-UP COVERED COVERS)**
Ps 91:4 He will *c* you with his feathers,
Jas 5:20 and *c* over a multitude of sins.

**COVER-UP (COVER)**
1Pe 2:16 but do not use your freedom as a *c*

**COVERED (COVER)**
Ps 32:1 whose sins are *c*.
Isa 6:2 With two wings they *c* their faces,
Ro 4:7 whose sins are *c*.
1Co 11:4 with his head *c* dishonors his head.

**COVERS (COVER)**
Pr 10:12 but love *c* over all wrongs.
1Pe 4:8 love *c* over a multitude of sins.

**COVET**
Ex 20:17 You shall not *c* your neighbor's
Ro 13:9 "Do not steal," "Do not *c*,"

**COWARDLY***
Rev 21:8 But the *c*, the unbelieving, the vile,

**CRAFTINESS (CRAFTY)**
1Co 3:19 "He catches the wise in their *c*";

**CRAFTY (CRAFTINESS)**
Ge 3:1 the serpent was more *c* than any
2Co 12:16 *c* fellow that I am, I caught you

**CRAVE**
Pr 23:3 Do not *c* his delicacies,
1Pe 2:2 newborn babies, *c* pure spiritual

**CREATE (CREATED CREATION CREATOR)**
Ps 51:10 *C* in me a pure heart, O God,
Isa 45:18 he did not *c* it to be empty,

**CREATED (CREATE)**
Ge 1:1 In the beginning God *c* the heavens
1:21 God *c* the great creatures of the sea
1:27 So God *c* man in his own image,
Ps 148:5 for he commanded and they were *c*
Isa 42:5 he who *c* the heavens and stretched
Ro 1:25 and served *c* things rather
1Co 11:9 neither was man *c* for woman,
Col 1:16 For by him all things were *c:*
1Ti 4:4 For everything God *c* is good,
Rev 10:6 who *c* the heavens and all that is

**CREATION (CREATE)**
Mk 16:15 and preach the good news to all *c.*
Jn 17:24 me before the *c* of the world.
Ro 8:19 The *c* waits in eager expectation
8:39 depth, nor anything else in all *c,*
2Co 5:17 he is a new *c;* the old has gone,
Col 1:15 God, the firstborn over all *c.*
1Pe 1:20 chosen before the *c* of the world,
Rev 13:8 slain from the *c* of the world.

**CREATOR (CREATE)**
Ge 14:22 God Most High, *C* of heaven
Ro 1:25 created things rather than the *C*—

**CREATURE (CREATURES)**
Lev 17:11 For the life of a *c* is in the blood,

**CREATURES (CREATURE)**
Ge 6:19 bring into the ark two of all living *c,*
Ps 104:24 the earth is full of your *c.*

**CREDIT (CREDITED)**
Ro 4:24 to whom God will *c* righteousness
1Pe 2:20 it to your *c* if you receive a beating

**CREDITED (CREDIT)**
Ge 15:6 and he *c* it to him as righteousness.
Ro 4:5 his faith is *c* as righteousness.
Gal 3:6 and it was *c* to him as righteousness
Jas 2:23 and it was *c* to him as righteousness

**CRIED (CRY)**
Ps 18:6 I *c* to my God for help.

**CRIMSON**
Isa 1:18 though they are red as *c,*

**CRIPPLED**
Mk 9:45 better for you to enter life *c*

**CRITICISM**
2Co 8:20 We want to avoid any *c*

**CROOKED**
Pr 10:9 he who takes *c* paths will be found
Php 2:15 children of God without fault in a *c*

**CROSS**
Mt 10:38 and anyone who does not take his *c*
Lk 9:23 take up his *c* daily and follow me.
Ac 2:23 to death by nailing him to the *c.*
1Co 1:17 lest the *c* of Christ be emptied
Gal 6:14 in the *c* of our Lord Jesus Christ,
Php 2:8 even death on a *c!*
Col 1:20 through his blood, shed on the *c.*
2:14 he took it away, nailing it to the *c.*
2:15 triumphing over them by the *c.*
Heb 12:2 set before him endured the *c,*

**CROWD**
Ex 23:2 Do not follow the *c* in doing wrong.

**CROWN (CROWNED CROWNS)**
Pr 4:9 present you with a *c* of splendor."
10:6 Blessings *c* the head
12:4 noble character is her husband's *c,*
17:6 Children's children are a *c*
Isa 61:3 to bestow on them a *c* of beauty
Zec 9:16 like jewels in a *c.*
Mt 27:29 then twisted together a *c* of thorns
1Co 9:25 it to get a *c* that will last forever.
2Ti 4:8 store for me the *c* of righteousness,
Rev 2:10 and I will give you the *c* of life.

**CROWNED (CROWN)**
Ps 8:5 and *c* him with glory and honor.
Pr 14:18 the prudent are *c* with knowledge.
Heb 2:7 you *c* him with glory and honor

**CROWNS (CROWN)**
Rev 4:10 They lay their *c* before the throne
19:12 and on his head are many *c.*

**CRUCIFIED (CRUCIFY)**
Mt 20:19 to be mocked and flogged and *c.*
27:38 Two robbers were *c* with him,
Lk 24:7 be *c* and on the third day be raised
Jn 19:18 Here they *c* him, and with him two
Ac 2:36 whom you *c,* both Lord and Christ
Ro 6:6 For we know that our old self was *c*
1Co 1:23 but we preach Christ *c:* a stumbling
2:2 except Jesus Christ and him *c.*
Gal 2:20 I have been *c* with Christ
5:24 Christ Jesus have *c* the sinful

**CRUCIFY (CRUCIFIED CRUCIFYING)**
Mt 27:22 They all answered, "*C* him!" "Why
27:31 Then they led him away to *c* him.

**CRUCIFYING* (CRUCIFY)**
Heb 6:6 to their loss they are *c* the Son

**CRUSH (CRUSHED)**
Ge 3:15 he will *c* your head,
Isa 53:10 it was the LORD 's will to *c* him
Ro 16:20 The God of peace will soon *c* Satan

**CRUSHED (CRUSH)**
Ps 34:18 and saves those who are *c* in spirit.
Isa 53:5 he was *c* for our iniquities;
2Co 4:8 not *c;* perplexed, but not in despair;

**CRY (CRIED)**
Ps 34:15 and his ears are attentive to their *c;*
40:1 he turned to me and heard my *c.*
130:1 Out of the depths I *c* to you,

**CUP**
Ps 23:5 my *c* overflows.
Mt 10:42 if anyone gives even a *c* of cold water
23:25 You clean the outside of the *c*
26:39 may this *c* be taken from me.
1Co 11:25 after supper he took the *c,* saying,

**CURSE (CURSED)**
Dt 11:26 before you today a blessing and a *c*
21:23 hung on a tree is under God's *c.*
Lk 6:28 bless those who *c* you, pray
Gal 3:13 of the law by becoming a *c* for us,
Rev 22:3 No longer will there be any *c.*

**CURSED (CURSE)**
Ge 3:17 "*C* is the ground because of you;
Dt 27:15 "*C* is the man who carves an image
27:16 "*C* is the man who dishonors his
27:17 "*C* is the man who moves his
27:18 "*C* is the man who leads the blind
27:19 *C* is the man who withholds justice
27:20 "*C* is the man who sleeps
27:21 "*C* is the man who has sexual
27:22 "*C* is the man who sleeps
27:23 "*C* is the man who sleeps
27:24 "*C* is the man who kills his
27:25 "*C* is the man who accepts a bribe
27:26 "*C* is the man who does not uphold
Ro 9:3 I could wish that I myself were *c*
Gal 3:10 "*C* is everyone who does not

**CURTAIN**
Ex 26:33 The *c* will separate the Holy Place
Lk 23:45 the *c* of the temple was torn in two.
Heb 10:20 opened for us through the *c,*

**CYMBAL***
1Co 13:1 a resounding gong or a clanging *c.*

**DANCE (DANCING)**
Ecc 3:4 a time to mourn and a time to *d,*
Mt 11:17 and you did not *d;*

**DANCING (DANCE)**
Ps 30:11 You turned my wailing into *d;*
149:3 Let them praise his name with *d*

**DANGER**
Pr 27:12 The prudent see *d* and take refuge,
Ro 8:35 famine or nakedness or *d* or sword?

**DANIEL**
Hebrew exile to Babylon, name changed to Belteshazzar (Da 1:6-7). Refused to eat unclean food (Da 1:8-21). Interpreted Nebuchadnezzar's dreams (Da 2; 4), writing on the

wall (Da 5). Thrown into lion's den (Da 6). Visions of (Da 7-12).

**DARK (DARKNESS)**

Job 34:22 There is no *d* place, no deep
Pr 31:15 She gets up while it is still *d;*
Ro 2:19 a light for those who are in the *d,*
2Pe 1:19 as to a light shining in a *d* place,

**DARKNESS (DARK)**

Ge 1:4 he separated the light from the *d.*
2Sa 22:29 the LORD turns my *d* into light.
Jn 3:19 but men loved *d* instead of light
2Co 6:14 fellowship can light have with *d?*
Eph 5:8 For you were once *d,* but now you
1Pe 2:9 out of *d* into his wonderful light.
1Jn 1:5 in him there is no *d* at all.
2:9 but hates his brother is still in the *d.*

**DAUGHTERS**

Joel 2:28 sons and *d* will prophesy,

**DAVID**

Son of Jesse (Ru 4:17-22; 1Ch 2:13-15), ancestor of Jesus (Mt 1:1-17; Lk 3:31).

Anointed king by Samuel (1Sa 16:1-13). Musician to Saul (1Sa 16:14-23; 18:10). Killed Goliath (1Sa 17). Relation with Jonathan (1Sa 18:1-4; 19-20; 23:16-18; 2Sa 1). Disfavor of Saul (1Sa 18:6-23:29). Spared Saul's life (1Sa 24; 26). Among Philistines (1Sa 21:10-14; 27-30). Lament for Saul and Jonathan (2Sa 1).

Anointed king of Judah (2Sa 2:1-11); of Israel (2Sa 5:1-4; 1Ch 11:1-3). Promised eternal dynasty (2Sa 7; 1Ch 17; Ps 132). Adultery with Bathsheba (2Sa 11-12). Absalom's revolt (2Sa 14-18). Last words (2Sa 23:1-7). Death (1Ki 2:10-12; 1Ch 29:28).

**DAWN**

Ps 37:6 your righteousness shine like the *d,*
Pr 4:18 is like the first gleam of *d,*

**DAY (DAYS)**

Ge 1:5 God called the light "*d,*"
Ex 20:8 "Remember the Sabbath *d*
Lev 23:28 because it is the *D* of Atonement,
Nu 14:14 before them in a pillar of cloud by *d*
Jos 1:8 meditate on it *d* and night,
Ps 84:10 Better is one *d* in your courts
96:2 proclaim his salvation *d* after *d.*
118:24 This is the *d* the LORD has made;
Pr 27:1 not know what a *d* may bring forth.
Joel 2:31 and dreadful *d* of the LORD.
Ob :15 The *d* of the LORD is near
Lk 11:3 Give us each *d* our daily bread.
Ac 17:11 examined the Scriptures every *d*
2Co 4:16 we are being renewed *d* by *d.*
1Th 5:2 for you know very well that the *d*
2Pe 3:8 With the Lord a *d* is like

**DAYS (DAY)**

Dt 17:19 he is to read it all the *d,* of his life
Ps 23:6 all the *d* of my life,
90:10 The length of our *d* is seventy years
Ecc 12:1 Creator in the *d* of your youth,
Joel 2:29 I will pour out my Spirit in those *d.*
Mic 4:1 In the last *d*
Heb 1:2 in these last *d* he has spoken to us
2Pe 3:3 that in the last *d* scoffers will come,

**DEACONS**

1Ti 3:8 *D,* likewise, are to be men worthy

**DEAD (DIE)**

Dt 18:11 or spiritist or who consults the *d.*
Mt 28:7 'He has risen from the *d*
Ro 6:11 count yourselves *d* to sin
Eph 2:1 you were *d* in your transgressions
1Th 4:16 and the *d* in Christ will rise first.
Jas 2:17 is not accompanied by action, is *d.*
2:26 so faith without deeds is *d.*

**DEATH (DIE)**

Nu 35:16 the murderer shall be put to *d.*
Ps 23:4 the valley of the shadow of *d,*
116:15 is the *d* of his saints.
Pr 8:36 all who hate me love *d.*"
14:12 but in the end it leads to *d.*
Ecc 7:2 for *d* is the destiny of every man;
Isa 25:8 he will swallow up *d* forever.
53:12 he poured out his life unto *d,*
Jn 5:24 he has crossed over from *d* to life.

Ro 5:12 and in this way *d* came to all men,
6:23 For the wages of sin is *d*,
8:13 put to *d* the misdeeds of the body,
1Co 15:21 For since *d* came through a man,
15:55 Where, O *d*, is your sting?"
Rev 1:18 And I hold the keys of *d* and Hades
20:6 The second *d* has no power
20:14 The lake of fire is the second *d*.
21:4 There will be no more *d*

**DEBAUCHERY**
Ro 13:13 not in sexual immorality and *d*,
Eph 5:18 drunk on wine, which leads to *d*.

**DEBORAH**
Prophetess who led Israel to victory over Canaanites (Jdg 4-5).

**DEBT (DEBTORS DEBTS)**
Ro 13:8 Let no *d* remain outstanding,
13:8 continuing *d* to love one another,

**DEBTORS (DEBT)**
Mt 6:12 as we also have forgiven our *d*.

**DEBTS (DEBT)**
Dt 15:1 seven years you must cancel *d*.
Mt 6:12 Forgive us our *d*,

**DECAY**
Ps 16:10 will you let your Holy One see *d*.
Ac 2:27 will you let your Holy One see *d*.

**DECEIT (DECEIVE)**
Mk 7:22 greed, malice, *d*, lewdness, envy,
1Pe 2:1 yourselves of all malice and all *d*,
2:22 and no *d* was found in his mouth."

**DECEITFUL (DECEIVE)**
Jer 17:9 The heart is *d* above all things
2Co 11:13 men are false apostles, *d* workmen,

**DECEITFULNESS (DECEIVE)**
Mk 4:19 the *d* of wealth and the desires
Heb 3:13 of you may be hardened by sin's *d*.

**DECEIVE (DECEIT DECEITFUL DECEITFULNESS DECEIVED DECEIVES DECEPTIVE)**
Lev 19:11 " 'Do not *d* one another.
Pr 14:5 A truthful witness does not *d*,
Mt 24:5 'I am the Christ,' and will *d* many.
Ro 16:18 and flattery they *d* the minds
1Co 3:18 Do not *d* yourselves.
Eph 5:6 Let no one *d* you with empty words
Jas 1:22 to the word, and so *d* yourselves.
1Jn 1:8 we *d* ourselves and the truth is not

**DECEIVED (DECEIVE)**
Ge 3:13 "The serpent *d* me, and I ate."
Gal 6:7 Do not be *d*: God cannot be
1Ti 2:14 And Adam was not the one *d*;
2Ti 3:13 to worse, deceiving and being *d*.
Jas 1:16 Don't be *d*, my dear brothers.

**DECEIVES (DECEIVE)**
Gal 6:3 when he is nothing, he *d* himself.
Jas 1:26 he *d* himself and his religion is

**DECENCY***
1Ti 2:9 women to dress modestly, with *d*

**DECEPTIVE (DECEIVE)**
Pr 31:30 Charm is *d*, and beauty is fleeting;
Col 2:8 through hollow and *d* philosophy,

**DECLARE (DECLARED DECLARING)**
1Ch 16:24 *D* his glory among the nations,
Ps 19:1 The heavens *d* the glory of God;
96:3 *D* his glory among the nations,
Isa 42:9 and new things I *d*;

**DECLARED (DECLARE)**
Mk 7:19 Jesus *d* all foods "clean.")
Ro 2:13 the law who will be *d* righteous.
3:20 no one will be *d* righteous

**DECLARING (DECLARE)**
Ps 71:8 *d* your splendor all day long.
Ac 2:11 we hear them *d* the wonders

**DECREED (DECREES)**
La 3:37 happen if the Lord has not *d* it?
Lk 22:22 Son of Man will go as it has been *d*,

**DECREES (DECREED)**
Lev 10:11 Israelites all the *d* the LORD has

Ps 119:112 My heart is set on keeping your *d*

**DEDICATE (DEDICATION)**

Nu 6:12 He must *d* himself to the LORD
Pr 20:25 for a man to *d* something rashly

**DEDICATION (DEDICATE)**

1Ti 5:11 sensual desires overcome their *d*

**DEED (DEEDS)**

Col 3:17 you do, whether in word or *d*,

**DEEDS (DEED)**

1Sa 2:3 and by him *d* are weighed.
Ps 65:5 with awesome *d* of righteousness,
66:3 "How awesome are your *d!*
78:4 the praiseworthy *d* of the LORD,
86:10 you are great and do marvelous *d;*
92:4 For you make me glad by your *d*,
111:3 Glorious and majestic are his *d*,
Hab 3:2 I stand in awe of your *d*, O LORD.
Mt 5:16 that they may see your good *d*
Ac 26:20 prove their repentance by their *d*.
Jas 2:14 claims to have faith but has no *d?*
2:20 faith without *d* is useless?
1Pe 2:12 they may see your good *d*

**DEEP (DEPTH)**

1Co 2:10 all things, even the *d* things
1Ti 3:9 hold of the *d* truths of the faith

**DEER**

Ps 42:1 As the *d* pants for streams of water,

**DEFEND (DEFENSE)**

Ps 74:22 Rise up, O God, and *d* your cause;
Pr 31:9 *d* the rights of the poor and needy
Jer 50:34 He will vigorously *d* their cause

**DEFENSE (DEFEND)**

Ps 35:23 Awake, and rise to my *d!*
Php 1:16 here for the *d* of the gospel.
1Jn 2:1 speaks to the Father in our *d*—

**DEFERRED***

Pr 13:12 Hope *d* makes the heart sick,

**DEFILE (DEFILED)**

Da 1:8 Daniel resolved not to *d* himself

**DEFILED (DEFILE)**

Isa 24:5 The earth is *d* by its people;

**DEFRAUD**

Lev 19:13 Do not *d* your neighbor or rob him.

**DEITY***

Col 2:9 of the *D* lives in bodily form,

**DELIGHT (DELIGHTS)**

1Sa 15:22 "Does the LORD *d*
Ps 1:2 But his *d* is in the law of the LORD
16:3 in whom is all my *d*.
35:9 and *d* in his salvation.
37:4 *D* yourself in the LORD
43:4 to God, my joy and my *d*.
51:16 You do not *d* in sacrifice,
119:77 for your law is my *d*.
Pr 29:17 he will bring *d* to your soul.
Isa 42:1 my chosen one in whom I *d;*
55:2 and your soul will *d* in the richest
61:10 I *d* greatly in the LORD;
Jer 9:24 for in these I *d*,"
15:16 they were my joy and my heart's *d*,
Mic 7:18 but *d* to show mercy.
Zep 3:17 He will take great *d* in you,
Mt 12:18 the one I love, in whom I *d;*
1Co 13:6 Love does not *d* in evil
2Co 12:10 for Christ's sake, I *d* in weaknesses,

**DELIGHTS (DELIGHT)**

Ps 22:8 since he *d* in him."
35:27 who *d* in the well-being
36:8 from your river of *d*.
37:23 if the LORD *d* in a man's way,
Pr 3:12 as a father the son he *d* in.
12:22 but he *d* in men who are truthful.
23:24 he who has a wise son *d* in him.

**DELILAH***

Woman who betrayed Samson (Jdg 16:4-22).

**DELIVER (DELIVERANCE DELIVERED DELIVERER DELIVERS)**

Ps 72:12 For he will *d* the needy who cry out

Ps 79:9 *d* us and forgive our sins
Mt 6:13 but *d* us from the evil one.'
2Co 1:10 hope that he will continue to *d* us,

**DELIVERANCE (DELIVER)**
Ps 3:8 From the LORD comes *d.*
32:7 and surround me with songs of *d.*
33:17 A horse is a vain hope for *d;*

**DELIVERED (DELIVER)**
Ps 34:4 he *d* me from all my fears.
Ro 4:25 He was *d* over to death for our sins

**DELIVERER (DELIVER)**
Ps 18:2 is my rock, my fortress and my *d;*
40:17 You are my help and my *d;*
140:7 O Sovereign LORD, my strong *d,*
144:2 my stronghold and my *d,*

**DELIVERS (DELIVER)**
Ps 34:17 he *d* them from all their troubles.
34:19 but the LORD *d* him from them all
37:40 The LORD helps them and *d* them
37:40 he *d* them from the wicked

**DEMANDED**
Lk 12:20 This very night your life will be *d*
12:48 been given much, much will be *d;*

**DEMONS**
Mt 12:27 And if I drive out *d* by Beelzebub,
Mk 5:15 possessed by the legion of *d,*
Ro 8:38 neither angels nor *d,* neither
Jas 2:19 Good! Even the *d* believe that—

**DEMONSTRATE (DEMONSTRATES)**
Ro 3:26 he did it to *d* his justice

**DEMONSTRATES* (DEMONSTRATE)**
Ro 5:8 God *d* his own love for us in this:

**DEN**
Da 6:16 and threw him into the lions' *d.*
Mt 21:13 you are making it a '*d* of robbers.'"

**DENARIUS**
Mk 12:15 Bring me a *d* and let me look at it."

**DENIED (DENY)**
1Ti 5:8 he has *d* the faith and is worse

**DENIES (DENY)**
1Jn 2:23 No one who *d* the Son has

**DENY (DENIED DENIES DENYING)**
Ex 23:6 "Do not *d* justice to your poor
Job 27:5 till I die, I will not *d* my integrity.
La 3:35 to *d* a man his rights
Lk 9:23 he must *d* himself and take up his
Tit 1:16 but by their actions they *d* him.

**DENYING* (DENY)**
Eze 22:29 mistreat the alien, *d* them justice.
2Ti 3:5 a form of godliness but *d* its power.
2Pe 2:1 *d* the sovereign Lord who bought

**DEPART (DEPARTED)**
Ge 49:10 The scepter will not *d* from Judah,
Job 1:21 and naked I will *d.*
Mt 25:41 '*D* from me, you who are cursed,
Php 1:23 I desire to *d* and be with Christ,

**DEPARTED (DEPART)**
1Sa 4:21 "The glory has *d* from Israel"—
Ps 119:102 I have not *d* from your laws,

**DEPOSIT**
2Co 1:22 put his Spirit in our hearts as a *d,*
5:5 and has given us the Spirit as a *d,*
Eph 1:14 who is a *d* guaranteeing our
2Ti 1:14 Guard the good *d* that was

**DEPRAVED (DEPRAVITY)**
Ro 1:28 he gave them over to a *d* mind,
Php 2:15 fault in a crooked and *d* generation,

**DEPRAVITY (DEPRAVED)**
Ro 1:29 of wickedness, evil, greed and *d.*

**DEPRIVE**
Dt 24:17 Do not *d* the alien or the fatherless
Pr 18:5 or to *d* the innocent of justice.
Isa 10:2 to *d* the poor of their rights
29:21 with false testimony *d* the innocent
1Co 7:5 Do not *d* each other

**DEPTH (DEEP)**
Ro 8:39 any powers, neither height nor *d,*
11:33 the *d* of the riches of the wisdom

**DESERT**
Nu 32:13 wander in the *d* forty years,
Ne 9:19 you did not abandon them in the *d.*
Ps 78:19 "Can God spread a table in the *d?*
78:52 led them like sheep through the *d.*
Mk 1:13 and he was in the *d* forty days,

**DESERTED (DESERTS)**
Ezr 9:9 our God has not *d* us
Mt 26:56 all the disciples *d* him and fled.
2Ti 1:15 in the province of Asia has *d* me,

**DESERTING (DESERTS)**
Gal 1:6 are so quickly *d* the one who called

**DESERTS (DESERTED DESERTING)**
Zec 11:17 who *d* the flock!

**DESERVE (DESERVES)**
Ps 103:10 he does not treat us as our sins *d*
Jer 21:14 I will punish you as your deeds *d,*
Mt 22:8 those I invited did not *d* to come.
Ro 1:32 those who do such things *d* death,

**DESERVES (DESERVE)**
2Sa 12:5 the man who did this *d* to die!
Lk 10:7 for the worker *d* his wages.
1Ti 5:18 and "The worker *d* his wages."

**DESIRABLE (DESIRE)**
Pr 22:1 A good name is more *d*

**DESIRE (DESIRABLE DESIRES)**
Ge 3:16 Your *d* will be for your husband,
Dt 5:21 You shall not set your *d*
1Ch 29:18 keep this *d* in the hearts
Ps 40:6 Sacrifice and offering you did not *d*
40:8 I *d* to do your will, O my God;
73:25 earth has nothing I *d* besides you
Pr 3:15 nothing you *d* can compare
10:24 what the righteous *d* will be
11:23 The *d* of the righteous ends only
Isa 26:8 are the *d* of our hearts.
53:2 appearance that we should *d* him.
55:11 but will accomplish what I *d*
Hos 6:6 For I *d* mercy, not sacrifice,
Mt 9:13 learn what this means: 'I *d* mercy,
Ro 7:18 For I have the *d* to do what is good,
1Co 12:31 But eagerly *d* the greater gifts.
14:1 and eagerly *d* spiritual gifts,
Php 1:23 I *d* to depart and be with Christ,
Heb 13:18 *d* to live honorably in every way.
Jas 1:15 Then, after *d* has conceived,

**DESIRES (DESIRE)**
Ge 4:7 at your door; it *d* to have you,
Ps 34:12 and *d* to see many good days,
37:4 he will give you the *d* of your heart.
103:5 satisfies your *d* with good things,
145:19 He fulfills the *d* of those who fear
Pr 11:6 the unfaithful are trapped by evil *d.*
19:22 What a man *d* is unfailing love;
Mk 4:19 and the *d* for other things come in
Ro 8:5 set on what that nature *d;*
13:14 to gratify the *d* of the sinful nature.
Gal 5:16 and you will not gratify the *d*
5:17 the sinful nature *d* what is contrary
1Ti 3:1 an overseer, he *d* a noble task.
6:9 and harmful *d* that plunge men
2Ti 2:22 Flee the evil *d* of youth,
Jas 1:20 about the righteous life that God *d.*
4:1 from your *d* that battle within you?
1Pe 2:11 to abstain from sinful *d,* which war
1Jn 2:17 The world and its *d* pass away,

**DESOLATE**
Isa 54:1 are the children of the *d* woman

**DESPAIR**
Isa 61:3 instead of a spirit of *d.*
2Co 4:8 perplexed, but not in *d;* persecuted,

**DESPISE (DESPISED DESPISES)**
Job 42:6 Therefore I *d* myself
Pr 1:7 but fools *d* wisdom and discipline.

Pr 3:11 do not *d* the LORD's discipline
23:22 do not *d* your mother
Lk 16:13 devoted to the one and *d* the other.
Tit 2:15 Do not let anyone *d* you.

**DESPISED (DESPISE)**
Ge 25:34 So Esau *d* his birthright.
Isa 53:3 He was *d* and rejected by men,
1Co 1:28 of this world and the *d* things—

**DESPISES (DESPISE)**
Pr 14:21 He who *d* his neighbor sins,
15:20 but a foolish man *d* his mother.
15:32 who ignores discipline *d* himself,
Zec 4:10 "Who *d* the day of small things?

**DESTINED (DESTINY)**
Lk 2:34 "This child is *d* to cause the falling

**DESTINY (DESTINED PREDESTINED)**
Ps 73:17 then I understood their final *d*.
Ecc 7:2 for death is the *d* of every man;

**DESTITUTE**
Pr 31:8 for the rights of all who are *d*.
Heb 11:37 *d*, persecuted and mistreated—

**DESTROY (DESTROYED DESTROYS DESTRUCTION)**
Pr 1:32 complacency of fools will *d* them;
Mt 10:28 of the One who can *d* both soul

**DESTROYED (DESTROY)**
Job 19:26 And after my skin has been *d*,
Isa 55:13 which will not be *d*."
1Co 8:11 for whom Christ died, is *d*
15:26 The last enemy to be *d* is death.
2Co 5:1 if the earthly tent we live in is *d*,
Heb 10:39 of those who shrink back and are *d*,
2Pe 3:10 the elements will be *d* by fire,

**DESTROYS (DESTROY)**
Pr 6:32 whoever does so *d* himself.
11:9 mouth the godless *d* his neighbor,
18:9 is brother to one who *d*.
28:24 he is partner to him who *d*.
Ecc 9:18 but one sinner *d* much good.
1Co 3:17 If anyone *d* God's temple,

**DESTRUCTION (DESTROY)**
Pr 16:18 Pride goes before *d*,
Hos 13:14 Where, O grave, is your *d*?
Mt 7:13 broad is the road that leads to *d*,
Gal 6:8 from that nature will reap *d*;
2Th 1:9 punished with everlasting *d*
1Ti 6:9 that plunge men into ruin and *d*.
2Pe 2:1 bringing swift *d* on themselves.
3:16 other Scriptures, to their own *d*.

**DETERMINED (DETERMINES)**
Job 14:5 Man's days are *d*;
Isa 14:26 This is the plan *d* for the whole
Da 11:36 for what has been *d* must take place
Ac 17:26 and he *d* the times set for them

**DETERMINES* (DETERMINED)**
Ps 147:4 He *d* the number of the stars
Pr 16:9 but the LORD *d* his steps.
1Co 12:11 them to each one, just as he *d*.

**DETESTABLE (DETESTS)**
Pr 21:27 The sacrifice of the wicked is *d*—
28:9 even his prayers are *d*.
Isa 1:13 Your incense is *d* to me.
Lk 16:15 among men is *d* in God's sight.
Tit 1:16 They are *d*, disobedient

**DETESTS (DETESTABLE)**
Dt 22:5 LORD your God *d* anyone who
23:18 the LORD your God *d* them both.
25:16 LORD your God *d* anyone who
Pr 12:22 The LORD *d* lying lips,
15:8 The LORD *d* the sacrifice
15:9 The LORD *d* the way
15:26 The LORD *d* the thoughts
16:5 The LORD *d* all the proud of heart
17:15 the LORD *d* them both.

Pr 20:23 The LORD *d* differing weights,

**DEVIL (DEVIL'S)**

Mt 13:39 the enemy who sows them is the *d.*
25:41 the eternal fire prepared for the *d*
Lk 4:2 forty days he was tempted by the *d.*
8:12 then the *d* comes and takes away
Eph 4:27 and do not give the *d* a foothold.
2Ti 2:26 and escape from the trap of the *d,*
Jas 4:7 Resist the *d,* and he will flee
1Pe 5:8 Your enemy the *d* prowls
1Jn 3:8 who does what is sinful is of the *d,*
Rev 12:9 that ancient serpent called the *d*

**DEVIL'S* (DEVIL)**

Eph 6:11 stand against the *d* schemes.
1Ti 3:7 into disgrace and into the *d* trap.
1Jn 3:8 was to destroy the *d* work.

**DEVOTE (DEVOTED DEVOTING DEVOTION DEVOUT)**

Job 11:13 "Yet if you *d* your heart to him
Jer 30:21 for who is he who will *d* himself
Col 4:2 *D* yourselves to prayer, being
1Ti 4:13 *d* yourself to the public reading
Tit 3:8 may be careful to *d* themselves

**DEVOTED (DEVOTE)**

Ezr 7:10 For Ezra had *d* himself to the study
Ac 2:42 They *d* themselves
Ro 12:10 Be *d* to one another
1Co 7:34 Her aim is to be *d* to the Lord

**DEVOTING (DEVOTE)**

1Ti 5:10 *d* herself to all kinds of good deeds.

**DEVOTION (DEVOTE)**

1Ch 28:9 and serve him with wholehearted *d*
Eze 33:31 With their mouths they express *d,*
1Co 7:35 way in undivided *d* to the Lord.
2Co 11:3 from your sincere and pure *d*

**DEVOUR**

2Sa 2:26 "Must the sword *d* forever?
Mk 12:40 They *d* widows' houses
1Pe 5:8 lion looking for someone to *d.*

**DEVOUT (DEVOTE)**

Lk 2:25 Simeon, who was righteous and *d.*

**DIE (DEAD DEATH DIED DIES)**

Ge 2:17 when you eat of it you will surely *d*
Ex 11:5 Every firstborn son in Egypt will *d,*
Ru 1:17 Where you *d* I will *d,* and there I
2Ki 14:6 each is to *d* for his own sins."
Pr 5:23 He will *d* for lack of discipline,
10:21 but fools *d* for lack of judgment.
15:10 he who hates correction will *d.*
23:13 with the rod, he will not *d.*
Ecc 3:2 a time to be born and a time to *d,*
Isa 66:24 their worm will not *d,* nor will their
Eze 3:18 that wicked man will *d* for his sin,
18:4 soul who sins is the one who will *d.*
33:8 'O wicked man, you will surely *d,*'
Mt 26:52 "for all who draw the sword will *d*
Jn 11:26 and believes in me will never *d.*
Ro 5:7 Very rarely will anyone *d*
14:8 and if we *d,* we *d* to the Lord.
1Co 15:22 in Adam all *d,* so in Christ all will
15:31 I *d* every day—I mean that,
Php 1:21 to live is Christ and to *d* is gain.
Heb 9:27 Just as man is destined to *d* once,
Rev 14:13 Blessed are the dead who *d*

**DIED (DIE)**

Ro 5:6 we were still powerless, Christ *d*
6:2 By no means! We *d* to sin;
6:8 if we *d* with Christ, we believe that
14:15 brother for whom Christ *d.*
1Co 8:11 for whom Christ *d,* is destroyed
15:3 that Christ *d* for our sins according
2Co 5:14 *d* for all, and therefore all *d.*
Col 3:3 For you *d,* and your life is now
1Th 5:10 He *d* for us so that, whether we are
2Ti 2:11 If we *d* with him,
Heb 9:15 now that he has *d* as a ransom

1Pe 3:18 For Christ *d* for sins once for all,
Rev 2:8 who *d* and came to life again.

**DIES (DIE)**
Job 14:14 If a man *d,* will he live again?
Pr 11:7 a wicked man *d,* his hope perishes;
Jn 11:25 in me will live, even though he *d;*
1Co 15:36 does not come to life unless it *d.*

**DIFFERENCE (DIFFERENT)**
Ro 10:12 For there is no *d* between Jew

**DIFFERENT (DIFFERENCE)**
1Co 12:4 There are *d* kinds of gifts,
2Co 11:4 or a *d* gospel from the one you

**DIGNITY**
Pr 31:25 She is clothed with strength and *d;*

**DIGS**
Pr 26:27 If a man *d* a pit, he will fall into it;

**DILIGENCE (DILIGENT)**
Heb 6:11 to show this same *d* to the very end

**DILIGENT (DILIGENCE)**
Pr 21:5 The plans of the *d* lead to profit
1Ti 4:15 Be *d* in these matters; give yourself

**DIRECT (DIRECTS)**
Ps 119:35 *D* me in the path of your
119:133 *D* my footsteps according
Jer 10:23 it is not for man to *d* his steps.
2Th 3:5 May the Lord *d* your hearts

**DIRECTS (DIRECT)**
Ps 42:8 By day the LORD *d* his love,
Isa 48:17 who *d* you in the way you should

**DIRGE**
Mt 11:17 we sang a *d,*

**DISAPPEAR**
Mt 5:18 will by any means *d* from the Law
Lk 16:17 earth to *d* than for the least stroke

**DISAPPOINT* (DISAPPOINTED)**
Ro 5:5 And hope does not *d* us,

**DISAPPOINTED (DISAPPOINT)**
Ps 22:5 in you they trusted and were not *d.*

**DISASTER**
Ps 57:1 wings until the *d* has passed.
Pr 3:25 Have no fear of sudden *d*
17:5 over *d* will not go unpunished.
Isa 45:7 I bring prosperity and create *d;*
Eze 7:5 An unheard-of *d* is coming.

**DISCERN (DISCERNING DISCERNMENT)**
Ps 19:12 Who can *d* his errors?
139:3 You *d* my going out and my lying
Php 1:10 you may be able to *d* what is best

**DISCERNING (DISCERN)**
Pr 14:6 knowledge comes easily to the *d.*
15:14 The *d* heart seeks knowledge,
Pr 17:24 A *d* man keeps wisdom in view,
17:28 and *d* if he holds his tongue.
19:25 rebuke a *d* man, and he will gain

**DISCERNMENT (DISCERN)**
Pr 17:10 A rebuke impresses a man of *d*
28:11 a poor man who has *d* sees

**DISCIPLE (DISCIPLES)**
Mt 10:42 these little ones because he is my *d,*
Lk 14:27 and follow me cannot be my *d.*

**DISCIPLES (DISCIPLE)**
Mt 28:19 Therefore go and make *d*
Jn 8:31 to my teaching, you are really my *d*
13:35 men will know that you are my *d*
Ac 11:26 The *d* were called Christians first

**DISCIPLINE (DISCIPLINED DISCIPLINES)**
Ps 38:1 or *d* me in your wrath.
39:11 You rebuke and *d* men for their sin;
94:12 Blessed is the man you *d,* O LORD
Pr 1:7 but fools despise wisdom and *d.*
3:11 do not despise the LORD 's *d*
5:12 You will say, "How I hated *d!*
5:23 He will die for lack of *d,*
6:23 and the corrections of *d*
10:17 He who heeds *d* shows the way
12:1 Whoever loves *d* loves knowledge,

Pr 13:18 He who ignores *d* comes to poverty
13:24 who loves him is careful to *d* him.
15:5 A fool spurns his father's *d*,
15:32 He who ignores *d* despises himself,
19:18 *D* your son, for in that there is hope
22:15 the rod of *d* will drive it far
23:13 Do not withhold *d* from a child;
29:17 *D* your son, and he will give you
Heb 12:5 do not make light of the Lord's *d*,
12:7 as *d*; God is treating you
12:11 No *d* seems pleasant at the time,
Rev 3:19 Those whom I love I rebuke and *d*.

**DISCIPLINED (DISCIPLINE)**

Pr 1:3 for acquiring a *d* and prudent life,
Jer 31:18 'You *d* me like an unruly calf,
1Co 11:32 we are being *d* so that we will not
Tit 1:8 upright, holy and *d*.
Heb 12:7 For what son is not *d* by his father?

**DISCIPLINES (DISCIPLINE)**

Dt 8:5 your heart that as a man *d* his son,
Pr 3:12 the LORD *d* those he loves,
Heb 12:6 because the Lord *d* those he loves,
12:10 but God *d* us for our good,

**DISCLOSED**

Lk 8:17 is nothing hidden that will not be *d*,

**DISCOURAGED**

Jos 1:9 Do not be terrified; do not be *d*,
10:25 "Do not be afraid; do not be *d*.
1Ch 28:20 or *d*, for the LORD God,
Isa 42:4 he will not falter or be *d*
Col 3:21 children, or they will become *d*.

**DISCREDITED**

2Co 6:3 so that our ministry will not be *d*.

**DISCRETION***

1Ch 22:12 May the LORD give you *d*
Pr 1:4 knowledge and *d* to the young—
2:11 *D* will protect you,
5:2 that you may maintain *d*
8:12 I possess knowledge and *d*.
11:22 a beautiful woman who shows no *d*.

**DISCRIMINATED***

Jas 2:4 have you not *d* among yourselves

**DISFIGURED**

Isa 52:14 his appearance was so *d*

**DISGRACE (DISGRACEFUL DISGRACES)**

Pr 11:2 When pride comes, then comes *d*,
14:34 but sin is a *d* to any people.
19:26 is a son who brings shame and *d*.
Ac 5:41 of suffering *d* for the Name.
Heb 13:13 the camp, bearing the *d* he bore.

**DISGRACEFUL (DISGRACE)**

Pr 10:5 during harvest is a *d* son.
17:2 wise servant will rule over a *d* son,

**DISGRACES (DISGRACE)**

Pr 28:7 of gluttons *d* his father.
29:15 but a child left to itself *d* his mother

**DISHONEST**

Pr 11:1 The LORD abhors *d* scales,
29:27 The righteous detest the *d*;
Lk 16:10 whoever is *d* with very little will
1Ti 3:8 wine, and not pursuing *d* gain.

**DISHONOR (DISHONORS)**

Lev 18:7 " 'Do not *d* your father
Pr 30:9 and so *d* the name of my God.
1Co 15:43 it is sown in *d*, it is raised in glory;

**DISHONORS (DISHONOR)**

Dt 27:16 Cursed is the man who *d* his father

**DISMAYED**

Isa 28:16 the one who trusts will never be *d*.
41:10 do not be *d*, for I am your God.

**DISOBEDIENCE (DISOBEY)**

Ro 5:19 as through the *d* of the one man
11:32 to *d* so that he may have mercy
Heb 2:2 and *d* received its just punishment,
4:6 go in, because of their *d*.
4:11 fall by following their example of *d*.

**DISOBEDIENT (DISOBEY)**
2Ti 3:2 proud, abusive, *d* to their parents,
Tit 1:6 to the charge of being wild and *d.*
1:16 *d* and unfit for doing anything

**DISOBEY (DISOBEDIENCE DISOBEDIENT)**
Dt 11:28 the curse if you *d* the commands
2Ch 24:20 'Why do you *d* the LORD 's
Ro 1:30 they *d* their parents; they are

**DISORDER**
1Co 14:33 For God is not a God of *d*
2Co 12:20 slander, gossip, arrogance and *d.*
Jas 3:16 there you find *d* and every evil

**DISOWN**
Pr 30:9 I may have too much and *d* you
Mt 10:33 I will *d* him before my Father
26:35 to die with you, I will never *d* you."
2Ti 2:12 If we *d* him,

**DISPLAY (DISPLAYS)**
Eze 39:21 I will *d* my glory among the nations
1Ti 1:16 Christ Jesus might *d* his unlimited

**DISPLAYS (DISPLAY)**
Isa 44:23 he *d* his glory in Israel.

**DISPUTE (DISPUTES)**
Pr 17:14 before a *d* breaks out.
1Co 6:1 If any of you has a *d* with another,

**DISPUTES (DISPUTE)**
Pr 18:18 Casting the lot settles *d*

**DISQUALIFIED**
1Co 9:27 I myself will not be *d* for the prize.

**DISREPUTE***
2Pe 2:2 will bring the way of truth into *d.*

**DISSENSION***
Pr 6:14 he always stirs up *d.*
6:19 and a man who stirs up *d*
10:12 Hatred stirs up *d,*
15:18 A hot-tempered man stirs up *d,*
16:28 A perverse man stirs up *d,*
28:25 A greedy man stirs up *d,*
29:22 An angry man stirs up *d,*
Ro 13:13 debauchery, not in *d* and jealousy.

**DISSIPATION***
Lk 21:34 will be weighed down with *d,*
1Pe 4:4 with them into the same flood of *d,*

**DISTINGUISH**
1Ki 3:9 and to *d* between right and wrong.
Heb 5:14 themselves to *d* good from evil.

**DISTORT**
2Co 4:2 nor do we *d* the word of God.
2Pe 3:16 ignorant and unstable people *d,*

**DISTRESS (DISTRESSED)**
Ps 18:6 In my *d* I called to the LORD;
Jnh 2:2 "In my *d* I called to the LORD,
Jas 1:27 after orphans and widows in their *d*

**DISTRESSED (DISTRESS)**
Ro 14:15 If your brother is *d*

**DIVIDED (DIVISION)**
Mt 12:25 household *d* against itself will not
Lk 23:34 they *d* up his clothes by casting lots
1Co 1:13 Is Christ *d?* Was Paul crucified

**DIVINATION**
Lev 19:26 " 'Do not practice *d* or sorcery.

**DIVINE**
Ro 1:20 his eternal power and *d* nature—
2Co 10:4 they have *d* power
2Pe 1:4 you may participate in the *d* nature

**DIVISION (DIVIDED DIVISIONS DIVISIVE)**
Lk 12:51 on earth? No, I tell you, but *d.*
1Co 12:25 so that there should be no *d*

**DIVISIONS (DIVISION)**
Ro 16:17 to watch out for those who cause *d*
1Co 1:10 another so that there may be no *d*
11:18 there are *d* among you,

**DIVISIVE* (DIVISION)**
Tit 3:10 Warn a *d* person once,

**DIVORCE**
Mal 2:16 "I hate *d,*" says the LORD God
Mt 19:3 for a man to *d* his wife for any
1Co 7:11 And a husband must not *d* his wife.
7:27 Are you married? Do not seek a *d.*

**DOCTOR**

Mt 9:12 "It is not the healthy who need a *d*,

**DOCTRINE**

1Ti 4:16 Watch your life and *d* closely.
Tit 2:1 is in accord with sound *d*.

**DOMINION**

Ps 22:28 for *d* belongs to the LORD

**DOOR**

Ps 141:3 keep watch over the *d* of my lips.
Mt 6:6 close the *d* and pray to your Father
7:7 and the *d* will be opened to you.
Rev 3:20 I stand at the *d* and knock.

**DOORKEEPER**

Ps 84:10 I would rather be a *d* in the house

**DOUBLE-EDGED**

Heb 4:12 Sharper than any *d* sword,
Rev 1:16 of his mouth came a sharp *d* sword.
2:12 of him who has the sharp, *d* sword.

**DOUBLE-MINDED (MIND)**

Ps 119:113 I hate *d* men,
Jas 1:8 he is a *d* man, unstable

**DOUBT**

Mt 14:31 he said, "why did you *d?*"
21:21 if you have faith and do not *d*,
Mk 11:23 and does not *d* in his heart
Jas 1:6 he must believe and not *d*,
Jude :22 Be merciful to those who *d;*

**DOWNCAST**

Ps 42:5 Why are you *d*, O my soul?
2Co 7:6 But God, who comforts the *d*,

**DRAW (DRAWING DRAWS)**

Mt 26:52 "for all who *d* the sword will die
Jn 12:32 up from the earth, will *d* all men
Heb 10:22 let us *d* near to God

**DRAWING (DRAW)**

Lk 21:28 because your redemption is *d* near

**DRAWS (DRAW)**

Jn 6:44 the Father who sent me *d* him,

**DREADFUL**

Heb 10:31 It is a *d* thing to fall into the hands

**DRESS**

1Ti 2:9 I also want women to *d* modestly,

**DRINK (DRUNK DRUNKARDS DRUNKENNESS)**

Pr 5:15 *D* water from your own cistern,
Lk 12:19 Take life easy; eat, *d* and be merry
Jn 7:37 let him come to me and *d*.
1Co 12:13 were all given the one Spirit to *d*.
Rev 21:6 to *d* without cost from the spring

**DRIVES**

1Jn 4:18 But perfect love *d* out fear,

**DROP**

Pr 17:14 so *d* the matter before a dispute
Isa 40:15 Surely the nations are like a *d*

**DRUNK (DRINK)**

Eph 5:18 Do not get *d* on wine, which leads

**DRUNKARDS (DRINK)**

Pr 23:21 for *d* and gluttons become poor,
1Co 6:10 nor the greedy nor *d* nor slanderers

**DRUNKENNESS (DRINK)**

Lk 21:34 weighed down with dissipation, *d*
Ro 13:13 and *d*, not in sexual immorality
Gal 5:21 factions and envy; *d*, orgies,
1Pe 4:3 living in debauchery, lust, *d*, orgies,

**DRY**

Isa 53:2 and like a root out of *d* ground.
Eze 37:4 '*D* bones, hear the word

**DUST**

Ge 2:7 man from the *d* of the ground
Ps 103:14 he remembers that we are *d*.
Ecc 3:20 all come from *d*, and to *d* all return.

**DUTY**

Ecc 12:13 for this is the whole *d* of man.
Ac 23:1 I have fulfilled my *d* to God
1Co 7:3 husband should fulfill his marital *d*

**DWELL (DWELLING)**

1Ki 8:27 "But will God really *d* on earth?
Ps 23:6 I will *d* in the house of the LORD
Isa 43:18 do not *d* on the past.
Eph 3:17 so that Christ may *d* in your hearts

Col 1:19 to have all his fullness *d* in him,
3:16 the word of Christ *d* in you richly

**DWELLING (DWELL)**
Eph 2:22 to become a *d* in which God lives

**EAGER**
Pr 31:13 and works with *e* hands.
1Pe 5:2 greedy for money, but *e* to serve;

**EAGLE'S (EAGLES)**
Ps 103:5 your youth is renewed like the *e*.

**EAGLES (EAGLE'S)**
Isa 40:31 They will soar on wings like *e*;

**EAR (EARS)**
1Co 2:9 no *e* has heard,
12:16 if the *e* should say, "Because I am

**EARNED**
Pr 31:31 Give her the reward she has *e*,

**EARS (EAR)**
Job 42:5 My *e* had heard of you
Ps 34:15 and his *e* are attentive to their cry;
Pr 21:13 If a man shuts his *e* to the cry
2Ti 4:3 to say what their itching *e* want

**EARTH (EARTHLY)**
Ge 1:1 God created the heavens and the *e*.
Ps 24:1 *e* is the LORD 's, and everything
108:5 and let your glory be over all the *e*.
Isa 6:3 the whole *e* is full of his glory."
51:6 the *e* will wear out like a garment
55:9 the heavens are higher than the *e*,
66:1 and the *e* is my footstool.
Jer 23:24 "Do not I fill heaven and *e?*"
Hab 2:20 let all the *e* be silent before him."
Mt 6:10 done on *e* as it is in heaven.
16:19 bind on *e* will be bound
24:35 Heaven and *e* will pass away,
28:18 and on *e* has been given to me.
Lk 2:14 on *e* peace to men
1Co 10:26 The *e* is the Lord's, and everything
Php 2:10 in heaven and on *e* and under the *e*,
2Pe 3:13 to a new heaven and a new *e*,

**EARTHLY (EARTH)**
Php 3:19 Their mind is on *e* things.
Col 3:2 on things above, not on *e* things.

**EAST**
Ps 103:12 as far as the *e* is from the west,

**EASY**
Mt 11:30 For my yoke is *e* and my burden is

**EAT (EATING)**
Ge 2:17 but you must not *e* from the tree
Isa 55:1 come, buy and *e!*
65:25 and the lion will *e* straw like the ox,
Mt 26:26 "Take and *e;* this is my body."
Ro 14:2 faith allows him to *e* everything,
1Co 8:13 if what I *e* causes my brother to fall
10:31 So whether you *e* or drink
2Th 3:10 man will not work, he shall not *e*."

**EATING (EAT)**
Ro 14:17 kingdom of God is not a matter of *e*

**EDICT**
Heb 11:23 they were not afraid of the king's *e*.

**EDIFIES**
1Co 14:4 but he who prophesies *e* the church

**EFFECT**
Isa 32:17 *e* of righteousness will be quietness
Heb 9:18 put into *e* without blood.

**EFFORT**
Lk 13:24 "Make every *e* to enter
Ro 9:16 depend on man's desire or *e*,
14:19 make every *e* to do what leads
Eph 4:3 Make every *e* to keep the unity
Heb 4:11 make every *e* to enter that rest,
12:14 Make every *e* to live in peace
2Pe 1:5 make every *e* to add
3:14 make every *e* to be found spotless,

**ELAH**
Son of Baasha; king of Israel (1Ki 16:6-14).

**ELDERLY* (ELDERS)**
Lev 19:32 show respect for the *e*

**ELDERS (ELDERLY)**
1Ti 5:17 The *e* who direct the affairs

**ELECTION**

Ro 9:11 God's purpose in *e* might stand:
2Pe 1:10 to make your calling and *e* sure.

**ELI**

High priest in youth of Samuel (1Sa 1-4). Blessed Hannah (1Sa 1:12-18); raised Samuel (1Sa 2:11-26).

**ELIJAH**

Prophet; predicted famine in Israel (1Ki 17:1; Jas 5:17). Fed by ravens (1Ki 17:2-6). Raised Sidonian widow's son (1Ki 17:7-24). Defeated prophets of Baal at Carmel (1Ki 18:16-46). Ran from Jezebel (1Ki 19:1-9). Prophesied death of Azariah (2Ki 1). Succeeded by Elishah (1Ki 19:19-21; 2Ki 2:1-18). Taken to heaven in whirlwind (2Ki 2:11-12). Return prophesied (Mal 4:5-6); equated with John the Baptist (Mt 17:9-13; Mk 9:9-13; Lk 1:17). Appeared with Moses in transfiguration of Jesus (Mt 17:1-8; Mk 9:1-8).

**ELISHA**

Prophet; successor of Elijah (1Ki 19:16-21); inherited his cloak (2Ki 2:1-18). Miracles of (2Ki 2-6).

**ELIZABETH***

Mother of John the Baptist, relative of Mary (Lk 1:5-58).

**EMBITTER***

Col 3:21 Fathers, do not *e* your children,

**EMPTY**

Eph 5:6 no one deceive you with *e* words,
1Pe 1:18 from the *e* way of life handed

**ENABLE (ABLE)**

Lk 1:74 to *e* us to serve him without fear
Ac 4:29 *e* your servants to speak your word

**ENABLED (ABLE)**

Lev 26:13 *e* you to walk with heads held high.
Jn 6:65 unless the Father has *e* him."

**ENABLES (ABLE)**

Php 3:21 by the power that *e* him

**ENCAMPS***

Ps 34:7 The angel of the LORD *e*

**ENCOURAGE (ENCOURAGEMENT)**

Ps 10:17 you *e* them, and you listen
Isa 1:17 *e* the oppressed.
Ac 15:32 to *e* and strengthen the brothers.
Ro 12:8 if it is encouraging, let him *e;*
1Th 4:18 Therefore *e* each other
2Ti 4:2 rebuke and *e*— with great patience
Tit 2:6 *e* the young men to be
Heb 3:13 But *e* one another daily, as long
10:25 but let us *e* one another—

**ENCOURAGEMENT (ENCOURAGE)**

Ac 4:36 Barnabas (which means Son of *E*),
Ro 15:4 *e* of the Scriptures we might have
15:5 and *e* give you a spirit of unity
1Co 14:3 to men for their strengthening, *e*
Heb 12:5 word of *e* that addresses you

**END**

Ps 119:33 then I will keep them to the *e.*
Pr 14:12 but in the *e* it leads to death.
19:20 and in the *e* you will be wise.
23:32 In the *e* it bites like a snake
Ecc 12:12 making many books there is no *e,*
Mt 10:22 firm to the *e* will be saved.
Lk 21:9 but the *e* will not come right away
Ro 10:4 Christ is the *e* of the law
1Co 15:24 the *e* will come, when he hands

**ENDURANCE (ENDURE)**

Ro 15:4 through *e* and the encouragement
15:5 May the God who gives *e*
2Co 1:6 which produces in you patient *e*
Col 1:11 might so that you may have great *e*
1Ti 6:11 faith, love, *e* and gentleness.
Tit 2:2 and sound in faith, in love and in *e.*

**ENDURE (ENDURANCE ENDURES)**

Ps 72:17 May his name *e* forever;
Pr 12:19 Truthful lips *e* forever,
27:24 for riches do not *e* forever,
Ecc 3:14 everything God does will *e* forever;
Mal 3:2 who can *e* the day of his coming?
2Ti 2:3 *E* hardship with us like a good
2:12 if we *e,* / we will also reign
Heb 12:7 *E* hardship as discipline; God is

Rev 3:10 kept my command to *e* patiently,

**ENDURES (ENDURE)**
Ps 112:9 his righteousness *e* forever;
136:1 *His love e forever.*
Da 9:15 made for yourself a name that *e*

**ENEMIES (ENEMY)**
Ps 23:5 in the presence of my *e*.
Mic 7:6 a man's *e* are the members
Mt 5:44 Love your *e* and pray
Lk 20:43 hand until I make your *e*

**ENEMY (ENEMIES ENMITY)**
Pr 24:17 Do not gloat when your *e* falls;
25:21 If your *e* is hungry, give him food
27:6 but an *e* multiplies kisses.
1Co 15:26 The last *e* to be destroyed is death.
1Ti 5:14 and to give the *e* no opportunity

**ENJOY (JOY)**
Dt 6:2 and so that you may *e* long life.
Eph 6:3 and that you may *e* long life
Heb 11:25 rather than to *e* the pleasures of sin

**ENJOYMENT (JOY)**
Ecc 4:8 and why am I depriving myself of *e*
1Ti 6:17 us with everything for our *e*.

**ENLIGHTENED* (LIGHT)**
Eph 1:18 that the eyes of your heart may be *e*
Heb 6:4 for those who have once been *e*,

**ENMITY* (ENEMY)**
Ge 3:15 And I will put *e*

**ENOCH**
Walked with God and taken by him (Ge 5:18-24; Heb 11:5). Prophet (Jude 14).

**ENTANGLED (ENTANGLES)**
2Pe 2:20 and are again *e* in it and overcome,

**ENTANGLES* (ENTANGLED)**
Heb 12:1 and the sin that so easily *e*,

**ENTER (ENTERED ENTERS ENTRANCE)**
Ps 100:4 *E* his gates with thanksgiving
Mt 5:20 will certainly not *e* the kingdom
7:13 "*E* through the narrow gate.
18:8 It is better for you to *e* life maimed
Mk 10:15 like a little child will never *e* it."
10:23 is for the rich to *e* the kingdom

**ENTERED (ENTER)**
Ro 5:12 as sin *e* the world through one man,
Heb 9:12 but he *e* the Most Holy Place once

**ENTERS (ENTER)**
Mk 7:18 you see that nothing that *e* a man
Jn 10:2 The man who *e* by the gate is

**ENTERTAIN**
1Ti 5:19 Do not *e* an accusation
Heb 13:2 Do not forget to *e* strangers,

**ENTHRALLED***
Ps 45:11 The king is *e* by your beauty;

**ENTHRONED (THRONE)**
1Sa 4:4 who is *e* between the cherubim.
Ps 2:4 The One *e* in heaven laughs;
102:12 But you, O LORD, sit *e* forever;
Isa 40:22 He sits *e* above the circle

**ENTICE**
Pr 1:10 My son, if sinners *e* you,
2Pe 2:18 they *e* people who are just escaping

**ENTIRE**
Gal 5:14 The *e* law is summed up

**ENTRUSTED (TRUST)**
1Ti 6:20 guard what has been *e* to your care.
2Ti 1:12 able to guard what I have *e* to him
1:14 Guard the good deposit that was *e*
Jude :3 once for all *e* to the saints.

**ENVY**
Pr 3:31 Do not *e* a violent man
14:30 but *e* rots the bones.
1Co 13:4 It does not *e*, it does not boast,

**EPHRAIM**
1. Second son of Joseph (Ge 41:52; 46:20). Blessed as firstborn by Jacob (Ge 48).
2. Synonymous with Northern Kingdom (Isa 7:17; Hos 5).

**EQUAL**
Isa 40:25 who is my *e*?" says the Holy One.

Jn 5:18 making himself *e* with God.
1Co 12:25 that its parts should have *e* concern

**EQUIP* (EQUIPPED)**
Heb 13:21 *e* you with everything good

**EQUIPPED (EQUIP)**
2Ti 3:17 man of God may be thoroughly *e*

**ERROR**
Jas 5:20 Whoever turns a sinner from the *e*

**ESAU**
Firstborn of Isaac, twin of Jacob (Ge 25:21-26). Also called Edom (Ge 25:30). Sold Jacob his birthright (Ge 25:29-34); lost blessing (Ge 27). Reconciled to Jacob (Gen 33).

**ESCAPE (ESCAPING)**
Ro 2:3 think you will *e* God's judgment?
Heb 2:3 how shall we *e* if we ignore such

**ESCAPING (ESCAPE)**
1Co 3:15 only as one *e* through the flames.

**ESTABLISH**
Ge 6:18 But I will *e* my covenant with you,
1Ch 28:7 I will *e* his kingdom forever
Ro 10:3 God and sought to *e* their own,

**ESTEEMED**
Pr 22:1 to be *e* is better than silver or gold.
Isa 53:3 he was despised, and we *e* him not.

**ESTHER**
Jewess who lived in Persia; cousin of Mordecai (Est 2:7). Chosen queen of Xerxes (Est 2:8-18). Foiled Haman's plan to exterminate the Jews (Est 3-4; 7-9).

**ETERNAL (ETERNALLY ETERNITY)**
Ps 16:11 with *e* pleasures at your right hand.
111:10 To him belongs *e* praise.
119:89 Your word, O LORD, is *e*;
Isa 26:4 LORD, the LORD, is the Rock *e*.
Mt 19:16 good thing must I do to get *e* life?"
25:41 into the *e* fire prepared for the devil
25:46 they will go away to *e* punishment,
Jn 3:15 believes in him may have *e* life.
3:16 him shall not perish but have *e* life.
3:36 believes in the Son has *e* life,
4:14 spring of water welling up to *e* life."
5:24 believes him who sent me has *e* life
6:68 You have the words of *e* life.
10:28 I give them *e* life, and they shall
17:3 this is *e* life: that they may know
Ro 1:20 his *e* power and divine nature—
6:23 but the gift of God is *e* life
2Co 4:17 for us an *e* glory that far outweighs
4:18 temporary, but what is unseen is *e*.
1Ti 1:16 believe on him and receive *e* life.
1:17 Now to the King *e*, immortal,
Heb 9:12 having obtained *e* redemption.
1Jn 5:11 God has given us *e* life,
5:13 you may know that you have *e* life.

**ETERNALLY (ETERNAL)**
Gal 1:8 let him be *e* condemned! As we

**ETERNITY (ETERNAL)**
Ps 93:2 you are from all *e*.
Ecc 3:11 also set *e* in the hearts of men;

**ETHIOPIAN**
Jer 13:23 Can the *E* change his skin

**EUNUCHS**
Mt 19:12 For some are *e* because they were

**EVANGELIST (EVANGELISTS)**
2Ti 4:5 hardship, do the work of an *e*,

**EVANGELISTS* (EVANGELIST)**
Eph 4:11 some to be prophets, some to be *e*,

**EVE**
2Co 11:3 as *E* was deceived by the serpent's
1Ti 2:13 For Adam was formed first, then *E*

**EVEN-TEMPERED***
Pr 17:27 and a man of understanding is *e*.

**EVER (EVERLASTING FOREVER)**
Ex 15:18 LORD will reign for *e* and *e*."
Dt 8:19 If you *e* forget the LORD your

Ps 5:11 let them *e* sing for joy.
10:16 The LORD is King for *e* and *e;*
25:3 will *e* be put to shame,
26:3 for your love is *e* before me,
45:6 O God, will last for *e* and *e;*
52:8 God's unfailing love for *e* and *e.*
89:33 nor will I *e* betray my faithfulness.
145:1 I will praise your name for *e* and *e.*
Pr 4:18 shining *e* brighter till the full light
5:19 may you *e* be captivated
Isa 66:8 Who has *e* heard of such a thing?
Jer 31:36 the descendants of Israel *e* cease
Da 7:18 it forever—yes, for *e* and *e.*'
12:3 like the stars for *e* and *e.*
Mk 4:12 *e* hearing but never understanding;
Jn 1:18 No one has *e* seen God,
Rev 1:18 and behold I am alive for *e* and *e!*
22:5 And they will reign for *e* and *e.*


## EVER-INCREASING* (INCREASE)


Ro 6:19 to impurity and to *e* wickedness,
2Co 3:18 into his likeness with *e* glory,


## EVERLASTING (EVER)


Dt 33:27 and underneath are the *e* arms.
Ne 9:5 your God, who is from *e* to *e.*"
Ps 90:2 from *e* to *e* you are God.
139:24 and lead me in the way *e.*
Isa 9:6 *E* Father, Prince of Peace.
33:14 Who of us can dwell with *e* burning
35:10 *e* joy will crown their heads.
45:17 the LORD with an *e* salvation;
54:8 but with *e* kindness
55:3 I will make an *e* covenant with you,
63:12 to gain for himself *e* renown,
Jer 31:3 "I have loved you with an *e* love;
Da 9:24 to bring in *e* righteousness,
12:2 some to *e* life, others to shame
Jn 6:47 the truth, he who believes has *e* life.
2Th 1:9 punished with *e* destruction
Jude :6 bound with *e* chains for judgment


## EVER-PRESENT*


Ps 46:1 an *e* help in trouble


## EVIDENCE (EVIDENT)


Jn 14:11 on the *e* of the miracles themselves.


## EVIDENT (EVIDENCE)


Php 4:5 Let your gentleness be *e* to all.


## EVIL


Ge 2:9 of the knowledge of good and *e.*
Job 1:1 he feared God and shunned *e.*
1:8 a man who fears God and shuns *e.*"
Job 34:10 Far be it from God to do *e,*
Ps 23:4 I will fear no *e,*
34:14 Turn from *e* and do good;
51:4 and done what is *e* in your sight,
97:10 those who love the LORD hate *e,*
101:4 I will have nothing to do with *e.*
Pr 8:13 To fear the LORD is to hate *e;*
10:23 A fool finds pleasure in *e* conduct,
11:27 *e* comes to him who searches for it.
24:19 Do not fret because of *e* men
24:20 for the *e* man has no future hope,
Isa 5:20 Woe to those who call *e* good
13:11 I will punish the world for its *e,*
55:7 and the *e* man his thoughts.
Hab 1:13 Your eyes are too pure to look on *e;*
Mt 5:45 He causes his sun to rise on the *e*
6:13 but deliver us from the *e* one.'
7:11 If you, then, though you are *e,*
12:35 and the *e* man brings *e* things out
Jn 17:15 you protect them from the *e* one.
Ro 2:9 for every human being who does *e:*
12:9 Hate what is *e;* cling
12:17 Do not repay anyone *e* for *e.*
16:19 and innocent about what is *e.*
1Co 13:6 Love does not delight in *e*

1Co 14:20 In regard to *e* be infants,
Eph 6:16 all the flaming arrows of the *e* one.
1Th 5:22 Avoid every kind of *e*.
1Ti 6:10 of money is a root of all kinds of *e*.
2Ti 2:22 Flee the *e* desires of youth,
Jas 1:13 For God cannot be tempted by *e*,
1Pe 2:16 your freedom as a cover-up for *e*;
3:9 Do not repay *e* with *e* or insult

**EXACT**
Heb 1:3 the *e* representation of his being,

**EXALT (EXALTED EXALTS)**
Ps 30:1 I will *e* you, O LORD,
34:3 let us *e* his name together.
118:28 you are my God, and I will *e* you.
Isa 24:15 *e* the name of the LORD, the God

**EXALTED (EXALT)**
2Sa 22:47 *E* be God, the Rock, my Savior!
1Ch 29:11 you are *e* as head over all.
Ne 9:5 and may it be *e* above all blessing
Ps 21:13 Be *e*, O LORD, in your strength;
46:10 I will be *e* among the nations,
57:5 Be *e*, O God, above the heavens;
97:9 you are *e* far above all gods.
99:2 he is *e* over all the nations.
108:5 Be *e*, O God, above the heavens,
Ps 148:13 for his name alone is *e*;
Isa 6:1 *e*, and the train of his robe filled
12:4 and proclaim that his name is *e*.
33:5 The LORD is *e*, for he dwells
Eze 21:26 The lowly will be *e* and the *e* will be
Mt 23:12 whoever humbles himself will be *e*.
Php 1:20 always Christ will be *e* in my body,
2:9 Therefore God *e* him

**EXALTS (EXALT)**
Ps 75:7 He brings one down, he *e* another.
Pr 14:34 Righteousness *e* a nation,
Mt 23:12 For whoever *e* himself will be

**EXAMINE (EXAMINED)**
Ps 26:2 *e* my heart and my mind;
Jer 17:10 and *e* the mind,
La 3:40 Let us *e* our ways and test them,
1Co 11:28 A man ought to *e* himself
2Co 13:5 *E* yourselves to see whether you

**EXAMINED (EXAMINE)**
Ac 17:11 *e* the Scriptures every day to see

**EXAMPLE (EXAMPLES)**
Jn 13:15 have set you an *e* that you should
1Co 11:1 Follow my *e*, as I follow
1Ti 4:12 set an *e* for the believers in speech,
Tit 2:7 In everything set them an *e*
1Pe 2:21 leaving you an *e*, that you should

**EXAMPLES* (EXAMPLE)**
1Co 10:6 Now these things occurred as *e*
10:11 as *e* and were written down
1Pe 5:3 to you, but being *e* to the flock.

**EXASPERATE***
Eph 6:4 Fathers, do not *e* your children;

**EXCEL (EXCELLENT)**
1Co 14:12 to *e* in gifts that build up the church
2Co 8:7 But just as you *e* in everything—

**EXCELLENT (EXCEL)**
1Co 12:31 now I will show you the most *e* way
Php 4:8 if anything is *e* or praiseworthy—
1Ti 3:13 have served well gain an *e* standing
Tit 3:8 These things are *e* and profitable

**EXCHANGED**
Ro 1:23 *e* the glory of the immortal God
1:25 They *e* the truth of God for a lie,

**EXCUSE (EXCUSES)**
Jn 15:22 they have no *e* for their sin.
Ro 1:20 so that men are without *e*.

**EXCUSES* (EXCUSE)**
Lk 14:18 "But they all alike began to make *e*.

**EXISTS**
Heb 2:10 and through whom everything *e*,
11:6 to him must believe that he *e*

**EXPECT (EXPECTATION)**
Mt 24:44 at an hour when you do not *e* him.

**EXPECTATION (EXPECT)**
Ro 8:19 waits in eager *e* for the sons
Heb 10:27 but only a fearful *e* of judgment

**EXPEL***
1Co 5:13 *E* the wicked man from among you

**EXPENSIVE**
1Ti 2:9 or gold or pearls or *e* clothes,

**EXPLOIT**
Pr 22:22 Do not *e* the poor because they are
2Co 12:17 Did I *e* you through any

**EXPOSE**
1Co 4:5 will *e* the motives of men's hearts.
Eph 5:11 of darkness, but rather *e* them.

**EXTENDS**
Pr 31:20 and *e* her hands to the needy.
Lk 1:50 His mercy *e* to those who fear him,

**EXTINGUISHED**
2Sa 21:17 the lamp of Israel will not be *e.*"

**EXTOL***
Job 36:24 Remember to *e* his work,
Ps 34:1 I will *e* the LORD at all times;
68:4 *e* him who rides on the clouds—
95:2 and *e* him with music and song.
109:30 mouth I will greatly *e* the LORD;
111:1 I will *e* the LORD with all my heart
115:18 it is we who *e* the LORD,
Ps 117:1 *e* him, all you peoples.
145:2 and *e* your name for ever and ever.
145:10 your saints will *e* you.
147:12 *E* the LORD, O Jerusalem;

**EXTORT***
Lk 3:14 "Don't *e* money and don't accuse

**EYE (EYES)**
Ex 21:24 you are to take life for life, *e* for *e*,
Ps 94:9 Does he who formed the *e* not see?
Mt 5:29 If your right *e* causes you to sin,
5:38 '*E* for *e*, and tooth for tooth.'
7:3 of sawdust in your brother's *e*
1Co 2:9 "No *e* has seen,
Col 3:22 not only when their *e* is on you
Rev 1:7 and every *e* will see him,

**EYES (EYE)**
Nu 33:55 remain will become barbs in your *e*
Jos 23:13 on your backs and thorns in your *e*,
2Ch 16:9 For the *e* of the LORD range
Job 31:1 "I made a covenant with my *e*
36:7 He does not take his *e*
Ps 119:18 Open my *e* that I may see
121:1 I lift up my *e* to the hills—
141:8 But my *e* are fixed on you,
Pr 3:7 Do not be wise in your own *e;*
Pr 4:25 Let your *e* look straight ahead,
15:3 The *e* of the LORD are everywhere
Isa 6:5 and my *e* have seen the King,
Hab 1:13 Your *e* are too pure to look on evil;
Jn 4:35 open your *e* and look at the fields!
2Co 4:18 So we fix our *e* not on what is seen,
Heb 12:2 Let us fix our *e* on Jesus, the author
Jas 2:5 poor in the *e* of the world to be rich
1Pe 3:12 For the *e* of the Lord are
Rev 7:17 wipe away every tear from their *e.*"
21:4 He will wipe every tear from their *e*

**EZEKIEL**
Priest called to be prophet to the exiles (Eze 1-3).

**EZRA**
Priest and teacher of the Law who led a return of exiles to Israel to reestablish temple and worship (Ezr 7-8). Corrected intermarriage of priests (Ezr 9-10). Read Law at celebration of Feast of Tabernacles (Neh 8).

**FACE (FACES)**
Ge 32:30 "It is because I saw God *f* to *f*,
Ex 34:29 was not aware that his *f* was radiant
Nu 6:25 the LORD make his *f* shine
1Ch 16:11 seek his *f* always.
2Ch 7:14 and seek my *f* and turn
Ps 4:6 Let the light of your *f* shine upon us
27:8 Your *f*, LORD, I will seek.

Ps 31:16 Let your *f* shine on your servant;
105:4 seek his *f* always.
119:135 Make your *f* shine
Isa 50:7 Therefore have I set my *f* like flint,
Mt 17:2 His *f* shone like the sun,
1Co 13:12 mirror; then we shall see *f* to *f*.
2Co 4:6 the glory of God in the *f* of Christ.
1Pe 3:12 but the *f* of the Lord is
Rev 1:16 His *f* was like the sun shining

**FACES (FACE)**

2Co 3:18 who with unveiled *f* all reflect

**FACTIONS**

Gal 5:20 selfish ambition, dissensions, *f*

**FADE**

1Pe 5:4 of glory that will never *f* away.

**FAIL (FAILING FAILINGS FAILS)**

1Ch 28:20 He will not *f* you or forsake you
2Ch 34:33 they did not *f* to follow the LORD,
Ps 89:28 my covenant with him will never *f*.
Pr 15:22 Plans *f* for lack of counsel,
Isa 51:6 my righteousness will never *f*.
La 3:22 for his compassions never *f*.
2Co 13:5 unless, of course, you *f* the test?

**FAILING (FAIL)**

1Sa 12:23 sin against the LORD by *f* to pray

**FAILINGS (FAIL)**

Ro 15:1 ought to bear with the *f* of the weak

**FAILS (FAIL)**

1Co 13:8 Love never *f*.

**FAINT**

Isa 40:31 they will walk and not be *f*.

**FAIR**

Pr 1:3 doing what is right and just and *f*;
Col 4:1 slaves with what is right and *f*,

**FAITH (FAITHFUL FAITHFULLY FAITHFULNESS FAITHLESS)**

2Ch 20:20 Have *f* in the LORD your God
Hab 2:4 but the righteous will live by his *f*—
Mt 9:29 According to your *f* will it be done
17:20 if you have *f* as small as a mustard
24:10 many will turn away from the *f*
Mk 11:22 "Have *f* in God," Jesus answered.
Lk 7:9 I have not found such great *f*
12:28 will he clothe you, O you of little *f*!
17:5 "Increase our *f*!" He replied,
18:8 will he find *f* on the earth?"
Ac 14:9 saw that he had *f* to be healed
14:27 the door of *f* to the Gentiles.
Ro 1:12 encouraged by each other's *f*.
1:17 is by *f* from first to last,
1:17 "The righteous will live by *f*."
Ro 3:3 What if some did not have *f*?
3:22 comes through *f* in Jesus Christ
3:25 a sacrifice of atonement, through *f*
4:5 his *f* is credited as righteousness.
5:1 we have been justified through *f*,
10:17 *f* comes from hearing the message,
14:1 Accept him whose *f* is weak,
14:23 that does not come from *f* is sin.
1Co 13:2 and if I have a *f* that can move
13:13 And now these three remain: *f*,
16:13 stand firm in the *f*; be men
2Co 5:7 We live by *f*, not by sight.
13:5 to see whether you are in the *f*;
Gal 2:16 Jesus that we may be justified by *f*
2:20 I live by *f* in the Son of God,
3:11 "The righteous will live by *f*."
3:24 that we might be justified by *f*.
Eph 2:8 through *f*—and this not
4:5 one Lord, one *f*, one baptism;
6:16 to all this, take up the shield of *f*,
Col 1:23 continue in your *f*, established
1Th 5:8 on *f* and love as a breastplate,
1Ti 2:15 if they continue in *f*, love
4:1 later times some will abandon the *f*

1Ti 5:8 he has denied the *f* and is worse
6:12 Fight the good fight of the *f*.
2Ti 3:15 wise for salvation through *f*
4:7 finished the race, I have kept the *f*.
Phm :6 may be active in sharing your *f*,
Heb 10:38 But my righteous one will live by *f*.
11:1 *f* is being sure of what we hope for
11:3 By *f* we understand that
11:5 By *f* Enoch was taken from this life
11:6 And without *f* it is impossible
11:7 By *f* Noah, when warned about
11:8 By *f* Abraham, when called to go
11:17 By *f* Abraham, when God tested
11:20 By *f* Isaac blessed Jacob
11:21 By *f* Jacob, when he was dying,
11:22 By *f* Joseph, when his end was near
11:24 By *f* Moses, when he had grown up
11:31 By *f* the prostitute Rahab,
12:2 the author and perfecter of our *f*,
Jas 2:14 if a man claims to have *f*
2:17 In the same way, *f* by itself,
2:26 so *f* without deeds is dead.
2Pe 1:5 effort to add to your *f* goodness;
1Jn 5:4 overcome the world, even our *f*.
Jude :3 to contend for the *f* that was once

**FAITHFUL (FAITH)**

Nu 12:7 he is *f* in all my house.
Dt 7:9 your God is God; he is the *f* God,
32:4 A *f* God who does no wrong,
2Sa 22:26 "To the *f* you show yourself *f*,
Ps 25:10 of the LORD are loving and *f*
31:23 The LORD preserves the *f*,
33:4 he is *f* in all he does.
37:28 and will not forsake his *f* ones.
97:10 for he guards the lives of his *f* ones
145:13 The LORD is *f* to all his promises
146:6 the LORD, who remains *f* forever.
Pr 31:26 and *f* instruction is on her tongue.
Mt 25:21 'Well done, good and *f* servant!
Ro 12:12 patient in affliction, *f* in prayer.
1Co 4:2 been given a trust must prove *f*.
10:13 And God is *f*; he will not let you be
1Th 5:24 The one who calls you is *f*
2Ti 2:13 he will remain *f*,
Heb 3:6 But Christ is *f* as a son
10:23 for he who promised is *f*.
1Pe 4:19 themselves to their *f* Creator
1Jn 1:9 he is *f* and just and will forgive us
Rev 1:5 who is the *f* witness, the firstborn
2:10 Be *f*, even to the point of death,
19:11 whose rider is called *F* and True.

**FAITHFULLY (FAITH)**

Dt 11:13 if you *f* obey the commands I am
1Sa 12:24 and serve him *f* with all your heart;
1Ki 2:4 and if they walk *f* before me
1Pe 4:10 *f* administering God's grace

**FAITHFULNESS (FAITH)**

Ps 57:10 your *f* reaches to the skies.
85:10 Love and *f* meet together;
86:15 to anger, abounding in love and *f*.
89:1 mouth I will make your *f* known
89:14 love and *f* go before you.
91:4 his *f* will be your shield
117:2 the *f* of the LORD endures forever.
119:75 and in *f* you have afflicted me.
Pr 3:3 Let love and *f* never leave you;
Isa 11:5 and *f* the sash around his waist.
La 3:23 great is your *f*.
Ro 3:3 lack of faith nullify God's *f*?
Gal 5:22 patience, kindness, goodness, *f*,

**FAITHLESS (FAITH)**

Ps 119:158 I look on the *f* with loathing,
Jer 3:22 "Return, *f* people;
Ro 1:31 they are senseless, *f*, heartless,
2Ti 2:13 if we are *f*,

**FALL (FALLEN FALLING FALLS)**

Ps 37:24 though he stumble, he will not *f*,
55:22 he will never let the righteous *f*.
69:9 of those who insult you *f* on me.
Pr 11:28 Whoever trusts in his riches will *f*,
Lk 11:17 a house divided against itself will *f*.
Ro 3:23 and *f* short of the glory of God,
Heb 6:6 if they *f* away, to be brought back

**FALLEN (FALL)**

2Sa 1:19 How the mighty have *f*!
Isa 14:12 How you have *f* from heaven,
1Co 15:20 of those who have *f* asleep.
Gal 5:4 you have *f* away from grace.
1Th 4:15 precede those who have *f* asleep.

**FALLING (FALL)**

Jude :24 able to keep you from *f*

**FALLS (FALL)**

Pr 24:17 Do not gloat when your enemy *f*;
Jn 12:24 a kernel of wheat *f* to the ground
Ro 14:4 To his own master he stands or *f*.

**FALSE (FALSEHOOD FALSELY)**

Ex 20:16 "You shall not give *f* testimony
23:1 "Do not spread *f* reports.
Pr 13:5 The righteous hate what is *f*,
19:5 A *f* witness will not go unpunished,
Mt 7:15 "Watch out for *f* prophets.
19:18 not steal, do not give *f* testimony,
24:11 and many *f* prophets will appear
Php 1:18 whether from *f* motives or true,
1Ti 1:3 not to teach *f* doctrines any longer
2Pe 2:1 there will be *f* teachers among you.

**FALSEHOOD (FALSE)**

Ps 119:163 I hate and abhor *f*
Pr 30:8 Keep *f* and lies far from me;
Eph 4:25 each of you must put off *f*

**FALSELY (FALSE)**

Lev 19:12 " 'Do not swear *f* by my name
Lk 3:14 and don't accuse people *f*—
1Ti 6:20 ideas of what is *f* called knowledge,

**FALTER***

Pr 24:10 If you *f* in times of trouble,
Isa 42:4 he will not *f* or be discouraged

**FAMILIES (FAMILY)**

Ps 68:6 God sets the lonely in *f*,

**FAMILY (FAMILIES)**

Pr 15:27 greedy man brings trouble to his *f*,
31:15 she provides food for her *f*
Lk 9:61 go back and say good-by to my *f*."
12:52 in one *f* divided against each other,
1Ti 3:4 He must manage his own *f* well
3:5 how to manage his own *f*,
5:4 practice by caring for their own *f*
5:8 and especially for his immediate *f*,

**FAMINE**

Ge 41:30 seven years of *f* will follow them.
Am 8:11 but a *f* of hearing the words
Ro 8:35 or persecution or *f* or nakedness

**FAN***

2Ti 1:6 you to *f* into flame the gift of God,

**FAST**

Dt 13:4 serve him and hold *f* to him.
Jos 22:5 to hold *f* to him and to serve him
23:8 to hold *f* to the LORD your God,
Ps 119:31 I hold *f* to your statutes, O LORD;
139:10 your right hand will hold me *f*.
Mt 6:16 "When you *f*, do not look somber
1Pe 5:12 Stand *f* in it.

**FATHER (FATHER'S FATHERLESS FATHERS FOREFATHERS)**

Ge 2:24 this reason a man will leave his *f*
17:4 You will be the *f* of many nations.
Ex 20:12 "Honor your *f* and your mother,
21:15 "Anyone who attacks his *f*
21:17 "Anyone who curses his *f*
Lev 18:7 " 'Do not dishonor your *f*
19:3 you must respect his mother and *f*,

Dt 5:16 “Honor your *f* and your mother,
21:18 son who does not obey his *f*
Ps 27:10 Though my *f* and mother forsake
68:5 A *f* to the fatherless, a defender
Pr 10:1 A wise son brings joy to his *f*,
17:21 there is no joy for the *f* of a fool.
23:22 Listen to your *f*, who gave you life,
23:24 *f* of a righteous man has great joy;
28:7 of gluttons disgraces his *f*.
29:3 loves wisdom brings joy to his *f*,
Isa 9:6 Everlasting *F*, Prince of Peace.
Mt 6:9 “ ‘Our *F* in heaven,
10:37 “Anyone who loves his *f*
15:4 ‘Honor your *f* and mother’
19:5 this reason a man will leave his *f*
Lk 12:53 *f* against son and son against *f*,
23:34 Jesus said, “*F*, forgive them,
Jn 6:44 the *F* who sent me draws him,
6:46 No one has seen the *F*
8:44 You belong to your *f*, the devil,
10:30 I and the *F* are one.”
14:6 No one comes to the *F*
14:9 who has seen me has seen the *F*.
Ro 4:11 he is the *f* of all who believe
2Co 6:18 “I will be a *F* to you,
Eph 6:2 “Honor your *f* and mother”—
Heb 12:7 what son is not disciplined by his *f*?

**FATHER'S (FATHER)**

Pr 13:1 A wise son heeds his *f* instruction,
15:5 A fool spurns his *f* discipline,
19:13 A foolish son is his *f* ruin,
Lk 2:49 had to be in my *F* house?”
Jn 2:16 How dare you turn my *F* house
10:29 can snatch them out of my *F* hand.
14:2 In my *F* house are many rooms;

**FATHERLESS (FATHER)**

Dt 10:18 He defends the cause of the *f*
24:17 Do not deprive the alien or the *f*
24:19 Leave it for the alien, the *f*
Ps 68:5 A father to the *f*, a defender
Pr 23:10 or encroach on the fields of the *f*,

**FATHERS (FATHER)**

Ex 20:5 for the sin of the *f* to the third
Lk 11:11 “Which of you *f*, if your son asks
Eph 6:4 *F*, do not exasperate your children;
Col 3:21 *F*, do not embitter your children,

**FATHOM***

Job 11:7 “Can you *f* the mysteries of God?
Ps 145:3 his greatness no one can *f*.
Ecc 3:11 yet they cannot *f* what God has
Isa 40:28 and his understanding no one can *f*
1Co 13:2 and can *f* all mysteries and all

**FAULT (FAULTS)**

Mt 18:15 and show him his *f*, just
Php 2:15 of God without *f* in a crooked
Jas 1:5 generously to all without finding *f*,
Jude :24 his glorious presence without *f*

**FAULTFINDERS***

Jude :16 These men are grumblers and *f*;

**FAULTS (FAULT)**

Ps 19:12 Forgive my hidden *f*.

**FAVORITISM***

Ex 23:3 and do not show *f* to a poor man
Lev 19:15 to the poor or *f* to the great,
Ac 10:34 true it is that God does not show *f*
Ro 2:11 For God does not show *f*.
Eph 6:9 and there is no *f* with him.
Col 3:25 for his wrong, and there is no *f*.
1Ti 5:21 and to do nothing out of *f*.
Jas 2:1 Lord Jesus Christ, don't show *f*.
2:9 But if you show *f*, you sin

**FEAR (AFRAID FEARS)**

Dt 6:13 *F* the LORD your God, serve him
10:12 but to *f* the LORD your God,
31:12 and learn to *f* the LORD your God

Ps 19:9 The *f* of the LORD is pure,
23:4 I will *f* no evil,
27:1 whom shall I *f*?
91:5 You will not *f* the terror of night,
111:10 *f* of the LORD is the beginning
Pr 8:13 To *f* the LORD is to hate evil;
9:10 *f* of the LORD is the beginning
10:27 The *f* of the LORD adds length
14:27 The *f* of the LORD is a fountain
15:33 *f* of the LORD teaches a man
16:6 through the *f* of the LORD a man
19:23 The *f* of the LORD leads to life:
29:25 *F* of man will prove to be a snare,
Isa 11:3 delight in the *f* of the LORD.
41:10 So do not *f*, for I am with you;
Lk 12:5 I will show you whom you should *f*:
Php 2:12 to work out your salvation with *f*
1Jn 4:18 But perfect love drives out *f*,

**FEARS (FEAR)**
Job 1:8 a man who *f* God and shuns evil."
Ps 34:4 he delivered me from all my *f*.
Pr 31:30 a woman who *f* the LORD is
1Jn 4:18 The one who *f* is not made perfect

**FEED**
Jn 21:15 Jesus said, "*F* my lambs."
21:17 Jesus said, "*F* my sheep.
Ro 12:20 "If your enemy is hungry, *f* him;
Jude :12 shepherds who *f* only themselves.

**FEET (FOOT)**
Ps 8:6 you put everything under his *f*:
22:16 have pierced my hands and my *f*.
40:2 he set my *f* on a rock
110:1 a footstool for your *f*."
119:105 Your word is a lamp to my *f*
Ro 10:15 "How beautiful are the *f*
1Co 12:21 And the head cannot say to the *f*,
15:25 has put all his enemies under his *f*.
Heb 12:13 "Make level paths for your *f*,"

**FELLOWSHIP**
2Co 6:14 what *f* can light have with darkness
13:14 and the *f* of the Holy Spirit be
Php 3:10 the *f* of sharing in his sufferings,
1Jn 1:6 claim to have *f* with him yet walk
1:7 we have *f* with one another,

**FEMALE**
Ge 1:27 male and *f* he created them.
Gal 3:28 *f*, for you are all one in Christ Jesus

**FERVOR**
Ro 12:11 but keep your spiritual *f*, serving

**FIELD (FIELDS)**
Mt 6:28 See how the lilies of the *f* grow.
Mt 13:38 *f* is the world, and the good seed
1Co 3:9 you are God's *f*, God's building.

**FIELDS (FIELD)**
Lk 2:8 were shepherds living out in the *f*
Jn 4:35 open your eyes and look at the *f*!

**FIG (FIGS)**
Ge 3:7 so they sewed *f* leaves together

**FIGHT (FOUGHT)**
Ex 14:14 The LORD will *f* for you; you need
Dt 1:30 going before you, will *f* for you,
3:22 the LORD your God himself will *f*
Ne 4:20 Our God will *f* for us!"
Ps 35:1 *f* against those who *f* against me.
Jn 18:36 my servants would *f*
1Co 9:26 I do not *f* like a man beating the air.
2Co 10:4 The weapons we *f*
1Ti 1:18 them you may *f* the good *f*,
6:12 Fight the good *f* of the faith.
2Ti 4:7 fought the good *f*, I have finished

**FIGS (FIG)**
Lk 6:44 People do not pick *f*

**FILL (FILLED FILLS FULL FULLNESS FULLY)**
Ge 1:28 and increase in number; *f* the earth
Ps 16:11 you will *f* me with joy
81:10 wide your mouth and I will *f* it.

Pr 28:19 who chases fantasies will have his *f*
Hag 2:7 and I will *f* this house with glory,'
Jn 6:26 you ate the loaves and had your *f*.
Ac 2:28 you will *f* me with joy
Ro 15:13 the God of hope *f* you with all joy

**FILLED (FILL)**
Ps 72:19 may the whole earth be *f*
119:64 The earth is *f* with your love,
Eze 43:5 the glory of the LORD *f* the temple
Hab 2:14 For the earth will be *f*
Lk 1:15 and he will be *f* with the Holy Spirit
1:41 and Elizabeth was *f* with the Holy
Jn 12:3 the house was *f* with the fragrance
Ac 2:4 All of them were *f*
4:8 Then Peter, *f* with the Holy Spirit,
9:17 and be *f* with the Holy Spirit."
13:9 called Paul, *f* with the Holy Spirit,
Eph 5:18 Instead, be *f* with the Spirit.
Php 1:11 *f* with the fruit of righteousness

**FILLS (FILL)**
Nu 14:21 of the LORD *f* the whole earth,
Ps 107:9 and *f* the hungry with good things.
Eph 1:23 fullness of him who *f* everything

**FILTHY**
Isa 64:6 all our righteous acts are like *f* rags;
Col 3:8 and *f* language from your lips.
2Pe 2:7 by the *f* lives of lawless men

**FIND (FINDS FOUND)**
Nu 32:23 be sure that your sin will *f* you out.
Dt 4:29 you will *f* him if you look for him
1Sa 23:16 and helped him *f* strength in God.
Ps 36:7 *f* refuge in the shadow
91:4 under his wings you will *f* refuge;
Pr 14:22 those who plan what is good *f* love
31:10 A wife of noble character who can *f*
Jer 6:16 and you will *f* rest for your souls.
Mt 7:7 seek and you will *f*; knock
11:29 and you will *f* rest for your souls.
16:25 loses his life for me will *f* it.
Lk 18:8 will he *f* faith on the earth?"
Jn 10:9 come in and go out, and *f* pasture.

**FINDS (FIND)**
Ps 62:1 My soul *f* rest in God alone;
112:1 who *f* great delight
119:162 like one who *f* great spoil.
Pr 18:22 He who *f* a wife *f* what is good
Mt 7:8 he who seeks *f*; and to him who
10:39 Whoever *f* his life will lose it,
Lk 12:37 whose master *f* them watching
15:4 go after the lost sheep until he *f* it?

**FINISH (FINISHED)**
Jn 4:34 him who sent me and to *f* his work.
5:36 that the Father has given me to *f*,
Ac 20:24 if only I may *f* the race
2Co 8:11 Now *f* the work, so that your eager
Jas 1:4 Perseverance must *f* its work

**FINISHED (FINISH)**
Ge 2:2 seventh day God had *f* the work he
Jn 19:30 the drink, Jesus said, "It is *f*."
2Ti 4:7 I have *f* the race, I have kept

**FIRE**
Ex 13:21 in a pillar of *f* to give them light,
Lev 6:12 *f* on the altar must be kept burning;
Isa 30:27 and his tongue is a consuming *f*.
Jer 23:29 my word like *f*," declares
Mt 3:11 you with the Holy Spirit and with *f*.
5:22 will be in danger of the *f* of hell.
25:41 into the eternal *f* prepared
Mk 9:43 where the *f* never goes out.
Ac 2:3 to be tongues of *f* that separated
1Co 3:13 It will be revealed with *f*,
1Th 5:19 Do not put out the Spirit's *f*;
Heb 12:29 for our "God is a consuming *f*. "
Jas 3:5 set on *f* by a small spark.
2Pe 3:10 the elements will be destroyed by *f*,
Jude :23 snatch others from the *f*

Rev 20:14 The lake of *f* is the second death.

**FIRM**
Ex 14:13 Stand *f* and you will see
2Ch 20:17 stand *f* and see the deliverance
Ps 33:11 of the LORD stand *f* forever,
37:23 he makes his steps *f*;
40:2 and gave me a *f* place to stand.
89:2 that your love stands *f* forever,
119:89 it stands *f* in the heavens.
Pr 4:26 and take only ways that are *f*.
Zec 8:23 nations will take *f* hold of one Jew
Mk 13:13 he who stands *f* to the end will be
1Co 16:13 on your guard; stand *f* in the faith;
2Co 1:24 because it is by faith you stand *f*.
Eph 6:14 Stand *f* then, with the belt
Col 4:12 that you may stand *f* in all the will
2Th 2:15 stand *f* and hold to the teachings
2Ti 2:19 God's solid foundation stands *f*,
Heb 6:19 an anchor for the soul, *f* and secure
1Pe 5:9 Resist him, standing *f* in the faith,

**FIRST**
Isa 44:6 I am the *f* and I am the last;
48:12 I am the *f* and I am the last.
Mt 5:24 *F* go and be reconciled
6:33 But seek *f* his kingdom
Mt 7:5 *f* take the plank out
20:27 wants to be *f* must be your slave—
22:38 This is the *f* and greatest
23:26 *F* clean the inside of the cup
Mk 13:10 And the gospel must *f* be preached
Ac 11:26 disciples were called Christians *f*
Ro 1:16 *f* for the Jew, then for the Gentile.
1Co 12:28 in the church God has appointed *f*
2Co 8:5 they gave themselves *f* to the Lord
1Ti 2:13 For Adam was formed *f*, then Eve.
Jas 3:17 comes from heaven is *f* of all pure;
1Jn 4:19 We love because he *f* loved us.
3Jn :9 but Diotrephes, who loves to be *f*,
Rev 1:17 I am the *F* and the Last.
2:4 You have forsaken your *f* love.

**FIRSTBORN (BEAR)**
Ex 11:5 Every *f* son in Egypt will die,

**FIRSTFRUITS**
Ex 23:19 "Bring the best of the *f* of your soil

**FISHERS**
Mk 1:17 "and I will make you *f* of men."

**FITTING***
Ps 33:1 it is *f* for the upright to praise him.
147:1 how pleasant and *f* to praise him!
Pr 10:32 of the righteous know what is *f*,
Pr 19:10 It is not *f* for a fool to live in luxury
26:1 honor is not *f* for a fool.
1Co 14:40 everything should be done in a *f*
Col 3:18 to your husbands, as is *f* in the Lord
Heb 2:10 sons to glory, it was *f* that God,

**FIX**
Dt 11:18 *F* these words of mine
Pr 4:25 *f* your gaze directly before you.
2Co 4:18 we *f* our eyes not on what is seen,
Heb 3:1 heavenly calling, *f* your thoughts
12:2 Let us *f* our eyes on Jesus,

**FLAME (FLAMES FLAMING)**
2Ti 1:6 you to fan into *f* the gift of God,

**FLAMES (FLAME)**
1Co 3:15 only as one escaping through the *f*.
13:3 and surrender my body to the *f*,

**FLAMING (FLAME)**
Eph 6:16 you can extinguish all the *f* arrows

**FLASH**
1Co 15:52 in a *f*, in the twinkling of an eye,

**FLATTER (FLATTERING FLATTERY)**
Job 32:21 nor will I *f* any man;
Jude :16 *f* others for their own advantage.

**FLATTERING (FLATTER)**
Ps 12:2 their *f* lips speak with deception.

Ps 12:3 May the LORD cut off all *f* lips
Pr 26:28 and a *f* mouth works ruin.

**FLATTERY (FLATTER)**
Ro 16:18 and *f* they deceive the minds
1Th 2:5 You know we never used *f*,

**FLAWLESS***
2Sa 22:31 the word of the LORD is *f*.
Job 11:4 You say to God, 'My beliefs are *f*
Ps 12:6 And the words of the LORD are *f*,
18:30 the word of the LORD is *f*.
Pr 30:5 "Every word of God is *f*;
SS 5:2 my dove, my *f* one.

**FLEE**
Ps 139:7 Where can I *f* from your presence?
1Co 6:18 *F* from sexual immorality.
10:14 my dear friends, *f* from idolatry.
1Ti 6:11 But you, man of God, *f* from all this
2Ti 2:22 *F* the evil desires of youth,
Jas 4:7 Resist the devil, and he will *f*

**FLEETING**
Ps 89:47 Remember how *f* is my life.
Pr 31:30 Charm is deceptive, and beauty is *f*

**FLESH**
Ge 2:23 and *f* of my *f*;
2:24 and they will become one *f*.
Job 19:26 yet in my *f* I will see God;
Eze 11:19 of stone and give them a heart of *f*.
36:26 of stone and give you a heart of *f*.
Mk 10:8 and the two will become one *f*.'
Jn 1:14 The Word became *f* and made his
6:51 This bread is my *f*, which I will give
1Co 6:16 "The two will become one *f*."
Eph 5:31 and the two will become one *f*."
6:12 For our struggle is not against *f*

**FLOCK (FLOCKS)**
Isa 40:11 He tends his *f* like a shepherd:
Eze 34:2 not shepherds take care of the *f*?
Zec 11:17 who deserts the *f*!
Mt 26:31 the sheep of the *f* will be scattered.'
Ac 20:28 all the *f* of which the Holy Spirit
1Pe 5:2 Be shepherds of God's *f* that is

**FLOCKS (FLOCK)**
Lk 2:8 keeping watch over their *f* at night.

**FLOG**
Ac 22:25 to *f* a Roman citizen who hasn't

**FLOODGATES**
Mal 3:10 see if I will not throw open the *f*

**FLOURISHING**
Ps 52:8 *f* in the house of God;

**FLOW (FLOWING)**
Nu 13:27 and it does *f* with milk and honey!
Jn 7:38 streams of living water will *f*

**FLOWERS**
Isa 40:7 The grass withers and the *f* fall,

**FLOWING (FLOW)**
Ex 3:8 a land *f* with milk and honey—

**FOLDING**
Pr 6:10 a little *f* of the hands to rest—

**FOLLOW (FOLLOWING FOLLOWS)**
Ex 23:2 Do not *f* the crowd in doing wrong.
Lev 18:4 and be careful to *f* my decrees.
Dt 5:1 Learn them and be sure to *f* them.
Ps 23:6 Surely goodness and love will *f* me
Mt 16:24 and take up his cross and *f* me.
Jn 10:4 his sheep *f* him because they know
1Co 14:1 *F* the way of love and eagerly
Rev 14:4 They *f* the Lamb wherever he goes.

**FOLLOWING (FOLLOW)**
1Ti 1:18 by *f* them you may fight the good

**FOLLOWS (FOLLOW)**
Jn 8:12 Whoever *f* me will never walk

**FOOD (FOODS)**
Pr 20:13 you will have *f* to spare.
22:9 for he shares his *f* with the poor.
25:21 If your enemy is hungry, give him *f*
31:15 she provides *f* for her family
Da 1:8 to defile himself with the royal *f*
Jn 6:27 Do not work for *f* that spoils,

Ro 14:14 fully convinced that no *f* is unclean
1Co 8:8 But *f* does not bring us near to God
1Ti 6:8 But if we have *f* and clothing,
Jas 2:15 sister is without clothes and daily *f*.

**FOODS (FOOD)**
Mk 7:19 Jesus declared all *f* "clean.")

**FOOL (FOOLISH FOOLISHNESS FOOLS)**
Ps 14:1 The *f* says in his heart,
Pr 15:5 A *f* spurns his father's discipline,
17:28 Even a *f* is thought wise
18:2 A *f* finds no pleasure
26:5 Answer a *f* according to his folly,
28:26 He who trusts in himself is a *f*,
Mt 5:22 But anyone who says, 'You *f*!'

**FOOLISH (FOOL)**
Pr 10:1 but a *f* son grief to his mother.
17:25 A *f* son brings grief to his father
Mt 7:26 practice is like a *f* man who built
25:2 of them were *f* and five were wise.
1Co 1:27 God chose the *f* things of the world

**FOOLISHNESS (FOOL)**
1Co 1:18 of the cross is *f* to those who are
1:25 For the *f* of God is wiser
2:14 for they are *f* to him, and he cannot
1Co 3:19 of this world is *f* in God's sight.

**FOOLS (FOOL)**
Pr 14:9 *F* mock at making amends for sin,
1Co 4:10 We are *f* for Christ, but you are

**FOOT (FEET FOOTHOLD)**
Jos 1:3 every place where you set your *f*,
Isa 1:6 From the sole of your *f* to the top
1Co 12:15 If the *f* should say, "Because I am

**FOOTHOLD (FOOT)**
Eph 4:27 and do not give the devil a *f*.

**FORBEARANCE***
Ro 3:25 because in his *f* he had left the sins

**FORBID**
1Co 14:39 and do not *f* speaking in tongues.

**FOREFATHERS (FATHER)**
Heb 1:1 spoke to our *f* through the prophets

**FOREKNEW* (KNOW)**
Ro 8:29 For those God *f* he
11:2 not reject his people, whom he *f*.

**FOREVER (EVER)**
1Ch 16:15 He remembers his covenant *f*,
16:34 his love endures *f*.
Ps 9:7 The LORD reigns *f*;
23:6 dwell in the house of the LORD *f*.
33:11 the plans of the LORD stand firm *f*
86:12 I will glorify your name *f*.
92:8 But you, O LORD, are exalted *f*.
Ps 110:4 "You are a priest *f*,
119:111 Your statutes are my heritage *f*;
Jn 6:51 eats of this bread, he will live *f*.
14:16 Counselor to be with you *f*—
1Co 9:25 it to get a crown that will last *f*.
1Th 4:17 And so we will be with the Lord *f*.
Heb 13:8 same yesterday and today and *f*.
1Pe 1:25 but the word of the Lord stands *f*."
1Jn 2:17 who does the will of God lives *f*.

**FORFEIT**
Lk 9:25 and yet lose or *f* his very self?

**FORGAVE (FORGIVE)**
Ps 32:5 and you *f*
Eph 4:32 just as in Christ God *f* you.
Col 2:13 He *f* us all our sins, having
3:13 Forgive as the Lord *f* you.

**FORGET (FORGETS FORGETTING)**
Dt 6:12 that you do not *f* the LORD,
Ps 103:2 and *f* not all his benefits.
137:5 may my right hand *f* its skill
Isa 49:15 "Can a mother *f* the baby
Heb 6:10 he will not *f* your work

**FORGETS (FORGET)**
Jn 16:21 her baby is born she *f* the anguish
Jas 1:24 immediately *f* what he looks like.

**FORGETTING (FORGET)**
Php 3:13 *F* what is behind and straining

**FORGIVE (FORGAVE FORGIVENESS FORGIVING)**
2Ch 7:14 will *f* their sin and will heal their
Ps 19:12 *F* my hidden faults.
Mt 6:12 *F* us our debts,
6:14 For if you *f* men when they sin
18:21 many times shall I *f* my brother
Mk 11:25 in heaven may *f* you your sins."
Lk 11:4 *F* us our sins,
23:34 Jesus said, "Father, *f* them,
Col 3:13 *F* as the Lord forgave you.
1Jn 1:9 and just and will *f* us our sins

**FORGIVENESS (FORGIVE)**
Ps 130:4 But with you there is *f*;
Ac 10:43 believes in him receives *f* of sins
Eph 1:7 through his blood, the *f* of sins,
Col 1:14 in whom we have redemption, the *f*
Heb 9:22 the shedding of blood there is no *f*.

**FORGIVING (FORGIVE)**
Ne 9:17 But you are a *f* God, gracious
Eph 4:32 to one another, *f* each other,

**FORMED**
Ge 2:7 And the LORD God *f* man
Ps 103:14 for he knows how we are *f*,
Isa 45:18 but *f* it to be inhabited—
Ro 9:20 "Shall what is *f* say to him who *f* it,
1Ti 2:13 For Adam was *f* first, then Eve.
Heb 11:3 understand that the universe was *f*

**FORSAKE (FORSAKEN)**
Jos 1:5 I will never leave you nor *f* you.
24:16 "Far be it from us to *f* the LORD
2Ch 15:2 but if you *f* him, he will *f* you.
Ps 27:10 Though my father and mother *f* me
Isa 55:7 Let the wicked *f* his way
Heb 13:5 never will I *f* you."

**FORSAKEN (FORSAKE)**
Ps 22:1 my God, why have you *f* me?
37:25 I have never seen the righteous *f*
Mt 27:46 my God, why have you *f* me?"
Rev 2:4 You have *f* your first love.

**FORTRESS**
Ps 18:2 The LORD is my rock, my *f*
71:3 for you are my rock and my *f*.

**FOUGHT (FIGHT)**
2Ti 4:7 I have *f* the good fight, I have

**FOUND (FIND)**
1Ch 28:9 If you seek him, he will be *f* by you;
Isa 55:6 Seek the LORD while he may be *f*;
Da 5:27 on the scales and *f* wanting.
Lk 15:6 with me; I have *f* my lost sheep.'
15:9 with me; I have *f* my lost coin.'
Ac 4:12 Salvation is *f* in no one else,

**FOUNDATION**
Isa 28:16 a precious cornerstone for a sure *f*;
1Co 3:11 For no one can lay any *f* other
Eph 2:20 built on the *f* of the apostles
2Ti 2:19 God's solid *f* stands firm,

**FOXES**
Mt 8:20 "*F* have holes and birds

**FRAGRANCE**
2Co 2:16 of death; to the other, the *f* of life.

**FREE (FREED FREEDOM FREELY)**
Ps 146:7 The LORD sets prisoners *f*,
Jn 8:32 and the truth will set you *f*."
Ro 6:18 You have been set *f* from sin
Gal 3:28 slave nor *f*, male nor female,
1Pe 2:16 *f* men, but do not use your freedom

**FREED (FREE)**
Rev 1:5 has *f* us from our sins by his blood,

**FREEDOM (FREE)**
Ro 8:21 into the glorious *f* of the children
2Co 3:17 the Spirit of the Lord is, there is *f*.
Gal 5:13 But do not use your *f* to indulge
1Pe 2:16 but do not use your *f* as a cover-up

**FREELY (FREE)**
Isa 55:7 and to our God, for he will *f* pardon
Mt 10:8 Freely you have received, *f* give.

Ro 3:24 and are justified *f* by his grace
Eph 1:6 which he has *f* given us

**FRIEND (FRIENDS)**
Ex 33:11 as a man speaks with his *f*.
Pr 17:17 A *f* loves at all times,
18:24 there is a *f* who sticks closer
27:6 Wounds from a *f* can be trusted,
27:10 Do not forsake your *f* and the *f*
Jas 4:4 Anyone who chooses to be a *f*

**FRIENDS (FRIEND)**
Pr 16:28 and a gossip separates close *f*.
Zec 13:6 given at the house of my *f*.'
Jn 15:13 that he lay down his life for his *f*.

**FRUIT (FRUITFUL)**
Ps 1:3 which yields its *f* in season
Pr 11:30 The *f* of the righteous is a tree
Mt 7:16 By their *f* you will recognize them.
Jn 15:2 branch in me that bears no *f*,
Gal 5:22 But the *f* of the Spirit is love, joy,
Rev 22:2 of *f*, yielding its *f* every month.

**FRUITFUL (FRUIT)**
Ge 1:22 "Be *f* and increase in number
Ps 128:3 Your wife will be like a *f* vine
Jn 15:2 prunes so that it will be even more *f*.

**FULFILL (FULFILLED FULFILLMENT)**
Ps 116:14 I will *f* my vows to the LORD
Mt 5:17 come to abolish them but to *f* them.
1Co 7:3 husband should *f* his marital duty

**FULFILLED (FULFILL)**
Pr 13:19 A longing *f* is sweet to the soul,
Mk 14:49 But the Scriptures must be *f*."
Ro 13:8 loves his fellowman has *f* the law.

**FULFILLMENT (FULFILL)**
Ro 13:10 Therefore love is the *f* of the law.

**FULL (FILL)**
Ps 127:5 whose quiver is *f* of them.
Pr 31:11 Her husband has *f* confidence
Isa 6:3 the whole earth is *f* of his glory."
11:9 for the earth will be *f*
Jn 10:10 may have life, and have it to the *f*.
Ac 6:3 known to be *f* of the Spirit

**FULLNESS (FILL)**
Col 1:19 to have all his *f* dwell in him,
2:9 in Christ all the *f* of the Deity lives

**FULLY (FILL)**
1Ki 8:61 your hearts must be *f* committed
2Ch 16:9 whose hearts are *f* committed
Ps 119:4 that are to be *f* obeyed.
119:138 they are *f* trustworthy.

1Co 15:58 Always give yourselves *f*

**FUTURE**
Ps 37:37 there is a *f* for the man of peace.
Pr 23:18 There is surely a *f* hope for you,
Ro 8:38 neither the present nor the *f*,

**GABRIEL***
Angel who interpreted Daniel's visions (Da 8:16-26; 9:20-27); announced births of John (Lk 1:11-20), Jesus (Lk 1:26-38).

**GAIN (GAINED)**
Ps 60:12 With God we will *g* the victory,
Mk 8:36 it for a man to *g* the whole world,
1Co 13:3 but have not love, I *g* nothing.
Php 1:21 to live is Christ and to die is *g*.
3:8 that I may *g* Christ and be found
1Ti 6:6 with contentment is great *g*.

**GAINED (GAIN)**
Ro 5:2 through whom we have *g* access

**GALILEE**
Isa 9:1 but in the future he will honor *G*

**GALL**
Mt 27:34 mixed with *g*; but after tasting it,

**GAP**
Eze 22:30 stand before me in the *g* on behalf

**GARDENER**
Jn 15:1 true vine, and my Father is the *g*.

**GARMENT (GARMENTS)**
Ps 102:26 they will all wear out like a *g*.

Mt 9:16 of unshrunk cloth on an old *g*,
Jn 19:23 This *g* was seamless, woven

**GARMENTS (GARMENT)**
Ge 3:21 The LORD God made *g* of skin
Isa 61:10 me with *g* of salvation
63:1 with his *g* stained crimson?
Jn 19:24 "They divided my *g* among them

**GATE (GATES)**
Mt 7:13 For wide is the *g* and broad is
Jn 10:9 I am the *g*; whoever enters

**GATES (GATE)**
Ps 100:4 Enter his *g* with thanksgiving
Mt 16:18 the *g* of Hades will not overcome it

**GATHER (GATHERS)**
Zec 14:2 I will *g* all the nations to Jerusalem
Mt 12:30 he who does not *g* with me scatters
23:37 longed to *g* your children together,

**GATHERS (GATHER)**
Isa 40:11 He *g* the lambs in his arms
Mt 23:37 a hen *g* her chicks under her wings,

**GAVE (GIVE)**
Ezr 2:69 According to their ability they *g*
Job 1:21 LORD *g* and the LORD has taken
Jn 3:16 so loved the world that he *g* his one
2Co 8:5 they *g* themselves first to the Lord
Gal 2:20 who loved me and *g* himself for me
1Ti 2:6 who *g* himself as a ransom

**GAZE**
Ps 27:4 to *g* upon the beauty of the LORD
Pr 4:25 fix your *g* directly before you.

**GENEALOGIES**
1Ti 1:4 themselves to myths and endless *g*.

**GENERATIONS**
Ps 22:30 future *g* will be told about the Lord
102:12 your renown endures through all *g*.
145:13 dominion endures through all *g*.
Lk 1:48 now on all *g* will call me blessed,
Eph 3:5 not made known to men in other *g*

**GENEROUS**
Ps 112:5 Good will come to him who is *g*
Pr 22:9 A *g* man will himself be blessed,
2Co 9:5 Then it will be ready as a *g* gift,
1Ti 6:18 and to be *g* and willing to share.

**GENTILE (GENTILES)**
Ro 1:16 first for the Jew, then for the *G*.
10:12 difference between Jew and *G*—

**GENTILES (GENTILE)**
Isa 42:6 and a light for the *G*,
Ro 3:9 and *G* alike are all under sin.
11:13 as I am the apostle to the *G*,
1Co 1:23 block to Jews and foolishness to *G*,

**GENTLE (GENTLENESS)**
Pr 15:1 A *g* answer turns away wrath,
Zec 9:9 *g* and riding on a donkey,
Mt 11:29 for I am *g* and humble in heart,
21:5 *g* and riding on a donkey,
1Co 4:21 or in love and with a *g* spirit?
1Pe 3:4 the unfading beauty of a *g*

**GENTLENESS* (GENTLE)**
2Co 10:1 By the meekness and *g* of Christ,
Gal 5:23 faithfulness, *g* and self-control.
Php 4:5 Let your *g* be evident to all.
Col 3:12 kindness, humility, *g* and patience.
1Ti 6:11 faith, love, endurance and *g*.
1Pe 3:15 But do this with *g* and respect,

**GETHSEMANE**
Mt 26:36 disciples to a place called *G*,

**GIDEON***
Judge, also called Jerub-Baal; freed Israel from Midianites (Jdg 6-8; Heb 11:32). Given sign of fleece (Jdg 8:36-40).

**GIFT (GIFTS)**
Pr 21:14 A *g* given in secret soothes anger,
Mt 5:23 if you are offering your *g*
Ac 2:38 And you will receive the *g*
Ro 6:23 but the *g* of God is eternal life
1Co 7:7 each man has his own *g* from God;
2Co 8:12 the *g* is acceptable according

2Co 9:15 be to God for his indescribable *g!*
Eph 2:8 it is the *g* of God—not by works,
1Ti 4:14 not neglect your *g,* which was
2Ti 1:6 you to fan into flame the *g* of God,
Jas 1:17 and perfect *g* is from above,
1Pe 4:10 should use whatever *g* he has

**GIFTS (GIFT)**
Ro 11:29 for God's *g* and his call are
12:6 We have different *g,* according
1Co 12:4 There are different kinds of *g,*
12:31 But eagerly desire the greater *g.*
14:1 and eagerly desire spiritual *g,*
14:12 excel in *g* that build up the church.

**GILEAD**
Jer 8:22 Is there no balm in *G?*

**GIVE (GAVE GIVEN GIVER GIVES GIVING)**
Nu 6:26 and *g* you peace." '
1Sa 1:11 then I will *g* him to the LORD
2Ch 15:7 be strong and do not *g* up,
Pr 21:26 but the righteous *g* without sparing
23:26 My son, *g* me your heart
30:8 but *g* me only my daily bread.
31:31 *G* her the reward she has earned,
Isa 42:8 I will not *g* my glory to another
Eze 36:26 I will *g* you a new heart
Mt 6:11 *G* us today our daily bread.
10:8 Freely you have received, freely *g.*
22:21 "*G* to Caesar what is Caesar's,
Mk 8:37 Or what can a man *g* in exchange
Lk 6:38 *G,* and it will be given to you.
11:13 Father in heaven *g* the Holy Spirit
Jn 10:28 I *g* them eternal life, and they shall
13:34 "A new commandment I *g* you:
Ac 20:35 blessed to *g* than to receive.' "
Ro 12:8 let him *g* generously;
13:7 *G* everyone what you owe him:
14:12 each of us will *g* an account
2Co 9:7 Each man should *g* what he has
Rev 14:7 "Fear God and *g* him glory,

**GIVEN (GIVE)**
Nu 8:16 are to be *g* wholly to me.
Ps 115:16 but the earth he has *g* to man.
Isa 9:6 to us a son is *g,*
Mt 6:33 and all these things will be *g* to you
7:7 "Ask and it will be *g* to you;
Lk 22:19 saying, "This is my body *g* for you;
Jn 3:27 man can receive only what is *g* him
Ro 5:5 the Holy Spirit, whom he has *g* us.
1Co 4:2 those who have been *g* a trust must
12:13 we were all *g* the one Spirit to drink
Eph 4:7 to each one of us grace has been *g*

**GIVER* (GIVE)**
Pr 18:16 A gift opens the way for the *g*
2Co 9:7 for God loves a cheerful *g.*

**GIVES (GIVE)**
Ps 119:130 The unfolding of your words *g* light;
Pr 14:30 A heart at peace *g* life to the body,
15:30 good news *g* health to the bones.
28:27 He who *g* to the poor will lack
Isa 40:29 He *g* strength to the weary
Mt 10:42 if anyone *g* even a cup of cold water
Jn 6:63 The Spirit *g* life; the flesh counts
1Co 15:57 He *g* us the victory
2Co 3:6 the letter kills, but the Spirit *g* life.

**GIVING (GIVE)**
Ne 8:8 *g* the meaning so that the people
Ps 19:8 *g* joy to the heart.
Mt 6:4 so that your *g* may be in secret.
2Co 8:7 also excel in this grace of *g.*

**GLAD (GLADNESS)**
Ps 31:7 I will be *g* and rejoice in your love,
46:4 whose streams make *g* the city
97:1 LORD reigns, let the earth be *g;*
118:24 let us rejoice and be *g* in it.
Pr 23:25 May your father and mother be *g;*
Zec 2:10 and be *g,* O Daughter of Zion.
Mt 5:12 be *g,* because great is your reward

**GLADNESS (GLAD)**

Ps 45:15 They are led in with joy and *g;*
51:8 Let me hear joy and *g;*
100:2 Serve the LORD with *g;*
Jer 31:13 I will turn their mourning into *g;*

**GLORIFIED (GLORY)**

Jn 13:31 Son of Man *g* and God is *g* in him.
Ro 8:30 those he justified, he also *g.*
2Th 1:10 comes to be *g* in his holy people

**GLORIFY (GLORY)**

Ps 34:3 *G* the LORD with me;
86:12 I will *g* your name forever.
Jn 13:32 God will *g* the Son in himself,
17:1 *G* your Son, that your Son may

**GLORIOUS (GLORY)**

Ps 45:13 All *g* is the princess
111:3 *G* and majestic are his deeds,
145:5 of the *g* splendor of your majesty,
Isa 4:2 the LORD will be beautiful and *g,*
12:5 for he has done *g* things;
42:21 to make his law great and *g.*
63:15 from your lofty throne, holy and *g.*
Mt 19:28 the Son of Man sits on his *g* throne,
Lk 9:31 appeared in *g* splendor, talking
Ac 2:20 of the great and *g* day of the Lord.
2Co 3:8 of the Spirit be even more *g?*
Php 3:21 so that they will be like his *g* body.
4:19 to his *g* riches in Christ Jesus.
Tit 2:13 the *g* appearing of our great God
Jude :24 before his *g* presence without fault

**GLORY (GLORIFIED GLORIFY GLORIOUS)**

Ex 15:11 awesome in *g,*
33:18 Moses said, "Now show me your *g*
1Sa 4:21 "The *g* has departed from Israel"—
1Ch 16:24 Declare his *g* among the nations,
16:28 ascribe to the LORD *g*
29:11 and the *g* and the majesty
Ps 8:5 and crowned him with *g* and honor
19:1 The heavens declare the *g* of God;
24:7 that the King of *g* may come in.
29:1 ascribe to the LORD *g*
72:19 the whole earth be filled with his *g.*
96:3 Declare his *g* among the nations,
Pr 19:11 it is to his *g* to overlook an offense.
25:2 It is the *g* of God to conceal
Isa 6:3 the whole earth is full of his *g.*"
48:11 I will not yield my *g* to another.
Eze 43:2 and the land was radiant with his *g.*
Mt 24:30 of the sky, with power and great *g.*
25:31 the Son of Man comes in his *g,*
Mk 8:38 in his Father's *g* with the holy
13:26 in clouds with great power and *g.*
Lk 2:9 and the *g* of the Lord shone
2:14 saying, "*G* to God in the highest,
Jn 1:14 We have seen his *g,* the *g* of the One
17:5 presence with the *g* I had with you
17:24 to see my *g,* the *g* you have given
Ac 7:2 The God of *g* appeared
Ro 1:23 exchanged the *g* of the immortal
3:23 and fall short of the *g* of God,
8:18 with the *g* that will be revealed
9:4 theirs the divine *g,* the covenants,
1Co 10:31 whatever you do, do it all for the *g*
11:7 but the woman is the *g* of man.
15:43 it is raised in *g;* it is sown
2Co 3:10 comparison with the surpassing *g.*
3:18 faces all reflect the Lord's *g,*
4:17 us an eternal *g* that far outweighs
Col 1:27 Christ in you, the hope of *g.*
3:4 also will appear with him in *g.*
1Ti 3:16 was taken up in *g.*
Heb 1:3 The Son is the radiance of God's *g*
2:7 you crowned him with *g* and honor
1Pe 1:24 and all their *g* is like the flowers

Rev 4:11 to receive *g* and honor and power,
21:23 for the *g* of God gives it light,

**GLUTTONS**
Tit 1:12 always liars, evil brutes, lazy *g*."

**GNASHING**
Mt 8:12 where there will be weeping and *g*

**GNAT***
Mt 23:24 You strain out a *g* but swallow

**GOAL**
2Co 5:9 So we make it our *g* to please him,
Gal 3:3 to attain your *g* by human effort?
Php 3:14 on toward the *g* to win the prize

**GOAT (GOATS SCAPEGOAT)**
Isa 11:6 the leopard will lie down with the *g*

**GOATS (GOAT)**
Nu 7:17 five male *g* and five male lambs

**GOD (GOD'S GODLINESS GODLY GODS)**
Ge 1:1 In the beginning *G* created
1:2 and the Spirit of *G* was hovering
1:26 Then *G* said, "Let us make man
1:27 So *G* created man in his own image
1:31 *G* saw all that he had made,
2:3 And *G* blessed the seventh day
2:22 Then the LORD *G* made a woman
3:21 The LORD *G* made garments
3:23 So the LORD *G* banished him
Ge 5:22 Enoch walked with *G* 300 years
6:2 sons of *G* saw that the daughters
9:16 everlasting covenant between *G*
17:1 "I am *G* Almighty; walk before me
21:33 name of the LORD, the Eternal *G*.
22:8 "*G* himself will provide the lamb
28:12 and the angels of *G* were ascending
32:28 because you have struggled with *G*
32:30 "It is because I saw *G* face to face,
35:10 *G* said to him, "Your name is Jacob
41:51 *G* has made me forget all my
50:20 but *G* intended it for good
Ex 2:24 *G* heard their groaning
3:6 because he was afraid to look at *G*.
6:7 own people, and I will be your *G*.
8:10 is no one like the LORD our *G*.
13:18 So *G* led the people
15:2 He is my *G*, and I will praise him,
17:9 with the staff of *G* in my hands."
19:3 Then Moses went up to *G*,
20:2 the LORD your *G*, who brought
20:5 the LORD your *G*, am a jealous *G*,
20:19 But do not have *G* speak to us
22:28 "Do not blaspheme *G*
Ex 31:18 inscribed by the finger of *G*.
34:6 the compassionate and gracious *G*,
34:14 name is Jealous, is a jealous *G*.
Lev 18:21 not profane the name of your *G*.
19:2 the LORD your *G*, am holy.
26:12 walk among you and be your *G*,
Nu 22:38 I must speak only what *G* puts
23:19 *G* is not a man, that he should lie,
Dt 1:17 for judgment belongs to *G*.
3:22 LORD your *G* himself will fight
3:24 For what *g* is there in heaven
4:24 is a consuming fire, a jealous *G*.
4:31 the LORD your *G* is a merciful *G*;
4:39 heart this day that the LORD is *G*
5:11 the name of the LORD your *G*,
5:14 a Sabbath to the LORD your *G*.
5:26 of the living *G* speaking out of fire,
6:4 LORD our *G*, the LORD is one.
6:5 Love the LORD your *G*
6:13 the LORD your *G*, serve him only
6:16 Do not test the LORD your *G*
7:9 your *G* is *G*; he is the faithful *G*,
7:12 the LORD your *G* will keep his
7:21 is a great and awesome *G*.

| | | |
|---|---|---|
| Dt | 8:5 | the LORD your *G* disciplines you. |
| | 10:12 | but to fear the LORD your *G*, |
| | 10:14 | the LORD your *G* belong |
| | 10:17 | For the LORD your *G* is *G* of gods |
| | 11:13 | to love the LORD your *G* |
| | 13:3 | The LORD your *G* is testing you |
| | 13:4 | the LORD your *G* you must |
| | 15:6 | the LORD your *G* will bless you |
| | 19:9 | to love the LORD your *G* |
| | 25:16 | the LORD your *G* detests anyone |
| | 29:29 | belong to the LORD our *G*, |
| | 30:2 | return to the LORD your *G* |
| | 30:16 | today to love the LORD your *G*, |
| | 30:20 | you may love the LORD your *G*, |
| | 31:6 | for the LORD your *G* goes |
| | 32:3 | Oh, praise the greatness of our *G*! |
| | 32:4 | A faithful *G* who does no wrong, |
| | 33:27 | The eternal *G* is your refuge, |
| Jos | 1:9 | for the LORD your *G* will be |
| | 14:8 | the LORD my *G* wholeheartedly. |
| | 22:5 | to love the LORD your *G*, |
| | 22:34 | Between Us that the LORD is *G*. |
| | 23:11 | careful to love the LORD your *G*. |
| | 23:14 | the LORD your *G* gave you has |
| Jdg | 16:28 | O *G*, please strengthen me just |
| Ru | 1:16 | be my people and your *G* my *G*. |
| 1Sa | 2:2 | there is no Rock like our *G*. |
| | 2:3 | for the LORD is a *G* who knows, |
| | 2:25 | another man, *G* may mediate |
| | 10:26 | men whose hearts *G* had touched. |
| | 12:12 | the LORD your *G* was your king. |
| | 17:26 | defy the armies of the living *G*?" |
| | 17:46 | world will know that there is a *G* |
| | 30:6 | strength in the LORD his *G*. |
| 2Sa | 14:14 | But *G* does not take away life; |
| | 22:3 | my *G* is my rock, in whom I take |
| | 22:31 | "As for *G*, his way is perfect; |
| 1Ki | 4:29 | *G* gave Solomon wisdom |
| | 8:23 | there is no *G* like you in heaven |
| | 8:27 | "But will *G* really dwell on earth? |
| | 8:61 | committed to the LORD our *G*, |
| | 18:21 | If the LORD is *G*, follow him; |
| | 18:37 | are *G*, and that you are turning |
| | 20:28 | a *g* of the hills and not a *g* |
| 2Ki | 19:15 | *G* of Israel, enthroned |
| 1Ch | 16:35 | Cry out, "Save us, O *G* our Savior; |
| | 28:2 | for the footstool of our *G*, |
| | 28:9 | acknowledge the *G* of your father, |
| | 29:10 | *G* of our father Israel, |
| | 29:17 | my *G*, that you test the heart |
| 2Ch | 2:4 | for the Name of the LORD my *G* |
| | 5:14 | of the LORD filled the temple of *G* |
| | 6:18 | "But will *G* really dwell on earth |
| | 18:13 | I can tell him only what my *G* says |
| | 20:6 | are you not the *G* who is in heaven? |
| | 25:8 | for *G* has the power to help |
| | 30:9 | for the LORD your *G* is gracious |
| | 33:12 | the favor of the LORD his *G* |
| Ezr | 8:22 | "The good hand of our *G* is |
| | 9:6 | "O my *G*, I am too ashamed |
| | 9:13 | our *G*, you have punished us less |
| Ne | 1:5 | the great and awesome *G*, |
| | 8:8 | from the Book of the Law of *G*, |
| | 9:17 | But you are a forgiving *G*, |
| | 9:32 | the great, mighty and awesome *G*, |
| Job | 1:1 | he feared *G* and shunned evil. |
| | 2:10 | Shall we accept good from *G*, |
| | 4:17 | a mortal be more righteous than *G*? |
| | 5:17 | is the man whom *G* corrects; |
| | 11:7 | Can you fathom the mysteries of *G* |
| | 19:26 | yet in my flesh I will see *G*; |
| | 22:13 | Yet you say, 'What does *G* know? |
| | 25:4 | can a man be righteous before *G*? |
| | 33:14 | For *G* does speak—now one way, |

| | | |
|---|---|---|
| Job | 34:12 | is unthinkable that *G* would do |
| | 36:26 | is *G*—beyond our understanding! |
| | 37:22 | *G* comes in awesome majesty. |
| Ps | 18:2 | my *G* is my rock, in whom I take |
| | 18:28 | my *G* turns my darkness into light. |
| | 19:1 | The heavens declare the glory of *G;* |
| | 22:1 | *G,* my *G,* why have you forsaken |
| | 29:3 | the *G* of glory thunders, |
| | 31:14 | I say, "You are my *G.*" |
| | 40:3 | a hymn of praise to our *G.* |
| | 40:8 | I desire to do your will, O my *G;* |
| | 42:2 | thirsts for *G,* for the living *G.* |
| | 42:11 | Put your hope in *G,* |
| | 45:6 | O *G,* will last for ever and ever; |
| | 46:1 | *G* is our refuge and strength, |
| | 46:10 | "Be still, and know that I am *G;* |
| | 47:7 | For *G* is the King of all the earth; |
| | 50:3 | Our *G* comes and will not be silent; |
| | 51:1 | Have mercy on me, O *G,* |
| | 51:10 | Create in me a pure heart, O *G,* |
| | 51:17 | O *G,* you will not despise. |
| | 62:7 | my honor depend on *G;* |
| | 65:5 | O *G* our Savior, |
| | 66:1 | Shout with joy to *G,* all the earth! |
| | 66:16 | listen, all you who fear *G;* |
| Ps | 68:6 | *G* sets the lonely in families, |
| | 71:17 | my youth, O *G,* you have taught |
| | 71:19 | reaches to the skies, O *G,* |
| | 71:22 | harp for your faithfulness, O my *G;* |
| | 73:26 | but *G* is the strength of my heart |
| | 77:13 | What *g* is so great as our God? |
| | 78:19 | Can *G* spread a table in the desert? |
| | 81:1 | Sing for joy to *G* our strength; |
| | 84:2 | out for the living *G.* |
| | 84:10 | a doorkeeper in the house of my *G* |
| | 86:12 | O Lord my *G,* with all my heart; |
| | 89:7 | of the holy ones *G* is greatly feared; |
| | 90:2 | to everlasting you are *G.* |
| | 91:2 | my *G,* in whom I trust." |
| | 95:7 | for he is our *G* |
| | 100:3 | Know that the LORD is *G.* |
| | 108:1 | My heart is steadfast, O *G;* |
| | 113:5 | Who is like the LORD our *G,* |
| | 139:23 | Search me, O *G,* and know my |
| Pr | 3:4 | in the sight of *G* and man. |
| | 25:2 | of *G* to conceal a matter; |
| | 30:5 | "Every word of *G* is flawless; |
| Ecc | 3:11 | cannot fathom what *G* has done |
| | 11:5 | cannot understand the work of *G,* |
| Ecc | 12:13 | Fear *G* and keep his |
| Isa | 9:6 | Wonderful Counselor, Mighty *G,* |
| | 37:16 | you alone are *G* over all |
| | 40:3 | a highway for our *G.* |
| | 40:8 | the word of our *G* stands forever." |
| | 40:28 | The LORD is the everlasting *G,* |
| | 41:10 | not be dismayed, for I am your *G.* |
| | 44:6 | apart from me there is no *G.* |
| | 52:7 | "Your *G* reigns!" |
| | 55:7 | to our *G,* for he will freely pardon. |
| | 57:21 | says my *G,* "for the wicked." |
| | 59:2 | you from your *G;* |
| | 61:10 | my soul rejoices in my *G.* |
| | 62:5 | so will your *G* rejoice over you. |
| Jer | 23:23 | "Am I only a *G* nearby," |
| | 31:33 | I will be their *G,* |
| | 32:27 | "I am the LORD, the *G* |
| Eze | 28:13 | the garden of *G;* |
| Da | 3:17 | the *G* we serve is able to save us |
| | 9:4 | O Lord, the great and awesome *G,* |
| Hos | 12:6 | and wait for your *G* always. |
| Joel | 2:13 | Return to the LORD your *G,* |
| Am | 4:12 | prepare to meet your *G,* O Israel." |
| Mic | 6:8 | and to walk humbly with your *G.* |
| Na | 1:2 | LORD is a jealous and avenging *G;* |
| Zec | 14:5 | Then the LORD my *G* will come, |

| | | |
|---|---|---|
| Mal | 3:8 | Will a man rob *G*? Yet you rob me. |
| Mt | 1:23 | which means, "*G* with us." |
| | 5:8 | for they will see *G*. |
| | 6:24 | You cannot serve both *G* |
| | 19:6 | Therefore what *G* has joined |
| | 19:26 | but with *G* all things are possible." |
| | 22:21 | and to *G* what is God's." |
| | 22:37 | " 'Love the Lord your *G* |
| | 27:46 | which means, "My *G*, my *G*, |
| Mk | 12:29 | the Lord our *G*, the Lord is one. |
| | 16:19 | and he sat at the right hand of *G*. |
| Lk | 1:37 | For nothing is impossible with *G*." |
| | 1:47 | my spirit rejoices in *G* my Savior, |
| | 10:9 | 'The kingdom of *G* is near you.' |
| | 10:27 | " 'Love the Lord your *G* |
| | 18:19 | "No one is good—except *G* alone. |
| Jn | 1:1 | was with *G*, and the Word was *G*. |
| | 1:18 | seen *G*, but *G* the One and Only, |
| | 3:16 | "For *G* so loved the world that he |
| | 4:24 | *G* is spirit, and his worshipers must |
| | 14:1 | Trust in *G*; trust also in me. |
| | 20:28 | "My Lord and my *G*!" |
| Ac | 2:24 | But *G* raised him from the dead, |
| | 5:4 | You have not lied to men but to *G* |
| Ac | 5:29 | "We must obey *G* rather than men! |
| | 7:55 | to heaven and saw the glory of *G*, |
| | 17:23 | TO AN UNKNOWN *G*. |
| | 20:27 | to you the whole will of *G*. |
| | 20:32 | "Now I commit you to *G* |
| Ro | 1:17 | a righteousness from *G* is revealed, |
| | 2:11 | For *G* does not show favoritism. |
| | 3:4 | Let *G* be true, and every man a liar. |
| | 3:23 | and fall short of the glory of *G*, |
| | 4:24 | to whom *G* will credit |
| | 5:8 | *G* demonstrates his own love for us |
| | 6:23 | but the gift of *G* is eternal life |
| | 8:28 | in all things *G* works for the good |
| | 11:22 | the kindness and sternness of *G*: |
| | 14:12 | give an account of himself to *G*. |
| 1Co | 1:20 | Has not *G* made foolish |
| | 2:9 | what *G* has prepared |
| | 3:6 | watered it, but *G* made it grow. |
| | 6:20 | Therefore honor *G* with your body. |
| | 7:24 | each man, as responsible to *G*, |
| | 8:8 | food does not bring us near to *G*; |
| | 10:13 | *G* is faithful; he will not let you be |
| | 10:31 | do it all for the glory of *G*. |
| | 14:33 | For *G* is not a *G* of disorder |
| | 15:28 | so that *G* may be all in all. |
| 2Co | 1:9 | rely on ourselves but on *G*, |
| | 2:14 | be to *G*, who always leads us |
| | 3:5 | but our competence comes from *G*. |
| | 4:7 | this all-surpassing power is from *G* |
| | 5:19 | that *G* was reconciling the world |
| | 5:21 | *G* made him who had no sin |
| | 6:16 | we are the temple of the living *G*. |
| | 9:7 | for *G* loves a cheerful giver. |
| | 9:8 | *G* is able to make all grace abound |
| Gal | 2:6 | *G* does not judge by external |
| | 6:7 | not be deceived: *G* cannot be |
| Eph | 2:10 | which *G* prepared in advance for us |
| | 4:6 | one baptism; one *G* and Father |
| | 5:1 | Be imitators of *G*, therefore, |
| Php | 2:6 | Who, being in very nature *G*, |
| | 4:19 | And my *G* will meet all your needs |
| 1Th | 2:4 | trying to please men but *G*, |
| | 4:7 | For *G* did not call us to be impure, |
| | 4:9 | taught by *G* to love each other. |
| | 5:9 | For *G* did not appoint us |
| 1Ti | 2:5 | one mediator between *G* and men, |
| | 4:4 | For everything *G* created is good, |
| | 5:4 | for this is pleasing to *G*. |

Tit 2:13 glorious appearing of our great *G*
Heb 1:1 In the past *G* spoke
4:12 For the word of *G* is living
6:10 *G* is not unjust; he will not forget
10:31 to fall into the hands of the living *G*
11:6 faith it is impossible to please *G*,
12:10 but *G* disciplines us for our good,
12:29 for our "*G* is a consuming fire."
13:15 offer to *G* a sacrifice of praise—
Jas 1:13 For *G* cannot be tempted by evil,
2:19 You believe that there is one *G*.
2:23 "Abraham believed *G*,
4:4 the world becomes an enemy of *G*.
4:8 Come near to *G* and he will come
1Pe 4:11 it with the strength *G* provides,
2Pe 1:21 but men spoke from *G*
1Jn 1:5 *G* is light; in him there is no
3:20 For *G* is greater than our hearts,
4:7 for love comes from *G*.
4:9 This is how *G* showed his love
4:11 Dear friends, since *G* so loved us,
4:12 No one has ever seen *G*;
4:16 *G* is love.
Rev 4:8 holy is the Lord *G* Almighty,
Rev 7:17 *G* will wipe away every tear
19:6 For our Lord *G* Almighty reigns.


## GOD-BREATHED* (BREATHED)


2Ti 3:16 All Scripture is *G* and is useful


## GOD'S (GOD)


2Ch 20:15 For the battle is not yours, but *G*.
Job 37:14 stop and consider *G* wonders.
Ps 52:8 I trust in *G* unfailing love
69:30 I will praise *G* name in song
Mk 3:35 Whoever does *G* will is my brother
Jn 7:17 If anyone chooses to do *G* will,
10:36 'I am *G* Son'? Do not believe me
Ro 2:3 think you will escape *G* judgment?
2:4 not realizing that *G* kindness leads
3:3 lack of faith nullify *G* faithfulness?
7:22 in my inner being I delight in *G* law
9:16 or effort, but on *G* mercy.
11:29 for *G* gifts and his call are
12:2 and approve what *G* will is—
12:13 Share with *G* people who are
13:6 for the authorities are *G* servants,
1Co 7:19 Keeping *G* commands is what
2Co 6:2 now is the time of *G* favor,
Eph 1:7 riches of *G* grace that he lavished
1Th 4:3 It is *G* will that you should be
5:18 for this is *G* will for you
1Ti 6:1 so that *G* name and our teaching
2Ti 2:19 *G* solid foundation stands firm,
Tit 1:7 overseer is entrusted with *G* work,
Heb 1:3 The Son is the radiance of *G* glory
9:24 now to appear for us in *G* presence.
11:3 was formed at *G* command,
1Pe 2:15 For it is *G* will that
3:4 which is of great worth in *G* sight.
1Jn 2:5 *G* love is truly made complete


## GODLINESS (GOD)


1Ti 2:2 and quiet lives in all *g* and holiness.
4:8 but *g* has value for all things,
6:6 *g* with contentment is great gain.
6:11 and pursue righteousness, *g*, faith,


## GODLY (GOD)


Ps 4:3 that the LORD has set apart the *g*
2Co 7:10 *G* sorrow brings repentance that
11:2 jealous for you with a *g* jealousy.
2Ti 3:12 everyone who wants to live a *g* life
2Pe 3:11 You ought to live holy and *g* lives


## GODS (GOD)


Ex 20:3 "You shall have no other *g*
Ac 19:26 He says that man-made *g* are no *g*

## GOLD

| | | |
|---|---|---|
| Job | 23:10 | tested me, I will come forth as *g*. |
| Ps | 19:10 | They are more precious than *g*, |
| | 119:127 | more than *g*, more than pure *g*, |
| Pr | 22:1 | esteemed is better than silver or *g*. |

## GOLGOTHA

| | | |
|---|---|---|
| Jn | 19:17 | (which in Aramaic is called *G*). |

## GOLIATH

Philistine giant killed by David (1Sa 17; 21:9).

## GOOD

| | | |
|---|---|---|
| Ge | 1:4 | God saw that the light was *g*, |
| | 1:31 | he had made, and it was very *g*. |
| | 2:18 | "It is not *g* for the man to be alone. |
| | 50:20 | but God intended it for *g* |
| Job | 2:10 | Shall we accept *g* from God, |
| Ps | 14:1 | there is no one who does *g*. |
| | 34:8 | Taste and see that the LORD is *g*; |
| | 37:3 | Trust in the LORD and do *g*; |
| | 84:11 | no *g* thing does he withhold |
| | 86:5 | You are forgiving and *g*, O Lord |
| | 103:5 | satisfies your desires with *g* things, |
| | 119:68 | You are *g*, and what you do is *g*; |
| | 133:1 | How *g* and pleasant it is |
| | 147:1 | How *g* it is to sing praises |
| Pr | 3:4 | you will win favor and a *g* name |
| Pr | 11:27 | He who seeks *g* finds *g* will, |
| | 17:22 | A cheerful heart is *g* medicine, |
| | 18:22 | He who finds a wife finds what is *g* |
| | 22:1 | A *g* name is more desirable |
| | 31:12 | She brings him *g*, not harm, |
| Isa | 5:20 | Woe to those who call evil *g* |
| | 52:7 | the feet of those who bring *g* news, |
| Jer | 6:16 | ask where the *g* way is, |
| | 32:39 | the *g* of their children after them. |
| Mic | 6:8 | has showed you, O man, what is *g*. |
| Mt | 5:45 | sun to rise on the evil and the *g*, |
| | 7:17 | Likewise every *g* tree bears *g* fruit, |
| | 12:35 | The *g* man brings *g* things out |
| | 19:17 | "There is only One who is *g*. |
| | 25:21 | 'Well done, *g* and faithful servant! |
| Mk | 3:4 | lawful on the Sabbath: to do *g* |
| | 8:36 | What *g* is it for a man |
| Lk | 6:27 | do *g* to those who hate you, |
| Jn | 10:11 | "I am the *g* shepherd. |
| Ro | 8:28 | for the *g* of those who love him, |
| | 10:15 | feet of those who bring *g* news!" |
| | 12:9 | Hate what is evil; cling to what is *g*. |
| 1Co | 10:24 | should seek his own *g*, but the *g* |
| | 15:33 | Bad company corrupts *g* character |
| 2Co | 9:8 | you will abound in every *g* work. |
| Gal | 6:9 | us not become weary in doing *g*, |
| | 6:10 | as we have opportunity, let us do *g* |
| Eph | 2:10 | in Christ Jesus to do *g* works, |
| Php | 1:6 | that he who began a *g* work |
| 1Th | 5:21 | Hold on to the *g*. |
| 1Ti | 3:7 | have a *g* reputation with outsiders, |
| | 4:4 | For everything God created is *g*, |
| | 6:12 | Fight the *g* fight of the faith. |
| | 6:18 | them to do *g*, to be rich in *g* deeds, |
| 2Ti | 3:17 | equipped for every *g* work. |
| | 4:7 | I have fought the *g* fight, I have |
| Heb | 12:10 | but God disciplines us for our *g*, |
| 1Pe | 2:3 | you have tasted that the Lord is *g*. |
| | 2:12 | Live such *g* lives among the pagans |

## GOSPEL

| | | |
|---|---|---|
| Ro | 1:16 | I am not ashamed of the *g*, |
| | 15:16 | duty of proclaiming the *g* of God, |
| 1Co | 1:17 | to preach the *g*—not with words |
| | 9:16 | Woe to me if I do not preach the *g*! |
| | 15:1 | you of the *g* I preached to you, |
| Gal | 1:7 | a different *g*—which is really no *g* |
| Php | 1:27 | in a manner worthy of the *g* |

## GOSSIP

| | | |
|---|---|---|
| Pr | 11:13 | A *g* betrays a confidence, |

Pr 16:28 and a *g* separates close friends.
18:8 of a *g* are like choice morsels;
26:20 without *g* a quarrel dies down.
2Co 12:20 slander, *g,* arrogance and disorder.

**GRACE (GRACIOUS)**
Ps 45:2 lips have been anointed with *g,*
Jn 1:17 *g* and truth came through Jesus
Ac 20:32 to God and to the word of his *g,*
Ro 3:24 and are justified freely by his *g*
5:15 came by the *g* of the one man,
5:17 God's abundant provision of *g*
5:20 where sin increased, *g* increased all
6:14 you are not under law, but under *g.*
11:6 if by *g,* then it is no longer by works
2Co 6:1 not to receive God's *g* in vain.
8:9 For you know the *g*
9:8 able to make all *g* abound to you,
12:9 "My *g* is sufficient for you,
Gal 2:21 I do not set aside the *g* of God,
5:4 you have fallen away from *g.*
Eph 1:7 riches of God's *g* that he lavished
2:5 it is by *g* you have been saved.
2:7 the incomparable riches of his *g,*
2:8 For it is by *g* you have been saved,
Php 1:7 all of you share in God's *g* with me.
Col 4:6 conversation be always full of *g,*
2Th 2:16 and by his *g* gave us eternal
2Ti 2:1 be strong in the *g* that is
Tit 2:11 For the *g* of God that brings
3:7 having been justified by his *g,*
Heb 2:9 that by the *g* of God he might taste
4:16 find *g* to help us in our time of need
4:16 the throne of *g* with confidence,
Jas 4:6 but gives *g* to the humble."
2Pe 3:18 But grow in the *g* and knowledge

**GRACIOUS (GRACE)**
Nu 6:25 and be *g* to you;
Pr 22:11 a pure heart and whose speech is *g*
Isa 30:18 Yet the LORD longs to be *g* to you

**GRAIN**
1Co 9:9 ox while it is treading out the *g.*"

**GRANTED**
Php 1:29 For it has been *g* to you on behalf

**GRASS**
Ps 103:15 As for man, his days are like *g,*
1Pe 1:24 "All men are like *g,*

**GRAVE (GRAVES)**
Pr 7:27 Her house is a highway to the *g,*
Hos 13:14 Where, O *g,* is your destruction?

**GRAVES (GRAVE)**
Jn 5:28 are in their *g* will hear his voice
Ro 3:13 "Their throats are open *g;*

**GREAT (GREATER GREATEST GREATNESS)**
Ge 12:2 "I will make you into a *g* nation
Dt 10:17 the *g* God, mighty and awesome,
2Sa 22:36 you stoop down to make me *g.*
Ps 19:11 in keeping them there is *g* reward.
89:1 of the LORD's *g* love forever;
103:11 so *g* is his love for those who fear
107:43 consider the *g* love of the LORD.
108:4 For *g* is your love, higher
119:165 *G* peace have they who love your
145:3 *G* is the LORD and most worthy
Pr 23:24 of a righteous man has *g* joy;
Isa 42:21 to make his law *g* and glorious.
La 3:23 *g* is your faithfulness.
Mk 10:43 whoever wants to become *g*
Lk 21:27 in a cloud with power and *g* glory.
1Ti 6:6 with contentment is *g* gain.
Tit 2:13 glorious appearing of our *g* God
Heb 2:3 if we ignore such a *g* salvation?
1Jn 3:1 How *g* is the love the Father has

**GREATER (GREAT)**
Mk 12:31 There is no commandment *g*
Jn 1:50 You shall see *g* things than that."

Jn 15:13 *G* love has no one than this,
1Co 12:31 But eagerly desire the *g* gifts.
Heb 11:26 as of *g* value than the treasures
1Jn 3:20 For God is *g* than our hearts,
4:4 is in you is *g* than the one who is

**GREATEST (GREAT)**
Mt 22:38 is the first and *g* commandment.
Lk 9:48 least among you all—he is the *g*."
1Co 13:13 But the *g* of these is love.

**GREATNESS (GREAT)**
Ps 145:3 his *g* no one can fathom.
150:2 praise him for his surpassing *g*.
Isa 63:1 forward in the *g* of his strength?
Php 3:8 compared to the surpassing *g*

**GREED (GREEDY)**
Lk 12:15 on your guard against all kinds of *g*
Ro 1:29 kind of wickedness, evil, *g*
Eph 5:3 or of any kind of impurity, or of *g*,
Col 3:5 evil desires and *g*, which is idolatry
2Pe 2:14 experts in *g*—an accursed brood!

**GREEDY (GREED)**
Pr 15:27 A *g* man brings trouble
1Co 6:10 nor thieves nor the *g* nor drunkards
Eph 5:5 No immoral, impure or *g* person—
1Pe 5:2 not *g* for money, but eager to serve;

**GREEN**
Ps 23:2 makes me lie down in *g* pastures,

**GREW (GROW)**
Lk 2:52 And Jesus *g* in wisdom and stature,
Ac 16:5 in the faith and *g* daily in numbers.

**GRIEF (GRIEVE)**
Ps 10:14 O God, do see trouble and *g*;
Pr 14:13 and joy may end in *g*.
La 3:32 Though he brings *g*, he will show
Jn 16:20 but your *g* will turn to joy.
1Pe 1:6 had to suffer *g* in all kinds of trials.

**GRIEVE (GRIEF)**
Eph 4:30 do not *g* the Holy Spirit of God,
1Th 4:13 or to *g* like the rest of men,

**GROUND**
Ge 3:17 "Cursed is the *g* because of you;
Ex 3:5 where you are standing is holy *g*."
Eph 6:13 you may be able to stand your *g*,

**GROW (GREW)**
Pr 13:11 by little makes it *g*.
1Co 3:6 watered it, but God made it *g*.
2Pe 3:18 But *g* in the grace and knowledge

**GRUMBLE (GRUMBLING)**
1Co 10:10 And do not *g*, as some of them did
Jas 5:9 Don't *g* against each other,

**GRUMBLING (GRUMBLE)**
Jn 6:43 "Stop *g* among yourselves,"
1Pe 4:9 to one another without *g*.

**GUARANTEE (GUARANTEEING)**
Heb 7:22 Jesus has become the *g*

**GUARANTEEING (GUARANTEE)**
2Co 1:22 as a deposit, *g* what is to come.
Eph 1:14 who is a deposit *g* our inheritance

**GUARD (GUARDS)**
Ps 141:3 Set a *g* over my mouth, O LORD;
Pr 4:23 Above all else, *g* your heart,
Isa 52:12 the God of Israel will be your rear *g*
Mk 13:33 Be on *g*! Be alert! You do not know
1Co 16:13 Be on your *g*; stand firm in the faith
Php 4:7 will *g* your hearts and your minds
1Ti 6:20 *g* what has been entrusted

**GUARDS (GUARD)**
Pr 13:3 He who *g* his lips *g* his life,
19:16 who obeys instructions *g* his life,
21:23 He who *g* his mouth and his tongue
22:5 he who *g* his soul stays far

**GUIDE**
Ex 13:21 of cloud to *g* them on their way
15:13 In your strength you will *g* them
Ne 9:19 cease to *g* them on their path,

Ps 25:5 *g* me in your truth and teach me,
43:3 let them *g* me;
48:14 he will be our *g* even to the end.
67:4 and *g* the nations of the earth.
73:24 You *g* me with your counsel,
139:10 even there your hand will *g* me,
Pr 4:11 I *g* you in the way of wisdom
6:22 When you walk, they will *g* you;
Isa 58:11 The LORD will *g* you always;
Jn 16:13 comes, he will *g* you into all truth.

**GUILTY**
Ex 34:7 does not leave the *g* unpunished;
Jn 8:46 Can any of you prove me *g* of sin?
Heb 10:22 to cleanse us from a *g* conscience
Jas 2:10 at just one point is *g* of breaking all

**HADES**
Mt 16:18 the gates of *H* will not overcome it.

**HAGAR**
Servant of Sarah, wife of Abraham, mother of Ishmael (Ge 16:1-6; 25:12). Driven away by Sarah while pregnant (Ge 16:5-16); after birth of Isaac (Ge 21:9-21; Gal 4:21-31).

**HAGGAI***
Post-exilic prophet who encouraged rebuilding of the temple (Ezr 5:1; 6:14; Hag 1-2).

**HAIR (HAIRS)**
Lk 21:18 But not a *h* of your head will perish
1Co 11:6 for a woman to have her *h* cut

**HAIRS (HAIR)**
Mt 10:30 even the very *h* of your head are all

**HALLELUJAH***
Rev 19:1,3,4,6

**HALLOWED (HOLY)**
Mt 6:9 *h* be your name,

**HAND (HANDS)**
Ps 16:8 Because he is at my right *h*,
37:24 the LORD upholds him with his *h*.
139:10 even there your *h* will guide me,
Ecc 9:10 Whatever your *h* finds to do,
Mt 6:3 know what your right *h* is doing,
Jn 10:28 one can snatch them out of my *h*.
1Co 12:15 I am not a *h*, I do not belong

**HANDS (HAND)**
Ps 22:16 they have pierced my *h*
24:4 He who has clean *h* and a pure
31:5 Into your *h* I commit my spirit;
31:15 My times are in your *h*;
Pr 10:4 Lazy *h* make a man poor,
31:20 and extends her *h* to the needy.
Isa 55:12 will clap their *h*.
65:2 All day long I have held out my *h*
Lk 23:46 into your *h* I commit my spirit."
1Th 4:11 and to work with your *h*,
1Ti 2:8 to lift up holy *h* in prayer,
5:22 hasty in the laying on of *h*,

**HANNAH***
Wife of Elkanah, mother of Samuel (1Sa 1). Prayer at dedication of Samuel (1Sa 2:1-10). Blessed (1Sa 2:18-21).

**HAPPY**
Ps 68:3 may they be *h* and joyful.
Pr 15:13 A *h* heart makes the face cheerful,
Ecc 3:12 better for men than to be *h*
Jas 5:13 Is anyone *h*? Let him sing songs

**HARD (HARDEN HARDSHIP)**
Ge 18:14 Is anything too *h* for the LORD?
Mt 19:23 it is *h* for a rich man
1Co 4:12 We work *h* with our own hands.
1Th 5:12 to respect those who work *h*

**HARDEN (HARD)**
Ro 9:18 he hardens whom he wants to *h*.
Heb 3:8 do not *h* your hearts

**HARDHEARTED* (HEART)**
Dt 15:7 do not be *h* or tightfisted

**HARDSHIP (HARD)**
Ro 8:35 Shall trouble or *h* or persecution
2Ti 2:3 Endure *h* with us like a good
4:5 endure *h*, do the work
Heb 12:7 Endure *h* as discipline; God is

**HARM**
Ps 121:6 the sun will not *h* you by day,
Pr 3:29 not plot *h* against your neighbor,

Pr 31:12 She brings him good, not *h*,
Ro 13:10 Love does no *h* to its neighbor.
1Jn 5:18 and the evil one cannot *h* him.

**HARMONY**

Ro 12:16 Live in *h* with one another.
2Co 6:15 What *h* is there between Christ
1Pe 3:8 live in *h* with one another;

**HARVEST**

Mt 9:37 *h* is plentiful but the workers are
Jn 4:35 at the fields! They are ripe for *h*.
Gal 6:9 at the proper time we will reap a *h*
Heb 12:11 it produces a *h* of righteousness

**HASTE (HASTY)**

Pr 21:5 as surely as *h* leads to poverty.
29:20 Do you see a man who speaks in *h*?

**HASTY* (HASTE)**

Pr 19:2 nor to be *h* and miss the way.
Ecc 5:2 do not be *h* in your heart
1Ti 5:22 Do not be *h* in the laying

**HATE (HATED HATES HATRED)**

Lev 19:17 " 'Do not *h* your brother
Ps 5:5 you *h* all who do wrong.
45:7 righteousness and *h* wickedness;
97:10 those who love the LORD *h* evil,
139:21 Do I not *h* those who *h* you,
Pr 8:13 To fear the LORD is to *h* evil;
Am 5:15 *H* evil, love good;
Mal 2:16 "I *h* divorce," says the LORD God
Mt 5:43 your neighbor and *h* your enemy.'
10:22 All men will *h* you because of me,
Lk 6:27 do good to those who *h* you,
Ro 12:9 *H* what is evil; cling to what is good

**HATED (HATE)**

Ro 9:13 "Jacob I loved, but Esau I *h*."
Eph 5:29 no one ever *h* his own body,
Heb 1:9 righteousness and *h* wickedness;

**HATES (HATE)**

Pr 6:16 There are six things the LORD *h*,
13:24 He who spares the rod *h* his son,
Jn 3:20 Everyone who does evil *h* the light,
1Jn 2:9 *h* his brother is still in the darkness.

**HATRED (HATE)**

Pr 10:12 *H* stirs up dissension,
Jas 4:4 with the world is *h* toward God?

**HAUGHTY**

Pr 16:18 a *h* spirit before a fall.

**HAY**

1Co 3:12 costly stones, wood, *h* or straw,

**HEAD (HEADS HOTHEADED)**

Ge 3:15 he will crush your *h*,
Ps 23:5 You anoint my *h* with oil;
Pr 25:22 will heap burning coals on his *h*,
Isa 59:17 and the helmet of salvation on his *h*
Mt 8:20 of Man has no place to lay his *h*."
Ro 12:20 will heap burning coals on his *h*."
1Co 11:3 and the *h* of Christ is God.
12:21 And the *h* cannot say to the feet,
Eph 5:23 For the husband is the *h* of the wife
2Ti 4:5 keep your *h* in all situations,
Rev 19:12 and on his *h* are many crowns.

**HEADS (HEAD)**

Lev 26:13 you to walk with *h* held high.
Isa 35:10 everlasting joy will crown their *h*.

**HEAL (HEALED HEALING HEALS)**

2Ch 7:14 their sin and will *h* their land.
Ps 41:4 *h* me, for I have sinned against you
Mt 10:8 *H* the sick, raise the dead,
Lk 4:23 to me: 'Physician, *h* yourself!
5:17 present for him to *h* the sick.

**HEALED (HEAL)**

Isa 53:5 and by his wounds we are *h*.
Mt 9:22 he said, "your faith has *h* you."
14:36 and all who touched him were *h*.
Ac 4:10 this man stands before you *h*.

| | | |
|---|---|---|
| Ac | 14:9 | saw that he had faith to be *h* |
| Jas | 5:16 | for each other so that you may be *h* |
| 1Pe | 2:24 | by his wounds you have been *h*. |

**HEALING (HEAL)**

| | | |
|---|---|---|
| Eze | 47:12 | for food and their leaves for *h*." |
| Mal | 4:2 | rise with *h* in its wings. |
| 1Co | 12:9 | to another gifts of *h* |
| | 12:30 | Do all have gifts of *h*? Do all speak |
| Rev | 22:2 | are for the *h* of the nations. |

**HEALS (HEAL)**

| | | |
|---|---|---|
| Ex | 15:26 | for I am the LORD, who *h* you." |
| Ps | 103:3 | and *h* all your diseases; |
| | 147:3 | He *h* the brokenhearted |

**HEALTH (HEALTHY)**

| | | |
|---|---|---|
| Pr | 3:8 | This will bring *h* to your body |
| | 15:30 | and good news gives *h* to the bones |

**HEALTHY (HEALTH)**

| | | |
|---|---|---|
| Mk | 2:17 | "It is not the *h* who need a doctor, |

**HEAR (HEARD HEARING HEARS)**

| | | |
|---|---|---|
| Dt | 6:4 | *H*, O Israel: The LORD our God, |
| | 31:13 | must *h* it and learn |
| 2Ch | 7:14 | then will I *h* from heaven |
| Ps | 94:9 | he who implanted the ear not *h*? |
| Isa | 29:18 | that day the deaf will *h* the words |
| | 65:24 | while they are still speaking I will *h* |
| Mt | 11:15 | He who has ears, let him *h*. |
| Jn | 8:47 | reason you do not *h* is that you do |
| 2Ti | 4:3 | what their itching ears want to *h*. |

**HEARD (HEAR)**

| | | |
|---|---|---|
| Job | 42:5 | My ears had *h* of you |
| Isa | 66:8 | Who has ever *h* of such a thing? |
| Mt | 5:21 | "You have *h* that it was said |
| | 5:27 | "You have *h* that it was said, |
| | 5:33 | you have *h* that it was said |
| | 5:38 | "You have *h* that it was said, |
| | 5:43 | "You have *h* that it was said, |
| 1Co | 2:9 | no ear has *h*, |
| 1Th | 2:13 | word of God, which you *h* from us, |
| 2Ti | 1:13 | What you *h* from me, keep |
| Jas | 1:25 | not forgetting what he has *h*, |

**HEARING (HEAR)**

| | | |
|---|---|---|
| Ro | 10:17 | faith comes from *h* the message, |

**HEARS (HEAR)**

| | | |
|---|---|---|
| Jn | 5:24 | whoever *h* my word and believes |
| 1Jn | 5:14 | according to his will, he *h* us. |
| Rev | 3:20 | If anyone *h* my voice and opens |

**HEART (BROKENHEARTED HARDHEARTED HEARTS WHOLEHEARTEDLY)**

| | | |
|---|---|---|
| Ex | 25:2 | each man whose *h* prompts him |
| Lev | 19:17 | Do not hate your brother in your *h*. |
| Dt | 4:29 | if you look for him with all your *h* |
| | 6:5 | LORD your God with all your *h* |
| Dt | 10:12 | LORD your God with all your *h* |
| | 15:10 | and do so without a grudging *h*; |
| | 30:6 | you may love him with all your *h* |
| | 30:10 | LORD your God with all your *h* |
| Jos | 22:5 | and to serve him with all your *h* |
| 1Sa | 13:14 | sought out a man after his own *h* |
| | 16:7 | but the LORD looks at the *h*." |
| 2Ki | 23:3 | with all his *h* and all his soul, |
| 1Ch | 28:9 | for the LORD searches every *h* |
| 2Ch | 7:16 | and my *h* will always be there. |
| Job | 22:22 | and lay up his words in your *h*. |
| | 37:1 | "At this my *h* pounds |
| Ps | 14:1 | The fool says in his *h*, |
| | 19:14 | and the meditation of my *h* |
| | 37:4 | will give you the desires of your *h*. |
| | 45:1 | My *h* is stirred by a noble theme |
| | 51:10 | Create in me a pure *h*, O God, |
| | 51:17 | a broken and contrite *h*, |
| | 66:18 | If I had cherished sin in my *h*, |
| | 86:11 | give me an undivided *h*, |
| | 119:11 | I have hidden your word in my *h* |
| | 119:32 | for you have set my *h* free. |
| | 139:23 | Search me, O God, and know my *h* |
| Pr | 3:5 | Trust in the LORD with all your *h* |
| | 4:21 | keep them within your *h*; |

Pr 4:23 Above all else, guard your *h*,
7:3 write them on the tablet of your *h*.
13:12 Hope deferred makes the *h* sick,
14:13 Even in laughter the *h* may ache,
15:30 A cheerful look brings joy to the *h*,
17:22 A cheerful *h* is good medicine,
24:17 stumbles, do not let your *h* rejoice,
27:19 so a man's *h* reflects the man.
Ecc 8:5 wise *h* will know the proper time
SS 4:9 You have stolen my *h*, my sister,
Isa 40:11 and carries them close to his *h*;
57:15 and to revive the *h* of the contrite.
Jer 17:9 The *h* is deceitful above all things
29:13 when you seek me with all your *h*.
Eze 36:26 I will give you a new *h*
Mt 5:8 Blessed are the pure in *h*,
6:21 treasure is, there your *h* will be
12:34 of the *h* the mouth speaks.
22:37 the Lord your God with all your *h*
Lk 6:45 overflow of his *h* his mouth speaks.
Ro 2:29 is circumcision of the *h*,
10:10 is with your *h* that you believe
1Co 14:25 the secrets of his *h* will be laid bare.
Eph 5:19 make music in your *h* to the Lord,
6:6 doing the will of God from your *h*.
Col 3:23 work at it with all your *h*,
1Pe 1:22 one another deeply, from the *h*.

**HEARTS (HEART)**

Dt 11:18 Fix these words of mine in your *h*
1Ki 8:39 for you alone know the *h* of all men
8:61 your *h* must be fully committed
Ps 62:8 pour out your *h* to him,
Ecc 3:11 also set eternity in the *h* of men;
Jer 31:33 and write it on their *h*.
Lk 16:15 of men, but God knows your *h*.
24:32 "Were not our *h* burning within us
Jn 14:1 "Do not let your *h* be troubled.
Ac 15:9 for he purified their *h* by faith.
Ro 2:15 of the law are written on their *h*,
2Co 3:2 written on our *h*, known
3:3 but on tablets of human *h*.
4:6 shine in our *h* to give us the light
Eph 3:17 dwell in your *h* through faith.
Col 3:1 set your *h* on things above,
Heb 3:8 do not harden your *h*
10:16 I will put my laws in their *h*,
1Jn 3:20 For God is greater than our *h*,

**HEAT**

2Pe 3:12 and the elements will melt in the *h*.

**HEAVEN (HEAVENLY HEAVENS)**

Ge 14:19 Creator of *h* and earth.
1Ki 8:27 the highest *h*, cannot contain you.
2Ki 2:1 up to *h* in a whirlwind,
2Ch 7:14 then will I hear from *h*
Isa 14:12 How you have fallen from *h*,
66:1 "*H* is my throne,
Da 7:13 coming with the clouds of *h*.
Mt 6:9 " 'Our Father in *h*,
6:20 up for yourselves treasures in *h*,
16:19 bind on earth will be bound in *h*,
19:23 man to enter the kingdom of *h*.
24:35 *H* and earth will pass away,
26:64 and coming on the clouds of *h*."
28:18 "All authority in *h*
Mk 16:19 he was taken up into *h*
Lk 15:7 in *h* over one sinner who repents
18:22 and you will have treasure in *h*.
Ro 10:6 'Who will ascend into *h*?' " (that is,
2Co 5:1 an eternal house in *h*, not built
12:2 ago was caught up to the third *h*.
Php 2:10 *h* and on earth and under the earth,
3:20 But our citizenship is in *h*.
1Th 1:10 and to wait for his Son from *h*,
Heb 8:5 and shadow of what is in *h*.

Heb 9:24 he entered *h* itself, now to appear
2Pe 3:13 we are looking forward to a new *h*
Rev 21:1 Then I saw a new *h* and a new earth

**HEAVENLY (HEAVEN)**

Ps 8:5 him a little lower than the *h* beings
2Co 5:2 to be clothed with our *h* dwelling,
Eph 1:3 in the *h* realms with every spiritual
1:20 at his right hand in the *h* realms,
2Ti 4:18 bring me safely to his *h* kingdom.
Heb 12:22 to the *h* Jerusalem, the city

**HEAVENS (HEAVEN)**

Ge 1:1 In the beginning God created the *h*
1Ki 8:27 The *h,* even the highest heaven,
2Ch 2:6 since the *h,* even the highest
Ps 8:3 When I consider your *h,*
19:1 The *h* declare the glory of God;
102:25 the *h* are the work of your hands.
108:4 is your love, higher than the *h;*
119:89 it stands firm in the *h.*
139:8 If I go up to the *h,* you are there;
Isa 51:6 Lift up your eyes to the *h,*
55:9 "As the *h* are higher than the earth,
65:17 new *h* and a new earth.
Joel 2:30 I will show wonders in the *h*
Eph 4:10 who ascended higher than all the *h,*
2Pe 3:10 The *h* will disappear with a roar;

**HEBREW**

Ge 14:13 and reported this to Abram the *H.*

**HEEDS**

Pr 13:1 wise son *h* his father's instruction,
13:18 whoever *h* correction is honored.
15:5 whoever *h* correction shows
15:32 whoever *h* correction gains

**HEEL**

Ge 3:15 and you will strike his *h.*"

**HEIRS (INHERIT)**

Ro 8:17 then we are *h*—*h* of God
Gal 3:29 and *h* according to the promise.
Eph 3:6 gospel the Gentiles are *h* together
1Pe 3:7 as *h* with you of the gracious gift

**HELL**

Mt 5:22 will be in danger of the fire of *h.*
Lk 16:23 In *h,* where he was in torment,
2Pe 2:4 but sent them to *h,* putting them

**HELMET**

Isa 59:17 and the *h* of salvation on his head;
Eph 6:17 Take the *h* of salvation
1Th 5:8 and the hope of salvation as a *h.*

**HELP (HELPED HELPER HELPING HELPS)**

Ps 18:6 I cried to my God for *h.*
30:2 my God, I called to you for *h*
46:1 an ever-present *h* in trouble.
79:9 *H* us, O God our Savior,
121:1 where does my *h* come from?
Isa 41:10 I will strengthen you and *h* you;
Jnh 2:2 depths of the grave I called for *h,*
Mk 9:24 *h* me overcome my unbelief!"
Ac 16:9 Come over to Macedonia and *h* us
1Co 12:28 those able to *h* others, those

**HELPED (HELP)**

1Sa 7:12 "Thus far has the LORD *h* us."

**HELPER (HELP)**

Ge 2:18 I will make a *h* suitable for him."
Ps 10:14 you are the *h* of the fatherless.
Heb 13:6 Lord is my *h;* I will not be afraid.

**HELPING (HELP)**

Ac 9:36 always doing good and *h* the poor.
1Ti 5:10 *h* those in trouble and devoting

**HELPS (HELP)**

Ro 8:26 the Spirit *h* us in our weakness.

**HEN**

Mt 23:37 as a *h* gathers her chicks

**HERITAGE (INHERIT)**

Ps 127:3 Sons are a *h* from the LORD,

**HEROD**

1. King of Judea who tried to kill Jesus (Mt 2; Lk 1:5).
2. Son of 1. Tetrarch of Galilee who arrested and beheaded John the Baptist (Mt 14:1-12; Mk 6:14-29; Lk 3:1, 19-20; 9:7-9); tried Jesus (Lk 23:6-15).
3. Grandson of 1. King of Judea who killed James (Ac 12:2); arrested Peter (Ac 12:3-19). Death (Ac 12:19-23).

**HERODIAS**

Wife of Herod the Tetrarch who persuaded her daughter to ask for John the Baptist's head (Mt 14:1-12; Mk 6:14-29).

**HEZEKIAH**

King of Judah. Restored the temple and worship (2Ch 29-31). Sought the LORD for help against Assyria (2Ki 18-19; 2Ch 32:1-23; Isa 36-37). Illness healed (2Ki 20:1-11; 2Ch 32:24-26; Isa 38). Judged for showing Babylonians his treasures (2Ki 20:12-21; 2Ch 32:31; Isa 39).

**HID (HIDE)**

Ge 3:8 and they *h* from the LORD God
Ex 2:2 she *h* him for three months.
Jos 6:17 because she *h* the spies we sent.
Heb 11:23 By faith Moses' parents *h* him

**HIDDEN (HIDE)**

Ps 19:12 Forgive my *h* faults.
119:11 I have *h* your word in my heart
Pr 2:4 and search for it as for *h* treasure,
Isa 59:2 your sins have *h* his face from you,
Mt 5:14 A city on a hill cannot be *h*.
13:44 of heaven is like treasure *h*
Col 1:26 the mystery that has been kept *h*
2:3 in whom are *h* all the treasures
3:3 and your life is now *h* with Christ

**HIDE (HID HIDDEN)**

Ps 17:8 *h* me in the shadow of your wings
143:9 for I *h* myself in you.

**HILL (HILLS)**

Mt 5:14 A city on a *h* cannot be hidden.

**HILLS (HILL)**

Ps 50:10 and the cattle on a thousand *h*.
121:1 I lift up my eyes to the *h*—

**HINDER (HINDERS)**

1Sa 14:6 Nothing can *h* the LORD
Mt 19:14 come to me, and do not *h* them,
1Co 9:12 anything rather than *h* the gospel
1Pe 3:7 so that nothing will *h* your prayers.

**HINDERS (HINDER)**

Heb 12:1 let us throw off everything that *h*

**HINT***

Eph 5:3 even a *h* of sexual immorality,

**HOLD**

Ex 20:7 LORD will not *h* anyone guiltless
Lev 19:13 " 'Do not *h* back the wages
Jos 22:5 to *h* fast to him and to serve him
Ps 73:23 you *h* me by my right hand.
Pr 4:4 "Lay *h* of my words
Isa 54:2 do not *h* back;
Mk 11:25 if you *h* anything against anyone,
Php 2:16 as you *h* out the word of life—
3:12 but I press on to take *h* of that
Col 1:17 and in him all things *h* together.
1Th 5:21 *H* on to the good.
1Ti 6:12 Take *h* of the eternal life
Heb 10:23 Let us *h* unswervingly

**HOLINESS (HOLY)**

Ex 15:11 majestic in *h*,
Ps 29:2 in the splendor of his *h*.
96:9 in the splendor of his *h*;
Ro 6:19 to righteousness leading to *h*.
2Co 7:1 perfecting *h* out of reverence
Eph 4:24 God in true righteousness and *h*.
Heb 12:10 that we may share in his *h*.
12:14 without *h* no one will see the Lord.

**HOLY (HALLOWED HOLINESS)**

Ex 19:6 kingdom of priests and a *h* nation.'
20:8 the Sabbath day by keeping it *h*.
Lev 11:44 and be *h*, because I am *h*.
20:7 " 'Consecrate yourselves and be *h*,
20:26 You are to be *h* to me because I,
21:8 Consider them *h*, because I

Lev 22:32 Do not profane my *h* name.
Ps 16:10 will you let your *H* One see decay.
24:3 Who may stand in his *h* place?
77:13 Your ways, O God, are *h*.
99:3 he is *h*.
99:5 he is *h*.
99:9 for the LORD our God is *h*.
111:9 *h* and awesome is his name.
Isa 5:16 the *h* God will show himself *h*
6:3 *H*, *h*, *h* is the LORD Almighty;
40:25 who is my equal?" says the *H* One.
57:15 who lives forever, whose name is *h*:
Eze 28:25 I will show myself *h* among them
Da 9:24 prophecy and to anoint the most *h*.
Hab 2:20 But the LORD is in his *h* temple;
Ac 2:27 will you let your *H* One see decay.
Ro 7:12 and the commandment is *h*,
12:1 as living sacrifices, *h* and pleasing
Eph 5:3 improper for God's *h* people.
2Th 1:10 to be glorified in his *h* people
2Ti 1:9 saved us and called us to a *h* life—
3:15 you have known the *h* Scriptures,
Tit 1:8 upright, *h* and disciplined.
1Pe 1:15 But just as he who called you is *h*,
1:16 is written: "Be *h*, because I am *h*."
1Pe 2:9 a royal priesthood, a *h* nation,
2Pe 3:11 You ought to live *h* and godly lives
Rev 4:8 "*H*, *h*, *h* is the Lord God

**HOME (HOMES)**

Dt 6:7 Talk about them when you sit at *h*
Ps 84:3 Even the sparrow has found a *h*,
Pr 3:33 but he blesses the *h* of the righteous
Mk 10:29 "no one who has left *h* or brothers
Jn 14:23 to him and make our *h* with him.
Tit 2:5 to be busy at *h*, to be kind,

**HOMES (HOME)**

Ne 4:14 daughters, your wives and your *h*."
1Ti 5:14 to manage their *h* and to give

**HOMOSEXUAL***

1Co 6:9 male prostitutes nor *h* offenders

**HONEST**

Lev 19:36 Use *h* scales and *h* weights,
Dt 25:15 and *h* weights and measures,
Job 31:6 let God weigh me in *h* scales
Pr 12:17 truthful witness gives *h* testimony,

**HONEY**

Ex 3:8 a land flowing with milk and *h*—
Ps 19:10 than *h* from the comb.
119:103 sweeter than *h* to my mouth!

**HONOR (HONORABLE HONORABLY HONORED HONORS)**

Ex 20:12 "*H* your father and your mother,
Nu 25:13 he was zealous for the *h* of his God
Dt 5:16 "*H* your father and your mother,
1Sa 2:30 Those who *h* me I will *h*,
Ps 8:5 and crowned him with glory and *h*.
Pr 3:9 *H* the LORD with your wealth,
15:33 and humility comes before *h*.
20:3 It is to a man's *h* to avoid strife,
Mt 15:4 '*H* your father and mother'
Ro 12:10 *H* one another above yourselves.
1Co 6:20 Therefore *h* God with your body.
Eph 6:2 "*H* your father and mother"—
1Ti 5:17 well are worthy of double *h*,
Heb 2:7 you crowned him with glory and *h*
Rev 4:9 *h* and thanks to him who sits

**HONORABLE (HONOR)**

1Th 4:4 body in a way that is holy and *h*,

**HONORABLY (HONOR)**

Heb 13:18 and desire to live *h* in every way.

**HONORED (HONOR)**

Ps 12:8 when what is vile is *h* among men.
Pr 13:18 but whoever heeds correction is *h*.
1Co 12:26 if one part is *h*, every part rejoices
Heb 13:4 Marriage should be *h* by all,

**HONORS (HONOR)**
Ps 15:4 but *h* those who fear the LORD,
Pr 14:31 to the needy *h* God.

**HOOKS**
Isa 2:4 and their spears into pruning *h*.
Joel 3:10 and your pruning *h* into spears.

**HOPE (HOPES)**
Job 13:15 Though he slay me, yet will I *h*
Ps 42:5 Put your *h* in God,
62:5 my *h* comes from him.
119:74 for I have put my *h* in your word.
130:7 O Israel, put your *h* in the LORD,
147:11 who put their *h* in his unfailing love
Pr 13:12 *H* deferred makes the heart sick,
Isa 40:31 but those who *h* in the LORD
Ro 5:4 character; and character, *h*.
8:24 But *h* that is seen is no *h* at all.
12:12 Be joyful in *h*, patient in affliction,
15:4 of the Scriptures we might have *h*.
1Co 13:13 now these three remain: faith, *h*
15:19 for this life we have *h* in Christ,
Col 1:27 Christ in you, the *h* of glory.
1Th 5:8 and the *h* of salvation as a helmet.
1Ti 6:17 but to put their *h* in God,
Tit 2:13 while we wait for the blessed *h*—
Heb 6:19 We have this *h* as an anchor
Heb 11:1 faith is being sure of what we *h* for
1Jn 3:3 Everyone who has this *h*

**HOPES (HOPE)**
1Co 13:7 always *h*, always perseveres.

**HORSE**
Ps 147:10 not in the strength of the *h*,
Pr 26:3 A whip for the *h*, a halter
Zec 1:8 before me was a man riding a red *h*
Rev 6:2 and there before me was a white *h*!
6:4 Come!" Then another *h* came out,
6:5 and there before me was a black *h*!
6:8 and there before me was a pale *h*!
19:11 and there before me was a white *h*,

**HOSANNA**
Mt 21:9 "*H* in the highest!"

**HOSHEA**
Last king of Israel (2Ki 15:30; 17:1-6).

**HOSPITABLE* (HOSPITALITY)**
1Ti 3:2 self-controlled, respectable, *h*,
Tit 1:8 Rather he must be *h*, one who loves

**HOSPITALITY (HOSPITABLE)**
Ro 12:13 Practice *h*.
1Ti 5:10 as bringing up children, showing *h*,
1Pe 4:9 Offer *h* to one another

**HOSTILE**
Ro 8:7 the sinful mind is *h* to God.

**HOT**
1Ti 4:2 have been seared as with a *h* iron.
Rev 3:15 that you are neither cold nor *h*.

**HOT-TEMPERED**
Pr 15:18 A *h* man stirs up dissension,
19:19 A *h* man must pay the penalty;
22:24 Do not make friends with a *h* man,
29:22 and a *h* one commits many sins.

**HOTHEADED (HEAD)**
Pr 14:16 but a fool is *h* and reckless.

**HOUR**
Ecc 9:12 knows when his *h* will come:
Mt 6:27 you by worrying can add a single *h*
Lk 12:40 the Son of Man will come at an *h*
Jn 12:23 The *h* has come for the Son of Man
12:27 for this very reason I came to this *h*

**HOUSE (HOUSEHOLD STOREHOUSE)**
Ex 20:17 shall not covet your neighbor's *h*.
Ps 23:6 I will dwell in the *h* of the LORD
84:10 a doorkeeper in the *h* of my God
122:1 "Let us go to the *h* of the LORD."
127:1 Unless the LORD builds the *h*,
Pr 7:27 Her *h* is a highway to the grave,

Pr 21:9 than share a *h* with a quarrelsome
Isa 56:7 a *h* of prayer for all nations."
Zec 13:6 given at the *h* of my friends.'
Mt 7:24 is like a wise man who built his *h*
12:29 can anyone enter a strong man's *h*
21:13 My *h* will be called a *h* of prayer,'
Mk 3:25 If a *h* is divided against itself,
Lk 11:17 a *h* divided against itself will fall.
Jn 2:16 How dare you turn my Father's *h*
12:3 the *h* was filled with the fragrance
14:2 In my Father's *h* are many rooms;
Heb 3:3 the builder of a *h* has greater honor

**HOUSEHOLD (HOUSE)**
Jos 24:15 my *h*, we will serve the LORD."
Mic 7:6 are the members of his own *h*.
Mt 10:36 will be the members of his own *h*.'
12:25 or *h* divided against itself will not
1Ti 3:12 manage his children and his *h* well.
3:15 to conduct themselves in God's *h*,

**HUMAN (HUMANITY)**
Gal 3:3 to attain your goal by *h* effort?

**HUMANITY* (HUMAN)**
Heb 2:14 he too shared in their *h* so that

**HUMBLE (HUMBLED HUMBLES HUMILIATE HUMILITY)**
2Ch 7:14 will *h* themselves and pray
Ps 25:9 He guides the *h* in what is right
Pr 3:34 but gives grace to the *h*.
Isa 66:2 he who is *h* and contrite in spirit,
Mt 11:29 for I am gentle and *h* in heart,
Eph 4:2 Be completely *h* and gentle;
Jas 4:10 *H* yourselves before the Lord,
1Pe 5:6 *H* yourselves,

**HUMBLED (HUMBLE)**
Mt 23:12 whoever exalts himself will be *h*,
Php 2:8 he *h* himself

**HUMBLES (HUMBLE)**
Mt 18:4 whoever *h* himself like this child is
23:12 whoever *h* himself will be exalted.

**HUMILIATE* (HUMBLE)**
Pr 25:7 than for him to *h* you
1Co 11:22 and *h* those who have nothing?

**HUMILITY (HUMBLE)**
Pr 11:2 but with *h* comes wisdom.
15:33 and *h* comes before honor.
Php 2:3 but in *h* consider others better
Tit 3:2 and to show true *h* toward all men.
1Pe 5:5 clothe yourselves with *h*

**HUNGRY**
Ps 107:9 and fills the *h* with good things.
Ps 146:7 and gives food to the *h*.
Pr 25:21 If your enemy is *h*, give him food
Eze 18:7 but gives his food to the *h*
Mt 25:35 For I was *h* and you gave me
Lk 1:53 He has filled the *h* with good things
Jn 6:35 comes to me will never go *h*,
Ro 12:20 "If your enemy is *h*, feed him;

**HURT (HURTS)**
Ecc 8:9 it over others to his own *h*.
Mk 16:18 deadly poison, it will not *h* them
Rev 2:11 He who overcomes will not be *h*

**HURTS* (HURT)**
Ps 15:4 even when it *h*,
Pr 26:28 A lying tongue hates those it *h*,

**HUSBAND (HUSBAND'S HUSBANDS)**
1Co 7:3 The *h* should fulfill his marital duty
7:10 wife must not separate from her *h*.
7:11 And a *h* must not divorce his wife.
7:13 And if a woman has a *h* who is not
7:39 A woman is bound to her *h* as long
2Co 11:2 I promised you to one *h*, to Christ,
Eph 5:23 For the *h* is the head of the wife
5:33 and the wife must respect her *h*.
1Ti 3:2 the *h* of but one wife, temperate,

**HUSBAND'S (HUSBAND)**
Pr 12:4 of noble character is her *h* crown,
1Co 7:4 the *h* body does not belong

**HUSBANDS (HUSBAND)**
Eph 5:22 submit to your *h* as to the Lord.
5:25 *H,* love your wives, just
Tit 2:4 the younger women to love their *h*
1Pe 3:1 same way be submissive to your *h*
3:7 *H,* in the same way be considerate

**HYMN**
1Co 14:26 everyone has a *h,* or a word

**HYPOCRISY (HYPOCRITE HYPOCRITES)**
Mt 23:28 but on the inside you are full of *h*
1Pe 2:1 *h,* envy, and slander of every kind.

**HYPOCRITE (HYPOCRISY)**
Mt 7:5 You *h,* first take the plank out

**HYPOCRITES (HYPOCRISY)**
Ps 26:4 nor do I consort with *h;*
Mt 6:5 when you pray, do not be like the *h*

**HYSSOP**
Ps 51:7 with *h,* and I will be clean;

**IDLE (IDLENESS)**
1Th 5:14 those who are *i,* encourage
2Th 3:6 away from every brother who is *i*
1Ti 5:13 they get into the habit of being *i*

**IDLENESS* (IDLE)**
Pr 31:27 and does not eat the bread of *i.*

**IDOL (IDOLATRY IDOLS)**
Isa 44:17 From the rest he makes a god, his *i;*
1Co 8:4 We know that an *i* is nothing at all

**IDOLATRY (IDOL)**
Col 3:5 evil desires and greed, which is *i.*

**IDOLS (IDOL)**
1Co 8:1 Now about food sacrificed to *i:*

**IGNORANT (IGNORE)**
1Co 15:34 for there are some who are *i* of God
Heb 5:2 to deal gently with those who are *i*
1Pe 2:15 good you should silence the *i* talk
2Pe 3:16 which *i* and unstable people distort

**IGNORE (IGNORANT IGNORES)**
Dt 22:1 do not *i* it but be sure
Ps 9:12 he does not *i* the cry of the afflicted
Heb 2:3 if we *i* such a great salvation?

**IGNORES (IGNORE)**
Pr 10:17 whoever *i* correction leads others
15:32 He who *i* discipline despises

**ILLUMINATED***
Rev 18:1 and the earth was *i* by his splendor.

**IMAGE**
Ge 1:26 "Let us make man in our *i,*
1:27 So God created man in his own *i,*
1Co 11:7 since he is the *i* and glory of God;
Col 1:15 He is the *i* of the invisible God,
3:10 in knowledge in the *i* of its Creator.

**IMAGINE**
Eph 3:20 more than all we ask or *i,*

**IMITATE (IMITATORS)**
1Co 4:16 Therefore I urge you to *i* me.
Heb 6:12 but to *i* those who through faith
13:7 of their way of life and *i* their faith.
3Jn :11 do not *i* what is evil but what is

**IMITATORS* (IMITATE)**
Eph 5:1 Be *i* of God, therefore,
1Th 1:6 You became *i* of us and of the Lord
2:14 became *i* of God's churches

**IMMANUEL**
Isa 7:14 birth to a son, and will call him *I.*
Mt 1:23 and they will call him *I*"—

**IMMORAL* (IMMORALITY)**
Pr 6:24 keeping you from the *i* woman,
1Co 5:9 to associate with sexually *i* people
5:10 the people of this world who are *i,*
5:11 but is sexually *i* or greedy,
6:9 Neither the sexually *i* nor idolaters

Eph 5:5 No *i*, impure or greedy person—
Heb 12:16 See that no one is sexually *i*,
13:4 the adulterer and all the sexually *i*.
Rev 21:8 the murderers, the sexually *i*,
22:15 the sexually *i*, the murderers,

**IMMORALITY (IMMORAL)**
1Co 6:13 The body is not meant for sexual *i*,
6:18 Flee from sexual *i*.
10:8 We should not commit sexual *i*,
Gal 5:19 sexual *i*, impurity and debauchery;
Eph 5:3 must not be even a hint of sexual *i*,
1Th 4:3 that you should avoid sexual *i*;
Jude :4 grace of our God into a license for *i*

**IMMORTAL* (IMMORTALITY)**
Ro 1:23 glory of the *i* God for images made
1Ti 1:17 Now to the King eternal, *i*,
6:16 who alone is *i* and who lives

**IMMORTALITY (IMMORTAL)**
Ro 2:7 honor and *i*, he will give eternal life
1Co 15:53 and the mortal with *i*.
2Ti 1:10 and *i* to light through the gospel.

**IMPERISHABLE**
1Pe 1:23 not of perishable seed, but of *i*,

**IMPORTANCE* (IMPORTANT)**
1Co 15:3 passed on to you as of first *i*:

**IMPORTANT (IMPORTANCE)**
Mt 6:25 Is not life more *i* than food,
23:23 have neglected the more *i* matters
Mk 12:29 "The most *i* one," answered Jesus,
12:33 as yourself is more *i* than all burnt
Php 1:18 The *i* thing is that in every way,

**IMPOSSIBLE**
Mt 17:20 Nothing will be *i* for you."
Lk 1:37 For nothing is *i* with God."
18:27 "What is *i* with men is possible
Heb 6:18 things in which it is *i* for God to lie,
11:6 without faith it is *i* to please God,

**IMPROPER***
Eph 5:3 these are *i* for God's holy people.

**IMPURE (IMPURITY)**
Ac 10:15 not call anything *i* that God has
Eph 5:5 No immoral, *i* or greedy person—
1Th 4:7 For God did not call us to be *i*,
Rev 21:27 Nothing *i* will ever enter it,

**IMPURITY (IMPURE)**
Ro 1:24 hearts to sexual *i* for the degrading
Eph 5:3 or of any kind of *i*, or of greed,

**INCENSE**
Ex 40:5 Place the gold altar of *i* in front
Ps 141:2 my prayer be set before you like *i*;
Mt 2:11 him with gifts of gold and of *i*

**INCOME**
Ecc 5:10 wealth is never satisfied with his *i*.
1Co 16:2 sum of money in keeping with his *i*,

**INCOMPARABLE***
Eph 2:7 ages he might show the *i* riches

**INCREASE (EVER-INCREASING INCREASED INCREASES INCREASING)**
Ge 1:22 "Be fruitful and *i* in number
Ps 62:10 though your riches *i*,
Isa 9:7 Of the *i* of his government
Lk 17:5 said to the Lord, "*I* our faith!"
1Th 3:12 May the Lord make your love *i*

**INCREASED (INCREASE)**
Ac 6:7 of disciples in Jerusalem *i* rapidly,
Ro 5:20 But where sin *i*, grace *i* all the more

**INCREASES (INCREASE)**
Pr 24:5 and a man of knowledge *i* strength;

**INCREASING (INCREASE)**
Ac 6:1 when the number of disciples was *i*,
2Th 1:3 one of you has for each other is *i*.
2Pe 1:8 these qualities in *i* measure,

**INDEPENDENT***
1Co 11:11 however, woman is not *i* of man,
11:11 of man, nor is man *i* of woman.

**INDESCRIBABLE***
2Co 9:15 Thanks be to God for his *i* gift!

**INDISPENSABLE***
1Co 12:22 seem to be weaker are *i*,

**INEFFECTIVE***
2Pe 1:8 they will keep you from being *i*

**INEXPRESSIBLE***
2Co 12:4 He heard *i* things, things that man
1Pe 1:8 are filled with an *i* and glorious joy,

**INFANTS**
Mt 21:16 " 'From the lips of children and *i*
1Co 14:20 In regard to evil be *i*,

**INFIRMITIES**
Isa 53:4 Surely he took up our *i*

**INHERIT (CO-HEIRS HEIRS HERITAGE INHERITANCE)**
Ps 37:11 But the meek will *i* the land
37:29 the righteous will *i* the land
Mt 5:5 for they will *i* the earth.
Mk 10:17 "what must I do to *i* eternal life?"
1Co 15:50 blood cannot *i* the kingdom of God

**INHERITANCE (INHERIT)**
Dt 4:20 to be the people of his *i*,
Pr 13:22 A good man leaves an *i*
Eph 1:14 who is a deposit guaranteeing our *i*
5:5 has any *i* in the kingdom of Christ
Heb 9:15 receive the promised eternal *i*—
1Pe 1:4 and into an *i* that can never perish,

**INIQUITIES (INIQUITY)**
Ps 78:38 he forgave their *i*
103:10 or repay us according to our *i*.
Isa 59:2 But your *i* have separated
Mic 7:19 and hurl all our *i* into the depths

**INIQUITY (INIQUITIES)**
Ps 51:2 Wash away all my *i*
Isa 53:6 the *i* of us all.

**INJUSTICE**
2Ch 19:7 the LORD our God there is no *i*

**INNOCENT**
Pr 17:26 It is not good to punish an *i* man,
Mt 10:16 shrewd as snakes and as *i* as doves.
27:4 "for I have betrayed *i* blood."
1Co 4:4 but that does not make me *i*.

**INSCRIPTION**
Mt 22:20 And whose *i*?" "Caesar's,"

**INSOLENT**
Ro 1:30 God-haters, *i*, arrogant

**INSTITUTED**
Ro 13:2 rebelling against what God has *i*,
1Pe 2:13 to every authority *i* among men:

**INSTRUCT (INSTRUCTION)**
Ps 32:8 I will *i* you and teach you
Pr 9:9 *I* a wise man and he will be wiser
Ro 15:14 and competent to *i* one another.
2Ti 2:25 who oppose him he must gently *i*,

**INSTRUCTION (INSTRUCT)**
Pr 1:8 Listen, my son, to your father's *i*
4:1 Listen, my sons, to a father's *i*;
4:13 Hold on to *i*, do not let it go;
8:10 Choose my *i* instead of silver,
8:33 Listen to my *i* and be wise;
13:1 A wise son heeds his father's *i*,
13:13 He who scorns *i* will pay for it,
16:20 Whoever gives heed to *i* prospers,
16:21 and pleasant words promote *i*.
19:20 Listen to advice and accept *i*,
23:12 Apply your heart to *i*
1Co 14:6 or prophecy or word of *i*?
14:26 or a word of *i*, a revelation,
Eph 6:4 up in the training and *i* of the Lord.
1Th 4:8 he who rejects this *i* does not reject
2Th 3:14 If anyone does not obey our *i*
1Ti 1:18 I give you this *i* in keeping
6:3 to the sound *i* of our Lord Jesus
2Ti 4:2 with great patience and careful *i*.

**INSULT**
Pr 9:7 corrects a mocker invites *i*;

Pr 12:16 but a prudent man overlooks an *i.*
Mt 5:11 Blessed are you when people *i* you,
Lk 6:22 when they exclude you and *i* you
1Pe 3:9 evil with evil or *i* with *i,*

**INTEGRITY**
1Ki 9:4 if you walk before me in *i* of heart
Job 2:3 And he still maintains his *i,*
27:5 till I die, I will not deny my *i.*
Pr 10:9 The man of *i* walks securely,
11:3 The *i* of the upright guides them,
29:10 Bloodthirsty men hate a man of *i*
Tit 2:7 your teaching show *i,* seriousness

**INTELLIGENCE**
Isa 29:14 the *i* of the intelligent will vanish."
1Co 1:19 *i* of the intelligent I will frustrate."

**INTELLIGIBLE**
1Co 14:19 I would rather speak five *i* words

**INTERCEDE (INTERCEDES INTERCESSION)**
Heb 7:25 he always lives to *i* for them.

**INTERCEDES (INTERCEDE)**
Ro 8:26 but the Spirit himself *i* for us

**INTERCESSION* (INTERCEDE)**
Isa 53:12 and made *i* for the transgressors.
1Ti 2:1 *i* and thanksgiving be made

**INTERESTS**
1Co 7:34 his wife—and his *i* are divided.
Php 2:4 only to your own *i,* but also to the *i*
2:21 everyone looks out for his own *i,*

**INTERMARRY (MARRY)**
Dt 7:3 Do not *i* with them.

**INVENTED***
2Pe 1:16 We did not follow cleverly *i* stories

**INVESTIGATED**
Lk 1:3 I myself have carefully *i* everything

**INVISIBLE**
Ro 1:20 of the world God's *i* qualities—
Col 1:15 He is the image of the *i* God,
1Ti 1:17 immortal, *i,* the only God,

**INVITE (INVITED INVITES)**
Lk 14:13 you give a banquet, *i* the poor,

**INVITED (INVITE)**
Mt 22:14 For many are *i,* but few are chosen
25:35 I was a stranger and you *i* me in,

**INVITES (INVITE)**
1Co 10:27 If some unbeliever *i* you to a meal

**INVOLVED**
2Ti 2:4 a soldier gets *i* in civilian affairs—

**IRON**
1Ti 4:2 have been seared as with a hot *i.*
Rev 2:27 He will rule them with an *i* scepter;

**IRREVOCABLE***
Ro 11:29 for God's gifts and his call are *i.*

**ISAAC**
Son of Abraham by Sarah (Ge 17:19; 21:1-7; 1Ch 1:28). Offered up by Abraham (Ge 22; Heb 11:17-19). Rebekah taken as wife (Ge 24). Fathered Esau and Jacob (Ge 25:19-26; 1Ch 1:34). Tricked into blessing Jacob (Ge 27). Father of Israel (Ex 3:6; Dt 29:13; Ro 9:10).

**ISAIAH**
Prophet to Judah (Isa 1:1). Called by the LORD (Isa 6).

**ISHMAEL**
Son of Abraham by Hagar (Ge 16; 1Ch 1:28). Blessed, but not son of covenant (Ge 17:18-21; Gal 4:21-31). Sent away by Sarah (Ge 21:8-21).

**ISRAEL (ISRAELITES)**
1. Name given to Jacob (see JACOB).
2. Corporate name of Jacob's descendants; often specifically Northern Kingdom.
Dt 6:4 Hear, O *I:* The LORD our God,
1Sa 4:21 "The glory has departed from *I*"—
Isa 27:6 *I* will bud and blossom
Jer 31:10 'He who scattered *I* will gather
Eze 39:23 of *I* went into exile for their sin,
Mk 12:29 'Hear, O *I,* the Lord our God,
Lk 22:30 judging the twelve tribes of *I.*
Ro 9:6 all who are descended from *I* are *I.*
11:26 And so all *I* will be saved,
Eph 3:6 Gentiles are heirs together with *I,*

**ISRAELITES (ISRAEL)**
Ex 14:22 and the *I* went through the sea

| | | |
|---|---|---|
| Pr | 16:35 | The *I* ate manna forty years, |
| Hos | 1:10 | "Yet the *I* will be like the sand |
| Ro | 9:27 | the number of the *I* be like the sand |

**ITCHING***

| | | |
|---|---|---|
| 2Ti | 4:3 | to say what their *i* ears want to hear |

**JACOB**

Second son of Isaac, twin of Esau (Ge 26:21-26; 1Ch 1:34). Bought Esau's birthright (Ge 26:29-34); tricked Isaac into blessing him (Ge 27:1-37). Abrahamic covenant perpetuated through (Ge 28:13-15; Mal 1:2). Vision at Bethel (Ge 28:10-22). Wives and children (Ge 29:1-30:24; 35:16-26; 1Ch 2-9). Wrestled with God; name changed to Israel (Ge 32:22-32). Sent sons to Egypt during famine (Ge 42-43). Settled in Egypt (Ge 46). Blessed Ephraim and Manasseh (Ge 48). Blessed sons (Ge 49:1-28; Heb 11:21). Death (Ge 49:29-33). Burial (Ge 50:1-14).

**JAMES**

1. Apostle; brother of John (Mt 4:21-22; 10:2; Mk 3:17; Lk 5:1-10). At transfiguration (Mt 17:1-13; Mk 9:1-13; Lk 9:28-36). Killed by Herod (Ac 12:2).
2. Apostle; son of Alphaeus (Mt 10:3; Mk 3:18; Lk 6:15).
3. Brother of Jesus (Mt 13:55; Mk 6:3; Lk 24:10; Gal 1:19) and Judas (Jude 1). With believers before Pentecost (Ac 1:13). Leader of church at Jerusalem (Ac 12:17; 15; 21:18; Gal 2:9, 12). Author of epistle (Jas 1:1).

**JAPHETH**

Son of Noah (Ge 5:32; 1Ch 1:4-5). Blessed (Ge 9:18-28).

**JARS**

| | | |
|---|---|---|
| 2Co | 4:7 | we have this treasure in *j* of clay |

**JEALOUS (JEALOUSY)**

| | | |
|---|---|---|
| Ex | 20:5 | the LORD your God, am a *j* God, |
| | 34:14 | whose name is Jealous, is a *j* God. |
| Dt | 4:24 | God is a consuming fire, a *j* God. |
| Joel | 2:18 | the LORD will be *j* for his land |
| Zec | 1:14 | I am very *j* for Jerusalem and Zion, |
| 2Co | 11:2 | I am *j* for you with a godly jealousy |

**JEALOUSY (JEALOUS)**

| | | |
|---|---|---|
| 1Co | 3:3 | For since there is *j* and quarreling |
| 2Co | 11:2 | I am jealous for you with a godly *j*. |
| Gal | 5:20 | hatred, discord, *j*, fits of rage, |

**JEHOAHAZ**

1. Son of Jehu; king of Israel (2Ki 13:1-9).
2. Son of Josiah; king of Judah (2Ki 23:31-34; 2Ch 36:1-4).

**JEHOASH**

Son of Jehoahaz; king of Israel (2Ki 13-14; 2Ch 25).

**JEHOIACHIN**

Son of Jehoiakim; king of Judah exiled by Nebuchadnezzar (2Ki 24:8-17; 2Ch 36:8-10; Jer 22:24-30; 24:1). Raised from prisoner status (2Ki 25:27-30; Jer 52:31-34).

**JEHOIAKIM**

Son of Josiah; king of Judah (2Ki 23:34-24:6; 2Ch 36:4-8; Jer 22:18-23; 36).

**JEHORAM**

Son of Jehoshaphat; king of Judah (2Ki 8:16-24).

**JEHOSHAPHAT**

Son of Asa; king of Judah (1Ki 22:41-50; 2Ki 3; 2Ch 17-20).

**JEHU**

King of Israel (1Ki 19:16-19; 2Ki 9-10).

**JEPHTHAH**

Judge from Gilead who delivered Israel from Ammon (Jdg 10:6-12:7). Made rash vow concerning his daughter (Jdg 11:30-40).

**JEREMIAH**

Prophet to Judah (Jer 1:1-3). Called by the LORD (Jer 1). Put in stocks (Jer 20:1-3). Threatened for prophesying (Jer 11:18-23; 26). Opposed by Hananiah (Jer 28). Scroll burned (Jer 36). Imprisoned (Jer 37). Thrown into cistern (Jer 38). Forced to Egypt with those fleeing Babylonians (Jer 43).

**JEROBOAM**

1. Official of Solomon; rebelled to become first king of Israel (1Ki 11:26-40; 12:1-20; 2Ch 10). Idolatry (1Ki 12:25-33); judgment for (1Ki 13-14; 2Ch 13).
2. Son of Jehoash; king of Israel (1Ki 14:23-29).

**JERUSALEM**

| | | |
|---|---|---|
| 2Ki | 23:27 | and I will reject *J*, the city I chose, |
| 2Ch | 6:6 | now I have chosen *J* for my Name |
| Ne | 2:17 | Come, let us rebuild the wall of *J*, |
| Ps | 122:6 | Pray for the peace of *J*: |
| | 125:2 | As the mountains surround *J*, |
| | 137:5 | If I forget you, O *J*, |
| Isa | 40:9 | You who bring good tidings to *J*, |
| | 65:18 | for I will create *J* to be a delight |
| Joel | 3:17 | *J* will be holy; |
| Zep | 3:16 | On that day they will say to *J*, |
| Zec | 2:4 | '*J* will be a city without walls |

Zec 8:8 I will bring them back to live in *J;*
14:8 living water will flow out from *J,*
Mt 23:37 "O *J, J,* you who kill the prophets
Lk 13:34 die outside *J!* "O *J, J,*
21:24 *J* will be trampled
Jn 4:20 where we must worship is in *J.*"
Ac 1:8 and you will be my witnesses in *J,*
Gal 4:25 corresponds to the present city of *J*
Rev 21:2 I saw the Holy City, the new *J,*

**JESUS**

LIFE: Genealogy (Mt 1:1-17; Lk 3:21-37). Birth announced (Mt 1:18-25; Lk 1:26-45). Birth (Mt 2:1-12; Lk 2:1-40). Escape to Egypt (Mt 2:13-23). As a boy in the temple (Lk 2:41-52). Baptism (Mt 3:13-17; Mk 1:9-11; Lk 3:21-22; Jn 1:32-34). Temptation (Mt 4:1-11; Mk 1:12-13; Lk 4:1-13). Ministry in Galilee (Mt 4:12-18:35; Mk 1:14-9:50; Lk 4:14-13:9; Jn 1:35-2:11; 4; 6), Transfiguration (Mt 17:1-8; Mk 9:2-8; Lk 9:28-36), on the way to Jerusalem (Mt 19-20; Mk 10; Lk 13:10-19:27), in Jerusalem (Mt 21-25; Mk 11-13; Lk 19:28-21:38; Jn 2:12-3:36; 5; 7-12). Last supper (Mt 26:17-35; Mk 14:12-31; Lk 22:1-38; Jn 13-17). Arrest and trial (Mt 26:36-27:31; Mk 14:43-15:20; Lk 22:39-23:25; Jn 18:1-19:16). Crucifixion (Mt 27:32-66; Mk 15:21-47; Lk 23:26-55; Jn 19:28-42). Resurrection and appearances (Mt 28; Mk 16; Lk 24; Jn 20-21; Ac 1:1-11; 7:56; 9:3-6; 1Co 15:1-8; Rev 1:1-20).

MIRACLES. Healings: official's son (Jn 4:43-54), demoniac in Capernaum (Mk 1:23-26; Lk 4:33-35), Peter's mother-in-law (Mt 8:14-17; Mk 1:29-31; Lk 4:38-39), leper (Mt 8:2-4; Mk 1:40-45; Lk 5:12-16), paralytic (Mt 9:1-8; Mk 2:1-12; Lk 5:17-26), cripple (Jn 5:1-9), shriveled hand (Mt 12:10-13; Mk 3:1-5; Lk 6:6-11), centurion's servant (Mt 8:5-13; Lk 7:1-10), widow's son raised (Lk 7:11-17), demoniac (Mt 12:22-23; Lk 11:14), Gadarene demoniacs (Mt 8:28-34; Mk 5:1-20; Lk 8:26-39), woman's bleeding and Jairus' daughter (Mt 9:18-26; Mk 5:21-43; Lk 8:40-56), blind man (Mt 9:27-31), mute man (Mt 9:32-33), Canaanite woman's daughter (Mt 15:21-28; Mk 7:24-30), deaf man (Mk 7:31-37), blind man (Mk 8:22-26), demoniac boy (Mt 17:14-18; Mk 9:14-29; Lk 9:37-43), ten lepers (Lk 17:11-19), man born blind (Jn 9:1-7), Lazarus raised (Jn 11), crippled woman (Lk 13:11-17), man with dropsy (Lk 14:1-6), two blind men (Mt 20:29-34; Mk 10:46-52; Lk 18:35-43), Malchus' ear (Lk 22:50-51). Other Miracles: water to wine (Jn 2:1-11), catch of fish (Lk 5:1-11), storm stilled (Mt 8:23-27; Mk 4:37-41; Lk 8:22-25), 5,000 fed (Mt 14:15-21; Mk 6:35-44; Lk 9:10-17; Jn 6:1-14), walking on water (Mt 14:25-33; Mk 6:48-52; Jn 6:15-21), 4,000 fed (Mt 15:32-39; Mk 8:1-9), money from fish (Mt 17:24-27), fig tree cursed (Mt 21:18-22; Mk 11:12-14), catch of fish (Jn 21:1-14).

MAJOR TEACHING: Sermon on the Mount (Mt 5-7; Lk 6:17-49), to Nicodemus (Jn 3), to Samaritan woman (Jn 4), Bread of Life (Jn 6:22-59), at Feast of Tabernacles (Jn 7-8), woes to Pharisees (Mt 23; Lk 11:37-54), Good Shepherd (Jn 10:1-18), Olivet Discourse (Mt 24-25; Mk 13; Lk 21:5-36), Upper Room Discourse (Jn 13-16).

PARABLES: Sower (Mt 13:3-23; Mk 4:3-25; Lk 8:5-18), seed's growth (Mk 4:26-29), wheat and weeds (Mt 13:24-30, 36-43), mustard seed (Mt 13:31-32; Mk 4:30-32), yeast (Mt 13:33; Lk 13:20-21), hidden treasure (Mt 13:44), valuable pearl (Mt 13:45-46), net (Mt 13:47-51), house owner (Mt 13:52), good Samaritan (Lk 10:25-37), unmerciful servant (Mt 18:15-35), lost sheep (Mt 18:10-14; Lk 15:4-7), lost coin (Lk 15:8-10), prodigal son (Lk 15:11-32), dishonest manager (Lk 16:1-13), rich man and Lazarus (Lk 16:19-31), persistent widow (Lk 18:1-8), Pharisee and tax collector (Lk 18:9-14), payment of workers (Mt 20:1-16), tenants and the vineyard (Mt 21:28-46; Mk 12:1-12; Lk 20:9-19), wedding banquet (Mt 22:1-14), faithful servant (Mt 24:45-51), ten virgins (Mt 25:1-13), talents (Mt 25:1-30; Lk 19:12-27).

DISCIPLES see APOSTLES. Call of (Jn 1:35-51; Mt 4:18-22; 9:9; Mk 1:16-20; 2:13-14; Lk 5:1-11, 27-28). Named Apostles (Mk 3:13-19; Lk 6:12-16). Twelve sent out (Mt 10; Mk 6:7-11; Lk 9:1-5). Seventy sent out (Lk 10:1-24). Defection of (Jn 6:60-71; Mt 26:56; Mk 14:50-52). Final commission (Mt 28:16-20; Jn 21:15-23; Ac 1:3-8).

Ac 2:32 God has raised this *J* to life,
9:5 "I am *J,* whom you are persecuting
15:11 of our Lord *J* that we are saved,
16:31 "Believe in the Lord *J,*
Ro 3:24 redemption that came by Christ *J.*
5:17 life through the one man, *J* Christ.
8:1 for those who are in Christ *J,*
1Co 2:2 except *J* Christ and him crucified.
8:6 and there is but one Lord, *J* Christ,
12:3 and no one can say, "*J* is Lord,"

2Co 4:5 not preach ourselves, but *J* Christ
Gal 2:16 but by faith in *J* Christ.
3:28 for you are all one in Christ *J*.
5:6 in Christ *J* neither circumcision
Eph 2:10 created in Christ *J*
2:20 with Christ *J* himself as the chief
Php 1:6 until the day of Christ *J*.
2:5 be the same as that of Christ *J*:
2:10 name of *J* every knee should bow,
Col 3:17 do it all in the name of the Lord *J*,
2Th 2:1 the coming of our Lord *J* Christ
1Ti 1:15 Christ *J* came into the world
2Ti 3:12 life in Christ *J* will be persecuted,
Tit 2:13 our great God and Savior, *J* Christ,
Heb 2:9 But we see *J*, who was made a little
3:1 fix your thoughts on *J*, the apostle
4:14 through the heavens, *J* the Son
7:22 *J* has become the guarantee
7:24 but because *J* lives forever,
12:2 Let us fix our eyes on *J*, the author
2Pe 1:16 and coming of our Lord *J* Christ,
1Jn 1:7 and the blood of *J*, his Son,
2:1 *J* Christ, the Righteous One.
2:6 to live in him must walk as *J* did.
1Jn 4:15 anyone acknowledges that *J* is
Rev 22:20 Come, Lord *J*.

**JEW (JEWS JUDAISM)**
Zec 8:23 of one *J* by the edge of his robe
Ro 1:16 first for the *J*, then for the Gentile.
10:12 there is no difference between *J*
1Co 9:20 To the Jews I became like a *J*,
Gal 3:28 There is neither *J* nor Greek,

**JEWELRY (JEWELS)**
1Pe 3:3 wearing of gold *j* and fine clothes.

**JEWELS (JEWELRY)**
Isa 61:10 as a bride adorns herself with her *j*.
Zec 9:16 like *j* in a crown.

**JEWS (JEW)**
Mt 2:2 who has been born king of the *J*?
27:11 "Are you the king of the *J*?" "Yes,
Jn 4:22 for salvation is from the *J*.
Ro 3:29 Is God the God of *J* only?
1Co 1:22 *J* demand miraculous signs
9:20 To the *J* I became like a Jew,
12:13 whether *J* or Greeks, slave or free
Gal 2:8 of Peter as an apostle to the *J*,
Rev 3:9 claim to be *J* though they are not,

**JEZEBEL**
Sidonian wife of Ahab (1Ki 16:31). Promoted Baal worship (1Ki 16:32-33). Killed prophets of the LORD (1Ki 18:4, 13). Opposed Elijah (1Ki 19:1-2). Had Naboth killed (1Ki 21). Death prophesied (1Ki 21:17-24). Killed by Jehu (2Ki 9:30-37).

**JOASH**
Son of Ahaziah; king of Judah. Sheltered from Athaliah by Jehoiada (2Ki 11; 2Ch 22:10-23:21). Repaired temple (2Ki 12; 2Ch 24).

**JOB**
Wealthy man from Uz; feared God (Job 1:1-5). Righteousness tested by disaster (Job 1:6-22), personal affliction (Job 2). Maintained innocence in debate with three friends (Job 3-31), Elihu (Job 32-37). Rebuked by the LORD (Job 38-41). Vindicated and restored to greater stature by the LORD (Job 42). Example of righteousness (Eze 14:14, 20).

**JOHN**
1. Son of Zechariah and Elizabeth (Lk 1). Called the Baptist (Mt 3:1-12; Mk 1:2-8). Witness to Jesus (Mt 3:11-12; Mk 1:7-8; Lk 3:15-18; Jn 1:6-35; 3:27-30; 5:33-36). Doubts about Jesus (Mt 11:2-6; Lk 7:18-23). Arrest (Mt 4:12; Mk 1:14). Execution (Mt 14:1-12; Mk 6:14-29; Lk 9:7-9). Ministry compared to Elijah (Mt 11:7-19; Mk 9:11-13; Lk 7:24-35).
2. Apostle; brother of James (Mt 4:21-22; 10:2; Mk 3:17; Lk 5:1-10). At transfiguration (Mt 17:1-13; Mk 9:1-13; Lk 9:28-36). Desire to be greatest (Mk 10:35-45). Leader of church at Jerusalem (Ac 4:1-3; Gal 2:9). Elder who wrote epistles (2Jn 1; 3Jn 1). Prophet who wrote Revelation (Rev 1:1; 22:8).
3. Cousin of Barnabas, co-worker with Paul, (Ac 12:12-13:13; 15:37), see MARK.

**JOIN (JOINED)**
Pr 23:20 Do not *j* those who drink too much

| | | |
|---|---|---|
| Pr | 24:21 | and do not *j* with the rebellious, |
| Ro | 15:30 | to *j* me in my struggle by praying |
| 2Ti | 1:8 | *j* with me in suffering for the gospel |

## JOINED (JOIN)

| | | |
|---|---|---|
| Mt | 19:6 | Therefore what God has *j* together, |
| Mk | 10:9 | Therefore what God has *j* together, |
| Eph | 2:21 | him the whole building is *j* together |
| | 4:16 | *j* and held together |

## JOINTS

| | | |
|---|---|---|
| Heb | 4:12 | even to dividing soul and spirit, *j* |

## JOKING

| | | |
|---|---|---|
| Eph | 5:4 | or coarse *j*, which are out of place, |

## JONAH

Prophet in days of Jeroboam II (2Ki 14:25). Called to Nineveh; fled to Tarshish (Jnh 1:1-3). Cause of storm; thrown into sea (Jnh 1:4-16). Swallowed by fish (Jnh 1:17). Prayer (Jnh 2). Preached to Nineveh (Jnh 3). Attitude reproved by the LORD (Jnh 4). Sign of (Mt 12:39-41; Lk 11:29-32).

## JONATHAN

Son of Saul (1Sa 13:16; 1Ch 8:33). Valiant warrior (1Sa 13-14). Relation to David (1Sa 18:1-4; 19-20; 23:16-18). Killed at Gilboa (1Sa 31). Mourned by David (2Sa 1).

## JORAM

1. Son of Ahab; king of Israel (2Ki 3; 8-9; 2Ch 22).

## JORDAN

| | | |
|---|---|---|
| Nu | 34:12 | boundary will go down along the *J* |
| Jos | 4:22 | Israel crossed the *J* on dry ground.' |
| Mt | 3:6 | baptized by him in the *J* River. |

## JOSEPH

1. Son of Jacob by Rachel (Ge 30:24; 1Ch 2:2). Favored by Jacob, hated by brothers (Ge 37:3-4). Dreams (Ge 37:5-11). Sold by brothers (Ge 37:12-36). Served Potiphar; imprisoned by false accusation (Ge 39). Interpreted dreams of Pharaoh's servants (Ge 40), of Pharaoh (Ge 41:4-40). Made greatest in Egypt (Ge 41:41-57). Sold grain to brothers (Ge 42-45). Brought Jacob and sons to Egypt (Ge 46-47). Sons Ephraim and Manasseh blessed (Ge 48). Blessed (Ge 49:22-26; Dt 33:13-17). Death (Ge 50:22-26; Ex 13:19; Heb 11:22). 12,000 from (Rev 7:8).

2. Husband of Mary, mother of Jesus (Mt 1:16-24; 2:13-19; Lk 1:27; 2; Jn 1:45).

3. Disciple from Arimathea, who gave his tomb for Jesus' burial (Mt 27:57-61; Mk 15:43-47; Lk 24:50-52).

4. Original name of Barnabas (Ac 4:36).

## JOSHUA

1. Son of Nun; name changed from Hoshea (Nu 13:8, 16; 1Ch 7:27). Fought Amalekites under Moses (Ex 17:9-14). Servant of Moses on Sinai (Ex 24:13; 32:17). Spied Canaan (Nu 13). With Caleb, allowed to enter land (Nu 14:6, 30). Succeeded Moses (Dt 1:38; 31:1-8; 34:9).

Charged Israel to conquer Canaan (Jos 1). Crossed Jordan (Jos 3-4). Circumcised sons of wilderness wanderings (Jos 5). Conquered Jericho (Jos 6), Ai (Jos 7-8), five kings at Gibeon (Jos 10:1-28), southern Canaan (Jos 10:29-43), northern Canaan (Jos 11-12). Defeated at Ai (Jos 7). Deceived by Gibeonites (Jos 9). Renewed covenant (Jos 8:30-35; 24:1-27). Divided land among tribes (Jos 13-22). Last words (Jos 23). Death (Jos 24:28-31).

2. High priest during rebuilding of temple (Hag 1-2; Zec 3:1-9; 6:11).

## JOSIAH

Son of Amon; king of Judah (2Ki 22-23; 2Ch 34-35).

## JOTHAM

Son of Azariah (Uzziah); king of Judah (2Ki 15:32-38; 2Ch 26:21-27:9).

## JOY (ENJOY ENJOYMENT JOYFUL OVERJOYED REJOICE REJOICES REJOICING)

| | | |
|---|---|---|
| Dt | 16:15 | and your *j* will be complete. |
| 1Ch | 16:27 | strength and *j* in his dwelling place. |
| Ne | 8:10 | for the *j* of the LORD is your |
| Est | 9:22 | their sorrow was turned into *j* |
| Job | 38:7 | and all the angels shouted for *j*? |
| Ps | 4:7 | have filled my heart with greater *j* |
| | 21:6 | with the *j* of your presence. |
| | 30:11 | sackcloth and clothed me with *j*, |
| | 43:4 | to God, my *j* and my delight. |
| | 51:12 | to me the *j* of your salvation |
| | 66:1 | Shout with *j* to God, all the earth! |
| | 96:12 | the trees of the forest will sing for *j*; |
| | 107:22 | and tell of his works with songs of *j* |
| | 119:111 | they are the *j* of my heart. |
| Pr | 10:1 | A wise son brings *j* to his father, |

Pr 10:28 The prospect of the righteous is *j*,
12:20 but *j* for those who promote peace.
Isa 35:10 everlasting *j* will crown their heads
51:11 Gladness and *j* will overtake them,
55:12 You will go out in *j*
Lk 1:44 the baby in my womb leaped for *j*.
2:10 news of great *j* that will be
Jn 15:11 and that your *j* may be complete.
16:20 but your grief will turn to *j*.
2Co 8:2 their overflowing *j* and their
Php 2:2 then make my *j* complete
4:1 and long for, my *j* and crown,
1Th 2:19 For what is our hope, our *j*,
Phm :7 Your love has given me great *j*
Heb 12:2 for the *j* set before him endured
Jas 1:2 Consider it pure *j*, my brothers,
1Pe 1:8 with an inexpressible and glorious *j*
2Jn :4 It has given me great *j* to find some
3Jn :4 I have no greater *j*

## JOYFUL (JOY)

Ps 100:2 come before him with *j* songs.
Hab 3:18 I will be *j* in God my Savior.
1Th 5:16 Be *j* always; pray continually;

## JUDAH

1. Son of Jacob by Leah (Ge 29:35; 35:23; 1Ch 2:1). Tribe of blessed as ruling tribe (Ge 49:8-12; Dt 33:7).
2. Name used for people and land of Southern Kingdom.

Jer 13:19 All *J* will be carried into exile,
Zec 10:4 From *J* will come the cornerstone,
Heb 7:14 that our Lord descended from *J*,

## JUDAISM (JEW)

Gal 1:13 of my previous way of life in *J*,

## JUDAS

1. Apostle (Lk 6:16; Jn 14:22; Ac 1:13). Probably also called Thaddaeus (Mt 10:3; Mk 3:18).
2. Brother of James and Jesus (Mt 13:55; Mk 6:3), also called Jude (Jude 1).
3. Apostle, also called Iscariot, who betrayed Jesus (Mt 10:4; 26:14-56; Mk 3:19; 14:10-50; Lk 6:16; 22:3-53; Jn 6:71; 12:4; 13:2-30; 18:2-11). Suicide of (Mt 27:3-5; Ac 1:16-25).

## JUDGE (JUDGED JUDGES JUDGING JUDGMENT)

Ge 18:25 Will not the *J* of all the earth do
1Ch 16:33 for he comes to *j* the earth.
Ps 9:8 He will *j* the world in righteousness
Joel 3:12 sit to *j* all the nations on every side.
Mt 7:1 Do not *j*, or you too will be judged.
Jn 12:47 For I did not come to *j* the world,
Ac 17:31 a day when he will *j* the world
Ro 2:16 day when God will *j* men's secrets
1Co 4:3 indeed, I do not even *j* myself.
6:2 that the saints will *j* the world?
Gal 2:6 not *j* by external appearance—
2Ti 4:1 who will *j* the living and the dead,
4:8 which the Lord, the righteous *J*,
Jas 4:12 There is only one Lawgiver and *J*,
4:12 who are you to *j* your neighbor?
Rev 20:4 who had been given authority to *j*.

## JUDGED (JUDGE)

Mt 7:1 "Do not judge, or you too will be *j*.
1Co 11:31 But if we *j* ourselves, we would not
Jas 3:1 who teach will be *j* more strictly.
Rev 20:12 The dead were *j* according

## JUDGES (JUDGE)

Jdg 2:16 Then the LORD raised up *j*,
Ps 58:11 there is a God who *j* the earth."
Heb 4:12 it *j* the thoughts and attitudes
Rev 19:11 With justice he *j* and makes war.

## JUDGING (JUDGE)

Mt 19:28 *j* the twelve tribes of Israel.
Jn 7:24 Stop *j* by mere appearances,

## JUDGMENT (JUDGE)

Dt 1:17 of any man, for *j* belongs to God.
Ps 1:5 the wicked will not stand in the *j*,
119:66 Teach me knowledge and good *j*,
Pr 6:32 man who commits adultery lacks *j*;
12:11 but he who chases fantasies lacks *j*.

Ecc 12:14 God will bring every deed into *j*,
Isa 66:16 the LORD will execute *j*
Mt 5:21 who murders will be subject to *j*.'
10:15 on the day of *j* than for that town.
12:36 have to give account on the day of *j*
Jn 5:22 but has entrusted all *j* to the Son,
7:24 appearances, and make a right *j*."
16:8 to sin and righteousness and *j*:
Ro 14:10 stand before God's *j* seat.
14:13 Therefore let us stop passing *j*
1Co 11:29 body of the Lord eats and drinks *j*
2Co 5:10 appear before the *j* seat of Christ,
Heb 9:27 to die once, and after that to face *j*,
10:27 but only a fearful expectation of *j*
1Pe 4:17 For it is time for *j* to begin
Jude :6 bound with everlasting chains for *j*

**JUST (JUSTICE JUSTIFICATION JUSTIFIED JUSTIFY JUSTLY)**

Dt 32:4 and all his ways are *j*.
Ps 37:28 For the LORD loves the *j*
111:7 of his hands are faithful and *j*;
Pr 1:3 doing what is right and *j* and fair;
2:8 for he guards the course of the *j*
Da 4:37 does is right and all his ways are *j*.
Ro 3:26 as to be *j* and the one who justifies
Heb 2:2 received its *j* punishment,
1Jn 1:9 and *j* and will forgive us our sins
Rev 16:7 true and *j* are your judgments."

**JUSTICE (JUST)**

Ex 23:2 do not pervert *j* by siding
23:6 "Do not deny *j* to your poor people
Job 37:23 in his *j* and great righteousness,
Ps 9:8 he will govern the peoples with *j*.
9:16 The LORD is known by his *j*;
11:7 he loves *j*;
45:6 a scepter of *j* will be the scepter
101:1 I will sing of your love and *j*;
106:3 Blessed are they who maintain *j*,
Pr 21:15 When *j* is done, it brings joy
28:5 Evil men do not understand *j*,
29:4 By *j* a king gives a country stability
29:26 from the LORD that man gets *j*.
Isa 9:7 it with *j* and righteousness
28:17 I will make *j* the measuring line
30:18 For the LORD is a God of *j*.
42:1 and he will bring *j* to the nations.
42:4 till he establishes *j* on earth.
56:1 "Maintain *j*
61:8 "For I, the LORD, love *j*;
Jer 30:11 I will discipline you but only with *j*;
Eze 34:16 I will shepherd the flock with *j*.
Am 5:15 maintain *j* in the courts.
5:24 But let *j* roll on like a river,
Zec 7:9 'Administer true *j*; show mercy
Lk 11:42 you neglect *j* and the love of God.
Ro 3:25 He did this to demonstrate his *j*,

**JUSTIFICATION (JUST)**

Ro 4:25 and was raised to life for our *j*.
5:18 of righteousness was *j* that brings

**JUSTIFIED (JUST)**

Ac 13:39 him everyone who believes is *j*
Ro 3:24 and are *j* freely by his grace
3:28 For we maintain that a man is *j*
5:1 since we have been *j* through faith,
5:9 Since we have now been *j*
8:30 those he called, he also *j*; those he *j*,
1Co 6:11 you were *j* in the name
Gal 2:16 observing the law no one will be *j*.
3:11 Clearly no one is *j* before God
3:24 to Christ that we might be *j* by faith
Jas 2:24 You see that a person is *j*

**JUSTIFY (JUST)**

Gal 3:8 that God would *j* the Gentiles

**JUSTLY (JUST)**

Mic 6:8 To act *j* and to love mercy

**KEEP (KEEPER KEEPING KEEPS KEPT)**

Ge 31:49 "May the LORD *k* watch
Ex 20:6 and *k* my commandments.
Nu 6:24 and *k* you;
Ps 18:28 You, O LORD, *k* my lamp burning
19:13 *K* your servant also from willful
119:9 can a young man *k* his way pure?
121:7 The LORD will *k* you
141:3 *k* watch over the door of my lips.
Pr 4:24 *k* corrupt talk far from your lips.
Isa 26:3 You will *k* in perfect peace
Mt 10:10 for the worker is worth his *k*.
Lk 12:35 and *k* your lamps burning,
Gal 5:25 let us *k* in step with the Spirit.
Eph 4:3 Make every effort to *k* the unity
1Ti 5:22 *K* yourself pure.
2Ti 4:5 *k* your head in all situations,
Heb 13:5 *K* your lives free from the love
Jas 1:26 and yet does not *k* a tight rein
2:8 If you really *k* the royal law found
Jude :24 able to *k* you from falling

**KEEPER (KEEP)**

Ge 4:9 I my brother's *k?*" The LORD

**KEEPING (KEEP)**

Ex 20:8 the Sabbath day by *k* it holy.
Ps 19:11 in *k* them there is great reward.
Mt 3:8 Produce fruit in *k* with repentance.
Lk 2:8 *k* watch over their flocks at night.
1Co 7:19 *K* God's commands is what counts.
2Pe 3:9 Lord is not slow in *k* his promise,

**KEEPS (KEEP)**

Pr 17:28 a fool is thought wise if he *k* silent,
Am 5:13 Therefore the prudent man *k* quiet
1Co 13:5 is not easily angered, it *k* no record
Jas 2:10 For whoever *k* the whole law

**KEPT (KEEP)**

Ps 130:3 If you, O LORD, *k* a record of sins,
2Ti 4:7 finished the race, I have *k* the faith.
1Pe 1:4 spoil or fade—*k* in heaven for you,

**KEYS**

Mt 16:19 I will give you the *k* of the kingdom

**KILL (KILLS)**

Mt 17:23 They will *k* him, and on the third

**KILLS (KILL)**

Lev 24:21 but whoever *k* a man must be put
2Co 3:6 for the letter *k*, but the Spirit gives

**KIND (KINDNESS KINDS)**

Ge 1:24 animals, each according to its *k*."
2Ch 10:7 "If you will be *k* to these people
Pr 11:17 A *k* man benefits himself,
12:25 but a *k* word cheers him up.
14:21 blessed is he who is *k* to the needy.
14:31 whoever is *k* to the needy honors
19:17 He who is *k* to the poor lends
Da 4:27 by being *k* to the oppressed.
Lk 6:35 because he is *k* to the ungrateful
1Co 13:4 Love is patient, love is *k*.
15:35 With what *k* of body will they
Eph 4:32 Be *k* and compassionate
1Th 5:15 but always try to be *k* to each other
2Ti 2:24 instead, he must be *k* to everyone,
Tit 2:5 to be busy at home, to be *k*,

**KINDNESS (KIND)**

Ac 14:17 He has shown *k* by giving you rain
Ro 11:22 Consider therefore the *k*
Gal 5:22 peace, patience, *k*, goodness,
Eph 2:7 expressed in his *k* to us
2Pe 1:7 brotherly *k;* and to brotherly *k*,

**KINDS (KIND)**

1Co 12:4 There are different *k* of gifts,
1Ti 6:10 of money is a root of all *k* of evil.

**KING (KINGDOM KINGS)**

1. Kings of Judah and Israel: see Saul, David, Solomon.

2. Kings of Judah: see Rehoboam, Abijah, Asa, Jehoshaphat, Jehoram, Ahaziah, Athaliah (Queen), Joash, Amaziah, Uzziah, Jotham, Ahaz, Hezekiah, Manasseh, Amon, Josiah, Jehoahaz, Jehoiakim, Jehoiachin, Zedekiah.

3. Kings of Israel: see Jeroboam I, Nadab, Baasha, Elah, Zimri, Tibni, Omri, Ahab, Ahaziah, Joram, Jehu, Jehoahaz, Jehoash, Jeroboam II, Zechariah, Shallum, Menahem, Pekah, Pekahiah, Hoshea.

Jdg 17:6 In those days Israel had no *k;*
1Sa 12:12 the LORD your God was your *k.*
Ps 24:7 that the *K* of glory may come in.
Isa 32:1 See, a *k* will reign in righteousness
Zec 9:9 See, your *k* comes to you,
1Ti 6:15 the *K* of kings and Lord of lords,
1Pe 2:17 of believers, fear God, honor the *k.*
Rev 19:16 *K OF KINGS AND LORD*

**KINGDOM (KING)**

Ex 19:6 you will be for me a *k* of priests
1Ch 29:11 Yours, O LORD, is the *k;*
Ps 45:6 justice will be the scepter of your *k.*
Da 4:3 His *k* is an eternal *k;*
Mt 3:2 Repent, for the *k* of heaven is near
5:3 for theirs is the *k* of heaven.
6:10 your *k* come,
6:33 But seek first his *k* and his
7:21 Lord,' will enter the *k* of heaven,
11:11 least in the *k* of heaven is greater
13:24 "The *k* of heaven is like a man who
13:31 *k* of heaven is like a mustard seed,
13:33 "The *k* of heaven is like yeast that
Mt 13:44 *k* of heaven is like treasure hidden
13:45 the *k* of heaven is like a merchant
13:47 *k* of heaven is like a net that was let
16:19 the keys of the *k* of heaven;
18:23 the *k* of heaven is like a king who
19:24 for a rich man to enter the *k* of God
24:7 rise against nation, and *k* against *k.*
24:14 gospel of the *k* will be preached
25:34 the *k* prepared for you
Mk 9:47 better for you to enter the *k* of God
10:14 for the *k* of God belongs to such
10:23 for the rich to enter the *k* of God!"
Lk 10:9 'The *k* of God is near you.'
12:31 seek his *k,* and these things will be
17:21 because the *k* of God is within you
Jn 3:5 no one can enter the *k* of God
18:36 "My *k* is not of this world.
1Co 6:9 the wicked will not inherit the *k*
15:24 hands over the *k* to God the Father
Rev 1:6 has made us to be a *k* and priests
11:15 of the world has become the *k*

**KINGS (KING)**

Ps 2:2 The *k* of the earth take their stand
72:11 All *k* will bow down to him
Da 7:24 ten horns are ten *k* who will come
1Ti 2:2 for *k* and all those in authority,
Rev 1:5 and the ruler of the *k* of the earth.

**KINSMAN-REDEEMER (REDEEM)**

Ru 3:9 over me, since you are a *k.*"

**KISS**

Ps 2:12 *K* the Son, lest he be angry
Pr 24:26 is like a *k* on the lips.
Lk 22:48 the Son of Man with a *k?*"

**KNEE (KNEES)**

Isa 45:23 Before me every *k* will bow;
Ro 14:11 'every *k* will bow before me;
Php 2:10 name of Jesus every *k* should bow,

**KNEES (KNEE)**

Isa 35:3 steady the *k* that give way;
Heb 12:12 your feeble arms and weak *k.*

**KNEW (KNOW)**

Job 23:3 If only I *k* where to find him;
Jnh 4:2 I *k* that you are a gracious
Mt 7:23 tell them plainly, 'I never *k* you.

**KNOCK**

Mt 7:7 *k* and the door will be opened
Rev 3:20 I am! I stand at the door and *k.*

**KNOW (FOREKNEW KNEW KNOWING KNOWLEDGE KNOWN KNOWS)**

Dt 18:21 "How can we *k* when a message

Job 19:25 I *k* that my Redeemer lives,
42:3 things too wonderful for me to *k*.
Ps 46:10 "Be still, and *k* that I am God;
139:1 and you *k* me.
139:23 Search me, O God, and *k* my heart;
Pr 27:1 for you do not *k* what a day may
Jer 24:7 I will give them a heart to *k* me,
31:34 his brother, saying, '*K* the LORD,'
Mt 6:3 let your left hand *k* what your right
24:42 you do not *k* on what day your
Lk 1:4 so that you may *k* the certainty
Jn 3:11 we speak of what we *k*,
4:22 we worship what we do *k*,
9:25 One thing I do *k*.
10:14 I *k* my sheep and my sheep *k* me—
17:3 that they may *k* you, the only true
21:24 We *k* that his testimony is true.
Ac 1:7 "It is not for you to *k* the times
Ro 6:6 For we *k* that our old self was
7:18 I *k* that nothing good lives in me,
8:28 we *k* that in all things God works
1Co 2:2 For I resolved to *k* nothing
6:15 Do you not *k* that your bodies are
6:19 Do you not *k* that your body is
13:12 Now I *k* in part; then I shall *k* fully,
1Co 15:58 because you *k* that your labor
Php 3:10 I want to *k* Christ and the power
2Ti 1:12 because I *k* whom I have believed,
Jas 4:14 *k* what will happen tomorrow.
1Jn 2:4 The man who says, "I *k* him,"
3:14 We *k* that we have passed
3:16 This is how we *k* what love is:
5:2 This is how we *k* that we love
5:13 so that you may *k* that you have

**KNOWING (KNOW)**

Ge 3:5 and you will be like God, *k* good
Php 3:8 of *k* Christ Jesus my Lord,

**KNOWLEDGE (KNOW)**

Ge 2:9 the tree of the *k* of good and evil.
Job 42:3 obscures my counsel without *k*?'
Ps 19:2 night after night they display *k*.
73:11 Does the Most High have *k*?"
139:6 Such *k* is too wonderful for me,
Pr 1:7 of the LORD is the beginning of *k*,
10:14 Wise men store up *k*,
12:1 Whoever loves discipline loves *k*,
13:16 Every prudent man acts out of *k*,
19:2 to have zeal without *k*,
Isa 11:9 full of the *k* of the LORD
Hab 2:14 filled with the *k* of the glory
Ro 11:33 riches of the wisdom and *k* of God!
1Co 8:1 *K* puffs up, but love builds up.
8:11 Christ died, is destroyed by your *k*.
13:2 can fathom all mysteries and all *k*,
2Co 2:14 everywhere the fragrance of the *k*
4:6 light of the *k* of the glory of God
Eph 3:19 to know this love that surpasses *k*
Col 2:3 all the treasures of wisdom and *k*.
1Ti 6:20 ideas of what is falsely called *k*,
2Pe 3:18 grow in the grace and *k* of our Lord

**KNOWN (KNOW)**

Ps 16:11 You have made *k* to me the path
105:1 make *k* among the nations what he
Isa 46:10 *k* the end from the beginning,
Mt 10:26 or hidden that will not be made *k*.
Ro 1:19 since what may be *k* about God is
11:34 "Who has *k* the mind of the Lord?
15:20 the gospel where Christ was not *k*,
2Co 3:2 written on our hearts, *k*
2Pe 2:21 than to have *k* it and then

**KNOWS (KNOW)**

1Sa 2:3 for the LORD is a God who *k*,
Job 23:10 But he *k* the way that I take;
Ps 44:21 since he *k* the secrets of the heart?

Ps 94:11 The LORD *k* the thoughts of man;
Ecc 8:7 Since no man *k* the future,
Mt 6:8 for your Father *k* what you need
24:36 "No one *k* about that day or hour,
Ro 8:27 who searches our hearts *k* the mind
1Co 8:2 who thinks he *k* something does
2Ti 2:19 The Lord *k* those who are his," and

**LABAN**

Brother of Rebekah (Ge 24:29-51), father of Rachel and Leah (Ge 29-31).

**LABOR**

Ex 20:9 Six days you shall *l* and do all your
Isa 55:2 and your *l* on what does not satisfy
Mt 6:28 They do not *l* or spin.
1Co 3:8 rewarded according to his own *l*.
15:58 because you know that your *l*

**LACK (LACKING LACKS)**

Pr 15:22 Plans fail for *l* of counsel,
Ro 3:3 Will their *l* of faith nullify God's
Col 2:23 *l* any value in restraining sensual

**LACKING (LACK)**

Ro 12:11 Never be *l* in zeal, but keep your
Jas 1:4 and complete, not *l* anything.

**LACKS (LACK)**

Pr 6:32 who commits adultery *l* judgment;
12:11 he who chases fantasies *l* judgment
Jas 1:5 any of you *l* wisdom, he should ask

**LAID (LAY)**

Isa 53:6 and the LORD has *l* on him
1Co 3:11 other than the one already *l*,
1Jn 3:16 Jesus Christ *l* down his life for us.

**LAKE**

Rev 19:20 into the fiery *l* of burning sulfur.
20:14 The *l* of fire is the second death.

**LAMB (LAMB'S LAMBS)**

Ge 22:8 "God himself will provide the *l*
Ex 12:21 and slaughter the Passover *l*.
Isa 11:6 The wolf will live with the *l*,
53:7 he was led like a *l* to the slaughter,
Jn 1:29 *L* of God, who takes away the sin
1Co 5:7 our Passover *l*, has been sacrificed.
1Pe 1:19 a *l* without blemish or defect.
Rev 5:6 Then I saw a *L*, looking
5:12 "Worthy is the *L*, who was slain,
14:4 They follow the *L* wherever he

**LAMB'S (LAMB)**

Rev 21:27 written in the *L* book of life.

**LAMBS (LAMB)**

Lk 10:3 I am sending you out like *l*
Jn 21:15 Jesus said, "Feed my *l*."

**LAMENT**

2Sa 1:17 took up this *l* concerning Saul

**LAMP (LAMPS)**

2Sa 22:29 You are my *l*, O LORD;
Ps 18:28 You, O LORD, keep my *l* burning;
119:105 Your word is a *l* to my feet
Pr 31:18 and her *l* does not go out at night.
Lk 8:16 "No one lights a *l* and hides it
Rev 21:23 gives it light, and the Lamb is its *l*.

**LAMPS (LAMP)**

Mt 25:1 be like ten virgins who took their *l*
Lk 12:35 for service and keep your *l* burning,

**LAND**

Ge 1:10 God called the dry ground "*l*,"
1:11 "Let the *l* produce vegetation:
12:7 To your offspring I will give this *l*."
Ex 3:8 a *l* flowing with milk and honey—
Nu 35:33 Do not pollute the *l* where you are.
Dt 34:1 LORD showed him the whole *l*—
Jos 13:2 "This is the *l* that remains:
14:4 Levites received no share of the *l*
2Ch 7:14 their sin and will heal their *l*.
7:20 then I will uproot Israel from my *l*,
Eze 36:24 and bring you back into your own *l*.

**LANGUAGE**

Ge 11:1 Now the whole world had one *l*

Ps 19:3 There is no speech or *l*
Jn 8:44 When he lies, he speaks his native *l*
Ac 2:6 heard them speaking in his own *l*.
Col 3:8 slander, and filthy *l* from your lips.
Rev 5:9 from every tribe and *l* and people

**LAST (LASTING LASTS LATTER)**
2Sa 23:1 These are the *l* words of David:
Isa 44:6 I am the first and I am the *l*;
Mt 19:30 But many who are first will be *l*,
Mk 10:31 are first will be *l*, and the *l* first."
Jn 15:16 and bear fruit—fruit that will *l*.
Ro 1:17 is by faith from first to *l*,
2Ti 3:1 will be terrible times in the *l* days.
2Pe 3:3 in the *l* days scoffers will come,
Rev 1:17 I am the First and the *L*.
22:13 the First and the *L*, the Beginning

**LASTING (LAST)**
Ex 12:14 to the LORD—a *l* ordinance.
Lev 24:8 of the Israelites, as a *l* covenant.
Nu 25:13 have a covenant of a *l* priesthood,
Heb 10:34 had better and *l* possessions.

**LASTS (LAST)**
Ps 30:5 For his anger *l* only a moment,
2Co 3:11 greater is the glory of that which *l*!

**LATTER (LAST)**
Job 42:12 The LORD blessed the *l* part

**LAUGH (LAUGHS)**
Ecc 3:4 a time to weep and a time to *l*,

**LAUGHS (LAUGH)**
Ps 2:4 The One enthroned in heaven *l*;
37:13 but the Lord *l* at the wicked,

**LAVISHED**
Eph 1:8 of God's grace that he *l* on us
1Jn 3:1 great is the love the Father has *l*

**LAW (LAWS)**
Dt 31:11 you shall read this *l* before them
31:26 "Take this Book of the *L*
Jos 1:8 of the *L* depart from your mouth;
Ne 8:8 from the Book of the *L* of God,
Ps 1:2 and on his *l* he meditates day
19:7 The *l* of the LORD is perfect,
119:18 wonderful things in your *l*.
119:72 *l* from your mouth is more precious
119:97 Oh, how I love your *l*!
119:165 peace have they who love your *l*,
Isa 8:20 To the *l* and to the testimony!
Jer 31:33 "I will put my *l* in their minds
Mt 5:17 that I have come to abolish the *L*
7:12 sums up the *L* and the Prophets.
22:40 All the *L* and the Prophets hang
Lk 16:17 stroke of a pen to drop out of the *L*.
Jn 1:17 For the *l* was given through Moses;
Ro 2:12 All who sin apart from the *l* will
2:15 of the *l* are written on their hearts,
5:13 for before the *l* was given,
5:20 *l* was added so that the trespass
6:14 because you are not under *l*,
7:6 released from the *l* so that we serve
7:12 *l* is holy, and the commandment is
8:3 For what the *l* was powerless to do
10:4 Christ is the end of the *l*
13:10 love is the fulfillment of the *l*.
Gal 3:13 curse of the *l* by becoming a curse
3:24 So the *l* was put in charge to lead us
5:3 obligated to obey the whole *l*.
5:4 justified by *l* have been alienated
5:14 The entire *l* is summed up
Heb 7:19 (for the *l* made nothing perfect),
10:1 The *l* is only a shadow
Jas 1:25 intently into the perfect *l* that gives
2:10 For whoever keeps the whole *l*

**LAWLESSNESS***
2Th 2:3 and the man of *l* is revealed,
2:7 power of *l* is already at work;
1Jn 3:4 sins breaks the law; in fact, sin is *l*.

**LAWS (LAW)**
Lev 25:18 and be careful to obey my *l*,
Ps 119:30 I have set my heart on your *l*.
119:120 I stand in awe of your *l*.
Heb 8:10 I will put my *l* in their minds
10:16 I will put my *l* in their hearts,

**LAY (LAID LAYING)**
Job 22:22 and *l* up his words in your heart.
Isa 28:16 "See, I *l* a stone in Zion,
Mt 8:20 of Man has no place to *l* his head."
Jn 10:15 and I *l* down my life for the sheep.
15:13 that he *l* down his life
1Co 3:11 no one can *l* any foundation other
1Jn 3:16 And we ought to *l* down our lives
Rev 4:10 They *l* their crowns

**LAYING (LAY)**
1Ti 5:22 Do not be hasty in the *l* on of hands
Heb 6:1 not *l* again the foundation

**LAZARUS**
1. Poor man in Jesus' parable (Lk 16:19-31).
2. Brother of Mary and Martha whom Jesus raised from the dead (Jn 11:1-12:19).

**LAZY**
Pr 10:4 *L* hands make a man poor,
Heb 6:12 We do not want you to become *l*,

**LEAD (LEADERS LEADERSHIP LEADS LED)**
Ex 15:13 "In your unfailing love you will *l*
Ps 27:11 *l* me in a straight path
61:2 *l* me to the rock that is higher
139:24 and *l* me in the way everlasting.
143:10 *l* me on level ground.
Ecc 5:6 Do not let your mouth *l* you
Isa 11:6 and a little child will *l* them.
Da 12:3 those who *l* many to righteousness,
Mt 6:13 And *l* us not into temptation,
1Jn 3:7 do not let anyone *l* you astray.

**LEADERS (LEAD)**
Heb 13:7 Remember your *l*, who spoke
13:17 Obey your *l* and submit

**LEADERSHIP (LEAD)**
Ro 12:8 if it is *l*, let him govern diligently;

**LEADS (LEAD)**
Ps 23:2 he *l* me beside quiet waters,
Pr 19:23 The fear of the LORD *l* to life:
Isa 40:11 he gently *l* those that have young.
Mt 7:13 and broad is the road that *l*
15:14 If a blind man *l* a blind man,
Jn 10:3 sheep by name and *l* them out.
Ro 14:19 effort to do what *l* to peace
2Co 2:14 always *l* us in triumphal procession

**LEAH**
Wife of Jacob (Ge 29:16-30); bore six sons and one daughter (Ge 29:31-30:21; 34:1; 35:23).

**LEAN**
Pr 3:5 *l* not on your own understanding;

**LEARN (LEARNED LEARNING)**
Isa 1:17 *l* to do right!
Mt 11:29 yoke upon you and *l* from me,

**LEARNED (LEARN)**
Php 4:11 for I have *l* to be content whatever
2Ti 3:14 continue in what you have *l*

**LEARNING (LEARN)**
Pr 1:5 let the wise listen and add to their *l*,
2Ti 3:7 always *l* but never able

**LED (LEAD)**
Ps 68:18 you *l* captives in your train;
Isa 53:7 he was *l* like a lamb to the slaughter
Am 2:10 and I *l* you forty years in the desert
Ro 8:14 those who are *l* by the Spirit
Eph 4:8 he *l* captives in his train

**LEFT**
Jos 1:7 turn from it to the right or to the *l*,
Pr 4:27 Do not swerve to the right or the *l*;
Mt 6:3 do not let your *l* hand know what
25:33 on his right and the goats on his *l*.

**LEGION**
Mk 5:9 "My name is *L*," he replied,

**LEND (LENDS)**
Dt 15:8 freely *l* him whatever he needs.

Ps 37:26 are always generous and *l* freely;
Lk 6:34 if you *l* to those from whom you

**LENDS (LEND)**
Pr 19:17 to the poor *l* to the LORD,

**LENGTH (LONG)**
Ps 90:10 The *l* of our days is seventy years—
Pr 10:27 The fear of the LORD adds *l* to life

**LEPROSY**
2Ki 7:3 men with *l* at the entrance

**LETTER (LETTERS)**
Mt 5:18 not the smallest *l*, not the least
2Co 3:2 You yourselves are our *l*, written
3:6 for the *l* kills, but the Spirit gives
2Th 3:14 not obey our instruction in this *l*,

**LETTERS (LETTER)**
2Co 3:7 which was engraved in *l* on stone,
10:10 "His *l* are weighty and forceful,
2Pe 3:16 His *l* contain some things that are

**LEVEL**
Ps 143:10 lead me on *l* ground.
Pr 4:26 Make *l* paths for your feet
Isa 26:7 The path of the righteous is *l*;
Heb 12:13 "Make *l* paths for your feet,"

**LEVI (LEVITES)**
1. Son of Jacob by Leah (Ge 29:34; 46:11; 1Ch 2:1). Tribe of blessed (Ge 49:5-7; Dt 33:8-11), chosen as priests (Nu 3-4), numbered (Nu 3:39; 26:62), allotted cities, but not land (Nu 18; 35; Dt 10:9; Jos 13:14; 21), land (Eze 48:8-22), 12,000 from (Rev 7:7).
2. See MATTHEW.

**LEVITES (LEVI)**
Nu 1:53 The *L* are to be responsible
8:6 "Take the *L* from among the other
18:21 I give to the *L* all the tithes in Israel

**LEWDNESS**
Mk 7:22 malice, deceit, *l*, envy, slander,

**LIAR (LIE)**
Pr 19:22 better to be poor than a *l*.
Jn 8:44 for he is a *l* and the father of lies.
Ro 3:4 Let God be true, and every man a *l*.

**LIBERATED***
Ro 8:21 that the creation itself will be *l*

**LIE (LIAR LIED LIES LYING)**
Lev 19:11 " 'Do not *l*.
Nu 23:19 God is not a man, that he should *l*,
Dt 6:7 when you *l* down and when you get
Ps 23:2 me *l* down in green pastures,
Isa 11:6 leopard will *l* down with the goat,
Eze 34:14 they will *l* down in good grazing
Ro 1:25 exchanged the truth of God for a *l*,
Col 3:9 Do not *l* to each other,
Heb 6:18 which it is impossible for God to *l*,

**LIED (LIE)**
Ac 5:4 You have not *l* to men but to God."

**LIES (LIE)**
Ps 34:13 and your lips from speaking *l*.
Jn 8:44 for he is a liar and the father of *l*.

**LIFE (LIVE)**
Ge 2:7 into his nostrils the breath of *l*,
2:9 of the garden were the tree of *l*
9:11 Never again will all *l* be cut
Ex 21:23 you are to take *l* for *l*, eye for eye,
Lev 17:14 the *l* of every creature is its blood.
24:18 must make restitution—*l* for *l*.
Dt 30:19 Now choose *l*, so that you
Ps 16:11 known to me the path of *l*;
23:6 all the days of my *l*,
34:12 Whoever of you loves *l*
39:4 let me know how fleeting is my *l*.
49:7 No man can redeem the *l*
104:33 I will sing to the LORD all my *l*;
Pr 1:3 a disciplined and prudent *l*,
6:23 are the way to *l*,
7:23 little knowing it will cost him his *l*.
8:35 For whoever finds me finds *l*
11:30 of the righteous is a tree of *l*,
21:21 finds *l*, prosperity and honor.
Jer 10:23 that a man's *l* is not his own;

Eze 37:5 enter you, and you will come to *l.*
Da 12:2 some to everlasting *l,* others
Mt 6:25 Is not *l* more important than food,
7:14 and narrow the road that leads to *l,*
10:39 Whoever finds his *l* will lose it,
16:25 wants to save his *l* will lose it,
20:28 to give his *l* as a ransom for many."
Mk 10:45 to give his *l* as a ransom for many."
Lk 12:15 a man's *l* does not consist
12:22 do not worry about your *l,*
14:26 even his own *l*—he cannot be my
Jn 1:4 In him was *l,* and that *l* was
3:15 believes in him may have eternal *l.*
3:36 believes in the Son has eternal *l,*
4:14 of water welling up to eternal *l.*"
5:24 him who sent me has eternal *l*
6:35 Jesus declared, "I am the bread of *l*
6:47 he who believes has everlasting *l.*
6:68 You have the words of eternal *l.*
10:10 I have come that they may have *l,*
10:15 and I lay down my *l* for the sheep.
10:28 I give them eternal *l,* and they shall
11:25 "I am the resurrection and the *l.*
14:6 am the way and the truth and the *l.*
Jn 15:13 lay down his *l* for his friends.
20:31 that by believing you may have *l*
Ac 13:48 appointed for eternal *l* believed.
Ro 4:25 was raised to *l* for our justification.
6:13 have been brought from death to *l;*
6:23 but the gift of God is eternal *l*
8:38 convinced that neither death nor *l,*
1Co 15:19 If only for this *l* we have hope
2Co 3:6 letter kills, but the Spirit gives *l.*
Gal 2:20 The *l* I live in the body, I live
Eph 4:1 I urge you to live a *l* worthy
Php 2:16 as you hold out the word of *l*—
Col 1:10 order that you may live a *l* worthy
1Th 4:12 so that your daily *l* may win
1Ti 4:8 for both the present *l* and the *l*
4:16 Watch your *l* and doctrine closely.
6:19 hold of the *l* that is truly *l.*
2Ti 3:12 to live a godly *l* in Christ Jesus will
Jas 1:12 crown of *l* that God has promised
3:13 Let him show it by his good *l,*
1Pe 3:10 "Whoever would love *l*
2Pe 1:3 given us everything we need for *l*
1Jn 3:14 we have passed from death to *l,*
5:11 has given us eternal *l,* and this *l* is
Rev 13:8 written in the book of *l* belonging
20:12 was opened, which is the book of *l.*
21:27 written in the Lamb's book of *l.*
22:2 side of the river stood the tree of *l,*

**LIFT (LIFTED)**

Ps 121:1 I *l* up my eyes to the hills—
134:2 *L* up your hands in the sanctuary
La 3:41 Let us *l* up our hearts and our
1Ti 2:8 everywhere to *l* up holy hands

**LIFTED (LIFT)**

Ps 40:2 He *l* me out of the slimy pit,
Jn 3:14 Moses *l* up the snake in the desert,
12:32 when I am *l* up from the earth,

**LIGHT (ENLIGHTENED)**

Ge 1:3 "Let there be *l,*" and there was *l.*
2Sa 22:29 LORD turns my darkness into *l.*
Job 38:19 "What is the way to the abode of *l?*
Ps 4:6 Let the *l* of your face shine upon us
19:8 giving *l* to the eyes.
27:1 LORD is my *l* and my salvation—
56:13 God in the *l* of life.
76:4 You are resplendent with *l,*
104:2 He wraps himself in *l*
119:105 and a *l* for my path.
119:130 The unfolding of your words gives *l;*
Isa 2:5 let us walk in the *l* of the LORD.
9:2 have seen a great *l;*

Isa 49:6 also make you a *l* for the Gentiles,
Mt 4:16 have seen a great *l*;
5:16 let your *l* shine before men,
11:30 yoke is easy and my burden is *l*."
Jn 3:19 but men loved darkness instead of *l*
8:12 he said, "I am the *l* of the world.
2Co 4:6 made his *l* shine in our hearts
6:14 Or what fellowship can *l* have
11:14 masquerades as an angel of *l*.
1Ti 6:16 and who lives in unapproachable *l*,
1Pe 2:9 of darkness into his wonderful *l*.
1Jn 1:5 God is *l*; in him there is no
1:7 But if we walk in the *l*,
Rev 21:23 for the glory of God gives it *l*,

## LIGHTNING

Da 10:6 his face like *l*, his eyes like flaming
Mt 24:27 For as the *l* that comes from the east
28:3 His appearance was like *l*,

## LIKENESS

Ge 1:26 man in our image, in our *l*,
Ps 17:15 I will be satisfied with seeing your *l*
Isa 52:14 his form marred beyond human *l*—
Ro 8:3 Son in the *l* of sinful man
8:29 to be conformed to the *l* of his Son,
2Co 3:18 his *l* with ever-increasing glory,
Php 2:7 being made in human *l*.
Jas 3:9 who have been made in God's *l*.

## LILIES

Lk 12:27 "Consider how the *l* grow.

## LION

Isa 11:7 and the *l* will eat straw like the ox.
1Pe 5:8 around like a roaring *l* looking
Rev 5:5 See, the *L* of the tribe of Judah,

## LIPS

Ps 8:2 From the *l* of children and infants
34:1 his praise will always be on my *l*.
119:171 May my *l* overflow with praise,
Pr 13:3 He who guards his *l* guards his life,
27:2 someone else, and not your own *l*.
Isa 6:5 For I am a man of unclean *l*,
Mt 21:16 " 'From the *l* of children
Col 3:8 and filthy language from your *l*.

## LISTEN (LISTENING LISTENS)

Dt 30:20 *l* to his voice, and hold fast to him.
Pr 1:5 let the wise *l* and add
Jn 10:27 My sheep *l* to my voice; I know
Jas 1:19 Everyone should be quick to *l*,
1:22 Do not merely *l* to the word,

## LISTENING (LISTEN)

1Sa 3:9 Speak, LORD, for your servant is *l*
Pr 18:13 He who answers before *l*—

## LISTENS (LISTEN)

Pr 12:15 but a wise man *l* to advice.

## LIVE (ALIVE LIFE LIVES LIVING)

Ex 20:12 so that you may *l* long
33:20 for no one may see me and *l*."
Dt 8:3 to teach you that man does not *l*
Job 14:14 If a man dies, will he *l* again?
Ps 119:175 Let me *l* that I may praise you,
Isa 55:3 hear me, that your soul may *l*.
Eze 37:3 can these bones *l*?" I said,
Hab 2:4 but the righteous will *l* by his faith
Mt 4:4 'Man does not *l* on bread alone,
Ac 17:24 does not *l* in temples built by hands
17:28 'For in him we *l* and move
Ro 1:17 "The righteous will *l* by faith."
2Co 5:7 We *l* by faith, not by sight.
Gal 2:20 The life I *l* in the body, I *l* by faith
5:25 Since we *l* by the Spirit, let us keep
Php 1:21 to *l* is Christ and to die is gain.
1Th 5:13 *L* in peace with each other.
2Ti 3:12 who wants to *l* a godly life
Heb 12:14 Make every effort to *l* in peace
1Pe 1:17 *l* your lives as strangers here

**LIVES (LIVE)**

| | | |
|---|---|---|
| Job | 19:25 | I know that my Redeemer *l*, |
| Isa | 57:15 | he who *l* forever, whose name is |
| Da | 3:28 | to give up their *l* rather than serve |
| Jn | 14:17 | for he *l* with you and will be in you. |
| Ro | 7:18 | I know that nothing good *l* in me, |
| | 14:7 | For none of us *l* to himself alone |
| 1Co | 3:16 | and that God's Spirit *l* in you? |
| Gal | 2:20 | I no longer live, but Christ *l* in me. |
| Heb | 13:5 | Keep your *l* free from the love |
| 2Pe | 3:11 | You ought to live holy and godly *l* |
| 1Jn | 3:16 | to lay down our *l* for our brothers. |
| | 4:16 | Whoever *l* in love *l* in God, |

**LIVING (LIVE)**

| | | |
|---|---|---|
| Ge | 2:7 | and man became a *l* being. |
| Jer | 2:13 | the spring of *l* water, |
| Mt | 22:32 | the God of the dead but of the *l*." |
| Jn | 7:38 | streams of *l* water will flow |
| Ro | 12:1 | to offer your bodies as *l* sacrifices, |
| Heb | 4:12 | For the word of God is *l* and active. |
| | 10:31 | to fall into the hands of the *l* God. |
| Rev | 1:18 | I am the *L* One; I was dead, |

**LOAD**

| | | |
|---|---|---|
| Gal | 6:5 | for each one should carry his own *l*. |

**LOCUSTS**

| | | |
|---|---|---|
| Mt | 3:4 | His food was *l* and wild honey. |

**LOFTY**

| | | |
|---|---|---|
| Ps | 139:6 | too *l* for me to attain. |
| Isa | 57:15 | is what the high and *l* One says— |

**LONELY**

| | | |
|---|---|---|
| Ps | 68:6 | God sets the *l* in families, |

**LONG (LENGTH LONGED LONGING LONGS)**

| | | |
|---|---|---|
| 1Ki | 18:21 | "How *l* will you waver |
| Jn | 9:4 | As *l* as it is day, we must do |
| Eph | 3:18 | to grasp how wide and *l* and high |
| 1Pe | 1:12 | Even angels *l* to look |

**LONGED (LONG)**

| | | |
|---|---|---|
| Mt | 13:17 | righteous men *l* to see what you see |
| | 23:37 | how often I have *l* |
| 2Ti | 4:8 | to all who have *l* for his appearing. |

**LONGING (LONG)**

| | | |
|---|---|---|
| Pr | 13:19 | A *l* fulfilled is sweet to the soul, |
| 2Co | 5:2 | *l* to be clothed with our heavenly |

**LONGS (LONG)**

| | | |
|---|---|---|
| Isa | 30:18 | Yet the LORD *l* to be gracious |

**LOOK (LOOKING LOOKS)**

| | | |
|---|---|---|
| Dt | 4:29 | you will find him if you *l* for him |
| Job | 31:1 | not to *l* lustfully at a girl. |
| Ps | 34:5 | Those who *l* to him are radiant; |
| Pr | 4:25 | Let your eyes *l* straight ahead, |
| Isa | 60:5 | Then you will *l* and be radiant, |
| Hab | 1:13 | Your eyes are too pure to *l* on evil; |
| Zec | 12:10 | They will *l* on me, the one they |
| Mk | 13:21 | '*L*, here is the Christ!' or, '*L*, |
| Lk | 24:39 | *L* at my hands and my feet. |
| Jn | 1:36 | he said, "*L*, the Lamb of God!" |
| | 4:35 | open your eyes and *l* at the fields! |
| | 19:37 | "They will *l* on the one they have |
| Jas | 1:27 | to *l* after orphans and widows |
| 1Pe | 1:12 | long to *l* into these things. |

**LOOKING (LOOK)**

| | | |
|---|---|---|
| 2Co | 10:7 | You are *l* only on the surface |
| Rev | 5:6 | I saw a Lamb, *l* as if it had been |

**LOOKS (LOOK)**

| | | |
|---|---|---|
| 1Sa | 16:7 | Man *l* at the outward appearance, |
| Lk | 9:62 | and *l* back is fit for service |
| Php | 2:21 | For everyone *l* out |

**LORD† (LORD'S† LORDING)**

| | | |
|---|---|---|
| Ne | 4:14 | Remember the *L*, who is great |
| Job | 28:28 | 'The fear of the *L*—that is wisdom, |
| Ps | 54:4 | the *L* is the one who sustains me. |
| | 62:12 | and that you, O *L*, are loving. |
| | 86:5 | You are forgiving and good, O *L*, |
| | 110:1 | The LORD says to my *L*: |
| | 147:5 | Great is our *L* and mighty in power |
| Isa | 6:1 | I saw the *L* seated on a throne, |

Da 9:4 "O *L*, the great and awesome God,
Mt 3:3 'Prepare the way for the *L*,
4:7 'Do not put the *L* your God
7:21 "Not everyone who says to me, '*L*,
22:37 " 'Love the *L* your God
22:44 For he says, " 'The *L* said to my *L*:
Mk 12:11 the *L* has done this,
12:29 the *L* our God, the *L* is one.
Lk 2:9 glory of the *L* shone around them,
6:46 "Why do you call me, '*L*, *L*,'
10:27 " 'Love the *L* your God
Ac 2:21 on the name of the *L* will be saved.'
16:31 replied, "Believe in the *L* Jesus,
Ro 10:9 with your mouth, "Jesus is *L*,"
10:13 on the name of the *L* will be saved
12:11 your spiritual fervor, serving the *L*.
14:8 we live to the *L*; and if we die,
1Co 1:31 Let him who boasts boast in the *L*."
3:5 the *L* has assigned to each his task.
7:34 to be devoted to the *L* in both body
10:9 We should not test the *L*,
11:23 For I received from the *L* what I
12:3 "Jesus is *L*," except by the Holy
15:57 victory through our *L* Jesus Christ.
16:22 If anyone does not love the *L*—
2Co 3:17 Now the *L* is the Spirit,
8:5 they gave themselves first to the *L*
10:17 Let him who boasts boast in the *L*."
Gal 6:14 in the cross of our *L* Jesus Christ,
Eph 4:5 one *L*, one faith, one baptism;
5:10 and find out what pleases the *L*.
5:19 make music in your heart to the *L*,
Php 2:11 confess that Jesus Christ is *L*,
3:1 my brothers, rejoice in the *L*!
4:4 Rejoice in the *L* always.
Col 2:6 as you received Christ Jesus as *L*,
3:17 do it all in the name of the *L* Jesus,
3:23 as working for the *L*, not for men,
4:17 work you have received in the *L*."
1Th 3:12 May the *L* make your love increase
5:2 day of the *L* will come like a thief
5:23 at the coming of our *L* Jesus Christ.
2Th 2:1 the coming of our *L* Jesus Christ
2Ti 2:19 "The *L* knows those who are his,"
Heb 12:14 holiness no one will see the *L*.
13:6 *L* is my helper; I will not be afraid.
Jas 4:10 Humble yourselves before the *L*,
1Pe 1:25 the word of the *L* stands forever."
1Pe 2:3 you have tasted that the *L* is good.
3:15 in your hearts set apart Christ as *L*.
2Pe 1:16 and coming of our *L* Jesus Christ,
2:1 the sovereign *L* who bought
3:9 The *L* is not slow in keeping his
Jude :14 the *L* is coming with thousands
Rev 4:8 holy, holy is the *L* God Almighty,
4:11 "You are worthy, our *L* and God,
17:14 he is *L* of lords and King of kings—
22:20 Come, *L* Jesus.

**LORD'S† (LORD†)**

Ac 21:14 and said, "The *L* will be done."
1Co 10:26 "The earth is the *L*, and everything
11:26 you proclaim the *L* death
2Co 3:18 faces all reflect the *L* glory,
2Ti 2:24 And the *L* servant must not quarrel
Jas 4:15 you ought to say, "If it is the *L* will,

**LORDING* (LORD†)**

1Pe 5:3 not *l* it over those entrusted to you,

**LORD‡ (LORD'S‡)**

Ge 2:4 When the *L* God made the earth
2:7 the *L* God formed the man
3:21 The *L* God made garments of skin
7:16 Then the *L* shut him in.
15:6 Abram believed the *L*,
18:14 Is anything too hard for the *L*?

| | | |
|---|---|---|
| Ge | 31:49 | “May the *L* keep watch |
| Ex | 3:2 | the angel of the *L* appeared to him |
| | 9:12 | the *L* hardened Pharaoh’s heart |
| | 14:30 | That day the *L* saved Israel |
| | 20:2 | “I am the *L* your God, who |
| | 33:11 | The *L* would speak to Moses face |
| | 40:34 | glory of the *L* filled the tabernacle. |
| Lev | 19:2 | ‘Be holy because I, the *L* your God, |
| Nu | 8:5 | *L* said to Moses: “Take the Levites |
| | 14:21 | glory of the *L* fills the whole earth, |
| Dt | 2:7 | forty years the *L* your God has |
| | 5:9 | the *L* your God, am a jealous God, |
| | 6:4 | The *L* our God, the *L* is one. |
| | 6:5 | Love the *L* your God |
| | 6:16 | Do not test the *L* your God |
| | 10:14 | To the *L* your God belong |
| | 10:17 | For the *L* your God is God of gods |
| | 11:1 | Love the *L* your God and keep his |
| | 28:1 | If you fully obey the *L* your God |
| | 30:16 | today to love the *L* your God, |
| | 30:20 | For the *L* is your life, and he will |
| | 31:6 | for the *L* your God goes with you; |
| Jos | 22:5 | to love the *L* your God, to walk |
| | 24:15 | my household, we will serve the *L* |
| 1Sa | 1:28 | So now I give him to the *L*. |
| 1Sa | 2:2 | “There is no one holy like the *L*; |
| | 7:12 | “Thus far has the *L* helped us.” |
| | 12:22 | his great name the *L* will not reject |
| | 15:22 | “Does the *L* delight |
| 2Sa | 22:2 | “The *L* is my rock, my fortress |
| 1Ki | 2:3 | and observe what the *L* your God |
| | 8:11 | the glory of the *L* filled his temple. |
| | 8:61 | fully committed to the *L* our God, |
| | 18:21 | If the *L* is God, follow him; |
| 2Ki | 13:23 | But the *L* was gracious to them |
| 1Ch | 16:8 | Give thanks to the *L*, call |
| | 16:23 | Sing to the *L*, all the earth; |
| | 28:9 | for the *L* searches every heart |
| | 29:11 | O *L*, is the greatness and the power |
| 2Ch | 5:14 | the glory of the *L* filled the temple |
| | 16:9 | of the *L* range throughout the earth |
| | 19:6 | judging for man but for the *L*, |
| | 30:9 | for the *L* your God is gracious |
| Ne | 1:5 | Then I said: “O *L*, God of heaven, |
| Job | 1:21 | *L* gave and the *L* has taken away; |
| | 38:1 | the *L* answered Job out |
| | 42:9 | and the *L* accepted Job’s prayer. |
| Ps | 1:2 | But his delight is in the law of the *L* |
| | 9:9 | The *L* is a refuge for the oppressed, |
| Ps | 12:6 | And the words of the *L* are flawless |
| | 16:8 | I have set the *L* always before me. |
| | 18:30 | the word of the *L* is flawless. |
| | 19:7 | The law of the *L* is perfect, |
| | 19:14 | O *L*, my Rock and my Redeemer. |
| | 23:1 | The *L* is my shepherd, I shall not be |
| | 23:6 | I will dwell in the house of the *L* |
| | 27:1 | The *L* is my light and my salvation |
| | 27:4 | to gaze upon the beauty of the *L* |
| | 29:1 | Ascribe to the *L*, O mighty ones, |
| | 32:2 | whose sin the *L* does not count |
| | 33:12 | is the nation whose God is the *L*, |
| | 33:18 | But the eyes of the *L* are |
| | 34:3 | Glorify the *L* with me; |
| | 34:7 | The angel of the *L* encamps |
| | 34:8 | Taste and see that the *L* is good; |
| | 34:18 | The *L* is close to the brokenhearted |
| | 37:4 | Delight yourself in the *L* |
| | 40:1 | I waited patiently for the *L*; |
| | 47:2 | How awesome is the *L* Most High, |
| | 48:1 | Great is the *L*, and most worthy |
| | 55:22 | Cast your cares on the *L* |
| | 75:8 | In the hand of the *L* is a cup |
| | 84:11 | For the *L* God is a sun and shield; |

Ps 86:11 Teach me your way, O *L*,
89:5 heavens praise your wonders, O *L*,
91:2 I will say of the *L*, "He is my refuge
95:1 Come, let us sing for joy to the *L*;
96:1 Sing to the *L* a new song;
98:4 Shout for joy to the *L*, all the earth,
100:1 Shout for joy to the *L*, all the earth.
103:1 Praise the *L*, O my soul;
103:8 The *L* is compassionate
104:1 O *L* my God, you are very great;
107:8 to the *L* for his unfailing love
110:1 The *L* says to my Lord:
113:4 *L* is exalted over all the nations,
115:1 Not to us, O *L*, not to us
116:15 Precious in the sight of the *L*
118:1 Give thanks to the *L*, for he is good
118:24 This is the day the *L* has made;
121:2 My help comes from the *L*,
121:5 The *L* watches over you—
125:2 so the *L* surrounds his people
127:1 Unless the *L* builds the house,
127:3 Sons are a heritage from the *L*,
130:3 If you, O *L*, kept a record of sins,
135:6 The *L* does whatever pleases him,

Ps 136:1 Give thanks to the *L*, for he is good
139:1 O *L*, you have searched me
144:3 O *L*, what is man that you care
145:3 Great is the *L* and most worthy
145:18 The *L* is near to all who call on him

Pr 1:7 The fear of the *L* is the beginning
3:5 Trust in the *L* with all your heart
3:9 Honor the *L* with your wealth,
3:12 the *L* disciplines those he loves,
3:19 By wisdom the *L* laid the earth's
5:21 are in full view of the *L*,
6:16 There are six things the *L* hates,
10:27 The fear of the *L* adds length to life
11:1 The *L* abhors dishonest scales,
12:22 The *L* detests lying lips,
14:26 He who fears the *L* has a secure
15:3 The eyes of the *L* are everywhere,
16:2 but motives are weighed by the *L*.
16:4 The *L* works out everything
16:9 but the *L* determines his steps.
16:33 but its every decision is from the *L*.
18:10 The name of the *L* is a strong tower
18:22 and receives favor from the *L*.
19:14 but a prudent wife is from the *L*.

Pr 19:17 to the poor lends to the *L*,
21:3 to the *L* than sacrifice.
21:30 that can succeed against the *L*.
21:31 but victory rests with the *L*.
22:2 The *L* is the Maker of them all.
24:18 or the *L* will see and disapprove
31:30 a woman who fears the *L* is

Isa 6:3 holy, holy is the *L* Almighty;
11:2 The Spirit of the *L* will rest on him
11:9 full of the knowledge of the *L*
12:2 The *L*, the *L*, is my strength
24:1 the *L* is going to lay waste the earth
25:8 The Sovereign *L* will wipe away
29:15 to hide their plans from the *L*,
33:6 the fear of the *L* is the key
35:10 the ransomed of the *L* will return.
40:5 the glory of the *L* will be revealed,
40:7 the breath of the *L* blows on them.
40:10 the Sovereign *L* comes with power,
40:28 The *L* is the everlasting God,
40:31 but those who hope in the *L*
42:8 "I am the *L*; that is my name!
43:11 I, even I, am the *L*,
44:24 I am the *L*,
45:5 I am the *L*, and there is no other;
45:21 Was it not I, the *L*?

Isa 51:11 The ransomed of the *L* will return.
53:6 and the *L* has laid on him
53:10 and the will of the *L* will prosper
55:6 Seek the *L* while he may be found;
58:8 of the *L* will be your rear guard.
58:11 The *L* will guide you always;
59:1 the arm of the *L* is not too short
61:3 a planting of the *L*
61:10 I delight greatly in the *L*;
Jer 1:9 Then the *L* reached out his hand
9:24 I am the *L*, who exercises kindness,
16:19 O *L*, my strength and my fortress,
17:7 is the man who trusts in the *L*,
La 3:40 and let us return to the *L*.
Eze 1:28 of the likeness of the glory of the *L*.
Hos 1:7 horsemen, but by the *L* their God."
3:5 They will come trembling to the *L*
6:1 "Come, let us return to the *L*.
Joel 2:1 for the day of the *L* is coming.
2:11 The day of the *L* is great;
3:14 For the day of the *L* is near
Am 5:18 long for the day of the *L*?
Jnh 1:3 But Jonah ran away from the *L*
Mic 4:2 up to the mountain of the *L*,
6:8 And what does the *L* require of you?
Na 1:2 The *L* takes vengeance on his foes
1:3 The *L* is slow to anger
Hab 2:14 knowledge of the glory of the *L*,
2:20 But the *L* is in his holy temple;
Zep 3:17 The *L* your God is with you,
Zec 1:17 and the *L* will again comfort Zion
9:16 The *L* their God will save them
14:5 Then the *L* my God will come,
14:9 The *L* will be king
Mal 4:5 and dreadful day of the *L* comes.

**LORD'S‡ (LORD‡)**

Ex 34:34 he entered the *L* presence
Nu 14:41 you disobeying the *L* command?
Dt 6:18 is right and good in the *L* sight,
32:9 For the *L* portion is his people,
Jos 21:45 Not one of all the *L* good promises
Ps 24:1 The earth is the *L*, and everything
32:10 but the *L* unfailing love
89:1 of the *L* great love forever;
103:17 *L* love is with those who fear him,
Pr 3:11 do not despise the *L* discipline
Isa 24:14 west they acclaim the *L* majesty.
62:3 of splendor in the *L* hand,
Jer 48:10 lax in doing the *L* work!
La 3:22 of the *L* great love we are not
Mic 4:1 of the *L* temple will be established

**LOSE (LOSES LOSS LOST)**

1Sa 17:32 "Let no one *l* heart on account
Mt 10:39 Whoever finds his life will *l* it,
Lk 9:25 and yet *l* or forfeit his very self?
Jn 6:39 that I shall *l* none of all that he has
Heb 12:3 will not grow weary and *l* heart.
12:5 do not *l* heart when he rebukes you

**LOSES (LOSE)**

Mt 5:13 But if the salt *l* its saltiness,
Lk 15:4 you has a hundred sheep and *l* one
15:8 has ten silver coins and *l* one.

**LOSS (LOSE)**

Ro 11:12 and their *l* means riches
1Co 3:15 he will suffer *l*; he himself will be
Php 3:8 I consider everything a *l* compared

**LOST (LOSE)**

Ps 73:2 I had nearly *l* my foothold.
Jer 50:6 "My people have been *l* sheep;
Eze 34:4 the strays or searched for the *l*.
34:16 for the *l* and bring back the strays.
Mt 18:14 any of these little ones should be *l*.
Lk 15:4 go after the *l* sheep until he finds it?
15:6 with me; I have found my *l* sheep.'
15:9 with me; I have found my *l* coin.'

Lk 15:24 is alive again; he was *l* and is found
19:10 to seek and to save what was *l*."
Php 3:8 for whose sake I have *l* all things.

**LOT (LOTS)**

Nephew of Abraham (Ge 11:27; 12:5). Chose to live in Sodom (Ge 13). Rescued from four kings (Ge 14). Rescued from Sodom (Ge 19:1-29; 2Pe 2:7). Fathered Moab and Ammon by his daughters (Ge 19:30-38).

Est 3:7 the *l*) in the presence of Haman
9:24 the *l*) for their ruin and destruction.
Pr 16:33 The *l* is cast into the lap,
18:18 Casting the *l* settles disputes
Ecc 3:22 his work, because that is his *l*.
Ac 1:26 Then they drew lots, and the *l* fell

**LOTS (LOT)**

Ps 22:18 and cast *l* for my clothing.
Mt 27:35 divided up his clothes by casting *l*.

**LOVE (BELOVED LOVED LOVELY LOVER LOVERS LOVES LOVING)**

Ge 22:2 your only son, Isaac, whom you *l*,
Ex 15:13 "In your unfailing *l* you will lead
20:6 showing *l* to a thousand generations
20:6 of those who *l* me
34:6 abounding in *l* and faithfulness,
Lev 19:18 but *l* your neighbor as yourself.
19:34 *L* him as yourself,
Nu 14:18 abounding in *l* and forgiving sin
Dt 5:10 showing *l* to a thousand generations
5:10 of those who *l* me
6:5 *L* the LORD your God
7:13 He will *l* you and bless you
10:12 to walk in all his ways, to *l* him,
11:13 to *l* the LORD your God
13:6 wife you *l*, or your closest friend
30:6 so that you may *l* him
Jos 22:5 to *l* the LORD your God, to walk
1Ki 3:3 Solomon showed his *l*
8:23 you who keep your covenant of *l*
2Ch 5:13 his *l* endures forever."
Ne 1:5 covenant of *l* with those who *l* him
Ps 18:1 I *l* you, O LORD, my strength.
23:6 Surely goodness and *l* will follow
25:6 O LORD, your great mercy and *l*,
31:16 save me in your unfailing *l*.
32:10 but the LORD 's unfailing *l*
33:5 the earth is full of his unfailing *l*.
33:18 whose hope is in his unfailing *l*,
36:5 Your *l*, O LORD, reaches
36:7 How priceless is your unfailing *l*!
45:7 You *l* righteousness and hate
51:1 according to your unfailing *l*;
Ps 57:10 For great is your *l*, reaching
63:3 Because your *l* is better than life,
66:20 or withheld his *l* from me!
70:4 may those who *l* your salvation
77:8 Has his unfailing *l* vanished forever
85:7 Show us your unfailing *l*, O LORD
85:10 *L* and faithfulness meet together;
86:13 For great is your *l* toward me;
89:1 of the LORD's great *l* forever;
89:33 but I will not take my *l* from him,
92:2 to proclaim your *l* in the morning
94:18 your *l*, O LORD, supported me.
100:5 is good and his *l* endures forever;
101:1 I will sing of your *l* and justice;
103:4 crowns you with *l* and compassion.
103:8 slow to anger, abounding in *l*.
103:11 so great is his *l* for those who fear
107:8 to the LORD for his unfailing *l*
108:4 For great is your *l*, higher
116:1 I *l* the LORD, for he heard my
118:1 his *l* endures forever.
119:47 because I *l* them.
119:64 The earth is filled with your *l*,
119:76 May your unfailing *l* be my
119:97 Oh, how I *l* your law!

Ps 119:119 therefore I *l* your statutes.
119:124 your servant according to your *l*
119:132 to those who *l* your name.
119:159 O LORD, according to your *l*.
119:163 but I *l* your law.
119:165 peace have they who *l* your law,
122:6 "May those who *l* you be secure.
130:7 for with the LORD is unfailing *l*
136:1 *His l endures forever.*
143:8 of your unfailing *l*,
145:8 slow to anger and rich in *l*.
145:20 over all who *l* him,
147:11 who put their hope in his unfailing *l*
Pr 3:3 Let *l* and faithfulness never leave
4:6 *l* her, and she will watch over you.
5:19 you ever be captivated by her *l*.
8:17 I *l* those who *l* me,
9:8 rebuke a wise man and he will *l* you
10:12 but *l* covers over all wrongs.
14:22 those who plan what is good find *l*
15:17 of vegetables where there is *l*
17:9 over an offense promotes *l*,
19:22 What a man desires is unfailing *l*;
20:6 claims to have unfailing *l*,
20:13 Do not *l* sleep or you will grow
Pr 20:28 through *l* his throne is made secure
21:21 who pursues righteousness and *l*
27:5 rebuke than hidden *l*.
Ecc 9:6 Their *l*, their hate
9:9 life with your wife, whom you *l*,
SS 2:4 and his banner over me is *l*.
8:6 for *l* is as strong as death,
8:7 Many waters cannot quench *l*;
8:7 all the wealth of his house for *l*,
Isa 5:1 I will sing for the one I *l*
16:5 In *l* a throne will be established;
38:17 In your *l* you kept me
54:10 yet my unfailing *l* for you will not
55:3 my faithful *l* promised to David.
61:8 "For I, the LORD, *l* justice;
63:9 In his *l* and mercy he redeemed
Jer 5:31 and my people *l* it this way.
31:3 you with an everlasting *l*;
32:18 You show *l* to thousands
33:11 his *l* endures forever."
La 3:22 of the LORD's great *l* we are not
3:32 so great is his unfailing *l*.
Eze 33:32 more than one who sings *l* songs
Da 9:4 covenant of *l* with all who *l* him
Hos 2:19 in *l* and compassion.
Hos 3:1 Go, show your *l* to your wife again,
11:4 with ties of *l*;
12:6 maintain *l* and justice,
Joel 2:13 slow to anger and abounding in *l*,
Am 5:15 Hate evil, *l* good;
Mic 3:2 you who hate good and *l* evil;
6:8 To act justly and to *l* mercy
Zep 3:17 he will quiet you with his *l*,
Zec 8:19 Therefore *l* truth and peace."
Mt 3:17 "This is my Son, whom I *l*;
5:44 *L* your enemies and pray
6:24 he will hate the one and *l* the other,
17:5 "This is my Son, whom I *l*;
19:19 and '*l* your neighbor as yourself.'"
22:37 "'*L* the Lord your God
Lk 6:32 Even 'sinners' *l* those who *l* them.
7:42 which of them will *l* him more?"
20:13 whom I *l*; perhaps they will respect
Jn 13:34 I give you: *L* one another.
13:35 disciples, if you *l* one another."
14:15 "If you *l* me, you will obey what I
15:13 Greater *l* has no one than this,
15:17 This is my command: *L* each other.
21:15 do you truly *l* me more than these
Ro 5:5 because God has poured out his *l*

Ro 5:8 God demonstrates his own *l* for us
8:28 for the good of those who *l* him,
8:35 us from the *l* of Christ?
8:39 us from the *l* of God that is
12:9 *L* must be sincere.
12:10 to one another in brotherly *l.*
13:8 continuing debt to *l* one another,
13:9 "*L* your neighbor as yourself."
13:10 Therefore *l* is the fulfillment
13:10 *L* does no harm to its neighbor.
1Co 2:9 prepared for those who *l* him"—
8:1 Knowledge puffs up, but *l* builds up
13:1 have not *l,* I am only a resounding
13:2 but have not *l,* I am nothing.
13:3 but have not *l,* I gain nothing.
13:4 Love is patient, *l* is kind.
13:4 *L* is patient, *l* is kind.
13:6 *L* does not delight in evil
13:8 *L* never fails.
13:13 But the greatest of these is *l.*
13:13 three remain: faith, hope and *l.*
14:1 way of *l* and eagerly desire spiritual
16:14 Do everything in *l.*
2Co 5:14 For Christ's *l* compels us,
8:8 sincerity of your *l* by comparing it
8:24 show these men the proof of your *l*
Gal 5:6 is faith expressing itself through *l.*
5:13 rather, serve one another in *l.*
5:22 But the fruit of the Spirit is *l,* joy,
Eph 1:4 In *l* he predestined us
2:4 But because of his great *l* for us,
3:17 being rooted and established in *l,*
3:18 and high and deep is the *l* of Christ,
3:19 and to know this *l* that surpasses
4:2 bearing with one another in *l.*
4:15 Instead, speaking the truth in *l,*
5:2 loved children and live a life of *l,*
5:25 *l* your wives, just as Christ loved
5:28 husbands ought to *l* their wives
5:33 each one of you also must *l* his wife
Php 1:9 that your *l* may abound more
2:2 having the same *l,* being one
Col 1:5 *l* that spring from the hope that is
2:2 in heart and united in *l,*
3:14 And over all these virtues put on *l,*
3:19 *l* your wives and do not be harsh
1Th 1:3 your labor prompted by *l,*
4:9 taught by God to *l* each other.
5:8 on faith and *l* as a breastplate,
2Th 3:5 direct your hearts into God's *l*
1Ti 1:5 The goal of this command is *l,*
1Ti 2:15 *l* and holiness with propriety.
4:12 in life, in *l,* in faith and in purity.
6:10 For the *l* of money is a root
6:11 faith, *l,* endurance and gentleness.
2Ti 1:7 of power, of *l* and of self-discipline.
2:22 and pursue righteousness, faith, *l*
3:10 faith, patience, *l,* endurance,
Tit 2:4 women to *l* their husbands
Phm :9 yet I appeal to you on the basis of *l.*
Heb 6:10 and the *l* you have shown him
10:24 may spur one another on toward *l*
13:5 free from the *l* of money
Jas 1:12 promised to those who *l* him.
2:5 he promised those who *l* him?
2:8 "*L* your neighbor as yourself,"
1Pe 1:22 the truth so that you have sincere *l*
1:22 *l* one another deeply,
2:17 *L* the brotherhood of believers,
3:8 be sympathetic, *l* as brothers,
3:10 "Whoever would *l* life
4:8 Above all, *l* each other deeply,
4:8 *l* covers over a multitude of sins.
5:14 Greet one another with a kiss of *l.*
2Pe 1:7 and to brotherly kindness, *l.*

2Pe 1:17 "This is my Son, whom I *l;*

1Jn 2:5 God's *l* is truly made complete

2:15 Do not *l* the world or anything

3:1 How great is the *l* the Father has

3:10 anyone who does not *l* his brother.

3:11 We should *l* one another.

3:14 Anyone who does not *l* remains

3:16 This is how we know what *l* is:

3:18 let us not *l* with words or tongue

3:23 to *l* one another as he commanded

4:7 Dear friends, let us *l* one another,

4:7 for *l* comes from God.

4:8 Whoever does not *l* does not know

4:9 This is how God showed his *l*

4:10 This is *l:* not that we loved God,

4:11 we also ought to *l* one another.

4:12 and his *l* is made complete in us.

4:16 God is *l.*

4:16 Whoever lives in *l* lives in God,

4:17 *l* is made complete among us

4:18 But perfect *l* drives out fear,

4:19 We *l* because he first loved us.

4:20 If anyone says, "I *l* God,"

4:21 loves God must also *l* his brother.

5:2 we know that we *l* the children

1Jn 5:3 This is *l* for God: to obey his

2Jn :5 I ask that we *l* one another.

:6 his command is that you walk in *l.*

:6 this is *l:* that we walk in obedience

Jude :12 men are blemishes at your *l* feasts,

:21 Keep yourselves in God's *l*

Rev 2:4 You have forsaken your first *l.*

3:19 Those whom I *l* I rebuke

12:11 they did not *l* their lives so much

**LOVED (LOVE)**

Ge 24:67 she became his wife, and he *l* her;

29:30 and he *l* Rachel more than Leah.

37:3 Now Israel *l* Joseph more than any

Dt 7:8 But it was because the LORD *l* you

1Sa 1:5 a double portion because he *l* her,

20:17 because he *l* him as he *l* himself.

Ps 44:3 light of your face, for you *l* them.

Jer 2:2 how as a bride you *l* me

31:3 "I have *l* you with an everlasting

Hos 2:23 to the one I called 'Not my *l* one.'

3:1 though she is *l* by another

9:10 became as vile as the thing they *l.*

11:1 "When Israel was a child, I *l* him,

Mal 1:2 "But you ask, 'How have you *l* us?'

Mk 12:6 left to send, a son, whom he *l.*

Jn 3:16 so *l* the world that he gave his one

3:19 but men *l* darkness instead of light

11:5 Jesus *l* Martha and her sister

12:43 for they *l* praise from men more

13:1 Having *l* his own who were

13:23 the disciple whom Jesus *l,*

13:34 As I have *l* you, so you must love

14:21 He who loves me will be *l*

15:9 the Father has *l* me, so have I *l* you.

15:12 Love each other as I have *l* you.

19:26 the disciple whom he *l* standing

Ro 8:37 conquerors through him who *l* us.

9:13 "Jacob I *l,* but Esau I hated."

9:25 her 'my *l* one' who is not my *l* one,"

11:28 they are *l* on account

Gal 2:20 who *l* me and gave himself for me.

Eph 5:2 as Christ *l* us and gave himself up

5:25 just as Christ *l* the church

2Th 2:16 who *l* us and by his grace gave us

2Ti 4:10 for Demas, because he *l* this world,

Heb 1:9 You have *l* righteousness

1Jn 4:10 This is love: not that we *l* God,

4:11 Dear friends, since God so *l* us,

4:19 We love because he first *l* us.

**LOVELY (LOVE)**

Ps 84:1 How *l* is your dwelling place,
SS 2:14 and your face is *l*.
5:16 he is altogether *l*.
Php 4:8 whatever is *l*, whatever is

**LOVER (LOVE)**

SS 2:16 *Beloved* My *l* is mine and I am his;
7:10 I belong to my *l*,
1Ti 3:3 not quarrelsome, not a *l* of money.

**LOVERS (LOVE)**

2Ti 3:2 People will be *l* of themselves,
3:3 without self-control, brutal, not *l*
3:4 *l* of pleasure rather than *l* of God—

**LOVES (LOVE)**

Ps 11:7 he *l* justice;
33:5 The LORD *l* righteousness
34:12 Whoever of you *l* life
91:14 Because he *l* me," says the LORD,
127:2 for he grants sleep to those he *l*.
Pr 3:12 the LORD disciplines those he *l*,
12:1 Whoever *l* discipline *l* knowledge,
13:24 he who *l* him is careful
17:17 A friend *l* at all times,
17:19 He who *l* a quarrel *l* sin;
22:11 He who *l* a pure heart and whose
Ecc 5:10 whoever *l* wealth is never satisfied
Mt 10:37 anyone who *l* his son or daughter
Lk 7:47 has been forgiven little *l* little."
Jn 3:35 Father *l* the Son and has placed
10:17 reason my Father *l* me is that I lay
12:25 The man who *l* his life will lose it,
14:21 obeys them, he is the one who *l* me.
14:23 Jesus replied, "If anyone *l* me,
Ro 13:8 for he who *l* his fellowman has
2Co 9:7 for God *l* a cheerful giver.
Eph 5:28 He who *l* his wife *l* himself.
5:33 must love his wife as he *l* himself,
Heb 12:6 the Lord disciplines those he *l*,
1Jn 2:10 Whoever *l* his brother lives
2:15 If anyone *l* the world, the love
4:7 Everyone who *l* has been born
4:21 Whoever *l* God must also love his
5:1 who *l* the father *l* his child
3Jn :9 but Diotrephes, who *l* to be first,
Rev 1:5 To him who *l* us and has freed us

**LOVING (LOVE)**

Ps 25:10 All the ways of the LORD are *l*
62:12 and that you, O Lord, are *l*.
145:17 and *l* toward all he has made.
Heb 13:1 Keep on *l* each other as brothers.
1Jn 5:2 by *l* God and carrying out his

**LOWLY**

Job 5:11 The *l* he sets on high,
Pr 29:23 but a man of *l* spirit gains honor.
Isa 57:15 also with him who is contrite and *l*
Eze 21:26 *l* will be exalted and the exalted
1Co 1:28 He chose the *l* things of this world

**LUKE***

Co-worker with Paul (Col 4:14; 2Ti 4:11; Phm 24).

**LUKEWARM***

Rev 3:16 So, because you are *l*—neither hot

**LUST**

Pr 6:25 Do not *l* in your heart
Col 3:5 sexual immorality, impurity, *l*,
1Th 4:5 not in passionate *l* like the heathen,
1Jn 2:16 the *l* of his eyes and the boasting

**LYING (LIE)**

Pr 6:17 a *l* tongue,
26:28 A *l* tongue hates those it hurts,

**MACEDONIA**

Ac 16:9 "Come over to *M* and help us."

**MADE (MAKE)**

Ge 1:16 He also *m* the stars.
1:25 God *m* the wild animals according
2:22 Then the LORD God *m* a woman
2Ki 19:15 You have *m* heaven and earth.
Ps 95:5 The sea is his, for he *m* it,

Ps 100:3 It is he who *m* us, and we are his;
118:24 This is the day the LORD has *m;*
139:14 I am fearfully and wonderfully *m;*
Ecc 3:11 He has *m* everything beautiful
Mk 2:27 "The Sabbath was *m* for man,
Jn 1:3 Through him all things were *m;*
Ac 17:24 "The God who *m* the world
Heb 1:2 through whom he *m* the universe.
Rev 14:7 Worship him who *m* the heavens,

**MAGI**
Mt 2:1 *M* from the east came to Jerusalem

**MAGOG**
Eze 38:2 of the land of *M,* the chief prince
39:6 I will send fire on *M*
Rev 20:8 and *M*—to gather them for battle.

**MAIDEN**
Pr 30:19 and the way of a man with a *m.*
Isa 62:5 As a young man marries a *m,*
Jer 2:32 Does a *m* forget her jewelry,

**MAIMED**
Mt 18:8 It is better for you to enter life *m*

**MAJESTIC (MAJESTY)**
Ex 15:6 was *m* in power.
15:11 *m* in holiness,
Ps 8:1 how *m* is your name in all the earth
29:4 the voice of the LORD is *m.*
111:3 Glorious and *m* are his deeds,
SS 6:10 *m* as the stars in procession?
2Pe 1:17 came to him from the *M* Glory,

**MAJESTY (MAJESTIC)**
Ex 15:7 In the greatness of your *m*
Dt 33:26 and on the clouds in his *m.*
1Ch 16:27 Splendor and *m* are before him;
Est 1:4 the splendor and glory of his *m.*
Job 37:22 God comes in awesome *m.*
40:10 and clothe yourself in honor and *m*
Ps 45:4 In your *m* ride forth victoriously
93:1 The LORD reigns, he is robed in *m*
110:3 Arrayed in holy *m,*
145:5 of the glorious splendor of your *m,*
Isa 53:2 or *m* to attract us to him,
Eze 31:2 can be compared with you in *m?*
2Pe 1:16 but we were eyewitnesses of his *m.*
Jude :25 only God our Savior be glory, *m,*

**MAKE (MADE MAKER MAKES MAKING)**
Ge 1:26 "Let us *m* man in our image,
2:18 I will *m* a helper suitable for him."
12:2 "I will *m* you into a great nation
Ex 22:3 thief must certainly *m* restitution,
Nu 6:25 the LORD *m* his face shine
Ps 108:1 *m* music with all my soul.
Isa 14:14 I will *m* myself like the Most High
29:16 "He did not *m* me"?
Jer 31:31 "when I will *m* a new covenant
Mt 3:3 *m* straight paths for him.' "
28:19 and *m* disciples of all nations,
Mk 1:17 "and I will *m* you fishers of men."
Lk 13:24 "*M* every effort to enter
14:23 country lanes and *m* them come in,
Ro 14:19 *m* every effort to do what leads
2Co 5:9 So we *m* it our goal to please him,
Eph 4:3 *M* every effort to keep the unity
Col 4:5 *m* the most of every opportunity.
1Th 4:11 *M* it your ambition
Heb 4:11 *m* every effort to enter that rest,
12:14 *M* every effort to live in peace
2Pe 1:5 *m* every effort to add
3:14 *m* every effort to be found spotless,

**MAKER (MAKE)**
Job 4:17 Can a man be more pure than his *M*
36:3 I will ascribe justice to my *M.*
Ps 95:6 kneel before the LORD our *M;*
Pr 22:2 The LORD is the *M* of them all.
Isa 45:9 to him who quarrels with his *M,*

Isa 54:5 For your *M* is your husband—
Jer 10:16 for he is the *M* of all things,

**MAKES (MAKE)**
1Co 3:7 but only God, who *m* things grow.

**MAKING (MAKE)**
Ps 19:7 *m* wise the simple.
Ecc 12:12 Of *m* many books there is no end,
Jn 5:18 *m* himself equal with God.
Eph 5:16 *m* the most of every opportunity,

**MALE**
Ge 1:27 *m* and female he created them.
Gal 3:28 slave nor free, *m* nor female,

**MALICE (MALICIOUS)**
Ro 1:29 murder, strife, deceit and *m*.
Col 3:8 *m*, slander, and filthy language
1Pe 2:1 rid yourselves of all *m*

**MALICIOUS (MALICE)**
Pr 26:24 A *m* man disguises himself
1Ti 3:11 not *m* talkers but temperate
6:4 *m* talk, evil suspicions

**MAN (MEN WOMAN WOMEN)**
Ge 1:26 "Let us make *m* in our image,
2:7 God formed the *m* from the dust
2:18 for the *m* to be alone
2:23 she was taken out of *m*.
9:6 Whoever sheds the blood of *m*,
Dt 8:3 *m* does not live on bread
1Sa 13:14 a *m* after his own heart
15:29 he is not a *m* that he
Job 14:1 *M* born of woman is of few
14:14 If a *m* dies, will he live
Ps 1:1 Blessed is the *m* who does
8:4 what is *m* that you are
119:9 can a young *m* keep his
127:5 Blessed is the *m* whose quiver
Pr 14:12 that seems right to a *m*,
30:19 way of a *m* with a maiden.
Isa 53:3 a *m* of sorrows,
Mt 19:5 a *m* will leave his father
Mk 8:36 What good is it for a *m*
Lk 4:4 '*M* does not live on bread
Ro 5:12 entered the world through one *m*
1Co 7:2 each *m* should have his own
11:3 head of every *m* is Christ,
11:3 head of woman is *m*
13:11 When I became a *m*,
Php 2:8 found in appearance as a *m*,
1Ti 2:5 the *m* Christ Jesus,
2:11 have authority over a *m*;
Heb 9:27 as *m* is destined to die

**MANAGE**
Jer 12:5 how will you *m* in the thickets
1Ti 3:4 He must *m* his own family well
3:12 one wife and must *m* his children
5:14 to *m* their homes and to give

**MANASSEH**
1. Firstborn of Joseph (Ge 41:51; 46:20). Blessed (Ge 48).
2. Son of Hezekiah; king of Judah (2Ki 21:1-18; 2Ch 33:1-20).

**MANGER**
Lk 2:12 in strips of cloth and lying in a *m*."

**MANNA**
Ex 16:31 people of Israel called the bread *m*.
Dt 8:16 He gave you *m* to eat in the desert,
Jn 6:49 Your forefathers ate the *m*
Rev 2:17 I will give some of the hidden *m*.

**MANNER**
1Co 11:27 in an unworthy *m* will be guilty
Php 1:27 conduct yourselves in a *m* worthy

**MARITAL* (MARRY)**
Ex 21:10 of her food, clothing and *m* rights.
Mt 5:32 except for *m* unfaithfulness,
19:9 except for *m* unfaithfulness,
1Co 7:3 husband should fulfill his *m* duty

**MARK (MARKS)**
Cousin of Barnabas (Col 4:10; 2Ti 4:11; Phm 24; 1Pe 5:13), see JOHN.
Ge 4:15 Then the LORD put a *m* on Cain
Rev 13:16 to receive a *m* on his right hand

**MARKS (MARK)**
Jn 20:25 Unless I see the nail *m* in his hands
Gal 6:17 bear on my body the *m* of Jesus.

**MARRED**
Isa 52:14 his form *m* beyond human likeness

**MARRIAGE (MARRY)**
Mt 22:30 neither marry nor be given in *m;*
24:38 marrying and giving in *m,*
Ro 7:2 she is released from the law of *m.*
Heb 13:4 by all, and the *m* bed kept pure,

**MARRIED (MARRY)**
Ro 7:2 by law a *m* woman is bound
1Co 7:27 Are you *m?* Do not seek a divorce.
7:33 But a *m* man is concerned about
7:36 They should get *m.*

**MARRIES (MARRY)**
Mt 5:32 and anyone who *m* the divorced
19:9 and *m* another woman commits
Lk 16:18 the man who *m* a divorced woman

**MARRY (INTERMARRY MARITAL MARRIAGE MARRIED MARRIES)**
Mt 22:30 resurrection people will neither *m*
1Co 7:1 It is good for a man not to *m.*
7:9 control themselves, they should *m,*
1Ti 5:14 So I counsel younger widows to *m,*

**MARTHA***
Sister of Mary and Lazarus (Lk 10:38-42; Jn 11; 12:2).

**MARVELED**
Lk 2:33 mother *m* at what was said about

**MARY**
1. Mother of Jesus (Mt 1:16-25; Lk 1:27-56; 2:1-40). With Jesus at temple (Lk 2:41-52), at the wedding in Cana (Jn 2:1-5), questioning his sanity (Mk 3:21), at the cross (Jn 19:25-27). Among disciples after Ascension (Ac 1:14).
2. Magdalene; former demoniac (Lk 8:2). Helped support Jesus' ministry (Lk 8:1-3). At the cross (Mt 27:56; Mk 15:40; Jn 19:25), burial (Mt 27:61; Mk 15:47). Saw angel after resurrection (Mt 28:1-10; Mk 16:1-9; Lk 24:1-12); also Jesus (Jn 20:1-18).
3. Sister of Martha and Lazarus (Jn 11). Washed Jesus' feet (Jn 12:1-8).

**MASQUERADES***
2Co 11:14 for Satan himself *m* as an angel

**MASTER (MASTERED MASTERS)**
Mt 10:24 nor a servant above his *m.*
23:8 for you have only one *M*
24:46 that servant whose *m* finds him
25:21 "His *m* replied, 'Well done,
Ro 6:14 For sin shall not be your *m,*
14:4 To his own *m* he stands or falls.
2Ti 2:21 useful to the *M* and prepared

**MASTERED* (MASTER)**
1Co 6:12 but I will not be *m* by anything.
2Pe 2:19 a slave to whatever has *m* him.

**MASTERS (MASTER)**
Mt 6:24 "No one can serve two *m.*
Eph 6:5 obey your earthly *m* with respect
6:9 And *m,* treat your slaves
Tit 2:9 subject to their *m* in everything,

**MATTHEW***
Apostle; former tax collector (Mt 9:9-13; 10:3; Mk 3:18; Lk 6:15; Ac 1:13). Also called Levi (Mk 2:14-17; Lk 5:27-32).

**MATURE (MATURITY)**
Eph 4:13 of the Son of God and become *m,*
Php 3:15 of us who are *m* should take such
Heb 5:14 But solid food is for the *m,*
Jas 1:4 work so that you may be *m*

**MATURITY* (MATURE)**
Heb 6:1 about Christ and go on to *m,*

**MEAL**
Pr 15:17 Better a *m* of vegetables where
1Co 10:27 some unbeliever invites you to a *m*
Heb 12:16 for a single *m* sold his inheritance

**MEANING**
Ne 8:8 and giving the *m* so that the people

**MEANS**
1Co 9:22 by all possible *m* I might save some

**MEAT**
Ro 14:6 He who eats *m,* eats to the Lord,
14:21 It is better not to eat *m*

**MEDIATOR**
1Ti 2:5 and one *m* between God and men,
Heb 8:6 of which he is *m* is superior
9:15 For this reason Christ is the *m*
12:24 to Jesus the *m* of a new covenant,

**MEDICINE***
Pr 17:22 A cheerful heart is good *m*,

**MEDITATE (MEDITATES MEDITATION)**
Jos 1:8 from your mouth; *m* on it day
Ps 119:15 I *m* on your precepts
119:78 but I will *m* on your precepts.
119:97 I *m* on it all day long.
145:5 I will *m* on your wonderful works.

**MEDITATES* (MEDITATE)**
Ps 1:2 and on his law he *m* day and night.

**MEDITATION* (MEDITATE)**
Ps 19:14 of my mouth and the *m* of my heart
104:34 May my *m* be pleasing to him,

**MEDIUM**
Lev 20:27 " 'A man or woman who is a *m*

**MEEK (MEEKNESS)**
Ps 37:11 But the *m* will inherit the land
Mt 5:5 Blessed are the *m*,

**MEEKNESS* (MEEK)**
2Co 10:1 By the *m* and gentleness of Christ,

**MEET (MEETING)**
Ps 85:10 Love and faithfulness *m* together;
Am 4:12 prepare to *m* your God, O Israel."
1Th 4:17 them in the clouds to *m* the Lord

**MEETING (MEET)**
Heb 10:25 Let us not give up *m* together,

**MELCHIZEDEK**
Ge 14:18 *M* king of Salem brought out bread
Ps 110:4 in the order of *M*."
Heb 7:11 in the order of *M*, not in the order

**MELT**
2Pe 3:12 and the elements will *m* in the heat.

**MEMBERS**
Mic 7:6 a man's enemies are the *m*
Ro 7:23 law at work in the *m* of my body,
12:4 of us has one body with many *m*,
1Co 6:15 not know that your bodies are *m*
12:24 But God has combined the *m*
Eph 4:25 for we are all *m* of one body.
Col 3:15 as *m* of one body you were called

**MEN (MAN)**
Mt 4:19 will make you fishers of *m*
5:16 your light shine before *m*
12:36 *m* will have to give account
Jn 12:32 will draw all *m* to myself
Ac 5:29 obey God rather than *m*!
Ro 1:27 indecent acts with other *m*,
5:12 death came to all *m*,
1Co 9:22 all things to all *m*
2Co 5:11 we try to persuade *m*.
1Ti 2:4 wants all *m* to be saved
2Ti 2:2 entrust to reliable *m*
2Pe 1:21 but *m* spoke from God

**MENAHEM**
King of Israel (2Ki 15:17-22).

**MERCIFUL (MERCY)**
Dt 4:31 the LORD your God is a *m* God;
Ne 9:31 for you are a gracious and *m* God.
Mt 5:7 Blessed are the *m*,
Lk 6:36 Be *m*, just as your Father is *m*.
Heb 2:17 in order that he might become a *m*
Jude :22 Be *m* to those who doubt; snatch

**MERCY (MERCIFUL)**
Ex 33:19 *m* on whom I will have *m*,
Ps 25:6 O LORD, your great *m* and love,
Isa 63:9 and *m* he redeemed them;
Hos 6:6 For I desire *m*, not sacrifice,
Mic 6:8 To act justly and to love *m*
Hab 3:2 in wrath remember *m*.
Mt 12:7 'I desire *m*, not sacrifice,' you
23:23 justice, *m* and faithfulness.
Ro 9:15 "I will have *m* on whom I have *m*,

Eph 2:4 who is rich in *m*, made us alive
Jas 2:13 *M* triumphs over judgment!
1Pe 1:3 In his great *m* he has given us new

**MESSAGE**

Isa 53:1 Who has believed our *m*
Jn 12:38 "Lord, who has believed our *m*
Ro 10:17 faith comes from hearing the *m*,
1Co 1:18 For the *m* of the cross is
2Co 5:19 to us the *m* of reconciliation.

**MESSIAH***

Jn 1:41 "We have found the *M*" (that is,
4:25 "I know that *M*" (called Christ) "is

**METHUSELAH**

Ge 5:27 Altogether, *M* lived 969 years,

**MICHAEL**

Archangel (Jude 9); warrior in angelic realm, protector of Israel (Da 10:13, 21; 12:1; Rev 12:7).

**MIDWIVES**

Ex 1:17 The *m*, however, feared God

**MIGHT (ALMIGHTY MIGHTY)**

Jdg 16:30 Then he pushed with all his *m*,
2Sa 6:14 before the LORD with all his *m*,
Ps 21:13 we will sing and praise your *m*.
Zec 4:6 'Not by *m* nor by power,
1Ti 6:16 To him be honor and *m* forever.

**MIGHTY (MIGHT)**

Ex 6:1 of my *m* hand he will drive them
Dt 7:8 he brought you out with a *m* hand
2Sa 1:19 How the *m* have fallen!
23:8 the names of David's *m* men:
Ps 24:8 The LORD strong and *m*,
50:1 The *M* One, God, the LORD,
89:8 You are *m*, O LORD,
136:12 with a *m* hand and outstretched
147:5 Great is our Lord and *m* in power;
Isa 9:6 Wonderful Counselor, *M* God,
Zep 3:17 he is *m* to save.
Eph 6:10 in the Lord and in his *m* power.

**MILE***

Mt 5:41 If someone forces you to go one *m*,

**MILK**

Ex 3:8 a land flowing with *m* and honey—
Isa 55:1 Come, buy wine and *m*
1Co 3:2 I gave you *m*, not solid food,
Heb 5:12 You need *m*, not solid food!
1Pe 2:2 babies, crave pure spiritual *m*,

**MILLSTONE (STONE)**

Lk 17:2 sea with a *m* tied around his neck

**MIND (DOUBLE-MINDED MINDFUL MINDS)**

1Sa 15:29 Israel does not lie or change his *m*;
1Ch 28:9 devotion and with a willing *m*,
Ps 26:2 examine my heart and my *m*;
Isa 26:3 him whose *m* is steadfast,
Mt 22:37 all your soul and with all your *m*.'
Ac 4:32 believers were one in heart and *m*.
Ro 7:25 I myself in my *m* am a slave
8:7 the sinful *m* is hostile to God.
12:2 by the renewing of your *m*.
1Co 2:9 no *m* has conceived
14:14 spirit prays, but my *m* is unfruitful.
2Co 13:11 be of one *m*, live in peace.
Php 3:19 Their *m* is on earthly things.
1Th 4:11 to *m* your own business
Heb 7:21 and will not change his *m*:

**MINDFUL* (MIND)**

Ps 8:4 what is man that you are *m* of him,
Lk 1:48 God my Savior, for he has been *m*
Heb 2:6 What is man that you are *m* of him,

**MINDS (MIND)**

Ps 7:9 who searches *m* and hearts,
Jer 31:33 "I will put my law in their *m*
Eph 4:23 new in the attitude of your *m*;
Col 3:2 Set your *m* on things above,
Heb 8:10 I will put my laws in their *m*
Rev 2:23 I am he who searches hearts and *m*,

**MINISTERING (MINISTRY)**
Heb 1:14 Are not all angels *m* spirits sent

**MINISTRY (MINISTERING)**
Ac 6:4 to prayer and the *m* of the word."
2Co 5:18 gave us the *m* of reconciliation:
2Ti 4:5 discharge all the duties of your *m*.

**MIRACLES (MIRACULOUS)**
1Ch 16:12 his *m*, and the judgments he
Ps 77:14 You are the God who performs *m*;
Mt 11:20 most of his *m* had been performed,
11:21 If the *m* that were performed
24:24 and perform great signs and *m*
Mk 6:2 does *m!* Isn't this the carpenter?
Jn 10:32 "I have shown you many great *m*
14:11 the evidence of the *m* themselves.
Ac 2:22 accredited by God to you by *m*,
19:11 God did extraordinary *m*
1Co 12:28 third teachers, then workers of *m*,
Heb 2:4 it by signs, wonders and various *m*,

**MIRACULOUS (MIRACLES)**
Jn 3:2 could perform the *m* signs you are
9:16 "How can a sinner do such *m* signs
20:30 Jesus did many other *m* signs
1Co 1:22 Jews demand *m* signs and Greeks

**MIRE**
Ps 40:2 out of the mud and *m*;
Isa 57:20 whose waves cast up *m* and mud.

**MIRIAM**
Sister of Moses and Aaron (Nu 26:59). Led dancing at Red Sea (Ex 15:20-21). Struck with leprosy for criticizing Moses (Nu 12). Death (Nu 20:1).

**MIRROR**
Jas 1:23 a man who looks at his face in a *m*

**MISERY**
Ex 3:7 "I have indeed seen the *m*
Jdg 10:16 he could bear Israel's *m* no longer.
Hos 5:15 in their *m* they will earnestly seek
Ro 3:16 ruin and *m* mark their ways,
Jas 5:1 of the *m* that is coming upon you.

**MISLED**
1Co 15:33 Do not be *m:* "Bad company

**MISS**
Pr 19:2 nor to be hasty and *m* the way.

**MIST**
Hos 6:4 Your love is like the morning *m*,
Jas 4:14 You are a *m* that appears for a little

**MISUSE***
Ex 20:7 "You shall not *m* the name
Dt 5:11 "You shall not *m* the name
Ps 139:20 your adversaries *m* your name.

**MOCK (MOCKED MOCKER MOCKERS MOCKING)**
Ps 22:7 All who see me *m* me;
Pr 14:9 Fools *m* at making amends for sin,
Mk 10:34 who will *m* him and spit on him,

**MOCKED (MOCK)**
Mt 27:29 knelt in front of him and *m* him.
27:41 of the law and the elders *m* him.
Gal 6:7 not be deceived: God cannot be *m*.

**MOCKER (MOCK)**
Pr 9:7 corrects a *m* invites insult;
9:12 if you are a *m*, you alone will suffer
20:1 Wine is a *m* and beer a brawler;
22:10 Drive out the *m*, and out goes strife

**MOCKERS (MOCK)**
Ps 1:1 or sit in the seat of *m*.

**MOCKING (MOCK)**
Isa 50:6 face from *m* and spitting.

**MODEL***
Eze 28:12 " 'You were the *m* of perfection,
1Th 1:7 And so you became a *m*
2Th 3:9 to make ourselves a *m* for you

**MOMENT**
Job 20:5 the joy of the godless lasts but a *m*.
Ps 30:5 For his anger lasts only a *m*,
Isa 66:8 or a nation be brought forth in a *m?*
Gal 2:5 We did not give in to them for a *m*,

**MONEY**
Ecc 5:10 Whoever loves *m* never has *m*

| | | |
|---|---|---|
| Isa | 55:1 | and you who have no *m*, |
| Mt | 6:24 | You cannot serve both God and *M*. |
| Lk | 9:3 | no bread, no *m*, no extra tunic. |
| 1Co | 16:2 | set aside a sum of *m* in keeping |
| 1Ti | 3:3 | not quarrelsome, not a lover of *m*. |
| | 6:10 | For the love of *m* is a root |
| 2Ti | 3:2 | lovers of *m*, boastful, proud, |
| Heb | 13:5 | free from the love of *m* |
| 1Pe | 5:2 | not greedy for *m*, but eager to serve |

## MOON

| | | |
|---|---|---|
| Ps | 121:6 | nor the *m* by night. |
| Joel | 2:31 | and the *m* to blood |
| 1Co | 15:41 | *m* another and the stars another; |

## MORNING

| | | |
|---|---|---|
| Ge | 1:5 | and there was *m*—the first day. |
| Dt | 28:67 | In the *m* you will say, "If only it |
| Ps | 5:3 | In the *m*, O LORD, |
| 2Pe | 1:19 | and the *m* star rises in your hearts. |
| Rev | 22:16 | of David, and the bright *M* Star." |

## MORTAL

| | | |
|---|---|---|
| 1Co | 15:53 | and the *m* with immortality. |

## MOSES

Levite; brother of Aaron (Ex 6:20; 1Ch 6:3). Put in basket into Nile; discovered and raised by Pharaoh's daughter (Ex 2:1-10). Fled to Midian after killing Egyptian (Ex 2:11-15). Married to Zipporah, fathered Gershom (Ex 2:16-22).

Called by the LORD to deliver Israel (Ex 3-4). Pharaoh's resistance (Ex 5). Ten plagues (Ex 7-11). Passover and Exodus (Ex 12-13). Led Israel through Red Sea (Ex 14). Song of deliverance (Ex 15:1-21). Brought water from rock (Ex 17:1-7). Raised hands to defeat Amalekites (Ex 17:8-16). Delegated judges (Ex 18; Dt 1:9-18).

Received Law at Sinai (Ex 19-23; 25-31; Jn 1:17). Announced Law to Israel (Ex 19:7-8; 24; 35). Broke tablets because of golden calf (Ex 32; Dt 9). Saw glory of the LORD (Ex 33-34). Supervised building of tabernacle (Ex 36-40). Set apart Aaron and priests (Lev 8-9). Numbered tribes (Nu 1-4; 26). Opposed by Aaron and Miriam (Nu 12). Sent spies into Canaan (Nu 13). Announced forty years of wandering for failure to enter land (Nu 14). Opposed by Korah (Nu 16). Forbidden to enter land for striking rock (Nu 20:1-13; Dt 1:37). Lifted bronze snake for healing (Nu 21:4-9; Jn 3:14). Final address to Israel (Dt 1-33). Succeeded by Joshua (Nu 27:12-23; Dt 34). Death (Dt 34:5-12).

"Law of Moses" (1Ki 2:3; Ezr 3:2; Mk 12:26; Lk 24:44). "Book of Moses" (2Ch 25:12; Ne 13:1). "Song of Moses" (Ex 15:1-21; Rev 15:3). "Prayer of Moses" (Ps 90).

## MOTH

| | | |
|---|---|---|
| Mt | 6:19 | where *m* and rust destroy, |

## MOTHER (MOTHER'S)

| | | |
|---|---|---|
| Ge | 2:24 | and *m* and be united to his wife, |
| | 3:20 | because she would become the *m* |
| Ex | 20:12 | "Honor your father and your *m*, |
| Lev | 20:9 | " 'If anyone curses his father or *m*, |
| Dt | 5:16 | "Honor your father and your *m*, |
| | 21:18 | who does not obey his father and *m* |
| | 27:16 | who dishonors his father or his *m*." |
| 1Sa | 2:19 | Each year his *m* made him a little |
| Ps | 113:9 | as a happy *m* of children. |
| Pr | 23:25 | May your father and *m* be glad; |
| | 29:15 | child left to himself disgraces his *m*. |
| | 31:1 | an oracle his *m* taught him: |
| Isa | 49:15 | "Can a *m* forget the baby |
| | 66:13 | As a *m* comforts her child, |
| Mt | 10:37 | or *m* more than me is not worthy |
| | 15:4 | 'Honor your father and *m*' |
| | 19:5 | and *m* and be united to his wife, |
| Mk | 7:10 | 'Honor your father and your *m*,' |
| | 10:19 | honor your father and *m*.' " |
| Jn | 19:27 | to the disciple, "Here is your *m*." |

## MOTHER'S (MOTHER)

| | | |
|---|---|---|
| Job | 1:21 | "Naked I came from my *m* womb, |
| Pr | 1:8 | and do not forsake your *m* teaching |

## MOTIVES*

| | | |
|---|---|---|
| Pr | 16:2 | but *m* are weighed by the LORD. |
| 1Co | 4:5 | will expose the *m* of men's hearts. |
| Php | 1:18 | whether from false *m* or true, |
| 1Th | 2:3 | spring from error or impure *m*, |
| Jas | 4:3 | because you ask with wrong *m*, |

## MOUNTAIN (MOUNTAINS)

| | | |
|---|---|---|
| Mic | 4:2 | let us go up to the *m* of the LORD, |

Mt 17:20 say to this *m*, 'Move from here

**MOUNTAINS (MOUNTAIN)**
Isa 52:7 How beautiful on the *m*
55:12 the *m* and hills
1Co 13:2 if I have a faith that can move *m*,

**MOURN (MOURNING)**
Ecc 3:4 a time to *m* and a time to dance,
Isa 61:2 to comfort all who *m*,
Mt 5:4 Blessed are those who *m*,
Ro 12:15 *m* with those who *m*.

**MOURNING (MOURN)**
Jer 31:13 I will turn their *m* into gladness;
Rev 21:4 There will be no more death or *m*

**MOUTH**
Jos 1:8 of the Law depart from your *m;*
Ps 19:14 May the words of my *m*
40:3 He put a new song in my *m*,
119:103 sweeter than honey to my *m!*
Pr 16:23 A wise man's heart guides his *m*,
27:2 praise you, and not your own *m;*
Isa 51:16 I have put my words in your *m*
Mt 12:34 overflow of the heart the *m* speaks.
15:11 into a man's *m* does not make him
Ro 10:9 That if you confess with your *m*,

**MUD**
Ps 40:2 out of the *m* and mire;
Isa 57:20 whose waves cast up mire and *m*.
2Pe 2:22 back to her wallowing in the *m*."

**MULTITUDE (MULTITUDES)**
Isa 31:1 who trust in the *m* of their chariots
1Pe 4:8 love covers over a *m* of sins.
Rev 7:9 me was a great *m* that no one could

**MULTITUDES (MULTITUDE)**
Joel 3:14 *M*, *m* in the valley of decision!

**MURDER (MURDERER MURDERERS)**
Ex 20:13 "You shall not *m*.
Mt 15:19 *m*, adultery, sexual immorality,
Ro 13:9 "Do not *m*," "Do not steal,"
Jas 2:11 adultery," also said, "Do not *m*."

**MURDERER (MURDER)**
Nu 35:16 he is a *m;* the *m* shall be put
Jn 8:44 He was a *m* from the beginning,
1Jn 3:15 who hates his brother is a *m*,

**MURDERERS (MURDER)**
1Ti 1:9 for *m*, for adulterers and perverts,
Rev 21:8 the *m*, the sexually immoral,

**MUSIC**
Jdg 5:3 I will make *m* to the LORD,
Ps 27:6 and make *m* to the LORD.
95:2 and extol him with *m* and song.
98:4 burst into jubilant song with *m;*
108:1 make *m* with all my soul.
Eph 5:19 make *m* in your heart to the Lord,

**MUSTARD**
Mt 13:31 kingdom of heaven is like a *m* seed,
17:20 you have faith as small as a *m* seed,

**MUZZLE**
Dt 25:4 Do not *m* an ox while it is treading
Ps 39:1 I will put a *m* on my mouth
1Co 9:9 "Do not *m* an ox while it is

**MYRRH**
Mt 2:11 of gold and of incense and of *m*.
Mk 15:23 offered him wine mixed with *m*,

**MYSTERY**
Ro 16:25 to the revelation of the *m* hidden
1Co 15:51 I tell you a *m:* We will not all sleep,
Eph 5:32 This is a profound *m*—
Col 1:26 the *m* that has been kept hidden
1Ti 3:16 the *m* of godliness is great:

**MYTHS**
1Ti 4:7 Have nothing to do with godless *m*

**NADAB**
Son of Jeroboam I; king of Israel (1Ki 15:25-32).

**NAIL* (NAILING)**
Jn 20:25 "Unless I see the *n* marks

**NAILING* (NAIL)**

Ac 2:23 him to death by *n* him to the cross.
Col 2:14 he took it away, *n* it to the cross.

**NAKED**

Ge 2:25 The man and his wife were both *n*,
Job 1:21 *N* I came from my mother's womb,
Isa 58:7 when you see the *n*, to clothe him,
2Co 5:3 are clothed, we will not be found *n*.

**NAME**

Ex 3:15 This is my *n* forever, the *n*
20:7 "You shall not misuse the *n*
Dt 5:11 "You shall not misuse the *n*
28:58 this glorious and awesome *n*—
1Ki 5:5 will build the temple for my *N*.'
2Ch 7:14 my people, who are called by my *n*,
Ps 34:3 let us exalt his *n* together.
103:1 my inmost being, praise his holy *n*.
147:4 and calls them each by *n*.
Pr 22:1 A good *n* is more desirable
30:4 What is his *n*, and the *n* of his son?
Isa 40:26 and calls them each by *n*.
57:15 who lives forever, whose *n* is holy:
Jer 14:7 do something for the sake of your *n*
Da 12:1 everyone whose *n* is found written
Joel 2:32 on the *n* of the LORD will be saved
Zec 14:9 one LORD, and his *n* the only *n*.
Mt 1:21 and you are to give him the *n* Jesus,
6:9 hallowed be your *n*,
18:20 or three come together in my *n*,
Jn 10:3 He calls his own sheep by *n*
16:24 asked for anything in my *n*.
Ac 4:12 for there is no other *n*
Ro 10:13 "Everyone who calls on the *n*
Php 2:9 him the *n* that is above every *n*,
Col 3:17 do it all in the *n* of the Lord Jesus,
Heb 1:4 as the *n* he has inherited is superior
Rev 20:15 If anyone's *n* was not found written

**NAOMI**

Mother-in-law of Ruth (Ru 1). Advised Ruth to seek marriage with Boaz (Ru 2-4).

**NARROW**

Mt 7:13 "Enter through the *n* gate.

**NATHANAEL**

Apostle (Jn 1:45-49; 21:2). Probably also called Bartholomew (Mt 10:3).

**NATION (NATIONS)**

Ge 12:2 "I will make you into a great *n*
Ps 33:12 Blessed is the *n* whose God is
Pr 14:34 Righteousness exalts a *n*,
Isa 65:1 To a *n* that did not call on my name
1Pe 2:9 a royal priesthood, a holy *n*,
Rev 7:9 from every *n*, tribe, people

**NATIONS (NATION)**

Ge 17:4 You will be the father of many *n*.
18:18 and all *n* on earth will be blessed
Ex 19:5 of all *n* you will be my treasured
Ne 1:8 I will scatter you among the *n*,
Ps 96:3 Declare his glory among the *n*,
Isa 40:15 Surely the *n* are like a drop
Eze 36:23 *n* will know that I am the LORD,
Hag 2:7 and the desired of all *n* will come,
Zec 8:23 *n* will take firm hold of one Jew
14:2 I will gather all the *n* to Jerusalem
Mt 28:19 and make disciples of all *n*,
Rev 21:24 The *n* will walk by its light,

**NATURAL (NATURE)**

Ro 6:19 you are weak in your *n* selves.
1Co 15:44 If there is a *n* body, there is

**NATURE (NATURAL)**

Ro 8:4 do not live according to the sinful *n*
8:8 by the sinful *n* cannot please God.
Gal 5:19 The acts of the sinful *n* are obvious:
5:24 Jesus have crucified the sinful *n*
Php 2:6 Who, being in very *n* God,

**NAZARENE**

Mt 2:23 prophets: "He will be called a *N*."

**NAZIRITE**

Jdg 13:7 because the boy will be a *N* of God

**NECESSARY**

Ro 13:5 it is *n* to submit to the authorities,

**NEED (NEEDS NEEDY)**

Ps 116:6 when I was in great *n*, he saved me.
Mt 6:8 for your Father knows what you *n*
Ro 12:13 with God's people who are in *n*.
1Co 12:21 say to the hand, "I don't *n* you!"
1Jn 3:17 sees his brother in *n* but has no pity

**NEEDLE**

Mt 19:24 go through the eye of a *n*

**NEEDS (NEED)**

Isa 58:11 he will satisfy your *n*
Php 4:19 God will meet all your *n* according

**NEEDY (NEED)**

Pr 14:21 blessed is he who is kind to the *n*.
14:31 to the *n* honors God.
31:20 and extends her hands to the *n*.
Mt 6:2 "So when you give to the *n*,

**NEGLECT (NEGLECTED)**

Ne 10:39 We will not *n* the house of our God
Ps 119:16 I will not *n* your word.
Ac 6:2 for us to *n* the ministry of the word
1Ti 4:14 Do not *n* your gift, which was

**NEGLECTED (NEGLECT)**

Mt 23:23 But you have *n* the more important

**NEHEMIAH**

Cupbearer of Artaxerxes (Ne 2:1); governor of Israel (Ne 8:9). Returned to Jerusalem to rebuild walls (Ne 2-6). With Ezra, reestablished worship (Ne 8). Prayer confessing nation's sin (Ne 9). Dedicated wall (Ne 12).

**NEIGHBOR (NEIGHBOR'S)**

Ex 20:16 give false testimony against your *n*.
Lev 19:13 Do not defraud your *n* or rob him.
19:18 but love your *n* as yourself.
Pr 27:10 better a *n* nearby than a brother far
Mt 19:19 and 'love your *n* as yourself.' "
Lk 10:29 who is my *n?*" In reply Jesus said:
Ro 13:10 Love does no harm to its *n*.

**NEIGHBOR'S (NEIGHBOR)**

Ex 20:17 You shall not covet your *n* wife,
Dt 5:21 not set your desire on your *n* house
19:14 not move your *n* boundary stone
Pr 25:17 Seldom set foot in your *n* house—

**NEW**

Ps 40:3 He put a *n* song in my mouth,
Ecc 1:9 there is nothing *n* under the sun.
Isa 65:17 *n* heavens and a *n* earth.
Jer 31:31 "when I will make a *n* covenant
Eze 36:26 give you a *n* heart and put a *n* spirit
Mt 9:17 Neither do men pour *n* wine
Lk 22:20 "This cup is the *n* covenant
2Co 5:17 he is a *n* creation; the old has gone,
Eph 4:24 and to put on the *n* self, created
2Pe 3:13 to a *n* heaven and a *n* earth,
1Jn 2:8 Yet I am writing you a *n* command;

**NEWBORN (BEAR)**

1Pe 2:2 Like *n* babies, crave pure spiritual

**NEWS**

Isa 52:7 the feet of those who bring good *n*,
Mk 1:15 Repent and believe the good *n!*"
16:15 preach the good *n* to all creation.
Lk 2:10 I bring you good *n*
Ac 5:42 proclaiming the good *n* that Jesus
17:18 preaching the good *n* about Jesus
Ro 10:15 feet of those who bring good *n!*"

**NICODEMUS***

Pharisee who visited Jesus at night (Jn 3). Argued fair treatment of Jesus (Jn 7:50-52). With Joseph, prepared Jesus for burial (Jn 19:38-42).

**NIGHT**

Job 35:10 who gives songs in the *n*,
Ps 1:2 on his law he meditates day and *n*.
91:5 You will not fear the terror of *n*,
Jn 3:2 He came to Jesus at *n* and said,
1Th 5:2 Lord will come like a thief in the *n*.
5:5 We do not belong to the *n*
Rev 21:25 for there will be no *n* there.

**NOAH**
Righteous man (Eze 14:14, 20) called to build ark (Ge 6-8; Heb 11:7; 1Pe 3:20; 2Pe 2:5). God's covenant with (Ge 9:1-17). Drunkenness of (Ge 9:18-23). Blessed sons, cursed Canaan (Ge 9:24-27).

**NOBLE**
Ru 3:11 you are a woman of *n* character.
Ps 45:1 My heart is stirred by a *n* theme
Pr 12:4 of *n* character is her husband's
31:10 A wife of *n* character who can find?
31:29 "Many women do *n* things,
Isa 32:8 But the *n* man makes *n* plans,
Lk 8:15 good soil stands for those with a *n*
Ro 9:21 of clay some pottery for *n* purposes
Php 4:8 whatever is *n*, whatever is right,
2Ti 2:20 some are for *n* purposes

**NOTHING**
Ne 9:21 in the desert; they lacked *n*,
Jer 32:17 *N* is too hard for you
Jn 15:5 apart from me you can do *n*.

**NULLIFY**
Ro 3:31 Do we, then, *n* the law by this faith

**OATH**
Dt 7:8 and kept the *o* he swore

**OBEDIENCE (OBEY)**
2Ch 31:21 in *o* to the law and the commands,
Pr 30:17 that scorns *o* to a mother,
Ro 1:5 to the *o* that comes from faith.
6:16 to *o*, which leads to righteousness?
2Jn :6 that we walk in *o* to his commands.

**OBEDIENT (OBEY)**
Lk 2:51 with them and was *o* to them.
Php 2:8 and became *o* to death—
1Pe 1:14 As *o* children, do not conform

**OBEY (OBEDIENCE OBEDIENT OBEYED)**
Ex 12:24 "*O* these instructions as a lasting
Dt 6:3 careful to *o* so that it may go well
13:4 Keep his commands and *o* him;
21:18 son who does not *o* his father
30:2 and *o* him with all your heart
32:46 children to *o* carefully all the words
1Sa 15:22 To *o* is better than sacrifice,
Ps 119:34 and *o* it with all my heart.
Mt 28:20 to *o* everything I have commanded
Jn 14:23 loves me, he will *o* my teaching.
Ac 5:29 "We must *o* God rather than men!
Ro 6:16 slaves to the one whom you *o*—
Gal 5:3 obligated to *o* the whole law.
Eph 6:1 *o* your parents in the Lord,
6:5 *o* your earthly masters with respect
Col 3:20 *o* your parents in everything,
1Ti 3:4 and see that his children *o* him
Heb 13:17 *O* your leaders and submit
1Jn 5:3 love for God: to *o* his commands.

**OBEYED (OBEY)**
Ps 119:4 that are to be fully *o*.
Jnh 3:3 Jonah *o* the word of the LORD
Jn 17:6 and they have *o* your word.
Ro 6:17 you wholeheartedly *o* the form
Heb 11:8 *o* and went, even though he did not
1Pe 3:6 who *o* Abraham and called him her

**OBLIGATED**
Ro 1:14 I am *o* both to Greeks
Gal 5:3 himself be circumcised that he is *o*

**OBSCENITY**
Eph 5:4 Nor should there be *o*, foolish talk

**OBSOLETE**
Heb 8:13 he has made the first one *o*;

**OBTAINED**
Ro 9:30 not pursue righteousness, have *o* it,
Php 3:12 Not that I have already *o* all this,
Heb 9:12 having *o* eternal redemption.

**OFFENDED (OFFENSE)**
Pr 18:19 An *o* brother is more unyielding

**OFFENSE (OFFENDED OFFENSIVE)**
Pr 17:9 over an *o* promotes love,
19:11 it is to his glory to overlook an *o*.

**OFFENSIVE (OFFENSE)**
Ps 139:24 See if there is any *o* way in me,

**OFFER (OFFERED OFFERING OFFERINGS)**
Ro 12:1 to *o* your bodies as living sacrifices,
Heb 13:15 therefore, let us continually *o*

**OFFERED (OFFER)**
Heb 7:27 once for all when he *o* himself.
11:4 By faith Abel *o* God a better

**OFFERING (OFFER)**
Ge 22:8 provide the lamb for the burnt *o*,
Ps 40:6 Sacrifice and *o* you did not desire,
Isa 53:10 the LORD makes his life a guilt *o*,
Mt 5:23 if you are *o* your gift at the altar
Eph 5:2 as a fragrant *o* and sacrifice to God.
Heb 10:5 "Sacrifice and *o* you did not desire,

**OFFERINGS (OFFER)**
Mal 3:8 do we rob you?' "In tithes and *o*.
Mk 12:33 is more important than all burnt *o*

**OFFICER**
2Ti 2:4 wants to please his commanding *o*.

**OFFSPRING**
Ge 3:15 and between your *o* and hers;
Ge 12:7 "To your *o* I will give this land."

**OIL**
Ps 23:5 You anoint my head with *o*;
Isa 61:3 the *o* of gladness
Heb 1:9 by anointing you with the *o* of joy."

**OLIVE (OLIVES)**
Zec 4:3 Also there are two *o* trees by it,
Ro 11:17 and you, though a wild *o* shoot,
Rev 11:4 These are the two *o* trees

**OLIVES (OLIVE)**
Jas 3:12 a fig tree bear *o*, or a grapevine bear

**OMEGA**
Rev 1:8 "I am the Alpha and the *O*,"

**OMRI**
King of Israel (1Ki 16:21-26).

**OPINIONS***
1Ki 18:21 will you waver between two *o*?
Pr 18:2 but delights in airing his own *o*.

**OPPORTUNITY**
Ro 7:11 seizing the *o* afforded
Gal 6:10 as we have *o*, let us do good
Eph 5:16 making the most of every *o*,
Col 4:5 make the most of every *o*.
1Ti 5:14 to give the enemy no *o* for slander.

**OPPOSES**
Jas 4:6 "God *o* the proud
1Pe 5:5 because, "God *o* the proud

**OPPRESS (OPPRESSED)**
Ex 22:21 "Do not mistreat an alien or *o* him,
Zec 7:10 Do not *o* the widow

**OPPRESSED (OPPRESS)**
Ps 9:9 The LORD is a refuge for the *o*,
Isa 53:7 He was *o* and afflicted,
Zec 10:2 *o* for lack of a shepherd.

**ORDAINED**
Ps 8:2 you have *o* praise

**ORDERLY**
1Co 14:40 done in a fitting and *o* way.
Col 2:5 and delight to see how *o* you are

**ORGIES***
Ro 13:13 not in *o* and drunkenness,
Gal 5:21 drunkenness, *o*, and the like.
1Pe 4:3 *o*, carousing and detestable

**ORIGIN**
2Pe 1:21 For prophecy never had its *o*

**ORPHANS**
Jn 14:18 will not leave you as *o*; I will come
Jas 1:27 to look after *o* and widows

**OUTCOME**
Heb 13:7 Consider the *o* of their way of life
1Pe 4:17 what will the *o* be for those who do

**OUTSIDERS***
Col 4:5 wise in the way you act toward *o*;
1Th 4:12 daily life may win the respect of *o*
1Ti 3:7 also have a good reputation with *o*,

**OUTSTANDING**
SS 5:10 *o* among ten thousand.

Ro 13:8 no debt remain *o*,

**OUTSTRETCHED**
Ex 6:6 and will redeem you with an *o* arm
Jer 27:5 and *o* arm I made the earth
Eze 20:33 an *o* arm and with outpoured wrath

**OUTWEIGHS**
2Co 4:17 an eternal glory that far *o* them all.

**OVERCOME (OVERCOMES)**
Mt 16:18 and the gates of Hades will not *o* it.
Mk 9:24 I do believe; help me *o* my unbelief
Jn 16:33 But take heart! I have *o* the world."
Ro 12:21 Do not be *o* by evil, but *o* evil
1Jn 5:4 is the victory that has *o* the world,
Rev 17:14 but the Lamb will *o* them

**OVERCOMES* (OVERCOME)**
1Jn 5:4 born of God *o* the world.
5:5 Who is it that *o* the world?
Rev 2:7 To him who *o*, I will give the right
2:11 He who *o* will not be hurt at all
2:17 To him who *o*, I will give some
2:26 To him who *o* and does my will
3:5 He who *o* will, like them, be
3:12 Him who *o* I will make a pillar
3:21 To him who *o*, I will give the right
21:7 He who *o* will inherit all this,

**OVERFLOW (OVERFLOWS)**
Ps 119:171 May my lips *o* with praise,
Lk 6:45 out of the *o* of his heart his mouth
Ro 15:13 so that you may *o* with hope
2Co 4:15 to *o* to the glory of God.
1Th 3:12 *o* for each other and for everyone

**OVERFLOWS* (OVERFLOW)**
Ps 23:5 my cup *o*.
2Co 1:5 also through Christ our comfort *o*.

**OVERJOYED* (JOY)**
Da 6:23 The king was *o* and gave orders
Mt 2:10 they saw the star, they were *o*.
Jn 20:20 The disciples were *o*
Ac 12:14 she was so *o* she ran back
1Pe 4:13 so that you may be *o*

**OVERSEER (OVERSEERS)**
1Ti 3:1 anyone sets his heart on being an *o*,
3:2 Now the *o* must be above reproach,
Tit 1:7 Since an *o* is entrusted

**OVERSEERS* (OVERSEER)**
Ac 20:28 the Holy Spirit has made you *o*.
Php 1:1 together with the *o* and deacons:
1Pe 5:2 as *o*—not because you must,

**OVERWHELMED**
Ps 38:4 My guilt has *o* me
65:3 When we were *o* by sins,
Mt 26:38 "My soul is *o* with sorrow
Mk 7:37 People were *o* with amazement.

**OWE**
Ro 13:7 If you *o* taxes, pay taxes; if revenue
Phm :19 to mention that you *o* me your very

**OX**
Dt 25:4 Do not muzzle an *o*
Isa 11:7 and the lion will eat straw like the *o*
1Co 9:9 "Do not muzzle an *o*

**PAGANS**
Mt 5:47 Do not even *p* do that? Be perfect,
1Pe 2:12 such good lives among the *p* that,

**PAIN (PAINFUL)**
Ge 3:16 with *p* you will give birth
Job 33:19 may be chastened on a bed of *p*
Jn 16:21 woman giving birth to a child has *p*

**PAINFUL (PAIN)**
Ge 3:17 through *p* toil you will eat of it
Heb 12:11 seems pleasant at the time, but *p*.
1Pe 4:12 at the *p* trial you are suffering,

**PALMS**
Isa 49:16 you on the *p* of my hands;

**PANTS**
Ps 42:1 As the deer *p* for streams of water,

**PARADISE***
Lk 23:43 today you will be with me in *p*."
2Co 12:4 God knows—was caught up to *p*.

Rev 2:7 of life, which is in the *p* of God.

**PARALYTIC**
Mk 2:3 bringing to him a *p,* carried by four

**PARDON (PARDONS)**
Isa 55:7 and to our God, for he will freely *p.*

**PARDONS* (PARDON)**
Mic 7:18 who *p* sin and forgives

**PARENTS**
Pr 17:6 and *p* are the pride of their children
Lk 18:29 left home or wife or brothers or *p*
21:16 You will be betrayed even by *p,*
Ro 1:30 they disobey their *p;* they are
2Co 12:14 for their *p,* but *p* for their children.
Eph 6:1 Children, obey your *p* in the Lord,
Col 3:20 obey your *p* in everything,
2Ti 3:2 disobedient to their *p,* ungrateful,

**PARTIALITY**
Dt 10:17 who shows no *p* and accepts no
2Ch 19:7 our God there is no injustice or *p*
Lk 20:21 and that you do not show *p*

**PARTICIPATION**
1Co 10:16 is not the bread that we break a *p*

**PASS**
Ex 12:13 and when I see the blood, I will *p*
La 1:12 to you, all you who *p* by?
Lk 21:33 Heaven and earth will *p* away,
1Co 13:8 there is knowledge, it will *p* away.

**PASSION (PASSIONS)**
1Co 7:9 better to marry than to burn with *p.*

**PASSIONS (PASSION)**
Gal 5:24 crucified the sinful nature with its *p*
Tit 2:12 to ungodliness and worldly *p,*

**PASSOVER**
Ex 12:11 Eat it in haste; it is the LORD's *P.*
Dt 16:1 celebrate the *P* of the LORD your
1Co 5:7 our *P* lamb, has been sacrificed.

**PAST**
Isa 43:18 do not dwell on the *p.*
Ro 15:4 in the *p* was written to teach us,
Heb 1:1 In the *p* God spoke

**PASTORS***
Eph 4:11 and some to be *p* and teachers,

**PASTURE (PASTURES)**
Ps 37:3 dwell in the land and enjoy safe *p.*
100:3 we are his people, the sheep of his *p*
Jer 50:7 against the LORD, their true *p,*
Eze 34:13 I will *p* them on the mountains
Jn 10:9 come in and go out, and find *p.*

**PASTURES (PASTURE)**
Ps 23:2 He makes me lie down in green *p,*

**PATCH**
Mt 9:16 No one sews a *p* of unshrunk cloth

**PATH (PATHS)**
Ps 27:11 lead me in a straight *p*
Ps 119:105 and a light for my *p.*
Pr 15:19 the *p* of the upright is a highway.
15:24 The *p* of life leads upward
Isa 26:7 The *p* of the righteous is level;
Lk 1:79 to guide our feet into the *p* of peace
2Co 6:3 no stumbling block in anyone's *p,*

**PATHS (PATH)**
Ps 23:3 He guides me in *p* of righteousness
25:4 teach me your *p;*
Pr 3:6 and he will make your *p* straight.
Ro 11:33 and his *p* beyond tracing out!
Heb 12:13 "Make level *p* for your feet,"

**PATIENCE (PATIENT)**
Pr 19:11 A man's wisdom gives him *p;*
2Co 6:6 understanding, *p* and kindness;
Gal 5:22 joy, peace, *p,* kindness, goodness,
Col 1:11 may have great endurance and *p,*
3:12 humility, gentleness and *p.*

**PATIENT (PATIENCE PATIENTLY)**
Pr 15:18 but a *p* man calms a quarrel.
Ro 12:12 Be joyful in hope, *p* in affliction,
1Co 13:4 Love is *p,* love is kind.
Eph 4:2 humble and gentle; be *p,*
1Th 5:14 help the weak, be *p* with everyone.

**PATIENTLY (PATIENT)**
Ps 40:1 I waited *p* for the LORD;
Ro 8:25 we do not yet have, we wait for it *p*.

**PATTERN**
Ro 5:14 who was a *p* of the one to come.
12:2 longer to the *p* of this world,
2Ti 1:13 keep as the *p* of sound teaching,

**PAUL**
Also called Saul (Ac 13:9). Pharisee from Tarsus (Ac 9:11; Php 3:5). Apostle (Gal 1). At stoning of Stephen (Ac 8:1). Persecuted Church (Ac 9:1-2; Gal 1:13). Vision of Jesus on road to Damascus (Ac 9:4-9; 26:12-18). In Arabia (Gal 1:17). Preached in Damascus; escaped death through the wall in a basket (Ac 9:19-25). In Jerusalem; sent back to Tarsus (Ac 9:26-30).

Brought to Antioch by Barnabas (Ac 11:22-26). First missionary journey to Cyprus and Galatia (Ac 13-14). Stoned at Lystra (Ac 14:19-20). At Jerusalem council (Ac 15). Split with Barnabas over Mark (Ac 15:36-41).

Second missionary journey with Silas (Ac 16-20). Called to Macedonia (Ac 16:6-10). Freed from prison in Philippi (Ac 16:16-40). In Thessalonica (Ac 17:1-9). Speech in Athens (Ac 17:16-33). In Corinth (Ac 18). In Ephesus (Ac 19). Return to Jerusalem (Ac 20). Farewell to Ephesian elders (Ac 20:13-38). Arrival in Jerusalem (Ac 21:1-26). Arrested (Ac 21:27-36). Addressed crowds (Ac 22), Sanhedrin (Ac 23:1-11). Transferred to Caesarea (Ac 23:12-35). Trial before Felix (Ac 24), Festus (Ac 25:1-12). Before Agrippa (Ac 25:13-26:32). Voyage to Rome; shipwreck (Ac 27). Arrival in Rome (Ac 28).

**PAY (REPAID REPAY)**
Lev 26:43 They will *p* for their sins
Pr 22:17 *P* attention and listen
Mt 22:17 Is it right to *p* taxes to Caesar
Ro 13:6 This is also why you *p* taxes,
2Pe 1:19 you will do well to *p* attention to it,

**PEACE (PEACEMAKERS)**
Nu 6:26 and give you *p*." '
Ps 34:14 seek *p* and pursue it.
85:10 righteousness and *p* kiss each other
119:165 Great *p* have they who love your
122:6 Pray for the *p* of Jerusalem:
Pr 14:30 A heart at *p* gives life to the body,
17:1 Better a dry crust with *p* and quiet
Isa 9:6 Everlasting Father, Prince of *P*.
26:3 You will keep in perfect *p*
48:22 "There is no *p*," says the LORD,
Zec 9:10 He will proclaim *p* to the nations.
Mt 10:34 I did not come to bring *p*,
Lk 2:14 on earth *p* to men on whom his
Jn 14:27 *P* I leave with you; my *p*
16:33 so that in me you may have *p*.
Ro 5:1 we have *p* with God
1Co 7:15 God has called us to live in *p*.
14:33 a God of disorder but of *p*.
Gal 5:22 joy, *p*, patience, kindness,
Eph 2:14 he himself is our *p*, who has made
Php 4:7 the *p* of God, which transcends all
Col 1:20 by making *p* through his blood,
3:15 Let the *p* of Christ rule
1Th 5:3 While people are saying, "*P*
2Th 3:16 the Lord of *p* himself give you *p*
2Ti 2:22 righteousness, faith, love and *p*,
1Pe 3:11 he must seek *p* and pursue it.
Rev 6:4 power to take *p* from the earth

**PEACEMAKERS* (PEACE)**
Mt 5:9 Blessed are the *p*,
Jas 3:18 *P* who sow in peace raise a harvest

**PEARL* (PEARLS)**
Rev 21:21 each gate made of a single *p*.

**PEARLS (PEARL)**
Mt 7:6 do not throw your *p* to pigs.
13:45 like a merchant looking for fine *p*.
1Ti 2:9 or gold or *p* or expensive clothes,
Rev 21:21 The twelve gates were twelve *p*,

**PEKAH**
King of Israel (2Ki 15:25-31; Isa 7:1).

**PEKAHIAH***
Son of Menahem; king of Israel (2Ki 15:22-26).

**PEN**
Mt 5:18 letter, not the least stroke of a *p*,

**PENTECOST**
Ac 2:1 of *P* came, they were all together

**PEOPLE (PEOPLES)**
Dt 32:9 the LORD's portion is his *p*,
Ru 1:16 Your *p* will be my *p*
2Ch 7:14 if my *p*, who are called
Jer 24:7 They will be my *p*,
Zec 2:11 and will become my *p*.
Lk 2:10 joy that will be for all the *p*.
Ac 15:14 from the Gentiles a *p*.
2Co 6:16 and they will be my *p*."
Tit 2:14 a *p* that are his very own,
1Pe 2:9 you are a chosen *p*,
Rev 21:3 They will be his *p*,

**PEOPLES (PEOPLE)**
Da 7:14 all *p*, nations and men
Mic 4:1 and *p* will stream to it.

**PERCEIVING**
Isa 6:9 be ever seeing, but never *p*.'

**PERFECT (PERFECTER PERFECTION)**
SS 6:9 but my dove, my *p* one, is unique,
Isa 26:3 You will keep in *p* peace
Mt 5:48 as your heavenly Father is *p*.
Ro 12:2 his good, pleasing and *p* will.
2Co 12:9 for my power is made *p*
Col 1:28 so that we may present everyone *p*
3:14 binds them all together in *p* unity.
Heb 9:11 and more *p* tabernacle that is not
10:14 he has made *p* forever those who
Jas 1:17 Every good and *p* gift is from above
1:25 into the *p* law that gives freedom,
3:2 he is a *p* man, able
1Jn 4:18 But *p* love drives out fear,

**PERFECTER* (PERFECT)**
Heb 12:2 the author and *p* of our faith,

**PERFECTION (PERFECT)**
Ps 119:96 To all *p* I see a limit;
2Co 13:11 Aim for *p*, listen to my appeal,
Heb 7:11 If *p* could have been attained

**PERFORMS**
Ps 77:14 You are the God who *p* miracles;

**PERISH (PERISHABLE)**
Ps 1:6 but the way of the wicked will *p*.
102:26 They will *p*, but you remain;
Lk 13:3 unless you repent, you too will all *p*
Jn 10:28 eternal life, and they shall never *p*;
Col 2:22 These are all destined to *p* with use,
Heb 1:11 They will *p*, but you remain;
2Pe 3:9 not wanting anyone to *p*,

**PERISHABLE (PERISH)**
1Co 15:42 The body that is sown is *p*,

**PERJURERS**
1Ti 1:10 for slave traders and liars and *p*—

**PERMISSIBLE (PERMIT)**
1Co 10:23 "Everything is *p*"— but not

**PERMIT (PERMISSIBLE)**
1Ti 2:12 I do not *p* a woman to teach

**PERSECUTE (PERSECUTED PERSECUTION)**
Mt 5:11 *p* you and falsely say all kinds
Jn 15:20 they persecuted me, they will *p* you
Ac 9:4 why do you *p* me?" "Who are you,
Ro 12:14 Bless those who *p* you; bless

**PERSECUTED (PERSECUTE)**
1Co 4:12 when we are *p*, we endure it;
2Ti 3:12 life in Christ Jesus will be *p*,

**PERSECUTION (PERSECUTE)**
Ro 8:35 or hardship or *p* or famine

**PERSEVERANCE (PERSEVERE)**
Ro 5:3 we know that suffering produces *p*;
5:4 *p*, character; and character, hope.
Heb 12:1 run with *p* the race marked out
Jas 1:3 the testing of your faith develops *p*.
2Pe 1:6 *p*; and to *p*, godliness;

**PERSEVERE* (PERSEVERANCE PERSEVERED PERSEVERES)**
1Ti 4:16 *P* in them, because if you do,
Heb 10:36 You need to *p* so that

**PERSEVERED* (PERSEVERE)**

Heb 11:27 he *p* because he saw him who is
Jas 5:11 consider blessed those who have *p*.
Rev 2:3 You have *p* and have endured

**PERSEVERES* (PERSEVERE)**

1Co 13:7 trusts, always hopes, always *p*.
Jas 1:12 Blessed is the man who *p*

**PERSUADE**

2Co 5:11 is to fear the Lord, we try to *p* men.

**PERVERSION (PERVERT)**

Lev 18:23 sexual relations with it; that is a *p*.
Jude :7 up to sexual immorality and *p*.

**PERVERT (PERVERSION PERVERTS)**

Gal 1:7 are trying to *p* the gospel of Christ.

**PERVERTS* (PERVERT)**

1Ti 1:10 for murderers, for adulterers and *p*,

**PESTILENCE**

Ps 91:6 nor the *p* that stalks in the darkness

**PETER**

Apostle, brother of Andrew, also called Simon (Mt 10:2; Mk 3:16; Lk 6:14; Ac 1:13), and Cephas (Jn 1:42). Confession of Christ (Mt 16:13-20; Mk 8:27-30; Lk 9:18-27). At transfiguration (Mt 17:1-8; Mk 9:2-8; Lk 9:28-36; 2Pe 1:16-18). Caught fish with coin (Mt 17:24-27). Denial of Jesus predicted (Mt 26:31-35; Mk 14:27-31; Lk 22:31-34; Jn 13:31-38). Denied Jesus (Mt 26:69-75; Mk 14:66-72; Lk 22:54-62; Jn 18:15-27). Commissioned by Jesus to shepherd his flock (Jn 21:15-23).

Speech at Pentecost (Ac 2). Healed beggar (Ac 3:1-10). Speech at temple (Ac 3:11-26), before Sanhedrin (Ac 4:1-22). In Samaria (Ac 8:14-25). Sent by vision to Cornelius (Ac 10). Announced salvation of Gentiles in Jerusalem (Ac 11; 15). Freed from prison (Ac 12). Inconsistency at Antioch (Gal 2:11-21). At Jerusalem Council (Ac 15).

**PHARISEES**

Mt 5:20 surpasses that of the *P*

**PHILIP**

1. Apostle (Mt 10:3; Mk 3:18; Lk 6:14; Jn 1:43-48; 14:8; Ac 1:13).
2. Deacon (Ac 6:1-7); evangelist in Samaria (Ac 8:4-25), to Ethiopian (Ac 8:26-40).

**PHILOSOPHY***

Col 2:8 through hollow and deceptive *p*,

**PHYLACTERIES***

Mt 23:5 They make their *p* wide

**PHYSICAL**

1Ti 4:8 For *p* training is of some value,
Jas 2:16 but does nothing about his *p* needs,

**PIECES**

Ge 15:17 and passed between the *p*.
Jer 34:18 and then walked between its *p*.

**PIERCED**

Ps 22:16 they have *p* my hands and my feet.
Isa 53:5 But he was *p* for our transgressions,
Zec 12:10 look on me, the one they have *p*,
Jn 19:37 look on the one they have *p*."

**PIGS**

Mt 7:6 do not throw your pearls to *p*.

**PILATE**

Governor of Judea. Questioned Jesus (Mt 27:1-26; Mk 15:15; Lk 22:66-23:25; Jn 18:28-19:16); sent him to Herod (Lk 23:6-12); consented to his crucifixion when crowds chose Barabbas (Mt 27:15-26; Mk 15:6-15; Lk 23:13-25; Jn 19:1-10).

**PILLAR**

Ge 19:26 and she became a *p* of salt.
Ex 13:21 ahead of them in a *p* of cloud
1Ti 3:15 the *p* and foundation of the truth.

**PIT**

Ps 40:2 He lifted me out of the slimy *p*,
103:4 who redeems your life from the *p*
Mt 15:14 a blind man, both will fall into a *p*."

**PITIED**

1Co 15:19 we are to be *p* more than all men.

**PLAGUE**

2Ch 6:28 "When famine or *p* comes

**PLAIN**

Ro 1:19 what may be known about God is *p*

**PLAN (PLANNED PLANS)**

Job 42:2 no *p* of yours can be thwarted.
Pr 14:22 those who *p* what is good find love
Eph 1:11 predestined according to the *p*

**PLANK**

Mt 7:3 attention to the *p* in your own eye?

Lk 6:41 attention to the *p* in your own eye?

**PLANNED (PLAN)**
Ps 40:5 The things you *p* for us
Isa 46:11 what I have *p*, that will I do.
Heb 11:40 God had *p* something better for us

**PLANS (PLAN)**
Ps 20:4 and make all your *p* succeed.
33:11 *p* of the LORD stand firm forever,
Pr 20:18 Make *p* by seeking advice;
Isa 32:8 But the noble man makes noble *p*,

**PLANTED (PLANTS)**
Ps 1:3 He is like a tree *p* by streams
Mt 15:13 Father has not *p* will be pulled
1Co 3:6 I *p* the seed, Apollos watered it,

**PLANTS (PLANTED)**
1Co 3:7 So neither he who *p* nor he who
9:7 Who *p* a vineyard and does not eat

**PLATTER**
Mk 6:25 head of John the Baptist on a *p*."

**PLAYED**
Lk 7:32 " 'We *p* the flute for you,
1Co 14:7 anyone know what tune is being *p*

**PLEADED**
2Co 12:8 Three times I *p* with the Lord

**PLEASANT (PLEASE)**
Ps 16:6 for me in *p* places;
133:1 How good and *p* it is
147:1 how *p* and fitting to praise him!
Heb 12:11 No discipline seems *p* at the time,

**PLEASE (PLEASANT PLEASED PLEASES PLEASING PLEASURE PLEASURES)**
Pr 20:23 and dishonest scales do not *p* him.
Jer 6:20 your sacrifices do not *p* me."
Jn 5:30 for I seek not to *p* myself
Ro 8:8 by the sinful nature cannot *p* God.
15:2 Each of us should *p* his neighbor
1Co 7:32 affairs—how he can *p* the Lord.
10:33 I try to *p* everybody in every way.
2Co 5:9 So we make it our goal to *p* him,
Gal 1:10 or of God? Or am I trying to *p* men
1Th 4:1 how to live in order to *p* God,
2Ti 2:4 wants to *p* his commanding officer.
Heb 11:6 faith it is impossible to *p* God,

**PLEASED (PLEASE)**
Mt 3:17 whom I love; with him I am well *p*
1Co 1:21 God was *p* through the foolishness
Col 1:19 For God was *p* to have all his
Heb 11:5 commended as one who *p* God.
2Pe 1:17 whom I love; with him I am well *p*

**PLEASES (PLEASE)**
Ps 135:6 The LORD does whatever *p* him,
Pr 15:8 but the prayer of the upright *p* him.
Jn 3:8 The wind blows wherever it *p*.
8:29 for I always do what *p* him."
Col 3:20 in everything, for this *p* the Lord.
1Ti 2:3 This is good, and *p* God our Savior,
1Jn 3:22 his commands and do what *p* him.

**PLEASING (PLEASE)**
Ps 104:34 May my meditation be *p* to him,
Ro 12:1 *p* to God—which is your spiritual
Php 4:18 an acceptable sacrifice, *p* to God.
Heb 13:21 may he work in us what is *p* to him,

**PLEASURE (PLEASE)**
Ps 5:4 You are not a God who takes *p*
147:10 His *p* is not in the strength
Pr 21:17 He who loves *p* will become poor;
Eze 18:32 For I take no *p* in the death
Eph 1:5 in accordance with his *p* and will—
1:9 of his will according to his good *p*,
2Ti 3:4 lovers of *p* rather than lovers

**PLEASURES (PLEASE)**
Ps 16:11 with eternal *p* at your right hand.
Heb 11:25 rather than to enjoy the *p* of sin
2Pe 2:13 reveling in their *p* while they feast

**PLENTIFUL**
Mt 9:37 harvest is *p* but the workers are

**PLOW (PLOWSHARES)**
Lk 9:62 "No one who puts his hand to the *p*

**PLOWSHARES (PLOW)**
Isa 2:4 They will beat their swords into *p*
Joel 3:10 Beat your *p* into swords

**PLUNDER**
Ex 3:22 And so you will *p* the Egyptians."

**POINT**
Jas 2:10 yet stumbles at just one *p* is guilty

**POISON**
Mk 16:18 and when they drink deadly *p*,
Jas 3:8 It is a restless evil, full of deadly *p*.

**POLLUTE* (POLLUTED)**
Nu 35:33 " 'Do not *p* the land where you are.
Jude :8 these dreamers *p* their own bodies,

**POLLUTED* (POLLUTE)**
Ezr 9:11 entering to possess is a land *p*
Pr 25:26 Like a muddied spring or a *p* well
Ac 15:20 to abstain from food *p* by idols,
Jas 1:27 oneself from being *p* by the world.

**PONDER**
Ps 64:9 and *p* what he has done.
119:95 but I will *p* your statutes.

**POOR (POVERTY)**
Dt 15:4 there should be no *p* among you,
15:11 There will always be *p* people
Ps 34:6 This *p* man called, and the LORD
82:3 maintain the rights of the *p*
112:9 scattered abroad his gifts to the *p*,
Pr 10:4 Lazy hands make a man *p*,
13:7 to be *p*, yet has great wealth.
14:31 oppresses the *p* shows contempt
19:1 Better a *p* man whose walk is
19:17 to the *p* lends to the LORD,
22:2 Rich and *p* have this in common:
22:9 for he shares his food with the *p*.
28:6 Better a *p* man whose walk is
31:20 She opens her arms to the *p*
Isa 61:1 me to preach good news to the *p*.
Mt 5:3 saying: "Blessed are the *p* in spirit,
11:5 the good news is preached to the *p*.
19:21 your possessions and give to the *p*,
26:11 The *p* you will always have
Mk 12:42 But a *p* widow came and put
Ac 10:4 and gifts to the *p* have come up
1Co 13:3 If I give all I possess to the *p*
2Co 8:9 yet for your sakes he became *p*,
Jas 2:2 and a *p* man in shabby clothes

**PORTION**
Dt 32:9 For the LORD's *p* is his people,
2Ki 2:9 "Let me inherit a double *p*
La 3:24 to myself, "The LORD is my *p*;

**POSSESS (POSSESSING POSSESSION POSSESSIONS)**
Nu 33:53 for I have given you the land to *p*.
Jn 5:39 that by them you *p* eternal life.

**POSSESSING* (POSSESS)**
2Co 6:10 nothing, and yet *p* everything.

**POSSESSION (POSSESS)**
Ge 15:7 to give you this land to take *p* of it
Nu 13:30 "We should go up and take *p*
Eph 1:14 of those who are God's *p*—

**POSSESSIONS (POSSESS)**
Lk 12:15 consist in the abundance of his *p*."
2Co 12:14 what I want is not your *p* but you.
1Jn 3:17 If anyone has material *p*

**POSSIBLE**
Mt 19:26 but with God all things are *p*."
Mk 9:23 "Everything is *p* for him who
10:27 all things are *p* with God."
Ro 12:18 If it is *p*, as far as it depends on you,
1Co 9:22 by all *p* means I might save some.

**POT (POTSHERD POTTER POTTERY)**
2Ki 4:40 there is death in the *p*!"
Jer 18:4 But the *p* he was shaping

**POTSHERD (POT)**

Isa 45:9 a *p* among the potsherds

**POTTER (POT)**

Isa 29:16 Can the pot say of the *p*,
45:9 Does the clay say to the *p*,
64:8 We are the clay, you are the *p*;
Jer 18:6 "Like clay in the hand of the *p*,
Ro 9:21 Does not the *p* have the right

**POTTERY (POT)**

Ro 9:21 of clay some *p* for noble purposes

**POUR (POURED)**

Ps 62:8 *p* out your hearts to him,
Joel 2:28 I will *p* out my Spirit on all people.
Mal 3:10 *p* out so much blessing that you
Ac 2:17 I will *p* out my Spirit on all people.

**POURED (POUR)**

Ac 10:45 of the Holy Spirit had been *p* out
Ro 5:5 because God has *p* out his love

**POVERTY (POOR)**

Pr 14:23 but mere talk leads only to *p*.
21:5 as surely as haste leads to *p*.
30:8 give me neither *p* nor riches,
Mk 12:44 out of her *p*, put in everything—
2Co 8:2 and their extreme *p* welled up
8:9 through his *p* might become rich.

**POWER (POWERFUL POWERS)**

1Ch 29:11 LORD, is the greatness and the *p*
2Ch 32:7 for there is a greater *p* with us
Job 36:22 "God is exalted in his *p*.
Ps 63:2 and beheld your *p* and your glory.
68:34 Proclaim the *p* of God,
147:5 Great is our Lord and mighty in *p*;
Pr 24:5 A wise man has great *p*,
Isa 40:10 the Sovereign LORD comes with *p*
Zec 4:6 nor by *p*, but by my Spirit,'
Mt 22:29 do not know the Scriptures or the *p*
24:30 on the clouds of the sky, with *p*
Ac 1:8 you will receive *p* when the Holy
4:33 With great *p* the apostles
10:38 with the Holy Spirit and *p*,
Ro 1:16 it is the *p* of God for the salvation
1Co 1:18 to us who are being saved it is the *p*
15:56 of death is sin, and the *p*
2Co 12:9 for my *p* is made perfect
Eph 1:19 and his incomparably great *p*
Php 3:10 and the *p* of his resurrection
Col 1:11 strengthened with all *p* according
2Ti 1:7 but a spirit of *p*, of love
Heb 7:16 of the *p* of an indestructible life.
Rev 4:11 to receive glory and honor and *p*,
19:1 and glory and *p* belong to our God,
20:6 The second death has no *p*

**POWERFUL (POWER)**

Ps 29:4 The voice of the LORD is *p*;
Lk 24:19 *p* in word and deed before God
2Th 1:7 in blazing fire with his *p* angels.
Heb 1:3 sustaining all things by his *p* word.
Jas 5:16 The prayer of a righteous man is *p*

**POWERLESS**

Ro 5:6 when we were still *p*, Christ died
8:3 For what the law was *p* to do

**POWERS (POWER)**

Ro 8:38 nor any *p*, neither height nor depth
1Co 12:10 to another miraculous *p*,
Col 1:16 whether thrones or *p* or rulers
2:15 And having disarmed the *p*

**PRACTICE**

Lev 19:26 " 'Do not *p* divination or sorcery.
Mt 23:3 for they do not *p* what they preach.
Lk 8:21 hear God's word and put it into *p*."
Ro 12:13 *P* hospitality.
1Ti 5:4 to put their religion into *p* by caring

**PRAISE (PRAISED PRAISES PRAISING)**

Ex 15:2 He is my God, and I will *p* him,

Dt 32:3 Oh, *p* the greatness of our God!
Ru 4:14 said to Naomi: "*P* be to the LORD,
2Sa 22:47 The LORD lives! *P* be to my Rock
1Ch 16:25 is the LORD and most worthy of *p;*
2Ch 20:21 and to *p* him for the splendor
Ps 8:2 you have ordained *p*
33:1 it is fitting for the upright to *p* him.
34:1 his *p* will always be on my lips.
40:3 a hymn of *p* to our God.
48:1 the LORD, and most worthy of *p,*
68:19 *P* be to the Lord, to God our Savior
89:5 The heavens *p* your wonders,
100:4 and his courts with *p;*
105:2 Sing to him, sing *p* to him;
106:1 *P* the LORD.
119:175 Let me live that I may *p* you,
139:14 I *p* you because I am fearfully
145:21 Let every creature *p* his holy name
146:1 *P* the LORD, O my soul.
150:2 *p* him for his surpassing greatness.
150:6 that has breath *p* the LORD.
Pr 27:2 Let another *p* you, and not your
27:21 man is tested by the *p* he receives.
31:31 let her works bring her *p*
Mt 5:16 and *p* your Father in heaven.
Mt 21:16 you have ordained *p*'?"
Jn 12:43 for they loved *p* from men more
Eph 1:6 to the *p* of his glorious grace,
1:12 might be for the *p* of his glory.
1:14 to the *p* of his glory.
Heb 13:15 offer to God a sacrifice of *p*—
Jas 5:13 happy? Let him sing songs of *p.*

**PRAISED (PRAISE)**

1Ch 29:10 David *p* the LORD in the presence
Ne 8:6 Ezra *p* the LORD, the great God;
Da 2:19 Then Daniel *p* the God of heaven
Ro 9:5 who is God over all, forever *p!*
1Pe 4:11 that in all things God may be *p*

**PRAISES (PRAISE)**

2Sa 22:50 I will sing *p* to your name.
Ps 47:6 Sing *p* to God, sing *p;*
147:1 How good it is to sing *p* to our God,
Pr 31:28 her husband also, and he *p* her:

**PRAISING (PRAISE)**

Ac 10:46 speaking in tongues and *p* God.
1Co 14:16 If you are *p* God with your spirit,

**PRAY (PRAYED PRAYER PRAYERS PRAYING)**

Dt 4:7 is near us whenever we *p* to him?
1Sa 12:23 the LORD by failing to *p* for you.
2Ch 7:14 will humble themselves and *p*
Job 42:8 My servant Job will *p* for you,
Ps 122:6 *P* for the peace of Jerusalem:
Mt 5:44 and *p* for those who persecute you,
6:5 "And when you *p,* do not be like
6:9 "This, then, is how you should *p:*
26:36 Sit here while I go over there and *p*
Lk 6:28 *p* for those who mistreat you.
18:1 them that they should always *p*
22:40 "*P* that you will not fall
Ro 8:26 do not know what we ought to *p,*
1Co 14:13 in a tongue should *p* that he may
1Th 5:17 Be joyful always; *p* continually;
Jas 5:13 one of you in trouble? He should *p.*
5:16 *p* for each other so that you may be

**PRAYED (PRAY)**

1Sa 1:27 I *p* for this child, and the LORD
Jnh 2:1 From inside the fish Jonah *p*
Mk 14:35 *p* that if possible the hour might

**PRAYER (PRAY)**

2Ch 30:27 for their *p* reached heaven,
Ezr 8:23 about this, and he answered our *p.*
Ps 6:9 the LORD accepts my *p.*
86:6 Hear my *p,* O LORD;
Pr 15:8 but the *p* of the upright pleases him
Isa 56:7 a house of *p* for all nations."

Mt 21:13 house will be called a house of *p*,'
Mk 11:24 whatever you ask for in *p*,
Jn 17:15 My *p* is not that you take them out
Ac 6:4 and will give our attention to *p*
Php 4:6 but in everything, by *p* and petition
Jas 5:15 *p* offered in faith will make the sick
1Pe 3:12 and his ears are attentive to their *p*,

**PRAYERS (PRAY)**
1Ch 5:20 He answered their *p*, because they
Mk 12:40 and for a show make lengthy *p*.
1Pe 3:7 so that nothing will hinder your *p*.
Rev 5:8 which are the *p* of the saints.

**PRAYING (PRAY)**
Mk 11:25 And when you stand *p*,
Jn 17:9 I am not *p* for the world,
Ac 16:25 and Silas were *p* and singing hymns
Eph 6:18 always keep on *p* for all the saints.

**PREACH (PREACHED PREACHING)**
Mt 23:3 they do not practice what they *p*.
Mk 16:15 and *p* the good news to all creation.
Ac 9:20 At once he began to *p*
Ro 10:15 how can they *p* unless they are sent
15:20 to *p* the gospel where Christ was
1Co 1:17 to *p* the gospel—not with words
1:23 wisdom, but we *p* Christ crucified:
9:14 that those who *p* the gospel should
9:16 Woe to me if I do not *p* the gospel!
2Co 10:16 so that we can *p* the gospel
Gal 1:8 from heaven should *p* a gospel
2Ti 4:2 I give you this charge: *P* the Word;

**PREACHED (PREACH)**
Mk 13:10 And the gospel must first be *p*
Ac 8:4 had been scattered *p* the word
1Co 9:27 so that after I have *p* to others,
15:1 you of the gospel I *p* to you,
2Co 11:4 other than the Jesus we *p*,
Gal 1:8 other than the one we *p* to you,
Php 1:18 false motives or true, Christ is *p*.
1Ti 3:16 was *p* among the nations,

**PREACHING (PREACH)**
Ro 10:14 hear without someone *p* to them?
1Co 9:18 in *p* the gospel I may offer it free
1Ti 4:13 the public reading of Scripture, to *p*
5:17 especially those whose work is *p*

**PRECEPTS**
Ps 19:8 The *p* of the LORD are right,
111:7 all his *p* are trustworthy.
Ps 111:10 who follow his *p* have good
119:40 How I long for your *p*!
119:69 I keep your *p* with all my heart.
119:104 I gain understanding from your *p*;
119:159 See how I love your *p*;

**PRECIOUS**
Ps 19:10 They are more *p* than gold,
116:15 *P* in the sight of the LORD
Pr 8:11 for wisdom is more *p* than rubies,
Isa 28:16 a *p* cornerstone for a sure
1Pe 1:19 but with the *p* blood of Christ,
2:6 a chosen and *p* cornerstone,
2Pe 1:4 us his very great and *p* promises,

**PREDESTINED* (DESTINY)**
Ro 8:29 *p* to be conformed to the likeness
8:30 And those he *p*, he also called;
Eph 1:5 In love he *p* us to be adopted
1:11 having been *p* according

**PREDICTION***
Jer 28:9 only if his *p* comes true."

**PREPARE (PREPARED)**
Ps 23:5 You *p* a table before me
Am 4:12 *p* to meet your God, O Israel."
Jn 14:2 there to *p* a place for you.
Eph 4:12 to *p* God's people for works

**PREPARED (PREPARE)**

Mt 25:34 the kingdom *p* for you
1Co 2:9 what God has *p* for those who love
Eph 2:10 which God *p* in advance for us
2Ti 4:2 be *p* in season and out of season;
1Pe 3:15 Always be *p* to give an answer

**PRESENCE (PRESENT)**

Ex 25:30 Put the bread of the *P* on this table
Ezr 9:15 one of us can stand in your *p*."
Ps 31:20 the shelter of your *p* you hide them
89:15 who walk in the light of your *p*,
90:8 our secret sins in the light of your *p*
139:7 Where can I flee from your *p?*
Jer 5:22 "Should you not tremble in my *p?*
Heb 9:24 now to appear for us in God's *p*.
Jude :24 before his glorious *p* without fault

**PRESENT (PRESENCE)**

2Co 11:2 so that I might *p* you as a pure
Eph 5:27 and to *p* her to himself
2Ti 2:15 Do your best to *p* yourself to God

**PRESERVES**

Ps 1 19:50 Your promise *p* my life.

**PRESS (PRESSED PRESSURE)**

Php 3:14 I *p* on toward the goal

**PRESSED (PRESS)**

Lk 6:38 *p* down, shaken together

**PRESSURE (PRESS)**

2Co 1:8 We were under great *p*, far
11:28 I face daily the *p* of my concern

**PREVAILS**

1Sa 2:9 "It is not by strength that one *p;*

**PRICE**

Job 28:18 the *p* of wisdom is beyond rubies.
1Co 6:20 your own; you were bought at a *p*.
7:23 bought at a *p;* do not become slaves

**PRIDE (PROUD)**

Pr 8:13 I hate *p* and arrogance,
16:18 *P* goes before destruction,
Da 4:37 And those who walk in *p* he is able
Gal 6:4 Then he can take *p* in himself,
Jas 1:9 ought to take *p* in his high position.

**PRIEST (PRIESTHOOD PRIESTS)**

Heb 4:14 have a great high *p* who has gone
4:15 do not have a high *p* who is unable
7:26 Such a high *p* meets our need—
8:1 We do have such a high *p*,

**PRIESTHOOD (PRIEST)**

Heb 7:24 lives forever, he has a permanent *p*.
1Pe 2:5 into a spiritual house to be a holy *p*,
2:9 you are a chosen people, a royal *p*,

**PRIESTS (PRIEST)**

Ex 19:6 you will be for me a kingdom of *p*
Rev 5:10 to be a kingdom and *p*

**PRINCE**

Isa 9:6 Everlasting Father, *P* of Peace.
Jn 12:31 now the *p* of this world will be
Ac 5:31 as *P* and Savior that he might give

**PRISON (PRISONER)**

Isa 42:7 to free captives from *p*
Mt 25:36 I was in *p* and you came to visit me
1Pe 3:19 spirits in *p* who disobeyed long ago
Rev 20:7 Satan will be released from his *p*

**PRISONER (PRISON)**

Ro 7:23 and making me a *p* of the law of sin
Gal 3:22 declares that the whole world is a *p*
Eph 3:1 the *p* of Christ Jesus for the sake

**PRIVILEGE***

2Co 8:4 pleaded with us for the *p* of sharing

**PRIZE**

1Co 9:24 Run in such a way as to get the *p*.
Php 3:14 on toward the goal to win the *p*

**PROCLAIM (PROCLAIMED PROCLAIMING)**

1Ch 16:23 *p* his salvation day after day.
Ps 19:1 the skies *p* the work of his hands.
50:6 the heavens *p* his righteousness,
68:34 *P* the power of God,

Ps 118:17 will *p* what the LORD has done.
Zec 9:10 He will *p* peace to the nations.
Ac 20:27 hesitated to *p* to you the whole will
1Co 11:26 you *p* the Lord's death

**PROCLAIMED (PROCLAIM)**
Ro 15:19 I have fully *p* the gospel of Christ.
Col 1:23 that has been *p* to every creature

**PROCLAIMING (PROCLAIM)**
Ro 10:8 the word of faith we are *p:*

**PRODUCE (PRODUCES)**
Mt 3:8 *P* fruit in keeping with repentance.
3:10 tree that does not *p* good fruit will

**PRODUCES (PRODUCE)**
Pr 30:33 so stirring up anger *p* strife."
Ro 5:3 that suffering *p* perseverance;
Heb 12:11 it *p* a harvest of righteousness

**PROFANE**
Lev 22:32 Do not *p* my holy name.

**PROFESS***
1Ti 2:10 for women who *p* to worship God.
Heb 4:14 let us hold firmly to the faith we *p*.
10:23 unswervingly to the hope we *p*,

**PROMISE (PROMISED PROMISES)**
1Ki 8:20 The LORD has kept the *p* he made
Ac 2:39 The *p* is for you and your children
Gal 3:14 that by faith we might receive the *p*
1Ti 4:8 holding *p* for both the present life
2Pe 3:9 Lord is not slow in keeping his *p*,

**PROMISED (PROMISE)**
Ex 3:17 And I have *p* to bring you up out
Dt 26:18 his treasured possession as he *p*,
Ps 119:57 I have *p* to obey your words.
Ro 4:21 power to do what he had *p*.
Heb 10:23 for he who *p* is faithful.
2Pe 3:4 "Where is this 'coming' he *p?*

**PROMISES (PROMISE)**
Jos 21:45 one of all the LORD's good *p*
Ro 9:4 the temple worship and the *p*.
2Pe 1:4 us his very great and precious *p*,

**PROMPTED**
1Th 1:3 your labor *p* by love, and your
2Th 1:11 and every act *p* by your faith.

**PROPHECIES (PROPHESY)**
1Co 13:8 where there are *p*, they will cease;
1Th 5:20 do not treat *p* with contempt.

**PROPHECY (PROPHESY)**
1Co 14:1 gifts, especially the gift of *p*.
2Pe 1:20 you must understand that no *p*

**PROPHESY (PROPHECIES PROPHECY PROPHESYING PROPHET PROPHETS)**
Joel 2:28 Your sons and daughters will *p*,
Mt 7:22 Lord, did we not *p* in your name,
1Co 14:39 my brothers, be eager to *p*,

**PROPHESYING (PROPHESY)**
Ro 12:6 If a man's gift is *p*, let him use it

**PROPHET (PROPHESY)**
Dt 18:18 up for them a *p* like you
Am 7:14 "I was neither a *p* nor a prophet's
Mt 10:41 Anyone who receives a *p*
Lk 4:24 "no *p* is accepted in his hometown.

**PROPHETS (PROPHESY)**
Ps 105:15 do my *p* no harm."
Mt 5:17 come to abolish the Law or the *P;*
7:12 for this sums up the Law and the *P*.
24:24 false Christs and false *p* will appear
Lk 24:25 believe all that the *p* have spoken!
Ac 10:43 All the *p* testify about him that
1Co 12:28 second *p*, third teachers, then
14:32 The spirits of *p* are subject
Eph 2:20 foundation of the apostles and *p*,
Heb 1:1 through the *p* at many times
1Pe 1:10 Concerning this salvation, the *p*,
2Pe 1:19 word of the *p* made more certain,

**PROSPER (PROSPERITY PROSPERS)**
Pr 28:25 he who trusts in the LORD will *p.*

**PROSPERITY (PROSPER)**
Ps 73:3 when I saw the *p* of the wicked.
Pr 13:21 but *p* is the reward of the righteous.

**PROSPERS (PROSPER)**
Ps 1:3 Whatever he does *p.*

**PROSTITUTE (PROSTITUTES)**
1Co 6:15 of Christ and unite them with a *p?*

**PROSTITUTES (PROSTITUTE)**
Lk 15:30 property with *p* comes home,
1Co 6:9 male *p* nor homosexual offenders

**PROSTRATE**
Dt 9:18 again I fell *p* before the LORD

**PROTECT (PROTECTS)**
Ps 32:7 you will *p* me from trouble
Pr 2:11 Discretion will *p* you,
Jn 17:11 *p* them by the power of your name

**PROTECTS (PROTECT)**
1Co 13:7 It always *p,* always trusts,

**PROUD (PRIDE)**
Pr 16:5 The LORD detests all the *p*
Ro 12:16 Do not be *p,* but be willing
1Co 13:4 it does not boast, it is not *p.*

**PROVE**
Ac 26:20 *p* their repentance by their deeds.
1Co 4:2 been given a trust must *p* faithful.

**PROVIDE (PROVIDED PROVIDES)**
Ge 22:8 "God himself will *p* the lamb
Isa 43:20 because I *p* water in the desert
1Ti 5:8 If anyone does not *p*

**PROVIDED (PROVIDE)**
Jnh 1:17 But the LORD *p* a great fish
4:6 Then the LORD God *p* a vine
4:7 dawn the next day God *p* a worm,
4:8 God *p* a scorching east wind,

**PROVIDES (PROVIDE)**
1Ti 6:17 who richly *p* us with everything
1Pe 4:11 it with the strength God *p,*

**PROVOKED**
Ecc 7:9 Do not be quickly *p* in your spirit,

**PRUDENT**
Pr 14:15 a *p* man gives thought to his steps.
19:14 but a *p* wife is from the LORD.
Am 5:13 Therefore the *p* man keeps quiet

**PRUNING**
Isa 2:4 and their spears into *p* hooks.
Joel 3:10 and your *p* hooks into spears.

**PSALMS**
Eph 5:19 Speak to one another with *p,*
Col 3:16 and as you sing *p,* hymns

**PUBLICLY**
Ac 20:20 have taught you *p* and from house
1Ti 5:20 Those who sin are to be rebuked *p,*

**PUFFS**
1Co 8:1 Knowledge *p* up, but love builds up

**PULLING**
2Co 10:8 building you up rather than *p* you

**PUNISH (PUNISHED PUNISHES)**
Ex 32:34 I will *p* them for their sin."
Pr 23:13 if you *p* him with the rod, he will
Isa 13:11 I will *p* the world for its evil,
1Pe 2:14 by him to *p* those who do wrong

**PUNISHED (PUNISH)**
La 3:39 complain when *p* for his sins?
2Th 1:9 be *p* with everlasting destruction
Heb 10:29 to be *p* who has trampled the Son

**PUNISHES (PUNISH)**
Heb 12:6 and he *p* everyone he accepts

**PURE (PURIFIES PURIFY PURITY)**
2Sa 22:27 to the *p* you show yourself *p,*
Ps 24:4 who has clean hands and a *p* heart,
51:10 Create in me a *p* heart, O God,
119:9 can a young man keep his way *p?*

Pr 20:9 can say, "I have kept my heart *p;*
Isa 52:11 Come out from it and be *p,*
Hab 1:13 Your eyes are too *p* to look on evil;
Mt 5:8 Blessed are the *p* in heart,
2Co 11:2 I might present you as a *p* virgin
Php 4:8 whatever is *p,* whatever is lovely,
1Ti 5:22 Keep yourself *p.*
Tit 1:15 To the *p,* all things are *p,*
2:5 to be self-controlled and *p,*
Heb 13:4 and the marriage bed kept *p,*
1Jn 3:3 him purifies himself, just as he is *p.*

**PURGE**
Pr 20:30 and beatings *p* the inmost being.

**PURIFIES* (PURE)**
1Jn 1:7 of Jesus, his Son, *p* us from all sin.
3:3 who has this hope in him *p* himself,

**PURIFY (PURE)**
Tit 2:14 to *p* for himself a people that are
1Jn 1:9 and *p* us from all unrighteousness.

**PURITY (PURE)**
2Co 6:6 in *p,* understanding, patience
1Ti 4:12 in life, in love, in faith and in *p.*

**PURPOSE**
Pr 19:21 but it is the LORD's *p* that prevails
Isa 55:11 and achieve the *p* for which I sent it
Ro 8:28 have been called according to his *p.*
Php 2:2 love, being one in spirit and *p.*

**PURSES**
Lk 12:33 Provide *p* for yourselves that will

**PURSUE**
Ps 34:14 seek peace and *p* it.
2Ti 2:22 and *p* righteousness, faith,
1Pe 3:11 he must seek peace and *p* it.

**QUALITIES (QUALITY)**
2Pe 1:8 For if you possess these *q*

**QUALITY (QUALITIES)**
1Co 3:13 and the fire will test the *q*

**QUARREL (QUARRELSOME)**
Pr 15:18 but a patient man calms a *q.*
17:14 Starting a *q* is like breaching a dam;
17:19 He who loves a *q* loves sin;
2Ti 2:24 And the Lord's servant must not *q;*

**QUARRELSOME (QUARREL)**
Pr 19:13 a *q* wife is like a constant dripping.
1Ti 3:3 not violent but gentle, not *q,*

**QUICK-TEMPERED**
Tit 1:7 not *q,* not given to drunkenness,

**QUIET (QUIETNESS)**
Ps 23:2 he leads me beside *q* waters,
Zep 3:17 he will *q* you with his love,
Lk 19:40 he replied, "if they keep *q,*
1Ti 2:2 we may live peaceful and *q* lives
1Pe 3:4 beauty of a gentle and *q* spirit,

**QUIETNESS (QUIET)**
Isa 30:15 in *q* and trust is your strength,
32:17 the effect of righteousness will be *q*
1Ti 2:11 A woman should learn in *q*

**QUIVER**
Ps 127:5 whose *q* is full of them.

**RACE**
Ecc 9:11 The *r* is not to the swift
1Co 9:24 that in a *r* all the runners run,
2Ti 4:7 I have finished the *r,* I have kept
Heb 12:1 perseverance the *r* marked out

**RACHEL**
Daughter of Laban (Ge 29:16); wife of Jacob (Ge 29:28); bore two sons (Ge 30:22-24; 35:16-24; 46:19).

**RADIANCE (RADIANT)**
Heb 1:3 The Son is the *r* of God's glory

**RADIANT (RADIANCE)**
Ex 34:29 he was not aware that his face was *r*
Ps 34:5 Those who look to him are *r;*
SS 5:10 *Beloved* My lover is *r* and ruddy,
Isa 60:5 Then you will look and be *r,*
Eph 5:27 her to himself as a *r* church,

**RAIN (RAINBOW)**
Mt 5:45 and sends *r* on the righteous

**RAINBOW (RAIN)**
Ge 9:13 I have set my *r* in the clouds,

**RAISED (RISE)**
Ro 4:25 was *r* to life for our justification.
10:9 in your heart that God *r* him
1Co 15:4 that he was *r* on the third day

**RAN (RUN)**
Jnh 1:3 But Jonah *r* away from the LORD

**RANSOM**
Mt 20:28 and to give his life as a *r* for many."
Heb 9:15 as a *r* to set them free

**RAVENS**
1Ki 17:6 The *r* brought him bread
Lk 12:24 Consider the *r:* They do not sow

**READ (READS)**
Jos 8:34 Joshua *r* all the words of the law—
Ne 8:8 They *r* from the Book of the Law
2Co 3:2 known and *r* by everybody.

**READS (READ)**
Rev 1:3 Blessed is the one who *r* the words

**REAL (REALITY)**
Jn 6:55 is *r* food and my blood is *r* drink.

**REALITY* (REAL)**
Col 2:17 the *r,* however, is found in Christ.

**REAP (REAPS)**
Job 4:8 and those who sow trouble *r* it.
2Co 9:6 generously will also *r* generously.

**REAPS (REAP)**
Gal 6:7 A man *r* what he sows.

**REASON**
Isa 1:18 "Come now, let us *r* together,"
1Pe 3:15 to give the *r* for the hope that you

**REBEKAH**
Sister of Laban, secured as bride for Isaac (Ge 24). Mother of Esau and Jacob (Ge 25:19-26). Taken by Abimelech as sister of Isaac; returned (Ge 26:1-11). Encouraged Jacob to trick Isaac out of blessing (Ge 27:1-17).

**REBEL**
Mt 10:21 children will *r* against their parents

**REBUKE (REBUKED REBUKING)**
Pr 9:8 *r* a wise man and he will love you.
27:5 Better is open *r*
Lk 17:3 "If your brother sins, *r* him,
2Ti 4:2 correct, *r* and encourage—
Rev 3:19 Those whom I love I *r*

**REBUKED (REBUKE)**
1Ti 5:20 Those who sin are to be *r* publicly,

**REBUKING (REBUKE)**
2Ti 3:16 *r,* correcting and training

**RECEIVE (RECEIVED RECEIVES)**
Ac 1:8 you will *r* power when the Holy
20:35 'It is more blessed to give than to *r*.'
2Co 6:17 and I will *r* you."
Rev 4:11 to *r* glory and honor and power,

**RECEIVED (RECEIVE)**
Mt 6:2 they have *r* their reward in full.
10:8 Freely you have *r,* freely give.
1Co 11:23 For I *r* from the Lord what I
Col 2:6 just as you *r* Christ Jesus as Lord,
1Pe 4:10 should use whatever gift he has *r*

**RECEIVES (RECEIVE)**
Mt 7:8 everyone who asks *r;* he who seeks
10:40 he who *r* me *r* the one who sent me.
Ac 10:43 believes in him *r* forgiveness of sins

**RECKONING**
Isa 10:3 What will you do on the day of *r,*

**RECOGNIZE (RECOGNIZED)**
Mt 7:16 By their fruit you will *r* them.

**RECOGNIZED (RECOGNIZE)**
Mt 12:33 for a tree is *r* by its fruit.
Ro 7:13 in order that sin might be *r* as sin,

**RECOMPENSE**
Isa 40:10 and his *r* accompanies him.

**RECONCILE (RECONCILED RECONCILIATION)**
Eph 2:16 in this one body to *r* both of them

**RECONCILED (RECONCILE)**
Mt 5:24 First go and be *r* to your brother;
Ro 5:10 we were *r* to him through the death
2Co 5:18 who *r* us to himself through Christ

**RECONCILIATION* (RECONCILE)**
Ro 5:11 whom we have now received *r.*
11:15 For if their rejection is the *r*
2Co 5:18 and gave us the ministry of *r:*
5:19 committed to us the message of *r.*

**RECORD**
Ps 130:3 If you, O LORD, kept a *r* of sins,

**RED**
Isa 1:18 though they are *r* as crimson,

**REDEEM (KINSMAN-REDEEMER REDEEMED REDEEMER REDEMPTION)**
2Sa 7:23 on earth that God went out to *r*
Ps 49:7 No man can *r* the life of another
Gal 4:5 under law, to *r* those under law,

**REDEEMED (REDEEM)**
Gal 3:13 Christ *r* us from the curse
1Pe 1:18 or gold that you were *r*

**REDEEMER (REDEEM)**
Job 19:25 I know that my *R* lives,

**REDEMPTION (REDEEM)**
Ps 130:7 and with him is full *r.*
Lk 21:28 because your *r* is drawing near."
Ro 8:23 as sons, the *r* of our bodies.
Eph 1:7 In him we have *r* through his blood
Col 1:14 in whom we have *r,* the forgiveness
Heb 9:12 having obtained eternal *r.*

**REFLECT**
2Co 3:18 unveiled faces all *r* the Lord's

**REFUGE**
Nu 35:11 towns to be your cities of *r,*
Dt 33:27 The eternal God is your *r,*
Ru 2:12 wings you have come to take *r.*"
Ps 46:1 God is our *r* and strength,
91:2 "He is my *r* and my fortress,

**REHOBOAM**
Son of Solomon (1Ki 11:43; 1Ch 3:10). Harsh treatment of subjects caused divided kingdom (1Ki 12:1-24; 14:21-31; 2Ch 10-12).

**REIGN**
Ex 15:18 The LORD will *r*
Ro 6:12 Therefore do not let sin *r*
1Co 15:25 For he must *r* until he has put all
2Ti 2:12 we will also *r* with him.
Rev 20:6 will *r* with him for a thousand years

**REJECTED (REJECTS)**
Ps 118:22 The stone the builders *r*
Isa 53:3 He was despised and *r* by men,
1Ti 4:4 nothing is to be *r* if it is received
1Pe 2:4 *r* by men but chosen by God
2:7 "The stone the builders *r*

**REJECTS (REJECTED)**
Lk 10:16 but he who *r* me *r* him who sent me
Jn 3:36 whoever *r* the Son will not see life,

**REJOICE (JOY)**
Ps 2:11 and *r* with trembling.
66:6 come, let us *r* in him.
118:24 let us *r* and be glad in it.
Pr 5:18 may you *r* in the wife of your youth
Lk 10:20 but *r* that your names are written
15:6 '*R* with me; I have found my lost
Ro 12:15 Rejoice with those who *r;* mourn
Php 4:4 *R* in the Lord always.

**REJOICES (JOY)**
Isa 61:10 my soul *r* in my God.
Lk 1:47 and my spirit *r* in God my Savior,
1Co 12:26 if one part is honored, every part *r*
13:6 delight in evil but *r* with the truth.

**REJOICING (JOY)**
Ps 30:5 but *r* comes in the morning.
Lk 15:7 in the same way there will be more *r*
Ac 5:41 *r* because they had been counted

**RELIABLE**
2Ti 2:2 witnesses entrust to *r* men who will

**RELIGION**
1Ti 5:4 all to put their *r* into practice
Jas 1:27 *R* that God our Father accepts

**REMAIN (REMAINS)**
Nu 33:55 allow to *r* will become barbs
Jn 15:7 If you *r* in me and my words
Ro 13:8 Let no debt *r* outstanding,
1Co 13:13 And now these three *r:* faith,
2Ti 2:13 he will *r* faithful,

**REMAINS (REMAIN)**
Ps 146:6 the LORD, who *r* faithful forever.
Heb 7:3 Son of God he *r* a priest forever.

**REMEMBER (REMEMBERS REMEMBRANCE)**
Ex 20:8 "*R* the Sabbath day
1Ch 16:12 *R* the wonders he has done,
Ecc 12:1 *R* your Creator
Jer 31:34 and will *r* their sins no more."
Gal 2:10 we should continue to *r* the poor,
Php 1:3 I thank my God every time I *r* you.
Heb 8:12 and will *r* their sins no more."

**REMEMBERS (REMEMBER)**
Ps 103:14 he *r* that we are dust.
111:5 he *r* his covenant forever.
Isa 43:25 and *r* your sins no more.

**REMEMBRANCE (REMEMBER)**
1Co 11:24 which is for you; do this in *r* of me

**REMIND**
Jn 14:26 will *r* you of everything I have said

**REMOVED**
Ps 30:11 you *r* my sackcloth and clothed me
103:12 so far has he *r* our transgressions
Jn 20:1 and saw that the stone had been *r*

**RENEW (RENEWED RENEWING)**
Ps 51:10 and *r* a steadfast spirit within me.
Isa 40:31 will *r* their strength.

**RENEWED (RENEW)**
Ps 103:5 that your youth is *r* like the eagle's.
2Co 4:16 yet inwardly we are being *r* day

**RENEWING (RENEW)**
Ro 12:2 transformed by the *r* of your mind.

**RENOUNCE (RENOUNCES)**
Da 4:27 *R* your sins by doing what is right,

**RENOUNCES (RENOUNCE)**
Pr 28:13 confesses and *r* them finds

**RENOWN**
Isa 63:12 to gain for himself everlasting *r*,
Jer 32:20 have gained the *r* that is still yours.

**REPAID (PAY)**
Lk 14:14 you will be *r* at the resurrection
Col 3:25 Anyone who does wrong will be *r*

**REPAY (PAY)**
Dt 32:35 It is mine to avenge; I will *r*.
Ru 2:12 May the LORD *r* you
Ps 116:12 How can I *r* the LORD
Ro 12:19 "It is mine to avenge; I will *r*,"
1Pe 3:9 Do not *r* evil with evil

**REPENT (REPENTANCE REPENTS)**
Job 42:6 and *r* in dust and ashes."
Jer 15:19 "If you *r*, I will restore you
Mt 4:17 "*R*, for the kingdom of heaven is
Lk 13:3 unless you *r*, you too will all perish.
Ac 2:38 Peter replied, "*R* and be baptized,
17:30 all people everywhere to *r*.

**REPENTANCE (REPENT)**
Lk 3:8 Produce fruit in keeping with *r*.
5:32 call the righteous, but sinners to *r*."
Ac 26:20 and prove their *r* by their deeds.
2Co 7:10 Godly sorrow brings *r* that leads

**REPENTS (REPENT)**
Lk 15:10 of God over one sinner who *r*."
17:3 rebuke him, and if he *r*, forgive him

**REPROACH**
1Ti 3:2 Now the overseer must be above *r*,

**REPUTATION**
1Ti 3:7 also have a good *r* with outsiders,

**REQUESTS**
Ps 20:5 May the LORD grant all your *r*.
Php 4:6 with thanksgiving, present your *r*

**REQUIRE**
Mic 6:8 And what does the LORD *r* of you

**RESCUE (RESCUES)**
Da 6:20 been able to *r* you from the lions?"
2Pe 2:9 how to *r* godly men from trials

**RESCUES (RESCUE)**
1Th 1:10 who *r* us from the coming wrath.

**RESIST**
Jas 4:7 *R* the devil, and he will flee
1Pe 5:9 *R* him, standing firm in the faith,

**RESOLVED**
Ps 17:3 I have *r* that my mouth will not sin.
Da 1:8 But Daniel *r* not to defile himself
1Co 2:2 For I *r* to know nothing while I was

**RESPECT (RESPECTABLE)**
Lev 19:3 " 'Each of you must *r* his mother
19:32 show *r* for the elderly and revere
Pr 11:16 A kindhearted woman gains *r*,
Mal 1:6 where is the *r* due me?" says
1Th 4:12 so that your daily life may win the *r*
5:12 to *r* those who work hard
1Ti 3:4 children obey him with proper *r*.
1Pe 2:17 Show proper *r* to everyone:
3:7 them with *r* as the weaker partner

**RESPECTABLE* (RESPECT)**
1Ti 3:2 self-controlled, *r*, hospitable,

**REST**
Ex 31:15 the seventh day is a Sabbath of *r*,
Ps 91:1 will *r* in the shadow
Jer 6:16 and you will find *r* for your souls.
Mt 11:28 and burdened, and I will give you *r*.

**RESTITUTION**
Ex 22:3 "A thief must certainly make *r*,
Lev 6:5 He must make *r* in full, add a fifth

**RESTORE (RESTORES)**
Ps 51:12 *R* to me the joy of your salvation
Gal 6:1 are spiritual should *r* him gently.

**RESTORES (RESTORE)**
Ps 23:3 he *r* my soul.

**RESURRECTION**
Mt 22:30 At the *r* people will neither marry
Lk 14:14 repaid at the *r* of the righteous."
Jn 11:25 Jesus said to her, "I am the *r*
Ro 1:4 Son of God by his *r* from the dead:
1Co 15:12 some of you say that there is no *r*
Php 3:10 power of his *r* and the fellowship
Rev 20:5 This is the first *r*.

**RETRIBUTION**
Jer 51:56 For the LORD is a God of *r*;

**RETURN**
2Ch 30:9 If you *r* to the LORD, then your
Ne 1:9 but if you *r* to me and obey my
Isa 55:11 It will not *r* to me empty,
Hos 6:1 "Come, let us *r* to the LORD.
Joel 2:12 "*r* to me with all your heart,

**REVEALED (REVELATION)**
Dt 29:29 but the things *r* belong to us
Isa 40:5 the glory of the LORD will be *r*,
Mt 11:25 and *r* them to little children.
Ro 1:17 a righteousness from God is *r*,
8:18 with the glory that will be *r* in us.

**REVELATION (REVEALED)**
Gal 1:12 I received it by *r* from Jesus Christ.
Rev 1:1 *r* of Jesus Christ, which God gave

**REVENGE (VENGEANCE)**
Lev 19:18 " 'Do not seek *r* or bear a grudge
Ro 12:19 Do not take *r*, my friends,

**REVERE (REVERENCE)**
Ps 33:8 let all the people of the world *r* him

**REVERENCE (REVERE)**
Lev 19:30 and have *r* for my sanctuary.
Ps 5:7 in *r* will I bow down
Col 3:22 of heart and *r* for the Lord.
1Pe 3:2 when they see the purity and *r*

**REVIVE (REVIVING)**
Ps 85:6 Will you not *r* us again,
Isa 57:15 to *r* the spirit of the lowly

**REVIVING (REVIVE)**
Ps 19:7 *r* the soul.

**REWARD (REWARDED)**
Ps 19:11 in keeping them there is great *r*.

- Ps 127:3 children a *r* from him.
- Pr 19:17 he will *r* him for what he has done.
- 25:22 and the LORD will *r* you.
- 31:31 Give her the *r* she has earned,
- Jer 17:10 to *r* a man according to his conduct
- Mt 5:12 because great is your *r* in heaven,
- 6:5 they have received their *r* in full.
- 16:27 and then he will *r* each person
- 1Co 3:14 built survives, he will receive his *r*.
- Rev 22:12 I am coming soon! My *r* is with me

### REWARDED (REWARD)

- Ru 2:12 May you be richly *r* by the LORD,
- Ps 18:24 The LORD has *r* me according
- Pr 14:14 and the good man *r* for his.
- 1Co 3:8 and each will be *r* according

### RICH (RICHES)

- Pr 23:4 Do not wear yourself out to get *r*;
- Jer 9:23 or the *r* man boast of his riches,
- Mt 19:23 it is hard for a *r* man
- 2Co 6:10 yet making many *r*; having nothing
- 8:9 he was *r*, yet for your sakes he
- 1Ti 6:17 Command those who are *r*

### RICHES (RICH)

- Ps 119:14 as one rejoices in great *r*.
- Pr 30:8 give me neither poverty nor *r*,
- Isa 10:3 Where will you leave your *r*?
- Ro 9:23 to make the *r* of his glory known
- 11:33 the depth of the *r* of the wisdom
- Eph 2:7 he might show the incomparable *r*
- 3:8 to the Gentiles the unsearchable *r*
- Col 1:27 among the Gentiles the glorious *r*

### RID

- Ge 21:10 "Get *r* of that slave woman
- 1Co 5:7 Get *r* of the old yeast that you may
- Gal 4:30 "Get *r* of the slave woman

### RIGHT (RIGHTS)

- Ge 18:25 the Judge of all the earth do *r*?"
- Ex 15:26 and do what is *r* in his eyes,
- Dt 5:32 do not turn aside to the *r*
- Ps 16:8 Because he is at my *r* hand,
- 19:8 The precepts of the LORD are *r*,
- 63:8 your *r* hand upholds me.
- 110:1 "Sit at my *r* hand
- Pr 4:27 Do not swerve to the *r* or the left;
- 14:12 There is a way that seems *r*
- Isa 1:17 learn to do *r*!
- Jer 23:5 and do what is just and *r* in the land
- Hos 14:9 The ways of the LORD are *r*;
- Mt 6:3 know what your *r* hand is doing,
- Jn 1:12 he gave the *r* to become children
- Ro 9:21 Does not the potter have the *r*
- 12:17 careful to do what is *r* in the eyes
- Eph 1:20 and seated him at his *r* hand
- Php 4:8 whatever is *r*, whatever is pure,
- 2Th 3:13 never tire of doing what is *r*.

### RIGHTEOUS (RIGHTEOUSNESS)

- Ps 34:15 The eyes of the LORD are on the *r*
- 37:25 yet I have never seen the *r* forsaken
- 119:137 *R* are you, O LORD,
- 143:2 for no one living is *r* before you.
- Pr 3:33 but he blesses the home of the *r*.
- 11:30 The fruit of the *r* is a tree of life,
- 18:10 the *r* run to it and are safe.
- Isa 64:6 and all our *r* acts are like filthy rags
- Hab 2:4 but the *r* will live by his faith—
- Mt 5:45 rain on the *r* and the unrighteous.
- 9:13 For I have not come to call the *r*,
- 13:49 and separate the wicked from the *r*
- 25:46 to eternal punishment, but the *r*
- Ro 1:17 as it is written: "The *r* will live
- 3:10 "There is no one *r*, not even one;
- 1Ti 1:9 that law is made not for the *r*
- 1Pe 3:18 the *r* for the unrighteous,
- 1Jn 3:7 does what is right is *r*, just as he is *r*.

Rev 19:8 stands for the *r* acts of the saints.)

**RIGHTEOUSNESS (RIGHTEOUS)**

Ge 15:6 and he credited it to him as *r*.
1Sa 26:23 LORD rewards every man for his *r*
Ps 9:8 He will judge the world in *r*;
23:3 He guides me in paths of *r*
45:7 You love *r* and hate wickedness;
85:10 *r* and peace kiss each other.
89:14 *R* and justice are the foundation
111:3 and his *r* endures forever.
Pr 14:34 *R* exalts a nation,
21:21 He who pursues *r* and love
Isa 5:16 will show himself holy by his *r*.
59:17 He put on *r* as his breastplate,
Eze 18:20 The *r* of the righteous man will be
Da 9:24 to bring in everlasting *r*,
12:3 and those who lead many to *r*,
Mal 4:2 the sun of *r* will rise with healing
Mt 5:6 those who hunger and thirst for *r*,
5:20 unless your *r* surpasses that
6:33 But seek first his kingdom and his *r*
Ro 4:3 and it was credited to him as *r*."
4:9 faith was credited to him as *r*.
6:13 body to him as instruments of *r*.
2Co 5:21 that in him we might become the *r*
Gal 2:21 for if *r* could be gained
3:6 and it was credited to him as *r*."
Eph 6:14 with the breastplate of *r* in place,
Php 3:9 not having a *r* of my own that
2Ti 3:16 correcting and training in *r*,
4:8 is in store for me the crown of *r*,
Heb 11:7 became heir of the *r* that comes
2Pe 2:21 not to have known the way of *r*,

**RIGHTS (RIGHT)**

La 3:35 to deny a man his *r*
Gal 4:5 that we might receive the full *r*

**RISE (RAISED)**

Isa 26:19 their bodies will *r*.
Mt 27:63 'After three days I will *r* again.'
Jn 5:29 those who have done good will *r*
1Th 4:16 and the dead in Christ will *r* first.

**ROAD**

Mt 7:13 and broad is the *r* that leads

**ROBBERS**

Jer 7:11 become a den of *r* to you?
Mk 15:27 They crucified two *r* with him,
Lk 19:46 but you have made it 'a den of *r*.' "
Jn 10:8 came before me were thieves and *r*,

**ROCK**

Ps 18:2 The LORD is my *r*, my fortress
40:2 he set my feet on a *r*
Mt 7:24 man who built his house on the *r*.
16:18 and on this *r* I will build my church
Ro 9:33 and a *r* that makes them fall,
1Co 10:4 the spiritual *r* that accompanied

**ROD**

Ps 23:4 your *r* and your staff,
Pr 13:24 He who spares the *r* hates his son,
23:13 if you punish him with the *r*,

**ROOM (ROOMS)**

Mt 6:6 But when you pray, go into your *r*,
Lk 2:7 there was no *r* for them in the inn.
Jn 21:25 the whole world would not have *r*

**ROOMS (ROOM)**

Jn 14:2 In my Father's house are many *r*;

**ROOT**

Isa 53:2 and like a *r* out of dry ground.
1Ti 6:10 of money is a *r* of all kinds of evil.

**ROYAL**

Jas 2:8 If you really keep the *r* law found
1Pe 2:9 a *r* priesthood, a holy nation,

**RUBBISH***

Php 3:8 I consider them *r*, that I may gain

**RUDE***

1Co 13:5 It is not *r*, it is not self-seeking,

**RUIN (RUINS)**

Pr 18:24 many companions may come to *r*,

1Ti 6:9 desires that plunge men into *r*

**RUINS (RUIN)**
Pr 19:3 A man's own folly *r* his life,
2Ti 2:14 and only *r* those who listen.

**RULE (RULER RULERS RULES)**
1Sa 12:12 'No, we want a king to *r* over us'—
Ps 2:9 You will *r* them with an iron
119:133 let no sin *r* over me.
Zec 9:10 His *r* will extend from sea to sea
Col 3:15 the peace of Christ *r* in your hearts,
Rev 2:27 He will *r* them with an iron scepter;

**RULER (RULE)**
Ps 8:6 You made him *r* over the works
Eph 2:2 of the *r* of the kingdom of the air,
1Ti 6:15 God, the blessed and only *R*,

**RULERS (RULE)**
Ps 2:2 and the *r* gather together
Col 1:16 or powers or *r* or authorities;

**RULES (RULE)**
Ps 103:19 and his kingdom *r* over all.
Lk 22:26 one who *r* like the one who serves.
2Ti 2:5 he competes according to the *r*.

**RUMORS**
Mt 24:6 You will hear of wars and *r* of wars,

**RUN (RAN)**
Isa 40:31 they will *r* and not grow weary,
1Co 9:24 *R* in such a way as to get the prize.
Heb 12:1 let us *r* with perseverance the race

**RUST**
Mt 6:19 where moth and *r* destroy,

**RUTH***
Moabitess; widow who went to Bethlehem with mother-in-law Naomi (Ru 1). Gleaned in field of Boaz; shown favor (Ru 2). Proposed marriage to Boaz (Ru 3). Married (Ru 4:1-12); bore Obed, ancestor of David (Ru 4:13-22), Jesus (Mt 1:5).

**SABBATH**
Ex 20:8 "Remember the *S* day
Dt 5:12 "Observe the *S* day
Col 2:16 a New Moon celebration or a *S* day

**SACKCLOTH**
Mt 11:21 would have repented long ago in *s*

**SACRED**
Mt 7:6 "Do not give dogs what is *s;*
1Co 3:17 for God's temple is *s*, and you are

**SACRIFICE (SACRIFICED SACRIFICES)**
Ge 22:2 *S* him there as a burnt offering
Ex 12:27 'It is the Passover *s* to the LORD,
1Sa 15:22 To obey is better than *s*,
Hos 6:6 For I desire mercy, not *s*,
Mt 9:13 this means: 'I desire mercy, not *s*.'
Heb 9:26 away with sin by the *s* of himself.
13:15 offer to God a *s* of praise—
1Jn 2:2 He is the atoning *s* for our sins,

**SACRIFICED (SACRIFICE)**
1Co 5:7 our Passover lamb, has been *s*.
8:1 Now about food *s* to idols:
Heb 9:28 so Christ was *s* once

**SACRIFICES (SACRIFICE)**
Ps 51:17 The *s* of God are a broken spirit;
Ro 12:1 to offer your bodies as living *s*,

**SADDUCEES**
Mk 12:18 *S*, who say there is no resurrection,

**SAFE (SAVE)**
Ps 37:3 in the land and enjoy *s* pasture.
Pr 18:10 the righteous run to it and are *s*.

**SAFETY (SAVE)**
Ps 4:8 make me dwell in *s*.
1Th 5:3 people are saying, "Peace and *s*,"

**SAINTS**
Ps 116:15 is the death of his *s*.
Ro 8:27 intercedes for the *s* in accordance
Eph 1:18 of his glorious inheritance in the *s*,
6:18 always keep on praying for all the *s*
Rev 5:8 which are the prayers of the *s*.
19:8 for the righteous acts of the *s*.)

**SAKE**

Ps 44:22 Yet for your *s* we face death all day
Php 3:7 loss for the *s* of Christ.
Heb 11:26 He regarded disgrace for the *s*

**SALT**

Ge 19:26 and she became a pillar of *s*.
Mt 5:13 "You are the *s* of the earth.

**SALVATION (SAVE)**

Ex 15:2 he has become my *s*.
1Ch 16:23 proclaim his *s* day after day.
Ps 27:1 The LORD is my light and my *s*—
51:12 Restore to me the joy of your *s*
62:2 He alone is my rock and my *s*;
85:9 Surely his *s* is near those who fear
96:2 proclaim his *s* day after day.
Isa 25:9 let us rejoice and be glad in his *s*."
45:17 the LORD with an everlasting *s*;
51:6 But my *s* will last forever,
59:17 and the helmet of *s* on his head;
61:10 me with garments of *s*
Jnh 2:9 *S* comes from the LORD."
Zec 9:9 righteous and having *s*,
Lk 2:30 For my eyes have seen your *s*,
Jn 4:22 for *s* is from the Jews.
Ac 4:12 *S* is found in no one else,
13:47 that you may bring *s* to the ends
Ro 11:11 *s* has come to the Gentiles
2Co 7:10 brings repentance that leads to *s*
Eph 6:17 Take the helmet of *s* and the sword
Php 2:12 to work out your *s* with fear
1Th 5:8 and the hope of *s* as a helmet.
2Ti 3:15 wise for *s* through faith
Heb 2:3 escape if we ignore such a great *s*?
6:9 case—things that accompany *s*.
1Pe 1:10 Concerning this *s*, the prophets,
2:2 by it you may grow up in your *s*,

**SAMARITAN**

Lk 10:33 But a *S*, as he traveled, came where

**SAMSON**

Danite judge. Birth promised (Jdg 13). Married to Philistine (Jdg 14). Vengeance on Philistines (Jdg 15). Betrayed by Delilah (Jdg 16:1-22). Death (Jdg 16:23-31). Feats of strength: killed lion (Jdg 14:6), 30 Philistines (Jdg 14:19), 1,000 Philistines with jawbone (Jdg 15:13-17), carried off gates of Gaza (Jdg 16:3), pushed down temple of Dagon (Jdg 16:25-30).

**SAMUEL**

Ephraimite judge and prophet (Heb 11:32). Birth prayed for (1Sa 1:10-18). Dedicated to temple by Hannah (1Sa 1:21-28). Raised by Eli (1Sa 2:11, 18-26). Called as prophet (1Sa 3). Led Israel to victory over Philistines (1Sa 7). Asked by Israel for a king (1Sa 8). Anointed Saul as king (1Sa 9-10). Farewell speech (1Sa 12). Rebuked Saul for sacrifice (1Sa 13). Announced rejection of Saul (1Sa 15). Anointed David as king (1Sa 16). Protected David from Saul (1Sa 19:18-24). Death (1Sa 25:1). Returned from dead to condemn Saul (1Sa 28).

**SANCTIFIED (SANCTIFY)**

Ac 20:32 among all those who are *s*.
Ro 15:16 to God, *s* by the Holy Spirit.
1Co 6:11 But you were washed, you were *s*,
7:14 and the unbelieving wife has been *s*
Heb 10:29 blood of the covenant that *s* him,

**SANCTIFY (SANCTIFIED SANCTIFYING)**

1Th 5:23 *s* you through and through.

**SANCTIFYING (SANCTIFY)**

2Th 2:13 through the *s* work of the Spirit

**SANCTUARY**

Ex 25:8 "Then have them make a *s* for me,

**SAND**

Ge 22:17 and as the *s* on the seashore.
Mt 7:26 man who built his house on *s*.

**SANDALS**

Ex 3:5 off your *s*, for the place where you
Jos 5:15 off your *s*, for the place where you

**SANG (SING)**

Job 38:7 while the morning stars *s* together
Rev 5:9 And they *s* a new song:

## SARAH

Wife of Abraham, originally named Sarai; barren (Ge 11:29-31; 1Pe 3:6). Taken by Pharaoh as Abraham's sister; returned (Ge 12:10-20). Gave Hagar to Abraham; sent her away in pregnancy (Ge 16). Name changed; Isaac promised (Ge 17:15-21; 18:10-15; Heb 11:11). Taken by Abimelech as Abraham's sister; returned (Ge 20). Isaac born; Hagar and Ishmael sent away (Ge 21:1-21; Gal 4:21-31). Death (Ge 23).

## SATAN

Job 1:6 and *S* also came with them.
Zec 3:2 said to *S*, "The LORD rebuke you,
Mk 4:15 *S* comes and takes away the word
2Co 11:14 for *S* himself masquerades
12:7 a messenger of *S*, to torment me.
Rev 12:9 serpent called the devil, or *S*,
20:2 or *S*, and bound him for a thousand
20:7 *S* will be released from his prison

## SATISFIED (SATISFY)

Isa 53:11 he will see the light of life and be *s*

## SATISFIES (SATISFY)

Ps 103:5 who *s* your desires with good things,

## SATISFY (SATISFIED SATISFIES)

Isa 55:2 and your labor on what does not *s*?

## SAUL

1. Benjamite; anointed by Samuel as first king of Israel (1Sa 9-10). Defeated Ammonites (1Sa 11). Rebuked for offering sacrifice (1Sa 13:1-15). Defeated Philistines (1Sa 14). Rejected as king for failing to annihilate Amalekites (1Sa 15). Soothed from evil spirit by David (1Sa 16:14-23). Sent David against Goliath (1Sa 17). Jealousy and attempted murder of David (1Sa 18:1-11). Gave David Michal as wife (1Sa 18:12-30). Second attempt to kill David (1Sa 19). Anger at Jonathan (1Sa 20:26-34). Pursued David: killed priests at Nob (1Sa 22), went to Keilah and Ziph (1Sa 23), life spared by David at En Gedi (1Sa 24) and in his tent (1Sa 26). Rebuked by Samuel's spirit for consulting witch at Endor (1Sa 28). Wounded by Philistines; took his own life (1Sa 31; 1Ch 10).

2. See PAUL

## SAVE (SAFE SAFETY SALVATION SAVED SAVIOR)

Isa 63:1 mighty to *s*."
Da 3:17 the God we serve is able to *s* us
Zep 3:17 he is mighty to *s*.
Mt 1:21 he will *s* his people from their sins
16:25 wants to *s* his life will lose it,
Lk 19:10 to seek and to *s* what was lost."
Jn 3:17 but to *s* the world through him.
1Ti 1:15 came into the world to *s* sinners—
Jas 5:20 of his way will *s* him from death

## SAVED (SAVE)

Ps 34:6 he *s* him out of all his troubles.
Isa 45:22 "Turn to me and be *s*,
Joel 2:32 on the name of the LORD will be *s*;
Mk 13:13 firm to the end will be *s*.
Mk 16:16 believes and is baptized will be *s*,
Jn 10:9 enters through me will be *s*.
Ac 4:12 to men by which we must be *s*."
16:30 do to be *s*?" They replied,
Ro 9:27 only the remnant will be *s*.
10:9 him from the dead, you will be *s*.
1Co 3:15 will suffer loss; he himself will be *s*,
15:2 By this gospel you are *s*,
Eph 2:5 it is by grace you have been *s*.
2:8 For it is by grace you have been *s*,
1Ti 2:4 who wants all men to be *s*

## SAVIOR (SAVE)

Ps 89:26 my God, the Rock my *S*.'
Isa 43:11 and apart from me there is no *s*.
Hos 13:4 no *S* except me.
Lk 1:47 and my spirit rejoices in God my *S*,
2:11 of David a *S* has been born to you;
Jn 4:42 know that this man really is the *S*
Eph 5:23 his body, of which he is the *S*.
1Ti 4:10 who is the *S* of all men,
Tit 2:10 about God our *S* attractive.
2:13 appearing of our great God and *S*,
3:4 and love of God our *S* appeared,
1Jn 4:14 Son to be the *S* of the world.
Jude :25 to the only God our *S* be glory,

**SCALES**
Lev 19:36 Use honest *s* and honest weights,
Da 5:27 You have been weighed on the *s*

**SCAPEGOAT (GOAT)**
Lev 16:10 by sending it into the desert as a *s*.

**SCARLET**
Isa 1:18 "Though your sins are like *s*,

**SCATTERED**
Jer 31:10 'He who *s* Israel will gather them
Ac 8:4 who had been *s* preached the word

**SCEPTER**
Rev 19:15 "He will rule them with an iron *s*."

**SCHEMES**
2Co 2:11 For we are not unaware of his *s*.
Eph 6:11 stand against the devil's *s*.

**SCOFFERS**
2Pe 3:3 that in the last days *s* will come,

**SCORPION**
Rev 9:5 sting of a *s* when it strikes a man.

**SCRIPTURE (SCRIPTURES)**
Jn 10:35 and the *S* cannot be broken—
1Ti 4:13 yourself to the public reading of *S*,
2Ti 3:16 All *S* is God-breathed
2Pe 1:20 that no prophecy of *S* came about

**SCRIPTURES (SCRIPTURE)**
Lk 24:27 said in all the *S* concerning himself.
Jn 5:39 These are the *S* that testify about
Ac 17:11 examined the *S* every day to see

**SCROLL**
Eze 3:1 eat what is before you, eat this *s*;

**SEA**
Ex 14:16 go through the *s* on dry ground.
Isa 57:20 the wicked are like the tossing *s*,
Mic 7:19 iniquities into the depths of the *s*.
Jas 1:6 who doubts is like a wave of the *s*,
Rev 13:1 I saw a beast coming out of the *s*.

**SEAL (SEALS)**
Jn 6:27 God the Father has placed his *s*
2Co 1:22 set his *s* of ownership on us,
Eph 1:13 you were marked in him with a *s*,

**SEALS (SEAL)**
Rev 5:2 "Who is worthy to break the *s*
6:1 opened the first of the seven *s*.

**SEARCH (SEARCHED SEARCHES SEARCHING)**
Ps 4:4 *s* your hearts and be silent.
139:23 *S* me, O God, and know my heart;
Pr 2:4 and *s* for it as for hidden treasure,
Jer 17:10 "I the LORD *s* the heart
Eze 34:16 I will *s* for the lost and bring back
Lk 15:8 and *s* carefully until she finds it?

**SEARCHED (SEARCH)**
Ps 139:1 O LORD, you have *s* me

**SEARCHES (SEARCH)**
Ro 8:27 And he who *s* our hearts knows
1Co 2:10 The Spirit *s* all things,

**SEARCHING (SEARCH)**
Am 8:12 *s* for the word of the LORD,

**SEARED**
1Ti 4:2 whose consciences have been *s*

**SEASON**
2Ti 4:2 be prepared in *s* and out of *s*;

**SEAT (SEATED SEATS)**
Ps 1:1 or sit in the *s* of mockers.
Da 7:9 and the Ancient of Days took his *s*.
2Co 5:10 before the judgment *s* of Christ,

**SEATED (SEAT)**
Ps 47:8 God is *s* on his holy throne.
Isa 6:1 I saw the Lord *s* on a throne,
Col 3:1 where Christ is *s* at the right hand

**SEATS (SEAT)**
Lk 11:43 you love the most important *s*

**SECRET (SECRETS)**
Dt 29:29 The *s* things belong
Jdg 16:6 Tell me the *s* of your great strength
Ps 90:8 our *s* sins in the light
Pr 11:13 but a trustworthy man keeps a *s*.
Mt 6:4 so that your giving may be in *s*.
2Co 4:2 we have renounced *s* and shameful
Php 4:12 I have learned the *s*

**SECRETS (SECRET)**
Ps 44:21 since he knows the *s* of the heart?
1Co 14:25 the *s* of his heart will be laid bare.

**SECURE (SECURITY)**
Ps 112:8 His heart is *s*, he will have no fear;
Heb 6:19 an anchor for the soul, firm and *s*.

**SECURITY (SECURE)**
Job 31:24 or said to pure gold, 'You are my *s*,'

**SEED (SEEDS)**
Lk 8:11 of the parable: The *s* is the word
1Co 3:6 I planted the *s*, Apollos watered it,
2Co 9:10 he who supplies *s* to the sower
Gal 3:29 then you are Abraham's *s*,
1Pe 1:23 not of perishable *s*,

**SEEDS (SEED)**
Jn 12:24 But if it dies, it produces many *s*.
Gal 3:16 Scripture does not say "and to *s*,"

**SEEK (SEEKS SELF-SEEKING)**
Dt 4:29 if from there you *s* the LORD your
1Ch 28:9 If you *s* him, he will be found
2Ch 7:14 themselves and pray and *s* my face
Ps 119:10 I *s* you with all my heart;
Isa 55:6 *S* the LORD while he may be
65:1 found by those who did not *s* me.
Mt 6:33 But *s* first his kingdom
Lk 19:10 For the Son of Man came to *s*
Ro 10:20 found by those who did not *s* me;
1Co 7:27 you married? Do not *s* a divorce.

**SEEKS (SEEK)**
Jn 4:23 the kind of worshipers the Father *s*.

**SEER**
1Sa 9:9 of today used to be called a *s*.)

**SELF-CONTROL (CONTROL)**
1Co 7:5 you because of your lack of *s*.
Gal 5:23 faithfulness, gentleness and *s*.
2Pe 1:6 and to knowledge, *s*; and to *s*,

**SELF-CONTROLLED* (CONTROL)**
1Th 5:6 are asleep, but let us be alert and *s*.
5:8 let us be *s*, putting on faith and love
1Ti 3:2 *s*, respectable, hospitable,
Tit 1:8 who is *s*, upright, holy
2:2 worthy of respect, *s*, and sound
2:5 to be *s* and pure, to be busy at home
2:6 encourage the young men to be *s*.
2:12 to live *s*, upright and godly lives
1Pe 1:13 prepare your minds for action; be *s*;
4:7 and *s* so that you can pray.
5:8 Be *s* and alert.

**SELF-INDULGENCE**
Mt 23:25 inside they are full of greed and *s*.

**SELF-SEEKING (SEEK)**
1Co 13:5 it is not *s*, it is not easily angered,

**SELFISH***
Ps 119:36 and not toward *s* gain.
Pr 18:1 An unfriendly man pursues *s* ends;
Gal 5:20 fits of rage, *s* ambition, dissensions,
Php 1:17 preach Christ out of *s* ambition,
2:3 Do nothing out of *s* ambition
Jas 3:14 and *s* ambition in your hearts,
3:16 you have envy and *s* ambition,

**SEND (SENDING SENT)**
Isa 6:8 *S* me!" He said, "Go and tell this
Mt 9:38 to *s* out workers into his harvest
Jn 16:7 but if I go, I will *s* him to you.

**SENDING (SEND)**
Jn 20:21 Father has sent me, I am *s* you."

**SENSES***
Lk 15:17 "When he came to his *s*, he said,
1Co 15:34 Come back to your *s* as you ought,
2Ti 2:26 and that they will come to their *s*

**SENSUAL**
Col 2:23 value in restraining *s* indulgence.

**SENT (SEND)**
Isa 55:11 achieve the purpose for which I *s* it.
Mt 10:40 me receives the one who *s* me.

Jn 4:34 "is to do the will of him who *s* me
Ro 10:15 can they preach unless they are *s*?
1Jn 4:10 but that he loved us and *s* his Son

**SEPARATE (SEPARATED SEPARATES)**

Mt 19:6 has joined together, let man not *s*."
Ro 8:35 Who shall *s* us from the love
1Co 7:10 wife must not *s* from her husband.
2Co 6:17 and be *s*, says the Lord.

**SEPARATED (SEPARATE)**

Isa 59:2 But your iniquities have *s*

**SEPARATES (SEPARATE)**

Pr 16:28 and a gossip *s* close friends.

**SERPENT**

Ge 3:1 the *s* was more crafty than any
Rev 12:9 that ancient *s* called the devil

**SERVANT (SERVANTS)**

1Sa 3:10 "Speak, for your *s* is listening."
Mt 20:26 great among you must be your *s*,
25:21 'Well done, good and faithful *s*!
Lk 16:13 "No *s* can serve two masters.
Php 2:7 taking the very nature of a *s*,
2Ti 2:24 And the Lord's *s* must not quarrel;

**SERVANTS (SERVANT)**

Lk 17:10 should say, 'We are unworthy *s*;
Jn 15:15 longer call you *s*, because a servant

**SERVE (SERVICE SERVING)**

Dt 10:12 to *s* the LORD your God
Jos 22:5 and to *s* him with all your heart
24:15 this day whom you will *s*,
Mt 4:10 Lord your God, and *s* him only.' "
6:24 "No one can *s* two masters.
20:28 but to *s*, and to give his life
Eph 6:7 *S* wholeheartedly,

**SERVICE (SERVE)**

1Co 12:5 There are different kinds of *s*,
Eph 4:12 God's people for works of *s*,

**SERVING (SERVE)**

Ro 12:11 your spiritual fervor, *s* the Lord.
Eph 6:7 as if you were *s* the Lord, not men,
Col 3:24 It is the Lord Christ you are *s*.
2Ti 2:4 No one *s* as a soldier gets involved

**SEVEN (SEVENTH)**

Ge 7:2 Take with you *s* of every kind
Jos 6:4 march around the city *s* times,
1Ki 19:18 Yet I reserve *s* thousand in Israel—
Pr 6:16 *s* that are detestable to him:
24:16 a righteous man falls *s* times,
Isa 4:1 In that day *s* women
Da 9:25 comes, there will be *s* 'sevens,'
Mt 18:21 Up to *s* times?" Jesus answered,
Lk 11:26 takes *s* other spirits more wicked
Ro 11:4 for myself *s* thousand who have not
Rev 1:4 To the *s* churches in the province
6:1 opened the first of the *s* seals.
8:2 and to them were given *s* trumpets.
10:4 And when the *s* thunders spoke,
15:7 to the *s* angels *s* golden bowls filled

**SEVENTH (SEVEN)**

Ge 2:2 By the *s* day God had finished
Ex 23:12 but on the *s* day do not work,

**SEXUAL (SEXUALLY)**

1Co 6:13 body is not meant for *s* immorality,
6:18 Flee from *s* immorality.
10:8 should not commit *s* immorality,
Eph 5:3 even a hint of *s* immorality,
1Th 4:3 that you should avoid *s* immorality

**SEXUALLY (SEXUAL)**

1Co 5:9 to associate with *s* immoral people
6:18 he who sins *s* sins against his own

**SHADOW**

Ps 23:4 through the valley of the *s* of death,
36:7 find refuge in the *s* of your wings.
Heb 10:1 The law is only a *s*

**SHALLUM**

King of Israel (2Ki 15:10-16).

**SHAME (ASHAMED)**
Ps 34:5 their faces are never covered with *s*
Pr 13:18 discipline comes to poverty and *s*,
Heb 12:2 endured the cross, scorning its *s*,

**SHARE (SHARED)**
Ge 21:10 that slave woman's son will never *s*
Lk 3:11 "The man with two tunics should *s*
Gal 4:30 the slave woman's son will never *s*
6:6 in the word must *s* all good things
Eph 4:28 something to *s* with those in need.
1Ti 6:18 and to be generous and willing to *s*.
Heb 12:10 that we may *s* in his holiness.
13:16 to do good and to *s* with others,

**SHARED (SHARE)**
Heb 2:14 he too *s* in their humanity so that

**SHARON**
SS 2:1 I am a rose of *S*,

**SHARPER***
Heb 4:12 *S* than any double-edged sword,

**SHED (SHEDDING)**
Ge 9:6 by man shall his blood be *s*;
Col 1:20 through his blood, *s* on the cross.

**SHEDDING (SHED)**
Heb 9:22 without the *s* of blood there is no

**SHEEP**
Ps 100:3 we are his people, the *s*
119:176 I have strayed like a lost *s*.
Isa 53:6 We all, like *s*, have gone astray,
Jer 50:6 "My people have been lost *s*;
Eze 34:11 I myself will search for my *s*
Mt 9:36 helpless, like *s* without a shepherd.
Jn 10:3 He calls his own *s* by name
10:15 and I lay down my life for the *s*.
10:27 My *s* listen to my voice; I know
21:17 Jesus said, "Feed my *s*.
1Pe 2:25 For you were like *s* going astray,

**SHELTER**
Ps 61:4 take refuge in the *s* of your wings.
91:1 in the *s* of the Most High

**SHEM**
Son of Noah (Ge 5:32; 6:10). Blessed (Ge 9:26). Descendants (Ge 10:21-31; 11:10-32).

**SHEPHERD (SHEPHERDS)**
Ps 23:1 LORD is my *s*, I shall not be in want.
Isa 40:11 He tends his flock like a *s*:
Jer 31:10 will watch over his flock like a *s*.'
Eze 34:12 As a *s* looks after his scattered
Zec 11:17 "Woe to the worthless *s*,
Mt 9:36 and helpless, like sheep without a *s*.
Jn 10:11 The good *s* lays down his life
10:16 there shall be one flock and one *s*.
1Pe 5:4 And when the Chief *S* appears,

**SHEPHERDS (SHEPHERD)**
Jer 23:1 "Woe to the *s* who are destroying
Lk 2:8 there were *s* living out in the fields
Ac 20:28 Be *s* of the church of God,
1Pe 5:2 Be *s* of God's flock that is

**SHIELD**
Ps 28:7 LORD is my strength and my *s*;
Eph 6:16 to all this, take up the *s* of faith,

**SHINE (SHONE)**
Ps 4:6 Let the light of your face *s* upon us,
80:1 between the cherubim, *s* forth
Isa 60:1 "Arise, *s*, for your light has come,
Da 12:3 are wise will *s* like the brightness
Mt 5:16 let your light *s* before men,
13:43 the righteous will *s* like the sun
2Co 4:6 made his light *s* in our hearts
Eph 5:14 and Christ will *s* on you."

**SHIPWRECKED***
2Co 11:25 I was stoned, three times I was *s*,
1Ti 1:19 and so have *s* their faith.

**SHONE (SHINE)**
Mt 17:2 His face *s* like the sun,
Lk 2:9 glory of the Lord *s* around them,
Rev 21:11 It *s* with the glory of God,

**SHORT**
Isa 59:1 of the LORD is not too *s* to save,

Ro 3:23 and fall *s* of the glory of God,

**SHOULDERS**

Isa 9:6 and the government will be on his *s*
Lk 15:5 he joyfully puts it on his *s*

**SHOWED**

1Jn 4:9 This is how God *s* his love

**SHREWD**

Mt 10:16 Therefore be as *s* as snakes and

**SHUN***

Job 28:28 and to *s* evil is understanding.' "
Pr 3:7 fear the LORD and *s* evil.

**SICK**

Pr 13:12 Hope deferred makes the heart *s*,
Mt 9:12 who need a doctor, but the *s*.
25:36 I was *s* and you looked after me,
Jas 5:14 of you *s?* He should call the elders

**SICKLE**

Joel 3:13 Swing the *s*,

**SIDE**

Ps 91:7 A thousand may fall at your *s*,
124:1 If the LORD had not been on our *s*
2Ti 4:17 But the Lord stood at my *s*

**SIGHT**

Ps 90:4 For a thousand years in your *s*
116:15 Precious in the *s* of the LORD
2Co 5:7 We live by faith, not by *s*.
1Pe 3:4 which is of great worth in God's *s*.

**SIGN (SIGNS)**

Isa 7:14 the Lord himself will give you a *s:*

**SIGNS (SIGN)**

Mk 16:17 these *s* will accompany those who
Jn 20:30 Jesus did many other miraculous *s*

**SILENT**

Pr 17:28 a fool is thought wise if he keeps *s*,
Isa 53:7 as a sheep before her shearers is *s*,
Hab 2:20 let all the earth be *s* before him."
1Co 14:34 women should remain *s*
1Ti 2:12 over a man; she must be *s*.

**SILVER**

Pr 25:11 is like apples of gold in settings of *s*.
Hag 2:8 'The *s* is mine and the gold is mine,'
1Co 3:12 *s*, costly stones, wood, hay or straw

**SIMON**

1. See PETER.
2. Apostle, called the Zealot (Mt 10:4; Mk 3:18; Lk 6:15; Ac 1:13).
3. Samaritan sorcerer (Ac 8:9-24).

**SIN (SINFUL SINNED SINNER SINNERS SINNING SINS)**

Nu 5:7 and must confess the *s* he has
32:23 be sure that your *s* will find you
Dt 24:16 each is to die for his own *s*.
1Ki 8:46 for there is no one who does not *s*
2Ch 7:14 and will forgive their *s* and will heal
Ps 4:4 In your anger do not *s;*
32:2 whose *s* the LORD does not count
32:5 Then I acknowledged my *s* to you
51:2 and cleanse me from my *s*.
66:18 If I had cherished *s* in my heart,
119:11 that I might not *s* against you.
119:133 let no *s* rule over me.
Isa 6:7 is taken away and your *s* atoned
Mic 7:18 who pardons *s* and forgives
Mt 18:6 little ones who believe in me to *s*,
Jn 1:29 who takes away the *s* of the world!
8:34 everyone who sins is a slave to *s*.
Ro 5:12 as *s* entered the world
5:20 where *s* increased, grace increased
6:11 count yourselves dead to *s*
6:23 For the wages of *s* is death,
14:23 that does not come from faith is *s*.
2Co 5:21 God made him who had no *s* to be *s*
Gal 6:1 if someone is caught in a *s*,
Heb 9:26 to do away with *s* by the sacrifice
11:25 the pleasures of *s* for a short time.
12:1 and the *s* that so easily entangles,
1Pe 2:22 "He committed no *s*,
1Jn 1:8 If we claim to be without *s*,

| | | |
|---|---|---|
| 1Jn | 3:4 | in fact, *s* is lawlessness. |
| | 3:5 | And in him is no *s*. |
| | 3:9 | born of God will continue to *s*, |
| | 5:18 | born of God does not continue to *s*; |

**SINCERE**

| | | |
|---|---|---|
| Ro | 12:9 | Love must be *s*. |
| Heb | 10:22 | near to God with a *s* heart |

**SINFUL (SIN)**

| | | |
|---|---|---|
| Ps | 51:5 | Surely I was *s* at birth |
| | 51:5 | *s* from the time my mother |
| Ro | 7:5 | we were controlled by the *s* nature, |
| | 8:4 | not live according to the *s* nature |
| | 8:9 | are controlled not by the *s* nature |
| Gal | 5:19 | The acts of the *s* nature are obvious |
| | 5:24 | Jesus have crucified the *s* nature |
| 1Pe | 2:11 | abstain from *s* desires, which war |

**SING (SANG SINGING SONG SONGS)**

| | | |
|---|---|---|
| Ps | 30:4 | *S* to the LORD, you saints of his; |
| | 47:6 | *S* praises to God, *s* praises; |
| | 59:16 | But I will *s* of your strength, |
| | 89:1 | I will *s* of the LORD's great love |
| | 101:1 | I will *s* of your love and justice; |
| Eph | 5:19 | *S* and make music in your heart |

**SINGING (SING)**

| | | |
|---|---|---|
| Ps | 63:5 | with *s* lips my mouth will praise |
| Ac | 16:25 | Silas were praying and *s* hymns |

**SINNED (SIN)**

| | | |
|---|---|---|
| 2Sa | 12:13 | "I have *s* against the LORD." |
| Job | 1:5 | "Perhaps my children have *s* |
| Ps | 51:4 | Against you, you only, have I *s* |
| Da | 9:5 | we have *s* and done wrong. |
| Mic | 7:9 | Because I have *s* against him, |
| Lk | 15:18 | I have *s* against heaven |
| Ro | 3:23 | for all have *s* and fall short |
| 1Jn | 1:10 | claim we have not *s*, we make him |

**SINNER (SIN)**

| | | |
|---|---|---|
| Ecc | 9:18 | but one *s* destroys much good. |
| Lk | 15:7 | in heaven over one *s* who repents |
| | 18:13 | 'God, have mercy on me, a *s*.' |
| 1Co | 14:24 | convinced by all that he is a *s* |
| Jas | 5:20 | Whoever turns a *s* from the error |
| 1Pe | 4:18 | become of the ungodly and the *s*?" |

**SINNERS (SIN)**

| | | |
|---|---|---|
| Ps | 1:1 | or stand in the way of *s* |
| Pr | 23:17 | Do not let your heart envy *s*, |
| Mt | 9:13 | come to call the righteous, but *s*." |
| Ro | 5:8 | While we were still *s*, Christ died |
| 1Ti | 1:15 | came into the world to save *s*— |

**SINNING (SIN)**

| | | |
|---|---|---|
| Ex | 20:20 | be with you to keep you from *s*." |
| 1Co | 15:34 | stop *s*; for there are some who are |
| Heb | 10:26 | If we deliberately keep on *s* |
| 1Jn | 3:6 | No one who lives in him keeps on *s* |
| | 3:9 | go on *s*, because he has been born |

**SINS (SIN)**

| | | |
|---|---|---|
| 2Ki | 14:6 | each is to die for his own *s*." |
| Ezr | 9:6 | our *s* are higher than our heads |
| Ps | 19:13 | your servant also from willful *s*; |
| | 32:1 | whose *s* are covered. |
| | 103:3 | who forgives all your *s* |
| | 130:3 | O LORD, kept a record of *s*, |
| Pr | 28:13 | who conceals his *s* does not |
| Isa | 1:18 | "Though your *s* are like scarlet, |
| | 43:25 | and remembers your *s* no more. |
| | 59:2 | your *s* have hidden his face |
| Eze | 18:4 | soul who *s* is the one who will die. |
| Mt | 1:21 | he will save his people from their *s* |
| | 18:15 | "If your brother *s* against you, |
| Lk | 11:4 | Forgive us our *s*, |
| | 17:3 | "If your brother *s*, rebuke him, |
| Ac | 22:16 | be baptized and wash your *s* away, |
| 1Co | 15:3 | died for our *s* according |
| Eph | 2:1 | dead in your transgressions and *s*, |
| Col | 2:13 | us all our *s*, having canceled |
| Heb | 1:3 | he had provided purification for *s*, |

Heb 7:27 He sacrificed for their *s* once for all
8:12 and will remember their *s* no more
10:12 for all time one sacrifice for *s*,
Jas 4:17 ought to do and doesn't do it, *s*.
5:16 Therefore confess your *s*
5:20 and cover over a multitude of *s*.
1Pe 2:24 He himself bore our *s* in his body
3:18 For Christ died for *s* once for all,
1Jn 1:9 If we confess our *s*, he is faithful
Rev 1:5 has freed us from our *s* by his blood

## SITS

Ps 99:1 *s* enthroned between the cherubim,
Isa 40:22 He *s* enthroned above the circle
Mt 19:28 of Man *s* on his glorious throne,
Rev 4:9 thanks to him who *s* on the throne

## SKIN

Job 19:20 with only the *s* of my teeth.
19:26 And after my *s* has been destroyed,
Jer 13:23 Can the Ethiopian change his *s*

## SLAIN (SLAY)

Rev 5:12 "Worthy is the Lamb, who was *s*,

## SLANDER (SLANDERED SLANDERERS)

Lev 19:16 " 'Do not go about spreading *s*
1Ti 5:14 the enemy no opportunity for *s*.
Tit 3:2 to *s* no one, to be peaceable

## SLANDERED (SLANDER)

1Co 4:13 when we are *s*, we answer kindly.

## SLANDERERS (SLANDER)

Ro 1:30 They are gossips, *s*, God-haters,
1Co 6:10 nor the greedy nor drunkards nor *s*
Tit 2:3 not to be *s* or addicted

## SLAUGHTER

Isa 53:7 he was led like a lamb to the *s*,

## SLAVE (SLAVERY SLAVES)

Ge 21:10 "Get rid of that *s* woman
Mt 20:27 wants to be first must be your *s*—
Jn 8:34 everyone who sins is a *s* to sin.
1Co 12:13 whether Jews or Greeks, *s* or free
Gal 3:28 *s* nor free, male nor female,
4:30 Get rid of the *s* woman and her son
2Pe 2:19 a man is a *s* to whatever has

## SLAVERY (SLAVE)

Ro 6:19 parts of your body in *s* to impurity
Gal 4:3 were in *s* under the basic principles

## SLAVES (SLAVE)

Ro 6:6 that we should no longer be *s* to sin
6:22 and have become *s* to God,

## SLAY (SLAIN)

Job 13:15 Though he *s* me, yet will I hope

## SLEEP (SLEEPING)

Ps 121:4 will neither slumber nor *s*.
1Co 15:51 We will not all *s*, but we will all be

## SLEEPING (SLEEP)

Mk 13:36 suddenly, do not let him find you *s*.

## SLOW

Ex 34:6 and gracious God, *s* to anger,
Jas 1:19 *s* to speak and *s* to become angry,
2Pe 3:9 The Lord is not *s* in keeping his

## SLUGGARD

Pr 6:6 Go to the ant, you *s*;
20:4 A *s* does not plow in season;

## SLUMBER

Ps 121:3 he who watches over you will not *s*;
Pr 6:10 A little sleep, a little *s*,
Ro 13:11 for you to wake up from your *s*,

## SNAKE (SNAKES)

Nu 21:8 "Make a *s* and put it up on a pole;
Pr 23:32 In the end it bites like a *s*
Jn 3:14 Moses lifted up the *s* in the desert,

## SNAKES (SNAKE)

Mt 10:16 as shrewd as *s* and as innocent
Mk 16:18 they will pick up *s* with their hands;

## SNATCH

Jn 10:28 no one can *s* them out of my hand.
Jude :23 *s* others from the fire and save

## SNOW

Ps 51:7 and I will be whiter than *s*.

**SOAR**
Isa 40:31 They will *s* on wings like eagles;

**SODOM**
Ge 19:24 rained down burning sulfur on *S*
Ro 9:29 we would have become like *S*,

**SOIL**
Ge 4:2 kept flocks, and Cain worked the *s*.
Mt 13:23 on good *s* is the man who hears

**SOLDIER**
1Co 9:7 as a *s* at his own expense?
2Ti 2:3 with us like a good *s* of Christ Jesus

**SOLE**
Dt 28:65 place for the *s* of your foot.
Isa 1:6 From the *s* of your foot to the top

**SOLID**
2Ti 2:19 God's *s* foundation stands firm,
Heb 5:12 You need milk, not *s* food!

**SOLOMON**
Son of David by Bathsheba; king of Judah (2Sa 12:24; 1Ch 3:5, 10). Appointed king by David (1Ki 1); adversaries Adonijah, Joab, Shimei killed by Benaiah (1Ki 2). Asked for wisdom (1Ki 3; 2Ch 1). Judged between two prostitutes (1Ki 3:16-28). Built temple (1Ki 5-7; 2Ch 2-5); prayer of dedication (1Ki 8; 2Ch 6). Visited by Queen of Sheba (1Ki 10; 2Ch 9). Wives turned his heart from God (1Ki 11:1-13). Jeroboam rebelled against (1Ki 11:26-40). Death (1Ki 11:41-43; 2Ch 9:29-31).

Proverbs of (1Ki 4:32; Pr 1:1; 10:1; 25:1); psalms of (Ps 72; 127); song of (SS 1:1).

**SON (SONS)**
Ge 22:2 "Take your *s*, your only *s*, Isaac,
Ex 11:5 Every firstborn *s* in Egypt will die,
Dt 21:18 rebellious *s* who does not obey his
Ps 2:7 He said to me, "You are my *S*;
2:12 Kiss the *S*, lest he be angry
Pr 10:1 A wise *s* brings joy to his father,
13:24 He who spares the rod hates his *s*,
29:17 Discipline your *s*, and he will give
Isa 7:14 with child and will give birth to a *s*,
Hos 11:1 and out of Egypt I called my *s*.
Mt 2:15 "Out of Egypt I called my *s*."
3:17 "This is my *S*, whom I love;
11:27 one knows the *S* except the Father,
16:16 "You are the Christ, the *S*
17:5 "This is my *S*, whom I love;
20:18 and the *S* of Man will be betrayed
24:30 They will see the *S* of Man coming
24:44 the *S* of Man will come at an hour
27:54 "Surely he was the *S* of God!"
28:19 and of the *S* and of the Holy Spirit,
Mk 10:45 even the *S* of Man did not come
14:62 you will see the *S* of Man sitting
Lk 9:58 but the *S* of Man has no place
18:8 when the *S* of Man comes,
Lk 19:10 For the *S* of Man came to seek
Jn 3:14 so the *S* of Man must be lifted up,
3:16 that he gave his one and only *S*,
17:1 Glorify your *S*, that your *S* may
Ro 8:29 conformed to the likeness of his *S*,
8:32 He who did not spare his own *S*,
1Co 15:28 then the *S* himself will be made
Gal 4:30 rid of the slave woman and her *s*,
1Th 1:10 and to wait for his *S* from heaven,
Heb 1:2 days he has spoken to us by his *S*,
10:29 punished who has trampled the *S*
1Jn 1:7 his *S*, purifies us from all sin.
4:9 only *S* into the world that we might
5:5 he who believes that Jesus is the *S*
5:11 eternal life, and this life is in his *S*.

**SONG (SING)**
Ps 40:3 He put a new *s* in my mouth,
96:1 Sing to the LORD a new *s*;
149:1 Sing to the LORD a new *s*,
Isa 49:13 burst into *s*, O mountains!
55:12 will burst into *s* before you,
Rev 5:9 And they sang a new *s*:
15:3 and sang the *s* of Moses the servant

**SONGS (SING)**
Job 35:10 who gives *s* in the night,

- Ps 100:2 come before him with joyful *s*.
- Eph 5:19 with psalms, hymns and spiritual *s*.
- Jas 5:13 Is anyone happy? Let him sing *s*

**SONS (SON)**
- Joel 2:28 Your *s* and daughters will prophesy
- Jn 12:36 so that you may become *s* of light."
- Ro 8:14 by the Spirit of God are *s* of God.
- 2Co 6:18 and you will be my *s* and daughters
- Gal 4:5 we might receive the full rights of *s*.
- Heb 12:7 discipline; God is treating you as *s*.

**SORROW (SORROWS)**
- Jer 31:12 and they will *s* no more.
- Ro 9:2 I have great *s* and unceasing
- 2Co 7:10 Godly *s* brings repentance that

**SORROWS (SORROW)**
- Isa 53:3 a man of *s*, and familiar

**SOUL (SOULS)**
- Dt 6:5 with all your *s* and with all your
- 10:12 all your heart and with all your *s*,
- Jos 22:5 with all your heart and all your *s*."
- Ps 23:3 he restores my *s*.
- 42:1 so my *s* pants for you, O God.
- 42:11 Why are you downcast, O my *s*?
- 103:1 Praise the LORD, O my *s*;
- Pr 13:19 A longing fulfilled is sweet to the *s*,
- Isa 55:2 your *s* will delight in the richest
- Mt 10:28 kill the body but cannot kill the *s*.
- 16:26 yet forfeits his *s*? Or what can
- 22:37 with all your *s* and with all your
- Heb 4:12 even to dividing *s* and spirit,

**SOULS (SOUL)**
- Pr 11:30 and he who wins *s* is wise.
- Jer 6:16 and you will find rest for your *s*.
- Mt 11:29 and you will find rest for your *s*.

**SOUND**
- 1Co 14:8 if the trumpet does not *s* a clear call
- 15:52 the trumpet will *s*, the dead will
- 2Ti 4:3 men will not put up with *s* doctrine.

**SOVEREIGN**
- Da 4:25 that the Most High is *s*

**SOW (SOWS)**
- Job 4:8 and those who *s* trouble reap it.
- Mt 6:26 they do not *s* or reap or store away
- 2Pe 2:22 and, "A *s* that is washed goes back

**SOWS (SOW)**
- Pr 11:18 he who *s* righteousness reaps a sure
- 22:8 He who *s* wickedness reaps trouble
- 2Co 9:6 Whoever *s* sparingly will
- Gal 6:7 A man reaps what he *s*.

**SPARE (SPARES)**
- Ro 8:32 He who did not *s* his own Son,
- 11:21 natural branches, he will not *s* you

**SPARES (SPARE)**
- Pr 13:24 He who *s* the rod hates his son,

**SPEARS**
- Isa 2:4 and their *s* into pruning hooks.
- Joel 3:10 and your pruning hooks into *s*.
- Mic 4:3 and their *s* into pruning hooks.

**SPECTACLE**
- 1Co 4:9 We have been made a *s*
- Col 2:15 he made a public *s* of them,

**SPIN**
- Mt 6:28 They do not labor or *s*.

**SPIRIT (SPIRIT'S SPIRITS SPIRITUAL SPIRITUALLY)**
- Ge 1:2 and the *S* of God was hovering
- 6:3 "My *S* will not contend
- 2Ki 2:9 inherit a double portion of your *s*,"
- Job 33:4 The *S* of God has made me;
- Ps 31:5 Into your hands I commit my *s*;
- 51:10 and renew a steadfast *s* within me.
- 51:11 or take your Holy *S* from me.
- 51:17 sacrifices of God are a broken *s*;
- 139:7 Where can I go from your *S*?
- Isa 57:15 him who is contrite and lowly in *s*,

Isa 63:10 and grieved his Holy *S*.
Eze 11:19 an undivided heart and put a new *s*
36:26 you a new heart and put a new *s*
Joel 2:28 I will pour out my *S* on all people.
Zec 4:6 but by my *S*,' says the LORD
Mt 1:18 to be with child through the Holy *S*
3:11 will baptize you with the Holy *S*
3:16 he saw the *S* of God descending
4:1 led by the *S* into the desert
5:3 saying: "Blessed are the poor in *s*,
26:41 *s* is willing, but the body is weak."
28:19 and of the Son and of the Holy *S*,
Lk 1:80 child grew and became strong in *s*;
11:13 Father in heaven give the Holy *S*
Jn 4:24 God is *s*, and his worshipers must
7:39 Up to that time the *S* had not been
14:26 But the Counselor, the Holy *S*,
16:13 But when he, the *S* of truth, comes,
20:22 and said, "Receive the Holy *S*.
Ac 1:5 will be baptized with the Holy *S*."
2:4 of them were filled with the Holy *S*
2:38 will receive the gift of the Holy *S*.
6:3 who are known to be full of the *S*
19:2 "Did you receive the Holy *S*
Ro 8:9 And if anyone does not have the *S*
Ro 8:26 the *S* helps us in our weakness.
1Co 2:10 God has revealed it to us by his *S*.
2:14 man without the *S* does not accept
6:19 body is a temple of the Holy *S*,
12:13 baptized by one *S* into one body—
2Co 3:6 the letter kills, but the *S* gives life.
5:5 and has given us the *S* as a deposit,
Gal 5:16 by the *S*, and you will not gratify
5:22 But the fruit of the *S* is love, joy,
5:25 let us keep in step with the *S*.
Eph 1:13 with a seal, the promised Holy *S*,
4:30 do not grieve the Holy *S* of God,
5:18 Instead, be filled with the *S*.
6:17 of salvation and the sword of the *S*,
2Th 2:13 the sanctifying work of the *S*
Heb 4:12 even to dividing soul and *s*,
1Pe 3:4 beauty of a gentle and quiet *s*,
2Pe 1:21 carried along by the Holy *S*.
1Jn 4:1 Dear friends, do not believe every *s*

**SPIRIT'S (SPIRIT)**

1Th 5:19 not put out the *S* fire; do not treat

**SPIRITS (SPIRIT)**

1Co 12:10 to another distinguishing between *s*,
14:32 The *s* of prophets are subject
1Jn 4:1 test the *s* to see whether they are

**SPIRITUAL (SPIRIT)**

Ro 12:1 this is your *s* act of worship.
12:11 but keep your *s* fervor, serving
1Co 2:13 expressing *s* truths in *s* words.
3:1 I could not address you as *s* but
12:1 Now about *s* gifts, brothers,
14:1 of love and eagerly desire *s* gifts,
15:44 a natural body, it is raised a *s* body.
Gal 6:1 you who are *s* should restore him
Eph 1:3 with every *s* blessing in Christ.
5:19 with psalms, hymns and *s* songs.
6:12 and against the *s* forces of evil
1Pe 2:2 newborn babies, crave pure *s* milk,
2:5 are being built into a *s* house

**SPIRITUALLY (SPIRIT)**

1Co 2:14 because they are *s* discerned.

**SPLENDOR**

1Ch 16:29 the LORD in the *s* of his holiness.
29:11 the glory and the majesty and the *s*,
Job 37:22 of the north he comes in golden *s*;
Ps 29:2 in the *s* of his holiness.
45:3 clothe yourself with *s* and majesty.
96:6 *S* and majesty are before him;
96:9 in the *s* of his holiness;
104:1 you are clothed with *s* and majesty.
145:5 of the glorious *s* of your majesty,

Isa 61:3 the LORD for the display of his *s.*
63:1 Who is this, robed in *s,*
Lk 9:31 appeared in glorious *s,* talking
2Th 2:8 and destroy by the *s* of his coming.

**SPOIL**
Ps 119:162 like one who finds great *s.*

**SPOTLESS**
2Pe 3:14 make every effort to be found *s,*

**SPREAD (SPREADING)**
Ac 12:24 of God continued to increase and *s.*
19:20 the word of the Lord *s* widely

**SPREADING (SPREAD)**
1Th 3:2 God's fellow worker in *s* the gospel

**SPRING**
Jer 2:13 the *s* of living water,
Jn 4:14 in him a *s* of water welling up
Jas 3:12 can a salt *s* produce fresh water.

**SPUR***
Heb 10:24 how we may *s* one another

**SPURNS***
Pr 15:5 A fool *s* his father's discipline,

**STAFF**
Ps 23:4 your rod and your *s,*

**STAKES**
Isa 54:2 strengthen your *s.*

**STAND (STANDING STANDS)**
Ex 14:13 *S* firm and you will see
2Ch 20:17 *s* firm and see the deliverance
Ps 1:5 Therefore the wicked will not *s*
40:2 and gave me a firm place to *s.*
119:120 I *s* in awe of your laws.
Eze 22:30 *s* before me in the gap on behalf
Zec 14:4 On that day his feet will *s*
Mt 12:25 divided against itself will not *s.*
Ro 14:10 we will all *s* before God's judgment
1Co 10:13 out so that you can *s* up under it.
15:58 Therefore, my dear brothers, *s* firm
Eph 6:14 *S* firm then, with the belt
2Th 2:15 *s* firm and hold to the teachings we
Jas 5:8 You too, be patient and *s* firm,
Rev 3:20 Here I am! I *s* at the door

**STANDING (STAND)**
Ex 3:5 where you are *s* is holy ground."
Jos 5:15 the place where you are *s* is holy."
1Pe 5:9 Resist him, *s* firm in the faith,

**STANDS (STAND)**
Ps 89:2 that your love *s* firm forever,
119:89 it *s* firm in the heavens.
Mt 10:22 but he who *s* firm to the end will be
2Ti 2:19 God's solid foundation *s* firm,
1Pe 1:25 but the word of the Lord *s* forever

**STAR (STARS)**
Nu 24:17 A *s* will come out of Jacob;
Rev 22:16 and the bright Morning *S.*"

**STARS (STAR)**
Da 12:3 like the *s* for ever and ever.
Php 2:15 in which you shine like *s*

**STATURE**
Lk 2:52 And Jesus grew in wisdom and *s,*

**STEADFAST**
Ps 51:10 and renew a *s* spirit within me.
Isa 26:3 him whose mind is *s,*
1Pe 5:10 and make you strong, firm and *s.*

**STEAL**
Ex 20:15 "You shall not *s.*
Mt 19:18 do not *s,* do not give false
Eph 4:28 has been stealing must *s* no longer,

**STEP (STEPS)**
Gal 5:25 let us keep in *s* with the Spirit.

**STEPS (STEP)**
Pr 16:9 but the LORD determines his *s.*
Jer 10:23 it is not for man to direct his *s.*
1Pe 2:21 that you should follow in his *s.*

**STICKS**
Pr 18:24 there is a friend who *s* closer

**STIFF-NECKED**
Ex 34:9 Although this is a *s* people,

**STILL**
Ps 46:10 "Be *s,* and know that I am God;

Zec 2:13 Be *s* before the LORD, all mankind

**STIRS**

Pr 6:19 and a man who *s* up dissension
10:12 Hatred *s* up dissension,
15:1 but a harsh word *s* up anger.
15:18 hot-tempered man *s* up dissension,
16:28 A perverse man *s* up dissension,
28:25 A greedy man *s* up dissension,
29:22 An angry man *s* up dissension,

**STONE (CAPSTONE CORNERSTONE MILLSTONE)**

1Sa 17:50 the Philistine with a sling and a *s*;
Isa 8:14 a *s* that causes men to stumble
Eze 11:19 remove from them their heart of *s*
Mk 16:3 "Who will roll the *s* away
Lk 4:3 tell this *s* to become bread."
Jn 8:7 the first to throw a *s* at her."
2Co 3:3 not on tablets of *s* but on tablets

**STOOP**

2Sa 22:36 you *s* down to make me great.

**STORE**

Pr 10:14 Wise men *s* up knowledge,
Mt 6:19 not *s* up for yourselves treasures

**STOREHOUSE (HOUSE)**

Mal 3:10 Bring the whole tithe into the *s*,

**STRAIGHT**

Pr 3:6 and he will make your paths *s*.
4:25 Let your eyes look *s* ahead,
15:21 of understanding keeps a *s* course.
Jn 1:23 'Make *s* the way for the Lord.' "

**STRAIN**

Mt 23:24 You *s* out a gnat but swallow

**STRANGER (STRANGERS)**

Mt 25:35 I was a *s* and you invited me in,
Jn 10:5 But they will never follow a *s*;

**STRANGERS (STRANGER)**

1Pe 2:11 as aliens and *s* in the world,

**STREAMS**

Ps 1:3 He is like a tree planted by *s*
46:4 is a river whose *s* make glad
Ecc 1:7 All *s* flow into the sea,
Jn 7:38 *s* of living water will flow

**STRENGTH (STRONG)**

Ex 15:2 The LORD is my *s* and my song;
Dt 6:5 all your soul and with all your *s*.
2Sa 22:33 It is God who arms me with *s*
Ne 8:10 for the joy of the LORD is your *s*."
Ps 28:7 The LORD is my *s* and my shield;
46:1 God is our refuge and *s*,
96:7 ascribe to the LORD glory and *s*.
118:14 The LORD is my *s* and my song;
147:10 not in the *s* of the horse,
Isa 40:31 will renew their *s*.
Mk 12:30 all your mind and with all your *s*.'
1Co 1:25 of God is stronger than man's *s*.
Php 4:13 through him who gives me *s*.
1Pe 4:11 it with the *s* God provides,

**STRENGTHEN (STRONG)**

2Ch 16:9 to *s* those whose hearts are fully
Ps 119:28 *s* me according to your word.
Isa 35:3 *S* the feeble hands,
41:10 I will *s* you and help you;
Eph 3:16 of his glorious riches he may *s* you
2Th 2:17 and *s* you in every good deed
Heb 12:12 *s* your feeble arms and weak knees.

**STRENGTHENING (STRONG)**

1Co 14:26 done for the *s* of the church.

**STRIFE**

Pr 20:3 It is to a man's honor to avoid *s*,
22:10 out the mocker, and out goes *s*;

**STRIKE (STRIKES)**

Ge 3:15 and you will *s* his heel."
Zec 13:7 "*S* the shepherd,
Mt 26:31 " 'I will *s* the shepherd,

**STRIKES (STRIKE)**

Mt 5:39 If someone *s* you on the right

**STRONG (STRENGTH STRENGTHEN STRENGTHENING)**

Dt 31:6 Be *s* and courageous.
1Ki 2:2 "So be *s*, show yourself a man,
Pr 18:10 The name of the LORD is a *s* tower
31:17 her arms are *s* for her tasks.
SS 8:6 for love is as *s* as death,
Lk 2:40 And the child grew and became *s;*
Ro 15:1 We who are *s* ought to bear
1Co 1:27 things of the world to shame the *s*.
16:13 in the faith; be men of courage; be *s*
2Co 12:10 For when I am weak, then I am *s*.
Eph 6:10 be *s* in the Lord and in his mighty

**STRUGGLE**

Ro 15:30 me in my *s* by praying to God
Eph 6:12 For our *s* is not against flesh
Heb 12:4 In your *s* against sin, you have not

**STUDY**

Ezr 7:10 Ezra had devoted himself to the *s*
Ecc 12:12 and much *s* wearies the body.
Jn 5:39 You diligently *s* the Scriptures

**STUMBLE (STUMBLING)**

Ps 37:24 though he *s*, he will not fall,
119:165 and nothing can make them *s*.
Isa 8:14 a stone that causes men to *s*
Jer 31:9 a level path where they will not *s*,
Eze 7:19 for it has made them *s* into sin.
1Co 10:32 Do not cause anyone to *s*,
1Pe 2:8 and, "A stone that causes men to *s*

**STUMBLING (STUMBLE)**

Ro 14:13 up your mind not to put any *s* block
1Co 8:9 freedom does not become a *s* block
2Co 6:3 We put no *s* block in anyone's path,

**SUBDUE**

Ge 1:28 in number; fill the earth and *s* it.

**SUBJECT (SUBJECTED)**

1Co 14:32 of prophets are *s* to the control
15:28 then the Son himself will be made *s*
Tit 2:5 and to be *s* to their husbands,
2:9 slaves to be *s* to their masters
3:1 Remind the people to be *s* to rulers

**SUBJECTED (SUBJECT)**

Ro 8:20 For the creation was *s*

**SUBMISSION (SUBMIT)**

1Co 14:34 but must be in *s*, as the Law says.
1Ti 2:11 learn in quietness and full *s*.

**SUBMISSIVE (SUBMIT)**

Jas 3:17 then peace-loving, considerate, *s*,
1Pe 3:1 in the same way be *s*
5:5 in the same way be *s*

**SUBMIT (SUBMISSION SUBMISSIVE SUBMITS)**

Ro 13:1 Everyone must *s* himself
Ro 13:5 necessary to *s* to the authorities,
1Co 16:16 to *s* to such as these
Eph 5:21 *S* to one another out of reverence
Col 3:18 Wives, *s* to your husbands,
Heb 12:9 How much more should we *s*
13:17 Obey your leaders and *s*
Jas 4:7 *S* yourselves, then, to God.
1Pe 2:18 *s* yourselves to your masters

**SUBMITS* (SUBMIT)**

Eph 5:24 Now as the church *s* to Christ,

**SUCCESSFUL**

Jos 1:7 that you may be *s* wherever you go.
2Ki 18:7 he was *s* in whatever he undertook.
2Ch 20:20 in his prophets and you will be *s*."

**SUFFER (SUFFERED SUFFERING SUFFERINGS SUFFERS)**

Isa 53:10 to crush him and cause him to *s*,
Mk 8:31 the Son of Man must *s* many things
Lk 24:26 the Christ have to *s* these things
24:46 The Christ will *s* and rise
Php 1:29 to *s* for him, since you are going
1Pe 4:16 However, if you *s* as a Christian,

**SUFFERED (SUFFER)**

Heb 2:9 and honor because he *s* death,
2:18 Because he himself *s*

1Pe 2:21 Christ *s* for you, leaving you

**SUFFERING (SUFFER)**
Isa 53:3 of sorrows, and familiar with *s*.
Ac 5:41 worthy of *s* disgrace for the Name.
2Ti 1:8 But join with me in *s* for the gospel,
Heb 2:10 of their salvation perfect through *s*.

**SUFFERINGS (SUFFER)**
Ro 8:17 share in his *s* in order that we may
8:18 that our present *s* are not worth
2Co 1:5 as the *s* of Christ flow
Php 3:10 the fellowship of sharing in his *s*,

**SUFFERS (SUFFER)**
Pr 13:20 but a companion of fools *s* harm.
1Co 12:26 If one part *s*, every part *s* with it;

**SUFFICIENT**
2Co 12:9 said to me, "My grace is *s* for you,

**SUITABLE**
Ge 2:18 I will make a helper *s* for him."

**SUN**
Ecc 1:9 there is nothing new under the *s*.
Mal 4:2 the *s* of righteousness will rise
Mt 5:45 He causes his *s* to rise on the evil
17:2 His face shone like the *s*,
Rev 1:16 His face was like the *s* shining
21:23 The city does not need the *s*

**SUPERIOR**
Heb 1:4 he became as much *s* to the angels
8:6 ministry Jesus has received is as *s*

**SUPERVISION**
Gal 3:25 longer under the *s* of the law.

**SUPREMACY* (SUPREME)**
Col 1:18 in everything he might have the *s*.

**SUPREME (SUPREMACY)**
Pr 4:7 Wisdom is *s*; therefore get wisdom.

**SURE**
Nu 32:23 you may be *s* that your sin will find
Dt 6:17 Be *s* to keep the commands
14:22 Be *s* to set aside a tenth
Isa 28:16 cornerstone for a *s* foundation;
Heb 11:1 faith is being *s* of what we hope for
2Pe 1:10 to make your calling and election *s*.

**SURPASS* (SURPASSES SURPASSING)**
Pr 31:29 but you *s* them all."

**SURPASSES (SURPASS)**
Mt 5:20 unless your righteousness *s* that
Eph 3:19 to know this love that *s* knowledge

**SURPASSING* (SURPASS)**
Ps 150:2 praise him for his *s* greatness.
2Co 3:10 in comparison with the *s* glory.
9:14 of the *s* grace God has given you.

Php 3:8 the *s* greatness of knowing Christ

**SURROUNDED**
Heb 12:1 since we are *s* by such a great cloud

**SUSPENDS***
Job 26:7 he *s* the earth over nothing.

**SUSTAINING* (SUSTAINS)**
Heb 1:3 *s* all things by his powerful word.

**SUSTAINS (SUSTAINING)**
Ps 18:35 and your right hand *s* me;
146:9 and *s* the fatherless and the widow,
147:6 The LORD *s* the humble
Isa 50:4 to know the word that *s* the weary.

**SWALLOWED**
1Co 15:54 "Death has been *s* up in victory."
2Co 5:4 so that what is mortal may be *s* up

**SWEAR**
Mt 5:34 Do not *s* at all: either by heaven,

**SWORD (SWORDS)**
Ps 45:3 Gird your *s* upon your side,
Pr 12:18 Reckless words pierce like a *s*,
Mt 10:34 come to bring peace, but a *s*.
26:52 all who draw the *s* will die by the *s*.
Lk 2:35 a *s* will pierce your own soul too."
Ro 13:4 for he does not bear the *s*
Eph 6:17 of salvation and the *s* of the Spirit,
Heb 4:12 Sharper than any double-edged *s*,
Rev 1:16 came a sharp double-edged *s*.

**SWORDS (SWORD)**

Isa 2:4 They will beat their *s*

Joel 3:10 Beat your plowshares into *s*

**SYMPATHETIC***

1Pe 3:8 in harmony with one another; be *s*,

**SYNAGOGUE**

Lk 4:16 the Sabbath day he went into the *s*,

Ac 17:2 custom was, Paul went into the *s*,

**TABERNACLE**

Ex 40:34 the glory of the LORD filled the *t*.

**TABLE (TABLES)**

Ps 23:5 You prepare a *t* before me

**TABLES (TABLE)**

Ac 6:2 word of God in order to wait on *t*.

**TABLET (TABLETS)**

Pr 3:3 write them on the *t* of your heart.

7:3 write them on the *t* of your heart.

**TABLETS (TABLET)**

Ex 31:18 he gave him the two *t*

Dt 10:5 and put the *t* in the ark I had made,

2Co 3:3 not on *t* of stone but on *t*

**TAKE (TAKEN TAKES TAKING TOOK)**

Dt 12:32 do not add to it or *t* away from it.

31:26 "*T* this Book of the Law

Job 23:10 But he knows the way that I *t*;

Ps 49:17 for he will *t* nothing with him

Ps 51:11 or *t* your Holy Spirit from me.

Mt 10:38 anyone who does not *t* his cross

11:29 *T* my yoke upon you and learn

16:24 deny himself and *t* up his cross

**TAKEN (TAKE)**

Lev 6:4 must return what he has stolen or *t*

Isa 6:7 your guilt is *t* away and your sin

Mt 24:40 one will be *t* and the other left.

Mk 16:19 he was *t* up into heaven

1Ti 3:16 was *t* up in glory.

**TAKES (TAKE)**

1Ki 20:11 should not boast like one who *t* it

Ps 5:4 You are not a God who *t* pleasure

Jn 1:29 who *t* away the sin of the world!

Rev 22:19 And if anyone *t* words away

**TAKING (TAKE)**

Ac 15:14 by *t* from the Gentiles a people

Php 2:7 *t* the very nature of a servant,

**TALENT**

Mt 25:15 to another one *t*, each according

**TAME***

Jas 3:8 but no man can *t* the tongue.

**TASK**

Mk 13:34 each with his assigned *t*,

Ac 20:24 complete the *t* the Lord Jesus has

1Co 3:5 the Lord has assigned to each his *t*.

2Co 2:16 And who is equal to such a *t*?

**TASTE (TASTED)**

Ps 34:8 *T* and see that the LORD is good;

Col 2:21 Do not *t*! Do not touch!"?

Heb 2:9 the grace of God he might *t* death

**TASTED (TASTE)**

1Pe 2:3 now that you have *t* that the Lord

**TAUGHT (TEACH)**

Mt 7:29 he *t* as one who had authority,

1Co 2:13 but in words *t* by the Spirit,

Gal 1:12 nor was I *t* it; rather, I received it

**TAXES**

Mt 22:17 Is it right to pay *t* to Caesar or not

Ro 13:7 If you owe *t*, pay *t*; if revenue,

**TEACH (TAUGHT TEACHER TEACHERS TEACHES TEACHING)**

Ex 33:13 *t* me your ways so I may know you

Dt 4:9 *T* them to your children

8:3 to *t* you that man does not live

11:19 *T* them to your children, talking

1Sa 12:23 I will *t* you the way that is good

Ps 32:8 *t* you in the way you should go;

51:13 I will *t* transgressors your ways,

90:12 *T* us to number our days aright,

143:10 *T* me to do your will,

Jer 31:34 No longer will a man *t* his neighbor
Lk 11:1 said to him, "Lord, *t* us to pray,
Jn 14:26 will *t* you all things and will remind
1Ti 2:12 I do not permit a woman to *t*
3:2 respectable, hospitable, able to *t*,
Tit 2:1 You must *t* what is in accord
Heb 8:11 No longer will a man *t* his neighbor
Jas 3:1 know that we who *t* will be judged
1Jn 2:27 you do not need anyone to *t* you.

**TEACHER (TEACH)**
Mt 10:24 "A student is not above his *t*,
Jn 13:14 and *T*, have washed your feet,

**TEACHERS (TEACH)**
1Co 12:28 third *t*, then workers of miracles,
Eph 4:11 and some to be pastors and *t*,
Heb 5:12 by this time you ought to be *t*,

**TEACHES (TEACH)**
1Ti 6:3 If anyone *t* false doctrines

**TEACHING (TEACH)**
Pr 1:8 and do not forsake your mother's *t*.
Mt 28:20 *t* them to obey everything I have
Jn 7:17 whether my *t* comes from God or
14:23 loves me, he will obey my *t*.
1Ti 4:13 of Scripture, to preaching and to *t*.
2Ti 3:16 is God-breathed and is useful for *t*,
Tit 2:7 In your *t* show integrity,

**TEAR (TEARS)**
Rev 7:17 God will wipe away every *t*

**TEARS (TEAR)**
Ps 126:5 Those who sow in *t*
Php 3:18 and now say again even with *t*,

**TEETH (TOOTH)**
Mt 8:12 will be weeping and gnashing of *t*."

**TEMPERATE***
1Ti 3:2 *t*, self-controlled, respectable,
3:11 not malicious talkers but *t*
Tit 2:2 Teach the older men to be *t*,

**TEMPEST**
Ps 55:8 far from the *t* and storm."

**TEMPLE (TEMPLES)**
1Ki 8:27 How much less this *t* I have built!
Hab 2:20 But the LORD is in his holy *t*;
1Co 3:16 that you yourselves are God's *t*
6:19 you not know that your body is a *t*
2Co 6:16 For we are the *t* of the living God.

**TEMPLES (TEMPLE)**
Ac 17:24 does not live in *t* built by hands.

**TEMPT (TEMPTATION TEMPTED)**
1Co 7:5 again so that Satan will not *t* you

**TEMPTATION (TEMPT)**
Mt 6:13 And lead us not into *t*,
26:41 pray so that you will not fall into *t*.
1Co 10:13 No *t* has seized you except what is

**TEMPTED (TEMPT)**
Mt 4:1 into the desert to be *t* by the devil.
1Co 10:13 he will not let you be *t*
Heb 2:18 he himself suffered when he was *t*,
4:15 but we have one who has been *t*
Jas 1:13 For God cannot be *t* by evil,

**TEN (TENTH TITHE TITHES)**
Ex 34:28 covenant—the *T* Commandments.
Ps 91:7 *t* thousand at your right hand,
Mt 25:28 it to the one who has the *t* talents.
Lk 15:8 suppose a woman has *t* silver coins

**TENTH (TEN)**
Dt 14:22 Be sure to set aside a *t*

**TERRIBLE (TERROR)**
2Ti 3:1 There will be *t* times

**TERROR (TERRIBLE)**
Ps 91:5 You will not fear the *t* of night,
Lk 21:26 Men will faint from *t*, apprehensive
Ro 13:3 For rulers hold no *t*

**TEST (TESTED TESTS)**
Dt 6:16 Do not *t* the LORD your God
Ps 139:23 *t* me and know my anxious
Ro 12:2 Then you will be able to *t*
1Co 3:13 and the fire will *t* the quality
1Jn 4:1 *t* the spirits to see whether they are

**TESTED (TEST)**
Ge 22:1 Some time later God *t* Abraham.
Job 23:10 when he has *t* me, I will come forth
Pr 27:21 man is *t* by the praise he receives.
1Ti 3:10 They must first be *t;* and then

**TESTIFY (TESTIMONY)**
Jn 5:39 are the Scriptures that *t* about me,
2Ti 1:8 ashamed to *t* about our Lord,

**TESTIMONY (TESTIFY)**
Isa 8:20 and to the *t!* If they do not speak
Lk 18:20 not give false *t,* honor your father

**TESTS (TEST)**
Pr 17:3 but the LORD *t* the heart.
1Th 2:4 but God, who *t* our hearts.

**THADDAEUS**
Apostle (Mt 10:3; Mk 3:18); probably also known as Judas son of James (Lk 6:16; Ac 1:13).

**THANKFUL (THANKS)**
Heb 12:28 let us be *t,* and so worship God

**THANKS (THANKFUL THANKSGIVING)**
1Ch 16:8 Give *t* to the LORD, call
Ne 12:31 assigned two large choirs to give *t.*
Ps 100:4 give *t* to him and praise his name.
1Co 15:57 *t* be to God! He gives us the victory
2Co 2:14 *t* be to God, who always leads us
9:15 *T* be to God for his indescribable
1Th 5:18 give *t* in all circumstances,

**THANKSGIVING (THANKS)**
Ps 95:2 Let us come before him with *t*
100:4 Enter his gates with *t*
Php 4:6 by prayer and petition, with *t,*
1Ti 4:3 created to be received with *t*

**THIEF (THIEVES)**
Ex 22:3 A *t* must certainly make restitution
1Th 5:2 day of the Lord will come like a *t*
Rev 16:15 I come like a *t!* Blessed is he who

**THIEVES (THIEF)**
1Co 6:10 nor homosexual offenders nor *t*

**THINK (THOUGHT THOUGHTS)**
Ro 12:3 Do not *t* of yourself more highly
Php 4:8 praiseworthy—*t* about such things

**THIRST (THIRSTY)**
Ps 69:21 and gave me vinegar for my *t.*
Mt 5:6 Blessed are those who hunger and *t*
Jn 4:14 the water I give him will never *t.*

**THIRSTY (THIRST)**
Isa 55:1 "Come, all you who are *t,*
Jn 7:37 "If anyone is *t,* let him come to me
Rev 22:17 Whoever is *t,* let him come;

**THOMAS**
Apostle (Mt 10:3; Mk 3:18; Lk 6:15; Jn 11:16; 14:5; 21:2; Ac 1:13). Doubted resurrection (Jn 20:24-28).

**THONGS**
Mk 1:7 *t* of whose sandals I am not worthy

**THORN (THORNS)**
2Co 12:7 there was given me a *t* in my flesh,

**THORNS (THORN)**
Nu 33:55 in your eyes and *t* in your sides.
Mt 27:29 then twisted together a crown of *t*
Heb 6:8 But land that produces *t*

**THOUGHT (THINK)**
Pr 14:15 a prudent man gives *t* to his steps.
1Co 13:11 I talked like a child, I *t* like a child,

**THOUGHTS (THINK)**
Ps 94:11 The LORD knows the *t* of man;
139:23 test me and know my anxious *t.*
Isa 55:8 "For my *t* are not your *t,*
Heb 4:12 it judges the *t* and attitudes

**THREE**
Ecc 4:12 of *t* strands is not quickly broken.
Mt 12:40 *t* nights in the belly of a huge fish,
18:20 or *t* come together in my name,
27:63 'After *t* days I will rise again.'
1Co 13:13 And now these *t* remain: faith,
14:27 or at the most *t*—should speak,
2Co 13:1 testimony of two or *t* witnesses."

**THRESHING**
2Sa 24:18 an altar to the LORD on the *t* floor

**THRONE (ENTHRONED)**
2Sa 7:16 your *t* will be established forever
Ps 45:6 Your *t*, O God, will last for ever
47:8 God is seated on his holy *t*.
Isa 6:1 I saw the Lord seated on a *t*,
66:1 "Heaven is my *t*
Heb 4:16 Let us then approach the *t* of grace
12:2 at the right hand of the *t* of God.
Rev 4:10 They lay their crowns before the *t*
20:11 Then I saw a great white *t*
22:3 *t* of God and of the Lamb will be

**THROW**
Jn 8:7 the first to *t* a stone at her."
Heb 10:35 So do not *t* away your confidence;
12:1 let us *t* off everything that hinders

**THWART***
Isa 14:27 has purposed, and who can *t* him?

**TIBNI**
King of Israel (1Ki 16:21-22).

**TIME (TIMES)**
Est 4:14 come to royal position for such a *t*
Da 7:25 to him for a *t*, times and half a *t*.
Hos 10:12 for it is *t* to seek the LORD,
Ro 9:9 "At the appointed *t* I will return,
Heb 9:28 and he will appear a second *t*,
10:12 for all *t* one sacrifice for sins,
1Pe 4:17 For it is *t* for judgment to begin

**TIMES (TIME)**
Ps 9:9 a stronghold in *t* of trouble.
31:15 My *t* are in your hands;
62:8 Trust in him at all *t*, O people;
Pr 17:17 A friend loves at all *t*,
Am 5:13 for the *t* are evil.
Mt 18:21 how many *t* shall I forgive my
Ac 1:7 "It is not for you to know the *t*
Rev 12:14 *t* and half a time, out

**TIMIDITY***
2Ti 1:7 For God did not give us a spirit of *t*

**TIMOTHY**
Believer from Lystra (Ac 16:1). Joined Paul on second missionary journey (Ac 16-20). Sent to settle problems at Corinth (1Co 4:17; 16:10). Led church at Ephesus (1Ti 1:3). Co-writer with Paul (1Th 1:1; 2Th 1:1; Phm 1).

**TIRE (TIRED)**
2Th 3:13 never *t* of doing what is right.

**TIRED (TIRE)**
Ex 17:12 When Moses' hands grew *t*,
Isa 40:28 He will not grow *t* or weary,

**TITHE (TEN)**
Lev 27:30 " 'A *t* of everything from the land,
Dt 12:17 eat in your own towns the *t*
Mal 3:10 the whole *t* into the storehouse,

**TITHES (TEN)**
Mal 3:8 'How do we rob you?' "In *t*

**TITUS**
Gentile co-worker of Paul (Gal 2:1-3; 2Ti 4:10); sent to Corinth (2Co 2:13; 7-8; 12:18), Crete (Tit 1:4-5).

**TODAY**
Mt 6:11 Give us *t* our daily bread.
Lk 23:43 *t* you will be with me in paradise."
Heb 3:13 daily, as long as it is called *T*,
13:8 Christ is the same yesterday and *t*

**TOIL**
Ge 3:17 through painful *t* you will eat of it

**TOLERATE**
Hab 1:13 you cannot *t* wrong.
Rev 2:2 that you cannot *t* wicked men,

**TOMB**
Mt 27:65 make the *t* as secure as you know
Lk 24:2 the stone rolled away from the *t*,

**TOMORROW**
Pr 27:1 Do not boast about *t*,
Isa 22:13 "for *t* we die!"
Mt 6:34 Therefore do not worry about *t*,
Jas 4:13 "Today or *t* we will go to this

**TONGUE (TONGUES)**
Ps 39:1 and keep my *t* from sin;
Pr 12:18 but the *t* of the wise brings healing.
1Co 14:2 speaks in a *t* does not speak to men

1Co 14:4 He who speaks in a *t* edifies himself
14:13 in a *t* should pray that he may
14:19 than ten thousand words in a *t*.
Php 2:11 every *t* confess that Jesus Christ is
Jas 1:26 does not keep a tight rein on his *t*,
3:8 but no man can tame the *t*.

**TONGUES (TONGUE)**
Isa 28:11 with foreign lips and strange *t*
66:18 and gather all nations and *t*,
Mk 16:17 in new *t*; they will pick up snakes
Ac 2:4 and began to speak in other *t*
10:46 For they heard them speaking in *t*
19:6 and they spoke in *t* and prophesied
1Co 12:30 Do all speak in *t*? Do all interpret?
14:18 speak in *t* more than all of you.
14:39 and do not forbid speaking in *t*.

**TOOK (TAKE)**
1Co 11:23 the night he was betrayed, *t* bread,
Php 3:12 for which Christ Jesus *t* hold of me.

**TOOTH (TEETH)**
Ex 21:24 eye for eye, *t* for *t*, hand for hand,
Mt 5:38 'Eye for eye, and *t* for *t*.'

**TORMENTED**
Rev 20:10 They will be *t* day and night

**TORN**
Gal 4:15 you would have *t* out your eyes

Php 1:23 I do not know! I am *t*

**TOUCH (TOUCHED)**
Ps 105:15 "Do not *t* my anointed ones;
Lk 24:39 It is I myself! *T* me and see;
2Co 6:17 *T* no unclean thing,
Col 2:21 Do not taste! Do not *t*!"?

**TOUCHED (TOUCH)**
1Sa 10:26 men whose hearts God had *t*.
Mt 14:36 and all who *t* him were healed.

**TOWER**
Ge 11:4 with a *t* that reaches to the heavens
Pr 18:10 of the LORD is a strong *t*;

**TOWNS**
Nu 35:2 to give the Levites *t* to live
35:15 These six *t* will be a place of refuge

**TRACING***
Ro 11:33 and his paths beyond *t* out!

**TRADITION**
Mt 15:6 word of God for the sake of your *t*.
Col 2:8 which depends on human *t*

**TRAIN (TRAINING)**
Pr 22:6 *T* a child in the way he should go,
Eph 4:8 he led captives in his *t*

**TRAINING (TRAIN)**
1Co 9:25 in the games goes into strict *t*.
2Ti 3:16 correcting and *t* in righteousness,

**TRAMPLED**
Lk 21:24 Jerusalem will be *t*
Heb 10:29 to be punished who has *t* the Son

**TRANCE**
Ac 10:10 was being prepared, he fell into a *t*.

**TRANSCENDS***
Php 4:7 which *t* all understanding,

**TRANSFIGURED**
Mt 17:2 There he was *t* before them.

**TRANSFORM* (TRANSFORMED)**
Php 3:21 will *t* our lowly bodies

**TRANSFORMED (TRANSFORM)**
Ro 12:2 be *t* by the renewing of your mind.
2Co 3:18 are being *t* into his likeness

**TRANSGRESSION (TRANSGRESSIONS TRANSGRESSORS)**
Isa 53:8 for the *t* of my people he was
Ro 4:15 where there is no law there is no *t*.

**TRANSGRESSIONS (TRANSGRESSION)**
Ps 32:1 whose *t* are forgiven,
51:1 blot out my *t*.
103:12 so far has he removed our *t* from us
Isa 53:5 But he was pierced for our *t*,
Eph 2:1 you were dead in your *t* and sins,

**TRANSGRESSORS (TRANSGRESSION)**

Ps 51:13 Then I will teach *t* your ways,
Isa 53:12 and made intercession for the *t*.
53:12 and was numbered with the *t*.

**TREADING**

Dt 25:4 an ox while it is *t* out the grain.
1Co 9:9 an ox while it is *t* out the grain."

**TREASURE (TREASURED TREASURES)**

Isa 33:6 of the LORD is the key to this *t*.
Mt 6:21 For where your *t* is, there your
2Co 4:7 But we have this *t* in jars of clay

**TREASURED (TREASURE)**

Dt 7:6 to be his people, his *t* possession.
Lk 2:19 But Mary *t* up all these things

**TREASURES (TREASURE)**

Mt 6:19 up for yourselves *t* on earth,
Col 2:3 in whom are hidden all the *t*
Heb 11:26 of greater value than the *t* of Egypt,

**TREAT**

Lev 22:2 sons to *t* with respect the sacred
1Ti 5:1 *T* younger men as brothers,
1Pe 3:7 and *t* them with respect

**TREATY**

Dt 7:2 Make no *t* with them, and show

**TREE**

Ge 2:9 and the *t* of the knowledge of good
2:9 of the garden were the *t* of life
Dt 21:23 hung on a *t* is under God's curse.
Ps 1:3 He is like a *t* planted by streams
Mt 3:10 every *t* that does not produce good
12:33 for a *t* is recognized by its fruit.
Gal 3:13 is everyone who is hung on a *t*."
Rev 22:14 they may have the right to the *t*

**TREMBLE (TREMBLING)**

1Ch 16:30 *T* before him, all the earth!
Ps 114:7 *T*, O earth, at the presence

**TREMBLING (TREMBLE)**

Ps 2:11 and rejoice with *t*.
Php 2:12 out your salvation with fear and *t*,

**TRESPASS**

Ro 5:17 For if, by the *t* of the one man,

**TRIALS**

1Th 3:3 one would be unsettled by these *t*.
Jas 1:2 whenever you face *t* of many kinds,
2Pe 2:9 how to rescue godly men from *t*

**TRIBES**

Ge 49:28 All these are the twelve *t* of Israel,
Mt 19:28 judging the twelve *t* of Israel.

**TRIBULATION***

Rev 7:14 who have come out of the great *t*;

**TRIUMPHAL* (TRIUMPHING)**

Isa 60:11 their kings led in *t* procession.
2Co 2:14 us in *t* procession in Christ

**TRIUMPHING* (TRIUMPHAL)**

Col 2:15 of them, *t* over them by the cross.

**TROUBLE (TROUBLED TROUBLES)**

Job 14:1 is of few days and full of *t*.
Ps 46:1 an ever-present help in *t*.
107:13 they cried to the LORD in their *t*,
Pr 11:29 He who brings *t* on his family will
24:10 If you falter in times of *t*,
Mt 6:34 Each day has enough *t* of its own.
Jn 16:33 In this world you will have *t*.
Ro 8:35 Shall *t* or hardship or persecution

**TROUBLED (TROUBLE)**

Jn 14:1 "Do not let your hearts be *t*.
14:27 Do not let your hearts be *t*

**TROUBLES (TROUBLE)**

1Co 7:28 those who marry will face many *t*
2Co 1:4 who comforts us in all our *t*,
4:17 and momentary *t* are achieving

**TRUE (TRUTH)**

Dt 18:22 does not take place or come *t*,
1Sa 9:6 and everything he says comes *t*.

Ps 119:160 All your words are *t*;
Jn 17:3 the only *t* God, and Jesus Christ,
Ro 3:4 Let God be *t*, and every man a liar.
Php 4:8 whatever is *t*, whatever is noble,
Rev 22:6 These words are trustworthy and *t*.

**TRUMPET**
1Co 14:8 if the *t* does not sound a clear call,
15:52 For the *t* will sound, the dead will

**TRUST (ENTRUSTED TRUSTED TRUSTS TRUSTWORTHY)**
Ps 20:7 we *t* in the name of the LORD our
37:3 *T* in the LORD and do good;
56:4 in God I *t*; I will not be afraid.
119:42 for I *t* in your word.
Pr 3:5 *T* in the LORD with all your heart
Isa 30:15 in quietness and *t* is your strength,
Jn 14:1 *T* in God; *t* also in me.
1Co 4:2 been given a *t* must prove faithful.

**TRUSTED (TRUST)**
Ps 26:1 I have *t* in the LORD
Isa 25:9 we *t* in him, and he saved us.
Da 3:28 They *t* in him and defied the king's
Lk 16:10 *t* with very little can also be *t*

**TRUSTS (TRUST)**
Ps 32:10 surrounds the man who *t* in him.
Pr 11:28 Whoever *t* in his riches will fall,
Pr 28:26 He who *t* in himself is a fool,
Ro 9:33 one who *t* in him will never be put

**TRUSTWORTHY (TRUST)**
Ps 119:138 they are fully *t*.
Pr 11:13 but a *t* man keeps a secret.
Rev 22:6 "These words are *t* and true.

**TRUTH (TRUE TRUTHFUL TRUTHS)**
Ps 51:6 Surely you desire *t*
Isa 45:19 I, the LORD, speak the *t*;
Zec 8:16 are to do: Speak the *t* to each other,
Jn 4:23 worship the Father in spirit and *t*,
8:32 Then you will know the *t*,
8:32 and the *t* will set you free."
14:6 I am the way and the *t* and the life.
16:13 comes, he will guide you into all *t*.
18:38 "What is *t*?" Pilate asked.
Ro 1:25 They exchanged the *t* of God
1Co 13:6 in evil but rejoices with the *t*.
2Co 13:8 against the *t*, but only for the *t*.
Eph 4:15 Instead, speaking the *t* in love,
6:14 with the belt of *t* buckled
2Th 2:10 because they refused to love the *t*
1Ti 2:4 to come to a knowledge of the *t*.
3:15 the pillar and foundation of the *t*.
2Ti 2:15 correctly handles the word of *t*.
2Ti 3:7 never able to acknowledge the *t*.
Heb 10:26 received the knowledge of the *t*,
1Pe 1:22 by obeying the *t* so that you have
2Pe 2:2 the way of *t* into disrepute.
1Jn 1:6 we lie and do not live by the *t*.
1:8 deceive ourselves and the *t* is not

**TRUTHFUL (TRUTH)**
Pr 12:22 but he delights in men who are *t*.
Jn 3:33 it has certified that God is *t*.

**TRUTHS (TRUTH)**
1Co 2:13 expressing spiritual *t*
1Ti 3:9 hold of the deep *t* of the faith
Heb 5:12 to teach you the elementary *t*

**TRY (TRYING)**
Ps 26:2 Test me, O LORD, and *t* me,
Isa 7:13 enough to *t* the patience of men?
1Co 14:12 *t* to excel in gifts that build up
2Co 5:11 is to fear the Lord, we *t*
1Th 5:15 always *t* to be kind to each other

**TRYING (TRY)**
2Co 5:12 We are not *t* to commend ourselves
1Th 2:4 We are not *t* to please men but God

**TUNIC**
Lk 6:29 do not stop him from taking your *t*.

**TURN (TURNED TURNS)**
Ex 32:12 *T* from your fierce anger; relent

Dt 5:32 do not *t* aside to the right
28:14 Do not *t* aside from any
Jos 1:7 do not *t* from it to the right
2Ch 7:14 and *t* from their wicked ways,
30:9 He will not *t* his face from you
Ps 78:6 they in *t* would tell their children.
Pr 22:6 when he is old he will not *t* from it.
Isa 29:16 You *t* things upside down,
30:21 Whether you *t* to the right
45:22 "*T* to me and be saved,
55:7 Let him *t* to the LORD,
Eze 33:11 *T! T* from your evil ways!
Mal 4:6 He will *t* the hearts of the fathers
Mt 5:39 you on the right cheek, *t*
10:35 For I have come to *t*
Jn 12:40 nor *t*—and I would heal them."
Ac 3:19 Repent, then, and *t* to God,
26:18 and *t* them from darkness to light,
1Ti 6:20 *T* away from godless chatter
1Pe 3:11 He must *t* from evil and do good;

**TURNED (TURN)**
Ps 30:11 You *t* my wailing into dancing;
40:1 he *t* to me and heard my cry.
Isa 53:6 each of us has *t* to his own way;
Hos 7:8 Ephraim is a flat cake not *t* over.
Joel 2:31 The sun will be *t* to darkness
Ro 3:12 All have *t* away,

**TURNS (TURN)**
2Sa 22:29 the LORD *t* my darkness into light
Pr 15:1 A gentle answer *t* away wrath,
Isa 44:25 and *t* it into nonsense,
Jas 5:20 Whoever *t* a sinner from the error

**TWELVE**
Ge 49:28 All these are the *t* tribes of Israel,
Mt 10:1 He called his *t* disciples to him

**TWINKLING***
1Co 15:52 in a flash, in the *t* of an eye,

**UNAPPROACHABLE***
1Ti 6:16 immortal and who lives in *u* light,

**UNBELIEF (UNBELIEVER UNBELIEVERS UNBELIEVING)**
Mk 9:24 help me overcome my *u!*"
Ro 11:20 they were broken off because of *u*,
Heb 3:19 able to enter, because of their *u*.

**UNBELIEVER* (UNBELIEF)**
1Co 7:15 But if the *u* leaves, let him do so.
10:27 If some *u* invites you to a meal
14:24 if an *u* or someone who does not
2Co 6:15 have in common with an *u?*
1Ti 5:8 the faith and is worse than an *u*.

**UNBELIEVERS (UNBELIEF)**
1Co 6:6 another—and this in front of *u!*
2Co 6:14 Do not be yoked together with *u*.

**UNBELIEVING (UNBELIEF)**
1Co 7:14 For the *u* husband has been
Rev 21:8 But the cowardly, the *u*, the vile,

**UNCERTAIN***
1Ti 6:17 which is so *u*, but to put their hope

**UNCHANGEABLE***
Heb 6:18 by two *u* things in which it is

**UNCIRCUMCISED**
1Sa 17:26 Who is this *u* Philistine that he
Col 3:11 circumcised or *u*, barbarian,

**UNCIRCUMCISION**
1Co 7:19 is nothing and *u* is nothing.
Gal 5:6 neither circumcision nor *u* has any

**UNCLEAN**
Isa 6:5 ruined! For I am a man of *u* lips,
Ro 14:14 fully convinced that no food is *u*
2Co 6:17 Touch no *u* thing,

**UNCONCERNED***
Eze 16:49 were arrogant, overfed and *u;*

**UNCOVERED**
Heb 4:13 Everything is *u* and laid bare

**UNDERSTAND (UNDERSTANDING UNDERSTANDS)**
Job 42:3 Surely I spoke of things I did not *u*,
Ps 73:16 When I tried to *u* all this,
119:125 that I may *u* your statutes.

Lk 24:45 so they could *u* the Scriptures.
Ac 8:30 "Do you *u* what you are reading?"
Ro 7:15 I do not *u* what I do.
1Co 2:14 and he cannot *u* them,
Eph 5:17 but *u* what the Lord's will is.
2Pe 3:16 some things that are hard to *u*,

### UNDERSTANDING (UNDERSTAND)

Ps 119:104 I gain *u* from your precepts;
147:5 his *u* has no limit.
Pr 3:5 and lean not on your own *u*;
4:7 Though it cost all you have, get *u*.
10:23 but a man of *u* delights in wisdom.
11:12 but a man of *u* holds his tongue.
15:21 a man of *u* keeps a straight course.
15:32 whoever heeds correction gains *u*.
23:23 get wisdom, discipline and *u*.
Isa 40:28 and his *u* no one can fathom.
Da 5:12 a keen mind and knowledge and *u*,
Mk 4:12 and ever hearing but never *u*;
12:33 with all your *u* and with all your
Php 4:7 of God, which transcends all *u*,

### UNDERSTANDS (UNDERSTAND)

1Ch 28:9 and *u* every motive
1Ti 6:4 he is conceited and *u* nothing.

### UNDIVIDED*

1Ch 12:33 to help David with *u* loyalty—
Ps 86:11 give me an *u* heart,
Eze 11:19 I will give them an *u* heart
1Co 7:35 way in *u* devotion to the Lord.

### UNDOING

Pr 18:7 A fool's mouth is his *u*,

### UNDYING*

Eph 6:24 Lord Jesus Christ with an *u* love.

### UNFADING*

1Pe 3:4 the *u* beauty of a gentle

### UNFAILING

Ps 33:5 the earth is full of his *u* love.
119:76 May your *u* love be my comfort,
143:8 bring me word of your *u* love,
Pr 19:22 What a man desires is *u* love;
La 3:32 so great is his *u* love.

### UNFAITHFUL (UNFAITHFULNESS)

Lev 6:2 is *u* to the LORD by deceiving his
1Ch 10:13 because he was *u* to the LORD;
Pr 13:15 but the way of the *u* is hard.

### UNFAITHFULNESS (UNFAITHFUL)

Mt 5:32 except for marital *u*, causes her
19:9 for marital *u*, and marries another

### UNFOLDING

Ps 119:130 the *u* of your words gives light;

### UNGODLINESS

Tit 2:12 It teaches us to say "No" to *u*

### UNIT

1Co 12:12 body is a *u*, though it is made up

### UNITED (UNITY)

Ro 6:5 If we have been *u* with him
Php 2:1 from being *u* with Christ,
Col 2:2 encouraged in heart and *u* in love,

### UNITY (UNITED)

Ps 133:1 is when brothers live together in *u*!
Ro 15:5 a spirit of *u* among yourselves
Eph 4:3 effort to keep the *u* of the Spirit
4:13 up until we all reach *u* in the faith
Col 3:14 them all together in perfect *u*.

### UNIVERSE

Php 2:15 which you shine like stars in the *u*
Heb 1:2 and through whom he made the *u*.

### UNKNOWN

Ac 17:23 TO AN *U* GOD.

### UNLEAVENED

Ex 12:17 "Celebrate the Feast of *U* Bread,

### UNPROFITABLE

Tit 3:9 because these are *u* and useless.

### UNPUNISHED

Ex 34:7 Yet he does not leave the guilty *u*;
Pr 19:5 A false witness will not go *u*,

### UNREPENTANT*

Ro 2:5 stubbornness and your *u* heart,

**UNRIGHTEOUS***

Zep 3:5 yet the *u* know no shame.
Mt 5:45 rain on the righteous and the *u*.
1Pe 3:18 the righteous for the *u*, to bring you
2Pe 2:9 and to hold the *u* for the day

**UNSEARCHABLE**

Ro 11:33 How *u* his judgments,
Eph 3:8 preach to the Gentiles the *u* riches

**UNSEEN**

2Co 4:18 on what is seen, but on what is *u*.
4:18 temporary, but what is *u* is eternal.

**UNSTABLE***

Jas 1:8 he is a double-minded man, *u*
2Pe 2:14 they seduce the *u*; they are experts
3:16 ignorant and *u* people distort,

**UNTHINKABLE***

Job 34:12 It is *u* that God would do wrong,

**UNVEILED***

2Co 3:18 with *u* faces all reflect the Lord's

**UNWORTHY**

Job 40:4 "I am *u*—how can I reply to you?
Lk 17:10 should say, 'We are *u* servants;

**UPRIGHT**

Job 1:1 This man was blameless and *u*;
Pr 2:7 He holds victory in store for the *u*,
15:8 but the prayer of the *u* pleases him.
Tit 1:8 who is self-controlled, *u*, holy
2:12 *u* and godly lives in this present

**UPROOTED**

Jude :12 without fruit and *u*—twice dead.

**USEFUL**

2Ti 2:21 *u* to the Master and prepared
3:16 Scripture is God-breathed and is *u*

**USELESS**

1Co 15:14 our preaching is *u*
Jas 2:20 faith without deeds is *u*?

**USURY**

Ne 5:10 But let the exacting of *u* stop!

**UTTER**

Ps 78:2 I will *u* hidden things, things from of

**UZZIAH**

Son of Amaziah; king of Judah also known as Azariah (2Ki 15:1-7; 1Ch 6:24; 2Ch 26).

**VAIN**

Ps 33:17 A horse is a *v* hope for deliverance;
Isa 65:23 They will not toil in *v*
1Co 15:2 Otherwise, you have believed in *v*.
15:58 labor in the Lord is not in *v*.
2Co 6:1 not to receive God's grace in *v*.

**VALLEY**

Ps 23:4 walk through the *v* of the shadow
Isa 40:4 Every *v* shall be raised up,
Joel 3:14 multitudes in the *v* of decision!

**VALUABLE (VALUE)**

Lk 12:24 And how much more *v* you are

**VALUE (VALUABLE)**

Mt 13:46 When he found one of great *v*,
1Ti 4:8 For physical training is of some *v*,
Heb 11:26 as of greater *v* than the treasures

**VEIL**

Ex 34:33 to them, he put a *v* over his face.
2Co 3:14 for to this day the same *v* remains

**VENGEANCE (AVENGE REVENGE)**

Isa 34:8 For the LORD has a day of *v*,

**VICTORIES (VICTORY)**

Ps 18:50 He gives his king great *v*;
21:1 great is his joy in the *v* you give!

**VICTORIOUSLY* (VICTORY)**

Ps 45:4 In your majesty ride forth *v*

**VICTORY (VICTORIES VICTORIOUSLY)**

Ps 60:12 With God we will gain the *v*,
1Co 15:54 "Death has been swallowed up in *v*
15:57 He gives us the *v* through our Lord
1Jn 5:4 This is the *v* that has overcome

**VINDICATED**

1Ti 3:16 was *v* by the Spirit,

**VINE**

Jn 15:1 "I am the true *v*, and my Father is

**VINEGAR**
Mk 15:36 filled a sponge with wine *v*,

**VIOLATION**
Heb 2:2 every *v* and disobedience received

**VIOLENCE**
Isa 60:18 No longer will *v* be heard
Eze 45:9 Give up your *v* and oppression

**VIPERS**
Ro 3:13 "The poison of *v* is on their lips."

**VIRGIN**
Isa 7:14 The *v* will be with child
Mt 1:23 "The *v* will be with child
2Co 11:2 that I might present you as a pure *v*

**VIRTUES***
Col 3:14 And over all these *v* put on love,

**VISION**
Ac 26:19 disobedient to the *v* from heaven.

**VOICE**
Ps 95:7 Today, if you hear his *v*,
Isa 30:21 your ears will hear a *v* behind you,
Jn 5:28 are in their graves will hear his *v*
10:3 and the sheep listen to his *v*.
Heb 3:7 "Today, if you hear his *v*,
Rev 3:20 If anyone hears my *v* and opens

**VOMIT**
Pr 26:11 As a dog returns to its *v*,
2Pe 2:22 "A dog returns to its *v*," and,

**VOW**
Nu 30:2 When a man makes a *v*

**WAGES**
Lk 10:7 for the worker deserves his *w*.
Ro 4:4 his *w* are not credited to him
6:23 For the *w* of sin is death,

**WAILING**
Ps 30:11 You turned my *w* into dancing;

**WAIST**
2Ki 1:8 with a leather belt around his *w*."
Mt 3:4 he had a leather belt around his *w*.

**WAIT (WAITED WAITS)**
Ps 27:14 *W* for the LORD;
130:5 I *w* for the LORD, my soul waits,
Isa 30:18 Blessed are all who *w* for him!
Ac 1:4 *w* for the gift my Father promised,
Ro 8:23 as we *w* eagerly for our adoption
1Th 1:10 and to *w* for his Son from heaven,
Tit 2:13 while we *w* for the blessed hope—

**WAITED (WAIT)**
Ps 40:1 I *w* patiently for the LORD;

**WAITS (WAIT)**
Ro 8:19 creation *w* in eager expectation

**WALK (WALKED WALKS)**
Dt 11:19 and when you *w* along the road,
Ps 1:1 who does not *w* in the counsel
23:4 Even though I *w*
89:15 who *w* in the light of your presence
Isa 2:5 let us *w* in the light of the LORD.
30:21 saying, "This is the way; *w* in it."
40:31 they will *w* and not be faint.
Jer 6:16 ask where the good way is, and *w*
Da 4:37 And those who *w* in pride he is able
Am 3:3 Do two *w* together
Mic 6:8 and to *w* humbly with your God.
Mk 2:9 'Get up, take your mat and *w*'?
Jn 8:12 Whoever follows me will never *w*
1Jn 1:7 But if we *w* in the light,
2Jn :6 his command is that you *w* in love.

**WALKED (WALK)**
Ge 5:24 Enoch *w* with God; then he was no
Jos 14:9 which your feet have *w* will be your
Mt 14:29 *w* on the water and came toward

**WALKS (WALK)**
Pr 13:20 He who *w* with the wise grows wise

**WALL**
Jos 6:20 *w* collapsed; so every man charged
Ne 2:17 let us rebuild the *w* of Jerusalem,
Rev 21:12 It had a great, high *w*

**WALLOWING**
2Pe 2:22 back to her *w* in the mud."

**WANT (WANTED WANTING WANTS)**
1Sa 8:19 "We *w* a king over us.

Ps 23:1 is my shepherd, I shall not be in *w.*
Lk 19:14 'We don't *w* this man to be our king
Ro 7:15 For what I *w* to do I do not do,
Php 3:10 I *w* to know Christ and the power

**WANTED (WANT)**
1Co 12:18 of them, just as he *w* them to be.

**WANTING (WANT)**
Da 5:27 weighed on the scales and found *w.*
2Pe 3:9 with you, not *w* anyone to perish,

**WANTS (WANT)**
Mt 20:26 whoever *w* to become great
Mk 8:35 For whoever *w* to save his life will
Ro 9:18 he hardens whom he *w* to harden.
1Ti 2:4 who *w* all men to be saved

**WAR (WARS)**
Isa 2:4 nor will they train for *w* anymore.
Da 9:26 *W* will continue until the end,
2Co 10:3 we do not wage *w* as the world does
Rev 19:11 With justice he judges and makes *w*

**WARN (WARNED WARNINGS)**
Eze 3:19 But if you do *w* the wicked man
33:9 if you do *w* the wicked man to turn

**WARNED (WARN)**
Ps 19:11 By them is your servant *w;*

**WARNINGS (WARN)**
1Co 10:11 and were written down as *w* for us,

**WARS (WAR)**
Ps 46:9 He makes *w* cease to the ends
Mt 24:6 You will hear of *w* and rumors of *w,*

**WASH (WASHED WASHING)**
Ps 51:7 *w* me, and I will be whiter
Jn 13:5 and began to *w* his disciples' feet,
Ac 22:16 be baptized and *w* your sins away,
Rev 22:14 Blessed are those who *w* their robes

**WASHED (WASH)**
1Co 6:11 you were *w,* you were sanctified,
Rev 7:14 they have *w* their robes

**WASHING (WASH)**
Eph 5:26 cleansing her by the *w* with water
Tit 3:5 us through the *w* of rebirth

**WATCH (WATCHES WATCHING WATCHMAN)**
Ge 31:49 "May the LORD keep *w*
Jer 31:10 will *w* over his flock like a shepherd
Mt 24:42 "Therefore keep *w,* because you do
26:41 *W* and pray so that you will not fall
Lk 2:8 keeping *w* over their flocks at night
1Ti 4:16 *W* your life and doctrine closely.

**WATCHES (WATCH)**
Ps 1:6 For the LORD *w* over the way
Ps 121:3 he who *w* over you will not slumber

**WATCHING (WATCH)**
Lk 12:37 whose master finds them *w*

**WATCHMAN (WATCH)**
Eze 3:17 I have made you a *w* for the house

**WATER (WATERED WATERS)**
Ps 1:3 like a tree planted by streams of *w,*
22:14 I am poured out like *w,*
Pr 25:21 if he is thirsty, give him *w* to drink.
Isa 49:10 and lead them beside springs of *w.*
Jer 2:13 broken cisterns that cannot hold *w.*
Zec 14:8 On that day living *w* will flow out
Mk 9:41 anyone who gives you a cup of *w*
Jn 4:10 he would have given you living *w.*"
7:38 streams of living *w* will flow
Eph 5:26 washing with *w* through the word,
1Pe 3:21 this *w* symbolizes baptism that now
Rev 21:6 cost from the spring of the *w* of life.

**WATERED (WATER)**
1Co 3:6 I planted the seed, Apollos *w* it,

**WATERS (WATER)**
Ps 23:2 he leads me beside quiet *w,*
Ecc 11:1 Cast your bread upon the *w,*
Isa 58:11 like a spring whose *w* never fail.

1Co 3:7 plants nor he who *w* is anything,

**WAVE (WAVES)**

Jas 1:6 he who doubts is like a *w* of the sea,

**WAVES (WAVE)**

Isa 57:20 whose *w* cast up mire and mud.
Mt 8:27 Even the winds and the *w* obey him
Eph 4:14 tossed back and forth by the *w*,

**WAY (WAYS)**

Dt 1:33 to show you the *w* you should go.
2Sa 22:31 "As for God, his *w* is perfect;
Job 23:10 But he knows the *w* that I take;
Ps 1:1 or stand in the *w* of sinners
37:5 Commit your *w* to the LORD;
119:9 can a young man keep his *w* pure?
139:24 See if there is any offensive *w* in me
Pr 14:12 There is a *w* that seems right
16:17 he who guards his *w* guards his life.
22:6 Train a child in the *w* he should go,
Isa 30:21 saying, "This is the *w*; walk in it."
53:6 each of us has turned to his own *w*;
55:7 Let the wicked forsake his *w*
Mt 3:3 'Prepare the *w* for the Lord,
Jn 14:6 "I am the *w* and the truth
1Co 10:13 also provide a *w* out so that you can
12:31 will show you the most excellent *w*.
Heb 4:15 who has been tempted in every *w*,
9:8 was showing by this that the *w*
10:20 and living *w* opened for us

**WAYS (WAY)**

Ex 33:13 teach me your *w* so I may know
Ps 25:10 All the *w* of the LORD are loving
51:13 I will teach transgressors your *w*,
Pr 3:6 in all your *w* acknowledge him,
Isa 55:8 neither are your *w* my *w*,"
Jas 3:2 We all stumble in many *w*.

**WEAK (WEAKER WEAKNESS)**

Mt 26:41 spirit is willing, but the body is *w*."
Ro 14:1 Accept him whose faith is *w*,
1Co 1:27 God chose the *w* things
8:9 become a stumbling block to the *w*.
9:22 To the *w* I became *w*, to win the *w*.
2Co 12:10 For when I am *w*, then I am strong.
Heb 12:12 your feeble arms and *w* knees.

**WEAKER (WEAK)**

1Co 12:22 seem to be *w* are indispensable,
1Pe 3:7 them with respect as the *w* partner

**WEAKNESS (WEAK)**

Ro 8:26 the Spirit helps us in our *w*.
1Co 1:25 and the *w* of God is stronger
2Co 12:9 for my power is made perfect in *w*
Heb 5:2 since he himself is subject to *w*.

**WEALTH**

Pr 3:9 Honor the LORD with your *w*,
Mk 10:22 away sad, because he had great *w*.
Lk 15:13 and there squandered his *w*

**WEAPONS**

2Co 10:4 The *w* we fight with are not

**WEARIES (WEARY)**

Ecc 12:12 and much study *w* the body.

**WEARY (WEARIES)**

Isa 40:31 they will run and not grow *w*,
Mt 11:28 all you who are *w* and burdened,
Gal 6:9 Let us not become *w* in doing good,

**WEDDING**

Mt 22:11 who was not wearing *w* clothes.
Rev 19:7 For the *w* of the Lamb has come,

**WEEP (WEEPING WEPT)**

Ecc 3:4 a time to *w* and a time to laugh,
Lk 6:21 Blessed are you who *w* now,

**WEEPING (WEEP)**

Ps 30:5 *w* may remain for a night,
126:6 He who goes out *w*,
Mt 8:12 where there will be *w* and gnashing

**WELCOMES**

Mt 18:5 whoever *w* a little child like this

2Jn :11 Anyone who *w* him shares

**WELL**

Lk 17:19 your faith has made you *w*."

Jas 5:15 in faith will make the sick person *w*

**WEPT (WEEP)**

Ps 137:1 of Babylon we sat and *w*

Jn 11:35 Jesus *w*.

**WEST**

Ps 103:12 as far as the east is from the *w*,

**WHIRLWIND (WIND)**

2Ki 2:1 to take Elijah up to heaven in a *w*,

Hos 8:7 and reap the *w*.

Na 1:3 His way is in the *w* and the storm,

**WHITE (WHITER)**

Isa 1:18 they shall be as *w* as snow;

Da 7:9 His clothing was as *w* as snow;

Rev 1:14 hair were *w* like wool, as *w* as snow,

3:4 dressed in *w*, for they are worthy.

20:11 Then I saw a great *w* throne

**WHITER (WHITE)**

Ps 51:7 and I will be *w* than snow.

**WHOLE**

Mt 16:26 for a man if he gains the *w* world,

24:14 will be preached in the *w* world

Jn 13:10 to wash his feet; his *w* body is clean

21:25 the *w* world would not have room

Ac 20:27 proclaim to you the *w* will of God.

Ro 3:19 and the *w* world held accountable

8:22 know that the *w* creation has been

Gal 3:22 declares that the *w* world is

5:3 obligated to obey the *w* law.

Eph 4:13 attaining to the *w* measure

Jas 2:10 For whoever keeps the *w* law

1Jn 2:2 but also for the sins of the *w* world.

**WHOLEHEARTEDLY (HEART)**

Dt 1:36 because he followed the Lord *w*

Eph 6:7 Serve *w*, as if you were serving

**WICKED (WICKEDNESS)**

Ps 1:1 walk in the counsel of the *w*

1:5 Therefore the *w* will not stand

73:3 when I saw the prosperity of the *w*.

Pr 10:20 the heart of the *w* is of little value.

11:21 The *w* will not go unpunished,

Isa 53:9 He was assigned a grave with the *w*

55:7 Let the *w* forsake his way

57:20 But the *w* are like the tossing sea,

Eze 3:18 that *w* man will die for his sin,

18:23 pleasure in the death of the *w*?

33:14 to the *w* man, 'You will surely die,'

**WICKEDNESS (WICKED)**

Eze 28:15 created till *w* was found in you.

**WIDE**

Isa 54:2 stretch your tent curtains *w*,

Mt 7:13 For *w* is the gate and broad is

Eph 3:18 to grasp how *w* and long and high

**WIDOW (WIDOWS)**

Dt 10:18 cause of the fatherless and the *w*,

Lk 21:2 saw a poor *w* put in two very small

**WIDOWS (WIDOW)**

Jas 1:27 look after orphans and *w*

**WIFE (WIVES)**

Ge 2:24 and mother and be united to his *w*,

24:67 she became his *w*, and he loved her;

Ex 20:17 shall not covet your neighbor's *w*,

Dt 5:21 shall not covet your neighbor's *w*.

Pr 5:18 in the *w* of your youth.

12:4 *w* of noble character is her

18:22 He who finds a *w* finds what is

19:13 quarrelsome *w* is like a constant

31:10 *w* of noble character who can find?

Mt 19:3 for a man to divorce his *w* for any

1Co 7:2 each man should have his own *w*,

7:33 how he can please his *w*—

Eph 5:23 the husband is the head of the *w*

5:33 must love his *w* as he loves himself,

1Ti 3:2 husband of but one *w*, temperate,
Rev 21:9 I will show you the bride, the *w*

**WILD**
Lk 15:13 squandered his wealth in *w* living.
Ro 11:17 and you, though a *w* olive shoot,

**WILL (WILLING WILLINGNESS)**
Ps 40:8 I desire to do your *w*, O my God;
143:10 Teach me to do your *w*,
Isa 53:10 Yet it was the LORD's *w*
Mt 6:10 your *w* be done
26:39 Yet not as I *w*, but as you *w*."
Jn 7:17 If anyone chooses to do God's *w*,
Ac 20:27 to you the whole *w* of God.
Ro 12:2 and approve what God's *w* is—
1Co 7:37 but has control over his own *w*,
Eph 5:17 understand what the Lord's *w* is.
Php 2:13 for it is God who works in you to *w*
1Th 4:3 God's *w* that you should be
5:18 for this is God's *w* for you
Heb 9:16 In the case of a *w*, it is necessary
10:7 I have come to do your *w*, O God
Jas 4:15 "If it is the Lord's *w*,
1Jn 5:14 we ask anything according to his *w*,
Rev 4:11 and by your *w* they were created

**WILLING (WILL)**
Ps 51:12 grant me a *w* spirit, to sustain me.
Da 3:28 were *w* to give up their lives rather
Mt 18:14 Father in heaven is not *w* that any
23:37 her wings, but you were not *w*.
26:41 The spirit is *w*, but the body is weak

**WILLINGNESS (WILL)**
2Co 8:12 For if the *w* is there, the gift is

**WIN (WINS)**
Php 3:14 on toward the goal to *w* the prize
1Th 4:12 your daily life may *w* the respect

**WIND (WHIRLWIND)**
Jas 1:6 blown and tossed by the *w*.

**WINE**
Pr 20:1 *W* is a mocker and beer a brawler;
Isa 55:1 Come, buy *w* and milk
Mt 9:17 Neither do men pour new *w*
Lk 23:36 They offered him *w* vinegar
Ro 14:21 not to eat meat or drink *w*
Eph 5:18 on *w*, which leads to debauchery.

**WINESKINS**
Mt 9:17 do men pour new wine into old *w*.

**WINGS**
Ru 2:12 under whose *w* you have come
Ps 17:8 hide me in the shadow of your *w*
Isa 40:31 They will soar on *w* like eagles;
Mal 4:2 rise with healing in its *w*.
Lk 13:34 hen gathers her chicks under her *w*,

**WINS (WIN)**
Pr 11:30 and he who *w* souls is wise.

**WIPE**
Rev 7:17 God will *w* away every tear

**WISDOM (WISE)**
1Ki 4:29 God gave Solomon *w* and very
Ps 111:10 of the LORD is the beginning of *w*;
Pr 31:26 She speaks with *w*,
Jer 10:12 he founded the world by his *w*
Mt 11:19 But *w* is proved right by her actions
Lk 2:52 And Jesus grew in *w* and stature,
Ro 11:33 the depth of the riches of the *w*
Col 2:3 are hidden all the treasures of *w*
Jas 1:5 of you lacks *w*, he should ask God,

**WISE (WISDOM WISER)**
1Ki 3:12 give you a *w* and discerning heart,
Job 5:13 He catches the *w* in their craftiness
Ps 19:7 making *w* the simple.
Pr 3:7 Do not be *w* in your own eyes;
9:8 rebuke a *w* man and he will love
10:1 A *w* son brings joy to his father,
11:30 and he who wins souls is *w*.
13:20 He who walks with the *w* grows *w*,
17:28 Even a fool is thought *w*
Da 12:3 Those who are *w* will shine like

Mt 11:25 hidden these things from the *w*
1Co 1:27 things of the world to shame the *w;*
2Ti 3:15 able to make you *w* for salvation

**WISER (WISE)**
1Co 1:25 of God is *w* than man's wisdom,

**WITHER (WITHERS)**
Ps 1:3 and whose leaf does not *w.*

**WITHERS (WITHER)**
Isa 40:7 The grass *w* and the flowers fall,
1Pe 1:24 the grass *w* and the flowers fall,

**WITHHOLD**
Ps 84:11 no good thing does he *w*
Pr 23:13 Do not *w* discipline from a child;

**WITNESS (WITNESSES)**
Jn 1:8 he came only as a *w* to the light.

**WITNESSES (WITNESS)**
Dt 19:15 by the testimony of two or three *w.*
Ac 1:8 and you will be my *w* in Jerusalem,

**WIVES (WIFE)**
Eph 5:22 *W*, submit to your husbands
5:25 love your *w*, just as Christ loved
1Pe 3:1 words by the behavior of their *w*,

**WOE**
Isa 6:5 "*W* to me!" I cried.

**WOLF**
Isa 65:25 *w* and the lamb will feed together,

**WOMAN (MAN)**
Ge 2:22 God made a *w* from
Ge 3:15 between you and the *w*,
Lev 20:13 as one lies with a *w*,
Dt 22:5 *w* must not wear men's
Ru 3:11 a *w* of noble character
Pr 31:30 a *w* who fears the LORD
Mt 5:28 looks at a *w* lustfully
Jn 8:3 a *w* caught in adultery.
Ro 7:2 a married *w* is bound to
1Co 11:3 the head of the *w* is man,
11:13 a *w* to pray to God with
1Ti 2:11 A *w* should learn in

**WOMEN (MAN)**
Lk 1:42 Blessed are you among *w*,
1Co 14:34 *w* should remain silent in
1Ti 2:9 want *w* to dress modestly
Tit 2:3 teach the older *w* to be
1Pe 3:5 the holy *w* of the past

**WOMB**
Job 1:21 Naked I came from my mother's *w*,
Jer 1:5 you in the *w* I knew you,
Lk 1:44 the baby in my *w* leaped for joy.

**WONDER (WONDERFUL WONDERS)**
Ps 17:7 Show the *w* of your great love,

**WONDERFUL (WONDER)**
Job 42:3 things too *w* for me to know.
Ps 31:21 for he showed his *w* love to me
119:18 *w* things in your law.
119:129 Your statutes are *w;*
139:6 Such knowledge is too *w* for me,
Isa 9:6 *W* Counselor, Mighty God,
1Pe 2:9 out of darkness into his *w* light.

**WONDERS (WONDER)**
Job 37:14 stop and consider God's *w.*
Ps 119:27 then I will meditate on your *w.*
Joel 2:30 I will show *w* in the heavens
Ac 2:19 I will show *w* in the heaven above

**WOOD**
Isa 44:19 Shall I bow down to a block of *w?*"
1Co 3:12 costly stones, *w*, hay or straw,

**WORD (WORDS)**
Dt 8:3 but on every *w* that comes
2Sa 22:31 the *w* of the LORD is flawless.
Ps 119:9 By living according to your *w.*
119:11 I have hidden your *w* in my heart
119:105 Your *w* is a lamp to my feet
Pr 12:25 but a kind *w* cheers him up.
25:11 A *w* aptly spoken
30:5 "Every *w* of God is flawless;
Isa 55:11 so is my *w* that goes out
Jn 1:1 was the *W*, and the *W* was
1:14 The *W* became flesh and made his

2Co 2:17 we do not peddle the *w* of God
4:2 nor do we distort the *w* of God.
Eph 6:17 of the Spirit, which is the *w* of God.
Php 2:16 as you hold out the *w* of life—
Col 3:16 Let the *w* of Christ dwell
2Ti 2:15 and who correctly handles the *w*
Heb 4:12 For the *w* of God is living
Jas 1:22 Do not merely listen to the *w*,
2Pe 1:19 And we have the *w* of the prophets

**WORDS (WORD)**
Dt 11:18 Fix these *w* of mine in your hearts
Ps 119:103 How sweet are your *w* to my taste
119:130 The unfolding of your *w* gives light;
119:160 All your *w* are true;
Pr 30:6 Do not add to his *w*,
Jer 15:16 When your *w* came, I ate them;
Mt 24:35 but my *w* will never pass away.
Jn 6:68 You have the *w* of eternal life.
15:7 in me and my *w* remain in you,
1Co 14:19 rather speak five intelligible *w*
Rev 22:19 And if anyone takes *w* away

**WORK (WORKER WORKERS WORKING WORKMAN WORKMANSHIP WORKS)**
Ex 23:12 "Six days do your *w*,
Nu 8:11 ready to do the *w* of the LORD.
Dt 5:14 On it you shall not do any *w*,
Ecc 5:19 his lot and be happy in his *w*—
Jer 48:10 lax in doing the LORD 's *w!*
Jn 6:27 Do not *w* for food that spoils,
9:4 we must do the *w* of him who sent
1Co 3:13 test the quality of each man's *w*.
Php 1:6 that he who began a good *w*
2:12 continue to *w* out your salvation
Col 3:23 Whatever you do, *w* at it
1Th 5:12 to respect those who *w* hard
2Th 3:10 If a man will not *w*, he shall not eat
2Ti 3:17 equipped for every good *w*.
Heb 6:10 he will not forget your *w*

**WORKER (WORK)**
Lk 10:7 for the *w* deserves his wages.
1Ti 5:18 and "The *w* deserves his wages."

**WORKERS (WORK)**
Mt 9:37 is plentiful but the *w* are few.
1Co 3:9 For we are God's fellow *w;*

**WORKING (WORK)**
Col 3:23 as *w* for the Lord, not for men,

**WORKMAN (WORK)**
2Ti 2:15 a *w* who does not need

**WORKMANSHIP* (WORK)**
Eph 2:10 For we are God's *w*, created

**WORKS (WORK)**
Pr 31:31 let her *w* bring her praise
Ro 8:28 in all things God *w* for the good
Eph 2:9 not by *w*, so that no one can boast.
4:12 to prepare God's people for *w*

**WORLD (WORLDLY)**
Ps 50:12 for the *w* is mine, and all that is in it
Isa 13:11 I will punish the *w* for its evil,
Mt 5:14 "You are the light of the *w*.
16:26 for a man if he gains the whole *w*,
Mk 16:15 into all the *w* and preach the good
Jn 1:29 who takes away the sin of the *w!*
3:16 so loved the *w* that he gave his one
8:12 he said, "I am the light of the *w*.
15:19 As it is, you do not belong to the *w*,
16:33 In this *w* you will have trouble.
18:36 "My kingdom is not of this *w*.
Ro 3:19 and the whole *w* held accountable
1Co 3:19 the wisdom of this *w* is foolishness
2Co 5:19 that God was reconciling the *w*
10:3 For though we live in the *w*,
1Ti 6:7 For we brought nothing into the *w*,
1Jn 2:2 but also for the sins of the whole *w*.
2:15 not love the *w* or anything in the *w*.
Rev 13:8 slain from the creation of the *w*.

**WORLDLY (WORLD)**
Tit 2:12 to ungodliness and *w* passions,

**WORM**
Mk 9:48 " 'their *w* does not die,

**WORRY (WORRYING)**
Mt 6:25 I tell you, do not *w* about your life,
10:19 do not *w* about what to say

**WORRYING (WORRY)**
Mt 6:27 of you by *w* can add a single hour

**WORSHIP**
1Ch 16:29 *w* the LORD in the splendor
Ps 95:6 Come, let us bow down in *w*,
Mt 2:2 and have come to *w* him."
Jn 4:24 and his worshipers must *w* in spirit
Ro 12:1 this is your spiritual act of *w*.

**WORTH (WORTHY)**
Job 28:13 Man does not comprehend its *w*;
Pr 31:10 She is *w* far more than rubies.
Mt 10:31 are *w* more than many sparrows.
Ro 8:18 sufferings are not *w* comparing
1Pe 1:7 of greater *w* than gold,
3:4 which is of great *w* in God's sight.

**WORTHLESS**
Pr 11:4 Wealth is *w* in the day of wrath,
Jas 1:26 himself and his religion is *w*.

**WORTHY (WORTH)**
1Ch 16:25 For great is the LORD and most *w*
Eph 4:1 to live a life *w* of the calling you
Php 1:27 in a manner *w* of the gospel
3Jn :6 on their way in a manner *w* of God.
Rev 5:2 "Who is *w* to break the seals

**WOUNDS**
Pr 27:6 *W* from a friend can be trusted,
Isa 53:5 and by his *w* we are healed.
Zec 13:6 'What are these *w* on your body?'
1Pe 2:24 by his *w* you have been healed.

**WRATH**
2Ch 36:16 scoffed at his prophets until the *w*
Ps 2:5 and terrifies them in his *w*, saying,
76:10 Surely your *w* against men brings
Pr 15:1 A gentle answer turns away *w*,
Jer 25:15 filled with the wine of my *w*
Ro 1:18 The *w* of God is being revealed
5:9 saved from God's *w* through him!
1Th 5:9 God did not appoint us to suffer *w*
Rev 6:16 and from the *w* of the Lamb!

**WRESTLED**
Ge 32:24 and a man *w* with him till daybreak

**WRITE (WRITING WRITTEN)**
Dt 6:9 *W* them on the doorframes
Pr 7:3 *w* them on the tablet of your heart.
Heb 8:10 and *w* them on their hearts.

**WRITING (WRITE)**
1Co 14:37 him acknowledge that what I am *w*

**WRITTEN (WRITE)**
Jos 1:8 careful to do everything *w* in it.
Da 12:1 everyone whose name is found *w*
Lk 10:20 but rejoice that your names are *w*
Jn 20:31 these are *w* that you may believe
1Co 4:6 "Do not go beyond what is *w*."
2Co 3:3 *w* not with ink but with the Spirit
Col 2:14 having canceled the *w* code,
Heb 12:23 whose names are *w* in heaven.

**WRONG (WRONGDOING WRONGED WRONGS)**
Ex 23:2 Do not follow the crowd in doing *w*
Nu 5:7 must make full restitution for his *w*,
Job 34:12 unthinkable that God would do *w*,
1Th 5:15 that nobody pays back *w* for *w*,

**WRONGDOING (WRONG)**
Job 1:22 sin by charging God with *w*.

**WRONGED (WRONG)**
1Co 6:7 not rather be *w*? Why not rather

**WRONGS (WRONG)**
Pr 10:12 but love covers over all *w.*
1Co 13:5 angered, it keeps no record of *w.*

**YEARS**
Ps 90:4 For a thousand *y* in your sight
90:10 The length of our days is seventy *y*
2Pe 3:8 the Lord a day is like a thousand *y,*
Rev 20:2 and bound him for a thousand *y.*

**YESTERDAY**
Heb 13:8 Jesus Christ is the same *y*

**YOKE (YOKED)**
Mt 11:29 Take my *y* upon you and learn

**YOKED (YOKE)**
2Co 6:14 Do not be *y* together

**YOUNG (YOUTH)**
Ps 119:9 How can a *y* man keep his way
1Ti 4:12 down on you because you are *y,*

**YOUTH (YOUNG)**
Ps 103:5 so that your *y* is renewed like
Ecc 12:1 Creator in the days of your *y,*
2Ti 2:22 Flee the evil desires of *y,*

**ZEAL**
Pr 19:2 to have *z* without knowledge,
Ro 12:11 Never be lacking in *z,*

**ZECHARIAH**
1. Son of Jeroboam II; king of Israel (2Ki 15:8-12).
2. Post-exilic prophet who encouraged rebuilding of temple (Ezr 5:1; 6:14; Zec 1:1).
3. Father of John the Baptist (Lk 1:13; 3:2).

**ZEDEKIAH**
Mattaniah, son of Josiah (1Ch 3:15), made king of Judah by Nebuchadnezzar (2Ki 24:17-25:7; 2Ch 36:10-14; Jer 37-39; 52:1-11).

**ZERUBBABEL**
Descendant of David (1Ch 3:19; Mt 1:3). Led return from exile (Ezr 2-3; Ne 7:7; Hag 1-2; Zec 4).

**ZIMRI**
King of Israel (1Ki 16:9-20).

**ZION**
Ps 137:3 "Sing us one of the songs of *Z!*"
Jer 50:5 They will ask the way to *Z*
Ro 9:33 I lay in *Z* a stone that causes men
11:26 "The deliverer will come from *Z;*

**REVEREND ESTRELDA ALEXANDER** is Associate Dean for Community Life at Wesley Theological Seminary, and co-founder and president of the Association of Full Gospel Women Clergy. She is also an Adjunct Professor of Theology at Trinity College. She is a graduate of Wesley Theological Seminary (M.Div.), Columbia University (M.A.), and is a Ph.D. candidate in Political Theology at the Catholic University of America.

**PROFESSOR LINDA L. AMMONS** is Associate Professor of Law at the Cleveland-Marshall College of Law in Cleveland, OH, where she teaches Administrative Law, Legislation, and Women and the Law. She has also served as a legal expert for the California legislature and numerous organizations on the subject of battered women. She has published numerous articles for national scholarly and popular press publications.

**DR. PAMELA JUNE ANDERSON** is a graduate of Johns Hopkins University (B.S.), Howard University Divinity School (M.Div.), and United Theological Seminary (D.Min.). She is the National Secretary for Ministers for Racial and Social Justice, Jeremiah A. Wright, Jr./Molefi K. Asante/Cornell West Scholar, author, and highly acclaimed seminar/workshop leader, preacher and pastor. Dr. Anderson has contributed to a number of publications and is the author of *Heavenly Hints/Earthly Events: A Chat with Churchfolk*.

**REVEREND CHESTINA M. ARCHIBALD**, lecturer, educator, editor and author, is pastor of Braden United Methodist Church and serves as Director of the Wesley Foundation at Fisk University. She is the editor of *Say Amen: The African-American Family's Book of Prayers*, co-editor of *Divine Inspiration*, and author of *Secret of the Psalms*.

**MRS. MARCIA B. ARMSTEAD** is founder and president of the Complete Family Seminars, a consulting service to improve the spiritual, psychosocial and physical quality of life for families. She authors, designs and conducts seminars nationally and internationally. She is scriptwriter and producer of an employee training video, a former columnist for an Orlando business magazine, and a talk-show guest on two television programs.

**REVEREND ANGELA D. AUBRY** is a public school teacher. She also teaches at the Greater St. Stephen College of Ministry and Theological Seminary and the Victory Bible School. She has Master's degrees in Theological/Historical Studies and in Biblical Literature from Oral Roberts University. She is a member of Victory Fellowship, where she is a leader in the Singles' and Women's Ministries, Music Ministry and Evangelism Ministry.

**REVEREND LISA MILLER AUTRY** was ordained in January 2004 and continues to preach and teach locally, nationally and abroad. She is the co-founder of Eirene Christian Fellowship, where she serves under the leadership of her husband, who also serves as pastor. She is also the founder and president of The Autry Consulting Group, Inc., a financial consulting firm to banks, small businesses and churches.

**REVEREND KAREN E. MOSBY-AVERY**, writer, consultant and the mother of twins, is former pastor of Good News Community Church United Church of Christ in Chicago, IL, a multiracial, multicultural, bilingual inner city congregation. She is a graduate of Garrett-Evangelical Theological Seminary (M.Div.) and a Ph.D. candidate at Garrett. She serves on various local and national committees and advisory boards for the United Church of Christ, the National Council of Churches of Christ, and the Center for the Church and the Black Experience at Garrett-Evangelical Theological Seminary.

**REVEREND MARY ANNE ALLEN BELLINGER** is an advisor, consultant and a member of numerous local and national programs and boards, who has traveled widely as a preacher for political observation and religious dialogue in Cuba, West Africa, England, Guyana and other countries. She is an ordained minister in the Baptist church and an ordained Itinerant Elder in the A.M.E. church. She is a graduate of Andover Newton Theological School (M.Div.).

**REVEREND CYNTHIA B. BELT** is pastor of Mt. Tabor United Methodist Church in Gambrills, MD, and New Beginnings Fellowship United Methodist Church in Severn, MD. Reverend Belt is a graduate of Wesley Theological Seminary (M.Div.) and is currently enrolled in the Doctor of Ministry program with an emphasis on The African-American Church and Its Ministries.

**MS. KEYA BELT** is the daughter of Reverend Cynthia B. Belt. Ms. Belt serves on the leadership team of her church, New Beginnings Fellowship United Methodist Church, where her mother is the pastor. She also serves on the Youth Council for the Annapolis District.

**MS. JETOLA ANDERSON-BLAIR** is a Regional Human Resources Advisor for a major chemical company in Houston, TX. She holds a Bachelor's in Psychology from the State University of New York at Plattaburgh and an M.B.A. in Management from Villanova University. Ms. Anderson-Blair is a member of Friendship Community Bible Church in Houston, where she is a member of the teaching and ushering staff.

**REVEREND WINFRED BLAGMOND** is a graduate of Wesley Theological Seminary (M.Div.), with a focus on Urban Ministry. She is pastor of Strawbridge United Methodist Church in New Windsor, Maryland.

**REVEREND MICHELE COTTON BOHANON** is an Assistant in the Prayer Ministry at the First Institutional Baptist Church in Phoenix, AZ, and is involved in the social justice and civic organizations for the Paradise Valley School District.

**REVEREND TONI R. BOOKER** is the youth minister at Martin Luther King, Jr. Memorial Baptist Church in Renton, WA. Her ministry involves educating young people about God and their accountability to him. She has a B.A. in Psychology from Portland State University, Portland, OR.

**DR. ANN BOUIE** is Visiting Scholar for the U.S. Department of Education National Institute on the Education of At-Risk Students in Washington, DC. She assists policy makers and practitioners in designing and implementing programs and support services in the area of education. She holds a Ph.D in Policy Administration and Analysis, an M.A. in Secondary Education, and an M.A. in African and African-American History from Stanford University.

**REVEREND COOKIE FRANCES LEE BRACEY** is a pastor, chaplain and professor. She serves as pastor of the St. Matthew United Methodist Church in Trevose, PA, chaplain of the United States Air Force Civil Air Patrol, the Methodist Hospital and Pennsylvania Hospital in Philadelphia. She is a graduate of Temple University and Wesley Theological Seminary.

**REVEREND NINA BRYANT** is a chaplain and a clinical pastoral educator, serving in ministry at Alta Bates Medical Center in Oakland, CA. She is a trainer of seminary students, lay leaders and clergy in grief counseling and other compassionate care ministries. She is a graduate of San Francisco Theological Seminary (M.Div.).

**REVEREND MARION WYVETTA BULLOCK** is the Executive Director of the Division for Congregational Ministries (DCM) of the Evangelical Lutheran Church in America (ELCA). Her duties include directing churchwide ministries in the areas of worship, Christian education, evangelism, youth, social ministry, hunger education and multicultural and language/culture-specific resources. She is a graduate of the Lutheran School of Theology and Hartford Seminary.

**ATTORNEY CANDACE LORELLE BYRD** received her law degree from Howard University. She has been active in the State Bar of Georgia's Moot Court Committee and the High School Mock Trial Program, a program in which high school students conduct a trial and compete on the local and state level. She is an active member of the music ministry at World Changers Church International in College Park, GA.

**MINISTER TERRI L. BYRD** is a graduate of Southern University A & M College. She is a member of Church Point Ministries, Inc. Minister Byrd is a writer of short stories, poems, songs and plays.

**REVEREND LAJUANA D. CALDWELL** is a minister with the Church of God. She holds a Master of Theology degree from the International Seminary, Plymouth, FL. Reverend Caldwell is the Director of Christian Education at Harvest Temple Church of God in Forestville, MD.

**DR. IVA E. CARRUTHERS** is general secretary of the Samuel Dewitt Proctor Conference. She is a noted researcher, historian and published writer. She is a graduate of Northwestern University with an M.A. in Counselor Education and a Ph.D. in Sociology. She also holds a master of theological studies from Garrett-Evangelical Theological Seminary.

**REVEREND JACQUETTA CHAMBERS** is pastor of McMillian United Methodist Church in Fort Worth, TX. She is a graduate of Texas Christian University Brite School of Divinity with a Master of Divinity degree in Pastoral Care and Counseling and has currently completed the course work for her Doctor of Divinity degree.

**REVEREND MONICA ANITA COLEMAN** is a pastoral assistant at Metropolitan Interdenominational Church in Nashville, TN. She is founder and coordinator of "The Dinah Project," an organized church response to the crisis of sexual violence in the community. She is a graduate of Vanderbilt Divinity School (M.Div.) and certified the study of religion, gender and sexuality.

**DR. SUZAN D. JOHNSON COOK** is the founder and senior pastor of the Bronx Christian Fellowship. She also serves as the first woman president of the historic Hampton Minister's Conference. She is a graduate of New York's Columbia University Teacher's College and Union Theological Seminary (M.A. and M.Div.) and United Theological Seminary (D.Min.). She is the author or editor of several books, including *Sister to Sister: Devotions for and from African American Women.*

**REVEREND CHARMAYNE COOKE** is a native of Boston, MA, who has worked in the field of broadcasting for the last 25 years. An ordained Baptist minister, Reverend Cooke resides in the Washington, D.C., area.

**REVEREND MARIA-ALMA RAINEY COPELAND** is pastor of Mizpah Lutheran Church in St. Louis, MO. She is a graduate of Pacific Lutheran University (B.A.) and Luther Northwestern Theological Seminary (M.Div.). She has completed her academic studies for the Doctor of Ministry degree at Eden Theological Seminary.

**DR. A. ELAINE CRAWFORD** is a graduate of Virginia Union University School of Theology (M.Div.). She earned her Ph.D. in Historical/Theological Studies from Union Theological Seminary. Currently she serves as Program Coordinator for the Womanist Scholars Program, in the Office of Black Women in Church and Society at the ITC, and as Adjunct Professor in the Religion and Philosophy Department at Spelman College.

**REVEREND ALICE J. BURNETTE DAVIS,** attorney, is the Minister of Community Outreach, Executive Director of the Family Life Center Foundation, Sunday School teacher, Bible Study teacher and member of the Economic and Community Development Corporation. She is responsible for working with various church and community groups to plan and implement church-related community activities. She earned her Master of Divinity degree from Wesley Theological Seminary.

**REVEREND KATHERINE J. DAVIS** is an ordained Elder, Central Texas Conference, United Methodist Church, and associate pastor of First United Methodist Church, Arlington, TX. Her areas of responsibility include the Singles Ministry, Commission on Religion and Race, Church and Society, AIDS Care Team, and Better Home Ministry to Homeless Families. She is a graduate of the Interdenominational Theological Center at Gammon Theological Seminary (M.Div.).

**REVEREND SANDRA DEMBY** is pastor of the Hereford Charge in Baltimore County, MD. She is a graduate of Morgan University (B.S.) and Wesley Theological Seminary (M.Div.).

**REVEREND ALICE DISE** is a member of Vernon Park Church of God, Chicago, IL, where she is a member of the ministerial staff and Superintendent of Sunday School. Reverend Dise is author of *Black Women in Ministry in the Church of God, Preparation For Teaching: The Inner Life,* and contributing author in *Called To Minister, Empowered To Serve.*

**REVEREND TROY JANEL HARRISON-DIXON** is pastor of Calvary Presbyterian Church in Wilson, NC. She earned a Masters of Divinity degree and a Masters of Theology degree from Eastern Theological Seminary. She is a Bible study teacher, Christian educator and seminar/workshop leader.

**REVEREND LASANDRA MELTON-DOLBERRY** is associate minister, New Creation Church, where she enjoys a multi-faceted ministry as director in the areas of children, youth, young adult and women's ministries. She is a certified crisis counselor, completing the Crisis Intervention Counseling Program at University of California, San Diego. She is a contributing author in the second volume of *Sister to Sister: Devotions for and from African American Women.*

**REVEREND MARCIA L. DYSON** is a social and cultural critic, writer and public relations and marketing specialist. A graduate of Chicago State University, her most provocative essay to date is her honest, self-critical and deeply probing examination of ministerial misconduct, sexual exploitation and gender oppression in the black church, which was featured in *Essence Magazine,* entitled "When Preachers Prey."

**DR. VIOLET LUCINDA FISHER** is currently an ordained elder and serves as associate pastor at St. Daniel's United Methodist Church in Chester, PA. Her ministry has extended throughout the islands of Bermuda, Jamaica and Haiti, and in Africa where she served as a missionary in Kenya, Uganda and Tanzania.

**DR. LEAH GASKIN FITCHUE** is the first woman to serve as president of Payne Theological Seminary. She holds a Bachelor's degree from Rutgers University, a Master of Science from the University of Michigan, a Master of Divinity from Princeton Theological Seminary, and a Doctor of Education from Harvard University. Dr. Fitchue is also a published poet and a licensed marriage and family therapist.

**DR. MARGARET ELAINE MCCOLLINS FLAKE** is an Itinerant Elder in the AME Church and is copastor at Allen AME Church, Jamaica, New York. She is also the Educational Director of Allen Christian School, which she co-founded with her husband and pastor, Dr. Floyd H. Flake. She received a M.A. in English from Boston University, a M.Div. from Union Theological Seminary, and a D.Min. from Union Theological Seminary.

**DR. ABENA SAFIYAH FOSUA** is a pastor, professor, speaker and author, who has written for Upper Room Publications, Cokesbury's Daily Bible Study, and for Urban Ministries. Her first book was *Mother Wit: 365 Meditations for African-American Women.* She earned a Master of Divinity Degree from Oral Roberts Seminary and a Doctor of Ministry Degree from United Theological Seminary in Afrocentric pastoring and preaching.

**REVEREND BEVERLY JACKSON GARVIN** is Minister to Youth at Christ United Methodist Church in Detroit, MI, and she is Executive Director of Lifelines Ministries, Inc., International, a womanist ministry for mother-daughter relationships. She is a graduate of Garrett Evangelical Theological Seminary (M.Div.).

**MS. PORTIA GEORGE** has been active in Christian education for more than 25 years. She is founder of "Kingdom Kids," a program designed to help children of all ages in their journey to know Christ. She is also the sole proprietor of PG Enterprises, the author of three African-American Christian children's books and director of the American Baptist Mission Speakers Bureau.

**MS. SHÁ GIVENS** is an author, motivational speaker, licensed minister and global humanitarian. As the president and founder of I Can Fly International, Givens established two adult literacy schools and children learning centers within drought-stricken villages in Kenya, East Africa, and set up food programs that feed over 1,000 villagers each month. She works diligently for equality and human rights for underprivileged women and children living in third world countries around the world.

**DR. ARLENE W. GORDON** is Associate for Resource Center Development and Educational Ministry Advocates Support in the Congregational Ministries Division of the Presbyterian Church (USA). She has mentored and worked with youth and young adults and led numerous workshops across denominations. She is a graduate of United Theological Seminary (D.Min.) and San Francisco Theological Seminary (M.Div.).

**DR. CYNTHIA L. HALE** is the founding pastor of the Ray of Hope Christian Church in Decatur, GA. Dr. Hale's natural talent in music led her to study at Hollins College in Virginia. She holds a Master of Divinity degree from Duke University and a Doctor of Ministry degree from

United Theological Seminary. Dr. Hale was listed on *Ebony* magazine's Honor Roll of Great Black Women Preachers.

**REVEREND CECLIA SWAFFORD HARRIS** is pastor of the Hazel Crest Community Church and an ordained Elder in the United Methodist Church. Reverend Harris has designed curriculum and taught at Pembroke Institute. She received her M.Div. from Garrett-Evangelical Theological Seminary.

**MRS. HATTIE G. HARRIS** is a retired educator who received her formal training from Benedict College, Columbia, SC, and Furman University, Greenville, SC. She is pursuing a Master of Christian Education degree from Erskine Theological Seminary, Due West, SC. She is a member of the Cedar Grove Baptist Church, Simpsonville, SC, where she serves as Director of Christian Education.

**MS. VANESSA HARTSFIELD,** author, speaker, seminar leader and massage therapist, has a Physics degree from Spelman College, a Mechanical Engineering degree from the Georgia Institute of Technology, and a Certificate in Massage Therapy from the Atlanta School of Massage. She is also certified in Deep Tissue, Neuromuscular Therapy, Sports Massage and Cranial Sacral Balancing. She studied Tuina in Beijing, China, and has taught at the Atlanta School of Massage.

**REVEREND KELLIE V. HAYES** is co-pastor of New Liberation AME Church in Landover, MD. She is a graduate of Hampton University where she studied Fashion Merchandising/Marketing and received her B.A. She received her Master's of Theological Studies with an emphasis in Systematic Theology from Wesley Theological Seminary. While serving as Assistant Youth Pastor at Ebenezer AME Church, along with her husband, they were instrumental in the development and implementation of a Manhood/Womanhood Adolescent Rites of Passage Ministry.

**REVEREND RAYE EVELYN HAYNES** is an active member of Second Baptist Church in Vallejo, CA, where her goal is to establish a Christian counseling center for women. She is a graduate of California State University, Sacramento, with an M.S. degree in Counseling and Pupil Personnel. She is active in mission work in Senegal, West Africa.

**REVEREND BARBARA ANN HEARD** is associate pastor at Trinity United Church of Christ, where she is active in the community. Reverend Heard is a supporter of "Family Rescue," a shelter for abused women and children. She was previously employed as Instructor of Clinical Pastoral Education at the University of Chicago Medical Center. She is a graduate of Garrett-Evangelical Theological Seminary (M.Div.).

**MS. KELLY HILL** is the author of *Destined For Greatness—12 Keys to an Extraordinary Life*. Her mission is to help people uncover their purpose, take action on their dreams and live with passion. As a speaker and success coach, she travels across the country inspiring audiences to reach their full potential. She is also an award-winning filmmaker and has appeared as a guest expert on major television and radio shows.

**DR. LOTTIE JONES HOOD** is the pastor of First Congregational Church in Detroit, MI, where she lives with her husband, the Honorable Harold Hood, judge on the Bench of the Michigan Court of Appeals. She is the author of numerous books, including *Stigma, Its Effect on the Woman Alcoholic* and *The Role of the African-American Church in the Prevention of Drug Abuse.* She has a Masters in Management, Supervision and Public Administration, a Master of Social Work, a Master of Divinity, a Doctor of Education, Human Services Administration, and a Doctor of Divinity.

**DR. JANET HOPKINS** pastors two churches on the west side of Chicago. She received her doctorate from McCormick Theological Seminary and is an ordained elder in the United Methodist Church.

**MS. ARNESA A. HOWELL** is a freelance writer and health care reporter in Washington, DC. She is a graduate of Howard University with a B.A. in Journalism.

**REVEREND DARLENE MOORE-JAMES** is the first female pastor of Hartzell Mount Zion United Methodist Church in Slidell, LA, a member of the St. Tammany Ministerial Alliance and a mentoring pastor for incoming pastors for the St. Tammany Ministerial Alliance.

She is a speaker and workshop leader and the recipient of the "Women Who Have Made a Difference" Award. She is a graduate of Gammon Theological Seminary at the Interdenominational Theological Center (M.Div.). She is the author of "Sista Pearl" and "I am the Preacher's Child."

**REVEREND DEBORAH L. SHUMAKE JAPHIA**, author, playwright, producer, director, retreat coordinator, is a member of the Greater Christ Baptist Church in Detroit, MI. She is Founder/CEO of *God's Woman, The Magazine For Women Who Love and Serve Jesus Christ,* the radio talk show of *God's Woman* Magazine "On The Air," and proprietor of God's Woman Publishing, Inc., Company. She is currently enrolled at the University of Chicago, Graham School of Publishing.

**DR. DIANE H. JOHNSON** serves as Associate Minister at Galilee A.M.E. Church. She and her husband own Gospel Notes Records and Books in Oxon Hill, MD. She earned an M.A. in Education, an M.B.A. and an M.Div. from Howard University, and a D.Min. from United Theological Seminary.

**REVEREND FRANKYE ANTHEA SOURIE JOHNSON** is an ordained Elder and member of the Oklahoma Annual Conference of the United Methodist Church. She is the pastor of the Warren Memorial United Methodist Church in Ardmore, OK, where she is leading the church in reaching out to all those, especially African-American women, who have been overlooked by the church and society.

**REVEREND KATURAH WORRILL JOHNSON** is currently serving as Associate Pastor at College Avenue United Methodist Church. Reverend Johnson received her M.Div., concentrating in Biblical Studies, from Gammon Theological Seminary at Interdenominational Theological Center, and holds a B.A. in Journalism from Georgia State University. She is a member of the Mayor's Steering Committee Against Domestic Violence and serves as co-workshop leader of Children Coping with Divorce for the county's divorcing parents.

**REVEREND WILMA R. JOHNSON** currently serves as pastor of New Prospect Baptist Church in Detroit, MI. She is the first woman in the city of Detroit to pastor a prominent, traditional black Baptist church. She has taught, conducted workshops and preached for more than 25 years. She and her husband David have two sons. She is a graduate of Marygrove College with a Masters of Arts degree in Pastoral Ministry.

**REVEREND JOLENE JOSEY**, Associate Minister at Eastside Baptist Church in Tacoma, WA, has worked for 22 years in a non-traditional job for women, commonly called "The Trades," where she has been the only African-American female in the "The Trades" in the Tacoma area. She is also working with other women who are interested in entering "The Trades," and women in transition, whose lives have been ones of drugs, alcohol, prostitution and abuse.

**MRS. MARJORIE L. KIMBROUGH** holds a Masters Degree in Christian Education from Interdenominational Theological Center. She held the positions of Instructor in Christian Education for ITC and Professor of Religion at Clark Atlanta University. Her book, *Accept No Limitations: A Black Woman Encounters Corporate America,* won the 1991 Georgia Author of the Year Award in the area of non-fiction.

**REVEREND BONITA A. KITT** is a graduate of The American Baptist Seminary of West, Berkeley, CA, where she earned two Masters Degrees. Reverend Kitt is the Minister of Comfort at the Allen Temple Baptist Church in Oakland, CA. This ministry provides grief support to the congregation and the community through counseling and referrals. Reverend Kitt is also a Hospice Chaplain and Volunteer Coordinator with GranCare Home Health and Hospice.

**MARJORIE H. LAWSON** was the editor for the original *Women of Color Study Bible.*

**DR. LINDA LEE**, a pastor's wife, is currently the District Superintendent of the Detroit East District Annual Conference. Previously, for three years she was the Pastor of the Covenant Avenue Methodist Church in Detroit, MI. Dr. Lee holds a D.Min. Degree and a M.Div. from the United Theological Seminary in Dayton, OH. She is the mother of three children.

**REVEREND GINGER D. LONDON**, Bible study teacher, author and counselor, is the founder and host of "Heart

To Heart," a Christian radio talk show. She earned two Masters of Arts Degrees from Oral Roberts University Graduate School of Theology and Missions. For several years she worked with battered women's programs as a telephone crisis counselor and an outpatient counselor for abused women and their families. She is the author of *Understanding Your Calling, Discerning Your Boaz,* and *The Making of a Spiritual Diamond.*

**DR. CAROLYN B. LOVE** co-pastors with her husband at the Truth For Living Ministries in Jacksonville, FL, where her personal deliverance from drugs, alcohol and depression are all tremendous witnesses to the awesome power of God. She is president and founder of Truth Bible College and Seminary, president and founder of Fresh Word Outreach Ministries, and she serves as a local host for the Trinity Broadcasting Network (TBN).

**MS. VICTORIA LOWE** is a nationally recognized, respected and celebrated teacher, speaker and entrepreneur. She is the author of *10 Spiritual Principles of Successful Women.*

**MRS. DINAH PAGE MANNES**, volunteer counselor, high school teacher and director of a halfway house, is the Assistant Director of the Educational Opportunity Center at Rogers State University. She earned a Masters degree in Counseling from Oral Roberts University and is a doctoral candidate in Adult Education at Oklahoma State University.

**MRS. ANN SHENETHIA MANUEL** holds a degree in Social Studies and Education from the University of Oklahoma and a Juris Doctorate from the University of Texas. She is currently an administrator at Carl Albert State College and is pursuing a limited license in the ministry.

**DR. DOLORES E. LEE MCCABE**, Minister of Evangelism at Zion Baptist Church of Ardmore, PA, is also Assistant Professor of Social Justice and Counseling and Assistant to the Provost for Multicultural Affairs at Eastern College in St. Davids, PA. She received a Master of Education in Counseling from Antioch University, a Master of Divinity degree and a Doctor of Ministry degree in Marriage and Family Counseling from Eastern Baptist Theological Seminary. She also studied at the Jungian Institute in Switzerland, specializing in dream interpretation.

**CHAPLAIN EMMA LOUISE MCNAIR** is the mother of six children and the grandmother of eight. She is Staff Chaplain at the Methodist Medical Center. She is the first black woman in the Mississippi Conference and the state of Mississippi to receive a certificate as a certified chaplain (fellow) of the College Chaplains, Inc.

**REVEREND BERNADINE GRANT MCRIPLEY** is a writer for PC (USA) *Stewardship of Public Life (SPL) Health Care Quarterly* and editor for *EcoJustice Quarterly Magazine.* She is a graduate of Princeton Theological Seminary (M.Div.) and an ordained clergywoman in the Presbyterian Church (USA).

**REVEREND ANDREA L. MIDDLETON** is pastor of John Wesley United Methodist Church in Clarksburg, MD. She is a graduate of Wesley Theological Seminary (M.Div.) and The Citadel, The Military College of South Carolina (Master of Education). She has worked in the field of telecommunications as a tutor of English composition and literature, and as a word processing instructor.

**DR. ELLA PEARSON MITCHELL**, former Dean of the Chapel at Spelman College, has preached and taught across America for over five decades. She holds an M.A. in Religious Education from Columbia University Teachers College and Union Theological Seminary and a D.Min. from School of Theology, Claremont, California. She is the editor of three volumes of "Those Preaching Women," a contributor to "Black Church Lifestyles," and a writer of various articles for church-related publications.

**DR. SHERRY DAVIS MOLOCK**, author and speaker, is Associate Professor of Psychology at The George Washington University in Washington, D.C. She conducts research in the area of suicidal behaviors, and on infertility and adoption in the African-American community. She earned a Master's degree and a Ph.D. in Psychology from the University of Maryland, College Park, and is working on her Masters of Divinity at Howard University Divinity School.

**EVANGELIST ALBERIENE RIENE ADAMS-MORRIS**, poet and licensed missionary in the Church of God in Christ in Gary, IN, holds a degree in Culinary Arts. She is also a teacher in the Gary school system, program counselor for the mentally and physically challenged in various group homes in the area. She is a contributing author in the *Sister to Sister* devotional series.

**MS. VICTORIA CHRISTOPHER MURRAY** is a renowned author of Christian fiction. She self-published her first book, *Temptation,* which was later published by Walk Worthy Press. Murray has won numerous awards for *Temptation* and her subsequent books. Her work has been on the Essence Bestseller List and has been nominated for an NAACP Image Award.

**REVEREND NAOMI E. PEETE**, author, evangelist, preacher, artist and singer is Associate Minister at Mount Zion Baptist Church in Seattle, WA, and Senior Faculty Member and Professor of Biology at City University Graduate School of Education in Tacoma, WA. She received a Master of Science degree from Morgan State University in Science Education and a Master of Pastoral Studies from Seattle University.

**REVEREND ANITA ADAMS POWELL** is an Associate Pastor/Minister of Faith Development who previously served as Associate Director of Admissions and Adjunct Professor at Eastern Baptist Theological Seminary. She holds a Master of Arts degree from Wesleyan University and a Master of Divinity degree from Eastern Baptist Theological Seminary.

**MS. CONSTANCE RICHARDS** is a junior high and high school teacher. She holds a Bachelor of Science in Physics from the University of the West Indies. She holds a Master of Music degree from Howard University in Piano Performance and is presently completing another M.A. in Vocal Performance.

**MS. SHEWANDA RILEY** has been a producer for Armed Forces Radio and Television, radio host and announcer, and writer. She is an executive assistant/scheduler for a Texas congresswoman. Previously she was Adjunct Professor in writing at Richland Community College, Assistant Director of Communications for New Creation Christian Fellowship. She is a member of The Potter's House and works with PHASE, the singles ministry.

**REVEREND MONIQUE ROBINSON**, a native of Los Angeles, CA, is the pastor of women's discipleship and a pastoral counselor at Faithful Central Bible Church in Inglewood, CA, where she was ordained as a minister of the gospel. She is a graduate of Dallas Theological Seminary, where she earned her Master of Arts in Biblical Counseling. She is the author of the book, *Longing for Daddy: Healing the Pain of an Absent or Emotionally Distant Father.*

**REVEREND SHEILA FORD ROBINSON**, director of religious programming and a religious announcer, is the creator of an audiotape and book of Christian poems and songs for children. She is an active member of the Bible Way Christian Center in San Jose, CA, where she is director of the singles ministry.

**REVEREND JANNAH SCOTT** is Assistant in Evangelism and Community Outreach Ministry at First Institutional Baptist Church, and Research and Statistical Analysis Chief for the Arizona Department of Health Services. She received both undergraduate and graduate degrees from the University of California, Berkeley, in Health Policy Studies. She also completed doctoral course work in Political Science at Brown University.

**REVEREND ANGELA STEWART SIMS** is an accounting manager in Bethesda, MD. She is a graduate of Howard University School of Divinity (M.Div.).

**DR. KATHRYN R. SMALLWOOD** is a widow with three adult children and three granddaughters. She is a graduate of Pittsburgh Theological Seminary (M.Div.) and an ordained minister in the Presbyterian Church, USA. She has designed a mentoring program for Family Resources and East End Cooperative Ministries, and served as interim pastor in Richwood, WV.

**MINISTER TERRI MCFADDIN-SOLOMON** is an ordained minister, author, speaker and songwriter with two Grammy Awards to her credit. She is the author of *God Made Me Beauty-Full, Only A Woman* and *Sapphires and Other Precious Jewels.* Minister McFaddin-Solomon attended Temple University and later graduated from Virginia Union University. She also holds a Masters degree in Theology from Fuller Theological Seminary.

**DR. MALVINA V. STEPHENS** is a native of Port Arthur, TX. She is a full time staff member of Allen Temple Baptist Church in Oakland, CA. She is the Director of Prison Ministry and Coordinator of Congregational Care. She earned her Masters of Divinity from The American Baptist Seminary of the West and her Doctor of Ministry from San Francisco Theological Seminary.

**REVEREND DOROTHEA J. BELT STROMAN**, a pastor's wife, is an ordained Deacon and Elder presently serving as pastor of Albright Memorial United Methodist Church in Washington, DC. She is a graduate of Howard University Divinity School (M.Div.).

**REVEREND DEBORAH TINSLEY TAYLOR**, registered nurse, poet, singer and liturgist, writes and performs original works that celebrate God's love. She has conducted Bible studies based on the "Silent Voices of Women in the Bible, Woman's Word," a monthly discussion of writings by women Biblical scholars and theologians. She writes workshop-based curriculums for inter-generational Sunday Schools, and is an advocate for women. Several of her poems were published in *Taking Back My Yesterdays*, edited by Dr. Linda H. Hollies.

**REVEREND MERIANN TAYLOR** is an author, psychotherapist and family therapist, who specializes in pastoral care, counseling, couples and family therapy, HIV/AIDS, and women's health. Reverend Taylor is director of The Black Church HIV/AIDS National Technical Assistance Center of The Balm in Gilead, Inc., Instructor of Pastoral Care and Counseling at Blanton-Peale Institute and New York Theological Seminary. She is a graduate of Vanderbilt University Divinity School (M.Div.).

**REVEREND JACQUELINE THOMPSON** is a graduate of Howard University School of Divinity where she earned a Master's of Divinity degree. While at Howard she received numerous honors and awards for exhibiting qualities of excellence in scholarship, preaching and ministry. Currently she serves as the Minister of Youth at Shiloh Baptist Church in Washington, DC.

**DR. LA VERNE TOLBERT** is founder of Teaching Like Jesus Ministries, a Christian education training group. Dr. Tolbert earned both her Masters and Doctor of Philosophy degrees from Talbot School of Theology/Biola University. She continues her role in higher education as an adjunct professor at Biola University and at Haggard School of Theology/Azusa Pacific University. She is also Director of Christian Education Ministries at Crenshaw Christian Center in Los Angeles.

**TOGETTA S. ULMER** is first lady of the Faith Central Bible Church. She is a leader with a proven track record in both spiritual and secular arenas. She is a conference convener and received her Bachelor of Arts degree in Business Education from Southern Illinois University.

**REVEREND TANYA S. WADE** is the first African-American female ordained in the Presbytery of Baltimore. She also became the first female assistant pastor ordained and installed in the Madison Avenue Presbyterian Church's 149 year history. Currently she is Director of the Baltimore County Delta Community Outreach Center in Randallstown, MD, and the Parish Associate of Cherry Hill Presbyterian Church. She has developed, written and implemented several enrichment curriculums, Christian education studies and Christian plays.

**REVEREND N. S. "ROBIN" WALKER** is administrator at Beth Eden Housing Development in Oakland, CA. Reverend Walker is a graduate of the American Baptist Seminary of the West (M.Div.). She is an active member of Allen Temple Baptist Church, where she serves as Research Assistant to the senior pastor and the co-pastor.

**REVEREND ELAINE P. WALTERS** is assistant pastor and church administrator for St. Paul AME Church in Indianapolis, IN, consultant to Indiana University Purdue University School of Social Work, and Executive Director of Indiana One Church, One Child Program, Inc, a program that prepares families for foster care licensing and adoption. A pastor's wife, mother of three, grandmother of seven, and great grandmother of one, she holds a Master of Arts degree in Urban Ministry.

**REVEREND CHERYL D. WARD**, a native of Oakland, CA, was called to preach at the age of twelve. She is founder and pastor of New Liberation Community

Church in Oakland, CA. The church is non-denominational and ethnically diverse. She is the author of *I Have Fallen and I Can Get Up.* She holds a Master of Arts degree in Preaching from the Pacific School of Religion in Berkeley and plans to pursue a Ph.D. in Homiletics.

**MINISTER KATARA A. WASHINGTON** is a writer, editor and Christian education trainer. She is the co-executive editor of *The African American Pulpit*, a preaching journal. She holds a B.A. from Dillard University, a Master's degree in Journalism from Northwestern University, and a Master's of Divinity from Garrett-Evangelical Theological Seminary.

**DR. ELIZABETH D. WATSON** is Associate Professor of Social Work and the Director of Admissions in the Department of Social Work at Andrews University in Berrien Springs, MI. She teaches at both the graduate and undergraduate levels. She earned a Master's degree in Social Work from Howard University and is currently in the dissertation stage of a Ph.D. program in Educational Leadership. She has written for several magazines and contributed to a series of women's devotional books.

**REVEREND JOAN C. WEBSTER** is a worship leader, intercessor, teacher/preacher, counselor and church administrator. She earned an M.Div. and M.A. in Christian Education from Oral Roberts University. In 1993 she began Shalom (Peace) Family Fun Camp, a violence prevention summer camp. Shalom has grown and is now a year-round program under the umbrella of Operation 2008 Bridges for Youth, Inc.

**DR. JOAN L. WHARTON** served as the first woman secretary of the historic AME Ministerial Alliance of Baltimore and Vicinity. She received a Master's degree from Howard University Divinity School and a Doctorate degree from United Theological Seminary. She is an ordained Itinerant Elder in the African Methodist Episcopal Church and serves a pastor of Mt. Zion AME Church in Long Green, MD.

**REVEREND BARBARA J. WHIPPLE** is Associate Minister at the Mt. Zion Baptist Church, where she is also a part of the Prayer Ministry, Missionary Outreach Ministry and the Evangelism Ministry. She is a graduate of Coppin State College, Family Bible Institute College and Seminary and the College of Notre Dame.

**REVEREND BESSIE WHITAKER** is the Assistant Bible Study teacher at Allen Temple Baptist Church in Oakland, CA, where she is a member. She completed her undergraduate studies at Southern University, her graduate studies in engineering at Tuskegee Institute, and her M.Th. from Fuller Theological Seminary.

**DR. LEAH ELIZABETH MOSLEY WHITE**, while serving the Greater Faith Baptist Church, also serves as the administrator of the New Psalmist Christian School, the largest accredited African-American Christian School in the Baltimore area. She is the first African-American woman to be called to pastor a Baptist church in Baltimore. She earned a Master of Science degree from Johns Hopkins University, a M.Th. from Saint Mary's Seminary and University, and a D.Min. from United Theological Seminary.

**DR. BERNADETTE GLOVER-WILLIAMS** is a graduate of Eastern College, Eastern Baptist Theological Seminary, and Blanton-Peal Institute, and holds a D.Min. from United Theological Seminary. She serves as assistant pastor of the Second Baptist Church, Perth Amboy, NJ.

**REVEREND MARY NEWBERN-WILLIAMS** is Associate for Racial Ethnic Schools and Colleges for the Presbyterian Church (USA). She is a graduate of Princeton Theological Seminary with a Master of Arts degree in Christian Education and a Master of Divinity degree. She is a writer and has performed in a number of plays and theatrical productions.

**YOLANDA WILLIAMS** is the Chief Administrative Officer of Faithful Central Bible Church led by Bishop Kenneth C. Ulmer. She oversees the 10,000+ member church's Information Technology, Facilities, Media and Human Resource functions. Williams received a Bachelor's degree in Accounting from Hampton University and a Masters of Arts degree in Organizational Leadership from Antioch University.

**REVEREND PORTIA TURNER WILLIAMSON** has been Professor of Biblical studies at the university and graduate school level, graduate school teaching assistant, professor of New Testament and Associate Dean of the Master of Divinity Program at several universities and divinity schools. She earned the M.Div. degree from Virginia Union and has completed course work for a Ph.D. in religion at Duke University.

**MS. CHERYL WILSON** is an active member of Valley Kingdom Ministries, Int, in South Holland, IL, where she is the contributing editor for *GRACE TODAY* Magazine. She is also an Assistant Editor for an independent Christian curriculum publisher. She is a graduate of Roosevelt University with a B.S. in Organizational Communication and is currently pursing a M.S. in Training and Development.

**REVEREND JANE E. WOOD** is the first African-American to serve as Associate Pastor of St. Paul-Lusby United Methodist Church. She is a graduate of Wesley Seminary Course of Study School and continues to work toward her degree in Sociology with a concentration in Family Studies at the University of Maryland University College. She is also a volunteer in the Rockville Detention Center as well as the Homeless Program for the Women in Rockville.

**REVEREND LOIS A. WOODEN** is Associate Minister at Metropolitan Baptist Church in Washington, DC. She is also a retreat facilitator, revivalist, teacher, counselor and Chaplain of the Chevy Chase Chapter of the Order of Saint Luke the Physician. She is a graduate of Virginia Union University School of Theology (M.Div.).

**REVEREND CYNTHIA E. WOODS** is the Protestant Chaplain at Georgetown University and Associate Pastor of the National Memorial Church of God, a growing multicultural congregation in Washington, D.C. She holds a B.S. in Human Development from Virginia Polytechnic Institute and State University and a M.Div. from Wesley Theological Seminary with distinction as a Benjamin E. Mays Fellow.

**MRS. BEVERLY YATES**, pastor's wife, mother and grandmother, is a retired registered nurse. She is past president of Chicagoland Christian Women's Conference.

Other contributors include: Kenya Moore, Aladrian Elmore and Kimberly Yancy.

| DAY | PASSAGE |
|---|---|
| January 1 | Genesis 1—4 |
| January 2 | Genesis 5—8 |
| January 3 | Genesis 9—12 |
| January 4 | Genesis 13—17 |
| January 5 | Genesis 18—20 |
| January 6 | Genesis 21—23 |
| January 7 | Genesis 24—25 |
| January 8 | Genesis 26—28 |
| January 9 | Genesis 29—31 |
| January 10 | Genesis 32—35 |
| January 11 | Genesis 36—38 |
| January 12 | Genesis 39—41 |
| January 13 | Genesis 42—43 |
| January 14 | Genesis 44—46 |
| January 15 | Genesis 47—50 |
| January 16 | Exodus 1—4 |
| January 17 | Exodus 5—7 |
| January 18 | Exodus 8—10 |
| January 19 | Exodus 11—13 |
| January 20 | Exodus 14—16 |
| January 21 | Exodus 17—20 |
| January 22 | Exodus 21—23 |
| January 23 | Exodus 24—27 |
| January 24 | Exodus 28—30 |
| January 25 | Exodus 31—34 |
| January 26 | Exodus 35—37 |
| January 27 | Exodus 38—40 |
| January 28 | Leviticus 1—4 |
| January 29 | Leviticus 5—7 |
| January 30 | Leviticus 8—10 |
| January 31 | Leviticus 11—13 |
| February 1 | Leviticus 14—45 |
| February 2 | Leviticus 16—18 |
| February 3 | Leviticus 19—21 |
| February 4 | Leviticus 22—23 |
| February 5 | Leviticus 24—25 |
| February 6 | Leviticus 26—27 |
| February 7 | Numbers 1—2 |
| February 8 | Numbers 3—4 |
| February 9 | Numbers 5—6 |
| February 10 | Numbers 7 |
| February 11 | Numbers 8—10 |
| February 12 | Numbers 11—13 |
| February 13 | Numbers 14—15 |

| DAY | PASSAGE |
|---|---|
| February 14 | Numbers 16—18 |
| February 15 | Numbers 19—21 |
| February 16 | Numbers 22—24 |
| February 17 | Numbers 25—26 |
| February 18 | Numbers 27—29 |
| February 19 | Numbers 30—32 |
| February 20 | Numbers 33—36 |
| February 21 | Deuteronomy 1—2 |
| February 22 | Deuteronomy 3—4 |
| February 23 | Deuteronomy 5—8 |
| February 24 | Deuteronomy 9—11 |
| February 25 | Deuteronomy 12—15 |
| February 26 | Deuteronomy 16—19 |
| February 27 | Deuteronomy 20—23 |
| February 28 | Deuteronomy 24—27 |
| March 1 | Deuteronomy 28—29 |
| March 2 | Deuteronomy 30—32 |
| March 3 | Deuteronomy 33—34 |
| March 4 | Joshua 1—4 |
| March 5 | Joshua 5—7 |
| March 6 | Joshua 8—10 |
| March 7 | Joshua 11—13 |
| March 8 | Joshua 14—17 |
| March 9 | Joshua 18—20 |
| March 10 | Joshua 21—22 |
| March 11 | Joshua 23—24 |
| March 12 | Judges 1—3 |
| March 13 | Judges 4—5 |
| March 14 | Judges 6—8 |
| March 15 | Judges 9—10 |
| March 16 | Judges 11—13 |
| March 17 | Judges 14—16 |
| March 18 | Judges 17—19 |
| March 19 | Judges 20—21 |
| March 20 | Ruth 1—4 |
| March 21 | 1 Samuel 1—3 |
| March 22 | 1 Samuel 4—7 |
| March 23 | 1 Samuel 8—12 |
| March 24 | 1 Samuel 13—14 |
| March 25 | 1 Samuel 15—16 |
| March 26 | 1 Samuel 17—18 |
| March 27 | 1 Samuel 19—21 |
| March 28 | 1 Samuel 22—24 |
| March 29 | 1 Samuel 25—27 |

| DAY | PASSAGE |
|---|---|
| March 30 | 1 Samuel 28—31 |
| March 31 | 2 Samuel 1—3 |
| April 1 | 2 Samuel 4—7 |
| April 2 | 2 Samuel 8—11 |
| April 3 | 2 Samuel 12—13 |
| April 4 | 2 Samuel 14—16 |
| April 5 | 2 Samuel 17—19 |
| April 6 | 2 Samuel 20—22 |
| April 7 | 2 Samuel 23—24 |
| April 8 | 1 Kings 1—2 |
| April 9 | 1 Kings 3—5 |
| April 10 | 1 Kings 6—7 |
| April 11 | 1 Kings 8—9 |
| April 12 | 1 Kings 10—12 |
| April 13 | 1 Kings 13—15 |
| April 14 | 1 Kings 16—18 |
| April 15 | 1 Kings 19—20 |
| April 16 | 1 Kings 21—22 |
| April 17 | 2 Kings 1—3 |
| April 18 | 2 Kings 4—5 |
| April 19 | 2 Kings 6—8 |
| April 20 | 2 Kings 9—10 |
| April 21 | 2 Kings 11—13 |
| April 22 | 2 Kings 14—16 |
| April 23 | 2 Kings 17—18 |
| April 24 | 2 Kings 19—21 |
| April 25 | 2 Kings 22—23 |
| April 26 | 2 Kings 24—25 |
| April 27 | 1 Chronicles 1—2 |
| April 28 | 1 Chronicles 3—4 |
| April 29 | 1 Chronicles 5—6 |
| April 30 | 1 Chronicles 7—9 |
| May 1 | 1 Chronicles 10—12 |
| May 2 | 1 Chronicles 13—16 |
| May 3 | 1 Chronicles 17—19 |
| May 4 | 1 Chronicles 20—23 |
| May 5 | 1 Chronicles 24—26 |
| May 6 | 1 Chronicles 27—29 |
| May 7 | 2 Chronicles 1—4 |
| May 8 | 2 Chronicles 5—7 |
| May 9 | 2 Chronicles 8—11 |
| May 10 | 2 Chronicles 12—16 |
| May 11 | 2 Chronicles 17—20 |
| May 12 | 2 Chronicles 21—24 |

| DAY | PASSAGE |
|---|---|
| May 13 | 2 Chronicles 25—28 |
| May 14 | 2 Chronicles 29—31 |
| May 15 | 2 Chronicles 32—34 |
| May 16 | 2 Chronicles 35—36 |
| May 17 | Ezra 1—4 |
| May 18 | Ezra 5—7 |
| May 19 | Ezra 8—10 |
| May 20 | Nehemiah 1—3 |
| May 21 | Nehemiah 4—7 |
| May 22 | Nehemiah 8—9 |
| May 23 | Nehemiah 10—11 |
| May 24 | Nehemiah 12—13 |
| May 25 | Esther 1—3 |
| May 26 | Esther 4—7 |
| May 27 | Esther 8—10 |
| May 28 | Job 1—4 |
| May 29 | Job 5—8 |
| May 30 | Job 9—12 |
| May 31 | Job 13—16 |
| June 1 | Job 17—20 |
| June 2 | Job 21—24 |
| June 3 | Job 25—30 |
| June 4 | Job 31—34 |
| June 5 | Job 35—38 |
| June 6 | Job 39—42 |
| June 7 | Psalms 1—8 |
| June 8 | Psalms 9—17 |
| June 9 | Psalms 18—21 |
| June 10 | Psalms 22—27 |
| June 11 | Psalms 28—33 |
| June 12 | Psalms 34—37 |
| June 13 | Psalms 38—42 |
| June 14 | Psalms 43—49 |
| June 15 | Psalms 50—55 |
| June 16 | Psalms 56—61 |
| June 17 | Psalms 62—68 |
| June 18 | Psalms 69—72 |
| June 19 | Psalms 73—77 |
| June 20 | Psalms 78—80 |
| June 21 | Psalms 81—88 |
| June 22 | Psalms 89—94 |
| June 23 | Psalms 95—103 |
| June 24 | Psalms 104—106 |
| June 25 | Psalms 107—111 |

| DAY | PASSAGE |
|---|---|
| June 26 | Psalms 112—118 |
| June 27 | Psalm 119 |
| June 28 | Psalms 120—133 |
| June 29 | Psalms 134—140 |
| June 30 | Psalms 141—150 |
| July 1 | Proverbs 1—3 |
| July 2 | Proverbs 4—7 |
| July 3 | Proverbs 8—11 |
| July 4 | Proverbs 12—14 |
| July 5 | Proverbs 15—17 |
| July 6 | Proverbs 18—20 |
| July 7 | Proverbs 21—23 |
| July 8 | Proverbs 24—26 |
| July 9 | Proverbs 27—29 |
| July 10 | Proverbs 30—31 |
| July 11 | Ecclesiastes 1—4 |
| July 12 | Ecclesiastes 5—8 |
| July 13 | Ecclesiastes 9—12 |
| July 14 | Song of Songs 1—4 |
| July 15 | Song of Songs 5—8 |
| July 16 | Isaiah 1—3 |
| July 17 | Isaiah 4—8 |
| July 18 | Isaiah 9—11 |
| July 19 | Isaiah 12—14 |
| July 20 | Isaiah 15—19 |
| July 21 | Isaiah 20—24 |
| July 22 | Isaiah 25—28 |
| July 23 | Isaiah 29—31 |
| July 24 | Isaiah 32—34 |
| July 25 | Isaiah 35—37 |
| July 26 | Isaiah 38—40 |
| July 27 | Isaiah 41—43 |
| July 28 | Isaiah 44—46 |
| July 29 | Isaiah 47—49 |
| July 30 | Isaiah 50—52 |
| July 31 | Isaiah 53—56 |
| August 1 | Isaiah 57—59 |
| August 2 | Isaiah 60—63 |
| August 3 | Isaiah 64—66 |
| August 4 | Jeremiah 1—3 |
| August 5 | Jeremiah 4—5 |
| August 6 | Jeremiah 6—8 |
| August 7 | Jeremiah 9—11 |
| August 8 | Jeremiah 12—14 |

| DAY | PASSAGE |
|---|---|
| August 9 | Jeremiah 15—17 |
| August 10 | Jeremiah 18—21 |
| August 11 | Jeremiah 22—24 |
| August 12 | Jeremiah 25—27 |
| August 13 | Jeremiah 28—30 |
| August 14 | Jeremiah 31—33 |
| August 15 | Jeremiah 34—36 |
| August 16 | Jeremiah 37—39 |
| August 17 | Jeremiah 40—43 |
| August 18 | Jeremiah 44—46 |
| August 19 | Jeremiah 47—48 |
| August 20 | Jeremiah 49 |
| August 21 | Jeremiah 50 |
| August 22 | Jeremiah 51—52 |
| August 23 | Lamentations 1—2 |
| August 24 | Lamentations 3—5 |
| August 25 | Ezekiel 1—4 |
| August 26 | Ezekiel 5—8 |
| August 27 | Ezekiel 9—12 |
| August 28 | Ezekiel 13—15 |
| August 29 | Ezekiel 16—17 |
| August 30 | Ezekiel 18—20 |
| August 31 | Ezekiel 21—22 |
| September 1 | Ezekiel 23—24 |
| September 2 | Ezekiel 25—27 |
| September 3 | Ezekiel 28—30 |
| September 4 | Ezekiel 31—32 |
| September 5 | Ezekiel 33—35 |
| September 6 | Ezekiel 36—38 |
| September 7 | Ezekiel 39—40 |
| September 8 | Ezekiel 41—43 |
| September 9 | Ezekiel 44—46 |
| September 10 | Ezekiel 47—48 |
| September 11 | Daniel 1—3 |
| September 12 | Daniel 4—5 |
| September 13 | Daniel 6—8 |
| September 14 | Daniel 9—12 |
| September 15 | Hosea 1—4 |
| September 16 | Hosea 5—9 |
| September 17 | Hosea 10—14 |
| September 18 | Joel 1—3 |
| September 19 | Amos 1—4 |
| September 20 | Amos 5—9 |
| September 21 | Obadiah and Jonah |

| DAY | PASSAGE |
|---|---|
| September 22 | Micah 1—4 |
| September 23 | Micah 5—7 |
| September 24 | Nahum 1—3 |
| September 25 | Habakkuk 1—3 |
| September 26 | Zephaniah 1—3 |
| September 27 | Haggai |
| September 28 | Zechariah 1—5 |
| September 29 | Zechariah 6—10 |
| September 30 | Zechariah 11—14 |
| October 1 | Malachi 1—4 |
| October 2 | Matthew 1—4 |
| October 3 | Matthew 5—6 |
| October 4 | Matthew 7—9 |
| October 5 | Matthew 10—11 |
| October 6 | Matthew 12—13 |
| October 7 | Matthew 14—17 |
| October 8 | Matthew 18—20 |
| October 9 | Matthew 21—22 |
| October 10 | Matthew 23—24 |
| October 11 | Matthew 25—26 |
| October 12 | Matthew 27—28 |
| October 13 | Mark 1—3 |
| October 14 | Mark 4—5 |
| October 15 | Mark 6—7 |
| October 16 | Mark 8—9 |
| October 17 | Mark 10—11 |
| October 18 | Mark 12—13 |
| October 19 | Mark 14 |
| October 20 | Mark 15—16 |
| October 21 | Luke 1—2 |
| October 22 | Luke 3—4 |
| October 23 | Luke 5—6 |
| October 24 | Luke 7—8 |
| October 25 | Luke 9—10 |
| October 26 | Luke 11—12 |
| October 27 | Luke 13—15 |
| October 28 | Luke 16—18 |
| October 29 | Luke 19—20 |
| October 30 | Luke 21—22 |
| October 31 | Luke 23—24 |
| November 1 | John 1—2 |
| November 2 | John 3—4 |
| November 3 | John 5—6 |
| November 4 | John 7—8 |

| DAY | PASSAGE |
|---|---|
| November 5 | John 9—10 |
| November 6 | John 11—12 |
| November 7 | John 13—15 |
| November 8 | John 16—17 |
| November 9 | John 18—19 |
| November 10 | John 20—21 |
| November 11 | Acts 1—3 |
| November 12 | Acts 4—5 |
| November 13 | Acts 6—7 |
| November 14 | Acts 8—9 |
| November 15 | Acts 10—11 |
| November 16 | Acts 12—13 |
| November 17 | Acts 14—15 |
| November 18 | Acts 16—17 |
| November 19 | Acts 18—19 |
| November 20 | Acts 20—21 |
| November 21 | Acts 22—23 |
| November 22 | Acts 24—26 |
| November 23 | Acts 27—28 |
| November 24 | Romans 1—3 |
| November 25 | Romans 4—7 |
| November 26 | Romans 8—10 |
| November 27 | Romans 11—14 |
| November 28 | Romans 15—16 |
| November 29 | 1 Corinthians 1—4 |
| November 30 | 1 Corinthians 5—9 |
| December 1 | 1 Corinthians 10—13 |
| December 2 | 1 Corinthians 14—16 |
| December 3 | 2 Corinthians 1—4 |
| December 4 | 2 Corinthians 5—9 |
| December 5 | 2 Corinthians 10—13 |
| December 6 | Galatians 1—3 |
| December 7 | Galatians 4—6 |
| December 8 | Ephesians 1—6 |
| December 9 | Philippians 1—4 |
| December 10 | Colossians 1—4 |
| December 11 | 1 Thessalonians 1—5 |
| December 12 | 2 Thessalonians 1—3 |
| December 13 | 1 Timothy 4—6 |
| December 14 | 2 Timothy 1—4 |
| December 15 | Titus and Philemon |
| December 16 | Hebrews 1—4 |
| December 17 | Hebrews 5—8 |
| December 18 | Hebrews 9—10 |

| DAY | PASSAGE |
|---|---|
| December 19 | Hebrews 11—13 |
| December 20 | James 1—5 |
| December 21 | 1 Peter 1—5 |
| December 22 | 2 Peter 1—3 |
| December 23 | 1 John 1—5 |
| December 24 | 2, 3 John, Jude |
| December 25 | Revelation 1—3 |
| December 26 | Revelation 4—7 |
| December 27 | Revelation 8—11 |
| December 28 | Revelation 12—14 |
| December 29 | Revelation 15—17 |
| December 30 | Revelation 18—19 |
| December 31 | Revelation 20—22 |

| DAY | THEME | PASSAGE |
|---|---|---|
| ☐ | In the Beginning | Genesis 1:1—2:25 |
| ☐ | Sin Enters the Picture | Genesis 3:1–24 |
| ☐ | Water, Water Everywhere | Genesis 6:1—9:29 |
| ☐ | God's Promise to Abraham | Genesis 12:1—18:15; 20:1—22:19 |
| ☐ | Goodbye, Sodom and Gomorrah | Genesis 18:16—19:29 |
| ☐ | Isaac Loves Rebekah | Genesis 24:1–67 |
| ☐ | Between Brothers | Genesis 25:19–34; 27:1—33:20 |
| ☐ | Joseph's Egyptian Adventure | Genesis 37:1–36; 39:1—50:26 |
| ☐ | A Man Named Moses | Exodus 1:1—7:7 |
| ☐ | Escape From Egypt | Exodus 7:8—14:31 |
| ☐ | Life in the Wilderness | Exodus 15:22—18:27 |
| ☐ | Ten Commandments | Exodus 19:1–21 |
| ☐ | Calf Worship | Exodus 32:1–35 |
| ☐ | Assignment From God | Exodus 33:1—40:38 |
| ☐ | Moses Loses His Cool—and a Lot More | Numbers 20:1–13 |
| ☐ | Joshua Takes Command | Joshua 1:1—6:27 |
| ☐ | Destination: Promised Land | Joshua 8:1—12:24 |
| ☐ | Gideon, the Reluctant Leader | Judges 6:1—8:35 |
| ☐ | The Weak Strong Man | Judges 13:1—16:31 |
| ☐ | Calling Samuel | 1 Samuel 1:1—3:21 |
| ☐ | Israel Gets Its King | 1 Samuel 8:1—11:15 |
| ☐ | Rejected | 1 Samuel 15:1—16:23 |
| ☐ | David Versus Goliath | 1 Samuel 17:1–58 |
| ☐ | King David | 2 Samuel 1:1—8:14 |
| ☐ | Wise Guy | 1 Kings 1:1—4:34 |
| ☐ | Building the Temple | 1 Kings 5:1—8:66 |
| ☐ | Elijah and the Battle Royale | 1 Kings 17:1—19:18 |
| ☐ | The Exile of Israel | 2 Kings 17:1–41 |
| ☐ | The Fall of Jerusalem | 2 Kings 25:1–30 |
| ☐ | Return to Jerusalem | Ezra 1:1—8:36 |
| ☐ | Rebuilding the Walls | Nehemiah 1:1—7:3 |
| ☐ | Esther Saves Her People | Esther 2:1—8:17 |
| ☐ | Job, the Noble Sufferer | Job 1:1—2:10; 42:1–17 |
| ☐ | The Shepherd's Psalm | Psalm 23:1–6 |
| ☐ | A Prayer of Forgiveness | Psalm 51:1–19 |
| ☐ | The Coming Messiah | Isaiah 52:13—53:12 |
| ☐ | A Night in the Lions' Den | Daniel 6:1–28 |
| ☐ | The Ultimate Fish Story | Jonah 1:1—4:11 |
| ☐ | The First Christmas | Matthew 1:18—2:23; Luke 2:1–52 |
| ☐ | The Sermon on the Mount | Matthew 5:1—7:29 |
| ☐ | Miracle After Miracle | Matthew 8:1—9:38; Mark 5:1—6:56 |
| ☐ | Parable After Parable | Matthew 13:1–58; 18:1–35; 21:28—25:46 |
| ☐ | The Lord's Prayer | Luke 11:1–13 |
| ☐ | The Raising of Lazarus | John 11:1–44 |

| DAY | THEME | PASSAGE |
| --- | --- | --- |
| ☐ | The Passion of the Christ | John 18:1—19:42 |
| ☐ | He Lives! | John 20:1—21:25 |
| ☐ | Welcome, Holy Spirit | Acts 2:1–47 |
| ☐ | The First Martyr | Acts 6:8—7:60 |
| ☐ | Saul Sees the Light | Acts 9:1–31 |
| ☐ | Good News for Gentiles | Acts 10:1—11:18 |
| ☐ | Hit the Road, Paul | Acts 13:1—28:31 |
| ☐ | Sin and Salvation | Romans 2:1—8:39 |
| ☐ | Love Is . . . | 1 Corinthians 13:1–13 |
| ☐ | Arm Yourself | Ephesians 6:10–20 |
| ☐ | Jesus Is Coming | 1 Thessalonians 4:13—5:11 |
| ☐ | The Faith Hall of Fame | Hebrews 11:1–40 |
| ☐ | Just Do It | James 1:2–27 |
| ☐ | Love, Love, Love | 1 John 3:11–24 |
| ☐ | Judgment Day | Revelation 20:1–15 |
| ☐ | Forever and Ever | Revelation 21:1—22:21 |

| DAY | DESCRIPTION | PASSAGE |
|---|---|---|
| ☐ | The Fall of Humanity | Genesis 3:1–19 |
| ☐ | A People for God | Genesis 28:10–15; 32:22–28 |
| ☐ | The Ten Commandments | Exodus 20:1–17 |
| ☐ | Sacrifices Required Under Law | Leviticus 5:14–19 |
| ☐ | Punishments for Sin Under Law | Leviticus 20:7–27 |
| ☐ | Obedience From Love | Deuteronomy 11:13–21 |
| ☐ | Cycles of Disobedience | Judges 2:10–19 |
| ☐ | The People Demand a King | 1 Samuel 8:1–22 |
| ☐ | Saul Fails and Is Rejected | 1 Samuel 15:17–23 |
| ☐ | Many Kings Fail | Jeremiah 1—17 |
| ☐ | The Sin of the People | Ezekiel 20:5–26 |
| ☐ | An Eternal King Promised | Jeremiah 23:1–6; Isaiah 9:6–7; Zechariah 9:9–10 |
| ☐ | The Promised King Is Born | Luke 2:1–20 |
| ☐ | The Word Became Flesh | John 1:1–18 |
| ☐ | Signs and Miracles of Authority | Matthew 9:1–8; Luke 13:10–17 |
| ☐ | Jesus Fulfills the Law | Matthew 5:17–20; Romans 8:1–4 |
| ☐ | Jesus Teaches About New Life | John 3:1–36 |
| ☐ | Jesus Willingly Taken | John 18:1–11 |
| ☐ | Jesus' Death and Resurrection | Luke 23:44—24:12 |
| ☐ | Christ a Sacrifice for All | Hebrews |
| ☐ | God's Wrath Explained | Romans 1:18–32 |
| ☐ | God's Judgment Explained | Romans 2:5–11 |
| ☐ | Righteousness by Faith | Romans 3:9–26 |
| ☐ | Life Through Christ | Romans 5:12–21 |
| ☐ | Life by the Spirit | Romans 8:1–17; Galatians 5:16–26 |
| ☐ | Living Sacrifices | Romans 12:1–21 |
| ☐ | Walking in the Light | 1 John 1—2 |
| ☐ | Living for God | 1 Peter 1–11 |
| ☐ | Love for One Another | 1 John 3:11–24 |
| ☐ | Promise of Eternity | 2 Corinthians 5:1–10; Revelation 21:1–4 |

| DAY | DESCRIPTION | PASSAGE |
|---|---|---|
| ☐ | Jesus' coming is predicted. | Isaiah 7:14; 9:1–9; Luke 1:26–38 |
| ☐ | Jesus is born. | Matthew 1:18—2:23; Luke 2:1–20 |
| ☐ | Jesus is baptized by John the Baptist. | Matthew 3:1–17 |
| ☐ | Jesus begins his public ministry. | Matthew 4:1–17; Luke 4:14–44 |
| ☐ | Jesus calls his disciples. | Luke 5:1–11; 6:12–16; John 1:35–51 |
| ☐ | Jesus talks to a Pharisee and a Samaritan. | John 3:1—4:42 |
| ☐ | Jesus delivers the Sermon on the Mount. | Matthew 5:1—7:29 |
| ☐ | Jesus heals people in need. | Matthew 8:1—9:8 |
| ☐ | Jesus tangles with the Pharisees. | Matthew 12:1–45 |
| ☐ | Jesus teaches his disciples using parables. | Matthew 13:1–52 |
| ☐ | Jesus demonstrates his power over nature. | Mark 6:45–52; Luke 8:22–25 |
| ☐ | Jesus heals many. | Mark 5:1–43 |
| ☐ | Jesus feeds 5,000 followers. | John 6:1–15 |
| ☐ | Jesus is identified as the Christ. | Matthew 16:13—17:13 |
| ☐ | Jesus casts out an evil spirit. | Mark 9:14–32 |
| ☐ | Jesus teaches on forgiveness. | Matthew 18:15–35 |
| ☐ | Jesus teaches on the kingdom of heaven. | Matthew 13:24–52 |
| ☐ | Jesus confronts the rich young man. | Mark 10:17–31 |
| ☐ | Jesus sends out his disciples. | Luke 10:1–24 |
| ☐ | Jesus teaches how to love and pray. | Luke 10:25—11:13 |
| ☐ | Jesus teaches about himself. | John 10:1–42 |
| ☐ | Jesus raises Lazarus from the dead. | John 11:1–44 |
| ☐ | Jesus travels to Jerusalem. | Matthew 21:1–27 |
| ☐ | Jesus eats the Last Supper. | Matthew 26:17–30; John 13:1–17 |
| ☐ | Jesus comforts his disciples. | John 14:1—16:33 |
| ☐ | Jesus is arrested. | Matthew 26:36–75 |
| ☐ | Jesus is put on trial. | John 18:19—19:16 |
| ☐ | Jesus is crucified and buried. | John 19:17–42 |
| ☐ | Jesus rises from the dead. | John 20:1—21:25 |
| ☐ | Jesus ascends to heaven. | Matthew 28:16–20; Luke 24:36–53 |

| DAY | DESCRIPTION | PASSAGE |
|---|---|---|
| ☐ | Blessing | Psalms 67, 72, 84, 128 |
| ☐ | Calling to God | Psalms 4, 5, 22 |
| ☐ | Confidence | Psalms 27, 36, 71, 125 |
| ☐ | Deeds of God | Psalms 9, 18, 118 |
| ☐ | Doubt | Psalms 42, 73, 77 |
| ☐ | Faithfulness of God | Psalms 105, 119:137—144, 146 |
| ☐ | Fear | Psalms 37, 49, 91 |
| ☐ | Glory of God | Psalms 19, 24, 29 |
| ☐ | God Is a Helper | Psalms 54, 115, 119:169—176 |
| ☐ | Identity | Psalms 8, 139 |
| ☐ | Justice of God | Psalms 7, 26, 82 |
| ☐ | Meditation | Psalms 119:9—16, 41—48 |
| ☐ | Mercy | Psalms 13, 28, 86 |
| ☐ | Music | Psalms 6, 149, 150 |
| ☐ | Nature | Psalms 50, 104, 147, 148 |
| ☐ | Peace | Psalms 23, 133, 119:161—168 |
| ☐ | Power of God | Psalms 68, 93, 135 |
| ☐ | Praise | Psalms 65, 98, 138 |
| ☐ | Prayer | Psalms 17, 20, 102 |
| ☐ | Protection | Psalms 59, 62, 124 |
| ☐ | Safety in God | Psalms 11, 16, 142, 46 |
| ☐ | Rejoicing | Psalms 30, 47, 97 |
| ☐ | Righteousness | Psalms 1, 15, 112 |
| ☐ | Salvation | Psalms 3, 14, 121 |
| ☐ | Sin and Repentance | Psalms 25, 32, 38, 51 |
| ☐ | Thanksgiving | Psalms 75, 106, 136 |
| ☐ | Trust | Psalms 31, 40, 56 |
| ☐ | Victory | Psalms 21, 76, 144 |
| ☐ | Wisdom | Psalms 90, 107, 111 |
| ☐ | Worship | Psalms 33, 34, 145 |

| DAY | PASSAGE |
|---|---|
| ☐ | Proverbs 1 |
| ☐ | Proverbs 2 |
| ☐ | Proverbs 3 |
| ☐ | Proverbs 4 |
| ☐ | Proverbs 5 |
| ☐ | Proverbs 6 |
| ☐ | Proverbs 7 |
| ☐ | Proverbs 8 |
| ☐ | Proverbs 9 |
| ☐ | Proverbs 10 |
| ☐ | Proverbs 11 |
| ☐ | Proverbs 12 |
| ☐ | Proverbs 13 |
| ☐ | Proverbs 14 |
| ☐ | Proverbs 15 |
| ☐ | Proverbs 16 |
| ☐ | Proverbs 17 |
| ☐ | Proverbs 18 |
| ☐ | Proverbs 19 |
| ☐ | Proverbs 20 |
| ☐ | Proverbs 21 |
| ☐ | Proverbs 22 |
| ☐ | Proverbs 23 |
| ☐ | Proverbs 24 |
| ☐ | Proverbs 25 |
| ☐ | Proverbs 26 |
| ☐ | Proverbs 27 |
| ☐ | Proverbs 28 |
| ☐ | Proverbs 29 |
| ☐ | Proverbs 30–31 |

| DAY | DESCRIPTION | PASSAGE |
|---|---|---|
| ☐ | Fire and Birds: God Lays Down the Law | Numbers 11 |
| ☐ | Miriam: Leprous as Snow | Numbers 12 |
| ☐ | Korah, Dathan and Abiran | Numbers 16 |
| ☐ | Aaron: A Budding Leader | Numbers 17 |
| ☐ | Moses Strikes Out | Numbers 20:1–13 |
| ☐ | Afraid of Snakes? | Numbers 21:4–9 |
| ☐ | Balaam and his donkey | Numbers 22 |
| ☐ | | Numbers 23—24 |
| ☐ | Laws for a Special People in a Special Time | Deuteronomy 21 |
| ☐ | Moses: End of an Era | Deuteronomy 31 |
| ☐ | | Deuteronomy 32:44–52; 34 |
| ☐ | Solar Stand Still | Joshua 10:1–15 |
| ☐ | Ehud: Left Handed Wonder | Judges 3:12–30 |
| ☐ | David and Abigail: Wisdom in a Tough Situation | 1 Samuel 25 |
| ☐ | Mephibosheth: Rags to Riches | 2 Samuel 9 |
| ☐ | Elisha: Miracle Man | 2 Kings 2:23–25; 4:8–37 |
| ☐ | | 2 Kings 6:1–23 |
| ☐ | Asa: But if You Forsake Him . . . | 2 Chronicles 15 |
| ☐ | | 2 Chronicles 16 |
| ☐ | Joash: Kindness Forgotten | 2 Chronicles 22:10—23:21 |
| ☐ | | 2 Chronicles 24 |
| ☐ | Josiah: Youthful Ruler | 2 Chronicles 34 |
| ☐ | | 2 Chronicles 35 |
| ☐ | Nehemiah: Homesickness | Nehemiah 1 |
| ☐ | | Nehemiah 2 |
| ☐ | Jerusalem Falls: Judgment Arrives | Jeremiah 52 |
| ☐ | The Writing on the Wall | Daniel 5 |

| DAY | THEME | PASSAGE |
|---|---|---|
| ☐ | Elusive righteousness | Romans 3:9–26 |
| ☐ | Peace and joy | Romans 5:1–11 |
| ☐ | Sin and death | Romans 5:12–21 |
| ☐ | Alive in Christ | Romans 6:1–14 |
| ☐ | Battle with sin | Romans 7:7–25 |
| ☐ | Being a conqueror | Romans 8:28–39 |
| ☐ | A living sacrifice | Romans 12:1–8 |
| ☐ | Running the race | 1 Corinthians 9:19–27 |
| ☐ | One body | 1 Corinthians 12:12–31 |
| ☐ | Love | 1 Corinthians 13:1–13 |
| ☐ | Resurrection | 1 Corinthians 15:12–34 |
| ☐ | Longing for heaven | 2 Corinthians 5:1–10 |
| ☐ | Christian hardships | 2 Corinthians 6:3–13 |
| ☐ | Weakness | 2 Corinthians 12:1–10 |
| ☐ | Christian freedom | Galatians 5:1–15 |
| ☐ | Fruit of the Spirit | Galatians 5:16–26 |
| ☐ | Incomparable grace | Ephesians 2:1–10 |
| ☐ | Christian unity | Ephesians 4:1–16 |
| ☐ | People of light | Ephesians 4:17—5:21 |
| ☐ | Family dynamics | Ephesians 5:22—6:4 |
| ☐ | Armor of God | Ephesians 6:10–20 |
| ☐ | Imitating Jesus | Philippians 2:1–11 |
| ☐ | Reaching the ultimate goal | Philippians 3:12—4:1 |
| ☐ | Christ the head | Colossians 1:15–23 |
| ☐ | Pleasing God | 1 Thessalonians 4:1–12 |
| ☐ | Jesus is coming | 1 Thessalonians 4:13—5:11 |
| ☐ | Avoiding idleness | 2 Thessalonians 3:6–18 |
| ☐ | Instructions for a young believer | 1 Timothy 4:1–16 |
| ☐ | Money | 1 Timothy 6:3–10 |
| ☐ | Staying strong | 2 Timothy 3:10—4:8 |

| DAY | THEME | PASSAGE |
|---|---|---|
| ☐ | When you're discouraged | Deuteronomy 31:1–8 |
| ☐ | When you're looking for direction | Psalm 32:1–11 |
| ☐ | When you're scared | Psalm 34:1–22 |
| ☐ | When you're facing troubling circumstances | Psalm 49:1–20 |
| ☐ | When you're tempted to cut corners | Proverbs 28:1–28 |
| ☐ | When you need peace of mind | Isaiah 26:1–21 |
| ☐ | When you're uncertain about the future | Jeremiah 29:4–14 |
| ☐ | When you don't think you can change | Ezekiel 36:22–32 |
| ☐ | When you can't let go of a grudge | Matthew 6:5–15 |
| ☐ | When you've reached the end of your rope | Matthew 11:25–30 |
| ☐ | When you're feeling cocky | Matthew 23:1–12 |
| ☐ | When you're tempted to seek revenge | Luke 6:27–36 |
| ☐ | When you need to reprioritize your life | Luke 12:22–34 |
| ☐ | When a situation seems hopeless | Luke 18:18–30 |
| ☐ | When you're facing persecution | Luke 21:8–19 |
| ☐ | When you're tired of the way you're living | John 8:12–30 |
| ☐ | When you're questioning your faith | John 10:22–42 |
| ☐ | When you need a glimpse of eternity | John 14:1–7 |
| ☐ | When you have a major request of God | John 14:8–14 |
| ☐ | When you're memorizing Scripture | John 14:25–31 |
| ☐ | When you're sharing your faith | Romans 10:1–13 |
| ☐ | When temptation won't let go | 1 Corinthians 10:1–13 |
| ☐ | When you wonder whether you can trust God's promises | 2 Corinthians 1:12–22 |
| ☐ | When Satan targets you | 2 Thessalonians 3:1–5 |
| ☐ | When you're facing a tough decision | James 1:2–18 |
| ☐ | When you're feeling distant from God | James 4:1–9 |
| ☐ | When you're trying to get ahead | James 4:10–17 |
| ☐ | When you need forgiveness | 1 John 1:1–9 |
| ☐ | When you're waiting for an answer to prayer | 1 John 5:13–21 |
| ☐ | When you're overwhelmed by death, sorrow or pain | Revelation 21:1–27 |

| DAY | THEME | PASSAGE |
|---|---|---|
| ☐ | Responding to an unusual assignment | Genesis 6:1—7:24 |
| ☐ | Relocating | Genesis 12:1–9 |
| ☐ | Preparing for lean times | Genesis 41:41–57 |
| ☐ | Leading an exodus | Exodus 13:17—14:31 |
| ☐ | Delegating responsibility | Exodus 18:1–27 |
| ☐ | Dealing with wrongdoers | Exodus 32:1–35 |
| ☐ | Handling opposition | Numbers 12:1–16 |
| ☐ | Facing down challengers | Numbers 16:1–50 |
| ☐ | Motivating followers | Deuteronomy 11:1–32 |
| ☐ | Appointing a successor | Deuteronomy 31:1–8 |
| ☐ | Succeeding a legend | Joshua 1:1–18 |
| ☐ | Identifying cause of failure | Joshua 7:1–26 |
| ☐ | Saying goodbye | Joshua 23:1–16 |
| ☐ | Recognizing a call | Judges 6:1–40 |
| ☐ | Giving a necessary rebuke | 1 Samuel 12:1–15 |
| ☐ | Doing what no one else will | 1 Samuel 17:1–54 |
| ☐ | Mending fences | 2 Samuel 9:1–13 |
| ☐ | Accepting responsibility | 2 Samuel 12:1–25 |
| ☐ | Recognizing what's important | 1 Kings 3:1–15 |
| ☐ | Putting wisdom to use | 1 Kings 3:16–28 |
| ☐ | Tackling a huge project | 1 Kings 6:1–14 |
| ☐ | Avoiding critical mistakes | 1 Kings 11:1–39 |
| ☐ | Learning from the example of a predecessor | 1 Kings 15:9–24 |
| ☐ | Understanding what it means to be first and last | Matthew 19:16–30 |
| ☐ | Dealing with ambitious subordinates | Mark 10:35–45 |
| ☐ | Managing shrewdly | Luke 16:1–15 |
| ☐ | Entering into partnerships | 2 Corinthians 6:3–13 |
| ☐ | Practicing generosity | 2 Corinthians 9:6–15 |
| ☐ | Living a holy life | Colossians 3:1–17 |
| ☐ | Qualifying for leadership | 1 Timothy 3:1–16 |

| DAY | THEME | PASSAGE |
|---|---|---|
| ☐ | Abraham's plea for Sodom | Genesis 18:16–33 |
| ☐ | A servant's plea for success | Genesis 24:12–27 |
| ☐ | The song of Moses and Miriam | Exodus 15:1–18 |
| ☐ | Moses' desperate request | Deuteronomy 3:23–29 |
| ☐ | The song of Deborah | Judges 5:1–31 |
| ☐ | Hannah's rejoicing | 1 Samuel 2:1–10 |
| ☐ | A king's prayer | 2 Samuel 7:18–29 |
| ☐ | David's song of praise | 2 Samuel 22:1–51 |
| ☐ | Solomon's prayer of dedication | 1 Kings 8:22–53 |
| ☐ | A nation's prayer promise | 2 Chronicles 7:11–22 |
| ☐ | Nehemiah's request | Nehemiah 1:5–11 |
| ☐ | Appreciating God's majesty | Psalm 8:1–9 |
| ☐ | David's plea for mercy | Psalm 51:1–19 |
| ☐ | The God who answers prayer | Psalm 65:1–13 |
| ☐ | A song of praise | Isaiah 26:1–21 |
| ☐ | Words from a fish's belly | Jonah 2:1–10 |
| ☐ | The Lord's prayer | Matthew 6:5–15 |
| ☐ | Jesus' prayer in Gethsemane | Matthew 26:36–46 |
| ☐ | Asking, seeking and knocking | Luke 11:7–13 |
| ☐ | Jesus prays for himself | John 17:1–5 |
| ☐ | Jesus prays for his disciples | John 17:6–19 |
| ☐ | Jesus prays for all believers | John 17:20–26 |
| ☐ | Help from the Holy Spirit | Romans 8:18–27 |
| ☐ | Paul prays for the Ephesian believers | Ephesians 1:15–23 |
| ☐ | Paul prays for the Colossian believers | Colossians 1:3–14 |
| ☐ | Paul thanks God for the Thessalonian believers | 1 Thessalonians 1:2–10 |
| ☐ | Paul prays for the Thessalonian believers | 2 Thessalonians 1:3–12 |
| ☐ | Paul requests prayer for himself | 2 Thessalonians 3:1–5 |
| ☐ | Praying for others | 1 Timothy 2:1–7 |
| ☐ | Prayer of faith | James 5:13–20 |

| DAY | THEME | PASSAGE |
|---|---|---|
| ☐ | Maker of covenants | Genesis 9:8–17 |
| ☐ | Thwarter of evil ambition | Genesis 11:1–8 |
| ☐ | Wrestler | Genesis 32:22–32 |
| ☐ | Bestower of talents | Genesis 41:1–39 |
| ☐ | Master of the unexpected | Exodus 3:1–17 |
| ☐ | Protector of the faithful | Exodus 12:1–30 |
| ☐ | Caterer par excellence | Exodus 16:1–18 |
| ☐ | Lawgiver | Exodus 20:1–21 |
| ☐ | Punisher of rebellion | Numbers 14:1–45 |
| ☐ | Opener of eyes | Numbers 22:21–41 |
| ☐ | Initiator of vengeance | Numbers 31:1–24 |
| ☐ | One and only | Deuteronomy 4:32–40 |
| ☐ | Sole object of worship | Deuteronomy 13:1–18 |
| ☐ | Offerer of proof | Judges 6:1–40 |
| ☐ | Protector of widows | Ruth 4:1–12 |
| ☐ | Hearer of prayers | 1 Samuel 1:1–30 |
| ☐ | Late night caller | 1 Samuel 3:1–21 |
| ☐ | Rejecter of the unfaithful | 1 Samuel 15:1–29 |
| ☐ | Supporter of the underdog | 1 Samuel 17:1–54 |
| ☐ | Provider of wisdom | 1 Kings 3:1–15 |
| ☐ | Sustainer | 1 Kings 17:1–24 |
| ☐ | Undefeated competitor | 1 Kings 18:16–40 |
| ☐ | Gentle whisperer | 1 Kings 19:9–18 |
| ☐ | Orchestrator of perfect justice | Esther 6:1—7:10 |
| ☐ | Holder of Satan's reins | Job 1:1–12 |
| ☐ | Rewarder of faithfulness | Job 42:7–17 |
| ☐ | Refuge | Psalm 18:1–50 |
| ☐ | Shepherd | Psalm 23:1–6 |
| ☐ | Originator of prophecy | Isaiah 53:1–12 |
| ☐ | Provider of salvation | John 3:1–21 |

| DAY | THEME | PASSAGE |
|---|---|---|
| ☐ | Noah builds an ark. | Genesis 6:1—7:24 |
| ☐ | Abram moves to a strange land. | Genesis 12:1–20 |
| ☐ | Abram trusts God's promise. | Genesis 15:1–21 |
| ☐ | Abraham offers Isaac. | Genesis 22:1–19 |
| ☐ | Abraham's servant chooses a wife for Isaac. | Genesis 24:1–67 |
| ☐ | Jacob works 14 years in order to marry Rachel. | Genesis 29:15–30 |
| ☐ | Joseph flourishes in an Egyptian prison. | Genesis 39:20—40:16 |
| ☐ | Joseph reveals God's plan to his brothers. | Genesis 45:1–20 |
| ☐ | Moses' mother trusts God to take care of her baby. | Exodus 2:1–10 |
| ☐ | Moses reveals himself as an Israelite. | Exodus 2:11–25 |
| ☐ | Moses and Aaron confront Pharaoh. | Exodus 6:28—7:13 |
| ☐ | Moses parts the Red Sea. | Exodus 14:5–31 |
| ☐ | Moses coaxes water from a rock. | Exodus 17:1–7 |
| ☐ | Caleb recommends invading the promised land. | Numbers 13:26–33 |
| ☐ | Rahab hides Israelite spies. | Joshua 2:1–24 |
| ☐ | Joshua defeats the Amorites. | Joshua 10:1–15 |
| ☐ | Gideon leads his men against the Midianites. | Judges 7:1–25 |
| ☐ | Ruth accompanies her mother–in–law. | Ruth 1:1–22 |
| ☐ | Hannah dedicates her son to God's service. | 1 Samuel 1:1–28 |
| ☐ | David confronts Goliath. | 1 Samuel 17:1–54 |
| ☐ | Solomon asks for wisdom. | 1 Kings 3:1–15 |
| ☐ | Elijah challenges the prophets of Baal and Asherah. | 1 Kings 18:16–40 |
| ☐ | Job continues to trust God in the midst of tragedy. | Job 1:6–22 |
| ☐ | Shadrach, Meshach and Abednego face death. | Daniel 3:1–30 |
| ☐ | Daniel refuses to give up prayer. | Daniel 6:1–28 |
| ☐ | Peter walks on water. | Matthew 14:22–36 |
| ☐ | Mary trusts God | Luke 1:26–56 |
| ☐ | Zacchaeus changes his ways. | Luke 19:1–10 |
| ☐ | Stephen loses his life. | Acts 6:8–15; 7:54–60 |
| ☐ | Saul meets Christ. | Acts 9:1–31 |

*Aspire: The New Women of Color Study Bible*

Concept by: Mel Banks II, Urban Spirit
General Editor: Katara A. Washington
Contributing Editor: Victoria Christopher Murray
Production Editor: Cheryl Wilson
Editor: Crystal McDowell
Project Management and Editorial: Shari Vanden Berg
Editorial Assistance: Dawn Anderson, Amy Ballor, Natalie Block
Theological Review:
Vanessa L. Lovelace, adjunct professor, Elmhurst College
Andrew Sloan, M.Div., Oral Roberts University
Production Management: Phil Herich
Art Direction: Jamie DeBruyn
Cover Design: Dogeared Design—Kirk DouPonce
Interior Design: Dogeared Design—Kirk DouPonce; Blackbird Creative—Robin Black; Jamie DeBruyn
Proofreading: Peachtree Editorial and Proofreading Service, Peachtree City, GA
Interior Typesetting: The Livingstone Corporation, Carol Stream, IL

### *GUARANTEE*

Thank you for choosing a Zondervan product. We want to make sure you're satisfied with the quality of your purchase. We stand behind every product we make; that's why we guarantee each one for a lifetime against manufacturing defects. For more information on our quality guarantee and product care instructions, visit us at www.zondervan.com/guarantee.

# Map 1: **WORLD OF THE PATRIARCHS**

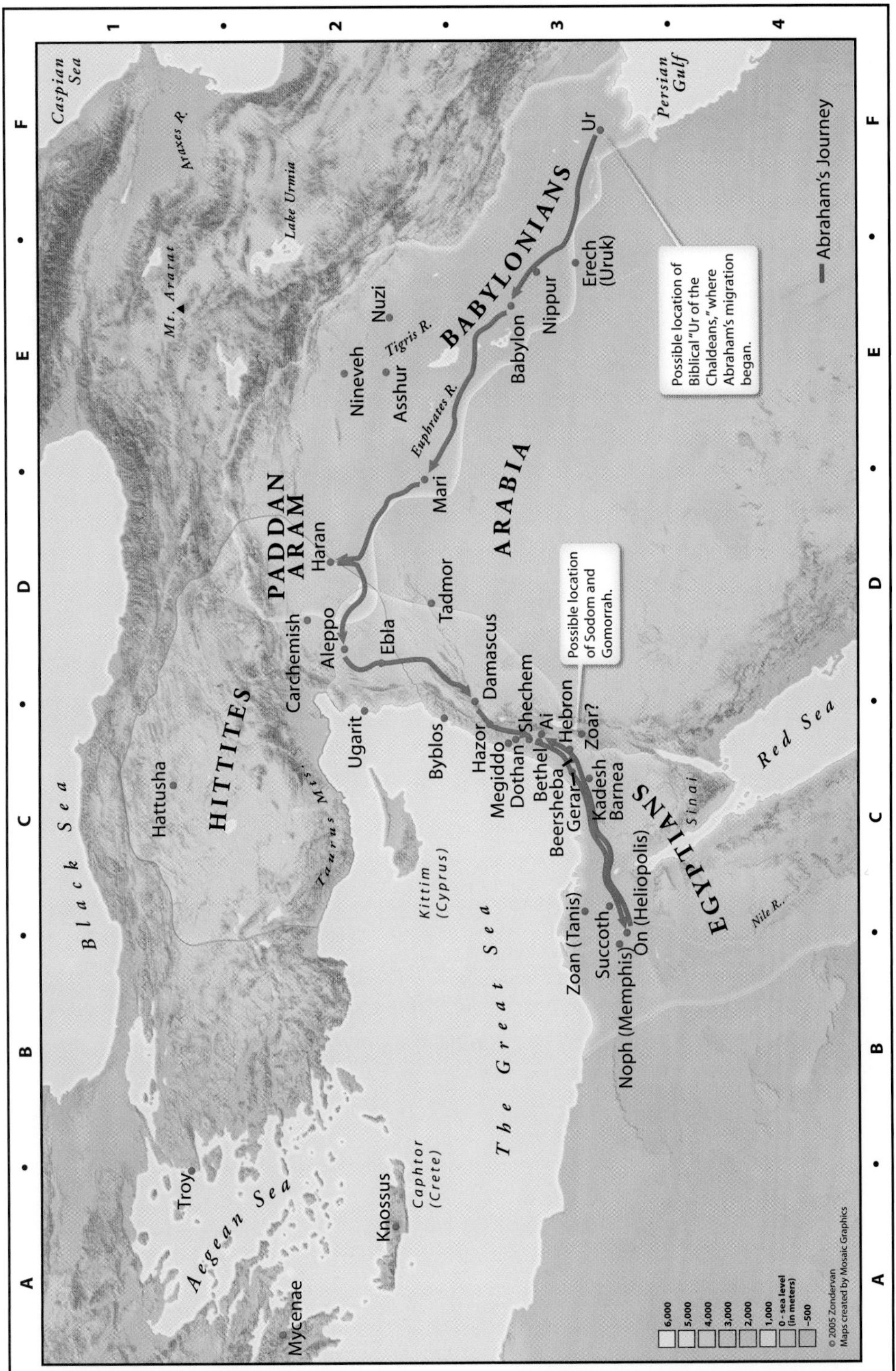

## Map 2: **EXODUS AND CONQUEST OF CANAAN**

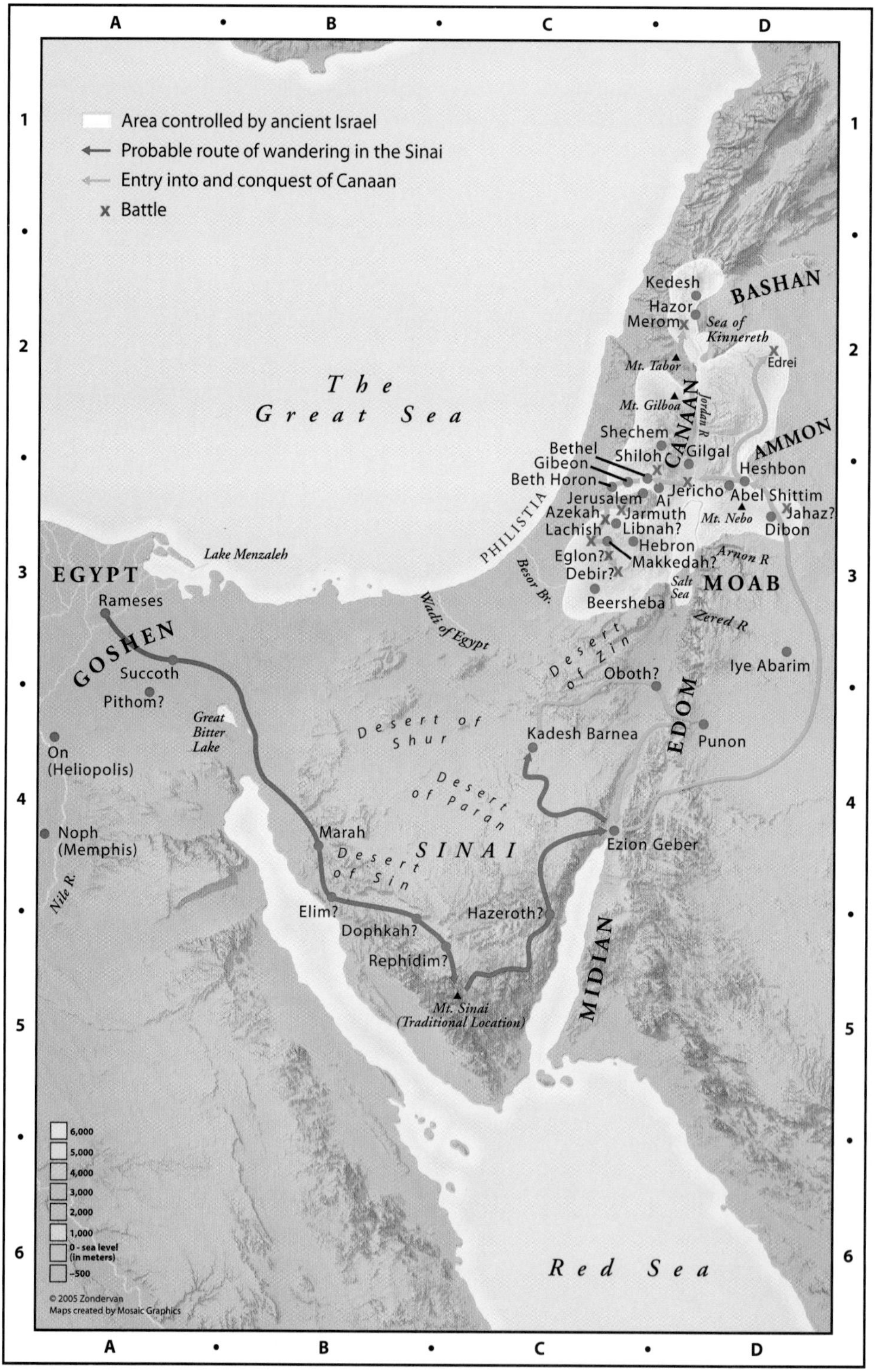

# Map 3: **LAND OF THE TWELVE TRIBES**

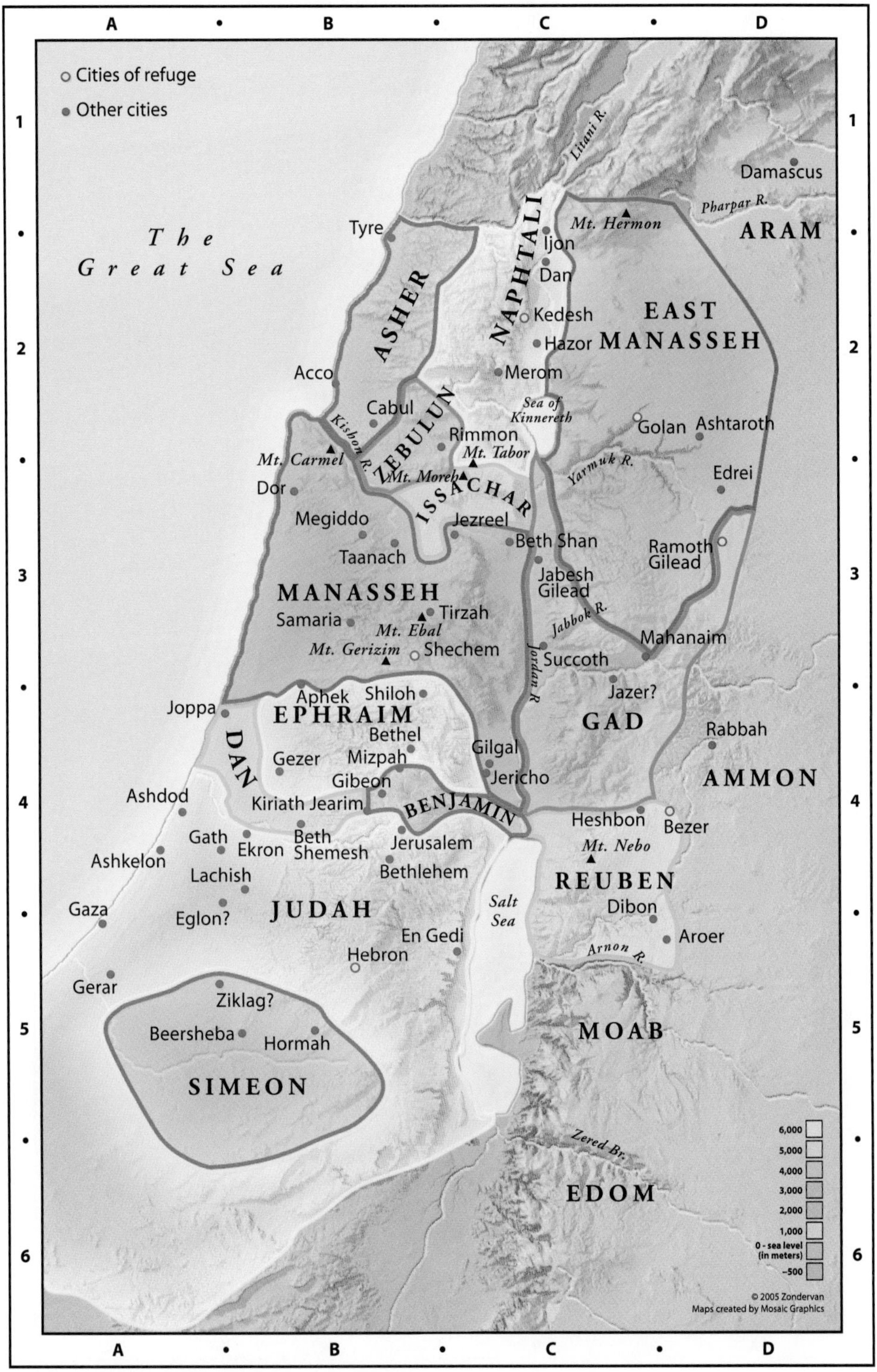

# Map 4: **KINGDOM OF DAVID AND SOLOMON**

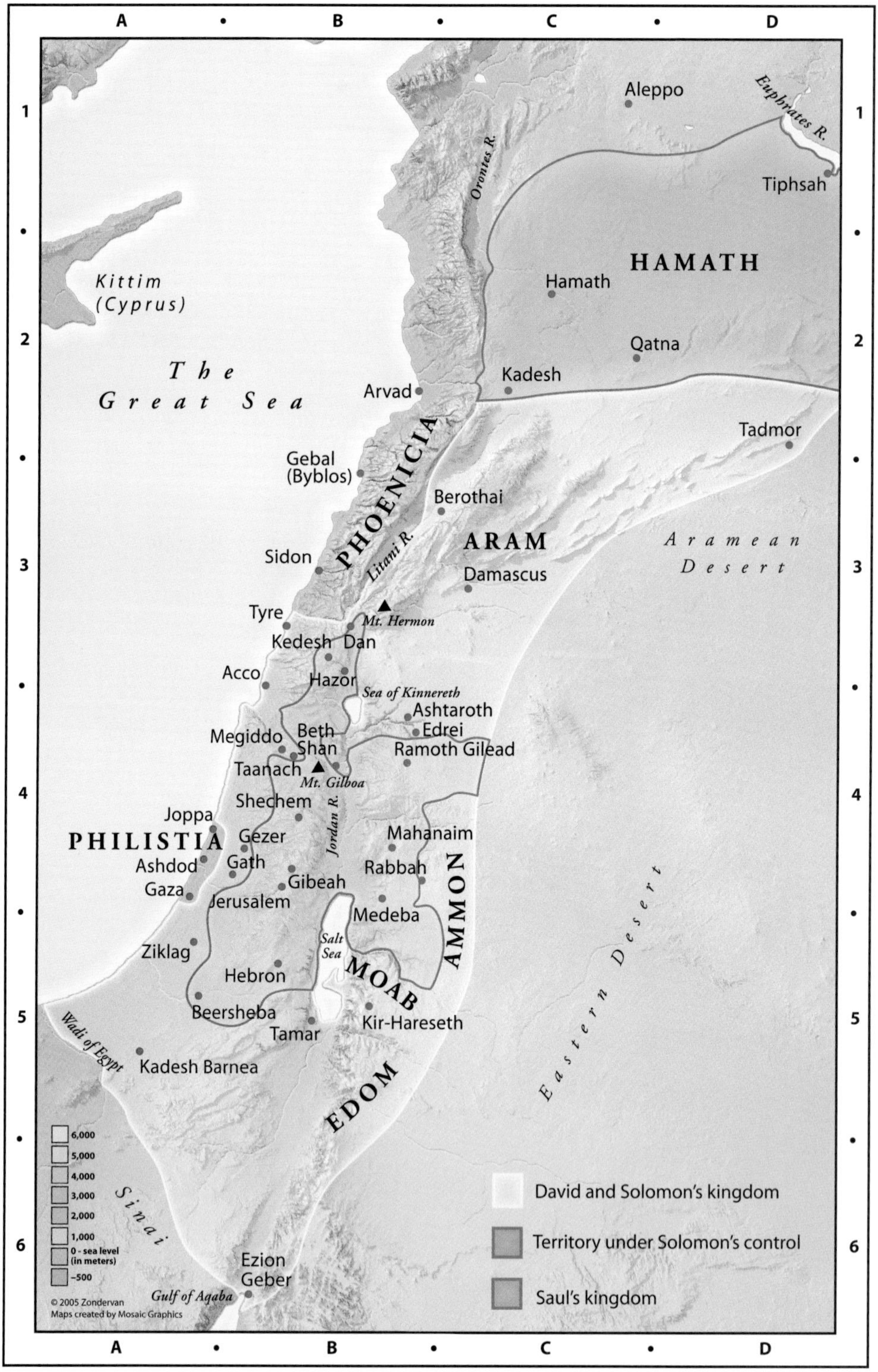

## Map 5: **JESUS' MINISTRY**

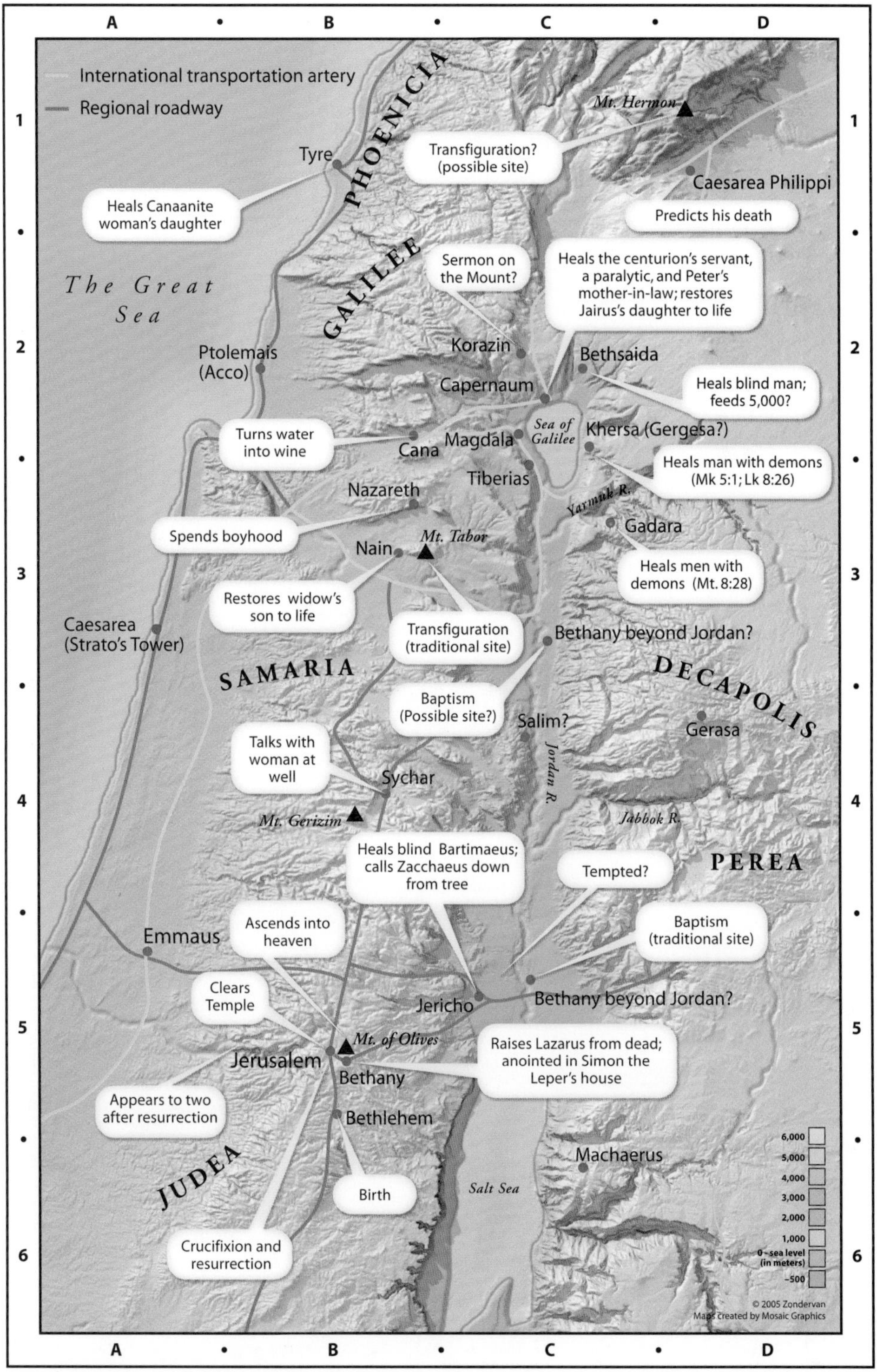

## Map 6: **PAULS' MISSIONARY JOURNEYS**

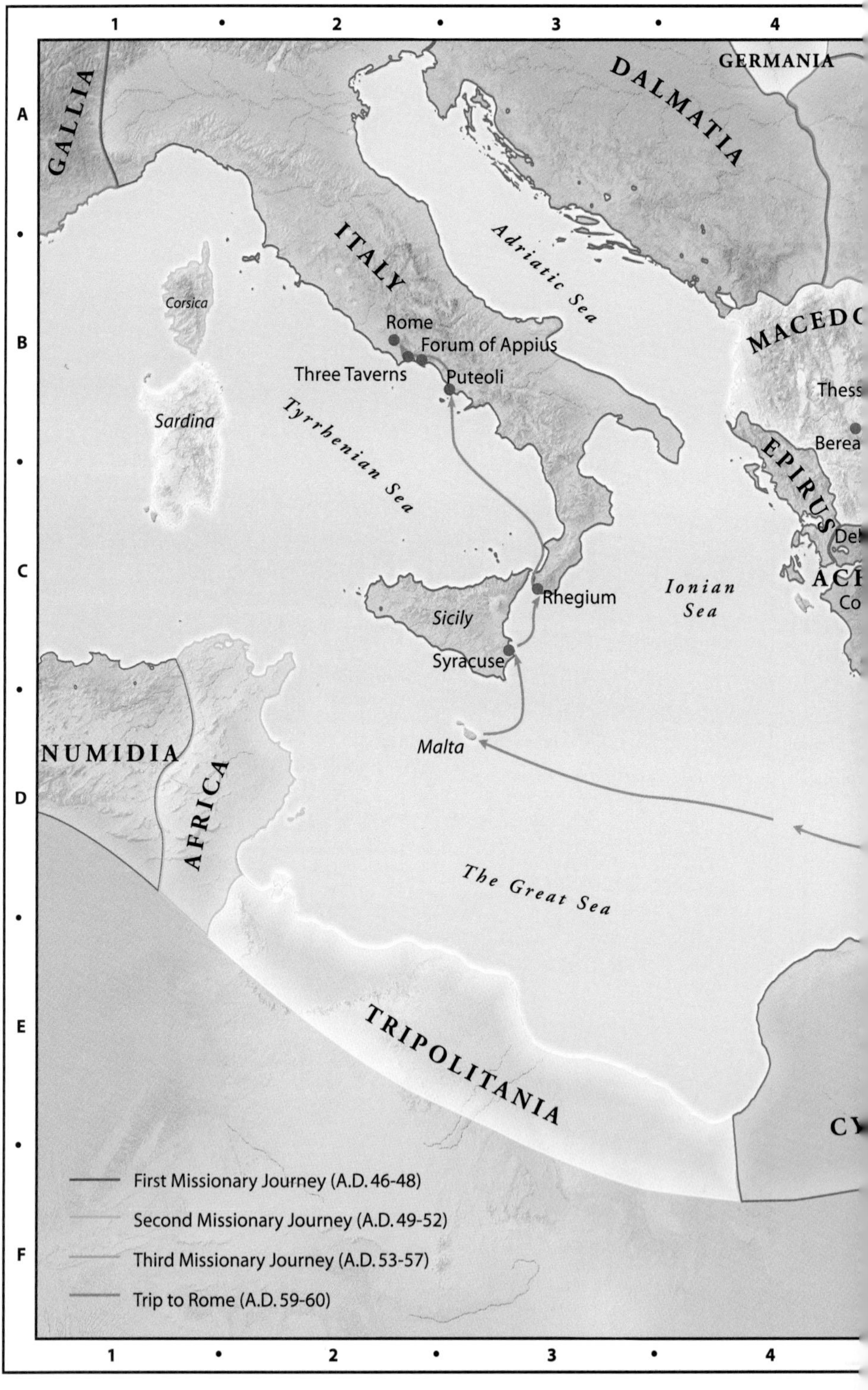

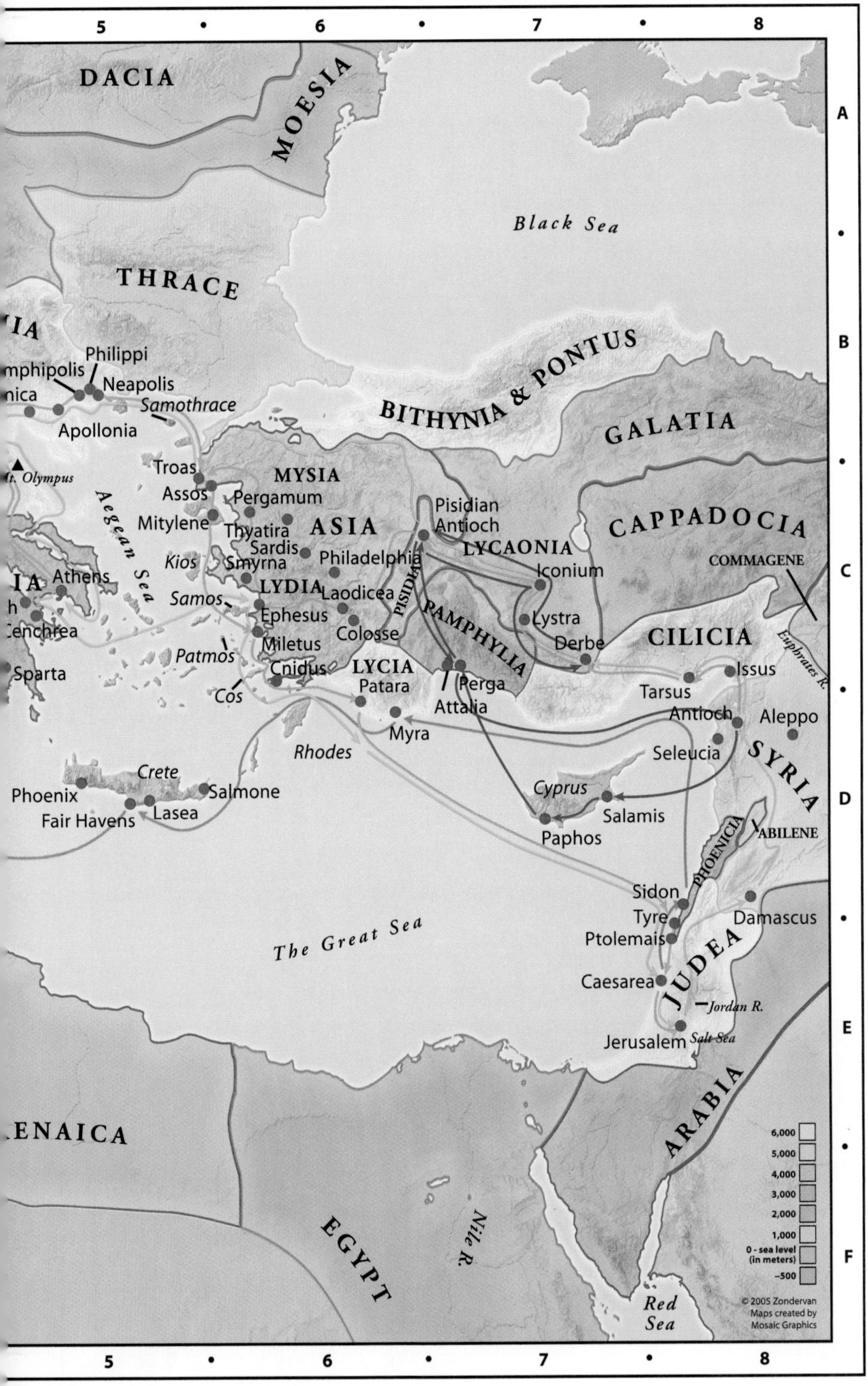
5
6
7
8
A
B
C
D
E
F
DACIA
MOESIA
Black Sea
THRACE
BITHYNIA & PONTUS
GALATIA
CAPPADOCIA
COMMAGENE
MYSIA
ASIA
LYCAONIA
LYDIA
PISIDIA
PAMPHYLIA
LYCIA
CILICIA
SYRIA
PHOENICIA
ABILENE
JUDEA
ARABIA
EGYPT
Philippi
Neapolis
Samothrace
Apollonia
Troas
Assos
Pergamum
Mitylene
Thyatira
Sardis
Smyrna
Philadelphia
Kios
Athens
Samos
Ephesus
Laodicea
Colosse
Miletus
Patmos
Cnidus
Cos
Sparta
Aegean Sea
Pisidian Antioch
Iconium
Lystra
Derbe
Perga
Attalia
Patara
Myra
Rhodes
Crete
Phoenix
Fair Havens
Lasea
Salmone
Tarsus
Issus
Antioch
Aleppo
Seleucia
Cyprus
Salamis
Paphos
Sidon
Tyre
Ptolemais
Damascus
Caesarea
Jordan R.
Jerusalem
Salt Sea
Euphrates R.
The Great Sea
Nile R.
Red Sea
6,000
5,000
4,000
3,000
2,000
1,000
0 - sea level (in meters)
–500
© 2005 Zondervan
Maps created by Mosaic Graphics

# Map 7: **JERUSALEM IN THE TIME OF JESUS**

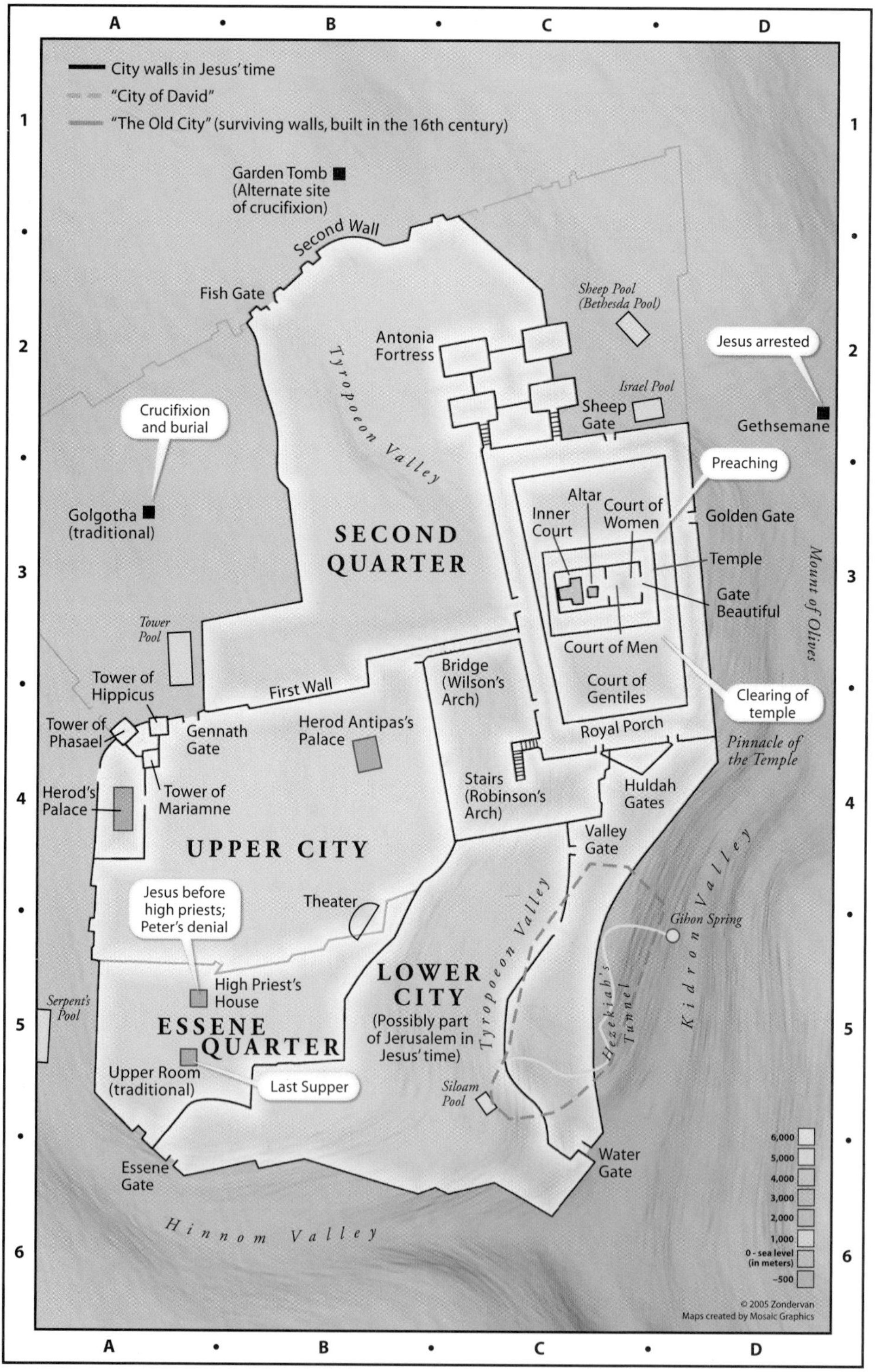